# PRODUCTS LIABILITY LAW

### David G. Owen
*Carolina Distinguished Professor of Law*
*University of South Carolina*

**HORNBOOK SERIES®**

Mat #13347549

*Hornbook Series*, *Westlaw*, and West Group are trademarks registered in the U.S. Patent and Trademark Office.

© 2005 West, a Thomson business
    610 Opperman Drive
    P.O. Box 64526
    St. Paul, MN 55164–0526
    1–800–328–9352

**ISBN** 0–314–21175–6

TEXT IS PRINTED ON 10% POST CONSUMER RECYCLED PAPER

*For Wendy and Ethan*

\*

# Preface

This book explores, describes, explains, and selectively critiques products liability law in America in the early stages of the 21st century. Over the last half century, modern products liability law was born, matured, and "reformed" by legislatures around America and the world. Many aspects of products liability law are still shifting and transmogrifying around the nation and the globe, but some of its features are beginning to focus and others even to resolve. My goal here is to trace the evolution of products liability law in America, to examine how legislatures and courts presently define and apply the law, and to explore an array of problematic issues on which courts and commentators disagree.

In recent decades, tumultuous litigation has arisen over the proper allocation of responsibility for harm caused by a variety of specific products—asbestos, cigarettes, handguns, silicone breast implants, and the diet drug, phen-fen, to name just a few of the more notorious. Litigations involving these types of products raise a host of complex procedural issues, such as the availability of class actions, which lie beyond the scope of this book. Nor does this volume address, except indirectly, the regulation of product safety by administrative agencies. What this book does explore are substantive issues of liability, defense, and damages involved in fixing responsibility for product injuries.

As addressed more particularly in the Acknowledgments, early versions of various sections and chapters intended for this volume first appeared as articles in law journals and as my chapters in Madden & Owen on Products Liability (3 vols., West 2000). Such materials have been reworked and updated for this book.

Over the last century, commentators have chronicled and critiqued the developing products liability law propounded by courts and legislatures in the United States, and, more recently, abroad. Cobbling together many aspects of these developments, this volume seeks to bring some order to the melange of common law decisions and statutes (tort and contract) which combine to create this befuddling field of law that so often appears out of focus, as if viewed through air currents shimmering over a baking summer road. The grist for any commentator, as others have observed, is the scholarship of others who came before. Particularly in a work that seeks principally to organize and explain, little room remains for designing new pathways of development. Credit belongs to William Prosser for observing that such chroniclers essentially are packrats, "unblushingly" collecting and assembling bits and pieces from other scholars, judicial and academic.*

---

* See The Law of Torts (4th ed. 1971), preface, at xi. Or, "dwarfs perched on the shoulders of giants," to borrow a twelfth-century metaphor of Bernard of Chartres. See Jacques Le Goff, Intellectuals in the Middle Ages 12 (1957, 1985) (T. Fagan trans., Blackwell, 1993), citing Stephen C. Ferrulolo, The Origins of the University: The Schools of Paris and Their Critics, 1100-1215, at 154 (Stanford, 1985).

Even if products liability law for a moment would stand still, perfection in such a work, like proximate cause, would be as elusive as a butterfly. In an effort to make the next edition of this book better than its predecessor, I invite corrections, suggestions, and comments on any aspect of this work: owen@sc.edu.

DAVID G. OWEN

Kiawah Island, South Carolina
November 2004

# Acknowledgments

Appreciation is due to many whose contributions made this book possible. First are the generations of research and editorial assistants who labored with skill and dedication over many years on this book and the progenitor treatise from which many chapters draw. My deep appreciation for such assistance goes to Anne Kearse, René LeBlanc-Allman, Sarah Berry Fellona, Denise Bessellieu, Stephen Hall, Suzanne Guitar Odom, Huntley Crouch, Matthew Richardson, Jason Dennis, Thad Westbrook, James Callahan, David Scott, Scott Taylor, Sara Centioni, Cathy Lightsey Weaver, Thomas Andrews, Rangeley Bailey Chewning, Stephanie Borsanyi, James Burns, Natalie Byars, Racheal Dain, Michael Dirnbauer, Scott Johnson, Candy Kern-Fuller, Trent Kirk, Nikki Lee, James Mayberry, Forrest Norvell, Dave Smith, Terri Vincent, Jennifer Young, Carrie Fisher, Dayton Stout, Van Anderson, Amanda Bailey, John Bell, Julia Ebert, Dana Pagän, Anne Ross, David Watkins, Danielle Evans, Jay A'Hearn, David Hoyle, Tod Williams, Eric Zaiser, Rochelle Oldfield, Adam Whitsett, Mary Gruenhagen, Emily Howard, David Marshall, and Eric Tonnsen. Special thanks are owed to the finish editors, John Harvey, David Kusa, Taylor Lacy, Richard Miller, and Emma Thomas and particularly to the final team of managing editors, Aaron Dias, Amy Neuschafer, and Alyson Campbell, who skillfully steered the book through final editing. I am especially grateful to an accomplished products liability litigator and scholar, Robert Hill, who as my research assistant long ago helped update Page Keeton's chapter on products liability in Prosser and Keeton on Torts, for once more lending his keen update skills on several of the chapters here.

Much of the research and writing on this book was done during visits to various other universities, including the Universities of Nebraska, Texas, Indiana, Alabama, and the University of Oxford (Corpus Christi and University Colleges) in England, and Santa Anna University in Pisa, Italy, and I thank my friends at each of them for their good support. But by far the greatest labors occurred at the University of South Carolina, and the project would not have seen the light of day but for the substantial and unremitting encouragement and support of John Montgomery, now Dean Emeritus, over many years. Thanks also to Associate Dean Philip Lacy for his enthusiastic and creative support of the project for many years in untold ways.

A number of scholars deserve special comment. Thanks to Michael Green for guidance on topical coverage and for helpful comments on the prescrription drug design defect materials; Mary Davis and Richard Ausness for their helpful review of the preemption materials; and Jim Gash for his suggestions on the ever-mushrooming topic of punitive damages. I am indebted to my coauthors of various other books from which I draw, including Dan Dobbs, Robert Keeton, John Montgomery, Mike Green, Stuart Madden, Mary Davis, Page Keeton, and William Prosser. The early products liability scholarship of the latter two, together with that of John Wade, Fleming James, Dix Noel, and others, tilled this field of law with inspiration in the early years in preparation for its explosion in modern times.

My special appreciation goes to Stuart Madden, Mary Davis, and West, for allowing me to place early versions of certain chapters intended eventually for this volume first in Madden & Owen on Products Liability. In addition, many paragraphs in this volume began as paragraphs in journal articles I published elsewhere over the years, and I thank those journals for the return of my prior musings. Most recently, I am grateful to various journals for publishing certain sections of this book as articles: *Special Defenses in Products Liability Law*, 70 Mo. L. Rev. __ (No. 1, 2005); *Proof of Product Defect*, 93 Ky. L.J. __ (No. 3, 2005); *Proving Negligence in Modern Products Liability Litigation*, 36 Ariz. St. L. Rev. __ (No. 3, Fall 2004); *Inherent Product Hazards*, 93 Ky. L.J. __ (No. 2, 2004); *The Puzzle of Comment j*, 55 Hastings L.J. 1377 (2004); *Federal Preemption of Products Liability Claims*, 55 S.C. L. Rev. 411 (2003); *A Decade of Daubert*, 80 Denver U. L. Rev. 345 (2003); *Manufacturing Defects*, 54 S.C. L. Rev. 851 (2002); *Products Liability: User Misconduct Defenses*, 52 S.C. L. Rev. 1 (2000); *Products Liability Law in America*, 11 Danno e Responsabilita 1999 (Italian trans.); *Products Liability Law Restated*, 49 S.C. L. Rev. 273 (1998); and *American Products Liability Law Restated*, 6 Consumer L.J. 161 (1998).

Abroad, several scholars in particular stand out for special thanks—Geraint Howells, John Miller, Richard Goldberg, Jane Stapleton, Peter Cane, and Martin Matthews. The first four, I thank for providing me (as others) with an insightful body of scholarship on international products liability law which has helped to shrink the globe. They also deserve special thanks for providing helpful comments on the section entitled "foreign law." I am particularly in the debt of the latter three for their support at the University of Oxford, now quite long ago, which gave me the opportunity to explore the moral foundations of this field of law rather than working, as my friends at West might have preferred, more directly on this book. In addition, my thanks go to Giovanni Comandé of Santa Anna University, Pisa, Italy, Erwin Deutsch of the University of Göttingen, Germany, and Jean-Sebastien Borghetti, of the Université Panthéon-Sorbonne (Paris I), for providing portals for my inquiries into the products liability law of mainland Europe. To Akio Morishima of Nagoya University, and Michitaro Urakawa of Waseda University, I am grateful for a first-hand view of Japan's march into modern products liability law.

Closer to home, I am grateful to Rebecca Maxwell and Sara Krome for many hours of help on the intricacies of computer research and WordPerfect, from WP5.1 to WP11.0. For many years of discussions on the intricacies of products liability law and theory, I am indebted to John Montgomery, Bob Felix (who also critiqued the discussion here on choice of law), and, for his tireless (if not entirely successful) efforts to guide me in the rudiments of how economic theory applies to tort law, John Lopatka. And I should thank Pat Hubbard, I suppose, for the reference to the butterfly.

My particular thanks go to West for its patience while this hornbook project was deferred as I explored the philosophical foundations of tort and products liability law, then was bound up in the products liability and other tort law Restatement projects, and, finally, contributed to a multi-volume treatise on the topic of this book. In particular, my thanks go to the late Roger Noreen who, with his characteristically gracious enthusiasm, endorsed the project of a then-young commentator in this then-new field of law; next to John Hodson, whose persistent prodding was instrumental in keeping this project's first stage moving forward; and, finally, to Doug Powell, who, with genial encouragement, helped nurture the project of an aging commentator to its eventual completion. I should also note my appreciation for the good efforts of Roxanne Birkel and Louis Higgins in production and marketing, respectively.

Acknowledgments would not be complete without my recognition of the many talented commentators, now scattered about the globe, whose mushrooming scholarship on all aspects of products liability law has played a major role in defining and enriching this legal discipline. In particular, I should note the debt I share with others for the major contributions to the development of this field of law made by James Henderson and Aaron Twerski—not only in their prodigious scholarship, but in their monumental Restatement (Third) of Torts: Products Liability, a project deftly managed by ALI Director Geoffrey Hazzard, that consumed a large proportion of the Reporters' labors over much of the 1990s. Their overarching vision on the structure and essence of products liability law, though inevitably controversial, has already begun to reshape this field of law for the new millennium.

My largest debt is to my family, first and foremost Joan, Wendy, Ethan, and Megan, and also to my golfing buddy, Don, all of whom long and cheerfully ceded unto me this project's most vital ingredient, boundless time.

\*

# WESTLAW® Overview

*Products Liability Law* offers a detailed and comprehensive treatment of the basic rules, principles, and issues relating to the law of products liability. To supplement the information contained in this book, you can access Westlaw, West's computer-assisted legal research service. Westlaw contains a broad array of legal resources, including case law, statutes, expert commentary, current developments, and various other types of information.

Learning how to use these materials effectively will enhance your legal research abilities. To help you coordinate the information in the book with your Westlaw research, this volume contains an appendix listing Westlaw databases, search techniques, and sample problems.

The instructions and features described in this Westlaw overview are based on accessing Westlaw via westlaw.com® at **www.westlaw.com**.

THE PUBLISHER

\*

# Summary of Contents

\*

# Table of Contents

## PART III.  CAUSATION

## PART IV.  DEFENSES

## PART V.  SPECIAL ISSUES

# Abbreviated Citations

**2 Am. Law Prod. Liab. 3d**

American Law of Products Liability 3d

**Anderson on the UCC; Lawrence's Anderson on the UCC**

Ronald Anderson, Anderson on the Uniform Commercial Code (3d ed. 1994-1997); Lary Lawrence, Anderson on the Uniform Commercial Code (3d ed. 2001-02 rev. ed.)

**Clark and Smith, Product Warranties 2d**

Barkley Clark and Christopher Smith, The Law of Product Warranties (2d ed. 2002)

**Dobbs, Law of Torts**

Dan B. Dobbs, The Law of Torts (2000)

**Frumer and Friedman, Products Liability**

Louis R. Frumer, Melvin I. Friedman, and Cary Stewart Sklaren, Products Liability

**Harper, James, and Gray, Law of Torts**

Fowler V. Harper, Fleming James, Jr., and Oscar S. Gray, The Law of Torts (2d ed. 1986)

**Hawkland, UCC Series**

William D. Hawkland, Uniform Commercial Code Series (CBC)

**Madden & Owen on Products Liability**

David G. Owen, M. Stuart Madden, and Mary J. Davis, Madden & Owen on Products Liability (3d ed. 2000)

**McCormick on Evidence**

McCormick on Evidence (John Strong 5th ed. 1999)

**Products Liability Restatement**

Restatement (Third) of Torts: Products Liability (1998)

## Restatement (3d) Torts: Liability for Physical Harm

Restatement (Third) of Torts: Liability for Physical Harm (Tentative Drafts)

## Prosser and Keeton on Torts

W. Page Keeton, Dan B. Dobbs, Robert E. Keeton, and David G. Owen, Prosser and Keeton on the Law of Torts (5th ed. 1984)

## White and Summers, UCC

James J. White and Robert S. Summers, Uniform Commercial Code (5th Student ed. 2000) and (5th Pract. ed. 2002)

# PRODUCTS LIABILITY LAW

*

# Chapter 1

# INTRODUCTION

*Table of Sections*

---

## § 1.1 PRODUCTS LIABILITY LAW

Products liability law governs liability for the sale or other commercial transfer of a product that causes harm because it was defective or its properties were falsely represented. While this definition is at once too narrow and too broad, it captures the great bulk of cases normally viewed as falling under the "products liability" umbrella, and not too many more. The definition is too narrow, for example, because it does not include a limited category of cases at the fringe of products liability law that involve various types of improper marketing. And the definition is too broad because it is defined in terms of "harm," whereas products liability law generally includes only claims for personal injury, death, and property damage; many cases involving purely commercial loss—such as profits lost by an industrial enterprise when a defect in a punch press halts production—often are viewed more properly as commercial contractual disputes rather than as "products liability" cases. And no doubt the definition here includes other types of cases that fall outside this area of law and excludes others that properly belong within this legal category. But this field of law is new, with borders still in flux, so the definition given here is good enough for now.

### Product Safety Law Distinguished

What products liability law is *not* is "product safety" law. "Products liability" and "product safety" are phrases used to describe the law that broadly covers product-related accidents and illnesses. A central issue in both products liability law and product safety law is establishing how products should be classified as "excessively" or "unduly" hazardous, "unreasonably" dangerous, or "defective." Both areas of law seek to reduce the toll of accidents from such hazards, to improve product safety. But there they begin to diverge.

1

### Product Safety Law

The law of product safety is *regulatory* law—the systems of rules established by legislatures and administrative agencies of federal, state, and occasionally municipal governments to regulate the safety of products sold to the public. Product safety law operates *ex ante*, seeking to prevent product-caused accidents and diseases before they occur.

Municipal authorities regulate the safety of certain building products through building codes and sometimes prohibit the sale of miscellaneous other types of dangerous products. At the state level, departments of health, employment safety, fire boards, consumer protection and other agencies administer safety laws on a variety of diverse products, such as glue, architectural glass, industrial tools and machinery, fireworks, mattresses, refrigerators, household chemicals, life preservers, power tools, toys, elevators, BB guns, sling shots, unvented gas heaters, food and drugs, blood, plastic bags and, in Connecticut (until not too long ago), used hats.[1] These state and local laws have aptly been described as "a hodgepodge of tragedy-inspired responses" to the product safety problem and are generally characterized by "narrow scope, diffuse jurisdiction, minuscule budgets, absence of enforcement, mild sanctions, and casual administration."[2]

Product safety law at the federal level is much more significant, although regulation even at this level has so far proved to be of questionable effectiveness in many areas. Nevertheless, various federal agencies do exert considerable control over product safety on a national scale. The Consumer Product Safety Commission (CPSC) has broad jurisdiction to regulate consumer product safety under the Consumer Product Safety Act[3] and various other federal product safety statutes.[4] Authority for other major safety regulation is vested in the National Highway Traffic Safety Administration (NHTSA) of the Department of Transportation,[5] the Food and Drug Administration (FDA) of the Department of Health and Human Services,[6] the Occupational Safety and Health Administration (OSHA) of the Department of Labor,[7] the Federal Aviation Administration (FAA) of the Department of Transportation,[8] and the Environmental Protection Agency (EPA).[9] These and other

---

**§ 1.1**

**1.** Conn. Gen. Stat. Ann. § 19–425, repealed.

**2.** Final Report, National Commission on Product Safety 2, 81–88 (1970). Municipal laws of these types often are administered more through education than enforcement. See id.

**3.** 15 U.S.C. § 2051 et seq. See, e.g., Southland Mower Co. v. Consumer Product Safety Commission, 619 F.2d 499 (5th Cir. 1980) (upholding CPSC design requirement for walk-behind power lawn mowers).

**4.** These include the Federal Hazardous Substances Act, 15 U.S.C. § 1261 et seq.; the Poison Prevention Packaging Act, 15 U.S.C. § 1471 et seq.; the Flammable Fabrics Act, 15 U.S.C. § 1191 et seq., and the Refrigerator Safety Act, 15 U.S.C. § 1211 et seq.

**5.** This agency administers the National Traffic and Motor Vehicle Safety Act of 1966, 15 U.S.C. § 1381 et seq.

**6.** This agency administers the Federal Food, Drug, and Cosmetic Act, 21 U.S.C. § 301 et seq.

**7.** This agency administers the Occupational Safety and Health Act of 1970, 29 U.S.C. § 651 et seq.

**8.** This agency administers the safety provisions of the Federal Aviation Act of 1958, 49 U.S.C. § 1301 et seq.

**9.** This agency administers the Toxic Substances Control Act, 15 U.S.C. § 2601 et seq., the Federal Insecticide, Fungicide, and Rodenticide Act, 7 U.S.C. § 135 et seq., and the Clean Air Act, particularly the regulation of asbestos removal in 42 U.S.C. § 7412.

federal agencies also regulate the safety of pesticides, fungicides, meat, poultry, eggs, perishable agricultural commodities, railroad safety appliances, firearms, cigarette labeling, and boat safety. Federal regulation of product safety has an impact on products liability litigation in a number of ways considered at various points in this book.

### Products Liability Law

In contrast to product safety law, products liability law governs the private *litigation* of product accidents. Operating *ex post*, after a product accident has occurred, its rules define the legal responsibility of sellers and other commercial transferors of products for damages resulting from product defects and misrepresentations about a product's safety or performance capabilities.

A typical products liability case involves a claim for damages against the manufacturer or retailer of a product by a person injured while using the product. The plaintiff seeks to prove that the injury was caused by some deficiency in the way the product was made or marketed—that the product was in some manner "defective" or falsely described. In addition, the plaintiff will attempt to demonstrate that he or she was using the product properly or at least foreseeably. Typically, damage claims include medical expenses, disability and disfigurement, pain and suffering, lost earnings and earning capacity, perhaps emotional harm, and possibly some kind of property damage, perhaps to the product itself. The defendant usually attempts to show that the product was *not* defective—that it was in fact reasonably made and properly marketed. Further, the defendant often seeks to establish that the plaintiff's injuries resulted principally because the plaintiff or some other person improperly used the product, or perhaps that something other than the product caused the harm. These are the central issues in a typical products liability case.

Some products liability cases involve transactions other than a sale. Products are sometimes merely leased, licensed, or simply bailed. Or the injury-producing "product" may be something other than a typical, mass-produced chattel—such as a house, a toxic substance, a recipe, electricity, a truckload of sand, an internet game, transfused blood, or a poisonous spider in a pair of pants. Or the defendant may be a wholesaler, a component part manufacturer, a successor corporation, an employer, a publisher, a dentist, a trademark owner, or a plumber. All of these examples raise questions about the outer boundaries of products liability law—how to define a "product"; how to decide what kinds of defendants and transactions should be covered by products liability principles; and how to draw lines between products liability and such overlapping fields of law as professional malpractice, environmental law, and workers' compensation.[10]

These are some of the issues of products liability law, the topic of this book.

---

**10.** As discussed below, the difficulty of drawing boundaries of this type has led some scholars to question whether "products liability" really defines a field of law at all.

### Mixed Sources of Products Liability Law

Products liability law is full of mixtures. It is a mixture of tort law—negligence, strict liability in tort, and deceit—and of the contract law of sales—mostly warranty. It is a mixture of common law, now mostly on its tort side, and statutory law, generally on its contract side—notably the Uniform Commercial Code. In addition, many state legislatures (and Congress, to a lesser extent) have enacted products liability "reform" acts which address products liability matters, often functionally, apart from tort and contract. Because of these hybrid characteristics of products liability law, plaintiffs in such actions often have a variety of available claims. Negligence, breach of implied warranty, and strict liability in tort are all based on the notion that something was wrong with the product, that it was unduly dangerous or "defective." Remedies for breach of express warranty and fraud (and possibly other forms of tortious misrepresentation) may be available when a product is more dangerous than it was said to be, even if it was not defective or unfit by standards of negligence, implied warranty, or strict liability in tort.

As seen throughout this book, many of the most difficult products liability issues in modern products liability law spring from the doctrinal mixture of tort and contract. Just to name a few of the many issues of this type, the clash of tort and contract doctrines has generated perplexing questions about the standard of liability, the test for design defectiveness, defenses, statutes of limitations, and recoverable damages.

### The "Field" of Products Liability Law

The discussion so far has assumed that products liability is a proper field of law. Yet, the fact that products liability law involves a blend of tort and contract doctrines raises a question of whether it really is a field of law at all, or whether products liability might best be viewed merely as a hodgepodge category that borrows principles from true fields of law (like tort and contract) and applies them to problems involving the sale of defective and falsely represented chattels that cause harm. A number of respected scholars have made the claim, mostly some time ago, that products liability is only one of many types of litigation existing inside tort (and warranty) law—that it is not a separate field of law, and that efforts to make it so should be abandoned.[11]

**11.** One of the first challenges to products liability as a field of law was by a warranty law scholar, Richard Speidel, critically reviewing W.P. Keeton, D. Owen, and J. Montgomery, Products Liability and Safety—Cases and Materials (1980), Book Review, 33 Vand. L. Rev. 813 (1980) (questioning whether products liability is a legitimate topic for a law school course, and concluding that "[t]he common law string in products cases barely holds its own weight and is in danger of breaking"). One of the first tort law scholars in the modern era to raise serious questions about the viability of products liability as a legitimate legal category was William Powers. See

Powers, A Modest Proposal to Abandon Strict Products Liability, 1991 U. Ill. L. Rev. 639, 639 (1991). Jane Stapleton has most vigorously articulated this thesis. See J. Stapleton, Product Liability ch. 13, at 341 et seq. (1994); Stapleton, Bugs in Anglo–American Products Liability, 53 S.C. L. Rev. 1225, 1254 (2002) (questioning "why in the Restatement Third and the Directive we tolerate a special tort rule for injuries that happened to have been caused by commercially supplied products," observing that "there does not seem to be any particular moral, economic, or social reason why the victims of such injuries should have

Much power resides inside this argument, and determining when a sub-field in fact becomes its own field of law, or when it *should* be viewed as having achieved this status, is a complex project. It certainly is true that products liability law could have developed perfectly well within the law of obligations which has quite comfortably contained both tort and warranty law for at least two thousand years.[12] There is no good reason why negligence doctrine from the law of torts, and (if less comfortably) implied warranty principles from the law of contracts, cannot handle design and warnings cases with perfect ease. Nor do strong reasons exist why warranty and strict liability in tort cannot smoothly continue to regulate the law on manufacturing defects, nor why tortious misrepresentation, together with express warranty, cannot well manage the treatment of misstatements of product safety. But the substantial overlap of tort and contract rules in all these areas continues to stir up problems, and the doctrinal niceties of the two proud branches of the law of obligations—niceties that deserve respect—continue in products liability cases to be cast aside by attempts to force products liability issues into the tort or contract tents where such matters sometimes do not fit. For these reasons, many courts, scholars, state legislatures, and the American Law Institute in the *Restatement (Third) of Torts: Products Liability* all have begun a major shift away from conceptualizing products liability problems as "tort" or "contract" and toward viewing these problems as functionally distinct.[13]

An enormous amount of products liability law has accumulated in recent years, just in terms of case decisions—roughly 15,000 products liability decisions of some significance now reported in the United States.[14] While the sheer number of cases on a topic ought not alone

been accorded any more special treatment than the victims of medical misadventures or environmental disasters," and concluding that "the creation of special rules for injuries associated with commercially supplied products warps our laws of obligation for little if any benefit and blinkers us to important common themes that run through all personal injury cases generally"). See also Bernstein, Restatement Redux, 48 Vand. L. Rev. 1663, 1681 (1995) (in reviewing Stapleton's Product Liability, sympathetically acknowledging Professor Stapleton's criticisms of the incoherence of the products liability topic, and observing that even "the Third Restatement lacks a conception of products liability as a discrete area of the law"). *But see* Bernstein, How Can a Product Be Liable?, 45 Duke L.J. 1, 4, 83 (1995) (drawn to the criticism of products liability as a legal category, but ultimately, powerfully, rejecting it).

**12.** See § 1.2, below.

**13.** See, e.g., Bernstein, How Can a Product Be Liable?, 45 Duke L.J. 1, 4 (1995) (acknowledging, but rejecting, the argument that products liability is not a

proper, discrete field of law, and arguing that how we make and what we do with products define ourselves and our cultures in a manner that gives content to this field of law). "Too limber for the Procrustean beds that commentators build, products liability continually reasserts its autonomy.... Once acknowledged to be an independent doctrine, products liability can enlighten and provoke." Id. at 83. See also Owen, The Moral Foundations of Products Liability Law: Toward First Principles, 68 Notre Dame L. Rev. 427 (1993). See generally Reimann, Liability for Defective Products at the Beginning of the Twenty–First Century: Emergence of a Worldwide Standard?, 51 Am. J. Comp. L. 751, 753 n.3 (2003) (noting "the vast and fast-growing mass of products liability literature").

**14.** The approximation here is based on an August 2004 study of the three comprehensive products liability reporters in the United States: the CCH Products Liability Reporter, Westlaw, and Lexis. At that time, the CCH reporter, which includes most significant products liability court opinions, contained about 12,000 decisions. The Westlaw and Lexis products liability databases included far more cases at that time:

determine whether an independent field of law truly has emerged (thousands of vehicular accidents do not a "field" make), the mushrooming complexity of products liability rules and principles, of doctrine and sub-doctrine; the increasingly distinctive "products liability" way of thinking about the goals, principles, and doctrine for resolving cases of this type; and the increasing number of products liability statutes enacted by the states, all combine with the enormous amount of litigation on these sets of products liability issues to suggest that this area of the law might appropriately be called a "field." In addition, beginning in the 1960s, scholars and practitioners increasingly began to view products liability as a separate field of law and practice. Finally, this area of the law has become codified and internationalized. Many American states, and many nations (and the European Community), have enacted statutes recognizing products liability disputes as raising distinctive problems that require specialized treatment, and "products liability law as a subject in its own right has spread throughout the world."[15]

There simply is no arguing that products liability draws heavily from tort, contract, and other fields of law. Yet, its separate treatment by courts, academics, practitioners, and legislatures around the world dispels the view that modern products liability simply is bits and pieces of other fields of law, that it has no separate identity of its own. Academics may argue this point until the cows come home, but products liability is a field of law distinct unto itself.

### The Moral Foundations of Products Liability Law

Products liability law lies at the center of the modern world. To a large extent, persons accomplish their individual and collective objectives, and relate to one another, through the products of technology—

Westlaw had about 24,000 cases in its multi-state products liability case database (MPL–CS), and over 25,000 cases in its federal products liability cases database (FPL–CS), for a total of nearly 50,000 cases; the Lexis database for federal and state products liability decisions (MEGAPL) reportedly included about 95,000 cases. Our review of each of the first 150 cases reported by these online services in August 2004 revealed that most cases in the databases addressed procedural matters almost exclusively, were trivial, or were not a products liability case of any type. In short, the products liability databases of Westlaw and Lexis were both vastly overinclusive (which may be necessary to the proper design of a comprehensive electronic database for a legal category). In all, our review of each case in the Westlaw sample revealed that slightly more than 30% were significant substantive law decisions, and our review of each case in the Lexis sample revealed that slightly more than 15% were significant substantive law decisions. Extrapolating these yields to the total databases suggests that the Westlaw products liability databas-

es then contained about 15,100, and Lexis about 14,500, significant substantive law cases. The 15,000 approximation may be a little high because our bias was to err on inclusion when in doubt on whether to classify a decision as involving a significant discussion of a substantive issue of products liability law. Because our sample size was quite small, and because our criteria for excluding "insignificant" cases were subjective, our results should be viewed as rough approximations. Nevertheless, a consideration of all this data suggests to us that 15,000 is a reasonable estimate of the number of significant products liability decisions reported in the United States as of August 2004.

**15.** Reimann, Liability for Defective Products at the Beginning of the Twenty–First Century: Emergence of a Worldwide Standard?, 51 Am. J. Comp. L. 751, 756–57 (2003) (concluding that products liability is a separate area of private law because of specialized legislation governing it and recognition of it by scholars and practitioners "as a particular field with (at least) its own rules and principles").

automobiles, punch presses, drain cleaners, tractors, prescription drugs, frozen dinners, tennis rackets, perfumes, computers, and airplanes (civilian and military).[16] Matters concerning the creation and exchange of such products of science and technology are addressed by the law of property, patents, contracts, and commerce. Products liability law instead concerns the consequences of modern science and technology gone awry—when products, or the interactions between people and their products, fail.

But products liability law deals with matters of much greater import than merely the relationship between people and their machines. This rather sterile conception of the subject matter has dominated the thinking about products liability law since it arose in modern form four decades in the past. When a person is injured by a product, the principal question of interest in products liability law is whether the product was too dangerous, according to some standard of product safety. This focus of modern products liability law expressly upon the products—both the one which caused the injury, and some hypothetical one of proper safety—thus tends to direct the liability issue into a barren, technologically-based determination.

Yet the most essential question in any products liability case is not whether certain engineering, production, or informational psychology standards were met or breached. Rather, the relationship between the maker of a product and the victim of a product accident implicates fundamental issues of moral philosophy. By choosing to expose product users and others to certain types and degrees of risk, manufacturers appropriate to themselves certain interests in safety and bodily integrity that may belong to those other persons. Similarly, by choosing to purchase products with certain inherent risks or by choosing to use such products in certain risky ways, and then by choosing to make claims against manufacturers for harm resulting from such risks or uses, victims of product accidents seek to appropriate to themselves economic interests that may belong to manufacturers and other consumers. Both situations involve important questions of how people should treat one another. Ethical and political theory thus have much to say about whether responsibility for product accidents lies (in part or in whole) with the manufacturer, the user, or the victim. At bottom, product accidents are moral—not technological—events.[17]

## Products Liability Resources

Many works have been written on products liability law, and the most useful scholarship often resides in law journals. Following is a list of some of the most helpful general reference works in this field of law.

**16.** This idea is developed in Owen, Products Liability: Principles of Justice for the 21st Century, 11 Pace L. Rev. 63, 64–66 (1990).

**17.** These observations are adapted from Owen, The Moral Foundations of Products Liability Law: Toward First Principles, 68 Notre Dame L. Rev. 427, 429–30 (1993).

*American Law*

**Frumer, Friedman, and Sklaren, Products Liability.** Any discussion of products liability resources must begin with Louis Frumer and Melvin Friedman's classic treatise on products liability law, published by Matthew Bender. First published in 1960, Frumer and Friedman originally was structured around the law of negligence (and, to a lesser extent, warranty law). As products liability was redefined by strict liability in tort and other modern principles during the 1970s and 1980s, the organization of this treatise hindered its development. But Cary Sklaren took on the editorship during the 1980s, and the treatise since that time has been reinvigorated, and much of it rewritten. Now containing 11 volumes, Frumer, Friedman, and Sklaren has once again regained its rightful place as the leading treatise in the field. It explores products liability law and litigation widely, in great depth, and with sensitivity, such that courts and lawyers ignore this treatise at their peril.

**American Law of Products Liability 3d.** This is another comprehensive treatise on products liability law that has some helpful, often exhaustive, treatments of a vast range of products liability topics. Under the general editorship of John Hodson, the American Law of Products Liability 3d, which now contains 25 volumes, is published by Thomson–West. Many topics are addressed in encyclopedic fashion, and the discussions on some subjects are more complete and useful than those in other treatises. On Westlaw, the American Law of Products Liability 3d is available at ALPL.

**Madden & Owen on Products Liability Law (3d ed. 2000).** This is the successor to William Kimble and Robert Lesher, Products Liability (1979), and M. Stuart Madden, Products Liability (2d ed. 1988). Published by Thomson–West, and authored by Stuart Madden, Mary Davis, and myself, Madden & Owen provides a short treatise treatment of a wide range of products liability and litigation topics. This 3–volume treatise contains two volumes of substantive discussion and one volume containing products liability statutes, Restatements, and similar resource materials. On Westlaw, Madden and Owen is available at MOPL.

**Shapo, The Law of Products Liability (4th ed. 2002).** This scholarly 2–volume work by Marshall Shapo, published by CCH, examines the body of products liability jurisprudence through the distinctive lens of America's senior academic statesman in this field. Often more theoretical than the other treatises, it presents a cultural window on how society addresses product accidents that provides insightful, academic perspectives on this field of law.

**Restatement (Third) of Torts: Products Liability (1998).** This invaluable digest and restatement of the principles of modern American products liability law was written by two of the field's leading scholars since the 1970s, James Henderson and Aaron Twerski. Their Reporters' Notes contain a wealth of scholarship on the major issues in the field. Though viewed by some as driven by a "reform" agenda, many of the more recent products liability decisions adopt, reject, and otherwise address its various provisions. This monumental work, published in 1998 after five years of intense debate, may be the single most important resource in this field.

**Products Liability Reporter (CCH).** This reporter contains short summaries of the law and carries full reports of most important cases and products liability statutes. Prior to Westlaw's development of online research, this reporter was an invaluable resource for a products liability lawyer. Because it provides full and timely reports of important cases in hard copy, this Reporter remains a helpful resource for those interested in staying current in this field.

**BNA Product Safety and Liability Reporter.** This reporter summarizes some of the most important judicial decisions, reports on various product safety agency regulatory matters, and contains the full text of safety statutes and regulations. Always a helpful way to stay current on product safety as well as products liability law, this reporter's usefulness has been enhanced by its availability online.

**Casebooks.** The American casebooks are David Owen, John Montgomery, and Mary Davis, Products Liability and Safety (Foundation Press, 4th ed. 2004); James Henderson and Aaron Twerski, Products Liability (Aspen, 5th ed. 2004); David Fischer, Michael Green, William Powers, and Joseph Sanders, Products Liability (West 3d ed. 2002); Jerry Phillips, Nicolas Terry, Frank Vandall, and Ellen Wertheimer, Products Liability (Matthew Bender, 2d ed. 2002). See also M. Kotler, Products Liability and Basic Tort Law (Carolina Academic Press, 2004).

**Other books.** Earlier works of significance, among others, include A. Weinstein, A. Twerski, H. Piehler, and W. Donaher, Products Liability and the Reasonably Safe Product (John Wiley, 1978); R. Epstein, Modern Products Liability Law (Quorum, 1980); P. Sherman, Products Liability (Shepard's/McGraw-Hill, 1981); and F. Vandall, Strict Liability (Greenwood, 1989). There is also a large collection of useful books that provide a more focused look at various aspects of products liability law, litigation, governmental regulation of product safety, and the science and engineering of product safety. There are several very useful state-specific books on products liability and litigation which would be an important resource for lawyers practicing products liability law in such a state. See, e.g., W. Powers, Texas Products Liability Law (Butterworths, 2nd ed. 1992); J. Thorpe, D. Venderbush, and J. Neal, Georgia Products Liability, 3d (Harrison, 2002); R. Eades, Products Liability—The Law in Kentucky (Harrison, 2003); D. King and M. Murray, Missouri Products Liability, 2d (Harrison, 2002); J. McGoldrick and F. Smith, New Jersey Product Liability Law (N.J. L.J. 1997); M. Weinberger, New York Products Liability, 2d (Lawyers Coop., 1982); G. Spahn, R. Draim, D. Carr, S. Otero, and M. Levin, Virginia Law of Products Liability with Forms, 2d (2004, Harrison).

A concise overview of the field is J. Phillips and D. Owen, Products Liability in a Nutshell (Thomson–West, 7th ed. 2005).

### Foreign Law

**Stapleton, Product Liability (1994).** This is Jane Stapleton's scholarly study of products liability law, published by Butterworth. Written by one of the world's great scholars of products liability law, this remains the best critical, theoretical inquiry into this field of law.

**Miller and Goldberg, Product Liability (2d ed. 2004).** This comprehensive, modern, enormously useful one-volume treatise was written by two of Britain's leading products liability scholars, C. John Miller and Richard Goldberg. Published by Oxford, this excellent book provides helpful comparisons between British and American developments in the field.

**Howells, ed., The Law of Product Liability (2000).** This collection of studies on various aspects of the law, litigation, and regulation of products liability and product safety is edited by Geraint Howells, one of Europe's leading comparative law experts on products liability and consumer law. The essays in this useful volume extend beyond substantive products liability law to jurisdiction, choice of law, class actions, and the regulation of product safety.

**Whittaker, Liability for Products (2005).** This forthcoming book, to be published by Oxford, is written by Simon Whittaker, one of Oxford University's leading scholars. As yet unseen, this book on English, French, and European law promises to be an important work.

**European Law.** On European law, the reader is directed to Application of the EC Product Liability Directive–Quinquennial Reports to the Council. A vast, immensely valuable portal into European case and statutory law is available electronically, in English, from the British Institute on International and Comparative Law, at the BIICL Product Liability and Product Safety Database: www.biicl.org.

**Foreign Law—In General.** Canadian products liability resources include Stephen Waddams, Products liability (Carswell/Thomson, 4th ed. 2002); Dean Edgell, Product Liability Law in Canada (Butterworths, LexisNexis Canada, 2000); and Lawrence Theall, et al., Product Liability: Canadian Law and Practice (Canada Law Book, looseleaf with annual supplements). Many other sources of European and other foreign products liability law are cited in the section on that topic.[18]

## § 1.2  EARLY LAW

Products liability law, as a broad and coherent set of legal principles for the recovery of product-caused harm, is of recent origin. As late as 1955, one commentator remarked, "Products liability does not yet rank as a term of art in the courts of law."[1] With the exception of a few cases involving fraud and the sale of defective medicines and food, the appearance of products liability cases in the law reports coincides with the rise of the Industrial Revolution in the late 1800s. By 1900, such cases began to appear with some frequency. Despite its recency in Anglo–American law, the roots of modern products liability law reach deep into history, as far back as the law of ancient Rome.[2] The early origins of products liability law are mostly located in the tort-contract hybrid warranties of quality, both express and implied, although there are early signs of seller liability in negligence as well.

---

**18.** See § 1.4, below.

**§ 1.2**

**1.** Wilson, Products Liability (pt. 1), 43 Cal. L. Rev. 614 (1955).

**2.** The pertinent, original texts of Roman law, the British Sales of Goods Act, and the Uniform Sales Act, are reproduced in Francis de Zulueta, The Roman Law of Sale—Introduction and Select Texts 61–222 (reprint from corr. 1st ed. 1966)(1945).

## Roman Law

The products liability law of ancient Rome lies shrouded in the mists of history.[3] Neither the law of tort (*delict*) nor the law of sales (*emptio venditio*) provided much assistance to the disappointed purchaser under the early classical law as set forth in the Twelve Tables of 450 B.C.: "The original principle [although not the maxim] of the civil law was *caveat emptor* . . . [let the buyer beware]. The seller was not liable for any defects in the thing unless he had by *stipulation* expressly undertaken such liability."[4] Beginning roughly 300–200 B.C., however, some basic principles of seller responsibility for certain aspects of certain sales began to emerge, and the law of sales continued to develop, albeit haltingly, through its flowering in Justinian's *Digest* in 533 A.D.

The law of tort was quite undeveloped in early Roman law and appears to have afforded little, if any, protection to a person injured by a defective product. By the time of Justinian in the sixth century A.D., however, product sellers were being held responsible for certain losses attributable to their failure to exercise the greatest of care.[5] The standard of care for sellers as it eventually developed was quite rigorous: "[N]egligence due to the absence of the greatest care is a failure to observe such diligence as a good man of business or a very prudent man would exercise."[6] A person who held himself out as an expert in his occupation was deemed to be culpably negligent if he failed to use such skill.[7] Liability in negligence, in Roman law, was offset by the victim's own contributory negligence.[8]

The Roman law of fraud (*dolus*), in addition to covering express statements known to be false, broadly included the mere failure to disclose to the buyer such latent defects as the seller knew the product to possess.[9] Apart from fraud, the seller was also responsible for a product's

**3.** Attempting to piece together a Roman law of products liability is fraught with difficulty. Especially for the early law of Rome, legal sources are few (and some unreliable), incomplete, and ambiguous, and scholars of Roman law disagree on various aspects of the nature and extent of liability for losses associated with defective products. For an excellent scholarly inquiry illustrating the necessary guesswork involved in attempting to unravel the nature and scope of recovery for defective products under the various Roman law forms of action, see Honoré, The History of the Aedilitian Actions from Roman to Roman–Dutch Law, in Studies in the Roman Law of Sale 132 (David Daube ed., reprint 1977)(1959). Helpful summaries of the Roman law of sales are J. A. C. Thomas, Textbook of Roman Law 15, 16, 286–88 (1976), and Francis de Zulueta, The Roman Law of Sale—Introduction and Select Texts 46–51 (reprint from corr. 1st ed. 1966) (1945). See W. Buckland, A Text–Book of Roman Law from Augustus to Justinian 491–94 (3d ed. Stein rev. 1966); R. Lee, The Elements of Roman Law 13, 15, 314–16 (4th ed. 1956).

**4.** Barry Nicholas, An Introduction to Roman Law 181 (1962).

**5.** See Charles Phineas Sherman, 2 Roman Law in the Modern World 345 (2d ed., reprint 1994) (1922).

**6.** Id. at 299 (citing *Digest* 19, 2, 25, § 7 and *Digest* 18, 6, 13). The extra-high standard of care for sellers in Roman law may be the origin of the modern doctrine that a product seller is bound to exercise care at the level of an expert in the field. This doctrine appears in modern American products liability law both in negligence, see, e.g., § 2.2, and "strict" products liability. See, e.g., Vassallo v. Baxter Healthcare Corp., 696 N.E.2d 909 (1998) (under Massachusetts' implied warranty of merchantability, that state's products liability doctrine akin to *Restatement (Second) of Torts* § 402A, manufacturers are "held to the standard of knowledge of an expert in the appropriate field").

**7.** " 'Want of skill is reckoned as negligence,' is the Roman jurist Gaius' famous interpretation of negligence." Sherman, above, at 382 (citing *Digest* 50, 17, 132; *Digest* 9, 2, 8).

**8.** Id. at 383 (citing *Digest* 50, 17, 203; *Digest* 9, 2, 9, § 4; J. Inst. 4, 3 § 5; Hunter, Roman Law 246–7).

**9.** "[D]uring the last century of the Republic the notion of *dolus* was extended to failure to conform to express promises of quality that were innocently made, whether by formal stipulation (*stipulatio*) or by other description of the product.[10] Liability for express misrepresentations were limited to factual assertions, however, and sellers were not responsible for "puffing" the quality of their wares.[11]

The developing law of an implied warranty of quality—akin to the modern notion of strict products liability for the sale of a defective product—is perhaps the most interesting aspect of the Roman law of products liability. From 367 B.C., the curule aediles were magistrates charged with policing the public markets. From the Edict of the Aediles,[12] which regulated the public sale of slaves and certain livestock, the aediles required that the seller warrant the soundness of the subject of the sale.[13] If the seller did not expressly so warrant, he was liable for the defects in any event, whether or not he was aware of them.[14] The extent to which this implied warranty of quality was extended beyond the sale of slaves and livestock prior to Justinian is entirely unclear.[15] Nevertheless, Justinian in his *Digest* announces a basic implied warranty of quality applicable to the sale of all products: "All sellers of all sorts of thing[s] are liable for defects."[16] This is a general rule of strict liability

cover both the statement by the seller that the thing sold possessed or did not possess some quality when he knew this was untrue and also the case when the seller knowingly concealed a defect." Honoré, above, at 135. See also Rogerson, Implied Warranty Against Latent Defects in Roman and English Law, in Studies in the Roman Law of Sale 112, 113 (David Daube ed., reprint 1977)(1959).

**10.** See Rogerson, above.

**11.** See, e.g., Honoré, above, at 141 (liability was restricted to "such statements or promises . . . which it is right to enforce as opposed to mere puffs or commendations for which it would be inappropriate to impose legal liability"). Justinian's *Digest* provides:

> What a seller says in order to puff his wares is to be considered neither as a statement nor as a promise. But if it was said in order to deceive the buyer, it must be held that, though here too there is no action for contravention of a statement or a promise, there is the action *de dolo*.

*Digest* 4, 3, 37, reprinted in de Zulueta, above, at 158.

**12.** The Aedilician Edict may have been promulgated in 199 B.C. See Honoré, above, at 134.

**13.** See Thomas, above, at 287.

**14.** See *Digest*, above, at 21, 1, 1, 1.

**15.** "[T]here are texts which indicate that the civil law was developing its own implied warranty of quality, outside, though in all probability influenced by the example of, the Edictal developments. The texts deal mainly with sales of land or its accessories, but there are others on movables. There is not a great deal of authority, and perhaps there was not any great need for a general warranty of quality." Rogerson, above, at 117–18 (footnotes omitted). Compare Sherman, above, at 347 n.55 (edictal provisions spread from slaves and cattle to all products in first century A.D.) with Honoré, above, at 139–40 (textual evidence for such surmise is thin).

**16.** Rogerson, above, at 115 (footnotes omitted)(relying on *Digest* 21, 1, 1, which provides in part: "Labeo writes that the edict of the curule aediles applies as well to sales of land as to sales of chattels inanimate or animate.")

*Digest* 21, 1, 1, 2 explains why sellers should be responsible for defects in their wares:

> The motive for the proposition of this edict is to defeat the artifices of sellers and to assist buyers whenever they are cheated by sellers. It is, however, to be understood that a seller, even though he was unaware of the existence of faults, . . . must nevertheless be held liable. Nor is this unfair; for the seller was in a position to inform himself on these matters, while to the buyer it makes no difference whether his deception is due to the seller's ignorance or to his guile.

*Digest* 21, 1, 1, 2, reprinted in de Zulueta, above at 139–140. Consider also *Digest* 21, 1, 63: "It should be understood that this edict relates only to sales, though to sales not of slaves only, but of everything else." Id. at 147.

for the sale of a defective product,[17] for "liability exists independently of the seller's knowledge of the defect and in Justinian's law extends to sales of all kinds of things."[18]

Responsibility for obvious defects in a product lay with the buyer, not with the seller. This was true even with respect to the seller's express assertions of product quality which might otherwise be interpreted as denying the existence of the defect.[19] Moreover, the parties could negate all warranty responsibility by express agreement.[20]

Damages at Roman law depended upon the basis of liability. If the buyer could establish fraud (*dolus*), which included the seller's failure to disclose a latent defect known to the seller, the buyer was entitled to full recovery of his consequential damages. To recover under the strict liability rule of breach of the implied warranty of quality, however, the buyer's remedies were more restricted[21]—to rescind the sale, within six months thereafter, or, within twelve months, to adjust the price to the actual value of the defective thing.[22]

### Early English Law

From the laws of Justinian to early medieval English law, the legal system degenerated from a moderately sophisticated system of sales law to one that was crude at best. Indeed, private law, under which an aggrieved purchaser might sue the seller for damages caused by defective

**17.** "I have not found in the texts any discussion whether a seller who could not reasonably discover the existence of the defect is excused. It seems to be universally thought that he was not.... [I]t may be thought that, by a gradual development, a seller became liable for defects whether he could have discovered them or not, a form of strict liability familiar in the case of a stipulation." Honoré, above, at 136 (footnote omitted).

**18.** Rogerson, above, at 113.

**19.** "[P]atent defects, as in modern legal systems, were taken to be accepted by the buyer and even express warranties were deemed not to cover them—if, for instance, a one-eyed dog was sold as sound, it was as a sound one-eyed dog." Thomas, above, at 286 (footnote omitted).

**20.** de Zulueta, above, at 51.

**21.** "The bases of Justinian's law seem to be [that] [t]here is fault, though not as serious as *dolus*, in not knowing the thing one sells. The buyer wants and is entitled to a thing as free from faults as it appears to be. The seller does not perform his side of the contract by supplying a faulty thing. The compilers, wishing for these reasons to create a general implied warranty against defects, did so by extending the principle of the Edict to cover all sales and effected a fusion of these principles with civil law fraud liability and the much more meager civil law liability in the absence of fraud,

making the award of consequential damages the feature differentiating between the liability of the fraudulent and the nonfraudulent seller." Rogerson, above, at 129–30.

**22.** See, e.g., Rogerson, above, at 123; Thomas, above, at 287. The basic distinction in damages available for the innocent sale of a defective product, on the one hand, and fraudulent nondisclosure of a defect, on the other, is described in Book 19, Tit. 1, Lex 13 of Justinian's *Digest* (533 A.D.):

> In the matter of damages in the action *ex empto* [*actio empti*] Julian, book 15, distinguishes between one who has sold with knowledge and one who has sold in ignorance. For, he says, the unwitting seller of a diseased herd or of unsound timber will have to make good in the action *ex empto* only the amount by which the price would have been reduced had the buyer known the truth, whereas, if the seller knew, but was silent and so deceived the buyer, he will have to make good to the buyer all losses that have fallen on him in consequence of the purchase: thus, if a house has collapsed owing to the unsound timber, he must make good the value of the house, or if the buyer's beasts have perished through being infected by the diseased herd, the damage sustained.

de Zulueta, above, at 124 (footnote omitted).

goods, was largely unknown in early England.[23] In time, guilds of the various crafts developed an elaborate system of localized criminal regulation of product quality by statutes which often developed into ordinances of the town. But such local statutes were designed principally to protect the public more from being cheated than from being injured. The late Roman law's insistence on the fair quality of goods sold was largely absent from the rustic local law of medieval England, but certain aspects of Justinian's law wended their way to a limited extent into early English law through the dominant role in society of the church, the scholars of which were trained in the civil law.

In the thirteenth century, Thomas Acquinas (1225?–1274 A.D.) in his *Summa Theologica*[24] outlined the basic mercantile obligations consistent with those expressed by Justinian in his *Digest*. Thus, the seller was bound to disclose secret flaws: it was sin and fraud to sell a product containing a latent defect known to the seller and not the buyer, and the sale was void. If the seller was unaware of the defect, the sale was not a sin, but the seller was obligated to return to the buyer any excess in the price attributable to the defect.[25] The buyer was responsible for obvious defects, according to Acquinas, so that the seller was not bound to disclose such defects from "any duty of justice," but to do so would reflect "the more exuberant virtue."[26]

Despite the obvious virtues of the ecclesiastical doctrine of seller responsibility for defective products, the early English common law over time developed the notion of *caveat emptor*, or "let the buyer beware." The buyer's duty to protect himself against obvious defects was extended to embrace an obligation to protect himself against hidden defects as well, and any lingering notion of an implied warranty of quality from the late Roman law withered away into oblivion in English law. In 1562, "[a]n ordinance of Lancaster, relating to the purchase of malt, ignored the distinction between obvious and latent defects and restated an old proverb, 'let their eye be their chapman.' "[27] By 1600, the basic notion that the risk of product defects lay on the buyer had become well established in English law. A much-quoted passage attributed to Coke on Littleton (1633) noted: "[B]y the civil law every man is bound to warrant the thing he selleth or conveyeth, albeit there be no express warranty, either in deed or in law; but the common law bindeth him not, for *caveat emptor*."[28]

**23.** On the early history of products liability law in England and America, see, e.g., Bohlen, The Basis of Affirmative Obligations in the Law of Tort (pts. 2 & 3), 53 U. Pa. L. Rev. 273, 337 (1905); Hamilton, The Ancient Maxim Caveat Emptor, 40 Yale L.J. 1133 (1931); Llewellyn, On Warranty of Quality, and Society (pts. 1 & 2), 36 Colum. L. Rev. 699 (1936), 37 Colum. L. Rev. 341 (1937); Prosser, The Implied Warranty of Merchantable Quality, 27 Minn. L. Rev. 117, 118–22 (1943); Murphy, Medieval Theory and Products Liability, 3 B.C. Indus. & Com. L. Rev. 29 (1961).

**24.** Thomas Acquinas, Summa Theologica, Ethicus, II, II, question 77, arts. 2–4.

**25.** See generally Hamilton, above note 23, at 1136–64.

**26.** Id. at 1138 (quoting Acquinas, Summa Theologica, Ethicus, II, II, question 77, Art. 4 (Rickaby trans., 2d ed. 1896)).

**27.** Id. at 1164. "It was proverbial in France, 'qui n'ouvre pas yeux doit ouvrir la bourse.' " Id. at n.208 (quoting 2 Borough Customs 183 (Mary Bateson ed., 1906)).

**28.** Id. at 1165.

The maxim of *caveat emptor* first appears in the law reports in the early 1600s.[29] In 1603, the judges and barons of the Exchequer–Chamber decided the celebrated case of the bezoar stone,[30] *Chandler v. Lopus*.[31] Plaintiff alleged that the defendant goldsmith sold him a stone "which he affirmed to Lopus to be a bezoar-stone ... for one hundred pounds; *ubi revera* it was not a bezoar-stone: the defendant pleaded not guilty, and verdict was given and judgment entered for the plaintiff in the King's Bench." Holding the declaration deficient, the Exchequer–Chamber reversed, writing: "[T]he bare affirmation that it was a bezar-stone, without warranting it to be so, is no cause of action: and although he knew it to be no bezar-stone, it is not material; for every one in selling his wares will affirm that his wares are good, or the horse which he sells is sound; yet if he does not warrant them to be so, it is no cause of action...."

As *Chandler v. Lopus* came to be interpreted, it announced a simple rule governing the rights of the buyer of inferior goods:

> He had a cause of action if he had exacted an express warranty at the time of the sale from a seller who knew his representations to be false. An affirmation, no matter how many holy saints were invoked, fell short of a warranty; latent defects, however impervious to ordinary vision, were the purchaser's own lookout. When in time writs were accommodated more sharply to specific complaints, ... the buyer had the alternative of a suit in assumpsit on express warranty or in deceit by proving a *scienter*. The exactions of a ceremonial were set down as an injunction to the buyer to look to himself for protection.[32]

For the next two centuries, except for cases of fraud and breach of express warranty, the doctrine of *caveat emptor* ruled supreme.

In 1810, the English courts finally replaced the *caveat emptor* rule— that the buyer takes the risks of hidden product defects—with its opposite doctrine, the implied warranty of quality—that the seller impliedly warrants that its products contain no hidden defects.[33] Five years

**29.** See Moore v. Hussey, 80 Eng. Rep. 243 (K. B. 1601 or 1609).

**30.** Analogous to pearls, bezoar stones were valuable "stones" created in the digestive tracts of goats, llamas, and certain other animals by the layering of animal matter around some foreign object. See Oxford English Dictionary 163 (2d ed. 1989). These stones were thought to possess mystical medicinal powers, particularly in combatting the effects of poison or venom. Webster's New Int'l Dictionary 261 (2d ed. 1936). In addition to such curative uses, the stones were sometimes used as preventative "medicine" and are said to have been "used by royalty to detect poison in wine" by changing colors when they came into contact with a poison. RareEnds (visited Nov. 16, 1998), at <http://www.rareends.com/html/atocha.html>. Due to their rarity and unique features, bezoar stones have always been highly valued, and their historical and ornamental value continues to increase. For example, one gold-encased bezoar stone, recently salvaged from a shipwreck, has been advertised for sale for $6.8 million. Id. See also Fisher, Featured Artifacts: Bezoar Stone Pendant (visited Nov. 16, 1998), at <http://www.melfisher.com/artifact.html>. For further discussions on the history of the bezoar stone, see generally Bezoar, or *Bezaar*: First Aid for Poisoning (visited Nov. 17, 1998), at <http://www.fortunecity.com/victorian/canterbury/228/Monardes.html>.

**31.** 79 Eng. Rep. 3 (K.B. 1603).

**32.** Hamilton, above, at 1168–69.

**33.** See Holcombe v. Hewson, 2 Camp. 391, 170 Eng. Rep. 1194 (N.P. 1810).

later, in the leading case of *Gardiner v. Gray*,[34] Lord Ellenborough explained the fundamental notion of the implied warranty of merchantable quality:

> [T]he purchaser has a right to expect a saleable article answering the description in the contract. Without any particular warranty, this is an implied term in every such contract. Where there is no opportunity to inspect the commodity, the maxim of *caveat emptor* does not apply. He cannot without a warranty insist that it shall be of any particular quality or fineness, but the intention of both parties must be taken to be, that it shall be saleable in the market under the denomination mentioned in the contract between them. The purchaser cannot be supposed to buy goods to lay them on a dunghill.[35]

Subsequent cases established that this basic warranty of quality requires "not only that the goods delivered must be genuine according to the name, kind or description specified, but that they must be of a quality to pass in the market under that description, and this in turn to mean that they must be reasonably fit for the ordinary uses to which such goods are put."[36] The implied warranty of fitness for a *particular* purpose evolved as a separate and independent implied warranty,[37] distinct from the implied warranty of merchantability which included the concept that the good was fit for its *ordinary* purposes. In short, the implied warranty of merchantable quality reflected the view that sellers should be held accountable, as a matter of law rather than of the seller's intent, for defects in the products that they sold.[38] Parliament eventually codified the common-law implied warranty of merchantability in the Sale of Goods Act of 1893.[39]

The other major development in English products liability law in the nineteenth century, the inception of the privity of contract defense to negligence claims, served to shield remote sellers from legal responsibility for negligently caused harm from defects in their products. It was 1842 that the Exchequer–Chamber decided the celebrated case of *Winterbottom v. Wright*,[40] which held that an injury victim could not maintain a negligence action against a seller in the absence of privity of contract.[41]

**34.** 4 Camp. 144, 171 Eng. Rep. 46 (N.P. 1815). See also Laing v. Fidgeon, 6 Taunt. 108, 4 Camp. 169, 128 Eng. Rep. 974 (C.P. 1815).

**35.** *Gardiner*, 171 Eng. Rep. at 47.

**36.** Prosser, above, at 121 (footnotes omitted).

**37.** See Jones v. Bright, 5 Bing. 533, 130 Eng. Rep. 1167 (C.P. 1829); Randall v. Newson, 2 Q.B.D. 102 (1877). The developed common law of implied warranty at the time was usefully summarized in Jones v. Just, 9 B. & S. 141, 3 L.R.-Q.B. 197 (1868).

**38.** Perhaps the development of the implied warranty of merchantable quality reflected "the development of modern notions of policy, based upon the increasing practice of reputable sellers to assume responsibility for defective good[s] sold, together with the feeling that such responsibility is best placed upon the seller as a cost of his business, which he may distribute to the public at large as a part of the price. As a result, it is often said that implied warranties of quality arise by operation of law and are independent of any intention to agree upon their terms as a matter of fact...." Prosser, above, at 122 (footnotes omitted).

**39.** Sale of Goods Act, 1893, 56 & 57 Vict., ch. 71, § 14(2).

**40.** 10 M. & W. 109, 152 Eng. Rep. 402 (Ex. 1842).

**41.** *Winterbottom* is discussed further in § 4.5, below.

The defendant, Wright, a manufacturer and repairer of stagecoaches, supplied a stagecoach to the Postmaster General under a contract to keep it in good repair. The coach subsequently broke down and overturned, injuring the driver, Winterbottom, who sued for damages. The court gave judgment for the defendant. In an opinion reflecting the views of the other judges, Lord Abinger, C.B., remarked that to allow such claims would open up "an infinity of actions.... Unless we confine the operation of such contracts as this to the parties who entered into them, the most absurd and outrageous consequences, to which I can see no limit, would ensue."[42] It was not until 1932 that England finally abolished the privity of contract defense to negligence claims, in *Donoghue v. Stevenson*,[43] in which the plaintiff was sickened by the decomposed remains of a snail in a bottle of ginger beer purchased by a friend.[44]

## Early American law

### *Warranty*

**Caveat emptor.** The English doctrine of *caveat emptor* was embraced widely in the American colonies.[45] In 1804, Chancellor Kent of New York proclaimed that *caveat emptor* applied to latent defects,[46] and other early nineteenth-century American courts latched on to the rule with a gusto reflecting the new nation's devotion to individualism and free enterprise.[47] In 1850, the Supreme Court summarized the American

---

**42.** 152 Eng. Rep. at 404–05.

**43.** 1932 App. Cas. 562 (appeal taken from Scot.). On *Donoghue*, See C.J. Miller and R. Goldberg, Product Liability 9–12 and 536–40 (Oxford, 2d ed. 2004); G. Howells and S. Wetherill, Consumer Protection § 4.2.4.2, at 217 (Ashgate, 2d ed. 2004); J. Stapleton, Product Liability 20 (Butterworth, 1994); G. Howells, Comparative Product Liability 69–72 (Dartmouth, 1993).

**44.** *Donoghue* was preceded by George v. Skivington, 5 L.R.-Ex. 1 (Ex. Ch. 1869), in which a pharmacist was held liable to the buyer's wife for defective shampoo, and Heaven v. Pender, 11 Q.B.D. 503 (1883), in which a dry-dock owner was held liable for injuries to a worker injured by defective staging that broke. *Donoghue* was followed by Grant v. Australian Knitting Mills, Ltd., 1936 App. Cas. 85 (appeal taken from Austl.), which extended the principle of *Donoghue* beyond food to products generally. For a helpful summary of these developments, see G. Howells, Comparative Product Liability 69–72 (1993).

**45.** For discussions on the early history of products liability in England and America, see, e.g., Bohlen, The Basis of Affirmative Obligations in the Law of Tort (pts. 2 & 3), 53 U. Pa. L. Rev. 273, 337 (1905); Hamilton, The Ancient Maxim Caveat Emptor, 40 Yale L.J. 1133 (1931); Llewellyn, On Warranty of Quality, and Society (pts. 1 & 2), 36 Colum. L. Rev. 699 (1936), 37 Colum. L. Rev. 341 (1937); Prosser, The Implied Warranty of Merchantable Quality, 27 Minn. L. Rev. 117, 118–22 (1943); Murphy, Medieval Theory and Products Liability, 3 B.C. Indus. & Com. L. Rev. 29 (1961); Wade, Strict Tort Liability for Products: Past, Present and Future, 13 Cap. U. L. Rev. 335 (1984) (excellent discussion of nineteenth and early twentieth century English and American cases).

**46.** Seixas v. Woods, 2 Cai. R. 48, 2 Am. Dec. 215 (N.Y. 1804).

**47.** That the doctrine of *caveat emptor* was the prevailing legal ethic during the seventeenth and eighteenth centuries is the conventional historical wisdom. See, e.g., Prosser, above. At least in the eighteenth and early nineteenth centuries, however, there is evidence of some pockets of resistance to the doctrine in the form of support for an implied warranty of quality in a few American jurisdictions and possibly in England, perhaps reflecting aberrational mercantile customs in certain areas. Yet once the nineteenth century was well under way, apparently all American jurisdictions except South Carolina adhered to the principle of *caveat emptor*. See generally M. Horwitz, The Transformation of American Law, 1780–1860, at 167, 180, 330 n.106 (1977). Horwitz argues, however, that a "sound price" rule *generally* prevailed during the seventeenth and eighteenth century and that the *caveat emptor* notion did not take hold until about 1800.

view of the *caveat emptor* doctrine in *Barnard v. Kellogg:*[48]

> No principle of the common law has been better established, or more often affirmed, both in this country and in England, than that in sales of personal property, in the absence of express warranty, where the buyer has an opportunity to inspect the commodity, and the seller is guilty of no fraud, and is neither the manufacturer nor grower of the article he sells, the maxim of *caveat emptor* applies. Such a rule, requiring the purchaser to take care of his own interests, has been found best adapted to the wants of trade in the business transactions of life. And there is no hardship in it, because if the purchaser distrusts his judgment he can require of the seller a warranty that the quality or condition of the goods he desires to buy corresponds with the sample exhibited.... Of such universal acceptance is the doctrine of *caveat emptor* in this country, that the courts of all the States in the Union where the common law prevails, with one exception (South Carolina), sanction it.[49]

Toward the end of the century, some courts finally began imposing an implied warranty of quality on manufacturers (and growers), but the *caveat emptor* principle persisted in most states in retailer cases even into the twentieth century.[50]

Notwithstanding the widespread acceptance of the *caveat emptor* doctrine in America in the early nineteenth century, various states, following the lead of South Carolina and England, began to abandon the doctrine during the latter part of the century in favor of the implied warranty of merchantable quality.

Under the rule of *caveat venditor,* a sale "raises an implied warranty (against latent defects) from the fairness and fullness of the price paid, upon this clear and reasonable ground, that in the contract of sale, the purchaser is not supposed to part with his money, but in expectation of an adequate advantage, or recompense.... Selling for a sound price raises an implied warranty that the thing sold is free from defects, known and unknown (to the seller)."[51] By the turn of the twentieth century, enough American states had adopted a common law implied warranty of quality that the doctrine was reduced to statutory form in the Uniform Sales Act of 1906,[52] patterned after the English Sales of Goods Act.[53]

---

**48.** 77 U.S. (10 Wall.) 383 (1870).

**49.** Id. at 388–89.

**50.** See, e.g., National Oil Co. v. Rankin, 68 Kan. 679, 75 P. 1013 (1904).

**51.** Lane v. Trenholm Bldg. Co., 229 S.E.2d 728, 730 (S.C.1976) (quoting Champneys v. Johnson, 4 S.C.L. (2 Brev.) 268, 273 (S.C. 1809), and Southern Iron & Equip. Co. v. Bamberg E & W Ry. Co., 149 S.E. 271, 278 (S.C. 1929)).

**52.** Promulgated in 1906, the American Uniform Sales Act (predecessor to the Uniform Commercial Code) provided, in

§ 15(2), for an implied warranty of merchantability in sales by description:

> Where the goods are bought by description from a seller who deals in goods of that description (whether he be the grower or manufacturer or not), there is an implied warranty that the goods shall be of merchantable quality.

Unif. Sales Act § 15(2) (superseded by UCC § 2–314 (1962)), 1 U.L.A. 7 (1950).

**53.** Section 15(2) of the Uniform Sales Act adopts, almost verbatim, § 14(2) of the English Sale of Goods Act, which provided:

**Privity of contract.** As courts began imposing implied warranties of quality on manufacturers in the latter part of the nineteenth century, manufacturers increasingly were spinning off the retail function to third party dealers. This meant that the typical consumer began to deal contractually only with the retailer. Thus, manufacturers sued in warranty by consumers of defective products in the late 1800s had available the ready-made defense of no privity of contract, a defense that was proving its effectiveness in actions brought in negligence. But the harshness of the rule in cases of consumer injury was readily apparent, and courts began to riddle it with exceptions at an early date.[54]

The first cases to abolish outright the manufacturer's privity defense in implied warranty were decided at the turn of the century and involved defective foodstuffs.[55] The court in *Jacob E. Decker & Sons, Inc. v. Capps*[56] explained that liability in such cases is based on "the broad principle of the public policy to protect human health and life." Producers place food products in the channels of commerce "with the intention that they shall pass from hand to hand until they are finally used by some remote consumer" who is ill-equipped to determine whether such food is fit to eat. When it is not in fact fit for human consumption, "there is such an utter failure of the purpose for which the food is sold, and the consequences of eating unsound food are so disastrous to human health and life, that the law imposes a warranty of purity in favor of the ultimate consumer as a matter of public policy."[57]

The breakdown of the remote seller's privity defense in implied warranty cases spread in the 1950s from human food to animal food and products for intimate bodily use, such as soap, hair dye, and permanent wave solution. Then, in the late 1950s and early 1960s, several courts in

---

Where goods are bought by description from a seller who deals in goods of that description (whether he be the manufacturer or not), there is an implied condition that the goods shall be of merchantable quality; provided that if the buyer has examined the goods, there shall be no implied condition as regards defects which such examination ought to have revealed.

Sale of Goods Act, 1893, 56 & 57 Vict., Ch. 71, § 14(2).

**54.** See Gillam, Products Liability in a Nutshell, 37 Or. L. Rev. 119, 153–55 (1958) (listing 29 such exceptions).

**55.** See Mazetti v. Armour & Co., 135 P. 633 (Wash. 1913); Parks v. G.C. Yost Pie Co., 144 P. 202 (Kan. 1914). See also Jackson Coca–Cola Bottling Co. v. Chapman, 64 So. 791, 791 (Miss. 1914): "A 'sma' mousie' caused the trouble in this case. The 'wee, sleekit, cow'rin', tim'rous beastie' drowned in a bottle of coca-cola.... [The consumer] did not get joy from the anticipated refreshing drink. He was in the frame of mind to approve the poet's [Robert Burns'] words:

'The best-laid schemes o' mice an' men
        Gang aft aglay
An' lea'e us nought but grief an' pain
        For promis'd joy!' "

However, even some of the later cases denied warranty recovery to users injured by food products which they had not bought themselves. E.g., Chysky v. Drake Bros. Co., 139 N.E. 576 (N.Y. 1923). In *Chysky*, a waitress bit into a nail baked into a cake purchased by her employer from defendant. In determining that there was no liability, the court stated: "If there were an implied warranty which inured to the benefit of the plaintiff it must be because there was some contractual relation between her and the defendant, and there was no such contact .... [U]nless there be privity of contract, there can be no implied warranty." Id. at 577–78. Especially in the context of food purchases for other family members, some courts employed agency principles to avoid the privity problem and allow recovery. See, e.g., Greenberg v. Lorenz, 173 N.E.2d 773 (N.Y.1961) (presumption that father purchased food for all members of household).

**56.**   164 S.W.2d 828 (Tex. 1942).

**57.**   Id. at 829.

rapid succession extended nonprivity recovery to durable goods. The year was 1960, and the case was *Henningsen v. Bloomfield Motors, Inc.*,[58] in which the privity bar was forcefully repudiated in a landmark implied warranty case involving injuries from a defective automobile. Justice Francis spoke for the New Jersey Supreme Court: "We see no rational doctrinal basis for differentiating between a fly in a bottle of beverage and a defective automobile. The unwholesome beverage may bring illness to one person, the defective car, with its great potentiality for harm to the driver, occupants, and others, demands even less adherence to the narrow barrier of privity."[59] In the words of Dean William Prosser, *Henningsen* marked the "fall of the citadel of privity."[60]

The issue of privity of contract had also presented a stumbling block for plaintiffs relying on *express* warranties. Because sellers affirmatively create such warranties in an effort to induce remote consumers to purchase the goods, the policy arguments against a privity defense in this context were stronger than in the implied warranty situation. The 1958 Ohio Supreme Court decision of *Rogers v. Toni Home Permanent Co.*[61] is the landmark case abolishing the privity bar in express warranty cases. Noting that the express warranty action derived originally from tort (deceit) rather than contract,[62] the *Rogers* court relied upon *Baxter v. Ford Motor Co.*[63] in extending the privity exception recognized in food cases to products generally, reasoning that it is only proper to permit consumers to recover for false advertising statements "aimed squarely" at them.[64] It is now a widely accepted tenet of American products liability law that express warranties as well as implied warranties run directly to the purchaser, despite the absence of privity of contract.[65]

### *Negligence and the Privity Obstacle*

As the functions of manufacturing and retailing separated in the 1800s during the course of industrialization, American law borrowed from England the formidable obstacle to consumer recovery for injuries from defective products by adopting the doctrine of *Winterbottom v.*

**58.** 161 A.2d 69 (N.J. 1960).

**59.** Id. at 83.

**60.** Prosser, The Fall of the Citadel (Strict Liability to the Consumer), 50 Minn. L. Rev. 79 (1966).

**61.** 147 N.E.2d 612 (Ohio 1958).

**62.** Id. at 614. On this point, see generally Ames, History of Assumpsit, 2 Harv. L. Rev. 1, 8 (1888); Prosser, The Assault Upon the Citadel (Strict Liability to the Consumer), 69 Yale L.J. 1099, 1126 (1960); Prosser, above, 23, at 118–25; 1 T. Street, Foundations of Legal Liability 377 (1906); 2 Williston on Sales § 15–1 (5th ed. 1995).

**63.** 12 P.2d 409 (Wash. 1932). *Baxter* is discussed in § 3.4, below.

**64.** *Rogers*, 147 N.E.2d at 615 ("The warranties made by the manufacturer in his advertisements and by the labels on his products are inducements to the ultimate consumers, and the manufacturer ought to be held to strict accountability to any consumer who buys the product in reliance on such representations and later suffers injury [as a result].").

**65.** That express warranties run directly to remote purchasers, see, e.g., Reid v. Volkswagen of Am., Inc., 512 F.2d 1294 (6th Cir. 1975)(Mich. Law); Hauter v. Zogarts, 534 P.2d 377 (Cal. 1975); Hamon v. Digliani, 174 A.2d 294 (Conn. 1961); Kinlaw v. Long Mfg. N.C., Inc., 259 S.E.2d 552 (N.C. 1979). *Rogers* is noted in 58 Colum. L. Rev. 1092 (1958); 19 Ohio St. L.J. 733 (1958); 44 Iowa L. Rev. 229 (1958); 11 Vand. L. Rev. 1459 (1958); 44 Va. L. Rev. 1002 (1958); Annot., 75 A.L.R.2d 112 (1961).

The extent to which third parties may take the benefits of warranties, as well as most other aspects of the law of warranty, is now covered to a large extent by Uniform

*Wright*, previously discussed, which prohibited negligence actions against "remote" manufacturers with whom plaintiffs had no "privity of contract." The privity requirement was an effective instrument of social policy for a nation bent on promoting the development of its infant industries. As explained by the Supreme Court of Pennsylvania, if a manufacturer of a boiler, machine, or steam-ship "owes a duty to the whole world" that the product contains no hidden defects, "it is difficult to measure the extent of his responsibility, and no prudent man would engage in such occupations upon such conditions. It is safer and wiser to confine such liabilities to the parties immediately concerned."[66] Despite occasional rumblings of discontent,[67] other American courts in the late nineteenth and early twentieth centuries, widely agreeing with the sentiment expressed by the Pennsylvania Supreme Court, staunchly applied the privity of contract doctrine to bar negligence claims in defective product cases.[68]

By 1900, dissatisfaction with the privity-bar rule had generated certain exceptions, summarized in *Huset v. J.I. Case Threshing Mach. Co.*[69]: (1) "an act of negligence of a manufacturer or vendor which is imminently dangerous to the life or health of mankind [in preparing] an article intended to preserve, destroy, or affect human life"; (2) a property owner's negligence that injures a person invited "to use his defective appliance upon the owner's premises"; and (3) providing an article known to be "imminently dangerous to life or limb to another without notice of its qualities."[70] Although there were minor variations in the formulation of the exceptions among the cases, the three *Huset* exceptions were widely accepted at the time. To recover against a negligent manufacturer or other remote vendor, a plaintiff had to squeeze his case into one of the three exceptions—which usually was quite hard to do, since most courts at the time interpreted the exceptions narrowly. Clearly the most important exceptions were the first and third, which involved the sale of "imminently" or "inherently" dangerous products. Yet when *Huset* was decided in 1903, courts confined these exceptions to products like poisons, drugs, guns, explosives, and foodstuffs.

Seven years after *Huset* was decided, Donald MacPherson, a stone cutter and gravestone dealer from a small village near Saratoga Springs,

---

Commercial Code § 2–318. See § 4.5, below.

**66.** Curtain v. Somerset, 21 A. 244, 245 (Pa. 1891).

**67.** At least one early scholar disagreed with the privity of contract doctrine: "To encourage commerce and industry by removing all duty and incentive to protect the public is to invite wholesale sacrifice of individual rights on the altar of commercial greed.... [I]t cannot be to the interest of any community to encourage carelessness and disregard of human life and property therein." Bohlen, above, at 355.

**68.** E.g., Loop v. Litchfield, 42 N.Y. 351 (1870); Lebourdais v. Vitrified Wheel Co., 80 N.E. 482 (Mass. 1907).

For historical studies of the privity defense to products liability claims brought in negligence, see generally C. J. Miller & P. Lovell, Product Liability 171–75 (1977); Bohlen, The Basis of Affirmative Obligations in the Law of Tort (pts. 2 & 3), 53 U. Pa. L. Rev. 273, 337 (1905); Bohlen, Liability of Manufacturers to Persons Other than Their Immediate Vendees, 45 L. Q. Rev. 343 (1929); Feezer, Tort Liability of Manufacturers and Vendors, 10 Minn. L. Rev. 1 (1925); Russell, Manufacturers' Liability to the Ultimate Consumer, 21 Ky. L. J. 388 (1933); Gillam, Products Liability in a Nutshell, 37 Or. L. Rev. 119, 131 (1958).

**69.** 120 F. 865 (8th Cir. 1903) (Sanborn, J.).

**70.** Id. at 870–71.

New York, purchased a new Buick runabout from the local automobile dealer. In late July, 1911, while Mr. MacPherson was driving a sick neighbor to the hospital, the wooden spokes on his Buick's left rear wheel broke, causing the wheel to collapse and the car to go out of control and into a ditch—pinning Mr. MacPherson under the axle. The dealer probably did not have sufficient assets to pay MacPherson's damages claim, and so MacPherson's lawyer decided to sue Buick Motor Company and fight the privity doctrine head on. Despite the fact that MacPherson lacked privity of contract with the defendant manufacturer, the trial judge refused to bar the claim, and the jury returned a verdict of $5,000 for MacPherson. The intermediate appellate court affirmed,[71] and Buick appealed to the New York Court of Appeals.[72]

In a case that in many respects began the modern era of products liability law, *MacPherson v. Buick Motor Co.*,[73] the New York Court of Appeals affirmed the decision for the plaintiff. Judge Benjamin Cardozo, writing for the majority, held that the imminent danger rule was not limited to poisons, explosives, and other products which "in their normal operation are implements of destruction. If the nature of a thing is such that it is reasonably certain to place life and limb in peril when negligently made, it is then a thing of danger. Its nature gives warning of the consequences to be expected."[74] If the manufacturer of such a foreseeably dangerous product knows that it "will be used by persons other than the purchaser, and used without new tests, then, irrespective of contract, the manufacturer of this thing of danger is under a duty to make it carefully." Explaining the liberation of tort law from the law of contracts, Judge Cardozo proclaimed: "We have put aside the notion that the duty to safeguard life and limb, when the consequences of negligence may be foreseen, grows out of contract and nothing else. We have put the source of the obligation where it ought to be. We have put its source in the law."[75]

While many courts quickly followed *MacPherson*, others did not, and by 1933 the case law on the scope of the "imminently dangerous" exception was in a state of utter confusion.[76] One by one, however, courts

**71.** MacPherson v. Buick Motor Co., 145 N.Y.S. 462 (App. Div. 1914).

**72.** For detailed and colorful accounts of the *MacPherson* case, see David W. Peck, Decision at Law 40 et seq. (1961); Henderson, MacPherson v. Buick Motor Company: Simplifying the Facts While Reshaping the Law, in Torts Stories 41 (R. Rabin & S. Sugarman eds., Foundation Press, 2003). See also Probert, Applied Jurisprudence: A Case Study in *MacPherson v. Buick* and Its Precedents, 21 U.C. Davis L. Rev. 789 (1988). *MacPherson* was noted in 29 Harv. L. Rev. 866 (1916) and 25 Yale L.J. 679 (1916).

England's *MacPherson* came in 1932 in Donoghue v. Stevenson, [1932] A.C. 562 (H.L.). See C.J. Miller and R. Goldberg, Product Liability 9–12 and 536–40 (Oxford, 2d ed. 2004); G. Howells and S. Wetherill,

Consumer Protection § 4.2.4.2, at 217 (Ashgate, 2d ed. 2004); J. Stapleton, Product Liability 20 (Butterworth, 1994); G. Howells, Comparative Product Liability 69–72 (Dartmouth, 1993).

**73.** 111 N.E. 1050 (N.Y. 1916).

**74.** Id. at 1053.

**75.** Id. at 1053. "Subtle distinctions are drawn by the defendant between things inherently dangerous and things imminently dangerous, but the case does not turn upon these verbal niceties. If danger was to be expected as reasonably certain, there was a duty of vigilance, and this whether you call the danger inherent or imminent." Id. at 1054–55. Chief Justice Bartlett dissented.

**76.** See Russell, Manufacturers' Liability to the Ultimate Consumer, 21 Ky. L.J. 388, 397–99 (1933).

swung over to *MacPherson*.[77] By 1955, Professor Fleming James could write that "[t]he citadel of privity has crumbled, and today the ordinary tests of duty, negligence and liability are applied widely to the man who supplies a chattel for the use of another."[78] Lingering in some states longer than others, the privity requirement in negligence actions was finally abolished in Maine in 1982.[79] "This trend was responsive to ever-growing pressure for protection of the consumer coupled with a realization that liability would not unduly inhibit the enterprise of manufacturers and that they were well placed both to profit from its lessons and to distribute its burdens."[80] The *MacPherson* rule has been extended to property damage; to non-purchasers, including mere bystanders; to non-manufacturer suppliers; and even to repairmen and building contractors. In the words of Dean Prosser: "It has become, in short, a general rule imposing negligence liability upon any supplier, for remuneration, of any chattel."[81]

## § 1.3   MODERN AMERICAN LAW

Once *MacPherson v. Buick Motor Co.*[1] gave birth to negligence claims against manufacturers, products liability claims slowly began to spread across the nation.[2] By the 1950s, courts were beginning to apply warranty claims to manufacturers of defective food, cosmetics, and similar products. Truly modern products liability law in America arose in the early 1960s, beginning with *Henningsen v. Bloomfield Motors*,[3] in 1960, which allowed a non-purchaser injured in an accident caused by a defective car to sue the manufacturer despite the absence of two linchpins of the law of warranty: privity of contract and a disclaimer that barred such claims. Three years later, in 1963, the Supreme Court of California decided *Greenman v. Yuba Power Products, Inc.*,[4] which declared that manufacturers of defective products should be strictly liable in tort to persons injured by such products, irrespective of any contract limitations that might inhere in the law of warranty. In 1964, the American Law Institute memorialized the rule of strict products liability in tort in § 402A of the *Restatement (Second) of Torts*, and officially promulgated it in 1965. For the rest of the 1960s, the doctrine of strict products liability in tort, together with a miscellany of secondary principles, spread like wildfire around the nation. This was the birth of modern products liability law in America.

---

**77.** See, e.g., Carter v. Yardley & Co., 64 N.E.2d 693, 700 (Mass. 1946) ("The doctrine of the MacPherson case is now generally accepted.... [It] caused the exception to swallow the asserted general rule of non-liability, leaving nothing upon which that rule could operate."). See generally Peairs, The God in the Machine, 29 B.U. L. Rev. 37 (1949).

**78.** James, Products Liability (pt. 1), 34 Tex. L. Rev. 44, 44 (1955).

**79.** Adams v. Buffalo Forge Co., 443 A.2d 932 (Me. 1982).

**80.** James, above, at 44.

**81.** Prosser, The Assault Upon the Citadel (Strict Liability to the Consumer), 69 Yale L.J. 1099, 1102 (1960). See also Prosser, The Fall of the Citadel (Strict Liability to the Consumer), 50 Minn. L. Rev. 791 (1966). "Probably no other case has been as frequently cited in following decisions or has made as great an impact on industry." David W. Peck, Decision at Law 69 (1961).

### § 1.3

**1.** 111 N.E. 1050 (N.Y. 1916).

**2.** See § 1.2, above.

**3.** 161 A.2d 69 (N.J. 1960).

**4.** 377 P.2d 897 (Cal. 1963).

Yet the products liability law that prevails in the United States in the early twenty-first century is a much different creature than the simple story just related might suggest. First of all, the law has become much more complex, having evolved and transmogrified in myriad diffuse directions, by many thousands of cases and a proliferation of state statutes altering various aspects of this area of the law, since those early days of the 1960s. Also, the significance of products liability law has mushroomed from the 1960s and early 1970s when the development of this curious new legal subject was little more than an academic curiosity. Today, products liability occupies a central role in American law: products liability litigation and prevention figure prominently in corporate and legal decisionmaking as plaintiffs' lawyers across the nation file thousands of products liability suits each year. In an effort to prevent and manage such high stakes litigation, many major corporations and law firms have established separate teams or departments for products liability matters.

## Reform

From the time manufacturers and insurers first began to feel the impact of modern products liability in practice during the 1970s, they began to push for its "reform," arguing that the products liability system had developed certain excesses that unfairly increased liability at the expense of everyone except plaintiffs and their lawyers. Since the late 1970s, products liability reform efforts have taken center stage in many state legislatures, the United States Congress, the courts themselves, federal regulatory agencies (like the FDA, which has revised its traditional stance on federal preemption to advance a tort reform agenda), and the American Law Institute. In 1996, President Clinton vetoed an act of Congress[5] that would have significantly altered certain aspects of this area of the law, and Congress regularly continues to address selected issues of products liability and safety. In 1998, the American Law Institute provided products liability with its own *Restatement*—the *Restatement (Third) of Torts: Products Liability*. And state legislatures continue each year to reform this area of the law in varying ways.

To date, most legislative reform has been in the states, several of which have enacted broad products liability statutes, codifying the basic principles of products liability law. Topics subject to statutory reform have included theories of liability; definitions of defects in manufacture, design, and warnings; available defenses, including the effect of a user's fault or assumption of risk, obvious dangers, product alteration and misuse, state of the art, compliance with custom, compliance with statutes and regulations, and statutes of limitation and repose; retailer liability; pleading compensatory damages; punitive damages; and special rules governing various topics, such as the effect of using seatbelts and child restraint devices, and various types of products, such as tobacco,

---

**5.** See Common Sense Product Liability Legal Reform Act of 1996, H.R. 956, 104th Cong. (1996).

alcohol, guns, asbestos, prescription drugs and medical devices, and breast implants.[6]

## Anatomy of Modern Products Liability Litigation

Several studies provide useful empirical information on products liability law in action. The following statistics are gathered from a 1976–78 study by a federal Interagency Task Force on Product Liability, a 1986 report of insurance organizations, a 1995 study by the Department of Justice, and a 2003 report by a jury research firm.

### *Interagency Task Force Study*

The federal Interagency Task Force on Product Liability conducted an in-depth study of products liability law in the mid–1970s,[7] revealing the following statistics about products liability litigation at that time. Although the data now are somewhat dated, they present a helpful picture of modern products liability law in its first decade.

*The Forum*—78% of the cases were tried in state court, 22% in federal court. Suit usually was brought in the state where the injury occurred, usually *not* where the product was manufactured, and almost always in the plaintiff's home state. Juries heard 86% of the cases tried.

*Increase in Cases*—The number of products liability cases reported in the eight states doubled from 1965–70 to 1971–76.

*Type of Product*—About ⅓ of the cases involved automobiles, followed in frequency by industrial machinery.

**6.** The broadest statutes are Ind. Code Ann. § 34–20–1–1 et seq.; La. Rev. Stat. Ann. § 9:2800.51 et seq.; Miss. Code Ann. § 11–1–63 et seq.; N.J. Rev. Stat. § 2A:58C–1 et seq.; N.C. Gen. Stat. § 99B–1 et seq.; Ohio Rev. Code Ann. § 2307.71 et seq.; and Wash. Rev. Code Ann. § 7.72.010 et seq.

Significant but more narrow products liability statutes include Conn. Gen. Stat. §§ 52–572l, 52–572m et seq.; Idaho Code § 6–1401 et seq.; Kan. Rev. Stat. Ann. § 60–3301 et seq.; Mich. Stat. Ann. § 600.2945 et seq.; Or. Rev. Stat. § 30.900 et seq.; and Tex. Stat. Ann. § 82.001 et seq.

More narrow still are Ariz. Rev. Stat. Ann. § 12–681 et seq.; Colo. Rev. Stat. § 13–21–401 et seq.; Iowa Code Ann. § 613.18 and § 668.12; Ky. Rev. Stat. Ann. § 411.300 et seq.; Mo. Rev. Stat. § 537.760 et seq.; and Tenn. Code Ann. § 29–28–101 et seq.

Some states have very narrow legislation, directed at only one or two issues. See, e.g., Cal. Health & Saf. Code § 1714.4 (defectiveness of guns and ammunition), § 1714.45 (defectiveness of tobacco, alcohol, and sugar); D.C. Code § 6–2381 et seq. (firearms), § 6–2391 et seq. (assault rifles); R.I. Gen. Laws § 9–1–13 (10–year period of repose), § 9–1–32 (effect of alteration or modifica-

tion); S.C. Code § 15–73–10 et seq. (adopting § 402A).

Almost all states have "blood shield" statutes, shielding blood banks from strict products liability, a number have statutes of repose for products liability actions, and various states have special statutes governing certain aspects of a wide variety of products liability issues, such as asbestos and breast implant litigation. Products liability statutes are compiled in volume 3 of Madden & Owen on Products Liability.

**7.** A comprehensive study of products liability litigation was conducted under the auspices of the Interagency Task Force on Product Liability, formed in 1976 to study the increase in products liability litigation and resulting insurance premiums. Under the direction of Professor Victor Schwartz, working out of The Department of Commerce, the Task Force analyzed hundreds of products liability decisions from 1965–76. The statistics here are from Product Liability: Final Report of the Legal Study, vol. 3 (Interagency Task Force on Product Liability: U.S. Dept. of Comm., 1977), summarized in id., vol. 1, at 17–18. In addition to the Final Report, see also Selected Papers, Interagency Task Force on Product Liability (1978).

*Parties*—Manufacturers were defendants in 79% of the cases, retailers in 33%, wholesalers 5%, manufacturers' suppliers 5%, employers 4%, lessors 3%, and installers 5%. Manufacturers were third-party plaintiffs in 15% of the cases in which they were original defendants. Manufacturers were third-party defendants in about 10% of the cases; employers in 8%.

*Age of Product*—About 10% of the products were over 20 years old. Excluding automobiles, 21% of the products were over 20 years old.

*Industrial Products*—In 1971–76, 50% of the cases involved work-related injuries from machinery and tools.

*Type of Defect*—The bases of liability asserted were manufacturing (and inadequate inspection) defects in 42% of the cases, design defects in 39%, and warning defects in 21%.[8] Most automotive and container cases alleged defective manufacture, most machinery and recreational product cases alleged defective design, and most chemical cases alleged inadequate warnings.

*Prevailing Party*—Plaintiffs prevailed in 50% of all the cases, defendants in 50%.[9] Of cases decided on the merits, plaintiffs prevailed 41% of the time in Arizona, 44% in Illinois, 58% in California, and 63% in Texas. Plaintiffs won 60% of the jury trials but only 44% of the non-jury trials. From the 1965–70 period to 1971–76, the rate of successful plaintiff cases rose 4%.

*Damages*—The average damage award in cases in which the plaintiff ultimately prevailed rose from $104,000 in 1965–70 to $222,000 in 1971–76, for an average over the entire period of $181,000. By state, average damage awards for the entire period were as follows: California ($272,-000), Texas ($221,000), New York ($170,000), Pennsylvania ($137,000), and Illinois ($119,000). Much of the increase in awards between the two periods was attributable to inflation, especially the cost of medical care which is often the largest component of products liability claims.

### Insurance Industry Study

The following statistics are from an insurance industry study of large (in excess of $100,000) products liability claims closed in 1985.[10] While such claims represent only 1–2% of all products liability claims, they account for 50–60% of insurer payments.

*Payments at Various Stages of Litigation*—In the 4% of large claims where no suit was filed, the average payment was $232,000. In the 71% of claims where suit was filed, but where settlement was reached before trial, payments averaged $441,000. Where settlement was reached dur-

---

**8.** By comparison, a 1973 survey indicated the following breakdown of 222 cases brought in strict tort: manufacturing defects—28%; design defects—46%; warning defects—25%; and misrepresentation—1%.

**9.** A comprehensive insurance industry survey in 1977 found that less than 4% of all products liability claims went all the way to verdict and, in contrast to the findings of the Task Force, fewer than 25% of the defendants in these cases were found liable. Highlights, Insurance Services Office Product Liability Closed Claim Survey: A Technical Analysis of Survey Results 6 (1977).

**10.** See A Study of Large Product Liability Claims Closed in 1985, a joint study of the Alliance of American Insurers (L. Soular, Research Dept.) and the American Insurance Association (1986).

ing trial (14% of the cases), payments averaged $649,000. In cases that went to verdict (11%), payments averaged $532,000.

*Theory of Liability*—Strict liability was the only theory alleged in 22% of the claims; negligence the only theory in 15%; and breach of warranty the only theory in 3%. All three theories of liability were alleged in 30% of the claims. Strict liability was the main theory relied upon in settlement in 60% of the cases, negligence in 31%, and warranty in 8%.

*Type of Defect*—Where strict liability was the main theory of liability, defective design was the applicable theory in 75% of the claims, and warning defects in 18%.

*Punitive Damages*—Punitive damages were demanded in 18% of the incidents; separate payments for such damages were awarded by a jury or paid for in settlement in 1% of the cases. Yet the threat of such damages probably increased the size of other settlements.

*Number of Defendants*—There was only one defendant in 56% of the cases. There were two defendants in 22%, three defendants in 9%, four defendants in 6%, and more than four in 7%.

*Miscellaneous Issues*—In the opinion of the claim reviewers, the question of product defect was too technical for the jury to understand and decide in 17% of the incidents; alteration, modification, or misuse was a cause of the accident in 34% of the incidents; and 12% of the products failed to comply with governmental safety standards.[11]

### Department of Justice Study

In 1995, the Bureau of Justice Statistics of the U.S. Department of Justice released a study of state court jury verdicts in all types of civil damages cases during 1991–92 in the 75 largest counties in the nation. The study included a total of 358 *ordinary* product cases and 287 involving *toxic* substances, asbestos in particular.[12]

*Proportion of Total*—Ordinary products liability cases represented 3% of the total civil cases, *toxic* substance product cases 2.4%. (By comparison, auto cases were 33% of the total, premises liability 17%, and medical malpractice 11%.)

*Time to Verdict*—The periods from filing of the civil complaint to verdict for *ordinary* products, was 32 months on average; 17% of the cases took 4 years or longer to verdict. For *toxic* substance cases, the average time was 38 months, and 27% took 4 years or longer.

*Plaintiff Success Rates*—Plaintiffs won 41% of the *ordinary* product cases, 74% of the *toxic* substance cases.

**11.** Another study, based on cases from the late 1970s, found that 19% of products liability claims filed were dropped, and 95% of the remainder were settled. Of the 5% that went to verdict, plaintiffs won 37% and lost 63%. Viscusi, The Determinants of the Disposition of Product Liability Claims and Compensation for Bodily Injury, 15 J. Leg. Stud. 321 (1986). By contrast, a Rand Corporation study indicated that plaintiffs won about 50% of the products liability trials in San Francisco and Cook County, Illinois in the early 1980s. D. Hensler, Summary of Research Results on Products Liability (Institute for Civil Justice, Oct. 1986).

**12.** See Civil Justice Survey of State Courts, 1992—Civil Jury Cases and Verdicts in Large Counties, NCJ–154346 (July 1995).

*Compensatory Damage Awards*—For *ordinary* products, the median award was $260,000, and the mean was $727,000. For *toxic* substances, the median was $101,000, and the mean was $526,000. Of the awards won by plaintiffs, 15% involving *ordinary* products exceeded $1 million, compared to 13% of those involving *toxic* substances.

*Punitive Damage Awards*—Punitive damages were awarded in a total of three (2%) and thirteen (6%) of the *ordinary* product and *toxic* substance cases in which the plaintiff won, respectively. Punitive awards averaged $12,000 in the *ordinary* cases, compared to $2 million in *toxic* substance cases.

*Jurisdictional Effects*—Verdicts vary considerably around the nation, including the rate at which plaintiffs win awards, median awards, mean awards, and in the percentage of verdicts that equal or exceed $1 million. In Honolulu, for example, results for plaintiffs are quite modest (37% plaintiff success, $50,000 median, $130,000 mean, and 0% at $1 million or more). Modest awards were found as well in Hartford, Connecticut (53%, $30,000, $90,000, and 0%, respectively) and St. Louis, Missouri (46%, $20,000, $60,000, and 0%). By comparison, juries appeared more generous to plaintiffs in such locations as Los Angeles (51% plaintiff success, $120,000 median, $970,000 mean, and 18% at $1 million or more), Cook (Chicago) (58%, $60,000, $580,000, and 11%), and New York (60%, $150,000, $1,200,000, and 17%).[13]

### Jury Verdict Research Study

In 2003, Jury Verdict Research published a study on products liability verdicts and settlements, which compiled statistical data on recoveries in such cases.[14]

*Products Liability Cases of All Types*—Probability of plaintiff recovery, 44%; median award, $700,000; awards of $1 million or greater, 44%.

*Industrial, Construction, Commercial and Farm Products*—Probability of plaintiff recovery, 53%; median award, $800,000; awards of $1 million or greater, 44%.

*Transportation Products*—Probability of plaintiff recovery, 47%; median award, $1.4 million; awards of $1 million or greater, 59%.

*General Consumer Products*—Probability of plaintiff recovery, 35%; median award, $168,000; awards of $1 million or greater, 21%.

*Medical Products*—Probability of plaintiff recovery, 51%; median award, $1 million; awards of $1 million or greater, 54%.

One should be cautious in interpreting these data, not only because of the mysteries of statistics and the partisan nature of this field of law, but also because of changes over time. Products liability studies covering the late 1980s and most of the 1990s showed moderation and, in some instances, declines in case filings (at least in non-asbestos cases), verdicts, and plaintiff success rates.[15] But products liability costs and

---

**13.** These data are for accident cases of all types, not just product cases.

**14.** See Products Liability: Verdicts, Settlements and Statistical Analysis (Jury Verdict Research, R. Kaiman ed., 2003).

**15.** See, e.g., Message from the Chair, ABA TIPS Newsletter 1 (Spring/Summer 1995)(noting that products liability filings in federal court, apart from asbestos cases, declined 36% between 1985 and 1991);

insurance tend to move in waves, sometimes up and sometimes down. In the early 2000s the wave appears to be on the rise. A quite recent study revealed that fewer products liability cases now are being brought, but the size of awards has substantially increased—from about $500,000 in 1993 to over $1.8 million in 1999—and that the rate of increase in such awards is accelerating at the fastest pace in two decades.[16] The study's research suggested that the plaintiff's bar is increasingly limiting its clients to those with serious injuries and a greater likelihood of success, and that it is refining its litigation techniques and skills, including the effective use of expert witnesses.

## Theories of Recovery

### Negligence

Negligence is the classic claim in American products liability law, and it remains a fundamentally important theory of recovery. Even as its doctrinal significance slipped into the shadows as various "strict" theories of manufacturer liability emerged and developed in recent decades, negligence retained a vital role in modern products liability law. Negligence is still the principal theory of tort recovery in several states that chose not to adopt strict products liability in tort. In the vast majority of states that do recognize strict liability in tort claims, empirical studies show that juries are more likely to find for plaintiffs, and in higher amounts, on negligence rather than strict liability. Since the 1980s, there has been a growing movement to return to negligence in design, warnings, and other types of cases, leading some state legislatures, courts, and the *Restatement (Third) of Torts: Products Liability* to return to negligence principles, and in some cases negligence doctrine, as the basis of liability in various products liability contexts.

Negligence may occur at any stage of the design, manufacturing, or marketing process. To prove any products liability claim sounding in negligence, whether negligent design, negligent manufacture, or negligent failure to provide adequate warnings or instructions, a plaintiff must establish: (1) that the seller owed a duty to the plaintiff; (2) that the seller breached that duty; (3) that the breach of duty was a cause in fact of the plaintiff's injury; (4) that the cause in fact was a proximate cause of the injury; and (5) that the harm is recoverable in negligence. In any case, the standard of care to which a manufacturer must conform is the standard of reasonable care for an expert manufacturer of such a product. But a manufacturer's responsibility in negligence is limited to such risks, uses, and persons as are reasonably foreseeable at the time a product is made and sold.

Hunter, Product Liability Insurance—Report of the Insurance Group of Consumer Federation of America (June 1998) (showing products liability insurance costs "minute" and declining, from 25¢ per $100 of retail product sales in 1985 to 16¢ in 1996).

**16.** See Winter, Jury Awards Soar as Lawsuits Decline on Defective Goods, www.nytimes.com (Jan. 30, 2001) (reporting on study of 2,751 products liability verdicts by LRP Publications, reportedly a nonpartisan organization that collects data on products liability case outcomes in several states).

Sometimes the negligence standard of care—reasonable care under the circumstances—may inhere in a statute, in which case a defendant's breach of the statute may amount to negligence per se. Other times, an industry code or standard may be a good gauge of reasonable care, but rarely is industry custom strictly the measure of that care. And sometimes the breach of the standard of care, and causation, suggest themselves circumstantially by the way in which an accident occurs which may activate the doctrine of res ipsa loquitur. Yet, ordinarily, negligence is determined by balancing the burden ("costs") of safety precautions against the safety benefit the precautions seek to prevent. The type and amount of care reasonably required is generally a function of the type, likelihood, and amount of harm (together viewed as the risk) that precautions (of a particular cost) may be expected to prevent. If the risk posed by the sale and use of a product in a certain condition is great, due care requires that great precautions be taken to avert the risk; if the risk is small, reasonable care requires only small precautionary measures in response. Stated simply, a manufacturer in the exercise of due care is obligated to exercise an amount of care in avoiding risk that is proportionate to the expected risk.

This principle of balance, sometimes referred to as the "calculus of risk," was expressed in a celebrated formulation by Judge Learned Hand in *United States v. Carroll Towing Co.*[17] There, Judge Hand reasoned that a determination of the degree of care appropriate to an occasion often reflects a calculus of three factors: the burden of taking precautions to avoid a risk of harm, on the one side, balanced against the likelihood that the actor's conduct will produce the harm multiplied by the seriousness of the harm, on the other. Expressed algebraically, negligence is suggested if $B < P \times L$, where B is the burden (cost) of avoiding accidental loss that foreseeably may result if B is not undertaken, P is the increase in probability of loss if B is not undertaken, and L is the probable magnitude (expected cost) of such loss. This is the so-called "Hand formula," which more fully reads: $B < P \times L \Rightarrow N$: if the cost of taking a particular safety precaution (B) is less than the precaution's expected safety benefits ($P \times L$), then the manufacturer's failure to adopt the precaution implies its negligence ($\Rightarrow N$). Thus, in making and marketing its products, a manufacturer is obligated to exercise an amount of care in avoiding risk that is proportionate to the expected risk.

### Tortious Misrepresentation

Misrepresentation is the communication of false or misleading information to another. A tortious misrepresentation claim may arise in a products liability context if a manufacturer or other seller communicates false and material words about a product to a person who is harmed by reasonably relying on the truth of that communication. For example, a manufacturer may claim that its cranes can lift 20,000 pounds of weight, when lifting that amount of weight will actually break the crane's boom, causing the load to fall on workers underneath; or a drug manufacturer may promote a medication as free of dangerous side effects, when it does cause side effects in many people. Misrepresentation claims therefore require no "defect" in the product but are based on the communication of words that are false.

---

**17.**   159 F.2d 169, 173 (2d Cir. 1947).

Three separate claims for tortious misrepresentation may arise under the common law, theories of liability that differ principally according to the defendant's state of mind in making the representation. The elements of fraudulent misrepresentation, or "deceit," are expressed many ways but almost always include some version of the following elements: (1) a representation; (2) its falsity; (3) its materiality; (4) the speaker's knowledge of its falsity or ignorance of its truth; (5) the speaker's intent that the hearer will act in reliance on the representation; (6) the hearer's ignorance of its falsity; (7) the hearer's reliance on its truth; (8) the justifiability of that reliance; and (9) the hearer's resulting harm. In place of the defendant's *scienter* (that the speaker knew the matter represented to be false and intended it to mislead the plaintiff), negligent misrepresentation substitutes the defendant's negligence in not knowing the falsity of the representations, or, less commonly, communicating them in a negligent manner. Finally, under *Restatement (Second) of Torts* § 402B, a handful of jurisdictions allow claims of strict liability in tort for innocently making public misrepresentations about a product's safety, notwithstanding the seller's belief that the representations are true, the seller's good faith, and the seller's exercise of all due care.

### Breach of Warranty

Like tortious misrepresentation, warranty law concerns the legal obligations that arise from representations connected with transactions. In the products liability context, the law of warranty prescribes the legal effect accorded assertions associated with the transfer of a product for value, usually through a sale. Such representations about a product may be express, through a seller's affirmative communications concerning the product's attributes, or they may be implied by the nature of the sales transaction.

While most products liability law today is based in tort, warranty law is ordinarily conceived as part of the modern law of contract because the relevant representations arise out of the sale and purchase of a product. Several states that never did adopt the doctrine of strict liability in tort for the sale of defective products (notably Delaware, Massachusetts, Michigan, and Virginia) have constructed their modern products liability jurisprudence largely upon an implied warranty of quality.

The source of modern products liability warranty law is the article on sales law in the Uniform Commercial Code, Article 2, which prescribes how warranties arise and are defined, to whom they extend, and remedies for their breach. In 2002, the National Conference of Commissioners on Uniform State Laws adopted a substantial revision of Article 2, and, in 2003, the American Law Institute added its endorsement to their joint revision project. Yet, adoption by state legislatures will surely take a number of years, as was true with the UCC which took about a decade to be enacted by state legislatures nationwide during the 1950s and 1960s. In the meantime, courts will continue to apply the current provisions of UCC Article 2 to products liability warranty cases as they have since the 1960s.

Article 2 defines three types of warranties applicable to products liability litigation: express warranties, under UCC § 2–313; the implied warranty of merchantability, under UCC § 2–314; and the implied warranty of fitness for particular purpose, under UCC § 2–315. Claims for breach of express warranty under UCC § 2–313 are similar in many respects to strict liability claims for misrepresentation under *Restatement (Second) of Torts* § 402B, except that an express warranty claim requires that the buyer, rather than proving reliance on the representation, prove that the representation was part of the basis of the bargain. Products liability claims for breach of the implied warranty of merchantability under UCC § 2–314 in products liability cases normally are based on a product's failure to be fit for the ordinary purposes of such a product, as when the brakes on a new car fail, causing it to leave the highway and hit a tree. The essential basis of liability in such cases is that the product was not reasonably safe, that it was in fact defective, which makes the basis of the merchantability warranty essentially the same as the basis of liability for strict liability in tort under § 402A of the *Restatement (Second) of Torts*. The implied warranty of fitness for particular purpose, which only infrequently arises in products liability litigation, is something of a hybrid, lying part way between an express warranty and an implied warranty of merchantability. This warranty is most likely to arise in the products liability setting in a retail transaction when a seller has reason to know that a buyer is relying on the seller's skill or judgment to select a product for the buyer that will serve the buyer's special needs.

Various contractual doctrines limit the availability of breach of warranty claims under Article 2. If the person claiming breach of warranty was not the purchaser, then the plaintiff will not be in privity of contract with the seller and so must qualify as a third party beneficiary under UCC § 2–318 which describes which parties other than buyers may benefit from a seller's breach of warranty. Moreover, a plaintiff may not sue for breach of warranty unless he or she has promptly notified the seller, under UCC § 2–607, of the supposed breach. But the most powerful limitation on warranty claims in Article 2 is the seller's ability contractually to avoid warranty responsibility by disclaimers, under UCC § 2–316, and to limit damages for breach of warranty, under UCC § 2–719. While the law has placed substantial limitations on a seller's ability to disclaim responsibility[18] and limit damages for breach of warranty,[19] these limitations on warranty responsibility remain important obstacles to recovery in many instances.

### *Strict Liability in Tort*

The doctrine of strict liability in tort is widely viewed as the prime theory of recovery in modern products liability law. Indeed, the development and growth of the doctrine of strict products liability in tort was

---

**18.** Particularly under the Magnuson–Moss Federal Warranty Act, 15 U.S.C. § 2301 et seq.

**19.** Particularly with respect to personal injuries in the case of consumer goods.

the centerpiece around which the rest of modern products liability law was constructed. In *Henningsen v. Bloomfield Motors, Inc.*,[20] the New Jersey Supreme Court in 1960 held the manufacturer of a defective car strictly liable for injuries to a driver with whom it had no contractual relations, nominally on the basis of the manufacturer's breach of its implied warranty of quality but without regard to the purchase contract's warranty exclusions or remedy limitations, and despite the fact that the injured driver had no contractual relationship (no "privity of contract") with the manufacturer. On the footings of *Henningsen*, the Supreme Court of California in 1963 constructed the new theory of strict products liability in tort in *Greenman v. Yuba Power Products, Inc.*[21] The next year, Dean William Prosser, Reporter for the *Restatement (Second) of Torts*, included this new liability principle in § 402A of that *Restatement*, which the American Law Institute approved that year and promulgated the following year, in 1965. With a gusto unparalleled by any development in the law of torts, the new doctrine swept across the face of America during the late 1960s and 1970s as courts and legislatures embraced § 402A and the bold new doctrine that it proclaimed—"strict" liability in tort for physical harm caused by defective products.

Liability under § 402A was defined as "strict" because it rests not on a manufacturer's fault in producing a defective product, but on the frustration of consumer expectations of product safety when a latent defect in a product causes harm. However, as more and more courts during the 1970s and 1980s broadly extended the new principle beyond manufacturing errors to design and warning cases, the truly strict consumer expectations test increasingly gave way to the principles of foreseeability and risk-utility balancing that underlie the law of negligence. While courts continued to assert that they were applying "strict" liability, and while such liability was indeed strict when applied to manufacturers in cases involving manufacturing defects (and to retailers in any type of case), it became increasingly clear that the principles governing liability in design and warnings cases were truly based on fault.

In 1992, the American Law Institute began work on a new *Restatement (Third) of Torts* on the specific topic of products liability law, approving the new *Restatement* in 1997 and publishing it in 1998 as the *Restatement (Third) of Torts: Products Liability*. While the *Third Restatement* continues to base liability for manufacturing defects in terms that are strict, it abandons any pretense of "strict" responsibility for design and warning defects which it grounds explicitly in principles of negligence. Yet modern products liability law in most states still rests squarely on the "strict liability" language of § 402A. Thus, while a number of courts have adopted certain key provisions of the *Products Liability Restatement*, and while many courts acknowledge that the principles applied to design and warning cases are similar to negligence, most courts continue to parrot traditional § 402A jurisprudence that calls modern products liability law "strict." In this way, courts have created a disjunction between what they say and what they do. Be that

**20.**  161 A.2d 69 (N.J. 1960) (Francis, J.).

**21.**  377 P.2d 897 (Cal. 1963) (Traynor, J.).

as it may, the principle of inertia suggests that courts for many years will continue to apply principles of negligence to design and warning defect issues while purporting to apply the accumulated "strict" liability doctrine spawned by § 402A.

## Product Defectiveness

### *In General*

Regardless of the underlying cause of action, the plaintiff in nearly every products liability case must prove that the defendant's product contained an unnecessary hazard that caused the harm.[22] Almost every type of product is dangerous to some extent, at least when put to certain uses. But many product dangers are impractical, if not impossible, to avoid. For such inherent product risks, *users* rather than makers or suppliers properly must avoid and insure against the possibility of injury. But sometimes products carry excessive risks that users and consumers should not have to bear, either because users and consumers do not expect the risks or because manufacturers can cost-effectively and practicably avoid them. In such cases, manufacturers properly bear responsibility for such excessive harm their products cause to users and third parties. Products that carry excessive risk are called "defective."

While most jurisdictions still require plaintiffs in most cases to rely upon one or more traditional causes of action (negligence, breach of implied warranty, and/or strict liability in tort), a developing trend subordinates the formal aspects—the *doctrine*—of these traditional liability theories to a *functional* consideration of whether the product was "defective." Virtually every American jurisdiction now divides product defect cases into three categories, which are further discussed below:

(1) *manufacturing defects*—production mistakes or flaws that a manufacturer did not intend;

(2) *design defects*—undue hazards in how a product was engineered, because a safety mechanism was not included or because the product's conceptual formulation included risks which otherwise could reasonably have been designed away; and

(3) *warning defects*—the absence of sufficient information on product hazards or how to avoid them.

These types of defect, and a manufacturer's obligations to avoid them, are separate and distinct.

Conceptualizing product defects and proving them are two very different things. The key to proof of product defect has long been understood to rest on the effective use of experts to explain how a product's dangers are excessive, how the defect reasonably could have been removed, and how its presence caused the plaintiff's harm. Particularly since the Supreme Court in 1993 sought to rid the law of "junk science" in *Daubert v. Merrell Dow Pharmaceuticals, Inc.*,[23] which placed

---

**22.**　This puts aside cases where a defendant's false statements cause the harm.

**23.**　509 U.S. 579 (1993).

on courts a "gatekeeping" responsibility to evaluate the reliability and relevance of scientific expert testimony offered by the parties before allowing it in evidence, courts and lawyers have been striving to figure out how science and engineering may properly be used to help determine whether a product is defective and, if so, whether the product defect caused the plaintiff's harm.

Various evidentiary doctrines affect proof of product defect and causation in modern products liability litigation. For example, if the cause of a product accident is a mystery, but its circumstances suggest the probability that the product was defective, then the "malfunction doctrine," a close cousin to res ipsa loquitur, may establish the product's defectiveness. In other cases, proof that a product violated or complied with a safety standard adopted by industry or the government may help establish whether the product was or was not defective. Sometimes a product's defectiveness may be proved in part by similar failures of the same kind of product, while at other times a long safe history will go to show a product's nondefectiveness. Finally, in an effort not to discourage product safety, most courts apply the "repair doctrine" to exclude evidence that a manufacturer adopted remedial measures to improve a product's safety after an accident has occurred.

### The Products Liability Restatement

In 1998, the American Law Institute adopted the *Restatement (Third) of Torts: Products Liability*. As a guide to courts (not a statute), the *Third Restatement* is designed to replace the *Second Restatement*'s treatment of products liability law in § 402A and certain other sections. Under the *Products Liability Restatement*, liability generally arises from selling a product that is defective in one of the three ways mentioned earlier, or from making a misrepresentation of product safety. A product contains a *manufacturing defect* under the *Third Restatement* if it "departs from its intended design even though all possible care was exercised in the preparation and marketing of the product." A product contains a *design defect*, if the product's hazard could have been reduced with "a reasonable alternative design," meaning that the danger could have been designed away cost-effectively without unduly diminishing the product's usefulness. A product contains a *warning or instruction defect* if it was not, but reasonably could have been, equipped with adequate warning of foreseeable product hazards or instruction on how to avoid them. Special provisions govern special products, transactions, defendants, and duties, such as food, used products, prescription drugs and medical devices, successor corporations, and post-sale duties to warn or recall.

### Product Defects in Modern Law

Although plaintiffs' lawyers widely viewed the *Third Restatement* as a conservative reformation of products liability law, and while it did abandon the *Second Restatement*'s idea in § 402A of applying one general principle of "strict" liability for defective products of all types, the *Third Restatement* largely mirrors the paths that many American courts had begun to trod in the 1980s and 1990s as the expansionary doctrines adopted during the 1960s and 1970s began to falter. Today, while recovery for product accidents is still formally based on the underlying theories of recovery—negligence, breach of the implied warranty of merchantability, and strict liability in tort—liability principally rests on proof that a product was defective in manufacture, design, or warnings.

**Manufacturing defects.** Manufacturers and other suppliers normally are liable for injuries caused by manufacturing defects in products that they sell. When strict liability principles are applied to defects of this type, liability is *truly* strict, based on proof of some error in production that caused the product to contain some unintended flaw. Most litigation over defectively manufactured goods concerns questions of causation rather than the defectiveness vel non of the accident product. If a product allegedly malfunctions in a manner that causes an accident, as when a vehicle's steering locks, causing it to leave the road and crash into a tree, the steering mechanism may be damaged in the accident. In such a case, it is difficult or impossible to determine specifically why the steering failed, if it really did at all. Where a product is damaged or destroyed in the accident, or possibly lost thereafter, the "malfunction doctrine" may help a plaintiff who is unable to establish the specific defect. Quite like res ipsa, the malfunction doctrine comes to play when the circumstances of an accident suggest that it probably was caused by some defect in the product, and the plaintiff's evidence eliminates other normal causes of such accidents, such as an errant mechanic or driver error.

Defective food cases present the most unappetizing types of manufacturing defect cases, where mice turn up in soft drinks, glass in cans of spinach, clam shells in clam chowder, and maggots in dried pea soup. Today, food is considered defective in its "manufacture" if it contains a hazard the consumer did not reasonably expect, and a food supplier is strictly liable for resulting injuries.

**Design defects.** Manufacturers are subject to liability for unreasonable design hazards that injure users and other persons. Because product users may put any type of product to a dangerous use, no matter how safely it is designed, it is crucially important to fix upon a definition of design defect that divides products designed with reasonable safety from those that are not. While courts in the 1960s and 1970s widely applied the *Second Restatement*'s definition of design defect—whether the product was more dangerous than an ordinary consumer would contemplate (the "consumer expectations" test)—courts in recent years increasingly have abandoned this test, mostly because it fails to provide a meaningful standard for complex designs, and because it eliminates responsibility for obvious dangers of design. Today, most courts use some form of cost-benefit analysis, often referred to as a "risk-utility" or "risk-benefit" test of liability, to make design defect determinations.

Even when cost-benefit principles are applied to design defect determinations, many courts still purport to be applying some principle of "strict" liability. Yet the risk-utility test they employ is nothing more or less than the risk-utility test applied in negligence, based on Judge Learned Hand's formula from the *Carroll Towing* case, discussed above.

That negligence formula, it will be recalled, is $B < P \times L \Rightarrow N$. In modern products liability law, courts have substituted "defect" for "negligence" (D for N), which adapts the test to the "strict" products liability task of determining design defectiveness. So reformulated, the defectiveness "equation" becomes $B < P \times L \Rightarrow D$, which, in cost-benefit terms, means this: Costs < (Safety) Benefits $\Rightarrow$ Defect. In ordinary language, this means that a design defect is implied if the safety benefits of an untaken design precaution foreseeably exceed its costs, including any diminished usefulness or safety. This risk-utility test for design defectiveness, which ties the measure of precaution to the measure of risk, grounds design safety determinations in fairness and utility.

A number of secondary design issues create special problems, such as whether a manufacturer may offer safety devices as optional equipment or must install them as a mandatory part of every product. The decisions are split on this issue, but the result usually turns on the extent to which the safety device will interfere with the product's usefulness and whether the buyer is a better party to evaluate the costs and benefits of using the device in the buyer's particular situation. The normal rules of design defectiveness fit awkwardly when applied to prescription drugs (and, to a lesser extent, medical devices) because most drugs cannot be redesigned more safely, and because of the FDA's heavy involvement in their evaluation before they are marketed at all. For these reasons, most courts ordinarily do not subject drug designs to judicial review.

**Warning defects.** A product is defective if the manufacturer does not provide adequate information about its hidden dangers (warnings) and, if not evident, how to avoid them (instructions). Warnings and instructions must be adequate not only in their content (substantive adequacy), but in the means by which they are communicated to users and consumers (procedural adequacy). If a hazard is substantial, prudence may require that the warning be placed directly on the product rather than in product literature that may become separated from the product. Sometimes foreign language warnings or symbols would help communicate warnings information, but American courts generally do not condition a warning's adequacy on these special ways to warn. If a product may be expected to cause serious allergic reactions in a substantial number of people, a manufacturer must disclose the product's allergenic tendencies.

The "sophisticated purchaser" and "bulk supplier" doctrines sometimes exempt manufacturers from their normal obligation to provide warnings of product hazards directly to users and consumers. Thus, when selling a product (like a chemical) to a "sophisticated user" (like a large manufacturing enterprise), or selling the product in bulk (like transporting chemicals by truck or railroad tanker car) to purchasers who understand the risks, these doctrines often relieve the seller of its duties to warn the product's end users, often employees of the purchasing enterprise which itself may understand the product risk full well. Finally, manufacturers of prescription drugs and medical devices in most cases have a duty to warn only the physician, not the patient, because the doctor stands as a "learned intermediary" between the drug supply and patients, with responsibility for connecting appropriate drugs and devices to appropriate patients, and for passing along whatever information may be appropriate for their patients to know.

### Limitations on Defectiveness

Although a product may be hazardous, one or more factors may cut against classifying the product as "defective" and so may shield a manufacturer from responsibility for accidental harm. The obviousness of a product hazard does not relieve a manufacturer from taking reasonable steps to design the danger from the product, perhaps by incorporating some safety device that does not cost much and that does not diminish the product's usefulness. But, in most states, there is no duty to warn of obvious or widely known product hazards—that sharp knives cut, that cigarettes are addictive, that alcohol causes intoxication, that guns can kill, and that fast food causes obesity—because little good is served by telling people what they already know. Not only are the hazards of such products obvious, but they also are inherent, meaning they cannot be designed away. Thus, while their manufacturers remain responsible for production errors and warning of any hidden dangers, such products are not defective for their obvious, inherent risks.

When § 402A of the *Restatement (Second) of Torts* was being widely adopted during the 1960s and 1970s, many believed that "strict" products liability in tort meant that manufacturers were liable for harm from product accidents, even if that risk of harm was unforeseeable or otherwise could not reasonably be prevented. This was the holding in *Beshada v. Johns–Manville Products Corporation*[24] in which the New Jersey Supreme Court in 1982 unanimously held that a product was defective for not bearing a warning against an unforeseeable risk. After a storm of academic protest, the court reversed its position two years later, in *Feldman v. Lederle Laboratories*,[25] where it ruled that manufacturers must only warn of risks they reasonably can foresee (dangers within the "state of the art") at the time they sell a product. Together, these two cases marked the pivotal point in modern American products liability law, when courts began to shift their perspective away from trying to fashion truly strict standards of manufacturer liability to imposing standards of responsibility to which manufacturers reasonably might conform. Today, no matter how dangerous a product may be, it is not "defective" (in all but a couple of states) if the manufacturer could not reasonably foresee the risk when the product was sold, nor is it defective if there was no reasonable way to remove its hazards. A product's design and warnings, in other words, need only be as safe as reasonably possible under the prevailing "state of the art." These two propositions—that manufacturers must guard against risks only if they are *foreseeable*, and that manufacturers must guard against those risks only by precautions that are *reasonable*—are the two pillars of modern products liability law in America.

Prenatal and preconception harm caused by drugs and chemicals, the effects of which can ripple through generations of offspring, raise

**24.**  447 A.2d 539 (N.J. 1982).        **25.**  479 A.2d 374, 376 (N.J. 1984).

issues of foreseeability and the proper reach of tort law. Manufacturers of such products bear responsibility, of course, for failing to provide reasonable warnings of foreseeable risks of harm, even if that harm is caused prenatally—and possibly even if the harm is caused before conception, as when a chemical damages a woman's reproductive system which later injures a child who was unconceived when the mother's injuries were sustained. Courts have not yet decided many cases of this type, but several, reasoning that liability must stop somewhere, have applied no-duty rules (such as no duty to third-generation plaintiffs) to serve as bright-line liability boundaries for the remote effects of prenatal harm to future generations from toxic substances.

Another natural limitation on a manufacturer's responsibility for making its products safe reflects the fact that all products, like all lawyers and judges, eventually wear out. Courts widely hold that dangers arising from a product's natural deterioration normally do not render the product defective, particularly if the dangers arise out of the disposal and dismantling of the product (perhaps releasing dangerous chemicals) at the end of the product's life.

The law on a manufacturer's *post-sale* responsibilities for product safety, once it learns that its products are causing injuries not expected when the product first was sold, has long been in a muddle. Thanks in part to the *Third Restatement*, at least the issues now are clear. While federal product safety agencies may require manufacturers to recall products to repair unreasonable dangers, there normally is no common-law duty to recall and fix a product. But courts increasingly are imposing a post-sale duty of reasonable care on manufacturers to provide whatever *warnings* may be reasonable in the circumstances when they discover dangerous defects in products already in consumers' hands.

## Causation

Causation, or "proximate causation," is comprised of two separate issues: (1) cause in fact, and (2) proximate cause. Courts sometimes confuse the two, by referring to a *factual* causation issue as one involving "proximate cause," so a reader of the law reports must cautiously study decisions on these topics to be certain which of these distinct issues is truly involved in the particular case.

### *Cause in Fact*

Cause in fact is the actual connection between a product defect and the plaintiff's harm. Although this physical (or metaphysical) nexus is not controverted in most cases, a plaintiff must always link his or her injury or disease to a defect in a product which the manufacturer made and sold. The first causal requirement in every case is to show that the challenged product was manufactured by the defendant. Establishing the identity of the manufacturer of many products (like toasters, punch presses, SUVs, and butane lighters) usually is a simple task. Yet, after a serious accident, sometimes butane lighters and other products disappear, and memories fade. Many other kinds of products (like cleaning solvents, dish towels, and industrial chemicals) may have come from sources not remembered or quite unknown. And so the plaintiff's first, important causation task is to prove that it was the defendant who made or sold the subject product.

Connecting a plaintiff's injury to a product defect causally involves the same hypothetical inquiry involved in other tort law contexts, based on the same "but-for" test of cause in fact. A product defect thus may be a cause in fact of the plaintiff's harm if the defect was a *sine qua non* of the harm, a necessary antecedent without which the harm would not have occurred. Although California has substituted the "substantial factor" test for the but-for test in tort law generally, most states reserve the substantial factor test for situations where multiple products (such as several chemicals) combine to cause an injury which would have occurred even if one of them were removed. In such cases, a defendant's product will be considered a cause in fact of the plaintiff's harm so long as it was a substantial factor in producing it.

Toxic substance cases present plaintiffs with a variety of causation problems, and the substantial factor test helps plaintiffs in only a limited number of cases of this type. Tracing harmful consequences to asbestos fibers, drugs, and other kinds of chemicals involves perplexing causation problems both in science and the law. Science itself often does not fully understand the biological mechanisms involved in disease causation, rendering it difficult for the law to be confident of evidence that a plaintiff's cancer or other disease was caused by the plaintiff's exposure to a particular product. While the but-for test remains at the center of legal causation, and while the substantial-factor test assists in some respects, plaintiffs in toxic substance cases normally must provide certain special types of proofs to establish factual causation: (1) *exposure*— that the plaintiff was exposed to the toxic substance; (2) *general causation*—that the substance is capable of causing the particular disease in humans; and (3) *specific causation*—that the substance actually caused the disease in the plaintiff. General causation sometimes is hotly contested, as was the case for many years with harms suspected to be caused by Bendectin and silicone-gel breast implants. Yet, for many diseases, exposure and general causation will be clear, in which case causal inquires will revolve around the plaintiff's proofs of specific causation. In asbestos cases, where the connections between asbestos and certain lung diseases are well established, a "frequency, regularity, and proximity" standard is often used to prove that a particular defendant's asbestos product was a cause of a plaintiff's lung disease.

A special kind of multiple defendant causation problem arises when a plaintiff who is injured by a fungible product, such as a generic drug taken long ago, is unable to identify the manufacturer. The most distinctive products liability theory developed for cases of this type is the "market share" approach for establishing causation, whereby each manufacturer of the fungible product must contribute a proportion of the plaintiff's damages equal to its market share.[26] While a number of courts in major states adopted versions of this doctrine in the 1980s for use in

---

**26.** This theory was first adopted in Sindell v. Abbott Labs., 607 P.2d 924 (Cal. 1980).

cases involving a drug called DES, many courts have rejected this causation theory altogether, and most courts that have applied market share liability to DES have refused to extend it to other types of products. Plaintiffs have tried to induce the courts to adopt a number of other theories of collective responsibility on industries for harms that cannot be traced to particular manufacturers—alternative liability, enterprise liability, concert of action, and civil conspiracy—but these theories have mostly failed.

Warnings claims present special causation problems. Whether an untaken precaution on a machine, like a guard, probably would have prevented the plaintiff's injury usually can be sensibly determined, even if it requires hypothetical deductions. Yet, trying to decide if a plaintiff (or someone responsible for the plaintiff's interests) would even have seen an adequate warning and, if so, whether he or she would have acted in a way to avoid the harm, raise questions that barely are justiciable. By forcing plaintiffs to provide self-serving hypothetical testimony, causal inquiries in this context place speculation at the heart of every defective warnings case. To avoid this problem, many courts have adopted a "heeding presumption" by which the law presumes—by a presumption the defendant may rebut, depending on the circumstances—that an adequate warning would have been read and heeded.

### Proximate Cause

Proximate cause is a reasonably close connection between the plaintiff's injury and a product defect, a connection that is not "remote." Proximate causation principles applicable to tort law generally apply to products liability cases also, including the central limitation of responsibility to *foreseeable* types of risks. Normal principles of superseding causation also apply to products liability cases, principles that arise when third parties deliberately put products to unfair, possibly criminal, uses. When a manufacturer unbolts a machine guard (that arguably should have been welded permanently to the machine) to accelerate production, injuring a worker, or an assailant attacks the driver of a vehicle stranded in the wilderness due to a defective tire, whether the manufacturer's responsibility for the harm is broken by the intervening force depends on whether the type of intervention was a reasonably foreseeable consequence of the product defect, or, whether legal responsibility is more fairly cast entirely upon the intervening agency.

## Defenses

### Misconduct Defenses

If a product accident is caused in whole or in part by a user's behavior that was improper, or that was informed and voluntary, the manufacturer may avoid responsibility for some or all of the resulting damages even if the product was defective. This is because manufacturers are properly responsible for injuries proximately caused by defects in their products, not for injuries caused by a user's improper or deliberately-risky product use. While the role of contributory negligence is diminished in certain strict tort contexts, this doctrine remains a powerful defense to products liability claims. This is so even in comparative fault states, most of which bar recovery for that portion of a plaintiff's injuries attributable to his or her fault, and for *all* damages when the plaintiff's fault exceeds the defendant's. Although the assumption of risk doctrine is dwindling to some extent, this defense still bars recovery entirely in many states. In many other states, its merger into comparative fault has converted the plaintiff's deliberate and voluntary risk engagement into a damages-reducing factor. Product misuse widely bars recovery altogether, provided the misuse was unforeseeable.

The law is quite confused on just what misconduct defenses apply to warranty claims, and how they may apply, and generalizations on this issue are not much help. Since warranty claims lie in contract, one might think that their defenses should derive from contract, too. Article 2 of the UCC indeed makes some scattered comments on a buyer's careless use, stating that, if a buyer purchases or uses a product knowing it to contain a dangerous defect, any resulting injuries may be the proximate result of the plaintiff's use rather than of any unmerchantable condition in the product. But many courts apply the standard tort law misconduct defenses of contributory (and comparative) negligence, assumption of risk, and product misuse to claims for breach of implied warranty, as to claims of negligence and strict liability in tort. In fraud and other tortious misrepresentation actions, the basic misconduct issue is whether the plaintiff's reliance was "justifiable" or "reasonable," whether the plaintiff had a "right to rely" (based on reasonableness principles) on the particular representation.

### *Special Defenses*

Several special defenses are sometimes available to products liability claims. One, sometimes called the "regulatory compliance defense," is based on a manufacturer's compliance with statutory or, more commonly, regulatory standards. Most courts hold that products liability claims are not automatically barred by proof of such compliance, but that the trier of fact may consider a product's conformance to government safety standards as evidence of nondefectiveness. The doctrine of "federal preemption," however, if applicable, will bar a products liability claim if the safety issue, such as the "adequacy" of warnings on cigarettes, has already been resolved by Congress or a federal agency. The "contract specifications defense" protects a manufacturer from design defect claims for merely fabricating a product according to design specifications provided by another enterprise, unless the defect was obvious to the fabricator. A special application of this principle is the "government contractor defense," which normally bars defective design claims against contractors who build products according to designs provided or approved by the government.

Finally, every state has statutes of limitations for tort claims, and some for products liability claims in particular, requiring that such actions be filed within some specified period—from one to six years, typically two or three—from the date the plaintiff reasonably should have discovered the injury, and perhaps its cause. Under the UCC, warranty claims must be brought within four years from when the product first is sold. Some states have statutes of "repose," designed to put products liability claims ultimately to rest, whether they have been discovered or not, within some fairly long period of time. Most such statutes terminate claims after a specified period of time, anywhere from six to fifteen years (often ten years) after the date of sale. The time periods of a few repose statutes are more vague, based on the product's "useful life." Some states have realty improvement statutes of repose, ranging from five to twenty years in length, which apply to products liability claims involving buildings and other products attached to realty.

## Special Defendants, Transactions, Products, and Litigation

Most products liability principles are directed primarily at manufacturers who design, manufacture, and sell new chattels and who often are in the best position to provide warnings and instructions to users and consumers. When this products liability paradigm falters, there may or may not be reason to apply products liability principles to special types of defendants, special types of products, and special types of transactions. Negligence principles usually apply in each of these special situations, and sometimes warranty principles as well, so the predominant question in these cases is whether the doctrine of strict products liability in tort applies to these special types of defendants, products, and transactions.

### *Special Defendants*

When the defendant in a products liability case is not a manufacturer, it ordinarily has less control over product safety than does the enterprise that manufactured the product, raising the question of whether it is logical or fair to hold a nonmanufacturing supplier strictly responsible for injuries from defects in the products it sells.

**Retailers.** Although retailers usually play no role in a product's design or manufacture, or in providing warnings and instructions, they normally are subject to strict liability in tort. In recent years, however, some states have enacted statutes protecting retailers from suit if the manufacturer is solvent and within the jurisdiction of the court, but subjecting retailers to strict liability if no solvent manufacturer is available to the plaintiff.

**Raw material and component part suppliers.** Suppliers of products of these types are subject to liability for injuries caused by defects in the materials or components they provide, but they generally are not responsible for defects in the design of the finished product unless they substantially participate in that design.

**Parent corporations.** Parent corporations normally are not responsible for harm caused by defective products manufactured by their subsidiaries, because of fundamental principles of corporate law shielding shareholders from the debts of the corporation they own. Yet a court may allow a parent's "corporate veil" to be "pierced" on certain limited grounds, including agency and apparent agency, apparent manufacturer, concerted tortious action, and, most importantly, alter ego.

**Trademark-holders and franchisers.** Consumers may think that the owner of a trademark or a franchise is the manufacturer of products that bear its name, or sold by retailers by that name, but trademark owners and franchisers are accountable for a defective product manufactured by a trademark licensee or franchisee only if the trademark owner or franchiser had substantial control over the product's safety.

**Successor corporations.** When one company (the successor) purchases the assets of another (the predecessor), the successor normally is not responsible, under general corporate law principles, for the predecessor's debts, including products liability claims after the sale of assets has occurred. Yet, courts widely recognize four exceptions to this rule, situations in which a successor corporation is responsible for the liabilities of its predecessor. These situations are: (1) when the purchaser expressly or impliedly assumes such liability; (2) when the transaction amounts to a consolidation or merger of the two companies; (3) when the purchaser is a mere continuation of the seller; and (4) when the transaction is a fraudulent attempt to avoid such liability. Several states have broadened this list with one or two new exceptions: (5) when the successor continues the predecessor's product line; and (6) when there is a continuity of enterprise after the transaction.

**Employers.** Sometimes employers manufacture machinery and other products for use in their own enterprises, and sometimes employees are injured by defects in such products. Normally, the "exclusive remedy" principle of workers' compensation precludes employees in this situation from suing their employers as manufacturers of defective products. While early cases in California and Ohio allowed such products liability claims under the "dual capacity" doctrine, this doctrine was rejected in other jurisdictions and now is dead as well in the two states which gave it life for several years.

### *Special Transactions and Products*

In addition to being centered on the manufacturer, the products liability paradigm also rests on the sale of a new chattel. But some products liability litigation involves transactions at the border or outside this paradigm which also raises the question of whether the doctrine of strict products liability should be extended from the new chattel sale situation to other transactional contexts in which other policies and principles predominate.

**Leased, bailed, and licensed products.** Products may be leased, loaned, or licensed rather than sold outright. Courts have viewed commercial leases, such as rental cars, as involving largely the same policy issues as commercial sales, and so have applied strict liability in tort (and warranty) to such leases. Courts have had more trouble determining whether to apply strict liability principles to commercial bailments or licenses for use of a product for a short time—such as ice skates at a rink, a go-cart at a fair, a grocery cart at a supermarket, a washing machine at a laundromat, or a wine glass at a restaurant. Only if the licensed or bailed product is necessary or "integral" to the sale of some other product (as a wine glass for the sale of wine), in which case it becomes a "tie-in" product, do most courts hold that it may be subject to strict liability in tort.

**Sales-service transactions.** A doctor who uses a hypodermic needle to inject a serum into a patient's arm will probably include as part of the medical fee a charge for the hypodermic needle and the serum. If the needle breaks while in the patient's arm, or if the serum is defective, the patient may wish to make a products liability claim against the doctor for "selling" a defective product that caused an injury. Sales-service transactions also arise with architects, engineers, building contractors, plumbers, and electricians who may select or install a defective water heater for or in a home. In sales-service hybrid cases of this type, most courts search for the "essence" of the transaction, to ascertain whether the sale or service aspect predominates, and then apply strict liability principles only if the essence of the transaction involved a sale rather than a service.

**Repaired, refurbished, reconditioned, rebuilt, and remanufactured products.** In deciding whether to apply strict liability principles to these different product-improvement situations, courts generally apply some rough form of the essence-of-the-transaction or predominant-factor test mentioned above. This issue often depends on whether the product that comes out from service is essentially the one that went in, in which case only negligence principles will apply, or whether an essentially different product is being introduced into the stream of commerce, in which case strict liability principles may apply.

**Used products.** On whether strict liability principles should apply to used products, the courts are widely split. The majority view is that strict liability in tort ordinarily does *not* apply to the sale of used products, but a substantial minority rules the other way.

**Electricity.** A majority of courts hold that electricity is a "product" that may subject its suppliers, electrical utility companies, to strict liability in tort for selling it in a defective condition, once it has passed through a customer's meter and thus sold into the stream of commerce. Such cases typically involve power surges, causing personal injury or property loss by the excessive flow of electricity into a building. Yet many other courts refuse to apply strict liability to such cases, reasoning that the provision of electricity is a service rather than the sale of a product.

**Real estate.** Most courts refuse to apply the doctrine of strict products liability in tort to claims involving defects in land, houses, and other structures attached to the land, reasoning that products liability law properly applies only to *products*, which are chattels or personal property, not *real* property. But many courts have applied such principles to component fixtures installed in houses and other structures, and a handful of early decisions applied strict liability in tort to builder-vendors of mass-produced residential homes and to manufacturers of prefabricated homes and structures.

**Publications.** A number of claims have been brought against publishers for injuries attributable to books, magazine articles, films, records, computer games, websites, and aeronautical charts. Except for aeronautical charts containing false information, courts refuse to apply strict liability to the provision of information, reasoning that the message (as distinct from its packaging) is not a "product," and often mentioning but putting aside the difficult First Amendment issues such claims would raise.

**Blood.** Infected blood and blood products can cause AIDS or hepatitis, but almost all states have enacted "blood shield statutes" that protect blood banks and other suppliers from strict liability in tort or warranty, leaving victims to their proof of negligence in how the blood was gathered or tested for disease.

**Animals.** The decisions are split on whether strict liability in tort applies to animals, most courts holding that living things are not "products" within the scope of the strict tort doctrine, because an animal's nature is not fixed when it leaves the seller's control. Courts have been particularly reluctant to hold sellers subject to strict liability for an animal's natural proclivities, such as the tendency of a dog to bite.

### Special Types of Litigation

**Special product litigation.** Litigation has become quite specialized in connection with various types of products—cigarettes, asbestos, and certain prescription drugs are good examples—where procedural considerations (such as rules on consolidation) tend to dominate litigation. These products often are inherently hazardous, requiring special thought as to whether and how the normal principles of design defectiveness may need to be adjusted. Otherwise, the fundamental principles of liability and defense in these cases are basically the same as those applied in other types of products liability litigation. While it would be useful to isolate and separately examine the recurring doctrinal and litigation issues related to these and other specific types of products, the only special type of products liability litigation segregated for separate treatment here concerns automotive vehicles.

**Motor vehicles.** Automotive manufacturers must produce their vehicles free of manufacturing defects (in steering and braking systems, for example) and must provide users with reasonable warnings of hidden dangers (such as the possibility that an airbag might explosively inflate with sufficient force to kill a child). In addition to these normal responsibilities applicable to manufacturers of most types of products, certain special liability principles govern automotive products liability litigation. The most significant special rule of this type is the principle of crashworthiness, that automotive manufacturers must anticipate the possibility that their vehicles may crash and so must design them with reasonable safety for the crash environment. A manufacturer thus is subject to liability for "enhanced injuries" to occupants caused by uncrashworthy aspects of their vehicle designs, injuries over and above those that would have occurred had the vehicle been designed with reasonable safety for such accidents. When an occupant suffers indivisible injuries (such as paraplegia or death) in a vehicular accident, determining how to apportion the harm between the uncrashworthy aspect of the vehicle and the crash itself is often difficult if not impossible. While some courts require the plaintiff to prove apportionment in such situations, a growing majority of courts hold manufacturers of uncrashworthy vehicles responsible for indivisible injuries.

Ordinary principles of user misconduct govern most aspects of automotive products liability litigation, but some special issues of driver fault arise in cases of this type. A difficult issue on which the courts are sharply split is whether a driver's fault in causing an accident may be considered, as a matter of proximate cause or comparative fault, in apportioning damages for enhanced injuries in cases where the driver challenges the crashworthiness of the vehicle. Some courts rule that a plaintiff's fault in causing the first collision (such as running a red light) simply is irrelevant to a manufacturer's duty to protect occupants against unreasonable "second-collision" risks in a vehicle's design (such as sharp protrusions on a dashboard, a propensity to roll over, or a flimsy frame), since automotive collisions from one source or another are the very risk that manufacturers must reasonably attempt to avoid under the crashworthiness doctrine. Other courts reason that a plaintiff's fault logically deserves the same treatment in crashworthiness cases as in any other context.

A driver's intoxication may be relevant to contributory and comparative negligence, assumption of risk, and possibly misuse and proximate causation. Manufacturers attempt to use the "seat-belt defense" to establish that the plaintiff, rather than the defendant, is responsible for those injuries which a seatbelt would have prevented. But the law concerning this defense is fragmented, largely because the states have enacted various types of statutes that govern the effect of seatbelt nonuse in civil litigation—some permitting and others prohibiting nonuse evidence to reduce a plaintiff's damages, while some states leave the matter to the courts.

## Damages

### *Compensatory Damages*

Principles of compensatory damages in products liability cases largely track the rules of compensatory damages applied in ordinary tort cases. In particular, the same types of damages normally are recoverable in strict liability in tort as in negligence, including damages for personal injuries, wrongful death, and, in most states, property damage. But claims for pure economic loss normally are recoverable only in warranty, and not in either negligence or strict liability in tort. Some courts allow claims for an increased risk of disease, but most do not. Damages for emotional distress are often allowed in claims for strict products liability in tort, both by direct victims and bystanders, under rules similar to those applied under the law of negligence. Some courts have allowed recovery for fear of diseases such as cancer ("cancerphobia") from contact with a harmful substance, sometimes on narrow rules, while other courts deny such claims. Recovery for lost consortium by spouses, parents, and children are generally the same in strict liability in tort as in negligence. Finally, courts have divided on whether to allow recovery for medical monitoring of victims exposed to some toxic substance, or defective medical device, where future harm is possible but difficult to detect.

### Punitive Damages

The most interesting damages questions in products liability litigation concern the availability and measurement of awards of punitive damages. Such damages first appeared in scattered cases during the late 1960s and the 1970s, and punitive damages have been awarded from time to time thereafter (on average, in about 3% of all products liability cases), particularly in asbestos litigation. Punitive damages are available in claims for negligence, fraud, or strict liability in tort (but not warranty), on proof that a manufacturer was guilty of flagrantly disregarding consumer safety. Examples of such gross misconduct include fraudulently marketing unsafe products, or selling a product known to contain a serious, hidden hazard without disclosing it to consumers, in order to promote the product's sale. Among the functions of such damages are: (1) to punish such manufacturers and thereby provide retribution to victims and society; (2) to deter the knowing or reckless sale of dangerously defective products; (3) to help enforce the common law rules of product safety; (4) to educate manufacturers on the importance of product safety; and (5) to assure that consumers injured by flagrantly improper conduct by manufacturers are fully compensated for their injuries, including the costs of litigation.

Punitive damages are subject to criticism on various fronts, including the vague standards for their recovery and for determining their amount, standards which can be employed to heap enormous punishments on manufacturers whose guilty conduct may amount to little more than simple negligence inflated into gross consumer abuse by the oratory of a plaintiff's lawyer who beguiles a jury sympathetic to an injured plaintiff and hostile to large manufacturing enterprises. In an effort to impose some control on awards of punitive damages, most states have adopted one or more statutory reforms, the most common being an increase in the standard of proof from "preponderance of the evidence" to "clear and convincing" proof. Beginning with *Pacific Mutual Life Insurance Co. v. Haslip*[27] in 1991, to *BMW of North America, Inc. v. Gore*[28] in 1996, through *State Farm Mutual Automobile Insurance Co. v. Campbell* in 2003,[29] the Supreme Court has rendered a series of decisions imposing due process constraints on punitive damages. These decisions require that trial courts instruct juries properly on the functions of punitive damages, that trial and appellate courts review such awards with studied care to assure that they are awarded on rational grounds, that punitive awards are not assessed for conduct outside the state that may be legal elsewhere, and that the ratio of punitive to compensatory awards be reasonable, not unduly large. The Supreme Court decisions appear to be having some effect, for appellate courts have substantially reduced some number of high punitive damage awards in products liability cases on the basis of these decisions.

**27.** 499 U.S. 1 (1991).

**28.** 517 U.S. 559 (1996).

**29.** 538 U.S. 408 (2003).

## § 1.4　Foreign Law

Until the 1980s, other nations around the globe had not experienced the major legal jolt felt in America during the 1960s and early 1970s with the rapid adoption of strict liability in tort and other modern products liability doctrines. Yet, over the last decade or two of the twentieth century, and the beginning years of the current century, modern products liability law and litigation has begun to spread its wings around the world. Put differently, America no longer has a corner on the market of modern products liability law, and the resolution of products liability problems in the years ahead increasingly will be facilitated by a comparative law approach. Scholars for some time have been comparing the products liability law of the U.S., the U.K., Europe, and other nations.[1] In 1985, the European Community organized the law of EU nations under a single legislative umbrella, in an approach followed by many other nations.[2] Modern principles of products liability law have been developing elsewhere around the globe, all of which is touched on briefly below. Studying products liability from a truly global perspective has just begun,[3] yet it is a perspective that soon may predominate in a world where products are manufactured, distributed, fail, and injure human beings without regard to the boundaries of nation states.

The topic of products liability law outside of the United States is now far too broad to describe in any detail in a book like this devoted to products liability law in America. Yet products liability problems share similarities wherever they may arise, and so a lawyer, judge, scholar, or student examining a products liability problem in the United States should be aware that the courts or legislatures of Europe and other nations may have addressed and perhaps resolved the same or a similar issue. All that can be done here is to sketch out the framework of European products liability law and alert the reader to the existence of "the vast and fast-growing mass of products liability literature"[4] that is sprouting up around the world.

### § 1.4

**1.** Early treatments of comparative products liability included J. Stapleton, Product Liability (Butterworths, 1994) (comparing the law of Europe, the United Kingdom, and the U.S.), and G. Howells, Comparative Product Liability (Dartmouth, 1993) (Europe, the U.K., France, Germany, Scandinavia, the U.S., Canada, Australia, and New Zealand). More recent works include S. Whittaker, Liability for Products–English Law, French Law, and European Harmonization (Oxford, 2005); C.J. Miller & R. Goldberg, Product Liability (Oxford, 2d ed. 2004) (U.K., U.S., Australia, New Zealand, Canada, France, Germany, and E.U.); Taylor, The Harmonisation of European Product Liability Rules: French and English Law, 48 Int'l & Comp. L.Q. 419 (1999); J. Kellam, The Contract–Tort Dichotomy and Theoretical Framework for Product Liability Law: A Comparison of the Elements of Liability in Australia, France and Germany (Baden–Baden, Nomoes, 2000); J.-S. Borghetti, La Responsabilité du Fait des Produits—Étude de Droit Comparé (LGDJ, 2005) (U.S., England, France, and Europe); Product Liability in the European Union (Lovells, Feb. 2003, MARKT/2001/11/D).

The British Institute on International and Comparative Law (BIICL) has an especially useful database describing the case and statutory products liability law of separate European nations. See www.biicl.org.

**2.** For current developments in products liability law in Europe, see European Product Liability Review (Lovells, London, www.lovells.com).

**3.** Most notably by Reimann, Liability for Defective Products at the Beginning of the Twenty–First Century: Emergence of a Worldwide Standard?, 51 Am. J. Comp. L. 751, 836–38 (2003); Reimann, Product Liability in a Global Context: The Hollow Victory of the European Model, 11 Eur. Rev. Priv. L. 128 (2003).

**4.** Reimann, 51 Am. J. Comp. L. at 753 n.3.

Before addressing foreign products liability law, a note of caution is in order. In considering the law of other nations, it is important to remember that the substantive legal rules are only as effective as allowed by the rules of damages, procedure, and law practice (including methods for funding litigation), all of which reflect the cultural tradition of the particular nation and its legal system.[5] Japan, for example, in 1995 enacted a products liability law patterned closely after Europe's *Products Liability Directive*.[6] Yet Japan has few lawyers in general and even fewer plaintiffs' lawyers, in particular, and products liability litigation there, conflicting with that nation's cultural traditions, confronts numerous structural and procedural hurdles.[7] Europe may be somewhat more comfortable with litigation than Japan, but it views *ex ante* governmental regulation as a preferable way to achieve product safety, to deter product accidents, than litigation *ex post*.[8] Moreover, public health care in much of Europe reduces the need for litigation to recover a victim's medical bills from product accidents.[9] In short, other nations are less dependent than America on the twin pillars of tort litigation in this nation—deterrence and compensation. For these reasons, even though the laws of Europe, Japan, Australia, and most other developed nations now declare the availability of remedies for harm caused by defective products, procedural and damages restrictions, together with rules on attorneys fees (loser pays), substantially diminish the practical rights of injured persons in many nations to recover for their injuries. It is easy for American lawyers to forget that the products liability law in action in other nations may be much less useful than the law in theory,[10] and there is some real question whether recent products liability develop-

**5.** See Reimann, Liability for Defective Products at the Beginning of the Twenty–First Century: Emergence of a Worldwide Standard?, 51 Am. J. Comp. L. 751, 836–38 (2003).

**6.** See, e.g., Kobayashi & Furuta, Products Liability Act and Transnational Litigation in Japan, 34 Tex. Int'l L.J. 93, 99–100 (1999); L. Nottage, Product Safety and Liability Law in Japan 126 (RoutledgeCurzon, 2004).

**7.** See, e.g., Marcuse, Why Japan's New Products Liability Law Isn't, 5 Pac. Rim & Pol'y J. 365 (1996) (explaining structural and procedural barriers to suit); Behrens & Raddock, Japan's New Product Liability Law: The Citadel of Strict Liability Falls, But Access to Recovery is Limited by Formidable Barriers, 16 U. Pa. J. Int'l Bus. L. 669 (1995) (cultural and legal barriers).

**8.** See General Product Safety Directive, 2001/95/EC, [2002] O.J. L 11/4. See generally Howells and Wilhelmsson, EC Consumer Law: Has It Come of Age?, 28 European L. Rev. 370 (2003); Howells, The Relationship Between Product Liability and Product Safety—Understanding a Necessary Element in a European Product Liability Through a Comparison with the U.S. Position, 39 Washburn L.J. 305, 308 (2000) (explaining "the European commitment to regulation, rather than litigation, as a means of promoting product safety"); G. Howells and S. Wetherill, Consumer Protection ch. 10 (Ashgate, 2d ed. 2004).

**9.** See, e.g., Howells, The Relationship Between Product Liability and Product Safety—Understanding a Necessary Element in European Product Liability Comparison with the U.S. Position, 39 Washburn L.J. 305, 307 (2000) ("Litigation in the U.S. is widely recognized as a surrogate for the European welfare state."); Howells and Mildred, Is European Products Liability More Protective Than the Restatement (Third) of Torts: Products Liability?, 65 Tenn. L. Rev. 985, 992–93 (1998).

**10.** See Reimann, Product Liability in a Global Context: The Hollow Victory of the European Model, 11 Eur. Rev. Priv. L. 128 (2003) (notant la "disparité entre l'influence de la Directive en théorie et son inefficacité en pratique"); Reimann, Liability for Defective Products at the Beginning of the Twenty–First Century: Emergence of a Worldwide Standard?, 51 Am. J. Comp. L. 751, 838 (2003) (concluding that "the United States is still the only country where product liability really matters on a grand scale").

ments around the globe have accomplished much at all.[11] As so well put by one of the world's leading scholars on the subject, "Comparative products liability law is a dangerous business."[12]

## Europe

### Pre-Directive Law

Prior to 1985, products liability law in Europe varied from nation to nation, but it was largely based on negligence and warranty law,[13] as was true in many other nations.[14] In the United Kingdom,[15] the House of Lords in 1932 abandoned the privity of contract bar to negligence claims in *Donoghue v. Stevenson*,[16] the famous case of a snail in a bottle of ginger beer,[17] and it later applied principles of circumstantial evidence, not unlike res ipsa loquitur, to facilitate recovery in products liability cases.[18] In the 1960s and early 1970s, tort law's failure satisfactorily to address the consequences of a major drug tragedy in which thousands of women who took the drug Thalidomide during pregnancy gave birth to severely deformed children,[19] led to the creation of three commissions each of which recommended the adoption of strict manufacturer responsibility for harm from defective products. England also had a Sales of Goods Act, which created warranties of quality for buyers that amounted to a form of strict liability.[20] Products liability law in Germany also was

**11.** "After decades of reform and heroic rhetoric about 'strict' liability and the advancement of consumer rights against manufacturers, the humiliating truth for the United Kingdom and Continental consumer lobbyists and law reform bodies alike is that, were a new Thalidomide disaster to occur today, the victims would have no stronger remedies against the manufacturers than were present in the 1960s." Stapleton, The Conceptual Imprecision of "Strict" Product Liability, 6 Torts L.J. 260, 275 (1998).

**12.** Stapleton, Products Liability in the United Kingdom: The Myths of Reform, 34 Tex. Int'l L.J. 45, 46 (1999). See also G. Howells, Comparative Product Liability vii (Dartmouth, 1993) (noting the risk of embarrassment from revealing incomplete knowledge of foreign legal systems).

**13.** Much of this subsection draws from Taschner, Harmonization of Product Liability Law in the European Community, 34 Tex. Int'l L.J. 21, 25–28 (1999). Dr. Taschner played a prominent role in drafting Europe's Product Liability Directive.

**14.** See, e.g., Waddams, The Canadian Law of Products Liability, 34 Tex. Int'l L.J. 119 (1999); S. Waddams, Products Liability (Carswell, 4th ed. 2002).

**15.** See, e.g., Stapleton, Products Liability in the United Kingdom: The Myths of Reform, 34 Tex. Int'l L.J. 45, 48–51 (1999).

**16.** 1932 App. Cas. 562 (H.L., appeal from Scot.).

**17.** On *Donoghue*, see C.J. Miller and R. Goldberg, Product Liability 9–12 and 536–40 (Oxford, 2d ed. 2004); G. Howells and S. Wetherill, Consumer Protection § 4.2.4.2, at 217 (Ashgate, 2d ed. 2004); J. Stapleton, Product Liability 20 (1994); G. Howells, Comparative Product Liability 69–72 (1993).

**18.** Grant v. Australian Knitting Mills, Ltd., 1936 App. Cas. 85 (appeal from Austl.). See C.J. Miller and R. Goldberg, Product Liability 602–04 (Oxford, 2d. ed. 2004).

**19.** Thalidomide, used as a sleeping aid and for morning sickness throughout the world in the 1950s and 1960s, caused limb deformities in children born to women who took the drug while pregnant. The FDA's protracted review of the drug saved most Americans from this terrible tragedy. See Sanders, The Bendectin Litigation: A Case Study in the Life Cycle of Mass Torts, 43 Hastings L.J. 301, 313–14 (1992) (characterizing Thalidomide as "one of the most potent human teratogens ever found"). See also Bernstein, Formed by Thalidomide: Mass Torts as a False Cure for Toxic Exposure, 97 Colum. L. Rev. 2153 (1997).

**20.** On sales law in the U.K., see C.J. Miller and R. Goldberg, Product Liability ch. 4 (Oxford, 2d ed. 2004); Benjamin's Sale of Goods (A. Guest, ed., Sweet and Maxwell, 6th ed. 2002).

then developing in a pro-consumer direction.[21] In 1968, the German Supreme Court reversed the burden of proof, in the *Chicken-Pest Case*,[22] and the law in practice thereafter began to approach a principle of liability without fault. The Thalidomide experience led the German Parliament to enact a Pharmaceutical Act, holding manufacturers strictly liable for harm caused by defective pharmaceuticals. The law of Ireland, the Netherlands, and Denmark[23] evolved in a similar fashion, drifting in various ways toward strict manufacturer liability.

Products liability law in France, Belgium, and Luxembourg is based on a statutory framework based on the *Code Civil* of 1804.[24] This system allowed products liability claims in both warranty and tort. While the basic tort provision of the *Code Civil* requires fault, courts began to apply other doctrines during this period, such as *garantie des vices cachés*, *garde de la structure*,[25] and *manquement à l'obligation de sécurité*,[26] in a manner that amounted to strict liability for sellers of defective products. Products liability law in Italy,[27] Greece, Spain,[28] and Portugal, although formally derived from the French *Code Civil*, at this time was less generous to victims of accidents caused by product defects; if such persons were unable to prove the seller's fault, they generally were left without a remedy.

### *The Directive*

Spurred by the Thalidomide tragedy and the widespread adoption of § 402A of the Restatement (Second) of Torts in America,[29] and after nearly a decade of study, debate, and raw political horse-trading, the European Economic Community (the EEC or Common Market) in 1985 adopted a *Directive on Liability for Defective Products*.[30] The *Products Liability Directive* sought to harmonize the laws of member states that governed liability for defective products in order to facilitate free trade

---

**21.** See Wandt, German Approaches to Products Liability, 34 Tex. Int'l L.J. 71 (1999). See also Möllers, European Directives on Civil Law—Shaping a New German Civil Code, 18 Tulane Eur. & Civ. L. F. 1 (2003) (effect on German law of EC directives, including Product Liability *Directive* (Produkthaftungsgesetz)).

**22.** BGHZ 51, 91 (1968), in 2 B. Markesinis, The German Law of Obligations—The Law of Torts: A Comparative Introduction 493 (Clarendon Oxford, 3d ed. 1997).

**23.** See Hansen, Product Liability Legislation in Denmark—A Danish Lawyer Looks at the Directive, Prod. Liab. Int'l 146 (Oct. 1986).

**24.** See J.-S. Borghetti, La Responsabilité du Fait des Produits—Étude de Droit Comparé (LGDJ, 2005).

**25.** See Reimann, Liability for Defective Products at the Beginning of the Twenty–First Century: Emergence of a Worldwide Standard?, 51 Am. J. Comp. L. 751, 758 (2003).

**26.** See J.-S. Borghetti, La Responsabilité du Fait des Produits–Étude de Droit Comparé (LGDJ, 2005).

**27.** See Rajneri, Interaction Between the European Directive on Product Liability and the Former Liability Regime in Italy, 4 Global Jurist Topics, www.bepress.com (2004); Dreyfuss, The Italian Law on Strict Products Liability, 17 N.Y.L. Sch. J. Int'l & Comp. L. 37 (1997); Bernstein and Fanning, Heirs of Leonardo: Cultural Obstacles to Strict Products Liability in Italy, 27 Vand. J. Transnat'l L. 1 (1994).

**28.** See Vela Sánchez, Products Liability in Spain, 32 Tex. Tech. L. Rev. 979 (2001).

**29.** See Howells and Mildred, Is European Products Liability More Protective Than the Restatement (Third) of Torts: Products Liability?, 65 Tenn. L. Rev. 985, 992–93 (1998).

**30.** Council Directive 85/374/EEC of 25 July 1985 on the Approximation of the Laws, Regulations and Administrative Provisions of the Member States Concerning Liability for Defective Products, 1985 O.J. (L 210) 29.

within the Common Market.[31] Each member state in the Economic Community, now including all 25 members of the European Union, is obligated to enact national legislation "approximating" EC Directives.[32] What this means, of course, is that the wording and interpretation of the various states' national legislation differs in some respects from the *Directive*,[33] a problem that occasionally leads to challenges of national laws in the European Court of Justice.[34]

The basic pillar of the *Directive* is that "liability without fault on the part of the producer is the sole means of adequately [protecting] the consumer against damage caused by a defective product."[35] Article 1 of the *Directive* provides, "The producer shall be liable for damage caused by a defect in his product." Articles 2 and 3 define "product" and "producer"; Article 4 places the burden of proof on plaintiffs to establish damage, defect, and causation; and Article 5 endorses the principle of joint and several liability when two or more producers are liable for the same damage.[36]

**"Defective."** The heart of the *Directive* is Article 6, which states when a product will be deemed "defective" and hence subject its producer to liability:

*Article 6*

1. A product is defective when it does not provide the safety which a person is entitled to expect, taking all circumstances into account, including:

    (a) the presentation of the product;

    (b) the use to which it could reasonably be expected that the product would be put;

    (c) the time when the product was put into circulation.

2. A product shall not be considered defective for the sole reason that a better product is subsequently put into circulation.

---

**31.** See Taschner, Harmonization of Product Liability Law in the European Community, 34 Tex. Int'l L.J. 21, 22–25 (1999).

**32.** Id.

**33.** See C. van Dam, European Tort Law § 1502–2 (2005) ("Substantial differences remain because of the options in the Directive, the remaining differences in the national laws of damages and the application of pre-existing liability regimes next to the Directive.").

**34.** See, e.g., European Comm'n v. United Kingdom, C–300/95, E.C.R. I–2649 [1997], [1997] All E.R. 481, discussed in Stapleton, Bugs in Anglo–American Products Liability, 53 S.C. L. Rev. 1225, 1246–52 (2002); Taschner, Harmonization of Product Liability Law in the European Community, 34 Tex. Int'l L.J. 21, 33–34 (1999); G.

Howells and S. Wetherill, Consumer Protection § 4.2.4.3, at 234 (Ashgate, 2d ed. 2004). See also Sánchez v. Medicina Asturiana SA, C–183/00, E.C.R. I–3901 [2002 Spain]; Commission v. France, C–52/00, E.C.R. I–3827 [2002]; Commission v. Greece, C–154/00, E.C.R. I–3879 [2002]; Veedfald v. Arhus Reg'l Auth., C–203/99, E.C.R. I–3569 [2001] (Danish organ transplant solution case).

**35.** Preamble to the Directive.

**36.** For a helpful recent overview of the United Kingdom's version of the Directive, the Consumer Protection Act of 1987, see G. Howells and S. Wetherill, Consumer Protection § 4.2.4.3 (Ashgate, 2d ed. 2004). For helpful early critiques, see Stapleton, Products Liability Reform—Real or Illusory?, 6 Oxford J. Legal Stud. 392, 405 (1986); J. Stapleton, Stapleton, Product Liability 236–42 (Butterworths, 1994).

So defining defectiveness in terms of "the safety which a person is entitled to expect" opens a host of interpretative questions.[37] At first glance, Europe's consumer-entitlement test suggests a strong resemblance to the consumer expectations test of § 402A of the *Restatement (Second) of Torts*,[38] America's traditional, if fading, standard for design defectiveness.[39] But this interpretation is too facile and most certainly incorrect. While there is as yet little European case law developing the meaning of product defectiveness, the standard is clearly one of consumer "entitlement" rather than consumer "expectations." Whereas America's original standard of defectiveness, set forth in the comments to § 402A of the *Restatement (Second) of Torts*, plainly defined the norm of product safety in terms of the *actual* expectations of consumers,[40] the European *Directive* in Article 6 just as plainly rests its safety standard on the level of safety that people are *entitled* to expect. Under such a standard, the actual expectations of consumers are secondary to the true question of what safety norm, under all the circumstances, is appropriate—a norm which surely is informed by actual consumer expectations, but which often rests more fully on the practicalities of manufacturing and marketing.

One should be cautious in predicting how European law will develop on this important issue, but one might reasonably suppose that European courts in the long run will be drawn to interpret the consumer-entitlement standard as requiring, at least in cases involving durable goods,[41] a cost-benefit evaluation of a product's safety.[42] Whether looked at normatively, from the view that consumers are "entitled" to expect no

---

**37.** See C.J. Miller and R. Goldberg, Product Liability chs. 10–12 (Oxford, 2d ed. 2004).

**38.** For such an interpretation, see, e.g., Henderson and Twerski, What Europe, Japan, and Other Countries Can Learn from the New American Restatement of Products Liability, 34 Tex. Int'l L.J. 1 (1999).

**39.** On the consumer expectations test, see §§ 5.6 and 8.3, below.

**40.** See Restatement (2d) Torts § 402A cmt. *g* (defining "defective condition" as "a condition not contemplated by the ultimate consumer, which will be unreasonably dangerous to him"), and cmt. *i* (defining "unreasonably dangerous" as "dangerous to an extent beyond that which would be contemplated by the ordinary consumer who purchases it, with the ordinary knowledge common to the community as to its characteristics").

**41.** A U.K. decision applied an absolute, rather than risk-utility, standard to infected blood. See In re Hepatitis C Litigation (A v. National Blood Authority), 3 All E.R. 289 (Q.B. 2001). As discussed below, cases involving such special products as blood, drugs, food, and toxic chemicals will surely receive the special treatment they deserve.

**42.** This is the firm position of a leading scholar on European and Anglo–American products liability law, Professor Jane Sta-

pleton. See, e.g., Stapleton, Bugs in Anglo–American Products Liability, 53 S.C. L. Rev. 1225 (2002); Stapleton, Products Liability in the United Kingdom: The Myths of Reform, 34 Tex. Int'l L.J. 45, 53–54 (1999) ("Despite the lack of a definition of defect, it seems most likely that the approach European judges will take will be the sort of broad balancing of costs and benefits which underlies the judicial resolution of the standard of care in negligence."); Stapleton, Products Liability Reform—Real or Illusory?, 6 Oxford J. Legal Stud. 392, 405 (1986); J. Stapleton, Product Liability 236 (1994). See also Stapleton, The Restatement (Third) of Torts: Products Liability, An Anglo–Australian Perspective, 39 Washburn L.J. 363, 376–79 (2000) (the interpretation of the "entitled to expect" standard as a consumer-expectations test is "both widespread and dangerous," but "it is highly unlikely that European and Australian courts will interpret these provisions as mandating the consumer expectations test"); Owen, Strict Products Liability in America and Europe, in Festschrift für Erwin Deutsch 305, 309–10 (1999); Lord Griffiths, De Val, and Dormer, Developments in English Product Liability Law: A Comparison with the American System, 62 Tul. L. Rev. 353, 382 (1988).

more safety than manufacturers reasonably can deliver, or textually, from the fact that Article 6 requires "taking all circumstances into account" including the use to which the product "could reasonably be expected" to be put[43] "at the time when the product was put into circulation,"[44] Article 6 leads naturally to a risk-utility balancing test in conventional product cases involving defects in design.[45]

    **Development risks.** The other central provision of the *Directive*, Article 7, sets forth defenses to products liability claims.[46] Of greatest interest to American lawyers, from a conceptual point of view, is the "development risk" defense in Article 7(e), which applies to most European nations.[47] Not unlike the state-of-the-art defense in America,[48] the development risk defense shields a producer from liability if "the state of scientific and technical knowledge at the time when he put the product into circulation was not such as to enable the existence of the defect to be discovered." Exactly what this means is difficult to say, for this provision has spawned a diversity of results: a Dutch court has ruled that the development risk defense protects sellers of HIV-infected blood;[49] an English court has held that the defense does not protect

---

**43.** Article 6(b).

**44.** Article 6(c)

**45.** See authorities cited above and §§ 5.7 and 8.4, below.

**46.** In full, this section of the Product Liability Directive provides:

*Article 7*

The producer shall not be liable as a result of this Directive if he proves:

    (a) that he did not put the product into circulation; or

    (b) that, having regard to the circumstances, it is probable that the defect which caused the damage did not exist at the time when the product was put into circulation by him or that this defect came into being afterwards; or

    (c) that the product was neither manufactured by him for sale or any form of distribution for economic purpose nor manufactured or distributed by him in the course of his business; or

    (d) that the defect is due to compliance of the product with mandatory regulations issued by the public authorities; or

    (e) that the state of scientific and technical knowledge at the time when he put the product into circulation was not such as to enable the existence of the defect to be discovered; or

    (f) in the case of a manufacturer of a component, that the defect is attributable to the design of the product in which the component has been fitted or to the instructions given by the manufacturer of the product.

**47.** Article 15(1)(b) permits member states to opt out of this provision. Of the fifteen EU members in early 2004, only Luxembourg and Finland opted to omit this defense entirely, under Article 15(1)(b). Spain excludes from this defense liability for the sale of defective medicines and food, Germany for pharmaceuticals, and France for products (like blood) derived from the human body.

**48.** Some commentators on European law distinguish the development risk defense from the state-of-the-art defense. See, e.g., Taschner, Harmonization of Product Liability Law in the European Community, 34 Tex. Int'l L.J. 21, 31 (1999); G. Howells and S. Wetherill, Consumer Protection § 4.1.3, at 201 (Ashgate, 2d ed. 2004). Other commentators appear to equate the two. See Wandt, German Approaches to Product Liability, 34 Tex. Int'l L.J. 71 (1999). See generally Howells and Mildred, Infected Blood: Defect and Discoverability—A First Exposition of the EC Product Liability Directive, 65 Mod. L. Rev. 95, 98 (2002); Stapleton, Bugs in Anglo–American Products Liability, 53 S.C. L. Rev. 1225, 1243–52 (2002); Stapleton, Products Liability in the United Kingdom: The Myths of Reform, 34 Tex. Int'l L.J. 45, 53–61 (1999); Newdick, Risk, Uncertainty and "Knowledge" in the Development Risk Defence, 20 Anglo–Am. L. Rev. 309 (1991); C.J. Miller and R. Goldberg, Product Liability ch. 13, at 489–528 (Oxford, 2d ed. 2004); J. Stapleton, Product Liability 236–42 (Butterworths, 1994).

**49.** Scholten v. The Foundation Sanquin of Blood Supply, Amsterdam, Feb. 3, 1999, NJ 621 (ann. DJV), discussed in Stapleton, Bugs in Anglo–American Products Liability, 53 S.C. L. Rev. 1225, 1252–53 (2002).

suppliers of infected blood, while it does apply to manufacturing defects—but only until a risk is actually discovered;[50] a German court has concluded that the defense does not apply to manufacturing defects;[51] and the European Court of Justice has held that the defense applies even if knowledge of the defect exists but is not "accessible."[52]

### Directions in European Law

The future path of European products liability law is quite uncertain.[53] Hazarding a prediction on how European courts will define defectiveness in cases involving ordinary, durable types of products should make any sensible American lawyer tremble. Yet attempting to predict how a court in any European nation will define the term "defective" and apply the development risk defense in cases involving special types of product dangers—such as toxic chemicals, natural food hazards, electrical surges, infected blood, and side effects of drugs— would be sheer folly. The *Directive* gives no hint at how such cases should be resolved, and both Europe's and America's experience with quagmires such as these suggest that the underlying tensions in these special situations will be resolved according to the varying cultural contexts of each European state.[54]

**50.** In re Hepatitis C Litigation (A v. National Blood Authority), 3 All E.R. 289 (Q.B. 2001). See Howells and Mildred, Infected Blood: Defect and Discoverability—A First Exposition of the EC Product Liability Directive, 65 Mod. L. Rev. 95, 98 (2002). See generally Feldman, Blood Justice: Courts, Conflicts, and Compensation in Japan, France, and the United States, 34 Law & Society Rev. 651 (2000).

**51.** BGHZ 129, 353, discussed in Hodges, The Case of the Exploding Bottle of Water, 18 Prod. Liab. Int'l 73 (1996).

**52.** As, perhaps, where it resides only in a remote Manchurian scientific journal. See European Comm'n v. United Kingdom, C–300/95, E.C.R. I–2649 (1997), [1997] All E.R. 481. Compare the decision of an Australian court, interpreting a similar provision, which ruled that the development risk defense applies where the general risk is known but its discovery in a particular product is impossible to detect. See Ryan v. Great Lakes Council, 78 F.C.R. 309 (1999) (hepatitis-infected oysters), on appeal, Graham Barclay Oysters Pty v. Ryan, 102 F.C.R. 307 (2000), on further appeal on other grounds, [2002] H.C.A. 54 (5 Dec. 2002).

**53.** After a Green Paper, a White Paper, and a major research study, it appears that the European Commission is content for now to leave the *Directive* in its present form, and calls in Europe for further harmonization of products liability law (as by negating the effect of separate national laws on sales and other branches of products liability law) appear to have abated. See Liability for Defective Products: Green Paper from the European Commission, COM (99) 396 final; Comm'n Report on the Application of Directive 85/374 on Liability for Defective Products, COM (2000) 893 final (Jan. 31, 2001, the "White Paper"); Product Liability in the European Union (Lovells, Feb. 2003) (the major research study). See generally Stapleton, Bugs in Anglo-American Products Liability, 53 S.C. L. Rev. 1225, 1226–27 (2002); Stapleton, Products Liability in the United Kingdom: The Myths of Reform, 34 Tex. Int'l L.J. 45, 67–70 (1999) (predicting the future course of products liability law in the UK and the EU); G. Howells and S. Wetherill, Consumer Protection § 4.2.5, at 240 (Ashgate, 2d ed. 2004).

**54.** As simply one example, an English court has ruled that contaminated blood was "defective" under Article 6, subjecting its supplier to strict liability. See In re Hepatitis C Litigation (A v. National Blood Authority), 3 All E.R. 289 (Q.B. 2001). American law is directly to the contrary. See § 16.9, below.

## Other Nations

In recent years, other nations have begun to tackle products liability law in a serious manner. Put otherwise, products liability law has gone global.[55] At least Japan,[56] Australia,[57] Taiwan, Israel,[58] Brazil, and several of the recently admitted EU nations—Hungary and Latvia, among others[59]—have enacted (or introduced) "clones" of the *European Directive* which is rapidly becoming the worldwide model for products liability legislation outside of the United States.[60] And many other nations in recent years have adopted various types of products liability laws, sometimes as independent products liability statutes, other times as portions of consumer protection acts, and still other times as part of the torts or sales law chapters of a civil code.[61] Such other nations with important products liability legislation include Korea, Russia, Poland, Argentina, Peru,[62] China,[63] India, Malaysia, Philippines,[64] Taiwan,[65] and

**55.** See Reimann, Liability for Defective Products at the Beginning of the Twenty–First Century: Emergence of a Worldwide Standard?, 51 Am. J. Comp. L. 751, 836–38 (2003); Reimann, Product Liability in a Global Context: The Hollow Victory of the European Model, 11 Eur. Rev. Priv. L. 128 (2003).

**56.** See, e.g., Kelemen & Sibbitt, The Americanization of Japanese Law, 23 U. Pa. J. Int'l Econ. L. 269 (2002); Rothenberg, Japan's New Product Liability Law: Achieving Modest Success, 31 Law & Pol'y Int'l Bus. 453 (2000); Easton, The Path for Japan?: An Examination of Product Liability Laws in the United States, The United Kingdom, and Japan, 23 B.C. Int'l & Comp. L. Rev. 311 (2000); Kobayashi and Furuta, Products Liability Act and Transnational Litigation in Japan, 34 Tex. Int'l L. J. 93 (1999); Nottage, The Present and Future of Product Liability Dispute Resolution in Japan, 27 Wm. Mitchell L. Rev. 215 (2000); Behrens & Raddock, Japan's New Product Liability Law: The Citadel of Strict Liability Falls, But Access to Recovery is Limited by Formidable Barriers, 16 U. Pa. J. Int'l Bus. L. 669 (1995); L. Nottage, Product Safety and Liability Law in Japan: From Minamata to Mad Cows (Routledge, 2004).

**57.** See, e.g., Stapleton, Restatement (Third) of Torts: Products Liability, an Anglo–Australian Perspective, 39 Washburn L. J. 363 (2000); Kellam & Arste, Current Trends and Future Directions in Product Liability in Australia, 27 Wm. Mitchell L. Rev. 141 (2000); J. Kellam, Product Liability in the Asia–Pacific (2d ed. 1999); H. Beerworth, Product Liability in Australia (Butterworth, 2001).

**58.** See Westermann, Product Liability in Germany and Israel Against the Background of European Standardization, 13 Tel Aviv U. Stud. in Law 205 (1997).

**59.** See Gödölle, Being Liable for Your Product: Central and Eastern Europe, 26 Int'l Bus. Law 73 (1998).

**60.** See Reimann, Product Liability in a Global Context: The Hollow Victory of the

European Model, 11 Eur. Rev. Priv. L. 128 (2003) (observing that, as products liability law has spread to the four corners of the globe in the last two decades, the European Directive, rather than the American model, has become the blueprint for new laws, but also noting that these new products liability laws have had little real-word effect). See also Reimann, Liability for Defective Products at the Beginning of the Twenty–First Century: Emergence of a Worldwide Standard?, 51 Am. J. Comp. L. 751 (2003) (same).

**61.** See, e.g., Maestroni, Overview of the Study Undertaken by the National Law Center for Inter–American Free Trade, 20 Ariz. J. Int'l & Comp. L. 1 (2003) (brief comparative overview of Latin American products liability doctrine in Argentina, Brazil, Chile, Uruguay, Mexico, Costa Rica, and Colombia); Velazquez, Preview of Problems in Product Liability: U.S. and Mexico, 8 U.S.-Mex. L.J. 117 (2000); Van Eeden and Van Wyk, Product Liability in South Africa, 26 Int'l Bus. Law 63 (1998).

**62.** See Olenka Woolcott Oyague, Univ. de Lima–Peru, La Responsabilidad del Productor (Pontificia Univ. Católica del Perú, 2003).

**63.** See, e.g., Li Han, The Product Quality Law in China: A Proper Balance Between Consumers and Producers?, 6 J. Chinese & Comp. L. 1 (2003); Zhao, Chinese Product Liability Law: Can China Build Another Great Wall to Protect Its Consumers?, 1 Wash. U. Global Stud. L. Rev. 581 (2002); Jansson and Riley, Product Liability in China, 10 I.C.C.L.R. 129 (1999); Hongjie, The Legal System of Product Liability in the People's Republic of China, 6 Consumer L.J. 213 (1998).

**64.** See J. Kellam, Product Liability in the Asia–Pacific (2d ed. 1999).

**65.** See Juang, The Taiwan Consumer Protection Law: Attempt to Protect Consumers Proves Ineffective, 6 Pac. Rim L. & Pol'y J. 219 (1997).

also the province of Quebec. And the law of products liability in Canada, while mostly common law, is quite developed.[66]

The literature on products liability law in other nations around the world is so vast, and is expanding so rapidly, that a reader interested in finding resources on the products liability law of a particular foreign nation is best directed to a library or the internet.

**66.** See, e.g., Morritt & Bjorkquist, Product Liability in Canada: Principles and Practice North of the Border, 27 Wm. Mitchell L. Rev. 177 (2000); Waddams, The Canadian Law of Products Liability, 34 Tex. Int'l L.J. 119 (1999); S. Waddams, Products Liability (Carswell, 4th ed. 2002). See generally Reimann, above.

# PART I

## THEORIES OF RECOVERY

# Chapter 2

# NEGLIGENCE

*Table of Sections*

## § 2.1 NEGLIGENCE—GENERALLY

Negligence is the classic products liability claim. Historically, it was the principal basis of recovery in products liability cases during the beginning and much of the middle part of the twentieth century. Even as its doctrinal significance slipped into the shadows as various "strict" theories of manufacturer liability emerged and developed in recent decades, negligence retained a vital role in modern products liability law. It remains the principal theory of tort recovery in the five states that have refused to adopt the theory of strict products liability in tort.[1] In the great majority of other states, there may be good reasons for a plaintiff to emphasize the manufacturer's fault and so to base recovery at least in part on negligence. Tactically, perhaps because the rhetoric of negligence is "hotter" than strict liability, juries are more likely to find for plaintiffs, and in higher amounts, on negligence rather than strict liability claims.[2] In terms of evidence, some jurisdictions bar certain

---

**§ 2.1**

**1.** Delaware, Massachusetts, Michigan, North Carolina, and Virginia. See, e.g., In re September 11 Litig., 280 F.Supp.2d 279, 306 (S.D.N.Y. 2003) (Va. law) (no strict products liability in tort in Virginia); Smith v. DaimlerChrysler Corp., 2002 WL 31814534, at *2 (Del. Super. Ct. 2002); Commonwealth v. Johnson Insulation, 682 N.E.2d 1323 (Mass. 1997) (no strict products liability in tort in Massachusetts); Ryan v. Brunswick, 557 N.W.2d 541 (Mich. 1997), citing Prentis v. Yale Mfg. Co., 365 N.W.2d 176 (Mich. 1984); N.C. Gen. Stat. 99B–1.1.

**2.** See, e.g., Trull v. Volkswagen of Am., Inc., 320 F.3d 1 (1st Cir. 2002) (N.H. law) (affirming jury verdict in crashworthiness case for defendant on strict liability claim and for plaintiff, for $9 million, on negligence claim). See generally Cupp and Polage, The Rhetoric of Strict Products Liability Versus Negligence: An Empirical Analysis, 77 N.Y.U. L. Rev. 874, 924 (2002) (empirical study finding that "jurors respond more favorably to negligence language than to strict liability language"); Rheingold, The Expanding Liability of the Product Supplier: A Primer, 2 Hofstra L. Rev. 521, 531–32 (1974) (trial lawyer's similar experience).

types of proof in strict liability in tort that may be allowed in negligence, such as evidence that a risk was foreseeable or that the manufacturer failed to follow an industry safety standard.[3] At least in one state, a negligence or other fault-based claim is necessary to support a punitive damages claim,[4] and, although unusual, a negligence claim sometimes is available when a strict tort claim is not.[5] Since about 1980, there has been a growing movement to return to negligence in design, warnings, and other types of cases, leading some state legislatures, courts, and the *Restatement (Third) of Torts: Products Liability*[6] to reassert the central role of negligence principles, and in some cases negligence doctrine, in a variety of products liability contexts.[7] For these and other reasons, the negligence cause of action remains a vital theory of recovery in products liability litigation.[8]

Negligence may occur at any stage of the design, manufacturing, or marketing process. To prove any products liability claim sounding in negligence, whether negligent design, negligent manufacture, or a negligent failure to provide adequate warnings or instructions, a plaintiff must establish: (1) that the seller owed a duty to the plaintiff;[9] (2) that the seller breached that duty; (3) that the breach of duty was a cause in fact of the plaintiff's injury;[10] (4) that the cause in fact was a proximate cause of the injury;[11] and (5) that damages for the harm suffered are recoverable in negligence.[12] The plaintiff has the burden of proof on each element of the negligence cause of action.[13]

### Duty

The preliminary element in every negligence claim is the defendant's duty of care to protect the plaintiff from harm.[14] Broadly stated,

---

**3.** See § 2.3, below.

**4.** See, e.g., Barnwell v. Barber–Colman Co., 393 S.E.2d 162 (S.C. 1989) (3–2 decision).

**5.** See, e.g., Tillman v. R.J. Reynolds Tobacco Co., 871 So.2d 28 (Ala. 2003) (cigarette smoker could not recover under strict liability in tort, but might in negligence); Trull v. Volkswagen of Am., Inc., 320 F.3d 1, 6 (1st Cir. 2002) (N.H. law) (jury's answers on general verdict form finding negligence but not strict liability were not inconsistent); Griggs v. BIC Corp., 981 F.2d 1429, 1433 (3d Cir. 1992) (Pa. law) (design of non-childproof disposable butane cigarette lighter used by small child to start fire not defective under strict liability, because lighter was not "unreasonably dangerous to intended users," but negligent design claim was sufficient); High v. Westinghouse Elec. Corp., 610 So.2d 1259 (Fla. 1992) (no strict liability in tort because dismantling of transformers containing PCB's substantially altered product, but duty to warn in negligence of foreseeable risks). See § 5.9, below.

**6.** See § 6.5, below.

**7.** See § 2.6, below.

**8.** For a comparison of negligence to strict liability, see § 5.9, below.

**9.** Various duty issues are examined in ch. 10, below.

**10.** Cause in fact is examined in ch. 11, below.

**11.** Proximate cause is examined in ch. 12, below.

**12.** See 2 Madden & Owen on Products Liability ch. 17 for a discussion of damages recoverable in negligence.

**13.** See, e.g., Birch v. Midwest Garage Door Sys., 790 N.E.2d 504, 509 (Ind. Ct. App. 2003); Roach v. Ivari Int'l Ctrs., Inc., 822 A.2d 316, 322 (Conn. App. Ct. 2003); Jay v. Moog Auto., Inc., 652 N.W.2d 872, 880 (Neb. 2002); D'Olier v. General Motors Corp., 495 N.E.2d 1040, 1043–44 (Ill. App. Ct. 1986) (burden of proof is not met where plaintiff shows only "possibilities" and not "competent evidence" to support negligence claim).

**14.** See, e.g., Phillips v. Cricket Lighters, 841 A.2d 1000 (Pa. 2003), characterizing duty as the "primary" element and noting that duty rests on a balance of (1)

manufacturers have a duty to exercise reasonable care to refrain from selling products that contain unreasonable risks of harm. Once American courts repudiated the rule of *Winterbottom v. Wright* in *MacPherson v. Buick* and its progeny, as previously discussed,[15] the duty of manufacturers became defined in terms of foreseeable risks to foreseeable victims from the failure to exercise reasonable care. That is, in the design, manufacture, and marketing of products, manufacturers have a duty of reasonable care to protect foreseeable victims from foreseeable risks of harm.

Due care in the *design* of a product requires that a manufacturer exercise reasonable care in a variety of different functions: that the general product concept be conceived and formulated carefully for its foreseeable uses and abuses;[16] that proper attention be devoted to selecting appropriate materials and components to be assembled together into the finished product; that safety devices for the product's expected uses be adopted as appropriate; and that prototypes of the product be tested, as appropriate, in contexts duplicating the harshest circumstances of expected use.[17] Due care in a product's *manufacture* requires a manufacturer to exercise reasonable care in the product's assembly.[18] This duty requires the manufacturer to exercise reasonable care at two distinct stages of the manufacturing process prior to distribution of the product: (1) during the actual process of manufacturing the product, including the selection, inspection, and assembly of raw materials and component parts;[19] and (2) after production, in the process of quality control (or "quality assurance") designed to limit the output of defective products to the smallest reasonable level.[20] Finally, in *marketing* its products, a manufacturer must exercise reasonable care to instruct consumers on

---

the parties' relationship; (2) the social utility of the defendant's conduct; (3) the nature of the risk and foreseeability of the harm; (4) the consequences of imposing a duty in the circumstances; and (5) the public interest in imposing a duty on the defendant. See also Blue v. Environmental Eng'g, Inc., 803 N.E.2d 187 (Ill. App. Ct. 2003). See generally Goldberg and Zipursky, The Restatement (Third) and the Place of Duty in Negligence Law, 54 Vand. L. Rev. 657 (2001); Owen, Duty Rules, 54 Vand. L. Rev. 767 (2001); Rabin, The Duty Concept in Negligence Law, 54 Vand. L. Rev. 787 (2001); Weirib, The Passing of Palsgraf?, 54 Vand. L. Rev. 803 (2001).

**15.** Winterbottom v. Wright, 10 M. & W. 109, 152 Eng. Rep. 402 (Ex. 1842); MacPherson v. Buick Motor Co., 111 N.E. 1050 (N.Y. 1916). See § 1.2, above.

**16.** Restatement (2d) Torts § 398.

**17.** See Blue v. Environmental Eng'g, Inc., 803 N.E.2d 187, 194 (Ill. App. Ct. 2003) ("it is generally the duty of the manufacturer 'to design a product so that it will be reasonably safe for its intended use and for any reasonably foreseeable use' ").

**18.** Restatement (2d) Torts § 395.

**19.** See, e.g., Jenkins v. General Motors Corp., 446 F.2d 377 (5th Cir. 1971) (Ga. law) (jury could find that GM assembly line worker had improperly torqued nut on bolt in suspension system causing nut to work loose, bolt to drop out, wheel to cant out, and resultant loss of steering).

**20.** See, e.g., Ford Motor Co. v. Zahn, 265 F.2d 729, 731 (8th Cir. 1959) (Minn. law) (jury could find negligent quality control where jagged burr on ash tray penetrated plaintiff's eye during sudden stop):

[T]here is imposed upon the manufacturer of an article for sale or use the duty to exercise reasonable care to prevent defective conditions caused by a miscarriage in the manufacturing process. This duty requires reasonable skill and care in the process of manufacture and for reasonable inspection or tests to discover defects.

Id. See generally Prod. Liab. Rep. (CCH) ¶ 1130 (1997); Annot., Manufacturer's Duty to Test or Inspect as Affecting His Liability for Product–Caused Injury, 6 A.L.R. 3d 91 (1966).

how to use its products safely and to warn them of hidden dangers that the products may contain.[21]

In considering the scope of a manufacturer's duty under negligence law, it is important not to substitute the notion of duty for negligence itself.[22] But it is also important to note that duty shares with negligence the limiting principles of foreseeability, cost-effectiveness, and balance.[23] Rather than being absolute, as would be a truly "strict" theory of liability, the duty under negligence law is limited to requiring only *reasonable* care—not perfect care; to protecting only persons *foreseeably* placed at risk—not all persons; and to avoiding only risks that are *foreseeable*—not all risks. In short, the negligence duty is one of reasonableness—not perfection.

In addition to defining the scope of a manufacturer's obligations in general terms to persons put at risk by product dangers, duty serves another sharper role of limitation. As a threshold issue of law in every negligence case,[24] the duty element provides courts with an effective screening device for dividing cases into two broad categories—those properly embraced by the negligence system and those properly excluded. Drawing from a broad range of considerations of fairness, justice, and social policy,[25] the duty issue provides courts with an opportunity to consider the appropriateness of applying negligence law to various types of cases at the category level.[26] For example, courts have employed no-

---

**21.** Restatement (2d) Torts § 388, Chattel Known to Be Dangerous for Intended Use, provides that product sellers who have reason to know that their products are dangerous and, further, that users may not recognize the dangers, have a duty of reasonable care to inform users of those dangers.

**22.** See Goldberg and Zipursky, The Restatement (Third) and the Place of Duty in Negligence Law, 54 Vand. L. Rev. 657 (2001); Restatement (3d) Torts: Liability for Physical Harm § 7 and comments thereto.

**23.** See id.

**24.** Whether a duty exists is a question of law for the court. See, e.g., Friedman v. Merck & Co., 131 Cal.Rptr.2d 885, 891 (Ct. App. 2003); Roach v. Ivari Int'l Ctrs., Inc., 822 A.2d 316, 321 (Conn. App. Ct. 2003). See generally Prosser and Keeton on Torts § 37 at 236; Dobbs, Law of Torts § 226. *But see* Birch v. Midwest Garage Door Sys., 790 N.E.2d 504, 510 (Ind. Ct. App. 2003) (duty is ordinarily to be determined by court, but there may be factual issues interwoven with question of duty that make it "a mixed question of law and fact to be determined by the factfinder").

**25.** See, e.g., Friedman v. Merck & Co., 131 Cal.Rptr.2d 885, 891 (Ct. App. 2003) (major considerations include " 'the foreseeability of harm to the plaintiff, the degree of certainty that the plaintiff suffered injury, the closeness of the connection between the defendant's conduct and the injury suffered, the moral blame attached to the defendant's conduct, the policy of preventing future harm, the extent of the burden to the defendant and consequences to the community of imposing a duty to exercise care with resulting liability for breach, and the availability, cost, and prevalence of insurance for the risk involved' "); Hamilton v. Beretta U.S.A. Corp., 750 N.E.2d 1055, 1060 (N.Y. 2001) (duty determinations involve " 'balancing factors, including the reasonable expectations of parties and society generally, the proliferation of claims, the likelihood of unlimited or insurer-like liability, disproportionate risk and reparation allocation, and public policies affecting the expansion or limitation of new channels of liability' "). See also Prosser and Keeton on Torts § 53, at 359 (duty includes such factors as "convenience of administration, capacity of the parties to bear the loss, a policy of preventing future injuries, the moral blame attached to the wrongdoer, and many others").

**26.** " 'The foreseeability of a particular kind of harm plays a very significant role in this calculus, but a court's task—in determining "duty"—is not to decide whether a particular plaintiff's injury was reasonably foreseeable in light of a particular defendant's conduct, but rather to evaluate more generally whether the category of negligent conduct at issue is sufficiently likely to result in the kind of harm experienced that

duty rationales in denying claims against fast food retailers for selling fattening foods to customers who get fat;[27] against pharmacists for failing to warn clients of side effects in prescription drugs;[28] and against manufacturers for failing to equip each product with a safety feature sold as optional,[29] failing to warn of obvious dangers,[30] and failing to recall dangerous products;[31] and for selling alcohol to persons who get ill or cause an accident,[32] selling products that may be dangerous when disposed of or dismantled,[33] selling drugs that cause birth defects in the grandchild of the drug's recipient,[34] and selling handguns in such quantities and other circumstances as to facilitate handgun crime.[35]

## Breach

In addition to duty, a plaintiff must also prove its breach. Simply stated, a breach of duty is established by proving that a manufacturer or other product seller failed to conform to the standard of reasonable care which defines the duty. The standard of care required varies with the risk and circumstances, as discussed below.[36]

As mentioned above, it is important to note that duty in negligence law is limited to a duty of reasonable care, not a duty to produce goods without defects. Even the most careful manufacturers who follow all tenets of good manufacturing practices sometimes produce products that are defective. Thus, because the duty under negligence law is only to act with reasonable care not to produce defective products, the mere fact that a manufactured good is defective ordinarily will not establish breach. Indeed, in order to establish breach, the plaintiff in a negligence case generally must prove both defect *and* negligence: that is, (1) that the product was defective (in its design, manufacture, or marketing), and (2) that the manufacturer was negligent in some manner in allowing the product to be manufactured and sold in that defective condition.[37] While it is readily apparent that a negligence claim requires establishing this second aspect of breach, negligence,[38] the first aspect of breach, defectiveness, is not so widely understood to be required in negligence claims as it

liability may appropriately be imposed on the negligent party.'" Friedman v. Merck & Co., 131 Cal.Rptr.2d 885, 891 (Ct. App. 2003). Although the factors relevant to duty substantially overlap those relevant to both negligence and proximate cause, the fact that duty is decided at the category level distinguishes it from the other two elements which involve fact-specific inquiries into the propriety of applying negligence doctrine to particular claims. See Restatement (3d) Torts: Liability for Physical Harm § 7 and comments thereto.

**27.** See § 10.3, below.

**28.** See § 9.6, below.

**29.** See § 8.9, below.

**30.** See § 10.2, below.

**31.** See § 10.8, below.

**32.** See § 10.3, below.

**33.** See § 10.7, below.

**34.** See § 10.5, below.

**35.** See § 10.3, below.

**36.** See § 2.2, below.

**37.** "In negligent design claims it is well established that a manufacturer or seller is not liable in the absence of proof that a product is defective.... Thus, an element of a negligent design case is that the product is defective [such that a plaintiff in such cases must prove two elements:] [1] that the defendants failed to use reasonable care in designing the [product] and [2] that such failure resulted in a defective product." Oanes v. Westgo, Inc. 476 N.W.2d 248, 253 (N.D. 1991).

**38.** Note, however, that the proof of negligence in manufacturing flaw cases often may be inferred from defectiveness, as discussed in §§ 2.2 and 2.5, below.

is in strict liability in tort. Yet, except in certain limited contexts,[39] it is perfectly clear that a manufacturer or other seller cannot be negligent for making or selling a product that is good.[40]

### Cause in Fact

Cause in fact is a necessary element in products liability claims brought in negligence, as it is in negligence law more generally.[41] Thus, a plaintiff ordinarily must prove that the breach of duty of which he or she complains was a necessary antecedent to the harm at issue—that the harm would not have occurred but for the breach of duty. However, it is important to note that the breach need only be shown to have been one cause among others, that it was "a" cause of the harm, not "the" cause of the harm. So long as the breach is shown to have been a substantial contributing factor to the plaintiff's injury, this element generally will be established. These and other causation issues are examined in depth below.[42]

### Proximate Cause

In addition to establishing a factual connection between the harm and the manufacturer's breach of duty, the plaintiff must also establish that the connection was reasonably close, that it was "proximate." This means that the resulting harm must have resulted from one of the risks that the defendant negligently failed to prevent, and that the risk and the plaintiff were both of a reasonably foreseeable type.[43] In addition, for the harm to result proximately from the defendant's negligence, it must flow from the breach without any unforeseeable, intervening interruptions.[44] These and other principles of proximate cause are also treated below.[45]

### Damage

Finally, a plaintiff in a products liability action brought in negligence must establish that the damage proximately caused by the manufacturer's breach of duty was a type of harm for which the plaintiff may recover under negligence. For example, certain plaintiffs may recover in negligence for certain types of pure emotional harm, whereas other plaintiffs may not.[46] And, particularly in products liability actions which

---

**39.** The principal exceptions are misrepresentation and negligent entrustment. See ch. 3 and § 15.2, below.

**40.** See, e.g., Austin v. Will–Burt Co., 232 F.Supp.2d 682, 691 (N.D. Miss. 2002) (negligence claim failed due to plaintiff's failure to prove product defect), aff'd, 361 F.3d 862 (5th Cir. 2002). See generally § 5.9, below.

**41.** See Prosser and Keeton on Torts § 41.

**42.** See ch. 11, below.

**43.** See, e.g., Jones v. Amazing Prods., Inc., 231 F.Supp.2d 1228, 1241 (N.D. Ga. 2002) (foreseeable that consumer might at- tempt to transfer sulfuric acid drain cleaner to container that could melt; foreseeability "means that which would be foreseeably probable or objectively reasonable to expect, not merely what might occur").

**44.** See, e.g., Stahlecker v. Ford Motor Co., 667 N.W.2d 244 (Neb. 2003) (rape and murder of motorist stranded when tire failed due to alleged negligence of manufacturers of vehicle and tires; *held*, criminal assault was "an efficient intervening cause" which precludes negligence from being the proximate cause of the harm).

**45.** See ch. 12, below.

**46.** See Frumer and Friedman, Products Liability § 13.03[9].

implicate the law of contracts, negligence law generally does not provide recovery for pure economic loss.[47] Yet punitive damages may be recoverable in products liability cases brought in negligence, provided that the plaintiff introduces additional evidence showing aggravated fault. With the special exception of punitive damages, examined in depth below,[48] the principles governing the recovery of various types of damages in negligence actions are treated elsewhere.[49]

## § 2.2 THE STANDARD OF CARE

### In General

Most courts apply ordinary negligence parlance in defining the standard of care applicable to negligence claims in products liability cases. When courts do define the standard, they generally go no further than to state that the duty is one of "reasonable," "ordinary," or "due" care.[1] Sometimes a court will be more explicit, such as: "[N]egligence is the doing of something that a person of ordinary prudence would not have done in the same or similar circumstances or a failure to do something that a person of ordinary prudence would have done in the same or similar circumstances."[2] And some courts tailor these principles to the products liability context by measuring the defendant's conduct against that of a mythical "manufacturer of ordinary prudence in the exercise of ordinary care."[3] Finally, courts sometimes focus on the particular industry of the defendant and apply the standard prevailing in this particular business,[4] such as "a press manufacturer of ordinary prudence."[5] This kind of particularized focus would seem to be helpful to juries attempting to apply the general standard of care to particularized industry contexts in which the technical knowledge and skill fairly expected of manufacturers acting reasonably is frequently specific to the industry.

**47.** See Frumer and Friedman, Products Liability § 13.07[1].

**48.** See ch. 18, below.

**49.** For discussions of compensatory damages in products liability litigation, see Frumer and Friedman, Products Liability ch. 13; 2 Madden & Owen on Products Liability ch. 17; Am. Law Prod. Liab. 3d ch. 60; C.J. Miller and R. Goldberg, Product Liability ch. 16 (Oxford, 2d ed. 2004).

### § 2.2

**1.** See, e.g., Stahlecker v. Ford Motor Co., 667 N.W.2d 244, 253 (Neb. 2003) ("In a products liability case premised upon negligence, the issue is whether a manufacturer's conduct was reasonable in view of the foreseeable risk of injury."); Andrade v. General Motors Corp., 785 N.E.2d 214, 218 (Ill. App. Ct. 2003) ("ordinary care"; seats); Jarvis v. Ford Motor Co., 283 F.3d 33, 44 (2d Cir. 2002) (N.Y. law) ("reasonable care"; cruise control); Ford Motor Co. v. Burdeshaw 661 So.2d 236, 238 (Ala. 1995) (conduct of "reasonably prudent" person; automobile); Short v. Estwing Mfg., 634 N.E.2d 798 (Ind. Ct. App. 1994) ("due care"; hammer); King v. National Spa & Pool Inst., Inc., 570 So.2d 612 (Ala. 1990) ("due care"; swimming pool); Atkins v. American Motors Corp., 335 So.2d 134 (Ala. 1976) ("due care"; automobile); Ulrich v. Kasco Abrasives Co., 532 S.W.2d 197 (Ky. 1976) ("ordinary care"; grinding machine).

**2.** Rhoads v. Service Mach. Co., 329 F.Supp. 367, 373 (E.D. Ark. 1971). See also Roach v. Ivari Int'l Ctrs., Inc., 822 A.2d 316 (Conn. Ct. App. 2003) (a "reasonably prudent person under the same circumstances").

**3.** Rhoads v. Service Mach. Co., 329 F.Supp. at 376.

**4.** See, e.g., Morden v. Continental AG, 611 N.W.2d 659, 675 (Wis. 2000) (manufacturers held to "reasonable person" standard of customary methods of manufacture in similar industry).

**5.** Rhoads v. Service Mach. Co., 329 F.Supp. at 377.

### Manufacturers Held to Standard of "Expert in the Field"

One of the most fundamental propositions of negligence law in the products liability context is that a manufacturer is held to the level of an expert in its field.[6] Because the manufacturer is the maker of the product who designs, produces, and markets the product for purchase and use, the manufacturer is presumed to be an expert in the field in which it has chosen to do business. As such an expert, its conduct thus is fairly measured against that of a reasonable manufacturer which is an expert in manufacturing that particular type of product.[7] Accordingly, a manufacturer is charged with the duty of design, manufacture, and marketing commensurate with an expert's awareness of the particular product's foreseeable environments of use and special dangers within that environment. This doctrine is especially relevant to the duty of reasonable care to warn of foreseeable risks of harm.[8] For example, the manufacturer of a weed killer made of arsenic will be deemed to know of its long-lasting nature, invisibility, and toxic risk to a homeowner who, some time after applying the poison in the yard, forgets to protect herself against its insidious dangers.[9]

Large and experienced manufacturers normally are the true experts in their fields, so holding them to this standard amounts to nothing more than ordinary care. However, holding smaller and newer manufacturers to such a standard may amount to a kind of strict liability, for it establishes a standard of knowledge and responsibility that smaller and less experienced manufacturers may be incapable of meeting even if they exercise "all due care," as it ordinarily is defined. Now that strict products liability doctrines have spread across the land, courts might be

---

**6.** See, e.g., Olson v. Prosoco, Inc., 522 N.W.2d 284, 289 (Iowa 1994) ("In testing the defendant's liability for negligence in failing to warn, the defendant should be held to the standard of care of an expert in its field."). See also Miles v. Ford Motor Co., 922 S.W.2d 572, 594 (Tex. App. 1996), rev'd in part on other grounds, 967 S.W.2d 377 (Tex. 1998) (a manufacturer is held to be an expert in his field; seat belt harness failed); Stahlheber v. American Cyanamid Co., 451 S.W.2d 48, 61 (Mo. 1970) (manufacturer of polio vaccine "knew or, by using the skill of an expert in defendant's business, could have known of the dangerous potentiality of said product" when administered to adults). See generally 5 Harper, James, and Gray, Law of Torts 350–51:

> [A manufacturer] will be held to the skill of an expert in that business and to an expert's knowledge of the arts, materials, and processes. Thus manufacturers must keep reasonably abreast of scientific knowledge and discoveries touching their products and of techniques and devices used by practical people in their trade.

See also Noel, Manufacturer's Negligence of Design or Directions for Use of a Product, 71 Yale L.J. 816, 847 (1962) ("anyone who enters a special field of manufacturing will

be held to possess the knowledge and skill of an expert in that field").

**7.** See, e.g., Trull v. Volkswagen of Am., Inc., 320 F.3d 1, 8 (1st Cir. 2002) (N.H. law) (automotive manufacturer); Chretien v. General Motors, 959 F.2d 231 (4th Cir. 1992) (Va. law) (same).

**8.** See, e.g., Strothkamp v. Chesebrough–Pond's Inc., 1993 WL 79239 (Mo. Ct. App. 1993) (manufacturer should have warned of risk that child could be injured by placing cotton swab too far inside ear). A failure to warn may be negligent, of course, only if the danger is reasonably foreseeable to the manufacturer. See generally Comment, Foreseeability in Product Design and Duty to Warn Cases—Distinctions and Misconceptions, 1968 Wis. L. Rev. 228. But foreseeability is often viewed from the perspective of an expert in the business who is held to know the characteristics of its products and the uses to which they possibly may be applied. Put another way, the manufacturer is deemed to possess the knowledge of an expert in the field.

**9.** Boyl v. California Chem. Co., 221 F.Supp. 669, 674 (D. Or. 1963) (toxic chemical manufacturers must warn users of its long-lasting dangers arising out of use, storage, and disposal).

wise to rethink the logic and equity of the "expert in the field" doctrine that sometimes unfairly stretches negligence law beyond its natural boundaries.[10]

## Responsibility Limited By Reasonable Foreseeability

One of the most fundamental notions of all of negligence law is that an actor's responsibility is limited to those risks and extends only to those potential victims which the conduct foreseeably threatens. In other words, if a risk or potential victim lies outside of the realm of reasonable foreseeability, the manufacturer or other actor cannot be faulted for failing to take steps to avert the risk or protect the victim.

Especially before the advent of strict products liability in tort, courts sometimes stretched the ordinary notion of foreseeability in negligence cases in order to cover certain risks or persons that sometimes lay outside the normal boundaries of reasonable foreseeability. Sometimes this kind of foreseeability stretching was accomplished by means of the doctrine that a manufacturer is held to the knowledge and skill of an "expert in its field," as just discussed. Another device used by courts in negligence cases confronting claims of unforeseeability is the doctrine of "constructive knowledge."[11] This doctrine holds that a manufacturer will not be heard to challenge the foreseeability of a risk (or victim) if a manufacturer in the same position acting reasonably should have foreseen the risk (or victim). In such cases, a court simply implies, or "constructs," the knowledge based on the reasonable foreseeability of the risk.[12]

That foreseeability inheres in the concept of negligence is evident in the formulations of negligence in the *Second* and *Third Restatements of Torts*. In defining the basic negligence concept applicable to manufacturers, the *Restatement (Second) of Torts* § 395 employs the foreseeability concept in separate ways, each of which places an outer limit on a manufacturer's responsibility for harm caused by its negligent mistakes. First, in order to be "unreasonable," a *risk of harm* from a product must be foreseeable.[13] Second, a manufacturer is properly liable in negligence only if the *use* to which the article was put was foreseeable.[14] Finally, the plaintiff must fall within the *class of persons* foreseeably placed at risk

---

**10.** See, e.g., Sternhagen v. Dow Co., 935 P.2d 1139 (Mont. 1997) (cancer from herbicide exposure). The "issues of reasonableness and foreseeability [are] concepts fundamental to negligence law—to determine a manufacturer's liability." Id. at 1144. "Under the imputation of knowledge doctrine, which is based on strict liability's focus on the product and not on the manufacturer's conduct, knowledge of a product's undiscovered or undiscoverable dangers shall be imputed to the manufacturer." Id. at 1143.

**11.** " 'Negligence based on the failure to warn requires actual or constructive knowledge of the danger on the part of the manufacturer, and the lack of a warning no-

tice.' " Smith v. United States, 155 F.Supp. 605, 609 (E.D. Va. 1957).

**12.** " 'Constructive knowledge' refers to knowledge that one has the opportunity to possess by the exercise of ordinary care." First Nat'l Bank v. Nor–Am Agric. Prod., 537 P.2d 682, 690 (N.M. Ct. App. 1975).

**13.** The justification for a manufacturer's responsibility in negligence rests in part upon "the foreseeability of harm if proper care is not used." Restatement (2d) Torts § 395 cmt. *b*.

**14.** Liability does not extend to "unforeseeable use or manner of use." Id. cmt. *j*. See also cmt. *k*.

by the manufacturer's negligence.[15] These basic foreseeability limitations are carried forward into the *Restatement (Third) of Torts*.[16]

In negligence, therefore, a manufacturer is required to exercise reasonable care to make the product safe only if, and to the extent that, it is foreseeable that a failure to do so will create an unreasonable risk of physical harm to a person, or class of persons, foreseeably at risk. Liability does not require that a manufacturer divine the precise manner in which an accident may occur; it only requires that a defendant should have foreseen the general type of risk that caused the accident.[17] For example, in an exploding soda bottle case, the plaintiff's injury did not occur directly from the exploding glass but rather from his fall as he attempted to clean up the resulting spill. The court ruled that the manufacturer of a defective bottle containing liquid under pressure that explodes should foresee not only broken glass and a spill but also normal efforts to clean up the consequences of the spill.[18] Here, as elsewhere, the problem of establishing whether foreseeability of the particular type of harm should limit liability is troublesome, to say the least. How far any court will follow the chain of consequences in any case is a function of the particular facts, the particular court's view of fairness, and the policy implications in the circumstances.[19]

If a use or misuse is not in fact reasonably foreseeable, the manufacturer has no responsibility to protect persons against it.[20] However, a manufacturer's duty to anticipate harm may extend to harm resulting from product misuse or use of the product in a way or for a purpose for which it was not designed, built, or sold. Many products are commonly used for purposes for which they are not sold. For instance, the manufacturer of a chair may be required to anticipate that it will be stood as well

---

**15.** Liability extends to "those who use [the product] . . . and to those whom [the manufacturer] should expect to be endangered by its probable use." Restatement (2d) Torts § 395. See also id. cmts. *h*, *i*, and *j*.

**16.** "To establish the actor's negligence, it is not enough that there be a likelihood of harm; the likelihood must be foreseeable to the actor at the time of conduct." Restatement (3d) Torts: Liability for Physical Harm § 3 cmt. *g*. See also Products Liability Restatement §§ 2(b) and 2(c), defining defective design and warnings, respectively, in terms of "foreseeable risks." See id. cmt. *m*. These "functional" definitions of product defect are applicable to negligence claims. See id. cmt. *n*.

**17.** See, e.g., Moran v. Faberge, Inc., 332 A.2d 11 (Md. 1975) (although cologne manufacturer could not foresee that teenage girls would attempt to scent lit candle with cologne, it should have foreseen general risk that cologne might come in contact with ignition source such as match to light cigarette or candle on vanity).

**18.** Wallace v. Owens–Illinois, Inc., 389 S.E.2d 155 (S.C. Ct. App. 1989) (Bell, J.).

**19.** On proximate cause, see ch. 12, below.

**20.** See, e.g., Jones v. Amazing Prods., Inc., 231 F.Supp.2d 1228, 1240–41 (N.D. Ga. 2002) (manufacturers not liable for injuries from abnormal, unforeseeable use of product); Wolfe v. Stork RMS–Protecon Inc., 683 N.E.2d 264, 268 (Ind. Ct. App. 1997) (manufacturer not liable for damages caused by unforeseeable alteration of product by employer); Anderson v. ALFA–LA-VAL AGRI, Inc., 564 N.W.2d 788 (Wis. Ct. App. 1997) (manufacturer of milk line cleaning system not liable for injuries to child who drank milk line cleaning solution); Beer v. Upjohn Co., 943 S.W.2d 691 (Mo. Ct. App. 1997) (manufacturer of prescription drug not liable for suicide of consumer); Romito v. Red Plastic Co., 44 Cal. Rptr.2d 834 (Ct. App. 1995) (manufacturer of skylight not responsible for making skylight durable enough to withstand falling person); National Bank of Bloomington v. Westinghouse Elec. Corp., 600 N.E.2d 1275 (Ill. App. Ct. 1992) (manufacturer of water heater not liable for injuries incurred by unattended child burned by hot water).

as sat upon.[21] Where it is reasonably foreseeable that a product will be used for some purpose other than that for which it is sold, the manufacturer will be required to use due care to make it reasonably safe for that purpose, and where it is reasonably foreseeable that the product will be misused, the manufacturer is generally required to reduce the risk consistent with principles of reasonable foreseeability and reasonable care.[22]

Finally, it should be stressed that foreseeability is a rule of limitation, not a sufficient basis in itself for liability. From the premise that liability in negligence may be imposed only for injuries the risk of which is reasonably foreseeable, it does not follow that negligence liability should be assigned for *all* risks that are foreseeable. Thus, as is true in tort law generally, foreseeability is a necessary but not sufficient criterion for negligence liability in products liability cases. Such liability may be imposed only where, in addition to being reasonably foreseeable, a risk is also unreasonable.[23]

### Determining Due Care—Cost–Benefit Analysis

The negligence standard of care, reasonable care in the circumstances, ordinarily may be determined by balancing the burden ("costs") of safety precautions against the safety benefit the precautions seek to prevent. That is, the type and amount of care that reason requires is generally a function of the type, likelihood, and amount of harm (together viewed as the magnitude of the risk) that precautions (of a particular cost) may be expected to prevent.[24] If the risk posed by the sale and use of a product in a certain condition is great, due care therefore requires that great precautions be taken to avert the risk; if the risk is small, reasonable care requires only small precautionary measures in response.

For example, if the risk at issue concerns the possible failure of an automobile's steering, brakes, or tires at highway speeds, or the possibili-

---

**21.** See, e.g., Phillips v. Ogle Aluminum Furniture, Inc., 235 P.2d 857 (Cal. Ct. App. 1951).

**22.** See, e.g., Hiner v. Deere and Co., Inc., 340 F.3d 1190, 1199 (10th Cir. 2003) (Kan. law) (alteration of tractor front-end loader was reasonably foreseeable); In re September 11 Litig., 280 F.Supp.2d 279, 313 (S.D.N.Y. 2003) (Va. law) (airplane manufacturer had duty to design secure cockpit because hijacking was foreseeable risk); Short v. Estwing Mfg. Corp., 634 N.E.2d 798 (Ind. Ct. App. 1994) (manufacturer's duty to use due care in making hammer was undisputed where hammer broke while being used to dislodge rock from ground). See § 13.5 (misuse), below.

**23.** "In order that an act may be negligent it is necessary that the actor should realize that it involves a risk of causing harm to some interest of another, such as the interest in bodily security, which is protected against unintended invasion. But this is not of itself sufficient to make the act negligent. Not only must the act involve a risk which the actor realizes or should realize, but the risk which is realized or should be realized must be unreasonable." Restatement (2d) Torts § 289, cmt. *b.* See also Prosser and Keeton on Torts 170 ("In the light of the recognizable risk, the conduct, to be negligent, must be unreasonable.").

**24.** Section 3 of the Restatement (3d) Torts: Liability for Physical Harm formulates negligence in cost-benefit terms:

A person acts with negligence if the person does not exercise reasonable care under all the circumstances. Primary factors to consider in ascertaining whether the person's conduct lacks reasonable care are the foreseeable likelihood that it will result in harm, the foreseeable severity of the harm that may ensue, and the burden that would be borne by the person and others if the person takes precautions that eliminate or reduce the possibility of harm.

ty that a punch press ram may unexpectedly depress upon an operator's hand, "reasonable" care will demand the utmost precautions by the manufacturer to avert the risk. Yet, if the foreseeable risk is relatively minimal, reasonably appearing to involve at most the risk of minor harm to person or property—a scratch, a fabric tear, or a harmless product malfunction—then there is little reason for a manufacturer to devote more than the smallest amount of attention, expense, or other resources to reducing such a trivial risk of harm. This principle of balance, inherent in tort law generally and negligence law in particular, is sometimes referred to as the "calculus of risk."

The most celebrated formulation of the calculus-of-risk approach for evaluating conduct under the negligence standard of care was offered by Judge Learned Hand in *United States v. Carroll Towing Co.*[25] In *Carroll Towing*, Judge Hand reasoned that a determination of the degree of care appropriate to an occasion often reflects a calculus of three factors: the burden of taking precautions to avoid a risk of harm, on the one side, balanced against the likelihood that the actor's conduct will produce the harm multiplied by the seriousness of the harm, on the other. Negligence is implied if an actor fails to shoulder a burden of precaution of less magnitude than the harm it is likely to prevent. Judge Hand expressed this concept algebraically: Negligence is suggested if $B < P \times L$, where B is the burden (cost) of avoiding accidental loss that foreseeably may result if B is not undertaken, P is the increase in probability of loss if B is not undertaken, and L is the probable magnitude of such loss. This is the so-called "Hand formula." If the formula is supplemented with a symbol for the implication ( $\Rightarrow$ ) of negligence, N, the full formula[26] reads:

$$B < P \times L \Rightarrow N$$

Thus conceived and applied to the products liability context, the Hand formula may be explained as follows: if the cost of taking a particular safety precaution (B) is less than the precaution's expected safety benefits ($P \times L$), the manufacturer's failure to adopt the precaution implies its negligence ( $\Rightarrow N$).

The Hand formula expresses algebraically the commonsense idea that people may fairly be required to contemplate the possible consequences of important actions before so acting. That is, nearly all reasoned decisions involve a weighing of the costs and benefits expected to

**25.**  159 F.2d 169, 173 (2d Cir. 1947) (N.Y. law). Hand first employed this approach in Conway v. O'Brien, 111 F.2d 611 (2d Cir. 1940) (Vt. law), rev'd on other grounds, 312 U.S. 492 (1941), and he subsequently reexamined this approach in Moisan v. Loftus, 178 F.2d 148, 149 (2d Cir. 1949) (Vt. law). On *Carroll Towing*, see Gilles, United States v. Carroll Towing Co.: The Hand Formula's Home Port, in Torts Stories 11 (R. Rabin & S. Sugarman, eds., Foundation Press, 2003).

**26.**  The formula may be further refined by indicating the *change* ($\Delta$) and *foreseeability* (*f*) of the risk that B is expected to reduce. So enhanced, the formula reads:

$$B < \Delta \, (f) \, (P \times L) \Rightarrow N$$

where B is the cost of taking a precaution that is expected to reduce by a certain extent ($\Delta$) a foreseeable (*f*) risk of harm (P x L). A failure to take a precaution implies negligence if its cost is less than its expected benefit, that is, if its cost is less than the expected reduction in risk.

flow from a contemplated course of action,[27] and the decisions of product manufacturers are no different.[28] Thus, prior to making important design, manufacturing, and marketing decisions, a responsible manufacturer should fairly weigh the risks of injury to consumers and bystanders when considering its own interests in maximizing profits. In making particular design, production, and marketing decisions, manufacturers may properly consider product usefulness, consumer cost, and profitability. But the point of the Hand calculus-of-risk formula is that manufacturers acting reasonably are also duty-bound to include in the balance a properly proportionate consideration of the various risks of harm that fairly may be expected to result when the product is put to real-world use.

In sum, a manufacturer in the exercise of due care is obligated to exercise an amount of care in avoiding risk that is proportionate to the expected risk. This simple yet fundamental principle of reasonableness, which ties the measure of care to the measure of risk, grounds the manufacturer's duty of care. And, after an accident, the Hand formula provides an appropriate and convenient method for a court and jury to evaluate a manufacturer's failure to employ the particular safety feature the plaintiff claims should have been adopted. These important calculus-of-risk principles are applicable to each of the three contexts (production, design, and marketing) where a manufacturer's failure adequately to consider product risks may unreasonably endanger consumer safety.

## Due Care in Manufacture

Manufacturers sometimes make negligent mistakes at some stage of the production process, and such mistakes occasionally cause harm to

---

**27.** See, e.g., Benjamin Franklin, *Letter* (Sept. 19, 1772), reproduced in E. Gramlich, Benefit–Cost Analysis of Government Programs 1–2 (1981) (suggesting, as an aid to rendering difficult decisions, that one list and consider "all the reasons pro and con" and contemplate "where the balance lies"):

> [T]hough the weight of reasons cannot be taken with the precision of algebraic quantities, yet when each is thus considered, separately and comparatively, and the whole lies before me, I think I can judge better, and am less liable to make a rash step, and in fact I have found great advantage from this kind of equation, in what may be called moral or prudential algebra.

Consider also Oliver W. Holmes, The Path of Law, 10 Harv. L. Rev. 457, 474 (1897) ("for everything[,] we have to give up something else, and we [must] set the advantage we gain against the other advantage we lose"). The moral foundation of the Hand formula is explained in Owen, Philosophical Foundations of Fault in Tort Law, in Philosophical Foundations of Tort Law 201, 214–15 (Oxford, D. Owen ed. 1995).

**28.** For the Hand formula's relevance to products liability law, see, e.g., M. Green, Negligence = Economic Efficiency: Doubts, 75 Tex. L. Rev. 1605 (1997); Owen, Toward a Proper Test for Design Defectiveness: "Micro–Balancing" Costs and Benefits, 75 Tex. L. Rev. 1661 (1997); M. Green, The Schizophrenia of Risk–Benefit Analysis in Design Defect Litigation, 48 Vand. L. Rev. 609, 615–16 (1995); Gilles, The Invisible Hand Formula, 80 Va. L. Rev. 1015, 1025 (1994); Owen, The Moral Foundations of Products Liability Law: Toward First Principles, 68 Notre Dame L. Rev. 427, 479 (1993); Miller, Design Defect Litigation in Iowa: The Myths of Strict Liability, 40 Drake L. Rev. 465, 476 (1991); White, Risk–Utility Analysis and the Learned Hand Formula: A Hand that Helps or a Hand that Hides?, 32 Ariz. L. Rev. 77 (1990); Viscusi, Wading Through the Muddle of Risk–Utility Analysis, 39 Am. U. L. Rev. 573 (1990); Epstein, The Risks of Risk/Utility, 48 Ohio St. L.J. 469 (1987). See also R. Posner, Economic Analysis of Law §§ 6.1 and 6.6 (6th ed. 2003).

consumers and other persons foreseeably placed at risk.[29] Beginning with the careful selection and testing of raw materials and component parts, the manufacturing process involves all aspects of the maker's construction, assembly, and preparation of the product for distribution. The manufacturer is bound to exercise reasonable care at each step to reduce the risk of dangerous defects in its products. Although the manufacturer of a mass-produced product has exercised the utmost care in production, it is inevitable that some small percentage of products—from time to time and for one reason or another—will be produced with manufacturing flaws dangerous to users or third parties. For this reason, manufacturers must exercise reasonable care to catch such defects by designing and implementing quality control ("quality assurance") systems appropriate to the nature and degree of risk. Due care in the manufacturing process therefore often requires the sampling and testing of products off the assembly line, for "[p]ernicious products should be scrapped in the factory rather than dodged in the home."[30] In short, manufacturers must exercise reasonable prudence in all aspects of the production and preparation of products for commercial distribution.

The proportionality principles of the Hand formula previously discussed are helpful in resolving the issue of negligence in the manufacture of a defective product. The *Restatement (Second) of Torts* § 395, Negligent Manufacture of Chattel Dangerous Unless Carefully Made, provides:

> A manufacturer who fails to exercise reasonable care in the manufacture of a chattel which, unless carefully made, he should recognize as involving an unreasonable risk of causing physical harm . . . is subject to liability for physical harm caused . . . by its lawful use in a manner and for a purpose for which it is supplied.

How a manufacturer (or jury) is to determine how much care is "reasonable" in particular cases is described in comment *g*, which provides that "the amount of care which the manufacturer must exercise is proportionate to the extent of the risk involved in using the article if manufactured without the exercise of these precautions." So, "[w]here, as in the case of an automobile or high speed machinery or high voltage electrical devices, there is danger of serious bodily harm or death unless the article is substantially perfect, it is reasonable to require the manufacturer to exercise almost meticulous precautions . . . in order to secure substantial perfection."[31] However, "it would be ridiculous to demand equal care of

**29.** See, e.g., Johnson Controls Battery Group, Inc. v. Runnels, 2003 WL 21191063 (Tex. App. 2003) (defective battery exploded); McGuire v. Davidson Mfg. Corp., 258 F.Supp. 2d 945 (N.D. Iowa 2003) (defective ladder broke).

**30.** Morris, Negligence in Tort Law— With Emphasis on Automobile Accidents and Unsound Products, 53 Va. L. Rev. 899, 909 (1967).

**31.** Restatement (2d) Torts § 395, cmt. *g*. Comment *d* to § 395 refers the "unrea-

sonableness" of risk determination to § 291, which provides:

§ 291. Unreasonableness; How Determined; Magnitude of Risk and Utility of Conduct

Where an act is one which a reasonable man would recognize as involving a risk of harm to another, the risk is unreasonable and the act is negligent if the risk is of such magnitude as to outweigh what the law regards as the utility of the act or

the manufacturer of an article which, no matter how imperfect, is unlikely to do more than ... trivial harm."[32]

Yet, with limited exceptions,[33] the courts are rarely explicit in applying calculus of risk principles to negligent manufacturing cases. Instead, once an accident is proved to have been caused by a manufacturing defect, courts routinely assume (or allow a jury to conclude) that the manufacturer was negligent for making and selling the product in a defective condition.[34] In such cases, courts seem to be applying the doctrine of res ipsa loquitur, but they are doing so *sub silentio*. The res ipsa doctrine is a perfectly respectable one in a great majority of jurisdictions, and there is no good reason for a court not to apply the doctrine explicitly if the evidence of negligence is insufficient to support a complete explanation of how the accident occurred and the doctrine otherwise is appropriate on the facts.[35] If the evidence does in fact reveal the circumstances of the accident, it would seem that the normal calculus-of-risk principles of reasonableness and balance ordinarily should be applied to determine whether the manufacturer was negligent in allowing the defect to occur. These and other aspects of a manufacturer's obligations to market products free of manufacturing defects are explored below in a chapter on this topic.[36]

## Due Care in Design

Only in recent decades have courts in any significant number begun to examine the reasonableness of the design of products involved in accidents.[37] Yet the formulation of the product concept is the first, and in many ways most important, safety function of manufacturers. It is at this crucial stage of the manufacturing process that a manufacturer makes decisions that will affect the safety of the entire product line: decisions concerning the types and strengths of raw materials and component parts, the manner in which they are to be combined into the finished product, whether safety devices are to be incorporated into the product, the overall product concept, and the type and extent of prototype testing to assure that the product works safely when put to use.[38] A

of the particular manner in which it is done.

**32.** Restatement (2d) Torts § 395, cmt. g.

**33.** See, e.g., Ford Motor Co. v. Zahn, 265 F.2d 729 (8th Cir. 1959) (Minn. law).

**34.** See, e.g., Klinke v. Mitsubishi Motors Corp., 556 N.W.2d 528 (Mich. Ct. App. 1996) (negligent manufacture; fracture of automobile steering knuckle); Pouncey v. Ford Motor Co., 464 F.2d 957 (5th Cir. 1972) (Ala. law) (negligent manufacture and design; automobile fan blade broke); Jenkins v. General Motors Corp., 446 F.2d 377 (5th Cir. 1971) (Ga. law) (negligent manufacture; improper inspection of automobile rear suspension system).

**35.** See § 2.5, below.

**36.** See ch. 7, below.

**37.** See, e.g., Jones v. Amazing Prods., Inc., 231 F.Supp.2d 1228, 1240 (N.D. Ga. 2002) (evidence sufficient to establish negligent design of drain cleaner container); Ford Motor Co. v. Burdeshaw, 661 So.2d 236 (Ala. 1995) (evidence sufficient to establish negligent design; driver pinned between truck and loading dock).

**38.** Just as there is a duty to test and inspect products for manufacturing flaws, so too does the manufacturer have a duty of reasonable care to test the product prototype for hidden dangers in design. Consider Dalehite v. United States, 346 U.S. 15, 51–52 (1953) (Jackson, J., dissenting):

This is a day of synthetic living, when to an ever-increasing extent our population is dependent upon mass producers for its food and drink, its cures and complexions, its apparel and gadgets. These

determination of whether the design of any particular product was "adequately" safe—or was, instead, "unreasonably" hazardous—is often a difficult task, particularly since the process may well involve second-guessing (with the benefit of hindsight) the defendant's professional design engineers. Yet, "mistakes" of this type sometimes are made, and resulting injuries are sometimes traceable to the manufacturer's failure to exercise reasonable care in product design.[39]

The usefulness of the Hand cost-benefit formula is most evident in design cases. Here, design engineers regularly consider the various trade-offs between product usefulness, cost, and safety. As a general proposition, the more safety that is designed into a product, the greater is the sacrifice of usefulness and affordability. That is, safety generally comes at a cost in terms of both utility and price—safety devices may interfere with the proper functioning of the product, and they usually add to the product's monetary costs. Thus, in making the often difficult decisions of how much safety should be designed into any particular product, the duty of due care generally requires that a manufacturer's engineers be guided by the Hand formula's principles of proportionality: the greater the foreseeable risk of harm, the greater should be the precautions to avoid the harm. In this manner, the Hand formula, based on principles of reasonableness, optimality, and balance, is especially useful in determining whether a particular design decision was reasonable or unreasonable—whether the manufacturer, in adopting the design, was negligent or not.

A case in which the court explicitly applied these Hand principles of balance is *Griggs v. BIC Corp.*,[40] which involved a negligent design claim for injuries in a fire started by a 3-year-old boy who used a BIC disposable butane cigarette lighter that did not contain the kind of childproof design now required by the Consumer Product Safety Commission. The CPSC estimated that, in the early 1980s, 120 people were killed and 750 persons injured each year in residential fires started by

no longer are natural or simple products but complex ones whose compositions and qualities are often secret. Such a dependent society must exact greater care than in more simple days and must require from manufacturers or producers increased integrity and caution as the only protection of its safety and well-being. Purchasers cannot try out drugs to determine whether they kill or cure. Consumers cannot test the youngster's cowboy suit or the wife's sweater to see if they are apt to burst into fatal flames. Carriers, by land or by sea, cannot experiment with the combustibility of goods in transit. Where experiment or research is necessary to determine the presence or the degree of danger, the product must not be tried out on the public, nor must the public be expected to possess the facilities or the technical knowledge to learn for itself of inherent but latent dangers.

See also Banks v. Koehring Co., 538 F.2d 176, 179 (8th Cir. 1976) (Iowa law) ("When a manufacturer offers a machine or equipment to the public . . . , the user is entitled to presume that the manufacturer has fully tested the mechanism.").

**39.** Restatement (2d) Torts § 398, Chattel Made Under Dangerous Plan or Design, provides:

A manufacturer of a chattel made under a plan or design which makes it dangerous for the uses for which it is manufactured is subject to liability to others whom he should expect to use the chattel or to be endangered by its probable use for physical harm caused by his failure to exercise reasonable care in the adoption of a safe plan or design.

Section 398 is "a special application of the rule stated in § 395," id. cmt. *a*, such that it adopts the proportionality principles of § 395 cmt. *g*.

**40.** 981 F.2d 1429, 1436–37 (3d Cir. 1992) (Pa. law).

children playing with lighters, for a national cost of lighter fires of $300–375 million. This amounted to an accident cost of $.60–.75 per lighter, which at the time cost under $1.00 apiece. The district court gave summary judgment to BIC on the plaintiff's negligent design claim, but the Court of Appeals reversed, remarking, "As the gravity of the possible harm increases, the apparent likelihood of its occurrence need be correspondingly less to generate a duty of precaution." The appeals court reasoned that the lighter's injury costs without a childproof design were unreasonable because of "the high social value placed on the safety of people and property threatened by childplay fires, the high gravity of risk, the considerable probability of risk, and the likelihood of a reasonably available [safer] alternative [design feature] may outweigh BIC's interest in producing its lighters without childproofing features."[41] While specific evidence on the components of the negligence calculus of risk may rarely be available to this degree,[42] *Griggs* nevertheless is helpful in illustrating how the injury costs may be balanced against injury-prevention costs in negligent design cases.

Proof of negligence in a design case often centers around the availability of a feasible, alternative design that would have prevented the accident and would have been safer overall.[43] As a general proposition, if there is no reasonable, feasible way to design a particular danger out of a product, the manufacturer cannot be held negligent for the product's design. This and other aspects of a manufacturer's design responsibilities are examined in depth below in a chapter devoted to that topic.[44]

### Due Care in Marketing—Warnings and Instructions

A product may be designed and produced exactly as the manufacturer intended yet still be unduly hazardous to consumers who do not appreciate its dangerous characteristics. This is increasingly true as consumers confront a burgeoning variety of mechanical, electrical, and chemical products of ever-increasing technological complexity. Accordingly, consumers are increasingly dependent upon the expert manufacturer to supply them with information on product dangers and how to avoid them. In order to "apprise a party of a danger of which he is not aware, and thus enable him to protect himself against it,"[45] due care may require a manufacturer "to speak out if the product is capable of harm

---

**41.** See id. at 1437.

**42.** More typical is Metzgar v. Playskool Inc., 30 F.3d 459, 461 (3d Cir. 1994) (Pa. law), where on less specific information on the costs of injury and its prevention a jury was permitted to find that the defendant manufacturer had negligently designed a toy block of a "size and shape which made the block susceptible of being swallowed and causing a child to choke."

**43.** Compare Richards v. Michelin Tire Corp., 21 F.3d 1048 (11th Cir. 1994) (Ala. law) (plaintiff's alternative design might have decreased overall safety: not negligent), and Garst v. General Motors Corp., 484 P.2d 47 (Kan. 1971) (design of 40–ton earthmover that could neither be turned nor braked quickly: not negligent), with South Austin Drive–In Theatre v. Thomison, 421 S.W.2d 933 (Tex. App. 1967) (failure to provide $3 shield to cover rear of power mower: negligent); Calkins v. Sandven, 129 N.W.2d 1 (Iowa 1964) (absence of simple, inexpensive shield over exposed conveyor mechanism on power farm wagon, where shield would not interfere with operation: negligent).

**44.** See ch. 8, below.

**45.** Jonescue v. Jewel Home Shopping Serv., 306 N.E.2d 312, 316 (Ill. App. Ct. 1973).

and does not itself carry a message of danger."[46] Thus, in passing along a finished product to the ultimate consumer, a prudent manufacturer must attach whatever information reasonably appears necessary to permit the consumer to use the product with reasonable safety. A manufacturer consequently may be negligent if it fails to provide consumers with adequate *warnings* of dangers in its product or *instructions* on methods for its safe use.[47] The duty to warn and instruct is independent of the manufacturer's duty to design and manufacture its products safely.[48]

The cost-benefit principles of the Hand formula apply in an interesting way to the duty to warn, and courts occasionally are quite explicit in applying this form of analysis to warnings cases. In an early case involving the manufacturer's failure to warn of skin irritation from a herbicide, the court remarked: "In determining the duty of care required of defendant in the case at hand, the likelihood of harm, and the gravity of harm if it happens, must be weighed against the burden of precaution which would be effective to avoid the harm."[49] Perhaps the clearest application of the Hand formula to the negligent warnings context is *Moran v. Faberge, Inc.*,[50] where the defendant failed to warn that its perfume was flammable:

> [A] manufacturer's duty to produce a safe product, with appropriate warnings and instructions when necessary, is no different from the responsibility each of us bears to exercise due care to avoid unreasonable risks of harm to others. Whether any such unreasonable risk exists in a given situation depends on balancing the probability and seriousness of harm, if care is not exercised, against the costs of taking appropriate precautions. [Yet] the cost of giving an adequate warning is usually so minimal, amounting only to the expense of adding some more printing to a label, that this balancing process will almost always weigh in favor of an obligation to warn of latent dangers, if the manufacturer is otherwise required to do so.

Despite the clarity of the *Moran* court's reasoning, it should be noted that its explicit discussion of cost-benefit principles is unusual in a negligent warnings case. Instead, as in cases involving claims of negligent manufacture, courts more often appear simply to assume a manufacturer is negligent for failing to provide adequate warnings of a

---

**46.** Dillard and Hart, Product Liability: Directions for Use and the Duty to Warn, 41 Va. L. Rev. 145, 147 (1955).

**47.** See, e.g., Hunter v. Werner Co., 574 S.E.2d 426 (Ga. Ct. App. 2002) (danger of improperly transporting fiberglass ladder); Jones v. Amazing Prods., Inc., 231 F.Supp. 2d 1228, 1240 (N.D. Ga. 2002) (dangers of transferring "Liquid Fire" drain cleaner to another container).

**48.** "It is not necessary that the product be negligently designed or manufactured; the failure to warn of hazards associated with foreseeable uses of a product is itself negligence, and if that negligence proxi-

mately results in a plaintiff's injuries, the plaintiff may recover." Laaperi v. Sears, Roebuck & Co., 787 F.2d 726, 729 (1st Cir. 1986) (Mass. law).

**49.** Holladay v. Chicago, Burlington & Quincy R.R., 255 F.Supp. 879, 884 (S.D. Iowa 1966). See also Jonescue v. Jewel Home Shopping Serv., 306 N.E.2d 312 (Ill. App. Ct. 1973) (child drank all-purpose cleaner); Boyl v. California Chem. Co., 221 F.Supp. 669 (D. Or. 1963) (no warning of long lasting toxicity of weed killer; plaintiff sunbathed on treated area).

**50.** 332 A.2d 11 (Md. 1975).

significant hidden danger.[51] These and many other aspects of a manufacturer's warnings obligations are explored below in a chapter on that topic.[52]

## § 2.3 PROOF OF NEGLIGENCE—INDUSTRY STANDARDS

### Proof of Negligence—In General

Proving negligence in a products liability case involves proving that the product supplier failed to exercise reasonable care for the plaintiff's safety. If the defendant is a manufacturer, negligence proof ordinarily involves evidence that the manufacturer acted unreasonably in developing, producing, or marketing a defective product. Evidence of this type normally will establish, directly or circumstantially, the components of the negligence calculus—the nature, magnitude, and likelihood of a particular risk of harm, on the one hand, weighed against the various costs and practicality of mitigating the risk, on the other.[1]

Many aspects of proving negligence are similar or identical to proving other types of products liability claims and so are treated in other chapters that focus on the common features of such types of proof. For example, expert testimony, as important to proving negligence as it is to proving strict products liability in tort and breach of implied warranty, is addressed in the context of proving defectiveness;[2] proof of other similar accidents and subsequent remedial measures, relevant to other types of claims as well as negligence, is also treated in that context;[3] proof in cases involving defective food or drink[4] or automotive crashworthiness[5] is quite similar regardless of the cause of action, and so is examined in those contexts; and proof of compliance with a statute or regulation, while relevant to negligence, spans all theories of products liability and so is examined principally as a special defense.[6]

This and the next two sections address three major forms of proof that may be especially germane to a negligence claim: industry custom, safety statutes and regulations, and res ipsa loquitur.[7] A plaintiff's negligence claim ordinarily will be enhanced by proof that a defendant violated a relevant safety standard set by industry in a code or by the government in a statute or regulation, whereas a defendant's defense to such a claim typically will be strengthened by proof that it complied with all industry and governmental safety standards. In cases where a plaintiff is unable to prove precisely how an accident happened, the doctrine

---

**51.** See Restatement (2d) Torts § 388, Chattel Known to Be Dangerous for Intended Use, which addresses a manufacturer's responsibility for negligent failure to warn. Except for cmt. *n* (warnings to third persons), which is richly grounded in calculus-of-risk principles, § 388 contains little discussion of cost-benefit concepts.

**52.** See ch. 9, below. For modern types of negligent marketing claims, see Ausness, Tort Liability for the Sale of Non–Defective Products: An Analysis and Critique of the Concept of Negligent Marketing, 53 S.C. L.Rev. 907 (2002).

**§ 2.3**

**1.** See § 2.2, above.

**2.** See § 6.3, below.

**3.** See § 6.4, below.

**4.** See § 7.5, below.

**5.** See § 17.3, below.

**6.** See § 14.3, below. This form of evidence is also treated briefly here.

**7.** The discussion here on proof also appears in Owen, Proving Negligence in Modern Products Liability Litigation, 36 Ariz. St. L.Rev. ___ (2004).

of res ipsa loquitur may provide a method for the plaintiff to establish the defendant's negligence by circumstantial evidence.

### Industry Standards as Custom—In General

Custom—how a community addresses particular situations according to prevailing social norms—is one of the most rudimentary and powerful sources of law.[8] Because the standard of reasonable behavior in negligence law is grounded in community norms,[9] whether a person who has caused harm to another acted or failed to act as similar persons customarily act in the same situation goes to the heart of negligence determinations. Thus, it is not surprising that one of the traditional definitions of negligence is the failure to exercise "ordinary" care.[10] This definition reflects the thought that most actors most of the time seek to act in a sensible, prudent manner, reasonably balancing the costs and benefits to others as well as to themselves. And actors, in attempting to make rational choices about how to act in given situations, necessarily frame those decisions against a backdrop of the expected environment of their actions, including the customary behavior of others.

Yet people tend to be self-centered and imperfect, and persons working in a complex world to achieve certain primary goals are often distracted by having to take steps to protect others from risks ancillary to the achievement of the actors' objectives. In such situations, it is not uncommon for people to devote less care and attention to protecting others from the risks of their activities than warranted by ordinary prudence. In such a case, a person would be negligent for *failing* to conform to the customary level of care. In many other situations, the converse can be true: the community over time may allow the ordinary level of care for protecting others to fall below the level of care that a reasonable prudent person would provide. Here, an actor would be negligent for *conforming* to the customary level of care. In short, while the standard of customary prudence often is the standard of reasonable prudence, sometimes it is not. In the famous *T.J. Hooper* case, Judge Learned Hand articulated the rule, by then well established,[11] that industry practice or custom is important evidence of the reasonableness of its members' conduct but that it is generally not conclusive on due care, since the industry as a whole may have been derelict in failing to adopt precautionary measures dictated by reasonable prudence.[12] This

**8.** See Symposia, The Legal Construction of Norms, 86 Va. L. Rev. 1577 (2000); Social Norms, Social Meaning, and the Economic Analysis of Law, 27 J. Legal Stud. 537 (1998); Law, Economics, & Norms, 144 U. Pa. L. Rev. 1643 (1996).

**9.** See, e.g., Prosser and Keeton on Torts § 33, at 193 et seq.

**10.** The person of "ordinary prudence" standard in negligence law can be traced at least to Vaughn v. Menlove, 3 Bing. N.C. 468, 132 Engl. Rep. 490 (1837). It still is sometimes employed. See, e.g., Morden v. Continental AG, 611 N.W.2d 659, 675 (Wis. 2000). See generally Prosser and Keeton on Torts § 32, at 174.

**11.** Judge Hand drew from Texas & Pac. Ry. Co. v. Behymer, 189 U.S. 468, 470 (1903), in which Oliver Wendell Holmes, Jr. observed, "What usually is done may be evidence of what ought to be done, but what ought to be done is fixed by a standard of reasonable prudence, whether it usually is complied with or not."

**12.** See The T.J. Hooper, 60 F.2d 737, 740 (2d Cir. 1932) (N.Y. law) (L. Hand, C.J.) ("[I]n most cases reasonable prudence is in fact common prudence; but strictly it is never its measure; a whole calling may have unduly lagged in the adoption of new and available devices. It never may set its own tests, however persuasive be its usages.

conclusion leads to the universal rule[13] in negligence law that a defendant's conformance to or violation of applicable customary standards of care ordinarily is some evidence, but rarely conclusive, of whether a particular defendant in fact exercised due care in a particular situation.[14]

## Industry Standards in Products Liability Law

These negligence law principles concerning evidence of custom[15] apply to negligence claims in products liability litigation.[16] That is, evidence that a defendant failed to or did adopt a standard for a product's design, warning, or manufacturing process customarily used by manufacturers of similar products normally is relevant evidence that, if otherwise admissible,[17] the defendant was or was not negligent in the

Courts must in the end say what is required; there are precautions so imperative that even their universal disregard will not excuse their omission.").

**13.** See Restatement (3d) Torts: Liability for Physical Harm § 13, Custom, which provides:

(a) An actor's compliance with the custom of the community, or of others in like circumstances, is evidence that the actor's conduct is not negligent but does not preclude a finding of negligence.

(b) An actor's departure from the custom of the community, or of others in like circumstances, in a way that increases risk is evidence of the actor's negligence but does not require a finding of negligence.

On the role of evidence of custom in negligence law, there is no minority view. See Restatement (3d) Torts: Liability for Physical Harm § 13, Reporter's Note to cmt. *b*.

**14.** See Hetcher, Creating Safe Social Norms in a Dangerous World, 73 S. Cal. L. Rev. 1 (1999); Epstein, The Path to The T.J. Hooper: The Theory and History of Custom in the Law of Tort, 21 J. Legal Stud. 1 (1992); Morris, Custom and Negligence, 42 Colum. L. Rev. 1145 (1942) (classic article); Prosser and Keeton on Torts § 33, at 193–96; Dobbs, Law of Torts § 17.3; Harper, James, and Gray, Law of Torts § 17.3; Restatement (3d) Torts: Liability for Physical Harm § 13; Restatement (2d) Torts § 295.

**15.** The terms "custom" and "state of the art" are sometimes interchanged and often confused. See Products Liability Restatement § 2 Reporters' Note to cmt. *c*, at 81–84; Boyd and Ingberman, Should "Relative Safety" Be a Test of Product Liability?, 26 J. Legal Stud. 433 (1997). "Custom" is customarily used to mean the prevailing practices in an industry. See, e.g., Carter v. Massey–Ferguson, Inc., 716 F.2d 344, 347 (5th Cir. 1983) (Tex. law) (custom means "the usual practice of the manufacturer, that is, what is done"); Chown v. USM

Corp., 297 N.W.2d 218, 221 (Iowa 1980) (custom means "what was being done in the industry"). While "state of the art" may mean largely the same thing as custom to business managers and engineers, the latter phrase, although variously defined, has evolved into a term of art in products liability law that essentially means the best science or technology reasonably available at the time of manufacture, in contrast to the customary, prevailing use of science or technology. See, e.g., Potter v. Chicago Pneumatic Tool Co., 694 A.2d 1319, 1347 (Conn. 1997) ("state of the art refers to what is technologically feasible, rather than merely industry custom").

Perhaps the best summary of the difference between the two concepts is Lohrmann v. Pittsburgh Corning Corp., 782 F.2d 1156, 1164 (4th Cir. 1986) (Md. law): "Industry standards are the practices common to a given industry.... often set forth in some type of code, such as a building code or electrical code, or they may be adopted by the trade organization of a given industry. State of the art is a higher standard because scientific knowledge expands much more rapidly than industry can assimilate the knowledge and adopt it as a standard." See also Hollingsworth & Vose Co. v. Connor, 764 A.2d 318, 334–35 (Md. Ct. Spec. App. 2000). On state of the art, see § 10.4, below.

**16.** See Boyd and Ingberman, Should "Relative Safety" Be a Test of Product Liability?, 26 J. Legal Stud. 433 (1997); Comment, Custom's Proper Role in Strict Product Liability Actions Based on Design Defect, 38 UCLA L. Rev. 439 (1990); Frumer and Friedman, Products Liability § 18.04[1]; 2 Madden & Owen on Products Liability Law § 2.7 and § 27:6; Am. Law. Prod. Liab. § 30:47; Products Liability Restatement § 2, cmt. *d*. On the very similar rules applied in most jurisdictions to strict liability in tort, see § 6.4, below.

**17.** To avoid the rule against hearsay and otherwise be admissible, Federal Rule

manufacture and sale of its own products. Either way, evidence of applicable customs may tend to show the foreseeability of the risk as well as the cost, feasibility, utility, and acceptability among consumers of the particular safety measures the plaintiff asserts the defendant negligently failed to adopt. While a jury thus may normally consider evidence of customary safety standards as bearing on the standard of care and whether it was breached, such evidence is usually only part of the package of evidence offered by the parties on the particularities of the case. In addition to evidence of custom, a plaintiff generally will want to introduce specific evidence as to the foreseeability and magnitude of the risk, its hidden nature, and the feasibility, utility, and cost-effectiveness of means to avoid it; a manufacturer, on the other hand, will seek to show the opposite: that the risk was remote, open and obvious, and impracticable and costly to remove. Evidence of custom, then, usually will supplement these more basic types of proof as to how and why, particularly, the defendant was or was not negligent in terms of the individual elements of the calculus of risk.[18]

Industry customs are often developed over time and informally as a matter of trial and error by engineers working in the field.[19] Many formal product safety standards are promulgated by standard-setting organizations, such as the American National Standards Institute (ANSI),[20] the American Standards Association (ASA),[21] the National Safety Council (NSC),[22] Underwriters Laboratories (UL),[23] the Society of Automotive Engineers (SAE),[24] the National Fire Protection Association,[25] and other specialized organizations, such as the National Spa and Pool Institute,[26] the Scaffolding and Shoring Institute,[27] the Industrial

of Evidence 803(18) requires that published industry standards be reliable, meaning deemed trustworthy by other professionals in the field, and be called to the attention of or relied upon by an expert who can assist the fact finder by explaining the materials. See 2 McCormick on Evidence § 321 (J. Strong, ed., 5th ed. 1999). See generally Brown v. Clark Equip. Co., 618 P.2d 267, 275–76 (Haw. 1980) (discussing hearsay problem); Annot., 58 A.L.R.3d 153 (1974) (admissibility of safety codes and standards); Comment, 37 Tenn. L. Rev. 581, 582 (1970) (same). Additionally, evidence meeting these requirements may still be excluded under Federal Rule of Evidence 403 if its probative value is outweighed by its prejudicial impact or likelihood of confusing or misleading the jury.

**18.** "[S]tanding alone [proof of compliance with custom] does not justify a verdict on behalf of the actor." Restatement (3d) Torts: Liability for Physical Harm § 13, Reporter's Note to cmt. *b*.

**19.** See, e.g., Tri–Pak Mach., Inc. v. Hartshorn, 644 So.2d 118, 120 (Fla. Dist. Ct. App. 1994) (by implication).

**20.** See, e.g., Clarke v. LR Sys., 219 F.Supp.2d 323, 334 (E.D.N.Y. 2002) (guarding standard for grinders); DiCarlo v. Keller Ladders, Inc., 211 F.3d 465, 468 (8th Cir. 2000) (Mo. law) (stepladder standards); Potter v. Chicago Pneumatic Tool Co., 694 A.2d

1319 (Conn. 1997) (vibration limits for tools).

**21.** See, e.g., Poches v. J.J. Newberry Co., 549 F.2d 1166 (8th Cir. 1977) (S.D. law) (specifications for speed and angle of power mower blade).

**22.** See, e.g., Hutchison v. Urschel Labs., Inc., 157 F.3d 613, 615 (8th Cir. 1998) (Mo. law) (guarding standards for chicken dicer); Brown v. Clark Equip. Co., 618 P.2d 267, 275–76 (Haw. 1980).

**23.** See, e.g., McKinnon v. Skil Corp., 638 F.2d 270, 276–77 (1st Cir. 1981) (Mass. law) (lower-blade guard standards for power saw).

**24.** See, e.g., Alfred v. Caterpillar, Inc., 262 F.3d 1083 (10th Cir. 2001) (Okla. law) (design of asphalt paver speed control as lever rather than as counterintuitive rotary dial).

**25.** See Soproni v. Polygon Apt. Partners, 971 P.2d 500, 505–06 (Wash. 1999) (window standards).

**26.** See Ryan v. KDI Sylvan Pools, Inc., 579 A.2d 1241, 1243–44 (N.J. 1990) (pool depth standards).

**27.** See McNeal v. Hi–Lo Powered Scaffolding, Inc., 836 F.2d 637, 642–43 (D.C. Cir. 1988) (D.C. law) (standards for scaffolding clips).

Stapling and Nailing Technical Association,[28] the American Conference of Governmental and Industrial Hygienists,[29] and many others.[30] Such organizations typically work closely with industry to assure that the safety standards they establish, safety "codes," are practicable as well as useful. Although some of these organizations are more independent than others,[31] safety standards contained in the codes of organizations generally represent the industry's consensus on the most appropriate balance of safety and practicality.[32] And because the organizations that issue such standards and codes may be heavily influenced (if not controlled) by industry, courts generally treat the admissibility of such standards the same as any other industry standards.[33] But the formal way in which such standards may be developed and formulated into specific codes and industry's commensurate reliance upon them suggest that they sometimes should be accorded greater weight.[34]

As proof of the negligence of a manufacturer's product design, courts have admitted evidence of a defendant's failure to abide by industry standards governing the design of such products as a toy action figure,[35] a tire,[36] a meat grinder,[37] a vehicle such as a front-end loader,[38] a cigarette lighter,[39] and various machinery and equipment that is un-

**28.** See Baier v. Bostitch, 611 N.E.2d 1103 (Ill. App. Ct. 1993) (contact trip on nailer should prevent tool from discharging under its own weight).

**29.** See Potter v. Chicago Pneumatic Tool Co., 694 A.2d 1319 (Conn. 1997) (vibration limits for tools). These and other standards-setting organizations are described in 7 Frumer and Friedman, Products Liability § 91.15.

**30.** See 6 Frumer and Friedman, Products Liability § 76.03.

**31.** See, e.g., Fayerweather v. Menard, Inc., 659 N.W.2d 506 (Wis. Ct. App. 2003) (ANSI's ladder committee membership ⅓ from industry, ⅓ users, and ⅓ chosen from CPSC, OSHA, labor organizations, and "outside specialists").

**32.** See Hansen v. Abrasive Eng'g & Mfg., 856 P.2d 625, 628 (Or. 1993) (ANSI standards are helpful in determining whether defendant was negligent because they may represent consensus on what reasonable member of industry would do).

**33.** However, because some standards-setting groups are comprised of members outside the industry, and because their standards are voluntary guidelines of minimum safety, they are not to be equated with "industry custom," as such. See Fayerweather v. Menard, Inc., 659 N.W.2d 506 (Wis. Ct. App. 2003) (because ⅔ of ANSI ladder standards committee members came from outside industry, "the standards are not evidence of 'custom and usage' within an industry as contemplated" by standard

jury instruction, so that court's failure to give it was not error).

**34.** See Vermett v. Fred Christen & Sons Co., 741 N.E.2d 954, 971 (Ohio Ct. App. 2000) ("compliance with ANSI is a compelling factor"). See also Tri–Pak Mach., Inc. v. Hartshorn, 644 So.2d 118, 120 (Fla. Dist. Ct. App. 1994) (trial court did not err in failing to instruct on effect of violating "engineering industry and organizational standards" which plaintiff's expert only generally described and which had not been reduced to "any formal industry standard or any published regulation").

**35.** See Lugo ex rel. Lopez v. LJN Toys, Ltd., 552 N.E.2d 162 (N.Y. 1990) (plaintiff's eye injured when 8–pointed detachable star from Voltron–Defender of the Universe was thrown just as on TV; expert's testimony, based on customs and standards in toy safety community, that detachable star rendered design defective because Voltron would throw his star on TV was sufficient to create question for jury and withstand defendant's summary judgment motion).

**36.** See Morden v. Continental AG, 611 N.W.2d 659, 675–76 (Wis. 2000).

**37.** See De Pree v. Nutone, Inc., 422 F.2d 534, 535–36 (6th Cir. 1970) (Mich. law) (U.L. standards for cutter plate).

**38.** See Brown v. Clark Equip. Co., 618 P.2d 267, 275–76 (Haw. 1980) (National Safety Council standards).

**39.** See Glover v. BIC Corp., 987 F.2d 1410, 1417 (9th Cir. 1993) (Or. law) (ASTM standards for extinguishment).

guarded[40] or not equipped with an emergency stop device.[41] So, too, have courts admitted, as proof of due care, a manufacturer's *compliance* with design standards for a grinder,[42] a tractor,[43] a press,[44] and a car.[45]

In negligence claims that a manufacturer has failed to provide adequate warnings or instructions, courts have allowed plaintiffs to introduce evidence that the defendant failed to conform to industry practices governing appropriate warnings or instructions with respect to the assembly of a floor lamp[46] and the location of warnings on containers holding explosive materials.[47] Similarly, as evidence of due care, courts have allowed defendants to show their compliance with the customary types of warnings or instructions used for a trampoline[48] and asbestos products.[49] While most of the cases involving evidence of industry safety standards pertain to a product's design, and occasionally to a product's warnings or instructions, as just discussed, such evidence may bear also on a product's defective manufacture.[50]

Evidence of compliance or noncompliance with an industry standard of care is almost always admissible evidence on whether the defendant exercised due care,[51] assuming the standard is applicable to the dangerous aspect of the product in question,[52] but it rarely is conclusive of a

**40.** See, e.g., Cigna Ins. Co. v. Oy Saunatec, Ltd., 241 F.3d 1, 12 (1st Cir. 2001) (Mass. law); Cacevic v. Simplimatic Eng'g Co., 645 N.W.2d 287, 291–92 (Mich. Ct. App. 2001) (ANSI standards for guarding pallitizer); Wallner v. Kitchens of Sara Lee, Inc., 419 F.2d 1028, 1032 (7th Cir. 1970) (Ill. law) (American Safety Standards Institute standards for guarding conveyor).

**41.** See Almazan v. CTB, Inc., 2000 WL 33348244, at *10 (W.D. Tex. 2000) (ASME standards).

**42.** See Clarke v. LR Sys., 219 F.Supp.2d 323, 334 (E.D.N.Y. 2002) (ANSI guarding standard for grinders).

**43.** See Spieker v. Westgo, Inc., 479 N.W.2d 837, 843–44 (N.D. 1992) (power take-off driveline).

**44.** See Vermett v. Fred Christen & Sons Co., 741 N.E.2d 954, 971 (Ohio Ct. App. 2000) (ANSI safeguards for press).

**45.** See Hasson v. Ford Motor Co., 650 P.2d 1171, 1182–83 (Cal. 1982) (SAE standards for automotive brakes).

**46.** See Creadore v. Shades of Light, 2003 WL 152003, at *3 (S.D.N.Y. 2003) (UL guidelines).

**47.** See Beadling v. William Bowman Assocs., 809 A.2d 188, 191 (N.J. Super. Ct. App. Div. 2002).

**48.** See Anderson v. Hedstrom Corp., 76 F.Supp.2d 422, 450 (S.D.N.Y. 1999).

**49.** See Horne v. Owens–Corning Fiberglas Corp., 4 F.3d 276, 281–82 (4th Cir. 1993) (N.C. law).

**50.** See, e.g., Holder v. Keller Indus., 2000 WL 141070 (Tex. App. 2000) (ladder that broke constructed of low-density wood in violation of ANSI standards); Short v. Estwing Mfg. Corp., 634 N.E.2d 798, 802 (Ind. Ct. App. 1994) (whether hammer that broke met ANSI standards for hardness of steel). See also Doe v. American Nat'l Red Cross, 848 F.Supp. 1228, 1233 (S.D. W. Va. 1994) (whether Red Cross met collection standards of blood-banking industry to protect against risk that donor might have AIDS). One of the earliest cases concerning manufacturing defect claims was Grant v. Graham Chero–Cola Bottling Co., 97 S.E. 27, 28–29 (N.C. 1918) (bottle of ginger ale exploded because it was too highly charged or bottle was defective).

**51.** See, e.g., Fidalgo v. Columbus McKinnon Corp., 775 N.E.2d 803 (Mass. App. Ct. 2002) (dictum); Kent Village Assocs. Joint Venture v. Smith, 657 A.2d 330, 337 (Md. Ct. Spec. App. 1995) ("where relevant to the case and upon a proper evidentiary foundation, safety standards promulgated by organizations such as ANSI may be admitted to show an accepted standard of care, the violation of which may be regarded as evidence of negligence"); Mich. Comp. Laws § 600.2946(1) (evidence of compliance admissible); Wash. Rev. Code 7.72.050 (compliance or noncompliance). See generally Frumer and Friedman, Products Liability 18.04[1] ("almost every jurisdiction").

**52.** See, e.g., Fidalgo v. Columbus McKinnon Corp., 775 N.E.2d 803, 809 (Mass. App. Ct. 2002).

defendant's negligence.[53] Nevertheless, some courts view certain industry safety codes particularly persuasive on whether a manufacturer was[54] or was not[55] negligent, and an argument may be made for holding compliance[56] or noncompliance[57] with clear and important industry standards to be dispositive of product defectiveness in special situations.

## § 2.4 PROOF OF NEGLIGENCE—VIOLATION OF STATUTE

### Statutory and Regulatory Safety Standards in Negligence Law

In negligence actions, the trier of fact normally sets the applicable standard of care by applying the general common law standard of reasonable care and prudence to the facts and circumstances of the particular case. Products liability claims for negligence are usually adjudicated in this manner. Yet legislatures sometimes specify by statute, and regulatory agencies sometimes specify by regulation, particular safety measures required in certain situations or particular dangerous conditions prohibited in others. Such statutes (or regulations) may provide explicitly for civil damages arising from their breach.[1] More typically, however, safety statutes[2] provide criminal or quasi-criminal penalties for their violation. If a manufacturer, retailer, or other prod-

**53.** See, e.g., Gable v. Village of Gates Mills, 784 N.E.2d 739 (Ohio Ct. App. 2003) (compliance with federal standards admissible as guide in determining liability, but compliance alone is not conclusive); Rufer v. Abbott Labs., 2003 WL 22430193, at *7 (Wash. Ct. App. 2003) (compliance with custom evidence of due care, but does not conclusively disprove negligence); Brooks v. Beech Aircraft Corp., 902 P.2d 54, 64 (N.M. 1995) ("industry standards, while probative of what a reasonably prudent manufacturer would do, should not be conclusive"); Hillrichs v. Avco Corp., 514 N.W.2d 94, 98 (Iowa 1994) (custom of cornpicker manufacturers not to equip them with $50 emergency stop device no defense to claim of negligent design); Short v. Estwing Mfg. Corp., 634 N.E.2d 798, 802 (Ind. Ct. App. 1994); Meseck v. General Elec. Co., 600 N.Y.S.2d 384 (App. Div. 1993) (noncompliance with industry standards is some evidence of negligence, sufficient to raise factual question and hence avoid summary judgment, but is not conclusive on defendant's failure to exercise reasonable care); Hasson v. Ford Motor Co., 650 P.2d 1171, 1182–83 (Cal. 1982) (industry standards are "minimal," such that compliance with them does not establish due care).

In Kentucky, compliance with customary industry standards results in a rebuttable presumption that the product was not defectively designed or manufactured, applicable to any products liability action. See Ky. Rev. Stat. Ann. § 411.310(2). The opposite is true in Nevada. See M & R Inv. Co. v. Anzalotti, 773 P.2d 729, 730 (Nev. 1989) (manufacturer presumptively negligent if elevator violated ANSI standards).

**54.** See, e.g., Morden v. Continental AG, 611 N.W.2d 659, 675–76 (Wis. 2000).

**55.** See, e.g., Vermett v. Fred Christen & Sons Co., 741 N.E.2d 954, 971 (Ohio Ct. App. 2000) ("compliance with ANSI is a compelling factor"); McKee v. Cutter Laboratories, Inc., 866 F.2d 219, 224 (6th Cir. 1989) (Ky. law).

**56.** See, e.g., Lamb v. Kysor Indus. Corp., 759 N.Y.S.2d 266 (App. Div. 2003) (evidence that saw guard met industry standards at time of manufacture sufficient to establish product was not defective as matter of law); Wilder v. Toyota Motor Sales, U.S.A., 23 Fed. Appx. 155, 157 (4th Cir. 2001) (Va. law) ("While conformity with industry custom does not absolve a manufacturer or seller of a product from liability, such compliance may be conclusive when there is no evidence to show that the product was not reasonably safe.").

**57.** See Henderson and Twerski, *Achieving Consensus on Defective Product Design*, 83 Cornell L. Rev. 867 (1998) (arguing that defendant's violation of clear industry standard should be conclusive proof of product's defectiveness).

**§ 2.4**

**1.** On civil damages acts, see 3 Harper, James, and Gray, Law of Torts § 17.6.

**2.** "By 'statute' is meant both state and federal legislative and administrative enactments." Lukaszewicz v. Ortho Pharm. Corp., 510 F.Supp. 961, 964 (E.D. Wis. 1981).

ucts liability defendant fails to comply with a safety statute in a manner that harms a plaintiff, the doctrine of negligence per se may permit the plaintiff to establish the defendant's duty of care and breach thereof by proving the statutory violation.[3] In such situations, a court borrows the specific standard of conduct set forth in the statute,[4] deferring to the legislative determination of proper behavior, in substitution for the general definition of due care.[5]

### Negligence Per Se—The Two–Pronged Test

All safety rules, whether statutory, regulatory, or common law, are adopted to protect certain types of persons against certain types of risk of harm, and the scope of all such rules is limited to this extent.[6] Accordingly, most courts will adopt a standard of behavior set by a statute or regulation for use in a negligence action only if they determine that (1) the plaintiff was injured by a type of risk[7] the statute (or regulation) was intended to prevent, and (2) the plaintiff was in the class of persons the statute (or regulation) was intended to protect.[8] This is

**3.** "[T]he violation of a statute, or regulation having the force of statute, enacted for the safety of others is negligence in law or negligence per se." Price v. Blood Bank of Del., Inc., 790 A.2d 1203, 1212–13 (Del. 2002).

See generally 2 Frumer and Friedman, Products Liability §§ 10.03 and 55.02[3]; 2 Madden & Owen on Products Liability § 27.7; 1 Am. Law Prod. Liab. § 12:10–38; D'Angelo, Effect of Compliance or Noncompliance with Applicable Governmental Product Safety Regulations on a Determination of Product Defect, 36 S. Tex. L. Rev. 453 (1995); Wheeler, The Use of Criminal Statutes to Regulate Product Safety, 13 J. Legal Stud. 593 (1984); Note, Products Liability Based Upon Violation of Statutory Standards, 64 Mich. L. Rev. 1388 (1966) (classic treatment); Products Liability Restatement § 4(a).

More generally, see Prosser and Keeton on Torts § 36; Dobbs, Law of Torts §§ 133–42; 3 Harper, James, and Gray, Law of Torts § 17.6; Restatement (3d) Torts: Liability for Physical Harm § 14; Morris, The Role of Criminal Statutes in Negligence Actions, 49 Colum. L. Rev. 21 (1949); Lowndes, Civil Liability Created by Criminal Legislation, 16 Minn. L. Rev. 361 (1932); Thayer, Public Wrong and Private Action, 27 Harv. L. Rev. 317 (1914).

The effect of violation or compliance with statute on proving defectiveness, a closely related issue, is examined in § 6.4, below.

**4.** If a statutory standard is not specific, but merely restates a general safety principle of tort law, the statute will have borrowed from the common law in which case there is no reason for a state to borrow the standard back again. Thus, the doctrine of negligence per se applies only to safety standards that are specific rather than vague and general. See, e.g., Sikora v. Wenzel, 727 N.E.2d 1277, 1280 (Ohio 2000); Shanks v. Upjohn Co., 835 P.2d 1189, 1201 (Alaska 1992).

**5.** "When the doctrine of negligence per se applies, the general standard of a reasonable man is replaced by a specific rule of conduct established in a statute or regulation." Dougherty v. Santa Fe Marine, Inc., 698 F.2d 232, 234 (5th Cir. 1983) (La. law). Compare Lukaszewicz v. Ortho Pharm. Corp., 510 F.Supp. 961, 964 (E.D. Wis. 1981) ("A finding of 'negligence per se' serves to relieve a plaintiff in a products liability case from proving specific acts of negligence.").

If the relevant statutes and regulations are numerous and complex, a plaintiff may need expert testimony to explain the standards they establish and their breach in order to show their applicability to the litigation. See, e.g., McNeil Pharm. v. Hawkins, 686 A.2d 567, 580–85 (D.C. 1996).

**6.** See Hill v. Lundin & Assocs., Inc., 256 So.2d 620 (La. 1972); Malone, Ruminations on Cause–In–Fact, 9 Stan. L. Rev. 60, 73 (1956); Restatement (3d) Torts: Liability for Physical Harm § 14 (comments).

**7.** Note that courts and commentators often use the term "harm" for "risk of harm." See, e.g., Prosser and Keeton on Torts § 36. The Third Restatement changes type of "harm" to type of "accident." Restatement (3d) Torts: Liability for Physical Harm § 14.

**8.** Restatement (3d) Torts: Liability for Physical Harm § 14, Statutory Violations as Negligence Per Se, provides:

An actor is negligent if, without excuse, the actor violates a statute that is de-

the classic two-pronged test for deciding whether a safety standard in a criminal safety statute may properly be used as the standard of care in a negligence action under the doctrine of negligence per se.[9]

### Risks Prevented

As for the types of risk sought to be prevented, courts have ruled that the federal Motor Vehicle Safety Act, enacted to reduce traffic accidents and deaths, sought to prevent deaths in an accident caused by a manufacturer's deficient recall of a car with defective steering in violation of the Act's recall provisions;[10] that an FDA regulation requiring drug manufacturers to report adverse reactions to the agency was intended to prevent just such reactions;[11] and that a state housing standards act was designed to protect against the risks of unsafe construction and installation of mobile homes, including failing to anchor them to the ground.[12] On the other hand, a statute requiring motor vehicles to be equipped with turn signals does not apply to a road grader which is statutorily exempted therefrom;[13] a statute prohibiting the sale of cars equipped with hood ornaments that protrude beyond the face of the radiator grill applies only to the hazard of hood ornaments on moving cars piercing people, not the risk of people piercing themselves on the hood ornament of a car at rest;[14] a statute requiring that gasoline be dispensed only into safe containers is intended to prevent the risk of leaks, not the risk that gasoline bought in a cup might be used to throw on a person to facilitate catching her on fire;[15] a statute that prohibits false statements to the government[16] is a "truth" statute, not a "safety statute" protecting users against risks from prescription drugs;[17] and an act requiring insurers of total-loss vehicles to send their titles and plates to the Department of Revenue is an "anti-theft" act, not a safety statute designed to prevent such vehicles from being defectively rebuilt and thereafter causing accidents.[18]

signed to protect against the type of accident the actor's conduct causes, and if the accident victim is within the class of persons the statute is designed to protect.

Restatement (2d) Torts § 286 formulates the doctrine in a four-part test, including class of persons, interest, harm, and hazard.

**9.** Many courts and commentators state the two-pronged test in reverse order, asking first if the plaintiff is included in the protected class. Yet, because the class of plaintiffs intended to be protected by a statute is largely a subset of the hazards the legislature sought to prevent, the Third Restatement's ordering is preferable in suggesting that analysis begin with an inquiry into the risks prevented, from which the class of protected victims tumbles easily.

**10.** See Lowe v. General Motors Corp., 624 F.2d 1373, 1379 (5th Cir. 1980) (Ala. law) (violation of NHTSA regulations governing automotive recalls).

**11.** See Stanton v. Astra Pharm. Prods., Inc., 718 F.2d 553, 564 (3d Cir. 1983) (Pa. law) (Becker, J.) (drug manufacturer failed

to file adverse reaction reports required by FDA regulation).

**12.** See Gem Homes, Inc. v. Contreras, 861 S.W.2d 449, 453 (Tex. App. 1993) (home rolled over in storm).

**13.** See Cook v. Caterpillar, Inc., 849 S.W.2d 434 (Tex. App. 1993).

**14.** See Hatch v. Ford Motor Co., 329 P.2d 605, 608 (Cal. Ct. App. 1958).

**15.** See Walcott v. Total Petroleum, Inc., 964 P.2d 609, 613 (Colo. Ct. App. 1998).

**16.** "Whoever ... knowingly or wilfully falsifies ... a material fact, or makes any false, fictitious or fraudulent statements or representations ... shall be [in violation of this statute]." 18 U.S.C. § 1001.

**17.** See McNeil Pharm. v. Hawkins, 686 A.2d 567, 580 (D.C. 1996) (action on behalf of patient who died of severe liver failure following administration of defendant's pharmaceutical).

**18.** See Treadwell Ford, Inc. v. Campbell, 485 So.2d 312, 317–18 (Ala. 1986).

### *Plaintiffs Protected*

As for the class of plaintiffs sought to be protected, the federal Motor Vehicle Safety Act, enacted to reduce traffic accidents and deaths, was intended to protect the driver and passenger in a car that was dangerously defective in violation of the act;[19] an FDA regulation prohibiting the use of sulfites on raw fruits and vegetables seeks to protect sulfite-sensitive individuals from consuming food so treated;[20] and a state statute requiring manufacturers of toxic products to supply purchasers with a material safety data sheet (MSDS) is designed to protect users of the product, often the purchaser's employees.[21] But an act requiring insurers to return titles and licenses of total-loss vehicles to the Department of Revenue seeks to protect owners of vehicles from thefts, not pedestrians injured by runaway vehicles defectively rebuilt;[22] a driving permit requiring paraplegic drivers to be accompanied by co-drivers is intended to protect persons on the highways, not the paraplegic driver himself while using a defective wheelchair lift on a vehicle at rest;[23] a state statute barring hood ornaments from protruding beyond the front hood is intended to protect persons who might be struck by moving cars, not those who impale themselves on an ornament on a car at rest;[24] and a statute prescribing standards for the use of LP gas is intended to protect users in commercial settings, not contractors using such gas to heat houses they are building.[25]

## Other Negligence Per Se Requirements

An essential element of every negligence per se action is that the defendant actually *violated* the pertinent statute or regulation, as proof that the safety standard contained therein was breached.[26] Indeed, a court confronting a negligence per se claim sometimes may choose to reverse the normal duty-breach order of decisionmaking by first considering the issue of breach. If the statute was not breached, there is no reason to proceed to the sometimes more difficult analytical task of applying the two-pronged relevancy test. Further, even if a plaintiff establishes that a statute was breached and meets the two-pronged test, so that it may be used to set the relevant standard of care, the plaintiff still must also prove each of the other elements of a negligence claim.[27] So, a court will not apply a statutory standard if the violation was not a

---

**19.** See Lowe v. General Motors Corp., 624 F.2d 1373, 1380 (5th Cir. 1980) (Ala. law).

**20.** See Allen v. Delchamps, Inc., 624 So.2d 1065 (Ala. 1993) (sale of celery hearts treated with sodium bisulfite in violation of FDA regulation).

**21.** Byrne v. SCM Corp., 538 N.E.2d 796, 813 (Ill. App. Ct. 1989).

**22.** See Treadwell Ford, Inc. v. Campbell, 485 So.2d 312, 317–18 (Ala. 1986).

**23.** See Keegan v. Joytech Int'l, Inc., 2002 WL 982643, at *5 (Cal. Ct. App. 2002).

**24.** See Hatch v. Ford Motor Co., 329 P.2d 605, 608 (Cal. Ct. App. 1958).

**25.** See Trinity Universal Ins. Co. v. Streza, 8 P.3d 613, 616–17 (Colo. Ct. App. 2000).

**26.** See, e.g., In re Meridia Products Liability Litigation, 328 F.Supp.2d 791 (N.D. Ohio 2004); McNeil Pharm. v. Hawkins, 686 A.2d 567, 582 (D.C. 1996); Cook v. Caterpillar, Inc., 849 S.W.2d 434 (Tex. App. 1993).

**27.** See, e.g., Gaines–Tabb v. ICI Explosives, USA, Inc., 160 F.3d 613, 622 (10th Cir. 1998) (Okla. law) ("The violation of a statute constitutes negligence per se only if the other elements of negligence are present.").

cause in fact,[28] or not a proximate cause,[29] of the plaintiff's harm. Moreover, application of the negligence per se doctrine to any particular case is discretionary, and a court usually should decline to adopt a statutory standard that is obsolete, arcane, trivial, amounts to little more than a general common law rule of reasonable care, is otherwise vague and of little help to the judicial branch in setting a standard of reasonable care in a particular situation,[30] or "if sufficient policy considerations militate against it."[31]

## Licensing Statutes

Whether on grounds of proximate causation or scope of risk, a defendant's violation of a licensing statute generally does not amount to negligence per se.[32] Thus, a restaurant's failure to obtain an operating license from the health department, a drug manufacturer's failure to obtain proper FDA approval of a new drug or medical device,[33] or an aircraft manufacturer's failure to obtain proper certification from the FAA for a new airplane, may each subject the manufacturer to administrative penalty, but none of these violations converts the defendant into an outlaw subject to absolute liability. Food sold by an unlicensed

**28.** See, e.g., Alexander v. Smith & Nephew, P.L.C., 98 F.Supp.2d 1310, 1319–20 (N.D. Okla. 2000) (negligence per se claim failed in part on causation grounds because plaintiff's orthopedic surgeon knew that medical device had not been approved for inserting bone screws in vertebral pedicles but relied on his own judgment in recommending the surgery); Harden v. Danek Med., Inc., 985 S.W.2d 449, 453 (Tenn. Ct. App. 1998) (same; surgeon chose to make "off-label" use of product, relying on his own experience and judgment).

**29.** See, e.g., Brooks v. Howmedica, Inc., 236 F.3d 956, 967 (8th Cir. 2001) (Minn. law); Walcott v. Total Petroleum, Inc., 964 P.2d 609, 611–13 (Colo. Ct. App. 1998) (filling station's sale of gasoline in paper cup to customer not proximate cause of injuries to person on whom customer threw gasoline to set on fire); Gaines–Tabb v. ICI Explosives, USA, Inc., 160 F.3d 613, 623 (10th Cir. 1998) (Okla. law) (defendant's manufacture and sale of ammonium nitrate used by terrorists to bomb federal building in Oklahoma City not proximate cause of injuries due to "the intervention of a supervening cause—the unforeseeable, nearly unprecedented, criminal bombing of the Murrah Building. Absent proximate cause there can be no negligence, per se or otherwise.").

**30.** See, e.g., In re Shigellosis Litig., 647 N.W.2d 1 (Minn. Ct. App. 2002) (no negligence per se in food poisoning case for violation of federal Food, Drug and Cosmetic Act prohibition against sale of adulterated food because act fails to particularize any affirmative standard of care); Jones v. GMRI, Inc., 551 S.E.2d 867, 873 (N.C. Ct.

App. 2001) (same—metal in meatball; state pure food act); Sikora v. Wenzel, 727 N.E.2d 1277, 1280 (Ohio 2000) (negligence per se applies where statute sets out "positive and definite standard of care" but not where it "contains a general, abstract description of a duty"); Shanks v. Upjohn Co., 835 P.2d 1189, 1201 (Alaska 1992) (trial court did not abuse discretion in refusing to adopt standard of state drug misbranding statute that merely requires labeling to contain adequate warnings and instructions). See also Dougherty v. Santa Fe Marine, Inc., 698 F.2d 232, 234 (5th Cir. 1983) (La. law) (violation of one Coast Guard regulation not negligence per se where it was contradicted by another).

**31.** McNeil Pharm. v. Hawkins, 686 A.2d 567, 579 (D.C. 1996).

**32.** See Prosser and Keeton on Torts § 36, at 226; Gregory, Breach of Criminal Licensing Statutes in Civil Litigation, 36 Cornell L.Q. 622, 630–42 (1951).

**33.** See, e.g., King v. Danek Med., Inc., 37 S.W.3d 429, 453–60 (Tenn. Ct. App. 2000) (pedicle screws sold for unapproved purposes; FDA pre-marketing approval regulations are administrative in nature and do not establish a standard of care or quality); Talley v. Danek Med., Inc., 179 F.3d 154 (4th Cir. 1999) (Va. law) (same). See generally Beck and Valentine, Challenging the Viability of FDCA–Based Causes of Action in the Tort Context: The Orthopedic Bone Screw Experience, 55 Food & Drug L.J. 389 (2000).

Breach of federal statutes and regulations also raise issues of federal preemption. See § 14.4, below.

restaurant may be just as tasty and pure as food sold by a restaurant that licensing officials grade as "A." A drug or medical device may be reasonably safe despite not being approved for use by the FDA. An uncertified plane may be entirely airworthy and equally as safe as a plane approved by the FAA. In such cases, a plaintiff may not rest upon the defendant's violation of a certification rule but must prove the defendant's negligence another way.[34]

### Excuses

Treating a defendant's violation of a statute as a breach of duty amounts to a form of "strict" liability: liability flows merely from the defendant's breach of statute rather than from particularized proof of how the defendant was at fault. That is, a plaintiff may establish a breach of the duty of care without specific evidence showing how the defendant's actions were unreasonable, in how they foreseeably exposed the plaintiff to an undue risk of harm.[35] Yet this strictness in the basis of liability usually is fleeting, for most courts in most situations reset liability back on a fault foundation by providing a broad range of excuses that cover most situations in which a defendant could not reasonably have avoided the violation or the harm.[36] Many courts accept the list of excuses set forth in the *Restatement of Torts* which relieves a defendant of liability in negligence for a violation of a statute or administrative regulation if the violation is due to the defendant's incapacity, unawareness of a need for compliance,[37] inability to comply,[38] an emergency not due to the defendant's own misconduct, or if compliance would have presented a greater risk of harm than violation.[39] While these traditional negligence per se excuses may not be relevant to most products liability litigation,[40] they sometimes are germane[41] in which case they should be available as in any other context.[42]

**34.** See, e.g., *King* and *Talley*, above; Keegan v. Joytech Int'l, Inc., 2002 WL 982643 (Cal. Ct. App. 2002) (paraplegic truck driver's violation of special licensing statute).

**35.** See, e.g., Magna Trust Co. v. Illinois Cent. R.R. Co., 728 N.E.2d 797, 805–06 (Ill. App. Ct. 2000); Ross Labs. v. Thies, 725 P.2d 1076, 1081 (Alaska 1986) (retailer's unknowing violation of misbranding provisions of state food, drug, and cosmetic act: "the basis for the retailer's liability perhaps could as aptly be called strict liability per se"). See also Elliott v. City of New York, 747 N.E.2d 760, 762 (N.Y. 2001) (observing that violation of statute that creates specific duty "constitutes negligence per se, or may even create absolute liability").

**36.** See Sikora v. Wenzel, 727 N.E.2d 1277, 1281 (Ohio 2000); Prosser and Keeton on Torts § 36, at 227–29; Dobbs, Law of Torts §§ 140 and 141. And sometimes courts simply refuse to apply negligence per se. See, e.g., Mehlman v. Diamond Sparklers, Inc., 2002 WL 32096585 (E.D.N.Y. 2002) (court refused to rule that violation of

statute criminalizing sale of fireworks in New York resulted in strict or absolute liability).

**37.** See, e.g., Sikora v. Wenzel, 727 N.E.2d 1277, 1280 (Ohio 2000). *But see* Ross Labs. v. Thies, 725 P.2d 1076, 1080–81 (Alaska 1986); Dura Corp. v. Harned, 703 P.2d 396 (Alaska 1985) (manufacturer's ignorance of standards of nationally recognized safety code no excuse).

**38.** See, e.g., Roth v. I & M Rail Link, L.L.C., 179 F.Supp.2d 1054, 1063 (S.D. Iowa 2001) (impossibility of compliance, meaning "not reasonably practicable").

**39.** See Restatement (2d) Torts § 288A.

**40.** See Products Liability Restatement § 4, cmt. *d*.

**41.** As when a drug or other chemical's risk is unforeseeable.

**42.** See D'Angelo, Effect Of Compliance Or Noncompliance With Applicable Governmental Product Safety Regulations On A Determination Of Product Defect, 36 S. Tex. L. Rev. 453 (1995).

### Procedural Effect

Jurisdictions vary in the procedural effect accorded to a statutory or regulatory violation.[43] Some courts, possibly a majority,[44] hold that such a violation conclusively establishes the defendant's negligence—that an unexcused violation of a statute or regulation is negligence in itself, or negligence "per se."[45] While such a procedural effect powerfully stamps the violation as a breach of duty as a matter of law, it nevertheless leaves open all other issues involved in a negligence cause of action, such as cause in fact, proximate cause, the plaintiff's damage, and any affirmative defenses that might apply.[46] Many other jurisdictions treat a violation merely as evidence of negligence,[47] perhaps the best approach,[48] which the trier of fact may accept or reject as it sees fit. In a small number of jurisdictions, by common law or statute, a violation of a safety statute or regulation creates a rebuttable presumption of negligence.[49] And some jurisdictions that give conclusive status to violations of a legislature's statutes give a lesser, mere-evidence effect to violations of a city's ordinances[50] or regulations of administrative agencies,[51] both con-

**43.** See Prosser and Keeton on Torts § 36, at 229–31.

**44.** Commentators have long asserted that the conclusive effect proclaimed by Judge Cardozo in Martin v. Herzog, 126 N.E. 814, 815 (N.Y. 1920), that "jurors have no ... power ... [to] relax" the standard set by the legislature, is the majority rule. See, e.g., Note, Products Liability Based Upon Violation of Statutory Standards, 64 Mich. L. Rev. 1388, 1393–94 (1966) (citing sources mostly prior to 1950). See also Restatement (3d) Torts: Liability for Physical Harm § 14 Reporter's Note to cmt. c (Martin v. Herzog's conclusive effect approach is "the strong majority rule"). Yet, because of the different meanings of the phrase "negligence per se," 64 Mich. L. Rev. at 1396; because of the absence of a methodical study of every jurisdiction; and because many of the more recent cases treat statutory violations as mere evidence of negligence, it is unclear whether most jurisdictions still treat the violation of statute as conclusive of negligence.

**45.** See, e.g., McNeil Pharm. v. Hawkins, 686 A.2d 567, 578 (D.C. 1996) (an unexcused violation renders defendant negligent as a matter of law); Peek v. Oshman's Sporting Goods, Inc., 768 S.W.2d 841 (Tex. App. 1989); Stanton v. Astra Pharm. Prods., Inc., 718 F.2d 553, 564–65 (3d Cir. 1983) (Pa. law) (Becker, J.); Harned v. Dura Corp., 665 P.2d 5, 12–13 (Alaska 1983) (failure of tank to conform to ASME standards, incorporated into state law, was negligence per se). This is the rule of Restatement (2d) Torts § 288B.

**46.** See Solo v. Trus Joint MacMillan, 2004 WL 524898, at *6 (D. Minn. 2004) ("[N]egligence per se, however, is not liability per se. There remain (the defenses of)

assumption of risk, contributory negligence and proximate cause ...."); Prosser and Keeton on Torts § 36, at 229–31.

**47.** See, e.g., Berish v. Bornstein, 770 N.E.2d 961, 979 (Mass. 2002); King v. Danek Med., Inc., 37 S.W.3d 429 (Tenn. Ct. App. 2000); Horstmeyer v. Golden Eagle Fireworks, 534 N.W.2d 835 (N.D. 1995).

**48.** According a breach of statute any greater weight confronts a number of theoretical obstacles. See Prosser and Keeton on Torts § 36, at 220–22.

**49.** See, e.g., Ramirez v. Plough, Inc., 863 P.2d 167, 172 (Cal. 1993) (dictum, citing evidence code); Klanseck v. Anderson Sales & Serv., Inc., 393 N.W.2d 356 (Mich. 1986); or "prima facie" evidence thereof, raising such a presumption but allowing an excuse. See, e.g., Magna Trust Co. v. Illinois Cent. R.R. Co., 728 N.E.2d 797, 804–05 (Ill. App. Ct. 2000) ("Since the violation is only *prima facie* evidence of negligence, a defendant may prevail by showing that he acted reasonably under the circumstances."); Bacon v. Lascelles, 678 A.2d 902 (Vt. 1996). See also Colo. Rev. Stat. § 13–21–403(2) (rebuttable presumption); Kan. Stat. Ann. § 60–3304(b) (product deemed defective unless manufacturer shows violation was reasonably prudent action). The rebuttable presumption approach is further discussed at § 14.3, below.

**50.** See, e.g., Elliott v. City of New York, 747 N.E.2d 760 (N.Y. 2001).

**51.** See, e.g., Montalvo v. Rheem Textile Sys., Inc., 1991 WL 52777 (S.D.N.Y. 1991) (violation of state workplace safety agency regulation requiring that presses be

sidered "subordinate rule-making bod[ies]."[52]

## Federal Law and Federal Courts

Negligence per se claims, being creatures of state tort law, must be distinguished from the federal doctrine prescribing when a private cause of action may be implied into a federal statute.[53] More narrow than negligence per se, the federal implication doctrine allows private claims only when Congress clearly so intended.[54] While the federal implication doctrine may be its cousin, negligence per se is an independent, substantive doctrine of state tort law applicable in both state courts[55] and federal diversity actions[56] for violations of both state[57] and federal[58] statutes and

equipped with, and operable by, two separate push-buttons was merely evidence of negligent design; not conclusive).

**52.** See Elliott v. City of New York, 747 N.E.2d 760, 762 (N.Y. 2001), citing inter alia Martin v. Herzog, 126 N.E. 814 (N.Y. 1920). See generally Prosser and Keeton on Torts § 36, at 231.

**53.** See Sherman, Use of Federal Statutes in State Negligence Per Se Actions, 13 Whittier L. Rev. 831 (1992).

**54.** Compare Swenson v. Emerson Elec. Co., 374 N.W.2d 690 (Minn. 1985) (allowing private claim for violation of CPSC's substantial product hazard reporting regulations), with Drake v. Honeywell, Inc., 797 F.2d 603 (8th Cir. 1986) (contra). See also Gibson v. Wal–Mart Stores, Inc., 189 F.Supp.2d 443, 448 (W.D. Va. 2002) (disallowing private claims under Federal Hazardous Substances Act and Poison Prevention Packaging Act). See generally Comment, Private Causes of Action Under the Reporting Rules of the Consumer Product Safety Act, 70 Minn. L. Rev. 955 (1986). Consider also National Bank of Commerce v. Kimberly–Clark Corp., 38 F.3d 988 (8th Cir. 1994) (estate of woman killed by toxic shock syndrome may sue manufacturer for non-compliance with warning requirement of Medical Device Amendments to Food, Drug & Cosmetic Act—type size too small, not written to 6th–to–8th grade level, and absence of boldface or different colors for certain portions demanded by FDA prominence requirement). Contra, Martin v. Ortho Pharm., 661 N.E.2d 352 (Ill. 1996) (risk of birth limb reductions from pills used in first trimester of pregnancy; disallowing private claim for violation of FDA consumer information regulations).

"Like substantive federal law itself, private rights of action to enforce federal law must be created by Congress. The judicial task is to interpret the statute Congress has passed to determine whether it displays an intent to create not just a private right but also a private remedy. Statutory intent on this latter point is determinative. Without

it, a cause of action does not exist and courts may not create one, no matter how desirable that might be as a policy matter, or how compatible with the statute." Alexander v. Sandoval, 532 U.S. 275, 286–87 (2001) (describing how implication doctrine narrowed from J.I. Case Co. v. Borak, 377 U.S. 426, 433 (1964), to Cort v. Ash, 422 U.S. 66, 78 (1975), to present; citations omitted). Cort's four-factor test has effectively been conflated back into the one determinative factor of Congressional intent. See Jackson v. Birmingham Bd. of Educ., 309 F.3d 1333, 1338 n.5 (11th Cir. 2002).

**55.** See, e.g., Nissan Motor Co. v. Armstrong, 32 S.W.3d 701, 711 (Tex. App. 2000) (car manufacturer's failure to report safety defect under federal law; dictum), rev'd on other grounds, 145 S.W.3d 131 (Tex.2004); Wallace v. Parks Corp., 629 N.Y.S.2d 570, 575–76 (App. Div. 1995) (notwithstanding federal preemption of inadequate warnings claims, negligence claim allowed for violating labeling requirements of Federal Hazardous Substances Act).

**56.** Milanese v. Rust–Oleum Corp., 244 F.3d 104, 109–10 (2d Cir. 2001) (N.Y. law) (allowing negligent "misbranding" claim for violating labeling requirements of Federal Hazardous Substances Act, although federal preemption precluded inadequate warnings claim that asserted manufacturer should have provided warnings additional to those required by Act); Loewy v. Stuart Drug & Surgical Supply, Inc., 1999 WL 216656 (S.D.N.Y. 1999) (pedicle screw case; violation of Medical Device Amendments to Federal Food, Drug, and Cosmetic Act); Sharp v. Artifex, Ltd., 110 F.Supp.2d 388 (W.D. Pa. 1999) (same); Stanton v. Astra Pharm. Prods., Inc., 718 F.2d 553, 564 (3d Cir. 1983) (Pa. law) (Becker, J.) (drug manufacturer failed to file adverse reaction reports required by FDA regulation).

Some courts disagree, mistakenly believing that to allow such state law claims, even in a diversity action, is somehow inconsistent with a ruling that the statute does not allow a private right of action under the

**57.–58.** See notes 57–58 on page 92.

regulations, regardless of whether the implication doctrine would also allow a private claim.[59] If the negligence per se issue concerns a federal statute or regulation, an unrelated but important issue will be whether the federal law preempts the claim for negligence per se together with some or all of the plaintiff's other products liability claims, an issue of growing significance in products liability litigation.[60]

### Compatibility with Ordinary Negligence Claims

Finally, it is important to note that negligence per se claims are separate and independent from ordinary negligence claims, yet the two claims are quite compatible. Indeed, plaintiffs typically and properly include counts for both ordinary negligence and negligence per se in the same complaint, and a plaintiff may prevail by establishing the defendant's breach of its duty of care on either form of negligence claim.[61]

implication doctrine as a matter of federal law. See e.g., Hackett v. G.D. Searle & Co., 246 F.Supp.2d 591, 594 (W.D. Tex. 2002) ("Because the FDCA does not provide for a private cause of action, many courts have held plaintiffs cannot seek to enforce it through negligence per se tort actions."); Rodriguez v. American Cyanamid Co., 858 F.Supp. 127, 129–31 (D. Ariz. 1994) (manufacturer of exploding bug bombs failed to comply with adverse incidents reporting requirements of FIFRA; negligence per se claim disallowed for not meeting standards for implying cause of action into statute). See generally Beck and Valentine, Challenging the Viability of FDCA–Based Causes of Action in the Tort Context: The Orthopedic Bone Screw Experience, 55 Food & Drug L.J. 389 (2000). But these courts and commentators miss the point: that negligence per se, as a matter of state common-law doctrine, borrows the standard of proper behavior from a state or federal statute not because the legislature intended to create a private cause of action for breach of the statute but because a standard of behavior specified in a statute may provide a better standard of conduct for a court to employ in a negligence case than the general tort law standard of reasonable prudence. See, e.g., Lowe v. General Motors Corp., 624 F.2d 1373, 1381 (5th Cir. 1980) (Ala. law) (violation of federal automotive safety statute in diversity action was negligence per se; because no private right of action or federal question was involved, "Cort v. Ash was not at all at issue in this case"). See generally James, Statutory Standards and Negligence in Accident Cases, 11 La. L. Rev. 95, 106 (1950–51); Thayer, Public Wrong and Private Action, 27 Harv. L. Rev. 317, 322 (1913).

**57.** See, e.g., Gaines–Tabb v. ICI Explosives, USA, Inc., 160 F.3d 613, 623 (10th Cir. 1998) (Okla. law) (state statute and regulations governing sale of explosives) (by implication); Montalvo v. Rheem Textile Sys., Inc., 1991 WL 52777 (S.D.N.Y. 1991) (state workplace safety agency regulation requiring presses to be equipped with, and operable by, two separate push-buttons).

**58.** See, e.g., Price v. Blood Bank of Del., Inc., 790 A.2d 1203, 1212–13 (Del. 2002) (violation of FDA blood donor screening regulations); Sharp v. Artifex, Ltd., 110 F.Supp.2d 388 (W.D. Pa. 1999) (violations of FDCA and MDA by pedicle screw manufacturer); Allen v. Delchamps, Inc., 624 So.2d 1065 (Ala. 1993) (selling celery hearts treated with sodium bisulfite in violation of FDA regulation).

**59.** "The mere fact that the law which evidences negligence is Federal while the negligence action itself is brought under State common law does not mean that the state law claim metamorphoses into a private right of action under Federal regulatory law." Lowe v. General Motors Corp., 624 F.2d 1373, 1379 (5th Cir. 1980) (Ala. law) (violation of Motor Vehicle Safety Act provisions governing automotive recalls). See also In re StarLink Corn Prods. Liab. Litig., 212 F.Supp.2d 828, 836 (N.D. Ill. 2002) (violation of FIFRA labeling requirements could support negligence per se claims even though there is no federal private right of action under statute).

**60.** The doctrine of federal preemption is examined at § 14.4, below.

**61.** Indeed, because of the possibility that a court will exercise its discretion to deny a negligence per se claim, or find an applicable excuse, a plaintiff's lawyer who limits the complaint to a negligence per se claim and thereby loses the suit risks a subsequent action for malpractice.

## Compliance with Statutory Standards—Evidence of Due Care

Since a manufacturer or other product seller may be found negligent per se if it *violates* an applicable product safety statute or regulation, a defendant in a products liability case might fairly ask to be shielded from negligence liability if it *complies* with an applicable safety statute or regulation.[62] Yet, because "the lawmaking process can sometimes be insufficiently attentive to the interests of potential victims,"[63] a product seller's compliance with a statutory or regulatory safety standard in a negligence action is proper evidence of a product's nondefectiveness but is not conclusive of that issue.[64] In very unusual situations, where no special circumstances suggest the need for greater caution, a court may rule as a matter of law that a defendant's conformity to a statutory or regulatory safety standard amounts to due care as a matter of law.[65] A few state products liability reform statutes provide that compliance with a statute or regulation gives rise to a rebuttable presumption that the manufacturer was not negligent.[66] In the great majority of cases, however, because legislatures and regulatory agencies normally set safety standards at minimally acceptable levels, a jury is free to find that a manufacturer was negligent for failing to take further steps to improve the product's warnings,[67] design,[68] or manufacture[69] beyond the level of

---

**62.** See Symposium, Regulatory Compliance as a Defense to Products Liability, 88 Geo. L.J. 2049 (2000); Ausness, The Case for a "Strong" Regulatory Compliance Defense, 55 Md. L. Rev. 1210, 1241–47 (1996); D'Angelo, Effect of Compliance and Noncompliance with Applicable Governmental Product Safety Regulations on a Determination of Product Defect, 36 S. Tex. L. Rev. 453 (1995); § 14.3, below.

**63.** Restatement (3d) Torts: Liability for Physical Harm § 16 cmt. *b*. See T. Schwartz, The Role of Federal Safety Regulations in Products Liability Actions, 41 Vand. L. Rev. 1121 (1988).

**64.** "[C]ompliance with a statutory standard is evidence of due care, [but] it is not conclusive on the issue. Such a standard is no more than a minimum, and it does not necessarily preclude a finding that the actor was negligent in failing to take additional precautions." Prosser and Keeton on Torts § 36, at 233; Restatement (3d) Torts: Liability for Physical Harm § 16 cmt. *b* ("compliance is evidence of nonnegligence but is not conclusive"). Historically, this principle was perhaps first applied in Bradley v. Boston & Me. R.R., 56 Mass. 539 (1848), and was restated by the Supreme Court in Grand Trunk Ry. Co. v. Ives, 144 U.S. 408 (1892). "In modern years, the rule has been frequently applied in products-liability cases where the defendant has complied with a federal regulatory standard." Restatement (3d) Torts: Liability for Physical Harm § 16, Reporter's Note to cmt. *b*.

**65.** See, e.g., Ramirez v. Plough, Inc., 863 P.2d 167, 172 and 176–77 (Cal. 1993) (compliance with FDA's English language only warning requirement shielded drug

manufacturer from also having to warn in Spanish that giving aspirin to children suffering flu might cause Reyes Syndrome); Beatty v. Trailmaster Prods., Inc., 625 A.2d 1005 (Md. 1993) (compliance with bumper height statute was complete defense). See Restatement (3d) Torts: Liability for Physical Harm § 16 cmt. *e* (in "unusual situations," statutory or regulatory compliance may be conclusive).

**66.** See, e.g., Colo. Rev. Stat. § 13–21–403(1); Ind. Code § 34–20–5–1. Compare McClain v. Chem–Lube Corp., 759 N.E.2d 1096 (Ind. Ct. App. 2001) (presumption not rebutted; summary judgment for manufacturer), with Cansler v. Mills, 765 N.E.2d 698 (Ind. Ct. App. 2002) (presumption rebutted; summary judgment for manufacturer reversed).

**67.** See, e.g., Caraker v. Sandoz Pharm. Corp., 172 F.Supp.2d 1018, 1033 (S.D. Ill. 2001) ("the FDA's drug labeling decisions impose only 'minimum' standards that are open to supplementation by state law through a jury's verdict enforcing a manufacturer's common law duty to warn"); Moss v. Parks Corp., 985 F.2d 736 (4th Cir. 1993) (S.C. law) (CPSC labeling regulations for paint thinner, under Federal Hazardous Substances Act); Ferebee v. Chevron Chem. Co., 736 F.2d 1529 (D.C. Cir. 1984) (Md. law) (EPA-approved label for paraquat herbicide, under Federal Insecticide, Fungicide, and Rodenticide Act); Burch v. Amsterdam Corp., 366 A.2d 1079 (D.C. 1976) (Federal Hazardous Substances Act labeling requirements); Stevens v. Parke, Davis & Co., 507

---

**68.–69.** See notes 68–69 on page 94.

safety required by the government. The *Third Restatement of Torts* is in accord.[70] The topic of compliance with governmental safety statutes and regulations is addressed later in depth as a matter of special defense.[71] Also examined later is the special defense of federal preemption,[72] a distant cousin to the compliance-with-statute defense.

## § 2.5  PROOF OF NEGLIGENCE—RES IPSA LOQUITUR

### Nature of Doctrine

#### *Purpose*

To establish a defendant's negligence, a plaintiff usually must prove, with specificity, the manner in which the defendant was negligent in making or selling the product that injured the plaintiff. Proof merely that a product malfunctioned and caused an accident normally will not suffice.[1] Stated otherwise, a plaintiff typically cannot make out a prima facie case if he or she fails to establish just *how* the defendant was negligent and *how* that negligence caused the harm. The absence of direct evidence establishing precisely how or why a product was defective may be due to circumstances beyond the plaintiff's control, as where the product is destroyed in the accident or because there simply is no way for the plaintiff to uncover what went wrong on the assembly line long ago. Sometimes, as when the plaintiff encounters a bug[2] or a mouse[3] in his Coke or a toe in his chewing tobacco,[4] the circumstantial evidence

---

P.2d 653, 661 (Cal. 1973) (FDA warnings requirements).

**68.** See, e.g., Brooks v. Beech Aircraft Corp., 902 P.2d 54, 63 (N.M. 1995) (crashworthiness of aircraft design: evidence of defendant's compliance with applicable government regulations is relevant to whether it was negligent but does not conclusively establish its non-negligence).

**69.** Cf. Reiter v. Zimmer Inc., 897 F.Supp. 154 (S.D.N.Y. 1995) (manufacturing procedures for prosthesis implant cement allegedly failed to meet FDA "good manufacturing processes").

**70.** Section 4(b) of the Products Liability Restatement provides that, in connection with liability for defective designs and warnings, "a product's compliance with an applicable product safety statute or administrative regulation is properly considered in determining whether the product is defective with respect to the risks sought to be reduced by the statute or regulation, but such compliance does not preclude as a matter of law a finding of product defect." While this provision is framed in terms of product defects, it draws from and embraces products liability negligence claims as well. See § 4 cmt. *e* and Reporters' Note thereto.

Restatement (3d) Torts: Liability for Physical Harm § 16(a), Statutory Compliance, provides:

An actor's compliance with a pertinent statute, while evidence of non-negligence, does not preclude a finding that the actor is negligent under § 3 for failing to adopt precautions in addition to those mandated by the statute.

**71.** See § 14.3, below.

**72.** See § 14.4, below.

**§ 2.5**

**1.** See Prosser and Keeton on Torts § 32, at 242; Dobbs, Law of Torts § 154, at 370.

**2.** See, e.g., Oklahoma Coca–Cola Bottling Co. v. Newton, 237 P.2d 627 (Okla. 1951) (fly); Birmingham Coca–Cola Bottling Co. v. Sellers, 39 So.2d 706, 707 (Ala. Ct. App. 1949) ("a cockroach or bug of some kind").

**3.** See, e.g., Harris v. Coca–Cola Bottling Co., 183 N.E.2d 56 (Ill. App. Ct. 1962); Trembley v. Coca–Cola Bottling Co., 138 N.Y.S.2d 332 (App. Div. 1955); Moss v. Coca–Cola Bottling Co. 229 P.2d 802 (Cal. Ct. App. 1951); Eisenbeiss v. Payne, 25 P.2d 162 (Ariz. 1933). See generally Annot., 52 A.L.R.2d 117 (1957).

**4.** "We can imagine no reason why, with ordinary care, human toes could not be left out of chewing tobacco, and if toes are found in chewing tobacco, it seems to us that somebody has been very careless." Pillars v. R.J. Reynolds Tobacco Co., 78 So. 365, 366 (Miss. 1918).

surrounding the misadventure quite strongly suggests that the product's defective condition resulted from some negligent act or omission of the manufacturer or other supplier.[5] In situations such as these, negligence law contains a doctrine that allows a plaintiff to establish a prima facie case without direct evidence of how specifically the product failed or how the defendant may have been negligent—"res ipsa loquitur."

Res ipsa loquitur ("res ipsa") is an established doctrine of circumstantial evidence,[6] applied by name in nearly every state,[7] that may assist a plaintiff in proving a negligence claim in a products liability case as in any other type of case.[8] The doctrine originated from a casual remark by Chief Baron Pollock during argument with counsel in *Byrne v. Boadle*,[9] where a pedestrian, hit on the head by a barrel of flour that rolled out of a second-story window over the defendant's shop beside the street where the plaintiff was walking, sought recovery from the defendant without introducing affirmative proof of why the barrel fell from the window. To the defendant's argument that the plaintiff's case must be dismissed because he failed to prove specifically how the defendant was negligent in allowing the barrel to tumble from the window, Chief Baron Pollock remarked, "res ipsa loquitur," the thing speaks for itself, and allowed the plaintiff's verdict. This remark promptly evolved into a full-blown doctrine[10]—that a plaintiff may establish a defendant's breach of duty indirectly, in situations where an accident's specific cause is unknown but where the circumstances indicate that some negligence by the defendant probably was its cause—that was warmly embraced by (and has complicated)[11] the Anglo–American law of negligence.[12]

---

**5.** "Some circumstantial evidence is very strong, as when you find a trout in the milk." Henry David Thoreau, Nov. 11, 1850, in 2 The Journal of Henry David Thoreau 94 (Bradford Torry and Frances H. Allen eds., 1984).

**6.** "The doctrine of res ipsa loquitur is neither procedural nor substantive, but 'only a shorthand expression for circumstantial proof of negligence—a rule of evidence.'" Waering v. BASF Corp., 146 F.Supp.2d 675, 687 (M.D. Pa. 2001). See Prosser and Keeton on Torts §§ 39 and 40; Dobbs, Law of Torts §§ 155–161; Harper, James, and Gray, Law of Torts § 19.5–.12; Cal. Evid. Code § 646; Restatement (2d) Torts § 328D. See also 9 Wigmore, Evidence § 2509 (3d ed. 1940); McCormick on Evidence § 342 (J. Strong 5th ed. 1999).

**7.** South Carolina takes perverse pride in eschewing the doctrine by name while applying largely similar principles of circumstantial evidence. Compare Legette v. Smith, 220 S.E.2d 429 (S.C. 1975) (rejecting doctrine), with McQuillen v. Dobbs, 204 S.E.2d 732 (S.C. 1974) (applying similar circumstantial evidence principles).

**8.** See Hoffman, Res Ipsa Loquitur And Indeterminate Product Defects: If They Speak For Themselves, What Are They Saying?, 36 S. Tex. L. Rev. 353 (1995). Frumer and Friedman, Products Liability § 10.04;

Madden & Owen on Products Liability § 7:9; Am. Law Prod. Liab. § 15:01 et seq. For a discussion of the "malfunction doctrine" (or, informally, "*defect* ipsa loquitur"), a parallel theory of proof in strict products liability, see § 7.4, below. *But see* Lauder v. Teaneck Volunteer Ambulance Corps., 845 A.2d 1271, 1277 (N.J. Super.A.D. 2004) ("The res ipsa loquitur doctrine is not available to product liability plaintiffs, however.").

**9.** 2 H. & C. 722, 159 Eng. Rep. 299 (1863). See also Prosser and Keeton on Torts § 39, at 243; Dobbs, Law of Torts § 155, at 372.

**10.** *But see* Jackson v. Millar, 1 S.C.R. 225, 235–36 (Can. 1975) (not a "doctrine"); Ballard v. North British Ry. Co., 1923 S.L.T. 219, 227 (Scot. 1923) (Lord Shaw) ("If that phrase had not been in Latin, nobody would have called it a principle.").

**11.** Res ipsa loquitur is "a thing of fearful and wonderful complexity and ramifications, and the problems of its application and effect have filled the courts of all our states with a multitude of decisions, baffling and perplexing alike to students, attorneys and judges." Prosser, Res Ipsa Loquitur in California, 37 Cal. L. Rev. 183, 183 (1949).

**12.** Two years after Byrne v. Boadle, the res ipsa doctrine was described by Chief

Especially prior to the development of strict liability theories of products liability law in the 1960s, res ipsa served in certain cases as an important mechanism for unburdening plaintiffs from having to establish specifically how a manufacturer or other supplier had been negligent in the production or sale of a defective product. Particularly in manufacturing defect cases, where the product violently malfunctioned, res ipsa thus provided a bridge between the difficulties of proving negligence by direct evidence and modern products liability claims based on product defect that relieve a plaintiff, at least in theory, from having to prove a manufacturer's fault at all. A prime example is *Escola v. Coca Cola Bottling Co.*,[13] a negligence case against the bottler by a waitress injured when a bottle of Coke exploded in her hand. Today, *Escola* is remembered for Justice Traynor's celebrated concurring opinion in which he outlined the various reasons for favoring a rule of "absolute liability" for manufacturers of defective products,[14] reasons which provided the theoretical basis for his opinion for the court in *Greenman v. Yuba Power Products, Inc.*,[15] nearly two decades later.[16] Now largely forgotten is the fact that the *Escola* majority, on the basis of res ipsa loquitur, upheld a judgment for the waitress despite her inability to prove specifically how the defendant bottler may have been negligent.[17] With the advent of strict products liability in tort and warranty, and strict liability's parallel "malfunction doctrine" in particular,[18] res ipsa in most jurisdictions has lost considerable importance. Yet it remains a valid doctrine that continues to be pled and on which plaintiffs continue to win products liability claims.

### *Limitations*

It may be helpful to note some attributes of the res ipsa doctrine that limit its applicability. First, the doctrine applies only in situations where the circumstances surrounding the accident are mysterious and unknown. That is, there is neither need nor room for a doctrine of circumstantial evidence that is designed to allow plausible guesses as to how an accident occurred where direct evidence clearly identifies both the nature of the product's defect and the defendant's conduct that allowed the defect to occur and harm the plaintiff. So, while many courts allow a plaintiff to rely on res ipsa even when the plaintiff pleads and offers specific evidence on negligence and causation on how and why a product accident occurred,[19] the doctrine assuredly must vanish, like a

---

Justice Erle: "There must be reasonable evidence of negligence; but where the thing is shown to be under the management of the defendant or his servants, and the accident is such as in the ordinary course of things does not happen if those who have the management use proper care, it affords reasonable evidence, in the absence of explanation by the defendants, that the accident arose from want of care." Scott v. London & St. Katherine Docks Co., 3 H. & C. 596, 159 Eng. Rep. 665 (1865).

**13.** 150 P.2d 436 (Cal. 1944).

**14.** Id. at 440.

**15.** 377 P.2d 897 (Cal. 1963)

**16.** See § 5.2, below.

**17.** See 150 P.2d at 438.

**18.** See § 7.4, below.

**19.** See, e.g., Weyerhaeuser Co. v. Thermogas Co., 620 N.W.2d 819, 831 (Iowa 2000). See generally Frumer and Friedman, Products Liability § 10.04[4].

bat in the proverbial light, once the plaintiff's evidence fully and specifically explains how the product failed and the steps the defendant could have taken to prevent the failure.[20] Ordinarily, however, a plaintiff's proof of how an accident occurred will not be so specific and complete, in which case the plaintiff should be entitled to rely upon res ipsa in addition to more specific proof.[21]

Second, it should be stressed that res ipsa loquitur normally is little more than an application of ordinary principles of circumstantial evidence to the accident law context, albeit in crystallized form tailored to the law of negligence.[22] The principal benefit the res ipsa doctrine provides a plaintiff is to supply an indirect means by which a jury may infer the defendant's breach of duty. While causation is also frequently established by the res ipsa inferences,[23] a plaintiff relying on res ipsa still has the burden of proving, in almost all states, *all* the elements of a negligence case—the defendant's duty, breach, cause in fact, proximate cause, and damage.[24] That is, as discussed below, the procedural effect of res ipsa in most jurisdictions is merely to provide some evidence of breach which a jury may accept or reject as it sees fit, such that the plaintiff retains the burden of proof on this as well as the other elements of the tort of negligence.

Third, one should also remember that res ipsa loquitur is a rule of *negligence*, not strict products liability, such that the inferences (or presumptions) must point to a probability that defendant was *negligent* in allowing a product to *become* defective, not merely that the product was defective.[25] So, the doctrine establishes both defect and negligence, as where a product's specific defect is unknown, and the product's failure destroys evidence of its cause—as when a new car's engine compartment suddenly catches fire; or where the presence of the defect is crystal clear, but its precise origin is a matter of conjecture—as when a mouse shows up in a bottle of Coke. In either case, what must be inferred is the defendant's negligence in allowing the defect into the product and in selling it in that condition. And proof, no matter how strong, of the product's defectiveness alone—whether direct or circum-

---

**20.** See, e.g., Stahlecker v. Ford Motor Co., 667 N.W.2d 244, 252 (Neb. 2003) ("if specific acts of negligence are alleged or there is direct evidence of the precise cause of the accident, the doctrine of res ipsa loquitur is not applicable"); Dover Elevator Co. v. Swann, 638 A.2d 762 (Md. 1994) (res ipsa inapplicable where plaintiff's expert fully explained why elevator misleveled). See generally Prosser and Keeton on Torts at 260; Dobbs, Law of Torts at 372 and 387.

**21.** See, e.g., Weyerhaeuser Co. v. Thermogas Co., 620 N.W.2d 819, 830 (Iowa 2000) (specific negligence and res ipsa may be pleaded and submitted to jury in the alternative).

**22.** See, e.g., Waering v. BASF Corp., 146 F.Supp.2d 675, 687 (M.D. Pa. 2001); Weyerhaeuser Co. v. Thermogas Co., 620 N.W.2d 819, 831 (Iowa 2000). See generally Prosser and Keeton on Torts § 39.

**23.** See, e.g., Knight v. Just Born, Inc., 2000 WL 924624, at *13 (D. Or. 2000) (allowing res ipsa for both negligence and causation); Dover Elevator Co. v. Swann, 638 A.2d 762, 765 (Md. 1994) ("Res ipsa loquitur is 'merely a short way of saying that the circumstances attendant upon an accident are themselves of such a character as to justify a [court or] jury in inferring negligence as the cause of that accident.'"). See generally Prosser and Keeton on Torts § 39, 247–48.

**24.** See, e.g., Dover Elevator Co. v. Swann, 638 A.2d 762, 765 (Md. 1994).

**25.** *But see* Parsons v. Ford Motor Co., 85 S.W.3d 323, 331 (Tex.App. 2002) ("The doctrine of res ipsa loquitur can apply to both negligence and strict liability cases to provide a presumption of product defect and causation.").

stantial—simply will not suffice. For the latter, there is a closely similar, newer doctrine of circumstantial evidence, the "malfunction doctrine," specifically tailored to proof of defect for purposes of establishing strict products liability.[26]

## Elements

Although res ipsa is properly not a cause of action but merely a method of proof, it nevertheless has two or three definite elements. Most traditional formulations of res ipsa in America derive from the first edition of Wigmore on Evidence, which divided the doctrine into three elements:

(1) the event must be of a kind which ordinarily does not occur in the absence of someone's negligence; (2) it must be caused by an agency or instrumentality within the exclusive control of the defendant; and (3) it must not have been due to any voluntary action or contribution on the part of the plaintiff.[27]

In order, these elements raise inferences (1) that *someone* was negligent; (2) that the someone *was* the defendant; and (3) that the someone was *not* the plaintiff. In combination, these elements provide that a plaintiff may rely on res ipsa where the circumstances of an accident suggest that it probably resulted from the defendant's negligence and not from the actions of the plaintiff or another.

Recently, however, prompted by the widespread adoption of comparative fault, many courts have eliminated the third element, an element which suggests an absence of the plaintiff's contributory fault. Thus, while many courts continue to define the doctrine in terms of the traditional three elements,[28] sounder formulations of res ipsa today limit the essential elements to the first two.[29] In terms of inferences, these elements establish that the accident probably resulted from someone's negligence, and that the negligent person was probably the defendant.[30] Whether the elements of res ipsa loquitur are established in any given case, and whether it otherwise applies to the facts, are questions of law for the court.[31]

It is sometimes said that res ipsa, which provides an incentive for a defendant to come forward with evidence of how an accident occurred, cannot be applied unless the plaintiff shows that the evidence is more accessible to the defendant than to the plaintiff.[32] It is true enough that

**26.** See § 7.4, below.

**27.** See 4 Wigmore, Evidence § 2509 (1st ed. 1905), quoted in Prosser and Keeton on Torts 244. More currently, see 9 Wigmore, Evidence § 2509 (3d ed. 1940). See also McCormick on Evidence § 342.

**28.** See cases cited below.

**29.** See, e.g., McGuire v. Davidson Mfg. Corp., 258 F.Supp.2d 945, 953 (N.D. Iowa 2003) (comparative fault act "abrogates the requirement that the plaintiff show his actions did not contribute to the injury"); Turbines, Inc. v. Dardis, 1 S.W.3d 726, 741 (Tex. App. 1999); Barretta v. Otis Elevator

Co., 698 A.2d 810, 812 (Conn. 1997). See also cases cited below.

**30.** See, e.g., Turbines, Inc. v. Dardis, 1 S.W.3d 726, 741 (Tex. App. 1999) ("The first factor is necessary to support the inference of negligence and the second to support the inference that the defendant was the negligent party."). See generally Dobbs, Law of Torts § 154, at 370–71.

**31.** See, e.g., Barretta v. Otis Elevator Co., 698 A.2d 810, 811 (Conn. 1997).

**32.** See Prosser and Keeton on Torts § 39, at 254; Dobbs, Law of Torts § 160.

providing such an incentive to defendants is one secondary function of the doctrine.[33] Yet few courts today explicitly treat this secondary purpose as a formal requirement, for to do so would confusingly erect a "cardboard defense" that does little more than parrot the second element's requirement that the plaintiff show the defendant controlled the instrumentality that caused the harm.[34]

It should be helpful to examine the individual elements in more detail.

### Accident of Type that Normally Results Only from Negligence

The purpose of the first res ipsa element, that the accident was a type that ordinarily does not occur without someone's negligence, is to determine if the accident was probably caused by a negligent act or omission. For example, it may be that the negligence of someone is the most likely cause of a mouse or bug in a Coke,[35] a toe in chewing tobacco,[36] a trout in the milk,[37] a candy that burned the plaintiff's mouth, so that it felt on fire,[38] a new motor home that in fact catches on fire,[39] a hand grenade with visible defects that explodes too quickly,[40] or the steering[41] or brakes[42] of an automobile that suddenly fail.

Looked at from the other direction, limiting the res ipsa doctrine's operation to situations in which someone probably was negligent properly excludes from coverage true accidents most likely caused by no one's fault. While many product misadventures are attributable to someone's failure to exercise reasonable care—the manufacturer, the user, or someone else—many others are an inevitable result of imperfect humans using imperfect machines in an uncertain world. Thus, it may be most likely that a product accident is attributable to no one's negligence when injury results from a new motor home that catches fire,[43] a vehicle that suddenly loses its steering,[44] a blood transfusion that causes serum hepatitis,[45] an escalator that malfunctions,[46] an airbag that fails to

**33.** See, e.g., Turbines, Inc. v. Dardis, 1 S.W.3d 726, 740 (Tex. App. 1999) ("The purpose of res ipsa loquitur is to relieve the plaintiff of the burden of proving a specific act of negligence by the defendant when it is impossible for the plaintiff to determine the sequence of events, or when the defendant has superior knowledge or means of information to determine the cause of the accident.").

**34.** Professor Dan Dobbs must be credited with this apt metaphor. See Dobbs, Law of Torts § 160, at 386.

**35.** See, e.g., Harris v. Coca–Cola Bottling Co., 183 N.E.2d 56 (Ill. App. Ct. 1962) (mouse); Oklahoma Coca–Cola Bottling Co. v. Newton, 237 P.2d 627 (Okla. 1951) (fly).

**36.** See Pillars v. R.J. Reynolds Tobacco Co., 78 So. 365 (Miss. 1918).

**37.** See Henry David Thoreau, Nov. 11, 1850, in 2 The Journal of Henry David Thoreau 94 (Bradford Torry and Frances H. Allen, eds. 1984).

**38.** See Knight v. Just Born, Inc., 2000 WL 924624 (D. Or. 2000).

**39.** See Hinckley v. La Mesa R.V. Ctr., Inc., 205 Cal.Rptr. 22 (Ct. App. 1984).

**40.** See McGonigal v. Gearhart Indus., 788 F.2d 321 (5th Cir. 1986) (Tex. law).

**41.** See General Motors Corp. v. Dillon, 367 A.2d 1020 (Del. 1976).

**42.** See, e.g., Holman v. Ford Motor Co., 239 So.2d 40 (Fla. Dist. Ct. App. 1970).

**43.** See Rocky Mountain Fire & Cas. Co. v. Biddulph Oldsmobile, 640 P.2d 851 (Ariz. 1982).

**44.** See, e.g., Beatty v. Ford Motor Co., 574 S.E.2d 803, 807–08 (W. Va. 2002); Brothers v. General Motors Corp., 658 P.2d 1108 (Mont. 1983).

**45.** See Schmaltz v. St. Luke's Hosp., 521 P.2d 787 (Colo. Ct. App. 1974).

**46.** See, e.g., Ellis v. Sears Roebuck & Co., 388 S.E.2d 920 (Ga. Ct. App. 1989).

deploy,[47] or an underground gas tank that springs a leak.[48] In each such case, because the product might well have failed for reasons other than someone's negligent act or omission, res ipsa did not apply.

### Defendant's Exclusive Control

**In general.** No matter how clearly the plaintiff establishes the first element, that someone was negligent in making or handling the product, a res ipsa case will fail unless the plaintiff further shows that the defendant is the particular party who most probably was responsible for the negligence. Traditionally, and quite roughly, this inference is established by showing that the manufacturer or other defendant had exclusive control of the instrumentality that caused the accidental harm—the product in question—at the relevant time. That is, the "exclusive control" requirement is simply another way of assuring that the injury is traceable to a specific instrumentality or cause for which the defendant was responsible.[49]

It is of upmost importance in products liability cases whether the relevant *time* of exclusive control over the instrumentality is viewed as the time of the accident that caused the plaintiff's injury or the time of the probable negligence.[50] Basing res ipsa on the defendant's control at the time of the accident makes good sense in conventional types of tort cases where res ipsa has long been employed, such as a passenger's claim against the driver where a car leaves the highway and goes into a ditch— a type of case where common sense suggests that the operator of the vehicle at the time of the accident was most likely responsible for the car's misadventure. But ascertaining who had control of the instrumentality at the time of the accident makes no sense in other contexts, including those involving products liability claims. No matter how powerful the circumstantial evidence that a defective or malfunctioning product resulted from some negligence by the manufacturer, the manufacturer will have relinquished control of the product to a retail dealer or someone else long before a product accident occurs. Indeed, plaintiffs themselves often are in control of products at the time they are injured. So, if a car-in-a-ditch case is brought by the driver's estate against the manufacturer of the car, and the plaintiff proves that the car was new, the weather was clear, the roadway was empty, and the driver was awake and sober, the relevant time of control in such a products liability case would seem to be the time when the product was designed and manufactured, not at the time of the accident. To take another example, a person drinking a bottle of Coke who suddenly encounters a bug or a mouse surely has control of the product at the time of the misadventure. But the circumstantial evidence in such a case is very strong that the relevant negligence was that of the bottler—who surely had control of

**47.** See Batiste v. General Motors Corp., 802 So.2d 686 (La. Ct. App. 2001).

**48.** See Mitchell v. Suburban Propane Gas Corp., 581 N.Y.S.2d 927 (App. Div. 1992).

**49.** See Weyerhaeuser Co. v. Thermogas Co., 620 N.W.2d 819, 832 (Iowa 2000); Prosser and Keeton on Torts § 39, at 248. "Exclusive control is merely one fact which establishes the responsibility of the defendant; and if it can be established otherwise, exclusive control is not essential to a res ipsa loquitur case." Restatement (2d) Torts § 328D cmt. *g*.

**50.** See Prosser and Keeton on Torts § 39, at 250; Dobbs, Law of Torts § 157.

the product at the time of bottling, the time of the probable negligence, and who just as surely had not a wit of control at the extraneous time of consumption.

Thus, if a court were to insist on applying the exclusive control element in a products liability case mechanically to mean control-at-the-time-of-injury, res ipsa almost never would be applied in this type of litigation.[51] For many years, however, a trend has been afoot to interpret the exclusive control element more liberally in a way that promotes its purpose in identifying the party most likely responsible for the negligence already inferred by element number one.[52] As early as *Escola v. Coca Cola Bottling Co.*,[53] discussed above, many courts were construing the control test in this more logical manner. There, the court decisively held that exclusive control may properly be determined at the time of the probable negligence, rather than at the time of the accident.[54] Many other courts have similarly interpreted the time of control in this commonsense fashion.[55]

The probability that a defect is attributable to the manufacturer, retailer, or other supplier diminishes over time after a product is first manufactured and sold as it suffers ordinary wear and tear, deterioration from the elements, abuse by users and mechanics, repairs, accidents, and other misadventures.[56] By the same token, as such incidents mount over the life of a product, the likelihood increases that a defect causing a product malfunction is attributable to such an event rather than to an original defect present at the time of sale. Thus, the longer a product is out and about in the hurly-burly world, the more likely it is that a product failure cannot be traced to the doorstep of the original product suppliers. In such cases, once it becomes more likely than not that causes other than the defendant supplier's negligence were responsible for a product's misbehavior, the exclusive control element shields the defendant from the rigors of res ipsa. Hence, courts have refused to apply res ipsa loquitur to a high-mileage vehicle that malfunctioned,[57]

---

**51.** A few courts still do apply the exclusive control test narrowly in this manner. See, e.g., Harris v. General Motors Corp., 34 Fed. Appx. 487 (7th Cir. 2002) (Ill. law) (late deployment of airbag on one-year-old car; res ipsa inapplicable because of absence of defendant's exclusive control); McConchie v. Samsung Elec. Am., Inc., 2000 WL 1513777 (D. N.H. 2000) (res ipsa inapplicable to 6½ month old microwave that caught fire because it was installed in plaintiffs' kitchen and so was not under defendant's exclusive control).

**52.** See, e.g., Pavon v. Rudin, 679 N.Y.S.2d 27, 30 (App. Div. 1998). See generally Frumer and Friedman, Products Liability § 10.04[3][a]; Restatement (2d) Torts § 328D cmt. *g*.

**53.** 150 P.2d 436 (Cal. 1944).

**54.** See id. at 438: "Many authorities state that the happening of the accident does not speak for itself where it took place some time after defendant had relinquished control of the instrumentality causing the injury. Under the more logical view, however, the doctrine may be applied upon the theory that defendant had control at the time of the alleged negligent act, although not at the time of the alleged accident, provided plaintiff first proves that the condition of the instrumentality had not been changed after it left the defendant's possession."

**55.** See, e.g., McGuire v. Davidson Mfg. Corp., 258 F.Supp.2d 945, 954 (N.D. Iowa 2003); Weyerhaeuser Co. v. Thermogas Co., 620 N.W.2d 819, 831 (Iowa 2000). See also Turbines, Inc. v. Dardis, 1 S.W.3d 726, 741–42 (Tex. App. 1999) (dictum). See generally Prosser and Keeton on Torts § 39, at 250 ("there is now quite general agreement" to this effect).

**56.** See § 10.6, below.

**57.** See, e.g., Beatty v. Ford Motor Co., 574 S.E.2d 803, 808 (W. Va. 2002) (alleged steering failure on van driven 110,000

tires that blew out,[58] an old ladder that buckled,[59] a car[60] or tractor that caught fire,[61] a folding chair that collapsed,[62] and to many other cases where causes outside of the defendant's control best explain a product mishap.

**Multiple defendants.** The exclusive control element is problematic for plaintiffs in cases with multiple defendants.[63] If more than one defendant handles a product in a way that could cause the injury, no one defendant will have had exclusive control over the product and a res ipsa case ordinarily should fail.[64] To make out a res ipsa case against any one defendant in such a successive control situation, a plaintiff usually will have to show that the probable negligence was attributable to a particular defendant and not the others—by evidence that implicates the particular defendant, exonerates the other parties, or some combination of the two.[65] But a number of courts, in varying situations, have allowed plaintiffs to rely on res ipsa against multiple defendants who separately or jointly controlled the product before it caused the injury.[66]

miles: "[O]ther responsible causes, including the conduct of the appellant and third persons, [were] not sufficiently eliminated by the evidence. The record shows it was not clear how the van had been operated or maintained over the many miles that the van had accumulated, suggesting that the conduct of unknown third persons could have caused the accident."); Mosesian v. Ford Motor Co., 2002 WL 31009208 (Cal. Ct. App. 2002) ("No less than seven years elapsed between the time Ford relinquished possession of the car and occurrence of the fire. During this time, the car underwent a series of repairs, both major and minor, some of which involved the electrical system. Three days before the fire, the car was in fact taken to a repair shop for an apparent electrical malfunction. There was no evidence linking the fire to the original condition of the car or rebutting the possibility that the problem arose from a modification of the motor or electrical system or from a faulty repair by a third party. [T]he requirement of exclusive control would be rendered meaningless if it could be applied to the present case.").

**58.** Goodyear Tire & Rubber Co. v. Hughes Supply, Inc., 358 So.2d 1339 (Fla. 1978).

**59.** See Crawford v. Sears Roebuck & Co., 295 F.3d 884 (8th Cir. 2002) (Ark. law) (ladder was 20–28 years old).

**60.** See Parsons v. Ford Motor Co., 85 S.W.3d 323 (Tex. App. 2002) (ignition switch had been replaced before fire).

**61.** See U.S. Fidelity & Guar. Co. v. J. I. Case Co., 432 S.E.2d 654 (Ga. Ct. App. 1993) (drivers used tractor for 300 hours without following instruction manual on cooling engine down).

**62.** See Rivera–Emerling v. M. Fortunoff of Westbury Corp., 721 N.Y.S.2d 653 (App. Div. 2001) (chair had been on sales

floor to which innumerable shoppers had access).

**63.** See Frumer and Friedman, Products Liability § 10.04[3][c]; Prosser and Keeton on Torts § 39, at 251.

**64.** See, e.g., Waering v. BASF Corp., 146 F.Supp.2d 675, 687 (M.D. Pa. 2001) ("The employment of res ipsa loquitur is problematic where, as here, there are several defendants who had successive control over the harm-causing instrumentality and there is no reason to believe that more than one defendant is responsible for the harm. In such cases, the other defendants are 'other responsible causes' that must be sufficiently eliminated in order for it to be more likely than not that the remaining defendant is responsible for the harm.").

**65.** See id. at 688 (evidence of prior negligent packaging by hazardous chemical's manufacturer, with no evidence of prior negligent shipping by distributors, sufficed to implicate manufacturer and exonerate distributors).

**66.** See, e.g., National Union Fire Ins. Co. v. Harrington, 854 So.2d 880, 891–92 (La. Ct. App. 2003) (res ipsa appropriate against only possible tortfeasors, operator of vehicle and manufacturer, where former controlled vehicle at time it caught fire in plaintiff's carport and latter controlled vehicle when it was manufactured); Knight v. Just Born, Inc., 2000 WL 924624 (D. Or. 2000) (defective candy–manufacturer and seller); Samansky v. Rush–Presbyterian–St. Luke's Med. Ctr., 567 N.E.2d 386 (Ill. 1990) (catheter line that broke and remained in plaintiff's body during bypass surgery—manufacturer, hospital, and doctors all had "consecutive" control); Ruiz v. Otis Elevator, 703 P.2d 1247 (Ariz. Ct. App. 1985) (elevator that squashed plaintiff–owner and party who manufactured, installed, and

### *Plaintiff's Noninvolvement*

The third traditional res ipsa element is that the plaintiff did not participate in causing the accident. Like the exclusive-control requirement, if this element were applied literally, a plaintiff using a product at the time it malfunctions could never recover under the res ipsa doctrine. Such a result would sap res ipsa of much of its proper power. While some courts and commentators have viewed the third element as a surrogate for contributory negligence, albeit as part of the plaintiff's case in chief, the third conventional element may more logically be viewed as a subset of and check on the second element. That is, if the defendant at the relevant time had *exclusive* control of the product, then the plaintiff must have had none—and so could not have participated in causing the accident.[67] From either perspective, the third element (as is true with the second) bears a distinctly antiquarian appearance of a search for an accident's sole responsible cause.[68] Yet modern principles of joint causation and comparative fault have decisively discarded the notion that a plaintiff's case against a negligent defendant is demolished if the plaintiff in some minor way contributed to the accident's causation.[69]

Today, while many courts continue to include the absence of voluntary action by the plaintiff as part of the litany of the conventional three-element res ipsa rule,[70] many other courts have dropped the third Wigmorian element, as previously discussed, reducing res ipsa to its two principal elements: (1) the accident being of a type that normally results only from negligence, and (2) the defendant's exclusive control.[71] Perhaps

maintained it); Stalter v. Coca–Cola Bottling Co. of Ark., 669 S.W.2d 460 (Ark. 1984) (soft drink bottle that fell through bottom of carton–bottler and retailer, who shared control of display); Holliday v. Peden, 359 So.2d 640 (La. Ct. App. 1978) (surgical needle that broke in plaintiff's throat during tonsillectomy—manufacturer, hospital, and surgeon).

**67.** See Dobbs, Law of Torts § 159.

**68.** See Prosser and Keeton on Torts § 38.

**69.** See, e.g., Barretta v. Otis Elevator Co., 698 A.2d 810, 812 (Conn. 1997); Montgomery Elevator Co. v. Gordon, 619 P.2d 66, 70 (Colo. 1980) (the no-plaintiff-contribution element is "in direct contravention to the concept of comparative negligence" because "[a] plaintiff who . . . had to rely on res ipsa and who was only slightly negligent would be barred from recovery since his contributory negligence would deny him the application of the res ipsa loquitur doctrine"). See generally Dobbs, Law of Torts § 159; chs. 11, 12, and 13, below.

**70.** See, e.g., Nat'l Union Fire Ins. Co. v. Harrington, 854 So.2d 880, 891 (La. Ct. App. 2003); Mosesian v. Ford Motor Co., 2002 WL 31009208, at *3 (Cal. Ct. App. 2002); Williams v. American Med. Sys., 548 S.E.2d 371, 374 (Ga. Ct. App. 2001); Darms v. Bunce Rental, Inc., 2000 WL 1174548, at

*6 (Wash. Ct. App. 2000). See also Beatty v. Ford Motor Co., 574 S.E.2d 803, 808 (W. Va. 2002) (blending conduct of plaintiff or third persons into single element and including duty as a separate element); Searle v. Suburban Propane Div. of Quantum Chem. Corp., 700 N.Y.S.2d 588, 592 (App. Div. 2000) (including a fourth element: "evidence as to the true explanation of the event must be more readily accessible to the defendant than the plaintiff").

**71.** See, e.g., McGuire v. Davidson Mfg. Corp., 258 F.Supp.2d 945, 951 (N.D. Iowa 2003) ("Two elements must be present for the doctrine to apply: '(1) the injury is caused by an instrumentality under the exclusive control of the defendant, and (2) the occurrence is such as in the ordinary course of things would not happen if reasonable care had been used.' "); Parsons v. Ford Motor Co., 85 S.W.3d 323, 332 (Tex. App. 2002) ("'(1) the character of the injury is such that it would not have occurred in the absence of negligence; and (2) the instrumentality which caused the injury is shown to have been under the sole management and control of the defendant' "); Weyerhaeuser Co. v. Thermogas Co., 620 N.W.2d 819, 831 (Iowa 2000). Some courts add a duty element. See, e.g., Beatty v. Ford Motor Co., 574 S.E.2d 803, 808 (W. Va. 2002); Waering v. BASF Corp., 146 F.Supp.2d 675 (D. Pa.

in recognition that the plaintiff-noninvolvement element is logically subsumed by the exclusive-control element, some courts rely upon the latter element in barring res ipsa claims where the plaintiff is using the product at the time of injury.[72]

## Procedural Effect

The importance of res ipsa loquitur lies in its procedural effect. Like any other type of circumstantial evidence, a large majority of courts hold that res ipsa provides nothing more than an inference that the defendant was negligent, an inference the jury is free to accept or reject.[73] Yet an inference of this type may be exceedingly important to a plaintiff deprived by circumstances of direct proof of negligence and causation, saving him from summary judgment or a directed verdict for the defendant.[74] In these mere-inference states, a defendant confronted with res ipsa may choose to introduce no evidence at all, and simply argue that the plaintiff's circumstantial evidence is insufficient to make a case. In a few states, however, res ipsa provides the plaintiff with a "presumption" of negligence, or makes out a prima facie case, that shifts the burden of going forward with the evidence (or the "burden of proof") to the defendant who thereupon must produce some evidence that it was not negligent or lose the case.[75] Few terms are more slippery than "presumption" and "burden of proof,"[76] and a lawyer must look closely and skeptically at res ipsa opinions using those words to be certain precisely what procedural effect the court has in mind.[77]

2001) (negligence in question must be within defendant's scope of duty to plaintiff).

**72.** See, e.g., Darms v. Bunce Rental, Inc., 2000 WL 1174548 (Wash. Ct. App. 2000). Compare Beatty v. Ford Motor Co., 574 S.E.2d 803, 808 (W. Va. 2002) ("[T]here is a substantial possibility that the rain-soaked highway and/or the appellant's carelessness in operating the van may have been, at the very least, a contributing factor to the accident. Accordingly, the appellant has not shown that the accident was of a kind that ordinarily would not have occurred in the absence of the [defendant's] negligence.").

**73.** See, e.g., Barretta v. Otis Elevator Co., 698 A.2d 810, 812 (Conn. 1997) ("The doctrine permits, but does not compel, such an inference. The doctrine has no evidential force, does not shift the burden of proof and does not give rise to a presumption. It is but a specific application of the general principle that negligence can be proved by circumstantial evidence.").

**74.** See, e.g., Knight v. Just Born, Inc., 2000 WL 924624 (D. Or. 2000) (denying summary judgment); Williams v. Emerson Elec. Co., 909 F.Supp. 395 (M.D. La. 1995) (same); Jurls v. Ford Motor Co., 752 So.2d 260 (La. Ct. App. 2000) (reversing directed verdict).

**75.** See, e.g., Stalter v. Coca–Cola Bottling Co. of Ark., 669 S.W.2d 460, 462 (Ark. 1984) ("the burden shifts to the defendant to go forward with evidence to offset the inference of negligence").

**76.** When courts say that res ipsa shifts the "burden of proof," they usually mean only that the doctrine shifts to the defendant the burden of producing evidence, not the ultimate burden of persuasion. See McCormick on Evidence § 342.

**77.** See, e.g., National Union Fire Ins. Co. v. Harrington, 854 So.2d 880, 892 (La. Ct. App. 2003) (variously describing res ipsa as allowing fact-finder to "infer negligence," as creating a "presumption of negligence," and as requiring defendant to "rebut an inference of negligence"); McGuire v. Davidson Mfg. Corp., 258 F.Supp.2d 945, 952 (N.D. Iowa 2003) (res ipsa doctrine permits "inference of negligence," yet defendant must present "rebutting evidence"); Opelika Coca–Cola Bottling Co. v. Johnson, 241 So.2d 327, 328 (Ala. Ct. App. 1970) (explaining how Alabama courts, in addressing the procedural effect of res ipsa, variously state that the doctrine creates an *inference* of negligence; that it makes out a *prima facie case* of negligence, shifting the burden of going forward to the defendant; and that it creates a *presumption* of negligence). See McCormick on Evidence § 342.

## § 2.6  THE RESURGENCE OF NEGLIGENCE

Beginning in the 1980s, negligence theory has experienced a resurgence in American products liability law. This development is visible in some states much more than others, although it still appears to be resisted in Europe and elsewhere in the world.[1] The shift away from strict products liability back to negligence has occurred, albeit sporadically, in both courts and legislatures, a general development that has been observed and encouraged by some commentators[2] while lamented by others.[3]

### Resurgence in the Courts

In most jurisdictions, the doctrine of strict liability in tort never fully displaced the law of negligence in products liability cases. It is certainly true that many courts, in adopting strict liability in tort during the 1960s and 1970s, stated or suggested that the new strict products liability doctrine eliminated the need for a separate theory of liability in negligence. But as courts applied the new "strict" liability doctrine to manufacturers and other defendants in an increasing array of contexts, many courts and legislatures began to recognize that liability for the manufacture and sale of products containing design and warnings defects is best defined in terms of the principles of negligence law, centered on the balance of foreseeable risk, cost, utility, reasonableness, and optimality.[4]

This resurgence of negligence principles is evident in "strict liability" cases involving defects in *design*. As discussed below,[5] the now-dominant risk-utility test for determining liability in design defect cases is ordinarily little or nothing more than the Learned Hand negligence calculus discussed above.[6] Many courts have acknowledged this close

### § 2.6

**1.** Europe, Japan, and other nations, which began their modern development of products liability law systems more recently than America, still appear to be attempting to ground this field of law on a truly "strict" liability foundation. See § 1.4, above.

**2.** See, e.g., Cupp and Polage, The Rhetoric of Strict Products Liability Versus Negligence: An Empirical Analysis, 77 N.Y.U. L. Rev. 874 (2002); Owen, Defectiveness Restated: Exploding the "Strict" Products Liability Myth, 1996 U. Ill. L. Rev. 743; Owen, The Moral Foundations of Products Liability Law: Toward First Principles, 68 Notre Dame L. Rev. 427 (1993); Henderson and Twerski, A Proposed Revision of Section 402A of the Restatement (Second) of Torts, 77 Cornell L. Rev. 1512 (1992); Powers, A Modest Proposal to Abandon Strict Products Liability, 1991 U. Ill. L. Rev. 639, 639 (1991); Birnbaum, Unmasking the Test for Design Defect: From Negligence [to Warranty] to Strict Liability to Negligence, 33 Vand. L. Rev. 593 (1980); Epstein, Prod-

ucts Liability: The Search for the Middle Ground, 56 N.C. L. Rev. 643 (1976).

**3.** See, e.g., Phillips, Consumer Expectations, 53 S.C. L. Rev. 1047 (2002); Shapo, In Search of the Law of Products Liability: The ALI Restatement Project, 48 Vand. L. Rev. 631 (1995); Vandall, The Restatement (Third) of Torts: Products Liability Section 2(b): The Reasonable Alternative Design Requirement, 61 Tenn. L. Rev. 1407 (1994); Corboy, The Not–So–Quiet Revolution—Rebuilding Barriers to Jury Trial in the Proposed Restatement (Third) of Torts: Products Liability, 61 Tenn. L. Rev. 1043 (1994); Wertheimer, Unknowable Dangers and the Death of Strict Products Liability: The Empire Strikes Back, 60 U. Cin. L. Rev. 1183, 1206–41 (1992).

**4.** See Owen, Defectiveness Restated: Exploding the "Strict" Products Liability Myth, 1996 U. Ill. L. Rev. 743.

**5.** See §§ 5.7 and 8.4, below.

**6.** "The risk-utility balancing test is merely a detailed version of Judge Learned Hand's negligence calculus. See United

similarity, or "functional equivalence," of negligence and "strict" liability in the design context, and a small number boldly insist upon applying negligence principles explicitly, rather than those of "strict" liability, in design defect cases.[7] But most courts so far have refused to take the final step and acknowledge that negligence doctrine should entirely displace strict liability as the single, proper liability standard for rendering risk-utility determinations in design defect cases.[8]

Courts have most forthrightly admitted the central role of negligence principles in "strict" liability claims in the context of the duty to warn. In the words of Justice Mosk of the California Supreme Court: "In no area of strict products liability has the impact of principles of negligence become more pronounced than in failure-to-warn cases."[9] Courts increasingly agree with the Supreme Court of Ohio's assertion in *Crislip v. TCH Liquidating Co.*[10] that "the standard imposed upon the defendant in a strict liability claim grounded upon an inadequate warning is the same as that imposed in a negligence claim based upon inadequate warning."[11] In *Olson v. Prosoco, Inc.*,[12] the Supreme Court of Iowa took the final step of recognizing that, because negligence is indeed a better doctrine than strict liability in warnings cases, negligence should formally displace the doctrine of strict liability in tort in this context.[13]

States v. Carroll Towing Co., 159 F.2d 169, 173 (2d Cir. 1947). As Dean Prosser has pointed out, the liability of the manufacturer rests 'upon a departure from proper standards of care, so that the tort is essentially a matter of negligence.'" Prentis v. Yale Mfg. Co., 365 N.W.2d 176, 184 (Mich. 1984) (negligence only proper basis for liability in design defect case). See § 2.2, above.

**7.** The best recent example of this trend may be Wright v. Brooke Group Ltd., 652 N.W.2d 159 (Iowa 2002) (explicitly replacing § 402A with the negligence-based principles of § 2(b) of the Third Restatement). Prentis v. Yale Mfg. Co., 365 N.W.2d 176, 185–186 (Mich. 1984), may be the best early example. Refusing to apply the strict liability principles of implied warranty doctrine to the design defect context, the *Prentis* court concluded: "Imposing a negligence standard for design defect litigation is only to define in a coherent fashion what our litigants in this case are in fact arguing and what our jurors are in essence analyzing. Thus we adopt, forthrightly, a pure negligence, risk-utility test in products liability actions against manufacturers of products, where liability is predicated upon defective design."

**8.** Banks v. ICI Ams., Inc. 450 S.E.2d 671, 674 n.3 (Ga. 1994), is typical:

While we recognize that the determination of whether a product was defective (involving the reasonableness of a manufacturer's design decisions), which is a basic inquiry for strict liability purposes, generally will overlap the determination of whether the manufacturer's conduct was reasonable, which is a basic inquiry for negligence purposes, we cannot agree that the use of negligence principles to determine whether the design of a product was "defective" necessarily obliterates under every conceivable factual scenario the distinction Georgia law has long recognized between negligence and strict liability theories of liability. Hence, we see no reason to conclude definitively that the two theories merge in design defect cases.

**9.** Anderson v. Owens–Corning Fiberglas Corp., 810 P.2d 549, 561 (Cal. 1991) (Mosk, J., concurring and dissenting).

**10.** 556 N.E.2d 1177 (Ohio 1990) (failure to instruct on strict liability failure to warn claim was harmless error).

**11.** Id. at 1183. See also McConnell v. Cosco, Inc., 238 F.Supp.2d 970, 976 (S.D. Ohio 2003) ("the same standard applies for both strict liability and negligence claims for inadequate warning").

**12.** 522 N.W.2d 284 (Iowa 1994).

**13.** The court remarked, at 289–90:

[T]he correct submission of instructions regarding a failure to warn claim for damages is under a theory of negligence and the claim should not be submitted as a theory of strict liability. In testing the defendant's liability for negligence in failing to warn, the defendant should be held

Nevertheless, even while acknowledging that liability in design and warnings cases is really nothing more than negligence, most courts continue to pretend that it really *is* something more. Thus, even in the warnings context, most courts still call liability "strict." *Crislip* is one case in point, the Ohio Supreme Court there taking care to explain that "[w]e do not mean to suggest that a cause of action for negligent failure to warn or warn adequately is identical to one brought under strict liability."[14] *Anderson v. Owens–Corning Fiberglas Corp.*[15] is another example of a court struggling to apply negligence principles under the guise of "strict" liability. In deciding that a defendant in a warnings case may present evidence on state of the art, the majority of the California Supreme Court noted that, "while a manufacturing or design defect *can be* evaluated without reference to the conduct of the manufacturer, the giving of a warning cannot."[16] Nevertheless, the majority asserted (but failed convincingly to explain)[17] that "despite its roots in negligence, failure to warn in strict liability differs markedly from failure to warn in the negligence context."[18]

These developments in the courts are mirrored by the *Products Liability Restatement* which acknowledges that liability for both defective design and defective warnings is based on principles of negligence. In § 2(b), design defectiveness is defined as follows:

> [A] product is defective in design when the foreseeable risks of harm posed by the product could have been reduced or avoided by the adoption of a reasonable alternative design ... and the omission of the alternative design renders the product not reasonably safe.

Comment *d* recognizes that this liability formulation is essentially a negligence standard of liability because it "adopts a reasonableness ('risk-utility balancing') test as the standard for judging the defectiveness of product designs. More specifically, the test is whether a reasonable alternative design would, at reasonable cost, have reduced the foreseeable risks of harm posed by the product and, if so, whether the

to the standard of care of an expert in its field. The relevant inquiry therefore is whether the reasonable manufacturer knew or should have known of the danger, in light of the generally recognized and prevailing best scientific knowledge, yet failed to provide adequate warning to users or consumers.

**14.** *Crislip*, 556 N.E.2d at 1183 (Ohio 1990) (explaining that the causes of action are not identical principally because plaintiff's comparative fault may not reduce damages in a strict liability claim in Ohio).

**15.** 810 P.2d 549 (Cal. 1991).

**16.** Id. at 558 (emphasis added).

**17.** The frailty of the majority's efforts to explain the supposed differences between negligence and strict tort liability in the warnings context rang hollow on the ears of Justice Stanley Mosk, a member of the California Supreme Court since 1964 who per-

sonally helped develop "[t]he pure concepts of products liability so pridefully fashioned and nurtured" by that court in the 1960s and 1970s. Id. at 561. Nevertheless, Justice Mosk rebelled at continuing the subterfuge. Noting that the strict liability focus "has become blurred through the years," he observed that "our past acquiescence in this muddled state of affairs does not justify making matters worse. Misconception compounded cannot result in authenticity." Id. He concluded that the court "should consider the possibility of holding that failure-to-warn actions lie solely on a negligence theory." 810 P.2d at 563. (Mosk, J., concurring and dissenting). When the court was later so asked, it refused. See Carlin v. Superior Court, 920 P.2d 1347 (Cal. 1996) (strict liability in tort proper theory for warnings claim in prescription drug case).

**18.** Anderson v. Owens–Corning Fiberglas Corp., 810 P.2d 549, 558 (Cal. 1991).

omission of the alternative design rendered the product not reasonably safe." The necessary "comparison between an alternative design and the product design that caused the injury [is] undertaken from the viewpoint of a reasonable person. That standard is also used in administering the traditional reasonableness standard in negligence."[19] Section 2(c) similarly "adopts a reasonableness test for judging the adequacy of product instructions and warnings [and so] parallels Subsection (b)."[20]

Thus, American products liability law increasingly recognizes that negligence principles properly control the determinations in both design and warnings cases. While most courts have not yet explicitly repudiated "strict" liability doctrine in favor of negligence in these two contexts, more courts in the years ahead may be expected to see the merits of such a forthright approach to legal doctrine.

### Resurgence in Reform Statutes

Negligence principles and rules also figure prominently in the products liability reform statutes passed in a number of states. A prominent feature of many such statutes is the definition of liability in negligence terms. Several of the statutes define design defectiveness in classic risk-utility language, which, as discussed above, is simply an application in the product design context of Learned Hand's negligence formula from the *Carroll Towing* case.[21] In addition, many of the statutes define the liability standard for warnings and instructions defects in conventional negligence terms.[22]

First to be mentioned are a small number of state statutes which have quite definitively reapplied negligence doctrine to both design and warnings cases. Indiana, in 1978, adopted strict products liability in tort legislatively by codifying § 402A of the *Restatement (Second) of Torts* essentially verbatim. On its face, it is clear that § 402A imposes liability that purports to be truly strict, rejecting any intimation that a manufacturer or other seller may defend on the ground that it exercised all due care in the preparation or sale of the product. In 1996, however, the Indiana legislature amended its § 402A statute by adding the following proviso: "However, in any action based on an alleged design [or warnings defect], the [plaintiff] must establish that the manufacturer or seller failed to exercise reasonable care under the circumstance in designing the product or in providing the warnings or instructions."[23] Washington's reform statute similarly declares in part that "[a] product manufacturer is subject to liability to a claimant if the claimant's harm was proximately caused by the negligence of the manufacturer in that the

---

**19.** Products Liability Restatement § 2, cmt. *d*.

**20.** Products Liability Restatement § 2(c), cmt. *i*.

**21.** United States v. Carroll Towing Co., 159 F.2d 169 (2d Cir. 1947). See § 2.2, above.

**22.** See, e.g., Ohio Rev. Code Ann. § 2307.76(A)(1) (manufacturer subject to liability if it knew or reasonably should have known of a risk and "failed to provide the warning or instruction that a manufacturer exercising reasonable care would have provided"). See McConnell v. Cosco, Inc., 238 F.Supp.2d 970 (S.D. Ohio 2003).

**23.** Ind. Code § 34–20–2–2, recodifying Ind. Code § 33–1–1.5–3(b)(2).

product was not reasonably safe as designed or not reasonably safe because adequate warnings or instructions were not provided."[24]

Some products liability reform statutes, while not so explicitly redefining liability in negligence *doctrine*, redefine the standard of liability in negligence *terms*. Thus, a number of state reform statutes quite clearly use negligence calculus-of-risk principles in defining liability for defects in *design*. Louisiana's statute, for example, formulates its standard for design defect liability largely in terms of whether "[t]he likelihood that the product's design would cause the claimant damage and the gravity of that damage outweighed the burden on the manufacturer of adopting [an] alternative design and the adverse effect, if any, of such alternative design on the utility of the product."[25] And a small number of products liability reform statutes are quite explicit about applying negligence doctrine to design defect litigation. In addition to the Indiana and Washington statutes examined above, North Carolina's statute expressly reaffirms its rejection of the strict liability in tort doctrine[26] and provides in part that a manufacturer may not be liable for design defects "unless the claimant proves that . . . the manufacturer acted unreasonably in designing or formulating the product. . . . "[27]

A larger number of state legislatures, mirroring the common law development in the courts, have turned quite explicitly to negligence doctrine to define a manufacturer's liability for failing adequately to *warn* or *instruct*. So, in addition to the Indiana and Washington statutes mentioned above, the Louisiana statute provides that "[a] product is unreasonably dangerous because an adequate warning about the product has not been provided if . . . the product possessed a characteristic that may cause damage and the manufacturer failed to use reasonable care to provide an adequate warning of such characteristic and its danger to users and handlers of the product."[28] Mississippi's statute provides that "[a]n adequate product warning or instruction is one that a reasonably prudent person in the same or similar circumstances would have provided. . . . "[29] New Jersey's statutory return to negligence principles in warnings cases is similarly clear, providing that "[a]n adequate product warning or instruction is one that a reasonably prudent person in the same or similar circumstances would have provided. . . . "[30] A manufacturer or other seller is liable in a warnings case in North Carolina only if the defendant "acted unreasonably in failing to provide [a] warning or instruction."[31] And Ohio limits recovery in warnings cases to circumstances where the manufacturer knew or should have known of the risk and failed to provide the warning or instruction that a manufacturer exercising reasonable care would have provided.[32]

**24.** Wash. Rev. Code Ann. § 7.72.030(1). Note, however, that the statute ambiguously adds, in subsection (3): "In determining whether a product was not reasonably safe under this section, the trier of fact shall consider whether the product was unsafe to an extent beyond that which would be contemplated by the ordinary consumer."

**25.** La. Rev. Stat. Ann. § 9:2800.56(2).

**26.** N.C. Gen. Stat. § 99B–1.1 ("There shall be no strict liability in tort in product liability actions.").

**27.** Id. at 99B–6(a).

**28.** La. Rev. Stat. Ann. § 9:2800.57A.

**29.** Miss. Code Ann. § 11–1–63(c)(ii).

**30.** N.J. Stat. Ann. § 2A.58c–4.

**31.** N.C. Gen. Stat. § 99B–5.

**32.** Ohio Rev. Code Ann. § 2307.76.

Thus, in an increasing number of states, negligence principles are returning to the law of products liability as the dominant (and sometimes exclusive) tort law standard of liability in design and warnings cases. As examined above, this development is endorsed by the *Restatement (Third) of Torts: Products Liability*[33] and it is a trend, building sound doctrine on sound policy,[34] that may be expected to continue in both courts and legislatures in the years ahead.

---

**33.** See § 6.5, below.

**34.** The policy and ethical reasons supporting the use of negligence principles in design and warnings cases are explored in Owen, The Moral Foundations of Products Liability Law: Toward First Principles, 68 Notre Dame L. Rev. 427 (1993).

# Chapter 3

# TORTIOUS MISREPRESENTATION

*Table of Sections*

## § 3.1  MISREPRESENTATION—GENERALLY

Misrepresentation is the communication of false or misleading information to another. Three separate claims for tortious misrepresentation[1] may arise under the common law, theories of liability that differ principally according to the defendant's state of mind in making the representation.[2] The classic tortious misrepresentation claim, deceit (now more commonly called "fraud"), requires a showing of *scienter*—that the defendant knew the matter represented to be false and intended it to mislead the plaintiff, or some similar state of mind. Negligent misrepresentation requires proof only that the defendant was negligent in not knowing the falsity of the representations, or, less commonly, that the defendant communicated them in a negligent manner. Finally, some jurisdictions allow claims of strict liability in tort for innocently making public misrepresentations about a product's safety, notwithstanding the

### § 3.1

**1.** Liability for contractual misrepresentation lies in UCC § 2–313 (Express Warranty). See § 4.2, below.

**2.** See, e.g., In re Tobacco Cases II, 113 Cal.Rptr.2d 120, 130 (Ct. App. 2001), review granted and opinion superseded, 39 P.3d 511 (2002) ("intentional fraud and negligent misrepresentation ... involve fundamentally different state of mind requirements"); Cummings v. HPG Int'l, Inc., 244 F.3d 16, 22–23 (1st Cir. 2001) (Mass. law) (hypothesizing that the confusion in cases as to knowledge required for deceit may derive from failure of courts to distinguish between intentional and negligent misrepresentation).

Section 9 of the Products Liability Restatement, entitled "Liability of Commercial Product Seller or Distributor for Harm Caused by Misrepresentation," provides:

> One engaged in the business of selling or otherwise distributing products who, in connection with the sale of a product, makes a fraudulent, negligent, or innocent misrepresentation of material fact concerning the product is subject to liability for harm to persons or property caused by the misrepresentation.

See § 6.5, below. An early, classic article on the topic is Bohlen, Misrepresentation as Deceit, Negligence, or Warranty, 42 Harv. L. Rev. 733 (1929). More recent treatments of tortious misrepresentation include Dobbs, Law of Torts ch. 35; 2 Harper, James, and Gray, Law of Torts ch. 7; Prosser and Keeton on Torts ch. 18.

seller's belief that the representations are true, the seller's good faith, or the seller's exercise of all due care. Other differences between these three separate theories of recovery are considered below.

Products liability claims of misrepresentation generally are grounded in a manufacturer's or other seller's communication of false and material words about a product to a plaintiff who is harmed by relying on the truth of that communication.[3] Such claims therefore require no "defect" in the product but only the communication of words that are false. Hinging in this manner upon particular words written or spoken by the defendant, misrepresentation claims thus require the precise identification and close scrutiny of particular, offending language. Thus, a lawyer or judge considering a misrepresentation claim must first and foremost isolate the exact words challenged, framing the particular context in which they were communicated, in order to assess whether they properly give rise to a misrepresentation claim.[4]

## § 3.2 FRAUD

The action of fraudulent misrepresentation or "deceit," often referred to as "fraud" or "intentional misrepresentation," may be traced in old English law to the writ of deceit, dating at least to 1201,[1] which most likely evolved from the concept of *dolus* (fraud) in Roman law.[2] One of the earliest reported English cases allowing recovery for personal

---

**3.** The classic study of how misrepresentation shapes products liability is Shapo, A Representational Theory of Consumer Protection: Doctrine, Function and Legal Liability for Product Disappointment, 60 Va. L. Rev. 1109 (1974). For a helpful discussion of various misrepresentation issues in the products liability context, see 1 Frumer and Friedman, Products Liability § 2.05. See also Phillips, Product Misrepresentation and the Doctrine of Causation, 2 Hofstra L. Rev. 561 (1974); Annot., 75 A.L.R.2d 112, 140 (1961) (advertising statements as affecting manufacturer's or seller's liability for product injury).

**4.** See, e.g., Tuttle v. Lorillard Tobacco Co., 377 F.3d 917 (8th Cir. 2004) (Minn. law) (negligent misrepresentation claim dismissed because plaintiff "fail[ed] to identify any misrepresentation he actually read and relied upon in using smokeless tobacco."); In re Kings Cty. Tobacco Litig., 727 N.Y.S.2d 241 n.8 (Sup. Ct. 2000) (misrepresentation claim dismissed because of plaintiff's failure to identify particular representations, merely relying on television ads that "made smoking seem cool"); Sanchez v. Liggett & Myers Inc., 187 F.3d 486, 491 (5th Cir. 1999) (Tex. law) (no specific representations); Small v. Lorillard Tobacco Co., 679 N.Y.S.2d 593, 604–05 (App. Div. 1998) (same), aff'd, 698 N.Y.S.2d 615 (N.Y. 1999); Rowan Cty. Bd. of Educ. v. U.S. Gypsum Co., 418 S.E.2d 648, 659 (N.C. 1992) ("Requiring proof of a specific representation facilitates courts in distinguishing mere

puffing, guesses, or assertions of opinions from representations of material facts."); G & M Farms v. Funk Irrigation Co., 808 P.2d 851 (Idaho 1991) (studied analysis of several different representations).

*But see* Boeken v. Philip Morris Inc., 2004 WL 2095334, at *2–*14 (Cal.Ct.App. 2004) (plaintiff's memory of Marlboro advertising themes was sufficient proof of reliance); Williams v. Philip Morris Inc., 48 P.3d 824, 831–35 (Or. Ct. App. 2002), vacated on other grounds, Philip Morris USA Inc. v. Williams, 124 S.Ct. 56 (2003), which allowed a fraud claim against a cigarette manufacturer despite the plaintiff's inability to identify particular statements, based on the defendant's advertising over many years that was intended to create an impression in the public of a legitimate controversy over the safety of cigarette smoking. The court rejected the defendant's vilification of such a claim as a "fraud on the American public" similar to "fraud on the market." "[A] defendant may be liable for fraud for a misrepresentation that creates a false impression even though it is impossible to identify the specific misrepresentation on which a person relied." Id. at 830–31.

### § 3.2

**1.** See 1 T. Street, The Foundations of Legal Liability 374–77 (1906).

**2.** See id.; J. Thomas, Textbook of Roman Law 288–90 (1976).

injuries in a products liability case was based in fraud,[3] and such claims continue to figure prominently (if not particularly frequently) in modern American products liability litigation.[4] Depending on the jurisdiction, proof of fraud may advantage a plaintiff's case with respect to privity,[5] federal preemption,[6] a statute of limitations, the effect of a disclaimer, contributory negligence, and, possibly, punitive damages. In some jurisdictions, however, fraud claims do not survive the death of a party.[7]

The contemporary cause of action for intentional or fraudulent misrepresentation requires the plaintiff to establish each of a number of elements, which together comprise the intentional tort of fraud, or deceit. Although the precise specification of elements varies somewhat from state to state, most courts agree in substance that a plaintiff must establish elements similar to the following in order to prevail in a claim for fraud:

> (1) a representation; (2) its falsity; (3) its materiality; (4) the speaker's knowledge of its falsity or ignorance of its truth; (5) his intent that it should be acted on by the person and in the manner reasonably contemplated; (6) the hearer's ignorance of its falsity; (7) his reliance on its truth; (8) his right to rely thereon; and (9) his consequent and proximate injury.[8]

In formulating these requirements for the tort of deceit, some courts condense them into as few as three,[9] four,[10] or five elements.[11] For

---

**3.** Langridge v. Levy, 150 Eng. Rep. 863 (1836), aff'd, 150 Eng. Rep. 1458 (1838).

**4.** By way of example, fraud claims figure prominently in the current litigation against cigarette manufacturers. See, e.g., Williams v. Philip Morris Inc., 48 P.3d 824 (Or. Ct. App. 2002), vacated, Philip Morris USA Inc. v. Williams, 124 S.Ct. 56 (2003) verdict adhered to on remand, 92 P.3d 126 (Or. Ct. App. 2004); In re Simon II Litig., 211 F.R.D. 86, 139 (E.D.N.Y. 2002) (Weinstein, J.) (certifying national tobacco class action seeking punitive damages for fraud: "The ingenuity of humanity in devising frauds, and the need to deter them, has led to the creation of a common law and statutory net sufficiently wide to ensnare an enormous and ever-expanding universe of frauds."). See generally Motley and Player, Issues in "Crime–Fraud" Practice and Procedure: The Tobacco Litigation Experience, 49 S.C. L. Rev. 187 (1998).

**5.** See Wright v. Brooke Group Ltd., 652 N.W.2d 159, 175–76 (Iowa 2002) (privity of contract unnecessary to fraud claim).

**6.** See, e.g., Williams v. Philip Morris Inc., 48 P.3d 824, 830 (Or. Ct. App. 2002) (federal labeling act preempted warnings and fraudulent concealment but not fraud claims), vacated on other grounds, Philip Morris USA Inc. v. Williams, 124 S.Ct. 56 (2003); In re Simon II Litig., 211 F.R.D. 86, 141–43 (E.D.N.Y. 2002) (Weinstein, J.) (class action fraud claims against tobacco companies not preempted).

**7.** See, e.g., Faircloth v. Finesod, 938 F.2d 513 (4th Cir. 1991) (S.C. law) (*Held*, constitutional).

**8.** Williams v. Philip Morris Inc., 48 P.3d 824, 830 (Or. Ct. App. 2002), vacated on other grounds, Philip Morris USA Inc. v. Williams, 124 S.Ct. 56 (2003).

**9.** See, e.g., Cummings v. HPG Int'l, Inc., 244 F.3d 16, 22 (1st Cir. 2001) (Mass. law) ("a plaintiff must show that the defendant: [1] made a false representation of material fact; [2] for the purpose of inducing reliance; and [3] that plaintiff relied upon the representation to his or her detriment").

**10.** See, e.g., Lewis v. Lead Indus. Ass'n, Inc., 793 N.E.2d 869, 876 (Ill. App. Ct. 2003); Mason v. Chrysler Corp., 653 So.2d 951, 953 (Ala. 1995) (advertising and salesman's representations concerning defective new car):

> To establish a cause of action for fraudulent representation or fraud, the [plaintiffs] must show (1) that the defendant made a misrepresentation, (2) that misrepresentation concerned a material existing fact, . . . (3) that the plaintiff relied on the representation, and (4) that the reliance was to the plaintiff's detriment.

**11.** See, e.g., Smith v. DaimlerChrysler Corp., 2002 WL 31814534, at *6 (Del. Super. 2002) (fraudulent misrepresentation requires plaintiff to show "(1) a false repre-

example, elements (7) and (8) in the above formulation may easily be combined into a single element designated "justifiable reliance." In contrast, other courts splinter the various requirements into as many as eleven elements,[12] which is easily accomplished by pulling apart element (1) into its separate components of "representation," "existing," and "fact." Regardless of how the elements are divided, courts widely agree that the substance of these components are necessary to establish a claim for fraudulent misrepresentation.

Fraud claims are bounded by certain restrictive principles of pleading and proof. In many states,[13] and under the Federal Rules of Civil Procedure,[14] a plaintiff must plead with specificity the facts constituting a fraud. Moreover, because of the accompanying stigma associated with the commission of a fraud,[15] many jurisdictions apply a "clear and convincing evidence" standard of proof to claims of fraudulent misrepre-

sentation, or deliberate concealment, of a material fact, by the defendant; (2) the defendant acted with scienter; (3) an intent to induce plaintiff's reliance on the misrepresentation or concealment; (4) causation; and (5) damage resulting from the misrepresentation or concealment"); In re Simon II Litig., 211 F.R.D. 86, 139 (E.D.N.Y. 2002) (summarizing fraud elements as "1) representation of a material fact; 2) falsity; 3) scienter; 4) reasonable reliance; and 5) damages"); Board of Educ. of City of Chicago v. A, C & S, Inc., 546 N.E.2d 580, 591 (Ill. 1989) ((1) a false statement of material fact, (2) knowledge or belief of the falsity by the party making it, (3) intention to induce the other party to act, (4) action by the other party in reliance on the truth of the statements, and (5) damage to the other party resulting from such reliance.

**12.** See, e.g., Yost v. Millhouse, 373 N.W.2d 826, 829–830 (Minn. Ct. App. 1985), reciting the elements of fraudulent misrepresentation as follows:

(1) There must be a representation; (2) That representation must be false; (3) It must have to do with a past or present fact; (4) That fact must be material; (5) It must be susceptible of knowledge; (6) The representor must know it to be false, or in the alternative, must assert it as of his own knowledge without knowing whether it is true or false; (7) The representor must intend to have the other person induced to act, or justified in acting upon it; (8) That person must be so induced to act or so justified in acting; (9) The person's action must be in reliance upon the representation; (10) That person must suffer damage; (11) That damage must be attributable to the misrepresentation, that is, the statement must be the proximate cause of the injury.

**13.** See, e.g., Board of Educ. v. A, C & S, Inc., 546 N.E.2d 580, 593–94 (Ill. 1989):

The facts which constitute an alleged fraud must be pleaded with sufficient specificity, particularity and certainty to apprise the opposing party of what he is called upon to answer. The pleadings must contain specific allegations of facts from which fraud is the necessary or probable inference.... Even under the more lenient Federal rules ... a plaintiff must at least plead with sufficient particularity facts establishing the elements of fraud, including what misrepresentations were made, when they were made, who made [them] and to whom they were made.

Note that most states have now adopted rules of civil procedure patterned on the federal rules.

**14.** Fed. R. Civ. P. 9(b) provides in part: "In all averments of fraud or mistake, the circumstances constituting fraud or mistake shall be stated with particularity." See, e.g., Gilleon v. Medtronic USA, Inc., 2002 WL 31300694, at *6 (N.D. Cal. 2002) ("[T]he misrepresentation claims are not sufficiently pleaded under Rule 9, and the 'who, what, when and where' facts are wholly absent. Thus, it is appropriate to dismiss those claims, with leave to amend to plead the claims with the specificity required by Rule 9."); Sanchez v. Liggett & Myers Inc., 187 F.3d 486, 491 (5th Cir. 1999) (Tex. law) (affirming judgment for defendants on misrepresentation claims because plaintiff failed to identify specific representations).

**15.** "[I]n civil cases involving ... fraud or some other quasi-criminal wrongdoing by the defendant[,] [t]he interests at stake ... are ... more substantial than mere loss of money[,] and some jurisdictions accordingly reduce the risk to the defendant of having his reputation tarnished erroneously by increasing plaintiff's burden of proof." Rodriguez v. Suzuki Motor Corp., 936 S.W.2d 104 (Mo. 1996) (en banc).

sentation.[16] The plaintiff's burden of proof applies to each element of fraudulent misrepresentation, and such a claim will fail if the plaintiff fails to establish any one of the separate elements of the tort. For these reasons, recovery on fraudulent misrepresentation claims is often particularly difficult,[17] and plaintiffs often shy away from this tort if relief appears available on some other theory of recovery with fewer elements and less stringent requirements of proof.[18]

### Representation

By its very nature, a misrepresentation consists of the defendant's communication of information to the plaintiff or another. As discussed above,[19] the plaintiff in a fraudulent misrepresentation case must identify with specificity a particular representation, and the failure to do so will result in dismissal of the claim. Information usually is communicated by spoken or written word, but it may also be conveyed pictorially or by conduct. Hence, a manufacturer or other seller may be liable in deceit for printing a picture of the product performing tasks it cannot safely perform or for physically preventing a prospective buyer from discovering a dangerous defect, as by covering over it with paint or grease.[20]

More difficult conceptually is the question of whether a defendant may be liable in fraud for mere *silence*, for failing to communicate information about some hidden defect or danger lurking within a product. This issue also may be phrased as whether the law of deceit[21] imposes on defendants a "duty of disclosure"—whether liability ever may attach for *non*disclosure—with respect to dangers hidden in the

**16.** "A plaintiff must prove each element of the tort by clear and convincing evidence, or evidence that establishes that the truth of the facts alleged is highly probable." Williams v. Philip Morris Inc., 48 P.3d 824, 830 (Or. Ct. App. 2002), vacated on other grounds, Philip Morris USA Inc. v. Williams, 124 S.Ct. 56 (2003). See also Rodriguez v. Suzuki Motor Corp., 936 S.W.2d 104 (Mo. 1996) (en banc); G & M Farms v. Funk Irrigation Co., 808 P.2d 851 (Idaho 1991).

For an extensive study of the origins and nature of the clear and convincing standard of proof, see Riley Hill Gen. Contractor v. Tandy Corp., 737 P.2d 595, 605 (Or. 1987) ("[T]he standard of proof in a civil action for common law deceit must be 'clear and convincing.' ... [T]he evidence must be free from confusion, fully intelligible, distinct and establish to the jury that the defendant intended to deceive the plaintiff or did so with a reckless disregard for the truth. To be both clear and convincing, the truth of the facts asserted must be highly detailed.").

**17.** "Of all civil liabilities, fraud is the most difficult to establish." Dobbin v. Pacific Coast Coal Co., 170 P.2d 642, 648 (Wash. 1946) (distributor of defective furnace not liable in fraud).

**18.** Assuming no problems with privity, disclaimers, or notice, probably the easiest parallel theory on which to recover is for breach of express warranty under the Uniform Commercial Code, a doctrine available in every state. See § 4.2, below.

**19.** See § 3.1, above.

**20.** See, e.g., Kuelling v. Roderick Lean Mfg. Co., 75 N.E. 1098, 1099 (N.Y. 1905) (beam on farm machine made of unfit, cross-grained wood with knothole): "[D]efendant concealed this knothole with a plug of soft wood nailed in, and then the knot, the plug, the hole, the cross-grain of the wood, and the kind of wood used were covered up and concealed by the defendant with putty and paint...." This amounted to "an affirmative representation that the [beam] was sound...." Id. at 1101. See also Woodward v. Miller & Karwisch, 46 S.E. 847 (Ga. 1904) (large crack in axle of buggy covered over with grease). See generally Keeton, Fraud—Concealment and Nondisclosure, 15 Tex. L. Rev. 1 (1936).

**21.** As opposed to the duty to warn, which by its very nature imposes an affirmative obligation to communicate danger and safe-use information to persons likely to need such information. For a thorough examination of the duty to warn, see ch. 9, below.

products they sell. Because the tort of misrepresentation rests on the idea that the defendant in fact communicated a false and damaging idea to another person, the traditional general rule is that the mere *nondisclosure* of information will not support an action of deceit. Viewed doctrinally, a defendant's failure to disclose a fact will not ordinarily satisfy the "representation" element of a claim for fraud.[22] This general rule is eminently sound, of course, for otherwise any failure to warn would amount ipso facto to a misrepresentation.

The no-duty-to-disclose rule, however, has sometimes proven harsh in application, and courts at an early date began to create exceptions to it for special situations.[23] One exception applicable to the products liability context is the duty to disclose information necessary to cure a misconception caused by a defendant's representation that is literally true but which implies facts that themselves are untrue—in other words, a "half-truth."[24] Thus, "a statement which is technically true as far as it goes may nevertheless be fraudulent, where it is misleading because it does not state matters which materially qualify the statement as made. In other words, a half-truth is sometimes more misleading than an outright lie."[25] Another exception to the no-duty-to-disclose general rule

**22.** "It has commonly been stated as a general rule, particularly in the older cases, that the action will not lie for such tacit nondisclosure." Prosser and Keeton on Torts § 106, at 737. "When the parties to a transaction deal with each other at arm's length, with no confidential relationship, no obligation to disclose information arises when the information is not requested." Mason v. Chrysler Corp., 653 So.2d 951, 955 (Ala. 1995).

**23.** For example, a duty of disclosure may exist "where the seller actively conceals a defect or where he prevents investigation; where the seller has told a half truth or has made an ambiguous statement if the seller's intent is to create a false impression and he does so; where there is a fiduciary relationship between the parties; or where the facts are peculiarly or exclusively within the knowledge of one party to the transaction and the other party is not in a position to discover the facts for himself." Ollerman v. O'Rourke Co., 288 N.W.2d 95, 102 (Wis. 1980) (purchaser of lot claimed he would not have purchased it at stipulated price if he had been alerted to underground well which he alleged vendor was aware of prior to sale).

**24.** "The most obvious [exception] is that if the defendant does speak, he must disclose enough to prevent his words from being misleading, and that there is fraud in a statement [when he does not do so]. In other words, half of the truth may obviously amount to a lie, if it is understood to be the whole." Prosser and Keeton on Torts § 106, at 738.

**25.** St. Joseph Hosp. v. Corbetta Constr. Co., 316 N.E.2d 51, 71 (Ill. App. Ct. 1974).

General Electric's Textolite wall paneling failed the Underwriters Laboratories' flame spread fire tunnel test, registering a 255. UL refused to give Textolite a rating because it considered any product testing in excess of 200 to be dangerously flammable. In selling the Textolite to a contractor for use in the construction of a hospital in Chicago, which by code required that paneling be rated no higher than 15, GE represented that the paneling did not have a flame spread rating. However, GE failed to mention that the reason it was not rated was that, if it were, its rating would be 17 times the maximum permitted by the city. The court agreed with the plaintiff's characterization of GE's nondisclosure of the true full facts as fraudulent, despite the literal truth of the "no-flame-spread-rating" representation. "Regardless of how many times General Electric might say, either orally or in writing, that 'Our material is not flame rated,' the statement is still a 'gross deception' covering up the real truth namely that General Electric was proposing for installation in this hospital a material which it actually knew was utterly unfit for use in such an institution." Id. at 70–71.

See also Boeken v. Philip Morris Inc., 2004 WL 2095334, at *4 (Cal.Ct.App. 2004) ("a duty to speak may arise when necessary to clarify misleading 'half-truths.'"); Wright v. Brooke Group Ltd., 652 N.W.2d 159, 175–76 (Iowa 2002) ("a manufacturer has a duty to a consumer under Restatement (Second) of Torts § 551(2)(b) to disclose 'matters known to [the manufacturer] that [it] knows to be necessary to prevent [its] partial or ambiguous statement of the

sometimes applicable to products liability cases is the duty to correct information believed by the speaker to be true at the time it was communicated but which is subsequently discovered to be false.[26] In addition, the existence of a fiduciary or confidential relationship may impose an affirmative duty on the person holding the position of power to provide the other with information necessary to protect the other's interests.[27] But the normal relationship between manufacturers and consumers can hardly be characterized as fiduciary or confidential, no matter how shoddy the products sold may be, so that some other exception to the general no-duty-to-disclose rule must be found to support a misrepresentation claim[28] for failing to disclose defects in the goods sold.[29] These and various other exceptions[30] to the general no-duty-

facts from being misleading' and under § 551(2)(c) to disclose subsequently acquired information that would prevent a prior statement from being false or misleading"); In re Simon II Litig., 211 F.R.D. 86, 140 (E.D.N.Y. 2002):

> A partial disclosure accompanied by a willful concealment of material and qualifying facts can constitute a misrepresentation. Even if everything one says is true, if something is omitted which would qualify the assertion, then it may amount to a false representation. Moreover, if the defendant speaks at all, it is obliged to make a full and fair disclosure.

**26.** "[W]here one has made a statement which at that time is true but subsequently acquires new information which makes it untrue or misleading, he must disclose such information to anyone whom he knows to be acting on the basis of the original statement—or be guilty of fraud or deceit." Id. at 71; Prosser and Keeton on Torts § 106, at 738. See also Wright v. Brooke Group Ltd., 652 N.W.2d 159 (Iowa 2002), previous note.

**27.** See Prosser and Keeton on Torts § 106, at 738.

**28.** Apart from tortious misrepresentation, of course, manufacturers normally have a duty to warn consumers of any dangerous defects their products might contain. See ch. 9, below.

**29.** See, e.g., Wright v. Brooke Group Ltd., 652 N.W.2d 159, 177 (Iowa 2002) ("'[A] manufacturer's failure to warn or to disclose material information does not give rise to a fraud claim when the relationship between a plaintiff and a defendant is solely that of a customer/buyer and manufacturer with two exceptions. Those exceptions are limited to instances where the manufacturer (1) has made misleading statements of fact intended to influence consumers, or (2) has made true statements of fact designed to influence consumers and subsequently acquires information rendering the prior statements untrue or misleading.'"). See also Jeter ex rel. Estate of Smith v. Brown & Williamson Tobacco Corp., 294 F.Supp.2d

681, 687–88 (W.D. Pa. 2003); Estate of White v. R.J. Reynolds Tobacco Co., 109 F.Supp.2d 424, 431 (D. Md. 2000) (refusing to impose duty to disclose based on mere relationship of manufacturer and buyer); Dow Chem. Co. v. Mahlum, 970 P.2d 98, 110–11 (Nev. 1998) (for purposes of fraudulent concealment claim, parent corporation of manufacturer of silicone breast implants did not have duty to disclose risks to users); Connick v. Suzuki Motor Co., 675 N.E.2d 584, 593 (Ill. 1996) (owners of Suzuki Samurais that were prone to roll over could not maintain fraudulent concealment claim against manufacturer with whom they had no fiduciary or confidential relationship); Mason v. Chrysler Corp., 653 So.2d 951 (Ala. 1995) (sale of shoddily manufactured car to consumers does not give rise to fiduciary or other special relationship, on the part of either manufacturer or dealer, sufficient to give rise to duty to speak; nor does the dealer's repair of the car on several occasions).

*A fortiori*, a manufacturer has no duty to disclose information to third parties who buy a competitor's products. See, e.g., Flynn v. American Home Prods. Corp., 627 N.W.2d 342, 350 (Minn. Ct. App. 2001) (manufacturer of brand-name phen-fen weight loss drug had no duty to disclose risks to purchasers of generic drug: "there is no fiduciary relationship here").

**30.** For example, a defendant may have a duty to speak if the plaintiff requests particular information from the defendant. See Mason v. Chrysler Corp., 653 So.2d 951, 954 (Ala. 1995). See also University Sys. of New Hampshire v. U.S. Gypsum Co., 756 F.Supp. 640, 651 (D.N.H. 1991) ("A duty to disclose arises when a seller knows of a concealed defect which is unknown to the buyer and not capable of detection by the buyer, provided the defect is dangerous to life or property."). This latter dangerous-defect exception would appear to embrace every instance where there is a duty to warn and, thus, seems overly broad for a

to-speak rule might be framed as recognizing "a duty to speak whenever justice, equity, and fair dealing demand it,"[31] but a description of the duty in such a broad manner is too vague for principled application in specific cases.[32]

Courts sometimes allow claims for "fraudulent concealment."[33] Unfortunately, judicial references to fraudulent concealment are often ambiguous and do not distinguish clearly between a defendant's mere failure to disclose facts that may be important to a product purchaser or user,[34] which amounts to nothing more than failing to warn,[35] and a

description of the circumstances giving rise to a duty to speak under the law of fraud.

**31.** See Keeton, Fraud—Concealment and Non-disclosure, 15 Tex. L. Rev. 1, 31 (1936), where Dean Keeton observed:

In the present stage of the law, the decisions show a drawing away from this idea [that nondisclosure is not actionable], and there can be seen an attempt by many courts to reach a just result insofar as possible, but yet maintaining the degree of certainty which the law must have. The statement may often be found that if either party to a contract of sale conceals or suppresses a material fact which he is in good faith bound to disclose then his silence is fraudulent.

The attitude of the courts toward nondisclosure ... in these cases should be to impose on parties to the transaction a duty to speak whenever justice, fair dealing, or equity demand it. This statement is made only with reference to instances where the party to be charged is an actor in the transaction. This duty to speak does not result from an implied representation by silence, but exists only because a refusal to speak constitutes unfair conduct.

**32.** See Note, Silence as Fraudulent Concealment—Vendor and Purchaser—Duty to Disclose, 36 Wash. L. Rev. 202, 204 (1961) ("A somewhat nebulous standard, praiseworthy as looking toward more stringent business ethics, but possibly difficult of practical application.").

**33.** See, e.g., Steele v. Depuy Orthopaedics, Inc., 295 F.Supp.2d 439, 456–57 (D.N.J. 2003) (stating elements and denying defendant's motion for summary judgment). Or, "fraudulent suppression." Mason v. Chrysler Corp., 653 So.2d 951, 954–55 (Ala. 1995). In a few jurisdictions, the law is unambiguous, and fraudulent concealment is clearly defined with elements of its own. See, e.g., Loughridge v. Goodyear Tire & Rubber Co., 192 F.Supp.2d 1175, 1184 (D. Colo. 2002):

The elements of fraudulent concealment are: (1) concealment of a material existing fact that in equity and good con-

science should be disclosed; (2) knowledge on the part of the party against whom the claim is asserted that such a fact is being concealed; (3) ignorance of that fact on the part of the one from whom the fact is concealed; (4) the intention that concealment be acted upon; and (5) action on the concealment resulting in damages.

**34.** See, e.g., Smith v. DaimlerChrysler Corp., 2002 WL 31814534, at *6 (Del. Super. Ct. 2002) (failure to warn dwarf-like individuals of special hazards they confront from airbags); Holmes v. Wegman Oil Co., 492 N.W.2d 107, 114 (S.D. 1992), in which the manufacturer of a thermostatic control for gas water heaters discovered a dangerous design defect in the control five years after it first marketed the control. Once the company learned of the problem, it began to develop a safer design for the control and eventually replaced the dangerous design with the safe design. Although the company thereupon destroyed its inventory of defective valves and implemented a recall campaign to replace them, the company failed to warn customers of the risk prior to the recall and failed to recall as vigorously as it might have. *Held*, evidence supported finding of "fraudulent concealment" under statute which provides that deceit may be established by "the suppression of a fact by one who is bound to disclose it."

See also Nicolet, Inc. v. Nutt, 525 A.2d 146, 149 (Del. 1987), in which the Delaware Supreme Court held that plaintiffs stated a claim for fraudulent concealment by alleging that the defendant asbestos manufacturers (1) knowingly and falsely asserted that it was safe to work in close proximity to asbestos materials, and (2) suppressed from the workers medical and scientific data on potential health hazards of asbestos inhalation. Such "fraudulent concealment" claims are quite common in asbestos litigation. See also Rowan Cty. Bd. of Educ. v. U.S. Gypsum Co., 418 S.E.2d 648, 661 (N.C. 1992).

**35.** In the cigarette litigation, for example, plaintiffs often allege that the defendants "fraudulently concealed" the industry's increasing awareness of the

defendant's affirmative action to hide facts from such a person—as by painting over a crack in the product[36] or by physically destroying documents to which the plaintiff has a preexisting right.[37] Courts quite frequently use the "fraudulent concealment" term in cases involving one of the particular, independent situations giving rise to a duty to speak under the traditional exceptions previously discussed.[38] In such cases, however, it seems better to avoid the use of polemical terms that mean other than what they say and to address instead the particular "half-truth," subsequently-acquired information, or other exception which may (or may not) give rise to the duty to speak in a particular situation. Loose talk about "fraudulent concealment" tends to interfere with sound analysis in a complicated context where such analysis is especially needed. Much confusion would be avoided if the "fraudulent conceal-ment" term were not substituted for the duty to warn and if the term were restricted to its traditional context in which a defendant has affirmatively acted to conceal a danger from the plaintiff, that is, where the defendant engaged in conduct designed to hide facts about a prod-uct's dangers from someone with a right to that information.

### Fact

To support a fraud claim, a representation must be of an existing *fact*. The fact represented must exist at the time of the representation, and a fraudulent misrepresentation claim will not lie with respect to predictions of future conditions or events,[39] unless such predictions imply

addictiveness and other health risks of cigarettes. Claims of this type, that amount to little more than claims of failure to warn, aim at a loophole in Ci-pollone v. Liggett Group, Inc., 505 U.S. 504 (1992), where the Supreme Court ruled that federal preemption broadly bars warnings claims but not most claims of fraud or fraudulent conceal-ment. But the transparency of merely changing the label on a claim from "failure to warn" to "fraudulent con-cealment" is not lost on many courts. See, e.g., DeLuca v. Liggett & Myers, Inc., 2003 WL 1798940, at *3–*5 (N.D. Ill. 2003); In re Kings Cty. Tobacco Li-tig., 727 N.Y.S.2d 241, 245 n.8 (Sup. Ct. 2000); Small v. Lorillard Tobacco Co., 679 N.Y.S.2d 593, 602–04 (App. Div. 1998), aff'd, 698 N.Y.S.2d 615 (N.Y. 1999). *But see* Glassner v. R.J. Reynolds Tobacco Co., 223 F.3d 343 (6th Cir. 2000) (Ohio law).

**36.** See discussion of fraudulent acts as representations, above.

**37.** See, e.g., Nicolet, Inc. v. Nutt, 525 A.2d 146, 149 (Del. 1987), where the court characterizes "concealment" as sufficient to establish a prima facie case of intentional misrepresentation where plaintiff proves:

(1) Deliberate concealment by the defen-dant of a material past or present fact, or silence in the face of a duty to speak;

(2) That the defendant acted with scien-ter;

(3) An intent to induce plaintiff's reli-ance upon the concealment;

(4) Causation; and

(5) Damages resulting from the conceal-ment.

**38.** See, e.g., Cheney Bros. v. Batesville Casket Co., 47 F.3d 111, 115 (4th Cir. 1995) (S.C. law) (breach of the duty to disclose, giving rise to a "fraudulent concealment" claim, requires a specific fiduciary-type rela-tion between the parties); Mason v. Chrys-ler Corp., 653 So.2d 951, 954–55 (Ala. 1995) (rejecting claim for "fraudulent suppres-sion" and explaining that such claims are allowable only when plaintiff establishes a traditional exception to general rule that there is no affirmative duty to speak); Khan v. Shiley Inc., 266 Cal.Rptr. 106 (1990) (duty might arise from misleadingly incom-plete advertisements by manufacturer of defective heart valve; by implication); Zim-merman v. Northfield Real Estate, Inc., 510 N.E.2d 409, 413 (Ill. App. Ct. 1987) ("Where a person has a duty to speak, his failure to disclose material information con-stitutes fraudulent concealment.").

**39.** See, e.g., Champion Home Builders Co. v. ADT Sec. Servs., 179 F.Supp.2d 16, 23 (N.D.N.Y. 2001); Mason v. Chrysler Corp., 653 So.2d 951, 953–54 (Ala. 1995) ("predictions as to events to occur in the

the existence of facts which presently exist.[40] A promise of future performance made with no present intention of keeping it constitutes a misstatement of an existing fact.[41]

The misrepresentation must concern a *fact* as opposed to an *opinion*.[42] That is, the matter misrepresented must be specific and capable of objective determination. Interpretation of a representation as fact or opinion may depend upon the expertise of the manufacturer: "Where the party making the representations has superior knowledge regarding the subject matter of his representations, and the other party is so situated that he may reasonably rely on such supposed superior knowledge or special information, the representations may be construed as fact and not opinion."[43]

By definition, a "puff" is not a representation of fact. The seller's subjective beliefs concerning the value or quality of the product, including general commendatory characterizations—such as "good," "excellent," "high quality,"[44] or "terrific"—ordinarily are considered by everyone to be mere sales talk, "puffery" not intended or taken to be factual assertions, and so are ordinarily insufficient to support an action of fraud.[45] Normally, the more specific the assertion, the more likely that it fairly may be regarded as a factual assertion, and the more general it is, the more likely that it should be characterized as an opinion.[46] Thus, to

future are not statements concerning material facts upon which individuals have a right to act and, therefore, will not support a fraud claim").

**40.** See, e.g., Cummings v. HPG Int'l, Inc., 244 F.3d 16, 22 (1st Cir. 2001) (Mass. law) (manufacturer's assertion that roof would last 20 years implied that manufacturer "knew facts to justify its statement").

**41.** See Willard v. Chrysler Corp., 148 S.E.2d 867 (S.C. 1966) (plaintiff stated cause of action for fraud by alleging that car manufacturer knew of the particular latent defect and entered into a warranty with the plaintiff knowing the defect could not be remedied).

**42.** See, e.g., Crowther v. Guidone, 441 A.2d 11, 13 (Conn. 1981) (court should focus on "whether, under the circumstances surrounding the statement, the representation was intended and understood as one of fact distinguished from one of opinion").

**43.** Toole v. Richardson–Merrell, Inc., 60 Cal.Rptr. 398, 411 (1967) (drug that produced serious eye damage to defendant's test animals, and later to humans, was advertised as "virtually non-toxic," "safe," and free of "significant side effects"). Compare Goldwater v. Ollie's Garage, 1995 WL 348236 (Conn. Super. Ct. 1995) (defendant represented defective camper as being in "excellent condition," and "suitable and fit for use"). *Held*, the representations "may have been intended by the defendant and understood by the plaintiff as statements of

fact regarding the condition of the vehicle." Id. at *2. See generally Keeton, Fraud: Misrepresentations of Opinion, 21 Minn. L. Rev. 643 (1937).

**44.** See Tatum v. Cordis Corp., 758 F.Supp. 457, 463 (M.D. Tenn. 1991) (pacemaker was produced with "the highest degree of dedication and skill").

**45.** See, e.g., Champion Home Builders Co. v. ADT Sec. Servs., 179 F.Supp. 2d 16, 23–25 (N.D.N.Y. 2001) (fire alarm provider was an "industry leader"); Holley v. Central Auto Parts, 347 S.W.2d 341 (Tex. App. 1961) (tire rim was "a good one"); Lambert v. Sistrunk, 58 So.2d 434 (Fla. 1952) (stepladder would "last a lifetime" and customer would "never break it"). See also Mason v. Chrysler Corp., 653 So.2d 951, 952–53 (Ala. 1995) (buyers of new car assured that it was "a smooth-riding, luxury car" that was comparable to Cadillacs and Lincolns but "much less expensive," that its warranty was "the best," that buyers "were making a good deal" and "couldn't get a better deal any place"). *Held*, summary judgment for Chrysler and dealer affirmed: "[S]tatements of opinion amounting to 'puffery' . . . are not statements concerning material facts upon which individuals have a right to act and, therefore, will not support a fraud claim." The comments and advertisements made about this car "were statements commonly made in the course of selling cars and do not amount to misstatements of a material fact." Id. at 953–54.

**46.** See, e.g., Cummings v. HPG Int'l, Inc., 244 F.3d 16, 22 (1st Cir. 2001) (Mass.

say that a crane is "capable of safely lifting 40,000 pounds" is a statement of fact, but to say that it is "a mighty strong crane" is a statement of opinion.

### Falsity

In any misrepresentation claim, the plaintiff of course must prove that a fact represented was false. In ascertaining a representation's truth or falsity, its fair meaning must first be established. The second step is to ascertain whether that meaning deviates substantially from the truth, the actual facts concerning the matter represented. In order to determine whether a representation should be considered substantially true or substantially false, the words should be construed in the total context surrounding their utterance by the defendant and their communication to the plaintiff. As previously discussed, a statement (a "half-truth") may be literally true but properly viewed as false because it is misleading by implying facts which themselves are untrue. Interpreting particular words as true or false is crucially important to the analysis of a misrepresentation claim and typically is the threshold step in determining the viability of such a claim.

### Materiality

To support a claim for fraud, the misrepresentation must be *material*, as distinguished from trivial or irrelevant.[47] One is not likely to rely, nor does one have a right to rely, on information truly insignificant to the transaction. "There are misstatements which are so trivial, or so far unrelated to anything of real importance in the transaction, that the plaintiff will not be heard to say that they substantially affected his decision."[48] In the words of the *Restatement (Second) of Torts*, "[r]eliance upon a fraudulent misrepresentation is not justifiable unless the matter misrepresented is material."[49] The *Restatement* classifies a fact as "material" either if a reasonable person would consider it important *or* if the speaker expects the recipient to so consider it.[50]

### "Scienter"—Knowledge of Falsity and Intent to Deceive

The central elements of the tort of fraud or deceit, the elements that distinguish this tort from negligent and innocent misrepresentation, are a defendant's *knowledge* that its representation is false and its *intent* to

---

law) (manufacturer's assertion that roof would last 20 years "was specific and verifiable, not a mere expression of opinion or estimate," and implied that manufacturer "knew facts to justify its statement").

**47.** "Where the fact represented would not influence the reasonable person, either because of its triviality or because of its irrelevance to the subject dealt with, the law will ordinarily regard that fact as immaterial and reliance on it unjustified." 2 Harper, James, and Gray, Law of Torts 437–38.

**48.** Prosser and Keeton on Torts at 753.

**49.** Restatement (2d) Torts § 538.

**50.** A fact is material if: "(a) a reasonable man would attach importance to its existence or nonexistence in determining his choice of action in the transaction in question; or (b) the maker of the representation knows or has reason to know that its recipient regards or is likely to regard the matter as important in determining his choice of action, although a reasonable man would not so regard it." Restatement (2d) Torts § 538.

deceive the plaintiff thereby. Because of the difficulties in proving this guilty state of mind, plaintiffs in fraud cases often have difficulty establishing this important "scienter" component to an intentional misrepresentation claim.[51]

In recent decades, many courts have liberalized the scienter requirement, holding that "deliberate deception or scienter is not a necessary element of the cause of action for fraud. . . . It is sufficient if the speaker makes the statement as of his own knowledge without knowing whether it is true or false."[52] Thus, while such a defendant may not know that what he says is false, he *does* know that he does *not* know whether the assertion be true or false.[53] In such a case, the "[d]efendant has lied about the extent of his knowledge of the facts in question; he has in effect represented that he knew a thing to be true when he knew that he only believed or surmised it to be true,"[54] or when he knew that he had no idea whether it was true or not. In sum, " 'fraud' includes pretense of knowledge, where there is no knowledge."[55] While some courts squeeze this type of state of mind into the "intent" mold, others classify it merely as "recklessness."[56] Characterized either way, such a state of mind normally is considered adequate scienter to support a claim for fraud.

## Justifiable Reliance

The plaintiff, or someone acting on the plaintiff's behalf (such as a parent, employer, or physician), must in fact learn about and then act somehow in *reliance* upon the misrepresentation—as by purchasing the product, using it in a particular manner, or failing to take certain precautions. If a plaintiff fails to establish such reliance on the defen-

---

**51.** See, e.g., Limited Flying Club, Inc. v. Wood, 632 F.2d 51 (8th Cir. 1980) (Iowa law) (scienter and intent to deceive were not established by statements that airplane was "airworthy" and a "good little airplane," although the defendant was aware of prior damage and repairs and failed to report repairs in logbook).

**52.** Clements Auto Co. v. Service Bureau Corp., 298 F.Supp. 115, 126 (D. Minn. 1969), aff'd in part, rev'd in part on other grounds, 444 F.2d 169 (8th Cir. 1971) (Minn. law).

**53.** See, e.g., Cummings v. HPG Int'l, Inc., 244 F.3d 16, 23 (1st Cir. 2001) (Mass. law) (reciting Restatement (2d) Torts § 526:

A misrepresentation is fraudulent if the maker (a) knows or believes that the matter is not as he represents it to be, (b) does not have the confidence in the accuracy of his representation that he states or implies, or (c) knows that he does not have the basis for his representation that he states or implies.)

**54.** 2 Harper, James, and Gray, Law of Torts § 7.3, at 394.

**55.** Sgarlata v. Carioto, 201 N.Y.S.2d 384, 385 (Albany City Ct. 1960). See Aaron v. Hampton Motors, Inc., 124 S.E.2d 585, 588 (S.C. 1962). Cf. Cooper v. R.J. Reynolds Tobacco Co., 234 F.2d 170, 174–75 (1st Cir. 1956) (Mass. law) (Magruder, J., concurring) (lung cancer from Camel cigarettes advertised as "healthful" and "harmless to the respiratory system"). See generally Keeton, Fraud: The Necessity for an Intent to Deceive, 5 UCLA L. Rev. 583 (1958).

**56.** See, e.g., Guiggey v. Bombardier, 615 A.2d 1169, 1173 (Me. 1992) (no recovery for intentional misrepresentation unless plaintiff establishes that "statements were made with knowledge of falsity or reckless disregard of truth or falsity"); Limited Flying Club, Inc. v. Wood, 632 F.2d 51, 54–55 (8th Cir. 1980) (Iowa law) (scienter requires at least a showing that misrepresentations were made "in reckless disregard of their truth or falsity"); Aaron v. Hampton Motors, Inc., 124 S.E.2d 585, 588 (S.C. 1962) (actual knowledge that misrepresentation is false unnecessary if speaker makes representation "as of his personal knowledge, with reckless disregard of his lack of information as to its truth").

dant's misrepresentation, the case will fail.[57] A plaintiff's reliance normally provides the crucial causal link between the defendant's wrongful act and the plaintiff's harm, establishing that the wrong somehow generated the harmful consequences for which recovery is sought.[58] Thus, a person who takes no action on account of a misrepresentation usually is not harmed by it. Typically, causation is embedded in reliance, and proof of the former often establishes the latter.[59] The converse is also widely true: a plaintiff's proof of reliance on a misrepresentation normally establishes a causal link between the defendant's misrepresentation and the plaintiff's harm. But this connection does not always exist, and reliance on a misrepresentation does not uniformly prove causation.[60] For example, a long-time smoker seriously considering stopping may continue smoking because he sees, believes, and relies upon particular fraudulent advertisements of a cigarette manufacturer; but, if the smoker dies from lung cancer soon after first seeing the advertisements, his death most probably is not causally attributable to those ads.[61]

A plaintiff who does not hear or see a misrepresentation at all generally will be unable to establish reliance upon it.[62] Yet, the reliance

**57.** See, e.g., Fitzgerald v. Liberty Safe and Security Products, 80 Fed. Appx. 897 (5th Cir. 2003) (Miss. law) (fraud claim as to ability of safe to withstand fire not sustainable where plaintiff bought safe for protection from burglaries, not fire); Lewis v. Lead Indus. Ass'n, Inc., 793 N.E.2d 869, 876 (Ill. App. Ct. 2003) (fraud claim failed because parents did not allege that they relied on manufacturers' representations in exposing their children to lead paint); Brown ex rel. Estate of Brown v. Philip Morris Inc., 228 F.Supp.2d 506, 518–20 (D.N.J. 2002) (rejecting fraud-on-the-market theory where no proof deceased smoker ever saw defendant's ads); Glassner v. R.J. Reynolds Tobacco Co., 223 F.3d 343 (6th Cir. 2000) (Ohio law) (affirming dismissal of fraud claim for failure to state a claim because plaintiff failed to allege facts that decedent relied on defendant's misrepresentations); Bay Summit Cmty. Ass'n v. Shell Oil Co., 59 Cal.Rptr.2d 322, 324 (1996) (fraudulent misrepresentation claims failed for want of proof of reliance). On justifiable reliance and other defenses to misrepresentation claims, see § 13.7, below.

**58.** "Justifiable reliance exists when the misrepresentation or nondisclosure was an immediate cause of the plaintiff's conduct which alters his legal relations, and when without such misrepresentation or nondisclosure he would not, in all reasonable probability, have entered into the contract or other transaction." Pritchett v. Avon Prods., Inc., 2002 WL 31547045 (Cal. Ct. App. 2002).

**59.** See, e.g., Tetuan v. A.H. Robins Co., 738 P.2d 1210, 1230–31 (Kan. 1987):

[T]he magic word "reliance" was not used, but the effect was the same: the jury was required to find that Robins' misrepresentations caused Dr. Pfuetze to use the Dalkon Shield which, in turn, caused [the plaintiff's] injuries. The jury was thus required to find reliance....

See also Learjet Corp. v. Spenlinhauer, 901 F.2d 198, 200 (1st Cir. 1990) (Kan. law) ("If the aircraft would not have been put into commerce without the FAA certificate of airworthiness, it follows that a purchaser necessarily relied on the certificate, since a sale could not have occurred but for the FAA certificate.").

**60.** See, e.g., Dillon v. Zeneca Corp., 42 P.3d 598, 603 (Ariz. Ct. App. 2002) (plaintiffs relied on manufacturer's statement that herbicide effectively controlled weeds, but representation, even if false, did not cause damage from herbicide's killing crops); Small v. Lorillard Tobacco Co., 679 N.Y.S.2d 593, 601 (App. Div. 1998) (noting absence of evidence of "reliance and causation elements," suggesting their independence), aff'd, 698 N.Y.S.2d 615 (N.Y. 1999).

**61.** Cf. Cooper v. R.J. Reynolds Tobacco Co., 256 F.2d 464, 466 (1st Cir. 1958) (Mass. law).

**62.** See, e.g., DeLuca v. Liggett & Myers, Inc., 2003 WL 1798940, at *5 (N.D. Ill. 2003) ("There is no evidence that [plaintiff] saw or much less relied on the 'Frank Statement.' There is also no evidence that he was aware of the 1994 testimony [by the defendants' CEOs, before Congress, that they did not believe nicotine was addictive] let alone that it affected his actions in any

need not be by the plaintiff personally, so long as it is by someone acting on his or her behalf.[63] Thus, "where a patient relies on a physician for treatment or advice as to an ethical or prescription device, justifiable reliance by the physician ... constitutes justifiable reliance by the patient."[64] Formerly, courts applied the same principle to situations where a manufacturer made fraudulent representations to a government agency, such as the FDA or the FAA, to get approval to market a new product, such as a new prescription drug or a new model aircraft. In such cases, while the fraud is aimed at the government agency, the fraudfeasor knows full well that its harmful effects may come to rest on the consuming public, which itself relies upon the integrity of the approval process administered by the agency. So, where the purchaser of an airplane relies upon an FAA airworthiness certificate which the manufacturer procured from the FAA by means of fraudulent represen-

way."); Miller v. Pfizer Inc. (Roerig Division), 196 F.Supp.2d 1095 (D. Kan. 2002) (no reliance where patient's doctor never read the representations), aff'd on point, 356 F.3d 1326 (2004); Insolia v. Philip Morris Inc., 53 F. Supp. 2d 1032, 1044–45 (W.D. Wis. 1999) (granting summary judgment to defendants on fraud-based claims because "[a]s a matter of logic, plaintiffs cannot argue they relied on statements that they never heard"), aff'd in part, rev'd in part on other grounds, 216 F.3d 596 (7th Cir. 2000).

Courts generally reject the argument that a plaintiff who personally did not see and rely on a misrepresentation can establish reliance by proving reliance by other consumers in the market, the so-called "fraud-on-the-market" theory drawn from securities law. See, e.g., Brown ex rel. Estate of Brown v. Philip Morris Inc., 228 F.Supp.2d 506, 518–20 (D.N.J. 2002) (rejecting fraud-on-the-market theory where no proof deceased smoker ever saw defendant's ads). But see Williams v. Philip Morris Inc., 48 P.3d 824, 830–31 (Or. Ct. App. 2002) (allowing fraud claim against cigarette manufacturer despite plaintiff's inability to identify particular statements on which he relied, based on defendant's claim over many years of advertising to the effect that there was a legitimate controversy over the safety of cigarette smoking; rejecting defendant's argument that claim was based on a "fraud on the American public" similar to "fraud on the market"), vacated on other grounds, Philip Morris USA Inc. v. Williams, 124 S.Ct. 56 (2003), verdict adhered to on remand, 92 P.3d 126 (Or. Ct. App. 2004).

**63.** See, e.g., Miller v. Pfizer Inc. (Roerig Division), 196 F.Supp.2d 1095 (D. Kan. 2002) (doctor, by implication), aff'd, 356 F.3d 1326 (10th Cir. 2004); Potts v. UAP–GA AG CHEM, Inc., 567 S.E.2d 316, 319 (Ga. Ct. App. 2002) ("[T]he misrepresentation need not be to the plaintiff, but may be to someone on whom the plaintiff relies. 'We hold that the requirement of reliance is satisfied where ... A, having as his objective to defraud C, and knowing that C will rely upon B, fraudulently induces B to act in some manner on which C relies, and whereby A's purpose of defrauding C is accomplished.'"); Ernst & Young, L.L.P. v. Pacific Mut. Life Ins. Co., 51 S.W.3d 573, 580 (Tex. 2001), rejecting Kanon v. Methodist Hosp., 9 S.W.3d 365, 372–73 (Tex. App. 1999) (representations as to quality of TMJ jaw implant made to medical community at large, rather than specifically to injured patient, could not support representation claim: "For a misrepresentation to be actionable, the maker must intend to influence the very person to whom he makes the representation."). But see Wilson v. Dryvit Sys., Inc., 206 F.Supp.2d 749 (E.D.N.C. 2002) (homeowners could not base fraud claim on fraudulent statements made by manufacturer of building materials to such "third parties" as builders, trade associations, and government entities), aff'd, 71 Fed.Appx. 960 (4th Cir. 2003); Nichols v. General Motors Corp., 1999 WL 33292839, at *4 (N.H. Super. 1999) (used car buyer not in privity of contract with manufacturer not entitled to rely on manufacturer's representations to buyers). See generally Phillips, Product Misrepresentation and the Doctrine of Causation, 2 Hofstra L. Rev. 561 (1974); Owen, The Highly Blameworthy Manufacturer: Implications on Rules of Liability and Defense in Products Liability Actions, 10 Ind. L. Rev. 769, 781–84 (1977).

**64.** Tetuan v. A.H. Robins Co., 738 P.2d 1210, 1228 (Kan. 1987) (upholding awards of $1.7 million compensatory and $7.5 million punitive damages for fraudulently marketing dangerous Dalkon Shield IUD). See also Albertson v. Richardson–Merrell, Inc., 441 So.2d 1146 (Fla. Dist. Ct. App. 1983); Wechsler v. Hoffman–La Roche, Inc., 198 Misc. 540, 99 N.Y.S.2d 588, 590 (Sup. Ct. 1950) (prescription drug alleged to have been fraudulently marketed to doctors).

tations, a fraud claim brought by the purchaser against the manufacturer logically should rest upon the FAA's reliance on the misrepresentations made to it by the manufacturer.[65] Notwithstanding the soundness of this general principle, the Supreme Court has dubiously declared that such "fraud-on-the-agency" claims violate the principles of federal preemption.[66]

In contrast to the entirely subjective nature of the element of reliance, involving as it does the issue of whether the plaintiff or other representee in fact believed the representation and took action, at least in part, as a result thereof, the *justifiability* of the reliance is based in many ways on an *objective* standard of reasonableness in all the circumstances.[67] Thus, for a fraud to be actionable, a plaintiff must not only rely on the misrepresentation, but the reliance must be justifiable or reasonable. Yet, since justifiability is an element of a claim for *intentional* misrepresentation, courts often are understandably loathe to allow a plaintiff's careless trust on a defendant's calculated fraud to bar a claim for this intentional tort.[68] But a plaintiff in the end must have had a "right to rely" on the defendant's misrepresentation, and a case for fraud will fail if the plaintiff cannot prove the justifiability of his or her reliance.[69]

Bound together with this broad issue of the reasonableness or justifiability of the plaintiff's reliance—whether the plaintiff had a "right to rely"—are the more specific issues involving the fact/opinion distinction and the element of materiality,[70] both examined earlier. In making

**65.** See, e.g., Learjet Corp. v. Spenlinhauer, 901 F.2d 198 (1st Cir. 1990) (Kan. law). See also Toole v. Richardson–Merrell, Inc., 60 Cal.Rptr. 398 (1967) (misrepresentations of drug's safety made to FDA to obtain approval to market new drug).

**66.** Buckman Co. v. Plaintiffs' Legal Comm., 531 U.S. 341 (2001) (fraud-on-the-FDA claim federally preempted). Federal preemption is addressed in § 14.4, below.

**67.** Courts often define "justifiability" or "right to rely" in terms of reasonableness. See, e.g., In re Simon II Litig., 211 F.R.D. 86, 139 (E.D.N.Y. 2002) (Weinstein, J., restating element (4) of fraud, "plaintiff justifiably relied on the misrepresentation," as "reasonable reliance"); Cheney Bros., Inc. v. Batesville Casket Co., 47 F.3d 111, 115 (4th Cir. 1995) (S.C. law):

Related to the "right to rely" element is the necessity that the reliance be reasonable. See Thomas v. American Workmen, 14 S.E.2d 886, 887–88 (S.C. 1941) ("[T]he right of reliance is closely bound up with a duty on the part of the representee to use some measure of protection and precaution to safeguard his interest [and whether this condition is met depends] upon the various circumstances involved, such as the form and materiality of the representations, the respective intelligence, experience, age, and mental

and physical condition of the parties, and the relation and respective knowledge and means of knowledge of the parties.").

**68.** For a discussion of the tendency of courts to push justifiability toward a more subjective approach in cases involving true fraud, see § 13.7, below.

**69.** See, e.g., Soliman v. Philip Morris, Inc., 311 F.3d 966, 975 (9th Cir. 2002) (Cal. law) ("A necessary element of a fraud claim is justifiable reliance on the defendant's misrepresentation or omission.... California law presumes a plaintiff's awareness that smoking causes addiction and other health problems. Purported reliance on the industry's failure to disclose those facts is therefore not justifiable. Fraud that 'should be apparent even to the plaintiff[ ]' is not actionable.").

**70.** See 2 Harper, James, and Gray, Law of Torts §§ 7.7 and 7.8; Prosser and Keeton on Torts §§ 108 and 109. Representative factors to be considered in evaluating the justifiability of a plaintiff's reliance upon a defendant's fraudulent representations are set forth in Sippy v. Cristich, 609 P.2d 204 (Kan. Ct. App. 1980) (home purchasers claimed seller concealed defective roof):

Many factors must be considered in determining whether a statement is a matter of fact or a matter of opinion and

significant purchase decisions, buyers ordinarily do not accept as factual truth a seller's general commendations of its product or general assurances of the product's great value or extraordinary usefulness. Representations of this sort properly are viewed merely as the seller's opinion rather than as statements of fact. Nor do buyers ordinarily make important purchase decisions on the basis of the seller's assurances concerning matters that are trivial.

At bottom, it makes little difference whether one views puffs, as well as irrelevant and trivial representations, from the objective viewpoint that buyers have no *right* to rely on such representations in making important decisions, or, instead, from the subjective perspective that buyers in such cases very probably do not *in fact* rely on such representations. In either case, the law should not provide an injured buyer with an easy way to escape responsibility for an injury principally caused by his or her own careless use of the product rather than by some insignificant misstatement that played little or no role in either the buyer's decision to purchase the product or in how it should be used. Thus, a plaintiff must establish that the reliance was "justifiable" not because fraudfeasors should be shielded from responsibility by a plaintiff's gullibility or contributory negligence[71] but because such proof provides additional, objective assurance that the plaintiff in fact truly did rely upon the defendant's representation.

## Resulting Damage

A plaintiff may recover damages that result from relying upon a defendant's fraudulent misrepresentation.[72] While the type, scope, and measure of such damages present special considerations of damages law

---

whether or not plaintiff has a right to rely on the statement. Among the facts the court will take into consideration are the intelligence, education, business experience and relative situation of the parties; the general information and experience of the persons involved as to the nature and use of the property; the habits and methods of those in the industry or profession involved; the opportunity for both parties to make an independent investigation as well as the nature, extent, and result of any investigation so made; and any contract the parties knowingly and understandingly entered into.... "A recipient of a fraudulent misrepresentation is justified in relying upon its truth without investigation, unless he knows or has reason to know of facts which make his reliance unreasonable." ... [T]he test is whether the recipient has "information which would serve as a danger signal and a red light to any normal person of his intelligence and experience."

Id. at 208 (quoting from, inter alia, Restatement (2d) Torts § 540 and comments thereto).

**71.** In misrepresentation claims by individuals against institutions, most modern courts no longer hold the plaintiff to a duty of care to investigate the truth of the defendant's representation. See, e.g., Kavarco v. T.J.E., Inc., 478 A.2d 257 (Conn. App. Ct. 1984) (plaintiff is not required to independently investigate personal injury defendant's representation to determine if it be true). This development would seem especially apt in the typical personal injury products liability case against the manufacturer. The softening of the justifiability element in cases of fraudulent misrepresentation is examined in § 13.7, below.

In claims between major enterprises dealing with one another at arm's length, however, the requirement of justifiability of reliance still has considerable force. See, e.g., Cheney Bros. v. Batesville Casket Co., 47 F.3d 111, 115 (4th Cir. 1995) (S.C. law).

**72.** See, e.g., Dillon v. Zeneca Corp., 42 P.3d 598, 603 (Ariz. Ct. App. 2002) (plaintiffs' damages did not result from their reliance on claim of herbicide's effectiveness in weed control but from herbicide's killing crops).

beyond the scope of this text,[73] it should be noted here that a claim for deceit is completed by proof of this final element—actual damages resulting from the misrepresentation. In the absence of proof of present injury, an intentional misrepresentation claim will fail.[74]

## Other Issues

### Statutes

Some states have statutes that broadly prohibit false, misleading, unfair, or deceptive trade practices.[75] As with the federal odometer tampering statute,[76] which prohibits and provides redress for a particular form of fraudulent behavior, deceptive trade practices laws often provide for treble damages and attorneys' fees.[77] However, because such statutes generally were not enacted to provide remedies to persons suffering physical injuries from defective products, the statutes' remedies may not be available in such cases.[78] In situations where federal preemption of state products liability law is an issue, as in the cigarette litigation, fraud claims may avoid preemption if fraudulent conduct falls outside the realm of conduct addressed by Congress.[79] Yet, depending on the particular federal statute, even fraud claims sometimes do not escape the grasp of federal preemption.[80]

**73.** For example, some courts hold that the economic loss rule bars certain fraud and other tortious misrepresentation claims for pure economic loss. See, e.g., Werwinski v. Ford Motor Co., 286 F.3d 661 (3d Cir. 2002) (Pa. law); AKA Distrib. Co. v. Whirlpool Corp., 137 F.3d 1083 (8th Cir. 1998) (Minn. law). *But see* Tietsworth v. Harley–Davidson, Inc., 661 N.W.2d 450, 454 (Wis. Ct. App. 2003) (allowing fraudulent concealment claim in class action for economic losses to buyers of motorcycles with defective engines), rev'd on other grounds, 677 N.W.2d 233 (Wis. 2004). Note that the Uniform Commercial Code remedies for breach of warranty are available for fraudulent breach. UCC § 2–721. For the role of fraud in recovering punitive damages, see §§ 18.3 and 18.4, below.

**74.** See, e.g., Tietsworth v. Harley–Davidson, Inc., 677 N.W.2d 233, 240 (Wis. 2004) (in "no injury" products liability fraud case "[d]iminished value premised upon a mere possibility of future product failure is too speculative and uncertain to support a fraud claim"); Ziegelmann v. DaimlerChrysler Corp., 649 N.W.2d 556, 565 (N.D. 2002) ("no-injury" fraudulent concealment products liability lawsuit, seeking diminution-in-value damages for vehicle design hazard that might cause future injury, was "simply too speculative to constitute a legally cognizable tort injury"); Frank v. DaimlerChrysler Corp., 741 N.Y.S.2d 9, 16 (App. Div. 2002) (same: "Public policy concerns, in our view, also dictate that we reject plaintiffs' claims, for it would be manifestly unfair to require a manufacturer to become, in essence, an indemnifier for a loss that may never occur.").

**75.** See, e.g., Delahunt v. Cytodyne Techs., 241 F.Supp.2d 827, 836 (S.D. Ohio 2003) (denying motion to dismiss unfair trade practices class action, against manufacturer and retailer of dietary supplement containing ephedrine, for engaging in unfair or deceptive practices in sale of supplement with misrepresentations or omissions on supplement's label).

**76.** 49 U.S.C.A. § 32710.

**77.** See Utica Mut. Ins. Co. v. Denwat Corp., 778 F.Supp. 592 (D. Conn. 1991) (separate products liability claim maintainable under such a statute notwithstanding state products liability statute that purports to govern all product actions).

**78.** See Boswell, Stagg, and Myers, Deceptive Trade Practice—Consumer Protection Acts and Their Effect on Product Liability Litigation, 15 Forum 716 (Spring 1980). *But see* Maldonado v. Nutri/System, Inc., 776 F.Supp. 278 (E.D. Va. 1991) ("loss" under statute included loss of gall bladder caused by defendant's weight loss food advertised as safe).

**79.** Most of the plaintiff's fraud claims escaped preemption in Cipollone v. Liggett Group, Inc., 505 U.S. 504 (1992), and such claims continue to figure prominently in claims against the tobacco industry.

**80.** See, e.g., Lewis v. Brunswick Corp., 107 F.3d 1494 (11th Cir. 1997) (Ga. law) (in suit rising from fatal injury caused by boat

Mail or wire fraud (including fraud by telephone, television, and radio) that establishes a "pattern of racketeering activity" may give rise to treble damages and attorneys' fees under the Racketeer Influenced and Corrupt Organizations Act ("RICO"), enacted by Congress in 1970.[81] The Supreme Court has interpreted the RICO statute restrictively, however, and courts now require a massive and ongoing scheme perpetrated by repeated and intensive use of the mails and wires.[82] Moreover, RICO claims are probably unavailable in ordinary products liability actions for personal injuries, since the statute provides only that civil damages are available for injuries to a person's "business or property."[83]

Fraud claims ordinarily are governed by their own statutes of limitations, rather than by the contract statute of limitations contained in the Uniform Commercial Code,[84] at least where the claim for fraud is separately cognizable.[85]

### *Disclaimers*

Because fraud and deceit are grounded in conduct which normally is intentionally harmful, the law attempts to discourage persons from devising ways to engage in this type of antisocial behavior without legal accountability. Accordingly, contractual waivers and disclaimers against liability for fraud normally are held to be void as against public policy.[86]

## § 3.3  NEGLIGENT MISREPRESENTATION

### In General

If a person injured as a result of misrepresentation is unable to prove fraud for lack of scienter,[1] the injured party nevertheless may be

---

propeller blade, claim that outboard engine manufacturer fraudulently misrepresented to Coast Guard differences between guarded and unguarded engines held preempted by Federal Boat Safety Act). On federal preemption, see § 14.4, below.

**81.** 18 U.S.C.A. § 1961 et seq.

**82.** See, e.g., H.J. Inc. v. Northwestern Bell Tel. Co., 492 U.S. 229 (1989); cf. Reves v. Ernst & Young, 507 U.S. 170 (1993), noted, 108 Harv. L. Rev. 1405 (1995). See generally GE Inv. Private Placement Partners II v. Parker, 247 F.3d 543 (4th Cir. 2001); Efron v. Embassy Suites (Puerto Rico), Inc., 223 F.3d 12 (1st Cir. 2000); Walker and Tanner, RICO Claims: The Challenge of Alleging the "Pattern" Element, 76–May Fla. B.J. 34 (2002).

**83.** See 18 U.S.C.A. § 1964(c); Annot., 96 A.L.R. Fed. 881 (1990). On RICO civil damages actions, see generally Marple, "Pattern" Requirement Renders RICO Inapplicable to Ordinary Business Disputes, 14 Rev. Litig. 343 (1995); Camp, Dual Construction of RICO: The Road Not Taken in Reves, 51 Wash. & Lee L. Rev. 61 (1994); Note, Stretching RICO to the Limit and Beyond, 45 Duke L.J. 819 (1996); Annot., 70 A.L.R. Fed. 538 (1984) (civil action under RICO for damages caused by racketeering activity).

**84.** See UCC § 2–725; § 14.5, below.

**85.** That is, where the fraud claim is distinct from a claim for fraudulent nonperformance of the contract. See Triangle Underwriters, Inc. v. Honeywell, Inc., 604 F.2d 737, 747–48 (2d Cir. 1979) (N.Y. law) ("The case at bar does not involve any ... attempt to dress up a contract claim in a fraud suit of clothes. The fraud Triangle alleges in Count I consisted of independent false representations, made before there ever was a contract between the parties, which led Triangle to enter into it. In other words, Triangle clearly alleges fraud that was extraneous to the contract, rather than any fraudulent nonperformance of the contract itself."). Id. at 747.

**86.** See, e.g., Werremeyer v. K.C. Auto Salvage Co., 2003 WL 21487311, at *4 (Mo. Ct. App. 2003); Cummings v. HPG Int'l, Inc., 244 F.3d 16, 21 (1st Cir. 2001) (Mass. law); First Nat'l Bank v. Brooks Farms, 1990 WL 6386 (Tenn. Ct. App. 1990) (good discussion), aff'd on this point, 821 S.W.2d 925 (Tenn. 1991). *But see* Champion Home Builders Co. v. ADT Sec. Servs., 179 F.Supp.2d 16, 25 (N.D.N.Y. 2001).

**§ 3.3**

**1.** "Scienter" refers to the defendant's knowledge of falsity and intent to deceive. See §§ 3.1 and 3.2, above.

able to establish a claim for *negligent* misrepresentation.[2] The prima facie claim for negligent misrepresentation, a quite uncommon cause of action in products liability cases, closely resembles the claim for intentional misrepresentation,[3] except that the elements of duty and negligence replace the element of fraudulent intent.[4] Thus, negligent misrepresentation partakes of two quite different torts—negligence and deceit—a union that injects confusion into an understanding of the contours of this particular type of claim.[5] Although negligent misrepresentation claims are not allowed by all states for all types of harm,[6]

---

**2.** See Fahey v. R.J. Reynolds Tobacco Co., 1995 WL 809837 (Mass. Super. Ct. 1995) (plaintiff did not have to prove that cigarette manufacturer intentionally deceived him about the hazardous effects of smoking; sufficient evidence on negligent misrepresentation for jury).

**3.** See, e.g., Jimenez v. DaimlerChrysler Corp., 269 F.3d 439 (4th Cir. 2001) (S.C. law) ("to prove a claim for negligent misrepresentation, the plaintiff must establish that (1) the defendant negligently made a false statement, (2) the plaintiff suffered an injury or loss as a consequence of relying on the misrepresentation, and (3) the misrepresentation induced the plaintiff to enter into a contract or business transaction"); Maneely v. General Motors Corp., 108 F.3d 1176, 1181 (9th Cir. 1997) (Cal. law): "To establish a negligent misrepresentation claim, a plaintiff must prove: (1) that defendant had a duty to exercise reasonable care in giving information, (2) that defendant negligently provided false information, (3) that plaintiff reasonably relied on the false information, and (4) that plaintiff was injured as a result." See also Foster v. American Home Prods. Corp., 29 F.3d 165, 171 (4th Cir. 1994) (Md. law), stating the elements of negligent misrepresentation:

1) [T]he defendant, owing a duty of care to the plaintiff, negligently asserts a false statement;

2) the defendant intends that his statement will be acted on by the plaintiff;

3) the defendant has knowledge that the plaintiff will probably rely on the statement which, if erroneous, will cause loss or injury;

4) the plaintiff, justifiably, takes action in reliance on the statement; and

5) the plaintiff suffers damage proximately caused by the defendant's negligence.

**4.** See, e.g., Board of Educ. v. A, C & S, Inc., 546 N.E.2d 580, 591 (Ill. 1989) ("Negligent misrepresentation has essentially the same elements [as deceit], except that the

defendant's mental state is different. The defendant need not know that the statement is false. His own carelessness or negligence in ascertaining its truth will suffice for a cause of action."); Snelten v. Schmidt Implement Co., 647 N.E.2d 1071, 1076 (Ill. Ct. App. 1995):

To state a cause of action for negligent misrepresentation, the complaint must again allege a duty to plaintiff, a breach of the duty and injury proximately resulting from such breach.... Restatement (Second) of Torts § 311 (1965) provides there may be liability for negligently giving false information to another if the information causes some physical harm to the person who justifiably relies on the information.... [T]he elements of a cause of action for negligent misrepresentation are essentially the same as those for fraudulent misrepresentation except the defendant need not know or believe the statement to be false; instead, the plaintiff need only allege the defendant was careless or negligent in ascertaining the truth of the statement made.

**5.** See, e.g., Cummings v. HPG Int'l, Inc., 244 F.3d 16 (1st Cir. 2001) (Mass. law) ("Massachusetts courts treat negligent misrepresentation claims more as negligence actions than deceit actions, focusing on the degree of care exercised by the speaker in making the statement"); In re Tobacco Cases II, 113 Cal.Rptr.2d 120 (Ct. App. 2001) (negligent misrepresentation claims normally are viewed in California as a form of fraud, but they nevertheless are subject to negligence law's remoteness doctrine).

**6.** See, e.g., Friedman v. Merck & Co., 131 Cal.Rptr.2d 885, 899–900 (Ct. App. 2003) (plaintiff failed to state a claim for negligent misrepresentation because misrepresentation only posed a risk of emotional injury); Daye v. General Motors Corp., 720 So.2d 654, 659 (La. 1998) ("We find no Louisiana case which allows a plaintiff to sue a defendant manufacturer for damages arising out of the negligent misrepresenta-

this type of claim is available in many states in a products liability case in which its elements can be established.[7]

Most of the older cases of negligent misrepresentation involve retailers.[8] However, manufacturers have also been held responsible for negligent misrepresentation, usually in connection with representations on a product's label or in advertising.[9] On occasion, certifiers of product quality are also held subject to liability for negligent misrepresentation. The most prominent case of this type is *Hanberry v. Hearst Corp.*,[10] an early California case against the publisher of Good Housekeeping magazine brought by the purchaser of slippery shoes accorded the "Good Housekeeping's Consumers' Guaranty Seal." The court ruled that a product endorser "may be liable to a purchaser who, relying on the endorsement, buys the product and is injured because it is defective and not as represented in the endorsement."[11] Reasoning that the very purpose of the seal is to induce consumers to rely upon its assertions of quality, the court held that negligent misrepresentation, but not implied warranty or strict liability in tort, was the appropriate remedy for a consumer injured by reliance upon such an endorsement.[12] In similar situations, Underwriters Laboratories has also been held liable for negligent misrepresentation.[13]

tions about its product."); Driver v. Burlington Aviation, Inc., 430 S.E.2d 476 (N.C. Ct. App. 1993) (passenger injured in aircraft that crashed due to carburetor icing denied recovery for negligent misrepresentation; such claims are available in North Carolina only for pecuniary loss, not for recovery of damages for personal injury); Flynn v. American Home Prods. Corp., 627 N.W.2d 342, 351 (Minn. Ct. App. 2001) (Minnesota: same).

**7.** See 1 Frumer and Friedman, Products Liability § 2.05[3].

**8.** The defendant's negligence in the retailer cases usually consists of its failure to exercise reasonable care to ascertain the accuracy of its representation. Typical are the used car cases. E.g., Boos v. Claude, 9 N.W.2d 262 (S.D. 1943) (car with defective steering said to be in "perfect mechanical condition," yet "defendants had not used reasonable care in making tests for the purpose of ascertaining defects"); Flies v. Fox Bros. Buick Co., 218 N.W. 855 (Wis. 1928) (Owen, J.) (dealer representing car, restored after wreck, to be "in perfect operating condition" negligent in not discovering defective brakes).

**9.** In early manufacturer cases, the product typically was labeled or advertised to be "harmless" or "safe" when it in fact contained a hidden danger. Thus, the manufacturer's failure to warn of the danger in such cases often will support a claim for recovery independent of the manufacturer's affirmative misrepresentation of safety. See, e.g., La Plant v. E.I. Du Pont de Nemours

& Co., 346 S.W.2d 231 (Mo. Ct. App. 1961) (plaintiff's cattle died from eating willows sprayed with defendant's weed killer labeled "not hazardous to livestock"); Crist v. Art Metal Works, 243 N.Y.S. 496 (App. Div. 1930), aff'd, 175 N.E. 341 (N.Y. 1931) (toy revolver, advertised as "absolutely harmless," ignited plaintiff's Santa Claus beard and costume during demonstration of product in department store window); Henry v. Crook, 195 N.Y.S. 642 (App. Div. 1922) (sparklers advertised as "A harmless and delightful amusement for children" ignited seven-year-old plaintiff's dress).

**10.** 81 Cal.Rptr. 519 (1969).

**11.** Id. at 521.

**12.** Noting that the defendant permitted sellers of products approved by the magazine to advertise the fact of that approval and to use the defendant's seal in such ads, the court remarked: "Implicit in the seal and certification is the representation that respondent has taken reasonable steps to make an independent examination of the product endorsed, with some degree of expertise, and found it satisfactory.... [T]he very purpose of respondent's seal and certification is to induce consumers to purchase products so endorsed...." Because the defendant "loaned its reputation" to market such products, reasoned the court, it had a duty to exercise reasonable care in the issuance of its seal of approval and certification of quality. Id. at 522.

**13.** See, e.g., U.S. Lighting Serv., Inc. v. Llerrad Corp., 800 F.Supp. 1513, 1517 (N.D. Ohio 1992) (defective lighting equip-

A typical negligent misrepresentation case against a retail seller is *Pabon v. Hackensack Auto Sales, Inc.*[14] The plaintiff was injured when the steering on his new automobile locked, causing the car to crash. He had noticed a "clicking" and "chopping" sensation in the steering and had brought it to the attention of the defendant's service manager on three occasions prior to the accident. Each time, without checking the problem, the service manager said something like, "It's a new car. Don't worry about it. It'll wear out." The court held that a jury could find the defendant car dealer liable for negligent misrepresentation on these facts because the service manager made positive assertions without a reasonable basis to know them to be true.[15]

As with claims for fraudulent misrepresentation, the plaintiff claiming negligent misrepresentation must prove the elements of deceit apart from scienter: that the defendant made a false representation of material fact which was justifiably and detrimentally relied upon by the plaintiff[16] or someone acting on the plaintiff's behalf.[17] Thus, a negligent misrepre-

---

ment approved by Underwriters Laboratories, a nonprofit testing organization, which was negligent in applying its own internal testing procedures): "The raison d'etre of the UL mark is to show that a product has met safety standards. By offering its mark to manufacturers, UL has placed itself into the stream of commerce.... The UL seal does not guarantee that a manufacturer has acted with ordinary care but sound public policy requires that UL act with ordinary care in the conduct of its own business—the certification process." The court emphasized, however, that liability against a product endorsement service is limited to negligence, and that it should not extend to strict liability. See also Hempstead v. General Fire Extinguisher Corp., 269 F.Supp. 109 (D. Del. 1967), where UL allowed the use of its inspection and testing label on a manufacturer's fire extinguishers. *Held,* UL could be held liable, for injuries from the explosion of an extinguisher carrying its label, for negligent approval of its design.

See generally Babij, Liability of a Product Endorser as Certifier: A Tort Whose Time Has Come and Gone, 20 Trial 38 (April 1984); Note, Publisher Liability for Material that Invites Reliance, 66 Tex. L. Rev. 1155 (1988); Note, Tort Liability for Non-libelous Negligent Statements: First Amendment Considerations, 93 Yale L.J. 744 (1984); Annot., 1 A.L.R.5th 431 (1992) (products liability of endorsers, trade associations, certifiers, and similar parties).

**14.** 164 A.2d 773 (N.J. Super. Ct. App. Div. 1960).

**15.** See id. at 784, where the court observed:

A false statement negligently made, and on which justifiable reliance is placed, may be the basis for the recovery of dam-

ages for injury sustained as a consequence of such reliance. The statement need not be a factual report, but may consist of an expert opinion. Justification for the imposition of a duty of care upon the speaker is found in the respective positions of the one making the representation and the relying party, the former purporting to exercise the skill and competency compatible with his profession or calling, the latter openly placing his faith on such reputed skill. There must be knowledge, or reason to know, on the part of the speaker that the information is desired for a serious purpose, that the seeker of the information intends to rely upon it, and that if the information or opinion is false or erroneous, the relying party will be injured in person or property. While privity of contract is generally thought to be a prerequisite to the right to recover for financial loss caused by a negligent statement, where the resulting damage is physical in nature the test becomes one of foreseeability rather than contractual privity.

**16.** "To establish a claim for both negligent misrepresentation and strict responsibility for misrepresentation the plaintiff must show that the defendant made a representation of fact, that the representation was untrue, and that the plaintiff believed the representation and relied upon it to his or her detriment." Consolidated Papers, Inc. v. Dorr–Oliver, Inc., 451 N.W.2d 456, 459 (Wis. Ct. App. 1989).

**17.** Some courts limit negligent misrepresentation claims to persons to whom the representation was made, or to those in privity with the defendant. See, e.g., Soule v. Norton, 750 N.Y.S.2d 692 (App. Div. 2002) (patients could not maintain negli-

sentation claim will fail if there is no representation,[18] if the representation cannot fairly be construed as an affirmation of fact,[19] if the representation is not material,[20] or if it is more a prediction of the product's future performance than a representation of existing fact.[21] Also, a claim for negligent misrepresentation cannot be sustained if the plaintiff fails to rely,[22] or does so without justification,[23] upon the defendant's representation, or if the plaintiff's reliance on the representation did not cause the plaintiff's harm.[24]

In addition, particularly in the context of claims for damages other than personal injury or property damage, courts often state that a negligent misrepresentation claimant must show the additional element that the defendant owed a *duty* to the claimant to impart accurate

gent misrepresentation claim against manufacturer of surgical laser because they did not have "actual privity of contract . . . or a relationship so close as to approach that of privity"); Nichols v. General Motors Corp., 1999 WL 33292839, at *4 (N.H. Super. 1999) (used car buyer not in privity of contract with manufacturer not entitled to rely on manufacturer's representations to buyers). See also Yanas v. Albany Med. Ctr. Hosp., 744 N.Y.S.2d 514 (App. Div. 2002). *But see* Gilleon v. Medtronic USA, Inc., 2002 WL 31300694, at *4 (N.D. Cal. 2002) (misrepresentations made to the general public, physicians, the patient-plaintiffs and plaintiffs' physicians).

**18.** See, e.g., Krueger Assocs., Inc. v. American Dist. Tel. Co., 247 F.3d 61, 67 (3d Cir. 2001) (Pa. law); Jimenez v. Daimler-Chrysler Corp., 269 F.3d 439 (4th Cir. 2001) (S.C. law) (plaintiff could not identify specific, relevant representation of safety, and defendant had no affirmative duty to disclose safety facts); Lacy v. State Accident Ins. Fund, Inc., 832 P.2d 1268 (Or. Ct. App. 1992) (after accident, workers' compensation insurer has no duty to advise injured employee that he might have claim against manufacturer of product involved).

**19.** See, e.g., Maneely v. General Motors Corp., 108 F.3d 1176, 1181 (9th Cir. 1997) (Cal. law) (plaintiffs riding in cargo bed of pickup truck paralyzed when truck crashed into palm tree; advertisements showing people in cargo bed of defendant's pick-up trucks "do not make any affirmations of fact or promises regarding the safety of riding in the cargo bed").

**20.** See, e.g., Ward Dev. Co. v. Ingrao, 493 A.2d 421 (Md. Ct. Spec. App. 1985).

**21.** See Consolidated Papers, Inc. v. Dorr–Oliver, Inc., 451 N.W.2d 456 (Wis. Ct. App. 1989). Compare Champion Home Builders Co. v. ADT Security Services, 179 F.Supp.2d 16 (N.D.N.Y. 2001) (no negligent misrepresentation claim for statements of future intent).

**22.** See, e.g., Krueger Assocs., Inc. v. American Dist. Tel. Co., 247 F.3d 61, 67 (3d Cir. 2001) (Pa. law) ("By definition any representation on which a party has purportedly relied has to be known to that party—else how could reliance take place?"). A plaintiff's failure to rely on a defendant's false advertisements precludes a causal link between the defendant's wrong and plaintiff's harm, which is fatal to the claim. See Lowe v. Sporicidin Int'l, 47 F.3d 124, 131 (4th Cir. 1995) (Md. law) ("She never alleged that she relied on the advertisements and that this reliance caused her to use [the product] and so resulted in her injuries.").

**23.** See, e.g., Village of Cross Keys v. U.S. Gypsum Co., 556 A.2d 1126 (Md. 1989), where the architects followed some but not all of defendant U.S. Gypsum's construction design specifications, including use of certain specialized materials it manufactured; the structure leaked, and architects sued for negligent misrepresentation, arguing they had relied on defendant's design which was faulty. *Held*, plaintiffs' claim failed because they had not adhered to defendant's specifications and so could not show reasonable reliance on the design publication. Compare Board of Educ. v. A, C & S, Inc., 546 N.E.2d 580 (Ill. 1989) (questioning ability of school districts on remand to prove the justifiability of their reliance on safety representations made by suppliers of asbestos materials used in plaintiffs' buildings during entire time period of 1946 to 1972). On justifiable reliance and other defenses to misrepresentation claims, see § 13.7, below.

**24.** See, e.g., Daye v. General Motors Corp., 720 So.2d 654 (La. 1998) (driver's high speed driving and imprudent application of brakes were sole cause of accident, not his reliance on promotional information); Foster v. American Home Prods. Corp., 29 F.3d 165, 168 (4th Cir. 1994) (Md. law) (causation necessary to negligent misrepresentation claim).

information.[25] With respect to the risk of personal injury and property damage, the duty to refrain from negligent misrepresentation is generally defined in terms of reasonable foreseeability,[26] whereas the duty to protect against the risk of pure economic loss is ordinarily defined more narrowly.[27] If the relationship between the defendant and plaintiff is too remote, the manufacturer may have no duty at all.[28]

In place of the element of fraudulent intent or scienter, a plaintiff asserting a negligent misrepresentation claim must prove that the defendant was negligent in some way in making the representation.[29] In such claims, negligence ordinarily is established by proof that the defendant communicated the matter represented without possessing a reasonable basis to ascertain the truth or falsity of the matter, but a negligent misrepresentation claim may also lie for the communication of information in some negligent manner.[30]

**25.**  Foster v. American Home Prods. Corp., 29 F.3d 165, 171 (4th Cir. 1994) (Md. law) ("An action for negligent misrepresentation will not lie unless the defendant owes the plaintiff a duty of care."); Board of Educ. v. A, C & S, Inc., 546 N.E.2d 580, 591 (Ill. 1989) (same; claim by school districts against suppliers of asbestos materials for costs of removal).

**26.**  See, e.g., Nichols v. General Motors Corp., 1999 WL 33292839, at *4 (N.H. Super. 1999) (no duty to subsequent purchasers); Foster v. American Home Prods. Corp., 29 F.3d 165, 171 (4th Cir. 1994) (Md. law) (to impose duty on manufacturer of name-brand pharmaceutical for representations on labels copied by manufacturer of generic equivalent administered to decedent "would be to stretch the concept of foreseeability too far"). *But see* In re Rezulin Prods. Liab. Litig., 2002 WL 31852826, *3 (S.D.N.Y. 2002) (Mississippi law requires a misrepresentation made to plaintiffs, as opposed to others).

**27.**  See, e.g., Moore Excavating, Inc. v. Consolidated Supply Co., 63 P.3d 592, 598 (Or. Ct. App. 2003) (parties did not form requisite special relationship on which plaintiff could base a claim of negligent misrepresentation); Wilson v. Dryvit Sys., Inc., 206 F.Supp.2d 749 (E.D.N.C. 2002) (homeowners could not base negligent misrepresentation claim on statements made by manufacturer of building materials to such "third parties" as builders, trade associations, and government entities), aff'd, 71 Fed.Appx. 960 (4th Cir. 2003); Board of Educ. v. A, C & S, Inc., 546 N.E.2d 580, 591 (Ill. 1989) (allowing negligent misrepresentation claim by school districts against suppliers of asbestos materials for the costs of removal and repair; court characterized school district's damages as property damage rather than economic loss, noting narrower ambit of duty for negligently caused pecuniary loss, under Restatement (2d)

Torts § 552, than for negligently caused personal injury and property loss, under Restatement (2d) Torts § 311)

Compare Learjet Corp. v. Spenlinhauer, 901 F.2d 198 (1st Cir. 1990) (Kan. law), where the court rejected a claim for negligent misrepresentation by the owner of a jet aircraft against the manufacturer for the costs of certain modifications required by the FAA in order for jet to fly at a ceiling of 51,000 feet, a ceiling capability the manufacturer had represented to the FAA in obtaining original approval of the plane's design. *Held*, a claim for negligent rather than fraudulent misrepresentation would lie only for representations made by the defendant directly to the plaintiff.

**28.**  See, e.g., Soule v. Norton, 750 N.Y.S.2d 692 (App. Div. 2002) (patients could not maintain negligent misrepresentation claim against manufacturer of surgical laser because they did not have "actual privity of contract . . . or a relationship so close as to approach that of privity"); In re Tobacco Cases II, 113 Cal.Rptr.2d 120 (Ct. App. 2001) (medical expenses paid by union too remote to be recoverable under negligent misrepresentation); Foster v. American Home Prods. Corp., 29 F.3d 165, 171 (4th Cir. 1994) (Md. law) (manufacturer of brand-name generic drug had no duty to users of other manufacturer's drugs and so not liable for labeling misrepresentations copied by other manufacturers).

**29.**  See, e.g., Board of Educ. v. A, C & S, Inc., 546 N.E.2d 580 (Ill. 1989). Thus, a negligent misrepresentation claim will fail in the absence of proof that, in making the representation, the defendant failed to exercise reasonable care. See, e.g., Cummings v. HPG Int'l, Inc., 244 F.3d 16, 25 (1st Cir. 2001) (Mass. law); Byrd Motor Lines, Inc. v. Dunlop Tire & Rubber Corp., 304 S.E.2d 773 (N.C. Ct. App. 1983).

**30.**  See, e.g., Cummings v. HPG Int'l, Inc., 244 F.3d 16 (1st Cir. 2001) (Mass. law)

Negligent misrepresentation claims may not be subject to federal preemption,[31] although one must be cautious in generalizing this complex and statute-specific issue of products liability law.[32] Also complex is the issue of whether a defendant may contractually disclaim responsibility for damages arising out of negligent misrepresentations. Some courts in some contexts allow contracting parties to disclaim responsibility for negligent misrepresentation,[33] but this issue is multi-layered and fact-specific, and other courts in other contexts invalidate clauses seeking to avoid responsibility for negligent misrepresentation.[34]

### Misrepresentation as a Violation of Statute—Negligence Per Se

If a defendant's misrepresentation violates a statute or administrative regulation designed to protect consumers from harm, a consumer injured as a result may have a claim against the defendant based on the violation. If the statute or regulation itself provides for civil redress,[35] the consumer will have a claim directly under the statute or regulation. If the statute or regulation is in the nature of a quasi-criminal safety measure, however, with no damages provision for persons harmed by its violation, an injured consumer may have a claim against the defendant under the common-law doctrine of negligence per se.[36] Thus, false labeling or advertising concerning a product's safety that contravenes a

(plaintiff must show that defendant "failed to exercise reasonable care in obtaining or communicating the information"). See generally Restatement (2d) Torts § 552, comment *e* ("the defendant is subject to liability if . . . he has failed to exercise the care or competence of a reasonable man in obtaining or communicating the communication").

**31.** See, e.g., Gorton v. American Cyanamid Co., 533 N.W.2d 746 (Wis. 1995) (labeling requirements of Federal Insecticide, Fungicide, and Rodenticide Act (FIFRA) did not preempt claim based on negligent misrepresentations that herbicide was safe for certain products). See also Goeb v. Tharaldson, 615 N.W.2d 800 (Minn. 2000) (FIFRA preempts claim for label warnings, but not a negligent misrepresentation claim against insecticide manufacturer for hotline assurances made directly to consumer). *But see* M & H Enters. v. Tri–State Delta Chems., Inc., 35 S.W.3d 899 (Mo. Ct. App. 2001) (claim preempted under FIFRA).

**32.** On federal preemption, see § 14.4, below.

**33.** At least with respect to misrepresentations other than those inducing the plaintiff to enter into the contract containing the disclaimer. See, e.g., Houghland v. Security Alarms & Servs., Inc., 755 S.W.2d 769 (Tenn. 1988). *But see* Agristor Leasing v. A.O. Smith Harvestore Prods., Inc., 869 F.2d 264, 268 (6th Cir. 1989) ("Tennessee law . . . gives no effect to disclaimers in the presence of fraud or negligent misrepresentations.").

**34.** See, e.g., Snelten v. Schmidt Implement Co., 647 N.E.2d 1071 (Ill. App. Ct. 1995), arising out of injuries to the plaintiff who was run over by his new used tractor that he started while it was in gear. The purchase order, which included an "as is" clause, also represented that the tractor had been serviced, adjusted, and inspected according to specific representations, and that it had not been modified or altered. The plaintiff alleged that the seller had failed to inspect the tractor (properly) and that someone had altered it by bypassing the neutral safety switch. *Held*, "when a written contract contains a specific, written, affirmative representation, the inclusion of general 'as is,' 'with all faults' or like language does not, in and of itself, relieve the party making the statement of a duty arising from the statement." 647 N.E.2d at 1075. The court reasoned convincingly as follows: "The same policy underlying [UCC] section 2–213's prohibition on the exclusion of express warranties, *i.e.*, people have a right to the benefit of what the seller has agreed to sell, should be applied to negligent misrepresentation actions; people should have the benefit of duties that the seller has agreed to undertake based on the express representations included in their final contract." Id.

**35.** As does, for example, the Federal Odometer Tampering Act, 49 U.S.C.A. § 32710.

**36.** See § 2.4, above.

misbranding, false advertising, or unfair and deceptive trade practices act may support a claim for damages either directly under the statute or under the common law doctrine of negligence per se.[37]

An early, prominent decision allowing recovery for breach of such a statute was *Wright v. Carter Prods., Inc.*[38] In this case, although the defendant manufacturer had received over 373 complaints of skin irritation over a four year period, it continued to advertise its deodorant, Arrid, as "safe" and "harmless," and that it "does not irritate the skin." Suffering a skin disorder from using Arrid, the plaintiff alleged that the defendant had misrepresented and falsely advertised its product. Applying conventional negligence per se principles, the court allowed the claim, observing that "a statutory violation may be the basis for civil liability if the injured person is a member of the class for whose express benefit the statute was enacted and the harm resulting from the violation is of the type that the statute was designed to prevent."[39] Subsequent decisions have similarly allowed state law negligence per se claims for misrepresentations that result in violations of state statutes.[40] In limited situations, courts sometimes permit a claim for statutory violation by implying a private cause of action into the statute.[41] Negligence per se claims may also be maintained, as a matter of state law, for violation of a federal safety statute or regulation.[42]

Material misrepresentations knowingly made to a federal governmental agency are criminalized by federal statute.[43] However, this statute may be viewed more in the nature of a "truth" rather than a "safety" statute, such that its violation may not amount to a breach of a standard of care sufficient to trigger the doctrine of negligence per se.[44]

## § 3.4   STRICT LIABILITY FOR MISREPRESENTATION

### In General

A manufacturer or other seller that innocently makes a false statement about a product's quality or safety that results in harm is not subject to liability for deceit or negligent misrepresentation, but such a defendant may be subject to liability in contract for breach of an express warranty.[1] Some states provide an additional claim for such strict or no-

---

**37.** See, e.g., Soule v. Norton, 750 N.Y.S.2d 692 (App. Div. 2002) (suit for "deceptive practices" under General Business Law § 349(a) requires plaintiff to prove that defendant engaged in "consumer oriented" conduct that is deceptive or misleading in a material way that caused injury to the plaintiff).

**38.** 244 F.2d 53 (2d Cir. 1957) (Mass. law).

**39.** Id. at 61.

**40.** See, e.g., Tetuan v. A.H. Robins Co., 738 P.2d 1210 (Kan. 1987) (false advertising of dangerous Dalkon Shield IUD).

**41.** See, e.g., Bob Godfrey Pontiac, Inc. v. Roloff, 630 P.2d 840 (Or. 1981) (excellent analysis).

**42.** See Prosser and Keeton on Torts § 36, at 221 n.9; § 2.4, above.

**43.** "Whoever . . . knowingly or wilfully falsifies . . . a material fact, or makes any false, fictitious or fraudulent statements or representations . . . shall be [in violation of this statute]." 18 U.S.C.A. § 1001.

**44.** See McNeil Pharm. v. Hawkins, 686 A.2d 567 (D.C. 1996) (action on behalf of patient who died of severe liver failure following administration of defendant's pharmaceutical).

§ 3.4

**1.** On express warranty generally, see ch. 4, below. For a comparison of express warranty and strict liability in tort for misrepresentation, see § 4.2, below.

fault liability for misrepresentation under a parallel cause of action in tort.[2] The modern claim for strict products liability in tort for misrepresentation is formulated in *Restatement (Second) Torts* § 402B.[3] This section provides as follows:

> § 402B. Misrepresentation by Seller of Chattels to Consumer
>
> One engaged in the business of selling chattels who, by advertising, labels, or otherwise, makes to the public a misrepresentation of material fact concerning the character or quality of a chattel sold by him is subject to liability for physical harm to a consumer of the chattel caused by justifiable reliance upon the misrepresentation, even though
>
> (a) it is not made fraudulently or negligently, and
>
> (b) the consumer has not bought the chattel from or entered into any contractual relation with the seller.

Underlying § 402B is the concept of a kind of "non-contractual 'express warranty' made to the consumer in the form of the representation to the public upon which he relies."[4] But liability is grounded in principles of tort, not contract, law.[5] Probably because it trespasses deeply into the express warranty domain that is statutorily defined today in the Uniform Commercial Code,[6] and notwithstanding its solid foundation in moral theory,[7] judicial support for § 402B has been weak.[8] The courts of most states have never adopted or applied the doctrine at all,[9] and case authority for the doctrine in states in which the doctrine at one time or another has been discussed is generally sparse and often dated. Nevertheless, this section of the *Restatement (Second) of Torts* was reaffirmed by the *Restatement (Third) of Torts: Products Liability* with little analysis, debate, or fanfare,[10] and the doctrine seems quite firmly

---

**2.** See Freeman v. Hoffman–LaRoche, Inc., 618 N.W.2d 827, 844 (Neb. 2000).

**3.** On § 402B, see Sales, The Innocent Misrepresentation Doctrine: Strict Tort Liability under Section 402B, 16 Houston L. Rev. 239 (1979); L. Green, Strict Liability Under Sections 402A and 402B: A Decade of Litigation, 54 Tex. L. Rev. 1185 (1976); Shapo, A Representational Theory of Consumer Protection: Doctrine, Function and Legal Liability for Product Disappointment, 60 Va. L. Rev. 1109 (1974); Comment, Interpreting the Restatement of Torts Section 402B After the Changes to Section 402A, 28 Cumb. L. Rev. 177 (1997–98).

**4.** Restatement (2d) Torts § 402B cmt. *d.*

**5.** Id.

**6.** See, e.g., Hauter v. Zogarts, 534 P.2d 377, 388 (Cal. 1975) (Clark, J., concurring).

**7.** See Owen, The Moral Foundations of Products Liability Law, 68 Notre Dame L. Rev. 427, 463–64 (1993) (explaining how powerful reasons based on autonomy, truth, equality, and utility support a rule of strict liability for accidental harm resulting from

innocent but false assertions of product quality).

**8.** Appendices to Restatement (2d) Torts § 402B digest state court opinions which appear to apply § 402B in Arizona, California, Colorado, Illinois, Pennsylvania, Tennessee, Texas, and Washington, and opinions from several other states (including Nebraska, New Jersey, and Wyoming) which appear to refer favorably to this doctrine. A law journal student comment cites cases thought to show support for the doctrine in eighteen states: Arizona, California, Colorado, Illinois, Kansas, Maryland, Mississippi, New Mexico, New Jersey, New York, North Dakota, Ohio, Oregon, Pennsylvania, Tennessee, Texas, Washington, and Wyoming. See Comment, 28 Cumb. L. Rev. 177, 178 n.5 (1997–98).

**9.** See, e.g., Prohaska v. Sofamor, S.N.C., 138 F.Supp.2d 422, 447–48 (W.D.N.Y. 2001) (striking § 402B claim because New York has never adopted that approach).

**10.** Section 9 of the Products Liability Restatement, entitled "Liability of Com-

established—even if infrequently used—in such major jurisdictions as California, Illinois, Pennsylvania, and Texas.[11]

## Background

Like so much of modern products liability law, the doctrine of strict products liability in tort for misrepresentation grew out of the law's impatience with the limitation imposed by the doctrine of privity of contract, applied in this context to the express warranty cause of action in cases involving personal injuries.[12] The classic case widely credited with paternity of the doctrine of strict products liability in tort for misrepresentation is *Baxter v. Ford Motor Co.*[13] While plaintiff was driving his Model A Ford, a pebble from a passing car struck his windshield, causing small pieces of glass to fly into his eye, which he lost as a result. Plaintiff sued Ford Motor Company for misrepresenting the windshield's characteristics in its advertising catalogues, which stated: "TRIPLEX SHATTER-PROOF GLASS WINDSHIELD. All of the new Ford cars have a Triplex shatter-proof glass windshield—so made that it will not fly or shatter under the hardest impact.... Its extra margin of safety is something that every motorist should look for in the purchase of a car—especially where there are women and children." Ford defended the case on the basis there could be no claim for "express warranty" in the absence of privity of contract, but the Supreme Court of Washington rejected such a narrow, doctrinal perspective:

> The rule in such cases does not rest upon contractual obligations, but rather on the principle that the original act of delivering an article is wrong, when, because of the lack of those qualities which the manufacturer represented it as having, the absence of which could not be readily detected by the consumer, the article is not safe for the purposes for which the consumer would ordinarily use it.[14]

mercial Product Seller or Distributor for Harm Caused by Misrepresentation," provides:

> One engaged in the business of selling or otherwise distributing products who, in connection with the sale of a product, makes a fraudulent, negligent, or innocent misrepresentation of material fact concerning the product is subject to liability for harm to persons or property caused by the misrepresentation.

Rather than "restating" § 402B in a black letter section of its own, § 9 of the Third Restatement seemingly affirms and readopts § 402B in comment *b*: "The rules governing liability for innocent product misrepresentation are stated in the Restatement, Second, of Torts § 402B."

**11.** See, e.g., Hollenbeck v. Selectone Corp., 476 N.E.2d 746 (Ill. App. Ct. 1985); Klages v. General Ordnance Equip. Corp., 367 A.2d 304 (Pa. Super. Ct. 1976); Hauter

v. Zogarts, 534 P.2d 377 (Cal. 1975); Crocker v. Winthrop Lab., 514 S.W.2d 429 (Tex. 1974).

The Tennessee courts endorsed § 402B in an important early decision, Ford Motor Co. v. Lonon, 398 S.W.2d 240, 250 (Tenn. 1966), and have reaffirmed the doctrine more recently. Ritter v. Custom Chemicides, Inc., 912 S.W.2d 128, 131–32 (Tenn. 1995); Ladd v. Honda Motor Co., 939 S.W.2d 83 (Tenn. Ct. App. 1996) (extensive analysis of doctrine's history and application).

**12.** For an excellent historical discussion of this cause of action, see Sales, The Innocent Misrepresentation Doctrine: Strict Tort Liability under Section 402B, 16 Houston L. Rev. 239 (1979). See also American Safety Equip. Corp. v. Winkler, 640 P.2d 216, 219–20 (Colo. 1982).

**13.** 12 P.2d 409 (Wash. 1932).

**14.** Id. at 412.

The court reasoned that it simply is not equitable to allow a manufacturer to create demand for its products by means of false statements in mass advertising and then to hide behind the privity of contract defense when consumers, induced by the false statements to purchase the products, were injured as a result.[15] Affirming a plaintiff's verdict on second appeal, the court ruled that the seller's belief in the truth of its representations and its evidence that the windshield was as good as any made were irrelevant.[16]

*Baxter* thus held that liability for misrepresentation was truly strict, like liability for express warranty, yet it ignored the warranty law rules concerning privity of contract and other contractual limitations. Scholars at the time astutely observed that, in *Baxter*, they were witnessing the birth of a new tort.[17] Prior to the inclusion of § 402B in the *Restatement (Second) of Torts*, a small number of other decisions followed the lead of *Baxter* by allowing recovery for personal injuries on similar principles.[18]

## Nature of Liability

It is fundamental that the § 402B action presaged in *Baxter* is not dependent on culpable conduct by the seller. Material representations concerning the character or quality of a product are made to the public at the seller's peril; if the representations are false, and if injury follows from justifiable reliance thereon, the seller is liable.[19] Liability under § 402B, therefore, is truly "strict"—liability will attach regardless of the seller's total inability to discover that its representations are false.[20]

**15.** "Radio, bill boards and the products of the printing press have become the means of creating a large part of the demand that causes goods to depart from factories to the ultimate consumer. It would be unjust to recognize a rule that would permit manufacturers of goods to create a demand for their products by representing that they possess qualities which they, in fact, do not possess; and then, because there is no privity of contract existing between the consumer and the manufacturer, deny the consumer the right to recover if damages result from the absence of those qualities, when such absence is not readily noticeable." Id.

**16.** "If a person states as true material facts susceptible of knowledge to one who relies and acts thereon to his injury, if the representations are false, it is immaterial that he did not know they were false, or that he believed them to be true." Baxter v. Ford Motor Co., 35 P.2d 1090, 1092 (Wash. 1934).

**17.** "As to this general field—negligence, deceit, warranty, or whatever the *Baxter* case may really involve—I take it we are feeling our way.... Perhaps we are actually witnessing the birth of a new type of tort liability." Leidy, Another New Tort?, 38 Mich. L. Rev. 964, 986 (1940). See also Feezer, Manufacturer's Liability for Injuries Caused by His Products: Defective Automobiles, 37 Mich. L. Rev. 1, 26 (1938).

**18.** See Worley v. Proctor & Gamble Mfg. Co., 253 S.W.2d 532 (Mo. Ct. App. 1952), in which the defendant manufacturer represented that "Tide is kind to your hands." *Held,* representation could support non-contractual warranty action imposing strict liability for its breach on manufacturer despite absence of privity. Another important, foundational case for the incipient innocent misrepresentation in tort claim was Rogers v. Toni Home Permanent Co., 147 N.E.2d 612 (Ohio 1958). The plaintiff had suffered hair loss and severe scalp irritation after using defendant's product, which was labeled "safe" and "harmless." Reiterating *Baxter*'s rationales, the court imposed strict liability for misrepresentation: "The warranties made by the manufacturer in his advertisements and by the labels on his products are inducements to the ultimate consumers, and the manufacturer ought to be held to strict accountability to any consumer who buys the product in reliance upon such representations." See id. at 615–16.

**19.** Section 402B makes this point clear in black letter. See § 402B(a).

**20.** See Crocker v. Winthrop Labs., 514 S.W.2d 429 (Tex. 1974), where the decedent

Thus, the § 402B claim defined in the *Restatement (Second) of Torts* eliminates the difficulties in proving scienter and fault that inhere in actions for deceit and negligent misrepresentation. Unlike liability under § 402A, however, § 402B bases recovery on an improper communication. Accordingly, liability under § 402B is grounded in the defendant's communication of false words that harm the plaintiff and so does not require that the product contain a "defect" unless the manufacturer falsely states that the product is free thereof.[21]

Apart from the absence of seller fault, the elements of a § 402B cause of action for innocent misrepresentation closely track the elements of deceit.[22] Thus, as in deceit, the defendant must affirmatively communicate information bearing on the product's safety, such that a buyer's reliance on the manufacturer's good name alone will not suffice.[23] The plaintiff also must prove, of course, that the representation was *false*, so that if it fairly may be interpreted as true, or at least as not being false with respect to the relevant facts, then no misrepresentation claim will lie. Consequently, it is vital that the particular words be closely interpreted, in context with any warnings, to determine if they were actually true or false.[24] For example, in *General Motors Corp. v. Howard*,[25] the plaintiff truck driver sustained injuries to his head and chest when another truck hit the side of his vehicle thrusting him against the steering wheel. Plaintiff claimed that the steering column, advertised as

became addicted to a drug that the defendant drug company had represented as being nonaddictive:

> Whatever the danger and state of medical knowledge, and however rare the susceptibility of the user, when the drug company positively and specifically represents its product to be free and safe from all dangers of addiction, and when the treating physician relies upon that representation, the drug company is liable when the representation proves to be false and harm results.

Id. at 433.

**21.** See Freeman v. Hoffman–LaRoche, Inc., 618 N.W.2d 827, 844 (Neb. 2000); Products Liability Restatement § 9 cmt. *d*.

**22.** See, e.g., Baughn v. Honda Motor Co., 727 P.2d 655 (Wash. 1986):

> Three requirements must be met in order to establish a prima facie case under § 402B: (1) there must be a misrepresentation of a material fact concerning the character or quality of a chattel; (2) the misrepresentation must be made to the public; and (3) physical harm must have resulted to a consumer from justifiable reliance upon the misrepresentation.

Id. at 667. See also Ladd v. Honda Motor Co., 939 S.W.2d 83, 97 (Tenn. Ct. App. 1996): "In order to create liability under Section 402B, there must be proof of a misrepresentation of a material fact, made to the public, with respect to the character and quality of the product, which is false

and upon which the consumer is expected to justifiably rely.... The representations must be more than mere statements of opinion or the kind of loose general sales talk commonly referred to as 'puffing.'"

While § 402B claims are basically no-fault versions of the fault-based causes of action for misrepresentation, strict liability claims for "public" misrepresentation may be narrower than deceit and negligent misrepresentation claims in certain respects. As discussed below, recovery in strict liability probably precludes recovery for misrepresentations made privately to the plaintiff, and for those that cause pure economic loss. Moreover, at least in some jurisdictions, innocent misrepresentation claims may be available to a smaller class of plaintiffs than are the fault-based claims.

**23.** See Gower v. Savage Arms, Inc., 166 F.Supp.2d 240 (E.D. Pa. 2001) (strangely appearing to reason that there might be a strict liability duty to disclose known hazards).

**24.** See, e.g., Chandler v. Gene Messer Ford, Inc., 81 S.W.3d 493, 500 (Tex. App. 2002) (general advertisements showing children riding in front seat should be interpreted together with warnings about dangers of airbags to children in front seat and instruction to restrain them in rear seat if possible).

**25.** 244 So.2d 726 (Miss. 1971), overruled on other grounds by, Toliver v. G.M.C., 482 So.2d 213 (Miss. 1986).

"telescopic," failed to telescope adequately, contrary to the representation. Noting that the column would have telescoped more had the collision been head-on, and that it had telescoped somewhat even though plaintiff had been hit at an angle, the court concluded that the representation was not false: "The statement of appellant . . . never asserted that the steering column would telescope under any and all circumstances and conditions."[26]

If a manufacturer advertises its products generally as possessing certain characteristics, then the failure of any model to possess such characteristics may fairly be found to render the advertisement false.[27] But an advertisement that a particular product model possesses certain traits may not necessarily be construed as meaning that other models of the product possess those same features.[28] And if the product is claimed to possess a certain trait—even the most important general trait of being "safe"—when used in a particular manner or under other specified conditions, then its failure to possess the trait in the absence of those conditions simply is not false.[29]

The matter misrepresented must be *factual*, and the § 402B doctrine "does not apply to statements of opinion, and, in particular, it does not apply to the kind of loose general praise of wares [which may be] considered to be 'sales talk,' and is commonly called 'puffing.' "[30] So, representations that a helicopter is "easy to fly" for beginners,[31] or that

---

**26.**   244 So.2d at 729.

**27.**   See, e.g., Ladd v. Honda Motor Co., 939 S.W.2d 83 (Tenn. Ct. App. 1996) (advertisements showing young children using minibikes). Contrast Haynes v. American Motors Corp., 691 F.2d 1268, 1270–71 (8th Cir. 1982) (Ark. law), where the court excluded plaintiff's proffer of evidence of Jeep advertisements where they involved a different model than that driven by plaintiffs, and where the advertisements portrayed off-road settings whereas plaintiffs' vehicle slid off a rain-slick pavement.

**28.**   In American Safety Equip. Corp. v. Winkler, 640 P.2d 216, 223 (Colo. 1982) (4–3 decision), the plaintiff, an off-duty, general duty policeman riding his personal motorcycle, received head injuries when he collided with a truck and his helmet popped off before he hit the ground. The helmet he was wearing was a general duty model 1601, designed with a special snap harness for quick release to permit an officer to remove the helmet easily in a riot if someone grabbed his head. The police department issued a different helmet (model 1602) to the motorcycle police, as plaintiff knew. Both models were packaged in the same type box, with illustrations on both sides of the box depicting a motorcyclist wearing a helmet. In an action against the manufacturer under § 402B, the plaintiff claimed that he relied upon the illustrations on the box in deciding to use his model 1601 helmet for personal motorcycle riding.

*Held*, the claim was rejected because the model was different. Although the majority's reasoning emphasized the absence of justifiable reliance, rather than the truth or falsity of the representations, the plaintiff's claim failed just the same.

**29.**   See, e.g., Baughn v. Honda Motor Co., 727 P.2d 655 (Wash. 1986), where two eight-year-old children were injured when they rode a Honda mini-trail bike through a stop sign and into a truck on a public road. A warning attached to the bike conspicuously stated that the bike was sold only for off-road use. The plaintiffs' § 402B claim relied upon assertions in the owner's manual which stated that the bike could be equipped with a throttle control device that could lower the maximum speed, a *"feature that assures safe riding for a beginner."* *Held*, no misrepresentation under § 402B. The manual statements were "not particularly relevant here since the throttle device never was installed on [the] bike. In addition, all of these statements are qualified by the explicit manual instructions that the mini-trail bike is for trail use only and not for use on the streets and roadways. The statements referred to do not guarantee safety; they say that the mini-trail bike will be safe if the device is installed." Id. at 668.

**30.**   Restatement (2d) Torts § 402B, cmt. g (entitled *"Material fact"*).

**31.**   Berkebile v. Brantly Helicopter Corp., 337 A.2d 893 (Pa. 1975). See also

a truck's braking device offers "unprecedented safety,"[32] or that "You meet the nicest people on a Honda" mini-trail bike,[33] or advertising "to protect your dreams" and showing children riding in a vehicle's front seat,[34] are all such vague and general commendations that they are properly interpreted as "puffs" rather than as assertions of fact.[35] In contrast, a representation that a golfing practice device is "completely safe—ball will not hit player" is the kind of specific assurance of an ascertainable safety characteristic that should be construed as fact rather than as opinion.[36]

In addition, the fact misrepresented must be *material*, which means that it would be important to a normal purchaser, who therefore would be justified in relying upon it in buying or using the product.[37]

As with other misrepresentation claims, those based on innocent misrepresentations require that the plaintiff prove a causal link between the wrong (the misrepresentation) and the injury.[38] That is, no matter how false a statement may be, a claim for misrepresentation will fail if the statement does not have some untoward effect, if it does not in some manner cause the plaintiff's harm. Hence, there exists the element of *reliance*, which usually, but not always, establishes this imperative causal connection.[39] Thus, the strict liability for misrepresentation doctrine does not apply if the representation is never seen, or otherwise learned about, and acted upon by the plaintiff or someone acting on the plaintiff's behalf.[40] As with express warranty, the necessary reliance is often established by proof that the plaintiff or another decided to purchase the product because of the quality misrepresented, at least in

Hittle v. Scripto–Tokai Corp., 166 F.Supp.2d 142 (M.D. Pa. 2001).

**32.** Hoffman v. A.B. Chance Co., 339 F.Supp. 1385, 1388 (M.D. Pa. 1972).

**33.** Baughn v. Honda Motor Co., 727 P.2d 655, 668 (Wash. 1986).

**34.** Chandler v. Gene Messer Ford, Inc., 81 S.W.3d 493, 500 (Tex. App. 2002).

**35.** See id. (salesman's assertion that dual airbags made Ford Aspire safer than a Geo Metro—opinion, not statement of fact).

**36.** Hauter v. Zogarts, 534 P.2d 377 (Cal. 1975) (the celebrated case of the "Golfing Gizmo").

**37.** Restatement (2d) Torts § 402B cmt. g. Cf. Chandler v. Gene Messer Ford, Inc., 81 S.W.3d 493, 499 (Tex. App. 2002) (fact that Aspire, sold by Ford with a "Ford" warranty, was actually made by Kia, could not support § 402B claim).

**38.** In addition to the more typically relevant issue of cause in fact, proximate cause must also be established. See Hollenbeck v. Selectone Corp., 476 N.E.2d 746 (Ill. App. Ct. 1985) (police officer's pager failed when he sought to use it to summon assistance; *held*, criminal attack not unforeseeable risk breaking causal connection between pager manufacturer's representations and officer's injuries); § 12.3, below.

**39.** See Baker v. Danek Med., Inc., 35 F.Supp.2d 875, 878 (N.D. Fla. 1998) (noting that a defendant is subject to liability under § 402B for harm caused by reliance on a representation).

**40.** The rule "does not apply where the misrepresentation is not known, or there is indifference to it, and it does not influence the purchase or subsequent conduct.... Since the liability here is for misrepresentation, the rules as to what will constitute justifiable reliance [for the action of deceit] are applicable to this Section, so far as they are pertinent." Restatement (2d) Torts § 402B cmt. j. See, e.g., Miller v. Pfizer Inc., 196 F.Supp.2d 1095 (D. Kan. 2002) (reliance not established because plaintiff's prescribing doctor never read and would simply throw away promotional materials containing misrepresentations), aff'd, 356 F.3d 1326 (10th Cir. 2004); Estate of White v. R.J. Reynolds Tobacco Co., 109 F.Supp.2d 424, 429–30 (D. Md. 2000) (because no evidence that deceased ever saw or heard any of defendants' statements, he could not have relied on them; also refusing to *presume* such reliance); Bean v. Baxter Healthcare Corp., 965 S.W.2d 656 (Tex. App. 1998) (no reliance if representations unknown to plaintiff); Baker v. Danek Med., Inc., 35 F. Supp. 2d 875 (N.D. Fla. 1998) (same).

part.[41] But, because the misrepresentation claim lies in tort, the harm need not be linked to the purchase decision if it can be sufficiently connected to a decision as to how the product may be used.[42] Nor does it matter, also because the action lies in tort, whether the reliance is by the purchaser himself, or whether it is by the consumer who is injured, provided that the requisite causal linkage is established.[43] Thus, a prescribing doctor's reliance on misrepresentations by a pharmaceutical company that its drug is nonaddictive will support a claim by the doctor's patient who is injured by the drug;[44] a mother's decision to purchase a product advertised as "absolutely safe" will support her child's claim for injuries;[45] an adult's decision to loan his ATV to his friend's young son, on the strength of advertisements showing young children safely riding such vehicles, will establish reliance for a claim on behalf of the injured boy;[46] the reliance of a retailer on a manufacturer's representations will support a claim by the customer;[47] and an employer's decision to purchase equipment on the strength of a manufacturer's misrepresentations should support an employee's claim against the manufacturer.

Even the strongest reliance, of course, must also be *justified*, and the principles concerning the plaintiff's (or another's) right to rely on the representation applicable to deceit claims are also applicable to claims for innocent misrepresentation.[48] So, if the plaintiff relies on obvious puffs or clearly dubious assertions, or if he unreasonably claims to rely on representations he has reason to doubt are true or apply to his particular model, then the reliance may not be justifiable and a claim under § 402B will not lie.[49]

---

**41.** Comment *j* to § 402B notes that "the misrepresentation need not be the sole inducement to purchase, or to use the chattel, and it is sufficient that it has been a substantial factor in that inducement."

**42.** Comment *j* to § 402B (entitled "*Justifiable reliance*") requires that the misrepresentation either "influence the purchase *or* subsequent conduct." (Emphasis added.) See, e.g., Ladd v. Honda Motor Co., 939 S.W.2d 83 (Tenn. Ct. App. 1996).

**43.** "[The reliance] may be that of the ultimate purchaser of the chattel, who because of such reliance passes it on to the consumer who is in fact injured, but is ignorant of the misrepresentation." Restatement (2d) Torts § 402B cmt. *j*.

**44.** See, e.g., Crocker v. Winthrop Labs., 514 S.W.2d 429 (Tex. 1974).

**45.** Hauter v. Zogarts, 534 P.2d 377 (Cal. 1975) (the Golfing Gizmo case).

**46.** Ladd v. Honda Motor Co., 939 S.W.2d 83 (Tenn. Ct. App. 1996).

**47.** See, e.g., Westlye v. Look Sports, Inc., 22 Cal.Rptr.2d 781 (Ct. App. 1993); Baughn v. Honda Motor Co., 727 P.2d 655 (Wash. 1986) (en banc).

**48.** See § 402 B cmt. *j*. See, e.g., Gawloski v. Miller Brewing Co., 644 N.E.2d 731, 736 (Ohio Ct. App. 1994), a claim against Miller Brewing Company by incarcerated criminals who claimed that their criminal behavior resulted from their addiction to Miller beer which the defendant had misrepresented as safe, thereby negating any common knowledge of the dangers of alcohol consumption. *Held*, the plaintiffs' reliance was not justified; judgment on pleadings for manufacturer affirmed. On justifiable reliance and other defenses to misrepresentation claims, see § 13.7, below.

**49.** See, e.g., Herzog v. Arthrocare Corp., 2003 WL 1785795, at *7 (D. Me. 2003) (summary judgment for seller of surgical tool because plaintiff was physician who, due to his medical knowledge, could not have justifiably relied on defendant's assertions); American Safety Equip. Corp. v. Winkler, 640 P.2d 216, 223 (Colo. 1982) (4–3 decision) ("Justifiable reliance contemplates the reasonable exercise of knowledge and intelligence in assessing the represented facts. Unsupportable subjective reliance is inadequate.")

Although the *Second Restatement* explicitly takes no position on whether the strict liability doctrine should apply to private misrepresentations,[50] the rule is formulated explicitly in terms of *public* misrepresentations—and that is how the courts have applied it.[51] Thus, the misrepresentation must be made "by public advertising in newspapers or television, by literature distributed to the public through dealers, by labels on the product sold, or leaflets accompanying it," or by any other public means of communication.[52]

### Damages

Section 402B provides for "liability for physical harm to a consumer," and the *Second Restatement* defines "physical harm" to mean "physical impairment of the human body, or of land or chattels."[53] While this general *Restatement* definition suggests an intent to include liability for property damage as well as personal injury, all the cases cited in the comments and all four illustrations involve personal injuries. Moreover, when § 402B's damages language is compared with that of § 402A,[54] a solid argument may be made that the American Law Institute intended § 402B to be restricted to cases involving personal injury or death. There is a paucity of judicial authority on whether the section supports recovery of property damage. At least one case reads § 402B restrictively, though not unreasonably, as excluding recovery for such losses.[55]

As for the recovery of pure economic loss under § 402B, the law is much more clear. An early, prominent Tennessee decision, *Ford Motor Company v. Lonon*,[56] did impose strict tort liability for misrepresentation for economic loss upon the defendant on the basis of § 402B and its reference, in comment *a*, to a draft parallel rule applicable to pecuniary loss in a then-proposed § 552D.[57] But the ALI never adopted the pro-

**50.** Restatement (2d) Torts § 402B Caveat (1). Compare Products Liability Restatement § 9 cmt. *b* ("This question remains open.").

**51.** See, e.g., Chandler v. Gene Messer Ford, Inc., 81 S.W.3d 493, 499 (Tex. App. 2002) (salesman's private representations not covered by § 402B); Freeman v. Hoffman–LaRoche, Inc., 618 N.W.2d 827 (Neb. 2000); Lewis & Lambert Metal Contractors, Inc. v. Jackson, 914 S.W.2d 584, 590 (Tex. App. 1994) (§ 402B "does not apply to private misrepresentations"), vacated upon settlement without reference to merits, 938 S.W.2d 716 (Tex. 1997). Indeed, at least one court has included the public nature of the misrepresentation as an element of this tort. See Baughn v. Honda Motor Co., 727 P.2d 655 (Wash. 1986).

**52.** Restatement (2d) Torts § 402B cmt. *h* (entitled "*To the public*"). Notwithstanding Caveat (1), which provides that the ALI takes no position on whether the rule may apply "where the representation is not made to the public, but to an individual," comment *h* plainly states that the doctrine "is limited to misrepresentations which are made by the seller to the public at large."

**53.** Restatement (2d) Torts § 7(3).

**54.** In contrast to § 402B's language of "physical harm to a consumer," § 402A speaks in terms of "physical harm thereby caused to the ultimate user or consumer, or to his property." Restatement (2d) Torts § 402A.

**55.** See Fischbach & Moore Int'l Corp. v. Crane Barge R–14, 632 F.2d 1123, 1127 (4th Cir. 1980) (Md. law) ("Section 402B, in contrast to § 402A, provides liability for misrepresentation ... for physical harm to the consumer, not for property damage."). *But see* Ritter v. Custom Chemicides, Inc., 912 S.W.2d 128 (Tenn. 1995); Westric Battery Co. v. Standard Elec. Co., 482 F.2d 1307 (10th Cir. 1973) (Colo. law).

**56.** 398 S.W.2d 240 (Tenn. 1966).

**57.** The proposed provision, entitled "Misrepresentation by Seller of Chattels to Public" mirrored the language of § 402B, except that it rendered the defendant "subject to liability for pecuniary loss caused to another...." Restatement (2d) Torts, Council Draft No. 17, p. 76, quoted in *Lonon*, 398 S.W.2d at 246–47.

posed § 552D, and Tennessee long stood as the solitary state allowing recovery in such cases for pure economic loss. Eventually coming to its senses, the Tennessee Supreme Court[58] in time repudiated the *Lonon* holding.[59] Apart from *Lonon* and its progeny in Tennessee,[60] the courts have universally rejected claims for pure economic loss based on § 402B.[61]

**58.** With some help by the legislature. See Tenn. Code Ann. § 29–28–101 et seq.

**59.** First Nat'l Bank of Louisville v. Brooks Farms, 821 S.W.2d 925, 929–31 (Tenn. 1991). See also Ritter v. Custom Chemicides, Inc., 912 S.W.2d 128 (Tenn. 1995).

**60.** See, e.g., Vicon, Inc. v. CMI Corp., 657 F.2d 768 (5th Cir. 1981) (Tenn. law).

**61.** See, e.g., Rice v. Bell Tel. Co., 524 A.2d 522, 523 (Pa. Super. Ct. 1987); Roxalana Hills, Ltd. v. Masonite Corp., 627 F.Supp. 1194, 1198 (S.D. W. Va. 1986), aff'd, 813 F.2d 1228 (4th Cir. 1987) (W. Va. law).

# Chapter 4

# WARRANTY

*Table of Sections*

## § 4.1  WARRANTY—GENERALLY

Warranty law concerns the legal obligations arising from assertions or promises connected with transactions.[1] In the products liability context, the law of warranty prescribes the legal effect accorded assertions associated with the transfer of a product for value, usually through a sale.[2] The assertions about a product may be express,[3] through the seller's affirmative communications concerning the product's attributes, or they may be implied by the nature of the sales transaction.[4] The roots of warranty law reach back deep into history, at least to the law of Rome.[5]

---

**§ 4.1**

**1.** Helpful general treatments on the law of warranty under the Uniform Commercial Code include R. Anderson, Anderson on the Uniform Commercial Code (3d ed. 1994–97); L. Lawrence, Lawrence's Anderson on the Uniform Commercial Code (3d ed. 2001–02 rev. ed.); J. White and R. Summers, Uniform Commercial Code (5th Pract. Ed. 2002) and (5th student ed. 2000); UCC Case Digest (Callaghan, West); B. Clark and C. Smith, The Law of Product Warranties (2d ed. 2002); R. Nordstrom, Law of Sales (1970); O. Harris and A. Squillante, Warranty Law in Tort and Contract Actions (1989); W. Hawkland, 1 and 2 UCC Series (2000 rev. ed.); D. Nelson and J. Howicz, 2 Williston on Sales (5th ed. 1995); and M. Foran, 3 Williston on Sales (5th ed. 1996). Useful shorter works include C. Gillette and S. Walt, Sales Law (1999); and W.

Lawrence and W. Henning, Understanding Sales and Leases of Goods (1995). See also Frumer and Friedman, Products Liability ch. 9; 1 Madden & Owen on Products Liability ch. 4; 2 Am. Law Prod. Liab. 3d chs. 18–24; C.J. Miller and R. Goldberg, Product Liability chs. 2–6 (Oxford, 2d ed. 2004) (British law).

**2.** For an historical overview of warranty law in the products liability context, see § 1.2, above.

**3.** Uniform Commercial Code (UCC) § 2–313; see § 4.2, below.

**4.** Uniform Commercial Code (UCC) §§ 2–314 (merchantability) and 2–315 (fitness for particular purpose); see §§ 4.3 and 4.4, below.

**5.** For an historical sketch of early products liability warranty law, see § 1.2, above.

In contrast to most of products liability law, which today is generally based in tort, the law of warranty is associated with promises arising out of sales transactions and so is ordinarily conceived as part of the modern law of contract. In fact, however, warranty law sprang from the law of torts,[6] and it was the direct progenitor of the doctrine of strict products liability in tort.[7] A small number of states which never did adopt the doctrine of strict liability in tort for the sale of defective products (notably Delaware, Massachusetts, Michigan, and Virginia) have constructed their modern products liability jurisprudence upon an implied warranty of quality. But much of the common-law "warranty" doctrine of such states has been patterned after the developed tort law jurisprudence of negligence doctrine and the *Restatement (Second) of Torts* § 402A[8] and so in essence, if not totally in doctrine, is part of the larger law of tort.[9]

Warranty law governing the sale of chattels, which evolved as a matter of common law in both England and America, was first codified by the Sale of Goods Act of 1893 in Great Britain and by the Uniform Sales Act of 1906 in the United States.[10] Article 2 (Sales) of the Uniform Commercial Code (UCC), promulgated in the 1950s and legislatively

**6.** See Ames, The History of Assumpsit, 2 Harv. L. Rev. 1, 8 (1888); Prosser, The Implied Warranty of Merchantable Quality, 27 Minn. L. Rev. 117, 118–22 (1943); Prosser, Assault on the Citadel (Strict Liability to the Consumer), 69 Yale L.J. 1099, 1103–1110, 1124–27 (1960).

**7.** See § 5.2, below.

**8.** See, e.g., Vassallo v. Baxter Healthcare Corp., 696 N.E.2d 909, 923 (Mass. 1998) ("liability under the implied warranty of merchantability in Massachusetts is 'congruent in nearly all respects with the principles expressed in Restatement (Second) of Torts § 402A' "); Jeld–Wen, Inc. v. Gamble, 501 S.E.2d 393, 396 (Va. 1998) (level of required safety "is essentially the same whether the theory of liability is labeled warranty or negligence," both requiring proof that the product was "unreasonably dangerous" for a foreseeable use); Gregory v. Cincinnati, Inc., 538 N.W.2d 325 (Mich. 1995); Graham v. Pittsburgh Corning Corp., 593 A.2d 567, 571 (Del. Super. Ct. 1990) (warnings; duty based on conduct of manufacturer of reasonable prudence).

**9.** The law of warranty, which in early English times appears to have arisen out of the tort law action of deceit, preceded the development of assumpsit and contract law. See Ames, The History of Assumpsit, 2 Harv. L. Rev. 1, 8 (1888). Beginning with Stuart v. Wilkins, 1 Dougl. 18 Eng. Rep. 15 (1778), warranty law was increasingly absorbed into the branch of contract law dealing with the law of sales. See Prosser, The

Implied Warranty of Merchantable Quality, 27 Minn. L. Rev. 117, 118–22 (1943). Nevertheless, a good number of courts throughout the nineteenth and twentieth centuries continued to apply a special, tort-like warranty of quality to the sale of food. See, e.g., Van Bracklin v. Fonda, 12 Johns. 468, 468, (N.Y. 1815) (Blackstone states that, in sales of foodstuffs, "it is always implied that they are wholesome; and if they are not, case lies to recover damages for the deceit"); Jacob E. Decker & Sons v. Capps, 164 S.W.2d 828 (Tex. 1942). See generally Prosser, The Assault on the Citadel (Strict Liability to the Consumer), 69 Yale L.J. 1099, 1103–10 (1960). Several courts in the late 1950s expanded the "tort" food warranty to sales of pet food and products for intimate bodily use, and this development lay the foundation for the extension of the tort warranty to durable products and for its transformation in the early 1960s into the doctrine of strict products liability in tort. See § 5.2, below.

**10.** The Uniform Sales Act, patterned after the British Sales of Goods Act, was written by Samuel Williston. D. Nelson and J. Howicz, 1 Williston on Sales § 1–5, at 6 (5th ed. 1994) (hereinafter 1 Williston on Sales). Pertinent provisions of both acts, together with their sources from Justinian's Digest, are set forth in F. de Zulueta, The Roman Law of Sale—Introduction and Select Texts, pt. II at 61 et. seq. (corr. 1st ed. 1945).

adopted across the United States during the late 1950s and the 1960s, supplanted the Uniform Sales Act.[11] Thus, the modern products liability law of warranty generally concerns the interpretation and application of various sections of UCC Article 2.[12] In 2002, after nearly two decades of travail, the National Conference of Commissioners on Uniform State Laws finally adopted a revision of Article 2 of the Uniform Commercial Code and, in 2003, the American Law Institute added its endorsement to their joint revision project.[13] Yet, adoption by state legislatures will surely take a number of years, as was true with the UCC which took about a decade for its adoption nationwide during the 1950s and 1960s.[14] In the meantime, courts will continue to apply the current provisions of UCC Article 2 to products liability warranty cases as they have since the 1960s.

There is substantial overlap, but also considerable difference, between products liability law in tort and in warranty under the UCC.[15] Claims for breach of express warranty under UCC § 2–313 are similar in many respects to strict liability claims for product misrepresentation under *Restatement (Second) of Torts* § 402B;[16] also, claims for breach of the implied warranty of merchantability under UCC § 2–314 are cousin,

**11.** In 1940, the idea of a uniform commercial code was conceived, overseen by a joint Editorial Board of the National Conference of Commissioners on Uniform State Laws and the American Law Institute. Judge Herbert Goodrich (Chairman), Professor Karl Llewellyn (Chief Reporter), Professor Soia Mentschikoff (Associate Chief Reporter), and numerous committees began work on the Code, unofficially in 1942 and officially in 1945. A final first draft appeared four years later, the "1949 Official Text," comprised of nine articles with notes and comments. This draft was substantially critiqued and debated, resulting in a revised 1952 edition, enacted by Pennsylvania in 1953 to take effect in 1954. The several other states into whose legislatures this version of the Code was introduced referred it to study commissions, notably the New York Law Review Commission. The Editorial Board studied the critiques of various state commissions and offered a new version of the Code in late 1956, the "1957 Official Text," which was enacted by Massachusetts in 1957 and Kentucky in 1958, after which a further revised "1958 Official Text" was successively enacted in Connecticut, New Hampshire, Rhode Island, Wyoming, Arkansas, New Mexico, Ohio, Oregon, Oklahoma, Illinois, New Jersey, Georgia, Alaska, New York, Michigan, and Pennsylvania (which substituted the 1958 version for the original version). Thereafter, because of the large number of individual state amendments, a newly constituted Permanent Editorial Board promulgated a revised "1962 Official Text," the version (as amended in 1966) which the

other states subsequently enacted. See generally, 1 Uniform Laws Annotated xv-xl (2004); 1 Williston on Sales § 1–5.

**12.** As examined below, the warranties generally at issue in products liability litigation are UCC § 2–313 (express warranties), UCC § 2–314 (implied warranties of merchantability), and, occasionally, UCC § 2–315 (implied warranties of fitness for particular purpose). For a case reviewing the applicability of each of these three warranties to a defective automobile airbag claim, see Sipes v. General Motors Corp., 946 S.W.2d 143, 157–59 (Tex. App. 1997).

**13.** The revision was a joint project of the National Conference of Commissioners on Uniform State Laws (NCCUSL) and The American Law Institute (ALI). See 25 ALI Reporter 1 (Summer 2003). For a description of the revisions (called "amendments"), see Rusch, Is the Saga of the Uniform Commercial Code Article 2 Revisions Over? A Brief Look at What NCCUSL Finally Approved, 6 Del. L. Rev. 41 (2003).

**14.** The UCC, as approved in 1952 and revised in 1958 (and further revised in 1962 and 1966) was first adopted in Pennsylvania in 1953, Massachusetts in 1957, Kentucky in 1958, and Connecticut and New Hampshire in 1959, and it was last adopted in Arizona and Idaho in 1967, and Louisiana (selected articles, *not* including Article 2) in 1974. See 1 UCC 1 (Master ed. cum. ann. pocket pt. 2004).

**15.** For a comparison of UCC § 2–313 and Restatement (2d) Torts § 402B, see § 4.2, below.

**16.** See § 3.4, above.

if not sister, theories of recovery to claims for the sale of defective products under § 402A of the *Restatement (Second) of Torts*.[17] Because of the fundamental similarities in these separate claims under the UCC and in tort, a plaintiff's lawyer contemplating the applicability of one such products liability theory of recovery almost invariably should examine the possible applicability of the other, at least as a matter of initial consideration.

Tort and warranty claims, however, possess a variety of important distinctions. Warranty claims often are restricted by contract law limitations, such as privity, disclaimers, limitations on remedies, and notice. But the Code's uniform statute of limitations is a generous four years (normally from the date of sale),[18] which is longer than typical tort statutes of limitations of two or three (or, as in California, one) years (normally from the date when the injury or claim should have been discovered). In addition, as discussed below, § 402B is drafted more narrowly in certain respects than is UCC § 2–313,[19] and, at least in New York, an implied warranty of merchantability claim may lie in circumstances where a § 402A claim does not.[20] Finally, defenses based upon user misconduct (and, to a lesser extent, third party misconduct) may vary between actions brought in tort and those brought in contract under Article 2 of the UCC.[21]

This chapter separately examines the major topics of Article 2 of the Uniform Commercial Code applicable to products liability cases. First considered are each of the three applicable warranties—express warranties, under UCC § 2–313; implied warranties of merchantability, under UCC § 2–314; and implied warranties of fitness for particular purpose, under UCC § 2–315. Next examined is the issue of privity of contract, under UCC § 2–318, which concerns the question of which parties other than the buyer are able to benefit from a seller's breach of warranty. The buyer's obligation to promptly notify the seller of a breach of warranty, under UCC § 2–607, is then briefly explored. Next considered is the seller's ability contractually to avoid warranty responsibility by disclaimers, under UCC § 2–316, and to limit damages for breach of warranty, under UCC § 2–719. Then examined are the various warranty reform measures designed to protect consumers from unfair and unbargained-for disclaimers—both under state law and the Magnuson–Moss Federal Warranty Act. Throughout, the recent amendments to Article 2, while not yet the law in any jurisdiction, are addressed as appropriate.

**17.** See § 5.3, below.

**18.** UCC § 2–725. The limitations period may exceed four years if the warranty extends to future performance, in which case the claim accrues when the breach is or should have been discovered. Weiss v. Herman, 597 N.Y.S.2d 52 (App. Div. 1993) (breast implants); Nationwide Ins. Co. v. General Motors Corp., 625 A.2d 1172 (Pa. 1993) (automobile manufacturer's 12–month/12,000–mile warranty).

**19.** See § 4.2, below.

**20.** Denny v. Ford Motor Co., 662 N.E.2d 730 (N.Y. 1995) (manufacturer of SUV not strictly liable where design necessary for vehicle's off-road capability increased its tendency to roll over during highway use; but manufacturer did breach implied warranty of merchantability where vehicle was advertised for general highway and family use). *Denny* is examined in § 5.9, below.

**21.** See chapter 13, below.

## § 4.2 EXPRESS WARRANTY

Express warranties are affirmative assertions, made by a seller in connection with a sales transaction, that a product possesses certain characteristics of quality, construction, performance capability, durability, or safety. This form of warranty is predicated on a seller's provision of information about a product, by words or other means of communication, rather than any inherent characteristic of the product itself. Hence, as with tortious misrepresentation,[1] claims for breach of express warranty rest on the falsity of such information rather than any deficiency in the product itself. Stated otherwise, a plaintiff need not prove that a product was "defective," or that the seller was at fault, to prove that the seller made and breached an express warranty.[2]

Such warranties may be written, oral,[3] or communicated by some other means and, as discussed below, they generally must precede or accompany the sale. Legal responsibility follows from breach of an express warranty because the manufacturer or other seller[4] is deemed to have assumed responsibility for the harmful consequences of false representations made to consumers in an effort to sell the product.[5] For centuries, law and custom have provided a remedy if a seller fractures a buyer's "frame of reference" and equal freedom interests by a false claim of product quality that causes injury to the buyer.[6]

### § 4.2

**1.** See § 3.1, above.

**2.** See, e.g., Austin v. Will–Burt Co., 232 F.Supp.2d 682, 687 (N.D. Miss. 2002) (fault unnecessary to establish breach), aff'd, 361 F.3d 862 (5th Cir. 2004); Bell Sports, Inc. v. Yarusso 759 A.2d 582, 594 (Del. 2000) (jury could find motorcycle helmet manufacturer made and breached express warranty while also finding that helmet was not defective and manufacturer was not negligent); McCarty v. E.J. Korvette, Inc., 347 A.2d 253, 264 (Md. Ct. Spec. App. 1975) ("no 'defect' other than a failure to conform to the warrantor's representations need be shown in order to establish a breach of an express warranty"). Courts sometimes loosely refer to the breach of an express warranty as a kind of "defect," an unfelicitous linguistic practice. See, e.g., *McCarty*, above; Genetti v. Caterpillar, Inc., 621 N.W.2d 529, 541 (Neb. 2001) (for breach of express warranty plaintiff "must show, among other things, that 'the goods did not comply with the warranty, that is, that they were defective,'" such that, without evidence "that a defect in a product caused the plaintiff's damages, he or she cannot recover for breach of warranty").

**3.** See, e.g., Paper Mfrs. Co. v. Rescuers, Inc., 60 F.Supp.2d 869, 882–83 (N.D. Ind. 1999) (that ink was suitable for use on label of container of bone cement powder); Crothers v. Cohen, 384 N.W.2d 562 (Minn. Ct. App. 1986) (that used car, which next day went out of control and crashed into a tree, was a "good runner"). See also Connick v. Suzuki Motor Co., 656 N.E.2d 170 (Ill. App. Ct. 1995) (that vehicle, which was subject to rollovers, was safe), rev'd in part on other grounds, 675 N.E.2d 584 (Ill. 1996); Weiss v. Keystone Mack Sales, Inc., 456 A.2d 1009 (Pa. Super. Ct. 1983) (salesman's oral statements concerning truck).

**4.** In addition to bearing responsibility for its own express warranties, a retail seller may also bear responsibility for those of the manufacturer which the retailer "adopts." This principle is treated in § 15.2, below.

**5.** See Huebert v. Federal Pac. Elec. Co., 494 P.2d 1210, 1214 (Kan. 1972) (advertising claims may assure buyers "that the product will operate in a manner on which the purchaser can rely and no injury will occur"). "A manufacturer may by express warranty assume responsibility in connection with its products which extends beyond liability for defects. All express warranties must be reasonably construed taking into consideration the nature of the product, the situation of the parties, and surrounding circumstances." Id. at 1215. Moreover, liability is based on whether the product operates as warranted by the manufacturer, not on whether it is defective. Id.

**6.** See Owen, The Moral Foundations of Products Liability Law: Toward First Principles, 68 Notre Dame L. Rev. 427, 463–65 (1993).

The language or other form of communication is to be fairly interpreted in light of the context of the particular sales transaction. Questions of interpretation—as to whether or not a particular assertion amounted to an express warranty, its scope and meaning, and whether the assertion was true or false—are generally factual questions to be determined by the trier of fact.[7]

Two examples illustrate the inherently factual nature of interpreting communications and ascertaining whether such interpretations are true or false. In *Sylvestri v. Warner & Swasey Co.*,[8] the plaintiff was thrown from the operator's seat of a backhoe manufactured by the defendant. The vehicle tipped when its stabilizing outriggers shifted while it was being used to lift boulders and swing them around to different locations. An advertising brochure showed the backhoe lifting a length of pipe and stated that the "hydraulic system provides powerful lift force for material handling."[9] Upholding a verdict for the plaintiff for breach of express warranty, the court remarked: "While Sylvestri apparently did not attach the rock to the backhoe in exactly the same manner that the pipe was attached in the brochure picture, and while lifting rock may in some way be different from lifting pipe, [the jury was properly left to] determine . . . whether the brochure picture and statements as a whole represented an affirmation of fact or promise that the machine could be used as Sylvestri used it. It is the 'essential idea' conveyed by the advertising representations which is relevant. . . ."[10]

In contrast is *Salk v. Alpine Ski Shop, Inc.*,[11] where the court denied the plaintiff's express warranty claim. There, a skier who broke his leg when his ski bindings failed to release sued the bindings manufacturer for breach of express warranty for advertisements which stated: "Cubco is the precise binding . . . that releases when it's supposed to. . . . Both heel and toe release at the exact tension you set. And release whichever way you fall."[12] Stating that, to be liable, Cubco would have had to state that its bindings "would release in every situation presenting a danger

---

**7.** See, e.g., Bell Sports, Inc. v. Yarusso, 759 A.2d 582, 593 (Del. 2000) (jury properly could conclude that statements that motorcycle helmet was designed "to reduce the harmful effects of a blow to the head" and to absorb and spread the force of a blow to the head as much as possible were express warranty to motorcyclist who suffered neck injury and paralysis from blow to helmet, notwithstanding warning that helmets cannot protect against all impacts); Husky Spray Service, Inc. v. Patzer, 471 N.W.2d 146, 150 (S.D. 1991) (airplane "is ready to go"; "You can get in it and go to work."); Yuzwak v. Dygert, 534 N.Y.S.2d 35 (App. Div. 1988) (representation that horse, which kicked plaintiff's daughter in face while she was leading it to barn, was good for children).

If a term is susceptible to two meanings, its interpretation ordinarily is a question for the finder of fact. See McLaughlin v.

Denharco, Inc., 129 F.Supp.2d 32, 38 (D. Me. 2001) (whether ambiguous affirmation was express warranty for jury). In Bud Wolf Chevrolet, Inc. v. Robertson, 496 N.E.2d 771 (Ind. Ct. App. 1986), modified on other grounds, 508 N.E.2d 567 (Ind. Ct. App. 1987), vacated in part on other grounds, 519 N.E.2d 135 (Ind. 1988), a truck sold as "new" had been previously damaged on the lot. "Although . . . the evidence is susceptible to reasonably differing interpretations, the jury could have inferred that the truck . . . was not 'new' as the term is commonly understood by the general public. . . ." Id. at 775–76.

**8.** 398 F.2d 598 (2d Cir. 1968) (N.Y. law).

**9.** Id. at 602.

**10.** Id. (footnote and citations omitted).

**11.** 342 A.2d 622 (R.I. 1975).

**12.** Id. at 626.

to the user's limbs," the court noted that the defendant's advertising fell short of such a "blanket guarantee." Trial had revealed that the Cubco multi-directional release bindings could be adjusted to release at varying tensions and that no binding could be set to release during slow falls yet also be set not to release during normal skiing operations. The court concluded that the defendant's advertisements had done no more than affirm these uncontroverted facts.[13] Many other cases similarly demonstrate the preliminary importance in express warranty litigation of interpreting the meaning, scope, and truth or falsity of the defendant's representations alleged to comprise a warranty.[14]

### Manner of Communication

There is no determinative manner by which an express warranty must be created,[15] and such a warranty may arise from any affirmative means by which information is conveyed. Thus, an express warranty may arise from statements on a product's packaging or label,[16] a seller's assurances to a buyer's pilots that a used plane is "ready to go,"[17] a sales clerk's assertion that a pressure cooker would not explode,[18] a label on a can of chicken stating "Boned Chicken" read in conjunction with newspaper advertisements representing that the chicken contained "No Bones,"[19] or an "off" designation for a control handle on an electrical panel which was alive with current.[20] Advertisements, catalogues, and circulars containing statements of fact may be interpreted as creating express warranties.[21] Statements contained in a Dear Doctor letter[22] or

**13.** Id.

**14.** See, e.g., Beyette v. Ortho Pharm. Corp., 823 F.2d 990 (6th Cir. 1987) (Mich. law) (IUD manufacturer's representations as to (1) estimate of pelvic inflammatory disease rate, and (2) statement that more than one million women had used IUDs successfully; *held*, no recovery for such disease: first representation was merely a future prediction, and second was true, not a warranty of risk-free use); Whitmer v. Schneble, 331 N.E.2d 115, 118 (Ill. App. Ct. 1975) (female Doberman Pinscher, represented by sellers to be "docile," bit child viewing dog's new puppies 2½ years after sale; *held*, no recovery: "Even a docile dog is known and expected to bite under certain circumstances"; moreover, statement pertained to dog's personality at time of sale and did not mean that its personality could not change); Whittington v. Eli Lilly & Co., 333 F.Supp. 98 (S.D. W. Va. 1971) (birth control pills said to "offer virtually 100% protection" in fact offered 98.1% protection; *held*, no promise of *absolute* protection).

**15.** In particular, the formation of an express warranty does not require the use of magic words such as "warranty" or "guarantee." UCC § 2–313(2). See Cipollone v. Liggett Group, Inc., 893 F.2d 541 (3d Cir. 1990), rev'd in part on other grounds, 505 U.S. 504 (1992).

**16.** See, e.g., Michael v. Shiley, Inc., 46 F.3d 1316, 1321 (3d Cir. 1995) (Pa. law) (packaging label for artificial heart valve stating that "reasonable care ha[d] been used in manufactur[ing]").

**17.** Husky Spray Service, Inc. v. Patzer, 471 N.W.2d 146 (S.D. 1991).

**18.** Joseph v. Sears Roebuck & Co., 77 S.E.2d 583 (S.C. 1953).

**19.** Lane v. C.A. Swanson & Sons, 278 P.2d 723 (Cal. Ct. App. 1955).

**20.** Huebert v. Federal Pac. Elec. Co., 494 P.2d 1210 (Kan. 1972).

**21.** See, e.g., Imperia v. Marvin Windows of N.Y., Inc., 747 N.Y.S.2d 35, 37 (App. Div. 2002) (product literature can create express warranty); Duvall v. Bristol–Myers–Squibb Co., 103 F.3d 324 (4th Cir. 1996) (Md. law) (express warranty claims based on statements in advertising brochure for penile prosthesis not preempted by federal law); Connick v. Suzuki Motor Co., 656 N.E.2d 170 (Ill. App. Ct. 1995) (express warranties may be created by representations in documents, brochures, and advertisements), aff'd in part and rev'd in part on other grounds, 675 N.E.2d 584 (Ill. 1996); Huebert v. Federal Pac. Elec. Co., 494 P.2d 1210 (Kan. 1972) (advertisements).

**22.** See, e.g., Friedman v. Medtronic, Inc., 345 N.Y.S.2d 637 (App. Div. 1973) (expert testimony required to establish

package insert,[23] and even an assurance that a blood provider had exercised "utmost care" in donor selection on a container which also expressly rejected any warranty against the danger of infection,[24] have all been held to create express warranties.

In addition to the more common forms of representations in advertisements, labels, and brochures, express warranties have been found to be created by pamphlets and circulars,[25] owners manuals,[26] specification sheets,[27] and tags attached to products.[28] Express warranties need not be in words, for a description of an article may be pictoral,[29] or presented by blueprint, technical specifications,[30] samples, models, or even by past deliveries which have set a standard that fairly may be considered a description of the article.[31] General representations of safety may support an express warranty action,[32] as may generalized guarantees.[33] But a claim for breach of express warranty asserts a communicative wrong, such that it requires a plaintiff to plead and prove that the defendant affirmatively conveyed information by words or other express form of affirmation, without which such a claim collapses and will be dismissed.[34]

meaning doctors would attach to representations in promotional letter).

**23.** See, e.g., Rosci v. AcroMed, Inc., 669 A.2d 959 (Pa. Super. Ct. 1995).

**24.** Jackson v. Muhlenberg Hospital, 232 A.2d 879 (N.J. Super. Ct. 1967), rev'd on other grounds, 249 A.2d 65 (N.J. 1969).

**25.** See, e.g., Smith v. Gates Rubber Co., 47 Cal.Rptr. 307 (1965).

**26.** See, e.g., Bell Sports, Inc. v. Yarusso, 759 A.2d 582, 593 (Del. 2000).

**27.** See, e.g., Huebert v. Federal Pac. Elec. Co., 494 P.2d 1210 (Kan. 1972) (electrician's action against manufacturer of electrical panel boards).

**28.** See, e.g., Pegasus Helicopters, Inc. v. United Techs. Corp., 35 F.3d 507 (10th Cir. 1994) (Colo. law) (aircraft part repaired by manufacturer carried tag stating that part conformed to original specifications).

**29.** See, e.g., McLaughlin v. Denharco, Inc., 129 F.Supp.2d 32, 39 (D. Me. 2001) (statements in promotional videos); Sylvestri v. Warner & Swasey Co., 398 F.2d 598 (2d Cir. 1968) (N.Y. law). *But see* Maneely v. General Motors Corp., 108 F.3d 1176 (9th Cir. 1997) (Cal. law) (television and print ads showing young people standing and sitting in open cargo bed of pickup trucks, where most portrayals were of stationary trucks without a driver, did not create express warranty that it was safe to ride in trucks in this manner).

**30.** See, e.g., Sullivan v. Young Bros. & Co., 91 F.3d 242 (1st Cir. 1996) (Me. law) (express warranty created by manufacturer's product specification sheet accompanying fiberglass tubing used in lobster boat's exhaust system).

**31.** See UCC § 2–313 cmt. 5; Unicomp, Inc. v. Elementis Pigments, Inc., 1999 WL 1995400, at *15 (D. Me. 1999) (" 'Past deliveries may set the description of quality, either expressly or impliedly by course of dealing.' ").

**32.** See, e.g., Carlin v. Superior Ct., 38 Cal.Rptr.2d 576 (Ct. App. 1995); Cipollone v. Liggett Group, Inc., 893 F.2d 541 (3d Cir. 1990), rev'd in part on other grounds, 505 U.S. 504 (1992) (advertisements that long-term smoking of defendant's cigarettes would not endanger smoker's health); Drayton v. Jiffee Chem. Corp., 395 F.Supp. 1081 (N.D. Ohio 1975), modified on other grounds, 591 F.2d 352 (6th Cir. 1978) (advertising claims that particularly caustic drain cleaner was safe for household use).

**33.** Jones v. Cranman's Sporting Goods, 237 S.E.2d 402 (Ga. Ct. App. 1977) (explosion of "fully guaranteed" rifle). While an express warranty may state generally that a product "is merchantable" or that it "will fit the buyer's particular needs," such general warranties usually add nothing of substance to the implied warranties that normally arise by operation of law. See, e.g., Freeman v. Hoffman–La Roche, Inc., 618 N.W.2d 827, 844 (Neb. 2000).

**34.** See, e.g., Pulte Home Corp. v. Parex, Inc., 579 S.E.2d 188, 190–91 (Va. 2003); Schneidman v. Whitaker Co., 758 N.Y.S.2d 142 (App. Div. 2003) (express warranty claim properly dismissed because plaintiff failed to present evidence that defendant made any specific statement of fact); Thongchoom v. Graco Children's Prods., Inc., 71 P.3d 214, 219 (Wash. Ct. App. 2003) (express warranty claim failed where no proof of representation); Anthony v. Country Life Mfg., LLC, 70 Fed. Appx. 379, 383 (7th Cir. 2003) (Ill. law) ("While an express warranty need not be formed by words,

### Uniform Commercial Code § 2–313

The Uniform Commercial Code addresses the creation of express warranties in § 2–313, which provides:

> § 2–313. Express Warranties by Affirmation, Promise, Description, Sample.
>
> (1) Express warranties by the seller are created as follows:
>
> (a) Any affirmation of fact or promise made by the seller to the buyer which relates to the goods and becomes part of the basis of the bargain creates an express warranty that the goods shall conform to the affirmation or promise.
>
> (b) Any description of the goods which is made part of the basis of the bargain creates an express warranty that the goods shall conform to the description.
>
> (c) Any sample or model which is made part of the basis of the bargain creates an express warranty that the whole of the goods shall conform to the sample or model.
>
> (2) It is not necessary to the creation of an express warranty that the seller use formal words such as "warrant" or "guarantee" or that he have a specific intention to make a warranty, but an affirmation merely of the value of the goods or a statement purporting to be merely the seller's opinion or commendation of the goods does not create a warranty.

### Compared to Strict Liability in Tort for Misrepresentation

The cause of action for breach of an express warranty under UCC § 2–313 is closely similar to that for misrepresentation under *Restatement (Second) of Torts* § 402B.[35] A seller makes an express warranty under UCC § 2–313 by "[a]ny affirmation of fact or promise" or by "[a]ny description of the goods." *Restatement (Second) of Torts* § 402B, in turn, provides a similar cause of action for "a misrepresentation of a material fact concerning the character or quality" of the product. Both causes of action require the plaintiff to prove the representation was made and that it was false, and both impose a form of "strict" liability upon the seller which requires no showing of fault.[36]

Express warranty claims under the Code do differ in certain material respects from misrepresentation claims under § 402B of the *Torts*

there must nonetheless be some affirmation."); Johnson v. Brown & Williamson Tobacco Corp., 122 F.Supp.2d 194, 206 (D. Mass. 2000); Wajda v. R.J. Reynolds Tobacco Co., 103 F.Supp.2d 29 (D. Mass. 2000) ("The plaintiff at no point pleads the existence of anything remotely resembling an express warranty. No affirmation of fact or promise is ever mentioned or even proposed to exist.").

**35.** Strict liability in tort for product misrepresentation, under Restatement (2d) Torts § 402B, is treated in § 3.4, above.

**36.** It is axiomatic that breach of express warranty requires no showing of fault and thus is truly "strict" liability. Moreover, "no 'defect' other than a failure to conform to the warrantor's representations need be shown in order to establish a breach of an express warranty." Voelkel v. General Motors Corp., 846 F.Supp. 1468, 1476 (D. Kan. 1994) (seatbelt buckle described as "trouble-free, safe"); McCarty v. E.J. Korvette, Inc., 347 A.2d 253, 264 (Md. Ct. Spec. App. 1975) (tire guaranteed against blowouts).

*Restatement*, which is drawn more narrowly than UCC § 2–313. Under the *Restatement (Second) Torts* § 402B, a plaintiff must establish actual reliance by himself or by the purchaser,[37] whereas an express warranty claimant under the Code may be entitled to a presumption that he relied upon seller representations which became "part of the basis of the bargain."[38] Section 402B is generally deemed to apply only to public forms of representation, such as in advertising and manuals accompanying the product, whereas UCC § 2–313 express warranties apply as well to private misrepresentations between individual sales clerks and customers. Further, § 402B by its terms applies only to merchants "engaged in the business of selling chattels," whereas UCC § 2–313 (in contrast to UCC § 2–314) applies more widely to merchant and nonmerchant sellers alike. In addition, § 402B applies only to representations of "material" fact, whereas UCC § 2–313 claimants in some situations might be able to show that ordinarily trivial words became part of the basis of a particular bargain. Moreover, UCC § 2–313 allows recovery of all types of damages available under Article 2, including pure economic loss,[39] whereas § 402B provides for recovery only of "physical harm." Finally, it is important to note that warranty claims under the Uniform Commercial Code are controlled by a very different set of doctrines that concern a large variety of secondary issues, such as the requirements of privity of contract and notice of breach, statutes of limitations, special defenses based on disclaimers and limitations of remedy, user misconduct, and the non-availability of punitive damages, to name a few.

### Representations of Fact *vs.* Opinion and "Puffs"

To create an express warranty, a seller's affirmation ordinarily must be one of fact, which is to say that such a statement must convey more information than simply the seller's opinion of the product's worth. In the course of selling products to consumers, sellers often make exaggerated statements of opinion acclaiming their products' virtues, a form of salesmanship consumers generally recognize as devoid of content. Such embellished claims of product value have long and widely been dubbed mere "puffing." Even to the extent that such hollow commendations of value and quality may be true, they ordinarily contain no content other than, at best, an expression of the seller's subjective and inflated perception of the product's worth. Reasonable buyers generally recognize such puffs merely as sales pitch, designed to bend the buyer's will and encourage a sale.[40] A representation is likely to be construed as fact, on the other hand, when it describes certain specific traits of quality, construction, performance capability, durability, or safety possessed by the product, known to the seller but not to the buyer, which communi-

---

**37.** Section 402B states explicitly that the claimed harm must have been caused by "justifiable reliance."

**38.** See UCC § 2–313 cmt. 3 ("no particular reliance on such statements need be shown in order to weave them into the fabric of the agreement"). The "basis of the bargain" requirement in UCC § 2–313 is further discussed below.

**39.** See UCC §§ 2–714 and 2–715.

**40.** See, e.g., Chic Promotion v. Middletown Sec. Sys., Inc., 688 N.E.2d 278, 282 (Ohio Ct. App. 1996) (general assertions in sales brochure "did not cross the line from puffing to warranty"; brochure was deemed a pre-sale inducement "which is the very purpose of advertising").

cates a message of real value on which a prospective buyer may justifiably be expected to rely.[41]

Section 2–313(1)(a) of the Uniform Commercial Code states that express warranties are created by "[a]ny affirmation of fact." Section 2–313(2) further provides in part that "an affirmation merely of the value of the goods or a statement purporting to be merely the seller's opinion or commendation of the goods does not create a warranty." However, the "purporting to be" language suggests that the fact/opinion distinction in § 2–313 is intended to be read narrowly, such that commendations which purport to have some factual basis may be made part of the basis of a bargain, a suggestion reinforced by comment 8 to this section.[42]

If the information communicated is specific, technically based, and clearly important to the buyer ("this crane can support loads up to 20,000 pounds") or is, by contrast, highly vague praise ("this used car is terrific"), one may conclude with some confidence that the statement should be deemed a fact (as in the first example) or an opinion (as in the second). But many cases involve assertions much closer to the middle, where it is exceedingly difficult to isolate clear principles for determining whether a particular representation should be classified as fact or opinion. In such cases, the fact/opinion determination rests not only on the words at issue but also on a host of other considerations concerning the parties, including their corporate or personal identities, the nature of any pre-existing relationship they may have had, their respective power, their knowledge of and ability to discover information related to the matter asserted, their likely expectations, their actions and statements surrounding the transaction, and many other factors.[43] In such a murky sea, predicting whether a particular statement will be construed as fact or opinion is risky business, to say the least, particularly now that many courts have turned away from continuing to expand consumer rights. "Only a foolish lawyer will be quick to label a seller's statement as puffs or not puffs, and only a reckless one will label a seller's statement at all without carefully examining such factors as the nature of the defect (was it obvious or not) and the buyer's and seller's relative knowledge."[44]

---

**41.** See, e.g., Bobb Forest Prods., Inc. v. Morbark Indus., Inc., 783 N.E.2d 560, 574–75 (Ohio Ct. App. 2002); Scott v. Illinois Tool Works, Inc., 550 N.W.2d 809 (Mich. Ct. App. 1996) (breaking strength of 800 pounds).

**42.** UCC § 2–313 cmt. 8 provides in part:

Concerning affirmations of value or a seller's opinion or commendation under subsection (2), the basic question remains the same: What statements of the seller have in the circumstances and in objective judgment become part of the basis of the bargain? As indicated above, all of the statements of the seller do so unless good reason is shown to the contrary. The provisions of subsection (2) are included, however, since common experience discloses that some statements or predic-

tions cannot fairly be viewed as entering into the bargain.

**43.** "Certainly the specificity of the statement is important" and "[c]ertainly a written statement is less likely to pass as a puff than an oral one, and a written statement in the contract of the parties is less likely to pass as a puff than a written statement in an advertisement." White and Summers, UCC § 9–4, at 347–349. Other factors of importance include all aspects of the "context" in which the words are spoken, the reasonableness of the plaintiff's reliance, and whether the seller hedges in making the representation. Id. at 349–350. See Federal Signal Corp. v. Safety Factors, Inc., 886 P.2d 172 (Wash. 1994) (outlining relevant factors).

**44.** White and Summers, UCC § 9–4 at 348. See also R. Nordstrom, The Law of

Seller representations that are specific and unambiguous, particularly if they concern the safety of the product, are likely to be construed as factual. Thus, express warranties have been found to be created by an "off" designation on a high-voltage electrical panel switch;[45] an advertisement that a skin cream was "safe";[46] a tire manufacturer's advertisement, "If it saves your life once, it's a bargain," where plaintiff's decedent was killed when his tire blew out;[47] a booklet accompanying a steam vaporizer stating that it was safe to be used all night and featuring a picture of the appliance in use near a baby's crib, where a toddler was badly burned when the vaporizer overturned;[48] representations that a tree hunting stand was "probably the safest one on the market" and "there is no way [one] can fall" from it, where the plaintiff did;[49] a nightclub server's statement that the club's special drink that night was "good," where the plaintiffs were mistakenly served glasses of dishwashing liquid containing highly toxic lye;[50] statements in the owner's manual for an off-road motorcycle helmet that "the primary function of a helmet is to reduce the harmful effects of a blow to the head," where a rider's neck was injured when he was thrown from his motorcycle and struck his head;[51] and a representation that a Golfing Gizmo training device was "Completely Safe—Ball Will Not Hit Player," where a boy hit beneath the ball, catching the attached cord and causing the ball to fly back and hit him in the head—as opposed to another statement by the manufacturer that practice with the Gizmo could permit the user to challenge Jack Nicklaus.[52]

In contrast to such specific factual assertions, a seller's vague and general representations which appear merely to express the seller's personal views on a product's characteristics, worth, or quality, do not ordinarily constitute material facts. Such statements of seller opinion are known as "puffs." An illustrative case in which the statements were held to be only the seller's opinion or commendation about a product, and thus insufficient to create an express warranty, is *Carpenter v. Alberto*

Sales 219 (1970) ("In one sense, every statement made by a seller is nothing more than his opinion as to the goods or how the goods will operate; yet at some point he makes his statement in a manner and under such conditions that the buyer does not understand that *only* this seller's opinion is involved."). Compare Carney v. Sears, Roebuck & Co., 309 F.2d 300 (4th Cir. 1962) (Va. law) ("good quality ladder"; *held,* opinion), with Turner v. Central Hardware Co., 186 S.W.2d 603, 606 (Mo. 1945) (ladder "mighty strong and durable"; *held,* fact: "the seller's protection lies in the fact that his is the choice of language and action"). Compare also Jenkins v. Landmark Chevrolet, Inc., 575 So.2d 1157 (Ala. Civ. App. 1991) (used car "in good shape"; *held,* puff), with Jones v. Kellner, 451 N.E.2d 548, 550 (Ohio Ct. App. 1982) (used car "mechanically A–1"; *held,* fact) ("although it was unclear how long this warranty would have lasted, it should have lasted at least long enough for the appellee to get the car home").

**45.** Huebert v. Federal Pac. Elec. Co., 494 P.2d 1210 (Kan. 1972).

**46.** Spiegel v. Saks 34th St., 252 N.Y.S.2d 852 (1964), aff'd, 272 N.Y.S.2d 972 (App. Div. 1966) ("[T]he warranty was *express,* that the [skin cream] was 'safe' for anyone who purchased it; the warranty in effect stated that ... there would be no allergic reaction.").

**47.** Collins v. Uniroyal, Inc., 315 A.2d 16 (N.J. 1974).

**48.** McCormack v. Hankscraft Co., 154 N.W.2d 488 (Minn. 1967).

**49.** Moore v. Berry, 458 S.E.2d 879, 880 (Ga. Ct. App. 1995).

**50.** Cott v. Peppermint Twist Mgmt. Co., 856 P.2d 906 (Kan. 1993).

**51.** Bell Sports, Inc. v. Yarusso, 759 A.2d 582, 593 (Del. 2000).

**52.** Hauter v. Zogarts, 534 P.2d 377, 379 (Cal. 1975).

*Culver Co.*,[53] where the plaintiff suffered an adverse skin reaction from hair dye. The selling clerk had assured the plaintiff that she, the clerk, had used the same product; that her own hair came out "very nice" and "very natural"; and that the plaintiff "would get very fine results." Concluding that the sales clerk's statement was puffing and not a representation of fact creating an express warranty, the court noted the importance of considering whether the seller "assumes to assert a fact of which the buyer is ignorant, or merely states an opinion or judgment upon a matter of which the seller has no special knowledge, and on which the buyer may be expected also to have an opinion and to exercise his judgment."[54]

A seller's commendations of its product's worth ordinarily are merely puffs intended to enhance the product's attractiveness for prospective buyers rather than to assert a fact. So, statements that a Suzuki Samurai "never lets you down," has "fun written all over it," and is "nifty,"[55] are the kind of loose and general "sales talk" that should be viewed as puffing rather than as an affirmation of fact that the vehicle was not prone to roll over.[56] Other examples of statements held to be puffery rather than factual include claims that a truck, the roof of which collapsed after it fell nearly 30 feet, was "rock-solid" and its roof was "strong";[57] that an automotive manufacturer believed that "Quality is job one";[58] that a used car was in good shape;[59] that a fondue pot, which tipped over and burned a young child caught in its cord, was the "finest product of its kind available" and was "engineered to give [an] extra measure of satisfaction";[60] that computer modeling and laboratory tests resulted in "great road cars," including the plaintiff's which contained a defective seatbelt;[61] that a defective gas heater, that burned down the plaintiffs' house, was from "America's most complete line of reliable, economical gas heating appliances";[62] that heavy equipment tires were good and had been used successfully on prior occasions;[63] that a bungee cord was of "premium quality" and "made in the U.S.A.";[64] and that

**53.** 184 N.W.2d 547 (Mich. Ct. App. 1970).

**54.** Id. at 548.

**55.** Connick v. Suzuki Motor Co., 656 N.E.2d 170, 183 (Ill. App. Ct. 1995), rev'd in part on other grounds, 675 N.E.2d 584 (Ill. 1996) ("Whether you're on the job, or on the town, the Samurai never lets you down.... Nothing else comes close to giving you a better run for your money"; [it is a] "funmobile," with "fun written all over it" and "a million laughs"; "It won't spoil the fun knowing that the Samurai handles differently than any ordinary passenger car"; [it] "has a nifty, go-getter engine, ... and all the goodies of 4–wheel drive.")

**56.** Although the fact/opinion distinction in *Connick* was discussed in the specific context of fraud, the case involved various misrepresentation claims including breach of express warranty to which the fact/opinion discussion would be relevant as well.

**57.** Jordan v. Paccar, Inc., 37 F.3d 1181 (6th Cir. 1994) (Ohio law).

**58.** Martin v. Ford Motor Co., 914 F.Supp. 1449 (S.D. Tex. 1996).

**59.** Jenkins v. Landmark Chevrolet, Inc., 575 So.2d 1157 (Ala. Civ. App. 1991).

**60.** Rock v. Oster Corp., 810 F.Supp. 665, 667 (D. Md. 1991).

**61.** Voelkel v. General Motors Corp., 846 F.Supp. 1482 (D. Kan. 1994).

**62.** Warzynski v. Empire Comfort Sys., Inc., 401 S.E.2d 801, 803 (N.C. Ct. App. 1991).

**63.** McLaughlin v. Michelin Tire Corp., 778 P.2d 59 (Wyo. 1989).

**64.** Anderson v. Bungee Int'l Mfg. Corp., 44 F.Supp.2d 534, 541–42 (S.D.N.Y. 1999).

" 'You meet the nicest people on a Honda' and a Honda bike is a good one for children.''[65]

Ascertaining whether a particular representation is a statement of fact, such that it may create an express warranty, or whether instead it is merely an opinion and puff, is often highly fact-specific. Accordingly, fact/opinion determinations are peculiarly suited for the jury to resolve.[66]

## Basis of the Bargain; Reliance

In order for a seller's affirmation of fact to become an express warranty under Uniform Commercial Code § 2–313(1), it must become "part of the basis of the bargain."[67] The drafters introduced the "basis of the bargain" requirement into § 2–313 to replace the "reliance" requirement contained in its predecessor, § 12 of the Uniform Sales Act. Section 12 stated in part: "Any affirmation of fact or any promise by the seller relating to the goods is an express warranty if the natural tendency of such affirmation or promise is to induce the buyer to purchase the goods, and if the buyer purchases the goods relying thereon."

### *Nature of the Reliance Debate*

During the nineteenth century, warranty law grew out of the tort law misrepresentation action of "deceit."[68] Tortious misrepresentation has always required the plaintiff to prove reliance on the defendant's misrepresentation as a causal link between the defendant's false statement and the plaintiff's harm.[69] By contrast, under traditional contract

**65.** Federal Signal Corp. v. Safety Factors, Inc., 886 P.2d 172, 179 (Wash. 1994), citing Baughn v. Honda Motor Co., 727 P.2d 655 (Wash. 1986).

**66.** See, e.g., McLaughlin v. Denharco, Inc., 129 F.Supp.2d 32, 38–39 (D. Me. 2001); Yuzwak v. Dygert, 534 N.Y.S.2d 35 (App. Div. 1988) (horse, that kicked plaintiff's daughter in face, was said to be good for children; whether statement was fact or opinion was for jury).

**67.** On the role of the "basis of the bargain" requirement in UCC § 2–313, and the extent to which reliance may be required to create an express warranty under this section of the Code, see White, Freeing the Tortious Soul of Express Warranty Law, 72 Tul. L. Rev. 2089 (1998) (thorough review, analysis, and classification of all cases decided between 1965 and 1998, citing journal literature on the basis of the bargain requirement at 2096 n.21).

**68.** Although now frequently forgotten, tort law's paternity of warranty law has long been acknowledged by scholars of contract and commercial law as well as the law of torts. See S. Williston, The Law Governing Sales of Goods at Common Law and Under the Uniform Sales Act 251 (1909): "[T]he action upon a warranty was in its origin a pure action of tort ... [and its tortious character] was recognized by

Blackstone, [a perspective that] has been lost sight of by some courts...." See also White, 72 Tul. L. Rev. at 2111, noting that "[w]arranty law started as tort but progressively, from sometime in the nineteenth century, has moved step-by-step from tort to contract," deducing from the decided cases "that there is an irrepressible minimum of tort buried in express warranty," and concluding properly and boldly, for a scholar of contract and commercial law, that "we should let it out."

Tort scholars, of course, have long agreed. See, e.g., Prosser, The Implied Warranty of Merchantable Quality, 27 Minn. L. Rev. 117, 118–19 (1943):

In its inception, breach of warranty was a tort. The action was upon the case, for breach of an assumed duty, and the wrong was conceived to be a form of misrepresentation, in the nature of deceit and not at all clearly distinguished from deceit.... Warranty has never entirely lost this tort character which it had in the beginning; and this may have important consequences at the present day.

**69.** See the discussion of the reliance element in claims for fraud and deceit, § 3.2, above. For a case suggesting that the "basis of the bargain" requirement in § 2–

law doctrine, a contracting party was bound to the terms of a contract whether or not the other party had relied upon them.[70] As express warranty law was absorbed over time into the law of contracts, first into the common law and then into § 12 of the Uniform Sales Act, it carried with it the tort law element of reliance. Karl Llewyllen and other contract law scholars who drafted the UCC, vexed that a major section of sales law was anchored by a concept that belonged to tort,[71] sought to move express warranty doctrine back toward contract law by rejecting "reliance" as a formal element. But the novel phrase selected to replace reliance, "[part of the] basis of the bargain," proved infelicitous, to say the least.[72] Just how the drafters intended the new concept to be interpreted, and the extent to which reliance still might play a role, was left quite unclear.[73] Thus, the basic issue in ascertaining the meaning of "basis of the bargain" in UCC § 2–313 is to determine how that contract-based standard may differ, in varying contexts, from the tort-based notion of reliance.

There are basically two approaches to interpreting the "basis of the bargain" requirement of § 2–313.[74] The first, "strong" interpretation assumes that drafters of Article 2, in switching to the "basis of the bargain" language from "reliance," intended to make a major shift in warranty law, to redirect the focus away from the deal the buyer thought he or she was getting to the deal the seller's affirmations reasonably and objectively appeared to make.[75] This view finds support in comment 4 to UCC § 2–313, which provides, "In view of the principle that the whole purpose of the law of warranty is to determine what it is that the seller has in essence agreed to sell, the policy is adopted of those cases which refuse except in unusual circumstances to recognize a material deletion of the seller's obligation. Thus, a contract is normally a contract for a sale of something describable and described."[76] Simply put, if the seller makes a factual statement about the product, the statement becomes

---

313 serves the same causal linkage function in express warranty doctrine as does reliance in tortious misrepresentation doctrine, see Lowe v. Sporicidin Int'l, 47 F.3d 124, 131–32 (4th Cir. 1995) (Md. law) (plaintiff's misrepresentation and express warranty claims both were deficient because she failed to allege that she had relied on defendant's advertisements or other representations).

**70.** See 1 J. Perillo, Corbin on Contracts § 1.1 (1993 rev. ed.).

**71.** And distraught, perhaps, by the fundamental superiority of tort law to the law of contracts.

**72.** See White, 72 Tul. L. Rev. at 2094–95 and 2106–07.

**73.** In his study of the UCC for the New York Law Revision Commission in 1955, Professor Honnold noted the novelty of the "basis of the bargain" language, opined that its meaning was "less than clear," and suggested that "for lack of any other meaningful standard, courts must employ the test of whether buyer relied on the affirma-

tion or promise, the test presently employed in Section 12 of the Uniform Sales Act." Study of Uniform Commercial Code: Article 2–Sales, reprinted in 1 State of New York Report of The Law Revision Commission for 1955, Study of the Uniform Commercial Code at 355, 392, as cited in White, above, at 2095 n.20.

**74.** Both approaches are well summarized in Hauter v. Zogarts, 534 P.2d 377, 383–84 (Cal. 1975) (the Golfing Gizmo case), from which the textual discussion draws.

**75.** See, e.g., Note, 34 U. Pitt. L. Rev. 145, 150 (1972); R. Nordstrom, Law of Sales §§ 66–68 (1970).

**76.** See also comment 8, which states in part that "the basic question remains the same: What statements of the seller have in the circumstances and in objective judgment become part of the basis of the bargain? As indicated above, all of the statements of the seller do so unless good reason is shown to the contrary."

part of the deal purchased by the buyer, and the seller must stand behind the statement.[77]

The second, "weak" interpretation of "basis of the bargain" postulates that reliance remains an important consideration, although its absence now must be proven by the seller. This conception of § 2–313, that it merely shifts the burden of proving non-reliance to the seller,[78] finds support in comment 3 to UCC § 2–313, which provides that "no particular reliance ... need be shown in order to weave [the seller's affirmations of fact] into the fabric of the agreement. Rather, any fact which is to take such affirmations, once made, out of the agreement requires clear affirmative proof."

Courts and commentators have had enormous difficulty in deciding between these two views.[79] Many courts steer clear of any explicit use of the traditional reliance requirement whatsoever. Perhaps on the theory that the drafters of § 2–313 would not have altered the language of such a fundamental element of express warranty law without a purpose, such courts and commentators might plausibly reason that requiring an affirmation of fact to be part of the basis of a bargain, which sounds in contract, must somehow appreciably differ from requiring the buyer to rely on such an affirmation, which sounds in tort. Abandoning the reliance requirement altogether has some logical appeal, for it holds the seller to the deal the seller thought it was making—a deal which, viewed broadly, might reasonably be deemed to include whatever promises the seller made in an effort to merchandise its product.[80] In pricing its product, a seller might fairly be expected to include as a reserved expense the cost of fulfilling its claims of product description, quality, and performance. So, whether or not the buyer relies upon or even knows about a particular warranty, and regardless of whether it was made specifically to him or to the public at large, he arguably has paid

**77.** "[T]he seller must show by clear affirmative proof either that the statement was retracted by him before the deal was closed or that the parties understood that the goods would not conform to the affirmation or description. Under such an interpretation, the affirmation, once made, is a part of the agreement, and lack of reliance by the buyer is not a fact which would take the affirmation out of the agreement." Note, "Basis of the Bargain"—What Role Reliance?, 34 U. Pitt. L. Rev. 145, 151 (1972).

**78.** See, e.g., Boyd, Representing Consumers—The Uniform Commercial Code and Beyond, 9 Ariz. L. Rev. 372, 385 (1968). On this view, Article 2 relegates "the metaphysical 'buyer's reliance' requirement to secondary status, where it properly belongs." Ezer, The Impact of the Uniform Commercial Code on the California Law of Sales Warranties, 8 UCLA L. Rev. 281, 285 (1961). Ezer also notes: "The Code's implicit premise is that buyer's reliance is prima facie established from the fact that he made the purchase. If the seller can establish that the buyer in fact did not rely on the seller, that the affirmation or promise was not the

'basis of the bargain,' to use the Code language, then there is no express warranty." Id. at 285, n.30.

**79.** For thorough analyses of the entire issue, see White, Freeing the Tortious Soul of Express Warranty Law, 72 Tul. L. Rev. 2089 (1998) (analysis and classification of cases decided between 1965 and 1998); and Cipollone v. Liggett Group, Inc., 893 F.2d 541, 563–70 (3d Cir. 1990) (N.J. law) (Becker, J.), rev'd in part on other grounds, 505 U.S. 504 (1992). For a consideration of the problem shortly after the Code was promulgated, see Professor Honnold's analysis for the New York Law Revision Commission, quoted at length in White and Summers, UCC § 9–5, at 350.

**80.** See Nordstrom, Law of Sales 209 ("The 'basis of the bargain' includes the dickered terms, but is not limited to them. The 'basis of the bargain' is also the item purchased, and a part of that bargain includes the statements which the seller made about what he sold.").

for and bought it as part of the sales transaction.[81] Moreover, the seller might fairly be estopped from denying that the total product package included the seller's promises about the product. For these reasons and others, many courts have held that a plaintiff need not establish reliance in order to recover for breach of express warranty under UCC § 2–313.[82]

Other courts and commentators, unable to disengage themselves from the intuitively reasonable and long-established requirement of reliance, have refused to abandon it as part of express warranty responsibility, at least in certain contexts. Such an approach is based at least in part on the apparent unfairness of allowing a buyer to obtain redress for damage that in a real sense did not result from the seller's misstatement. Allowing a buyer who did not rely upon a warranty to recover damages on account of its breach might be seen as holding the seller as a kind of outlaw, responsible for any harm to anyone who bought and suffered damage from the seller's goods, and as providing a windfall to the buyer who has no true cause to charge the seller for his loss. "Why should one who has not relied on the seller's statement have the right to sue? That plaintiff is asking for greater protection than he would get under the warranty of merchantability, far more than he bargained for."[83] Thus, many courts indicate that the plaintiff's reliance is an implicit or explicit element in express warranty litigation under § 2–313, often by implying or asserting that the plaintiff's awareness of and reliance on the seller's representation may or must be established[84] to show that a representation was part of the "basis of the bargain" and amounted to a warranty.[85]

---

**81.** However, one might question whether such buyers actually or fairly expect that they have purchased in the bargain a full policy of accident insurance for all harmful consequences if such representations prove false.

**82.** See, e.g., Weng v. Allison, 678 N.E.2d 1254, 1256 (Ill. App. Ct. 1997) (trial court erred in ruling that seller's statements could not have been part of basis of bargain because no reasonable person could have relied on statements); Martin v. American Med. Sys., Inc., 116 F.3d 102, 105 (4th Cir. 1997) (Va. law); Comp–U–Aid, Inc. v. Berk–Tek, Inc., 547 N.W.2d 640 (Mich. 1995); Lutz Farms v. Asgrow Seed Co., 948 F.2d 638, 645 (10th Cir. 1991) (Colo. law) (asserting that a majority of jurisdictions no longer require proof of reliance, citing cases); Pack & Process, Inc. v. Celotex Corp., 503 A.2d 646 (Del. Super. Ct. 1985); Keith v. Buchanan, 220 Cal.Rptr. 392 (Ct. App. 1985). See also White, 72 Tul. L. Rev. at 2099 n.30 (collecting cases that explicitly state that reliance is not a condition of recovery in express warranty claims).

**83.** White and Summers, UCC § 9–5 at 356.

**84.** See Cipollone v. Liggett Group, Inc., 893 F.2d 541, 564 (3d Cir. 1990) (N.J. law), rev'd in part on other grounds, 505 U.S. 504 (1992) ("Although a few courts have

held that reliance is not a necessary element of section 2–313, the more common view has been that it is, and that either a buyer must prove reliance in order to recover on an express warranty or the seller must be permitted to rebut a presumption of reliance in order to preclude recovery.").

**85.** "Upon analyzing these cases, one senses that the courts, though divided, are loath to give up the reliance requirement of § 12 of the U.S.A. and continue it via the 'basis of bargain' test of 2–313(1)." White and Summers, UCC § 9–5 at 352 n.2. See, e.g., Austin v. Will–Burt Co., 232 F.Supp.2d 682, 687 (N.D. Miss. 2002) (no express warranty without reliance), aff'd, 361 F.3d 862 (5th Cir. 2004); American Tobacco Co. v. Grinnell, 951 S.W.2d 420, 436 (Tex. 1997) ("the fraud, fraudulent concealment, negligent misrepresentation, and express warranty claims all share the common element of reliance"); Sprague v. Upjohn Co., 1995 WL 376934 (D. Mass. 1995) ("in an express warranty claim, plaintiff must show reliance on such warranty"); State Farm Ins. Co. v. Nu Prime Roll–A–Way of Miami, Inc., 557 So.2d 107, 108 (Fla. Dist. Ct. App. 1990); Wendt v. Beardmore Suburban Chevrolet, Inc., 366 N.W.2d 424, 428 (Neb. 1985) ("Since an express warranty must have been made 'part of the basis of the

### Advertisements and Brochures

Probably the strongest case for requiring reliance may be made for assertions in advertisements, brochures, and the like which the buyer never sees or reads before the bargain, or even before the product accident. Such statements are typically far removed from the time and place of the actual contract, and including them therein stretches the contract notion to great lengths. In such cases, many courts understandably take the view that unseen or unread statements simply cannot form the basis for an express warranty claim, whether on "basis of the bargain" or "reliance" grounds.[86]

### Post-Sale Statements

Like advertisements, post-sale statements—promises or representations made after a sales transaction has been concluded—present an especially strong case for requiring reliance. One might reasonably think that a seller's post-sale statements about a product, generally unsupported by consideration, should not be viewed as part of the bargain or as something on which the buyer relied in making the deal. For this reason, some commentators on Article 2 sensibly argue that reliance should be required in such cases where a representation was distanced from the conclusion of the deal.[87] But assurances and other statements made shortly after a deal is formally concluded, while it is still "warm," involve a limited class of cases in which the buyer possesses certain equities. Comment 7 to § 2–313 states that the "precise time" when a statement is made is unimportant, and that what matters is only whether the statement is "fairly to be regarded as part of the contract," such that assurances by a seller made shortly after a sales transaction often may be properly viewed as part of that transaction.[88]

bargain,' it is essential that the plaintiffs prove reliance upon the warranty."); Scaringe v. Holstein, 477 N.Y.S.2d 903, 904 (App. Div. 1984) ("A necessary element in the creation of an express warranty is the buyer's reliance upon the seller's affirmations or promises."). See also White, 72 Tul. L. Rev. at 2100 n.31 (collecting cases that appear to condition express warranty recovery on showing of reliance).

**86.** See, e.g., Judge Becker's scholarly analysis in Cipollone v. Liggett Group, Inc., 893 F.2d 541, 567–68 (3d Cir. 1990) (N.J. law), rev'd in part on other grounds, 505 U.S. 504 (1992), in which he reconciles the various conflicting aspects of the reliance/basis of the bargain debate by requiring that the plaintiff prove:

that she read, heard, saw or knew of the advertisement containing the affirmation of fact or promise. Such proof will suffice "to weave" the affirmation of fact or promise "into the fabric of the agreement," U.C.C. Comment 3, and thus make it part of the basis of the bargain. We hold that once the buyer has become aware of the affirmation of fact or promise, the statements are presumed to be

part of the "basis of the bargain" unless the defendant, by "clear affirmative proof," shows that the buyer knew that the affirmation of fact or promise was untrue.

See also In re Bridgestone/Firestone, Inc., 205 F.R.D. 503, 526–28 (S.D. Ind. 2001) (Tenn. and Mich. law) (advertising must be seen by plaintiff to become part of basis of bargain), rev'd on other grounds, In re Bridgestone/Firestone, Inc., 288 F.3d 1012 (7th Cir. 2002). See generally White, 72 Tul. L. Rev. at 2106–11 (finding many cases supporting sound proposition that reliance be required for advertisements and post-sale representations and promises).

**87.** See White and Summers, UCC § 9–5 at 354–356, arguing that such post-sale statements made once the deal is no longer warm should require reliance unless they can be established as modifications under § 2–209; White, above, at 2106–11.

**88.** Comment 7 provides as follows:

The precise time when words of description or affirmation are made or samples are shown is not material. The sole question is whether the language or samples

Appearing to ignore the explicit language of comment 7, at least one court has refused to allow recovery for such a post-sale statement. In *Stang v. Hertz Corp.*,[89] a tire blew out on a car that had been rented by a nun, killing another nun who was a passenger. An express warranty claim was made against the rental agency, Hertz, for two statements: (1) the rental agreement's provision that the vehicle was in good mechanical condition, and (2) the rental agent's comment that "you have got good tires." Upholding a directed verdict for Hertz, the court reasoned that there was "no evidence that any of the nuns relied on, or in any way considered, the terms of the rental agreement before agreeing to the rental [and the] comment concerning 'good tires' was made after the car had been rented."[90] Despite some cases of this sort, the plain language of comment 7 has led the commentators reasonably to conclude that a seller's statements made shortly after a transaction is formally completed are to be considered part of the basis of the broader bargain.[91]

### *Bargaining Statements*

Probably the weakest case for requiring reliance is in the case of representations made in written contracts and oral representations made while the contract is being negotiated. Comment 3 to § 2–313, which speaks in terms of representations made "during a bargain,"[92] arguably appears to contemplate face-to-face bargaining in which context one may reasonably presume that both parties relied on the truth of the bargaining promises of the other. And comment 3 comes close to saying, and reasonably may be interpreted to mean, that the affirmations of a seller in a bargaining context may rebuttably be presumed to be part of the deal, part of the "basis of the buyer's bargain."[93] Although buyers often do in fact rely upon such representations, such statements are so clearly part of the contract that it is neither fair nor logical to require the tort-based notion of reliance in this express warranty context.[94] And so, even the staunchest advocates of retaining the reliance requirement in express warranty doctrine agree that reliance may be presumed, rebutt-

or models are fairly to be regarded as part of the contract. If language is used after the closing of the deal (as when the buyer when taking delivery asks and receives an additional assurance), the warranty becomes a modification, and need not be supported by consideration if it is otherwise reasonable and in order (Section 2–209).

**89.** 490 P.2d 475 (N.M. Ct. App. 1971), rev'd on other grounds, 497 P.2d 732 (N.M. 1972).

**90.** *Stang,* 490 P.2d at 477.

**91.** See White and Summers, UCC § 9–5; Nordstrom, Law of Sales at 205–07.

**92.** Comment 3 to UCC § 2–313 provides in full:

The present section deals with affirmations of fact by the seller, descriptions of the goods or exhibitions of samples, exactly as any other part of a negotiation which ends in a contract is dealt with. No

specific intention to make a warranty is necessary if any of these factors is made part of the basis of the bargain. In actual practice affirmations of fact made by the seller about the goods during a bargain are regarded as part of the description of those goods; hence no particular reliance on such statements need be shown in order to weave them into the fabric of the agreement. Rather, any fact which is to take such affirmations, once made, out of the agreement requires clear affirmative proof. The issue normally is one of fact.

**93.** Judge Becker explains the rebuttable presumption approach in Cipollone v. Liggett Group, Inc., 893 F.2d 541, 563–71 (3d Cir. 1990) (N.J. law), rev'd in part on other grounds, 505 U.S. 504 (1992).

**94.** As part of the contract-based law of sales in UCC Article 2, one might think that situations such as this, that involve purely contractual analysis, should be resolved with purely contractual doctrine.

ably,[95] in the case of statements made in written contracts and oral contract negotiations.[96]

### *Contextualizing Reliance*

After canvassing all basis of the bargain cases decided from 1965 through early 1998, Professor James White concluded that the best solution to the question of whether reliance should be required for express warranty claims under the Code is to "unbundle" the issue by acknowledging that the different considerations at play in different contexts call for different doctrine.[97] Thus, he proposes that reliance not be required for representations and promises that are truly part of the contract, such as terms in a written contract and oral terms that were part of a negotiated deal, nor should reliance be required in writings that are closely connected to the contract, such as product labels, the owner's manual, and other literature delivered with the product. However, Professor White asserts that reliance should be required in the case of representations far removed from the actual deal, such as most advertisements and post-sale representations and promises.[98] Such a simple decoupling of representational situations, which widely span the contract/tort horizon and therefore raise quite different problems, would go a long way toward resolving the basis of the bargain/reliance conundrum that has confounded the courts and commentators for so long.

### Amendments to UCC § 2–313

After nearly two decades of toil, a revision of Article 2 of the Uniform Commercial Code is now complete.[99] Although the revisions (called "amendments") are not effective until enacted into law by a state's legislature, it may be expected that the legislatures soon will begin the process of enactment. Some of the most significant revisions to Article 2 concern express warranties, § 2–313. Indeed, this section now is divided to differentiate a seller's express warranty responsibilities to buyers with whom it has a direct contractual relationship, on the one hand, and a seller's obligations to remote purchasers, on the other.

**95.** Reliance may be rebutted if the buyer admits that he already believed in the truth of the matter represented and so was not affected by the representation. Compare Putensen v. Clay Adams, Inc., 91 Cal.Rptr. 319 (Ct. App. 1970) (whether representation was "part of the basis of the bargain" was jury question), with McDaniel v. McNeil Labs., Inc., 241 N.W.2d 822 (Neb. 1976), and Ball v. Mallinkrodt Chem. Works, 381 S.W.2d 563 (Tenn. Ct. App. 1964) (no reliance on representation if buyer possesses independent knowledge of matter represented).

**96.** See White and Summers, UCC § 9–5 at 352. To this short list, Professor White adds manuals, labels, and the like attached to or delivered with the goods. White, above, at 2106–11.

**97.** After reviewing all the cases, Professor White observes: "[M]y cases show that not all warranty claims are the same: some are contract plain and simple; some are special and some really are tort or, in the words of Williston, quasi-tort. I believe that the law will be more certain, more predictable, and subject to smaller manipulation if we unbundle these liabilities." White, above, at 2110.

**98.** See White, above, at 2110–11.

**99.** In 2002, the National Conference of Commissioners on Uniform State Laws (NCCUSL) approved the revision of Article 2, as did the American Law Institute (ALI) in 2003. See UCC—Proposed Amendments to Article 2. Sales (Apr. 18, 2003); 25 ALI Reporter 1 (Summer 2003) (noting ALI membership's approval at annual meeting in May). After final revisions to the comments, Amended Article 2 should be formally promulgated.

Thus, while Amended UCC § 2–313 remains largely unchanged from the old § 2–313, the Amended version is narrowed to cover only express warranties made to an "immediate buyer." In addition, a new section specifies that a seller's "remedial promise" to an immediate buyer "creates an obligation that the promise will be performed upon the happening of the specified event."[100] Obligations arising from a seller's representations to persons other than immediate buyers are now spun off into two new sections, Amended §§ 2–313A (representations accompanying the product) and 2–313B (advertisements).

Amended UCC § 2–313A, entitled "Obligation to Remote Purchaser Created by Record Packaged with or Accompanying Goods," governs a seller's obligations to "remote purchasers" arising out of "pass through warranties," affirmations and remedial promises made in a "record" packaged with or otherwise accompanying the sale of new goods—such as a label on a product's container, or a card, sheet, or booklet accompanying the goods at the time of sale. In substitution for the basis-of-the-bargain requirement of § 2–313, § 2–313A substitutes a "reasonable belief" test: goods must conform to a seller's promises "unless a reasonable person in the position of the remote purchaser would not believe that the affirmation . . . created an obligation."[101] A seller may modify or limit remedies for breach if this fact is included in the record or otherwise provided to the buyer at the time of purchase.[102]

Amended UCC § 2–313B, entitled "Obligation to Remote Purchaser Created by Communication to the Public," largely tracks § 2–313A except that it governs a seller's obligations arising out of affirmations made to remote purchasers of new goods in advertising and similar communications to the public. Moreover, in substitution for the basis-of-the-bargain requirement of § 2–313, § 2–313B substitutes what amounts to an actual-and-reasonable reliance standard. More specifically, an obligation to the remote purchaser arises under this section if the purchaser (1) buys a product with knowledge of the affirmation, (2) expects the goods to conform to the affirmation, and (3) that expectation is reasonable.[103] Thus, in addition to the objective reasonable buyer standard of § 2–313A, § 2–313B adds a subjective requirement that the remote purchaser actually know of and believe the seller's affirmation. In short, this new requirement is one of reasonable reliance, no more no less.

---

**100.** Amended UCC § 2–313(4). A "remedial promise" is defined in Amended UCC § 2–103(1) as "a promise by the seller to repair or replace the goods or to refund all or part of the price of goods upon the happening of a specified event."

**101.** This test is similar to, but independent of, the basis of the bargain requirement of § 2–313. More clearly than basis of the bargain, the reasonable-belief concept places the burden of proof on the seller to establish that any factual affirmations about the contract were not part of the contract.

**102.** Amended UCC § 2–313A(5)(a).

**103.** Amended UCC § 2–313B(3).

## § 4.3 IMPLIED WARRANTY OF MERCHANTABILITY

The basic implied warranty of quality in the sale of goods, now referred to as the implied warranty of "merchantability," developed in late Roman law nearly two thousand years ago.[1] After a long period of stagnation, this warranty evolved in Anglo–American common law over the centuries, first in cases involving defective foodstuffs[2] and much later (during the nineteenth century) as a broad repudiation of the long-entrenched doctrine of *caveat emptor*.[3] The renewed doctrine of *caveat venditor* required a seller to take responsibility for damage caused by any latent defects in goods sold, on the theory that fair dealing implied into the sale of a product a fundamental guarantee of fair quality—that the product would conform to the general description under which it was sold.[4] In short, fair quality received became a legal quid pro quo for a fair price paid. In the colorful words of Lord Ellenborough, "The purchaser cannot be supposed to buy goods to lay them on a dunghill."[5]

Thus, the implied warranty of merchantability is an assurance, imposed by law upon the seller, that a product is reasonably suitable for the general uses for which it is purchased and sold.[6] This warranty does not arise out of any express agreement or intention between the buyer and the seller but is created instead, at the point of sale, by operation of law. Its foundation is in public policy, in the interest of promoting fair dealing in sales transactions.

As the central and most important warranty in the Uniform Commercial Code, the implied warranty of merchantability can be a vital theory of liability in products liability litigation.[7] Because liability for breach of such a warranty generally is based merely upon a product's inadequate condition or malfunction without regard to the seller's fault, it truly is a form of "strict" liability. Consequently, proof of the seller's negligence is not only unnecessary but also irrelevant. Generally, proof that a product is "defective" under strict liability in tort will establish

---

**§ 4.3**

**1.** For a brief history of warranty law aspects to products liability law, see § 1.2, above.

**2.** See §§ 5.2 and 7.5, below.

**3.** "It has been said that the concept of implied warranty rests upon the foundation of business ethics and constitutes an exception to the maxim 'let the buyer beware,' itself encompassing the idea that there is no warranty implied with respect to the quality of the goods being sold." Lambert v. Sistrunk, 58 So.2d 434–35 (Fla. 1952). On the development of the implied warranty of merchantability, see Prosser, Assault on the Citadel (Strict Liability to the Consumer), 69 Yale L.J. 1099, 1103–1110 and 1124–27 (1960); Prosser, The Implied Warranty of Merchantable Quality, 27 Minn. L. Rev. 117, 118–22 (1943); Llewellyn, On Warranty of Quality, and Society (pts. 1 and 2), 36 Colum. L. Rev. 699 (1936), 37 Colum. L. Rev. 341 (1937).

**4.** See Lane v. Trenholm Bldg. Co., 229 S.E.2d 728, 730 (S.C. 1976): "Under the rule of *caveat venditor,* a sale 'raises an implied warranty (against latent defects) from the fairness and fullness of the price paid, upon this clear and reasonable ground, that in the contract of sale, the purchaser is not supposed to part with his money, but in expectation of an adequate advantage, or recompense.' Champneys v. Johnson, [2 Brevard 268, 272 (1809)]. 'Selling for a sound price raises an implied warranty that the thing sold is free from defects, known and unknown (to the seller).' "

**5.** Gardiner v. Gray, (1815) 4 Camp. 144, 171 Eng. Rep. 46, 47. See Prosser, The Implied Warranty of Merchantable Quality, 27 Minn. L. Rev. 117 (1943).

**6.** See, e.g., McCabe v. L.K. Liggett Drug Co., 112 N.E.2d 254 (Mass. 1953).

**7.** "The implied warranty of merchantability in 2–314 is an important warranty. It is a first cousin to strict tort liability, and 'products liability' cases are often tried under the merchantability banner." White and Summers, UCC § 9–7, at 510.

that a product is not merchantable, and vice versa.[8] In this respect, these two theories of products liability recovery are essentially co-extensive. But some courts, for varying purposes, distinguish between the two liability theories. For example, a few courts have dubiously ruled that the merchantability warranty, unlike strict liability in tort, does not require proof that a product is inherently deficient or "defective."[9] In addition, claims for breach of implied warranty of merchantability lie for pure economic loss,[10] unlike tort actions, and warranty claims often have longer statutes of limitations than claims for negligence or strict liability in tort.[11] Consequently, injured plaintiffs in some cases can recover for breach of the implied warranty of merchantability where relief is unavailable under the law of tort. In short, the implied warranty of merchantability is sometimes a powerful products liability law claim.

### Uniform Commercial Code § 2–314

The implied warranty of merchantability was first codified in America in § 15(2) of the Uniform Sales Act, which provided, "Where the goods are bought by description from a seller who deals in goods of that description (whether he be the grower or manufacturer or not), there is an implied warranty that the goods shall be of merchantable quality." In the 1950s, this warranty was rewritten into § 2–314 of the Uniform Commercial Code as follows:

**8.** See, e.g., Fritz v. White Consol. Indus., 762 N.Y.S.2d 711, 713–14 (App. Div. 2003) (verdicts for plaintiff on strict liability and for defendant on breach of implied warranty were inconsistent; concept of defect is normally the same in both causes of action); Wright v. Brooke Group Ltd., 652 N.W.2d 159, 182 (Iowa 2002) ("conduct that gives rise to a warranty claim based on fitness for ordinary purposes mirrors conduct that gives rise to tort liability for a defective product"); Ford Motor Co. v. General Accident Ins. Co., 779 A.2d 362, 369 (Md. 2001) ("We consistently have held that a plaintiff must prove the existence of a defect at the time the product leaves the manufacturer to recover on an implied warranty claim as well as with regard to strict liability and negligence claims."); Hyundai Motor Co. v. Rodriguez, 995 S.W.2d 661, 665 (Tex. 1999) ("in a crashworthiness case involving a claim for personal injuries . . . strict liability's and breach-of-warranty's concepts of 'defect' are functionally identical"); Larsen v. Pacesetter Sys., Inc., 837 P.2d 1273, 1284–85 (Haw. 1992), amended on reconsideration in part by 843 P.2d 144 (Haw. 1992) ("to bring an action in implied warranty for personal injury a plaintiff is required to show product unmerchantability sufficient to avoid summary judgment on the issue of defectiveness in a tort strict products liability suit"); Lariviere v. Dayton Safety Ladder Co., 525 A.2d 892 (R.I. 1987)

(ladder that collapsed). See also Freeman v. Hoffman–La Roche, Inc., 618 N.W.2d 827, 842–44 (Neb. 2000) (merging implied warranty into design and manufacturing defect claims). See generally § 5.9, below.

**9.** See, e.g., Denny v. Ford Motor Co., 662 N.E.2d 730 (N.Y. 1995) (rollover case involving Ford Bronco II; *held*, cause of action for breach of implied warranty of merchantability may support design deficiency claim where strict liability in tort did not); Malawy v. Richards Mfg. Co., 501 N.E.2d 376, 383 (Ill. App. Ct. 1986) (implied warranty requires that product is "unmerchantable" whereas strict liability in tort requires that product be "defective"). See generally 3 Lawrence's Anderson on the UCC § 2–314:164 at 396. *Denny* is examined in § 5.9, below, and in White, Reverberations from the Collision of Tort and Warranty, 53 S.C. L. Rev. 1067, 1072–73 (2002) (noting "the need to draw the line between injury to life, limb and property— the domain of both tort and warranty—and injury that is purely economic, the exclusive domain of warranty").

**10.** See 1 Clark and Smith, Product Warranties 2d ch. 7.

**11.** Under UCC § 2–725 the statute of limitations is 4 years from the date of sale. In most states, the statute of limitations for tort claims is 2 or 3 years from the date of discovery. See § 14.5, below.

§ 2–314. Implied Warranty: Merchantability; Usage of Trade

(1) Unless excluded or modified (Section 2–316), a warranty that the goods shall be merchantable is implied in a contract for their sale if the seller is a merchant with respect to goods of that kind. Under this section the serving for value of food or drink to be consumed either on the premises or elsewhere is a sale.

(2) Goods to be merchantable must be at least such as

(a) pass without objection in the trade under the contract description; and

(b) in the case of fungible goods, are of fair average quality within the description; and

(c) are fit for the ordinary purposes for which such goods are used; and

(d) run, within the variations permitted by the agreement, of even kind, quality and quantity within each unit and among all units involved; and

(e) are adequately contained, packaged, and labeled as the agreement may require; and

(f) conform to the promises or affirmations of fact made on the container or label if any.

(3) Unless excluded or modified (Section 2–316) other implied warranties may arise from course of dealing or usage of trade.

The comments to § 2–314 point out the importance of custom and usage to a determination of merchantability. Comment 6 states that the listing of merchantability standards in subsection (2) "does not purport to exhaust the meaning of 'merchantable' nor to negate any of its attributes ... arising by usage of trade or through case law" and explains that "the intention is to leave open other possible attributes of merchantability." This section of the Code applies only to sales by "merchants," i.e., people in the business of selling products of that kind.[12] It does not apply to isolated sales made by persons not fitting that description, "isolated sales" being such as occur only once or very infrequently in the course of a seller's ordinary business.

Subsection (2) particularizes a concept that often is expressed more simply. To many courts, "merchantability" simply means reasonable fitness for the general purposes for which an article is sold and used. It does not imply absolute perfection; it does not require the seller to provide an article that will not wear out; it does not even imply high quality. The fitness need not, in other words, be absolute, and the warranty is met when an article is free of major imperfections, conforms to ordinary standards, and is of the average grade, quality, and value of similar goods sold commercially.[13] As with all warranties, the breach of

---

**12.** See UCC § 2–104.

**13.** See, e.g., Phillips v. Cricket Lighters, 852 A.2d 365, 370–71 (Pa. Super. Ct. 2004) ("The concept of 'merchantability' does not require that the goods be the best quality, or the best obtainable, but it does require that they have an inherent soundness which makes them suitable for the purpose for which they are designed, that they be free from significant defects, that they perform in the way that goods of that kind should perform, and that they be of

this warranty does not require that the manufacturer or other seller was negligent, nor did it traditionally require that the product was "defective" or "unreasonably dangerous" by the standards of the law of tort.[14] Yet it is difficult to untangle merchantability from defectiveness, and at least in products liability cases involving personal injuries, the concepts of "unmerchantable" and "defective" appear largely if not entirely congruent.[15] Indeed, it is important to note that Amended § 2–314 explicitly adopts this latter view by providing that "merchantability" is defined in personal injury cases by the products liability tort law of the state.[16]

### Requirements of "Merchant" and "Sale"

In contrast to warranty claims under §§ 2–313 and 2–315, claims for breach of implied warranty of merchantability under Uniform Commercial Code § 2–314 require that the seller be a "merchant" of such products in the ordinary course of trade.[17] An isolated sale of a product does not render a person a merchant for purposes of the Code.[18] Accordingly, it has been held that volunteer parent organizations providing food at school functions are not merchants as that term is used in UCC § 2–314,[19] nor are persons engaged in isolated sales of a fishing boat,[20] a used saw,[21] a used car,[22] or an entire business including its machinery.[23]

reasonable quality within expected variations and for the ordinary purpose for which they are used.").

**14.** See, e.g., Phillips v. Cricket Lighters, 852 A.2d 365, 371 (Pa. Super. Ct. 2004) ("a product need not be defective, for purposes of strict products liability, in order to be unfit for ordinary purposes" under implied warranty of merchantability); Denny v. Ford Motor Co., 662 N.E.2d 730 (N.Y. 1995) (causes of action for strict liability and for breach of implied warranty of merchantability not identical); 3 Lawrence's Anderson on the UCC § 2–314:743 (a plaintiff needs to prove only breach of warranty "and is not required to prove that the warranty was breached by a defect that made the product dangerously defective").

**15.** See, e.g., Solo v. Trus Joist MacMillan, 2004 WL 524898, *14 (D. Minn. 2004) (" 'This warranty is breached when the product is defective to a normal buyer making ordinary use of the product.' "); Johnson v. Brown & Williamson Tobacco Corp., 122 F. Supp. 2d 194, 206 (D. Mass. 2000) ("Goods are not fit for their ordinary purposes if, from the consumer's perspective, the absence of a warning makes the good unreasonably dangerous."); Foster v. Ford Motor Co., 621 F.2d 715, 719 (5th Cir. 1980) (Tex. law) ("The negative implication of the warranty requirement that goods be 'fit for the ordinary purposes for which such goods are used' is that the goods not be unreasonably dangerous"). "For a product to flunk the merchantability test, it must contain an inherent defect." 1 Clark and Smith, Product Warranties 2d § 5:5

(stating that "the courts find goods to be unfit for their ordinary purposes when they can identify one of three general types of defects: manufacturing defects, design defects, and failure to give the buyer proper instructions with respect to the goods" and noting that the test for unmerchantability is essentially the same as under strict liability in tort except that unmerchantability does not require a product to be "unreasonably dangerous").

**16.** See Amended UCC § 2–314 cmt. 7.

**17.** UCC § 2–314(1). See UCC § 2–104 ("merchant" defined).

**18.** See cmt. 3 to § 2–314: "A person making an isolated sale of goods is not a 'merchant' within the meaning of the full scope of this section. . . ."

**19.** Samson v. Riesing, 215 N.W.2d 662 (Wis. 1974) (salmonella food poisoning from turkey salad).

**20.** Prince v. LeVan, 486 P.2d 959 (Alaska 1971).

**21.** Downs v. Shouse, 501 P.2d 401 (Ariz. Ct. App. 1972).

**22.** Ballou v. Trahan, 334 A.2d 409 (Vt. 1975) (private person who sold used Porsche to plaintiff not "merchant").

**23.** See Olson v. U.S. Indus., Inc., 649 F.Supp. 1511, 1514 (D. Kan. 1986), where the court found that a manufacturer which sold its assets, including machinery, was not a "merchant" of machinery used in the manufacturing process, such that the sale

However, a seller need not deal regularly in the particular type of good sold if the seller in the regular course of business deals in goods of the same general type.[24] But the defendant must be a merchant *with respect to the type of goods sold to the plaintiff.*[25] So, a bank which sells a repossessed boat to a plaintiff in an isolated transaction, may not be a "merchant" with respect to such a product for purposes of § 2–314.[26]

As is true of all warranty claims under UCC Article 2,[27] breach of the implied warranty of merchantability generally requires there to be a product "sale." So, some courts hold that Article 2 warranties do not apply where the product is merely leased, as is the case with a rental car,[28] or where the plaintiff is merely a bailee of the product.[29] Many other courts, however, have applied the Code principles directly or by analogy to lease transactions.[30] The general application of warranties (including the implied warranty of merchantability) to lease transactions

did not give rise to an implied warranty of merchantability.

**24.** See, e.g., Stachurski v. K–Mart Corp., 447 N.W.2d 830 (Mich. Ct. App. 1989) (seller deemed merchant for purposes of implied warranty of merchantability where it requested manufacturer to produce copy of car seat cover using fasteners already sold by seller; although seller later decided not to market this prototype, it sold allegedly defective product to plaintiff through its sample store); McHugh v. Carlton, 369 F.Supp. 1271 (D.S.C. 1974) (service station operator who kept stock of new and used tires held to be merchant with respect to recapped tires, although he did not keep stock of recapped tires and ordered them only on specific request).

**25.** See, e.g., Gavula v. ARA Serv., Inc., 756 A.2d 17, 21 (Pa. Super. Ct. 2000) (company that sold corporate assets, including van from which plaintiff was thrown, was not a "merchant" under UCC); Siemen v. Alden, 341 N.E.2d 713 (Ill. App. Ct. 1975) (sawmill operator, who sold used power saw to plaintiff after replacing it with new one, not merchant with respect to goods of that kind).

**26.** Donald v. City Nat. Bank of Dothan, 329 So.2d 92 (Ala. 1976). See Annot., 91 A.L.R.3d 876 (1979) (UCC § 2–314 "merchant" defined).

**27.** Article 2, of course, is entitled "Sales."

**28.** See, e.g., Bechtel v. Paul Clark, Inc., 412 N.E.2d 143 (Mass. App. Ct. 1980) (car overturned due to brake defect).

**29.** In Watford v. Jack LaLanne Long Island, Inc., 542 N.Y.S.2d 765, 767 (App. Div. 1989), the court affirmed the health club defendant's motion for summary judgment as to plaintiff's warranty and strict tort liability claims arising from injuries

sustained during use of a rowing machine. Even though the health club's contract with its patron referred to the parties as buyer and seller, the court noted that no sales transaction in the rowing equipment occurred or was contemplated, adding: "We have recently held that 'liability may not be imposed for breach of warranty or strict products liability upon a party that is outside the manufacturing, selling or distributive chain.' In this case, the deposition testimony established that Jack LaLanne was not the manufacturer, seller, or distributor of the equipment.... In particular, the plaintiffs failed to submit any evidence as to any involvement by Jack LaLanne in the manufacturing, selling, or distributive chain of the exercise equipment."

Compare Levondosky v. Marina Assoc., 731 F.Supp. 1210 (D.N.J. 1990), holding that plaintiff stated a cause of action in implied warranty of merchantability against a casino in connection with the casino's provision of a complimentary drink to a patron. See also Hurley v. Larry's Water Ski School, 762 F.2d 925 (11th Cir. 1985) (Fla. law), where plaintiff was injured while taking water skiing lessons from the defendant when the wooden tow handle he was holding broke. In plaintiff's action against the ski school, the court held that since the tow rope and handle were at all times attached to the boat, he never had complete possession and control over them and so never had a bailment. Although plaintiff's strict liability in tort claim thus would not lie, the court held that his breach of warranty claim could. Implicit in the defendant's agreement to provide ski lessons to the plaintiff was "an implied warranty that the equipment supplied by Larry's was fit for the purpose of teaching an individual to ski." Id. at 929.

**30.** See, e.g., Januse v. U–Haul Co., 399 So.2d 402 (Fla. Dist. Ct. App. 1981) (steer-

is now routine, inasmuch as almost all states have adopted UCC Article 2A ("Leases"), first promulgated in 1987 and amended in 2003.[31] Article 2A's warranty provisions closely mimic those concerning Sales in Article 2, amendments to which also were finally approved in 2003.

The precise moment in time when a sale occurs and an implied warranty of merchantability attaches has been litigated in the context of shopper injuries occurring after a shopper takes a product from the shelf, but prior to payment and a technical sale at the checkout counter. Typical are cases involving beverage bottles that explode or fragment in the shopper's hands, or in the shopping cart. Noting that comment 1 to § 2–314 provides that "[t]he seller's obligation applies to present sales *as well as to contracts to sell,*"[32] many courts conclude that the merchant's placement of the product on the shelf constitutes an offer of sale, and the buyer's removal of the product from the shelf constitutes an acceptance, creating a contract sufficient for application of UCC § 2–314.[33] In such cases, the bottle and the contents are both covered by the merchantability warranty.[34]

### Fitness for Ordinary Purpose

As seen above, Uniform Commercial Code § 2–314(2) provides a long and nonexclusive list of tests for the merchantability of a product.[35] Yet the heart of the implied warranty of merchantability, as provided in subsection (c), is that a product is warranted to be "fit" for its "ordinary purposes," a notion that has deep roots in the law. An early example of a court applying the merchantability concept to the products liability context involved a new coffee maker that exploded, injuring the plaintiff.[36] Ruling for the plaintiff, the court remarked: "If the coffee maker was so imperfect in design that it could not be used without the

---

ing defect caused truck to overturn). See generally White and Summers, UCC § 9–2.

**31.** See Proposed Amendments to UCC—Article 2A. Leases (ALI, April 18, 2003), later that year approved by both the ALI and NCCUSL.

**32.** Emphasis added.

**33.** See Giant Food, Inc. v. Washington Coca–Cola Bottling Co., 332 A.2d 1 (Md. 1975). In Fender v. Colonial Stores, Inc., 225 S.E.2d 691 (Ga. Ct. App. 1976), plaintiff was injured when a bottle of Coca–Cola exploded as she was placing it on the defendant grocer's check-out counter. Defendant argued that UCC § 2–314 did not apply since a "contract for sale" had not yet been formed at the time of injury. *Held,* that defendant had offered the beverage for sale by placing it on the shelf; that plaintiff had accepted the offer by taking physical possession of the item; and that § 2–314 was thereafter applicable. See Keaton v. A.B.C. Drug Co., 467 S.E.2d 558 (Ga. 1996) (plaintiff's action of grasping the product to remove it from high store shelf with intent to purchase was sufficient "possession" of product to allow claim of breach of implied

warranty of merchantability). See UCC § 2–106(1).

Compare McQuiston v. K–Mart Corp., 796 F.2d 1346, 1350 (11th Cir. 1986) (Fla. law) (no claim for injuries incurred during inspection of cookie jar by shopper who had not formed intention to purchase); Favors v. Firestone Tire & Rubber Co., 309 So.2d 69 (Fla. Dist. Ct. App. 1975) (bailment for mutual benefit not similar to sale).

**34.** See Sheeskin v. Giant Food, Inc., 318 A.2d 874 (Md. Ct. Spec. App. 1974), judgment aff'd sub nom. Giant Food, Inc. v. Washington Coca–Cola Bottling Co., Inc., 332 A.2d 1 (Md. 1975); 78 A.L.R.3d 682 (1975).

**35.** So, for example, a product may be unmerchantable if it is not adequately contained under UCC § 2–314(2)(e). See, e.g., Keaton v. A.B.C. Drug Co., 467 S.E.2d 558, 560 (Ga. 1996) (plaintiff's eye injured from bleach spilled from container as she sought to remove it from high shelf in store: "bleach which spills via a loose cap is not adequately contained or packaged").

**36.** McCabe v. L.K. Liggett Drug Co., 112 N.E.2d 254 (Mass. 1953).

likelihood of an explosion it could be found that the appliance was not reasonably fit for making coffee and therefore not merchantable."[37] The important message of this and many other cases is that "merchantability" and "fitness for ordinary purposes" in the products liability context mean that products must be *reasonably safe* for their ordinary uses.[38] "The warranty of merchantability is broader than that the goods will do the ordinary job for which they were made. They must also, unless the further warranty is disclaimed, do the job safely."[39]

For example, shoes may be expected to have their heels firmly attached so they will not fall off in normal use;[40] a ladder may be expected not to collapse;[41] hair lotion may be expected not to burn the user's scalp;[42] a cookie may be expected to be free from foreign objects;[43] and an SUV marketed for ordinary driving may be expected to be reasonably stable and not roll over in normal use.[44] Similarly, insulation that emits noxious fumes will not be considered merchantable,[45] nor a clothes dryer that overheats and catches fire,[46] nor a flash cube,[47] coffee maker,[48] or stove[49] that explodes in the user's face.

On the other hand, insignificant flaws or irregularities do not render a product unmerchantable. "Merchantable," in other words, does not mean perfect, flawless, completely satisfactory, nor that the product will precisely fulfill the buyer's expectations.[50] It follows, therefore, that the

**37.** Id. at 257.

**38.** See, e.g., In re September 11 Litigation 280 F.Supp.2d 279, 306 (S.D.N.Y. 2003) (Va. law) ("an implied warranty of merchantability . . . guarantees that a product 'was reasonably safe for its intended use' "); Lewis v. Ariens Co., 751 N.E.2d 862, 864 (Mass. 2001) (jury found that "snow blower was not reasonably safe for its intended or reasonably foreseeable use (in breach of its implied warranty of merchantability)"). See generally 1 Clark and Smith, Product Warranties 2d § 5:5 ("not reasonably safe").

**39.** R. Nordstrom, Law of Sales § 76, at 236 (1970) ("Thus, fitness for ordinary purpose is a broader concept than just that of doing a single job; it contains ideas of doing that job safely."). But see Whitson v. Safeskin Corp., 313 F.Supp.2d 473, 480 (M.D. Pa. 2004) ("ordinary purpose" of defendants' latex gloves was to protect health care workers from transmitting or being exposed to blood-borne pathogens, so that merchantability warranty did not protect against latex allergies caused by gloves).

**40.** Chairaluce v. Stanley Warner Mgt. Corp., 236 F.Supp. 385 (D. Conn. 1964).

**41.** Lariviere v. Dayton Safety Ladder Co., 525 A.2d 892 (R.I. 1987).

**42.** Newmark v. Gimbel's, Inc., 258 A.2d 697 (N.J. 1969).

**43.** Otis Spunkmeyer, Inc. v. Blakely, 30 S.W.3d 678 (Tex. App. 2000).

**44.** Denny v. Ford Motor Co., 662 N.E.2d 730 (N.Y. 1995).

**45.** Shooshanian v. Wagner, 672 P.2d 455 (Alaska 1983).

**46.** Crandell v. Larkin & Jones Appliance Co., 334 N.W.2d 31 (S.D. 1983).

**47.** Maybank v. S.S. Kresge Co., 266 S.E.2d 409 (N.C. Ct. App. 1980), modified on other grounds and affirmed, 273 S.E.2d 681 (N.C. 1981).

**48.** McCabe v. L.K. Liggett Drug Co., 112 N.E.2d 254 (Mass. 1953).

**49.** Logan v. Montgomery Ward & Co., 219 S.E.2d 685 (Va. 1975).

**50.** " '[M]erchantable' is not synonymous with 'perfect.' Likewise, fitness for ordinary purposes does not mean that the product will fulfill buyer's every expectation." 1 White and Summers, UCC § 9–8, at 523 (4th Practitioners' ed. 1995) (hereinafter 1 White and Summers (Prac. ed.)). See also Connick v. Suzuki Motor Co., 656 N.E.2d 170, 182 (Ill. App. Ct. 1995), rev'd in part on other grounds, 675 N.E.2d 584 (Ill. 1996) ("The implied warranty of merchantability 'does not impose a general requirement that goods precisely fulfill the expectation of the buyer.' Instead, § 2–314(2)(c) provides for a minimum level of quality— that the goods 'are fit for the ordinary purposes for which such goods are used.' "). See also Chandler v. Gene Messer Ford, 81 S.W.3d 493, 503 (Tex. App. 2002) (child injured by front-seat airbag: "A product

presence of one small bone in a fish filet will not breach an implied warranty of merchantability,[51] nor will slight damage to a new car that does not affect the vehicle's "usefulness or drivability."[52] Similarly, the implied warranty will not be breached where minor repairs will make the product fit for normal use, and the seller has offered to undertake such repairs.[53]

Likewise, if a product characteristic is "open and obvious," posing risks apparent to the ordinary consumer, the product generally will not be considered unfit for its ordinary purposes.[54] Article 2 addresses the obviousness issue in the section on disclaimers, § 2–316(3)(b), which provides that a buyer who examines goods prior to purchase (or who refuses to so examine them) obtains "no implied warranty with regard to defects which an examination ought in the circumstances to have revealed to him." That is, the warranty of merchantability extends only to defects that are *latent*; conversely, there is no implied warranty of merchantability with respect to defects which are obvious, whether or not the buyer in fact discovers them.[55]

The implied warranty of merchantability may be breached only if a product failure or mishap occurs during the product's "ordinary" use.[56] Consistent with this requirement, there is no breach of that implied warranty where safety glasses fail after being subjected to force exceeding what should reasonably have been expected,[57] or where sliding glass doors leak upon exposure to unusual wind and spray conditions at an ocean-front property.[58] Determining whether a particular product use that results in injury is or is not "ordinary" sometimes is quite simple. A beer bottle thrown against a telephone pole for the very purpose of smashing it is not an ordinary use of the bottle.[59] And a plaintiff's failure

which performs its ordinary function adequately does not breach the implied warranty of merchantability merely because it does not function as the buyer would prefer."); General Motors Corp. v. Brewer, Prod. Liab. Rep. (CCH) ¶ 15,148 (Tex. 1998) (implied warranty of merchantability not breached if product "does not function as well as the buyer would like, or even as well as it could").

**51.** Ex parte Morrison's Cafeteria of Montgomery, Inc., 431 So.2d 975, 979 (Ala. 1983), on remand 431 So.2d 979 (Ala. Civ. App. 1983) (it was "undisputed that, in light of the process used to mass produce fillets, it was commercially impractical to remove all bones.").

**52.** Horne v. Claude Ray Ford Sales, Inc., 290 S.E.2d 497, 499 (Ga. Ct. App. 1982).

**53.** Hannon v. Original Gunite Aquatech Pools, Inc., 434 N.E.2d 611 (Mass. 1982).

**54.** See, e.g., Darrell Wood v. Bass Pro Shops, Inc., 462 S.E.2d 101, 103 (Va. 1995) ("a plaintiff may not recover damages for breach of an implied warranty if the purported defect . . . was 'known, visible or obvious' to him"); Toney v. Kawasaki

Heavy Indus., Ltd., 975 F.2d 162 (5th Cir. 1992) (Miss. law) (absence of leg protection on motorcycle did not render it either unreasonably dangerous or unfit for ordinary purpose because ordinary motorcycle rider would appreciate risk of leg injury in side collision with automobile).

**55.** "A failure to notice defects which are obvious cannot excuse the buyer." UCC § 2–316 cmt. 8. See, e.g., American Tobacco Co. v. Grinnell, 951 S.W.2d 420 (Tex. 1997) (common knowledge of health risks of cigarette smoking is defense barring claim for breach of implied warranty).

**56.** The development of seller liability for injuries occasioned by the foreseeable misuse of a product has not enjoyed the development in warranty that is seen in negligence and strict liability. On misuse generally, see § 13.5, below.

**57.** American Optical Co. v. Weidenhamer, 457 N.E.2d 181 (Ind. 1983).

**58.** Festa v. Closure Co., 436 N.E.2d 977 (Mass. App. Ct. 1982).

**59.** Venezia v. Miller Brewing Co., 626 F.2d 188, 190–91 (1st Cir. 1980): "Under Massachusetts law the question of fitness

to follow instructions in using the product, assuming the danger of nonobservance is warned of or obvious, may reasonably be considered not an ordinary use.[60]

But characterizing uses as "ordinary" requires careful consideration within each separate context of how the seller and the user fairly might expect the product to perform in each particular situation. Thus, the manufacturer of paint used for submerged murals on the walls of swimming pools may not breach an implied warranty of merchantability where the variegated coloring of the walls hampers detection of a drowning person.[61] Nor may the manufacturer of a toy ball breach an implied warranty of merchantability where a child dies from choking on the ball.[62] Yet, where a child sprays flammable hair spray on her dress and hair because of the pleasant fragrance, a jury might be permitted to find that such a use could be expected and so was "ordinary."[63] Such decisions, rooted in the fair expectations of the parties, are multi-faceted, fact specific, and peculiarly suited for jury determination.[64]

In a typical case involving a claim for breach of implied warranty of merchantability, the plaintiff will attempt to establish the precise manner in which the product failed. However, sometimes the product will be destroyed in the accident, or proof of how the product failed to operate safely will otherwise be unavailable. In such "malfunction" cases, the plaintiff still may rely on the merchantability warranty and need not necessarily show with particularity the precise nature of the defect or the precise physical mechanism which caused the product to fail.[65] For example, if the steering on a new car suddenly fails, causing the car to

---

for ordinary purposes is largely one centering around reasonable consumer expectations.... No reasonable consumer would expect anything but that a glass beer bottle, apparently well suited for its immediate intended use, would fail to safely withstand the type of purposeful abuse involved here."

**60.** See, e.g., Watson v. Uniden Corp. of Am., 775 F.2d 1514 (11th Cir. 1985) (Ga. law) (failure to follow instructions not "normal" use for purposes of warranty, but jury issue existed on adequacy of warning for negligence and strict liability in tort claims).

**61.** Kelly v. Koppers Co., 293 So.2d 763 (Fla. Dist. Ct. App. 1974).

**62.** Brazier v. Hasbro, Inc., 2004 WL 1497607, at *4 (S.D.N.Y. 2004) ("[N]o reasonable jury could conclude that a toy ball is performing an ordinary purpose when a child inserts it into his mouth. Because the implied warranty of merchantability for the [ball] does not include a warranty that the product is fit for safe insertion into a child's mouth, [plaintiff] cannot maintain a cause of action for breach of implied warranty based on the contention that the ball was not minimally safe for this purpose."

**63.** See Hardman v. Helene Curtis Indus., Inc., 198 N.E.2d 681, 691 (Ill. App. Ct. 1964), where the court remarked: "The essential question presented by a claim of breach of implied warranty of merchantability is whether the product failed to safely and adequately satisfy the uses to which such products are ordinarily put." See also Lakeview Country Club Inc. v. Superior Prod., 926 S.W.2d 428 (Ark. 1996) (absence of proof of what was ordinary purpose for latex coating used to paint swimming pool precluded implied warranty of merchantability claim when coating cracked and peeled).

**64.** More generally, "merchantability" is recognized as a question of fact. See 3 Lawrence's Anderson on the UCC § 2–314:765.

**65.** See, e.g., Genetti v. Caterpillar, Inc., 621 N.W.2d 529, 541 (Neb. 2001); Alvarez v. American Isuzu Motors, 749 N.E.2d 16, 22–23 (Ill. App. Ct. 2001) (defect may be proven circumstantially, such that plaintiff not required to prove specific defect); Red Hill Hosiery Mill, Inc. v. Magnetek, Inc., 530 S.E.2d 321, 327 (N.C. Ct. App. 2000) ("in a products liability action, based on tort or warranty, a product defect may be inferred from evidence of the product's malfunction, if there is evidence the product had been put to its ordinary use").

smash at high speed into a tree with such force that the steering mechanism is damaged so badly that the cause of the steering failure cannot be determined, the plaintiff may still prevail: it is sufficient in such a case for the plaintiff merely to show the malfunction, regardless of the cause.[66] As expressed by one court, "When machinery 'malfunctions,' it obviously lacks fitness regardless of the cause of the malfunction. Under the theory of warranty, the 'sin' is the lack of fitness as evidenced by the malfunction itself rather than some specific dereliction by the manufacturer in constructing or designing the machinery."[67]

### Amendments to UCC § 2–314

The Code amendments have left the black letter of § 2–314 virtually unchanged.[68] Importantly, however, comment 7 to Amended § 2–314 addresses "the tension between warranty law and tort law where goods cause personal injury or property damage." In particular, this comment clarifies the relationship between the concepts of "defective" in tort law and "unmerchantable" in warranty law: "When recovery is sought for injury to person or property, whether goods are merchantable is to be determined by applicable state products liability law." In plain language, this means that a court must define "merchantability" in products liability cases involving personal injury as the particular state defines "defectiveness" under strict liability in tort (or negligence, in states with no strict liability in tort). Yet the comment further provides that warranty law, while subordinated to tort law for purposes of UCC § 2–314, continues to support recovery, independent of tort law, for breach of express warranty (under § 2–313) and implied warranty of fitness for particular purpose (under § 2–315):[69]

> To illustrate, suppose that the seller makes a representation about the safety of a lawn mower that becomes part of the basis of the buyer's bargain. The buyer is injured when the gas tank cracks and a fire breaks out. If the lawnmower without the representation is not defective under applicable tort law, it is not unmerchantable under this section. On the other hand, if the lawnmower did not conform to the representation about safety, the seller made and breached an express warranty and the buyer may sue under Article 2.[70]

While comment 7 may not have the power of law in most jurisdictions, it does significantly resolve the knotty tension between tort and warranty

---

**66.** On the malfunction doctrine, see § 7.4. below.

**67.** Greco v. Bucciconi Eng'g Co., 283 F.Supp. 978, 982 (W.D. Pa. 1967), aff'd, 407 F.2d 87 (3d Cir. 1969). See also DeWitt v. Eveready Battery Co., Inc., 565 S.E.2d 140, 150 (N.C. 2002) (battery fluid leaked from battery); Collins v. Sears, Roebuck & Co., 583 N.E.2d 873 (Mass. App. Ct. 1992) (fire in dryer's electrical system).

**68.** The only change in black letter is the substitution of "goods of that description" for "such goods" in § 2–314(2)(c).

**69.** "When, however, a claim for injury to person or property is based on an implied warranty of fitness under Section 2–315 or an express warranty under Section 2–313 or an obligation arising under Section 2–313A or 2–313B, this Article determines whether an implied warranty of fitness or an express warranty was made and breached, as well as what damages are recoverable under Section 2–715." Amended UCC § 2–314 cmt. 7.

**70.** Id.

law on the fundamental question of how product deficiency should be defined.[71]

## § 4.4  IMPLIED WARRANTY OF FITNESS FOR PARTICULAR PURPOSE

The implied warranty of fitness for a particular purpose is a narrow and somewhat peculiar warranty,[1] sandwiched conceptually between express warranty and the implied warranty of merchantability. Some courts and commentators refer to the implied warranty of fitness for a particular purpose as the implied warranty of "fitness of purpose" or, simply, of "fitness." The precise designation perhaps should be of little consequence, except that some courts occasionally confuse the matter by referring to the implied warranty of *merchantability* as the "fitness" warranty—probably because of the central definition of "merchantability" in terms of "fitness" for ordinary purposes.[2] Although these two separate implied warranties (and express warranties) may sometimes overlap,[3] they are defined entirely differently and are conceptually distinct from one another.

In its essence, the implied warranty of fitness is an implied promise by the seller that the product sold will meet the buyer's *particular* needs. It has some similarities with express warranty, in that it is premised on a kind of representation by the seller: a representation that the product is suitable for the special purposes of the buyer made known to the seller. More specifically, the seller's implicit representation in this context is that the seller is aware of and promises to respect the buyer's trust that the seller has special skills or judgment which the seller will use in selecting a particular product that will promote the buyer's satisfaction of a particular, unusual type. The fitness warranty is therefore quite different from the implied warranty of merchantability, which is based on the seller's implicit representation that the product will safely and effectively perform the *normal* functions for which that type of product is ordinarily bought and sold. The fitness warranty typically arises from a one-on-one dealing between the buyer and the seller calculated to create quite explicit expectations in the buyer that the product selected by the seller will safely accomplish the buyer's particular task. Yet the fitness warranty (like the merchantability warranty) does not depend on an express seller affirmation, such that the fitness warranty (also like the merchantability warranty) truly is *implied*.

The distinction between the implied warranties of fitness and merchantability is well explained in comment 2 to Uniform Commercial Code § 2–315:

---

**71.** It also should be viewed as repudiating Denny v. Ford Motor Co., 662 N.E.2d 730 (N.Y. 1995). *Denny* is examined in § 5.9, below.

### § 4.4

**1.** On the implied warranty of fitness for a particular purpose, see generally An-

not., 83 A.L.R.3d 669 (1978) ("particular purpose" defined for UCC § 2–315).

**2.** UCC § 2–314(2)(c).

**3.** See UCC § 2–317 (cumulation and conflict of warranties).

A "particular purpose" differs from the ordinary purpose for which the goods are used in that it envisages a specific use by the buyer which is peculiar to the nature of his business whereas the ordinary purposes for which goods are used are those envisaged in the concept of merchantability and go to uses which are customarily made of the goods in question. For example, shoes are generally used for the purpose of walking upon ordinary ground, but a seller may know that a particular pair was selected to be used for climbing mountains.

Although the implied warranty of fitness for a particular purpose is invoked only infrequently in products liability litigation,[4] occasionally this special warranty is especially appropriate in this context. For example, the buyer may ask a hardware store salesman for a chain saw to cut out tree stumps below the level of the soil, requiring the saw to endure frequent encounters with dirt and rocks. If the salesman, after selecting the saw from several in stock, simply plunked it down on the counter saying, "That will be two hundred dollars," the implied warranty of fitness will likely have been made; and, if the saw's chain breaks from this particularly taxing use, the fitness warranty will likely have been breached. If, as occurs more frequently in such face-to-face encounters, the salesman were to add, "Oh, sure; this one will work just fine," he will have made an express warranty as well. Thus, express warranties often co-exist with implied warranties of fitness for a particular purpose.[5]

## Uniform Commercial Code § 2–315

Section 2–315 of the Uniform Commercial Code provides as follows:

§ 2–315. Implied Warranty: Fitness for Particular Purpose

Where the seller at the time of contracting has reason to know any particular purpose for which the goods are required and that the buyer is relying on the seller's skill or judgment to select or furnish suitable goods, there is unless excluded or modified under the next section an implied warranty that the goods shall be fit for such purpose.

To establish a claim for *breach* of the fitness warranty under § 2–315, the plaintiff must establish five elements:

**4.** See White and Summers, UCC § 9–10, at 371.

**5.** On the overlap between express and implied warranties of fitness for a particular purpose, see, e.g., Klein v. Sears Roebuck and Co., 773 F.2d 1421, 1424–25 (4th Cir. 1985) (Md. law), discussed in the text below. See also, Filler v. Rayex Corp., 435 F.2d 336, 338 (7th Cir. 1970) (Ind. law) (sunglasses advertised as "Baseball Sun-glasses," that splintered when hit by baseball, "not fit for baseball playing, the particular purpose for which they were sold"). See generally UCC § 2–317; Ezer, The Impact of the Uniform Commercial Code on the California Law of Sales Warranties, 8 UCLA L. Rev. 281, 299 (1961); Annot., 83 A.L.R.3d 656 (1978) (overlap of UCC express and implied warranties).

(1) That the seller had reason to know that the buyer intended to use the product for a particular purpose of which the seller was aware;

(2) That the seller had reason to know that the buyer was relying on the seller's skill or judgment to select or furnish a product suitable for that purpose;

(3) That the buyer did thereby rely on the seller;

(4) That the product was not in fact fit for the particular purpose; and

(5) That the unfitness for this purpose caused the plaintiff harm.

From these five elements for breach of the fitness warranty, two issues often predominate in importance: (1) the seller's knowledge, and (2) the buyer's reliance, which together comprise the first three elements from the list above. The fourth element, breach, is often uncontroverted in cases involving product failures producing substantial personal injury;[6] and the issues in the fifth element, causation and damage, are treated elsewhere.[7]

An example of a products liability case where the plaintiffs proved each element of their implied warranty of fitness claim is *Klein v. Sears Roebuck and Co.*[8] Plaintiffs bought a particular model riding mower upon the recommendation of the defendant's salesman for use on their hilly property, subject to the salesman's inspection of the property to confirm that the mower was appropriate. When the salesman delivered the mower, he inspected the property and pronounced the mower suitable, provided it was driven vertically up the steepest hills. Plaintiff husband was injured when the mower tipped over backwards while he was mowing vertically up one of the steeper slopes. On these facts, the court affirmed a verdict for the plaintiff husband for breach of an implied warranty of fitness (and breach of express warranty).

A plaintiff, of course, has the burden of proof on each element of his or her claim, and an implied warranty of fitness case will fail in the absence of sufficient proof of any element. *Rynders v. E.I. DuPont de Nemours & Co.*[9] was one of many actions against DuPont for selling Teflon to a small manufacturer, Vitek, which used Teflon to manufacture jaw implants marketed to help alleviate the wearing problems of TMJ syndrome. DuPont advised Vitek of studies suggesting the unsuitability of Teflon for human implants, but Vitek wrote DuPont that later studies showed solutions to the earlier problems and accepted responsibility for using Teflon in its implants. Teflon turned out to be drastically unsuited for this use, thousands of people suffered resulting injuries, Vitek went bankrupt, and its founder fled the country. There had been no breach of the implied warranty of merchantability, of course, because Teflon was a perfectly safe and sound product for most uses. As for the fitness warranty, the court held that (1) DuPont had no reason to

**6.** A products liability claim for breach of the fitness warranty is proper only if a product is dangerously unsuited for a particular purpose.

**7.** Causation issues are examined in chapters 11 and 12, below, and damages are addressed by UCC §§ 2–714 and 2–715.

**8.** 773 F.2d 1421 (4th Cir. 1985) (Md. law).

**9.** 21 F.3d 835 (8th Cir. 1994) (S.D. law).

suspect that Vitek was relying on DuPont's skill or judgment, and (2) Vitek did not in fact so rely.[10]

### Seller's Knowledge

In order for the fitness warranty to arise, a seller must be aware (or have reason to know) that a buyer plans to put a product to some special use known to the seller which is different from the ordinary uses for which the product usually is sold. The seller must further have reason to know that the buyer is relying on the seller's skill or judgment to select a product appropriate for this special purpose. The requirement that a seller be aware of these facts is a necessary predicate for the seller's (implicit) representation that the goods are suitable for a special use; a seller can hardly make a specific promise about something of which it is entirely unaware.

The seller's knowledge of the buyer's particular use and of the buyer's reliance on the seller's skill or judgment sometimes is very clear, as when an ordinary consumer requests a product with sophisticated characteristics from a dealer in such products who purports to have expertise in the product's special characteristics. So, when a prospective buyer of a riding lawnmower seeks and obtains an assurance from the selling dealer that a particular type and model lawnmower will be suited safely to mow uphill slopes inspected by the dealer, as in the *Klein* case discussed above, the dealer will know full well that the buyer is relying for his safety on the dealer's skill and judgment in the selection of a proper mower.[11]

The source of the seller's knowledge is unimportant, so long as it in fact exists. Although a buyer ordinarily will personally inform the seller of his or her intended use of the product, a communication from the buyer is unnecessary if the seller already has acquired the information from some other source, or if the buyer's intended use is evident from the context of the transaction.[12]

An implied warranty of fitness claim will fail if the plaintiff is unable to prove any aspect of the seller's required knowledge.[13] Thus, the fitness warranty will not apply to the sale of a stove, if the distributor is unaware of the buyer's particular heating needs;[14] or of retreaded tires for a pickup truck, if the seller is unaware that the truck will be used in the buyer's construction business;[15] or of a truck cab chassis, if the manufacturer did not know it would be put to use as a tow truck.[16]

---

**10.** See also Kalinowski v. E.I. Du Pont de Nemours & Co., 851 F.Supp. 149 (E.D. Pa. 1994).

**11.** See *Klein*, 773 F.2d at 1424–25.

**12.** See cmt. 1 to UCC § 2–315. See, e.g., Miller v. Andy Burger Motors, Inc., 370 S.W.2d 654 (Mo. Ct. App. 1963) (auto).

**13.** See West's Ann. Cal. Civ. Code § 1792.1, .2.

**14.** See Dalton v. Stanley Solar & Stove, Inc., 629 A.2d 794 (N.H. 1993).

**15.** See Jones v. Marcus, 457 S.E.2d 271 (Ga. Ct. App. 1995).

**16.** See Ford Motor Co. v. General Accident Ins. Co., 779 A.2d 362, 374–79 (Md. 2001) (implied warranty of fitness for particular purpose claim against manufacturer failed because no proof that it knew that cab chassis would be converted to tow truck).

**Buyer's Reliance**

As discussed above, the fitness warranty partakes of some aspects of express warranty. As is true generally for misrepresentation claims, including those based on express warranty, the buyer's reliance is a fundamental aspect of the claim.[17] The fitness warranty arises when, in dealings between a buyer and a seller, the seller renders an implicit assurance that a particular product selected by the seller will fulfill a specific need designated by the buyer. Even in the absence of an express representation to this effect, such dealings can create the same kinds of expectations of specific satisfaction. If, once the seller makes such implicit assurances of suitability, the buyer fails to rely upon them, any harm suffered by the buyer cannot have resulted from the product's failure to conform to the assurances. Thus, implied warranty of fitness claims require the buyer's reliance to provide a causal link between the seller's misconduct (the false message) and the buyer's harm.

A plaintiff's reliance or non-reliance on the seller's skill and judgment is sometimes very clear. Examples of self-evident reliance include a beauty shop customer who relies on the beautician to select an appropriate permanent wave solution, not one that will cause injuries to her scalp and loss of hair,[18] and purchasers of a casket and vault who rely on a funeral home to select a casket that will fit in the vault.[19] The reliance may be made by a prior party in the distributive chain, so that a patient in whom a prosthetic device is implanted may take the benefit of the hospital's reliance on the skill and judgment of the manufacturer of the device.[20] Sometimes evidence on the reliance issue points clearly the other way, that the buyer made an independent decision to buy and put a product to a particular use. So, if the buyer purchases a lawnmower of a particular type because his neighbor has one, and he fails to seek advice from or discuss the purchase decision with anyone, the absence of reliance will defeat a warranty of fitness claim.[21]

Certain types of situations suggest the absence of reliance. In early sales law, various specific rules developed that were designed to assure the buyer's reliance and to weed out cases where it did not exist. For example, a buyer's inspection of the product, or in some jurisdictions even his or her opportunity to inspect, negated both the implied warranties of fitness and merchantability. Section 15(3) of the Uniform Sales Act restricted this exclusion to actual examinations and defects which ought to have been revealed thereby, a restriction that has continued under UCC § 2–316(3)(b). A buyer's reliance was also assured by another rule that precluded implied warranties of fitness for a particular purpose in the case of articles that were "known, described and definite."[22] One application of this restriction was the more specific provision

**17.** That the reliance element is now cast in terms of "basis of the bargain" in § 2–313 is unimportant inasmuch as the basic concept is the same.

**18.** Newmark v. Gimbel's, Inc., 246 A.2d 11 (N.J. Super. Ct. 1968), aff'd, 258 A.2d 697 (N.J. 1969).

**19.** Caldwell v. Brown Serv. Funeral Home, 345 So.2d 1341 (Ala. 1977).

**20.** Perfetti v. McGhan Med., 662 P.2d 646 (N.M. Ct. App. 1983).

**21.** Freeman v. Case Corp., 924 F.Supp. 1456 (W.D. Va. 1996), rev'd on other grounds, 118 F.3d 1011 (4th Cir. 1997).

**22.** 1 Williston on Sales § 235 at 607 (1948 rev. ed.).

of Uniform Sales Act § 15(4) that precluded such warranties "[i]n the case of a contract to sell or a sale of a specified article under its patent or other trade name."[23] Now, the buyer's designation of a product by name is only one factor to be considered on the ultimate factual issue of reliance.[24] Finally, where the buyer rather than the seller prepares specifications for the product, it is well established that a product made to those specifications carries no warranty of fitness for the particular purpose, even when that purpose is in fact known to the seller.[25]

A buyer who inspects the product, or otherwise participates in its selection, may have some difficulty in establishing reliance on the seller's judgment in selecting the product. So, where a plaintiff looked over various step-ladders and chose the one recommended by a salesman, the court held that a fitness warranty did not arise because the selection was not "exclusively within the control of" the salesman and the buyer's "discretion and judgment played a major part in the selection."[26] Generally, however, a buyer's inspection should not conclusively establish nonreliance. In *Peters v. Lyons*,[27] the buyer asked for a dog chain strong enough to restrain his 100– to 120–pound German shepherd. The saleswoman selected the strongest chain, which she and the buyer both inspected and agreed would be sufficient. It was not, and the plaintiff was attacked and injured by the dog. The court held that the buyer had established his reliance on the seller's skill and judgment: " 'The buyer's reliance on the seller need not be total reliance. The buyer may rely on his own judgment as to some matters and on the seller's skill and judgment as to others.' "[28]

### Compared to Implied Warranty of Merchantability

Unlike the implied warranty of merchantability in UCC § 2–314, which requires that the seller be a "merchant" of such goods, UCC § 2–315 applies to any seller.[29] While buyers normally rely for selection advice on knowledgeable merchants, a warranty under UCC § 2–315 can

---

**23.** See 1 Williston on Sales, above, §§ 234–36a.

**24.** Compare UCC § 2–315 cmt. 5:

The elimination of the "patent or other trade name" exception constitutes the major extension of the warranty of fitness.... [T]he existence of a patent or other trade name and the designation of the article by that name, or indeed in any other definite manner, is only one of the facts to be considered on the question of whether the buyer actually relied on the seller, but it is not of itself decisive of the issue. If the buyer himself is insisting on a particular brand he is not relying on the seller's skill and judgment and so no warranty results. But the mere fact that the article purchased has a particular patent or trade name is not sufficient to indicate nonreliance if the article has been recommended by the seller as adequate for the buyer's purposes.

**25.** See, e.g., Singleton v. L.P. Anderson Supply Co., 943 P.2d 968 (Mont. 1997) (buyer ordered exact item of particular size); Fisher v. Monsanto Co., 863 F.Supp. 285 (W.D. Va. 1994) (buyer's specifications). See also Jacobs v. E.I. du Pont de Nemours & Co., 67 F.3d 1219 (6th Cir. 1995) (Tenn. law) (no implied warranty of fitness where buyer merely orders specified goods).

**26.** See Carney v. Sears, Roebuck & Co., 309 F.2d 300 (4th Cir. 1962) (Va. law).

**27.** 168 N.W.2d 759 (Iowa 1969).

**28.** Id. at 764, quoting Drager v. Carlson Hybrid Corn Co., 56 N.W.2d 18, 22 (Iowa 1952).

**29.** Under the prior Uniform Sales Act, the language referring to this warranty affirmed its scope as including the seller "whether he be the grower or the manufacturer or not." See UCC § 2–315 cmt. 4.

arise "as to non-merchants where this is justified by the particular circumstances."[30]

Another important distinction between these two implied warranties concerns the issue of reliance. Reliance is a crucially important element of the fitness warranty, as discussed above. But reliance is simply not an issue with respect to the warranty of merchantability, of basic quality for ordinary uses, which arises solely from the product's sale.

More fundamentally, as noted earlier, the fitness warranty is entirely distinct and independent from the implied warranty of merchantability. As lucidly explained in comment 2 to § 2–315, above, this distinction is so perfectly clear that one might reasonably conclude that an "ordinary" use by definition must be separate and distinct from a purpose which is "particular" to a buyer. Indeed, most courts have logically so concluded, ruling that an ordinary use cannot also be a special use.[31] For example, in *Miles v. Ford Motor Co.*,[32] the passenger in a Ford Ranger pickup truck was paralyzed in an accident by a defectively designed shoulder harness. Noting that all of the state's previous fitness warranty cases had involved evidence that the seller was aware of "peculiar or extraordinary uses to which the buyer intended to put the product that were at least somewhat out of the ordinary," the court concluded that "the better rule is that a particular purpose must be a particular nonordinary purpose."[33] Thus, the sale of an ordinary pickup truck did not include a warranty of fitness for the particular purpose of carrying passengers, since this was one of the ordinary purposes of such trucks.[34]

Notwithstanding the logic of this view, some courts remain confused.[35] Perhaps led astray by comment 2 to § 2–315,[36] a few courts have

**30.** UCC § 2–315 cmt. 4. See, e.g., Barb v. Wallace, 412 A.2d 1314 (Md. Ct. Spec. App. 1980) (sale of old lawnmower motor for use in go-cart).

**31.** See, e.g., Ford Motor Co. v. General Accident Ins. Co., 779 A.2d 362, 376–79 (Md. 2001) (use of truck cab chassis); Doe v. Miles, Inc., 2000 WL 667383, at *5–8 (Mo. Ct. App. 2000) (hemophiliac who contracted HIV and then AIDS from use of blood factor concentrate to replace clotting proteins could not recover under implied warranty of fitness for particular purpose because this was ordinary purpose of product); McCabe v. Allied Products Corp., 2000 WL 1805687, at *7 (D. Me. 2000) ("proof of breach of the implied warranty of fitness for a particular purpose requires proof that the purchaser had 'a particular purpose *outside* the scope or ordinary purposes' "); Coghlan v. Aquasport Marine Corp., 73 F.Supp.2d 769, 774 (S.D. Tex. 1999) ("the particular purpose must be some unusual, out of the ordinary purpose peculiar to the needs of an individual buyer"), aff'd, 240 F.3d 449 (5th Cir. 2001); Stones v. Sears, Roebuck & Co., 558 N.W.2d 540 (Neb. 1997) (ordinary, not particular, purpose of propane grill was to grill); Wilson v. Brown & Williamson Tobacco Corp., 968 F.Supp. 296 (S.D. W. Va.

1997) (smoking not particular purpose of tobacco); Curry v. Sile Distribs., 727 F.Supp. 1052, 1054 (N.D. Miss. 1990) ("Mississippi follows the comment to Uniform Commercial Code § 2–315 and does not imply a warranty of fitness for a particular use when the good is purchased for the ordinary use of a good of that kind.").

**32.** 922 S.W.2d 572 (Tex. App. 1996), rev'd in part on other grounds, Ford Motor Co. v. Miles, 967 S.W.2d 377 (Tex. 1998).

**33.** *Miles*, 922 S.W.2d at 587.

**34.** "Even if [the buyer] had expressly told either Ford or the dealership that he intended to carry passengers in his truck, that is the ordinary purpose of a passenger truck, rather than a particular purpose.... [T]here was no warranty for a particular purpose...." Id.

See also American Suzuki Motor Corp. v. Superior Ct., 44 Cal.Rptr.2d 526 (Ct. App. 1995) (consumer's purpose for buying automobile not a "particular purpose").

**35.** See, e.g., Lariviere v. Dayton Safety Ladder Co., 525 A.2d 892 (R.I. 1987).

**36.** Comment 2 states in part, "A contract may of course include both a warranty

ruled that an ordinary use under § 2–314 can also amount to a particular purpose under § 2–315.[37] "Such confusion under the Code is inexcusable. Sections 2–314 and 2–315 make plain that the warranty of fitness for a particular purpose is narrower, more specific, and more precise."[38] It is true, of course, that a product's unmerchantability may also render it unfit for some particular purpose for which it was specially warranted. In such a case, however, a claim for breach of implied warranty of fitness for a particular purpose will lie only if the buyer establishes each aspect of such a claim including the particularity of the purpose for which the product was warranted.

The converse is also true: the implied warranty of fitness for a particular purpose may be breached even if the product is entirely merchantable and "nondefective." While a product sold in breach of the fitness warranty may be "defective" or unmerchantable for its ordinary uses, many products that normally are entirely safe may be dangerous and entirely unfit when put to other uses for which those products were not designed. The point is that the fitness warranty has no concern with a product's safety sufficiency for its *general* uses, but only those *particular* uses made part of the buyer's and seller's special deal. Thus, the fitness warranty may be breached when a product properly made and merchantable is simply the wrong one for the buyer's particular use.[39]

## § 4.5  PRIVITY OF CONTRACT AND THIRD PARTY BENEFICIARIES

The privity of contract issue was examined earlier from the perspective of its availability as a defense to *negligence* claims, as established in *Winterbottom v. Wright*.[1] In repudiating the privity defense for negligence claims, *MacPherson v. Buick*[2] emphasized the irrelevance of contractual relationships to the independent obligations imposed on sellers by the law of torts. In the words of Judge Cardozo:

> We have put aside the notion that the duty to safeguard life and limb, when the consequences of negligence may be foreseen, grows out of contract and nothing else. We have put the source of the obligation where it ought to be. We have put its source in the law.[3]

of merchantability and one of fitness for a particular purpose."

**37.** See, e.g., Soaper v. Hope Indus., Inc., 424 S.E.2d 493, 495 (S.C. 1992) (concluding that the two implied warranties may "merge and are cumulative, such that a plaintiff may proceed upon either theory"); Great Dane Trailer Sales, Inc. v. Malvern Pulpwood, Inc., 785 S.W.2d 13, 17 (Ark. 1990) (the two implied warranties merge "[i]f the particular purpose for which goods are to be used coincides with their general functional use"); Nelson v. Wilkins Dodge, Inc., 256 N.W.2d 472 (Minn. 1977) (particular as well as ordinary use of pickup truck was to be driven at sustained high rates of speed); Knab v. Alden's Irving Park, Inc., 199 N.E.2d 815 (Ill. App. Ct. 1964) (child's trousers).

**38.** White and Summers, UCC § 9–10 at 369–70.

**39.** See, e.g., McLaughlin v. Michelin Tire Corp., 778 P.2d 59, 66 (Wyo. 1989) (affirming proposition).

### § 4.5

**1.** 10 M. & W. 109, 152 Eng. Rep. 402 (Ex. 1842).

**2.** 111 N.E. 1050 (N.Y. 1916). *MacPherson* and *Winterbottom* are discussed in § 1.2, above.

**3.** Id. at 1051. By "law," Judge Cardozo meant "tort law," the law of obligations toward other persons imposed on every person regardless of consent, as distinguished from the law of contracts which enforces

It was at this place and time, New York in 1916, that tort law took one of its most important detours away from the law of contract, especially in products liability actions, by stripping away the privity defense from actions that lay in negligence. In explaining the elemental difference between tort and contract law in respect to privity, Judge Cardozo indirectly revealed the logical power of the defense of privity in its own domain, contract cases involving claims for breach of warranty. That is, while a contractual relationship between a seller and a victim of a product accident may be irrelevant to a negligence claim, such a relationship is fundamental to whether the victim has a claim for breach of a contractual warranty.

In the early part of the twentieth century, the law of contracts quite firmly restricted the enforcement of contractual undertakings to the contracting parties themselves. In denying recovery to a person claiming as a contract beneficiary in one early case, Lord Haldane remarked that "[i]n the law of England certain principles are fundamental. One is that only a person who is a party to a contract can sue on it."[4] Contractual rights were extended to nonparties to the contract ("third party beneficiaries") only in limited situations where the contracting parties clearly intended to confer benefits on such other persons "remote" from the contract.[5] So, it is evident that the absence of a contractual relationship between the parties (the absence of "privity of contract") is a significant obstacle to a breach of warranty or other *contract* claim.

In examining the privity of contract issue in products liability claims brought in warranty, the problem may helpfully be considered in terms of the separate notions of "vertical" and "horizontal" privity. The unifying question in both contexts involves the determination of the proper parties to breach of warranty actions: What defendants are bound by warranties, and what plaintiffs obtain their benefits?

"Vertical privity" refers to the contractual relationship between the parties up and down the chain of distribution, from suppliers of raw materials and component parts, at the top, through manufacturers, distributors, wholesalers, retailers, and, at the bottom of the chain, the purchasers. The vertical privity issue may be framed as, *Who can be sued?* "Horizontal privity," on the other hand, involves the rights of nonpurchasing persons who may be affected by the product and who seek to stand in the purchaser's shoes to obtain the benefits of whatever warranties flowed to the purchaser by virtue of his or her contract of purchase. Such nonpurchasers, extending horizontally away from the purchaser in diminishing order of affinity, include the purchaser's family, members of the purchaser's household and household guests, the

private agreements which people consensually undertake.

**4.** Dunlop Pneumatic Tyre Co. v. Selfridge & Co., [1914–15] All E.R.Rep. 333, 334 (H.L. 1915).

**5.** See J. Perillo, Calamari and Perillo on Contracts ch. 17 (5th ed. 2003).

purchaser's employees, and others often referred to as "bystanders." The horizontal privity issue may be framed as, *Who can sue?*[6]

## Vertical Privity

Until the industrial revolution, consumers often bought their limited products—lamps, guns, leather goods, and garden and dairy produce—directly from the parties who manufactured them, the smiths or farmers who produced the goods.[7] Yet, just as courts in this nation began to impose implied warranties of quality on manufacturers in the latter part of the nineteenth century, manufacturers increasingly were spinning off the retail function to third party dealers. This meant, of course, that the typical consumer began to deal contractually only with the retailer. Of course, if the retailer were found to be an agent of the manufacturer the buyer could satisfy the privity requirement. In most cases, however, manufacturers sued in warranty by consumers of defective products in the late 1800s and early 1900s had available the ready-made defense of "no privity of contract," a defense that was proving its effectiveness in actions brought in negligence, at least before *MacPherson*. The harshness of this defense in cases of consumer injury was readily apparent, and the courts began to riddle it with exceptions at an early date.[8]

The first decisions to abolish outright the manufacturer's privity defense in implied warranty personal injury cases were made at the turn of the twentieth century and involved defective foodstuffs.[9] By mid-century, the weakening privity defense in implied warranty cases began to spread to products for intimate bodily use such as soap, hair dye, and

---

**6.** The distinction between vertical and horizontal privity is well summarized in Dalton v. Stanley Solar & Stove, Inc., 629 A.2d 794, 796–97 (N.H. 1993):

> The term vertical privity describes the relationship between adjoining parties in a marketing chain. *See* Hawkland, 1 UCC Series § 2–218:01, at 421 (1984). Vertical privity exists, for example, between a wholesaler and retailer, and between a retailer and the ultimate buyer, but not between a wholesaler and the ultimate buyer. Vertical privity is readily distinguishable from horizontal privity, which denotes the relationship between the retailer and one who uses or consumes the goods. Where a dealer sells goods to a buyer, and a third party is injured due to a defect in the goods, whether the third party can sue the dealer is an issue of horizontal privity.

**7.** "In earlier times the one who made the article generally sold it directly to the ultimate user, and thus the consumer, being in privity of contract with the manufacturer, was allowed to recover on the usual warranties for losses caused by defective workmanship." Jeanblanc, Manufacturers' Liability to Persons Other Than Their Immediate Vendees, 24 Va. L. Rev. 134, 134 (1937).

**8.** See Gillam, Products Liability in a Nutshell, 37 Or. L. Rev. 119, 152–55 (1958) (listing 29 such exceptions).

**9.** See Mazetti v. Armour & Co., 135 P. 633 (Wash. 1913); Parks v. G.C. Yost Pie Co., 144 P. 202 (Kan. 1914). See also Jackson Coca–Cola Bottling Co. v. Chapman, 64 So. 791, 791 (Miss. 1914); Jacob E. Decker & Sons, Inc. v. Capps, 164 S.W.2d 828, 829 (Tex. 1942):

> Liability in such case is [based] on the broad principle of the public policy to protect human health and life. It is a well-known fact that articles of food are manufactured and placed in the channels of commerce, with the intention that they shall pass from hand to hand until they are finally used by some remote customer. It is usually impracticable, if not impossible, for the ultimate customer to analyze the food and ascertain whether or not it is suitable for human consumption. . . . [W]here food products sold for human consumption are unfit for that purpose, there is such an utter failure of the purpose for which the food is sold, and the consequences of eating unsound food are so disastrous to human health and life, that the law imposes a warranty of purity in favor of the ultimate consumer as a matter of public policy.

permanent wave solution.[10] Then, in the late 1950s and early 1960s, several courts in rapid succession extended the idea to durable goods. In 1960, in *Henningsen v. Bloomfield Motors, Inc.*,[11] the privity bar was emphatically repudiated in a landmark implied warranty case involving injuries from a defective automobile manufactured by defendant, Chrysler Corporation, sold to a dealer, Bloomfield Motors, which sold it to Mr. Henningsen. The car had a steering defect, and Mr. Henningsen's wife was injured ten days after purchase when the car went off the road. Speaking for the New Jersey Supreme Court, Justice Francis explained why the demise of the privity defense in food and drink cases compelled its demise in a case involving a defective car: "We see no rational doctrinal basis for differentiating between a fly in a bottle of beverage and a defective automobile. The unwholesome beverage may bring illness to one person, the defective car, with its great potentiality for harm to the driver, occupants, and others, demands even less adherence to the narrow barrier of privity."[12]

In the view of Dean William Prosser, *Henningsen* marked the end of the privity defense in products liability claims brought in implied warranty, the "fall of the citadel of privity."[13] Finding the vertical privity requirement for implied warranty claims outmoded and bad policy, many courts have now abandoned it in cases of personal injury,[14] some in cases of property damage,[15] and a few even for economic loss.[16] Nevertheless, because implied warranty claims lie in contract, many courts still require vertical privity for implied warranty claims for economic loss,[17] and some

---

**10.** The breakdown of the privity defense is recounted in Prosser, Assault Upon the Citadel (Strict Liability to the Consumer), 69 Yale L.J. 1099 (1960).

**11.** 161 A.2d 69 (N.J. 1960).

**12.** Id. at 83.

**13.** Prosser, The Fall of the Citadel (Strict Liability to the Consumer), 50 Minn. L. Rev. 791, 791 (1966).

**14.** See, e.g., AgGrow Oils, L.L.C. v. National Union Fire Ins. Co. of Pittsburgh, 276 F.Supp.2d 999, 1014 (D.N.D. 2003) (dictum, distinguishing economic loss cases; Colon v. BIC USA, Inc., 199 F.Supp.2d 53, 95 (S.D.N.Y. 2001) ("No showing of privity is required in a personal injury action for breach of express or implied warranty."); Bouverette v. Westinghouse Elec. Corp., 628 N.W.2d 86, 91 (Mich. Ct. App. 2001) (privity unnecessary for injured bystanders suing manufacturer for breach of warranty or negligence); R.R. Donnelley & Sons Co. v. North Texas Steel Co., 752 N.E.2d 112, 124–25 (Ind. Ct. App. 2001); Berry v. G.D. Searle & Co., 309 N.E.2d 550 (Ill. 1974) (implied warranty of fitness for a particular purpose).

**15.** See, e.g., Kassab v. Central Soya, 246 A.2d 848 (Pa. 1968) (property damage), overruled on other grounds, AM/PM Franchise Ass'n v. Atlantic Richfield Co., 584 A.2d 915 (Pa. 1990). See generally Israel

Phoenix Assur. Co. v. SMS Sutton, Inc., 787 F.Supp. 102 (W.D. Pa. 1992).

**16.** See, e.g., Spagnol Enters., Inc. v. Digital Equip. Corp., 568 A.2d 948, 952 (Pa. Super. Ct. 1989) (economic loss; state high court's prior abolition of vertical privity "was intended to apply to all breach of warranty cases brought under the warranty provision of the Uniform Commercial Code for all types of damages, whether they be personal injuries, damage to property or economic loss"); Patty Precision Prod. Co. v. Brown & Sharpe Mfg. Co., 846 F.2d 1247, 1253–54 (10th Cir. 1988) (Okla. law) (Oklahoma rejects majority view requiring vertical privity which inefficiently requires plaintiffs to sue their immediate vendors who then have to sue their immediate vendors and so on up the chain of distribution until the responsible vendor eventually is reached: "It defies common sense to require such an endless chain of litigation in order to hold the party at fault responsible.").

**17.** See, e.g., Allstate Ins. Co. v. Daimler Chrysler, 2004 WL 442679, at *2 (N.D. Ill. 2004); Pulte Home Corp. v. Parex, Inc., 579 S.E.2d 188 (Va. 2003) (privity required for recovery of consequential damages); Norcold, Inc. v. Gateway Supply Co., 798 N.E.2d 618, 626–28 (Ohio Ct. App. 2003); Superior Kitchen Designs, Inc. v. Valspar Indus. (U.S.A.), 263 F.Supp.2d 140 (D. Mass. 2003); Szajna v. General Motors

(because of the availability of tort law claims) even in cases involving personal injuries.[18]

The vertical privity issue long presented a stumbling block for plaintiffs relying on *express* warranties, especially in earlier years. Yet, because the seller affirmatively creates such warranties in an effort to induce persons to purchase the goods, the fairness and policy arguments supporting a privity defense in this context are especially weak. That is, warranty law might reasonably hold a manufacturer responsible for harmful consequences of false advertisements, which it composes and directs at consumers to convince them to buy its products, regardless of the fact that a consumer thereby injured will virtually never have contracted directly with the manufacturer responsible for the injury.[19]

*Rogers v. Toni Home Permanent Co.*[20] is the landmark case abolishing the privity defense in express warranty cases.[21] Noting that the express warranty action derived originally from tort (deceit) rather than from contract, the court relied upon *Baxter v. Ford Motor Co.*[22] to extend the privity exception recognized in food cases to products generally, reasoning that basic fairness requires that such claims be allowed.[23] It is now widely accepted that express warranties arising from advertisements, labels, brochures, and owner's manuals run with the goods directly to "remote" purchasers who in reliance on the truth of such assertions thereby suffer harm,[24] especially consumers who suffer personal injury,[25] but sometimes also consumers[26] and even business enter-

---

Corp., 503 N.E.2d 760, 762–70 (Ill. 1986) (thorough analysis).

**18.** See, e.g., Baughn v. Honda Motor Co., 727 P.2d 655 (Wash. 1986); Gowen v. Cady, 376 S.E.2d 390 (Ga. Ct. App. 1988).

**19.** See, e.g., Dravo Equip. Co. v. German, 698 P.2d 63, 65 (Or. Ct. App. 1985) ("A seller, as the master of a warranty's destiny, is free to make it as broad or as narrow as it chooses. Express warranties can be limited in effect, duration and transferability. Because the seller is free to create an express warranty in any fashion it chooses, there is no reason why the warranty should not extend to remote purchasers when it is not so limited.").

**20.** 147 N.E.2d 612 (Ohio 1958). *Rogers* is noted in 58 Colum. L. Rev. 1092 (1958); 19 Ohio St. L.J. 733 (1958); 44 Iowa L. Rev. 229 (1958); 11 Vand. L. Rev. 1459 (1958); 44 Va. L. Rev. 1002 (1958); 75 A.L.R.2d 112 (1961).

**21.** Other important early cases were Silverman v. Samuel Mallinger Co., 100 A.2d 715 (Pa. 1953), and Hamon v. Digliani, 174 A.2d 294 (Conn. 1961). Note that the issue in these cases, how no privity affects express warranty claims, is to be distinguished from how no privity affects implied warranty claims, the issue in *Henningsen*.

**22.** 12 P.2d 409 (Wash. 1932).

**23.** See *Rogers*, 147 N.E.2d at 615:

The consuming public ordinarily relies exclusively on the representations of the manufacturer in his advertisements. What sensible or sound reason then exists as to why, when the goods purchased by the ultimate consumer on the strength of the advertisements aimed squarely at him do not possess their described qualities and goodness and cause him harm, he should not be permitted to move against the manufacturer to recoup his loss.... The warranties made by the manufacturer in his advertisements and by the labels on his products are inducements to the ultimate consumers, and the manufacturer ought to be held to strict accountability to any consumer who buys the product in reliance on such representations and later suffers injury [as a result].

**24.** This issue is now addressed explicitly in Amended UCC §§ 2–313A and 2–313B, as discussed in § 4.2, above.

**25.** See, e.g., Whitman v. Consolidated Aluminum Corp., 637 S.W.2d 405 (Mo. Ct. App. 1982); Kinlaw v. Long Mfg. N.C., Inc., 259 S.E.2d 552 (N.C. 1979); Reid v. Volkswagen of Am., Inc., 512 F.2d 1294 (6th Cir. 1975) (Mich. law); Hauter v. Zogarts, 534 P.2d 377 (Cal. 1975); Hamon v. Digliani, 174 A.2d 294 (Conn. 1961). *Contra* Oats v. Nissan Motor Corp., 879 P.2d 1095, 1102 (Idaho 1994).

**26.** Some courts have allowed remote consumers to recover for breach of express

prises[27] who suffer purely economic loss.[28]

It is important to note, however, that many states which have abolished the requirement of vertical privity in *express* warranty cases have retained it in the case of *implied* warranties, such that the absence of privity may bar an implied warranty claim in the same case in which an express warranty claim is allowed.[29] For example, *Connick v. Suzuki Motor Co.*[30] was a claim for economic loss by purchasers against the manufacturer of Suzuki Samurai sport utility vehicles based on the tendency of the vehicles to roll over. Having bought their vehicles from dealers, who were not agents of the manufacturer, the purchasers were not in privity with the manufacturer. Allowing the express warranty claim because "a manufacturer which extends a written warranty to a consumer establishes privity between it and the consumer,"[31] the court nevertheless dismissed one group of plaintiffs' merchantability and fitness implied warranty claims for want of vertical privity.[32]

In addition to the many state court decisions that have abolished the privity defense in various contexts involving warranty claims by purchasers against remote sellers, a few state legislatures have taken hold of the vertical privity requirement and expressly abolished it without regard to the type of injury suffered by the plaintiff.[33] Moreover, some courts and commentators have taken the position that the Magnuson–Moss Federal Warranty Act,[34] in cases where a manufacturer issues an express warranty and the Act otherwise applies, effectively abolishes the vertical privity

warranty that results only in economic loss. See, e.g., Kinlaw v. Long Mfg. N.C. Inc., 259 S.E.2d 552 (N.C. 1979) (absence of privity of contract between buyer and seller of tractor no bar to buyer's claim for economic losses due to tractor's continual breaking down, where buyer relied on statements in owner's manual).

**27.** Many courts allow such claims brought by non-privity corporations. See, e.g., Larrison v. Moving Floors, Inc., 873 P.2d 1092 (Or. Ct. App. 1994); Fullerton Aircraft Sales & Rentals, Inc. v. Beech Aircraft Corp., 842 F.2d 717 (4th Cir. 1988) (Kan. law); Prairie Prod., Inc. v. Agchem Div'n–Pennwalt Corp., 514 N.E.2d 1299 (Ind. Ct. App. 1987); Campus Sweater & Sportswear Co. v. M. B. Kahn Const. Co., 515 F.Supp. 64 (D.S.C. 1979), aff'd, 644 F.2d 877 (4th Cir. 1981). Yet, some courts still require privity in pure economic loss cases even for express warranty claims. See, e.g., Carcone v. Gordon Heating & Air Conditioning Co., 623 N.Y.S.2d 679 (App. Div. 1995).

**28.** See Vermont Plastics, Inc. v. Brine, Inc., 79 F.3d 272 (2d Cir. 1996) (Vt. law) (vertical privity unnecessary in express warranty cases involving personal injury, property damage, or Magnuson–Moss Federal Warranty Act claims by consumers).

**29.** See, e.g., Evraets v. Intermedics Intraocular, Inc., 34 Cal.Rptr.2d 852 (Ct. App. 1994).

**30.** 656 N.E.2d 170 (Ill. App. Ct. 1995), rev'd in part on other grounds, 675 N.E.2d 584 (Ill. 1996).

**31.** *Connick,* 656 N.E.2d at 177.

**32.** Id. at 180.

**33.** See, e.g., Virginia's "anti-privity" statute, a non-uniform version of UCC § 2–318. Va. Code Ann. § 8.2–318. Similar legislation exists in Maine, Massachusetts, and New Hampshire. At least Virginia's statute does not apply to consequential damages, however, because UCC § 2–715(2)(a) suggests that such damages are available only to parties in privity of contract. See Pulte Home Corp. v. Parex, Inc., 579 S.E.2d 188 (Va. 2003).

At least a couple of states have held that UCC § 2–318 Alternative B by its terms eliminates vertical as well as horizontal privity. See Bishop v. Sales, 336 So.2d 1340 (Ala. 1976). See also Gasque v. Eagle Mach. Co., 243 S.E.2d 831 (S.C. 1978). New Hampshire's enactment of a provision similar to Alternative C "removed both horizontal and vertical privity as defenses to implied warranty claims." Dalton v. Stanley Solar & Stove, Inc., 629 A.2d 794, 797 (N.H. 1993).

**34.** Enacted in 1975, the Act is codified at 15 U.S.C. § 2301 et seq. See § 4.9, below.

bar to consumers seeking to maintain implied warranty claims against remote manufacturers.[35] A close reading of the Act, however, suggests that courts reasoning to the contrary are correct in concluding that the Act leaves state privity rules intact.[36]

Finally, it should be noted that a state's abolition of the *vertical* privity defense, involving the issue of whether the actual purchaser in the stream of distribution may maintain a warranty action upstream against a remote seller (usually the manufacturer), does not affect the separate question of whether a non-purchaser who is injured, such as a family member or a bystander, can make a valid warranty claim against a product seller.[37] This latter question involves the issue of *horizontal* privity, which now is addressed statutorily under the UCC.

### Horizontal Privity—Third Party Beneficiaries Under § 2–318

Because of the absence of privity of contract, early cases denied warranty recovery to users injured by products purchased by others.[38] Especially in cases of food purchases for other family members, some courts employed agency principles to avoid the problem and allow recovery.[39] The issue of horizontal privity (and, perhaps, vertical privity to some extent) is now addressed explicitly in § 2–318 of the Uniform Commercial Code, entitled "Third Party Beneficiaries of Warranties Express or Implied."[40] By the mid–1960s, as the pro-consumer movement rapidly gained momentum in many states, substantial differences appeared in the development of the privity doctrine in the common law of the various states. Accordingly, in 1966, § 2–318 was amended and promulgated for adoption in three separate forms, allowing each state to choose whichever form best conformed to its own law and public policy on a matter which had become a fast-moving and controversial issue— the proper reach of strict products liability law in warranty.[41]

---

**35.** See, e.g., Szajna v. General Motors Corp., 503 N.E.2d 760, 769 (Ill. 1986): "[I]f a Magnuson–Moss written warranty (either 'full' or 'limited') is given . . . , the nonprivity 'consumer' should be permitted to maintain an action on an implied warranty against the 'warrantor.' "

**36.** See, e.g., Walsh v. Ford Motor Co., 588 F.Supp. 1513, 1524–27 (D.D.C. 1984), in which multiple plaintiffs brought claims under the Act. Because the Act defines "implied warranty" as "an implied warranty arising under State law," reasoned the court, it must respect the state law's privity rules which help determine whether it arises under state law, quoting Feinstein v. Firestone Tire & Rubber Co., 535 F.Supp. 595, 606 n.13 (S.D.N.Y. 1982): "[I]f state law requires vertical privity to enforce an implied warranty and there is none, then, like the yeastless souffle, the warranty does not 'arise.' "

**37.** The distinction between the two different forms of privity is considered in a number of decisions. For an in-depth treat-

ment, see, e.g., Szajna v. General Motors Corp., 503 N.E.2d 760, 762–70 (Ill. 1986).

**38.** See, e.g., Chysky v. Drake Bros. Co., 139 N.E. 576 (N.Y. 1923) (waitress bit into nail baked into cake purchased by her employer from defendant).

**39.** See, e.g., Greenberg v. Lorenz, 173 N.E.2d 773 (N.Y. 1961) (presumption that food purchase by father was made for all members of household).

**40.** As discussed above, the amended version of Article 2 now divides UCC § 2–313 into separate sections based on whether the plaintiff was (§ 2–313, "immediate buyers") or was not (§§ 2–313A and B, "remote purchasers") in privity with the seller.

**41.** Commentary to § 2–318 explained the rationale for amending the section and offering it in alternative form:

This section as drawn in 1950 was substantially in the form of the new Alternative B. The form shown as Alternative A was substituted in 1951, limiting beneficiaries to the family, household and

The three alternatives of § 2–318 are as follows:

### Alternative A

A seller's warranty whether express or implied extends to any natural person who is in the family or household of his buyer or who is a guest in his home if it is reasonable to expect that such person may use, consume or be affected by the goods and who is injured in person by breach of the warranty. A seller may not exclude or limit the operation of this section.

### Alternative B

A seller's warranty whether express or implied extends to any natural person who may reasonably be expected to use, consume or be affected by the goods and who is injured in person by breach of the warranty. A seller may not exclude or limit the operation of this section.

### Alternative C

A seller's warranty whether express or implied extends to any person who may reasonably be expected to use, consume or be affected by the goods and who is injured by breach of the warranty. A seller may not exclude or limit the operation of this section with respect to injury to the person of an individual to whom the warranty extends.

Each of the three alternatives to § 2–318 describes the extent to which warranty protection is extended beyond the purchaser in sales transactions. As stated in comment 2, the broad purpose of § 2–318 "is to give certain beneficiaries the benefit of the same warranty which the buyer received in the contract of sale, thereby freeing any such beneficiaries from any technical rules as to 'privity.' "[42] Accordingly, "any beneficiary of a warranty may bring a direct action for breach of warranty against the seller whose warranty extends to him."[43] The requirement of vertical privity had substantially begun to crumble in the pre-Code law, as described above, and § 2–318 was directed principally at the horizon-

---

guests of the buyer. Beyond this, according to Comment 3, the section was neutral and was not intended to enlarge or restrict "the developing case law." The section was criticized in California as "a step backward," and was omitted from the Code as enacted in California and in Utah. Nonuniform versions were enacted in ten states, and proposals for amendment have been made elsewhere. There appears to be no national consensus as to the scope of warranty protection which is proper, but the promulgation of alternatives may prevent further proliferation of separate variations in state after state. Alternative B is therefore promulgated in substantially the 1950 form, and Alternative C is drawn to reflect the trend of more recent decisions as indicated by Restatement of Torts 2d § 402A (Tentative Draft No. 10, 1965) extending the rule beyond personal injuries.

[Conforming changes were made in pars. 2 and 3 of the Comment, infra, in 1966].

1A Uniform Laws Annotated, Uniform Commercial Code 557 (2004).

**42.** See, e.g., Rynders v. E.I. Du Pont De Nemours & Co., 21 F.3d 835 (8th Cir. 1994) (S.D. law) (third party beneficiaries who can be reasonably anticipated are placed in shoes of buyer for purposes of enforcing express and implied warranties made by seller).

**43.** UCC § 2–318 cmt. 2.

tal privity question[44] in implied warranty cases[45] of what types of plaintiffs receive the benefit of the warranties received by the purchaser.[46]

Alternatives A and B conclude with the sentence, "A seller may not exclude or limit the operation of this section," to which Alternative C adds "with respect to injury to the person of an individual to whom the warranty extends." As discussed below in connection with disclaimers,[47] this language requires that all warranties received by the purchaser extend as well to persons who qualify as third party beneficiaries under this section.[48]

Most American jurisdictions, including half the states, have adopted Alternative A, or something similar.[49] About eight jurisdictions have adopted Alternative B, or a close approximation,[50] and about thirteen have adopted Alternative C, or a close equivalent.[51] California omitted § 2–318 from its version of the UCC and requires privity in implied warranty cases as a matter of common law.[52] Texas also leaves the matter to its courts,[53] Louisiana never did adopt Article 2, and several states have nonuniform provisions on privity.[54]

**44.** For authority that at least Alternative A of UCC § 2–318 is directed to the issue of horizontal privity alone, and not to vertical privity, and that vertical privity therefore still may be required, see, e.g., Thomaston v. Fort Wayne Pools, Inc., 352 S.E.2d 794, 796 (Ga. Ct. App. 1987) ("Nothing contained in [UCC § 2–318, Alternative A], which extends the seller's warranties to family members and guests in the buyer's home who may reasonably be expected to use the product and who are injured thereby, eliminates the requirement that the buyer and the defendant be in privity.").

**45.** Section 2–318 is directed primarily at the implied warranty of merchantability, "resting primarily upon the merchant-seller's warranty under this Article that the goods sold are merchantable and fit for the ordinary purposes for which such goods are used." UCC § 2–318 cmt. 2. As previously discussed, the privity defense finds little support in modern cases involving express warranty claims based on public advertising, labels, and brochures. Accordingly, even in the absence of privity of contract, many courts in personal injury cases have allowed such claims. See, e.g., Anderson v. Olmsted Utility Equip., Inc., 573 N.E.2d 626 (Ohio 1991).

**46.** Amended UCC § 2–318 retains these three alternative approaches to defining the scope of third party beneficiaries but expands them to include the newly formulated express warranty obligations under §§ 2–313, 2–313A, and 2–313B, discussed above.

**47.** See § 4.7, below.

**48.** This provision is well explained in comment 1 to § 2–318.

**49.** Alternative A or a similar provision was adopted in Alaska, Arizona, Connecti-

cut, District of Columbia, Florida, Georgia, Idaho, Illinois, Indiana, Kentucky, Michigan, Missouri, Montana, Nebraska, Nevada, New Jersey, New Mexico, North Carolina, Ohio, Oklahoma, Oregon, Pennsylvania, Tennessee, Washington, West Virginia, and Wisconsin.

**50.** Alternative B or a similar provision was adopted in Alabama, Delaware, Kansas, Maryland, New York, South Carolina, Vermont, and the Virgin Islands.

**51.** Alternative C or a similar provision was adopted in Arkansas, Colorado, Hawaii, Iowa, Maine, Massachusetts, Minnesota, New Hampshire, North Dakota, Rhode Island, South Dakota, Utah, and Wyoming.

**52.** See, e.g., Nissan Motor Co. v. Armstrong, 2004 WL 1908326 (Tex. 2004); Evraets v. Intermedics Intraocular, Inc., 34 Cal.Rptr.2d 852 (Ct. App. 1994) (injuries from intraocular lens surgically implanted in eye; absence of privity barred warranty claim); In re Air Crash Disaster at Sioux City Iowa on July 19, 1989, 760 F.Supp. 1283 (N.D. Ill. 1991). But California has an exception for warranty claims arising out of the sale of food and drugs, where privity is not required. See, e.g., Arnold v. Dow Chem. Co., 110 Cal.Rptr.2d 722, 739 (Ct. App. 2001) (extending exception to pesticides).

**53.** By statute. See, e.g., Hou–Tex, Inc. v. Landmark Graphics, 26 S.W.3d 103 (Tex. App. 2000); Garcia v. Texas Instruments, Inc., 610 S.W.2d 456 (Tex. 1980).

**54.** Nonuniform provisions on privity and third-party beneficiary warranty claims were adopted in Mississippi, Texas, and Virginia (Maine, New Hampshire, and Rhode Island have adopted provisions which are

Alternative A is the most restrictive of the three alternatives. Most importantly, Alternative A limits recovery to a person who "is in the family or household of his buyer or who is a guest in his home," whereas Alternatives B and C broadly extend the benefits of a purchaser's warranties to a "person who may reasonably be expected to use, consume or be affected by the goods," an extension which appears to embrace all persons who might foreseeably be harmed by the warranty's breach.[55] As with Alternative B, Alternative A includes only "natural" or human persons within its reach, whereas Alternative C, by extending warranty protection to "any person," includes "legal" persons such as business enterprises.[56] Similar to Alternatives B and C, even the narrow categories of persons designated in Alternative A may recover only "if it is reasonable to expect that such person may use, consume or be affected by the goods." Finally, Alternatives A and B both limit recovery to cases in which the plaintiff "is injured in person," a limitation which should preclude claims solely for property loss[57] and economic loss, at least where privity has not otherwise been abolished.[58]

**Alternative A Categories—In General**

Deciding what types of plaintiffs fall into a purchaser's "family," "household," or "guest[s] in his home," the categories specified in Alternative A, has generated considerable litigation. With some exceptions, the courts have interpreted such categories in a commonsense manner. So, a mother who does not live with her married daughter may not be in her daughter's "family";[59] a church member, trapped inside the church's walk-in freezer, is not a member of the church's "family," nor

similar in effect to Alternative C). See also Tenn. Code Ann. § 29–34–104, which provides: "In all causes of action for personal injury or property damage brought on account of negligence, strict liability, or breach of warranty . . . privity shall not be a requirement to maintain said action." Several states make various less significant modifications to the language in the various alternatives. See 1A Uniform Laws Annotated, Uniform Commercial Code 558–60 (2004) (classifying states under the three Alternatives). Classification errors by the ULA are corrected in the jurisdictional lists set forth above.

**55.** This assumes that the Code's notion of reasonable expectations, reflecting the nature and reach of contract law, see Hadley v. Baxendale, [1843–60] All E. R. Rep. 461 (Ex. 1854), is the equivalent of the tort law concept of reasonable foreseeability. Thus, Alternative C covers employees injured by defective business equipment purchased by their employers. See, e.g., Mills v. Allegiance Healthcare Corp., 178 F.Supp.2d 1, 7 (D. Mass. 2001) (seller should have foreseen and expected nurse employee of purchasing hospitals to use latex gloves); Lariviere v. Dayton Safety Ladder Co., 525 A.2d 892 (R.I. 1987).

**56.** See, e.g., TCF Bank & Savings, F.A. v. Marshall Truss Sys., Inc., 466 N.W.2d 49 (Minn. Ct. App. 1991), overruled on other grounds, Lloyd F. Smith Co. v. Den–Tal–Ez, Inc., 491 N.W.2d 11 (Minn. 1992).

**57.** See, e.g., Wellcraft Marine v. Zarzour, 577 So.2d 414 (Ala. 1990) (no implied warranty claim against manufacturer for property damage without privity of contract).

**58.** See 3A Lawrence's Anderson on the UCC § 2–318:42, at 352.

**59.** See Lane v. Barringer, 407 N.E.2d 1173, 1178 (Ind. Ct. App. 1980) (concurring and dissenting opinion) ("There are no facts shown here which would bring Lane within the coverage of Alternative A (the Indiana statute). Lane was not in the family or household of her daughter—they had separate families and residences, the daughter was emancipated and married; nor was Lane a guest in her daughter's home at the time of her injury. Perhaps Lane would have been covered under Alternative B or C, but Indiana has not adopted them. It is not the function of the court to adopt by decision an alternative statute which the legislature declined to enact.").

in its "household" nor a guest in its "home";[60] a customer injured by a patio chair on display in a store is not in the store's "family" nor in its "household" nor a "guest" in its home;[61] passengers in automobiles,[62] boats,[63] and airplanes[64] are not "guests" in the vehicle buyer's "home"; a patron in a shop is not a "guest in the home";[65] and a maid, whose finger was amputated by her employer's garage door, "simply does not fall into the category of persons benefitting from" Alternative A.[66]

Other persons who also have been excluded from warranty recovery under Alternative A include bystanders, such as a school girl struck in the eye by a rock thrown by a rotary lawnmower through an open classroom window;[67] a driver killed when his car collided with a defective truck stalled on a freeway;[68] business invitees who are injured on escalators in department stores and shopping malls;[69] a tenant injured by a defective table purchased by the landlord;[70] and patients injured by defective drugs or medical products provided by their doctors or hospitals—one who suffered side effects from a drug sample provided by her doctor,[71] another who contracted polio from a vaccine,[72] and one who had a defective surgical nail implanted in his femur.[73]

On the other hand, courts have sometimes stretched the interpretation of the "family," "household," and "guest in his home" categories to include certain persons who might not literally be included in those

---

**60.** Crews v. W.A. Brown & Son, Inc., 416 S.E.2d 924 (N.C. Ct. App. 1992).

**61.** Denton v. Sam Blount, Inc., 669 So.2d 951 (Ala. Civ. App. 1995) (N.C. law).

**62.** Thompson v. Reedman, 199 F.Supp. 120, 121 (E.D. Pa. 1961) ("It is too much of a leap, it seems, to classify a guest passenger in an automobile as a guest in the *home*"; warranty nevertheless ran to plaintiff under "the developing case law" of Pennsylvania); Oats v. Nissan Motor Corp., 879 P.2d 1095 (Idaho 1994) (no claim under UCC, but passenger allowed to maintain action for breach of warranty under tort law which was not time barred under state's products liability act).

**63.** Smith v. Mitlof, 198 F.Supp.2d 492, 506–07 (S.D.N.Y. 2002) (Conn. law); Curlee v. Mock Enters., Inc., 327 S.E.2d 736 (Ga. Ct. App. 1985) (even though boat owner and passenger had made preparations in owner's home to go to boat where passenger was injured by defective gun).

**64.** Driver v. Burlington Aviation, Inc., 430 S.E.2d 476 (N.C. Ct. App. 1993) (passengers in private plane, manual of which failed to alert pilot to risk of carburetor icing); Alexander v. Beech Aircraft Corp., 952 F.2d 1215 (10th Cir. 1991) (Ind. law). See also In re Air Crash Disaster at Sioux City Iowa on July 19, 1989, 760 F.Supp. 1283 (N.D. Ill. 1991) (under California common law, implied warranty claims not allowable in absence of privity between the parties).

**65.** Miller v. Sears, Roebuck and Co., 500 N.E.2d 557 (Ill. App. Ct. 1986), overruled in part by Whitaker v. Lian Feng Mach. Co., 509 N.E.2d 591 (Ill. Ct. 1987).

**66.** Verddier v. Neal Blun Co., 196 S.E.2d 469, 470 (Ga. Ct. App. 1973).

**67.** Stovall & Co. v. Tate, 184 S.E.2d 834 (Ga. Ct. App. 1971).

**68.** General Motors Corp. v. Davis, 233 S.E.2d 825 (Ga. Ct. App. 1977).

**69.** See, e.g., Hayes v. Otis Elevator Co., 946 F.2d 1272 (7th Cir. 1991) (Ill. law) (woman not warned of necessity for egress fell at intermediate stop); Westinghouse Corp. v. Ruiz, 537 So.2d 596 (Fla. Dist. Ct. App. 1988) (4-year-old child caught hand in escalator).

**70.** Barry v. Ivarson Inc., 249 So.2d 44 (Fla. Dist. Ct. App. 1971).

**71.** Bryant v. Hoffmann–La Roche, Inc., 585 S.E.2d 723 (Ga. Ct. App. 2003) (patient who did not purchase drug from manufacturer but obtained sample from doctor could not sue under Alternative A).

**72.** Snawder v. Cohen, 749 F.Supp. 1473 (W.D. Ky. 1990).

**73.** Munn v. Pfizer Hosp. Prods. Group, Inc., 750 F.Supp. 244 (W.D. Ky. 1990). By contrast, a patient who receives a defective implant in an Alternative C state has no such problem. See, e.g., Larsen v. Pacesetter Sys., Inc., 837 P.2d 1273 (Haw. 1992), amended in part on reconsideration, 843 P.2d 144 (Haw. 1992) (pacemaker).

designations. For example, a guest *outside* the home is a guest *"in the home"*;[74] and a niece not living in the household nevertheless is in the buyer's *"family,"*[75] as is the nephew of the purchaser of a vaporizer-humidifier which shot boiling water on the nephew.[76] In addition, courts that have not felt restricted by the specifically designated categories have extended coverage under Alternative A to various types of other persons.[77]

### Alternative A Categories—Employees

The courts are split on whether an employee injured by a defective product purchased by his or her employer may maintain a warranty claim under Alternative A against the supplier of the defective product.[78] Probably most courts preclude such claims, ruling that employees fit within none of the specifically designated categories, namely, the purchaser's "family," "household," and "guests in the home."[79] Other courts, as in *Whitaker v. Lian Feng Machine Co.*,[80] reason that the categories of included beneficiaries are merely statutory *minima* which do not prevent a court from allowing other persons lacking privity to take the benefit of the buyers' warranties.[81] Such courts rely upon comment 3 to § 2–318, which provides in part:

> The first alternative [Alternative A] expressly includes as beneficiaries within its provisions the family, household, and guests of the purchaser. Beyond this, the section in this form is neutral and is not intended to enlarge or restrict the developing case law on whether the seller's warranties, given to his buyer who resells, extend to other persons in the distributive chain.

Emphasizing the beginning of the second sentence, "Beyond this, the section in this form is neutral and is not intended to enlarge or

---

**74.** Handrigan v. Apex Warwick, Inc., 275 A.2d 262 (R.I. 1971) (plaintiff, friend of purchaser of ladder, fell while helping paint friend's house).

**75.** See Wolfe v. Ford Motor Co., 376 N.E.2d 143, 149 (Mass. App. Ct. 1978) (niece, not in household, was within buyer's family; "family" interpreted broadly to include persons of common progenitor to help distinguish word from "household"). Accord Chastain v. Fuqua Indust., 275 S.E.2d 679 (Ga. Ct. App. 1980).

**76.** Miller v. Preitz, 221 A.2d 320 (Pa. 1966), overruled on other grounds, Kassab v. Central Soya, 246 A.2d 848 (Pa. 1968).

**77.** See, e.g., Reed v. City of Chicago, 263 F.Supp.2d 1123 (N.D. Ill. 2003) (prison inmate, known to be suicidal, who hanged himself with paper isolation gown that failed to tear away, was proper beneficiary of seller's warranty).

**78.** Of course such employees may maintain such warranty claims in states which have adopted the broader Alternatives B and C. See, e.g., Atkinson v. Ormont

Mach. Co., 423 N.Y.S.2d 577 (Sup. Ct. Spec. Term 1979).

**79.** See, e.g., Halderman v. Sanderson Forklifts Co., 818 S.W.2d 270 (Ky. Ct. App. 1991); Hester v. Purex Corp., 534 P.2d 1306 (Okla. 1975).

**80.** 509 N.E.2d 591 (Ill. App. Ct. 1987).

**81.** See, e.g., Salvador v. Atlantic Steel Boiler Co., 319 A.2d 903 (Pa. 1974); McNally v. Nicholson Mfg. Co., 313 A.2d 913, 920 (Me. 1973), held that employees are in the "business family" of their employers for purposes of Alternative A. With some difficulty of expression, the *McNally* court explained why employees are proper beneficiaries of Code warranties although they do not fall within any of the categories specifically described in Alternative A: "The literal specifications of Section 2–318 are the guideposts of a fundamental course of policy flow adaptable to encompass other relationships which, policy-wise, may be fairly regarded as functionally equivalent to those textually designated." Webber, J., sat at argument but retired before the decision was rendered.

restrict the developing case law ...,"[82] the *Whitaker* court reasoned that the legislature thereby left the judiciary to determine whether to expand the class of beneficiaries specifically designated. The problem with this interpretation is that it ignores the remainder of the second sentence, which modifies the type of developing case law that remains permissible: " ... on whether the seller's warranties, given to the buyer who resells, extend to other persons in the distributive chain."[83] This second half of the sentence may be paraphrased to read: "on whether *vertical* privity should nevertheless remain a requirement." If so, the comment should be interpreted to mean that the legislature was authorizing the courts to continue to erode the doctrine of *vertical* privity, but that the legislature had defined with exclusive particularity the categories of third party beneficiaries for whom the doctrine of horizontal privity would be relaxed.[84] The *Whitaker* court also relied on the third sentence of comment 3, which begins, "The second alternative [Alternative B] is designed for states where the case law has already developed further...."[85] However, this sentence continues, " ... and for those that desire to expand the class of beneficiaries." Arguably, this latter phrase implies that state legislatures which did *not* wish to expand the beneficiary categories would opt for Alternative A, where the categories are specifically and exclusively set forth.[86]

While there surely may be some interpretative room in comment 3 for a court to reason that the legislature left the judiciary power to expand the categories of non-privity plaintiffs beyond those listed in Alternative A, such an interpretation appears quite strained.[87] More fundamentally, in construing a state statute enacted in 1961 (as it was in Illinois), it might be better to ignore an "Official Comment" rewritten by national law revision entities (the ALI and the NCCUSL[88]) five years later. To the extent that the actual intent of state legislators is relevant, one might reasonably conclude that those who actually read this section before voting on enactment probably interpreted the language of Alternative A as it reads, which appears to describe the *only* categories of non-privity plaintiffs allowed to take the benefits of a buyer's warranties.

**82.** *Whitaker*, 509 N.E.2d at 594.

**83.** Id.

**84.** This interpretation is suggested by an Illinois Supreme Court opinion rendered several months prior to *Whitaker*, Szajna v. General Motors Corp., 503 N.E.2d 760 (Ill. 1986), in which the high court decided to retain the *vertical* privity requirement in economic loss cases. Stating that "in Illinois section 2–318 ... is concerned only with horizontal privity," the Supreme Court observed that comment 3 "professes neutrality insofar as vertical privity and developing case law in that area are concerned." Id. at 766.

**85.** *Whitaker*, 509 N.E.2d at 594.

**86.** This was the reasoning of the court in Miller v. Sears, Roebuck & Co., 500 N.E.2d 557 (Ill. App. Ct. 1986), overruled by

Whitaker v. Lian Feng Mach. Co., 509 N.E.2d 591 (Ill. App. Ct. 1987), in concluding that Alternative A did not extend protection to business customers of a purchaser.

**87.** Illinois courts have been reluctant to expand *Whitaker*, ruling that non-employee truck drivers and other service providers of purchasers are too remote to fall inside Alternative A. See, e.g., Frank v. Edward Hines Lumber Co., 761 N.E.2d 1257 (Ill. App. Ct. 2001); Lukwinski v. Stone Container Corp., 726 N.E.2d 665 (Ill. App. Ct. 2000).

**88.** National Conference of Commissioners on Uniform State Laws.

### Damage Claims Available

Considerable litigation surrounds the issue of whether non-privity plaintiffs should be permitted to recover for different types of harm—personal injury, property damage, and direct economic loss (such as loss of bargain, where a product's defects diminish its value, and the cost of repair or replacement) or consequential economic loss (such as loss of profits, goodwill, and business reputation).[89] As previously discussed, Alternative A extends the buyer's warranty claims only to persons in the designated categories who are "injured in person." A spouse who loses the consortium of his or her spouse should probably be considered "injured in person."[90] However, courts are not likely to allow non-privity warranty claims for pure emotional distress, independent of an underlying physical injury.[91] Even more clearly, neither property damage[92] nor pure economic loss[93] is an injury to the plaintiff's person, and so neither should be recoverable to non-privity plaintiffs under Alternative A or Alternative B. By contrast, there are no restrictions on types of damages recoverable to non-privity plaintiffs under Alternative C.[94]

At the opposite end of the damages spectrum from consumers suffering personal injuries lie commercial enterprises suffering consequential economic loss. The privity of contract restriction is most at home in terms of logic and equity in this context. Especially with respect to consequential damages, the arguments are cogent for precluding plaintiffs in most such cases from exploiting other parties' bargains to recover such damages from firms with whom they had no contractual relations.[95] By way of example, warranty claims against manufacturers have been denied for lack of vertical privity in the case of a swimming pool contractor who purchased allegedly defective paint from a nonmanufacturing seller and who sought to recover from the manufacturer the cost of repainting a customer's pool;[96] a roofing contractor who purchased defective roofing materials from an intermediary seller;[97] a shop-

---

**89.** See 1 White and Summers (Prac. ed.) § 11.

**90.** See Phipps v. General Motors Corp., 363 A.2d 955 (Md. 1976) (recovery allowed under Alternative A).

**91.** See Carcone v. Gordon Heating & Air Conditioning Co., 623 N.Y.S.2d 679, 680 (App. Div. 1995) ("extreme emotional and mental trauma" from breakdown or nonperformance of product).

**92.** See, e.g., Wellcraft Marine v. Zarzour, 577 So.2d 414 (Ala. 1990) (no implied warranty claim against manufacturer for property damage without privity of contract).

**93.** See, e.g., Morris v. Osmose Wood Preserving, 667 A.2d 624 (Md. 1995); Rhodes v. General Motors Corp., 621 So.2d 945 (Ala. 1993).

**94.** See Dalton v. Stanley Solar & Stove, Inc., 629 A.2d 794 (N.H. 1993), where the court noted that the New Hampshire legislature had removed both horizontal and vertical privity as defenses to implied war-

ranty claims by its enactment of a version of § 2–318 that resembles Alternative C. See also Jacobs v. Yamaha Motor Corp. U.S.A., 649 N.E.2d 758 (Mass. 1995) (manufacturer liable to buyer of defective motorcycle which could not be repaired; statutory provision similar to Alternative C).

**95.** For a cogent summary of the arguments against non-privity claims for such damages between business enterprises, see 1 White and Summers (Prac. ed.) § 11–6, at 595–97. See generally Speidel, Products Liability, Economic Loss and the UCC, 40 Tenn. L. Rev. 309 (1973). For one court's criticism of the effort to distinguish between direct and consequential economic loss for purposes of privity, see Szajna v. General Motors Corp., 503 N.E.2d 760, 767 (Ill. 1986).

**96.** McCrary v. Kelly Tech. Coatings, Inc., Prod. Liab. Rep. (CCH) ¶ 10,666 (Tenn. Ct. App. 1985).

**97.** GAF Corp. v. Zack Co., 445 So.2d 350 (Fla. Dist. Ct. App. 1984).

keeper who purchased atrium doors through a retailer but sought to recover damages for deterioration of the doors and water damage to flooring from the manufacturer;[98] a cattle feeder who purchased an ineffective growth hormone from veterinarians instead of the manufacturer;[99] and a subcontractor, required to replace plumbing fittings installed in a number of new homes, who purchased the fittings from intermediate suppliers rather than from the manufacturers.[100]

Contrary authority can be found in other jurisdictions. In *Spring Motors Distributors, Inc. v. Ford Motor Co.*,[101] the New Jersey Supreme Court held that a commercial buyer seeking economic loss sustained from the purchase of defective goods may recover for breach of warranty from the remote seller as well as from the immediate seller. Other courts, sometimes under the authority of Alternative C, have similarly permitted commercial buyers to bring warranty claims against remote sellers where the damage is purely economic. For example, where a subcontractor manufactured and sold wooden trusses to a general contractor to support a canopy over a drive-through window at a savings and loan, and the canopy collapsed, the successor bank was permitted to maintain a breach of warranty claim for the costs of redesign and repair of the facility against the subcontractor, notwithstanding the absence of privity between the bank and the subcontractor.[102] Similarly, courts have allowed warranty claims against remote manufacturers for economic losses to a purchaser of a defective paving machine[103] and to a buyer of numerical controls.[104] Even under Alternative C, however, some courts refuse to allow recovery for economic loss, because they interpret "injury" in that Alternative as inconsistent with economic loss[105] or when a plaintiff has never even used the product and so may simply be outside the remedy contemplated by the legislature.[106]

In jurisdictions where the out-of-privity buyer suffering economic loss might be denied warranty recovery, resourceful parties may be able to prevail by showing that the manufacturer was aware of the particular purpose to be made of the product yet proceeded nevertheless to provide a product unsuited to that use. It has been held, therefore, that when a remote manufacturer knows "the identity, purpose, and requirements of [a] dealer's customer and manufactured or delivered the goods specifical-

**98.** Gregory v. Atrium Door & Window Co., 415 S.E.2d 574 (N.C. Ct. App. 1992).

**99.** Tomka v. Hoechst Celanese Corp., 528 N.W.2d 103 (Iowa 1995) (consequential economic loss).

**100.** Beard Plumbing & Heating, Inc. v. Thompson Plastics, Inc., 491 S.E.2d 731 (Va. 1997).

**101.** 489 A.2d 660 (N.J. 1985).

**102.** TCF Bank & Savings, F.A. v. Marshall Truss Sys., Inc., 466 N.W.2d 49 (Minn. Ct. App. 1991) (Alternative C).

**103.** Moscatiello v. Pittsburgh Contractors Equip. Co., 595 A.2d 1198 (Pa. Super. Ct. 1991).

**104.** Patty Precision Prods. Co. v. Brown & Sharpe Mfg. Co., 846 F.2d 1247, 1254 (10th Cir. 1988) (Okla. law) (noting that Oklahoma has "rejected the majority view that a 'vertical' non-privity plaintiff . . . cannot maintain an action for breach of implied warranty").

**105.** Nebraska Innkeepers, Inc. v. Pittsburgh–Des Moines Corp., 345 N.W.2d 124, 129 (Iowa 1984) (Alternative C's reference to a person "injured" suggests physical harm to plaintiff or his property, not economic loss).

**106.** See Minnesota Mining and Mfg. Co. v. Nishika Ltd., 565 N.W.2d 16 (Minn. 1997).

ly to meet those requirements,'' recovery of economic losses should be permitted even absent privity.[107]

In products liability cases, recovery of damages for pure economic loss is a complicated issue that is treated elsewhere extensively.[108] Commercial disputes involving only economic loss, which often involve complex issues of commercial law, are covered in treatises which address in detail the interrelationships between privity of contract, various types of economic loss, and related problems from a specialized commercial law perspective.[109]

## § 4.6 NOTICE OF BREACH

After purchase and acceptance of a product, a buyer who is injured by breach of warranty—a defect in the goods or the falsity of a representation—must promptly notify the seller of the breach. The buyer's penalty for failing to so inform the seller is the loss of his or her rights to recover damages for the breach. Prompt notification of breach has long been an established requirement for breach of warranty claims in sales law, and such a requirement was included in the Uniform Sales Act.[1] Today notice is required by Uniform Commercial Code § 2–607(3), which provides:

Where a tender has been accepted

(a) the buyer must within a reasonable time after he discovers or should have discovered any breach notify the seller of breach or be barred from any remedy.... [2]

Because the consequence of a failure to comply with the notice requirement is severe—the buyer is barred from any recovery for breach of warranty[3]—and because some courts hold that the provision of timely notice must be pleaded as an element of or condition precedent to maintaining a warranty claim,[4] the lawyer representing a products

---

**107.** Crest Container Corp. v. R.H. Bishop, Co., 445 N.E.2d 19 (Ill. App. Ct. 1982).

**108.** See Frumer and Friedman, Products Liability § 13.07; 2 Madden & Owen on Products Liability ch. 17; 2 Am. Law Prod. Liab. 3d §§ 60:36–60:38.

**109.** See, e.g., J. Feinman, Economic Negligence ch. 13 (1995); 1 White and Summers (Prac. ed.) §§ 11–5 (privity and direct economic loss) and 11–6 (privity and consequential economic loss); 1 Clark and Smith, Product Warranties 2d §§ 10:17–:21, § 10:23.

**§ 4.6**

**1.** Uniform Sales Act § 49 provides: "[I]f ... the buyer fail[s] to give notice to the seller of the breach of any promise or warranty within a reasonable time after the buyer knows, or ought to know of such breach, the seller shall not be liable therefor.'' See also USA § 69(3) (rescission conditioned on notice within reasonable time).

**2.** See Reitz, Against Notice: A Proposal to Restrict the Notice of Claims Rule in U.C.C. § 2–607(3)(a), 73 Cornell L. Rev. 534 (1988).

**3.** Amended UCC § 2–607(3)(a) relaxes this provision, barring a buyer's claim only if and to the extent that the seller is prejudiced by the buyer's failure to give timely notice.

**4.** See, e.g., Allstate Ins. Co. v. Daimler Chrysler, 2004 WL 442679 (N.D. Ill. 2004) (express warranty claim dismissed because plaintiff did not allege notice in complaint); Hays v. General Elec. Co., 151 F.Supp.2d 1001, 1010 (N.D. Ill. 2001) (notice is not affirmative defense but an element on which plaintiff bears burden of proof); Radford v. Daimler Chrysler Corp., 168 F.Supp.2d 751, 754 (N.D. Ohio 2001) (implied warranty of merchantability claim dismissed because plaintiff did not allege notice to defendant in her complaint); Williams v. Mozark Fire Extinguisher Co., 888 S.W.2d 303 (Ark. 1994); Schnabl v.

liability claimant should focus closely on this requirement at the outset of representation. For example, in *Buford v. Toys R' Us, Inc.*,[5] a boy was seriously injured when a defective weld caused the steer tube on his bicycle to separate from the front fork, throwing him to the pavement. His parents sued the retailer of the defective bicycle for strict liability in tort, negligence, and breach of the implied warranty of merchantability. The trial court granted summary judgment to the retailer on all three claims, which was affirmed on appeal. The appellate court ruled that there was no claim for strict liability in tort because the state products liability statute provides that such liability applies only to manufacturers, not retailers. Because the defective weld had been painted over during the course of manufacture, the retailer could not have been negligent in failing to discover it. As for the implied warranty of merchantability, which surely had been breached by the retailer's sale of a dangerously defective bike, the court ruled that the parents' failure to notify the seller of the claim until it filed a complaint two years after the accident was "unreasonable" as a matter of law, which barred the one claim against the retailer that surely would have succeeded on the merits.

A general warranty-law requirement that a buyer notify the seller promptly that a product defect (or false warranty) caused an injury promotes several goals.[6] First, prompt notice permits the seller to act quickly to try to cure the problem to minimize resulting losses for the buyer and damages for the seller. Moreover, if the product contains a design or warnings problem, or if an express warranty is dangerously misleading, early notification of the problem permits the seller to remedy the danger promptly and thus minimize the risk of loss to others. Second, prompt notice of defect and injury allows a seller to gather information about the product defect or representational problem, which should promote fairness, efficiency, and justice by increasing the probability of informed settlement or principled litigation based on facts which are true and complete.[7] Third, requiring prompt notice promotes the

---

Ford Motor Co., 198 N.W.2d 161 (Wis. 1972) (warranty complaint is defective if it does not allege that notice of breach was given). See also Allen v. G.D. Searle & Co., 708 F.Supp. 1142, 1160 (D. Or. 1989) (granting defendant's motion for summary judgment on express and implied warranty claims where injured plaintiff offered no evidence she had given notice of claims). As discussed below, however, this rule of pleading does not apply in many jurisdictions that allow a personal injury victim to satisfy the notice requirement by filing a timely complaint.

**5.** 458 S.E.2d 373 (Ga. Ct. App. 1995).

**6.** See, e.g., Bryant v. Adams, 448 S.E.2d 832 (N.C. Ct. App. 1994):

The policies behind the notice provision are (1) to enable the seller to make efforts to cure the breach by making ad-justments or replacements in order to minimize the buyer's damages and the seller's liability; (2) to afford the seller a reasonable opportunity to learn the facts so that he may adequately prepare for negotiation and defend himself in a suit; and (3) to provide a seller with a terminal point in time for liability.

Id. at 844. See generally 1 White and Summers (Prac. ed.) § 11–10, at 554–55.

**7.** Sufficient notice "opens the way for normal settlement through negotiation." UCC § 2–607 cmt. 4. See Perona v. Volkswagen of Am., Inc., 684 N.E.2d 859, 863 (Ill. App. Ct. 1997) ("The purpose of the notice is to allow the defendant an opportunity to gather evidence, investigate facts, and negotiate a possible settlement.")

expeditious resolution of controversies and so serves the several goals of finality, much like statutes of limitations.[8]

Although certain policies behind the notice requirement are applicable to consumers and bystanders injured in product accidents, others are not, and the notice requirement can become a "booby trap for the unwary," as colorfully expressed by Dean Prosser.[9] Indeed, the notice requirement was one of the "big three" warranty defenses[10] that frustrated products liability claimants and led in the 1960s to the adoption of the doctrine of strict products liability in tort.[11] In fact, two states have amended their versions of the UCC to ban the notice requirement in personal injury cases.[12] While the notice doctrine may appear strangely out of place to the personal injury lawyer who usually fishes in the waters of tort law,[13] a number of its policies designed to promote a sound functioning of commerce may also have some relevance, if diminished, to warranty claims brought by victims of product accidents.[14]

### "Reasonable" Time

In recognition of a proper but reduced role for the notice requirement in personal injury products liability litigation, the comments to UCC § 2–607 state that the notification rule *does* apply to victims of product accidents but that the allowable "reasonable" time for notification is *stretched* for consumers[15] and bystanders[16] beyond that which normally would apply to merchant buyers. By so extending the notice time period for such persons, § 2–607 eases the burden for persons

---

**8.** See § 14.5, below.

**9.** See Prosser and Keeton on Torts § 97, at 691.

**10.** The other two big warranty defenses were the requirement of privity of contract, discussed above, and contractual disclaimers, discussed below.

**11.** See, e.g., Henningsen v. Bloomfield Motors, Inc., 161 A.2d 69 (N.J. 1960) (court bypassed privity and disclaimer defenses to warranty claims); Greenman v. Yuba Power Prod., Inc., 377 P.2d 897 (Cal. 1963) (court bypassed notice defense to warranty claims by adopting doctrine of strict liability in tort). See §§ 5.2 and 5.3, below.

**12.** Maine's version of § 2–607(7) provides that 2–607(3)(a) "shall not apply where the remedy is for personal injury resulting from any breach." Me. Rev. Stat. Ann. tit. 11, § 2–607(7). South Carolina's addition to 2–607(3)(a) provides: "however, no notice of injury to the person in the case of consumer goods shall be required." S.C. Code Ann. § 36–2–607(3)(a).

**13.** Many jurisdictions impose similar, and often very short, notice obligations on accident victims contemplating suits against local and state governments. See, Prosser and Keeton on Torts § 131, at 1045–46 (discussing notice-of-claim statutes).

**14.** See comments 4 and 5 to § 2–607, below.

**15.** Comment 4 provides in part:

The time of notification is to be determined by applying commercial standards to a merchant buyer. "A reasonable time" for notification from a retail consumer is to be judged by different standards so that in his case it will be extended, for the rule of requiring notification is designed to defeat commercial bad faith, not to deprive a good faith consumer of his remedy.

**16.** Comment 5 provides:

Under this Article various beneficiaries are given rights for injuries sustained by them because of the seller's breach of warranty. Such a beneficiary does not fall within the reason of the present section in regard to discovery of defects and the giving of notice within a reasonable time after acceptance, since he has nothing to do with acceptance. However, the reason of this section does extend to requiring the beneficiary to notify the seller that an injury has occurred. What is said above, with regard to the extended time for reasonable notification from the lay consumer after the injury is also applicable here; but even a beneficiary can be properly held to the use of good faith in notifying, once he has had time to become aware of the legal situation.

whose injuries may limit for some time their ability to focus on the cause of their accidents or legal responsibility therefor. A determination of what may be a "reasonable time" within which notice must be provided rests peculiarly upon the specific factual context and particular equities of each case, and so it normally is a question of fact for the jury to resolve.[17] As with any question of fact, however, a court may rule on the reasonableness of the time for notice if the time period was clearly adequate or clearly inadequate, so that a jury could come to only one conclusion.[18] A determination regarding the reasonable time issue requires weighing the reasons for allowing a particular plaintiff to pursue a possibly meritorious claim against the reasons for protecting the particular defendant (and the court) from having to litigate a claim on evidence that may be insufficient to permit principled adjudication.

The courts generally have been quite lenient in interpreting what may be a "reasonable" time period in litigation involving persons injured by defective products. Reflecting the balance of fairness between the plaintiff and defendant discussed above, courts concluding that the time of a plaintiff's notice is reasonable often point to the lack of prejudice to the defendant from the delay.[19] Courts have allowed warranty claims for personal injuries when the delay in notice after the accident or discovery of the harm amounted to two days,[20] four months,[21] ten months;[22] and two,[23] three,[24] and nearly four years.[25]

---

**17.** See, e.g., Smith v. DaimlerChrysler Corp., 2002 WL 31814534, *4 (Del. Super. Ct. 2002); Hays v. General Elec. Co., 151 F.Supp.2d 1001, 1013 (N.D. Ill. 2001); Dudley v. Business Exp., Inc., 882 F.Supp. 199 (D.N.H. 1994) (passenger injured while boarding airplane); Bryant v. Adams, 448 S.E.2d 832, 844 (N.C. Ct. App. 1994) (reasonableness of 3–year delay from date 14–year-old boy fell from trampoline and was rendered quadriplegic was jury issue) ("Whether a prima facie showing that the notice was given 'within a reasonable time' has been made can be determined only by examining the particular facts and circumstances of each case and the policies behind the notice requirement. If plaintiff's evidence shows that the policies behind the requirement have not been frustrated and, instead, have been fulfilled, the evidence is sufficient to withstand a directed verdict motion.").

**18.** See, e.g., Wal–Mart Stores, Inc. v. Wheeler, 586 S.E.2d 83, 85 (Ga. Ct. App. 2003); Bryant v. Adams, 448 S.E.2d 832, 844 (N.C. Ct. App. 1994); Paper Mfrs. Co. v. Rescuers, Inc., 60 F.Supp.2d 869, 882 (N.D. Ind. 1999) (plaintiff sent manufacturer letter describing problems with manufacturer's ink approximately four months after ink contaminated plaintiff's product; time reasonable as matter of law); Hebron v. American Isuzu Motors, Inc., 60 F.3d 1095 (4th Cir. 1995) (Va. law) (2–year delay unreasonable as a matter of law where plaintiff failed to preserve evidence); Lariviere v.

Dayton Safety Ladder Co., 525 A.2d 892 (R.I. 1987) (letter plaintiff's attorney sent to manufacturer, one month after worker fell from stepladder, was timely).

**19.** See, e.g., Wal–Mart Stores, Inc. v. Wheeler, 586 S.E.2d 83, 85 (Ga. Ct. App. 2003); Chapman v. Bernard's, Inc., 167 F.Supp.2d 406, 415–16 (D. Mass. 2001); Maldonado v. Creative Woodworking Concepts, Inc., 694 N.E.2d 1021 (Ill. App. Ct. 1998); Maybank v. S. S. Kresge Co., 273 S.E.2d 681 (N.C. 1981).

**20.** Bailey v. Jordan Marsh Co., 6 Mass. App. Dec. 17 (1953) (after collapse of ladder).

**21.** Bonker v. Ingersoll Prod. Corp., 132 F.Supp. 5 (D. Mass. 1955) (plaintiff, who swallowed bone from can of boneless chicken fricassee, had several operations before giving notice).

**22.** See, e.g., Pritchard v. Liggett & Myers Tobacco Co., 295 F.2d 292 (3d Cir. 1961) (Pa. law) (letter sent to manufacturer 10 months after plaintiff's cancerous lung removed).

**23.** Palmer v. A.H. Robins Co., 684 P.2d 187 (Colo. 1984).

**24.** Maybank v. S. S. Kresge Co., 273 S.E.2d 681 (N.C. 1981).

**25.** Maldonado v. Creative Woodworking Concepts, Inc., 694 N.E.2d 1021 (Ill. App. Ct. 1998).

However, in a number of cases, courts have barred warranty claims of product accident victims for delays of one to twenty-eight years.[26] As illustrated below, the usual basis for barring a claim for the unreasonableness of a delay in providing notice is prejudice—that the time lapse has unfairly disadvantaged the defendant seller by occasioning the loss, deterioration, or destruction of physical evidence, often the product itself.[27] Sometimes, however, courts hold that a delay in notice bars a warranty claim simply because it has caused the claim to grow stale.

*Hebron v. American Isuzu Motors, Inc.*[28] illustrates the type of case where a warranty claim is barred because of the unfairness in forcing the defendant to defend a case when the delay has resulted in the loss of crucial evidence. The court ruled that a two-year delay after an accident was unreasonable where the plaintiff truck owner failed to take pictures, had no inspection conducted, and disposed of the truck before notifying the manufacturer of the matter. Thus, the manufacturer was prejudiced by the delay because it was unable to inspect the truck to determine the cause of the accident. The court further noted that prompt notice also would have promoted settlement of the claim.

*Sacramona v. Bridgestone/Firestone, Inc.*[29] is another loss-of-evidence case. Plaintiff gas station worker was injured by the explosion of a 16–inch tire he was attempting to inflate, which he had mounted on a 16– or 16½–inch wheel of a van to replace a leaking tire. After the accident, the wheel and tire were stored outside in the van owner's yard for three months before the plaintiff's attorney collected them. They were subsequently sent to a consulting engineer, who extensively cleaned the wheel, which rendered it impossible for the defendants to check for markings that might have revealed whether the original leaking tire had been mismatched on a larger wheel. Later, the plaintiff's expert subjected the wheel to a "somewhat destructive" examination. Three years after the accident, the worker finally filed a breach of warranty claim against the manufacturers of the tire and the wheel, asserting that both the tire and the wheel should have been designed to avoid the risk of

---

**26.** See, e.g., Hearn v. R.J. Reynolds Tobacco Co., 279 F.Supp.2d 1096, 1116 (D. Ariz. 2003) (almost 2 years); Sacramona v. Bridgestone/Firestone, Inc., 106 F.3d 444 (1st Cir. 1997) (Mass. law) (3 years); Hebron v. American Isuzu Motors, Inc., 60 F.3d 1095 (4th Cir. 1995) (Va. law) (2 years); Buford v. Toys R' Us, Inc., 458 S.E.2d 373, 375 (Ga. Ct. App. 1995) (2 years; no notice until complaint served on seller of defective bicycle); Leeper v. Banks, 487 S.W.2d 58 (Ky. 1972) (1 year); Castro v. Stanley Works, 864 F.2d 961 (1st Cir. 1989) (Mass. law) (1⅔ years); Ratkovich v. Smithkline, 711 F.Supp. 436, 438 (N.D. Ill. 1989) (28 years; plaintiff allegedly suffered brain damage from drug, Dexadrine, ingested by mother during pregnancy; in dismissing warranty claims, court remarked that it was "virtually impossible to believe that plaintiff's parents were unaware of the possibility of Smithkline's breach of its implied warranties until 28 years after plaintiff was born with brain damage [and that the] parents must have been considering the various possible causes of plaintiff's injury from the moment she was born"); Wagmeister v. A.H. Robins Co., 382 N.E.2d 23 (Ill. App. Ct. 1978) (2½ years; plaintiff learned IUD failed on Oct. 31, 1972, delivered stillborn baby on February 19, 1973, gave notice of breach on September 26, 1975).

**27.** See, e.g., Smith v. Robertshaw Controls Co., 2003 WL 23142189, at *4–5 (D. Mass 2003) (summary judgment granted for defendant prejudiced by 3–year delay in notice by which time crucial evidence under plaintiff's control had been lost).

**28.** 60 F.3d 1095 (4th Cir. 1995) (Va. law).

**29.** 106 F.3d 444 (1st Cir. 1997) (Mass. law).

mismatching tires and wheels. Sometime previously, the gas station had been sold and the original leaking tire, the mounting machine, and various safety and equipment manuals were lost. Affirming summary judgment for the defendants, the court ruled that the delay was unreasonable and thereby prejudiced the defendants.[30]

An example of a case based on the staleness of the claim rather than deterioration or loss of the subject product is *Williams v. Mozark Fire Extinguisher Co.*[31] In this case, the plaintiff restaurant owner sued the manufacturer of an allegedly defective fire extinguisher system for fire damage to her restaurant, amending her complaint five years after the fire (with no prior notice of breach) to add a warranty claim to her claims in tort. *Held*, the warranty claim was insufficient for failure to provide timely notice. The court pointed to two goals of the notice requirement: (1) giving the seller an opportunity to minimize damages, by correcting the defect, and (2) protecting the seller from stale claims. While the time delay did not diminish the manufacturer's ability to minimize its damages, because the fire extinguisher system had been destroyed in the fire, the manufacturer was entitled to be protected from stale claims.

### Bystanders and Other Non–Purchasers; Sellers to Whom Notice Should Be Given

A common question is whether the notice requirements of § 2–607 apply beyond the actual buyer to those who take the benefits of the buyer's warranties under § 2–318.[32] As mentioned earlier, a comment to § 2–607 provides quite clearly that the notice requirement applies to bystanders and other non-purchasers as well as to the purchasing consumer;[33] and occasionally a court has barred warranty claims brought by such third parties for failure to provide a timely notice.[34] But most courts take the position that third parties physically injured by defective products are not bound by the notice requirement of § 2–607,[35] frequent-

**30.** "[T]he requirement of prompt notice allows the defendant to gather evidence in timely fashion; without such notice, a defendant could easily be surprised by a lawsuit many years after selling its products." Id. at 449.

**31.** 888 S.W.2d 303 (Ark. 1994).

**32.** See Stallworth, An Analysis of Warranty Claims Instituted by Non–Privity Plaintiffs in Jurisdictions that Have Adopted Uniform Commercial Code Section 2–318 (Alternative A), 20 Pepp. L. Rev. 1215 (1993); Prince, Overprotecting the Consumer? Section 2–607(3)(a) Notice of Breach in Nonprivity Contexts, 66 N.C. L. Rev. 107 (1987).

**33.** Comment 5 to § 2–607 provides in pertinent part that "the reason of this section does extend to requiring the [third party] beneficiary [of a warranty under § 2–318] to notify the seller that an injury has occurred [because] even a beneficiary

can be properly held to the use of good faith in notifying, once he has had time to become aware of the legal situation."

**34.** Compare Sacramona v. Bridgestone/Firestone, Inc., 106 F.3d 444 (1st Cir. 1997) (Mass. law) (gas station manager, inflating tire for van owner, injured by explosion of allegedly defective tire he had mounted on allegedly defective wheel). Note that *Sacramona* should be viewed cautiously because the nonuniform Massachusetts version of UCC § 2–318 includes the following sentence: "Failure to give notice shall not bar recovery under this section unless the defendant proves that he was prejudiced thereby." See Cameo Curtains, Inc. v. Philip Carey Corp., 416 N.E.2d 995, 998 (Mass. App. Ct. 1981).

**35.** See, e.g., Morgan v. Sears, Roebuck & Co., 700 F.Supp. 1574 (N.D. Ga. 1988) (third party burn victim who did not buy

ly reasoning that the black letter language of § 2–607 explicitly pertains to "buyers" and no one else.[36]

In the commercial plaintiff context, the courts split over whether a buyer seeking recovery against a remote manufacturer must provide notice to that seller as well as to the immediate seller.[37] But when the plaintiff is personally injured in a product accident, he or she may give notice to the retailer or other immediate seller who is then expected to pass it along upstream to the manufacturer.[38] In *Palmer v. A.H. Robins Co.*,[39] for example, a woman injured by a defective IUD was able to pursue her warranty claim against the manufacturer even though before the litigation she had only informed her immediate seller, the doctor. The court ruled that her notice to this party was sufficient to support her claim against the manufacturer: "[A]s long as the buyer has given notice of the defect to his or her immediate seller, no further notification to those distributors beyond the immediate seller is required."[40]

### Method and Form of Notice; Filing of Complaint

Comment 4 to § 2–607 provides that notification need not specify the buyer's objections to the goods nor that the buyer is making, or intends to make, a claim for damages. Instead, "[t]he content of the notification need merely be sufficient to let the seller know that the transaction is still troublesome and must be watched [and to inform] the seller that the transaction is claimed to involve a breach, and thus opens the way for normal settlement through negotiation."[41] Oral notification may be sufficient,[42] and an attorney's letter stating that he is representing a person injured by the manufacturer's faulty product provides the defendant with adequate notice.[43] There is, in short, no magic form in which notice must be made.

Further, if a defendant is already aware of the general product deficiency that caused the plaintiff's injury from other lawsuits or

garment); Carlson v. Armstrong World Indus., 693 F.Supp. 1073 (S.D. Fla. 1987) (painter who did not buy paint). See also Cole v. Keller Indus., 132 F.3d 1044, 1048 (4th Cir. 1998) (Va. law) (noting that all but one case rule that personally injured non-purchasers are not bound by warranty notice requirements of § 2–607).

**36.** See, e.g., Yates v. Pitman Mfg., Inc., 514 S.E.2d 605, 607 (Va. 1999) (laborer injured by crane) ("only buyers . . . must give notice of breach of warranty to the seller as a prerequisite to recovery"); Carlson v. Armstrong World Indus., 693 F.Supp. 1073 (S.D. Fla. 1987); McKnelly v. Sperry Corp., 642 F.2d 1101 (8th Cir. 1981) (Iowa law); Simmons v. Clemco Indus., 368 So.2d 509 (Ala. 1979); Frericks v. General Motors Corp., 363 A.2d 460 (Md. 1976) (criticizing cmt. 5).

**37.** See Cooley v. Big Horn Harvestore Sys., Inc., 813 P.2d 736, 742 (Colo. 1991), discussing the split and holding that even a commercial buyer "is not required to give notice of such injury to a remote manufac-

turer prior to initiating litigation against such manufacturer."

**38.** See, e.g., Ragland Mills, Inc. v. General Motors Corp., 763 S.W.2d 357 (Mo. Ct. App. 1989); Firestone Tire & Rubber Co. v. Cannon, 452 A.2d 192 (Md. Ct. Spec. App. 1982), aff'd on op. below, 456 A.2d 930 (Md. 1983); Goldstein v. G. D. Searle & Co., 378 N.E.2d 1083 (Ill. App. Ct. 1978).

**39.** 684 P.2d 187 (Colo. 1984).

**40.** Id. at 206.

**41.** UCC § 2–607 cmt. 4.

**42.** See, e.g., Atwood v. Southeast Bedding Co., 485 S.E.2d 217 (Ga. Ct. App. 1997); Bennett v. United Auto Parts, Inc., 315 So.2d 579 (Ala. 1975); Sullivan v. H.P. Hood & Sons, Inc., 168 N.E.2d 80 (Mass. 1960) (son told president of milk supplier that mother should bring suit because she encountered dead mouse while drinking milk from container).

**43.** Lariviere v. Dayton Safety Ladder Co., 525 A.2d 892 (R.I. 1987).

otherwise,[44] some courts hold that the notice requirement is satisfied or unnecessary. Yet, courts are divided on how particular this type of indirect notice must be. In a split decision, a majority of the Illinois Supreme Court held that a vehicle manufacturer's generalized knowledge of a possible roll-over problem—from newspaper reports, magazines, and lawsuits brought by attorneys general of several states and by a consumer group—does not satisfy the notice requirements of § 2–607, which contemplates that the manufacturer be apprised of the trouble with a particular product of a particular buyer.[45] On this authority, a lower Illinois court subsequently ruled that car buyers are not excused from the notice requirement by the manufacturer's issuance of a federally mandated recall notice and accompanying press releases.[46]

A significant issue in products liability personal injury litigation is whether a plaintiff, in order to comply with the requirement of § 2–607, must provide the seller with some separate notice of breach prior to instituting the lawsuit, or whether the complaint itself will suffice. Many, perhaps most, courts have held in cases between commercial parties that the filing of a complaint does not satisfy the notice requirement.[47] In cases involving personal injuries,[48] however, most courts have held that the complaint alone satisfies the notice requirements of § 2–607,[49] particularly where the policies behind the notice rule have not been frustrated by the delay.[50] Even in personal injury cases, however, where the delay is substantial, the complaint itself may not suffice.[51]

**44.** See, e.g., Ragland Mills, Inc. v. General Motors Corp., 763 S.W.2d 357 (Mo. Ct. App. 1989) (buyer had car technically examined on immediate seller's premises after wreck); Malawy v. Richards Mfg. Co., 501 N.E.2d 376 (Ill. App. Ct. 1986) (employees of hospital vendor of metal bone plate learned plate had broken when they removed it from plaintiff's broken leg); Palmer v. A.H. Robins Co., 684 P.2d 187 (Colo. 1984) (prior lawsuits over same problem with IUD; no prejudice by delay).

**45.** Connick v. Suzuki Motor Co., 675 N.E.2d 584 (Ill. 1996).

**46.** Perona v. Volkswagen of Am., Inc., 684 N.E.2d 859 (Ill. App. Ct. 1997).

**47.** See, e.g., Armco Steel Corp. v. Isaacson Structural Steel Co., 611 P.2d 507 (Alaska 1980).

**48.** Even consumer cases may require notice prior to the filing of a complaint in the absence of personal injury damages. See, e.g., Connick v. Suzuki Motor Co., 675 N.E.2d 584 (Ill. 1996) (Ill. and Pa. law), where the court observed that, for purposes of notice, plaintiffs are divided into three categories: merchant buyers, consumer buyers who did not suffer personal injuries, and consumer buyers who did suffer personal injuries. Only plaintiffs in the last category may satisfy the notice requirement by filing a complaint against the seller.

**49.** See, e.g., Allstate Ins. Co. v. Daimler Chrysler, 2004 WL 442679, at *2 (N.D. Ill. 2004).

**50.** See, e.g., Bryant v. Adams, 448 S.E.2d 832 (N.C. Ct. App. 1994) (complaint filed 3 years after trampoline accident; because warranty claim was based on failure to warn, which did not require visual inspection of particular trampoline, reasonableness of delay left to jury), quoting Maybank v. S.S. Kresge Co., 273 S.E.2d 681, 685 (N.C. 1981); Bednarski v. Hideout Homes & Realty, Inc., 709 F.Supp. 90 (M.D. Pa. 1988). See also Hearn v. R.J. Reynolds Tobacco Co., 279 F.Supp.2d 1096, 1116 (D. Ariz. 2003) (complaint sufficed, but 2 year delay was unreasonable).

**51.** See, e.g., Sacramona v. Bridgestone/Firestone, Inc., 106 F.3d 444 (1st Cir. 1997) (Mass. law) (3 years); Buford v. Toys R' Us, Inc., 458 S.E.2d 373 (Ga. Ct. App. 1995) (2 years); Hebron v. American Isuzu Motors, Inc., 60 F.3d 1095 (4th Cir. 1995) (Va. law) (2 years); Wagmeister v. A.H. Robins Co., 382 N.E.2d 23 (Ill. App. Ct. 1978) (2½ years); Leeper v. Banks, 487 S.W.2d 58 (Ky. 1972) (1 year).

## § 4.7 DISCLAIMERS

A free marketplace contemplates that buyers and sellers generally may strike whatever deals they choose—that they may define the terms of their transactions however they decide. If the parties to a sale transaction choose to exchange cash for a product (perhaps a used car or lawnmower) containing certain flaws, for a price reflecting their view of the product's worth in that condition, they normally may do so. This approach to sales law suggests that buyers and sellers should be able to bargain on which between them will be responsible for unknown problems in the product and, if the seller is the one responsible, the type and extent of remedy for breach the buyer will receive. Allowing buyers and sellers to so define all aspects of their transaction unfettered by social control of law is grounded in two fundamental assumptions: (1) that they both have full access to information about the product, and (2) that they both can bargain effectively to protect their respective interests.

In the real world, of course, product manufacturers and other sellers usually know much more about the general characteristics of their products than buyers do, and power to define transaction terms usually is skewed heavily toward the top of the chain of distribution. This is particularly true, of course, in the case of consumer transactions where buyers generally know much less than manufacturers about the nature and extent of product dangers[1] and usually have no power to bargain for more or less safety in particular products. Manufacturers and other sellers are often motivated to increase short-term revenues by making consumers believe that products are safer and that warranties are wider (that both are more valuable) than they are in fact. Correspondingly, sellers are often motivated to decrease short-term expenses by avoiding responsibility for product accidents. A principal means for avoiding such responsibility is to exclude warranties and limit remedies for their breach in contracts of sale. Such contractual avoidance provisions can be especially effective in consumer transactions where consumers frequently have little information on the nature of dangerous defects that products may contain, how properly to value warranties provided by a seller, or what cost to place on the contractual exclusion of warranties or on the limitation of remedies for their breach.

In the interest of a free marketplace, but in recognition of the shortcomings of actual markets, Article 2 of the Uniform Commercial Code establishes a framework for parties to structure their deals freely within certain guidelines. Article 2 works most fairly and efficiently in transactions between merchant buyers and sellers, the types of parties most likely to be fully informed and capable of bargaining effectively. But the Code also contemplates and allows for, if in a plainly secondary fashion, certain frailties in the market for consumer goods. In certain important respects, Amended UCC § 2–316 further protects consumers from unfair and unbargained for reductions in warranty protection, as discussed below.

---

**§ 4.7**

**1.** However, consumers do often have more information than product sellers about how products may perform in particular settings when put to particular uses.

See Priest, The Current Insurance Crisis and Modern Tort Law, 96 Yale L.J. 1521 (1987); Priest, Theory of the Consumer Product Warranty, 90 Yale L.J. 1297, 1311 (1981).

Article 2 of the Code provides two principal means for sellers to avoid responsibility for the consequences of product defects and false warranties: (1) disclaimers of warranties, in § 2–316, and (2) limitations on remedies for breach of warranty, in §§ 2–718 and 2–719.[2] While disclaimers and remedy limitations serve the same ultimate objective, they operate independently and are conceptually distinct.[3] Section 2–316 allows sellers contractually to disclaim responsibility for express and implied warranties, and §§ 2–718 and 2–719 allow sellers to define and limit the type of remedy and amount of damages a buyer will receive in the event a warranty is breached. An effective disclaimer under § 2–316 prevents a warranty from ever arising, so that there is nothing for the seller to breach. By contrast, §§ 2–718 and 2–719, which assume that a valid warranty exists and was breached, concern only the nature and extent of remedy for the breach. An effective damages limitation under § 2–718 "liquidates" the buyer's damages at a predetermined, set amount; an effective limitation under § 2–719 typically limits the buyer's recovery for breach to repair or replacement of the product and allows no recovery for the buyer's incidental or consequential damages.

While Article 2 generally allows buyers and sellers to agree to shift the normal responsibility for breach of warranty from the seller to the buyer, and so to reintroduce the doctrine of *caveat emptor* into a sales contract, the Code seeks to assure that such changes in the normal allocation of responsibility are made apparent to the buyer. Comment 1 to § 2–316 explains this point:

> This section is designed principally to deal with those frequent clauses in sales contracts which seek to exclude "all warranties, express or implied." It seeks to protect a buyer from unexpected and unbargained language of disclaimer by denying effect to such language when inconsistent with language of express warranty and permitting the exclusion of implied warranties only by conspicuous language or other circumstances which protect the buyer from surprise.

Thus, the Code's goal is to assure that buyers know when a product sold does not in fact carry a warranty that ordinarily would attach to such a transaction. In this way, the Code seeks to mandate that sales transactions, as much as reasonably possible, reflect consensual "bargains" between the parties.

### Limiting Rights of Third–Party Beneficiaries by Disclaimer or Limitation

A plaintiff not in privity with a seller may sometimes step into the shoes of the buyer under § 2–318, as previously discussed. Because of

---

**2.** As discussed below, however, the Code does not permit a seller to limit a buyer's remedy so far as to avoid *all* warranty responsibility. See cmt. 1 to § 2–719; § 4.8, below.

**3.** See, e.g., Fleming Farms v. Dixie Ag Supply, Inc., 631 So.2d 922, 925 n.4 (Ala. 1994) ("A disclaimer of warranties and a limitation of remedies are in substance the same, although they are conceptually different. A disclaimer of warranties reduces the circumstances in which the seller would be liable for breach of contract; a limitation of remedies restricts the remedies available upon once a breach is established.").

the derivative nature of such a person's warranty claims, he or she has no greater right than the buyer to recover on a warranty.[4] Accordingly, limitations on and exclusions of warranties, and limitations on remedies for breach of warranty, logically carry over from the buyer to third party beneficiaries.[5] For example, an express warranty's time limitation will apply to third party beneficiaries as well as to the buyer.[6] And if the buyer never received a warranty in the first place, because it was effectively disclaimed in the sales contract between the seller and the buyer, then a third party harmed by a defect in the product will have no warranty upon which to base a claim for breach.[7]

While a third party beneficiary logically may take no *greater* warranty rights than the buyer, may he or she be given any *less*? In an effort to cut liability costs, a seller may wish to provide certain warranties only to the purchaser and to cut off responsibility at that point, excluding warranties (and remedies for breach of warranty) for all third party beneficiaries. A split disclaimer or limitation arrangement of this type may also please the buyer who personally receives warranty protection and may pay a lower price reflecting the seller's lower warranty costs. This temptation of sellers and buyers to conspire to deprive third party beneficiaries of warranty protection for personal injuries is specifically precluded by the last sentence to each of the three Alternative provisions in § 2–318, which all provide: "A seller may not exclude or limit the operation of this section."[8] Comment 1 to § 2–318 explains:

> To the extent that the contract of sale contains provisions under which warranties are excluded or modified, or remedies for breach are limited, such provisions are equally operative against beneficiaries of warranties under this section. What this last sentence forbids is exclusion of liability by the seller to the persons to whom the warranties which he has made to his buyer would extend under this section.

Attempts to split disclaimers and remedy limitations in this manner are quite unusual, and they should be denied effect under this provision of § 2–318.[9]

---

**4.** See 3A Lawrence's Anderson on the UCC § 2–318:13 et seq.

**5.** See id. § 2–316:146 et seq.

**6.** See, e.g., Ford Motor Co. v. Moulton, 511 S.W.2d 690 (Tenn. 1974).

**7.** See, e.g., Buettner v. R.W. Martin & Sons, Inc. 47 F.3d 116 (4th Cir. 1995) (Va. law) (valid "as is" disclaimer in employer's purchase contract also bound employee); Transport Corp. of Am. v. IBM Corp., 30 F.3d 953 (8th Cir. 1994) (Minn. law) (third party beneficiaries under § 2–318 bound by disclaimers binding on buyer); Rynders v. E.I. Du Pont de Nemours & Co., 21 F.3d 835 (8th Cir. 1994) (S.D. law) (warranties effectively disclaimed in original contract give third persons no warranty rights); Shell v. Union Oil Co., 489 So.2d 569 (Ala.

1986). *Contra* Wright v. Dow Chem. U.S.A., 845 F.Supp. 503, 511 (M.D. Tenn. 1993) (homeowners injured by pesticide applied by pest control company not bound by label disclaimers they never saw).

**8.** Alternative C further adds to the end of this sentence: "with respect to injury to the person of an individual to whom the warranty extends."

**9.** See, e.g., Hydra–Mac, Inc. v. Onan Corp., 430 N.W.2d 846 (Minn. Ct. App. 1988), rev'd in part on other grounds, 450 N.W.2d 913 (Minn. 1990). *But cf.* Marshall v. Wellcraft Marine, 103 F.Supp.2d 1099, 1113–14 (S.D. Ind. 1999) (Fla. law) (express warranty limited to first retail purchaser of boat; absence of privity barred recovery).

## Disclaimers of Express Warranties

### *In General*

The very notion of a disclaimer of an *express* warranty appears unprincipled. Why should a seller be permitted to avoid responsibility for making a promise for which the buyer paid, on which the buyer relied, and which constituted part of the basis of the buyer's bargain? For this reason, South Carolina simply prohibits the disclaimer of express warranties.[10] In other states, which do permit express warranties to be disclaimed, such disclaimers are disfavored by the courts.[11]

Article 2 of the Uniform Commercial Code does permit such disclaimers in a limited way, which makes good sense. Section 2–316(1) provides:

> Words or conduct relevant to the creation of an express warranty and words or conduct tending to negate or limit warranty shall be construed wherever reasonable as consistent with each other; but subject to the provisions of this Article on parol or extrinsic evidence (Section 2–202) negation or limitation is inoperative to the extent that such construction is unreasonable.

The first clause of § 2–316(1), which permits "consistent" express warranty limitations, is designed to permit sellers to define express warranties with specificity. All express warranties, of course, logically must have *some* definitional borders, some scope, for dividing product failures that fall within the warranty from those that fall without. So, a manufacturer of a new tire may expressly warrant it against "blowouts." But any such warranty will have some limitations to its scope—for time (3 years),[12] mileage (36,000 miles), type of use (normal, non-commercial passenger car road and highway driving), and manner of use or hazard (no coverage for tires run flat or damaged from off-road driving, fire, collision, vandalism, misalignment, mechanical defects in the vehicle, or deliberate misuse).[13] Surely sellers must be permitted to define the scope of their express warranties in this manner—whether by defining the scope of warranty under § 2–313 or, alternatively, by limiting or excluding warranty under § 2–316. By their nature, border definitions serve to exclude as well as to include.

---

**10.** See S.C. Code Ann. § 36–2–316(1): "If the agreement creates an express warranty words disclaiming it are inoperative."

**11.** See, e.g., Woodruff v. Clark Cty. Farm Bureau Coop. Ass'n, 286 N.E.2d 188, 200 (Ind. Ct. App. 1972) (noting the "judicial aversion to negation of express warranties"). On disclaimers of express warranties, see generally 3A Lawrence's Anderson on the UCC § 2–316:102 et seq.

**12.** See, e.g., Hahn v. Ford Motor Co., 434 N.E.2d 943 (Ind. Ct. App. 1982) (durational limitation effective). Although such "time warranties" occasionally have been invalidated as unreasonable, e.g., Community Television Serv., Inc. v. Dresser Indus.,

435 F.Supp. 214 (D.S.D. 1977), aff'd, 586 F.2d 637 (8th Cir. 1978), they are a standard method for defining the scope of a seller's responsibility, which buyers understand. Accordingly, assuming compliance with the Magnuson–Moss Federal Warranty Act, discussed in § 4.9, below, such time limitations generally should be viewed as permissible under § 2–316. See generally 1 Clark and Smith, Product Warranties 2d § 8:2, at 8–4 and 8–5; 1 White and Summers (Prac. ed.) § 12.2, at 624 n.6.

**13.** See McCarty v. E.J. Korvette, Inc., 347 A.2d 253, 259 (Md. Ct. Spec. App. 1975).

If a disclaimer cannot reasonably be construed as consistent with an express warranty, the disclaimer is void.[14] This is the basic purpose of the second clause in § 2–316(1), which invalidates attempts to limit or disclaim an express warranty where the disclaimer contradicts an essential aspect of the warranty, involving such basic features as a product's safety,[15] or its express description[16] as new,[17] or the descriptions and pictures in advertisements and brochures.[18] *Realmuto v. Straub Motors, Inc.*[19] illustrates the operation of § 2–316's unreasonable construction clause.[20] Plaintiff was injured when the accelerator-carburetor linkage malfunctioned on the used car he had purchased six days earlier from the defendant dealer. The salesman had written "30 day warranty" on the face of the purchase agreement. A printed clause on the back provided in part: "It is expressly agreed that there are no warranties, express or implied, made by either the selling dealer or the manufacturer...." Citing § 2–316(1), the court concluded that "[t]his attempted disclaimer of any express warranties is inoperative since to give effect to the disclaimer would be unreasonable in view of the writing on the face."[21]

A disclaimer of an express warranty is ineffectual if it does not become part of the basis of the bargain. Thus, if a disclaimer is printed in a writing not provided to the buyer until after the time of sale, it will have no effect.[22] For example, if a seller attempts to condition an express warranty on the return of a "warranty registration card" by a writing located inside a product's packaging,[23] or to limit or exclude express

**14.** See, e.g., Snelten v. Schmidt Implement Co., 647 N.E.2d 1071 (Ill. App. Ct. 1995); Ciba–Geigy Corp. v. Alter, 834 S.W.2d 136 (Ark. 1992); Barksdale v. Van's Auto Sales, Inc., 577 N.E.2d 426 (Ohio Ct. App. 1989).

**15.** See, e.g., Bell Sports, Inc. v. Yarusso, 759 A.2d 582, 593 (Del. 2000) (disclaimer stating that bike helmet could not guard against all injuries dubiously held to be ineffective where it also stated that its primary function was to reduce harmful effects of a blow to the head); Schlenz v. John Deere Co., 511 F.Supp. 224, 229 (D. Mont. 1981) (disclaimer was "ineffective to destroy the express warranty of safety made in the operator's manual").

**16.** See Fundin v. Chicago Pneumatic Tool Co., 199 Cal.Rptr. 789, 794–95 (Ct. App. 1984) (disclaimer construed so as not to disclaim express description that could not reasonably be disclaimed); H. G. Fischer X–Ray Co. v. Meredith, 433 A.2d 1306 (N.H. 1981) (description prevailed over disclaimer). If a description is mere puffing or not otherwise part of the basis of the bargain, of course, it does not amount to an express warranty so there is nothing to disclaim. See, e.g., Cuthbertson v. Clark Equip. Co., 448 A.2d 315 (Me. 1982) (holding that various descriptions were not part of basis of bargain).

**17.** See, e.g., Rivers v. BMW of N. Am., Inc., 449 S.E.2d 337 (Ga. Ct. App. 1994); Century Dodge, Inc. v. Mobley, 272 S.E.2d 502 (Ga. Ct. App. 1980) (express warranty, describing car as new, could not reasonably be negated by disclaimer).

**18.** See Grady, Inadvertent Creation of Express Warranties: Caveats for Pictorial Product Representations, 15 U.C.C. L.J. 268 (1983).

**19.** 322 A.2d 440 (N.J. 1974).

**20.** See also Woodruff v. Clark Cty. Farm Bureau Coop. Ass'n, 286 N.E.2d 188, 200 (Ind. Ct. App. 1972) (noting "judicial aversion to negation of express warranties").

**21.** *Realmuto*, 322 A.2d at 442 n.2.

**22.** See, e.g., Dorman v. International Harvester Co., 120 Cal.Rptr. 516, 522 (Ct. App. 1975). Post-sale duties ase discussed below.

**23.** Of course, if the parties' original agreement specifically conditions an express warranty on the return of a warranty registration card, such a condition may be valid. See 1 Clark and Smith, Product Warranties 2d § 8:4, at 8–13. But such a condition may be invalidated if it is principally a marketing information tool. See Van Den Broeke v.

warranties by a form placed inside the glove compartment of a new car delivered after execution of the sales contract, neither post-sale attempt at a disclaimer will be part of the original agreement and so neither will be effective.[24]

### *Disclaimers of Oral Warranties*

What has been said so far concerns a seller's attempts to disclaim express *written* warranties. But a buyer may assert that a salesperson *orally* promised that a product would perform in a certain manner, or that it could be used safely under certain specified conditions. After the fact, such claims of oral warranties raise obvious problems of proof, depending as they do on the veracity of the buyer and memories that tend to fade and evolve into one's subjective recollection of a negotiation that often looks quite different from opposite sides of a sales transaction, especially one that transpired long ago. In pre-sale negotiations, a salesperson may well overstate a product's virtues, and a buyer may well misinterpret the seller's comments about a product and so mistakenly conclude that the product is stronger or safer than it truly is. After the fact, when a product failure causes injury, the buyer's claim of an oral warranty can be quite nettlesome to a retail seller.

The Code addresses the problem of oral express warranties indirectly in § 2–316(1)'s reference to "parol or extrinsic evidence": "The seller is protected under this Article against false allegations of oral warranties by its provisions on parol and extrinsic evidence and against unauthorized representations by the customary 'lack of authority' clauses."[25] Probably a seller's most effective defense to oral warranties is to insert a merger clause in the contract of sale, stating that any oral representations made about the product during negotiations have no effect and are merged into the written contract which is the complete, exclusive, and final expression of the parties' agreement. If properly drafted, conspicuously presented, and acknowledged by the buyer's signature, such an agreement may serve effectively to disclaim express oral warranties, possibly even when a buyer has a claim for personal injuries, and so to prevent misunderstanding and litigation.[26]

## Disclaimers of Implied Warranties

### *In General*

Implied warranties, obligations that arise merely from the sale of goods, are generally easier to disclaim than express warranties a seller made as part of a specific agreement. In the context of commercial

Bellanca Aircraft Corp., 576 F.2d 582 (5th Cir. 1978) (Miss. law). Or it may be proscribed by statute. See, e.g., Cal. Commercial Code § 2801 (preventing seller from voiding warranty solely for failure to complete and return form to manufacturer or retail seller).

On the treatment of warranty registration cards under the Magnuson–Moss Warranty Act, see 2 Clark and Smith, Product Warranties 2d § 17:16, at 17–15 et seq.; C. Reitz, Consumer Protection Under the Magnuson–Moss Warranty Act 33 (ALI 1978, and rev. ed. 1987); § 4.9, below.

**24.** Post-sale disclaimers are more extensively examined below.

**25.** UCC § 2–316 cmt. 2.

**26.** On oral warranties and merger clauses, and for an example of a clear and complete merger clause, see 1 White and Summers (Prac. ed.) § 12.4.

transactions, the parties normally should be permitted to shape the nature of the deal as they desire. The normal inability of consumers to evaluate and bargain over the content of warranties accompanying the sale of new products was discussed above. In this context, permitting a seller to exclude the implied warranty of merchantability, the basic warranty of product quality and safety, seems singularly inappropriate. For this reason, there are a number of restrictions on such disclaimers. Section 2–316 of the Uniform Commercial Code attaches certain requirements on such disclaimers,[27] and a number of state statutes and the Magnuson–Moss Federal Warranty Act prohibit or substantially restrict the ability of manufacturers and other sellers to disclaim implied warranties or to limit damages for breach of warranty in sales of consumer products, as discussed below.[28] Where state law permits the complete exclusion of implied warranties under § 2–316, as most states do, courts disfavor such disclaimers and interpret them narrowly in favor of consumers.[29]

Notwithstanding the general oppressiveness of implied warranty disclaimers in sales of new consumer goods, however, most states long ago adopted the uniform version of § 2–316, which allows manufacturers and other sellers to disclaim completely both types of implied warranties: the implied warranty of merchantability, that otherwise would arise under § 2–314, and the implied warranty of fitness for particular purpose, that otherwise might arise under § 2–315. Accordingly, a disclaimer drafted to comport with the requirements of § 2–316 operates under the Code to prevent a consumer from recovering damages against a manufacturer or other seller even if the consumer is killed or seriously injured by a dangerously defective product.[30]

For example, in *Ford Motor Co. v. Moulton*,[31] the plaintiff was severely injured when a steering defect in his 14–month-old car caused it to veer off a bridge and fall to the street below. His 12–month/12,000–mile express warranty had expired, and the contract of sale disclaimed the implied warranty of merchantability in accordance with § 2–316(2). The plaintiff's tort law claims were barred by a one-year statute of limitations, and the court ruled that the properly drawn disclaimer barred his claim for breach of the warranty of merchantability. In short, the law provided no redress to a consumer severely injured by a dangerous defect in a car that was nearly new.

Implied warranties may be disclaimed in several ways under § 2–316(2), which describes a pre-approved disclaimer method—a "safe harbor"—for manufacturers and other sellers of new products:

**27.** These requirements are modified by Amended UCC § 2–316, as discussed below.

**28.** See § 4.9, below.

**29.** "The courts do not look with great favor on disclaimers; unless every *i* is dotted and every *t* crossed, the disclaimer will be nullified." 1 Clark and Smith, Product Warranties 2d § 8:6, at 8–17. See 3A Lawrence's Anderson on the UCC §§ 2–316:12,-:13 and :34–39.

**30.** See, e.g., Buettner v. Super Laundry Mach., 857 F.Supp. 471, 476–77 (E.D. Va. 1994), aff'd sub nom., Buettner v. R.W. Martin & Sons, Inc., 47 F.3d 116 (4th Cir. 1995) (Va. law); Bennett v. Matt Gay Chevrolet Oldsmobile, Inc., 408 S.E.2d 111, 114 (Ga. Ct. App. 1991); Ford Motor Co. v. Moulton, 511 S.W.2d 690 (Tenn. 1974).

**31.** 511 S.W.2d 690 (Tenn. 1974).

Subject to subsection (3), to exclude or modify the implied warranty of merchantability or any part of it the language must mention merchantability and in case of a writing must be conspicuous, and to exclude or modify any implied warranty of fitness the exclusion must be by a writing and conspicuous. Language to exclude all implied warranties of fitness is sufficient if it states, for example, that "There are no warranties which extend beyond the description on the face hereof."

Subsection (2), it should be noted, is subordinate to subsection (3). As discussed below, subsection (3) permits alternative methods by which implied warranties may be disclaimed. That said, sellers of new products usually employ subsection (2) to disclaim implied warranties. Under this approach, a disclaimer of the implied warranty of merchantability must specifically mention the word "merchantability."[32] To exclude implied warranties of fitness, the seller may use general language,[33] such as "no warranties of any kind accompany the sale of this product."

In addition, disclaimers of both types of implied warranties must be *conspicuous*. Disclaimers of implied warranties also must be written rather than oral—the fitness warranty, as explicitly required by § 2–316(2), and the merchantability warranty as a practical matter in most cases involving the sale of new consumer goods, especially those which prove dangerously defective.[34]

### Conspicuousness

**In general.** Disclaimers of implied warranties generally must be conspicuous to assure as much as possible that a buyer will know that a product is being sold "naked," without any implied warranties of quality or performance.[35] If such warranties are effectively disclaimed, the risk that a product may contain latent defects is shifted from the seller to the buyer, a significant reversal of the risk-of-loss rule of *caveat venditor* that normally governs the sale of goods. Thus, disclaimers of implied warranties under Uniform Commercial Code § 2–316(2) must be conspicuous to prevent a buyer's surprise.[36]

"Conspicuous" is defined in UCC § 1–201(10):

> "Conspicuous": A term or clause is conspicuous when it is so written that a reasonable person against whom it is to

---

**32.** See UCC § 2–316 cmt. 3.

**33.** See UCC § 2–316 cmt. 4.

**34.** By conflicting with the text of § 2–316, the assertion in the text here that merchantability disclaimers must be written, in most sales of new consumer goods, admittedly is bold. But it probably is an accurate statement of how most modern courts will see the issue, perhaps on grounds of conscionability, particularly in the case of defects in new products injuring consumers. By contrast, retail sellers of *used* products on occasion might plausibly attempt to disclaim such warranties in oral rather than written form. See 1 White and Summers (Prac. ed.) § 12–5. Even in the

used product context, however, it is difficult to imagine that a court would rule that, by uttering the words "this car comes with no warranty of merchantability," a used car dealer effectively protects itself against responsibility for injuries caused shortly after the sale by a latent defect in the car's steering which the seller unreasonably chose not to repair. As discussed below, Amended § 2–316(2) and (3) now require that all merchantability disclaimers of consumer goods be in writing and conspicuous.

**35.** See 3A Lawrence's Anderson on the UCC § 2–316:118 et seq.

**36.** See UCC § 2–316 cmt. 1

operate ought to have noticed it. A printed heading in capitals (as: Non-negotiable Bill of Lading) is conspicuous. Language in the body of a form is "conspicuous" if it is in larger or other contrasting type or color.... Whether a term or clause is "conspicuous" or not is for decision by the court.

Thus, an exclusion of an implied warranty must be made to stand out from the rest of the sales contract, by means of larger, bolder, or different color or style of typeface; by a heading, such as **DISCLAIMER OF IMPLIED WARRANTIES** which specifically calls the buyer's attention to the fact of the disclaimer; by location of the disclaimer in a prominent place in the agreement, as immediately above the principal signature line for the buyer, or with a separate buyer signature or initial line accompanying the disclaimer and asserting that the buyer has read and understands the resulting forfeiture of rights; and by any other means which helps assure that a buyer will be protected from "unexpected and unbargained language of disclaimer."[37]

While a seller should include as many features of conspicuousness mentioned in § 1–201(10) as feasible, § 2–316(2) does not require sellers to adopt each and every one of these separate techniques so long as, taken as a whole, the disclaimer is prominently displayed and likely to draw the attention of a reasonable person.[38] In addition to comprehensibility, discussed below, the seller normally should focus particularly upon three elements of prominence: font (size and style), heading, and location.[39] If a seller fails to make a disclaimer conspicuous, the result is clear: it will be void and of no effect, and a buyer's claim for breach of warranty will be unaffected by the purported words of disclaimer.[40]

A case illustrating how an implied warranty of merchantability disclaimer may fail on conspicuousness grounds is *Dorman v. International Harvester Co.*[41] There, a tractor manufacturer's form contract provided that "no other warranties, express or implied, including without limitation, the implied warranties of *merchantability and fitness for a particular purpose shall apply.*" In deciding whether this attempted disclaimer met the conspicuousness requirement under § 2–316, the court acknowledged that the language was indeed located near the

---

**37.** Id.

**38.** See, e.g., Alcan Aluminum Corp. v. BASF Corp., 133 F.Supp.2d 482, 497 (N.D. Tex. 2001) (test is whether attention can reasonably be expected to be called to disclaimer); McLaughlin v. Denharco, Inc., 129 F.Supp.2d 32, 40 (D. Me. 2001) (whether reasonable person would notice disclaimer, considering terms of warranty as a whole); Paper Mfrs. Co. v. Rescuers, Inc., 60 F.Supp.2d 869, 879 (N.D. Ind. 1999) (disclaimer in small type and difficult to read was not conspicuous); Basic Adhesives, Inc. v. Robert Matzkin Co., 420 N.Y.S.2d 983, 987 (City Civ. Ct. 1979) ("considering all factors—the size, prominence and contrast of the capitalized words—the disclaimer on the label was sufficiently conspicuous"), aff'd as modified, 1980 WL 98464 (N.Y. Sup. App. Term 1980) (but "microscopic

print" disclaimer was inconspicuous and ineffective). See generally Special Project, Article Two Warranties in Commercial Transactions: An Update, 72 Cornell L. Rev. 1159 (1987) (hereinafter Cornell II).

**39.** Cornell II, at 1269, suggests the following general guidelines: "Disclaimers should be written in large, noticeable print, set off from the rest of the page, and placed below a heading that clearly indicates that a *disclaimer* follows; sellers should ensure that the disclaimer or a noticeable reference to it appears near the buyer's signature."

**40.** See, e.g., Cate v. Dover Corp., 790 S.W.2d 559 (Tex. 1990); Dorman v. International Harvester Co., 120 Cal.Rptr. 516 (Ct. App. 1975).

**41.** 120 Cal.Rptr. 516 (Ct. App. 1975).

buyer's signature line, that it was printed in slightly larger type than the preceding paragraph, and that it was printed partially in italics. However, citing § 1–201(10), the court reasoned that the language was not conspicuous because it was not presented "in clear and distinct language and prominently set forth in large, bold print in such position as to compel notice."[42] In concluding that the disclaimer was not conspicuous, the court also noted the form's failure to carry a prominent "DISCLAIMER OF WARRANTIES" heading to call the buyer's attention to the content of this important clause.[43]

The *Dorman* court provided an important, additional reason for invalidating the seller's attempted disclaimer—that the phrasing and partial italics rendered it ambiguous and, hence, difficult to comprehend. Indeed, the court observed that the emphasized portion of the disclaimer—"*merchantability and fitness for a particular purpose shall apply*"— actually suggested that the contract was *including* such warranties rather than the other way around. Thus, the fact of disclaimer was not comprehensibly conveyed; its meaning was not clear, definite, nor specific. Although the court did not refer to the comprehensibility issue as one of "conspicuousness," and while strictly speaking it probably is not,[44] the Code's stated purpose of conspicuousness is to prevent the reasonable buyer's surprise at an unexpected bargain.[45] For this reason alone, stated the court, the attempted disclaimer was ineffective.

**Back-side disclaimers.** Disclaimers appearing on the back side or an interior page of a sales contract form are particularly suspect.[46] In *Koellmer v. Chrysler Motors Corp.*,[47] the buyer of a new Dodge truck sued the dealer and manufacturer for breach of the implied warranty of merchantability. The plaintiff had signed a purchase order form on the back of which was a disclaimer in the 7th of 10 separate paragraphs, printed in the same size and style type, in the same color, totaling over 800 words, and with nothing characteristic about the disclaimer clause to distinguish it from the other paragraphs. The court held that the disclaimer clause did not satisfy the conspicuousness requirement of § 2–316(2). As explained by another court,[48] "it is the policy of the law to look with disfavor upon semi-concealed or obscured self-protective provisions of a contract prepared by one party, which the other is not likely to notice."[49] Yet, a disclaimer located other than on the front page of a sales agreement is not invalid per se, provided that the buyer's attention is

---

**42.** Id. at 522.

**43.** Id.

**44.** In § 1–102(10), "conspicuous" is defined in terms of physical prominence, not comprehensibility. See Cornell II, at 1269– 70 (arguing that the conspicuous notion should not include the notion of "understandable," despite some authority for so broadening the concept).

**45.** See cmt. 1 to § 2–316. Compare the *Dorman* court's reliance on authority requiring such language to be "clear" in order to effectuate the parties' intent. 120 Cal.Rptr. at 521.

**46.** See 3A Lawrence's Anderson on the UCC § 2–316:126.

**47.** 276 A.2d 807 (Conn. App. Ct. 1970).

**48.** Christopher v. Larson Ford Sales, Inc., 557 P.2d 1009, 1012 (Utah 1976) (such a disclaimer should not bind a buyer "unless it is shown that the provision [on the back of the form] was actually called to his attention").

**49.** Id. See also Ressallat v. Burglar & Fire Alarms, Inc., 606 N.E.2d 1001 (Ohio Ct. App. 1992).

effectively directed to the clause and the clause is otherwise prominently displayed.[50]

**Disclaimers known to buyer.** A particularly thorny issue is whether an inconspicuous disclaimer should be invalidated even if the buyer admits that he or she read or otherwise knew about it at the time of contracting.[51] Comment 1 to § 2–316 states that the conspicuousness requirement is designed to prevent sellers from sneaking unbargained-for disclaimers into agreements that may surprise a buyer. This suggests that the ultimate question behind the conspicuousness requirement is the subjective issue of the buyer's knowledge. If this be so, then perhaps a court should enforce an inconspicuous disclaimer if a particular buyer at the time of purchase is in fact aware that the product carries no implied warranties. On the other hand, the "conspicuous" definition in § 1–201(10) is crafted in terms that are plainly objective: "A term or clause is conspicuous when *so written* that a *reasonable* person against whom it is to operate *ought to have* noticed it."[52]

Courts and commentators have split over the effect of a buyer's pre-sale knowledge of a disclaimer that is inconspicuous. Some courts, supported by some commentators,[53] hold that at least commercial buyers aware of such disclaimers should be bound to the deal they believe exists.[54] Other courts, supported by other commentators,[55] hold to the contrary that an inconspicuous disclaimer should have no effect even if the buyer knows it exists.[56] In the case of ordinary products liability litigation involving personal injuries, courts would do well to hold sellers strictly to the conspicuousness requirement in § 2–316(2). Allowing sellers to disclaim the basic warranty of reasonable quality in new consumer products is almost always contrary to the true expectations of most consumers and is hence unjust.[57] In such a context, there simply is no good reason to shield a seller from the plain meaning of § 2–316(2)'s admonition that such disclaimers "must be conspicuous" nor to protect a seller from the plainly objective definition of "conspicuous" in § 1–201(10).

**50.** See, e.g., Brown v. Range Rover of N.A., Inc., 24 UCC Rep. 2d 418 (Va. Cir. Ct. 1993); Houck v. DeBonis, 379 A.2d 765, 773 (Md. Ct. Spec. App. 1977), where a reverse-side disclaimer was held conspicuous: "The face of the contract mentions in two separate places that additional terms and conditions are contained on its reverse side. Furthermore, the disclaimer language is separately underscored in Item No. 7, and a heading in capital letters ['DIS-CLAIMER OF IMPLIED WARRANTY'] demarcates the section." See also Collins Radio Co. v. Bell, 623 P.2d 1039 (Okla. Ct. App. 1980), discussed approvingly in Cornell II, at 1268–69.

**51.** See 3A Lawrence's Anderson on the UCC § 2–316:127.

**52.** Emphasis added.

**53.** See, e.g., 1 White and Summers (Prac. ed.) § 12–5, at 638; Weintraub, Dis-

claimer of Warranties and Limitation of Damages for Breach of Warranty Under the UCC, 53 Tex. L. Rev. 60 (1974).

**54.** See, e.g., Imperial Stamp & Engraving Co. v. Bailey, 403 N.E.2d 294 (Ill. App. Ct. 1980).

**55.** See, e.g., Cornell II, at 1271 ("Courts should abide by [§ 2–316(2)'s] language and only enforce disclaimers that are objectively conspicuous.").

**56.** See, e.g., Rehurek v. Chrysler Credit Corp., 262 So.2d 452 (Fla. Dist. Ct. App. 1972).

**57.** The difficulty for consumers in acquiring and properly evaluating information on the risk of product defects is an important fact of life that the law should acknowledge. See C. Gillette and S. Walt, Sales Law 266–67, 271–72 (1999).

### Post-Sale Disclaimers

Sellers frequently include disclaimers in owners' manuals, postcards, and invoices; inside product packaging; on information delivered with a product; or otherwise in a manner inaccessible to buyers until after purchase.[58] Such disclaimers bear a practically insurmountable obstacle to validity if they purport to affect contracts of sale which have already been formed.[59] "In all of these cases, it is as though the seller were determined that the buyer not see the disclaimer until after the fact. Given this seller perversity, it is not surprising that the courts generally nullify such post-contract disclaimers."[60]

Courts hold such disclaimers invalid for a number of reasons.[61] Some courts reason that such a disclaimer should not be viewed as "conspicuous" under UCC § 1–201(10) because it is "not so written that a reasonable person against whom it is to operate ought to have noticed it," at least not at the time of contracting.[62] A more basic and perhaps preferable reason for invalidating post-sale disclaimers is that they are not part of the contract agreed to by the parties.[63] For this reason, to validate such a disclaimer, a seller generally will have to satisfy the modification conditions of § 2–209, which require the seller's good faith, the buyer's agreement to the modification, and possibly the buyer's signature thereon.[64] It seems inconceivable that a seller could satisfy each of these requirements in a typical consumer sales transaction, so that it appears virtually impossible for sellers to bind consumers to post-sale disclaimers in such transactions. Thus, a post-sale disclaimer normally has no effect on a warranty claim by a consumer personally injured by a defective product.[65]

**58.** See 3A Lawrence's Anderson on the UCC § 2–316:53 et seq.

**59.** See, e.g., G.W. White & Son, Inc. v. Gosier, 632 N.Y.S.2d 910 (App. Div. 1995) (no effect unless parties agree to modification of sales contract). See generally 1 White and Summers (Prac. ed.) § 12–5(c); Cornell II, at 1273.

**60.** 1 Clark and Smith, Product Warranties 2d § 8.8, at 8–36. Examples of judicial nullification of such disclaimers include Hornberger v. General Motors Corp., 929 F.Supp. 884 (E.D. Pa. 1996); G.W. White & Son, Inc. v. Gosier, 632 N.Y.S.2d 910 (App. Div. 1995) (no effect unless parties agree to modification of sales contract); Dorman v. International Harvester Co., 120 Cal.Rptr. 516, 522 (Ct. App. 1975) ("a disclaimer in a warranty given to the buyer *after* he signs the contract is *not* binding").

**61.** See, e.g., Whitaker v. Farmhand, Inc., 567 P.2d 916 (Mont. 1977); Rehurek v. Chrysler Credit Corp., 262 So.2d 452 (Fla. Dist. Ct. App. 1972). See generally 1 Clark and Smith, Product Warranties 2d § 8:8, at 8–36 to 8–38.

**62.** See, e.g., Uganski v. Little Giant Crane & Shovel, Inc., 192 N.W.2d 580 (Mich. Ct. App. 1971).

**63.** See, e.g., Paper Mfrs. Co. v. Rescuers, Inc., 60 F.Supp.2d 869, 880 (N.D. Ind. 1999) (post-sale disclaimers represent a "unilateral attempt by the seller to avoid warranty obligations that have already arisen"); Hornberger v. General Motors Corp., 929 F.Supp. 884 (E.D. Pa. 1996); Dorman v. International Harvester Co., 120 Cal.Rptr. 516, 522 (Ct. App. 1975): "A disclaimer of warranties must be specifically bargained for so that a disclaimer in a warranty given to the buyer *after* he signs the contract is *not* binding."

**64.** See UCC § 2–209. "Thus, a warranty booklet stuffed in a glove compartment of a new car would not be binding on a buyer who receives the car three days after signing the sales agreement—unless the buyer 'agreed' to the modification." 1 White and Summers (Prac. ed.) § 12–5, at 640.

**65.** *But see* Temple v. Velcro USA, Inc., 196 Cal.Rptr. 531, 533 (Ct. App. 1983), which involved the crash of a hot-air balloon after the manufacturer of a hook and loop closure issued warnings against the use of its product to hold in place the deflation panels on such balloons: "If the warning was adequate it certainly would be a proper disclaimer to any express or implied

### "As is" and Other Language

**In general.** Uniform Commercial Code § 2–316(3) provides three alternative methods for eliminating implied warranties that a seller may use in lieu of the safe-harbor techniques provided in UCC § 2–316(2). Comment 6 to § 2–316 provides in part:

> The exceptions to the general rule set forth in paragraphs (a), (b) and (c) of subsection (3) are common factual situations in which the circumstances surrounding the transaction are in themselves sufficient to call the buyer's attention to the fact that no implied warranties are made or that a certain implied warranty is being excluded.

Section 2–316 establishes the relative priority of subsection (3) by making subsection (2) "[s]ubject to subsection (3)" and by beginning subsection (3) with the phrase, "Notwithstanding subsection (2),...." What this priority means is that the safe-harbor approach to disclaimer nullification in subsection (2) is optional, that disclaimers may be drafted in other ways that work as well, provided they effectively communicate the fact that the buyer takes the risk of product defects. Thus, if a merchantability disclaimer satisfies subsection (3), it need not mention "merchantability." Nevertheless, many courts have construed subsection (3) narrowly to prevent its "exceptions" from swallowing the more specific procedures of subsection (2), an approach applauded by some commentators.[66]

Subsection (3)(a) permits a seller to disclaim implied warranties by using "as is"[67] or similar language:[68]

> [U]nless the circumstances indicate otherwise, all implied warranties are excluded by expressions like "as is," "with all faults" or other language which in common understanding calls the buyer's attention to the exclusion of warranties and makes plain that there is no implied warranty.

The thrust of this subsection is to permit a product seller to exclude implied warranties by making it clear to the buyer, without using the magic language of "merchantability" and "fitness" required in subsection (2), that no such warranties accompany the sale. The common expression "as is," and other language which plainly states that the buyer takes the risk that a product may contain latent defects, may thus exclude any implied warranties from the sales transaction. As discussed below, however, subsection (3) contains an important initial caveat which invalidates "as is" and similar disclaimers if "the circumstances indicate otherwise."

**Type of buyer and type of product.** In commercial sales transactions involving buyers who are knowledgeable business enterprises, "as is" and similar language of disclaimer generally serve effectively to

warranties...." The court offered no analysis for this conclusion.

**66.** See, e.g., Special Project, Article Two Warranties in Commercial Transactions: An Update, 72 Cornell L. Rev. 1159,

1278 (1987) ("We continue to urge courts to read section 2–316(3)(a) narrowly.").

**67.** See 3A Lawrence's Anderson on the UCC §§ 2–316:156–172.

**68.** See id. §§ 2–318:213–33.

exclude implied warranties,[69] even if the buyer's employee is injured by a defect in the product.[70] However, even in this context, "as is" disclaimers ordinarily may be expected only for sales of goods which are *used*, so that a court may refuse to enforce such a disclaimer where the goods sold are *new*.[71] Moreover, while subsection (3)(a) may properly be applied in many consumer transactions involving used products,[72] courts may conclude that "the circumstances indicate otherwise" in particular consumer sale situations.[73]

The commentators disagree on the proper effect of "as is" disclaimers in consumer sales transactions, some arguing that such disclaimers should effectively exclude implied warranties even in the consumer context,[74] others suggesting to the contrary that such disclaimers should be valid only in commercial sales,[75] and some taking a middle view dependent on the circumstances of the particular case.[76] One reasonable middle view might be to protect consumers generally from "as is" and similar disclaimers in new product cases, but to hold them to such disclaimers in used goods cases, with the result in either situation being rebuttable upon clear proof that the circumstances of the particular transaction call for other treatment.

An "as is" disclaimer will not shield a seller from fraud,[77] or from obligations arising from a service contract[78] or an express warranty,[79] but

---

**69.** See, e.g., Pelc v. Simmons, 620 N.E.2d 12 (Ill. App. Ct. 1993).

**70.** See, e.g., Buettner v. Super Laundry Mach., 857 F.Supp. 471 (E.D. Va. 1994), aff'd sub nom., Buettner v. R.W. Martin & Sons, Inc., 47 F.3d 116 (4th Cir. 1995) ("as is" disclaimer not unconscionable toward injured employee because employer was sophisticated business buyer).

**71.** See, e.g., Gindy Mfg. Corp. v. Cardinale Trucking Corp., 268 A.2d 345 (N.J. Super. 1970).

**72.** For example, see the used car cases cited below.

**73.** See, e.g., Knipp v. Weinbaum, 351 So.2d 1081, 1084 (Fla. Dist. Ct. App. 1977) ("the clause 'unless the circumstances indicate otherwise' ... precludes a finding that automatic absolution can be achieved in the sale of used consumer goods merely by the inclusion in a bill of sale of the magic words 'as is' ").

**74.** See, e.g., Honnold, 1 N.Y. State Law Revision Comm'n, 1955 Report 409, referenced in 1 White and Summers (Prac. ed.) § 12–6, at 642 n.6; Cornell II, at 1278 (backtracking from the consumer-friendly view of Special Project, Article Two Warranties in Commercial Transactions, 64 Cornell L. Rev. 30, 195–96 (1978) ("Cornell I"); 1 Clark and Smith, Product Warranties 2d § 8:10, at 8–44 and 8–45:

If the seller uses the buzz phrases set out in the statute, the court should not inquire into the characteristics of the buyer

in question.... Otherwise, the courts are drawn into ticklish questions of fact with great resulting uncertainty.... [T]here is simply no justification in the statute for such line-drawing.

**75.** See, e.g., Cornell I, at 195–96.

**76.** Although Professors White and Summers appear to lean toward universal enforcement of such clauses, they may be read to be equivocal on the consumer issue on which one might well conclude they would favor some middle-road approach. See 1 White and Summers (Prac. ed.) § 12–6, at 641–44.

**77.** See, e.g., Oakwood Mobile Homes, Inc. v. Cabler, 73 S.W.3d 363, 371–72 (Tex. App. 2002); Maybee v. Jacobs Motor Co., 519 N.W.2d 341 (S.D. 1994); Danley v. Murphy, 658 So.2d 483 (Ala. Civ. App. 1994) (used car dealer said car that had been totaled had been "smacked" in front); Leavitt v. Stanley, 571 A.2d 269 (N.H. 1990). See also Lou Bachrodt Chevrolet, Inc. v. Savage, 570 So.2d 306 (Fla. Dist. Ct. App. 1990).

**78.** Patton v. McHone, 822 S.W.2d 608 (Tenn. Ct. App. 1991).

**79.** See, e.g., Safadi v. Thompson, 487 S.E.2d 457 (Ga. Ct. App. 1997) ("as is" language does not disclaim express warranty that car had not been wrecked); Barksdale v. Van's Auto Sales, Inc., 577 N.E.2d 426 (Ohio Ct. App. 1989). However, courts occasionally assert that "as is" disclaimers

most courts hold in the absence of such circumstances that sellers of used cars may effectively exclude implied warranties by means of such disclaimers.[80] Most of the used car cases, however, involve claims for repair costs for unexpected mechanical problems, and a court confronted with a personal injury claim excluded by an "as is" disclaimer is likely to scrutinize quite closely the "circumstances" of the particular case to see if they might "indicate otherwise."

**Conspicuousness.** Must "as is" and similar subsection (3)(a) disclaimers be conspicuous? The explicit requirement of conspicuousness in subsection (2) and its omission in (3)(a) suggest that the drafters of § 2–316 did *not* intend to require that subsection (3)(a) disclaimers be conspicuous to be effective. A few courts take this view.[81] Alternatively, perhaps the drafters believed that the language "unless the circumstances indicate otherwise" should be used to invalidate inconspicuous subsection (3)(a) disclaimers, especially in consumer transactions, at least in cases where the buyer was unaware of the provision. Troubled by the anomaly of requiring conspicuousness for subsection (2) but not (3)(a) disclaimers, and influenced by § 2–316's underlying goal of preventing buyers from surprise, probably most courts hold that "as is" disclaimers must be conspicuous.[82] Except, perhaps, when a particular buyer truly understands the consequences of such exclusionary language, requiring "as is" disclaimers to be conspicuous in consumer products liability cases is the better view,[83] a requirement that is now explicitly included in Amended § 2–316(3)(a).

### *Prior Inspection*

Implied warranties may be disclaimed by the buyer's prior inspection, or the seller's demand that the buyer conduct such an inspection, of a product.[84] Uniform Commercial Code § 2–316(3)(b) provides:

> [W]hen the buyer before entering into the contract has examined the goods or the sample or model as fully as he desired or has refused to examine the goods there is no implied warranty with regard to defects which an examination ought in the circumstances to have revealed to him. . . .

This provision specifies two separate ways in which implied warranties may be disclaimed: (1) by the buyer's *actual* inspection of a product, and

---

*do* exclude liability for express as well as implied warranties, at least between commercial parties. See, e.g., Welch Sand & Gravel, Inc. v. O & K Trojan, Inc., 668 N.E.2d 529 (Ohio Ct. App. 1995). See generally 3A Lawrence's Anderson on the UCC § 2–316:164.

**80.** See, e.g., David [not Owen] v. Davenport, 656 So.2d 952 (Fla. Dist. Ct. App. 1995); Jenkins v. Landmark Chevrolet, Inc., 575 So.2d 1157 (Ala. Civ. App. 1991); DeVoe Chevrolet–Cadillac, Inc. v. Cartwright, 526 N.E.2d 1237 (Ind. Ct. App. 1988); Richardson v. Mast, 560 N.W.2d 488 (Neb. 1997).

**81.** See, e.g., Auburn Ford, Lincoln Mercury, Inc. v. Norred, 541 So.2d 1077, 1080 (Ala. 1989).

**82.** See, e.g., Basselen v. General Motors Corp., 792 N.E.2d 498, 508 (Ill. App. Ct. 2003) (by implication); Lumber Mut. Ins. Co. v. Clarklift of Detroit, Inc., 569 N.W.2d 681 (Mich. Ct. App. 1997); Patton v. McHone, 822 S.W.2d 608 (Tenn. Ct. App. 1991); Hillcrest Country Club v. N.D. Judds Co., 461 N.W.2d 55 (Neb. 1990); Fernandez v. Western Rail Road Builders, Inc., 736 P.2d 1361 (Idaho Ct. App. 1987).

**83.** See 1 Clark and Smith, Product Warranties 2d § 8:7, at 8–25 to 8–26.

**84.** See 3A Lawrence's Anderson on the UCC §§ 2–316:197–212.

(2) by the buyer's *refusal* of the seller's *demand* that the buyer inspect a product. In the first situation, the buyer is deemed to discover any obvious flaws in the product and so to understand that there is no implied assurance that such flaws do not exist.[85] As previously discussed,[86] obvious dangers are excluded from the scope of the condition that is warranted, whether the buyer actually discovers them or not.[87] In the second situation, by refusing a seller's demand, the buyer simply takes the risk of such flaws: "The seller by the demand puts the buyer on notice that he is assuming the risk of defects which the examination ought to reveal."[88]

Subsection (3)(c) disclaimers apply only to "defects which an examination ought in the circumstances to have revealed." Thus, in most cases, only defects which are truly obvious are covered by this form of disclaimer, for a buyer cannot be expected to uncover latent defects in an ordinary examination.[89] For example, if a used car dealer tells a prospective purchaser to examine a car carefully before buying it, the buyer's refusal to so inspect the car, or his inspection which fails to reveal that the tires are worn completely through to the fabric, probably will amount to a disclaimer of an implied warranty of the tires' merchantable quality.[90] Similarly, if a diver were to ask a seller for a water-resistant watch good to 100 meters and, while examining the watch handed to him in response, notices a sticker on the back of it which states "Water Resistant to 30 meters," any implied warranty of fitness to 100 meters probably would be disclaimed under § 2–316(3)(b). But neither warranty would be disclaimed if the defect were latent: if, in the first situation, the car's frame were dangerously defective,[91] or if, in the second, the watch had no depth indication whatsoever. Consumers generally will be responsible for discovering only the most glaring flaws.[92] On the other hand, sophisticated commercial buyers who know precisely what to look for

---

**85.** See, e.g., Darrell Wood v. Bass Pro Shops, Inc., 462 S.E.2d 101, 103 (Va. 1995) ("a plaintiff may not recover damages for breach of an implied warranty if the purported defect ... was 'known, visible or obvious' to him"); Toney v. Kawasaki Heavy Indus., Ltd., 975 F.2d 162 (5th Cir. 1992) (Miss. law) (absence of leg protection on motorcycle did not render it either unreasonably dangerous or unfit for ordinary purpose because ordinary motorcycle rider would appreciate risk of leg injury in side collision with automobile).

**86.** See § 4.3, above.

**87.** "A failure to notice defects which are obvious cannot excuse the buyer." UCC § 2–316 cmt. 8.

**88.** UCC § 2–316 cmt. 8. The seller must explicitly "demand ... that the buyer examine the goods fully." Id. See Hays v. General Elec. Co., 151 F.Supp.2d 1001, 1013–14 (N.D. Ill. 2001) (buyers held to objective standard of what a buyer of particular product in field should know).

**89.** See, e.g., Whitehouse v. Lange, 910 P.2d 801 (Idaho Ct. App. 1996).

**90.** However limited the warranty in this situation might be. See UCC § 2–314 cmt. 3.

**91.** See Twin Lakes Mfg. v. Coffey, 281 S.E.2d 864, 867 (Va. 1981), involving defects in the frame of a mobile home: "[The] defects ... did not become apparent, even to experienced workmen, until pressure was applied to join the two sections [of the house].... Such latent defects are not those contemplated by [subsection (3)(b)]," such that the buyer's inspection did not waive implied warranties concerning those defects.

**92.** See 1 Clark and Smith, Product Warranties 2d § 8:13, at 8–59: "If the buyer is a consumer without any special knowledge of the goods, the court will not find a disclaimer by inspection unless the defect reaches out and bites the buyer. This is particularly the case where automobiles are involved."

and how to conduct an effective examination of a particular type of product are held to a higher standard of discovery.[93]

### Course of Dealing

The third and final alternative method by which a disclaimer may arise is described in Uniform Commercial Code § 2–316(3)(c):

> [A]n implied warranty can also be excluded or modified by course of dealing or course of performance or usage of trade.[94]

The Code defines "course of dealing" as a "sequence of previous conduct between the parties to a particular transaction which is fairly to be regarded as establishing a common basis of understanding for interpreting their expressions and other conduct."[95] It defines "usage of trade" as "any practice or method of dealing having such regularity of observance in a place, vocation or trade as to justify an expectation that it will be observed with respect to the transaction in question."[96]

Subsection (3)(c) warranty exclusions are rarely litigated in the products liability context, but they can arise. For example, such exclusions might arise when a manufacturer of dangerous chemicals or machinery regularly supplies an industrial company with its products. These two parties may have an arrangement whereby the manufacturer sells the product "raw" to the buying company, with no warnings or guards, because the buying company adds such safety enhancements to the product in a way best suited to the peculiarities of each setting and, hence, is most efficient and effective in protecting the safety of its employees. While a manufacturer's duty to warn and to provide safety devices sometimes may be nondelegable,[97] a course of dealing like the one described normally should serve to exclude any implied warranty that the product could be safely used as sold.

Consumer transactions involving dangerously defective products rarely are affected by implied warranty exclusions under § 2–316(3)(c), but such exclusions can occur in this context, too. Suppose, for example, that a farmer regularly buys used tractor tires from a tire dealer who keeps a large pile of such tires behind his shop. The first time they do business, the tire dealer may inform the farmer that he has no idea which of the used tires may be good or bad, and that he sells these tires for $20 each on condition that the buyer personally inspect the tire and bear the entire risk that it may be defective. Thereafter, the dealer may sell many such tires to the farmer over the years while never uttering these words again,[98] and the farmer may simply discard and replace any such tires that after purchase turn out to be bad. If one day the farmer is injured when one such tire blows out, he might sue the dealer for breach of an implied warranty. In a case like this, a court may well hold that

---

**93.** See UCC § 2–316 cmt. 8 (distinguishing between professional and lay buyers).

**94.** See 3A Lawrence's Anderson on the UCC § 2–316:73 et seq.

**95.** UCC § 1–205(1).

**96.** UCC § 1–205(2).

**97.** See §§ 8.9 (design) and 9.5 (warnings), below.

**98.** The dealer's argument would be even stronger, of course, if the dealer frequently had reminded the buyer of the disclaimer. See Tolmie Farms, Inc. v. J.R. Simplot Co., 862 P.2d 299 (Idaho 1993).

subsection (3)(c) excludes any implied warranties from arising in this situation because of the parties' "course of dealing." If tire dealers and farmers commonly address the risk of loss from defective used tractor tires in this same manner, implied warranties might also be excluded by "usage of trade."

## Unconscionability

A question which has long vexed courts and commentators is whether a disclaimer drafted in compliance with Uniform Commercial Code § 2–316 can ever be struck down for being "unconscionable."[99] More specifically, may a disclaimer of the implied warranty of merchantability that is properly drafted under § 2–316(2) (by conspicuously mentioning merchantability) or § 2–316(3) (by conspicuously stating "as is") ever be invalidated as unconscionable under the Code? Those who reason that the Code's unconscionability principles apply to disclaimers draw upon one or two sections of Article 2: (1) the general provision on unconscionability in § 2–302, and (2) the specific application of unconscionability doctrine to consequential damages limitations in § 2–719(3).[100]

### Section 2–302

Article 2's general unconscionability provision, § 2–302, provides as follows:

§ 2–302. Unconscionable Contract or Clause

(1) If the court as a matter of law finds the contract or any clause of the contract to have been unconscionable at the time it was made the court may refuse to enforce the contract, or it may enforce the remainder of the contract without the unconscionable clause, or it may so limit the application of any unconscionable clause as to avoid any unconscionable result.

Despite the prominence of the important concept "unconscionability" in § 2–302 and various other sections, Article 2 never really defines the term. Whether this is because the notion is too vague or perhaps too complicated to permit a meaningful definition, courts and commentators have spilled considerable ink over the years wrestling with the meaning and effect of unconscionability in contract law, generally, and sales law under Article 2 of the UCC in particular. Comment 1 to § 2–302

---

**99.** The classic article arguing against applying the Code's unconscionability provisions to § 2–316 disclaimers is Leff, Unconscionability and the Code—The Emperor's New Clause, 115 U. Pa. L. Rev. 485, 516–28 (1967). This is supported by 1 N.Y. State Law Revision Comm'n, 1955 Report 586 (1955). For early statements of the opposite view, favoring the application of the Code's unconscionability principles to disclaimers, see, e.g., Ellinghaus, In Defense of Unconscionability, 78 Yale L.J. 757 (1969); Weintraub, Disclaimer of Warranties and Limitation of Damages for Breach of Warranty Under the UCC, 53 Tex. L. Rev. 60, 75–83 (1974). Modern commentators appear to have concluded that the exclusion of warranties cannot be per se unconscionable but that at least some courts will apply the Code's general unconscionability provision to invalidate disclaimers in particular cases where its inclusion in the contract and/or its operation appears one-sided and oppressive. See generally 3A Lawrence's Anderson on the UCC §§ 2–316:84–:92; White and Summers, UCC § 12–11, at 462 (splitting on propriety of this result).

**100.** See Annot., 38 A.L.R.4th 25 (1985) (unconscionability of disclaimers and limitations).

provides at best a hint of what the term might mean, referring to unconscionable clauses as being particularly "one-sided" and to the goal of § 2–302 as "the prevention of oppression and unfair surprise," but *not* the disturbance of "allocation of risks" arising from "superior bargaining power."[101] Many courts, usually outside the products liability context,[102] have defined and applied the term more fully in a wide variety of situations.[103]

**101.** Comment 1 provides more fully:

The basic test is whether, in the light of the general commercial background and the commercial needs of the particular trade or case, the clauses involved are so one-sided as to be unconscionable under the circumstances existing at the time of the contract.... The principle is one of the prevention of oppression and unfair surprise ... and not of disturbance of allocation of risks because of superior bargaining power.

**102.** The most significant products liability case, of course, was Henningsen v. Bloomfield Motors, Inc., 161 A.2d 69, 97 (N.J. 1960) (Francis, J.), involving a claim for personal injuries caused by a steering defect in a new Chrysler, where the court concluded that a disclaimer of the implied warranty of merchantability and a limitation of remedy to repair or replacement in a standardized form sales contract were "violative of public policy and void." *Henningsen* was decided the year before New Jersey's adoption of the UCC.

**103.** By way of example, consider Brunsman v. DeKalb Swine Breeders, Inc., 952 F.Supp. 628, 633 (N.D. Iowa 1996), aff'd, 138 F.3d 358 (8th Cir. 1998) (bargain unconscionable if "such as no person in his senses and not under delusion would make on the one hand, and as no honest and fair person would accept on the other"; relevant factors include "assent, unfair surprise, notice, disparity of bargaining power, and substantive unfairness"). See also Auto–Owners Ins. Co. v. Toole, 947 F.Supp. 1557 (M.D. Ala. 1996) (also defining in no-man-in-his-senses-and-not-under-delusion terms, and considering the following factors: whether one party was unsophisticated and/or uneducated; whether one party had no meaningful choice; whether terms unreasonably favored one party; whether there was unequal bargaining power; and whether the contract contained oppressive, one-sided, or patently unfair terms).

Consider Wayman v. Amoco Oil Co., 923 F.Supp. 1322, 1341 (D. Kan. 1996), aff'd, 145 F.3d 1347 (10th Cir. 1998) (Kan. law), in which the court noted that the doctrines of both unconscionability and adhesion "are concerned with unfairness and one-sidedness in a contract as a result of unequal bargaining power":

An adhesion contract is a "[s]tandardized contract form offered to consumers of goods and services on essentially 'take it or leave it' basis without affording consumer realistic opportunity to bargain and under such conditions that consumer cannot obtain desired product or services except by acquiescing in form contract."

Quoting the "basic test" of unconscionability in cmt. 1 to § 2–302 set forth in the text above, the court referred to other Kansas courts' formulation of this issue as whether a provision is "so outrageous and unfair in its wording or its application that it shocks the conscience or offends the sensibilities of the court," involving such considerations as: use of printed boilerplate drafted by stronger party; excessive price; denial of basic rights and remedies to consumers; penalty clauses; circumstances of contract execution and effect; hiding disadvantageous clauses in inconspicuous location or in mass of fine-print trivia; phrasing language incomprehensibly or misleadingly; imbalance of bargain's rights and responsibilities; exploitation of the unsophisticated and uneducated; and unequal bargaining power. Id. at 1342.

Many courts rely upon Professor Leff's classic distinction between "substantive" and "procedural" unconscionability. See Leff, 115 U. Pa. L. Rev. at 487. See, e.g., Nelson v. McGoldrick, 896 P.2d 1258, 1262 (Wash. 1995) ("substantive unconscionability": terms are one-sided or "monstrously harsh"; "procedural unconscionability": one party's lack of meaningful choice, as from inability to discover or understand terms); Walker v. American Cyanamid Co., 948 P.2d 1123 (Idaho 1997) (invalidating disclaimer on both substantive and procedural grounds). See also Allan v. Snow Summit, Inc., 59 Cal.Rptr.2d 813, 825 (Ct. App. 1996) (also examining nature of adhesion contracts), where the court defined "substantive inadequacy," as not only a one-sided result, but also the absence of justification for that result, or the unreasonable or unexpected reallocation of risks of bargain. The court defined "procedural unconscionability" as based either on (1) *oppression*, from unequal bargaining power precluding negotiation and choice; or (2) *surprise*, from supposedly agreed-upon terms being hidden in a prolix printed form.

Whether a disclaimer should be invalidated as unconscionable is particularly important in products liability cases in which manufacturers frequently attempt by contract to define the full extent of their legal responsibility for product accidents and to exclude as much responsibility as possible for implied warranties. Although much has been changed by state reform statutes,[104] the Magnuson–Moss Federal Warranty Act,[105] and the recent Amendments to Article 2,[106] manufacturers of automobiles and many other types of products have conventionally attempted to disclaim *all* implied warranties, especially the merchantability warranty, by mentioning merchantability conspicuously in the contract of sale. This return to the now-discredited doctrine of *caveat emptor* raises the question, answered powerfully in favor of consumers in *Henningsen v. Bloomfield Motors*,[107] whether such complete disclaimers of the basic warranty of safety can ever be conscionable in the context of the sale of new consumer products.

The issue that confronts a court adjudicating a claim for breach of warranty under Article 2 of the Uniform Commercial Code is one of statutory interpretation: Is § 2–316 entirely independent and self-contained, so that the validity of a disclaimer can be tested solely by whether it meets the requirements of this one section, which thus may be seen to "preempt" § 2–302? This might be called the "preemption" view. Alternatively, must disclaimers jump through *two* separate validity hoops: (1) § 2–316's specific disclaimer requirements, *and* (2) § 2–302's general policing filter, which requires that contract terms be conscionable? This might be called the "two-hoop" view.[108]

Strong arguments support both views.[109] Proponents of the preemption view argue, first, that § 2–316 clearly and specifically authorizes disclaimers and nowhere, in the text or comments, makes any mention of unconscionability. By contrast, § 2–316's cousin section that addresses limitations of consequential damages, § 2–719(3), specifically conditions such limitations on their conscionability.[110] Indeed, comment 3 to § 2–719 distinguishes that section from § 2–316 on the ground that, unlike § 2–719(3), "[t]he seller in *all* cases is free to disclaim warranties in the manner provided in Section 2–316."[111] Further, the principal purpose of § 2–316 is to protect buyers from "unbargained language of disclaimer" and "surprise," a policy which overlaps § 2–302's own goals of preventing "oppression and unfair surprise." This suggests that § 2–316 contains within itself as much internal policing of the fairness of disclaimers as useful, such that it can do without assistance from the general policing provisions of § 2–302.

Proponents of the two-hoop view observe that § 2–302 by its terms applies to "*any* clause of the contract,"[112] and nowhere does it suggest

---

**104.** See § 4.9, below.

**105.** See id.

**106.** See discussions above and below.

**107.** 161 A.2d 69 (N.J. 1960).

**108.** See 1 Clark and Smith, Product Warranties 2d § 8:12, at 8–51 et seq.

**109.** Both sets of arguments are well summarized in Clark and Smith, above, and White and Summers, UCC § 12–11(a).

**110.** See § 4.8, below.

**111.** UCC § 2–719 cmt. 3 (emphasis added).

**112.** UCC § 2–302(1) (emphasis added).

that disclaimers under § 2–316 are somehow out of bounds. Moreover, seven of the ten illustrative cases in comment 1 to § 2–302 involve disclaimers denied full effect. And while § 2–316 may protect buyers from "surprise," it does not protect them from one-sided contractual "oppression" of the type that the automotive industry imposed on consumers in *Henningsen v. Bloomfield Motors, Inc.*[113]

Like the commentators, the courts are split on whether § 2–316 disclaimers may be found unconscionable under § 2–302. There is clear judicial support for the preemption view that § 2–316 disclaimers simply may not be declared unconscionable.[114] However, a number of cases suggest[115] that § 2–302 may invalidate disclaimers that comply with § 2–316.[116]

### Section 2–719(3)

Rather than invoke the general unconscionability provision of § 2–302, some plaintiffs ask courts to nullify § 2–316 disclaimers under the remedy limitation provision, § 2–719(3), which provides:

> Consequential damages may be limited or excluded unless the limitation or exclusion is unconscionable. Limitation of consequential damages for injury to the person in the case of consumer goods is prima facie unconscionable but limitation of damages where the loss is commercial is not.

The argument is that if a disclaimer drafted in compliance with § 2–316 operates so as to deny a plaintiff the right to consequential damages for injury to person, it is (prima facie) invalid on grounds of unconscionability under § 2–719.

While a couple of courts have accepted this kind of "reasoning,"[117] it squarely contradicts the structure and wording of Article 2. In comments to both § 2–316 and § 2–719, the Code makes clear as a bell that § 2–316, which addresses whether a warranty's creation was nullified by a

---

**113.** 161 A.2d 69 (N.J. 1960). Professor Weintraub favors applying § 2–302 to certain disclaimers valid under 2–316, concluding that it "seems consistent with Code policy that section 2–302 be used to police against unconscionable warranty disclaimers, even those that have meticulously adhered to the formal requirements of section 2–316." Weintraub, above, at 83 (suggesting the relevance to the unconscionability determination of such factors as (1) type of remedy excluded—lost profits vs. personal injury, (2) advertence—whether the buyer understood the disclaimer's meaning and practical consequences, and (3) adhesion—whether the buyer could bargain for better terms).

**114.** See, e.g., Ford Motor Co. v. Moulton, 511 S.W.2d 690 (Tenn. 1974); Avery v. Aladdin Prods. Div., Nat'l Serv. Indus., 196 S.E.2d 357 (Ga. Ct. App. 1973); Marshall v. Murray Oldsmobile Co., 154 S.E.2d 140 (Va. 1967) (new car sale to consumer; pre-Code case).

**115.** However, finding a case which actually *holds* a disclaimer invalid on this basis may be difficult. See White and Summers, UCC § 12–11, at 460: "[W]e have found no cases that find a disclaimer conforming to 2–316 to be unconscionable [under 2–302]."

**116.** See, e.g., Murray v. Holiday Rambler, Inc., 265 N.W.2d 513 (Wis. 1978); Hiigel v. General Motors Corp., 544 P.2d 983 (Colo. 1976) (emphasizing consumer/commercial distinction); Haugen v. Ford Motor Co., 219 N.W.2d 462 (N.D. 1974); Zabriskie Chevrolet, Inc. v. Smith, 240 A.2d 195 (N.J. Super. Ct. Law Div. 1968). Cf. Henningsen v. Bloomfield Motors, Inc., 161 A.2d 69 (N.J. 1960) (new automobile; pre-Code case). See also Schmaltz v. Nissen, 431 N.W.2d 657 (S.D. 1988); Martin v. Joseph Harris Co., 767 F.2d 296 (6th Cir. 1985) (Mich. law), overruled on other grounds, 499 U.S. 225 (1991).

**117.** See, e.g., Ford Motor Co. v. Tritt, 430 S.W.2d 778 (Ark. 1968).

disclaimer, is totally independent of the entirely separate issue in § 2–719(3) of whether a seller may limit personal injury damages recoverable for a breach of a warranty that has *not* been nullified under § 2–316. In particular, comment 2 to § 2–316 provides:

> This Article treats the limitation or avoidance of consequential damages as a matter of limiting remedies for breach, separate from the matter of creation of liability under a warranty. *If no warranty exists, there is of course no problem of limiting remedies for breach of warranty.* Under [§ 2–316(4)] the question of limitation of remedy is governed by [§ 2–719 and related sections] rather than by this section.[118]

Professors White and Summers succinctly explain the meaning of this comment: "The comment's reasoning is elementary: there can be no consequential damages if there is no breach; there can be no breach of warranty if there is no warranty; there can be no warranty if the seller has disclaimed them pursuant to 2–316.... [I]t seems clear that the scheme of the Code does not permit a court to disregard [a] disclaimer on the basis that it operates to exclude consequential damages that [may] not be excluded under 2–719(3)."[119]

Not only does comment 2 to § 2–316 make entirely clear that § 2–719(3)'s unconscionability provision cannot be used to invalidate a warranty disclaimer that is good under § 2–316, but this point is underscored by comment 3 to § 2–719. After recognizing that unconscionability constrains the extent to which a seller may limit damages, the comment proceeds to declare that a seller "in *all* cases is free to disclaim warranties" under § 2–316.[120] Surely this must mean that § 2–316 disclaimers in all cases are free from the unconscionability restraints of § 2–719(3).[121]

The independence of § 2–316 and § 2–719(3) from one another, and the resulting impropriety of applying § 2–719(3) to invalidate disclaimers that are properly drawn under § 2–316, thus seems evident. Some courts have so held.[122] Curiously, a small number of courts,[123] and even some commentators,[124] have disagreed. The explanation for such an apparent breach of the Code's integrity in several of the cases appears to spring from confusion in how the Code is structured.[125] Another explana-

---

**118.** Emphasis added.

**119.** White and Summers, UCC § 12–12, at 464.

**120.** The comment states in full:

Subsection (3) recognizes the validity of clauses limiting or excluding consequential damages but makes it clear that they may not operate in an unconscionable manner. Actually such terms are merely an allocation of unknown or undeterminable risks. *The seller in all cases is free to disclaim warranties in the manner provided in Section 2–316.* (Emphasis added.)

**121.** White and Summers again capture the point with brilliant clarity: "The last sentence [of comment 3] seems to be telling the seller, 'If you really want to limit your liability, why don't you disclaim all warranties? Then you won't have to worry about limiting damages.'" White and Summers, UCC § 12–12, at 464.

**122.** See, e.g., Ford Motor Co. v. Moulton, 511 S.W.2d 690 (Tenn. 1974).

**123.** See Walsh v. Ford Motor Co., 298 N.Y.S.2d 538 (Sup. Ct. 1969); Ford Motor Co. v. Tritt, 430 S.W.2d 778 (Ark. 1968).

**124.** See, e.g., Note, 63 Va. L. Rev. 791 (1977).

**125.** See, e.g., Ford Motor Co. v. Tritt, 430 S.W.2d 778 (Ark. 1968).

tion for why a few courts have mistakenly applied the § 2–719 unconscionability provision to § 2–316 disclaimers may be an effort to ameliorate the harshness of denying any remedy to a consumer injured by a defective product.[126] While a court might well be tempted to adopt a chancellor mantle to render justice in such cases, it would seem that a state legislature's adoption of meticulously structured and precisely drafted sections of a commercial code should be respected. Creative justice in products liability judging appears more appropriately directed to the realm of tort law where judicial doctrines of tortious misrepresentation, negligence, and strict liability in tort provide courts in most cases ample room to protect deserving persons injured by defective products. And in cases where tort law closes its doors on such persons, perhaps because of a short tort law statute of limitations, a court faced with an oppressive disclaimer of a warranty claim might turn in good conscience to the general unconscionability provisions of § 2–302.

### Amendments to § 2–316

Amended UCC § 2–316 improves consumer protection against unbargained-for disclaimers of implied warranties in a number of ways. First, Amended § 2–316(2) provides that, in consumer contracts, a disclaimer of the implied warranty of merchantability must (1) be in writing, (2) be conspicuous, and (3) state "The seller undertakes no responsibility for the quality of the goods except as otherwise provided in this contract." Although sellers of new products virtually always put disclaimers in writing anyway, and while the conspicuousness requirement is not new, the third requirement is significant. This new "safe-harbor" language for sellers goes much further in alerting buyers to what an implied warranty disclaimer takes away than the previous safe-harbor technique of merely stating that the product carries no implied warranty of merchantability.

As for disclaimers of implied warranties of fitness for particular purpose, Amended § 2–316(2) similarly specifies safe-harbor language that clearly describes the effect of such a disclaimer: "The seller assumes no responsibility that the goods will be fit for any particular purpose for which you may be buying these goods, except as otherwise provided in the contract."

Finally, § 2–316(3) is substantively amended in two ways. First, "as is" and other disclaimers searching for legitimacy under subsection (3)(a) now must be conspicuous, provided that the sale includes a written contract. Second, subsection (3)(b) makes clear that a buyer who fails to inspect a (usually second-hand) product prior to purchase is not responsible for defects such an inspection should reveal unless the seller demands the buyer to so inspect the product. Although this form of disclaimer previously rested on a seller's demand to inspect, the demand requirement was buried in a comment,[127] and it now is elevated to formal black-letter status.

**126.** See White and Summers, UCC § 12–12, at 464–65.

**127.** See UCC § 2–316 cmt. 8.

## § 4.8  LIMITATIONS OF REMEDY

As with any damages claim, a products liability action consists of two major components: (1) a breach of legal duty, and (2) resulting damage. In warranty law, a seller breaches a legal duty by making and breaching a warranty that has not been disclaimed. As previously discussed, a disclaimer is an explicit means by which a seller may contractually nullify warranties, particularly implied warranties, that otherwise might arise from the sale of a product.[1] One might view disclaimers as a seller's front-door method for avoiding warranty responsibility for product accidents.

A second and equally effective method by which a seller at least theoretically may contractually avoid such responsibility is to exclude or limit a buyer's remedies for breach of warranty. In a world of perfect freedom of contract, a buyer and seller might agree to a sale in which (1) the product carries various (undisclaimed) express and implied warranties, but (2) the buyer's only remedy for breach would be one dollar.[2] More plausibly, a dealer might sell a used car with a 30–day express warranty against mechanical defects but with an exclusion of damages for personal injuries and a limitation of the buyer's remedy to repair or replacement of defective parts. This type of limitation-of-remedy provision in a sales contract might be viewed as a seller's back-door method for avoiding substantial warranty responsibility for product accidents.

As examined earlier, Uniform Commercial Code § 2–316, located in the "General Obligation" portion of Article 2,[3] authorizes and imposes various controls upon warranty *disclaimers*.[4] Section 2–719, located in the "Remedies" portion of Article 2,[5] authorizes and controls the *limitations* a seller may place on a buyer's *remedies* for breach of warranty. While proclaiming the separate and independent status of these two provisions, the Code suggests the tandem nature of how they may interrelate in sales transactions. The Code's warranty disclaimer section, in § 2–316(4), cross-references the Code's remedy limitation provisions:

> Remedies for breach of warranty can be limited in accordance with the provisions of this Article on liquidation or limitation of damages and on contractual modification of remedy (Sections 2–718 and 2–719).

Correspondingly, comment 3 to the Code's remedy limitation section, while noting the unconscionability restriction on such limitations in § 2–719(3), explains that § 2–316 warranty disclaimers, uncontrolled by the principles of § 2–719, are not so fettered.[6] Thus, while operating inde-

---

**§ 4.8**

**1.**  See § 4.7, above.

**2.**  Note that this kind of agreement is forbidden by UCC § 2–719's requirement that "it is of the very essence of a sales contract that at least minimum adequate remedies be available. If the parties intend to conclude a contract for sale within this Article they must accept the legal consequence that there be at least a fair quantum of remedy for breach of the obligations

or duties outlined in the contract." Cmt. 1 to § 2–719.

**3.**  Part 3, General Obligation and Construction of Contract, begins with § 2–301.

**4.**  See § 4.7, above.

**5.**  Part 7, Remedies, begins with § 2–701.

**6.**  "The seller in all cases is free to disclaim warranties in the manner provided in Section 2–316." UCC § 2–719 cmt. 3.

pendently, disclaimers and limitations form the horse and buggy of a product seller's responsibility-avoidance measures.[7]

The predicates to the § 2–719 limitations-of-remedy provisions are the Code's general provisions for a buyer's breach of warranty damages in §§ 2–714 and 2–715. Section 2–714(3) authorizes awards of "consequential damages" for breach of warranty, and § 2–715(2)(b) defines such damages to include "injury to person or property proximately resulting from any breach of warranty."

As with certain other provisions in Article 2,[8] §§ 2–714 and 2–715 operate principally as "default" provisions—provisions which take effect only if the parties' contract does not otherwise address the issue. That is, if a buyer and seller fail to specify in their agreement what damages will be available for breach of warranty, a buyer may recover the types of damages prescribed in §§ 2–714 and 2–715. Operating within a framework of freedom of contract, such default provisions serve to "fill in" contracts which fail to specify an important term with the kind of term most parties normally would agree to if they freely bargained and were informed.[9]

Thus, § 2–719 authorizes and conditions the *alteration* of a buyer's remedies otherwise available under §§ 2–714 and 2–715. Consistent with Article 2's objective of allowing parties to a sales transaction to shape their particular deals as they may agree, subject only to controls to help assure that their decisions are informed and truly free, the purpose of § 2–719 is to allow sellers and buyers to frame the remedy provisions of their sales contracts consistent with informed free choice.[10] Comment 1 to § 2–719 explains:

> Under this section parties are left free to shape their remedies to their particular requirements and reasonable agreements limiting or modifying remedies are to be given effect.
>
> However, it is of the very essence of a sales contract that at least minimum adequate remedies be available. If the parties intend to conclude a contract for sale within this Article they must accept the legal consequence that there be at least a fair quantum of remedy for breach of the obligations or duties outlined in the contract. Thus any clause purporting to modify or limit the remedial provisions of this Article in an unconscionable manner is subject to deletion and in that event the remedies made available by this Article are applicable as if the stricken clause had never existed. Similarly, under subsection (2), where an apparently fair and reasonable clause because of circumstances fails in its purpose or operates to deprive either

---

**7.** See § 4.7, above.

**8.** Other notable default provisions in Article 2 are those on implied warranties in §§ 2–314 and 2–315. These two provisions may arise by default in sales contracts which do not contain a term creating or excluding them.

**9.** Implementation of the "agreement of the parties" is a principal policy of the Uniform Commercial Code. See UCC § 1–102(2)(b)(3): "The effect of provisions of this Act may be varied by agreement, except as otherwise provided in this Act and except that the obligations of good faith, diligence, reasonableness and care prescribed by this Act may not be disclaimed by agreement...."

**10.** See id.

party of the substantial value of the bargain, it must give way to the general remedy provisions of this Article.

Each of the three subsections to § 2–719 reflects these general principles.

## Limitation of Remedies Generally; Repair or Replacement

Section 2–719(1) provides:

(1) Subject to the provisions of subsections (2) and (3) of this section and of the preceding section on liquidation and limitation of damages,

(a) the agreement may provide for remedies in addition to or in substitution for those provided in this Article and may limit or alter the measure of damages recoverable under this Article, as by limiting the buyer's remedies to return of the goods and repayment of the price or to repair and replacement of non-conforming goods or parts; and

(b) resort to a remedy as provided is optional unless the remedy is expressly agreed to be exclusive, in which case it is the sole remedy.

Subsection (1) generally allows a seller to limit a buyer's remedies to repair or replacement of the goods or defective parts, or otherwise to alter the types or amounts of damages normally available for breach, provided the contract makes clear that the limited or modified remedy is the sole and exclusive remedy available to the buyer.[11] If the exclusivity of an attempted limitation-of-remedy provision is at all ambiguous, the remedy provided will be deemed to *supplement*, rather than to displace, the Article 2 general remedy provisions.[12] Thus, a contract that limits a seller's "warranties," "obligations," or "liability," rather than the buyer's "remedies," may well be interpreted to be an invalid disclaimer of liability rather than a valid limitation of remedies.[13]

## Failure of Essential Purpose

Section 2–719(2) provides:

(2) Where circumstances cause an exclusive or limited remedy to fail of its essential purpose, remedy may be had as provided in this Act.

Courts generally apply subsection (2)'s failure-of-essential-purpose provision to cases involving products which are "lemons," not to ordinary products liability claims for personal injuries. The paradigm subsection (2) consumer case involves a car with many recurring defects the seller cannot or will not repair within a reasonable period of time, thereby indefinitely depriving the owner of its full and effective use. In such a

---

**11.** "If the parties intend the term to describe the sole remedy under the contract, this must be clearly expressed." Section 2–719 cmt. 2.

**12.** "Subsection (1)(b) creates a presumption that clauses prescribing remedies

are cumulative rather than exclusive." Section 2–719 cmt. 2.

**13.** See, e.g., Stream v. Sportscar Salon, Ltd., 397 N.Y.S.2d 677 (City Civ. Ct. 1977); Ford Motor Co. v. Reid, 465 S.W.2d 80 (Ark. 1971).

case, a limitation of the buyer's remedy to "repair or replacement of defective parts" fails its essential purpose of guaranteeing that the seller will, within a reasonable period of time, cure the defects and put the product into workable condition.[14] Thus, notwithstanding a seller's effort to limit remedies to repair or replacement, the buyer of such a lemon product may be entitled to revoke acceptance of the product under UCC § 2–608 if its value is "substantially impair[ed]."[15]

*Riley v. Ford Motor Co.*[16] is an early example of this type of irreparable new car case, where an exclusive repair or replacement provision was held to deprive the buyer of the "substantial value of the bargain."[17] There, the car in the first few weeks had over 14 defects which the dealer did not satisfactorily repair. A more recent example is *Ex parte Miller*,[18] where the seller, over a 21–month period, attempted to repair a large variety of different problems in a new tractor-type vehicle. Striking an exclusive repair-or-replacement clause on failure-of-essential-purpose grounds, the court observed that "the seller does not have an unlimited time" to cure defects in the products that it sells.[19] The problem of irreparable products is now also addressed by the Magnuson–Moss Federal Warranty Act[20] and various state "lemon laws."[21]

---

**14.** See, e.g., Bailey v. Skipperliner Indus., Inc., 278 F.Supp.2d 945 (N.D. Ind. 2003) (defendant made several unsuccessful attempts to fix boat engine, and jury could reasonably conclude that limited warranty had failed of its essential purpose); King v. Taylor Chrysler–Plymouth, Inc., 457 N.W.2d 42 (Mich. Ct. App. 1990) (purchaser took car to dealer to repair stalling problems seven times over nine months of unsuccessful repairs). Compare Ford Motor Co. v. Mayes, 575 S.W.2d 480, 485 (Ky. Ct. App. 1978), where the seller of a truck provided the buyers with a limited repair or replacement of defective parts warranty at the time of sale. The buyers made eight or nine fruitless efforts to have the truck repaired, during which time the frame had twisted and "diamonded" to the point that it would cause excessive wear and tear on various parts of the truck. *Held*, the vehicle's limited repair or replacement warranty, having failed of its essential purpose, would not confine the buyers' remedies.

**15.** On revocation of acceptance under § 2–608, see generally 1 Clark and Smith, Product Warranties 2d § 7:9; White and Summers, UCC § 8–4.

**16.** 442 F.2d 670 (5th Cir. 1971) (Ala. law).

**17.** UCC § 2–719 cmt. 1.

**18.** 693 So.2d 1372 (Ala. 1997).

**19.** Id. at 1378. More fully, the court remarked: " '[A]t some point after the purchase of a new [product], the same should be put in good running condition, that is, the seller does not have an unlimited time for the performance of the obligation to replace and repair parts. This is no more than saying that at some point in time, it must become obvious to all people that a particular [product] cannot be repaired or parts replaced so that the same is made free from defect.' " Id.

**20.** See § 4.9, below.

**21.** Almost all states now have automobile "lemon laws," first enacted in 1982, that typically permit buyers of new cars to receive a replacement of the car or a refund of the purchase price (less the value of its use) after the dealer has made three or four unsuccessful attempts to repair a substantial defect ("impairment") within one or (as in New York) two years after purchase. A few states, notably California (the Song–Beverly Consumer Warranty Act) but also Kansas and Minnesota, apply various warranty protections to consumer products more generally. See Cal. Civ. Code § 1790 et seq.; Kan. Stat. Ann. § 50–623 et seq. (Kansas Consumer Protection Act); Minn. Stat. Ann. § 325F.01 et seq. (Consumer Protection; Products and Sales).

For the citations to the lemon laws of nearly every state, see 1 Clark and Smith, Product Warranties 2d § 7:19, at 7–86 and 7–87; Consumer Product Warranty Acts, 17 Am. Jur. 2d § 68, at 355–56 (1990). On lemon laws generally, see, e.g., 1 Clark and Smith, Product Warranties 2d § 7:19; Honigman, The New "Lemon Laws" Expanding U.C.C. Remedies, 17 UCC L.J. 116 (1984); Kegley and Hiller, "Emerging" Lemon Car Laws, 24 Am Bus. L.J. 87 (1986); Reitz, What You Should Know About State "Lemon Laws," 34 Prac. Law. 83 (1988); Con-

## Personal Injury Damage Exclusions—Unconscionability

### *In General*

Section 2–719(3), particularly the second sentence thereof, is far and away the most important aspect of § 2–719 for consumer products liability litigation involving personal injuries. This subsection provides in full:

> Consequential damages may be limited or excluded unless the limitation or exclusion is unconscionable. Limitation of consequential damages for injury to the person in the case of consumer goods is prima facie unconscionable but limitation of damages where the loss is commercial is not.

Because subsection (3) takes priority over subsection (1),[22] the second sentence of § 2–719(3) means that sellers of consumer goods may not contractually limit damages for personal injuries, to repair or replacement or otherwise, unless the seller can show that such a limitation is not "unconscionable."[23] At the very least, such showings will be rare,[24]

sumer Product Warranty Acts, 17 Am. Jur. 2d §§ 66–68 (1990); Annot., 51 A.L.R.4th 872 (1987) (auto lemon laws).

**22.** UCC § 2–719(1) begins: "Subject to the provisions of subsections (2) and (3) . . . ."

**23.** As with disclaimers, see § 4.7, above, unconscionability determinations for § 2–719(3), per § 2–302, frequently refer to the noted distinction between *procedural* unconscionability, which precludes a buyer's meaningful choice in accepting a contractual provision, and *substantive* unconscionability, which denotes a one-sided provision that unreasonably favors the seller. See, e.g., Hornberger v. General Motors Corp., 929 F.Supp. 884, 891 (E.D. Pa. 1996). Some courts consider a potpourri of relevant factors. See, e.g., NEC Techs., Inc. v. Nelson, 478 S.E.2d 769 (Ga. 1996) ("unconscionability" under § 2–302 is a flexible doctrine which embraces a variety of factors rather than a formulaic concept). Observing that procedural unconscionability addresses "the process of making the contract," whereas substantive unconscionability focuses on "the contractual terms themselves," the *NEC* court offered a "non-inclusive" list of *procedural* unconscionability factors, including "age, education, intelligence, business acumen and experience of the parties, their relative bargaining power, the conspicuousness and comprehensibility of the contract language, the oppressiveness of the terms, and the presence or absence of a meaningful choice." *Substantive unconscionability*, on the other hand, focuses on such matters as "the commercial reasonableness of the contract terms, the purpose and effect of the terms, the allocation of the risks between the parties, and similar public policy concerns." Id. at 771–72. Holding that the ex-

clusion of consequential damages for property loss in the sale of a television set was not unconscionable, the *NEC* court, id. at 774, adopted the analysis of Fotomat Corp. of Fla. v. Chanda, 464 So.2d 626, 630 (Fla. Dist. Ct. App. 1985):

> People should be entitled to contract on their own terms without the indulgence of paternalism by courts in the alleviation of one side or another from the effects of a bad bargain. Also, they should be permitted to enter into contracts that actually may be unreasonable or which may lead to hardship on one side. It is only where it turns out that one side or the other is to be penalized by the enforcement of the terms of a contract so unconscionable that no decent, fairminded person would view the ensuing result without being possessed of a profound sense of injustice, that equity will deny the use of its good offices in the enforcement of such unconscionability.

**24.** An unusual case that did enforce a contractual avoidance of a personal injury claim under § 2–719 is Mullan v. Quickie Aircraft Corp., 797 F.2d 845 (10th Cir. 1986) (Colo. law), which involved the sale of a home-built aircraft kit that included a contractual waiver of claims arising from defects or safety in the aircraft. The plane crashed on take-off, and the pilot purchaser of the kit sued the manufacturer for his injuries. Upholding the waiver of such claims against a charge of prima facie unconscionability under § 2–719, the court reasoned that the "disclaimer provision" was not unconscionable in view of the plaintiff's expertise with respect to aircraft and woodworking, his thorough investigation of the aircraft before ordering it, and his modification of the sales agreement and "other circumstances surrounding the formation of

and it is safe to say that limitations on personal injury damages in consumer goods cases will be held unconscionable and void in almost every case.[25]

Nevertheless, one may imagine situations where a seller might reasonably and fairly attempt to limit its responsibility for personal injuries, such as where a seller provides consumers with an *extra* warranty over and above the kind of coverage against defects that other sellers normally provide consumers. For example, assume that most tire manufacturers warrant tires of a certain type and price against defects in materials and workmanship for 36 months/36,000 miles. During this warranty period, consumers injured in accidents caused by tire defects may recover personal injury damages under § 2–715, and any attempt by tire sellers to limit damages to repair or replacement in such cases would be void under § 2–719(3). Now, suppose that Acme Tire Company wishes to offer consumers an extra, broader warranty that covers not only all damages caused by defects but that also provides a limited remedy for damages from other sources such as road hazards like nails and glass. Acme will be responsible, of course, for personal injuries caused by tire defects during the warranty period, but it may be willing to broaden the warranty beyond defects to include all-hazard coverage only if it can limit its remedy for such extra coverage to repair or replacement of the non-defective tire. Assuming that this remedy limitation on the extra warranty is made entirely clear in the sales agreement, there appears to be no good reason why a seller should be discouraged from offering, and consumers precluded from receiving, this kind of extra benefit.

The argument for allowing personal injury damages limitations for such "extra" warranties was made by the dissenting judge in *Collins v. Uniroyal, Inc.*,[26] a warranty case involving the failure of a nondefective

---

the contract." Id. at 852. Note, however, that *Mullan*, while purporting to interpret § 2–719, involved a general waiver clause that looked as much like a disclaimer of warranties as a limitation of remedies.

**25.** "[I]t is virtually impossible to imagine what the disclaiming party can do or show to overcome the 'prima facie' language. In effect we probably have an absolute bar in section 2–719." Franklin, When Worlds Collide: Liability Theories and Disclaimers in Defective–Product Cases, 18 Stan. L. Rev. 974, 1013 (1966). See also 4B Lawrence's Anderson on the UCC § 2–719:103, at 94 ("It would appear that the only way to overcome the prima facie unconscionability is for the seller to show that the consumer had some type of choice regarding inclusion of the limitation on the consequential damages or was at least clearly aware of it and chose, in spite of the awareness, to proceed with the transaction.").

For examples of personal injury damages exclusions ruled unconscionable, see, e.g., Larsen v. Pacesetter Sys., Inc., 837 P.2d 1273 (Haw. 1992), amended in part on re-

consideration, 843 P.2d 144 (Haw. 1992) (heart pacemaker); Tuttle v. Kelly–Springfield Tire Co., 585 P.2d 1116 (Okla. 1978) (express warranty against tire blowouts); McCarty v. E.J. Korvette, Inc., 347 A.2d 253 (Md. Ct. Spec. App. 1975) (express warranty against tire blowouts); Collins v. Uniroyal, Inc., 315 A.2d 16 (N.J. 1974); Matthews v. Ford Motor Co., 479 F.2d 399 (4th Cir. 1973) (Va. law) (defective car).

**26.** 315 A.2d 16 (N.J. 1974). In Collins, the purchaser of a tire manufactured by the defendant and guaranteed against blowouts was killed when the tire blew out. Since the warranty guaranteed against blowouts from external causes as well as from defects in the tires, and since no defect was shown in this case, Judge Clifford argued in dissent that the manufacturer's limitation of remedy to repair or replacement should be enforced: "The drafters presumably had something in mind when they chose the expression 'prima facie unconscionable' instead of 'per se unconscionable' or simply 'unconscionable'. . . ." Id. at 20. Judge Clifford concluded that "where the express

tire, and its logic has been endorsed in a prominent law review article.[27] But the dissent's reasoning failed to impress the *Collins* majority, which held such a limitation to be "patently unconscionable."[28] While the *Collins* dissent had the better argument, courts in personal injury cases involving consumer goods simply have refused to penetrate the thicket of conscionability in ruling on purported exclusions of responsibility for personal injuries.[29]

### Consumer Goods

One vital limitation on the scope of the unconscionability provision in § 2–719(3) bears special attention: it applies only to *consumer* goods. This restriction to consumer goods means that sellers of *commercial* products *may* exclude responsibility for consequential damages, including personal injuries to a buyer's workers, without such exclusions being held prima facie unconscionable under § 2–719(3).

For example, *Reibold v. Simon Aerials, Inc.*[30] involved a claim by a mechanic, Reibold, employed by Hertz Equipment, a lessor of industrial and construction equipment, for injuries to his hand, which was struck by an unshielded engine cooling fan on an aerial lift manufactured by the defendant. Hertz had purchased the lift from the defendant manufacturer with a warranty that excluded liability for consequential damages, including injury to person. In response to Reibold's warranty claim, the defendant asserted the damages exclusion in its sales contract with Hertz Equipment, Reibold's employer. Reibold contended that the exclusion was unconscionable and void under § 2–719(3). Granting summary judgment for the defendant on plaintiff's warranty claim (but denying summary judgment on the tort claims), Judge Doumar reasoned persuasively that commercial parties are free to apportion the risk of loss from commercial products as they see fit. Moreover, because unconscionability "can only be examined with reference to the original parties to the bargain," "[n]o agreement can possibly be unconscionable with regard to a third party who may benefit from the agreement but who was not a party to the agreement in the first place."[31] Noting that employers are responsible under the workers' compensation laws for on-the-job injuries to their employees caused by third parties, the court concluded that it should not interfere with allocation-of-risk bargains struck by employers and the suppliers of their machinery.[32]

---

warranty goes beyond what is required by the Code and the common law of this state, and where the product is found to be free from defect, the prima facie unconscionability contemplated by the Code has been overcome. I would so hold. I emphasize that I would limit this holding to the 'extra' guarantee case." Id. at 21.

**27.** See Note, 50 N.Y.U. L. Rev. 148, 174–75 (1975) (limitation of remedies for *nondefective* failures might be viewed as *not* prima facie unconscionable because "such limitations simply do not seem to be unfair if the consumer is given an understanding of their operation and effect").

**28.** *Collins*, 315 A.2d at 18.

**29.** One unusual and dubious exception is Mullan v. Quickie Aircraft Corp., 797 F.2d 845 (10th Cir. 1986) (Colo. law), discussed above.

**30.** 859 F.Supp. 193 (E.D. Va. 1994).

**31.** Id. at 199.

**32.** Id. at 200:

[I]t makes good policy sense to allow employer-purchasers to negotiate warranties with manufacturers, because the employer is in an excellent position to measure and control the risks of employees injuring themselves while using such goods. Especially in a case such as this one, where Hertz maintains its own me-

"Consumer goods" are defined in the Code as goods "used or bought for use primarily for personal, family or household purposes."[33] This definition may suggest a subjective test based on the buyer's intended or actual use,[34] which is sometimes problematic. Under a subjective definition, a real estate salesperson's car, were it to crash due to a steering defect during a family drive to the beach, would *not* be a consumer good if the salesperson had bought and used the car principally for driving clients around town. At least in this context, it would be more reasonable to interpret the phrase "consumer goods" in § 2–719 *objectively* in terms of the primary use to which people generally put this type of product, that is, whether it is "normally used for personal, family, or household purposes."[35] Viewed this way, because cars normally are bought and used primarily as consumer products, a salesperson's car reasonably would be considered a "consumer good." An objective definition of consumer products avoids the anomaly of basing responsibility for identical products solely on the fortuity of a particular buyer's predominant use of a product, which often has little relation to the logic or fairness of allowing a damages exclusion.[36]

### Property Damage

Courts have split on whether limitations and exclusions of consequential damages should be stricken as unconscionable in consumer cases if the damages claim is for *property* loss. A few courts have held such limitations unconscionable, particularly if the limitations are part of a broad exclusion of all consequential damages including personal injuries.[37] Perhaps most courts, noting that § 2–719(3) classifies as *prima facie* unconscionable only the exclusion of personal injury damages, hold that limitations and exclusions of property damages, although they may be proved unconscionable on particular facts, are generally allowable under this section of the Code.[38]

chanics and engages in extensive company-wide safety training, it makes sense for Hertz to bear the risks of employee injuries in exchange for a cut in the price from the manufacturer. In any case, where two sophisticated and relatively equal parties enter such bargains— whether the bargain appears to make sense or not after the fact—it is not for the court or for juries to second-guess and rewrite such bargains.

**33.** UCC § 9–109(1). This definition applies to Article 2. See UCC § 2–103(3).

**34.** See, for example, the pick-up truck example in White and Summers, UCC § 12–11, at 457.

**35.** See Magnuson–Moss Federal Warranty Act, 15 U.S.C.A. § 2301(1) ("consumer product").

**36.** Note, however, that an objective definition of "consumer goods" hinders the case of a consumer who buys for personal use a pick-up truck of a type normally used by contractors. But the hindrance of such actions, arising out of the general commercial nature of such products, is more justified than the kind of unpredictable and haphazard product differentiations that would result from a subjective definition. Moreover, applying an objective definition to all cases—consumer purchasers of commercial goods as well as commercial purchasers of consumer goods—appears consistent with the Code's practice of characterizing specially-protected sales transactions as involving consumer "goods" rather than consumer "transactions."

**37.** See, e.g., Fischer v. General Elec. Hotpoint, 438 N.Y.S.2d 690 (Dist. Ct. 1981); McCarty v. E.J. Korvette, Inc., 347 A.2d 253 (Md. Ct. Spec. App. 1975) (breach of express tire warranty against blowouts caused damage to car as well as personal injury). See also Adams v. American Cyanamid Co., 498 N.W.2d 577 (Neb. Ct. App. 1992) (herbicide causing crop loss was both procedurally and substantively unconscionable).

**38.** See, e.g., Gladden v. Cadillac Motor Car Div'n, General Motors Corp., 416 A.2d 394 (N.J. 1980); Lobianco v. Property Prot., Inc., 437 A.2d 417 (Pa. Super. Ct. 1981);

## § 4.9  ANTI-DISCLAIMER AND OTHER WARRANTY REFORM LEGISLATION

### Disclaiming Responsibility for Personal Injuries to Consumers

Disclaimers of warranties and limitations of remedies for personal injuries in sales transactions involving new consumer products are inherently perverse. Manufacturers and other sellers should not be permitted to shield themselves from warranty responsibility for personal injuries resulting from explicit or implicit misrepresentations concerning the essential quality and safety of new consumer products. Thus, a seller's effort to avoid such responsibility by fine-print legalese buried in a form sales contract should be considered contrary to public policy and void.

In the landmark case of *Henningsen v. Bloomfield Motors, Inc.*,[1] decided in 1960, the New Jersey Supreme Court reached this eminently sensible conclusion. Even though half a century now has passed, *Henningsen* still powerfully illuminates the reasons for disallowing boilerplate disclaimers and limitations of remedies in consumer sales transactions. While Mrs. Henningsen was driving a new 1955 Plymouth sedan her husband had purchased ten days earlier from Bloomfield Motors, the car's steering failed due to a mechanical defect, whereupon the car veered sharply off the highway and crashed into a brick wall, injuring Mrs. Henningsen. Mr. and Mrs. Henningsen sued the dealer and manufacturer, the Chrysler Corporation, for breach of the implied warranty of merchantability, and the defendants presented the language of disclaimer and remedy limitation in the purchase order in defense.

Included among the ten fine-print paragraphs called "Conditions" on the reverse side of the sales contract was number 7, which Mr. Henningsen testified he did not read. Paragraph 7 provided that the manufacturer warranted the car against defects in materials or workmanship for 90 days or 4,000 miles; that its only responsibility was to repair or replace defective parts; and that this warranty was "expressly in lieu of all other warranties expressed or implied, and all other obligations or liabilities...."[2]

The *Henningsen* jury returned verdicts against both defendants in favor of the plaintiffs, and the defendants appealed. In one of America's classic judicial decisions, Justice Francis affirmed the plaintiffs' verdicts for a unanimous court. He observed that the carefully crafted "warranty" was "a sad commentary upon the automobile manufacturers' marketing practices" by converting a "warranty," developed by the law to protect consumers, into an instrument of oppression to abolish consumer

---

NEC Techs., Inc. v. Nelson, 478 S.E.2d 769 (Ga. 1996) (property damage to house from fire caused by television set; upholding trial court's partial summary judgment for manufacturer on warranty claim because exclusion of all incidental and consequential damages was not unconscionable): "The Legislature could have provided that a limitation on consequential property damages in the case of consumer goods is prima facie unconscionable, as it did with consequential damages for personal injuries, but it chose not to do so." 478 S.E.2d at 771.

§ 4.9

**1.** 161 A.2d 69 (N.J. 1960).

**2.** Id. at 74.

rights.[3] The standardized fine-print form imposed on all car buyers, a one-sided contract of adhesion reflecting the "gross inequality of bargaining position" of consumers, was "inimical to the public welfare."[4] Even had Mr. Henningsen read the fine print, it did not explain that he was surrendering all warranty claims for personal injury damages if his car proved defective, thereby consigning him to negligence law's formidable challenge of having to prove the seller's fault in making or selling the car in a defective condition.[5] In its adoption of the Uniform Sales Act, the New Jersey legislature had declared that sales of automobiles, like other products, should carry implied warranties of merchantability as a form of economic protection for consumers against the risk of injuries from defective products, and Chrysler's disclaimer and remedy limitation revealed "a studied effort to frustrate that protection."[6] In sum, Chrysler's attempts in the sales contract to exclude the implied warranty of merchantability and to exclude responsibility for personal injury damages were unconscionable, "violative of public policy and void."[7]

On its appearance in 1960, *Henningsen* was immediately applauded for its logic, fairness, and the brilliance of the light it cast into dark

---

**3.** The court observed:

The terms of the warranty are a sad commentary upon the automobile manufacturers' marketing practices. Warranties developed in the law in the interest of and to protect the ordinary consumer who cannot be expected to have the knowledge or capacity or even the opportunity to make adequate inspection of mechanical instrumentalities, like automobiles, and to decide for himself whether they are reasonably fit for the designed purpose. But the ingenuity of the Automobile Manufacturers Association, by means of its standardized form, has metamorphosed the warranty into a device to limit the maker's liability. . . .

Id. at 78. "The language gave little and withdrew much. In return for the delusive remedy of replacement of defective parts at the factory, the buyer is said to have accepted the exclusion of the maker's liability for personal injuries arising from the breach of the warranty. . . ." Id. at 85.

**4.** Id. at 87. "The warranty before us is a standardized form designed for mass use. It is imposed upon the automobile consumer. He takes it or leaves it, and he must take it to buy an automobile. No bargaining is engaged in with respect to it." Id.

**5.** The court, id. at 92–93, further remarked:

[The disclaimer and limitation were hidden in the fine print on the back of the form, but there is more than this. Even had Mr. Henningsen read the language,] can it be said that an ordinary layman would realize what he was relinquishing in return for what he was being granted? Under the law, breach of warranty against defective parts or workmanship which caused personal injuries would entitle a buyer to damages even if due care were used in the manufacturing process. Because of the great potential for harm if the vehicle was defective, that right is the most important and fundamental one arising from the relationship. Difficulties so frequently encountered in establishing negligence in manufacture in the ordinary case make this manifest. . . . [O]nly the abandonment of all sense of justice would permit us to hold that, as a matter of law, the phrase "its obligation under this warranty being limited to making good at its factory any part or parts thereof" signifies to an ordinary reasonable person that he is relinquishing any personal injury claim that might flow from the use of a defective automobile.

**6.** More fully, id. at 95, the court explained:

[The legislature] has imposed an implied warranty of merchantability as a general incident of sale of an automobile by description. The warranty does not depend upon the affirmative intention of the parties. It is a child of the law; it annexes itself to the contract because of the very nature of the transaction. The judicial process has recognized a right to recover damages for personal injuries arising from a breach of that warranty. The disclaimer of the implied warranty and exclusion of all obligations except those specifically assumed by the express warranty signify a studied effort to frustrate that protection.

**7.** Id. at 97.

corners of sharp commercial practices that undercut basic consumer rights. Yet *Henningsen* ran headlong into the Uniform Commercial Code, which had begun to be adopted around America about this time.[8] Although the practice of burying ambiguous disclaimers in pages of fine print was invalidated by the conspicuousness requirement of UCC § 2–316(2), that same section explicitly authorized conspicuous disclaimers of the implied warranty of merchantability by doing little more than mentioning "merchantability."[9] And as the Uniform Commercial Code (including § 2–316) was adopted by one state legislature after another in the early 1960s, the brightness of the *Henningsen* beacon of judicial protection for consumers dimmed steadily into oblivion.

From the inception of Article 2 of the Uniform Commercial Code, many commentators observed that its disclaimer provisions were unsatisfactory for consumer transactions.[10] This should have come as no surprise, for Article 2 was based to a large extent on sales law principles of the 1800s,[11] and, to some extent, even the 1700s.[12] As interest in consumer rights spread across America during the 1960s and early 1970s, so too did criticisms of the Code's treatment of disclaimers. In the words of one commentator, the disclaimer section was "the most controversial and ambiguous" section in all of Article 2. Although the Code claimed its interest in protecting buyers from unexpected and unbargained-for language of disclaimer, "its requirement that any disclaimer must mention 'merchantability' almost ensures failure of this purpose because the term conveys so little information to the average consumer." Indeed, § 2–316(2) empowers merchants "to continue shifting the risk of loss back to consumers while camouflaging their action with legal jargon."[13]

Targeting the specific problem of disclaimers in consumer sales transactions, some state legislatures and the federal Congress eventually passed legislation that effectively curtailed the widespread manipulation by product sellers of consumer warranty rights. Tipping the fairness scales significantly toward consumers, several states enacted legislation that completely prohibited the disclaimer of implied warranties (and

---

**8.** See § 4.1, above.

**9.** See § 4.7, above. Consider, for example, Marshall v. Murray Oldsmobile Co., 154 S.E.2d 140 (Va. 1967), where the Virginia Supreme Court explicitly rejected the *Henningsen* approach. Pointing to the legislative approval of disclaimers in § 2–316 of the Uniform Commercial Code, adopted in Virginia in 1966 after the case sub judice had arisen, the court reaffirmed its commitment to the principles of freedom of contract.

**10.** See, e.g., Peters, Remedies for Breach of Contracts Relating to the Sale of Goods Under the Uniform Commercial Code: A Roadmap for Article Two, 73 Yale L.J. 199, 282–83 (1963).

**11.** "The warranty provisions in Article 2 of the U.C.C. largely reenact the princi-ples that Chalmers had found in nineteenth-century common law and codified in the British Sale of Goods Act of 1893." C. Reitz, Consumer Protection Under the Magnuson–Moss Warranty Act 14 (1978).

**12.** See Wiseman, The Limits of Vision: Karl Llewellyn and the Merchant Rules, 100 Harv. L. Rev. 465 (1987) (noting that the Uniform Sales Act "was based on the English Sales of Goods Act of 1893, which itself was based on the nineteenth-century English sales law that reflected the organization of nineteenth and even eighteenth-century commerce").

**13.** Rothschild, The Magnuson–Moss Warranty Act: Does It Balance Warrantor and Consumer Interests?, 44 Geo. Wash. L. Rev. 335, 343–44 (1976) (also arguing that the "unconscionability" restriction on remedy limitations in § 2–719(3) is too vague to offer consumers much protection).

some that prohibited the limitation of remedies) in consumer sales transactions. As part of a broad consumer warranty effort, the United States Congress in 1976 enacted the Magnuson–Moss Federal Warranty Act, which sharply limited a seller's ability to disclaim implied warranties in most significant consumer sales transactions.

### State Anti–Disclaimer Statutes

At least fifteen states and the District of Columbia have now enacted legislation prohibiting or limiting disclaimers and/or limitations of remedies in sales transactions involving consumer products.[14] Most states have achieved this result by amending their versions of UCC §§ 2–316 and/or 2–719, but others have included such provisions in broader consumer warranty statutes. The first variety of legislation, amending a state's version of § 2–316, § 2–719, or both, is illustrated by Connecticut's addition of a fifth subsection to its version of § 2–316, addressing both disclaimers and remedy limitations in sales of consumer goods:

> (5) The provisions of subsections (2), (3) and (4) shall not apply to sales of new or unused consumer goods, except for those goods clearly marked "irregular," "factory seconds" or "damaged." Any language, oral or written, used by a seller or manufacturer of consumer goods, which attempts to exclude or modify any implied warranties of merchantability and fitness for a particular purpose or to exclude or modify the consumer's remedies for breach of those warranties, shall be unenforceable.[15]

In addition to Connecticut, other jurisdictions which have amended one or both of their commercial codes' disclaimer or remedy limitation provisions include Alabama,[16] the District of Columbia,[17] Maine,[18] Maryland,[19] Massachusetts,[20] Mississippi,[21] New Hampshire,[22] Rhode Island,[23] Vermont,[24] and Washington.[25]

---

**14.** See 1 Clark and Smith, Product Warranties 2d § 8:34; Clark and Davis, Beefing Up Product Warranties: A New Dimension in Consumer Protection, 23 U. Kan. L. Rev. 567 (1975). See especially Professor Donald Clifford's informative overview and analysis of the state provisions in Clifford, Non–UCC Statutory Provisions Affecting Warranty Disclaimers and Remedies in Sales of Goods, 71 N.C. L. Rev. 1011 (1993).

**15.** Conn. Gen. Stat. § 42a–2–316(5).

**16.** Alabama adds a subsection (5) to § 2–316: "Nothing in subsection (2) or subsection (3)(a) or in [the succeeding section] shall be construed so as to limit or exclude the seller's liability for damages for injury to the person in the case of consumer goods." Ala. Code § 7–2–316(5). And it further adds a subsection (4) to Ala. Code § 7–2–719(4): "Nothing in this section or in [the preceding section] shall be construed so as to limit the seller's liability for damages for injury to the person in the case of consumer goods."

**17.** District of Columbia adds a § 2–316.1 which excludes consumer goods from § 2–316 and substitutes new provisions which prohibit disclaimers of warranties in sales of consumer goods except for conspicuous notations of particular defect. D.C. Code Ann. § 28.2–316.1.

**18.** Maine adds a subsection (5) to § 2–316 which reads in part that subsections (2), (3), and (4) "do not apply to sales of consumer goods or services." Me. Rev. Stat. Ann. tit. 11 § 2–316(5).

**19.** See § 2–316.1, which excludes consumer goods from § 2–316 and substitutes new provisions which prohibit disclaimers of warranties in sales of consumer goods, except for sales of certain old cars if the buyer is properly notified. Md. Code Ann. § 2–316.1.

**20.** See § 2–316A, which excludes consumer goods from § 2–316 and substitutes new provisions which prohibit disclaimers of warranties in sales of consumer goods. Mass. Gen. Laws Ann. ch. 106, § 2–316A.

---

**21–25.** See notes 21–25 on page 241.

In addition to such statutes that have curtailed disclaimer and remedy limitations abuses by amending the commercial code, at least California, Kansas, Maryland, Minnesota, Oregon, and West Virginia have special warranty protection legislation outside the commercial code that offers consumers broad protection in sales transactions and (except for Maryland) specifically curtails the ability of a product seller to disclaim implied warranties.[26]

### The Magnuson–Moss Federal Warranty Act

In an effort to improve the clarity, truth, and strength of consumer product warranties, Congress enacted the Magnuson–Moss Warranty— Federal Trade Commission Improvement Act of 1975.[27] The Act does not

**21.** Mississippi omits § 2–316 and adds a § 2–315.1 which prohibits disclaimers of warranties in consumer goods sales except for certain old cars if the buyer is properly notified, Miss. Code Ann. § 75–2–315.1, and adds a subsection (4) to § 2–719 providing that limitations of remedy for breach of implied warranty are prohibited. Miss. Code Ann. § 75–2–719(4).

**22.** New Hampshire renumbers § 2–316(4) as § 2–316(5) and adds a new subsection (4) which renders ineffective disclaimers of implied warranties with respect to personal, family, and household goods unless the seller provides the buyer with a clear, simple, concise, and conspicuous writing, signed by the buyer, informing the buyer, before or at the time of the sale, that (a) the goods are sold "as is" or "with all faults"; (b) the entire risk as to quality and performance of the goods is with the buyer; and (c), if the goods are defective, the buyer assumes the entire cost of repair. N.H. Rev. Stat. Ann. 382–A:2–316(4).

**23.** Rhode Island adds a § 2–329(2), which provides that every "consumer sale" is accompanied by an implied warranty of merchantability and, if the circumstances warrant, a fitness warranty; that disclaimers of implied warranties in "as is" and "with all faults" consumer sales are effective only if a conspicuous writing clearly informs the buyer, prior to the sale, in simple and concise language that the goods are sold on such a basis and that the entire risk as to quality and performance lies with the buyer; and that express warranties in the sale of new consumer goods cannot disclaim implied warranties. R.I. Gen. Laws § 6A–2–329(2) through (3)(a).

**24.** Vermont adds a subsection (5) to § 2–316, which provides that subsections (2), (3), and (4) do not apply to sales of new consumer goods and that attempts to disclaim implied warranties and limit remedies for breach of such warranties are unenforceable. Vt. Stat. Ann. tit. 9A § 2–316(5).

**25.** Washington substitutes a subsection (4) in 62A.2–316, which provides that "where goods are purchased primarily for personal, family or household use and not for commercial or business use, disclaimers of the warranty of merchantability or fitness for particular purpose shall not be effective to limit the liability of merchant sellers except insofar as the disclaimer sets forth with particularity the qualities and characteristics which are not being warranted. Remedies for breach of warranty can be limited in accordance with [UCC §§ 2–718 and 2–719]." Rev. Code Wash. Ann. 62A.2–316(4).

**26.** See Cal. Civ. Code § 1790 et seq. (Song–Beverly Consumer Warranty Act); Kan. Stat. Ann. § 50–623 et seq. (Consumer Protection Act) and § 50–639 (anti-disclaimer provision); Md. Code Ann. Com. Law § 14–401 et seq. (Consumer Products Guaranty Act) and § 13–101 et seq. (Consumer Protection Act); Minn. Stat. Ann. § 325F.01 et seq. (Consumer Protection; Products and Sales); Minn. Stat. Ann. § 325G.17 et seq. (anti-disclaimer provisions); Or. Rev. Stat. § 72.8010 et seq. (Consumer Warranty Act) and Or. Rev. Stat. § 72.8050 (anti-disclaimer provision); W. Va. Code § 46A (Consumer Credit and Protection Act); W. Va. Code § 46A–6–107 (anti-disclaimer provision); R.I. Gen. Laws § 62–2–329 (various consumer warranty protections, including prohibition of disclaimers, included in commercial code).

**27.** 15 U.S.C. § 2301 et seq. On the Magnuson–Moss Warranty Act, see, e.g., 2 Clark and Smith, Product Warranties 2d chs. 14–21; C. Reitz, Consumer Protection Under the Magnuson–Moss Warranty Act (1978); C. Reitz, Consumer Product Warranties Under Federal and State Laws (2nd ed. 1987); Squillante, Remedies Provided by the Magnuson–Moss Warranty Act, 92 Com. L.J. 366 (1987); Miller and Kanter, Litigation Under Magnuson–Moss: New Opportunities in Private Actions, 13 UCC L.J. 10

require product sellers to issue warranties but imposes certain obligations on suppliers who do provide written warranties[28] for consumer products[29] costing more than $10 or $15.[30] Written warranties must be labeled either "full (statement of duration) warranty," requiring the warrantor to provide consumers with a designated spectrum of warranty rights, or "limited warranty," which requires full, clear, and nondeceptive presale disclosure of the warranty's terms, prohibits tie-in conditions, and protects consumers from unfair and unexpected disclaimers.[31] Written warranties for covered products must disclose fully, conspicuously, clearly, and without deception the warranty's terms and conditions;[32] warranty terms must be disclosed to consumers before purchase;[33] warrantors ordinarily may not condition warranties on the consumer's use of any other product or service;[34] disclaimers of implied warranties under UCC § 2–316 are severely restricted;[35] and providers of

(1980); Roberts and Mann, The Magnuson–Moss Federal Warranty Act and Uniform Commercial Code Section 2–719: Further Reflections and Recent Developments, 1979 Ariz. St. L.J. 765 (1979); Schroeder, Private Actions under the Magnuson–Moss Warranty Act, 66 Cal. L. Rev. 1 (1978); Eddy, Effects of the Magnuson–Moss Act Upon Consumer Product Warranties, 55 N.C. L. Rev. 835 (1977); Rothschild, The Magnuson–Moss Warranty Act: Does it Balance Warrantor & Consumer Interests?, 44 Geo. Wash. L. Rev. 335 (1976); Strasser, Magnuson–Moss Warranty Act: An Overview and Comparison with UCC Coverage, Disclaimer, and Remedies in Consumer Warranties, 27 Mercer L. Rev. 1111 (1976); Denicola, The Magnuson–Moss Warranty Act: Making Consumer Product Warranty a Federal Case, 44 Fordham L. Rev. 273 (1975); Note, 62 Cornell L. Rev. 738 (1977); Jovanovic, Consumer Product Warranty Acts, 17 Am. Jur. 2d § 1 et seq. (1990); Annot., 59 A.L.R. Fed 461 (Magnuson–Moss Act claims in federal court).

**28.** Or if the seller provides a service contract. 15 U.S.C. § 2308(a).

**29.** The Warranty Act applies only to *consumer* products, defined as products "normally used for personal, family, or household purposes" in § 2301(1); 16 CFR § 700.1. See, e.g., Essex Ins. Co. v. Blount, Inc., 72 F.Supp.2d 722, 723 (E.D. Tex. 1999) (heavy timber equipment not consumer product, precluding protection under Act). Compare Chrysler Financial Co., L.L.C. v. Flynn, 88 S.W.3d 142 (Mo. Ct. App. 2002) (whether dump truck, used by farmer for household purposes, was consumer product was question of fact for jury).

**30.** Notwithstanding a $5 trigger in 15 U.S.C. § 2302(e), FTC regulations governing disclosure of warranty terms, 16 CFR § 701 et seq., and presale availability of warranty information, id. at § 7:02 et seq.,

apply only to products costing more than $15. See 2 Clark and Smith, Product Warranties 2d § 17:3. The designations of warranties as "full" or "limited" apply to consumer products costing more than $10. 15 U.S.C. § 2303(d). See 16 CFR at § 700.6.

**31.** Warranties must be labeled "full" or "limited." 15 U.S.C. § 2303(a). The minimum requirements for warranties designated as "full" are set forth in 15 U.S.C. § 2304. On both types of warranty, see 2 Clark and Smith, Product Warranties 2d ch. 16.

**32.** See 15 U.S.C. § 2302. Particular disclosure requirements are mandated by FTC rules. See 16 CFR § 701. On the Act's disclosure requirements, see 2 Clark and Smith, Product Warranties 2d ch. 17. The Act defines and prohibits "deceptive warranties" in 15 U.S.C. § 2310(c).

**33.** 15 U.S.C. § 2302(b)(1)(A). On the Act's requirements for presale disclosure of written warranty terms, see generally 2 Clark and Smith, Product Warranties 2d ch. 18.

If a warranty is conditioned on the consumer's return of a warranty registration card, that fact must be disclosed. While such a condition is permissible for "limited" warranties, the FTC has ruled that it is an unreasonable duty and, hence, impermissible for "full" warranties. See 16 CFR at § 700.7; 2 Clark and Smith, Product Warranties 2d § 17:16 et seq.; C. Reitz, Consumer Protection Under the Magnuson–Moss Warranty Act 33 (1978); § 4.7, above.

**34.** 15 U.S.C. 2302(c). For example, a manufacturer of a new car may ordinarily not condition its warranty on the buyer's use of its own brand of oil or repair parts.

**35.** As discussed below, the Act prohibits complete disclaimers of implied warranties. Id. at § 2308(a).

full warranties must provide consumers with effective procedures for repairing or replacing defective products in a timely manner or provide a refund of the purchase price.[36] Thus, the Magnuson–Moss Act is a consumer protection statute designed to improve the truthfulness, strength, and comprehensibility of warranties that accompany consumer products and to provide consumers of products that carry "full" warranties with effective mechanisms for resolving warranty complaints. The Act does not provide new remedies for injured plaintiffs to use in ordinary products liability litigation.[37]

The Magnuson–Moss Warranty Act contains one provision that profoundly alters warranty responsibility for product accidents: § 108 of the Act outlaws implied warranty disclaimers notwithstanding the fact that such disclaimers are authorized by state law in most sales of major consumer goods. For consumer products costing more than $10[38] for which a written warranty is provided,[39] the Act nullifies implied warranty disclaimers, notwithstanding the fact that such disclaimers are authorized by state law in UCC § 2–316.[40] While the Act prohibits all implied warranty limitations for products carrying "full" warranties,[41] it does permit a supplier who provides a "limited" warranty to restrict the *duration* of implied warranties to the period of the written warranty, provided that this restriction is reasonable, conscionable, and clearly communicated to consumers on the face of the warranty.[42]

The Magnuson–Moss Warranty Act's disclaimer provisions are set forth in § 108[43] of the Act, which provides as follows:

§ 2308.   Implied warranties

(a) Restrictions on disclaimers or modifications

No supplier may disclaim or modify (except as provided in subsection (b) of this section) any implied warranty to a consumer with respect to such consumer product if (1) such supplier makes any written warranty to the consumer with respect to such consumer product, or (2) at the time of sale, or within 90

---

**36.**  Id. at § 2304(a)(4).

**37.**  Because the Magnuson–Moss Act leaves most of state warranty law unaffected, a state's requirement of privity of contract for implied warranty claims would seem to be unaffected by the Act. "If state law requires vertical privity to enforce an implied warranty and there is none, then, like the yeastless souffle, the warranty does not 'arise.'" Feinstein v. Firestone Tire & Rubber Co., 535 F.Supp. 595, 606 n.13 (S.D.N.Y. 1982). See 2 Clark and Smith, Product Warranties 2d § 20:39. But Illinois courts have held that an implied warranty claim brought under Magnuson–Moss may circumvent a vertical privity bar. See Connick v. Suzuki Motor Co., 656 N.E.2d 170, 180 (Ill. App. Ct. 1995), rev'd in part on other grounds, 675 N.E.2d 584 (Ill. 1996); Rothe v. Maloney Cadillac, Inc., 518 N.E.2d 1028, 1031 (Ill. 1988).

**38.**  The FTC's cost threshold is set forth in 16 CFR § 700.6.

**39.**  Or for which a service contract is provided. 15 U.S.C. § 2308(a).

**40.**  See § 4.7, above. Thus, by virtue of the Supremacy Clause, Congress has rewritten state disclaimer law to this extent.

**41.**  See 15 U.S.C. § 2304(a)(2), which provides that the duration of implied warranties may not be limited in "full" warranties. See also § 2308(a), which prohibits disclaimers of implied warranties, and § 2308(b), which excludes "fully" warranted products from the authorization of durational limitations on implied warranties.

**42.**  15 U.S.C. § 2308(b).

**43.**  As codified at 15 U.S.C. § 2308.

days thereafter, such supplier enters into a service contract with the consumer which applies to such consumer product.

(b) Limitation on duration

For purposes of this chapter (other than section 2304(a)(2) of this title), implied warranties may be limited in duration to the duration of a written warranty of reasonable duration, if such limitation is conscionable and is set forth in clear and unmistakable language and prominently displayed on the face of the warranty.

(c) Effectiveness of disclaimers, modifications, or limitations

A disclaimer, modification, or limitation made in violation of this section shall be ineffective for purposes of this chapter and State law.

Although the Act does not directly address products liability litigation, it does indirectly affect such litigation in several important ways. First and foremost, by nullifying complete disclaimers otherwise allowable under UCC § 2–316 in most substantial consumer product cases,[44] the Magnuson–Moss Warranty Act removes the most deadly arrow from the product seller's quiver of contractual defenses in products liability warranty litigation. Also important for products liability plaintiffs is the Act's requirement that limitations on an implied warranty's *duration* meet a rigorous fourfold test.[45] Any such durational limitation must be (1) reasonable in length, (2) conscionable, (3) set forth in clear and unmistakable language, and (4) prominently displayed on the face of the warranty.[46] A limitation that violates any of these rules is simply void and of no effect.[47]

## Private Claims under the Act; Jurisdiction and Attorneys' Fees

The Magnuson–Moss Act appears to provide that any breach of warranty, express or implied, is a violation of the Act—which thus would give rise to federal jurisdiction and the possibility of attorneys' fees in most serious products liability cases.[48] The Act states that a consumer damaged by a supplier's failure "to comply with any obligation under this chapter, or under a written warranty, implied warranty, or service contract," may (1) sue for damages in state court or, if the amount in

---

**44.** The Act does *not* apply to non-consumer products, nor do the § 108 disclaimer restrictions apply to products (1) for which no written warranty (or service contract) has been provided, or (2) which cost $10 or less. See 16 CFR § 700.6 (cost threshold).

**45.** 15 U.S.C. § 2308(b).

**46.** Id. For an important ruling on whether a car manufacturer's limitation of implied warranties to the duration of its 2/3–year 24,000/36,000–mile express warranties was "reasonable" and "conscionable," in a class action over defective diesel engines which gave out after the warranted period, see Carlson v. General Motors Corp., 883 F.2d 287 (4th Cir. 1989). Compare Abraham v. Volkswagen of Am., Inc., 795 F.2d 238 (2d Cir. 1986); Hahn v. Ford Motor Co., 434 N.E.2d 943, 947 (Ind. Ct. App. 1982) (upholding 12–month/12,000– mile limitation on implied warranty).

**47.** 15 U.S.C. § 2308(c).

**48.** For a thorough discussion of private claims under the Magnuson–Moss Warranty Act, see generally 2 Clark and Smith, Product Warranties 2d ch. 20, and Miller and Kanter, Litigation Under Magnuson–Moss: New Opportunities in Private Actions, 13 UCC L.J. 10 (1980).

controversy is at least $50,000, in federal court; and (2) recover attorneys' fees if he finally prevails.[49] Early commentators read this section of the Act to federalize products liability warranty claims: "[C]onsumers suddenly have a federal forum, as well as the prospect of recovering their attorneys' fees, for a violation of UCC section 2–314! In many respects, this 'muscling up' of the UCC could be one of the most important aspects of the Federal Act."[50] But the Act suffers from serious ambiguity on its applicability to products liability plaintiffs with personal injuries, for it elsewhere provides (with certain exceptions) that it does not "affect the liability of, or impose liability on, any person for personal injury."[51]

*Boelens v. Redman Homes, Inc.*[52] was a claim under state law and the Magnuson–Moss Warranty Act against the retailer and manufacturer of a mobile home for chemical hepatitis and other injuries caused by formaldehyde fumes from materials used to construct the home. Plaintiffs did not allege a breach of any substantive provision of the Federal Warranty Act, such as the prohibition against disclaiming implied warranties, but based their claim under the Act solely upon the defendants' breach of warranty under state law.[53] The jury awarded the plaintiffs substantial compensatory and punitive damages, the federal district judge awarded the plaintiffs $237,000 in attorneys' fees and other litigation expenses, and the defendants appealed to the United States Court of Appeals. The issue before the Fifth Circuit was whether a personal injury claim arising from a product supplier's breach of state warranty law may be brought under the Magnuson–Moss Act in the absence of a separate and independent violation of the Act.

The Fifth Circuit vacated the plaintiffs' judgment, ruling that personal injury claims based on breach of warranty are *not* cognizable under the Magnuson–Moss Warranty Act unless the supplier also violated an important substantive provision of the Act.[54] Carefully reviewing the history and purposes of the Act, Judge Wisdom observed that permitting ordinary warranty claims under the Act "would allow virtually any state products liability action for personal injury damages into federal court, subject only to the amount-in-controversy requirement."[55] To the contrary, reasoned Judge Wisdom, "Congress was content to let the question of personal injury products liability remain a matter of state-law

---

**49.** 15 U.S.C. § 2310(d).

**50.** Clark and Davis, Beefing Up Product Warranties: A New Dimension in Consumer Protection, 23 Kan. L. Rev. 567, 616 (1975).

**51.** 15 U.S.C. § 2311(b)(2) provides:

Nothing in this chapter (other than sections 2308 and 2304(a)(2) and (4) of this title) shall (A) affect the liability of, or impose liability on, any person for personal injury, or (B) supersede any provision of State law regarding consequential damages for injury to the person or other injury.

Note that the reference to subsection 2304(a)(4) was probably a mistaken drafting attempt to refer to subsection (a)(3).

See Boelens v. Redman Homes, Inc., 748 F.2d 1058, 1065 n.10 (5th Cir. 1984) (Tex. law).

**52.** 748 F.2d 1058 (5th Cir. 1984) (Tex. law) (Wisdom, J.).

**53.** Both under the state UCC and a state deceptive practices act.

**54.** *Boelens*, 748 F.2d at 1060 and 1071.

**55.** Id. at 1067. The Federal Warranty Act specifies that, for federal court jurisdiction, the amount in controversy be at least $50,000. 15 U.S.C. § 2310(d)(3)(B). See Grant v. Cavalier Mfg. Inc., 229 F.Supp.2d 1332, 1334 (M.D. Ala. 2002) (in determining amount in controversy, courts should consider only actual claim brought under the Act).

causes of action, except to the extent that certain substantive provisions in the Magnuson–Moss Act overrule contrary state laws relating to the warrantor's ability to disclaim personal injury liability."[56] Thus, the court concluded that § 2311(b)(2) of the Act "prohibits claims arising from personal injury based solely on a breach of warranty, express or implied," but that a plaintiff might recover personal injury damages for the violation of a substantive provision of § 2308 (that prohibits all warrantors from disclaiming implied warranties) and § 2304(a) (that prohibits full warrantors from limiting the duration of implied warranties and from excluding or limiting consequential damages without conspicuously so stating on the face of the warranty).[57]

Other courts have agreed that "an action for personal injury may be maintained only for substantive violations of §§ 2308 and 2304(a)(2) and (3)."[58] These sections of the Act (1) prohibit disclaimers of implied warranties, and (2) regulate (a) limitations on the duration of implied warranties, and (b) exclusions or limitations of consequential damages for breach of warranty.[59] In sum, the Act appears to say that a consumer of a covered product may bring an action under the Act to recover personal injuries caused by a breach of warranty under state law only if the product supplier violated the Act's disclaimer or consequential damages rules.

While the Act may be read in this manner to allow personal injury claims if a seller violates a substantive disclaimer provision, such claims are peculiar because there appears to be no requirement of a causal connection between such a violation and the plaintiff's personal injury claim.[60] Indeed, much may be said for simply prohibiting personal injury

---

**56.** *Boelens*, 748 F.2d at 1068, quoting Gorman v. Saf–T–Mate, Inc., 513 F.Supp. 1028, 1035 (N.D. Ind. 1981).

**57.** *Boelens,* 748 F.2d at 1068.

**58.** Voelkel v. General Motors Corp., 846 F.Supp. 1468, 1474 (D. Kan. 1994). "In short, § 2311(b)(2) does not directly impose personal injury liability but may have the effect of creating the same under state law in the event that a warranty disclaimer or modification or limitation is struck down." Id. at 1474 n.2. See also Oliver v. Homes of Legend, Inc., 2000 WL 1092130 (M.D. Ala. 2000) (no claim for emotional distress damages); Santarelli v. BP America, 913 F.Supp. 324, 333 (M.D. Pa. 1996) (injuries from eating contaminated salmon) ("The Act does not create a private, independent cause of action for personal injuries which are otherwise state law claims for breach of warranty."); Woodson v. McGeorge Camping Ctr., Inc., 974 F.2d 1333 (4th Cir. 1992) (Va. law); Rubin v. Marshall Field & Co., 597 N.E.2d 688 (Ill. App. Ct. 1992) (injuries from eye makeup remover); Walsh v. Ford Motor Co., 627 F.Supp. 1519 (D.D.C. 1986); Bush v. American Motors Sales Corp., 575 F.Supp. 1581 (D. Colo. 1984); Gorman v. Saf–T–Mate, Inc., 513 F.Supp. 1028 (N.D. Ind. 1981).

*But see* Hughes v. Segal Enters., Inc., 627 F.Supp. 1231, 1237 (W.D. Ark 1986) (acknowledging *Boelens* rule, but allowing class action under Magnuson–Moss for personal injury and economic loss claims for mobile home seller's failure to conspicuously label warranted homes as "full" or "limited") (sharply criticized in 2 Clark and Smith, Product Warranties 2d § 20:31.

**59.** Note that exclusions and limitations of consequential damages are only regulated, not prohibited, by § 108 of the Act. Indeed, such exclusions and limitations are specifically permitted by § 104(a)(3) of the Act, so long as the "exclusion or limitation conspicuously appears on the face of the warranty." In the case of personal injuries, however, the drafters quite clearly intended to leave UCC § 2–719(3) intact. See § 111(b) of the Act, 15 U.S.C.A. § 2311(b). Consequently, the Act does not address attempts by sellers to exclude responsibility for personal injuries arising from breach of warranty which are still essentially prohibited by UCC § 2–719(3). See § 4.8, above.

**60.** See 2 Clark and Smith, Product Warranties 2d § 20:31, at 20–50 ("[t]here is no real connection between a personal injury claim and unrelated violations of Magnuson–Moss in the sales documentation").

claims under the Act even where a supplier has breached the Act's disclaimer requirements.[61] Nevertheless, allowing personal injury claims in such cases might well be justified on the ground that the Act's disclaimer provisions are so important that they should offer as much federal protection for personal injury claims as for economic loss claims.

Although attorneys' fees and other costs of litigation theoretically are available to a prevailing plaintiff in the discretion of the court, one might expect many courts to exercise this discretion narrowly in personal injury cases.[62] The Magnuson–Moss Act was designed to protect consumers from sharp warranty practices that diminish the value of consumer products, not to provide attorneys' fees to plaintiffs injured by defective products, as Judge Wisdom noted in his decision in the *Boelens* case discussed above. Accordingly, even an injured consumer who can prove a technical breach of a relevant substantive provision on disclaimers or remedy limitations should expect a cold judicial shoulder to a Magnuson–Moss claim for attorneys' fees in the absence of convincing proof that the defendant supplier clearly ignored or deliberately flouted an important disclaimer or other provision of the Act.

---

**61.** See id. (noting that one might well "conclude that Section 2311 excludes personal injury claims from the scope of Magnuson–Moss, even if a substantive violation of the federal statute is involved").

**62.** See, e.g., Rubin v. Marshall Field & Co., 597 N.E.2d 688 (Ill. App. Ct. 1992) (no attorneys' fees for Magnuson–Moss warranty claim for injuries from eye makeup remover). A court that does allow attorneys' fees may limit them to recorded time specifically attributable to the narrow Magnuson–Moss Act issues. Such a limitation would exclude recovery for the great bulk of a plaintiff's counsel's time spent in preparing and trying the many state law issues of law and fact involved in a normal (warranty law) products liability action. Compare Hibbs v. Jeep Corp., 666 S.W.2d 792 (Mo. Ct. App. 1984) (attorneys' fees disallowed where billings did not clearly differentiate between Magnuson–Moss and other work on case), with Drouin v. Fleetwood Enters., 209 Cal.Rptr. 623 (Ct. App. 1985) (fees allowed; apportionment not required where plaintiff's claims arise from common core of facts or involve related legal theories).

# Chapter 5

---

# STRICT LIABILITY IN TORT

*Table of Sections*

---

## § 5.1  STRICT LIABILITY IN TORT—GENERALLY

The doctrine of strict liability in tort is widely considered the premier theory of recovery in modern products liability law. Indeed, lawyers and judges untutored in the finer points of products liability law sometimes casually interchange the terms "strict liability" and "products liability."[1] Such usage is imprecise and should be avoided, because it equates a single theory of liability with an entire field of law. But there can be no doubt that the development and growth of the doctrine of strict products liability in tort was the centerpiece around which the rest of modern products liability law was formed. This chapter describes the origins, evolution, nature, rationales, and tests for the doctrine of strict products liability in tort. In particular, it examines the development of § 402A of the *Restatement (Second) of Torts*, published in 1965. Consideration of the *Restatement (Third) of Torts: Products Liability*, published in 1998, is deferred to the next chapter because it largely abandons the doctrine of "strict" products liability for design and warning cases, which comprise the bulk of products liability litigation.[2] The many particulars of modern products liability law are addressed in depth in subsequent chapters.

**§ 5.1**

1. See, e.g., Romo v. Ford Motor Co., 122 Cal.Rptr.2d 139, 145 (Ct.App. 2002), vacated, 538 U.S. 1028 (2003).

2. See § 1.3, above. The Products Liability Restatement is examined in § 6.5, below.

After more than a century of slow and tortured growth in warranty, culminating in 1960 in *Henningsen v. Bloomfield Motors, Inc.*,[3] strict manufacturer liability for defective products swept into the American law of torts during the 1960s.[4] On the footings of *Henningsen*, as detailed below, Judge Traynor in 1963 constructed a new doctrine of strict products liability in tort in *Greenman v. Yuba Power Products, Inc.*;[5] in 1964, Dean Prosser, Reporter for the *Second Restatement*, endorsed the principle in § 402A of the *Restatement (Second) of Torts*, published by the American Law Institute the following year; and, shortly thereafter, a flood of jurisdictions rapidly adopted the new tort-law doctrine of strict liability for selling defective products that cause harm.[6]

Liability under § 402A is "strict" because it is based not on the manufacturer's fault in producing a defective product, but on the frustration of consumer expectations of product safety when a latent defect in a product causes harm. However, as more and more courts during the 1970s and 1980s broadly extended the new principle to design and warnings cases,[7] the truly strict consumer expectations test increasingly gave way to principles of foreseeability and risk-utility balancing that underlie the law of negligence.[8] While the courts continued to claim that they were applying liability that was "strict," it became increasingly clear that the standards actually applied were truly based on fault.[9]

In 1992 the American Law Institute began work on a new *Restatement of Torts* on the specific topic of products liability law, approving the new *Restatement* in 1997 and publishing it in 1998 as the *Restatement (Third) of Torts: Products Liability*.[10] While the new *Restatement* continues to base liability for manufacturing defects in terms that are strict, it abandons any pretense of "strict" responsibility for design and warnings defects which it grounds explicitly in principles of negligence.[11]

The *Third Restatement* was carefully conceived, debated, constructed, and approved,[12] and a number of courts have already adopted some of its key provisions.[13] Yet modern products liability law in most states was built squarely upon § 402A of the *Second Restatement* which, in various important respects, the *Third Restatement* largely dismantles. For this

**3.** 161 A.2d 69 (N.J. 1960).

**4.** See § 5.2, below.

**5.** 377 P.2d 897 (Cal. 1963).

**6.** See § 5.3, below.

**7.** Some courts had begun in earnest to examine manufacturers' design and warnings choices during the 1950s, but the cases were based on negligence or warranty. See, e.g., Matthews v. Lawnlite Co., 88 So.2d 299, 301 (Fla. 1956) (unguarded mechanism under arm rest of aluminum lounge chair's handle clipped off plaintiff's finger "with the ease that one clips a choice flower with pruning shears"; negligent design). See generally Noel, Manufacturer's Negligence of Design or Directions for Use of a Product, 71 Yale L.J. 816 (1962); Noel, Recent Trends in Manufacturer's Negligence as to Design, Instructions or Warnings, 19 Sw. L.J. 43 (1965).

**8.** See § 5.7, below.

**9.** See Owen, Defectiveness Restated: Exploding the "Strict" Products Liability Myth, 1996 U. Ill. L. Rev. 743.

**10.** See § 6.5, below.

**11.** See id. and § 5.9, below.

**12.** See Owen, Products Liability Law Restated, 49 S.C. L. Rev. 273 (1998).

**13.** See, e.g., Wright v. Brooke Group Ltd., 652 N.W.2d 159 (Iowa 2002) (adopting Third Restatement's manufacturing defect (§ 2(a)) and design defect (§ 2(b)) definitions); Hamilton v. Emerson Elec. Co., 133 F.Supp.2d 360 (M.D. Pa. 2001) (§ 2(a)); Myrlak v. Port Auth., 723 A.2d 45 (N.J. 1999) (§ 2(a); also relying on New Jersey statute); Vassallo v. Baxter Healthcare Corp., 696 N.E.2d 909 (Mass. 1998) (§ 2(c)); Freeman v. Hoffman–La Roche, Inc., 618 N.W.2d 827 (Neb. 2000) (§§ 2(c) and 6(d)).

reason, courts in some states have simply ignored the product defect standards of the new *Restatement*[14] while courts in other states have rejected the new liability formulations out of hand.[15] It thus is likely to be some years before most courts explicitly displace their evolved § 402A jurisprudence with the liability standards articulated in the new *Restatement*. Accordingly, the principles of "strict" products liability in tort spawned by § 402A may be expected to control products liability litigation in most jurisdictions, at least formally, for many years to come.

## § 5.2  THE PATH TO STRICT LIABILITY IN TORT

The path to strict products liability in tort was long, tortured, and tortuous.[1] This lengthy journey involved the intertwining of parts of two major branches of the law of obligations: tort law and contract law.[2] Each field of law separately contributed a central feature to the development of strict manufacturer liability for harm caused by defective products, and they combined to contribute a third. Tort law's major contribution, launched by *MacPherson v. Buick Motor Co.*[3] in 1916, was its rejection of the privity of contract requirement in tort law claims. In so doing, tort law championed the view that manufacturers are obligated to "remote" consumers by a public duty, independent of any private

---

**14.** See, e.g., Beatty v. Ford Motor Co., 574 S.E.2d 803 (W. Va. 2002); Merrill v. Navegar, Inc., 28 P.3d 116 (Cal. 2001); McCathern v. Toyota Motor Corp., 23 P.3d 320 (Or. 2001); Mercer v. Pittway Corp., 616 N.W.2d 602, 620 n.4 (Iowa 2000) (attorneys argued and court applied only § 402A, not Third Restatement); Soproni v. Polygon Apt. Partners, 971 P.2d 500 (Wash. 1999).

**15.** See, e.g., Halliday v. Sturm, Ruger & Co., 792 A.2d 1145 (Md. 2002) (rejecting design defect definition in § 2(b)); Green v. Smith & Nephew AHP, Inc., 629 N.W.2d 727, 750–52 (Wis. 2001) (rejecting definition of design defect in § 2(b) because it limits liability to foreseeable risks, bases liability on a risk-utility standard that approaches negligence, and requires plaintiffs to prove a "reasonable alternative design"); Vautour v. Body Masters Sports Indus., 784 A.2d 1178, 1182–84 (N.H. 2001) (rejecting § 2(b)'s design defect definition because of its rigidity).

**§ 5.2**

**1.** "Tortured," "tortuous," and "tort," the latter from the French for injury or wrong, all derive etymologically from the same Latin *tortus*, meaning twisted or crooked. See Prosser and Keeton on Torts § 1, at 2. See also Birks, The Concept of a Civil Wrong, in Philosophical Foundations of Tort Law 39 (D. Owen ed., Oxford 1995) (citing C. Onions ed., Oxford 1966): " 'Wrong' and 'tort', like 'crook' and 'bent', play on the same metaphor which contrasts to 'right' and 'straight'. Wrong conduct, or, using the French word, 'tort', is twisted, a metaphor for condemned or disapproved."

**2.** For early commentary on the path to strict products liability, see, e.g., Gillam, Products Liability in a Nutshell, 37 Or. L. Rev. 119 (1958); Jaeger, Privity of Warranty: Has the Tocsin Sounded?, 1 Duq. L. Rev. 1 (1963); James, Products Liability (pts. 1 and 2), 34 Tex. L. Rev. 44, 192 (1955); James, General Products—Should Manufacturers Be Liable Without Negligence?, 24 Tenn. L. Rev. 923 (1957); Keeton, Products Liability: Liability Without Fault and the Requirement of a Defect, 41 Tex. L. Rev. 855 (1963); Keeton, Products Liability—The Nature and Extent of Strict Liability, 1964 U. Ill. L. F. 693; Noel, Manufacturers of Products—The Drift Toward Strict Liability, 24 Tenn. L. Rev. 963 (1957); Prosser, The Assault Upon the Citadel (Strict Liability to the Consumer), 69 Yale L.J. 1099 (1960); Roberts, Implied Warranties—The Privity Rule and Strict Liability, 27 Mo. L. Rev. 194 (1962); Traynor, The Ways and Meanings of Defective Products and Strict Liability, 32 Tenn. L. Rev. 363 (1965); Wade, Strict Tort Liability of Manufacturers, 19 Sw. L.J. 5 (1965); Prosser, The Fall of the Citadel (Strict Liability to the Consumer), 50 Minn. L. Rev. 791 (1966); Wilson, Products Liability (pts. 1 and 2), 43 Cal. L. Rev. 614, 809 (1965); Wade, On the Nature of Strict Tort Liability for Products, 44 Miss. L.J. 825 (1973). See also Restatement (2d) Torts § 402A cmt. *b* (brief historical sketch). Commentary on the theoretical path to strict products liability is collected in § 5.4, below.

**3.** 111 N.E. 1050 (N.Y. 1916).

contractual obligations that may exist between them. To this, contract law contributed the idea that liability should be "strict," contrary to the general tort law notion that breach of duty generally must be based on a supplier's negligence or other form of fault. In combination, tort law and contract law furnished the legal concept that eventually developed into the doctrine of strict manufacturer liability in tort: the law of warranty. Although warranty law is conceived today as part of the law of sales, which is a branch of the law of contracts, it developed out of the tort action of deceit and remained a tort-type action, at least in food cases, until quite recently.[4] Even modern courts have occasionally turned to common-law tort law warranties for products liability and other types of claims.[5]

The story of the origins of strict products liability in tort is largely a tale of warranty law, which began in ancient Rome with the development of the principles of sales law, warranty, and deceit.[6] It suffices here, however, to consider more recent developments in American law over the last couple of centuries. The brief narration below describes how certain limbs of warranty and tort law grew increasingly toward one another for a century or so and then, in the early 1960s, suddenly and spectacularly conjoined to beget the radical new doctrine of strict products liability in tort.

The tort law action of deceit, with its ancient heritage,[7] spawned the law of warranty long before the law of assumpsit or contract was even born.[8] However, beginning with a late eighteenth century English case,[9] warranty in Anglo–American law gradually merged during the nineteenth century into the branch of contract law dealing with the law of sales.[10] Well into the twentieth century, however, a particular pocket of warranty law remained protected, shielded from contract law's predatory clutch: in cases involving unwholesome food and drink, American courts

---

**4.** See Ames, The History of Assumpsit, 2 Harv. L. Rev. 1, 8 (1888); Prosser, The Implied Warranty of Merchantable Quality, 27 Minn. L. Rev. 117, 118–22 (1943); Prosser, Assault on the Citadel (Strict Liability to the Consumer), 69 Yale L.J. 1099, 1103–10, 1124–27 (1960).

**5.** See, e.g., Goldberg v. Kollsman Instrument Corp., 191 N.E.2d 81, 82 (N.Y. 1963) ("[a] breach of warranty, it is now clear, is not only a violation of the sales contract out of which the warranty arises but is a tortious wrong suable by a noncontracting party"). See also Payne v. Soft Sheen Prod., Inc., 486 A.2d 712, 719–20 (D.C. App. 1985); Lonzrick v. Republic Steel Corp., 218 N.E.2d 185 (Ohio 1966) (applying "implied warranty in tort" to products liability claim); Temple v. Wean United, Inc., 364 N.E.2d 267 (Ohio 1977) (moving from "implied warranty in tort theory" to § 402A). See generally W. Prosser, Handbook of the Law of Torts § 95, at 635 (4th ed. 1971). See § 4.1, above.

**6.** See § 1.2, above.

**7.** See §§ 1.2 and 3.2, above.

**8.** See Ames, The History of Assumpsit, 2 Harv. L. Rev. 1, 8 (1888); Prosser, The Implied Warranty of Merchantable Quality, 27 Minn. L. Rev. 117, 118–22 (1943).

**9.** Stuart v. Wilkins, 1 Dougl. 18, 99 Eng. Rep. 15 (1778). While *Stuart v. Wilkins* appears to have been the first judicial pronouncement that assumpsit would lie for breach of warranty, if it were express (but not yet if it were implied), the opinion in this case may merely have certified the understanding and practice among lawyers since 1750 or shortly thereafter. See Prosser, The Implied Warranty of Merchantable Quality, 27 Minn. L. Rev. 117, 119–20 (1943).

**10.** See Prosser, The Implied Warranty of Merchantable Quality, 27 Minn. L. Rev. 117, 118–22 (1943).

continued persistently to apply the ancient tort-like warranty of quality.[11]

Throughout the history of Anglo–American law, food suppliers have always been held closely accountable for the wholesomeness of their provisions.[12] A series of early English statutes, beginning in 1266, criminalized the sale of "corrupt" food and drink for immediate consumption, and, as of 1431, "[a] taverner or vintner was bound as such to sell wholesome food and drink."[13] Whether this special duty amounted to a common law warranty of the wholesomeness of food is uncertain,[14] but American courts from an early date assumed that it was, holding sellers of food strictly liable for harm to their direct consumers.[15] As early as 1815, a New York court, relying on Blackstone, noted that a warranty of quality is always implied into the sale of foodstuffs because "the preservation of health and life" requires the seller to be "bound to know that they are sound and wholesome at his peril."[16] A century later, the New York Court of Appeals reaffirmed the necessity of a strict liability rule for the sale of food, stating that it was necessary to the public health and welfare.[17]

From at least 1913,[18] courts in food cases began to extend the strict liability rule to third persons.[19] By the middle of the twentieth century, although the courts were divided,[20] many jurisdictions enforced a special

---

**11.** See, e.g., Jacob E. Decker & Sons, Inc. v. Capps, 164 S.W.2d 828, 831–32 (Tex. 1942) (noting that the warranty in food cases was not the modern contractual warranty but the tort law warranty derived from the action of deceit which is "not dependent on any provision of the contract").

**12.** On the evolution of the tort-like warranty applied to food cases, see H. Melick, The Sale of Food and Drink (1936); R. Dickerson, Products Liability and the Food Consumer (1951); Perkins, Unwholesome Food as a Source of Liability (pts. 1 and 2), 5 Iowa L. Bull. 6, 86 (1919–1920); Waite, Retail Responsibility and Judicial Law Making, 34 Mich. L. Rev. 494 (1936); Brown, The Liability of Retail Dealers for Defective Food Products, 23 Minn. L. Rev. 585 (1939). See especially Prosser, The Assault on the Citadel (Strict Liability to the Consumer), 69 Yale L.J. 1099, 1103–10 (1960), from which much of this discussion is derived.

**13.** Ames, The History of Assumpsit, 2 Harv. L. Rev. 1, 9 (1888).

**14.** Compare Melick, The Sale of Food and Drink 10 (1936) (yes), with Perkins, Unwholesome Food as a Source of Liability, 5 Iowa L. Bull. 6, 8–9 (1919).

**15.** See Van Bracklin v. Fonda, 12 Johns. 468, 7 Am. Dec. 339 (N.Y. 1815), below. But note that the facts suggest fraudulent concealment of contamination and possibly an express representation that the beef was good and sound.

**16.** See Van Bracklin v. Fonda, 12 Johns. 468, 7 Am. Dec. 339 (N.Y. 1815) (seller failed to disclose that beef cow had been diseased prior to slaughter).

**17.** Race v. Krum, 118 N.E. 853, 854 (N.Y. 1918) ("This rule is based upon the high regard which the law has for human life. The consequences to the consumer resulting from consumption of articles of food sold for immediate use may be so disastrous that an obligation is placed upon the seller to see to it, at his peril, that the articles sold are fit for the purpose for which they are intended. The rule is an onerous one, but public policy, as well as the public health, demand such obligation should be imposed.").

**18.** Prosser reports that the first third-party case was Mazetti v. Armour & Co., 135 P. 633 (Wash. 1913), Prosser, Assault Upon the Citadel (Strict Liability to the Consumer), 69 Yale 1099, 1106 (1960), yet *Mazetti* relies on earlier cases which suggests an even earlier origin of this principle.

**19.** For a more expansive discussion of all of these developments, see Prosser, The Assault on the Citadel (Strict Liability to the Consumer), 69 Yale L.J. 1099, 1103–10 (1960).

**20.** In 1941, although noting a trend in the opposite direction, Prosser observed that "[t]he majority of courts still refuse to find a strict liability even as to food." W. Prosser, Handbook of the Law of Torts § 83, at 692 (4th ed. 1971).

food warranty running to remote consumers that lay outside of contract law and hence was one of tort. In a 1942 case from Texas, *Jacob E. Decker & Sons v. Capps*,[21] a producer sold contaminated sausage to a retail merchant, who sold it to Mr. Capps. The Capps family consumed the sausage, which killed one of the children and seriously sickened the rest of the family. In an action against the producer, the court noted that the food manufacturer's duty to consumers rested on "the broad principle of the public policy to protect human health and life."[22] The court noted that food items are placed in the channel of commerce with the intention that they pass from hand to hand until they find their way to some remote consumer who usually is unable to analyze the food to determine if it is safe. So, in the case of defective food, "there is such an utter failure of the purpose for which the food is sold, and the consequences of eating unsound food are so disastrous to human health and life, that the law imposes a warranty of purity in favor of the ultimate consumer as a matter of public policy."[23]

For products other than food, the path to strict products liability in tort took much longer. Over the first half of the twentieth century, tort law moved slowly in expanding a manufacturer's responsibility for product-caused harm to remote consumers. In particular, the *MacPherson* doctrine, which banished the no-privity-of-contract defense from negligence actions against manufacturers,[24] took decades to spread across the nation[25] and did nothing to relieve an injured consumer of the burden of proving the supplier's fault.

In the first edition of his celebrated tort law treatise in 1941, Dean William Prosser succinctly catalogued the variety of arguments favoring strict liability for remote sellers of defective products and why that liability should lie in tort.[26] Three years later, in *Escola v. Coca Cola Bottling Co.*,[27] the Supreme Court of California upheld a res ipsa loquitur verdict for a waitress injured when a Coke bottle exploded in her hand. In perhaps the most renowned concurring opinion in all of American tort law, Justice Roger Traynor elegantly elaborated each of Dean Prosser's arguments for strict products liability in tort.[28] Reasoning that "the manufacturer's negligence should no longer be singled out as the basis of a plaintiff's right to recover in cases like the present one," Traynor concluded that "it should now be recognized that a manufacturer incurs an absolute liability when an article that he has placed on the market,

**21.** 164 S.W.2d 828 (Tex. 1942).

**22.** Id. at 829.

**23.** Id.

**24.** See § 1.2, above.

**25.** As late as 1937, commenting on *MacPherson*, Francis Bohlen remarked, "Admirable as is the result, convincing as is the reasoning, the doctrine in that case has not gained the acceptance which its merits deserve." Bohlen, Fifty Years of Torts (pts. 1 and 2), 50 Harv. L. Rev. 725, 1225, 1234 (1937).

**26.** W. Prosser, Handbook of the Law of Torts 688–93 (4th ed. 1971). For one study of Dean Prosser's contributions to the development of strict products liability in tort,

see G. White, Tort Law in America—An Intellectual History 168–73 and 198–200 (1980) (chronicling Dean Prosser's contributions to the development of strict products liability in tort).

**27.** 150 P.2d 436 (Cal. 1944). On *Escola*, see Geistfeld, Escola v. Coca Cola Bottling Co.: Strict Products Liability Unbounded, in Torts Stories 229 (R. Rabin & S. Sugarman, eds., Foundation Press, 2003).

**28.** See G. White, Tort Law in America—An Intellectual History 198–200 (1980) (detailed comparison of arguments in Prosser's hornbook and Traynor's opinion).

knowing that it is to be used without inspection, proves to have a defect that causes injury to human beings." Regardless of fault, "public policy demands that responsibility be fixed wherever it will most effectively reduce the hazards to life and health inherent in defective products that reach the market." Manufacturers can test their products for defects in ways that consumers cannot, and the consequences of an injury from a defective product "may be an overwhelming misfortune to the person injured, and a needless one, for the risk of injury can be insured by the manufacturer and distributed among the public as a cost of doing business." Moreover, manufacturers rather than consumers are best situated to provide the most effective public protection against the "menace" of defective products.[29]

Justice Traynor reasoned further that a rule imposing strict liability to remote consumers on manufacturers of defective products would result in judicial economies since manufacturers were already indirectly subject to strict liability to consumers for selling defective products—an injured consumer could sue the retailer for breach of the implied warranty of merchantability; the retailer could then recover against the wholesaler for selling an unmerchantable product; and the wholesaler could in turn recover back against the manufacturer. But such a tortuous path "is needlessly circuitous and engenders wasteful litigation. Much would be gained if the injured person could base his action directly on the manufacturer's warranty."[30]

Observing that manufacturers of defective foods are held to a warranty of quality running to remote consumers, and that the rights of such persons to legal protection do not depend "upon the intricacies of the law of sales," Justice Traynor asserted that the same protection should be extended to consumers of all types of defective products: "Dangers to life and health inhere in other consumers' goods that are defective and there is no reason to differentiate them from the dangers of defective food products." There is no need for the courts to resort to the kinds of fictions they created in food product cases to rationalize extending the manufacturer's warranty to remote consumers "if the warranty is severed from the contract of sale between the dealer and the consumer and based on the law of torts[31] as a strict liability."[32] Justice Traynor reasoned that such a result was necessary to adjust the law to the vast changes in how products are manufactured and merchandised in the modern world. "As handicrafts have been replaced by mass production with its great markets and transportation facilities, the close relationship between the producer and consumer of a product has been altered." In marketing complex machines and chemicals, modern manufacturers urge remote consumers to trust in the safety of such products and to relinquish the consumer's historical self-protective role in evaluating a product's safety prior to purchase and use.[33] For these many

**29.** *Escola*, 150 P.2d at 440–41.

**30.** Id. at 442.

**31.** Citing Jacob E. Decker & Sons, Inc. v. Capps, 164 S.W.2d 828 (Tex. 1942); W. Prosser, Law of Torts 689 (1941).

**32.** *Escola*, 150 P.2d at 442–43.

**33.** Id. at 443–44.

reasons, Justice Traynor concluded that manufacturers should be strictly responsible to consumers for injuries caused by defects in the products that they sell.

Although Justice Traynor's *Escola* opinion attracted a bit of notoriety,[34] it received little more than passing notice[35] for a number of years.[36] During the 1950s, a number of courts expanded the "tort" food warranty to sales of dog[37] and fish[38] food,[39] and to products for intimate bodily use,[40] and scholars increasingly argued for strict manufacturer liability for defective products generally.[41] This was the legal landscape in 1960 when the New Jersey Supreme Court was asked to decide *Henningsen v. Bloomfield Motors, Inc.*[42] Ten days after Bloomfield Motors sold a new 1955 Plymouth sedan to Mr. Henningsen, the buyer's wife was injured when a defect in the car's steering caused the car to veer off the highway and crash into a brick wall. In Mr. and Mrs. Henningsen's suit for breach of the implied warranty of merchantability against the dealer and manufacturer, Chrysler Corporation, the defendants relied upon the disclaimer and remedy limitation clauses in the purchase order in defense. Verdicts were returned in favor of the plaintiffs, and the defendants appealed, claiming that the case should have been dismissed on grounds of lack of privity of contract and because of the disclaimer of implied warranties and limitations of remedies in the sales contract that Mr. Henningsen signed.

**34.** Compare Dean William Prosser's brief but favorable reference to Traynor's *Escola* opinion, in Prosser, Res Ipsa Loquitur in California, 37 Cal. L. Rev. 183, 224 n. 235 (1949), with Dean Roscoe Pound's extensive criticism of the opinion for expressing sentiments Pound viewed to be Marxist. R. Pound, New Paths of the Law 45 (1950), and Law in the Service State: Freedom v. Equality, 36 A.B.A. J. 977, 981 (1950). *But see* Pound, The Problem of the Exploding Bottle, 40 B.U. L. Rev. 167, 180–81 and 185–86 (1960), by which time Dean Pound had become converted to Traynor's views.

**35.** See, e.g., James, Accident Liability: Some Wartime Developments, 55 Yale L.J. 365 n.4 (1946) (Traynor's opinion given a *cf.* cite in article's introductory paragraph). In the 1955 edition of his treatise, Prosser merely cited but did not discuss Traynor's *Escola* opinion. See W. Prosser, Handbook of the Law of Torts 19 n.47 and 506 n.1 (1955). While he quoted from Traynor's opinion five years later in his "Assault" article, Prosser there remarked that "the question remains whether our courts, our legislators, and public sentiment in general, are yet ready to adopt so sweeping a legal philosophy, and to impose so heavy a burden abruptly and all at once upon all producers." Prosser, Assault Upon the Citadel (Strict Liability to the Consumer), 69 Yale L.J. 1099, 1120 (1960).

**36.** See Priest, The Invention of Enterprise Liability: A Critical History of the Intellectual Foundations of Modern Tort Law, 14 J. Legal Stud. 461, 498–99 (1985).

**37.** See McAfee v. Cargill, Inc., 121 F.Supp. 5 (S.D. Cal. 1954).

**38.** See Midwest Game Co. v. M.F.A. Milling Co., 320 S.W.2d 547 (Mo. 1959).

**39.** See Prosser, Assault on the Citadel (Strict Liability to the Consumer), 69 Yale 1099, 1111 (1960) ("apparently on the theory that food is food").

**40.** See Worley v. Proctor & Gamble Mfg. Co., 253 S.W.2d 532 (Mo. Ct. App. 1952) (detergent) (dictum); Kruper v. Proctor & Gamble Co., 113 N.E.2d 605 (Ohio Ct. App. 1953), rev'd on other grounds, 117 N.E.2d 7 (Ohio 1954) (soap); Graham v. Bottenfield's, Inc., 269 P.2d 413 (Kan. 1954) (hair dye); Rogers v. Toni Home Permanent Co., 147 N.E.2d 612 (Ohio 1958), and Markovich v. McKesson & Robbins, Inc., 149 N.E.2d 181 (Ohio App. 1958) (permanent wave solution); Ross v. Philip Morris Co., 164 F.Supp. 683 (W.D. Mo. 1958) (cigarettes). All are chronicled in Prosser, Assault on the Citadel (Strict Liability to the Consumer), 69 Yale 1099, at 1110–14 (1960), and W. Prosser, Handbook on the Law of Torts 510 (2d ed. 1955). See also Dean Prosser's Notes to the Restatement (2d) Torts § 402A at 9–14 (Tent. Draft No. 7, April 16, 1962).

**41.** See § 5.4, below.

**42.** 161 A.2d 69 (N.J. 1960).

The New Jersey Supreme Court, in a unanimous opinion, affirmed the plaintiffs' verdict. Drawing on the reasoning of the food warranty cases, Dean Prosser, Justice Traynor, and Justice Francis observed that implied warranties are a necessary protection for consumers unable effectively to inspect products for latent defects. "Warranties developed in the law in the interest of and to protect the ordinary consumer who cannot be expected to have the knowledge or capacity or even the opportunity to make adequate inspection of mechanical instrumentalities, like automobiles, and to decide for himself whether they are reasonably fit for the designed purpose."[43] Building from the right of consumers of defective food to recover from manufacturers despite the absence of privity of contract, Justice Francis saw "no rational doctrinal basis for differentiating between a fly in a bottle of beverage and a defective automobile. The unwholesome beverage may bring illness to one person, the defective car, with its great potentiality for harm to the driver, occupants, and others, demands even less adherence to the narrow barrier of privity."[44] And thus, in the immortal words of Dean Prosser, marked the "fall of the citadel of privity."[45]

Remarkably,[46] just a few weeks after *Henningsen* was handed down,[47] Dean Prosser published his groundbreaking article, "Assault on the Citadel,"[48] that argued for and predicted precisely such a result. Tracing the development of a manufacturer's warranty responsibility to consumers for injuries caused by defective products, Prosser related the variety of ingenious methods devised by the courts to avoid contract law obstacles to recovery, such as privity, disclaimers, and the requirement that a buyer promptly notify the seller of a breach. Prosser argued that the "warranty" rule of strict liability should be extended beyond cases of unwholesome food and other products for bodily use. "The public interest in the safety of products which the public must buy certainly extends to a great many other things. The wedge has entered, and we are on our way.... Ultimately, ... we may arrive at a 'general rule' of strict liability for all products."[49] Such would be the correct rule, but the "warranty" label was wrong. "If there is to be strict liability in tort," contended Prosser, "let there be strict liability in tort, declared outright, without an illusory contract mask."[50]

---

**43.** Id. at 78.

**44.** Id. at 83. Compare the observation of Professor Fleming James, three years earlier: "Surely greater danger lurks in a defective automobile wheel than in a pebble in a can of beans." James, General Products—Should Manufacturers Be Liable Without Negligence?, 24 Tenn. L. Rev. 923, 926 (1957).

**45.** Prosser, The Fall of the Citadel (Strict Liability to the Consumer), 50 Minn. L. Rev. 791 (1966).

**46.** "This simultaneity of prediction and confirmation is extraordinary and is unknown even in scientific work." Priest, The Invention of Enterprise Liability: A Critical

History of the Intellectual Foundations of Modern Tort Law, 14 J. Legal Stud. 461, 507 (1985).

**47.** George Priest notes that *Henningsen* was announced on May 9, 1960, and Dean Prosser's "Assault" article was published in the June 1960 issue of the Yale Law Journal. Priest, above, 14 J. Legal Stud. at 506 n.292.

**48.** Prosser, Assault on the Citadel (Strict Liability to the Consumer), 69 Yale L.J. 1099 (1960).

**49.** Id. at 1140.

**50.** Id. at 1134.

Now that a few courts,[51] supported by the leading tort law scholars,[52] were urging a generalized doctrine of strict manufacturer liability for selling defective products, the stage was set for judicial adoption of a doctrine of strict products liability that lay explicitly in tort. When Dean Prosser wrote his "Assault Upon the Citadel" article in 1960, however, he erred in one prediction: that the courts were not then ready for so novel a theory which, he opined, might take until the year 2010 before it was accepted.[53]

Quite the contrary, it was a scant three years later, in 1963, that the California Supreme Court handed down the landmark case of *Greenman v. Yuba Power Products, Inc.*[54] While using his combination power tool as a lathe, Mr. Greenman was injured when the tailstock of the lathe vibrated loose and the piece of wood he was shaping flew out and struck him on the head. He sued the manufacturer and retailer for negligence and breach of warranty, and he received a verdict and judgment against the manufacturer on his express warranty claim which the manufacturer challenged on appeal, arguing that the plaintiff had failed to provide timely notice of breach.[55]

Justice Traynor, who in 1944 had offered an eloquent, lone voice for strict products liability in *Escola v. Coca Cola Bottling Co.*,[56] authored an opinion in *Greenman*, too; but this time he spoke for a unanimous court. Affirming the plaintiff's judgment, the *Greenman* court ruled that, because the commercial code's requirement of prompt notice is inappropriate in cases involving injured consumers,[57] even an untimely notice would not bar such a consumer's express warranty claim. But Justice Traynor did not stop there. "Moreover, to impose strict liability on the manufacturer under the circumstances of this case, it was not necessary for plaintiff to establish an express warranty [under the commercial code]. A manufacturer is strictly liable in tort when an article he places on the market, knowing that it is to be used without inspection for defects, proves to have a defect that causes injury to a human being."[58] Tracing the development of the strict products liability doctrine under the warranty umbrella—from the food cases, through products for intimate bodily use, to durable products, such as the car in *Henningsen*— Justice Traynor explained that the rejection of the requirement of privity of contract, "the recognition that the liability is not assumed by agreement but imposed by law, and the refusal to permit the manufacturer to define the scope of its own responsibility for defective products make clear that the liability is not one governed by the law of contract warranties but by the law of strict liability in tort."[59]

**51.** In addition to *Henningsen*, see, e.g., Picker X–Ray Corp. v. General Motors Corp., 185 A.2d 919 (D.C. 1962).

**52.** Dean Prosser was by no means alone. See § 5.4, below.

**53.** "Thus far there has been relatively little indication that the time is yet ripe for what may very possibly be the law of fifty years ahead." Prosser, Assault on the Citadel (Strict Liability to the Consumer), 69 Yale 1099, 1120 (1960).

**54.** 377 P.2d 897 (Cal. 1963).

**55.** For a discussion of the buyer's duty to provide the seller with a timely notice of breach of warranty under UCC § 2–607, see § 4.6, above.

**56.** 150 P.2d 436, 440–44 (Cal. 1944).

**57.** See § 4.6, above.

**58.** *Greenman*, 377 P.2d at 900.

**59.** Id. at 901.

There was no reason to "recanvass the reasons for imposing strict liability on the manufacturer" which had already been "fully articulated,"[60] declared Traynor, citing his concurring opinion in *Escola*,[61] Prosser's "Assault Upon the Citadel" article,[62] and the Harper and James torts treatise:[63] "The purpose of such liability is to insure that the costs of injuries resulting from defective products are borne by the manufacturers that put such products on the market rather than by the injured persons who are powerless to protect themselves. Sales warranties serve this purpose fitfully at best."[64] For example, in the present case, the plaintiff could rely on an express warranty only because he happened to have read and relied on representations of the Shopsmith's ruggedness in the manufacturer's brochure. "Implicit in the machine's presence on the market, however, was a representation that it would safely do the jobs for which it was built." Thus, "it should not be controlling whether plaintiff selected the machine because of the statements in the brochure, or because of the machine's own appearance of excellence that belied the defect lurking beneath the surface, or because he merely assumed that it would safely do the jobs it was built to do."[65]

In *Greenman*, the path to strict manufacturer liability for defective products led home to the law of tort.

## § 5.3  RESTATEMENT (SECOND) OF TORTS § 402A

### The Progression of § 402A Drafts

In the 1950s and 1960s, the American Law Institute was in the midst of a quarter century revision of the *Restatement of Torts*, which it had originally promulgated in the 1930s. The Reporter for the new *Restatement (Second) of Torts* was none other than Dean William Prosser of the University of California at Berkeley. In the late 1950s, prior to *Henningsen v. Bloomfield Motors, Inc.*,[1] Dean Prosser began to revise chapter 14 of the old *Restatement*, which covered rules of negligence law governing the liability of product suppliers.[2] Revising the negligence sections in conventional form, he then turned to the special tort warran-

---

**60.** Id.

**61.** Escola v. Coca Cola Bottling Co., 150 P.2d 436, 440 (Cal. 1943).

**62.** Prosser, Assault Upon the Citadel (Strict Liability to the Consumer), 69 Yale L.J. 1099 (1960); *Greenman*, 377 P.2d at 901.

**63.** 2 F. Harper and F. James, Law of Torts §§ 28.15–28.16, pp. 1569–74; *Greeman, 377 P.2d at 901.

**64.** *Greenman*, 377 P.2d at 901 (citing Prosser, Assault Upon the Citadel (Strict Liability to the Consumer), 69 Yale L.J. 1099, 1124–1134 (1960)).

**65.** *Greenman*, 377 P.2d. at 901. Nor should it matter whether an implied warranty arose, because " '[t]he remedies of injured consumers ought not to be made to depend upon the intricacies of the law of sales.' Ketterer v. Armour & Co., D.C., 200 F. 322, 323.... To establish the manufacturer's liability it was sufficient that plaintiff proved that he was injured while using the Shopsmith in a way it was intended to be used as a result of a defect in design and manufacture of which plaintiff was not aware that made the Shopsmith unsafe for its intended use."

**§ 5.3**

**1.** 161 A.2d 69 (N.J. 1960).

**2.** In both the first and second Restatements, chapter 14 (beginning with § 388, a supplier's duty to warn third parties of certain risks) is entitled "Liability of Persons Supplying Chattels for the Use of Others."

ty that had been evolving for some time in the context of the sale of food.[3] Crafting a special section, new § 402A, to serve as a vehicle for the specialized development of "strict" tort liability for the sale of food "in a dangerous condition to the consumer," Prosser included the provision in a *Preliminary Draft* of the new *Restatement* in 1958,[4] and subsequently in a *Council Draft* in 1960.[5] And so began the journey of § 402A, quite modestly at the start, which propagated and mushroomed as it quickly progressed.[6]

After initially sprouting in foodstuff form in 1958 and 1960, § 402A then proceeded, in April 1961, to Tentative Draft No. 6, which recommended adoption of a new section, § 402A, strict liability for the sale of "food for human consumption." But events were moving rapidly and, in April 1962, in Tentative Draft No. 7, Dean Prosser expanded coverage of § 402A to include "products intended for intimate bodily use." A comment to § 402A explained that "intimate bodily use" also included "products intended for external application or contact" where it was "of an intimate character," such as chewing gum, chewing tobacco, snuff, cigarettes, drugs, clothing, soap, cosmetics, liniments, hair dye, and permanent wave solutions. By 1964, even this broadened version was obsolete, and the American Law Institute approved the final draft of § 402A which made the rule applicable to all products.[7]

Section 402A was published the next year, 1965, in volume 2 of the *Restatement (Second) of Torts*:

> § 402A. Special Liability of Seller of Product for Physical Harm to User or Consumer
>
> (1) One who sells any product in a defective condition unreasonably dangerous to the user or consumer or to his property is subject to liability for physical harm thereby caused to the ultimate user or consumer, or to his property, if
>
> (a) the seller is engaged in the business of selling such a product, and
>
> (b) it is expected to and does reach the user or consumer without substantial change in the condition in which it is sold.
>
> (2) The rule stated in Subsection (1) applies although
>
> (a) the seller has exercised all possible care in the preparation and sale of his product, and
>
> (b) the user or consumer has not bought the product from or entered into any contractual relation with the seller.

**3.** See § 5.2, above.

**4.** Restatement (2d) Torts § 402A (Prelim. Draft No. 6, 1958).

**5.** Restatement (2d) Torts § 402A (Council Draft No. 8, 1960).

**6.** For a discussion of how comments *i*, *j*, and *k* were drafted to apply only to food, drugs, and other inherently dangerous products, see § 6.2, below.

**7.** See Putnam v. Erie City Mfg. Co., 338 F.2d 911, 918–19 (5th Cir. 1964) (Tex. law) (reciting the evolution of § 402A).

Stripped of its prolixity, the liability principle of § 402A is short and simple: manufacturers and other suppliers are subject to strict liability in tort for injuries caused by defects in the products that they sell.

## Nature of Strict Products Liability in Tort

### *"Strict" Liability*

Section 402A provides that commercial sellers of products are strictly liable for harm to users caused by defects in their products. Stated otherwise, a manufacturer or other product seller is subject to liability for selling a defective product that proximately causes harm.[8] Because liability is "strict," a seller is liable even if it was not negligent, even if it exercised all due care. "The rule is one of strict liability, making the seller subject to liability to the user or consumer even though he has exercised all possible care in the preparation and sale of the product."[9]

All courts agree, however, that the doctrine of strict liability in tort is constrained by certain definite limitations[10]—that a manufacturer or other seller is not an insurer of its product's safety,[11] and that a supplier is not required to provide only the very safest of products,[12] nor those that represent only the "ultimate in safety"[13] or are accident-proof.[14] The

---

**8.** See discussion of elements, below.

**9.** Restatement (2d) Torts § 402A cmt. *m.* This point is made in black letter: "The rule stated in Subsection (1) applies although (a) the seller has exercised all possible care in the preparation and sale of his product." § 402A(2).

**10.** See Spieker v. Westgo, Inc., 479 N.W.2d 837, 845 (N.D. 1992), which approved the following "argumentative" instruction: "1) manufacturers are not insurers of the safety of persons who use the product, 2) manufacturers are under no duty to make an accident-proof or fool-proof product, 3) manufacturers are not required by law to guarantee their products cannot be used in such a way to cause injury, 4) so long as the product is reasonably safe for its intended use, manufacturers have done all that the law requires, even though other possible designs might be safer, and 5) manufacturers have no legal duty to produce products incorporating only the ultimate in safety."

**11.** See, e.g., Verchot v. General Motors Corp., 812 So.2d 296, 301 (Ala. 2001) ("the manufacturer of a product is not an insurer against all harm that might be caused by the use of the product"); Potter v. Chicago Pneumatic Tool Co., 694 A.2d 1319, 1328 (Conn. 1997) ("strict tort liability does not transform manufacturers into insurers, nor does it impose absolute liability"); Zimmerman v. Volkswagen of Am., Inc., 920 P.2d 67, 73 (Idaho 1996) ("strict liability is not absolute liability because a manufacturer is not an insurer or guarantor that no one will be injured in using his product"); Webb v. Navistar Int'l. Transp. Corp., 692 A.2d 343,

350 (Vt. 1996) ("Strict liability is not absolute liability; manufacturers are not insurers of user safety."); Engberg v. Ford Motor Co., 205 N.W.2d 104, 109 (S.D. 1973) ("the concept does not make the manufacturer an absolute insurer against any injuries caused by his product"). See generally Traynor, The Ways and Meanings of Defective Products and Strict Liability, 32 Tenn. L. Rev. 363, 366–67 (1965) ("the manufacturer is not an insurer for all injuries caused by his products").

**12.** See, e.g., Irion v. Sun Lighting, Inc., 2004 WL 746823 (Tenn. Ct. App. 2004) ("A manufacturer is not required to incorporate the ultimate safety features into a product."); Ford Motor Co. v. Miles, 967 S.W.2d 377, 386 (Tex. 1998) ("[a] manufacturer or distributor of products is not an insurer," and "a manufacturer is not required to design the safest possible product"); Graham v. Sprout–Waldron and Co., 657 So.2d 868, 870 (Ala. 1995) ("[t]he manufacturer of a product is not required to produce the safest product, but only to produce a product that is reasonably safe when put to its intended use"); Dutsch v. Sea Ray Boats, Inc., 845 P.2d 187, 191–92 (Okla. 1992) ("the manufacturer is not required to make a perfect product, but only manufacture and place into the stream of commerce a safe product").

**13.** See, e.g., Irion v. Sun Lighting, Inc., 2004 WL 746823 (Tenn. Ct. App. 2004) (product need not be "accident-proof or incapable of causing injury"); Nguyen v. F.L. Smithe Machine Co., 2000 WL 968815, at *2 (N.D. Ill. 2000) (manufacturer " 'had no

---

**14.** See note 14 on page 261.

obligation imposed on product sellers under § 402A is to provide products that are not "unreasonably dangerous" or "defective," not to provide products that are perfectly safe. This means that something must be *wrong* with a product before a seller is held responsible for harm.[15] Just how the law should make this determination, and how the standard of "defectiveness" should be defined, are complex questions that require the selection of an appropriate test of liability, as examined at length below.[16]

### Elements of a Strict Tort Claim

There usually is little reason to state the "elements" of a claim for strict products liability in tort, since the nature of such claims is so simple and clear. Yet because some courts do so, the topic will be considered here. While courts vary in their definitions of this cause of action, the formulations share a common core. Stated simply, the rule in almost every state is that manufacturers are subject to liability in tort for injuries caused by defects in products that they sell.[17] Although variously expressed, all courts require a plaintiff to prove two core elements: (1) that the defendant sold a defective product; and (2) that the defect proximately caused the plaintiff's harm.[18] These two elements

duty to produce a product which represented the ultimate in safety' "); Morrison v. Kubota Tractor Corp., 891 S.W.2d 422, 426 (Mo.App.1994) ("A manufacturer is not obligated to adopt only those features which represent the ultimate in safety or design."); Patton v. Hutchinson Wil–Rich Mfg. Co., 861 P.2d 1299, 1308 (Kan. 1993) ("All courts agree a manufacturer is not obligated to adopt features which represent the ultimate in safety or design."); Oanes v. Westgo, Inc., 476 N.W.2d 248, 252 (N.D. 1991) ("The manufacturer is under no duty to design the safest possible product, or one as safe as others make, or a safer product than the one designed, so long as the design adopted is reasonably safe. In other words, the manufacturer is under no duty to design the product so as to render it wholly incapable of producing an injury; nor is he required to adopt features representing the 'ultimate in safety.' ").

**14.** See, e.g., Verchot v. General Motors Corp., 812 So.2d 296, 301 (Ala. 2001) ("the manufacturer or designer is not obligated to produce an accident-proof or injury-proof product"); Cooper v. General Motors Corp., 702 So.2d 428, 442–43 (Miss. 1997) ("[M]anufacturers are not insurers ... '[o]ur law demands that products be reasonably fit, not perfectly so' [nor does our law] 'require that every manufacturer incorporate into his product every innovation which ... might have rendered the product more safe.' "); Conder v. Hull Lift Truck, Inc., 435 N.E.2d 10, 16 (Ind. 1982) (approving instruction that stated: "[the defendant manufacturer] was not and is not an insurer or guarantor in regard to the quality of its product and is not required to manufac-

ture or produce a product which is perfect or accident proof. Neither is the defendant ... liable for any and all accidents or damage which arise out of or which may occur by reason of the use of its products. The law only requires that the defendant ... produce a product which at the time of its manufacture and sale to a third person is reasonably safe for the use for which it was intended."). *But see* Indianapolis Athletic Club, Inc. v. Alco Std. Corp., 709 N.E.2d 1070, 1075–77 (Ind. Ct. App. 1999) (while instruction on the absence of such a duty may not be reversible error, it may provide misleading emphasis and should be avoided).

**15.** "There has to be something wrong with the product." 38 ALI Proceedings 88 (1961) (remarks of Reporter for Restatement (2d) Torts, Dean William Prosser, on § 402A draft).

**16.** See §§ 5.5–5.8, below.

**17.** The general rule is stated in terms of manufacturers, the paradigm products liability defendant. While many principles of strict products liability in tort apply as well to retailers and other commercial sellers, nonmanufacturing defendants are treated in chs. 15 and 16, below.

**18.** See, e.g., Brown v. Sears, Roebuck & Co., 328 F.3d 1274 (10th Cir. 2003) (Utah law); Klootwyk v. DaimlerChrysler Corp., 2003 WL 21038417 (N.D. Ill. 2003); Parsons v. Ford Motor Co., 85 S.W.3d 323 (Tex. App. 2002); Jonas v. Isuzu Motors Ltd., 210 F.Supp.2d 1373, 1377 (M.D. Ga. 2002); Vautour v. Body Masters Sports Indus., Inc., 784 A.2d 1178 (N.H. 2001); Smith v.

imply the product's defectiveness at the time of sale, a requirement many courts make explicit in their formulations of the elements.[19]

Despite the clarity and simplicity of a strict tort products liability claim, some courts do get entangled, understandably, in the prolix language of § 402A which imposes strict liability for the sale of an injury-producing product in a "defective condition unreasonably dangerous" to the user or consumer. The history of this clumsy phrase is just one part of § 402A's tortuous path from conception to completion,[20] and there is widespread understanding that this bulky liability phraseology really means just one thing—that a product is more dangerous than it properly should be.[21] Today, most courts (and almost all commentators) capture that single concept in a single word: "defective."[22]

Bryco Arms, 33 P.3d 638 (N.M. Ct. App. 2001); Norton Co. v. Fergestrom, 2001 WL 1628302 (Nev. 2001); Bray v. Marathon Corp., 553 S.E.2d 477 (S.C. Ct. App. 2001), aff'd on point, rev'd on other grounds, 588 S.E.2d 93 (S.C. 2003); Zaza v. Marquess & Nell, Inc., 675 A.2d 620 (N.J. 1996).

**19.** See, e.g., Taylor v. National R.R. Passenger Corp., 310 F.Supp.2d 727 (E.D. Pa. 2004) (plaintiff must prove that "the defect existed at the time the product left the manufacturer"); Bruner v. Anheuser–Busch, Inc., 153 F.Supp.2d 1358, 1358 (S.D. Fla. 2001) (a "product is defective when it 'is, at the time it leaves the seller's hands, in a condition not contemplated by the ultimate consumer, but which will be unreasonably dangerous to him,'" citing § 402A cmt. g); American Family Ins. Group v. JVC Americas Corp., 2001 WL 1618454, at *5 (D. Minn. 2001) (plaintiff must prove "the defect existed when the product left the defendant's control"); Vautour v. Body Masters Sports Indus., Inc., 784 A.2d 1178, 1181 (N.H. 2001) (plaintiff must prove "the condition existed when the product was sold by a seller"); Myrlak v. Port Auth. of N.Y., 723 A.2d 45, 52 (N.J. 1999) ("a plaintiff must prove that the product was defective, that the defect existed when the product left the manufacturer's control, and that the defect proximately caused injuries to the plaintiff, a reasonably foreseeable or intended user"); Moss v. Crosman Corp., 136 F.3d 1169, 1169 (7th Cir. 1998) (Ind. law) (plaintiff must prove "the defect existed at the time the product left the defendant's control"); Potter v. Chicago Pneumatic Tool Co., 694 A.2d 1319, 1330 (Conn. 1997) (plaintiff must prove "the defect existed at the time of the sale").

**20.** The phrase resulted from Dean Prosser's overreaction to the ALI Council's complaint that the "dangerous condition" language he initially proposed was overbroad. See § 5.8, below.

**21.** See, e.g., McAlpine v. Rhone–Poulenc Ag Co., 16 P.3d 1054, 1058 (Mont. 2000), quoting Dean W. Page Keeton of Texas, one of the ALI Advisers for the Second Restatement:

> It is unfortunate perhaps that Section 402A of the Restatement (Second) of Torts provides that as a basis for recovery it must be found that the product was both "defective" and "unreasonably dangerous" when as a matter of fact the term "unreasonably dangerous" was meant only as a definition of defect. The phrase was not intended as setting forth two requirements but only one.

W.P. Keeton, Product Liability and the Meaning of Defect, 5 St. Mary's L.J. 30, 32 (1973). *McAlpine* held that the trial court erred in instructing the jury that liability depended on the product having been in a "defective condition unreasonably dangerous," rather than only in a "defective condition," because the full Restatement phrase could mislead the jury into thinking that liability was based on two requirements rather than just one.

**22.** See, e.g., Webster v. Pacesetter, Inc., 259 F.Supp.2d 27 (D.D.C. 2003); Sprung v. MTR Ravensburg Inc., 788 N.E.2d 620 (N.Y. 2003); Gramex Corp. v. Green Supply, Inc., 89 S.W.3d 432 (Mo. 2002); Chandler v. Gene Messer Ford, Inc., 81 S.W.3d 493 (Tex. App. 2002); Bruner v. Anheuser–Busch, Inc., 153 F.Supp.2d 1358 (S.D. Fla. 2001); Vautour v. Body Masters Sports Indus., Inc., 784 A.2d 1178 (N.H. 2001); Smith v. Bryco Arms, 33 P.3d 638 (N.M. Ct. App. 2001); McAlpine v. Rhone–Poulenc Ag Co., 16 P.3d 1054, 1058 (Mont. 2000); General Motors Corp. v. Farnsworth, 965 P.2d 1209 (Alaska 1998); Taylor v. General Motors Corp., 707 So.2d 198 (Ala. 1997); Ohio Rev. Code Ann. § 2307.73(A)(1).

A few jurisdictions base liability on other single-concept phrases, such as "not reasonably safe" or "unreasonably dangerous." See, e.g., Wash. Rev. Code § 7.72.030 (2) ("not reasonably safe"); La. Rev. Stat. Ann. § 9:2800.54 ("unreasonably dangerous"); Sollami v. Eaton, 772 N.E.2d 215 (Ill. 2002) ("unreasonably dangerous").

Notwithstanding this general agreement about strict products liability in tort, some courts still attribute more meaning to the language of § 402A than it deserves. Thus, some courts nominally divide § 402A's "defective condition unreasonably dangerous" language into two separate elements, "defective" and "unreasonably dangerous,"[23] and a fair number of jurisdictions more ambiguously suggest two separate elements.[24] Yet it is difficult to find a case where a court in such a jurisdiction explicitly addresses the differences between the two elements,[25] perhaps because the comments to § 402A define both phrases

**23.** Some jurisdictions do so quite explicitly. See, e.g., Haase v. Badger Mining Corp. 682 N.W.2d 389, 395 (Wis. 2004) (strict liability in tort requires proof that product was (1) defective, and (2) unreasonably dangerous); McCoy v. Whirlpool Corp. 2003 WL 21554950, at *6 (D. Kan. 2003) ("Kansas courts require 'that the product be both defective and unreasonably dangerous' "); Halliday v. Sturm, Ruger & Co., Inc., 792 A.2d 1145, 1150 (Md. 2002) ("for a seller to be liable under § 402A, the product must be both in a 'defective condition' and 'unreasonably dangerous' at the time it was placed on the market"); American Family Ins. Group v. JVC Ams. Corp., 2001 WL 1618454, at *5 (D. Minn. 2001) ("a plaintiff in a products liability case must establish that the defendant's product was in a defective condition and unreasonably dangerous for its intended use"); Lee v. Martin, 45 S.W.3d 860, 864 (Ark. Ct. App. 2001) ("a plaintiff in a strict-liability case must prove that the product is unreasonably dangerous *and* defective"); Farnham v. Bombardier, Inc., 640 A.2d 47, 48 (Vt. 1994) ("To establish strict liability in a products liability action, a plaintiff must show that the defendant's product (1) is defective; (2) is unreasonably dangerous to the consumer in normal use; (3) reached the consumer without undergoing any substantial change in condition; and (4) caused injury to the consumer because of its defective design."). See § 5.6, below.

See also Tenn. Code Ann. § 29–28–105 (a), which seemingly grounds liability on *either* a product's defective *or* unreasonably dangerous condition, separately defined: "A manufacturer or seller of a product shall not be liable for any injury to a person or property caused by the product unless the product is determined to be in a defective condition or unreasonably dangerous at the time it left the control of the manufacturer or seller." Indiana's curious statute adopts the "defective condition unreasonably dangerous" language of § 402A, Ind. Code § 34–20–2–1, and then defines "defective condition" as a condition (1) not contemplated by consumers, and (2) that is "unreasonably dangerous." Ind. Code § 34–20–4–1.

**24.** Some jurisdictions state that a defect must "render" or "make" the product unreasonably dangerous. See, e.g., Johnson v. Ford Motor Co., 45 P.3d 86, 91 (Okla. 2002) ("plaintiff must prove ... that the product was defective when it left the control of the manufacturer, and that the defect made the product unreasonably dangerous"); Dillon v. Zeneca Corp., 42 P.3d 598 (Ariz. Ct. App. 2002) ("For a prima facie case of strict product liability, the plaintiff must demonstrate that the product was in a defective condition that made it unreasonably dangerous"); Raimbeault v. Takeuchi Mfg. (U.S.), Ltd., 772 A.2d 1056, 1063 (R.I. 2001) (plaintiff must prove defect and that " 'defect rendered the product unreasonably dangerous' "); Norton Co. v. Fergestrom, 2001 WL 1628302, at *3 (Nev. 2001) (plaintiff must prove that "the product was defective, which rendered it unreasonably dangerous"); Haag v. Bongers, 589 N.W.2d 318, 321 (Neb. 1999) ("the defect, if existent, rendered the product unreasonably dangerous and unsafe for its intended use"); Tabieros v. Clark Equip. Co., 944 P.2d 1279, 1297 (Haw. 1997) (plaintiff must prove " '(1) a defect in the product which rendered it unreasonably dangerous for its intended or reasonably foreseeable use; and (2) a causal connection between the defect and [the] plaintiff's injuries' "); Ark. Code Ann. § 4–86–102 ("the product was supplied ... in a defective condition which rendered it unreasonably dangerous"); Miss. Code Ann. § 11–1–63(a)(ii) ("[t]he defective condition rendered the product unreasonably dangerous"); N.D. Cent. Code § 28–.01.3–06 ("a defect or defective condition in the product which made the product unreasonably dangerous to the user or consumer"). Compare Allenberg v. Bentley Hedges Travel Serv., Inc., 22 P.3d 223, 227 (Okla. 2001) ("the seller of a product in a defective condition, which is unreasonably dangerous to the user or consumer, is strictly liable" for harm); Campbell v. Studer, Inc., 970 P.2d 389, 392 (Wyo. 1998) ("A defective product is a product which is 'not reasonably safe,' or is 'unreasonably dangerous' to the user or consumer.").

**25.** Statutes that seemingly do so include Ark. Code Ann. § 16–116–102(4), (7);

congruently, as dangerous beyond a consumer's expectations.[26] In states that have legislated products liability doctrine, the basis of liability is often formulated in terms of a product's being "defective," "unreasonably dangerous," or some other single-pronged terminology without the burden of a second prong.[27] Even courts in some jurisdictions whose legislatures adopted § 402A statutorily[28] have avoided the trap of dividing the "defective condition unreasonably dangerous" concept into two separate elements,[29] and there simply is no good reason to perpetuate a linguistic error grounded in a *Restatement* that has now been superseded.[30]

### Warranty Law Defenses

Although most of the cases which generated § 402A were nominally decided under the law of warranty,[31] liability under this section is "purely one of tort."[32] Accordingly, liability under § 402A is unaffected by warranty law defenses.[33] Thus, contrary to the requirements of the Uniform Commercial Code,[34] a buyer owes no duty to provide the seller with prompt notice of breach after an accident. Similarly, liability under § 402A is unaffected by whether or not there is any privity of contract

Ind. Code § 34–20–4–1; and Tenn. Code Ann. §§ 29–28–101, 105 (2002).

**26.** See Restatement (2d) Torts § 402A cmts. *g* and *i*. See § 5.6, below.

**27.** See, e.g., Ohio Rev. Code Ann. § 2307.73 (A) (manufacturer subject to liability if product "defective" and defect proximately caused claimant's harm); Tex. Code Ann. 82.001(2) ("defective"); N.J. Stat. Ann. § 2A:58C–2 ("designed in a defective manner"); La. Rev. Stat. Ann. § 9:2800.54 ("unreasonably dangerous"); Wash. Rev. Code § 7.72.030 (2) ("not reasonably safe"). *But cf.* Ga. Code Ann. § 51–1–11 (b)(1) (manufacturer subject to liability if product was "not merchantable and reasonably suited to the use intended").

**28.** See, e.g., Me. Rev. Stat. Ann. Tit. 14 § 221; Mont. Code Ann. § 27–1–719; Or. Rev. Stat. § 30.920; S.C. Code Ann. § 15–73–10.

**29.** See, e.g., McAlpine v. Rhone–Poulenc Ag Co., 16 P.3d 1054, 1058 (Mont. 2000) ("a plaintiff is not required to show that a product is defective and also that it is unreasonably dangerous because establishing that a product is unreasonably dangerous is merely a means of proving that it is defective"). See also McCathern v. Toyota Motor Corp., 23 P.3d 320, 329–32 (Or. 2001) (statutory consumer expectations test is sole standard for assessing whether product is in a "defective condition unreasonably dangerous" to user).

**30.** Section 402A of the Second Restatement is superseded by the Products Liability Restatement. See § 6.5, below. The history and problem of § 402A's apparently two-headed liability definition is further addressed in §§ 5.6 and 5.8, below.

**31.** See § 5.2, above. For a comparison of the strict liability in tort doctrine to the implied warranty of merchantability, see § 5.9, below.

**32.** Restatement (2d) Torts § 402A cmt. *m*. More fully, the comment observes that "[t]here is nothing in this Section which would prevent any court from treating the rule stated as a matter of 'warranty' to the user or consumer. But if this is done, it should be recognized and understood that the 'warranty' is a very different kind of warranty from those usually found in the sale of goods, and that it is not subject to the various contract rules which have grown up to surround such sales."

**33.** Comment *m* to § 402A makes this clear:

The rule stated in this Section is not governed by the provisions of the Uniform Sales Act, or those of the Uniform Commercial Code, as to warranties.... Nor is the consumer required to give notice to the seller of his injury within a reasonable time after it occurs, as is provided by the Uniform Act. The consumer's cause of action does not depend upon the validity of his contract with the person from whom he acquires the product, and it is not affected by any disclaimer or other agreement.... In short, "warranty" must be given a new and different meaning if it is used in connection with this Section. It is much simpler to regard the liability here stated as merely one of strict liability in tort.

**34.** See § 4.6, above.

relationship between the victim and the defendant.[35] Moreover, a seller's contractual efforts to disclaim liability or limit damages are simply null and void.[36]

### Time When Defect Must Exist

Section 402A(1)(b) conditions liability on proof that the product "is expected to and does reach the user or consumer without substantial change in the condition in which it is sold." Thus, plaintiff must establish not only that a defect caused his or her harm, but also that the product contained the defect at the time the product left the defendant's control.[37] As earlier discussed, this requirement is often stated as an explicit element of a strict tort claim. Elaborating on this requirement, usually pertinent only to manufacturing defects,[38] comment *g* to § 402A observes that the strict liability rule "applies only where the product is, at the time it leaves the seller's hands, in a condition not contemplated by the ultimate consumer, which will be unreasonably dangerous to him." A seller is not liable if the product is safe at the time of sale and thereafter becomes defective due to subsequent events. Moreover, the burden of proof that the product was defective at the time the defendant sold it rests upon the injured plaintiff.[39]

Comment *g* also makes clear that, if a manufacturer fails to take adequate precautions to insure that its products will remain in a safe condition for a reasonable length of time, the manufacturer will not be relieved of liability simply because one of its products was not actively dangerous at the time it left his possession.[40] A manufacturer, in other words, must take reasonable steps to protect users from a product's dangerously unexpected deterioration.[41] Thus, a producer must ensure

---

**35.** Section 402A(2) in black letter states that the strict liability rule "applies although ... (b) the user or consumer has not bought the product from or entered into any contractual relation with the seller." Privity of contract is still a significant consideration under the UCC. See § 4.5, above.

**36.** See, e.g., Curtis v. Hoosier Racing Tire Corp., 299 F.Supp.2d 777 (N.D. Ohio 2004); Ruzzo v. LaRose Enters., 748 A.2d 261 (R.I. 2000); McGraw–Edison Co. v. Northeastern Rural Elec. Membership Corp., 678 N.E.2d 1120 (Ind. 1997) (statute patterned substantially on § 402A); Wheelock v. Sport Kites, Inc., 839 F.Supp. 730 (D. Haw. 1993). Most of the difficult problems with disclaimers in strict tort involve their effectiveness in commercial contexts involving economic loss. See McNichols, Who Says that Strict Tort Disclaimers Can Never Be Effective? The Courts Cannot Agree, 28 Okla. L. Rev. 494 (1975); Note, 10 Tulsa L.J. 612 (1975).

**37.** Numerous cases are in accord. See, e.g., Levine v. Sears Roebuck & Co., 200 F.Supp.2d 180 (E.D.N.Y. 2002) (manufacturing defect claim dismissed where no evidence that alleged defect existed at time of sale); Cincinnati Cos. v. Ford Motor Co., 2001 WL 227362 (Ohio Ct. App. 2001)

(plaintiff failed to prove that electrical short-circuit that caused fire existed when car left manufacturer's control); York v. American Med. Sys., Inc., 166 F.3d 1216 (6th Cir. 1998) (Ohio law) (no proof that pinpoint hole in cylinder of inflatable penile prosthesis was caused by manufacturer); Southwire Co. v. Beloit Eastern Corp., 370 F.Supp. 842 (E.D. Pa. 1974) (plaintiff did not negate the substantial change alleged by manufacturer).

**38.** The principle could apply to a warnings defect if a third party forcibly removed a securely attached warning tag from the product after it left the defendant's control.

**39.** Restatement (2d) Torts § 402A cmt. *g.*

**40.** "Safe condition at the time of delivery by the seller will, however, include proper ... precautions required to permit the product to remain safe for a normal length of time when handled in a normal manner." Id.

**41.** Thus, if deterioration is likely to cause a product eventually to fail without warning in a dangerous manner, the manufacturer has a duty to warn users of this fact. See, e.g., Strauch v. Gates Rubber Co.,

that its product is safe—that its food is pure, that its vehicles steer properly, and that its other products are free of other untoward danger— not only at the time of sale but also for a reasonable period of time thereafter, perhaps for many years. This requirement, identical to that long employed in negligence, is not an exception to the rule that a defect must exist at the time the product leaves the defendant's hands, for it recognizes that a product may be defective at the time of sale if it then harbors a latent danger that eventually erupts.[42]

### Types of Plaintiffs

Section 402A makes clear that liability in no way depends on privity of contract between the plaintiff and the product supplier, as discussed above.[43] A passive user or consumer, such as a passenger in a defective automobile, a customer in a beauty shop whose hair is treated with a dangerously defective solution, or a repairer of a defective product, are all covered by the doctrine.[44] Yet, whether § 402A covers non-users and non-consumers, such as a person injured by a buyer's exploding soft drink bottle or a pedestrian hit by a defective car, is another question.[45] While "users" and "consumers" are defined broadly in comment *l*, the question of whether liability under § 402A extends to "innocent by-standers" (persons who are *not* "users" or "consumers") is a question that caveat (1) expressly leaves unresolved.[46]

While cases prior to § 402A may not have supported the extension of strict liability in tort to bystanders,[47] subsequent decisions have almost unanimously allowed foreseeable bystanders,[48] including res-

---

879 F.2d 1282 (5th Cir. 1989) (La. law). See § 10.6, below.

**42.** See § 10.6, below.

**43.** See Restatement (2d) Torts § 402A(2)(b). Comment *l* to that section explains that "it is not necessary that the ultimate user or consumer have acquired the product directly from the seller, although the rule applies equally if he does so. He may have acquired it through one or more intermediate dealers. It is not even necessary that the consumer have purchased the product at all. He may be a member of the family of the final purchaser, or his employee, or a guest at his table, or a mere donee from the purchaser."

**44.** Id.

**45.** On the extension of strict tort protection to bystanders, see Howes v. Hansen, 201 N.W.2d 825 (Wis. 1972); Cochran, Dangerous Products and Injured Bystanders, 81 Ky. L.J. 687, 725 (1993); Note, 38 U. Chi. L. Rev. 625 (1971); Annot., 33 A.L.R.3d 415 (1970) (extension of strict liability to bystanders).

**46.** This is explained in Restatement (2d) Torts § 402A cmt. *o*, which provides in part:

There may be no essential reason why such plaintiffs should not be brought within the scope of the protection afford-

ed, other than that they do not have the same reasons for expecting such protection as the consumer who buys a marketed product; but the social pressure which has been largely responsible for the development of the rule stated has been a consumers' pressure, and there is not the same demand for the protection of casual strangers.

**47.** See Restatement (2d) Torts § 402A cmt. *o*, which provides in part:

Thus far the courts, in applying the rule stated in this Section, have not gone beyond allowing recovery to users and consumers.... Casual bystanders ... have been denied recovery.

**48.** See, e.g., Stegemoller v. ACandS, Inc., 767 N.E.2d 974 (Ind. 2002) (spouse who developed disease due to exposure to asbestos residue on husband's clothing was domestic bystander with standing to sue asbestos manufacturers); Jones v. Nordic-Track, Inc., 550 S.E.2d 101 (Ga. 2001) (plaintiff who tripped over exercise machine was owed duty as one who might use, consume, or reasonably be affected by it); Kennedy v. Southern Cal. Edison Co., 219 F.3d 988 (9th Cir. 2000) (Cal. law) (jury issue whether decedent, whose leukemia allegedly caused by exposure to radiation from defective fuel rods at husband's work-

cuers,[49] to recover for their injuries caused by defective products.[50] Since bystanders have no choice in selecting products (and hence have no control over whether safety or price should be preferred in choosing between products), nor any control over inspecting products (no opportunity to "kick the tires") or the manner of their use, courts from an early date have reasoned that such plaintiffs deserve protection at least as much as users and consumers.[51] The extension of strict tort liability to bystanders normally does not burden manufacturers with additional precautions "for the reason that the same precautions required to protect the buyer or user would generally do the same for the bystander."[52] Assuming that a manufacturer or other seller can foresee a risk to bystanders,[53] the doctrine of strict liability in tort logically and fairly extends to such persons. Put simply, "[t]he price of dangerous products should include the losses that they cause to bystanders."[54] Similarly,

place, was foreseeable bystander), opinion withdrawn, 265 F.3d 1080 (9th Cir. 2001); Owens–Corning Fiberglas Corp. v. Garrett, 682 A.2d 1143 (Md. 1996) (decedent, who did not work directly with asbestos products but was exposed to them, was owed duty as bystander); Osborne v. International Harvester Co., 688 P.2d 390, 397 (Or. Ct. App. 1984) (plaintiff's car struck by defective truck; "Innocent victims should not be required to bear the burden of injuries caused by defective products."); Haumersen v. Ford Motor Co., 257 N.W.2d 7 (Iowa 1977) (car went out of control in school yard and ran over child); Passwaters v. General Motors Corp., 454 F.2d 1270 (8th Cir. 1972) (motorcycle passenger's leg lacerated by Ben–Hur-type ornamental wheel cover protrusions on car manufactured by defendant). In Caruth v. Mariani, 458 P.2d 371 (Ariz. Ct. App. 1969), modified, 463 P.2d 83 (Ariz. Ct. App. 1970), the court first held that bystanders could not recover and then, on a motion for rehearing after a change in composition of the court, held that they could.

**49.** See, e.g., Holloway v. Midland Risk Ins. Co., 832 So.2d 1004 (La. Ct. App. 2002) (professional rescuer's doctrine not applicable to firefighter suing manufacturer of rescue equipment for injuries from failure of equipment); McKernan ex rel. McKernan v. General Motors Corp., 3 P.3d 1261 (Kan. 2000) (policy reasons for "firefighter rule," precluding recovery by firemen against person whose negligence caused fire, do not apply in products liability context); McCoy v. American Suzuki Motor Corp., 961 P.2d 952 (Wash. 1998) (en banc) (motorist, struck by hit-and-run driver while stopped to help passengers in defectively designed vehicle that overturned on highway, could maintain products liability claim under rescue doctrine); Court v. Grzelinski, 379 N.E.2d 281 (Ill. 1978) (4–3 decision) (fire fighter injured when gas tank of burning car manufactured by defendant exploded;

"fireman's rule," prohibiting recovery by fireman against person whose negligence caused fire, held not to apply to strict tort products liability action); Fedorchick v. Massey–Ferguson, Inc., 438 F.Supp. 60 (E.D. Pa. 1977) (plaintiff struck by runaway crawler loader while attempting to rescue co-worker from being run over by vehicle); Buehler v. Whalen, 355 N.E.2d 99 (Ill. App. Ct. 1976) (rescuer burned while removing occupants from uncrashworthy car).

**50.** One curious exception is Pennsylvania, where § 402A operates only if a product is unsafe for its intended user, *not* for foreseeable victims. Hence, the doctrine does not protect victims of fires started by young children with disposable butane cigarette lighters, not equipped with a child-proof design, that are intended for adults. See Phillips v. Cricket Lighters, 841 A.2d 1000 (Pa. 2003).

**51.** See, e.g., Elmore v. American Motors Corp., 451 P.2d 84 (Cal. 1969).

**52.** Giberson v. Ford Motor Co., 504 S.W.2d 8, 12 (Mo. 1974) (court permitted strict tort suit by occupants of car involved in pile-up that occurred when engine in police car manufactured by defendant exploded in traffic, creating dense smoke that obscured vision).

**53.** See Kirk v. Michael Reese Hosp. & Med. Ctr., 513 N.E.2d 387, 394 (Ill. 1987) (passenger injured when driver, who consumed alcohol after taking prescription drugs, lost control of car; *held,* on inadequate warnings claim, that manufacturers "[could not] have reasonably foreseen that their drugs would be dispensed without warnings by the physicians, that the patient would be discharged from the hospital, drink alcohol, drive a car, lose control of his car, hit a tree, and injure the passenger [all] on the same day").

**54.** Cochran, Dangerous Products and Injured Bystanders, 81 Ky. L.J. 687, 725 (1993).

responsibility extends to other types of users, consumers, and other types of persons foreseeably placed at risk by a product defect.[55]

### Types of Defendants

Strict products liability in tort applies to all parties in the commercial chain of a product's distribution,[56] from manufacturers,[57] through intermediate dealers,[58] to retailers.[59] While the strict liability rule generally applies to a commercial business that provides products incidental to its principal business,[60] such as a movie theater which sells popcorn, and while it may apply to the sale by a specialty shop of a custom-designed product in the ordinary course of business,[61] it does not apply to the occasional private seller, such as a private individual who sells his or her used car.[62]

Because the question of whether manufacturers of defective component parts should be subject to strict products liability was an open question at the time § 402A was drafted and promulgated in the 1960s,[63]

---

**55.** See, e.g., Levey v. Yamaha Motor Corp., 825 A.2d 554 (N.J. Super. App. Div. 2003) (dealer's salesmen expected to demonstrate jet boat's operation to prospective customers).

**56.** See Restatement (2d) Torts § 402A cmt. *f* ("The rule stated in this Section applies to any person engaged in the business of selling products for use or consumption. It therefore applies to any manufacturer of such a product, to any wholesale or retail dealer or distributor, and to the operator of a restaurant.").

**57.** Manufacturers, who usually are responsible for causing a product to be defective, are the paradigmatic defendants in products liability cases. Manufacturers are defendants in a large majority of cases cited in this volume.

**58.** See ch. 15, below.

**59.** Note, however, that many states now have special statutes protecting retailers from strict products liability unless the manufacturer is bankrupt or outside the jurisdiction of the court. See § 15.2, below.

**60.** See Restatement (2d) Torts § 402A cmt. *f* ("It is not necessary that the seller be engaged solely in the business of selling such products. Thus the rule applies to the owner of a motion picture theater who sells popcorn or ice cream, either for consumption on the premises or in packages to be taken home."). Verily, the jurisprudence of products liability law now includes a popcorn case. See Tombank v. National Amusements, Inc., 1996 WL 240445, at *2 (Conn. Super. Ct. 1996) ("[i]t is not necessary that the seller be engaged solely in the business of selling such products").

**61.** See Sprung v. MTR Ravensburg Inc., 788 N.E.2d 620, 623 (N.Y. 2003) (while " 'casual' or 'occasional' sales are not subject to claims of strict liability," custom

fabricator of retractable floor sold in ordinary course of business subject to strict liability).

**62.** See Restatement (2d) Torts § 402A cmt. *f*:

> The rule does not ... apply to the occasional seller of food or other such products who is not engaged in that activity as a part of his business. Thus it does not apply to the housewife who, on one occasion, sells to her neighbor a jar of jam or a pound of sugar. Nor does it apply to the owner of an automobile who, on one occasion, sells it to his neighbor, or even sells it to a dealer in used cars, and this even though he is fully aware that the dealer plans to resell it. The basis for the rule is the ancient one of the special responsibility for the safety of the public undertaken by one who enters into the business of supplying human beings with products which may endanger the safety of their persons and property, and the forced reliance upon that undertaking on the part of those who purchase such goods. This basis is lacking in the case of the ordinary individual who makes the isolated sale, and he is not liable to a third person, or even to his buyer, in the absence of his negligence.

See, e.g., Allenberg v. Bentley Hedges Travel Serv., Inc., 22 P.3d 223 (Okla. 2001); Griffin Indus., Inc. v. Jones, 975 S.W.2d 100 (Ky. 1998). Compare Products Liability Restatement § 1 cmt. *c* (defect rule applies to manufacturers and other commercial sellers and distributors engaged in the business of distributing the type of product that harmed the plaintiff, including movie theater's sale of popcorn, but not to "casual sales").

**63.** See Goldberg v. Kollsman Instrument Corp., 191 N.E.2d 81 (N.Y. 1963) (as-

the ALI explicitly left this issue unresolved in a caveat.[64] Modern courts, however, uniformly hold manufacturers of such products strictly liable in tort where the risk is foreseeable and an intermediate assembler merely includes a defective component into a larger product.[65] But the case is otherwise where the assembler merges a nondefective component into a larger product in a manner that creates an unforeseeable danger to consumers.[66]

Many cases have examined the suitability of the doctrine of strict liability in tort under § 402A for particular types of defendants engaged in a large variety of miscellaneous sale and non-sale transactions involving a diversity of products. For example, courts have ruled on whether § 402A liability should be applied to raw material suppliers, bulk suppliers, repairers, successor corporations, governmental entities, employers, financiers, product lease transactions, bailments, licenses, franchises, services (including medical) in which products are provided incidentally, used products, electricity, real estate, publications of dangerous information, blood, and diseased or dangerous animals. Whether strict products liability is and should be allowed in each of these distinct situations requires examination of factors that are specific to each particular context, and each is separately considered below.[67]

### Types of Damages

By its terms, § 402A provides that a seller of a defective product "is subject to liability for physical harm thereby caused to the ultimate user or consumer, or to his property...."[68] All courts thus allow recovery under this doctrine for personal injury and death,[69] and the widely prevailing view is that recovery is allowable under strict products liability in tort for property damage alone.[70] Claims for suffering merely an increased risk of disease generally have failed.[71] Cases involving claims

sembler-manufacturer of airplane, but not supplier of defective component, an altimeter, held liable for crash).

**64.** See Restatement (2d) Torts § 402A caveat (3). But cmt. q remarks: "It is no doubt to be expected that where there is no change in the component part itself, but it is merely incorporated into something larger, the strict liability will be found to carry through to the ultimate user or consumer."

**65.** See § 15.3, below.

**66.** See id.

**67.** See chapters 15 and 16, below. The responsibility of other, miscellaneous types of defendants is treated contextually in various places throughout this book, such as the warnings duties of pharmacists and manufacturers of prescription drugs and medical devices, in § 9.6, below.

**68.** Restatement (2d) Torts § 402A(1).

**69.** On damages for personal injury and death in products liability actions, see 2 Frumer and Friedman, Products Liability § 13.03; 2 Madden & Owen on Products Liability ch. 17; 4A Am. Law Prod. Liab. 3d §§ 60:1, 60:10.

**70.** See, e.g., Jimenez v. Superior Court, 58 P.3d 450, 451 (Cal. 2002) ("a manufacturer, distributor, or retailer of a defective product is strictly liable in tort for any resulting harm to a person or to property other than the product itself"); Oasis Oil Corp. v. Koch Refining Co. L.P., 60 S.W.3d 248, 254 (Tex. App. 2001) (strict products liability causes of action are "for recovery of damages arising out of personal injury, death, or property damage allegedly caused by a defective product"); Calloway v. City of Reno, 993 P.2d 1259, 1270 (Nev. 2000). See also Seely v. White Motor Co., 403 P.2d 145, 152 (Cal. 1965) (Traynor, C.J.) ("Physical injury to property is so akin to personal injury that there is no reason for distinguishing them."). On damages for property damage in products liability actions, see generally 2 Frumer and Friedman, Products Liability § 13.02; 2 Madden & Owen on Products Liability § 17:11 and 17:12; 4A Am. Law Prod. Liab. 3d § 60:13.

**71.** See, e.g., Klein, A Model for Enhanced Risk Recovery in Tort, 56 Wash. & Lee L. Rev. 1173 (1999).

for damages under § 402A for emotional distress arise in a variety of contexts and sometimes are complex, but many courts allow recovery of such damages, to both direct victims[72] and bystanders,[73] under rules similar to those applied under the law of negligence.[74] Fear of cancer ("cancerphobia") or other disease, from contact with a harmful substance, is a special variety of claim for emotional distress.[75] Some courts have similarly allowed recovery for lost consortium to spouses of victims

**72.** Accordingly, most courts require a plaintiff to establish that the emotional distress was caused by—or that *it* caused— some injury, illness or other physical condition. See, e.g., Zeigler v. Fisher–Price, Inc., 261 F.Supp.2d 1047, 1053 (N.D. Iowa 2003) (homeowner could not recover emotional distress damages from manufacturer of defective toy that caused home to catch on fire where homeowner not injured in fire); Palmer v. Nan King Restaurant, Inc., 798 A.2d 583, 583 (N.H. 2002) (to recover for emotional distress from biting into used bandage in food served by defendant restaurant, plaintiff "must demonstrate physical symptoms of her distress"); Slaton v. Vansickle, 872 P.2d 929 (Okla. 1994) (owner of defective gun could not recover for emotional distress from accidentally killing person while handling gun because owner suffered no injury); Payton v. Abbott Labs., 437 N.E.2d 171, 181 (Mass. 1982) (DES daughters, not yet suffering vaginal cancer, could not recover for emotional distress from increased likelihood that they would incur such cancer in the future).

**73.** See, e.g., Ortiz v. HPM Corp., 285 Cal.Rptr. 728 (Ct. App. 1991) (plaintiff found the limp but alive, oxygen-depleted and bleeding body of her co-worker husband, who had been fixing a plastic injection molding machine, still being squashed between giant cylinder and stationary part of machine; recovery allowed under rules of Thing v. La Chusa, 771 P.2d 814 (Cal. 1989)); Pearsall v. Emhart Indus., 599 F.Supp. 207 (E.D. Pa. 1984) (mother-wife allowed to recover in strict tort against manufacturer of defective smoke alarm for distress at discovering smoldering bodies of two children and husband shortly after their deaths in burning house); Gnirk v. Ford Motor Co., 572 F.Supp. 1201 (D.S.D. 1983); Kennedy v. McKesson Co., 448 N.E.2d 1332 (N.Y. 1983) (dentist, who killed patient, could not recover for emotional distress against repairer of anesthetic machine for reversing oxygen and nitrous oxide decals). *Contra,* Blackmon v. American Home Prods. Corp., 267 F.Supp.2d 667, 676–77 (S.D. Tex. 2003)(parents could not recover emotional distress damages against vaccine manufacturers for children's serious neurological injuries from mercury used as preservative in vaccines; no recovery of

emotional distress as bystanders because distress did not result from "shocking accident" but from "routine vaccination"); Straub v. Fisher and Paykel Health Care, 990 P.2d 384 (Utah 1999) (respiratory therapist could not recover for emotional distress from witnessing defective ventilator kill patient because therapist was never personally in danger); Compare Bray v. Marathon Corp., 553 S.E.2d 477 (S.C. Ct. App. 2001) (same; employee operating trash compactor in which co-worker crushed to death), aff'd in part, rev'd in part, 588 S.E.2d 93 (S.C. 2003); Maldonado v. National Acme Co., 73 F.3d 642 (6th Cir. 1996) (Mich. law) (worker, almost hit by deadly metal part flung viciously from machine into co-worker's head, could not sue as bystander but could sue as direct victim who feared for his own safety).

**74.** At least one court has held that damages for emotional distress are not recoverable in strict liability because such damages are based on fault. See Pasquale v. Speed Prod. Eng'g, 654 N.E.2d 1365 (Ill. 1995) (clutch parts on race car burst through defective bellhousing and flew into crowd of spectators, partially decapitating plaintiff's wife, revealing interior of her head including backs of her eyeballs, and spewing bone marrow, blood, and brain matter on plaintiff's face with such force as to leave marks for weeks; held, no recovery in strict tort for emotional distress). On damages for emotional distress in products liability actions, see 2 Frumer and Friedman, Products Liability § 13.03 [9]; 2 Madden & Owen on Products Liability §§ 17:8 and 17:9; 4A Am. Law Prod. Liab. 3d §§ 60:20–60:35.

**75.** See, e.g., Redick, Twenty–First Century Toxicogenomics Meets Twentieth Century Mass Tort Precedent: Is There a Duty to Warn of a Hypothetical Harm to an "Eggshell" Gene?, 42 Washburn L.J. 547 (2003); Klein, Fear of Disease and the Puzzle of Futures Cases in Tort, 35 U.C. Davis L. Rev. 965 (2002); Henderson and Twerski, Asbestos Litigation Gone Mad: Exposure–Based Recovery for Increased Risk, Mental Distress, and Medical Monitoring, 53 S.C. L. Rev. 815, 823 (2002); T. Dworkin, Fear of Disease and Delayed Manifestation Injuries: A Solution or a Pandora's Box?, 53 Fordham L. Rev. 527, 576 (1984).

killed or injured by defective products.[76] Yet many courts have refused, in this context as in others, to permit claims by parents and by children for the loss of companionship arising out of injury to the other.[77] Another type of damages claim seeks recovery of damages for medical monitoring of victims exposed to some toxic substance, or defective medical device, where future harm is possible but difficult to detect.[78]

Since the inception of § 402A, a minor debate has swirled around the issue of whether recovery in strict liability in tort should be allowed for pure economic loss,[79] including damage a defective product causes to

**76.** See, e.g., John Crane, Inc. v. Jones, 586 S.E.2d 26 (Ga. Ct. App. 2003) (death from asbestos exposure); Jones v. General Motors Corp., 2002 WL 31956941 (Mich. Ct. App. 2002) (serious injuries from seatbelt malfunction in rollover); Knight v. Just Born, Inc., 2000 WL 924624, at *15 (D. Or. 2000) (husband's mouth burned by defective candy); Timms v. Verson Allsteel Press Co., 520 F.Supp. 1147 (N.D. Ga. 1981) (husband's fingers crushed in press). Compare General Motors Corp. v. McGee, 837 So.2d 1010 (Fla. Dist. Ct. App. 2002) (severely-burned husband and wife each recovered loss of consortium in action against manufacturer of their vehicle that exploded when its gas tank was pierced in collision); Klein v. Sears Roebuck & Co., 773 F.2d 1421 (4th Cir. 1985) (Md. law) (wife's recovery of $104,000 for loss of husband's consortium from hand injury in lawn mower reversed for insufficient evidence).

**77.** See, e.g., Hosler v. Caterpillar, Inc., 710 N.E.2d 193 (Ind. Ct. App. 1999) (denying minor child's loss of consortium claim for loss of worker father killed when caught under and crushed by dump truck); Green v. A.B. Hagglund & Soner, 634 F.Supp. 790 (D. Idaho 1986) (same); Kershner v. Beloit Corp., 611 F.Supp. 943 (D. Me. 1985) (denying children's claim for loss of injured parent's society); Siciliano v. Capitol City Shows, Inc., 475 A.2d 19 (N.H. 1984) (4–1 decision) (denying parents' claim for loss of society of minor children injured and killed on amusement ride). But see, e.g., allowing such recovery, Owens v. American Home Products Corp., 203 F.Supp.2d 748, 757 (S.D. Tex. 2002) (allowing parents' claims for loss of consortium of children injured by mercury-contaminated vaccines); Darbone v. State, 815 So.2d 943 (La. Ct. App. 2002) (allowing parents' claims for loss of consortium of three daughters injured in car accident).

**78.** Medical monitoring has been defined as "the expense related to the periodic diagnostic evaluation of an individual or group of individuals in order to detect and/or prevent an anticipated medical outcome. It can also include scientific research necessary to determine the root cause of a particular product failure, as well as, re-search exploring more efficient methods of diagnosis." Gallacher, Medical Monitoring of Medical Devices: An Industry–Based Solution Provides the Best Results, 10 Loy. Consumer L. Rev. 239, 239–40 (1998). See, e.g., Bower v. Westinghouse Elec. Co., 522 S.E.2d 424 (W. Va. 1999); Burns v. Jaquays Mining Corp., 752 P.2d 28 (Ariz. Ct. App. 1987); Harbour and Splittgerber, Making the Case Against Medical Monitoring: Has The Shine Faded on This Trend?, 70 Def. Couns. J. 315 (2003) (discussing cases rejecting such claims and problems with class certification); Henderson and Twerski, Asbestos Litigation Gone Mad: Exposure–Based Recovery for Increased Risk, Mental Distress, and Medical Monitoring, 53 S.C. L. Rev. 815, 836 (2002); Geistfeld, The Analytics of Duty: Medical Monitoring and Related Forms of Economic Loss, 88 Va. L. Rev. 1921 (2002); DeVries and Gallacher, Medical Monitoring in Drug and Medical Device Cases: Taking the Temperature of a New Theory, 68 Def. Couns. J. 163 (2001); Gallacher, Maskin, Cailteux, and McLaren, Medical Monitoring: A Viable Remedy for Deserving Plaintiffs or Tort Law's Most Expensive Consolation Prize?, 27 Wm. Mitchell L. Rev. 521 (2000); Garner et al., Medical Monitoring: The Evolution of a Cause of Action, 30 Envtl. L. Rep. 10024 (2000); V. Schwartz, Behrens, Burton, and Groninger, Medical Monitoring: Should Tort Law Say Yes?, 34 Wake Forest L. Rev. 1057 (1999); Klein, Rethinking Medical Monitoring, 64 Brook. L. Rev. 1 (1998); Comment, 82 Or. L. Rev. 529 (2003) (viability of such claims); Note, 102 Colum. L. Rev. 1659 (2002) (class certification of medical monitoring claims); Note, 17 Rev. Litig. 551 (1998) (medical monitoring and Daubert); Note, 7 U. Fla. J.L. & Pub. Pol'y 127 (1995) (as remedy in power line radiation cases).

**79.** "In the context of products liability cases, economic loss generally means pecuniary damage that occurs through loss of value or use of the goods sold or the cost of repair together with consequential lost profits when there has been no claim of personal injury or damage to other property." Cooperative Power Assn. v. Westing-

itself.[80] In time, spearheaded by a decision of the United States Supreme Court,[81] a great majority of courts have come to apply the "economic loss rule" to such cases, denying recovery in strict products liability (or negligence) for pure economic loss.[82] Some courts, however, do allow a limited exception to the general bar of recovery for pure economic loss when such damages result from product defects that present a hazard to property or human safety.[83] In a new form of class action litigation,

house Elec. Corp., 493 N.W.2d 661, 663 n.5 (N.D. 1992). On damages for economic loss in products liability actions, see, e.g., Rusch, Products Liability Trapped by History: Our Choices of Rules Rules Our Choices, 76 Temple L. Rev. 739 (2003); 2 Frumer and Friedman, Products Liability §§ 9.05[1][c] and 13.07 [1]; 2 Madden & Owen on Products Liability § 17:13; 4A Am. Law Prod. Liab. 3d § 60:36–60; White and Summers, UCC § 10–5; Products Liability Restatement § 21.

**80.** See, e.g., Tennessee Farmers Mut. Ins. Co. v. Ford Motor Co., 2002 WL 1332492 (Tenn. Ct. App. 2002) (no strict products liability recovery where spontaneous combustion destroyed vehicle but did not cause personal injuries nor damage to other property); Progressive Ins. Co. v. General Motors Corp., 749 N.E.2d 484, 486 (Ind. 2001) ("there is no recovery . . . where the claim is based on damage to the defective product itself"); Saratoga Fishing Co. v. J.M. Martinac & Co., 520 U.S. 875 (1997) (*East River*'s bar of damages to "product itself" under economic loss rule does not apply to equipment owner later purchases and attaches to original product, which instead is "other property"). Compare Santor v. A & M Karagheusian, Inc., 207 A.2d 305 (N.J. 1965) (recoverable), with Seely v. White Motor Co., 403 P.2d 145 (Cal. 1965) (Traynor, C.J.) (not recoverable). See generally Annot., 72 A.L.R.4th 12 (1989) (recovery in strict tort for damages to product alone).

**81.** See East River Steamship Corp. v. Transamerica Delaval, Inc., 476 U.S. 858, 871 (1986).

**82.** See, e.g., Herbert A. Sullivan, Inc. v. Utica Mut. Ins. Co., 788 N.E.2d 522, 543 (Mass. 2003) ("purely economic losses are unrecoverable in tort and strict liability actions in the absence of personal injury or property damage"); Catalano v. Heraeus Kulzer, Inc., 759 N.Y.S.2d 159 (App. Div. 2003) (dentist whose patients were injured by defective dental restorations could not recover for loss of professional reputation); Russell v. Deere & Co., 61 P.3d 955, 959 (Or. Ct. App. 2003) ("mere economic loss unaccompanied by physical injury to property will not suffice for a product liability claim"); Jimenez v. Superior Court, 58 P.3d 450, 456 (Cal. 2002) ("damages available under strict products liability do not include

economic loss"); Calloway v. City of Reno, 993 P.2d 1259, 1270 (Nev. 2000) (strict products liability unavailable for purely economic loss); Alloway v. General Marine Indus., 695 A.2d 264 (N.J. 1997); Airport Rent–A–Car, Inc. v. Prevost Car, Inc., 660 So.2d 628 (Fla. 1995) (rejecting exceptions for "no alternative remedy," "sudden calamitous events," and post-sale duties to warn); Rockport Pharmacy, Inc. v. Digital Simplistics, Inc., 53 F.3d 195 (8th Cir. 1995) (Mo. law) (lost data in defective computer system merely commercial loss, not "other property"); Casa Clara Condominium Ass'n, Inc. v. Charley Toppino & Sons, 620 So.2d 1244 (Fla. 1993); Cooperative Power Assn. v. Westinghouse Elec. Corp., 493 N.W.2d 661 (N.D. 1992) (good discussion of various approaches). *Contra*, Alaskan Oil, Inc. v. Central Flying Serv., Inc., 975 F.2d 553 (8th Cir. 1992) (applying Arkansas' minority rule allowing strict tort liability for purely economic damages). On the economic loss rule, see Rusch, Products Liability Trapped by History: Our Choice of Rules Rules Our Choices, 76 Temp. L. Rev. 739 (2003).

Some products liability statutes explicitly exclude recovery for economic loss. See, e.g., Cincinnati v. Beretta U.S.A. Corp., 768 N.E.2d 1136, 1146 (Ohio 2002) (applying Ohio Rev. Code § 2307.71(M), excluding economic loss from definition of "product liability claim"); Wash. Rev. Code § 7.72.010(6) (economic loss excluded from definition of recoverable "harm").

**83.** See, e.g., Heritage Harbour, L.L.C. v. John J. Reynolds, Inc., 795 A.2d 806, 812 (Md. Ct. App. 2002) ("to circumvent the Economic Loss Doctrine, appellants must allege the existence of a serious risk of injury to persons or property"); Morris v. Osmose Wood Preserving, 667 A.2d 624 (Md. 1995) (tort recovery precluded without "a clear, serious, and unreasonable risk of death or personal injury"); Tioga Pub. Sch. Dist. #15 v. United States Gypsum Co., 984 F.2d 915 (8th Cir. 1993) (N.D. law) (recovery of asbestos abatement costs allowed); 80 South Eighth St. Ltd. P'ship v. W.R. Grace Co., 486 N.W.2d 393 (Minn. 1992) (same); Touchet Valley Grain Growers, Inc. v. Opp & Seibold Gen. Constr., 831 P.2d 724 (Wash. 1992). See also Martin Rispens & Son v. Hall Farms, Inc., 601 N.E.2d 429 (Ind. Ct. App. 1992) (recovery allowable un-

courts in recent years have been asked to allow recovery for the reduction in value of a product because it contains a dangerous condition, such as a particular type of tire likely to blow out or SUV likely to roll over. The courts have been singularly unreceptive to these "no-injury" claims, whether grounded in strict liability in tort or other theory of recovery.[84]

Punitive damages, despite the controversy they engender, are recoverable in most states on claims for strict products liability in tort upon sufficient proof of fraud or recklessness.[85] Although such damages are a creature of the common law, they increasingly are subject to judicial, statutory, and constitutional reform.[86]

## Adoption of § 402A

The American Law Institute approved *Restatement (Second) of Torts* § 402A at its annual meeting in 1964[87] and published it the following year in volume 2 of the *Second Restatement*. With a gusto unmatched in the annals of Restatements of the Law,[88] the new doctrine swept across the face of America as courts and legislatures embraced § 402A and the bold new doctrine that it proclaimed: "strict" liability in tort for harm caused by defective products.[89] Tort law has probably never witnessed such a rapid, widespread, and altogether explosive change in a rule and theory of legal responsibility.[90]

der state statute for "sudden, major damage to property," but not for "gradually evolving damage to property or economic losses from such damage"). See generally Ausness, Tort Liability for Asbestos Removal Costs, 73 Or. L. Rev. 505 (1994).

**84.** See, e.g., Frank v. DaimlerChrysler Corp., 741 N.Y.S.2d 9, 16 (Sup. Ct. App. Div. 2002) (rejecting "no-injury" claims based on strict liability and other causes of action because "it would be manifestly unfair to require a manufacturer to become, in essence, an indemnifier for a loss that may never occur"). See also Ziegelmann v. DaimlerChrysler Corp., 649 N.W.2d 556, 565 (N.D. 2002) (based on negligence, fraud, and deceit, recovery of diminution-in-value damages for vehicle design hazard that might cause future injury was "simply too speculative to constitute a legally cognizable tort injury"); In re Bridgestone/Firestone, Inc. Tires Prod. Liab. Litig., 155 F.Supp.2d 1069, 1087 (S.D. Ind. 2001) (plaintiffs could not recover for emotional distress from possibility that their defective tires might suffer future tread separations causing their vehicles to roll over, nor for the resulting lower resale price they might one day receive for their vehicles, because "[t]hese simply are not cognizable tort injuries"). See generally White, Reverberations from the Collision of Tort and Warranty, 53 S.C. L. Rev. 1067 (2002).

**85.** See § 18.4, below.

**86.** See §§ 18.6 and 18.7, below.

**87.** The ALI Reporter, Dean Prosser, presented this section for consideration by the Institute in Restatement (Second) of Torts, Tentative Draft No. 10, April 20, 1964.

**88.** At the June 8, 1993 meeting of the Consultative Group on the Products Liability Restatement, Professor Geoffrey Hazard, then Director of the ALI, reported that § 402A had been cited in judicial opinions more than any other section of any Restatement.

**89.** In 1963, of course, California had already adopted strict products liability in tort in *Greenman*, and New York had more or less followed suit in *Goldberg v. Kollsman Instrument Corp.*, 191 N.E.2d 81, 83 (N.Y. 1963) (4–3 decision), decided three and a half months after *Greenman*. Leaning heavily on *Greenman* for support, the New York Court of Appeals in *Goldberg* held an aircraft manufacturer strictly liable to a passenger killed in a crash due to a defective altimeter in the plane. Basing its decision on breach of implied warranty in *tort*, the court held that privity of contract was not required.

**90.** See, e.g., Prosser, The Fall of the Citadel (Strict Liability to the Consumer), 50 Minn. L. Rev. 791, 793–94 (1966) (characterizing the adoption of strict products liability in the early 1960s as "the most rapid and altogether spectacular overturn of an established rule in the entire history of the law of torts"). See also V. Nolan and

Connecticut, Illinois, Kentucky, and New Jersey all adopted the principles of § 402A in 1965.[91] In 1966, four more states embraced the doctrine—Mississippi, Ohio, Pennsylvania, and Tennessee[92]—as did four more in 1967—Minnesota, Oregon, Texas, and Wisconsin.[93] By the time of Dean Prosser's death in 1971, twenty-eight states had adopted the doctrine, and, by the mid–1970s, over forty states had embraced the principle of strict manufacturer liability in tort for the sale of defective products.[94] The last state to adopt the doctrine was Wyoming, in 1986,[95] by which time a total of forty-five states, the District of Columbia, and the Virgin Islands had all embraced a doctrine of strict products liability in tort.[96] As of 2005, the only states that still formally reject the doctrine

E. Ursin, Understanding Enterprise Liability 105 (1995) (characterizing the spread of § 402A doctrine as "the strict products liability 'revolution,' the most spectacular episode of judicial creativity in the history of American tort law").

**91.** See Garthwait v. Burgio, 216 A.2d 189 (Conn. 1965); Suvada v. White Motor Co., 210 N.E.2d 182, 187 (Ill. 1965); Dealers Transp. Co. v. Battery Distrib. Co., 402 S.W.2d 441, 446–47 (Ky. 1965, as modified 1966); Santor v. A. & M. Karagheusian, Inc., 207 A.2d 305 (N.J. 1965).

**92.** See State Stove Mfg. Co. v. Hodges, 189 So.2d 113, 119 (Miss. 1966); Lonzrick v. Republic Steel Corp., 218 N.E.2d 185, 192–93 (Ohio 1966); Webb v. Zern, 220 A.2d 853 (Pa. 1966); Ford Motor Co. v. Lonon, 398 S.W.2d 240 (Tenn. 1966).

**93.** See McCormack v. Hankscraft Co., 154 N.W.2d 488, 501 (Minn. 1967) (dictum); Heaton v. Ford Motor Co., 435 P.2d 806, 808 (Or. 1967); McKisson v. Sales Affiliates, Inc., 416 S.W.2d 787 (Tex. 1967); Dippel v. Sciano, 155 N.W.2d 55 (Wis. 1967).

**94.** See Priest, The Invention of Enterprise Liability: A Critical History of the Intellectual Foundations of Modern Tort Law, 14 J. Legal Stud. 461, 518 (1985).

**95.** In Ogle v. Caterpillar Tractor Co., 716 P.2d 334 (Wyo. 1986).

**96.** The adopting decisions and statutes were as follows: *Alabama*: Casrell v. Altec Indus., Inc., 335 So.2d 128 (Ala. 1976), and Atkins v. American Motors Corp. 335 So.2d 134 (Ala. 1976); *Alaska*: Clary v. Fifth Ave. Chrysler Ctr., Inc., 454 P.2d 244 (Alaska 1969); *Arizona*: O.S. Stapley Co. v. Miller, 447 P.2d 248 (Ariz. 1968), and also Shannon v. Butler Homes, Inc., 428 P.2d 990, 993 (Ariz. 1967) (en banc) (dictum); *Arkansas*: Ark. Code. Ann. § 4–86–102 (1973); *California*: Greenman v. Yuba Power Prods., Inc., 377 P.2d 897 (Cal. 1963); *Colorado*: Hiigel v. General Motors Corp., 544 P.2d 983 (Colo. 1975); *Connecticut*: Garthwait v. Burgio, 216 A.2d 189 (Conn. 1965); *District of Columbia*: The early tangled case law on strict liability in tort in the District of Columbia never expressly adopts the doc-

trine, but it surely exists by 1985: Picker X–Ray Corp. v. General Motors Corp., 185 A.2d 919 (D.C. 1962), Cottom v. McGuire Funeral Serv., Inc., 262 A.2d 807 (D.C. 1970) (dictum), and Payne v. Soft Sheen Prods., Inc., 486 A.2d 712 (D.C. 1985); *Florida*: West v. Caterpillar Tractor Co., Inc. 336 So.2d 80, 87 (Fla. 1976); *Georgia*: Ga. Code Ann. § 105–106 (1968), subsequently recodified at § 51–1–11 (1975); *Hawaii*: Stewart v. Budget Rent–A–Car Corp., 470 P.2d 240 (Haw. 1970); *Idaho*: Shields v. Morton Chem. Co., 518 P.2d 857 (Idaho 1974); *Illinois*: Suvada v. White Motor Co., 210 N.E.2d 182 (Ill. 1965); *Indiana*: Cornette v. Searjeant Metal Prods., Inc., 258 N.E.2d 652 (Ind. Ct. App. 1970); *Iowa*: Hawkeye–Security Ins. Co. v. Ford Motor Co., 174 N.W.2d 672 (Iowa 1970); *Kansas*: Brooks v. Dietz, 545 P.2d 1104 (Kan. 1976); *Kentucky*: Dealers Transp. Co. v. Battery Distrib. Co., 402 S.W.2d 441 (Ky.App. 1965, as modified 1966); *Louisiana*: Weber v. Fidelity & Cas. Ins. Co., 250 So.2d 754 (La. 1971); *Maine*: Me. Rev. Stat. Ann. tit. 14 § 221 (1973); *Maryland*: Phipps v. General Motors Corp., 363 A.2d 955 (Md. 1976); *Minnesota*: McCormack v. Hankscraft Co., 154 N.W.2d 488 (Minn. 1967); *Mississippi*: State Stove Mfg. Co. v. Hodges, 189 So.2d 113 (Miss. 1966); *Missouri*: Keener v. Dayton Elec. Mfg. Co., 445 S.W.2d 362 (Mo. 1969); *Montana*: Brandenburger v. Toyota Motor Sales, U.S.A., Inc., 513 P.2d 268 (Mont. 1973); *Nebraska*: Kohler v. Ford Motor Co., 191 N.W.2d 601 (Neb. 1971); *Nevada*: Shoshone Coca–Cola Bottling Co. v. Dolinski, 420 P.2d 855 (Nev. 1966); *New Hampshire*: Buttrick v. Arthur Lessard & Sons, 260 A.2d 111 (N.H. 1969); *New Jersey*: Santor v. A & M Karagheusian, Inc., 207 A.2d 305 (N.J. 1965); *New Mexico*: Stang v. Hertz Corp., 497 P.2d 732 (N.M. 1972); *New York*: Codling v. Paglia, 298 N.E.2d 622 (N.Y. 1973); *North Dakota*: Johnson v. American Motors Corp., 225 N.W.2d 57 (N.D. 1974); *Ohio*: Lonzrick v. Republic Steel Corp., 218 N.E.2d 185 (Ohio 1966); *Oklahoma*: Marathon Battery Co. v. Kilpatrick, 418 P.2d 900 (Okla. 1965); *Ore-*

of strict products liability in tort are Delaware, Massachusetts, Michigan, North Carolina, and Virginia, as discussed below. Although these states still refuse to join the strict tort bandwagon, each applies the great bulk of developed § 402A jurisprudence, either through the law of warranty or the law of negligence, to sellers of defective products.

In Delaware, the court refused to adopt § 402A in *Cline v. Prowler Industries of Maryland, Inc.*[97] because it believed that the legislature's adoption of Article 2 of the Uniform Commercial Code preempted the products liability issue. Yet, by basing warranty liability in products liability cases on tort law standards of ordinary and reasonable prudence and care, Delaware courts have implicitly adopted the core precepts applied to design and warnings responsibility in both negligence law and *Restatement (Second) of Torts* § 402A.[98]

In Massachusetts, the courts formally apply Article 2 to products liability cases, but they use § 402A cases for guidance, if not authority. In *Vassallo v. Baxter Healthcare Corp.*,[99] for example, the court observed that "liability under the implied warranty of merchantability in Massachusetts is 'congruent in nearly all respects with the principles expressed in Restatement (Second) of Torts § 402A.'"[100]

In Michigan, the courts have indicated in a number of decisions the practical congruence in that state between negligence, warranty, and strict products liability in tort.[101] In *Owens v. Allis–Chalmers Corp.*,[102] for

*gon*: Heaton v. Ford Motor Co., 435 P.2d 806 (Or. 1967); *Pennsylvania*: Webb v. Zern, 220 A.2d 853 (Pa. 1966); *Puerto Rico*: Mendoza v. Cerveceria Corona, Inc., 97 D.P.R. 499 (1969); *Rhode Island*: Ritter v. Narragansett Elec. Co., 283 A.2d 255 (R.I. 1971); *South Carolina*: S.C. Code Ann. § 15–73–10 et seq. (1974); *South Dakota*: Engberg v. Ford Motor Co., 205 N.W.2d 104 (S.D. 1973); *Tennessee*: Ford Motor Co. v. Lonon, 398 S.W.2d 240 (Tenn. 1966); *Texas*: McKisson v. Sales Affiliates, Inc., 416 S.W.2d 787 (Tex. 1967); *Utah*: Ernest W. Hahn, Inc. v. Armco Steel Co., 601 P.2d 152 (Utah 1979); *Vermont*: Zaleskie v. Joyce, 333 A.2d 110 (Vt. 1975); *Virgin Islands*: Gumbs v. International Harvester, Inc., 718 F.2d 88 (3d Cir. 1983) (V.I. law); *Washington*: Ulmer v. Ford Motor Co., 452 P.2d 729, 735 (Wash. 1969); *West Virginia*: Morningstar v. Black & Decker Mfg. Co., 253 S.E.2d 666 (W.Va. 1979); *Wisconsin*: Dippel v. Sciano, 155 N.W.2d 55 (Wisc. 1967); *Wyoming*: Ogle v. Caterpillar Tractor Co., 716 P.2d 334 (Wyo. 1986).

For other collections of citations to adopting cases and statutes, see 1 Frumer and Friedman, Products Liability § 8.03[1]; 2 Am. Law of Prod. Liab. 3d §§ 16:8–16:27; Annot., 13 A.L.R.3d 1057, § 4 (1967); Prod. Liab. Rep. (CCH) ¶¶ 4060–70; West v. Caterpillar Tractor Co., Inc., 336 So.2d 80, 87 n.1 (Fla. 1976).

**97.** 418 A.2d 968 (Del. 1980).

**98.** See Graham v. Pittsburgh Corning Corp., 593 A.2d 567, 571 (Del. Super. Ct. 1990) (warnings; duty based on conduct of manufacturer of reasonable prudence); Nacci v. Volkswagen of Am., Inc., 325 A.2d 617, 620 (Del. Super. Ct. 1974) (defective design; reasonable fitness determined by whether ordinarily prudent manufacturer would have adopted alternative design).

**99.** 696 N.E.2d 909 (Mass. 1998).

**100.** Id. at 923 (citing Commonwealth v. Johnson Insulation, 682 N.E.2d 1323 (Mass. 1997), quoting Back v. Wickes Corp., 378 N.E.2d 964 (Mass. 1978)).

See also *Vassallo*, 696 N.E.2d at 924 n.19, quoting Hayes v. Ariens Co., 462 N.E.2d 273 (Mass. 1984) ("defendant cannot be found negligent without also breaching implied warranty of merchantability").

**101.** See Owens v. Allis–Chalmers Corp., 268 N.W.2d 291, 293 (Mich. Ct. App. 1978), aff'd, 326 N.W.2d 372 (Mich. 1982) ("the requisite elements for a cause of action based upon strict liability in tort are congruent to those for breach of warranty"). See also Smith v. E.R. Squibb & Sons, 273 N.W.2d 476 (Mich. 1979) (issue of warnings adequacy identical under implied warranty and negligence). *But cf.* Lagalo v. Allied Corp., 577 N.W.2d 462 (Mich. 1998) (noting differences between negligence and implied warranty).

**102.** *Owens*, 268 N.W.2d at 293.

example, the court remarked that "the requisite elements for a cause of action based upon strict liability in tort are congruent to those for breach of warranty."

The North Carolina courts never have adopted § 402A or anything resembling it, and they probably never will. In the height of tort reform in the mid–1990s, a coalition of medical and other enterprises, funded in part by the tobacco industry, steered a bill through the legislature which, among other things, assured that North Carolina courts could not adopt the doctrine of strict liability in tort. In no uncertain terms, the statute declares that "[t]here shall be no strict liability in tort in product liability actions."[103] However, the North Carolina statute, which provides a fairly comprehensive set of rules governing products liability law, adopts a number of plaintiff-protective principles of modern products liability law put in place by courts from other states which operate under the strict tort doctrine.[104] Moreover, because the statute makes no effort to displace warranty law under the state's commercial code,[105] North Carolina's composite products liability law in action may not be too far removed from the law of other jurisdictions.

In Virginia, the court seemingly equates the negligence basis of liability with that of warranty, in terms that sound remarkably like strict liability in tort. In *Jeld-Wen, Inc. v. Gamble*,[106] for example, the court observed that " 'the standard of safety of goods imposed on . . . the manufacturer of a product is essentially the same whether the theory of liability is labeled warranty or negligence.' " Under both theories of recovery, " 'a plaintiff must show (1) that the [product was] unreasonably dangerous either for the use to which [it] would ordinarily be put or for some other reasonably foreseeable purpose, and (2) that the unreasonably dangerous condition existed when the goods left the manufacturer's hands.' "[107]

Many courts have pointed to the functional equivalence of strict tort liability and negligence in design and warnings cases,[108] and, at least the Iowa Supreme Court has followed the *Third Restatement*'s approach of discarding reference to such doctrinal categories and speaking solely in terms of design or warnings defect claims.[109] In most states, in design

---

**103.** See N.C. Gen. Stat. § 99B–1.1.

**104.** For example, the statute imposes a post-sale duty on manufactures to warn consumers of defects discovered in their products after initial distribution. See N.C. Gen. Stat. § 99B–5(a)(2). The duty is one of due care, the standard of responsibility normally adopted even in "strict" tort states.

**105.** See N.C. Gen. Stat. § 99B–1.2.

**106.** 501 S.E.2d 393 (Va. 1998).

**107.** Id. at 396 (citing Morgen Indus., Inc. v. Vaughan, 471 S.E.2d 489 (Va. 1996)). In *Morgen Industries*, the court observed that a product may be "unreasonably dangerous if it is defective in assembly or manufacture, unreasonably dangerous in design, or unaccompanied by adequate warnings

concerning its hazardous properties." 471 S.E.2d at 492.

**108.** See, e.g., Banks v. ICI Am., Inc., 450 S.E.2d 671, 673 n.3 (Ga. 1994) (design); Olson v. Prosoco, Inc., 522 N.W.2d 284, 289 (Iowa 1994) ("any posited distinction between strict liability and negligence principles is illusory"; warnings claims lie in negligence, not strict liability in tort); Crislip v. TCH Liquidating Co., 556 N.E.2d 1177, 1183 (Ohio 1990) ("the standard imposed upon the defendant in a strict liability claim grounded upon an inadequate warning is the same as that imposed in a negligence claim based upon inadequate warning").

**109.** See Wright v. Brooke Group Limited, 652 N.W.2d 159, 164–69 (Iowa 2002) (design defect claims stand on their own

and warnings cases alike, both the process and results of litigation are generally unaffected by whether the basis of tort recovery is formally called "negligence" or "strict."[110] The same may be said with respect to implied warranty as the basis of products liability recovery, except for secondary doctrine on such matters of disclaimers, privity, notice, and statutes of limitations.[111] This suggests that, despite some real variations in secondary doctrine,[112] the fundamentals of modern products liability law and litigation should continue broadly to evolve in quite similar respects across America, even in the five renegade states which formally have refused to follow that aspect of the products liability revolution which classifies the basis of liability in tort as "strict."

## Variations on § 402A

### *Judicial Variations*

Most states embraced the theory of strict products liability in tort by simply "adopting" § 402A.[113] Since that time, however, the products liability jurisprudence of every state has moved far beyond the original formulation of the doctrine as described in § 402A and its comments.[114] Some states, on various aspects of products liability doctrine, have headed off in rather strange directions. Pennsylvania, for example, while beginning its 402A jurisprudence with all normalcy,[115] subsequently veered off the common pathways for defining defectiveness into a doctrinal thicket that still ensnares whoever attempts to understand its strict

without reference to strict liability in tort or negligence).

**110.** See § 5.9, below. Formerly, a major difference between the two theories was that a plaintiff's simple contributory negligence barred recovery in negligence but not in strict liability in tort. In most jurisdictions today, however, comparative fault operates equally on both types of claim. See ch. 13, below.

**111.** See § 5.9, below.

**112.** One state supreme court judge has critically characterized the products liability law system in this nation as "the peculiarly American system of fifty uncoordinated, separate schemes of tort law coexisting within one industrial nation." Blankenship v. General Motors Corp., 406 S.E.2d 781, 785 (W. Va. 1991) (Neely, J.).

**113.** See, e.g., Heaton v. Ford Motor Co., 435 P.2d 806, 808 (Or. 1967) ("we now adopt Section 402A"); Hawkeye–Security Ins. Co. v. Ford Motor Co., 174 N.W.2d 672, 684 (Iowa 1970) ("[w]e now adopt the principles found in Restatement, Second, Torts § 402A"); Ritter v. Narragansett Elec. Co., 283 A.2d 255, 261 (R.I. 1971) ("the adoption of § 402A will well serve to promote the cause of justice"); Engberg v. Ford Motor Co., 205 N.W.2d 104, 109 (S.D. 1973) ("We hereby adopt strict liability as expressed in § 402A."); Shields v. Morton

Chem. Co., 518 P.2d 857, 859 (Idaho 1974) (a review of "the better reasoned cases leads us today to the adoption of the rule of strict liability in tort as it appears in the Restatement of the Law, Torts 2d § 402A"); Hiigel v. General Motors Corp., 544 P.2d 983, 987 (Colo. 1975) ("We hereby expressly adopt the doctrine of strict liability in tort which is stated in § 402A."); Brooks v. Dietz, 545 P.2d 1104, 1108 (Kan. 1976) ("the time has come for this court to adopt the rule of strict liability as set out in § 402A"); Phipps v. General Motors Corp., 363 A.2d 955, 963 (Md. 1976) ("we adopt the theory of strict liability as expressed in § 402A of the Restatement (Second) of Torts [which] [a]lmost all of the courts of our sister states have adopted").

**114.** For the diversity of approaches, see J. Beasley, Products Liability and the Unreasonably Dangerous Requirement 23 (1981): "Prosser's apprehension that the strict liability section would soon become outmoded was well-founded. Today, it is grossly out-of-date. Despite his constant effort in the first half of the 1960s to keep pace with new developments in the case law, strict tort liability has gone well beyond the confines, however flexibly they were written, of Section 402A."

**115.** See Webb v. Zern, 220 A.2d 853 (Pa. 1966) (adopting § 402A).

tort doctrine.[116] But the products liability law of most states has developed a peculiarity here and there, and the remaining chapters of this book attempt to make sense of such variations in secondary doctrine.

A number of states took a rather independent route from the start of modern products liability law, refusing simply to "adopt" § 402A yet adhering to the general principles of the developing jurisprudence of strict products liability in tort. One such state was Oklahoma where, in *Kirkland v. General Motors Corp.*,[117] the state supreme court adopted an extensively described theory of strict products liability in tort, called "Manufacturers' Products Liability."[118] Alabama also followed an independent path, in *Casrell v. Altec Indus., Inc.*[119] and *Atkins v. American Motors Corp.*,[120] by adopting a strict products liability in tort doctrine labeled the "Alabama Extended Manufacturer's Liability Doctrine (AEMLD)," likening the doctrine to negligence per se. In *Halphen v. Johns–Manville Sales Corp.*,[121] Louisiana adopted separate classifications of unreasonably dangerous products, although this development was largely superseded by the legislature's subsequent adoption of a comprehensive products liability reform statute.[122]

New York, which was at the forefront of the charge toward strict manufacturer liability to remote consumers in its *Goldberg v. Kollsman Instrument Corp.*[123] decision in 1963, did not formally adopt the doctrine of strict products liability,[124] nor make it clear that liability lay in tort,[125] until 1973. From the start, the New York decisions wove a somewhat distinctive pattern to the texture of strict products liability in tort, a singularity that has continued to mark the decisions of that state's high court.[126]

The California Supreme Court, which in 1963 gave birth to strict liability in tort in *Greenman v. Yuba Power Products, Inc.*,[127] seemed to adopt § 402A in 1970, in *Pike v. Frank G. Hough Co.*[128] However, in 1972, the California high court repudiated the *Restatement* formulation of the liability standard, "defective condition unreasonably dangerous," and reaffirmed the *Greenman* characterization of the basis of liability as merely "defective," in *Cronin v. J.B.E. Olson Corp.*[129]

---

**116.** See Surace v. Caterpillar, Inc., 111 F.3d 1039 (3d Cir. 1997) (Becker, J., struggling to make sense of Azzarello v. Black Bros. Co., 391 A.2d 1020 (Pa. 1978)). See generally Thomas, Defining "Design Defect" in Pennsylvania: Reconciling Azzarello and the Restatement (Third) of Torts, 71 Temp. L. Rev. 217 (1998). *Azzarello* is examined in § 5.8, below.

**117.** 521 P.2d 1353 (Okla. 1974).

**118.** See McNichols, The Kirkland v. General Motors Manufacturers' Products Liability Doctrine—What's In a Name?, 27 Okla. L. Rev. 347 (1974).

**119.** 335 So.2d 128 (Ala. 1976).

**120.** 335 So.2d 134 (Ala. 1976).

**121.** 484 So.2d 110 (La. 1986).

**122.** See The Louisiana Products Liability Act, La. Rev. Stat. Ann. § 9:2800.56 (liability for design dangers).

**123.** 191 N.E.2d 81 (N.Y. 1963) (assembler-manufacturer of airplane, but not supplier of defective component, an altimeter, held strictly liable to passenger killed in crash).

**124.** In Codling v. Paglia, 298 N.E.2d 622 (N.Y. 1973).

**125.** In Velez v. Craine & Clark Lumber Corp., 305 N.E.2d 750, 756 (N.Y. 1973).

**126.** See, e.g., Denny v. Ford Motor Co., 662 N.E.2d 730 (N.Y. 1995).

**127.** 377 P.2d 897 (Cal. 1963).

**128.** 467 P.2d 229 (Cal. 1970).

**129.** 501 P.2d 1153 (Cal. 1972). *Cronin* is examined in § 5.8, below

### Products Liability Reform Statutes

Several state legislatures enacted the doctrine of strict products liability in tort statutorily. Statutes enacted in Indiana, Maine, Montana, Oregon, and South Carolina were nearly verbatim restatements of § 402A.[130] Statutes in Arkansas and Georgia both provide variations on the same theme, but the Georgia statute in particular deviates substantially from the language and substance of § 402A.[131] Other state legislatures have enacted products liability reform codes which quite comprehensively extend well beyond the provisions of § 402A, as by formulating in some detail the bases of recovery in different contexts, defenses, and various procedural aspects of such litigation. These states include Connecticut,[132] Indiana,[133] Louisiana,[134] Mississippi,[135] New Jersey,[136] Ohio,[137] Texas,[138] and Washington.[139]

The Illinois legislature enacted a comprehensive products liability statute,[140] but the statute was struck down in 1997 as unconstitutional by the state supreme court,[141] the same fate that met New Hampshire's products liability statute 14 years earlier.[142] North Carolina's statute,[143] while expressly rejecting the doctrine of strict liability in tort, broadly adopts many of the secondary liability principles of modern products liability law. Many other states have enacted products liability reform statutes covering a miscellany of topics, as by adopting "state of the art" defenses, statutes of repose, shielding manufacturers of guns, protecting retailers (entirely or conditionally) from strict liability, and a host of other secondary issues.[144] These and many other topics receive detailed treatment in subsequent chapters.

**130.** See Ind. Code § 33–1–1.5–3 (superseded by Ind. Code § 34–20.2–1 which limits strict liability in tort to manufacturers and precisely redefines the basis of a manufacturer's liability); Me. Rev. Stat. Ann. tit. 14 § 221; Mont. Code Ann. § 27–1–719; Or. Rev. Stat. § 30.920; S.C. Code Ann. § 15–73–10 et seq.

**131.** See Ark. Code Ann. § 4–86–102; Ga. Code Ann. § 51–1–11 (manufacturers of new chattels strictly liable for injuries from unmerchantable products).

**132.** See Conn. Gen. Stat. § 52–572h et seq.

**133.** See Ind. Code § 34–20–2–1 et seq.

**134.** The Louisiana Products Liability Act, La. Rev. Stat. Ann. § 9:2800.51 et seq.

**135.** See Miss. Code Ann. § 11–1–63 et seq.

**136.** See N.J. Stat. Ann. § 2A.58c–1 et seq.

**137.** See Ohio Rev. Code Ann. § 2305.10 et seq. A major products liability reform statute was declared unconstitutional in State ex rel. Ohio Acad. of Trial Lawyers v. Sheward, 86 Ohio St.3d 451, 715 N.E.2d 1062 (1999), but Ohio still has a number of products liability provisions enacted prior thereto and in 2001. See Ohio Rev. Code Ann. § 2307.71 et seq.

**138.** See Tex. Civ. Prac. & Rem. Code Ann. § 82.001 et seq.

**139.** See Wash. Rev. Code Ann. § 7.72.010 et seq.

**140.** See 735 Ill. Comp. Stat. 5/2–621 et seq.

**141.** Best v. Taylor Mach. Works, 689 N.E.2d 1057 (Ill. 1997) (Illinois Civil Justice Reform Act of 1995 held unconstitutional).

**142.** See Heath v. Sears, Roebuck & Co., 464 A.2d 288 (N.H. 1983).

**143.** See Gen. Stat. § 99B–1 et seq.

**144.** The statutes are collected in 3 Madden & Owen on Products Liability 207 et seq.

## § 5.4  POLICIES AND RATIONALES

### Background

For half a century before the doctrine of strict manufacturer liability in tort burst forth in the 1960s, commentators had been examining the general question of whether enterprises should be strictly liable for injuries caused by their operations.[1] More particularly, several decades prior to § 402A, American commentators began to explain and justify (usually in the warranty law context, often arguing against the privity doctrine) why manufacturers of defective products should be liable for injuries to consumers.[2] Conceptual explorations into strict manufacturer liability are discernable in the 1920s with one commentator's call for the seller's implied warranty, termed "insurer's liability," to be viewed in terms of "risk-bearing."[3] The rationalization of such liability developed more fully in the 1930s, especially in writings by warranty law scholar Karl Llewellyn who argued that the law should impose strict liability on large manufacturers (and large retailers) who are "equipped to spread, and indeed to reduce, risks" to consumers from defective products that they sell.[4] As discussed above,[5] Dean William Prosser in 1941 catalogued the reasons for strict manufacturer liability in the first edition of his

### § 5.4

**1.** In the early 1900s, the scholarship centered on an employer's strict liability for injury to its employees under the new workers' compensation statutes which swept the nation in the first two decades of the century. This particular literature is discussed generally in the commentary cited in the following note.

**2.** There is now a rich literature on the evolution of the theoretical underpinnings to a rule of strict liability for manufacturers of defective products. See, e.g., Kysar, The Expectations of Consumers, 103 Colum. L. Rev. 1700, 1708 (2003) (collecting the literature); Witt, Speedy Fred Taylor and the Ironies of Enterprise Liability, 103 Colum. L. Rev. 1 (2003); Keating, The Theory of Enterprise Liability and Common Law Strict Liability, 54 Vand. L. Rev. 1285 (2001); Hackney, Jr., The Intellectual Origins of American Strict Products Liability: A Case Study in American Pragmatic Instrumentalism, 29 Am. J. Legal Hist. 443 (1995) (describing its origins in pragmatism, institutional economics, and legal realism, collectively referred to as "pragmatic instrumentalism"); Gray, Reflections on the Historical Context of Section 402A, 10 Touro L. Rev. 75 (1993); Priest, The Invention of Enterprise Liability: A Critical History of the Intellectual Foundations of Modern Tort Law, 14 J. Legal Stud. 461 (1985); V. Nolan and E. Ursin, Understanding Enterprise Liability (1995); M. Rahdert, Covering Accident Costs (1995); G. White, Tort Law in America (1980).

**3.** See, e.g., Patterson, The Apportionment of Business Risks Through Legal Devices, 24 Colum. L. Rev. 333, 358 (1924).

**4.** See, e.g., Llewellyn, On Warranty of Quality, and Society (pt. 1), 36 Colum. L. Rev. 699, 704 n.14 (1936). Professor Llewellyn had more fully expounded on this theme in his celebrated casebook, where he argued that there was a twofold need to hold manufacturers of defective products strictly liable to injured consumers: "to shift the immediate incidence of the hazard of life in an industrial society away from the individual over to a group which can distribute the loss; and to place the loss where the most pressure will be exerted to keep down future losses." K. Llewellyn, Cases and Materials on the Law of Sales 341 (1930). "The consumer, barring his own fault in use, should have no negligence to prove; that the article was not up to its normal character should be enough. . . . Under such an ideal system of law the loss would lie ultimately where it belongs, on the consumers of the article concerned *en masse*, in competition with other articles each carrying its own true costs in human life and effort. . . ." Id. at 341–42. On Llewellyn's influence, see generally Clutterbuck, Karl Llewellyn and the Intellectual Foundations of Enterprise Liability Theory, 97 Yale L.J. 1131 (1987); Wiseman, The Limits of Vision: Karl Llewellyn and the Merchant Rules, 100 Harv. L. Rev. 465 (1987). See also Feezer, Manufacturer's Liability for Injuries Caused by His Products: Defective Automobiles, 37 Mich. L. Rev. 1, 5–6, 22 n.58 (1938) (quoting from Llewellyn's casebook, and arguing in products liability cases for warranty without privity "as a basis for shifting the burden where it can be distributed and so can best be borne").

**5.** See § 5.2, above.

torts treatise,[6] and Judge Traynor elaborated upon those reasons in his famous concurring opinion in *Escola v. Coca Cola Bottling Co.* in 1943.[7] These were largely the same rationales relied upon by scholars in the 1950s as the march toward strict manufacturer liability accelerated,[8] and drawn upon by commentators in the 1960s, notably Dean Prosser in his "Assault Upon the Citadel" article, in 1960, and in his comment *c* to § 402A of the *Restatement (Second) of Torts*, in 1964,[9] to justify the doctrine that exploded upon the tort law landscape during that decade.

Comment *c* to *Restatement (Second) of Torts* § 402A summarized the rationales for strict products liability in tort as perceived by the Reporter, Dean Prosser, at the time he drafted this provision in the early 1960s: that manufacturers assume a "special responsibility" toward consumers who may be injured by their products; that consumers properly expect that reputable sellers will stand behind their goods; that the burden of injuries from product accidents will be borne by sellers and treated as a cost of production that may be insured against by liability insurance; and that consumers are "entitled to the maximum of protection at the hands of someone, and the proper persons to afford it are those who market the products."

### Rationales—In General

Prior to § 402A, courts and commentators had offered a variety of rationales for a manufacturer's strict products liability, generally predicating such liability on the increasing intricacy and danger of modern products comprised of complex mechanical and chemical substances, the safety of which, in contrast to simple products of previous generations,

---

**6.** W. Prosser, Handbook of the Law of Torts § 83, at 688–89 (1941). Prosser noted the increased impetus "to find some ground for strict liability which would make [the manufacturer] in effect a guarantor of his product, even though he had exercised all reasonable care," a development fueled by "an increased feeling that social policy demands that the burden of accidental injuries caused by defective chattels be placed upon the producer, since he is best able to distribute the risk to the general public by means of prices and insurance." In addition, Prosser observed, was "the difficulty of proving negligence in many cases where it exists, even with the aid of res ipsa loquitur, together with the wastefulness and uncertainty of a series of warranty actions carrying liability back through retailer and jobber to the original maker, the practice of reputable manufacturers to stand behind their goods as good business policy, and a recognition that the intermediate seller is usually a mere conduit to market the product. There is an obvious argument that in the public interest the consumer is entitled to the maximum of protection at the hands of some one, and that the producer, practically and morally, is the one to provide it."

**7.** See § 5.2, above.

**8.** See, e.g., Pound, The Problem of the Exploding Bottle, 40 B.U. L. Rev. 167, 180–

81 and 185–86 (1960) (embracing the *Escola* concurrence rationales); James, General Products—Should Manufacturers Be Liable without Negligence?, 24 Tenn. L. Rev. 923 (1957); Noel, Manufacturers of Defective Products—the Drift Toward Strict Liability, 24 Tenn. L. Rev. 963 (1957); James, Products Liability (pt. 2), 34 Tex. L. Rev. 192 (1955); Wilson, Products Liability (pts. 1 and 2), 43 Calif. 614, 809 (1955).

A number of leading scholars during this time expounded more broadly upon the benefits of enterprise responsibility for accidental harm based on broad loss distribution objectives. See, e.g., Ehrenzweig, Negligence Without Fault (1951), reprinted in 54 Cal. L. Rev. 1422 (1966); Ehrenzweig, A Psychoanalysis of Negligence, 47 Nw. U. L. Rev. 855 (1953); L. Green, The Individual's Protection Under Negligence Law: Risk Sharing, 47 Nw. U. L. Rev. 751 (1953); Morris, Hazardous Enterprises and Risk–Bearing Capacity, 61 Yale L.J. 1172 (1952). See generally G. Schwartz, The Beginning and the Possible End of the Rise of Modern American Tort Law, 26 Ga. L. Rev. 601, 635 (1992).

**9.** Less so in his celebrated article, Prosser, Assault Upon the Citadel (Strict Liability to the Consumer), 69 Yale L.J. 1099 (1960), where he disparaged both the insurance (risk-spreading) and deterrence rationales.

modern consumers had no practical way to detect.[10] From this premise, arguments for strict manufacturer liability centered on the propriety of relieving individual consumers of the economic consequences of injuries caused by defective products by shifting such losses to the enterprises that manufactured those products. Holding manufacturers liable for losses caused by defects in their products would force such firms to "internalize" these accident costs as they must absorb the other costs of production—materials, labor, and capital.[11] Manufacturers would then "spread" these costs, just as a kind of third-party insurer, by "passing them on" to those who benefitted from the enterprise[12]—the owners (through lower profits) and consumers (through higher prices).[13] An important additional aspect of this cost-internalization process is that it motivates manufacturers to eliminate defects in their products, in an effort to minimize accident costs which otherwise they must absorb, thus promoting public safety.[14]

**10.** See, e.g., Escola v. Coca Cola Bottling Co., 150 P.2d 436, 443 (Cal. 1944):

> As handicrafts have been replaced by mass production with its great markets and transportation facilities, the close relationship between the producer and consumer of a product has been altered. Manufacturing processes, frequently valuable secrets, are ordinarily either inaccessible to or beyond the ken of the general public. The consumer no longer has means or skill enough to investigate for himself the soundness of a product, even when it is not contained in a sealed package, and his erstwhile vigilance has been lulled by the steady efforts of manufacturers to build up confidence by advertising and marketing devices such as trademarks. Consumers no longer approach products warily but accept them on faith, relying on the reputation of the manufacturer or the trademark.

The extent to which humans are dependent on myriad complex products is sketched out in Owen, Products Liability: Principles of Justice for the 21st Century, 11 Pace L. Rev. 63, 64–66 (1990).

**11.** Important early articles promoting the general concept of cost internalization include Smith, Sequel to Workmen's Compensation Acts (pts. 1 and 2), 27 Harv. L. Rev. 235, 344 (1914); Thayer, Liability Without Fault, 29 Harv. L. Rev. 801 (1916); L. Green, The Duty Problem in Negligence Cases, 28 Colum. L. Rev. 1014 (1928); Morris, Rough Justice and Some Utopian Ideas, 24 Ill. L. Rev. 730 (1930); Feezer, Capacity to Bear Loss as a Factor in the Decision in Certain Types of Tort Cases (pt. 1), 78 U. Pa. L. Rev. 805 (1930); id. (pt. 2), 79 U. Pa. L. Rev. 742 (1931); Bohlen, Fifty Years of Torts, 50 Harv. L. Rev. 1225 (1937). An important later work is Cowan, Some Policy Bases of Products Liability, 17 Stan. L. Rev. 1077 (1965). See generally Priest, The Invention of Enterprise Liability: A Critical History of the Intellectual Foundations of Modern Tort Law, 14 J. Legal Stud. 461, 481 (1985).

**12.** Thus, the "benefit theory" of tort liability, prevalent during the first part of the twentieth century, provides important theoretical support to cost-internalization and risk-spreading. The leading exponent of this theory was Francis Bohlen. See Bohlen, The Basis of Affirmative Obligations in the Law of Torts (pts. 1–3), 53 Am. L. Reg. 209, 273, 337 (1905). See generally Priest, The Invention of Enterprise Liability: A Critical History of the Intellectual Foundations of Modern Tort Law, 14 J. Legal Stud. 461, 465–70 (1985).

**13.** See, e.g., Escola v. Coca Cola Bottling Co., 150 P.2d 436, 441 (Cal. 1944) ("The cost of an injury and the loss of time or health may be an overwhelming misfortune to the person injured, and a needless one, for the risk of injury can be insured by the manufacturer and distributed among the public as a cost of doing business."). Influential early treatments of the risk-spreading rationale were Thayer, Liability Without Fault, 29 Harv. L. Rev. 801 (1916); Douglas, Vicarious Liability and Administration of Risk (pts. 1 & 2), 38 Yale L. J. 534, 720 (1929); Feezer, Capacity to Bear Loss as a Factor in the Decision in Certain Types of Tort Cases (pt. 1), 78 U. Pa. L. Rev. 805 (1930); James, Contribution Among Joint Tort Feasors: A Pragmatic Criticism, 54 Harv. L. Rev. 1156, 1157 (1941) (a rule which can "effect loss distribution over a large segment of society [generally should predominate over] a rule which will bring about a less effective distribution"); Prosser, The Implied Warranty of Merchantable Quality, 27 Minn. L. Rev. 117, 122–25 (1943); Friedmann, Social Insurance and the Principles of Tort Liability, 63 Harv. L. Rev. 241 (1949); Morris, Hazardous Enterprises and Risk-bearing Capacity, 61 Yale L.J. 1172 (1952); L. Green, The Individual's Protection under Negligence Law: Risk Sharing, 47 Nw. U. L. Rev. 751 (1953).

**14.** See, e.g., Escola v. Coca Cola Bottling Co., 150 P.2d 436, 440–41 (Cal. 1944)

## Consumer Expectations

Another major rationale for holding manufacturers strictly liable in tort to consumers was to protect the consumer's fair expectations of safety in goods mass merchandised by reputable manufacturers.[15] This particular justification was borrowed from warranty law which, by the middle of the twentieth century, was generally considered a branch of contract law grounded in the protection of the parties' expectations.[16]

## Judicial Efficiency

A further argument for holding manufacturers directly liable to consumers for product accidents, perhaps best viewed as a procedural rather than a substantive justification, was the promotion of judicial efficiency: retailers were strictly liable to consumers anyway, via the implied warranty of merchantability; retailers held liable would obtain indemnity for their litigation losses back against their own suppliers; and these suppliers themselves would recover back against the manufacturer. To avoid this type of wasteful circuity of litigation, went the argument, consumers injured by defective products should simply be allowed to skip over retailers (and other intermediate sellers) and maintain their actions directly against product manufacturers.[17]

(Judge Traynor remarked that even without negligence, "public policy demands that responsibility be fixed wherever it will most effectively reduce the hazards to life and health inherent in defective products that reach the market," and that "[i]t is to the public interest to discourage the marketing of products having defects that are a menace to the public.").

**15.** See, e.g., Jacob E. Decker & Sons v. Capps, 164 S.W.2d 828, 832–33 (Tex. 1942) (noting that the modern manufacturer "uses the newspapers, magazines, billboards, and the radio to build up the psychology to buy and consume his products [and thereby acts to] create a demand for his products by inducing a belief that they are suitable for human consumption"). See also Prosser, Assault Upon the Citadel (Strict Liability to the Consumer), 69 Yale 1099, 1123 (1960): "The supplier, by placing the goods upon the market, represents to the public that they are suitable and safe for use; and by packaging, advertising or otherwise, he does everything that he can to induce that belief. He intends and expects that the product will be purchased and used in reliance upon this assurance of safety; and it is in fact so purchased and used." For an early discussion of this rationale, see Prosser, The Implied Warranty of Merchantable Quality, 27 Minn. L. Rev. 117, 122–25 (1943). For a rich exploration of this basis of products liability, see the monumental inquiry by Professor Marshall Shapo, A Representational Theory of Consumer Protection: Doctrine, Function and

Legal Liability for Product Disappointment, 60 Va. L. Rev. 1109 (1974).

**16.** See, e.g., R. Pound, Social Control Through Law 114 (1942, 1968 Reprint) ("[i]n civilized society men must be able to assume that [others] will make good reasonable expectations which their promises or other conduct reasonably create"); 1 J. Perillo, Corbin on Contracts § 1, at 2 (rev. ed. 1993) (the "main underlying purpose" of contract law is to enforce "the realization of reasonable expectations that have been induced by the making of a promise"). See § 5.6, below.

**17.** See, e.g., Escola v. Coca Cola Bottling Co., 150 P.2d 436, 442 (Cal. 1944) ("Such a procedure, however, is needlessly circuitous and engenders wasteful litigation. Much would be gained if the injured person could base his action directly on the manufacturer's warranty."). Prosser explained: "It is already possible to enforce strict liability by resort to a series of actions, in which the retailer is first held liable on a warranty to his purchaser, and indemnity on a warranty is then sought successively from other suppliers, until the manufacturer finally pays the damages, with the added costs of repeated litigation." Thus, "[w]hat is needed is a blanket rule which makes any supplier in the chain liable directly to the ultimate user, and so short-circuits the whole unwieldy process." Prosser, Assault Upon the Citadel (Strict Liability to the Consumer) 69 Yale 1099, 1123–24 (1960).

## Probable Negligence

Finally, some commentators reasoned that defective products usually result from a manufacturer's negligence, such that holding a manufacturer strictly liable serves as a proxy for the doctrine of res ipsa loquitur in the many cases in which the manufacturer probably was negligent in producing a defective product but where proof of negligence is unavailable to a person injured by the defect.[18]

## Deterrence and Risk–Spreading

Although courts and commentators offered a host of justifications for the doctrine of strict manufacturer liability in tort for harm caused by defective products, both before[19] and after[20] the promulgation of § 402A, it is important to note that two substantive rationales mentioned briefly above predominated: (1) "deterrence" (or, "safety"), and (2) "risk-spreading" (or "cost-spreading," "loss distribution," or "insurance").[21] Some courts and commentators emphasized deterrence, and

**18.** See, e.g., Phipps v. General Motors Corp., 363 A.2d 955, 958 (Md. 1976) ("the requirement of proof of a defect rendering a product unreasonably dangerous is a sufficient showing of fault on the part of the seller to impose liability without placing an often impossible burden on the plaintiff of proving specific acts of negligence"). See generally Cowan, Some Policy Bases of Products Liability, 17 Stan. L. Rev. 1077, 1087 (1965), observing that courts recognize "the great expense that plaintiffs would have to undergo to prove negligent manufacture of one out of a million products of the defendant [and] that if plaintiff were sufficiently well-heeled he would probably succeed in a surprisingly large number of cases in proving that the manufacturer was indeed negligent in the ordinary sense of the word." Thus, "implied warranty becomes 'presumed negligence.' Needless to say, this is really not very far from *res ipsa loquitur*. It merely extends its use." Compare Dean Wade's early, undeveloped idea that the sale of a defective product is akin to negligence per se. See Wade, Strict Tort Liability of Manufactures, 19 Sw. L.J. 5, 14 (1965).

**19.** See especially the cataloguing of rationales by Dean Prosser, in his treatise, and their elaboration by Justice Traynor, in *Greenman*, discussed above.

**20.** See, e.g., Brandenburger v. Toyota Motor Sales, U.S.A., Inc., 513 P.2d 268 (Mont. 1973). The various rationales for § 402A liability are summarized in Montgomery and Owen, Reflections on the Theory and Administration of Strict Tort Liability for Defective Products, 27 S.C. L. Rev. 803, 809–10 (1976):

  (1) Manufacturers convey to the public a general sense of product quality through the use of mass advertising and merchandising practices, causing consumers to rely for their protection upon the skill and expertise of the manufacturing community.

  (2) Consumers no longer have the ability to protect themselves adequately from defective products due to the vast number and complexity of products which must be "consumed" in order to function in modern society.

  (3) Sellers are often in a better position than consumers to identify the potential product risks, to determine the acceptable levels of such risks, and to confine the risks within those levels.

  (4) A majority of product accidents not caused by product abuse are probably attributable to the negligent acts or omissions of manufacturers at some stage of the manufacturing or marketing process, yet the difficulties of discovering and proving this negligence are often practicably insurmountable.

  (5) Negligence liability is generally insufficient to induce manufacturers to market adequately safe products.

  (6) Sellers almost invariably are in a better position than consumers to absorb or spread the costs of product accidents.

  (7) The costs of injuries flowing from typical risks inherent in products can fairly be put upon the enterprises marketing the products as a cost of their doing business, thus assuring that these enterprises will fully "pay their way" in the society from which they derive their profits.

**21.** See Owen, The Moral Foundations of Products Liability Law: Toward First Principles, 68 Notre Dame L. Rev. 427, 430–31 (1993):

others emphasized risk-spreading, but both rationales were and continue to be widely cited in support of holding manufacturers of defective products responsible for consumer injuries.

### Deterrence

As for deterrence, the case has seemed clear. Although there has been no shortage of skeptics,[22] many courts[23] and commentators[24] are persuaded that raising the standard of liability for manufacturers from negligence to strict liability will improve product safety.[25] To them, it has seemed self-evident that forcing producers to internalize the accident costs resulting from defects in their products will force them to take

During the 1960s and 1970s, as modern products liability doctrine first swept across the land, most of the theorizing that sought to justify and explain these developments [invoked two rationales]: (1) the need to provide compensation to injured consumers, through the mechanism of risk-spreading, by means of a third-party accident insurance system imposed on manufacturers by the courts, and (2) the need to improve product safety and restrain the power of manufacturers through rules designed to deter the production of dangerous products.

For earlier musings on tort law's "Siamese twin functions" of punishment and deterrence, on the one hand, and compensation and risk-spreading, on the other, see Morris, Rough Justice and Some Utopian Ideas, 24 U. Ill. L. Rev. 730 (1930). For a more modern Canadian perspective, see Trebilcock, The Social Insurance–Deterrence Dilemma of Modern North American Tort Law: A Canadian Perspective of the Liability Insurance Crisis, 24 San Diego L. Rev. 929 (1987).

**22.** A considerable body of literature questions whether a move from negligence to a strict basis of products liability in fact improves product safety. See, e.g., Williams, Second Best: The Soft Underbelly of Deterrence Theory in Tort, 106 Harv. L. Rev. 932 (1993) (economic critique of deterrence rationale); Posner, Strict Liability: A Comment, 2 J. Legal Stud. 205, 211–12 (1973) ("whether a general substitution of strict for negligence liability would improve efficiency seems at this stage hopelessly conjectural; the question is at bottom empirical and the empirical work has not been done"). Compare Sugarman, Doing Away with Tort Law, 73 Calif. L. Rev. 555, 566 (1985) (citing 1983 Rand study by Eads and Reuter which found that some manufacturers treat specific case outcomes as "random noise").

Defense lawyers argue that the standard of legal "defectiveness," at least in design cases, is too *vague* to be a meaningful deterrent and so instead is often simply ignored.

See Raleigh, The "State of the Art" in Product Liability: A New Look at an Old "Defense," 4 Ohio N. L. Rev. 249, 250–52 (1977) (General Motors' chief products liability lawyer's criticism of prevailing rules of products liability). Others have argued that manufacturers are generally as careful as reasonably possible anyway, regardless of the theory of liability, in order to safeguard their valuable reputations. See Plant, Strict Liability of Manufacturers for Injuries Caused by Defects in Products—An Opposing View, 24 Tenn. L. Rev. —938 (1957).

**23.** See, e.g., Fuchsgruber v. Custom Accessories, Inc., 628 N.W.2d 833, 839 (Wis. 2001); Perkins v. Wilkinson Sword, Inc., 700 N.E.2d 1247, 1252 (Ohio 1998); Larsen v. Pacesetter Sys., Inc., 837 P.2d 1273, 1287 (Haw. 1992) ("imposing liability on Pacesetter will promote product safety by encouraging manufacturers to anticipate and test for foreseeable defects likely to cause severe injury").

**24.** See, e.g., Shavell, Strict Liability v. Negligence, 9 J. Legal Stud. 1 (1980); Tietz, Strict Products Liability, Design Defects and Corporate Decision–Making: Greater Deterrence Through Stricter Process, 38 Vill. L. Rev. 1361, 1365 (1993) ("Courts and commentators generally agree that strict products liability creates incentives for manufacturers to ensure greater product safety."). On deterrence generally, see G. Schwartz, Reality in the Economic Analysis of Tort Law: Does Tort Law Really Deter?, 42 UCLA L. Rev. 377 (1994).

**25.** It appears quite clear that the increasing impact of products liability has caused many manufacturers to devote more attention, personnel, and money to product safety, and that products today are generally safer as a result. See Final Report, Interagency Task Force on Product Liability VI–47 (1977); N. Weber, Product Liability: The Corporate Response (Conf. Bd. 1987); The Benefits of the Modernization of the Tort Law in the Context of the Social Movement for Improved Safety and Quality in the National Economy (Cons. Fed. of Am. Sept.

such costs into account and, hence, induce them to reduce or eliminate defects in their products as much as reasonably possible. Safety, so important to the public, would thereby be improved.

For example, in an early case from New Mexico, *First National Bank v. Nor–Am Agricultural Products, Inc.*,[26] Mr. Huckleby fed his hogs grain that had been treated with a chemical seed disinfectant that contained mercury. The Huckleby family ate one of the hogs that had eaten the treated grain, and the children suffered blindness and paralysis from mercury poisoning. In the Hucklebys' strict liability action against the disinfectant manufacturer for inadequately warning of the danger, the trial court gave summary judgment to the defendant, and the plaintiffs appealed. Holding that the § 402A claim was proper, the court of appeals reversed, remarking that "[p]ublic interest in human life, health and safety requires that the law give consumers maximum protection against dangerous product defects."[27] The court reasoned that allowing plaintiffs to proceed on the basis of strict liability in tort, without being required to prove negligence, "will cause manufacturers to take cautionary steps to prevent the marketing of dangerously defective products."[28]

### Risk-Spreading

The other major rationale, risk-spreading, has also been instrumental in the development of strict products liability in tort.[29] Manufacturers forced to absorb the costs of product accidents will strive to pass along at least some portion of those costs to consumers through increased prices. In the process, manufacturers will relieve injured consumers of the possibly crushing financial burdens and, at the same time, spread such losses widely among the consuming public. Because modern science and technology benefit society as a whole, all consumers can fairly be asked

---

1987); Fuchsgruber v. Custom Accessories, Inc., 628 N.W.2d 833, 839 (Wis. 2001).

**26.** 537 P.2d 682 (N.M. Ct. App. 1975).

**27.** Id. at 695.

**28.** Id., quoting Phillips v. Kimwood Mach. Co., 525 P.2d 1033, 1042 (Or. 1974), to the effect that "in the final analysis, the imposition of liability has a beneficial effect on manufacturers of defective products both in the care they take and in the warning they give." Note, however, that the *First Nat'l Bank* court takes the *Phillips* court's remarks somewhat out of context.

**29.** See, e.g., W.P. Keeton, Products Liability—The Nature and Extent of Strict Liability, 1964 Ill. L. F. 693, 695 (1964):

The principal reason that has now gained undisputed acceptance for shifting losses from users and consumers to manufacturers is the capacity of those engaged in the manufacturing enterprise to distribute the losses of the few to the many who purchase the products. Thus, the assumption is that the greater part of these losses suffered by the few victims will be shifted to the many consumers by way of higher prices for the products.

Even the Supreme Court of Michigan, which never did adopt § 402A, acknowledges the widespread acceptance of the risk-spreading rationale. See Prentis v. Yale Mfg. Co., 365 N.W.2d 176, 181 (Mich. 1984) (courts "have agreed that manufacturers can most effectively distribute the costs of injuries"). On the risk-spreading function of modern products liability law, see generally M. Rahdert, Covering Accident Costs—Insurance, Liability, and Tort Reform (1995). Compare Priest, The Invention of Enterprise Liability: A Critical History of the Intellectual Foundations of Modern Tort Law, 14 J. Legal Stud. 461 (1985) (risk-distribution rationale played decisive role in development of strict products liability in tort), with G. Schwartz, The Beginning and the Possible End of the Rise of Modern American Tort Law, 26 Ga. L. Rev. 601, 634–47 (1992) (loss-distribution rationale played important, but not decisive, role in development of strict products liability in tort). Quite possibly the most discerning article ever written on this subject was penned by then Assistant Professor Guido Calabresi, Some Thoughts on Risk Distribution and the Law of Torts, 70 Yale L.J. 499 (1961).

to pay slightly higher prices as premiums for insurance against the risk of often random harm when science and technology go awry. By spreading the costs of product accidents in this manner, manufacturers thus provide all consumers, albeit indirectly, with mandatory accident insurance for harm from product defects. Moreover, because competition often prevents manufacturers from raising prices significantly, some portion of the accident costs will be spread, not unfairly, to the owners of the enterprise that made and sold the defective product.

Most courts and commentators in the 1960s and 1970s uncritically embraced deterrence, risk-spreading, and the other rationales for the doctrine of strict liability in tort for defective products,[30] frequently overlooking the doctrine's important limitations.[31] Even from the start, however, some judges[32] and commentators[33] found fault with the new

**30.** As for the courts, see, e.g., Santor v. A & M Karagheusian, Inc., 207 A.2d 305, 311 (N.J. 1965); McCormack v. Hankscraft Co. 154 N.W.2d 488 (Minn. 1967); Phillips v. Kimwood Mach. Co., 525 P.2d 1033 (Or. 1974); First Nat'l Bank v. Nor–Am Agricultural Prod., Inc., 537 P.2d 682, 695 (N.M. Ct. App. 1975); Phipps v. General Motors Corp., 363 A.2d 955, 958 (Md. 1976).

As for the commentators, see, e.g., W.P. Keeton, Products Liability—The Nature and Extent of Strict Liability, 1964 Ill. L. F. 693 (1964); Traynor, The Ways and Meanings of Defective Products and Strict Liability, 32 Tenn. L. Rev. 363 (1965); Wade, Strict Tort Liability of Manufacturers, 19 Sw. L.J. 5 (1965); W.P. Keeton, Products Liability—Some Observations About Allocation of Risks, 64 Mich. L. Rev. 1329 (1966); Wade, On the Nature of Strict Tort Liability for Products, 44 Miss. L.J. 825 (1973); Vetri, Products Liability: The Developing Framework for Analysis, 54 Or. L. Rev. 293 (1975); Montgomery and Owen, Reflections on the Theory and Administration of Strict Tort Liability for Defective Products, 27 S.C. L. Rev. 803, 810 (1976) ("In combination, [the articulated rationales] present a compelling case for basing the liability of product sellers on some foundation other than fault.").

**31.** Forgotten now by most courts and commentators was the conjunctive link, in early products liability theorizing by tort law scholars, between the expansion of a manufacturer's liability and a commensurate reduction of tort law *damages*. In 1955, Fleming James urged the adoption of "a rational scheme of strict liability for injurious products." James, Products Liability (pt. 2), 34 Tex. L. Rev. 192, 228 (1959). Yet such an enterprise liability scheme would have to be funded, which in James' view meant that victims might have to surrender their common-law right to damages for pain and suffering which he considered predicated on a defendant having been a true "wrongdoer." James, Damages in Accident Cases, 41 Cornell L.Q. 582, 583 (1956). Further, a rational enterprise liability scheme might require victims to surrender compensation even for some of their *pecuniary* losses, because "accidents bring a net pecuniary loss to society . . . so that if the victim is made entirely whole, he will fare better than society and will not himself share the economic burden he is asking society to distribute." Id. at 584. The idea of limiting pain and suffering damages was shared by other scholars of the day, including such notables as Albert Ehrenzweig, Louis Jaffe, Leon Green, Marcus Plant, Clarence Morris, and Roger Traynor. See also Prosser, Assault on the Citadel (Strict Liability to the Consumer), 69 Yale L.J. 1099, 1121 (1960). See generally Virginia E. Nolan and Edmund Ursin, Understanding Enterprise Liability ch. 15 (1995).

**32.** See, e.g., Bailey v. Montgomery Ward & Co., 431 P.2d 108, 119 (Ariz. Ct. App. 1967) (Molloy, J., dissenting: "The all-inclusive ring of 'strict liability' will cause an overextension (as here) of what is conceived by its progenitors to be a limited concept."). See also Markle v. Mulholland's Inc., 509 P.2d 529, 546 (Or. 1973) (Bryson, J., dissenting) ("I am not willing to place the court in a position of adopting a law based on a socialistic theory"); Cline v. Prowler Indus., 418 A.2d 968 (Del. Sup. Ct. 1980).

**33.** See, e.g., Speidel, The Virginia "Anti–Privity" Statute: Strict Products Liability Under the Uniform Commercial Code, 51 Va. L. Rev. 804 (1965); Smyser, Products Liability and the American Law Institute: A Petition for Rehearing, 42 U. Det. L.J. 343 (1965); Lange, Compensation of Victims—A Pious and Misleading Platitude, 54 Cal. L. Rev. 1559 (1966). See generally Titus, Restatement (Second) of Torts Section 402A and The Uniform Commercial Code, 22 Stan. L. Rev. 713, 714–15 (1970) (summarizing criticisms). At least a couple of com-

strict products liability in tort doctrine and its underlying rationales, and, as the initial flush of excitement over the new strict liability doctrine subsided, commentators increasingly questioned the wisdom and logic of the doctrine's traditional rationales.[34] But the conventional justifications for strict manufacturer liability have not yet been consigned to the trash heap, and some courts[35] and commentators[36] still

mentators saw the doctrine coming, and opposed it before it arrived. See, e.g., Peairs, The God in the Machine—A Study in Precedent, 29 B.U. L. Rev. 37 (1949); Plant, Strict Liability of Manufacturers for Injuries Caused by Defects in Products—An Opposing View, 24 Tenn. L. Rev. 938, 946 (1957) ("what is sometimes euphemistically called 'social engineering' . . . frequently turns out to be crass expediency seeking its ends without any particular regard for basic principles").

**34.** See, e.g., Klemme, The Enterprise Liability Theory of Torts, 47 Colo. L. Rev. 153, 191–92 (1976); A. Schwartz, Products Liability and Judicial Wealth Redistribution, 51 Ind. L.J. 558 (1976); Epstein, Products Liability: The Search for the Middle Ground, 56 N.C. L. Rev. 643, 661 (1978) ("[t]o allow loss spreading issues covertly to dominate the structure of the tort law will only produce unsound results and bad general principles [and] will only bring the law into disrepute as the courts say one thing and do yet another"); Birnbaum, Unmasking the Test for Design Defect: From Negligence [to Warranty] to Strict Liability to Negligence, 33 Vand. L. Rev. 593 (1980); R. Epstein, Modern Products Liability Law ch. 4 (1980); Owen, Rethinking the Policies of Strict Products Liability, 33 Vand. L. Rev. 681, 703–07 (1980); Epstein, Products Liability as an Insurance Market, 14 J. Legal Stud. 645 (1985); Priest, The Invention of Enterprise Liability: A Critical History of the Intellectual Foundations of Modern Tort Law, 14 J. Legal Stud. 461 (1985); Weinrib, The Insurance Justification and Private Law, 14 J. Legal Stud. 681 (1985); Huber, Safety and the Second Best: The Hazards of Public Risk Management in the Courts, 85 Colum. L. Rev. 277 (1985); Smith, The Critics and the "Crisis": A Reassessment of Current Conception of Tort Law, 72, Cornell L. Rev. 765 (1987); Epstein, The Unintended Revolution in Product Liability Law, 10 Cardozo L. Rev. 2193, 2202 (1989) ("the anticontractual bias of both *Henningsen* and *Greenman* has proved to have devastating long-term consequences for the soundness of the product liability system"); Owen, Products Liability:

Principles of Justice for the 21st Century, 11 Pace L. Rev. 63 (1990); Powers, A Modest Proposal to Abandon Strict Products Liability, 1991 U. Ill. L. Rev. 639, 639 (1991); Owen, The Moral Foundations of Products Liability Law: Toward First Principles, 68 Notre Dame L. Rev. 427, 484–93 (1993); V. Nolan and E. Ursin, Understanding Enterprise Liability (1995); M. Rahdert, Covering Accident Costs (1995); Ausness, An Insurance–Based Compensation System for Product–Related Injuries, 58 U. Pitt. L. Rev. 669 (1997); Feldman, Harm and Money: Against the Insurance Theory of Tort Compensation, 75 Tex. L. Rev. 1567 (1997); Ausness, Replacing Strict Liability with a Contract–Based Products Liability Regime, 71 Temp. L. Rev. 171 (1998); Owen, Defectiveness Restated: Exploding the "Strict" Products Liability Myth, 1996 U. Ill. L. Rev. 743, 754–55; Ausness, Replacing Strict Liability with a Contract–Based Products Liability Regime, 71 Temp. L. Rev. 171 (1998); Ausness, An Insurance–Based Compensation System for Product–Related Injuries, 58 U. Pitt. L. Rev. 669 (1997); Henderson, Why Negligence Dominates Tort, 50 UCLA L. Rev. 377 (2002); Henderson, Echoes of Enterprise Liability in Product Design and Marketing Litigation, 87 Cornell L. Rev. 958 (2002). For an explanation of problems with the risk-spreading rationale, see § 8.4, below.

**35.** See, e.g., Green v. Smith & Nephew AHP, Inc., 629 N.W.2d 727, 743–51 (Wis. 2001); Sternhagen v. Dow, 935 P.2d 1139, 1145–46 (Mont. 1997); Potter v. Chicago Penumatic Tool Co., 694 A.2d 1319 (Conn. 1997); Brooks v. Beach Aircraft Corp., 902 P.2d 54, 59 (N.M. 1995).

**36.** See, e.g., Korzec, Dashing Consumer Hopes: Strict Products Liability and the Demise of the Consumer Expectations Test, 20 B.C. Int'l & Comp. L. Rev. 227 (1997); Phillips, Achilles' Heel, 61 Tenn. L. Rev. 1265, 1274 (1994) (manufacturer "is usually in a better position to prevent the injury and to spread the risk of loss"); Prentice and Roszkowski, "Tort Reform" and the Liability "Revolution": Defending Strict Liability in Tort for Defective Products, 27 Gonz. L. Rev. 251 (1991–92).

cling tenaciously, sometimes with a modern theoretical spin,[37] to the traditional rationales.[38]

## § 5.5 LIABILITY TESTS

"Strict" liability may tend to connote responsibility that is absolute, liability for which there is no excuse. Indeed, in tort law theorizing during the early decades of the twentieth century, long before *Greenman v. Yuba Power Products, Inc.*[1] and *Restatement (Second) of Torts* § 402A swept into the limelight in the 1960s, the terms "strict" and "absolute" were frequently interchanged in general discussions of enterprise liability for causing harm.[2] For example, in his famous concurring opinion in *Escola v. Coca Cola Bottling Co.*,[3] Justice Traynor remarked: "In my opinion it should now be recognized that a manufacturer incurs an absolute liability when an article that he has placed on the market, knowing that it is to be used without inspection, proves to have a defect that causes injury to human beings."[4] In truth, however, tort law provides no home for a ground of liability so extreme as to be truly "absolute."[5] Modern tort law understands the simple fact that absolute safety is generally an impossible technological goal; and that, even when perfect safety is possible, it often is too expensive.[6]

**37.** See, e.g., Keating, Rawlsian Fairness and Regime Choice in the Law of Accidents, 72 Fordham L. Rev. 1858 (2004); Kysar, The Expectations of Consumers, 103 Colum. L. Rev. 1700, 1790 (2003) ("allowing design defect liability to rest on the frustrated expectations of consumers provides an avenue for judicial expression of legitimate public values that are not readily captured by risk-utility analysis"); Keating, Pressing Precaution Beyond the Point of Cost–Justification, 56 Vand. L. Rev. 653 (2003); Keating, The Theory of Enterprise Liability and Common Law Strict Liability, 54 Vand. L. Rev. 1285 (2001); Hanson and Kysar, Taking Behavioralism Seriously: A Potential Response to Market Manipulation, 6 Roger Williams L. Rev. 259 (2000); Hanson and Kysar, Taking Behavioralism Seriously: Some Evidence of Market Manipulation, 112 Harv. L. Rev. 1420 (1999); Hanson and Logue, The Costs of Cigarettes: The Economic Case for Ex Post Incentive–Based Regulation, 107 Yale L.J. 1163, 1263 (1998); Keating, The Idea of Fairness in the Law of Enterprise Liability, 95 Mich. L. Rev. 1266 (1997); Williams, Second Best: The Soft Underbelly of Deterrence Theory in Tort, 760 Harv. L. Rev. 932 (1993); Croley and Hanson, Rescuing the Revolution: The Revived Case for Enterprise Liability, 91 Mich. L. Rev. 683 (1993) (enterprise liability may help diminish imperfections in consumer product markets); Hanson and Logue, The First Party Insurance Externality: An Economic Justification for Enterprise Liability, 76 Cornell L. Rev. 129 (1990); Attanasio, The Principle of Aggregate Autonomy and the Calabresian Approach to Products Liability, 74 Va. L. Rev. 677 (1988). Cf. Guthrie, Prospect Theory,

Risk Preference, and the Law, 97 Nw. U. L. Rev. 1115 (2003); Geistfeld, Reconciling Cost–Benefit Analysis with the Principle That Safety Matters More Than Money, 76 N.Y.U. L. Rev. 114 (2001).

**38.** For sensitive evaluations of some of the conventional rationales, see V. Nolan and E. Ursin, Understanding Enterprise Liability (1995); M. Rahdert, Covering Accident Costs—Insurance, Liability, and Tort Reform (1995); G. Schwartz, Mixed Theories of Tort Law: Affirming Both Deterrence and Corrective Justice, 75 Tex. L. Rev. 1801 (1997).

**§ 5.5**

**1.** 377 P.2d 897 (Cal. 1963) (Traynor, J.).

**2.** See the discussion in Ehrenzweig, Negligence Without Fault (1951), reprinted, 54 Cal. L. Rev. 1422, 1450 n.1 (1966).

**3.** 150 P.2d 436, 440 (Cal. 1944).

**4.** Id.

**5.** See Winfield, The Myth of Absolute Liability, 42 L. Q. Rev. 37 (1926).

**6.** See Owen, Defectiveness Restated: Exploding the "Strict" Products Liability Myth, 1996 U. Ill. L. Rev. 743, 754–55; Huber, Safety and the Second Best: The Hazards of Public Risk Management in the Courts, 85 Colum. L. Rev. 277 (1985); Calabresi, The Costs of Accidents 17–18 (1970). For explanations in moral theory, see Owen, Philosophical Foundations of Fault in Tort Law, in Philosophical Foundations of Tort Law 201 (D. Owen ed., Oxford University Press 1995); Owen, The Moral Foundations of Products Liability Law: Toward First Principles, 68 Notre Dame L. Rev. 427 (1993).

Although some theorists in the 1950s still archaically equated liability without fault and "absolute" liability,[7] most tort law commentators by that time had begun distinguishing "strict" from "absolute" liability.[8] While absolute liability implies the complete absence of excuse, "strict" liability properly suggests only that responsibility is predicated on some basis other than the actor's fault, thus permitting defenses on such grounds as the victim's contributory fault or assumption of risk, the absence of proximate causation, and possibly even the actor's inability to prevent the harm.[9] "Manufacturers," it was understood by the 1950s, "are not expected to subsidize every act of carelessness on the part of consumers, nor compensate for every injury remotely connected with the use of a product."[10]

"Strict" products liability in tort, indisputably, is *not* absolute liability. The doctrine of strict products liability in tort does not require manufacturers to ensure perfect product safety nor guarantee that consumers are never injured by their products, as discussed above.[11] Since absolute safety is not to be the rule, the task is normally one of line drawing between degrees of safety—of deciding how to separate products that are unacceptably dangerous from those that are safe enough. In designing products, manufacturers are properly required only to make reasonable trade-offs between safety, utility, and cost; once a product causes harm, courts do not demand safety perfection but merely assess the soundness of the manufacturer's trade-offs to ascertain whether they were reasonable. In short, the central liability question in most products liability cases can often be reduced to "How safe is safe enough?"

The *Restatement (Second) of Torts* § 402A presents this cardinal issue of products liability law in terms of whether a product was sold in a "defective condition unreasonably dangerous" to the user or consumer. In litigation under § 402A, therefore, the question of whether a particular injury-producing product was too dangerous, or instead was safe enough, depends upon the meaning of the phrase "defective condition unreasonably dangerous." One of the most insightful early products liability decisions attempting to decode this central liability phrase in § 402A was *Phillips v. Kimwood Machine Co.*,[12] where the court noted that "courts continue to flounder while attempting to determine how one decides whether a product is 'in a defective condition unreasonably dangerous to the user.'" Observing that "[t]he problem with strict liability of products has been one of limitation," the court remarked, "No one wants absolute liability where all the article has to do is to cause injury. To impose liability there has to be something about the article which makes it dangerously defective without regard to whether the manufacturer was or was not at fault for such condition. A test for

---

**7.** See, e.g., Gregory, Trespass to Negligence to Absolute Liability, 37 Va. L. Rev. 359 (1951).

**8.** See Ehrenzweig, Negligence Without Fault (1951), reprinted, 54 Cal. L. Rev. 1422, 1450 n.1 (1966).

**9.** See Winfield, The Myth of Absolute Liability, 42 L. Q. Rev. 37 (1926).

**10.** Wilson, Products Liability (pt. 2), 43 Cal. L. Rev. 809, 809 (1955).

**11.** See § 5.3, above.

**12.** 525 P.2d 1033 (Or. 1974).

unreasonable danger is therefore vital."[13] And so the courts began to search for an appropriate yardstick or "test" of liability, a standard to apply to particular injury-producing products to determine if their level of safety was adequate or, instead, if they were sold in a "defective condition unreasonably dangerous" to persons foreseeably put at risk.

As liability under § 402A was beginning to be worked out in the 1960s and 1970s, courts and commentators generally sought a unitary liability standard or defect test—a single, general test that could determine defectiveness in every type of case. However, as products liability law and litigation matured in the 1980s and 1990s, and as its complexities were better understood, it became increasingly clear that liability standards should be contextually based, that is, that an appropriate test of liability depended upon the particular manner in which a product was unsafe. In recent years, therefore, courts have moved toward using separate liability tests for manufacturing defects, design defects, and warnings defects. As discussed below, it has been the search for a proper definition of *design* defectiveness that has most confounded courts and commentators, and the evolution of strict tort liability tests has centered on judging the adequacy of a product's design.

The next three sections examine the progression of liability tests for strict products liability in tort, from the early 1960s, under *Greenman v. Yuba Power Products, Inc.* and § 402A of the *Restatement (Second) of Torts*, through the late 1990s when the *Restatement (Third) of Torts: Products Liability* reformulated those tests, to the present time. Section 5.6 first explores the development, meaning, and problems of the "consumer expectations" test, the first principal test of products liability. Section 5.7 examines the "risk-utility" test, which in design and warnings cases has displaced the consumer expectations test in many states. Since the risk-utility test has evolved principally in the area of defective design, its meaning and evolution are treated in general terms in § 5.7, leaving detailed analysis of this test to the chapter on defects in design.[14] The last liability test section, § 5.8, investigates a variety of alternative liability tests that courts have used as products liability law has evolved and matured since its initial birth. This last section considers the various ways in which the courts have altered § 402A's verbal standard of "defective condition unreasonably dangerous," examines how some courts have combined the two principal tests into a single liability standard, and notes the trend toward defect-specific tests of liability. Detailed examination of the specific liability tests increasingly applied by courts in the various contexts of defective manufacture, design, and warnings is left for treatment in the chapters on those particular topics.[15] The standards in the *Third Restatement* are treated in §§ 5.10–5.12 and in the chapters addressing particular types of defect.[16]

---

**13.** Id. at 1035–36.

**14.** See ch. 8, below.

**15.** See chs. 7 (manufacturing defects), 8 (design defects), and 9 (warning defects), below.

**16.** See id.

## § 5.6  THE CONSUMER EXPECTATIONS TEST

In attempting to ascertain the meaning of § 402A's liability standard, "defective condition unreasonably dangerous," the first place the courts looked for guidance was in the Reporter's Comments that Dean Prosser wrote to that section of the *Restatement (Second) of Torts*. There, in comments *g* and *i*, lies the basis for the first important test for establishing strict products liability in tort, the consumer expectations test.[1] Comment *g* to § 402A, entitled "defective condition," states in part as follows:

> The rule stated in this Section applies only where the product is, at the time it leaves the seller's hands, *in a condition not contemplated by the ultimate consumer*, which will be unreasonably dangerous to him. (emphasis added)

Thus, according to the *Second Restatement*, the term "defective condition" in § 402A means "a condition not contemplated by the ultimate consumer, which will be unreasonably dangerous to him." Comment *i*, entitled "unreasonably dangerous," explains the meaning of that phrase:

> The rule stated in this Section applies only where the defective condition of the product makes it unreasonably dangerous to the user or consumer. Many products cannot possibly be made entirely safe.... That is not what is meant by "unreasonably dangerous" in this Section. The article sold must be *dangerous to an extent beyond that which would be contemplated by the ordinary consumer who purchases it*, with the ordinary knowledge common to the community as to its characteristics.[2]

The last phrase of the definition in comment *g* and the first sentence in comment *i*, both set out above, suggest that the terms "defective condition" and "unreasonably dangerous" mean different things, and that a plaintiff must separately prove each in order to prevail. Indeed, the compound black-letter phrase, "defective condition unreasonably dangerous," itself suggests such a two-part interpretation, as an array of courts,[3] at least two state statutes,[4] and a number of leading products liability lawyers[5] have suggested.

### § 5.6

**1.** See Kysar, The Expectations of Consumers, 103 Colum. L. Rev. 1700, 1790 (2003); Phillips, Consumer Expectations, 53 S.C. L. Rev. 1047 (2002); Korzec, Dashing Consumer Hopes: Strict Products Liability and the Demise of the Consumer Expectations Test, 20 B.C. Int'l & Comp. L. Rev. 227 (1997); Little, The Place of Consumer Expectations in Product Strict Liability Actions for Defectively Designed Products, 61 Tenn. L. Rev. 1189 (1994); Kennedy, The Role of the Consumer Expectations Test Under Louisiana's Products Liability Tort Doctrine, 69 Tulane L. Rev. 117, 162 (1994); Montal, The Consumer Expectations Test in New Jersey: What Can Consumers Expect Now?, 54 Brooklyn L. Rev. 1381 (1989); Bernacchi, A Behavioral Model for Imposing Strict Liability in Tort: The Importance of Analyzing Product Performance in Relation to Consumer Expectation and Frustration, 47 U. Cinn. L. Rev. 43

(1978); Hubbard, Reasonable *Human* Expectations: A Normative Model For Imposing Strict Liability for Defective Products, 29 Mercer L. Rev. 465 (1978); Fischer, Products Liability—The Meaning of Defect, 39 Mo. L. Rev. 339, 348–52 (1974); Shapo, A Representational Theory of Consumer Protection: Doctrine, Function and Legal Liability for Product Disappointment, 60 Va. L. Rev. 1109 (1974); Dickerson, Products Liability: How Good Does a Product Have to Be?, 42 Ind. L.J. 301 (1967); Rheingold, What Are the Consumer's "Reasonable Expectations"?, 22 Bus. Law. 589 (1967).

**2.** Restatement (2d) Torts § 402A cmt. *i* (emphasis added).

**3.** See, e.g., Sollami v. Eaton, 772 N.E.2d 215, 219 (Ill. 2002) ("plaintiff must plead and prove that the injury resulted from a condition of the product, [and] that the condition was an unreasonably danger-

**4–5.**  See notes 4–5 on page 293.

But the view that § 402A's liability test requires two separate showings, as previously discussed,[6] is decidedly mistaken. The second sentence in comment *i*, quoted above, cuts against such a bifurcated definition, for it defines "unreasonably dangerous" as "dangerous to an extent beyond that which would be contemplated by the ordinary consumer who purchases it."[7] Quite plainly, the "unreasonably dangerous" definition in comment *i* is virtually identical to the "defective condition" definition in comment *g*. Because both halves of § 402A's "defective condition unreasonably dangerous" liability standard ultimately are defined in terms of *dangerous beyond a consumer's contemplations*, many courts interpreting § 402A in the 1960s and 1970s assumed that the full definitional phrase established a *single* test of liability based on a single standard of product safety measured by "consumer expectations."[8] This quite plainly is the better view.

ous one"); Johnson v. Ford Motor Co., 45 P.3d 86, 91 (Okla. 2002) ("plaintiff must prove ... that the product was defective when it left the control of the manufacturer, and that the defect made the product unreasonably dangerous"); Dillon v. Zeneca Corp., 42 P.3d 598 (Ariz. Ct. App. 2002) ("For a *prima facie* case of strict product liability, the plaintiff must demonstrate that the product was in a defective condition that made it unreasonably dangerous"); Lee v. Martin, 45 S.W.3d 860, 864 (Ark. Ct. App. 2001) ("A plaintiff in a strict-liability case must prove that the product is unreasonably dangerous *and* defective"); Tabieros v. Clark Equip. Co., 944 P.2d 1279, 1297 (Haw. 1997) (plaintiff must prove "a defect in the product which rendered it unreasonably dangerous"); Stinson v. E.I. DuPont de Nemours & Co., 904 S.W.2d 428 (Mo. Ct. App. 1995) (trial court appeared to believe that liability was based on a two-part test); Patterson v. F.W. Woolworth Co., 786 F.2d 874 (8th Cir. 1986) (Iowa law); Phipps v. General Motors Corp. 363 A.2d 955, 958 (Md. 1976) ("For recovery, it must be established that (1) the product was in defective condition [and] (2) that it was unreasonably dangerous.... "); Early–Gary, Inc. v. Walters, 294 So.2d 181, 186 (Miss. 1974) (one of § 402A's three elements is that "the injury resulted from a defect in the product which rendered it unreasonably dangerous"). *But see* McAlpine v. Rhone–Poulenc AG Co., 16 P.3d 1054 (Mont. 2000) (jury verdict overturned because "defective condition unreasonably dangerous" language in jury instructions created vague and imprecise dual test).

**4.** Tennessee permits a plaintiff to recover upon a showing that the product was in a defective condition *or* unreasonably dangerous. See Smith v. Detroit Marine Eng'g Corp., 712 S.W.2d 472, 474 (Tenn. Ct. App. 1985), and the Arkansas statute that requires the plaintiff to prove a product was supplied "in a defective condition which *rendered* it unreasonably dangerous." See Tenn. Code Ann. § 29–28–105; Ark. Code Ann. § 4–86–102.

**5.** That some products liability lawyers so interpret § 402A may be seen by reviewing two products liability anthologies which contain state-by-state descriptions of products liability law written by practitioners from each state. See Products Liability—50 State Handbook 471 (Jerome H. Kahnke and James H. Price eds., 1994–95) (*Missouri*: "Under both manufacturing defect and design defect theories, plaintiffs are required to prove that a product was both defective AND unreasonably dangerous."); Product Liability Desk Reference—A Fifty-State Compendium 180 (Morton F. Daller ed., 2004) (*Idaho*: "Idaho has adopted [§ 402A] which gives rise to a cause of action ... if a product is defective *and* is unreasonably dangerous....").

**6.** See § 5.3 (elements), above, and § 5.8, below.

**7.** Comment *i* is qualified as follows: "with the ordinary knowledge common to the community as to its characteristics." Restatement (2d) Torts § 402A cmt. *i*.

**8.** Many early courts defined "defective condition unreasonably dangerous" in the consumer expectations terms of comments *g* and *i*. See, e.g., Vincer v. Esther Williams All–Aluminum Swimming Pool Co., 230 N.W.2d 794 (Wis. 1975); Lunt v. Brady Mfg. Corp., 475 P.2d 964 (Ariz. Ct. App. 1970); Dunham v. Vaughan & Bushnell Mfg. Co., 247 N.E.2d 401 (Ill. 1969).

### Basis of the Test

Consumer expectation protection was a logical choice as the foundation of strict products liability under § 402A. It will be recalled that modern products liability law, and § 402A in particular, evolved out of the law of warranty which by the twentieth century had been absorbed into the law of sales and contracts.[9] One of the most basic goals of law in general,[10] and the most fundamental pillar of contract law, is the protection of the expectations—the *reasonable* expectations—of the contracting parties.[11] Warranty law is based upon a manufacturer's explicit and implicit representations made to consumers in sales transactions, and the law reasonably protects consumer expectations that are predictably generated from such representations.[12] Because the warranty law cases that paved the way for § 402A aimed to protect a consumer's ordinary or reasonable expectations, this was the natural liability test for the new tort doctrine.[13]

Powerful reasons support a rule protecting a consumer's expectations of product safety that arise from the safety representations of a manufacturer or other seller, whether those representations be express or implied.[14] When making safety "promises" in an effort to sell its products, a manufacturer seeks to convince potential buyers that its affirmations are both important and true. Safety information is impor-

---

**9.** See § 5.2, above.

**10.** See R. Pound, Social Control Through Law 114 (1942, 1968 reprint):

In civilized society men must be able to assume that those with whom they deal in the general intercourse of society will act in good faith and hence

(a) will make good reasonable expectations which their promises or other conduct reasonably create; [and]

(b) will carry out their undertakings according to the expectations which the moral sentiment of the community attaches thereto. . . .

**11.** See 1 J. Perillo, Corbin on Contracts § 1.1 (rev. ed. 1993):

§ 1.1 The Main Purpose of Contract Law is the Realization of Reasonable Expectations Induced by Promises

The underlying purpose of law and government is human happiness and contentment, to be brought about by the satisfaction of human desires in the highest practicable degree. . . .

That portion of the field of law that is classified and described as the law of contracts attempts the realization of reasonable expectations that have been induced by the making of a promise. . . .

The law does not attempt the realization of every expectation that has been induced by a promise; the expectation must be a reasonable one. . . .

Id. at 2–4.

**12.** See, e.g., Markle v. Mulholland's Inc., 509 P.2d 529, 532 (Or. 1973), where the majority remarked that consumer ex-

pectations are "the result of the manufacturer's or seller's placing the article in the stream of commerce with the intention that it be purchased. This expectation is given legal sanction by the law through an assumption that the seller, by so placing the article in the stream of commerce, has represented that the article is not unreasonably dangerous if put to its intended use." Further, "[o]ne can only determine what a purchaser has a right to expect by the implications express or inherent in the sale to him. These implications are analogous to those underlying a representation of merchantable quality." Id. at 534. Consider also the powerful article by Marshall Shapo, A Representational Theory of Consumer Protection: Doctrine, Function and Legal Liability for Product Disappointment, 60 Va. L. Rev. 1109, 1370 (1974) ("liability should center initially and principally on the portrayal of the product which is made, caused to be made or permitted by the seller. . . . viewed in the context of the impression reasonably received by the consumer from . . . advertising, [the product's appearance, its usual functions, and] other ways in which the product projects an image on the mind of the consumer").

**13.** See Fischer, Products Liability—The Meaning of Defect, 39 Mo. L. Rev. 339, 348 (1974). Judge Roger Traynor thought the consumer contemplation test reflected the "surprise element of danger." Traynor, The Ways and Meanings of Defective Products and Strict Liability, 32 Tenn. L. Rev. 363, 370 (1965).

**14.** See Owen, The Moral Foundations of Products Liability Law: Toward First Principles, 68 Notre Dame L. Rev. 427, 463–65 (1993).

tant and, hence, valuable to users because it provides a "frame of reference" that permits a user to shift his or her limited cognitive and other resources away from self-protection toward the pursuit of other goals—which in turn shifts responsibility for protecting the user to the manufacturer. In this manner, true safety information adds value to the product by enhancing the user's autonomy, for which value the consumer fairly pays a price. So, if the information is not true but false, the purchaser loses significant autonomy as well as the benefit of the bargain. Since an important purpose of the law is to promote autonomy, and the equality of the buyer to the seller as reflected in their deal, the law fairly may demand that the seller rectify the underlying falsity and resulting inequality in the exchange transaction if harm results.

Like most other standards of tort law, the consumer expectations test is an *objective* test: it is based on the average, normal, or "ordinary" expectations of a reasonable person.[15] This follows from § 402A's grounding in warranty and contract law, where the law protects only the "reasonable" or "justified" expectations of the contracting parties, as previously mentioned, and not those that arise from idiosyncratic fits of fancy. An objective standard is plainly necessary,[16] because a manufacturer in its design decisions is bound to "legislate" an amount of safety that is optimal for all consumers as a class, and it cannot be expected to design products separately for every user's secret preferences.[17]

An early example of a court seizing on the consumer expectations test as the test of liability under § 402A was *Vincer v. Esther Williams All–Aluminum Swimming Pool Co.*[18] There, a two-year-old child climbed up the ladder of an above-ground swimming pool, fell in, and was brain-damaged in the water. In the strict tort claim against the manufacturer of the pool, the plaintiff claimed that the design of the pool was defective because the manufacturer failed to take the simple step of adding a self-closing and self-latching gate at the top of the ladder to prevent small children from entering the pool. On appeal from a dismissal of the plaintiff's claim, the Wisconsin Supreme Court, relying on the portions of comments *g* and *i* set out above, remarked that "the test in Wisconsin of whether a product contains an unreasonably dangerous defect depends upon the reasonable expectations of the ordinary consumer concerning the characteristics of this type of product. If the average consumer would reasonably anticipate the dangerous condition of the product and fully appreciate the attendant risk of injury, it would not be unreasonably dangerous and defective."[19] Noting that "[t]his is an objec-

---

**15.** Comment *i* is phrased in terms of the "ordinary" consumer "with the ordinary knowledge common to the community." See, e.g., Benjamin v. Wal–Mart Stores, Inc., 61 P.3d 257, 268 (Or. Ct. App. 2002) ("The relevant question is not what consumers *should* expect or how a product *should* perform; rather, the jury is to determine 'the basically factual question of what reasonable consumers *do* expect from the product.' ").

**16.** *But see* L. Green, Strict Liability Under Sections 402A and 402B: A Decade of Litigation, 54 Texas L. Rev. 1185, 1211

(1976) ("[Are] not the expectations of the specific injured consumer enough? He must be given credit for expecting a product that was reasonably safe. He certainly did not expect an unreasonably dangerous product.").

**17.** See Owen, The Moral Foundations of Products Liability Law: Toward First Principles, 68 Notre Dame L. Rev. 427, 468–84 (1993).

**18.** 230 N.W.2d 794 (Wis. 1975).

**19.** Id. at 798.

tive test and is not dependent upon the knowledge of the particular injured consumer,"[20] the court affirmed the dismissal of the plaintiff's claim. The pool was not defective, reasoned the court, because an average consumer could not help but comprehend the danger to young children from the obvious absence of a self-latching gate.[21]

The consumer expectations test was quite clearly the dominant standard of defectiveness used by courts in the 1960s and 1970s, despite a growing number that rejected it as the sole or principal test of strict products liability.[22] And despite the drawbacks of using consumer expectations as a liability standard, many courts continue to use this test either by itself or combined in some fashion with risk-utility.[23]

## Obvious Dangers

As *Vincer* illustrates, obvious product dangers are ipso facto "contemplated" by consumers. Put another way, because consumers' safety expectations are almost never frustrated by obvious product dangers, the expectancy test almost always precludes liability in such cases. For example, in *Hartman v. Miller Hydro Co.*,[24] the defendant manufactured and sold a bottle-washing machine with an unguarded drive shaft to plaintiff's employer, The Pepsi Cola Bottling Company. The plaintiff, an assistant manager responsible for plant safety, leaned over the revolving

**20.** Id. (also noting that a consumer's personal knowledge might bear on contributory negligence).

**21.** Id. at 799.

**22.** See Fischer, Products Liability—The Meaning of Defect, 39 Mo. L. Rev. 339, 348–52 (1974) (noting that its use as the sole test of defectiveness involves "serious drawbacks" and, "[a]s a consequence, an increasing number of courts ... have rejected this test in a number of situations").

**23.** See, e.g., Johnson v. Ford Motor Co., 45 P.3d 86, 91 (Okla. 2002) (plaintiff must prove that the "defect made the product unreasonably dangerous to an extent beyond which would be contemplated by the ordinary consumer who purchases it"); Vautour v. Body Masters Sports Indus., Inc., 784 A.2d 1178 (N.H. 2001) ("whether a product is unreasonably dangerous to an extent beyond that which would be contemplated by the ordinary consumer is determined by the jury using a risk-utility balancing test"); Allison v. Merck & Co., 878 P.2d 948, 952 (Nev. 1994) (measles, mumps, and rubella vaccine that caused blindness, deafness, and mental retardation did not perform as reasonably expected); Jarke v. Jackson Products, 631 N.E.2d 233 (Ill. App. Ct. 1994) (side rim of welding mask funneled molten welding slag into ear canal); Lester v. Magic Chef, Inc., 641 P.2d 353 (Kan. 1982). See also Utah Code Ann. § 78–6(2): " '[U]nreasonably dangerous' means that the product was dangerous to an extent beyond which would be contem-

plated by the ordinary and prudent buyer, consumer or user of that product in that community considering the product's characteristics ... together with any actual knowledge, training, or experience possessed by that particular buyer, user or consumer."

In a comprehensive review of the decisions from every state, John Vargo concluded that the consumer expectations test was then applied in some manner in half the states: Alabama, Alaska, Arizona, Arkansas, California, Connecticut, District of Columbia, Hawaii, Idaho, Illinois, Indiana, Iowa, Kansas, Maryland, Massachusetts, Nebraska, Ohio, Oklahoma, Rhode Island, South Carolina, Tennessee, Utah, Vermont, Washington, and Wisconsin. Vargo, The Emperor's New Clothes: The American Law Institute Adorns a "New Cloth" for Section 402A Products Liability Design Defects—A Survey of the States Reveals a Different Weave, 26 U. Memphis L. Rev. 493, 556 & 951 (1996) (index 2). The law in many of these states has been moving in the direction of risk-utility balancing, at least in certain types of cases. The Reporters for the Products Liability Restatement list Alaska, Arkansas, Hawaii, Nebraska, Oklahoma, and Wisconsin as states which still have an undiluted, independent consumer expectations basis for products liability in tort. See Products Liability Restatement § 2(b), Reporters' Notes on cmt. *d*, § II(D), at 76.

**24.** 499 F.2d 191 (10th Cir. 1974) (Kan. law).

shaft to set up some fallen bottles and was injured when his trousers were pulled into the machine. Applying the expectancy test of comment *i*, the court upheld a judgment for the defendant on the plaintiff's § 402A claim. Dismissing plaintiff's testimony that he did not comprehend the danger in leaning against the exposed drive shaft, the court noted that another employee had previously been caught in the same shaft. "Thus, it cannot be said that a danger existed which was beyond contemplation of an ordinary user. The danger was obvious."[25] Many other cases similarly have denied recovery under the consumer expectations test to plaintiffs injured by obvious product dangers.[26]

### Whose Expectations?

Special problems arise in determining whose expectations to protect. The first question in this regard concerns whether the expectations are those of the purchaser or the ultimate consumer, if the two are different. Under the law of contracts, the relevant expectations are, of course, those of the purchaser, a contracting party, which is the standard as set forth in comment *i*.[27] But, even though § 402A grew out of the law of warranty, it sets forth a liability standard for the law of *torts*, not contracts, and tort law duties normally extend to all foreseeable victims, as suggested by comment *g*.[28]

The expectations of persons whose safety is protected by others, such as children, patients, and employees, raise particular problems. The issue in such cases is whether the expectations of the ward (the child, patient, or employee) or those of the custodian (the parent, doctor, or employer) should govern. The user-bystander situation presents a similar problem.[29] Where the safety custodian, but not the ward, can best

---

**25.** Id. at 194.

**26.** See, e.g., Irion v. Sun Lighting, Inc., 2004 WL 746823 (Tenn. Ct. App. 2004) (summary judgment for defendants where plaintiff's son placed a pillowcase over halogen lamp thereby causing a fire and significant property damage because danger was obvious to the ordinary consumer); Ahrens v. Ford Motor Co., 340 F.3d 1142 (10th Cir. 2003) (Okla. law) (2003) (absence of seatbelt on tractor from which decedent was thrown); Halliday v. Sturm, Ruger & Co., 792 A.2d 1145 (Md. 2002) (plaintiff's decedent killed by self-inflicted gun shot wound: "There was no malfunction of the gun; regrettably, it worked exactly as it was designed and intended to work and as any ordinary consumer would have expected it to work."); Bruner v. Anheuser–Busch, Inc., 153 F.Supp.2d 1358 (S.D. Fla. 2001) (plaintiffs suffered harm from over-consumption of beer; because dangers of alcohol abuse are common knowledge, Budweiser beer is not dangerous beyond consumer's expectations); Vineyard v. Empire Mach. Co., 581 P.2d 1152, 1155 (Ariz. Ct. App. 1978) (absence of roll-over bar on large earth-moving scraper, which rolled over and crushed operator's leg, not a danger beyond consum-

er's expectations since its absence was "immediately evident"); Menard v. Newhall, 373 A.2d 505, 507 (Vt. 1977) (plaintiff's eye put out in BB gun fight: "A BB gun which is neither defectively designed nor manufactured is not dangerous beyond that which would be contemplated by the ordinary consumer.... A warning by the defendant Daisy that a BB gun, if fired at a person, could injure an eye, is nothing that even a seven-year-old child does not already know."). See § 10.2, below.

**27.** Comment *i* to § 402A states: "The article sold must be dangerous to an extent beyond that which would be contemplated by *the ordinary consumer who purchases it*." (emphasis added)

**28.** Comment *g* to § 402A refers to "a condition not contemplated by *the ultimate consumer*." (emphasis added)

**29.** On the bystander expectations issue, see, e.g., Ewen v. McLean Truck. Co., 706 P.2d 929 (Or. 1985) (pedestrian, struck by truck, could not recover as "consumer" under comment *i*); Cornelius v. Bay Motors Inc., 484 P.2d 299 (Or. 1971). See § 5.3 (types of plaintiffs), above.

evaluate and control the risk, as often is the case with parents, doctors, users, and sometimes employers, courts generally have applied the expectations of the custodian, rather than the ward whose safety expectations are usually vague or nonexistent. This surely is the proper result in most such cases, since responsibility in tort is frequently and properly placed on those responsible for controlling risk.[30]

A good example of the parent-child context is *Bellotte v. Zayre Corp.*,[31] in which a five-year old child was burned when his cotton pajama top ignited while he was playing with matches. In deciding whether the pajamas were "unreasonably dangerous to the user or consumer" because the fabric had not been treated with an effective fire-retardant substance, the court addressed the question of whether the safety characteristics of the pajamas should be measured according to the expectations of the "consuming" child or the "purchasing" parent. Plaintiffs contended that "the test should be whether they were dangerous to an extent beyond that which would be contemplated by the ordinary five-year old child." The court did not agree: "Children of that age do not contemplate even the unavoidable dangers of cotton pajamas and their flammable characteristics. There would therefore be no base from which to determine unreasonableness and the seller would become an insurer."[32] Thus, in cases involving injuries to young children, the parent or other adult buyer's (or user's) expectations ordinarily should control.[33]

In the doctor-patient situation, the expectations issue is likely to be more complicated and often depends upon the type of product that fails and the reason for its failure. If a surgical needle breaks while being inserted into the patient's body, the relevant expectations surely are the doctor's, not the patient's: it is the doctor (together with the manufacturer) who controls the risk; and it is the doctor, not the patient, who knows about the strength of such needles and what forces they fairly should be expected to withstand.[34] But if a patient is injured by the failure of a medical device or implant, such as a pacemaker or breast implant, the expectations issue is not so clear. Assuming that the doctor fully apprised the patient of all material risks and benefits of the medical device, the informed patient's reasonable expectations of the device's limitations seemingly should control.[35] But real-world medical care often

---

**30.** See, e.g., Owen, Rethinking the Policies of Strict Products Liability, 33 Vand. L. Rev. 681, 711–13 (1980).

**31.** 352 A.2d 723 (N.H. 1976).

**32.** Id. at 725.

**33.** See also Welch v. Scripto–Tokai Corp., 651 N.E.2d 810 (Ind. Ct. App. 1995) (3–year-old ignited his pajamas with disposable butane cigarette lighter; *held*, ordinary consumer is adult, and adults expect lighters to generate a flame); Brawner v. Liberty Indus., Inc., 573 S.W.2d 376 (Mo. Ct. App. 1978) (gasoline container lacking childproof lid not unreasonably dangerous beyond the expectations of the ordinary con-

sumer, because it was designed for adult use only).

**34.** See Ethicon, Inc. v. Parten, 520 S.W.2d 527, 533 (Tex. Civ. App. 1975) (surgical needle broke in patient's body).

**35.** See V. Mueller & Co. v. Corley, 570 S.W.2d 140 (Tex. Civ. App. 1978) (silicone breast implant broke in patient's body; "The defective condition in the prosthesis in question rendered it unreasonably dangerous to Mrs. Corley, not to her physician, Dr. Leeves. The appropriate question for the jury, therefore, was whether the defective condition was one which was not contemplated by the user, the 'ultimate consumer,' [such that the] trial court properly

differs quite materially from this model of ideal counseling, and in cases where the doctor, not the patient, makes the informed choice of risks and benefits, probably the doctor's expectations should be determinative. Not unfairly, in such a case, a patient may properly look solely to the doctor for proper counseling and recovery under the medical malpractice doctrine of informed consent.[36]

Employer-employee cases present other problems. While employees are in many respects dependent on employers to maintain workplaces that are safe, including the selection of safe industrial machinery and chemicals, manufacturers sometimes can best provide protection by warning employees directly of a risk. For example, in *Jackson v. Coast Paint & Lacquer Co.*,[37] the plaintiff, injured while spray-painting the inside of a tank car when the accumulated paint fumes ignited unexpectedly, sued the paint manufacturer for failing to warn of this risk. The defendant contended that no warning was necessary since plaintiff's employer knew of the risk, even if plaintiff did not. Holding for the plaintiff, the court reasoned that warnings could have been placed effectively upon the paint container labels. The "community" whose expectations were relevant, under comment *i*, consisted of the painters who would be exposed to the danger, not the employers who bought the paint.[38]

### Problems with the Test

Although the theoretical foundations of the consumer expectations test may be strong, the test has several serious, practical shortcomings if it is used as the sole test of strict products liability in every case. First, as previously discussed, the test undesirably bars consumers from recovery in virtually every case in which a danger was obvious, even if the manufacturer could easily and cheaply have removed a serious danger.[39] Also examined earlier, while the consumer expectations test may work satisfactorily in some cases where the plaintiff and the purchaser are the same person, it often fails to provide adequate guidance in cases involving other victims of product accidents, be they children, patients, employees, or bystanders. A third and especially problematic aspect of the consumer expectations test lies in the vagueness of consumer expectations in many contexts.[40] Particularly in considering the design adequacy

keyed its instructions to the mind of the person who would be injured by the dangerous condition of the product.").

**36.** See Prosser and Keeton on Torts § 32, at 189–93.

**37.** 499 F.2d 809, 812 (9th Cir. 1974) (Mont. law).

**38.** Note, however, that trained, experienced, professional workers will be held to understand the need to read and follow instructions with respect to products marketed for such professional purposes, and defectiveness will be determined according to such professional expectations. See, e.g., Hutchins v. Silicone Specialties, Inc., 881 P.2d 64 (Okla. 1993). On when a manufacturer must warn employees directly, see § 9.4, below.

**39.** This is conventionally recognized as an inherent weakness in this test. See Prosser and Keeton on Torts § 99, at 698 ("Under this test, a victim could never recover for harm suffered as a result of a design hazard that was open or obvious or one with respect to which the purchaser was adequately informed."). *But see* Phillips, Consumer Expectations, 53 S.C. L. Rev. 1047, 1049 (2002) (characterizing as "semantic" the consumer expectation test's foreclosure of relief to persons injured by obvious dangers).

**40.** See Montgomery and Owen, Reflections on the Theory and Administration of

of a complex product—such as an automobile, a pharmaceutical drug, or another chemical product—consumers have no idea how safely the product really ought to perform in various situations.[41] How can an ordinary consumer possibly know the extent of protection fairly to be expected when an automobile crashes into a tree at 10, 20, or even 40 miles per hour?[42] Lurking at the very heart of the consumer expectations test, the vagueness problem undermines the test in the most complex cases where a reliable standard of liability is needed most.[43]

For these and other reasons, courts increasingly are abandoning the consumer expectations test as the sole or principal means for determining defectiveness in most products liability cases.[44] Some courts, troubled at having to make the move from consumer expectations to risk-utility, do so furtively, by defining consumer expectations in risk-utility terms. One of the first decisions to do so was *Seattle–First Nat'l Bank v. Tabert*,[45] which finessed the inability of the consumer expectations test to resolve the complex design issues in an automotive liability case by converting consumer expectations to a risk-utility test: "In determining the reasonable expectations of the ordinary consumer, a number of factors must be considered [including t]he relative cost of the product,

Strict Tort Liability for Defective Products, 27 S.C. L. Rev. 803, 823 (1976) ("an attempt to determine the consumer's reasonable expectations of safety concerning a technologically complex product may well be an exercise in futility, for the consumer may have at most only a generalized expectancy—perhaps more accurately only an unconscious hope—that the product will not harm him if he treats it with a reasonable amount of care"). See also Prosser and Keeton on Torts at 699:

> In a sense the ordinary purchaser cannot reasonably expect anything more than that reasonable care in the exercise of the skill and knowledge available to design engineers has been exercised. The test can be utilized to explain most any result that a court or jury chooses to reach. The application of such a vague concept in many situations does not provide much guidance for a jury.

**41.** This problem springs from a variety of factors: "(1) humans lack the data necessary to form expectations; (2) humans are psychologically unable to contemplate injury to themselves and thus underestimate the importance of such injury in making decisions; and (3) people overvalue short-term gains and losses and undervalue long-range considerations." Hubbard, Reasonable *Human* Expectations: A Normative Model for Imposing Strict Liability for Defective Products, 29 Mercer L. Rev. 465, 475 (1978).

**42.** Or when a 5– to 6–inch rock strikes the wheel of a 4–wheel-drive pickup truck at normal highway speed. See Heaton v. Ford Motor Co., 435 P.2d 806 (Or. 1967). See Dickerson, Products Liability: How

Good Does a Product Have to Be?, 42 Ind. L.J. 301, 307 (1967): "The most troublesome situations are those in which consumer attitudes have not sufficiently crystallized to define an expected standard of performance. What, for instance, should the law do about tractors that overturn, surgical implants that break, and rear-engined automobiles that tend to swerve at high speeds?" See also Restatement (Third) of Torts § 2(b) cmt. *d*, Reporters' Notes, § III(A), at 79.

**43.** For discussions of problems with the consumer expectations test, see Davis, Design Defect Liability: In Search of a Standard of Responsibility, 39 Wayne L. Rev. 1217, 1236–37 (1993); Dickerson, Products Liability: How Good Does a Product Have to Be?, 42 Ind. L.J. 301 (1967); Fischer, Products Liability—The Meaning of Defect, 39 Mo. L. Rev. 339, 348–52 (1974).

**44.** For examples of movements away from consumer expectations toward risk-utility, see, e.g., Banks v. ICI Am., Inc., 450 S.E.2d 671 (Ga. 1994); St. Germain v. Husqvarna Corp., 544 A.2d 1283, 1286 (Me. 1988); Nichols v. Union Underwear Co., 602 S.W.2d 429 (Ky. 1980). In Sperry–New Holland v. Prestage, 617 So.2d 248, 255–56 (Miss. 1993), the court noted that it had followed "the trend in most federal and state jurisdictions" by moving "away from a 'consumer expectations' analysis" and "towards 'risk-utility'" because "[a] 'risk-utility' analysis best protects both the manufacturer and the consumer."

**45.** 542 P.2d 774 (Wash. 1975). See §§ 5.8 and 8.6, below.

the gravity of the potential harm from the claimed defect and the cost and feasibility of eliminating or minimizing the risk. . . . "[46]

The European Community's *Product Liability Directive* defines defectiveness in terms of consumer expectations.[47] Yet, the European liability standard is phrased in terms of what consumers are "entitled" to expect. Thus, consumers may be entitled to expect their products to be free of manufacturing flaws, and they probably are entitled to expect that the designs of most types of products are reasonably safe, not absolutely safe or accident-proof. Hence, the "entitled-to-expect" standard may require risk-utility analysis to determine how safe a manufacturer reasonably could have designed a product in lieu of fashioning a test from the actual contemplations of consumers.[48]

Although the consumer expectations test is withering as the true, sole test for strict products liability in tort, it remains an important consideration in many products liability cases. In some states it remains the principal, or only, test of liability;[49] in others, even if considered only as a factor in the risk-utility balance, it may be determinative in certain situations;[50] and in a small set of special product cases it remains the central liability consideration.[51]

## § 5.7   THE RISK-UTILITY TEST

### In General

Many courts, dissatisfied with the consumer expectations test and unwilling to abandon the calculus-of-risk principles of negligence law,[1] use some form of "risk-utility," "risk-benefit," or "cost-benefit" test for liability under strict products liability in tort.[2] Borrowed from the law of

---

**46.** Id. at 779.

**47.** Article 6(1) of the 1985 European Community Directive "Concerning Liability for Defective Products" provides that "[a] product is defective when it does not provide the safety which a person is entitled to expect, taking all circumstances into account, including: (a) the presentation of the product; (b) the use to which it could reasonably be expected that the product would be put; and (c) the time when the product was put into circulation." See § 1.4, above.

**48.** Professor Jane Stapleton has lucidly explained this point. See, e.g., Stapleton, Products Liability in the United Kingdom: The Myths of Reform, 34 Tex. Int'l L.J. 45 (1999); Stapleton, Products Liability Reform—Real or Illusory?, 6 Oxford J. Legal Stud. 392, 405 (1986). See also Owen, Strict Products Liability in America and Europe, in Festschrift für Erwin Deutsch 305, 309–10 (1999).

**49.** See, e.g., Green v. Smith & Nephew AHP, Inc., 629 N.W.2d 727, 741 (Wis. 2001) (noting that state's steadfast "devotion to the consumer-contemplation test").

**50.** See Products Liability Restatement § 2 cmt. *g.*

**51.** Id. at cmt. *h*: "With regard to two special product categories consumer expectations play a special role in determining product defect. See § 7 (food products) and § 8 (used products)."

**§ 5.7**

**1.** "It is necessary to remember that whether the doctrine of negligence . . . or strict liability is being used to impose liability, the same process is going on in each instance, i.e., weighing the utility of the article against the risk of its use." Phillips v. Kimwood Mach. Co., 525 P.2d 1033, 1039 (Or. 1974). See § 2.2 (cost-benefit analysis in negligence), above.

**2.** On the risk-utility test, see Gilles, United States v. Carroll Towing Co.: The Hand Formula's Home Port, in Torts Stories 11 (R. Rabin & S. Sugarman, eds., Foundation Press, 2003); Miller, Myth Surrenders to Reality: Design Defect Litigation in Iowa, 51 Drake L. Rev. 459 (2003); Owen, Toward a Proper Test for Design Defectiveness: "Micro–Balancing" Costs and Benefits, 75 Texas L. Rev. 1661 (1997); Owen, Risk–Utility Balancing in Design Defect Cases, 30 U. Mich. J.L. Ref. 239 (1997);

negligence, this test was converted to the realm of strict liability in tort at an early date.[3] For example, in *Helicoid Gage Div. of American Chain & Cable Co. v. Howell*,[4] a pressure gauge manufactured by the defendant burst, throwing a piece of the gauge lens into the plaintiff's eye. The jury rendered a verdict for the plaintiff, which the appellate court affirmed. "To determine whether a product is unreasonably dangerous," thought the court, "it is necessary to weigh the risk of harm against the utility of the product, considering whether safety devices would unreasonably raise the costs or diminish the utility of the product." The evidence revealed that shatterproof glass, which would have prevented the injury, would have increased the cost of each gauge by only one dollar without reducing its utility at all.[5] Moreover, an "inexpensive" safety shield, that would not have diminished the utility of the gauge, could have been added for about $2.50.

In another early case, *Dorsey v. Yoder Co.*,[6] the operator's hand and arm were caught and drawn into an unguarded metal slitter machine. On the defendant's motion for j.n.o.v. after a verdict for the plaintiff, the court observed that "a guard would not eliminate the machine's usefulness, nor would the cost of $200 to $500 on an $8,000 machine be unreasonable. Moreover, the seriousness of the potential harm was great. Ultimately, all of these facts were questions to be weighed by the jury in making their ultimate determination as to whether, under all of the circumstances, the machine was 'defective.'" Observing that the jury found that "the balance tipped in favor of plaintiff," the court remarked that it "could not possibly rule otherwise."[7]

By the mid–1970s, a number of products liability law scholars began to call for a shift away from § 402A's consumer expectations test toward a cost-benefit test, particularly in design defect cases. An early study of products liability law by a group of law and engineering professors reflects the beginnings of the shift toward evaluating product hazards in

M. Green, The Schizophrenia of Risk–Benefit Analysis in Design Defect Litigation, 48 Vand. L. Rev. 609 (1995); Miller, Design Defect Litigation in Iowa: The Myths of Strict Liability, 40 Drake L. Rev. 465 (1991); White, Risk–Utility Analysis and the Learned Hand Formula: A Hand that Helps or a Hand that Hides?, 32 Ariz. L. Rev. 77 (1990); Epstein, The Risks of Risk/Utility, 48 Ohio St. L. Rev. 469 (1987). For a useful practitioner perspective, see Rheingold, The Risk/Utility Test in Product Cases, 18 Trial Lawyers Quarterly 49 (1987).

For economic perspectives on risk-utility analysis, see, e.g., R. Posner, Economic Analysis of Law §§ 6.1 and 6.6 (6th ed. 2003); W. Viscusi, Reforming Products Liability ch. 4 (1991); Gilles, The Invisible Hand Formula, 80 Va. L. Rev. 1015, 1025 (1994); Viscusi, Wading Through the Muddle of Risk–Utility Analysis, 39 Am. U. L. Rev. 573 (1990); A. Schwartz, Proposals for Products Liability Reform: A Theoretical Synthesis, 97 Yale L.J. 353, 384–88 (1988); Epstein, The Risks of Risk/Utility, 48 Ohio

St. L.J. 469 (1987); Note, 73 Cornell L. Rev. 606 (1988); Comment, 84 Colum. L. Rev. 2045 (1984).

**3.** See, e.g., Roach v. Kononen, 525 P.2d 125 (Or. 1974), an action against Ford Motor Company for injuries from a crash occurring when the hood on a Ford automobile suddenly flew up and blocked the driver's vision. Experts testified that the hood could have been designed to permit substantially better visibility in such situations; that Ford was aware of six or seven inadvertent hood openings over a seven or eight year period; and that the proposed design would require adding certain reinforcements to the hood and its hinges that would cost $5–10 per car. *Held,* jury verdict for defendant affirmed.

**4.** 511 S.W.2d 573 (Tex. Civ.App. 1974).

**5.** Id. at 577.

**6.** 331 F.Supp. 753 (E.D. Pa. 1971), aff'd, 474 F.2d 1339 (3d Cir. 1973).

**7.** Id. at 760.

terms of the costs and benefits of remedying those hazards. "It is time to abandon the perspective of the reasonable consumer," they asserted, in order to "formulate the strict liability question for what it is. The issue in every products case is whether the product *qua* product meets society's standards of acceptability. The unreasonable danger question, then, is posed in terms of whether, given the risks and benefits of possible alternatives to the product, we as a society will live with it in its existing state or will require an altered, less dangerous form." In short, "the question is whether the product is a reasonable one given the reality of its use in contemporary society."[8] As more and more courts turned to some form of risk-benefit test in the 1980s and 1990s, and with the *Third Restatement*'s adoption of the risk-utility test for use in design and warnings cases,[9] cost-benefit analysis is now undoubtedly the dominant liability test in products liability law.[10]

### Nature of the Risk–Utility Test

The basic "risk-benefit," "cost-benefit," "risk-utility," or "calculus of risk" approach to products liability decision-making was explained in the context of negligence, above.[11] The fundamentals of this approach are identical in the strict tort context,[12] and they are worth restating here. "The basic notion of cost-benefit analysis is not new. Any individual decision is usually the consequence of the actor's assessment of the advantages (benefits) and disadvantages (costs) of the action."[13] As phrased in one early design case, a determination of whether a design hazard is "unreasonable" involves "a balancing of the probability and seriousness of harm against the costs of taking precautions. Relevant factors to be considered include the availability of alternative designs, the cost and feasibility of adopting alternative designs, and the frequency or infrequency of injury resulting from the design."[14] In short, a product

---

**8.** Donaher, Piehler, Twerski, and Weinstein, The Technological Expert in Products Liability Litigation, 52 Tex. L. Rev. 1303, 1307 (1974).

**9.** See §§ 6.5 and 8.8, below.

**10.** See a massive collection of authority to this effect by the Reporters for the new *Restatement*. Products Liability Restatement § 2, Reporters' Notes to cmt. *d*. For a dissenting view, canvassing the law of every state, see Vargo, The Emperor's New Clothes: The American Law Institute Adorns a "New Cloth" for Section 402A Products Liability Design Defects—A Survey of the States Reveals a Different Weave, 26 U. Mem. L. Rev. 493 (1996).

**11.** See § 2.2, above.

**12.** With the possible exception of the *foreseeability* of the costs and benefits, which many courts and commentators once believed distinguished strict from negligence-based liability. Because most courts and commentators now believe that a plaintiff must establish foreseeability in "strict" tort actions as well as in negligence, cost-

benefit or risk-utility analysis should normally be identical in both contexts. The foreseeability issue, which concerns the so-called Wade–Keeton test and often is examined under the "state of the art" umbrella, is addressed in §§ 8.7 and 10.4, below.

**13.** H. Green, Cost–Risk–Benefit Assessment and the Law: Introduction and Perspective, 45 Geo. Wash. L. Rev. 901, 903–04 (1977). Consider also Merrill, Risk–Benefit Decision–Making by the Food and Drug Administration, 45 Geo. Wash. L. Rev. 994, 996 (1977) (" 'Risk-benefit' ... includes any technique for making choices that explicitly or implicitly attempts to measure the potential adverse consequences of an activity and to predict its benefits. In its most refined form, such an analysis may make use of refined mathematical methods for calculating risks and benefits, attempting to assign uniform values, usually in dollars, to all factors, including human lives.").

**14.** Raney v. Honeywell, Inc., 540 F.2d 932, 935 (8th Cir. 1976) (Iowa law).

is considered "defective" under a risk-utility test if the costs of eliminating a particular hazard are less than the resulting safety benefits.[15]

The cost-benefit or risk-utility test, by balancing a particular risk of harm against the burden ("costs") of avoiding that risk, is most useful for ascertaining the safety or defectiveness of a product design.[16] Thus, the type and amount of safety required is generally a function of the type, likelihood, and amount of expected harm (together viewed as the magnitude of the risk) that precautions (of a particular cost) may be expected to prevent. If the risk posed by the sale and use of a product in a certain condition is great, substantial precautions must be taken to avert the risk; if the risk is small, precautions may be small as well. Thus, if the risk at issue concerns the possible failure of an automobile's steering, brakes, or tires at highway speeds, or the possibility that a punch press ram may unexpectedly depress upon an operator's hand, the manufacturer must employ the utmost precautions to avert the risk. Yet, if the risk is relatively minimal, reasonably appearing to involve at most the risk of minor harm to person or property—scratches, stains, or the harmless malfunction of the product—then a manufacturer need apply only minimal precautions to reduce such risks. This principle of balance that inheres in tort law generally is sometimes referred to as the "calculus of risk."

## The Hand Formula in the Strict Liability Context

### *In General*

The most celebrated formulation of the risk-benefit test, albeit in the context of negligence rather than "strict" products liability, was provided by Judge Learned Hand in the case of *United States v. Carroll Towing Co.*,[17] discussed above.[18] In *Carroll Towing*, Judge Hand reasoned that a determination of the extent of precaution appropriate to an occasion generally reflects a calculus of three factors: the burden of taking precautions to avoid a risk of harm, on the one side, balanced against the likelihood that the actor's conduct will produce the harm multiplied by the seriousness of the harm, on the other. Negligence is

---

**15.** On the formulation of such a test, see Owen, Toward a Proper Test for Design Defectiveness: "Micro–Balancing" Costs and Benefits, 75 Texas L. Rev. 1661, 1686–90 (1997).

**16.** Courts have found the risk-benefit test most helpful in making design defectiveness determinations and only marginally helpful in warnings cases. See ch. 8 (design defects) and ch. 9 (warnings defects), below. In manufacturing flaw cases decided in strict tort, where courts have sought to apply a truly "strict" basis of liability, cost-benefit analysis has been ignored. See ch. 7, below.

**17.** 159 F.2d 169, 173 (2d Cir. 1947). Hand first employed this approach in Conway v. O'Brien, 111 F.2d 611 (2d Cir. 1940),

rev'd on other grounds, 312 U.S. 492 (1941), and he subsequently reexamined this approach in Moisan v. Loftus, 178 F.2d 148, 149 (2d Cir. 1949).

**18.** The *Carroll Towing* case and the Hand formula are examined in the negligence context in § 2.2, above, and the design defect context, in § 8.4, below. Perhaps the most helpful accounts of both *Carroll Towing* and the Hand formula are Gilles, United States v. Carroll Towing Co.: The Hand Formula's Home Port, in Torts Stories 11 (R. Rabin & S. Sugarman, eds., Foundation Press, 2003), and Gilles, The Invisible Hand Formula, 80 Va. L. Rev. 1015, 1025 (1994). For other treatments, see n.2, above.

implied if an actor fails to adopt a burden of precaution of less magnitude than the harm it is likely to prevent. Judge Hand expressed this concept algebraically: Negligence is suggested if B < P x L, where B is the burden or cost of avoiding accidental loss expected to result if B is not undertaken, P is the increase in the probability of loss if B is not undertaken, and L is the probable magnitude (expected cost) of such loss if it does occur. This is the so-called "Hand formula." If the formula is supplemented with a symbol for the implication of negligence, ⇒ N the full formula reads: B < P x L ⇒ N. Thus, conceived and applied to negligence determinations in the products liability context, the Hand formula may be explained as follows: if the cost of adopting a particular safety precaution (B) is less than the safety gains expected to result therefrom (P x L), the manufacturer's failure to adopt the precaution implies its negligence ( ⇒ N).

By substituting "defect" for "negligence" (D for N), the Hand formula converts comfortably to the "strict" products liability task of determining defectiveness. So reformulated, the defectiveness "equation" looks like this:

$$B < P \text{ x } L \Rightarrow N$$

In cost-benefit terms, the formula states:

$$(Accident\ Prevention)\ Costs < (Safety)\ Benefits \Rightarrow Defect$$

In short, a product is defective if the safety benefits of a particular safety precaution the manufacturer fails to adopt foreseeably exceed the resulting costs, including any diminished usefulness or diminished safety.[19]

Most courts have formulated the risk-utility test in broader terms, whereby the product's risks are weighed against its benefits or utility.[20] Yet the formulation above (the Hand formula in cost-benefit terms) quite accurately describes the test as lawyers and judges properly put it to use in trial courtrooms around the nation.[21] That is, the issue actually litigated almost always concerns the narrow "*micro*-balance" of pros and cons of a manufacturer's failure to adopt some particular design feature that would have prevented the plaintiff's harm—whether the costs of changing the overall design in some particular (micro) manner would have been worth the resulting safety benefits.[22] Moreover, the more

**19.** See Owen, Toward a Proper Test for Design Defectiveness: "Micro–Balancing" Costs and Benefits, 75 Tex. L. Rev. 1661, 1690 (1997).

**20.** See Owen, Risk–Utility Balancing in Design Defect Cases, 30 U. Mich. L.J. Reform 239 (1997) (surveying risk-utility tests among the states).

**21.** Id. at 242.

**22.** The more narrow formulation of the test reflects how courts and lawyers actually proceed in assessing liability under the Hand formula. See, e.g., R. Heafey and D. Kennedy, Product Liability: Winning Strategies and Techniques §§ 4.04 and 4.05, and p. 4–9 (1994) (characterizing the manufac-

narrow formulation above avoids a number of quite serious problems inherent in the broader test.[23]

The Hand defectiveness formula succinctly captures the common-sense idea that products are unacceptably dangerous if they contain dangers that might cost-effectively (and practicably) be removed. A premise of the formula is that manufacturers may fairly be required to contemplate the consequences to consumers of dangers in their products' safety before they place those products on the market. Thus, in its design and marketing decisions, a responsible manufacturer should consider the risks of injury to consumers and bystanders and should weigh the interests of those parties equally to its own interest in maximizing profits. Manufacturers, of course, may also properly consider such factors as a product's usefulness, its cost, and profitability. But the point of the Hand formula is that manufacturers are also duty-bound to include in the balance a properly proportionate consideration of the various risks of harm that may be expected to result from the product when put to real-world use.

In sum, the risk-utility test demands that manufacturers adopt precautions proportionate to the magnitude of the expected risk. This simple yet fundamental principle of defectiveness, which ties the measure of precaution to the measure of risk, grounds the safety obligations of a manufacturer in strict liability as well as negligence.

Because the method for ascertaining responsibility is identical in both negligence and strict liability, many courts and commentators have recognized the "functional" equivalence of the two theories of liability in design and warnings cases,[24] causing the Iowa Supreme Court first to repeal its doctrine of strict products liability in tort in warnings cases in

turer's choice to forego a reasonable alternative design as "the heart of the plaintiff's case"). See also Rheingold, The Risk/Utility Test in Product Cases, 18 Trial Lawyers Quarterly 49, 50 (Spring/Fall 1987) ("The usual and proper approach for a plaintiff in a design defect case is to present evidence on an alternative design which the jury can find should have been adopted for the product in question.").

> The attorney for the plaintiff will try to find some act which, if the defendant had taken it, would have significantly reduced the probability of the accident at low cost [such] that the increment in the expected loss was greater than the cost of avoidance.... The defendant will try to respond that the expected benefits of the proposed act were, in fact, less than the costs of undertaking it. [The decision-maker is then] asked to compare the incremental expected benefits with the incremental costs.

Brown, Toward An Economic Theory of Liability, 2 J. Legal Stud. 323, 334–35 (1973).

**23.** See Brown, id.; Owen, Risk–Utility Balancing in Design Defect Cases, 30 U. Mich. J.L. Reform 239 (1997).

**24.** See, e.g., Mayor of Balt. v. Utica Mut. Ins. Co., 802 A.2d 1070, 1089 (Md. App. 2002) ("these two theories—negligence and strict liability failure to warn—have been described as nearly identical"); Cervelli v. Thompson/Center Arms, 183 F.Supp.2d 1032, 1040 (S.D. Ohio 2002) ("the standard imposed upon the defendant in a strict liability claim grounded upon an inadequate warning is the same as that imposed in a negligence claim based upon inadequate warning"); Jones v. Nordic-Track, Inc., 550 S.E.2d 101, 103 n.5 (Ga. 2001) (design: "no significant distinction between negligence and strict liability for purposes of the risk-utility analysis"); Olson v. Prosoco, Inc., 522 N.W.2d 284, 289 (Iowa 1994) (warnings: "we believe any posited distinction between strict liability and negligence principles is illusory"). See also Ackerman v. American Cyanamid Co., 586 N.W.2d 208, 220 (Iowa 1998) (" 'the strict liability claim depend[s] on virtually the same elements of proof as are required to establish the negligence claim' " and " 'a growing number of courts and commentators have found that, in cases in which the plaintiff's injury is caused by an alleged defect in the design of a product, there is no practical difference between theories of negligence and strict liability' ").

favor of plain negligence[25] and later to abandon liability theory labels altogether in design defect cases.[26] The virtual identity of the two doctrines in design and warnings cases, in jurisdictions which rely upon the risk-utility test, is examined further in this chapter[27] and in the chapters on defective design and warnings.[28]

## Risk–Utility Theory

The risk-utility test is constructed on solid theoretical footings.[29] Whereas the consumer expectations test seeks to protect the autonomy of potential product victims, the goal of the risk-utility test is to maximize the common good. By judging the sufficiency of a product's safety according to the balance of the costs and benefits of improving its safety in a particular manner, the test provides a powerful standard of responsibility: failure to adopt a safety feature is wrongful if the feature should have been expected to produce more good than harm, and such a failure is justified if such action might have been expected to produce more harm than good. This standard derives from utilitarian theory, which itself is grounded in the moral ideals of both freedom and equality. By judging a manufacturer's safety decision in terms of its expected costs and benefits, whether it would likely augment or diminish net communal welfare, the standard requires manufacturers to fairly respect the freedom interests of consumers generally, and potential accident victims in particular, by valuing them on an equal basis with the interests of its shareholders. By channeling a manufacturer's decisions in a cost-effective direction, the risk-utility test also helps to protect society's scarce resources and minimize waste, which generally advances social welfare. While the operation of a risk-utility rule in practice may only crudely assist the goal of optimizing product safety,[30] the test at least may help achieve a roughly efficient allocation of resources by discouraging manufacturers from marketing products containing excessive accident costs. Moreover, higher prices resulting from liability judgments and settlements should reduce consumption of such products by consumers. Finally, and perhaps most importantly, judicial use of an efficiency-based standard of liability may have important symbolic value in officially condemning the wasteful (unjustified) sacrifice of human life and limb.

---

**25.** See Olson v. Prosoco, Inc., 522 N.W.2d 284, 289 (Iowa 1994) ("[i]nevitably the conduct of the defendant in a failure to warn case becomes the issue").

**26.** See Wright v. Brooke Group Ltd., 652 N.W.2d 159, 169 (Iowa 2002) ("We question the need for or usefulness of any traditional doctrinal label in design defect cases because . . . a negligence claim and a strict liability claim . . . rest on an identical risk-utility evaluation."). See generally Miller, Myth Surrenders to Reality: Design Defect Litigation in Iowa, 51 Drake L. Rev. 549 (2003).

**27.** See § 5.9, below.

**28.** See chs. 8 (design) and 9 (warnings), below.

**29.** Its moral footings are examined in Owen, The Moral Foundations of Products Liability Law: Toward First Principles, 68 Notre Dame L. Rev. 427 (1993). Its economic footings are explained in Judge Posner's classic essay, Posner, A Theory of Negligence, 1 J. Legal Stud. 29 (1972), and sources cited in n.2, above.

**30.** See Calabresi, Optimal Deterrence and Accidents, 84 Yale L.J. 656 (1975); Calabresi and Hirschoff, Toward a Test for Strict Liability in Torts, 81 Yale L.J. 1055 (1972).

### Problems with the Risk–Utility Test

Despite the risk-utility test's solid theoretical foundation, and its effectiveness as a test of liability in design cases in particular, it has some weaknesses. Because many courts purport to balance a large miscellany of factors,[31] much broader than the direct costs and benefits discussed above, some critics charge that this type of balancing test is too indeterminate (and thus possibly unprincipled) to be of any use.[32] Other critics complain that risk-utility decisionmaking, based on stark economic efficiency, suffers from a lack of richness and humanism,[33] and even basic justice.[34]

There is, no doubt, some real truth to both of these challenges, but they fail to squarely hit the mark. Indeterminacy is a real problem for courts that try to balance a wide array of diverse factors. But the narrowly focused cost-benefit formulation of the test outlined above escapes this problem. Arguing that cost-benefit determinations lack humanism and justice misses a couple of important points as well. It is true that manufacturers are unable to bargain with consumers individually; if such individualization was possible, it would ideally permit each consumer to maximize (or optimize) his or her own preferences. Yet manufacturers are forced by circumstances to "legislate" safety decisions for consumers as a group. It may be true that manufacturers should give extra weight to the safety side of the scales, since they are forcing a collective cost-benefit tradeoff on all consumers, whether it meets their personal preferences or not.[35] Yet, a manufacturer which in good faith applies cost-benefit analysis to safety decisionmaking thereby necessarily respects the equality and safety rights of consumers as a group. Rather

**31.** Courts often draw on Dean John Wades's famous factors. See Wade, On the Nature of Strict Tort Liability for Products, 44 Miss. L.J. 825 (1973). The Wade factors are critiqued in the chapter on defects in design. See § 8.7, below.

**32.** See, e.g., Epstein, The Risks of Risk/Utility, 48 Ohio St. L. J. 469, 475–76 (1987) ("There is nothing in the disorganized array of [factors such as Wade's] that prevents a single headstrong jury from making fundamental decisions about what may be marketed and what may not be sold at all."). Professor Epstein reasons that "[w]ith variables so numerous, the ingenuity of lawyers should never be doubted when the stakes in litigation are very high and discovery underregulated. The test is couched in an offhand way that makes difficult matters [look simple]. It is a utilitarian nightmare. What starts out as a faithful application of the utilitarian calculus ends up as an unprincipled battle of the experts. Everything is admissible; nothing is quantifiable; nothing is dispositive." Id. at 476.

**33.** See, e.g., Klemme, The Enterprise Liability Theory of Torts, 47 U. Colo. L. Rev. 153, 191 n.106 (1976). Professor Balkin, in Too Good to Be True: The Positive Economic Theory of Law, 87 Colum. L. Rev.

1447, 1475–76 (1987), faults efficiency tests for being incomplete: "Human values and goals may take wealth maximization into account, but they may not be exclusively or even primarily concerned with it. Human action and human decision may rest only in part on [efficiency analysis. Thus,] the greatest problem with wealth maximization as a theory of human practical reason may be that it is insufficiently rich." See also Hubbard, Reasonable *Human* Expectations: A Normative Model for Imposing Strict Liability for Defective Products, 29 Mercer L.Rev. 465, 468–69 (1978) (human expectation should prevail over efficiency because we can afford some inefficiency, whereas a denial of expectations, negating a person's right to be viewed as an end rather than as a means, is fundamentally offensive).

**34.** Compare Wright, Hand, Posner, and the Myth of the "Hand Formula," 4 Theoretical Inquiries in Law 145, 201–02, 270 (2003) (arguing that risk-utility liability standards usually contravene principles of justice, but appearing to recognize an exception for products liability cases).

**35.** See Geistfeld, Reconciling Cost–Benefit Analysis with the Principle that Safety Matters More Than Money, 76 N.Y.U. L. Rev. 114 (2001).

than undercutting consumer safety, therefore, the risk-utility method of decisionmaking promotes the rights of all affected parties in equal measure.[36]

Because of the risk-utility test's special importance in judging defects in design, further aspects of this test, such as a consideration of Dean Wade's seven factors and the requirement that the plaintiff prove a feasible design alternative, are treated in the chapter on that topic.[37]

## § 5.8   ALTERNATIVE TESTS

The discussion of strict products liability in tort to this point has been based on *Restatement (Second) of Torts* § 402A's "defective condition unreasonably dangerous" formulation of the liability standard, and the discussion has addressed the two principal tests of liability, consumer expectations and risk-utility, as largely incompatible standards. This section explores various alternative approaches that some courts have applied to both the verbal and substantive standards of liability.

### Verbal Standards

The awkward "defective condition unreasonably dangerous" definitional language of § 402A resulted from pressure by the ALI Council on Dean William Prosser, the *Restatement* Reporter, to make clear that "strict" products liability has inherent limitations, that something must truly be *wrong* with a product before liability may be imposed.[1] Dean Prosser's early drafts of § 402A (in 1958[2] and 1960[3]), when the section still narrowly covered only food, defined the liability standard in terms of "a condition dangerous to the consumer." Responding to Council complaints that the "dangerous" "condition" phrasing of the standard was over-broad, Dean Prosser overreacted by modifying both "dangerous" with "unreasonably" and "condition" with "defective," thus setting § 402A's liability standard in its final form: *"defective condition unreasonably dangerous."*[4] When § 402A was first debated on the floor of the

---

**36.** Owen, The Moral Foundations of Products Liability Law: Toward First Principles, 68 Notre Dame L. Rev. 427 (1993).

**37.** See ch. 8, below.

**§ 5.8**

**1.** The objective was to foreclose the possibility that a manufacturer of such inherently dangerous products as butter, drugs, whiskey, cigarettes, and automobiles would become "automatically responsible for all the harm that such things do in the world." Prosser, Strict Liability to the Consumer in California, 18 Hastings L.J. 9, 23 (1966). The history of § 402A with respect to this objective is examined in detail in § 6.2, below. See, e.g., Buckingham v. R.J. Reynolds Tobacco Co., 713 A.2d 381, 384 (N.H. 1998) ("When the plaintiff cannot allege that something is 'wrong' with the product, strict liability should not be used as a tool of social engineering to mandate that manufacturers bear the entire risk and

costs of injuries caused by their products."). See also § 10.3 (liability for generically dangerous products).

**2.** See Restatement (2d) Torts § 402A (Prelim. Draft No. 6, 1958).

**3.** See Restatement (2d) Torts § 402A (Council Draft No. 8, 1960).

**4.** Prosser explained this point to the ALI membership at the 1961 meeting at which Tentative Draft No. 6 was reviewed. Noting the Council's objection to his original "dangerous" "condition" formulation (in fact, he misstated that his initial drafts had read *"unreasonably* dangerous"), Dean Prosser remarked:

> The Council then proceeded to raise the question of a number of products which, even though not defective, are in fact dangerous to the consumer—whiskey, for example [laughter]; cigarettes, which cause lung cancer; various types of drugs

American Law Institute in 1961, its double-headed definition of the liability standard in the black letter was uniformly criticized as confusing, "gilding the lily," and likely to cause mischief,[5] all of which have proved true.

The "defective condition unreasonably dangerous" standard appears to have two poles, "defective condition" and "unreasonably dangerous," such that the full phrase appears to establish a two-pronged test of liability.[6] This appearance is accentuated by the fact that the two sub-phrases are separately treated in different comments to the section—at least until one realizes, however, that both sub-phrases are defined in nearly identical consumer contemplation terms,[7] as discussed above.[8] But one is left to wonder whether the section's liability standard requires proof of one element or two, and, if two, how the elements may differ. Such linguistic confusion is regrettable, and it brings to mind the definition of a (two-humped) camel.[9] From the very start, and for many years, courts and commentators struggled valiantly with the meaning of this magic language.

The great definitional debate came to a head in 1972 in *Cronin v. J.B.E. Olson Corp.*[10] The issue before the California Supreme Court in *Cronin* was "whether the injured plaintiff seeking recovery upon the theory of strict liability in tort must establish, among other facts, not only that the product contained a defect which proximately caused his injuries but also that such defective condition made the product unreasonably dangerous to the user or consumer."[11] The court reviewed the development of the strict tort doctrine in California, particularly its 1963 decision in *Greenman v. Yuba Power Products, Inc.*,[12] which held that "[a] manufacturer is strictly liable in tort when an article he places on the market, knowing that it is to be used without inspection for defects, proves to have a defect that causes injury to a human being."[13] The court contrasted *Greenman*'s characterization of the requisite condition merely

which can be administered with safety up to a point but may be dangerous if carried beyond that—and they raised the question whether "unreasonably dangerous" was sufficient to protect the defendant against possible liability in such cases.

Therefore, they suggested that there must be something wrong with the product itself, and hence the word "defective" was put in; but the fact that the product itself is dangerous, or even unreasonably dangerous, to people who consume it is not enough. There has to be something wrong with the product.

38 ALI Proceedings 86–89 (1961). Earlier in the discussion Dean Prosser had indicated that the "*unreasonably* dangerous" language also had been added "to head off liability for a product which is sold where there is nothing wrong with the product as a product, but nevertheless it is going to injure some people. A good many individuals are allergic to strawberries and eggs. That doesn't mean that there is anything

wrong with the food. There is something wrong with the individual. 'Defective condition' and 'unreasonably dangerous' are deliberately designed to protect the defendant against undue liability." Id. at 55. See Viscusi, Wading Through the Muddle of Risk–Utility Analysis, 39 Am. U. L. Rev. 573 (1990); Wade, On the Nature of Strict Tort Liability for Products, 44 Miss. L.J. 825, 830 (1973).

**5.** See 38 ALI Proceedings 86–89 (1961).

**6.** See §§ 5.3 and 5.6, above.

**7.** "Defective condition," in § 402A cmt. *g* and "unreasonably dangerous," in § 402A cmt. *i*.

**8.** See §§ 5.3 and 5.6, above.

**9.** As a horse (defectively) designed by a committee.

**10.** 501 P.2d 1153 (Cal. 1972).

**11.** Id. at 1155.

**12.** 377 P.2d 897 (Cal. 1963).

**13.** Id. at 900.

as a "defect" to § 402A's "defective condition unreasonably dangerous" basis of liability. Acknowledging that the "unreasonably dangerous" phrase had been added to *Greenman*'s "defect" formulation as a limitation on a supplier's responsibility for harm from inherent product dangers, the court observed that this limitation has not only prevented sellers from becoming insurers of any harm caused by their products but "has burdened the injured plaintiff with proof of an element which rings of negligence." Noting "the susceptibility of Restatement section 402A to a literal reading which would require the finder of fact to conclude that the product is, first, defective and, second, unreasonably dangerous,"[14] the court observed that "[a] bifurcated standard is of necessity more difficult to prove than a unitary one. But merely proclaiming that the phrase 'defective condition unreasonably dangerous' requires only a single finding would not purge that phrase of its negligence complexion." Reasoning that "a requirement that a plaintiff also prove that the defect made the product 'unreasonably dangerous' places upon him a significantly increased burden and represents a step backward in the area pioneered by this court," the court forever banished the "unreasonably dangerous" language from California's strict products liability in tort jurisprudence.[15]

The *Cronin* court's concern that the full "defective condition unreasonably dangerous" phrase might lead courts to require proof of two separate elements was not misplaced: many early decisions,[16] at least two statutes,[17] and even some quite recent decisions[18] have defined the liability rule of § 402A in such a two-step way.

---

**14.** Citing Note, 55 Geo. L.J. 286, 296 (1966).

**15.** *Cronin*, 501 P.2d at 1161–63. "[T]o require an injured plaintiff to prove not only that the product contained a defect but also that such defect made the product unreasonably dangerous to the user or consumer would place a considerably greater burden upon him than that articulated in *Greenman*.... [T]he *Greenman* formulation is consonant with the rationale and development of products liability law in California because it provides a clear and simple test for determining whether the injured plaintiff is entitled to recovery." Id. at 1163.

**16.** See, e.g., Phipps v. General Motors Corp. 363 A.2d 955, 958 (Md. 1976) ("For recovery, it must be established that (1) the product was in a defective condition [and] (2) that it was unreasonably dangerous."); Early–Gary, Inc. v. Walters, 294 So.2d 181, 186 (Miss. 1974) (one of § 402A's three elements is that "the injury resulted from a defect in the product which rendered it unreasonably dangerous").

**17.** Tennessee permits a plaintiff to recover if a product was in a defective condition *or* unreasonably dangerous, and Arkansas requires a plaintiff to prove that a product was sold "in a defective condition which *rendered* it unreasonably dangerous." See Tenn. Code Ann. § 29–28–105; Ark. Code Ann. § 4–86–102.

**18.** See, e.g., Sollami v. Eaton, 772 N.E.2d 215, 219 (Ill. 2002) ("plaintiff must plead and prove that the injury resulted from a condition of the product, [and] that the condition was an unreasonably dangerous one"); Johnson v. Ford Motor Co., 45 P.3d 86, 91 (Okla. 2002) ("plaintiff must prove ... that the product was defective when it left the control of the manufacturer, and that the defect made the product unreasonably dangerous"); Dillon v. Zeneca Corp., 42 P.3d 598 (Ariz. Ct. App. 2002) ("the plaintiff must demonstrate that the product was in a defective condition that made it unreasonably dangerous"); Lee v. Martin, 45 S.W.3d 860, 864 (Ark. Ct. App. 2001) (plaintiff "must prove that the product is unreasonably dangerous *and* defective"); Tabieros v. Clark Equip. Co., 944 P.2d 1279, 1297 (Haw. 1997) (plaintiff must prove "a defect in the product which rendered it unreasonably dangerous"); Stinson v. E.I. DuPont de Nemours & Co., 904 S.W.2d 428 (Mo. Ct. App. 1995) (trial court appeared to believe that liability was based on a two-part test).

The California Supreme Court in *Cronin* was probably wise to select a single term to characterize "bad" products, and the single word "defective" is now used by the great majority of courts and commentators as a short-hand way of signifying that a product's undue dangers should make the seller liable for resulting harm. That is, "defective" frequently is used to express a legal conclusion that a product is unacceptably dangerous, not to provide a test for arriving at that conclusion.[19] However, while some courts followed *Cronin* in banishing the "unreasonably dangerous" phrase from the formal liability standard,[20] most did not.[21] A majority of courts simply ignored the *Cronin* decision and stuck with § 402A's "defective condition unreasonably dangerous" phraseology as the formal liability standard, despite its awkwardness. Other courts, while agreeing with the *Cronin* court's decision to select a single test of liability, recognized that the word "defective" was too narrow and mechanical to embrace the variety of complex issues which a liability test must address. While the word "defective" may quite well describe the simple concept of a manufacturing flaw, it fails entirely to capture the sensitive balance of usefulness, risk, and cost that lies at the center of design adjudication.[22] In recognition of this phenomenon, a few courts took an opposite approach to *Cronin*, banishing "defective" from the formal standard and selecting "unreasonably dangerous" as the better phrase to describe the balance and optimality concepts which frame design and warnings cases in particular.[23]

---

**19.** See Armentrout v. FMC Corp., 842 P.2d 175, 186 (Colo. 1992):

The word "defective" often is used to express a legal conclusion upon which liability may be based. See John W. Wade, On Product "Design Defects" and Their Actionability, 33 Vand. L. Rev. 551–52 (1980). When so used, "defective" is not a test for reaching the legal conclusion but is merely an abbreviation of the term "defective condition unreasonably dangerous" as used in Restatement (Second) of Torts § 402A.

**20.** See, e.g., following *Cronin*'s purge of the "unreasonably dangerous" phrase from the strict tort standard, Butaud v. Suburban Marine & Sporting Goods, Inc., 543 P.2d 209 (Alaska 1975); Berkebile v. Brantly Helicopter Corp., 337 A.2d 893 (Pa. 1975); Glass v. Ford Motor Co., 304 A.2d 562 (N.J. Super. Ct. Law. Div. 1973).

**21.** Noting that "*Cronin* has been widely criticized as providing no useful definition of an actionable defect, particularly in relation to a case of a product of unsafe design," the Supreme Court of New Jersey repudiated *Glass* on this point in Cepeda v. Cumberland Engineering Co., Inc., 386 A.2d 816, 829 (N.J. 1978), overruled on other grounds by Suter v. San Angelo Foundry & Mach. Co., 406 A.2d 140 (N.J. 1979). Like *Cepeda,* most courts that have passed on

the question have rejected the *Cronin* approach. See, e.g., Byrns v. Riddell, Inc., 550 P.2d 1065 (Ariz. 1976); Heldt v. Nicholson Mfg. Co., 240 N.W.2d 154 (Wis. 1976). Law review commentary on *Cronin* was generally critical. See, e.g., Fischer, Products Liability—The Meaning of Defect, 39 Mo. L. Rev. 339 (1974); Keeton, Product Liability and the Meaning of Defect, 5 St. Mary's L.J. 30 (1973); Wade, On the Nature of Strict Tort Liability for Products, 44 Miss. L.J. 825 (1973).

**22.** See, e.g., Cepeda v. Cumberland Eng'g Co., 386 A.2d 816 (N.J. 1978) (overruled on other grounds by Suter v. San Angelo Foundry & Mach. Co., 406 A.2d 140 (N.J. 1979)). See generally Owen, Defectiveness Restated: Exploding the "Strict" Products Liability Myth, 1996 U. Ill. L. Rev. 743, 754 ("the goal of both design engineers and the law should be to promote in products an ideal balance of product usefulness, cost, and safety").

**23.** The good sense of such an approach was observed by Judge Wisdom in his pre-*Cronin* decision in Ross v. Up–Right, Inc., 402 F.2d 943, 947 (5th Cir. 1968) ("to speak in terms of 'defect' only causes confusion. . . . The key . . . is whether the product is 'unreasonably dangerous'."). For cases using the "unreasonably dangerous" phrase alone, see, e.g., Brooks v. Dietz, 545 P.2d 1104, 1107 (1976). See also Lietz v.

In time, most courts eventually came to understand that the full *Restatement* phrase, "defective condition unreasonably dangerous," signifies a unitary concept that may be dubbed "defective"—convenient for general discussion but unhelpful as a liability "test" for ascertaining whether a particular product is or was adequately safe. Yet, many courts (and some statutes) continue to employ the full *Restatement* phrase which unfortunately continues to lead some courts (and probably some juries) to the false conclusion that the phrase must mean two things.[24]

Other courts from time to time have experimented with a variety of other definitional phrases, such as "not reasonably safe," "unduly unsafe," "not reasonably fit, suitable and safe," and "dangerously defective." In *Azzarello v. Black Bros. Co.*,[25] the Pennsylvania Supreme Court endorsed the following standard jury instruction:

> The [supplier] of a product is the guarantor of its safety. The product must, therefore, be provided with every element necessary to make it safe for [its intended] use, and without any condition that makes it unsafe for [its intended] use. If you find that the product, at the time it left the defendant's control, lacked any element necessary to make it safe for [its intended] use or contained any condition that made it unsafe for [its intended] use, then the product was defective, and the defendant is liable for all harm caused by such defect.

This standard, that the supplier is a "guarantor" of product safety, has frightening implications, and it has elsewhere properly been rejected as too extreme and as running counter to the universally accepted notion, even in Pennsylvania,[26] that a manufacturer is not an "insurer" of the safety of its products.[27]

### Combining Tests—Consumer Expectations and Risk–Utility

The discussion to this point of the consumer expectations and risk-utility tests, which has examined their pros and cons as discrete and independent tests, has shown that both tests have much merit: the consumer expectancy test of contract law protects vital interests of

Snyder Mfg. Co., 475 S.W.2d 105, 109 (Mo. 1972) (once product is shown to be unreasonably dangerous, it is "deemed" to be defective); Suvada v. White Motor Co., 210 N.E.2d 182 (Ill. 1965).

**24.** The trial court appears to have been so misled in Stinson v. E.I. DuPont de Nemours & Co., 904 S.W.2d 428 (Mo. Ct. App. 1995) (by implication). Compare McAlpine v. Rhone–Poulenc Ag Co., 16 P.3d 1054 (Mont. 2000) (jury verdict overturned because "defective condition unreasonably dangerous" language in jury instructions created vague and imprecise dual test). See Owen, Defectiveness Restated: Exploding the "Strict" Products Liability Myth, 1996 U. Ill. L. Rev. 743, 776–77.

**25.** 391 A.2d 1020, 1027 n.12 (Pa. 1978).

**26.** See Dambacher v. Mallis, 485 A.2d 408, 429 (Pa. Super. Ct. 1984) ("A guaran-

tor is not an insurer. An insurer of a product is responsible if the user . . . is injured by the product in some way. But a guarantor of a product is responsible only if the user of the product is injured as a result of a defect in the product."). See generally Thomas, Defining "Design Defect" in Pennsylvania: Reconciling *Azzarello* and the Restatement (Third) of Torts, 71 Temp. L. Rev. 217, 236–37 (1998).

**27.** For discussions of this standard, see Thomas, Defining "Design Defect" in Pennsylvania: Reconciling *Azzarello* and the Restatement (Third) of Torts, 71 Temp. L. Rev. 217 (1998) (critical of *Azzarello*'s rash language, but reconciling decision with mainstream law); Wertheimer, *Azzarello* Agonistes: Bucking the Strict Products Liability Tide, 66 Temp. L. Rev. 419 (1993) (favoring *Azzarello*); Notes, 81 Dick. L. Rev. 374 (1977); 21 Vill. L. Rev. 794 (1976).

buyers and sellers who strike private contractual bargains involving certain implied warranties of quality and safety, and the risk-utility test of tort law protects the general public by requiring product sellers to accord proper respect to the safety interests of persons put at risk by defective products. Recognizing the validity of both of these goals and the dual origins of strict products liability in warranty law and tort, the Supreme Court of California embraced *both* such tests in an important decision decided in 1978. In *Barker v. Lull Engineering Co.*,[28] discussed in detail below in the chapter on design defects,[29] the California high court, reasoning that a proper test of strict products liability should reflect its dual origins, *combined* the consumer expectations and risk-utility tests into a single, two-pronged test, and shifted the burden of proof on risk-utility to the manufacturer:

> [A] trial judge may properly instruct the jury that a product is defective in design (1) if the plaintiff demonstrates that the product failed to perform as safely as an ordinary consumer would expect when used in an intended or reasonably foreseeable manner, or (2) if the plaintiff proves that the product's design proximately caused his injury and the defendant fails to prove, in light of the relevant factors [the gravity of the danger, the likelihood of harm, the feasibility of altering the design to eliminate the danger, and the cost and other adverse effects of so altering the design], that on balance the benefits of the challenged design outweigh the risk of danger inherent in such design.[30]

A handful of courts have explicitly followed *Barker*'s two-pronged definition of product defect,[31] but generally not its shift in the burden of proof,[32] and at least a couple of courts have explicitly rejected the *Barker*

---

**28.** 573 P.2d 443 (Cal. 1978).

**29.** See ch. 8, below.

**30.** *Barker*, 573 P.2d at 457–58. See also Merrill v. Navegar, Inc., 28 P.3d 116, 125 (Cal. 2001).

**31.** See Dart v. Wiebe Mfg., Inc., 709 P.2d 876 (Ariz. 1985); Ontai v. Straub Clinic & Hosp., Inc., 659 P.2d 734 (Haw. 1983); Knitz v. Minster Mach. Co., 432 N.E.2d 814 (Ohio 1982); Caterpillar Tractor Co. v. Beck, 593 P.2d 871 (Alaska 1979). See also Lamkin v. Towner, 563 N.E.2d 449 (Ill. 1990). Washington's curious statute also generates such a two-pronged liability standard. See, e.g., Thongchoom v. Graco Children's Products, Inc., 71 P.3d 214, 217 (Wash. Ct. App. 2003).

**32.** Except for *Beck* (Alaska), and *Lamkin* (Illinois), the courts have rejected *Barker*'s second-prong shift in the burden of proof. See, e.g., Armentrout v. FMC Corp., 842 P.2d 175 (Colo. 1992) (overruling prior case on point); Kallio v. Ford Motor Co., 407 N.W.2d 92 (Minn. 1987); Hayes v. Ariens Co., 462 N.E.2d 273 (Mass. 1984); Ontai v. Straub Clinic & Hosp. Inc., 659 P.2d 734 (Haw. 1983); Cremeans v. International

Harvester Co., 452 N.E.2d 1281 (Ohio 1983); Wilson v. Piper Aircraft Corp. (on rehearing), 579 P.2d 1287 (Or. 1978). The commentators have been critical of *Barker*'s shift in the burden of proof:

> The rule places an enormous burden on the concept of a "product design that proximately causes injury," a burden which the concept seems ill-equipped to handle.... People fall off ladders all the time, and the fact that ladders are both high and in some general way unstable enables these falls to occur. Does it or doesn't it follow that in every case of a person's falling off a ladder, the ladder's design proximately causes the fall?

G. Schwartz, Foreword: Understanding Products Liability, 67 Calif. L. Rev. 435, 466–67 (1979). See also Prosser and Keeton on Torts 702; Wade, On Product "Design Defects" and Their Actionability, 33 Vand. L. Rev. 551, 573 (1980).

The California courts have had difficulty in applying the second-prong burden shift to real cases. See, e.g., Pietrone v. American Honda Motor Co., 235 Cal.Rptr. 137 (Ct. App. 1987).

test.[33] A few courts have danced around the issue, seemingly adopting the *Barker* two-pronged approach, but without saying so explicitly.[34] Perhaps most importantly, an increasing number of jurisdictions follow a *de facto Barker* approach, variously applying the consumer expectations and risk-utility tests in different cases, often without explanation as to why one test is applied in one situation and the other test in some other.[35] While many of the decisions may be faulted for failing clearly to specify when and how the two separate tests should be applied, much may be said for a liability regime which intelligibly blends, in some manner or another, both standards of liability.[36]

Two other developments, also examined further in the design defect chapter,[37] are also worthy of note. First is the redefinition of consumer expectations in risk-utility terms, at least in certain types of cases,[38] based apparently on the predicate that consumers can expect manufacturers to make their products as safe as reasonably possible in view of the relevant costs and benefits.[39] The second judicial development is the movement toward applying the *consumer expectations* test to cases involving the design of a *simple* mechanism, such as an unguarded fan, but a *risk-utility* test to a product with a *complex* design, such as a car. Although earlier cases had so held,[40] the California Supreme Court adopted such a test in an automobile crashworthiness case in 1994. In *Soule v. General Motors Corp.*,[41] the court restricted *Barker*'s consumer expectations prong to simple product cases where consumers from every-day experience are able to acquire meaningful expectations about the product's performance and safety characteristics, especially in cases where expert testimony is for this reason unnecessary and perhaps improper: "the consumer expectations test is reserved for cases in which the *everyday experience* of the product's users permits a conclusion that the product's design violated minimum safety assumptions, and is thus

---

**33.** See, e.g., Kallio v. Ford Motor Co. 407 N.W.2d 92, 95 (Minn. 1987); Lester v. Magic Chef, Inc., 641 P.2d 353 (Kan. 1982).

**34.** See, e.g., Soproni v. Polygon Apt. Partners, 971 P.2d 500, 504 (Wash. 1999); Ortho Pharm. Corp. v. Heath, 722 P.2d 410 (Colo. 1986) (overruled in part on other grounds by Armentrout v. FMC Corp., 842 P.2d 175 (Colo. 1992)) (by implication); Dart v. Wiebe Mfg., Inc., 709 P.2d 876 (Ariz. 1985).

**35.** See, e.g., Halliday v. Sturm, Ruger & Co., 792 A.2d 1145 (Md. 2002); Bragg v. Hi–Ranger, Inc., 462 S.E.2d 321, 328 (S.C. Ct. App. 1995).

**36.** See, e.g., Kennedy, The Role of the Consumer Expectations Test Under Louisiana's Products Liability Tort Doctrine, 69 Tul. L. Rev. 117, 162–63 (1994) ("it will be prudent in some cases to employ the consumer expectation test in conjunction with the risk-utility balancing test in the form of a 'risk-utility consumer expectation test.' Fusing the test often will make good sense given the complexity of products and products liability tort litigation today; the mor-

al, social, economic, and jurisprudential values sought to be advanced by tort liability; and the superiority of the risk-utility balancing test in serving these interests and in resolving many of the tough issues presented in most products liability disputes").

**37.** See § 8.6, below.

**38.** Notably complex cases, as next discussed.

**39.** See, e.g., McCathern v. Toyota Motor Corp., 23 P.3d 320, 331 (Or. 2001); Vautour v. Body Masters Sports Indus., 784 A.2d 1178, 1182 (N.H. 2001) (unreasonably dangerous defined in terms of consumer expectations defined in terms of risk-utility); Potter v. Chicago Pneumatic Tool Co., 694 A.2d 1319 (Conn. 1997); Seattle–First Nat'l Bank v. Tabert, 542 P.2d 774 (Wash. 1975).

**40.** See, e.g., Scoby v. Vulcan–Hart Corp., 569 N.E.2d 1147 (Ill. App. Ct. 1991) (only the consumer expectations test should be applied when a mechanism is simple and the danger is obvious).

**41.** 882 P.2d 298 (Cal. 1994).

defective *regardless of expert opinion about the merits of the design.*"[42] Courts and commentators increasingly are seeing the good sense in moving in this direction, which puts both of the traditional tests to their highest use.[43]

### Defect-Specific Tests

A major judicial development in connection with products liability defect tests in recent years is the trend toward separate tests for separate types of defect.[44] Except in food cases, there has been little need to define the nature of a production flaw (or "manufacturing defect"), for the fact of "defectiveness" and the resulting violation of a consumer's expectations are both generally self-evident in such cases. Accordingly, the courts have rarely bothered to define this form of defect.[45] Recently, however, a number of courts and state legislatures have begun defining manufacturing defects in terms of a deviation from the manufacturer's design.[46] This is the liability standard adopted by the new *Restatement*,[47] and it makes such good sense that it should be expected to spread far and wide.

Neither the consumer expectations nor risk-utility test is generally very helpful in determining whether a particular danger deserves a warning or whether a particular warning adequately conveys information about the risk. A product with an inadequate warning of danger quite obviously violates a consumer's expectations, and the safety benefits of adding a sufficient warning virtually always exceed its monetary costs.[48] For this reason, the warnings defect issue is generally posited merely in terms of the "adequacy" or "sufficiency" of the information provided and of the method by which it was conveyed.[49] Most courts have

---

**42.** Id. at 308 (emphasis in original). See also Pruitt v. General Motors Corp., 86 Cal.Rptr.2d 4 (Ct. App. 1999) (consumer expectations test did not apply to defective design of airbag claim).

**43.** See, e.g., Delaney v. Deere & Co., 999 P.2d 930, 944 (Kan. 2000) ("recogniz[ing] the validity of risk/utility analysis as a guide in determining the expectations of consumers in complex cases"); Potter v. Chicago Pneumatic Tool Co., 694 A.2d 1319 (Conn. 1997). See also McCathern v. Toyota Motor Corp., 23 P.3d 320, 331 (Or. 2001). See generally Kennedy, The Role of the Consumer Expectations Test Under Louisiana's Products Liability Tort Doctrine, 69 Tulane L. Rev. 117 (1994).

**44.** See §§ 6.2 and 6.5, below.

**45.** The more typical litigation problem in manufacturing defect cases concerns the problem of *proving* that the cause of a product malfunction was a production defect rather than something else. The malfunction theory of recovery addresses this problem, as discussed below. See § 7.1 and ch. 18, below.

**46.** See, e.g., Jones v. Amazing Prods., Inc., 231 F.Supp.2d 1228 (N.D. Ga. 2002);

Shreve v. Sears, Roebuck & Co., 166 F.Supp.2d 378 (D. Md. 2001); Morton Int'l v. Gillespie, 39 S.W.3d 651, 656 (Tex. App. 2001); Allstate Ins. Co. v. Ford Motor Co., 772 So.2d 339, 344 (La. Ct. App. 2000) (La. Code: if "product deviated in a material way from the manufacturer's specifications or performance standards for the product or from otherwise identical products manufactured by the same manufacturer"). See § 7.2, below.

**47.** See Products Liability Restatement § 2(a). See § 6.5, below.

**48.** See, e.g., Moran v. Faberge, Inc., 332 A.2d 11, 15 (Md. 1975) (noting that a risk almost always exceeds the small expense of a warning). See § 2.2, above. But other safety costs arise from over-warning, sometimes referred to as warnings pollution, which also should be considered. See § 9.3, below.

**49.** See, e.g., Lewis v. Sea Ray Boats, Inc., 65 P.3d 245, 249 (Nev. 2003) (" 'strict liability may be imposed if it was unreasonably dangerous to place the product in the hands of the user without suitable and adequate warning concerning safe and proper use' "); Needham v. Coordinated Apparel

turned to general negligence principles for guidance in such cases,[50] and at least one court has abolished the claim for strict tort liability in such cases and returned outright to the claim for negligence.[51]

Design defects were formerly defined in most jurisdictions in terms of consumer expectations. However, with the maturity of products liability law and litigation, many courts have been shifting to the risk-utility test for resolving design defectiveness, sometimes combining the test with some form of consumer expectancy analysis. The use of these tests in design defect litigation, described above, are examined further in detail in the chapter on defects in design.[52]

The trend toward separately defining the liability standard by type of defect has now been validated by the *Third Restatement* which, while defining design and warnings defects in similar risk-utility terms, trifurcates defectiveness into the three separate types of defect, each with its own separate definition.[53] The defect-specific definitions of strict products liability in tort are provided separate treatment below in their respective chapters.[54]

## § 5.9    COMPARISON WITH OTHER LIABILITY THEORIES

The doctrine of strict products liability in tort for selling defective products[1] may usefully be compared to the other two principal theories of products liability, negligence and warranty, in two respects: (1) how the underlying theories of liability compare and contrast, and (2) how other aspects of such claims, such as causation, damages, defenses, and statutes of limitations, correspond and differ. The first comparison, between the respective theories of liability, is treated here. How different liability theories affect other aspects of a products liability action is detailed in subsequent chapters devoted to those special topics. Before the strict products liability in tort doctrine is compared to negligence and warranty, it may be helpful to contrast it to the other major strict liability in tort doctrine—strict liability for abnormally dangerous activities.

### Strict Products Liability *vs.* Strict Liability for Abnormally Dangerous Activities

One might think that the two major strict liability in tort doctrines, one for selling a dangerously defective product and the other for conduct-

Group, Inc., 811 A.2d 124, 129 (Vt. 2002) ("[t]o establish strict liability for an inadequate warning, a plaintiff must prove that the inadequate warning made the product unreasonably dangerous"). See § 9.3, below.

**50.** See, e.g., Anderson v. Owens–Corning Fiberglas Corp., 810 P.2d 549, 561 (Cal. 1991) (Mosk, J., concurring and dissenting); Crislip v. TCH Liquidating Co., 556 N.E.2d 1177, 1183 (Ohio 1990).

**51.** See Olson v. Prosoco, Inc., 522 N.W.2d 284 (Iowa 1994). Note as well that some states have achieved this result by legislation. See § 9.2, below.

**52.** See ch. 8, below.

**53.** See §§ 6.2 and 6.5, below.

**54.** See ch. 7 (manufacturing defects), ch. 8 (design defects), and ch. 9 (warnings and instructions defects), below.

#### § 5.9

**1.** Strict products liability in tort for misrepresentation and express warranty are compared and contrasted in the chapters on those topics. See chs. 3 and 4, above.

ing an abnormally dangerous activity,[2] might have much in common. In fact, however, the two doctrines are fundamentally distinct.[3] Strict products liability in tort concerns the responsibility of a supplier for making or selling a product containing an excessive and often unexpected danger, such as the manufacturer of a car with defective brakes, which injures the user or someone else. By contrast, strict liability for an abnormally dangerous activity involves the responsibility of an actor, such as a contractor who sets off a large charge of dynamite in a city, for the harmful consequences of introducing a substantial, unavoidable danger into a setting where, because of the special characteristics of the particular location, the hazard is palpably out of place.

In the products liability context, strict liability follows the creation and sale of a product that in a condition that is unreasonably dangerous because it was made improperly or bears insufficient warnings of its dangers, such that the hazard could and reasonably should have been avoided, so that it should not have been *sold* in that condition at all. By contrast, strict liability for an abnormally dangerous activity arises out of an actor's *use* of a product or other activity whose dangers, though large, are reasonable when the activity is conducted in an appropriate environment where the hazard may be properly contained.[4] Such an actor is strictly liable for creating an unreasonable ("abnormal") danger by choosing to *use* (not sell) a product in a manner and context where the danger is substantial, unavoidable, and out of place.[5]

With almost no exceptions, the courts have steadfastly kept these two theories of strict tort liability separate and distinct. In refusing to extend the abnormally dangerous or utltrahazardous activity doctrine to the products liability context, courts have emphasized that product defect cases normally fail to satisfy the doctrine's basic requirements that the hazard be both unavoidable and uncommon, conditions which strongly suggest that this particular version of strict tort liability has no role to play in products liability litigation.[6]

**2.** See ch. 6, below.

**3.** See, e.g., Cantu, Distinguishing the Concept of Strict Liability for Ultrahazardous Activities from Strict Products Liability under Section 402A of the Restatement (Second) of Torts: Two Parallel Lines of Reasoning that Should Never Meet, 35 Akron L. Rev. 31, 56 (2001) ("the concept of strict liability for ultra-hazardous activities is entirely different from strict liability under Section 402A"); Montgomery and Owen, Reflections on the Theory and Administration of Strict Tort Liability for Defective Products, 27 S.C. L. Rev. 803, 825–28 (1976).

**4.** In the words of one court, "abnormal dangerousness in the context of sections 519 and 520 of the Restatement (Second) of Torts is a property of *activities* and not of substances." U.S. v. Union Corp., 277 F.Supp.2d 478, 494 (E.D. Pa. 2003).

**5.** See 1 Madden & Owen on Products Liability ch. 6 (describing strict liability for

abnormally dangerous activities); Restatement (3d) Torts: Liability for Physical Harm § 20 (strict liability for abnormally dangerous activities whose risks are "highly significant," foreseeable, unavoidable, and uncommon).

**6.** See, e.g., U.S. v. Union Corp. 277 F.Supp.2d 478, 495 (E.D. Pa. 2003) (manufacture and sale of PCBs is not an abnormally dangerous activity); Ehlis v. Shire Richwood, Inc., 233 F.Supp.2d 1189, 1191–93 (D.N.D. 2002) (strict liability for abnormally dangerous or ultrahazardous activity doctrine does not apply to sale of prescription drugs), aff'd, 367 F.3d 1013 (8th Cir. 2004); Merrill v. Navegar, Inc., 89 Cal. Rptr.2d 146, 190–92 (Ct. App. 1999), superseded on other grounds, 991 P.2d 755 (Cal. 2000) (same: sale of guns); Copier By and Through Lindsey v. Smith & Wesson Corp., 138 F.3d 833 (10th Cir. 1998 ) (Utah law) (same); Gaines–Tabb v. ICI Explosives USA, Inc., 995 F.Supp. 1304, (W.D. Okla.

### Strict Liability *vs.* Negligence

#### *In General*

How strict liability differs from fault-based liability, and which is preferable, may be the most fundamental issue in all of tort law.[7] It is elemental that the very basis of negligence liability, whether in products liability or other tort law context, is grounded on fault.[8] In contrast, the very basis of strict products liability in tort is the supplier's responsibility for harm caused by product defects *regardless* of fault. Thus, *Restatement (Second) of Torts* § 402A "applies although (a) the seller has exercised all possible care in the preparation and sale of his product."[9] Liability is called "strict" because the basis of responsibility for sellers of defective products is "no-fault" liability, meaning that liability is assessed in the absence of the seller's fault. Unlike negligence, it has been said many times, strict products liability focuses on the condition of the product rather than on the conduct of the manufacturer.[10]

The fundamental divide between negligence and strict liability in tort is manifest in manufacturing flaw cases, where even the most careful supplier is subject to liability under § 402A for injuries from a stone in a can of peas, an air bubble in a tire, or a crossed wire in the electrical system of a punch press.[11] Even in these cases, however, once the plaintiff proves the existence of a defect, establishing an inference of negligence requires very little proof,[12] and the courts in such cases generally presume that the manufacturer's failure to detect or remove

---

1996) (same: ammonium nitrate, labeled as fertilizer, used as explosive); Cavan v. General Motors Corp., 571 P.2d 1249, 1252 (Or. 1977) ("The fact that a product may create an 'ultrahazardous' condition by virtue of defective design or manufacture is thus of no moment under our present law."); First Nat'l Bank in Albuquerque v. Nor–Am Agricultural Prod., Inc., 537 P.2d 682 (N.M. Ct. App. 1975) (same: sale of liquid seed disinfectant ingested by hogs ingested by humans). See also Sprankle v. Bower Ammonia & Chem. Co., 824 F.2d 409 (5th Cir. 1987) (Miss. law); Morningstar v. Black and Decker Mfg. Co., 253 S.E.2d 666 (W. Va. 1979). On guns, see McNicholas and McNicholas, Ultrahazardous Products Liability: Providing Victims of Well–Made Firearm Ammunition to Fire Back at Gun Manufacturers, 30 Loy. L.A. L. Rev. 1599 (1997) (proposing theory of "ultrahazardous products liability" that would hold manufacturers of certain assault rifles liable for all damages caused by their products).

**7.** See Owen, Philosophical Foundations of Fault in Tort Law, in Philosophical Foundations of Tort Law 201 (D. Owen ed., Oxford, 1995). On the differences and parallels between negligence and strict liability in products liability law, see 2 Am. Law Prod. Liab. 3d § 28:8.

**8.** See § 2.1, above.

**9.** Restatement (2d) Torts § 402A(2).

**10.** See, e.g., Phillips v. Cricket Lighters, 841 A.2d 1000, 1007 (Pa. 2003) ("Strict liability focuses solely on the product, and is divorced from the conduct of the manufacturer."); Green v. Smith & Nephew AHP, Inc., 629 N.W.2d 727, 745 (Wis. 2001) ("unlike negligence liability, strict products liability focuses not on the defendant's conduct, but on the nature of the defendant's product"); Roach v. Kononen, 525 P.2d 125, 129 (Or. 1974) ("in strict liability we are talking about the condition (dangerousness) of an article . . . while in negligence we are talking about the reasonableness of the manufacturer's actions in designing and selling the article"). *But see* Wright v. Brooke Group Ltd., 652 N.W.2d 159, 166 (Iowa 2002) (noting that the court had earlier "abandoned the analysis that differentiated strict liability from negligence on the basis that negligence focuses on the defendant's conduct while strict liability focuses on the condition of the product").

**11.** See § 7.2, below.

**12.** Dean Prosser thought that proof that a defect was a result of the manufacturer's negligence "is by far the easiest" of the plaintiff's tasks, "and it is one in which the plaintiff almost never fails." Prosser, Assault on the Citadel (Strict Liability to the Consumer), 69 Yale L.J. 1099, 1114 (1960).

the defect was a result of negligence.[13] For this reason, Dean Prosser supposed in such cases that "there is not one case in a hundred in which strict liability would result in recovery where negligence does not."[14]

When the issue shifts away from manufacturing defects to dangers in a product's design or inadequate warnings and instructions, there can be little difference between negligence and strict liability because the plaintiff in each such case is required to show effectively the same thing—that the product contained a danger that is *unreasonable*. If the question of whether a particular danger is unreasonable is determined by the consumer expectations test,[15] the results may vary from a determination under principles of negligence. But as courts turn increasingly to the risk-utility test, which balances the costs and benefits of avoiding the danger, the method for determining "defect" or "unreasonable danger" is almost exactly the same as it is for establishing the supplier's fault in negligence law, as discussed above.[16]

At an early date, perceptive products liability scholars recognized the necessity for evaluating design and (to a lesser extent) warnings defect claims by means of a "negligence" cost-benefit approach. In an article written in 1957, as the push toward strict products liability of manufacturers was beginning to accelerate, Professor Leon Green observed that the rule of negligence, rather than strict liability, was best suited to such cases.[17] "Negligence law here," he reasoned, "is in its ancestral environment."[18] Products liability theorizing was in its infancy at the time, and so the essence of his observation may fairly be distilled. What he really meant of course, was that cost-benefit analysis, inherent in negligence law, is the basic analytical tool used by engineers in designing products, and it is the method by which the "reasonableness" of those decisions fairly and logically may be judged. In time, the necessity for risk-utility or "negligence-type" reasoning was also realized by some early courts attempting to apply the new strict products liability in tort doctrine in litigation.

Together with the commentators, many courts have come to appreciate the substantial equivalence in most products liability cases of negligence and strict liability in tort. The court in one early case perceptively observed that "the distinction between the so-called strict liability principle and negligence is of no practical significance so far as the standard of conduct required of the defendant is concerned. In either event the

**13.** The courts make the inference or presumption either formally, under the doctrine of res ipsa loquitur or the malfunction doctrine, or informally, as needing no discussion. See, e.g., Pouncey v. Ford Motor Co., 464 F.2d 957 (5th Cir. 1972) (Ala. law); Jenkins v. General Motors Corp., 446 F.2d 377 (5th Cir. 1971) (Ga. law). See generally § 2.5 (res ipsa), above, and § 7.4 (malfunction doctrine), below.

**14.** Prosser, Assault on the Citadel (Strict Liability to the Consumer), 69 Yale L.J. 1099, 1114 (1960).

**15.** This test is examined in § 5.6, above.

**16.** See § 5.7, above.

**17.** Although addressing only "mechanical products," as distinguished from food and chemical products where he thought a rule of strict liability was proper, Professor Green's case examples indicate that he was envisaging design and warnings problems with such mechanical machines. See L. Green, Should the Manufacturer of General Products Be Liable Without Negligence?, 24 Tenn. L. Rev. 928 (1957).

**18.** Id. at 934.

standard required is reasonable care."[19] While most early judges did not appreciate this important point, and while there are still a few stubborn holdouts,[20] modern courts increasingly recognize that the basis of liability in both design[21] and warnings cases[22] is virtually, or completely, equivalent in negligence and strict liability in tort. This recognition has finally reached the point that a few courts, usually indirectly but sometimes explicitly, have ruled that the equivalence of strict liability in tort and negligence in design and warnings cases supports a single cause of action. In an insightful splash of candor, the Iowa Supreme Court, in *Olson v. Prosoco, Inc.*,[23] boldly repealed its rule of "strict" liability for warnings cases, returning to a formal rule of negligence. In a later case, the same court adopted the *Third Restatement*'s approaches of applying cost-benefit analysis to design defect determinations and of abandoning in such cases doctrinal labels and distinctions between negligence and strict liability.[24] But there remains a dwindling, yet stubborn, contingent of courts that cling tenaciously to the view that the doctrines of negligence and strict liability in tort are and must be kept conceptually distinct.[25]

### *Juries, Strategy, and Inconsistent Verdicts*

The near or complete equivalence of negligence and strict liability in tort in design and warnings cases raises a couple of interesting trial issues, one strategic and the other theoretical. One aspect of the strategic issue concerns whether a lawyer should plead both theories, covering all bases, but risk confusing the jury which may, unless precisely guided by court and counsel, mistakenly believe that liability requires a finding of all the elements of both types of claims. If, on the other hand, the plaintiff's lawyer chooses to use a rifle shot approach by providing the jury with a single claim, which should it be, negligence or strict liability? Common sense would seem to suggest that a plaintiff's lawyer should simply abandon the negligence claim for the simpler and easier-to-prove

**19.**  Jones v. Hutchinson Mfg., Inc., 502 S.W.2d 66, 69–70 (Ky. 1973).

**20.**  See, e.g., Phillips v. Cricket Lighters, 841 A.2d 1000, 1007 (Pa. 2003) ("strict liability is not a type of mongrel derivative of negligence").

**21.**  See, e.g., Higginbotham v. KCS Int'l, Inc., 85 Fed.Appx. 911, 917 (4th Cir. 2004) (Md. law) ("the elements of proof are the same whether the claim be for strict liability or negligence," such that the plaintiffs' failure to establish defect and causation caused all their negligence, breach of warranty, and strict liability claims to fail); Jones v. NordicTrack, Inc., 550 S.E.2d 101, 103, n.5 (Ga. 2001) (design: "no significant distinction between negligence and strict liability for purposes of the risk-utility analysis").

**22.**  See, e.g., Mayor of Balt. v. Utica Mut. Ins. Co., 802 A.2d 1070, 1089 (Md. App. 2002) ("these two theories—negligence and strict liability failure to warn—have been described as nearly identical");

Cervelli v. Thompson/Center Arms, 183 F.Supp.2d 1032, 1040 (S.D. Ohio 2002) ("the standard imposed upon the defendant in a strict liability claim grounded upon an inadequate warning is the same as that imposed in a negligence claim based upon inadequate warning"); Olson v. Prosoco, Inc., 522 N.W.2d 284, 289 (Iowa 1994) (warnings: "we believe any posited distinction between strict liability and negligence principles is illusory"). See § 2.6, above.

**23.**  522 N.W.2d 284 (Iowa 1994).

**24.**  Wright v. Brooke Group Ltd., 652 N.W.2d 159, 169 (Iowa 2002) ("We question the need for or usefulness of any traditional doctrinal label in design defect cases because ... a negligence claim and a strict liability claim ... rest on an identical risk-utility evaluation.").

**25.**  See, e.g., Phillips v. Cricket Lighters, 841 A.2d 1000, 1007 (Pa. 2003) ("we can, and do, reaffirm that in this jurisdiction, negligence concepts have no place in strict liability law").

claim for strict liability in tort, and that it would almost be malpractice to assert a negligence claim alone. Yet seasoned plaintiff's counsel[26] and an important recent empirical jury study[27] both conclude that juries respond much more favorably to plaintiffs, in verdict likelihood and size, on the "hot" rhetoric of negligence than the "cold" logic of strict liability.

The theoretical issue arising from the closeness of the theories of negligence and strict liability concerns a thorny problem involving inconsistent jury verdicts. Suppose that a court submits a case to the jury on both negligence and strict liability in tort claims, and, by special interrogatories, the jury decides for the plaintiff on the negligence claim but for the defendant on the strict liability claim. The problem, of course, is that the two verdicts may be logically inconsistent: the strict liability claim requires a finding that the product is defective, and the negligence claim requires two implicit findings: (1) that the product was "bad" ("defective"), and (2) that the defendant was at fault in supplying the product in that condition.[28] A manufacturer or other supplier can hardly be faulted for supplying consumers with a "good" product, one that is *not* defective. So, a finding that a product is not defective for purposes of strict liability in tort logically precludes a finding that the manufacturer or other supplier was negligent in making or selling it in that condition.[29] An early Minnesota decision succinctly captured the essence of this point: "If a product is not ... defective ... , it is not negligence to manufacture it that way."[30] Hence, the two findings—that a product is not defective but that the defendant was negligent in making or selling it—are normally contradictory and cannot be harmonized or reconciled.[31]

Despite a curiously large number of decisions to the contrary,[32] most courts have convincingly reasoned that a negligence finding is necessari-

**26.** See Rheingold, The Expanding Liability of the Product Supplier: A Primer, 2 Hofstra L. Rev. 521, 531–32 (1974) (plaintiff's counsel would prefer to argue in "hot" negligence terms that a drug company concealed side effects from consumers than that the warning label was inadequate).

**27.** See Cupp and Polage, The Rhetoric of Strict Products Liability Versus Negligence: An Empirical Analysis, 77 N.Y.U. L. Rev. 874, 936–37 (2002) (in mock trials of same case, 26% of jurors in strict liability trial awarded damages whereas 38% of jurors in negligence trial awarded damages; damages for pain and suffering awarded by jurors in strict liability trial averaged $27,571 compared to $49,750 by jurors in negligence trial).

**28.** See, e.g., Merrill v. Navegar, Inc., 28 P.3d 116, 124 (Cal. 2001) (under both negligence and strict liability, plaintiff must prove a defect caused the injury and, under negligence, plaintiff must also prove "an additional element, namely, that the defect in the product was due to negligence of the defendant," citing Prosser, Strict Liability to the Consumer, 18 Hastings L.J. 9, 50–51 (1966)); Oanes v. Westgo, Inc., 476 N.W.2d

248, 253 (N.D. 1991) ("In negligent design claims it is well established that a manufacturer or seller is not liable in the absence of proof that a product is defective. Thus, an element of a negligent design case is that the product is defective or unsafe."). See generally § 2.1 above.

**29.** "Ordinarily, strict liability, which was developed to ease a claimant's burden of proof, requires proof of fewer elements than negligence, making a positive verdict on the latter difficult to explain if strict liability cannot be found." Annot., 41 A.L.R.4th 9, 13–14 (1985) (inconsistent products liability verdicts).

**30.** Halvorson v. American Hoist & Derrick Co., 240 N.W.2d 303, 307 (Minn. 1976).

**31.** See Annot., 41 A.L.R.4th 9, 13 (1985) (inconsistent products liability verdicts) ("if the alleged faults underlying the negligence and strict liability claims are clearly the same, the courts have commonly ruled that a finding of negligence but no strict liability cannot be sustained").

**32.** See, e.g., Phillips v. Cricket Lighters, 841 A.2d 1000, 1008–10 (Pa. 2003) (because the elements of the two torts are

ly inconsistent with a finding that a product was not defective.[33] In such a case, a jury's rendering of two fatally inconsistent findings normally invalidates the verdict, requiring that the verdict be vacated and a new trial granted.[34] Such verdicts are inconsistent, of course, only when the two claims pertain to the same particular fault or defect in the product. Thus, there is nothing inconsistent in a jury finding that a product was negligently designed, but that its warnings were sufficient; or that the manufacturer negligently failed to provide an adequate instruction or warning, but that the design itself, perhaps burdened with an unavoidable latent danger, was reasonably safe.[35] In such cases, the separate findings may be harmonized, and the plaintiff's verdict should be sustained.[36]

distinct, it would be "illogical" to reject a negligence claim solely because of the failure of the claim for strict liability in tort); Connelly v. Hyundai Motor Co., 351 F.3d 535 (1st Cir. 2003) (N.H. law) (no inconsistency in jury's finding of no defective design but negligence in testing or design); Sharp ex rel. Gordon v. Case Corp. 595 N.W.2d 380, 387 (Wis. 1999); Talkington v. Atria Reclamelucifers Fabrieken BV, 152 F.3d 254, 261–62 (4th Cir. 1998) (S.C. law) ("Strict liability and negligence are not mutually exclusive theories of recovery; that is, an injury may give rise to claims that can be established either under principles of strict liability or negligence, and failure to prove one theory does not preclude proving the other"); Brown v. Yamaha Motor Corp., 691 P.2d 577 (Wash. Ct. App. 1984); Robertson v. General Tire & Rubber Co., 462 N.E.2d 706 (Ill. App. Ct. 1984); Randall v. Warnaco, Inc., 677 F.2d 1226 (8th Cir. 1982) (N.D. law); Barry v. Manglass, 432 N.E.2d 125 (N.Y. 1981); Hasson v. Ford Motor Co., 564 P.2d 857 (Cal. 1977) (overruled in part on other grounds by Soule v. General Motors Corp., 882 P.2d 298 (Cal. 1994)); Greiten v. LaDow, 235 N.W.2d 677, 685–86 (Wis. 1975) (concurring opinion of Hefferman, J., subsequently elevated to "majority" status) ("there may be recovery for the negligent design of a product even though it is not unreasonably dangerous in the 402A sense").

**33.** See, e.g., Golonka v. General Motors Corp., 65 P.3d 956, 965 (Ariz. Ct. App. 2003) ("when a plaintiff's claims for strict liability design and negligent design are factually identical, and the jury employs a risk/benefit analysis to determine that the manufacturer is not at fault for strict liability design, the jury cannot consistently find the product manufacturer at fault for negligent design"); Lecy v. Bayliner Marine Corp., 973 P.2d 1110, 1113 (Wash. Ct. App. 1999) ("Federal and state case law in other jurisdictions is generally in agreement that a jury's rejection of strict liability for design defect precludes a finding of negligent design."); Lambert v. General Motors, 79 Cal.

Rptr.2d 657 (Ct. App. 1998) (jury's finding that Blazer was not defectively designed precluded it from finding that vehicle was negligently designed); Tipton v. Michelin Tire Co., 101 F.3d 1145, 1150–51 (6th Cir. 1996) (Ky. law) (jury could not find tire negligently designed but not defective); Halvorson v. American Hoist & Derrick Co., 240 N.W.2d 303, 307 (Minn. 1976). See also Voelkel v. General Motors Corp., 846 F.Supp. 1468, 1475 (D. Kan. 1994) (proof of defect is required under negligence, implied warranty, and strict liability in tort); Repola v. Morbark Indus., 934 F.2d 483 (3d Cir. 1991) (jury finding of no strict liability for failure to warn under N.J. products liability act negated finding of negligent failure to warn); Garrett v. Hamilton Std. Controls, Inc., 850 F.2d 253, 257 (5th Cir. 1988); Sprankle v. Bower Ammonia & Chemical Co., 824 F.2d 409, 413 (5th Cir. 1987) (any "theoretical error" in failing to instruct jury on negligent failure to warn theory was harmless in view of jury's rejection of strict tort failure to warn theory); Consolidated Aluminum Corp. v. Braun, 447 So.2d 391 (Fla. Dist. Ct. App. 1984); Lundgren v. McColgin, 464 N.Y.S.2d 317 (App. Div. 1983).

**34.** See, e.g., Golonka v. General Motors Corp., 65 P.3d 956, 965 (Ariz. Ct. App. 2003) (inconsistent verdict requires new trial); Lecy v. Bayliner Marine Corp., 973 P.2d 1110, 1117 (Wash. Ct. App. 1999) (same; otherwise, judge's judgement is substituted for jury's); Witt v. Norfe, Inc., 725 F.2d 1277 (11th Cir. 1984) (Fla. law). But see Eagle–Picher Indus. v. Balbos, 578 A.2d 228 (Md. App. 1990) (because inconsistent verdict may reflect lenity, mistake, or compromise, new trial would interfere with jury's decisional role), rev'd in part on other grounds, 604 A.2d 445 (Md. 1992).

**35.** On the independence of the three separate types of defect, see § 6.2, below.

**36.** See, e.g., Perry v. Red Wing Shoe Co., 597 So.2d 821 (Fla. Dist. Ct. App. 1992); Peterson v. Little–Giant Glencoe

It is difficult to understand why a jury might return inconsistent findings of this type. It may simply be because the jury does not fully understand the true meaning of the legal term of art, "defective"; perhaps the jury believes that even an inadequately designed product, or one carrying inadequate warnings, is not "defective" if it contains no loose screws or broken parts.[37] Or it may be because the phrase "unreasonably dangerous" may sound to the jury "as if the requisite proof for a product defect is some form of 'extraordinary' danger."[38] In addition to such confusion, it may be, as suggested by one court, that such inconsistencies reflect a jury's desire to be lenient with the plaintiff or to effect a kind of compromise between the parties. But, whatever the reason, such findings logically make no sense, are offensive to sound jurisprudence, and ordinarily should not be tolerated.

One solution to all this would be to require the plaintiff to elect a single theory, strict liability or negligence, upon which to submit the case to the jury, yet most courts do not require such a choice.[39] Yet a few courts have withdrawn the negligence count from the jury on grounds that it would be "superfluous and would tend to confuse the jurors" if included with a count for strict liability in tort,[40] and a few other courts have gone the other way, ruling that juries should be instructed only on negligence, and not on strict liability in tort.[41] Or a court could avoid the problem altogether by adopting the *Third Restatement*'s approach of abandoning distinctions between negligence and strict liability and submitting cases to juries according to the type of proof required for the type of defect plaintiff has alleged.[42]

### Strict Liability in Tort *vs.* Warranty

#### *In General*

Many courts and commentators in the 1960s agreed with Dean Prosser's view that the merger of warranty and tort into a new tort doctrine of strict products liability was a legal inevitability, as seen

---

Portable Elevator Div. of Dynamics Corp. of Am., 349 N.W.2d 280 (Minn. Ct. App. 1984), aff'd in part, rev'd in part on other grounds, 366 N.W.2d 111 (Minn. 1985) (jury findings of negligence but not strict liability were consistent when based on claims of separate conduct). Compare Hasson v. Ford Motor Co., 564 P.2d 857 (Cal. 1977) (overruled in part on other grounds by Soule v. General Motors Corp., 882 P.2d 298 (Cal. 1994)) (negligence finding not inconsistent with finding of no strict liability where defect arose after sale prompting subsequent duty to warn). See generally Annot., 41 A.L.R. 4th 9, 16 (1985) (inconsistent products liability verdicts).

**37.** Cf. Rinker v. Ford Motor Co., 567 S.W.2d 655, 659–60 (Mo. Ct. App. 1978).

**38.** Twerski, From Defect to Cause to Comparative Fault—Rethinking Some Product Liability Concepts, 60 Marq. L. Rev. 297, 334 (1977), relied upon in Hansen

v. Cessna Aircraft Co., 578 F.2d 679 (7th Cir. 1978) (Wis. law).

**39.** Hansen v. Cessna Aircraft Co., 578 F.2d 679 (7th Cir. 1978) (Wis. law); Howes v. Deere & Co., 238 N.W.2d 76 (Wis. 1976). Compare comment *a*.

**40.** See, e.g., Mather v. Caterpillar Tractor Corp., 533 P.2d 717, 719 (Ariz. Ct. App. 1975). The cases are collected in Annot., 52 A.L.R.3d 101 (1974) (necessity and propriety of instructing on alternative theories in products liability cases). See generally Slattery, Terschan and Griffin, Product Liability Verdict Formulation in Wisconsin, 61 Marq. L. Rev. 381 (1978).

**41.** See, e.g., Olson v. Prosoco, Inc., 522 N.W.2d 284, 289 (Iowa 1994) (warning defect).

**42.** See, e.g., Wright v. Brooke Group Ltd., 652 N.W.2d 159, 169 (Iowa 2002) (design defect).

above.[43] But a substantial segment of the legal academy always has been troubled by the overlap between the two strict products liability doctrines—the one doctrine standing proudly in tort while the other crouches shamelessly in contract, disparate branches of the law competing for coverage of a single social problem.[44] As both tort and contract law during the 1960s tried to stamp their brands on strict manufacturer liability for product accidents, scholars from different sides of the academy viewed the matter from quite different windows.

One leading commercial law scholar, Richard Speidel, argued that "nagging doubts about the propriety of a judicial imposition of strict products liability, recurring attacks upon the bases of liability itself, the complexity of the underlying problems of cost allocation among the various enterprises and individuals involved, and a suspicion that in a zealous attempt to protect the consumer interest the courts may have created more problems than they can solve all dictate against the type of 'unrealistic absolutism displayed in Section 402A of the *Restatement of Torts, Second*." Professor Speidel expressed the view that the warranty principles, embraced by the law of contract, allowed individuals to make whatever purchase and sales transactions that suited their particular needs and preferences and so were preferable to "the treacherous uncertainties of strict products liability" in tort.[45] Tort law scholars broadly disagreed. Mark Franklin, for example, was "left with regret that the Code, devoted so extensively to dealings within the business community, decided to try its hand at the products liability problem. That it did so is clear. That it should have is much less clear. The considerations involved in the products cases are so different from traditional commercial dealings that the Code's insistence on covering all of an abstract 'commercial' area may unfortunately lead to similar treatment for dissimilar problems."[46]

Such arguments fail sufficiently to embrace the important historical fact that the doctrine of strict products liability in tort sprang from the law of warranty, as seen above.[47] Once the decisions in *Henningsen v.*

---

**43.**  See §§ 5.2–5.4, above.

**44.**  See, e.g., Owen, Defectiveness Restated: Exploding the "Strict" Products Liability Myth, 1996 U. Ill. L. Rev. 743, 756 (observing that, in modern design defect theory, "the utilitarian, fault-based negligence principles of tort law and the expectational, strict liability principles of the law of contracts are conjoined" and opining that "[w]hether this conjunction is proper may well be doubted, for the separate spheres of tort and contract law serve distinct functions and derive from disparate policies and ethics").

**45.**  Speidel, The Virginia "Anti–Privity" Statute: Strict Products Liability Under The Uniform Commercial Code, 51 Va. L. Rev. 804, 851 (1965):

The value of some contractual risk allocation is that the alternatives for private decision-making are both strengthened and expanded under controlled conditions. The small enterprise which does not conform to the paradigm upon which strict liability is based may attempt to shift its risk to the consumer rather than simply absorb the loss or go out of business. The informed consumer can choose to accept the risk or not. Whatever the outcome of this choice, the result is more attuned to the needs and capabilities of the particular parties. Until an ultimate legislative solution to the problem is formulated and enacted into law, the treacherous uncertainties of strict products liability imposed by courts can be reduced by at least one firm anchor to the traditional values of freedom of contract.

**46.**  Franklin, When Worlds Collide: Liability Theories and Disclaimers in Defective–Product Cases, 18 Stan. L. Rev. 974, 1019–20 (1966).

**47.**  See § 5.2, above.

*Bloomfield Motors, Inc.*[48] and *Greenman v. Yuba Power Products, Inc.*[49] stripped the implied warranty claim of its traditional contract law defenses based on privity, disclaimers, and notice, what remained, in all its naked glory, was the doctrine of strict products liability in tort.[50] Thus, it often is noted that strict liability in tort "is essentially the liability of implied warranty divested of the contract doctrines of privity, disclaimer, and notice."[51] Despite the different manner in which the tort and implied warranty liability standards are phrased—"defective condition unreasonably dangerous"[52] versus "fit for the ordinary purposes for which such goods are used"[53]—courts often recite the virtual or complete equivalence of the two standards of liability, requiring the same types of proof.[54] Thus, most courts today properly view the defectiveness concept inherent in unmerchantability to be the equivalent of the defectiveness concept in both negligence and strict products liability in tort.[55]

That strict liability in tort derived largely from warranty law's inability to provide injured consumers with an effective mode of recovery—due to the restrictions of privity, disclaimer, and notice—raises an interesting question of whether courts could properly "legislate" around carefully crafted warranty law principles enacted by the state legislatures in their adoptions of Article 2 of the UCC. Thus, in *Cline v. Prowler Industries of Maryland, Inc.*,[56] the Delaware Supreme Court refused to adopt § 402A as the law of that state because of the legislature's then-recent enactment of the UCC. "[T]he General Assembly did not intend to permit the adoption of a competing theory of liability in cases involving the sales of goods and, thus, preempted the field."[57] But most courts were little concerned with the argument that strict products liability in tort might impermissibly invade a field preempted by the UCC, and the issue is now of little more than historical interest.[58]

---

**48.** 161 A.2d 69 (N.J. 1960).

**49.** 377 P.2d 897 (Cal. 1963).

**50.** See § 5.2, above.

**51.** Nave v. Rainbo Tire Service, Inc., 462 N.E.2d 620, 625 (Ill. App. Ct. 1984). "To recover on either theory—implied warranty or strict liability—the plaintiff in a products liability case must satisfy three basics from an evidentiary standpoint: (1) the existence of a defect, (2) the attribution of the defect to the seller, and (3) a causal relation between the defect and the injury." Virgil v. "Kash N' Karry" Service Corp., 484 A.2d 652, 656 (Md. Ct. Spec. App. 1984). Accord, Voelkel v. General Motors Corp., 846 F.Supp. 1468, 1475–76 (D. Kan. 1994) (implied warranty, strict products liability in tort, and negligence).

**52.** Restatement (2d) Torts § 402A.

**53.** UCC § 2–314(2)(c).

**54.** "[T]o bring an action in implied warranty for personal injury a plaintiff is required to show product unmerchantability sufficient to avoid summary judgment on the issue of defectiveness in a tort strict products liability suit." Larsen v. Pacesetter Sys., Inc., 837 P.2d 1273, 1284–85 (Haw.

1992), amended on reconsideration in part, 843 P.2d 144 (Haw. 1992).

**55.** See, e.g., Wright v. Brooke Group Ltd., 652 N.W.2d 159, 181 (Iowa 2002) ("under Iowa law a seller's warranty that goods are fit for the ordinary purposes for which such goods are used gives rise to the same obligation owed by manufacturers under tort law with respect to the avoidance of personal injury to others").

**56.** 418 A.2d 968 (Del. 1980).

**57.** Id. at 980.

**58.** Arguing that the preemption view was wrong, Dean John Wade had the last word in a decade-long debate with Professor Reed Dickerson on whether tort law had improperly invaded the field of warranty and contracts. See Wade, Tort Liability for Products Causing Physical Injury and Article 2 of the U.C.C., 48 Mo. L. Rev. 1 (1983) (arguing that tort law properly applies to this field of law). Revised Article 2 puts the matter to rest, in UCC Rev. § 2–314 cmt. 7, by explicitly addressing the interrelation between warranty law under the Code and products liability in tort. See § 4.3, above.

### *Inconsistent Jury Verdicts—Denny v. Ford Motor Co.*

The virtual or complete identity between the concept of defectiveness under § 402A and the notion of unmerchantability under UCC § 2–314 has led some courts to hold that conflicting jury verdicts on the two theories must be irreconcilable and, hence, the basis for reversal. On such reasoning, for example, an extension cord found *not* to be defective can hardly also be found to be unmerchantable.[59] Further, if the two claims are in fact redundant, a court may not be in error for refusing to instruct a jury on both doctrines.[60]

For many years, the inconsistency of jury verdicts was little more than a footnote to the developing body of products liability jurisprudence. In 1995, however, the New York Court of Appeals decided *Denny v. Ford Motor Co.*[61] in which it ruled that claims of strict products liability in tort and breach of implied warranty are not always co-extensive. Nancy Denny was injured when she slammed on the brakes of her Ford Bronco II SUV to avoid hitting a deer and the vehicle rolled over. Ms. Denny sued Ford in federal court, challenging the vehicle's design for rolling over too easily due to its relatively narrow track width, high center of gravity, and short wheel base and suspension system, and Ford's failure to warn of the vehicle's propensity to roll over. While these characteristics of the Bronco II made the vehicle less stable for normal suburban highway driving, for which Ford marketed the car, they were necessary to make the vehicle useful for driving over irregular off-road terrain, the supposed purpose of such a "sport utility vehicle."

Plaintiff asserted the same design and failure to warn claims in separate counts of (1) strict liability in tort, for selling a product in a defective condition, and (2) breach of the implied warranty of merchantability, for marketing a car that was not fit for its ordinary purposes. Despite the defendant's objections that the claims were identical, the trial court submitted the case to the jury on both claims. Without objection, the court instructed the jury that the tort law claim required the plaintiff to prove that the vehicle was "defective" or "not reasonably safe," to be determined by a risk-utility evaluation of the costs and benefits of designing out the danger. The court further explained that the implied warranty claim required the plaintiff to prove that the vehicle was not "reasonably fit for the ordinary purposes for which it was intended."

The jury returned a split verdict, concluding that (1) the Bronco was *not* "defective," so that Ford was not liable for strict products liability in tort, but that (2) Ford *had* breached an implied warranty of merchantability and so was liable on that basis for plaintiff's injuries. On defendant's appeal, the Second Circuit Court of Appeals certified certain questions to the New York high court, asking whether the two claims

---

**59.**  State Farm Fire & Cas. Co. v. Miller Elec. Co., 562 N.E.2d 589 (Ill. App. Ct. 1990). See also Gumbs v. International Harvester, Inc., 718 F.2d 88 (3d Cir. 1983). *Contra*, Malawy v. Richards Mfg. Co., 501 N.E.2d 376 (Ill. App. Ct. 1986) (distinguishing the two theories).

**60.**  See, e.g., Goblirsch v. Western Land Roller Co., 246 N.W.2d 687, 690 (Minn. 1976).

**61.**  662 N.E.2d 730 (N.Y. 1995).

were identical, and, if not, whether the jury's finding of no defect was reconcilable with its finding of a breach of warranty. *Held*, the claims are *not* identical and, on the facts, the jury's findings *were* reconcilable: defectiveness in strict liability in tort contains a "negligence-like risk/benefit component," which rests on the manufacturer's reasonableness in not adopting feasible alternative designs, whereas the implied warranty of merchantability rests on whether a product is "fit for ordinary purposes," measured by consumer expectations of how the product should operate in foreseeable situations.[62] The court reasoned that the jury could reasonably have concluded that the Bronco II was not "defective" for tort law purposes because its utility as an off-road vehicle outweighed the risk of rollovers, while also concluding that the vehicle was *not* safe under warranty law for the "ordinary purpose" of every-day on-road driving for which it was marketed and sold. These conclusions could have led the jury to conclude simultaneously that the strict products-liability claim failed but that the defendant had breached its implied warranty of merchantability of "fitness" for "ordinary purpose." The case was distinctive, thought the court, because the "ordinary purpose" for which the product was marketed and sold, the basis for the implied warranty claim, was different from the utility against which the risk was weighed, which supported the tort claim.

In a subsequent federal opinion applying New York law, the Second Circuit characterized *Denny* as adopting a doctrine that "can aptly be called the 'dual purpose' requirement."[63] The *Denny* dual-purpose rationale is clever, and in rare cases it may improve the fairness of a particular result. But by opening up a whole new representational doctrine that skirts around the conventional rules of tortious misrepresentation and express warranty, and which applies to only a tiny subset of cases, *Denny* may have concocted a cannon to kill a fly. The commentators generally have been unkind to *Denny*,[64] in part because it contra-

---

**62.** See id. at 736:

It is [the] negligence-like risk/benefit component of the defect element that differentiates strict-products-liability claims from UCC-based breach-of-implied-warranty claims in cases involving design defects. While the strict products concept of a product that is "not reasonably safe" requires a weighing of the product's dangers against its overall advantages, the UCC's concept of a "defective" product requires an inquiry only into whether the product in question was "fit for the ordinary purposes for which such goods are used" (UCC § 2–314[2][c]). The latter inquiry focused on the expectations for the performance of the product when used in the customary, usual and reasonably foreseeable manners. The cause of action is one involving true "strict" liability, since recovery may be had upon a showing that the product was not minimally safe for its expected purpose—without regard to the feasibility of alternative designs or the manufacturer's "reasonableness" in marketing it in that unsafe condition.

**63.** Castro v. QVC Network, Inc., 139 F.3d 114, 118 (2d Cir. 1998) (Calabresi, J.), following *Denny* ("in *Denny*, the Court of Appeals pointed out that the fact that a product's overall benefits might outweigh its overall risks does not preclude the possibility that consumers may have been misled into using the product in a context in which it was dangerously unsafe ... even though the benefits in other uses might make the product sufficiently reasonable so that it passed the risk/utility test."). On the *Denny* "dual purpose" test, see Ausili, Ramifications of Denny v. Ford Motor Co., 15 Touro L. Rev. 735 (1999).

**64.** See, e.g., White, Reverberations from the Collision of Tort and Warranty, 53 S.C. L. Rev. 1067, 1072–75 (2002); Ausili, Ramifications of Denny v. Ford Motor Co., 15 Touro L. Rev. 735 (1999); Schwartz and Behrens, An Unhappy Return to Confusion in the Common Law of Products Liability—Denny v. Ford Motor Company Should Be Overturned, 17 Pace L. Rev. 359, 377 (1997) ("the Court should overrule *Denny*

venes a strong majority rule,[65] and it has been rejected by the Supreme Court of Texas[66] and the American Law Institute, both in the *Products Liability Restatement*[67] and in its approval of Amended Article 2 of the UCC.[68]

and the Court's opinion should be ignored by courts of other states"); Note, 62 Mo. L. Rev. 381 (1997).

**65.** For citations, see Ausili, Ramifications of Denny v. Ford Motor Co., 15 Touro L. Rev. 735 (1999).

**66.** Hyundai Motor Co. v. Rodriguez, 995 S.W.2d 661 (Tex. 1999).

**67.** Products Liability Restatement § 2 cmt. *n*, at 34–35 ("two or more factually identical defective-design claims or two or more factually identical failure-to-warn claims should not be submitted to the trier of fact in the same case under different doctrinal labels").

**68.** See Amended UCC § 2–314 cmt. 7. See § 4.3, above.

*

# PART II

## PRODUCT DEFECTIVENESS

# Chapter 6

---

# NATURE AND PROOF OF
# DEFECTIVENESS

*Table of Sections*

---

## § 6.1 DEFECTIVENESS—GENERALLY

Defectiveness lies at the center of products liability law. Merely making and selling a product that causes accidental harm fails to provide a sufficient basis for moral or legal responsibility.[1] Instead, the essence of accountability in products liability law is that the defendant supplied a product that was *deficient* in some respect, that the product was "defective." In Roman law, responsibility for product harm rested to a large extent on the notion of product defect, as it did under medieval Church law and the law of early America.[2] Defectiveness continues to provide the core concept of modern products liability law around the world.[3]

Since the rise of modern products liability law in America during the 1960s, determining how defectiveness should be defined[4] and proved[5] has preoccupied the courts, commentators, and products liability lawyers. Apart from special types of claims (such as those involving misrepresentation,[6] negligent entrustment,[7] and certain others[8]), every products

---

### § 6.1

**1.** "The fact that a manufacturer makes and sells products, which generally are good, is an insufficient reason for requiring a manufacturer to compensate a victim of a product accident. . . . [M]oral philosophy requires more than action, related in some manner to another's harm, for the actor to be held accountable for the harm." Owen, The Moral Foundations of Products Liability Law: Toward First Principles, 68 Notre Dame L. Rev. 427, 461 (1993).

**2.** For an overview of products liability history, see §§ 1.2 and 5.2, above.

**3.** For an overview of modern products liability law in other nations, see § 1.4, above.

**4.** See § 4.3 (implied warranty), and §§ 5.5–5.9 (strict liability in tort), above, and §§ 7.2, 8.2 and 9.2, below.

**5.** See §§ 6.3 and 6.4, below.

**6.** See ch. 3, above.

**7.** See § 15.2, below.

**8.** Such as those based on the implied warranty of fitness for particular purpose, under UCC § 2–315, or possibly on the violation of a product safety statute, such as

---

liability claim requires proof that the injury was caused by an unnecessary hazard in the defendant's product. Regardless of the underlying cause of action, plaintiffs in products liability cases ordinarily must establish that something was *wrong* with the product. Virtually every product is dangerous in some manner and to some extent, at least when put to certain uses. But most such dangers are a simple fact of physics, chemistry, or biology which there is no reasonable way to avoid. For such natural risks of life, product users rather than product suppliers properly bear responsibility for avoiding and insuring against any injuries that may result.[9] But some products carry excessive risk which users and consumers should not fairly be required to shoulder, either because the risks are unexpected or because they can be economically avoided by manufacturers or other product suppliers. And so the law properly requires that a product contain some type of *excessive* danger before the risk of loss is shifted to the seller. The label which the law attaches to products carrying such excessive risks is "defective."[10]

At least implicitly, each of the three major causes of action in products liability law requires that the product be defective. Negligence claims are predicated on the defectiveness of a product, because its supplier ordinarily cannot be faulted for selling a product that is good (i.e. not defective).[11] The implied warranty of merchantability typically is based on the idea that a product is "unfit" for ordinary use, meaning virtually the same thing as "defective."[12] And strict liability in tort, of course, is explicitly based on the sale of a defective product.[13] The centrality of the concept of defectiveness to products liability law is reflected in the *Second* and *Third Restatements of Torts*, both of which ground liability on the notion of product defect.[14] In short, product defectiveness is the heart of products liability law.

a prohibition on the sale of fireworks to children or unlicensed persons (a species of unlawful entrustment). Yet many products liability statutes, such as pure food acts, are designed to prevent the sale of defective products. See § 7.5, below.

**9.** See Owen, The Moral Foundations of Products Liability Law: Toward First Principles, 68 Notre Dame L. Rev. 427 (1993).

**10.** See, e.g., Prentis v. Yale Mfg. Co., 365 N.W.2d 176, 182 (Mich. 1984) ("the plaintiff must, *in every case, in every jurisdiction*, show that the product was defective"); Phillips v. Kimwood Mach. Co., 525 P.2d 1033, 1036 (Or. 1974) ("To impose liability there has to be something about the article which makes it dangerously defective."). Products Liability Restatement § 1 (liability for harm from commercial sale of "defective" product).

**11.** See, e.g., Merrill v. Navegar, Inc., 28 P.3d 116, 124 (Cal. 2001) (under both negligence and strict liability, plaintiff must prove a defect caused the injury and, under negligence, plaintiff must also prove "an additional element, namely, that the defect

in the product was due to negligence of the defendant," citing Prosser, Strict Liability to the Consumer, 18 Hastings L.J. 9, 50–51 (1966)); Oanes v. Westgo, Inc., 476 N.W.2d 248, 253 (N.D. 1991) ("In negligent design claims it is well established that a manufacturer or seller is not liable in the absence of proof that a product is defective. Thus, an element of a negligent design case is that the product is defective or unsafe."); Garrett v. Hamilton Standard Controls, Inc., 850 F.2d 253 (5th Cir. 1988) (Tex. law) (electric blanket allegedly caused house fire). The new Restatement makes this point. "Negligence rests on a showing of fault leading to product defect. Strict liability rests merely on a showing of product defect." Products Liability Restatement § 2 cmt. *n*. See also §§ 2.1 and 5.9, above.

**12.** See, e.g., Spectron Dev. Lab. v. American Hollow Boring Co., 936 P.2d 852 (N.M. Ct. App. 1997) (manufacturing defect). See §§ 4.3 and 5.9, above.

**13.** See ch. 5, above.

**14.** See Restatement (2d) Torts § 402A; Products Liability Restatement §§ 1 and 2.

Chapters 6–10 explore in depth various aspects of product defectiveness. The present chapter addresses recurring issues concerning defects of all types, such as the independent nature of the three separate forms of defect, the special rules governing expert testimony, recurring issues of proof, and ends with an overview of the *Products Liability Restatement*, which centers on the concept of product defect. Chapter 7 examines manufacturing defectiveness, including the applicable liability tests[15] and the special issues involved in defective food and drink.[16] Chapter 8 considers design defects, including the twisted evolution of defect tests in this context,[17] and the special issues of optional safety devices,[18] prescription drugs, and medical devices.[19] Chapter 9 explores the topic of warning defects, including defect tests,[20] the notion of a warning's adequacy,[21] the parties to whom warnings must be provided,[22] and special rules governing prescription drugs and medical devices.[23] Finally, Chapter 10 examines a wide range of limiting doctrines on the defect concept, including the role of obvious dangers,[24] generic risk and product category liability,[25] the many strands of state of the art,[26] liability for prenatal harm,[27] product deterioration,[28] disposal and salvage,[29] and the developing law of post-sale duties to warn or recall.[30]

## § 6.2   The Three Types of Defect

### The Distinctness of the Defect Concepts

Both the *Second* and *Third Restatements of Torts* base liability on the concept of product defect. Section 402A of the *Second Restatement* provides liability for selling a product in a "defective condition unreasonably dangerous"[1] and § 1 of the *Third Restatement* provides liability for selling "a defective product." Notwithstanding this common grounding, the two *Restatements* treat the defect concept differently. When Dean Prosser crafted § 402A of the *Second Restatement* in the late 1950s and early 1960s, products liability law was in its infancy.[2] At this very early stage in the development of this branch of law, the defect concept was only roughly understood and conceived of quite naively as a unitary concept: products were either too dangerous (defective) or safe enough (nondefective).[3] As courts in the 1960s and 1970s applied the principles of § 402A to an ever-widening array of products in an ever-widening range of contexts, the disparities among the various forms of product dangers increasingly revealed themselves. Over time, courts and commentators came to understand the fundamental distinctions between the

---

15.   See §§ 7.2–7.4, below.

16.   See § 7.5, below.

17.   See §§ 8.2–8.8, below.

18.   See § 8.9, below.

19.   See § 8.10, below.

20.   See § 9.2, below.

21.   See § 9.3, below.

22.   See §§ 9.4 and 9.5, below.

23.   See § 9.6, below.

24.   See §§ 10.2 and 10.3, below.

25.   See § 10.3, below.

26.   See § 10.4, below.

27.   See § 10.5, below.

28.   See § 10.6, below.

29.   See § 10.7, below.

30.   See § 10.8, below.

**§ 6.2**

1.   Restatement (2d) Torts § 402A.

2.   See §§ 5.2 and 5.3, above. The discussion here also appears in Owen, The Puzzle of Comment *j*, 55 Hastings L.J. 1377 (2004).

3.   See §§ 5.3 and 5.5, above.

three very different forms of product defect: (1) manufacturing flaws—unintended physical irregularities that occur during the production process;[4] (2) design inadequacies—hazards lurking in a product's engineering or scientific conception that may reasonably be avoided by a different design or formula;[5] and (3) insufficient warnings of danger and instructions on safe use—the absence of information needed by users to avoid product hazards.[6] Misrepresentation, the fourth principal basis of products liability, is not generally classified as a product "defect."[7] In the decades since § 402A first roughly sketched a general doctrine of strict products liability in tort, the need to accord separate treatment to the liability issues distinctive to each of these very different defect contexts has become a well-accepted axiom. Today, the independent existence of each of these three separate types of defect is a fundamental premise of American products liability law.[8]

Section 402A of the *Second Restatement*, as mentioned above, provided a single rule of liability for the sale of defective products.[9] Because the *Third Restatement* in § 1 begins quite similarly in providing that a seller of a "defective product" is subject to liability for resulting harm,[10] it might at first glance appear to restate the *Second Restatement*'s no-fault doctrine of "strict liability" that has dominated products liability doctrine since the 1960s. But § 2 of the *Third Restatement* radically departs from § 402A by splintering the defect notion into the three separate forms of defect—defects in manufacture,[11] design,[12] and instruc-

---

**4.** See ch. 7, below.

**5.** See ch. 8, below.

**6.** See ch. 9, below.

**7.** By convention, although it would be as logical to attach the "defective" description to products carrying safety misrepresentations as to products carrying insufficient safety information. At least Ohio does so, imposing liability if a product "was defective because it did not conform to a representation made by its manufacturer." Ohio Rev. Code Ann. § 2307.73(A)(1). See id. at § 2307.77.

**8.** See, e.g., In re Coordinated Latex Glove Litig., 121 Cal.Rptr.2d 301 (Ct. App. 2002) (defectively manufactured latex gloves); Chandler v. Gene Messer Ford, Inc., 81 S.W.3d 493 (Tex. App. 2002) (airbag without adequate warnings); Jay v. Moog Auto., Inc., 652 N.W.2d 872 (Neb. 2002) (defectively designed compressor); Ritchie v. Glidden Co., 242 F.3d 713 (7th Cir. 2001) (Ind. law); McLennan v. American Eurocopter Corp., 245 F.3d 403 (5th Cir. 2001) (Tex. law); Vitanza v. Upjohn Co., 778 A.2d 829 (Conn. 2001). See Products Liability Restatement § 1 Reporters' Note to cmt. *a*, and § 2 cmt. *a*.

Early in the development of modern products liability theory, some courts and commentators classified defects into two categories, defects of manufacture or design, and

conceived of the duty to warn as a subcategory of the duty to design. See, e.g., LaGorga v. Kroger Co., 275 F.Supp. 373, 380 (W.D. Pa. 1967). For remnants of this conceptualization, see, e.g., Chellman v. Saab–Scania AB, 637 A.2d 148, 150–51 (N.H. 1993) ("[t]he duty to warn is part of the general duty to design, manufacture and sell products that are reasonably safe"); Glover v. BIC Corp., 6 F.3d 1318, 1323 (9th Cir. 1993) (Or. law) (warnings are part of the duty of safe design; see Or. Rev. Stat. §§ 30.900–.920); Wade, On the Effect in Products Liability of Knowledge Unavailable Prior to Marketing, 58 N.Y.U. L. Rev. 734, 740 (1983) ("although 'failure to warn' is usually treated as a separate basis for finding a product actionable, 'failure to warn' cases may be properly viewed as 'defective design' cases").

**9.** See § 5.3, above.

**10.** "One engaged in the business of selling or otherwise distributing products who sells or distributes a defective product is subject to liability for harm to persons or property caused by the defect." Products Liability Restatement § 1.

**11.** See Products Liability Restatement § 2(a).

**12.** See Products Liability Restatement § 2(b).

tions or warnings[13]—each with separate doctrine of its own.[14] By so trifurcating defectiveness, § 2 affords separate vessels for separate liability standards: § 2(a) defines liability for manufacturing defects in terms of departure-from-intended-design, whereas §§ 2(b) and (c) define liability for design and warnings defects in the foreseeable risk-utility terms of fault-based liability.[15] Liability in § 2 of the new *Restatement* thus is truly "strict" for manufacturing defects but is based on negligence for design and warnings defects.[16] The *Restatement (Third) of Torts: Products Liability* is premised upon the substantial independence of these three forms of defect, not only in the tripartite division of defectiveness in § 2, but also in the various provisions governing a product seller's obligations in different contexts.[17]

While variations among the liability standards may be the most fundamental distinction between the separate types of defects, other consequences flow from the particular type of defect alleged and proved. By way of illustration, the obviousness of a danger in most jurisdictions precludes, as a matter of law, a finding of warning,[18] but not design,[19] defectiveness.[20] Further, certain types of evidence may be proper in proving one type of defect but not another. For example, evidence of subsequent design changes may be admissible in some states to help establish a manufacturing defect, whereas such evidence ordinarily may not be used to prove a defect in a warning or design case.[21] In addition, some jurisdictions provide for special defenses tailored to particular types of defect.[22]

Thus, the three different types of product defectiveness generate three separate, independent sets of obligations for product sellers.

---

**13.** See Products Liability Restatement § 2(c).

**14.** See, e.g., Wright v. Brooke Group Ltd., 652 N.W.2d 159 (Iowa 2002) (applying the separate manufacturing and design defect concepts of Products Liability Restatement § 2); Hollister v. Dayton Hudson Corp., 201 F.3d 731, 740 (6th Cir. 2000) (Mich. law) ("design defect claims and failure to warn claims are governed by distinct analyses"). See Products Liability Restatement § 1 Reporters' Note 1 to cmt. *a*.

**15.** Notwithstanding the strict-sounding language of "defectiveness" in which the definitions are cast. See Products Liability Restatement § 1 cmt. *a*, § 2 cmts. *a, c, d, i,* and *m*. Note that the Third Restatement uses §§ 1–4 to describe liability rules applicable to products generally and that it addresses liability standards applicable to special defendants, such as sellers of component parts (§ 5), prescription drugs (§ 6), food (§ 7), and used products (§ 8), in later sections.

**16.** See Owen, Defectiveness Restated: Exploding the "Strict" Products Liability Myth, 1996 U. Ill. L. Rev. 743.

**17.** See, e.g., Products Liability Restatement § 6 (sellers of prescription drugs and medical devices subject to different standards for manufacturing defects, design defects, and warnings defects).

**18.** See § 10.4, below.

**19.** See § 10.3, below.

**20.** See, e.g., Lamb v. Kysor Indus. Corp., 759 N.Y.S.2d 266, 267–68 (App. Div. 2003) (obviousness of danger precluded liability for warning defect, but triable issue remained as to whether failure to provide "kill switch" constituted design defect); Delaney v. Deere & Co., 999 P.2d 930 (Kan. 2000).

**21.** See, e.g., Demirovski v. Skil Corp., 610 N.Y.S.2d 551 (App. Div. 1994); Cover v. Cohen, 461 N.E.2d 864 (N.Y. 1984).

**22.** See, e.g., Cacciola v. Selco Balers, Inc., 127 F.Supp.2d 175, 185–88 (E.D.N.Y. 2001) (substantial modification defense may preclude liability for design, but not warning, defect); N.J. Stat. Ann. §§ 2A:58C–3 (certain state-of-the-art defenses apply only to design dangers).

### The Puzzle of Comment *j*

That the three types of defect beget distinct and largely independent obligations would seem to be so obvious as to be beyond dispute. Yet, from time to time, this fundamental principle of products liability law escapes an unwary court. Typically, this confusion springs from a curious puzzle that lies at the heart of § 402A of the *Restatement (Second) of Torts*, the fountainhead of modern products liability law. The puzzle is this: § 402A, crafted by Dean William Prosser, generated the expansive, plaintiff-friendly doctrine of strict liability in tort for the sale of products that are defective in any of three very different ways—in manufacturing, warnings, or design. Yet a sentence in one comment to § 402A, comment *j*, can be read quite literally to mean that a manufacturer who provides a warning—*any* type of warning, no matter how deficient—eludes the duty of safe design. If this be true, if warnings trump design as a number of courts have held, then § 402A is a much weaker doctrine than generally believed. Dean Prosser, that is, in a single sentence of a single comment to a single section of the *Restatement*, may have stripped the doctrine of strict products liability in tort of much of its intrinsic power.

In attempting to ascertain the proper relationship between a manufacturer's duty to warn and its duty of safe design, most courts and commentators have side-stepped the enigmatic sentence in comment *j* simply by ignoring it. And the commentators who have studied the comment most closely, including the Reporters for the *Third Restatement of Torts*, have interpreted it as meaning that a manufacturer's warnings somehow cancel out its duty of safe design.[23] But this interpretation is wrong. In fact, the riddle of comment *j* has a key that really is quite simple, discoverable from examining the history of § 402A within the context of the times, that is consistent with the way products liability law has in fact evolved for the last half century.

Comment *j* basically sets forth, in a largely noncontroversial manner, a product seller's duty to warn of foreseeable hazards.[24] However,

---

**23.** See, e.g., Products Liability Restatement § 2 cmt. *l*; Henderson and Twerski, The Politics of the Products Liability Restatement, 26 Hofstra L. Rev. 667, 689 (1998); Latin, "Good" Warnings, Bad Products, and Cognitive Limitations, 41 UCLA L. Rev. 1193, 1294–95 (1994); Priest, Strict Products Liability: The Original Intent, 10 Cardozo L. Rev. 2301, 2303 (1989).

**24.** Comment *j* to § 402A provides in full:

> *j. Directions or warning.* In order to prevent the product from being unreasonably dangerous, the seller may be required to give directions or warning, on the container, as to its use. The seller may reasonably assume that those with common allergies, as for example to eggs or strawberries, will be aware of them, and he is not required to warn against them. Where, however, the product contains an ingredient to which a substantial number of the population are allergic, and the ingredient is one whose danger is not generally known, or if known is one which the consumer would reasonably not expect to find in the product, the seller is required to give warning against it, if he has knowledge, or by the application of reasonable, developed human skill and foresight should have knowledge, of the presence of the ingredient and the danger. Likewise in the case of poisonous drugs, or those unduly dangerous for other reasons, warning as to use may be required.

> But a seller is not required to warn with respect to products, or ingredients in them, which are only dangerous, or potentially so, when consumed in excessive quantity, or over a long period of time, when the danger, or potentiality of danger, is generally known and recognized. Again the dangers of alcoholic beverages are an example, as are also those

the comment concludes with the following "unfortunate language:"[25]

> Where warning is given, the seller may reasonably assume that it will be read and heeded; and a product bearing such a warning, which is safe for use if it is followed, is not in [a] defective condition, nor is it unreasonably dangerous.

This language is indeed "unfortunate" because its ambiguity permits it to be interpreted in any number of significantly different ways. For example, it may be read as meaning that *any* warning, no matter how inadequate, satisfies the *informational* obligations addressed in comment *j*; or that a warning *if adequate* satisfies those obligations; or that *any* warning, no matter how inadequate, satisfies *every* duty of whatever type owed by the seller to the user; or that an *adequate* warning will satisfy *every* duty of whatever type owed by the seller to the user. The proper interpretation of this sentence, as explained below, is really none of these,[26] but the much narrower proposition that the only obligation of sellers of inherently dangerous products like food, alcohol, tobacco, and drugs, in addition to supplying them free of impurities, is to warn consumers of the unavoidable, latent dangers such products foreseeably may contain. Understanding why this narrow interpretation is correct requires deconstructing comment *j* by reading it in the context of other comments, examining the "legislative history" of those comments, considering the relevant policies, and reviewing related products liability developments over time.

### Deconstructing Comment j

In attempting to unravel the inscrutable meaning of this clause of comment *j*, one needs to read it in context by considering the comments that precede and follow it and the narrow subject matter these comments in fact addressed. In examining this context, it must be remembered that the Restatement Reporter, Dean William Prosser, researched and drafted comment *j* in the late 1950s and early 1960 to accompany a narrow draft of § 402A of the *Second Restatement* limited to defective food and related products—such as drugs, alcoholic beverages, and tobacco—several years before a general doctrine of strict liability in tort applicable to all products ever saw the light of day.

of foods containing such substances as saturated fats, which may over a period of time have a deleterious effect upon the human heart.

Where warning is given, the seller may reasonably assume that it will be read and heeded; and a product bearing such a warning, which is safe for use if it is followed, is not in defective condition, nor is it unreasonably dangerous.

**25.** This is the characterization by the Reporters for the Third Restatement. See Products Liability Restatement § 2 Reporters' Note to cmt. *j*.

**26.** Most courts avoid this interpretive problem simply by ignoring it, which makes good sense. After all, this problem resides in a single sentence of a single comment to a single Restatement section that has now been superseded. Of the interpretations offered above, the best is the second: that a manufacturer satisfies its duty to provide safety information to purchasers and users—and only this duty—by providing them with warnings and instructions adequately explaining the risk and how to avoid it. Such an interpretation may be largely tautological, but it is the only interpretation that makes sense today. Yet, even this interpretation falsely assumes that comment *j* applies to the effect of warnings on the general duty to design any type of product, whereas comments *i*, *j*, and *k* in fact apply only to products possessing inherent, unavoidable dangers that cannot be designed away.

A close reading of comments *i, j*, and *k* to the *Restatement (Second) of Torts* § 402A, together with their "legislative history," reveals that these comments were directed exclusively to a narrow set of issues pertinent to a limited class of products, to wit, the liability (and limits of liability) of sellers of certain types of products—food, drugs, whiskey, cigarettes, and similar products that contain unavoidable dangers. While the titles to comments *i* ("*Unreasonably dangerous*") and *j* ("*Directions or warning*") unfortunately suggest that they might have general application to *all* products, these comments, together with comment *k* ("*Unavoidably unsafe products*"), in fact are limited to a single narrow topic: the responsibility of sellers of products like food, alcoholic beverages, tobacco, and drugs containing inherent product dangers that cannot be designed away.

The premise of each of these three comments is that strict liability under § 402A does not apply unless a manufacturer has a reasonable way to eliminate a product's hazards. Based on this premise, the main point of these particular comments is that the only duty of manufacturers of food, whiskey, cigarettes, drugs, and similar products containing inherent dangers is to warn consumers of hidden dangers. The comments thus explain that this limited class of products, accompanied by proper warnings, are not in a "defective condition unreasonably dangerous" with respect to the unavoidable dangers inherent in products of this type.

**Comment *i*.** Comment *i* explains why the ALI added the phrase "defective condition" to modify the "(unreasonably) dangerous" term used in an earlier, preliminary draft of § 402A. The "defective condition" language was added (at the urging of the ALI Council) to make clear that the new "strict" liability in tort would *not* give rise to design liability for the sale of products like food, whiskey, and cigarettes that contain inherent dangers that cannot be eliminated.[27] Comment *i* thus makes the single point that the strict liability principle of § 402A is inappropriate for some products that are widely known to be inherently dangerous such that consumers who choose to use such products are deemed to accept those inherent risks.[28]

**Comment *j*.** Comment *j*, first attached to the 1961 draft of § 402A that applied only to food and similar products, also discusses and applies only to dangerous foods, alcoholic beverages, and drugs—products that by their nature cannot be rendered safe except by warnings. This comment makes three points: first, continuing the reasoning of the previous comment, sellers of food, tobacco, alcohol, drugs, and similar products widely known to be inherently dangerous are *not* generally subject to strict liability for such dangers because consumers understand that products of these types necessarily include such risks; second, but that sellers of such products *do* have a duty to warn consumers of any latent risks of which consumers generally are unaware; and third, because there simply is no way *other than by warning* that sellers of such

**27.** See American Law Institute Proceedings 87–89 (1961).

**28.** "Many products cannot possibly be made entirely safe...." Restatement (2d) Torts § 402A cmt. *i*.

products can minimize their inherent risks, that the only reasonable duty for manufacturers of such products is to warn consumers of any hidden dangers.[29]

The premise here is that sellers of *generically dangerous products* may trust[30] that users, properly informed of any hidden dangers, will read and heed any (adequate) warnings and take responsibility for such inherent risks. Thus, properly interpreted, comment *j*'s concluding sentence actually means:

> Where [adequate] warning [of any hidden dangers] is given, the seller [of inherently dangerous products like food, drugs, alcoholic beverages, and cigarettes] may reasonably assume that [the warning] will be read and heeded [because there is nothing else the manufacturer can do to avoid the danger]; and [such] a product bearing such a warning, which is safe for use if it is followed, is not in [a] defective condition, nor is it unreasonably dangerous.

Comment *j* actually addresses only the narrow issue of a seller's duties with respect to food, tobacco, drugs, alcoholic beverages, and similar products containing inherent and unavoidable risks that cannot be designed away.[31] Conversely, comment *j* simply does not address how warnings affect the duty of safe design for *other* types of products whose dangers *can* reasonably be designed away.[32]

**Comment *k*.** Reiterating the overarching theme of all three comments—that a limited class of inherently and unavoidably dangerous products should be exempt from any design obligations in the strict liability rule of § 402A—comment *k* explains how, in particular, the principles of comments *i* and *j* apply to prescription drugs. In the context of this special type of unavoidably dangerous product, comment *k* makes the dual points that a seller does have a duty to provide proper warnings but that it is not otherwise liable for any inherent risks that cannot be designed away.[33]

In sum, a careful reading of comments *i*, *j*, and *k* makes clear that they are addressed *only* to the narrow unavoidable danger issue with

---

**29.** Putting aside, of course, the duties to produce a product without manufacturing defects and not to misrepresent a product's safety.

**30.** Indeed, manufacturers *must* trust in the good sense of users of such products, for there is nothing else to be done.

**31.** This interpretation of comment *j* is further supported by its direction that any required warnings be placed on the product's "container," surely the best place to warn of inherent dangers in food, drugs, whiskey, and cigarettes, but nonsensical when applied to the vast array of durable products that come without containers—tools, clothing, power mowers, automobiles, vacuum cleaners, and punch presses—for which the law requires that warnings against significant hidden dangers be locat-

ed in the most appropriate place. See ch. 9, below.

**32.** Dangers that *can* reasonably be designed out of products are by definition neither "inherent" nor "unavoidable."

**33.** Comment *k* provides in pertinent part:

> There are some products which, in the present state of human knowledge, are quite incapable of being made safe for their intended and ordinary use.... The seller of such products [particularly drugs], again with the qualification that they are properly prepared and marketed, and proper warning is given, where the situation calls for it, is not to be held to strict liability for unfortunate consequences [from] a known but apparently reasonable risk.

respect to inherently dangerous products like foods, cigarettes, whiskey, and drugs.[34] Everything in the comments points to their limited applicability, and nothing[35] suggests that they were intended to limit a seller's duty to design its products safely if there is a reasonable way to do so.[36]

**Comment *j*'s "legislative history."** The above contextual interpretation of comment *j* is confirmed by an examination of the evolution of § 402A drafts from 1961 through 1964, together with the contemporaneous scholarship of Dean Prosser and several key *Restatement* Advisers. Preceded by at least a couple of committee drafts,[37] § 402A was formally presented to the American Law Institute three times, beginning with Tentative Draft No. 6 in 1961. In this draft, § 402A imposed strict liability in tort upon sellers of "food in a defective condition unreasonably dangerous to consumers." In three small paragraphs, a single comment f (entitled *"Unreasonably dangerous"*) contained the entire discussion of the issues that in the final, published version eventually spanned three comments—*i, j,* and *k*. Although the § 402A black letter spoke only in terms of "food," comment *c* defined that word to embrace "all products intended for internal human consumption," including beverages, candy, chewing gum, chewing tobacco, snuff, unground coffee beans, and drugs. The next year, 1962, in order to embrace these non-food items more comfortably, the black letter of § 402A was expanded in Tentative Draft No. 7 to cover, in addition to food, "other products for intimate bodily use." In this draft, the discussions in comment f of the previous draft (Tent. Draft No. 6) were expanded upon and divided into comments *i, j,* and *k*. In 1964, after Justice Traynor's landmark ruling in *Greenman v. Yuba Power Products, Inc.,*[38] the black letter of § 402A was expanded again, in Tentative Draft No. 10,[39] to broaden the applicability of strict liability in tort to the sale of *all* products in a "defective condition unreasonably dangerous to the user or consumer." In this final draft, which Dean Prosser hurriedly rewrote to accommodate *Greenman,*[40] comments *i, j,* and *k* (all three of which sprang from comment f

---

**34.** The *only* examples in comments *i—k* are, in order: sugar (diabetes), castor oil (used by Mussolini for torture), whiskey (drunkenness), tobacco (cancer), butter (cholesterol and heart attacks), eggs (allergies), strawberries (allergies), alcohol (drunkenness), fatty foods (heart attacks), Pasteur rabies vaccine (allergic reactions), and other drugs and vaccines (side effects).

**35.** Except possibly for the unfortunate generality of their titles, left over from early tentative drafts of § 402A that applied only to food, and then food, drug, and bodily use products. Once Greenman v. Yuba Power Prods., Inc., 377 P.2d 897 (Cal. 1963), was decided, Dean Prosser promptly expanded the black letter of § 402A from food and products for "intimate bodily use" to *all* products. In his haste to revise the draft in this manner, as discussed below, Prosser neglected to adapt most of the comments to their now much broader scope, leaving most of them in the form in which they had originally been drafted with a much more limited type of product in mind.

Had he had more time, no doubt he would have added a major heading over comments *i, j,* and *k,* entitled "UNAVOIDABLY UNSAFE PRODUCTS," and then changed the title of comment *k* to *"Prescription drugs."*

**36.** In short, the comments simply recognize that you can't put a safety device on a stick of butter.

**37.** See Preliminary Draft No. 6, for review by the Advisory Committee (Jan. 3, 1958), and Council Draft No. 8 (Nov. 1, 1960). These early versions contained no direct reference to the unavoidable danger issues eventually addressed in comments *i, j,* and *k*.

**38.** 377 P.2d 897 (Cal. 1963).

**39.** Tentative Draft No. 10 was approved by the American Law Institute in 1964 and promulgated in final, published form the next year.

**40.** Once *Greenman* was rendered in 1963, Dean Prosser had to scramble to convert § 402A from its prior, narrow coverage

which had been written to accompany the "food" black-letter draft of 1961)[41] remained essentially unchanged.[42]

The contemporaneous scholarship of Dean Prosser and key ALI Advisers also suggests that comment *j* was intended only to address the narrow unavoidable danger issue in foods, drugs, cigarettes, whiskey, and the like. In his only three products liability articles published after § 402A was promulgated in 1965,[43] and in the next edition of his hornbook,[44] Dean Prosser examined the unavoidable danger issue, using the same examples and reasoning as he had used in comments *i, j*, and *k*. The only salient difference of his treatment of these issues in his scholarship[45] (distinguished from the comments) is that he reverted in his scholarship to lumping the inherent danger issues all together, under a single "unavoidable danger" umbrella, as he had originally done in comment *f* of Tentative Draft No. 6.[46] This suggests that Prosser, the Reporter for § 402A, intended the narrow, contextual interpretation of comment *j* discussed above. Although it appears that Dean Prosser never directly addressed the availability of design defect claims under § 402A for failing to adopt a reasonable alternative design, his writings indicate

to *all* products. Apart from his many other duties as Torts Restatement Reporter, dean, and professor, he had to prepare Tentative Draft No. 10 for circulation, first, to the Advisers, then to the Council, and finally to the whole ALI membership in time for the May 1964 annual meeting.

**41.** And which he had fleshed out in the 1962 draft to accommodate other products for intimate bodily use.

**42.** Apart from the addition of a butter example to comment *i*, and corrections of technical errors throughout, the comments in Tentative Drafts 7 and 10 are substantially the same.

There is only sparse discussion of the comment *j* issue in the Restatement debates, but nothing there suggests that Dean Prosser or anyone else contemplated that limiting a seller's responsibility to a duty to warn extended beyond the inherently dangerous food-type products then being considered; certainly there is no intimation that this limited duty might apply to manufacturers of durable goods whose dangers may reasonably be designed away. In discussing a manufacturer's duty to warn, Dean Prosser noted: "It is not correct to say that [the manufacturer] can always avoid liability by giving reasonable notice." ALI Proceedings 68 (1961). While the meaning of this sentence is somewhat unclear in its context, Dean Prosser's general remarks do make clear that the last sentence of then comment $\underline{f}$ (now comment *j*) only addressed the kind̄s of inherent, unavoidable risks dealt with in the food and drug examples covered by then comment $\underline{f}$ (now comments *i, j*, and *k*).

**43.** Prosser, Products Liability in Perspective, 5 Gonz. L. Rev. 157, 164 et seq. (1970); Prosser, The Fall of the Citadel (Strict Liability to the Consumer), 50 Minn. L. Rev. 791, 807 et seq. (1966); Prosser, Strict Liability to the Consumer in California, 18 Hastings L.J. 9 et seq. (1966).

**44.** W. Prosser, Handbook of the Law of Torts § 99, at 660 (4th ed. 1971) (beginning, "The second, and more important, question concerns [whether 402A should apply to] products that in the present state of human skill and knowledge are unavoidably dangerous, and cannot be made safe.").

**45.** In his last (and least formal) article, Dean Prosser explained that sellers of food, drugs, and other useful products containing unavoidable dangers are subject only to duties to warn and keep their products pure: "You cannot impose strict liability upon a man who sells what appears to be a perfectly reputable product and is actually extremely beneficial to the human race; you cannot make him strictly liable because once in a while something goes wrong with it in a way which he cannot prevent." Prosser, Products Liability in Perspective, 5 Gonz. L. Rev. 157, 166 (1970).

**46.** In all three articles and the hornbook, Prosser states that the question whether § 402A should apply to unavoidably dangerous products is one of the two or three most important issues on the proper reach of strict liability, and he organizes this discussion (that the final draft of § 402A had splintered into comments *i, j*, and *k*) under the general heading, "Type of Product" (in the articles) and "Unsafe Products" (in the hornbook).

that he believed that § 402A properly applied to such cases without regard to whether the danger was obvious or a warning had been given.[47]

The scholarship of at least four key ALI Advisers, Professor James, Deans Keeton and Wade, and Justice Traynor,[48] confirms that the duty of safe design is largely independent of the duty to warn. A decade prior to § 402A, Professor James wrote, "the risk that warning will not be heeded, and the danger likely to ensue if it is not, may be so great as to call for some safety device or even for abandonment of the process or the product if its utility is outweighed by the danger. Surely an automobile manufacturer would be negligent in marketing cars without brakes, even if that fact were known to all the world."[49] Dean Keeton's scholarship reveals that products liability scholars at the time were concerned principally with whether strict liability should be applied to manufacturing defects and, much more controversially, to inherently dangerous products such as food, drugs, cosmetics, whiskey, and tobacco.[50] As for more usual kinds of products, Dean Keeton rejected the view that a manufacturer's duty of safe design somehow vanishes if the danger is obvious or the user otherwise (as by a warning) is aware of the danger.[51] Dean Wade was more explicit, explaining that "a warning will not

---

**47.** In the only edition of his hornbook after § 402A was published in 1965, Dean Prosser addressed the meaning of § 402A's key phrase, "defective condition unreasonably dangerous," noting that it applies to design defects as well as manufacturing defects. W. Prosser, Law of Torts § 99, at 659 (4th ed. 1971). For this proposition, Prosser cites a safety device case, Pike v. Frank G. Hough Co., 467 P.2d 229 (Cal. 1970). *Pike* explains why strict liability applies to design defects as well as warnings defects, and it explicitly repudiated the "patent danger rule" ("the obviousness of peril is relevant to the manufacturer's defenses, not to the issue of duty," 467 P.2d at 234) and with it the defendant's argument that the manufacturer had no duty to design away dangers which were known to the user. The court quoted long passages from Harper and James, Law of Torts, and Noel, Manufacturer's Negligence of Design or Directions for Use of a Product, 71 Yale L.J. 816, 838 (1962) (the latter of which concluded, "Under the modern rule, even though the absence of a particular safety precaution is obvious, there ordinarily would be a question for the jury as to whether or not a failure to install the device creates an unreasonable risk."). *Pike* also relies substantially on Garcia v. Halsett, 82 Cal.Rptr. 420 (Ct. App. 1970), which permitted a design defect claim under strict liability in tort for injuries that the defendant should have prevented by equipping the machine with an electrical interlock (a "micro switch") that would have automatically cut off the electricity to the machine. Prosser in this manner endorsed the applicability of § 402A to design dangers which manufacturers reasonably can avoid.

**48.** Professor Fleming James (Harper and James on Torts) of Yale, Dean W. Page Keeton of the University of Texas, and Dean John W. Wade of Vanderbilt University were prominent tort law scholars of the day. Chief Justice Roger Traynor authored the principal judicial authority for § 402A, Greenman v. Yuba Power Prods., Inc., 377 P.2d 897 (Cal. 1963), theoretically grounded in his concurring opinion in Escola v. Coca–Cola Bottling Co., 150 P.2d 436, 439 (Cal. 1944).

**49.** James, Products Liability, 34 Tex. L. Rev. 44, 58 (1955).

**50.** See W.P. Keeton, Products Liability—Liability Without Fault and the Requirement of a Defect, 41 Tex. L. Rev. 855 (1963). See generally Priest, Strict Products Liability: The Original Intent, 10 Cardozo L. Rev. 2301, 2303 (1989). Cf. Wade, Strict Tort Liability of Manufacturers, 19 Sw. L.J. 5, 22 (1965).

**51.** "[T]he proposition that the user's knowledge of a particular hazard involved in the use of a product should necessarily preclude recovery by him if victimized by that hazard is rejected...." W.P. Keeton, Products Liability—Inadequacy of Information, 48 Tex. L. Rev. 398, 401 (1970) (also rejecting an economic argument "that a consumer and others who are injured through the use of a product do not have any right to be secure from harm from dangerous products apart from a right to be informed or apart from safety legislation") (emphasis omitted).

always be sufficient.''[52] Chief Justice Traynor, an ALI Adviser for § 402A as well as the author of *Greenman*, addressed this issue head-on in an article published the same year as § 402A. Observing that the last sentence of comment *j* was directed at inherently dangerous products such as poison and cigarettes, products with dangers that cannot be designed away,[53] he specifically noted that comment *j* in no way insulates manufacturers who provide warnings from liability for the other two types of product defects—manufacturing defects and defects in design. That is, manufacturers cannot use warnings to shift responsibility to consumers for these other, independent types of defects.[54]

It is evident that the comments to § 402A were not provided as a complete products liability "code" but in fact addressed only certain limited aspects of the new doctrine of strict products liability in tort. The comments do not directly address, outside of the narrow context of unavoidably dangerous products, the broader issue of the relationship between the general duties of warnings and safe design. As seen above, however, contemporaneous scholarship of Dean Prosser and his key ALI Advisers quite firmly suggests that comments *i, j*, and *k* were intended to address only the narrow issue of the limited manner in which the new strict liability section applied to unavoidably dangerous products whose inherent risks cannot be designed away. Their scholarship suggests, and the comments to § 402A imply, that the new strict liability doctrine in fact requires manufacturers to physically remove substantial dangers—even if they are warned about, obvious, or generally known—if there is a reasonable way to do so.[55]

**52.** Wade, On the Nature of Strict Tort Liability for Products, 44 Miss. L.J. 825, 842 (1973). Dean Wade provided some examples: "An electrical appliance with uninsulated wires would not be made duly safe by attaching a warning to look out for the danger of electric shock." Id. n.56 "A rotary lawn mower, for example, which had no housing to protect a user from the whirling blade would not be treated as duly safe, despite the obvious character of the danger." Id. at 843. He also notes the similarity of issues in cases where a danger is *warned* about and where it is *obvious*. Id.

**53.** See Traynor, The Ways and Meanings of Defective Products and Strict Liability, 32 Tenn. L. Rev. 363, 367–73 (1965) (examining the cases on food, drugs, tobacco, and similar products). "Some dangers are generic to the goods, so that people regard the goods as fit for ordinary use even with such qualities. The manufacturer would not be liable, under the *Restatement* test, for harm caused by generic dangers." Id. at 370 (referring to comment *i*). See also id. at 367 (§ 402A "would impose no strict liability for what are classified as 'unavoidably unsafe products' ") (citing comment *k*); id. at 372 (warnings "cannot be used, however, to mask a disclaimer of responsibility that would shift the risk to the consumer") (referring to comment *j*).

**54.** See id. at 372:

What is the effect of warning or notice? The *Restatement* provides: "Where warning is given, the seller may reasonably assume that it will be read and heeded; and a product bearing such a warning which is safe for use if the warning is heeded, is not in a defective condition. . . ." [Citing cmt. *j*.] Example: poison. A warning or notice cannot be used, however, to mask a disclaimer of responsibility that would shift the risk to the consumer. Thus, a notice by a manufacturer of soft drinks listing the possible foreign substances that might be contained in a bottle of its beverage, or a notice by an automobile manufacturer listing possible difficulties that might be encountered by the user of the car, would not preclude liability.

**55.** Scholarship on the origins of § 402A concludes that the Reporter, the Advisers, and the ALI were focused at the time on the narrow issue of liability for injuries from products containing inherent unavoidable dangers, *not* on the general duty of manufacturers of ordinary products to design them safely. See G. Schwartz, Considering the Proper Federal Role in American Tort Law, 38 Ariz. L. Rev. 917, 947 and id. n.185 (1996) ("402A is obtuse [in] dealing

### *Policy*

It makes good sense to interpret comment *j* narrowly, as limiting the duties of sellers of inherently dangerous products like drugs, cigarettes, and alcoholic beverages to providing products that are uncontaminated and possess adequate warnings of hidden dangers. Because there is no way (other than by providing warnings) that manufacturers of such products can minimize the inherent dangers of such products without also destroying their utility, there is no good reason in corrective justice or economics to force manufacturers to insure consumers against risks of harm they have chosen to accept by purchasing products with inherent risks of which they are fully aware. But if a product contains substantial risks that *can* reasonably be designed away, then a manufacturer that does not do so should be faulted, in both fairness and economics, for failing to respect the rights of consumers to reasonable product safety. These fundamental precepts, explored elsewhere in greater depth,[56] support the logic and fairness of keeping the manufacturer's duty of safe design largely independent of the duty to warn. To hold that warnings immunize manufacturers from the duty of safe design (or the duty of safe manufacture) would unreasonably and regressively subordinate the interests of consumers to the interests of manufacturers.[57]

A rule that fulfilling *one* of several independent tort law duties fulfills them *all* is quite preposterous. Surely a driver has a duty of reasonable care to give warning, by honking the horn, to all pedestrians endangered by the car's approach, even if they are at fault for being in the roadway. But a driver also has duties to maintain a proper lookout, to operate the car soberly and with reasonable skill, to obey traffic

---

with design issues only indirectly and by implication" and noting the section's "failure to focus on design issues"). See also Priest, Strict Products Liability: The Original Intent, 10 Cardozo L. Rev. 2301 (1989).

**56.** See Owen, The Moral Foundations of Products Liability Law: Toward First Principles, 68 Notre Dame L.Rev. 427 (1993).

**57.** See Latin, "Good" Warnings, Bad Products, and Cognitive Limitations, 41 UCLA L. Rev. 1193, 1294–95 (1994) (thoroughly critiquing interpretation of comment *j* as meaning that warnings trump manufacturer's duty of safe design):

> [T]he comment j presumption is unrealistic from a behavioral perspective, inefficient from an accident-prevention perspective, and inequitable from a normative perspective.... Good product warnings may be useful, indeed necessary, in many accident-prevention settings but their value is inherently limited and they consequently should not be treated as legally acceptable alternatives to safer product designs and marketing strategies.

See also Henderson and Twerski, A Proposed Revision of Section 402A of the Re-

statement (Second) of Torts, 77 Cornell L. Rev. 1512, 1538 (1992) ("Product warnings cannot bear the full burden of ensuring that products will be used safely. If a sensible design alternative can significantly reduce risk, the law will demand that the manufacturer design out the risk rather than merely warn against it."). See generally § 10.2 (Obvious Dangers), below.

The issue was debated by Professors Phillips and Ausness. See Phillips, Products Liability: Beyond Warnings, 26 N. Ky. L. Rev. 595, 602 (1999) ("It seems too late ... to return to an unbridled doctrine of laissez faire or caveat emptor, in the modern-day of complex products, advertising blandishments, and clearly foreseeable human frailty."). Compare Ausness, When Warnings Alone Won't Do: A Reply to Professor Phillips, 26 N. Ky. L. Rev. 627, 646 (1999) (Professor Phillips "rightly criticizes" comment *j*, but the Third Restatement's approach in comment *l* to § 2 goes too far the other way). See also Weissman, A "Comment J" Parry to Howard Latin's "Good" Warnings, Bad Products, and Cognitive Limitations, 70 St. John's L. Rev. 629 (1996).

signals, and not to speed. It would be absurd to interpret an ambiguous traffic rule in a manner that would relieve a driver of all responsibilities to pedestrians so long as the driver, though violating all the other duties, honked the horn. Applying this principle to the products liability situation here at issue, it makes no sense to relieve a manufacturer of all its other duties—notably its duties to design and manufacture its products safely—simply because it places a warning on its products. Such a rule would senselessly allow a manufacturer of household fans to substitute a warning on the base of the fan for the fan's protective cage; it would allow a manufacturer of power mowers to attach a warning on the engine and then remove the protective housing around the blade; and it would permit a manufacturer of industrial machinery a simple but completely unsatisfactory means to avoid its basic duty to equip dangerous industrial products with simple guards and electric interlocks when such safety devices are reasonably demanded in the circumstances to avoid substantial harm.

### The Evolving Products Liability Jurisprudence

Comment *j*, as previously explained, was intended to address only the limited issue of a seller's responsibility under § 402A for harm caused by unavoidable dangers inherent in a narrow class of products. Reading comment *j* more broadly, as according warnings the power of a shield against the duty of safe design applicable to products generally, conflicts not only with its intended scope but also with sound policy. Such an approach also contrasts starkly with products liability law over the past half century. When Prosser researched and initially drafted comment *j* in 1959 and 1960, products liability law was still dominated by many strictures from the early 1900s: liability was rarely imposed for a manufacturer's conscious design choices;[58] the patent danger doctrine still reigned supreme in limiting a manufacturer's design responsibility to only latent dangers;[59] consumer expectations were the only gauge of strict products liability (in warranty and, later, under § 402A);[60] consumer carelessness in any degree, even in the face of an egregiously dangerous product design, served to bar recovery altogether;[61] and the intended use doctrine barred liability for most forms of consumer misuse ("abnormal use"), including the failure to follow a seller's instructions, on the ground that it superseded the manufacturer's responsibility.[62] Yet, soon after § 402A (with its comments, including comment *j*) was published in 1965, the law took several sharp turns the other way. By the 1970s, courts began with a gusto to apply judicial oversight to manufacturer design choices;[63] the patent danger doctrine began a precipitous decline into virtual extinction;[64] the risk-utility standard began to swallow up the consumer expectation test for evaluating the safety of a product's design;[65] the total bar for user carelessness was rapidly giving way to

**58.** See § 8.1, below.

**59.** See § 10.2, below.

**60.** See §§ 5.6, above, and 8.3, below.

**61.** See § 13.2, below.

**62.** See § 13.5, below; Prosser on Torts § 102, at 669 (4th ed. 1971); Prosser, The Fall of the Citadel (Strict Liability to the Consumer), 50 Minn. L. Rev. 791, 824–26 (1966).

**63.** See § 8.1, below.

**64.** See § 10.2, below.

**65.** See §§ 5.6, 5.7, above, and 8.2–8.8, below.

damages apportionment based on comparative fault;[66] and the scope of a manufacturer's responsibility for product safety was widening broadly from intended uses to all foreseeable uses.[67]

In the twenty-first century, the most sensible way to interpret comment *j*'s ambiguous last sentence is according to its original intent—that it applies only to the narrow category of inherently dangerous products with unavoidable dangers like food, drugs, alcoholic beverages, and tobacco. If for some reason a court feels impelled to interpret this sentence more broadly, as applicable to *all* types of products, then the sentence should be interpreted as meaning nothing more than that a manufacturer may fulfill its informational obligations to consumers by providing adequate warnings and instructions.[68] According any greater import to comment *j*, as meaning that a warning cancels the fundamental duty of manufacturers of ordinary products to take reasonable steps to design away serious hazards, would elevate consumer responsibility for accidents to the archaic position it has not occupied for almost half a century,[69] and it would revive a host of discredited doctrines that long ago were properly put to rest.[70]

**66.** See § 13.3, below.

**67.** See § 13.5, below.

**68.** See, e.g., Moulton v. Rival Co., 116 F.3d 22, 28 (1st Cir. 1997) (Me. law) (comment *j* restricted to cases involving only duty to warn); see also Evridge v. American Honda Motor Co., 685 S.W.2d 632, 636 (Tenn. 1985); Uptain v. Huntington Lab, Inc., 723 P.2d 1322, 1331–33 (Colo. 1986) (Quinn, C.J., dissenting); Cf. Delaney v. Deere & Co., 999 P.2d 930, 941–42 (Kan. 2000) (ironically, the *defendant* proposed this interpretation but it was rejected by the court).

**69.** Imposing absolute responsibility on consumers ignores real-world limitations on human cognition:

The Comment *j* presumption embodies the behavioral assumption that "reasonable" users can be expected to receive, correctly interpret, and obey every comprehensible warning accompanying every product they use or encounter. Yet, people are exposed each day to innumerable risks created by appliances that may malfunction or be mishandled; by potentially toxic pollutants, food additives, and other chemical substances; by cosmetics, drugs, and cleansing agents that may be improperly applied and are inherently dangerous for some sensitive individuals; by machine tools, presses, and other industrial or occupational equipment; and by hazardous transportation and recreation devices. Indeed, almost all products present substantial risks if improperly manufactured, designed, or used. People would have to read, understand, remember, and follow innumerable product warnings to protect themselves from all product-related risks they may confront.

Latin, "Good" Warnings, Bad Products, and Cognitive Limitations, 41 UCLA L. Rev. 1193, 1206 (1994) (cognitive theory shows that warnings should only be used to supplement reasonable designs, not to substitute therefore). See also Twerski et al., The Use and Abuse of Warnings in Products Liability: Design Defect Comes of Age, 61 Cornell L. Rev. 495, 506 (1976); Products Liability Restatement § 2 Reporters' Note to cmt. *l*.

**70.** Defense lawyers, who are quite happy to try to revive the old defendant-protective rules, argue that comment *j* should be interpreted to mean that a manufacturer which provides a warning should be relieved of its duty of safe design. See, e.g., Silvergate, The Restatement (Third) of Torts: Products Liability—The Tension Between Product Design and Product Warnings, 75–DEC Fla. B.J. 10, 11 (2001); Morrison, Warning v. Design in Products Litigation: Third Time's Not Always a Charm, 10 Kan. J.L. & Pub. Pol'y 86 (2000); V. Schwartz, See No Evil, Hear No Evil: When Clear and Adequate Warnings Do Not Prevent the Imposition of Product Liability, 68 U. Cin. L. Rev. 47 (1999). Yet even Mr. Schwartz is reluctant to endorse this extreme position. See 68 U. Cin. L. Rev. at 59–60 (recognizing the Third Restatement's "legitimate concern" that people may not in fact read and heed all warnings, and noting the possibility that "courts could 'over-read' Comment *j* . . . to mean that a manufacturer who warns about a risk is not liable"—giving example of power lawnmower, which carries warning to stay away from unguarded blade, as

### Present Status of Comment j

With the exception of a handful of misguided decisions that have misinterpreted comment *j* as negating the general duty of safe design,[71] a great majority of courts, some explicitly rejecting comment *j* on this point,[72] hold that the separate forms of defect give rise to separate obligations that may independently support a products liability claim.[73] Thus, except in certain limited contexts,[74] it is abundantly clear that a manufacturer is subject to liability for a product's *manufacturing* defects, no matter how clear the product's warnings or how perfect its design;[75] for *warning* defects, no matter how perfect the product's manufacture or how impeccable its design;[76] and for *design* defects, no

situation where warning would not protect manufacturer from duty to add guard).

**71.** Interpreting comment *j* to mean that a warning eliminates the manufacturer's duty to provide a safe design, see, e.g., Curcio v. Caterpillar, Inc., 543 S.E.2d 264 (S.C. Ct. App. 2001), rev'd on other grounds, 585 S.E.2d 272 (S.C. 2003); Ferguson v. F.R. Winkler GMBH & Co., 79 F.3d 1221 (D.C. Cir. 1996); Freas v. Prater Constr. Corp., 573 N.E.2d 27 (Ohio 1991); Simpson v. Standard Container Co., 527 A.2d 1337 (Md. Ct. Spec. App. 1987). Cf. Dugan v. Sears, Roebuck & Co., 447 N.E.2d 1055 (Ill. App. Ct. 1983) (jury issue on whether user's ignoring warning was sole proximate cause, based largely upon its foreseeability).

**72.** Until recently, most courts have basically ignored the offending language of comment *j* as saying anything serious about the relationship between warnings and design. The Third Restatement's explicit rejection of this aspect of the Second Restatement's comment *j*, however, has focused courts and lawyers specifically on this point. For examples of recent cases explicitly rejecting the warnings-trump-design interpretation of comment *j*, see, e.g., Delaney v. Deere & Co., 999 P.2d 930, 942 (Kan. 2000) ("just because there is a warning on a piece of equipment does not prevent the equipment from being dangerous"); Uniroyal Goodrich Tire Co. v. Martinez, 977 S.W.2d 328, 335–37 (Tex. 1998); Rogers v. Ingersoll–Rand Co., 144 F.3d 841, 844 (D.C. Cir. 1998). See also Leaf v. Goodyear Tire & Rubber Co., 590 N.W.2d 525, 529 (Iowa 1999) (dictum critical of cmt. *j*).

**73.** Even critics of the Third Restatement's rejection of the warnings-trump-design approach acknowledge that the Third Restatement position is widely embraced by the courts. See, e.g., Ausness, When Warnings Alone Won't Do: A Reply to Professor Phillips, 26 N. Ky. L. Rev. 627, 638 (1999).

**74.** As with pharmaceutical drugs containing unavoidable dangers, where warnings normally are the only way to eliminate the risk. See Restatement (2d) Torts § 402A cmt. *k*. On generic risks and un-

avoidable dangers, see §§ 10.3 and 10.4, below.

**75.** See, e.g., Falada v. Trinity Indus. Inc., 642 N.W.2d 247, 251 (Iowa 2002) ("defective design and defective workmanship are separate concepts"); Chapman v. Maytag Corp., 297 F.3d 682, 689 (7th Cir. 2002) (Ind. law) (" 'adequate warnings will not render a product with a manufacturing defect non-defective,' regardless of whether compliance with the warning would have rendered the product safe"); Glover v. BIC Corp., 987 F.2d 1410, 1416 (9th Cir. 1993) (Or. law) (same).

**76.** See, e.g., Lewis v. Sea Ray Boats, Inc., 65 P.3d 245 (Nev. 2003) (" 'Strict liability may be imposed even though the product is faultlessly made if it was unreasonably dangerous to place the product in the hands of the user without suitable and adequate warning concerning safe and proper use.' "); Hiner v. Deere & Co., 340 F.3d 1190, 1193 (10th Cir. 2003) (Kan. law) (a "product, though perfectly designed and manufactured, may be defective if not accompanied by adequate warnings of its dangerous characteristics"); Hanus v. Texas Utils. Co., 71 S.W.3d 874, 879 (Tex. App. 2002) ("Texas law clearly provides that a lack of adequate warnings or instructions can render an otherwise adequate product unreasonably dangerous."); Stahl v. Novartis Pharms. Corp., 283 F.3d 254 (5th Cir. 2002) (La. law) ("Even if a product is not defectively designed or constructed, a manufacturer may still have a duty to warn consumers about any characteristic of the product that unreasonably may cause damage."); Wilkinson v. Duff, 575 S.E.2d 335 (W. Va. 2002) ("A failure to warn cause of action covers situations when a product may be safe as designed and manufactured, but which becomes defective because of the failure to warn of dangers which may be present when the product is used in a particular manner."); Wabash Metal Prods., Inc. v. AT Plastics Corp., 575 S.E.2d 683 (Ga. Ct. App. 2002) ("A duty to warn can arise even if a product is not defective."); Hennegan v. Cooper/T. Smith Stevedoring

matter the precision of its manufacture or the abundance of its warnings.[77] This latter point is the most significant, because of the lingering, perverse effects of comment *j*'s long tentacles in a number of jurisdictions.[78]

"Decisively" repudiating the "primitive" interpretation of comment *j* that would accord warnings the power to override a manufacturer's

Co., 837 So.2d 96 (La. Ct. App. 2002) ("The lack of an adequate warning renders a product defective and unreasonably dangerous even if there is no manufacturing or design defect in the product."); Wheeler v. HO Sports, 232 F.3d 754 (10th Cir. 2000) (Okla. law) (although no evidence that flotation vest was not properly manufactured or designed, jury could find that manufacturer should have warned that vest would not keep wearer afloat); Wilson v. U.S. Elevator Corp., 972 P.2d 235, 237 (Ariz. Ct. App. 1998) (" 'A product faultlessly made may be deemed defective if it is unreasonably dangerous to place the product in the hands of a user without a suitable warning.' "); Richter v. Limax Int'l, Inc., 45 F.3d 1464 (10th Cir. 1995) (Kan. law) (failure to warn of risk of stress fractures to ankles from repetitive use of exercise trampoline; "even if a product does not have a design defect, failure to warn of a foreseeable danger arising from the product's normal use makes the product defective"); Deines v. Vermeer Mfg. Co., 755 F.Supp. 350, 353 (D. Kan. 1990) ("A product may be perfectly manufactured and meet every requirement for its designed utility and still be rendered unreasonably dangerous through failure to warn of its dangerous characteristics."). See also Emery v. Federated Foods, Inc., 863 P.2d 426 (Mont. 1993) (no warning of risk to young children from ingesting marshmallows); Ayers v. Johnson & Johnson Baby Prods. Co., 818 P.2d 1337 (Wash. 1991) (no warning that baby could be paralyzed from ingesting "Baby Oil").

**77.** See, e.g., Delaney v. Deere & Co., 999 P.2d 930, 942 (Kan. 2000) ("just because there is a warning on a piece of equipment does not prevent the equipment from being dangerous"); White v. ABCO Eng'g Corp., 221 F.3d 293, 305–06 (2d Cir. 2000) (N.J. law) (notwithstanding clearly adequate warnings, conveyor manufacturer was subject to liability for failing to provide side guarding); Lewis v. American Cyanamid Co., 715 A.2d 967, 977 (N.J. 1998); Rogers v. Ingersoll–Rand Co., 144 F.3d 841, 844 (D.C. Cir. 1998); Crow v. Manitex, Inc., 550 N.W.2d 175 (Iowa Ct. App. 1996) (manufacturer of improperly used crane, contrary to adequate warnings and instructions that would have prevented accident if heeded, subject to liability for failing to design crane so as to prevent the accident); Glittenberg v. Doughboy Recreational Indus., 491

N.W.2d 208, 216 (Mich. 1992) ("A warning is not a Band–Aid to cover a gaping wound, and a product is not safe simply because it carries a warning."); Robinson v. G.G.C., Inc. 808 P.2d 522, 525 (Nev. 1991) ("a warning is not an adequate replacement when a safety device will eliminate the need for the warning"); Evridge v. American Honda Motor Co., 685 S.W.2d 632, 636 (Tenn. 1985) (interpreting comment *j* to allow simultaneous warnings and design claims); Uloth v. City Tank Corp., 384 N.E.2d 1188 (Mass. 1978) ("If a slight change in design would prevent serious, perhaps fatal, injury, the designer may not avoid liability by simply warning of the possible injury. We think that in such a case the burden to prevent needless injury is best placed on the designer or manufacturer rather than on the individual user of a product."). For early recognition that a manufacturer has a duty of safe design independent of any warnings, see, e.g., James, Products Liability (pt. 1), 34 Tex. L. Rev. 44, 49, 58–59 (1955).

**78.** See note 72, above. To the extent that comment *j* retains any beneficial vitality in the modern world, it is as a source of consumer protection on an entirely separate issue. Indeed, most courts addressing the last paragraph of comment *j* have applied it in a consumer-*friendly* way—ruling, in cases where adequate warnings are not provided, that comment *j* supports the creation of a presumption in favor of consumers that, had the manufacturer provided an adequate warning, the plaintiff (or someone acting on the plaintiff's behalf) would have read and heeded it. This widely adopted "heeding presumption" is used to satisfy the consumer's burden of proof on cause in fact. See, e.g., Coffman v. Keene Corp., 628 A.2d 710 (N.J. 1993). After *Coffman*, a manufacturer that had warned of a danger asked the New Jersey court to apply comment *j* in *its* favor to bar the plaintiff's design defect claim. The court would not allow this nonsense: "Allowing such a warning to defeat a design-defect claim. . . . would frustrate the imposition of liability when a product's design fails to take into account an injured party's objectively foreseeable misuse of the product." Lewis v. American Cyanamid Co., 715 A.2d 967, 977 (N.J. 1998). On this use of the heeding presumption, see § 11.4, below.

design responsibilities,[79] the *Third Restatement* declares in no uncertain terms that the law does not permit a manufacturer to hide behind a warning in an attempt to insulate itself from its independent duty of safe design:

> In general, when a safer design can reasonably be implemented and risks can reasonably be designed out of a product, adoption of the safer design is required over a warning that leaves a significant residuum of such risks.... Warnings are not ... a substitute for the provision of a reasonably safe design.[80]

The courts have quite colorfully expressed the same idea. For example, the Michigan Supreme Court has observed that "[a] warning is not a Band–Aid to cover a gaping wound, and a product is not safe simply because it carries a warning."[81] And the United States Court of Appeals for the District of Columbia Circuit has concluded, that "[i]t is thus not correct that a manufacturer may ... merely slap a warning onto its dangerous product, and absolve itself of any obligation to do more."[82] More succinctly, warnings do not trump design.

## Overlap of Safety Obligations

### *Proper Role of Warnings in Design Defect Determinations*

While the three forms of defect generate independent safety obligations, such that the satisfaction of one obligation does not ipso facto satisfy the others, fulfilling one duty sometimes helps to satisfy another. This overlap of safety responsibilities is clearest in the area of design and warnings. The safer a manufacturer *designs* its products, the fewer dangers there will be about which to *warn*. As seen above, however, the issue usually is posed the other way: how may a *warning* affect a manufacturer's duty of safe *design*? Although warnings will only rarely satisfy a manufacturer's duty of safe design, as previously discussed, warnings sometimes are the only practical way to reduce a risk, particularly in the case of pharmaceutical drugs and other chemical and inherently toxic products.[83]

For example, a furniture polish that is very harmful if swallowed by young children would clearly be defective if sold without adequate

---

**79.** The Restatement Reporters frequently have castigated this interpretation of comment *j*. For example, after the completion of the Third Restatement, the Reporters commented on their treatment of this aspect of comment *j*: "The Products Restatement rejects this primitive notion decisively." Henderson and Twerski, The Politics of the Products Liability Restatement, 26 Hofstra L. Rev. 667, 689 (1998).

**80.** Products Liability Restatement § 2 cmt. *l*. See Twerski, In Defense of the Products Liability Restatement: Part I, 8 Kan. J.L. & Pub. Pol'y 27, 29 (1998) ("[C]omment *j* took the position that a product whose dangers are warned against, is not defective. We took the position in section 2 comment *l* of the Restatement (Third) of Torts that one cannot warn one's way out

of a defective design case. If there is a reasonable design which would make the product safer, the mere fact that one warned against it does not insulate the seller from liability.... We vehemently disagree with the Second Restatement."); Henderson and Twerski, The Politics of the Products Liability Restatement, 26 Hofstra L. Rev. 667, 689 (1998).

**81.** Glittenberg v. Doughboy Recreational Indus., 491 N.W.2d 208, 216 (Mich. 1992).

**82.** Rogers v. Ingersoll–Rand Co., 144 F.3d 841, 844 (D.C. Cir. 1998).

**83.** This is particularly so in the case of many generic product risks, as discussed in comment *j*. See also § 10.3 below.

warnings of the danger.[84] Assuming there is no way to change the chemical formulation of the polish to reduce the risk without sacrificing its effectiveness, a manufacturer who warns of such an unavoidable hazard might also be seen as having thereby satisfied any design obligations as well. In truth, however, such a manufacturer has no relevant duty of safe design, because there is no duty to do the impossible, to design away an unavoidable risk.[85] So, cases like this are properly viewed as involving purely a duty to warn and not a duty to design away a danger inherent in the product.

Because warnings and instructions may in fact serve to reduce design hazards,[86] at least to some extent, the provision of such information may have *some* bearing on design defectiveness. Just as the obviousness of a hazard reduces the likelihood of resulting harm,[87] so, too, do warnings and instructions.[88] Thus, because warnings reduce the risk of injury from design hazards, the presence of a warning is one factor—sometimes an important one—to be balanced in the calculus of considerations involved in a determination of design defectiveness. Stated otherwise, in balancing the risk factors relevant to design defectiveness, a trier of fact should consider among other factors whether the design hazard was obvious, warned about, or generally known.[89]

### *Compatibility of Separate Defect Claims*

While the three types of defect are conceptually distinct, separate claims for each often are compatible. Thus, in an appropriate case, the plaintiff may claim and attempt to prove that a product was defective according to two, or, albeit infrequently, all three different types of defect.[90] Stated otherwise, the different types of defect claims are not intrinsically exclusive.[91] Indeed, design and warning defect claims with respect to the same danger are commonly asserted and allowed in cases in which a manufacturer allegedly failed to warn of a significant hidden

---

**84.** See, e.g., Spruill v. Boyle–Midway, Inc., 308 F.2d 79 (4th Cir. 1962) (Va. law).

**85.** See §§ 10.3 and 10.4, below.

**86.** See § 9.1, below.

**87.** See § 10.2, below.

**88.** See § 9.1, below.

**89.** See §§ 8.8 and 10.3, below. The Third Restatement makes this point in describing the "broad range of factors" that may be relevant to the defectiveness of a product's design, including "the magnitude and probability of the foreseeable risks of harm, the instructions and warnings accompanying the product, and the nature and strength of consumer expectations regarding the product ..." Products Liability Restatement § 2 cmt. *f*. See, e.g., Wright v. Brooke Group Ltd., 652 N.W.2d 159 (Iowa 2002) (adopting and applying Products Liability Restatement § 2 cmts. *g* and *j* on the role of consumer expectations in the Re-

statement's risk-utility analysis to a case involving cigarettes).

**90.** See, e.g., Anderson v. Owens–Corning Fiberglas Corp., 810 P.2d 549, 553 n.7 (Cal. 1991) ("In most instances, as here, the plaintiff alleges both design and warning defects."). However, the facts of a particular case often preclude the assertion of particular defect claims. See, e.g., Dierks v. Mitsubishi Motors Corp., 256 Cal.Rptr. 230, 231 (Ct. App. 1989) (where plaintiff tried auto roll-over case as a design case, claiming that the roof collapsed too easily, trial court properly refused to instruct jury on manufacturing defect claim: "A defect in manufacture is, of course, quite different from a defect in design.").

**91.** See, e.g., Caterpillar Tractor Co. v. Beck, 593 P.2d 871, 878 n.15 (Alaska 1979) ("Manufacturing defects and design errors are not mutually exclusive."). See also Colt Indus. Operation Corp. v. Frank W. Murphy Mfr., Inc., 822 P.2d 925, 930 (Alaska 1991).

danger that reasonably could have been designed away.[92] For example, an SUV that rolls over too easily on particular steering maneuvers may be defective in design, because its center of gravity is too high and its track width too narrow, and it may also be defective because of the absence of a warning of this tendency.[93] And while manufacturing defect claims usually stand on their own, they may be combined with design and even warnings claims on appropriate facts. So, if an occasional flashcube explodes when defectively manufactured, the seller may have a duty to warn of this tendency.[94] Sometimes the evidence is quite unclear as to whether a product was defective in manufacture or design,[95] and a plaintiff with credible evidence should be allowed to try to make out a case on both.[96] For example, a product's wires or cables may be mistakenly crossed during manufacture because the engineers did not design a sufficient separation to minimize this production risk. And if the engineers should have foreseen this hazard, perhaps they should have warned about the resulting danger. Malfunction cases present another example of how defect theories fairly may overlap: while the circumstances of a product malfunction ordinarily may suggest a manufacturing defect, sometimes a design defect may just as likely be the culprit.[97]

## § 6.3   PROOF OF DEFECT—EXPERT TESTIMONY

### In General

Proof of defectiveness and causation often requires scientific and technical experts to explain the relevant science and engineering of product safety and accidents to a lay jury and the court.[1] Understanding

**92.** See Anderson v. Owens–Corning Fiberglas Corp., 810 P.2d 549, 553 n.7 (Cal. 1991) ("In most instances, as here, the plaintiff alleges both design and warning defects."); Evridge v. American Honda Motor Co., 685 S.W.2d 632, 636 (Tenn. 1985) (interpreting comment *j* to allow simultaneous warnings and design claims).

**93.** See, e.g., Bericochea–Cartagena v. Suzuki Motor Co., 7 F.Supp.2d 109 (D.P.R. 1998) (Suzuki Sidekick); Purvis v. American Motors Corp., 538 So.2d 1015 (La. Ct. App. 1988) (Jeep CJ–5).

**94.** See Maybank v. S.S. Kresge, 266 S.E.2d 409 (N.C. Ct. App. 1980), modified on other grounds and affirmed, 273 S.E.2d 681 (N.C. 1981).

**95.** See, e.g., Stazenski v. Tennant Co., 617 So.2d 344 (Fla. Dist. Ct. App. 1993) (worker cut on sharp edge of industrial sweeper).

**96.** See, e.g., Richcreek v. General Motors Corp., 908 S.W.2d 772, 777 (Mo. Ct. App. 1995), in which a car's seat hinge pin, which may have been too short and may have needed welding rather than pounding into place, may have been pounded into place improperly: "In the case at bar, there appears a very fine line between design and manufacturing defects under strict liability. To limit a plaintiff to one theory where no inconsistency exists with others is too restrictive."

**97.** See, e.g., Morden v. Continental AG, 611 N.W.2d 659, 664 (Wis. 2000) (upholding verdict for plaintiff finding that tire manufacturer was negligent in design *or* manufacture of tires); Smith v. Ford Motor Co., 215 F.3d 713, 716 (7th Cir. 2000) (Ind. law) (reversing dismissal of plaintiff's claim, although plaintiff's expert, who concluded that steering failed due to defect in a van's steering gearbox, was unable to determine whether defect was due to design or manufacture). On the malfunction doctrine, see § 7.4, below.

**§ 6.3**

**1.** See, e.g., Anderson v. Raymond Corp., 340 F.3d 520 (8th Cir. 2003) granting summary judgment for defendant where plaintiff's expert on product's defectiveness was not qualified and his opinion was not reliable); Rivera Pomales v. Bridgestone Firestone, Inc., 217 F.R.D. 290 (D.P.R. 2003) (dismissing plaintiff's claims after striking plaintiff's expert testimony); Bruno v. Toyotomi U.S.A., Inc., 203 F.R.D. 77 (N.D.N.Y. 2001) (granting summary judgment for defendant where plaintiff failed to produce qualified and reliable expert testimony on defectiveness and causation); Mozes v. Medtronic, Inc., 14 F. Supp. 2d 1124 (D. Minn. 1998) (same); (Alevromagiros v. Hechinger, 993 F.2d 417 (4th Cir.

the various aspects of the design, manufacture, and labeling of products normally involves a host of complex, technical considerations requiring specialized expertise. Mechanical, chemical, and materials engineers, chemists, physicists, pharmacologists, epidemiologists, and other technical specialists are often necessary to help the fact finder comprehend how a product was made, how it was supposed to operate, whether and how it may have malfunctioned or otherwise caused an accident, and how it could have been made differently to avoid accidents of that type. Thus, involving as it does the inner workings of science and technology, products liability litigation often resolves into a "battle of the experts."[2]

### The Significance of Expert Testimony

Expert testimony has special significance in products liability litigation for several reasons. Most fundamentally, it is the means by which juries and judges in most products liability cases are provided with the decisional tools to decide whether a particular product was defective and whether a product defect caused the plaintiff's injury. Some products, and some product failures, are quite simple to understand, such as the explosion of a thermos bottle[3] or the presence of a cockroach in a sandwich.[4] In such cases, there is little "beyond the ken" of the judge or jury on which expert counsel is required.[5] But the mechanisms of most product failures are more complex. In such cases, courts and juries generally are dependent on the information and opinions provided by scientific and technical specialists on the technical issues that typically lie at the heart of a products liability case. In this respect, judges and juries, who by hypothesis are incapable of understanding without assistance the technical aspects of such a case, are at the mercy of the experts. In addition, the law of evidence gives experts especially wide latitude to offer opinions not available to ordinary witnesses.[6] For these reasons, expert testimony can be particularly powerful, and it has a particular power to mislead.[7] While the rules governing the admissibility of expert testimony on science and technology are treated extensively

1993) (upholding directed verdict for defendant where plaintiff's expert did not perform any tests on the product, but only introduced a single example of a similar product in attempt to establish an industry standard); Sears, Roebuck & Co. v. Haven Hills Farm, Inc., 395 So.2d 991, 995 (Ala. 1981) ("Ordinarily, expert testimony is required" in cases based on strict products liability in tort.).

**2.** See, e.g., Ferebee v. Chevron Chem. Co., 736 F.2d 1529, 1535 (D.C. Cir. 1984) (conflicting expert conclusions result in a "classic battle of the experts, a battle in which the jury must decide the victor"); Jenkins v. General Motors Corp., 446 F.2d 377, 380 (5th Cir. 1971) ("It all boils down to a battle of experts."). This simple fact of products liability litigation has long been true. See generally D. Peck, Decision at Law 40–64 (1961) (detailing expert testimony on nature of break, hickory grain of spoke, and tests and inspections of broken automobile wheel involved in MacPherson v. Buick Motor Co., 111 N.E. 1050 (N.Y. 1916)). An earlier version of this section was published as Owen, A Decade of Daubert, 80 Denv. U. L. Rev. 345 (2002).

**3.** See, e.g., Virgil v. "Kash N' Karry" Serv. Corp., 484 A.2d 652, 656 (Md. Ct. Spec. App. 1984) ("The general rule is well established that expert testimony is only required when the subject of the inference is so particularly related to some science or profession that it is beyond the ken of the average layman.").

**4.** See Bullara v. Checker's Drive–In Rest., Inc., 736 So.2d 936 (La. Ct. App. 1999) (chili dog).

**5.** Faryniarz v. Nike, Inc., 2002 WL 530997 (S.D.N.Y. 2002) (expert testimony unnecessary for jury to find running shoes defectively designed because of excessively long laces that could get caught on pull-tab).

**6.** See Federal Rules of Evidence 701, 702, 703, 705 and similar state evidentiary rules; Daubert v. Merrell Dow Pharm., Inc., 509 U.S. 579 (1993).

**7.** See, e.g., Rypkema v. Time Mfg. Co., 263 F.Supp.2d 687 (S.D.N.Y. 2003) (plaintiff's expert offered only "a flat opinion, lacking scientific or engineering basis" that

elsewhere,[8] the topic is so centrally important to products liability litigation that it deserves special treatment in this context.

Expert testimony is often necessary to establish defectiveness in manufacture, design, and warnings and instructions. As mentioned earlier, juries normally need the guidance of expert testimony to understand the technical aspects of both defectiveness and causation. Without such testimony, juries would be left to assumption, conjecture, and speculation on these central elements of every case. Thus, a products liability

was "bereft of any engineering methodology," as contrasted to defendant's "equally qualified expert who had performed tests on the product at issue"); Garcia v. BRK Brands, Inc., 266 F.Supp.2d 566 (S.D. Tex. 2003) (plaintiff's experts failed to perform "even the most basic scientific testing of their timely alarm theory").

"Judge Weinstein has explained: 'Expert evidence can be both powerful and misleading because of the difficulty in evaluating it.'" (citation omitted) *Daubert*, 509 U.S. at 595; Mendez, Expert Testimony and the Opinion Rule: Conforming the Evidence Code to the Federal Rules, 37 U.S.F. L. Rev. 411, 411 (2003) ("opening the door to expert testimony [has led to a concern] that testimony by experts with impressive credentials will overwhelm the jurors"); A. Schwartz, A "Dogma of Empiricism" Revisited: Daubert v. Merrell Dow Pharmaceuticals, Inc. and the Need to Resurrect the Philosophical Insight of Frye v. United States, 10 Harv. J.L. & Tech. 149, 196–98 (1997); Black et al., Science and the Law in the Wake of *Daubert*: A New Search for Scientific Knowledge, 72 Tex. L. Rev. 715, 789 (1994) ("[M]ost commentators believe ostensibly scientific testimony may sway a jury even when as science it is palpably wrong. Science can be greatly distorted by the pressures of litigation, but once it is admitted into evidence, it has an imprimatur of legitimacy and validity, and cross-examination often will not expose its flaws.").

**8.** See D. Faigman, D. Kaye, M. Saks, and J. Sanders, Science in the Law—Standards, Statistics and Research Issues (2002) (in-depth coverage of admissibility, nature of expertise, ethical issues, scientific method, statistical proof, survey research, epidemiology, and toxicology); Scientific Evidence Reference Manual (Federal Judicial Center 2000); Weinstein's Federal Evidence ch. 702 (2d ed. 1997); McCormick on Evidence §§ 10–18 (5th ed. 1999) (J. Strong ed.); Frumer and Friedman, Products Liability § 18.06; 2 Madden & Owen on Products Liability §§ 27:8–:9; R. Park, Evidence Law ch. 10 (1998). There are hundreds of articles on the topic. See, e.g., Sharko and

Lyons, Once Upon a *Daubert* Hearing: The Admissibility of Novel Theories, 3 Expert Evid. Rep. 369 (BNA Aug. 4, 2003); Owen, A Decade of *Daubert*, 80 Denv. L. Rev. 345 (2002); Pena, The Effective Evaluation of Expert Reliability, 20 Rev. Litig. 743 (2001); Stilwell, *Kumho Tire*: The Battle of the Experts Continues, 19 Rev. Litig. 193 (2000); Saks, The Aftermath of *Daubert*: An Evolving Jurisprudence of Expert Evidence, 40 Jurimetrics 229 (2000); Graham, The Expert Witness Predicament: Determining "Reliable" Under the Gatekeeping Test of *Daubert*, *Kumho*, and Proposed Amended Rule 702 of the Federal Rules of Evidence, 54 Minn. L. Rev. 317 (2000); Walker and Monahan, Scientific Authority: The Breast Implant Litigation and Beyond, 86 Va. L. Rev. 801 (2000) (examining causation study by National Science Panel); Brew, Where the Rubber Hits the Road: Steering the Trial Court Through a Post-*Kumho* Tire Evaluation of Expert Testimony, 27 Wm. Mitchell L. Rev. 467 (2000); Patterson, Conflicts of Interest in Scientific Expert Testimony, 40 Wm. & Mary L. Rev. 1314 (1999); Capra, The *Daubert* Puzzle, 32 Ga. L. Rev. 699 (1998); A. Schwartz, A "Dogma of Empiricism" Revisited: Daubert v. Merrell Dow Pharmaceuticals, Inc. and the Need to Resurrect the Philosophical Insight of Frye v. United States, 10 Harv. J.L. & Tech. 149 (1997); Damaska, Truth In Adjudication, 49 Hastings L.J. 289 (1997); Gross, Substance & Form in Scientific Evidence: What *Daubert* Didn't Do, in Reforming the Civil Justice System (L. Kramer ed., 1996); Fenner, The *Daubert* Handbook: The Case, Its Essential Dilemma, and Its Progeny, 29 Creighton L. Rev. 939 (1996); M. Green, Expert Witnesses and Sufficiency of Evidence in Toxic Substances Litigation: The Legacy of Agent Orange and Bendectin Litigation, 86 Nw. U. L. Rev. 643, 661 (1992); Annot., 177 A.L.R. Fed. 77 (2002) (Supreme Court cases on expert testimony); Note, 76 Ind. L.J. 465 (2001) (difficulties in attempting to apply *Daubert* criteria to warning label testimony); Symposium, 57 Wash. & Lee L. Rev. 661 (2000).

case usually will fail without proof of defect by expert testimony.[9] While the Federal Rules of Evidence have abolished the "ultimate issue" rule, barring witnesses from testifying on the ultimate issue in a case, some states still apply the rule, in one form or another, to products liability litigation.[10]

Manufacturing defects are sometimes so self-evident that expert proof will not be required, but expert testimony ordinarily will be necessary to establish that an accident product deviated from the manufacturer's design specifications.[11] And while reliance on the malfunction doctrine can sometimes assist a plaintiff when the precise cause of a product failure cannot be shown,[12] expert proof is often necessary even under this theory of recovery to rule out other possible causes of the accident.[13]

Simple warnings issues sometimes are entirely comprehensible by a jury and thus may not be appropriate for expert testimony.[14] But the science of how to communicate danger and safety information most effectively is evolving in sophistication such that expert testimony on warnings and instructions is often helpful, and sometimes mandatory, as

**9.** See, e.g., Brown v. Crown Equip. Corp., ___ S.W.3d ___, 2004 WL 350658 (Tenn. Ct. App. 2004) (summary judgment for defendant proper where neither of plaintiff's two experts on forklift design were qualified to testify); Anderson v. Raymond Corp., 340 F.3d 520 (8th Cir. 2003) (Ark. law) (summary judgment for defendant proper where plaintiff failed to produce reliable expert witness); Rivera Pomales v. Bridgestone Firestone, Inc., 217 F.R.D. 290, 295 (D.P.R. 2003) (directed verdict for defendant after plaintiff's only expert witness was excluded); Cantrell v. Weber–Stephen Prods. Co., 38 Fed. Appx. 921 (4th Cir. 2002) (Md. law) (summary judgment for defendant proper where plaintiff failed to provide expert testimony on why gas grill exploded; without such testimony "[a] jury could only infer the presence of a defect in the grill by engaging in 'surmise, conjecture, or speculation' "); Hochen v. Bobst Group, Inc., 290 F.3d 446 (1st Cir. 2002) (Mass. law) (affirming summary judgment against plaintiff who failed to designate expert under Fed. R. Civ. P. 26(a)(2) in complex case involving allegedly defective design and manufacture of printing press); Lessard v. Caterpillar, Inc., 737 N.Y.S.2d 191 (App. Div. 2002) ("The court properly granted defendant's motion for a directed verdict, given the inability of plaintiff to establish a prima facie case of design defect in the absence of expert testimony"); Moisenko v. Volkswagenwerk Ak., 100 F.Supp.2d 489 (W.D. Mich. 2000) ("Without expert evidence comparing a striker plate with a flat-ending to one with a rolling-ball

ending, Mr. Moisenko cannot meet the risk-utility test, and thus cannot establish a design defect.... As to the manufacturing defect claim, it is well-settled that such a claim cannot be proven without expert testimony." Defendant's motion for summary judgment granted); Brooks v. Colonial Chevrolet–Buick, Inc., 579 So.2d 1328 (Ala. 1991) ("because of the complex and technical nature of the product and in order to present evidence from which a lay jury may reasonably infer that a defective condition of the product was the cause of the product's failure and the cause of the resultant injury to the plaintiff, expert testimony is usually essential and, therefore, usually required"). See also Weisgram v. Marley Co., 528 U.S. 440 (2000), discussed in § 6.3, below.

**10.** See Vaughn v. Daniels Co., 777 N.E.2d 1110 (Ind. Ct. App. 2002) (holding inadmissible portions of expert's affidavit which opined that coal sump was unreasonably dangerous and that sump manufacturer failed to use reasonable care).

**11.** Stahl v. Novartis Pharm. Corp., 283 F.3d 254 (5th Cir. 2002) (absence of expert testimony on how particular pills of prescription toenail fungus medication Lamisil deviated from manufacturer's specifications was fatal to plaintiff's manufacturing defect claim). See § 7.3, below.

**12.** See § 7.4, below.

**13.** See id.

**14.** See, e.g., Robertson v. Norton Co., 148 F.3d 905 (8th Cir. 1998) (noting issue).

in many cases involving the labeling of dangerous machinery,[15] pharmaceutical drugs,[16] and in other specialized labeling situations.[17]

Most jurisdictions define design defectiveness in terms of risk-utility analysis, an analytical approach that requires an evaluation of the feasibility, costs, and benefits of altering a design to avoid an injury.[18] Such claims almost always require expert proof,[19] sometimes on the mechanisms of how the accident occurred and almost always on how the accident feasibly could have been designed away.[20] However, if design defectiveness is defined purely in consumer expectation terms,[21] whether expert testimony is appropriate may depend upon the type of product whose design is under scrutiny. A jury might well need expert guidance on the safety expectations of users of industrial, professional, or other products designed for use by specialists in a field. But consumer goods, particularly simple ones, are another matter: it is difficult to see how the opinion of a technical or other expert on ordinary consumer expectations about the safety of a simple consumer product could assist a jury, which would seem to preclude expert testimony on defectiveness in such cases.[22] Even design cases may be simple, however, in which case expert testimony is unnecessary.[23]

Regardless of the type of defect, expert testimony often is necessary to prove causation, the link that connects the product defect to the

**15.** A sophisticated system is described in Product Safety Sign and Label System (FMC Corp. 1993).

**16.** See, e.g., Handbook of Nonprescription Drugs (A.Ph.A., R. Berardi 13th ed., 2002) (U.S.); Patient Information in Medicine (R. Mann ed., 1991) (Europe).
*But cf.* Stahl v. Novartis Pharm. Corp., 283 F.3d 254 (5th Cir. 2002), holding that a treating physician's testimony that certain drug warnings were adequate is not "expert testimony" and thus need not meet *Daubert* standards.

**17.** Such as how tires should be labeled. See, e.g., Goodyear Tire & Rubber Co. v. Rios, 143 S.W.3d 107, 118 (Tex. App. 2004) ("A jury could not have determined, without the benefit of expert testimony, which, among many, warnings and instructions should be printed on a sidewall."). See generally ch. 9, below. On applying *Daubert* to warning-label testimony, see Note, 76 Ind. L.J. 465 (2001).

**18.** See ch. 8, below.

**19.** See, e.g., Brown v. Crown Equip. Corp., ___ S.W.3d ___, 2004 WL 350658 (Tenn. Ct. App. 2004) (summary judgment for defendant proper where neither of plaintiff's two experts on forklift design were qualified to testify); Anderson v. Raymond Corp., 340 F.3d 520 (8th Cir. 2003) (Ark. law) (summary judgment for defendant proper where plaintiff failed to produce reliable expert witness explaining safer alternative design); Lessard v. Caterpillar, Inc., 737 N.Y.S.2d 191 (App. Div. 2002) ("The court properly granted defendant's motion for a directed verdict, given

the inability of plaintiff to establish a prima facie case of design defect in the absence of expert testimony"); Moisenko v. Volkswagenwerk Ak., 100 F.Supp.2d 489 (W.D. Mich. 2000) (defendant's motion for summary judgment granted: "Without expert evidence comparing a striker plate with a flat-ending to one with a rolling-ball ending, Mr. Moisenko cannot meet the risk-utility test, and thus cannot establish a design defect.").

**20.** See ch. 8, below.

**21.** Id.

**22.** Because an expert normally could not assist the jury in determining consumer expectations. See e.g., Soule v. General Motors Corp., 882 P.2d 298 (Cal. 1994) ("[W]here the minimum safety of a product is within the common knowledge of lay jurors, expert witnesses may not be used to demonstrate what an ordinary consumer would or should expect. Use of expert testimony for that purpose would invade the jury's function ..."); Campbell v. General Motors Corp., 649 P.2d 224, (Cal. 1982) (quoting G. Schwartz, Foreword: Understanding Products Liability, 67 Cal. L. Rev. 435, 480 (1979), " '[O]ne can hardly imagine what credentials a witness must possess before he can be certified as an expert on the issue of *ordinary* consumer expectations.' ").

**23.** Faryniarz v. Nike, Inc., 2002 WL 530997 (S.D.N.Y. 2002) (expert testimony unnecessary for jury to find running shoes defectively designed because of excessively long laces that could get caught on pull-tab).

plaintiff's harm.[24] Causation is most typically in issue in toxic substance cases, where expert testimony on causation (and defectiveness) almost invariably is necessary.[25] Even in cases involving durable goods, where proofs of defectiveness and causation are often linked together closely, expert evidence on how the defect caused the harm is usually necessary to the plaintiff's case.[26]

To give but a few examples, judges and juries surely will need expert tutelage on defectiveness if the issue in dispute is whether the speed control mechanism for a paver should have been in the form of a lever rather than a rotary dial;[27] whether a sport utility vehicle should have been equipped with a barrier between the front seats and cargo area, together with a warning, to make it safe for occupants in the rear;[28] whether the strength of a corn chip rendered the corn chip unreasonably dangerous;[29] whether and how the steering gearbox in a vehicle may have been improperly assembled or designed;[30] whether the operator compartment on a forklift should have been equipped with a door[31] or wire mesh;[32] whether cigarettes could have been made more safely;[33] whether a hay baler should have had a guard;[34] or whether a lift truck was defectively designed because it had an open cockpit with no operator restraints.[35] Similarly, on causation, expert testimony will almost certainly be necessary if the parties disagree on whether a causal link exists between a plaintiff's ingestion of Viagra and his heart attack;[36] an allegedly defective product and a house fire that starts nearby;[37] the absence of a kill switch on an outboard motor and injuries to the plaintiff's hand;[38] an anti-depressant drug taken by a teenager and his

---

**24.** See ch. 11, below.

**25.** See, e.g., Rutigliano v. Valley Bus. Forms, 929 F.Supp. 779, 783 (D.N.J. 1996) (claim of "formaldehyde sensitization" from exposure to chemical in carbonless carbon paper; summary judgment granted). See generally Note, 10 Rev. Litig. 117, 119–23 (1990) (examining expert witness problems in toxic substance cases). Causation in toxic substance litigation is treated generally at § 11.2, below.

**26.** See, e.g., Cantrell v. Weber–Stephen Prods. Co., 38 Fed.Appx. 921 (4th Cir. 2002) (Md. law) (summary judgment for defendant proper where plaintiff failed to provide expert testimony on why gas grill exploded; without such testimony "[a] jury could only infer the presence of a defect in the grill by engaging in 'surmise, conjecture, or speculation'"); Booth v. Black & Decker, Inc., 166 F.Supp.2d 215 (E.D. Pa. 2001) (fire allegedly caused by toaster oven), discussed below.

**27.** See Alfred v. Caterpillar, Inc., 262 F.3d 1083 (10th Cir. 2001).

**28.** See Bowersfield v. Suzuki Motor Corp., 151 F.Supp.2d 625 (E.D. Pa. 2001).

**29.** See Grady v. Frito–Lay, Inc., 839 A.2d 1038 (Pa. 2003).

**30.** See Smith v. Ford Motor Co., 215 F.3d 713 (7th Cir. 2000).

**31.** See, e.g., Dhillon v. Crown Controls Corp., 269 F.3d 865 (7th Cir. 2001); Berry v. Crown Equip. Corp., 108 F.Supp.2d 743 (E.D. Mich. 2000).

**32.** See Bourelle v. Crown Equip. Corp., 220 F.3d 532 (7th Cir. 2000).

**33.** See LaBelle v. Philip Morris, Inc., 243 F.Supp.2d 508 (D.S.C. 2001).

**34.** See Masters v. Hesston Corp., 2001 WL 567736 (N.D. Ill. 2001), aff'd, 291 F.3d 985 (7th Cir. 2002).

**35.** See Anderson v. Raymond Corp., 340 F.3d 520 (8th Cir. 2003) (Ark. law).

**36.** See Brumley v. Pfizer, Inc., 200 F.R.D. 596 (S.D. Tex. 2001).

**37.** See, e.g., Booth v. Black & Decker, Inc., 166 F.Supp.2d 215 (E.D. Pa. 2001) (fire allegedly caused by toaster oven); Travelers Prop. & Cas. Corp. v. General Elec. Co., 150 F. Supp. 2d 360 (D. Conn. 2001) (clothes dryers); Weisgram v. Marley Co., 528 U.S. 440 (2000) (electric baseboard heater); Pride v. BIC Corp., 218 F.3d 566 (6th Cir. 2000) (cigarette lighter); Pappas v. Sony Elec., Inc., 136 F.Supp.2d 413 (W.D. Pa. 2000) (television).

**38.** See Brooks v. Outboard Marine Corp., 234 F.3d 89, 92 (2d Cir. 2000).

suicide;[39] a spinal rod implanted in the plaintiff's back to eliminate a painful condition and his quite similar post-operative pain;[40] or exposure to various chemical substances and many illnesses and disease.[41] In short, experts are crucial to both the prosecution and defense of a products liability case.

### Qualifications and Sources of Expert Witnesses

To serve as an expert witness, an individual must first be *qualified*—"by knowledge, skill, experience, training, or education"[42]—to offer opinions on the particular specialized matter before the court.[43] The bulk of experienced and otherwise qualified specialists in most fields of product design, manufacturing, and labeling are employed by private industry, often by the manufacturing enterprises who are defendants in products liability litigation. Thus, because such persons are already in its employ, a manufacturer usually has little difficulty in finding appropriate engineering and other experts to help defend a products liability case. Indeed, such experts may include the very persons who designed the accident product, advised on appropriate warnings, and designed and supervised the assembly process by which it was produced. Plaintiffs' lawyers, on the other hand, generally are limited to two principal resource pools for expert witness talent: universities and private consulting expert firms.[44]

**39.** See Miller v. Pfizer Inc., 196 F.Supp.2d 1095 (D. Kan. 2002) (Zoloft; excluding the testimony of plaintiff's expert, a psychologist and psychopharmacologist, on specific and general causation, noting that "[t]he flaws in Healy's methodology ... are glaring, overwhelming and unexplained"), aff'd, 356 F.3d 1326 (10th Cir. 2004).

**40.** See Alexander v. Smith & Nephew, P.L.C., 98 F.Supp.2d 1310 (N.D. Okla. 2000).

**41.** See, e.g., Mattis v. Carlon Elec. Prod., 114 F.Supp.2d 888 (D.S.D. 2000) (whether vapors from PVC cement caused reactive airways dysfunction syndrome); Heller v. Shaw Indus., 167 F.3d 146 (3d Cir. 1999) (whether carpet caused respiratory illnesses); Westberry v. Gislaved Gummi AB, 178 F.3d 257 (4th Cir. 1999) (whether inhaling talcum powder lubricant on gaskets aggravated sinus condition).

**42.** Fed. R. Evid. 702. See, e.g., Clark v. Safety–Kleen Corp., 845 A.2d 587 (N.J. 2004) (on the basis of education, training, or experience, chemist was qualified to testify on medical causation of plaintiff's injury).

**43.** See, e.g., Bryant v. Hoffmann–La Roche, Inc., 585 S.E.2d 723 (Ga. Ct. App. 2003) (doctors not qualified to testify on adequacy of manufacturer's testing and evaluation of heart drug with respect to whether FDA should have approved the drug); Green v. Smith & Nephew AHP, Inc., 629 N.W.2d 727 (Wis. 2001) (chemist

not qualified to testify on whether latex gloves caused allergic reaction); Goodwin v. MTD Prods., Inc., 232 F.3d 600 (7th Cir. 2000) (in case involving lawn mower that discharged wing nut into plaintiff's eye, engineer not qualified to give expert opinion on nature, scope, or cause of eye injury); Polaino v. Bayer Corp., 122 F.Supp.2d 63 (D. Mass. 2000) (chemist not qualified to testify on defectiveness of x-ray chemical mixer); Alexander v. Smith & Nephew, P.L.C., 98 F.Supp.2d 1310, 1315 (N.D. Okla. 2000) (proposed expert was board-certified doctor of family medicine: "The simple possession of a medical degree is insufficient to qualify a physician to testify as to the advantages of a spinal fixation device, the medical causation of spine-related ailments, or the mechanical functioning of an orthopedic implantation device."); Robertson v. Norton Co., 148 F.3d 905 (8th Cir. 1998) (in case involving explosion of ceramic grinding wheel, ceramics engineer not qualified to testify on adequacy of warnings).

**44.** Sources for the latter include expert books—i.e., H. Philo, D. Robb and R. Goodman, Lawyers Desk Reference: Technical Sources for Conducting a Personal Injury Action (9th ed. 2001); the ATLA Products Liability Exchange at www.atlanet.org; and Technical Advisory Service for Attorneys ("TASA"), an expert referral service at www.tasanet.com. Among the many engineering and other expert consulting firms are Triodyne Inc. at www.triodyne.com and Engineering Design & Testing Corp. at www.edtengineers.com.

### *The Rise of the "Professional" Expert Witness; The Problem of "Junk Science"*

As products liability litigation began to mushroom in the late 1960s and the 1970s, so too did the plaintiff's need for experts to battle a manufacturer's engineers and other experts over issues of product defectiveness and causation—in expert reports, depositions, and ultimately at trial. Straining the pool of then-existing technical talent, a surge in demand for expert testimony in the 1970s and 1980s spawned a whole new industry of "professional" expert engineers and other consulting specialists who mostly, but not exclusively,[45] supported the plaintiff's bar. Many such experts were of course entirely competent to testify on the issues they agreed to evaluate. But others advertised a willingness to testify, for a fee, on the defectiveness (and even the appropriateness of punitive damages) of just about anything,[46] "from toys to airplanes."[47]

The very idea of a *professional* expert witness is problematic. "Expertise" in any field requires substantial time to accumulate and to stay abreast of current developments—by reading, experimenting, writing, perhaps teaching, and otherwise pursuing knowledge in the specialized field of study. The problem is that much of a professional expert's time is spent in courtrooms and preparing for trial rather than in pursuing expertise. Moreover, because most professional experts are economically dependent on being retained by lawyers to testify that particular products were (or were not) defective and caused (or did not cause) particular injuries, they have a natural bias to arrive at conclusions that favor their employers. Without a steady moral compass, grounded in a personal reservoir of knowledge, judgment, and professional conviction, a professional witness will be tempted to tell the employing lawyer what the expert thinks the lawyer *wants* to hear, rather than what he or she *needs* to hear. Whether working for the plaintiff or defense, this temptation for professional witnesses to mold their findings and conclusions to make the case for their employer is persistent and strong; and it is insidious, in part because they may hide weaknesses in their testimony from their own employer.

The kind of twisted testimony[48] that too easily results from a hired expert's natural bias provides one explanation of why professional wit-

---

**45.** While manufacturers substantially rely on their own in-house technical experts, they frequently use outside consultants for accident reconstruction and the development of other proofs for trial. One such firm of engineering and scientific consultants drawn upon by defendants, at least in automotive products liability litigation, is Exponent at www.exponent.com.

**46.** See, e.g., Huber, Safety and the Second Best: The Hazards of Public Risk Management in the Courts, 85 Colum. L. Rev. 277 (1985) ("a Ph.D. can be found to swear to almost any 'expert' proposition, no matter how false or foolish"). See generally Note, 10 Rev. Litig. 117, 119–23 (1990) (examining seamy side of expert witness business).

**47.** One "system safety and human factors enginee[r]" listed in an early technical expert directory was advertised as having testified "in over 100 cases with products ranging from toys to airplanes." Products Liability and Transportation Directory 196 (1983). On problems with professional expert witnesses, see Richmond, The "Professional Expert" Witness: Doctor Lichtor, I Presume?, 17 J. Prod. & Toxics Liab. 197, 223 (1995).

**48.** For one expert's primer on how to mislead a jury, see Sanchez v. Black Bros. Co., 423 N.E.2d 1309 (Ill. App. Ct. 1981) (excerpting speech given by defendant's witness to engineering group on how to manipulate juries and obfuscate answers on cross examination).

nesses sometimes contradict themselves in different cases, a strategic Achilles heel which an opposing attorney may discover by diligent research. If the opposing attorney does not reveal such conflicting testimony until the trial, both the expert and the employing attorney will find themselves in the dreadful predicament of trying to explain the contradiction on the spot. On occasion, professional witnesses provide knowingly false, perjurious testimony which, if discovered, will likely devastate the party's entire case.[49]

The explosion of expert testimony in products liability litigation during the 1970s and 1980s, fueled by an expanding plaintiffs' bar fed by contingent fees, quite naturally led to a rather rapid increase of products liability lawsuits based on novel, untested, abstract, and occasionally quite fantastic theories of science and technology propounded by "experts" who sometimes were dubiously qualified to testify on issues on which they claimed expertise. As products liability litigation during this period marched along, courts[50] and commentators,[51] always skeptical of this form of witness,[52] increasingly decried a perceived growth in abuses of expert testimony—of "junk science" run amok.[53]

**49.** See, e.g., Harre v. A.H. Robins Co., 750 F.2d 1501 (11th Cir. 1985) (judgment for defendant reversed and remanded since verdict based in part on perjured testimony by defense expert). See also Jenkins v. General Motors Corp., 446 F.2d 377 (5th Cir. 1971) (holding that trial court properly excluded one of plaintiff's experts who was under indictment for perjury). See generally Richmond, The "Professional Expert" Witness: Doctor Lichtor, I Presume?, 17 J. Prod. & Toxics Liab. 197 (1995).

**50.** See, e.g., Lamon v. McDonnell Douglas Corp., 576 P.2d 426, 435 (Wash. Ct. App. 1978) (Anderson, J., dissenting), aff'd, 588 P.2d 1346 (Wash. 1979). More recently, see Rivera Pomales v. Bridgestone Firestone, Inc., 217 F.R.D. 290 (D.P.R. 2003) ("the use of professional expert witnesses has become rampant.... [I]nstead of utilizing professionals that work in a specific field to comment and give learned opinions on certain subjects, attorneys turn to 'guns for hire' whose main job or means of living is generated from giving expert testimony [which can result] in supposed experts not utilizing scientific methods to render an opinion but rather by twisting scientific methods to produce a result that will support the case of those footing the bill.").

**51.** The "junk science" concept was promoted and popularized by Peter W. Huber who worked for the Manhattan Institute, a conservative think-tank. See, e.g., P. Huber, Galileo's Revenge: Junk Science in the Courtroom (1991); P. Huber, Liability: The Legal Revolution and Its Consequences (1988); Huber, Safety and the Second Best: The Hazards of Public Risk Management in

the Courts, 85 Colum. L. Rev. 277, 333 (1985). For a powerful rebuttal, see Chesebro, Galileo's Retort: Peter Huber's Junk Scholarship, 42 Am. U. L. Rev. 1637 (1993).

**52.** See, e.g., Ferguson v. Hubbell, 97 N.Y. 507, 514 (1884) ("The expert witnesses' views cannot fail generally to be warped by a desire to promote the cause in which they are enlisted."); Friedman, Expert Testimony, Its Abuse and Reformation, 19 Yale L.J. 247, 247 (1910) (noting "a constant complaining and mistrust on the part of judges, juries and lawyers of the expert witness").

**53.** See P. Huber, Galileo's Revenge: Junk Science in the Courtroom 3 (1991):

Junk science cuts across chemistry and pharmacology, medicine and engineering.... It is a catalog of every conceivable kind of error: data dredging, wishful thinking, truculent dogmatism, and, now and again, outright fraud.

On the legal side [is] a speculative theory that expects lawyers, judges, and juries to search for causes at the far fringes of science and beyond. The legal establishment has adjusted rules of evidence accordingly, so that almost any self-styled scientist, no matter how strange or iconoclastic his views, will be welcome to testify in court. The same scientific questions are litigated again and again, in one courtroom after the next, so that error is almost inevitable.

Junk science is impelled through our courts by a mix of opportunity and incentive. "Let-it-all-in" legal theory creates the opportunity. The incentive is money: the prospect that the Midas-like touch of

### Early Limitations on Expert Testimony—*Frye*

At early common law,[54] the only real limitation on expert testimony was that the person proffered as an expert be *qualified* as an expert in the field. The courts generally allowed such experts to provide relevant testimony about technical matters as a matter of course: once a person was qualified as an expert, the judge simply admitted into evidence his or her relevant opinion testimony.[55] This liberal approach to expert testimony reflected the thought that a reliable test of the quality of expertise is the market from which an expert makes a living.[56] While the marketplace test generally may have worked satisfactorily to determine whether a carriage maker or pharmacist acted with reasonable care in making a carriage or mixing a medicine, this test was unhelpful when applied to expert opinions about *new* science or technology where an existing market for such expertise did not yet exist.

This was the situation confronting the court in *Frye v. United States*[57] in which the defendant in a murder case offered the results of an early polygraph test to show his innocence. In passing on the merits of a new form of science or technology, ruled the court, the test is whether it is "sufficiently established to have gained general acceptance in the particular field in which it belongs."[58] Shifting the fulcrum of decision from the expert to the expertise,[59] the *Frye* "general acceptance" test tended to exclude testimony on cutting-edge science and technology since new ideas become accepted wisdom only over time. During the next half century, *Frye*'s general acceptance standard, although increasingly criticized,[60] evolved into the prevailing test for admissibility of expert testimony.[61]

As modern products liability and other technical litigation expanded in the late 1960s and early 1970s, coincident with the debate over the

---

a credulous jury will now and again transform scientific dust into gold. See generally Black, A Unified Theory of Scientific Evidence, 56 Fordham L. Rev. 595, 597–98 nn.1–3 (1988).

**54.** On early expert testimony, see Chapin, Experts and Expert Testimony, 22 Alb. L.J. 365 (1880); Learned Hand, Historical and Practical Considerations Regarding Expert Testimony, 15 Harv. L. Rev. 40 (1901). See also Landsman, Of Witches, Madmen, and Products Liability: An Historical Survey of the Use of Expert Testimony, 13 Behav. Sci. & L. 131 (1995); Faigman, Porter and Saks, Check Your Crystal Ball at the Courthouse Door, Please: Exploring the Present, and Worrying About the Future of Scientific Evidence, 15 Cardozo L. Rev. 1799, 1803–09 (1994); D. Faigman, D. Kaye, M. Saks, and J. Sanders, Science in the Law: Standards, Statistics, and Research Issues (2002).

**55.** See D. Faigman, D. Kaye, M. Saks, and J. Sanders, Science in the Law: Standards, Statistics, and Research Issues 3–5 (2002).

**56.** "The assurance of expertise was implied by the expert's success in an occupa-

tion or profession that embraced that knowledge.... In effect, the marketplace determined whether valid knowledge existed by endowing it with commercial value." Id. at 4.

**57.** 293 F. 1013 (D.C. Cir. 1923).

**58.** Id. at 1014.

**59.** See Faigman, Porter and Saks, Check Your Crystal Ball at the Courthouse Door, Please: Exploring the Present, and Worrying About the Future of Scientific Evidence, 15 Cardozo L. Rev. 1799, 1805–09 (1994).

**60.** Criticisms often centered on its conservatism and its vagueness. See, e.g., D. Faigman, D. Kaye, M. Saks, and J. Sanders, Science in the Law: Standards, Statistics, and Research Issues 7–10 (2002) (examining criticisms of the *Frye* test). See also Note, 78 Chi.-Kent L. Rev. 861, 886–95 (2003) (criticizing *Frye* and urging Illinois to adopt *Daubert* or Federal Rule of Evidence 702).

**61.** See Giannelli, The Admissibility of Novel Scientific Evidence: Frye v. United States, a Half–Century Later, 80 Colum. L.

Federal Rules of Evidence then under consideration, the *Frye* test suddenly became quite "trendy."[62] In 1975, the Federal Rules of Evidence were adopted, including Rule 702, which provided for the admission of scientific and technical evidence by a qualified expert if such testimony will "assist the trier of fact"—if it is helpful to the jury,[63] and Rule 703, which allows an expert to rely upon facts and data "reasonably relied upon by experts" in the field.[64] Neither Rule 702 nor the Advisory Committee's comment on it made any reference to the *Frye* test, but most jurisdictions interpreted this rule to incorporate *Frye*'s general acceptance standard.[65]

During the 1980s and early 1990s, the logic and fairness of *Frye*'s general acceptance test came under increasing scrutiny as courts increasingly debated whether and to what extent this test made sense and whether it was truly consistent with Rule 702.[66] During this period, the courts struggled to find a balance between the need to open courtrooms to new science, on the one hand, with the problems of allowing experts to propound bad science, on the other. Increasingly, courts began to strike this balance by partially shifting the focus away from whether the science was "generally accepted," the *Frye* approach, to evaluating the methodology by which the expert reached his or her conclusion.[67]

Rev. 1197, 1204 (1980); Comment, 29 Hous. L. Rev. 1029, 1034 (1992).

**62.** Faigman, Porter and Saks, Check Your Crystal Ball at the Courthouse Door, Please: Exploring the Present, and Worrying About the Future of Scientific Evidence, 15 Cardozo L. Rev. 1799, 1808 (1994). But not all courts and commentators approved of the general acceptance test of admissibility. See McCormick on Evidence § 203, at 491 (2d ed. 1972) ("General scientific acceptance is a proper condition for taking judicial notice of scientific facts, but not a criterion for the admissibility of scientific evidence.").

**63.** Fed. R. Evid. 702 at the time provided: "If scientific, technical, or other specialized knowledge will assist the trier of fact to understand the evidence or to determine a fact in issue, a witness qualified as an expert by knowledge, skill, experience, training, or education, may testify thereto in the form of an opinion or otherwise." As discussed below, Rule 702 was amended in 2000 to reflect the holding in *Daubert*.

**64.** Fed. R. Evid. 703 provides: "The facts or data in the particular case upon which an expert bases an opinion or inference may be those perceived by or made known to him at or before the hearing. If a type reasonably relied upon by experts in the particular field in forming opinions or inferences upon the subject, the facts or data need not be admissible evidence."

**65.** See Faigman, Porter and Saks, Check Your Crystal Ball at the Courthouse Door, Please: Exploring the Present, and Worrying About the Future of Scientific Evidence, 15 Cardozo L. Rev. 1799, 1803–09 (1994).

**66.** See Comment, Liars, Damn Liars, and Expert Witnesses: Unhelpful Approaches to Unreliable Scientific Testimony in the Third and Fifth Circuits, 29 Hous. L. Rev. 1029 (1992).

**67.** See, e.g., Brock v. Merrell Dow Pharm., Inc., 874 F.2d 307, 310 (5th Cir. 1989), modified, 884 F.2d 166 (5th Cir. 1989) (difficult questions such as whether Bendectin caused birth defects compel courts to "critically evaluate the reasoning process by which the experts connect data to their conclusions ... in order to consistently and rationally resolve the disputes before them"); Christophersen v. Allied–Signal Corp., 939 F.2d 1106, 1110 (5th Cir. 1990) (en banc) (for an expert's scientific conclusions to be admissible, they must, inter alia, be based on "a well-founded methodology"), cert. denied, 503 U.S. 912, 912 (1992) (White, J., dissenting); United States v. Downing, 753 F.2d 1224, 1237 (3d Cir. 1985). See generally Comment, 29 Hous. L. Rev. 1029 (1992).

## *Daubert* and Its Progeny

### *Daubert*

In *Daubert v. Merrell Dow Pharmaceuticals*,[68] after several years of avoiding the issue,[69] the Supreme Court in 1993 finally decided to examine the admissibility of expert testimony on novel scientific theories and the relationship of the *Frye* test to Rule 702. *Daubert* involved the drug Bendectin, an anti-nausea medicine that, from 1956 until 1983, was widely prescribed to pregnant women for morning sickness.[70] From the first Bendectin case filed in 1979, which claimed that the drug had caused the plaintiff's missing and malformed fingers, nearly 2000 similar cases eventually were filed claiming damages for birth defects from the drug. In *Daubert,* filed late in the life cycle of the litigation, the plaintiffs claimed that their birth defects were caused by Bendectin administered to their mothers during pregnancy. The defendant moved for summary judgment, arguing that there was no causal link between Bendectin and birth defects. In affidavits from its expert scientists, the defendant showed that none of the thirty-eight epidemiological studies of Bendectin published at that time had found a causal connection between birth defects and the drug.[71] In opposition, plaintiffs offered affidavits from eight witnesses who concluded—on the basis of chemical structure analysis, *in vitro* (test tube) studies of animal cells, *in vivo* (live) animal studies, and a "reanalysis" of the previous epidemiological studies—that Bendectin can in fact cause birth defects. Concluding that the plaintiffs' proffered expert evidence did not meet *Frye*'s "general acceptance" standard of admissibility, the district court granted the defendant's summary judgment motion, and the Ninth Circuit affirmed.[72]

In the Supreme Court, the petitioning plaintiffs argued that the *Frye* "general acceptance" standard had been superseded by the Federal Rules of Evidence. Vacating and remanding, the Supreme Court agreed that the Rules do not allow a court to use the degree of acceptance of a subject of scientific testimony as the sole determinant of admissibility.[73] Because Rule 702 allows qualified experts to testify about "scientific . . .

---

**68.** 509 U.S. 579 (1993).

**69.** See, e.g., Justice White's dissents to the denial of certiorari in Mustafa v. United States, 479 U.S. 953, 953–54 (1986), and Christophersen v. Allied Signal Corp., 503 U.S. 912, 912 (1992). Prior to *Daubert*, the *Frye* test, which had been used almost exclusively in criminal cases, was increasingly subject to criticism. See Gross, Substance & Form in Scientific Evidence: What *Daubert* Didn't Do, in Reforming the Civil Justice System 234, 242–46 (L. Kramer, ed. 1996).

**70.** See M. Green, Expert Witnesses and Sufficiency of Evidence in Toxic Substances Litigation: The Legacy of Agent Orange and Bendectin Litigation, 86 Nw. U. L. Rev. 643, 661 (1992) (prescribed, during the 1960s and 1970s, to upwards of 25% of all pregnant women in U.S.). On the Bendectin litigation, see generally J. Sanders, Bendectin on Trial: A Study of Mass Tort Litigation (1998); M. Green, Bendectin and Birth Defects: The Challenges of Mass Toxic Substances Litigation (1996); Sanders, From Science to Evidence: The Testimony on

Causation in the Bendectin Cases, 46 Stan. L. Rev. 1 (1993); Sanders, The Bendectin Litigation: A Case Study in the Life Cycle of Mass Torts, 43 Hastings L.J. 301 (1992); Gross, Substance & Form in Scientific Evidence at 234–44 (summarizing the Bendectin litigation).

**71.** Four types of scientific studies commonly are used to determine the toxicity of a substance—(1) *chemical structure* analyses of the substance comparing it to known toxins; (2) *in vitro* tests on how the substance affects human or animal cells in the lab; (3) *in vivo* studies on how the substance affects live animals in the lab; and (4) *epidemiological* studies that examine its effects on human beings. Scientists normally consider epidemiological studies on large populations of humans the best test of the substance's toxicity. See Gross, Substance & Form in Scientific Evidence, at 238–39.

**72.** 951 F.2d 1128 (9th Cir. 1991), aff'g 727 F.Supp. 570 (S.D. Cal. 1989).

**73.** *Daubert*, 509 U.S. at 587–89.

knowledge," the Court reasoned that a trial judge must determine that proposed expert testimony is both "scientific" and "knowledge"—that the subject of the testimony is "ground[ed] in the methods and procedures of science," that it be "derived by the scientific method." An expert's proposed testimony must be "supported by appropriate validation—i.e., 'good grounds'. . . ." In short, expert testimony must be *reliable*.[74] In addition to requiring that expert testimony be reliable, the Court further reasoned that Rule 702 requires that such testimony be *relevant,* since the rule provides that expert scientific or technical testimony "assist the trier of fact to understand the evidence or to determine a fact in issue." This is the "helpfulness" requirement of Rule 702, requiring that expert testimony be sufficiently related to disputed facts to help the jury resolve facts or issues in dispute, a requirement that may be simply described as "fit."[75] Thus, when a party proffers expert scientific testimony, the trial court must make a preliminary determination of both the (1) *reliability* (validity), and (2) *relevance* (fit) of the expert's reasoning or methodology underlying the testimony proposed.[76]

Among the factors a court may usefully employ in assessing the validity of an expert's proffered testimony on scientific evidence, the Court noted five:[77]

(1) *Testability*: whether the theory or technique is testable and has been tested—its ability to withstand objective, verifiable challenge and scientific trial;[78]

(2) *Peer review*: whether it has been subjected to peer review and publication;

(3) *Error rate*: whether it has an acceptable known or potential rate of error;

(4) *Control standards*: whether its operation has been subjected to appropriate standards of control; and

(5) *General acceptance*: whether it is widely accepted in the relevant scientific community.

These are *Daubert*'s now-familiar reliability factors. In determining the admissibility of expert testimony under 702, the Court emphasized that the inquiry into pertinent reliability considerations should be flexible, and that the focus of inquiry "must be solely on principles and methodol-

---

**74.** Id. at 589–90.

**75.** Id. at 591–92.

**76.** Id. at 592–593. Thus, "a trial judge must evaluate the proffered testimony to assure that it is at least minimally reliable; concerns about expert testimony cannot simply be referred to the jury as a question of weight." Capra, The *Daubert* Puzzle, 32 Ga. L. Rev. 699, 701–02 (1998).

**77.** See *Daubert*, 509 U.S. at 593–94. Although the Court lumps factors (3) and (4) together, which has led most observers to a four-factor count, the separation of these two different considerations clarifies analysis. The following five-factor list is

adapted from Capra, The *Daubert* Puzzle, 32 Ga. L. Rev. 699, 702 (1998), which is the basis for the formulation in Federal Rule of Evidence 702, Advisory Committee Note to 2000 Amendment. Headings are added here.

**78.** The Advisory Committee version of this factor is more prolix: "whether the expert's theory or technique can be or has been tested—that is, whether the expert's theory can be challenged in some objective sense, or whether it is instead simply a subjective, conclusory approach that cannot reasonably be assessed for reliability."

ogy, not on the conclusions that they generate."[79] Because the lower courts had based their decisions in this case almost exclusively on *Frye*'s general acceptance standard, rather than on the broader reliability and fit requirements of Federal Rule of Evidence 702, the Supreme Court remanded the judgment to the Court of Appeals.[80]

### Supreme Court Progeny

Since *Daubert*, the Supreme Court has revisited the expert testimony issue a number of times. In *General Electric Co. v. Joiner*,[81] a district court applied *Daubert* to exclude expert testimony that purported to link the plaintiff's exposure to PCBs to his lung cancer, and the court of appeals reversed. Reinstating the district court's ruling, the Supreme Court emphasized that federal trial courts have wide discretion to exclude expert testimony, holding that such determinations are only subject to a permissive "abuse of discretion" standard of review. The Court further noted that *Daubert*'s direction that courts focus on an expert's *methodology* in no way precluded a trial judge from scrutinizing the quality of an expert's *conclusions*.[82]

Next came *Kumho Tire Co. v. Carmichael*,[83] a tire blowout case involving a worn tire containing at least two punctures that previously had been inadequately repaired. In a suit against the tire manufacturer, the plaintiffs claimed, on the basis of deposition testimony of an expert in tire failure analysis, that the blowout had been caused by a defect in the tire rather than abuse. Although the expert's testimony might have been viewed as "technical" rather than "scientific," the trial court applied the gatekeeping principles of *Daubert*, closely scrutinizing the reliability of the expert's hypotheses, methodology, and conclusions. Concluding that they failed each of the *Daubert* factors, and that their reliability had not been established on any other ground, the district court excluded the expert's testimony and granted the defendant's motion for summary judgement. The circuit court reversed, ruling that *Daubert* applied only to experts relying on "scientific" principles rather than on the kind of skill—or experience—based observation of the type relied upon by the plaintiff's expert. Reversing the circuit court, the Supreme Court held that Rule 702's broad reference to expert testimony on "scientific, technical, or other specialized knowledge" means that the *Daubert* gatekeeping principles apply to *all* expert testimony.[84] Further, the Court reaffirmed the flexibility of the reliability inquiry and noted

---

**79.** *Daubert*, 509 U.S. at 593–95.

**80.** On remand, applying the *Daubert* analysis, the Ninth Circuit ruled again that the district court had properly excluded the plaintiffs' expert testimony, concluding that the testimony of one of the plaintiffs' experts was not reliable and that the testimony of the others was not relevant because they would only testify that Bendectin is "capable of causing" birth defects, not that the drug *in fact* (more likely than not) caused the plaintiffs' birth defects. Daubert v. Merrell Dow Pharm., Inc., 43 F.3d 1311 (9th Cir. 1995).

**81.** 522 U.S. 136 (1997).

**82.** The Court remarked:

[C]onclusions and methodology are not entirely distinct from one another. Trained experts commonly extrapolate from existing data. But nothing in either *Daubert* or the Federal Rules of Evidence requires a district court to admit opinion evidence which is connected to existing data only by the *ipse dixit* of the expert. A court may conclude that there is simply too great an analytical gap between the data and the opinion preferred. Id. at 146.

**83.** 526 U.S. 137 (1999).

**84.** 526 U.S. at 147–49.

that the trial court has wide latitude, subject to review only for abuse of discretion, to determine what reliability factors are appropriate to the particular expert testimony under examination.[85]

The final Supreme Court decision to date on expert testimony is *Weisgram v. Marley Co.*,[86] a wrongful death action against the manufacturer of a heater arising out of a house fire. On testimony by three experts that the heater was defective and that the defect caused the fire, the plaintiffs obtained a judgment on a jury verdict, over the defendant's objection that the testimony was unreliable and therefore inadmissible under Rule 702 and *Daubert*. The circuit court reversed, agreeing with the defendant that the plaintiffs' expert testimony offered mere speculation as to the heater's defectiveness, making it scientifically unsound. Rather than remanding for a retrial, and reasoning that the plaintiffs had had a fair opportunity to prove their claim and so did not deserve a second chance, the circuit court directed judgment for the defendant manufacturer. The Supreme Court affirmed. Rejecting an argument that a plaintiff might hold certain expert testimony in reserve to shore up the claim if the proffered expert testimony were to be found insufficient, the Court noted that *Daubert* put parties relying on expert evidence on notice of "the exacting standards of reliability" demanded of such evidence. "It is implausible to suggest, post-*Daubert*, that parties will initially present less than their best expert evidence in the expectation of a second chance should their first try fail."[87] Reminding parties (usually plaintiffs) that they may well not get a second chance, *Weisgram* underscores *Daubert*'s basic message: parties bear responsibility for presenting expert testimony that is rigorously grounded in good science and technology and relevant to the particular issues in the case.

### *Amendment to Federal Rule of Evidence 702*

In 2000,[88] the Supreme Court approved certain amendments to the Rules of Evidence on opinion evidence and expert testimony to conform them to the principles of *Daubert* and its progeny.[89] In addition to making certain minor changes to Rules 701 and 703, the amendments added an important proviso to Rule 702 that permits expert testimony only if such testimony is grounded on "sufficient facts and data" and is the result of "reliable principles and methods" which are themselves reliably applied to the facts of the case.[90] The Advisory Committee's helpful Note to the 2000 Amendment observes that the amendment requires only that the data, principles, and methods used by an expert are reliable and reliably applied, and that the quality of expert testimony

---

**85.** Id. at 149–53.

**86.** 528 U.S. 440 (2000).

**87.** Id. at 455–56.

**88.** The amendments were effective December 1, 2000, a quarter century after the Rules were first adopted in 1975.

**89.** See Fed. R. Evid. 702 Advisory Committee's Note (2000 amendment).

**90.** With the amended language italicized, Federal Rule of Evidence 702 now provides in full:

If scientific, technical, or other specialized knowledge will assist the trier of fact to understand the evidence or to determine a fact in issue, a witness qualified as an expert by knowledge, skill, experience, training, or education, may testify thereto in the form of an opinion or otherwise *if (1) the testimony is based on sufficient facts and data, (2) the testimony is the product of reliable principles and methods, and (3) the witness has applied the principles and methods reliably to the facts of the case.*

is still largely to be tested by cross examination and the other safeguards of the adversary system. Observing that "[a] review of the caselaw after *Daubert* shows that the rejection of expert testimony is the exception rather than the rule," the Committee Note adds that the amendment "is not intended to provide an excuse for an automatic challenge to the testimony of every expert."

As for *Daubert*'s reliability factors, the Advisory Committee's Note reiterates *Daubert*'s five-factor list set forth above and further enumerates several additional factors courts have found useful in varying contexts:

> (1) Whether experts are "proposing to testify about matters growing naturally and directly out of research they have conducted independent of the litigation, or whether they have developed their opinions expressly for purposes of testifying."

> (2) Whether the expert has unjustifiably extrapolated from an accepted premise to an unfounded conclusion.

> (3) Whether the expert has adequately accounted for obvious alternative explanations.

> (4) Whether the expert "is being as careful as he would be in his regular professional work outside his paid litigation consulting."

> (5) Whether the field of expertise claimed by the expert is known to reach reliable results for the type of opinion the expert would give.[91]

While recognizing the importance of these and the original *Daubert* factors, the Committee observed that the Amendments make no attempt to "codify" the factors, which the Supreme Court has emphasized are not exclusive. Instead, the new standards added to Rule 702 are "broad enough to require consideration of any or all of the specific *Daubert* factors where appropriate." In sum, the amendment (including the Committee Note) to Federal Rule of Evidence 702 does not provide a conclusive roadmap for each specific aspect of expert testimony, but it does provide helpful guidance on the fundamental *Daubert* reliability principles.[92]

### *Daubert in the Lower Federal Courts*

*Daubert* has had its intended effect of forcing courts to examine expert testimony more closely. Since *Daubert*, the federal district courts, exercising their newly appointed "gatekeeper" function, have plainly heightened their scrutiny of expert testimony, often holding rigorous pre-trial "*Daubert* hearings"—that are often outcome-determinative—to determine the admissibility of proffered expert testimony.[93] But height-

---

**91.**  Citations omitted.

**92.**  Pointing to the Supreme Court's admonition that *Daubert*'s reliability factors are not exclusive, the Advisory Committee Note observes that the amendments do not attempt to "codify" the factors but instead set forth standards that are "broad enough

to require consideration of any or all of the specific *Daubert* factors where appropriate."

**93.**  See, e.g., Brasher v. Sandoz Pharm. Corp., 160 F.Supp.2d 1291, 1295 n.12 (N.D. Ala. 2001); Rudlin, The Judge as Gatekeeper: What Hath *Daubert-Joiner-Kumho*

ened judicial scrutiny of expert testimony does not mean that a court will necessarily exclude a plaintiff's expert, even if his testimony is unusual: the circuit courts sometimes affirm plaintiff verdicts in novel contexts in which the traditional scientific indicia of defectiveness or causation is marginal at best,[94] and they will reverse a district court for excluding a plaintiff's expert testimony with excessive zeal.[95] But *Daubert* decisions quite frequently go the other way, by excluding a plaintiff's expert testimony as unreliable or irrelevant. Thus, the lower federal courts have disallowed expert testimony on *Daubert* grounds because the expert proposed to testify on novel causal theory, not generally accepted or subjected to peer review, that was developed only for the litigation;[96] relied too heavily on the temporal proximity of harm to its alleged cause;[97] failed sufficiently to inspect or test the accident product or a proposed alternative design;[98] failed faithfully to reconstruct

Wrought?, 29 Prod. Saf. & Liab. Rep. 329 (BNA Apr. 2, 2001):

> [T]he *Daubert* hearing and ruling have effectively become virtually as case outcome determinative as a class certification hearing and ruling: once decided, a case either shrivels up and goes away, or becomes more dangerous to try. *Daubert* hearings are often every bit as case dispositive, practically speaking, as a summary judgment hearing. Thus, practitioners whose cases rely in any material way on expert testimony must [be] prepared for a full-blown *"trial within a trial"* that the *Daubert* hearing often becomes.

**94.** See, e.g., Bonner v. ISP Techs., Inc., 259 F.3d 924 (8th Cir. 2001) (affirming award for assembly line worker, exposed to defendant's organic solvent, who suffered psychological injuries, cognitive impairment, and Parkinsonian symptoms).

**95.** See, e.g., Smith v. B.M.W. N. Am., Inc., 308 F.3d 913 (8th Cir. 2002) (rejecting testimony from forensic pathologist for being outside pathologist's field is abuse of discretion where other information within his field supported his opinion that the allegedly defective airbag caused the death); Lauzon v. Senco Prods., Inc., 270 F.3d 681 (8th Cir. 2001) (only three published articles supported expert's theory that bottomfire pneumatic nailers are defective, but limited peer review not fatal because such nailers are new product); Smith v. Ford Motor Co., 215 F.3d 713 (7th Cir. 2000) (rejecting expert testimony on single ground of lack of peer review is abuse of discretion; no single factor is conclusive in determining reliability of expert's methodology); Kennedy v. Collagen Corp., 161 F.3d 1226 (9th Cir. 1998) (trial court failed properly to consider reasoning and methodology of plaintiff's expert).

**96.** See, e.g., Grant v. Bristol–Myers Squibb, 97 F.Supp.2d 986 (D. Ariz. 2000) (concluding that the conclusions of plain-

tiffs' experts—that silicone breast implants cause various systemic diseases—was developed for the litigation, had not gained acceptance in the relevant scientific community, and that their scientific methods were not practiced by a recognized minority in the field); Nelson v. American Home Prods. Corp., 92 F.Supp.2d 954 (W.D. Mo. 2000) (none of plaintiff's experts had conducted independent research, outside context of litigation, on whether defendant's heart medication caused damage to optic nerve and vision); Daubert v. Merrell Dow Pharm., Inc., 43 F.3d 1311 (9th Cir. 1995) (on remand) (ruling that testimony of plaintiffs' experts, on link between Bendectin and birth defects, was not reliable or relevant).

**97.** See, e.g., Wynacht v. Beckman Instruments, Inc., 113 F.Supp.2d 1205 (E.D. Tenn. 2000) (expert opinion on causation based solely on temporal relationship was unreliable, given complex nature of facts and expert's failure to identify biochemical, medical, or toxicological basis for opinion); Polaino v. Bayer Corp., 122 F.Supp.2d 63 (D. Mass. 2000) (expert's hypothesis, resting on temporal proximity rather than scientific principles, is classic illustration of fallacy of *post hoc ergo propter hoc*); Heller v. Shaw Indus., Inc., 167 F.3d 146 (3d Cir. 1999) (causation testimony unreliable when symptoms did not appear for two weeks after carpet installed and remained after it was removed). But the immediacy of acute symptoms to exposure may buttress the reliability of an expert's causation hypothesis. See, e.g., Bonner v. ISP Techs., Inc., 259 F.3d 924 (8th Cir. 2001) (strong temporal connection is sometimes powerful evidence of causation); Westberry v. Gislaved Gummi AB, 178 F.3d 257 (4th Cir. 1999) (same; temporal relationship between exposure to talcum powder, used as lubricant on rubber gaskets, and plaintiff's sinus infection).

**98.** See, e.g., Zaremba v. General Motors Corp., 360 F.3d 355 (2d Cir. 2004)

the circumstances of the accident;[99] failed to provide a theory of causation supported by sufficient confirmatory studies;[100] failed to conduct a differential diagnosis to rule out alternative potential causes,[101] or applied such an approach improperly;[102] failed to show the relevance ("fit")

(expert failed to test 2–rail alternative to accident car's 1–rail T-top design); Masters v. Hesston Corp., 291 F.3d 985 (7th Cir. 2002) (plaintiff's engineering expert failed to test hay balers lacking the allegedly defective feed roll design or balers equipped with the expert's proposed guard); Dhillon v. Crown Controls Corp., 269 F.3d 865, 870 (7th Cir. 2001) (no testing of forklift with rear door added; "hands-on testing is not an absolute prerequisite to the admission of expert testimony, but the theory here easily lends itself to testing and substantiation by this method, such that conclusions based only on personal opinion and experience do not suffice"); LaBelle v. Philip Morris, Inc., 243 F.Supp.2d 508 (D.S.C. 2001) (no testing of supposedly safer cigarette design); Shanks v. Home Depot, Inc., 2001 WL 1837829 (W.D. Mich. 2001) (examination, but no testing, of ladder for load-bearing capacity); Booth v. Black & Decker, Inc., 166 F.Supp.2d 215 (E.D. Pa. 2001); Brooks v. Outboard Marine Corp., 234 F.3d 89, 92 (2d Cir. 2000) (plaintiff's expert failed to test his theory that lanyard-activated kill switch would have disengaged motor boat engine under circumstances of accident to user's hand: "The failure to test a theory of causation can justify a trial court's exclusion of the expert's testimony."); Pride v. BIC Corp., 218 F.3d 566 (6th Cir. 2000) (defendant's expert subjected cigarette lighter that allegedly malfunctioned to replicable laboratory tests, but plaintiff's experts did not); Polaino v. Bayer Corp., 122 F.Supp.2d 63, 68–69 (D. Mass. 2000); Berry v. Crown Equip. Corp., 108 F.Supp.2d 743, 754 (E.D. Mich. 2000) ("courts interpreting *Daubert* have considered testability of the expert's theory to be the most important of the four factors, and this is especially true in cases involving allegations of defect in product design"). *But see* Travelers Prop. & Cas. Corp. v. General Elec. Co., 150 F.Supp.2d 360 (D. Conn. 2001) (although theory was not tested, it was capable of being tested; testimony admitted).

**99.** See, e.g., J.B. Hunt Transp., Inc. v. General Motors Corp., 243 F.3d 441, 444 (8th Cir. 2001); Brooks v. Outboard Marine Corp., 234 F.3d 89 (2d Cir. 2000).

**100.** See, e.g., Glastetter v. Novartis Pharm. Corp., 252 F.3d 986, 992 (8th Cir. 2001) (proposed expert testimony insufficient to show that Parlodel can cause intracerebral hemorrhages); Turner v. Iowa Fire Equip., 229 F.3d 1202, 1208 (8th Cir. 2000) (expert's differential diagnosis identified condition, not the cause); Wynacht v. Beck-

man Instruments, Inc., 113 F.Supp.2d 1205 (E.D. Tenn. 2000) (treating clinical physician failed to explain in scientifically reliable manner how wastewater discharge from lab analyzer caused plaintiff's respiratory, neurological, digestive, cardiovascular, and urinary problems that followed the discharge).

Note, however, that courts generally hold that epidemiological studies are not required to prove causation. See, e.g., Rider v. Sandoz Pharm. Corp., 295 F.3d 1194 (11th Cir. 2002) (epidemiological studies not necessary to prove causal link between Parodel, a prescription medication taken to suppress lactation after childbirth, and plaintiff's stroke); Westberry v. Gislaved Gummi AB, 178 F.3d 257 (4th Cir. 1999) (epidemiological studies not necessary to prove causal link between talcum powder, used as lubricant in rubber gaskets, and plaintiff's sinus infection). Any confirmatory studies that are proffered, however, must be reliable. See, e.g., Rider v. Sandoz Pharm. Corp., 295 F.3d 1194 (11th Cir. 2002) ("case reports alone ordinarily cannot prove causation," although they may support other proof of causation).

**101.** Differential diagnosis is an accepted scientific method for establishing causation in certain circumstances. See, e.g., Mattis v. Carlon Elec. Prods., 295 F.3d 856 (8th Cir. 2002) (differential diagnosis admissible to prove causal link between polyvinyl chloride (PVC) cement and the plaintiff's airways dysfunction syndrome); Westberry v. Gislaved Gummi AB, 178 F.3d 257 (4th Cir. 1999) (treating physician's differential diagnosis admissible to prove link between talcum powder used as lubricant in rubber gaskets and plaintiff's sinus infection). In some situations, an expert's failure to apply this diagnostic approach will undercut the validity of his or her conclusions. See, e.g., Turner v. Iowa Fire Equip. Co., 229 F.3d 1202 (8th Cir. 2000) (expert made no attempt to exclude possible causes of respiratory problems, allegedly caused by accidental discharge of substance from fire suppression equipment, until only one remained). See also Schafersman v. Agland Coop., 631 N.W.2d 862 (Neb. 2001) (applying *Frye* test to facts, but adopting *Daubert* prospectively).

**102.** See, e.g., Glastetter v. Novartis Pharm. Corp., 252 F.3d 986 (8th Cir. 2001) (although differential diagnosis is presumptively admissible, experts lacked basis for "ruling in" Parlodel, drug for suppressing postpartum lactation, as cause of stroke);

of accepted principles to the plaintiff's case;[103] or otherwise failed to proffer reliable and relevant testimony—supported by reliable data, methods, or conclusions—that was likely to be helpful to the trier of fact.[104] Quite often, an expert's testimony will fail *Daubert* scrutiny for many of these reasons.[105]

It may well be that the experts in each case in which the testimony was excluded propounded bad science, or perhaps the plaintiffs' attorneys simply failed to adequately prepare their experts on the *Daubert* requirements before the trial, or perhaps they failed at trial (or at a *Daubert* hearing) to provide the court with a sufficient offer of proof. Yet, the cases show that *Daubert* provides federal trial judges with a powerful operating manual for excluding expert testimony that, in the court's sound discretion, does not meet current criteria for "good science."[106]

Alexander v. Smith & Nephew, 98 F.Supp.2d 1310 (N.D. Okla. 2000) (expert's failure to explain why he eliminated other possible causes rendered methodology unreliable). See Sanders & Machal–Fulks, The Admissibility of Differential Diagnosis Testimony to Prove Causation in Toxic Tort Cases: The Interplay of Adjective and Substantive Law, 64 Law & Contemp. Probs. 107 (2001); Latimer, A Good Bedside Manner Wouldn't Be Enough, Either: Differential Diagnosis Under *Daubert*, 1 Expert Evid. Rep. 33 (BNA Aug. 1, 2001).

**103.** See, e.g., Rapp v. Singh, 152 F.Supp.2d 694 (E.D. Pa. 2001) (crashworthiness experts rigorously analyzed how plaintiff's car was propelled under defendant's tractor trailer, but data insufficient on how absence of vertical attachment to bumper made design defective); Cipollone v. Yale Indus. Prods., Inc., 202 F.3d 376 (1st Cir. 2000) (expert's testimony on dangerously narrow gap between fixed and moving handrail of loading dock lift was based on supposition that person's hand was widened by holding object, but plaintiff was holding nothing when accident occurred); Groome v. Matsushita Elec. Corp. of Am., 2000 WL 341134 (E.D.N.Y. 2000) (plaintiff's expert had to loosen safety switches to get microwave to operate with door open; his testimony that "it would be a 'very easy mistake' to install them improperly" did not "fit" because there was no factual basis for his opinion); Daubert v. Merrell Dow Pharm., Inc., 43 F.3d 1311 (9th Cir. 1995) (on remand, Bendectin birth defect case dismissed because plaintiff's experts could not testify that relative risk was more than the 2.0 necessary to show probability of causal connection).

**104.** See, e.g., Allen v. LTV Steel Co., 68 Fed. Appx. 718, 721 (7th Cir. 2003) (Ind. law) (expert unreliable because his methodology had not been "verified by testing, subjected to peer review, nor evaluated for its potential rate of error"); Calhoun v. Yamaha Motor Corp., 350 F.3d 316 (3d Cir.

2003) (Pa. law); Rivera Pomales v. Bridgestone Firestone, Inc., 217 F.R.D. 290, 294 (D.P.R. 2003) (mechanical engineer, who testified that common methodology and protocols were "silly," used unreliable methodology in rendering his opinion); Chapman v. Maytag Corp., 297 F.3d 682 (7th Cir. 2002) (expert's testimony that kitchen range was defectively designed failed all reliability factors where his opinions "amounted to nothing more than unverified statements unsupported by scientific methodology" or by any article, text, study, scientific literature, or data produced by others in the field); J.B. Hunt Transp., Inc. v. General Motors Corp., 243 F.3d 441 (8th Cir. 2001) (crashworthiness case; excluding testimony on crash theory by accident reconstructionist, based on photographs alone and dubious testimony of expert "foamologist"); Cacciola v. Selco Balers, Inc., 127 F.Supp.2d 175, 183 (E.D.N.Y. 2001) (having neither inspected machine itself nor interviewed injured worker, engineer's deposition testimony that machine's safety interlock switch was too accessible, based on photographs alone, "rests upon unsubstantiated generalizations, speculative hypotheses and subjective evaluation that are based neither upon any professional study or experience-based observation"); Mitchell v. Gencorp Inc., 165 F.3d 778 (10th Cir. 1999) (chemicals allegedly caused leukemia).

**105.** See, e.g., Milanowicz v. The Raymond Corp., 148 F.Supp.2d 525 (D.N.J. 2001) (testimony of consulting engineer on forklift truck design failed each of nine reliability indicia court reconfigured from *Daubert* for engineering cases); Oddi v. Ford Motor Co., 234 F.3d 136, 145 (3d Cir. 2000) (the "haphazard, intuitive inquiry" of plaintiff's expert engineer, who conducted no tests nor calculated forces involved in vehicle accident, failed each of eight reliability factors).

**106.** See, e.g., Brooks v. Outboard Marine Corp., 234 F.3d 89 (2d Cir. 2000) (ex-

There is indeed some logic to the view, suggested by the Supreme Court itself in *Daubert*,[107] that its ruling is balanced in its effect: while closing the door to testimony based on unreliable theories and methodologies, it opens the door to expert testimony on cutting-edge science and technology.[108] But the fact remains that only infrequently is *Daubert* invoked to exclude expert testimony proffered by defendants.[109] Instead, courts almost always apply its principles (often with good reason) to exclude a plaintiff's experts and, hence, to bar the plaintiff's claim.

*Booth v. Black & Decker, Inc.*,[110] an example of a court applying *Daubert* to *exclude* a plaintiff's expert testimony, involved claims of defective manufacture and design against the manufacturer of a toaster oven for negligence, breach of warranty, and strict liability in tort for fire damage to the plaintiffs' house. Although the Fire Marshall determined that the fire was caused by a recently-repaired microwave that had been used shortly before the fire, the plaintiffs' expert, Thomas, determined that the fire originated in the defendant's toaster oven located in the same portion of the kitchen. The defendant moved for summary judgment, which hinged on the admissibility of plaintiffs' expert testimony that the toaster oven was defective and caused the fire.

The court held a two-day *Daubert* hearing on Thomas' qualifications and the reliability of his opinion that the toaster oven was defective and caused the fire. The court first concluded that Thomas was qualified to offer expert testimony on the electrical aspects of consumer appliances, including toaster ovens, and that he was qualified to interpret the results of a scanning electron microscope examination he had conducted on the oven. On the issues of manufacturing defect and causation, Thomas hypothesized that while the toaster oven was being operated, its power contacts spontaneously welded together, causing the toaster oven to overheat and catch fire. Attempting to confirm this hypothesis, Thomas testified that he used an electron microscope to examine the contacts

---

pert testimony that outboard motor, propeller of which injured plaintiff's hand, should have been equipped with kill switch was inadmissible because plaintiff's expert had never seen boat or motor, either in person or in photographs; did not know boat's configuration or dimensions; had not spoken to boys involved in accident nor otherwise knew precisely how accident happened; nor attempted to reconstruct the accident to test his theory that a lanyard-activated kill switch would have disengaged motor under circumstances of accident); Berry v. Crown Equip. Corp., 108 F.Supp.2d 743, 754 (E.D. Mich. 2000) (even if proffered expert witness had been qualified to testify on forklift design safety, his opinions were "quite simply unsupported by any reasonable measure of technical data or foundation and are wholly unreliable"). See cf. Brasher v. Sandoz Pharm. Corp., 160 F.Supp. 1291, 1295 n.12 (N.D. Ala. 2001) (noting a busy trial court's natural temptation to apply *Daubert* "heavy-handedly" to reduce a heavy caseload).

**107.** See *Daubert*, 509 U.S. at 595–97.

**108.** " 'The first several victims of a new toxic tort should not be barred from having their day in court simply because the medical literature, which will eventually show the connection between the victims' condition and the toxic substance, has not yet been completed.' " Bonner v. ISP Techs., Inc., 259 F.3d 924, 928 (8th Cir. 2001), citing Turner v. Iowa Fire Equip. Co., 229 F.3d 1202, 1208–09 (8th Cir. 2000).

**109.** See, e.g., Harris v. General Motors Corp., 201 F.3d 800, 804 n.2 (6th Cir. 2000) (reversing summary judgment for defendant, granted on basis of affidavits of defendant's expert witnesses; on remand, proposed testimony of defendant's experts should be subjected to *Daubert* scrutiny); Edwards v. Safety–Kleen Corp., 61 F.Supp.2d 1354 (S.D. Fla. 1999) (excluding defendant's and plaintiff's experts alike).

**110.** 166 F.Supp.2d 215 (E.D. Pa. 2001) (Reed, J.).

which showed indications of melting and scoring, which suggested to him that the surfaces had welded together. The toaster oven was defectively designed, in Thomas' view, for two reasons: (1) because it lacked a thermal cut-off device, to cut off power when the oven reached a certain temperature, to prevent it from overheating, and (2) because it contained an excessive amount of plastic with a low melting point.

Applying the Third Circuit's version of the *Daubert* factors,[111] the court ruled that the evidence failed to establish that Thomas' methodology was reliable. Thomas' manufacturing defect theory was testable, but he had not attempted to get the power contacts of a similar toaster oven to weld together. While his microscopic investigation was a form of test, he failed to adequately explain why indications of melting and scoring mean that welding has occurred, nor did he offer any other basis for his conclusion other than his personal experience and "broad and circular assertions that such markings simply are what happens when welding occurs." Thomas asserted that his fire investigation methods were generally used by others in the field, but he failed to produce persuasive objective evidence to this effect. Prompted by defense counsel, Thomas claimed to have followed the fire investigation Guidelines of the National Fire Protection Association, but he did not point to any specific procedures in the guidelines that he had followed. Nor was there any credible evidence to show that Thomas' examination method was subject to peer review, had a known or potential rate of error, could be measured by existing standards, or was generally accepted. In short, because Thomas "did not take sufficient care in supporting the credibility or reliability of the methodology he applied, despite the best efforts of counsel to elicit it," his testimony that the toaster oven contained a manufacturing defect was not admissible. Similarly, Thomas' design defectiveness theories, on which he offered no methodology whatsoever, were equally deficient: he neither sketched nor produced an example of the kind of thermal cut-off device he recommended, nor did he install one on an exemplar toaster oven to test its ability to prevent overheating. While he claimed that such a device was used on a Black & Decker toaster oven sold in Canada, he failed to produce the Canadian model. As for his theory of excessive plastic materials, Thomas never explained how the fire might have been caused or affected by the plastic.

Thus, whether or not Thomas in fact conducted a reasonable investigation into the cause of the fire, he failed to provide the court with "enough basic, objective information" on the reliability of the investigation and his opinions based thereon.[112] "Thomas performed no tests of his own to determine whether his hypotheses were indeed true; he merely examined the toaster oven and concluded it could have been safer. His testimony ... seemed wholly based on his own training and experience, and he provided the Court with no objective anchor for his

---

**111.** See Oddi v. Ford Motor Co., 234 F.3d 136, 145 (3d Cir. 2000) (listing eight factors: the traditional five *Daubert* factors, plus "(6) the relationship of the technique to methods which have been established to be reliable; (7) the qualifications of the expert witness ...; and (8) the non-judicial uses to which the method has been put."

**112.** Booth v. Black & Decker, Inc., 166 F.Supp.2d 215, 222 (E.D. Pa. 2001).

conclusions."[113] Based on a review of Thomas' expert reports, deposition testimony, and testimony during the *Daubert* hearing, the court found his inquiry into whether the toaster oven contained a defect that caused the fire to be "intuitive and haphazard, his methodology to be unreliable, and, consequently, his conclusions to be suspect."[114] Since the plaintiffs had failed to meet their burden of establishing the reliability of Thomas' testimony under the principles of Rule 702, *Daubert*, and *Kumho Tire,* Thomas' expert testimony on defectiveness and causation was inadmissible. Because plaintiffs had no other evidence to establish that the fire probably was caused by a defect in the toaster oven, the court granted summary judgment for the defendant.[115]

But *Daubert* seeks to exclude only evidence which is invalid or irrelevant, and even a rigorous application of its principles does not compel the exclusion of expert testimony that is merely inconclusive or otherwise only marginally helpful to the trier of fact. Many product accidents leave few and ambiguous clues of accident causation, especially if the product is severely damaged in the accident or lost thereafter,[116] and the issue of design defectiveness is by nature vague and indeterminate.[117] In such cases, courts should allow plausible expert hypotheses, provided they are based on sound methodology and reasoning, that attempt to reconstruct the origins of an accident and how it might have been prevented.

*Rudd v. General Motors Corp.*[118] is an example of a case that allowed a plaintiff's expert testimony after rigorous *Daubert* scrutiny. The plaintiff was injured when a fan blade on his pickup truck broke loose and struck him while he stood in front of the truck's open hood twisting the distributor housing to adjust the engine's timing. Plaintiff sued the vehicle manufacturer, claiming that the fan blade had been made of defective metal, based largely on the testimony of his expert, Edmondson, a mechanical engineer with extensive experience in failure analysis. GM moved for summary judgment, arguing that plaintiff had offered no admissible evidence of a manufacturing defect.

Choosing not to hold a *Daubert* hearing,[119] the court ruled on the admissibility of Edmondson's testimony on the basis of his expert report

---

**113.** Id.

**114.** Id.

**115.** Id. at *6. Nor would the malfunction theory help the plaintiffs, since even that theory required reasonable inferences that the particular product had malfunctioned and caused the harm. Because of the multiple possible causes of the fire in this case, expert testimony on causation was necessary on the malfunction theory, too. Id. at *4, n.5.

**116.** On the malfunction theory, see § 7.4, below.

**117.** On design defectiveness, see ch. 8, below.

**118.** 127 F.Supp.2d 1330 (M.D. Ala. 2001).

**119.** Normally, the decision whether to hold a *Daubert* hearing is entirely discretionary with the trial court. There may be no need for such a hearing if the parties have developed an extensive evidentiary record, including expert reports, depositions, and the literature that supports the expert opinions, and assuming that the issues are well briefed. See id. at 1334, n.3 (citing authorities); Anderson v. Raymond Corp., 340 F.3d 520, 524 (8th Cir. 2003) (trial court's striking of expert's testimony without holding a Fed. R. Evid. § 104(a) hearing was not abuse of discretion; quoting *Kumho Tire*, 526 U.S. 137, 152); Schafersman v. Agland Coop, 631 N.W.2d 862, 877 (Neb. 2001); Nelson v. American Home Prods. Corp., 92 F.Supp.2d 954, 967 (W.D. Mo. 2000). As with any discretionary mat-

and deposition testimony. Edmondson found no direct evidence of a physical flaw in the fan blade but arrived at his conclusion circumstantially by excluding other possible explanations of how the fan blade might have broken. In particular, he first determined that the plaintiff's use of the vehicle at the time the fan blade broke was entirely proper: the plaintiff's technique in adjusting the timing, while running the engine at 1,200 to 1,500 rpms, was entirely normal and specifically recommended by GM's tune-up manuals. Next, based on Edmondson's visual examination, his "total indicator reading" measurements of the accident fan and fan assembly, and his background reading, he determined that prior to the accident the fan blade had not been bent, at the site of the fracture origin or elsewhere, and that there was no visible damage to the blade that might have caused the fatigue fracture and break.[120] Had the fan blade been subjected to a sudden trauma during operation, Edmondson testified that it would have left physical indicia of the trauma, such as broken paint, scarring, or denting, none of which were visible. The absence of any indications that the fan had been subjected to abnormal forces during operation led him to conclude its break was due to a metal-fatigue fracture resulting from a microscopic manufacturing defect, such as a scratch, grind mark, gas bubble, or an inclusion. The court concluded that Edmondson's systematic elimination of alternative causes led to circumstantial proof of defectiveness that was *relevant* to a jury's determination of that issue.[121]

Although the *reliability* of Edmondson's expert evidence was a closer question, the court concluded that it met each of the three specific reliability standards of new Rule 702—that it was based on (1) sufficient data, (2) reliable principles and methods, and (3) reliable application of the methods to the facts. First, the factual basis of Edmondson's testimony was sufficient—based on his visual inspection of the accident fan blade and other fans, his account of the use history of the truck and fan blade, his "total indicator reading" measurements, his reliance on two failure-analysis publications (which included a case study of a car fan fatigue fracture) and GM tune-up manuals, and his background and training analyzing metal fractures,[122] including automotive fan fatigue fractures. Second, the court ascertained that Edmondson's method for determining the cause of the fatigue fracture—by eliminating ("ruling out") other possible causes—is a well-established and reliable scientific method for determining causation.[123] Moreover, because a specialty publi-

---

ter, however, a trial court's failure to hold a *Daubert* hearing in particular circumstances, whether or not requested by the losing party, may be an abuse of discretion, particularly if the admissibility issue turns on factual issues and will be determinative of summary judgment. See Padillas v. Stork–Gamco, Inc., 186 F.3d 412, 418 (3d Cir. 1999).

**120.**   127 F.Supp.2d at 1340.

**121.**   Id. at 1342.

**122.**   The court quoted the Advisory Committee Note to Rule 702 to the effect that an expert's *experience* (alone or in con-

junction with other knowledge, skill, training or education) may provide a sufficient foundation for the expert's testimony if the witness explains "how that experience leads to the conclusion reached, why that experience is a sufficient basis for the opinion, and how that experience is reliably applied to the facts." 127 F.Supp.2d at 1336.

**123.**   In the medical context, experts quite often apply this well-accepted method for determining causation, called "differential diagnosis" (or "differential etiology"). See, e.g., Castillo v. E.I. Du Pont De Nemours & Co., 854 So.2d 1264, 1270–71 (Fla.

cation had employed the process-of-elimination method in a failure analysis model, which included a case history of a fatigue fracture in an automobile fan, this method further satisfied *Daubert*'s reliability factors on publication and acceptance within a relevant community of experts. Third, and finally, the court found that Edmondson reliably applied this method to the accident fan—by determining that the fan's history did not include improper operation and by closely inspecting the fan blade metal for physical indicia of other causes. Noting that Edmondson could not fairly be expected to assign a particular error rate to his techniques, the court concluded that his testimony was reliable, and hence admissible, "because he provides a step-by-step and transparent account" of "reasoning processes and data sources" on which he relies, "the physical indicia he associates with each possible alternative cause, and his reasons for excluding each of the alternative causes."[124] By fully revealing the grounds of his opinions, Edmondson's testimony thus supplied the defendant with a fair basis to challenge his opinions by cross examination and the presentation of contrary evidence, the fundamental tools of the adversary process.[125]

### *Daubert in the State Courts*

Because *Daubert* interprets Federal Rule of Evidence 702, it applies by its terms only to the federal courts. For this and other reasons, quite a few state courts, still trusting in *Frye* and other conventional rules governing the admissibility of expert testimony, have refused to adopt the *Daubert* principles.[126] Yet, prior to the Supreme Court's decision in *Daubert* in 1993, many courts had already adopted reliability principles

2003) (expert's use of differential diagnosis, to prove causal link between agricultural fungicide and birth defect, is generally accepted method in the relevant community under *Frye* test for admissibility); Mattis v. Carlon Elec. Prods., 295 F.3d 856 (8th Cir. 2002) (differential diagnosis admissible to prove causal link between polyvinyl chloride (PVC) cement and the plaintiff's airways dysfunction syndrome); Westberry v. Gislaved Gummi AB, 178 F.3d 257 (4th Cir. 1999) (differential diagnosis admissible to prove link between talcum powder used as lubricant in rubber gaskets and plaintiff's sinus infection). See generally Sanders and Machal–Fulks, The Admissibility of Differential Diagnosis Testimony to Prove Causation in Toxic Tort Cases: The Interplay of Adjective and Substantive Law, 64 Law & Contemp. Prob. 107 (2001); Brew, Where the Rubber Hits the Road: Steering the Trial Court Through a Post-*Kuhmo Tire* Evaluation of Expert Testimony, 27 Wm. Mitchell L. Rev. 467 (2000).

**124.** 127 F.Supp.2d at 1344.

**125.** Id.

**126.** As of 2004, roughly fifteen states still purport to follow *Frye*. See, e.g., Howerton v. Arai Helmet, Ltd., 597 S.E.2d 674 (N.C. 2004); Grady v. Frito–Lay, Inc., 839 A.2d 1038 (Pa. 2003) (rejecting *Daubert*; in applying *Frye*, proponent must prove that expert's *methodology* is generally accepted as a method for reaching a conclusion, not that the conclusion itself is generally accepted); Castillo v. E.I. Du Pont De Nemours & Co., 854 So.2d 1264, 1276 (Fla. 2003) (reaffirming *Frye* and rejecting *Daubert*); Goeb v. Tharaldson, 615 N.W.2d 800 (Minn. 2000) (same; thoroughly examining policy issues). See also Bagley v. Mazda Motor Corp., 864 So.2d 301 (Ala. 2003); Donaldson v. Central Illinois Public Serv. Co., 767 N.E.2d 314 (Ill. 2002); Byrum v. Superior Ct., 2002 WL 243565 (Cal. Ct. App. 2002); Anderson v. Combustion Eng'g, Inc., 647 N.W.2d 460 (Wis. Ct. App. 2002); Krause, Inc. v. Little, 34 P.3d 566 (Nev. 2001); Kansas City S. Ry. Co. v. Johnson, 798 So.2d 374 (Miss. 2001); Logerquist v. McVey, 1 P.3d 113 (Ariz. 2000) (en banc, 3–2 decision); Kuhn v. Sandoz Pharm. Corp., 14 P.3d 1170 (Kan. 2000); Mercer v. Pittway Corp., 616 N.W.2d 602 (Iowa 2000).

See generally Hamilton, The Movement from *Frye* to *Daubert*: Where Do the States Stand?, 38 Jurimetrics J. 201 (1998); States Move to *Daubert*, Even When They Say They're Stuck on *Frye*, 2 Expert Evid. Rep. 161 (BNA March 18, 2002).

quite similar to *Daubert*'s,[127] and since that time an increasing number of states have rejected *Frye* and swung over to the *Daubert* point of view.[128] In addition, a large majority of states have adopted codes of evidence patterned on the Federal Rules of Evidence, including Rule 702 on which *Daubert* is based.[129] Moreover, to the extent that *Daubert*'s precepts are grounded in reasoned principles of logic and fair play for adjudicating disputes involving principles of science and technology, those precepts have a certain logical and moral power that is difficult for state courts to ignore. For these reasons, a growing number of state courts, probably a majority, have now adopted the *Daubert* principles of reliability and relevance for expert testimony.[130]

### The Legacy of Daubert

In *Daubert* and its progeny, the Supreme Court attempted to bridge the yawning gap between how reality is perceived and described, and how problems are resolved, in science and the law.[131] In particular, the Court has sought to improve the legitimacy of judicial determinations

**127.** See Hamilton, The Movement from *Frye* to *Daubert*: Where Do the States Stand?, 38 Jurimetrics 201, 210–13 (1998) (listing twenty-one such states).

**128.** As of 1998, Hamilton counts thirty-three states that had adopted *Daubert*, id. at 209, to which tally at least five additional states should be added. See Mills v. States Sales, Inc., 824 A.2d 461 (R.I. 2003) (applying *Daubert* and *Kumho* to exclude causation testimony on link between carpet fumes and the plaintiff's injuries); Baker Valley Lumber, Inc. v. Ingersoll–Rand Co., 813 A.2d 409 (N.H. 2002) (replacing *Frye* test with *Daubert* reliability standards in case involving expert testimony on existence of design defect in air compressor's hose or fittings); People v. Shreck, 22 P.3d 68 (Colo. 2001) (replacing *Frye* test with *Daubert* reliability standards); Schafersman v. Agland Coop., 631 N.W.2d 862 (Neb. 2001) (same); Rogers v. Cosco, Inc., 737 N.E.2d 1158 (Ind. Ct. App. 2000) (applying *Daubert* "as instructive" in case involving expert's proposed design alternatives to child restraint seat).

Note, however, that some states that have adopted *Daubert* or a similar reliability test have declined to adopt *Kumho*. See Alder v. Bayer Corp., AGFA Division, 61 P.3d 1068 (Utah 2002) (limiting Utah's reliability test to expert testimony based on newly discovered principles and allowing differential diagnosis of chronic fatigue syndrome from exposure to chemicals allegedly emanating from x-ray machine); Watson v. Inco Alloys Int'l, Inc., 545 S.E.2d 294 (W. Va. 2001) (declining to apply West Virginia's reliability test to engineer's testimony that lift truck was defectively designed and had inadequate warnings because opinions were based on engineer's technical experience and observations; citing state court cases).

**129.** Hamilton reports that, as of 1998, only Connecticut, Massachusetts, New York, and Pennsylvania had not adopted Rule 702 and observes that Massachusetts had adopted *Daubert* judicially. Note, however, that few if any states have yet adopted the December 2000 amendment to Rule 702 that explicitly incorporates the *Daubert* principles. *But see* Safeco Ins. Co. of Am. v. Carrier Corp., 2003 WL 458959 (Mich. Ct. App. 2003) (excluding as unreliable electrical engineer's testimony about purported design defect in furnace and noting that Michigan had enacted MCL 600.2955 in an apparent effort to codify *Daubert*); Wood v. Toyota Motor Corp., 760 A.2d 315 (Md. Ct. Spec. App. 2000) (excluding as unreliable mechanical engineer's testimony that airbag caused plaintiff's chemical burns and observing that Maryland's case law "is consistent" with the federal rule as amended in December 2000).

**130.** The counts of states vary wildly. Compare Hamilton, at 209 (counting thirty-three states embracing *Daubert* principles), and States Move to *Daubert*, Even When They Say They're Stuck on *Frye*, 2 Expert Evid. Rep. 161 (2002) (counting twenty-six), with D. Faigman, D. Kaye, M. Saks, and J. Sanders, Science in the Law: Standards, Statistics, and Research Issues (2002), at 12–13 n.8 (counting twenty-one). See generally Eaton, Special Report: *Frye/Daubert* in the 50 States, 30 Prod. Safety & Liab. Rep. 333 (BNA Apr. 15, 2002) (listing standards in every state).

**131.** For a smattering of cerebration on the baffling borderland between law and science, see, e.g., A. Porat and A. Stein, Tort Liability under Uncertainty (2001); Feldman, Science & Uncertainty in Mass Exposure Litigation, 73 Tex. L. Rev. 1 (1995); Brennan, Causal Chains and Statistical Links: The Role of Scientific Uncer-

involving science and technology by forcing courts to rigorously scrutinize the foundations of an expert's scientific or technological opinions. This is a messy task which requires both courts and lawyers to do the kind of rigorous science they may have entered law to avoid.[132] By abandoning *Frye*'s "general acceptance" standard, which was based on the precept that courts should defer to scientific communities to decide for themselves whether a particular type of scientific approach should be recognized as useful, *Daubert* switched the basic responsibility for making such decisions to the courts, which on balance appears to make good sense. It is hard to gainsay the Court's decision that trial judges should serve as "gatekeepers" for expert testimony, as preliminary decision-makers of whether a qualified expert witness has devoted as much rigor, and has applied the same exacting methodologies, to the matter before the court as the expert devotes to his or her own professional projects.[133] But courts must sedulously avoid using this important gate-keeping function to bar evidence that actually may be sound.[134]

*Daubert* requires trial courts to look seriously at the quality of the science or technology of a witness proffered as an expert. Courts can no longer simply pass along to juries the principal task of determining the validity of expert testimony on difficult questions at the margin of established science. As door-closing rules governing the admissibility of expert testimony, the *Daubert* principles are capable of being applied oppressively to smother the judicial airing of legitimate disputes.[135] Instead, the courts need to apply the principles even-handedly—excluding expert testimony that is insufficiently grounded in sound methodology while allowing such testimony that reasonably, if boldly, reaches into uncharted waters of evolving knowledge.[136] By requiring experts to provide reasoned bases for their opinions, and by requiring that such opinions be relevant to the legal issues in the case and grounded in reliable methodology, the reliability and relevancy principles of *Daubert*, used properly, provide a firm foundation for the fair and rational resolution of the scientific and technological issues which lie at the heart of products liability adjudication.

tainty in Hazardous–Substances Litigation, 73 Cornell L. Rev. 469 (1988).

**132.** See Beecher–Monas, The Heuristics of Intellectual Due Process: A Primer for Triers of Science, 75 N.Y.U. L. Rev. 1563 (2000) (questioning courts' ability to comprehend genuine scientific inquiry); Comment, Proposals for Reform in the Evaluation of Expert Testimony in Pharmaceutical Mass Tort Cases, 13 Alb. L.J. Sci. & Tech. 517, 542 (2003) ("the *Daubert* standard . . . is flawed in vesting additional authority to evaluate science in a nonscientific judiciary").

**133.** See *Kumho*, at 152; Fed. R. Evid. 702 Adv. Comm. Note, supplemental reliability factor (4).

**134.** "Courts must be especially careful not to hobble the jury system by excluding potential evidence. Prematurely cutting off the flow of evidence to the jury generally favors defendants, who do not have the burden of proof on most issues, leading not only to a violation of the Constitution, but a tilting of the scales of justice." In re Simon II Litig., 211 F.R.D. 86, 156 (E.D.N.Y. 2002) (Weinstein, J.).

**135.** See, e.g., Schafersman v. Agland Coop., 631 N.W.2d 862 (Neb. 2001); Capra, The *Daubert* Puzzle, 32 Ga. L. Rev. 699 (1998); Graham, The *Daubert* Dilemma—At Last a Viable Solution, 179 F.R.D. 1 (1998).

**136.** Moreover, trial judges must conduct their *Daubert* duties impartially and avoid giving an appearance that they disbelieve a party's expert witnesses. See, e.g., Price v. Blood Bank of Del., Inc., 790 A.2d 1203 (Del. 2002).

## § 6.4  PROOF OF DEFECT—RECURRING ISSUES

In most products liability cases, the plaintiff's basic claim is that a defective condition in a product sold by the defendant proximately caused the plaintiff's harm. The plaintiff has the burden of proof on each element of such a case, including of course the product's defectiveness.[1] Sometimes the precise reasons for a product accident will be a mystery but its circumstances may logically suggest that the product was probably defective, and perhaps that the manufacturer probably was negligent in selling it in that condition. In such cases, the doctrines of product malfunction[2] or res ipsa loquitur[3] may help the plaintiff establish the product's defectiveness. In other cases, a plaintiff may introduce evidence that the product violated a safety standard—adopted by industry or the government—to establish the product's defectiveness[4] and possibly the manufacturer's negligence.[5] Similarly, although often with a different procedural effect, the defendant may rely on its *compliance* with such standards as evidence of its product's *non*defectiveness.[6] In proving defectiveness, sometimes a plaintiff may rely in part upon similar failures of other similar products made by the defendant, and sometimes a defendant may prove the *absence* of similar accidents—the product's record of safe performance—to help prove the converse. Finally, a plaintiff may try to prove a product's defectiveness or the defendant's negligence by showing that the defendant itself acknowledged the problem by remedying the hazard after the plaintiff's injury. These are the recurring issues of proof covered here.

### Safety Standards

Proof that a product violates or conforms to certain safety standards pertaining to the risk that caused the plaintiff's harm may be probative that the product was or was not defective. Such standards may be adopted by industry itself, perhaps through a standards-setting organization such as the American National Standards Institute (ANSI), the National Safety Council (NSC), or the Society of Automotive Engineers (SAE). Or safety standards may be promulgated by the government, by statute or regulatory standard of some governmental product safety agency, such as the federal food and drug agency (the FDA) or the federal automotive safety agency (NHTSA). In general, evidence that a products liability defendant violated or complied with an applicable safety standard is admissible on the issue of defectiveness. The role of such evidence in proving or disproving defectiveness derives from and parallels the law governing its use in proving and disproving negligence, a topic examined earlier.[7]

**§ 6.4**

**1.** See Products Liability Restatement § 2 cmts. *c* (manufacturing defects), *d* and *f* (design defects), and *i* (instruction and warning defects).

**2.** See § 7.4, below.

**3.** See § 2.5, above.

**4.** See discussion below.

**5.** The effect on a negligence claim of proof that a defendant violated a safety statute or regulation, often referred to as the doctrine of negligence per se, is addressed in § 2.4, above.

**6.** Or to help disprove the defendant's negligence. See Id.

**7.** See §§ 2.3 and 2.4, above.

## Industry Standards—Custom

A common type of evidence introduced to show that a product is or is not defective is the industry's prevailing safety standard with respect to the particular issue in dispute.[8] A plaintiff may seek to show, in an effort to prove a product's defectiveness, that other manufacturers in the industry regularly use a safer design or warning that the defendant failed to adopt. Conversely, a defendant manufacturer may seek to introduce evidence, in an effort to show that its product is not defective, that other manufacturers customarily use the same design or warnings approach followed by defendant for the product on trial in the case. The admissibility of evidence on customary standards in an industry to help determine whether a product is or is not defective grew out of and draws heavily from the use of this type of evidence in negligence law for nearly two centuries, a good place to start in attempting to unravel an evidence-of-custom conundrum in the context of strict liability in tort.[9]

Industry safety standards for products often develop informally over time, as a matter of custom, as engineers and other technical experts around the nation (and the world) migrate between companies and exchange ideas in papers, at conferences, and otherwise. Many industry safety provisions are spawned more formally by standards-setting organizations that specialize in developing practicable standards of efficacy and safety, including the American National Standards Institute (ANSI),[10] the American Standards Association (ASA),[11] the National Safety Council (NSC),[12] Underwriters Laboratories (UL),[13] the Society of Automotive Engineers (SAE),[14] and a host of more arcane and specialized organizations, such as the American Society of Agricultural Engineers,[15] the National Spa and Pool Institute,[16] the Scaffolding and Shoring Institute,[17] the Industrial Stapling and Nailing Technical Association,[18] and

**8.** See Hetcher, Creating Safe Social Norms in a Dangerous World, 73 S. Cal. L. Rev. 1 (1999); Boyd and Ingberman, Should "Relative Safety" Be a Test of Products Liability?, 26 J. Legal Stud. 433 (1997); Comment, Custom's Proper Role in Strict Products Liability Actions Based on Design Defect, 38 UCLA L. Rev. 439 (1990); Frumer and Friedman, Products Liability § 18.04[1]; 2 Madden & Owen on Products Liability Law § 27:6; Am. Law. Prod. Liab. § 30:47A; Products Liability Restatement § 2, Comment d. On the very similar rules applied in most jurisdictions to strict liability in tort, see § 6.4, below.

**9.** See § 2.3, above.

**10.** See, e.g., Clarke v. LR Sys., 219 F.Supp.2d 323, 334 (E.D.N.Y. 2002) (guarding standard for grinders); DiCarlo v. Keller Ladders, Inc., 211 F.3d 465, 468 (8th Cir. 2000) (Mo. law) (stepladder standards); Potter v. Chicago Pneumatic Tool Co., 694 A.2d 1319 (Conn. 1997) (vibration limits for tools).

**11.** See, e.g., Poches v. J.J. Newberry Co., 549 F.2d 1166 (8th Cir. 1977) (S.D. law) (specifications for speed and angle of power mower blade).

**12.** See, e.g., Hutchison v. Urschel Labs., Inc., 157 F.3d 613, 615 (8th Cir.

1998) (Mo. law) (guarding standards for chicken dicer); Brown v. Clark Equip. Co., 618 P.2d 267, 275–76 (Haw. 1980).

**13.** See, e.g., Brodsky v. Mile High Equip. Co., 69 Fed.Appx. 53, 57 (3d Cir. 2003) (Pa. law); Moulton v. Rival Co., 116 F.3d 22, 26 (1st Cir. 1997) (Me. law).

**14.** See, e.g., Alfred v. Caterpillar, Inc., 262 F.3d 1083 (10th Cir. 2001) (Okla. law) (design of asphalt paver speed control as lever rather than as counterintuitive rotary dial).

**15.** See Masters v. Hesston Corp., 291 F.3d 985, 991 (7th Cir. 2002) (Ill. law) (American Society of Agricultural Engineers standards relevant to setting standard of design safety for hay baler).

**16.** See Ryan v. KDI Sylvan Pools, Inc., 579 A.2d 1241, 1243–44 (N.J. 1990) (pool depth standards).

**17.** See McNeal v. Hi–Lo Powered Scaffolding, Inc., 836 F.2d 637, 642–43 (D.C. Cir. 1988) (D.C. law) (standards for scaffolding clips).

**18.** See Baier v. Bostitch, 611 N.E.2d 1103 (Ill. App. Ct. 1993) (contact trip on nailer should prevent tool from discharging under its own weight).

the American Conference of Governmental and Industrial Hygienists.[19] Although sometimes referred to as "quasi-public," these are actually private organizations many of which derive from and are basically controlled by the industries they serve. Thus, while some of these organizations can be quite independent of the industries they serve,[20] the standards of others are little more than formalized industry standards. Though industry may rely on this type of standard as setting proper types and levels of safety,[21] most courts treat evidence of such standards largely the same as less formal types of industry standards.[22]

A great majority of courts allow applicable evidence of industry custom.[23] To be applicable, a standard normally must have existed at the time the defendant manufactured the product[24] and must otherwise be directed to the particular aspect of the particular type of product involved in the dispute.[25] Thus, to prove a design defect, a plaintiff may introduce that the defendant manufacturer failed to comply with an applicable industry standard for the design of a speed control mechanism of an asphalt paver,[26] aircraft actuators that could be installed backwards by mistake,[27] a grader back-up alarm that was not tamper-proof,[28] power tools that vibrated excessively,[29] or the guarding of pinch points on industrial machinery.[30] Similarly, in seeking to prove a warnings defect,

**19.** See Potter v. Chicago Pneumatic Tool Co., 694 A.2d 1319 (Conn. 1997) (vibration limits for tools). These and other standards-setting organizations are described in 6 Frumer and Friedman, Products Liability §§ 76.01 and 76.03.

**20.** See, e.g., Fayerweather v. Menard, Inc., 659 N.W.2d 506 (Wis. Ct. App. 2003) (ANSI's ladder committee membership ⅓ from industry, ⅓ users, and ⅓ chosen from CPSC, OSHA, labor organizations, and "outside specialists").

**21.** See Del Cid v. Beloit Corp., 901 F.Supp. 539, 545 (E.D.N.Y. 1995) ("ANSI standards are relied upon by the manufacturers of machinery and by experts in various fields to conduct evaluations of the safety of machinery and processes.").

**22.** However, because some standards-setting groups are comprised of members outside the industry, and because their standards are voluntary guidelines of minimum safety, they are not to be equated with "industry custom," as such. See Fayerweather v. Menard, Inc., 659 N.W.2d 506 (Wis. Ct. App. 2003) (because ⅔ of ANSI ladder standards committee members came from outside industry, "the standards are not evidence of 'custom and usage' within an industry as contemplated" by standard jury instruction, so that court's failure to give it was not error).

**23.** See Frumer and Friedman, Products Liability § 18.04. Industry "custom," meaning prevailing use of technology, dif-

fers from "state of the art," meaning the best technology reasonably available at the time, a higher standard. See § 2.3, above, and § 10.4, below.

**24.** See, e.g., Hutchison v. Urschel Labs., Inc., 157 F.3d 613, 615 (8th Cir. 1998) (Mo. law); Bottignoli v. Ariens Co., 560 A.2d 1261, 1266 (N.J. Super. Ct. App. Div. 1989).

**25.** See, e.g., Chapman v. Bernard's Inc., 167 F.Supp.2d 406 (D. Mass. 2001) (industry standards plaintiff sought to use as evidence pertained to cribs, toddler beds, and bunk beds, not day beds like the one causing baby's death when he slipped between its mattress and side rail).

**26.** See Alfred v. Caterpillar, Inc., 262 F.3d 1083 (10th Cir. 2001) (Okla. law) (SAE standards called for such a control to be a lever rather than a rotary dial; operator backed up, squishing plaintiff into tree, rather than proceeding forward as he intended).

**27.** See Nesselrode v. Executive Beechcraft, Inc., 707 S.W.2d 371 (Mo. 1986).

**28.** See Bohnstedt v. Robscon Leasing L.L.C., 993 P.2d 135 (Okla. Civ. App. 1999).

**29.** See Potter v. Chicago Pneumatic Tool Co., 694 A.2d 1319 (Conn. 1997).

**30.** See, e.g., Masters v. Hesston Corp., 291 F.3d 985, 991 (7th Cir. 2002) (Ill. law ) (hay baler); Del Cid v. Beloit Corp., 901 F.Supp. 539, 545–49 (E.D.N.Y. 1995) (plastic injection molding machine).

a plaintiff may show that a product's warnings are inadequate for failing to comply with industry standards with respect to a risk that a crane operator might be shocked if the crane were to hit electrical wires,[31] that a kitchen floor cleaning chemical might cause severe burns,[32] or that a winch should use a safety-latched hook.[33]

By the same token, a manufacturer seeking to establish that its product's design is reasonably safe, that it is not defective for failing to meet the safety standard of some alternative design,[34] may show that its product complied with applicable industry standards for a stepladder,[35] a chair,[36] the fuel system of a pickup truck,[37] or the protective guard of a log skidder[38] or a grinder;[39] or, in an attempt to refute a defective warnings claim, that its compliance with industry standards for warnings and instructions was adequate for the product, such as a hot water heater[40] or a trampoline;[41] or, that its product was free of manufacturing defects.[42]

A great majority of jurisdictions maintain that a manufacturer's compliance or non compliance with custom is some evidence that the product was[43] or was not[44] defective,[45] while an occasional court appears

---

**31.** See Evanoff v. Grove Mfg. Co., 650 N.E.2d 914 (Ohio Ct. App. 1994)

**32.** See Westley v. Ecolab, Inc., 2004 WL 1068805 (E.D. Pa. 2004).

**33.** See Beneway v. Superwinch, Inc., 216 F.Supp.2d 24, 30 (N.D.N.Y. 2002).

**34.** Comment *d* to the Products Liability Restatement § 2(b) explains the relevance of industry custom to the feasibility requirement of design defect determinations:

This Section states that a design is defective if the product could have been made safer by the adoption of a reasonable alternative design. If such a design could have been practically adopted at time of sale and if the omission of such a design rendered the product not reasonably safe, the plaintiff establishes defect under Subsection (b). When a defendant demonstrates that its product design was the safest in use at the time of sale, it may be difficult for the plaintiff to prove that an alternative design could have been practically adopted. The defendant is thus allowed to introduce evidence with regard to industry practice that bears on whether an alternative design was practicable. Industry practice may also be relevant to whether the omission of an alternative design rendered the product not reasonably safe. While such evidence is admissible, it is not necessarily dispositive. If the plaintiff introduces expert testimony to establish that a reasonable alternative design could practically have been adopted, a trier of fact may conclude that the product was defective notwithstanding that such a design was not adopted by

any manufacturer, or even considered for commercial use, at the time of sale.

**35.** See DiCarlo v. Keller Ladders, Inc., 211 F.3d 465 (8th Cir. 2000) (Mo. law) (ANSI standards; affirming judgment on verdict for manufacturer).

**36.** See Delery v. Prudential Ins. Co. of Am., 643 So.2d 807, 813 (La. Ct. App. 1994) (ANSI standards).

**37.** See Ake v. General Motors Corp., 942 F.Supp. 869, 874 (W.D.N.Y. 1996).

**38.** See Westfall v. Caterpillar, Inc., 821 P.2d 973, 976 (Idaho 1991).

**39.** See Clarke v. LR Sys., 219 F.Supp.2d 323, 334 (E.D.N.Y. 2002) (ANSI guarding standard for grinders).

**40.** See Moore v. Mississippi Valley Gas Co., 863 So.2d 43, 46 (Miss. 2003) (scald warnings, American Gas Association and ANSI standards).

**41.** See Ford v. Nairn, 717 N.E.2d 525 (Ill. App. Ct. 1999) (ASTM Standard F381–84; summary judgment for defendant affirmed); Anderson v. Hedstrom Corp., 76 F.Supp.2d 422, 450 (S.D.N.Y. 1999).

**42.** See, e.g., Emody v. Medtronic, Inc., 238 F.Supp.2d 1291, 1294 (N.D. Ala. 2003) (rod in spinal fusion device met ASTM standards for chemistry, hardness, and microstructure).

**43.** See, e.g., Alfred v. Caterpillar, Inc., 262 F.3d 1083, 1088 (10th Cir. 2001) (Okla. law). Compare Hobson v. Waggoner Eng'g, Inc., 878 So.2d 68, 80 (Miss. Ct. App. 2003) (affirming summary judgment for defendant where plaintiff offered no evidence of industry standards, customs, or expert tes-

---

**44.–45.** See notes 44–45 on page 382.

to give such evidence somewhat greater weight.[46] A couple of state products liability reform statutes address the topic, at least one providing that evidence of industry custom and nongovernmental standards is admissible[47] while another accords a presumption of nondefectiveness to products that "conformed to the generally recognized and prevailing standards."[48] But a small number of courts go in the opposite direction by refusing altogether to allow evidence of industry custom on the issue of product defect for strict liability in tort, reasoning that evidence of the customary behavior of manufacturers with respect to safety issues improperly injects into a strict liability case issues of conduct and due care that have no relevance to the legal standard of product defectiveness, whether measured by consumer expectations or something else.[49] Finally, courts in strict tort cases, borrowing from negligence law's *T.J. Hooper* rule,[50] almost universally maintain that evidence of a defendant's compli-

timony as to availability of safer alternative design).

**44.** See, e.g., Ake v. General Motors Corp., 942 F.Supp. 869, 874 (W.D.N.Y. 1996); Wash. Rev. Code Ann. § 7.72.050.

**45.** See Frumer and Friedman, Products Liability § 18.04[1] ("almost every jurisdiction").

**46.** See, e.g., Vermett v. Fred Christen & Sons Co., 741 N.E.2d 954, 971 (Ohio Ct. App. 2000) ("compliance with ANSI is a compelling factor"); Jordan v. Massey–Ferguson, Inc., 100 F.3d 956 (6th Cir. 1996) (Ky. law) ("a manufacturer rarely 'will be held liable for failing to do what no one in his position has ever done before.' "); Del Cid v. Beloit Corp., 901 F.Supp. 539, 545–49 (E.D.N.Y. 1995); Mears v. General Motors Corp., 896 F.Supp. 548 (E.D. Va. 1995) (while compliance with industry practices does not conclusively establish product's safety, manufacturer will seldom be liable for failing to adopt safety measures no other member of industry employs). See also Products Liability Restatement § 2(b) cmt. *d*, at 20: "When a defendant demonstrates that its product design was the safest in use at the time of sale, it may be difficult for the plaintiff to prove that an alternative design [required for a finding of design defect] could have been practically adopted."

**47.** See Wash. Rev. Code Ann. § 7.72.050(1) (trier of fact may consider such evidence with respect to design, warnings, or manufacturing defects).

**48.** See Ky. Rev. Stat. Ann. § 411.310(2) ("it shall be presumed, until rebutted by a preponderance of the evidence to the contrary, that the product was not defective if the design, methods of manufacture, and testing conformed to the generally recognized and prevailing standards or the state of the art in existence at the

time the design was prepared, and the product was manufactured").

**49.** See, e.g., McCoy v. Whirlpool Corp., 2003 WL 21554950, *8 (D. Kan. 2003) (compliance with industry standards relevant only to a defendant's negligence, not to whether it is subject to strict liability in tort); Lay v. P & G Health Care, Inc., 37 S.W.3d 310, 332 (Mo. Ct. App. 2000); Lewis v. Coffing Hoist Div., Duff–Norton Co., 528 A.2d 590 (Pa. 1987) (evidence of customary design of control box for hoist not admissible in strict products liability action because such evidence introduces concepts of negligence and focuses on manufacturer's conduct rather than condition of product distracts jury; concurring judge, id. at 595, remarked that "a manufacturer cannot avoid liability to its consumers that it injures or maims through its defective designs by showing that 'the other guys do it too;' " dissents argued that evidence that 90% of industry used similar switch should be allowed to show, not conclude, that product was safe, and that courts should follow negligence approach allowing such evidence to help illuminate environment in which products are made and used); Rexrode v. American Laundry Press Co., 674 F.2d 826, 831–32 (10th Cir. 1982) (Kan. law); Grimshaw v. Ford Motor Co., 174 Cal.Rptr. 348, 378 (Ct. App. 1981) ("In a strict products liability case, industry custom or usage is irrelevant to the issue of defect.").

New York cannot make up its mind. Compare Jemmott v. Rockwell Mfg. Co., 628 N.Y.S.2d 184, 185 (App. Div. 1995) (ANSI standards inadmissible for strict liability in tort claim), with Ake v. General Motors Corp., 942 F.Supp. 869, 874 (W.D.N.Y. 1996) (admissible); Anderson v. Hedstrom Corp., 76 F.Supp.2d 422, 450 (S.D.N.Y. 1999) (same).

**50.** See The T.J. Hooper, 60 F.2d 737, 740 (2d Cir. 1932), discussed at § 2.4, above.

ance[51] or noncompliance[52] with industry safety standards does not alone conclusively establish whether a product is defective.[53] Yet, in unusual cases, proof of a defendant's compliance[54] or noncompliance[55] with a clear and vital industry custom, may conceivably be a proper basis for a dispositive determination of a product's defectiveness.

### Governmental Standards

**Violation.** The effect of a manufacturer's violation of a safety statute or regulation on a negligence determination was examined earlier in connection with the doctrine of negligence per se. It was there seen that a defendant's breach of an applicable statute or regulation—one addressing the type of risk that harmed the plaintiff to a person like the plaintiff—is at least evidence (and possibly conclusive) of the negligence issue.[56] The question examined here is whether the law recognizes an equivalent method of proving product defectiveness for purposes of strict products liability in tort, a doctrine that might be labeled "defectiveness per se."[57]

It is useful to remember that a finding of product defect is normally a kind of "lesser included offense" in a negligence determination since the latter normally requires a conclusion that the defendant negligently made or sold a product that was defective in some respect.[58] Stated

**51.**  See, e.g., Clarke v. LR Systems, 219 F.Supp.2d 323, (E.D.N.Y. 2002) (compliance with ANSI standard not dispositive of design defect issue and other evidence on design and safety of machine may be considered); Brooks v. Beech Aircraft Corp., 902 P.2d 54, 64 (N.M. 1995) ("In assessing whether a manufacturer was negligent in adopting a particular product design or whether the product design poses an unreasonable risk of injury, a court should not be restricted to determining whether the manufacturer's design complied with any applicable government regulations and industry standards. Such regulations and standards, while probative of what a reasonably prudent manufacturer would do, should not be conclusive.").

**52.**  See, e.g., Alfred v. Caterpillar, Inc., 262 F.3d 1083 (10th Cir. 2001) (Okla. law); Poches v. J.J. Newberry Co., 549 F.2d 1166 (8th Cir. 1977) (S.D. law).

**53.**  See, e.g., Allen v. Long Mfg. NC, Inc., 505 S.E.2d 354, 358 (S.C. Ct. App. 1998) (suggestion that compliance with an industry safety standard conclusively establishes product's nondefectiveness is "unsound since it would allow the industry to set its own standard of safety, a proposition which finds no support from other jurisdictions, and which is antithetical to the underlying premise of strict liability"); Del Cid v. Beloit Corp., 901 F.Supp. 539, 545 (E.D. N.Y. 1995) ("Compliance or lack of compliance with industry standards ... is not dispositive of the issue of a design defect and other evidence concerning the design

and safety of the machine may be considered."). See generally Frumer and Friedman, Products Liability § 18.04[1].

**54.**  See Wilder v. Toyota Sales, U.S.A., 23 Fed.Appx. 155, 157 (4th Cir. 2001) (Va. law) ("While conformity with industry custom does not absolve a manufacturer or seller of a product from liability, such compliance may be conclusive when there is no evidence to show that the product was not reasonably safe.").

**55.**  See Henderson and Twerski, Achieving Consensus on Defective Product Design, 83 Cornell L. Rev. 867 (1998) (arguing that a defendant's violation of a clear industry standard should be conclusive proof of a product's defectiveness).

**56.**  See § 2.4, above.

**57.**  See 2 Frumer and Friedman, Products Liability §§ 10.03 and 55.02[3]; 2 Madden & Owen on Products Liability § 27.7; 1 Am. Law Prod. Liab. § 12:10–38; D'Angelo, Effect Of Compliance With Applicable Governmental Product Safety Regulations On A Determination Of Product Defect, 36 S. Tex. L. Rev. 453 (1995); Wheeler, The Use of Criminal Statutes to Regulate Product Safety, 13 J. Legal Stud. 593 (1984); Note, Products Liability Based Upon Violation of Statutory Standards, 64 Mich. L. Rev. 1388 (1966) (classic treatment); Products Liability Restatement § 4(a).

**58.**  This is especially true with defendant manufacturers. Other types of negligence claims that are much less common

otherwise, a finding of negligence (whether by normal proofs or negligence per se) usually implies a finding of defectiveness. So, if a plaintiff establishes negligence per se—that a product was in violation of a safety statute or regulation that sought to protect persons like the plaintiff from risks like those that caused the plaintiff's harms—then the plaintiff logically has also made a case that the product was defective.[59] This is the premise of the *Products Liability Restatement* which states a defectiveness per se principle in traditional negligence per se terms.[60] Section 4(a) of the *Restatement* provides that "a product's noncompliance with an applicable product safety statute or administrative regulation renders the product defective with respect to the risks sought to be reduced by the statute or regulation."[61] Acknowledging that the rule derives from the doctrine of negligence per se,[62] the *Restatement* extends the principle across products liability theories to strict liability theories based on defectiveness as well as traditional negligence.[63]

While a doctrine of defectiveness per se might appear logically embedded in the concept of negligence per se, as previously discussed, the underlying rationale of *any* type of per se liability in tort for breach of statute is unclear. Negligence per se itself has always been theoretically suspect,[64] and just why a statutory or regulatory violation should be deemed to establish a product defect, if intuitively appealing, is unclear. The idea may be that governmental product safety standards necessarily take into account consumer expectations and the costs and benefits of alternative safety approaches, thereby resting on implicit determinations of product defectiveness; or perhaps it is the opposite, that consumers can reasonably expect that manufacturers will obey the law, and can reasonably expect no more.[65] But rationales like these seem contrived to make a point. The *Restatement*'s purported "policy" explanation for the rule is tautological,[66] which may reflect the fact that most courts that have applied the per se principle to proof of defectiveness in strict liability have borrowed this approach from negligence law without criti-

---

include negligent misrepresentation and negligent entrustment. See §§ 3.3 and 5.9, above, and § 15.2, below.

**59.** See Elsworth v. Beech Aircraft Corp., 691 P.2d 630, 632 (Cal. 1984) (applying negligence per se doctrine to find defective design).

**60.** The formulation is traditional except that it conflates the conventional two-pronged test into a single scope-of-risk prong.

**61.** Products Liability Restatement § 4(a).

**62.** See id. Reporters' Note to cmt. *d*.

**63.** Treating products liability doctrine broadly, without regard to distinctions between the traditional claims (negligence, implied warranty, and strict liability in tort), is consistent with the Third Restatement's "functional" approach to products liability which seeks to transcend the differ-

ent causes of action, reducing them to simple products liability claims. See Products Liability Restatement §§ 1–4. See § 6.5, below.

**64.** See, e.g., Prosser and Keeton on Torts § 36, at 220–22.

**65.** Cf. Soproni v. Polygon Apartment Partners, 971 P.2d 500, 505–06 (Wash. 1999) ("whether or not a product was in compliance with legislative or administrative regulatory standards is merely relevant evidence that may be considered by the trier of fact [together with the availability of feasible alternative designs, in determining] if the product was unsafe to an extent beyond that which would be expected by an ordinary consumer"). See also Eriksen v. Mobay Corp., 41 P.3d 488 (Wash. Ct. App. 2002).

**66.** "The rule in [§ 4(a)] is based on the policy judgment that designs and warnings that fail to comply with applicable safety

cal consideration.[67] Case law on the issue is sparse, and most of the few courts that apply the doctrine are federal courts sitting in diversity, sometimes drawing support dubiously from one another. In short, the doctrine of defectiveness per se, by which a violation of a safety statute or regulation establishes that a product is defective, rests on a slender case law reed. But a couple of state statutes,[68] a large handful of scattered opinions,[69] and the *Products Liability Restatement* do support this type of proof of product defect. In the final analysis, and for whatever reason, a product's failure to meet minimal government safety rules does seem somehow relevant—perhaps very relevant—to a defectiveness determination.[70]

To be admissible on the issue of product defect, a statutory violation must be *relevant* to that issue, which is another way of stating that the plaintiff must have been injured by the risk the statute sought to prevent.[71] Probably the most contentious issue in this regard concerns OSHA regulations that regulate the guarding of machinery and a myriad other workplace safety matters.[72] While OSHA's machinery guarding regulations are directed solely at *employers* rather than manufacturers, rendering such regulations immensely suspect in the halls of relevance,[73] both plaintiffs and defendants may seek to have such standards admitted into evidence in a products liability case. A plaintiff quite naturally will want to show that the manufacturer failed to adopt whatever guarding or other pertinent standards OSHA has required. Although machine guarding and most other OSHA safety regulations are not directed at manufacturers,[74] so that their breach (by employers) cannot establish a

standards established by statute or regulations are ... defective." Id. at cmt. *d*.

**67.** The courts are not alone in simply assuming that the per se principle for breach of statute may be transferred from negligence law to strict products liability. See, e.g., Rabin, Reassessing Regulatory Compliance, 88 Geo. L.J. 2049, 2051 (2000) ("If, in fact, a regulation is taken to set a minimum standard of safety, a violation can surely be taken to import responsibility as a matter of law.").

**68.** See Colo. Rev. Stat. § 13–21–403(2) (violation creates rebuttable presumption of defectiveness); Kan. Stat. Ann. § 60–3304(b) (violation renders product defective unless manufacturer establishes that violation was appropriate).

**69.** See, e.g., Stanton v. Astra Pharm. Prods., Inc., 718 F.2d 553 (3d Cir. 1983) (Pa. law) (manufacturer of Xylocaine anesthetic negligent per se for failing to file adverse reaction reports required by FDA regulation; violation also rendered drug defective under § 402A, since FDA was unable to assure that warnings of adverse reactions were disseminated to doctors); Lukaszewicz v. Ortho Pharm. Corp., 510 F.Supp. 961 (E.D. Wis. 1981) (manufacturer of Ortho–Novum birth control pills negligent per se, and liable under § 402A, for failure to warn user directly of side effects

pursuant to FDA regulation, 21 CFR § 310.501).

**70.** "Indeed, it seems anomalous to accord such a standard of conduct, promulgated by the community through its elected representatives, anything less than the force of law ... in the context of a civil suit." Note, 64 Mich. L. Rev. 1388, 1391 (1966).

**71.** See, e.g., Hagan v. Gemstate Mfg., Inc., 982 P.2d 1108 (Or. 1999).

**72.** See Frumer and Friedman, Products Liability § 18.05[3].

**73.** See, e.g., Gray v. Navistar Int'l Corp., 630 N.Y.S.2d 596 (App. Div. 1995) (truck not equipped with back-up beeping device; OSHA standards inadmissible); Jemmott v. Rockwell Mfg. Co., 628 N.Y.S.2d 184 (App. Div. 1995) (press guarding; OSHA standards inadmissible).

**74.** Note that other OSHA regulations, such as the OSHA Hazard Communication Standard, 29 C.F.R. § 1910.1200(g)(6)(I), requiring manufacturers and importers of chemicals to supply purchasers with Material Safety Data Sheets, are indeed directed at employers. See, e.g., Messer v. Amway Corp. 210 F.Supp.2d 1217, 1230 (D. Kan. 2002), aff'd 106 Fed.Appx. 678 (10th Cir. 2004).

manufacturer's liability per se, such standards may prescribe the types of safety devices the federal workplace safety agency deems necessary for the safety of particular machinery and so help define the standard of acceptable safety practices—the prevailing custom—in the industry of machinery manufacturers.[75] While plaintiffs therefore sometimes introduce evidence of OSHA standards, manufacturers themselves sometimes seek to introduce such standards.[76] Standing behind the shield that it cannot violate a safety regulation that applies only to employers, a manufacturer of industrial machinery may seek to use such a regulation to inform the jury, if indirectly, of a couple of important points: (1) that the employer, which is not a party in a products liability action,[77] owed and breached a duty under federal law to protect the worker and so in a sense was primarily responsible for the accident;[78] and (2) that the injured worker is already being compensated by workers' compensation benefits and so will not be left destitute if the jury finds the product not defective. Deciding how best to mesh workers' compensation and products liability law is exceedingly complex,[79] but violations of OSHA regulations applicable only to employers simply cannot establish product defectiveness per se.[80] Some courts bar the admission of such evidence, as being irrelevant[81] or as introducing more confusion into a products liability case than it is worth,[82] while others allow it against manufacturers as helping to draw a full and accurate portrayal of the environment into which industrial machines are sold and used.[83]

Most strict liability in tort cases involving noncompliance with safety statutes and regulations concern claims of defects in a product's

**75.** See, e.g., Couch v. Astec Indus., 53 P.3d 398, 403–04 (N.M. 2002) (OSHA standards admissible on this ground); Hannah v. Gregg, Bland & Berry, Inc., 840 So.2d 839 (Ala. 2002) (OSHA standards admissible to show that defendant, who reconfigured machinery, should have noticed that absence of barrier guard was safety hazard). *But cf.* 29 U.S.C. § 653(b)(4), providing that the OSHA statute does not affect the common law "rights, duties, or liabilities of employers and employees." See generally Dobbs, Law of Torts § 133, at 313.

**76.** See, e.g., Slisze v. Stanley–Bostitch, 979 P.2d 317, 321 (Utah 1999); Sims v. Washex Mach. Corp., 932 S.W.2d 559, 565 (Tex. App. 1995) (machine's compliance with OSHA regulations was "strong evidence" that it was not defective).

**77.** Due to the workers' compensation statutes which protect employers from tort suits by employees in exchange for workers compensation insurance benefits. See § 15.6, below.

**78.** See, e.g., Brodsky v. Mile High Equip. Co., 69 Fed.Appx. 53, 56–57 (3d Cir. 2003) (Pa. law) (evidence that OSHA imposed fines upon decedent's employer for failing to properly train employee was admissible to show that employer's intervening negligence was a superseding cause of

employee's death); Porchia v. Design Equip. Co., 113 F.3d 877, 881 (8th Cir. 1997) (Ark. law) (admissible on whether employer's actions were sole proximate cause of injury). *Contra*, Colegrove v. Cameron Mach. Co., 172 F.Supp.2d 611 (W.D. Pa. 2001) (irrelevant and inadmissible).

**79.** See § 15.6, below.

**80.** See, e.g., Jemmott v. Rockwell Mfg. Co., 628 N.Y.S.2d 184 (App. Div. 1995) (OSHA press guarding standards inadmissible).

**81.** See, e.g., Colegrove v. Cameron Mach. Co., 172 F.Supp.2d 611 (W.D. Pa. 2001).

**82.** See, e.g., Byrne v. Liquid Asphalt Sys., Inc., 238 F.Supp.2d 491 (E.D.N.Y. 2002) (inadmissible; OSHA standards not intended to impose duties upon manufacturers and they would likely mislead or confuse jury).

**83.** See, e.g., Couch v. Astec Indus., Inc., 53 P.3d 398, 403–04 (N.M. Ct. App. 2002); Messer v. Amway Corp., 210 F.Supp.2d 1217, 1230 (D. Kan. 2002), aff'd, 106 Fed. Appx. 678 (10th Cir. 2004); Hagan v. Gemstate Mfg., Inc., 982 P.2d 1108 (Or. 1999). For a discussion of a manufacturer's use of OSHA standards against plaintiffs, see § 14.3, below.

warnings[84] or design,[85] and the *Restatement* limits the per se principle to these types of cases. But a safety statute or regulation may pertain to manufacturing defects, as by prescribing the maximum level of contamination or flaws allowable in products such as food,[86] drugs,[87] or lumber,[88] or appropriate manufacturing processes for a medical material,[89] in which context the defectiveness per se principle would seem to apply with equal force and logic.

Jurisdictions vary in the procedural effect they accord a finding of noncompliance with a governmental safety standard. Most of the few opinions on point treat the violation of a safety statute or regulation as evidence of the product's defectiveness.[90] In a few states, such a violation

**84.** See, e.g., Stanton v. Astra Pharm. Prods., Inc., 718 F.2d 553 (3d Cir. 1983) (Pa. law) (manufacturer of Xylocaine anesthetic failed to file adverse reaction reports required by FDA regulation rendering drug defective under § 402A, since FDA was unable to assure that warnings of adverse reactions were disseminated to doctors); Toole v. Richardson–Merrell Inc., 60 Cal. Rptr. 398 (Ct. App. 1967) (same; MER/29); Lukaszewicz v. Ortho Pharm. Corp., 510 F.Supp. 961 (E.D. Wis. 1981) (manufacturer of Ortho–Novum birth control pills negligent per se, and liable under § 402A, for failure to warn user directly of side effects pursuant to FDA regulation, 21 CFR § 310.501).

**85.** See, e.g., Bennett v. PRC Public Sector, Inc., 931 F.Supp. 484, 501 (S.D. Tex. 1996) (NIOSH standards as to design of work station that caused repetitive motion); Brooks v. Beech Aircraft Corp., 902 P.2d 54, 64 (N.M. 1995) (absence of shoulder harnesses in private airplane allegedly rendered it uncrashworthy); Hall v. Fairmont Homes, Inc., 664 N.E.2d 546, 556 (Ohio Ct. App. 1995) (whether levels of formaldehyde fumes emitted by mobile home construction materials exceeded HUD regulations); McGee v. Cessna Aircraft Co., 188 Cal.Rptr. 542 (Ct. App. 1983) (aircraft firewalls between engine and passenger compartment failed to meet FAA requirement that they resist flame penetration for at least fifteen minutes); Ellis v. K–Lan Co., 695 F.2d 157, 161–62 and 162 n.5 (5th Cir. 1983) (Tex. law) (dictum) (whether drain cleaner cap design complied with or violated Special Packaging of Household Substances for Protection of Children Act, 15 U.S.C. §§ 1471–76, and regulations thereunder; such evidence was admissible but not conclusive on design defectiveness).

**86.** Cf. Coffer v. Standard Brands, Inc. 226 S.E.2d 534 (N.C. Ct. App. 1976) (plaintiff injured teeth when bit down on unshelled nut in bottle of shelled nuts; statute and regulation allowed for 1.00% to 2.50% unshelled peanuts per unit of shelled peanuts).

**87.** Cf. St. Louis Univ. v. United States, 182 F.Supp.2d 494 (D. Md. 2002) (polio vaccine did not meet federal "neurovirulence" standards), aff'd 336 F.3d 307 (4th Cir. 2003).

**88.** Cf. Holder v. Keller Indus., 2000 WL 141070 (Tex. App. 2000) (low density wood may have violated ANSI standards).

**89.** Cf. Reiter v. Zimmer Inc., 897 F.Supp. 154 (S.D.N.Y. 1995) (blending times for loads of prosthesis implant cement allegedly failed to meet FDA "good manufacturing processes").

**90.** See, e.g., Gibson v. Wal–Mart Stores, Inc., 189 F.Supp.2d 443, (W.D. Va. 2002) (federal regulations governing packaging of charcoal lighter fluid; but no showing of violation: " 'In determining what constitutes an unreasonably dangerous defect, a court will consider safety standards promulgated by the government or the relevant industry, as well as the reasonable expectations of consumers.' "); Quay v. Crawford, 788 So.2d 76 (Miss. Ct. App. 2001) (federal trucking regulation requiring effective rear-underride guard); Redman v. John D. Brush & Co., 111 F.3d 1174, 1177–78 (4th Cir. 1997) (Va. law) (dictum); Bennett v. PRC Public Sector, Inc., 931 F.Supp. 484, 501 (S.D. Tex. 1996) (government standards relevant to, but not conclusive on, worker's claim that work station that caused repetitive motion disorders was defectively designed); Hall v. Fairmont Homes, Inc., 664 N.E.2d 546, 551 (Ohio Ct. App. 1995) (formaldehyde emissions from materials used in mobile home exceeded HUD standards; by implication); Ellis v. K–Lan Co., 695 F.2d 157, 161 (5th Cir. 1983) (Tex. law) (federal child-proof packaging rules for household substances) (violation or compliance with rules "while plainly relevant, would not have been conclusive of its product's defectiveness or fitness"; trial court did not abuse discretion by instructing jury that they could give such evidence as much weight as any other evidence, "or [it] may be disregarded by you in its entirety," id. at

gives rise to a presumption of defectiveness that may shift the burden of proof.[91] At least one or two courts hold that breach of such a provision conclusively establishes that the product is defective,[92] a position endorsed by the *Products Liability Restatement*[93] which parallels what was conventionally said to be the majority rule in negligence per se.[94] But the *Restatement* further provides that a products liability defendant generally may not avail itself of the array of excuses or justifications for violating a statute or regulation allowed in negligence law,[95] reasoning that excuses are not applicable to most products liability situations where a manufacturer has occasion to know the facts and the law and time to conform its behavior to the safety standard's provisions.[96] It is true that valid justifications for violating safety statutes and regulations will arise less frequently in the products liability context than in ordinary accident situations where emergencies and reasonable mistakes more commonly occur. But case authority for the *Restatement*'s dual position—holding such violations to be conclusive on defectiveness, and allowing no excuses—is ephemeral, to say the least,[97] and courts might well be leery of adopting a truly "strict" form of liability for design and warnings cases without allowing in some manner for truly justifiable violations.[98]

In sum, the doctrine of "defectiveness per se," if such there be, is undeveloped and ethereal, with little real law to give it legs. To the extent that this doctrine does exist, the cases suggest that a defendant's noncompliance with an applicable product safety statute or regulation may be considered evidence, though not dispositive, that a product was defective.

---

162 n.5). See also Wash. Rev. Code Ann. § 7.72.050(1).

**91.** See, e.g., McGee v. Cessna Aircraft Co., 188 Cal.Rptr. 542 (Ct. App. 1983) (FAA specification that aircraft firewalls between engine and passenger compartment resist flame penetration for at least fifteen minutes); Colo. Rev. Stat. Ann. § 13–21–403(2) (rebuttable presumption); Kan. Stat. Ann. § 60–3304(b) (product deemed defective unless manufacturer shows that violation was reasonably prudent action). The rebuttable presumption approach is discussed below in the context of the regulatory compliance defense, at § 14.3.

**92.** See Stanton v. Astra Pharm. Prods., Inc., 718 F.2d 553, 569–71 (3d Cir. 1983) (Pa. law) (Becker, J.) (manufacturer of Xylocaine anesthetic failed to file adverse reaction reports required by FDA regulation rendering drug defective under § 402A, since FDA was unable to assure that warnings of adverse reactions were disseminated to doctors).

**93.** See Products Liability Restatement § 4(a).

**94.** See § 2.4, above. Most assertions to this effect draw their support from other sources from the 1940s, 1930s, or earlier. Research has uncovered no recent jurisdictional tally.

**95.** See Products Liability Restatement § 4(a) cmt. *d.*

**96.** Products Liability Restatement § 4 cmt. *d.*

**97.** See D'Angelo, Effect of Compliance or Noncompliance with Applicable Governmental Product Safety Regulations on a Determination of Product Defect, 36 S. Tex. L. Rev. 453, 469 (1995) (asserting that only one state, Alaska, accords such violations conclusive effect). The Reporters cite *Bachner v. Rich*, 554 P.2d 430 (Alaska 1976), but this is a workplace safety action against a contractor in which the court acknowledges the general availability of excuses to negligence per se but finds them inapplicable to the facts.

**98.** Cf. St. Louis Univ. v. United States, 182 F.Supp.2d 494 (D. Md. 2002) (some of nation's best scientists, employed by NIH to enforce polio vaccine "neurovirulence" standards, approved vaccine that did not comply with such standards because they believed the standards, subsequently abolished, were unreasonably high), aff'd, 336 F.3d 307 (4th Cir. 2003).

**Compliance.** The rule as to a manufacturer's compliance with a governmental safety standard set forth in a statute or regulation largely mimics the rule on violation: compliance with a regulated safety standard, such as a mandated warning, is widely considered proper evidence of a product's nondefectiveness but is not conclusive of that issue.[99] Notwithstanding such compliance, a jury normally is free to find a warning or design "defective" because governmental safety requirements generally are set at minimally acceptable levels.[100] Section 4(b) of the *Products Liability Restatement* is in accord, providing that, in connection with liability for defective design or warnings, "a product's compliance with an applicable product safety statute or administrative regulation is properly considered in determining whether the product is defective with respect to the risks sought to be reduced by the statute or regulation, but such compliance does not preclude as a matter of law a finding of product defect." Some states go further, providing that a manufacturer's compliance with an applicable statute or regulation gives rise to a rebuttable presumption that the product is not defective.[101] In very unusual situations, where no special circumstances suggest the need for greater caution, a court may rule in a negligence case that a defendant's conformity to a statutory or regulatory safety standard amounts to due care as a matter of law,[102] and this principle of special

**99.** See, e.g., Gable v. Village of Gates Mills, 784 N.E.2d 739, 747–48 (Ohio Ct. App. 2003) (compliance with airbag regulation, FMVSS 208, may be a guide but is not conclusive on nonliability); Clark v. Chrysler Corp., 310 F.3d 461, 473–74 (6th Cir. 2002) (Ky. law) (compliance with door latch test, FMVSS 206, did not exempt defendant from liability), vacated on other grounds, 540 U.S. 801 (2003); Quintana–Ruiz v. Hyundai Motor Corp., 303 F.3d 62, 74 (1st Cir. 2002) (P.R. law) ("states may impose liability under their products liability statutes even if the manufacturer or seller meets the minimum federal standards"); Soproni v. Polygon Apartment Partners, 971 P.2d 500 (Wash. 1999) (design of window, through which child fell, that complied with building and fire codes; compliance merely evidence of nondefectiveness); Contini v. Hyundai Motor Co., 840 F.Supp. 22, 23 (S.D.N.Y. 1993) (compliance with NHTSA seatbelt regulations); Moss v. Parks Corp., 985 F.2d 736 (4th Cir. 1993) (CPSC labeling regulations for paint thinner, under Federal Hazardous Substances Act); Lorenz v. Celotex Corp., 896 F.2d 148, 152 (5th Cir. 1990) (Tex. law); O'Gilvie v. International Playtex, Inc., 821 F.2d 1438, 1442 (10th Cir. 1987) (compliance with FDA mandated warning of toxic shock syndrome on tampons was evidence of nondefectiveness, but not conclusive); Ferebee v. Chevron Chem. Co., 736 F.2d 1529 (D.C. Cir. 1984) (EPA-approved label for paraquat herbicide, under Federal Insecticide, Fungicide, and Rodenticide Act); Burch v.

Amsterdam Corp., 366 A.2d 1079 (D.C. 1976) (Federal Hazardous Substances Act); Stevens v. Parke, Davis & Co., 507 P.2d 653, 661 (Cal. 1973) (FDA). See also Wash. Rev. Code § 7.72.050(1).

**100.** See, e.g., Kurer v. Parke, Davis & Co., 679 N.W.2d 867, 875 (Wis. Ct. App. 2004) (drug warnings). Perhaps the classic instances of extraordinarily minimal standards in a federal "safety" act are the flammability standards in the Flammable Fabrics Act. See, e.g., Needham v. Coordinated Apparel Group, 811 A.2d 124, 131 (Vt. 2002); Gryc v. Dayton–Hudson Corp., 297 N.W.2d 727, 733–35 (Minn. 1980); Raymond v. Riegel Textile Corp., 484 F.2d 1025 (1st Cir. 1973) (N.H. law).

**101.** See, e.g., General Motors Corp. v. Harper, 61 S.W.3d 118, 124 (Tex. App. 2001) (design of seatbelt restraint system in 1990 GM pickup truck in which driver's spine was fractured in head-on collision) ("Compliance with NHTSA regulations provides a presumption of no design defect."); Colo. Rev. Stat. § 13–21–403(1); Ind. Code Ann. § 34–20–5–1; Kan. Stat. Ann. § 60–3304(a). Compare McClain v. Chem–Lube Corp., 759 N.E.2d 1096 (Ind. Ct. App. 2001) (presumption not rebutted; summary judgment for manufacturer), with Cansler v. Mills, 765 N.E.2d 698 (Ind. Ct. App. 2002) (presumption rebutted; summary judgment for manufacturer reversed).

**102.** See, e.g., Ramirez v. Plough, Inc., 863 P.2d 167, 172 and 176–77 (Cal. 1993) (compliance with FDA's English language only warning requirement shielded drug

applicability surely applies to claims for strict liability in tort as well. The topic of compliance with governmental safety statutes and regulations is addressed later in depth as a matter of special defense.[103] Also examined later is the special defense of federal preemption,[104] a distant cousin to the defense of compliance with statute.

## Other Similar Accidents

A common, often quite persuasive, form of proof in products liability litigation is proof of other similar accidents.[105] Plaintiffs commonly offer evidence of other similar accidents to help prove, circumstantially, a product's dangerous or defective condition, the defendant's notice of it, or that it caused the plaintiff's injury. Less commonly, defendants offer converse evidence of this type—the *absence* of other similar accidents—in an attempt to prove the contrary: that a product's condition was *not* especially dangerous, that the defendant had no reason to know about it, or that it did *not* cause the plaintiff's harm. In addition, such evidence is sometimes allowed to rebut or impeach the other party's witness.[106] Plaintiff attorneys consider other-accident evidence to be an especially powerful form of proof,[107] while defense attorneys often view it as largely, if not entirely, irrelevant and prejudicial to the fair and rational adjudication of a products liability case.[108]

manufacturer from also having to warn in Spanish that giving aspirin to children suffering flu might cause Reyes Syndrome); Beatty v. Trailmaster Prods., Inc., 625 A.2d 1005 (Md. 1993) (compliance with bumper height statute was complete defense). See Products Liability Restatement § 16 cmt. *e* (in "unusual situations," statutory or regulatory compliance may be conclusive). Cf. Taylor v. Smithkline Beecham Corp., 658 N.W.2d 127, 131 (Mich. 2003) (upholding as constitutional Michigan statute shielding drug manufacturers from liability if their drugs comply with FDA regulations).

**103.** See § 14.3, below.

**104.** See § 14.4, below.

**105.** See 2 Weinstein's Federal Evidence § 401.08[2] (2d ed. 2002); McCormick on Evidence § 200 (J. Strong ed., 5th ed. 1999); G. Lilly, An Introduction to the Law of Evidence § 5.17 (3d ed. 1996); 2 J. Wigmore on Evidence § 458 (Chadbourn rev. 1979); C. Wright and K. Graham, Jr., 22 Fed. Prac. & Proc. § 5170 (2001) (cases on admissibility of similar incident evidence in state of hopeless disorder); Frumer and Friedman, Products Liability § 18.02; 2 Madden & Owen on Products Liability Law § 27:4; 2 Am. Law Prod. Liab. 3d § 14:28–46; Sachs, "Other Accident" Evidence in Product Liability Actions: Highly Probative or an Accident Waiting to Happen?, 49 Okla. L. Rev. 257 (1996); Morris, Proof of Safety History in Negligence Cases, 61 Harv. L. Rev. 205 (1948); Annot., 51 A.L.R. 4th 1186 (1987).

**106.** See, e.g., Samuel v. Ford Motor Co., 112 F.Supp.2d 460 (D. Md. 2000), aff'd, 95 Fed.Appx. 520 (4th Cir. 2004); Hale v. Firestone Tire & Rubber Co., 820 F.2d 928, 934–35 (8th Cir. 1987) (evidence of other explosions of identical multi-piece tire rims allowed to impeach defendant's expert), critically noted, 53 Mo. L. Rev. 547 (1988).

**107.** See, e.g., Hare, Admissibility of Evidence Concerning Other Similar Incidents in a Defective Design Product Case: Courts Should Determine "Similarity" by Reference to the Defect Involved, 21 Am. J. Trial Advoc. 491 (1998). See also Turner, Proving Design Defects with Other Similar Incidents Evidence, 35 Trial 42 (1999) (techniques for finding and using such evidence in auto cases).

**108.** See, e.g., Reynolds and Kirschman, The Ten Myths of Product Liability, 27 Wm. Mitchell L. Rev. 551 (2000) (other-accident evidence peculiarly subject to misuse by jury; discussing limiting instructions and strategy for exclusion). See generally Carlson, Is Revised Expert Witness Rule 703 a Critical Modernization for the New Century?, 52 Fla. L. Rev. 715 (2000); Sachs, "Other Accident" Evidence in Product Liability Actions: Highly Probative or an Accident Waiting to Happen?, 49 Okla. L. Rev. 257 (1996).

An analogous evidentiary issue concerns "comparative risk" evidence. Defense attorneys in ATV and other high-risk product cases sometimes attempt to introduce comparative risk studies comparing the risks of

### Relevance

Other-accident evidence may be relevant to one or more of three basic factual matters commonly in dispute in products liability litigation: (1) the nature and extent of a product's dangerous condition,[109] (2) the defendant's awareness of that condition,[110] and (3) the causal relationship between the condition and the plaintiff's harm. Each of these matters might be controverted, for example, in an action against the manufacturer of a sport utility vehicle for injuries in a rollover that occurred during a particular steering maneuver on a particular grade at a particular speed.[111] Evidence that there have been 100 accidents involving the same model SUV under similar circumstances might tend to show all three facts: (1) that this model SUV is especially prone to rolling over under these particular conditions; (2) that the manufacturer, because of the large number of similar accidents, had likely become informed of this danger in the vehicle; and (3) that certain aspects of the vehicle's design (and perhaps the absence of adequate warnings and instructions) may have contributed to cause the accidents. In short, other-accident evidence may be probative of a product's dangerous condition,[112] notice,[113] or causation.[114] In addition, because punitive damages may be based upon a defendant's failure to take simple steps to

ATVs to other off-road recreational vehicles, such as snowmobiles, minibikes, and trail bikes, and sometimes to such dissimilar products and activities as flying, skydiving, scuba diving, swimming, skiing, boating, bicycling, and horseback riding. Some courts have allowed such evidence for some purposes. See, e.g., Kava v. American Honda Motor Co., 48 P.3d 1170, 1173–76 (Alaska 2002); Bittner v. American Honda Motor Co., 533 N.W.2d 476, 479–87 (Wis. 1995). See generally Frumer and Friedman, Products Liability § 18.01.

**109.** These factors comprise the P x L side of the Hand risk-utility formula for negligence and defectiveness, examined in chapters 2 and 5, above, and 8, below.

**110.** More particularly, this is the issue of "notice," actual or constructive (that defendant knew or should have known), which commonly includes foreseeability.

**111.** Compare McCathern v. Toyota Motor Corp., 23 P.3d 320 (Or. 2001) (Toyota 4Runner rollover; fact of 15 other substantially similar incidents relevant to understanding expert's opinion).

**112.** See, e.g., Lovick v. Wil–Rich, 588 N.W.2d 688 (Iowa 1999) (cultivator wing fell on plaintiff after he removed a pin; evidence of other accidents showing collapse of wing on workers showed dangerousness of location of wing lock bracket subjecting operator to risk from collapse); Santos v. Chrysler Corp., 715 N.E.2d 47 (Mass. 1999) (rear of minivan skidded when brakes applied hard; relevant to dangerousness, defect, and notice).

**113.** See, e.g., Jones v. Ford Motor Co., 559 S.E.2d 592 (Va. 2002) (sudden acceleration of vehicle); Waddill v. Anchor Hocking, Inc., 27 P.3d 1092 (Or. Ct. App. 2001) (notice that fish bowl might shatter in one's hands; failure to warn of necessity to inspect fish bowl for small dings or cracks); Toole v. Baxter Healthcare Corp., 235 F.3d 1307 (11th Cir. 2000) (92 breast implant complaints relevant to fragility of product, although only 13 resulted from rupture by closed capsulotomy); Gerow v. Mitch Crawford Holiday Motors, 987 S.W.2d 359, 364–65 (Mo. Ct. App. 1999) (crashworthiness). See also McClure v. Walgreen Co., 613 N.W.2d 225 (Iowa 2000) (34 incident reports of misfilled prescriptions over 3–year period admissible for punitive damages to show notice of problem without effort to cure it).

**114.** See, e.g., Arabian Agric. Servs. Co. v. Chief Indus., Inc., 309 F.3d 479, 485 (8th Cir. 2002) (Neb. law) (allowing evidence that other silos of manufacturer also collapsed; " '[e]vidence of other accidents may be relevant to prove the defendant's notice of defects, the defendant's ability to correct known defects, the magnitude of the danger, the product's lack of safety for intended uses, or causation' "); Newman v. Ford Motor Co., 975 S.W.2d 147 (Mo. 1998) (evidence of 5 other rear-end collisions properly admitted, in case involving ejection from seat that collapsed despite passenger's wearing seatbelt, with limiting instruction that jury consider the evidence only for determining effect of seatbelt in restraining occupants in rear-impact crash, not for deciding whether seat was defective).

address a serious hazard of which it is aware,[115] evidence of other similar accidents may be relevant to this issue.[116]

Sometimes courts admit other-accident evidence as proof of a product's *defectiveness* or the manufacturer's *negligence*.[117] While this form of evidence may indeed help to prove part of defectiveness or negligence, other-accident evidence logically establishes (in addition to foreseeability or notice) only the type and level of danger in those other products.[118] To the extent that the products and other circumstances involved in the other accidents were similar to those involved in the plaintiff's lawsuit, such evidence at best provides circumstantial evidence that a particular design feature or absence of warning shared in common by the products (including the one that harmed the plaintiff) was *dangerous*, and that the danger was a common *cause* of the accidents. But to prevail in a strict products liability action, a plaintiff must prove more than that the product that injured him was dangerous—he must also prove that the product's design (or absence of warning) was *defective*. And in a negligence action, the plaintiff must further prove that the defendant, by selling the product in such a dangerous condition, was negligent.[119] In addition to evidence that a product's condition was dangerous, both negligence and strict liability in tort generally require additional proof that the dangerous condition was both (1) foreseeable, and (2) reasonably preventable.[120] Other-accident evidence may help to establish the first requirement, foreseeability, because a manufacturer is likely to learn about such accidents, particularly if numerous and severe. Indeed, the more numerous and serious the similar accidents caused by a product, the more likely it is that the manufacturer became aware or at least should have become aware of the product's danger—providing the manufacturer with "notice" of the danger, actual or constructive. But other-accident evidence in no way helps establish the second requirement, the availability of a reasonable alternative design (or warning) that could have prevented the plaintiff's accident. For this, the plaintiff must rely upon other types of proof.[121]

### *Substantial Similarity*

The most fundamental requirement of other-accident evidence is that the other accidents be "substantially similar" to the plaintiff's

---

**115.** See ch. 18, below.

**116.** See, e.g., Preston v. Montana Eighteenth Judicial Dist. Court, Gallatin Cty., 936 P.2d 814 (Mont. 1997). *But see* Kopczick v. Hobart Corp., 721 N.E.2d 769 (Ill. App. Ct. 1999) (reversing $20 million punitive damages verdict against manufacturer of meat saw; while notice of prior accidents relevant to punitive damages, 30 prior accidents not sufficient to put manufacturer of widely used, inherently dangerous product on notice that it was unreasonably dangerous).

**117.** See, e.g., Carballo–Rodriguez v. Clark Equip. Co., 147 F.Supp.2d 66 (D.P.R. 2001) (design defect, warnings defect, negligence, and notice); Smith v. Ingersoll–Rand

Co., 214 F.3d 1235 (10th Cir. 2000) (N.M. law) (defectiveness); Santos v. Chrysler Corp., 715 N.E.2d 47 (Mass. 1999) (defectiveness).

**118.** See, e.g., Melton v. Deere & Co., 887 F.2d 1241, 1245 (5th Cir. 1989) (Miss. law) ("the question is not simply danger itself but unreasonable dangerousness as measured by consumer expectations").

**119.** See ch. 2, above.

**120.** See chs. 2 and 5, above, and § 10.4, below.

**121.** In particular, proof by expert testimony that a reasonable alternative design or warning was available when the product was made and sold. See, § 8.5 below.

accident.[122] First, of course, the products involved in the other accidents must be the same as, or similar to, the product claimed to have injured the plaintiff.[123] But the relevance of such evidence also rests on a similarity in the principal causative facts and circumstances involved in the other accidents with those involved in the plaintiff's case. Accordingly, evidence of other accidents generally is admissible if the plaintiff establishes their substantial similarity to the plaintiff's accident,[124] and it will be excluded in the absence of such proof.[125] But "similar" does not mean identical,[126] and evidence of other accidents is admissible if the facts and circumstances surrounding the other accidents are shown to be reasonably similar to those surrounding the plaintiff's case,[127] and the

**122.** "In products liability cases, the 'rule of substantial similarity' prohibits the admission into evidence of other transactions, occurrences, or claims unless the proponent first shows that there is a 'substantial similarity' between the other transactions, occurrences, or claims and the claim at issue in the litigation." Cooper Tire & Rubber Co. v. Crosby, 543 S.E.2d 21, 23 (Ga. 2001). See also Lovick v. Wil-Rich, 588 N.W.2d 688, 697 (Iowa 1999) ("a foundational showing must indicate the prior accidents occurred under substantially the same circumstances").

**123.** See, e.g., Ray v. Ford Motor Co., 514 S.E.2d 227, 230–31 (Ga. Ct. App. 1999) (546 other incidents of inadvertent vehicle movement properly excluded where database not limited to any year or model of vehicle). *But see* Smith v. Ingersoll–Rand Co., 214 F.3d 1235, 1248 (10th Cir. 2000) (different models, but with same design problem: "The substantial similarity requirement does not require identical products; nor does it require us to compare the products in their entireties [but only as to] variables relevant to the plaintiff's theory of defect."); Santos v. Chrysler Corp., 715 N.E.2d 47, 53 (Mass. 1999) (6 other incidents of rear-wheel lockup in minivan; other incident evidence admissible although 5 minivans were from different model years and 4 had braking systems with different design features). See also Preston v. Montana Eighteenth Judicial Dist. Ct., 936 P.2d 814 (Mont. 1997) (trial court erred in restricting discovery of similar accidents to those involving specific model involved in plaintiff's accident).

**124.** *Allowed*: See, e.g., Jones v. Ford Motor Co., 559 S.E.2d 592 (Va. 2002) (prior accidents from cars accelerating without warning); Arabian Agric. Servs. Co. v. Chief Indus., Inc., 309 F.3d 479 (8th Cir. 2002) (Neb. law) (other silos manufactured by defendant collapsed in similar manner as plaintiff's); McCathern v. Toyota Motor Corp., 23 P.3d 320 (Or. 2001) (Toyota 4Runner rollover; expert testimony based on information from 15 other similar incidents admitted to explain expert's opinion);

Santos v. Chrysler Corp., 715 N.E.2d 47 (Mass. 1999) (on hard application of brakes, rear of minivan skidded; other incidents also on wet roads and otherwise essentially the same); Newman v. Ford Motor Co., 975 S.W.2d 147 (Mo. 1998) (other occupant also thrown from seats that collapsed in rear-end collisions, despite wearing seatbelts); Uniroyal Goodrich Tire Co. v. Martinez, 977 S.W.2d 328 (Tex. 1998).

**125.** *Excluded*: See, e.g., Gable v. Village of Gates Mills, 784 N.E.2d 739, 744–45 (Ohio Ct. App. 2003) (airbag injury incidents to be similar must involve victim of similar size, gender, and position in same seat; evidence of previous airbag injury involved female driver rather than male passenger); Palmer v. Volkswagen of Am., Inc., 2003 WL 22006296, *28 (Miss. Ct. App. 2003) (two other accidents in which person was killed by airbag were not substantially similar to plaintiff's accident); Cooper Tire & Rubber Co. v. Crosby, 543 S.E.2d 21 (Ga. 2001) (tire failure from separation of radial belting; adjustment data for all types of tires manufactured at same plant over 9 years with no showing of substantial similarity of design, manufacturing process, defect, or causation); Pickel v. Automated Waste Disposal, Inc., 782 A.2d 231, 237 (Conn. App. Ct. 2001) (other incident of lid suddenly closing on person using dumpster); Lovett v. Union Pac. R.R. Co., 201 F.3d 1074 (8th Cir. 2000) (4 other vehicular accidents); Mercer v. Pittway Corp., 616 N.W.2d 602 (Iowa 2000) (116 consumer complaints of failure of same model fire alarm).

**126.** See, e.g., Clark v. Chrysler Corp., 310 F.3d 461, 473 (6th Cir. 2002) (Ky. law) ("In order to prove that an accident occurred under similar circumstances, it is not necessary to prove that the prior accidents involved a vehicle identical to the one driven by [decedent] or that all of the circumstances of the accidents are identical."); Smith v. Ingersoll–Rand Co., 214 F.3d 1235 (10th Cir. 2000) (N.M. law).

**127.** See, e.g., Ulm v. Ford Motor Co., 750 A.2d 981 (Vt. 2000) (breakage of steer-

jury may consider any dissimilarities in evaluating the weight of the evidence.[128] It is sometimes noted that the substantial similarity requirement is heightened if the other incidents are offered to prove defectiveness or causation, and relaxed if the evidence is used to show merely the defendant's notice of the possibility that its product is dangerous or defective.[129]

The question of substantial similarity is a matter for the sound discretion of the trial court, reversible only for abuse of discretion.[130] As with other forms of evidence, a court should exclude other-accident evidence, even if relevant, "if its probative value is substantially outweighed by the danger of unfair prejudice, confusion of the issues, or misleading the jury, or by considerations of undue delay, waste of time, or needless presentation of cumulative evidence."[131] In balancing probative value against the various disadvantages of this form of evidence, a court may allow evidence of those other accidents deemed most similar and exclude the rest.[132]

### Absence of Other Accidents

Because plaintiffs normally are permitted to use other-accident evidence to prove dangerousness, notice, and causation, it seems only

ing gear sector shaft on Bronco caused loss of steering control; Ford's engineering investigations into complaints of accidents alleging loss of steering control relevant under business record exception of hearsay rule); Lovick v. Wil–Rich, 588 N.W.2d 688, 697–98 (Iowa 1999) (several prior instances of farm cultivator wings falling on farm workers); Moulton v. Rival Co., 116 F.3d 22, 26–27 (1st Cir. 1997) (Me. law) (reports to potpourri pot manufacturer of previous burns to young children admissible despite differences in circumstances).

**128.** Santos v. Chrysler Corp., 715 N.E.2d 47, 53 (Mass. 1999).

**129.** See, e.g., Smith v. Ingersoll–Rand Co., 214 F.3d 1235 (10th Cir. 2000) (N.M. law); Weir v. Crown Equip. Corp., 217 F.3d 453 (7th Cir. 2000). See generally 2 Weinstein's Federal Evidence § 401.08[2] (2d ed. 2002) (less similarity required for notice, while very high degree of similarity necessary to prove product was unreasonably dangerous); McCormick on Evidence § 200.

**130.** See, e.g., Palmer v. Volkswagen of Am., Inc., 2003 WL 22006296, *28 (Miss. Ct. App. 2003) (trial court was within its discretion); Cooper Tire & Rubber Co. v. Crosby, 543 S.E.2d 21, 25 (Ga. 2001) (tire failure; trial court did not abuse discretion in excluding adjustment data without a showing of substantial similarity) ("[a]bsent clear abuse, the trial courts' exercise of discretion in admitting or refusing to admit such evidence is entitled to deference"); Lovett v. Union Pac. R.R. Co., 201 F.3d 1074 (8th Cir. 2000) (no abuse of discretion in exclusion of other-accident evidence).

Compare with Andrews v. Harley Davidson, Inc., 796 P.2d 1092, 1096 (Nev. 1990) (error not to allow evidence of other accident where difference between motorcycle hitting parked vs. moving vehicle was trivial).

**131.** Fed. R. Evid. 403. See, e.g., Blevins v. New Holland N. Am., Inc., 128 F.Supp.2d 952 (W.D. Va. 2001) (excluding prior accident on hay baler under Rule 403 because "to explore the similarities and dissimilarities of the Hornsby case with the present accident will prolong the trial and risk jury confusion and prejudice"); Weir v. Crown Equip. Corp., 217 F.3d 453, 459 (7th Cir. 2000) (other brake failures on same type of forklift); General Motors Corp. v. Moseley, 447 S.E.2d 302 (Ga. Ct. App. 1994) (overturning jury punitive damages verdict of $101 million); Drabik v. Stanley–Bostitch, Inc., 997 F.2d 496 (8th Cir. 1993) (overturning $7.5 million punitive damages award); Brooks v. Chrysler Corp., 786 F.2d 1191, 1198 (D.C. Cir. 1986) (affirming trial court's exclusion of evidence of consumer complaints because of minimal probative value and substantial delay, court remarked that "Chrysler would have attempted to rebut the substance of each of the 330 complaints or to distinguish the nature of the complaints contained therein from the alleged defect in this case").

**132.** See, e.g., Jones v. Ford Motor Co., 559 S.E.2d 592 (Va. 2002); Carballo–Rodriguez v. Clark Equip. Co., 147 F.Supp.2d 66 (D.P.R. 2001) (other reports of false-latching problem in crane that dropped load on workers); Weir v. Crown Equip. Corp., 217 F.3d 453, 459 (7th Cir. 2000).

logical and fair to allow defendants to use the absence of such evidence to prove the opposite.[133] Accordingly, defendants generally may introduce the absence of other accidents to help establish that a product was not dangerous or defective, that the defendant had no notice of a danger or defect, or the absence of causation.[134] This reverse type of other-accident evidence—product *safe*-use evidence—also requires a proper foundation of substantial similarity: a defendant offering such proof must show the regular safe use[135] of the same type of product under substantially similar conditions to those of the plaintiff's accident.[136]

It may be that evidence of the absence of prior accidents is less probative than evidence of the existence of prior accidents since proof of the absence of accidents only really shows that none have been discovered, not that they did not occur.[137] It thus has been asserted "that proving a negative by the lack of accidents is 'more complex' than proving the happening of an accident."[138] While the case law on the admissibility of the absence of accidents is more sparse, a number of cases have allowed evidence of a product's good safety history to help refute a plaintiff's other-accident evidence,[139] or to help disprove dangerousness,[140] causation,[141] or notice.[142] But evidence of the absence of other accidents normally is relevant only in cases involving design and warnings defects and so generally should be excluded in manufacturing defect cases.[143]

---

**133.** See, e.g., Schaefer v. Cedar Fair, L.P., 791 A.2d 1056 (N.J. Super. Ct. App. Div. 2002); Schaffner v. Chicago & N. W. Transp. Co., 515 N.E.2d 298, 309 (Ill. App. Ct. 1987).

**134.** See, e.g., Varano v. Jabar, 197 F.3d 1 (1st Cir. 1999) (causation); Spino v. John S. Tilley Ladder Co., 696 A.2d 1169 (Pa. 1997) (same), noted, 60 U. Pitt. L. Rev. 297 (1998); Benson v. Honda Motor Co., 32 Cal. Rptr.2d 322 (Ct. App. 1994). See generally McCormick on Evidence § 200; Ross, A Good Accident Reporting System Can Help in Defending Product Liability Cases, 7 Prod. Liab. L. & Strategy 1 (2000) (admissibility may be dependent on existence of effective accident reporting system); Morris, Proof of Safety History in Negligence Cases, 61 Harv. L. Rev. 205 (1948); Annot., 51 A.L.R.4th 1186 (1987) (admissibility of absence of other product accidents).

**135.** The reliability of this kind of evidence requires similar use by a large number of other persons. See, e.g., Watkins v. Toro Co., 901 S.W.2d 917, 920 (Mo. Ct. App. 1995).

**136.** See, e.g., Pandit v. American Honda Motor Co., 82 F.3d 376, 380–81 (10th Cir. 1996); Espeaignnette v. Gene Tierney Co., 43 F.3d 1, 9–10 (1st Cir. 1994).

**137.** See McCormick on Evidence § 200; G. Lilly, An Introduction to the Law of Evidence § 5.17 (3d ed. 1996).

**138.** Schaffer v. Cedar Fair, L.P., 791 A.2d 1056, 1064 (N.J. Super. Ct. App. Div. 2002) (discussing the distinction between other-accident and no-accident evidence).

**139.** See id.

**140.** See, e.g., Espeaignnette v. Gene Tierney Co., 43 F.3d 1 (1st Cir. 1994); Emerson Elec. Co. v. Garcia, 623 So.2d 523 (Fla. Dist. Ct. App. 1993).

**141.** See Varano v. Jabar, 197 F.3d 1, 4–5 (1st Cir. 1999); Spino v. John S. Tilley Ladder Co., 696 A.2d 1169 (Pa. 1997).

**142.** See Jimenez v. Sears, Roebuck & Co., 885 P.2d 120 (Ariz. Ct. App. 1994) (defendant's detailed offer of proof on company's thorough accident information gathering system satisfied rigorous admissibility test).

**143.** See, e.g., McKenzie v. S K Hand Tool Corp., 650 N.E.2d 612, 619–20 (Ill. App. Ct. 1995) (in case involving alleged manufacturing defect of ratchet wrench, trial court erred in admitting evidence of absence of other accidents); Jones v. Pak–Mor Mfg. Co., 700 P.2d 819, 826 (Ariz. 1985) (safety history of entire line of products irrelevant to whether accident product was mismanufactured).

However, the safety history of the particular product unit claimed to have injured the plaintiff may be relevant to a manufacturing defect claim. See Stanley v. Schiavi Mobile Homes, Inc., 462 A.2d 1144, 1149 (Me. 1983) (absence of prior reports of stumbling by people going through mobile home).

### Subsequent Accidents

Most other-accident evidence admitted in products liability litigation involves accidents that occurred prior to the plaintiff's accident. While some courts disagree,[144] a number of courts go further and allow evidence of other accidents that occurred *after* the defendant's product was involved in the accident that injured the plaintiff.[145] These courts reason that the probative force of such evidence to show a product's dangerous (or defective) condition, or causation, in no way depends on when the other accidents occurred. It is clear, however, that evidence of subsequent accidents can have no relevance to the issue of notice,[146] and the relevance of subsequent-accident evidence rests upon the substantial similarity of such accidents to the accident in which the plaintiff was injured.[147] At least one jurisdiction allows evidence of subsequent similar accidents to show a defendant's culpability for purposes of punitive damages.[148]

## Subsequent Remedial Measures

The longer a product is on the market, the more a manufacturer learns about the product's hazards and how best to eliminate them. Thus, as the years progress, a manufacturer with due concern for product safety will tend to improve its manufacturing processes, enhance the design safety of its products, and provide consumers with better information on product dangers and how to avoid them. This natural evolution of product safety over time gives rise to an important evidentiary issue as to the admissibility of evidence that a manufacturer, after making and selling a product that injured the plaintiff, improved the product's safety in a manner that would have prevented the injury.

The fact that a manufacturer has eliminated the very danger responsible for a plaintiff's injury is powerful evidence that the particular safety enhancement was both practicable and otherwise reasonable at the time the safety change was made. So, by improving a product's design safety or by providing additional warnings or instructions, a manufacturer acknowledges the fact that, at that time, the benefits of the safety improvement exceeded their costs. Absent a technological breakthrough between the time the product is manufactured (or when

---

**144.** See, e.g., Mercer v. Pittway Corp., 616 N.W.2d 602, 615 (Iowa 2000) ("the rule allowing evidence of similar incidents is generally limited to incidents occurring prior to the one in question").

**145.** See, e.g., Van Slyke v. Sunterra Corp., 2001 WL 543419 (Va. Cir. Ct. 2001) (showerhead; causation); Carballo–Rodriguez v. Clark Equip. Co., 147 F.Supp.2d 66 (D.P.R. 2001) (latching defect in crane; notice and negligent design); Smith v. Ingersoll–Rand Co., 214 F.3d 1235, 1248 (10th Cir. 2000) (N.M. law) (defectiveness); Preston v. Montana Eighteenth Judicial Dist. Court, Gallatin Cty., 936 P.2d 814 (Mont. 1997); Simon v. Coppola, 876 P.2d 10, 14

(Colo. Ct. App. 1993); Robinson v. G.G.C., Inc., 808 P.2d 522 (Nev. 1991).

**146.** See, e.g., Smith v. Ingersoll–Rand Co., 214 F.3d 1235, 1248 (10th Cir. 2000).

**147.** Compare Crowston v. Goodyear Tire & Rubber Co., 521 N.W.2d 401, 411–12 (N.D. 1994) (upholding exclusion of evidence of subsequent accidents not shown to be substantially similar to plaintiff's accident), with Gowler v. Ferrell–Ross Co., 563 N.E.2d 773, 777–78 (Ill. App. Ct. 1990) (allowing such evidence where subsequent accidents similar, although not identical).

**148.** See Smith v. Ingersoll–Rand Co., 214 F.3d 1235, 1249 (10th Cir. 2000) (N.M. law). *Contra*, Burke v. Deere & Co., 6 F.3d 497, 507–09 (8th Cir. 1993) (Iowa law).

the plaintiff is injured) and the time the product's safety is improved, evidence of such a product safety enhancement may well suggest that prior to its improvement the product was defective and possibly that the manufacturer was negligent. Normally, therefore, evidence that a manufacturer adopted a subsequent remedial measure would appear to be relevant to liability and, hence, presumptively admissible in a products liability case.[149]

### *Common-Law Development of the Repair Doctrine*

Although evidence that an actor cured a dangerous condition after it injured a plaintiff may be generally relevant to the condition's defectiveness and the actor's negligence, such evidence does not itself establish either, and it may unjustly punish persons for their care and prudence. Moreover, allowing subsequent repair evidence may serve to diminish safety by providing parties in control of dangerous conditions with a disincentive to reduce or cure such hazards for fear that their repairs may be used against them in subsequent litigation.[150] For these reasons, courts at an early date developed a special rule of relevancy called the "repair doctrine,"[151] barring evidence of a defendant's post-accident repairs to show the defendant's negligence. Spreading from Britain[152] to America,[153] the doctrine was announced by the United States Supreme Court in 1892 in a case in which the Court explained that "it is now settled [that post-accident repair] evidence is incompetent, because the taking of such precautions against the future is not to be construed as an admission of responsibility for the past, has no legitimate tendency to prove that the defendant had been negligent before the accident happened, and is calculated to distract the minds of the jury from the real issue, and to create a prejudice against the defendant."[154]

Today, the rule barring evidence of subsequent remedial measures to prove negligence is the law in almost every state[155] by common law or formal rule of evidence.[156] It is a controversial rule, as much for the

---

**149.** See Fed. R. Evid. 402 ("[a]ll relevant evidence is admissible").

**150.** A post-accident repair "afford[s] no legitimate basis for construing such an act as an admission of previous neglect of duty. A person may have exercised all the care which the law required, and yet, in the light of his new experience, after an unexpected accident has occurred, and as a measure of extreme caution, he may adopt additional safeguards. The more careful a person is, the more regard he has for the lives of others, the more likely he would be to do so; and it would seem unjust that he could not do so without being liable to have such acts construed as an admission of prior negligence. We think such a rule puts an unfair interpretation upon human conduct, and virtually holds out an inducement for continued negligence." Morse v. Minneapolis & St. L. Ry. Co., 16 N.W. 358, 359 (Minn. 1883).

**151.** Also known as the "subsequent repair," "subsequent remedial measure," and

"post-accident corrective measure" rule or doctrine.

**152.** In Hart v. Lincolnshire & Yorkshire Ry., 21 L.T.R. 261, 263 (Ex. 1869), Lord Bramwell of the court of the exchequer explained that it would be "barbarous.... to hold that because the world gets wiser as it gets older, therefore it was foolish before."

**153.** See, e.g., Terre Haute & Indianapolis R.R. Co. v. Clem, 23 N.E. 965 (Ind. 1890).

**154.** Columbia & Puget Sound R.R. Co. v. Hawthorne, 144 U.S. 202, 207 (1892).

**155.** Rhode Island appears to be the only state that broadly allows the admission of evidence of subsequent remedial measures. See R.I. R. Evid., R. 407.

**156.** See, e.g., Ray v. American Nat'l Red Cross, 685 A.2d 411 (D.C. 1996) (evidence that, after plaintiff contracted HIV, Red Cross began to screen donors by ques-

breadth of its exceptions,[157] which can operate to swallow the general rule of exclusion, as for the logic of its premises, the ambiguity of its formulation, and its economic and other policy implications.[158] The repair doctrine applies to products liability litigation, barring evidence of subsequent safety improvements to prove negligence and, in some jurisdictions, product defectiveness.[159]

### *Federal Rule of Evidence 407*

The general rule prohibiting evidence of post-accident repairs to prove negligence was adopted in Federal Rule of Evidence 407, "Subsequent Remedial Measures," which originally provided:

> When, after an event, measures are taken which, if taken previously, would have made the event less likely to occur, evidence of the subsequent measures is not admissible to prove negligence or culpable conduct in connection with the event. This rule does not require the exclusion of evidence of subsequent measures when offered for another purpose, such as proving ownership, control, or feasibility of precautionary measures, if controverted, or impeachment.

In this original iteration, Rule 407 generated interpretative problems concerning (1) whether the rule barred evidence of subsequent remedial measures in strict products liability cases, or whether instead its exclusionary principle was limited to negligence claims;[160] and (2) whether, regardless of the theory of recovery, the rule applied to safety measures a manufacturer adopted after the date of manufacture and sale but before the plaintiff was injured or just to measures adopted after the plaintiff's

tioning them directly was not admissible to prove negligence); Fernandez v. Higdon Elevator Co., 632 N.Y.S.2d 546 (App. Div. 1995) (such evidence "is never admissible as proof of admission of negligence").

See generally C. Wright and K. Graham, 23 Fed. Prac. & Proc. Evid. § 5282 (2002); McCormick on Evidence § 267; 2 Wigmore on Evidence § 283 (J. Chadbourn rev. ed. 1979); 2 J. Weinstein and M. Berger, Weinstein's Federal Evidence ch. 407 (J. McLaughlin 2d ed. 2003); G. Lilly, An Introduction to the Law of Evidence § 5.18 (3d ed. 1996); D. Leonard, The New Wigmore, A Treatise on Evidence, Selected Rules of Limited Admissibility ch. 2 (2002); Annot., 158 A.L.R. Fed. 609 (1999) (Fed. R. Evid. 407); Annot., 15 A.L.R.5th 119 (1993) (repair doctrine–modern state cases).

**157.** See, e.g., 1 M. Graham, Modern State and Federal Evidence: A Comprehensive Reference Text 480 (1989) ("The opportunities for admissibility may fairly be said to come close to swallowing up the rule" of exclusion).

**158.** See, e.g., C. Wright and K. Graham, 23 Fed. Prac. & Proc. Evid. § 5282 (2002) (challenging Rule 407's justifications); J. Weinstein and M. Berger, Wein-

stein's Evidence Manual—§ 7.04[1] (same); Carver, Subsequent Remedial Measures 2000 and Beyond, 27 Wm. Mitchell L. Rev. 583, 587 (2000) (criticizing the rule on all these grounds and characterizing the current rule as "a post hoc litigation artifice for clever lawyers to use to their client's advantage").

**159.** See Frumer and Friedman, Products Liability § 18.06; 2 Madden & Owen on Products Liability § 27:5; Am. Law. Prod. Liab. 3d § 14:53 et seq. and §§ 54:9–11; Carver, Subsequent Remedial Measures 2000 and Beyond, 27 Wm. Mitchell L. Rev. 583 (2000) (citing the large body of literature, at n.5); Stewart and Andreas, Subsequent Remedial Measures: An Analytical Model for Product Liability Cases, 26 Tort & Ins. L.J. 74 (1990); Notes, 71 U. Colo. L. Rev. 757 (2000); 81 Va. L. Rev. 1141 (1995); 65 N.Y.U. L. Rev. 736 (1990); 1972 Duke L.J. 837; Annots., 74 A.L.R.3d 1001 (admissibility in products liability cases, generally); 38 A.L.R.4th 583 (1985) (admissibility of post-injury warnings); 84 A.L.R.3d 1220 (1978) (recall letters).

**160.** The interpretive question was whether "culpable conduct" included strict products liability.

injury. To resolve these questions, the first sentence of Rule 407 was amended in 1997 to read:

> When, after an injury or harm allegedly caused by an event, measures are taken that, if taken previously, would have made the injury or harm less likely to occur, evidence of the subsequent measures is not admissible to prove negligence, culpable conduct, a defect in a product, a defect in a product's design, or a need for a warning or instruction.[161]

The revised rule thus makes clear, in federal court,[162] (1) that the rule applies and so bars evidence of safety improvements in strict products liability as well as negligence, and that it applies to all three types of defect;[163] and (2) that the rule excludes only evidence of safety improvements adopted after the plaintiff's *injury*, leaving the admissibility of safety improvements made after manufacture but before the plaintiff's injury to the general rules of relevancy and prejudice.[164] While a large number of other issues remain unresolved,[165] the revisions to Federal Rule of Evidence 407 help considerably to clarify how the repair doctrine applies to products liability cases under federal law.

### Strict Liability Claims under State Law

While a few states already have adopted the clarifications of the new federal rule,[166] the evidence codes and common law of most states still track the repair doctrine's traditional formulation in terms of negligence and culpability.[167] The states agree that the repair doctrine applies to

**161.** Apart from the treatises cited above, the amendment is examined in Note, 16 Rev. Litig. 773 (1997); Comment, 45 Am. U. L. Rev. 1453 (1996) (criticizing proposed amendment).

**162.** Most federal courts hold that the federal rule applies, rather than state law, in diversity cases. The Tenth Circuit is an exception. See, e.g., Call v. State Indus., 221 F.3d 1351 (10th Cir. 2000) (Wyo. law); Garcia v. Fleetwood Enterprises, Inc., 200 F.Supp.2d 1302 (D.N.M. 2002) (N.M. law). See generally Frumer and Friedman, Products Liability § 18.06[3][g]; Casenote, 71 U. Colo. L. Rev. 757, 779–86 (2000) (excellent discussion); Note, 53 Fordham L. Rev. 1485 (1985).

**163.** See, e.g., Stahl v. Novartis Pharm. Corp., 283 F.3d 254, 270 n.10 (5th Cir. 2002) (warning added to package insert after plaintiff's injury not admissible to show that earlier warning was defective); J.B. Hunt Transport, Inc. v. General Motors Corp., 243 F.3d 441, 445 (8th Cir. 2001) (GM's subsequent safety improvements in seat integrity not admissible to show that earlier design was defective).

**164.** See, e.g., Caraballo–Rodriguez v. Clark Equip. Co., 147 F.Supp.2d 66, 77 (D.P.R. 2001) (evidence of pre-accident service bulletin and warning decal on crane not barred by Rule 407). Compare United States Fid. & Guar. Co. v. Baker Material

Handling Corp., 62 F.3d 24, 27 (1st Cir. 1995) (although evidence of pre-accident design change subject to Rule 403, Rule 407 did not apply). See generally Advisory Committee Note to the 1997 Amendments: "Evidence of subsequent measures that is not barred by Rule 407 may still be subject to exclusion on Rule 403 grounds when the dangers of prejudice or confusion substantially outweigh the probative value of the evidence."

**165.** On Fed. R. Evid. 407, see Annot., 158 A.L.R. Fed. 609 (1999).

**166.** See Fla. Stat. Ann.§ 90.407 (but omitting "defect in product's design, or a need for a warning or instruction"); Idaho R. Ev., R. 407; Me. R. Ev., R. 407; N.D. R. Ev., R. 407.

**167.** Although many states have some version of the federal rules of evidence, including rule 407, many have not yet formally amended their rules to conform to the 1997 change to federal rule 407 that explicitly applies it to strict products liability claims. See, e.g., Pa. R. Ev., R. 407, interpreted in Duchess v. Langston Corp., 769 A.2d 1131, 1137–50 (Pa. 2001) (traditional rule providing that evidence of subsequent remedial measures is not admissible to prove culpable conduct or negligence bars such evidence in strict products liability cases, too); Hyjek v. Anthony Indus., 944 P.2d 1036, 1038 (Wash. 1997) (same).

products liability claims based on negligence, but they split on whether the rule should be limited to such claims or instead should be expanded to shield manufacturers against evidence of subsequent remedial measures in strict products liability claims. Many states, by formal rule of evidence[168] or judicial opinion,[169] limit the exclusionary rule to negligence claims and so *allow* a plaintiff to introduce evidence of subsequent remedial measures in products liability cases based on strict liability. The classic case adopting this view is *Ault v. International Harvester Co.*,[170] which rejected the empirical assumptions underlying the rule in the modern products liability context:

> The contemporary corporate mass producer of goods, the normal products liability defendant, manufactures tens of thousands of units of goods; it is manifestly unrealistic to suggest that such a producer will forego making improvements in its product, and risk innumerable additional lawsuits and the attendant adverse effect upon its public image, simply because evidence of adoption of such improvement may be admitted in an action founded on strict liability for recovery on an injury that preceded the improvement.[171]

Ruling to the contrary, many other states have opted instead to broaden the rule beyond its traditional negligence basis so as to *exclude* evidence of subsequent remedial measures in the strict liability context as well.[172] These courts reason that the policies that support excluding such evidence in negligence cases—the questionable relevance of safety measures taken subsequent to a product's manufacture, the undesirability of discouraging safety improvements, and the risk of juror confusion—are

**168.** See, e.g., Alaska R. Ev., R. 407; Haw. Rev. St. Ann. § 626–1, R 407; Iowa Code Ann. R. 5.407; Ky. Stat. Rev., R. Ev. 407; Tex. R. Ev., R. 407(a), applied in Uniroyal Goodrich Tire Co. v. Martinez, 977 S.W.2d 328, 341 (Tex. 1998).

**169.** See, e.g., Green v. Smith & Nephew AHP, Inc., 617 N.W.2d 881, 892–93 (Wis. App. 2000), aff'd, 629 N.W.2d 727 (Wis. 2001); Call v. State Indus., 221 F.3d 1351, 1355, (10th Cir. 2000) (Wyo. law); Forma Scientific, Inc. v. Biosera, Inc., 960 P.2d 108, 111 (Colo. 1998) (rule 407 inapplicable to strict liability design defect claim); Wagner v. Clark Equip. Co., 700 A.2d 38 (Conn. 1997); Barnett v. La Societe Anonymous, 963 S.W.2d 639, 651–52 (Mo. App. 1997); General Motors Corp. v. Mosley, 447 S.E.2d 302, 310 (Ga. Ct. App. 1994), overruled on other grounds, 496 S.E.2d 459, 463 (1998); McFarland v. Bruno Mach. Corp., 626 N.E.2d 659, 664 (Ohio 1994); Ford Motor Co. v. Fulkerson, 812 S.W.2d 119 (Ky. 1991); Robinson v. G.G.C., Inc., 808 P.2d 522, 526 (Nev. 1991); D.L. by Friederichs v. Huebner, 329 N.W.2d 890, 907–08 (Wis. 1983); Klug v. Keller Indus., 328 N.W.2d 847 (S.D. 1982); Caldwell v. Yamaha Motor Co., Ltd., 648 P.2d 519 (Wyo. 1982); Ault v. International Harvester Co., 528 P.2d 1148

(Cal. 1974); Sutkowski v. Universal Marion Corp., 281 N.E.2d 749, 753 (Ill. App. Ct. 1972).

**170.** 528 P.2d 1148 (Cal. 1974).

**171.** Id. at 1152.

**172.** See, e.g., Garcia v. Fleetwood Enters., Inc., 200 F. Supp.2d 1302 (D.N.M. 2002); Duchess v. Langston Corp., 769 A.2d 1131, 1132–50 (Pa. 2001) (5–2 decision) (but allowing such evidence under both feasibility and impeachment exceptions); Lawhon v. Ayers Corp., 992 S.W.2d 162, 166 (Ark.App. 1999); Hyjek v. Anthony Indus., 944 P.2d 1036, 1038 (Wash. 1997); Smith v. Black & Decker (U.S.), Inc., 650 N.E.2d 1108, 1113 (Ill. App. Ct. 1995) (noting "potential chilling effect on safety improvements"); Cyr v. J.I. Case Co., 652 A.2d 685 (N.H. 1994); Krause v. American Aerolights, Inc., 762 P.2d 1011, 1013 (Or. 1988); Kallio v. Ford Motor Co., 407 N.W.2d 92 (Minn. 1987); Rix v. General Motors Corp., 723 P.2d 195 (Mont. 1986); Hallmark v. Allied Prods. Corp., 646 P.2d 319, 325–26 (Ariz. 1982); Moldovan v. Allis Chalmers Mfg. Co., 268 N.W.2d 656, 660 (Mich.Ct. App. 1978). See also Tenn. Stat. Rev., R. Ev. 407.

as applicable to products liability claims that rest on strict liability as those that rest on negligence.[173] New York quite oddly straddles the issue, excluding evidence of subsequent remedial measures in strict products liability cases in the normal context of design and warnings defects (unless feasibility is contested) while allowing such evidence in the much less typical context of manufacturing defects.[174]

### Feasibility, Impeachment, and Other Limitations

The repair doctrine, which as a general rule excludes evidence of post-accident repair evidence, is subject to various exceptions that allow a plaintiff to present evidence of a manufacturer's subsequent remedial measures in certain situations. That is, the post-accident repair rule bars the use of such evidence only for the purpose of proving the defendant's negligence, culpability or, in many jurisdictions, the product's defectiveness. By its terms, the doctrine does not affect the admissibility of post-accident repair evidence "when offered for another purpose."[175] In particular, the rule does *not* require the exclusion of evidence of subsequent remedial measures to prove "the feasibility of precautionary measures, if controverted,"[176] or to impeach a witness,[177] exceptions which often overlap.[178]

The significance of the "feasibility" and "impeachment" exceptions depends largely on how narrowly or widely they are interpreted and applied, and the integrity of this rule of evidence depends upon the exceptions not being applied so widely as to swallow the general rule of exclusion. A manufacturer, of course, must be deemed to controvert feasibility if it denies the *technological possibility* of a safety measure it subsequently adopts, even if it does so only implicitly, as by asserting that the product that injured the plaintiff was the safest possible.[179] So, too, a manufacturer "controverts" the "feasibility" of a safety measure if it explicitly denies that fact.[180] By the same token, if a manufacturer explicitly *admits* the feasibility of precautionary measures, proof that it

**173.** See, e.g., Duchess v. Langston Corp., 769 A.2d 1131, 1138–50 (Pa. 2001) (5–2 decision) (thoroughly examining applicability of traditional rationales to strict products liability).

**174.** See Demirovski v. Skil Corp., 610 N.Y.S.2d 551 (App. Div. 1994); Cover v. Cohen, 461 N.E.2d 864, 868 (N.Y. 1984).

**175.** Fed. R. Evid. 407.

**176.** Id. Note that the question of the *feasibility* of a safety improvement may give rise to another evidentiary issue concerning the admissibility of state-of-the-art evidence. In cases where technology has in fact advanced from the time the product was manufactured to when the manufacturer adopted a safety improvement, the state-of-the-art doctrine is likely to bar evidence of the safety enhancement if it was practically unavailable at the time of manufacture. See, e.g., Patton v. Hutchinson Wil–Rich Mfg. Co., 861 P.2d 1299, 1312–13 (Kan. 1993) (interpreting Kan. St. Ann. § 60–

3307(a)(1)). On state of the art, see § 10.4, below.

**177.** See, e.g., Wilson Foods Corp. v. Turner, 460 S.E.2d 532, 535 (Ga.Ct.App. 1995); Traylor v. Husqvarna Motor, 988 F.2d 729, 733–34 (7th Cir. 1993) (Ind. law).

**178.** The overlap is most pronounced when a witness for a manufacturer denies the feasibility of a safety measure it adopted shortly after the plaintiff's accident.

**179.** See Frumer and Friedman, Products Liability § 18.06[1][f].

**180.** See, e.g., Reese v. Mercury Marine Div. of Brunswick Corp., 793 F.2d 1416, 1428 (5th Cir. 1986) (defendant denied feasibility of warnings subsequently added to instruction manual); Dixon v. International Harvester Co., 754 F.2d 573, 584 (5th Cir. 1985) (defendant's witness asserted that plaintiff's proposed design was not feasible because it would block tractor operator's view).

subsequently adopted them normally should be excluded.[181] More difficult is the question of whether a manufacturer "controverts feasibility" of safety measures (or may have its witnesses impeached) because it defends the "safety," "reasonableness," or "acceptability" of its earlier design or warning. While a defendant's general arguments along these lines arguably might open the admissibility door under one or both exceptions, most courts have construed the exceptions more narrowly to prevent their swallowing the general rule of exclusion.[182] The repair doctrine rests on the premise that a defendant normally should be allowed to assert that its product and actions both were safe and reasonable at the time of manufacture without having to contend with proof that it decided to improve the product at some later time. This suggests that the exceptions should not be interpreted so broadly as to allow a plaintiff to use a back-door exception to introduce evidence of a type and for a purpose that the general rule bars at the front—that the controverting-feasibility and impeachment exceptions should not be used to let in evidence of post-accident safety improvements to prove that a product was defective and the defendant was negligent. So, if a manufacturer in fact concedes the economic and technological feasibility of a particular safety enhancement that it eventually adopted, it still may argue that "the safety problem was not great enough to warrant the trade-off of consumer frustration, increased complexity of the product, and risk of consumer efforts to disconnect the safety device" without opening the door to proof that it adopted the enhancement under the feasibility or impeachment exception.[183] Thus, the feasibility and impeachment exceptions normally should be applied, and evidence of a subsequent corrective measure admitted, only if a manufacturer asserts that the measure was at least impracticable at the time.[184]

A variety of other issues lurk within the subsequent repair doctrine that may restrict or expand its use, and the resolution of such issues in state court may rest upon the particular state's formulation of the repair doctrine. While a great majority of the subsequent repair cases involve design or warnings defects, the doctrine may also apply to defects in a

---

**181.** See, e.g., J.B. Hunt Transport, Inc. v. General Motors Corp., 243 F.3d 441, 445 n.3 (8th Cir. 2001) (defendant stipulated feasibility of stiffer seats by admitting that it had "tested proposed seating systems that were both stronger and not as strong as the seating system in the 1991 Camaro"); Kallio v. Ford Motor Co., 407 N.W.2d 92, 98 (Minn. 1987) (defendant conceded feasibility of altering transmission design).

But a manufacturer may be too clever in first admitting "feasibility" and then attempting to limit its definition to technological possibility. See Duchess v. Langston Corp., 769 A.2d 1131, 1145–50 (Pa. 2001) (rejecting defendant's effort to avoid evidence of subsequent safety measure by admitting its feasibility, but only in terms of technological possibility, and arguing that its use would preclude the product from functioning properly).

**182.** See Duchess v. Langston Corp., 769 A.2d 1131, 1145–50 (Pa. 2001); Frumer and Friedman, Products Liability § 18.06[1][f].

**183.** See, e.g., Gauthier v. AMF, Inc., 788 F.2d 634, 638 (9th Cir. 1986) (admission of evidence of subsequent remedial measures improper in view of manufacturer's concession of feasibility).

**184.** Compare Duchess v. Langston Corp., 769 A.2d 1131, 1145–50 (Pa. 2001) (applying both exceptions and holding that trial court erred in excluding evidence of subsequently adopted interlock safety device where defendant challenged practicability of that device), with Keating v. United Instruments, Inc., 742 A.2d 128, 130–31 (N.H. 1999) (trial court properly excluded evidence of subsequent safety measure in aircraft altimeter because measure did not "directly" impeach defendant's expert).

product's manufacture.[185] One important issue that still divides the states is whether the exclusionary rule should be limited to remedial measures adopted after the plaintiff's accident,[186] as under the revised federal rule, or whether it should be applied more broadly to exclude evidence of any safety improvements made after the date a product is manufactured or sold.[187] Another question is whether the repair rule applies to safety measures taken by a third party, such as an employer who adds a safety feature to a product after an employee is injured; most courts hold that the doctrine is limited to defendant manufacturers and so does not bar evidence of safety improvements by third parties, while at least a couple courts extend the exclusionary rule beyond manufacturers to remedial measures adopted by other parties.[188] A further issue on which the courts are split is whether the rule applies to remedial measures required by the government, such as mandatory safety improvements ordered by NHTSA or another federal agency in charge of safety regulation, since here the safety-disincentive rationale disappears.[189]

## § 6.5    RESTATEMENT (THIRD) OF TORTS: PRODUCTS LIABILITY

For most of the late twentieth century, § 402A of the *Restatement (Second) of Torts*, the fountainhead of modern products liability law, ruled supreme. With approval by the American Law Institute[1] of the

---

**185.** See, e.g., Rix v. General Motors Corp., 723 P.2d 195, 202 (Mont. 1986). See also Fed. R. Evid. 407, barring admission of subsequent remedial measures to prove, inter alia, *"a defect in a product*, a defect in a product's design, or a need for a warning or instruction" (emphasis added). For an early example, see Foley v. Coca–Cola Bottling Co., 215 S.W.2d 314 (Mo. Ct. App. 1948) (tacks in soft drink; implied warranty).

**186.** See, e.g., Myers v. Hearth Techs., Inc., 621 N.W.2d 787, 792 (Minn. Ct. App. 2001) (rule did not apply to, and so did not bar admission of, safety enhancement made before accident); Tucker v. Caterpillar, Inc., 564 N.W.2d 410 (Iowa 1997) (same).

**187.** See, e.g., Ariz. Rev. Stat. Ann. § 12–686(2) (rule applies to corrective measures adopted after sale); Brown v. Ford Motor Co., 714 N.E.2d 556, 559 (Ill. App. Ct. 1999) (after sale or manufacture; same policy considerations apply); Cover v. Cohen, 461 N.E.2d 864, 868 (N.Y. 1984) (after manufacture).

**188.** Compare Ford Motor Co. v. Nuckolls, 894 S.W.2d 897, 900 (Ark. 1995) (evidence that employer improved product's safety after accident was properly admitted), and Wagner v. Clark Equip. Co., 700 A.2d 38 (Conn. 1997) (same), with Torrens v. Delta Int'l Mach. Corp., 696 N.Y.S.2d 230 (App. Div. 1999) (evidence that employer, subsequent to accident, fashioned safety guard that would have prevented injury was properly excluded), and Padillas v. Stork–Gamco, Inc., 2000 WL 1470210 (E.D. Pa.

2000) (same). See generally Annot., 64 A.L.R.5th 119 (1998) (admissibility of evidence of subsequent repairs by non-defendant third party); Johnson, Subsequent Remedial Measures May Not Be Admissible to Establish Product Design Defect, 3 No. 7 Law. J. 6 (Apr. 6, 2001) (summarizing *Padillas*).

**189.** See Annot., 158 A.L.R. Fed. 609 § 5 (1999) (citing cases both ways on whether there is a "superior authority" exception to Rule 407); Note, 1991 U. Ill. L. Rev. 843.

Evidence of product recalls, which are sometimes voluntary and at other times ordered by a regulatory agency, raise various evidentiary issues including the subsequent repair doctrine. See J. Weinstein and M. Berger, Weinstein's Evidence Manual § 7.04[3] (student ed. 1999); Am. Law Prod. Liab. 3d §§ 14:64–14:66; Annot., 84 A.L.R.3d 1220 (1978) (admissibility of recall letter by defendant manufacturer). On product recalls, see § 10.8, below.

**§ 6.5**

**1.** The American Law Institute (the "ALI" or "Institute") was formed in 1923 to clarify, simplify, and improve the common law of this nation. See W. D. Lewis, How We Did It, in ALI, Restatement in the Courts: History of the American Law Institute and the First Restatement of the Law 1 (perm. ed. 1945). With an elected membership of more than 3,000 of the nation's

*Restatement (Third) of Torts: Products Liability*[2] in 1997, § 402A of the *Second Restatement* was effectively repealed.[3] In its place now sits an entire new *Restatement* dedicated solely to the topic of products liability law.[4] This section describes the process by which the law in this area was "restated" by the American Law Institute and outlines the structure of the new *Restatement*.

## Development

With the termination of its overly ambitious "enterprise responsibility" project in 1991,[5] the American Law Institute sensibly decided instead to restate the law of torts in more conventional form. Because tort law had grown so large and cumbersome, the ALI decided for *Restatement* purposes to subdivide the law on this topic into various components. Due to the explosive expansion of products liability law after the promulgation of § 402A in the *Second Restatement of Torts* in 1965, the ALI announced in 1991 that the first of the new tort law *Restatements* would be the *Restatement (Third) of Torts: Products Liability*. In 1992, Professor James Henderson and Professor Aaron Twerski were appointed Reporters for the project, and so began the process of

nearly one million practicing lawyers, judges, and law professors, the ALI's "Restatements" of various fields of law command broad respect.

For commentary on the American Law Institute and the Restatement process, see, e.g., Symposium on the American Law Institute: Process, Partisanship, and the Restatements of Law, 26 Hofstra L. Rev. 567 (1998); Frank, The American Law Institute, 1923–98, 26 Hofstra L. Rev. 615 (1998); Henderson and Twerski, The Politics of the Products Liability Restatement, 26 Hofstra L. Rev. 667 (1998); Howells, Is European Products Liability More Protective than the Restatement (Third) of Torts: Products Liability?, 65 Tenn. L. Rev. 985 (1998); Abrahamson, Refreshing Institutional Memories: Wisconsin and the American Law Institute, 17 Wis. L. Rev. 1, 1 n.60 (1995) (citing N.E.H. Hull, Restatement and Reform: A New Perspective on the Origins of the American Law Institute, 8 Law & Hist. Rev. 55, 60–65 (1990)); Shapo, In Search of the Law of Products Liability: The ALI Restatement Project, 48 Vand. L. Rev. 631 (1995); Linde, Courts and Torts: "Public Policy" Without Public Politics?, 28 Val. U. L. Rev. 821, 840, 844 (1994); Wechsler, Restatements and Legal Change: Problems of Policy in the Restatement Work of the American Law Institute, 13 St. Louis U. L.J. 185 (1968); L. Green, The Torts Restatement, 29 Ill. L. Rev. 582, 591–92 (1935).

Among the several state treatments of the new Restatement, see Steenson, A Comparative Analysis of Minnesota Products Liability Law and the Restatement (Third) of Torts: Products Liability, 24 Wm. Mitchell L. Rev. 1 (1998); Dreier, The Restatement

(Third) of Torts: Products Liability and New Jersey Law—Not Quite Perfect Together, 50 Rutgers L. Rev. 2059 (Summer, 1998); Thomas, Defining "Design Defect" in Pennsylvania: Reconciling *Azzarello* and The Restatement (Third) of Torts, 71 Temp. L. Rev. 217 (1998); Note, 101 W. Va. L. Rev. 285 (Fall 1998) (West Virginia).

**2.** In conformity with its standard practice, the ALI entitled the new Restatement the "Restatement of the Law Third, Torts: Products Liability," which here is usually cited as the "Products Liability Restatement."

**3.** The development of the Restatement (2d) Torts § 402A, is chronicled in § 5.3, above.

**4.** At its annual meeting in Washington, D.C., on May 20, 1997, the ALI membership voted to adopt the Proposed Final Draft of the Products Liability Restatement, subject to editorial revision and amendments debated and approved at the May 20 meeting.

**5.** Initially entitled "Compensation and Liability for Product and Process Injuries," the Enterprise Responsibility for Personal Injury Project results were published in 1991 in the form of a "Reporters' Study" which was never submitted to the ALI membership for approval. See ALI, Reporters' Study: Enterprise Responsibility for Personal Injury (1991). The project suffered from a variety of defects on which numerous observers, sometimes not unfairly, heaped their scorn. See, e.g., Phillips, Comments on the Reporters' Study of Enterprise Responsibility for Personal Injury, 30 San Diego L. Rev. 241 (1993).

converting a single section of the *Second Restatement,* § 402A, into an entire *Restatement* of its own.

Throughout the *Products Liability Restatement* project, the Reporters regularly met with and were advised by the ALI Council,[6] the ALI Advisers,[7] and the ALI Consultative Group comprised of interested members of the Institute.[8] In addition, the Reporters periodically met with and obtained advice from various other groups and persons interested in the *Restatement* project, including various interest groups representing a wide variety of defense, claimant, academic, and other interests. Over the course of the project, beginning with Preliminary Draft No. 1 in 1993, the Institute circulated drafts of various portions of the *Restatement* to these special interest groups for comment and critique.[9] Beginning with Tentative Draft No. 1 in 1994, the full ALI membership[10] debated and voted on Tentative Drafts of various provisions at each of its annual meetings until the Institute's final debate and adoption of the Proposed Final Draft in May 1997. Although debates on each successive draft at these four ALI meetings were vigorous and occasionally contentious, the membership's final vote to adopt the Proposed Final Draft was unanimous.

After the 1997 annual meeting at which the ALI voted to adopt the Proposed Final Draft, the Reporters folded in amendatory language from the final meeting,[11] and the *Restatement* as finally revised was reviewed for technical correctness and stylistic consistency.[12] To assure that the final amendatory revisions remained faithful to the approval vote of the ALI membership, the final revisions were reviewed by several designated members of the Institute. The *Restatement (Third) of Torts: Products Liability* was published in 1998.

**6.** Roughly sixty prominent lawyers, judges, and law professors comprise the ALI Council.

**7.** Nineteen lawyers, judges, and law professors comprised the basic Adviser group and one especially good-looking law professor served as Editorial Adviser.

**8.** Roughly three hundred lawyers, judges, and law professors who are members of the ALI comprised the Consultative Group.

**9.** Prior to publication of the final version of the Products Liability Restatement in 1998, the ALI published a total of twelve drafts of various portions of the work: Preliminary Draft No. 1 (April 20, 1993); Council Draft No. 1 (September 17, 1993); Council Draft No. 1A (January 4, 1994); Tentative Draft No. 1 (April 12, 1994); Preliminary Draft No. 2 (May 19, 1994); Council Draft No. 2 (September 2, 1994); Tentative Draft No. 2 (March 13, 1995); Preliminary Draft No. 3 (May 18, 1995); Council Draft No. 3 (November 15, 1995); Tentative Draft No. 3 (April 5, 1996); Proposed Final Draft (Preliminary Version), Volumes I and II (October 18,

1996); and the Proposed Final Draft (April 1, 1997).

**10.** The American Law Institute holds annual meetings in May for the principal purposes of debating and voting on drafts of Institute projects, including the various Restatements of the Law. Several hundred members attended the annual meetings from 1994 through 1997 at which the Products Liability Restatement drafts were considered, and, typically, some 200 to 300 members were present and voted on issues put to the membership. Each year the Institute publishes an edited transcript of the annual meeting proceedings.

**11.** During final debate on the Products Liability Restatement at the 1997 annual ALI meeting, the Proposed Final Draft was amended in various relatively minor respects. Some amendments were by formal vote while others were directed by the Director or agreed to by the Reporters to resolve problematic phraseology, mostly in the comments.

**12.** Final technical proofing was conducted by the Reporters, the Editorial Adviser, and Institute staff.

**Structure**

The *Products Liability Restatement* is divided into four broad chapters, some of which are further divided into sub-topics, for a total of 21 black-letter sections. The centerpiece of this new *Restatement* is Chapter 1, Topic 1, entitled "Liability Rules Applicable to Products Generally." Topic 1, comprising §§ 1–4, contains the basic liability standards and methods of proof. The first two sections within Topic 1 concern the basic principles of liability, based on the concept of defectiveness, that apply to products generally. Section 2, which contains definitions for defects in manufacture, design, and warnings and instructions, is the heart of the new *Restatement*. Section 3 describes a circumstantial evidence doctrine, akin to the doctrine of res ipsa loquitur, for establishing defectiveness where the manner in which the accident occurred renders it likely that the accident was caused by a product defect. Section 4, the final section in Topic 1, describes the effect of a product's violation of, or compliance with, governmental standards of product safety.

The second topic in Chapter 1, Liability Rules Applicable to Special Products or Product Markets, contains §§ 5–8. These sections set forth principles governing the liability of sellers of particular types of products: component parts, prescription drugs, food, and used products.

Chapters 2 (Liability of Commercial Product Sellers Not Based on Product Defects at Time of Sale) and 3 (Liability of Successors and Apparent Manufacturers), which include §§ 9–14, address other special duty issues: misrepresentation, post-sale duties to warn and recall, and the responsibilities of successor enterprises and apparent manufacturers. Chapter 4 (Provisions of General Applicability) first addresses, in §§ 15–18, causation issues and affirmative defenses based on user misconduct and contractual disclaimers. The final sections in Chapter 4, §§ 19–21, define "product," "seller," and "harm."

The most significant structural feature of the new *Restatement* is that its most important liability provisions, mostly contained in § 2, are configured in "functional" rather than "doctrinal" form. Rules, of course, may be formulated as they are *stated* by the courts ("doctrinal" form) or they may be restated as the courts in fact *apply* them ("functional" form). From the birth of § 402A of the *Second Restatement* in 1963–65, the hallmark of modern products liability law has been that liability is "strict." Yet the rhetoric of "strictness" proved so potent and uncompromising that it hampered the reasoned evolution of doctrine over time. The products liability law-in-action continued to develop, but the language of the law (its doctrine) failed to keep pace.

The most prominent example of how doctrine lagged behind function concerns the definition of liability for design and warnings dangers. Courts quickly discovered that they had no choice but to apply negligence principles of reasonableness to resolve the difficult issues of balance between product usefulness, safety, cost, practicality, and information dissemination inherent in such cases. Whether one calls this method for determining liability "strict" or "popcorn," it is at bottom negligence. And, once one admits that responsibility must be limited in such cases by principles of foreseeability, as most courts have done,[13] then the liability standard is plainly one of negligence, and nothing more.[14] Increasingly, in other words, whatever "strictness" there ever was in a manufacturer's design and warnings responsibility has inexorably been drained away. But most courts, while often acknowledging the application of negligence principles in such cases, have continued to insist on calling liability "strict," on calling a pig a mule.[15]

Many observers would have preferred that the *Third Restatement* preserve the form and language of the *Second Restatement*'s "strict" products liability doctrine as echoed by the courts in thousands of courtrooms and written decisions for over three decades.[16] Other observers would have liked for the doctrine to follow practice, which suggested that the liability rule in design and warnings cases formally be returned to the law of negligence.[17] Perhaps not unwisely, in view of the undiluted passion of the warring camps, the Reporters decided to ignore the conventional doctrinal labels of "strict liability" and "negligence" and, instead, to define liability functionally according to the required proof.[18]

## Basic Liability Provisions

Sections 1, 2, and 3 define the fundamental rules of defectiveness theory and proof applicable to most products liability cases.[19] Section 4 addresses how a product's compliance or noncompliance with a product

**13.** This development arose from the evolution of two doctrines in particular, both of which are addressed in later chapters: (1) the decline of the Wade–Keeton liability test, which presumes that the manufacturer knew at the time of manufacture the nature and extent of its product's hazards, and (2) the rise of the state-of-the-art defense. See chapters 8 (design defects) and 10 (limitations on defectiveness), below.

**14.** See Owen, Defectiveness Restated: Exploding the "Strict" Products Liability Myth, 1996 U. Ill. L. Rev. 743.

**15.** See id. at 749.

**16.** See, e.g., Shapo, A New Legislation: Remarks on the Draft Restatement of Products Liability, 30 U. Mich. J.L. Reform 215 (1997); Vandall, Constructing a Roof Before the Foundation Is Prepared: The Restatement (Third) of Torts: Products Liability Design Defect, 30 U. Mich. J.L. Reform 261 (1997); Vargo, The Emperor's New Clothes: The American Law Institute Adorns a "New Cloth" for Section 402A Products Liability Design Defects—A Survey of the States Reveals a Different Weave, 26 U. Mem. L. Rev. 493, 557 (1996); Shapo, In Search of the Law of Products Liability: The ALI Restatement Project, 48 Vand. L. Rev. 631 (1995); Phillips, Achilles' Heel, 61 Tenn. L. Rev. 1265 (1994).

**17.** See, e.g., Owen, Defectiveness Restated: Exploding the "Strict" Products Liability Myth, 1996 U. Ill. L. Rev. 743; Owen, The Graying of Products Liability Law: Paths Taken and Untaken in the New Restatement, 61 Tenn. L. Rev. 1241 (1994).

**18.** See Products Liability Restatement § 2 cmt. *n* (recommending that, because design and warnings claims rest on a risk-utility assessment regardless of doctrinal label, courts should not risk inconsistent verdicts by submitting such claims to juries on different causes of action, whether negligence, implied warranty, or strict liability in tort). At least one state supreme court agrees. See Wright v. Brooke Group Ltd., 652 N.W.2d 159, 169 (Iowa 2002) ("We question the need for or usefulness of *any* traditional doctrinal label in design defect cases because, as comment *n* points out, a court should not submit both a negligence claim and a strict liability claim based on the same design defect since both claims rest on an identical risk-utility evaluation. Moreover, to persist in using two names for the same claim only continues the dysfunction engendered by section 402A. Therefore, we prefer to label a claim based on a defective product design as a design defect claim without reference to strict liability or negligence.").

**19.** The great bulk of products liability law is loaded into the official Comments and Reporters' Notes to these three initial sections, particularly section 2.

safety statute or regulation affects a defectiveness determination.[20]

Grounding the *Restatement*, § 1 provides the overarching general principle of modern products liability law—that commercial enterprises are liable for harm caused by defects in products that they sell:

### § 1. Liability of Commercial Seller or Distributor for Harm Caused by Defective Products

One engaged in the business of selling or otherwise distributing products who sells or distributes a defective product is subject to liability for harm to persons or property caused by the defect.[21]

Basing liability on whether a product is "defective," § 1 is bound together with § 2, which defines the three ways in which a defect may occur:

### § 2. Categories of Product Defect

A product is defective when, at the time of sale or distribution, it contains a manufacturing defect, is defective in design, or is defective because of inadequate instructions or warnings. A product:

(a) contains a manufacturing defect when the product departs from its intended design even though all possible care was exercised in the preparation and marketing of the product;

(b) is defective in design when the foreseeable risks of harm posed by the product could have been reduced or avoided by the adoption of a reasonable alternative design by the seller or other distributor, or a predecessor in the commercial chain of distribution, and the omission of the alternative design renders the product not reasonably safe;

(c) is defective because of inadequate instructions or warnings when the foreseeable risks of harm posed by the product could have been reduced or avoided by the provision of reasonable instructions or warnings by the seller or other distributor, or a predecessor in the commercial chain of distribution, and the omission of the instructions or warnings renders the product not reasonably safe.[22]

The three liability standards in § 2 provide the foundation for most modern products liability law.[23]

Finally, § 3 provides a method for establishing defectiveness, useful primarily when the specific kind of proof contemplated by the § 2

---

**20.** Much of the following draws from Owen, Products Liability Law Restated, 49 S.C. L. Rev. 273 (1998), Owen, Defectiveness Restated: Exploding the "Strict" Products Liability Myth, 1996 U. Ill. L. Rev. 743 (hereinafter Defectiveness Restated), and Owen, The Graying of Products Liability Law: Paths Taken and Untaken in the New Restatement, 61 Tenn. L. Rev. 1241 (1994).

**21.** Products Liability Restatement § 1.

**22.** Id. § 2.

**23.** The Comments to § 2 canvass most of the central issues in products liability law, and the Reporters' Note to this section in particular provides a wealth of case, statutory, and secondary authority on these issues.

definitions has been destroyed in the accident or is otherwise practically unavailable. While plaintiffs ordinarily must prove their cases under the § 2 defectiveness provisions, § 3 provides a default mechanism for establishing liability in special cases where logic and fairness suggest that a plaintiff's inability to establish a specific defect according to conventional proof requirements should not preclude the claim. In such cases, proof of defect under § 3 is allowed when the very circumstances of the accident themselves suggest, more probably than not, that the accident was caused by a product defect rather than something else:

§ 3. Circumstantial Evidence Supporting Inference of Product Defect

It may be inferred that the harm sustained by the plaintiff was caused by a product defect existing at the time of sale or distribution, without proof of a specific defect, when the incident that harmed the plaintiff:

(a) was of a kind that ordinarily occurs as a result of product defect; and

(b) was not, in the particular case, solely the result of causes other than product defect existing at the time of sale or distribution.[24]

Section 3, roughly adapted from the res ipsa loquitur provision of the *Second Restatement of Torts*,[25] might fairly be termed a principle of "defect ipsa loquitur." This section adopts the so-called "malfunction doctrine" which a small number of states have explicitly adopted, and which most implicitly apply, to accommodate problems of proof that plague plaintiffs when events conspire to eliminate direct evidence of a specific defect but where circumstances suggest that the product's failure most probably resulted from a defect. For example, if a new electric coffee maker spontaneously ignites, burning its electrical components beyond recognition in the resulting fire, one may reasonably assume that the fire was caused by some manufacturing defect in its electrical mechanism. This is true even though, because of the nature of the product accident, direct proof of defect from an examination of the product itself is simply unavailable.

**Distinguishing the Separate Types of Defect**

When Dean William Prosser crafted § 402A of the *Second Restatement of Torts* in the early 1960s, products liability law was in its infancy. At this very early stage in the development of the law, the defect concept was only roughly understood and conceived of quite naively as a unitary concept: products were either too dangerous (defective) or safe enough (nondefective). As courts in the 1960s and 1970s applied the principles of § 402A to an ever-widening array of products in an ever-widening range of contexts, the disparities among the various forms of product dangers increasingly revealed themselves. Today, most courts and commentators

**24.** Products Liability Restatement § 3.

**25.** The Reporters drew § 3 from § 328D of the Restatement (2d) Torts; see Products Liability Restatement § 3 cmt. *a*.

accept as axiomatic the fundamental distinctions between three very different forms of product defect: (1) manufacturing flaws, (2) design inadequacies, and (3) insufficient warnings of danger and instructions on safe use.[26] Over the decades since § 402A was adopted by the ALI, the need to develop different doctrinal approaches to the problems in these three very different contexts has become a well-accepted premise of products liability law.

Although § 1 of the *Products Liability Restatement* sets the doctrinal stage somewhat deceptively, by establishing a single principle of liability for selling "defective" products, § 2 decisively splinters the notion into the three separate forms of defect.[27] Because the general principle of § 1 is rooted in the notion of a "defective product" rather than fault, it might appear simply to restate the no-fault doctrine of "strict liability" that has dominated products liability doctrine since the 1960s. However, apart from cases involving manufacturing flaws, the language of defectiveness is merely a cloak for a standard of design and warning "defect" liability that is grounded in fault. Indeed, the primary reason for trifurcating defectiveness in § 2 is to provide separate vessels for separate liability standards: subsection 2(a) defines liability for manufacturing defects in terms that are truly "strict," whereas subsections 2(b) and (c) define liability for design and warnings defects largely in terms of negligence principles, notwithstanding the strict-sounding language of "defectiveness" in which the definitions are cast.[28] In short, liability in § 2 of the new *Restatement* truly is strict for manufacturing defects but is based in negligence for design and warnings defects.[29]

### Manufacturing Defects

The new *Restatement* defines the standard of liability for manufacturing defects in the strict liability manner of the law of contract. Thus, as seen above, a product is deemed defective in manufacture under § 2(a) "when the product departs from its intended design even though all possible care was exercised in the preparation and marketing of the product."[30] Although only a small number of courts have explicitly used this type of deviation-from-blueprints form of definition, it is plainly implied by the word "defective" when applied to the manufacturing flaw context. Seeing no need to define the straight-forward notion of a

---

**26.** On the now-conventional nature of this tripartite classification, see Products Liability Restatement § 1 cmt. *a*, Reporters' Note. See also § 6.2, above.

**27.** The *Restatement* continues this form of segregation by type of defect in various contexts, as in § 6 which separately defines the various duties of sellers of prescription drugs and medical devices by type of defect.

**28.** The reasoning behind this move is explained in § 1, comment *a*. See Defectiveness Restated at 747–51.

**29.** Comment *a* to § 2 provides in part: "The rules set forth in this Section establish separate standards of liability for man-

ufacturing defects, design defects, and defects based on inadequate instructions or warnings." The comment explains that subsection (a) imposes "[s]trict liability without fault," and further provides: "Subsections (b) and (c), which impose liability for products that are defectively designed or sold without adequate warnings or instructions and are thus not reasonably safe, achieve the same general objectives as does liability predicated on negligence." It is important to note, however, that a retailer's liability under subsections 2(b) and 2(c), in contrast to the liability of a manufacturer, is truly strict. See Products Liability Restatement § 1 cmt. *e* and § 2 cmt. *o*.

**30.** Products Liability Restatement § 2(a).

manufacturing defect, courts probably have simply assumed this kind of commonsense definition.

The *Restatement's* standard of liability for manufacturing defects, quite explicitly stated to be strict, was noncontroversial during the ALI debates on the *Restatement* and for nearly two decades of debate in Congress over scores of products liability bills. Because of the special significance of the user's expectation interests in manufacturing flaw cases, grounded in philosophic principles of equal freedom,[31] contract law's strict-liability principle is plainly proper in this context. In short, true strict liability in this context is both logical and fair.

### Design and Warnings Defects

The liability standards for design and warnings (and instructions) defects are formulated in parallel fashion in § 2, as seen above. Neither liability standard is stated in traditional strict liability or negligence terms. Instead, § 2 defines both design and warnings defects in terms of the availability of some "reasonable alternative" design or warning. The Reporters chose this rather peculiar, "functional"[32] method of refashioning the basic liability tests because of the schizophrenic nature of design and warnings liability law which, in doctrine, speaks the language of "strict" liability but which, in practice, bespeaks the law of negligence.[33] Products liability judicial opinions are simply stuck in a no-man's-land somewhere between negligence and true strict liability.

As a way around this doctrinal dilemma, the Reporters focused on the type of proof courts require to establish a design or warnings defect case. What their research revealed, although hotly contested,[34] was that courts in these cases generally require the plaintiff to establish that the defendant reasonably could have adopted some alternative design or warning that would have prevented the plaintiff's harm.[35] Thus, in both design and warnings cases, the *Products Liability Restatement* defines liability functionally in terms of whether the manufacturer reasonably could have provided a safer product. Stripping the rather cumbersome *Restatement* language to its essentials, the standard of liability under

---

**31.** The policy reasons supporting strict liability in this context are summarized in the Products Liability Restatement in § 2 comment *a*. The reasons in moral theory are developed in Owen, The Moral Foundations of Products Liability Law: Toward First Principles, 68 Notre Dame L. Rev. 427, 467–68 (1993) (hereinafter Moral Foundations).

**32.** The Reporters aptly characterize their definitional approach as "functional," and cite widespread authority therefor. See § 1 cmt. *a* and § 2 cmt. *n*, and the Reporters' Note thereto.

**33.** See Defectiveness Restated at 747–51.

**34.** See, e.g., Vargo, The Emperor's New Clothes: The American Law Institute

Adorns a "New Cloth" for Section 402A Products Liability Design Defects—A Survey of the States Reveals a Different Weave, 26 U. Mem. L. Rev. 493 (1996) (comprehensive survey of the states); Klemme, Comments to the Reporters and Selected Members of the Consultative Group, Restatement of Torts (Third): Products Liability, 61 Tenn. L. Rev. 1173 (1994); Vandall, The Restatement (Third) of Torts: Products Liability Section 2(b): The Reasonable Alternative Design Requirement, 61 Tenn. L. Rev. 1407, 1413–18 (1994).

**35.** For an extended discussion of this point, see the Products Liability Restatement Reporters' Note to § 2 cmt. *d*.

subsections 2(b) and (c) for design and warnings defects may be translated[36] as follows:

> A product is defective if its foreseeable risks of harm could have been reduced by the adoption of a reasonable alternative design (or warning) the omission of which renders the product not reasonably safe.

Converted to the active voice, the *Restatement's* liability standard for design and warnings defects reduces essentially to this:

> A product is defective if the seller could have reduced its foreseeable risks of harm by adopting a reasonable alternative design (or warning) the omission of which renders the product not reasonably safe.

The requirements of "foreseeability" and "reasonableness" in subsections 2(b) and 2(c) effectively reconvert the products liability standard for these types of cases to one of negligence—a rather remarkable retreat from § 402A's explicitly "strict" standard of liability of the *Second Restatement* that most courts boldly purported to apply to design and warnings cases for thirty years. Thus, while reaffirming the doctrine of strict tort liability for manufacturing defects in subsection 2(a), subsections 2(b) and 2(c) of the *Third Restatement* abandon the strict liability concept and apply negligence principles to design and warning cases.[37] This point is clearly made in comment *a* to § 1:

> [The strict liability] rule developed for manufacturing defects is inappropriate for [design and warnings claims]. These latter categories of cases require determinations that the product could have reasonably been made safer by a better design or instruction or warning.... [The definitions of defect in these cases] rely on a reasonableness test traditionally used in determining whether an actor has been negligent.[38]

Thus, the *Products Liability Restatement* grounds liability for design and warnings defects in the reasonableness-balancing-negligence concepts that properly dominate the law of tort.[39] Particularly in the context of design dangers, most courts have come to employ a "risk-utility" test for ascertaining whether such dangers are excessive or acceptable.[40] In most cases, this determination is based upon a cost-benefit analysis of

---

**36.** The Restatement's liability formulations are linguistically deconstructed in Defectiveness Restated at 766–76.

**37.** Design and warnings claims comprise the bulk of products liability causes of action. Together, such claims were found to comprise 60% of all claims in one study and 71% in another. In a study of large claims (in excess of $100,000) in which strict liability was the main theory of liability, defective design was the theory in 75% of the claims, and warning defects was the theory in 18%. See § 1.3, above.

**38.** Products Liability Restatement § 1 cmt. *a*.

**39.** The moral propriety of these principles is explained elsewhere. See Owen, Philosophical Foundations of Fault in Tort Law, in Philosophical Foundations of Tort Law 201 (Oxford, D. Owen ed., 1995); Owen, The Fault Pit, 26 Ga. L. Rev. 703 (1992); Moral Foundations, above.

**40.** For surveys of how different states define the risk-utility test, see the Products Liability Restatement Reporters' Note to § 2 cmt. *d* (concluding that most courts use risk-utility test), Owen, Risk–Utility Balancing in Design Defect Cases, 30 U. Mich. J. L. Reform 239 (1997) (hereinafter Risk–Utility Balancing) (same), and Vargo, 26 U. Mem. L. Rev. 493 (1996) (querulously challenging this conclusion).

the manufacturer's choice to forego a safety improvement that the plaintiff claims was necessary to render the design reasonably safe.[41] This reasonable-safer-design concept lies at the heart of the new *Restatement's* definition of design defectiveness in subsection 2(b).

Consumer expectations remain entitled to important respect in evaluating design and warning defect claims, but the comments to § 2 unceremoniously relieve consumer expectations of their elevated status as the test of liability under § 402A. Instead, the *Third Restatement*, following the approach of most courts,[42] relegates consumer expectations to the balancing calculus.[43] Many commentators vociferously complained of these definitional changes to the basic liability tests in subsections 2(b) and (c) (and related comments), fearful that these provisions in the new *Restatement* would jettison decades of consumer protection progress in this area of the law.[44] Yet, by shifting from "strict" liability to negligence principles, the *Products Liability Restatement* merely "restates" what most courts have long been doing if rarely saying.

It has been an open secret for many years that while purporting to apply "strict" liability doctrine to design and warnings cases, courts in fact have been applying principles that look remarkably like negligence.[45] That is, most courts in most contexts have been basing the defectiveness determination in both design and warnings cases on the risk-utility principles of balance, reasonableness, and foreseeability. Except in certain very limited contexts, the courts have rejected efforts to make manufacturers guarantors of product safety, requiring only that manufacturers (1) make their products as safe as they are reasonably able to do, and (2) warn of foreseeably material risks, by methods that are reasonably available and reasonably likely to be effective.[46] This is negligence, pure and simple, in fact if not in name. Consequently, by grounding liability for design and warnings defects in the principles of negligence, the new *Restatement* truly "restates" the law—no doubt quite differently from how most courts have stated the law to be, but in

**41.** How the cost-benefit test is and should be formulated is closely examined in Risk–Utility Balancing, and Owen, Toward a Proper Test for Design Defectiveness: "Micro–Balancing" Costs and Benefits, 75 Tex. L. Rev. 1661 (1997).

**42.** Compare Potter v. Chicago Pneumatic Tool Co., 694 A.2d 1319 (Conn. 1997) (retaining consumer expectations test in name, but redefining it in cost-benefit terms), discussed at § 8.6, below.

**43.** Risk-utility balancing normally is used only in design cases. See Products Liability Restatement § 2 cmt. *f*. While it applies in some respects to warnings cases, such cases are by their nature more fundamentally based on the frustration of expectations. Nevertheless, for a variety of good reasons, negligence principles properly govern warnings cases, too. See Moral Foundations at 465–67.

**44.** See, e.g., Little, The Place of Consumer Expectations in Product Strict Lia-

bility Actions for Defectively Designed Products, 61 Tenn. L. Rev. 1189 (1994).

**45.** See, e.g., Davis, Design Defect Liability: In Search of a Standard of Responsibility, 39 Wayne L. Rev. 1217, 1238–48 (1993); Powers, Jr., A Modest Proposal to Abandon Strict Products Liability, 1991 U. Ill. L. Rev. 639; Henderson and Twerski, Doctrinal Collapse in Products Liability: The Empty Shell of Failure to Warn, 65 N.Y.U. L. Rev. 265, 277–78 (1990); Birnbaum, Unmasking the Test for Design Defect: From Negligence (to Warranty) to Strict Liability to Negligence, 33 Vand. L. Rev. 593, 601 (1980). This divergence between illusory strict liability doctrine and actual liability principles is diagrammatically portrayed in The Fault Pit, 26 Ga. L. Rev. at 706.

**46.** In addition, of course, manufacturers must not misrepresent the safety of their products.

fact quite closely to how most courts functionally have applied the law in litigation.[47]

### The Basic Limitations on Liability—In General

In the jurisprudence of products liability law, the basic limitations on liability have proved at least as significant, and their contours have been litigated at least as frequently, as the basic definitions of defectiveness. A review of the law in this area would be incomplete without at least mentioning four of the most important boundary issues of products liability law: foreseeability, obvious dangers, product misuse and alteration, and inherent product dangers.

#### *Foreseeability*

Whether manufacturers should or should not be responsible in "strict" products liability for unforeseeable risks is an issue that has long divided courts and commentators.[48] Prior to the mid–1980s, most courts and many commentators assumed that the "strictness" of liability under § 402A precluded a defense based on the unforeseeability of the risk.[49] But two decisions in the mid–1980s, the first in New Jersey[50] and the second in California,[51] boldly renounced the illogic and unfairness of holding pharmaceutical manufacturers liable for harm they could neither anticipate nor prevent, and the California court subsequently expanded this fault-based principle to producers generally.[52] In recent years, while an occasional court still clings tenaciously to the notion that strict liability for defective design and warnings should not depend upon the foreseeability of the risk,[53] most courts squarely confronting the issue have shielded manufacturers from liability for harm caused by unfore-

---

**47.** At least one state supreme court has followed the *Third Restatement*'s lead in defining design defectiveness functionally and ignoring traditional theories of recovery. See Wright v. Brooke Group Ltd., 652 N.W.2d 159, 169 (Iowa 2002).

**48.** This issue variously has been posed in terms of "undiscoverable dangers" or of whether the discoverability of the risk was within the "state of the art."

**49.** From the initial adoption of the doctrine of strict products liability in tort during the mid–1960s, courts routinely made this point. But, in cases where liability was established, negligence or warranty doctrine typically was sufficient for liability on the facts, for there were usually fairly simple steps that the manufacturer reasonably could have taken to prevent the harm. The first noteworthy decision to emphasize and explain the "strictness" of strict tort liability for selling defective products, on facts where liability turned on the foreseeability of the risk, was Beshada v. Johns–Manville Prods. Corp., 447 A.2d 539 (N.J. 1982).

**50.** Feldman v. Lederle Lab., 479 A.2d 374 (N.J. 1984) (restricting *Beshada*, 447 A.2d 539, an asbestos case, to its facts).

**51.** Brown v. Superior Court, 751 P.2d 470 (Cal. 1988). To some extent, the California court backtracked doctrinally from *Brown* in Carlin v. Superior Court, 920 P.2d 1347 (Cal. 1996).

**52.** The California Supreme Court extended its rejection of true strict liability beyond prescription drugs to other products in Anderson v. Owens–Corning Fiberglas Corp., 810 P.2d 549 (Cal. 1991) (asbestos). *But cf. Carlin*, 920 P.2d 1347 (reaffirming the strict liability label).

**53.** See, e.g., Green v. Smith & Nephew AHP, Inc., 617 N.W.2d 881 (Wis. Ct. App. 2000); Kuhn v. Sandoz Pharm. Corp., 14 P.3d 1170 (Kan. 2000); Sternhagen v. Dow Co., 935 P.2d 1139, 1142–45 (Mont. 1997) (knowledge of danger, whether or not discoverable, is to be imputed to manufacturer; state-of-the-art evidence is not admissible to show that manufacturer could not have known of danger). Cf. Potter v. Chicago Pneumatic Tool Co., 694 A.2d 1319, 1348–49 (Conn. 1997) (manufacturer's conformance to state-of-the-art relevant to, but not conclusive on, liability).

seeable product risks.[54] The new *Restatement*'s explicit limitation of liability to foreseeable risks of harm in § 2, based on logic and fairness, thus in fact restates the law applied by most courts.[55]

### *Obvious Dangers*

Courts also hold that manufacturers should be protected, at least to some extent, from responsibility for accidents attributable to dangers that are obvious.[56] Almost all courts agree that manufacturers have no duty to warn of obvious dangers for the simple reason that there is no need to inform people further of dangers that a product on its face already displays.[57] The proper role of a danger's obviousness in determining defectiveness in design is far more difficult and subtle. Although the old no-duty rule for obvious dangers is now properly defunct as an independent doctrine in almost all jurisdictions, courts that test a product's design defectiveness according to consumer expectations are logically compelled to shield manufacturers from design liability in cases where the danger is apparent on the product's face.[58] As discussed above, however, most courts now ascertain a design's defectiveness according to some form of risk-utility balancing of the costs and benefits of adopting a proposed alternative design. Within this calculus, obviousness of danger is properly considered to be an important—but not necessarily decisive—factor in the ultimate balance that determines product defectiveness. The new *Restatement* adopts these widely accepted limitations that courts place on recovery for injuries from dangers that are obvious.[59]

**54.** Even the California decision that reaffirmed the doctrine of "strict" products liability, Carlin v. Superior Court, 920 P.2d 1347 (Cal. 1996), limits liability to risks which are foreseeable.

**55.** Comment *a* to § 2 provides in part: "For the liability system to be fair and efficient, most courts agree that the balancing of risks and benefits in judging product design and marketing must be done in light of the knowledge of risks and risk-avoidance techniques reasonably attainable at the time of distribution.... [M]anufacturers may persuasively ask to be judged by a normative behavior standard to which it is reasonably possible for manufacturers to conform. For these reasons, Subsections (b) and (c) speak of products being defective only when risks were reasonably foreseeable." Products Liability Restatement § 2 cmt. *a*; cf. id. § 2 cmt. *m*. For the propriety of this approach in moral theory, see Moral Foundations at 465–67, 483–84 and 490–92.

**56.** See Products Liability Restatement, § 2 cmt. *j*. In addition to dangers that are obvious, most of the same limiting principles apply to dangers that generally are known.

**57.** "When a risk is obvious or generally known, the prospective addressee of a warning will or should already know of its existence." Products Liability Restatement § 2 cmt. *j*.

**58.** Manufacturers are not liable in such cases because purchasers and users can hardly expect a product to be free of danger that is apparent for all to see. See, e.g., Sollami v. Eaton, 772 N.E.2d 215 (Ill. 2002); Vincer v. Ester Williams All–Aluminum Swimming Pool Co., 230 N.W.2d 794 (Wis. 1975) (young child climbed ladder and fell into above-ground swimming pool not equipped with simple self-latching gate at top of ladder).

**59.** For the warnings context, see Products Liability Restatement § 2 cmt. *j*, which provides in part: "In general, a product seller is not subject to liability for failing to warn or instruct regarding risks and risk avoidance measures that should be obvious to, or generally known by, foreseeable product users." For the design context, see id. § 2 cmt. *d*, which provides in part: "Subsection (b) does not recognize the obviousness of a design-related risk as precluding a finding of defectiveness. The fact that a danger is open and obvious is relevant to the issue of defectiveness, but does not necessarily preclude a plaintiff from establishing that a reasonable alternative design should have been adopted that would have reduced or prevented injury to the plaintiff."

### Product Misuse and Alteration

When people choose to use and abuse products in ways that are unforeseeable and unreasonable, courts generally relieve manufacturers of at least partial responsibility for resulting harm.[60] Products can hardly be designed to do all things safely for all people, and so product misuse and alteration provide important limitations on liability for the sale of defective products. While courts widely hold that manufacturers have a duty to adopt reasonable precautions against uses, misuses, and alterations that in fact are reasonably foreseeable, in general there is no duty to protect against uses and abuses that are not foreseeable. Moreover, the doctrine of proximate cause may apply to cases of third party misuse, barring liability altogether if the misuse was unforeseeable, and principles of comparative responsibility generally reduce a manufacturer's responsibility proportionate to the user's own fault for putting a product to an improper type or extent of use.[61] The *Products Liability Restatement* adopts these widespread views on the role of product alteration and misuse.[62]

### Inherent Product Dangers

A perplexing issue in the law of products liability is whether manufacturers should be held responsible for injuries resulting from inherent product hazards that are incapable of being designed or warned away. Many products, from simple kitchen knives and matches to complex chemicals and aircraft, may be classified as possessing such inherent dangers. In most such cases, however, the product's benefits so clearly outweigh its risks that liability for the product's general inherent risk is never litigated. Of late, however, courts and commentators are beginning to reevaluate whether manufacturers of certain unavoidably dangerous products should be liable for the harm they inevitably cause.[63] Surely the most notorious product of this type today is the cigarette, but alcoholic beverages, cheap handguns, and certain other products all might be viewed as inherently defective because they arguably cause more social harm than good.

Producers of such generically dangerous products argue that they are merely providing lawful goods consumers demand and, accordingly, that they should not be held accountable for harm from danger that is unavoidably part and parcel of the demanded product design. Some consumer advocates argue to the contrary that, while products of this

---

**60.** "Product sellers ... are not required to foresee and take precautions against every conceivable mode of use and abuse to which their products might be put. Increasing the costs of designing and marketing products in order to avoid the consequences of unreasonable modes of use is not required." Products Liability Restatement § 2 cmt. *m.* See chapters 14 and 15, below.

**61.** See Products Liability Restatement § 2 cmt. *p.*

**62.** See id. § 2 cmts. *m* (foreseeability of risk), *p* (misuse, modification, and alteration); id. § 15 (legal causation); id. § 17 (apportionment of responsibility). Damages

apportionment, treated generally in § 17 as an issue of comparative responsibility, is addressed thoroughly in its own Restatement. See Restatement (3d) Torts: Apportionment of Liability (2000).

**63.** See, e.g., Emery v. Federated Foods, Inc., 863 P.2d 426 (Mont. 1993) (5–2 decision) (marshmallow stuck in young child's throat; summary judgment for supplier reversed and case remanded for trial). See generally D. Owen, J. Montgomery, and M. Davis, Products Liability and Safety 440–71 (4th ed. 2004); Symposium, Generic Products Liability, 72 Chi.-Kent L. Rev. 3 (1996).

type (say, cigarettes or cheap handguns) may be "demanded" by consumers, such "goods" are inherently bad (defective) if the aggregate social harm they produce exceeds their aggregate benefit.[64] At bottom, this debate involves fundamental questions of separation of powers between the legislative and judicial branches of government, for arguably the decision of whether the harm from cigarettes should be paid for by cigarette manufacturers is properly a legislative rather than a judicial decision, if properly a governmental decision at all. Attitudes and the law are presently in substantial flux on responsibility for cigarette-caused harm,[65] but the courts historically have almost universally shut their doors to claims arising from generic product dangers which unavoidably inhere in a product's design.[66] Yet, this area of products liability law is in ferment, and it is difficult to predict how courts and legislatures will resolve this issue in particular contexts in the years ahead. On this intriguing issue, the *Restatement* adopts the prevailing view that, except in extreme cases,[67] and putting aside the special case of cigarettes, the courts have no business legislating the overall desirability of necessarily dangerous but widely-consumed products.[68]

### Product Safety Statutes and Regulations

The final basic liability provision in the new *Restatement*, § 4, addresses how a product's compliance or noncompliance with statutory or regulatory rules of product safety affects defectiveness. Subsection 4(a) provides that a product is defective if its design, warning, or instruction violates a product safety statute or safety regulation and a person is injured by the risk which the statute or regulation attempts to reduce. This section effectively converts the widespread, conventional doctrine of "negligence per se" into a new doctrine of "defectiveness per se."

Subsection (b) addresses the opposite issue, whether a manufacturer may successfully *defend* a case if the product's design, warning, or instruction *conforms* to some safety statute or regulation. Following the approach of virtually all courts, the new *Restatement* provides that compliance with such safety provisions is merely some evidence that the

---

**64.** See Bogus, War on the Common Law: The Struggle at the Center of Products Liability, 60 Mo. L. Rev. 1, 8–9 (1995).

**65.** See, e.g., Rabin, The Third Wave of Tobacco Tort Litigation, in Regulating Tobacco 176 (R. Rabin and S. Sugarman eds., 2001); G. Schwartz, Cigarette Litigation's Offspring: Assessing Tort Issues Related to Guns, Alcohol, & Other Controversial Products In Light of the Tobacco Wars, 27 Pepp. L. Rev. 751, 751 (2000); LeBel and Ausness, Toward Justice in Tobacco Policymaking: A Critique of Hanson and Logue and an Alternative Approach to the Costs of Cigarettes, 33 Ga. L. Rev. 693 (1999), critiquing Hanson and Logue, The Costs of Cigarettes: The Economic Case for Ex Post Incentive–Based Regulation, 107 Yale L.J. 1163 (1998); Symposium, 24 N. Ky. L. Rev. 1

(1997); Notes, 79 Tex. L. Rev. 1727 (2001), 49 S.C. L. Rev. 311 (1998).

**66.** In the rare instances where courts have allowed liability in these cases, legislatures generally have overturned the judicial decisions. See Products Liability Restatement § 2 cmt. *d* Reporters' Note.

**67.** Extreme cases involve products of "manifestly unreasonable design." Products Liability Restatement § 2 cmt. *e*. Such a product may be ruled defective because "the extremely high degree of danger posed by its use or consumption so substantially outweighs its negligible social utility that no rational, reasonable person, fully aware of the relevant facts, would choose to use, or to allow children to use, the product." Id.

**68.** On inherent product hazards, see § 10.3, below.

product is not defective, such that a defectiveness determination is still possible in many cases. The reasoning for this limited role for compliance with safety statutes and regulations is that such provisions generally prescribe merely the absolute minimum levels of acceptable safety, below which a manufacturer's conduct is criminalized. Thus, because such safety provisions generally do not attempt to reach the optimal level of safety contemplated by the law of negligence and "strict" products liability, a product's design or warnings may comport with the minimum required by the criminal safety statute or regulation yet still be unacceptably dangerous under notions of cost-effectiveness and reasonableness inherent in the principles of products liability law, a branch of common law developed and applied by the courts independent of statutory and regulatory law. Section 4 provides:

> § 4. Noncompliance and Compliance with Product Safety Statutes or Regulations
>
> In connection with liability for defective design or inadequate instructions or warnings:
>
> (a) a product's noncompliance with an applicable product safety statute or administrative regulation renders the product defective with respect to the risks sought to be reduced by the statute or regulation; and
>
> (b) a product's compliance with an applicable product safety statute or administrative regulation is properly considered in determining whether the product is defective with respect to the risks sought to be reduced by the statute or regulation, but such compliance does not preclude as a matter of law a finding of product defect.

In sum, §§ 1 through 4 of the *Products Liability Restatement* together comprise a framework of principles that resolve the great bulk of liability issues in ordinary products liability litigation.

After establishing basic products liability doctrine in §§ 1–4, the *Products Liability Restatement* addresses, in §§ 5–8, special principles governing the liability of sellers of particular types of products: component parts, prescription drugs, food, and used products. Next, in §§ 9–14, the *Restatement* covers such other special duty issues as misrepresentation, post-sale duties to warn and recall, and the responsibilities of successor enterprises and apparent manufacturers. Then, in §§ 15–18, it treats causation issues and affirmative defenses based on user misconduct and contractual disclaimers. The final sections, §§ 19–21, define "product," "seller," and "harm."

## Component Parts and Raw Materials

The courts have had a difficult time determining just when the supplier of a raw material (such as iron ore or asbestos) or a component part (such as a motor in an industrial machine) should bear responsibility for injuries from a defective product into which the material or component is integrated by an assembling manufacturer. The new *Restatement* takes a commonsense approach to this problem, holding a supplier liable (1) if the material or component is itself defective, or (2) if the supplier so substantially participates in the design of the integrated product that he becomes in essence a co-designer of the assembled product. Section 5 provides:

> § 5.  Liability of Commercial Seller or Distributor of Product Components for Harm Caused by Products Into Which Components Are Integrated
>
> One engaged in the business of selling or otherwise distributing product components who sells or distributes a component is subject to liability for harm to persons or property caused by a product into which the component is integrated if:
>
> (a) the component is defective in itself, as defined in this Chapter, and the defect causes the harm; or
>
> (b)(1) the seller or distributor of the component substantially participates in the integration of the component into the design of the product; and
>
> (2) the integration of the component causes the product to be defective, as defined in this Chapter; and
>
> (3) the defect in the product causes the harm.

## Defective Drugs and Medical Devices

Consistent with the developing law, sellers of prescription drugs (and medical devices, such as pacemakers) are accorded special protection in § 6 of the new *Restatement*. Although this section is quite long and technical, its main points may be summarized succinctly. In short, manufacturers of such products are subject to true strict liability for manufacturing defects in their products, just as sellers of other types of products. But, because the safety (and efficacy) of prescription drugs and medical devices are heavily regulated by a powerful governmental agency, the Food and Drug Administration (the FDA), which scrutinizes and regulates the "design" of prescription drugs and medical devices and the appropriate warnings and instructions that should accompany such products, courts have tended to treat manufacturers of such products somewhat differently than producers of normal products.

Courts have only infrequently held prescription drug manufacturers liable for *design* defects, and the new *Restatement* mirrors this perspective by strictly limiting design liability in § 6(c) to cases where a drug is shown to have no net value for *any* class of patient. Section 6(d) restates the widely accepted "learned intermediary" doctrine for warnings cases, by which a manufacturer generally is obligated to provide a warning only to the prescribing physician, not directly to the patient. Finally, § 6(e) provides that pharmacists and other retail sellers are subject only to negligence liability for selling such products containing design or warnings defects. Section 6 provides:

§ 6. Liability of Commercial Seller or Distributor for Harm Caused by Defective Prescription Drugs and Medical Devices

(a) A manufacturer of a prescription drug or medical device who sells or otherwise distributes a defective drug or medical device is subject to liability for harm to persons caused by the defect. A prescription drug or medical device is one that may be legally sold or otherwise distributed only pursuant to a health-care provider's prescription.

(b) For purposes of liability under Subsection (a), a prescription drug or medical device is defective if at the time of sale or other distribution the drug or medical device:

(1) contains a manufacturing defect as defined in § 2(a); or

(2) is not reasonably safe due to defective design as defined in Subsection (c); or

(3) is not reasonably safe due to inadequate instructions or warnings as defined in Subsection (d).

(c) A prescription drug or medical device is not reasonably safe due to defective design if the foreseeable risks of harm posed by the drug or medical device are sufficiently great in relation to its foreseeable therapeutic benefits that reasonable health-care providers, knowing of such foreseeable risks and therapeutic benefits, would not prescribe the drug or medical device for any class of patients.

(d) A prescription drug or medical device is not reasonably safe due to inadequate instructions or warnings if reasonable instructions or warnings regarding foreseeable risks of harm are not provided to:

(1) prescribing and other health-care providers who are in a position to reduce the risks of harm in accordance with the instructions or warnings; or

(2) the patient when the manufacturer knows or has reason to know that health-care providers will not be in a position to reduce the risks of harm in accordance with the instructions or warnings.

(e) A retail seller or other distributor of a prescription drug or medical device is subject to liability for harm caused by the drug or device if:

(1) at the time of sale or other distribution the drug or medical device contains a manufacturing defect as defined in § 2(a); or

(2) at or before the time of sale or other distribution of the drug or medical device the retail seller or other distributor fails to exercise reasonable care and such failure causes harm to persons.

## Food

The principal effect of § 7, the special section on food products, is its explicit adoption of the so-called "consumer expectations" test of liability for food containing injurious matter, such as the proverbial mouse in a bottle of Coke or a nail or a fish bone in a can of fish soup. Some states formerly applied a more mechanical liability test, the "foreign-natural" test, which held the seller liable only if the injurious substance was "foreign" to the food item, as a nail in fish soup. By the same token, if a substance "naturally" occurred in the product, such as a bone in fish soup, then consumers might fairly be on the lookout for it, and so consumers should be responsible for any resulting harm. Although this "foreign-natural" test often worked efficiently, fairly, and consistently with reasonable consumer expectations, sometimes it did not. Accordingly, courts have largely switched to the more functional, and more flexible, consumer expectations test in food cases of this type. Thus, the *Restatement*'s adoption of this test is consistent with the developed law on liability for the sale of defective food products. Section 7 provides:

> **§ 7. Liability of Commercial Seller or Distributor for Harm Caused by Defective Food Products**
>
> One engaged in the business of selling or otherwise distributing food products who sells or distributes a food product that is defective under § 2, § 3, or § 4 is subject to liability for harm to persons or property caused by the defect. Under § 2(a), a harm-causing ingredient of the food product constitutes a defect if a reasonable consumer would not expect the food product to contain that ingredient.

## Used Products

Retail sellers of used products often are far less able than manufacturers of new products to eliminate defects in their products, especially defects in design. Moreover, buyers of used automobiles and other products usually do not expect the product to have the same level of safety in all respects as such products when they were new. Accordingly, courts often treat sellers of used products more leniently in products liability cases than manufacturers of new products. Reflecting this perspective, § 8(a) provides as a general rule that sellers of used products are generally liable only if they are negligent, with the following limited exceptions: where consumers fairly *do* expect the same degree of safety as a new product (such as the buyer of an automobile used only for one week), § 8(b); where products are sold as "remanufactured," § 8(c); and where a consumer's injuries are attributable to the seller's violation of an applicable safety statute or regulation, § 8(d). Section 8 provides:

> **§ 8. Liability of Commercial Seller or Distributor of Defective Used Products**
>
> One engaged in the business of selling or otherwise distributing used products who sells or distributes a defective used product is subject to liability for harm to persons or property caused by the defect if the defect:
>
> (a) arises from the seller's failure to exercise reasonable care; or
>
> (b) is a manufacturing defect under § 2(a) or a defect that may be inferred under § 3 and the seller's

marketing of the product would cause a reasonable person in the position of the buyer to expect the used product to present no greater risk of defect than if the product were new; or

(c) is a defect under § 2 or § 3 in a used product remanufactured by the seller or a predecessor in the commercial chain of distribution of the used product; or

(d) arises from a used product's noncompliance under § 4 with a product safety statute or regulation applicable to the used product.

A used product is a product that, prior to the time of sale or other distribution referred to in this Section, is commercially sold or otherwise distributed to a buyer not in the commercial chain of distribution and used for some period of time.

## Misrepresentation

Section 9 concerns the liability of suppliers for misrepresentation. This section of the *Products Liability Restatement* broadly provides that the general principles of tortious misrepresentation apply to products liability cases. All states agree that a product seller is liable in tort for wrongful misrepresentation, that is, for fraudulent (intentional) and negligent misrepresentation. And all states, under the Uniform Commercial Code § 2–313 provision on express warranties, hold sellers liable in *contract* for damages caused by misrepresentation, without regard to fault. What is more questionable is whether a seller should also be liable in *tort* for misrepresentation in the absence of the seller's fault—that is, whether product sellers should be strictly liable in tort for misrepresentation.

The *Restatement (Second) of Torts*, in § 402B, promulgated by the American Law Institute in 1965, did provide for such a strict liability rule for a seller's public misrepresentations, in a more narrow provision than § 9 of the *Third Restatement*:

§ 402B. Misrepresentation by Seller of Chattels to Consumer

One engaged in the business of selling chattels who, by advertising, labels, or otherwise, makes to the public a misrepresentation of a material fact concerning the character or quality of a chattel sold by him is subject to liability for physical harm to a consumer of the chattel caused by justifiable reliance upon the misrepresentation even though

(a) it is not made fraudulently or negligently, and

(b) the consumer has not bought the chattel from or entered into any contractual relation with the seller.

Courts in a few states, notably in California, Texas, and Pennsylvania, adopted § 402B, but most have not. Instead, most states have left the doctrine of strict seller liability for misrepresentations to the law of contract and, in particular, to § 2–313 of the Uniform Commercial Code.

So, while perhaps noncontroversial at a substantive level (almost everyone agrees that sellers should be strictly liable for harm from misrepresentations), § 9 of the new *Restatement* "restates" the law logically but more boldly than it actually exists in most states. Section 9 will require courts to confront anew the issue of whether the doctrine of product seller responsibility for misrepresentation without fault should be left exclusively to the law of contract or whether instead the law of torts should be broadened to embrace the doctrine as well. Section 9 provides:

> **§ 9.  Liability of Commercial Product Seller or Distributor for Harm Caused by Misrepresentation**
>
> One engaged in the business of selling or otherwise distributing products who, in connection with the sale of a product, makes a fraudulent, negligent, or innocent misrepresentation of material fact concerning the product is subject to liability for harm to persons or property caused by the misrepresentation.

## Post-Sale Duty to Warn

The liability of sellers for defects that become known after the product is first designed and placed on the market is covered in §§ 10 and 11. Once a product is already on the market and in the hands of consumers, a manufacturer who discovers a defective condition in the product can do only one of two things to remedy the danger: (1) it can attempt to provide warnings to consumers who own the product, and/or (2) it can recall the product, to fix the defect or destroy the product.

Section 10 concerns the liability of a supplier for failing to warn of a danger discovered after the product was sold. Responsibility for post-sale warnings, in § 10(a), is controlled by the rules of negligence: a seller must warn in situations where it is "reasonable" to do so. However, rather than leave the issue of reasonableness in this context open-ended, the *Restatement* in § 10(b) follows a number of well-reasoned judicial opinions which particularize when the duty to warn will arise in this context according to a balance of certain prescribed factual issues: the existence of a substantial danger of which the seller is or should be aware, the probability that consumers will be unaware of the danger, and the feasibility of identifying and providing warnings to persons who possess the product. Section 10 provides:

> **§ 10.  Liability of Commercial Product Seller or Distributor for Harm Caused by Post–Sale Failure to Warn**
>
> (a) One engaged in the business of selling or otherwise distributing products is subject to liability for harm to persons or property caused by the seller's failure to provide a warning after the time of sale or distribution of a product if a reasonable person in the seller's position would provide such a warning.
>
> (b) A reasonable person in the seller's position would provide a warning after the time of sale if:

(1) the seller knows or reasonably should know that the product poses a substantial risk of harm to persons or property; and

(2) those to whom a warning might be provided can be identified and can reasonably be assumed to be unaware of the risk of harm; and

(3) a warning can be effectively communicated to and acted on by those to whom a warning might be provided; and

(4) the risk of harm is sufficiently great to justify the burden of providing a warning.

## Post-Sale Duty to Recall

Section 11 concerns a supplier's liability for failing to recall a product to remedy a defect. Although a couple of early decisions imposed a duty to recall on manufacturers of defective products under principles of negligence, there is very little judicial support for any duty to recall in the absence of a governmental order to do so. The new *Restatement* conforms to the majority view of those few states that have ruled on this issue, holding that a manufacturer's only duty to recall is when an administrative agency specifically requires the recall, as occurs from time to time and probably most frequently in the automotive industry regulated by the National Highway Traffic Safety Administration. The Food and Drug Administration and the Consumer Product Safety Commission also occasionally require manufacturers to recall defective products. Although the *Restatement* thus prescribes no general duty to recall, it does acknowledge the general principle of the law of negligence that, once a person voluntarily chooses to act, the person must act with reasonable care—hence the principle of § 11(2) that a seller who recalls a product is liable for doing so negligently. Section 11 provides:

§ 11.     Liability of Commercial Product Seller or Distributor for Harm Caused by Post–Sale Failure to Recall Product

One engaged in the business of selling or otherwise distributing products is subject to liability for harm to persons or property caused by the seller's failure to recall a product after the time of sale or distribution if:

(a)(1) a governmental directive issued pursuant to a statute or administrative regulation specifically requires the seller or distributor to recall the product; or

(2) the seller or distributor, in the absence of a recall requirement under Subsection (a)(1), undertakes to recall the product; and

(b) the seller or distributor fails to act as a reasonable person in recalling the product.

## Liability of Successor Corporations

Sections 12 and 13 concern the liability of a successor corporation for injuries caused by products sold by a predecessor company. Section 12 restates the widely accepted rule in the U.S. that a successor company that has merely purchased the assets of the predecessor (as opposed to merging or consolidating with it) is generally not liable for defects in products sold by the predecessor, subject to the four conventional exceptions. Section 12 provides:

> ### § 12.   Liability of Successor for Harm Caused by Defective Products Sold Commercially by Predecessor
>
> A successor corporation or other business entity that acquires assets of a predecessor corporation or other business entity is subject to liability for harm to persons or property caused by a defective product sold or otherwise distributed commercially by the predecessor if the acquisition:
>
> (a) is accompanied by an agreement for the successor to assume such liability; or
>
> (b) results from a fraudulent conveyance to escape liability for the debts or liabilities of the predecessor; or
>
> (c) constitutes a consolidation or merger with the predecessor; or
>
> (d) results in the successor becoming a continuation of the predecessor.

## Successor Post–Sale Duty to Warn

Section 13 addresses the limited situation in which a successor manufacturer has a duty to warn persons who possess products manufactured and sold by a predecessor corporation. If the successor corporation services its predecessor's products or otherwise undertakes some responsibility with respect to those products, then it fairly may be expected to act with reasonable care. Thus, the successor company in such a situation is obligated, under § 13, to act reasonably to warn according to the same principles as in § 10(b). Section 13 provides:

> ### § 13.   Liability of Successor for Harm Caused by Successor's Own Post–Sale Failure to Warn
>
> (a) A successor corporation or other business entity that acquires assets of a predecessor corporation or other business entity, whether or not liable under the rule stated in § 12, is subject to liability for harm to persons or property caused by the successor's failure to warn of a risk created by a product sold or distributed by the predecessor if:
>
> > (1) the successor undertakes or agrees to provide services for maintenance or repair of the product or enters into a similar relationship with purchasers of the predecessor's products giving rise to actual or potential economic advantage to the successor, and

(2) a reasonable person in the position of the successor would provide a warning.

(b) A reasonable person in the position of the successor would provide a warning if:

(1) the successor knows or reasonably should know that the product poses a substantial risk of harm to persons or property; and

(2) those to whom a warning might be provided can be identified and can reasonably be assumed to be unaware of the risk of harm; and

(3) a warning can be effectively communicated to and acted on by those to whom a warning might be provided; and

(4) the risk of harm is sufficiently great to justify the burden of providing a warning.

**Product Sponsorship**

Section 14 concerns the liability of a supplier of a product made by another under the supplier's name. This section adopts the principle of § 400 of the *Restatement (Second) of Torts*, which provides that sellers, such as large retailers, which market under their own names products manufactured by others are liable as if they were the manufacturer. Although trademark licensors are not liable under this provision, they are liable for injuries from defects in products sold under their trademarks or logos if such licensors substantially participate in the design, manufacture, or distribution of the product. The reasoning underlying these principles is that a product carrying a particular company's name, trademark, or logo represents that the indicated company is responsible in some manner for the product's quality. Section 14 provides:

§ 14. Selling or Distributing as One's Own a Product Manufactured by Another

One engaged in the business of selling or otherwise distributing products who sells or distributes as its own a product manufactured by another is subject to the same liability as though the seller or distributor were the product's manufacturer.

**Causation in General**

Section 15 merely provides, in general terms, that causation between a product defect and the plaintiff's harm is an important element necessary to any products liability claim. The American Law Institute did not address most specific issues of causation in this *Products Liability Restatement* because the issue of causation is treated in detail in the separate *Restatement (Third) of Torts* on the topics of "Apportionment" and "Liability for Physical Harm (Basic Principles)." Section 15 provides:

### § 15. General Rule Governing Causal Connection Between Product Defect and Harm

Whether a product defect caused harm to persons or property is determined by the prevailing rules and principles governing causation in tort.

## Causation of Additional Harm

Section 16 concerns a manufacturer's responsibility for increased harm ("enhanced injuries") caused by a product defect, the one particular causation topic addressed by the *Products Liability Restatement*. Arising most frequently in vehicular products liability cases (including cars, tractors, snowmobiles, etc.), the enhanced injury issue concerns the liability of a vehicle manufacturer (and retailer) for injuries attributable to the so-called "second collision." For example, suppose that an otherwise nondefective automobile is rammed on the side of the driver's door by a truck (the first collision), causing the automobile to roll over. Assume further that the driver's left arm is broken by the force of the collision and his neck is broken when the roof collapses on his head in the rollover (the *second* collision, between the occupant and the interior of the vehicle). The truck driver, of course, may be liable for all such foreseeable damages under ordinary principles of tort law. Section 16 addresses the separate issue of the liability of the automobile manufacturer, who may share responsibility with the truck driver.

Section 16(a) states the general rule that manufacturers may be liable for certain enhanced injuries in such situations. Section 16(b) provides that the automobile manufacturer in the situation above may (or may not) be responsible for the broken neck injuries, depending on whether the roof was designed with adequate strength for rollovers under ordinary principles of design defectiveness in § 2(b). However, even if the roof design was defective under § 2(b), the roof design did not cause the broken arm, and so § 16(b) provides that the manufacturer will not be liable for that particular "divisible" injury. Section 16(c) addresses the situation where the evidence establishes that the defectively designed roof was probably a substantial factor in causing the roof to collapse as hard as it did on the plaintiff's head, breaking his neck, but where the evidence further shows that a properly designed roof also would have collapsed somewhat, so that the driver's head or neck would have been injured to some extent anyway. In such a case, where causation of the neck injury by the accident and the defect is "indivisible," § 16(c) provides that the manufacturer responsible for the defect is fully liable for the indivisible (broken neck) harm. Finally, § 16(d) provides that a manufacturer liable under the principles of §§ 16(b) or 16(c) is jointly and severally liable, or severally liable, under the jurisdiction's prevailing rules on joint and several liability. Thus, the truck driver, but not the automobile manufacturer, would be subject to liability for the divisible injury of the broken arm. If the roof design were proven defective, and if this defect were proven to be a substantial cause of the plaintiff's broken neck, then the automobile manufacturer, depending on the jurisdiction's rule on joint and several liability, would be severally or jointly and severally liable with the truck driver for the plaintiff's broken neck. Section 16 provides:

§ 16.   Increased Harm Due to Product Defect

(a) When a product is defective at the time of commercial sale or other distribution and the defect is a substantial factor in increasing the plaintiff's harm beyond that which would have resulted from other causes, the product seller is subject to liability for the increased harm.

(b) If proof supports a determination of the harm that would have resulted from other causes in the absence of the product defect, the product seller's liability is limited to the increased harm attributable solely to the product defect.

(c) If proof does not support a determination under Subsection (b) of the harm that would have resulted in the absence of the product defect, the product seller is liable for all of the plaintiff's harm attributable to the defect and other causes.

(d) A seller of a defective product that is held liable for part of the harm suffered by the plaintiff under Subsection (b), or all of the harm suffered by the plaintiff under Subsection (c), is jointly and severally liable or severally liable with other parties who bear legal responsibility for causing the harm, determined by applicable rules of joint and several liability.

### Apportionment of Damages

Section 17, which concerns the apportionment of damages between the plaintiff, defendant, and others, adopts for products liability cases the comparative fault rule by which a plaintiff's damages are reduced proportionate to fault. This principle is consistent with the law in all but a handful of jurisdictions. Because the question of how damages are to be apportioned between multiple parties is treated in depth in the new *Restatement (Third) of Torts: Apportionment*, the specifics of apportionment (and the doctrine of assumption of risk) are not treated separately in the *Products Liability Restatement*. Section 17 provides:

§ 17.   Apportionment of Responsibility Between or Among Plaintiff, Sellers and Distributors of Defective Products, and Others

(a) A plaintiff's recovery of damages for harm caused by a product defect may be reduced if the conduct of the plaintiff combines with the product defect to cause the harm and the plaintiff's conduct fails to conform to generally applicable rules establishing appropriate standards of care.

(b) The manner and extent of the reduction under Subsection (a) and the apportionment of plaintiff's recovery among multiple defendants are governed by generally applicable rules apportioning responsibility.

## Contractual Disclaimers

Section 18 restates the prevailing rule applied to strict products liability cases in tort that contractual disclaimers and limitations of remedy have no affect on claims brought by plaintiffs injured in person by defective products. Because this section is limited to injury to persons, who have limited bargaining power, corporate plaintiffs who bring claims for property damage may still be bound by such contractual provisions. Section 18 provides:

> § 18. Disclaimers, Limitations, Waivers, and Other Contractual Exculpations as Defenses to Products Liability Claims for Harm to Persons
>
> Disclaimers and limitations of remedies by product sellers or other distributors, waivers by product purchasers, and other similar contractual exculpations, oral or written, do not bar or reduce otherwise valid products liability claims against sellers or other distributors of new products for harm to persons.

## "Product" Defined

In the concluding definitional sections, §§ 19—21, the *Products Liability Restatement* defines its borders and, hence, who and what are subject to its provisions. Thus, in § 19, the word "product" is defined, consistent with the developed case law, to include most movable personal property, but to exclude services (such as a doctor's implantation of a defective pacemaker), blood, and human tissue. The *Restatement* leaves products such as real property (for example, a defectively designed swimming pool) and electricity, which some courts have held as controlled by the rules of products liability law in certain contexts, subject to case-by-case treatment depending on the context. Section 19 provides:

> § 19.  Definition of "Product"
>
> For purposes of this Restatement:
>
> (a) A product is tangible personal property distributed commercially for use or consumption. Other items, such as real property and electricity, are products when the context of their distribution and use is sufficiently analogous to the distribution and use of tangible personal property that it is appropriate to apply the rules stated in this Restatement.
>
> (b) Services, even when provided commercially, are not products.
>
> (c) Human blood and human tissue, even when provided commercially, are not subject to the rules of this Restatement.

## Sellers and Distributors

Section 20 applies the *Restatement* to manufacturers, wholesalers, retailers, and other commercial transferors of products for ultimate consumption. It covers commercial lessors (such as rental car companies) and commercial bailors (such as laundromats charging a fee for the use of washing machines). The *Restatement* does not apply to a supermarket which provides shopping carts merely as a convenience to its customers, nor institutions (such as banks) that merely provide financing for product purchases, nor to product advertisers or auctioneers. Section 20 provides:

§ 20.   Definition of "One Who Sells or Otherwise Distributes"

For purposes of this Restatement:

(a) One sells a product when, in a commercial context, one transfers ownership thereto either for use or consumption or for resale leading to ultimate use or consumption. Commercial product sellers include, but are not limited to, manufacturers, wholesalers, and retailers.

(b) One otherwise distributes a product when, in a commercial transaction other than a sale, one provides the product to another either for use or consumption or as a preliminary step leading to ultimate use or consumption. Commercial nonsale product distributors include, but are not limited to, lessors, bailors, and those who provide products to others as a means of promoting either the use or consumption of such products or some other commercial activity.

(c) One also sells or otherwise distributes a product when, in a commercial transaction, one provides a combination of products and services and either the transaction taken as a whole, or the product component thereof, satisfies the criteria in Subsection (a) or (b).

## Economic Loss

The final section of the *Products Liability Restatement*, § 21, addresses the responsibility of a supplier for economic loss. Courts have routinely permitted recovery in products liability tort actions for personal injury, property loss, and any accompanying economic loss (most typically, lost earnings) resulting from the injury. Increasingly, courts have also permitted spouses, and sometimes parents or children, to recover damages for their own relationship ("consortium") damages with the injured person. Courts also permit punitive damages in appropriate cases, but those damages lie outside the scope of the *Products Liability Restatement*.

In the early years of products liability in America, in the 1960s and 1970s, courts were split on whether the *Restatement (Second) of Torts* § 402A should apply to "pure" economic loss, as when a manufacturing company suffered production losses due to a defect in an industrial machine purchased from the manufacturer of such machines. Over time, courts have moved strongly toward the position that strict products liability in tort should *not* apply to such pure economic losses which instead should be addressed by the law of contract. Adopting this majority position, the *Products Liability Restatement* provides for the recovery of compensatory damages for personal injury, consortium losses to family members, property damage, and economic loss flowing therefrom, but not for pure economic loss. Section 21 provides:

> § 21.  Definition of "Harm to Persons or Property": Recovery for Economic Loss
>
> For purposes of this Restatement, harm to persons or property includes economic loss if caused by harm to:
>
> (a) the plaintiff's person; or
>
> (b) the person of another when harm to the other interferes with an interest of the plaintiff protected by tort law; or
>
> (c) the plaintiff's property other than the defective product itself.

## Conclusion

The *Restatement (Third) of Torts: Products Liability* provides an encyclopedia of products liability law in America as it stood at the threshold of the twenty-first century. The black letter provisions set forth above provide a skeleton of the law which is elaborated in copious comments and reporters' notes. There simply is no more fruitful place to begin a study of products liability law than in the *Products Liability Restatement*.

# Chapter 7

# MANUFACTURING DEFECTS

*Table of Sections*

## § 7.1   MANUFACTURING DEFECTS—GENERALLY

Manufacturing defects, flaws or irregularities in products arising from errors in production,[1] give rise to the most basic type of products liability claim. For example, the misalignment of a punch press may result in a jagged burr along a product's metal edge;[2] the misadjustment of a nut on a bolt may interfere with a machine's operation;[3] and the failure to prevent foreign matter from entering food or drink may cause its contamination.[4] Tire failures sometimes are the result of defective

---

**§ 7.1**

**1.** See, e.g., Colon ex rel. Molina v. BIC USA, Inc., 199 F.Supp.2d 53, 85 (S.D.N.Y. 2001) ("[T]he plaintiff must show that a specific product unit was defective as a result of 'some mishap in the manufacturing process itself, improper workmanship, or because defective materials were used in construction,' and that the defect was the cause of plaintiff's injury; in other words, a manufacturing flaw exists when the unit in question deviates in quality and other performance standards from all of the other identical units."); Wheeler v. HO Sports Inc., 232 F.3d 754, 757 (10th Cir. 2000) (Okla. law) ("A product is defective in manufacture if it 'deviates in some material way from its design or performance standards.'"); Wood v. Old Trapper Taxi, 952 P.2d 1375, 1379–80 (Mont. 1997) ("the central question is whether the product is flawed due to improper construction [generating] 'imperfections that inevitably occur in a typically small percentage of products of a given design as a result of the fallibility of the manufacturing process.'"); Lyall v.

Leslie's Poolmart, 984 F.Supp. 587, 593 (E.D. Mich. 1997) ("A manufacturing defect claim relates to quality control; it requires proof that the product was an anomaly that failed to conform to the manufacturer's own standards."); Miles v. Ford Motor Co., 922 S.W.2d 572, 585 (Tex. App. 1996) (product "does not conform to the manufacturer's design standards [or] blueprints"), rev'd in part on other grounds, 967 S.W.2d 377 (Tex. 1998).

Some state statutes provide liability for manufacturing defects, usually defining such defects in terms of departure from intended design. See § 7.3, below.

**2.** See, e.g., Ford Motor Co. v. Zahn, 265 F.2d 729 (8th Cir. 1959) (Minn. law) (jagged burr on car's dashboard ashtray).

**3.** See, e.g., Jenkins v. General Motors Corp., 446 F.2d 377 (5th Cir. 1971) (Ga. law) (inadequately torqued nut on bolt in suspension system that resulted in bolt falling out and loss of steering).

**4.** See, e.g., Brayman v. 99 W., Inc., 116 F.Supp.2d 225 (D. Mass. 2000) (piece of

manufacturing.[5] When the manufacturing process goes awry, the resulting products may fail to meet the manufacturer's own design specification standards. If such a product escapes the manufacturer's quality controls, its flawed condition may lead to its failure during use, to an accident, and possibly to an injury to the user or another.

Responsibility for manufacturing defects is the most fundamental obligation of product manufacturers. The law governing production errors is now quite settled, and it fairly may be viewed as the first pillar of modern products liability law.[6] In general, manufacturers and other suppliers are liable for injuries caused by manufacturing defects in products that they sell.[7]

*Keeler v. Richards Mfg. Co., Inc.*,[8] which involved a surgical compression screw, is an illustrative manufacturing defect case. The screw broke several months after a surgeon inserted it into the plaintiff's broken hip to assist the healing process. In the plaintiff's action against the manufacturer, her experts testified that the screw had four irregularities they considered manufacturing defects, any one of which could have caused the failure by increasing stress concentrations that could have led to fatigue failure in the screw: (1) the screw's internal threads were longer (1.1875 inches) than the maximum length (1.125 inches) specified in the blueprint specifications; (2) the screw contained excessive metal debris which could have interfered with the surgeon's ability to compress the screw properly, leading to excess movement of the bones; (3) its radius was slightly less than the exemplar screw furnished by the manufacturer; and (4) it failed to comply with the American Society of Testing Materials 35% ductility standard. The jury concluded that the screw was defectively manufactured, and the court upheld this determination on appeal.

In former times, from ancient Rome through medieval England and into early American law of the nineteenth and early twentieth centuries, the incipient law of products liability (much of which involved defective

---

glass in mashed potatoes), aff'd, 26 Fed. Appx. 24 (1st Cir. 2002); Cooper v. Borden, Inc., 709 So.2d 878 (La. Ct. App. 1998) (penicillin in milk).

**5.** See 7A Am. Law Prod. Liab. 3d § 98 (1999). For example, a rash of failures of Bridgestone/Firestone tires on Ford Explorers probably resulted in part from various irregularities in the production process. While manufacturing defects appear to have been involved in many of the failures, the evidence suggests that various design shortcomings also played a major role. See, e.g., Safety Assurance Office of Defects Investigation, Nat'l Highway Traffic Safety Admin., U.S. Dep't of Transp., Engineering Analysis Report and Initial Decision Regarding EA00–023: Firestone Wilderness AT Tires 29–30 (2001) (suggesting design defects in the Wilderness AT Tires); Kruegar and Mas, Strikes, Scabs, and Tread Separation: Labor Strike and The Production of Defective Bridgestone/Firestone

Tires (Jan. 9, 2002) (unpublished paper, Princeton Univ.) (finding a correlation between a labor dispute at the Decateur Bridgestone/Firestone plant and an inordinately high proportion of manufacturing defects during the period of the dispute).

**6.** Owen, The Moral Foundations of Products Liability Law: Toward First Principles, 68 Notre Dame L. Rev. 427, 467–68, 473–74, 502–03 (1993).

**7.** On liability for manufacturing defects, see 2 Frumer and Friedman, Products Liability § 11.02; 1 Madden & Owen on Products Liability Law ch. 7; 2 Am. Law Prod. Liab. ch. 31; C.J. Miller and R. Goldberg, Product Liability ch. 11 (Oxford, 2d ed. 2004) (British law); Products Liability Restatement §§ 2(a) and 3. For an earlier version of this chapter, see Owen, Manufacturing Defects, 53 S.C. L. Rev. 851 (2002).

**8.** 817 F.2d 1197 (5th Cir. 1987) (Tex. law).

food and drink) was largely comprised of cases involving physical flaws or defects.[9] With the advent of modern products liability law during the mid–1900s,[10] manufacturing defect cases for a variety of reasons began to occupy a decreasing proportion of products liability litigation as the plaintiffs' bar increasingly challenged the sufficiency of product designs and warnings.[11] This proportional decline in manufacturing defect cases in part reflects improvements in the technology of production engineering, including quality assurance. Moreover, as discussed below, the liability standards governing manufacturing flaw cases are generally quite clear and noncontroversial—there usually is little debate over whether a product containing a physical flaw is "defective." Thus, manufacturing flaw cases are more likely to settle than design and warnings defects cases which by nature involve normative judgments of safety sufficiency. Disputes in manufacturing defect cases normally involve the sufficiency of evidence of causation—whether the product in fact contained a manufacturing flaw attributable to the manufacturer, and, if so, whether that flaw caused the plaintiff's harm.[12] Such factual determinations are peculiarly committed to jury determination and usually are upheld on appeal.[13]

Manufacturing defect claims possess certain advantages for plaintiffs over claims involving design and warnings defects. First, neither the plaintiff nor the defendant will need to invest as much in litigating a manufacturing defect claim since it challenges only a single product unit

---

**9.** See, e.g., Lewis v. Terry, 43 P. 398 (Cal. 1896) (folding bed's legs failed to lock into place); Schubert v. J.R. Clark Co., 51 N.W. 1103 (Minn. 1892) (step ladder constructed of cross-grained and decaying lumber); Devlin v. Smith, 89 N.Y. 470 (1882) (planks on painter's scaffold nailed rather than lashed down); Langridge v. Levy, 150 Eng. Rep. 863 (Ex. 1837), aff'd, 150 Eng. Rep. 1458 (Ex. 1838) (defective gun fraudulently represented as safe); Osgood v. Lewis, 2 Harr. & G. 495, 519 (Md. 1829) (inferior cooking oil sold as higher grade oil); Van Bracklin v. Fonda, 12 Johns. 468 (N.Y. 1815) (contaminated beef). On early law generally, see § 1.2, above. The development of warranty law liability for selling defective foodstuffs is examined in § 5.2, above. See also § 7.5, below.

In the twentieth century, the classic products liability cases involved manufacturing defects. See, e.g., MacPherson v. Buick Motor Co., 111 N.E. 1050 (N.Y. 1916) (collapse of car's wheel made of defective wood—negligence); Henningsen v. Bloomfield Motors, Inc., 161 A.2d 69 (N.J. 1960) (defect in car's steering system—implied warranty). In Greenman v. Yuba Power Prods., Inc., 377 P.2d 897 (Cal. 1963), it is unclear whether the set screws were "inadequate" because of a defect in manufacture or design.

**10.** Even in the 1950s, manufacturing defects still dominated products liability lit-

igation. See Wilson, Products Liability (pt. 1): The Protection of the Injured Person, 43 Cal. L. Rev. 614, 636 (1955) ("The chief concern is, of course, negligent manufacture, the insecure attachment of a device on a machine, the introduction of a foreign substance in a loaf of bread, the use of a harmful chemical in a cosmetic.").

**11.** See Priest, Strict Products Liability: The Original Intent, 10 Cardozo L. Rev. 2301 (1989); Twerski, Weinstein, Donaher and Piehler, The Use and Abuse of Warnings in Products Liability: Design Defect Comes of Age, 61 Cornell L. Rev. 495 (1976); Henderson, Judicial Review of Manufacturers' Conscious Design Choices: The Limits of Adjudication, 73 Colum. L. Rev. 1531 (1973); Noel, Manufacturer's Negligence of Design or Directions for Use of a Product, 71 Yale L.J. 816 (1962).

**12.** On causation issues, see ch. 11, below.

**13.** See, e.g., Jenkins v. General Motors Corp., 446 F.2d 377 (5th Cir. 1971) (Ga. law) (upholding jury's determination that crash was caused by defective suspension system rather than by driver inattention); Shoshone Coca-Cola Bottling Co. v. Dolinski, 420 P.2d 855 (Nev. 1966) (upholding jury's rejection of bottler's theory that third-party tamperer put mouse in bottle of Squirt).

rather than the entire line of products.[14] In addition, and quite unlike design and warnings cases, the liability standards for manufacturing defects—departure from intended design[15] and product malfunction[16]— are still explicitly "strict."[17] Moreover, manufacturing defect claims may be immune from certain types of requirements, limitations, or defenses applicable to other types of claims.[18] Nor can it be doubted that moral imperatives normally favor recovery for plaintiffs injured by physical flaws in the products they buy and use. Manufacturers deliberately select the level of manufacturing flaws in their products by the level of investment they choose to make in the quality of their production and quality control processes.[19] For this reason, and because buyers reasonably expect that the products they purchase will be free of defects, principles of fairness, truth, and restitution all suggest manufacturers should compensate persons injured by production defects.[20]

For these reasons, and to avoid the cost and publicity of litigation with a low probability of success, a manufacturer persuaded that a physical flaw in one of its products injured a claimant normally will be amenable to settling the case. But a manufacturer is likely to litigate a case involving a physically flawed product if it believes (1) that its product was not in fact defective;[21] (2) that, even if the product was defective, the plaintiff's harm was caused by something other than the defect;[22] (3) that, even if a product defect caused the plaintiff's harm,

**14.** This difference gives rise to a rule in some jurisdictions exempting manufacturing defect claims from the rule that prohibits evidence of subsequent improvements in design. See, e.g., Cramer v. Toledo Scale Co., 551 N.Y.S.2d 718 (App. Div. 1990); Cover v. Cohen, 461 N.E.2d 864 (N.Y. 1984).

**15.** See § 7.3, below.

**16.** See § 7.4, below.

**17.** See §§ 6.2 and 6.5, above.

**18.** For example, a state-of-the-art defense may not be applicable to manufacturing defect claims. See, e.g., Falada v. Trinity Indus., Inc., 642 N.W.2d 247 (Iowa 2002) (state of the art was no defense to manufacturing defect claim that an ammonia tank was welded improperly); N.J. Stat. Ann. § 2A:58C–3 (certain state-of-the-art defenses applies only to design dangers). Nor, of course, do manufacturing defect claims require proof of alternative designs. See, e.g., Ridgway v. Ford Motor Co., 82 S.W.3d 26 (Tex. App. 2002) (plaintiff need not produce evidence of a reasonable alternative design to succeed on claim that automobile's ignition switch was defectively manufactured), rev'd on other grounds, 135 S.W.3d 598 (Tex. 2004); Colon ex rel. Molina v. BIC USA, Inc., 199 F.Supp.2d 53 (S.D.N.Y. 2001) (the existence of some better alternative design is "obviously" not an element in a case alleging that a butane lighter was defectively manufactured).

**19.** See Cowan, Some Policy Bases of Products Liability, 17 Stan. L. Rev. 1077, 1086–92 (1965).

**20.** See Owen, The Moral Foundations of Products Liability Law: Toward First Principles, 68 Notre Dame L. Rev. 427, 467–68, 473–74, 502–03 (1993) (explaining moral bases of manufacturer liability for manufacturing defects).

**21.** See cases in note 41, below.

**22.** See, e.g., Calhoun v. Honda Motor Co., 738 F.2d 126 (6th Cir. 1984) (Ky. law) (plaintiff failed to establish that defective brakes caused motorcycle accident). Compare Church v. Martin–Baker Aircraft Co., Ltd., 643 F.Supp. 499 (E.D. Mo. 1986) (death of fighter pilot who ejected from plane could have been caused by defective ejection seat or by external wind blasts); Crocker v. Sears, Roebuck & Co. 346 So.2d 921 (Miss. 1977) (fire that destroyed plaintiff's house could just as plausibly have been started by recent rewiring of house, or by defective installation of stove, as by defect in the stove itself); Price v. Ashby's Inc., 354 P.2d 1064, 1065 (Utah 1960) (hole in airlift line caused one side of automobile to sink lower than the other, but there was no proof that this defect—rather than driver error—caused car to continue straight at bend in road: "With two or more possible causes such as an inattentive driver and a mechanical defect ... proof that it may have been either is not proof that it was in fact either.").

someone or something other than the manufacturer caused the defect after the product left the manufacturer's control;[23] or (4) that the plaintiff's damages claim is unreasonable.[24]

A manufacturer may breach its duty to manufacture "nondefective" products in various ways. First, the raw materials or components used to construct the product may contain physical flaws. For example, the materials of which the product is comprised—such as the defective wooden spoke of the car wheel in *MacPherson v. Buick Motor Co.*[25]—may contain weaknesses or impurities.[26] Similarly, the product may become damaged[27] or contaminated[28] during construction. Third, although a

**23.** See, e.g., Cincinnati Cos. v. Ford Motor Co., 2001 WL 227362 (Ohio Ct. App. 2001) (electrical short-circuit in car caused fire; summary judgment for defendant affirmed as to manufacturing defect because plaintiff failed to show that defect existed when car left manufacturer's control); Maher v. General Motors Corp., 346 N.E.2d 833 (Mass. 1976) (steering suddenly locking failed to establish defect at time of sale since steering had been serviced on three occasions). See also note 42, below.

**24.** There is little other explanation for many of the cases, often involving defective foodstuffs, where proof of a true manufacturing defect causing plaintiff's harm (including emotional distress) is clear. See, e.g., Brayman v. 99 W., Inc., 116 F.Supp.2d 225 (D. Mass. 2000) (piece of glass in mashed potatoes; court rejected excessiveness challenge, with respect to verdict of $25,000, for cut in diner's throat), aff'd, 26 Fed.Appx. 24 (1st Cir. 2002); Kroger Co. v. Beck, 375 N.E.2d 640 (Ind. Ct. App. 1978) (hypodermic needle in beef; $2700 not excessive, despite absence of physical injury, for prick in housewife's throat).

**25.** 111 N.E. 1050 (N.Y. 1916). Compare Bell v. T.R. Miller Mill Co., Inc., 768 So.2d 953 (Ala. 2000) (telephone pole which broke, causing accident, was made of wood containing pre-manufacture decay and bursts).

**26.** See, e.g., Benitez v. Synthes, Inc., 199 F.Supp.2d 1339 (M.D. Fla. 2002) (surgical rod containing fractures and cracks); Rudd v. General Motors Corp., 127 F.Supp.2d 1330 (M.D. Ala. 2001) (defective steel in pickup truck's fan blade); Pouncey v. Ford Motor Co., 464 F.2d 957 (5th Cir. 1972) (Ala. law) (same).

**27.** See, e.g., Fillebrown v. Steelcase, Inc., 63 Fed.Appx. 54 (3d Cir. 2003) (N.J. law) (machining marks on metal spindle connecting base of chair to seat); Chapman v. Maytag Corp., 2000 WL 1038183 (S.D. Ind. 2000) (pinched wire in stove), aff'd, 297 F.3d 682 (7th Cir. 2002); Simon v. Coppola, 876 P.2d 10 (Colo. Ct. App. 1993) (crimp in hot tub thermostat actuator allowed water to overheat); Hewitt v. B.F. Goodrich Co.,

732 F.2d 1554 (11th Cir. 1984) (Fla. law) (tire bead bundle broke during manufacturing process).

**28.** See, e.g., Flagstar Enter., Inc. v. Davis, 709 So.2d 1132 (Ala. 1997) (biscuit and gravy contaminated with human blood); Glover v. BIC Corp., 6 F.3d 1318 (9th Cir. 1993) (Or. law) (brass chips left inside body of disposable lighter could cause it to fail to extinguish); Williams v. Volkswagenwerk AG, 226 Cal.Rptr. 306 (Ct. App. 1986) (foreign substance cluster in metal near break point); Simpson v. Logan Motor Co., 192 A.2d 122 (D.C. 1963) (foreign substance in hydraulic fluid); Trowbridge v. Abrasive Co. of Philadelphia, 190 F.2d 825 (3d Cir. 1951) (Pa. law) (abrasive wheel disintegrated due to trapped gases which generated internal fissures and cracks).

It is important to note that the mere presence of impurities in any amount does not automatically render a product legally defective. "[T]he concept of defect is not self-defining when a product contains a flaw. Since all products are flawed at some technological level, the decision must still be made as to when a flaw emerges as a defect. In order to make this decision, some judgmental standard must be utilized." Weinstein, Twerski, Piehler and Donaher, Product Liability: An Interaction of Law and Technology, 12 Duq. L. Rev. 425, 430–31 (1974). "To a metallurgist all metallic structures contain flaws or irregularities at some size level. They range from dislocations at the atomic size level to cracks visible to the naked eye.... Since these flaws [unfortunately sometimes called *defects* by metallurgists] can be identified in all products, the critical question to be asked is when can these deviations from structural perfection really lead to a conclusion of [legal] defect." Id. at n.11. "Materials processing and fabrication are thus based upon flaw or irregularity control to achieve an economically feasible trade-off among all the properties of the material which, together with proper design, serve to achieve a given performance requirement.... [Thus], the mere presence of an identifiable

product's components individually may be free of flaws, a mistake may be made in how they are assembled into final form. This is the most common type of manufacturing defect case. Thus, the ingredients in a particular batch may deviate from the specified formulation;[29] the rivets, welds, screws, bolts, or nuts used to hold components together may be improperly made, applied, inserted, or attached weakening the product's assembly;[30] or the product's components may otherwise be assembled improperly.[31] Fourth, after assembly, an otherwise properly produced product may not be finished sufficiently, leaving its edges too rough, too sharp, or otherwise hazardous.[32] Finally, a properly assembled and finished product may be rendered defective because of a dangerous flaw in its package or container.[33]

The quality control process is designed to catch such manufacturing mistakes, but sometimes it fails to do so. And while insufficient quality control may provide the basis for a claim of negligence,[34] a manufacturer's failure to adequately inspect or test its products is not itself a

---

irregularity or flaw in a metallic structure is in and of itself an insufficient basis for the establishment of defect." Id. at 432 n.11(4).

**29.** See, e.g., Reiter v. Zimmer Inc., 897 F.Supp. 154 (S.D.N.Y. 1995) (improper proportion of ingredients in batch of bone cement).

**30.** See, e.g., Dieker v. Case Corp., 73 P.3d 133 (Kan. 2003) (failure to fully tighten nut on combine's hydraulic valve caused fire); Benson v. Tennessee Valley Elec. Coop., 868 S.W.2d 630 (Tenn. Ct. App. 1993) (defective weld in aerial boom unit failed in part because repair weld too weak); Harley–Davidson Motor Co. v. Wisniewski, 437 A.2d 700 (Md. Ct. Spec. App. 1981) (cross-threaded screw on throttle clamp fractured); Jenkins v. General Motors Corp., 446 F.2d 377 (5th Cir. 1971) (Ga. law) (improperly tightened nut on bolt caused suspension assembly to fail); O'Donnell v. Geneva Metal Wheel Co., 183 F.2d 733 (6th Cir. 1950) (Ohio law) (wheel barrow tire exploded because metal rivets holding rim together were weakened during assembly by pressing the metal too thin which generated visible radial cracks).

**31.** See, e.g., Ford Motor Co. v. Massey, 855 S.W.2d 897 (Ark. 1993) (stiffness of truck throttle cable caused vehicle to lurch into plaintiff); Yamaha Motor Co. v. Thornton, 579 So.2d 619 (Ala. 1991) (motorcycle speed reduction plate left out in manufacture); Gasque v. Heublein, Inc., 315 S.E.2d 556 (S.C. Ct. App. 1984) (wire hood attached improperly to stopper in bottle of sparkling wine); Horne v. Liberty Furniture Co., 452 So.2d 204 (La. Ct. App. 1984) (chair parts improperly glued together); Willis v. Floyd Brace Co., 309 S.E.2d 295 (S.C. Ct. App. 1983) (leg brace locking mechanism, the component parts of which

were improperly aligned); Hall v. Chrysler Corp., 526 F.2d 350 (5th Cir. 1976) (La. law) (misrouted transmission cable on truck came into contact with exhaust manifold, which melted cable and caused transmission to lock in "drive" position although gear lever indicated "park").

**32.** See, e.g., Stazenski v. Tennant Co., 617 So.2d 344 (Fla. Dist. Ct. App. 1993) (worker cut on sharp edge of industrial sweeper); McBurnette v. Playground Equip. Corp., 130 So.2d 117 (Fla. Dist. Ct. App. 1960), rev'd in part on other grounds, 137 So.2d 563 (Fla. 1962) (child's finger cut off by sharp edge of swing). Compare Tibbetts v. Ford Motor Co., 358 N.E.2d 460 (Mass. Ct. App. 1976) (rough inner edges of wheel covers; not dangerous for intended purpose).

**33.** See, e.g., DeWitt v. Eveready Battery Co., 565 S.E.2d 140 (N.C. 2002) (acid leaked from battery case onto plaintiff); Helm v. Pepsi–Cola Bottling Co. of St. Louis, Inc., 723 S.W.2d 465 (Mo. Ct. App. 1986) (bottles fell through cardboard carton, and exploding glass injured plaintiff). See also Ebenhoech v. Koppers Indus., Inc., 239 F.Supp.2d 455 (D.N.J. 2002) (tank car is the "packaging" for hazardous chemical that left slippery residue on top of tank car from which plaintiff fell).

**34.** Because quality control procedures are an important component of the production process, employed to catch defectively manufactured products before distribution to users, evidence of inadequate quality control may be especially relevant to negligent manufacturing claims. See, e.g., Jones v. United Metal Recyclers, 825 F.Supp. 1288, 1298 (W.D. Mich. 1993) (negligent failure to inspect for defects; summary judgment denied); Ford Motor Co. v. Zahn, 265 F.2d 729, 731 (8th Cir. 1959) (Minn. law). See § 2.3, above.

products liability claim.[35] A manufacturer's evidence of *good* quality control might seem to be logically irrelevant to a strict products liability claim, since the issue in such cases is the defectiveness of the product and not the manufacturer's conduct in allowing the defect to arise.[36] Nevertheless, especially in cases involving allegations of foreign objects or contamination in foodstuffs, such evidence may be admissible, even on strict liability in tort or breach of warranty,[37] if it tends to show that the manufacturer is not responsible for the defect, to wit, that the defect (if any) probably arose after the product left the manufacturer's control.[38]

As mentioned earlier, issues related to causation rather than defectiveness typically dominate cases based on claims of manufacturing defects. Especially if the product accident destroys direct evidence of why an accident occurred, the crucial issue is often whether the plaintiff's proof sufficiently establishes that the accident was attributable to a manufacturing defect as opposed to some other plausible cause—such as normal wear and tear or the conduct of the user or someone else. In general, a plaintiff must establish, by a reasonable probability, that the product contained a defect attributable to the manufacturer and that such hypothesis is more likely than any other suggested by the evidence.[39] If a product dangerously malfunctions, but the plaintiff is unable to prove the existence of a specific defect, the malfunction doctrine may provide relief if the plaintiff can eliminate other normal causes of such malfunctions, as discussed below.[40] Yet an allegation of a manufacturing defect properly will be dismissed if the plaintiff fails to prove, one way or another, that the product contained a defect[41] that caused the

---

**35.** There is no separate claim for defective quality control. See, e.g., Valentine v. Baxter Healthcare Corp., 81 Cal.Rptr.2d 252, 264 (Ct. App. 1999); Kociemba v. G.D. Searle & Co., 707 F.Supp. 1517, 1527 (D. Minn. 1989).

**36.** See, e.g., Nave v. Rainbo Tire Serv., Inc., 462 N.E.2d 620 (Ill. App. Ct. 1984).

**37.** "In an action based on breach of warranty, it is of course necessary to show not only the existence of the warranty but the fact that the warranty was broken and that the breach of warranty was the proximate cause of the loss sustained. . . . [E]vidence indicating that the seller exercised care in the manufacture, processing or selection of the goods is relevant to the issue of whether the warranty was in fact broken." UCC § 2–314 cmt. 13.

**38.** See, e.g., Hazelton v. Safeway Stores, Inc., 745 P.2d 309 (Kan. Ct. App. 1987) (needle in baked bread; baker's evidence that it tested for metal contamination was proper); Johnesee v. Stop & Shop Cos., 416 A.2d 956 (N.J. Super. Ct. App. Div. 1980) (quality control evidence proper in case of possibly contaminated soup, going to improbability it was defective); Brown v. General Foods Corp., 573 P.2d 930 (Ariz. Ct. App. 1978) (manufacturer's quality con-

trol procedures admissible on improbability that banana peel entered cereal box during production).

**39.** See, e.g., Klinke v. Mitsubishi Motors Corp., 556 N.W.2d 528 (Mich. Ct. App. 1996), aff'd, 581 N.W.2d 272 (Mich. 1998); Triplett v. General Elec. Co., 954 F.Supp. 149, 151 (W.D. Mich. 1996) ("the plaintiff must provide direct or circumstantial evidence that 'adequately supports a reasonable inference that the accident was probably caused by a defect attributable to the manufacturer'.").

**40.** See § 7.4, below.

**41.** See, e.g., Henry v. Bridgestone/Firestone Inc., 63 Fed.Appx. 953 (7th Cir. 2003) (Okla. law) (affirming summary judgment for manufacturer where plaintiff's circumstantial evidence of manufacturing defect in tire did not support the claim with reasonable certainty and probability); Wright v. Brooke Group Ltd., 652 N.W.2d 159 (Iowa 2002) (cigarettes not manufactured defectively where they were in condition intended by manufacturer); In re Coordinated Latex Glove Litig., 121 Cal.Rptr.2d 301 (Ct. App. 2002) (claim that excessive protein levels in latex gloves were manufacturing defect failed absent evidence of set standard for protein levels within manufacturer's de-

harm,[42] and that the defect was in the product when it left the manufacturer's control.[43] In many manufacturing defect cases, as in products liability litigation generally, the plaintiff may,[44] and often must,[45] establish his case by competent expert testimony.

## § 7.2  THEORIES AND TESTS OF LIABILITY

A defendant's liability for manufacturing defects may give rise to any number of products liability claims. For example, a manufacturer may misrepresent the purity of its products[1] or a supplier of contaminated food or drink may be negligent per se for violating a pure food

sign specifications); Prohaska v. Sofamor, S.N.C., 138 F.Supp.2d 422, 444 (W.D.N.Y. 2001) (insufficient proof that defendant's pedicle bone screws were manufactured with "inadequate materials of construction, inadequate quality control in machining or critical components and poor finishing processes"); Freeman v. Hoffman–LaRoche, Inc., 618 N.W.2d 827, 841 (Neb. 2000) (manufacturing defect claim properly dismissed where plaintiff alleged manufacturing defect but no facts to support the allegations); Wheeler v. HO Sports, 232 F.3d 754 (10th Cir. 2000) (Okla. law) (insufficient proof that floatation vest contained a manufacturing defect); Holder v. Keller Indus., 2000 WL 141070 (Tex. App. 2000) (insufficient proof that ladder was defectively manufactured).

**42.** See, e.g., Booth v. Black & Decker, Inc., 166 F.Supp.2d 215 (E.D. Pa. 2001) (insufficient proof that manufacturing defect in toaster caused fire that burned down house).

**43.** See, e.g., Levine v. Sears Roebuck and Co., 200 F.Supp.2d 180 (E.D.N.Y. 2002) (manufacturing defect claim dismissed where no proof that defect existed at time of sale); Cincinnati Cos. v. Ford Motor Co., 2001 WL 227362 (Ohio Ct. App. 2001) (plaintiff failed to prove that electrical short-circuit that caused fire existed when car left manufacturer's control); York v. American Med. Sys., Inc., 166 F.3d 1216, (6th Cir. 1998) (Ohio law) (no proof that pinpoint hole in cylinder of inflatable penile prosthesis was caused by manufacturer). See Restatement (2d) Torts § 402A cmt. g:

> The rule ... applies only where the product is, at the time it leaves the seller's hands, in a [defective condition].... The burden of proof [on this point] is upon the injured plaintiff; and unless evidence can be produced which will support the conclusion that it was then defective, the burden is not sustained.

**44.** See, e.g., Benitez v. Synthes, Inc., 199 F.Supp.2d 1339 (M.D. Fla. 2002) (allowing expert testimony on machining process

to establish that surgical rod contained fractures and cracks). Compare Benzel v. Keller Indus., Inc., 567 N.W.2d 552 (Neb. 1997) (affirming plaintiff's verdict on expert testimony that collapse of ladder step was due to various defects attributable to improper assembly and that defendant's ladders failed to meet UL standards for gaps in steps and rails).

**45.** See, e.g., Emody v. Medtronic, Inc., 238 F.Supp.2d 1291 (N.D. Ala. 2003) (summary judgment appropriate where expert's criticism of spinal fusion rod was based solely on visual inspection and rod admittedly passed all objective tests); Cantrell v. Weber–Stephen Prods. Co., 38 Fed. Appx. 921 (4th Cir. 2002) (Md. law) (summary judgment for defendant proper where plaintiff failed to provide expert testimony on why gas grill exploded; without such testimony, "a jury could only infer the presence of a defect in the grill by engaging in 'surmise, conjecture, or speculation.' "); Clark v. Bohn Ford, Inc., 213 F.Supp.2d 957 (S.D. Ind. 2002) (dismissing manufacturing defect claim absent expert testimony that tire that failed was defective); Rudd v. General Motors Corp., 127 F.Supp.2d 1330 (M.D. Ala. 2001) (allowing expert testimony after careful scrutiny); Moisenko v. Volkswagenwerk AG, 100 F.Supp.2d 489 (W.D. Mich. 2000) (granting defendant's motion for summary judgment for manufacturing defect claims; "it is well settled that such a claim cannot be proven without expert testimony").

The expert testimony must be competent. See, e.g., Hamilton v. Emerson Elec. Co., 133 F.Supp.2d 360 (M.D. Pa. 2001) (excluding expert testimony that miter saw brake was defective because it did not work at time of accident, and granting defendant's motion for summary judgment, where expert failed to examine saw and had no reliable basis for opinion). On expert testimony generally, see § 6.3, above.

### § 7.2

**1.** On tortious misrepresentation, see ch. 3, above. On breach of express warranty, see § 4.2, above.

statute.[2] More commonly, however, a seller of a defectively manufactured product is subject to liability under one or more of the three primary products liability theories of recovery—negligence, breach of implied warranty, and strict liability in tort.

## Negligence

In earlier times, most products liability cases for manufacturing defects were brought in negligence.[3] A prominent case in point is *MacPherson v. Buick Motor Co.*,[4] which involved the crash of an automobile due to a defective wooden spoke in its wheel. Indeed, until the development of the doctrine of strict products liability in tort in the 1960s, most products liability cases were manufacturing defect cases brought in negligence.[5] Because negligence is much more difficult to prove than strict liability in manufacturing defect cases, negligence claims in such cases are less common today than formerly. Nevertheless, negligent manufacturing (including negligent testing and quality control) remains a viable basis of products liability recovery in almost every state.[6]

Negligence, it will be recalled,[7] is unreasonable conduct, as measured against the conduct of a reasonable, prudent manufacturer in the same or similar circumstances.[8] Ordinarily, reasonable care is ascertained according to a calculus of risk, balancing the burden or costs of improving safety against the foreseeable safety benefits of so doing. If the foreseeable risks from an occasional flaw are simply that a person may suffer a scratch or snag an article of clothing, then minimal quality control generally is sufficient.[9] Yet, if the foreseeable risks from a manufacturing flaw are substantial, as with defects in the steering or braking mechanisms of a car, then due care requires a manufacturer to devote considerable resources to preventing such errors during production and to catching resulting flaws thereafter through an effective system for quality control.[10]

**2.** See § 7.5, below.

**3.** One small category of cases to the contrary involved defective foodstuff claims against retailers which most commonly asserted breach of warranty. See F. R. Dickerson, Products Liability and the Food Consumer 69–70 (1951).

**4.** 111 N.E. 1050 (N.Y. 1916).

**5.** See, e.g., Wilson, Products Liability (pt. 1), 43 Cal. L. Rev. 614, 636 (1955).

**6.** A negligence claim is logically superfluous to a claim for strict liability in tort, since the former requires proof of all elements of the latter plus fault. See, e.g., Guilbeault v. R.J. Reynolds Tobacco Co., 84 F.Supp.2d 263 (D.R.I. 2000) ("it is unclear to this court why plaintiff would include a negligent manufacturing claim in their Complaint since strict liability will lie due to a manufacturing defect without ... the additional requirement that defendant knew or should have known of the defect"). See § 5.9, above. In addition, a few states

by statute have merged negligence, warranty, and strict liability claims into a single "product liability" claim. See, e.g., Conn. Gen. Stat. §§ 52–572m, 52–572n; Ind. Code Ann. § 34–6–2–115; La. Rev. Stat. Ann. § 9:2800.52; N.J. § 2A:58c–1(b)(3); Wash. Rev. Code Ann. § 7.72.010.

**7.** Negligence claims are addressed generally in chapter 2, above.

**8.** Holder v. Keller Indus., 2000 WL 141070, at *6 (Tex. App. 2000) (defendant ladder manufacturer's conduct must be measured against "standard of a reasonably prudent manufacturer of ladders rather than an ordinary prudent person").

**9.** This was the defendant's argument made and rejected in Ford Motor Co. v. Zahn, 265 F.2d 729 (8th Cir. 1959) (Minn. law).

**10.** "The obligation to inspect must vary with the nature of the thing to be inspected. The more probable the danger

Because of the difficulties in proving the specific manufacturing mistake that caused a production flaw in an accident product, together with the likelihood that any such mistake was the result of the manufacturer's negligence, courts commonly allow juries to infer negligence from proof of a manufacturing flaw alone.[11]

### Strict Liability

Even if manufacturers exercise due care, however, they generally are strictly liable—in warranty and in tort—for injuries caused by production defects in products that they make and sell.[12] The very essence of an ordinary exchange transaction involving a new product is the notion that the buyer is paying appropriate value for a certain *type* of "good" comprised of various utility and safety characteristics common to each unit of that type produced by the maker according to a single design. Both the manufacturer and the buyer contemplate (and hence contract for) an exchange of a standard, uniform monetary value for a standard, uniform package of utility and safety. At some level of abstract awareness most consumers know, of course, that manufacturers sometimes make mistakes and that the cost of perfect production for many types of products would be exorbitant. Yet, while consumers may abstractly comprehend the practical necessity of allowing imperfect production, their actual expectation when purchasing a new product is that its important attributes, including safety, will match those of other similar units.[13] When a purchaser pays full value for a product that appears to be the same as every other, only to receive a product with a dangerous hidden flaw, the product's price and appearance both generate false expectations of safety in the buyer. Buyers do not intend to pay fair value for a mismanufactured product only to be maimed or killed.[14] Nor, in the modern world, can a manufacturer reasonably expect to be

---

the greater the need of caution." MacPherson v. Buick Motor Co., 111 N.E. 1050, 1055 (N.Y. 1916) (Cardozo, J.). See Restatement (2d) Torts § 395 cmt. *e*:

> A garment maker is not required to subject the finished garment to anything like so minute an inspection for the purpose of discovering whether a basting needle has not been left in a seam as is required of the maker of an automobile or of high speed machinery or of electrical devices, in which the slightest inaccuracy may involve danger of death.

**11.** See, e.g., Klinke v. Mitsubishi Motors Corp., 556 N.W.2d 528 (Mich. Ct. App. 1996), aff'd, 581 N.W.2d 272 (Mich. 1998) (car's steering knuckle fractured); Pouncey v. Ford Motor Co., 464 F.2d 957, 961 (5th Cir. 1972) (Ala. law) (automobile fan blade made of dirty steel); Jenkins v. General Motors Corp., 446 F.2d 377 (5th Cir. 1971) (Ga. law) (improper tightening of nut on bolt in rear suspension system). On the doctrine of res ipsa loquitur, see § 2.5, above.

**12.** Similarly, retailers and other suppliers downstream from the manufacturer ordinarily are also strictly liable for harm from manufacturing defects in products they supply. See Products Liability Restatement § 1 cmt. *e*, and § 2 cmt. *c*. See also § 15.2, below.

**13.** See, e.g., Dico Tire, Inc. v. Cisneros, 953 S.W.2d 776, 783 (Tex. App. 1997) (due to defective bead bundle, tire exploded during repair; jury verdict for plaintiff affirmed) ("The manufacturing defect theory is based upon a consumer expectancy that a mass-produced product will not differ from its counterparts in a manner which makes it more dangerous than the other.").

**14.** In the leading English case explaining this notion of implied warranty, Lord Ellenborough colorfully explained the concept: "[T]he intention of both parties must be taken to be, that [the product] shall be saleable in the market under the denomination mentioned in the contract between them. The purchaser cannot be supposed to buy goods to lay them on a dunghill." Gardiner v. Gray, 171 Eng. Rep. 46, 47 (K.B. 1815).

relieved of responsibility for such harm from hidden production defects.[15] Thus, the expectations of the parties, buttressed by principles of fairness and restitution, support the maker's strict responsibility for harm from latent manufacturing defects.[16] For all of these reasons, courts and legislatures widely provide that strict liability is the appropriate standard of liability for injuries resulting from manufacturing defects.[17]

### Warranty

The earliest approach the modern law employed to enforce these expectations, which has now been in effect for about two centuries,[18] was to imply into the exchange transaction a promise or warranty by the seller of the basic, uniform soundness—safety, in this context—of its goods. Today, the implied warranty of merchantability provides buyers a general guarantee, enforceable under the Uniform Commercial Code, against manufacturing defects in the goods they buy.[19] Similarly, the sale of a defectively manufactured product may breach an express warranty[20] or the implied warranty of fitness for particular purpose.[21] While strict liability in tort in most states normally may be a preferable theory of recovery for personal injury damages, the implied warranty of merchantability offers a strict basis of liability for personal injuries in the few states that have not adopted the doctrine of strict liability in tort;[22] it provides a basis for economic losses in the many states that preclude recovery of such damages in tort;[23] and it offers a miscellany of other advantages in various situations.[24]

---

**15.** If the defect is obvious, rather than hidden, there is no untruth within the transaction to generate false safety expectations in the consumer nor, hence, to support the manufacturer's responsibility for resulting harm.

**16.** For a discussion of the policies underlying strict liability for manufacturing defects, see Products Liability Restatement § 2 cmt. *a.* For a discussion of the ethical bases for strict liability in this context, see Owen, The Moral Foundations of Products Liability Law: Toward First Principles, 68 Notre Dame L. Rev. 427, 467–74 (1993).

**17.** By defining liability for manufacturing defects in terms of departure from design specifications, both courts and legislatures are employing a basis of liability that is truly strict. See § 7.3, below.

**18.** It has been in effect longer in England than in most states in this nation. See Prosser, The Implied Warranty of Merchantable Quality, 27 Minn. L. Rev. 117 (1943).

**19.** UCC § 2–314; see § 4.3, above.

**20.** UCC § 2–313; see § 4.2, above. See, e.g., Spectron Dev. Lab. v. American Hollow Boring Co., 936 P.2d 852 (N.M. Ct. App. 1997).

**21.** UCC § 2–315; see § 4.4, above.

**22.** The states are Delaware, Massachusetts, Michigan, North Carolina, and Virgi-

nia. See, e.g., DeWitt v. Eveready Battery Co., 565 S.E.2d 140 (N.C. 2002) (battery leaked acid—implied warranty of merchantability); Triplett v. General Elec. Co., 954 F.Supp. 149 (W.D. Mich. 1996) (defective ballast in fluorescent light caused fire; common law implied warranty).

**23.** See, e.g., Russell v. Deere & Co., 61 P.3d 955 (Or. Ct. App. 2003) (economic loss doctrine barred strict liability in tort claim based on alleged manufacturing defect in combine); Dieker v. Case Corp., 73 P.3d 133 (Kan. 2003) (while economic loss doctrine barred negligence and strict liability in tort claims, plaintiff could recover for manufacturing defect in combine under implied warranty of merchantability); Spectron Dev. Lab. v. American Hollow Boring Co., 936 P.2d 852 (N.M. Ct. App. 1997) (economic losses and damage to defectively manufactured light-gas gun that exploded, and to owner's other property; implied and express warranty claims allowed, but negligence and strict liability in tort claims denied).

**24.** One advantage is the 4–year statute of limitations (from date of sale) under UCC § 2–725, compared to the 2 or 3 year statute of limitations normally provided in tort. See § 14.5, below. Some courts and juries may be more likely to find that a product malfunction alone establishes that a product was not "fit" for its ordinary

*Strict Liability in Tort*

The doctrine of strict liability in tort, which evolved out of warranty cases involving manufacturing defects,[25] is particularly well-suited to claims for injuries caused by manufacturing defects.[26] A majority of the earliest cases adopting § 402A of the *Restatement (Second) of Torts* in the mid–1960s involved manufacturing defects,[27] and strict liability in tort remains the preferred basis of recovery in manufacturing defect cases generally[28] and under § 2(a) of the *Restatement (Third) of Torts: Products Liability* in particular.[29]

Whether a product is in a "defective condition unreasonably dangerous" under § 402A, according to the Reporter's comments, depends upon whether it is dangerous beyond the safety expectations of ordinary consumers.[30] For this reason, and because the protection of reasonable consumer expectations is a basic rationale for imposing strict liability on sellers of defectively manufactured products, many of the earlier decisions involving manufacturing defects explained liability in terms of protecting consumer expectations.[31] Some decisions have not only explained but purported also to apply consumer expectations as a test of liability,[32] often with little success because of the vagueness inherent in

purposes, under UCC § 2–314(2)(b), than that the product was "defective" for purposes of strict liability in tort. See, e.g., Denny v. Ford Motor Co., 42 F.3d 106 (2d Cir. 1994) (N.Y. law) (upholding jury finding that SUV which rolled over was not defective but was unfit for its ordinary purpose).

**25.** See 1 Madden & Owen on Products Liability § 5:2.

**26.** "Commentators and courts agree that the manufacturing defect case presents the clearest and strongest case for applying both strict liability in tort and the consumer expectations test." Korzec, Dashing Consumer Hopes: Strict Products Liability and the Demise of the Consumer Expectations Test, 20 B.C. Int'l & Comp. L. Rev. 227, 243 n.120 (1997). See also Westerbeke, The Sources of Controversy in the New Restatement of Products Liability: Strict Liability Versus Products Liability, 8 Kan. J.L. & Pub. Pol'y 1 (1998); § 5.11, above. This point has long been acknowledged. See, e.g., Fischer, Products Liability—The Meaning of Defect, 39 Mo. L. Rev. 339 (1974).

**27.** Of the first eight cases adopting § 402A, all in 1965 and 1966, six appear to have involved manufacturing defect claims. See 1 Madden & Owen on Products Liability § 5.3, at 273 nn.59–66.

**28.** See, e.g., Riley v. De'Longhi Corp., 238 F.3d 414 (4th Cir. 2000) (Md. law); Independent Sch. Dist. 441 v. Bunn–O–Matic Corp., 1996 WL 689768 (Minn. Ct. App. 1996).

**29.** See, e.g., Hamilton v. Emerson Elec. Co., 133 F.Supp.2d 360 (M.D. Pa. 2001); Mylark v. Port Auth., 723 A.2d 45 (N.J.

1999) (quoting § 2(a) but decided under similar provision of products liability statute); Spectron Dev. Lab. v. American Hollow Boring Co., 936 P.2d 852 (N.M. Ct. App. 1997). See generally Products Liability Restatement § 1 cmt. *a*, and § 2 cmt. *a*. Today, many manufacturing defect cases are decided under the malfunction doctrine, as set forth in Products Liability Restatement § 3. See § 7.4, below.

**30.** See Restatement (2d) Torts § 402A comments *g* and *i*. See generally §§ 5.6 (in general), above and 8.3 (design defectiveness), below; Annot., Products Liability: Consumer Expectations Test, 73 A.L.R.5th 75 (1999).

**31.** See, e.g., Cassisi v. Maytag Co., 396 So.2d 1140 (Fla. Dist. Ct. App. 1981); Phipps v. General Motors Corp., 363 A.2d 955 (Md. 1976); Ford Motor Co. v. Darryl, 432 S.W.2d 569 (Tex. App. 1968); State Stove Mfg. Co. v. Hodges, 189 So.2d 113 (Miss. 1966).

**32.** See, e.g., Chapman v. Maytag Corp., 2000 WL 1038183, at *4 (S.D. Ind. 2000), aff'd, 297 F.3d 682 (7th Cir. 2002); Dico Tire, Inc. v. Cisneros, 953 S.W.2d 776 (Tex. App. 1997); Boy v. I.T.T. Grinnell Corp., 724 P.2d 612, 620 (Ariz. Ct. App. 1986) ("If something goes wrong in the manufacturing process, the result is a product which the manufacturer did not intend and which could hardly be contemplated by the consumer."). See also Independent Sch. Dist. 441 v. Bunn–O–Matic Corp., 1996 WL 689768, at *7 (Minn. Ct. App. 1996) (consumer expectation instruction is appropriate for manufacturing defect case).

the test.[33] Many other courts, apparently understanding that *rationales* for liability theories frequently serve poorly as liability *tests*, have tended to shy away from applying the consumer expectations standard as a formal test for establishing liability in manufacturing defect cases.[34] Recognizing that the risk-utility test is entirely inappropriate in a context which properly requires a strict liability standard,[35] most courts in the 1980s and early 1990s simply left the term manufacturing defect undefined without a liability "test" of its own.

Spurred in the 1990s by the liability definitions for manufacturing defects in the *Products Liability Restatement*, courts in recent years have increasingly based liability for manufacturing defects in two quite different ways. As a specific definition of manufacturing defect, recent decisions have turned to the *Products Liability Restatement*'s "departure from intended design."[36] And in cases involving product malfunctions under circumstances suggesting product defect, many courts have been applying the "malfunction doctrine," a principle of circumstantial evidence allowing recovery on evidence of this type.[37] These two bases of strict liability, examined in the following two sections, are now the principal liability tests for manufacturing defects.

## § 7.3  DEPARTURE FROM DESIGN SPECIFICATIONS

For many years, both courts and commentators considered the meaning of the "manufacturing defect" concept so self-evident as to be self-defining. A defect in manufacture simply meant that through some mistake in the production process the product was rendered "defective."[1] Thus, until quite recently, judicial decisions involving this form of defect generally failed to provide a definitional "test" of liability for such

**33.** See, e.g., Chapman v. Maytag Corp., 2000 WL 1038183 (S.D. Ind. 2000), aff'd, 297 F.3d 682 (7th Cir. 2002); Controlled Atmosphere, Inc. v. Branom Instrument Co., 748 P.2d 686 (Wash. Ct. App. 1988); Bhagvandoss v. Beiersdorf, Inc., 723 S.W.2d 392, 395–96 (Mo. 1987) (users of non-sterile bandage could not expect it to be free of microorganisms), affirming 1986 WL 141628, at *5 (Mo. Ct. App. 1986) (jury could find that users did not reasonably expect to find Rhizopus fungus on bandages); Fitzgerald Marine Sales v. LeUnes, 659 S.W.2d 917 (Tex. App. 1983). On the vagueness of the consumer expectations test, see § 5.6, above.

**34.** See, e.g., Dico Tire, Inc. v. Cisneros, 953 S.W.2d 776 (Tex. App. 1997).

However, if the relevant state's statute defines defectiveness in consumer expectation terms, a court is bound to use that standard in manufacturing defect as other cases. See, e.g., Chapman v. Maytag Corp., 2000 WL 1038183, at *4 (S.D. Ind. 2000) (Ind. statute; wire pinched between parts of stove during assembly), aff'd, 297 F.3d 682 (7th Cir. 2002).

**35.** "The risk-utility analysis applies to design defects cases, not manufacturing defect cases." Leverette v. Louisville Ladder Co., 183 F.3d 339, 342 (5th Cir. 1999) (Miss. law). For a rare exception to this nearly universal principle of strict products liability, see Controlled Atmosphere, Inc. v. Branom Instrument Co., 748 P.2d 686 (Wash. Ct. App. 1988).

**36.** See Products Liability Restatement § 2(a). See § 7.3, below.

**37.** See Products Liability Restatement § 3. See also § 7.4, below.

**§ 7.3**

**1.** See, e.g., Wade, Strict Tort Liability of Manufacturers, 19 Sw. L.J. 5, 14 (1965) ("[A] defective condition is easily understandable in the usual situation in which a particular article has something wrong with it. Because of a mistake in the manufacturing process, for example, the product was adulterated or one of its parts was broken or weakened or not properly attached...."); Wilson, Products Liability (pt. 2), 43 Cal. L. Rev. 809, 810 (1955).

defects.[2] If a plaintiff establishes a manufacturing defect from a common-sense perspective, and further proves that the manufacturer was responsible for the defect and that the defect injured the plaintiff, most defendants have no reason to contest the plaintiff's conception of manufacturing "defectiveness" such that, even today, most courts simply do not bother to define the term.[3]

### Development of the Departure–from–Design Test

During the 1960s, although little attention was devoted to the issue, products liability scholars began to develop a formulation of the manufacturing defect concept that evolved in pragmatic terms into a departure from the manufacturer's intended design standards, a deviation from the maker's "blueprint" specifications.[4] Manufacturing defectiveness was defined in this logical manner in a prominent law review article published by Professor James Henderson in 1973,[5] and, over the next couple of decades, a scattering of courts picked up and repeated variations of this formulation,[6] a number of them relying on Professor Henderson's article for authority.[7]

---

**2.** See, e.g., Hewitt v. B.F. Goodrich Co., 732 F.2d 1554 (11th Cir. 1984) (Fla. law) (tire bead bundle that broke during manufacturing process); Hall v. Chrysler Corp., 526 F.2d 350 (5th Cir. 1976) (Mich. law) (misrouted transmission cable on truck).

**3.** See, e.g., Bell v. T.R. Miller Mill Co., 768 So.2d 953 (Ala. 2000) (telephone pole made of rotten wood); Sanders v. Hartville Milling Co., 14 S.W.3d 188, 200 (Mo. Ct. App. 2000) (toxins in animal feed).

**4.** See, e.g., Nader and Page, Automobile Design and the Judicial Process, 55 Cal. L. Rev. 645, 649 (1967) (citing 1 Frumer and Friedman, Products Liability § 16.04(4)); Traynor, The Ways and Meanings of Defective Products and Strict Liability, 32 Tenn. L. Rev. 363, 367 (1965) ("A defective product may be defined as one that fails to match the average quality of like products, and the manufacturer is then liable for injuries resulting from deviations from the norm.... If a normal sample of defendant's product would not have injured plaintiff, but the peculiarities of the particular product did cause harm, the manufacturer is liable for injuries caused by this deviation."); W.P. Keeton, Products Liability–Liability Without Fault and the Requirement of a Defect, 41 Tex. L. Rev. 855, 859 (1963) ("a miscarriage in the manufacturing process" that made the product different from what "it was intended to be").

On the departure-from-design-specification standard for defining manufacturing defects, see 2 Frumer and Friedman, Products Liability § 11.02[3][a]; 1 Madden & Owen on Products Liability § 7.1; 2 Am. Law Prod. Liab. 3d § 31:3; 1 Products Liability Restatement § 2(a).

**5.** Henderson, Judicial Review of Manufacturers' Conscious Design Choices: The

Limits of Adjudication, 73 Colum. L. Rev. 1531, 1543 (1973):

> Manufacturing flaws are imperfections that inevitably occur in a typically small percentage of products of a given design as a result of the fallibility of the manufacturing process. A flawed product does not conform in some significant aspect to the intended design, nor does it conform to the great majority of products manufactured in accordance with that design.

**6.** The cases almost all involved design defects where the definition of manufacturing defects was dictum. See, e.g., Camacho v. Honda Motor Co., 741 P.2d 1240, 1247 (Colo. 1987) ("whether the product as produced conformed with the manufacturer's specifications"); Ford Motor Co. v. Pool, 688 S.W.2d 879, 881 (Tex. App. 1985) ("Manufacturing defect cases involve products which are flawed, i.e., which do not conform to the manufacturer's own specifications, and are not identical to their mass-produced siblings."), rev'd in part on other grounds, 715 S.W.2d 629 (Tex. 1986); Prentis v. Yale Mfg. Co., 365 N.W.2d 176, 182 (Mich. 1984) (in manufacturing defect cases, "the product may be evaluated against the manufacturer's own production standards, as manifested by that manufacturer's other like products"); Duke v. Gulf & W. Mfg. Co., 660 S.W.2d 404, 411 (Mo. Ct. App. 1983) ("jury can rather easily determine whether a single product conforms to the intended design"); Singleton v. International Harvester Co., 685 F.2d 112, 115 (4th Cir. 1981) (Md. law) ("In manufacturing defect cases, the plaintiff proves that the product is defective by simply showing that it does not conform to the manufacturer's specifications."); Caterpillar Tractor Co. v. Beck, 593 P.2d 871, 881 (Alaska

---

**7.** See note 7 on page 446.

From the first draft of the first sections of the *Products Liability Restatement* in 1993,[8] manufacturing defect was defined in terms of "a departure from the product's intended design," and § 2 of the *Restatement* as eventually published in 1998 provides:

> A product: (a) contains a manufacturing defect when the product departs from its intended design even though all possible care was exercised in the preparation and marketing of the product; . . . .

Since the American Law Institute's adoption of the departure-from-intended-design definition in the early 1990s, an increasing number of courts have used some form of this standard for defining manufacturing defectiveness,[9] some expressly relying on § 2(a) of the *Restatement*.[10] In

1979) ("Under the 'deviation from the norm' test, the product is classified as defective because it does not match the quality of most similar products."); Back v. Wickes Corp., 378 N.E.2d 964, 970 (Mass. 1978) ("jury might simply compare the propensities of the product as sold with those which the product's designer intended it to have and thereby reach a judgment as to whether the deviation from the design rendered the product unreasonably dangerous and therefore unfit for its ordinary purposes"); Barker v. Lull Eng'g Inc., 573 P.2d 443, 454 (Cal. 1978) ("manufacturing or production defect is readily identifiable because a defective product is one that differs from the manufacturer's intended result or from other ostensibly identical units of the same product line").

**7.** See, e.g., Rix v. General Motors Corp., 723 P.2d 195 (Mont. 1986); Caprara v. Chrysler Corp., 417 N.E.2d 545, 552 (N.Y. 1981) (dissent); Thibault v. Sears, Roebuck & Co., 395 A.2d 843 (N.H. 1978).

**8.** Products Liability Restatement § 101(2)(a), at 7 (Prelim. Draft No. 1, 1993).

**9.** See, e.g., McGuire v. Davidson Mfg. Corp., 258 F.Supp.2d 945 (N.D. Iowa 2003) ("manufacturing defect" defined as "a physical departure in the stepladder, as manufactured, from the stepladder's intended design, even if all possible care was exercised in manufacturing and distributing the stepladder"); Jones v. Amazing Prods., Inc., 231 F.Supp.2d 1228 (N.D. Ga. 2002) (dismissing claim that drain cleaner contained manufacturing defect for lack of evidence that product was not manufactured to design specifications); Shreve v. Sears, Roebuck & Co., 166 F.Supp.2d 378 (D. Md. 2001) (dismissing claim that dead man's switch on snow blower contained manufacturing defect for lack of evidence showing that switch did not meet manufacturer's specifications or that there was some error in product's assembly); Morton Int'l v. Gil-

lespie, 39 S.W.3d 651, 656 (Tex. App. 2001) ("a plaintiff has a manufacturing defect claim when a finished product deviates, in terms of its construction or quality, from the specifications or planned output in a manner that renders it unreasonably dangerous"); Allstate Ins. Co. v. Ford Motor Co., 772 So.2d 339, 344 (La. Ct. App. 2000) (La. Code: if "product deviated in a material way from the manufacturer's specifications or performance standards for the product or from otherwise identical products manufactured by the same manufacturer"); Perez–Trujillo v. Volvo Car Corp., 137 F.3d 50, 53 (1st Cir. 1998) (P.R. law) (manufacturing defect exists "if the product 'differs from manufacturer's intended result or from other ostensibly identical units of the same product line' "); Dico Tire, Inc. v. Cisneros, 953 S.W.2d 776, 783 (Tex. App. 1997) (manufacturing defect exists "when a product does not conform to the design standards and blueprints of the manufacturer and the flaw makes the product more dangerous and therefore unfit for its intended or foreseeable uses"); Wood v. Old Trapper Taxi, 952 P.2d 1375 (Mont. 1997); Miles v. Ford Motor Co., 922 S.W.2d 572, 585 (Tex. App. 1996) (manufacturing defect if accident product "does not conform to the manufacturer's design standards [or] blueprints"), rev'd in part on other grounds, 967 S.W.2d 377 (Tex. 1998); McKenzie v. S K Hand Tool Corp., 650 N.E.2d 612, 616 (Ill. App. Ct. 1995) (a manufacturing defect was established "because the measurements of the parts of the wrench were shown not to comply with the manufacturer's specifications").

**10.** See, e.g., Wright v. Brooke Group Ltd., 652 N.W.2d 159 (Iowa 2002) (adopting and applying § 2(a) to hold cigarettes that were in condition intended by manufacturer had no manufacturing defect); Hamilton v. Emerson Elec. Co., 133 F.Supp.2d 360 (M.D. Pa. 2001); Warren v. K–Mart Corp.,

addition, beginning with Washington in 1981,[11] several states have enacted statutes defining manufacturing defects by some formulation of the departure-from-design theme.[12] Mississippi's statute is the most concise, providing for liability if a product was "defective because it deviated in a material way from the manufacturer's specifications or from otherwise identical units manufactured to the same manufacturing specifications."[13] Under such a statute, at least one court has allowed the plaintiff to establish a manufacturing defect by circumstantial evidence that the product malfunctioned under circumstances suggesting that a defect in manufacture caused the malfunction.[14] On some basis or another, however, the plaintiff in a manufacturing defect case must prove the existence of a defect, that the product contained the defect at the time it left the defendant's control,[15] and that the defect caused the plaintiff's harm.[16] As mentioned earlier, many courts require such proof by expert testimony.[17]

One of the few reported decisions explicitly applying a deviation-from-design-specifications standard is *McKenzie v. S K Hand Tool Corp.*[18] While using a 3/4–inch ratchet wrench, the parts of which were held together by a snap ring, the plaintiff was injured when the wrench came apart causing him to fall upon the floor. In an action against the

---

765 So.2d 235 (Fla. Dist. Ct. App. 2000); Myrlak v. Port Auth., 723 A.2d 45 (N.J. 1999) (also relying on New Jersey statute); Spectron Dev. Lab. v. American Hollow Boring Co., 936 P.2d 852 (N.M. Ct. App. 1997); Parker v. St. Vincent Hosp., 919 P.2d 1104 (N.M. Ct. App. 1996).

**11.** Wash. Rev. Code Ann. § 7.72.030(2)(a) provides: "A product is not reasonably safe in construction if, when the product left the control of the manufacturer, the product deviated in some material way from the design specifications or performance standards of the manufacturer, or deviated in some material way from otherwise identical units of the same product line."

**12.** See also La. Rev. Stat. Ann. § 9:2800.55; Miss. Code Ann. § 11–1–63(a)(I); N.J. Stat. Ann. § 2A:58C–2; Ohio Rev. Code Ann. § 2307.74.

**13.** Miss. Code Ann. § 11–1–63(a)(i)(1).

**14.** See Jurls v. Ford Motor Co., 752 So.2d 260, 265–66 (La. Ct. App. 2000) (3–2 decision) (even under deviation-from-specifications statutory definition, product malfunction entitled plaintiff to jury consideration of manufacturing defect on basis of res ipsa loquitur).

**15.** See, e.g., Hamilton v. Emerson Elec. Co., 133 F.Supp.2d 360 (M.D. Pa. 2001) (summary judgment for manufacturer granted because plaintiff failed to prove that defect in miter saw's braking device was present when saw left manufacturer). Cf. Wood v. Old Trapper Taxi, 952 P.2d 1375, 1380–81 (Mont. 1997) (collapse of radio tower manufactured three decades earli-

er; evidence that manufacturing defect in tower was present before it left manufacturer, though weak, was sufficient).

**16.** "To recover for a manufacturing defect, the plaintiff must show a manufacturing flaw which renders the product unreasonably dangerous, that the defect existed at the time the product left the seller, and that the defect was the producing cause of the plaintiff's injuries." Dico Tire, Inc. v. Cisneros, 953 S.W.2d 776, 783 (Tex. App. 1997). Accord, Wood v. Old Trapper Taxi, 952 P.2d 1375, 1379 (Mont. 1997).

On the requirement of causation, see, e.g., Stewart v. Von Solbrig Hosp., Inc., 321 N.E.2d 428, 432 (Ill. App. Ct. 1974) (defective stainless steel surgical pin implanted in plaintiff's leg not designed to withstand weight of person; plaintiff walked on leg contrary to doctor's orders, breaking pin; pin would have broken even if it had not contained manufacturing defects which reduced its strength by one third). See also Lucas v. Texas Indus., 696 S.W.2d 372, 378 (Tex. 1984) (concrete beam, manufactured with one-inch inserts rather than the one and one-quarter inch inserts specified in plans, fell on plaintiff while being lifted with one and one-quarter inch lifting equipment; no evidence that beam's failure to be manufactured to specifications caused the danger or, by implication, the harm). On causation generally, see ch. 11, below.

**17.** See, e.g., Moisenko v. Volkswagenwerk AG., 100 F.Supp.2d 489, 493 (W.D. Mich. 2000).

**18.** 650 N.E.2d 612 (Ill. App. Ct. 1995).

wrench manufacturer, the plaintiff's expert theorized that the snap ring failed because of defective manufacture in both (1) the hardness of the snap ring, and (2) the diameter of the wrench handle groove in which the ring was seated. The manufacturer's blueprints contained specifications for the sizes of each component of the wrench together with specific tolerances (upper and lower limits) for each measurement. Each particular wrench was considered acceptable if its particular measurements fit within the tolerance limits, and if any measurement fell outside the upper or lower limits, the machinist knew that the part was unacceptable. As for the ring's hardness, the specifications called for a measurement of 48–52 on the Rockwell C scale, whereas the accident-wrench ring measurements ranged (in various places) from 45–51. As for the diameter of the handle groove, the specifications called for 2.290 inches, with a tolerance of .005 inches, providing an acceptable range of 2.285–2.295 inches. However, the diameter of the groove on the accident wrench measured appreciably larger, between 2.3125–2.3130 inches. Concluding that the evidence was relevant to defectiveness and causation, and that the trial court's exclusion of it therefore was erroneous, the *McKenzie* court ruled that the plaintiff had established a prima facie case of manufacturing defectiveness.

There are many slight variations in how courts and legislatures define the deviation-from-specification liability standard, although all mean essentially the same thing.[19] A possible benefit of the *Products Liability Restatement* formulation in departure-from-intended-design terms is that it provides a sound basis upon which the liability test's formulation may begin to standardize.[20] Of course, any such standard must allow for tolerances within which a product may be considered nondefective, as the tolerances mentioned above in *McKenzie* illustrate, since absolute perfection is not possible (because of limitations of science and technology), nor desirable (because of cost), nor necessary (for accident prevention). A straight-forward departure-from-design-standard definition occasionally may fail to capture a product hazard that properly should be considered a manufacturing defect, such that the normal definition from time to time may need to be supplemented in some respect. And most courts will certainly want to allow manufacturing defects to be established by the malfunction doctrine[21] and possibly by other forms of proof.[22] But courts should have little difficulty handling

---

**19.** Definitions vary over time even in the same jurisdiction. Compare Morton Int'l v. Gillespie, 39 S.W.3d 651, 656 (Tex. App. 2001) ("a plaintiff has a manufacturing defect claim when a finished product deviates, in terms of its construction or quality, from the specifications or planned output in a manner that renders it unreasonably dangerous"), with Dico Tire, Inc. v. Cisneros, 953 S.W.2d 776, 783 (Tex. App. 1997) ("A manufacturing defect exists when a product does not conform to the design standards and blueprints of the manufacturer and the flaw makes the product more dangerous and therefore unfit for its intended or foreseeable uses.").

**20.** The adoption of the standard by a number of courts suggests that this process has begun. Note 1, above. However, it should be noted that the Restatement itself appears unconcerned with uniformity of terminology. See Products Liability Restatement § 2(a) cmt. *c*, restating § 2(a) as meaning "a manufacturing defect is a departure from a product unit's design specifications."

**21.** See Jurls v. Ford Motor Co., 752 So.2d 260, 265–66 (La. Ct. App. 2000) (3–2 decision). On the malfunction doctrine generally, see § 7.4, below.

**22.** See Magnuson v. Kelsey–Hayes Co., 844 S.W.2d 448, 455 (Mo. Ct. App. 1992)

such special situations as they arise, and, for the bulk of manufacturing defect cases, it may safely be predicted that courts increasingly will define manufacturing defect in terms of departure from design specifications.

### Methods of Proof; Ethical Implications

The statutes and several judicial decisions mentioned above explicitly provide a two-pronged definition of manufacturing defect which allows a plaintiff to establish defectiveness by either of two alternative methods of proof: comparing the accident-product unit to the manufacturer's formal design specifications *or* to the dimensions and other parameters of some otherwise identical product. The result of either form of proof should be essentially the same, for the two approaches provide alternative routes to the same destination—a determination of whether the product in question was produced or assembled in a manner contrary to the manufacturer's intentions.

Permitting a plaintiff to establish an accident-product's defectiveness simply by comparing its characteristics to those of a like product unit found on a retailer's shelf[23] has interesting practical and ethical implications. As a practical matter, this liability standard means that the defectiveness of an accident product often may be determined prior to filing a lawsuit. The plaintiff's expert, after locating another product unit of the same make and model, may simply compare and contrast the two products to ascertain whether the accident is fairly traceable to some physical difference between the two product units resulting from some variation in the production process. In some cases, no doubt, an expert will be unable to reliably determine defectiveness or causation simply by comparing two product units.[24] Oftentimes, however, a simple comparative analysis will provide a firm basis for determining whether a product accident in fact was caused by a flaw in manufacture.

Certain strategic and ethical implications spring from this ready availability of a relatively simple test of manufacturing defectiveness. In particular, it would seem that plaintiffs' attorneys handling manufacturing defect cases must seek to obtain such comparative analyses prior to filing suit.[25] Similarly, once defense counsel gain access to accident products in manufacturing defect cases, they must compare those product units to the manufacturer's design specifications and conform the defense of such cases to the results of those comparisons.[26]

("a showing of non-conformity to design . . . is illustrative of one form of proof which may be presented"). See also McCabe v. American Honda Motor Co., 123 Cal. Rptr.2d 303 (Ct. App. 2002) (a manufacturing defect "is often demonstrated by showing that the product performed differently from other ostensibly identical units of the same product line").

**23.** Literally or metaphorically.

**24.** For example, in the *McKenzie* case discussed above, the measurements were so precise that a reliable defectiveness determination may have been possible only because the experts were able to compare the measurements of the accident product against the measurements and tolerances actually specified by the manufacturer. *McKenzie*, 650 N.E.2d at 614–15.

**25.** See Fed. R. Civ. P. 11.

**26.** Id.

## § 7.4 PRODUCT MALFUNCTION

### Nature of Doctrine

In modern products liability litigation, it is axiomatic that a plaintiff normally must prove that a product was defective, that the product contained the defect when it left the defendant's control, and that the defect proximately caused the plaintiff's harm.[1] A plaintiff who fails to establish each of these elements by a preponderance of the evidence fails to make a prima facie case.[2] If a manufacturing defect causes a product accident, usually the plaintiff can prove the defect and its causal relation to both the manufacturer and the accident largely by direct evidence—as by testimony from an expert that the product contained an identifiable production flaw, deviating from design specifications, that caused the product to fail in a particular manner.[3] Sometimes, however, a product may malfunction under circumstances suggesting a manufacturing defect (or possibly a design defect)[4] but without leaving any direct physical evidence as to how or why, specifically, the product failed to operate properly. In such cases, the absence of direct evidence of product defectiveness and causation hampers a plaintiff's efforts to establish a prima facie products liability case.

In negligence law, if the specific cause of a product malfunction is unknown, the doctrine of res ipsa loquitur allows a jury to infer the manufacturer's negligence when the circumstances of the accident suggest that the product was negligently manufactured or designed. However, because the res ipsa doctrine is designed to establish a defendant's *negligence* rather than a product's *defectiveness*, most courts consider the res ipsa doctrine technically inapplicable to strict liability in tort or breach of warranty, both of which are unconcerned with a defendant's conduct.[5] Although not entirely necessary,[6] the courts, in an effort to

---

**§ 7.4**

**1.** See, e.g., Myrlak v. Port Auth., 723 A.2d 45, 52 (N.J. 1999); Davis v. Berwind Corp., 690 A.2d 186 (Pa. 1997). See also Rone v. Sharp Elec. Corp., 2000 WL 133822, at *2 (D. Kan. 2000); Prosser and Keeton on Torts § 103, at 712–13.

**2.** This is certainly true for strict liability in tort. See § 5.3, above. It is also generally true as well for negligence and breach of the implied warranty of merchantability. See, e.g., Riley v. De'Longhi Corp., 238 F.3d 414 (4th Cir. 2000) (Md. law) (requirements apply to strict liability, negligence, and breach of warranty).

**3.** See §§ 6.3 and 7.3, above.

**4.** See, e.g., Rudd v. General Motors Corp., 127 F.Supp.2d 1330, 1340 (M.D. Ala. 2001) (pickup truck's fan blade broke due to fatigue fracture that might have resulted from low-strength alloy used to make fan); Products Liability Restatement § 3 cmt. *b*. However, the malfunction "doctrine is ill-suited to cases involving defective design for failure to include a safety device." Dan-

cy v. Hyster Co., 127 F.3d 649, 653 (8th Cir. 1997) (Ark. law).

**5.** See, e.g., Myrlak v. Port Auth., 723 A.2d 45, 53 (N.J. 1999) ("Res ipsa loquitur is a doctrine created under the fault theory of negligence as a means of circumstantially proving a defendant's lack of due care. Strict products liability, on the other hand, is a theory of liability based upon allocating responsibility regardless of a defendant's unreasonableness, negligence, or fault."). This is the majority rule. See also O'Connor v. General Motors Corp., 1997 WL 792996, at *3 (Conn. Super. Ct. 1997) ("Res ipsa loquitur relates to cases involving negligence and has no application to cases where a strict liability theory is advanced."); Tresham v. Ford Motor Co., 79 Cal.Rptr. 883, 886 (Ct. App. 1969) ("When a party relies on the rule of strict liability the requirement of showing a defect cannot be satisfied by reliance on the doctrine of res ipsa loquitur."). On the relationship between res ipsa loquitur and the malfunction doctrine, see, e.g., Cassisi v. Maytag Co., 396 So.2d 1140 (Fla. Dist. Ct. App. 1981).

---

**6.** See note 6 on page 451.

maintain a fundamental distinction between negligence and strict liability, began at an early date to tailor principles similar to those that underlie res ipsa loquitur[7] into a separate doctrine for proving claims in strict products liability.[8] Dubbed the "malfunction theory,"[9] these special principles of circumstantial evidence now provide a widely accepted means for proving defectiveness in cases where direct evidence of defectiveness is unavailable.[10]

Under the malfunction doctrine, a plaintiff may establish a prima facie case of product defect by proving that the product failed in normal use under circumstances suggesting a product defect. Put otherwise, a product defect may be inferred by circumstantial evidence that (1) the product malfunctioned, (2) the malfunction occurred during proper use, and (3) the product had not been altered or misused in a manner that probably caused the malfunction. The malfunction doctrine may be described less formally as providing that a plaintiff need not establish that a specific defect caused an accident if circumstantial evidence

A couple of courts allow plaintiffs to use res ipsa to establish defectiveness for purposes of strict products liability. See, e.g., Parsons v. Ford Motor Co. 85 S.W.3d 323, 331 (Tex. App. 2002) (res ipsa available in both negligence and strict liability to provide presumption of product defect and causation); Jurls v. Ford Motor Co., 752 So.2d 260 (La. Ct. App. 2000) (res ipsa may be used to establish liability under statute defining manufacturing defect as a deviation from manufacturer's design specifications).

**6.** Unnecessary because a negligence claim requires proof of each element of a strict products liability claim, including defectiveness, plus the additional element of fault. See §§ 2.1 and 5.9, above. Thus, proof of a manufacturer's negligence under res ipsa logically includes within itself proof that the product was defective.

**7.** "Strictly speaking, since proof of negligence is not in issue, res ipsa loquitur has no application to strict liability; but the inferences which are the core of the doctrine remain, and are no less applicable." W. Prosser, Law of Torts § 103, at 672–73 (4th ed. 1971). On res ipsa, see § 2.5, above.

**8.** Early examples of the doctrine in nascent form include MacDougall v. Ford Motor Co., 257 A.2d 676 (Pa. Super. Ct. 1969); Greco v. Bucciconi Eng'g Co., 283 F.Supp. 978, 982 (W.D. Pa. 1967), aff'd, 407 F.2d 87 (3d Cir. 1969); Marathon Battery Co. v. Kilpatrick, 418 P.2d 900 (Okla. 1965). For the doctrine's even earlier warranty law basis, see W. Prosser, Law of Torts § 103 (4th ed. 1971).

**9.** It is so called in several jurisdictions, including Pennsylvania which has the most developed jurisprudence on this doctrine. See, e.g., Dansak v. Cameron Coca–Cola Bottling Co., 703 A.2d 489 (Pa. Super. Ct.

1997); Ducko v. Chrysler Motors Corp., 639 A.2d 1204 (Pa. Super. Ct. 1994); Troy v. Kampgrounds of Am., Inc., 581 A.2d 665 (Pa. Super. Ct. 1990); Rogers v. Johnson & Johnson Prods., Inc., 565 A.2d 751 (Pa. 1989); Kuisis v. Baldwin–Lima–Hamilton Corp., 319 A.2d 914 (Pa. 1974).

A few courts refer to it as the "indeterminate defect theory," reflecting the fact that the doctrine applies when the circumstances surrounding an accident suggest a product defect but no direct evidence of a specific defect is available. See, e.g., Riley v. De'Longhi Corp., 238 F.3d 414 (Md. law); Myrlak v. Port Auth., 723 A.2d 45, 55 (N.J. 1999). The doctrine is also sometimes referred to as the "general defect" theory. See, e.g., Corcoran v. General Motors Corp., 81 F.Supp.2d 55, 66 (D.D.C. 2000); Hall v. General Motors Corp., 8 F.3d 27 (9th Cir. 1993) (Or. law). Without assigning a particular name to the doctrine, most courts refer to it simply as a principle of circumstantial evidence.

**10.** See 1 Frumer and Friedman Products Liability § 8.06 (in general) and 3 id. § 22.09 (automobiles); 1 Am. Law Prod. Liab. §§ 3:13, 17:68, & 31:19–31:28; Hoffman, Res ipsa loquitur and Indeterminate Product Defects: If They Speak for Themselves, What Are They Saying?, 36 S. Tex. L. Rev. 353 (1995); G. Schwartz, New Products, Old Products, Evolving Law, Retroactive Law, 58 N.Y.U. L. Rev. 796, 828 (1983); Note, Rolling the "Barrel" a Little Further: Allowing Res Ipsa Loquitur to Assist in Proving Strict Liability in Tort Manufacturing Defects, 38 Wm. & Mary L. Rev. 1197 (1997); Annot., 65 A.L.R. 4th 346 (1988) (malfunction doctrine); CCH Prod. Liab. Rep. ¶ 1740; Products Liability Restatement § 3.

permits an inference that the product, in one way or another, probably was defective.[11]

Since normal products liability doctrine requires a plaintiff to establish that a product was defective and that the defect caused his harm, requiring a plaintiff to prove that a specific defect caused the accident might appear to make good sense. But the very purpose of the malfunction doctrine is to allow a plaintiff to prove a case by circumstantial evidence when there simply is no direct evidence of precisely how or why the product failed. Sometimes the specific cause of a malfunction disappears in the accident when the product blows up, burns up, is otherwise severely damaged, or is thereafter lost.[12] Not infrequently, however, products simply malfunction, and mysteriously so, leaving no tangible trace of how or why they failed. In all such situations, where direct evidence is unavailable, the courts have properly refused to require the plaintiff to prove what specific defect caused the product to malfunction.[13]

Because the malfunction doctrine is merely a principle of circumstantial evidence rather than a formal definition of what constitutes a manufacturing defect, the doctrine is logically compatible with a definition of manufacturing defect in terms of a departure from the manufacturer's design specifications.[14]

## Applicability

The malfunction doctrine is frequently applied to cases involving cars and other automotive vehicles. In *Ducko v. Chrysler Motors Corp.*,[15]

---

**11.** Products Liability Restatement § 3, cmt. *c*, provides that "[t]he inference of defect may be drawn under this Section without proof of the specific defect. Furthermore, quite apart from the question of what type of defect was involved, the plaintiff need not explain specifically what constituent part of the product failed."

**12.** The loss of a product that is the subject of a products liability action raises issues of "spoliation" of evidence. See, e.g., Copenhagen Reinsurance Co. v. Champion Home Builders Co., 872 So.2d 848 (Ala. Civ. App. 2003); Torres v. Matsushita Elec. Corp., 762 So.2d 1014 (Fla. Dist. Ct. App. 2000) (malfunction doctrine not available where product was unavailable because of plaintiff's negligent destruction rather than malfunction); Tracy v. Cottrell, 524 S.E.2d 879, 887–90 (W. Va. 1999); Dansak v. Cameron Coca–Cola Bottling Co., 703 A.2d 489 (Pa. Super. Ct. 1997). See generally 2 McCormick on Evidence § 264–65 (1999); 2 Wigmore on Evidence § 277–81 (1979); Kindel and Richter, Spoliation of Evidence: Will the New Millennium See a Further Expansion of Sanctions for the Improper Destruction of Evidence?, 27 Wm. Mitchell L. Rev. 687 (2000); Volin, You Have No Evidence But You May Still Have a Case: The New Products Liability Spoliation Doctrine, 69 Pa. Bar Ass'n Q. 129 (1998); Note, Spoliation in the Product Liability Context, 27 U. Mem. L. Rev. 663, 663 (1997); Comment, Doctrinal Malfunction—Spoliation and Products Liability Law in Pennsylvania, 69 Temp. L. Rev. 899 (1996); Marquardt, Spoliation of Evidence, 23 Brief 9 (1994). See generally M. Koesel et al., Spoliation of Evidence: Sanctions and Remedies for Destruction of Evidence in Civil Litigation (A.B.A. 2000) (generally discussing the problem of spoliation in civil litigation).

**13.** See, e.g., Kenkel v. Stanley Works, 665 N.W.2d 490, 497 (Mich. Ct. App. 2003) (plaintiff, trapped between sliding glass doors, not required to identify specific defect); Stackiewicz v. Nissan Motor Corp. in U.S.A., 686 P.2d 925 (Nev. 1984); MacDougall v. Ford Motor Co., 257 A.2d 676 (Pa. Super. Ct. 1969).

**14.** See Jurls v. Ford Motor Co., 752 So.2d 260, 265–66 (La. Ct. App. 2000) (3–2 decision) (under deviation-from-specifications statutory definition of manufacturing defect, proof of product malfunction entitled plaintiff to jury determination of manufacturing defect on basis of res ipsa).

**15.** 639 A.2d 1204 (Pa. Super. Ct. 1994).

for example, the plaintiff was driving a new Chrysler Fifth Avenue[16] on a dry road at 55 mph when the car suddenly jerked to the right, the steering locked, and the brakes failed to respond. The car crashed, and the plaintiff broke her back. No specific defect could be found in the vehicle. The plaintiffs' expert concluded that the accident was caused by a transient malfunction of the power system for the steering and brakes, whereas Chrysler's expert postulated that the accident resulted from driver error. Because the plaintiff could not prove the specific defect that caused the crash, the trial court entered summary judgment for the defendant. Based on the malfunction doctrine, the superior court reversed and remanded for trial, holding that a plaintiff need not establish a specific defect to prove a manufacturing defect but may establish a case-in-chief by proving (1) that the product malfunctioned, and (2) the absence of likely causes other than product defect.[17] Because circumstantial evidence of this type would permit a jury to infer that the product probably was defective at the time of sale,[18] the trial court's grant of summary judgment to Chrysler improperly precluded the jury from determining the cause of the accident—whether driver error or, based on the plaintiff's testimony of steering and braking problems, some defect in the car.[19]

In addition to cases like *Ducko* that involve the sudden failure of a vehicle's steering[20] or brakes,[21] courts have applied the malfunction doctrine to other automotive cases in which a vehicle inexplicably accelerates,[22] changes gears,[23] catches fire,[24] or rolls over;[25] in which a tire

**16.** The car had been driven 1,655 miles since its purchase less than two months earlier. Id. at 1205.

**17.** The Pennsylvania courts characterize such alternative likely causes as "abnormal use or reasonable, secondary causes for the malfunction." See *Ducko*, 639 A.2d at 1205, citing Rogers v. Johnson & Johnson Prod., Inc., 565 A.2d 751, 754 (Pa. 1989).

**18.** Id. at 1205.

**19.** "Mrs. Ducko's testimony of the erratic performance of the vehicle's steering and braking systems, under the circumstances of this case, was sufficient to make out a prima facie case of a manufacturing defect in the vehicle. The issue of strict liability, therefore, was a disputed issue for the jury. Although a jury, after considering the testimony of appellee's expert witnesses, may find that the vehicle was not defective and that the accident was caused by operator error, it was improper for the trial court to make such a determination summarily and as a matter of law." Id. at 1207.

**20.** See, e.g., Stackiewicz v. Nissan Motor Corp. in U.S.A., 686 P.2d 925 (Nev. 1984) (steering on automobile with 2,400 total miles suddenly locked; routine maintenance performed at 1,000 miles); Millette v. Radosta, 404 N.E.2d 823 (Ill. App. Ct. 1980) (11,000 miles); Caprara v. Chrysler Corp., 423 N.Y.S.2d 694 (App. Div. 1979), aff'd on

other grounds, 417 N.E.2d 545 (N.Y. 1981); Stewart v. Ford Motor Co., 553 F.2d 130 (D.C. Cir. 1977) (12 days old; 1,400 miles); Hunt v. Ford Motor Co., 341 So.2d 614 (La. Ct. App. 1977); Farmer v. International Harvester Co., 553 P.2d 1306 (Idaho 1976) (truck: 116,000 miles); Moraca v. Ford Motor Co., 332 A.2d 599 (N.J. 1975) (11,000 miles); Stewart v. Budget Rent–A–Car Corp., 470 P.2d 240 (Haw. 1970) (2,829 miles); MacDougall v. Ford Motor Co., 257 A.2d 676 (Pa. Super. Ct. 1969) (less than 1 month old; 143 miles).

**21.** See, e.g., Vernon v. Stash, 532 A.2d 441 (Pa. Super. Ct. 1987) (parking brake); Joseph v. Bohn Ford, Inc., 483 So.2d 934 (La. 1986) (3,800 miles); Tweedy v. Wright Ford Sales, Inc., 357 N.E.2d 449 (Ill. 1976) (7,500 miles); Snider v. Bob Thibodeau Ford, Inc., 202 N.W.2d 727 (Mich. Ct. App. 1972) (truck); Darryl v. Ford Motor Co., 440 S.W.2d 630 (Tex. 1969) (truck: 3 months old; 600–700 miles).

**22.** See, e.g., Wakabayashi v. Hertz Corp., 660 P.2d 1309 (Haw. 1983) (1½ years old; 22,577 miles); Phipps v. General Motors Corp., 363 A.2d 955 (Md. 1976). See also Jurls v. Ford Motor Co., 752 So.2d 260 (La. Ct. App. 2000) (cruise control apparently failed to disengage).

**23.** See, e.g., Harrell Motors, Inc. v. Flanery, 612 S.W.2d 727 (Ark. 1981); Williams v. Deere & Co., 598 S.W.2d 609

**24–25.** See notes 24 and 25 on page 454.

fails;[26] or in which an airbag fails to deploy,[27] deploys improperly,[28] or spews acid on an occupant.[29] In addition to automobiles, the doctrine has been applied to malfunctions of a wide range of other products, as when a bottle of soda pop,[30] glass baby bottle,[31] transformer,[32] gas grill,[33] propane fuel canister,[34] an aerosol can of paint,[35] or an oxygen tank's glass humidifier[36] explodes; a bottle of ketchup,[37] jar of peanuts,[38] an automatic coffee maker's glass carafe,[39] or a silicone breast implant[40] breaks apart; a television,[41] clothes dryer,[42] dishwasher,[43] portable heater,[44] combine,[45] refrigerator,[46] or an electric blanket[47] catches fire; a

(Mo. App. 1980) (tractor: 2 years old). See also O'Connor v. General Motors Corp., 1997 WL 792996 (Conn. Super. Ct. 1997) (although clutch not engaged, truck lurched when ignition turned on).

**24.** See, e.g., TNT Road Co. v. Sterling Truck Corp., 2004 WL 1626254 (D. Me. 2004); Hall v. General Motors Corp., 8 F.3d 27 (9th Cir. 1993) (Or. law); Anderson v. Chrysler Corp., 403 S.E.2d 189 (W. Va. 1991); Cincinnati Ins. Co. v. Volkswagen of Am., Inc., 502 N.E.2d 651 (Ohio App. 1985); Hinckley v. La Mesa R.V. Center, Inc., 205 Cal.Rptr. 22 (Ct. App. 1984).

**25.** See, e.g., Perkins v. Trailco Mfg. & Sales Co., 613 S.W.2d 855 (Ky. 1981) (new dump truck, properly used and maintained, overturned).

**26.** See Taylor v. Cooper Tire & Rubber Co., 130 F.3d 1395 (10th Cir. 1997) (Utah law); Colboch v. Uniroyal Tire Co., 670 N.E.2d 1366 (Ohio Ct. App. 1996).

**27.** See, e.g., Silvestri v. General Motors Corp., 210 F.3d 240 (4th Cir. 2000) (N.Y. law).

**28.** See Perez–Trujillo v. Volvo Car Corp. (Swed.), 137 F.3d 50, 51 (1st Cir. 1998) (P.R. law).

**29.** See McEneaney v. Haywood, 687 N.Y.S.2d 547 (App. Div. 1999).

**30.** See, e.g., Dansak v. Cameron Coca–Cola Bottling Co., 703 A.2d 489 (Pa. Super. Ct. 1997); Robertson v. Gulf S. Beverage, Inc., 421 So.2d 877 (La. 1982); Embs v. Pepsi–Cola Bottling Co., 528 S.W.2d 703 (Ky. Ct. App. 1975); Lee v. Crookston Coca–Cola Bottling Co., 188 N.W.2d 426 (Minn. 1971).

**31.** See Patterson v. Foster Forbes Glass Co., 674 S.W.2d 599 (Mo. Ct. App. 1984).

**32.** See Bich v. General Elec. Co., 614 P.2d 1323 (Wash. Ct. App. 1980).

**33.** See Adkins v. K–Mart Corp., 511 S.E.2d 840 (W. Va. 1998).

**34.** See Eaton Corp. v. Wright, 375 A.2d 1122 (Md. 1977).

**35.** See Van Zee v. Bayview Hardware Store, 74 Cal.Rptr. 21 (Ct. App. 1968).

**36.** See James v. Keefe & Keefe, Inc., 377 N.Y.S.2d 991 (App. Div. 1975).

**37.** See Powers v. Hunt–Wesson Foods, Inc., 219 N.W.2d 393 (Wis. 1974).

**38.** See Welge v. Planters Lifesavers Co., 17 F.3d 209, 210 (7th Cir. 1994) (Ill. law) (Posner, C.J.).

**39.** See, e.g., Rizzo v. Corning Inc., 105 F.3d 338 (7th Cir. 1997) (Ill. law) (Posner, C.J.) ("A carafe designed to be used for years, not months, breaks in half without being dropped or banged or cleaned with abrasive cleansers or damaged in a flood or fire. In these unusual circumstances the accident itself is sufficient evidence of a defect to permit, though of course not compel, the jury to infer a defect. Whether these *were* the circumstances of the accident was a jury question."); Mondido v. Cory Corp., 483 F.Supp. 26 (E.D.N.Y. 1979).

**40.** See Baxter Healthcare Corp. v. Grimes, 1998 WL 548729 (Tex. App. 1998).

**41.** See, e.g., Rone v. Sharp Elec. Corp., 2000 WL 133822 (D. Kan. 2000); Union Ins. Co. v. RCA Corp., 724 P.2d 80 (Colo. Ct. App. 1986); Fain v. GTE Sylvania, Inc., 652 S.W.2d 163 (Mo. Ct. App. 1983); Liberty Mut. Ins. Co. v. Sears, Roebuck & Co., 406 A.2d 1254 (Conn. Super. Ct. 1979); Bombardi v. Pochel's Appliance & TV Co., 518 P.2d 202 (Wash. Ct. App. 1973).

**42.** See Weir v. Federal Ins. Co., 811 F.2d 1387 (10th Cir. 1987) (Colo. law); Cassisi v. Maytag Co., 396 So.2d 1140 (Fla. Dist. Ct. App. 1981) (thorough analysis of doctrine).

**43.** See McCoy v. Whirlpool Corp., 2003 WL 21554950 (D. Kan. 2003).

**44.** See Riley v. De'Longhi Corp., 238 F.3d 414 (4th Cir. 2000) (Md. law); Pearson Constr. Corp. v. Intertherm, Inc., 566 P.2d 575 (Wash. Ct. App. 1977).

**45.** See Dieker v. Case Corp., 73 P.3d 133 (Kan. 2003).

**46.** See Speller v. Sears, Roebuck & Co., 790 N.E.2d 252 (N.Y. 2003).

**47.** See, e.g., Henderson v. Sunbeam Corp., 46 F.3d 1151 (10th Cir. 1995) (Okla.

crutch,[48] grain auger,[49] football helmet,[50] or ladder collapses;[51] a crane drops a load;[52] the blade guard of a power circular saw fails to close;[53] a staple gun misfires a staple;[54] a winch cable snaps;[55] and many other situations in which products have inexplicably malfunctioned.[56]

### Limitations and Effect

While courts have applied the malfunction doctrine in many cases to help plaintiffs get to the jury when evidence of a specific defect is unavailable, plaintiffs have lost many other cases in which they have relied unreasonably upon this type of circumstantial proof.[57] The doctrine presents a seductive but faulty shelter for plaintiffs with insufficient proof of defect and causation, and the law reports brim with decisions that recite the propriety of the doctrine as a general proposition but hold it inapplicable to the facts.[58] The opinions in such cases frequently note that, while the malfunction doctrine provides a method for plaintiffs in proper cases to establish defectiveness and causation, the law will not allow plaintiffs or juries to rely on guess, conjecture, or speculation.[59]

Although the malfunction doctrine may come to a plaintiff's rescue when circumstances fairly suggest the responsibility of a product defect, it is hornbook law that proof of a product accident alone proves neither defectiveness nor causation.[60] Nor does further proof that the accident was caused by a malfunction suffice to prove these elements. The crucial additional showing required of a plaintiff in a malfunction case is the negation of causes for the malfunction other than a product defect.

While malfunctions are sometimes caused by defects for which the manufacturer is responsible, product failures also result from improper

---

law); Watson v. Sunbeam Corp., 816 F.Supp. 384 (D. Md. 1993).

**48.** See Varady v. Guardian Co., 506 N.E.2d 708 (Ill. Ct. App. 1987).

**49.** See Thudium v. Allied Prods. Corp., 36 F.3d 767 (8th Cir. 1994) (Mo. law).

**50.** See Rawlings Sporting Goods Co. v. Daniels, 619 S.W.2d 435 (Tex.Civ.App. 1981).

**51.** See, e.g., Gillespie v. R.D. Werner Co., 375 N.E.2d 1294 (Ill. 1978).

**52.** See Kuisis v. Baldwin–Lima–Hamilton Corp., 319 A.2d 914 (Pa. 1974) (brake-locking mechanism failed).

**53.** See, e.g., Skil Corp. v. Lugsdin, 309 S.E.2d 921 (Ga. Ct. App. 1983); Agostino v. Rockwell Mfg. Co., 345 A.2d 735 (Pa. Super. Ct. 1975).

**54.** See Senco Prods., Inc. v. Riley, 434 N.E.2d 561 (Ind. Ct. App. 1982).

**55.** See Lachney v. Motor Parts & Bearing Supply, Inc., 357 So.2d 1277 (La. Ct. App. 1978).

**56.** See, e.g., Dietz v. Waller, 685 P.2d 744, 748 (Ariz. 1984) (new speed boat "disintegrated" at high speed during normal operation); Lee's Hawaiian Islanders, Inc. v.

Safety First Prods., Inc., 480 A.2d 927 (N.J. Super. Ct. App. Div. 1984) (fire suppression system failed to operate); Marquez v. City Stores Co., 371 So.2d 810 (La. 1979) (child's shoe caught in side of escalator).

**57.** Cases both ways are collected in Annot., 65 A.L.R.4th 346 (1988).

**58.** See id.

**59.** See, e.g., Woodin v. J.C. Penney Co., 629 A.2d 974, 976–77 (Pa. Super. Ct. 1993); Willard v. BIC Corp., 788 F.Supp. 1059, 1064 (W.D. Mo. 1991); State Farm Fire & Cas. Co. v. Chrysler Corp., 523 N.E.2d 489, 496–97 (Ohio 1988); Thomas v. Amway Corp., 488 A.2d 716 (R.I. 1985) (irritation, red splotches, rash, and bleeding may have been caused by soap, but cause of condition could not be left to jury speculation).

**60.** See, e.g., Williams v. Smart Chevrolet Co., 730 S.W.2d 479 (Ark. 1987) (car door suddenly swinging open while car in motion does not alone prove car was defective; directed verdict for defendant affirmed). See generally W. Prosser, Law of Torts § 103, at 673 (4th ed. 1971); Annot., 65 A.L.R.4th 346, 363 § 4 (1988) (collecting cases).

treatment of products by users and repairers, and many products eventually simply wear out from a long and possibly rugged life. Tires, for example, when worn enough, will eventually blow out. Thus, if the plaintiff fails to show that he used the product properly;[61] or does not show that the product was not misused or tampered with by other parties (such as prior users and repairers) who had access to the product;[62] or cannot show that the product was properly maintained;[63] or does not establish that the product failed during a normal life span of safe use;[64] then a malfunction case will fail. So, the malfunction doctrine will not help a plaintiff injured when her butane lighter causes an explosion if she lights a cigarette while surrounded by gas fumes in a boat her husband has just fueled up;[65] nor will the doctrine assist a plaintiff injured when his grinding disc explodes if he does not show that the prior user had not abused it;[66] nor will it assist the owner of a used

**61.** See, e.g., Corcoran v. General Motors Corp., 81 F.Supp.2d 55, 69 (D.D.C. 2000) (alleged brake failure; because other evidence suggested driver error, summary judgment for defendant); Saieva v. Budget Rent–A–Car, 591 N.E.2d 507, 516 (Ill. App. Ct. 1992) (summary judgment for defendant affirmed where record supported inference that plaintiff was speeding over dark, wet, and bumpy rural highway and simply lost control of van); Cohen v. General Motors Corp., 427 So.2d 389 (Fla. Dist. Ct. App. 1983) (while car was sitting on an incline and in reverse gear, plaintiff reached inside and released parking brake, causing car to back over his leg).

**62.** See, e.g., Parsons v. Ford Motor Co., 85 S.W.3d 323 (Tex. App. 2002) (recognizing malfunction doctrine but holding that it did not apply where a dealer's intervening replacement and repair of the allegedly defective ignition switch negated the inference of a defect); Yielding v. Chrysler Motor Co., 783 S.W.2d 353 (Ark. 1990) (repairers); Farmer v. Ford Motor Co., 316 So.2d 140 (La. Ct. App. 1975) (use of car by prior owner); Scanlon v. General Motors Corp., 326 A.2d 673 (N.J. 1974) (dealer repairer and wife as other driver); Elliott v. Lachance, 256 A.2d 153 (N.H. 1969) (hair loss from permanent solution could result if beautician left solution on hair too long).

**63.** See, e.g., Schlier v. Milwaukee Elec. Tool Corp., 835 F.Supp. 839, 842 (E.D. Pa. 1993) (blade of power circular saw was dull and saw that was dirty).

**64.** See, e.g., Kourim v. Emerson Elec. Co., 2004 WL 1391747, at *4 (N.D.Tex. 2004) (where refrigerator leaked and caused damage, "any circumstantial evidence created merely by the valve's malfunction is rebutted by Defendants' evidence that the age of the filter ... could have caused the failure"); Corcoran v. General Motors Corp., 81 F.Supp.2d 55, 69 (D.D.C. 2000) ("although brake failure in a new car gives rise to the inference that a defect existed

when the car entered the stream of commerce, this inference is unavailable to the plaintiff, whose complaint involves a 7½ year-old car which he drove approximately 23,000 miles without incident."); Woodin v. J.C. Penney Co., 629 A.2d 974 (Pa. Super. Ct. 1993) (no evidence of defect in cord of freezer that had functioned flawlessly for 8 years of continuous operation); Mullen v. General Motors Corp., 336 N.E.2d 338 (Ill. App. Ct. 1975) (28 month old tire driven 24,000 miles, possibly driven on while underinflated). See generally Prosser and Keeton on Torts § 99, at 697 ("[t]he older the product, the less likely it is that evidence of malfunctioning will suffice as an inference of a construction flaw").

However, even if the product has had a long and full life, "[w]here a failure is caused by a defect in a relatively inaccessible part integral to the structure of the automobile not generally required to be repaired, replaced or maintained, it may be reasonable, absent misuse, to infer that the defect is attributable to the manufacturer." Holloway v. General Motors Corp., 271 N.W.2d 777, 782 (Mich. 1978) (4 year-old car, driven 47,000 miles, suddenly left highway and hit a utility pole; directed verdict for manufacturer reversed).

**65.** Willard v. BIC Corp., 788 F.Supp. 1059 (W.D. Mo. 1991).

**66.** See Jakubowski v. Minnesota Mining & Mfg., 199 A.2d 826, 831 (N.J. 1964) (plaintiff failed to show that grinding disc's failure was more likely caused by defect than by wearing out or misuse):

There is no hint in the record as to the manner and extent of use of the disc prior to plaintiff's use of it. Plaintiff failed to produce as a witness the workman he succeeded or to introduce other evidence which would exclude prior mishandling or overuse of the disc as a cause of the break. It is quite possible that a

pickup truck that caught fire, where the truck had been driven over 50,000 miles by two prior owners, one of whom had installed a spotlight on the door frame;[67] nor can homeowners rely upon the doctrine when their toaster-oven catches fire and burns down their home if the toaster-oven may well have lived out its useful life.[68] But a plaintiff must negate only the most likely alternative causes of malfunction, and only by a preponderance of the evidence, so that a plaintiff need not conclusively disprove every conceivable alternative theory of how the malfunction may possibly have occurred.[69]

By its very nature, the malfunction doctrine generally permits a plaintiff to establish a prima facie case—proof of a malfunction together with the absence of plausible causes other than the product's defectiveness—without resort to expert testimony.[70] But if the testimony of the parties and lay witnesses, together with common sense, do not remove the probability of other causes of a malfunction, then a plaintiff fairly may be required to exclude such other causes by expert testimony.[71]

weakness in the backing was created by inexpert or careless use during the preceding operation, causing the disc to break when plaintiff subsequently used it.

**67.** Ford Motor Co. v. Ridgway, 135 S.W.3d 598 (Tex. 2004) (plaintiff's expert "suspected" an electrical system malfunction caused the fire but could not rule out other causes).

**68.** Walker v. General Elec. Co., 968 F.2d 116 (1st Cir. 1992) (Me. law) (plaintiffs' expert admitted that shut-off mechanisms on toaster-ovens sometimes wear out and need to be replaced; plaintiffs' toaster-oven used daily for over six years).

**69.** In Welge v. Planters Lifesavers Co., 17 F.3d 209 (7th Cir. 1994) (Ill. law) (Posner, C.J.), the plaintiff was injured when a bottle of peanuts shattered as he attempted to replace the lid. The plaintiff testified that he did not mishandle the bottle, but the defendants asserted that the plaintiff had failed to exclude causes for the shattering apart from the bottle's defectiveness. "Elves may have played ninepins with the jar of peanuts while Welge and Godfrey were sleeping.... The plaintiff in a products liability suit is not required to exclude every possibility, however fantastic or remote, that the defect which led to the accident was caused by someone other than one of the defendants." Id. at 211. "Normal people do not lock up their jars and cans lest something happen to damage these containers while no one is looking. The probability of such damage is too remote. It is not only too remote to make a rational person take measures to prevent it; it is too remote to defeat a products liability suit should a container prove dangerously defective." Id. at 211–212. See also W. Prosser, Law of Torts § 103, at 673 (4th ed. 1971) ("The

plaintiff is not required to eliminate all other possibilities, and so prove his case beyond a reasonable doubt.... [I]t is enough that he makes out a preponderance of probability.").

**70.** Cf. Sundberg v. Keller Ladder, 189 F.Supp.2d 671 (E.D. Mich. 2002) (plaintiff need not proffer expert testimony to show that ladder which collapsed was defectively manufactured); Colon ex rel. Molina v. BIC USA, Inc., 199 F.Supp.2d 53 (S.D.N.Y. 2001) (plaintiff and other lay witnesses' account of event was sufficient for jury to decide if particular butane lighter was a "lemon"); Perez–Trujillo v. Volvo Car Corp. (Swed.), 137 F.3d 50, 55–56 (1st Cir. 1998) (P.R. law); O'Connor v. General Motors Corp., 1997 WL 792996, at *3 (Conn. Super. Ct. 1997). Compare Silvestri v. General Motors Corp., 210 F.3d 240 (4th Cir. 2000) (N.Y. law) (airbag did not deploy) ("in order to justify dismissing a case because the plaintiff has failed to present expert testimony, a court must find that the facts necessary to establish a prima facie case cannot be presented to any reasonably informed factfinder without the assistance of expert testimony").

**71.** See, e.g., Cantrell v. Weber–Stephen Prods. Co., 38 Fed.Appx. 921 (4th Cir. 2002) (Md. law) (summary judgment for defendant proper where plaintiff failed to provide expert testimony on why gas grill exploded; without such testimony, "a jury could only infer the presence of a defect in the grill by engaging in 'surmise, conjecture, or speculation.'"); Beatty v. Ford Motor Co., 574 S.E.2d 803 (W. Va. 2002) (dismissing claim that an automobile's drag line had a manufacturing defect because plaintiff did not show that a broken drag link would not ordinarily happen absent a defect); Clark v.

When a plaintiff successfully invokes the malfunction doctrine, a permissible inference arises that a defect caused the malfunction, an inference which the defendant has no obligation (and frequently has no evidence) to rebut.[72] The plaintiff still has the burden to prove both defectiveness and causation by a preponderance of the evidence; the doctrine merely provides a circumstantial method by which these elements may be proved in the limited class of cases in which direct evidence is unavailable for some good reason.[73] "The plaintiff still must satisfy the burden of proving that a defect is the most likely cause of the accident, and therefore must negate the likelihood of other reasonable causes."[74] Indeed, because of the vagueness of this ephemeral form of evidence built on circumstantial inferences, the plaintiff's burden of proof is especially important in malfunction cases to protect defendants from unfounded liability. Thus, a plaintiff must establish such a case by the *probabilities*, not just the possibilities,[75] and where there is an equal probability that an accident occurred for reasons other than a defect attributable to the defendant, the plaintiff's case will fail.[76]

Bohn Ford, Inc., 213 F.Supp.2d 957 (S.D. Ind. 2002) (dismissing claim that tire had manufacturing defect for lack of expert testimony because tire failure is not such an unusual event that a defect can be inferred solely from fact that accident occurred); Booth v. Black & Decker, Inc., 166 F.Supp.2d 215 (E.D. Pa. 2001) (toaster oven allegedly was defective and caught fire; plaintiff failed to present prima facie case because expert's methodology for determining defectiveness and causation failed *Daubert* standards); Corcoran v. General Motors Corp., 81 F.Supp.2d 55, 69 (D.D.C. 2000) (alleged brake failure; other evidence suggested driver error); White v. W.W. Grainger Co., 1988 WL 290663 (D. Mass. 1998) (dimmer switch started fire); Brooks v. Colonial Chevrolet–Buick, Inc., 579 So.2d 1328 (Ala. 1991) (brakes failed); Falcone v. Chrysler Motors Corp., 13 UCC Rep. Serv. 2d 734 (D. Md. 1990) (reclining mechanism on seat broke in rear-end collision).

**72.** "[T]he circumstantial evidence rules established in these malfunction theory cases merely establish a prima facie case and permit but do not require a finding for the plaintiff even in the absence of contrary evidence. Thus a defendant need not come forward with rebuttal evidence to avoid a directed verdict.... [T]he burden of production does not shift.... " O'Connor v. General Motors Corp., 1997 WL 792996, at *3 (Conn. Super. 1997). See also Cassisi v. Maytag Co., 396 So.2d 1140, 1151 (Fla. Dist. Ct. App. 1981). *But cf.* Graham v. Walter S. Pratt & Sons Inc., 706 N.Y.S.2d 242, 243 (App. Div. 2000) (the inference of defectiveness (and causation) raised by a product malfunction serves effectively to shift to the defendant the burden of coming

forward with the evidence (the "burden of production")).

**73.** See, e.g., Walker v. General Elec. Co., 968 F.2d 116 (1st Cir. 1992) (Me. law); Ocean Barge Transp. Co. v. Hess Oil Virgin Islands Corp., 726 F.2d 121, 124–25 (3d Cir. 1984) (V.I. law).

**74.** Ocean Barge Transp. Co. v. Hess Oil Virgin Islands Corp., 726 F.2d 121, 125 (3d Cir. 1984) (V.I. law).

**75.** "For circumstantial evidence to make out a prima facie case, it must tend to negate other reasonable causes, or there must be an expert opinion that the product was defective. Because liability in a products liability action cannot be based on mere speculation, guess or conjecture, the circumstances shown must justify an inference of probability as distinguished from mere possibility." Mateika v. LaSalle Thermogas Co., 418 N.E.2d 503, 505 (Ill. App. Ct. 1981). See also Henry v. Bridgestone/Firestone Inc., 63 Fed.Appx. 953 (7th Cir. 2003) (plaintiff need not produce the allegedly defective product to succeed on a manufacturing defect claim but must produce circumstantial evidence that tends to support the theory with reasonable certainty and probability).

**76.** "Evidence which points equally to a cause for which the defendants are responsible and to one for which the defendants are not responsible is not sufficient to make a case of strict liability in tort for submission to a jury." Willard v. BIC Corp., 788 F.Supp. 1059, 1064 (W.D. Mo. 1991). See also State Farm Fire & Cas. Co. v. Chrysler Corp., 523 N.E.2d 489, 496–97 (Ohio 1988); Mays v. Ciba–Geigy Corp., 661 P.2d 348 (Kan. 1983) (gas pipeline explosion).

## Acceptance

Having spread across the nation with little fanfare over the last half century, the malfunction doctrine has become a well established precept of modern products liability law.[77] A substantial and growing majority of American jurisdictions[78] (typically without the "malfunction doctrine" label) now accept this principle of circumstantial evidence for proving defectiveness in strict products liability.[79] Certifying the propriety of the doctrine's widespread acceptance, the American Law Institute in 1998 endorsed the principle in the *Products Liability Restatement* § 3.[80]

**77.** See Products Liability Restatement § 3, Reporters' Note to cmt. *b* ("A huge body of case law supports this proposition."). For the older case authority, see W. Prosser, Law of Torts § 103 (4th ed. 1971).

**78.** Many of the older cases are collected in Annot., 65 A.L.R.4th 346 (1988). Asserting that the doctrine is a minority rule, 1 Frumer and Friedman, Products Liability § 8.06[3] list the following jurisdictions as adhering to some version of the malfunction theory under whatever name: Alabama, Arizona, Arkansas, Connecticut, D.C., Florida, Idaho, Illinois, Kansas, Louisiana, Maryland, Michigan, Missouri, Nevada, New Hampshire, New York, North Carolina, Pennsylvania, Tennessee, Texas, West Virginia, and Wyoming. To this list should be added at least California, Colorado, Georgia, Hawaii, Indiana, Iowa, Kentucky, Maine, Massachusetts, Minnesota, Montana, New Jersey, Ohio, Oklahoma, Oregon, Puerto Rico, Rhode Island, Utah, the Virgin Islands, Washington, and Wisconsin. See, e.g., Myrlak v. Port Auth., 723 A.2d 45, 52 (N.J. 1999); Perez–Trujillo v. Volvo Car Corp. (Swed.), 137 F.3d 50, 55–56 (1st Cir. 1998) (P.R. law); White v. W.W. Grainger Co., 1988 WL 290663 (D. Mass. 1988); Ford Motor Co. v. Reed, 689 N.E.2d 751 (Ind. App. 1997); Taylor v. Cooper Tire & Rub. Co., 130 F.3d 1395 (10th Cir. 1997) (Utah law); Hall v. General Motors Corp., 8 F.3d 27 (9th Cir. 1993) (Or. law); State Farm Fire & Cas. Co. v. Chrysler Corp., 523 N.E.2d 489, 494 (Ohio 1988); Weir v. Federal Ins. Co., 811 F.2d 1387 (10th Cir. 1987) (Colo. law); Rix v. General Motors Corp., 723 P.2d 195, 203–04 (Mont. 1986); Thomas v. Amway Corp., 488 A.2d 716 (R.I. 1985); Ocean Barge Transp. Co. v. Hess Oil Virgin Islands Corp., 726 F.2d 121, 124–25 (3d Cir. 1984) (V.I. law); Hinckley v. La Mesa R.V. Center, Inc., 205 Cal.Rptr. 22 (Ct. App. 1984); Skil Corp. v. Lugsdin, 309 S.E.2d 921 (Ga. Ct. App. 1983); Perkins v. Trailco Mfg. & Sales Co., 613 S.W.2d 855 (Ky. 1981); Bombardi v. Pochel's Appliance & TV Co., 518 P.2d 202 (Wash. Ct. App. 1973); Jagmin v. Simonds Abrasive Co., 211 N.W.2d 810 (Wis. 1973); Lee v. Crookston Coca–Cola Bottling Co., 188 N.W.2d 426 (Minn. 1971); Stewart v. Budget Rent–A–Car Corp., 470

P.2d 240 (Haw. 1970); Marathon Battery Co. v. Kilpatrick, 418 P.2d 900 (Okla. 1965). While most courts are less explicit than New Jersey in formally adopting the doctrine, each decision above acknowledges this method of proof for use in appropriate cases.

**79.** Because strict liability in tort is the chief claim in modern products liability litigation, most applications of the malfunction doctrine have been in this context. But the malfunction theory is also especially applicable to claims for breach of the implied warranty of merchantability which are based upon a product's being "unfit" for the ordinary purposes for which such goods are used. See UCC § 2–314(2)(c) (1987). In Greco v. Bucciconi Eng'g Co., 283 F.Supp. 978, 982 (W.D. Pa. 1967), aff'd, 407 F.2d 87 (3d Cir. 1969), the court explained:

> When machinery 'malfunctions', it obviously lacks fitness regardless of the cause of the malfunction. Under the theory of warranty, the 'sin' is the lack of fitness as evidenced by the malfunction itself rather than some specific dereliction by the manufacturer in constructing or designing the machinery.

See also DeWitt v. Eveready Battery Co., 565 S.E.2d 140 (N.C. 2002); Genetti v. Caterpillar, Inc., 621 N.W.2d 529 (Neb. 2001) (thorough analysis); Sipes v. General Motors Corp., 946 S.W.2d 143, 158 (Tex. App. 1997) (airbag failed to deploy); Triplett v. General Elec. Co., 954 F.Supp. 149 (W.D. Mich. 1996); Estate of Triplett v. General Elec. Co., 954 F.Supp. 149 (W.D. Mich. 1996) (ballast in fluorescent light that allegedly caused fire); Collins v. Sears, Roebuck & Co., 583 N.E.2d 873 (Mass. App. Ct. 1992) (fire in dryer's electrical system).

**80.** Restatement (3d) of Torts: Products Liability § 3, "Circumstantial Evidence Supporting Inference of Product Defect," provides:

> It may be inferred that the harm sustained by the plaintiff was caused by a product defect existing at the time of sale or distribution, without proof of a specific defect, when the incident that harmed the plaintiff:

Courts and juries need to be cautious and apply the malfunction doctrine only in those limited situations where, first, the circumstances of the case conspire to prevent the plaintiff from establishing defectiveness and causation by ordinary methods of proof, and, second, where circumstantial evidence in the case points fairly to some defect attributable to the manufacturer as the cause of the accident.[81] In a proper case,[82] however, it is difficult to see how any jurisdiction could reject some properly formulated version[83] of such a well-established,[84] fair,[85] and logical[86] principle of proof. In short, the manifest merits of this simple canon of circumstantial evidence suggest that its acceptance should soon be universal.

## § 7.5  FOOD AND DRINK

From early times, people have relied on the skill and care of others to catch, grow, gather, preserve, prepare, and provide much of the food

(a) was of a kind that ordinarily occurs as a result of product defect; and

(b) was not, in the particular case, solely the result of causes other than product defect existing at the time of sale or distribution.

See Myrlak v. Port Auth., 723 A.2d 45 (N.J. 1999) (adopting § 3).

**81.** See Products Liability Restatement § 3 cmt. *b*; Henderson and Twerski, Intuition and Technology in Product Design Litigation: An Essay on Proximate Causation, 88 Geo. L.J. 659, 672 (2000) (malfunction cases "constitute a relatively narrow subset of products liability cases"); Hoffman, Res Ipsa Loquitur and Indeterminate Product Defects: If They Speak for Themselves, What Are They Saying?, 36 S. Tex. L. Rev. 353, 380 (1995) ("it will be up to the courts to ensure that [§ 3 of the Restatement] is appropriately limited to cases in which circumstantial evidence truly supports a reasonable inference that a defect existed in the product at the time it left the manufacturer's hands and is not simply a 'catchall' for cases in which plaintiffs are unable to sustain their burden of proof of a specific manufacturing or design defect").

**82.** Such as when a new appliance explodes or catches fire. See, e.g., Cassisi v. Maytag Co., 396 So.2d 1140, 1151–52 (Fla. Dist. Ct. App. 1981) (strength of inference of defectiveness from malfunction depends on particular type of product; stronger inference of defect arises from dangerous malfunction in self-operating products like televisions and dryers than in products, like cars leaving highway, whose dangers are to a large extent under driver's control).

**83.** The Restatement's formulation is not ideal, which reflects the difficulty of formulating a concise, general statement of the principle. A formulation of the malfunction doctrine like the following might be simpler:

If proof of a specific product defect is unavailable through no fault of the plaintiff, the factfinder may infer that a product which malfunctioned was defective at the time of sale if the plaintiff establishes that (1) the malfunction was of a kind that ordinarily does not occur unless the product is defective, and (2) any defect in the product was most likely attributable to the manufacturer and not to the plaintiff, a third party, normal wear and tear, or other causes.

Consider also the commonsense formulation of Chief Judge Richard Posner: "If it is the kind of accident that would not have occurred but for a defect in the product, and if it is reasonably plain that the defect was not introduced after the product was sold, the accident is evidence that the product was defective when sold." Welge v. Planters Lifesavers Co., 17 F.3d 209, 211 (7th Cir. 1994) (Ill. law).

**84.** See W. Prosser, Law of Torts § 103 (4th ed. 1971).

**85.** When a product "is lost or destroyed in the accident, direct evidence of specific defect may not be available" in this case the malfunction doctrine "may offer the plaintiff the only fair opportunity to recover." Products Liability Restatement § 3 cmt. *b*.

**86.** "When the jury reasonably can find that the product is unchanged from the condition it was in when sold and the unusual behavior of the product is not due to any conduct on the part of the plaintiff or anyone else who has a connection with the product, logic dictates that it is a distinct possibility that there is some defect in the product." Brownell v. White Motor Corp., 490 P.2d 184, 187 (Or. 1971).

and drink indispensable to survival. Whether paid for with a beaver pelt, a copper coin, or a modern dollar, food has always been the single most important product bought and sold by human beings. Both king and pauper live by food and drink, just as both may die by food or drink gone bad. And this essential fact of human life is as true today as it was a thousand years ago. Because pure food is necessary to survival, rendering most persons extraordinarily dependent for their health, safety, and very lives on the care and skill of food providers, the rules that govern liability for selling defective food and drink have long stood apart from those concerning other types of products.[1]

Defective food and drink can kill and injure human beings in myriad ways. The types of defects in different types of foods span the gamut, from spoiled meat,[2] particles of glass in ice cream,[3] ptomaine poison in a can of pork and beans,[4] a piece of metal in a meatball,[5] arsenic in biscuit flour,[6] tacks or wire in a loaf of bread,[7] clam shells in a bowl of chowder[8] and fried clam strips,[9] a crustaceous creature in a can of mackerel,[10] strychnine in a box of candy,[11] a metal screw in chewing gum,[12] and glass,[13] dead flies,[14] worms,[15] condoms,[16] and mice[17] in Coca–Cola and other soft drinks, not to mention contaminated water[18] and soft drink bottles that explode.[19] But the prize for the most repulsive "food" item

### § 7.5

**1.** "No man can justify selling corrupt victual, but an action on the case lies against the seller, whether the victual was warranted to be good or not. But if a man sells me cloth or other thing, [he must] *know the cloth to be bad* [to] be punished by writ on the case." Keilway's Report (Frowike) 91, 72 Eng. Rep. 254 (1507), quoted in F. R. Dickerson, Products Liability and the Food Consumer 20 (1951) (emphasis added).

**2.** See, e.g., Prejean v. Great Atl. & Pac. Tea Co., Inc., 457 So.2d 60 (La. Ct. App. 1984) (rotten roast was "green as grass"); Swift & Co. v. Wells, 110 S.E.2d 203 (Va. 1959) (food poisoning from pork shoulder containing staphylococci organisms); Salmon v. Libby, McNeill & Libby, 76 N.E. 573 (Ill. 1905).

**3.** See Minutilla v. Providence Ice Cream, 144 A. 884 (R.I. 1929).

**4.** See Davis v. Van Camp Packing Co., 176 N.W. 382 (Iowa 1920).

**5.** See Jones v. GMRI, Inc., 551 S.E.2d 867 (N.C. Ct. App. 2001).

**6.** See Ballard & Ballard Co. v. Jones, 21 So.2d 327 (Ala. 1945).

**7.** See Collins Baking Co. v. Savage, 150 So. 336 (Ala. 1933).

**8.** See Koperwas v. Publix Supermarkets, Inc., 534 So.2d 872 (Fla. Dist. Ct. App. 1988).

**9.** See Mitchell v. T.G.I. Friday's, 748 N.E.2d 89,90 (Ohio Ct. App. 2000).

**10.** See Johnson v. Epstein, 1998 WL 166805 (N.D.N.Y. 1998).

**11.** See Whitethorn v. Nash–Finch Co., 293 N.W. 859 (S.D. 1940).

**12.** See Hickman v. William Wrigley, Jr. Co., 768 So.2d 812 (La. Ct. App. 2000).

**13.** See Watson v. Augusta Brewing Co., 52 S.E. 152 (Ga. 1905) (particles of glass in bottle of soda).

**14.** See Floyd v. Florence Nehi Bottling Co., 198 S.E. 161 (S.C. 1938).

**15.** See Norfolk Coca–Cola Bottling Works v. Land, 52 S.E.2d 85 (Va. 1949) (worm in bottle of Coke).

**16.** See Hagan v. Coca–Cola Bottling Co., 804 So.2d 1234 (Fla. 2001).

**17.** See Eisenbeiss v. Payne, 25 P.2d 162 (Ariz. 1933) (remains of mouse in bottle of soft drink).

**18.** See Gash, Beyond Erin Brockovich and a Civil Action: Should Strict Products Liability Be the Next Frontier for Water Contamination Lawsuits?, 80 Wash. U. L.Q. 51 (2002).

**19.** See, e.g., Escola v. Coca Cola Bottling Co. of Fresno, 150 P.2d 436 (Cal. 1944). Because these cases do not involve risks from consuming the beverage itself, they are treated elsewhere. See generally 4 Frumer and Friedman, Products Liability § 48.24; Spangenberg, Exploding Bottles, 24 Ohio St. L.J. 516 (1963) (also examining bottle cases, including mice-in-bottle cases).

sold to a consumer probably should be awarded to the seller of a can of chewing tobacco containing a human toe.[20]

The great majority of defective food and drink cases involve claims that the foodstuffs contained "manufacturing" defects—hazardous objects, contaminants, and other deviations from the safe and wholesome condition intended by the seller and expected by the buyer.[21] Less frequently, foodstuff cases involve claims of defects in design or warnings, as from serving coffee at too high a temperature with insufficient warnings of the risks,[22] or failing to warn consumers of possible health risks from certain types of food.[23] This section examines the recurring issues that arise in the more typical manufacturing defect cases involving food and drink.[24]

**20.** See Pillars v. R.J. Reynolds Tobacco Co., 78 So. 365 (Miss. 1918).

**21.** See, e.g., Phillips v. Restaurant Mgmt. of Carolina, L.P., 552 S.E.2d 686 (N.C. Ct. App. 2001) (employee's saliva in nacho chips bought at Taco Bell); Hickman v. William Wrigley, Jr. Co., 768 So.2d 812 (La. Ct. App. 2000) (screw in gum); Otis Spunkmeyer, Inc. v. Blakely, 30 S.W.3d 678 (Tex. App. 2000) (hard object in cookie).

**22.** The hot coffee cases normally involve claims of defective design (too high a temperature) or warnings (failure to warn adequately of the high temperature and its capacity to burn), rather than manufacturing defects. See, e.g., McCroy v. Coastal Mart, Inc., 207 F.Supp.2d 1265 (D. Kan. 2002) (no duty to warn about severity of potential burns from hot chocolate; extensive review of hot beverage cases); Olliver v. Heavenly Bagels, Inc., 729 N.Y.S.2d 611 (Sup. Ct. 2001) (summary judgment for defendants; discussing other cases). Liability in such cases thus depends on rules that govern these other types of defects, discussed in chapters 8 and 9, below. See Products Liability Restatement § 7 and cmt. a. See generally Note, 10 Loy. Consumer L. Rev. 310 (1998) (discussing split in hot coffee burn cases); § 10.3, below. On punitive damages for coffee burns, see § 18.3, below.

**23.** See, e.g., Pelman v. McDonald's Corp., 237 F.Supp.2d 512 (S.D.N.Y. 2003) (restaurant's failure to warn of deleterious aspects of fast food; held, restaurants have no duty to warn patrons of open, obvious, and inherent dangers of consuming such foods); Livingston v. Marie Callender's, Inc., 85 Cal.Rptr.2d 528 (Ct. App. 1999) (failure to warn of risk of possible reaction to MSG in soup).

Some cases have imposed at least a duty to warn of the risk of a serious, possibly deadly, infection from contaminated oysters, even though the risk normally is only to persons with cirrhosis of the liver, hepa-

titis, diabetes, high iron content, or suppressed immune systems, which conditions diminish the ability of the body to destroy the bacteria. See, e.g., Simeon v. Doe, 618 So.2d 848 (La. 1993) (no strict liability, but may be duty in negligence to warn); Kilpatrick v. Superior Court, 11 Cal.Rptr.2d 323 (Ct. App. 1992); Cain v. Sheraton Perimeter Park S. Hotel, 592 So.2d 218 (Ala. 1991) (jury might find oyster eater did not reasonably expect contamination that could cause hepatitis).

**24.** For early treatments of the liability of purveyors of food and drink, see, e.g., F. R. Dickerson, Products Liability and the Food Consumer (1951); H. Melnick, The Sale of Food and Drink at Common Law and Under the Uniform Sales Act (1936), reviewed in 50 Harv. L. Rev. 553 (1937); Mintener, Product Liability Law, 5 Food Drug Cosm. L.J. 168 (1950); Guiher and Morris, Handling Food Products Liability Cases, 1 Food Drug Cosmetic L.Q. 109 (1946); Perkins, Unwholesome Food as a Source of Liability (pts. 1 and 2), 5 Iowa L. Bull. 6, 86 (1919, 1920); Note, 92 U. Pa. L. Rev. 306 (1944).

For more recent treatments, see Noah, One Decade of Food and Drug Law Scholarship: A Selected Bibliography, 55 Food Drug Cosm. L.J. 641 (2000); Notes, 74 Tul. L. Rev. 379 (1999) (foreign/natural doctrine); 10 Loy. Consumer L. Rep. 310 (1998) (judicial split in hot coffee burn cases); 18 S. Ill. U. L.J. 637 (1994) (same); Comment, 72 N.D. L. Rev. 481 (1996) (pleading and proving food foreign contaminant cases); Annots., 2 A.L.R.5th 1 (1992) (liability for spoiled or contaminated food); 2 A.L.R.5th 189 (1992) (liability for object related to but not intended to be in food). See generally 4 Frumer and Friedman § 48; CCH Prod. Liab. Rep. ¶¶ 30,002H, 30,007; Products Liability Restatement § 7. On English, Irish, and E.U. law, see, e.g., R. O'Rourke, Food Safety and Product Liability (Palladian 2000); R. O'Rourke, European Food Law (Palladian 1998); D. Jukes, Food Legislation of the UK (Butterworths 1996).

## Early Law

Early law provided criminal penalties and civil remedies for the sale of defective food and drink. Beginning in 1266, a series of early English statutes criminalized the sale of "corrupt" food and drink for immediate consumption,[25] and, by 1431, the civil law held purveyors of foodstuffs strictly accountable for the wholesomeness of their provisions.[26] Whether this special duty amounted to a common law warranty of the wholesomeness of food is uncertain,[27] but American courts from an early date assumed that it did. In an 1815 New York decision, *Van Bracklin v. Fonda*,[28] a seller of beef was held strictly liable for failing to disclose that the cow had been diseased prior to slaughter. Relying on Blackstone, the court observed that a warranty of quality is always implied into the sale of foodstuffs because "the preservation of health and life" requires the seller to be "bound to know that they are sound and wholesome at his peril."[29] A century later, recognizing the special vulnerability of food consumers, the New York court reaffirmed the view that the special importance of food safety fully justifies imposing strict liability on sellers of food and drink.[30]

Although American courts from an early date applied the ancient tort-like warranty of quality to sales of foodstuffs made directly to consumers,[31] the absence of privity of contract often obstructed recov-

**25.** See F. R. Dickerson, Products Liability and the Food Consumer 20 (1951).

**26.** "A taverner or vintner was bound as such to sell wholesome food and drink." Ames, The History of Assumpsit, 2 Harv. L. Rev. 1, 9 (1888). The case decided in 1431 provided: "[I]f I come into a tavern to eat and the taverner gives and sells me beer or food which is corrupt, by which I am put to great suffering, I shall clearly have an action against the taverner on the case even though he makes no warranty to me." Year Book, 9 Hen. VI, f. 53B, pl.37 (1431), quoted in F. R. Dickerson, Products Liability and the Food Consumer 20 (1951).

On the evolution of the tort-like warranty applied to food cases, see F. R. Dickerson, Products Liability and the Food Consumer (1951); Prosser, The Assault on the Citadel (Strict Liability to the Consumer), 69 Yale L.J. 1099, 1103–10 (1960) (from which much of this historical discussion is derived).

**27.** Compare Melick, The Sale of Food and Drink 10 (1936) (yes), with Perkins, Unwholesome Food as a Source of Liability, 5 Iowa L. Bull. 6, 8–9 (1919) (no).

**28.** 12 Johns. 468, 7 Am. Dec. 339 (N.Y. 1815).

**29.** More fully, the court remarked:

In 3 Black. Com. 165, it is stated as a sound and elementary proposition, that in contracts for provisions, it is always implied that they are wholesome; and if they are not, case lies to recover damages for the deceit.

In the sale of provisions for domestic use, the vendor is bound to know that they are sound and wholesome, at his peril. This is a principle, not only salutary, but necessary to the preservation of health and life.

In the present case, the concealment of the fact that the animal was diseased, is equivalent to the suggestion of a falsehood that she was sound.

*Van Bracklin*, 12 Johns. at 467–68.

**30.** Race v. Krum, 118 N.E. 853, 854 (N.Y. 1918):

This rule is based upon the high regard which the law has for human life. The consequences to the consumer resulting from consumption of articles of food sold for immediate use may be so disastrous that an obligation is placed upon the seller to see to it, at his peril, that the articles sold are fit for the purpose for which they are intended. The rule is an onerous one, but public policy, as well as the public health, demand such obligation should be imposed.

**31.** See, e.g., Van Bracklin v. Fonda, 12 Johns. 468, 7 Am. Dec. 339 (N.Y. 1815) (implication of fraudulent concealment of contamination, and possibly an express representation that the beef was edible). See generally Jacob E. Decker & Sons, Inc. v.

ery.[32] However, from the early 1900s,[33] some courts, often intermingling theories of negligence and implied warranty, began breaking through the privity barrier to hold food sellers liable to third parties.[34] By the middle of the twentieth century, many jurisdictions had abandoned the requirement of privity in food cases by enforcing a special food warranty in tort that ran to remote consumers.[35]

One such case was *Jacob E. Decker & Sons v. Capps*[36] in which a producer sold contaminated sausage to a retail merchant who sold it to Mr. Capps. The Capps family consumed the sausage, which killed one of the children and seriously sickened the remainder of the family. In an action against the remote producer, the court imposed an implied warranty in tort into the sale of food and drink running to those injured by the defective meat, reasoning that this kind of strict liability to remote food consumers is necessary as a deterrent to protect human health and life; that remote providers intend that the food they sell to intermediaries eventually will be consumed by someone; that most consumers, lacking the tools, skills, and time necessary to inspect their food for hazards, are unable to protect themselves effectively against dangerous defects in the foods they eat; and that legal incentives for improving food safety are best placed on food suppliers.[37] But it should be noted that *Capps* was in the vanguard of developing doctrine on the privity issue, and most jurisdictions continued for some time to prohibit warranty actions in the absence of privity, leaving negligence for some time as the only form of relief in cases of this type.[38]

Capps, 164 S.W.2d 828, 831–32 (Tex. 1942) (noting that the warranty in food cases was not the modern contractual warranty but the separate tort law warranty derived from the action of deceit).

**32.** For cases against retailers or restaurants, where the absence of privity was held to bar recovery, see, e.g., Borucki v. MacKenzie Bros. Co., 3 A.2d 224 (Conn. 1938) (purchaser's child—glass in liverwurst); Hazelton v. First Nat'l Stores, 190 A. 280 (N.H. 1937) (wife and two children—trichinosis); Bourcheix v. Willow Brook Dairy, 196 N.E. 617 (N.Y. 1935) (chauffeur—glass in milk); Shepard v. Beck Bros., 225 N.Y.S. 438, 440 (City Ct. 1927) (grandson—nail in coffee cake); Prinsen v. Russos, 215 N.W. 905 (Wis. 1927) (guest—trichinae in ham sandwich). For similar cases against manufacturers, see, e.g., Nelson v. Armour Packing Co., 90 S.W. 288 (Ark. 1905); Chysky v. Drake Bros. Co., 139 N.E. 576 (N.Y. 1923). See F. R. Dickerson, Products Liability and the Food Consumer §§ 1.22 (retailers and restaurants); 2.1–2.6 (manufacturers) (1951).

**33.** And possibly before. See, e.g., Mazetti v. Armour & Co., 135 P. 633 (Wash. 1913), and Tomlinson v. Armour & Co, 70 A. 314 (N.J. Ct. Err. & App. 1908) (both

citing earlier cases). See generally Prosser, The Assault Upon the Citadel (Strict Liability to the Consumer), 69 Yale L.J. 1099, 1106 (1960).

**34.** For a more expansive discussion of these developments, see Prosser, The Assault on the Citadel (Strict Liability to the Consumer), 69 Yale L.J. 1099, 1103–10 (1960).

**35.** But many courts still refused. Although noting a trend in favor of liability, Prosser in 1941 observed that "[t]he majority of courts still refuse to find a strict liability even as to food." W. Prosser, Handbook of the Law of Torts § 83, at 692 (1941).

**36.** 164 S.W.2d 828 (Tex. 1942).

**37.** "[W]here food products sold for human consumption are unfit for that purpose, there is such an utter failure of the purpose for which the food is sold, and the consequences of eating unsound food are so disastrous to human health and life, that the law imposes a warranty of purity in favor of the ultimate consumer as a matter of public policy." Id. at 829.

**38.** See Prosser, The Assault on the Citadel (Strict Liability to the Consumer), 69 Yale L.J. 1099, 1103–10 (1960).

## Theories of Recovery

### *Negligence*

Although most jurisdictions continued to require privity of contract in most negligence claims well into the twentieth century,[39] courts have long made an exception for products that were "imminently dangerous," initially as to a product's inherent condition[40] and later as to its condition if defective.[41] Food products were so classified from an early date, such that the absence of privity quickly dropped away as an obstacle to negligence claims.[42]

Because of society's special concern for food safety, some of the early negligence decisions held purveyors of food and drink to a standard of extraordinary or utmost care.[43] Today, however, consistent with the widespread repudiation of special levels of care,[44] modern courts hold sellers of food and drink, like sellers of other types of products, to the normal standard of reasonable care.[45]

Often, the easiest way for a plaintiff to establish negligence is by proof of a violation of a pure food act which in many states amounts to negligence per se.[46] But before a court may rule that a pure food act provides a basis for negligence per se, the defendant must have violated the statute, which typically requires a finding that the particular foodstuff was "adulterated"[47] and which may allow a defense for good faith

**39.** This was so until rejected by MacPherson v. Buick Motor Co., 111 N.E. 1050 (N.Y. 1916), and its progeny.

**40.** Such products include poisons, guns, and explosives. See Huset v. J.I. Case Threshing Mach. Co., 120 F. 865, 865, 871 (8th Cir. 1903) (Minn. law).

**41.** See MacPherson v. Buick Motor Co., 111 N.E. 1050 (N.Y. 1916).

**42.** See, e.g., Minutilla v. Providence Ice Cream Co., 144 A. 884 (R.I. 1929) (good summary); Freeman v. Schults Bread Co., 163 N.Y.S. 396, 397 (1916); see also Drury v. Armour & Co., 216 S.W. 40 (Ark. 1919); Comment, 4 Fordham L. Rev. 295, 296 n.7 (1935) (collecting cases).

**43.** See, e.g., Linker v. Quaker Oats Co., 11 F.Supp. 794 (D. Okla. 1935) (very high degree of care); Eisenbeiss v. Payne, 25 P.2d 162 (Ariz. 1933) (the "highest duty known to the law").

**44.** See Prosser and Keeton on Torts § 34.

**45.** See, e.g., Hyde v. Schlotzsky's, Inc., 561 S.E.2d 876 (Ga. Ct. App. 2002) (franchisor not liable in negligence to patrons who contracted Hepatitis A from eating tainted food at franchisee's restaurant where franchisor lacked the ability to control restaurant's day-to-day operations); Jones v. GMRI, Inc., 551 S.E.2d 867 (N.C. Ct. App. 2001); Bullara v. Checker's Drive–In Rest., Inc., 736 So.2d 936 (La. Ct. App. 1999); Porteous v. St. Ann's Cafe & Deli, 713 So.2d 454, 457–58 (La. 1998); Flagstar Enters., Inc. v. Davis, 709 So.2d 1132, 1139–41 (Ala. 1997).

**46.** See, e.g., Chambley v. Apple Rest., Inc., 504 S.E.2d 551 (Ga. Ct. App. 1998) (condom in chicken salad); Allen v. Delchamps, Inc., 624 So.2d 1065 (Ala. 1993) (prepackaged celery hearts treated with sulfites in violation of FDA regulations banning their use on fresh produce; asthmatic customer suffered anaphylactic reaction); Koster v. Scotch Assoc., 640 A.2d 1225 (N.J. Super. Ct. Law Div. 1993) (salmonella from Smuggler's Cove); Coward v. Borden Foods, Inc., 229 S.E.2d 262 (S.C. 1976) (hard object in Cracker Jack popcorn); Slonsky v. Phoenix Coca–Cola Bottling Co., 499 P.2d 741 (Ariz. Ct. App. 1972) (metallic filings in bottle of Coke). *Contra*, Jones v. GMRI, Inc., 551 S.E.2d 867 (N.C. Ct. App. 2001) (negligence per se doctrine inapplicable to food case).

On negligence per se, see § 2.4, above.

**47.** See, e.g., Jones v. GMRI, Inc., 551 S.E.2d 867 (N.C. Ct. App. 2001); Goodman v. Wenco Foods, Inc., 423 S.E.2d 444 (N.C. 1992) (small bone sliver in ground beef not "adulteration"); Allen v. Grafton, 164 N.E.2d 167 (Ohio Ct. App. 1960) (oysters containing shell were not adulterated); Norris v. Pig'n Whistle Sandwich Shop, 53 S.E.2d 718 (Ga. Ct. App. 1949) (barbecued pork sandwich containing piece of pig bone not adulterated).

efforts to comply.[48]

Without the assistance of a pure food act, a plaintiff may have difficulty proving the negligence of the purveyor of defective food.[49] This is particularly true in the case of a food-product retailer who purchases the food and then resells it in a sealed container, a situation which deprives the seller of any opportunity to inspect for defects.[50] But, in other cases, the seller's fault is clear.[51] Also, some courts allow juries to infer the negligence of a manufacturer or other seller merely from the presence of a defect in the food.[52]

In cases where direct evidence of responsibility and fault is unavailable, but where circumstantial evidence points to the defendant's probable negligence as the cause of defective food, plaintiffs in most jurisdictions can invoke the doctrine of res ipsa loquitur.[53] Speaking to this very point, Henry David Thoreau declared, "some circumstantial evidence is very strong, as when you find a trout in the milk."[54] In such cases, the circumstantial evidence surrounding the accident leads to inferences that the food would not have been defective without the negligence of someone, that the defendant's exclusive control over the foodstuff at the time of preparation suggests the negligence was that of the defendant,

**48.** For example, a criminal pure food act may provide an exception if the seller has acted in good faith, as by obtaining a guarantee of wholesomeness from its own supplier. See F. R. Dickerson, Products Liability and the Food Consumer 282 (1951).

**49.** See, e.g., Jones v. GMRI, Inc., 551 S.E.2d 867 (N.C. Ct. App. 2001) (affirming directed verdict in favor of restauranteur on negligence claim for serving meatball with a piece of metal lodged inside); Livingston v. Marie Callender's, Inc., 85 Cal.Rptr.2d 528 (Ct. App. 1999) (affirming judgment for defendant on negligence, but reversing on strict liability in tort, for failure to warn of possible allergic reaction to MSG in soup); Cain v. Winn–Dixie La., Inc., 757 So.2d 712 (La. Ct. App. 1999) (no proof that grocery store's bakery was negligent in allowing hair to get into baked cake); Porteous v. St. Ann's Cafe & Deli, 713 So.2d 454 (La. 1998) (reversing judgment for plaintiff on claim of restaurant's negligence for failing to find and remove pearl in oyster po-boy sandwich).

**50.** See, e.g., McCauley v. Manda Bros. Provisions Co., 211 So.2d 637 (La. 1968). At least in some jurisdictions, however, a food consumer injured by a deleterious substance purchased in a sealed container may recover against the seller for breach of an implied warranty of wholesomeness. See, e.g., Bonenberger v. Pittsburgh Mercantile Co., 28 A.2d 913 (Pa. 1942).

On the sealed-container (or "original-package") doctrine or defense, see § 15.2, below.

**51.** See, e.g., Bullara v. Checker's Drive–In Rest., Inc., 736 So.2d 936 (La. Ct. App. 1999) (allowing cockroach to enter chi-

li dog, failing to discover roach lurking in dog prior to sale, and making sale to customer of roach-infested dog); Flagstar Enters., Inc. v. Davis, 709 So.2d 1132 (Ala. 1997) (allowing blood from unbandaged cut to spill into take-out order of biscuit and gravy).

**52.** See, e.g., Bullara v. Checker's Drive–In Rest., Inc., 736 So.2d 936 (La. Ct. App. 1999) (by implication); Vamos v. Coca-Cola Bottling Co. of N.Y., Inc., 627 N.Y.S.2d 265, 270 (Civ. Ct. 1995) ("It has long been the rule that a prima facie case of negligence is made out merely upon proof of the presence of the foreign substance . . . sold in a sealed container"); Cohen v. Allendale Coca–Cola Bottling Co., 351 S.E.2d 897, 899 (S.C. Ct. App. 1986) (Bell, J.).

**53.** See, e.g., Santine v. Coca Cola Bottling Co., 591 P.2d 329 (Okla. Ct. App. 1978); Samson v. Riesing, 215 N.W.2d 662 (Wis. 1974); Leikach v. Royal Crown Bottling Co., 276 A.2d 81 (Md. 1971). *Contra*, Jones v. GMRI, Inc., 551 S.E.2d 867 (N.C. Ct. App. 2001) ("res ipsa loquitur does not apply in a case involving an injury from the ingestion of an adulterated food product"). See generally 4 Frumer and Friedman, Products Liability §§ 48.08[3] and 48.10[2].

On res ipsa loquitur, see § 2.5, above. On the related malfunction doctrine, see § 7.4, above.

**54.** Henry David Thoreau, Nov. 11, 1850, *in* 2 The Journal of Henry David Thoreau 94 (B. Torry and F. Allen, eds. 1984).

and that the plaintiff did not contribute to the injury.[55] Such inferences may be quite strong in cases in which the consumer is injured by a foreign object in food or drink, particularly if it is found in a package, can, or other container sealed at the defendant's place of business.[56] In an early case of this type, in which the plaintiff encountered a human toe in a can of chewing tobacco, the court had little difficulty in finding an inference of negligence: "We can imagine no reason why, with ordinary care, human toes could not be left out of chewing tobacco, and if toes are found in chewing tobacco, it seems to us that somebody has been very careless."[57]

### Warranty

In cases involving foodstuffs, as any type of product, warranty claims have the distinct advantage over negligence that proof of the defendant's fault is not necessary.[58] Although express warranty actions are unusual in foodstuff cases, occasionally they do arise.[59] Thus, when a seller of canned chicken advertises its product as "boned chicken" that contains "no bones," a consumer injured by a bone sliver lurking in the chicken may recover for the seller's false affirmations of fact.[60] Much more typical in food cases are claims for breach of the implied warranty of quality or wholesomeness.[61] This latter form of warranty, now encompassed by the implied warranty of merchantability, provides a strict, no-fault basis for liability under the Uniform Commercial Code.[62] While the sealed-container doctrine,[63] privity,[64] and other sales law restrictions may sometimes limit the reach of warranty law claims, the courts have long and widely used the law of warranty to provide relief to persons injured by defective food and drink.[65]

**55.** See, e.g., Knight v. Just Born, Inc., 2000 WL 924624 (D. Or. 2000) (severe chemical burns to mouth from eating Hot Tamale candy); Fender v. Colonial Stores, Inc., 225 S.E.2d 691 (Ga. Ct. App. 1976); Giant Food, Inc. v. Washington Coca–Cola Bottling Co., 332 A.2d 1 (Md. 1975). See generally 4 Frumer and Friedman, Products Liability § 48.08[3][a].

**56.** Res ipsa has long been applied in this situation. See, e.g., Dryden v. Continental Baking Co., 77 P.2d 833 (Cal. 1938); Richenbacher v. California Packing Corp., 145 N.E. 281 (Mass. 1924). See also Minutilla v. Providence Ice Cream, 144 A. 884 (R.I. 1929) (although res ipsa did not apply, inference of manufacturer's negligence arose from presence of glass in ice cream served in its original package).

**57.** Pillars v. R.J. Reynolds Tobacco Co., 78 So. 365, 366 (Miss. 1918).

**58.** See §§ 4.1, 4.3, and 5.9, above.

**59.** See, e.g., Cott v. Peppermint Twist Mgmt. Co., 856 P.2d 906 (Kan. 1993) (night club waitress told patrons that drink was "good" whereas it was dishwashing detergent containing lye).

**60.** See Lane v. C.A. Swanson & Sons, 278 P.2d 723 (Cal. Ct. App. 1955).

**61.** See, e.g., Elliot v. Kraft Foods N. Am., Inc., 118 S.W.3d 50 (Tex. App. 2003) (rocks in Grape Nuts cereal breached implied warranty of merchantability); CEF Enters., Inc. v. Betts, 838 So.2d 999 (Miss. Ct. App. 2003) (insect in biscuit from Burger King breached the implied warranty of merchantability); Jones v. GMRI, Inc., 551 S.E.2d 867 (N.C. Ct. App. 2001).

**62.** See UCC § 2–314; § 4.3, above.

**63.** This doctrine may preclude warranty claims against retailers. See, e.g., Jones v. GMRI, Inc., 551 S.E.2d 867, 870–71 (N.C. Ct. App. 2001) (upholding judgment for restaurant on implied warranty claim on basis of statutory sealed-container defense).

**64.** This doctrine may preclude warranty claims against remote sellers. See, e.g., Barnett v. Leiserv, Inc., 968 F.Supp. 690 (N.D. Ga. 1997) (warranty action brought by child, burned by hot coffee purchased and spilled by family friend in restaurant, barred by lack of privity); Minutilla v. Providence Ice Cream, 144 A. 884, 885 (R.I. 1929) ("there can be no warranty without privity of contract").

**65.** See, e.g., Creach v. Sara Lee Corp., 502 S.E.2d 923 (S.C. Ct. App. 1998); Cott v. Peppermint Twist Mgmt. Co., 856 P.2d 906

### *Strict Liability in Tort*

With the rise of the doctrine of strict products liability in tort in the 1960s and 1970s, problems of establishing negligence and satisfying the technical rules of warranty law fell away in cases involving foodstuffs as in other types of products.[66] While negligence and warranty claims are still frequently asserted in foodstuff cases,[67] various advantages of strict liability in tort[68] make this doctrine the preferred theory of recovery in most such cases. Thus, purveyors of food or drink have been held subject to strict liability in tort for injuries from mice and cigarettes in soft drink bottles,[69] contaminated oysters,[70] a metal screw in a stick of chewing gum,[71] a pebble in a biscuit,[72] MSG in soup,[73] human blood in a biscuit and gravy,[74] and many other situations involving defective food and drink.[75]

Regardless of the particular cause of action, two issues of proof frequently predominate in foodstuff cases: defectiveness and causation. The burden of proof on both issues, of course, resides on the plaintiff.[76]

(Kan. 1993); Clime v. Dewey Beach Enters., 831 F.Supp. 341, 348–49 (D. Del. 1993). See generally 4 Frumer and Friedman, Products Liability §§ 48.15–.19; F. R. Dickerson, Products Liability and the Food Consumer 19–170 (1951); ch. 4, above.

**66.** See § 5.2, above.

**67.** See, e.g., Knight v. Just Born, Inc., 2000 WL 924624 (D. Or. 2000) (negligence and strict liability in tort); Otis Spunkmeyer, Inc. v. Blakely, 30 S.W.3d 678 (Tex. App. 2000) (implied warranty and strict liability in tort); Holowaty v. McDonald's Corp., 10 F.Supp.2d 1078 (D. Minn. 1998) (negligence, implied warranty, and strict liability in tort); Creach v. Sara Lee Corp., 502 S.E.2d 923 (S.C. Ct. App. 1998) (same); Campbell Soup Co. v. Gates, 889 S.W.2d 750 (Ark. 1994) (same); Cott v. Peppermint Twist Mgmt. Co., 856 P.2d 906 (Kan. 1993) (negligence, implied warranty, express warranty, and strict liability in tort).

Negligence and breach of warranty are the only claims available in states that have never adopted the doctrine of strict products liability in tort. See, e.g., Jones v. GMRI, Inc., 551 S.E.2d 867 (N.C. Ct. App. 2001) (metal in meatball); Goldman v. Food Lion, Inc., 879 F.Supp. 33 (E.D. Va. 1995) (pit in canned peach); Clime v. Dewey Beach Enters., 831 F.Supp. 341, 348–49 (D. Del. 1993) (bacteria in clams).

**68.** See § 5.9, above.

**69.** See, e.g., Shoshone Coca–Cola Bottling Co. v. Dolinski, 420 P.2d 855 (Nev. 1966) (mouse); Pulley v. Pacific Coca–Cola Bottling Co., 415 P.2d 636 (Wash. 1966).

**70.** See Kilpatrick v. Superior Court, 277 Cal.Rptr. 230 (Ct. App. 1991).

**71.** See Hickman v. William Wrigley, Jr. Co., 768 So.2d 812 (La. Ct. App. 2000).

**72.** See Creach v. Sara Lee Corp., 502 S.E.2d 923 (S.C. Ct. App. 1998).

**73.** See Livingston v. Marie Callender's, Inc., 85 Cal.Rptr.2d 528 (Ct. App. 1999).

**74.** See Flagstar Enters., Inc. v. Davis, 709 So.2d 1132 (Ala. 1997).

**75.** See, e.g., Almquist v. Finley Sch. Dist. No. 53, 57 P.3d 1191 (Wash. Ct. App. 2002) (school district subject to strict liability under state Product Liability Act because it "manufactured" tacos tainted with E. coli bacteria); In re Shigellosis Litigation, 647 N.W.2d 1 (Minn. Ct. App. 2002) (distributor of bacteria-contaminated parsley can be strictly liable in tort even though distributor did not design or manufacture the parsley and had no reason to know of the bacteria); Knight v. Just Born, Inc., 2000 WL 924624 (D. Or. 2000) (chemical burns to mouth from piece of Hot Tamale cinnamon candy containing concentrated cinnamon oil). See generally Annots., 2 A.L.R.5th 1 (1992) (liability for spoiled or contaminated food); 2 A.L.R.5th 189 (liability for object related to but not intended to be in food).

**76.** See, e.g., Cooper v. Borden, Inc., 709 So.2d 878, 881 (La. Ct. App. 1998) (to establish manufacturer's liability for harm from food consumption, plaintiff must prove that: (1) defendant's product contained deleterious substance; (2) plaintiff consumed the substance; and (3) the consumption caused the plaintiff's injury); Valenti v. Great Atl. & Pac. Tea Co., 615 N.Y.S.2d 84, 85 (App. Div. 1994).

### Proving Defectiveness—In General

To recover for injuries from ingesting food or drink, a plaintiff must establish that the food contained some dangerous element that rendered it unwholesome or "defective."[77] The concept of defectiveness in food and drink cases is basically the same as in other contexts. Thus, a food or beverage item generally is defective, and a seller generally is subject to liability in negligence, warranty, and strict liability in tort for selling it, if the food product's condition is dangerous in a manner neither intended by the seller nor expected by the consumer. As with any other type of product, a person injured by food or drink must establish its defectiveness—in this context, that it was unwholesome,[78] unfit for human consumption,[79] adulterated,[80] or contained a foreign or otherwise dangerous substance of a type that consumers generally do not expect.[81]

Sometimes the defectiveness of a food or drink product is very clear, as when a soft drink contains slivers of glass,[82] a condom,[83] a slimy substance,[84] a moth,[85] or a mouse;[86] a meatball contains a piece of metal;[87] a can of pork and beans contains a condom;[88] a can of spinach,[89] a bowl of soup,[90] or a candy bar[91] is infested with worms; or a chili dog contains a

**77.** See, e.g., Anderson v. Piccadilly Cafeteria, Inc., 804 So.2d 75 (La. Ct. App. 2001) (plaintiff's testimony that fruit salad was discolored, malodorous, and made her nauseous insufficient to prove fruit salad was defective); Mann v. D.L. Lee & Sons, Inc., 537 S.E.2d 683 (Ga. Ct. App. 2000) (although plaintiffs probably suffered food poisoning, insufficient evidence that defendant's ham was defective).

**78.** See, e.g., Sowell v. Hyatt Corp., 623 A.2d 1221 (D.C. Ct. App. 1993) (worm in rice); Slonsky v. Phoenix Coca–Cola Bottling Co., 499 P.2d 741 (Ariz. Ct. App. 1972) (metallic filings in bottle of Coke).

**79.** See, e.g., Johnson v. Epstein, 1998 WL 166805, at *2 (N.D.N.Y. 1998) ("foreign substance that was revolting or unfit for human consumption"); Goldman v. Food Lion, Inc., 879 F.Supp. 33 (E.D. Va. 1995) (warranty that food is "fit for human consumption").

**80.** "Adulterated" is a common description of the condition in which food may not be sold under pure food acts. See, e.g., Chambley v. Apple Rests., Inc., 504 S.E.2d 551 (Ga. Ct. App. 1998) (condom in chicken salad).

**81.** See discussions of the foreign/natural and consumer expectations tests, below.

**82.** See Peryea v. Coca–Cola Bottling Co. of New England, 286 A.2d 877 (R.I. 1972).

**83.** See Hagan v. Coca–Cola Bottling Co., 804 So.2d 1234 (Fla. 2001).

**84.** See Cernes v. Pittsburg Coca Cola Bottling Co., 332 P.2d 258 (Kan. 1958) (jelly

substance in beverage, "slimy like serum, mud or a bug").

**85.** See Simmons v. Baton Rouge Coca–Cola Bottling Co., Ltd., 282 So.2d 827 (La. App. 1973) (decomposed moth in bottle of Tab).

**86.** The early soft drink intruder cases were collected in Bishop, Trouble in a Bottle, 16 Baylor L. Rev. 337 (1964), which classified the cases in various respects. Glass was the most frequent intruder into beverage bottles, followed by mice in the following conditions and numbers: dead—16; dead, fur oozing Coca–Cola—1; dead and putrid—2; dead, badly battered—1; decayed—2; decomposed—14; decomposed and swollen—1; skeleton only—1; small—1; unspecified—9. Flies, spiders, worms, and cockroaches also appeared with some frequency. Led by Louisiana, the "top" eight states (by number of reported cases) all were in the South.

**87.** See Jones v. GMRI, Inc., 551 S.E.2d 867 (N.C. Ct. App. 2001).

**88.** See Gentry v. Stokely–Van Camp, Prod. Liab. Rep. (CCH) ¶ 9259 (Tenn. Ct. App. 1982).

**89.** See Food Fair Stores of Fla., Inc. v. Macurda, 93 So.2d 860 (Fla. 1957).

**90.** See Campbell Soup Co. v. Gates, 889 S.W.2d 750 (Ark. 1994).

**91.** See Kassouf v. Lee Bros., Inc., 26 Cal.Rptr. 276, 277 (Ct. App. 1962). After eating part of a Mr. Goodbar, plaintiff "bit into a mushy worm. When she looked at the bar, she saw that it was covered with worms and webbing; worms were crawling out of the chocolate and the webbing had little eggs 'hanging onto it.'"

cockroach.[92] Where a food's defectiveness is plain, unless the danger was so open and obvious that it should have been apparent to the consumer,[93] its manifest deficiency renders it unwholesome, unfit, and defective by any standard. In such cases, unless causation is in doubt, food suppliers generally should want to avoid litigation unless the plaintiff's settlement demand is excessive. In other situations, the defectiveness of a food-stuff's dangerous condition may be in doubt. In the hot coffee cases, for example, most courts rule as a matter of law that a hot drink's propensity to burn is not a defective condition but an obvious risk that must be born by those who drink hot beverages.[94] Similarly, a food's defectiveness often is subject to challenge if the hazard naturally occurs in the particular food, as a chicken bone in chicken soup, an issue examined below.

A plaintiff must establish that the food product really did contain an improper substance, a fact which the plaintiff's testimony may establish.[95] But the plaintiff's uncorroborated testimony that he or she swallowed a bug is not the strongest type of evidence, and so a plaintiff who swallows or otherwise disposes of the objectionable item, such as a cockroach in a dish of beans and rice[96] or a piece of metal or other hard object in a meatball[97] or in a dish of barbecued spareribs,[98] may find the lawsuit traveling a route quite similar.[99] Yet, even if the plaintiff has no direct evidence of a defect in the food, defectiveness properly may be established by circumstantial evidence and credible expert testimony that the defendant's food probably was defective.[100]

---

**92.** See Bullara v. Checker's Drive–In Rest., Inc., 736 So.2d 936 (La. Ct. App. 1999) (customer bit into cockroach in chili dog).

**93.** In Harris–Teeter, Inc. v. Burroughs, 399 S.E.2d 801 (Va. 1991), the plaintiff's daughter-in-law went to the grocery store and bought a birthday cake decorated with two white plastic birds resting on white "clouds" which were part of the cake's design. Plaintiff ate a piece of the cake, white bird and all, swallowing it whole without chewing. Quite soon she realized that she had a problem, and the bird was surgically removed from her colon. Applying the plain view doctrine, the court held that there was no negligence in supplying a cake ornament the same color as the icing.

**94.** See, e.g., McCroy v. Coastal Mart, Inc., 207 F.Supp.2d 1265 (D. Kan. 2002) (no duty to warn about severity of potential burns from hot chocolate; extensive review of the hot beverage cases); Olliver v. Heavenly Bagels, Inc., 729 N.Y.S.2d 611 (Sup. Ct. 2001) (summary judgment for defendants; discussing other cases). On hot beverages as inherent risks, see § 10.3, below.

**95.** See, e.g., Johnson v. Epstein, 1998 WL 166805 (N.D.N.Y. 1998) (crustacean attached to mackerel in can shown to others).

**96.** See Wimberly v. B.P. Newman Invs., Inc., 805 So.2d 239 (La. Ct. App. 2001) (plaintiff's testimony that he was served beans and rice containing fully-in-

tact cockroach was inconceivable given manner in which the beans and rice were prepared and served by Popeye's).

**97.** See Jones v. GMRI, Inc., 551 S.E.2d 867 (N.C. Ct. App. 2001).

**98.** See Kneibel v. RRM Enters., 506 N.W.2d 664 (Minn. Ct. App. 1993).

**99.** See, e.g., Schafer v. JLC Food Systems, Inc., 2004 WL 78022 (Minn. Ct. App. 2004) (2–1 decision) (plaintiff's throat scratched by alleged foreign object in pumpkin muffin), review granted (Minn. 2004). The plaintiffs' testimony was also found insufficient in Farroux v. Denny's Rest., Inc., 962 S.W.2d 108 (Tex. App. 1997) (affidavit of restaurant patron, allegedly sickened from undercooked eggs, which conflicted with his own deposition, where medical records contained no evidence of food poisoning but only showed that he suffered from obesity and gout); Valenti v. Great Atl. & Pac. Tea Co., 615 N.Y.S.2d 84, 85 (App. Div. 1994) (flu-like symptoms after eating beans allegedly containing worm, where no mention of worm during visit to doctor next day).

**100.** See, e.g., Trapnell v. John Hogan Interests, Inc., 809 S.W.2d 606 (Tex. App. 1991) (expert testimony, based on reasonable medical probability, permitted conclusion that fatal allergic reaction was triggered by sulfite potato whiteners); Gant v. Lucy Ho's Bamboo Garden, Inc., 460 So.2d

### The Foreign/Natural and Consumer Expectations Tests

Defectiveness is clear enough, as mentioned earlier, when food or drink contains a foreign object, such as glass, steel, bugs, or when the food is spoiled[101] or otherwise contaminated.[102] Yet the parties' expectations and legal responsibility may be quite different with respect to hazards that are natural to certain types of food, such as clamshells in clam chowder, cherry pits in cherry pies, and fish bones in fish fillets. To the extent that such naturally occurring objects are dangerous, food purveyors ordinarily attempt to keep them out of the food and drink they sell. But sometimes their efforts are unsuccessful and a food consumer is injured by a naturally occurring object of this type. The question in such cases is whether the food should be considered defective or whether such naturally occurring objects should be expected, and thus the responsibility of the consumer.[103]

#### *The Rise of the Foreign/Natural Doctrine*

In *Mix v. Ingersoll Candy Co.*,[104] decided by the California Supreme Court in 1936, the plaintiff was injured from swallowing a fragment of a chicken bone contained in a chicken pie sold and served by the defendant restaurant to the plaintiff. The plaintiff sued the restaurant for negligence and breach of implied warranty, alleging that the food was not reasonably fit to eat. The trial court dismissed the claims, and the plaintiff appealed. Stating that the defendant's obligation in warranty was only to sell food that was *reasonably* fit, not perfect, the court upheld the dismissal of the complaint. While the court acknowledged that even slight deviations from perfection may sometimes cause a food to be legally unfit, it reasoned that "in certain instances a deviation from perfection, particularly if it is of such a nature as in common knowledge could be reasonably anticipated and guarded against by the consumer, may not be such a defect as to result in the food being not reasonably fit for human consumption." Observing that the warranty cases holding food unfit involved foreign substances such as glass, stones, wires, nails, or foods that were tainted, decayed, diseased, or infected, the court remarked that warranty law could not hold restaurateurs liable for serving a fish dish with a fish bone, a cherry pie with a cherry stone, or T-bone steaks or beef stew with bones "natural to the type of meat served." Hence, "[b]ones which are natural to the type of meat served cannot legitimately be called a foreign substance, and a consumer who

---

499 (Fla. Dist. Ct. App. 1984) (food poisoning from egg rolls; doctor testified that the bacteria involved is usually transmitted from fecal matter of infected person, and that the egg rolls were the probable source); Mushatt v. Page Milk Co., 262 So.2d 520 (La. Ct. App. 1972).

**101.** See, e.g., Prejean v. Great Atl. & Pac. Tea Co., Inc., 457 So.2d 60 (La. Ct. App. 1984) (rotten roast); Swift & Co. v. Wells, 110 S.E.2d 203 (Va. 1959) (staphylococci organisms in pork shoulder).

**102.** See, e.g., Cooper v. Borden, Inc., 709 So.2d 878, 881 (La. Ct. App. 1998) (penicillin in milk); Claxton Coca–Cola Bottling Co. v. Coleman, 22 S.E.2d 768 (Ga. Ct. App. 1942) (kerosene in Coke).

**103.** See Notes, 74 Tul. L. Rev. 379 (1999) (Louisiana court's repudiation of foreign/natural doctrine in *Porteous* is consistent with state Products Liability Act); Comment, 72 N.D. L. Rev. 481 (1996) (pleading and proving food contamination cases); 18 S. Ill. U. L.J. 637 (1994) (applauding repudiation of foreign/natural doctrine in *Nestle-Beich*); Annot., 2 A.L.R.5th 189 (1992) (liability for object related to but not intended to be in food); Products Liability Restatement § 7.

**104.** 59 P.2d 144 (Cal. 1936).

eats meat dishes ought to anticipate and be on his guard against the presence of such bones." Thus, because such naturally occurring risks are to be expected by the food consumer, neither implied warranty[105] nor negligence compels a restaurant to assure that its chicken pies are perfectly free of chicken bones.[106]

The *Mix* approach to liability for naturally occurring hazards in food and drink, which came to be known as the "foreign/natural" test or doctrine, held that sellers are subject to liability for injuries from objects that are "foreign" to a food's ingredients, but that consumers should expect and thereby bear the risks of hazards that are in some way "natural" to the food. At a time when rules of law were an accepted judicial method for avoiding jury trials in recurring situations where responsibility was clear,[107] the foreign/natural doctrine appeared to be a sensible way for courts to short-circuit needlessly repetitive litigation. As time went by, a number of jurisdictions adopted the doctrine and applied it to such perils as bones and bone slivers in dressing served with a roast turkey dinner,[108] a pork chop,[109] creamed chicken,[110] barbecue pork sausage,[111] and fish chowder;[112] a piece of broken prune pit in a jar of prune butter;[113] a crystallized grain of corn in a box of Corn Flakes;[114] and an unshelled filbert in a jar of shelled nuts.[115]

### The Shift to a Consumer Expectations Test

Although a number of courts applied the foreign/natural doctrine as a method for determining the defectiveness of food in certain types of cases, the test never was adopted in more than a handful of jurisdictions. In 1951, America's leading food-law scholar, Professor Reed Dickerson, argued that the foreign/natural inquiry should be rejected in favor of a determination of consumer expectations.[116] And during the 1950s, courts began to manifest their discontent with the doctrine's applicability to processed foods by refocusing the inquiry away from whether the offending object naturally and initially occurred in some ingredient of the food to whether it was appropriate to the food as it ultimately was served.

---

**105.** The result is different under express warranty if the seller affirms that the product is "boned chicken" which has "no bones." See Lane v. C.A. Swanson & Sons, 278 P.2d 723 (Cal. Ct. App. 1955).

**106.** *Mix,* 59 P.2d at 148.

**107.** See Prosser and Keeton on Torts § 35; Dobbs, Law of Torts § 132 (2000).

**108.** Silva v. F.W. Woolworth Co., 83 P.2d 76 (Cal. Ct. App. 1938).

**109.** Brown v. Nebiker, 296 N.W. 366 (Iowa 1941).

**110.** Goodwin v. Country Club of Peoria, 54 N.E.2d 612 (Ill. App. Ct. 1944).

**111.** Norris v. Pig'n Whistle Sandwich Shop, 53 S.E.2d 718 (Ga. Ct. App. 1949).

**112.** Webster v. Blue Ship Tea Room, Inc., 198 N.E.2d 309, 312 (Mass. 1964) (offering a history of, and several recipes for, New England chowder (a "gustatory adven-

ture") and observing: "We should be prepared to cope with the hazards of fish bones, the occasional presence of which in chowders is, it seems to us, to be anticipated, and which, in the light of a hallowed tradition, do not impair their fitness or merchantability.").

**113.** Courter v. Dilbert Bros., 186 N.Y.S.2d 334 (Sup. Ct. 1959).

**114.** Adams v. Great Atl. & Pac. Tea Co., 112 S.E.2d 92 (N.C. 1960).

**115.** See Coffer v. Standard Brands, Inc., 226 S.E.2d 534 (N.C. Ct. App. 1976).

**116.** "The better test of what is legally defective appears to be what consumers customarily expect and guard against. Canned foods are expected to be found already washed, cleaned, and trimmed, while the same foods in fresh form normally call for work of that sort by the consumer." F. R. Dickerson, Products Liability and the Food Consumer 185 (1951).

This shift in analytical approach narrowed the doctrine into oblivion by allowing claims for bones in chicken soup,[117] sausage,[118] and canned chicken labeled "boned."[119] Moreover, at least a couple of fairly early decisions rejected the foreign/natural test outright, reasoning that the decisive issue should not be whether an ingredient was natural or foreign to the food at some stage of preparation, but whether the consumer might reasonably expect to find such a substance in the type of food involved.[120]

As modern principles of products liability law established a foothold in the 1960s and 1970s, criticism of the foreign/natural doctrine accelerated.[121] During this period, courts and commentators began to recognize the inconsistency between the *caveat emptor* principles inherent in this doctrine and the consumer protection objectives of modern products liability law.[122] As time progressed, courts in the 1980s and 1990s increasingly adopted a reasonable[123] consumer expectations standard, often explicitly rejecting the foreign/natural doctrine, for determining the defectiveness of food.[124] Typical of these decisions was *Jackson v.*

**117.** Even if chicken bones were necessary to the preparation of chicken soup, "the question is not whether the substance may have been natural or proper at some time in the early stages of preparation of this kind of soup, but whether the presence of such substance, if it is harmful and makes the food unfit for human consumption, is natural and ordinarily expected to be in the final product which is impliedly represented as fit for human consumption." Wood v. Waldorf Sys., Inc., 83 A.2d 90, 93 (R.I. 1951).

**118.** Lore v. De Simone Bros., 172 N.Y.S.2d 829 (Sup. Ct. 1958).

**119.** Bryer v. Rath Packing Co., 156 A.2d 442 (Md. 1959).

**120.** See, e.g., Betehia v. Cape Cod Corp., 103 N.W.2d 64, 67 (Wis. 1960) (chicken bone in chicken sandwich); Bonenberger v. Pittsburgh Mercantile Co., 28 A.2d 913 (Pa. 1942) (oyster shell in can of oysters).

**121.** See, e.g., Hunt v. Ferguson–Paulus Enters., 415 P.2d 13 (Or. 1966) (cherry pit in pie; court noted criticism of the foreign/natural rule, but avoided the issue by deferring to the jury).

**122.** See, e.g., Jim Dandy Fast Foods, Inc. v. Carpenter, 535 S.W.2d 786, 790 (Tex. Civ.App. 1976) (piece of bone in chicken meat); Stark v. Chock Full O'Nuts, 356 N.Y.S.2d 403, 404 (App. Term 1974) (walnut shell in nutted cheese sandwich); Williams v. Braum Ice Cream Stores, Inc., 534 P.2d 700 (Okla. Ct. App. 1974) (cherry seed or pit in cherry-pecan ice cream); Hochberg v. O'Donnell's Rest., Inc., 272 A.2d 846, 848–49 (D.C. Ct. App. 1971) (pit in olive); Zabner v. Howard Johnson's, Inc., 201 So.2d 824, 826 (Fla. Dist. Ct. App. 1967) (walnut shell in maple walnut ice

cream: "Naturalness of the substance to any ingredients in the food served is important only in determining whether the consumer may reasonably expect to find such substance in the particular type of dish or style of food served."); Betehia v. Cape Cod Corp., 103 N.W.2d 64, 67–68 (Wis. 1960). Compare O'Dell v. DeJean's Packing Co., 585 P.2d 399, 401–02 (Okla. Ct. App. 1978) (whether plaintiff should have expected to find deleterious item in packaged food is defense for pleading and proof by seller). See generally Note, 37 Ohio St. L. Rev. 634 (1976); Annot., 2 A.L.R.5th 189 (1992).

**123.** Note that the standard is framed in terms of a *reasonable* consumer's expectations, which is an objective rather than a subjective test. See, e.g., Phillips v. Town of West Springfield, 540 N.E.2d 1331 (Mass. 1989). *But see* Williams v. Braum Ice Cream Stores, Inc., 534 P.2d 700 (Okla. Ct. App. 1974) (additional question of fact was whether individual plaintiff acted in a reasonable manner).

**124.** See, e.g., Langiulli v. Bumble Bee Seafood, Inc., 604 N.Y.S.2d 1020, 1021 (Sup. Ct. 1993); Clime v. Dewey Beach Enters., 831 F.Supp. 341, 348–49 (D. Del. 1993); Goodman v. Wenco Foods Inc., 423 S.E.2d 444, 451 (N.C. 1992) (thorough discussion); Jackson v. Nestle–Beich, Inc., 589 N.E.2d 547, 549 (Ill. 1992) (foreign-natural test is an "outdated and discredited doctrine"); Phillips v. Town of West Springfield, 540 N.E.2d 1331, 1332–33 (Mass. 1989); Yong Cha Hong v. Marriott Corp., 656 F.Supp. 445, 448–49 (D. Md. 1987) (noting that reasonable expectations test "had largely displaced the natural/foreign test"); Gates v. Standard Brands Inc., 719 P.2d 130, 134 (Wash. Ct. App. 1986) (adopt-

*Nestle–Beich, Inc.*,[125] a carefully reasoned decision of the Illinois Supreme Court which adopted a reasonable consumer expectations test. There, the court rebuffed the defendant's invitation to adopt Louisiana's then-existing[126] middle-of-the-road approach (subsequently adopted in California)[127] shielding food sellers from strict liability, but not negligence, for dangers naturally occurring in food products.[128] In the mid–1990s,[129] the propriety of the shift from the foreign/natural doctrine to a consumer expectations test was certified by the American Law Institute in the *Products Liability Restatement.*[130] In recent years, courts have rarely applied the foreign/natural doctrine as a liability determinative rule,[131]

ing "buyer oriented" consumer expectations test"); Morrison's Cafeteria of Montgomery, Inc. v. Haddox, 431 So.2d 975, 978 (Ala. 1983).

The legal commentators unanimously agree with the propriety of this development. See, e.g., F. R. Dickerson, Products Liability and the Food Consumer, §§ 4.2 and 4.3, at 184–90 (1951); Dobbs, Law of Torts, § 356, at 981; Spak, Bone of Contention: The Foreign–Natural Test and the Implied Warranty of Merchantability for Food Products, 12 J.L. & Com. 23 (1992); Notes, 74 Tul. L. Rev. 379 (1999); 71 N.C. L. Rev. 2163 (1993); 20 Mem. St. U. L. Rev. 377 (1990); 37 Ohio St. L. Rev. 634 (1976). See also W. Prosser, Law of Torts, § 99, at 660, n.76 (4th ed. 1971).

**125.** 589 N.E.2d 547 (Ill. 1992).

**126.** Louisiana abandoned this approach in Porteous v. St. Ann's Cafe & Deli, 713 So.2d 454 (La. 1998), which shifted to a negligence analysis that weighs the naturalness of an item's presence in food together with consumer expectations.

**127.** In Mexicali Rose v. Superior Court, 822 P.2d 1292, 1303 (Cal. 1992) (chicken bone in enchilada), the California Supreme Court replaced the *Mix* doctrine with the following:

> If the injury-producing substance is natural to the preparation of the food served, it can be said that it was reasonably expected by its very nature and the food cannot be determined unfit or defective. A plaintiff in such a case has no cause of action in strict liability or implied warranty. If, however, the presence of the natural substance is due to a restaurateur's failure to exercise due care in food preparation, the injured patron may sue under a negligence theory.

> If the injury-causing substance is foreign to the food served then the injured patron may also state a cause of action in implied warranty and strict liability, and the trier of fact will determine whether the substance (i) could be reasonably expected by the average consumer and (ii) rendered the food unfit or defective.

**128.** For the traditional Louisiana cases, see, e.g., Title v. Pontchartrain Hotel, 449 So.2d 677 (La. Ct. App. 1984) (restaurant not liable for allowing pearl to remain in fried oyster); Musso v. Picadilly Cafeterias, Inc., 178 So.2d 421 (La. Ct. App. 1965) (restaurant not negligent in failing to remove every pit in cherry pie).

**129.** In 1995, Tentative Draft No. 2 of the Products Liability Restatement, comment *g* to § 2, suggested that the consumer expectations test was the majority rule. The far more decisive rejection of the foreign/natural test in favor of the consumer expectations test first appeared as a separate section in the Proposed Final Draft in 1997, and the Restatement was published in final form in 1998.

**130.** Products Liability Restatement § 7, "Liability of Commercial Seller or Distributor for Harm Caused by Defective Food Products," provides:

> One engaged in the business of selling or otherwise distributing food products who sells or distributes a food product that is defective under § 2, § 3, or § 4 is subject to liability for harm to persons or property caused by the defect. Under § 2(a), a harm-causing ingredient of the food product constitutes a defect if a reasonable consumer would not expect the food product to contain that ingredient.

In comment *b*, the Reporters note: "A consumer expectations test in this context relies upon culturally defined, widely shared standards that food products ought to meet."

**131.** For remnants of the foreign/natural doctrine, see, e.g., Lewis v. Handel's Homemade Ice Cream & Yogurt, 2003 WL 21509258, at *3 (Ohio Ct. App. 2003) ("common sense dictates that the presence of a pistachio shell in a pistachio nut ice cream cone is a natural occurrence that appellant reasonably should have anticipated and guarded against"); Mitchell v. T.G.I. Friday's, 748 N.E.2d 89 (Ohio Ct. App. 2000) (schizophrenically applying both tests in line with Ohio's equivocal approach);

and the judicial march toward the reasonable consumer expectations test appears inexorable.

In summary, modern courts have rejected the foreign/natural distinction as too rigid a rule of law for assessing the defectiveness of food. While restricting liability for natural hazards to appropriate negligence claims[132] arguably strikes a nuanced balance between consumer and seller obligations, most courts today prefer the blunter but simpler consumer expectation protection approach of the type adopted by the *Products Liability Restatement*. Absent from most discussions of the battle between these two food defect tests is a recognition of the specially high protection the law historically has afforded food consumers, as discussed above. Perhaps the disappearance from common discourse of the high priority of food safety reflects the fact that consumers in the world today confront a host of deadly dangers—mechanical, chemical, and biological—which might suggest that food products no longer deserve an elevated level of protection. Yet, perhaps, food safety should still be viewed as a necessary first goal in the kind of broader human safety plan the law must now construct. Be that as it may, food safety remains a vital social goal that undoubtedly is better protected by the reasonable consumer expectations test, which now is plainly the prevailing legal doctrine,[133] than the foreign/natural doctrine which properly is on the run.

### *Court and Jury*

Even with the decline of the foreign/natural test, which is nearing extinction as a general test of liability, the "naturalness" of a dangerous item's presence in a food necessarily lingers on as an important sub-issue in assessing reasonable expectations in particular contexts—that is, in determining just what types of dangers consumers justifiably *should* be required to expect in certain types of foods.[134] While the task of ascertaining such expectations normally is peculiarly well suited for jury resolution,[135] reasonable consumer expectations sometimes are so clear that a court should take the issue from the jury. For example, in an early case that rejected the foreign/natural test and embraced the consumer expectations test as the formal liability standard, the court nevertheless ruled as a matter of law that the consumer should have expected to find an

---

Ford v. Miller Meat Co., 33 Cal.Rptr.2d 899 (Ct. App. 1994).

**132.** This is the former rule in Louisiana that is now applied in California. See notes 124–26, above.

**133.** See Products Liability Restatement § 7, Reporters' Note 1 to cmt. *b* ("strong majority of courts").

**134.** Reasonable expectations are also used in determinations of how carefully a consumer should chew. See, e.g., Hochberg v. O'Donnell's Rest., Inc., 272 A.2d 846 (D.C. Ct. App. 1971) (restaurant patron broke tooth on pit in olive served in vodka martini). Compare Scheller v. Wilson Certified Foods, Inc., 559 P.2d 1074 (Ariz. Ct. App. 1976) (seller of smoked pork not liable

for death from trichinosis because it is common knowledge that pork must be cooked prior to consumption; plaintiff thought pork already had been cooked).

**135.** See, e.g., Phillips v. Town of West Springfield, 540 N.E.2d 1331 (Mass. 1989) (trier of fact determines the reasonable expectations of ordinary high school student concerning the likely presence of a bone in his meal); Yong Cha Hong v. Marriott Corp., 656 F.Supp. 445, 448–49 (D. Md. 1987) (whether presence of worm-like trachea or aorta in fast-food fried chicken fell below reasonable consumer expectations was question of fact); Williams v. Braum Ice Cream Stores, Inc., 534 P.2d 700 (Okla. Ct. App. 1974). See generally Note, 18 S. Ill. U. L.J. 637 (1994).

oyster shell in a serving of fried oysters.[136] More recently, courts have held as a matter of law that consumers should expect that a fish fillet might contain a 1–centimeter bone,[137] that a can of clam chowder[138] or fried clam strip[139] might contain a piece of clam shell, that a raw clam served in a restaurant might contain harmful bacteria,[140] that a pistachio shell might reside in a pistachio nut ice cream cone,[141] and that a cake might contain a strand of human hair.[142] The contrary is also true: courts should rule as a matter of law for food consumers who have no reason to expect a particular food hazard, such as a lethally sharp sliver of bone in a fried strip of chicken, "natural" though it might be. Modern courts have begun to reassert control over juries in a variety of ways,[143] and the decline of the foreign/natural doctrine in favor of a consumer expectations test should not be viewed as a wholesale shift of power from judge to jury. Instead, the battle lines for judicial rulings in foodstuff cases have simply shifted—away from classifying food hazards as "foreign" vs. "natural," to case-specific judicial rulings on when consumers, as a matter of law, should be required to expect natural hazards in the foodstuffs that they eat.

## Proving Causation

Even if a plaintiff can establish that a food or drink ingested was dangerously defective, the plaintiff still must connect the defect both to the defendant and to the plaintiff's injury or illness.[144]

### Linking Foodstuff to Defendant

It is fundamental, of course, that a seller is responsible for an injury only if the seller was responsible for the defect—that is, only if the defect was in the product when it left the seller's control.[145] Thus, even if the plaintiff proves that a Baby Ruth candy bar contained a pin, the plaintiff still may be unable to meet his burden of proving that the pin was in the candy bar when it left the defendant's candy factory if the manufacturer

**136.** Allen v. Grafton, 164 N.E.2d 167 (Ohio 1960) (4–3 decision). See also Mathews v. Maysville Seafoods, Inc., 602 N.E.2d 764, 765–66 (Ohio Ct. App. 1991) (plaintiff's case failed under either test since "consumer must reasonably anticipate and guard against the presence of a fish bone in a fish fillet").

**137.** Morrison's Cafeteria of Montgomery, Inc. v. Haddox, 431 So.2d 975 (Ala. 1983). See also Ruvolo v. Homovich, 778 N.E.2d 661 (Ohio Ct. App. 2002) (customer should reasonably expect that chicken sandwich may contain chicken bone).

**138.** See Koperwas v. Publix Supermarkets, Inc., 534 So.2d 872 (Fla. Dist. Ct. App. 1988).

**139.** See Mitchell v. T.G.I. Friday's, 748 N.E.2d 89 (Ohio Ct. App. 2000).

**140.** See Clime v. Dewey Beach Enters., 831 F.Supp. 341 (D. Del. 1993). *But see* Ayala v. Bartolome, 940 S.W.2d 727 (Tex. App. 1997) (whether ordinary consumer would expect raw oysters to be contaminated with bacteria fatal to persons with liver disease is fact issue for jury).

**141.** See Lewis v. Handel's Homemade Ice Cream & Yogurt, 2003 WL 21509258 (Ohio Ct. App. 2003).

**142.** See Cain v. Winn–Dixie La., Inc., 757 So.2d 712 (La. Ct. App. 1999).

**143.** See Powers, Judge and Jury in the Texas Supreme Court, 75 Tex. L. Rev. 1699 (1997).

**144.** See, e.g., Meyer v. Super Disc. Mkts., Inc., 501 S.E.2d 2 (Ga. Ct. App. 1998); Cooper v. Borden, Inc., 709 So.2d 878, 881 (La. Ct. App. 1998).

**145.** See, e.g., Mears v. H.J. Heinz Co., 1995 WL 37344 (Tenn. Ct. App. 1995) (sliver of tin plate in bowl of soup could have come from sources other than defendant's control, even though expert testified that 90% of tin plate is used in manufacture of tin cans).

introduces evidence of the rigorous quality control procedures at its plant.[146] Often, time is of the essence in establishing causation of this type. If a plaintiff discovers maggots, "[l]ittle bitty worms with a black head," floating and squiggling in chicken-flavored soup made from a dry mix sold by the defendant manufacturer six weeks prior to the plaintiff's purchase, she cannot recover if the larvae might reasonably have entered the soup between the time when the defendant sold it and when her mother bought and prepared it.[147]

But a plaintiff need not prove the defendant's responsibility for the defect beyond all doubt; the plaintiff may recover if the evidence, including reasonable inferences from any circumstantial evidence, suggests the likelihood that the defect was in the product at the time the defendant sold it.[148] Thus, a plaintiff may recover if she bites into a cockroach in a chili dog she had purchased earlier at a fast-food restaurant if she establishes that she ate the dog shortly after she got home and before her own household roaches had time to crawl inside.[149] And while a jokester conceivably may cram a mouse into a soft drink bottle after it leaves the bottling plant, a jury may reasonably interpret dark fecal stains at the bottom of the bottle as suggesting that the mouse resided in the bottle long before that point.[150]

### Linking Foodstuff to Plaintiff's Harm

In order to link an injury or illness to a defective foodstuff, a plaintiff first must connect the injury or illness to a particular food item sold by the defendant, and further, show that the item was bad.[151] When a person becomes ill shortly after eating, the natural tendency is to associate the illness with the foods or beverages the person recently consumed. Often, any food remaining unconsumed is discarded, which means that no samples may be available in order to test and analyze to ascertain whether the food was good or bad. In such cases, courts properly allow plaintiffs to go to the jury if they offer reasonable circumstantial evidence of defectiveness, such as that a particular food item smelled or tasted strange.[152] Yet without credible evidence suggest-

**146.** See Tardella v. RJR Nabisco, Inc., 576 N.Y.S.2d 965 (App. Div. 1991) (pin in Baby Ruth candy bar; in view of defendant's detailed evidence of rigorous quality control procedures, plaintiff failed to meet burden of proof that pin was in candy bar when it left defendant's plant).

**147.** Campbell Soup Co. v. Gates, 889 S.W.2d 750 (Ark. 1994).

**148.** See, e.g., Cooper v. Borden, Inc., 709 So.2d 878, 881 (La. Ct. App. 1998) (penicillin in milk); Flagstar Enters., Inc. v. Davis, 709 So.2d 1132 (Ala. 1997) (blood in take-out order of biscuit and gravy); Cohen v. Allendale Coca–Cola Bottling Co., 351 S.E.2d 897, 899 (S.C. Ct. App. 1986) (Bell, J.) (plaintiff's testimony that the bug was lying on the bottom of the bottle, that it might have been partially decomposed, and that no bugs were flying around his office on the fateful October day was sufficient circumstantial evidence that bug was in

bottle at defendant's plant); Slonsky v. Phoenix Coca–Cola Bottling Co., 499 P.2d 741 (Ariz. Ct. App. 1972) (metallic filings in bottle of Coke; bottle appeared to be properly sealed, and no other evidence of tampering).

**149.** See Bullara v. Checker's Drive–In Rest., 736 So.2d 936 (La. Ct. App. 1999) (by implication).

**150.** See Shoshone Coca–Cola Bottling Co. v. Dolinski, 420 P.2d 855 (Nev. 1966).

**151.** See § 11.1, below.

**152.** See, e.g., Croteau v. Denny's Rest., Inc., 2002 Mass. App. Div. 81 (Dist. Ct. 2002) (salmonella poisoning; evidence that symptoms occurred during incubation period and that restaurant had been cited for violations of sanitary code sufficient to establish causation); Knight v. Just Born, Inc., 2000 WL 924624 (D. Or. 2000) (burned

ing that a particular food item was in fact defective, the plaintiff's case quite properly will fail.[153]

In addition to showing that a particular food item was defective, the plaintiff must also link the defective food product to the harm. In many cases, the causal link between defective foodstuff and a plaintiff's harm is undisputed, as when the plaintiff immediately is injured or sickened from consuming food that clearly is defective, as a sirloin steak containing the tip end of a hypodermic needle,[154] or a chili dog containing a cockroach.[155] But if the connection between defective food or drink and a person's illness is not self-evident, as often is the case, reliable[156] expert testimony may be required to establish the causal link between the defect and the harm.[157]

A plaintiff who proves all three elements—(1) that food or drink was defective, (2) that the manufacturer was responsible for the defect, and (3) that the defect proximately caused the harm—may recover damages for the harm.[158] If a plaintiff bites off the head of a mouse[159] or a cockroach[160] hiding in a sandwich, the plaintiff normally can recover

mouth; evidence sufficient to establish that one piece of Hot Tamale cinnamon candy produced chemical burns from concentrated cinnamon oil). See also Worthy v. Beautiful Rest., Inc., 556 S.E.2d 185 (Ga. Ct. App. 2001) (illness alone cannot establish causation but may be factor supporting causation if every other reasonable hypothesis of the injuries' cause can be excluded).

**153.** "A person claiming injury from consuming allegedly unwholesome food must show a causal link between that food and the resulting illness." Mann v. D.L. Lee & Sons, Inc., 537 S.E.2d 683, 684 (Ga. Ct. App. 2000) (although plaintiffs probably suffered food poisoning, insufficient evidence that defendant's ham was defective). "Given that no laboratory test performed on the Manns revealed any pathogen responsible for their symptoms, that the Manns consumed other foods at the same time they ate the ham, and that the ham itself was not available for testing but had not looked, smelled, or tasted bad, the Manns could not carry their burden of excluding every other reasonable hypothesis as to the cause of their illness." Id. at 684. See also Anderson v. Piccadilly Cafeteria, Inc., 804 So.2d 75 (La. Ct. App. 2001) (plaintiff's testimony that fruit salad was discolored, malodorous, and made her nauseous was insufficient by itself to prove fruit salad was defective); Fuggins v. Burger King, 760 So.2d 605 (La. Ct. App. 2000) (evidence insufficient to establish that defendant's illness was food poisoning and, if so, whether it had any connection to hamburger sold by defendant); Meyer v. Super Disc. Mkts., 501 S.E.2d 2, 4 (Ga. Ct. App. 1998) ("a mere showing that a person became sick subsequent to eating food is insufficient.).

**154.** See Kroger Co. v. Beck, 375 N.E.2d 640 (Ind. Ct. App. 1978) (prick in plaintiff's throat caused her to vomit).

**155.** See Bullara v. Checker's Drive-In Rest., 736 So.2d 936 (La. Ct. App. 1999). See also CEF Enters., Inc. v. Betts, 838 So.2d 999 (Miss. Ct. App. 2003) (expert testimony not necessary to show that eating a biscuit containing an insect makes one ill).

**156.** Such expert testimony must be reliable. See, e.g., Lassiegne v. Taco Bell Corp., 202 F.Supp.2d 512 (E.D. La. 2002) (excluding as unreliable expert testimony proffered to show that chicken bone in chicken dish caused consumer's migraine headaches, post-traumatic stress disorder, and impotency; summary judgment for restaurant granted).

**157.** See, e.g., Arbourgh v. Sweet Basil Bistro, Inc., 740 So.2d 186 (La. Ct. App. 1999) (in food poisoning case, testimony by treating doctors that plaintiff's infection probably was caused by ingestion of raw chicken at defendant restaurant was sufficient to establish causation).

**158.** See, e.g., Cooper v. Borden, Inc., 709 So.2d 878, 881 (La. Ct. App. 1998).

**159.** Plaintiff bought a barbecue sandwich from a vending machine, heated it in a microwave oven, and took a bite. She heard "an awful crunch," opened the sandwich and discovered a small mouse with a small tail, but no head. She sued, and the jury awarded damages of $10,000. Greenville News (S.C.), Feb. 24 & 25, 1993.

**160.** Bullara v. Checker's Drive-In Rest., Inc., 736 So.2d 936 (La. Ct. App. 1999) (customer bit into cockroach in chili dog).

damages for emotional distress.[161] Even if nothing is eaten of the intruder or even of the foodstuff, the plaintiff still may establish causation in most jurisdictions by proof that he or she was sickened by observing, touching, or smelling (and thinking about) the mouse, bug, spoilage, or other offending condition.[162] As with other types of products, damages for lost consortium are available on proper proofs.[163]

**161.** See, e.g., Brayman v. 99 W., Inc., 116 F.Supp.2d 225, 233–34 (D. Mass. 2000), aff'd, 26 Fed.Appx. 24 (1st Cir. 2002) (plaintiff, cut in throat by piece of glass hidden in mashed potatoes, could recover for past and future pain and suffering, emotional distress, anxiety, mental anguish, embarrassment and loss of enjoyment of life); Way v. Tampa Coca Cola Bottling Co., 260 So.2d 288 (Fla. Dist. Ct. App. 1972) (while sucking the partially frozen contents out of a bottle of Coke, plaintiff encountered a "rat with the hair sucked off"; damages for emotional distress allowed).

The emotional distress, however, must be reasonable. See, e.g., Coca–Cola Bottling Co. v. Hagan, 813 So.2d 167 (Fla. Dist. Ct. App. 2002) (plaintiffs who drank from a bottle that they thought contained a used condom could not recover for fear of AIDS absent basis for this fear; citing fear of AIDS cases).

**162.** See, e.g., Chambley v. Apple Rests., Inc., 504 S.E.2d 551 (Ga. Ct. App. 1998) (condom in chicken salad); Sowell v. Hyatt Corp., 623 A.2d 1221 (D.C. Ct. App. 1993) (worm in rice plaintiff almost ate); Prejean v. Great Atl. & Pac. Tea Co., 457 So.2d 60 (La. App. 1984) (rotten roast that was "green as grass"); Wallace v. Coca–Cola Bottling Plants, Inc., 269 A.2d 117 (Me. 1970) (unpackaged prophylactic in Coke). See also Cohen v. Allendale Coca–Cola Bottling Co., 351 S.E.2d 897 (S.C. Ct. App. 1986) (Bell, J.) ("psychic nausea" from discovering insect in soft drink).

To recover for emotional distress in most jurisdictions, the plaintiff must establish that the emotional distress caused, or was caused by, some injury, illness, or other physical condition. See, e.g., Ellington v. Coca Cola Bottling Co. of Tulsa, Inc., 717 P.2d 109 (Okla. 1986) (plaintiff permitted to recover for emotional distress from observing piece of Good-n-Plenty candy, which she thought was a worm, in her bottle of Coke because her distress caused nausea, diarrhea, dehydration, kidney infection, and fever). Compare Ford v. Aldi, Inc., 832 S.W.2d 1 (Mo. Ct. App. 1992), where the plaintiff, while eating spinach she had prepared, became ill and threw up after discovering a 3/4 inch insect on her fork. In Missouri, plaintiffs no longer must prove physical harm to recover for emotional distress, but the distress must be "medically diagnosable" or "medically significant." *Held*, because plaintiff admitted to having suffered no injury and to having had insufficient reason to consult a doctor, summary judgment affirmed. At least Florida and Maine have abolished the physical injury requirement for recovery in cases involving emotional distress caused by the consumption of contaminated food. See Hagan v. Coca–Cola Bottling Co., 804 So.2d 1234 (Fla. 2001); Culbert v. Sampson's Supermarkets Inc., 444 A.2d 433 (Me. 1982).

**163.** See, e.g., Knight v. Just Born, Inc., 2000 WL 924624, at *15 (D. Or. 2000) (husband suffered severe chemical burns to mouth from eating Hot Tamale candy); Bullara v. Checker's Drive–In Rest., 736 So.2d 936 (La. Ct. App. 1999) (for a few months after she bit into cockroach in chili dog, wife was not in mood for sex and husband had to cook and eat alone).

# Chapter 8

# DESIGN DEFECTS

*Table of Sections*

## § 8.1  DESIGN DEFECTS—GENERALLY

The concept of design defectiveness is the heart of products liability law. Yet judicial oversight of a manufacturer's design choices is a relatively new phenomenon. Design defect claims under any theory of liability were rarely entertained by courts early in the twentieth century,[1] and only in recent decades have courts with any frequency begun to adjudicate the reasonableness of product designs in accident litigation. Yet a product's design concept predetermines the extent to which use of the product will result in human injury, and a fundamental premise of modern products liability law is that manufacturers are fairly held to answer in the courts for the basic safety of their products' designs.

Finding an acceptable definition for what constitutes a "defective" design is a difficult task. Elusive as an elf, the true meaning of "design defect" has largely escaped capture by court or commentator, and the search therefor leads inexorably to consternation and confusion. The quest for understanding design defectiveness perennially vexes courts[2]

---

**§ 8.1**

**1.** For a small handful of early examples, see James, Products Liability (pt. 1), 34 Tex. L. Rev. 44, 50 (1955).

**2.** For the views of Chief Justice Roger Traynor, who should be credited with the judicial invention of strict products liability in tort in Greenman v. Yuba Power Prods., Inc., 377 P.2d 897 (Cal. 1963), see Traynor,

The Ways and Meanings of Defective Products and Strict Liability, 32 Tenn. L. Rev. 363 (1965). Judicial confusion was not just a phenomenon of early products liability law. From the 1970s, see, e.g., Phillips v. Kimwood Mach. Co., 525 P.2d 1033, 1035 (Or. 1974) ("courts continue to flounder while attempting to determine how one decides whether a product is 'in a defective

and accomplished products liability lawyers[3] attempting to unravel design defect problems; delights law clerks,[4] young associates,[5] and law students[6] furnished an occasion for displaying their erudition; and provides fertile grist for law professors[7] aspiring for the renown thought to

condition unreasonably dangerous to the user' ''). From the 1980s, see, e.g., Prentis v. Yale Mfg. Co., 365 N.W.2d 176, 182 (Mich. 1984) ("questions related to 'design defects' and the determination of when a product is defective, because of the nature of its design, appear to be the most agitated and controversial issues before the courts in the field of products liability"). From the 1990s, see, e.g., Denny v. Ford Motor Co., 662 N.E.2d 730, 739, 740 (N.Y. 1995) (Simons, J., dissenting) ("the word 'defect' has no clear legal meaning"). From the 2000s, see, e.g., Jarvis v. Ford Motor Co. 283 F.3d 33, 63 (2d Cir. 2002) (N.Y. law) (noting "the unsettled nature of the law in this area"); McCathern v. Toyota Motor Corp., 23 P.3d 320 (Or. 2001); Green v. Smith & Nephew AHP, Inc., 629 N.W.2d 727 (Wis. 2001).

**3.** For a small sampling of the large literature on design defectiveness written by the practicing bar, see, e.g., V. Schwartz and Tedesco, The Re–Emergence of "Super Strict" Liability: Slaying the Dragon Again, 71 U. Cin. L. Rev. 917 (2003) (Schwartz); Vargo, The Emperor's New Clothes: The American Law Institute Adorns a "New Cloth" for Section 402A Products Liability Design Defects—A Survey of the States Reveals a Different Weave, 26 U. Mem. L. Rev. 493 (1996); Corboy, The Not–So–Quiet Revolution: Rebuilding Barriers to Jury Trial in the Proposed Restatement (Third) of Torts: Products Liability, 61 Tenn. L. Rev. 1043, 1087–1099 (1994); Rheingold, The Risk/Utility Test in Product Cases, 18 Trial L.Q. 49 (Summer/Fall 1987); Rheingold, What are the Consumer's "Reasonable Expectations"?, 22 Bus. Law. 589 (1967); Freedman, "Defect" in the Product: The Necessary Basis for Products Liability, 33 Tenn. L. Rev. 323 (1966).

**4.** See, e.g., F. Vandall and J. Vandall, A Call for An Accurate Restatement (Third) of Torts: Design Defect, 33 U. Mem. L. Rev. 909 (2003) (J. Vandall law clerk to Chatham County Judge Ginsberg); Ausili, Ramifications of Denny v. Ford Motor Co., 15 Touro L. Rev. 735 (1999) (law clerk to Eastern District of New York Judge Wexler); Thompson, The Arkansas Products Liability Statute: What Does "Unreasonably Dangerous" Mean in Arkansas?, 50 Ark. L. Rev. 663 (1998) (law clerk to Eighth Circuit Court of Appeals Chief Judge Arnold); Price, Toward a Unified Theory of Products Liability: Reviving the Causative Concept of Legal Fault, 61 Tenn. L. Rev. 1277, 1319–

25 (1994) (law clerk to Fifth Circuit Court of Appeals Judge King).

**5.** See, e.g., V. Schwartz and Tedesco, The Re–Emergence of "Super Strict" Liability: Slaying the Dragon Again, 71 U. Cin. L. Rev. 917 (2003) (Tedesco).

**6.** The law reviews are filled with hundreds of student commentaries on the meaning of defectiveness in products liability law. Perhaps the most valuable student work was a two-part article, prepared for his LL.M. thesis by Richard Wilson under the supervision of Dean William Prosser and Professor Albert Ehrenzweig at the University of California, Berkeley. See Wilson, Products Liability (pts. 1 and 2), 43 Cal. L. Rev. 614, 809, 810–35 (1955) (exploring the meaning of product defectiveness).

**7.** For early excursions by the law professors into the quagmire of design defectiveness, see, e.g., Keeton, Products Liability—Current Developments, 40 Tex. L. Rev. 193, 210 (1961); Keeton, Products Liability: Liability Without Fault and the Requirement of a Defect, 41 Tex. L. J. 855 (1963); Wade, Strict Tort Liability of Manufacturers, 19 Sw. L. J. 5 (1965); Dickerson, Products Liability: How Good Does a Product Have to Be?, 42 Ind. L.J. 301 (1967); Wade, On the Nature of Strict Tort Liability for Products, 44 Miss. L.J. 825, 837–38 (1973) (setting forth his famous seven factors); Henderson, Judicial Review of Manufacturers' Conscious Design Choices: The Limits of Adjudication, 73 Colum. L. Rev. 1531, 1534, 1538 (1973). At a very early date, Professor Karl Llewellyn referred to design defects in defining "defect" in Revised Uniform Sales Act § 1(b), cmt. b, at 125 (2d draft 1941), cited in Wilson, Products Liability (pt. 2), 43 Cal. L. Rev. 809, 810 n.7 (1955).

For a sampling of recent additions to the ever-burgeoning literature on design defectiveness from legal academics, see, e.g., Kysar, The Expectations of Consumers, 103 Colum. L. Rev. 1700 (2003); Miller, Myth Surrenders to Reality: Design Defect Litigation in Iowa, 51 Drake L. Rev. 459 (2003); F. Vandall and J. Vandall, A Call for An Accurate Restatement (Third) of Torts: Design Defect, 33 U. Mem. L. Rev. 909 (2003); Owen, Toward a Proper Test for Design Defectiveness: "Micro–Balancing" Costs and Benefits, 75 Tex. L. Rev. 1661 (1997); Owen, Defectiveness Restated: Exploding the "Strict" Products Liability Myth, 1996 U. Ill. L. Rev. 743; Vandall, The Restate-

follow discovery of the key to any riddle wrapped in a mystery inside an enigma.[8]

Just as strict liability in tort is the dominant liability theory in major products liability litigation, design defectiveness is the dominant claim in most major products liability cases.[9] Manufacturer design determinations involve a multitude of safety-related choices, including decisions on the types and strengths of raw materials and component parts, the manner in which such materials and parts are combined, whether safety devices will be included, and the overall product concept. Perhaps the most frequent claim of design defectiveness is the absence of some type of adequate safety device, such as a housing surrounding a power lawnmower,[10] a mechanical guard or electrical interlock cut-off device on a dangerous machine,[11] or a "safety" on a gun.[12] Much automotive products liability litigation challenges the design of motor vehicles, including the extent to which their designs are sufficiently "crashworthy" to provide their occupants adequate protection in the event of a crash.[13] In addition to such typical design danger claims, numerous other forms of design hazards may give rise to claims of defectiveness—such as allergenic latex gloves, flammable fabrics not treated with flame retardant chemicals, drain cleaners comprised of chemicals that are unnecessarily caustic, products whose moving parts are made of metal too soft to last throughout the product's useful life, tampons that are too absorbent,

ment (Third) of Torts, Products Liability, Section 2(b): Design Defect, 68 Temple L. Rev. 167 (1995); M. Green, The Schizophrenia of Risk–Benefit Analysis in Design Defect Litigation, 48 Vand. L. Rev. 609 (1995); Tietz, Strict Products Liability, Design Defects and Corporate Decision–Making: Greater Deterrence Through Stricter Process, 38 Vill. L. Rev. 1361 (1993); Davis, Design Defect Liability: In Search of a Standard of Responsibility, 39 Wayne L. Rev. 1217 (1993); Henderson and Twerski, Closing the American Products Liability Frontier: The Rejection of Liability Without Defect, 66 N.Y.U. L. Rev. 1263 (1991); C.J. Miller and R. Goldberg, Product Liability ch. 11 (Oxford, 2d ed. 2004) (British law).

**8.** Design defectiveness in the early 2000s may be somewhat less inscrutable than was Russia in the late 1930s, but Winston Churchill's inimitable characterization nevertheless seems apt.

**9.** An insurance industry study of large claims (in excess of $100,000) revealed that strict liability was the principal liability theory, and that defective design was the principal claim in 75% of such cases. See A Study of Large Product Liability Claims Closed in 1985, a joint study of the Alliance of American Insurers (L. Soular, Research Dept.) and the American Insurance Association (1986).

**10.** See, e.g., Thibault v. Sears, Roebuck & Co., 395 A.2d 843 (N.H. 1978) (strict tort action against manufacturer of rotary lawn mower for injuries from slipping under mower that rear trailing guard could have prevented).

**11.** See, e.g., Burke v. Spartanics, Ltd., 252 F.3d 131 (2d Cir. 2001) (N.Y. law) (no rear guard on metal shearing machine); Daley v. Gemini Bakery Equip. Co., 643 N.Y.S.2d 106 (App. Div. 1996) (safety interlock on dough dividing machine would have turned machine off when door was opened); Knitz v. Minster Mach. Co., 1987 WL 6486 (Ohio Ct. App. 1987) (interlock gate guard on press would have prevented ram from descending on operator's hand).

**12.** See, e.g., Halliday v. Sturm, Ruger & Co., 792 A.2d 1145 (Md. 2002); Sturm, Ruger & Co. v. Day, 594 P.2d 38 (Alaska 1979), modified on other grounds, 615 P.2d 621 (Alaska 1980).

**13.** See, e.g., Connelly v. Hyundai Motor Co. 351 F.3d 535 (1st Cir. 2003) (N.H. law) (child killed by deployment of front-seat airbag); General Motors Corp. v. McGee, 837 So.2d 1010 (Fla. Dist. Ct. App. 2002) (fuel tank vulnerable to impact, fuel leakage, and fire); Compton v. Subaru of Am., Inc., 82 F.3d 1513 (10th Cir. 1996) (Kan. law) (roof crushed). Automotive products liability litigation is treated in ch. 17, below.

coffee that is too hot, raw asbestos comprised of toxic fibers, and tell-tale mechanical heart valves that emit excessive noise.[14]

The discussion of defectiveness in the chapter on strict liability in tort[15] focused on the quest by courts for a general definition of "defectiveness," commonly viewed in early products liability as embracing a single principle applicable to any type of case.[16] As products liability law has matured,[17] however, most courts[18] and commentators[19] have come to understand that meaningful evaluation of the acceptability of a product's dangers logically turns on considerations that vary contextually depending upon whether the problem was one of manufacture, design, or the absence of sufficient warning.[20] And early in the evolution of products liability law observers recognized that determining how and why a design danger should or should not be characterized as "defective" was at once the most important and baffling problem in this entire field of law.[21] For this reason, much of the search for a general definition of

---

**14.** See, e.g., Green v. Smith & Nephew AHP, Inc., 629 N.W.2d 727 (Wis. 2001) (allergic reactions to latex gloves possessing excessive levels of proteins and other toxic chemical substances); Morson v. Superior Court, 109 Cal. Rptr.2d 343 (Ct. App. 2001) (same); Arena v. Owens-Corning, 74 Cal. Rptr.2d 580 (Ct. App. 1998) (toxic raw asbestos dust inhaled by naval shipyard worker); Nadel v. Burger King Corp., 695 N.E.2d 1185 (Ohio Ct. App. 1997) (175° coffee caused second degree burns); Bravman v. Baxter Healthcare Corp., 984 F.2d 71 (2d Cir. 1993) (N.Y. law) (noisy mechanical heart valve); Strothkamp v. Chesebrough–Pond's, Inc., Prod. Liab. Rep. (CCH) ¶ 13,-456 (Mo. Ct. App. 1993) (failure to child-proof box of cotton swabs); Toner v. Lederle Lab., 828 F.2d 510 (9th Cir. 1987) (Idaho law) (DPT vaccine should have been formulated in safer manner); Boyer v. Empiregas, Inc. of Chillicothe, 734 S.W.2d 828 (Mo. Ct. App. 1987) (inadequately odorized propane gas exploded); Apels v. Murjani Int'l Ltd., Prod. Liab. Rep. (CCH) ¶ 11,229 (D. Kan. 1986) (composition of blouse fabric, 80% cotton and 20% polyester, excessively flammable); West v. Johnson & Johnson Prods., Inc., 220 Cal.Rptr. 437 (Ct. App. 1985) (extra-high absorbency tampons caused toxic shock syndrome); Hilliard v. A.H. Robins Co., 196 Cal.Rptr. 117 (Ct. App. 1983) (Dalkon Shield IUD, with multifilament tail string, facilitated migration of bacteria into uterus); Drayton v. Jiffee Chem. Corp., 395 F.Supp. 1081 (N.D. Ohio 1975), modified 591 F.2d 352 (6th Cir. 1978) (formulation of drain cleaner as 26% lye unnecessarily caustic).

**15.** See ch. 5, above.

**16.** Some early commentators recognized that design and manufacturing defects were conceptually distinct (and warning defects to a lesser extent, because such defects were sometimes viewed as a subset of design defectiveness), but such commen-

tators generally viewed the classification as having little or no doctrinal significance. See, e.g., James, Products Liability, 34 Tex. L. Rev. 44, 49 (1955) ("It is not suggested that this dichotomy [between design and manufacturing defects] has any automatic or uniform legal significance."). See generally § 6.2, above.

**17.** Although the distinctive nature of design, manufacturing, and warnings defects was overlooked by many courts and commentators during the burst of excitement surrounding the adoption of strict products liability in tort, both the First and the Second Restatements of Torts so divided the cases in the law of negligence. See Restatement (2d) Torts §§ 388 (duty to warn), 395 (manufacturing flaws), and 398 (dangerous design).

**18.** Some courts still appear to miss this point. See, e.g., Urena v. Biro Mfg. Co., 114 F.3d 359, 365 (2d Cir. 1997) (N.Y. law) (plaintiff's evidence that "design was unreasonably dangerous because it lacks adequate warnings and instructions was unrebutted. He therefore survives summary judgment on his design defect claim."); Sperry–New Holland v. Prestage, 617 So.2d 248 (Miss. 1993).

**19.** Some commentators also appear to miss this point. See, e.g., Shapo, In Search of the Law of Products Liability: The ALI Restatement Project, 48 Vand. L. Rev. 631, 659–60 (1995); Corboy, The Not–So–Quiet Revolution: Rebuilding Barriers to Jury Trial in the Proposed Restatement (Third) of Torts: Products Liability, 61 Tenn. L. Rev. 1043, 1089–92 (1994); Phillips, Achilles' Heel, 61 Tenn. L. Rev. 1265, 1267–70 (1994); Price, Toward a Unified Theory of Products Liability: Reviving the Causative Concept of Legal Fault, 61 Tenn. L. Rev. 1277, 1319–25 (1994).

**20.** See § 6.2, above.

**21.** For early law journal discussions of this point, see note 7, above.

"product defect," examined above,[22] was in essence a search for the meaning of defectiveness in design, as further discussed below.

Determining how to evaluate the acceptability or defectiveness of a product's design is difficult in part because a product's design is the essence of what the manufacturer decides to make and sell. A manufacturing defect is truly a mistake, one which results from some fault in the production process whereby a particular product deviates from the manufacturer's own "blueprint" specifications of the intended and correct design. Quite to the contrary, a charge that a product is defective in design challenges those very specifications on the ground that the design engineers, in their conceptual rendition of the product, failed to take safety into adequate account. Consequently, a challenge to a product design is a challenge to the quality of the manufacturer's engineering department as well as to the standards of its management in deciding to develop and sell a product containing a particular type and level of danger. Thus, unlike a manufacturing defect claim, which implicates merely a single product unit, a design defect claim challenges the integrity of the entire product line and so pierces to the very core of the manufacturer's enterprise. For this reason, design defect claims are of greatest concern to manufacturers, since a judicial declaration that the design of a particular product is "defective" condemns the entire product line.

Judicial evaluations of manufacturer design decisions encounter other difficulties, too. Far more than in manufacturing and warnings defect cases, design cases require courts to second-guess a manufacturer's analyses of consumer market preferences. Some commentators have challenged the propriety of courts displacing multi-faceted engineering and managerial determinations of this type with judicial fiats rendered in the litigation arena.[23] Be that as it may, courts around the nation have come to adjudicate the sufficiency of product designs on a regular basis.

This chapter examines in depth the tests of design defectiveness developed by the courts, particularly in applying the doctrine of *Restatement (Second) of Torts* § 402A. Although these tests were examined preliminarily in the chapter on strict liability in tort, their application in design defect cases is explored in greater depth in §§ 8.2–8.7, below. The *Third Restatement*'s definition of design defectiveness is examined in § 8.8. A manufacturer's liability for equipping its products with optional, rather than mandatory, safety features is examined in § 8.9, and a pharmaceutical manufacturer's special liability for prescription drugs and medical devices is addressed in § 8.10. Other topics of particular interest in design defect litigation are examined elsewhere, such as automotive crashworthiness;[24] how a warning may affect a manufactur-

---

**22.** See ch. 5, above.

**23.** See, e.g., Epstein, The Risks of Risk/Utility, 48 Ohio St. L. Rev. 469 (1987); Huber, Safety and the Second Best: The Hazards of Public Risk Management in the Courts, 85 Colum. L. Rev. 277 (1985); Henderson, Judicial Review of Manufactur-

ers' Conscious Design Choices: The Limits of Adjudication, 73 Colum. L. Rev. 1531, 1534, 1538 (1973) (characterizing such decisions by manufacturers as "polycentric" and "managerial").

**24.** See § 17.3, below.

er's duty of safe design;[25] proof of defect,[26] including the use of expert witnesses;[27] product misuse;[28] and certain limitations on liability affecting design defect determinations, such as obvious dangers, generic risks, state of the art, and product deterioration.[29]

## § 8.2   THEORIES AND TESTS OF LIABILITY

Manufacturers and other sellers[1] are subject to liability for defective design under each of the major theories of liability. Thus, as is true with respect to other types of defects, product suppliers are subject to liability in negligence, for negligently making and selling products that are defectively designed;[2] in implied warranty, for selling products that are not fit for ordinary purposes, and hence "unmerchantable," because they are defectively designed;[3] and in strict liability in tort for simply selling products that are defective in design.[4]

Regardless of the theory of liability, whether a design is "defective" is typically the central issue in litigation associated with a product's design. Indeed, the *Products Liability Restatement* proposes that liability in such cases be grounded solely on the notion of product defect rather than on traditional theories of liability such as negligence and strict liability in tort.[5] Strict liability in tort, of course, is defined principally in terms of a product's "defectiveness."[6] Yet proof of a defect in a product's design is just as important in cases brought in negligence inasmuch as a manufacturer hardly can be at fault for selling a product with a *safe* design, a design that is *not* defective.[7] Moreover, in the great majority of

---

**25.** See § 6.2, above.

**26.** See § 6.4, above.

**27.** See § 6.3, above.

**28.** See § 13.5, below.

**29.** See ch. 10, below.

### § 8.2

**1.** Some jurisdictions partially immunize retailers and other nonmanufacturers from liability for design defectiveness and other forms of strict liability. See § 15.2, below.

**2.** See, e.g., Connelly v. Hyundai Motor Co., 351 F.3d 535 (1st Cir. 2003) (N.H. law) (automobile); Phillips v. Cricket Lighters, 841 A.2d 1000 (Pa. 2003) (butane lighter).

**3.** See, e.g., Smith v. DaimlerChrysler Corp., 2002 WL 31814534 (Del. Super. Ct. 2002) (automobile); Chapman ex rel. Estate of Chapman v. Bernard's Inc., 167 F.Supp.2d 406, 415 (D. Mass. 2001) (day bed); Denny v. Ford Motor Co., 662 N.E.2d 730 (N.Y. 1995) (Bronco II).

**4.** See, e.g., Flock v. Scripto–Tokai Corp., 319 F.3d 231 (5th Cir. 2003) (Tex. law) (utility lighter not child-resistant); Vautour v. Body Masters Sports Indus., 784 A.2d 1178 (N.H. 2001) (leg press machine with fixed stops); McCathern v. Toyota Mo-

tor Co., 23 P.3d 320 (Or. 2001) (SUV rollover).

**5.** See Products Liability Restatement § 2 cmt. *n* (recommending that, because design claims rest on a risk-utility assessment regardless of doctrinal label, courts should not risk inconsistent verdicts by submitting such claims to juries on different causes of action, whether negligence, implied warranty, or strict liability in tort). At least one state supreme court agrees. See Wright v. Brooke Group Ltd., 652 N.W.2d 159, 169 (Iowa 2002) ("We question the need for or usefulness of *any* traditional doctrinal label in design defect cases because, as comment *n* points out, a court should not submit both a negligence claim and a strict liability claim based on the same design defect since both claims rest on an identical risk-utility evaluation. Moreover, to persist in using two names for the same claim only continues the dysfunction engendered by section 402A. Therefore, we prefer to label a claim based on a defective product design as a design defect claim without reference to strict liability or negligence.").

**6.** See § 5.3, above.

**7.** See, e.g., Bishop v. Gentec Inc., 48 P.3d 218, 226 (Utah 2002). See generally §§ 2.1 and 5.9, above.

states, and even in most cases brought in the Empire State,[8] proving that a product design is dangerously unmerchantable under UCC § 2–314 amounts to precisely the same thing as that the product is "defective" (or "unreasonably dangerous") under *Restatement (Second) of Torts* § 402A.[9]

In considering the concept of design defectiveness, it is crucial to remember that a manufacturer's liability for harm from a product's design characteristics, even if labeled "strict," is not absolute. As the strict manufacturer liability principles of *Greenman v. Yuba Power Products, Inc.*[10] and *Restatement (Second) of Torts* § 402A spread across the nation in the 1960s and 1970s,[11] courts and commentators searched mightily for standards or "tests" of liability that would stop liability well short of absolute.[12] Although early test formulations generally failed to distinguish between the various forms of defect, most of the cases struggling with the meaning of defectiveness involved dangers in design.[13] Consequently, the evolution of liability tests examined in chapter 5 (the consumer expectations test, the risk-utility test, combinations thereof, and alternative tests) generally involved a search for appropriate methods for separating product designs that were adequately safe from those that were not.

**8.** Denny v. Ford Motor Co., 662 N.E.2d 730 (N.Y. 1995), held that a product not defectively designed for purposes of strict products liability in tort could nevertheless be unmerchantable for purposes of UCC § 2–314(2). Yet even *Denny* recognized that in most cases the two standards will produce precisely the same result: "As a practical matter, the distinction between the defect concepts in tort law and in implied warranty theory may have little or no effect in most cases." Id. at 738. On *Denny*, see § 5.9, above.

**9.** Or under Products Liability Restatement § 2(b). See § 8.8, below. Courts often recite the virtual or complete equivalence of the warranty and tort law standards of liability: "[T]o bring an action in implied warranty for personal injury a plaintiff is required to show product unmerchantability sufficient to avoid summary judgment on the issue of defectiveness in a tort strict products liability suit." Larsen v. Pacesetter Sys., Inc., 837 P.2d 1273, 1284–85 (Haw. 1992), as amended on reconsideration, 843 P.2d 144 (Haw. 1992). See also State Farm Fire & Cas. Co. v. Miller Elec. Co., 562 N.E.2d 589 (Ill. App. Ct. 1990); Virgil v. "Kash N' Karry" Serv. Corp., 484 A.2d 652, 656 (Md. Ct. Spec. App. 1984):

To recover on either theory—implied warranty or strict liability—the plaintiff in a products liability case must satisfy three basics from an evidentiary standpoint: (1) the existence of a defect, (2) the attribution of the defect to the seller, and (3) a causal relation between the defect and the injury.

See also Gumbs v. International Harvester, Inc., 718 F.2d 88 (3d Cir. 1983) (V.I. law). Accord, Voelkel v. General Motors Corp., 846 F.Supp. 1468, 1475–76 (D. Kan. 1994) (for implied warranty, strict products liability, and negligence). Their equivalence is stated by Revised UCC § 2–314, Official Comment 7 ("When recovery is sought for injury to person or property, whether goods are merchantable is to be determined by applicable state products liability [tort] law."). See §§ 4.3 and 5.9, above.

**10.** 377 P.2d 897 (Cal. 1963) (Traynor, J.).

**11.** See § 5.2 et seq., above.

**12.** See § 5.3, above. Phillips v. Kimwood Mach. Co., 525 P.2d 1033, 1035–36 (Or. 1974), may have said it best. Noting that the "courts continue to flounder while attempting to determine how one decides whether a product is 'in a defective condition unreasonably dangerous to the user,'" the court observed: "The problem with strict liability of products has been one of limitation. No one wants absolute liability where all the article has to do is to cause injury. To impose liability there has to be something about the article which makes it dangerously defective without regard to whether the manufacturer was or was not at fault for such condition. A test for unreasonable danger is therefore vital."

**13.** See, e.g., id.

All courts judge the adequacy of a product's design upon one of two basic standards, or some combination thereof: (1) by determining whether the design meets the safety expectations of users or consumers, and/or (2) by conducting a risk-benefit evaluation of whether the safety benefits of designing away a foreseeable danger exceed the resulting costs. The following section reconsiders § 402A's original test, the consumer expectations test. The fundamentals of the risk-utility test are then reassessed in § 8.4 which explores the appropriate factors weighed in a risk-utility balance. Section 8.5 next considers the critical role of feasible design alternatives in risk-utility decisionmaking. The blending by some courts of the consumer expectations and risk-utility tests is investigated in § 8.6, and the Wade–Keeton prudent-seller hindsight test based on constructive knowledge of a product's design dangers is examined in § 8.7. How the *Products Liability Restatement* treats the concept of design defect is explored in § 8.8, followed by considerations of the special design issues involving optional safety devices and pharmaceutical drugs and medical devices, in §§ 8.9 and 8.10, respectively.

## § 8.3  THE CONSUMER EXPECTATIONS TEST

The consumer expectations test was the first standard for evaluating design defectiveness, and it remains a persistent, if embattled, liability test in at least certain types of design defect cases in many states.[1] In searching for a test for design defectiveness, courts turned first to the definitions of "defective condition unreasonably dangerous" provided in the comments to *Restatement (Second) of Torts* § 402A. Comment *g* defines "defective condition":

> The rule stated in this Section applies only where the product is, at the time it leaves the seller's hands, in a condition not contemplated by the ultimate consumer, which will be unreasonably dangerous to him.

Comment *i* defines the other half of the liability standard, "unreasonably dangerous":

> The article sold must be dangerous to an extent beyond that which would be contemplated by the ordinary consumer who purchases it, with the ordinary knowledge common to the community as to its characteristics.

Because "defective condition" and "unreasonably dangerous" are both defined as *dangerous beyond a consumer's contemplations*, most courts

---

**§ 8.3**

**1.** "The consumer expectations test for design defectiveness has become products liability's version of the rule against perpetuities: a doctrine nearly universally reviled but stubbornly and inexplicably persistent." Kysar, The Expectations of Consumers, 103 Colum. L. Rev. 1700, 1701 (2003). See also V. Schwartz and R. Tedesco, The Re–Emergence of "Super Strict" Liability: Slaying the Dragon Again, 71 U. Cin. L. Rev. 917 (2003); Phillips, Consumer Expectations, 53 S.C. L. Rev. 1047 (2002); Korzec, Dashing Consumer Hopes: Strict Products Liability and the Demise of the Consumer Expectations Test, 20 B.C. Int'l & Comp. L. Rev. 227 (1997); Little, The Place of Consumer Expectations in Product Strict Liability Actions for Defectively Designed Products, 61 Tenn. L. Rev. 1189 (1994); Kennedy, The Role of the Consumer Expectations Test Under Louisiana's Products Liability Tort Doctrine, 69 Tul. L. Rev. 117, 162 (1994). For additional citations, and further discussion, see § 5.6 n.1, above.

applying § 402A in the 1960s and 1970s concluded that design defectiveness under § 402A should be tested according to a standard of product safety gauged by "consumer expectations."[2]

Roughly two centuries in the past, warranty law broke away from the tort law action of deceit and migrated to the law of contracts,[3] a field of law which seeks at bottom to protect the reasonable expectations of the contracting parties.[4] Warranty law sensibly protects consumer expectations predictably generated by a manufacturer's representations about its products, both express and implied.[5] When the Reporter for the *Restatement (Second) of Torts*, Dean William Prosser, was drafting § 402A in the late 1950s and early 1960s,[6] virtually all of the scant case authority for strict manufacturer liability for injuries to remote consumers from the sale of defective products had been decided under the law of warranty.[7] The strongest authority for the new tort doctrine was a long line of cases involving defective food products, a context in which the law has long protected consumer expectations with special vigilance.[8] So, it was only natural that Dean Prosser would define strict products liability in the same consumer expectations terms that supported the warranty law cases which were his authority for the new tort doctrine. And it was also only natural for the courts, in beginning to apply the new doctrine to design defect cases in the early days of strict products liability in tort, to adopt the warranty-based definition of liability provided in the comments to § 402A.[9]

Although most modern courts have abandoned consumer expectations as the basic test of design defectiveness, as discussed below,[10] some courts still use this test in design defect cases[11] and some version of the

---

**2.** See id. For examples of early decisions defining § 402A's "defective condition unreasonably dangerous" in the consumer expectations terms of comments *g* and *i*, see, e.g., Rossignol v. Danbury Sch. of Aeronautics, Inc., 227 A.2d 418 (Conn. 1967); Dunham v. Vaughan & Bushnell Mfg. Co., 247 N.E.2d 401 (Ill. 1969); Lunt v. Brady Mfg. Corp., 475 P.2d 964 (Ariz. Ct. App. 1970); Vincer v. Esther Williams All–Aluminum Swimming Pool Co., 230 N.W.2d 794 (Wis. 1975).

**3.** See § 5.2, above.

**4.** See 1 A. Corbin, Corbin on Contracts 2 (1993 rev. ed.) ("the law of contracts attempts the realization of reasonable expectations").

On the warranty law background of strict products liability in tort, see § 5.2, above.

**5.** See, e.g., Denny v. Ford Motor Co., 662 N.E.2d 730, 736 (N.Y. 1995) (warranty law, originating in the law of contracts, "directs its attention to the purchaser's disappointed expectations"); Markle v. Mulholland's Inc., 509 P.2d 529, 532 and 534 (Or. 1973). See generally Owen, The Moral Foundations of Products Liability Law, 68 Notre Dame L. Rev. 427, 462–65 (1993); Shapo, A Representational Theory of Consumer Protection: Doctrine, Function and Legal Liability for Product Disappointment, 60 Va. L. Rev. 1109, 1370 (1974).

On warranty law under the Uniform Commercial Code, see ch. 4, above.

**6.** See §§ 5.2–5.6, above.

**7.** See § 5.2, above.

**8.** See § 5.2, above.

**9.** See § 5.6, above.

**10.** See also ch. 5, above.

**11.** See, e.g., Green v. Smith & Nephew AHP, Inc., 629 N.W.2d 727, 755 (Wis. 2001) (consumer expectations test appropriate for proof of latex glove's defectiveness based on ordinary consumer's ignorance that gloves could cause allergic reaction); Delaney v. Deere and Co., 999 P.2d 930, 944 (Kan. 2000) (consumer expectations proper test, but reasonable alternative design may be factor to consider). See also Wheeler v. John Deere Co., 935 F.2d 1090 (10th Cir. 1991) (Kan. law), which affirmed a judgment for a farm worker against the manufacturer of a combine for injuries to his arm which occurred when he reached into the combine's augur to remove a residual buildup of grain. On the consumer expectations

test is statutory in a small number of states.[12] Although the consumer expectations standard was conventionally viewed as more protective to plaintiffs than the risk-utility standard,[13] courts have used the consumer expectations test most frequently to *deny* recovery to plaintiffs in cases involving obvious design hazards.[14]

Among the few cases applying the consumer expectations standard to *allow* a design defect claim is *Jarke v. Jackson Products*,[15] which involved a welder's claim against the manufacturer of a welding mask for injuries from molten metal that spilled from the mask into his ear. The plaintiff was injured while squatting beneath an object he was welding overhead, with his head cocked to one side, when some molten metal dropped from above onto his mask, rolled down to the mask's side rim, which channeled it into his ear. The complaint alleged that the mask was defectively designed (1) because it did not provide protection for the user's ears, and (2) because its overall configuration, including its side rim, could channel molten metal into a user's ears. Reasoning that the danger to a user's ears was obvious, the trial court granted the defendant manufacturer's motion for summary judgment, and the plaintiff appealed. Although the appellate court agreed that the obvious absence of an ear guard precluded a finding of design defectiveness

---

issue, plaintiff had ten other farm workers, each of whom had also lost portions of their arms in augurs of this model combine, testify "as to unexpected danger when, in the process of manual cleanout, the auger suddenly was engaged while the engine was running." Id. at 1095. Moreover, plaintiff's expert in farm machinery design, a mechanical engineer, testified "that the combine was more dangerous than anticipated by ordinary consumers." Id. at 1100. *Held*, both forms of proof of consumer expectations were acceptable. For earlier cases, see, e.g., Lester v. Magic Chef, 641 P.2d 353 (Kan. 1982); Rahmig v. Mosley Mach. Co., 412 N.W.2d 56 (Neb. 1987); Woods v. Fruehauf Trailer Corp., 765 P.2d 770 (Okla. 1988).

**12.** A statute in North Dakota explicitly defines "unreasonably dangerous" in consumer contemplation terms; see Endresen v. Scheels Hardware & Sports Shop, Inc., 560 N.W.2d 225, 233 (N.D. 1997). An Oregon statute does so indirectly, by legislatively incorporating the comments to § 402A including comment *i*; see McCathern v. Toyota Motor Corp., 23 P.3d 320, 329–32 (Or. 2001). A Tennessee statute defines "unreasonably dangerous" alternatively in both consumer contemplations and prudent manufacturer terms; see Ray v. BIC Corp., 925 S.W.2d 527, 529 (Tenn. 1996). And Ohio's statute grounds defective design liability alternatively on consumer expectations or risk-benefit analysis; see Griffith v. Chrysler Corp., 2003 WL 21500037, *3 (Ohio Ct. App. 2003). The statutes are: N.D. Cent. Code § 28–01.3–01(4); Or. Rev. Stat. § 30.920; Tenn. Code Ann. § 29–28–102(8);

Ohio Rev. Code Ann. § 2307.75(A). See also S.C. Code § 15–73–30 (adopting comments to § 402A); Utah Code § 78–15–6(2) (setting forth *Barker*-like alternative, two-pronged test).

**13.** See, e.g., Shapo, In Search of the Law of Products Liability: The ALI Restatement Project, 48 Vand. L. Rev. 631 (1995); Phillips, Achilles' Heel, 61 Tenn. L. Rev. 1265 (1994). However, the plaintiff's bar appears to recognize the weaknesses in the consumer expectations test. See Vandall, The Restatement (Third) of Torts: Products Liability Section 2(b): The Reasonable Alternative Design Requirement, 61 Tenn. L. Rev. 1407 (1994).

**14.** See, e.g., Brown v. Sears, Roebuck & Co., 328 F.3d 1274, 1282–83 (10th Cir. 2003) (Utah law) (ordinary and prudent user would expect danger to toddler standing behind riding mower operated in reverse); Vineyard v. Empire Mach. Co., 581 P.2d 1152, 1155 (Ariz. Ct. App. 1978) (absence of roll-over bar on large earth-moving scraper, which rolled over and crushed operator's leg, not a danger beyond consumer's expectations since its absence was "immediately evident"); Menard v. Newhall, 373 A.2d 505, 507 (Vt. 1977) (plaintiff's eye put out in BB gun fight: "A BB gun which is neither defectively designed nor manufactured is not dangerous beyond that which would be contemplated by the ordinary consumer. . . . A warning by the defendant Daisy that a BB gun, if fired at a person, could injure an eye, is nothing that even a seven-year-old child does not already know.").

**15.** 631 N.E.2d 233 (Ill. App. Ct. 1994).

under the consumer expectations test on that particular ground, it reversed and remanded on the issue of whether an ordinary person would understand that the mask's design itself created the means for molten slag to be channelled into a user's ear.[16]

It will be recalled that the consumer expectations test is an *objective* test based on the average, normal, or "ordinary" expectations of a reasonable user or consumer.[17] Usually that person, whether a user or consumer, will be the person placed at risk by the product's danger in design.[18] However, purchasers and users sometimes control product risks to other persons, as discussed above. In such cases, when one person (such as a parent or a doctor) purchases a product with particular dangers or uses a product in a manner that injures a person under his or her control (such as the parent's child or the doctor's patient), the law frequently looks to the expectations of the risk controller rather than to those of the victim.[19]

The utility of the consumer expectations test is severely compromised when design dangers are obvious.[20] Because consumers acquire their safety and danger expectations most directly from a product's appearance, obvious dangers—such as the risk to human limbs from an unguarded power mower or industrial machine—are virtually always contemplated or expected by the user or consumer who thereby is necessarily unprotected by the consumer expectations test, no matter how probable or severe the likely danger nor how easy or cheap the means of avoiding it. In such cases, the buyer gets what he or she paid for, or the user engaged a danger that he or she expected, so that the risk of injury shifts to the buyer or user who chose to encounter it, or to a third-party victim who had no say in the matter at all.[21] Thus, while the consumer expectations test protects the autonomy of buyers and users by shielding them from unexpected harm, the flip side of this test requires users and consumers to be ever vigilant and take responsibility for the harmful consequences of their choices about risk. And a pure consumer expectations test perniciously rewards manufacturers for failing to adopt cost-effective measures to remedy obviously unnecessary dangers to human life and limb.[22] The failure of the consumer expecta-

**16.** Id. at 239.

**17.** Comment *i* is phrased in terms of the "ordinary" consumer "with the ordinary knowledge common to the community." See § 5.6, above.

**18.** See § 5.6, above.

**19.** See id.

**20.** On obvious dangers, see § 10.2, below.

**21.** Such as a toddler run over by a riding lawn mower. See Brown v. Sears, Roebuck & Co., 328 F.3d 1274, 1282–83 (10th Cir. 2003) (Utah law).

**22.** See, e.g., Chaney v. Hobart Int'l, Inc., 54 F.Supp.2d 677, 681 (E.D. La. 1999) ("As dangerous as the meat grinder may have been without a feed pan guard, it was clearly 'not dangerous to an extent beyond

that which would be contemplated by the ordinary user.' The possibility of injury is glaring.").

Relying on the strength of this important point, one court boldly circumvented the logically inescapable impact of an obvious design danger on the consumer expectations test. See Hansen v. New Holland N. Am., Inc., 574 N.W.2d 250 (Wis. Ct. App. 1997), where the plaintiff's hand was caught and injured in the mechanism of a hay baler while he was trying to cut away a buildup of hay on the rollers with a jack-knife. The trial court dismissed the plaintiff's design defect claim on the ground that the danger of placing one's hands near the moving mechanism presented an obvious danger which precluded recovery under the consumer expectations test. *Held*, reversing

tions test to deal adequately with the obvious danger problem profoundly weakens the usefulness of the test and effectively disqualifies it for principled use[23] as the sole basis for determining defects in design.[24]

Another significant limitation on the usefulness of consumer expectations as a liability standard in design cases concerns the vagueness of a consumer's expectations concerning most complex designs.[25] For example, consumers comprehend that automobiles are not completely crash-proof, but they have no meaningful expectations as to the extent to which a vehicle may, or may not, be compromised in the event of a collision at substantial speeds. The consumer expectations test thus was held to be an invalid gauge of design defectiveness in one case where a large rock hit the wheel of a vehicle traveling on the highway,[26] in another where the driver's airbag deployed and broke her jaw in a low-speed collision,[27] and in another where the passenger compartment collapsed in upon the driver's feet in a near head-on collision.[28] In such cases, the ordinary user of a vehicle "simply has 'no idea' how it should perform in all [such] situations."[29] For this reason, courts that use the consumer expectations test increasingly are limiting the applicability of the test to cases involving simple, rather than complex, product designs and accident mechanisms, as examined in detail below.[30]

and remanding, jury question presented on whether an average user would have fully appreciated the risk:

> [F]ocusing solely on the user's conduct will frustrate public policy considerations underlying product liability law. A danger that is open and obvious to a consumer is equally apparent to the manufacturer. Concentrating only on the user's conduct ignores the manufacturer's responsibility for producing that danger, and indeed creates an incentive for manufacturers to ensure that hazards are in fact open and obvious, possibly minimizing needed safeguards and exposure to liability for designing dangerous products.

Id. at 254.

**23.** True, it is possible to distort this as any test to avoid the harsh results of its principled application. See Phillips, Consumer Expectations, 53 S.C. L. Rev. 1047, 1049 (2002) (characterizing as "semantic" the consumer expectations test's foreclosure of relief to persons injured by obvious dangers).

**24.** See id. In switching from the consumer expectations test to the risk-utility standard in 1993, the Mississippi Supreme Court noted that its conversion to risk-utility permitted it to reject the patent danger rule which inhered in the consumer expectations test. Sperry–New Holland v. Prestage, 617 So.2d 248, 256 n.4 (Miss. 1993).

**25.** See Prosser and Keeton on Torts § 99, at 699. *But see* Phillips, Consumer Expectations, 53 S.C. L. Rev. 1047, 1052–61 (2002) (consumer expectations can be based

on risk-utility, informed by experts, as in the *Potter* case, discussed in § 8.6, below).

**26.** Heaton v. Ford Motor Co., 435 P.2d 806 (Or. 1967).

**27.** Pruitt v. General Motors Corp., 86 Cal.Rptr.2d 4 (Ct. App. 1999).

**28.** Soule v. General Motors Corp., 882 P.2d 298 (Cal. 1994).

**29.** Id. at 308.

**30.** See, e.g., Bates v. Richland Sales Corp., 803 N.E.2d 977 (Ill. App. Ct. 2004); Quintana–Ruiz v. Hyundai Motor Co., 303 F.3d 62, 77 (1st Cir. 2002) (P.R. law) ("the rule that consumer expectations cannot be the basis of liability in a case involving complex technical matters" precludes use of this test in airbag design defect case); Morson v. Superior Court, 109 Cal.Rptr.2d 343, 350–51 (Ct. App. 2001) (consumer expectations test inappropriate to determine design defectiveness of latex gloves that could trigger harmful allergic reactions in persons with nonexistent, dormant, or minor allergic conditions); Soule v. General Motors Corp., 882 P.2d 298 (Cal. 1994) (risk-utility test, not consumer expectations test, should be used when design danger is complex); Scoby v. Vulcan–Hart Corp., 569 N.E.2d 1147 (Ill. App. Ct. 1991). See also Coffey v. Dowley Mfg., Inc., 187 F.Supp.2d 958, 969 (M.D. Tenn. 2002), aff'd, 89 Fed. Appx. 927 (6th Cir. 2003) (although "technically applicable to all cases," consumer expectations test may be inadequate when product complex); Camacho v. Honda Motor Co., 741 P.2d 1240, 1246–47 (Colo. 1987). See § 8.6, below.

Some courts[31] and legislatures[32] are more generally blending the consumer expectations test with the risk-utility standard,[33] or replacing consumer expectations with risk-utility altogether, for determining design defectiveness.[34] Even in a risk-utility regime, however, consumer expectations may be considered together with the other evaluative factors[35] and occasionally can even be conclusive of design defect determinations.[36] In addition, the consumer expectations standard is still widely accepted as the most appropriate test for certain limited types of cases.[37] Finally, the consumer expectations test still plays some role as a liability standard for design defectiveness in roughly half of all the American states,[38] and a related standard, at least in name, exists in Europe.[39]

## § 8.4   THE RISK–UTILITY TEST

The risk-utility test is the principal standard for judging the safety or defectiveness of a product's design.[1] While liability for design defects

**31.** See, e.g., McCathern v. Toyota Motor Corp., 23 P.3d 320, 330–32 (Or. 2001) (risk-utility evidence may be required to prove consumer expectations); Vautour v. Body Masters Sports Indus., 784 A.2d 1178 (N.H. 2001) (consumer expectations defined in terms of risk-utility); Delaney v. Deere & Co., 999 P.2d 930, 944 (Kan. 2000) (recognizing "the validity of risk/utility analysis as a guide in determining the expectations of consumers in complex cases"); Potter v. Chicago Pneumatic Tool Co., 694 A.2d 1319 (Conn. 1997) (same); Nichols v. Union Underwear Co., 602 S.W.2d 429 (Ky. 1980); Seattle–First Nat'l Bank v. Tabert, 542 P.2d 774, 779 (Wash. 1975).

**32.** For example, in both Ohio and Tennessee, liability is alternatively defined in both consumer expectations and risk-utility terms. See Ohio Rev. Code Ann. § 2307.75(A); Tenn. Code Ann. § 29–28–102(8). A Washington statute blends the consumer expectations and risk-utility tests by providing (1) that a design is not reasonably safe if it fails the risk-utility test, and (2) that the trier of fact shall also consider whether the product's dangers exceeded the contemplations of the ordinary consumer. See Wash. Rev. Code Ann. § 7.72.030(1)(a) and (3).

**33.** See § 8.6, below.

**34.** See §§ 5.6 and 5.7, above, and §§ 8.4–8.6, below.

**35.** See, e.g., Products Liability Restatement § 2 cmt. g.

**36.** "Such expectations are often influenced by how products are portrayed and marketed and can have a significant impact on consumer behavior. Thus, although consumer expectations do not constitute an independent standard for judging the defectiveness of product designs, they may substantially influence or even be ultimately

determinative on risk-utility balancing...." Id. § 2(b) cmt. g, at 28.

**37.** Most notably in cases involving contaminated food and defects in used products. See Products Liability Restatement § 2 cmt. h, § 7 (food products), and § 8 (used products). Note, however, that food product cases virtually always involve "manufacturing" rather than design defects, and that used product cases normally do as well.

**38.** See § 5.6, above.

**39.** See the European Community's Directive "Concerning Liability for Defective Products," adopted in 1985, which provides in art. 6(1) as follows: "A product is defective when it does not provide the safety which a person is entitled to expect...." See generally J. Stapleton, Product Liability, ch. 10 (Butterworth, 1994); G. Howells, Comparative Product Liability, ch. 3 (Dartmouth, 1993). Note, however, that because this provision addresses the degree of safety a person is *entitled* to expect, the standard may be applied in risk-utility fashion. See Stapleton, Products Liability in the United Kingdom: The Myths of Reform, 34 Tex. Int'l L.J. 45 (1999); Owen, Strict Products Liability in America and Europe, in Festschrift für Erwin Deutsch 305, 309–10 (1999); Stapleton, Products Liability Reform–Real or Illusory?, 6 Oxford J. Legal Stud. 392, 405 (1986). See § 1.4, above.

### § 8.4

**1.** On the risk-utility test, see Miller, Myth Surrenders to Reality: Design Defect Litigation in Iowa, 51 Drake L. Rev. 459 (2003); Owen, Toward a Proper Test for Design Defectiveness: "Micro–Balancing" Costs and Benefits, 75 Tex. L. Rev. 1661 (1997); Owen, Risk–Utility Balancing in Design Defect Cases, 30 U. Mich. J.L. Reform 239 (1997); M. Green, The Schizophrenia of

was more commonly based on the consumer expectations test in the 1960s and early 1970s, even during these early years of products liability some courts saw the wisdom of assessing design defectiveness according to whether the safety benefits of remedying a design danger were worth the costs.[2] As courts over the decades have turned away from the consumer expectations test in design danger cases,[3] they have substitut-

Risk–Benefit Analysis in Design Defect Litigation, 48 Vand. L. Rev. 609 (1995); Miller, Design Defect Litigation in Iowa: The Myths of Strict Liability, 40 Drake L. Rev. 465 (1991); White, Risk–Utility Analysis and the Learned Hand Formula: A Hand that Helps or a Hand that Hides?, 32 Ariz. L. Rev. 77 (1990). For a useful practitioner perspective, see Rheingold, The Risk/Utility Test in Product Cases, 18 Trial Law. Q. 49 (Summer/Fall 1987); Gilles, United States v. Carroll Towing Co.: The Hand Formula's Home Port, in Torts Stories 11 (R. Rabin & S. Sugarman, eds., Foundation Press, 2003).

For economic perspectives on risk-utility analysis, see, e.g., Geistfeld, Reconciling Cost–Benefit Analysis with the Principle that Safety Matters More Than Money, 76 N.Y.U. L. Rev. 114 (2001); Gilles, The Invisible Hand Formula, 80 Va. L. Rev. 1015, 1025 (1994); Viscusi, Wading Through the Muddle of Risk–Utility Analysis, 39 Am. U. L. Rev. 573 (1990); A. Schwartz, Proposals for Products Liability Reform: A Theoretical Synthesis, 97 Yale L.J. 353, 384–88 (1988); Epstein, The Risks of Risk/Utility, 48 Ohio St. L.J. 469 (1987); Note, 73 Cornell L. Rev. 606 (1988); Comment, 84 Colum. L. Rev. 2045 (1984); R. Posner, Economic Analysis of Law §§ 6.1 and 6.6 (6th ed. 2003); W. Viscusi, Reforming Products Liability ch. 4 (1991).

For general discussions of the risk-utility test in negligence and strict liability in tort, see § 2.2 and § 5.7, above.

**2.** See, e.g., Helicoid Gage Div. of Am. Chain & Cable Co. v. Howell, 511 S.W.2d 573, 577 (Tex. App. 1974) (affirming verdict for plaintiff, where $2.50 safety shield could have prevented burst pressure gauge from throwing piece of lens into plaintiff's eye):

> To determine whether a product is unreasonably dangerous, ... it is necessary to weigh the risk of harm against the utility of the product, considering whether safety devices would unreasonably raise the cost or diminish the utility of the product. The evidence at trial showed that shatterproof glass would have increased the cost of each [gauge] by approximately one dollar and would not have reduced the gage's utility. Further, there was testimony that this injury would not have occurred had shatterproof glass been used.

See generally Dorsey v. Yoder Co., 331 F.Supp. 753 (E.D. Pa. 1971), aff'd, 474 F.2d 1339 (3d Cir. 1973) (jury properly found that $8,000 machine was defective for not being equipped with $200–$500 guard that would have protected operator's hand and arm from being caught and drawn into metal slitter machine); McCormack v. Hankscraft Co., 154 N.W.2d 488 (Minn. 1967) (jury could find that vaporizer top could have been screwed cheaply and without diminishing vaporizer's usefulness onto top of container of hot water that scalded infant plaintiff).

See also Roach v. Kononen, 525 P.2d 125 (Or. 1974), an action against Ford Motor Company for injuries from a crash occurring when the hood on a Ford automobile suddenly flew up and blocked the driver's vision. Plaintiff's expert testified that the hood could have been designed to permit substantially better visibility in such situations. Another witness testified that Ford was aware of only six or seven inadvertent hood openings occurring over a 7 or 8 year period. Ford's design engineer testified that the proposed design would require the addition of certain reinforcements to the hood and its hinges that would cost $5–10 per car. *Held,* jury verdict for defendant affirmed.

**3.** For examples of movements away from consumer expectations toward risk-utility, see, e.g., McCathern v. Toyota Motor Corp., 23 P.3d 320, 330–32 (Or. 2001) (risk-utility evidence may be required to prove consumer expectations); Vautour v. Body Masters Sports Indus., 784 A.2d 1178 (N.H. 2001) (consumer expectations defined in risk-utility terms); Delaney v. Deere & Co., 999 P.2d 930, 944 (Kan. 2000) (recognizing "the validity of risk/utility analysis as a guide in determining the expectations of consumers in complex cases"); Potter v. Chicago Pneumatic Tool Co., 694 A.2d 1319 (Conn. 1997) (redefining consumer expectations in risk-utility terms); Banks v. ICI Am., Inc., 450 S.E.2d 671 (Ga. 1994) (switching from consumer expectations to risk-utility); St. Germain v. Husqvarna Corp., 544 A.2d 1283, 1286 (Me. 1988); Nichols v. Union Underwear Co., 602 S.W.2d 429 (Ky. 1980); Seattle–First Nat'l Bank v. Tabert, 542 P.2d 774, 779 (Wash. 1975). In Sperry–New Holland v. Prestage, 617 So.2d 248, 255–56 (Miss. 1993), noting its own movement away from the consumer expectations test, the court switched to risk-utility for design defect determinations,

ed some form of cost-benefit (often referred to as "risk-utility" or "risk-benefit") standard of liability, which is the liability standard for design defectiveness adopted by the *Restatement (Third) of Torts: Products Liability*.[4] By the turn of the new millennium, despite the tenacity of consumer expectations in a decreasing number of jurisdictions,[5] the risk-utility test had indubitably become America's dominant test for design defectiveness.[6]

### Fundamentals of Cost–Benefit Analysis; The Hand Formula

The fundamentals of the risk-utility test were examined earlier, in the discussions of negligence[7] and strict liability in tort,[8] but they are worth restating here. An analytical technique explicitly relied upon by Benjamin Franklin and Oliver Wendell Holmes,[9] cost-benefit analysis is as old as rational thought. All deliberative decisions involve a weighing of the advantages (benefits) and disadvantages (costs) of a contemplated course of action.[10] Whether a particular design danger is "unreasonable,"

observing that the switch to risk-utility "has become the trend in most federal and state jurisdictions" because it "best protects both the manufacturer and the consumer."

**4.** For the prevalence of the risk-utility test in design defect cases, see Products Liability Restatement § 2, Reporters' Notes to cmt. *d*. See generally § 8.8, below.

**5.** See Kysar, The Expectations of Consumers, 103 Colum. L. Rev. 1700, 1701 (2003) (characterizing the consumer expectations test as "stubbornly and inexplicably persistent"). See also Phillips, Consumer Expectations, 53 S.C. L. Rev. 1047 (2002).

**6.** See, e.g., Wright v. Brooke Group Ltd., 652 N.W.2d 159 (Iowa 2002) (adopting Products Liability Restatement § 2(b)); In re Methyl Tertiary Butyl Ether Prods. Liab. Litig., 175 F.Supp.2d 593, 623 (S.D.N.Y. 2001) (Cal., Fla., Ill., and N.Y. law) ("Courts have generally utilized the 'risk-utility balancing' test to determine whether a product is defectively designed."); Ford Motor Co. v. Miles, 967 S.W.2d 377, 386 (Tex. 1998) (Owen, J., concurring) (instruction conflicted with "the risk versus utility analysis that lies at the core of products liability design defect law"); Warner Fruehauf Trailer Co. v. Boston, 654 A.2d 1272, 1276 (D.C. 1995) ("In design defect cases, most jurisdictions decide [strict liability in tort] by applying some form of a risk-utility balancing test."); Banks v. ICI Am., Inc., 450 S.E.2d 671 (Ga. 1994); Sperry–New Holland v. Prestage, 617 So.2d 248, 255 (Miss. 1993) ("Risk-utility has become the trend in most federal and state jurisdictions."). The dominance of the risk-utility test for determining design defectiveness has been clear for some time. See Foley v. Clark Equip. Co., 523 A.2d 379, 388 (Pa. Super. Ct. 1987) ("Although various tests

for design defectiveness have been proposed, there is general agreement among legal scholars that any evaluation of design defectiveness must invariably include some form of a risk/utility analysis.... Most courts employ a version of this balancing process in analyzing allegations of design defects.").

**7.** See § 2.2, above.

**8.** See § 5.7, above.

**9.** See, e.g., Letter, Benjamin Franklin (Sept. 19, 1772) (suggesting, as aid to rendering difficult decisions, that one list and consider "all the reasons pro and con" and contemplate "where the balance lies"), reprinted in Edward M. Gramlich, Benefit–Cost Analysis of Government Programs 1–2 (1981). Franklin said:

> [T]hough the weight of reasons cannot be taken with the precision of algebraic quantities, yet when each is thus considered, separately and comparatively, and the whole lies before me, I think I can judge better, and am less liable to make a rash step, and in fact I have found great advantage from this kind of equation, in what may be called moral or prudential algebra.

Id. at 2 (emphasis omitted). Consider also Oliver Wendell Holmes, Jr., The Path of the Law, 10 Harv. L. Rev. 457, 474 (1897) (advising that "for everything we have to give up something else, and we are taught to set the advantage we gain against the other advantage we lose").

**10.** See H. Green, Cost–Risk–Benefit Assessment and the Law: Introduction and Perspective, 45 Geo. Wash. L. Rev. 901, 903–04 (1977). Consider also Merrill, Risk–Benefit Decision–making by the Food and Drug Administration, 45 Geo. Wash. L. Rev.

that is, whether the design is "defective," involves "a balancing of the probability and seriousness of harm against the costs of taking precautions. Relevant factors to be considered include the availability of alternative designs, the cost and feasibility of adopting alternative designs, and the frequency or infrequency of injury resulting from the design."[11] In addition, courts and scholars increasingly recognize the importance of including a product's warnings and instructions, which serve to reduce the foreseeable risks of a design, as an important factor in design defect risk-utility analysis.[12]

A product's design is "defective" under a risk-utility test if the costs of avoiding a particular hazard are foreseeably less than the resulting safety benefits. In other words, if the safety benefits from preventing the danger that harmed the plaintiff were foreseeably greater than its precaution costs, the product's design is defective under the cost-benefit (or "risk-utility") standard of liability.[13] Costs and benefits should be limited to those that are foreseeable,[14] and both should be calculated for the entire product line[15] and for some substantial period of time.[16] The risk-utility test for establishing design defectiveness is unaffected by

---

994, 996 (1977) ("Risk-benefit analysis . . . includes any technique for making choices that explicitly or implicitly attempts to measure the potential adverse consequences of an activity and to predict its benefits. In its most refined form, such an analysis may make use of refined mathematical methods for calculating risks and benefits, attempting to assign uniform values, usually in dollars, to all factors, including human lives.").

**11.** Raney v. Honeywell, Inc., 540 F.2d 932, 935 (8th Cir. 1976) (Iowa law).

**12.** See Hansen v. Sunnyside Prod., Inc., 65 Cal.Rptr.2d 266 (Ct. App. 1997) (design defectiveness of household cleaner):

> We do not think that the risk to the consumer of the design of many household products can be rationally evaluated without considering the product's warnings. Thus, for example, what is the risk of the design of a power saw, or other power tools or equipment, without considering the product's directions and warnings? We dare say that the risk would be astronomically, and irrationally, high. The same could be said about common garden pesticides, or even the household microwave oven. [W]ere we to ask jurors to evaluate the risks of the design of many household products without considering their directions or warnings, the practical result would be the withdrawal from the market of many useful products that are dangerous in the abstract but safe when used as directed.

Id. at 278 (noting that Dean John Wade "expressly lists consideration of warnings or instructions as a factor relevant to the determination of whether a product is un-

reasonably dangerous," id. at 276 n.9, referring to Dean Wade's factor number six, discussed below). See generally Products Liability Restatement § 2(b) cmt. *f* (among "broad range of factors" relevant to design defectiveness are "the instructions and warnings accompanying the product"). See also id., at cmt. *l*.

**13.** See, e.g., Warner Fruehauf Trailer Co. v. Boston, 654 A.2d 1272, 1276 (D.C. 1995) (plaintiff must show " 'that the magnitude of the danger from the product outweighed the costs of avoiding the danger' "). On the formulation of such a test, see Owen, Toward a Proper Test for Design Defectiveness: "Micro–Balancing" Costs and Benefits, 75 Tex. L. Rev. 1661, 1686–90 (1997).

**14.** See, e.g., Coleman v. Cintas Sales Corp., 40 S.W.3d 544, 549 (Tex. App. 2001) (employee uniforms need not be flame retarded when there is no foreseeable risk that they will be exposed to fire); Products Liability Restatement § 2(b) and cmt. *a* (design may be defective "only when risks are reasonably foreseeable").

**15.** Courts should guard against the tendency of juries to narrowly compare the individuated costs of precaution and safety benefits of the particular accident in the case at hand which, of course, is never the proper form of cost-benefit calculation for establishing design defectiveness.

**16.** The period selected, whether one year or the projected lifetime of the product line, generally should not matter, provided that it is large enough to establish a standard rate and that both costs and benefits are measured over the same period.

whether the underlying theory of recovery is negligence, strict liability in tort,[17] or even implied warranty,[18] because the necessary balance between a particular design feature's safety, costs, and effect on product utility remains the same.[19]

The cost-benefit or risk-utility test,[20] which balances the safety benefits (from avoiding a particular risk) against the avoidance costs ("burdens"), is especially well suited to establishing the safety or defectiveness of a product design.[21] The type and degree of design safety required depends upon the type, likelihood, and amount of harm (together viewed as the magnitude of the risk) that a particular burden of precaution (of a particular cost) may be expected to prevent.[22] If the risk

**17.** See, e.g., Banks v. ICI Am., Inc., 450 S.E.2d 671, 674 n.3 (Ga. 1994) ("the determination of whether a product was defective (involving the reasonableness of a manufacturer's design decision), which is a basic inquiry for strict liability purposes, generally will overlap the determination of whether the manufacturer's conduct was reasonable, which is a basic inquiry for negligence purposes"); Phillips v. Kimwood Mach. Co., 525 P.2d 1033, 1039 (Or. 1974) ("It is necessary to remember that whether the doctrine of negligence ... or strict liability is being used to impose liability, the same process is going on in each instance, i.e., weighing the utility of the article against the risk of its use."). See also Ackerman v. American Cyanamid Co., 586 N.W.2d 208, 220 (Iowa 1998) ("a growing number of courts and commentators have found that, in cases in which the plaintiff's injury is caused by an alleged defect in the design of a product, there is no practical difference between theories of negligence and strict liability"); Foley v. Clark Equip. Co., 523 A.2d 379, 388–89 (Pa. Super. Ct. 1987) ("The risk/utility analysis is nothing more than a detailed version of the balancing process used in evaluating reasonable care in negligence cases.... Because strict liability and negligence employ the same balancing process to assess liability, proof sufficient to establish liability under one theory will in most instances be sufficient under the other.").

Note, however, that many courts formerly distinguished strict liability from negligence on the basis of the *foreseeability* of the costs and benefits of improving the product's design safety, and a few still do. Because most courts and commentators now believe that a plaintiff must establish the foreseeability of harm (manufacturers rarely challenge the foreseeability of precautionary costs) in "strict" tort actions as well as in negligence, cost-benefit (risk-utility) analysis should normally be identical in both contexts. The foreseeability issue is addressed in the discussion of the so-called Wade–Keeton constructive knowledge test

in § 8.7, below, and is further examined in the "state of the art" context in § 10.4, below.

**18.** See, e.g., Gregory v. Cincinnati Inc., 538 N.W.2d 325, 329 (Mich. 1995). The application of tort-like risk-utility principles to implied warranty claims is widely accepted. See Revised UCC § 2–314 cmt. 7; § 4.3, above. *But see* Denny v. Ford Motor Co., 662 N.E.2d 730 (N.Y. 1995).

**19.** At least in the absence of a manufacturer's specific safety representations which may give rise to specific consumer expectations protectable in warranty. See, e.g., Denny v. Ford Motor Co., 662 N.E.2d 730 (N.Y. 1995) (roll-over of Bronco II); Leichtamer v. American Motors Corp., 424 N.E.2d 568 (Ohio 1981) (pitch-over of Jeep). See generally Shapo, A Representational Theory of Consumer Protection: Doctrine, Function and Legal Liability for Product Disappointment, 60 Va. L. Rev. 1109 (1974).

**20.** Although the "risk-utility" term has been gaining ground in recent years over the more traditional "risk-benefit" phraseology, "cost-benefit" is the preferable term. See Owen, Toward a Proper Test for Design Defectiveness: "Micro–Balancing" Costs and Benefits, 75 Tex. L. Rev. 1661, 1692 (1997). The terms are used interchangeably here.

**21.** Courts have found the risk-benefit test most helpful in making design defectiveness determinations and only marginally helpful in warnings cases. In manufacturing flaw cases decided in strict tort, this method of analysis has been virtually ignored.

**22.** For example, if the risk at issue concerns the possible failure of an automobile's steering, brakes, or tires at highway speeds, or the possibility that a punch press ram may unexpectedly depress upon an operator's hand, the manufacturer must employ the utmost precautions to avert the risk. Yet, if the risk is relatively minimal, reasonably appearing to involve at most the

posed by the design of a product in a certain condition is great, greater precautions must be taken to avert the risk; if the risk is small, less precaution is required. This principle of balance, inherent in tort law generally, is sometimes referred to as the "calculus of risk."

The most celebrated formulation of the risk-benefit test was provided by Judge Learned Hand in *United States v. Carroll Towing Co.*,[23] previously discussed.[24] In *Carroll Towing*, Judge Hand reasoned that ascertaining an appropriate level of precaution is normally a function of three factors: the burden of taking precautions to avoid a risk of harm, on the one side, balanced against the likelihood of harm of a particular magnitude, on the other. Negligence is implied if an actor fails to adopt a precaution of less magnitude than the harm it is likely to prevent. Judge Hand expressed this concept algebraically: Negligence is suggested if B < P x L, where B is the burden or cost of adopting precautions against accidental loss that foreseeably might result if B is not undertaken, P is the increased probability of loss if B is not undertaken, and L is the probable magnitude (expected cost) of such loss if it does occur. This is the so-called "Hand formula."[25] If the formula is supplemented with a symbol for the implication ( ⇒ ) of negligence, N, the full formula becomes: B < P x L ⇒ N. Applied to negligence determinations in the products liability context, the Hand formula may be explained as follows: if the cost of adopting a particular safety precaution (B) is less than the safety gains expected to result therefrom (P x L), the manufacturer's failure to adopt the precaution implies its negligence ( ⇒ N).

By substituting "defect" for "negligence" (D for N), the Hand formula converts comfortably to the "strict" products liability task of determining design defectiveness, as discussed above.[26] So reformulated, the defectiveness "equation" may be stated as follows:

$$B < P \text{ x } L \Rightarrow D$$

In cost-benefit terms, the formula looks like this:

$$(\text{Accident Prevention}) \text{ Costs} < (\text{Safety}) \text{ Benefits} \Rightarrow \text{Defect}$$

In short, a product's design is defective if the safety benefits of an untaken design precaution foreseeably exceed its costs, including any diminished usefulness or diminished safety.[27]

---

risk of minor harm to person or property—scratches, stains, or the harmless malfunction of the product—then a manufacturer need apply only minimal precautions to reduce such risks.

**23.** 159 F.2d 169, 173 (2d Cir. 1947). Hand first employed this approach in Conway v. O'Brien, 111 F.2d 611 (2d Cir. 1940), rev'd on other grounds, 312 U.S. 492 (1941), and subsequently reexamined it in Moisan v. Loftus, 178 F.2d 148, 149 (2d Cir. 1949).

**24.** The *Carroll Towing* case is examined in the negligence context in § 2.2, and the strict liability in tort context in § 5.7, above.

**25.** Perhaps the most helpful accounts of *Carroll Towing* and the Hand formula are Gilles, United States v. Carroll Towing Co.: The Hand Formula's Home Port, in Torts Stories 11 (R. Rabin & S. Sugarman, eds., Foundation Press, 2003), and Gilles, The Invisible Hand Formula, 80 Va. L. Rev. 1015 (1994). For other treatments, see note 1, above.

**26.** See § 5.7, above. See generally Owen, Toward a Proper Test for Design Defectiveness: "Micro–Balancing" Costs and Benefits, 75 Tex. L. Rev. 1661, 1684–86 (1997).

**27.** See Owen, Toward a Proper Test for Design Defectiveness: "Micro–Balancing"

Based on certain imprecise language in some early scholarly explorations into the meaning of product defectiveness,[28] most appellate courts have formulated the risk-utility test more broadly in terms of whether a *product*'s risks are greater than its benefits or utility.[29] While this broader formulation may appear harmless at first glance, it is logically misleading and in fact conflicts with how the law is actually applied. As discussed below,[30] the proper issue that is almost always litigated in trial courtrooms is the narrow *"micro*-balance" of pros and cons of a manufacturer's failure to adopt some particular design *feature* that would have prevented the plaintiff's harm—that is, whether the costs of changing the design in some particular ("micro") manner would have been worth the resulting safety benefits.[31] Courts could avoid considerable confusion by formulating the risk-utility standard according to the proper cost-benefit terms of the Hand formula.[32]

The Hand defectiveness formula succinctly captures the common-sense idea that a product's design is unacceptably dangerous if it contains a danger that might cost-effectively (and practicably) be removed. More basically, the Hand formula requires manufacturers, in designing products, to consider risks of injury to consumers and bystanders and to weigh the interests of those parties equally to its own interest in maximizing profits.[33] Manufacturers, of course, properly consider such factors as the usefulness, cost, and profitability of designing a product in any particular way. Yet the Hand formula assures that manufacturers, in legislating for consumers the proper mix of a product's cost and benefits, include in the balance a proportionate consideration of the various hazards in the product's particular design. It may be true, of course, that manufacturers should give safety a greater weight than cold cost-benefit analysis might suggest, since individual consumers have little voice in the collective tradeoffs forced upon them.[34] Yet, the risk-utility test has the elasticity to absorb refinements of this type, demanding only that a manufacturer adopt design precautions proportionate to

Costs and Benefits, 75 Tex. L. Rev. 1661, 1690 (1997).

**28.** Notably, Keeton, Products Liability—Current Developments, 40 Tex. L. Rev. 193, 210 (1961); Wade, On the Nature of Strict Tort Liability for Products, 44 Miss. L.J. 825, 837 (1973) (first two factors framed in global terms). See generally Owen, Toward a Proper Test for Design Defectiveness: "Micro–Balancing" Costs and Benefits, 75 Tex. L. Rev. 1661, 1683 n.74 (1997).

**29.** See Owen, Risk–Utility Balancing in Design Defect Cases, 30 U. Mich. J.L. Reform 239 (1997) (surveying risk-utility tests among states).

**30.** See § 8.5, below.

**31.** Brown, Toward An Economic Theory of Liability, 2 J. Legal Stud. 323, 342 (1973); R. Heafey and D. Kennedy, Product Liability: Winning Strategies and Techniques §§ 4.04 and 4.05, and at 4–9 (1994) (characterizing the manufacturer's choice to forego a reasonable alternative design as

"the heart of the plaintiff's case"). See also Rheingold, The Risk/Utility Test in Product Cases, 18 Trial Law. Q. 49, 50 (Spring/Fall 1987) ("The usual and proper approach for a plaintiff in a design defect case is to present evidence on an alternative design which the jury can find should have been adopted for the product in question.").

**32.** See Owen, Risk-Utility Balancing, 30 U. Mich. J.L. Reform at 242.

**33.** See Owen, Philosophical Foundations of Fault in Tort Law, in Philosophical Foundations of Tort Law 201, 214–15 (1995); Owen, The Moral Foundations of Products Liability Law: Toward First Principles, 68 Notre Dame L. Rev. 427 (1993). The basic economics of this perspective are explained in Judge Posner's classic essay, A Theory of Negligence, 1 J. Legal Stud. 29 (1972).

**34.** See Geistfeld, Reconciling Cost–Benefit Analysis with the Principle that Safety Matters More Than Money, 76 N.Y.U. L. Rev. 114 (2001).

the magnitude of the expected risk. This simple yet fundamental principle of defectiveness, which ties the measure of precaution to the measure of risk, thus grounds the design safety obligations of a manufacturer in both fairness and utility.

### Burdens, Benefits, and Utility; the Wade Factors

In applying the risk-utility test, courts almost always properly restrict their analysis to the narrow costs and benefits of some particular untaken design precaution, as discussed in detail below.[35] Not infrequently, however, appellate courts open a Pandora's box by formulating the risk-utility calculus more widely. For example, in *Banks v. ICI Americas, Inc.*,[36] in adopting a risk-benefit test for evaluating design defectiveness, the Georgia Supreme Court remarked: "[N]o finite set of factors can be considered comprehensive or applicable under every factual circumstance, since such matters must necessarily vary according to the unique facts of each case. Such diverse matters as competing cost trade-offs, tactical market decisions, product development and research/testing demands, the idiosyncrasies of individual corporate management styles, and federal and other regulatory restrictions" can properly enter into the determination of the "reasonableness" of the manufacturer's design determination.[37] The court offered the following "non-exhaustive list of general factors," beginning with what might be labeled "risk factors":

> the usefulness of the product; the gravity and severity of the danger . . .; the likelihood of that danger; the avoidability of the danger, i.e., the user's knowledge of the product, publicity surrounding the danger, or the efficacy of warnings, as well as common knowledge and the expectation of danger; the user's ability to avoid danger; the state of the art . . . ; the ability to eliminate danger without impairing the usefulness of the product or making it too expensive; and the feasibility of spreading the loss in the setting of the product's price or by purchasing insurance.[38]

The court then listed the "[a]lternative safe design factors" also pertinent to the issue: "the feasibility of an alternative design; the availability of an effective substitute for the product which meets the same need but is safer; the financial cost of the improved design; and the adverse effects from the alternative."[39] Finally, the court set forth "benefit factors" that may also be considered in the balancing test: "the appearance and aesthetic attractiveness of the product; its utility for multiple uses; the convenience and extent of its use, especially in light of the period of time it could be used [safely]; and the collateral safety of a feature other than the one that harmed the plaintiff."[40]

No doubt many (perhaps most) of the factors from this long list[41] should be considered by manufacturers making fully informed good-faith

---

**35.**  See § 8.5, below.

**36.**  450 S.E.2d 671 (Ga. 1994).

**37.**  Id. at 675.

**38.**  Id. at n.6.

**39.**  Id.

**40.**  Id.

**41.**  Thirty-three, by one count.

design decisions about their products. And most of the listed factors will surely be legitimate issues in different kinds of design cases confronting courts over time. Indeed, the Georgia court's "alternative safe design" factors *usually* will be important for both manufacturers making design decisions and courts adjudicating the safety or defectiveness of particular designs after product accidents have occurred, as discussed below.[42] But such a wide and open-ended catalogue of factors provides little help for adjudicating the design defect issue in particular cases,[43] and a general "test" for design defectiveness must be formulated far more narrowly in terms of the particular types of costs and benefits normally at issue in typical design defect cases.

Over-broad formulations of risk-utility analysis for design decision-making are directly traceable to a widely quoted set of liability factors proposed in an early, influential article written by Dean John Wade,[44] *On the Nature of Strict Tort Liability for Products.*[45] Dean Wade proposed that a court[46] consider the following list of factors:

> (1) The usefulness and desirability of the product—its utility to the user and to the public as a whole.

> (2) The safety aspects of the product—the likelihood that it will cause injury, and the probable seriousness of the injury.

> (3) The availability of a substitute product which would meet the same need and not be as unsafe.

> (4) The manufacturer's ability to eliminate the unsafe character of the product without impairing its usefulness or making it too expensive to maintain its utility.

> (5) The user's ability to avoid danger by the exercise of care in the use of the product.

> (6) The user's anticipated awareness of the dangers inherent in the product and their avoidability, because of general public knowledge of the obvious condition of the product, or of the existence of suitable warnings or instructions.

> (7) The feasibility, on the part of the manufacturer, of spreading the loss by setting the price of the product or carrying liability insurance.

Searching for some guidance in the murky sea of design defectiveness, appellate courts grasped quickly onto the Wade factors for use in

---

**42.** See § 8.5, below.

**43.** For an effort, see Moore v. ECI Mgmt., 542 S.E.2d 115 (Ga. Ct. App. 2000) (applying multi-factor risk-utility test to washer/dryer design defect claim).

**44.** Indeed, the *Banks* court's first list of factors, the risk factors, was largely a restatement of Dean Wade's seven factors.

**45.** 44 Miss. L.J. 825, 837–38 (1973).

**46.** But Dean Wade believed that a court should *not* instruct the jury on the factors. Id. at 840. Courts largely have

agreed. See, e.g., Fiorino v. Sears Roebuck & Co., 707 A.2d 1053, 1057–58 (N.J. Super. Ct. App. Div. 1998) (including factor seven in jury instruction is reversible error because it improperly introduces insurance into case). *But see*, e.g., Potter v. Chicago Pneumatic Tool Co., 694 A.2d 1319 (Conn. 1997) (in risk-utility balancing, jury may consider Wade factors among others); Turner v. General Motors Corp., 584 S.W.2d 844, 848–49 (Tex. 1979).

ascertaining defects in design.[47] At least courts have *said* that these factors were somehow relevant to design defect cases.[48] However, while courts across the continent have authoritatively quoted these six or seven[49] factors for decades, only infrequently do courts actually try to *apply* the factors in assessing whether a particular product was defective in design. Even more rarely has an application of these factors actually *helped* a court determine design defectiveness;[50] more typically, a court attempting to apply the factors becomes ensnared in one of their many traps.[51]

Despite some early favorable commentary on the Wade factor approach,[52] commentators more recently view most of the Wade factors as problematic.[53] The first factor, the utility of the product, has been criticized on political grounds for allowing courts to second-guess the market as to the desirability of different kinds of products, and this factor seems to reflect "the fallacy that 'essentials' provide utility whereas 'luxuries' do not."[54] Factor two, on the other hand, which embraces the P x L (risk of harm) side of the Hand formula discussed above, is vital to intelligent cost-benefit decisionmaking.[55]

The third factor, the availability of a substitute product, is difficult to interpret. If it is read narrowly to mean the availability of a substitute design feature, then it properly introduces the necessarily central ques-

---

**47.** See, e.g., Cepeda v. Cumberland Eng'g Co., Inc., 386 A.2d 816 (N.J. 1978) (overruled in part on other grounds by, Suter v. San Angelo Foundry & Mach. Co., 406 A.2d 140 (N.J. 1979)); Roach v. Kononen, 525 P.2d 125, 129 (Or. 1974) ("We agree that these factors should be considered by a court before submitting a design defect case to the jury. Also, proof of these factors bears on the jury's determination of whether or not a given design is defective.").

For an inspired reduction of the Wade and other factors, see Montgomery and Owen, Reflections on the Theory and Administration of Strict Tort Liability for Defective Products, 27 S.C. L. Rev. 803, 818 (1976) (proposing four elegantly crafted factors).

**48.** For more recent recitations of the Wade factors, see, e.g., Akee v. Dow Chem. Co., 272 F.Supp.2d 1112, 1132 (D. Hawaii 2003); Smith v. Mack Trucks, Inc., 819 So.2d 1258, 1263 (Miss. 2002); Wortel v. Somerset Indus., 770 N.E.2d 1211, 1218 (Ill. App. Ct. 2002); LaBelle v. Philip Morris, Inc., 243 F.Supp.2d 508, 515 n.4 (D.S.C. 2001); Potter v. Chicago Pneumatic Tool Co., 694 A.2d 1319, 1333–34 (Conn. 1997); Barton v. Adams Rental, Inc., 938 P.2d 532, 537 (Colo. 1997); Ray v. BIC Corp., 925 S.W.2d 527, 533 n.10 (Tenn. 1996); Denny v. Ford Motor Co., 662 N.E.2d 730, 735 (N.Y. 1995).

**49.** Many courts have left out the seventh factor, loss-spreading, as discussed below.

**50.** Monahan v. Toro Co., 856 F.Supp. 955 (E.D. Pa. 1994) (astute application of factors).

**51.** See, e.g., Johansen v. Makita U.S.A., Inc., 607 A.2d 637, 645 (N.J. 1992) (court should have instructed jury not to consider evidence of plaintiff's lack of care in deciding question of product defect, because fifth factor pertained only to users generally, not to particular plaintiff's conduct). Compare Murphy ex rel. Murphy v. Playtex Family Products Corp., 176 F.Supp.2d 473, 490–91 (D. Md. 2001), aff'd, 69 Fed.Appx. 140 (4th Cir. 2003) where the court valiantly tried to apply the factors, yet ended up basing its determination on the reasonableness of the defendant's actions.

**52.** See, e.g., Montgomery and Owen, Reflections on the Theory and Administration of Strict Tort Liability for Defective Products, 27 S.C. L. Rev. 803 (1976).

**53.** See, e.g., R. Epstein, Simple Rules for a Complex World 239–45 (1995); W. Viscusi, Reforming Products Liability 62–86 (1991); M. Green, The Schizophrenia of Risk–Benefit Analysis in Design Defect Litigation, 48 Vand. L. Rev. 609, 615–16 (1995); Viscusi, Wading Through the Muddle of Risk–Utility Analysis, 39 Am. U. L. Rev. 573 (1990); Epstein, The Risks of Risk/Utility, 48 Ohio St. L.J. 469 (1987).

**54.** Viscusi, Wading Through the Muddle of Risk–Utility Analysis, 39 Am. U. L. Rev. 573, 582 (1990).

**55.** See id. at 583.

tion in design defect analysis of the availability of a feasible and otherwise reasonable alternative design feature, an important issue discussed below.[56] If, on the other hand, this factor is interpreted literally, as Dean Wade probably intended it,[57] the availability of substitute "products" falls victim to the flaw infecting the first factor by inviting a judge or jury to engage in social engineering of the highest (and most dubious) order. Factor four, the manufacturer's ability to eliminate the risk without unduly sacrificing price or utility, properly raises the relevant issues of the costs and benefits of altering the chosen design to eliminate the risk. Indeed, factors two and four together form the heart of proper cost-benefit analysis in design defect litigation.

Factor five, the user's ability to avoid the risk, importantly introduces the issue of consumer responsibility into the matrix. Its only fault lies in its tendency to mislead courts, and especially juries, into confusing the proper issue of how users generally may act with the improper issue of whether the particular plaintiff behaved appropriately in using the particular product in the manner that led to the accident being litigated.[58] The sixth factor, the user's awareness of the danger and avoidance techniques, is problematic. Its most reasonable interpretation appears to be subjective, which then introduces the plaintiff's conduct into the prima facie case of design defectiveness, rather than leaving it as an affirmative defense where it more properly belongs. If, on the other hand, this factor is interpreted with some strain as an objective inquiry into the extent to which consumers generally may be expected to comprehend a product's dangers, it would fit nicely with (although should precede) factor five, which in combination would present the important issues on the allocation of responsibility for product accidents between manufacturers and users.

The final Wade factor, number seven, is especially problematic as a factor for design liability decisionmaking. As a rationale for a generalized doctrine of strict tort liability for manufacturers, "loss-spreading" (insurance by another name) has been viewed in recent decades with increasing skepticism.[59] If the strict products liability litigation system is to serve as a substitute for private and social insurance, it must force people to buy types and levels of insurance they neither need nor want, and at excessive cost. By so requiring consumers to pay higher prices for products as a form of product accident insurance, loss-spreading may be seen as both unfair[60] and inefficient.[61] Poor people pay regressively unfair

---

**56.** See § 8.5, below.

**57.** This interpretation springs from the need to differentiate factor three from factor four which appears to cover the feasible alternative design issue.

**58.** See, e.g., Johansen v. Makita U.S.A., Inc., 607 A.2d 637 (N.J. 1992) (court should have instructed jury not to consider evidence of plaintiff's lack of care in deciding the question of product defect, because the fifth factor pertained only to users generally, not to particular plaintiff's conduct). While irrelevant to duty, the propriety of

the particular user's conduct is relevant to the conduct defenses. See ch. 13, below.

**59.** On the nature and problems of loss-spreading as a products liability rationale, see § 5.4, above.

**60.** See, e.g., Owen, The Moral Foundations of Products Liability Law: Toward First Principles, 68 Notre Dame L. Rev. 427, 484–93 (1993).

**61.** See, e.g., Viscusi, Wading Through the Muddle of Risk–Utility Analysis, 39 Amer. U. L. Rev. 573, 584–91 (1990); Priest, The Current Insurance Crisis and Modern Tort Law, 96 Yale L.J. 1521 (1987).

premiums (or "taxes," when the tort system substitutes for social welfare insurance) for this form of insurance,[62] and the litigation method for determining whether particular accidents are covered by the system (whether a product is "defective," whether jurisdiction is proper, whether any defenses apply, etc.) is exceedingly time-consuming, enervating, and expensive. For the most serious accidents, where a victim's compensation needs are immediate and immense, it not infrequently takes five or even ten years to complete the litigation compensation process. And in the end, the victim may lose the case and end up with no compensation whatsoever. In short, design defect liability is a poor means for society to spread the losses that result from product accidents.

As a factor for helping assess whether *particular* products are defective, loss-spreading is even more seriously flawed, because it will *always* point toward liability: a finding of design defectiveness resulting in a judgment for the plaintiff will always spread the plaintiff's loss, at least among the shareholders of the manufacturer.[63] But the rationale for properly limiting a manufacturer's liability to designs that are "defectively" designed is to distinguish between products whose design dangers are acceptable from those that are not, as discussed above.[64] Including loss-spreading, or any other factor that always weighs on the same side of the scales, can only subvert the process of fair and rational adjudication of design defectiveness.[65] As a result, this seventh, loss-spreading factor is often excluded from the list as simply inappropriate.[66]

It is understandable that in the early days of modern products liability courts looked for guidance to the Wade factors which had an aura of logic, fairness, and common sense. Indeed, modern products liability law has absorbed many of Dean Wade's factors in a variety of ways. But modern design defect jurisprudence has moved well beyond the place it was when Dean Wade conceived it at the time § 402A was just getting off the ground. Indeed, modern courts rarely do little more than pay lip service to the Wade factors, which are simply past their prime. Typically, a court will recite the factors and then move on to a far more narrow and appropriate cost-benefit analysis of some particular

---

**62.** George Priest has explained that the level of insurance "premiums" manufacturers add to product prices regressively penalizes the poor who stand to gain far less in damages for lost earnings than wealthy victims who pay the same premium for much higher coverage. See, e.g., Priest, The Current Insurance Crisis and Modern Tort Law, 96 Yale L.J. 1521, 1558–60 (1987).

**63.** See Owen, Products Liability: Principles of Justice for the 21st Century, 11 Pace L. Rev. 63, 71–72 (1990); G. Schwartz, Understanding Products Liability, 67 Cal. L. Rev. 435, 445 (1979):

[T]he loss-spreading criterion, when offered as a rationale for any tort law rule, seems inherently unstable, since it is in a basic sense promiscuous. If loss spreading is deemed the law's fundamental purpose, a compensation right should accordingly be extended to the victim of every serious

accident, without regard to the involvement in that accident of any product. Yet tort law as we know it is "tort law" instead of a compensation program exactly because it is selective—that is, because the liability rules it fashions exclude recovery for some accident victims while permitting recovery for others.

**64.** See § 8.1, above.

**65.** See Owen, The Moral Foundations of Products Liability Law: Toward First Principles, 68 Notre Dame L. Rev. 427, 492–93 (1993); Owen, Rethinking the Policies of Strict Products Liability, 33 Vand. L. Rev. 681, 703–07 (1980).

**66.** See, e.g., Nunnally v. R.J. Reynolds Tobacco Co., 869 So.2d 373, 380 (Miss. 2004).

design feature offered by the plaintiff as a safer and preferred alternative design.[67] In short, the design defect bus long ago left the "catalogue of factors" station and now rides comfortably on the wheels of costs and benefits of alternative designs.[68]

### The Products Liability Restatement

The *Products Liability Restatement* explicitly adopts risk-utility balancing as the test for design defectiveness, as previously discussed.[69] In essence, § 2(b) of the *Third Restatement* classifies a design as defective if the plaintiff suffered a foreseeable injury that could have been prevented by a reasonable alternative design.[70] Section 2(b) thus "adopts a reasonableness ('risk-utility balancing') test as the standard for judging the defectiveness of product designs."[71] Numerous factors may be relevant to "whether an alternative design is reasonable and whether its omission renders a product not reasonably safe" under § 2(b), including the likelihood and seriousness of foreseeable harm from the chosen design, warnings accompanying the product,[72] and the relative costs and benefits of the alternative design relative to the chosen design.[73] Finally, it is important to note that while the *Restatement* rejects consumer expectations as an independent basis for ascertaining the defectiveness of product designs, it includes consumer expectations as a factor in the calculus of risk-utility considerations.[74] The *Third Restatement*'s treatment of these and other aspects of design defectiveness is explored in greater depth below.[75]

## § 8.5    PROOF OF A REASONABLE ALTERNATIVE DESIGN

Just as design defectiveness lies at the center of products liability law,[1] cost-benefit analysis of an alternative design lies at the heart of design defectiveness.[2] As examined earlier,[3] design defectiveness is usual-

---

**67.** See, e.g., Nunnally v. R.J. Reynolds Tobacco Co., 869 So.2d 373, 380 (Miss. 2004); Irion v. Sun Lighting, Inc., 2004 WL 746823, *7 (Tenn. Ct. App. 2004); In re September 11 Litigation, 280 F.Supp.2d 279, 312–13 (S.D.N.Y. 2003); Barton v. Adams Rental, Inc., 938 P.2d 532, 537 (Colo. 1997); Denny v. Ford Motor Co., 662 N.E.2d 730, 735 (N.Y. 1995); Brooks v. Beech Aircraft Corp., 902 P.2d 54, 61 n.2 (N.M. 1995).

**68.** See § 8.5, below.

**69.** See § 6.5, above.

**70.** See id. The Restatement addresses the special problem of the generically dangerous product that may possess a manifestly unreasonable design in cmt. *e*. See § 10.3, below.

**71.** Products Liability Restatement § 2(b), cmt. *d*.

**72.** Id. cmt. *f*.

**73.** Including the effects the alternative design feature would likely have on production costs, product longevity, maintenance,

repair, aesthetics, and "the range of consumer choice." Id.

**74.** See id. cmt. *g*.

**75.** See § 8.8, below.

**§ 8.5**

**1.** See § 8.1, above.

**2.** See, e.g., Jones v. NordicTrack, Inc., 550 S.E.2d 101, 103 (Ga. 2001) ("The 'heart' of a design defect case is the reasonableness of selecting from among alternative product designs and adopting the safest feasible one."). See also Ford Motor Co. v. Miles, 967 S.W.2d 377, 386 (Tex. 1998) (Owen, J., concurring) (examining "the risk versus utility analysis that lies at the core of products liability design defect law").

**3.** See § 8.4, above. See also Products Liability Restatement § 1, cmt. *a*; § 2(b), cmt. *d*. The Third Restatement approach to design defectiveness, which requires the plaintiff in design defect cases to prove that a "reasonable alternative design" would have prevented the injury, is examined at § 6.5, above, and § 8.8, below.

ly best resolved by risk-utility analysis, the purpose of which is to determine "whether the risk of injury might have been reduced or avoided if the manufacturer had used a feasible alternative design."[4] In the words of a leading tort law scholar, "one simply cannot talk meaningfully about a risk-benefit defect until and unless one has identified some design alternative (including any design omission) that can serve as the basis for a risk-benefit analysis."[5]

Throughout the twentieth century, the great majority of design defect cases involved proof by the plaintiff of a feasible alternative design—proof of some practicable and cost-effective design alternative that would have prevented the plaintiff's harm.[6] The cases include, for example, a commercial coffee urn which exploded, where the explosion could have been prevented by a simple reducing valve;[7] a tractor steering wheel, made of rubber and fiber that broke in the driver's hands, causing him to fall into the path of the tractor, where a rim made of wood or metal would not have broken;[8] a vaporizer which overheated and caught fire when the water boiled away, where the fire could have been prevented by a simple cutoff device;[9] a moving metal mechanism under the arm-rest of a lawn chair which amputated a user's finger, where a simple housing could have shielded the mechanism;[10] a drain cleaner comprised of chemicals that were highly corrosive to human skin, where a change in the chemical formulation would have made it much safer and actually improved its efficacy at cleaning drains;[11] a Dalkon Shield IUD which had a multifilament tail string, facilitating migration of bacteria into the uterus, where a single filament would have minimized the risk;[12] an industrial machine with a sharp edge that cut a worker, where the sharp edge served no purpose and could easily have been rounded smooth;[13] a small Playskool play block that asphyxiated a baby, where slightly increasing the size of the cylindrical block would have made it too big to swallow;[14] and a truck liftgate equipped with a single

**4.** McCarthy v. Olin Corp., 119 F.3d 148, 155 (2d Cir. 1997) (N.Y. law).

**5.** G. Schwartz, Foreword: Understanding Products Liability, 67 Cal. L. Rev. 435, 468 (1979). One of the most prominent tort law scholars of the late twentieth century, Gary Schwartz was a professor at UCLA, an adviser for the Products Liability Restatement, and the initial Reporter for the Restatement (Third) of Torts: Liability for Physical Harm (Basic Principles). Most other products liability scholars agree. See, e.g., Owen, Defectiveness Restated: Exploding the "Strict" Products Liability Myth, 1996 U. Ill. L. Rev. 743, 774–75; M. Green, The Schizophrenia of Risk–Benefit Analysis in Design Defect Litigation, 48 Vand. L. Rev. 609 (1995); Henderson and Twerski, Closing the American Products Liability Frontier: The Rejection of Liability Without Defect, 66 N.Y.U. L. Rev. 1263 (1991).

**6.** See Noel, Manufacturer's Negligence of Design or Directions for Use of a Product, 71 Yale L.J. 816, 820 (1962).

**7.** Muller v. A.B. Kirschbaum Co., 148 A. 851 (Pa. 1930).

**8.** Goullon v. Ford Motor Co., 44 F.2d 310 (6th Cir. 1930) (Ky. law).

**9.** Lindroth v. Walgreen Co., 87 N.E.2d 307 (Ill. App. Ct. 1949), aff'd, 94 N.E.2d 847 (Ill. 1950).

**10.** Matthews v. Lawnlite Co., 88 So.2d 299 (Fla. 1956).

**11.** Drayton v. Jiffee Chem. Corp., 395 F.Supp. 1081 (N.D. Ohio 1975), judgment modified on other grounds, 591 F.2d 352 (6th Cir. 1978).

**12.** Hilliard v. A.H. Robins Co., 196 Cal. Rptr. 117 (Ct. App. 1983).

**13.** Stazenski v. Tennant Co., 617 So.2d 344 (Fla. Dist. Ct. App. 1993).

**14.** Metzgar v. Playskool Inc., 30 F.3d 459 (3d Cir. 1994) (Pa. law).

hydraulic cylinder that was prone to collapse unexpectedly, where the addition of a second cylinder would have eliminated the risk.[15]

Without affirmative proof of a feasible design alternative, a plaintiff usually cannot establish that a product's design is defective. Put otherwise, there typically is nothing wrong with a product that simply possesses inherent dangers which cannot feasibly be designed away.[16] For example, in *Blissenbach v. Yanko*,[17] a child was injured by scalding water from a hot water vaporizer when it tipped over, causing the lid to fall off the top of the container. The plaintiff alleged that the manufacturer's failure to secure the lid to the container was a negligent design, but the manufacturer defended on the ground that the lid was left unattached in order to provide a "natural safety valve" for the release of steam if the aperture for discharging medicated vapor became clogged.[18] In part because the plaintiff made no proof of a feasible alternative design method for releasing steam, the plaintiff's verdict was reversed on appeal.[19] *McCormack v. Hankscraft Co.*[20] was another vaporizer tip-over case decided on similar facts except that the plaintiff's experts established that the danger "could have been eradicated by the adoption of any one of several practical and inexpensive alternative designs which utilized simple and well known techniques to secure the top to the jar to the inside of the plastic top so it could screw onto the jar and the putting of two or three small holes in the top, which would take care of any danger that steam would build up inside the jar." Based on proof of such a feasible alternative design, the *McCormack* court ordered entry of judgment on a verdict for the plaintiff.

Recognizing the central role of an alternative design to design defectiveness, many courts, perhaps most,[21] hold that proof of a feasible design alternative is generally, or always, a necessary element of design defectiveness: "In order to prove defectiveness, the plaintiff must prove that a safer, practical, alternative design was available to the manufacturer."[22] Most courts properly hold that the plaintiff has the burden of

---

**15.** Warner Fruehauf Trailer Co. v. Boston, 654 A.2d 1272 (D.C. 1995).

**16.** See §§ 6.2, above, and 10.3, below.

**17.** 107 N.E.2d 409 (Ohio Ct. App. 1951).

**18.** Id. at 411.

**19.** See Noel, Manufacturer's Negligence of Design or Directions for Use of a Product, 71 Yale L.J. 816, 823 (1962).

**20.** 154 N.W.2d 488, 495 (Minn. 1967).

**21.** See Hernandez v. Tokai Corp., 2 S.W.3d 251 (Tex. 1999), stating that most states make proof of a reasonable alternative design a prerequisite to a determination of design defectiveness.

**22.** General Motors Corp. v. Edwards, 482 So.2d 1176, 1191 (Ala. 1985). Accord, Bagley v. Mazda Motor Corp., 864 So.2d 301 (Ala. 2003); Wankier v. Crown Equip. Corp., 353 F.3d 862 (10th Cir. 2003) (Utah

law) (trial court's failure to instruct jury on plaintiff's duty to establish safer alternative design was reversible error); Wright v. Brooke Group Ltd., 652 N.W.2d 159, 169 (Iowa 2002) (adopting Products Liability Restatement § 2(b)); Colon ex rel. Molina v. BIC USA, Inc., 199 F.Supp.2d 53, 83–84 (S.D.N.Y.2001).

For an exhaustive (if increasingly dated) collection of authority on the extent of each state's commitment to a feasible alternative design requirement in design defect cases, see Products Liability Restatement § 2(b), Reporters' Note to cmt. d. The Reporters' Note indicates that a large majority of courts, either expressly or by implication, require the plaintiff in a design defect case to prove a feasible alternative design. The cases on this point in many jurisdictions are jumbled and inconsistent, with the result that some commentators have interpreted them quite differently as generally not re-

proof on this issue,[23] and, that if a plaintiff fails to present sufficient evidence on this point, a design defect claim ordinarily will fail.[24] In some states, statutes require plaintiffs to prove a feasible alternative design, either in every case or with some limited exceptions.[25] Other states that employ a risk-utility test implicitly require such proof in most design defect cases.[26] And a number of jurisdictions—sometimes noting the value of proof of a feasible alternative design, other times observing how difficult and costly a requirement of such proof would be for plaintiffs—explicitly reject any idea that proof of an alternative design is a necessary element of a plaintiff's design defect case.[27]

quiring such proof. See, e.g., Vargo, The Emperor's New Clothes: The American Law Institute Adorns a "New Cloth" for Section 402A Products Liability Design Defects—A Survey of the States Reveals a Different Weave, 26 U. Mem. L. Rev. 493 (1996); Shapo, In Search of the Law of Products Liability: The ALI Restatement Project, 48 Vand. L. Rev. 631, 668–71 (1995); Klemme, Comments to the Reporters and Selected Members of the Consultative Group, Restatement of Torts (Third): Products Liability, 61 Tenn. L. Rev. 1173 (1994); Vandall, The Restatement (Third) of Torts: Products Liability Section 2(b): The Reasonable Alternative Design Requirement, 61 Tenn. L. Rev. 1407 (1994). As a matter of practical jurisprudence, the Reporters appear correct in their view that, in most states, the plaintiff appropriately will face a dismissal or directed verdict in most design defect cases in the absence of proof of a feasible alternative design.

**23.** Despite a contrary rule in California and a small number of other states, the plaintiff logically and fairly has the burden of proof on the feasibility and cost-effectiveness of the alternative design. See Products Liability Restatement § 2(b) cmt. *f*; Prosser and Keeton on Torts § 99, at 702; Wade, On Product "Design Defects" and Their Actionability, 33 Vand. L. Rev. 551, 573 (1980) (criticizing cases that shift the burden of proof to the defendant); G. Schwartz, Foreword: Understanding Products Liability, 67 Cal. L. Rev. 435, 466–67 (1979).

**24.** "Since plaintiff failed to present evidence that there was a safe and reasonably feasible alternative to defendants' product, the trial court properly concluded that there was no issue of design defect for the jury to determine." Macri v. Ames McDonough Co., 512 A.2d 548, 551 (N.J. Super. Ct. App. Div. 1986) (hammer that chipped). See also Smith v. Louisville Ladder Co., 237 F.3d 515 (5th Cir. 2001) (Tex. law); Smith v. Keller Ladder Co., 645 A.2d 1269 (N.J. Super. Ct. App. Div. 1994) (ladder expert performed no risk-utility analysis and offered no evidence of reasonably feasible alternative design, offering only conclusory testimony that design was defective; prima facie design defect case requires plaintiff to prove availability of technically feasible, al-

ternative practical design that would have reduced or prevented plaintiff's harm); Voss v. Black & Decker Mfg. Co., 450 N.E.2d 204 (N.Y. 1983).

See also Scarangella v. Thomas Built Buses, Inc., 717 N.E.2d 679 (N.Y. 1999); Lewis v. American Cyanamid Co., 715 A.2d 967 (N.J. 1998); Hollister v. Dayton Hudson Corp., 201 F.3d 731 (6th Cir. 2000) (Mich. law) (negligence and implied warranty; state has no doctrine of strict liability in tort); Warner Fruehauf Trailer Co. v. Boston, 654 A.2d 1272 (D.C. 1995); Whitted v. General Motors Corp., 58 F.3d 1200, 1206 (7th Cir. 1995) (Ind. law) (summary judgment on strict liability design defect claim was proper where plaintiff failed to prove a safer, more practicable, better product design that was cost-effective); Kallio v. Ford Motor Co., 407 N.W.2d 92, 96 (Minn. 1987); Rix v. General Motors Corp., 723 P.2d 195, 202 (Mont. 1986); Wilson v. Piper Aircraft Corp., 577 P.2d 1322, 1326–27 (Or. 1978).

**25.** Statutes in at least seven states require proof of a feasible alternative design to establish liability in all or most design defect cases. See La. Rev. Stat. Ann. § 9:2800.56; Miss. Code Ann. § 11–1–63(f)(ii); N.J. Stat. Ann. § 2A:58C–3a(1); N.C. Gen. Stat. § 99B–6; Ohio Rev. Code Ann. § 2307.75(F) (2001 reenactment); Tex. Civ. Prac. & Rem. Code Ann. § 82.005; Wash. Rev. Code §§ 7.72.030(1)(a) and (3). See, e.g., Honda of America Mfg., Inc. v. Norman 104 S.W.3d 600 (Tex. App. 2003). Washington's statute ambiguously provides for the jury to consider such proof together with a consumer's safety contemplations. See Couch v. Mine Safety Appliances Co., 728 P.2d 585 (Wash. 1986). The statutes in New Jersey and North Carolina make statutory exceptions for cases for egregiously dangerous products. Illinois had a provision that was part of a broad tort reform act that was held unconstitutional. See Best v. Taylor Mach. Works, 689 N.E.2d 1057 (Ill. 1997).

**26.** See, e.g., Products Liability Restatement § 2(b), Reporters' Notes to cmt. *d* (including Arizona, Florida, Kansas, Kentucky, Maine, Missouri, New Hampshire, New Mexico, South Carolina, and Virginia in this list).

**27.** See, e.g., Vautour v. Body Masters Sports Indus., 784 A.2d 1178, 1183 (N.H.

## Risk–Utility Analysis of an Alternative Design

Although the risk-utility issue in design defect cases is frequently framed vaguely in terms of a balance between the risks and benefits of the "product," as mentioned earlier and discussed further below, the true cost-benefit issue litigated in almost every case is much narrower: whether the safety benefits of altering the product's design in a particular manner would have (foreseeably) exceeded the costs of the alteration.[28] Risk-utility analysis is focused, in other words, on the costs and benefits of the specific alternative design feature proposed by the plaintiff. The relevant *benefits* of a proposed alternative design are limited to the aggregate safety benefits to people suffering injury and property damage in accidents of a similar type to that which harmed the plaintiff.[29] But the *costs* of an alternative design feature more diversely may include: (1) the monetary costs of adopting the alternative design for all such products; (2) any loss of usefulness in the product that the design alteration may cause; and (3) any new dangers that the design feature may introduce.

The risk-utility (cost-benefit) issue often is conceptually quite simple: whether the aggregate costs of adding some safety feature proposed by the plaintiff is or is not outweighed by the aggregate benefit of preventing foreseeable accidents like that which injured the plaintiff. So, if a proposed alternative safety feature would be expensive to adopt, and if it would be unlikely to produce substantial safety benefits, it is not required.[30] But a manufacturer will fail the risk-utility test if it does not adopt a relatively inexpensive safety feature that could appreciably improve a product's safety, such as by incorporating a child-resistant feature in a utility lighter for less than 5¢ per lighter;[31] installing a $2.50

2001) ("while proof of an alternative design is relevant in a design defect case, it should be neither a controlling factor nor an essential element that must be proved in every case"); McCathern v. Toyota Motor Corp., 23 P.3d 320, 331 (Or. 2001) (such evidence not always necessary); Boerner v. Brown & Williamson Tobacco Corp., 260 F.3d 837 (8th Cir. 2001) (Ark. law); Delaney v. Deere and Co., 999 P.2d 930, 944 (Kan. 2000); Potter v. Chicago Pneumatic Tool Co., 694 A.2d 1319, 1334 (Conn. 1997) ("The availability of a feasible alternative design is a factor that the plaintiff may, rather than must, prove in order to establish that a product's risks outweigh its utility."); Barton v. Adams Rental, Inc., 938 P.2d 532, 537 n.7 (Colo. 1997) (such evidence "may be a factor in the risk-benefit analysis"); Rahmig v. Mosley Mach. Co., 412 N.W.2d 56 (Neb. 1987) (such evidence important but unnecessary under consumer expectations test). See Note, Just What You'd Expect: Professor Henderson's Redesign of Products Liability, 111 Harv. L. Rev. 2366, 2373 (1998) (costs of alternative design

proof requirement place a "potentially insurmountable stumbling block in the way of those injured by badly designed products").

**28.** See Owen, Toward a Proper Test for Design Defectiveness: "Micro–Balancing" Costs and Benefits, 75 Tex. L. Rev. 1661, 1690 (1997).

**29.** Thus, a manufacturer may not introduce evidence of the collateral social benefits from the production of cigarettes, such as profits, employment, benefits to suppliers of goods and services, tax revenues paid, and charitable contributions made to the community. See Cipollone v. Liggett Group, Inc., 644 F.Supp. 283, 286 (D.N.J. 1986); Products Liability Restatement § 2(b) cmt. *f*; Note, 73 Cornell L. Rev. 606, 616–19 (1988).

**30.** See Products Liability Restatement § 2(b) cmt. *f* (noting that a court should consider "the likely effects of the alternative design on production costs").

**31.** Flock v. Scripto–Tokai Corp., 319 F.3d 231, 240 (5th Cir. 2003) (Tex. law) (at a total out-of-pocket cost to the company of $500,000).

shield made of shatterproof glass over a pressure gauge to protect a person's eyes;[32] including a $3 shield to cover the rear of a power mower;[33] or making a $5–10 alteration to a car's engine hood to shape it to provide the driver with visibility if an improperly latched hood flies open while driving.[34] Because the cost of a safety improvement is weighed against the risk of harm it should prevent, even safety features that substantially raise a product's cost and price will sometimes be required. If a guard costing $200 to $500 will protect an operator against a substantial risk of losing a hand and arm in an $8,000 machine, the cost of safety may be worth the benefit.[35] And even if adding a child-proof device to a disposable butane cigarette lighter increases its cost by as much as 60–75%, raising its price to that extent may be worth the benefit of substantially reducing the massive losses regularly caused by child's play fires from lighters not equipped with such a device.[36]

In addition to the actual dollar costs of enhancing a product's safety, risk-utility analysis of a plaintiff's proposed alternative design requires consideration of another significant cost—any reduction in the product's usefulness. Adding a guard to a punch press may help to keep out hands, but it may preclude the operator from feeding large sheets of metal into the press and may slow down production. Child-proofing tops of medicines and household cleansers will reduce the number of small children poisoned by such products, but childproof designs make life more difficult for older persons whose hands are weakened by arthritis. Adding flame repellant chemicals to fabrics used for clothing will protect against fabric fire injuries, but such chemicals may decrease a fabric's comfort and durability, may make it more difficult to wash out odors, and may make the fabric more prone to wrinkle and more difficult to dry. Many hazards are serious enough that sacrificing a little product usefulness in exchange for greater safety makes good sense. However, people buy and use products to help them with their labors and to give them satisfaction.[37] Thus, sacrifices in a product's utility are important costs that must be carefully evaluated in assessing the costs and benefits of a proposed alternative design.[38]

**32.** Helicoid Gage Div. of Am. Chain & Cable Co. v. Howell, 511 S.W.2d 573 (Tex. App. 1974).

**33.** South Austin Drive–In Theatre v. Thomison, 421 S.W.2d 933 (Tex. App. 1967).

**34.** Roach v. Kononen, 525 P.2d 125 (Or. 1974).

**35.** See Dorsey v. Yoder Co., 331 F.Supp. 753 (E.D. Pa. 1971), aff'd, 474 F.2d 1339 (3d Cir. 1973).

**36.** See Griggs v. BIC Corp., 981 F.2d 1429 (3d Cir. 1992) (Pa. law) (in early 1980s, increase of $.60–.75 per lighter then costing under $1 apiece; 120 people killed and 750 persons injured in such fires at annual national cost of $300–375 million). Compare Todd v. Societe BIC (Todd II), 9 F.3d 1216, 1221 n.† (7th Cir. 1993) (Ill. law) (noting CPSC estimates that childproofing

lighters would raise their unit market price by only 15–20 cents, but also noting the elusiveness of such statistics).

**37.** Satisfaction may come from the senses, as from a pleasurable taste, or smell, or touch; a motorcyclist's pleasure of feeling the rushing air through an open design of a motorcycle helmet might be worth the slightly increased dangers. And satisfaction may be aesthetic, such as the pleasure experienced by an owner of an especially sleek, small sports car that may be much less safe than larger cars. Assuming in both situations that the additional risks are widely known and appreciated, or fully disclosed to buyers, a trier of fact might well conclude that the benefits of the dangers exceed the risks.

**38.** See, e.g., Products Liability Restatement § 2(b) cmt. f ("evidence of the magnitude and probability of foreseeable harm

Another important, but less common, cost in the risk-utility evaluation of a plaintiff's proposed alternative design is the creation of additional dangers by the new design. For example, seatbelts and airbags of various designs protect the safety of many occupants in certain collisions, but in other situations both seatbelts and airbags may cause more harm than good.[39] Guarding motorboat propellers presents another example. *Fitzpatrick v. Madonna*[40] was one of a number of cases involving claims by swimmers injured or killed by motorboat propellers alleging that the propellers should have been shrouded with a guard. The benefit of such guards would be the large number of swimmers saved from harm. But such devices are not without their costs, including reduced speed, reduced fuel efficiency, and reduced maneuverability. In addition, propeller guards introduce a number of new risks, such as increasing the size of the motor that can hit and injure swimmers and creating a trap in which human limbs may become wedged near the moving propeller blades.[41] Any such new dangers that a proposed alternative design are likely to create are important costs which must be balanced against the alternative design's safety benefits, such that the ultimate safety issue in such cases becomes the overall *net* safety improvement from the alternative design.[42]

Costs and benefits of differing alternative designs vary considerably with the type of product, types of dangers, and available methods for reducing risk. But the basic risk-utility issue remains the same: whether the product reasonably could have been designed more safely so as to prevent the plaintiff's harm without unduly increasing the product's cost, decreasing its utility, or introducing other hazards. The *Products Liability Restatement* formulates the relevant balance of costs and benefits in design defectiveness by requiring that an alternative design be "reasonable"—that the safety advantages of the alternative design on balance are worth its risks and other disadvantages.[43]

may be offset by evidence that the proposed alternative design would reduce the efficiency and utility of the product").

**39.** See, e.g., Connelly v. Hyundai Motor Co., 351 F.3d 535, 541 (1st Cir. 2003) (N.H. law) (jury entitled to find either that front seat airbag should have been less aggressive or that its design was defective "because . . . on balance, the benefit to the public of including the overly aggressive airbag system in the Sonata outweighed the danger caused by the airbag system (because the system saved many more lives than it took)").

**40.** 623 A.2d 322 (Pa. Super. Ct. 1993).

**41.** Id. at 325.

**42.** See, e.g., Phatak v. United Chair Co., 756 A.2d 690, 695 (Pa. Super. Ct. 2000) (automobile resembling tank "might make its occupants safer, but if in so doing it creates an unacceptable hazard to other motorists or pedestrians, the risk-utility is negative and the product design feature should be thought of as a negative, not a positive."); Crespo v. Chrysler Corp., 75 F.Supp.2d 225, 228 (S.D.N.Y. 1999) ("This requirement that the alternative design be not only feasible but also safer for the relevant users is vital, for otherwise a plaintiff could recover simply by showing that a product could feasibly and without loss of utility be designed in such a way as to avoid injury to him alone even though the change would inflict injury on numerous others— an absurd position."). See cmt. *f* to § 2(b) of the Products Liability Restatement:

When evaluating the reasonableness of a design alternative, the overall safety of the product must be considered. It is not sufficient that the alternative design would have reduced or prevented the harm suffered by the plaintiff if it would also have introduced into the product other dangers of equal or greater magnitude.

**43.** See Products Liability Restatement § 2(b) and cmt. *f* thereto.

## The "Feasibility" of the Alternative Design

An "alternative" design implies a reasonable choice between available designs. A safety feature that a plaintiff claims a product should have carried can fairly be considered a design "alternative" only if there was a practical means by which a manufacturer reasonably could have adopted such a safety feature at the time the product was designed and sold. Thus, the plaintiff must prove that the alternative design, offered to show that the manufacturer's chosen design was defective, was "feasible."[44] Because the feasibility of an alternative design suggests that the design feature proposed by plaintiff was technologically and commercially practicable, feasibility is often bound up in the issue of "state of the art."[45] Feasibility requires at least technological capability,[46] but it is normally viewed more broadly to include cost, commercial practicability (including practicable availability of materials and components), and even the likelihood of consumer acceptance.[47] Viewed in this expanded fashion, "feasibility" really means "reasonable," such that the *Products Liability Restatement* defines design defectiveness in terms of the availability of a "reasonable alternative design."[48] All significant disadvantages of a proposed alternative design are properly embraced within the

**44.** See, e.g., Wankier v. Crown Equip. Co., 353 F.3d 862 (10th Cir. 2003) (Utah law) (plaintiff must prove "safer, feasible, alternative design"); Jeter ex rel. Estate of Smith v. Brown & Williamson Tobacco Corp., 294 F.Supp.2d 681, 686 (W.D. Pa. 2003) ("[p]laintiff must prove a feasible alternative design"); Rypkema v. Time Mfg. Co., 263 F.Supp.2d 687, 692 (S.D.N.Y. 2003) ("Under New York law, in a design defect case a plaintiff is required to prove the existence of a feasible alternative which would have prevented the accident."); Warner Fruehauf Trailer Co. v. Boston, 654 A.2d 1272, 1278 (D.C. Ct. App. 1995) ("In order to determine whether a safer design that would have prevented the injury should have been used, the trier of fact ordinarily must consider whether any safer alternative designs were commercially feasible.").

**45.** See, e.g., Cavanaugh v. Skil Corp., 751 A.2d 518, 523 (N.J. 2000) ("the absence of both a practical and technically feasible alternative device is a necessary predicate to barring liability under the state-of-the-art defense"); Potter v. Chicago Pneumatic Tool Co., 694 A.2d 1319, 1344–1349 (Conn. 1997); Robinson v. Audi Nsu Auto Union, 739 F.2d 1481, 1485–86 (10th Cir. 1984) (Okla. law) ("plaintiff could use state-of-the-art evidence to try to show the feasibility of other safer alternatives"); Boatland of Houston, Inc. v. Bailey, 609 S.W.2d 743, 748 (Tex. 1980) (state-of-the-art evidence "important in determining whether a safer design was feasible"); Lancaster Silo & Block Co. v. Northern Propane Gas Co., 427 N.Y.S.2d 1009, 1016 (App. Div. 1980) ("state of the art sets the parameters of

feasibility"). On state of the art, see § 10.4, below.

**46.** See, e.g., Martin v. Michelin N. Am., 92 F.Supp.2d 745, 754 (E.D. Tenn. 2000) (feasibility defined in terms of what manufacturer could have known under existing state of technological and scientific art at the time of manufacture).

**47.** See, e.g., Glover v. BIC Corp., 6 F.3d 1318 (9th Cir. 1993) (practicability means economic feasibility in terms of cost, overall design, and operation); Rix v. General Motors Corp., 723 P.2d 195 (Mont. 1986); Troja v. Black & Decker Mfg. Co., 488 A.2d 516 (Md. Ct. Spec. App. 1985); Oberst v. International Harvester Co., 640 F.2d 863 (7th Cir. 1980) (Ill. law).

An expert witness's mere concept of an alternative design, if it has never been developed, does not satisfy the feasibility requirement. See, e.g., Ballarini v. Clark Equip. Co., 841 F.Supp. 662 (E.D. Pa. 1993) (interlock device that would disable forklift when operator forgets to apply parking brake before dismounting); Allen v. Minnstar, Inc., 8 F.3d 1470 (10th Cir. 1993) (Utah law) (speculative prototype for motorboat propeller guard does not satisfy requirement that alternative design be practicable and available).

**48.** "A product . . . is defective in design when the foreseeable risks of harm posed by the product could have been reduced or avoided by the adoption of a reasonable alternative design . . . and the omission of the alternative design renders the product not reasonably safe." Products Liability Restatement § 2(b).

feasibility concept, including any increased cost, decreased utility, and increased dangers of other types.[49]

An early case that viewed feasibility in this broader sense was *Wilson v. Piper Aircraft Corp.*[50] *Wilson* involved the crash of a small plane possibly due to carburetor icing, a condition that could not have occurred if the plane's engine had been equipped with a fuel-injection rather than carburetor system. Although fuel injection systems were available at the time, some 80–90% of all small airplanes used carbureted engines which had various advantages approved by the FAA. Reversing jury verdicts for the plaintiffs, the court observed that the plaintiff in a design defect case must establish the availability of an "alternative, safer design, practicable under the circumstances," meaning that the alternative design is feasible "in terms of cost, practicality and technological possibility."[51] The trial court should not submit a design case to a jury unless the jury could find that the proposed alternative design is "not only technically feasible but also practicable in terms of cost and the over-all design and operation of the product."[52]

The cost-benefit method for evaluating proposed alternative designs may be logical and straight-forward, but the actual process of balancing the variety of intangible considerations involved in safety, cost, and utility trade-offs involves a complex conceptual balance which is as much political as it is "factual." Accordingly, the risk-utility balance determination, assuming that the plaintiff has offered credible evidence for the balance, almost always raises an issue of fact for jury determination.[53]

### Focusing the Risk–Utility Test on the Proposed Alternative Design

A particularly nettlesome aspect of defining the risk-utility standard for design defectiveness is deciding precisely what to balance against what.[54] Many courts have purported to lean heavily on Dean Wade's famous seven factors, as discussed in the previous section, and some of the problems with relying on such an open-ended catalogue of possibly relevant considerations were there examined. A similar problem, also previously noted, arises out of the broad way in which many courts phrase the risk-utility balance for design defectiveness—in terms of weighing the risks and utility of the "product" or the product's "design."[55] The process of design defect litigation would be rendered more

---

**49.** See, e.g., Caterpillar, Inc. v. Shears, 911 S.W.2d 379 (Tex. 1995) (front-end loader equipped with detachable rather than permanent rollover protective structure ("ROPS") was not defective; permanent structure was not "feasible" because it would have destroyed multi-purpose nature of loader); Monahan v. Toro Co., 856 F.Supp. 955 (E.D. Pa. 1994) (lawn tractor rolled over on steep slope; adding roll-bar and altering center of gravity might diminish utility); Hagans v. Oliver Mach. Co., 576 F.2d 97 (5th Cir. 1978) (Tex. law) (multipurpose table circular saw equipped with removable, rather than permanent, blade guard).

**50.** 577 P.2d 1322 (Or. 1978).

**51.** Id. at 1326.

**52.** Id. at 1327.

**53.** See id. at 1327 nn. 3 and 5.

**54.** Extensively examined in Owen, Toward a Proper Test for Design Defectiveness: "Micro–Balancing" Costs and Benefits, 75 Tex. L. Rev. 1661 (1997); Owen, Risk–Utility Balancing in Design Defect Cases, 30 U. Mich. J.L. Reform 239 (1997).

**55.** See, e.g., Halliday v. Sturm, Ruger & Co., 792 A.2d 1145, 1150 (Md. 2002) ("The risk-utility test ... regards a product as defective and unreasonably dangerous

comprehensible if courts were to narrow their formulations of the risk-utility test to correspond to the issues actually litigated in courtrooms across the nation,[56] but trial judges and lawyers seem to understand what the appellate judges mean when they speak of balancing the risks and utility of a product whose design is challenged by a plaintiff in a products liability case.[57]

In a design defect case, there are really two distinct designs that are separately on trial: (1) the manufacturer's chosen design, and (2) the alternative design proposed by the plaintiff that allegedly would have prevented the plaintiff's harm. The propriety of the first (chosen) design would seem to be the more important issue in such a case, and to a real extent it is: the "defectiveness" (vel non) of the chosen design remains the ultimate issue in the trial. Yet, it is no more than that—the ultimate

... if the danger presented by the product outweighs its utility."); Roberts v. Rich Foods, Inc., 654 A.2d 1365, 1371 (N.J. 1995) (characterizing *O'Brien* test for a product defective in design as whether "its risks outweighed its utility"); Denny v. Ford Motor Co., 662 N.E.2d 730, 735–36 (N.Y. 1995) (stating that ascertaining defectiveness requires "a weighing of the product's benefits against its risks" and "a weighing of the product's dangers against its over-all advantages"); Caterpillar, Inc. v. Shears, 911 S.W.2d 379, 384 (Tex. 1995) (determining design defectiveness "requires balancing the utility of the product against the risks involved in its use"); Hoyt v. Vitek, Inc., 894 P.2d 1225, 1231 (Or. Ct. App. 1995) (determining defectiveness "by balancing the product's utility against the magnitude of the risk associated with its use"); Haberkorn v. Chrysler Corp., 533 N.W.2d 373, 380 (Mich. Ct. App. 1995) ("In determining whether a defect exists, the trier of fact must balance the risk of harm occasioned by the design against the design's utility."); Soule v. General Motors Corp., 882 P.2d 298, 308 (Cal. 1994) (indicating that no design defect exists if " 'the benefits of the ... design outweigh the risk of danger inherent in such design'," quoting Barker v. Lull Eng'g Co., 573 P.2d 443, 454 (Cal. 1978)); Banks v. ICI Ams., Inc., 450 S.E.2d 671, 673 (Ga. 1994) (describing a consensus among jurisdictions that, in determining design defectiveness, "the risks inherent in a product design are weighed against the utility or benefit derived from the product"); Wagatsuma v. Patch, 879 P.2d 572, 584 (Haw. Ct. App. 1994) (stating that there is no design defect if "the benefits of the design outweigh the risk of danger inherent in that design"); Sperry–New Holland v. Prestage, 617 So.2d 248, 254 (Miss. 1993) (concluding that a design is defective if "the utility of the product is outweighed by the danger that the product creates"); Armentrout v. FMC Corp., 842 P.2d 175, 182 (Colo. 1992) (holding that jury was properly

instructed that a product is defective in design "if it creates a risk of harm to persons which is not outweighed by the benefits to be achieved from such design"); Guiggey v. Bombardier, 615 A.2d 1169, 1172 (Me. 1992) ("To determine whether a product is defectively dangerous, we balance the danger presented by the product against its utility.").

**56.** An example of a court focusing on the proper, narrow issue is Colon v. Bic USA, Inc., 199 F.Supp.2d 53, 91 n.32 (S.D.N.Y. 2001) (test of lighters defective in design because of their bright color is whether "the risk of bright color outweighs the utility of using a bright color compared to the risk versus utility of using a dull color"). The proper balance is explained in Owen, Toward a Proper Test for Design Defectiveness: "Micro–Balancing" Costs and Benefits, 75 Tex. L. Rev. 1661 (1997); Owen, Risk–Utility Balancing in Design Defect Cases, 30 U. Mich. J. L. Reform 239 (1997).

**57.** However, the courts in at least a couple of states, most notably New Jersey, appear to believe in the propriety of both broad and narrow forms of risk-utility balancing in design defect cases. See, e.g., Lewis v. American Cyanamid Co., 715 A.2d 967, 980 (N.J. 1998) ("A plaintiff must prove either that the product's risks outweighed its utility or that the product could have been designed in an alternative manner so as to minimize or eliminate the risk of harm. Plaintiffs who assert that the product could have been designed more safely must prove under a risk-utility analysis the existence of an alternative design that is both practical and feasible." New Jersey's statutory exception to the feasible alternative design requirement, for "egregiously unsafe or ultrahazardous" products and those with "little or no usefulness," suggests approval of broad risk-utility balancing in this narrow class of cases. See N.J. Stat. Ann. § 2A:58C–3(b).

legal determination that merely characterizes, but provides no guidelines for establishing, the outcome of a case. What typically is far more significant in the adjudication process is the second (alternative) design—more specifically, the reasons for and against the manufacturer's failure to adopt it. This is the design decision normally and properly at issue in the trial, requiring particularized cost-benefit proof by the parties and evaluative processing by the judge and jury, that lies at the heart of nearly every design defect case. Although the propriety of the manufacturer's chosen design remains of ultimate consequential interest in terms of legal outcome, it ordinarily is determinable only indirectly by evaluating the costs and benefits of the untaken design precaution proposed by the plaintiff.

Thus, regardless of how broadly appellate courts may formulate the risk-utility test, design defectiveness litigation almost invariably focuses on the costs and benefits related directly to a solution of the particular design problem asserted by the plaintiff. That is, the design defect issue actually litigated is a *micro*-balance of the pros and cons of the manufacturer's failure to adopt some design feature that could have prevented the plaintiff's harm—the balance of the safety benefits from changing the design in some particular manner weighed against the various costs of adopting the safety feature.[58] Most simply, the risk-utility balance truly at issue in design defect litigation is whether the safety benefits of an alternative design would have been worth the resulting costs.[59] More fully formulated, a product's design is defective if the safety benefits from improving its safety (by the plaintiff's proposed alternative design) would foreseeably have exceeded the resulting costs, including any diminished usefulness or diminished safety.[60]

When the risk-utility test normally applicable to design defectiveness is properly defined in terms of the costs and benefits of adopting the alternative design feature proposed by plaintiff, it fails to catch a limited class of unavoidably dangerous products—exploding cigars, lawn darts that are deadly sharp, and possibly guns, cigarettes, and alcohol whose inherent dangers cannot be designed away and which on balance argu-

---

**58.** See, e.g., R. Heafey and D. Kennedy, Product Liability: Winning Strategies and Techniques § 4.04, at 4–9 (1994) (characterizing the manufacturer's choice to forego a reasonable alternative design as "the heart of the plaintiff's case"); see also Rheingold, 18 Trial Law. Q. 49, 50 (Summer/Fall 1987) ("The usual and proper approach for a plaintiff in a design defect case is to present evidence on an alternative design which the jury can find should have been adopted for the product in question."). This is the manner in which design defectiveness is defined in the Products Liability Restatement § 2 comments *d* and *f*, and it reflects more generally how courts and lawyers actually proceed in assessing liability under the Hand formula. One scholar has noted that a plaintiff's attorney will "try to find some act which, if the defendant had taken it, would have significantly reduced the probability of the accident at low cost

[such] that the increment in the expected loss was greater than the cost of avoidance [and the defendant's attorney tries to show] that the expected benefits of the proposed act were, in fact, less than the costs of undertaking it. [The decision maker is then] asked to compare the incremental expected benefits with the incremental costs." Brown, Toward An Economic Theory of Liability, 2 J. Legal Stud. 323, 334–35 (1973).

**59.** "In sum, an alternative design is reasonable if its marginal benefits exceed its marginal costs." Products Liability Restatement § 2(b), Reporters' Note to cmt. *f.*

**60.** See Owen, Toward a Proper Test for Design Defectiveness: "Micro–Balancing" Costs and Benefits, 75 Tex. L. Rev. 1661, 1690 (1997).

ably cause more social harm than good. The difficult problem here is whether the law should impose product category liability for generically dangerous products,[61] an important issue examined in a later chapter.[62] A number of courts,[63] at least two state legislatures,[64] and the *Products Liability Restatement*,[65] all require plaintiffs in design cases to prove a feasible alternative design as a general rule but provide a special exception for a very small category of egregiously dangerous products which possess little redeeming value, a quite reasonable approach to a difficult problem.

## § 8.6   COMBINING CONSUMER EXPECTATIONS AND RISK-UTILITY

Evolving separately from the law of warranty and the law of negligence, the consumer expectations and risk-utility tests of design defectiveness developed largely as rival theories of design defect liability. Thus, for much of modern products liability law, most courts have determined design defectiveness exclusively by one or the other standard and have refused to recognize the validity of the other. In more recent years, however, in recognition of the combined warranty-tort heritage of products liability law, and because of inadequacies in consumer expectations as an exclusive standard,[1] many courts have begun to blend the two tests in one way or another. The two principal approaches for blending the two standards are: (1) by defining one test in terms of the other, or

**61.** As mentioned in the text, the classic examples are cigarettes, certain guns, and alcoholic beverages. See also Products Liability Restatement, § 2 comments *d* and *e*, and illus. 5 (exploding cigar). For a range of views on the appropriateness of using broad-based risk-utility analysis to find cigarettes defectively designed, see the three separate opinions, each concurring and dissenting, in Horton v. American Tobacco Co., 667 So.2d 1289 (Miss. 1995) (compare opinion of Hawkins, C.J., arguing that risk-utility analysis is inappropriate in such cases and noting that liability has been denied by every prior decision, with the opinions of Lee, P.J., and McRae, J., arguing that cigarette manufacturers properly may be held liable under a risk-utility test). For a case holding that the absence of an alternative design to hollow-point bullets, used in a shooting spree on a passenger train, precluded a finding of design defectiveness under the risk-utility test because the purpose of the hollow points was to make the bullets kill especially effectively, see McCarthy v. Olin Corp., 119 F.3d 148 (2d Cir. 1997) (N.Y. law) (2–1 decision, Calabresi, J., dissenting).

**62.** See § 10.3, below.

**63.** See, e.g., Armentrout v. FMC Corp., 842 P.2d 175, 185 n.8 (Colo. 1992) (en banc); Kallio v. Ford Motor Co., 407 N.W.2d

92, 97 n.8 (Minn. 1987); Rix v. General Motors Corp., 723 P.2d 195, 201 (Mont. 1986); Wilson v. Piper Aircraft Corp., 577 P.2d 1322, 1328 n.5 (Or. 1978).

**64.** New Jersey's statute provides that the plaintiff must prove a feasible alternative design or that the product was especially hazardous or practically useless. See N.J. Stat. Ann. § 2A:58c–3(b). North Carolina's statute provides that the plaintiff must prove a feasible alternative design or "that a reasonable person, aware of the relevant facts, would not use or consume a product of this design"). See N.C. Gen. Stat. § 99B–6(a).

**65.** See Products Liability Restatement § 2(b) cmt. *e*, entitled "Design defects: possibility of manifestly unreasonable design," which notes that a court might choose to abandon the alternative design requirement in special cases where "the extremely high degree of danger posed by [a product's] use or consumption so substantially outweighs its negligible social utility that no rational, reasonable person, fully aware of the relevant facts, would choose to use, or to allow children to use, the product"). Id.

**§ 8.6**

**1.** See G. Schwartz, Foreword: Understanding Products Liability, 67 Cal. L. Rev. 435, 471–82 (1979); § 8.3, above.

(2) by establishing each as separate liability "prongs,"[2] either one of which may independently support a design defect finding. Some jurisdictions which embrace the two-pronged approach have recently begun to narrow the applicability of the consumer expectations prong to product designs viewed as "simple."

### Defining One Test in Terms of the Other—The *Potter* Approach

Quite early in the development of modern products liability law, Judge Minor Wisdom recognized how the two basic liability tests might be viewed as partners in evaluating product dangers. In *Welch v. Outboard Marine Corp.*,[3] the plaintiff's minor son was injured while operating a power mower when a piece of wire was thrown out from behind the mower, injuring his ankle. Plaintiff sued, asserting that the mower was defectively designed because it lacked a guard plate hinged to the back. The trial court instructed the jury that it could find the mower defectively designed if "a reasonable man would not sell the product if he knew the risks involved. To put it another way, a product is unreasonably dangerous if it is dangerous to an extent beyond which would be contemplated by the ordinary consumer."[4] The jury gave a verdict for the defendant, and the plaintiff appealed, complaining that the instruction confused the jury by giving them two contradictory definitions of the liability standard. Affirming the judgment on the verdict, Judge Wisdom observed no inconsistency between the reasonable seller and reasonable buyer tests which he viewed as merely "two sides of the same standard."[5] Although this two-sides-of-the-same-coin perspective failed to achieve much of a judicial following, it was applauded by both courts and commentators as a novel but sound approach that appropriately reflected the hybrid evolution of strict manufacturer liability from warranty and tort.[6] Developing Judge Wisdom's concept further, commentators recommended interpreting the *Welch* definition not as a single liability "coin" or standard, but as a bifurcated test that would provide recovery *either* if a product failed a risk-benefit test *or* if the product's dangers exceeded consumer expectations.[7]

One year later, in 1974, the Supreme Court of Oregon entered the search for a design defect test in *Phillips v. Kimwood Machine Co.*,[8] a case involving the design of an industrial sanding machine that ejected a piece of fiberboard at the operator.[9] Although the Oregon court had

---

**2.** In Barker v. Lull Eng'g Co., 573 P.2d 443, 456 (Cal. 1978), the court aptly referred to the use of two alternative bases of liability as the "two-pronged definition of design defect." See G. Schwartz, Foreword: Understanding Products Liability, 67 Cal. L. Rev. 435, 436 (1979).

**3.** 481 F.2d 252 (5th Cir. 1973) (La. law).

**4.** Id. at 253–54.

**5.** "A product is defective and unreasonably dangerous when a reasonable seller would not sell the product if he knew of the risks involved or if the risks are greater

than a reasonable buyer would expect." Id. at 254.

**6.** See, e.g., Phillips v. Kimwood Mach. Co., 525 P.2d 1033, 1036–1037 (Or. 1974); Montgomery and Owen, Reflections on the Theory and Administration of Strict Tort Liability for Defective Products, 27 S.C. L. Rev. 803, 843–45 (1976).

**7.** 27 S.C. L. Rev. at 845 n.147.

**8.** 525 P.2d 1033 (Or. 1974).

**9.** The design defect claim was the machine's failure to be equipped with teeth which could have prevented regurgitation of the boards. Id. at 1035.

previously adopted the consumer expectations test for ascertaining design defectiveness, in *Heaton v. Ford Motor Co.*,[10] it had been troubled in that case with the vagueness of a consumer's safety expectations in view of the kinds of engineering tradeoffs between costs and benefits unknown to consumers that inhere in design decisionmaking.[11] In the process of switching from a consumer expectations test to risk-utility,[12] the *Phillips* court reiterated Judge Wisdom's view in *Welch* that the two tests may be the same "because a seller acting reasonably would be selling the same product which a reasonable consumer believes he is purchasing."[13] The Oregon court's assertion that buyers and sellers have the same safety expectations ignores its important criticism in *Heaton* of consumer expectations as a meaningless safety gauge for complex designs, but the court may have repeated the equivalency of the two tests as window-dressing for its switch away from the problematic consumer expectations test to the more felicitous risk-utility standard for design defect determinations. Be that as it may, by collapsing the former test into the latter, consumer expectations into risk-utility, *Phillips* abandoned the consumer expectations test entirely for risk-utility.

The following year, the Supreme Court of Washington decided *Seattle-First National Bank v. Tabert*,[14] a crashworthiness case involving the structural integrity of a snub-nosed Volkswagen van. A husband and wife were killed by the collapse of the front of their van back upon them when their van struck the rear of a flatbed truck. Reversing a summary judgment for the defendants, the court defined design defect liability under § 402A in terms of an ordinary consumer's reasonable safety expectations.[15] Observing that an ordinary consumer "evaluates a product in terms of safety, recognizing that virtually no product is or can be made absolutely safe,"[16] the *Tabert* court expressly collapsed the consumer expectations test into risk-utility analysis, stating that the reasonable expectations of ordinary consumers include the cost and feasibility of avoiding the risk.[17] Because the plaintiff's expert in his affidavit had applied risk-utility analysis to the weakness of the vehicle's forward structure, the court reversed the summary judgment.[18]

By defining the design defect test in terms of consumer expectations, and then "determining" consumer expectations in terms of the costs and

---

**10.**   435 P.2d 806 (Or. 1967).

**11.**   See id., at 809.

**12.**   Phillips v. Kimwood Mach. Co., 525 P.2d 1033, 1036 (Or. 1974).

**13.**   Id. at 1037. The court continued: "That is to say, a manufacturer who would be negligent in marketing a given product, considering its risks, would necessarily be marketing a product which fell below the reasonable expectations of consumers who purchase it. The foreseeable uses to which a product could be put would be the same in the minds of both the seller and the buyer unless one of the parties was not acting reasonably." Id. Note, however, the *Phillips* court also curiously remarked that the two tests "are not necessarily different standards." Id. at 1036.

**14.**   542 P.2d 774 (Wash. 1975).

**15.**   Id. at 779

**16.**   Id.

**17.**   Noting that "[t]he purchaser of a Volkswagen cannot reasonably expect the same degree of safety as would the buyer of the much more expensive Cadillac," the court remarked that a number of factors must be considered in determining an ordinary consumer's reasonable expectations: "The relative cost of the product, the gravity of the potential harm from the claimed defect and the cost and feasibility of eliminating or minimizing the risk may be relevant in a particular case." Id.

**18.**   See id. at 779–80.

benefits of eliminating or minimizing the danger, the *Tabert* court blended the two tests of design defectiveness. But how the blend should operate in practice is not made clear in the court's decision. While the court states that risk-utility factors are determinants of consumer expectations, it retains consumer expectations as the formal test of liability. At this early stage in the development of design defect theory, it is likely that the court was simply feeling its way and had not worked through precisely how the two standards relate to one another. It may be that the court was thinking that in crashworthiness and other complex design cases consumers only have a right to expect that a vehicle be reasonably designed according to the cost-benefit calculations of reasonable engineers. Yet by leaving room for "other factors" in other situations, the court implicitly left open the possibility of applying a consumer expectations test in other contexts, perhaps in cases involving simple designs.

Whatever the *Tabert* court may actually have had in mind, its definition of consumer expectations in risk-utility terms was ignored by courts in most other states for many years. In 1981, however, the Washington state legislature enacted a statute ambiguously basing liability for design dangers on the costs and benefits of a feasible alternative design *and* on the safety contemplations of an ordinary consumer.[19] A subsequent Washington decision interpreted the statute to mean that a plaintiff could prevail on *either* basis, which amounts to a two-pronged approach for defining design defectiveness,[20] a dubious interpretation of the statute which narrowly avoided being overruled in a 1999 en banc decision.[21]

Courts in most other jurisdictions largely ignored the *Welch* and *Tabert* approach combining the consumer expectations and risk-utility tests in some amorphous manner,[22] and the idea of mixing the two approaches to design defectiveness (or finding them equivalent) lay dormant[23] during the 1980s as the consumer expectations test gradually lost ground to risk-utility in their battle for supremacy as independent tests of design defectiveness. Then, as if awakening like Rip Van Winkle from a lengthy slumber, courts in a small number of states in the 1990s resurrected the nearly defunct idea[24] that the two independent design

**19.** See Couch v. Mine Safety Appliances Co., 728 P.2d 585 (Wash. 1986); Wash. Rev. Code §§ 7.72.030(1)(a) and (3).

**20.** Falk v. Keene Corp., 782 P.2d 974, 977–80 (Wash. 1989). *Falk*'s interpretation of the Washington statute converts it into a *Barker* standard, discussed below.

**21.** Soproni v. Polygon Apt. Partners, 971 P.2d 500 (Wash. 1999) (5–4 decision). Compare Eriksen v. Mobay Corp., 41 P.3d 488, 494 (Wash. Ct. App. 2002) (asserting unequivocally that a plaintiff may establish design defect liability by statute on either risk-utility or consumer expectations).

**22.** *But see* McCathern v. Toyota Motor Corp., 985 P.2d 804 (Or. Ct. App. 1999), aff'd, 23 P.3d 320, 330–32 (Or. 2001); Potter v. Chicago Pneumatic Tool Co., 694 A.2d 1319 (Conn. 1997), discussed below.

**23.** Or nearly so. See, e.g., Robinson v. Reed–Prentice Div. of Package Mach. Co., 403 N.E.2d 440, 443 (N.Y. 1980) ("a defectively designed product is one which, at the time it leaves the seller's hands, is in a condition not reasonably contemplated by the ultimate consumer and is unreasonably dangerous for its intended use; that is one whose utility does not outweigh the danger inherent in its introduction into the stream of commerce").

**24.** In Ray v. BIC Corp., 925 S.W.2d 527, 531 (Tenn. 1996), noting the error in viewing the two tests as equivalent, the court "decline[d] to weave the two tests into one." Even Oregon, which asserted in *Phillips* the equivalence of the two tests, now understands the naivete of that view. See McCathern v. Toyota Motor Corp., 23

defect standards are equivalent, merely representing "two sides of the same coin."[25]

The most notable decision in the 1990s to embrace the equivalency notion is *Potter v. Chicago Pneumatic Tool Co.*,[26] decided by the Supreme Court of Connecticut in 1997. This was a case brought by workers at a shipyard against the manufacturers of pneumatic hand tools for injuries the workers claimed were caused by excessive vibration of the tools. Although the consumer expectations test was "well established in Connecticut strict products liability decisions,"[27] the court was nevertheless troubled by the vagueness problem in consumer expectations concerning the safety of complex designs. Following jurisdictions like Washington "that have modified their formulation of the consumer expectation test by incorporating risk-utility factors into the ordinary consumer expectation analysis,"[28] the *Potter* court adopted the *Tabert* court's reformulation of the consumer expectations test in risk-utility terms.[29] The *Potter* court observed that this "modified formulation" of the consumer expectations test "would establish the product's risk and utility, and the inquiry would then be whether a reasonable consumer would consider the product design unreasonably dangerous."[30] Effectively moving the design defect liability test from consumer expectations to a balance of costs and benefits, other courts have followed *Potter*'s approach of defining the consumer expectations test in risk-utility terms.[31]

The *Potter* court and others following its approach of defining consumer expectations in risk-utility terms are obviously conflicted about abandoning consumer expectations altogether in favor of risk-utility as the basis for design defect liability, generally because they accept the now-suspect view that the consumer expectations test protects

P.3d 320, 330–32 (Or. 2001). Yet the fact that the equivalency notion is now largely discredited does not mean that courts do not occasionally muddle the developing products liability jurisprudence by dragging this obsolete notion from obscurity. See, e.g., Jackson v. Bomag GmbH, 638 N.Y.S.2d 819, 821 (App. Div. 1996).

**25.** The quote is from Ray v. BIC Corp., 925 S.W.2d 527, 530 (Tenn. 1996), which itself was quoting Estate of Ryder v. Kelly–Springfield Tire Co., 587 P.2d 160, 164 (Wash. 1978). It is important to note, however, that the Tennessee court merely noted this approach and criticized it as incorrect and obsolete. 925 S.E.2d at 531. Subsequent decisions resting on the idea include Potter v. Chicago Pneumatic Tool Co., 694 A.2d 1319 (Conn. 1997); Bragg v. Hi–Ranger, Inc., 462 S.E.2d 321, 328 (S.C. Ct. App. 1995) ("[W]e balance the utility of the risk inherent in the design of the product with the magnitude of the risk to determine the reasonableness of the manufacturer's action in designing the product. This 'balancing act' is also relevant to the determination that the product, as designed, is unreasonably dangerous in its failure to conform to the ordinary user's expectations."). See also

the confusing discussion of the relationship between consumer expectations and risk-utility in Flemister v. General Motors Corp., 723 So.2d 25 (Ala. 1998), in which consumer expectations appear to be redefined in risk-utility terms, and risk-utility appears to trump consumer expectations.

**26.** 694 A.2d 1319 (Conn. 1997).

**27.** Id. at 1330.

**28.** Id. at 1333.

**29.** Id.

**30.** Id. In determining what a consumer reasonably would expect, the court noted that a jury should consider most of the Wade risk-utility factors discussed at § 8.4, above. Id. at n. 15.

**31.** See, e.g., McCathern v. Toyota Motor Corp., 23 P.3d 320, 330–32 (Or. 2001) (risk-utility evidence may be required to prove consumer expectations); Vautour v. Body Masters Sports Indus., 784 A.2d 1178 (N.H. 2001) (consumer expectations defined in terms of risk-utility); Delaney v. Deere & Co., 999 P.2d 930, 944 (Kan. 2000) (recognizing "the validity of risk/utility analysis as a guide in determining the expectations of consumers in complex cases").

consumer interests better than risk-utility.[32] These courts have recognized, if reluctantly, the need to turn to a true risk-utility test for evaluating the safety of complex designs in order to provide a determinate standard for liability determinations. As discussed below, however, the clarity of design defect decisionmaking is probably improved by completely breaking with consumer expectations as an independent test for evaluating complex designs and switching to risk-utility as the exclusive liability standard for most such cases.[33]

### Two Liability "Prongs"—The *Barker* Approach

A more forthright and intelligible approach for accommodating the warranty and tort law foundations of strict manufacturer liability, which acknowledges the separate value of each, holds a manufacturer accountable for breaching its duties under either one by recognizing two independent bases or "prongs" of liability. By such a "two-pronged" approach to design defectiveness, a plaintiff injured by a product may establish a design defect if *either* (1) the design violates the consumer expectations test, *or* (2) the design fails a risk-utility test. This approach has logical appeal because it protects the essential interests furthered by each test: contract law's consumer expectancy test protects the expectations of buyers and sellers arising out of their private bargains, and tort law's risk-utility test protects the general public welfare by requiring sellers to accord due respect to the interests of persons put at risk by defective products.[34]

*Barker v. Lull Engineering Co.*,[35] decided by the California Supreme Court in 1978, was the first judicial formulation of an explicitly two-pronged definition of design defectiveness. The plaintiff, while operating a high-lift loader manufactured by the defendant, was struck by a piece of lumber when he leaped from the vehicle as his load began to shift. Plaintiff's strict liability in tort claim alleged that the loader's design was deficient because it was not equipped with stabilizing outriggers, a seatbelt, a roll bar, or an automatic locking device on the leveling lever, and was deficient in certain other respects as well. The trial court instructed the jury that strict liability for defective design is "based on a finding that the product was unreasonably dangerous," the jury found for the defendant, and the plaintiff appealed. Reversing because of defects in the design defect instruction, the Supreme Court of California adopted a two-pronged test for defects in design:

> [A] trial judge may properly instruct the jury that a product is defective in design (1) if the plaintiff demonstrates that the product failed to perform as safely as an ordinary consumer would expect when used in an intended or reasonably foresee-

---

**32.** For difficulties the consumer expectations test causes plaintiffs, see § 8.3, above.

**33.** While retaining use of the consumer expectations standard for addressing simple product failures, discussed below, and certain other specialized contexts. See Products Liability Restatement § 2 cmt. *h*, § 7 (food) and § 8(b) (used products).

**34.** The two-pronged approach may be traced doctrinally to Montgomery and Owen, Reflections on the Theory and Administration of Strict Tort Liability for Defective Products, 27 S.C. L. Rev. 803, 843–45 (1976).

**35.** 573 P.2d 443 (Cal. 1978).

able manner, or (2) if the plaintiff proves that the product's design proximately caused his injury and the defendant fails to prove, in light of the relevant factors, that on balance the benefits of the challenged design outweigh the risk of danger inherent in such design.[36]

Among other factors relevant to the risk-utility prong of this test, the court listed the likelihood and gravity of danger posed by the challenged design, "the mechanical feasibility of a safer alternative design, the financial cost of an improved design, and the adverse consequences to the product and to the consumer that would result from an alternative design."[37]

As for the burden of proof, the *Barker* court left it on the plaintiff for the first, consumer expectations, prong but shifted it to the manufacturer for the second, risk-utility, prong.[38] Observing that the doctrine of strict manufacturer liability in tort was designed to relieve injured plaintiffs of "the onerous evidentiary burdens" of proving a manufacturer's negligence, the court explained the shift in the burden of proof by noting that most risk-benefit evidence on the feasibility and cost of alternative designs involves "technical matters peculiarly within the knowledge of the manufacturer."[39]

A handful of courts have explicitly followed *Barker*'s two-pronged definition of product defect.[40] One state that has followed this approach is Washington, which has a confusing statutory definition of design defectiveness. The statute separately provides that a product design may be considered defective on a finding of the cost-effectiveness of a feasible alternative design and for violating the safety contemplations of an ordinary consumer, but the statute fails to state whether the two design defect standards are independent or whether one will trump the other.[41] As mentioned earlier, the Washington Supreme Court interpreted this statute as establishing a two-pronged standard,[42] a questionable interpretation which narrowly escaped reversal a decade later.[43] Unlike Washing-

---

**36.** Id. at 457–58.

**37.** Id. at 455.

**38.** Id. ("Once the plaintiff makes a prima facie showing that the injury was proximately caused by the product's design, the burden should appropriately shift to the defendant to prove, in light of the relevant factors, that the product is not defective"). See also id. at 456.

**39.** Id.

**40.** See Rivera Pomales v. Bridgestone Firestone, Inc., 217 F.R.D. 290, 295 (D.P.R. 2003); Ontai v. Straub Clinic & Hosp., Inc., 659 P.2d 734 (Haw. 1983); Knitz v. Minster Mach. Co., 432 N.E.2d 814 (Ohio 1982); Caterpillar Tractor Co. v. Beck, 593 P.2d 871 (Alaska 1979). See also Lamkin v. Towner, 563 N.E.2d 449 (Ill. 1990); Dart v. Wiebe Mfg., Inc., 709 P.2d 876 (Ariz. 1985). In 1982, Kansas, deciding to retain § 402A's consumer expectations standard, flatly rejected the *Barker* two-pronged ap-

proach. Lester v. Magic Chef, Inc., 641 P.2d 353 (Kan. 1982). But risk-utility evidence has crept into that state's method for determining defects in design. See Delaney v. Deere & Co., 999 P.2d 930, 944 (Kan. 2000) (recognizing "the validity of risk/utility analysis as a guide in determining the expectations of consumers in complex cases"); Jenkins v. Amchem Prods., Inc., 886 P.2d 869, 890 (Kan. 1994).

**41.** On this issue, see Wash. Rev. Code §§ 7.72.030(1)(a) and (3).

**42.** See Falk v. Keene Corp., 782 P.2d 974, 977–80 (Wash. 1989). See also Bruns v. PACCAR, Inc., 890 P.2d 469 (Wash. Ct. App. 1995).

**43.** See Soproni v. Polygon Apt. Partners, 971 P.2d 500 (Wash. 1999) (5–4 decision). Recent decisions unquestioningly accept the two-pronged standard. See, e.g., Thongchoom v. Graco Children's Products, Inc., 71 P.3d 214, 217 (Wash. Ct. App.

ton's legislation, statutes in Tennessee[44] and Ohio[45] clearly provide *Barker*-like, two-pronged standards for design defectiveness.

A few courts have danced around the issue, seemingly adopting the *Barker* two-pronged approach, but without saying so explicitly.[46] A number of jurisdictions follow a *de facto Barker* approach, variously applying the consumer expectations and risk-utility tests in different cases,[47] generally without explanation as to why one test is applied in one situation and the other test in some other.[48] And the *Potter* approach discussed above, which conflates consumer expectations and risk-utility, is itself a variation on the *Barker* two-pronged standard. While some of these decisions may be faulted for failing clearly to specify when and how the two separate tests should be applied, the courts are still feeling their way in the seemingly never-ending search for an ideal test for design defectiveness. And there is real value in the idea of intelligently combining, in some manner or another, both standards of liability.[49]

2003); Eriksen v. Mobay Corp., 41 P.3d 488, 494 (Wash. Ct. App. 2002).

**44.** See Tenn. Code Ann. § 29–28–102(8), defining an "unreasonably dangerous" product as "a product [that] is dangerous to an extent beyond that which would be contemplated by the ordinary consumer who purchases it, [or a product that] because of its dangerous condition would not be put on the market by a reasonably prudent manufacturer or seller assuming that [the manufacturer or seller] knew of its dangerous condition." See, e.g., Ray v. BIC Corp., 925 S.W.2d 527 (Tenn. 1996) (declining to weave the two standards into one, and holding that the prudent manufacturer prong requires risk-utility analysis).

**45.** Ohio Rev. Code Ann. § 2307.75(A) (reenacted 2001).

**46.** See, e.g., Ortho Pharm. Corp. v. Heath, 722 P.2d 410 (Colo. 1986) (by implication), overruled on other grounds by Armentrout v. FMC Corp., 842 P.2d 175 (Colo. 1992); Dart v. Wiebe Mfg., Inc., 709 P.2d 876 (Ariz. 1985). Compare Bredberg v. Pepsico, Inc., 551 N.W.2d 321, 325 n.3 (Iowa 1996) (pattern jury instruction appearing to present both standards as alternative tests); Baughn v. Honda Motor Co., 727 P.2d 655, 660 (Wash. 1986) (applying "consumer expectations test with a risk-utility base"); Phipps v. General Motors Corp., 363 A.2d 955, 957–63 (Md. 1976). Colorado courts appear now to have interpreted *Ortho* as joining the *Barker* camp. See, e.g., Bartholic v. Scripto–Tokai Corp., 140 F.Supp.2d 1098 (D. Colo. 2000).

**47.** See, e.g., Halliday v. Sturm, Ruger & Co., 792 A.2d 1145, 1153 (Md. 2002) (consumer expectations test applies to design cases unless product malfunctions in which case risk-utility test applies). This is now the de facto approach to design cases in New York whose courts apply a consumer expectations test to implied warranty claims and a risk-utility test to claims for strict liability in tort. See, e.g., Castro v. QVC Network, Inc., 139 F.3d 114, 118 (2d Cir. 1998) (N.Y. law) (Calabresi, J.) ("The imposition of strict liability for an alleged design 'defect' is determined by a risk-utility standard. The notion of 'defect' in a U.C.C.-based breach of warranty claim focuses, instead, on consumer expectations."); Denny v. Ford Motor Co., 662 N.E.2d 730 (N.Y. 1995).

**48.** See, e.g., Bragg v. Hi–Ranger, Inc., 462 S.E.2d 321, 328 (S.C. Ct. App. 1995); Warner Fruehauf Trailer Co. v. Boston, 654 A.2d 1272, 1276 (D.C. 1995) (truck liftgate suddenly collapsed because it had only one, rather than two, hydraulic cylinders). In *Warner*, following what it said was the majority approach, the court used a risk-utility test for the design defect determination in the case before it, "[g]iven the type of product," but observed that consumer expectations test is also frequently used.

**49.** See, e.g., Kennedy, The Role of the Consumer Expectation Test Under Louisiana's Products Liability Tort Doctrine, 69 Tul. L. Rev. 117, 162–63 (1994) ("it will be prudent in some cases to employ the consumer expectation test in conjunction with the risk-utility balancing test in the form of a 'risk-utility consumer expectation test.' . . . given the complexity of products and products liability tort litigation today; the moral, social, economic, and jurisprudential values sought to be advanced by tort liability; and the superiority of the risk-utility balancing test in serving these interests and in resolving many of the tough issues presented in most products liability disputes").

A small number of jurisdictions adopting *Barker*'s two-pronged approach for defining design defects have also followed that decision's reversal of the burden of proof.[50] However, most courts adopting a two-pronged approach have rejected this change in the balance of litigation responsibility and continue to require the plaintiff to prove the feasibility and cost-effectiveness of the alternative design, together with other components of the risk-utility analysis.[51] At a superficial level, *Barker*'s shift in the burden of proof seems fair and reasonable because at least some information on cost-benefit tradeoffs is likely to lie in the defendant's files. Yet it hardly seems unfair to require the plaintiff to offer and prove a hypothesis as to how, specifically, a product ought to have been more safely designed. And, requiring a defendant to prove why it did not adopt any of an infinite number of potential alternative designs unfairly requires it to prove a negative. For these and other reasons, leading commentators understandably have viewed *Barker*'s shift in the burden of proof as simply wrong.[52]

Putting aside the troublesome shift in the burden of proof on the risk-utility prong, *Barker*'s basic two-pronged approach to defining design defects in many respects makes good sense. And it is far more forthright and intelligible than artful definitions of consumer expectations and risk-utility in terms of one another. In addition to simple clarity, a major advantage of the two-pronged approach is that each test shores up the weaknesses of the other. When used alone as the exclusive test of design defectiveness, both the consumer expectations and risk-utility tests must be expanded past their fair limits to provide liability in some cases where it is appropriate. Thus, plaintiffs are helped by the

---

**50.** See, e.g., Quintana–Ruiz v. Hyundai Motor Corp., 303 F.3d 62 (1st Cir. 2002) (P.R. law); Ontai v. Straub Clinic & Hosp., Inc., 659 P.2d 734 (Haw. 1983); Caterpillar Tractor Co. v. Beck, 593 P.2d 871 (Alaska 1979). See also Lamkin v. Towner, 563 N.E.2d 449 (Ill. 1990), examined in Wortel v. Somerset Indus., 770 N.E.2d 1211 (Ill. App. Ct. 2002). Cf. Warner Fruehauf Trailer Co. v. Boston, 654 A.2d 1272, 1277 n.11 (D.C. 1995) (dictum, based on federal district court's interpretation of Colorado law subsequently changed by Colorado court).

In Ortho Pharm. Corp. v. Heath, 722 P.2d 410 (Colo. 1986), the Colorado court, which had already adopted the consumer expectations test for design defectiveness, adopted *Barker*'s two-pronged approach, including the shift in the burden of proof on risk-utility. Id. at 413. Several years later, however, the court reconsidered and overruled itself on the burden of proof issue. Armentrout v. FMC Corp., 842 P.2d 175, 183 (Colo. 1992).

In Soule v. General Motors Corp., 882 P.2d 298, 311 n.8 (Cal. 1994), the California Supreme Court revisited and reaffirmed *Barker*'s shift in the burden of proof.

**51.** Except for Alaska, Hawaii, Illinois, and Puerto Rico, the courts have rejected

*Barker*'s second-prong shift in the burden of proof. See, e.g., Armentrout v. FMC Corp., 842 P.2d 175 (Colo. 1992) (overruling prior case on point); Kallio v. Ford Motor Co., 407 N.W.2d 92 (Minn. 1987); Hayes v. Ariens Co., 462 N.E.2d 273 (Mass. 1984); Cremeans v. International Harvester Co., 452 N.E.2d 1281 (Ohio 1983); Wilson v. Piper Aircraft Corp. (on rehearing), 579 P.2d 1287 (Or. 1978). See also Ray v. BIC Corp., 925 S.W.2d 527, 532 (Tenn. 1996) (labeling *Barker*'s shift in the burden of proof "aberrant"); Dart v. Wiebe Mfg., Inc., 709 P.2d 876 (Ariz. 1985) (en banc) (by implication).

**52.** "The rule places an enormous burden on the concept of a 'product design that proximately causes injury,' a burden which the concept seems ill-equipped to handle.... People fall off ladders all the time, and the fact that ladders are both high and in some general way unstable enables these falls to occur. Does it or doesn't it follow that in every case of a person's falling off a ladder, the ladder's design proximately causes the fall?" G. Schwartz, Foreword: Understanding Products Liability, 67 Calif. L. Rev. 435, 466–67 (1979). See also Prosser and Keeton on Torts 702; Wade, On Product "Design Defects" and Their Actionability, 33 Vand. L. Rev. 551, 573 (1980).

two-pronged approach, for they get to bite the apple on both sides. But this test also provides benefits for defendants and the courts. Defendants may be advantaged by the paring down of both tests to their leanest forms, where the proofs may be clearer and results more predictable from each test. And courts will benefit in the same respect from the improvement in logic and clarity from narrowing down the tests to permit them to establish proper norms of responsibility for their own particular realms. Yet, despite its benefits, a two-pronged standard must be shaped carefully around such problems as the indeterminacy of the consumer expectations test in gauging the adequacy of complex designs as well as the need to assist plaintiffs injured by obvious dangers that could easily have been designed away.

### Complex Designs—The *Soule* Approach

From the very earliest days of modern products liability law, courts and commentators turned to the risk-utility test to avoid applying the consumer expectations test to cases involving vague expectations concerning complex designs.[53] In one early design defect case, *Heaton v. Ford Motor Co.*,[54] the driver of a pickup truck hit a 5–or 6–inch rock, damaging the wheel, which caused the truck to leave the road and tip over. In making a claim for design defectiveness under § 402A, the plaintiff introduced no risk-utility evidence of the costs or feasibility of designing a stronger wheel but relied exclusively upon the consumer expectations test to prove his case. Affirming a non-suit against the plaintiff, the Oregon Supreme Court ruled that the jury, without evidence on the costs and benefits of designing the wheel more strongly, did not have the necessary tools to render a principled decision: without such data, the jury could only speculate on the reasonableness of the wheel's design.[55] Put otherwise, the complexity of the engineering trade-offs involved in the wheel's design rendered consumer expectations unsuitable as a test of its adequacy. Instead, the risk-utility test's factors of feasibility, costs, and benefits were needed to ascertain the sufficiency of the design. Several years later, the Oregon courts took the final plunge by abandoning the consumer expectations test in favor of a risk-utility test requiring proof of a feasible alternative design.[56]

---

**53.** See, e.g., Wade, On the Nature of Strict Tort Liability for Products, 44 Miss. L.J. 825, 829 (1973) (criticizing use of consumer expectations test in cases where "the consumer would not know what to expect, because he would have no idea how safe the product could be made").

**54.** 435 P.2d 806 (Or. 1967).

**55.** "Where the jury has no experiential basis for knowing this, the record must supply a basis. In the absence of either common experience or evidence, any verdict would, in effect, be the jury's opinion of how strong the product *should* be. Such an opinion by the jury would be formed without the benefit of data concerning the cost or feasibility of designing and building stronger products. Without reference to relevant factual data, the jury has no special

qualifications for deciding what is reasonable." Id. at 809.

**56.** See, e.g., Roach v. Kononen, 525 P.2d 125 (Or. 1974); Phillips v. Kimwood Mach. Co., 525 P.2d 1033 (Or. 1974); Wilson v. Piper Aircraft Corp., 577 P.2d 1322, rehearing denied, 579 P.2d 1287 (Or. 1978); Willamette Essential Oils v. Herrold & Jensen Implement Co., 683 P.2d 1374 (Or. Ct. App. 1984); Wood v. Ford Motor Co., 691 P.2d 495 (Or. Ct. App. 1984). In 1979, the Oregon legislature essentially adopted Restatement (2d) Torts § 402A, including its comments defining "defective" and "unreasonably dangerous" in consumer contemplation terms. See Or. Stat. § 30.920(3). While at least one Oregon court interpreted the statute to require use of the consumer expectations test alone, Burns v. General

Once the California Supreme Court decided *Barker* in 1979, other courts began to view consumer expectations and risk-utility as compatible rather than mutually exclusive ways to define a defect in design.[57] Some courts which followed *Barker* in adopting a two-pronged test for design defectiveness began to limit the consumer expectations prong to contexts where consumers have meaningful expectations concerning product safety. For example, rather than abandoning the consumer expectations test altogether, the Supreme Court of Arizona, in a 1985 decision which adopted the *Barker* two-pronged approach, limited the consumer expectations test to cases where such expectations are well-defined, requiring the risk-utility test in cases where consumer expectations are vague.[58] The next year, the Supreme Court of Colorado adopted the *Barker* two-pronged test,[59] observing the following year that the consumer expectations test was inappropriate for judging the adequacy of complex designs.[60]

By the 1990s, it had become quite clear that the consumer expectations test was a poor gauge for ascertaining the adequacy of complex designs. In *Soule v. General Motors Corp.*,[61] the California Supreme Court in 1994 squarely confronted the vagueness problem inherent in *Barker*'s consumer expectations prong. The plaintiff's ankles were fractured when the Chevrolet Camaro she was driving collided with another vehicle at a closing speed of 50–60 miles per hour. She sued the manufacturer, asserting that the design of her automobile was defective because the left front wheel broke free, collapsed rearward, and smashed the toe pan and floorboard into her feet. In particular, she claimed that the configuration of the car's frame, and the bracket attaching the wheel assembly to it, were defectively designed because they did not limit the wheel's rearward travel in the event the bracket should fail. At trial, the parties disagreed on the angle and force of the impact and the extent to which the toe pan had actually deformed. Design defectiveness and causation were addressed by numerous experts on biomechanics, metallurgy, orthopedics, design engineering, crash-test simulation, and other matters. The plaintiff's experts, relying on crash tests, metallurgical analysis, and other evidence, explained how the damage to her car would have been minimized had it been properly designed. The defendant's

Motors Corp., 891 P.2d 1354 (Or. Ct. App. 1995), the resiliency of the risk-utility test has been illustrated by subsequent decisions reintroducing risk-utility analysis as a basis for design defectiveness in complex cases. See, e.g., McCathern v. Toyota Motor Corp., 23 P.3d 320, 330–32 (Or. 2001) (risk-utility evidence may be required to prove consumer expectations).

**57.** See, e.g., Biosera, Inc. v. Forma Scientific, Inc., 941 P.2d 284, 287 (Colo. Ct. App. 1996), aff'd on other grounds, 960 P.2d 108 (Colo. 1998) ("[W]e conclude that the two tests are not mutually exclusive. Rather, a court should review each to determine if it is an appropriate standard for judging the dangerous nature of the product at issue.").

**58.** Dart v. Wiebe Mfg., Inc., 709 P.2d 876 (Ariz. 1985).

**59.** In Ortho Pharm. Corp. v. Heath, 722 P.2d 410 (Colo. 1986) (by implication), overruled on other grounds by Armentrout v. FMC Corp., 842 P.2d 175 (Colo. 1992).

**60.** See Camacho v. Honda Motor Co., 741 P.2d 1240 (Colo. 1987) ("exclusive reliance upon consumer expectations is a particularly inappropriate means of determining [defectiveness] where both the unreasonableness of the danger in the design defect and the efficacy of alternative designs in achieving a reasonable degree of safety must be defined primarily by technical, scientific information").

**61.** 882 P.2d 298 (Cal. 1994).

experts attempted to refute these claims and explained how the plaintiff's ankle injuries were caused by the force of the collision and her failure to wear a seatbelt rather than any defect in the car. The trial court instructed the jury on the consumer expectations test, and the jury returned a verdict for the plaintiff.

On appeal, an important question was whether the trial court erred in instructing the jury on the consumer expectations test in a case in which the common experience of product users does not provide a basis for determining how safely the product should have performed. The intermediate appellate court affirmed the judgment for the plaintiff, and the defendant appealed to the California Supreme Court. Reversing, the Supreme Court held that the trial court erred in instructing the jury on the consumer expectations test on the facts of the case.[62] The court noted that it previously had explained, in *Barker v. Lull Engineering Co.*,[63] that a proper assessment of the costs, benefits, and practicality inherent in appropriate design defective determinations requires risk-utility balancing rather than a gauge of consumer expectations.[64] The court there had cited automotive crashworthiness litigation as an example of the kind of complex case in which the feasibility, costs, and benefits of particular designs are "implicit" in an evaluation of the quality of the manufacturer's design decision.[65] Distinguishing a case in which it had held that consumer expectations were a proper test for judging the design adequacy of a bus without a "grab bar" in easy reach of the plaintiff's seat,[66] the *Soule* court reasoned that the particular safety issue in that case was a matter of common understanding. Thus, the consumer expectations test of *Barker*'s first prong is appropriate, and expert testimony on defectiveness would invade the province of the jury, in cases involving simple product safety issues about which consumers and jurors have a common understanding of widely accepted minimum safety expectations.[67]

The court reasoned further, however, that cases involving complex products often involve risks of injury that do not intelligibly engage the reasonable minimum safety expectations of consumers.[68] And in automotive crashworthiness situations consumers typically simply have "no idea" how safely their vehicles should have performed in the particular circumstances of the crash. In such cases, "the jury must consider the manufacturer's evidence of competing design considerations, and the issue of design defect cannot fairly be resolved by standardless reference

---

**62.** Soule v. General Motors, 882 P.2d 298, 307–08 (Cal. 1994).

**63.** 573 P.2d 443 (Cal. 1978).

**64.** Soule v. General Motors, 882 P.2d 298, 305 (Cal. 1994).

**65.** Id.

**66.** Campbell v. General Motors Corp., 649 P.2d 224 (Cal. 1982).

**67.** As examples, the court pointed to situations where a car explodes while sitting at a stoplight, experiences sudden steering or brake failure as it leaves the

dealership, or rolls over and catches fire in a two-mile-per-hour collision. Soule v. General Motors, 882 P.2d 298, 308 n.3 (Cal. 1994). Thus, the consumer expectations test of *Barker*'s first prong must be reserved "for cases in which the *everyday experience* of the product's users permits a conclusion that the product's design violated minimum safety assumptions, and is thus defective *regardless of expert opinion about the merits of the design.*" Id. at 308.

**68.** Id.

to the 'expectations' of an 'ordinary consumer.' "[69] Because safety expectations in such cases are vague and safety performance mechanisms more complex, juries must turn to "the balancing of risks and benefits required by the second prong of *Barker*."[70] The *Soule* court thus concluded that the jury should *not* have been instructed on the consumer expectations test because the plaintiff's design defect theory involved complex technical and mechanical issues.[71]

*Soule*'s allocation of the consumer expectations and risk-utility tests to their best uses—the former to designs involving simple safety issues (where expert testimony may be improper) and the latter to designs involving complex cost-benefit tradeoffs (where expert testimony is required)—appears to make good sense.[72] Yet, this separation can also result in mischief if it is used to deprive plaintiffs of the right to employ the risk-utility test in cases where a simple risk is obvious, such as a lighter not equipped with a simple child-proof design.[73] Courts bifurcating design defect tests along *Soule* lines will need to make allowances for these types of cases to avoid resurrecting the patent danger rule which now is properly defunct.[74] Other courts have adopted *Soule*'s method of selecting design defect tests based on the complexity of the product's design,[75] sometimes citing *Soule*,[76] sometimes not.[77]

**69.** Id.

**70.** Id. at 308–09.

**71.** "An ordinary consumer of automobiles cannot reasonably expect that a car's frame, suspension, or interior will be designed to remain intact in any and all accidents. Nor would ordinary experience and understanding inform such a consumer how safely an automobile's design should perform under the esoteric circumstances of the collision at issue here. Indeed, both parties assumed that quite complicated design considerations were at issue, and that expert testimony was necessary to illuminate these matters. Therefore, injection of ordinary consumer expectations into the design defect equation was improper." Id. at 310. Nevertheless, because of the voluminous evidence presented on the costs and benefits of the Camaro's design, the court saw no reason to believe that the jury ignored the risk-utility issue and only relied upon the consumer expectations test. Id. at 311. Accordingly, the court held that the trial court's error in instructing the jury on the consumer expectations prong was harmless. Id.

**72.** See Kennedy, The Role of the Consumer Expectation Test Under Louisiana's Products Liability Tort Doctrine, 69 Tul. L. Rev. 117 (1994).

**73.** Compare Todd v. Societe Bic, 21 F.3d 1402 (7th Cir. 1994) (Ill. law) (holding that Illinois would use consumer expectations prong of its two-pronged test in judging design of simple products with obvious risks; a disposable butane cigarette lighter,

not equipped with a child-proof design, is not defective because consumers expect it to ignite when activated), with Robins v. Kroger Co., 80 S.W.3d 641 (Tex. App. 2002) (seller of lighter without child-proof design not entitled to summary judgment on risk-utility test which included consumer expectations as one factor in the balance).

Courts in Illinois and Michigan sometimes slip into this beastly trap. See, e.g., Bates v. Richland Sales Corp., 803 N.E.2d 977 (Ill. App. Ct. 2004) (risk from removing loader's roll bar); Miles v. S.C. Johnson & Son, Inc., 2002 WL 1303131 (N.D. Ill. 2002) (obvious danger to young child who eats crystal Drano drain cleaner). Compare Mills v. Curioni, Inc., 238 F.Supp.2d 876, 892 (E.D. Mich. 2002) ("It is only when a 'simple tool' is involved that the 'open and obvious danger' rule will relieve a manufacturer of liability on a design defect claim."), with Cacevic v. Simplimatic Eng'g Co., 617 N.W.2d 386, 392 (Mich. Ct. App. 2000) (concluding that "the open and obvious danger doctrine [does not] apply to obviate a manufacturer's duty in a case alleging defective design of a simple product").

**74.** See § 10.2, below.

**75.** *But see* Jackson v. General Motors Corp., 60 S.W.3d 800 (Tenn. 2001) (refusing to limit consumer expectations prong of two-pronged statutory design defect standard to simple product designs).

**76.** See, e.g., Potter v. Chicago Pneumatic Tool Co., 694 A.2d 1319, 1333–34

**77.** See note 77 on page 528.

Courts that have defined consumer expectations in terms of risk-utility, discussed above, have effectively chosen to follow the *Barker-Soule* approach, if by a crooked path. The Connecticut Supreme Court's experience in *Potter v. Chicago Pneumatic Tool Co.*[78] is a good example. There, reasoning that "a consumer's expectations may be viewed in light of various factors that balance the utility of the product's design with the magnitude of its risks,"[79] the court materially altered that state's design defect jurisprudence. Holding that this form of "modified consumer expectation test" should be used for complex design cases, the court held, citing *Soule*, that the "ordinary consumer expectation test" should be reserved for use "when the everyday experience of the particular product's users permits the inference that the product did not meet minimum safety expectations."[80] In so doing, *Potter* effectively established its own version of a two-pronged *Barker-Soule* test—with a first prong being an "ordinary" consumer expectations test, limited to simple design cases, and a second prong being a risk-utility test (window-dressed as a "modified consumer expectation test"), for application in complex cases. *Potter*'s basic result is sound, but tying the risk-utility prong to consumer expectations sows seeds of confusion for future design defect litigation. Yet *Potter* also contains an important insight: its recognition that risk-utility analysis should be turned to when "ordinary" consumer expectations fail to provide a rational basis for recovery.[81]

As cost-benefit analysis gathers strength around the globe as the dominant method for judging whether a product's design is adequately safe,[82] courts continue to search for ways to accommodate consumer expectations without banishing it altogether from design defect determinations. Even the *Products Liability Restatement*, though assigning consumer expectations to a secondary position as a mere factor in the risk-utility balance, recognizes that consumer expectations may sometimes play an important role in assessing design defectiveness.[83] The approach

---

(Conn. 1997); Ray v. BIC Corp., 925 S.W.2d 527, 533 (Tenn. 1996) (in *Barker* statute, "the consumer expectation test will be inapplicable, by definition, to certain products about which an ordinary consumer can have no expectation;" citing *Soule* at 531). See also General Motors Corp. v. Farnsworth, 965 P.2d 1209, 1221 (Alaska 1998) (passenger in car submarined under lap belt; consumers could form expectations concerning lap belt design).

**77.** See, e.g., Biosera, Inc. v. Forma Scientific, Inc., 941 P.2d 284 (Colo. Ct. App. 1996), aff'd on other grounds, 960 P.2d 108 (Colo. 1998).

**78.** 694 A.2d 1319 (Conn. 1997).

**79.** Potter v. Chicago Pneumatic Tool Co., 694 A.2d 1319, 1333 (Conn. 1997).

**80.** Id.

**81.** As, presumably, in obvious danger cases. *Potter* emphasized that only the risk-utility test (dubbed the "*modified* consumer expectations test"), not the ("ordinary")

consumer expectation test, should be used in cases where the consumer expectations test does not provide relief:

> [T]he jury should engage in the risk-utility balancing required by our modified consumer expectation test when the particular facts do not reasonably permit the inference that the product did not meet the safety expectations of the ordinary consumer. Furthermore, instructions based on the ordinary consumer expectation test would not be appropriate when, as a matter of law, there is insufficient evidence to support a jury verdict under that test. In such circumstances, the jury should be instructed solely on the modified consumer expectation test we have articulated today.

Id. at 1334.

**82.** This trend is not limited to the United States. See § 1.4, above.

**83.** See § 8.8, below.

of some courts in defining consumer expectations and risk-utility in terms of one another may accommodate both interests but does so through a sleight of hand that muddies products liability jurisprudence. The *Barker* two-pronged test for design defectiveness achieves the same objectives, more clearly and intelligibly, but the burden of proof should be left on plaintiffs for both prongs. Moreover, the consumer expectations prong should be limited to simple design dangers, as in *Soule* and *Potter*, except that the risk-utility prong should be retained for use in simple design cases in which the risks are obvious. Combining the consumer expectations and risk-utility tests along these lines may provide an optimal standard for judging design defectiveness.[84]

## § 8.7  CONSTRUCTIVE KNOWLEDGE—THE WADE–KEETON TEST

In holding manufacturers responsible for defects in design, courts and commentators have always sought to avoid absolute liability, recognizing that the concepts of design safety and design danger are matters of degree involving reasonable trade-offs between a product's usefulness, cost, and safety.[1] Put otherwise, the idea of a design defect has long been understood to rest on the idea of reasonable balance.[2] Because negligence itself is grounded on both reasonableness and balance, one is led to inquire whether and how negligence and strict liability may differ in design defect litigation. Accordingly, in the 1960s, products liability scholars began to search for a way to define strict liability for selling products with defects in design (and warnings) in a manner that distinguished the strict liability standard from mere negligence.

Other than Dean Prosser, the two most prominent tort law scholars in the 1960s who shared a special interest in products liability law were Dean Page Keeton of the University of Texas and Dean John Wade of Vanderbilt University. As modern products liability law was just beginning to emerge in the 1960s, the two deans, both advisors to the American Law Institute's *Restatement (Second) of Torts* which was then in progress, offered separate versions of a similar definition of product defectiveness which distinguished negligence-based responsibility from liability called "strict" in a fundamental way. At the time, courts and commentators were just beginning to feel their way around the new precept of holding manufacturers of defective products "strictly" accountable for injuries to remote consumers.[3] Little thought was being devoted to how the new field might be divided up, for purposes of the standard of liability, according to different types of defect.[4] Accordingly,

---

**84.**  One such test might look something like the following:

  A simple product design is defective if it fails to perform as safely as an ordinary consumer would expect, and any design is defective if it feasibly could have been designed more safely, in a way that would have prevented the plaintiff's injuries, and the safety benefits of such an alternative design foreseeably exceeded its costs, including any diminished usefulness or safety.

**§ 8.7**

**1.**  See ch. 5, above.

**2.**  See, e.g., Owen, Defectiveness Restated: Exploding the "Strict" Products Liability Myth, 1996 U. Ill. L. Rev. 743, 754–61.

**3.**  See §§ 5.3 and 5.4, above.

**4.**  See § 6.2, above. This is not to say that certain scholars of the day did not perceive a great divide between manufacturing and design defects, for they did. See,

as with most other scholars of the day, the search by Deans Keeton and Wade for an appropriate "test" of strict liability was a search for a single liability standard that alone would embrace most products liability problems of the day.[5]

The test developed by Deans Keeton and Wade, which in time became known as the "Wade–Keeton" test[6] quite simply was a negligence test stripped of its scienter.[7] That is, both scholars proposed defining defectiveness in terms of whether a manufacturer or other seller with full knowledge of its product's dangerous condition would be negligent in selling it in that condition. By requiring a seller to know its product's risks, which commensurately relieves an injured plaintiff of the burden of proving the foreseeability of those risks, this test imposes constructive knowledge on the seller of the dangers in its products.[8]

In 1961, two years before Judge Roger Traynor penned his opinion in *Greenman v. Yuba Power Products, Inc.*,[9] three years before Dean William Prosser submitted to the ALI his draft of *Restatement (Second) of Torts* § 402A applicable to products generally,[10] and four years before Dean Wade first offered a similar proposal, Dean Page Keeton authored a little article in the Texas Law Review in which he first articulated a liability test for product defects that was truly strict. At the conclusion of the article in which he examined the various techniques by which courts were holding manufacturers accountable for injuries from defective products, in both tort and warranty,[11] Dean Keeton proposed that a product should not be considered defective "if a reasonable man with full knowledge of all the properties and the danger therein, would continue to market the product because the utility of its use outweighs the danger."[12] Two years later, Dean Keeton hinted at this test in another article in the Texas Law Review,[13] and then, in 1964, in an article exploring the nature of strict products liability,[14] he explained that courts had imposed strict manufacturer liability when "the product was so

e.g., W. P. Keeton, Products Liability—Liability Without Fault and the Requirement of a Defect, 41 Tex. L. Rev. 854, 859 (1963).

**5.** Especially in the 1960s, the case law was quite limited, and, like other scholars of the time, both Deans Keeton and Wade drew on various examples of defects in manufacturing, design, and warnings.

**6.** See, e.g., Privette v. CSX Transp., Inc., 79 Fed.Appx. 879, 889 (6th Cir. 2003) (Tenn. law) (referring to this liability standard more fully as "the Wade–Keeton prudent manufacturer test"); Brooks v. Beech Aircraft Corp., 902 P.2d 54, 63 (N.M. 1995); Cupp and Polage, The Rhetoric of Strict Liability Versus Negligence: An Empirical Analysis, 77 N.Y.U. L. Rev. 874, 884 (2002). The Wade–Keeton test is further discussed at § 10.4, below.

**7.** The Wade–Keeton test is examined from a state-of-the-art perspective in § 10.4, below.

**8.** See, e.g., Phillips v. Kimwood Mach. Co., 525 P.2d 1033 (Or. 1974).

**9.** 377 P.2d 897 (Cal. 1963).

**10.** The ALI approved § 402A when Dean Prosser presented it in final form, applicable to products generally, in 1964. See § 5.3, above.

**11.** Keeton, Products Liability—Current Developments, 40 Tex. L. Rev. 193 (1961).

**12.** Id. at 210. "This is close to a negligence test but not the same [because] excusable ignorance of a defect or the properties of a product is immaterial. . . . " Id. In his full discussion, Dean Keeton mistakenly confuses the negative and positive formulations of the standard.

**13.** W. P. Keeton, Products Liability—Liability Without Fault and the Requirement of a Defect, 41 Tex. L. Rev. 854, 867–68 (1963).

**14.** W. P. Keeton, Products Liability—The Nature and Extent of Strict Liability, 1964 U. Ill. L. F. 693, 702.

dangerous to the user in the condition that it was in that a reasonable man would not have sold it in such condition with knowledge of such a condition and appreciation of the danger. The manufacturer would have been negligent except for his excusable ignorance of the danger."[15] In numerous other articles, from 1966 to at least 1980, Dean Keeton recommended and refined his test of design defectiveness. In his later articles, he emphasized that a design's risks should be determined at the date of trial, which of course simply imposes constructive knowledge on the manufacturer at the time of first design and sale: "A product is defectively designed [if] the magnitude of the danger in fact of the design as it is proved to be at the trial outweighs the utility of the design."[16]

In 1965, in an article[17] in which he cited both of Dean Keeton's Texas articles,[18] Dean John Wade offered a similar strict liability test for ascertaining whether a product is unreasonably dangerous: "Thus, assuming that the defendant had knowledge of the condition of the product, would he then have been acting unreasonably in placing it on the market?"[19] Further, Dean Wade remarked: "If the test is equivalent to that of whether a reasonable prudent man would put it on the market if he knew of the dangers of this particular article, then the elements for determining negligence are relevant. We have here again the problem of balancing the utility of the risk against the magnitude of the risk."[20] In his famous 1973 article in the Mississippi Law Journal,[21] Dean Wade restated his version of the test:

> The simplest and easiest way [to define defectiveness] is to assume that the defendant knew of the dangerous condition of the product and ask whether he was then negligent in putting it on the market or supplying it to someone else. In other words, the scienter is supplied as a matter of law, and there is no need for the plaintiff to prove its existence as a matter of fact. Once given this notice of the dangerous condition of the chattel, the question then becomes whether the defendant was negligent.... Another way of saying this is to ask whether the magnitude of the risk created by the dangerous condition of the product was outweighed by the social utility attained by putting it out in this fashion.[22]

---

**15.** Id.

**16.** W. P. Keeton, Products Liability—Design Hazards and the Meaning of Defect, 10 Cumb. L. Rev. 294, 313 (1979). In this article, Dean Keeton noted that his test "differs from negligence primarily because, as proposed, the danger in fact as proven at trial determines whether a product is good or bad.... When the negligence of the defendant is in issue, it is perceivable danger at the time the product was designed that is the basis for weighing danger against utility. Therefore, a clear difference between proof of negligence and proof of defect as a basis for recovery is apparent." Id. at 314–15. In a footnote, Dean Keeton pointed out that the difference between the two tests was the requirement for negligence that the danger be foreseeable, whereas, under his "strict" liability test, "it is irrelevant that the defendant did not know or had no reason to know of the danger." Id. at 315 n.87.

**17.** Wade, Strict Tort Liability of Manufacturers, 19 Sw. L.J. 5 (1965). The article arose out of a products liability symposium the year before in Dallas, Texas where both deans presented papers.

**18.** Id. at 12, 13 n.45.

**19.** Id. at 15.

**20.** Id. at 17.

**21.** Wade, On the Nature of Strict Tort Liability for Products, 44 Miss. L.J. 825 (1973).

**22.** Id. at 834–35. Dean Wade also recommended how the jury might be instructed on this test:

Just why the "Wade–Keeton" test was labeled precisely as it was is shrouded in the mists of time,[23] but its name is surely backwards. Not only does it appear to have been invented by Dean Keeton in 1961,[24] four years before Dean Wade first proposed it, but Dean Keeton spread the theory far and wide. Dean Wade, who appears to have borrowed the idea for the test from Dean Keeton,[25] may have offered the test in the law journals merely twice, in 1965 and 1973.[26] By contrast, Dean Keeton proposed and explained the test in law journals and his products liability casebook at least a dozen times, from 1961 at least to 1980.[27]

Be that as it may, a number of courts, themselves searching for a basis by which to distinguish strict liability design claims (and warnings claims) from those in negligence, picked up quite early on the Wade–Keeton hindsight test (sometimes referred to as the prudent-manufacturer test).[28] Perhaps the first such case was *Dorsey v. Yoder*,[29] in which the court stated that the proper test for strict products liability in tort is "whether a reasonable manufacturer would continue to market his product in the same condition as he sold it to the plaintiff *with* knowl-

---

A [product] is not duly safe if it is so likely to be harmful to person [or property] that a reasonable prudent manufacturer [supplier], who had actual knowledge of its harmful character would not place it on the market. It is not necessary to find that this defendant had knowledge of the harmful character of the [product] in order to determine that it was not duly safe.

Id. at 839–40.

**23.** The dual origins of the test were noted at least as early as 1974, see Phillips v. Kimwood Mach. Co., 525 P.2d 1033, 1036 n.6 (Or. 1974), and the "Wade–Keeton" moniker appeared in print no later than 1978. See Cepeda v. Cumberland Eng'g Co., Inc., 386 A.2d 816, 829 (N.J. 1978). See also Birnbaum, Unmasking the Test for Design Defect: From Negligence [to Warranty] to Strict Liability to Negligence, 33 Vand. L. Rev. 593, 619 n.125 (1980).

**24.** In W. P. Keeton, Products Liability—Current Developments, 40 Tex. L. Rev. 193, 210 (1961).

**25.** It should be noted, however, that Dean Wade reported that, at the time he wrote his Southwestern Law Journal article in 1964–65, he had not even read Dean Keeton's 1961 Texas article. Wade, On the Effect in Product Liability of Knowledge Unavailable Prior to Marketing, 58 N.Y.U. L. Rev. 734, 761 (1983) ("Postscript: An Excursus on the 'Wade–Keeton' Approach"). By 1983, Dean Wade must have forgotten that he cited both of Dean Keeton's 1961 and 1962 Texas articles in his own article in the Southwestern Law Journal. See Wade, Strict Tort Liability of Man-

ufacturers, 19 Sw. L.J. 5, at 12, 13 n.45 (1965).

**26.** My research on this point was not exhaustive, and it may have missed Dean Wade's recommendation of the test somewhere else.

**27.** In addition to Dean Keeton's articles cited elsewhere in this section, see, e.g., W. P. Keeton, D. Owen, and J. Montgomery, Products Liability and Safety 245 n.1 (1980); W. P. Keeton, The Meaning of Defect in Products Liability Law—A Review of Basic Principles, 45 Mo. L. Rev. 579, 592 (1980); W. P. Keeton, Product Liability and the Meaning of Defect, 5 St. Mary's L. J. 30, 37–38 (1973); W. P. Keeton, Products Liability—Drugs and Cosmetics, 25 Vand. L. Rev. 131, 144 (1972); W. P. Keeton, Product Liability—Inadequacy of Information, 48 Tex. L. Rev. 398, 402–03 (1970); W. P. Keeton, Manufacturer's Liability: The Meaning of "Defect" in the Manufacture and Design of Products, 20 Syracuse L. Rev. 559, 568 (1969); W. P. Keeton, Some Observations About the Strict Liability of the Maker of Prescription Drugs: The Aftermath of MER/29, 56 Cal. L. Rev. 149, 158 (1968); W. P. Keeton, Products Liability—Some Observations About Allocation of Risks, 64 Mich. L. Rev. 1329, 1336 (1966).

**28.** Early examples include Dorsey v. Yoder Co., 331 F.Supp. 753, 759–60 (E.D. Pa. 1971), aff'd, 474 F.2d 1339 (3d Cir. 1973); Phillips v. Kimwood Mach. Co., 525 P.2d 1033, 1036 (Or. 1974); Cepeda v. Cumberland Eng'g Co., Inc., 386 A.2d 816, 829 (N.J. 1978). See generally Dart v. Wiebe Mfg., Inc., 709 P.2d 876 (Ariz. 1985).

**29.** 331 F.Supp. 753 (E.D. Pa. 1971).

edge of the potential dangerous consequences the trial just revealed."[30] More prominently, in *Phillips v. Kimwood Machine Co.*,[31] the Supreme Court of Oregon embraced the test in 1974. A worker injured when a commercial sanding machine ejected a fiberboard sheet sued the manufacturer for failing to either warn of the danger or equip the machine with an inexpensive line of metal teeth that would have prevented the expulsion without interference with the functioning of the machine. Reversing a summary judgment for the manufacturer, the court formulated the test in the following terms:

> A dangerously defective article would be one which a reasonable person would not put into the stream of commerce *if he had knowledge of its harmful character*. The test, therefore, is whether the seller would be negligent if he sold the article *knowing of the risk involved*. Strict liability imposes what amounts to constructive knowledge of the condition of the product.[32]

By the 1980s, courts and commentators had begun to question the fairness and logic of attempting to impose strict liability for design defectiveness,[33] and the only other truly strict test of products liability, the consumer expectations test, had already begun its decline.[34] Recognizing the problems in forcing truly strict liability on manufacturers for dangers in design, Dean Wade and Dean Keeton, in the early 1980s, both repudiated the test(s) that bore their names: Dean Wade claimed that he never meant what he had said,[35] and Dean Keeton admitted that he no longer believed what he had said.[36] The *Products Liability Restatement*, adopting a negligence-type risk-utility standard of liability, based on risks which are *foreseeable* at the time of sale, explicitly rejects the Wade–Keeton test and notes with pith: "The idea has not worn well with time."[37]

Despite the rejection of the Wade–Keeton test by the scholars who gave it birth, courts continued to adopt the test after its "official" demise in the early 1980s,[38] and some have continued rotely to restate

---

**30.** Id. at 759–60, citing W. P. Keeton, Manufacturer's Liability: The Meaning of "Defect" in the Manufacture and Design of Products, 20 Syracuse L. Rev. 559, 568 (1969).

**31.** 525 P.2d 1033 (Or. 1974).

**32.** Id. at 1036 (emphasis in original). The court noted further that "[t]he advantage of describing a dangerous defect in the manner of Wade and Keeton is that it preserves the use of familiar terms and thought processes with which courts, lawyers, and jurors customarily deal." Id. at 1037. Moreover, "[w]hile apparently judging the seller's conduct, the test set out above would actually be a characterization of the product by a jury. If the manufacturer was not acting reasonably in selling the product, knowing of the risks involved, then the product would be dangerously defective when sold and the manufacturer would be

subject to liability." Id. See Vetri, Products Liability: The Developing Framework for Analysis, 54 Or. L. Rev. 293, 299 (1975).

**33.** See §§ 5.4, 8.1, and 8.4, above.

**34.** See §§ 5.4, 5.6, 8.3, and 8.4, above.

**35.** See Wade, On the Effect in Product Liability of Knowledge Unavailable Prior to Marketing, Postscript, 58 N.Y.U. L. Rev. 734, 761 (1983).

**36.** See W. P. Keeton et al., Prosser and Keeton on Torts 697–98 n.21 (5th ed. 1984).

**37.** See Reporters' Note to § 2, cmt. *l*.

**38.** See, e.g., Sternhagen v. Dow Co., 935 P.2d 1139, 1147 (Mont. 1997) (adopting Wade–Keeton constructive knowledge test for strict products liability, and holding that "knowledge of any undiscovered or undiscoverable dangers should be imputed to the manufacturer").

the test,[39] and even proudly to reaffirm allegiance to it while knowing it has died.[40] While one state legislature reversed the judicial adoption of the Wade–Keeton test,[41] another appears to have affirmatively adopted it,[42] and one wonders at its staying power around the nation. The ghost of the Wade–Keeton test continues to haunt judicial halls, but its time has come and gone.

## § 8.8     DESIGN DEFECTIVENESS IN THE THIRD RESTATEMENT

Effectively repealing § 402A of the *Restatement (Second) of Torts,* the *Restatement (Third) of Torts: Products Liability* substantially restructures the principles of responsibility for selling products containing defects in design.[1] Rather than using doctrinal labels of "strict" liability and "negligence," the *Products Liability Restatement* provides separate "functional" definitions of liability for each of the three forms of defect, including defects in design. Sections 1 and 2 set forth the basic principles of a seller's liability for design defectiveness. Section 3 provides a special rule of circumstantial evidence for proof of product defect in cases where

**39.** See, e.g., Irion v. Sun Lighting, Inc., 2004 WL 746823 (Tenn. Ct. App. 2004) (stating hindsight test, now ensconced in statutory form); Golonka v. General Motors Corp., 65 P.3d 956, 963–64 (Ariz. Ct. App. 2003) (applying hindsight test); Donald v. Shinn Fu Co. of Am., 2002 WL 32068351, at *10 (E.D.N.Y. 2002); Beneway v. Superwinch, Inc., 216 F.Supp.2d 24, 29 (N.D.N.Y. 2002); Murphy ex rel. Murphy v. Playtex Family Products Corp., 176 F.Supp.2d 473, 484 (D. Md. 2001), aff'd, 69 Fed.Appx. 140 (4th Cir. 2003) (test for design defectiveness is " 'whether a manufacturer, knowing the risks inherent in his product, acted reasonably in putting it on the market.' "); Sternhagen v. Dow Co., 935 P.2d 1139, 1144 (Mont. 1997) ("Strict liability imposes what amounts to constructive knowledge of the condition of the product."); Sipes v. General Motors Corp., 946 S.W.2d 143, 156 (Tex. App. 1997) ("Under strict liability, one may impute to the manufacturer constructive knowledge of the hazardous condition of the product."); Denny v. Ford Motor Co., 662 N.E.2d 730, 735 (N.Y. 1995) ("the New York standard for determining the existence of a design defect has required an assessment of whether 'if the design defect were known at the time of manufacture, a reasonable person would conclude that the utility of the product did not outweigh the risk inherent in marketing a product designed in that manner' "), citing Voss v. Black & Decker Mfg. Co., 450 N.E.2d 204 (N.Y. 1983). See also Sperry–New Holland v. Prestage, 617 So.2d 248, 254–55 (Miss. 1993).

**40.** See Brooks v. Beech Aircraft Corp., 902 P.2d 54, 63 (N.M. 1995), recognizing that the Wade–Keeton test is now a misnomer, but reaffirming it where the facts did

not show a true advancement in the technological state of the art: "[I]n those hypothetical instances in which technology known at the time of trial and technology knowable at the time of distribution differ—and outside of academic rationale we find little to suggest the existence in practice of unknowable design considerations— it is more fair that the manufacturers and suppliers who have profited from the sale of the product bear the risk of loss." The standard New Mexico jury instruction adopts the Wade–Keeton test from Keeton, Product Liability and the Meaning of Defect, 5 St. Mary's L.J. 30, 37–38 (1973). See *Brooks,* 902 P.2d at 62.

**41.** In 1979, the Oregon legislature abolished the Wade–Keeton test adopted by that state's Supreme Court in Phillips v. Kimwood Mach. Co., 525 P.2d 1033 (Or. 1974), by legislatively adopting Restatement (2d) Torts § 402A, including its comments which define defectiveness in consumer contemplation terms. See Or. Rev. Stat. 30.920; Burns v. General Motors Corp., 891 P.2d 1354 (Or. Ct. App. 1995) (statute inconsistent with instruction on *Phillips'* reasonable manufacturer test). See also McCathern v. Toyota Motor Corp., 23 P.3d 320, 331 (Or. 2001).

**42.** See Tenn. Code Ann. § 29–28–102(8). *But see* id. § 29–28–105. See also Irion v. Sun Lighting, Inc., 2004 WL 746823 (Tenn. Ct. App. 2004) (stating Wade–Keeton hindsight test); Jackson v. General Motors Corp., 60 S.W.3d 800 (Tenn. 2001) (same).

### § 8.8

**1.** For a consideration of the entire Products Liability Restatement, see § 6.5, above.

direct evidence of the cause of an accident is unavailable but where circumstances suggest the probability that a product defect caused the harm;[2] and § 4 concerns the effect on liability of compliance or noncompliance with product safety statutes and regulations.[3] The role of design defectiveness in prescription drug and medical device cases receives separate treatment both in the *Third Restatement* and here.[4]

### Design Defectiveness Under §§ 1 and 2

Section 1 of the *Products Liability Restatement* establishes the basic liability principle of products liability: one who sells "a defective product is subject to liability for harm to persons or property caused by the defect." Section 2, basing liability on the three separate types of defect, provides in subsection (b) that a product "is defective in design when the foreseeable risks of harm posed by the product could have been reduced or avoided by the adoption of a reasonable alternative design by the seller or other distributor, or a predecessor in the commercial chain of distribution, and the omission of the alternative design renders the product not reasonably safe." Stripped to its essence, § 2(b) provides:

> [A product] is defective in design when the foreseeable risks of harm posed by the product could have been reduced or avoided by the adoption of a reasonable alternative design ... and the omission of the alternative design renders the product not reasonably safe.

Paraphrased, § 2(b) provides:

> A product is defective in design if its foreseeable risks could have been avoided by a reasonable alternative design, the omission of which renders the product not reasonably safe.

And § 2(b) may be converted to the active voice:

> A product is defective in design if the seller could have reduced the foreseeable risk that harmed the plaintiff by adopting a reasonable alternative design, the omission of which renders the product not reasonably safe.[5]

By requiring that an alternative design be "reasonable," and basing liability on the manufacturer's failure to adopt such an alternative design only if it renders the product "not reasonably safe," the *Third Restatement* rejects absolute safety in favor of optimality: "Society does not benefit from products that are excessively safe ... any more than it

---

**2.** Although § 3 usually applies to accidents caused by manufacturing defects, it may apply to defects in design. See Rudd v. General Motors Corp., 127 F.Supp.2d 1330, 1340 (M.D. Ala. 2001) (pickup truck's fan blade broke due to fatigue fracture; such fractures might result from selection of low-strength alloy for use in constructing fan); Products Liability Restatement § 3 cmt. *b*. Section 3 of the Restatement and the "malfunction theory" are addressed in § 7.4, above.

**3.** The effect of a manufacturer's compliance and noncompliance with safety stat-

utes and regulations is addressed in § 14.3 (compliance), below, and §§ 2.3 (noncompliance, negligence) and 6.4 (noncompliance, strict liability), above.

**4.** See Products Liability Restatement § 6(c); § 8.10, below.

**5.** For a more complete linguistic deconstruction of § 2(b), see Owen, Defectiveness Restated: Exploding the "Strict" Products Liability Myth, 1996 U. Ill. L. Rev. 743, 766–77.

benefits from products that are too risky. Society benefits most when the right, or optimal, amount of product safety is achieved.''[6] The risk-utility balance prescribed in § 2(b) for defectiveness determinations ordinarily resolves to a negligence-style[7] evaluation of the foreseeable[8] costs and benefits of the manufacturer's decision to forego an alternative design:

> Subsection (b) adopts a reasonableness ("risk-utility balancing") test as the standard for judging the defectiveness of product designs. More specifically, the test is whether a reasonable alternative design would, at reasonable cost, have reduced the foreseeable risks of harm posed by the product and, if so, whether [its] omission ... rendered the product not reasonably safe.[9]

In making the relevant cost-benefit assessment, "[a] broad range of factors may be considered in determining whether an alternative design is reasonable and whether its omission renders a product not reasonably safe.''[10] The balance includes a wide variety of design considerations that often conflict with one another: the foreseeable risks of harm, consumer expectations, usefulness, cost, longevity, responsibility for maintenance, aesthetics, marketability, and other advantages and disadvantages of the chosen and alternative designs.[11] A judge or jury must evaluate these factors with respect to both the accident product as designed and the alternative design feature put forward by the plaintiff. A product's design is "not reasonably safe," and is hence "defective," if a comparison between the accident product without plaintiff's proposed safety feature and the alternative product with it demonstrates that the balance of costs and benefits of the alternative design is better than the balance of these same factors in the chosen design that resulted in the

---

**6.** Products Liability Restatement § 2 cmt. *a*. "Some sort of independent assessment of advantages and disadvantages, to which some attach the label "risk-utility balancing," is necessary.... [T]he various trade-offs need to be considered in determining whether accident costs are more fairly and efficiently borne by accident victims, on the one hand, or, on the other hand, by consumers generally through the mechanism of higher product prices attributable to liability costs imposed by courts on product sellers."

**7.** "Assessment of a product design in most instances requires a comparison between an alternative design and the product design that caused the injury, undertaken from the viewpoint of a reasonable person. That approach is also used in administering the traditional reasonableness standard in negligence. See Restatement (2d) Torts § 283, cmt. *c*. The policy reasons that support use of a reasonable-person perspective in connection with the general negligence standard also support its use in the products liability context." Id. cmt. *d*. See also id. § 1 cmt. *a*.

**8.** In the black-letter definition of design defectiveness in § 2(b), set forth above, the Third Restatement limits a seller's responsibility to risks that are "foreseeable," an important limitation explained in comment *a*:

> Most courts agree that, for the liability system to be fair and efficient, the balancing of risks and benefits in judging product design and marketing must be done in light of the knowledge of risks and risk-avoidance techniques reasonably attainable at the time of distribution. To hold a manufacturer liable for a risk that was not foreseeable when the product was marketed might foster increased manufacturer investment in safety. But such investment by definition would be a matter of guesswork. Furthermore, manufacturers may persuasively ask to be judged by a normative behavior standard to which it is reasonably possible for manufacturers to conform. For these reasons, Subsections (b) and (c) speak of products being defective only when risks are reasonably foreseeable.

**9.** Id., cmt. *d*.

**10.** Id., cmt. *f*.

**11.** See id.

accident.[12] And the converse is also true: if the balance of competing design considerations in the accident product without the proposed safety feature was as good as or better than the balance in the proposed alternative design, then the accident product's design will be deemed "reasonably safe" and "nondefective."[13] In short, "the requirement of Subsection (b) that a product is defective in design if the foreseeable risks of harm could have been reduced by a reasonable alternative design is based on the commonsense notion that liability for harm caused by product designs should attach only when harm is reasonably preventable."[14]

### Consumer Expectations

One of the most controversial aspects of the *Third Restatement*'s definition of design defectiveness concerns the elimination of consumer expectations as an independent test of liability and the relegation of those expectations to mere "factor" status in the list of risk-utility considerations.[15] Comment *g* declares: "Under Subsection (b), consumer expectations do not constitute an independent standard for judging the defectiveness of product designs."[16] Although not determinative in most cases, if consumer safety expectations are implicated by a particular design, they factor into an evaluation of whether the manufacturer should have adopted a reasonable alternative design.[17] Moreover, the *Restatement* makes clear that manufacturers and other sellers may not use consumer expectations as a defense when they fail to eliminate substantial hazards, even if obvious, which may easily be designed

---

**12.** The plaintiff, of course, must also prove causation–that the alternative product would have prevented or reduced his harm. See id. § 1; § 2, cmts. *f* and *q*; and § 15. Causation is treated generally in id. §§ 15 and 16.

**13.** A "better balance" definition of defective design is proposed in Owen, Defectiveness Restated: Exploding the "Strict" Products Liability Myth, 1996 U. Ill. L. Rev. 743, 775.

**14.** Products Liability Restatement § 2 cmt. *f*.

**15.** See, e.g., Shapo, A New Legislation: Remarks on the Draft Restatement of Products Liability, 30 U. Mich. J.L. Reform 215 (1997); Vandall, Constructing a Roof Before the Foundation Is Prepared: The Restatement (Third) of Torts: Products Liability Design Defect, 30 U. Mich. J.L. Reform 261 (1997); Vargo, The Emperor's New Clothes: The American Law Institute Adorns a "New Cloth" for Section 402A Products Liability Design Defects—A Survey of the States Reveals a Different Weave, 26 U. Mem. L. Rev. 493, 557 (1996); Shapo, In Search of the Law of Products Liability: The ALI Restatement Project, 48 Vand. L. Rev. 631 (1995); Phillips, Achilles' Heel, 61 Tenn. L. Rev. 1265 (1994).

**16.** Products Liability Restatement § 2 cmt. *g*.

**17.** See id.:

[C]onsumer expectations do not play a determinative role in determining defectiveness. See Comment *h*. Consumer expectations, standing alone, do not take into account whether the proposed alternative design could be implemented at reasonable cost, or whether an alternative design would provide greater overall safety. Nevertheless, consumer expectations about product performance and the dangers attendant to product use affect how risks are perceived and relate to foreseeability and frequency of the risks of harm, both of which are relevant under Subsection (b). See Comment *f*. Such expectations are often influenced by how products are portrayed and marketed and can have a significant impact on consumer behavior. Thus, although consumer expectations do not constitute an independent standard for judging the defectiveness of product designs, they may substantially influence or even be ultimately determinative on risk-utility balancing in judging whether the omission of a proposed alternative design renders the product not reasonably safe.

away.[18]

## Special Design Defect Issues

### *Inherently Dangerous Products*

While proof of a reasonable alternative design is normally required to establish design defectiveness under § 2(b), generic risks in certain products may be impossible to design away. Ordinarily, there can be no recovery for injuries from the "design" of such products because the plaintiff cannot prove the availability of a reasonable alternative design.[19] The *Second Restatement* immunized sellers of such products specifically from design defect liability, listing ordinary sugar (which can cause diabetes), castor oil (used by Mussolini as an instrument of torture), "good whiskey," "good tobacco," "good butter" (containing cholesterol which can lead to heart attacks), eggs and strawberries (to which some people are allergic), and prescription drugs, such as the Pasteur vaccine for rabies (which sometimes causes severe adverse reactions).[20] As examined elsewhere,[21] the *Third Restatement* takes a similar position, providing that "[c]ommon and widely distributed products such as alcoholic beverages, firearms, and above-ground swimming pools may be found to be defective" in design only if the plaintiff proves a reasonable alternative design under subsection 2(b).[22]

Noticeably absent in the *Third Restatement* from the special list of generically dangerous products protected from judicial scrutiny are tobacco products (cigarettes, in particular), and they just narrowly missed the boat. Yet "tobacco" was in fact on the list of protected products in the *Proposed Final Draft* of the *Third Restatement*, sandwiched between alcoholic beverages and firearms. At the final meeting of the American Law Institute on the *Third Restatement*, after five years of intense debate over thousands of particulars, during the closing moments of final discussion a member moved from the floor to strike "tobacco" from the short list of examples of protected products. Noting the increasing national crescendo of legal and political attacks against cigarette manufacturers then in progress, he argued that the American Law Institute should not go on record as providing favored treatment for this product.

---

**18.** "Subsection (b) likewise rejects conformance to consumer expectations as a defense. The mere fact that a risk presented by a product design is open and obvious, or generally known, and that the product thus satisfies expectations, does not prevent a finding that the design is defective.... [W]hile disappointment of consumer expectations may not serve as an independent basis for allowing recovery under Subsection (b), neither may conformance with consumer expectations serve as an independent basis for denying recovery. Such expectations may be relevant in both contexts, but in neither are they controlling." Id.

**19.** Id., cmt. *d*.

**20.** See Restatement (2d) Torts § 402A cmts. *i*, *j*, and *k*, discussed in §§ 6.2, above, and 10.3, below.

**21.** See id.

**22.** Products Liability Restatement cmt. *d*. In the absence of normal proof of a design or other defect, the comment notes that "courts have not imposed liability for categories of products that are generally available and widely used and consumed, even if they pose substantial risks of harm. Instead, courts generally have concluded that legislatures and administrative agencies can, more appropriately than courts, consider the desirability of commercial distribution of some categories of widely used and consumed, but nevertheless dangerous, products." Id.

The unscheduled motion caught almost everyone by surprise, and, after a brief debate in which the Reporters explained again that the court decisions to date supported leaving tobacco within the protected category, the motion to strike "tobacco" carried by a whisker. Thus, the *Restatement (Third) of Torts: Products Liability* takes no explicit position on whether sellers should be liable for the inherent dangers contained in tobacco products.[23]

Comment *e* to § 2 of the *Third Restatement* addresses the related, controversial issue of whether courts should hold manufacturers liable for selling products with generic risks so serious that they may be viewed as possessing "manifestly unreasonable designs."[24] Such products fortunately now are rare, but, in former times, lawn darts, highly flammable hula skirts, and similarly hazardous products containing substantial threats to safety but little social utility were no strangers to the market. There are a paucity of cases on the topic of whether courts should second-guess the market with respect to such manifestly unreasonable designs,[25] but comment *e* adopts the dicta from a small number of cases suggesting that a manufacturer might properly be subject to liability for harm from selling a product if "the extremely high degree of danger posed by its use or consumption so substantially outweighs its negligible social utility that no rational, reasonable person, fully aware of the relevant facts, would choose to use, or to allow children to use, the product."[26] The broader issue of products with generic risks is examined elsewhere in greater depth.[27]

### Obvious Dangers and Misuse

Two major issues of design defectiveness involve whether a product should be characterized as defectively designed if its dangers are obvious or result from product misuse and alteration. On these important issues, treated extensively below,[28] the new *Restatement* follows well-accepted judicial norms. The obviousness of a danger is relevant to design defectiveness because the obvious nature of the danger gives warning to persons who confront it so that they are likely to act to protect themselves.[29] But the new *Restatement* summarily rejects the long-discredited patent danger rule which barred recovery altogether in such cases.[30]

When people use and abuse products unreasonably and unforeseeably, courts generally relieve sellers of at least partial responsibility for resulting harm.[31] Products cannot be designed to be perfectly safe for

---

**23.** For a discussion of products containing generic risks, including cigarettes, see § 10.3, below.

**24.** This issue lies closely beside the problem of design defect liability for alcohol, certain types of guns, and cigarettes, but the Restatement segregates those products (except tobacco) in comment *d* and separately classifies this topic in comment *e*.

**25.** Products Liability Restatement § 2 Reporters' Note to cmt. *e*.

**26.** Products Liability Restatement § 2 cmt. *e*.

**27.** See §§ 6.2, above, and 10.3, below.

**28.** The issue of a seller's liability for obvious dangers is examined in § 10.2, below; the role of product misuse is treated in § 13.5, below; and product alteration is treated in § 12.3, below.

**29.** Products Liability Restatement § 2 cmt. *d*.

**30.** Id.

**31.** "Product sellers ... are not required to foresee and take precautions against every conceivable mode of use and abuse to which their products might be put.

every use, and so the doctrines of product misuse and alteration provide important limitations on liability for the sale of defective products. In general, manufacturers and other sellers have no duty to design against unintended uses, misuses, and alterations that cannot be foreseen, but the converse is also true: sellers must adopt reasonable design precautions against product uses and abuses which they reasonably should foresee.[32] Further, third party misuse raises principles of intervening and superseding causation that may bar liability altogether if a misuse was unforeseeable,[33] and principles of comparative responsibility generally reduce a manufacturer's responsibility proportionately to the user's fault in putting a product to an improper type or extent of use.[34] The *Third Restatement* adopts these widespread principles on the role of product alteration and misuse,[35] topics which are addressed below.[36]

## § 8.9 OPTIONAL SAFETY DEVICES

Sometimes manufacturers offer safety devices only as optional add-ons to their products rather than installing them as mandatory features of every product unit sold. For example, a manufacturer may sell a chain saw with an optional, rather than a mandatory, chain brake;[1] a radial arm saw with an optional, non-mandatory lower blade guard;[2] a forklift,[3] tractor,[4] loader,[5] or tractor loader,[6] with an optional rather than mandatory overhead guard; a truck chassis and cab,[7] forklift,[8] or bus[9] with an optional backup alarm; a concrete mixer truck with an optional platform guardrail;[10] an industrial machine with an optional aural start-up warn-

Increasing the costs of designing and marketing products in order to avoid the consequences of unreasonable modes of use is not required." Products Liability Restatement § 2 cmt. *m*.

**32.** Products Liability and Safety, at 471–87.

**33.** See id. at 613–37.

**34.** See Products Liability Restatement § 2 cmt. *p*.

**35.** See id. § 2 comments *m* (foreseeability of risk) and *p* (misuse, modification, and alteration); § 15 (legal causation); § 17 (apportionment of responsibility). Damages apportionment, treated generally in § 17 as an issue of comparative responsibility, is addressed thoroughly in its own Restatement. See Restatement (Third) of Torts: Apportionment of Liability (2000).

**36.** See § 12.3 (intervening and superseding causation) and ch. 13 (user misconduct defenses), below.

### § 8.9

**1.** See, e.g., Nettles v. Electrolux Motor AB, 784 F.2d 1574 (11th Cir. 1986) (Ala. law).

**2.** See, e.g., Sears, Roebuck & Co. v. Kunze, 996 S.W.2d 416 (Tex. App. 1999).

**3.** See, e.g., Geddes v. Crown Equip. Corp., 709 N.Y.S.2d 770 (App. Div. 2000);

Christopherson v. Hyster Co., 374 N.E.2d 858 (Ill. App. Ct. 1978).

**4.** See, e.g., Austin v. Clark Equip. Co., 48 F.3d 833 (4th Cir. 1995) (Va. law); Morrison v. Kubota Tractor Corp., 891 S.W.2d 422 (Mo. Ct. App. 1994); Davis v. Caterpillar Tractor Co., 719 P.2d 324 (Colo. Ct. App. 1985).

**5.** See, e.g., Biss v. Tenneco, Inc., 409 N.Y.S.2d 874 (App. Div. 1978).

**6.** See, e.g., Pahuta v. Massey–Ferguson, Inc., 170 F.3d 125 (2d Cir. 1999) (N.Y. law).

**7.** See, e.g., Ogletree v. Navistar Int'l Transp. Corp., 535 S.E.2d 545 (Ga. Ct. App. 2000); Verge v. Ford Motor Co., 581 F.2d 384 (3d Cir. 1978) (V.I. law).

**8.** See, e.g., Euclides Campos v. Crown Equip. Corp., 35 Fed.Appx. 31 (2d Cir. 2002) (N.Y. law); Dean v. Toyota Indus. Equip. Mfg., Inc., 540 S.E.2d 233 (Ga. Ct. App. 2000); Patane v. Thompson & Johnson Equip. Co., 649 N.Y.S.2d 547 (App. Div. 1996); Austin v. Clark Equip. Co., 48 F.3d 833 (4th Cir. 1995) (Va. law).

**9.** See, e.g., Scarangella v. Thomas Built Buses, Inc., 717 N.E.2d 679 (N.Y. 1999).

**10.** See, e.g., Pigliavento v. Tyler Equip. Corp., 669 N.Y.S.2d 747 (App. Div. 1998).

ing horn;[11] or a motorcycle, with or without leg-protective crash bars at the option of the buyer.[12] If a purchaser rejects an optional safety device, and the purchaser, user, or a third party is subsequently injured in a manner that the safety device would have prevented, the accident victim may seek recovery against the manufacturer for failing to incorporate the safety device as a standard feature of the product. Whether such a claim may lie is a question that has confounded courts and commentators.[13]

Cases involving the liability of a manufacturer for providing optional rather than mandatory safety devices raise issues of duty,[14] defectiveness (or negligence),[15] and actual and proximate causation.[16] More broadly, they raise fundamental questions of how far manufacturers should be required to design safety features into their products, raising their costs and diminishing their utility, which many purchasers do not want but which reduce the risks of certain types of injuries. In addition, whether the law prescribes a no-duty rule in certain types of optional safety device cases raises significant issues of allocation of power between courts and juries.

Whether a manufacturer is subject to liability for allowing buyers to decide whether or not a product should be equipped with a particular safety feature is part of the broader issue of design defectiveness, or the scope of a manufacturer's design responsibilities, previously discussed. As a general proposition, it may be said that if the safety of a product can be substantially enhanced by adding a practical, relatively inexpensive safety device that does not appreciably diminish the product's usefulness, then the manufacturer is obligated to add the feature, and to make it mandatory.[17] Thus, even if the manufacturer were to offer such a feature as optional equipment, a court normally would conclude that a product sold without such a feasible, safety-enhancing, inexpensive safe-

---

**11.** See, e.g., Davidson v. Besser Co., 70 F.Supp.2d 1020 (E.D. Mo. 1999).

**12.** See, e.g., Rainbow v. Albert Elia Bldg. Co., 436 N.Y.S.2d 480 (App. Div. 1981).

**13.** See Powell, Products Liability and Optional Safety Equipment—Who Knows More?, 73 Neb. L. Rev. 843, 866–67 (1994); Annot., 99 A.L.R.3d 693 (1980) (supplier's obligation to supply or recommend safety devices for industrial equipment).

**14.** Compare Bexiga v. Havir Mfg. Corp., 290 A.2d 281 (N.J. 1972) (general duty to supply safety devices), with Passante v. Agway Consumer Prods., 741 N.Y.S.2d 624, 626 (App. Div. 2002) (no duty to supply safety device where buyer is in superior position to manufacturer to conduct risk-utility analysis); Coleman v. Cintas Sales Corp., 40 S.W.3d 544 (Tex. App. 2001) (when seller offers buyers option of flame-retardant uniforms or flammable uniforms, depending on whether employees will be exposed to ignition sources, seller not liable for selling employer cheaper and more comfortable flammable uniforms); Biss v. Tenneco, Inc., 409 N.Y.S.2d 874 (App. Div. 1978) (no general duty to supply safety devices).

**15.** See, e.g., Tannebaum v. Yale Materials Handling Corp., 38 F.Supp.2d 425 (D. Md. 1999) (summary judgment for defendant; not defective as matter of law); Fernandez v. Ford Motor Co., 879 P.2d 101 (N.M. Ct. App. 1994) (reversing summary judgment for defendant; unreasonably dangerous issue for jury).

**16.** See, e.g., Ogletree v. Navistar Int'l Trans. Corp., 535 S.E.2d 545 (Ga. Ct. App. 2000) (no cause in fact or proximate causation as matter of law); Davidson v. Besser Co., 70 F.Supp.2d 1020, 1027 (E.D. Mo. 1999) ("in the face of the literature sent by the defendant," whether employer's failure to install purchased safety device was superseding cause of accident was question of fact for jury).

**17.** This conclusion is based on simple cost-benefit analysis, examined in § 8.4, above.

ty feature renders the product defective[18] and the manufacturer negligent for failing to equip the product with the feature as a standard part of the design.[19] For example, most courts would agree that a pressure gauge equipped with a lucite lens that foreseeably fractures, injuring a worker's eye, is defective, even if a safer, shatterproof lens is offered as an option at a slightly greater cost.[20] And the converse is also true: because some safety features may not be particularly effective, practical, or cost-effective, and may even increase various dangers, a product may *not* be defective for failing to include such a safety device as standard equipment.[21] Thus, although closing the rear opening of a forklift may reduce a very small risk that an operator may be ejected through the opening, a forklift without such a standard design feature is not defective because such a feature would diminish the convenience and safety of the forklift by eliminating a useful egress.[22]

Although manufacturers sometimes fail to incorporate safety devices into their products simply to improve their competitive position,[23] without regard to safety, manufacturers generally provide safety devices on an optional rather than mandatory basis in order to make a product more adaptable for a variety of uses. Overhead guards on forklifts, for example, are important safety enhancements for most purposes, but they may render such vehicles unusable for passing under low doorways;[24] motorcycle leg guards undoubtedly enhance safety for many uses, but they may diminish safety for others;[25] point-of-operation guards add vital safety to industrial presses put to certain uses, but they may interfere, possibly dangerously, with certain other functions;[26] and while roll-over protection structures (ROPS) add an important safety dimension to tractors used on hilly farms, they offer little protection, and add unnecessary cost and inconvenience, when used on flat terrain.[27] In short, safety features that are feasible, cost-effective, and vitally important in some contexts may be unnecessary, inconvenient, and even dangerous in

---

**18.**  See id.

**19.**  See § 2.2, above.

**20.**  See Helicoid Gage Div. of Am. Chain & Cable Co. v. Howell, 511 S.W.2d 573 (Tex. App. 1974).

**21.**  See, e.g., Banzhaf v. ADT Sec. Sys. Southwest, Inc., 28 S.W.3d 180 (Tex. App. 2000) (court refused to second-guess convenience store's decision not to add distress feature to security system for fear that it might endanger employees). See also Bates v. Richland Sales Corp., 803 N.E.2d 977 (Ill. App. Ct. 2004) (optional, removable roll bar on loader would have prevented death of operator; permanent roll bar had been removed to allow better access); Berczyk v. Emerson Tool Co., 291 F.Supp.2d 1004, 1007 (D. Minn. 2003) (optional lower blade guard for radial saw could increase risks).

**22.**  See Tannebaum v. Yale Materials Handling Corp., 38 F.Supp.2d 425 (D. Md. 1999) (forklift not defective under risk-utility test as matter of law; manufacturer's motion for summary judgment granted).

**23.**  See, e.g., Derrick v. Yoder Co., 410 N.E.2d 1030, 1038–39 (Ill. App. Ct. 1980).

**24.**  See, e.g., Bates v. Richland Sales Corp., 803 N.E.2d 977 (Ill. App. Ct. 2004) (optional, removable roll bar on loader would have prevented death of operator; permanent roll bar had been removed to allow better access); Christopherson v. Hyster Co., 374 N.E.2d 858 (Ill. App. Ct. 1978) (but duty to supply guards was nondelegable, notwithstanding buyer's insistence that forklift not have guards to permit its use in low-clearance areas, because of evidence that retractable overhead guards were then available).

**25.**  Rainbow v. Albert Elia Bldg. Co., 436 N.Y.S.2d 480, 483 (App. Div. 1981).

**26.**  See, e.g., Bexiga v. Havir Mfg. Corp., 290 A.2d 281 (N.J. 1972) (but two-button control would not so interfere).

**27.**  See, e.g., Morrison v. Kubota Tractor Corp., 891 S.W.2d 422 (Mo. Ct. App. 1994).

others. Just as consumers want and need vehicles and other products that come in varying size, shape, power, and even color, depending on their special needs and preferences, the type and amount of safety individual consumers may need and want also varies according to their special needs and preferences. One safety size, in short, may not fit all.

It is often asserted that there are two lines of conflicting authority on the optional safety device issue: one holding that a manufacturer cannot delegate important safety decisions to consumers and another holding that a manufacturer has no duty to equip its products with mandatory safety features if consumers are informed of the availability of such devices as optional equipment.[28] While this classification has some value, it glosses over the variations in the decisions and ignores the frequent overlap between the two approaches which undermines meaningful analysis of the cases. In truth, it is difficult to classify the cases on optional safety devices with clarity because the law in this area is muddled and quite sparse.

The debate over whether a manufacturer should be subject to design defect liability for offering consumers safety features on an optional rather than mandatory basis finds its origins in *Bexiga v. Havir Manufacturing Corp.*,[29] an important, early case examining the general duty of manufacturers to equip machinery with safety devices.[30] The plaintiff was injured while adjusting a piece of metal beneath the ram of an unguarded punch press when he mistakenly depressed the foot control. The trial and intermediate appellate courts held that the plaintiff could not maintain a design defect claim against the manufacturer of the press for failing to guard the machine because, by custom and state statute, responsibility for guarding industrial machinery lay with the employer-purchasers of such machinery rather than with the manufacturer.[31] Reversing, the Supreme Court of New Jersey ruled that the manufacturer was in a better position than the employer to install feasible safety devices on industrial machinery. The court reasoned that manufacturers can make better decisions about what types of safety devices are reasonably necessary on such machinery, and that the law should place responsibility for such devices on manufacturers rather than leaving such critical decisions about design safety to "the haphazard conduct" of buyers.[32]

**28.** See, e.g., Powell, Products Liability and Optional Safety Equipment—Who Knows More?, 73 Neb. L. Rev. 843, 866–67 (1994).

**29.** 290 A.2d 281 (N.J. 1972).

**30.** For an earlier case arriving at the same conclusion, see Rhoads v. Service Mach. Co., 329 F.Supp. 367 (E.D. Ark. 1971).

**31.** Bexiga v. Havir Mfg. Corp., 290 A.2d 281, 283–84 (N.J. 1972).

**32.** See id. at 285:

Where a manufacturer places into the channels of trade a finished product which can be put to use and which should be provided with safety devices because without such it creates an unreasonable risk of harm, and where such safety devices can feasibly be installed by the manufacturer, the fact that he expects that someone else will install such devices should not immunize him. The public interest in assuring that safety devices are installed demands more from the manufacturer than to permit him to leave such a critical phase of his manufacturing process to the haphazard conduct of the ultimate purchaser. The only way to be certain that such devices will be installed on all machines—which clearly the public interest requires—is to place the duty on the manufacturer where it is feasible for him to do so.

Although *Bexiga* did not directly involve the issue of optional safety devices, its holding that manufacturers may not delegate design safety decisions to purchasers lay the foundation for the optional safety device debate. Quickly becoming a landmark for the "nondelegable duty doctrine,"[33] *Bexiga* provided a beacon for the view that manufacturers, even if they have a reasonable basis for believing that purchasers normally will add appropriate safety devices to their products, should nevertheless bear ultimate responsibility for harm caused by a buyer's failure to add such design features as may be necessary to make its product reasonably safe. Sometimes citing *Bexiga*,[34] but often not,[35] a number of courts have ruled that a manufacturer may not delegate its safe-design responsibility by offering as optional equipment a safety device necessary to a product's safety.

Six years after *Bexiga*, two cases were decided quite the other way, shielding manufacturers from liability for delegating the choice of appropriate safety devices to purchasers down the chain of distribution. In the first, *Verge v. Ford Motor Co.*,[36] a garbage truck without a back-up buzzer backed into and squashed a garbage man against a garbage can. The garbage truck had been assembled by a company that installed a compactor unit on a multi-purpose flat-bed truck cab and chassis it had purchased from Ford Motor Company. In an action against Ford and the garbage truck assembler for failing to equip the vehicle with a back-up buzzer, the Third Circuit ruled that Ford had no duty to install the alarm. Reversing judgment on a verdict for the plaintiff, the court reasoned, based on (1) trade custom, (2) the relative expertise of the parties, and (3) feasibility, that the assembler alone should bear responsibility for the selection and installation of appropriate safety equipment on the final truck.[37]

Three months after *Verge*, a New York appellate court decided *Biss v. Tenneco, Inc.*,[38] which involved a multi-use loader that slid off a road, tipped over, and squashed the operator between the loader and a pole. A design defect claim was instituted against the manufacturer for failing to build into the vehicle a roll-over protective structure (ROPS), which might have saved the plaintiff's life, rather than offering it merely as optional equipment. When the plaintiff's employer purchased the loader for use in its logging operations, it knew that the ROPS was available as

If the absence of a safety device on a product subjects users to an unreasonable risk, then the product may be found defectively designed unless "the device would render the machine unusable for its intended purposes." Id. Because the jury might reasonably have concluded that the manufacturer could feasibly have used a safe two-button device for activating the press in lieu of the dangerous foot-pedal method without sacrificing any uses of the press, the court ruled that the trial judge should not have dismissed the plaintiff's strict liability design defect claim.

**33.** See, e.g., Note, 86 Harv. L. Rev. 923 (1973) (noting *Bexiga*).

**34.** See, e.g., Fernandez v. Ford Motor Co., 879 P.2d 101, 111–12 (N.M. Ct. App. 1994) (thorough discussion, citing numerous cases both ways); Bilotta v. Kelley Co., 346 N.W.2d 616 (Minn. 1984).

**35.** See, e.g., Sears, Roebuck & Co. v. Kunze, 996 S.W.2d 416 (Tex. App. 1999); Nettles v. Electrolux Motor AB, 784 F.2d 1574 (11th Cir. 1986) (Ala. law); Caterpillar v. Ford, 406 So.2d 854 (Ala. 1981); Helicoid Gage Div. of Am. Chain & Cable Co. v. Howell, 511 S.W.2d 573 (Tex. App. 1974).

**36.** 581 F.2d 384 (3d Cir. 1978) (V.I. law).

**37.** Id. at 387–90.

**38.** 409 N.Y.S.2d 874 (App. Div. 1978).

an option from the manufacturer. Affirming a dismissal of the plaintiff's claim, the New York court reasoned that the manufacturer's only duty was to assure that appropriate safety devices were made known and available to the purchaser because the danger of a roll-over varies with the nature of particular job sites where particular buyers use the loader, an issue on which the buyer has better information than the manufacturer. Consequently, a buyer informed of an available safety option like a ROPS is in a better position than the manufacturer to make an informed cost-benefit decision on whether the machine should be equipped with such a safety device.[39] Other courts, particularly in New York,[40] have followed the *Verge-Biss* approach of not holding manufacturers to an unwavering duty to equip their products with standard safety features if such features are available to purchasers as optional equipment.[41]

While the *Bexiga* nondelegable duty doctrine and the *Verge-Biss* no-duty to supply safety devices as standard equipment doctrine may be contrasted as "radically different point[s] of view"[42] if formulated in bluntest fashion, all three cases contain caveats that diminish their differences and lead toward middle ground. In *Bexiga*, for example, the New Jersey court carefully limited its holding in two respects: (1) to cases where it was "feasible" to install a particular safety device "on all machines," and (2) to those where "the device would [not] render the machine unusable for its intended purposes."[43] Thus, *Bexiga* "does not imply automatic manufacturers' liability" and is consistent with the view that the nondelegable duty applies only when no single safety device can be employed effectively for all the product's uses.[44] By the terms of *Bexiga* itself, it is not "feasible" for a manufacturer to install a one-size-fits-all safety device as standard equipment on a multi-purpose product if the device makes the product "unusable" for one of its functions.[45] Thus, even under *Bexiga*, a manufacturer does not have a

**39.** Id. at 876–77.

**40.** See, e.g., Bova v. Caterpillar, Inc., 761 N.Y.S.2d 85 (App. Div. 2003); Passante v. Agway Consumer Prods., Inc., 741 N.Y.S.2d 624 (App. Div. 2002) (3–2 opinion); Beneway v. Superwinch, Inc., 216 F.Supp.2d 24, 30 (N.D.N.Y. 2002); Geddes v. Crown Equip. Corp., 709 N.Y.S.2d 770 (App. Div. 2000); Rainbow v. Albert Elia Bldg. Co., 436 N.Y.S.2d 480 (App. Div. 1981). In Scarangella v. Thomas Built Buses, Inc., 717 N.E.2d 679, 683 (N.Y. 1999), affirming summary judgment for the defendant, the New York Court of Appeals held that a product is not defectively designed where the evidence reveals that: (1) the buyer is thoroughly knowledgeable about the product, its use, and the availability of the safety feature; (2) the product is safe for some normal use without the optional equipment; and (3) "the buyer is in a position, given the range of uses of the product, to balance the benefits and the risks of not having the safety device in the specifically contemplated circumstances of the buyer's use of the product." Id. at 683.

**41.** See, e.g., Ogletree v. Navistar Int'l Transp. Corp., 535 S.E.2d 545 (Ga. Ct. App.

2000) (no causation); Tannebaum v. Yale Materials Handling Corp., 38 F.Supp.2d 425 (D. Md. 1999) (no defect in design); Austin v. Clark Equip. Co., 48 F.3d 833 (4th Cir. 1995) (Va. law); Scallan v. Duriron Co., 11 F.3d 1249 (5th Cir. 1994) (La. law); Morrison v. Kubota Tractor Corp., 891 S.W.2d 422, 428–29 (Mo. Ct. App. 1994) (citing cases); Davis v. Caterpillar Tractor Co., 719 P.2d 324 (Colo. Ct. App. 1985) (no design defect); Gordon v. Niagra Mach. & Tool Works, 574 F.2d 1182 (5th Cir. 1978) (Miss. law).

**42.** See Powell, Products Liability and Optional Safety Equipment—Who Knows More?, 73 Neb. L. Rev. 843, 876 (1994).

**43.** Id.

**44.** Westbrock v. Marshalltown Mfg. Co., 473 N.W.2d 352, 357 (Minn. Ct. App. 1991).

**45.** Id. at 358. An earlier Minnesota decision, Bilotta v. Kelley Co., 346 N.W.2d 616, 624 (Minn. 1984), which adopted the *Bexiga* nondelegable duty doctrine, observed this limitation on the doctrine, noting that the *Biss* no-duty doctrine "can

duty to provide a guard that sacrifices a product's "multi-functional nature."[46] Since *Biss* itself involved a multi-purpose vehicle and *Verge* involved a multi-purpose cab and chassis flatbed truck, the *Bexiga* and *Biss-Verge* doctrines may be seen as converging into a single subdoctrine that manufacturers ordinarily may offer safety features as optional rather than standard equipment on multi-functional products if there is no standard safety feature that will allow each function to operate unimpeded.

Apart from whether a product has one or multiple uses, and whether or not a reasonable safety feature exists that is compatible with each use, courts have pointed to other factors relevant to whether a manufacturer may satisfy its design obligations by supplying safety features as optional equipment. Such factors include the relative expertise of the parties,[47] which party could more feasibly have installed the safety device,[48] the dangerousness of the product without the safety device,[49] the obviousness of the danger,[50] the cost of the safety feature,[51] industry custom,[52] and the sophistication of consumers of the particular type of product.[53] Consumer sophistication is an especially important factor, since the justification for allowing manufacturers to delegate some portion of design safety responsibility to purchasers is the assumption that purchasers can make better cost-benefit analyses of whether particular safety features are appropriate for their own particular needs.[54] For this reason, most of the cases protecting manufacturers from liability for offering optional safety devices involve industrial machines purchased by sophisticated commercial buyers. But there are contexts where ordinary consumers are likely to be well-informed about the risks and benefits of particular types of guards that may interfere with some ways in which a product may be used, such as complex wood-working saws, and there would appear to be no good reason to force all woodworkers to buy a

---

be justified only where multi-use equipment is involved and the optional device would impair the equipment's utility" for certain uses.

**46.** While *Bexiga* itself involved a multi-purpose press, the safety device at issue there, a two-button control mechanism, was consistent with all functions of the press.

**47.** See, e.g., Verge v. Ford Motor Co., 581 F.2d 384 (3d Cir. 1978) (V.I. law).

**48.** See, e.g., id.

**49.** See Annot., 99 A.L.R.3d 693, § 2 (1980).

**50.** See, e.g., Price v. Niagara Mach. & Tool Works, 136 Cal.Rptr. 535 (Ct. App. 1977).

**51.** See, e.g., Bilotta v. Kelley Co., 346 N.W.2d 616 (Minn. 1984); Helicoid Gage Div. of Am. Chain & Cable Co. v. Howell, 511 S.W.2d 573 (Tex. App. 1974).

**52.** See, e.g., Verge v. Ford Motor Co., 581 F.2d 384 (3d Cir. 1978) (V.I. law).

**53.** See, e.g., Rainbow v. Albert Elia Bldg. Co., 436 N.Y.S.2d 480, 483 (App. Div. 1981); Noonan v. Texaco, Inc., 713 P.2d

160, 163 (Wyo. 1986). See generally Powell, Products Liability and Optional Safety Equipment—Who Knows More?, 73 Neb. L. Rev. 843, 881–82 (1994) (endorsing "sophisticated consumer" approach).

**54.** See, e.g., Davis v. Caterpillar Tractor Co., 719 P.2d 324, 327 (Colo. Ct. App. 1985). See also Noonan v. Texaco, Inc., 713 P.2d 160 (Wyo. 1986); Wagner v. International Harvester Co., 611 F.2d 224 (8th Cir. 1979) (Ill. law) (appropriate safety device not offered to purchasers on facts of case, but protecting sellers who offer optional safety devices is "basically sound"):

> According to this theory, the purchaser of multi-use equipment knows best the dangers associated with its particular use, and so it should determine the degree of safety provided. That is to say, the purchaser may be in the best position to make the cost-benefit analysis implicit in the principles of general negligence. Imposing liability on such a purchaser would result in minimizing the sum of accident and preventive costs.

Id. at 231.

guard that interferes with a normal operation of such a machine. At least a couple decisions support this view, one holding that a manufacturer may sell a motorcycle with optional leg-protection crash bars to a buyer who is an experienced motorcycle enthusiast,[55] and another allowing a manufacturer to sell a tractor with an optional roll-over protection system to an experienced farmer.[56] Both reasoned that the plaintiff, not the manufacturer, "was in the best position to exercise an intelligent judgment in making the trade-off between cost and function" in order to decide whether the particular safety devices were reasonably necessary for the buyer's particular purposes.[57]

Perhaps the most significant distinction between the two "conflicting" doctrines on optional safety devices is whether the issue presents a duty question of law for the court or a factual question for the jury. But even here, there are cases in jurisdictions following the *Bexiga* approach that hold that a manufacturer has no duty to offer safety features only as standard equipment,[58] and cases in *Biss-Verge* jurisdictions holding that the matter is for the jury.[59] Indeed, the New York courts may be retreating from the no-duty aspect of the *Biss* line of cases.[60] Nor does the no-duty approach address the fact that the question of how responsibility over safety devices should be allocated between courts and juries is peculiarly fact-sensitive and hence appropriate for factual distinctions. Moreover, while the no-duty approach often appears to make most sense, it fails to recognize a purchasing employer's natural tendency to prefer an uncertain future risk to its employees, who bear substantial responsibility for their own safety and are covered by workers' compensation, over having to absorb a certain and immediate expense in purchasing an optional safety feature. Nor does the no-duty approach recognize the fact that the uses of construction equipment, punch presses, and other heavy machinery that may last for decades change over time, and a safety device that is unnecessary for the machine's immediate intended uses may be necessary for the uses of tomorrow.

If an important safety feature can reasonably be integrated as a standard feature without diminishing a product's utility, a manufacturer ordinarily should not be permitted to delegate the issue of whether to include the safety feature to purchasers likely to make improper cost-benefit safety decisions. But whether safety devices should be added to certain products, especially when those devices interfere with important functions of a multi-use product, is a decision that sometimes is better assessed by purchasers than manufacturers, particularly if the consumer

---

**55.** "[P]laintiff was an experienced motorcyclist and he had been a successful motorcycle racer for many years. He testified that he was familiar with crash bars and their availability and that in fact he had removed crash bars mounted on a previously owned motorcycle, finding them dangerous for his needs." Rainbow v. Albert Elia Bldg. Co., 436 N.Y.S.2d 480, 483 (App. Div. 1981).

**56.** Morrison v. Kubota Tractor Corp., 891 S.W.2d 422 (Mo. Ct. App. 1994).

**57.** Rainbow v. Albert Elia Bldg. Co., 436 N.Y.S.2d 480, 483 (App. Div. 1981). See

also Morrison v. Kubota Tractor Corp., 891 S.W.2d 422, 428 (Mo. Ct. App. 1994).

**58.** See, e.g., Westbrock v. Marshalltown Mfg. Co., 473 N.W.2d 352, 358 (Minn. Ct. App. 1991).

**59.** Pahuta v. Massey–Ferguson, Inc., 170 F.3d 125 (2d Cir. 1999) (N.Y. law).

**60.** See Scarangella v. Thomas Built Buses, Inc., 717 N.E.2d 679 (N.Y. 1999); Pahuta v. Massey–Ferguson, Inc., 170 F.3d 125 (2d Cir. 1999) (N.Y. law).

group is generally well-informed. If purchasers as a group are likely to have special needs or wants for which a standard safety feature may be unnecessary or inappropriate, and as long as they have access to appropriate safety features and understand the safety tradeoffs those features represent, courts generally should permit manufacturers to delegate to individual purchasers the decision of what, if any, safety features may best fit their special needs. A no-duty rule appears most appropriate in such cases, despite its problems, particularly when safety features are relatively expensive and may interfere substantially with a product's utility. The nondelegable duty principle works poorly in such cases, and juries normally should not be asked to decide these cases as questions of fact on general principles of liability. In optional safety device cases of this type, the law should step aside and leave decisions to individual product purchasers.

## § 8.10 PRESCRIPTION DRUGS AND MEDICAL DEVICES

Many have been bewitched, bedazzled, and bewildered in trying to understand just how principles of design defectiveness should be applied to prescription drugs[1] and, to a lesser extent, medical devices.[2] Whether

**§ 8.10**

**1.** See, e.g., Conk, The True Test: Alternative Safer Designs for Drugs and Medical Devices in a Patent–Constrained Market, 49 UCLA L. Rev. 737 (2002); Henderson and Twerski, Drug Designs Are Different, 111 Yale L.J. 151 (2001); Conk, Is There a Design Defect in the Restatement (Third) of Torts: Products Liability?, 109 Yale L.J. 1087 (2000); Cupp, The Continuing Search for Proper Perspective: Whose Reasonableness Should Be at Issue in a Prescription Product Design Defect Analysis?, 30 Seton Hall L. Rev. 233 (1999); M. Green, Prescription Drugs, Alternative Designs, and The Restatement (Third): Preliminary Reflections, 30 Seton Hall L. Rev. 207, 209 (1999); Gilhooley, When Drugs Are Safe for Some But Not Others: The FDA Experience and Alternatives for Products Liability, 36 Hous. L. Rev. 927 (1999); Henderson, Jr., Prescription Drug Design Liability Under the Proposed Restatement (Third) of Torts: A Reporter's Perspective, 48 Rutgers L. Rev. 471, 494 (1996); T. Schwartz, Prescription Products and the Proposed Restatement (Third), 61 Tenn. L. Rev. 1357 (1994); Cupp, Rethinking Conscious Design Liability for Prescription Drugs: The Restatement (Third) Standard Versus a Negligence Approach, 63 Geo. Wash. L. Rev. 76 (1994); Ausness, Unavoidably Unsafe Products and Strict Products Liability: What Liability Rule Should be Applied to the Sellers of Pharmaceutical Products? 78 Ky. L.J. 705 (1989–1990); Reilly, The Erosion of Comment k, 14 U. Dayton L. Rev. 255 (1989); V. Schwartz, Unavoidably Unsafe Products: Clarifying the Meaning and Policy Behind Comment k, 42 Wash. & Lee L. Rev. 1139 (1985); Page, Generic Product Risks: The Case Against Comment k and for Strict Tort Liability, 58 N.Y.U. L. Rev. 853 (1983); Willig, The Comment k Character: A Conceptual Barrier to Strict Liability, 29 Mercer L. Rev. 545 (1978); McClellan, Strict Liability For Drug Induced Injuries: An Excursion Through the Maze of Products Liability, Negligence and Absolute Liability, 25 Wayne L. Rev. 1 (1978); Merrill, Compensation for Prescription Drug Injuries, 59 Va. L. Rev. 1 (1973); Frumer and Friedman, Products Liability § 8.7; Frumer and Friedman, Products Liability § 8.07 and ch. 50; 2 Am. Law Prod. Liability § 28.12; 6 Am. Law Prod. Liability §§ 89.4–89.7.

**2.** Medical devices involve fewer special issues of design defectiveness than prescription drugs, and so they are touched on only briefly in this section. A major issue in medical device design litigation, federal preemption, is addressed in § 14.4, below. On medical device litigation generally, see McLean, Cybersurgery—An Argument for Enterprise Liability, 23 J. Legal Med. 167 (2002); Frank, An Assessment of the Regulations on Medical Devices in the European Union, 56 Food & Drug L.J. 99 (2001); M. Green and Schultz, Tort Law Deference to FDA Regulation of Medical Devices, 88 Geo. L.J. 2119 (2000); Chai, Medical Device Regulation in the United States and the European Union: A Comparative Study, 55 Food & Drug L.J. 57 (2000); Tumidolsky, How Medtronic v. Lohr Has Redefined Medical Device Regulation and Litigation, 65 Def. Couns. J. 268 (1998); Walsh and Pyrich, Rationalizing the Regulation of Prescription

and how prescription drugs in particular should be treated differently from other types of products has consumed more time and effort, and resulted in the gnashing of more teeth, than about any other particularized issue in all of products liability law. In addition to featuring two prominent *Restatement* provisions—comment *k* to § 402A of the *Restatement (Second) of Torts* and § 6(c) of the *Third Restatement*, the drug design defect story wends through two of the most prominent cases in products liability law history—*Feldman v. Lederle Laboratories*[3] and *Brown v. Superior Court*.[4] The issue is complex, involving the learned intermediary doctrine,[5] product category liability,[6] state of the art,[7] the battle for supremacy between the consumer expectations and risk-utility tests of liability for design defectiveness,[8] the never-ending struggle between negligence and strict liability, how design and warning defect notions fit together,[9] federal preemption,[10] and, at bottom, whether drugs in fact are different from other types of products, and whether they should be treated differently by products liability law. Yet, of all the many insights into this nearly impenetrable thicket of separate yet intertwined forays into distinct doctrinal quagmires, the one that transcends the rest in clarity and brilliance is this: [that] it simply doesn't matter—that, for drugs, "the liability game is with the warnings candle, not with design."[11] Understanding this important insight requires examining the nature of the drug design defect problem and then, if only briefly, the doctrinal battles that have long been fought, and still continue, on this war-weary terrain.

## The Problem

Prescription drugs are paradoxical: as one of the greatest triumphs of the twentieth century, their powerful chemicals and biologics save many millions of humans from suffering and death; yet, these same chemicals also cause great suffering and death. All prescription drugs, that is, possess substantial costs as well as benefits. This is because most drug hazards are inherent and unavoidable.[12] These dangers simply cannot be removed: the same chemical properties in drugs that can cause great harm are usually the very properties that are therapeutic. Put another way, if a drug's chemical structure were altered to avoid some adverse health effect, that same change would often also reduce or

Drugs and Medical Devices: Perspectives on Private Certification and Tort Reform, 48 Rutgers L. Rev. 883 (1996); Notes, 25 Cardozo L. Rev. 1159 (2004), 76 Ind. L.J. 443 (2001) (federal preemption of medical device claims), 30 U. Balt. L. Rev. 389 (2001) (surgically implanted medical devices, the Third Restatement, and preemption), 25 Del. J. Corp. L. 715 (2000) (affect of Biomaterials Access Assurance Act of 1998 on supplier liability); Frumer and Friedman, Products Liability chs. 52 (engineering aspects of medical devices) and 53 (liability for medical devices).

**3.** 479 A.2d 374, 382–83 (N.J. 1984).

**4.** 751 P.2d 470 (Cal. 1988).

**5.** See § 9.6, below.

**6.** See § 10.3, below.

**7.** See § 10.4, below.

**8.** See §§ 8.3–8.8, above.

**9.** See § 6.2, above.

**10.** To date, federal preemption has largely concerned medical devices, not prescription drugs, but the doctrine has begun to seep into prescription drug litigation. See § 14.4, below.

**11.** M. Green, Prescription Drugs, Alternative Designs, and The Restatement (Third): Preliminary Reflections, 30, Seton Hall L. Rev. 207, 209 (1999).

**12.** On inherent product hazards, see §§ 6.2, above, and 10.3, below.

eliminate the drug's beneficial health effects.[13] Thus, in general, the "design" of drugs cannot be changed.

Penicillin may be the classic example of a drug that, while highly beneficial to most people, can be hazardous, indeed lethal, to others.[14] But other examples abound. Accutane is a good modern example of a drug that combines great benefits with great risks of harm: it is highly effective in treating the most severe cases of acne; yet, it is a virulent teratogen that can cause birth defects when given to pregnant women. Surely the most impelling example is thalidomide, another teratogen, prescribed widely as a sedative and for morning sickness throughout much of the world (but not the U.S.) during the 1950s and 1960s.[15] Despite the havoc it then wreaked throughout the world, the federal Food and Drug Administration (the FDA) approved thalidomide in 1998 for fighting leprosy.[16] And the list of unavoidably unsafe drugs goes on and on.[17]

Outside of tort law, our medico-legal systems address this conundrum, the bad-comes-with-the-good aspect of prescription drugs, in two basic ways.[18] First, prior to being allowed onto the market, prescription

**13.** "Normally," because the hazard in some drugs may be reduced or eliminated by changing the prescribed dosage, the active ingredients in combination drugs, or the inert ingredients used in a drug. See M. Green, Prescription Drugs, Alternative Designs, and The Restatement (Third): Preliminary Reflections, 30, Seton Hall L. Rev. 207 (1999).

**14.** See W. Prosser, Handbook of the Law of Torts § 99, at 661 (4th ed. 1971).

**15.** Thalidomide caused severe limb deformities in children born to women who took the drug while pregnant. The FDA's protracted review of the drug barely saved most Americans from this terrible tragedy. See Sanders, The Bendectin Litigation: A Case Study in the Life Cycle of Mass Torts, 43 Hastings L.J. 301, 313–14 (1992) (characterizing thalidomide as "one of the most potent human teratogens ever found"). See also, Berstein, Formed by Thalidomide: Mass Torts as a False Cure for Toxic Exposure, 97 Colum. L. Rev. 2153 (1997).

**16.** "Thalidomide, the sedative that produced thousands of babies with flipperlike limbs and other gross deformities, was approved today for use in the United States for the first time, nearly four decades after it was stripped from pharmacy shelves around the world." Stolberg, Thalidomide Approved to Treat Leprosy, with Other Uses Seen, nytimes.com (July 17, 1998).

**17.** "The whole pharmacopeia is full of drugs which are not safe, and at present cannot be made safe." W. Prosser, Handbook of the Law of Torts § 99, at 661 (4th ed. 1971).

**18.** *National Childhood Vaccine Injury Act.* A third approach that lies outside the tort law system is the no-fault compensation system to compensate children suffering adverse reactions to vaccinations required by public health statutes. See National Childhood Vaccine Injury Act of 1986, 42 U.S.C. § 300aa–1 et seq. Claims are made in the Court of Claims against the Secretary of HHS, including recovery for economic losses, pain and suffering (limited to $250,000) and death (limited to $250,000). A claimant may accept or reject the court's award; if it is rejected, the claimant may then (and only then) initiate a products liability action against the manufacturer, except that the Act bars recovery in such actions for "side effects that were unavoidable even though the vaccine was properly prepared and was accompanied by proper directions and warnings." Id. at § 300aa–22. See Cheskiewicz v. Aventis Pasteur, Inc., 843 A.2d 1258 (Pa. Super. Ct. 2004) (Vaccine Act remedies must be exhausted before products liability claim is filed); Schafer v. American Cyanamid Co., 20 F.3d 1 (1st Cir. 1994) (Breyer, J.) (summarizing Act); Shalala v. Whitecotton, 514 U.S. 268 (1995).

See generally Calandrillo, Vanishing Vaccinations: Why Are So Many Americans Opting Out of Vaccinating Their Children?, 37 U. Mich. J.L. Reform 353 (2004); Noah, Triage in the Nation's Medicine Cabinet: The Puzzling Scarcity of Vaccines and Other Drugs, 54 S.C. L. Rev. 741 (2002); Hodge and Gostin, School Vaccination Requirements: Historical, Social, and Legal Perspectives, 90 Ky. L.J. 831 (2001–02); Ridgway, No–Fault Vaccine Insurance: Lessons from the National Vaccine Injury Compen-

drugs must undergo rigorous analysis, laboratory testing, and clinical trials, the results of which are closely scrutinized by the FDA, to assure both the safety and efficacy of all new drugs. Under the Food, Drug and Cosmetic Act of 1938, as amended,[19] Congress has vested more regulatory power in the FDA to regulate drug safety than it has vested in other agencies to regulate the safety of other products, mirroring the special role of prescription drugs in preserving life and health together with the special dangers they pose to life and health.[20] A key function of the FDA is to help assure that only drugs which are on balance beneficial to some class of patients ever reach the health care market.[21]

The second relevant feature of our medico-legal system is that it positions experts in diagnosis and drug therapy, doctors and nurse practitioners, between beneficial yet dangerous prescription drugs, on the one hand, and the lay public who need drug therapy, on the other. The role of such health care professionals, such "learned intermediaries," is to connect individual drugs and patients—to choose from among the panoply of available prescription drugs the one with the highest benefit-risk ratio for each particular patient's needs and wants. Thus, the very purpose of a doctor in drug therapy is to assure that the right prescription medicine, in view of its particular benefits and risks, is assigned to the right patient, in view of that patient's special needs.[22]

**The Question**

The question of interest here is what role, if any, does the medico-legal system just described leave for the law of torts and products

sation Program, 24 J. Health Care L. & Pol'y 59 (1999); Rabin, Some Thoughts on the Efficacy of a Mass Toxics Administrative Compensation Scheme, 52 Md. L. Rev. 951, 958 (1993); Sanzo, Vaccines and the Law, 19 Pepp. L. Rev. 29 (1991); Hagan, Vaccine Compensation Schemes, 45 Food Drug Cosm. L.J. 477 (1990); Dark, Is the National Childhood Vaccine Injury Act of 1986 the Solution for the DTP Controversy?, 19 U. Tol. L. Rev. 799 (1988); V. Schwartz and Mahshigian, National Childhood Vaccine Injury Act of 1986: An Ad Hoc Remedy or a Window for the Future?, 48 Ohio St. L.J. 387 (1987); Notes, 41 Wm. & Mary L. Rev. 309 (1999) ("a one shot deal"); 4 B.U. J. Sci. & Tech. L. 9 (1998); 63 Geo. Wash. L. Rev. 144 (1994); 42 Am. U. L. Rev. 199 (1992); 63 Wash. L. Rev. 149 (1988); Annot., 129 A.L.R. Fed. 1 (1996); 5 Harper, James, and Gray, Law of Torts § 28.8A (2004 Supp. at 132); Dobbs, Law of Torts § 399, at 1112–13.

**19.** 21 U.S.C.A. §§ 301–392. The Act's key provisions are § 331(a), prohibiting the sale of "any food, drug, device, or cosmetic that is adulterated or misbranded," and § 355, requiring FDA approval prior to the marketing of any new drug.

**20.** The Food, Drug, and Cosmetic Act and the FDA are discussed more fully in § 9.6, below.

**21.** On the drug regulation by the FDA, see, e.g., Gilhooley, When Drugs Are Safe for Some But Not Others: The FDA Experience and Alternatives for Products Liability, 36 Hous. L. Rev. 927 (1999); M. Green, Safety as an Element of Pharmaceutical Quality: The Respective Roles of Regulation and Tort Law, 42 St. Louis U. L.J. 163 (1998); T. Schwartz, Regulatory Standards and Products Liability: Striking the Right Balance Between the Two, 30 U. Mich. J.L. Reform 431 (1997); Merrill, The Architecture of Government Regulation of Medical Products, 82 Va. L. Rev. 1753 (1996); Walsh & Pyrich, Rationalizing the Regulation of Prescription Drugs and Medical Devices: Perspectives on Private Certification and Tort Reform, 48 Rutgers L. Rev. 883 (1996); Gilhooley, Innovative Drugs, Products Liability, Regulatory Compliance and Patient Choice, 24 Seton Hall L. Rev. 1481 (1994); T. Schwartz, The Role of Federal Safety Regulations in Products Liability Actions, 41 Vand. L. Rev. 1121 (1988); Merrill, Compensation for Prescription Drug Injuries, 59 Va. L. Rev. 1 (1973).

**22.** The "learned intermediary doctrine" is examined in § 9.6, below.

liability? Because the system just described breaks down in many ways in practice, the answer to the question must be that products liability law has a powerful role to play in compensating persons harmed unnecessarily by defective drugs, and some role (if a lesser one) in deterring their sale and promoting drug safety. The model of the perfect FDA, unfortunately, does not fit the real world closely. Legislative, budgetary, and political constraints mar the ideal of a perfect regulatory body that optimally protects the public from exposure to defective drugs.[23] Nor, as most people painfully well know, do doctors typically match prescription drugs to patients in a manner that approaches optimality.[24] Because of these and other shortcomings in the medico-legal structure for the production and distribution of prescription drugs, products liability law needs to play a significant role in compensating, and hopefully helping to protect, consumers of defective prescription drugs.

Because the answer to the question posed above was that there is a proper role for products liability when people suffer harm from prescription drugs, we must inquire into what that role should be. The following discussion focuses on the role of design defectiveness in drug products liability litigation. What the inquiry reveals is that courts, commentators, and the *Torts Restatements* widely agree that the products liability system should place its primary emphasis on assuring that doctors and (indirectly) patients receive adequate warnings and instructions about drug dangers, and that reevaluations of prescription drug designs should be quite limited. How these general propositions have evolved doctrinally in the *Restatements* and the courts, keeping the focus here on design defectiveness, now can be explored. The specifics of warning liability for prescription drugs and medical devices is examined later.[25]

## The Restatements and the Courts

### The Second Restatement—Comment k

An attempt to understand how the notion of a design defect fits together with prescription drugs ideally should begin with a study of the chemistry, manufacture, marketing approaches, and therapeutic applications of this peculiar type of product. Yet, because time and space require that such deep inquires be left to specialized texts on drugs,[26] and journal articles,[27] the best place to begin the inquiry here is with comment *k*, a controversial comment to § 402A of the *Restatement (Second) of Torts*.[28] In a nutshell, comment *k* provides that manufactur-

---

**23.** On weaknesses in the perfect FDA model, see, e.g., Rabin, Reassessing Regulatory Compliance, 88 Geo. L. J. 2049 (2000); T. Schwartz, The Role of Federal Safety Regulations in Products Liability Actions, 41 Vand. L. Rev. 1121 (1988); § 14.4, below.

**24.** Apart from the increasingly limited time doctors devote to treating each patient, doctors typically receive woefully limited education—from one to three semesters—on pharmaceuticals. See § 9.6, below. See generally M. Green, above, at 229 n.67 (explaining how the "idealized role of the physician is not borne out in practice").

**25.** See § 9.6, below.

**26.** See, e.g., 1 M. Dixon and F. Woodside, Drug Product Liability ch. 3 (2000) (principles of pharmacology). See also Frumer and Friedman, Products Liability ch. 50 (drug litigation).

**27.** See note 1, above.

**28.** See Cupp, Rethinking Conscious Design Liability for Prescription Drugs: The Restatement (Third) Standard Versus a Negligence Approach, 63 Geo. Wash. L. Rev. 76, 78 n.6 (1994) (asserting that comment *k* is "the most frequently debated

ers are not subject to strict liability in tort for harm caused by certain "unavoidably unsafe" but useful products, notably prescription drugs, solely on the basis of their inherent hazards that cannot feasibly be designed away.[29] The Reporter for the *Second Restatement* who drafted comment *k*, William Prosser, justified this exemption in a famous quote: "The argument that industries producing potentially dangerous products should make good the harm, distribute it by liability insurance, and add the cost to the price of the product, encounters reason for pause, when we consider that two of the greatest medical boons to the human race, penicillin and cortisone, both have their dangerous side effects, and that drug companies might well have been deterred from producing and selling them."[30] Drugs, in short, are different.[31] As a result, most courts agree that comment *k* properly exempts useful prescription drugs that

comment to 402A"). On comment *k*, see generally Frumer and Friedman, Products Liability § 8.07.

**29.** In fact, this is the theme of three companion comments to § 402A, comments *i, j,* and *k*. These three comments are examined in depth in § 6.2, above. In full, comment *k* provides:

> *k. Unavoidably unsafe products.* There are some products which, in the present state of human knowledge, are quite incapable of being made safe for their intended and ordinary use. These are especially common in the field of drugs. An outstanding example is the vaccine for the Pasteur treatment of rabies, which not uncommonly leads to very serious and damaging consequences when it is injected. Since the disease itself invariably leads to a dreadful death, both the marketing and the use of the vaccine are fully justified, notwithstanding the unavoidable high degree of risk which they involve. Such a product, properly prepared, and accompanied by proper directions and warning, is not defective, nor is it *unreasonably* dangerous. The same is true of many other drugs, vaccines, and the like, many of which for this very reason cannot legally be sold except to physicians, or under the prescription of a physician. It is also true in particular of many new or experimental drugs as to which, because of lack of time and opportunity for sufficient medical experience, there can be no assurance of safety, or perhaps even of purity of ingredients, but such experience as there is justifies the marketing and use of the drug notwithstanding a medically recognizable risk. The seller of such products, again with the qualification that they are properly prepared and marketed, and proper warning is given, where the situation calls for it, is not to be held to strict liability for unfortunate consequences attending their use, merely because he has undertaken to supply the public with an apparently use-

ful and desirable product, attended with a known but apparently reasonable risk.

**30.** W. Prosser, Handbook of the Law of Torts § 99, at 661 (4th ed. 1971).

**31.** See Henderson and Twerski, Drug Designs Are Different, 111 Yale L.J. 151 (2001); M. Green, above, at 232 ("Drugs are different.... "); Note, 27 Vt. L. Rev. 1017, 1049 (2003) ("Drugs are different."). Professor Green examines various claims as to how drugs are different: (1) that "they cannot be manipulated physically to provide marginally greater safety"; (2) that they are harmful for some people while beneficial for others; (3) that their adverse effects frequently are not discoverable through research and testing, such that these harmful effects are not revealed until they injure drug consumers; (4) that they are subject to especially heavy regulatory oversight, much of it pre-market, by the FDA; (5) that they are especially beneficial to mankind, sometimes even necessary to the preservation of health and life; (6) that learned intermediaries, doctors, stand between drug products and consumers, matching particular drugs to particular people. See Id. To these six claims of difference, a seventh might be added: (7) that they are extremely costly to bring to market, each new brand name prescription drug on average costing roughly $½ billion for research, development, laboratory testing, clinical testing, FDA submission work, and production. See, e.g., Glasgow, Stretching the Limits of Intellectual Property Rights: Has the Pharmaceutical Industry Gone Too Far?, 41 IDEA 227 (2001) ($250–500 million estimate, citing FTC Bur. of Econ. Staff Rpt.); Crimm, A Tax Proposal to Promote Pharmacologic Research, to Encourage Conventional Prescription Drug Innovation and Improvement, and to Reduce Product Liability Claims, 29 Wake Forest L. Rev. 1007, 1035 (1994) ($259 to $359 million, citing Office of Technology Assessment); Note, 3 J. Intell. Prop. 120, 142 n.24 (2003) ($800 million, citing economic report).

are unavoidably unsafe from strict products liability,[32] assuming always that they were properly prepared and carried adequate warnings.[33] And while design hazards in medical devices often can be designed away,[34] some courts have nevertheless extended comment *k*'s exemption from design defect liability to cases involving prescription medical devices.[35]

In addition to questioning comment *k*'s very premise, that prescription drug manufacturers deserve protection from the rigors of strict liability, courts and commentators disagree on a number of aspects of comment *k*, including (1) whether its application is confined to a limited class of drugs properly characterized as "unavoidably unsafe," or whether it applies to all prescription drugs; and (2) whether the exemption it affords from strict liability in tort applies as well to negligence. On the first question, the New Jersey Supreme Court in 1984 ruled in *Feldman v. Lederle Laboratories*[36] that only certain drugs qualify for comment *k*'s exemption from design defect liability—those proven on a case-by-case basis to be highly useful and unavoidably unsafe.[37] The year after *Feldman*, a California intermediate appellate court decided *Kearl v. Lederle Labs.*,[38] in which it adopted and elaborated upon the *Feldman* approach, prescribing a detailed "mini-trial" necessary before a judge could qualify a drug for exemption from strict liability under comment *k*.[39] Soon thereafter, however, the California Supreme Court rejected the

**32.** See generally 1 Frumer and Friedman, Products Liability § 8.07 (citing cases from 30 states and the District of Columbia applying comment *k*). A small number of courts have explicitly rejected comment *k*. See, e.g, Allison v. Merck & Co., 878 P.2d 948, 954 (Nev. 1994); Collins v. Eli Lilly Co., 342 N.W.2d 37, 52 (Wis. 1984). See also Shanks v. Upjohn Co., 835 P.2d 1189 (Alaska 1992) (refusing to adopt comment *k* but agreeing with its basic policy).

**33.** This important proviso, which leaves room for claims of defects in manufacture, warnings, and instructions, is from comment *k* itself.

**34.** See Larsen v. Pacesetter Sys., Inc., 837 P.2d 1273, 1286 (Haw. 1992) (pacemaker that had to be removed because of recall not exempt under comment *k* because it "was demonstrably capable of being made safer for its intended use").

**35.** See, e.g., Parkinson v. Guidant Corp., 315 F.Supp.2d 741 (W.D.Pa. 2004) (angioplasty guidewire); Transue v. Aesthetch Corp., 341 F.3d 911 (9th Cir. 2003) (Wash. law) (breast implants); Artiglio v. Superior Court, 27 Cal.Rptr.2d 589 (Ct. App. 1994) (same, as well as other implants); Tansy v. Dacomed Corp., 890 P.2d 881 (Okla. 1994) (penile implant); Hufft v. Horowitz, 5 Cal.Rptr.2d 377 (Ct. App. 1992) (same); Hill v. Searle Labs., 884 F.2d 1064 (8th Cir. 1989) (Ark. law) (IUDs).

**36.** 479 A.2d 374, 382–83 (N.J. 1984).

**37.** "Comment *k* immunizes from strict liability the manufacturers of some prod-

ucts, including certain drugs, that are unavoidably unsafe. However, we see no reason to hold as a matter of law and policy that all prescription drugs that are unsafe are unavoidably so. Drugs, like any other products, may contain defects that could have been avoided by better manufacturing or design. Whether a drug is unavoidably unsafe should be decided on a case-by-case basis; we perceive no justification [in policy or under comment *k* for immunizing prescription drug manufacturers from their safe manufacturing, warning, and risk-utility design obligations under strict liability in tort.]" Id. at 383.

**38.** 218 Cal.Rptr. 453 (Ct. App. 1985).

**39.** Sitting in this phase of the trial without a jury, the judge would determine "(1) whether, when distributed, the product was intended to confer an exceptionally important benefit that made its availability highly desirable; (2) whether the then-existing risk posed by the product both was 'substantial' and 'unavoidable'; and (3) whether the interest in availability (again measured as of the time of distribution) outweighs the interest in promoting enhanced accountability through strict liability design defect review." Id. at 829–30. See also Freeman v. Hoffman–La Roche, Inc., 618 N.W.2d 827, 840–41 (Neb. 2000) (exemption applies if (1) product is properly manufactured and adequate warnings are provided; (2) its benefits exceed its risks; and (3) it was incapable of being made safer).

*Feldman-Kearl* approach in *Brown v. Superior Court*,[40] interpreting comment *k* as embracing *all* prescription drugs within its unavoidably-unsafe safe harbor. The *Brown* court reasoned that forcing drug manufacturers to litigate whether their drugs deserve design-defect exemption in every case would emasculate comment *k*'s objective of shielding prescription drug manufacturers *ex ante* from the risks of design defect liability *ex post* in order to reduce the perils of overdeterrence, including higher drug prices and fewer new drugs. While a few courts have followed *Brown*'s general exemption of all prescription drugs from design defect liability,[41] most courts have taken the *Feldman-Kearl* case-by-case approach, reluctant to surrender judicial oversight of a drug manufacturer's responsibility for safety in design.[42]

Another aspect of comment *k* which engenders some debate is whether comment *k*, assuming (as almost all courts do) that it exempts manufacturers of at least some drugs from strict liability in tort, should exempt them also from liability in *negligence* for defects in design.[43] The language of comment *k*, of course, should not be parsed as if it were a statute,[44] but it should be noted that comment *k* does not address the question of a drug manufacturer's liability in negligence for defects in design. After all, this provision is a comment to § 402A, which addresses a seller's *strict* liability in tort—not negligence, which is a different topic the *Restatement* separately addresses in another section.[45] Apart from this quite obvious fact, the debate may be resolved quite simply[46]: if the design of a drug is not defective, for purposes of strict liability in tort, it cannot be negligent to sell it in that nondefective condition.[47] While this

---

**40.**  751 P.2d 470 (Cal. 1988).

**41.**  See, e.g., Transue v. Aesthetech Corp., 341 F.3d 911, 916 (9th Cir. 2003) (Wash. law); Grundberg v. Upjohn Co., 813 P.2d 89, 95 (Utah 1991). See also McKee v. Moore, 648 P.2d 21, 24 (Okla. 1982).

**42.**  See, e.g., Bryant v. Hoffmann–La Roche, Inc., 585 S.E.2d 723, 728 (Ga. Ct. App. 2003); Bennett v. Madakasira, 821 So.2d 794, 809 (Miss. 2002); Freeman v. Hoffman–La Roche, Inc., 618 N.W.2d 827, 837 (Neb. 2000); Glassman v. Wyeth Labs., 606 N.E.2d 338, 342 (Ill. 1992); West v. Searle & Co., 806 S.W.2d 608, 612 (Ark. 1991); Adams v. G.D. Searle & Co., 576 So.2d 728, 731 (Fla. Dist. Ct. App. 1991); Savina v. Sterling Drug, Inc., 795 P.2d 915, 923–29 (Kan. 1990); White v. Wyeth Labs., 533 N.E.2d 748 (Ohio 1988); Castrignano v. E.R. Squibb & Sons, Inc., 546 A.2d 775, 781 (R.I. 1988); Toner v. Lederle Labs., 732 P.2d 297 (Idaho 1987).

**43.**  Most courts hold that negligence liability in fact applies to the design of drugs. See, e.g., Toner v. Lederle Labs., 732 P.2d 297, 310 (Idaho 1987); Johnson v. American Cyanamid Co., 718 P.2d 1318, 1324–25 (Kan. 1986).

**44.**  Except, perhaps, in Oregon and South Carolina which adopted the comments to § 402A by statute. See § 5.4, above.

**45.**  The Second Restatement addressed negligent design in § 395 which makes no reference to liability for the sale of dangerous drugs.

**46.**  Dean Prosser appears to have believed that the answer to whether negligence claims should lie against drug manufacturers for selling drugs that were harmful as well as beneficial usually was simple: they should not. "Where only negligence liability is in question, the answer as to such products [inherently hazardous drugs] is usually a simple one. The utility and social value of the thing sold normally outweighs the known, and all the more so the unknown risk, and there is no negligence in selling it, provided always that proper warning and directions are given." W. Prosser, Handbook of the Law of Torts § 99, at 661 (4th ed. 1971). It is possible, however, that Dean Prosser only meant that because drugs normally are not defective, it normally is not negligent to sell them; not that, because drugs normally are not defective, courts should not inquire into whether they are or not, and, if they are defective, whether the manufacturer was negligent in marketing them in that condition.

**47.**  See §§ 2.1 and 5.9, above.

kind of doctrinal, set-theory reasoning normally is sound, it falters somewhat here because comment *k* exempts all prescription drugs from strict liability in tort, not because they all are truly nondefective, but because most drugs are (due to market competition and oversight by the FDA) and, also, because many courts have decided that a protective umbrella should shield all prescription drugs (including the defective ones) to avoid discouraging manufacturers from developing important new drugs (most of which will be nondefective) and from setting high drug prices. Thus, some prescription drugs probably are "defective" in design notwithstanding the comment *k* exemption, and the manufacturers of some of those defective drugs may well have been negligent in their development and sale.

Even if strict liability is allowed in prescription drug cases, its usefulness to consumers appears quite limited. Because the doctor is the "consumer" in prescription drug cases, under the learned intermediary rule,[48] the consumer expectations test provides no relief to patients suffering foreseeable drug injuries if the manufacturer adequately warned doctors of the risk that such injuries might result. And, if the drug contains foreseeable dangers that doctors do not expect, then failure-to-warn claims protect persons injured by such drugs. Finally, because almost every jurisdiction now protects manufacturers from liability from dangers that are unforeseeable under the prevailing state of the art,[49] a patient injured by an unforeseeable drug risk in most jurisdictions has no claim under any liability test or theory.

Under a risk-utility test, whether it be called "negligence," "strict liability," or simply "design defectiveness,"[50] a manufacturer is subject to liability for failing to adopt a particular design feature that would have prevented the plaintiff's harm, if the safety benefits of the design feature were greater than its costs.[51] But this suggests that a drug can be re-engineered to eliminate a particular design danger without sacrificing its health benefits, which normally is impossible, since the hazards in most drugs, as mentioned earlier, are inherent and unavoidable. This leaves only one narrow version of risk-benefit analysis available for properly assessing the defectiveness of a drug's design, the approach adopted by the *Third Restatement*.

### The Third Restatement

In 1998, the ALI promulgated a liability standard for defective drug designs that is unusual, to say the least. Section 6(c) of the *Products Liability Restatement* provides:

> (c) A prescription drug or medical device is not reasonably safe due to defective design if the foreseeable risks of harm posed by the drug or medical device are sufficiently great in relation to its foreseeable therapeutic benefits that reasonable health-care providers, knowing of such foreseeable risks and

---

**48.** See § 9.6, below.

**49.** On the state of the art, see § 10.4, below.

**50.** See §§ 2.2 (negligence), 5.7 (strict liability in tort), and 8.4 (design defect), above.

**51.** See §§ 8.4, 8.5, 8.8, above.

therapeutic benefits, would not prescribe the drug or medical device for any class of patients.

The most important thing to note about this standard, which has been judicially applied,[52] is that it leaves a very small window for design defect claims for prescription drugs, a window so tiny that almost no drug claim could fit through it. Even thalidomide would not be captured by the *Third Restatement* test, because of its value in treating leprosy. But thalidomide may prove the virtue of this test, rather than its frailty, for who reasonably can argue that lepers should be deprived of beneficial drug therapy because some doctors may improperly prescribe the drug for child-bearing women? In such a case, the defect, it would seem, would lie in the doctor rather than the drug. While not minimizing the tragedy of a child born deformed to a woman who was prescribed the drug improperly, perhaps tort (and possibly criminal) remedies against the prescribing doctor would be a better way to address the consequences, rather than forcing the manufacturer and lepers to bear the economic consequences of an untoward misuse of a beneficial pharmaceutical.

In a world in which the medico-legal scheme described earlier operates with perfection—where manufacturers carefully engage in good faith drug safety investigations, where a fully-funded and politically neutral FDA keeps drugs with foreseeable excess dangers from being sold, and where doctors perfectly match up individual drugs to individual patients—the § 6(c) formulation of design defectiveness for drugs would appear ideal. The problem, of course, is that the models of an ideal FDA and of ideal prescribing doctors are quite inaccurate. But the solution to imperfections in the medico-legal framework is not to allow juries to engage in risk-utility comparisons between different drugs used to treat the same condition. Assume that three drugs, A, B, and C, each are used to fight lung infections, and that drug A causes drowsiness in some persons, drug B causes birth defects when given to some women, and drug C causes acne in some teenage boys. A doctor presumably would prescribe B or possibly C to a male truck driver, drug A or B to a teenage boy, and drug A or C, to a woman capable of bearing children. Surely products liability law should not force substantial economic costs on manufacturers of any of these drugs because a prescribing doctor matches one drug to the wrong patient. Nor should these manufacturers have to litigate such cases of misprescription, over and over again in courtrooms around the nation, assuming, of course that they fully and properly performed their investigation and reporting duties to the FDA. Nor should consumers be deprived of one or two of these drugs because the litigation costs (including occasional lost verdicts) proved too much for the manufacturers of the drugs, particularly when juries began to classify one drug of the three as causing the least net harm to all these patient groups, considered as a whole.

This latter example reveals the perils of using a macro-balance approach to risk-utility analysis. Notwithstanding the frailties of doctors

---

**52.** See, e.g., Gebhardt v. Mentor Corp., 191 F.R.D. 180 (D. Ariz. 1999) (granting summary judgment for manufacturer be- cause plaintiff failed to prove that a reason- able health-care provider would not have prescribed an Angelchik for any class of

and the FDA, a drug's design should not be characterized as defective on the ground that its total harm to all users exceeds its total benefits to all users, assuming that the drug provides net benefits to any class of patients, and assuming further that the drug's excessive harm results from its improper use by doctors.[53] Applying such a macro-balance test to declare drug designs defective in such cases would be both "unfair and inefficient," in the words of the *Restatement* Reporters, because it "would require courts to deny classes of patients access to a particular drug that provides them unique benefits in order to protect other patients from the risks of misprescription by negligent physicians."[54]

Pointing to the weaknesses in the FDA and health care delivery systems, the natural profit motivations of drug manufacturers to skimp on research and design,[55] a patent system which artificially protects manufacturers from competition, and the industry's temptation to over-promote its products, some courts[56] and commentators[57] reject the *Third Restatement*'s narrow definition of design defectiveness for drugs. The basis for rejecting § 6(c) is the belief that drug designs should be subject to challenge on some basis or another—either by means of a normal risk-utility test (on proof of a safer alternative design) or a macro-balance test (on proof that a drug caused patients as a whole more harm than good). Yet neither approach works well in most drug cases, as previously discussed. The first simply does not work for the majority of drugs that cannot be redesigned because their hazards are inherent. As for the

patients), aff'd, 15 Fed.Appx. 540 (9th Cir. 2001).

**53.** This assumes that a manufacturer's sales reps do not promote the drug for such improper use, in which case the manufacturer should be subject to liability. On the prevalence of off-label use, see Noah, Constraints on the Off-Label Uses of Prescription Drug Products, 16 J. Prod. & Toxic Liab. 139 (1994).

**54.** Henderson and Twerski, Drug Designs Are Different, 111 Yale L.J. 151, 180–81 (2001). For commentators that agree that § 6(c) basically is sound, if in need of some improvement, see, e.g., M. Green, Prescription Drugs, Alternative Designs, and the Restatement (Third): Preliminary Reflections, 30 Seton Hall L. Rev. 207 (1999); Dreier, Manufacturers' Liability for Drugs and Medical Devices Under the Restatement (Third) of Torts: Products Liability, 30 Seton Hall L. Rev. 258 (1999); Notes, 82 Cornell L. Rev. 644, 692 (1997), 45 Syracuse L. Rev. 1291, 1305 (1995). See also Henderson, Prescription Drug Design Liability Under the Proposed Restatement (Third) of Torts: A Reporter's Perspective, 48 Rutgers L. Rev. 471 (1996).

**55.** See, e.g., Note, 82 Cornell L. Rev. 644, 692 (1997) ("in light of the enormous amounts of money at stake in the global pharmaceutical industry, manufacturers are inevitably tempted to market products that are clearly less effective and more dangerous than others").

**56.** See Bryant v. Hoffmann–La Roche, Inc., 585 S.E.2d 723, 725–28 (Ga. Ct. App. 2003); Freeman v. Hoffman–La Roche, Inc., 618 N.W.2d 827, 837 (Neb. 2000).

**57.** See, e.g., Conk, The True Test: Alternative Safer Designs for Drugs and Medical Devices in a Patent–Constrained Market, 49 UCLA L. Rev. 737 (2002); Conk, Is There a Design Defect in the Restatement (Third) of Torts: Products Liability?, 109 Yale L.J. 1087 (2000); Cupp, The Continuing Search for Proper Perspective: Whose Reasonableness Should Be at Issue in a Prescription Product Design Defect Analysis?, 30 Seton Hall L. Rev. 233 (1999); Cupp, Rethinking Conscious Design Liability for Prescription Drugs: The Restatement (Third) Standard Versus a Negligence Approach, 63 Geo. Wash. L. Rev. 76 (1994); Phillips, The Unreasonably Unsafe Product and Strict Liability, 72 Chi.-Kent L. Rev. 129, 130 (1996); T. Schwartz, Prescription Products and the Proposed Restatement (Third), 61 Tenn. L. Rev. 1357, 1378–85 (1994); T. Schwartz, Regulatory Standards and Products Liability: Striking the Right Balance Between the Two, 30 U. Mich. J.L. Reform 431, 459 (1997); Vandall, Constructing a Roof Before the Foundation Is Prepared: The Restatement (Third) of Torts: Products Liability Section 2(b) Design Defect, 30 U. Mich. J.L. Reform, 261, 270 (1997).

second test, it is true that any product which causes more harm than good is truly bad, "defective," from a utilitarian point of view. And, if there were an effective way to identify such products, their manufacturers ordinarily should have to pay for all the harm they cause, and the products normally should be banned. Yet, as discussed above, particular classes of patients (like lepers) deserve therapy from drugs, even if doctors sometimes do misuse those drugs on other classes of patients. Moreover, there is a devil residing in the process of distinguishing which drugs, on balance, have net value from those that produce net harm— the threat of repeated litigation over the ultimate social value of any type of drug that causes someone harm, because it did not suit that patient.

So the *Third Restatement*'s test for defective drug designs, though very narrow, and incomplete in failing to identify important exceptions,[58] seems basically correct. That is, by putting most drugs beyond the reach of design defect litigation, under any liability theory, the *Third Restatement* properly pours over most litigation concerning hazardous drugs into the defectiveness of their warnings and instructions.[59]

### Resolving the Dilemma: Empowering Warnings Claims

For the various reasons discussed above, design defectiveness has never been a favored theory of recovery for drug injuries. While strict liability in tort generally got off the ground in the 1960s, and while design defect claims for most types of products became prevalent in the 1970s, courts did not even begin imposing design defect liability on drug manufacturers until the 1980s and 1990s.[60] And even to the present, most courts are chary in allowing such claims, properly directing drug litigation away from design defect claims to warnings claims. While many courts do allow broad risk-utility challenges to a drug's design, as discussed above, this approach appears mistaken because of the availability of a preferable basis of recovery in most cases for injuries from harmful drugs.

Most prescription drug litigation properly is based on the adequacy of warnings and instructions provided to the doctor about the drug,[61] because the best place to locate a drug manufacturer's responsibility is in the information it provides to doctors—information which must be

---

**58.** For discussions of some exceptions, see M. Green, Prescription Drugs, Alternative Designs, and the Restatement (Third): Preliminary Reflections, 30 Seton Hall L. Rev. 207 (1999); Dreier, Manufacturers' Liability for Drugs and Medical Devices Under the Restatement (Third) of Torts: Products Liability, 30 Seton Hall L. Rev. 258 (1999).

**59.** While § 6(c) might seemingly be improved by including a proviso that allows claims for a manufacturer's failure to meet its research and reporting responsibilities to the FDA, a robust warnings approach appears a better way for products liability law

to perform its oversight of those responsibilities.

**60.** Brochu v. Ortho Pharm. Corp., 642 F.2d 652 (1st Cir. 1981) (N.H. law), is widely thought to be the first prescription drug case in which a defective drug design claim figured prominently. A small number of earlier cases also involved challenges to drug designs. See, e.g., Tinnerholm v. Parke Davis & Co., 285 F.Supp. 432 (S.D.N.Y. 1968), aff'd as modified, 411 F.2d 48 (2d Cir. 1969), and Stromsodt v. Parke Davis & Co., 257 F.Supp. 991 (D.N.D. 1966), aff'd, 411 F.2d 1390 (8th Cir. 1969) (N.D. law).

**61.** See § 9.6, below.

clear, complete, and properly conveyed.[62] In the great majority of cases, a challenge to a drug's design can easily be reformulated as a defect in a warning or instruction. If a drug's adverse effects are not reasonably foreseeable, the manufacturer should not be responsible for its untoward effects for reasons examined elsewhere.[63] If such adverse effects in fact are reasonably discoverable by a manufacturer properly performing its research and development obligations, then it will have a duty to provide adequate warnings to doctors of those effects. And if a doctor fails to provide this information to his or her patients, to provide them with informed consent to drug therapy, then a medical malpractice claim would seem the proper remedy, not a claim against the manufacturer for a supposed defect in the drug's design. As a final backstop to physician failures of this sort, courts might consider abandoning the learned intermediary doctrine and requiring that information about all prescription hazards be provided not only to physicians but also directly to the patients who will take the drugs.[64]

In sum, drugs are different from other types of products. Because the safety of prescription drugs is subjected to quite rigorous review by the FDA before they ever reach the market, it is best that drug designs remain exempt from scrutiny in courtrooms in all but special situations.[65] But as a counterweight to relieving manufacturers from judicial scrutiny of their drug designs, courts should insist that judicial review of drug warnings and instructions be robust. As one prominent tort law scholar concludes, litigation over injuries from prescription drugs lies properly in the sufficiency of their warnings and instructions, not in the sufficiency of their designs.[66]

---

**62.** See id.

**63.** See § 10.4, below.

**64.** See Gilhooley, When Drugs Are Safe for Some But Not Others: The FDA Experience and Alternatives for Products Liability, 36 Hous. L. Rev. 927 (1999).

**65.** Such as where a manufacturer failed to comply with all requirements for FDA approval, and that failure caused the plaintiff's harm, and, possibly, where practicable drug engineering in fact would have allowed a manufacturer to eliminate a drug's adverse effects while leaving its beneficial effects unchanged.

**66.** See M. Green, Prescription Drugs, Alternative Designs, and the Restatement (Third): Preliminary Reflections, 30 Seton Hall L. Rev. 207, 209 (1999).

# Chapter 9

## WARNING DEFECTS

*Table of Sections*

---

## § 9.1  WARNING DEFECTS—GENERALLY

Manufacturers and other sellers have a duty to provide consumers with warnings of hidden product dangers and instructions on how their products may be safely used.[1] Products that fail to carry sufficient informational "software" of this type are deemed "defective." If a user or consumer is injured as a result of a warning defect,[2] because such danger or safety information was not provided, the manufacturer is subject to liability for the harm.[3]

### § 9.1

**1.** Retail sellers and other product suppliers generally have a duty to warn buyers of product hazards. See, e.g, Swanson v. Burlington Construction, Inc., 2004 WL 1050866 (Conn. Super. Ct. 2004) (retail dealer had duty to warn). Yet, because warning defects normally originate with the manufacturer, this chapter addresses the law on warning defects principally in relation to the manufacturer.

**2.** The term "warning defects" is often used as an umbrella term to include instruction defects, too, as discussed below. In Texas, warning defects are referred to as "marketing defects." See, e.g., Daimler–Chrysler Corp. v. Hillhouse, ___ S.W.3d ___, ___, 2004 WL 1195687 (Tex. App. 2004); Dalton v. Barry–Wehmiller Design Group, Inc., 2003 WL 193467, at *5 (N.D. Tex. 2003).

**3.** On warnings generally, see Howells, Information Obligations and Product Liability—A Game of Russian Roulette?, in Information Rights and Obligations—A Challenge for Party Autonomy and Transactional Fairness (G. Howells, A. Janssen, and R. Schulze eds., Ashgate, 2004/05); Korzec, Restating the Obvious in Maryland Products Liability Law: The Restatement (Third) of Torts: Products Liability and Failure to Warn Defenses, 30 U. Balt. L. Rev. 341 (2001); Bowbeer, Lumish, and Cohen, Warning! Failure to Read This Article May Be Hazardous to Your Failure to Warn Defense, 27 Wm. Mitchell L. Rev. 439 (2000) (all caps in title removed); Flynn and Laravuso, The Existence of a Duty to Warn: A Question for the Court or the Jury?, 27 Wm. Mitchell L. Rev. 633 (2000); Viscusi, Using Warnings to Extend the Boundaries of Consumer Sovereignty, 23 Harv. J.L. & Pub. Pol'y 211 (1999); Geistfeld, Inadequate Product Warnings and Causation, 30 U. Mich. J.L. Ref. 309 (1997); Rheingold and Feinglass, Risk–Utility Analysis in the Failure to Warn Context, 30 U. Mich. J.L. Ref. 353 (1997); R. Keeton, Warning Defect: Origins, Policies, and Directions, 30 U. Mich. J.L. Ref. 367

## History

The manufacturer's duty to warn of hidden dangers in its products is ancient, with roots reaching back at least to Roman sales law. In early Rome, a seller who was aware of hidden defects in its products was guilty of fraud (*dolus*) if the seller did not disclose the defects to the buyer.[4] Later, Justinian pronounced that "if the seller knew, but was silent and so deceived the buyer, he will have to make good to the buyer all losses that have fallen on him in consequence of the purchase."[5] In the thirteenth century, Thomas Acquinas[6] outlined the responsibilities of merchants, in the *Summa Theologica,*[7] consistent with Justinian principles from the *Digest*. A seller was bound to disclose to the buyer any secret flaws the product might possess: it was a sin and fraud to sell a product containing a latent defect known to the seller and not the buyer, and such a sale was void. If the seller was unaware of the defect, the sale was not a sin, but the seller nevertheless had to return any excess price attributable to the defect.[8] A seller was not bound to disclose obvious defects from "any duty of justice," but to do so would reflect "the more exuberant virtue."[9]

In America, products liability claims based on a seller's failure to provide adequate warnings or instructions arose during the late 1800s, although claims for failure to warn, as products liability claims more generally, were uncommon until the 1900s.[10] The earliest warnings

(1997); Latin, Good Warnings, Bad Products, and Cognitive Limitations, 41 UCLA L. Rev. 1193 (1994); Noah, The Imperative to Warn: Disentangling the "Right to Know" from the "Need to Know" about Consumer Product Hazards, 11 Yale J. on Reg. 293 (1994); Hager, Don't Say I Didn't Warn You (Even Though I Didn't): Why the Pro–Defendant Consensus on Warning Law Is Wrong, 61 Tenn. L. Rev. 1125 (1994); Michael A. Pittenger, Reformulating the Strict Liability Failure to Warn, 49 Wash. & Lee L. Rev. 1509 (1992); Jacobs, Toward a Process Based Approach to Failure-to-Warn Law, 71 N.C. L. Rev. 121 (1992); Henderson and Twerski, Doctrinal Collapse in Products Liability: The Empty Shell of Failure to Warn, 65 N.Y.U. L. Rev. 265 (1990); Madden, The Duty to Warn in Products Liability: Contours and Criticism, 89 W.Va. L. Rev. 221 (1987); Twerski, Weinstein, Donaher & Piehler, The Use and Abuse of Warnings in Products Liability—Design Defect Litigation Comes of Age, 61 Cornell L.Rev. 495 (1976); W.P. Keeton, Products Liability—Inadequacy of Information, 48 Texas L. Rev. 398 (1970); Noel, Manufacturer's Negligence of Design or Directions for Use of a Product, 71 Yale L.J. 816 (1962); Dillard and Hart, Product Liability: Directions for Use and the Duty to Warn, 41 Va. L. Rev. 145 (1955); 1 Madden & Owen on Products Liability ch. 9; 5 Frumer and Friedman, Products Liability 50.01; 2 Am. Law Prod. Liab. 3d § 28.32; C.J. Miller and R. Goldberg, Product Liability ch. 12

(Oxford, 2d ed. 2004) (British and European law).

**4.** See J. Thomas, Textbook of Roman Law 286 (1976) ("The concern is with latent or hidden defects.... [I]f the vendor was aware of the defect and did not disclose it, he was guilty of *dolus* and would be liable in the *actio empti*...."); Honoré, The History of the Aedilitian Actions from Roman to Roman–Dutch Law, in Studies in the Roman Law of Sale 132, 135 (D. Daube ed., reprint 1977) (1959) ("during the last century of the Republic the notion of *dolus* was extended to cover both the statement by the seller that the thing sold possessed or did not possess some quality when he knew this was untrue and also the case when the seller knowingly concealed a defect"). See also Rogerson, Implied Warranty Against Latent Defects in Roman and English Law, in Studies in the Roman Law of Sale 112, 113 (1959) (D. Daube ed., reprint 1977).

**5.** Justinian's Digest, Book 19, Tit. 1, Lex 13 (533 A.D.).

**6.** 1225?–1274 A.D.

**7.** Thomas Acquinas, Summa Theologica, Ethicus, II, II, question 77, arts. 2–4.

**8.** See Hamilton, The Ancient Maxim Caveat Emptor, 40 Yale L.J. 1133 (1931).

**9.** Id. at 1138 (quoting Acquinas, Summa Theologica, Ethicus, II, II, question 77, Art. 4 (Rickaby trans., 2d ed. 1896)).

**10.** See Bohlen, The Basis of Affirmative Obligations in the Law of Tort, 53 U.

claims grew out of and intermingled notions of false representations and deceit,[11] the courts following the ancient approach of considering a merchant's failure to disclose a known defect to be fraudulent.[12] On this basis, early courts held sellers liable for failing to warn that sheep were diseased;[13] that lead paint had been spilled on hay sold for cow feed which killed the cow;[14] and that a painted step-ladder was made of defective wood.[15] A plaintiff seeking recovery on a warnings claim against a remote seller could be barred by the absence of privity of contract with the defendant,[16] and sometimes on the basis that the seller was not aware of the danger,[17] or that the plaintiff was.[18] But a number of early decisions permitted claims by remote parties, on principles made famous in *Huset v. J.I. Case Threshing Machine Co.,*[19] where the defendant sold "an article which he knows to be imminently dangerous to life or limb to another without notice of its qualities."[20]

Early cases alleged that a manufacturer or other seller had failed to provide adequate warnings about a variety of dangers—that naphtha sold for lamp oil could explode;[21] that a pull-out bed frame might fall if the legs were not secured;[22] that stove polish might ignite;[23] that coal oil sold for use in starting fires was mixed with gasoline and might explode;[24] that a car crank might kick back and break an arm;[25] that the

Pa. L. Rev. 273 (1905); Dillard and Hart, Product Liability: Directions for Use and the Duty to Warn, 41 Va. L. Rev. 145 (1955) (thorough historical review of duty to warn); Noel, Manufacturer's Negligence of Design or Directions for Use of a Product, 71 Yale L.J. 816 (1962).

**11.** Notably Langridge v. Levy, 2 M & W 518 (1837) (retailer subject to liability in tort for misrepresenting that poorly made gun, an inherently dangerous instrument, was made by a good manufacturer and was safe), and Thomas v. Winchester, 6 N.Y. 397 (1852) (medicine seller who falsely labels belladonna as extract of dandelion liable for resulting injuries, citing Langridge v. Levy).

**12.** *But see* Bohlen, The Basis of Affirmative Obligations in the Law of Tort, 53 U. Pa. L. Rev. 273 (1905) (mentioning vendor's positive duty to disclose known dangers to a buyer and distinguishing it from vendor's negative duty not to misrepresent).

**13.** Jeffrey v. Bigelow & Tracy, 13 Wend. 518, 28 Am. Dec. 476 (N.Y. Sup. Ct. 1835) (citing Evans' Pothier, pt. 1, ch. 2, art. 3, pl. 166).

**14.** French v. Vining, 102 Mass. 132 (1869) (if the defendant knew the hay was "dangerous or poisonous, it would plainly be a violation of good faith, and an illegal act, to sell it to the plaintiff without disclosing its condition," citing Thomas v. Winchester and Langridge v. Levy).

**15.** Schubert v. J.R. Clark Co., 51 N.W. 1103 (Minn. 1892) (cites Thomas v. Winchester and holds that the defendant had a duty to warn of the latent defect).

**16.** See § 1.2, above.

**17.** See, e.g., Peaslee–Gaulbert Co. v. McMath's Adm'r, 146 S.W. 770 (Ky. 1912) (sellers unaware of risk that painters would put candle close to can of paint, causing can to explode).

**18.** Leavitt v. Fiberloid Co., 82 N.E. 682 (Mass. 1907) (flammability of "fiberloid" used to make combs).

**19.** 120 F. 865 (8th Cir. 1903) (Minn. law), discussed in § 1.2, above. See, e.g., Wellington v. Downer Kerosene Oil Co., 104 Mass. 64 (1870); Schubert v. J.R. Clark Co., 51 N.W. 1103 (Minn. 1892). See also Heizer v. Kingsland & Douglass Mfg. Co., 19 S.W. 630, 633 (Mo. 1892) (dictum); Olds Motor Works v. Shaffer, 140 S.W. 1047, 1051 (Ky. 1911) (defective rumble seat on which plaintiff was sitting fell off car; dictum).

**20.** Id. at 871.

**21.** Wellington v. Downer Kerosene Oil Co., 104 Mass. 64 (1870).

**22.** Lewis v. Terry, 43 P. 398 (Cal. 1896).

**23.** Clement v. Crosby & Co., 111 N.W. 745 (Mich. 1907).

**24.** Waters–Pierce Oil Co. v. Deselms, 212 U.S. 159 (Okla. 1909).

**25.** Martin v. Maxwell–Brisco Motor Vehicle Co., 138 S.W. 65 (Mo. 1911).

dye in a coat's fur collar might cause allergies;[26] that a can of paint stain might ignite;[27] and that dehydrated milk might go bad.[28] While most of these early warnings claims remained partially rooted in deceit, by the middle of the twentieth century warnings claims stood solidly on their own.[29]

## Nature of Duty to Warn

The "duty to warn" is an umbrella term for describing a manufacturer's informational obligations to those who purchase and use its products. This duty is actually comprised of two quite separate obligations: the duty to warn—to inform buyers and users of hidden dangers in a product; and the duty to instruct—to inform them on how to avoid those dangers in order to use the product safely.[30] Together, these duties require that important information on product hazards and product safety are transferred from manufacturers, who possess the information, to buyers and users of products, who need it.[31]

From a manufacturer's perspective, it usually is less costly to warn of a danger than to improve quality assurance or to design the problem entirely out of the product. Courts also sometimes assume that supplying warnings and instructions is an easy and inexpensive way for manufacturers to fulfill their obligation to make their products reasonably safe. And injured plaintiffs often reinforce this view, sometimes frivolously adding warning defect claims to cases where they have no business, since proving a warning "defective" is often a far easier (and less expensive) task than successfully attacking a product's design.[32] Yet many courts look skeptically at warnings claims and do not lightly impose a duty to warn on manufacturers.[33]

It is true that the direct economic costs of providing warnings and instructions typically are minimal, but less obvious costs raise subtle and important issues. One is the danger of providing too *much* information— the risk of over-warning or "warnings pollution."[34] Moreover, the decision on how much and what types of information a manufacturer should provide with a product can only be answered intelligibly if the goals sought to be achieved by the legal requirements are fully understood. Probably the most generally accepted goal of products liability law is

---

**26.**  Gerkin v. Brown & Sehler Co., 143 N.W. 48 (Mich. 1913).

**27.**  Thornhill v. Carpenter–Morton Co., 108 N.E. 474 (Mass. 1915).

**28.**  Rosenbusch v. Ambrosia Milk Corp., 168 N.Y.S. 505 (App. Div. 1917).

**29.**  See, e.g., Orr v. Shell Oil Co., 177 S.W.2d 608 (Mo. 1943) (worker could maintain claim for failing to warn that contact with chemical could cause damage to kidneys and other injuries, citing Restatement of Torts § 388); Dillard and Hart, Product Liability: Directions for Use and the Duty to Warn, 41 Va. L. Rev. 145 (1955) (citing *Orr* as illustration of modern approach to duty to warn).

**30.**  See, e.g., Ontai v. Straub Clinic & Hosp. Inc., 659 P.2d 734, 743 (Haw. 1983).

**31.**  Warnings and instructions are distinguished in § 9.3, below.

**32.**  See, e.g., Richmond, Renewed Look at the Duty to Warn and Affirmative Defenses, 61 Def. Couns. J. 205 (1994) ("failure to warn claims are not technical and are relatively inexpensive to prosecute, unlike traditional design defect cases").

**33.**  See, e.g., Killeen v. Harmon Grain Products, Inc., 413 N.E.2d 767, 770–771 (Mass. App. Ct. 1980) (manufacturer of cinnamon-flavored toothpicks had no duty to warn of danger to child falling during play while holding one in mouth: duty to warn not imposed as "a mindless ritual").

**34.**  See § 9.3, below.

deterrence—risk reduction—predicated on the view that a consumer informed about product dangers and methods of safe use will use that information for self-protection. And deterrence rests on the more complex goal of economic efficiency, which seeks to maximize social resources by minimizing wasteful injuries.[35] There can be no doubt that warnings and instructions often are an efficient way to help protect consumers from latent product hazards.[36]

A related reason for requiring warnings and instructions, but one which is grounded in quite a different value, is the promotion of individual autonomy—by shifting cost-benefit decisionmaking on product hazards from manufacturers to individual consumers.[37] A consumer who is fully informed of a product's dangers and how to avoid them may choose to use the product in a particular, safer manner. Or the informed consumer may choose not to buy or use the product at all.[38] Unlike the risk-reduction rationale, which reflects a utilitarian perspective rooted in economic efficiency, this kind of informed consent value focuses on protecting a user's individual rights—specifically, the user's right of self-determination, the right "to determine his own fate."[39] The idea here is "that the user or consumer is entitled to make his own choice as to whether the product's utility or benefits justify exposing himself to the risks of harm. Thus, a true choice situation arises, and a duty to warn attaches, whenever a reasonable man would want to be informed of the risk in order to decide whether to expose himself to it."[40] On the obverse side of the individual freedom perspective lies the value of personal responsibility, and with it issues of paternalism.

Lurking within the duty to warn lies a paradox: The duty to warn is at once the most important, yet least effective, duty in the law of products liability. Its importance lies in its respect for the autonomy of consumers, as discussed above, together with its promotion of utility by helping to reduce the level of unnecessary product accidents. Its ineffectiveness springs from how easy it is to assert a warnings claim,[41] even if unjustified; how elusive such claims are to rationally adjudicate;[42] and what little impact warnings have on product safety—since mounting

**35.** See § 5.4, above.

**36.** See, e.g., Geistfeld, Inadequate Product Warnings and Causation, 30 U. Mich. J.L. Ref. 309, 314 (1997).

**37.** See Viscusi, Using Warnings to Extend the Boundaries of Consumer Sovereignty, 23 Harv. J.L. & Pub. Pol'y 211, 231 (1999) (noting that "there is typically substantial heterogeneity in individuals' willingness to bear risk and in the kinds of products they prefer" and that "[h]azard warnings enable consumers to make decentralized choices for the products that best promote their welfare").

**38.** See Products Liability Restatement § 2(c) cmt. *i*.

**39.** Pavlides v. Galveston Yacht Basin, Inc., 727 F.2d 330 (5th Cir.1984) (Tex. law).

**40.** Borel v. Fibreboard Paper Products Corp., 493 F.2d 1076, 1089 (5th Cir.1973)

(Tex. law) (asbestos insulation worker, not warned of risks, contracted asbestosis and mesothelioma).

**41.** See, e.g., Richmond, Renewed Look at the Duty to Warn and Affirmative Defenses, 61 Def. Couns. J. 205 (1994); Priest, Products Liability Law and the Accident Rate, in Liability: Perspectives and Policy, at 217–20 (R. Litan & C. Winston eds., 1988); A. Schwartz, Proposals for Products Liability Reform: A Theoretical Synthesis, 97 Yale L.J. 353, 398 (1988); P. Huber, Liability: The Legal Revolution and Its Consequences 51–58 (1988); R. Epstein, Modern Products Liability Law 93 (1980).

**42.** See, e.g., Henderson and Twerski, Doctrinal Collapse in Products Liability: The Empty Shell of Failure to Warn, 65 N.Y.U. L. Rev. 265 (1990).

studies reveal that they often are ignored.[43] If this latter point be true, if most warnings and instructions truly are ignored, then a manufacturer's duty to warn and instruct may be mostly sound and fury, signifying little. So, warnings are powerful because they transfer important safety information and decisionmaking to consumers, yet they are trivial because consumers often fail to process safety information rationally. This is the paradox of the duty to warn.

## Relationship Between Duty to Warn and Duty of Safe Design

A fundamental aspect of the duty to warn is its relationship to the duty of safe design. The duty to warn is undoubtedly linked to a product's design, in that a warning or instruction provides information about hazards that are inherent in a product's design and how those design hazards may be avoided. For this reason, some early courts and commentators viewed the duty to warn as a subsidiary obligation of the duty of safe design.[44] In modern products liability law, however, although design defect and warning defect claims often go hand in hand,[45] almost every jurisdiction views the duty to warn and the duty of safe design as separate obligations that are largely independent of one another.[46] Thus, even if a product's design is as safe as it can be, the manufacturer still has a duty to warn of hidden dangers in the product.[47] If a substantial danger could have been designed out of a product at little cost, a large majority of courts hold that even an "adequate" warning does not insulate a manufacturer who failed to employ the safer design.[48] "A warning is not a Band–Aid to cover a gaping wound, and a product is not

**43.** See, e.g., Sunstein, The Laws of Fear, 115 Harv. L. Rev. 1119, 1123 (2002) (reviewing P. Slovic, The Perception of Risk) ("ordinary people often deal poorly with the topic of risk"); Symposium: Rational Actors or Rational Fools? The Implications of Psychology for Products Liability, 6 Roger Williams U. L. Rev. 1 (2000); Hanson and Kysar, Taking Behavioralism Seriously: The Problem of Market Manipulation, 74 N.Y.U. L. Rev. 630, 724 (1999); Hanson and Kysar, Taking Behavioralism Seriously: Some Evidence of Market Manipulation, 112 Harv. L. Rev. 1420, 1425 (1999); Latin, Good Warnings, Bad Products, and Cognitive Limitations, 41 UCLA L.Rev. 1193 (1994). This matter is examined in the context of cause in fact. See § 11.4, below.

**44.** See Noel, Manufacturer's Negligence of Design or Directions for Use of a Product, 71 Yale L.J. 816 (1962). This thought still lingers in some minds. See, e.g., Colegrove v. Cameron Machine Co., 172 F.Supp.2d 611, 635 (W.D. Pa. 2001) (trial court did not err in allowing engineer's testimony that absence of guard on foot switch of machine and lack of warnings regarding the unguarded foot switch were both design defects).

**45.** See, e.g., McConnell v. Cosco, Inc., 238 F.Supp.2d 970 (S.D. Ohio 2003) (valid

claim for design defect and failure to warn that infant could get neck caught on the highchair's tray, and be strangled, while trying to get out of chair); Colegrove v. Cameron Machine Co., 172 F.Supp.2d 611, 635 (W.D. Pa. 2001) (allowing engineer's expert testimony, that absence of guard on foot switch of machine and lack of warnings regarding the unguarded foot switch were both design defects, was not improper); Watkins v. Ford Motor Co., 190 F.3d 1213 (11th Cir. 1999) (Ga. law) (valid claims that Bronco II, which had propensity to roll over, was designed defectively and that Ford should have warned of this condition).

**46.** See § 6.2, above.

**47.** See, e.g., Hollister v. Dayton Hudson Corp., 201 F.3d 731, 740–43 (6th Cir. 2000) (Mich. law).

**48.** See, e.g., Delaney v. Deere & Co., 999 P.2d 930, 942 (Kan. 2000) ("just because there is a warning on a piece of equipment does not prevent the equipment from being dangerous"); White v. ABCO Eng'g Corp., 221 F.3d 293, 305–06 (2d Cir. 2000) (N.J. law) (notwithstanding clearly adequate warnings, conveyor manufacturer was subject to liability for failing to provide side guarding).

safe simply because it carries a warning.''[49] This important issue is considered in the chapter on defectiveness.[50]

### Variety of Warnings Issues

Many important warnings issues lie scattered throughout this book, as they are scattered widely throughout products liability law. Addressed in other contexts are the role of expert testimony in proving that a warning was defective and that the defect caused the plaintiff's harm;[51] the absence, in most jurisdictions, of a duty to warn of obvious and widely known dangers;[52] the dwindling idea of a duty to warn of unknowable dangers;[53] the spreading acceptance of a manufacturer's post-sale duty to warn;[54] the duty, accepted in virtually every jurisdiction, to warn against foreseeable product misuse;[55] the circumstances in which a manufacturer's common law duty to warn may be preempted by a federal safety statute;[56] the duties to warn of parties other than manufacturers, such as retailers,[57] successor corporations,[58] and sellers of used products;[59] and circumstances in which a manufacturer's failure to warn of danger may result in punitive damages.[60]

This chapter considers the fundamental issues surrounding the duty to warn: what theories of recovery support the duty to warn, what types of information that duty requires manufacturers to convey, how that information must be communicated, and to whom it must be given. The chapter first addresses the theories and tests of liability in warnings cases,[61] and the central issue of whether a manufacturer's warnings and instructions for a particular product are ''adequate'' given its likely environments of use.[62] The inquiry then focuses on who, other than the purchaser, the manufacturer must warn,[63] an inquiry that includes consideration of the bulk supplier and sophisticated user doctrines.[64] The final topic in this chapter concerns warnings issues surrounding the sale of prescription drugs and medical devices, including the adequacy of drug warnings, the learned intermediary doctrine, and the evolving law on a pharmacist's duty to warn its customers.[65]

## § 9.2   THEORIES AND TESTS OF LIABILITY

Warning defect claims may be brought in most jurisdictions on the basis of negligence, breach of the implied warranty of merchantability, and strict liability in tort. While plaintiffs often plead two or all three causes of action to support a warnings claim in modern products liability

---

**49.** Glittenberg v. Doughboy Recreational Indus., 491 N.W.2d 208, 216 (Mich. 1992). See Products Liability Restatement § 2 cmt. *l*.

**50.** See § 6.2, above.

**51.** See § 6.3, above.

**52.** See § 10.2, below.

**53.** See § 10.4, below.

**54.** See § 10.8, below.

**55.** See § 13.5, below.

**56.** See § 14.4, below.

**57.** See § 15.2, below.

**58.** See § 15.5, below.

**59.** See § 16.5, below.

**60.** See § 18.3, below.

**61.** See § 9.2, below.

**62.** See § 9.3, below.

**63.** See § 9.4, below.

**64.** See § 9.5, below.

**65.** See § 9.6, below.

litigation,[1] the negligence cause of action traditionally has been viewed as the most natural basis for such claims.[2] To "apprise a party of a danger of which he is not aware, and thus enable him to protect himself against it,"[3] due care may require a manufacturer "to speak out if the product is capable of harm and does not itself carry a message of danger."[4] The law reports are filled with cases in which the warnings claim is based, entirely or in part, on negligence.[5] With increasing evidence that plaintiffs fare better in products liability claims based on negligence than on strict liability, both for likelihood of success and size of verdict,[6] negligence surely will continue to be a favored cause of action for warnings claims.

To recover on a warnings claim in negligence, the plaintiff must establish that the manufacturer failed to exercise reasonable care to provide adequate information in a reasonable manner to an appropriate person about a foreseeable risk that was significant enough to justify the costs of providing the information.[7] How much care is reasonable, as previously discussed, requires balancing the expected safety benefits of a warning against its expected costs.[8] Courts infrequently engage explicitly in this type of cost-benefit analysis in any type of case, much less in negligence cases involving warnings claims. But when they do, the conclusion appears inescapable that "the cost of giving an adequate warning is usually so minimal, amounting only to the expense of adding some more printing to a label, that this balancing process will almost always weigh in favor of an obligation to warn of latent dangers, if the

---

**§ 9.2**

**1.** See, e.g., Larkin v. Pfizer, Inc., 2004 WL 1361954 (Ky. 2004) (negligence, breach of warranty, and strict liability); Goehring v. Target, 91 Fed. Appx. 1 (9th Cir. 2004) (Idaho law) (negligence, breach of warranty, and strict liability); Gray v. Badger Mining Corp., 676 N.W.2d 268 (Minn. 2004) (negligence, breach of warranty, and strict liability); Fralish v. A.O. Smith Corp., 2004 WL 1587559 (Pa. Super. Ct. 2004) (negligence and strict liability); Needham v. Coordinated Apparel Group, Inc., 811 A.2d 124 (Vt. 2002) (negligence, breach of warranty, and strict liability in tort); McConnell v. Cosco, 238 F.Supp.2d 970 (S.D. Ohio 2003) (negligence and failure to warn statutory liability); McConnell v. Cosco, Inc., 238 F. Supp. 2d 970 (S.D. Ohio 2003) (negligence and strict liability); Jones v. Amazing Prods., Inc., 231 F.Supp.2d 1228, 1240 (N.D. Ga. 2002) (negligence and strict liability).

**2.** "[W]here directions for use and duty to warn are in the picture, as they are to an increasing extent nowadays, negligence has been, and still is, the favorite cause of action." Prosser, Products Liability in Perspective, 5 Gonz. L. Rev. 157, 158 (1970). See generally Henderson and Twerski, Doctrinal Collapse in Products Liability: The Empty Shell of Failure to Warn, 65 N.Y.U. L. Rev. 265, 269 (1990) (noting, but critiquing, the assumption "that the all-purpose negligence formula works well in failure-to-

warn cases"); Noel, Manufacturer's Negligence of Design or Directions for Use of a Product, 71 Yale L.J. 816 (1962); Dillard and Hart, Product Liability: Directions for Use and the Duty to Warn, 41 Va. L. Rev. 145 (1955); Prosser and Keeton on Torts § 99, at 697.

Deviations from this view, which found some favor prior to the mid–1980s, included the Wade–Keeton definition of liability, usually (but not always) applied to design defect cases, and early rejections of the state of the art defense in warnings cases. See W.P. Keeton, Products Liability—Inadequacy of Information, 48 Texas L. Rev. 398 (1970); § 8.7 (the Wade–Keeton test), above, and § 10.4 (state of the art), below.

**3.** Jonescue v. Jewel Home Shopping Serv., 306 N.E.2d 312, 316 (Ill. App. Ct. 1973).

**4.** Dillard and Hart, Product Liability: Directions for Use and the Duty to Warn, 41 Va. L. Rev. 145, 147 (1955).

**5.** See note 1, above.

**6.** See Cupp and Polage, The Rhetoric of Strict Products Liability Versus Negligence: An Empirical Analysis, 77 N.Y.U. L. Rev. 874 (2002).

**7.** See Restatement (Second) of Torts § 388. See generally § 2.2, above.

**8.** See id.

manufacturer is otherwise required to do so.'"[9] Yet the values and analytical inquiry at play in negligence determinations are more subtle and complex than such a simple weighing of economic costs and safety benefits implies,[10] and courts usually provide little explanation or justification of negligence determinations in defective warnings cases.

Since the 1980s, there has been a significant resurgence in negligence reasoning in products liability law—in case law, state reform legislation, and in the *Products Liability Restatement*. These developments have been particularly pronounced with respect to warnings claims which so comfortably rest on the principles of negligence, as mentioned earlier. As has been pointed out for many years, claims for warnings defects in negligence and strict liability in tort are nearly, or entirely, identical.[11] At least one state supreme court has abandoned strict liability for negligence in warnings cases,[12] as have several state statutes,[13] as examined elsewhere in greater detail.[14]

Breach of the implied warranty of merchantability is claimed less frequently than negligence in products liability litigation generally, and the same holds true in warnings cases.[15] Yet breach of implied warranty, usually on the ground that a product was unfit for its ordinary purposes,[16] is an entirely sound basis for recovery for injuries attributable to a manufacturer's failure to provide sufficient warnings or instructions.[17]

**9.** Moran v. Faberge, Inc., 332 A.2d 11, 15 (Md. 1975). See § 2.2, above.

**10.** See, e.g., Wright, The Standards of Care in Negligence Law, in Philosophical Foundations of Tort Law 249 (D. Owen ed., Oxford 1995); Henderson and Twerski, Doctrinal Collapse in Products Liability: The Empty Shell of Failure to Warn, 65 N.Y.U. L. Rev. 265 (1990).

**11.** See, e.g., Mohney v. U.S. Hockey, Inc., 300 F.Supp.2d 556, 578 (N.D. Ohio 2004) ("The standard imposed is the same whether such a claim sounds in negligence or strict liability."); Ex parte Chevron Chemical Co., 720 So.2d 922, 926–29 (Ala. 1998) (negligence and strict liability in tort claims for negligence essentially the same); Miller v. Upjohn Co., 465 So.2d 42, 45 (La. Ct. App. 1985) (warning of side effects from drugs: "negligence and strict liability become one and identical"); Feldman v. Lederle Labs., 479 A.2d 374, 386 (N.J. 1984) ("negligence and strict liability in warning cases may be deemed to be functional equivalents"); Werner v. Upjohn Co., 628 F.2d 848, 858 (4th Cir.1980) (Md. law) ("[T]he issue under either theory is essentially the same: was the warning adequate?"). See generally Anderson v. Owens–Corning Fiberglas Corp., 810 P.2d 549, 561 (Cal. 1991) (Mosk, J., concurring and dissenting) ("In no area of strict products liability has the impact of principles of negligence become more pronounced than in failure-to-warn cases."); 2 Frumer and Friedman, Products Liability § 12.02[1] (collecting cases). Some courts disagree.

See, e.g., Werckenthein v. Bucher Petrochemical Co., 618 N.E.2d 902, 907 (Ill. App. Ct. 1993) ("The two theories are not identical, however: strict liability for failure to warn requires evidence of the industry's knowledge of the product's dangerous propensity, and it turns on the nature of the product and the adequacy of the warning; negligence focuses on the particular defendant's knowledge and conduct.").

**12.** Olson v. Prosoco, Inc., 522 N.W.2d 284 (Iowa 1994).

**13.** At least Indiana, Louisiana, Mississippi, New Jersey, North Carolina (restating negligence principles for warnings cases), Ohio, and Washington.

**14.** See §§ 2.6 (negligence) and 5.9 (strict liability in tort), above.

**15.** See § 4.3, above.

**16.** See UCC § 2–314(2)(c). A defective warning claim may be supported by other subsections. See, e.g., Reid v. Eckerds Drugs, Inc., 253 S.E.2d 344 (N.C. Ct. App. 1979) (plaintiff liberally applied deodorant, lit a cigarette, and burst into blue flame; an inadequate warning of danger might render the product unmerchantable under subsections (c), (e), and (f)).

**17.** See, e.g., Wright v. Brooke Group Ltd., 652 N.W.2d 159, 179–83 (Iowa 2002) (sale of cigarettes without adequate warnings of danger may breach implied warranty of merchantability); DeWitt v. Eveready Battery Co., 550 S.E.2d 511, 517 (N.C. Ct.

After all, a product unequipped with the information necessary to make it reasonably safe is quite obviously "unfit" for its ordinary uses. More fundamentally, to the extent that the implied warranty of merchantability is grounded in protecting a purchaser's reasonable expectations of product safety,[18] a seller's failure to warn consumers of a product's hidden dangers will assuredly subvert the buyer's safety expectations. In such a case, having paid full value for a product that contained less safety than expected, the buyer would be deprived of the benefit of the bargain.

Strict liability in tort is the most common cause of action for defective warning claims. A product with inadequate information about product dangers and how to avoid them is "defective," plain and simple. Such claims are routine in modern products liability litigation and, not uncommonly, they are held to be a proper basis of recovery.[19]

It will be recalled that the two principal liability tests for design defectiveness in strict liability in tort are the consumer expectations test and the risk-utility test.[20] These tests might helpfully be employed to test the defectiveness of a product alleged to contain insufficient information on a product's danger.[21] Yet neither test is especially helpful for distinguishing between those dangers which should be warned about and those which should not, or for determining whether a particular warning adequately conveys information about a risk. If a product fails to have adequate warnings of a hidden danger, it plainly violates a consumer's expectations,[22] as the implied warranty discussion explains; and the

App. 2001), aff'd, 565 S.E.2d 140 (N.C. 2002) (failure to provide adequate warnings of a product's dangers may render a product unmerchantable); Hollister v. Dayton Hudson Corp., 201 F.3d 731, 740 (6th Cir. 2000) (Mich. law) (plaintiff established prima facie case that shirt was defective, and therefore sold in breach of the implied warranty of merchantability, because it lacked a warning of its extreme flammability); Johnson v. Brown & Williamson Tobacco Corp., 122 F.Supp.2d 194, 206 (D. Mass. 2000) (implied warranty of merchantability breached if adequate warnings about product dangers are not given to foreseeable users); Bryant v. Adams, 448 S.E.2d 832, 843 (N.C. Ct. App. 1994) (failure to warn and instruct concerning use of trampoline); Bly v. Otis Elevator Co., 713 F.2d 1040, 1045 (4th Cir. 1983) (Va. law) ("A manufacturer may breach its implied warranty of merchantability by failing to warn or instruct concerning dangerous propensities or characteristics of a product even if that product is flawless in design and manufacture."). See generally 3 Lawrence's Anderson on the UCC 2–314:219 (product without warning of hidden danger, or with inadequate warning, may be unmerchantable).

**18.** See § 4.3, above.

**19.** See, e.g., Fralish v. A.O. Smith Corp., 2004 WL 1587559 (Pa. Super. Ct.

2004) (no warning on hot water heater of serious risk of scald injuries if water heated to 150° F); Lewis v. Sea Ray Boats, Inc., 65 P.3d 245 (Nev. 2003) (warnings of danger of carbon monoxide exposure from engine exhaust caused by running boat's heater might not have adequately apprised users of risk of such poisoning from using air conditioner run by generator); McConnell v. Cosco, Inc., 238 F.Supp.2d 970 (S.D. Ohio 2003) (failing to warn that infant, trying to get out of high chair, could get strangled if neck caught on tray); Benjamin v. Wal–Mart Stores, Inc., 61 P.3d 257 (Or. 2002) (insufficient warnings of risk of asphyxiation from using propane heater in tent); Campagna ex rel. Greco v. American Cyanamid Co., 767 A.2d 996 (N.J. Super. Ct. App. Div. 2001).

**20.** See chs. 5 and 8, above.

**21.** The consumer expectations and risk-utility tests arose in the design context not because they innately and narrowly applied to design defect claims but because they were the general tests for breach of warranty and negligence, respectively, which combined to generate strict liability in tort. See ch. 5, above.

**22.** By paying fair value for products appearing to contain certain types and levels of risk, consumers expect to encounter those risks—not others, known to the seller

safety benefits of adding a sufficient warning virtually always exceed its monetary costs, as noted in the negligence discussion.[23] Thus, when applied to warning cases, both design defect tests point toward liability in every case in which a manufacturer fails to provide meaningful warnings of material hidden risks in its products. Not surprisingly, but without explanation, this is precisely the standard that courts apply in judging warning defects: if a hazard is foreseeable to manufacturers, if it is material to and hidden from consumers, and if there is a reasonable means to convey the information about the risk to users and consumers, a product is defective if the manufacturer fails to provide adequate warnings of the danger and instructions on how to avoid it. More concisely,[24] a manufacturer has a duty to provide adequate warnings of all material risks, and a manufacturer is subject to strict liability in tort for failing to supply adequate warnings and instructions with the products that it sells.[25]

Two related issues treated elsewhere should be noted here. Perhaps the most fundamental issue, when a warnings claim is brought in strict liability in tort, is whether the duty to warn is limited to foreseeable risks or whether the duty extends to risks which are unforeseeable, undiscoverable, or "unknowable" at the time the product is sold. A few courts[26] and commentators[27] in the developmental stages of modern products liability law took the position that the move to "strict" liability must mean that the risks of unforeseeable hazards shifted from consumers to manufacturers, so that a product without warnings of unforeseeable risks would be "defective" for purposes of strict liability in tort. Over the last couple of decades, however, American courts and commentators have widely (if not quite universally) rejected this kind of "superstrict" liability on grounds of fairness, logic, and practicality. The various strands of this important aspect of the duty to warn are examined later in the context of state of the art.[28]

The second related issue is how, if at all, strict liability in tort claims for warning defects differ from claims in negligence. As mentioned earlier in this section, most courts now agree that these types of claims

---

but undisclosed, which frustrate the consumers' reasonable expectations and deprive them of the fair value of their deals. See, e.g., Needham v. Coordinated Apparel Group, Inc., 811 A.2d 124 (Vt. 2002) (jury could find that clothing fabric which ignites some distance from a fire, and burns explosively, is more dangerous than a consumer would expect).

**23.** See, e.g., Moran v. Faberge, Inc., 332 A.2d 11, 15 (Md. 1975) (flammability risk of perfume exceeded small expense of printing a warning). See ch. 2, above. But other safety costs arise from over-warning, sometimes referred to as warnings pollution, which also should be considered.

**24.** Admittedly incomplete, this formulation is stated simply in a manner applicable to most cases. Two important limitations on the duty to warn, that are implied

in this formulation to keep it concise, are that the duty extends only to (1) risks which are foreseeable to the manufacturer, see § 10.4, below, and (2) latent risks of which consumers generally are unaware. See § 10.2, below.

**25.** See Gershonowitz, The Strict Liability Duty to Warn, 44 Wash. & Lee L. Rev. 71, (1987) (proposing such a standard). See also Note, 49 Wash. & Lee L. Rev. 1509 (1992) (proposing a more elaborate version of this standard).

**26.** See especially Beshada v. Johns–Manville Prods. Corp., 447 A.2d 539, 545 (N.J. 1982), examined in § 10.4, below.

**27.** See, e.g., W.P. Keeton, Products Liability–Inadequacy of Information, 48 Texas L. Rev. 398 (1970).

**28.** See § 10.4, below.

are nearly, or entirely, identical—that, in the words of the Ohio Supreme Court, "the standard imposed upon the defendant in a strict liability claim grounded upon an inadequate warning is the same as that imposed in a negligence claim based upon inadequate warning."[29] Nevertheless, even while acknowledging that "strict" liability in the warnings context is really nothing more than negligence, most courts continue to pretend that it really is something more, that liability (perhaps because of differing defenses and other secondary rules) is "strict."[30]

The *Third Restatement* rejects doctrinal labels—such as negligence, implied warranty, and strict liability in tort—in defining a seller's liability for warning defects.[31] In § 2(c), a mirror image of the design defect definition in § 2(b),[32] the *Products Liability Restatement* bases liability in warnings cases on principles of reasonableness:

> A product ... is defective because of inadequate instructions or warnings when the foreseeable risks of harm posed by the product could have been reduced or avoided by the provision of reasonable instructions or warnings ... and the omission of the instructions or warnings renders the product not reasonably safe.

While simplicity and elegance may be wanting,[33] this definition of a warning states a simple proposition: that a product without adequate ("reasonable") warnings or instructions (of foreseeable risks) is defective. Although resting on principles of negligence, the Restatement test for warning defects is compatible with the other two conventional causes of action (implied warranty and strict liability in tort) and, like warning claims based on the three conventional causes of action, rests on whether a seller provides adequate ("reasonable") safety information with a product.

Thus, the duty to warn in negligence, implied warranty, and strict liability in tort, under the *Third Restatement*, and under state products liability reform statutes,[34] centers on one central issue—whether "adequate" warnings and instructions were provided with a product: if so, the product supplier has fulfilled its duty to warn; if not, it has breached its duty and is subject to liability.[35] In short, the liability test for warnings claims, regardless of the theory of liability, is "adequacy."

---

**29.** Crislip v. TCH Liquidating Co., 556 N.E.2d 1177, 1183 (Ohio 1990) (failure to instruct on strict liability failure to warn claim was harmless error).

**30.** *Crislip* is a case in point, the court there explaining that "[w]e do not mean to suggest that a cause of action for negligent failure to warn or warn adequately is identical to one brought under strict liability," principally because a plaintiff's comparative fault may not reduce damages in a strict liability claim in Ohio. See also Anderson v. Owens–Corning Fiberglas Corp., 810 P.2d 549 (Cal. 1991) (unsuccessful attempt to distinguish strict liability in tort from negligence claims).

**31.** See Products Liability Restatement § 2 cmt. *n*.

**32.** The "reasonableness test for judging the adequacy of product instructions and warnings ... parallels § 2(b) which adopts a similar standard for judging the safety of product designs. Although the liability standard is formulated in identical terms, the concept is more difficult to apply in the warnings context." Products Liability Restatement § 2(c) cmt. *i*.

**33.** One reason for its complexity is that it unnecessarily includes causation in the definition of defectiveness.

**34.** See, e.g., Ohio Rev. Code Ann. § 2307.76; La. Rev. Stat. Ann. § 9:2800.57.

**35.** See, e.g., Clark v. Safety–Kleen Corp., 845 A.2d 587, 598 (N.J. 2004) ("a product is defective absent an adequate

## § 9.3   ADEQUACY

At the center of the duty to warn lies "adequacy." Each theory of liability supporting a warnings claim is premised on the defendant's failure to provide users and consumers adequate information about a product danger, or how to avoid it, as just discussed.[1] Unless a plaintiff can prove that a warning was inadequate, a defective warning claim will fail.[2]

"Adequacy" suggests a matter of degree, and most adequacy cases do involve products for which some warning of danger or instruction on safe use was provided. But the "adequacy" category sometimes quite easily elides into situations where no warning was provided whatsoever. While the issues in many no-warning cases overlap with adequacy, such as whether the nature and appearance of a product adequately telegraphed its dangers,[3] these cases often are more properly treated as "duty" cases—such as whether there is a duty to warn consumers that their clothing may ignite some distance from a fire, and burn explosively thereafter, or whether this hazard is only part of the fabric flammability risk of which consumers are aware.[4]

Many courts have stated what makes a warning "adequate." One frequently cited formulation is from *Pavlides v. Galveston Yacht Basin, Inc.*,[5] where the court explained that, to be adequate, a warning "must provide 'a complete disclosure of the existence and extent of the risk involved.' A warning must (1) be designed so it can reasonably be expected to catch the attention of the consumer; (2) be comprehensible and give a fair indication of the specific risks involved with the product; and (3) be of an intensity justified by the magnitude of the risk.'"[6] Another court observed that a warning's adequacy depends upon a balance of many factors, including "the severity of the danger; the likelihood that the warning will catch the attention of those who will foreseeably use the product and convey the nature of the danger to them; the intensity and form of the warning; and the cost of improving the strength or mode of the warning."[7] The *Products Liability Restate-*

---

warning"); Ohio Rev. Code Ann. § 2307.76 (liability for "inadequate" warning or instruction).

### § 9.3

**1.** See § 9.2, above.

**2.** See, e.g., Austin v. Will–Burt Co., 361 F.3d 862 (5th Cir. 2004) (Miss. law) (dismissing inadequate warnings claim for electrocution of news van worker killed when van's telescoping mast hit power lines; yellow labels on mast, with red and black lettering, stated: DANGER! PLEASE READ INSTRUCTIONS BEFORE RAISING!— DANGER. WATCH FOR WIRES. YOU CAN BE KILLED IF THIS PRODUCT COMES NEAR ELECTRICAL POWER LINES).

**3.** See, e.g., Fralish v. A.O. Smith Corp., 2004 WL 1587559 (Pa. Super. Ct. 2004) (no warning on water heater of scalding risk;

trial court improperly granted summary judgment for manufacturer).

**4.** Compare Needham v. Coordinated Apparel Group, Inc., 811 A.2d 124 (Vt. 2002) (duty to warn of cotton garment's explosive flammability), with Coleman v. Cintas Sales Corp., 100 S.W.3d 384 (Tex. App. 2002) (no duty to warn that non-flame retardant uniform would ignite when exposed to open flame and that flaming fabric would be difficult to extinguish). Duty issues associated with products containing obvious and commonly known hazards are addressed in § 10.2, below.

**5.** 727 F.2d 330 (5th Cir. 1984).

**6.** Id. at 338. Other courts still rely on this formulation. See, e.g., Lewis v. Sea Ray Boats, Inc., 65 P.3d 245, 248 (Nev. 2003).

**7.** Bloxom v. Bloxom, 512 So.2d 839, 844 (La. 1987). See also Gray v. Badger

*ment* notes that determining a warning's adequacy requires focusing on its "content and comprehensibility, intensity of expression, and the characteristics of expected user groups," but the *Restatement* emphasizes that courts must be sensitive to a large range of considerations that inform adequacy determinations in different situations.[8] More concisely, it might be said that a warning is adequate if it provides a reasonable amount and type of information about a product's material risks and how to avoid them in a manner calculated to reach and be understood by those likely to need the information.[9]

The adequacy of a warning is often bound up with the issue of who should be warned, so that a warning ordinarily will not be adequate unless it warns those persons who are threatened by a product hazard or others in the best position—such as parents, employers, and doctors—to act on warnings to protect those persons subject to the hazard.[10] This aspect of warning adequacy informs several issues examined in this section, such as whether warnings should be made in foreign languages (or by symbols) to warn persons who do not read English, and whether industrial machinery should be equipped with back-up bells or buzzers to warn bystanders whom operators cannot see. While the issue of whom the manufacturer should warn is touched on indirectly in this section, it is specifically addressed in later sections which inquire generally into the categories of persons to whom warnings should be given (including allergic users);[11] consider the sophisticated user and bulk supplier doctrines most applicable to the workplace;[12] and examine the learned

---

Mining Corp., 676 N.W.2d 268, 274 (Minn. 2004) ("To be legally adequate, the warning should (1) attract the attention of those that the product could harm; (2) explain the mechanism and mode of injury; and (3) provide instructions on ways to safely use the product to avoid injury.").

**8.** Products Liability Restatement § 2(c) cmt. *i.* Observing that warnings and instructions rarely can provide "all potentially relevant information" about product hazards, that there is no easy guideline for courts to turn to in assessing the adequacy of warnings and instructions, and that determining the appropriate level of detail in warnings is particularly problematic, the *Restatement* notes that courts should be sensitive to many factors, such as the possibility that "educated or experienced product users and consumers may benefit from inclusion of more information about the full spectrum of product risks, whereas less-educated or unskilled users may benefit from more concise warnings and instructions stressing only the most crucial risks and safe-handling practices," and that "products intended for special categories of users, such as children, may require more vivid and unambiguous warnings." Excessive detail in some cases may diminish a normal person's ability "to focus on the important aspects of the warnings," while

"reasonably full disclosure" may be necessary in other cases "to enable informed, efficient choices by product users." Product warnings and instructions rarely can communicate all potentially relevant information, and the ability of a plaintiff to imagine a hypothetical better warning in the aftermath of an accident does not establish that the warning actually accompanying the product was inadequate. No easy guideline exists for courts to adopt in assessing the adequacy of product warnings and instructions. In making their assessments, courts must focus on various factors, such as content and comprehensibility, intensity of expression, and the characteristics of expected user groups. Id.

**9.** The first half of this formulation concerns the "substantive" adequacy of the warning's informational content, and the latter half concerns the "procedural" adequacy of the form of its conveyance.

**10.** See Anderson v. Hedstrom Corp., 76 F.Supp.2d 422, 440 (S.D.N.Y. 1999) ("The factual determination of whether an adequate warning was given is 'often interwoven with the question of whether the defendant manufacturer has a duty to warn, and if so, to whom that duty is owed.' ")

**11.** See § 9.4, below.

**12.** See § 9.5, below.

intermediary doctrine applicable to warnings for prescription drugs and medical devices.[13]

Whether a manufacturer or other seller has provided sufficient information about a product's hazards is especially fact intensive, such that the adequacy of warnings and instructions normally, but not always,[14] is a factual question for the jury to decide.[15]

Depending on the nature of a product and its hazards, expert testimony may or may not be appropriate on the adequacy of a warning or instruction.[16] Expert testimony will not be allowed in a particular case if it is unhelpful to the jury because it has no need for expert guidance on the adequacy of a warning;[17] because the testimony is unreliable;[18] or because adequacy is the ultimate issue in the case.[19] Yet courts often admit testimony on the adequacy of a warning by experts with various backgrounds, such as pharmacological labeling, communications psychology, human factors engineering, and others.[20] In cases involving complex

---

**13.** See § 9.6, below.

**14.** See, e.g., Austin v. Will–Burt Co., 361 F.3d 862 (5th Cir. 2004) (Miss. law) (warning may be adequate as a matter of law when it specifically warns against risk which causes plaintiff's harm); Calhoun v. Hoffman–La Roche, Inc., 768 So.2d 57, 61 (La. Ct. App. 2000) (adequacy becomes a question of law when the warning is "accurate, clear, and unambiguous"). See generally 2 Frumer and Friedman, Products Liability § 12.03[1] [b].

**15.** See, e.g., Mohr v. Saint Paul Fire & Marine Ins. Co., 674 N.W.2d 576, 589 (Wis. Ct. App. 2003); Benjamin v. Wal–Mart Stores, Inc., 61 P.3d 257, 265 (Or. Ct. App. 2002); Tesmer v. Rich Ladder Co., 380 N.W.2d 203 (Minn. Ct. App. 1986); Edwards v. California Chem. Co., 245 So.2d 259 (Fla. Dist. Ct. App. 1971). See generally 2 Frumer and Friedman, Products Liability § 12.03[1] [a].

**16.** On expert testimony, see § 6.3, above.

**17.** See, e.g., Ferebee v. Chevron Chem. Co., 552 F.Supp. 1293, 1304 (D.D.C. 1982), aff'd, 736 F.2d 1529 (D.C. Cir. 1984) ("The Court can think of no question more appropriately left to a common sense lay judgment than that of whether a written warning gets its message across to an average person. After all, it is to the layman that the warning is addressed, not to the expert on labeling.").

**18.** See, e.g., Worthington v. Wal–Mart Stores, Inc., 257 F.Supp.2d 1339, 1344 (D. Kan. 2003) (testimony of plaintiff's human factors/ergonomics and labeling expert on need for flammability warning labels on flannel shirts properly excluded as unreliable); Kerrigan v. Maxon Ind., 223 F.Supp.2d 626, 634 (E.D. Pa. 2002) (driver of cement truck injured when mixer unexpectedly raised and struck overpass; expert not qual-

ified to testify as to in-cab warning light or buzzer that would have informed driver that mixer was rising while vehicle was in motion; nor was expert's proposed testimony reliable, since he had prepared no plans, drawings, or data showing how feature would work); Meyerhoff v. Michelin Tire Corp., 852 F.Supp. 933 (D. Kan. 1994).

**19.** See, e.g., Worthington v. Wal–Mart Stores, Inc., 257 F.Supp.2d 1339, 1343–44 (D. Kan. 2003) (plaintiff's textile expert could not testify on defendant's ultimate responsibility for failing to provide appropriate warnings); Shell Oil Co. v. Gutierrez, 581 P.2d 271 (Ariz. Ct. App. 1978) (expert opinion admissible on the properties of chemicals, but not on adequacy of warning).

**20.** See, e.g., Fralish v. A.O. Smith Corp., 2004 WL 1587559 (Pa. Super. Ct. 2004) (trial court improperly ignored report of safety engineer explaining why water heater was defective because it did not warn of scalding risk); Benjamin v. Wal–Mart Stores, Inc., 61 P.3d 257, 265 (Or. Ct. App. 2002) (mechanical engineering professor, specializing in human factors engineering, could explain how warning was inadequate: "A warning's adequacy is a proper subject of expert testimony."); Yamaha Motor Co., U.S.A. v. Arnoult, 955 P.2d 661, 668–69 (Nev. 1998) (industrial engineer specializing in human factors and ergonomics allowed to testify; *Daubert* did not apply); Surace v. Caterpillar, Inc., 1995 WL 303895 (E.D. Pa. 1995) (mechanical and safety engineer, and human factors psychologist, both could testify on adequacy of back-up alarm on pavement profiler); Prevatt v. Pennwalt Corp., 237 Cal.Rptr. 488 (Ct. App. 1987) (cognitive psychologist: labels failed to attract user's attention or to warn appropriately of the danger); Smith v. United States Gypsum Co., 612 P.2d 251

hazards, such as those involving warnings about toxic substances and prescription drugs, expert testimony may be necessary to explain the technical or scientific mechanisms or effects that make a particular type of warning necessary.[21]

## Content—"Substantive Adequacy"

### Warnings vs. Instructions

As noted earlier,[22] the duty to "warn" is really comprised of two separate duties: (1) the duty to *warn*, to provide information on hidden dangers in the product; and (2) the duty to *instruct*, to provide information on how to avoid those dangers and use the product safely.[23] Because these duties are largely separate and independent, fulfilling one normally does not fulfill the other. So, no matter how adequately a manufacturer may warn about a product's danger, consumers still may need instructions on how to use the product safely. Thus, a telescope that may be used for viewing the sun must include not only warnings of the dangers of viewing the sun without a proper filter, but it must further provide clear and complete directions on how to install the sun filter in a manner that will protect against the danger.[24]

The converse is also true: instructions ordinarily do not satisfy the duty to warn. While manufacturers often argue that their instructions amount to warnings, sometimes luring an unwary court into this deceptive trap, even the best instruction will not satisfy the manufacturer's duty to warn if it does not alert users to specific dangers hidden in the product.[25] However, some instructions do imply a seriousness of danger,

(Okla. 1980) (holding admissible testimony of chemical engineer and psychiatrist that manufacturer's warning of heptane flammability was "inadequate" and "vague").

**21.** See, e.g., Beadling v. William Bowman Associates, 809 A.2d 188, 193–94 (N.J. Super. Ct. App. Div. 2002) (explosion of methanol vapor in empty 55 gallon drum when worker was welding near by; expert testimony on warning inadequacy sufficient to withstand supplier's summary judgment motion); Campagna ex rel. Greco v. American Cyanamid Co., 767 A.2d 996 (N.J. Super. Ct. App. Div. 2001) (doctor's testimony on how polio vaccine warning was inadequate sufficient to withstand manufacturer's summary judgment motion).

**22.** See § 9.1, above.

**23.** See, e.g., Ontai v. Straub Clinic & Hosp. Inc., 659 P.2d 734, 743 (Haw. 1983) ("A duty to warn actually consists of two duties: One is to give adequate instructions for safe use, and the other is to give a warning as to dangers. . . ."). See also Products Liability Restatement § 2(c) cmt. *i*: "[S]ellers must provide reasonable instructions and warnings about risks of injury posed by products. Instructions inform persons how to use and consume products safely. Warnings alert users and consumers to

the existence and nature of product risks so that they can prevent harm either by appropriate conduct during use or consumption or by choosing not to use or consume."

**24.** See Midgley v. S.S. Kresge Co., 127 Cal.Rptr. 217 (Ct. App. 1976) (K–Mart telescope had inadequate written instructions, and no diagrammatic illustrations, on proper method of attaching sun filter). A plane may crash or a house may burn down if an airplane part or a woodstove chimney pipe is inadvertently installed upside down. See Duford v. Sears, Roebuck & Co., 833 F.2d 407 (1st Cir. 1987) (N.H. law) (wood stove); Nesselrode v. Executive Beechcraft, Inc., 707 S.W.2d 371 (Mo.1986) (plane). See also Piper v. Bear Med. Systems, Inc., 883 P.2d 407 (Ariz. Ct. App. 1993) (respirator patient died when therapist, not having been warned of risk, attached one-way valve backwards); Downing v. Overhead Door Corp., 707 P.2d 1027 (Colo. Ct. App. 1985).

**25.** "Instructions on the use of a product [do] not discharge a manufacturer's duty to warn." Shuras v. Integrated Project Services, Inc., 190 F.Supp.2d 194, 201 (D. Mass. 2002). Accord, McConnell v. Cosco, Inc., 238 F.Supp.2d 970 (S.D. Ohio 2003) (holding that a highchair's instruction to "secure baby with safety straps" does not

even if only indirectly, that in certain circumstances may sufficiently convey the spirit of the risk. Thus, if the label on a disposable butane cigarette lighter says, "Keep out of reach of children," it may just be that this is a sufficient "warning" of the risk that a young child might use the lighter to start a fire. On a small object such as a lighter, there is insufficient room to describe most dangers fully if at all. In such cases, particularly when adults already have a quite accurate impression of the risk, a "Keep out of reach of children" instruction may alone imply, sufficiently, that the product poses a serious risk to children that adults had better heed.[26]

### Nature and Degree of Specific Risk

To be adequate, a warning must clearly and comprehensibly describe the nature and degree of a product's specific risks. This formulation conflates at least three ideas. First, warnings must be expressed in terms that are clear and comprehensible, meaning that they use language that effectively communicates information about a product's hazards. If warning language is confusing and unclear, such that users cannot understand its meaning, then the warning is inadequate.[27] Second, a warning should describe, with reasonable precision, the particular way in which a product is dangerous, the specific risks from using or misusing it in different ways. A warning which describes these risks vaguely and too generally, or which describes a different risk from the one which harms a plaintiff, will likely be inadequate.[28] Third, a warning must effectively

warn of risk of strangulation); Fuentes v. Shin Caterpillar Mitsubishi, Ltd., 2003 WL 22205665, *4 (Cal. Ct. App. 2003, unpublished) ("!WARNING Use self-attaching air chuck and stand behind tire tread while inflating" was really an instruction and was an inadequate warning because "there was no description of the fact that the tire assembly or the rim could explode upon inflation or that death or other serious injury could result"); Brown v. Glade & Grove Supply, 647 So.2d 1033 (Fla. Dist. Ct. App. 1994) (advising driver to operate tractor with lock-out pins in place is instruction, not warning); Meisner v. Patton Elec. Co., 781 F.Supp. 1432 (D. Neb. 1990) (instruction to plug space heater directly into wall outlet did not warn of risk of short circuit and fire from using extension cord).

**26.** See Todd v. Societe BIC (*Todd II*), 9 F.3d 1216 (7th Cir. 1993) (Ill. law) (Easterbrook, J.).

**27.** See, e.g., Benjamin v. Wal–Mart Stores, Inc., 61 P.3d 257 (Or. Ct. App. 2002) (juxtaposing warning against using propane heater in unventilated area beside warning of the risk of fire might lead reader to believe that the heater posed a risk of fire in a tent, not that it would asphyxiate the occupants of the tent).

**28.** See, e.g., Lewis v. Sea Ray Boats, Inc., 65 P.3d 245 (Nev. 2003) (warning of carbon monoxide poisoning from using

boat's engines to run heater does not warn of risk of such poisoning from using generator to run air-conditioning); Hayes v. Spartan Chemical Co., 622 So.2d 1352 (Fla. Dist. Ct. App. 1993) (warning of general risks of cleaning fluids inadequate without mentioning risks from one brief exposure); Ayers v. Johnson & Johnson Baby Prod. Co., 818 P.2d 1337 (Wash. 1991) (warning that baby may get diarrhea from ingesting "Baby Oil" does not warn of paralysis); General Chem. Corp. v. De La Lastra, 815 S.W.2d 750 (Tex. App. 1991) ("toxic" inadequately describes death). *But see* Werckenthein v. Bucher Petrochemical Co., 618 N.E.2d 902 (Ill. Ct. App. 1993) (warning against "repeated exposure" to chemical adequately warned chemist who suffered cancer and stroke after using sniff test on chemicals for many years).

Compare Spillane v. Georgia Pacific Corp., 1995 WL 71183 (E.D. Pa. 1995), which involved a roofing compound which warned: "CAUTION, SLIPPERY WHEN WET. Do not walk on surface unless it is completely dry. Follow proper safety precautions, including using appropriate shoes and safety rope." Plaintiff, a roofer, slipped on the compound, fell off a roof, and sued the manufacturer for failing adequately to warn. *Held*, defendant's motion for summary judgment denied. Although the language "at first seems the epitome of unam-

communicate the degree of risk, the likelihood and severity of injury the risk may cause. If serious injury of a particular type, or death, may be a consequence, those potential consequences should be described—with an intensity proportionate to the risk—or the warning will be inadequate.[29]

An adequate warning should disclose all foreseeable, material risks from foreseeable ways in which a product may be used. To begin with, a manufacturer must provide adequate warnings of all material risks that may arise from a product's normal, intended uses, including the risk of allergic reactions discussed in a later section.[30] But a manufacturer must also warn adequately of risks from unintended uses (which a manufacturer may call "misuses"), provided they are reasonably foreseeable.[31] And a manufacturer must provide warnings and instructions on peripheral uses which reasonably may be expected, such as why a hazardous chemical may need to be disposed of safely, and how to do so.[32] Yet, there simply is no way to warn perfectly of every risk, and too much information presents dangers of its own, the "warnings pollution" problem discussed below.

## Form—"Procedural Adequacy"

### Form—In General

For a warning or instruction to be adequate, it must be conveyed in such a form that is likely to reach and be comprehended by those who buy and use the product. Because it deals with physical methods for delivering substantive information, this type of adequacy may be referred to as "procedural," to distinguish it from the information's substantive content. Procedural adequacy has various dimensions, from the conspicuousness of written warnings, including their placement in prominent locations, to the use of foreign language or nonverbal warnings when fairly called for in the circumstances.

biguous clarity," it failed to convey how "appallingly slick" the roof surface was. The court drew an analogy to warning "Beware of cat. Stay Away," which would fail adequately to warn a person "chomped" by "a full-grown, hungry cheetah." "The cheetah is the quickest land-animal in the world, and plaintiffs' papers suggest this was just about the slickest roof in the world."

**29.** See, e.g., Benjamin v. Wal–Mart Stores, Inc., 61 P.3d 257 (Or. Ct. App. 2002) (jury could find inadequate a warning on propane heater that stated: "WARNING: FOR OUTDOOR USE ONLY. Never use inside house, camper, tent, vehicle or other unventilated or enclosed areas." because it did not warn that user could suffer "serious injury" or "death," or be "killed"); Shuras v. Integrated Project Services, Inc., 190 F.Supp.2d 194, 201 (D. Mass. 2002) (a warning's strength " 'must be commensurate with the dangers involved' "); General Chem. Corp. v. De La Lastra, 815 S.W.2d

750 (Tex. App. 1991) ("toxic" inadequately describes death).

**30.** See § 9.4, below.

**31.** See, e.g., Benjamin v. Wal–Mart Stores, Inc., 61 P.3d 257 (Or. Ct. App. 2002) (jury properly found that manufacturer could foresee that propane heater, marketed only for outdoor use because of its carbon monoxide fumes, might be used to heat a tent). A manufacturer has no duty to warn of uses that are unforeseeable. See § 13.5, below.

**32.** See, e.g., Tucci v. Bossert, 385 N.Y.S.2d 328 (App. Div. 1976) (partially used can of Drano placed in trash bag in front of house because manufacturer had inadequately warned of risks); Boyl v. California Chemical Co., 221 F.Supp. 669 (D. Or. 1963) (inadequate warning on how and why to safely rinse highly toxic residue from spray tank used to dispense liquid weed killer). On a manufacturer's responsibility for dangers of disposal, see § 10.7, below.

**Conspicuousness.** Written warnings are most common, and the most significant procedural adequacy issue in this context is the conspicuousness of the warning. The conspicuousness of written warnings typically depends on the type size, its style or font, its color, whether it contrasts with other messages nearby, and whether it has a heading such as "WARNING!" or "CAUTION." Conspicuousness has long been a formal requirement of warranty disclaimers, and the considerations for determining whether a writing is conspicuous in that context translate well to cases involving the procedural adequacy of written warnings.[33] So, if a warning is written in yellow or red letters that are large and bold, and preceded by a large "WARNING!" heading,[34] it is more likely to be conspicuous than if the warning is black and white, small, and has no heading.[35]

**Location.** An important feature of conspicuousness is location. When warnings are set apart, and located in a prominent position, they are most likely to be observed and absorbed. Thus, warnings are more likely to be conspicuous if they are printed by themselves on the front of the product or its label, rather than together with other information on a product's side or back.[36] Similarly, warnings are more likely to catch the attention of the user if they are placed near the point of danger,[37] at eye level,[38] or at a place where the user normally focuses attention, such as

---

**33.** See § 4.7, above.

**34.** See, e.g., Austin v. Will–Burt Co., 361 F.3d 862 (5th Cir. 2004) (Miss. law) (dismissing inadequate warnings claim for electrocution of news van worker killed when van's telescoping mast hit power lines; yellow labels on mast, with red and black lettering, stated: DANGER! PLEASE READ INSTRUCTIONS BEFORE RAISING!—DANGER. WATCH FOR WIRES. YOU CAN BE KILLED IF THIS PRODUCT COMES NEAR ELECTRICAL POWER LINES.). Compare Beadling v. William Bowman Associates, 809 A.2d 188, 193–94 (N.J. Super. Ct. App. Div. 2002) (methanol vapor in empty 55 gallon drum exploded while worker was welding near by; flammability warning label on top of drum, obscured by dark oily residue, should also have been placed on sides of drum and had plastic coating—ANSI standard provides that label should be protected from "damage, fading or visual obstruction" from abrasion, ultra-violet light, lubricants, chemical, or dirt).

**35.** See, e.g., Jones v. Amazing Prods., Inc., 231 F.Supp.2d 1228, 1248 (N.D. Ga. 2002) (cautionary instruction on drain cleaner label was in such small print, "buried in the middle of a long paragraph," that even the judge, who was looking for this specific language, had to read the label twice to find the particular language; held, adequacy for jury); Jaurequi v. John Deere Co., 971 F.Supp. 416, 428 (E.D. Mo. 1997) (warnings on farm machine were inadequate because they were too small and lo-

cated far from the hazard); Spruill v. Boyle–Midway, Inc., 308 F.2d 79, 82 (4th Cir. 1962) (Va. law) (furniture polish ingested by small child; classic case in which warning printed in small, brown type was held inadequate).

**36.** Compare Falkner v. Para Chem, 2003 WL 21396693, *7 (Ohio Ct. App. 2003) (warning that carpet adhesive should not be used indoors because its vapors were flammable "could easily be missed," according to defendant's chemist, because it was located on side panel not read by carpet installers), with Mohney v. U.S. Hockey, Inc., 300 F.Supp.2d 556 (N.D. Ohio 2004) (location, form, and method of display of warnings on hockey helmet were adequate). See also Delery v. Prudential Ins. Co. of America, 643 So.2d 807, 814 (La. Ct. App. 1994) (warning that chair was unstable on carpeting, placed underneath chair rather than in sales brochure or shipping box that came with chair, was inadequate).

**37.** See, e.g., Jaurequi v. John Deere Co., 971 F.Supp. 416, 428 (E.D. Mo. 1997) (expert could testify that warnings on farm machine were inadequate because they were placed at a location remote from the hazard).

**38.** See, e.g., General Motors Corp. v. Saenz, 873 S.W.2d 353 (Tex. 1993) (warning against overloading truck that was located on doorjamb at eye level, in accordance with custom and federal regulations, was adequate); Gordon v. Niagara Machine & Tool Works, 574 F.2d 1182, 1194 (5th Cir. 1978)

near the controls and at the front of a machine.[39] Warnings are less likely to be seen, and thus may be inconspicuous, if they are buried deep inside an operator's manual.[40]

These principles of conspicuousness point to one of the most basic questions of location, whether a warning must be placed directly on the product itself—on its label, its container, or its body—or whether the warning may be included in a sheet, leaflet, manual, contract, or other form of conveyance intended to accompany the product. This issue is bound up with that of *who* must be warned of product hazards, since it often arises in the context of industrial products, such as punch presses or cranes, where the manufacturer fails to place a warning label directly on the product but includes danger warnings in an "operator's manual" that the people who actually operate the machine may never see.[41] Whether adequacy requires in any given case that warnings be placed directly on the product involves a balance of the significance of the hazard, the user's need for the information, the availability of a feasible means to place the warnings on the product, and other factors in the calculus of risk. If feasible, reason normally suggests that important warnings be placed on the product itself rather than in a pamphlet, booklet, or information sheet that can be damaged, lost, or destroyed.[42] Warnings normally can quite easily be located on a container's label, on a warning plate attached near the ram of a press or other danger point of a machine, etched into the body of the product, or printed on a tag attached somewhere likely to be seen.[43] Depending on the circumstances, however, a warning may still be adequate even if it is provided off the product in a manual or other writing.[44]

(Miss. law) ("a direct warning attached to the press and conspicuously displayed at eye level would surely be a more effective warning than [words in a] manual").

**39.** See, e.g., Vermett v. Fred Christen & Sons Co., 741 N.E.2d 954, 971 (Ohio Ct. App. 2000) (warnings were adequate when they were on front of press, directly in front of operator, at eye level, and stated: "NEVER PLACE ANY PART OF YOUR BODY AT THE POINT OF OPERATION (UNDER THE RAM OR WITHIN THE DIE AREA)" and "NEVER OPERATE MACHINE WITHOUT PINCH POINTS GUARDED AND WITHOUT ADEQUATE POINT OF OPERATION SAFEGUARDING.").

**40.** See, e.g., Easton v. Chevron Indus., 602 So.2d 1032, 1037 (La. Ct. App. 1992).

**41.** See §§ 9.4–9.6, below.

**42.** See Restatement (Second) of Torts § 402A cmt. *j* (a seller may be required to place warnings or instructions on a product's container).

**43.** See, e.g., Fuentes v. Shin Caterpillar Mitsubishi, Ltd. 2003 WL 22205665, *4 (Cal. Ct. App. 2003, unpublished) (warning of risk that tire rim might explode while putting air in tire should have been stamped on wheel of loader); Vermett v. Fred Christen & Sons Co., 741 N.E.2d 954, 971 (Ohio Ct. App. 2000) (warnings were adequate when they were on front of press, directly in front of operator, and at eye level); Gordon v. Niagara Machine & Tool Works, 574 F.2d 1182, 1194 (5th Cir. 1978) (Miss. law) ("a direct warning attached to the press and conspicuously displayed at eye level would surely be a more effective warning than [words in a] manual"); Griggs v. Firestone Tire & Rubber Co., 513 F.2d 851 (8th Cir. 1975) (Mo. law) (warning against mismatching multipiece tire rims to prevent violent explosions could have been stamped on rim components); West v. Broderick & Bascom Rope Co., 197 N.W.2d 202 (Iowa 1972) (metal tag with load limit could have been bonded to collar of metal rope or "sling" that broke).

**44.** See, e.g., Freas v. Prater Constr. Corp., 573 N.E.2d 27 (Ohio 1991) (crane manual adequately warned not to stand under boom, and warning need not have been placed on boom itself); Broussard v. Continental Oil Co., 433 So.2d 354 (La. Ct. App. 1983); cf. Westry v. Bell Helmets, Inc., 487 N.W.2d 781 (Mich. Ct. App. 1992) (warning stickers sufficed; no duty to emboss warnings permanently on helmet).

### Foreign Language Warnings

With the increasingly global marketplace for products manufactured in this nation, and with Spanish spoken on our southern borders, French spoken on our northeastern borders, and Oriental languages increasingly spoken in the West, one must wonder whether product warnings can possibly be adequate when they are limited to English. If manufacturers market their products heavily in southern portions of Florida, Texas, New Mexico, Arizona, and California, or in Northern Vermont and Maine (adjacent to Québec) the question is whether the law should require them to warn in Spanish, French, or Japanese as well as English. A second issue is whether the decision of whether products should carry multi-lingual warnings should be left to manufacturers or should be mandated by the government. And, if the government should intervene, one must decide which branch or branches of government should make and enforce that determination—the courts, legislatures, administrative agencies, or some combination of these three. So far, each branch of government has played some role in making these decisions. Yet, there has been surprisingly little debate on this important issue, perhaps reflecting the deep English-only tradition that has long prevailed in America, which is geographically isolated from most other cultures. But the world is rapidly going global, as is the law of products liability,[45] and the various branches of American government increasingly will need to address the multi-lingual question.

Only a handful of judicial decisions in America have examined whether a warning must be made in a foreign language to be adequate.[46] Two decisions have ruled that a warning is not inadequate because it is written in English only. In *Ramirez v. Plough, Inc.*,[47] an infant contracted Reye's Syndrome after his Spanish-speaking mother gave him St. Joseph's Aspirin for Children to relieve his cold symptoms. The aspirin's label warned of the Reye's Syndrome risk in English, but not in Spanish. Although the FDA specifically permitted English-only labeling, the plaintiff claimed that the label's failure to include a Spanish warning rendered it inadequate. The court reviewed a number of related factors, including the web of rules on foreign-language labeling requirements in various other contexts adopted by the California legislature; the FDA's quite specific rules governing foreign-language labeling that permitted, but did not require, such labeling; and the multiplicity of health, social, cost, and practicability factors. Considering all these factors, the court concluded that foreign-language labeling requirements were better determined by legislatures and regulatory agencies than by the courts. Because other branches of government had determined that English-only warnings were sufficient, the court decided that it should apply the same rule to the case.[48] On similar reasoning, a federal circuit court approved

**45.**  See § 1.4, above.

**46.**  See Richmond, When Plain English Isn't: Manufacturers' Duty to Warn in a Second Language, 29 Tort & Ins. L.J. 588 (1994); Notes, 47 Vand. L. Rev. 1107 (1994), 29 Ga. L. Rev. 197 (1994), 29 Ga. J. Int'l &

Comp. L. 573 (1994), 15 J. Legal Med. 129 (1994); Annot., 27 A.L.R.5th 697 (1995).

**47.**  863 P.2d 167 (Cal. 1993). *Ramirez* is also examined in § 14.3, below.

**48.**  Noting that the FDA stresses the importance of "uniformity of presentation and clarity of message," the court conclud-

the English-only flammability warnings on a 55–gallon drum of chemicals that exploded when Spanish-speaking workers in Puerto Rico used a welding torch near the drum.[49] Because OSHA regulations required employers to warn only in English, allowing but not requiring them to warn in other languages, the court was strongly influenced by the administrative policy to leave decisions on multi-lingual warnings to the discretion of employers and, inferentially, to the discretion of manufacturers. Thus, even though the chemical product was sold for use in Spanish-speaking Puerto Rico, the English-only warnings were held sufficient.[50]

Other cases point the opposite direction, suggesting that foreign-language warnings sometimes may be necessary to make a warning adequate.[51] In *Stanley Industries, Inc. v. W. M. Barr & Co.*,[52] the defendant manufactured and sold linseed oil in a can which warned in English that rags soaked with the oil could spontaneously combust. Spanish-speaking workers used the rags which ignited and caused a fire. Because the defendant marketed its product in an area with a substantial Spanish-speaking population, the court decided to allow the jury to decide if the warning was inadequate because it did not warn in Spanish.[53] In another case, a Spanish-speaking worker, who was not wearing safety goggles, was injured in the eye while using a pneumatic nailer.[54] The nailer's manual warned in English, but not Spanish, of the need for eye protection. Here, the court allowed a warning expert to testify that the warning was defective for being in English only when labor statistics revealed that 51% of non-fatal injuries by nail guns were caused to Hispanics, and when two of the defendant's competitors placed dual-language warnings on their pneumatic nailers. Quite the opposite question was raised by *Fuentes v. Shin Caterpillar Mitsubishi, Ltd.*,[55] where a Spanish-speaking driver of a loader tractor in California was injured when the tractor's tire exploded as he was inflating it with air. His suit against the Japanese manufacturer alleged that the warnings were inadequate because they should have been in English, not just Japanese. While agreeing that warnings for products made for a foreign market should be written in the language of that market, the court

ed: "To preserve that uniformity and clarity, to avoid adverse impacts upon the warning requirements mandated by the federal regulatory scheme, and in deference to the superior technical and procedural lawmaking resources of legislative and administrative bodies, we adopt the legislative/regulatory standard of care that mandates nonprescription drug package warnings in English only." Id. at 177.

**49.** Torres–Rios v. LPS Labs., 152 F.3d 11, 13–14 (1st Cir. 1998) (P.R. law).

**50.** Although perhaps not necessary to the decision, the court also noted that, in addition to the warnings in English, the drum prominently displayed a pictorial of a flame, "a universal symbol of flammability," which "filled any language gap." Id.

**51.** See, e.g., Arbaiza v. Delta Int'l Mach. Corp., 1998 WL 846773 (E.D.N.Y. 1998) (table saw warned in small print and English only; adequacy was jury question).

**52.** 784 F.Supp. 1570 (S.D. Fla. 1992).

**53.** "Given the advertising of defendants' product in the Hispanic media and the pervasive presence of foreign-tongued individuals in the Miami workforce, it is for the jury to decide whether a warning, to be adequate, must contain language other than English or pictorial warning symbols." Id. at 1576.

**54.** Ortiz v. Stanley–Bostitch, Inc., 2000 WL 640645 (S.D.N.Y. 2000).

**55.** 2003 WL 22205665 (Cal. Ct. App. 2003, unpublished).

dismissed the claim because the manufacturer had sold the tractor for use exclusively in Japan.[56]

### *Nonverbal Warnings—Pictures, Symbols, Bells, and Smells*

**General danger symbols—Adults.** A recurring (if secondary) theme in the foreign-language cases just discussed is that pictures or symbols, with or in lieu of foreign-language warnings, may be a particularly effective way to convey information on product dangers to people who read only foreign languages, or who cannot read at all.[57] In perhaps the earliest case involving the adequacy of warnings on a product used by foreign workers, *Hubbard-Hall Chemical Co. v. Silverman,*[58] two Spanish-speaking farm workers died from inhaling insecticide dust from bags that had English warnings only. After the jury was instructed that an adequate warning is one "calculated to bring home to a [reasonable user] the nature and extent of the danger of the product involved," it returned a verdict for the plaintiffs. The appellate court upheld the verdict, reasoning that the jury properly could have concluded that even the best of written warnings was inadequate because it was foreseeable that the insecticide would be used by illiterate farm workers who needed warnings conveyed by a skull and crossbones or other danger symbol.

The traditional skull and cross bones, like the one below, has long been viewed as an effective, if general, nonverbal way to communicate a danger.[59]

Empirical research confirms the inference that symbols, such as a skull and crossbones, often may be necessary to alert even literate adults to product dangers. Some studies suggest that it matters little how com-

---

**56.** "Determining whether a warning would be feasible and effective necessarily involves a consideration of the language in which a warning must be given. We certainly believe that if a Japanese manufacturer places a product in the stream of commerce, and it is reasonably foreseeable that the product will be used in United States, safety warnings regarding the risks of operation should be in English. However, plaintiff failed to prove manufacturer knew their product, made and sold in Japan, would be resold to a purchaser in U.S." Id. at *11.

**57.** See also Campos v. Firestone Tire & Rubber Co., 485 A.2d 305, 310 (N.J. 1984)

("In view of the unskilled or semi-skilled nature of the work and the existence of many in the work force who do not read English, warnings in the form of symbols might have been appropriate, since the employee's 'ability to take care of himself' was limited.").

**58.** 340 F.2d 402 (1st Cir. 1965) (Mass. law).

**59.** See, e.g., Mossrud v. Lee, 157 N.W. 758 (Wis. 1916) (jury could find that farm supplier was negligent for selling quack grass poison in containers that did not include skull and crossbones).

pletely a written warning is worded, or even whether it is given at all, since few people will read or heed it anyway.[60] More recent and sophisticated behavioral studies confirm the conclusion that consumers process information irrationally.[61] For whatever reasons, people frequently fail to process verbal danger information in a manner that will avoid accidents.

**General danger symbols—Children.** Research at the Pittsburgh Poison Center of the Children's Hospital of Pittsburgh in 1971 revealed that the traditional skull and crossbones symbol tended to *attract* rather than repel small children to hazardous substances so labeled. The children associated the symbol with cartoon pirates, adventure, excitement and, at least in Pittsburgh, with the Pittsburgh Pirates baseball team. So researchers sought a new symbol that would deter young children from playing with (or consuming) toxic substances in the home. Children at daycare centers were shown six bottles of mouthwash, separately labeled with different symbols, and asked to identify bottles they might not like to play with. The symbols included a red stop sign, a skull and crossbones, a scowling green face, and three others. The least popular was the scowling face, which one of the youngsters said "looks yukky," which gave rise to the famous "Mr. Yuk":

### Mr. Yuk

Green-faced Mr. Yuk stickers, for parents to affix to toxic substances around the home, are now widely available from poison control centers across the nation. He is a registered trademark and was copyrighted by the Children's Hospital of Pittsburgh. Mr. Yuk stickers are thought to be partially responsible for a substantial drop in child poisonings.[62]

**60.** See, e.g., Goldhaber and deTurk, Effects of Consumers' Familiarity With a Product on Attention To and Compliance With Warnings, 11 J. Prod. Liab. 29 (1988); Dorris and Purswell, Warnings and Human Behavior: Implications for the Design of Product Warnings, 1 J. Prod. Liab. 254 (1977).

**61.** See, e.g., Symposium: Rational Actors or Rational Fools? The Implications of Psychology for Products Liability, 6 Roger Williams U. L. Rev. 1 (2000); Hanson and Kysar, Taking Behavioralism Seriously: The Problem of Market Manipulation, 74 N.Y.U.

L. Rev. 630, 724 (1999); Hanson and Kysar, Taking Behavioralism Seriously: Some Evidence of Market Manipulation, 112 Harv. L. Rev. 1420, 1425 (1999). See generally Sunstein, The Laws of Fear, 115 Harv. L. Rev. 1119, 1123 (2002) (reviewing P. Slovic, The Perception of Risk) ("ordinary people often deal poorly with the topic of risk").

**62.** On the effectiveness of Mr. Yuk, see Strothkamp v. Chesebrough–Pond's, Inc., 1993 WL 79239, *7 (Mo. Ct. App. 1993) (5-year-old child who injured his ear with a Q-Tip from box that did not have Mr. Yuk

Whether making Mr. Yuk look even more revolted would be more likely to scare children away from toxic substances, and hence be more effective, is difficult to know. The variation on Mr. Yuk shown below, is a registered New Zealand trademark of Quick Stil International:

[E7579]

A large field trial revealed that the super-revolted Mr. Yuk shown immediately above would *not* be effective in preventing child poisonings. Many of the parents believed the symbol actually attracted children to the labeled substances.[63] Perhaps explaining why plaintiffs have not based defective warning claims on a manufacturer's failure to use danger symbols on drain cleaners, furniture polish, and other toxic household products is the difficulty of establishing the efficacy of such symbols in averting consumption by young children.

**Particularized danger symbols—Adults.** In an effort to increase attention to product warnings, both the government and private industry have explored the use of danger symbols to signify particular types and levels of particular product risks. A powerful anti-acne drug called Accutane, a synthetic derivative of Vitamin A, was found to cause birth defects in about 25% of children born to women taking the drug. Rather than totally banning the drug, the FDA required the manufacturer to provide emphatic written warnings and instructions, in both patient and physician information labeling, together with the following diagram on each page of the patient leaflet and on each side of the drug's packaging. In addition, the FDA directed that patient information labeling was to include a drawing of a deformed baby.[64]

---

sticker testified that he would not touch anything marked with a Mr. Yuk sticker).

**63.** See 5 Prod. Liab. Int'l 190 (Dec. 1983).

**64.** See Willis, New Warning About Accutane and Birth Defects, FDA Consumer 27 (Oct. 1988).

While warning symbols often help convey danger information, symbols by themselves sometimes will not be adequate to fully convey a danger and how to avoid it.[65] In such cases, a reasonable warning may require supplementing the picture or symbol with written warnings or instructions. Several companies and industry associations have researched how to improve communications on product hazards in the workplace. The leader in this area has long been FMC Corporation, which some time ago developed a sophisticated industrial product warnings system that combines particularized danger symbols with written warnings and instructions.[66] Its Product Safety Sign and Label System uses pictorials, combined with words and colors, in formats designed to present hazard information to industrial workers as effectively as possible.[67] The system uses 3–paneled rectangular labels to communicate: (1) the level of hazard seriousness, (2) the nature of the hazard; (3) the consequence of interaction with the hazard; and (4) instructions on how to avoid the hazard.

As seen below, the top panel in each warning contains a signal word (DANGER, WARNING or CAUTION) which communicates the level of hazard seriousness. (DANGER is printed in white letters, against a red background; WARNING, in black on orange; and CAUTION, in black on yellow.) The center panel contains the pictorial which communicates the nature of the hazard, and the likely consequence of human interaction with the hazard. Some pictorials also depict a method for avoiding the hazard, such as wearing protection for the eyes. The bottom panel provides an instruction on how to avoid the hazard and may further describe the hazard and/or its consequences to the worker. Sometimes a separate box, entitled SAFETY INSTRUCTIONS (white letters on green), provides more information on safe use.

---

**65.** See Fyssakis v. Knight Equip. Corp., 826 P.2d 570 (Nev. 1992) (symbol for corrosiveness on soap dispenser inadequately warned that dishwashing soap could blind).

**66.** See Product Safety Sign and Label System, © 1993 FMC Corporation.

**67.** The communication system was designed to meet or exceed the requirements of American National Standard Z535.4–1991, Products Safety Signs and Labels.

[E7580]

### Selected Pictorial Examples

Such pictorial warnings are undoubtedly more effective, in general, than written warnings alone. But the absence of case law addressing whether products liability law requires such sophisticated warning systems suggests that safety labeling experts are still uncertain as to just how effective such pictorial warnings may be. Even more difficult would be establishing causation—whether such a warning, had it been provided, would have prevented a particular product accident.[68]

**Other nonverbal warning methods.** Apart from pictorial warnings, danger information may be communicated to users in other nonverbal ways—even in non-visual ways, relying on other senses. A gauge or warning light may helpfully inform an operator that a crane is about to

---

**68.** However, a heeding presumption might be used in appropriate cases to by- pass this difficult causation problem. See § 11.4, below.

tip, that the fuel is low, that a parking brake is engaged, or that a rear mounted aircraft engine has stopped operating.[69] A buzzer, bell, rear-view mirror, or rear camera (with a viewing screen inside the cabin) may warn operators or potential victims of the risks from operating bulky vehicles in reverse.[70] Color may be added to a dangerous, clear, chemical fluid to distinguish it from water,[71] and odor may be added to propane gas to give notice of its presence.[72] And warnings may rely on the sense of touch, such as vibration in the seat of a crane about to tip over. There simply is no end to the kinds of creative ways warnings may be improved.

### Nullifying Warnings with Safety Assurances—"Overpromotion"

An otherwise adequate warning may be nullified by assurances of safety. The classic case on this issue is *Maize v. Atlantic Refining Co.*,[73] where a woman died from inhaling tetrachloride fumes in a cleaning fluid she used to clean her rugs. The label on the can twice stated, "CAUTION: Do not inhale fumes. Use only in a well ventilated place." However, in letters that were several times larger, the cleaner's name— "Safety–Kleen"—was emblazoned around the container. Affirming judgments for the plaintiffs, the court observed that "the conspicuous display on each of the four sides of a can of the words 'Safety–Kleen' would naturally lull the user [into] a false sense of security [so] as to make the word 'Caution' and the admonition against inhaling fumes and as to use only in a well ventilated place seem of comparatively minor import."[74] A small number of other decisions have applied the "overpromotion" principle to nullify a manufacturer's product warnings,[75] including one in which warnings and instructions provided by the manufacturer of a jet boat were cancelled out by a salesman's demonstration of the boat in ways contrary to those warnings.[76]

**69.** See, e.g., Hiser v. Bell Helicopter Textron Inc., 4 Cal.Rptr.3d 249 (Ct. App. 2003) (helicopter's low fuel warning light conflicted with fuel gauges); U.S. Xpress, Inc. v. Great Northern Ins. Co. as Subrogee of North American Communications Resource, 2003 WL 124021 (D. Minn. 2003) (rejecting claim that truck manufacturer's use of 1000–hour bulb instead of 5000–hour bulb in warning light was unreasonable); Kay v. Cessna Aircraft Co., 548 F.2d 1370 (9th Cir. 1977) (Cal. law) (warning light not necessary because engine gauges on Skymaster instrument panel would have indicated dead engine). See also Euclides Campos v. Crown Equipment Corp., 35 Fed. Appx. 31 (2d Cir. 2002) (N.Y. law) (forklift not defective for having back-up alarm and warning lights as optional, rather than standard, equipment).

*[handwritten margin note: but this is a defective DESIGN case...]*

**70.** See, e.g., Pike v. Frank G. Hough Co., 467 P.2d 229 (Cal. 1970).

**71.** See, e.g., Hayes v. Kay Chem. Co., 482 N.E.2d 611 (Ill. App. Ct. 1985) (McDonald's employee wiped face with towel saturated with caustic grill cleaner).

**72.** See, e.g., Donahue v. Phillips Petroleum Co., 866 F.2d 1008 (8th Cir. 1989) (Mo. law); Jones v. Hittle Service, Inc., 549 P.2d 1383 (Kan. 1976) (odorized to smell like rotten eggs or dead mice).

**73.** 41 A.2d 850 (Pa. 1945).

**74.** Id. at 852.

**75.** See Incollingo v. Ewing, 282 A.2d 206 (Pa. 1971) (pharmaceutical company's detail men minimized drug's hazards and stressed its benefits and widespread acceptance). Compare Ayers v. Johnson & Johnson Baby Prods. Co., 818 P.2d 1337 (Wash. 1991) (warning of diarrhea, but not paralysis, from ingesting "pure and gentle" Baby Oil).

**76.** See Levey v. Yamaha Motor Corp., 825 A.2d 554, 556 (N.J. Super. App. Div.

### Overwarning—"Warnings Pollution"

Cutting across the ideal formulations of adequacy, both substantive and procedural, is an important real-world limitation. As noted above, warnings, to be adequate, ideally should provide precise information about all specific dangers from all foreseeable uses, and this information ideally should be conveyed to users in a form most likely to catch their attention and help them understand the true nature and degree of risk. For example, in *Burch v. Amsterdam Corp.*,[77] the plaintiff was badly burned in an explosion and flash fire that occurred while he was applying a floor tile mastic adhesive sold by the defendant. The label on the can of mastic adhesive read, "DANGER! EXTREMELY FLAMMA-BLE—DO NOT USE NEAR FIRE OR FLAME—USE WITH ADE-QUATE VENTILATION." The plaintiff read the instructions on the label of the can, opened the windows, and turned on his fans and a large air conditioner. He checked the area to be sure there were no flames but did not think about the pilot light on a gas stove in the kitchen where he was working. After he had applied a first coat of adhesive to the floor, the vapors reached the pilot light and exploded. The plaintiff heard a "whoosh," "had a sense of time being elongated, felt searing heat and saw the skin peeling from his body."

The trial court granted summary judgment for defendant on plaintiff's inadequate warnings claim, but the Court of Appeals reversed, reasoning that the defendant had failed to warn of the *specific* risk that the fumes might explode when they came in contact with a pilot light.[78] Chief Judge Reilly dissented, arguing that requiring a duty to warn about pilot lights in particular, other than about "fire and flame" in general, suggested that a vendor would also have to warn about the risks from "lighted pipes, cigars and cigarettes, vigil lights, candles, sparks

---

2003) (the "seller vitiated the effectiveness of the printed instructions and warnings accompanying its product by providing a demonstration of the product to intended users in which the seller violated its own safety warnings").

**77.** 366 A.2d 1079 (D.C. App. 1976).

**78.** "[A]n ordinary user might not have realized that 'near fire or flame' included nearby pilot lights or that fumes and vapors, as well as the adhesive itself, were extremely flammable." Id. at 1087–88. At least one went even further than the *Burch* majority, ruling that a similar warning that contained a specific warning to extinguish pilot lights was not enough. See Murray v. Wilson Oak Flooring Co., 475 F.2d 129, 130–33 (7th Cir.1973) (Ill. law), where plaintiff was burned when the vapors from the mastic flooring adhesive he was applying were ignited by the pilot light of a water heater or stove. The label specifically warned, "KEEP AWAY From Fire, HEAT and OPEN flame LIGHTS—CAUTION: IN-FLAMMABLE MIXTURE—DO NOT USE NEAR FIRE OR FLAME—USE IN WELL VENTILATED AREA—Do not smoke—Extinguish flame—including pilots lights." In a negligent warning action against the manufacturer, the jury found for the plaintiff, the trial court granted the defendant's motion for j.n.o.v., and the Court of Appeals reversed, reinstating the plaintiff's verdict. Experts had agreed that the adhesive emits a heavy and highly explosive vapor that can travel for some distance along a floor, burn with explosive force when it comes in contact with a flame, and can transmit the flame back to spread adhesive. The Court of Appeals concluded that it could not hold as a matter of law that "near" adequately informed the plaintiff that spreading the adhesive "within four feet of a pilot light *located behind a closed door* and within eight feet of stove pilot lights three feet off the floor exposed him to the risk of an explosion."

from an electric lamp switch, a running fan or motor, and the other myriad of things which could possibly ignite vapors. If this is what the law requires, big lettering would have to be discarded for smaller print enumerating details at such length that few users would bother to read it—the warning then [being inadequate in] lacking the requisite 'intensity.' "[79]

*Burch* was decided in the mid–1970s, at the height of modern products law's expansion when courts were beguiled by the thought that products liability law could and should be used to the maximum extent to promote product safety incentives and loss-spreading principles.[80] As these principles have fallen out of favor in recent decades, courts and commentators have begun to recognize that there is such a thing as *too much* information—that information, like everything, can be an evil in excess. By the 1980s, courts began to acknowledge the dangers of over-warning, "warnings pollution," that had concerned Chief Judge Reilly in his dissent in *Burch*. This simple idea is that product warnings ideally should contain *optimal* types and levels of danger and safety information, not maximum information.[81]

One of the first cases decided on warning pollution principles was *Cotton v. Buckeye Gas Products Co.,*[82] decided in 1988. As a night heater watcher for a construction company, the plaintiff monitored heaters used to cure concrete in cold weather and changed the propane cylinders supplied by the defendant when they ran low on gas. The areas being cured were covered with polyethylene curtains to contain the heat. Despite warnings on the cylinders that they contained "flammable" gas and should not be used or stored in "living areas," plaintiff neglected to close the valves on the used cylinders and stored them near the active heaters within the polyethylene enclosed areas. Gas escaping from the used cylinders ignited and severely burned the plaintiff. In his suit against the suppliers, the plaintiff claimed that the warning was inadequate because it failed (1) to warn that propane was not only flammable but "explosive"; (2) to instruct users to shut the valves on used cylinders; (3) to advise users not to use or store the cylinders in enclosed,

---

**79.** Id. at 1089.

**80.** See §§ 5.3–5.5, above.

**81.** See Twerski, Weinstein, Donaher, Piehler, The Use and Abuse of Warnings in Products Liability—Design Defect Litigation Comes of Age, 61 Cornell L. Rev. 495, 514–16 (1976): "Warnings, in order to be effective, must be selective.... The warning process, in order to have impact, will have to select carefully the items which are to become part of the consumer's mental apparatus while using the product. Making the consumer account mentally for trivia or guard against risks that are not likely to occur imposes a very real societal cost...."

In short, when calculating the burden of precaution which is part of the risk–utility calculus, it will be necessary to focus on costs other than the cost of label printing."

Some commentators view warnings pollution claims skeptically. See Latin, Good Warnings, Bad Products, and Cognitive Limitations, 41 UCLA L. Rev. 1193 (1994); Grether, Schwartz & Wilde, The Irrelevance of Information Overload: An Analysis of Search and Disclosure, 59 S. Cal. L. Rev. 277 (1986). See generally Symposium, Rational Actors or Rational Fools? The Implications of Psychology for Products Liability, 6 Roger Williams U. L. Rev. 1 (2000).

**82.** 840 F.2d 935 (D.C. Cir. 1988).

unventilated areas; and (4) to warn that gas might escape from used cylinders believed to be empty. The jury agreed, but the trial court granted the defendant's motion for j.n.o.v., which the appellate court affirmed.

Debunking the assumption that keying warnings to every particular type of risk is "virtually cost free," the court noted that there is a real cost in the increased time and effort necessary to grasp the message. The court observed that each extra item included "dilutes the punch of every other item. Given short attention spans, items crowd each other out; they get lost in fine print." The defendant's warning approach was reasonable, thought the court, in providing brief "flammability" warnings on the cylinders and more detailed warnings in the pamphlet provided to the purchaser, which included an admonition to close the valves. Nor was the court persuaded that the warnings were inadequate because they merely said "flammable" rather than "explosive," noting that the plaintiff's injuries exclusively were burns. And while the pamphlet did not explicitly warn that the valves should be closed on cylinders after they were "empty" (because they might still contain some propane), this was common sense. "[A] warning need not dot every i,"[83] and the warnings given were adequate on the whole: "warnings need not spell out [every] risk in intricate detail"[84] for " 'the list of foolish practices warned against would be so long, it would fill a volume.' "[85] Many other courts have agreed that warnings and instructions should be judicious and selective, that they need not—should not—provide information on the details of every product hazard.[86]

Another case that made the point that more numerous and more prominent warnings are not always better, and not always required, was *General Motors Corp. v. Saenz*,[87] which involved a claim that GM's warning against overloading a truck was not specific enough. The court held that it was, reasoning that just because the warning could have been more prominent did not prove that it was not prominent enough.

**83.** Id. at 938.

**84.** Id. at 939.

**85.** Id. at 937–39, quoting Kerr v. Koemm, 557 F.Supp. 283, 288 n.2 (S.D.N.Y. 1983).

**86.** See, e.g., Aetna Casualty & Surety Co. v. Ralph Wilson Plastics Co., 509 N.W.2d 520 (Mich. Ct. App. 1993) (2–1 decision), where a glue manufacturer warned of the extreme flammability of its solvents and instructed users to turn off pilot lights, stoves, heaters, flames and electric motors, and not to smoke. Plaintiff was injured when static electricity from a solvent cleanup sponge set off an explosion. *Held*, the warning was adequate. "A spark is a spark, and a possible source of ignition of a highly flammable compound irrespective of the means by which the spark was generated, whether by static electricity or otherwise." The majority further noted that "excessive warnings on product labels may be counterproductive, causing 'sensory overload' which literally drowns crucial information in a sea of mind-numbing detail."

See also Todd v. Societe BIC (*Todd II*), 9 F.3d 1216, 1218–19 (7th Cir. 1993) (Ill. law) (Easterbrook, J.): "KEEP OUT OF REACH OF CHILDREN" was sufficient "warning" on BIC disposable butane lighter: among the problems with more extensive warnings is that "the more text must be squeezed onto the product, the smaller the type, and the less likely is the consumer to read or remember any of it. Only pithy and bold warnings can be effective. Long passages in capital letters are next to illegible, and long passages in lower case letters are treated as boilerplate. Plaintiff wants a warning in such detail that a magnifying glass would be necessary to read it."

**87.** 873 S.W.2d 353 (Tex. 1993).

"Every WARNING can always be made bigger, brighter and more obvious. GM could have placed the WARNING where it could not possibly have been overlooked, perhaps engraved upon the dashboard, or backlit on the instrument panel." But GM could not have placed every important warning on the dashboard, or any other place. Indeed, the more warnings and instructions that are located in one place—whether on the dashboard, a doorplate, or in the owner's manual—the less likely that users will notice any one. The court concluded that the issue was not whether GM should have put the overloading warning on a sticker near the gear shift, as the plaintiffs argued, but whether the warning that GM did provide offered "reasonable notice" against the risk of overloading.

*Saenz* is a good case to end with, because it illustrates the important point that warnings, to be "adequate," need not be perfect, only "reasonable." This crucial aspect of the law of warnings took many courts about a quarter century to understand, and it is the central message of the warning defect standard in the *Third Restatement*.[88]

## § 9.4 PERSONS TO BE WARNED

The duty to warn supposes that the warning will reach, be read by, and protect the safety of certain types of persons.[1] Deciding who those persons are—what categories of persons should be warned—raises important questions of duty and adequacy. The selection of the proper groups to warn is part of a lexical series of determinations: (1) whom the warning should protect, (2) who can best accomplish that protection, and (3) what type of warning will do it best. The last question is one of adequacy, the factual question just examined.[2] Although the first two questions sometimes mix law and fact, they basically are duty issues for a court.

Whom a manufacturer has a duty to protect, who has a right to be protected, normally is clear: persons a product foreseeably puts at risk. While the scope of a manufacturer's responsibility for product safety once was closely tied to contractual aspects of the purchasing transaction, and while transactional considerations to some extent still control the scope of obligations under the law of warranty,[3] privity of contract no longer binds the hands of duty in the law of torts.[4] So, the answer to the first question stated above is that the duty to warn is owed to persons foreseeably endangered by a product's use.[5]

Remaining to be resolved is: Who should protect the persons a product puts at risk? Normally, people quite obviously can best protect themselves, assuming that they recognize a hazard and can control it. Because users and consumers normally are the people threatened by a

---

**88.** See Products Liability Restatement § 2(c) and cmt. *i*. See also § 9.2, above.

**§ 9.4**

**1.** In the words of the Products Liability Restatement, warnings of product dangers must be provided to users or consumers so "they can prevent harm either by appropriate conduct during use or consumption or

by choosing not to use or consume." Section 2(c) cmt. *i*.

**2.** See § 9.3, above.

**3.** See § 4.5, above.

**4.** See §§ 1.2, 5.2, and 5.3, above.

**5.** See ch. 12, below.

product's hazards, they are usually the ones best situated to decide how best to protect themselves from harm. Even if real-world safety decisions of people often fall short on logic, giving users and consumers the opportunity to make product safety decisions that affect their welfare advances self-determination.[6] Accordingly, even when a manufacturer sells its products to intermediaries, it normally should provide warnings and instructions about product hazards directly to users and consumers if there is a reasonable way to do so.[7] One iteration of the warn-consumers-directly principle is the manufacturer's duty, previously discussed,[8] to place warnings directly on the product, if feasible. The principle rests on reason, rather than being absolute, because some products come in a form that precludes warnings on the body of the product, such as products that are very small or liquid sold in bulk. The bulk-supplier doctrine, discussed below,[9] addresses the latter point.

In other situations, where users and consumers rely on others for protection, warnings should be given to those other persons in addition to or, if appropriate, in substitution for warnings provided to users and consumers. Young children depend on parents to make informed safety decisions about their food, clothing, and toys; workers depend on supervisors to make informed safety decisions on what types of machinery to purchase and on safe procedures for operating and maintaining those machines; and patients depend on doctors to make informed decisions on prescription drugs. These and other special categories of persons charged with protecting others often can make better use of product safety information than the ultimate users and consumers, as discussed in later sections. Two special categories of persons treated briefly here are bystanders and persons who are allergic to certain products, both of whom need special warnings.

### Bystanders

Warnings play two different roles in protecting bystanders. Bystanders may well be placed at risk when products are used dangerously by other people, as when a crane operator uses a crane in a dangerous manner that threatens workers underneath the load. In such cases, warnings necessary to the safe operation of the crane protect persons foreseeably placed at risk, including the operator's fellow workers ("bystanders") who may be standing beneath the crane. The manufacturer of such a crane has a duty to warn the operator for the benefit of the operator and others foreseeably placed at risk, including bystanders. So, also, although the manufacturer of a car or plane normally has a duty to provide warnings and instructions concerning operational hazards only to the operator, not to passengers,[10] the breach of the duty to warn the operator will violate the safety rights of passengers and other bystanders

---

**6.** See Products Liability Restatement § 2(c) cmt. *i.*

**7.** See, e.g., Lee v. Martin, 45 S.W.3d 860, 865 (Ark. Ct. App. 2001) ("As a general rule, there is a duty to warn the ultimate user of a product of the risk of the product . . . . under either a negligence theory or a strict-liability theory.")

**8.** See § 9.3, above.

**9.** See § 9.5, below.

**10.** See, e.g., Stevens v. Cessna Aircraft Co., 170 Cal.Rptr. 925, 926 (Ct. App. 1981) (4–seat airplane crashed, allegedly because it was overloaded with pilot and three passengers; manufacturer did not have duty to post notice in passenger compartment of plane's load capacity): "[T]he passenger necessarily depends upon the skill and judg-

injured as a result of the operator's failure to have such safety information.[11] This is the normal type of bystander case in which a manufacturer's duty to bystanders is governed by ordinary principles of reasonable foreseeability, in tort,[12] and by third party beneficiary principles, in warranty.[13]

In addition to this form of indirect benefit from a manufacturer's provision of warnings and instructions to product users, bystanders sometimes are entitled to warnings directly to themselves.[14] For example, cranes sometimes must move in reverse, and a crane cab may make it impossible for the operator to see directly behind the crane. In this type of situation, the crane normally would need to be equipped with a horn or buzzer, and also perhaps with flashing lights, to warn bystanders behind the crane that it is being run in reverse by an operator with diminished visibility.[15] Surely rear-view mirrors also would be required, to increase the operator's range of vision as much as possible and, depending on the risk and feasibility, possibly a rear camera with a viewing screen inside the cab.[16]

## Allergic Persons

Some foods, drugs, cleansers, and lotions which are useful and entirely safe to the great majority of people can cause serious allergic

---

ment of the pilot to determine the load capacity of the airplane in light of the flying conditions to be encountered. Plaintiff's argument implies logically that numerous other bits of information should be posted in the passenger compartment to enable the passengers to second-guess the pilot on a myriad of flying decisions. It would be impossible ultimately to provide meaningful information to the passenger, and in the long run a rule requiring the manufacturer to provide such information directly to the passenger would not be in the interests of passenger safety." *But see* Bickram v. Case I.H., 712 F.Supp. 18, 22 (E.D.N.Y. 1989) (suggesting that bystanders might be entitled to effective written warnings).

**11.** See, e.g., Hisrich v. Volvo Cars of North America, Inc., 226 F.3d 445 (6th Cir. 2000) (Ohio law) (inadequate warning to operator that unbelted child passenger could be killed by airbag).

**12.** See § 5.3, above. *But see* Kirk v. Michael Reese Hosp. & Med. Ctr., 513 N.E.2d 387, 393 (Ill. 1987) (manufacturer's duty to warn doctors of risk of drinking alcohol while taking prescription drug might possibly extend to passengers in cars driven by persons who drank alcoholic beverages while on the drug, but such a combination of events was unforeseeable as a matter of law).

**13.** See § 4.5, above.

**14.** See, e.g., 2 Frumer and Friedman, Products Liability § 12.06[2]; see also § 5.3, above.

**15.** See, e.g., Bohnstedt v. Robscon Leasing L.L.C., 993 P.2d 135 (Okla. Civ. App. 1999) (backup alarm on grader needed to be maintained to protect bystanders). *But see* Vickery v. Waste Management of Ga., Inc., 549 S.E.2d 482, 484 (Ga. Ct. App. 2001) (truck manufacturer had no duty to warn purchaser or bystander that truck was not equipped with backup alarm).

**16.** Other cases in which the duty to warn was extended to bystanders include Georgia–Pacific Corp. v. Pransky, 800 A.2d 722 (Md. 2002) (mesothelioma victim exposed to dust while father worked with asbestos product in basement was a foreseeable bystander); Hayes v. Kay Chem. Co., 482 N.E.2d 611 (Ill. App. Ct. 1985) (McDonald's employee wiped face with towel saturated with colorless, odorless, caustic grill cleaner used by another employee; duty extended beyond user to foreseeable persons and "nonusers"); Karns v. Emerson Electric Co., 817 F.2d 1452, 1457 (10th Cir. 1987) (Okla. law) (hand-held "Weed Eater" brush-cutting device, with exposed 10–inch circular steel sawblade struck something near ground, causing machine to swing violently around and cut off arm of user's nephew standing 6–10 feet away); Givens v. Lederle, 556 F.2d 1341 (5th Cir. 1977) (Fla. law) (mother contracted polio, possibly from contact with diapers of child recently administered vaccine produced by defendant).

reactions in other persons. Peanuts,[17] aspirin,[18] strawberries,[19] penicillin,[20] oysters,[21] monosodium glutamate,[22] and latex gloves[23] are examples of products which many people enjoy or need but which cause some people to get very sick and even die. The defect in such situations might be seen to lie in the persons who incur idiosyncratic reactions, rather than in the product.[24] The question in these situations is whether the producer has a duty to warn that its product may cause allergic reactions.[25]

If the population of allergic users is foreseeably quite large, and if such users are not generally aware of the risk,[26] then the manufacturer

**17.** See, e.g., Thompson v. East Pacific Enterprises, Inc., 2003 WL 352914, *1 (Wash. Ct. App. 2003) (plaintiff suffered severe allergic reaction and heart attack from eating almond chicken dish that contained peanut or peanut residue). See generally Note, Suing for Peanuts, 75 Notre Dame L. Rev. 1269 (2000).

**18.** See Products Liability Restatement § 2 cmt. *k*, Illus. 13.

**19.** See Restatement (Second) of Torts § 402A cmt. *j*.

**20.** See, e.g., See, e.g., Thompson v. East Pacific Enterprises, Inc., 2003 WL 352914 (Wash. Ct. App. 2003) (plaintiff was allergic to penicillin as well as peanuts and other substances).

**21.** See, e.g., Gregor v. Argenot Great Central Ins. Co., 851 So.2d 959 (La. 2003) (raw oysters and other marine filter feeders may contain vibrio vulnificus, a naturally occurring salt water organism not dangerous to most people but dangerous, possibly fatal, to persons with chronic health problems including gastric disorders, liver diseases, and immune disorders; restaurant posted mandatory warning in oyster bar but not in dining room where plaintiff ate raw oysters from which he died); Edwards v. Hop Sin, Inc., 140 S.W.3d 13 (Ky. Ct. App. 2003) (jury might find that a reasonable consumer would expect to be warned of such a serious risk); Ayala v. Bartolome, 940 S.W.2d 727 (Tex. App. 1997) (same).

**22.** See, e.g., Livingston v. Marie Callender's, Inc., 85 Cal.Rptr.2d 528 (Ct. App. 1999) (MSG in soup).

**23.** See, e.g., Green v. Smith & Nephew AHP, Inc., 629 N.W.2d 727 (Wis. 2001) (latex gloves used by health workers).

**24.** "The term *allergy* or *hypersensitivity* refers to the condition or state of an individual who reacts specifically and with unusual symptoms to the administration of, or to contact with, a substance which when given in similar amounts to the majority of all other individuals proves harmless or innocuous." It is not so clear, therefore, that there is anything "defective" about a product which generates an allergic reaction: "A person suffering an allergic reaction to a product is, by definition, abnormal or hypersensitive. The resulting harm, therefore, is arguably more fairly attributable to some 'defect' in the person's body rather than to a 'defect' in the product—a product that is entirely safe for all normal ('nondefective') people." Panel Discussion, Medico–Legal Aspects of Allergies, 24 Tenn. L. Rev. 840–42 (1957).

See, e.g., Thompson v. East Pacific Enterprises, Inc., 2003 WL 352914, *1 (Wash. Ct. App. 2003) (plaintiff, who sued restaurant for contaminating its almond chicken dish with peanut or peanut residue to which plaintiff was allergic, was also allergic to penicillin, walnut, pine nut, sunflower seed, almond, soybean, pecan, hazelnut, brazil nut, sesame seed, and other substances). See also Henderson, Process Norms in Products Litigation: Liability for Allergic Reactions, 51 U. Pitt. L. Rev. 761, 804 (1990) ("[T]here is nothing defective about perfectly pure shampoo that happens to cause allergic reactions in a handful of abnormally sensitive individuals, assuming warnings describing the risks accompany the product. The consumer, rather than the product, is defective.").

**25.** See Barrett, Latex Gloves, 22 J. Legal Med. 263 (2001); Ortego, Allergic or Idiosyncratic Reactions as a Defense to Strict Products Liability: Recent Developments, 42 Fed'n Ins. & Corp. Couns. Q. 41 (1991); Henderson, Process Norms in Products Litigation: Liability for Allergic Reactions, 51 U. Pitt. L. Rev. 761 (1990); Major, Manufacturer's Failure to Warn Consumer of allergenic Nature of Product, 47 Am. Jur. Proof of Facts 2d 227 (1987); Mobilia, Allergic Reactions to Prescription Drugs: A Proposal for Compensation, 48 Alb. L. Rev. 343 (1984); Note, Suing for Peanuts, 75 Notre Dame L. Rev. 1269 (2000); Prosser and Keeton on Torts § 96, at 687–88.

**26.** "The ingredient that causes the allergic reaction must be one whose danger or whose presence in the product is not generally known to consumers. When both the presence of an allergenic ingredient in the product and the risks presented by such ingredient are widely known, instructions and warnings about that danger are unnec-

clearly must provide adequate warnings of a product's allergenic tendencies.[27] If the risk is not foreseeable, then there can be no duty to warn about it,[28] except in a couple jurisdictions.[29] If the group of allergic persons is small, the courts are split on whether the manufacturer has a duty to warn. Most courts require the manufacturer to warn only if it can foresee a risk of serious allergy to a *substantial* number of persons.[30] This was the position of the *Second Torts Restatement*,[31] and it is followed by the *Third Restatement* which notes that the "substantial number" concept logically should decrease as the risk of harm increases.[32]

essary." Products Liability Restatement § 2 cmt. *k*. See, e.g., Pelman v. McDonald's Corp., 237 F.Supp.2d 512, 536 (S.D.N.Y. 2003); Posey v. Warner Lambert Consumer Healthcare, 2001 WL 1776757 (W.D. Ky. 2001).

**27.** See, e.g., Green v. Smith & Nephew AHP, Inc., 629 N.W.2d 727 (Wis. 2001) (duty to warn health care users, 5–17% of whom were allergic, that proteins in powdered latex gloves might cause allergies).

**28.** See, e.g., Adelman–Tremblay v. Jewel Companies, Inc., 859 F.2d 517 (7th Cir. 1988) (Wis. law) (one million nail kits sold and plaintiff suffered first allergic reaction to glue in kit; state would follow general rule that sellers are not strictly liable for injuries from idiosyncratic or rare allergic reactions). See generally § 10.4, below.

**29.** This duty exists in Minnesota, and possibly in Montana and one or two other states. See Green v. Smith & Nephew AHP, Inc., 629 N.W.2d 727 (Wis. 2001) (duty to warn users allergic to proteins in powdered latex gloves, even if risk was unforeseeable).

**30.** See, e.g., Friedman v. Merck & Co., 131 Cal.Rptr.2d 885, 894 (Ct. App. 2003) ("a TB test distributor's negligent failure to warn that the test contains animal products is not ... sufficiently likely to result in serious harm to a sufficiently significant segment of the population" so as to impose a duty to so advise on defendants as a matter of law); Green v. Smith & Nephew AHP, Inc., 629 N.W.2d 727, 754–55 (Wis. 2001) (duty to warn 5–17% of users allergic to proteins in powdered latex gloves, even if risk were unforeseeable); Daley v. McNeil Consumer Products Co., 164 F.Supp.2d 367 (S.D.N.Y. 2001) (Lactaid); Posey v. Warner–Lambert Consumer Healthcare, 2001 WL 1776757 (W.D. Ky. 2001) (Lubriderm); Morris v. Pathmark Corp., 592 A.2d 331 (Pa. Super. Ct. 1991) (hair straightener); Griggs v. Combe, Inc., 456 So.2d 790 (Ala. 1984) (first known case of systemic illness from benzocaine in vaginal itch ointment); Kaempfe v. Lehn & Fink Products Corp., 249 N.Y.S.2d 840 (App. Div. 1964), aff'd 231 N.E.2d 294 (N.Y. 1967) (dermatitis from aluminum sulphate in deodorant; no liability where manufacturer received only 4 sensitivity complaints in 600,000 sales—plain-

tiff not one "of a substantial number or of an identifiable class" of allergic persons: "the manufacturer is [not] to be held under an absolute duty of giving special warning against a remote possibility of harm due to an unusual allergic reaction from use by a minuscule percentage of the potential customers").

**31.** "The seller may reasonably assume that those with common allergies, as for example to eggs or strawberries, will be aware of them, and he is not required to warn against them. Where, however, the product contains an ingredient to which a substantial number of the population are allergic, and the ingredient is one whose danger is not generally known, or if known is one which the consumer would reasonably not expect to find in the product, the seller is required to give warning against it, if he has knowledge, or by the application of reasonable, developed human skill and foresight should have knowledge, of the presence of the ingredient and the danger." Restatement (Second) of Torts § 402A cmt. *j*.

See also Restatement (Second) of Torts § 395 cmt. *k* ("the manufacturer may know, or may be under a duty to discover, that some possible users of the product are especially susceptible to harm from it, if it contains an ingredient to which any substantial percentage of the population are allergic or otherwise sensitive, and he fails to take reasonable precautions, by giving warning or otherwise, against harm to such persons").

**32.** See Products Liability Restatement § 2 cmt. *k* which provides in part: "The general rule in cases involving allergic reactions is that a warning is required when the harm-causing ingredient is one to which a substantial number of persons are allergic. The degree of substantiality is not precisely quantifiable. Clearly the plaintiff in most cases must show that the allergic predisposition is not unique to the plaintiff. In determining whether the plaintiff has carried the burden in this regard, however, the court may properly consider the severity of the plaintiff's harm. The more severe the harm, the more justified is a conclusion

Another line of cases rejects a strict no-duty approach for "insignificant" or "insubstantial" numbers of allergy victims and, instead, imposes a duty to warn of *any* foreseeable allergy that may be serious.[33] Assuming that the duty is restricted to allergic risks of which users generally are unaware, this latter formulation of the duty might be viewed as more fairly and flexibly tying the duty to warn to traditional tort law principles of reasonableness and foreseeability, rather than anchoring it to a wooden category of "substantial numbers," whatever that may mean. Yet the substantial or appreciable number of allergic persons requirement has the virtue of being somewhat less vague than the evanescent notion of "foreseeability,"[34] and it also contains a threshold of materiality that may be helpful in excluding trivial claims.[35]

If there *is* a duty to warn of an allergic reaction risk, the warning must be adequate.[36] This means that the manufacturer must warn not only of the possibility and type of allergic reaction that may occur, and identify the kinds of users who may be especially subject to the risk[37]— assuming those facts are not widely known—but also of the relevant consequences, if they are not widely known as well.[38]

that the number of persons at risk need not be large to be considered 'substantial' so as to require a warning. Essentially, this reflects the same risk-utility balancing undertaken in warnings cases generally. But courts explicitly impose the requirement of substantiality in cases involving adverse allergic reactions."

**33.** See, e.g., Kehm v. Procter & Gamble Mfg. Co., 724 F.2d 613 (8th Cir. 1983) (Iowa law) (user of defendant's extra absorbent Rely tampon died from toxic shock syndrome): "[L]iability does not turn on whether the risk of harm runs to a substantial number of persons. Rather, in determining whether a manufacturer has a duty to warn, courts inquire whether the manufacturer knew that there were even a relatively few persons who could not use its product without serious injury, and whether a proper warning would have helped prevent harm to them." Id. at 620. Cf. Goldman v. Walco Tool & Eng'g, 614 N.E.2d 42 (Ill. Ct. App. 1993) (no duty to warn idiosyncratic users of risks from over-the-counter products, but rule does not apply to other types of products like dangerous chemicals in rust-preventative oil).

**34.** For a critique of foreseeability on grounds of indeterminacy, see § 13.5, below.

**35.** In this respect, consider Friedman v. Merck & Co., 131 Cal.Rptr.2d 885, 894 (Ct. App. 2003), which used the "significant segment of the population" classification, together with the immateriality of the

harm, to deny a claim against a TB test distributor for failing to warn that the test contained animal products which vegans would find objectionable).

**36.** See, e.g., Mitchell v. VLI Corp., 786 F.Supp. 966 (M.D. Fla. 1992), in which the package insert for nonprescription "Today" contraceptive sponge stated that approximately 2% of users in studies "discontinued use because of allergic reactions." Plaintiff suffered a severe allergic reaction that ultimately led to a hysterectomy. *Held*, because it was unclear whether a lay person would understand "allergic reaction" to include a severe reaction requiring major surgery, the manufacturer's motion for summary judgment on warnings claim was denied. See also Tongate v. Wyeth Labs., 580 N.E.2d 1220 (Ill. App. Ct. 1991) (jury question as to whether manufacturer's inserts for tetanus toxoid contained adequate warnings of potential neurologic complications).

**37.** Such as when persons who are allergic to one substance, such as penicillin, are more likely to be allergic to another. See, e.g., Jacobs v. Dista Products Co., 693 F.Supp. 1029 (D. Wyo. 1988).

**38.** "When the presence of the allergenic ingredient would not be anticipated by a reasonable user or consumer, warnings concerning its presence are required. Similarly, when the presence of the ingredient is generally known to consumers, but its dangers are not, a warning of the dangers must be given." Products Liability Restatement § 2 cmt. *k*.

## § 9.5   SOPHISTICATED USERS AND BULK SUPPLIERS

Two doctrines that exempt manufacturers from their normal obligation to provide end-users and consumers with warnings of product hazards are the "sophisticated user doctrine" and the "bulk supplier doctrine." Both doctrines relieve an upstream seller of the duty to warn a downstream purchaser or user in circumstances where the purchaser already knows about the risk.[1] Because these two doctrines relieve manufacturers of the duty to warn in certain situations, they partake of a defense.[2] Yet, they more appropriately are seen as helping define the proper scope of a manufacturer's duty to warn in certain contexts, such that their application undermines the plaintiff's prima facie case. Because both doctrines rest on hazard information possessed by downstream purchasers, the two doctrines sometimes are blended together into a single doctrine.[3] Yet, while they often overlap,[4] most courts view them as legal doctrines that are related but quite distinct.[5]

### § 9.5

**1.** See Korzec, Restating the Obvious in Maryland Products Liability Law: The Restatement (Third) of Torts: Products Liability and Failure to Warn Defenses, 30 U. Balt. L. Rev. 341 (2001); Madden, Liability of Suppliers of Natural Raw Materials and the Restatement (Third) of Torts: Products Liability—A First Step Toward Sound Public Policy, 30 U. Mich. J.L. Ref. 281, 291–95 (1997); Mansfield, Reflection on Current Limits on Component and Raw Material Supplier Liability and the Proposed Third Restatement, 84 Ky. L.J. 221 (1996); Ausness, Learned Intermediaries and Sophisticated Users: Encouraging the Use of Intermediaries to Transmit Product Safety Information, 46 Syracuse L. Rev. 1185 (1996); Baker, Effects of Products Liability on Bulk Suppliers of Biomaterials, 50 Food & Drug L.J. 455 (1995); Slawotsky, The Learned Intermediary Doctrine: The Employer as Intermediary, 30 Torts & Ins. L.J. 1059 (1995); Hager, Don't Say I Didn't Warn You Even Though I Didn't: Why the Pro–Defendant Consensus on Warning Law Is Wrong, 61 Tenn. L. Rev. 1125 (1994); Faulk, Products Liability and the Chemical Manufacturer: Limitations on the Duty to Warn, 38 Okla. L. Rev. 233 (1985); Notes, 85 Nw. U. L. Rev. 562 (1991) (duty to warn of chemical suppliers), 74 Va. L. Rev. 579 (1988) (sophisticated user defense); 1 Madden & Owen on Products Liability § 9.8 (sophisticated users), § 9.9 (bulk suppliers); 2 Frumer and Friedman, Products Liability § 12.06[4] and [5]; Am. Law Prod. Liab. 3d § 32:75 § 33:19—:29.

**2.** See, e.g., Hoffman v. Houghton Chem. Corp., 751 N.E.2d 848, 852 (Mass. 2001) (adopting bulk supplier doctrine as affirmative defense); Higgins v. E.I. Dupont de Nemours & Co., 671 F.Supp. 1055 (D.

Md. 1987) (applying "sophisticated user/bulk supplier defense").

**3.** See, e.g., Higgens v. E.I. DuPont de Nemours & Co., 671 F.Supp. 1055 (D. Md. 1987), which applied a "sophisticated user/bulk supplier defense" to shield manufacturers of chemicals sold to Dupont for its use in making paint that allegedly was teratogenic: "There is no duty on product suppliers to warn ultimate users (whether employees or customers) of product-related hazards in products supplied in bulk to a knowledgeable user." Id. at 1061.

**4.** See, e.g., Gray v. Badger Mining Corp., 676 N.W.2d 268, 280–81 (Minn. 2004) (examining both doctrines).

**5.** See, e.g., Hoffman v. Houghton Chem. Corp., 751 N.E.2d 848, 854 (Mass. 2001); In re Silicone Gel Breast Implants Products Liability Litigation, 996 F.Supp. 1110, 1113–14 (N.D. Ala. 1997) (referring to the "raw material supplier defense" or the "bulk sales/sophisticated purchaser rule," observing that these "doctrines, though conceptually distinct, overlap and tend to merge," and stating that the strongest case for exempting a supplier from its duty to warn end users is when the doctrines overlap, "namely, when a supplier sells to a knowledgeable manufacturer raw materials in bulk, which are not themselves inherently dangerous and which are substantially changed during the manufacturing process before resale to consumers, and when the supplier has little or no role in the design of the end product").

Because the cases in which these doctrines arise often involve sand, chemicals, and other raw and component materials, cases in which these doctrines appear often address the special obligations of suppliers of raw materials and component parts. See § 15.3, below.

### Sophisticated User Doctrine

The sophisticated user doctrine[6] may arise if there is no *need* to warn, because of the expertise of the buyer or user.[7] A product supplier has no duty, under this doctrine, to warn employees of knowledgeable commercial buyers[8] about product hazards of which such buyers are aware.[9] Explained by the absence of a need to provide buyers with warning information they already possess, the sophisticated purchaser or user doctrine is a close cousin of the generally accepted principle that there is no duty to warn of obvious or commonly known dangers,[10] considered below.[11] The purpose of warnings, as previously discussed, is to provide information to people about hazards and safety information they do not know about so that they may avoid the product altogether or avoid the danger by careful use.[12] So, the failure to provide warnings about risks already known to a sophisticated purchaser usually is not a proximate cause of harm resulting from those risks suffered by the buyer's employees or downstream purchasers.[13]

Under the sophisticated user doctrine, a supplier of sheet metal has no duty to warn a building contractor that its metal may be slippery, or to warn about the dangers of working with metal at heights;[14] a chimney manufacturer has no duty to warn an installer of the risk of carbon

---

**6.** Among the various permutations of this doctrine are the "knowledgeable user" doctrine and the "sophisticated intermediary" defense. On the former, see, e.g., Donald v. Shinn Fu Co. of America, 2002 WL 32068351, at *8–*10 (E.D.N.Y. 2002). On the latter, see generally Gray v. Badger Mining Corp., 676 N.W.2d 268, 277–280 (Minn. 2004); Ritchie v. Glidden Co., 242 F.3d 713, 725 (7th Cir. 2001) (Ind. law). Sometimes, it is even referred to as the "learned intermediary" doctrine. See, e.g., Curtis v. M & S Petroleum, Inc., 174 F.3d 661, (5th Cir. 1999) (Miss. law). Subdividing the sophisticated user doctrine and referring to it by different labels can inject confusion and is best avoided.

**7.** An early, landmark case explaining this point is Littlehale v. E.I. DuPont de Nemours Co., 268 F.Supp. 791, 798 (S.D.N.Y. 1966), aff'd, 380 F.2d 274 (2d Cir. 1967), where the court stated that " '[t]here need be no warning to one in a particular trade or profession against a danger generally known to that trade or profession.' " Moreover, "[i]f no warning is required to be given by the manufacturer to a purchaser who is well aware of the inherent dangers of the product, there is no duty on the part of the manufacturer to warn an employee of that purchaser." Id. at 799.

**8.** Some jurisdictions apply similar principles to individual purchasers who themselves are sophisticated users. See, e.g., Smith v. Louisville Ladder Co., 237 F.3d 515, 521 (5th Cir. 2001) (Tex. law) (ladders were sold to individuals in the telecommunications industry who were familiar with

the risk of ladder slides; "a supplier may rely on the professional expertise of the user in tailoring its warning"); Crook v. Kaneb Pipe Line Operating P'ship, 231 F.3d 1098 (8th Cir. 2000) (Neb. law) (manager of farmer's coop killed in propane gas explosion could not recover against propane supplier because coop stored large quantities of propane gas and manager had specialized knowledge of propane hazards).

**9.** Goodbar v. Whitehead Bros., 591 F.Supp. 552, 559 (D. Va. 1984) ("there is no duty on product suppliers to warn employees of knowledgeable industrial purchasers as to product-related hazards"), aff'd sub nom. Beale v. Hardy, 769 F.2d 213 (4th Cir. 1985).

**10.** See, e.g., Donald v. Shinn Fu Co. of America, 2002 WL 32068351, at *8–*10 (E.D.N.Y. 2002) (applying "knowledgeable user" doctrine to bar failure to warn claim against manufacturer of fork lift jack by forklift operator who knew there was a risk of collapse from using jack without its stand).

**11.** See § 10.2, below.

**12.** See § 9.1, above.

**13.** See, e.g., Crook v. Kaneb Pipe Line Operating P'ship, 231 F.3d 1098, 1102–03 (8th Cir. 2000) (Neb. law).

**14.** See Contranchis v. Travelers Ins. Co., 839 So.2d 301, 304 (La. Ct. App. 2003) ("there is no duty to warn 'sophisticated users' of the dangers, which they may be presumed to know about because of their familiarity with the product").

monoxide poisoning if the chimney is not kept clean;[15] and a seller of diving platforms has no duty to warn a high school purchasing them that they are dangerous if used for diving in shallow water.[16] More typically, the doctrine shields a silica sand supplier of a duty to warn foundry workers that they can contract silicosis from breathing silica dust, if the supplier has reason to believe that the foundry which purchases the sand, being a "sophisticated user," already fully knows this risk and how to avoid it.[17] But the doctrine may not relieve a supplier of its warning responsibilities if the purchaser's awareness is limited to a general risk that does not include a specific hazard that results in harm.[18] Thus, if a supplier of silica sand knows that disposable respirators are not effective in guarding against the risk of silicosis, it has a duty to provide this specific safety information to a foundry that knows of the general risk of silicosis but which does not specifically know that the type of respirators its workers use are ineffective.[19]

At least three states have statutes bear, at least to some extent, on the sophisticated user doctrine. Connecticut's statute provides that a warning, to be adequate, must be provided to "the person best able to take or recommend precautions" to avoid harm;[20] Louisiana's statute states that a manufacturer need not warn of specific dangers of which the user already knows or should be expected to know;[21] and the Kansas statute eliminates the duty to warn of dangers and precautions of which the user or consumer should be aware.[22]

### Bulk Supplier Doctrine

The bulk supplier doctrine may arise if there is no *way* to warn, because of the nature of the product and the form in which it is sold.[23] This doctrine normally applies to liquids, sand, and other products sold

**15.** See Gajewski v. Pavelo, 652 A.2d 509 (Conn. App. 1994).

**16.** See Mohr v. St. Paul Fire & Marine Ins. Co., 674 N.W.2d 576 (Wis. Ct. App. 2003) (high school should realize this risk, possibly relieving seller of duty to warn; doctrine not limited to purchases by employers).

**17.** See, e.g., Haase v. Badger Mining Corp., 669 N.W.2d 737 (Wis. Ct. App. 2003) (silica sand supplier had no duty to warn foundry of risk that foundry workers might contract silicosis), aff'd on other grounds, 682 N.W.2d 389 (Wis. 2004) (manufacturer of silica sand was not subject to strict liability in tort because sand underwent substantial change by purchasing foundry which combined it with other materials to make molds for cast iron products like manhole covers, after which silica molds were broken off); Bergfeld v. Unimin Corp., 319 F.3d 350 (8th Cir. 2003) (Iowa law). Taylor v. Monsanto Co., 150 F.3d 806 (7th Cir. 1998) (Ind. law) (PCBs).

**18.** See, e.g., Swope v. Columbian Chems. Co., 281 F.3d 185 (5th Cir. 2002) (La. law) (sophisticated user defense does not apply unless user "already knew or reasonably should have been expected to

know of the product's dangerous characteristics"). *But see* Taylor v. Monsanto Co., 150 F.3d 806, 808–09 (7th Cir. 1998) (Ind. law) (questioning plaintiffs' "attempt to fine-tune the 'sophisticated intermediary' doctrine to make it require Westinghouse to have specific expertise on human health and employee safety issues related to PCBs" and noting that "there is often no easy way to select the particular 'level of abstraction' that governs" such an inquiry).

**19.** Gray v. Badger Mining Corp., 676 N.W.2d 268 (Minn. 2004) (reversing summary judgment for supplier).

**20.** See Conn. Gen. Stat. § 52–572q(d) (a "seller may not be considered to have provided adequate warnings or instructions unless they were devised to communicate with the person best able to take or recommend precautions against the potential harm"). See Gajewski v. Pavelo, 652 A.2d 509 (Conn. App. Ct. 1994).

**21.** See La. Rev. Stat. Ann. § 9:2800.57.

**22.** See Kan. Stat. Ann. § 60–3305.

**23.** This doctrine applies with extra force in many cases because the purchasers are knowledgeable users who usually do not

in bulk to commercial purchasers by railroad car or tanker truck. The difficulty with imposing a duty to warn on such bulk suppliers is that there normally is no practical way to place a warning on such a product to alert end-users of its dangers. Moreover, the purchaser may itself repackage the chemical or other product in drums or other containers for subsequent transport and distribution to users or consumers, or it may simply use it as it arrives in bulk for some manufacturing process.[24] In either event, there typically is little way for an upstream seller of such a product to provide warnings to the ultimate users or consumers of hazards that the product may contain.[25] Accordingly, if the purchaser knows of the product's hazards, from warnings provided to it by the bulk supplier or from general knowledge, the bulk supplier normally will have no duty to provide additional warnings to the ultimate user or consumer.[26] However, if the bulk supplier knows more about a product hazard or how to avoid it than its purchasers, it has a duty to provide this additional safety information to the purchaser of its materials, if there is some reasonable way to do so.[27]

In *Purvis v. PPG Industries, Inc.*,[28] a dry cleaner employee was poisoned by a cleaning solvent manufactured by the defendant, PPG,

need any warning, as discussed above. Because the doctrine applies to such materials as sand, chemicals, and other raw materials sold to other manufacturers, the doctrine sometimes is called the "raw material supplier" doctrine. See 2 Frumer and Friedman, Products Liability § 12.06[5].

Products Liability Restatement § 5, "Liability of Commercial Seller or Distributor of Product Components for Harm Caused by Products Into Which Components Are Integrated," provides that the supplier of a nondefective component (including a raw material) is subject to liability only if it "substantially participates in the integration of the component" into the integrated product, and the integration causes the product to be defective. Suppliers of "raw materials" do not have a duty to investigate end uses nor a duty to warn end users. See cmt. *c*. On the special duties of suppliers of raw materials, see § 15.3, below.

**24.** See, e.g., Gray v. Badger Mining Corp., 676 N.W.2d 268, 280–81 (Minn. 2004) (foundry used silica sand for making molds into which molten metal was poured, after which molds were knocked off castings, pulverizing sand into sub-micron sized particles of dust that workers could inhale unless protected by adequate respirators).

**25.** *But see* Gryc v. Dayton–Hudson Corp., 297 N.W.2d 727, 731 (Minn. 1980) (textile manufacturer, which made flammable fabric sold to manufacturer of nightgown, argued that any warnings it provided to garment manufacturers would not find their way to consumers; yet manufacturer used hang tags for other purposes, sent

through the chain of commerce, that did reach consumers).

**26.** See, e.g., Wood v. Phillips Petroleum Co., 119 S.W.3d 870, 874 (Tex. App. 2003) (supplier of benzene to petrochemical company had no duty to warn purchaser on why and how to protect workers from its well-known toxic effects: "In some instances, a bulk supplier, who has no package of its own on which to place a label, may satisfy its duty to warn ultimate users of its product by proving that the intermediary to whom it sells the product is adequately trained and warned, familiar with the propensities of the product and its safe use, and capable of passing its knowledge on to users in a warning.... The question in any case is whether a bulk supplier has a reasonable assurance that its warning will reach those endangered by the use of its product."); Tilton v. Union Oil Co. of California, 776 N.E.2d 455 (Mass. App. Ct. 2002) (buyer's employee injured when nearly empty drum of chemical solvent exploded as he tried to remove lid with acetylene torch; petroleum company that sold solvent could rely on bulk supplier defense); In re TMJ Implants Prods. Liab. Litig., 872 F.Supp. 1019, 1029 (D. Minn. 1995) (because DuPont sold Teflon in bulk to knowledgeable medical device manufacturer to make jaw implants, it had no duty to warn ultimate consumers that Teflon might not be suited for human implantation).

**27.** See, e.g., Gray v. Badger Mining Corp., 676 N.W.2d 268, 280–81 (Minn. 2004) (reversing summary judgment for supplier).

**28.** 502 So.2d 714 (Ala. 1987).

which shipped the solvent in tank trucks to various distributors who then resold the solvent in drums to users such as the plaintiff's employer. PPG provided its distributors with warning labels and all relevant danger information in Material Safety Data Sheets.[29] Plaintiff sued PPG, claiming that the company should have provided the warnings directly to her. Affirming summary judgment for the defendant, the court held that PPG had no duty to provide warnings directly to the plaintiff. The court reasoned that sometimes manufacturers, like PPG, have no effective way to convey information directly to ultimate users or consumers about dangers in products sold in bulk.

Whether due to bulk sales, repackaging, or product combinations, upstream manufacturers sometimes may properly rely on downstream distributors to perform the warning function, provided there is a reasonable basis for the supplier to believe that the purchasing distributors will pass along appropriate warnings to its vendees.[30] Hence, the bulk supplier doctrine may exempt manufacturers who sell in bulk from having to warn the ultimate user or consumer of hydrogen peroxide sold to a hospital;[31] of natural gas sold to a city;[32] of propane sold to a propane transporter;[33] of flammable chemicals sold to a manufacturer of ink;[34] or of chemicals with other kinds of hazards sold to a wood treating company[35] or to an automotive manufacturer.[36]

### The Restatements

Both the bulk supplier and sophisticated user doctrines are offshoots of a general principle expressed in *Restatement (Second) of Torts* § 388, the basic provision on a chattel supplier's duty to warn under the law of negligence in the *Second Restatement*. Addressing a seller's duty to warn when it sells a product to an intermediate supplier, comment *n* to § 388 provides that a seller may rely on the intermediary to provide warnings to the end-user if that reliance is reasonable in the circumstances.[37] Such reliance is reasonable only if the seller has reason to believe that the intermediary will faithfully discharge this obligation and, even then, the seller may have a duty to warn end users of particularly serious hazards if a feasible means of communication exists.[38] Section 388 is often relied upon for the principle that a manufacturer may not always rely on an

---

**29.** The Hazard Communication Standard promulgated by OSHA requires manufacturers and importers to label all containers of hazardous chemicals and to provide Material Safety Data Sheets to purchasing employers. In turn, employers must make the MSD Sheet information available to employees, and must train their employees in the safe handling of such substances. 29 C.F.R. § 1910.1200 (2004). See M. Green, When Toxic Worlds Collide: Regulatory and Common Law Prescriptions for Risk Communication, 13 Harv. Envt'l L. Rev. 209 (1989); O'Reilly, Risks of Assumptions: Impacts of Regulatory Label Warnings Upon Industrial Products Liability, 37 Cath. U. L. Rev. 85 (1987).

**30.** *Purvis*, 502 So.2d at 722.

**31.** See Cook–Pizzi v. Van Waters & Rogers, Inc., 94 S.W.3d 636 (Tex. App. 2002).

**32.** See Downs v. Panhandle E. Pipeline Co., 694 N.E.2d 1198 (Ind. Ct. App. 1998).

**33.** See Stoffel v. Thermogas Co., 998 F.Supp. 1021 (N.D. Iowa 1997) (Iowa law).

**34.** See Hoffman v. Houghton Chemical Corp., 751 N.E.2d 848 (Mass. 2001).

**35.** Coffey v. Chemical Specialities, Inc., 4 F.3d 984 (4th Cir. 1993) (S.C. law).

**36.** Adams v. Union Carbide Corp., 737 F.2d 1453 (6th Cir. 1984) (Ohio law).

**37.** See, e.g., Persons v. Salmon N. Am., Inc., 265 Cal.Rptr. 773 (Ct. App. 1990).

**38.** Comment *n* to § 388, entitled Warnings given to third person, provides in part:

intermediary to pass along warnings of a product hazard, but the other side of this coin—that a manufacturer may properly rely on an intermediary if there is a reasonable basis for such reliance—provides the basis for the exemption from the duty to warn for both the sophisticated user and bulk supplier doctrines.[39] While § 388 of the *Restatement (Second) of Torts* addresses the obligations of a supplier to warn in the law of negligence, most courts apply its principles to the duty to warn in strict products liability.[40]

But providing danger information to an intermediate buyer may not be enough if a reasonable supplier would supply the buyer with more or

Chattels are often supplied for the use of others.... In all such cases the question may arise as to whether the person supplying the chattel is exercising that reasonable care, which he owes to those who are to use it, by informing the third person through whom the chattel is supplied of its actual character.

Giving to the third person through whom the chattel is supplied all the information necessary to its safe use is not in all cases sufficient to relieve the supplier from liability. It is merely a means by which this information is to be conveyed to those who are to use the chattel. The question remains whether this method gives a reasonable assurance that the information will reach those whose safety depends upon their having it....

[I]f the danger involved in the ignorant use of a particular chattel is very great, it may be that the supplier does not exercise reasonable care in entrusting the communication of the necessary information even to a person whom he has good reason to believe to be careful. Many such articles can be made to carry their own message to the understanding of those who are likely to use them by the form in which they are put out, by the container in which they are supplied, or by a label or other device, indicating with a substantial sufficiency their dangerous character. Where the danger involved in the ignorant use of their true quality is great and such means of disclosure are practicable and not unduly burdensome, it may well be that the supplier should be required to adopt them.

**39.** See, e.g., McGhee v. Oryx Energy Co., 657 So.2d 853 (Ala. 1995) (house exploded from leak of propane gas not detected due to odor fade; producer, which sold gas through pipeline to distributors whom it warned, had no way to identify or warn individual consumers); Newson v. Monsanto Co., 869 F.Supp. 1255 (E.D. Mich. 1994) (suppliers of chemical to Ford Motor Co. used to make shatterproof windshields could reasonably assume that Ford had or would obtain information "abundantly available in the scientific literature"); Vines v. Beloit Corp., 631 So.2d 1003 (Ala. 1994) (papermaking machine manufacturer satisfied duty by warning sophisticated user of machine); Davis v. Avondale Indus., 975 F.2d 169 (5th Cir.1992) (La. law) (sale to sophisticated intermediate purchaser of welding brazing rods; no duty to warn ultimate user).

**40.** See, e.g., Hoffman v. Houghton Chem. Corp., 751 N.E.2d 848 (Mass. 2001) (§ 388 applies to strict products liability duty to warn in implied warranty); Phillips v. A.P. Green Refractories Co., 630 A.2d 874 (Pa. Super. Ct. 1993), aff'd on other grounds sub nom. Phillips v. A–Best Products Co., 665 A.2d 1167, 1172 (Pa. 1995); Smith v. Walter C. Best, Inc., 927 F.2d 736 (3d Cir. 1990) (Ohio law) (§ 388 applies to strict liability in tort duty to warn); Higgins v. E.I. DuPont de Nemours & Co., 671 F.Supp. 1055 (D. Md. 1987) (same).

Note that a few courts have refused to apply the sophisticated user and bulk supplier doctrines as no-duty rules in strict liability in tort, holding that the duty to warn in strict tort is nondelegable as a matter of law so that suppliers must directly warn ultimate users. See, e.g., Menschik v. Mid–America Pipeline Co., 812 S.W.2d 861 (Mo. Ct. App. 1991). See also Hall v. Ashland Oil Co., 625 F.Supp. 1515 (D. Conn. 1986); Neal v. Carey Canadian Mines, Ltd., 548 F.Supp. 357, 368 (E.D. Pa. 1982), aff'd sub nom. Van Buskirk v. Carey Canadian Mines, Ltd., 760 F.2d 481, 497 (3d Cir. 1985); Whitehead v. St. Joe Lead Co., 729 F.2d 238 (3d Cir.1984) (N.J. law).

Some courts hold that whether there is a duty to provide warnings directly to ultimate users is a factual question, for jury determination, based on a balance of risk versus feasibility. See, e.g., Bryant v. Technical Research Co., 654 F.2d 1337 (9th Cir. 1981) (Idaho law) (bulk supplier might have obtained distributor's customer list and directly warned end users); Shell Oil Co. v.

better information,[41] or would provide it directly to the ultimate users, considering the overall balance of costs and benefits, including the reliability of the intermediary, the magnitude of the hazard, and the feasibility of providing more effective warnings,[42] a principle well summarized in the *Third Restatement*.[43] Even if a supplier had a reasonable basis for trusting an intermediate purchaser in the past, discovering facts suggesting that the vendee is failing to pass on important warnings extinguishes the basis for relying on the vendee and restores the supplier's duty to provide warnings directly to end-users.[44] Moreover, when a product is a durable good on which a warning may be attached or embossed, the manufacturer usually has a ready means to provide warnings about serious hazards directly to end users—regardless of whether there is a knowledgeable or "sophisticated" employer or other intermediary involved.[45]

## § 9.6 PRESCRIPTION DRUGS AND MEDICAL DEVICES

Warnings issues in cases involving prescription drugs and medical devices in many ways parallel those issues in other types of cases. Yet, as seen in connection with design defectiveness,[1] prescription drugs and medical devices raise a variety of special issues for products liability litigation. Unlike most other types of products liability cases, inadequate

Gutierrez, 581 P.2d 271 (Ariz. Ct. App. 1978).

**41.** See, e.g., Union Carbide Corp. v. Kavanaugh, 879 So.2d 42, 45 (Fla. Dist. Ct. App. 2004) (asbestos supplier not protected by § 388 because, "although UCC provided information and some warning to Georgia–Pacific, it did not fully disclose the magnitude of the hazards then known to exist").

**42.** See, e.g., Gray v. Badger Mining Corp., 676 N.W.2d 268 (Minn. 2004) (reversing summary judgment for supplier; Provision of MSDS not necessarily enough); Little v. Liquid Air Corp., 939 F.2d 1293 (5th Cir. 1991) (Miss. law) (court should consider all aspects of the reasonableness of relying on a particular intermediate distributor in a particular situation, so that summary judgment for bulk supplier is improper solely on proof that it supplied its vendee with a MSDS containing the risk information).

**43.** Products Liability Restatement § 2(c) cmt. *i* provides: "There is no general rule as to whether one supplying a product for the use of others through an intermediary has a duty to warn the ultimate product user directly or may rely on the intermediary to relay warnings. The standard is one of reasonableness in the circumstances. Among the factors to be considered are the gravity of the risks posed by the product, the likelihood that the intermediary will convey the information to the ultimate user, and the feasibility and effectiveness of giving a warning directly to the user."

See also, Products Liability Restatement § 5, which addresses the duties of suppliers of component parts and raw materials. Comment *c* thereto provides that raw material suppliers do not have a duty to warn end users. See § 15.3, below.

**44.** See Lakeman v. Otis Elevator Co., 930 F.2d 1547 (11th Cir.1991) (Ala. law) (where manufacturer sold chemical in bulk to repackager who resold it to industrial customers with some warnings, but not the most important ones, bulk supplier had duty to warn ultimate users once it became aware of intermediate seller's inadequate warning labels).

**45.** "When the purchaser of machinery is the owner of a workplace who provides the machinery to employees for their use, and there is reason to doubt that the employer will pass warnings on to employees, the seller is required to reach the employees directly with necessary instructions and warnings if doing so is reasonably feasible." Products Liability Restatement § 2(c) cmt. *i*. See, e.g., Square D Co. v. Hayson, 621 So.2d 1373 (Fla. Dist. Ct. App. 1993) (manufacturer of electrical busway system should have placed label on system directly warning workers of backwards installation risks). *But see* Vines v. Beloit Corp., 631 So.2d 1003 (Ala.1994) (manufacturer of machine discharged its duty toward users of machinery by warning sophisticated employer). See generally §§ 9.3 and 9.4, above.

**§ 9.6**

**1.** See § 8.10, above.

warnings and instructions claims dominate prescription drug and medical device litigation.[2]

Several important warnings issues recur in cases involving drugs and medical devices. The first concerns the theories of liability applicable to this type of case. Another involves the regulatory backdrop to this area of the law, provided by the Federal Food, Drug, and Cosmetic Act of 1938, administered by the FDA. A further recurring question is whom a manufacturer of such products must warn, the patient or the doctor. Whether a warning or instruction about a drug or medical device is "adequate" is usually the principal issue in this type of litigation. Finally is the question of whether pharmacists should have a duty to warn patients about prescription drug risks at all, and, if so, what the scope of that duty should be. A wealth of information is available on each of these important issues,[3] and each will be briefly considered here.

Other issues bearing particularly on prescription drug and medical device litigation treated elsewhere include the liability of drug and medical device manufacturers for harm caused by design defectiveness;[4] the responsibility of drug manufacturers for side effects that are unavoidable[5] or unforeseeable under the prevailing state of the art;[6] the scope of a drug company's liability for prenatal harm;[7] and the limitations on litigation of this type, occasioned by a manufacturer's compliance with FDA regulations, under the common law,[8] and the federal preemption doctrine.[9]

### Theory of Liability

Settling on a proper theory of liability for inadequate warnings and instructions has been of greater interest in cases involving prescription drugs and medical devices than any other type of product. Courts widely apply all three theories of liability to cases of this type, negligence, breach of the implied warranty of merchantability, and strict liability in tort,[10] as well as special warning defect provisions of state products

---

**2.** "Failure to warn or instruct is the major basis of liability for manufacturers of prescription drugs and medical devices." Restatement (Third) Torts: Products Liability § 8 cmt. *d*.

**3.** See Hall, The Promise and Peril of Direct-to-Consumer Prescription Drug Promotion on the Internet, 7 De Paul J. Health Car L. 1 (2003); Ausness, Will More Aggressive Marketing Practices Lead to Greater Tort Liability for Prescription Drug Manufacturers, 37 Wake Forest L. Rev. 97 (2002); Madden, The Enduring Paradox of Products Liability Law Relating to Prescription Pharmaceuticals, 21 Pace L. Rev. 313 (2001); Furrow, Enterprise Liability for Bad Outcomes from Drug Therapy: The Doctor, The Hospital, The Pharmacy, and the Drug Firm, 44 Drake L. Rev. 377 (1996); Walsh and Pyrich, Rationalizing the Regulation of Prescription Drugs and Medical Devices: Perspectives on Private Certification and Tort Reform, 48 Rutgers L. Rev.

883 (1996); T. Schwartz, Prescription Products and the Proposed Restatement (Third), 61 Tenn. L. Rev. 1357 (1994); Note, 75 N.Y.U. L. Rev. 1452 (warnings liability for online prescribing); Products Liability Restatement § 6(d); 2 Madden & Owen on Products Liability ch. 22; 5 Frumer & Friedman, Products Liability § 50.01 et seq.; 3 S. Woodhouse, Drug Product Liability § 14.01 et seq. (liability of manufacturers), and § 14A.01 et seq. (liability of drug and medical device intermediaries).

**4.** See § 8.10, above.

**5.** See § 10.3, below.

**6.** See § 10.4, below.

**7.** See § 10.5, below.

**8.** See § 14.3, below.

**9.** See § 14.4, below.

**10.** See, e.g., Larkin v. Pfizer, Inc., 2004 WL 1361954 (Ky. 2004) (prescription drug;

liability statutes.[11] As earlier discussed, courts have been drawn to negligence principles in warnings cases more than in cases involving other types of defects.[12] This has been especially true in cases involving prescription drugs and medical devices. Except for cases of contamination, drugs (as food) were largely exempted from strict liability in tort from the very start of modern products liability law in § 402A of the *Restatement (Second) of Torts,*[13] and courts have continued to apply negligence principles—and to reject true strict liability principles—in landmark prescription drug and medical device cases over the years.[14]

The reasons for preferring negligence principles to true strict liability in drug warning cases run broad and deep,[15] but they are worth summarizing here. First is the fact that banning foreseeability from the liability calculus—the principal way in which strict liability distinguishes itself from negligence—does violence to basic principles of justice and fair play.[16] Another reason for preferring negligence principles in this context is that the extra deterrent effect of strict liability is needed less for products whose warnings must be specifically approved prior to marketing by a federal agency, the FDA.[17] And a related reason is the possibility that strict liability may result in too *much* deterrence, that pharmaceutical manufacturers may be discouraged from investing in new prescription drugs and medical devices, already extremely expensive to develop and bring to market,[18] for fear of financial ruin if the new product possesses unexpected problems.[19] For these and other reasons, while most courts in this context continue to apply "strict" liability by name to warnings cases, the principles that they in fact apply are nothing more than negligence. The *Third Restatement* follows this approach in limiting a manufacturer's warning responsibility in prescription drug and medical device cases to a duty to provide "reasonable instructions or warnings regarding foreseeable risks of harm."[20]

## Regulation by the FDA

Prescription drug and medical device litigation must be considered against the backdrop of the strict regulation provided by the federal

negligence, breach of warranty, and "strict liability"); Hansen v. Baxter Healthcare Corp., 764 N.E.2d 35 (Ill. 2002) (medical device; negligence and "product liability").

**11.** See, e.g., Graham v. American Cyanamid Co., 350 F.3d 496 (6th Cir. 2003) (Ohio law) (vaccine; statute defines duty to warn in negligence terms); Perez v. Wyeth Labs., 734 A.2d 1245 (N.J. 1999) (drug). Compare Marks v. Ohmeda, Inc., 871 So.2d 1148 (La. Ct. App. 2004) (anesthesia machine).

**12.** See § 9.2, above.

**13.** See Restatement (Second) of Torts § 402A cmts. *j* and *k*. See generally Madden, The Enduring Paradox of Products Liability Law Relating to Prescription Pharmaceuticals, 21 Pace L. Rev. 313 (2001).

**14.** See, e.g., Brown v. Superior Court, 751 P.2d 470 (Cal. 1988); Feldman v. Led-

erle Labs., 479 A.2d 374, 386 (N.J. 1984) (in warnings cases, negligence and strict liability are "functional equivalents").

**15.** See generally §§ 6.2 and 10.3, below.

**16.** See Owen, The Moral Foundations of Products Liability Law: Toward First Principles, 68 Notre Dame L. Rev. 427 (1993).

**17.** See, e.g., Brown v. Superior Court, 751 P.2d 470 (Cal. 1988).

**18.** See § 8.10, above.

**19.** Id.

**20.** See Products Liability Restatement § 6(d). See generally T. Schwartz, Prescription Products and the Proposed Restatement (Third), 61 Tenn. L. Rev. 1357 (1994).

Food and Drug Administration, the FDA. The FDA regulates both the safety and effectiveness of prescription pharmaceuticals and certain medical devices.[21] In addition to ascertaining that prescription drugs are safe and effective before they are sold in interstate commerce, the FDA must approve all information a manufacturer plans to provide physicians on a drug's recommended use, contraindications, risks, and side effects. Underlying the regulatory scheme are two assumptions that reflect the special types of dangers that inhere in drugs classified as prescription pharmaceuticals. First is the belief that the risks in many drugs are so complex and dangerous that the FDA must determine their safety and effectiveness before they can be marketed at all. The second premise is that the potential risks of improperly using many drugs are so substantial as to require professional medical judgment and supervision by doctors and nurse practitioners, rendering such products available to consumers only through prescriptions written by such health professionals.

The principal federal statute regulating the quality of drugs is the Federal Food, Drug and Cosmetic Act,[22] originally enacted by Congress in 1938. The Act's key provisions prohibit the sale of "any food, drug, device, or cosmetic that is adulterated or misbranded"[23] and require FDA approval of new drugs prior to the marketing.[24] The Act addresses warnings and instructions through its requirement that drug labels not be "misbranded."[25] The thrust of these sections is to require manufacturers to provide adequate information on purpose, proper dosage, and possible dangers to consumers, for over-the-counter (OTC) drugs, and to the medical professional, for prescription drugs. Labels for over-the-counter drugs must state the drug's active ingredients and established name;[26] must contain adequate directions for use, warnings against dangerous uses, dosages, and duration of use;[27] and must describe the drug's effectiveness, side effects, and contraindications.[28] A prescription drug is one which, "because of its toxicity or other potentiality for harmful effect, or the method of its use, or the collateral measures necessary to its use," is safe only when prescribed and used under the supervision of a licensed medical practitioner,[29] and such drugs must be labeled accordingly.[30]

---

**21.** "Drugs" over which the FDA has authority are defined in 21 U.S.C. § 321(g)(1)(C) as "articles (other than food) intended to affect the structure or any function of the body." A "device" subject to regulation is defined in § 321(g)(1)(C) as "an instrument, apparatus, implement, machine, contrivance, . . . or other similar or related article [that] is intended to affect the structure or any function of the body."

**22.** 21 U.S.C.A. §§ 301–392.

**23.** Id. at § 331(a).

**24.** Id. at § 355.

**25.** Id. at §§ 352 and 353.

**26.** Id. at § 352(e).

**27.** Id. at § 352(f).

**28.** Id. at § 352(n).

**29.** Id. at § 353(b)(1)(B). The process by which a drug may be determined to be an over-the-counter (OTC) drug as opposed to a prescription drug is described in 21 C.F.R. § 330.10, which provides a detailed process for determining a drug's safety and effectiveness that includes a benefit-to-risk ratio. See § 330.10(a)(4)(iii). See also 21 C.F.R. 330.10(a)(4)(vi) ("A drug shall be permitted for OTC sale and use by the laity unless, because of its toxicity or other potential for harmful effect or because of the method or collateral measures necessary to it use, it may safely be sold and used only under the supervision of a practitioner licensed by law to administer such drugs.").

**30.** Prescription drugs must bear labels stating, "CAUTION: Federal law prohibits dispensing without prescription," id. at § 353(b)(4), and must provide any special

## Who Must Be Warned—The "Learned Intermediary Doctrine"

### *In General*

In addition to the required pre-market approval by the FDA, a prescription drug's warnings and instructions must be provided to health professionals—doctors and nurse practitioners—rather than directly to patients. Such "learned intermediaries" stand between the drug manufacturer and the patient, dispensing what medications and information they deem best. Thus, like the sophisticated user and bulk supplier doctrines previously examined, the learned intermediary doctrine is an exception to the general requirement that manufacturers take all reasonable steps to provide warnings directly to a product's ultimate user or consumer.[31] Accordingly, under the "learned intermediary doctrine," the prescription drug manufacturer's duty to inform consumers runs only indirectly through physicians, rather than directly to consumers.[32]

The basic rationale for the learned intermediary doctrine is quite powerful: medical professionals, and only medical professionals, have the requisite knowledge, training, and judgment to properly match drugs, which carry distinctive benefits and dangers, to individual patients who possess distinctive constitutions and medical conditions—and to properly monitor the results thereafter.[33] If manufacturers fulfill their obligations to provide full and fair information to doctors and other health care professionals, those professionals should be able to make intelligent, reasonably safe, and effective treatment decisions.[34] In turn, the prescribing doctor is obliged under the law of torts to inform the patient of a

directions for use and cautionary statements contained in the prescription. Id. at § 353(b)(2).

**31.** See Vitanza v. Upjohn Co., 778 A.2d 829, 836 (Conn. 2001).

**32.** See Ausness, Will More Aggressive Marketing Practices Lead to Greater Tort Liability for Prescription Drug Manufacturers, 37 Wake Forest L. Rev. 97 (2002); Madden, The Enduring Paradox of Products Liability Law Relating to Prescription Pharmaceuticals, 21 Pace L. Rev. 313 (2001); Wiseman, Another Factor in the "Decisional Calculus": The Learned Intermediary Doctrine, The Physician–Patient Relationship, and Direct-to-Consumer Marketing, 52 S.C. L. Rev. 993 (2001); Lear, The Learned Intermediary Doctrine in the Age of Direct Consumer Advertising, 65 Mo. L. Rev. 1101 (2000); Plant, The Learned Intermediary Doctrine: Some New Medicine for an Old Ailment, 81 Iowa L. Rev. 1007 (1996); Ausness, Learned Intermediaries and Sophisticated Users: Encouraging the Use of Intermediaries to Transmit Product Safety Information, 46 Syracuse L. Rev. 1185 (1996); Walsh, Rowland, and Dorfman, The Learned Intermediary Doctrine: The Correct Prescription for Drug Labeling, 48 Rutgers L. Rev. 821 (1996); Ferguson, Liability for Pharmaceutical Products: A Critique of The Learned Intermediary Rule, 12

Oxford J. Legal Stud. 59 (1992); Notes, 51 Stan. L. Rev. 1543 (2001) (learned intermediary doctrine and patient package inserts); 75 N.Y.U. L. Rev. 1452 (2000) (failure to warn liability for online prescriptions); 2 Madden & Owen on Products Liability ch. 22.

**33.** Judge Wisdom provides one of the best descriptions of the rationale in Reyes v. Wyeth Laboratories, 498 F.2d 1264, 1276 (5th Cir. 1974) (Tex. law): "Prescription drugs are likely to be complex medicines, esoteric in formula and varied in effect. As a medical expert, the prescribing physician can take into account the propensities of the drug, as well as the susceptibilities of his patient. His is the task of weighing the benefits of any medication against its potential dangers. The choice he makes is an informed one, an individualized medical judgment bottomed on a knowledge of both patient and palliative. Pharmaceutical companies then, who must warn ultimate purchasers of dangers inherent in patent drugs sold over the counter, in selling prescription drugs are required to warn only the prescribing physician, who acts as a 'learned intermediary' between manufacturer and consumer."

**34.** For a good summary of the doctrine's rationales, see Larkin v. Pfizer, Inc., 2004 WL 1361954 (Ky. 2004).

drug's benefits and dangers (as well as the benefits and dangers of no treatment and alternative treatments), and to monitor how the drug affects the patient.[35]

Sprouting in the 1960s,[36] and becoming firmly planted in the early 1970s,[37] the learned intermediary doctrine is an established fixture in American products liability law, adopted now in almost every state.[38] In addition to prescription drugs, the learned intermediary doctrine has been applied to a cardiac pacemaker;[39] an intrauterine device;[40] a spinal fixation device;[41] a herniated disk plate;[42] a heart catheter;[43] spinal pedicle screws;[44] a morphine pump;[45] an x-ray machine;[46] an electroconvulsive therapy machine;[47] an anesthesia machine;[48] and nicotine chewing gum.[49] The New York Supreme Court seems to have drawn the line at extended-wear contact lenses fitted by an optometrist.[50] While efforts

**35.** See Smith, The Vagueness of Informed Consent, 1 Ind. Health L. Rev. 109 (2004); Prosser and Keeton on Torts § 32, at 189–93; Dobbs, Law of Torts § 250.

**36.** See, e.g., Stottlemire v. Cawood, 213 F.Supp. 897, 899 (D.C.D.C. 1963); Sterling Drug, Inc. v. Cornish, 370 F.2d 82, 85 (8th Cir. 1966) (Mo. law) (With prescription drugs, "the purchaser's doctor is a learned intermediary between the purchaser and the manufacturer. If the doctor is properly warned of the possibility of a side effect in some patients, and is advised of the symptoms normally accompanying the side effect, there is an excellent chance that injury to the patient can be avoided."); Davis v. Wyeth Laboratories, 399 F.2d 121, 130 (9th Cir. 1968) (Idaho law). See also Magee v. Wyeth Laboratories, Inc., 29 Cal.Rptr. 322, 327–28 (Ct. App. 1963).

**37.** See, e.g., Incollingo v. Ewing, 282 A.2d 206, 220 (Pa. 1971); Hoffman v. Sterling Drug, Inc., 485 F.2d 132 (3rd Cir. 1973) (Penn. law); Gravis v. Parke–Davis & Co., 502 S.W.2d 863, 870 (Tex. App. 1973) ("The entire system of drug distribution in America is set up so as to place the responsibility of distribution and use upon professional people. The laws and regulations prevent prescription type drugs from being purchased by individuals without the advice, guidance and consent of licensed physicians and pharmacists. These professionals are in the best position to evaluate the warnings put out by the drug industry."); Reyes v. Wyeth Laboratories, 498 F.2d 1264 (5th Cir. 1974) (Tex. law). See generally Merrill, Compensation for Prescription Drug Injuries, 59 Va. L. Rev. 1, 91 (1973).

**38.** See, e.g., Ehlis v. Shire Richwood, Inc., 367 F.3d 1013, 1017 (8th Cir. 2004) (N.D. law) ("an overwhelming majority of jurisdictions have adopted the learned intermediary doctrine"), citing In re Norplant Contraceptive Prods. Liab. Litig., 215 F. Supp. 2d 795, 806 (E.D. Tex. 2002) ("the doctrine either applies or is recognized . . .

in 48 states, the District of Columbia, and Puerto Rico"); Thom v. Bristol–Myers Squibb Co., 353 F.3d 848, 852 (10th Cir. 2003) (Wyo. law) (stating that 44 jurisdictions adhere to doctrine), citing Vitanza v. The Upjohn Co., 778 A.2d 829, 838 n.11 (Conn. 2001) (collecting cases).

**39.** See Brooks v. Medtronic, Inc., 750 F.2d 1227 (4th Cir. 1984) (S.C. law).

**40.** See McKee v. Moore, 648 P.2d 21 (Okla. 1982).

**41.** See Vaccariello v. Smith & Nephew Richards, Inc., 763 N.E.2d 160 (Ohio 2002). See also Emody v. Medtronic, Inc., 238 F.Supp.2d 1291 (N.D. Ala. 2003) (spinal fusion device).

**42.** See McCombs v. Synthes, 553 S.E.2d 17 (Ga. Ct. App. 2001).

**43.** See Phelps v. Sherwood Medical Indus., 836 F.2d 296 (7th Cir. 1987) (Me. law).

**44.** See King v. Danek Medical, Inc., 37 S.W.3d 429 (Tenn. Ct. App. 2000).

**45.** See Ellis v. C.R. Bard, Inc., 311 F.3d 1272 (11th Cir. 2002) (Ga. Law).

**46.** See Kirsch v. Picker Int'l, Inc., 753 F.2d 670 (8th Cir. 1985) (Mo. law).

**47.** See Andre v. Mecta Corp., 587 N.Y.S.2d 334 (App. Div. 1992).

**48.** See Marks v. Ohmeda, Inc., 871 So.2d 1148 (La. Ct. App. 2004).

**49.** See Tracy v. Merrell Dow Pharmaceuticals, Inc., 569 N.E.2d 875 (Ohio 1991). See also Jack v. Glaxo Wellcome, Inc., 239 F.Supp.2d 1308 (N.D. Ga. 2002) (Zyban, a smoking suppressant drug containing bupropion, an antidepressant).

**50.** See Bukowski v. CooperVision Inc., 592 N.Y.S.2d 807 (App. Div. 1993) (lenses caused corneal ulcers; no evidence that optometrist has ability to assimilate manufacturer's technical information to fulfill learned intermediary role).

to apply the doctrine outside the medical field have largely failed,[51] some courts, misled by the generality of the doctrine's name,[52] have used the "learned intermediary" label when applying principles of the "sophisticated user doctrine" to other types of products.[53] It may well be that the foundations of the learned intermediary rule are weakening,[54] but the rule was explicitly endorsed by the *Third Restatement* and appears quite firmly entrenched for now.[55] Because the doctrine defines the scope of a pharmaceutical manufacturer's duty to warn, application of the learned intermediary rule involves a question of law for the court, not a factual question of adequacy for a jury.[56]

### Exceptions

If a prescription drug is dispensed under circumstances where a health professional does not render the type of individualized balancing of risks and benefits contemplated by the learned intermediary doctrine, warnings may have to be provided directly to the patient. Thus, when the rationale for the learned intermediary doctrine falls away, the general rule requiring manufacturers to warn consumers directly reappears. This commonsense principle has spawned three exceptions, only one of which has much support.

**Mass immunization programs.** The best established exception to the learned intermediary rule is for mass immunization programs where no health professional mediates information about drug risks for the

The learned intermediary doctrine most certainly does not apply to over-the-counter medications, nor does it protect a retailer of such medicines from liability for selling such a product with defective warnings or instructions. See, e.g., Morales v. American Home Prods., 214 F.Supp.2d 723 (S.D. Tex. 2002) (Alka Selzer Plus).

**51.** See, e.g., Hall v. Ashland Oil Co., 625 F.Supp. 1515 (D. Conn. 1986) (differences between doctor-patient relationship and employer-employee relationship precluded application of learned intermediary doctrine to chemical manufacturer who warned decedent's employer but not decedent himself).

**52.** And perhaps these courts have felt the tug of the doctrine's historical roots in the more general principle that those who supply any type of product to expert purchasers normally should be able to rely upon them to pass on warnings to any employees or sub-vendees threatened by a product hazard. See, e.g., Magee v. Wyeth Labs., 29 Cal.Rptr. 322, 327–28 (Ct. App. 1963).

**53.** See, e.g., Coleman v. Cintas Sales Corp., 40 S.W.3d 544 (Tex. App. 2001) (flammable uniform); Burke v. Dow Chemical Co., 797 F.Supp. 1128, 1133 (E.D.N.Y. 1992) (supplier of toxic chemical in "Rid–A–Bug" household insecticide that may have caused brain damage to children of preg-

nant women). See also Gray v. Badger Mining Corp., 676 N.W.2d 268, 275–76 (Minn. 2004) (silica sand; noting that learned intermediary defense is properly limited to pharmaceutical products and refusing to extend it to the employer/employee relationship); Vitanza v. The Upjohn Co., 778 A.2d 829, 845–46 (Conn. 2001) (stating that the learned intermediary and sophisticated user doctrines are not appropriately analogized, because the learned intermediary doctrine applies specifically to the medical field).

**54.** See, e.g., Castagnera & Gerner, The Gradual Enfeeblement of the Learned Intermediary Rule and the Argument in Favor of Abandoning It Entirely, 36 Tort & Ins. L. J. 119, 120 (2000) (describing a weakening of the rule due to "(1) the rise in consumer awareness, (2) the complexity of pharmaceutical products, (3) the development of clinical pharmacies that bring their own special expertise to bear on consumer and patient choices, and (4) the reduced time spent by patients in doctors' offices.").

**55.** See Products Liability Restatement § 6(d).

**56.** Vitanza v. Upjohn Co., 778 A.2d 829 (Conn. 2001) (hence, claim that manufacturer (which did provide adequate warnings of Ansaid's risks to doctors) should have placed warnings on drug samples, could not be converted into a factual question of adequacy for a jury).

benefit of the patient.[57] Most courts confronted with the issue have thus refused to apply the learned intermediary rule to situations where patients are vaccinated in assembly-line fashion, often by persons other than physicians, with no opportunity for individualized medical assessments. When people line up like lemmings to receive a polio shot or flu vaccination at a school or other facility for mass distribution of a vaccine, the manufacturer must take all reasonable steps to assure that each patient is directly provided warnings and instructions on risks the manufacturer should know the drug possesses.[58] As an exception to the learned intermediary rule, which itself is an exception to the manufacturer's general obligation to warn consumers directly, the mass immunization doctrine restores the manufacturer's duty to provide warnings directly to recipients of the vaccine. This true exception was applied in early cases to the polio vaccine,[59] and later to the Swine Flu vaccine.[60] Although a court has wavered here or there,[61] there is every reason to believe that courts will continue to require direct warnings to consumers in similar instances of mass immunization programs.

**Birth control pills.** In *MacDonald v. Ortho Pharmaceutical Corp.*,[62] the plaintiff suffered a stroke leaving her partially paralyzed after taking the defendant's birth control pills for an extended period of time, during which she had seen her physician once each year. The manufacturer provided information to consumers via a package insert that included a warning of the risks of blood clots but that did not specifically mention the possibility of strokes. After suffering a stroke, the plaintiff claimed that the manufacturer had a duty to provide full and adequate warnings directly to her, the patient, and not just to

---

**57.** See Franklin & Mais, Tort Law and Mass Immunization Programs: Lessons from the Polio and Flu Episodes, 65 Cal. L. Rev. 754 (1977).

**58.** For suggestions on what those steps might be, see, e.g., Petty v. United States, 740 F.2d 1428, 1433–34 n.3 (8th Cir. 1984) (Iowa law).

**59.** See, e.g., Davis v. Wyeth Laboratories, 399 F.2d 121, 131 (9th Cir. 1968) (Idaho law) ("Here, however, although the drug was denominated a prescription drug it was not dispensed as such. It was dispensed to all comers at mass clinics without an individualized balancing by a physician of the risks involved. In such cases (as in the case of over-the-counter sales of nonprescription drugs) warning by the manufacturer to its immediate purchaser will not suffice.... In such cases, then, it is the responsibility of the manufacturer to see that warnings reach the consumer, either by giving warning itself or by obligating the purchaser to give warning. Here appellee knew that warnings were not reaching the consumer. Appellee had taken an active part in setting up the mass immunization clinic program for the society and well knew that the program did not make any such provision, either in advertising prior to the clinics or at

the clinics themselves. On the contrary, it attempted to assure all members of the community that they should take the vaccine."); Reyes v. Wyeth Laboratories, 498 F.2d 1264, 1276 (5th Cir. 1974) (Tex. law) ("the manufacturer of a prescription drug who knows or has reason to know that it will not be dispensed as such a drug must provide the consumer with adequate information so that he can balance the risks and benefits of a given medication himself"); Givens v. Lederle Labs., 556 F.2d 1341 (5th Cir.1977) (Fla. law).

**60.** See Brazzell v. United States, 788 F.2d 1352 (8th Cir. 1986) (Iowa law); Petty v. United States, 740 F.2d 1428 (8th Cir. 1984) (Iowa law).

**61.** Compare Mazur v. Merck & Co., 964 F.2d 1348 (3d Cir. 1992) (Pa. law) (oral rubella vaccine maker satisfied duty by providing information to U.S. Center for Disease Control), with Allison v. Merck & Co., 878 P.2d 948, 959 (Nev. 1994) (measles, mumps, and rubella vaccine manufacturer could *not* delegate its duty to warn to CDC whose information sheet made no mention of risks of blindness, deafness, and brain damage).

**62.** 475 N.E.2d 65 (Mass. 1985).

doctors. Although all but one of the fifteen prior reported judicial opinions had applied the learned intermediary doctrine to birth control pills, like other prescription drugs, the *McDonald* majority reinstated a jury verdict for the plaintiff, reasoning that oral contraceptives "stand apart" from other types of prescription medications because of the "heightened participation of patients in decisions relating to use of 'the pill'; the substantial risks affiliated with the product's use; the feasibility of direct warnings by the manufacturer to the user; the limited participation of the physician (annual prescriptions); and the possibility that oral communications between physicians and consumers may be insufficient or too scanty standing alone to apprise consumers fully of the product's dangers at the time the initial selection of a contraceptive method is made and at subsequent points when alternative methods may be considered."[63] For these reasons, the court concluded that the learned intermediary doctrine should not apply to birth control pill manufacturers who, therefore, must provide warnings directly to ultimate users on the nature, gravity, and likelihood of foreseeable side effects, and who must advise consumers to ask their doctors about any other matters about which they may be concerned. The dissenting justice, observing that manufacturers of prescription pharmaceuticals have a duty to provide full information on all material risks to prescribing physicians who, in turn, have a duty (under the informed consent doctrine, redressable in a malpractice action) to provide full information on all material risks to patients for whom they prescribe the drug, argued that this traditional division of responsibility most fairly and efficiently allocates risks and responsibilities among the parties.[64] While *MacDonald* frequently is cited as creating a new common-law exception to the learned intermediary rule for birth control pills, only a couple of federal judges followed it, while other courts have uniformly rejected this exception and continued to apply the learned intermediary doctrine to birth control pills as other types of prescription pharmaceuticals.[65]

**63.** Id. at 70.

**64.** "The rules place on drug manufacturers the duty to gather, compile, and provide to doctors data regarding the use of their drugs, tasks for which the manufacturers are best suited, and the rules place on doctors the burden of conveying those data to their patients in a useful and understandable manner, a task for which doctors are best suited. Doctors, unlike printed warnings, can tailor to the needs and abilities of an individual patient the information that that patient needs in order to make an informed decision whether to use a particular drug. Manufacturers are not in position to give adequate advice directly to those consumers whose medical histories and physical conditions, perhaps unknown to the consumers, make them peculiarly susceptible to risk. Prescription drugs—including oral contraceptives—differ from other products because their dangers vary widely depending on characteristics of individual consumers." Id. at 146.

**65.** See, e.g., In re Norplant Contraceptive Products Liability Litigation, 955 F.Supp. 700, 704 (E.D. Tex. 1997) ("Only a single jurisdiction, Massachusetts, recognizes an exception to the doctrine for prescription contraceptives.").

Note that an FDA regulation requires that birth control manufacturers provide warnings of dangers in lay language directly to the user. This means that a negligence per se action may be available against such a manufacturer who fails to provide adequate risk information directly to users. But the violation-of-regulation approach was explicitly rejected in Martin v. Ortho Pharmaceuticals, Corp., 661 N.E.2d 352 (Ill. 1996) (risk of birth limb reductions from pills used in first trimester of pregnancy).

Consider also that the *MacDonald* exception might create an "overwarning" problem for birth control pills, detrimental to women's health. A Gallup poll in 1985 showed that "Americans greatly overestimate the risks and understate the effective-

**Direct-to-consumer advertising.** It may be that the learned intermediary doctrine is out of touch with the way modern medicine is practiced and with a world where prescription drug manufacturers jump over health professionals to consumers via TV and other mass advertising.[66] In *Perez v. Wyeth Labs.*,[67] the plaintiff experienced problems after being implanted with the Norplant contraceptive device. Plaintiff sued Wyeth, which had properly warned her doctor of possible complications, for failing to provide warnings directly to her. The trial court granted summary judgment for the manufacturer, based on the learned intermediary doctrine as incorporated in a New Jersey statute, and the appellate division affirmed. In an important opinion, the New Jersey Supreme Court reversed, ruling that the learned intermediary doctrine should no longer insulate prescription drug manufacturers from their duty to warn consumers directly when they seek to influence a patient's choice of drugs through mass-marketing.

The *Perez* court reasoned that the learned intermediary doctrine is based on outmoded images of health care from a time when doctors gave medical advice in their offices, made house calls on request, charged only small sums for their advice, and prescribed medicines compounded by a neighborhood pharmacist—all at a time when "the prevailing attitude of law and medicine was that the 'doctor knows best.' "[68] Sadly, this picture is radically different from the health care world that presently exists. Today, managed health care organizations are mammoth businesses, dispensing medical care and prescriptions impersonally; and medicines are manufactured in distant places, sold in supermarket pharmacy departments, and often paid for by third-party providers. Against this back-drop, modern manufacturers of prescription drugs mass-market

ness of birth control methods, particularly the pill, leaving them vulnerable to unintended pregnancies." According to the American College of Obstetricians and Gynecologists, unwanted pregnancies and more than a million abortions each year needlessly threaten women's lives. "The society's survey found that people are particularly misinformed about the birth control pill, which the group said is the most effective and safest contraceptive for many women." Three quarters of the women surveyed thought that the pill presents substantial health risks, despite the fact that the risk of death from taking the pill is about half the mother's risk of death from childbirth. Pill Poll—National Survey Finds Many Have Bad Information, The State (Columbia, S.C.), March 6, 1985, p. 2A, col. 2.

**66.** See, e.g., Hall, The Promise and Peril of Direct-to-Consumer Prescription Drug Promotion on the Internet, 7 De Paul J. Health Car L. 1 (2003); Ausness, Will More Aggressive Marketing Practices Lead to Greater Tort Liability for Prescription Drug Manufacturers, 37 Wake Forest L. Rev. 97 (2002); Wiseman, Another Factor in the "Decisional Calculus": The Learned In-

termediary Doctrine, The Physician–Patient Relationship, and Direct-to-Consumer Marketing, 52 S.C. L. Rev. 993 (2001); Strain and Gaarder, Direct-to-Consumer Advertising and the Learned Intermediary Doctrine: Unsettling a Settled Doctrine, 30 U. Balt. L. Rev. 377 (2001); Heather, Liability for Direct-to-Consumer Advertising and Drug Information on the Internet, 68 Def. Couns. J. 412 (2001); Lear, The Learned Intermediary Doctrine in the Age of Direct Consumer Advertising, 65 Mo. L. Rev. 1101 (2000); Dreier, Direct-to-Consumer Advertising Liability: An Empty Gift to Plaintiffs, 30 Seton Hall L. Rev. 806 (2000); Tyler and Cooper, Blinded by the Hype: Shifting the Burden When Manufacturers Engage in Direct to Consumer Advertising of Prescription Drugs, 21 Vt. L. Rev. 1073 (1997); Noah, Advertising Prescription Drugs to Consumers: Assessing the Regulatory and Liability Issues, 32 Ga. L. Rev. 141 (1997); T. Schwartz, Consumer–Directed Prescription Drug Advertising and the Learned Intermediary Rule, 46 Food Drug Cosm. L.J. 829 (1991).

**67.** 734 A.2d 1245 (N.J. 1999).

**68.** Id. at 1247.

their wares directly to consumers by radio, television, the Internet, billboards on public transportation, and in magazines.[69] The court observed that the problems in these advertising practices are manifest, permitting manufacturers and advertisers to manipulate information on safety and effectiveness which, at best, presents a diluted picture of a product's risks.[70] Not all courts and commentators have agreed,[71] and it is still too early to predict whether *Perez* is a path-breaking case for a powerful, new exception to the learned intermediary rule or simply another decision like *MacDonald*, full of sound and fury, but which withers on the vine.

Note that of these three exceptions, only the one for mass immunization programs is generally accepted, and even it is applied infrequently.[72] Nonetheless, the *Products Liability Restatement* adopts the learned intermediary rule and provides a general exception wide enough to accommodate all three exceptions.[73] By comment, the *Restatement* specifically leaves open the question of whether a new exception should be created for drugs that are mass-marketed directly to consumers.[74]

## Adequacy of Warnings

### *Drugs*

The principles of adequacy applicable to warnings generally, discussed above,[75] apply as well to prescription drugs. All material information on possible risks must be conveyed to the doctor, comprehensible to the general practitioner as well as to the specialist, or to consumers, comprehensible to them, if the circumstances warrant.[76] For a drug warning to be "adequate," it must describe the scope of the danger; the effects of misuse, including the failure to follow instructions; and the physical aspects of the warning, and broader method of conveyance, must be likely to alert recipients to the danger.[77] Other aspects of a

---

**69.** Id. at 1246–47.

**70.** Id. at 1252–53, citing Hanson & Kysar, Taking Behaviorialism Seriously: Some Evidence of Market Manipulation, 112 Harv. L. Rev. 1420 (1999).

**71.** See, e.g., In re Norplant Contraceptive Products Liab. Litig., 165 F.3d 374 (5th Cir. 1999) (Ill. law) (learned intermediary doctrine shields Norplant manufacturer from having to warn patients of product's risks).

**72.** See Mazur v. Merck & Co., Inc., 742 F.Supp. 239, 253 (E.D. Pa. 1990) ("All of the vaccine cases recognize the theoretical validity of the 'mass immunization' exception' to the learned intermediary rule, but very few have found situations where its application is warranted.").

**73.** Products Liability Restatement § 6(d) provides that a prescription drug or medical device is defective if the manufacturer fails to provide reasonable warnings of foreseeable risks to: (1) the doctor or other health-care provider, or (2) the patient, if the manufacturer should know that

health-care providers are "not in a position to reduce the risks of harm in accordance with the instructions or warnings."

**74.** Id. cmt. *e*.

**75.** See § 9.3, above.

**76.** See, e.g., Perez v. Wyeth Labs., 734 A.2d 1245, 1257 (N.J. 1999) (warning must include all material risks, meaning those to which a reasonable patient would attach significance in deciding whether to take the drug); Wagner v. Roche Lab., 671 N.E.2d 252, 256 (Ohio 1996) (drug warnings were inadequate, meaning there was not a reasonable disclosure of "all risks inherent in the use of the drug of which the manufacturer, being held to the standards of an expert in the field, knew or should have known to exist").

**77.** See, e.g., Thom v. Bristol–Myers Squibb Co. 353 F.3d 848, 853 (10th Cir. 2003) (Wyo. law) (jury question whether manufacturer of Serzone antidepressant adequately warned of seriousness of risk of priapism, a persistent and painful erection of the penis).

warning's adequacy discussed above apply as well to prescription drugs, including whether warnings should be made in foreign languages,[78] and the effect of "overpromotion."[79]

An example of the adequacy issue at play in a drug case is *Martin v. Hacker*,[80] in which a doctor treated the decedent, Mr. Martin, for hypertension (high blood pressure) with two drugs manufactured by the defendant, including reserpine. Mr. Martin became severely depressed and fatally shot himself in the head, allegedly because of the reserpine. The issue was whether the information provided by the manufacturer to physicians about the drug's risks was adequate as a matter of law. The package insert specified among the drug's CONTRAINDICATIONS, "mental depression (especially with suicidal tendencies)"; and, among its WARNINGS, the package insert stated: "Extreme caution should be exercised in treating patients with a history of mental depression. Discontinue the drug at first sign of despondency, early morning insomnia, loss of appetite, impotence, or self-deprecation. Drug-induced depression may persist for several months after drug withdrawal and may be severe enough to result in suicide." Carefully applying a full list of adequacy factors, the court concluded that the warning was adequate: it was commensurate with the risk, including the possible consequences of use (death from suicide was specifically mentioned); the insert's language was accurate, clear, direct, unequivocal, sufficiently forceful, complete, consistent, devoid of contradiction, and the information was current;[81] and, when read as a whole, the meaning conveyed about the

---

**78.** See, e.g., Maciejewski, The Dilemma Over Foreign–Language Labeling of Over-the-Counter Drugs, 15 J. Legal Med. 129 (1994).

**79.** As with other types of products, risks in pharmaceuticals and medical devices must not be unduly downplayed, nor safety "overpromoted"; instead, a manufacturer's communications to doctors must present a reasonably balanced portrayal of the effectiveness and dangers of a drug. See Motus v. Pfizer Inc. 196 F.Supp.2d 984, 998 (C.D. Cal. 2001), aff'd, 358 F.3d 659 (9th Cir. 2004) ("An overpromotion theory is one way that a plaintiff in a failure-to-warn case can overcome the manufacturer's argument either (1) that it provided adequate warnings or (2) that the doctor's decision to prescribe a drug despite his awareness of its dangers was an intervening cause sufficient to vitiate the manufacturer's liability."). Compare Stevens v. Parke, Davis & Co., 507 P.2d 653 (Cal. 1973) (overpromotion of Chloromycetin, a broad-spectrum antibiotic, downplaying risk of fatal aplastic anemia), with Spinden v. Johnson & Johnson, 427 A.2d 597 (N.J. Super. Ct. App. Div. 1981) (AMA Journal ads did not amount to overpromotion). See generally Madden, The Enduring Paradox of Products Liability Law Relating to Prescription Pharmaceuticals, 21 Pace L. Rev. 313, 330 (2001) ("An other-

wise suitable warning may be vitiated by the conduct of the manufacturer or those acting at [its direction] if they promote the product in such a fashion as to obscure or lessen the cautionary impact of the seller's warnings."); Annot., 94 A.L.R.3d 1080 (1997) (effect of manufacturer's promotional efforts aimed at doctors).

**80.** 628 N.E.2d 1308 (N.Y. 1993).

**81.** To be adequate, a warning must be *timely*. A long series of cases involving Aralen, a drug used in the treatment of rheumatoid arthritis and eventually linked to irreversible eye damage in some users, established certain principles. To be timely, a warning of side effects must be made promptly upon discovery of the coexistence of the side effect and use of the drug, even though a causal relationship has not been clearly proved. See Basko v. Sterling Drug, Inc., 416 F.2d 417 (2d Cir. 1969) (Mo. law). The warning is required as soon as the side effect is documented even in only a very small percentage of users. See Sterling Drug, Inc. v. Cornish, 370 F.2d 82 (8th Cir. 1966) (Kan. law). Since the drug company is held to have the knowledge of an expert, a warning to be timely must be given as soon as the risks are pointed out in reputable scientific journals. See Schenebeck v. Sterling Drug, Inc., 423 F.2d 919 (8th Cir. 1970) (Ark. law).

possible consequences of taking the drug was unmistakable. The court thus determined that the warnings were adequate as a matter of law.

### Medical Devices

Medical devices involve many of the same adequacy issues.[82] For example, in *Phillips v. Baxter Healthcare Corp.*,[83] the plaintiff underwent breast augmentation surgery in which prostheses filled with silicone gel were implanted in her breasts. Several years later, when her doctor performed a closed capsulotomy, applying force to the breast to break up scar tissue that had formed around the implants, the implants broke. The implants were surgically removed and replaced, and the plaintiff sued the implant manufacturer on various theories including the failure to provide adequate warnings. The warning accompanying the implants stated that "[t]he silicone elastomer envelope of these products has a low tear strength and is thin to achieve desired prosthesis softness and mobility. For these reasons, the envelope may be easily cut by a scalpel or rupture by excessive stresses.... Care must be exercised during handling to prevent such events." It specifically provided that the manufacturer could not "guarantee the structural integrity of its implant should the surgeon elect to treat capsule firmness by forceful external stress." These warnings, held the court, were adequate.

By contrast, in *Hufft v. Horowitz*,[84] the plaintiff's penile implant malfunctioned, resulting in an almost constant erection with persistent pain and emotional distress, which required the plaintiff to have the implant surgically removed. The implant, which the plaintiff's surgeon viewed to be the "Cadillac of the industry," came with warnings of possible complications, such as malfunction of the pumping mechanism or cylinder, tubing kinks, and leakage of fluids, which might require removal. The court concluded that a jury might find this warning inadequate because it failed to warn that the implant was inappropriate for patients with well-muscled abdomens; that it could cause a continual and painful erection; and that scar tissue might encapsulate its reservoir, preventing it from functioning properly.

### Method of Conveyance

There are several standard avenues of communication between drug companies and physicians for transmitting information about drugs, and a manufacturer must select the best methods reasonably available to convey important new information on drug dangers to doctors who need the information. The Physician's Desk Reference (PDR), updated periodically, contains copies of package inserts for many prescription drugs. Other sources of information that are more complete than the PDR are Facts and Comparisons (updated monthly), and the annual United States Pharmacopeial Drug Information (USPDI) for the Health Care Professional (vol. IA & IB), and Advice for the Patient—Drug Information in

---

**82.** See, e.g., Ralston v. Smith & Nephew Richards, Inc., 275 F.3d 965, 976 (10th Cir. 2001) (Kan. law) (warnings of surgical nail's limitations were adequate); Bravman v. Baxter Healthcare Corp., 984 F.2d 71 (2d Cir. 1993) (N.Y. law) (jury question on whether manufacturer should have warned that heart valve might be noisy).

**83.** 1993 WL 524688 (Cal. Ct. App. 1993).

**84.** 5 Cal.Rptr.2d 377 (Ct. App. 1992).

Lay Language (vol. II). Information on warnings and contraindications is readily available to physicians from these reference works, and the warnings in package inserts and the PDR ordinarily are adequate to alert physicians to drug hazards. Yet the information provided in the PDR may become out of date due to new developments, and a manufacturer's failure promptly to update the medical profession may subject it to liability. If information is critical, the manufacturer may need to send "Dear Doctor" letters advising physicians individually of the new information.[85] However, the typically busy doctor may not regularly consult the PDR or even routinely read "Dear Doctor" letters. If the need to warn is compelling enough, reasonable care may require a company to use its salespersons who regularly call on doctors ("drug reps," formerly called "detail men"), to warn them personally of a particular risk.[86]

### The Products Liability Restatement

Unlike its controversial provision on design defects in prescription drugs and medical devices,[87] the *Third Restatement* defines a manufacturer's responsibility for warning defects in drugs and medical devices in conventional negligence terms that give no cause to cavil. In § 6(d), the *Third Restatement* provides that "[a] prescription drug or medical device is not reasonably safe due to inadequate instructions or warnings if reasonable instructions or warnings regarding foreseeable risks of harm are not provided to" health-care providers or patients, depending on the applicability of the learned intermediary doctrine,[88] as discussed above. Principles of adequacy discussed above are embraced by the requirement that warnings and instructions be "reasonable," and the limitation on responsibility to "foreseeable" risks reflects the now well-established principle, discussed above, that the law should not hold manufacturers of drugs, medical devices, or any other type of product responsible for harm which is unforeseeable or otherwise unavoidable under the prevailing state of the art, an important aspect of products liability law examined elsewhere in greater depth.[89]

### The Pharmacist's Duty to Warn

Pharmacists dispense millions of prescriptions for drugs in America each day.[90] While doctors prescribe pharmaceutical drugs, they typically know much less about such drugs, which they normally study for one to three semesters, than pharmacists, who study all aspects of drug therapy for five to seven years.[91] For whatever reasons, many doctors regularly prescribe inappropriate prescription drugs for their patients, causing

---

**85.** As to the standards of adequacy for such letters, see, e.g., Lawson v. G.D. Searle & Co., 356 N.E.2d 779 (Ill. 1976).

**86.** An early, leading case that examines factors bearing on whether a company must warn doctors in this manner is Sterling Drug, Inc. v. Yarrow, 408 F.2d 978 (8th Cir. 1969) (S.D. law) (Aralen; failure to use detail men to alert doctors of possible eye damage was unreasonable in light of the fact that the PDR and letters might not warn fast enough).

**87.** See § 8.10, above.

**88.** Products Liability Restatement § 6(d).

**89.** See § 10.4, below.

**90.** See Huang, The Omnibus Reconciliation Act of 1990: Redefining Pharmacists' Legal Responsibilities, 24 Am. J.L. & Med. 417, 418 (1998).

**91.** See Id.

numerous patients to suffer adverse drug reactions—many of which could be easily prevented if patients received adequate drug warnings, which often they do not. Studies show that a large proportion of drug prescriptions contain errors that result in adverse drug events,[92] and that most persons are inadequately warned, either by their doctors or pharmacists, of drug interactions and other hazards of prescription drugs.[93] These facts suggest that pharmacists, perhaps, should have a duty of reasonable care to warn patients of hazards in prescription drugs.[94]

Because pharmacists are more in the nature of service providers, like doctors, than retail merchants, like hatters, they are subject to liability for selling prescription drugs only in negligence, not strict liability.[95] In filling prescriptions, pharmacists are held to the highest standard of care, such that a pharmacist who makes a mistake in filling a prescription is almost certainly responsible for any resulting harm.[96] But pharmacists long have been held to have no duty other than to dispense drugs accurately according to the terms of a valid prescription.[97]

**92.** See, e.g., Hornish, Just What The Doctor Ordered—Or Was It?: Missouri Pharmacists' Duty Of Care In the 21st Century, 65 Mo. L. Rev. 1075, 1076 (2000) (noting that "courts have begun to recognize that pharmacists are the last chance that the system has to correct itself, and that pharmacists are experts in pharmaceutical science and should be treated as professionals").

**93.** See id. at 419.

**94.** See Fentiman, Internet Pharmacies and the Need for a New Federalism: Protecting Consumers While Increasing Access to Prescription Drugs, 56 Rutgers L. Rev. 119 (2003); Hornish, above, 65 Mo. L. Rev. 1075 (2000); Huang, The Omnibus Reconciliation Act of 1990: Redefining Pharmacists' Legal Responsibilities, 24 Am. J.L. & Med. 417 (1998); Termini, The Pharmacist Duty To Warn Revisited: The Changing Role of Pharmacy In Health Care And The Resultant Impact On the Obligation Of a Pharmacist To Warn, 24 Ohio N.U. L. Rev. 551 (1998); Brushwood, The Pharmacist's Duty Under OBRA–90 Standards, 18 J. Legal Med. 475 (1997); Furrow, Enterprise Liability for Bad Outcomes from Drug Therapy: The Doctor, The Hospital, The Pharmacy, and the Drug Firm, 44 Drake L. Rev. 377 (1996); Brushwood, The Professional Capabilities And Legal Responsibilities Of Pharmacists: Should "Can" Imply "Ought"?, 44 Drake L. Rev. 439 (1996); Baker, The OBRA 90 Mandate And Its Developing Impact On The Pharmacist's Standard Of Care, 44 Drake L. Rev. 503 (1996); Cacciatore, Computers, OBRA 90 and the Pharmacist's Duty to Warn, 5 J. Pharmacy & L. 103 (1996); Brushwood, The Pharmacist's Duty to Warn: Toward a Knowledge–Based Model of Professional Responsibility, 40 Drake L. Rev. 1 (1990); Comment, 40 Santa Clara L. Rev. 907 (2000); Note, 37

Ariz. L. Rev. 677 (1995) (noting *Lasley*); Annot., 44 A.L.R.5th 393 (1996) (pharmacist liability for harm caused by accurate prescriptions). See generally National Association of Boards of Pharmacy, Survey of Pharmacy Law (2000) (laws on drugs, licensing, census data, etc. from all U.S. jurisdictions).

**95.** See, e.g., Madison v. American Home Products Corp., 595 S.E.2d 493 (S.C. 2004) (pharmacy not subject to strict liability for properly filling prescription in accordance with doctor's orders); Schaerrer v. Stewart's Plaza Pharmacy, Inc., 79 P.3d 922 (Utah 2003); Parker v. St. Vincent Hosp., 919 P.2d 1104 (N.M. Ct. App. 1996); Coyle v. Richardson–Merrell, Inc., 584 A.2d 1383 (Pa. 1991); Murphy v. E.R. Squibb & Sons, Inc., 710 P.2d 247 (Cal. 1985); Pittman v. Upjohn Co., 890 S.W.2d 425 (Tenn. 1994); Annot., 3 A.L.R. 4th 270 (1981); Products Liability Restatement § 6(e) (pharmacists liable only for filling prescriptions incorrectly and for negligence; no strict liability for selling prescription drugs or medical devices with design or warnings defects). *Contra* Griffith v. Blatt, 51 P.3d 1256 (Or. 2002) (pharmacist who sold prescription lotion was "seller" under § 402A and, hence, subject to strict liability in tort for failing to warn); Heredia v. Johnson, 827 F.Supp. 1522 (D. Nev. 1993).

**96.** See, e.g., Troppi v. Scarf, 187 N.W.2d 511, 513 (Mich. Ct. App. 1971) (negligence in filling prescription for birth control pills resulting in unwanted child); Burke v. Bean, 363 S.W.2d 366, 368 (Tex. App. 1962) (sale of Oxsoralen capsules when Oxacholin tablets prescribed).

**97.** See, e.g., Kampe v. Howard Stark Prof'l Pharmacy, Inc., 841 S.W.2d 223 (Mo. Ct. App. 1992) (properly filling legal pre-

In particular, pharmacists simply have no general duty to warn patients—not even to pass along package inserts (intended for physicians) containing detailed warnings—of hazards or side effects in prescription drugs that they dispense.[98] The pharmacist's immunity from a general duty to warn patients has been justified on a number of grounds, including the learned intermediary doctrine's placement of warning responsibilities solely on doctors and nurse practitioners who theoretically are aware of a patient's treatment needs as well as the benefits and dangers of particular prescription drugs; the burdens on pharmacists of having to second-guess decisions of prescribing doctors; the confusion of patients receiving conflicting information from their doctors and pharmacists; and an assumption that doctors are simply better skilled than pharmacists at evaluating the possible consequences of prescription medications.[99]

But cracks are beginning to appear in the pharmacist's general immunity from a duty to warn, reflecting legislative requirements that pharmacists monitor and counsel their clients about prescription drugs,[100] a development which has stimulated increased education and professionalism in this field.[101] In a number of cases, courts have held that pharmacists may have a duty of reasonable care to warn in certain circumstances. First, pharmacists are subject to liability in negligence for failing to recognize a clear and obvious error present on the face of a prescription. So, if a prescription fails to state a medication's maximum dosage, it is patently defective on its face, and a pharmacist may be subject to liability in negligence for failing to check with the prescribing

scription fulfills pharmacist's duty). See generally Huang, The Omnibus Reconciliation Act of 1990: Redefining Pharmacists' Legal Responsibilities, 24 Am. J.L. & Med. 417 (1998); Comment, 40 Santa Clara L. Rev. 907 (2000).

**98.** See, e.g., Schaerrer v. Stewart's Plaza Pharmacy, 79 P.3d 922 (Utah 2003) (pharmacist compounded and sold phen-fen without warning of risks); Moore v. Memorial Hosp. of Gulfport, 825 So.2d 658 (Miss. 2002) (pharmacist did not warn pregnant woman that Diovan was contraindicated for pregnancy, and child suffered kidney failure as a result); In re Rezulin Products Liability Litigation, 133 F.Supp.2d 272 (S.D.N.Y. 2001) (16 actions from several states on diabetes medication; no general duty to warn in Alabama, Mississippi, Louisiana, Texas, or West Virginia); McKee v. American Home Products Corp., 782 P.2d 1045 (Wash. 1989) (5–4 decision) (pharmacists refilled potentially addictive amphetamine, prescribed as an appetite suppressant, for ten years without warning of addiction risk or passing on drug insert which warned about it); Laws v. Johnson, 799 S.W.2d 249, 251–55 (Tenn. Ct. App. 1990) (no liability for removing package insert which warned of risk of heart attack); Pysz v. Henry's Drug Store, 457 So.2d 561 (Fla. Dist. Ct. App. 1984) (doctor's responsibility, not

pharmacist's, to warn plaintiff of addiction risk in Quaaludes dispensed for more than 9 years); Stebbins v. Concord Wrigley Drugs, Inc., 416 N.W.2d 381 (Mich. Ct. App. 1987) (no duty to warn of drowsiness that caused car accident); Frye v. Medicare–Glaser Corp., 605 N.E.2d 557 (Ill. 1992) (no duty to warn).

**99.** See, e.g., Schaerrer v. Stewart's Plaza Pharmacy, 79 P.3d 922 (Utah 2003) (information may confuse consumers); Moore v. Memorial Hosp. of Gulfport, 825 So.2d 658 (Miss. 2002) (learned intermediary doctrine protects pharmacists); Moore v. Wyeth–Ayerst Lab., 236 F.Supp.2d 509, 512—513 (D. Md. 2002) ("it is unwise to impose liability on a pharmacist for filling a prescription signed by the physician, because the physician is in a better position to evaluate the patient's medical needs"); Morgan v. Wal–Mart Stores, Inc., 30 S.W.3d 455, 467 (Tex. App. 2000) (thorough review of a pharmacist's duty to warn, concluding that general no-duty rule should be retained).

**100.** See Huang, The Omnibus Reconciliation Act of 1990: Redefining Pharmacists' Legal Responsibilities, 24 Am. J.L. & Med. 417, 418 (1998).

**101.** See id.

physician or inform the patient of this important dosage fact.[102] Further, a pharmacist may have a duty to warn a customer or contact the physician if the pharmacist knows a drug is contraindicated for the customer, as when a pharmacist knows a customer is an alcoholic,[103] has an allergy,[104] or is taking another incompatible drug.[105] In addition, if a pharmacist undertakes to collect data on a client's allergies,[106] to monitor its clients prescriptions for drug interactions,[107] or, perhaps, to warn of side effects,[108] it normally will be bound to perform that undertaking with reasonable care.[109] In these and other situations where a pharmacist has special knowledge of a risk to a particular client, courts have sometimes broken through the traditional immunity and held pharmacists to a duty of reasonable care to warn of the risk of addiction,[110] potential drug interactions,[111] and other adverse effects of prescription drugs.[112]

How far these small cracks in the pharmacist's no-duty-to-warn wall eventually may propagate is impossible to say. There clearly is no stampede to break down the pharmacist's virtual immunity from a warning obligation.[113] But the face of the pharmacy profession is changing rapidly in ways that suggest that these strategically positioned experts in prescription pharmaceuticals might properly be required to bear a greater responsibility for warning patients of the hazards of such medications.

---

**102.** See Horner v. Spalitto, 1 S.W.3d 519 (Mo. Ct. App. 1999); Riff v. Morgan Pharmacy, 508 A.2d 1247 (Pa. Super. Ct. 1986).

**103.** See Hand v. Krakowski, 453 N.Y.S.2d 121 (App. Div. 1982).

**104.** See Happel v. Wal–Mart Stores, Inc., 766 N.E.2d 1118, 1124 (Ill. 2002) (pharmacy undertook to compile plaintiff's allergies, giving it superior knowledge and a duty to exercise reasonable care to warn of this foreseeable risk).

**105.** See Brienze v. Casserly, 2003 WL 23018810 (Mass. Super. Ct. 2003) (pharmacist has duty to warn particular customer of potentially adverse interaction of two drugs that pharmacist knows customer is taking).

**106.** See Happel v. Wal–Mart Stores, Inc., 766 N.E.2d 1118, 1124 (Ill. 2002) (pharmacy undertook to compile plaintiff's allergies, giving it superior knowledge and a duty to exercise reasonable care to warn of this foreseeable risk).

**107.** See Baker v. Arbor Drugs, Inc., 544 N.W.2d 727, 730 (Mich. Ct. App. 1996) (client died from adverse interaction of two drugs; "defendant voluntarily assumed a duty of care when it implemented the Arbortech Plus System and then advertised that this system would detect harmful drug interactions for its customers").

**108.** See, e.g., In re Propulsid Products Liability Litigation, 2002 WL 1446714 (E.D. La. 2002); Cottam v. CVS Pharmacy, 764

N.E.2d 814 (Mass. 2002) (by providing partial list of side effects, reasonable care might require including impotency). *Contra* Kasin v. Osco Drug, Inc., 728 N.E.2d 77 (Ill. App. Ct. 2000) (by listing some side effects, pharmacy did not have duty to list them all).

**109.** See Restatement (Third) of Torts: Liability for Physical Harm § 43 (liability for negligent undertakings, if risk increased or plaintiff relies on undertaking).

**110.** Hooks SuperX, Inc. v. McLaughlin, 642 N.E.2d 514 (Ind. 1994); Lasley v. Shrake's Country Club Pharmacy, Inc., 880 P.2d 1129 (Ariz. Ct. App. 1994).

**111.** See Baker v. Arbor Drugs, 544 N.W.2d 727 (Mich. Ct. App. 1996) (pharmacist assumed a duty to warn by advertising that its computerized drug detection system identified and prevented drug interactions); Dooley v. Everett, 805 S.W.2d 380 (Tenn. Ct. App. 1990) (antibiotic and asthma medication).

**112.** See Guillory v. Dr. X, 679 So.2d 1004, 1010 (La. Ct. App. 1996). See also Pittman v. Upjohn Co., 890 S.W.2d 425, 435 (Tenn. 1994) (but duty did not extend to patient's grandson).

**113.** See, e.g., Morgan v. Wal–Mart Stores, Inc., 30 S.W.3d 455, 467 (Tex. App. 2000) (thorough review of a pharmacist's duty to warn, concluding that general no-duty rule should be retained).

# Chapter 10

LIMITATIONS ON DEFECTIVENESS

*Table of Sections*

## § 10.1   LIMITATIONS ON DEFECTIVENESS—GENERALLY

The inquiry to this point has focused on when and why manufacturers *should* be held accountable for accidental harm caused by defective products. In this chapter, the focus reverses direction to a consideration of arguments and doctrine that *deny* a manufacturer's responsibility for harm from product accidents. While the underlying justifications for assigning responsibility in such cases remain largely the same—manufacturer accountability, feasibility, economic efficiency, consumer choice, personal responsibility, and judicial competency—the issues explored in this chapter look past the preliminary conditions and justifications for imposing liability to certain salient circumstances that delimit the normal principles of responsibility for selling defective products. In short, this chapter considers various factors that tend to *limit* a manufacturer's duty for harm from product hazards.

Most of the remaining chapters examine additional types of limitations on the responsibility of a manufacturer or other seller for product accidents. The chapters on actual and proximate causation focus on the necessary link between a defendant's wrongful conduct or a defective product and the plaintiff's harm. The chapters on defenses consider limitations that have crystallized into formal defenses limiting the responsibility of sellers of defective products. One topic treated there, product misuse, might comfortably have been included in the present chapter since most courts view the extent to which manufacturers must protect users against their own misuse to be an issue that defines the outer boundaries of a manufacturer's scope of duty.[1] Subsequent chapters examine how the law limits and otherwise adjusts the normal liability principles to fit a variety of special types of defendants, transactions, and products.

This chapter first inquires into the extent to which manufacturers and other sellers are responsible for obvious and inherent product hazards. The remaining sections consider when the normal principles of liability might be altered in certain situations affected by the passage of time: evolutions in the "state of the art" revealing a product hazard or how to avoid it; prenatal and preconception harm caused by drugs and other chemicals, the effects of which can ripple through generations; product deterioration over time; the special risks of product disposal and salvage; and the extent to which manufacturers may have post-sale duties to warn, repair, or recall when they discover hazards in their products in the field. The formal affirmative defenses arising out of the passage of time, statutes of limitations and repose, are treated elsewhere, in a chapter on special defenses.[2]

## § 10.2 OBVIOUS DANGERS

Hidden ("latent") product dangers are the most pernicious, for they deprive buyers and users of the opportunity to choose how best to address the danger, or even to avoid the product altogether, to avoid the risk of harm. In response, the law generally requires manufacturers and other sellers to provide purchasers and users with warnings of material hidden dangers and with instructions on how to avoid them.[1] Yet merely supplying a warning of danger often is not enough; if providing such information does not substantially eliminate a material risk, manufacturers ordinarily must take all reasonable steps to design the hidden danger away. A manufacturer's duty to provide warnings and instructions, in other words, is largely independent of its duty of safe design.[2]

But products frequently contain "open and obvious" dangers, hazards plainly appearing on a product's face which are manifest to those who buy and use the product. For example, the hazards to human limbs from power saws, power lawn mowers, and punch presses are evident for all to see. This section examines how the obviousness of a danger affects the determination of a manufacturer's responsibility for failing to design and warn against such obvious ("patent") hazards. In particular, the section reviews the rise and fall of the "open and obvious danger" doctrine, a no-duty doctrine that shields manufacturers from liability for harm caused by obvious dangers in their products, often called the "patent danger" rule.[3]

---

### § 10.1

**1.** But some courts, and those states that address product misuse statutorily, treat the issue as a matter of affirmative defense, similar to contributory and comparative negligence and assumption of risk. Because of the affinity between product misuse and these traditional misconduct defenses, misuse is treated in the chapter on that topic. See § 13.5, below.

**2.** See § 14.5, below.

### § 10.2

**1.** See ch. 9, above.

**2.** See § 6.2, above.

**3.** On the role of obviousness in products liability litigation, see Owen, Information Shields in Tort Law, in Exploring Tort Law ___ (S. Madden ed., Cambridge, 2005);

## The Rise and Fall of the Patent Danger Doctrine

### *Design Defects*

Prior to the 1970s, victims of accidents from obvious design dangers were broadly barred from recovery under the patent danger doctrine. The classic case was *Campo v. Scofield*,[4] decided by the New York Court of Appeals in 1950. The plaintiff, working on his son's farm, was dumping a crate of onions into an "onion topping" machine when his hands became caught in its revolving steel rollers and were so badly injured that they required amputation. He sued the manufacturers of the machine for negligently failing to equip it with a guard or stopping device. The trial court denied the defendants' motion to dismiss, the Appellate Division reversed, and the plaintiff appealed. *Held,* the plaintiff's failure to allege that the danger was latent or unknown was fatal to the complaint. Affirming the Appellate Division's order to dismiss the complaint, Judge Fuld spoke for a unanimous Court of Appeals:

> If a manufacturer does everything necessary to make the machine function properly for the purpose for which it is designed, if the machine is without any latent defect, and if its functioning creates no danger or peril that is not known to the user, then the manufacturer has satisfied the law's demands. We have not yet reached the state where a manufacturer is under the duty of making a machine accident proof or fool-proof.[5]

A manufacturer simply has no duty to protect people against "a patent peril or from a source manifestly dangerous." Otherwise, the manufacturer of an axe, buzz saw, or airplane with an exposed propeller would be subject to liability to a user cut by the blade or propeller. "In such cases, the manufacturer has the right to expect that such persons will do everything necessary to avoid such contact, for the very nature of the article gives notice and warning of the consequences to be expected, of the injuries to be suffered. In other words, the manufacturer is under no duty to render a machine or other article 'more' safe—as long as the danger to be avoided is obvious and patent to all."[6]

Bowbeer and Killoran, Liriano v. Hobart Corp.: Obvious Dangers, The Duty to Warn of Safer Alternatives, and the Heeding Presumption, 65 Brooklyn L. Rev. 717 (1999); Jacobs, Toward a Process–Based Approach to Failure to Warn, 71 N.C. L. Rev. 121, 128–37 (1992); Henderson and Twerski, Doctrinal Collapse in Products Liability: The Empty Shell of Failure-to-Warn Law, 65 N.Y.U. L. Rev. 265, 306 (1990); Pardieck and Hulbert, Is the Danger Really Open and Obvious?, 19 Ind. L. Rev. 383 (1986); Phillips, Products Liability: Obviousness of Danger Revisited, 15 Ind. L. Rev. 797 (1982); Darling, The Patent Danger Rule: An Analysis and a Survey of Its Vitality, 29 Mercer L. Rev. 583 (1978); Marschall, An Obvious Wrong Does Not Make A Right: Manufacturers' Liability for Patently Dangerous Products, 48 N.Y.U. L. Rev. 1065 (1973); Notes, 81 U. Det. Mercy L. Rev. 191 (2004) (Michigan's obvious danger rule); 88 Corn. L. Rev. 814 (2003) (noting *Liriano III*); 84 Marq. L. Rev. 445 (2000) (obvious dangers and comparative fault); 50 Mercer L. Rev. 643 (1999) (noting *Ogletree*); 1993 Det. C. L. Rev. 1357 (noting *Glittenberg II*); 25 Ind. L. Rev. 235 (1991) (relationship between obvious danger rule and consumer expectations test); 38 Emory L.J. 1189 (1989) (Alcoholic Beverage Labeling Act of 1988); 75 Cornell L. Rev. 158 (1989) (alcohol manufacturer's duty to warn); Annot., 35 A.L.R.4th 861 (1985) (status of patent or obvious danger liability rule).

**4.**   95 N.E.2d 802 (N.Y. 1950).

**5.**   Id. at 804.

**6.**   Id.

*Campo* was by no means the first case so holding,[7] but it anchored the patent danger doctrine like a rock. Its simple statement of individual responsibility for self protection struck a responsive chord throughout the nation, and, following *Campo*, many courts adopted the doctrine, or reaffirmed it if they had relied on it before.[8] In the 1950s and early 1960s, the *Campo* obvious danger rule was one of the most firmly entrenched doctrines in all of products liability law. Professor Fleming James, ever critical of rules that limited recovery for injured persons,[9] derided the absolutist no-duty nature of the rule as "a vestigial carry-over from pre-*MacPherson* days when deceit was needed for recovery."[10] Yet, even two decades after *Campo*, the Maryland Court of Appeals opted to align itself with other vestigial jurisdictions in adhering to the rule.[11]

Most design danger claims before the 1970s involved hidden or "latent" dangers,[12] and courts at the time exhibited little patience with claims involving design dangers that were obvious. For example, in *Bartkewich v. Billinger*,[13] decided in 1968, the hand of a glass-breaking machine operator was crushed when he reached into the machine to free a piece of glass that was jamming, and he thought damaging, the machine. Addressing the operator's design claim against the manufacturer for failing to provide guards or strategically located cut-off switches, the court held that the manufacturer had no such duty: "If he thought the machine was being damaged, what did he think would happen to his hand?"[14]

But not all courts were unsympathetic to the plight of workers and others injured by obvious product dangers, and as the consumer protectionist perspective of *Restatement (Second) of Torts* § 402A spread across America in the late 1960s, judicial attitudes toward the patent danger rule began to change as well. Some courts, persuaded by the safety, representational, and risk-spreading rationales thought to support the new strict tort doctrine, began to ignore defendants' pleas to apply the patent danger doctrine.[15] And, by 1970, courts had begun expressly to reject the obvious danger rule as outmoded and improper.

**7.** Earlier cases had also barred recovery in situations of obvious dangers. See, e.g., Stevens v. Allis–Chalmers Mfg. Co., 100 P.2d 723 (Kan. 1940); Yaun v. Allis–Chalmers Mfg. Co., 34 N.W.2d 853 (Wis. 1948).

**8.** See, e.g., Stevens v. Durbin–Durco, Inc., 377 S.W.2d 343 (Mo. 1964); Parker v. Heasler Plumbing & Heating Co., 388 P.2d 516 (Wyo. 1964); Tyson v. Long Mfg. Co., 107 S.E.2d 170 (N.C. 1959).

**9.** See V. Nolan and E. Ursin, Understanding Enterprise Liability (1995); Priest, The Invention of Enterprise Liability: A Critical History of the Intellectual Foundations of Modern Tort Law, 14 J. Leg. Stud. 461 (1985).

**10.** James, Products Liability (pt. 1), 34 Tex. L. Rev. 44, 52 (1955). See also 2 F.

Harper and F. James, The Law of Torts § 28.5, at 1544 (1956).

**11.** See Blankenship v. Morrison Mach. Co., 257 A.2d 430, 433 (Md. 1969). See also Halvorson v. American Hoist & Derrick Co., 240 N.W.2d 303 (Minn. 1976), overruled by Holm v. Sponco Mfg., Inc., 324 N.W.2d 207 (Minn. 1982).

**12.** See Luque v. McLean, 501 P.2d 1163, 1168 (Cal. 1972) ("the great majority of reported decisions dealing with products liability have involved defects classifiable as latent").

**13.** 247 A.2d 603 (Pa. 1968).

**14.** Id. at 605.

**15.** See, e.g., Wright v. Massey–Harris, Inc., 215 N.E.2d 465 (Ill. App. Ct. 1966).

One such case rejecting the patent danger rule, *Pike v. Frank G. Hough Co.*,[16] involved a design claim against the manufacturer of a large earth-moving machine, a paydozer, which backed over a worker. The paydozer had a large engine box in the rear that created a large blind spot behind the machine, and it was not equipped with rearview mirrors. Contending that the danger of being struck by the paydozer was obvious, the manufacturer claimed that it had no duty to install safety devices to protect against such a patent peril. Rejecting this defense, the California Supreme Court relied upon the analysis of the patent danger doctrine and the criticism of *Campo v. Scofield*,[17] by Professor Fleming James,[18] in his tort law treatise, who observed that "the bottom does not logically drop out of a negligence case against the maker when it is shown that the purchaser knew of the dangerous condition. Thus if the product is a carrot-topping machine with exposed moving parts,[19] or an electric clothes wringer dangerous to the limbs of the operator, and if it would be feasible for the maker of the product to install a guard or a safety release, it should be a question for the jury whether reasonable care demanded such a precaution, though its absence is obvious."[20] Reversing the nonsuit of the plaintiff, the *Pike* court concluded that "the obviousness of peril is relevant to the manufacturer's defenses, not to the issue of duty."[21]

Other courts at the time were also beginning to abandon the patent danger doctrine as contrary to the policies of the day. In *Palmer v. Massey–Ferguson, Inc.*,[22] for example, a farmer sued the manufacturer of a hay baler for injuries to his hand caught in the mechanism of the machine. Observing that the patent danger rule conflicted with the trend toward expanding manufacturer responsibility, the court thought that "a rule which excludes the manufacturer from liability if the defect in the design of his product is patent but applies the duty if such a defect is latent is somewhat anomalous. The manufacturer of the obviously defective product ought not to escape because the product was obviously a bad one. The law, we think, ought to discourage misdesign rather than encouraging it in its obvious form."[23]

Once the 1970s were under way, the expansionary principles of modern products liability law took hold quickly, and courts increasingly began to reevaluate the role that the obviousness of a danger should play in the determination of design defectiveness. For example, in *Luque v. McLean*,[24] the California Supreme Court in 1972 reexamined the applicability of the patent danger doctrine to design claims brought under § 402A in a case where the plaintiff was injured when he slipped on wet

**16.** 467 P.2d 229, 235 (Cal. 1970).

**17.** 95 N.E.2d 802 (N.Y. 1950).

**18.** Prior to publication in his treatise with Professor Harper, Fleming James first published his discussion of the obvious danger doctrine in James, Products Liability (pt. 1), 34 Tex. L. Rev. 44, 51–54 (1955).

**19.** Citing *Campo*. The product in *Campo* in fact was an onion-topping machine.

**20.** 2 F. Harper and F. James, The Law of Torts § 28.5, at 1542–1543 (1956). *Pike* quoted the Harper and James materials

quoted in this text, as well as some other excerpts. *Pike* also relied on similar conclusions by Dix Noel, in Manufacturer's Negligence of Design or Directions for Use of a Product, 71 Yale L.J. 816, 838 (1962). See *Pike*, 467 P.2d at 235.

**21.** *Pike*, 467 P.2d at 234.

**22.** 476 P.2d 713 (Wash. Ct. App. 1970).

**23.** Id. at 718–19. The fallacy here, of course, is that it is the *danger* that is obvious, not the defect.

**24.** 501 P.2d 1163 (Cal. 1972).

grass and his hand slid through an unguarded area in the front of a power lawn mower he was using. Relying on language in *Greenman v. Yuba Power Products, Inc.*[25] suggesting that a plaintiff must establish that he was not aware of the product's defective condition,[26] the trial court so instructed the jury, which returned a verdict for the defendant. Reversing for error in this instruction, the California court repudiated the patent danger rule in strict products liability.[27] As the decade of the 1970s progressed, more and more courts rejected the patent danger doctrine in design defect cases, holding that the obviousness of a danger is merely one factor in assessing the negligence or defectiveness of a design, not an absolute bar to liability.[28]

The landmark decision repudiating the obvious danger doctrine was decided in New York, in 1976, by the same court that in 1950 had provided the doctrine's bedrock decision of *Campo v. Scofield*. In *Micallef v. Miehle Co.*,[29] the New York Court of Appeals reconsidered its renowned *Campo* patent danger rule. The plaintiff, who operated a huge, photo-offset printing press, some 150 feet in length, discovered a foreign object on the printing plate, which was rotating at high speed. He proceeded to remove or "chase the hickie on the run," as was the custom in the industry, in order to avoid stopping the machine which took at least three hours to restart, by lightly touching the revolving plate with an eight inch wide piece of plastic. While so doing, the plastic and the plaintiff's hand were drawn together into the machine. The plaintiff's expert engineer testified that the machine should have been equipped with guards, which were available and would not have impeded hickie chasing, to prevent a user's hands from entering the machine. The defendant countered that the absence of guards was an open and obvious condition which it had no duty to correct. Judgment on a jury verdict for the plaintiff was reversed by the Appellate Division, relying in part on *Campo*'s patent danger doctrine, and the plaintiff appealed.

Reversing the Appellate Division, the Court of Appeals left no doubt as to its conclusion, beginning its decision: "The time has come to depart from the patent danger rule enunciated in Campo v. Scofield...."[30] In support of its decision to overrule *Campo*, the court noted the "sustained attack" on that opinion, stemming from "the belief that, in our highly complex and technological society, we fall victim to the manufacturer who holds himself out as an expert in his field." Further, the court pointed to charges that the patent danger rule was little more than an

---

**25.** 377 P.2d 897 (Cal. 1963).

**26.** "To establish the manufacturer's liability it was sufficient that plaintiff proved that he was injured while using the Shopsmith in a way it was intended to be used as a result of a defect in design and manufacture *of which plaintiff was not aware* that made the Shopsmith unsafe for its intended use." Id. at 901 (emphasis added).

**27.** As the *Luque* court pointed out, the California Supreme Court had repudiated the obvious danger rule in the *negligent* design context in Pike v. Frank G. Hough Co., 467 P.2d 229 (Cal. 1970). Other early

cases rejecting the patent danger doctrine in California are Thompson v. Package Mach. Co., 99 Cal.Rptr. 281 (Ct. App. 1971), and Buccery v. General Motors Corp., 132 Cal.Rptr. 605 (Ct. App. 1976).

**28.** See, e.g., Byrns v. Riddell, Inc., 550 P.2d 1065 (Ariz. 1976); Micallef v. Miehle Co., 348 N.E.2d 571 (N.Y. 1976); Stenberg v. Beatrice Foods Co., 576 P.2d 725 (Mont. 1978); Auburn Mach. Works Co. v. Jones, 366 So.2d 1167 (Fla. 1979).

**29.** 348 N.E.2d 571 (N.Y. 1976).

**30.** Id. at 573.

assumption of risk defense as a matter of law; that it was anomalous, for requiring manufacturers to develop reasonably safe products but then immunizing them from obvious dangers no matter how unreasonable; and that its rigidity produced harsh results for consumers who could not always recognize and appreciate obvious hazards. Accordingly, the court held that a manufacturer must design its products with reasonable care to avoid unreasonable risks of harm to persons who might be exposed to a foreseeable danger, dependent on "a balancing of the likelihood of harm, and the gravity of harm if it happens, against the burden of the precaution which would be effective to avoid the harm."[31] Thus, while the obviousness of a product danger might reduce the likelihood of accidents, and so factor into the calculus of risk, and while a danger's obviousness might affect the issues of contributory negligence and assumption of risk,[32] "the patent-danger doctrine should not, in and of itself, prevent a plaintiff from establishing his case."[33]

Once the *Campo* patent danger doctrine was repudiated in its own home state, the rule proceeded to collapse around the nation. One court after another, usually for claims in both negligence and strict liability in tort, abandoned the rule's absolute no-duty power and reduced the obviousness of danger to mere "factor" status in the cost-benefit evaluation of the safety of a product's design.[34] Some states continued the obvious danger rule into the 1980s,[35] and a few lingering offshoots of the

**31.** *Micallef*, 348 N.E.2d at 576–77.

**32.** See, e.g., Ford v. GACS, Inc., 265 F.3d 670, 676 (8th Cir. 2001) (Mo. law) (obviousness of defective design goes to comparative fault, not to duty).

**33.** 348 N.E.2d at 578.

**34.** One quite early case well explained the rationale:

> The patent danger doctrine encourages manufacturers to be outrageous in their design, to eliminate safety devices, and to make hazards obvious. For example, if the cage which is placed on an electric fan as a safety device were left off and someone put his hand in the fan, under this doctrine there would be no duty on the manufacturer as a matter of law.

Auburn Mach. Works Co. v. Jones, 366 So.2d 1167, 1170 (Fla. 1979). Also rejecting the patent danger doctrine, see, e.g., Flock v. Scripto–Tokai Corp., 319 F.3d 231, 242 (5th Cir. 2003) (Tex. law) (obvious danger of Aim n' Flame utility lighter did not preclude liability for defective design); Thongchoom v. Graco Children's Prods., Inc., 71 P.3d 214 (Wash. Ct. App. 2003) (plaintiff may prove design defect with either consumer expectations test or risk/utility test; obviousness does not preclude liability under the risk/utility analysis); Wortel v. Somerset Indus., Inc., 770 N.E.2d 1211, 1222 (Ill. App. Ct. 2002) (with possible exception of simple products, obviousness of danger does not preclude liability for defective design); Mills v. Curioni,

Inc., 238 F.Supp.2d 876 (E.D. Mich. 2002); Murphy v. Playtex Family Prods. Corp., 176 F.Supp.2d 473 (D. Md. 2001) (plaintiff may prove design defect under consumer expectation or risk/utility theory; under latter, obviousness of risk is merely one factor), aff'd, 69 Fed.Appx. 140 (4th Cir. 2003) (Md. law); Hernandez v. Tokai Corp., 2 S.W.3d 251 (Tex. 1999); Perkins v. Wilkinson Sword, Inc., 700 N.E.2d 1247 (Ohio 1998); LeBlanc v. American Honda Motor Co., 688 A.2d 556 (N.H. 1997); Seymour v. Brunswick Corp., 655 So.2d 892 (Miss. 1995); Morrison v. Kubota Tractor Corp., 891 S.W.2d 422 (Mo. Ct. App. 1994) (absence of rollover protection system on tractor); Holm v. Sponco Mfg., Inc., 324 N.W.2d 207 (Minn. 1982); Owens v. Allis–Chalmers Corp., 326 N.W.2d 372 (Mich. 1982) (restricting patent danger rule to cases involving simple tools and products); Stenberg v. Beatrice Foods Co., 576 P.2d 725 (Mont. 1978).

**35.** See, e.g., Miller v. Dvornik, 501 N.E.2d 160 (Ill. App. Ct. 1986); Gray v. Manitowoc Co., 771 F.2d 866 (5th Cir. 1985) (Miss. law) (refusing to abandon the patent danger rule, despite the fact that the rule has been the subject of much criticism); Coast Catamaran Corp. v. Mann, 321 S.E.2d 353 (Ga. Ct. App. 1984); Estrada v. Schmutz Mfg. Co., 734 F.2d 1218, 1220 (7th Cir. 1984) (Ind. law) (Posner, J.) (factory worker's hand caught while brushing ink on rollers: if you "go to the zoo and put your hand through the lion's cage, and the

doctrine still showed signs of life in five or six states even into the 1990s.[36] Perhaps the doctrine's last real stronghold was the state of Georgia,[37] and the Supreme Court of that state finally surrendered in 1998.[38]

Despite the formal collapse of the patent danger doctrine in recent decades, it is important to note that the obviousness of a product's risk still serves as a total bar to liability in some jurisdictions in special situations[39] and in other states under the guise of the consumer expectations test[40] or a misreading of § 402A's comment *j*.[41] That said, the rise and fall of the patent danger rule in design defect cases during the last half of the twentieth century is one of the fascinating tales of products

lion bites your hand off, ... you do not have an action against the zoo"); Hedgepeth v. Fruehauf Corp., 634 F.Supp. 93 (S.D. Miss. 1986).

**36.** Such as a no-duty rule with respect to simple product designs, which may still exist in both Illinois and Michigan. See, e.g., Mallard v. Hoffinger Indus., 564 N.W.2d 74 (Mich. Ct. App. 1997) (no duty to design away risk of injury from diving headfirst into above-ground swimming pool); Treadway v. Smith & Wesson Corp., 950 F.Supp. 1326 (E.D. Mich. 1996) (teenage boys playing with loaded revolver; no duty to warn or design out obvious danger of easy discharge); Adams v. Perry Furniture Co., 497 N.W.2d 514 (Mich. Ct. App. 1993) (child used disposable butane lighter, which was easy to ignite with one hand, to set fire which killed four children; no duty to warn of obvious risk that flame is dangerous or to design lighter with child-resistant cap); Scoby v. Vulcan–Hart Corp., 569 N.E.2d 1147 (Ill. App. Ct. 1991); Owens v. Allis–Chalmers Corp., 326 N.W.2d 372 (Mich. 1982). *But see* Boumelhem v. BIC Corp., 535 N.W.2d 574 (Mich. Ct. App. 1995) (similar facts; if not bound by *Adams'* no-duty ruling, court would have held that lighter manufacturer had duty to design out unreasonable risk of harm to children). See also Kearney v. Philip Morris, Inc., 916 F.Supp. 61 (D. Mass. 1996) (R. Keeton, J.) (suggesting that Massachusetts might endorse a similar approach).

In Indiana, while the patent danger doctrine does not apply to that state's statutory strict liability actions, it still applies to common law negligent design claims. See, e.g., Welch v. Scripto–Tokai Corp., 651 N.E.2d 810 (Ind. Ct. App. 1995) (pajamas of child playing with disposable butane lighter caught fire; no duty to warn of or make lighter child-resistant to obvious risk from flame; open and obvious doctrine precluded negligence claim, and statutory consumer contemplations test precluded strict liability claim); Miller v. Todd, 551 N.E.2d 1139 (Ind. 1990).

Although the Michigan Supreme Court has not yet so ruled, it appears that the

patent danger rule may still exist in that state in cases involving defects in design as well as warnings of risks of "simple" (vs. "complex") products, such as knives, guns, blenders, saws, drills, above-ground swimming pools, and possibly disposable butane cigarette lighters.

**37.** See, e.g., Vax v. Albany Lawn & Garden Ctr., 433 S.E.2d 364, 366 (Ga. Ct. App. 1993) (riding mower not equipped with smooth-start clutch or deadman control; "the fact that the defect was not latent but open and obvious constitutes an absolute legal defense," the court observing: "Despite criticism of the 'open and obvious' rule, it remains the law in this state."). See also Ream Tool Co. v. Newton, 433 S.E.2d 67 (Ga. Ct. App. 1993).

**38.** Ogletree v. Navistar Int'l Trans. Corp., 500 S.E.2d 570, 571–72 (Ga. 1998) ("The overwhelming majority of jurisdictions have held that the open and obvious nature of the danger does not preclude liability for design defects.").

**39.** Remaining offshoots of the patent danger rule for obvious design dangers still appear to exist in several states, as noted earlier.

**40.** Applying the consumer expectations test to deny recovery for obvious dangers of design, see, e.g., Tillman v. R.J. Reynolds Tobacco Co., 871 So.2d 28 (Ala. 2003) (harmful effects of smoking cigarettes: " 'certain products whose inherent danger is patent and obvious, do not, as a matter of law, involve defects of a sort that a jury should resolve' "); Ahrens v. Ford Motor Co., 340 F.3d 1142, 1146 (10th Cir. 2003) (Okla. law); Halliday v. Sturm, Ruger & Co., 792 A.2d 1145 (Md. 2002) (gunshot case); Greif v. Anheuser–Busch Cos., Inc., 114 F.Supp.2d 100 (D. Conn. 2000) (intoxicating effects of alcoholic beverages); Dickerson v. Cushman, Inc., 909 F.Supp. 1467 (M.D. Ala. 1995); Welch v. Scripto–Tokai Corp., 651 N.E.2d 810 (Ind. Ct. App. 1995); Griebler v. Doughboy Recreational, Inc., 466 N.W.2d 897 (Wis. 1991). See generally §§ 5.6 and 8.3, above.

**41.** See § 6.2, above.

liability law. Having now been entirely discredited as an absolute limitation on a manufacturer's duties of design in almost every state, the status of the patent danger doctrine as an independent no-duty rule in design defect cases may be stated simply: the rule essentially is dead.[42]

### Warning Defects

In contrast to design cases, where the obviousness of a danger is now generally viewed as merely one factor among many in the risk-utility defect balance, courts widely hold that there simply is no duty to warn of dangers that are obvious. Thus, while the patent danger no-duty rule has fallen into oblivion in design defect litigation, the "open and obvious danger rule" is alive and well in warnings cases where it precludes recovery in negligence,[43] implied warranty,[44] and strict liability in tort[45] for failing to warn of dangers that are evident. Although a very small number of courts flatly disagree,[46] the great majority of courts hold,[47] and statutes in several states provide,[48] that manufacturers and

**42.** This is the clear position of the *Products Liability Restatement*:

> Subsection (b) does not recognize the obviousness of a design-related risk as precluding a finding of defectiveness. The fact that a danger is open and obvious is relevant to the issue of defectiveness, but does not necessarily preclude a plaintiff from establishing that a reasonable alternative design should have been adopted that would have reduced or prevented injury to the plaintiff.

Products Liability Restatement § 2 cmt. *d*. See also Reporters' Note to id. ("A strong majority of courts have rejected the 'open and obvious' or 'patent danger' rule as an absolute defense to a claim of design defect. The obviousness of the danger is one factor among many to consider as to whether a product design meets risk-utility norms.").

**43.** Liability for negligent failure to warn arises only if a seller "has no reason to believe that those for whose use the chattel is supplied will realize its dangerous condition." Restatement (2d) Torts § 388(b).

**44.** The "fit for the ordinary purposes" standard of the implied warranty of merchantability, UCC § 2–314(2)(c), is based on the satisfaction of an ordinary buyer's reasonable expectations of safety and other quality. See, e.g., Scheibe v. Fort James Corp., 276 F.Supp.2d 246, 252 (D. Del. 2003) ("When a purchaser knows of the dangers of a product, or where that danger is obvious, . . . no implied warranty of merchantability arises."); American Tobacco Co. v. Grinnell, 951 S.W.2d 420, 435 (Tex. 1997). An implied warranty of merchantability does not arise with respect to dangers which the buyer observes before purchase, UCC § 2–316(3)(b) and cmt. 8, and the discovery of dangers after purchase bears

on whether breach was a cause of any injury. UCC § 2–314 cmt. 13. See § 4.3, above.

**45.** See Restatement (2d) Torts § 402A cmts. *j* and *k*.

**46.** See, e.g., Armentrout v. FMC Corp., 842 P.2d 175, 181 (Colo. 1992); Harnischfeger Corp. v. Gleason Crane Rentals, Inc., 585 N.E.2d 166 (Ill. App. Ct. 1991); Campos v. Firestone Tire & Rubber Co., 485 A.2d 305 (N.J. 1984).

**47.** "The rule that no duty is owed to warn of obvious and generally known dangers is supported by an overwhelming majority of jurisdictions." Products Liability Restatement § 2 Reporters' Note to cmt. *j*. See, e.g., Ahrens v. Ford Motor Co., 340 F.3d 1142, 1146 (10th Cir. 2003) (Okla. law) ("The duty to warn is only implicated where the manufacturer has no reason to expect ordinary users to discover the danger involved."); Hiner v. Deere & Co., 340 F.3d 1190, 1194 (10th Cir. 2003) (Kan. law) ("manufacturers should not be liable for failing to warn about risks that would be apparent to ordinary users"); Mohr v. St. Paul Fire & Marine Ins. Co., 674 N.W.2d 576, 585 (Wis. Ct. App. 2003); Scheibe v. Fort James Corp., 276 F.Supp.2d 246, 252 (D. Del. 2003); Needham v. Coordinated Apparel Group, Inc., 811 A.2d 124, 129 (Vt. 2002); Grover v. Superior Welding, Inc., 893 P.2d 500, 504 (Okla. 1995) ("the vast majority of courts have held that a manufacturer (supplier) of a product is not negligent when failing to warn against patent or open and obvious dangers"); Caterpillar, Inc. v. Shears, 911 S.W.2d 379, 382 (Tex. 1995) ("the law of products liability does not require a manufacturer or distribut[o]r to warn of obvious risks"); Hatch v. Maine Tank Co., 666 A.2d 90 (Me. 1995); Bavuso v. Caterpillar Indus., Inc., 563 N.E.2d 198 (Mass. 1990); Winterrowd v. Travelers Indem. Co., 462 So.2d 639, 642 (La. 1985).

**48.** See Kan. Stat. Ann. § 60–3305(c) (no duty to warn of "risks which are patent,

other sellers have no duty to warn of dangers that are open, obvious, or commonly known.[49]

Courts and commentators frequently observe that it is senseless to require warnings of dangers that are obvious.[50] A warning of a hidden danger provides users with useful information that enables them to act so as to reduce or avoid the risk.[51] Even with information about hidden dangers, however, users sometimes absent-mindedly or carelessly disregard such warnings and suffer accidental harm. For this reason, if a hidden danger is significant and may cheaply and easily be designed away, all but a handful of courts require the manufacturer to remove the residual risk (the risk remaining once a warning is provided) by adopting a practicable and cost-effective design solution.[52] For similar reasons, the priority of a manufacturer's design obligation remains the same with products involving obvious dangers, as previously discussed. Yet, if a product's danger is evident for all to see, it carries the warning of danger on its face, so to speak, so that adding a formal warning of the danger would duplicate information users already possess. Indeed, requiring such warnings trivializes warnings generally and thus may indirectly lead to an increase in product injuries rather than the other way around.[53]

open or obvious and which should have been realized by a reasonable user or consumer"); La. Rev. Stat. Ann. § 9:2800.57(B); Mich. Comp. Laws Ann. § 600.2948(2) (no duty to warn of risk which should be obvious to a reasonably prudent user or a matter of common knowledge to persons in plaintiff's position); Miss. Code Ann. § 11–1–63(e) (no duty to warn of known dangers or those that should have been obvious to user or consumer); N.C. Gen. Stat. § 99B–5(b) (no duty to warn of open and obvious risk or risk that is matter of common knowledge); Ohio Rev. Code Ann. § 2307.76(B) (no duty to warn of open and obvious risk or risk that is matter of common knowledge), Tenn. Code Ann. § 29–28–105(d). Compare Idaho Code § [6–1405] 6–1305(1)(b) (claimant's damages reduced for failing to observe an "obvious defective condition").

**49.** The Products Liability Restatement provides that sellers do not have a duty to warn of obvious dangers: "In general, a product seller is not subject to liability for failing to warn or instruct regarding risks and risk-avoidance measures that should be obvious to, or generally known by, foreseeable product users." Products Liability Restatement § 2 cmt. *j*.

**50.** See, e.g., First Nat'l Bank & Trust v. American Eurocopter Corp., 378 F.3d 682, 690 (7th Cir. 2004) (Ind. law) ("[T]here is no duty to warn of open and obvious dangers because a warning would be redundant."); House v. Armour of America, 929

P.2d 340, 343 (Utah 1996) ("Where the risks of the product are discernible by casual inspection, . . . the consumer is in just as good a position as the manufacturer to gauge the dangers associated with the product, and nothing is gained by shifting to the manufacturer the duty to warn."); Anderson v. F.J. Little Mach. Co., 68 F.3d 1113 (8th Cir. 1995) (Mo. law); Caterpillar, Inc. v. Shears, 911 S.W.2d 379, 382 (Tex. 1995) ("The fact that a risk is readily apparent serves the same function as a warning. Warnings about obvious hazards are not likely to reduce the chances of injury. Moreover, consumers are prone to ignore warnings of obvious dangers, thereby diminishing the importance given by users to warnings about non-obvious hazards."); Glittenberg v. Doughboy Recreational Industries, 491 N.W.2d 208 (Mich. 1992). See also Products Liability Restatement § 2 cmt. *j* (good summary of rationales).

**51.** See ch. 9, above.

**52.** See § 6.2, above.

**53.** See, e.g., Caterpillar, Inc. v. Shears, 911 S.W.2d 379 (Tex. 1995). See generally Products Liability Restatement § 2 cmt. *j* ("warnings that deal with obvious or generally known risks may be ignored by users and consumers and may diminish the significance of warnings about non-obvious, not-generally-known risks [such that] requiring warnings of obvious or generally known risks could reduce the efficacy of warnings generally").

The major divide between how the obviousness of a danger affects a manufacturer's design and warnings duties was astutely described by the Supreme Court of Michigan in *Glittenberg v. Doughboy Recreational Industries*,[54] which involved the question of whether the manufacturer should have warned of the risk of paralysis from diving headfirst into a shallow above-ground swimming pool. In design cases, the court noted, the obviousness of a danger does not eliminate the possibility that a cost-effective design feature could reduce the risk appreciably. In warnings cases, by contrast, "the obvious nature of the simple product's potential danger serves the core purpose of the claim, i.e., it functions as an inherent warning that the risk is present. Stated otherwise, if the risk is obvious from the characteristics of the product, the product itself telegraphs the precise warning that plaintiffs complain is lacking."[55] Because the condition that created the general danger, to wit, shallow water, was evident "upon casual inspection," the court concluded that the risk of hitting bottom in this simple product was obvious.[56] Refusing to impose a duty to warn of the specific risk of spinal injury or paralysis urged by the dissent,[57] the court reasoned that for patent hazards "warnings that parse the risk are not required. The general danger encompasses the risk of the specific injury sustained. In other words, the risk of hitting the bottom encompasses the risk of catastrophic injury."[58] Because the risk of diving into shallow water was obvious, and concluding that above-ground swimming pools are simple rather than complex products,[59] the court held that the manufacturers had no duty to warn of the obvious risk of injury from diving headfirst into such a pool.[60]

Another swimming pool case well illustrates the important distinction in how the obviousness of a hazard affects design defect claims, on the one hand, and warnings defect claims, on the other. In *Smith v. Hub Mfg., Inc.*,[61] while plaintiffs were at a party, their 4-year-old son climbed up the ladder of an above-ground pool, fell in, lost consciousness, and subsequently died of his injuries. In an action against the manufacturers of the pool and the ladder, in which the plaintiffs made both design and warnings claims, the defendants moved for summary judgment. *Held*, the defective design claim could go to the jury because of the plaintiffs' expert testimony "that other swimming pools have ladders that are more effective in preventing pool accidents."[62] However, the court ordered summary judgment on the failure-to-warn claim because the obviousness

---

**54.** 491 N.W.2d 208 (Mich. 1992) (4–3 decision).

**55.** *Glittenberg*, 491 N.W.2d at 215.

**56.** Id. at 217.

**57.** Faulting the majority for failing to understand that "[i]f there is a specific latent risk, there is an obligation to warn, even if there is a more general obvious risk," id. at 227, Judge Levin pointed to the hundreds of annual spinal injuries from such accidents and to the testimony of experts that most people do not appreciate "that diving in shallow water carries the potential for life-threatening injuries." Id. at 224–25.

**58.** Id. at 217–18.

**59.** "No one can mistake [above-ground pools] for other than what they are, i.e., large containers of water that sit on the ground, all characteristics and features of which are readily apparent or easily discernible upon casual inspection." Id. at 217. Michigan courts had previously limited the application of the no-duty to warn of obvious danger rule to simple, as opposed to complex, products. See Owens v. Allis–Chalmers Corp., 326 N.W.2d 372 (Mich. 1982).

**60.** *Glittenberg*, 491 N.W.2d, at 219.

**61.** 634 F.Supp. 1505 (N.D.N.Y. 1986).

**62.** Id. at 1508.

of the danger of swimming pools to young children left unattended rendered a warning "superfluous."[63]

Examples of courts applying the no-duty-to-warn rule in obvious danger cases abound. For example, courts have held that there is no duty to warn about the obvious and generally known risks of shooting a BB gun at a person's eye;[64] allowing an elastic strap on an automobile seat cover to snap back during installation, striking the installer in the eye;[65] riding a motorcycle with the kickstand down;[66] jump-starting a bulldozer while kneeling on its track;[67] allowing a 3–year-old child to ride on the running board of a tractor over bumpy ground;[68] driving into the side of a moving train;[69] suffering electrocution from a frayed extension cord,[70] a CB antenna,[71] an aluminum sailboat mast,[72] an aluminum mop handle,[73] an aluminum surveyor's prism pole,[74] an aluminum ladder,[75] or possibly a crane[76] coming in contact with a power line; sticking a hand into a potato chopper,[77] a drill press,[78] or under a power lawn mower;[79] playing with a loaded pistol;[80] allowing a revolver, that could be used in criminal assaults, to be stolen from one's house;[81] diving headfirst into a shallow above-ground swimming pool;[82] riding a tricycle-configured tractor up a steep hill covered with logs;[83] leaving a butane cigarette lighter[84] or

**63.** Id. "[T]here is no duty to warn if the plaintiff knows of the danger or if the danger is well known and should be obvious to anyone. In such situations a warning would be superfluous."

**64.** Marzullo v. Crosman Corp., 289 F.Supp.2d 1337 (M.D. Fla. 2003) (head); Moss v. Crosman Corp., 136 F.3d 1169, 1175 (7th Cir. 1998) (Ind. law); Koepke v. Crosman Arms Co., 582 N.E.2d 1000 (Ohio Ct. App. 1989); Sherk v. Daisy–Heddon, 450 A.2d 615, 618–20 (Pa. 1982). See also Haesche v. Kissner, 640 A.2d 89 (Conn. 1994) (since teenagers engaged in war games knew that BB guns could injure eyes, absence of warning was not cause of harm).

**65.** Van Dettum v. K–Mart Corp., 479 N.E.2d 1104 (Ill. App. Ct. 1985).

**66.** Emerick v. United States Suzuki Motor Corp., 750 F.2d 19 (3d Cir. 1984) (Pa. law).

**67.** Mach v. General Motors Corp., 315 N.W.2d 561 (Mich. Ct. App. 1982).

**68.** Kerr v. Koemm, 557 F.Supp. 283 (S.D.N.Y. 1983).

**69.** Morgan v. Bethlehem Steel Corp., 481 N.E.2d 836 (Ill. App. Ct. 1985) (no duty to light or add reflectors to train cars).

**70.** Brown v. Sears, Roebuck & Co., 667 P.2d 750 (Ariz. Ct. App. 1983).

**71.** Dickens v. Avanti Research & Dev., Inc., 515 N.E.2d 208 (Ill. App. Ct. 1987).

**72.** Complaint of Diehl, 610 F.Supp. 223 (D. Idaho 1985).

**73.** Putman v. Gulf States Utils., 588 So.2d 1223 (La. Ct. App. 1991).

**74.** Scaccianoce v. Hixon Mfg. & Supply Co., 57 F.3d 582 (7th Cir. 1995) (Ill. law).

**75.** Anderson v. Green Bull, Inc., 471 S.E.2d 708, 711 (S.C. Ct. App. 1996) ("the conductivity of an aluminum ladder is a condition commonly known and recognized").

**76.** Cf. FMC Corp. v. Brown, 526 N.E.2d 719 (Ind. Ct. App. 1988) (crane, not equipped with proximity warning devices or insulated link, hit power line; obviousness jury question where design of cab obstructed operator's view).

**77.** Plante v. Hobart Corp., 771 F.2d 617 (1st Cir. 1985) (Me. law).

**78.** Grover v. Superior Welding, Inc., 893 P.2d 500 (Okla. 1995).

**79.** Kuras v. International Harvester Co., 820 F.2d 15 (1st Cir. 1987) (R.I. law).

**80.** Raines v. Colt Indus., 757 F.Supp. 819 (E.D. Mich 1991) (handgun is "simple," not complex, product).

**81.** Resteiner v. Sturm, Ruger & Co., 566 N.W.2d 53 (Mich. Ct. App. 1997) (total absence of basis for claim, such that manufacturer entitled to attorneys' fees and other expenses of vexatious appeals).

**82.** Schremp v. Haugh's Prods., 1997 WL 760900 (Ohio Ct. App. 1997) (paralysis); Glittenberg v. Doughboy Recreational Indus., 491 N.W.2d 208 (Mich. 1992) (same); Belling v. Haugh's Pools, Ltd., 511 N.Y.S.2d 732 (App. Div. 1987) (same).

**83.** Lloyd v. John Deere Co., 922 F.2d 1192 (5th Cir. 1991) (Miss. law).

**84.** See, e.g., Welch v. Scripto–Tokai Corp., 651 N.E.2d 810 (Ind. Ct. App. 1995).

flammable gasoline[85] in the reach of young children; flying a private aircraft without locking the seat to prevent it from slipping back and depriving the pilot of control;[86] driving a car after drinking too much beer;[87] developing alcoholism and other debilitations from excessive drinking;[88] driving a Jeep with one bare foot resting on a step outside the vehicle;[89] colliding so severely with another vehicle that the seatbelts could not protect the occupants;[90] colliding head-on with another vehicle at speeds in excess of 100 miles per hour;[91] suffering leg injuries in a motorcycle collision;[92] riding unrestrained in the open cargo bed of a pickup truck;[93] suffering ill-effects from smoking cigarettes;[94] suffering ill-effects from lighting a cigarette minutes after being soaked with gasoline at the pump;[95] falling from a ladder;[96] sticking limbs into the rotating propeller of an outboard motor;[97] stacking glass cookware in a high pyramid on a cupboard shelf that slanted toward the floor;[98] loosening the bolts holding a ring, at top of a refinery tower, to which a scaffold's safety lanyard was attached;[99] operating a forklift or front-end loader without an overhead guard or removable roll-over protective structure (ROPS);[100] slipping when walking on the boom of a crane;[101] or spilling coffee served very hot.[102]

**85.** Donnelly v. Kerr–McGee Refining Corp., 1992 WL 208016 (W.D. Okla. 1992).

**86.** Argubright v. Beech Aircraft Corp., 868 F.2d 764 (5th Cir. 1989) (Tex. law) (student pilot supervised by flight instructor).

**87.** Morris v. Adolph Coors Co., 735 S.W.2d 578 (Tex. App. 1987).

**88.** See, e.g., Joseph E. Seagram & Sons, Inc. v. McGuire, 814 S.W.2d 385, 388 (Tex. 1991) (alcoholism); Garrison v. Heublein, Inc., 673 F.2d 189, 192 (7th Cir. 1982) (Ill. law) ("propensities" of alcohol). See also Pemberton v. American Distilled Spirits Co., 664 S.W.2d 690 (Tenn. 1984) (no duty to warn of risk of death from rapid over-consumption of grain alcohol in single sitting). Congress has now preempted the issue of warnings of the risks of alcoholic beverages. See 27 U.S.C. § 215, requiring that alcoholic beverages be labeled with certain specified warnings.

**89.** Smith v. American Motors Sales Corp., 576 N.E.2d 146 (Ill. App. Ct. 1991).

**90.** Mazda Motor of Am., Inc. v. Rogowski, 659 A.2d 391 (Md. Ct. Spec. App. 1995).

**91.** Timmons v. Ford Motor Co., 982 F.Supp. 1475, 1480 (S.D. Ga. 1997) (warning against this hazard would be a "foolish restatement of an obvious fact").

**92.** Nicholson v. Yamaha Motor Co., 566 A.2d 135 (Md. Ct. Spec. App. 1989).

**93.** Josue v. Isuzu Motors Am., Inc., 958 P.2d 535 (Haw. 1998); Maneely v. General Motors Corp., 108 F.3d 1176 (9th Cir. 1997) (Cal. law).

**94.** See, e.g., American Tobacco Co. v. Grinnell, 951 S.W.2d 420, 427 (Tex. 1997) (general ill-effects of cigarettes, but not addictive quality, generally known when deceased smoker began smoking in 1952).

**95.** Payne v. Quality Nozzle Co., 643 N.Y.S.2d 623 (App. Div. 1996).

**96.** Puckett v. Oakfabco, Inc., 979 P.2d 1174 (Idaho 1999) (no duty to warn of truly obvious risks notwithstanding statute providing that obvious risk shall reduce plaintiff's recovery).

**97.** See, e.g., Elliott v. Brunswick Corp., 903 F.2d 1505 (11th Cir. 1990) (Ala. law).

**98.** Jackson v. Corning Glass Works, 538 A.2d 666 (R.I. 1988).

**99.** Sauder Custom Fabrication, Inc. v. Boyd, 967 S.W.2d 349 (Tex. 1998).

**100.** Caterpillar, Inc. v. Shears, 911 S.W.2d 379 (Tex. 1995) (front-end loader); Bavuso v. Caterpillar Indus., Inc., 563 N.E.2d 198, 201 (Mass. 1990) (forklift). *But see* holding that a jury question on obviousness is raised by the absence of ROPS, Young v. Deere & Co., 818 F.Supp. 1420, 1423 (D. Kan. 1992); Gann v. International Harvester Co., 712 S.W.2d 100, 106 (Tenn. 1986); Caterpillar Tractor Co. v. Donahue, 674 P.2d 1276, 1283 (Wyo. 1983).

**101.** Campbell v. American Crane Corp., 60 F.3d 1329 (8th Cir. 1995) (Mo. law).

**102.** McMahon v. Bunn–O–Matic Corp., 150 F.3d 651 (7th Cir. 1998) (Ind. law) (because everyone knows that hot coffee will burn if spilled on skin, lack of knowledge that it can cause third-degree burns requires no warning). *Contra* Nadel v.

If there were any doubt as to the wisdom of the no-duty-to-warn rule in obvious danger cases, it should be laid to rest by the position taken on this issue by the courts of New York. It will be remembered that the New York Court of Appeals anchored the patent danger rule in design cases in *Campo v. Scofield*[103] which it later repudiated in *Micallef v. Miehle Co.*,[104] as mentioned earlier. *Micalleff* held that the patent danger doctrine should be abolished as a general no-duty rule in design cases and that the obviousness of a danger is only one factor in the risk-utility balance in weighing the costs and benefits of altering a design to eliminate a danger.[105] But the only-one-factor approach makes no sense in warnings cases, because the obviousness of a danger completely fulfills the purpose of a warning in most cases far better than any verbal communication could ever hope to do. In recognition of this fact and of the completely different purposes served by design and warnings obligations, New York courts have refused to extend the *Micallef* only-one-factor doctrine to warnings cases but, instead, have adhered to the widespread view that there simply is no duty to warn of dangers (and methods of avoiding dangers) that are truly obvious.[106] Other jurisdictions, which similarly have rejected the patent danger rule in design defect cases, have also adopted the logic of a bold no-duty-to-warn rule in obvious danger cases.[107]

Burger King Corp., 695 N.E.2d 1185 (Ohio Ct. App. 1997) (obviousness of risk that coffee served from drive-through window of fast-food restaurant, and spilled on child, would be so hot as to cause second-degree burns was question of fact for jury).

**103.** 95 N.E.2d 802 (N.Y. 1950).

**104.** 348 N.E.2d 571 (N.Y. 1976).

**105.** See id.

**106.** See, e.g., Lamb v. Kysor Indus. Corp., 759 N.Y.S.2d 266, 268 (App. Div. 2003) ("there is no duty to warn of an open and obvious danger of which the product user ... should be aware as a result of ordinary observation or as a matter of common sense"); Liriano v. Hobart Corp., 700 N.E.2d 303, 308 (N.Y. 1998) (*Liriano II*) (no duty to warn of obvious dangers; requiring manufacturers to warn of such risks "could greatly increase the number of warnings accompanying certain products" and trivialize, undermine, drown out, and neutralize cautions against important, latent dangers of which consumers need to be informed); Belling v. Haugh's Pools, Ltd., 511 N.Y.S.2d 732, 733 (App. Div. 1987) (risk of diving into above-ground pool; "there is no liability for failing to warn of obvious dangers"); Kerr v. Koemm, 557 F.Supp. 283, 287 n.1 (S.D.N.Y. 1983) ("[o]bviousness should not relieve manufacturers of the duty to eliminate dangers from their design if that can reasonably be done, but obviousness relieves the manufacturer of a duty to inform users of a danger").

But the distinction between warnings and instructions has muddied New York's jurisprudence. See Liriano v. Hobart Corp., 170 F.3d 264 (2d Cir. 1999) (N.Y. law) (*Liriano III*) (Calabresi, J.) (manufacturer had duty to inform users that guard was available, even though danger of using grinder without guard was obvious); Burke v. Spartanics, Ltd., 252 F.3d 131, 137 (2d Cir. 2001) (N.Y. law) (Calabresi, J.) (explaining how *Liriano III* was consistent with no-duty-to-warn-of-obvious-dangers rule: while there was no need to warn of obvious danger of unguarded grinder, jury could find that availability of guard to reduce risk was not obvious and so required instruction); Bowbeer and Killoran, Liriano v. Hobart Corp.: Obvious Dangers, The Duty to Warn of Safer Alternatives, and the Heeding Presumption, 65 Brooklyn L. Rev. 717 (1999) (critiquing *Liriano III*); Note, 88 Cornell L. Rev. 814 (2003) (same).

**107.** For example, compare Auburn Mach. Works Co. v. Jones, 366 So.2d 1167 (Fla. 1979) (rejecting patent danger doctrine in design defect context), with Knox v. Delta Int'l Mach. Corp., 554 So.2d 6, 7 (Fla. Dist. Ct. App. 1989) ("a manufacturer has no duty to warn consumers of ... an obvious danger"); and compare Holm v. Sponco Mfg., Inc., 324 N.W.2d 207 (Minn. 1982) (rejecting patent danger rule in design defect cases), with Mix v. MTD Prods., Inc., 393 N.W.2d 18, 19 (Minn. Ct. App. 1986) ("a manufacturer of a product has no duty to warn of dangers that are obvious to anyone using the product").

A few courts, however, have fallen into the trap of extending the *Micallef* only-one-factor approach to obviousness beyond defective design cases to warnings defect claims as well. Thus, decisions in Colorado,[108] Illinois,[109] New Jersey,[110] Mississippi,[111] and Montana[112] have espoused the only-one-factor approach rather than adopting the logical no-duty rule in obvious danger cases involving warnings defect claims. While the Illinois court was troubled, not unreasonably, by the no-duty rule's effect of denying the possibility of a duty to remind[113] in situations where a warning might reasonably serve that purpose well, other decisions have adopted the only-one-factor position in an offhand manner, without appearing to focus on the important distinctions between a manufacturer's design and warnings obligations discussed above. Courts can easily carve out meritorious exceptions to the no-duty rule, such as possibly providing a duty to remind in certain situations,[114] but the general rule should not fall victim to its failure to work perfectly in every type of case. In time, the few renegade jurisdictions that have rebuffed the no-duty-to-warn-of-obvious-dangers rule may be expected to see the logic and fairness of a general no-duty warning rule for risks that are truly obvious.

### Defining "Obvious"

A recurring, preliminary problem in obvious danger cases lies in determining how to define the relevant *risk*, how to determine what aspect of the product hazard must be obvious. For example, some courts have agreed with the *Glittenberg* court's conclusion, discussed above, that the general risk of injury from diving into a shallow above-ground pool is obvious and, hence, does not give rise to a duty to warn.[115] But the

---

**108.** Armentrout v. FMC Corp., 842 P.2d 175, 181 (Colo. 1992) (warning only factor, but no duty to warn of obvious danger "unless there is a substantial likelihood that the proposed warning would have prevented injury to the ordinary user").

**109.** Harnischfeger Corp. v. Gleason Crane Rentals, Inc., 585 N.E.2d 166 (Ill. App. Ct. 1991). But subsequent decisions suggest that Illinois in fact has adopted the widely accepted general doctrine that there is no duty to warn of obvious dangers. See, e.g., Lederman v. Pacific Indus., 119 F.3d 551 (7th Cir. 1997) (Ill. law). An Illinois statute eliminating the duty to warn of obvious product dangers, Ill. Rev. Stat. 735 § 5/2–2106(c), was part of a tort reform bill declared unconstitutional in its entirety. Best v. Taylor Mach. Works, 689 N.E.2d 1057 (Ill. 1997).

**110.** Campos v. Firestone Tire & Rubber Co., 485 A.2d 305 (N.J. 1984). But New Jersey now has a statute which suggests that there is no duty to warn of obvious dangers. See N.J. Stat. Ann. § 2A.58C–4.

**111.** Seymour v. Brunswick Corp., 655 So.2d 892, 895 (Miss. 1995) ("the open and obvious defense is simply a factor and not a complete bar in our jurisdiction applying comparative negligence principles"). But Mississippi now has a statute providing that there is no duty to warn of obvious product dangers. See Miss. Code Ann. § 11–1–63(e).

**112.** Tacke v. Vermeer Mfg. Co., 713 P.2d 527, 535 (Mont. 1986).

**113.** The few decisions on whether there should be a duty to *remind* of a known or obvious danger are split. Compare Tacke v. Vermeer Mfg. Co., 713 P.2d 527 (Mont. 1986) (duty to remind worker of specific risk of getting caught in machine's rollers), with Berry v. Eckhardt Porsche Audi, Inc., 578 P.2d 1195, 1196 (Okla. 1978) (seatbelt warning buzzer is "valiant attempt on part of the manufacturers to nag an occupant into fastening his seat belt," but its absence or failure is not a defect since function of seatbelts is generally known).

**114.** Compare Liriano v. Hobart Corp., 170 F.3d 264 (2d Cir. 1999) (N.Y. law) (*Liriano III*) (manufacturer had duty to remind users of the availability of a guard that could be removed).

**115.** See, e.g., Belling v. Haugh's Pools, Ltd., 511 N.Y.S.2d 732 (App. Div. 1987); Vallillo v. Muskin Corp., 514 A.2d 528 (N.J.

*Glittenberg* court was closely divided on this issue, and other courts have agreed with *Glittenberg*'s dissenting judges that the relevant, more particular risk in the case was far from obvious—involving aspects of physics, ergonomics, and anatomy related to the attempt to make a shallow dive from the wobbly edge of a pool, that could cause the diver to enter the water more steeply than intended which could result in catastrophic spinal injury, a hazard which most people only vaguely comprehend at best.[116] Yet the majority view seems sound, for manufacturers of above-ground pools should be entitled to expect that most people know and understand, at least in a general way, the serious consequences from a common hazard such as hitting one's head against the ground. From this perspective, it makes good sense to conclude that the manufacturer of such a pool should have no duty to warn of the "obvious" risk of diving into a shallow pool.

Once the proper risk is identified, the meaning of the word "obvious" is obviously important. A danger is "obvious" if it would be apparent to an ordinary or reasonable user or consumer of the type of product involved in the accident.[117] Many courts logically widen the doctrine to include hazards which may be classified as being widely, generally, or commonly known and recognized.[118] As one court observed, a danger is obvious if "the relevant condition or feature that creates the danger associated with use is fully apparent, widely known, commonly recognized, and anticipated by the ordinary user or consumer."[119] This sensible widening of the classification in an objective manner restates the doctrine in terms of the cognizant impact the danger is likely to make on product users. But the issue properly remains an *objective* determination of whether the risk is evident to ordinary or reasonable

---

Super. Ct. 1986). The cases are collected in Glittenberg v. Doughboy Recreational Indus., 491 N.W.2d 208, 211 nn. 4 and 5 (Mich. 1992).

**116.** See Glittenberg v. Doughboy Recreational Indus., 491 N.W.2d 208, 223 (Mich. 1992) (Levin, J., dissenting). See also Klen v. Asahi Pool, Inc., 643 N.E.2d 1360 (Ill. App. Ct. 1994) (obviousness should be determined by jury); Corbin v. Coleco Indus., 748 F.2d 411 (7th Cir. 1984) (Ind. law).

**117.** This definition is an adaptation of Restatement (2d) Torts § 343A cmt. *b*. See also Griebler v. Doughboy Recreational, Inc., 466 N.W.2d 897 (Wis. 1991) (interpreting § 343A as excluding appreciation of risk); Prosser and Keeton on Torts § 96, at 686–87 ("courts have usually meant by 'obvious danger' a condition that would ordinarily be seen and the danger of which would ordinarily be appreciated by those who would be expected to use the product").

**118.** See, e.g., Coleman v. Cintas Sales Corp. 100 S.W.3d 384 (Tex. App. 2002)

(common knowledge that non-flame retardant clothing would burn when exposed to open flame); Mills v. Curioni, Inc., 238 F.Supp.2d 876, 892 (E.D. Mich. 2002) (dangers associated with use must be "fully apparent, widely known, commonly recognized, and anticipated by the ordinary consumer"); House v. Armour of Am., 929 P.2d 340, 343 (Utah 1996) (citing Restatement (2d) Torts § 388(b) cmt. *j*, and observing: "if the danger posed by the use of a product is 'generally known and recognized,' then the seller is not required to warn about that danger"). North Carolina's statute speaks in terms of "open and obvious" risks and those which are "a matter of common knowledge." See N.C. Gen. Stat. § 99B–5(b). Compare Reiff v. Convergent Technologies, 957 F.Supp. 573 (D.N.J. 1997) (manufacturer of conventional computer keyboard had no duty to warn of risk of repetitive stress syndrome from use of keyboard at work).

**119.** Glittenberg v. Doughboy Recreational Indus., 491 N.W.2d 208, 213 (Mich. 1992) (citing many decisions using similar language, at 214 n.15).

persons in the plaintiff's position,[120] not whether the risk is perceived by the particular plaintiff.[121]

Some courts and at least one legislature, however, define the patent danger doctrine in terms of obvious dangers and those that are "known,"[122] a formulation which unfortunately suggests a *subjective* standard of a particular victim's state of mind, an issue which is extraneous in a formulation of such a duty of general applicability. That is, to the extent that the obviousness of a danger bears on a manufacturer's duty toward consumers, an identical duty should apply to each consumer. Characteristics of individual consumers, including their awareness of particular risks in particular circumstances, logically are relevant only to the issue of causation (especially in the warnings context),[123] and to affirmative defenses such as comparative fault and

---

**120.** Thus, the proper perspective is that of a normal (or average) *user* of the particular type of product, who may (or may not) be skilled and knowledgeable with respect to the product's proper use and limitations, not the perspective of a normal *person*. See Sauder Custom Fabrication, Inc. v. Boyd, 967 S.W.2d 349, 350 (Tex. 1998).

**121.** See, e.g., Swix v. Daisy Mfg. Co., 373 F.3d 678 (6th Cir. 2004) (Mich. law); Mohr v. St. Paul Fire & Marine Ins. Co., 674 N.W.2d 576, 585 (Wis. Ct. App. 2003) (issue is whether seller had reason to believe that plaintiff had knowledge, not whether plaintiff actually had knowledge); Mills v. Curioni, Inc., 238 F.Supp.2d 876, 892 (E.D. Mich. 2002) (rejecting subjective standard; "the focus is on the typical user's perception and knowledge"); Sauder Custom Fabrication, Inc. v. Boyd, 967 S.W.2d 349, 350 (Tex. 1998) ("whether a product has obvious dangers requires an objective standard"); Emory v. McDonnell Douglas Corp., 148 F.3d 347 (4th Cir. 1998) (Md. law); Powell Duffryn Terminals, Inc. v. Calgon Carbon Corp., 4 F.Supp.2d 1198 (S.D. Ga. 1998) (courts should use objective perspective, not subjective, since user's perceptions are irrelevant); Glittenberg v. Doughboy Recreational Indus., 491 N.W.2d 208 (Mich. 1992):

> Determination of the "obvious" character of a product-connected danger is objective. The focus is the typical user's perception and knowledge and whether the relevant condition or feature that creates the danger associated with use is fully apparent, widely know, commonly recognized, and anticipated by the ordinary user or consumer.

Id. at 213; Memphis Bank & Trust Co. v. Water Services, Inc., 758 S.W.2d 525 (Tenn. 1988) S.W.2d 525 (Tenn. 1988).

**122.** See, e.g., Hiner v. Deere & Co., Inc., 340 F.3d 1190, 1194 (10th Cir. 2003) (Kan. law) ("regardless of the ordinary

user's knowledge of the danger, there is no duty to warn of dangers actually known to the user of the product"); Lamb v. Kysor Indus. Corp., 759 N.Y.S.2d 266, 268 (Sup. Ct. App. Div. 2003) (same); Scheibe v. Fort James Corp., 276 F.Supp.2d 246, 252 (D. Del. 2003) (same); Sprankle v. Bower Ammonia & Chem. Co., 824 F.2d 409 (5th Cir. 1987) (Miss. law) (plaintiff had earlier refused to clean storage tanks because of hazards of inhaling ammonia gas); Sherk v. Daisy–Heddon, 450 A.2d 615 (Pa. 1982) (knowledge that BB gun fired into friend's head at close range could kill); Hagans v. Oliver Mach. Co., 576 F.2d 97 (5th Cir. 1978) (Tex. law) (known danger of cutting knotted wood with power circular saw).

Some courts lump the two no-duty rules together: "There is no duty to warn where risks are known and obvious to the plaintiff." Olson v. Prosoco, Inc., 522 N.W.2d 284, 291 (Iowa 1994). Idaho's products liability reform statute reduces a claimant's damages for injuries from obvious dangers and, in a separate subsection, from dangers of which the claimant knew. See Idaho Code §§ [6–1405] 6–1305(1)(b) (failure to observe obvious defective condition) and (2)(a) (voluntary use of product with known defective condition).

**123.** See, e.g., Burke v. Spartanics, Ltd., 252 F.3d 131, 137 (2d Cir. 2001) (N.Y. law) (Calabresi, J.) (carefully explaining distinction between duty and causation); Haesche v. Kissner III, 640 A.2d 89 (Conn. 1994) (since teenagers who engaged in war games knew that BB guns could injure eyes, absence of warning was not cause of harm); Campos v. Firestone Tire & Rubber Co., 485 A.2d 305, 311 (N.J. 1984) (user's knowledge relevant to whether absence of adequate warning was cause in fact of injury, but not to duty to warn): "Since the duty is to place on the market a product free of defects, and this duty attaches at the time the product is introduced into the stream of commerce, a particular user's subjective knowledge of a danger does not and cannot modify the manufacturer's duty."

assumption of risk which shift responsibility (in part or in whole) to individual consumers based on their personal choices and conduct.[124]

Courts occasionally speak loosely of whether a particular danger is "so obvious" that the manufacturer should not be liable.[125] While this parlance ordinarily is quite harmless, it is best to be avoided, for it suggests that the obviousness of a danger is a matter of degree. While the notion of obviousness may harmlessly be viewed on a sliding scale in common discourse, a finding or ruling that a danger is "obvious" has legal consequences. In short, it is a term of legal art, and, like product "defect," it simply exists or it does not. If a dangerous condition is somewhat evident, but not so evident as properly to trigger the consequences of concluding that it should be labeled open and obvious, then "obvious" it is not. There probably is less linguistic difficulty on the other side: once a danger is clearly in the obvious category, this usage is less problematic. So, a danger may harmlessly be spoken of as "so obvious" (so obviously obvious) that it requires this classification as a matter of law. Nevertheless, it is least confusing to speak of obviousness in absolute terms as a condition that either does or does not exist.

### Theory of Liability

The obvious nature of a danger properly bears on liability, but it by no means compels denial of recovery in every case for every type of claim. In negligence, the obviousness of a product danger reduces the risk of harm: if users perceive a significant product danger, they normally will want to take steps to protect themselves and others, hence reducing the likelihood that an accident will occur.[126] If a manufacturer tortiously misrepresents the safety of its products, an actor usually will not be justified in relying on a representation that obviously is false;[127] nor will an express warranty ordinarily be made or breached in such a case, because a statement the buyer knows is false usually cannot be part of the basis of the bargain.[128] For both types of claims, representations about a product's quality or safety long have been construed around obvious defects and dangerous conditions possessed by products. At Roman law, if a one-eyed dog was sold as "sound," the product sold was a sound one-eyed dog.[129] In modern law, if advertisements of a pickup truck show people sitting in its open cargo bed, the truck is sold as safe for such occupants under the conditions shown, not as safe when the truck is smashed into a tree.[130] And the same is true with respect to a

---

**124.** See W.P. Keeton, Personal Injuries Resulting from Open and Obvious Conditions, 100 U. Pa. L. Rev. 629, 648 (1952).

**125.** See, e.g., Scoby v. Vulcan–Hart Corp., 569 N.E.2d 1147, 1149 (Ill. App. Ct. 1991); Laaperi v. Sears, Roebuck & Co., 787 F.2d 726, 732 (1st Cir. 1986) (Mass. law).

**126.** See, e.g., Hughes v. Battenfeld Glouchester Eng'g Co., 2003 WL 22247195, at *3 (S.D. Ind. 2003) (open and obvious dangers bar recovery for negligent design and manufacture in Indiana, but not strict liability claims); Blue v. Environmental Eng'g, Inc., 803 N.E.2d 187, 195 (Ill. App. Ct. 2003). See generally James, Products

Liability, 34 Tex. L. Rev. 44, 51 (1955); Restatement (2d) Torts § 388(b).

**127.** "The recipient of a fraudulent misrepresentation is not justified in relying upon its truth if he knows that it is false or its falsity is obvious to him." Restatement (2d) Torts § 541. Compare Restatement (2d) Torts § 402B cmt. j; §§ 13.6 and 13.7, below.

**128.** See 3 Anderson on the UCC § 2–313.61 at 55.

**129.** See J. Thomas, Textbook of Roman Law 283–88 (1976).

**130.** See Maneely v. General Motors Corp., 108 F.3d 1176 (9th Cir. 1997) (Cal.

seller's implied representations, under the implied warranty of merchantability.[131] The law implies into a sales transaction such terms as the parties ordinarily understood to accompany the sale; if the buyer can see before the purchase that the product contains an obvious shortcoming, the buyer can hardly assume that the seller is promising that the shortcoming does not exist.[132] Instead, buyers ordinarily expect the price to reflect the presence of the flaw. Thus, under the Uniform Commercial Code, there are no warranties against a dangerously defective condition the buyer discovers before the purchase or against defects which the buyer's examination ought to have revealed.[133] If the buyer discovers it thereafter, or unreasonably ignores an obvious danger, any breach of warranty may not be considered the proximate cause of a resulting accident.[134]

In strict liability in tort, the obviousness of a danger plays either a greater or lesser role, depending on the theory of defectiveness. If design (or warnings) defectiveness is measured by consumer expectations, then a consumer injured by an obvious danger quite evidently must almost always lose.[135] Indeed, the consumer expectations test's failure to provide a satisfactory resolution to obvious danger cases is a major reason many courts have abandoned that standard as an exclusive test of design defectiveness.[136] The increasing majority of jurisdictions that employ a

---

law) (no claim for express warranty or for negligent misrepresentation).

**131.** See 3 Anderson on the UCC § 2–314.200 at 428.

**132.** See, e.g., American Tobacco Co. v. Grinnell, 951 S.W.2d 420, 435 (Tex. 1997) ("An implied warranty contrary to the community's common knowledge cannot exist. Because the general health dangers of cigarettes are commonly known by the community, no expectation of safety arises with respect to cigarettes when they are purchased.").

**133.** UCC § 2–316(3)(b). See also ch. 4, above.

**134.** UCC § 2–314 cmt. 13.; UCC § 2–715(2)(b) and cmt. 5.

**135.** See, e.g., Tillman v. R.J. Reynolds Tobacco Co., 871 So.2d 28, 34 (Ala. 2003) (obvious hazards of smoking cigarettes prevented recovery under consumer expectations test); Thongchoom v. Graco Children's Prods., Inc., 71 P.3d 214, 218 (Wash. Ct. App. 2003) (baby walker not defective under consumer expectations test because danger of baby's mobility was obvious); Wortel v. Somerset Indus., Inc., 770 N.E.2d 1211, 1222 (Ill. App. Ct. 2002) ("One shortcoming of the [consumer expectations test] is that a victim could never recover for harm suffered as a result of a design hazard that was open or obvious."); Sacks v. Philip Morris, Inc., 139 F.3d 892 (4th Cir. 1998) (Md. law) (obvious and commonly-known risk that cigarettes may start fires precludes liability under both consumer expectations and risk-utility tests); Dickerson v.

Cushman, Inc., 909 F.Supp. 1467 (M.D. Ala. 1995); Welch v. Scripto–Tokai Corp., 651 N.E.2d 810 (Ind. Ct. App. 1995) (consumer contemplations standard prevented strict tort claim); Griebler v. Doughboy Recreational, Inc., 466 N.W.2d 897 (Wis. 1991). *But see* Stenberg v. Beatrice Foods Co., 576 P.2d 725, 730–31 (Mont. 1978).

Many courts and commentators criticize the consumer expectations test for its unfairness to consumers injured by dangers which are obvious. See, e.g., Delvaux v. Ford Motor Co., 764 F.2d 469, 474 (7th Cir. 1985) (Wis. law) (rollover of convertible without roll bar) ("the consumer-contemplation approach reintroduces the discredited 'open and obvious' rule, now rejected by most jurisdictions"); W.P. Keeton, Products Liability—Design Hazards and the Meaning of Defect, 10 Cumb. L. Rev. 293, 300–05 (1979). *But see* Delaney v. Deere & Co., 999 P.2d 930, 946 (Kan. 2000) ("The fact that a hazard is open and obvious or has been warned against are factors to be considered in analyzing whether a product is defective or unreasonably dangerous [based upon] whether the product is defective and dangerous beyond a reasonable consumer's expectations."); Phillips, Consumer Expectations, 53 S.C. L. Rev. 1047, 1049–52 (2002) (heroic attempt to show that consumer expectations test does not bar recovery for obvious dangers). See generally §§ 5.6 and 8.3, above.

**136.** A number of courts cite this reason for abandoning consumer expectations as an independent test of liability. See, e.g.,

risk-utility balancing test for assessing design defectiveness consider the obviousness of a danger to be one factor in the balance, but only one, as discussed below. Also mentioned below is the approach in Illinois and Michigan of denying recovery altogether in cases of simple dangers which are obvious to the user.

Under all theories of liability, the obviousness of a danger is relevant not only to the issues of negligence and product defect but also to other elements of the plaintiff's prima facie case and to defenses based on the plaintiff's conduct.[137] As a general proposition, it may be said that the greater a user's awareness of a danger, the greater the user's care must be to avoid an accident. Yet, whether a plaintiff's choice to confront an obvious danger is viewed in terms of contributory negligence,[138] assumption of risk,[139] comparative fault,[140] misuse,[141] cause in fact, or proximate cause,[142] the obviousness of the danger plays an important role.[143] How a danger's obviousness affects these diverse issues is examined in the separate chapters on these topics.[144]

### Judge or Jury

In design cases, the obviousness of danger has lost its no-duty posture and melded with other risk-utility factors into the cost-benefit balance, an inquiry that is intrinsically factual.[145] Yet, the risks of some special types of products are so widely known and obviously part of the product's inherent nature that courts properly rule as a matter of law that their design is nondefective. Alcohol[146] and ciga-

---

Camacho v. Honda Motor Co., 741 P.2d 1240 (Colo. 1987) (motorcycle without crash bars; risk-utility, not consumer expectations, proper test); see also Seymour v. Brunswick Corp., 655 So.2d 892 (Miss. 1995) (swimmer's foot pulled into unguarded motorboat propeller while trying to climb on board). See generally §§ 5.6 & 8.3, above.

**137.** See W.P. Keeton, Personal Injuries Resulting from Open and Obvious Conditions, 100 U. Pa. L. Rev. 629, 648 (1952).

**138.** See, e.g., Tabieros v. Clark Equip. Co., 944 P.2d 1279 (Haw. 1997); Pike v. Frank G. Hough Co., 467 P.2d 229, 234 (Cal. 1970) "([T]he obviousness of the peril is relevant to the manufacturer's defenses, not to the issue of duty. If a bystander does not exercise due care to protect himself from an evident peril, he may be contributorily negligent.").

**139.** See, e.g., Luque v. McLean, 501 P.2d 1163 (Cal. 1972). Some state statutes provide that a plaintiff's knowledge of, and voluntary encounter with, a product risk may reduce a plaintiff's damages (Idaho) or will preclude liability altogether (Mississippi). See also Idaho Code § [6–1405] 6–1305(2)(a); Miss. Code Ann. § 11–1–63(d).

**140.** See, e.g., Mohr v. St. Paul Fire & Marine Ins. Co., 674 N.W.2d 576, 588 (Wis. Ct. App. 2003) (effect of plaintiff's confront-

ing obvious danger is factor for jury to consider in allocating fault); Byrnes v. Honda Motor Co., 845 F.Supp. 875 (S.D. Fla. 1994); Watson v. Navistar Int'l Transp. Corp., 827 P.2d 656 (Idaho 1992).

**141.** See, e.g., Joseph E. Seagram & Sons, Inc. v. McGuire, 814 S.W.2d 385 (Tex. 1991) (health risks of excessive consumption of alcohol).

**142.** See, e.g., Belling v. Haugh's Pools, Ltd., 511 N.Y.S.2d 732 (App. Div. 1987); Smith v. Hub Mfg. Inc., 634 F.Supp. 1505 (N.D.N.Y. 1986). See also UCC § 2–314 cmt. 13; UCC § 2–715(2)(b).

**143.** Although different courts take varying positions on the role of obviousness in particular cases, the open and obvious doctrine (in the absence of a statute so providing) is generally held not to be an affirmative defense. See, e.g., FMC Corp. v. Brown, 526 N.E.2d 719 (Ind. Ct. App. 1988) (crane, not equipped with proximity warning devices or insulated link, hit power line).

**144.** See chs. 12, 13, and 14, below.

**145.** See § 8.6, above.

**146.** See, e.g., Bruner v. Anheuser–Busch, Inc., 153 F.Supp.2d 1358 (S.D. Fla. 2001), aff'd, 31 Fed. Appx. 932 (11th Cir. 2002) (table); Joseph E. Seagram & Sons,

rettes,[147] for example, contain generic risks that are well known and unavoidable, a situation that raises a host of issues examined elsewhere.[148]

Whether the obviousness of a product danger is for court or jury determination is especially important in warnings cases.[149] In this context, courts sometimes baldly state that the obviousness of a danger is a matter of law for the court to decide,[150] a conclusion which makes some sense for no-duty issues that are properly for judicial resolution. Yet, the obviousness of a product's risk is so bound up in the facts and circumstances of human knowledge and risk perception surrounding particular hazards of particular products that most courts now hold that the obviousness of a risk is normally an issue of fact for the jury to decide.[151] As with any issue of fact, however, a court may rule that a risk in a particular case is obvious as a matter of law, because no reasonable jury could conclude to the contrary.[152] Perhaps for fear of omitting a possible basis of recovery, plaintiffs' counsel assert claims for failure to warn all

---

Inc. v. McGuire, 814 S.W.2d 385, 388 (Tex. 1991) ("From ancient times, the danger of alcoholism from prolonged and excessive consumption of alcoholic beverages has been widely known and recognized."). But the risks of moderate consumption may not be generally understood. See Hon v. Stroh Brewery Co., 835 F.2d 510 (3d Cir. 1987) (Pa. law) (26–year-old man died from pancreatitis as the result of drinking two or three cans of Old Milwaukee beer four nights per week for about five years). See generally Notes, 53 Mo. L. Rev. 555 (1988); 63 Wash. L. Rev. 979 (1988); 75 Cornell L. Rev. 158 (1989); 28 J. Fam. L. 71 (1990).

**147.** See, e.g., Tillman v. R.J. Reynolds Tobacco Co., 871 So.2d 28, 33 (Ala. 2003) ("there is a 'wealth of judicial precedence' recognizing that the dangers of cigarette smoking are well-known," citing cases); American Tobacco Co. v. Grinnell, 951 S.W.2d 420 (Tex. 1997) (no duty to warn of general health risks of cigarettes, which were commonly known; but addictive qualities of cigarettes not commonly known). Compare Sacks v. Philip Morris, Inc., 139 F.3d 892 (4th Cir. 1998) (Md. law) (obvious and commonly known risk that cigarettes may start fires precludes liability under both consumer expectations and risk-utility tests).

**148.** See § 10.3, below. See also § 6.2, above.

**149.** As illustrated by an early classic warnings case, Jamieson v. Woodward & Lothrop, 247 F.2d 23 (D.C. Cir. 1957), which involved the question of whether a jury should determine whether the common knowledge of a general risk should protect a manufacturer against the duty to remind users of either the general or a more specific risk. Plaintiff was injured while lying on the floor when defendant's rubber "Lithe–Line" exercise rope slipped off her feet and hit her in the eye. On a failure to warn

claim, *held* (5–4 decision), summary judgment for defendants affirmed: "Surely every adult knows that, if an elastic band, whether it be an office rubber band or a rubber rope exerciser, is stretched and one's hold on it slips, the elastic snaps back. There was no duty on the manufacturer to warn of that simple fact." Id. at 28. The dissenting judges thought there was a jury issue on the obviousness of the danger, reasoning that "the resiliency of rubber generally may be assumed to be a fact known to all, but reasonable minds can differ as to whether the danger that lurks in this condition in performing the [Tummy Flattener] exercise recommended by the manufacturer here—a striking force which can hit the eye and detach a retina—was readily apparent to all users of the device." Id. at 35.

**150.** See, e.g., Smith v. Hub Mfg., Inc., 634 F.Supp. 1505, 1508 (N.D.N.Y. 1986).

**151.** See Products Liability Restatement § 2 cmt. *j* (whether a risk was obvious or generally known is issue for trier of fact).

**152.** See, e.g., Tillman v. R.J. Reynolds Tobacco Co., 871 So.2d 28, 33–34 (Ala. 2003) (dangers from smoking cigarettes: " 'certain products whose inherent danger is patent and obvious, do not, as a matter of law, involve defects of a sort that a jury should resolve' "); Josue v. Isuzu Motors Am., Inc., 958 P.2d 535, 539 (Haw. 1998) (risks of riding unrestrained in open cargo bed of pickup truck: "faced with a plain and palpable danger for purposes of a failure to warn claim, a court may determine such danger to be open and obvious as a matter of law"); Maneely v. General Motors Corp., 108 F.3d 1176, 1180–81 (9th Cir. 1997) (Cal. law) ("the ordinary motoring public recognizes the dangers of riding unrestrained in the cargo bed of a moving pick-

too frequently in cases where the danger is evident and entirely clear in which the only legitimate claim is whether the danger should have been designed away.[153] If a risk is truly obvious, as are many of the risks mentioned above, then a court should not hesitate to rule that there is no duty to warn and dismiss the warnings claim.[154] But if the obviousness of a risk is fairly in doubt, if the discernability of risk is not entirely clear, then a duty to warn may exist and the obviousness of the risk should be submitted to the jury.[155]

## § 10.3　Inherent Product Hazards—Product Category Liability

### Limited Liability for Inherent Hazards

Every product is dangerous; each amalgamation of molecules involves some risk of harm. That is, some dangers inherent in every product are, as a practical matter, unavoidable—they cannot be eliminated without destroying the product's purpose or desirability. Conspiring with the frailty of human cognition and skill, gravity and other natural forces assure that thousands of children are injured and sometimes killed on bicycles, jungle gyms, and trampolines each year. Many thousands of adults die annually from misadventures with automobiles, prescription drugs, cigarettes, alcohol, and guns. But even the most

up truck [and] no reasonable jury could find to the contrary").

**153.** See Henderson and Twerski, Doctrinal Collapse in Products Liability: The Empty Shell of Failure to Warn, 65 N.Y.U. L. Rev. 265 (1990).

**154.** See, e.g., Maneely v. General Motors Corp., 108 F.3d 1176, 1180–81 (9th Cir. 1997) (Cal. law) (warnings—no reasonable jury could fail to conclude that people know danger of riding unrestrained in cargo bed of pickup truck; design—no reasonable jury could find that the absence of seatbelts in cargo bed was a design defect); Josue v. Isuzu Motors Am., Inc., 958 P.2d 535, 536 (Haw. 1998) ("riding unrestrained in the bed of a pickup truck ... is an open and obvious danger as a matter of law;" no duty to warn). See generally W.P. Keeton, Personal Injuries Resulting from Open and Obvious Conditions, 100 U. Pa. L. Rev. 629, 641–42 (1952) (recommending closer judicial control of cases involving obvious dangers).

**155.** See, e.g., Needham v. Coordinated Apparel Group, Inc., 811 A.2d 124, 129 (Vt. 2002) (danger of cotton turtleneck igniting three feet away from stove); House v. Armour of Am., Inc., 929 P.2d 340 (Utah 1996) (risk that bullet from high powered rifle could penetrate body armor vest and kill SWAT team point man); Maddox v. River & Sea Marine, Inc., 925 P.2d 1033 (Alaska 1996) (danger of lifting heavy boat and trailer from vehicle); FMC Corp. v. Brown, 526 N.E.2d 719 (Ind. Ct. App. 1988) (crane,

not equipped with proximity warning devices or insulated link, hit power line; obviousness of risk for jury where cab design obstructed operator's view); Laaperi v. Sears, Roebuck & Co., 787 F.2d 726 (1st Cir. 1986) (Mass. law) (risk that electrical fire could incapacitate AC-powered smoke detector); Melancon v. Western Auto Supply Co., 628 F.2d 395, 399 (5th Cir. 1980) (La. law) (risk that "mower's muffler could create a blowtorch effect when a fuel envelope is present as the mower is started").

Compare Nadel v. Burger King Corp., 695 N.E.2d 1185 (Ohio Ct. App. 1997) (jury question as to obviousness of risk that coffee served from drive-though window of fast-food restaurant, that spilled on child, would be so hot as to cause second degree burns), with McMahon v. Bunn–O–Matic Corp., 150 F.3d 651 (7th Cir. 1998) (Ind. law) (because everyone knows that hot coffee will burn if spilled on skin, lack of knowledge that it can cause third-degree burns requires no warning as matter of law). See Products Liability Restatement § 2 cmt. j ("When reasonable minds may differ as to whether the risk was obvious or generally known, the issue is to be decided by the trier of fact."). See generally Glittenberg v. Doughboy Recreational Indus., 491 N.W.2d 208, 217 (Mich. 1992) ("If reasonable minds cannot differ on the 'obvious' character of the product-connected danger, the court determines the question as a matter of law. If, on the other hand, the court determines that reasonable minds could dif-

innocuous products, under circumstances of extended or improper use, can become instruments of injury, disease, or death. Marshmallows and peanut butter can gag and suffocate young children;[1] baseballs hit with aluminum bats can strike pitchers in the head;[2] cotton garments can ignite and burn those who don them;[3] hot chocolate, tea, and coffee can scald those who drink them;[4] sleds can propel riders down snowy hills and into trees;[5] a computer keyboard can lead to carpal tunnel syndrome;[6] and butter and fast foods over time can cause obesity, diabetes, heart attacks and death.[7] In a world in which risk is a certain result of every step and breath, courts must be cautious in declaring entire categories of products—especially products widely understood to be inherently hazardous because of their inescapable, generic risks—to be on balance "good" or "bad." Whether courts should engage in such an enterprise has been characterized as the "last frontier" of products liability law: a borderland at the edge of law where fights erupt over whether manufacturers should be held responsible, without the usual proofs of defect, for selling products adjudged by a court or jury to be more bad than good.[8]

fer, the obviousness of risk must be determined by the jury.").

### § 10.3

**1.** See, e.g., Emery v. Federated Foods, Inc., 863 P.2d 426 (Mont. 1993) (child gagged on marshmallows); Fraust v. Swift & Co., 610 F.Supp. 711 (W.D. Pa. 1985) (child gagged on peanut butter).

**2.** Compare Vincer v. Esther Williams All–Aluminum Swimming Pool Co., 230 N.W.2d 794, 799 (Wis. 1975) (dissent citing baseball bat as unavoidably unsafe product), with Sanchez v. Hillerich & Bradsby Co., 128 Cal.Rptr.2d 529 (Ct. App. 2002) (pitcher allowed to pursue claim that bat was defectively designed).

**3.** See, e.g., Needham v. Coordinated Apparel Group, Inc., 811 A.2d 124, 129 (Vt. 2002) (cotton turtleneck); Ellsworth v. Sherne Lingerie, Inc., 495 A.2d 348 (Md. 1985) (adult's nightgown); Gryc v. Dayton–Hudson Corp., 297 N.W.2d 727 (Minn. 1980) (child's nightgown). Compare Coleman v. Cintas Sales Corp. 100 S.W.3d 384 (Tex. App. 2002) (35% cotton and 65% polyester).

**4.** See, e.g., McCroy v. Coastal Mart, Inc., 207 F.Supp.2d 1265 (D. Kan. 2002) (hot chocolate; extensive review of hot beverage cases); Garlinger v. Hardee's Food Systems, Inc., 16 Fed.Appx. 232 (4th Cir. 2001) (W. Va. law) (hot coffee); Immormino v. J & M Powers, Inc., 698 N.E.2d 516 (Ohio Ct. Com. Pl. 1998) (hot tea). On hot coffee and punitive damages, see § 18.1, below.

**5.** See, e.g., Jordon v. K–Mart Corp., 611 A.2d 1328 (Pa. Super. Ct. 1992).

**6.** See, e.g., Reiff v. Convergent Technologies, 957 F.Supp. 573 (D. N.J.1997) (no

duty to warn that physical manipulation inherent in use of certain objects can cause injuries to some persons in certain circumstances).

**7.** See Restatement (2d) Torts § 402A cmt. *i* (butter); Pelman v. McDonald's Corp., 237 F.Supp.2d 512 (S.D.N.Y. 2003) (fast food).

**8.** Criticizing product category liability, see, e.g., Ausness, Product Category Liability: A Critical Analysis, 24 N. Ky. L. Rev. 423 (1997); Grossman, Categorical Liability: Why the Gates Should Be Kept Closed, 36 S. Tex. L. Rev. 385 (1995); Henderson and Twerski, Closing the American Products Liability Frontier: The Rejection of Liability Without Defect, 66 N.Y.U. L. Rev. 1263 (1991) (coining the "last frontier" metaphor). Favoring product category liability, see, e.g., Bogus, War on the Common Law: The Struggle at the Center of Products Liability, 60 Mo. L. Rev. 1 (1995); Wertheimer, The Smoke Gets in Their Eyes: Product Category Liability and Alternative Feasible Designs in the Third Restatement, 61 Tenn. L. Rev. 1429, 1454 (1994). See generally Symposium on Generic Products Liability, 72 Chi.-Kent Law Rev. 3 (1996) (articles by Bogus, Bell, Page, Phillips, Powers, and Wertheimer). For additional articles, see discussions of specific product categories, below.

The notions of "generic risk" and "product category" liability have only recently begun to surface in the products liability literature, and the meaning and significance of the concepts are still in flux. Note that these concepts substantially overlap with those of "unavoidable danger" and "state of the art," examined in § 10.4, below. The "generic risk" phrase may be

In a legal world where responsibility is formally based on fault, the scope of a manufacturer's liability for supplying products of whatever type or degree of danger is quite clear: the manufacturer must take all reasonable measures proportionate to the risk to reduce foreseeable risks of harm.[9] Normally this means that the manufacturer must exercise reasonable care to eliminate from its products all substantial dangers that reasonably can be designed away, to warn consumers about all substantial, hidden dangers that remain, to produce its products carefully to minimize dangerous manufacturing flaws, and to act carefully to avoid misrepresenting its product's safety. If manufacturers exercise reasonable care in all these respects, consumers, under a negligence regime, must bear responsibility for any remaining dangers in the products used in daily life, whether those dangers be characterized as "defects" or "generic risks."

During the 1960s, the foundation of the legal regime governing product accidents in America nominally changed from fault to one called "strict."[10] At its inception, the doctrine of strict products liability appeared to accomplish a broad-based shift of responsibility for injuries associated with the use of products away from consumers and onto product suppliers, particularly manufacturers, who were viewed as more preferable risk bearers than the human victims of product accidents.[11] This far-reaching shift in the apparent basis of liability for product accidents, particularly when justified by insurance theory, raised fundamental questions of how far a manufacturer's liability should extend for the inevitably harmful results of generically hazardous products like butter, that causes high cholesterol and heart attacks; drugs, that cause dangerous side-effects; cigarettes that cause lung disease; and alcohol that causes liver damage, violence, and car accidents. Indeed, when the nascent concept of strict products liability in tort was first debated and developed in the 1950s and 1960s, this very question of the proper scope of supplier responsibility for such inherent or "generic" risks in certain limited categories of products—food, drugs, whiskey, and cigarettes—was one of the central issues of concern to Dean Prosser and other scholars of the day.[12]

To the scholars who were crafting a doctrine of strict products liability in tort in the early 1960s, particularly as they molded and debated § 402A of the *Restatement (Second) of Torts*, it was clear that manufacturers of unavoidably hazardous products could only be expected to assure that their products were free of production defects and contained warnings of hidden dangers they could foresee. To avoid the possibility that the new "strict liability" doctrine might be stretched further, and misconstrued as permitting a challenge to the *design* of products possessing such inherent dangers, Dean Prosser and the ALI explicitly excluded such an obligation from new strict tort doctrine. In

traced to an article by Joseph Page, Generic Product Risks: The Case Against Comment k and for Strict Tort Liability, 58 N.Y.U. L. Rev. 853 (1983), the first explicit foray into a variety of the interrelated and knotty issues here involved.

**9.** See ch. 2, above.

**10.** See § 5.2, above.

**11.** See § 5.4, above.

**12.** See § 6.2 (discussing development of comments *i, j*, and *k* to § 402A on liability for generic risks), above, and § 10.4 (unavoidable dangers and state of the art), below.

particular, comments $i, j$, and $k$ to § 402A of the *Restatement (Second) of Torts* made clear that the only duties of manufacturers of inherently dangerous products—such as alcoholic beverages, prescription drugs, cigarettes, certain foods, and other products whose dangers cannot be designed away—are to avoid manufacturing defects and to warn consumers of hidden dangers. Put otherwise, because such products by hypothesis are unavoidably unsafe precisely because their dangers cannot be removed without destroying their utility, such products cannot be defective in design.

### Judicial Rejection of Design Liability for Inherent Hazards

In recent decades, the underlying debate over liability for generic product risks has centered on whether a product can properly be viewed as legally "defective" because its overall social injury costs exceed its overall social benefits.[13] Two prominent, controversial examples are cheap handguns used by criminals to maim and kill while possessing little positive value, even for self defense, and cigarettes which sicken and kill hundreds of thousands of Americans each year for the "benefit" of satisfying an addiction.[14] A small handful of courts[15] and a number of

---

**13.** Professor Carl Bogus well explains the essence of the "generic liability" debate:

> Generic liability, or product category liability as it is also called, involves products that remain unreasonably dangerous despite the best possible construction, design and warnings. Some argue that products liability should end at this point, that a manufacturer who has done everything feasible to make its product reasonably safe ought not be subject to strict liability. Others contend that a manufacturer has a duty not to put unreasonably dangerous products, *i.e.*, products that have a greater social cost than social benefit, into the stream of commerce, and that a manufacturer who cannot feasibly make his product reasonably safe can elect not to distribute his product at all [or, Bogus might say, pay for its accident costs]. To many, generic liability is a radical concept: it raises the specter of courts deciding which products may and may not be distributed, and they perceive it as a judicial usurpation of legislative authority.

Bogus, War on the Common Law: The Struggle at the Center of Products Liability, 60 Mo. L. Rev. 1, 8–9 (1995).

**14.** As for cigarettes, compare Wertheimer, The Smoke Gets In Their Eyes: Product Category Liability and Alternative Feasible Designs in the Third Restatement, 61 Tenn. L. Rev. 1429, 1444 (1994) ("a product which is dangerous, useless, and without feasible alternative design is the cigarette"), with G. Schwartz, Cigarette Litigation's Offspring: Assessing Tort Issues

Related to Guns, Alcohol, & Other Controversial Products In Light of the Tobacco Wars, 27 Pepp. L. Rev. 751, 751 (2000) (noting such "undeniably significant benefits" of cigarettes as their flavor, ability to enhance concentration, and service as antidepressants and tranquilizers—making them, "[t]o that extent, a kind of miracle drug [that is] available without going through the costly intervention of any physician").

**15.** The Products Liability Restatement Reporters note three such cases: Halphen v. Johns–Manville Sales Corp., 484 So.2d 110 (La. 1986) (asbestos manufacturer subject to strict liability for products that fail broad social risk-utility test); Kelley v. R.G. Indus., 497 A.2d 1143 (Md. 1985) (manufacturer of "Saturday Night Special" cheap handgun subject to liability for criminal use of gun where its overall danger exceeded its overall benefits); and O'Brien v. Muskin Corp., 463 A.2d 298, 306 (N.J. 1983) (slippery vinyl bottom of above-ground swimming pool rendered pool defective even if no way to avoid risk). Each of these cases was overruled by statute. See Products Liability Restatement § 2 cmt. *d* Reporters' Note § IV(D).

One case that articulates the global risk-utility ("macro-balancing") approach to design liability in dictum (since the case involved warnings claims) and that distinguishes this approach from the conventional, narrower, micro-balance standard is Beshada v. Johns–Manville Prods. Corp., 447 A.2d 539, 545 (N.J. 1982) (asbestos):

> [W]e can distinguish two tests for determining whether a product is safe: (1) does

commentators[16] have taken the position that a product can fail a risk-utility test applied to a product considered *as a whole,* as distinguished from the normal risk-utility test based on proof that the manufacturer's failure to adopt a particular safety feature rendered the product defectively designed.[17] In some cases, the argument goes, even though there is no practicable way to design away the product's inherent danger, a product may be adjudged defective at a global level if it fails a "macro-balance" of its social costs and benefits—if, on balance and in the aggregate, the product is simply "bad." Yet the vast majority of courts have been markedly unreceptive to the call that they displace markets, legislatures, and governmental agencies by decreeing whole categories of products to be product "outlaws."[18]

Both the *Second* and *Third Restatements* endorse this highly restrained judicial approach. The *Second Restatement* addresses unavoidably dangerous products—such as food, alcohol, cigarettes, and drugs—in comments *i, j,* and *k.* These comments make clear that a manufacturer

its utility outweigh its risk? and (2) if so, has that risk been reduced to the greatest extent possible consistent with the product's utility? The first question looks to the product as it was in fact marketed. If that product caused more harm than good, it was not reasonably fit for its intended purposes. We can therefore impose strict liability for the injuries it caused without having to determine whether it could have been rendered safer. The second aspect of strict liability, however, requires that the risk from the product be reduced to the greatest extent possible without hindering its utility. Whether or not the product passes the initial risk-utility test, it is not reasonably safe if the same product could have been made or marketed more safely.

Also in dictum, other courts have opined that, in rare cases, a court may justifiably find that a product's overall dangers exceed its overall social benefits. See, e.g., Armentrout v. FMC Corp., 842 P.2d 175, 185 n.8 (Colo. 1992) (en banc); Kallio v. Ford Motor Co., 407 N.W.2d 92, 97 n.8 (Minn. 1987) ("Conceivably, rare cases may exist where the product may be judged unreasonably dangerous because it should be removed from the market rather than be redesigned...."); Rix v. General Motors Corp., 723 P.2d 195, 201 (Mont. 1986); Wilson v. Piper Aircraft Corp., 577 P.2d 1322, 1328 n.5 (Or. 1978).

**16.** See, e.g., Bogus, The Third Revolution in Products Liability, 72 Chi.-Kent L. Rev. 3 (1996); Bell, Children's Lives, Indonesians' Lives, and Generic Liability, 72 Chi.-Kent L. Rev. 21 (1996); Wertheimer, Unavoidably Unsafe Products: A Modest Proposal, 72 Chi.-Kent L. Rev. 189 (1996) Bogus, War on the Common Law: The

Struggle at the Center of Products Liability, 60 Mo. L. Rev. 1, 8–9 (1995). See also Page, Liability for Unreasonably and Unavoidably Unsafe Products: Does Negligence Doctrine Have a Role to Play?, 72 Chi.-Kent L. Rev. 87 (1996).

**17.** On the perils of judicial "macro-balancing," as contrasted to the properly more limited judicial task of "micro-balancing" the costs and benefits of particular design improvements, see Owen, Risk-Utility Balancing in Design Defect Cases, 30 U. Mich. L. Rev. 239 (1997); Owen, Toward a Proper Test for Design Defectiveness: "Micro-Balancing" Costs and Benefits, 75 Tex. L. Rev. 1661 (1997) (explaining that proper design defect determinations rest upon a balance of the marginal costs and benefits of particular alternative design features); Products Liability Restatement, cmt. *f* Reporter's Note.

**18.** See, e.g., Jones v. Amazing Prods., Inc., 231 F.Supp.2d 1228, 1248–51 (N.D. Ga. 2002) (drain cleaner containing 97% sulfuric acid). For individual products, see cases cited below. See generally Products Liability Restatement § 2(b), Reporters Note to comment *d,* IV(D), at 87 et seq. Judicial decisions do not of course truly outlaw the sale of such products because manufacturers may continue to sell the product and compensate persons injured thereby. See Owen, Product Outlaws, 10 Kans. J. L. & Pub. Pol'y 126 (2000). Manufacturers of cigarettes and cheap handguns could ill afford, of course, to pay for all the harm they cause without increasing the prices of these products considerably. But a judicial policy that would require manufacturers to internalize the full injury costs of such products, despite its inefficiency, does have a variety of social benefits to commend it. See § 5.4, above.

of such unavoidably dangerous products must avoid manufacturing defects (such as contamination) and must warn of hidden dangers. But the central message of the *Second Restatement*'s comments, responding to the central concern at the time over the reach of the new strict liability doctrine, is that a manufacturer of useful but unavoidably dangerous products is not liable for making them available to a public who desires them despite knowing of their inherent risks.[19]

The *Third Restatement* emphatically adheres to the principle that entire categories of products commonly understood to be inherently dangerous (such as alcoholic beverages, firearms, and above-ground swimming pools—but not cigarettes[20]) cannot as a general rule be judicially classified as "defective" in *design*. That is, the *Third Restatement* takes the position that plaintiffs in design defect cases generally must establish that the manufacturer failed to adopt a reasonable method for designing out the danger—an impossible task, of course, if a product's inherent risks are, by hypothesis, unavoidable.[21] Similar to the *Second Restatement*, however, the *Third Restatement* proclaims that provisional immunity from design liability in no way immunizes manufacturers of inherently dangerous products from the duties to *manufacture* such products free of dangerous defects or to *warn* consumers of any foreseeable, hidden dangers they may contain, for these are independent duties of manufacturers of every type of product.[22] In addition, the *Third Restatement* recognizes that some courts[23] have quite reasonably retained wiggle room to rule, in rare cases, that an "egregiously unacceptable" product may be of "manifestly unreasonable design," even if there is no reasonable way to design the danger away—cases where "the extremely high degree of danger posed by its use or consumption so substantially outweighs its negligible social utility that no rational, reasonable person, fully aware of the relevant facts, would choose to use, or to allow

---

**19.** See, e.g., Myers v. Philip Morris Cos., 50 P.3d 751, 755–56 (Cal. 2002). See also § 6.2, above.

**20.** Products Liability Restatement § 2 cmt. *d,* at 21 (Proposed Final Draft, April 1, 1997) included tobacco among the small category of products immunized from judicial scrutiny. During the American Law Institute debate on final approval, Professor Dratler of the University of Hawaii moved to strike the word "tobacco" from the list, arguing that the then escalating assault on the tobacco industry made ALI sanctuary for tobacco inappropriate. Over objection by the Reporters, who reasoned that the law did not justify removing tobacco from its protected position, the ALI membership voted narrowly to strike tobacco from the list of examples of generically dangerous products for which manufacturers are not subject to claims for defective design. See A.L.I. Proceedings 209–10 (1997); Henderson and Twerski, Achieving Consensus on Defective Product Design, 83 Cornell L. Rev. 867 (1998); Givelber, Cigarette Law,

73 Ind. L.J. 867, 871 (1998); ALI Membership Grants Final Approval to Influential Product Liability Treatise, 25 Prod. Safety and Liab. Rep. (BNA) No. 21, at 509 (May 23, 1997); § 8.8, above. The cigarette litigation is briefly discussed later in this section.

**21.** See, e.g., Jones v. Amazing Prods., Inc., 231 F.Supp.2d 1228, 1248–51 (N.D. Ga. 2002) (sulfuric acid drain cleaner). See generally Products Liability Restatement § 2 cmt. *d* (recognizing that "courts generally have concluded that legislatures and administrative agencies can, more appropriately than courts, consider the desirability of commercial distribution of some categories of widely used and consumed, but nevertheless dangerous, products").

**22.** See Products Liability Restatement § 2 cmt. *d;* § 6.2, above.

**23.** See Products Liability Restatement § 2(b), Reporters Note to comment *d,* IV(D), at 87 (entitled "Rejection by a Majority of Jurisdictions of Liability Based on Nondefective Products That Are Nevertheless Egregiously Dangerous").

children to use, the product."[24] This category of egregiously dangerous products is at once very narrow yet open-ended, and it might fairly include such products as toy guns that shoot hard pellets at high velocity,[25] exploding novelty cigars,[26] lawn darts,[27] and clothing made of highly flammable fabrics.[28] While it may well be that products like these should be banned altogether by legislatures or administrative safety agencies (as they sometimes are), it seems self-evident that courts should allow products liability claims by persons injured by products that in fact can be proven to produce far more social harm than good.[29] Yet the list of such products must properly be short, including only products that courts can be confident possess far greater risk than utility, such that they probably should not be sold at all. Moreover, courts should be wary of allowing such claims to go to the jury and so normally should bar such claims as a matter of law.[30]

## Particular Products

While commentators debate the desirability of a broad or narrow judicial role in cases involving design liability for inherent product risks, the courts have been busy handling expanding dockets involving litigation over products containing substantial inherent dangers of various types. Alcohol, cigarettes, and firearms might be singled out as prototypical products containing inherent risks that victims have sought to shift judicially to manufacturers. Many other types of products might be classified as inherently dangerous, some of which have generated very little litigation—such as marshmallows, peanut butter, snow sleds, jungle gyms, baby walkers, bullet-proof vests, and aluminum baseball bats;[31] other types of products whose dangers are great enough to trigger substantial litigation—such as ladders,[32] power boat motors,[33] and tram-

---

**24.** Id. cmt. *e*.

**25.** See id.

**26.** See id. Illus. 5.

**27.** See, e.g., Aimone by Aimone v. Walgreen's Co., 601 F.Supp. 507 (D.C. Ill. 1985). Lawn darts long ago were banned by the Consumer Product Safety Commission.

**28.** See, e.g., Abels v. Murjani Int'l, Ltd., Prod. Liab. Rep. (CCH) ¶ 11,229 (D. Kan. 1986) (blouse); Carter v. Joseph Bancroft & Sons Co., 360 F.Supp. 1103 (E.D. Pa. 1973) (dress); LaGorga v. Kroger Co., 275 F.Supp. 373 (W.D. Pa. 1967) (jacket); Chapman v. Brown, 198 F.Supp. 78 (D. Haw. 1961) (hula skirt). See generally Noel, Manufacturer's Negligence of Design or Directions for Use of a Product, 71 Yale L.J. 816, 844–45 (1962). Note, however, that flame retardants often can reduce the flammability of fabrics so that excessive flammability normally is not an unavoidable hazard. See, e.g., Gryc v. Dayton–Hudson Corp., 297 N.W.2d 727 (Minn. 1980); *LaGorga*, 275 F.Supp. at 380.

**29.** See Owen, The Graying of Products Liability Law: Paths Taken and Untaken in the New Restatement, 61 Tenn. L. Rev. 1241, 1253–57 (1994).

**30.** See, e.g., Jones v. Amazing Prods., Inc., 231 F.Supp.2d 1228, 1248–51 (N.D. Ga. 2002) (drain cleaner containing 97% sulfuric acid; manufacturer's motion for summary judgment granted on claim that product was too dangerous to sell at all).

**31.** See, e.g., Thongchoom v. Graco Children's Prods., Inc., 71 P.3d 214 (Wash. Ct. App. 2003) (baby walker); Sanchez v. Hillerich & Bradsby Co., 128 Cal.Rptr.2d 529 (Ct. App. 2002) (bat); Emery v. Federated Foods, Inc., 863 P.2d 426 (Mont. 1993) (marshmallow); Jordon v. K–Mart Corp., 611 A.2d 1328 (Pa. Super. Ct. 1992) (sled); Cozzi v. North Palos Elementary Sch. Dist., 597 N.E.2d 683 (Ill. App. Ct. 1992) (jungle gym); Linegar v. Armour of Am., Inc., 909 F.2d 1150 (8th Cir. 1990) (Mo. law) (vest); Fraust v. Swift & Co., 610 F.Supp. 711 (W.D. Pa. 1985) (peanut butter).

**32.** See, e.g., Fayerweather v. Menard, Inc., 659 N.W.2d 506 (Wis. Ct. App. 2003) (fall); Hoeft v. Louisville Ladder Co., 904 S.W.2d 298 (Mo. Ct. App. 1995) (aluminum ladder hit power line).

**33.** See, e.g., Sprietsma v. Mercury Marine, a Div. of Brunswick Corp., 537 U.S. 51

polines;[34] and some whose dangers are so substantial and widespread as to spawn a multitude of lawsuits around the nation—such as various prescription drugs, asbestos, lead paint, and, most recently, fast foods.[35] Except for the last type of case, which has just recently peeped onto the judicial landscape,[36] a court or lawyer confronting litigation concerning inherently dangerous products of latter types may draw from the enormous body of case law and commentary on each of these particular areas of litigation.[37]

Judicial decisions in cases involving the liability of manufacturers of such generically dangerous products as those described above involve a panoply of complex issues, substantive and procedural, and only rarely do they address the underlying social welfare question of whether such a product may be characterized as defective (in design) because its global injury costs exceed its global social benefits. Occasionally, however, courts do address issues of personal autonomy that lie close to the heart of these cases—concepts of free choice and individual responsibility— concepts which support the idea that consumers who choose to accept the benefits of an obviously and unavoidably dangerous product must accept responsibility for the product's risks as well. Sometimes this powerful ideal finds doctrinal expression in the consumer expectations test of product defectiveness, or in rules on assumption of risk or no duty to warn of commonly known dangers, but more often it lies hidden below discussions of unrelated legal doctrines. Embedded to some extent in the rules of products liability law,[38] the value of personal responsibility assuredly is the reason why plaintiffs have had such little success in convincing courts and juries that manufacturers should pay for the hundreds of thousands of American smokers who die each year.

The following discussions highlight a number of recurring issues that have arisen in litigation on several types of products whose notoriety springs from the substantial hazards they contain that are generic to such products. As discussed below, most of the litigation involving generically dangerous products has been brought by private plaintiffs (individually and collectively), but, increasingly, such claims also have been instituted by cities, states, and national governments.

### *Alcoholic Beverages*

While alcoholic beverages provide widespread pleasure and relaxation, they also wreak widespread harm. Alcoholism, liver and other

---

(2002) (boat passenger killed when he fell from boat and was struck by propeller blades of motor that was not equipped with propeller guard; *held*, federal preemption doctrine did not bar design defect claim).

**34.** See, e.g., Sollami v. Eaton, 772 N.E.2d 215 (Ill. 2002); Anderson v. Hedstrom Corp., 76 F.Supp.2d 422 (S.D.N.Y. 1999).

**35.** For prescription drugs, see §§ 8.10 and 9.6, above. For asbestos, lead paint, and fast foods, see discussions below.

**36.** See Pelman v. McDonald's Corp., 237 F.Supp.2d 512 (S.D.N.Y. 2003) (dis-

missing claims); Pelman v. McDonald's Corp., 2003 WL 22052778 (S.D.N.Y. 2003) (ditto, more emphatically). See generally Ausness, Tell Me What You Eat and I Will Tell You Who to Sue: Big Problems Ahead for "Big Food?", 39 Ga. L. Rev. No. 3 (2005).

**37.** Sources are compiled below by type of product.

**38.** See Owen, The Moral Foundations of Products Liability Law: Toward First Principles, 68 Notre Dame L. Rev. 427 (1993).

diseases, birth defects, car accidents, family discord, and violence follow all too frequently as direct results of alcohol consumption.[39] Put simply, "water is best."[40] Although one might plausibly argue that alcohol consumption causes society more harm than good—that its social costs exceed its social benefits—the courts and *Torts Restatements* reject this form of macro-balance risk-utility reasoning because the dangers of alcohol beverages are inherent, unavoidable, and widely known. Indeed, almost all adults know and understand, at least in a general way, the variety of serious risks that can result from the excessive consumption of alcohol. Accordingly, and because over-consumption is plainly product misuse,[41] ordinary alcoholic beverages cannot reasonably be viewed as defective.

The unavoidability of alcohol's inherent dangers—intoxication and disease—is highlighted in two comments to § 402A of the *Restatement (Second) of Torts*. Comment *i* uses alcoholic beverages as a prime example of how products that contain commonly known dangers cannot be classified as "unreasonably dangerous." Noting that "any food or drug necessarily involves some risk of harm, if only from over-consumption," comment *i* declares that the strict liability doctrine only applies to a product that is "dangerous to an extent beyond that which would be contemplated by the ordinary consumer who purchases it, with the ordinary knowledge common to the community as to its characteristics. Good whiskey is not unreasonably dangerous merely because it will make some people drunk, and is especially dangerous to alcoholics." The *Third Restatement* continues this safe harbor for alcoholic beverages from defectiveness in design.[42] Nor do manufacturers have a duty to *warn* consumers about the dangers of drinking alcoholic beverages in excess because these dangers already are widely known.[43] Accordingly,

---

**39.** See Cochran, From Cigarettes to Alcohol: The Next Step in Hedonic Product Liability?, 27 Pepp. L. Rev. 701 (2000); Le-Bel, John Barleycorn Must Pay—Compensating the Victims of Drinking Drivers (1992); Vaillant, The National History of Alcoholism: Causes, Patterns, and Paths to Recovery (1988); Novello, Underage Drinking—A Report from the Surgeon General, 268 JAMA 961 (1992); Holden, Probing the Complex Genetics of Alcoholism, 251 Science 163 (Jan. 11, 1991); Note, One Last Attempt at Liability for "Vice" Products: A Different Ending to the "Willie Story" Story?, 99 Com. L.J. 108 (1994); Note, Texas Supreme Court Refuses to Impose a Duty to Warn of Alcoholism Upon Beverage Alcohol Manufacturers: Joseph E. Seagram & Sons, Inc. v. McGuire, 22 Tex. Tech. L. Rev. 937 (1991); Note, Fetal Alcohol Syndrome: Liability for Failure to Warn—Should Liquor Manufacturers Pick Up the Tab?, 28 J. Fam. L. 71 (1990); Note, In Support of Hon v. Stroh Brewery Co.: A Brewing Debate Over Extending Liability to Manufacturers of Alcoholic Beverages, 51 U. Pitt. L. Rev. 197 (1989); Annot., Products Liability: Alcoholic Beverages, 42 A.L.R.4th 253 (1985); 2 Frumer and Friedman, Products Liability

§ 12.07; 5 Am. Law Prod. Liab. § 83:12 et seq.

**40.** Pindar, Olympian Odes, cited in Note, 31 Wm. & Mary L. Rev. 157 n.1 (1989). *But see* Gash, Beyond Erin Brockovich and a Civil Action: Should Strict Products Liability Be the Next Frontier for Water Contamination Lawsuits?, 80 Wash. U.L.Q. 51 (2002).

**41.** Although it is foreseeable and, hence, falls outside of the conventional definition of this "defense." See § 13.5, below.

**42.** See Products Liability Restatement § 2 cmt. *d*. See, e.g., Bruner v. Anheuser–Busch, Inc., 153 F.Supp.2d 1358 (S.D. Fla. 2001), aff'd, 31 Fed.Appx. 932 (11th Cir. 2002) (table).

**43.** See, e.g., Bruner v. Anheuser–Busch, Inc., 153 F.Supp.2d 1358, 1360 (S.D. Fla. 2001) (noting "the 'universal recognition of all potential dangers associated with alcohol' "), aff'd, 31 Fed.Appx. 932 (11th Cir. 2002) (table); Joseph E. Seagram & Sons, Inc. v. McGuire, 814 S.W.2d 385, 388 (Tex. 1991) ("From ancient times, the danger of alcoholism from prolonged and exces-

most decisions have held that manufacturers of uncontaminated alcoholic beverages simply are not subject to liability in negligence, implied warranty, or strict liability in tort for harm from their consumption.[44] But a couple of courts,[45] supported by some commentators,[46] have taken the not unreasonable position that manufacturers should have a duty to warn of dangers of alcohol consumption and disease that consumers only poorly understand, such as the risk of death from diseases other than of the liver or from a single act of over-consumption.[47] However, now that the duty to warn is mandated by federal statute, most warnings claims would appear to be barred by the doctrine of federal preemption,[48] as they may also be precluded by an inherent-risk provision of a state reform act, both of which are discussed below. For all of these reasons, it is safe to conclude as a general proposition that manufacturers of alcoholic beverages are not liable for injuries resulting from their consumption.[49]

sive consumption of alcoholic beverages has been widely known and recognized."); Morris v. Adolph Coors Co., 735 S.W.2d 578, 583 (Tex. Ct. App. 1987) ("The ordinary consumer in today's society ... knows of the dangers of driving while intoxicated."); Pemberton v. American Distilled Spirits Co., 664 S.W.2d 690, 693 (Tenn. 1984).

The Restatement (2d) Torts § 402A cmt. *j* provides that a seller does not have a duty to warn with respect to products that are dangerous only "when consumed in excessive quantity, or over a long period of time, when the danger, or potentiality of danger, is generally known and recognized. Again the dangers of alcoholic beverages are an example.... " The Third Restatement provides, in comment *j* to § 2, that sellers need not warn about risks "that should be obvious to, or generally known by, foreseeable product users."

**44.** See, e.g., Joseph E. Seagram & Sons, Inc. v. McGuire, 814 S.W.2d 385, 388 (Tex. 1991) (consolidated action by three alcoholics against manufacturers and distributors of various alcoholic beverages for failing to warn of risk of developing alcoholism from prolonged and excessive consumption of alcoholic beverages; no duty to warn of this widely known danger); Morris v. Adolph Coors Co., 735 S.W.2d 578, 583 (Tex. Ct. App. 1987) (injuries in car accident caused by driver drunk on beer; tort, warranty and statutory claims against manufacturer all dismissed); Maguire v. Pabst Brewing Co., 387 N.W.2d 565 (Iowa 1986) (no recovery against brewer for injuries from automobile collision caused by driver drunk on Pabst beer); Pemberton v. American Distilled Spirits Co., 664 S.W.2d 690 (Tenn. 1984) (death from single overdose of grain alcohol; no duty to warn of dangers apparent to ordinary user under Tennessee Products Liability Act); Garrison v. Heublein, Inc., 673 F.2d 189 (7th Cir. 1982) (Ill. law) (no liability for physical and mental

injuries from consumption of Smirnoff vodka over 20 years).

**45.** See Hon v. Stroh Brewery Co., 835 F.2d 510 (3d Cir. 1987) (Pa. law) (risk of death from pancreatitis caused by long-term moderate beer consumption); Brune v. Brown Forman Corp., 758 S.W.2d 827 (Tex. Ct. App. 1988) (risk of death to co-ed from acute alcohol poisoning from chugging tequila).

**46.** See, e.g., Notes, 22 Tex. Tech. L. Rev. 937 (1991) (noting *McGuire* disapprovingly); 51 U. Pitt. L. Rev. 179 (1989) (noting *Hon* approvingly); 31 Wm. & Mary L. Rev. 157 (1989); 38 Emory L.J. 1189, 1205–06 (1989) (concluding that "the Restatement's use of alcohol as an example of a product in which all of its dangers are common knowledge is out of step with medical advancement" and approving *Hon* and *Brune*); 11 Nova L. Rev. 1611, 1612 (1987) ("holding alcohol manufacturers liable for injuries and deaths caused by their products is both desirable and logical").

**47.** Another risk that still may not be fully appreciated, warned of by the Surgeon General, is the risk of fetal alcohol syndrome that may be caused by alcohol consumption during pregnancy, which may cause birth defects in the brain, nervous system, heart, limb, and face. See Prod. Saf. & Liab. Rep. (BNA) 11 (Jan. 1, 1988); Note, 28 J. Fam. L. 71 (1990). As discussed below, the Federal Labeling Act now requires a general warning of this risk.

**48.** See, e.g., Comment, 38 Emory L.J. 1189 (1989) (preempted); *but see* Note, 18 Hofstra L. Rev. 943 (1990); see generally § 14.4, below.

**49.** The proposition is limited to a general one to allow room for claims of contamination and fraudulent advertising. See Comment, 38 Emory L.J. 1189 (1989). The

### Cigarettes

**In general.** Few health hazards are as significant to the nation and world as cigarette smoking. Some 50 million Americans presently are smokers, over 400,000 of whom die from lung cancer, heart disease, and other tobacco-caused illnesses each year, as do another 4½ million people in other nations around the globe.[50] In the late 1990s and early 2000s, litigation against tobacco manufacturers—including the state health-care expense recoupment cases that resulted in a $246 billion settlement between the states and the tobacco industry,[51] and a $146 billion punitive damages verdict in a smoker class action in Florida,[52] now reversed[53] —figured among the most high-profile products liability litigation in America.[54]

During the early 1900s, when products liability was in its infancy, little thought was given to holding manufacturers of cigarettes liable for the illnesses they might cause. Indeed, during the 1930s, manufacturers advertised some cigarettes as "harmless" and even "healthful."[55] As the years progressed, however, knowledge about the harmful effects of smoking cigarettes mounted; by the 1950s, when about half of all American adults were smokers,[56] studies had begun to establish a clear link between cigarettes and disease.[57] Public disclosure of this connection promptly led to a ten percent drop in cigarette consumption over a two year period, spurring the industry to engage the services of a public relations firm to help it combat the growing concern over cigarettes and health.[58] The consultant's advice to the industry was to attack the health

courts have been unreceptive to deceptive advertising claims based on conventional "good life" advertising. See, e.g., Bruner v. Anheuser–Busch, Inc., 153 F. Supp. 2d 1358 (S.D. Fla. 2001), aff'd, 31 Fed.Appx. 932 (11th Cir. 2002); Overton v. Anheuser–Busch Co., 517 N.W.2d 308 (Mich. Ct. App. 1994) (Bud Lite ads showing "fantasies coming to life, fantasies involving tropical setting, and beautiful women and men engaged in unrestricted merriment" were merely puffs, not false statements of fact); Joseph E. Seagram & Sons, Inc. v. McGuire, 814 S.W.2d 385, 388 (Tex. 1991); Morris v. Adolph Coors Co., 735 S.W.2d 578, 583 (Tex. App. 1987).

**50.** See Langley, U.S. to Support World Tobacco—Control Treaty, www.nytimes.com (May 18, 2003) (citing national figure and WHO estimate of 4.9 million annual cigarette deaths around the world, a number it forecasts to double over the next 10 years); Birnbrich, Forcing Round Classes into Square Rules: Attempting Certification of Nicotine Addiction-as-Injury Class Actions under Federal Rule of Civil Procedure 23(B)(3), 29 U. Tol. L. Rev. 699, 699 (1998); Wertheimer, The Smoke Gets In Their Eyes: Product Category Liability and Alternative Feasible Designs in the Third Restatement, 61 Tenn. L. Rev. 1429, 1447–48 n.59 (1994) (450,000 deaths in U.S. per year).

**51.** This litigation is discussed below.

**52.** R.J. Reynolds Tobacco Co. v. Engle, 672 So.2d 39 (Fla. Dist. Ct. App. 1996) (upholding class certification).

**53.** Liggett Group Inc. v. Engle, 853 So.2d 434 (Fla. Dist. Ct. App. 2003).

**54.** See, e.g., Wertheimer, Pandora's Humidor: Tobacco Producer Liability in Tort, 24 N. Ky. L. Rev. 397 (1997); Wertheimer, The Smoke Gets In Their Eyes: Product Category Liability and Alternative Feasible Designs in the Third Restatement, 61 Tenn. L. Rev. 1469 (1994).

**55.** See, e.g., Pritchard v. Liggett & Myers Tobacco Co., 295 F.2d 292, 296–97 (3d Cir. 1961) (Pa. Law) (Chesterfields); Cooper v. R.J. Reynolds Tobacco Co., 234 F.2d 170, 174–75 (1st Cir. 1956) (Magruder, J., concurring), on reappeal 256 F.2d 464 (1st Cir. 1958) (Mass. law) (Camels).

**56.** See, Rabin, The Third Wave of Tobacco Tort Litigation, in Regulating Tobacco 176 (R. Rabin and S. Sugarman eds., 2001).

**57.** See Givelber, Cigarette Law, 73 Ind. L.J. 867, 889 (1998).

**58.** See id.; Rabin, A Sociolegal History of the Tobacco Tort Litigation, 44 Stan. L. Rev. 853, 858 (1992).

matter head-on by creating a supposedly independent organization, the Tobacco Industry Research Committee, for the supposed purpose of studying the relationship of tobacco smoking and disease. From this point forward, the industry's message to smokers was united, plain, and unequivocal: cigarettes do not cause cancer.[59]

As products liability litigation began to accelerate during the 1960s, the cigarette industry sought legal cover. Two powerful developments in this decade served to construct a strong fortress around the tobacco industry for most of the remainder of the twentieth century: the inclusion of tobacco in the safe harbor provided by the *Restatement (Second) of Torts* for certain inherently dangerous products[60] and federal labeling legislation mandating that manufacturers place certain warnings by the Surgeon General about smoking hazards on cigarette packages—an Act of Congress that served at once to provide the industry with an iron-clad assumption of risk defense together with a defense to inadequate warning claims based on federal preemption.[61]

**Smoker litigation.** Tobacco litigation, the subject of unrelenting scholarly debate,[62] has been divided into three waves: the first, from 1954 to the 1960s or early 1970s; the second, from the early 1980s to the early 1990s; and the third, beginning in the early to mid–1990s and continuing to the present.[63] Prior to the third wave, the tobacco industry was an "impenetrable fortress,"[64] litigating hard and boasting that it had never paid a dime in damages in the hundreds of lawsuits it had defended since

---

**59.** Id. See also Williams v. Philip Morris Inc., 48 P.3d 824 (Or. Ct. App. 2002) (reviewing history of cigarette marketing), vacated and remanded for reconsideration, Philip Morris USA, Inc. v. Williams, 124 S.Ct. 56 (2003), reconsidered and reinstated, 92 P.3d 126 (Or. Ct. App. 2004).

**60.** Restatement (2d) Torts § 402A cmt. i.

**61.** Givelber, above, at 889–90. The Supreme Court's holding on the preemptive effect of this legislation is examined in § 14.4, below.

**62.** See, e.g., LeBel and Ausness, Toward Justice in Tobacco Policymaking: A Critique of Hanson and Logue and an Alternative Approach to the Costs of Cigarettes, 33 Ga. L. Rev. 393 (1999) (moral theory suggests imposing an excise tax on cigarettes and allowing industry immunity from tort liability except for fraud), critiquing Hanson and Logue, The Costs of Cigarettes: The Economic Case for Ex Post Incentive–Based Regulation, 107 Yale L.J. 1163 (1998) (economic theory suggests strict tort liability and an administrative smokers compensation program).

**63.** See, e.g., Rabin, The Third Wave of Tobacco Tort Litigation, in Regulating Tobacco 176 (R. Rabin and S. Sugarman eds., 2001); Cupp, A Morality Play's Third Act: Revisiting Addiction, Fraud, and Consumer Choice in "Third Wave" Tobacco Litigation,

46 U. Kan. L. Rev. 465 (1998); Galligan, A Primer on Cigarette Litigation Under the Restatement (Third) of Torts: Products Liability, 27 Sw. U. L. Rev. 487 (1998); Vandall, The Legal Theory and the Visionaries that Led to the Proposed $368.5 Billion Tobacco Settlement, 27 Sw. U. L. Rev. 473, 473–76 (1998); Kelder and Daynard, The Role of Litigation in the Effective Control of the Sale and Use of Tobacco, 8 Stan. L. & Pol'y Rev. 63, 71 (1997); LeBel, "Of Deaths Put on by Cunning and Forced Cause"; Reality Bites the Tobacco Industry, 38 Wm. & Mary L. Rev. 605 (1997); Sarafa, Making Tobacco Companies Pay: The Florida Medicaid Third–Party Liability Act, 2 DePaul J. Health Care L. 123, 127–32 (1997); G. Schwartz, Tobacco Liability in the Courts, in Smoking Policy: Law, Politics, and Culture (R. Rabin and S. Sugarman eds., 1992) (describing first and second waves); Rabin, A Sociolegal History of the Tobacco Tort Litigation, 44 Stan. L. Rev. 853, 874 (1992); Daynard, The Third Wave of Tobacco Products Liability Cases, Trial 34 (Nov. 1992); Stein, Cigarette Products Liability Law in Transition, 54 Tenn. L. Rev. 631 (1987) (first wave); Edell, Cigarette Litigation: The Second Wave, 22 Tort & Ins. L.J. 90 (1986); Note, Legigation, 79 Tex. L. Rev. 1727 (2001); 5 Frumer and Friedman, § 56; 3 Am. Law Prod. Liab. 3d § 88.20.

**64.** Note, J. L. & Health 297, 298 (1999–2000).

the 1950s.[65] In the first wave, the plaintiffs' claims for negligence, breach of warranty,[66] and deceit were burdened by the absence of substantial scientific evidence linking smoking with disease. Sparing no expense and tenaciously defending each case, the tobacco lawyers were consistently victorious.[67] In the second wave, the plaintiffs had considerably better scientific evidence on causation, but their strict liability in tort design and warnings claims were encumbered by § 402A comment *i*'s safe haven for tobacco and by the freedom of choice argument that smokers knew that smoking could be dangerous yet voluntarily assumed the risk.[68] The tobacco lawyers ruthlessly fought on, relentlessly outspending every plaintiff's lawyer, and winning every case.[69]

In the third wave of tobacco litigation, spurred in part by new revelations of misleading and manipulative conduct by the tobacco industry, the cigarette industry's fortunes began to change. First, after several years in the lower courts, the Supreme Court in 1992 decided the carefully prosecuted case of *Cipollone v. Liggett Group, Inc.*[70] Although the Supreme Court ruled in *Cipollone* that the Congressionally mandated cigarette warnings preempted the plaintiffs' inadequate warning claims, the Court ruled that certain other claims (such as design defectiveness, breach of express warranty, and fraud) lay outside the federal labeling act's preemptive reach.[71] In 1994, documents and testimony provided by two whistle-blowers from the tobacco industry, made public in the newspapers and in Congressional hearings on tobacco, revealed stark new evidence on the industry's conspiracy to deceive the public about the hazards of smoking and, in particular, the addictive qualities of nicotine.[72] As early as 1963, for example, one of the industry's top

**65.** See Cupp, above, at 468 n.17 (industry by then had prevailed in over 800 lawsuits); Birnbrich, above, at 700 (not "a single dollar"); Rachlinski, Regulating in Foresight Versus Judging Liability in Hindsight: The Case of Tobacco, 33 Ga. L. Rev. 813, 813 (1999) (not "one dime"); Rabin, above, at 874 (not "a cent").

**66.** On the implied warranty of merchantability in cigarette litigation, see Note, 63 Ohio St. L.J. 1165 (2002).

**67.** See, e.g., Ross v. Philip Morris & Co., 328 F.2d 3 (8th Cir. 1964) (Mo. law); Cooper v. R.J. Reynolds Tobacco Co., 234 F.2d 170 (1st Cir. 1956) (Mass. law). See generally Birnbrich, above, at 700.

**68.** "[T]he most salient theme in the second wave litigation has been freedom of choice.... [T]obacco litigation is a last vestige of a perhaps idealized vision of nineteenth century tort law as an interpersonal morality play. The sophisticated plaintiffs' lawyers ... counted on the advent of comparative fault, buttressed by their ability to depict a socially irresponsible industry overpromoting a highly dangerous product, to counter—or, at least, blunt—the personal choice argument. In doing so, ... they simply failed to grasp how intensely most jurors would react to

damage claims by individuals who were aware of the risks associated with smoking and nonetheless chose to continue the activity over a long time period." Rabin, above, at 870–71.

**69.** See, e.g., Rogers v. R.J. Tobacco Co., 745 N.E.2d 793 (Ind. 2001) (affirming trial court judgment on verdict for defendant in case initiated in 1980s); Roysdon v. R.J. Reynolds Co., 849 F.2d 230 (6th Cir. 1988) (Tenn. law). See generally Birnbrich, above, at 700; Rabin, A Sociolegal History of the Tobacco Tort Litigation, 44 Stan. L. Rev. 853, 867–68 (1992) (detailing tobacco industry's "no-holds-barred defense of every claim"). "As a tobacco industry lawyer would put it, ... the industry's hardball tactics made the litigation 'extremely burdensome and expensive for plaintiffs' lawyers.... To Paraphrase Gen. [George] Patton, the way we won these cases was not by spending all of Reynolds' money, but by making [the enemy] spend all of his.' " Rabin at 868.

**70.** 505 U.S. 504 (1992).

**71.** See § 14.4, below.

**72.** Both whistleblowers had worked for Brown & Williamson—one a paralegal at the company's defense law firm, who copied

lawyers observed that "[w]e are, then, in the business of selling nicotine, an addictive product."[73] These revelations, combined with increasing public antipathy toward "Big Tobacco," prompted the plaintiffs' bar, newly enriched from the coffers of the (former) asbestos industry, to pool their resources and aggressively begin the third round of litigation that has continued to this day.

In the post-*Cipollone* world, plaintiffs continue to lose many cases altogether,[74] but other courts have allowed such claims as negligence, design defectiveness, fraud, conspiracy, and failure to warn prior to the 1966 federal labeling act.[75] A recurring defense in the third wave litigation is that the dangers of smoking were common knowledge. This defense has known some success,[76] but it has been roundly rejected by

internal documents prior to his dismissal, and the other the head of research and development for the company, fired after years of contention over the company's failure responsibly to address the perils of tobacco. See Rabin, The Third Wave of Tobacco Tort Litigation, in Regulating Tobacco, at 183–85 (R. Rabin and S. Sugarman eds., 2001).

**73.** Id.

**74.** See, e.g., Tillman v. R.J. Reynolds Tobacco Co., 871 So.2d 28 (Ala. 2003) (obvious hazards of smoking precluded liability under consumer expectations test); Brown v. Philip Morris Inc., 228 F.Supp.2d 506, 521–25 (D.N.J. 2002) (applying statutory state-of-the-art defense); LaBelle v. Philip Morris Inc., 243 F.Supp.2d 508 (D.S.C. 2001) (Pa. law) (plaintiff failed to prove feasible alternative design); Hughes v. The Tobacco Institute, Inc., 278 F.3d 417 (5th Cir. 2001) (applying Texas' "inherently unsafe product" defense); Glassner v. R.J. Reynolds Tobacco Co., 223 F.3d 343 (6th Cir. 2000) (Ohio law); Lacey v. Lorillard Tobacco Co., 956 F.Supp. 956 (N.D. Ala. 1997); Toole v. Brown & Williamson Tobacco Corp., 980 F.Supp. 419 (N.D. Ala. 1997); Allgood v. R.J. Reynolds Tobacco Co., 80 F.3d 168 (5th Cir. 1996) (Tex. law); Sonnenreich v. Philip Morris, Inc., 929 F.Supp. 416 (S.D. Fla. 1996); Brown v. R.J. Reynolds Tobacco Co., 852 F.Supp. 8 (E.D. La. 1994), aff'd, 52 F.3d 524 (5th Cir. 1995).

**75.** See, e.g., Williams v. Philip Morris Inc., 48 P.3d 824 (Or. Ct. App. 2002), vacated and remanded for reconsideration, Philip Morris USA, Inc. v. Williams, ___ U.S. ___, 124 S.Ct. 56 (2003), reconsidered and reinstated, 92 P.3d 126 (Or. Ct. App. 2004); Wright v. Brooke Group Ltd., 652 N.W.2d 159 (Iowa 2002) (fraud; design defect; civil conspiracy; answering certified questions as to requirements of such claims); Burton v. R.J. Reynolds Tobacco Co., 205 F.Supp.2d 1253 (D. Kan. 2002) (negligent testing and research; failure to warn and fraudulent

concealment of addictive nature); Boerner v. Brown and Williamson Tobacco Corp., 260 F.3d 837 (8th Cir. 2001) (Ark. law) (design defect and pre–1966 warnings); Insolia v. Philip Morris, Inc., 216 F.3d 596, 598 (7th Cir. 2000) (Wis. law) (negligence); Tompkin v. American Brands, 219 F.3d 566, 572 (6th Cir. 2000) (Ohio law) (implied warranty; design defect and pre–1965 failure to warn); Wright v. Brooke Group Ltd., 114 F.Supp.2d 797 (N.D. Iowa 2000) (strict liability and negligence); Cantley v. Lorillard Tobacco Co., 681 So.2d 1057 (Ala. 1996) (design defect). See also Naegele v. R.J. Reynolds Tobacco Co., 50 P.3d 769 (Cal. 2002) (immunity statute only barred claims for "inherent" risks in their product and so did not bar claim that companies fraudulently adulterated cigarettes by increasing their nicotine content); Myers v. Philip Morris Cos., 50 P.3d 751 (Cal. 2002) (state's tobacco immunity statute enacted in 1987 and repealed in 1997 does not bar claims with respect to tobacco company conduct before or after 10–year immunity period).

**76.** See, e.g., Spain v. Brown & Williamson Tobacco Corp., 363 F.3d 1183 (11th Cir. 2004) (Ala. law); Tillman v. R.J. Reynolds Tobacco Co., 871 So.2d 28, 33–34 (Ala. 2003); Glassner v. R.J. Reynolds Tobacco Co., 223 F.3d 343 (6th Cir. 2000) (Ohio law); Sanchez v. Liggett & Myers, Inc., 187 F.3d 486 (5th Cir. 1999) (Tex. law); Allgood v. R.J. Reynolds Tobacco Co., 80 F.3d 168, 172 (5th Cir. 1996) (Tex. law) (" 'tobacco has been used for over 400 years.... Knowledge that cigarette smoking is harmful to health is widespread and can be considered part of the common knowledge of the community.' "). See also Insolia v. Philip Morris, Inc., 216 F.3d 596 (7th Cir. 2000) (Wis. law) (because smokers probably understood health risks of smoking including fact that it is habit-forming when they began smoking in 1935 and early 1950s, strict liability claims precluded under consumer expectations test).

other courts on a variety of grounds—"moral estoppel;"[77] that knowing the general hazards of smoking does not amount to knowing that it can cause particular diseases or that it can be highly addictive; and that the user's awareness of a product risk is not dispositive of liability but is merely one factor for consideration in a risk-utility analysis of defectiveness.[78] On convincing evidence of fraud and conspiracy, a few juries have returned substantial verdicts, comprised mostly of punitive damages, with some favorable appellate results.[79]

Claims other than those brought by individual smokers have met with varying success. In *Castano v. American Tobacco Company*,[80] plaintiffs brought a national class action which was certified by the trial court but reversed on appeal. Plaintiffs' counsel thereafter brought a large number of state class actions, almost all of which eventually were lost.[81]

---

**77.** "If there were such a thing as moral estoppel, the outcome of this appeal would be plain. For decades tobacco companies have assured the public that there is nothing to fear from cigarettes, yet they now slough off lawsuits like this one by professing that everybody knew all along that smoking was risky." Insolia v. Philip Morris, Inc., 216 F.3d 596, 598 (7th Cir. 2000) (Wis. law).

**78.** See, e.g., id.; Henley v. Philip Morris, Inc., 9 Cal. Rptr. 3d 29 (Ct. App. 2004); Tompkin v. American Brands, 219 F.3d 566, 572 (6th Cir. 2000) (Ohio law) ("The pertinent issue here is not whether the public knew that smoking was hazardous to health at some undifferentiated level, but whether it knew of the specific linkages between smoking and lung cancer. Public awareness of a broad-based and ambiguous risk that smoking might be tenuously connected to lung cancer does not suggest 'common knowledge' of the known scientific fact that cigarette smoking is a strong precipitant of lung cancer."); Wright v. Brooke Group Ltd., 652 N.W.2d 159, 170–71 (Iowa 2002) (answering certified questions); Wright v. Brooke Group Ltd., 114 F.Supp.2d 797, 810 (N.D. Iowa 2000) (thorough analysis of whether various smoking claims were barred by common knowledge doctrine, and concluding that, because "there is a considerable difference between knowing that smoking is bad and knowing that smoking is addictive," the risk of addiction is not a "lesser included risk" of the risks of smoking).

**79.** In a half century of litigation prior to the state settlements in the late 1990s, only three smokers had ever prevailed in cigarette litigation, two of whose cases were reversed on appeal; in the first four years following the settlement of state claims, individual smokers won 9 cases. See, e.g., R.J. Reynolds Tobacco Co. v. Kenyon, 856 So.2d 998 (Fla. Dist. Ct. App. 2003) (affirming compensatory award; table), discussed in 32 Prod. Saf. & Liab. Rep. 126 (2004);

Henley v. Philip Morris, Inc., 5 Cal.Rptr.3d 42 (Ct. App. 2003) (further remitting punitive damages award to $9 million, earlier remitted by trial court from $50 million to $25 million), review granted, 88 P.3d 497 (Cal. 2004); Burton v. R.J. Reynolds Tobacco Co., 205 F.Supp.2d 1253 (D. Kan. 2002) (on jury's authorization, court assessed punitive damages of $15 million); Williams v. Philip Morris Inc., 48 P.3d 824 (Or. Ct. App. 2002) (fraud; reinstating $79.5 million punitive damages verdict remitted by trial court to $32.8 million), vacated and remanded for reconsideration, Philip Morris USA, Inc. v. Williams, 124 S.Ct. 56 (2003), reconsidered and reinstated, 92 P.3d 126 (Or. Ct. App. 2004) (concluding that $79.5 million punitive award comported with due process inasmuch as it was reasonable and proportionate to the wrong to the plaintiff and the public in the state); Boeken v. Philip Morris, Inc., 19 Cal. Rptr.3d 101 (Ct. App. 2004) (affirming punitive damages award but further reducing it to $50 million; trial court had reduced $3 billion verdict to $100 million). See also Whiteley v. Philip Morris Inc., 11 Cal.Rptr.3d 807 (Ct. App. 2004) (reversing and remanding judgment for plaintiff but ruling that substantial evidence supported finding of fraud).

**80.** 160 F.R.D. 544 (E.D. La. 1995), rev'd, 84 F.3d 734 (5th Cir. 1996) (decertifying class). See Rabin, The Third Wave of Tobacco Tort Litigation, in Regulating Tobacco 179–89 (R. Rabin and S. Sugarman eds., 2001).

**81.** See, e.g., Estate of Mahoney v. R.J. Reynolds Tobacco Co., 204 F.R.D. 150 (S.D. Iowa 2001) (denying certification of class of Iowa smokers). See generally Rabin, above, at 188. The lawsuits were grounded in theories developed in Gangarosa, Vandall, and Willis, Suits by Public Hospitals to Recover Expenditures for the Treatment of Disease, Injury and Disability Caused by Tobacco

*R.J. Reynolds Tobacco Co. v. Engle*,[82] a smoker's class action brought in Florida, led to a spectacular verdict of $145 billion,[83] but the judgment was reversed and the class decertified on appeal.[84] An Illinois smoker class action for economic losses resulted in a verdict for $10.1 billion which is presently on appeal.[85] In addition, Judge Weinstein has certified a class action seeking punitive damages for fraud on behalf of most injured smokers in the United States.[86] A few claims have been brought for second-hand smoke, which have met with varying success.[87] And at least one proposed class action was filed (also in Florida) on behalf of users of chewing tobacco who claim to have suffered various cancers from the product.[88]

**Litigation by states, nations, and insurers.** Probably the most significant development yet in the cigarette litigation was the tobacco industry's settlement of the health care reimbursement claims brought by the American states.[89] During the mid–1990s, beginning with Mississippi, the individual states sued the industry on a number of grounds, including public nuisance, unjust enrichment, and restitution[90] to recoup their accumulated expenses for Medicaid health care expenditures resulting from tobacco use.[91] In 1998, after settling with Mississippi for $3.6

and Alcohol, 22 Fordham Urb. L.J. 81 (1994).

**82.** 672 So.2d 39 (Fla. Dist. Ct. App. 1996) (upholding certification of 300,000 to 700,000 Florida smokers suffering from tobacco diseases), review denied, 682 So.2d 1100 (Fla. 1996), noted, 18 T.M. Cooley L. Rev. 201 (2001).

**83.** Rabin, above, at 188.

**84.** Liggett Group Inc. v. Engle, 853 So.2d 434 (Fla. Dist. Ct. App. 2003).

**85.** Price v. Philip Morris, 793 N.E.2d 942 (Ill. App. Ct. 2003): on verdict of $7.1 billion compensatory damages, to recompense class for cost of purchased cigarettes, and $3 billion punitive damages award, trial court erred in reducing $12 billion appeal bond; state-wide class action for fraudulently marketing "light," "low tar," and "mild" cigarettes as safer than ordinary cigarettes, while knowing they did not lower the risk of lung cancer. See O'Connell and Zuckerman, Altria Verdict Unleashes Worries, Wall St. J. at C1 (Apr. 1, 2003).

**86.** In re Simon II Litigation, 211 F.R.D. 86 (E.D.N.Y. 2002) (Weinstein, J.) (certifying national tobacco class action seeking punitive damages for fraud).

**87.** See, e.g., Badillo v. American Brands, Inc., 16 P.3d 435 (Nev. 2001) (class of smokers and non-smokers exposed to second-hand smoke; claim for medical monitoring costs denied); Wolpin v. Philip Morris, Inc., 974 F.Supp. 1465 (S.D. Fla. 1997) (denying motion to dismiss claims for failing to warn of dangers of second-hand smoke, fraud, and civil conspiracy); Broin v. Philip Morris Cos., 641 So.2d 888 (Fla. Dist. Ct.

App. 1994) (ordering trial court to certify flight attendant class action).

**88.** See Haggman, Tobacco Wars Are Going Smokeless, Nat'l L.J. A10 (Nov. 18, 2002).

**89.** See Ausness, Public Tort Litigation: Public Benefit or Public Nuisance?, 77 Temp. L. Rev. No. 4 (2005); Luka, The Tobacco Industry and The First Amendment, An Analysis of The 1998 Master Settlement Agreement, 14 J.L. & Health 297 (1999–2000); Ratliff, Parens Patriae: An Overview, 74 Tulane L. Rev. 1847 (2000); Rachlinski, Regulating in Foresight Versus Judging Liability In Hindsight: The Case of Tobacco, 33 Ga. L. Rev. 813 (1999); Galligan, A Primer on Cigarette Litigation Under the Restatement (Third) of Torts: Products Liability, 27 Sw. U. L. Rev. 487 (1998); Note, 66 Brook. L. Rev. 549 (2000) (comparing public entity tobacco and gun litigations); Appendix III–Tobacco Settlement Summary, 2 J. Health Care L. & Pol'y 167 (1998); R. Rabin, The Third Wave of Tobacco Tort Litigation, in Regulating Tobacco (R. Rabin and S. Sugarman eds., 2001).

**90.** Other claims include fraud, negligence, breach of warranty, strict liability in tort, and antitrust and consumer protection statutory violations.

**91.** See, e.g., State of Iowa v. Philip Morris Inc., 577 N.W.2d 401 (Iowa 1998) (claims too remote); State of Texas v. The American Tobacco Co., 14 F.Supp.2d 956 (E.D. Tex. 1997) (allowing most claims; not too remote); The American Tobacco Co. v. State of Florida, 697 So.2d 1249 (Fla. Dist. Ct. App. 1997) (discovery matters).

billion, Texas for $15.3 billion, Florida for $11.3 billion, and Minnesota for $7.1 billion,[92] all on the eve of or during trial, the tobacco industry saw the futility of continuing to fight the well-organized and well-funded state attorneys general and plaintiffs' lawyers and negotiated a global settlement with the states for a total of $246 billion, payable over 25 years.[93]

Following the highly successful tobacco litigation by the states, a number of health insurers, welfare funds, and hospitals filed similar "me-too suits" seeking recompense of the costs they had incurred from smokers' health care expenses.[94] None of these claims were successful, the courts reasoning generally that the costs to these types of institutional plaintiffs were too remote to give them standing to complain. In addition, the United States Department of Justice in 1999 filed its own suit against the tobacco industry, still active as a RICO lawsuit in 2003,[95] seeking a disgorgement of $289 billion in unlawful profits garnered by the tobacco industry over a half century of fraud and deceit.[96]

**92.** The total Minnesota recovery was comprised of $6.6 billion for the state and $469 million for Blue Cross–Blue Shield of Minnesota which had joined in the suit.

**93.** The figure of $246 billion is comprised of the four state settlements (also payable over 25 years) of roughly $40 billion together with a global settlement for the other 46 states plus the District of Columbia and four territories amounting to $206 billion, payable mostly from 2000 to 2025. See Ausness, Public Tort Litigation: Public Benefit or Public Nuisance?, 77 Temp. L. Rev. ___ (2004) (describing each state's litigation); R. Rabin, The Third Wave of Tobacco Tort Litigation, in Regulating Tobacco 189–93 (R. Rabin and S. Sugarman eds., 2001).

**94.** See, e.g., Regence Blueshield v. Philip Morris Inc., 5 Fed.Appx. 651, 653 (9th Cir. 2001) (Wash. law) ("Their claimed damages were not proximately caused by the Tobacco Firms' unlawful conduct, but were instead derivative of the personal injuries of smokers afflicted by tobacco-related illnesses."); Service Employees Int'l Union Health and Welfare Fund v. Philip Morris Inc., 249 F.3d 1068 (D.C. Cir. 2001) (claims too remote, not proximate, and employment health care funds lacked standing); Allegheny Gen. Hosp. v. Philip Morris, Inc., 228 F.3d 429 (3d Cir. 2000) (Pa. law) (common law and RICO claims dismissed because the unreimbursed health care costs incurred by the 16 hospital plaintiffs on behalf of indigent patients were injuries that were too remote to satisfy requirement of proximate cause); International Brotherhood of Teamsters, Local 734 Health & Welfare Trust Fund v. Philip Morris Inc., 196 F.3d 818, 824 (7th Cir. 1999) (Ill. law) ("[S]mokers (and their employers) pay for the medical costs, in advance, through higher insurance rates (or, equivalently, lower wages in a

medical-care-plus-wage compensation package). The Funds and the Blues are just financial intermediaries."); Steamfitters Local Union No. 420 Welfare Fund v. Philip Morris, Inc., 171 F.3d 912 (3d. Cir. 1999) (Pa. law) (remoteness; proximate cause). See generally Gangarosa, Vandall, and Willis, Suits by Public Hospitals to Recover Expenditures for the Treatment of Disease, Injury and Disability Caused by Tobacco and Alcohol, 22 Fordham Urb. L.J. 81 (1994).

**95.** See, e.g., United States v. Philip Morris Inc., 314 F.3d 612 (D.C. Cir. 2003) (granting stay of discovery order). See generally Lichtblau, U.S. Seeks $289 Billion in Cigarette Makers' Profits, nytimes.com (March 18, 2003) ("the Justice Department asserts in more than 1,400 pages of court documents that the major cigarette companies are running what amounts to a criminal enterprise by manipulating nicotine levels, lying to their customers about the dangers of tobacco and directing their multibillion-dollar advertising campaigns at children"). In recent filings, the Justice Department contends that the "defendants' scheme to defraud permeated and influenced all facets of defendants' conduct—research, product development, advertising, marketing, legal, public relations, and communications—in a manner that has resulted in extraordinary profits for the past half-century, but has had devastating consequences for the public's health." Id.

**96.** United States v. Philip Morris Inc., 116 F.Supp.2d 131 (D.D.C. 2000) (allowing RICO claim, but not others, to proceed). A 1971 Philip Morris research report purportedly refutes the industry's persistent denial of tobacco's addictive qualities in its acknowledgment of the depression, irritability

Several foreign nations have also sued the tobacco industry for their health care costs from tobacco diseases, but the cases have been dismissed on the ground that the plaintiffs' damages were too remote to satisfy the requirements of proximate cause and standing.[97] An entirely different type of litigation by foreign nations and the European Community[98] involves civil RICO[99] and tort law[100] claims that certain tobacco companies aided and abetted cigarette smuggling into their sovereign borders, black market operations typically bound up with money laundering, organized crime, and even terrorism.[101] Such operations are highly lucrative to manufacturers who can expand their markets by keeping the price of their cigarettes relatively low by avoiding the sometimes steep taxes imposed on cigarettes by foreign governments. Correspondingly, however, the plaintiff nations (and the EU) lose enormous tax revenues and must bear a variety of other costs, including the costs of maintaining anti-smuggling forces, and the economic and social costs of a sometimes violent criminal black market for cigarettes.[102]

In the first smuggling case to reach the courts, *Attorney General of Canada v. R.J. Reynolds Tobacco Holdings, Inc.*,[103] a federal district

and "neurotic symptoms" that can result from attempting to quit. The Justice Department's filings disclose that the cigarette manufacturer's research report "mocked an antismoking commercial that depicted an exuberant couple leaping for joy after they quit smoking" since a "more appropriate commercial would show a restless, nervous, constipated husband bickering viciously with his bitchy wife who is nagging him about his slothful behavior and growing waistline." Lichtblau, nytimes.com, above.

**97.** See, e.g., Service Employees Int'l Union Health and Welfare Fund v. Philip Morris Inc., 249 F.3d 1068 (D.C. Cir. 2001) (claims by Guatemala, Nicaragua, and Ukraine were essentially derivative, too remote, damages were not proximate, and defendants lacked standing), aff'g Republic of Guatemala v. Tobacco Institute, Inc., 83 F.Supp.2d 125 (D.D.C. 1999). Compare Republic of Panama v. American Tobacco Co., 217 F.3d 343 (5th Cir. 2000) (ordering trial court judge recused). See generally Note, 16 American U. Int'l L. Rev. 809 (2001) (parens patriae doctrine, unlike remoteness doctrine, would allow proper claims by foreign governments).

**98.** See European Cmty. v. Japan Tobacco, Inc., 186 F.Supp.2d 231 (E.D.N.Y. 2002), aff'd in part, vacated in part, 355 F.3d 123 (2d Cir. 2004).

**99.** The claims brought under the Racketeer Influenced and Corrupt Organizations Act ("RICO"), 18 U.S.C. § 1961 et seq., alleged that the defendant tobacco companies engaged in and directed a pattern of racketeering activity in conducting cigarette smuggling and money laundering activities.

**100.** The tort law claims alleged fraud, public nuisance, restitution for unjust en-

richment, negligence, and negligent misrepresentation.

**101.** See 147 Cong. Rec. S11028–29 (daily ed. Oct. 25, 2001) (remarks of Sen. Kerry) ("Smuggling, money laundering, and fraud against our allies are an important part of the schemes by which terrorism is financed."); D. Merriman, Understand, Measure, and Combat Tobacco Smuggling (Draft), www.worldbank.org/tobacco/pdf/ Smuggling.pdf, in Economics of Tobacco Toolkit (Yurekli & Beyer, eds.), Tool 7, Smuggling; Smuggling, Counterfeiting and Piracy: The Rising Tide of Contraband and Organized Crime in Europe, www.wcoipr.org/wcoipr/default. htm?/wcoipr/Menu_Alliance.htm (WCO IPR Strategic Group, Apr. 2001); Tobacco Companies Linked to Criminal Organizations in Lucrative Cigarette Smuggling, www.corpwatch.org/issues/PID.jsp? articleid=898 (Int'l Consortium of Invest. Journalists, March 3, 2001); BAT and Tobacco Smuggling: Submission to the House of Commons Health Select Committee, www.prn2.usm.my/mainsite/ tobacco/tinfo9.html (Feb. 14, 2000).

**102.** These harms are in addition to the evident health-care problems from increased consumption due to the enhanced availability of cigarettes to price-sensitive consumers at lower black-market prices.

**103.** 103 F.Supp.2d 134 (N.D.N.Y. 2000) (dismissing complaint alleging civil RICO violations and common law fraud), aff'd, 268 F.3d 103 (2d Cir. 2001) (2–1 decision). In a powerful dissent, Judge Calabresi reasoned: "It is manifest that the suit before us in no way requires our courts to enforce

court dismissed Canada's case on the basis of the "revenue rule," and, in a split decision, the Court of Appeals affirmed. The revenue rule is an archaic doctrine first promulgated by the English courts in the 1700s for the purpose of protecting the lucrative smuggling trade that British merchants then controlled around the world under the protection of the British navy which ruled the seven seas. In present form, the revenue rule has evolved into an abstention doctrine by which a court may choose whether or not to hear a tax claim brought by a foreign government seeking recovery from a foreign tax debtor on a tax debt under foreign law.[104] Parochially perverse from its inception, the revenue rule has been roundly criticized by modern courts and commentators and serves as an unseemly blight on American jurisprudence in a shrinking global environment where nations must cooperate in deterring trans-national criminal conspiracies hatched in, directed from, and carried out in different nations.[105] Despite its serious flaws, the rule has been applied by some courts in order to steer clear of international disputes that may enmesh them, if only indirectly, in enforcing the tax laws of other nations.[106]

Although *Canada* was largely denounced by the commentators,[107] it has led a couple of district judges to dismiss certain smuggling claims against tobacco companies, in one case brought by Ecuador[108] and another more significant consolidated action against certain cigarette manufacturers for smuggling, money laundering, and related tortious activi-

foreign judgments or claims; it simply is an action for damages provided for and brought under federal law." 268 F.3d at 136.

**104.** See, e.g., Milwaukee Cty. v. M.E. White Co., 296 U.S. 268, 272, 274 (1935).

**105.** See, e.g., European Community v. Japan Tobacco, Inc., 186 F.Supp.2d 231, 234 (E.D.N.Y. 2002) (noting criticism of rule), aff'd in part, vacated in part, 355 F.3d 123 (2d Cir. 2004); European Community v. RJR Nabisco, Inc., 150 F.Supp.2d 456, 472–86 (E.D.N.Y. 2001) (thoroughly examining basis for, defects in, and applicability of the rule); Banco Frances e Brasileiro S.A. v. John Doe, 331 N.E.2d 502, 505 (N.Y. 1975) (Jasen, J.) (the revenue rule is "justifiable neither precedentially nor analytically"); Note, 115 Harv. L. Rev. 2333, 2340 (2002). *But see* Dodge, Breaking the Public Law Taboo, 43 Harv. J. Int'l L.J. 161 (2002) (arguing that the revenue rule is justified on policy grounds because, unlike other branches of government, courts cannot ensure reciprocity in the enforcement of foreign tax laws).

**106.** "The revenue rule is a longstanding common law doctrine providing that courts of one sovereign will not enforce final tax judgments or unadjudicated tax claims of other sovereigns. It has been defended on several grounds, including respect for sovereignty, concern for judicial role and competence, and separation of powers." *Canada*, above, 268 F.3d at 103.

See also Republic of Ecuador v. Philip Morris Cos., 188 F.Supp.2d 1359 (S.D. Fla. 2002) (quoting earlier American decisions approving revenue rule), aff'd on point, 341 F.3d 1253 (11th Cir. 2003). *But see* Milwaukee Cty. v. M.E. White Co., 296 U.S. 268, 272, 274 (1935); King of Spain v. Oliver, 14 F. Cas. 577 (C.C.D.Pa. 1810).

**107.** See, e.g., Notes, 115 Harv. L. Rev. 2333, 2340 (2002) ("The court's reliance on the revenue rule oversimplifies complex questions of international policy and blunts the potential effectiveness of U.S. laws in tackling sophisticated, modern problems like international smuggling and global tax evasion."); 77 Wash. L. Rev. 843, 844–45 (2002) (*Canada* "was wrongly decided" because the civil claim under RICO did not raise separation of powers concerns, and the "court employed a novel expansion of the revenue rule that impermissibly restricted the scope of RICO"); 15 N.Y. Int'l L. Rev. 101 (2002) (noting that the decision "ultimately denied the legislative goal of the RICO act" inasmuch as the "court essentially permitted the defendants to retain the profits they made illegally"). *But see* Dodge, Breaking the Public Law Taboo, 43 Harv. J. Int'l L.J. 161, 233–34 (2002) (concluding that, on policy grounds, *Canada* was correctly decided).

**108.** See Republic of Equador v. Philip Morris Cos., 188 F.Supp.2d 1359 (S.D. Fla. 2002), aff'd on point, 341 F.3d 1253 (11th Cir. 2003).

ties brought by most states of the Republic of Colombia, the European Community, and most of its member states.[109] After the district court dismissed most of their claims on the basis of *Canada*, the plaintiffs in *European Community* refiled with an emphasis on the defendants' money laundering, racketeering, and various tortious activities, but once again the case was dismissed, and the dismissal affirmed,[110] albeit with a small window for the plaintiffs to file another lawsuit on their money laundering claims.[111] Apparently the window was big enough, for one defendant settled with the EU soon thereafter for $1.25 billion.[112]

### *Firearms*

**Background.** The menace of guns in American society, particularly handguns but also various assault rifles, has spawned a morass of litigation and debate.[113] Each year, tens of thousands of Americans are killed by guns—roughly the same number as are killed in car accidents.[114] While initially startling, this statistic reflects the fact that there are almost as many firearms in this nation as people.[115] While some

---

**109.** See European Cmty. v. Japan Tobacco, Inc., 186 F.Supp.2d 231 (E.D.N.Y. 2002) (holding that revenue rule required dismissal of smuggling claims seeking lost tax revenue but that money laundering claims seeking other types of damages might proceed), aff'd in part, vacated in part, 355 F.3d 123 (2d Cir. 2004).

**110.** European Community v. RJR Nabisco, Inc., 355 F.3d 123 (2d Cir. 2004).

**111.** See id. at 138.

**112.** See, e.g., EU Signs $1.25B Deal with Philip Morris, nytimes.com (AP, July 9, 2004).

**113.** See Ausness, Tort Liability For the Sale of Non–Defective Products: An Analysis and Critique of the Concept of Negligent Marketing, 53 S.C. L. Rev. 907 (2002); Culhane and Eggan, Gun Torts: Defining a Cause of Action for Victims in Suits Against Gun Manufacturers, 81 N.C. L. Rev. 115 (2002); Lytton, Lawsuits Against the Gun Industry: A Comparative Institutional Analysis, 32 Conn. L. Rev. 1247 (2000); Lowy, Litigating Against Gun Manufacturers, 36 Trial 42 (Nov. 2000); Lytton, Tort Claims Against Gun Manufacturers for Crime–Related Injuries: Defining a Suitable Role for the Tort System in Regulating the Firearms Industry, 65 Mo. L. Rev. 1 (2000); Twerski and Sebok, Liability Without Cause? Further Ruminations on Cause-in-Fact as Applied to Handgun Liability, 32 Conn. L. Rev. 1379 (2000); Bhowik, et al., A Sense of Duty: Retiring the "Special Relationship" Rule and Holding Gun Manufacturers Liable for Negligently Distributing Guns, 4 J. Health Care L. & Pol'y 42 (2000); Kairys, Legal Claims of Cities Against the Manufacturers of Handguns, 71 Temp. L. Rev. 1 (1998); Bogus, Pistols, Politics and Products Liability, 59 U. Cin. L. Rev. 1103, 1145–48 (1991); Hardy, Product Liability and Weapons Manufacture, 20 Wake Forest L. Rev. 541 (1984); Turley, Manufacturers' and Suppliers' Liability to Handgun Victims, 10 N. Ky. L. Rev. 41 (1982). See also Notes, a Good Predictor of What the Future Holds for Gun Manufacturers?, 34 Ind. L. Rev. 419 (2001) (noting Hamilton v. Accu–Tek); 60 Md. L. Rev. 441 (2001) (noting Valentine v. On Target); 9 Harv. J. L. and Pub. Pol'y 764 (1986) (noting Kelley v. R.G. Indus.); 97 Harv. L. Rev. 1912 (1984); 49 Mo. L. Rev. 834 (1984) (noting Richman v. Charter Arms); 24 Wm. & Mary L. Rev. 467 (1983) (noting *Barker*); 1 Frumer and Friedman, Products Liability §§ 3.05, 12.07. Compare Notes, 108 Harv. L. Rev. 1679 (1995) (proposing statute imposing absolute liability for manufacture of ammunition), with 97 Harv. L. Rev. 1912, 1928 (1984) (role of handguns in society is properly for legislatures, and courts should not use products liability law to usurp control over issue of handgun control).

**114.** Gun fatalities divide as follows: 48% suicides, 47% homicides, 4% accidents, and 1% legal justice system. In addition, another 125,000 people are injured by guns each year. Lytton, Tort Claims Against Gun Manufacturers for Crime–Related Injuries: Defining a Suitable Role for the Tort System in Regulating the Firearms Industry, 65 Mo. L. Rev. 1, 1 (2000).

**115.** See Barnes, Taking Aim: The Impetus Driving Suits Against Gun Manufacturers, 27 Pepp. L. Rev. 735, 736 (2000) (noting, also that about half of all American households possess at least one gun).

ninety-eight percent of all firearms are used lawfully,[116] the two to three million of those used illegally each year cause enormous injury and suffering.[117] The question whether products liability law should have anything to say about criminally inflicted losses of this type,[118] a topic that finds perennial debate in the elected legislatures around the nation, is a controversial issue that has been litigated with increasing frequency and intensity in recent years.

**Injury victim litigation.** A spate of decisions in the 1970s and 1980s, frequently pointing to the refusal of legislatures to ban handguns, were hostile to damages claims brought by shooting victims against handgun manufacturers alleging that such guns were inherently defective.[119] Two cases in the 1980s, however, were decided the other way. In the first case, *Richman v. Charter Arms Corp.*,[120] a federal district judge ruled that, while handguns are not defective under ordinary products liability principles, the sale of such a product might constitute an ultrahazardous activity. In the second case, *Kelley v. R.G. Industries, Inc.*,[121] an action against the manufacturer of the handgun used by a grocery store robber to shoot the assistant manager in the chest, the Maryland high court ruled that a manufacturer may be subject to strict liability for selling a general type of product that on balance is bad for society. *Kelley* held that strict tort liability could be imposed on sellers of "Saturday Night Specials" for harm to victims from the use of such guns.[122] In response to the holding in *Kelley*, the National Rifle Association conducted a multi-million dollar campaign to have the decision overturned, first by the Maryland legislature, and then by the people in a

**116.** Id.

**117.** The 9,390 gun-related homicides in the U.S. in 1996 contrast to 30 in Great Britain and 15 in Japan. See Vandall, Economic and Causation Issues in City Suits Against Gun Manufacturers, 27 Pepp. L. Rev. 719, 719 (2000). One American child dies from gunshot every 92 minutes, more than 15 on average each day. Id.

**118.** Of course manufacturers of firearms and ammunition, like other types of manufacturers, are subject to liability for misrepresentation, and defects in design, warnings and instructions, and manufacture. See, e.g., Halliday v. Sturm, Ruger & Co., 792 A.2d 1145 (Md. 2002); Smith ex rel. Smith v. Bryco Arms, 33 P.3d 638 (N.M. Ct. App. 2001).

**119.** See, e.g., Patterson v. Rohm Gesellschaft, 608 F.Supp. 1206, 1209 n.5 (N.D. Tex. 1985) (rejecting plaintiff's risk-utility argument under conventional strict products liability in tort, citing many cases in accord).

[D]espite this court's admiration for such a delightfully nonsensical claim: that a product which does not have a defect can nevertheless, under the law, be defective—the plaintiff's attorneys are simply wrong. Under Texas law, there can be no products liability recovery unless the

product does have a defect. Without this essential predicate, that something is wrong with the product, the risk/utility balancing test does not even apply.

Id. at 1210–11. The court further noted that "the theory advanced by the plaintiffs perverts the very purpose of the 'risk/utility balancing test' [which] incorporates the idea that a defect is something that can be remedied or changed." Id. at 1212. See also Burkett v. Freedom Arms, Inc., 704 P.2d 118 (Or. 1985) (rejecting strict liability claim based on manufacturer's conducting abnormally dangerous activity); Martin v. Harrington and Richardson, Inc., 743 F.2d 1200 (7th Cir. 1984) (Ill. law) (rejecting theory of manufacturer's strict liability under ultrahazardous activity theory); Mavilia v. Stoeger Indus., 574 F.Supp. 107, 111 (D. Mass. 1983) (rejecting tort claim for marketing handguns and holding "as a matter of law that at least with regard to the .38 caliber Llam automatic pistol, the gun is not inherently defective").

**120.** 571 F.Supp. 192 (E.D. La. 1983).

**121.** 497 A.2d 1143 (Md. 1985).

**122.** "Saturday Night Specials" are poorly made, cheap, small, inaccurate, and easily concealable handguns useful principally for criminal activity rather than self-protection or other legitimate activity.

referendum petition. In time, the gun lobby and gun control advocates agreed to compromise legislation that overturned *Kelley* but prohibited the sale of Saturday Night Specials in the state, and the voters by referendum approved the law.[123]

A number of subsequent handgun victim cases against manufacturers of handguns,[124] assault rifles,[125] and ammunition[126] have involved claims for design defect, negligent marketing, and strict liability for selling products that are abnormally dangerous. While plaintiffs had some initial success in a number of cases in the lower courts, and while an occasional court still allows such claims,[127] most of these gun-shot victim cases have been dismissed on such grounds as no duty, no defect (the guns or ammo only did what they were designed to do), and because of the superseding intervention of criminals putting them to improper use (the abuse of the guns by people, not the guns themselves, are the proximate cause of harm).[128]

**Municipality litigation.** Following the successful partnership in the cigarette litigation of state attorneys general and major plaintiffs' law firms, a number of municipalities filed claims against the gun industry for blanketing their cities with an oversupply of guns, particularly cheap handguns, that far exceeded the lawful market for firearms.[129] Following the first such suit by New Orleans in 1998, over 30

---

**123.** The referendum passed by a vote of 58% to 42%. See Bogus, Pistols, Politics and Products Liability, 59 U. Cin. L. Rev. 1103, 1145–48 (1991). See generally Halliday v. Sturm, Ruger & Co., 792 A.2d 1145 (Md. 2002) (child shot himself in head with father's gun; describing legislative developments and rejecting claim that gun was defective for failing to have child-proof design).

**124.** See, e.g., Halliday v. Sturm, Ruger & Co. 792 A.2d 1145 (Md. 2002) (no design defect under consumer expectations test); Hamilton v. Beretta U.S.A. Corp., 750 N.E.2d 1055 (N.Y. 2001) (no duty), answering certified question from id., 222 F.3d 36 (2d Cir. 2000). See also id., 264 F.3d 21 (2d Cir. 2001) (ordering that Weinstein, J., dismiss Hamilton v. Accu-Tek, 62 F.Supp.2d 802 (E.D.N.Y. 1999)).

**125.** See, e.g., Merrill v. Navegar, Inc., 28 P.3d 116 (Cal. 2001), rev'g 89 Cal. Rptr.2d 146 (Ct. App. 1999). See also Kromke, California's Legislative Response to Merrill v. Navegar: An Analysis, 24 Whittier L. Rev. 833 (2003).

**126.** See McCarthy v. Olin Corp., 119 F.3d 148 (2d Cir. 1997) (N.Y. law) (2–1 decision) (Black Talon hollow-point bullets not defectively designed; dissenting, Calabresi, J., reasoned that the bullets properly might be classified as egregiously unsafe and, hence, not immune from liability), rev'g McCarthy v. Sturm, Ruger & Co., 916 F.Supp. 366 (S.D.N.Y. 1996).

**127.** Ileto v. Glock Inc., 349 F.3d 1191 (9th Cir. 2003) (Cal. law) (2–1 decision) (allowing negligence and public nuisance claims, and noting legislature's actions to permit claims against gun manufacturers).

**128.** The Products Liability Restatement includes firearms in its short list of generically dangerous products that are not defective in design. See Products Liability Restatement § 2 cmt. *d.* On negligent marketing, see Ausness, Tort Liability For the Sale of Non–Defective Products: An Analysis and Critique of the Concept of Negligent Marketing, 53 S.C. L. Rev. 907, 962–64 (2002) (criticizing negligent marketing concept as paternalistic and elitist); McClurg, The Tortious Marketing of Handguns: Strict Liability Is Dead, Long Live Negligence, 19 Seton Hall Legis. J. 777, 806–18 (1996) (praising negligent marketing theory).

**129.** See generally Ausness, Public Tort Litigation: Public Benefit or Public Nuisance?, 77 Temple L. Rev. No. 4 (2004); Gifford, Public Nuisance as a Mass Products Liability Tort, 71 U. Cin. L. Rev. 743 (2003); Ausness, Tort Liability For the Sale of Non–Defective Products: An Analysis and Critique of the Concept of Negligent Marketing, 53 S.C. L. Rev. 907, 936 (2002); Kairys, The Origin and Development of the Governmental Handgun Cases, 32 Conn. L. Rev. 1163 (2000); Kairys, The Governmental Handgun Cases and the Elements and Underlying Policies of Public Nuisance, 32 Conn. L. Rev. 1175 (2000); Comment, 9

cities and counties instituted such "recoupment" lawsuits seeking to recover the various municipal costs associated with gun violence such as the increased expenses of law enforcement, emergency rescue services, medical care for gunshot victims, prosecutorial and prison services, social services, and lost tax revenues. Such lawsuits typically make claims against gun manufacturers, distributors, trade associations, and major retailers for defective design because of the absence of safety features; failure to provide adequate warnings; negligent marketing and negligent distribution; public nuisance; deceptive trade practices; and restitution for unjust enrichment. To date, most of these cases have been dismissed,[130] but a number have survived motions to dismiss and several have withstood appeal.[131] In view of the diminishing likelihood of success, the increasing costs of litigation, and the possibility that Congress may bar such lawsuits, at least a couple of cities have simply abandoned their cases against the gun industry.[132]

It is still too early to predict with confidence the ultimate outcome of the municipality gun litigation. While the public nuisance claim might be a viable basis of recovery, courts will have to find a way around a large variety of common law obstacles, including proximate cause (or remoteness), standing, no duty, the appropriateness of public nuisance and restitution in this new type of litigation,[133] and the persistent (if dubious) doctrine prohibiting public bodies from recovering the costs of emergency governmental services called, the "municipal cost recovery rule."[134] And a particularly formidable obstacle to recovery is the growing number

Geo. Mason L. Rev. 1127 (2001) (critiquing the litigation); Note, Recovering the Costs of Public Nuisance Abatement: The Public and Private City Sue the Gun Industry, 113 Harv. L. Rev. 1521 (2000).

**130.** See, e.g., District of Columbia v. Beretta, U.S.A., Corp., 847 A.2d 1127 (D.C. 2004) (no duty or standing); Philadelphia v. Beretta U.S.A. Corp., 277 F.3d 415 (3d Cir. 2002) (on grounds of no duty, proximate cause, remoteness, and standing); District of Columbia v. Beretta U.S.A. Corp., 2002 WL 31811717 (D.C. Super. Ct. 2002) (no duty, proximate cause, and remoteness under Holmes v. Securities Investor Protection Corp., 503 U.S. 258 (1992)); Mayor Baker & City of Wilmington v. Smith & Wesson Corp., 2002 WL 31741522 (Del. Super. Ct. 2002) (municipal cost recovery rule bars action); Ganim v. Smith & Wesson Corp., 780 A.2d 98 (Conn. 2001) (plaintiff lacked standing); Morial v. Smith & Wesson Corp., 785 So.2d 1 (La. 2001) (subsequently enacted statute barred New Orleans's lawsuit); Penelas v. Arms Tech., Inc., 778 So.2d 1042 (Fla. Dist. Ct. App. 2001); Camden Cty. Bd. v. Beretta, U.S.A. Corp., 273 F.3d 536 (3d Cir. 2001) (proximate cause and remoteness), aff'd in part on point, rev'd in part on other grounds, 847 A.2d 1127 (D.C. 2004).

**131.** See, e.g., James v. Arms Tech., Inc., 820 A.2d 27 (N.J. Super. Ct. App. Div. 2003) (allowing negligence, public nuisance, and punitive damages claims); Chicago and

Cty. of Cook v. Beretta U.S.A. Corp., 785 N.E.2d 16 (Ill. App. Ct. 2002) (allowing public nuisance claim); Cincinnati v. Beretta U.S.A. Corp., 768 N.E.2d 1136 (Ohio 2002) (rejecting defenses including municipal cost recovery rule); White v. Smith & Wesson, 97 F.Supp.2d 816 (N.D. Ohio 2000) (Cleveland) (same); City of Boston v. Smith & Wesson Corp., 2000 WL 1473568 (Mass. Super. Ct. 2000) (same).

**132.** See, e.g., Cincinnati Drops Suit Against Gun Industry; Suit Deemed Unwinnable and Wasteful, 71 Prod. Saf. & Liab. Rep. (BNA) 2750 (May 27, 2003) (noting Boston's similar action in 2002 and discussing current Congressional action to bar such litigation).

**133.** See Gifford, Public Nuisance as a Mass Products Liability Tort, 71 U. Cin. L. Rev. 741 (2003).

**134.** Also referred to as the "free public services doctrine." Compare James v. Arms Tech., Inc., 820 A.2d 27 (N.J. Super. Ct. App. Div. 2003) (rejecting doctrine and allowing action to proceed), with Baker v. Smith & Wesson Corp., 2002 WL 31741522 (Del. Super. Ct. 2002) (applying doctrine and dismissing action). See generally Lytton, Should Government Be Allowed to Recover the Costs of Public Services from Tortfeasors?: Tort Subsidies, the Limits of Loss Spreading, and the Free Public Services Doctrine, 76 Tulane L. Rev. 727, 728

of state statutes, mentioned below, that prohibit actions against gun manufacturers in general or, at least in one state, that broadly prohibits claims by local governments from suing manufacturers and other sellers for injuries caused by guns.[135]

### Other Products

Because every type of product is inherently dangerous in some respect, as mentioned at the outset, there is no end to the list of other types of products that might be included in this category.[136] But a small number of particular products may be mentioned briefly here because of the serious and widespread nature of their inherent risks.

**Drugs.** The largest category of generically dangerous products consists of prescription drugs[137] which are comprised of chemicals designed to alter the human body. Normally, the chemical compounds in prescription drugs are properly researched, designed, tested, produced, and labeled such that they accomplish their objectives of improving human pathologies effectively and with relatively minimal (or, at least, acceptable) harmful side effects. But drug manufacturers sometimes fail to discover or anticipate harmful side effects, and on occasion drug manufacturers may deliberately overlook or even conceal the risks of a profitable new drug.[138] Reports of new prescription drug side-effect problems appear with disturbing frequency, such as heart valve and other damage attributed to certain diet drugs called "fen-phen."[139] Apart

(2002) (arguing for the rule's abrogation because it "shields industrial tortfeasors from liability . . . , constitutes a tort subsidy to industry and functions as an insurance scheme for industrial accidents paid for by taxpayers"); Note, Tortfeasor Liability for Disaster Response Costs: Accounting for the True Cost of Accidents, 55 Fordham L. Rev. 1001 (1987).

**135.** See Va. Code Ann. § 15.2–915.1.

**136.** Silicone breast implants, for example, have led to many thousands of claims against their manufacturers. Plaintiffs have prevailed in some cases. See, e.g., Transue v. Aesthetech Corp., 341 F.3d 911, 919 (9th Cir. 2003) (Wash. law); Dow Chem. Co. v. Mahlum, 970 P.2d 98 (Nev. 1998); Baxter Healthcare Corp. v. Grimes, 1998 WL 548729 (Tex. App. 1998). See also In re Silicone Gel Breast Implants Prods. Liab. Litig. (MDL 926), 837 F.Supp. 1128 (N.D. Ala. 1993), vacated in part, 887 F.Supp. 1455 (N.D. Ala. 1995); In re Breast Implant Cases, 942 F.Supp. 958 (S.D.N.Y. 1996) (discussing possible transfer of thousands of cases). Defendants have prevailed in many others, often because the plaintiffs failed to prove causation. See, e.g., Meister v. Medical Eng'g Corp., 267 F.3d 1123 (D.C. Cir. 2002) (expert testimony on causation failed to meet *Daubert* admissibility standards); Allison v. McGhan Med. Corp., 184 F.3d 1300 (11th Cir. 1999) (Ga. law) (same). See Kolata, Company Making Case to Allow Breast Implants, nytimes.com (Sept. 6,

2003) (Institute of Medicine committee study in 2000 that reviewed epidemiological data found no evidence that breast implants cause any serious disease, including cancer, neurological diseases, autoimmune diseases like lupus, and connective tissue diseases like arthritis). As with asbestos, this massive litigation has bankrupted at least one manufacturer. See, e.g., In re Dow Corning Corp., 280 F.3d 648 (6th Cir. 2002). See generally Spanbauer, Breast Implants as Beauty Ritual: Woman's Sceptre and Prison, 9 Yale J.L. & Fem. 157 (1997); Stine, Silicone, Science and Settlements: Breast Implants and a Search for Truth, 63 Def. Couns. J. 491 (1996); Note, 29 Rutgers L.J. 121 (1997).

**137.** Dangers in over-the-counter drugs normally are less serious but nonetheless may be substantial in individual cases. See §§ 8.10 and 9.6, above.

**138.** See, e.g., Axen v. American Home Prods. Corp., 974 P.2d 224 (Or. Ct. App. 1999); Toole v. Richardson–Merrell, Inc., 60 Cal.Rptr. 398 (Ct. App. 1967). The same is sometimes true of medical devices. See Eichenwald, Guidant Admits That It Hid Problems of Artery Tool, www.nytimes.com (June 13, 2003). See generally § 18.1, below.

**139.** See, e.g., In re Diet Drugs (Phentermine, Fenfluramine, Dexfenfluramine) Products Liability Litigation, 2001 WL

from the typical issues of warnings adequacy in drug products liability litigation,[140] the most significant generic risk issue is whether a drug manufacturer may be subject to liability for *design* defectiveness, an issue treated elsewhere from a variety of perspectives.[141]

**Asbestos.** Asbestos has had a crushing effect on workers, manufacturers, and the courts.[142] Beginning in the 1970s, the courts have been barraged by hundreds of thousands of cases involving the ravages of asbestos, a mineral converted into insulation materials that can generate deadly asbestos dust that causes various lung diseases. Despite its highly useful insulation characteristics, asbestos has caused so much death and suffering that it fairly might be viewed as inherently defective in design on a "macro-balance" of its aggregate social costs and benefits.[143] From the start of the asbestos litigation, however, asbestos generally has been litigated not for being defective per se but for failing to carry sufficient warnings to alert asbestos workers to the lethal dangers of inhaling asbestos dust.[144]

The seminal asbestos case was *Borel v. Fibreboard Paper Products Corporation*,[145] the first strict products liability case to uphold a verdict for an installer of asbestos insulation materials against the manufacturers of those materials. Clarence Borel worked as an industrial insulation worker from 1936 until he was disabled in 1969 by asbestosis, a lung disease. Thereafter, he developed mesothelioma, an invariably fatal form of lung cancer, and died of that disease. Both diseases, asbestosis and mesothelioma, result from asbestos fibers lodging in the lungs of a

---

497313 (E.D. Pa. 2001) (describing fen-phen litigation and settlement); 2002 WL 32067308 (E.D. Pa. 2002) (ordering audit of certain settlement trust claims). See Texas Judge Upholds $1 Billion Verdict; Wyeth to Appeal, Says Award Not Justified, 32 Prod. Saf. & Liab. Rep. 488 (May 24, 2004); Abelson and Glater, Texas Jury Rules Against the Maker of Fen–Phen, a Diet Drug, nytimes.com (Apr. 28, 2004) (reporting $1 billion verdict to family of woman who died from lung disease, and that Wyeth had set aside $16 billion to cover costs of fen-phen litigation).

**140.** See § 9.6, above.

**141.** See § 8.10 (design liability), above, and § 10.4 (unavoidable dangers and state of the art), below. Prescription drug claims normally are not subject to the defense of federal preemption. See § 14.4, below.

**142.** On the asbestos litigation generally, see Am. Law Prod. Liab. ch. 122; S. Carroll, D. Hensler, et al., Asbestos Litigation Costs and Compensation: An Interim Report (RAND 2002) (comprehensive study); G. Bell, Asbestos Litigation and Judicial Leadership: The Courts' Duty to Help Solve the Asbestos Litigation Crisis (Nat'l Leg. Ctr. for Pub. Interest 2002); D. Hensler, Asbestos Litigation Costs and Compensation: An Interim Report (RAND 2002); McGovern, The Tragedy of the Asbestos

Commons, 88 Va. L. Rev. 1721 (2002); Edley and Weiler, Asbestos: A Multi–Billion Dollar Crisis, 30 Harv. J. on Legis. 383 (1993).

**143.** See Hennegan v. Cooper/T. Smith Stevedoring Co., Inc., 837 So.2d 96, 108 (La. Ct. App. 2002) (trial court properly found that "the utility of the asbestos products is vastly outweighed by the risk of death associated with their use"); Halphen v. Johns–Manville Sales Corp., 484 So.2d 110 (La. 1986). *But see* Owens–Corning Fiberglass Corp. v. Stone, 1996 WL 397435, at *2 (Tex. App. 1996) (jury found that defendant's asbestos product "was not defective, taking into consideration 'its utility and the risk involved in its use'"); Johnstone v. American Oil Co., 7 F.3d 1217, 1223 (5th Cir. 1993) (La. law) (approving jury finding that asbestos was not defective on proof that its effectiveness as heat insulator on Navy ships during World War II helped to win the war).

**144.** Inadequate warning remains the principal theory of defectiveness in these cases. See, e.g., In re Asbestos Litig., 832 A.2d 705 (Del. 2003); Garlock, Inc. v. Gallagher, 814 A.2d 1007 (Md. Ct. Spec. App. 2003); In re Asbestos Litig., 799 A.2d 1151 (Del. 2002).

**145.** 493 F.2d 1076 (5th Cir. 1973) (Tex. law) (Wisdom, J.).

person who inhales asbestos dust. In his employment, Borel was regularly and necessarily exposed to heavy concentrations of asbestos dust generated by insulation materials. Ruling that "[a] product must not be made available to the public without disclosure of those dangers that the application of reasonable foresight would reveal," [146] the court affirmed the verdict for the plaintiff.[147]

*Borel* opened the floodgates for asbestos litigation, and the resulting compensatory and punitive awards, together with the enormous litigation costs of defending hundreds of thousands of cases, have bankrupted much of the asbestos industry.[148] The litigation has swamped the dockets of many courts[149] which have sought to find ways to manage it efficiently, as by aggregating both claimants and defendants, while not sacrificing the rights of individual victims (present and future) to reasoned judicial resolution of their claims.[150] The courts and Congress continue to struggle to find ways to manage and resolve the many complicated issues of fairness, practicality, and bankruptcy, that surround this single type of product.[151]

**Lead paint.** An increasing type of litigation concerns lead poisoning.[152] For much of the twentieth century, until it was banned in 1978 by

**146.** Id. at 1090.

**147.** See id. at 1103.

**148.** Johns–Manville, the most prominent asbestos firm, declared bankruptcy in 1983, and about 60 more firms to date have followed in its wake, filing for Chapter 11 bankruptcy protection. Stiglitz et al., The Impact of Asbestos Liabilities on Workers in Bankrupt Firms, 12 J. Bankr. L. & Prac. 51, 52 (2003) (also noting that 47 states have experienced at least one asbestos-related bankruptcy). See also Slawotsky, New York's Article 16 and Multiple Defendant Product Liability Litigation: A Time To Rethink the Impact of Bankrupt Shares on Judgment Molding, 76 St. John's L. Rev. 397 (2002).

**149.** See, e.g., Harras, Asbestos Reform Summit Held on Capitol Hill; Congress, Business, Lawyers Seek Solution, 31 Prod. Saf. & Liab. Rep. (BNA) 298 (Apr. 7, 2003) (noting estimates that "[a]pproximately 250,000 asbestos claims are currently pending in courts across the country, with up to 3.1 million claims anticipated in the future," and that "the courts have adjudicated $30 billion in asbestos claims, with about $200 billion in claims pending or anticipated"). Compare RAND Report, above (roughly corroborating these figures and noting that more than 600,000 people have filed claims against 6,000 defendants and that estimates are for 1–3 million future claimants).

**150.** See, e.g., Ortiz v. Fibreboard Corp., 527 U.S. 815 (1999); Amchem Prods., Inc. v. Windsor, 521 U.S. 591 (1997). Another attempt to simplify this litigation was to col-

laterally estop defendants from continuing to litigate whether asbestos is defective, an attempt that failed. See Hardy v. Johns–Manville Sales Corp., 681 F.2d 334 (5th Cir. 1982) (Tex. law).

**151.** See, e.g., Chavers v. Gatke Corp., 132 Cal.Rptr.2d 198 (Ct. App. 2003) (neither civil conspiracy nor concert of action theory available to support claim against manufacturer of asbestos products to which plaintiff was not exposed); Asbestos Fund Negotiations Halted After No Compromise Found, 19 Liab. & Ins. Week 1 (May 10, 2004); Long–Awaited Asbestos Reform Bill Released; Hatch Proposes $108 Billion Trust Fund, 31 Prod. Saf. & Liab. Rep (BNA) 458 (May 26, 2003); Slawotsky, New York's Article 16 and Multiple Defendant Product Liability Litigation: A Time To Rethink the Impact of Bankrupt Shares on Judgment Molding, 76 St. John's L. Rev. 397 (2002).

**152.** See Smith, Turning Lead into Asbestos and Tobacco: Litigation Alchemy Gone Wrong, 71 Def. Coun. J. 119 (2004); Krauss, Regulation Masquerading as Judgment: Chaos Masquerading as Tort Law, 71 Miss. L.J. 631, 666–85 (2001); Cupp, State Medical Reimbursement Lawsuits After Tobacco: Is the Domino Effect for Lead Paint Manufacturers and Others Fair Game?, 27 Pepp. L. Rev. 685 (2000); Comment, Lead Paint Public Entity Lawsuits: Has the Broad Stroke of Tobacco and Firearms Litigation Painted a Troubling Picture for Lead Paint Manufacturers?, 28 Pepp. L. Rev. 915, 917–18 (2001); Comment, Private Causes of Action Against Manufacturers of

the federal government for use in household paints, lead pigment was an important ingredient of paint, increasing its durability and rendering it smooth and easy to wash. For many decades, the walls of much of the nation's residential housing were painted with coat upon coat of lead-based paint. As the century progressed, much of the housing began to deteriorate and the paint began to peel off the walls, leaving piles of lead paint chips in decaying housing around the nation. The problem is that lead, said to taste as "sweet as candy,"[153] is also highly toxic–particularly when ingested by toddlers ever on the lookout for objects to place in their mouths. As a result, approximately one million young American children currently have damaging levels of lead in their blood.[154] The consequences of ingestion can be severe, from speech impairment, decreased memory and intelligence, learning disabilities, brain damage, autism, kidney damage, and even death.[155] For at least a century, paint manufacturers have known of the hazards lead poses to human beings.[156] Indeed, other nations began banning the use of lead in residential paint as early as the 1920s.[157]

Beginning in the late 1980s, a number of products liability claims began to be brought against paint manufacturers for lead poisoning in children. To date, lead poisoning victims have faced the apparently insurmountable problem of identifying the particular manufacturers that made the particular pigments and paints in the particular chips eaten by particular victims. The plaintiffs' inability to meet their conventional burden of proof on causation has been fatal in these cases, most courts refusing to apply market share liability (or other theories of joint liability) to hold the industry liable as a whole.[158]

Following in the footsteps of the successful cigarette litigation, a large number of cities and the state of Rhode Island sued the industry on various grounds, seeking to recover the enormous costs of cleaning up the lead paint hazards, caring for children poisoned by the lead paint, and educating the public on the hazards of lead.[159] A couple of the early suits brought by Philadelphia and New Orleans ran into statute of limitations problems,[160] but New York's subsequent action had more

Lead–Based Paint: A Response to the Lead Paint Manufacturers' Attempt to Limit Their Liability by Seeking Abrogation of Parental Immunity, 18 B.C. Envtl. Aff. L. Rev. 381 (1991).

**153.** See Cupp, above, at 692.

**154.** See Comment, 28 Pepp. L. Rev. 915, 915–18 (2001) (noting varying estimates).

**155.** See id. at 918.

**156.** See Cupp, above, at 692 (noting that one manufacturer warned of lead paint's dangers in article published in 1904).

**157.** See id. at 692–93.

**158.** See, e.g. Lewis v. Lead Indus. Ass'n, 793 N.E.2d 869 (Ill. App. Ct. 2003); Brenner v. American Cyanamid Co., 732 N.Y.S.2d 799 (Sup. Ct. App. Div. 2001);

Skipworth v. Lead Industries Ass'n, 690 A.2d 169 (Pa. 1997); Jefferson v. Lead Indus. Ass'n, 106 F.3d 1245 (5th Cir. 1997) (La. law); Santiago v. Sherwin Williams Co., 3 F.3d 546 (1st Cir. 1993) (Mass. law) (2–1 decision). See also Sabater v. Lead Indus. Ass'n, 704 N.Y.S.2d 800 (Sup. Ct. 2000) (dismissing some claims). *But see* Jackson v. Glidden Co., 647 N.E.2d 879 (Ohio Ct. App. 1995) (allowing claims for alternative liability and market share liability).

**159.** See Comment, 28 Pepp. L. Rev. 915 (2001).

**160.** See City of Phila. v. Lead Indus. Ass'n, 994 F.2d 112 (3d Cir. 1993) (Pa. law) (also rejecting alternative liability and market share liability theories); Housing Authority of New Orleans v. Standard Paint and Varnish Company, 612 So.2d 916 (La. Ct. App. 1993).

success,[161] and additional cities have brought similar claims.[162] A number of claims in the Rhode Island suit, which included counts for public nuisance, other torts, and unfair trade practices, survived motions to dismiss for failure to state a claim,[163] but the trial judge declared a mistrial when the jury deadlocked.[164] The following week, the judge presiding over a lawsuit brought by two dozen New Jersey municipalities dismissed that action.[165] The trial judge in the Rhode Island suit subsequently ruled that the state may retry its public nuisance part of the case.[166] It is too early to predict whether the public-entity claims against lead paint manufacturers will ultimately prove successful, but the litigation results to date, reflecting the plaintiffs' difficulties with manufacturer identification and statutes of limitations, illustrate the significant problems confronting these claims.

**Fast food.** Whether fast food restaurants are responsible for burns to patrons who spill hot coffee and other hot drinks is an issue that American courts have been addressing for awhile.[167] Except for one celebrated aberration,[168] courts almost always dismiss these claims on the ground that the hazard of such spills is obvious and widely known, and that restaurants are simply serving a type of product that consumers want.[169] This type of claim has spread to England, where a class action of such claimants was dismissed.[170]

**161.** See City of New York v. Lead Indus. Ass'n, 644 N.Y.S.2d 919 (Sup. Ct. App. Div. 1996).

**162.** See Chicago Uses Public Nuisance Theory to Sue Paint Makers Over Lead–Based Risks, 30 Prod. Saf. & Liab. Rep. 808 (Sept. 16, 2002). Other major cities, such as New York, St. Louis, Milwaukee, and San Francisco filed similar actions.

**163.** State of Rhode Island v. Lead Indus. Ass'n, 2001 WL 345830 (R.I. Super. Ct. 2001).

**164.** See Judge Declares Mistrial in Lead–Paint Suit, N.Y. Times § A, p.20, col. 5, www.nytimes.com (Oct. 30, 2002); Kessler, Rhode Island Suit May Proceed After Judge's Denial of Post–Trial Motions, 31 Prod. Saf. & Liab. Rep. 324 (Apr. 14, 2003).

**165.** See Suit Dismissed Against Makers of Lead Paint, N.Y. Times, www.nytimes.com (Nov. 5, 2002).

**166.** See Lead Paint–State Judge Rules R.I. May Proceed with Nuisance Suit Against Manufacturers, 31 Prod. Saf. & Liab. Rep. 484 (June 9, 2003).

**167.** Recent cases include McCroy v. Coastal Mart, Inc., 207 F.Supp.2d 1265 (D. Kan. 2002) (hot chocolate; extensive review of hot beverage cases); Garlinger v. Hardee's Food Systems, Inc., 16 Fed.Appx. 232 (4th Cir. 2001) (W. Va. law) (hot coffee); Immormino v. J & M Powers, Inc., 698 N.E.2d 516 (Ohio Ct. Com. Pl. 1998) (hot tea).

**168.** Liebeck v. McDonald's Restaurants, P.T.S., Inc., No. CV–93–02419, 1995 WL 360309 (D. N.M. 1994). Mrs. Liebeck, a passenger in her grandson's car, spilled the coffee when she placed it between her legs and tried to remove the plastic lid. See Mead, Punitive Damages and the Spill Felt Round the World: A U.S. Perspective, 17 Loy. L.A. Int'l & Comp. L. Rev. 829 (1995); Gerlin, A Matter of Degree: How a Jury Decided that a Coffee Spill Is Worth $2.9 Million, Wall Street Journal A1 (Sept. 1, 1994); Morgan, McDonald's Burned Itself, Legal Times, Sept. 19, 1994, at 26; Two Hot Verdicts Were Distorted by Critics, 20 ATLA Advocate 3 (Oct. 1994). *Liebeck* is discussed in connection with punitive damages, in §§ 18.1 and 18.3, below. See also Greene v. Boddie–Noell Enters., Inc., 966 F.Supp. 416, 418 n.1 (W.D. Va. 1997) (discussing *Liebeck*).

**169.** Compare Nadel v. Burger King Corp., 695 N.E.2d 1185 (Ohio Ct. App. 1997) (jury question as to obviousness of risk that coffee served from drive-though window of fast-food restaurant, that spilled on child, would be so hot as to cause second degree burns, would be so hot as to cause second degree burns, with McMahon v. Bunn–O–Matic Corp., 150 F.3d 651 (7th Cir. 1998) (Ind. law) (Easterbrook, J.) (affirming dismissal of claim against manufacturer of coffee maker; because everyone knows that hot coffee will burn if spilled on skin, lack of knowledge that it can cause third-degree burns requires no warning as matter of law); Immormino v. J & M Powers, Inc., 698 N.E.2d 516 (Ohio Ct. Comm. Pl. 1998) (hot tea; defendant's motion for summary judgment granted because consumers are commonly aware of the dangers of hot liquid spills).

**170.** See B (A Child) v. McDonald's Restaurants Ltd., 2002 WL 347059 (Q.B. 2002)

The most recent (perhaps "ultimate") type of generic liability lawsuit is represented by a couple of putative class actions filed against fast food retailers for obesity and other health problems alleged to have resulted from the plaintiffs' consumption of too much "junk food" sold by the defendants.[171] The first suit filed, *Barber v. McDonald's Corp.*,[172] sought to certify a national class action against McDonald's, Burger King, KFC, and Wendy's for intentionally and negligently selling food that is high in fat, salt, sugar, and cholesterol without properly labeling the food or warning consumers of the risks.[173] The named plaintiff, 56–year-old Caesar Barber, stood 5 feet 11 inches and weighed 285 pounds at the time of his second heart attack after eating two or three fast food meals a day over an extended period of time. The class for which certification was sought consisted of persons who consumed the defendants' fast foods and became obese or developed coronary heart disease, diabetes, high blood pressure, high cholesterol levels, or other health problems from the defendants' foods. The lawyer for the plaintiffs reportedly decided not to pursue *Barber* but to focus instead upon *Pelman v. McDonald's Corp.*,[174] another class action against McDonald's brought on behalf of obese children, including one 400–pound 15–year-old suffering from Type 2 diabetes who claims to have eaten at McDonald's daily since he was 6.[175]

Observing that its failure to act decisively "could spawn thousands of similar 'McLawsuits,' "[176] the court promptly dismissed the *Pelman* complaint, with leave to amend, ruling that fast-food restaurants had no duty to warn consumers of the open, obvious, and well-known fact that such foods contain high levels of cholesterol, fat, salt, and sugar; that the complaint failed adequately to plead proximate cause because it failed to specify how often the children ate such foods and failed to account for factors other than diet that may have contributed to the children's health problems; that it failed to specify how the fats, sugars, and other substances may have been addictive; and that it failed to allege whether the defendants purposefully manufactured the fast foods with addictive qualities. At bottom, the court observed that the lawsuit raised vital

(people expect tea and coffee to be hot and know that, if they spill such beverages, they may be burned).

**171.** The litigation is championed by public interest law professor John Banzhaf of George Washington University Law School who teaches courses in Legal Activism, Tort Law, and Administrative Law. See www.banzhaf.net/obesitylinks. See generally Ausness, Tell Me What You Eat and I Will Tell You Who to Sue: Big Problems Ahead for "Big Food?", 39 Ga. L. Rev. ___ (2005).

**172.** N.Y. Sup. Ct., Bronx Cty., No. 23145/2002, filed July 24, 2002. See New York Man Files National Class Action Alleg-

ing Fast Food Chains Make People Fat, 30 Prod. Saf. & Liab. Rep. 674 (Aug. 5, 2002); Fountain, Living Large; Our Just (Burp!) Desserts, N.Y. Times § 4, p.6, col.1, www.nytimes.com (Oct. 13, 2002).

**173.** See Note, 63 Ohio St. L.J. 1165 (2002) (applicability of the implied warranty of merchantability to fast-food litigation).

**174.** 237 F.Supp.2d 512 (S.D.N.Y. 2003).

**175.** See Comment, Obesity Liability: A Supersized Problem or a Small Fry in the Inevitable Development of Product Liability?, 7 Chap. L. Rev. 239 (Spring 2004); Parloff, Is Fat the Next Tobacco?, N.Y. Times, www.fortune.com (Jan. 21, 2003).

**176.** 237 F.Supp.2d at 518.

questions of personal responsibility,[177] an issue highlighted by the derisive popular reactions to the filing of these lawsuits noted by the press.[178] Simply put, because the complaint failed to allege that consumers are unaware of "the potential ill health effects of eating at McDonald's, they cannot blame McDonald's if they, nonetheless, choose to satiate their appetite with a surfeit of supersized McDonald's products."[179] The plaintiffs refiled,[180] later abandoned their warnings claim, and the court dismissed the remaining claims of deceptive advertising under the state Consumer Protection Act.[181] The plaintiffs' bar has had more success with other food claims,[182] and they reportedly have decided to pursue such claims with vigor,[183] assuming that the legislatures do not interfere.[184] Time alone will tell whether plaintiffs' counsel in the future will be able to muster sufficiently weighty arguments for McLawsuits of this type.

## Reform Legislation

### Inherent Risk Legislation Generally

A number of states and the federal government have enacted legislation addressing in one way or another the issue of products that contain substantial inherent risks. Some state and federal statutes ban the sale to unauthorized persons of such dangerous products as fireworks, cigarettes, alcohol, and controlled substances,[185] while other states have

**177.** "The issue of determining the breadth of personal responsibility underlies much of the law: where should the line be drawn between an individual's own responsibility to take care of herself, and society's responsibility to ensure that others shield her?" Id. at 516.

**178.** See id. at 518, quoting, among others, the following reports: Goldman, Consumer Republic: Common Sense May Not Be McDonald's Ally for Long, Adweek, Ed. 14 (Dec. 12, 2002) ("[T]he masses have expressed their incredulity at and contempt for the litigious kids—and their parents—who won't take responsibility for a lifetime of chowing down Happy Meals. With much tongue-clucking, the vox populi bemoans yet another symptom of the decline of personal responsibility and the rise of the cult of victimhood."); Shlaes, Lawyers Get Fat on McDonald's, Chi. Trib. 25 (Nov. 27, 2002) ("Every now and then America draws a cartoon of herself for the amusement of the rest of the world. Last week's fat lawsuit against McDonald's is one of those occasions."). See also Turley, Editorial, Betcha Can't Sue Just One, L.A. Times, 2002 WL 2492444 (July 24, 2002) ("Finally, there is the question of personal responsibility, which seems often ignored in these massive lawsuits. We may soon see campaigns from the industry reminding us that 'Twinkies don't kill people, people kill people.' "); Parloff, Is Fat the Next Tobacco?, N.Y. Times, www.fortune.com (Jan. 21,

2003) ("News of the lawsuit drew hoots of derision.").

**179.** Id. at 517–18. It should be recalled that, in the 1960s, the ALI included butter in § 402A's safe harbor of inherently dangerous food products commonly known to produce cholesterol and increase the risk of heart attacks. See Restatement (2d) Torts § 402A cmt. i.

**180.** See Kaufmann, Franchising Fast Food Inanity, 229 N.Y.L.J. 3 (2003).

**181.** Pelman v. McDonald's Corp., 2003 WL 22052778 (S.D.N.Y. 2003).

**182.** See Zernike, Lawyers Shift Focus From Big Tobacco to Big Food, nytimes.com (April 9, 2004) (reporting that McDonald's paid $12 million to settle a claim for failing to disclose that its French fries contained beef fat; Kraft stopped using trans fats in Oreos; and the makers of a puffy cheese snack, Pirate's Booty, paid $4 million to settle a claim that it understated fat grams).

**183.** See Zernike, Lawyers Shift Focus From Big Tobacco to Big Food, nytimes.com (April 9, 2004).

**184.** Several states have already enacted legislation prohibiting such suits, and Congress held hearings on such a bill in 2004, as discussed in the section on reform legislation, below.

**185.** In addition to banning the sale of dangerous products, legislatures sometimes

enacted products liability reform legislation that limits a manufacturer's liability for generic product risks. North Carolina's provision, for example, shields manufacturers from design defect claims arising out of "an inherent characteristic of the product that cannot be eliminated without substantially compromising the product's usefulness or desirability and that is recognized by the ordinary person with the ordinary knowledge common to the community."[186] Statutes of this type quite clearly contemplate products such as alcohol and cigarettes. Other states have also enacted generic risk statutes, but often with important variations.[187] New Jersey's statute, for example, generally shields manufacturers of such products from design defect claims but allows such claims for industrial machinery and products whose design is "egregiously unsafe."[188] And California and Texas enacted nearly identical reform statutes adopting the safe harbor list of inherently dangerous products of comment *i* to § 402A of the *Restatement (Second) of Torts* which shelters manufacturers of such products from most products liability exposure.[189] In 1998, however, California's legislature deleted "tobacco" from the safe-harbor list of protected products and added new provisions specifically authorizing products liability suits against the tobacco industry.[190] Some statutory provisions are quite specific, such as a North Carolina provision that protects manufacturers of prescription drugs that are unavoidably unsafe if adequate warnings are provided.[191]

### *Alcoholic Beverages*

From the 1960s, and year after year during the 1970s and 1980s, the FDA, Senator Strom Thurmond of South Carolina, and other members of Congress pressed the alcoholic beverage industry to adopt a voluntary labeling program warning of the dangers of such beverages. One proposed statute would have required every alcoholic beverage container to be labeled, on a rotating basis, with warnings that alcohol consumption (1) during pregnancy can cause mental retardation and other birth defects to the baby; (2) impairs a person's ability to drive a car or operate machinery; (3) is particularly hazardous in combination with some drugs; (4) can increase the risk of developing hypertension, liver disease, and cancer; and (5) is a drug and may be addictive. An earlier

---

address their disposal. See, e.g., 15 U.S.C. § 1211 (prohibiting the disposal of refrigerators without first removing their latching doors); 42 U.S.C. § 9267 (batteries and other products containing toxic chemicals).

**186.** N.C. Gen. Stat. § 99B–6(c).

**187.** In addition to the North Carolina statute, see Cal. Health & Saf. Code § 1714.45(a) and (b); Mich. Comp. Laws § 600.2947(5); Miss. Code Ann. § 11–1–63(b); N.J. Stat. Ann. § 2A:58C–3; Tex. Code Ann. § 82.004.

**188.** N.J. Stat. Ann. § 2A:58C–3. Compare Products Liability Restatement § 2 cmt. *e*.

**189.** See Cal. Health & Saf. Code § 1714.45(a) and (b). Tex. Code Ann. § 82.004, entitled "Inherently Unsafe Prod-

ucts," provides that manufacturers and sellers are immunized from products liability, except for manufacturing defects and breach of express warranty, if:

(1) the product is inherently unsafe and the product is known to be unsafe by the ordinary consumer who consumes the product with the ordinary knowledge common to the community; and

(2) the product is a common consumer product intended for personal consumption, such as sugar, castor oil, alcohol, tobacco, and butter, as identified in Comment *i* to Section 402A of the Restatement (Second) Torts.

**190.** See Cal. Health & Saf. Code § 1714.45(e), (f), and (g).

**191.** See N.C. Gen. Stat. § 99B–6(d).

bill had substituted for (5) a warning that its rapid consumption can cause immediate death.[192]

By the late 1980s, proposed legislation of this type was widely debated in Congress, state legislatures, and the media. Bills were filed (and rejected) in at least Florida and California, and one passed the Massachusetts house in 1987. More than 60 national health organizations supported the federal bill summarized above, and a Gallup poll found that nearly 80% of Americans favored the labeling of alcoholic beverages with health warnings. A national editorial contended: "Consumers need to be able to make informed choices about everything they eat or drink or take as medicine. Especially alcoholic beverages. They need to know what's in them. And to be alerted to any possible hazards."[193] Citing statistics that 100,000 Americans die from alcohol use each year, that thousands of children are born each year with alcohol-related birth defects, that "18 million Americans and their families are torn apart by addiction and related problems," and that the annual loss to the nation exceeds $100 billion, the House and Senate sponsors of the warning label legislation—Congressman Conyers and Senator Thurmond—urged its passage.[194]

Finally, Congress enacted a compromise bill, the Alcoholic Beverage Labeling Act of 1988,[195] requiring that alcoholic beverages be labeled as follows:

> Government Warning: (1) According to the Surgeon General, women should not drink alcoholic beverages during pregnancy because of the risk of birth defects.

> (2) Consumption of alcoholic beverages impairs your ability to drive a car or operate machinery, and may cause health problems.

This legislation preempts products liability claims for warnings inadequacies, at least on beverage containers.[196]

### *Firearms*

In recent years, a number of states have enacted legislation seeking to protect makers and sellers of firearms and ammunition from products

---

**192.** S. 2047, 100th Cong., 2d Sess. (1988).

**193.** USA Today, April 8, 1988, at 10A, col. 1.

**194.** Noting that they had "waited more than a decade for the industry to heed the Food and Drug Administration's call for warning labels," they concluded: "What the alcohol marketers fear is information. What the public needs is that information. If marketers will not act responsibly to educate consumers about the real risks and costs, then Congress should." Conyers and Thurmond, We Can't Wait for Industry to Act, id. at col. 3.

**195.** Codified at 27 U.S.C. § 213–19.

**196.** 27 U.S.C. § 215, the act's preemption clause, provides that state law may not require any other warning to be placed on any alcoholic beverage container or package. See Note, 18 Hofstra L. Rev. 943 (1990); Comment, 38 Emory L.J. 1189 (1989). Claims for adulteration and fraudulent misrepresentation quite probably survive the Act, but warnings claims, even creative ones, are preempted. See Note, 99 Com. L.J. 108 (1994) (proposing implied warranty claims for allergic reaction). On federal preemption generally, see § 14.4, below.

A tragic footnote to this legislation concerns its Senatorial champion, Strom Thurmond, who fought for years for its enactment. In 1993, his daughter was struck and killed by a drunk driver.

liability exposure for injury and death resulting from their improper use. Many of the statutes bar the use of risk-benefit analysis for judging the defectiveness of guns and ammunition,[197] and some provide that it is their unlawful use, not their lawful manufacture and sale, that is the proximate cause of most resulting harm.[198] The National Rifle Association has lobbied vigorously for reform legislation along these lines, and many states have now enacted statutes of this general type.[199] Virginia has a statute that removes authority from localities to sue manufacturers and other sellers of firearms and ammunition for damages resulting from their lawful manufacture and sale, reserving the right to bring such actions to the Commonwealth.[200] Pointing in the other direction, toward gun control, an ordinance in the District of Columbia provides that sellers of assault weapons and machine guns are strictly liable in tort for injury or death caused by the discharge of such weapons in the District.[201]

### *Fast Food*

In 2004, the United States House of Representatives, but not the Senate, passed a "cheeseburger bill" banning obesity-related lawsuits against restaurants and other food sellers.[202] A flurry of similar "Baby McBills" were introduced in state legislatures across the nation and, by the end of the 2004 legislative session, about a dozen states had enacted such legislation.[203] The reasonableness of this type of statute suggests that legislatures in other states will take similar action in the future.[204]

**197.** See, e.g., Cal. Civ. Code § 1714.4(a) ("no firearm or ammunition shall be deemed defective in design on the basis that the benefits of the product do not outweigh the risk of injury, damage, or death when discharged"). In 2002, however, California's legislature repealed the protection of firearms from products liability in § 1714.4.

**198.** See, e.g., S.D. Stat. § 21–58–1 ("the unlawful use of firearms, rather than their lawful manufacture, distribution, or sale, is the proximate cause of any injury arising from their unlawful use").

**199.** See, e.g., Alaska Stat. § 09.65.155; Cal. Civ. Code § 1714.4; Idaho Code § 6–1410; 720 Ill. Comp. Stat. 5/24–1, La. Rev. Stat. Ann. § 9:2800.60; Mont. Code Ann. § 27–1–720; Nev. Rev. Stat. Ann. § 41.131; N.C. Gen. Stat. § 99B–11; S.C. Code Ann. § 15–73–40; S.D. Codified Laws § 21–58–1 to–4; Tex. Civ. Prac. & Rem. § 82.006; Wash. Rev. Code § 7.72.030.

**200.** See Va. Code Ann. § 15.2–915.1

**201.** See D.C. Code Ann. § 7–2551.02 formerly 6–2392.

**202.** See Zernike, Lawyers Shift Focus From Big Tobacco to Big Food, nytimes.com

(April 9, 2004); House Passes 'Cheeseburger Bill,' Bans Obesity–Related Suits Against Food Industry, 72 U.S. Law Week–Legal News 2547 (March 16, 2004). See H.R. Rep. No. 108–432, Personal Responsibility in Food Consumption Act, H.R. 339.

**203.** Louisiana's statute, perhaps the first and enacted in 2003, is typical: "[A]ny manufacturer, distributor or seller of a food or non-alcoholic beverage intended for human consumption shall not be subject to civil liability for personal injury or wrongful death where liability is premised upon an individual's weight gain, obesity or a health condition related to weight gain or obesity and resulting from his long term consumption of a food or non-alcoholic beverage." La. Rev. Stat. Ann. § 9:2799.6. See also Ariz. Rev. Stat. § 12–681; Colo. Rev. Stat. § 13–21–1101; Fla. Stat. Ann. § 768.37; Ga. Code Ann. § 26–2–430; Idaho Code § 39–8701; Mo. Rev. Stat. § 537.900; S.D. Codified Laws § 21–61–2; Tenn. Code Ann. § 39–17–1314; Utah Code Ann. § 78–27d–101; Wash. Rev. Code § 7.72.070.

**204.** At least California, Illinois, Nebraska, Ohio, and Wisconsin considered but did not enact such bills in 2004.

## § 10.4   STATE OF THE ART

In products liability law, "state of the art" is an unrefined concept whose meaning and proper role still continue to evolve.[1] The concept remains loosely and variously defined by courts and legislatures, and many courts have not yet crystallized the developing doctrine in this area into formal rules. Nevertheless, emerging from the cases and statutes is a common theme: reluctance to impose liability on manufacturers for dangers that were unknowable, or unpreventable, at the time their products were sold—reluctance to hold producers responsible for risks they cannot control.

State-of-the-art issues may be conveniently classified according to whether the asserted defect is one of warning or design.[2] In warning cases, the state-of-the-art issue involves a manufacturer's ability to foresee a product danger to enable it to warn consumers of its presence.[3] While manufacturers are at least generally aware of most hazards that lurk within their products before they are sold to consumers and cause harm, dangers are occasionally unknown or undiscoverable before a product is sold and put to use. Blood infected with serum hepatitis, a condition that is undetectable before blood is transfused into a person,[4] is a prime example, as was the presence of the AIDS virus in blood

### § 10.4

**1.** On the state-of-the-art issue in products liability law, see V. Schwartz and R. Tedesco, The Re–Emergence of "Super Strict" Liability: Slaying the Dragon Again, 71 U. Cin. L. Rev. 917 (2003); Ben–Shahar, Should Products Liability Be Based on Hindsight?, 14 J. L. Econ. & Org. 325 (1998); Cupp, Rethinking Conscious Design Liability for Prescription Drugs: The Restatement (Third) Standard Versus a Negligence Approach, 63 Geo. Wash. L. Rev. 76 (1994); Vandall, State-of-the-Art, Custom, and Reasonable Alternative Design, 28 Suffolk U. L. Rev. 1193 (1994); Wertheimer, Unknowable Dangers and the Death of Strict Products Liability: The Empire Strikes Back, 60 U. Cin. L. Rev. 1183 (1992); V. Schwartz, Unavoidably Unsafe Products: Clarifying the Meaning and Policy Behind Comment K, 42 Wash. & Lee. L. Rev. 1139 (1985); Birnbaum and Wrubel, "State of the Art" and Strict Products Liability, 21 Tort & Ins. L.J. 30 (1985); Wade, On the Effect in Product Liability of Knowledge Unavailable Prior to Marketing, 58 N.Y.U. L. Rev. 734 (1983); Page, Generic Product Risks: The Case Against Comment k and for Strict Tort Liability, N.Y.U. L. Rev. 853 (1983); Robb, A Practical Approach to Use of the State of the Art Evidence in Strict Products Liability Cases, 77 Nw. U. L. Rev. 1 (1982); O'Donnell, Design Litigation and the State of the Art: Terminology, Practice and Reform, 11 Akron L. Rev. 627 (1978); Willig, The Comment k Character: A Conceptual Barrier to Strict Liability, 29 Mercer L. Rev. 627 (1978); Newdick, Risk, Uncertainty and "Knowledge" in the Development Risk Defence, 20 Anglo–Am. L. Rev. 309 (1991); Annot. 33 A.L.R.4th 368 (1981) (state of the art in strict liability warnings cases; whether defendant must know of danger).

**2.** On rare occasions the issue arises in manufacturing defect cases. Compare Cunningham v. MacNeal Memorial Hospital, 266 N.E.2d 897, 902 (Ill. 1970) ("To allow a defense to strict liability on the ground that there is no way, either practical or theoretical, for a defendant to ascertain the existence of impurities in his product would be to emasculate the doctrine and in a very real sense would signal a return to a negligence theory."), with Indianapolis Athletic Club, Inc. v. Alco Standard Corp., 709 N.E.2d 1070 (Ind. Ct. App. 1999) (statutory state-of-the-art defense covered manufacturing defects as well as defects in warnings and design).

**3.** These cases usually involve claims of failure to warn rather than design defectiveness, but the unknowable risk issue occasionally does arise in a design defect claim. See, e.g., Dean v. General Motors Corp., 301 F.Supp. 187 (E.D. La. 1969) (foreseeability of thieves breaking into cars in certain way which could have been prevented by changing lock and key design).

**4.** See, e.g., Cunningham v. MacNeal Memorial Hosp., 266 N.E.2d 897, 902 (Ill. 1970) (rejecting state-of-the-art defense).

products prior to the development of reliable tests during the early 1980s.[5] Pork containing trichinae parasites, causing trichinosis in people who eat such pork without proper cooking, is another example of an undiscoverable product hazard.[6] Similarly, pharmaceutical drugs, chemicals, and other substances, such as asbestos, may be discovered to have toxic effects only after such products are marketed and harm consumers, sometimes generations later.[7] If such dangers prove to have been foreseeable, discoverable with appropriate pre-market testing or analysis, and if they were avoidable by appropriate warnings, processing, or redesign, then the manufacturers of such products may be held responsible for the harmful results of failing to discover or avoid those risks under ordinary principles of negligence, warranty, or strict liability in tort. But if the risks were in fact unknowable before consumers began to suffer harm, the question of responsibility for failing to warn about or otherwise address such unforeseeable risks becomes more complicated.

The second type of state of the art case involves the feasibility of adopting curative design measures to reduce or eliminate a risk of which the manufacturer is aware. Although manufacturers are well aware of most hazards in the durable products they make and sell, such hazards are often practicably unavoidable under the prevailing state of science and technology. Persons may be injured in countless ways: a person's foot may slip under a power lawnmower, a hand may be caught in a punch press or other industrial machine, a car may collide at high speed into a tree, and a kitchen stove burner may ignite a dish towel or a blouse. The science and technology of safety is constantly evolving—such as the development in recent years of guards, electrical interlocks, and other safety enhancements for power lawn mowers and industrial machinery; airbags for automobiles; and flame retardant chemicals for fabrics—to help reduce various risks of injury. But hands and feet still find ways to get under mowers and into machines, bones still get broken in car accidents, and fabrics still catch fire on kitchen stoves. Other kinds of products involve dangers which are entirely unavoidable under current science and technology, not just practicably so, such as the basic health risks of cigarettes and alcohol, and various side-effects of important pharmaceutical drugs, such as the Pasteur rabies vaccine.[8] The question in these types of cases is not whether the *risks* are known or knowable, for the hazards are well known, but whether the means of *avoiding* the risks, by designing them away, are known or reasonably knowable and feasible under the existing state of science and technology.

---

**5.** The contaminated blood issue is separately treated in § 16.9, below.

**6.** See, e.g., Kircos v. Holiday Food Ctr., Inc., 477 N.W.2d 130 (Mich. Ct. App. 1991) (public knows that pork must be cooked to be sure to avoid trichinosis); Hohn v. South Shore Serv., Inc., 529 N.Y.S.2d 129 (App. Div. 1988) (raw pork containing trichina spirulis not "adulterated"); Trabaudo v. Kenton Ruritan Club, Inc. 517 A.2d 706 (Del. Super. Ct. 1986) (no duty on sellers to inspect raw pork for trichinae infestation nor to warn consumers of need to cook properly); Hollinger v. Shoppers Paradise of N.J., Inc., 340 A.2d 687 (N.J. Super. Ct. Law Div. 1975) (seller not subject to liability because danger undetectable by seller and curable by proper cooking by buyer). See generally 4 Frumer and Friedman, Products Liability § 48.21[4][c].

**7.** See § 10.5, below.

**8.** See Restatement (2d) Torts § 402A cmt. *k.*

As science and technology evolve over time, permitting the development of new and improved methods for discovering product hazards and eliminating them prior to sale, public attitudes toward risk and responsibility also evolve. In the twenty-first century, people fairly expect much more safety in machine guarding, automotive crash protection, and fabric flammability than they did in 1900, or even in 1950. "A consumer would not expect a Model T to have the safety features which are incorporated in automobiles made today."[9] Whether manufacturers should be liable for failing to avert product-caused injuries that happen today, but which were unforeseeable or unpreventable (literally or practicably) at the time the products were designed and sold, raises difficult and important questions of logic, fairness, social policy, and legal doctrine.[10]

Penetrating to the heart of defectiveness and "strict" liability, the state-of-the-art issue forces courts and commentators to re-examine the goals of products liability law by raising a number of fundamental questions: Who should bear the risks and benefits of changes in science and technology that develop over time? How should the law deal with changes in public attitudes toward risk, manufacturers, individual responsibility, and products liability doctrine? Are juries capable of fairly judging products made before the jurors were born, according to the technology, standards, and values of long ago? Is the judicial system capable of resolving these problems in a principled manner, or is the legislature a preferable forum for drawing the basic liability lines? Courts, legislatures, and commentators must grapple with these perplexing questions that lie on the cutting edge of modern products liability law.

The state-of-the-art issue is treated generally in the materials that follow. Liability for the related issue of inherent or "generic" dangers in products such as cigarettes, handguns, and alcoholic beverages was examined in the previous section.[11]

## Definitions

As products liability law has developed, the terms "undiscoverable," "unknowable," "unavoidable," and "state of the art" have often been interchanged indiscriminately by courts and commentators attempting to describe certain kinds of risks that manufacturers and other sellers are unable to control. Increasingly, however, issues of this type are collected under the latter phrase, as in "state-of-the-art evidence" and "state-of-the-art defense." Due in part to the diffuse nature of the state-of-the-art concept, which embraces such diverse aspects of manufacturer responsibility as the foreseeability of risk, the feasibility of implementing a safer design, and the proper scope of "strict" liability, neither courts

**9.** Bruce v. Martin–Marietta Corp., 544 F.2d 442, 447 (10th Cir. 1976) (Md. law).

**10.** See, e.g., Henderson, Coping with the Time Dimension in Products Liability, 69 Cal. L. Rev. 919 (1981); Phillips, An Analysis of Proposed Reform of Products Liability Statutes of Limitations, 56 N.C. L. Rev. 663 (1978); and articles cited in note 1, above.

**11.** See § 10.3, above.

nor legislatures have agreed on a definition of the term.[12] Thus, "state of the art" means quite different things to different persons. To many manufacturers and some courts,[13] the phrase refers to customary practice in the industry. To many plaintiffs' counsel and some courts,[14] it means the ultimate in existing technology, including all knowledge pertinent to a problem existing at the time, regardless of its location or source, regardless of whether possessed by or accessible from industrial, governmental, or academic institutions, or even from the defendant's competitors.[15]

Neither of these extreme views of state of the art is a helpful definition for products liability law. To allow a manufacturer to hide behind the customary practices of an industry would create a shield stronger than that allowed by ordinary negligence law, where the *T. J. Hooper* rule[16] requires enterprises to conduct their affairs with reasonable prudence, even if the level of safety prevailing in the industry as a whole has lagged behind a standard of good behavior.[17] Thus, most courts properly distinguish state-of-the-art evidence from evidence of custom.[18] But to define state of the art in terms of the best science and

**12.** See, e.g., Lane v. Amsted Indus., Inc., 779 S.W.2d 754, 759 n.4 (Mo. Ct. App. 1989) ("The judicial decisions and some commentary employ the term *state of the art* without distinction to mean industry practice and custom, industry capability, industry or scientific knowability, and even compliance with government regulations."); Potter v. Chicago Pneumatic Tool Co., 694 A.2d 1319, 1345 (Conn. 1997) ("the term 'state of the art' has been the source of substantial confusion").

**13.** See, e.g., Lane v. Amsted Industries, Inc., 779 S.W.2d 754, 758 (Mo. Ct. App. 1989); Smith v. Minster Mach. Co., 669 F.2d 628, 633 (10th Cir. 1982) (Okla. law) (state of the art "is understood to mean simply the custom and practice in an industry"); Sturm, Ruger & Co. v. Day, 594 P.2d 38, 44–45 (Alaska 1979) ("Generally speaking, 'state of the art' refers to customary practice in the industry.").

**14.** See, e.g., Wiska v. St. Stanislaus Social Club, Inc., 390 N.E.2d 1133, 1138 n.8 (Mass. App. Ct. 1979) ("the level of pertinent scientific and technical knowledge existing at the time"); ACandS, Inc. v. Asner, 686 A.2d 250, 254 (Md. 1996) (" 'all of the available knowledge on a subject at a given time, and this includes scientific, medical, engineering, and any other knowledge that may be available' ").

**15.** See Owens–Illinois, Inc. v. Zenobia, 601 A.2d 633, 644–45 (Md. 1992).

**16.** Named, of course, after Judge Learned Hand's celebrated decision in The T.J. Hooper, 60 F.2d 737 (2d Cir. 1932) (Hand, J.). The *T. J. Hooper* rule provides that industry practice or custom, while important evidence of the reasonableness of a defendant's conduct, is not generally con-

clusive, since the industry as a whole may have been derelict in failing to adopt precautionary procedures dictated by ordinary prudence:

> [I]n most cases reasonable prudence is in fact common prudence; but strictly it is never its measure; a whole calling may have unduly lagged in the adoption of new and available devices. It never may set its own tests.... Courts must in the end say what is required; there are precautions so imperative that even their universal disregard will not excuse their omission.

Id. at 740. Judge Hand drew upon the wisdom of another giant, Justice Holmes, in Texas & Pacific Ry. Co. v. Behymer, 189 U.S. 468, 470 (1903): "What usually is done may be evidence of what ought to be done, but what ought to be done is fixed by a standard of reasonable prudence, whether it usually is complied with or not."

**17.** See, e.g., Hillrichs v. Avco Corp., 514 N.W.2d 94, 98 (Iowa 1994) (custom of cornpicker manufacturers not to equip them with $50 emergency stop device no bar to claim of negligent design); § 2.3 (evidence of custom to establish negligence), § 6.4 (evidence of custom to establish defectiveness), above.

**18.** See, e.g., Falada v. Trinity Indus., Inc., 642 N.W.2d 247, 250 (Iowa 2002) (" 'Custom refers to what was being done in the industry; state of the art refers to what feasibly could have been done.' "); Potter v. Chicago Pneumatic Tool Co., 694 A.2d 1319, 1347 (Conn. 1997) ("state of the art refers to what is technologically feasible, rather than merely industry custom");

technology in existence would go too far in the opposite direction: to require manufacturers to put new safety theories instantly into practice, when the theories may be locked away in arcane scientific journals (perhaps in another language) and are years removed from real-world application, is to ask manufacturers to perform a practical impossibility. Holding manufacturers to a standard so rigorous would in some cases force them to serve as guarantors or insurers of product safety, which for a variety of good reasons the law has never sought to do.[19]

Most statutes and judicial decisions define the state of the art idea more moderately along a middle ground, lying somewhere between these two extremes. For example, Nebraska's products reform act defines state of the art as "the best technology reasonably available at the time,"[20] and Missouri's statute states that the phrase "means that the dangerous nature of the product was not known and could not reasonably be discovered at the time the product was placed into the stream of commerce."[21] Arizona's statute is more prolix, but similar in its spirit: " 'state of the art' means the technical, mechanical and scientific knowledge of manufacturing, designing, testing or labeling the same or similar products which was in existence and reasonably feasible for use at the time of manufacture."[22]

Courts have variously stated that state of the art refers to "what feasibly could have been done,"[23] "the existing level of technological expertise and scientific knowledge relevant to a particular industry at the time a product is designed,"[24] "the technological feasibility of alternative safer designs in existence at the time the product was originally manufactured,"[25] "danger ... which [manufacturers] know or should have known on the basis of reasonably obtainable or available knowledge,"[26] whether "the particular risk was neither known nor knowable by the application of scientific knowledge available at the time of manufacture and/or distribution,"[27] "the best technology reasonably feasible at the time,"[28] whether "safety features ... were unknown or unavailable at the time the product" was sold,[29] and "the level of

---

ACandS, Inc. v. Asner, 686 A.2d 250, 254–55 (Md. 1996) ("Industry standards are the practices common to a given industry ... often set forth in some type of code [or] adopted by the trade organization of a given industry. State of the art is a higher standard because scientific knowledge expands much more rapidly than industry can assimilate the knowledge and adopt it as a standard."); Lenhardt v. Ford Motor Co., 683 P.2d 1097, 1099 (Wash. 1984); Carter v. Massey–Ferguson, Inc., 716 F.2d 344, 347 (5th Cir. 1983) (Wisdom, J.) (Tex. law) (evidence of industry custom that skidders are not equipped with back-up alarms is relevant to determination of risk or utility: " 'Custom' refers to the usual practice of the manufacturer, that is, what *is* done; 'state of the art' refers to the technological environment, that is, what *can* be done."); Bolm v. Triumph Corp., 422 N.Y.S.2d 969, 975 n.2 (App. Div. 1979).

**19.** See §§ 5.3 and 5.4, above.

**20.** See Neb. Rev. Stat. § 25–21,182.

**21.** See Mo. Ann. Stat. § 537.764.

**22.** See Ariz. Rev. Stat. § 12–681(8).

**23.** Falada v. Trinity Indus., Inc., 642 N.W.2d 247, 250 (Iowa 2002).

**24.** Crispin v. Volkswagenwerk A.G., 591 A.2d 966, 973 (N.J. Super. Ct. App. Div. 1991). See O'Brien v. Muskin Corp., 463 A.2d 298, 305 (N.J. 1983).

**25.** Lenhardt v. Ford Motor Co., 683 P.2d 1097, 1099 (Wash. 1984).

**26.** Feldman v. Lederle Labs., 479 A.2d 374, 376 (N.J. 1984).

**27.** Anderson v. Owens–Corning Fiberglas Corp., 810 P.2d 549, 559 (Cal. 1991).

**28.** Indianapolis Athletic Club, Inc. v. Alco Standard Corp., 709 N.E.2d 1070, 1074 (Ind. Ct. App. 1999).

**29.** Owens–Corning Fiberglas Corp. v. Golightly, 976 S.W.2d 409, 411 (Ky. 1998).

relevant scientific, technological and safety knowledge existing and reasonably feasible at the time of design."[30]

Moderate definitions such as these, based on reasonableness and practicability, appear most useful in drawing the state of the art line in a fair and pragmatic manner. An appropriate state of the art definition protects manufacturers who strive to stay abreast of (and perhaps advance) the developing science and technology of safety in their fields, and who implement such developments when practicable to do so, while properly ensnaring manufacturers unwilling to make such a commitment to product safety.

In sum, the precise manner in which "state of the art" definitions are formulated varies considerably, some leaning more toward industry custom, others leaning more toward theoretical technological capability, and the best ones lying somewhere in between. Some courts[31] and legislatures[32] simply use the term without defining it, which, while it avoids misdefining the term, provides decisionmakers with little guidance. Other courts[33] and legislatures[34] use the concepts but not the "state of the art" term, which has the benefit of providing appropriate limitations on liability while avoiding ambiguities in the term itself. But the "state of the art" term, which usefully describes a basic limitation of the law of products liability law, has a commonsense ring that may help to guide both courts and juries. It would seem hard to improve upon

**30.** Potter v. Chicago Pneumatic Tool Co., 694 A.2d 1319, 1346 (Conn. 1997) (quoting definitions from other cases, and stating that its definition is endorsed by a majority of courts).

**31.** See, e.g., Keogh v. W.R. Grasle, Inc., 816 P.2d 1343, 1349 n.10 (Alaska 1991). Compare Phillips v. Cameron Tool Corp., 950 F.2d 488 (7th Cir. 1991) (Ind. law) (because opposing lawyers defined the term differently in jury argument, trial judge's failure to define term was reversible error).

**32.** The statutes in Florida, Idaho, Indiana, Iowa, Kansas, and New Hampshire take this approach. See, e.g., Montgomery Ward & Co. v. Gregg, 554 N.E.2d 1145, 1155 (Ind. Ct. App. 1990); Phillips v. Cameron Tool Corp., 950 F.2d 488 (7th Cir. 1991) (Ind. law).

**33.** See, e.g., Flock v. Scripto–Tokai Corp., 319 F.3d 231, 239 (5th Cir. 2003) (Tex. law) (plaintiff required to prove availability of safer alternative design that was "economically and technologically feasible at the time the product left the control of the manufacturer or seller by the application of existing or reasonably achievable scientific knowledge"); McDaniel v. Trail King Indus., Inc., 248 F.Supp.2d 749, 757 (N.D. Ill. 2002) (alternative design must be "economical, practical and effective"); La-Belle v. Philip Morris Inc., 243 F.Supp.2d

508, 517 (D.S.C. 2001) (Pa. law) (alternative design must have been "feasible"); Cooper v. General Motors Corp., 702 So.2d 428, 443–44 (Miss. 1997) ("[I]mposing liability on a manufacturer for not installing an air bag in the early eighties, when air bags were new to the scene and still undergoing scientific testing, goes against the grain of public policy. The principles of law should not overlook the need for scientific development or bring manufacturers to their knees for choosing one restraint system over another, in light of what was known to them at the time of their manufacturing."). See also Artis v. Corona Corp., 703 A.2d 1214, 1217 (D.C. 1997) ("[A] safer alternative design may have been economically and technologically feasible at the time of the product's manufacture, but it may not have been commercially available. All that is required is that it be commercially feasible at the time of manufacture."); Young v. Key Pharm., Inc., 922 P.2d 59 (Wash. 1996) (unknown side-effect in drug).

**34.** Statutes in Louisiana, Michigan, Mississippi, and Tennessee take this approach. For example, the Michigan statute provides that a manufacturer is not liable for failing to warn unless it "knew or should have known about the risk of harm based on the scientific, technical, or medical information reasonably available at the time" of manufacture. Mich. Stat. Ann. § 600.2948(3).

Nebraska's simple, balanced definition of "the best technology reasonably available at the time."[35]

### Applicability to Different Types of Claims

State-of-the-art evidence is highly relevant to negligence claims, which are predicated on a manufacturer's ability to foresee and prevent product accidents. As discussed above, the state-of-the-art issue usually concerns either: (1) the foreseeability of a particular risk of which the plaintiff claims the defendant failed to warn, or (2) the feasibility of modifying a design in a particular manner to eliminate a risk of which the manufacturer was aware. In a negligent *warnings* case, if a risk is "unknowable," it is "unforeseeable" and so lies outside the manufacturer's duty to avoid.[36] In a negligent *design* case, if the manufacturer had no practical ability to eliminate a danger, then the burden on the manufacturer to avoid an injury outweighs virtually any risk of harm. For these reasons, perhaps all courts hold that state-of-the-art evidence is especially relevant to products liability claims brought in negligence.[37]

The relevance of the state-of-the-art issue to *strict* liability claims is more problematic. "Strict" liability implies that liability is imposed merely for selling a product which is too dangerous, according to some standard of excessive danger, not whether the manufacturer or other seller should be faulted for selling the product. Indeed, "strict liability" is often labeled "no-fault" liability.[38] If fault indeed is irrelevant to this form of liability, the state-of-the-art issue might appear to be irrelevant to whether a manufacturer is strictly liable for selling a product that is defective. This was the position of the court in *Johnson v. Raybestos–Manhattan, Inc.*,[39] which answered a certified question in an asbestos case on whether state-of-the-art evidence on the foreseeability of the risk is relevant to a strict tort claim. The court began by noting that a strict products liability action does not require a showing of defendant fault, but only that the defendant was a commercial seller, that the product was defective, and that the defect caused the plaintiff's harm.[40] The court thus concluded that "in a strict products liability action, the issue of whether the seller knew or reasonably should have known of the dangers inherent in his or her product is irrelevant to the issue of liability. Although highly relevant to a negligence action, it has absolutely no bearing on the elements of a strict product liability claim." Accordingly, the court ruled that "in a strict products liability action, state-of-the-art evidence is not admissible for the purpose of establishing whether the

---

**35.** See Neb. Rev. Stat. § 25–21,182.

**36.** See § 2.2, above.

**37.** See, e.g., Zavala v. Powermatic, Inc., 658 N.E.2d 371, 374 (Ill. 1995); Spieker v. Westgo, Inc., 479 N.W.2d 837 (N.D. 1992); Fell v. Kewanee Farm Equip. Co., 457 N.W.2d 911 (Iowa 1990); Johnson v. Raybestos–Manhattan, Inc., 740 P.2d 548, 549 (Haw. 1987) ("the issue of whether the seller knew or reasonably should have known of the dangers inherent in his or her product" is "highly relevant" to negligence

claims); Pontifex v. Sears, Roebuck & Co., 226 F.2d 909 (4th Cir. 1955) (Va. law). Compare Golonka v. General Motors Corp., 65 P.3d 956, 965 (Ariz. Ct. App. 2003) (jury could not consistently find that state of art defense protected manufacturer against design defect claim but not against negligent design claim).

**38.** See § 5.1, above.

**39.** 740 P.2d 548 (Haw. 1987).

**40.** See id. at 549.

seller knew or reasonably should have known of the dangerousness of his or her product."[41] A small handful of other courts have reasoned similarly that state-of-the-art evidence is simply irrelevant to products liability tort claims which are "strict." Most of these cases are older decisions,[42] the continued viability of which may be in doubt.[43] But at least a couple of courts in more recent decisions have reaffirmed their commitment to a truly "strict" products liability doctrine uncontaminated by principles of foreseeability, fault, negligence, or state of the art.[44]

From a strictly doctrinal perspective, barring state-of-the-art evidence is logical under a pure consumer expectations test for defectiveness because a manufacturer's knowledge of a danger or ability to eliminate it might well seem irrelevant to the degree of safety consumers actually expect.[45] Nevertheless, some courts allow state-of-the-art evi-

**41.** Id.

**42.** See, e.g., Cunningham v. MacNeal Mem'l Hosp., 266 N.E.2d 897, 902 (Ill. 1970) ("To allow a defense to strict liability on the ground that there is no way, either practical or theoretical, for a defendant to ascertain the existence of impurities in his product would be to emasculate the doctrine and in a very real sense would signal a return to a negligence theory."); Lunt v. Brady Mfg. Corp., 475 P.2d 964, 966 (Ariz. Ct. App. 1970) ("It does not matter if the seller has done 'the best he can' if the product is defective and unreasonably dangerous."); Elmore v. Owens–Illinois, Inc., 673 S.W.2d 434, 438 (Mo. 1984) ("[t]he manufacturer's standard of care is irrelevant because it relates to the reasonableness of the manufacturer's design choice; fault is an irrelevant consideration on the issue of liability in the strict liability context"); Carrecter v. Colson Equipment Co., 499 A.2d 326, 331 (Pa. Super. Ct. 1985) (state-of-the-art evidence would "inject negligence [principles] into a products liability case"); Kisor v. Johns–Manville Corp., 783 F.2d 1337 (9th Cir. 1986) (Wash. law); Connelly v. General Motors Corp., 540 N.E.2d 370 (Ill. App. Ct. 1989); Speiker v. Westgo, Inc., 479 N.W.2d 837 (N.D. 1992).

Compare Morton v. Owens–Corning Fiberglas Corp., 40 Cal.Rptr.2d 22 (Ct. App. 1995) (consumer expectations prong of Barker two-pronged standard); Crocker v. Winthrop Laboratories, 514 S.W.2d 429, 433 (Tex. 1974) (Restatement (2d) Torts § 402B: "Whatever the danger and state of medical knowledge, . . . when the drug company positively and specifically represents its product to be free and safe from all dangers of addiction, . . . the drug company is liable when the representation proves to be false and harm results.").

**43.** For example, Vassallo v. Baxter Healthcare Corp., 696 N.E.2d 909 (Mass. 1998), effectively overruled Hayes v. Ariens Co., 462 N.E.2d 273 (Mass. 1984), and stat-

utes in Arizona, Washington, and Missouri adopt some version of the state-of-the-art defense. Arizona's statute provides a general state-of-the-art defense, and Missouri's statute allows such a defense to strict tort warnings claims. The Washington statute defines liability for both warnings and design in terms of "negligence," specifically defines defective design partially in terms of the availability of a practical and feasible alternative design, and provides for the admissibility of evidence on custom and technological feasibility. See Ariz. Rev. Stat. § 12–683(1); Mo. Ann. Stat. § 537.764; Wash. Rev. Code Ann. §§ 7.72.030 & 7.72.050.

**44.** See, e.g., Golonka v. General Motors Corp., 65 P.3d 956, 963 (Ariz. Ct. App. 2003); Green v. Smith & Nephew AHP, Inc., 629 N.W.2d 727, 736–52 (Wis. 2001) (foreseeability of risk irrelevant to consumer expectations test for design defectiveness, which court reaffirmed as proper test to assure that costs of defective products are borne by manufacturers rather than consumers); Sternhagen v. Dow Co., 935 P.2d 1139, 1144–47 (Mont. 1997) (state-of-the-art defense rejected in strict products liability case because it raises reasonableness and foreseeability issues relevant to negligence which would abandon the core principles of modern products liability law: consumer protection against dangerous defects and compensation for resulting injuries, and making those who profit from sale of such products bear resulting costs; hence, focusing on product's condition rather than manufacturer's knowledge or conduct). Compare Uxa ex rel. Uxa v. Marconi, 128 S.W.3d 121, 131 (Mo. Ct. App. 2003) ("state-of-the-art" evidence, that really just shows custom, is irrelevant to claim alleging design defect).

**45.** See, e.g., Morton v. Owens–Corning Fiberglas Corp., 40 Cal.Rptr.2d 22 (Ct. App. 1995), in which plaintiff presented case on

dence even under the consumer expectations test, reasoning that such evidence "helps to determine the expectation of the ordinary consumer. A consumer would not expect a Model T to have the safety features which are incorporated in automobiles made today."[46] The Wade–Keeton constructive knowledge test of liability,[47] which imputes knowledge of all a product's dangers to the manufacturer, would seem to compel rejection of the state-of-the-art defense, at least in cases involving a failure to warn. By its nature, this test evaluates the safety of a product with the hindsight available at the time of trial and so leaves no room for evidence, much less a defense, that is based on the state of knowledge prevailing at the time the product was made and sold.[48]

As the risk-utility test of design defectiveness has increasingly displaced the consumer expectations standard around the nation,[49] and as the Wade–Keeton constructive knowledge test has fallen into desuetude,[50] the relevance of state-of-the-art evidence in design cases has become increasingly clear. In balancing the costs and benefits of a design feature that would have prevented the plaintiff's injury, the risk-utility test rests on the availability of a *feasible* alternative design.[51] Consequently, in the increasing number of jurisdictions that employ some form of risk-utility test for design defectiveness, courts widely hold that state-of-the-art evidence is admissible on the issue of the defectiveness of a product's design.[52]

consumer expectations prong of Barker's two-pronged standard. "[E]vidence as to what the scientific community knew about the dangers of asbestos and when they knew it is not relevant to show what the ordinary consumer of OCF's product reasonably expected in terms of safety at the time of Mr. Morton's exposure. It is the knowledge and reasonable expectations of the consumer, not the scientific community, that is relevant under the consumer expectations test. The fact that the scientific community was unaware of the dangers of asbestos, if that is a fact, would not make it any less reasonable for Mr. Morton or other consumers of OCF's products to expect that they could work with or near OCF's product without getting cancer." Id. at 25.

**46.** Bruce v. Martin–Marietta Corp., 544 F.2d 442, 447 (10th Cir. 1976) (Okla. law). See also Potter v. Chicago Pneumatic Tool Co., 694 A.2d 1319, 1346–48 (Conn. 1997) (collecting cases).

**47.** See § 8.7, above.

**48.** The classic holding to this effect was in Beshada v. Johns–Manville Prods. Corp., 447 A.2d 539 (N.J. 1982), restricted to its facts in Feldman v. Lederle Laboratories, 479 A.2d 374 (N.J. 1984). Both cases are discussed below.

**49.** See chapters 5 & 8, above.

**50.** See § 8.7, above.

**51.** See §§ 5.7, 8.4, & 8.5, above.

**52.** See, e.g., Falada v. Trinity Indus., Inc., 642 N.W.2d 247, 250 (Iowa 2002) (statutory defense); LaBelle v. Philip Morris Inc., 243 F.Supp.2d 508, 517–522 (D.S.C. 2001) (Pa. law) (no design defect if plaintiff unable to prove availability of technology to make safer cigarette); Potter v. Chicago Pneumatic Tool Co., 694 A.2d 1319, 1347 (Conn. 1997) (such evidence is "relevant and assists the jury in determining whether a product is defective and unreasonably dangerous"); Penick v. Christensen, 912 S.W.2d 276 (Tex. App. 1995) (such evidence may be considered on risk-utility balancing); Hughes v. Massey–Ferguson, Inc., 522 N.W.2d 294 (Iowa 1994); Fibreboard Corp. v. Fenton, 845 P.2d 1168, 1174 (Colo. 1993) ("State-of-the-art evidence is clearly admissible and is a factor to consider in determining whether a product is defective and unreasonably dangerous due to a defective design."); Keogh v. W.R. Grasle, Inc., 816 P.2d 1343 (Alaska 1991); Boatland of Houston, Inc. v. Bailey, 609 S.W.2d 743 (Tex. 1980).

Some courts allow defendants to introduce state-of-the-art evidence in rebuttal of a plaintiff's proofs of the feasibility of an alternative design. See, e.g., Murphy v. Chestnut Mountain Lodge, Inc., 464 N.E.2d 818 (Ill. App. Ct. 1984); Cantu v. John Deere Co., 603 P.2d 839 (Wash. Ct. App. 1979). This is only logical, since "state of the art refers to what *feasibly* could have been done." Mercer v. Pittway Corp., 616 N.W.2d 602, 622 (Iowa 2000).

In warnings cases involving "unknowable" risks of harm, state-of-the-art evidence plays a critical role. Notwithstanding the approach of a few decisions such as *Johnson*, discussed above, almost all courts allow state-of-the-art evidence in such cases to defeat strict liability claims. Otherwise stated, and as examined in detail below, the vast majority of courts today do not impose a duty on manufacturers to warn of unknowable risks.

### Procedural Effect of State-of-the-Art Evidence

Courts and legislatures that permit state-of-the-art evidence accord it one of three procedural effects: (1) as establishing an affirmative defense; (2) as creating a rebuttable presumption of non-defectiveness or non-negligence; or (3) as merely providing relevant evidence that a product was not defective or that a manufacturer or other supplier was not negligent. Most state statutes shield products liability defendants from liability, directly or indirectly, if they establish that the risk that injured the plaintiff was not reasonably foreseeable, or that the science or technology did not exist to prevent it.[53]

Several state statutes explicitly provide manufacturers with an affirmative state-of-the-art defense for products liability claims (either generally, or limited to warnings or other particular types of claims).[54] A handful of state statutes implicitly provide a state-of-the-art defense for design defectiveness by requiring a plaintiff to prove a feasible alternative design,[55] and courts in a number of states effectively provide such a defense in failure to warn cases by requiring a plaintiff to prove that the risk was foreseeable.[56] Statutes in Colorado, Indiana, and Kentucky create rebuttable presumptions—that the product was not defective or the defendant was not negligent—from proof that the defendant complied with the state of the art in a products liability case.[57]

Several statutes and the great majority of judicial opinions on state-of-the-art evidence take the position that this type of evidence, concern-

---

**53.** "In short, the state-of-the-art defense is a complete defense." Fell v. Kewanee Farm Equip. Co., 457 N.W.2d 911, 920 (Iowa 1990) (statutory defense). See also Falada v. Trinity Indus., 642 N.W.2d 247, 250 (Iowa 2002) (same); Brown v. Philip Morris Inc., 228 F.Supp.2d 506, 520–24 (D.N.J. 2002) (same); Fabian v. Minster Mach. Co., 609 A.2d 487, 492 (N.J. Super. Ct. App. Div. 1992) (feasible alternative design statute, referred to as a state-of-the-art statute, provides an "absolute defense" for design defect claims); Mo. Rev. Stat. § 537.764(2) ("The state of the art shall be a complete defense" for failure to warn claims.); N.H. Rev. Stat. Ann. § 507:8–g ("it is an affirmative defense that the risks complained of by the plaintiff were not discoverable using prevailing research and scientific techniques under the state of the art"). Statutory reform of the state-of-the-art issue is treated further, below.

**54.** See the statutes in Arizona, Iowa, Louisiana, Mississippi, Missouri, Nebraska, New Hampshire, and New Jersey. The statutes are set forth in 1 Madden & Owen on Products Liability § 10.7.

**55.** Statutes in at least Louisiana, Mississippi, New Jersey, North Carolina, and Texas require proof of a feasible alternative design to establish liability for a product's design in all or most design danger cases. See 1 Madden & Owen on Products Liability § 10.7 (excerpting the statutes).

**56.** See, e.g., Anderson v. Owens–Corning Fiberglas Corp., 810 P.2d 549 (Cal. 1991); Vassallo v. Baxter Healthcare Corp., 696 N.E.2d 909 (Mass. 1998); Brown v. Superior Court, 751 P.2d 470 (Cal. 1988); Feldman v. Lederle Labs., 479 A.2d 374 (N.J. 1984).

**57.** See Colo. Rev. Stat. § 13–21–403(1)(a); Ind. Code § 34–20–5–1; Ky. Rev. Stat. Ann. § 411.310(2).

ing the practical availability of safety technology at the time of manufacture and sale, is relevant and admissible on the issues of negligence and product defectiveness.[58] Florida's statute, for example, provides that "the finder of fact shall consider the state of the art of scientific and technical knowledge and other circumstances that existed at the time of manufacture, not at the time of loss or injury."[59] A statute in Tennessee contains a similar provision.[60] Idaho's statute prohibits evidence of changes in technological feasibility, state of the art, or the custom of the seller's industry that occurred after sale,[61] and Kansas has a similar provision.[62] A large majority of courts allow state-of-the-art evidence to show either the foreseeability of a risk of harm,[63] the feasibility of an alternative safer design,[64] or more generally hold that such evidence is relevant to a consumer's expectations, risk-utility, or simply to the issue of defectiveness.[65]

### Unknowable Dangers—Common Law Developments

Truly unknowable risks are a rarity in products liability law. Cases involving genuinely unforeseeable hazards surely must represent less than one in a hundred products liability cases, and probably less than one in a thousand. Manufacturers of durable products virtually always can foresee the harmful consequences of their products: that a punch press may crush a hand, that a defective electrical appliance may start a fire, or that a car will roll over in an accident.[66] Claims of unknowable risks are far more common in cases involving deleterious substances—pharmaceutical drugs, other chemical products, and certain natural substances such as asbestos and tobacco, all of which may cause cancer or other untoward harm. Even in such toxic substance cases, however, if manufacturers have conducted proper testing and analysis, truly unforeseeable dangers are exceedingly unusual. Not uncommonly, manufacturers of such products—such as some drugs, asbestos, and cigarettes—who

**58.** See Potter v. Chicago Pneumatic Tool Co., 694 A.2d 1319, 1346 (Conn. 1997) ("the overwhelming majority of courts have held that, in design defect cases, state-of-the-art evidence is relevant to determining the adequacy of the product's design").

**59.** See Fla. Stat. Ann. § 768.1257.

**60.** See Tenn. Code Ann. § 29–28–105(b).

**61.** See Idaho Code § [6–1406] 6–1306.

**62.** See Kan. Stat. Ann. § 60–3307(a)(1).

**63.** The seminal cases on this point were Feldman v. Lederle Labs., 479 A.2d 374 (N.J. 1984), and Brown v. Superior Court, 751 P.2d 470 (Cal. 1988), followed by Anderson v. Owens–Corning Fiberglas Corp., 810 P.2d 549 (Cal. 1991).

**64.** See, e.g., Falada v. Trinity Indus., Inc., 642 N.W.2d 247, 251 (Iowa 2002); LaBelle v. Philip Morris Inc., 243 F.Supp.2d 508, 515–22 (D.S.C. 2001) (Pa. law); Hughes v. Massey–Ferguson, Inc., 522 N.W.2d 294 (Iowa 1994); Fibreboard Corp.

v. Fenton, 845 P.2d 1168 (Colo. 1993); Boatland of Houston, Inc. v. Bailey, 609 S.W.2d 743 (Tex. 1980). See § 8.5, above.

**65.** See, e.g., Potter v. Chicago Pneumatic Tool Co., 694 A.2d 1319, 1346–48 (Conn. 1997) (collecting the cases, and emphasizing that "although state-of-the-art evidence may be dispositive on the facts of a particular case," it "does not constitute an affirmative defense that, if proven, would absolve the defendant from liability" but "is merely one factor for the jury to consider" on the issue of design defectiveness); Fibreboard Corp. v. Fenton, 845 P.2d 1168, 1174 (Colo. 1993); Crittenden v. Fibreboard Corp., 794 P.2d 554 (Wash. Ct. App. 1990).

**66.** See Brooks v. Beech Aircraft Corp., 902 P.2d 54, 63 (N.M. 1995) (referring to the "hypothetical instances in which technology known at the time of trial and technology knowable at the time of distribution differ" and noting that "outside of academic rationale we find little to suggest the existence in practice of unknowable design considerations").

persist in claiming (especially in early cases) that the risk was unforeseeable are subsequently deluged with punitive damages claims on proof that they not only could foresee the risks, but that they were well aware of, and fraudulently concealed, such risks.[67] Notwithstanding the rarity of legitimate claims that a product hazard was unknowable at the time of marketing, this issue does sometimes arise. And when it does arise, the question of whether a manufacturer has a duty to warn of unknowable dangers presents the starkest and most intriguing state-of-the-art issue of all.

In the early 1960s, before § 402A of the *Restatement (Second) of Torts* was promulgated and adopted by the courts, the few courts considering the issue generally had held that a manufacturer only had to warn of risks of which "the manufacturer knew, or by the application of reasonable developed human skill and foresight should have known."[68] This was true in both negligence and implied warranty.[69] And then, in

---

**67.** *Drugs.* Compare Cudmore v. Richardson–Merrell, Inc., 398 S.W.2d 640, 644 (Tex. App. 1965) (manufacturer of MER/29 not liable in implied warranty for cataracts: makers liable "only when such results or some similar results ought reasonably to have been foreseen"), with Toole v. Richardson–Merrell Inc., 60 Cal.Rptr. 398, 404–405 (Ct. App. 1967) (upholding punitive damages verdict: in seeking FDA approval to market drug, manufacturer submitted reports that omitted information that nine of ten rats in one test developed eye opacities, as did twenty-five of thirty-six in another, and that one dog went blind).

*Asbestos.* In the first asbestos case, Borel v. Fibreboard Paper Products Corp., 493 F.2d 1076 (5th Cir. 1973) (Tex. law), the manufacturers did not appear to rely upon the unforeseeability of the risk, and even defended on the ground that the plaintiff's employers knew of and had a duty to warn the plaintiffs of the hazards, and that the plaintiffs themselves knew of the hazards and assumed the risk. However, within a decade, the manufacturers had begun to rely heavily upon a state-of-the-art defense to claims that they had a duty to warn. See Beshada v. Johns–Manville Prods. Corp., 447 A.2d 539 (N.J. 1982) (rejecting the defense). Today, asbestos manufacturers continue to rely heavily on the state-of-the-art defense, even though they invariably lose on compensatory and often on punitive damages. See, e.g., Garlock, Inc. v. Gallagher, 814 A.2d 1007, 1023 (Md. Ct. Spec. App. 2003) (holding that dangers of asbestos were knowable when sold by defendant); Owens–Corning Fiberglas Corp. v. Golightly, 976 S.W.2d 409 (Ky. 1998) (upholding both compensatory and punitive damages against state-of-the-art defense). However, the state-of-the-art defense has operated to allow such a manufacturer to escape punitive damages in a jurisdiction that requires

clear and convincing proof of malice. See, e.g., ACandS, Inc. v. Asner, 686 A.2d 250 (Md. 1996) (insufficient proof of malice for punitive damages). On the asbestos litigation, see § 10.3, above

*Cigarettes.* Although there was one notable decision to the contrary, Green v. American Tobacco Co., 154 So.2d 169, 171 (Fla. 1963), cigarette manufacturers won most cases brought against them in the early and mid–1960s on the ground that the risk of cancer was unforeseeable. See, e.g., Ross v. Philip Morris & Co., 328 F.2d 3 (8th Cir. 1964) (Mo. law):

> [P]laintiff's position is ... that even though defendant may have had no reason to suspect that smoking its cigarettes could produce cancer ... and even though no developed human skill or foresight could afford knowledge of the cancer-smoking relationship, defendant should be held absolutely liable as an insurer if smoking its cigarettes caused or contributed to cause plaintiff's cancer. No Missouri case has imposed such a strict responsibility upon a manufacturer.

Id. at 10. Beginning in the 1990s, litigation against the cigarette industry, brought by state attorneys general and private parties alike, has established without a doubt that the industry knew full well the carcinogenic and addictive effects of cigarettes, and fraudulently concealed this information for the last half of the twentieth century. See, e.g., Whiteley v. Philip Morris Inc., 11 Cal. Rptr.3d 807 (Ct. App. 2004) (reversing and remanding judgment for plaintiff but ruling that substantial evidence supported finding of fraud). On the tobacco litigation, see § 10.3, above.

**68.** Howard v. Avon Prods., Inc., 395 P.2d 1007, 1011 (Colo. 1964) (unforeseeable risk from cosmetic).

**69.** See, e.g., id. (both claims); Ross v. Philip Morris & Co., 328 F.2d 3 (8th Cir.

1965, came § 402A.[70] The widespread adoption of § 402A was significant to the unknowable risk warnings problem in two respects. First, § 402A defined strict liability explicitly in no-fault form, so that the new liability standard on its face appeared to banish any possible defense based upon a manufacturer's best efforts to make its products safe. Such a definition seemed to preclude any possibility of a "state of the art" defense based on the unforeseeability of a product risk. For example, in *Wagner v. Coronet Hotel*,[71] the court rejected the manufacturer's arguments on its best efforts to make a rubber shower mat safe from the risk of slipping in a tub, which the court characterized as an irrelevant state of the art argument under § 402A.[72] "Implicit in the concept of strict liability is the idea that if the manufacturer produces a defective product which causes injury, he can be held legally liable despite his best efforts to make or design a safe product."[73] The next year, the same court rejected a trial court's jury instruction limiting a manufacturer's liability to "dangers reasonably to be foreseen,"[74] holding that it was fatally inconsistent with § 402A's black letter injunction that the strict liability rule applies "although ... the seller has exercised all possible care in the preparation and sale of his product."[75]

### Comments j and k

But there is a second aspect to § 402A that cuts the other way with respect to the issue of whether manufacturers should have a duty to warn of unknowable risks. Notwithstanding the general "strictness" prescribed by § 402A's black-letter liability standard, two comments to that section, comments *j* and *k*, address the duty to warn in negligence terms and effectively provide that the duty to warn under § 402A is limited to foreseeable risks. Both comments describe the general parameters of the duty to warn with respect to products containing inherent, unavoidable risks, with comment *k* considering the warnings obligation with respect to certain unavoidably dangerous products, particularly pharmaceutical drugs. Addressing the duty to warn consumers of the possibility of certain allergic reactions, comment *j* provides that if such a risk is significant and would be unexpected by consumers, "the seller is required to give warning against it, if he has knowledge, or by the application of reasonable, developed human skill and foresight should have knowledge, of the presence of the ingredient and the danger."[76] Comment *k* states that a seller of an unavoidably dangerous product, such as a new or experimental drug or vaccine, "is not to be held to strict liability for unfortunate consequences attending their use, merely because he has undertaken to supply the public with an apparently useful and desirable product, attended with a known but apparently reasonable risk."[77] Particularly when read with comment *j*'s limitation of

1964) (Mo. law) (both claims); Cudmore v. Richardson–Merrell, Inc., 398 S.W.2d 640, 644 (Tex. App. 1965) (implied warranty).

**70.** On this development, see ch. 5, above.

**71.** 458 P.2d 390 (Ariz. Ct. App. 1969).

**72.** See id. at 392.

**73.** Id. at 392–93.

**74.** Lunt v. Brady Mfg. Corp., 475 P.2d 964, 965 (Ariz. Ct. App. 1970).

**75.** Id. at 966.

**76.** Comment *j* to § 402A is examined and set forth in full in § 6.2, above.

**77.** Comment *k* to § 402A is examined and set forth in §§ 6.2 and 8.10, above. Although this comment conditions immuni-

the duty to warn only of foreseeable risks, and that comment's specific reference to the duty to warn of risks in dangerous drugs, comment *k* appears to immunize sellers of such unavoidably dangerous products from liability for failing to warn of unknowable product risks.

### The "Wade–Keeton" Test

Because of the intuitive logic and fairness of limiting the duty to warn to foreseeable risks, comments *j* and *k* probably would have effectively squelched any notion of a duty to warn of unknowable hazards were it not for another development which first appeared in the early 1960s. In 1961, Dean Page Keeton of the University of Texas first floated a new way to view the evolving standard of a manufacturer's responsibility to consumers for harm caused by defective products.[78] In order to differentiate the developing strict products liability doctrine from the law of negligence, Dean Keeton, and subsequently Dean John Wade of Vanderbilt University, annunciated the idea that "strict" liability should make manufacturers liable for selling products that turned out to be defective regardless of whether the product risks were foreseeable at the time of sale. Between 1961 and 1965, both scholars separately published their similar views that the law should base strict liability on *hindsight*, by imputing "constructive knowledge" to manufacturers of all subsequently discovered product dangers. Liability thus would depend on whether a manufacturer would be negligent in selling a product knowing of the risks it actually possessed. From 1961 through 1980, Dean Keeton published at least a dozen articles, and, in 1965 and 1973, Dean Wade published two especially influential articles, all urging that strict liability for product defects, particularly, but not limited to, defects in design, be defined in this special manner. In time, their similar definitional standard was labelled the "Wade–Keeton" hindsight or constructive knowledge test.[79] The sole distinction between the Wade–Keeton test and ordinary negligence was that the constructive knowledge aspect of the standard eliminated the requirement of the law of negligence that the risk of harm be known or knowable.[80]

And so, by the late 1960s, the stage was set for the courts to begin addressing the issue of whether there would be a duty in strict liability to warn of unknowable risks: comments *j* and *k* to § 402A provided that the strict liability duty, as in negligence, was limited to foreseeable risks; but the Wade–Keeton hindsight test, imputing knowledge of such risks to suppliers, required manufacturers to warn of hazards whether foreseeable or not. Cases addressing the unknowable risk issue were rare in the late 1960s, and so there was little early analysis of the unknowable risk warnings problem.

ty from strict liability upon the provision of a "proper warning," comment *j* makes clear that proper warnings are limited to risks which are foreseeable.

**78.** See W.P. Keeton, Products Liability–Current Developments, 40 Tex. L. Rev. 193, 210 (1961).

**79.** See § 8.7, above, citing and discussing the articles.

**80.** The rise and fall of the Wade–Keeton constructive knowledge test is examined in depth in § 8.7, above.

At least one case during this early period, *Helene Curtis Industries, Inc. v. Pruitt*,[81] cited both Dean Wade's and Dean Keeton's articles in which they proposed their liability standard.[82] In that case the plaintiff's scalp was burned by a combination of chemical bleaching products manufactured by the defendant. Endorsing Dean Wade's formulation of the test, the court remarked that a design, to be unreasonably dangerous, "must be so dangerous that a reasonable man would not sell the product if he knew the risks involved."[83] But, like so many other courts which in time endorsed the Wade–Keeton constructive knowledge standard, the *Helene Curtis* court seemed only to be doing so for academic purposes, for it failed to apply the test to the facts before it and instead reversed a plaintiff's judgment in part upon the unforeseeability of the risk.[84]

During the late 1960s, at least one case addressed the applicability of comment *j* to the unknowable danger warning question. In *Oakes v. Geigy Agricultural Chemicals*,[85] the plaintiff suffered a serious skin reaction to the defendant's weed-killing chemical products. The plaintiff alleged that the manufacturer's warning of "irritation" to the skin inadequately communicated the severe nature of his particular reaction, and the defendant demurred on the ground that the plaintiff failed to allege that the defendant knew or should have known that its products could cause the plaintiff's condition. The plaintiff refused to amend his complaint in this manner, and the trial court sustained the demurrer. On appeal, the California Court of Appeal affirmed, reasoning that a manufacturer was strictly liable only for risks of which it was or should have been aware, for "[t]o exact an obligation to warn the user of unknown and unknowable allergies . . . would be for the courts to recast the manufacturer in the role of an insurer beyond any reasonable application" of the strict liability rationales.[86] The court concluded that, to establish a claim for strict liability in tort, a plaintiff had to plead and prove the defendant's actual or constructive knowledge of the danger.[87]

As products liability litigation began to spread around the nation, courts increasingly adopted the Wade–Keeton constructive knowledge test for defining strict products liability in tort. At the same time, courts increasingly turned to comment *j*, and in the case of pharmaceutical drugs to comment *k*, for guidance on the scope of a manufacturer's duty to warn. The first clash of the two inconsistent standards arose with something of a whimper—in *Borel v. Fibreboard Paper Products Corporation*,[88] the first case to uphold a verdict for an installer of asbestos

---

**81.** 385 F.2d 841 (5th Cir. 1967) (Okla. law).

**82.** The court cited Dean Wade's article, Strict Tort Liability of Manufacturers, 19 Sw. L.J. 5 (1965), at 385 F.2d at 849–850, and Dean Keeton's article, Products Liability—The Nature and Extent of Strict Liability, 1964 U. Ill. L. Rev. 693, cited at note 3 on page 849.

**83.** *Helene Curtis*, 385 F.2d at 850. "This definition demonstrates that the only change from the traditional negligence analysis is that the maker cannot be excusably ignorant of the defect." Id.

**84.** See id. at 856 (citing Lartigue v. R. J. Reynolds Tobacco Co., 317 F.2d 19 (5th Cir. 1963)).

**85.** 77 Cal.Rptr. 709 (Ct. App. 1969).

**86.** Id. at 713.

**87.** Id.

**88.** 493 F.2d 1076 (5th Cir. 1973) (Tex. law) (Wisdom, J.).

insulation materials against the manufacturers of those materials. The plaintiff's claim was based on strict liability for failing to warn of the dangers involved in handling asbestos. Citing Dean Wade's early article and two articles of Dean Keeton, Judge Wisdom quoted the *Helene Curtis* court's adoption of the Wade–Keeton test, which defined § 402A's "unreasonably dangerous" concept as " 'so dangerous that a reasonable man would not sell the product if he knew the risk involved.' "[89] Moreover, citing Dean Keeton's 1970 article in the Texas Law Review, in which he once again urged the constructive knowledge standard, Judge Wisdom addressed the view of Dean Keeton and others that a seller should be strictly liable even if "the maker was excusably unaware of the extent of the danger."[90] But, when it came to resolving the knowability issues in the case, the *Borel* court ignored the Wade–Keeton test and applied the foreseeability-limitation principles of comment *j*.[91] On the facts of the case, the court applied these foreseeability limitations on liability, observing that the utility of asbestos insulation products should be weighed against "the known or foreseeable risk"[92] to the insulation installers, and that "[a] product must not be made available to the public without disclosure of those dangers that the application of reasonable foresight would reveal."[93] Because the jury was properly instructed,[94] the court affirmed the verdict for the plaintiff.[95]

As courts increasingly adopted and applied the foreseeability-limitation principles of comments *j* and *k*, a number of courts continued to purport to employ the Wade–Keeton constructive knowledge test for defining product defectiveness. In 1974, one year after *Borel*, the Oregon Supreme Court decided *Phillips v. Kimwood Machine Co.*,[96] an important case in which a factory worker was injured while feeding fiberboard into a sanding machine when the machine forcibly ejected a sheet back at the worker. The ejection occurred because a thin sheet had become mixed into a batch of thick sheets for which the sanding machine was set, the risk of which the manufacturer had failed to warn the plaintiff's employer. In the plaintiff's action against the manufacturer, the trial court directed a verdict for the defendant, and the plaintiff appealed. Citing

**89.** Id. at 1088.

**90.** Id. at 1088 n.22.

**91.** See id. at 1088 (emphasis removed):

Here, the plaintiff alleged that the defendants' product was unreasonably dangerous because of the failure to give adequate warnings of the known or knowable dangers involved. As explained in comment *j* to section 402A, a seller has a responsibility to inform users and consumers of dangers which the seller either knows or should know at the time the product is sold. The requirement that the danger be reasonably foreseeable, or scientifically discoverable, is an important limitation of the seller's liability. In general, "the rule of strict liability subjects the seller to liability to the user or consumer even though he has exercised all possible care in the

preparation and sale of the product." Section 402A, Comment *a*. This is not the case where the product is alleged to be unreasonably dangerous because of a failure to give adequate warnings. Rather, a seller is under a duty to warn of only those dangers that are reasonably foreseeable. The requirement of foreseeability coincides with the standard of due care in negligence cases in that a seller must exercise reasonable care and foresight to discover a danger in his product and to warn users and consumers of that danger.

**92.** Id. at 1089.

**93.** Id. at 1090.

**94.** See id. at 1090–92.

**95.** See id. at 1103.

**96.** 525 P.2d 1033 (Or. 1974).

both *Borel* and *Helene Curtis*,[97] the *Phillips* court reversed, carefully anticipating the Wade–Keeton test of defectiveness for defective warnings and design:

> A dangerously defective article would be one which a reasonable person would not put into the stream of commerce *if he had knowledge of its harmful character*. The test, therefore, is whether the seller would be negligent if he sold the article *knowing of the risk involved*. Strict liability imposes what amounts to constructive knowledge of the condition of the product.[98]

Noting that the Wade–Keeton test had the advantage of preserving familiar terms and concepts, the court reasoned that the test, while appearing to judge the manufacturer's conduct in terms of negligence, ultimately addressed the quality of the product. "If the manufacturer was not acting reasonably in selling the product, knowing of the risks involved, then the product would be dangerously defective when sold and the manufacturer would be subject to liability."[99] The court also quoted comment *j*'s limitation on the duty to warn to situations where the seller "had knowledge, or by the application of reasonable, developed human skill and foresight should have knowledge" of the danger.[100] But the *Phillips* court followed precisely the opposite approach taken by *Borel*, which had referred to, but ignored, the Wade–Keeton test and applied the foreseeability limiting principles of comment *j*. Instead, the *Phillips* court quoted, and then ignored, comment *j*, reversing the directed verdict for the defendant because the jury could find "that a reasonably prudent manufacturer, knowing that the machine would be fed manually and having the constructive knowledge of its propensity to regurgitate thin sheets when it was set for thick ones, which the courts via strict liability have imposed upon it, would have warned plaintiff's employer . . . , and that, in the absence of such a warning, the machine was dangerously defective."[101] Although the foreseeability that the sanding machine might regurgitate thin sheets was not really a disputed issue in *Phillips*, the Wade–Keeton test's triumph over comment *j* in this important judicial opinion was a pivotal event in the evolution of the duty to warn of unknowable product risks.

### The New Jersey Experience—Beshada and Feldman

Four years after the Oregon court decided *Phillips*, the New Jersey Supreme Court in 1978 adopted the Wade–Keeton standard as the test of design defectiveness in *Cepeda v. Cumberland Engineering Co.*,[102] citing *Phillips* and quoting substantially from articles by both Deans Wade and Keeton. Three years later, in *Freund v. Cellofilm Properties, Inc.*,[103] the New Jersey court revisited and reaffirmed the propriety of the Wade–Keeton test in the specific context of the duty to warn. Mr. Freund was burned in an industrial accident when a commercial chemical dust,

---

**97.** Id. at 1036 n.5.
**98.** Id. at 1036 (emphasis in original).
**99.** Id. at 1037.
100. Id. at 1038.
101. Id. at 1038–39.

**102.** 386 A.2d 816 (N.J. 1978), overruled on other grounds, Suter v. San Angelo Foundry & Mach. Co., 406 A.2d 140 (N.J. 1979).

**103.** 432 A.2d 925 (N.J. 1981).

nitrocellulose, suddenly ignited as it was being swept by a co-worker. In a suit against the manufacturer of the nitrocellulose, the plaintiff claimed that, in both negligence and strict liability in tort, the flammability warning was inadequate. The trial court refused to instruct on strict liability and submitted the case to the jury solely on the negligence claim. The jury found for the defendant, and the plaintiff appealed. Reversing, the New Jersey Supreme Court held that the trial court should have submitted the case to the jury on the strict liability claim. Relying on the "seminal" *Phillips* decision, and adopting the Wade–Keeton standard as the appropriate test for defining the duty to warn, the court ruled that the trial court, even though the defendant admitted knowing the dangers of nitrocellulose, should have relieved the plaintiffs of the burden of proving the defendant's knowledge of danger by imputing it to the defendant.[104]

One year later, the New Jersey Supreme Court had another strict liability failure to warn case, *Beshada v. Johns–Manville Products Corp.*,[105] one of the landmark cases in all of products liability law. In an important way, *Beshada* was different from *Freund* and other previous cases applying the Wade–Keeton test to the duty to warn. *Beshada* was the first state high court case in the United States involving the applicability of the Wade–Keeton test, and more generally the principles of strict products liability, to a warnings claim defended on the ground that the risk was unforeseeable—that is, the first such case squarely confronting the question of whether there should be a duty on manufacturers to warn of unknowable product risks. *Beshada* was another asbestos case brought by insulation workers who suffered asbestosis and mesothelioma from working with asbestos insulation products over many years. The workers claimed that the manufacturers breached their strict liability duty to warn of these dangers, and the defendants responded by asserting a state-of-the-art defense, claiming that no one knew or could have known that asbestos was so dangerous to insulation workers. The defendants conceded that they had known since the 1930s of the dangers of high-dose exposure of asbestos dust to workers in asbestos textile mills, but claimed that the danger to insulation workers who were exposed to much lower doses "was not discovered until recently."[106] The trial court denied the plaintiff's motion to strike the state-of-the-art defense, the plaintiffs appealed, and the New Jersey Supreme Court reversed, holding that compliance with the state-of-the-art is an improper defense to a strict liability failure to warn claim.[107]

The *Beshada* defendants claimed "that the danger of which they failed to warn was undiscovered at the time the product was marketed and that it was undiscoverable given the state of scientific knowledge at that time,"[108] and the court assumed the truth of this assertion for purposes of the appeal.[109] In response, the plaintiffs argued that the

---

**104.** "The plaintiffs were entitled to a strict liability charge that clearly and unmistakenly imputed knowledge of the dangers of the product to the defendant." Id. at 933.

**105.** 447 A.2d 539 (N.J. 1982).

**106.** Id. at 543.

**107.** See id. at 549.

**108.** Id. at 542.

**109.** See id. at 543.

court's earlier decision in *Freund* had "disposed of the state-of-the-art issue. Since defendant's knowledge of the dangers of the product is presumed, it is irrelevant whether the existence of such dangers was scientifically discoverable."[110] After reaffirming the Wade–Keeton constructive knowledge test that it had applied in *Freund* to warnings cases, the *Beshada* court examined the role of the state-of-the-art defense in the context of a strict liability duty to warn:

> As it relates to warning cases, the state-of-the-art defense asserts that distributors of products can be held liable only for injuries resulting from dangers that were scientifically discoverable at the time the product was distributed. Defendants argue that the question of whether the product can be made safer must be limited to consideration of the available technology at the time the product was distributed. Liability would be absolute, defendants argue, if it could be imposed on the basis of a subsequently discovered means to make the product safer since technology will always be developing new ways to make products safer. . . .

> In urging this position, defendants must somehow distinguish the *Freund* holding that knowledge of the dangers of the product is imputed to defendants as a matter of law. A state-of-the-art defense would contravene that by requiring plaintiffs to prove at least that knowledge of the dangers was scientifically available at the time of manufacture.[111]

The defendants argued that the knowledge of danger referred to in *Freund* was the knowledge existing at the time the product was manufactured and sold.[112] Conceding that *Freund* had not addressed the question of precisely what type of knowledge should be imputed to manufacturers, the *Beshada* court observed that state-of-the-art is essentially a negligence defense, and that the defendants' argument was that, by failing to warn of an unforeseeable risk, they were not at fault. "But in strict liability cases," the court explained, "culpability is irrelevant." That the product "was unsafe because of the state of technology does not change the fact that it was unsafe. Strict liability focuses on the product, not the fault of the manufacturer."[113]

After considering the duty to warn of unforeseeable risks from a doctrinal perspective, *Beshada* turned to a policy inquiry of the compatibility of the state's goals and policies underlying its strict products liability rules with a rule imposing liability on manufacturers for failing

---

**110.** Id.

**111.** Id. at 545–46.

**112.** Id. at 546.

**113.** Id., citing W. P. Keeton, Products Liability—Inadequacy of Information, 48 Tex. L. Rev. 398, 408 (1970). "When the defendants argue that it is unreasonable to impose a duty on them to warn of the unknowable, they misconstrue both the purpose and effect of strict liability. By imposing strict liability, we are not requir-

ing defendants to have done something that is impossible. In this sense, the phrase 'duty to warn' is misleading. It implies negligence concepts with their attendant focus on the reasonableness of defendant's behavior. However, a major concern of strict liability—ignored by defendants—is the conclusion that if a product was in fact defective, the distributor of the product should compensate its victims for the misfortune that it inflicted on them." Id.

to warn of dangers that were undiscoverable when the product was made and sold.[114] Concluding that the policies of strict products liability indeed supported such a rule,[115] the court explained how liability for harm caused by undiscoverable risks is consistent with the "risk spreading" rationale:

> [S]preading the costs of injuries among all those who produce, distribute and purchase manufactured products is far preferable to imposing it on the innocent victims who suffer illnesses and disability from defective products. This basic normative premise is at the center of our strict liability rules. It is unchanged by the state of scientific knowledge at the time of manufacture.[116]

As for the deterrence or "accident avoidance" goal of strict products liability, the defendants argued that manufacturers cannot protect against risks they cannot foresee. But the court reasoned that this argument missed the point that the "state-of-the-art" at any given time is a function of the level of resources industry invests in safety research. Accordingly, although a manufacturer may never foresee all the risks of harm its products in fact possess, its knowledge that it must eventually absorb the costs of all such harm, foreseeable or not, will spur its investment in safety research and thereby advance the state-of-the-art of product safety.[117]

Finally, the court turned to difficulties in the judiciary's ability to administer the "fact finding process" inherent in determining the scientific discoverability of particular product risks at any given time. The court saw good reason to avoid the "the vast confusion" that would arise from requiring plaintiffs to prove at trial "the concept of scientific knowability" inherent in the state-of-the-art defense. Such proof—on what kind of knowledge could have been discovered with more or better research—would require costly, confusing, and time-consuming expert testimony on "the history of science and technology to speculate as to what knowledge was feasible in a given year." The court doubted that juries would "be capable of even understanding the concept of scientific knowability, much less be able to resolve such a complex issue," and it was reluctant to allow the judicial system to become bloated with the resulting costs.[118]

Reaching back to the conventional rationale for strict products liability in tort,[119] the court concluded that fairness required that the costs of illnesses and injuries from dangerous products such as asbestos should be placed upon manufacturers who profit from their production and sale, and on society at large, rather than on the innocent victims of such harm. Barring the state-of-the-art defense would achieve not only this result, reasoned the court, but rejection of this defense should also "serve the salutary goals of increasing product safety research and

---

**114.** Id. at 547.

**115.** Id.

**116.** Id.

**117.** "By imposing on manufacturers the costs of failure to discover hazards, we

create an incentive for them to invest more actively in safety research." Id. at 548.

**118.** Id.

**119.** See § 5.4, above.

simplifying tort trials."[120] For all of these reasons, the Supreme Court of New Jersey in *Beshada v. Johns–Manville Products Corporation* ruled that strict liability in tort imposes a duty on manufacturers to warn of all significant product hazards, knowable and unknowable alike.

The New Jersey court may have expected its unanimous decision in *Beshada*, like most judicial decisions, to draw at best a modest amount of positive attention: after all, it merely applied the widely accepted Wade–Keeton test to a warnings claim, which other courts (like the Oregon court in *Phillips*, some eight years earlier) had done before; it applied the doctrine to defendants in a singularly unpopular industry; and it merely held that its rule of "strict" products liability was truly strict, rather than just negligence rehashed. But the opinion unleashed an immediate and powerful storm of academic protest[121] that appears to have caught the New Jersey Supreme Court completely unawares, but did not go unnoticed by that court. The commentators complained that, by imposing a duty on manufacturers to warn of unknowable dangers, the court had adopted an unfair standard which was impossible to meet; that it would lead to inefficient corporate behavior that could lead to strategic and unnecessary declarations of bankruptcy;[122] that the decision reflected a lack of understanding of how liability rules affect corporate behavior; and that the decision applied anachronistic strict liability rationales that had become discredited over time. At least in part because of *Beshada*, but also because the test had "not worn well with time,"[123] Dean Wade repudiated his half of the Wade–Keeton standard in a 1983 journal article,[124] and Dean Keeton repudiated the other half in his torts treatise the following year.[125]

A scant two years after rendering *Beshada*, the New Jersey Supreme Court in 1984 had an opportunity to reconsider this now-battered decision in another products liability case, *Feldman v. Lederle Laboratories*,[126] which involved a claim against a pharmaceutical manufacturer for a possibly unforeseeable risk that a tetracycline drug could discolor an infant's teeth. In one of the most striking reversals in the history of the law of torts, a unanimous court in *Feldman* effectively overruled *Besha-*

---

**120.** Id. at 549.

**121.** See, e.g., Wade, On the Effect in Product Liability of Knowledge Unavailable Prior to Marketing, 58 N.Y.U. L. Rev. 734, 754–56 (1983); Page, Generic Product Risks: The Case Against Comment K and for Strict Tort Liability, 58 N.Y.U. L. Rev. 853, 877–82 (1983); V. Schwartz, The Post-Sale Duty to Warn: Two Unfortunate Forks in the Road to a Reasonable Doctrine, 58 N.Y.U. L. Rev. 892, 901–05 (1983); Comment, Requiring Omniscience: The Duty to Warn of Scientifically Undiscoverable Product Defects, 71 Geo. L.J. 1635 (1983); Comment, Beshada v. Johns Manville Products Corp.: Adding Uncertainty to Injury, 35 Rutgers L. Rev. 982, 1008–15 (1983); Note, Products Liability—Strict Liability in Tort—State-of-the-Art Defense Inapplicable in Design Defect Cases, 13 Seton Hall L. Rev. 625 (1983).

**122.** See, e.g., A. Schwartz, Products Liability, Corporate Structure and Bankruptcy: Toxic Substances and the Remote Risk Relationship, 14 J. Leg. Stud. 689, 736 (1985). Indeed, Johns–Manville declared bankruptcy the year following *Beshada*, 1983, followed by the bankruptcy of scores of additional asbestos companies in due course. See § 10.3, above.

**123.** See Products Liability Restatement § 2 Reporters' Note 1 to cmt. *m*.

**124.** Wade, On the Effect in Product Liability of Knowledge Unavailable Prior to Marketing, Postscript, 58 N.Y.U. L. Rev. 734, 761 (1983).

**125.** See W. P. Keeton, D. Dobbs, R. Keeton & D. Owen, Prosser and Keeton on the Law of Torts 697–98 n.21 (5th ed. 1984).

**126.** 479 A.2d 374 (N.J. 1984).

*da*,[127] holding that "drug manufacturers have a duty to warn [only] of dangers of which they know or should have known on the basis of reasonably obtainable or available knowledge."[128] Turning *Beshada* completely on its head, the *Feldman* court not only ruled that state of the art was a good defense to a warnings claim but also substantially equated strict liability and negligence in the warnings context. *Feldman* endorsed comment *j*'s restriction of the warning duty to foreseeable risks and adopted the traditional negligence definition of "constructive knowledge"—what the defendant knew or should have known in view of knowledge available at the time—the same definition of constructive knowledge that the defendants had argued and the court had explicitly rejected in *Beshada*.

Following comment *j*, *Feldman* thus held that a manufacturer's duty to warn is limited to dangers which it knows or should know at the time the product is sold, which makes the relevant inquiry "Did the defendant know, or should he have known, of the danger, given the scientific, technological, and other information available when the product was distributed; or, in other words, did he have actual or constructive knowledge of the danger?"[129] Redefining "constructive knowledge" in traditional negligence terms—directly contrary to the special hindsight meaning the Wade–Keeton test accorded this term in the strict liability context—*Feldman* held that the term "embraces knowledge that should have been known based on information that was reasonably available or obtainable and should have alerted a reasonably prudent person to act."[130] The court correctly realized that this redefinition of the knowledge for which a defendant is responsible in warnings cases folds "strict liability" right back into the arms of negligence, reducing the two theories of liability essentially to one.[131]

In this way, the New Jersey Supreme Court in *Feldman* made a complete about-face on the unknowable danger warnings rule, holding that manufacturers have no duty to warn of risks which are unforeseeable. Reasoning that information on the knowability of risks in a particular field is more accessible to manufacturers than to plaintiffs, the court also ruled that the burden of proof should be reversed on the availability of information about the risk at the time the product is made and sold.[132]

In dramatic fashion, the *Beshada-Feldman* duo marks the rise and fall of the duty to warn of unknowable hazards—and even of the doctrine of strict manufacturer liability for warning (and indirectly

---

**127.** The court denied that it was "overruling" *Beshada*, but subjected it to house arrest (explicitly restricting it to its facts). Id. at 388.

**128.** Id. at 376.

**129.** Id. at 386.

**130.** Id.

**131.** "Under this standard negligence and strict liability in warning cases may be deemed to be functional equivalents." Id.

**132.** "As a matter of policy the burden of proving the status of knowledge in the field at the time of distribution is properly placed on the defendant." Id. at 388. The *Feldman* litigation saga continued for many years. See Feldman v. Lederle Labs., 625 A.2d 1066, 1070–71 (N.J. 1993) (once manufacturer learns of risk, it must warn "as soon as reasonably possible"; while manufacturer has burden of proof on state of knowledge, plaintiff must prove that any delay in warning was unreasonable).

design) dangers—in American products liability law. For a time, *Beshada* had reigned supreme as the first major decision in the nation to apply a truly strict manufacturer liability rule in a warnings or design context where the difference between strict liability and negligence really mattered. But *Beshada*'s moment in the sun was brief, and its fall from glory was precipitous and steep.

### *The Triumph of the State-of-the-Art Defense*

Four years after *Feldman*, across the continent, the California Supreme Court decided *Brown v. Superior Court*,[133] another pharmaceutical drug case, which involved the duty of manufacturers to warn of the possibly unforeseeable risks that a drug, DES, administered to pregnant women could cause certain birth defects in their unborn children. Following *Feldman* and the principles of comments *j* and *k*,[134] the California court held that manufacturers of the drug could not be held liable for failing to warn of risks "that were neither known by defendants nor scientifically knowable at the time the drug was distributed."[135] Three years later, the California Supreme Court completed the loop, in *Anderson v. Owens–Corning Fiberglas Corp.*,[136] by extending its holding in *Brown* beyond pharmaceutical drug products to products generally.[137] *Anderson* adopted "the requirement, as propounded by the Restatement Second of Torts and acknowledged by ... the majority of jurisdictions, that knowledge or knowability is a component of strict liability for failure to warn."[138]

A very small minority of states have refused to abandon the idea that strict liability should be defined so as to impute constructive knowledge to manufacturers of all product dangers, even risks that are entirely unknowable. In 1987, in a brief answer to a certified question in an asbestos case, the Hawaii Supreme Court ruled that "in a strict products liability action, state-of-the-art evidence is not admissible for the purpose of establishing whether the seller knew or reasonably should have known of the dangerousness of his or her product."[139] In 1995, the New Mexico Supreme Court reaffirmed the Wade–Keeton constructive knowledge definition of design defectiveness,[140] and a small handful of

---

**133.** 751 P.2d 470 (Cal. 1988).

**134.** The court interpreted comment *k* in the foreseeable risk terms of comment *j*:

[Comment *k*] provides that the producer of a properly manufactured prescription drug may be held liable for injuries caused by the product only if it was not accompanied by a warning of dangers that the manufacturer knew or should have known about.

Id. at 475.

**135.** Id. at 481. See also Carlin v. Superior Court, 920 P.2d 1347, 1354 (Cal. 1996) ("Drug manufacturers need only warn of risks that are *actually known or reasonably scientifically knowable*.").

**136.** 810 P.2d 549 (Cal. 1991).

**137.** "*Brown*'s logic and common sense are not limited to drugs." Id. at 556.

**138.** Id. at 557.

**139.** Johnson v. Raybestos–Manhattan, Inc., 740 P.2d 548, 549 (Haw. 1987).

**140.** See Brooks v. Beech Aircraft Corp., 902 P.2d 54, 63 (N.M. 1995):

[I]n those hypothetical instances in which technology known at the time of trial and technology knowable at the time of distribution differ—and outside of academic rationale we find little to suggest the existence in practice of unknowable design considerations—it is more fair that the manufacturers and suppliers who have profited from the sale of the product bear the risk of loss.... If in some future case we are confronted directly with a proffer of evidence on an advancement or change in the state of the art that was neither known nor knowable

other decisions have continued to state the definition of strict products liability in tort in hindsight form.[141] Each of these cases might be viewed as an aberration in the common law, which for many years has been attempting to purge itself of the Wade–Keeton liability standard and the imputed knowledge hindsight standard which it spawned, and rarely does a modern court attempt to justify the hindsight test in policy terms of whether a manufacturer should have a duty to warn of unknowable product risks.

But the appropriateness of a state-of-the-art defense based on the unforeseeability of a product risk was precisely the question raised in *Sternhagen v. Dow Co.*,[142] a 1997 Montana Supreme Court case involving an action against herbicide manufacturers for the death from cancer of a crop duster exposed to the herbicide 2,4–D from 1948 to 1950.[143] *Sternhagen* carefully reexamined the nature of and reasons for Montana's commitment to the doctrine of strict liability in tort, and it concluded that manufacturers should have a duty to warn of unknowable product risks.[144] The *Sternhagen* court's proud reaffirmation of a pure doctrine of strict products liability is reminiscent in many respects of the New Jersey court's ill-fated opinion in *Beshada v. Johns–Manville Products Corporation* decided now so many years ago. Whether *Sternhagen* eventually will suffer as sharp a collapse as *Beshada* is difficult to predict, but the tide has surely turned against a duty to warn of unknowable product risks. In the 1990s, the high courts of at least four other states studiously affirmed or reconfirmed the necessary role of foreseeability in duty to warn products liability cases, two with respect to prescription pharmaceutical products[145] and two with respect to products generally,[146] all four of which repudiated any notion of a duty to warn of unknowable risks. Of these four, the experience of the Massachusetts high court was the most significant.

The evolution of the unknowable risk warnings issue in Massachusetts appeared to mark the beginning of the final demise of the notion

at the time the product was supplied, we may at that time reconsider application of a state-of-the-art defense to those real circumstances. . . .

**141.** Other recent cases stating the Wade–Keeton test are cited and discussed in § 8.7, above.

**142.** 935 P.2d 1139 (Mont. 1997).

**143.** *Sternhagen* answered a question certified by a federal district court: "In a strict products liability case for injuries caused by an inherently unsafe product, is the manufacturer conclusively presumed to know the dangers inherent in his product, or is state-of-the-art evidence admissible to establish whether the manufacturer knew or through the exercise of reasonable human foresight should have known of the danger?" Id. at 1139.

**144.** The court answered as follows: "[W]e conclude that, in a strict products liability case, knowledge of any undiscovered or undiscoverable dangers should be imputed to the manufacturer. Further-

more, we conclude that, in a strict products liability case, state-of-the-art evidence is not admissible to establish whether the manufacturer knew or through the exercise of reasonable human foresight should have known of the danger." Id. at 1147.

**145.** Young v. Key Pharm., Inc., 922 P.2d 59 (Wash. 1996) (4-4 decision) (brain damage from administration of theophylline for asthma without warning of drug's risks to patients suffering viral illnesses); Wagner v. Roche Labs., 671 N.E.2d 252, 256 (Ohio 1996) (pseudotumor cerebri [PTC] from combining acne drug, Accutane, with certain antibiotics such as minocycline; reaffirming prior ruling).

**146.** Owens–Illinois, Inc. v. Zenobia, 601 A.2d 633, 641 n.8 (Md. 1992) (asbestos; burden of proof on knowability remains on plaintiff); Vassallo v. Baxter Healthcare Corp., 696 N.E.2d 909 (Mass. 1998) (silicone breast implants).

that manufacturers should have a duty to warn of unknowable risks. In 1984, in *Hayes v. Ariens Co.*,[147] the Supreme Judicial Court of Massachusetts specifically addressed the role of state-of-the-art evidence in warnings claims for breach of the implied warranty of merchantability.[148] Drawing on *Beshada, Phillips v. Kimwood Machine Co.*,[149] and Dean Wade's famous article on strict products liability in tort,[150] the court adopted the Wade–Keeton constructive knowledge test in no uncertain terms.[151] Although the Massachusetts high court reaffirmed this position in dictum in 1992,[152] it had occasion to confront the matter squarely once again in 1998, when it turned the corner as completely as New Jersey had in switching from *Beshada* to *Feldman* in the 1980s.

*Vassallo v. Baxter Healthcare Corporation*[153] was a negligence and implied warranty of merchantability action against the manufacturer of silicone breast implants for atypical autoimmune disease suffered by a woman in whom such products were implanted. The trial court denied the defendants' request for a jury instruction limiting its duty to warn to known or knowable risks, and the defendants appealed. While upholding the plaintiff's verdict on other grounds, the *Vassallo* court took the occasion to reevaluate its strict-liability (warranty) duty-to-warn rule which "presumes that a manufacturer was fully informed of all risks associated with the product at issue, regardless of the state of the art at the time of the sale."[154] Recognizing that it was "among a distinct minority of States that applies a hindsight analysis to the duty to warn;"[155] that most states follow the foreseeability limitation in *Restatement (Second) of Torts* § 402A cmt. *j*;[156] that the *Restatement (Third) of Torts: Products Liability* § 2(c) similarly limits the duty to warn to foreseeable risks;[157] that the goal of product safety is not advanced by a rule which requires the impossible;[158] that the minority approach "has

---

**147.**  462 N.E.2d 273 (Mass. 1984).

**148.**  Massachusetts, which never did adopt the doctrine of strict liability in tort, uses the implied warranty of merchantability as its vehicle for strict products liability. See Vassallo v. Baxter Healthcare Corp., 696 N.E.2d 909, 923 (Mass. 1998). See §§ 5.3 and 5.9, above.

**149.**  525 P.2d 1033 (Or. 1974).

**150.**  Wade, On the Nature of Strict Tort Liability for Products, 44 Miss. L.J. 825, 834–35 (1973).

**151.**  The court explained, at 462 N.E.2d at 277–78:

For strict liability purposes, and therefore for purposes of our warranty law, the adequacy of a warning is measured by the warning that would be given at the time of sale by an ordinarily prudent vendor *who, at that time, is fully aware of the risks presented by the product.* A defendant vendor is held to that standard regardless of the knowledge of risk that he actually had or reasonably should have had when the sale took place. The vendor is presumed to have been fully informed at the time of the sale of all risks. The state of the art is irrelevant, as is the culpability of the defendant. Goods that, from the consumer's perspective, are unreasonably dangerous due to lack of adequate warning, are not fit for the ordinary purposes for which such goods are used regardless of the absence of fault on the vendor's part.

**152.**  Simmons v. Monarch Mach. Tool Co., 596 N.E.2d 318, 320 n.3 (Mass. 1992).

**153.**  696 N.E.2d 909 (Mass. 1998).

**154.**  Id. at 922.

**155.**  Id.

**156.**  See id.

**157.**  See id. at 922–23. The duty to warn under § 2(c) is defined in black-letter terms of "foreseeable risks of harm," and comment *m* provides in part: "The harms that result from unforeseeable risks—for example, in the human body's reaction to a new drug, medical device, or chemical—are not a basis of liability."

**158.**  "The thin judicial support for a hindsight approach to the duty to warn is

received substantial criticism in the literature;"[159] and that an important basis of the Massachusetts court's original adoption of the hindsight approach, New Jersey's adoption of that approach in *Beshada*, had now disappeared;[160] the *Vassallo* court decided to revise its law to state that "a defendant will not be held liable under an implied warranty of merchantability for failure to warn or provide instructions about risks that were not reasonably foreseeable at the time of sale or could not have been discovered by way of reasonable testing prior to marketing the product."[161]

While the *Vassallo* court's decision to shield manufacturers from responsibility for unforeseeable product hazards appeared to signal an imminent demise of true strict products liability in American law (outside of manufacturing defect cases), the Supreme Court of Minnesota soon made clear that any such signal was premature. In 2001, the Minnesota high court decided *Green v. Smith and Nephew AHP, Inc.*,[162] in which a health care worker suffered a severe reaction to allergens in latex gloves manufactured by the defendant. Although the risk that users would suffer allergic reactions to the levels of proteins in such gloves was quite high,[163] the health care industry apparently did not know of the risk at the time the plaintiff's gloves were manufactured. The plaintiff's claim did not specify a type of defect, alleging only that the gloves were defective because the danger was not contemplated by ordinary users and consumers, and the court analyzed the case as if it involved a question of design defectiveness rather than a duty to warn. Reaffirming the consumer expectations test as the proper standard for determining a defendant's responsibility for harm under the doctrine of strict products liability in tort, the court in *Green* ruled that the foreseeability of risk was relevant only to negligence, not strict liability. "[U]nder no circumstance," said the court, "must the plaintiff prove that the risk of harm presented by the product that caused his or her injury was foreseeable."[164] The court justified its refusal to endorse a state-of-the-art defense on the conventional, if by now largely abandoned, rationales for strict products liability in tort: promoting product safety, protecting justified consumer expectations, and the perceived fairness of placing the loss on the party that created and profited from the risk.[165] While time has taken its toll on these tattered rationales,[166] their unabashed resurrection by the *Green* majority (as by the court in *Sternhagen*) shows that they may still possess a twitch of life before they finally bite the dust.

But for a few rogue jurisdictions,[167] American products liability law, like the law of most of Europe and Japan,[168] no longer holds manufactur-

easily explained. The goal of the law is to induce conduct that is capable of being performed. This goal is not advanced by imposing liability for failure to warn of risks that were not capable of being known." Id. at 922–23.

**159.** Id. at 923.

**160.** Id.

**161.** Id.

**162.** 629 N.W.2d 727 (Wis. 2001).

**163.** Stated by the court to be 5–17%. Id. at 731.

**164.** Id. at 746

**165.** Id. at 749–51.

**166.** See § 5.4, above.

**167.** See, e.g., Green v. Smith & Nephew AHP, Inc., 629 N.W.2d 727, 743–51 (Wis. 2001); Sternhagen v. Dow Co., 935 P.2d 1139, 1144–47 (Mont. 1997); Johnson v. Raybestos–Manhattan, Inc., 740 P.2d 548, 549 (Haw. 1987).

**168.** Foreign law is briefly discussed below.

ers responsible for unknowable product risks. The rise and fall of the duty to warn of unforeseeable hazards has played a decisive role in the more general rise and fall of "strict" products liability in America, a broader development examined in earlier chapters.[169] Infrequent cases involving egregiously dangerous products that never should have been marketed for widespread use, such as asbestos and Thalidomide, may appear to raise troubling problems for products liability law if manufacturers are exonerated for unknowable product risks. Yet, to the extent that such risks are truly unforeseeable, manufacturers cannot be faulted for placing such products on the market, nor can they be effectively encouraged by the law to protect against risks they cannot in fact foresee. While innocent victims of science and technology should not be left without any means of compensation, most courts and commentators reason that the laudable objective of spreading risks (insurance) is more fairly and efficiently administered by insurance institutions—private companies and public agencies designed to insure against and compensate for accidental loss—than by the law of torts.[170] In short, modern products liability law is quite surely better off without a duty to warn or otherwise protect against unknowable product risks.

## Statutory Reform

From the inception of the products liability statutory reform movement, many state legislatures have sought to afford products liability defendants with some protection from liability when a challenged product was designed, manufactured, labelled, and sold according to the state of scientific knowledge and reasonable technological capability prevailing in the industry at the time. Nebraska may have been the first state to enact such a provision, in 1978,[171] and Florida so far may be the latest, in 1999.[172] At present, some sixteen states have enacted some form of statute specifically addressing some aspect of the state-of-the-art issue, which concerns a products liability defendant's reasonable ability to prevent a particular injury based on the state of scientific knowledge and technology prevailing when the product is made and sold.

### *True State of the Art Statutes*

Many states have adopted "true" state-of-the-art statutes that address this topic directly.[173] Eight states (Arizona, Iowa, Louisiana, Michigan, Mississippi, Missouri, Nebraska, and New Hampshire) have statutes that either condition liability upon the defendant's ability to conform to the state of the art, which places the burden of proof on the plaintiff, or that create a state of the art affirmative defense, which places the

---

**169.** See chapters 5 and 8, above.

**170.** See Owen, The Moral Foundations of Products Liability Law: Toward First Principles, 68 Notre Dame L. Rev. 427 (1993).

**171.** See Neb. Rev. Stat. § 25–21,182, codifying Neb. Laws 1978, L.B. 665 § 4.

**172.** See Fla. Stat. Ann. § 768.1257.

**173.** The statutes are set out in 1 Madden & Owen on Products Liability § 10.7, at 661–68.

burden of proof on the defendant.[174] Three states (Colorado, Indiana, and Kentucky) have enacted rebuttable presumptions providing that products which conform to the state of the art are rebuttably presumed to be nondefective and that the manufacturers and sellers of such products are similarly presumed not negligent.[175] And eight states (Arizona, Colorado, Florida, Idaho, Kansas, Michigan, Tennessee, and Washington) have enacted products liability reform statutes that address the admissibility of state-of-the-art evidence, either by providing that a defendant may introduce evidence of the prevailing scientific knowledge or technology at the time of manufacture or sale, or that a claimant may not introduce evidence of improved science or technology that developed thereafter.[176]

### Evidentiary Provisions on Subsequent Remedial Measures

Closely related to products liability statutory provisions which prohibit the admission of evidence on improvements in scientific knowledge and technology is *Federal Rule of Evidence* 407, now also adopted in a large majority of states, which prohibits proof of subsequent remedial measures to prove that a defendant was negligent or that a product was defective.[177] Proof of subsequent remedial measures and Rule 407 were examined earlier.[178]

### Feasible Alternative Design Provisions

In proving design defectiveness, statutes in five or six states (Louisiana, Mississippi, New Jersey, North Carolina, Texas, and maybe Washington) require proof in design cases of a feasible alternative design,[179] as previously discussed.[180] In ordinary usage, "feasible" is widely defined as "capable of being done."[181] The Idaho statute defines "technological feasibility" rather unhelpfully as "the technological, mechanical and scientific knowledge relating to product safety that was reasonably

---

**174.** See Ariz. Rev. Stat. § 12–683; Iowa Code Ann. § 668.12; La. Rev. Stat. Ann. § 9:2800.59; Mich. Comp. Laws Ann. § 600.2948(3); Miss. Code Ann. § 11–1–63(b) and (c); Mo. Ann. Stat. § 537.764; Neb. Ann. Stat. § 25–21,182; and N.H. Rev. Stat. Ann. § 507:8–g.

**175.** See Colo. Rev. Stat. § 13–21–403(1); Ind. Code § 34–20–5–1; and Ky. Rev. Stat. Ann. § 411.310(2).

**176.** See Ariz. Rev. Stat. § 12–686; Colo. Rev. Stat. § 13–21–404; Fla. Stat. Ann. § 768.1257; Idaho Code § [6–1406] 6–1306; Kan. Stat. Ann. § 60–3307; Mich. Comp. Laws Ann. § 600.2946; Tenn. Code Ann. § 29–28–105; Wash. Rev. Code § 7.72.050.

**177.** The Kansas statute is patterned after, but deviates somewhat from, the federal rule. See Kan. Stat. Ann. § 60–3307.

**178.** See § 6.4, above.

**179.** Statutes in at least Illinois, Louisiana, Mississippi, New Jersey, North Carolina, Ohio, and Texas require proof of a feasible alternative design to establish liability for a product's design in all or most design cases. Washington has a statute that ambiguously provides for the jury to consider such proof together with a consumer's

safety contemplations. See Couch v. Mine Safety Appliances Co., 728 P.2d 585 (Wash. 1986). The statutes in New Jersey and North Carolina make statutory exceptions for cases for egregiously dangerous products. Illinois and Ohio both had similar provisions, 735 Ill. Comp. Stat. 5/2–2104 (West 1993 & Supp. 1996), Ohio Rev. Code Ann. § 2307.75 (F), but they were both invalidated when broad tort reform acts in both states were held unconstitutional. See Best v. Taylor Machine Works, 689 N.E.2d 1057 (Ill. 1997) (holding that tort reform act violated separation of powers and special legislation clause of Illinois Constitution); State ex rel. Ohio Academy of Trial Lawyers v. Sheward, 715 N.E.2d 1062 (Ohio 1999) (holding that tort reform act violated separation of powers and one-subject rule of Ohio Constitution). See La. Rev. Stat. Ann. § 9:2800.56; Miss. Code Ann. § 11–1–63; N.J. Stat. Ann. § 2A:58c–3; N.C. Gen. Stat. § 99B–6; Tex. Civ. Prac. & Rem. Code Ann. § 82.005; Wash. Rev. Code Ann. § 7.72.030.

**180.** See § 8.5, above.

**181.** See The Oxford English Dictionary 783 (R.W. Burchfield ed., Clarendon 2d ed. 1989).

feasible for use, in light of economic practicality, at the time of manufacture."[182] Mississippi's provision requires a plaintiff to prove that "[t]he product failed to function as expected and there existed a feasible design alternative that would have to a reasonable probability prevented the harm. A feasible design alternative is a design that would have ... prevented the harm without impairing the utility, usefulness, practicality or desirability of the product to users or consumers."[183] The Texas provision on design defectiveness requires the claimant to prove that "there was a safer alternative design"[184] which "was economically and technologically feasible at the time the product left the control of the manufacturer or seller by the application of existing or reasonably achievable scientific knowledge."[185]

### *Miscellaneous Statutory Provisions*

Finally, state reform statutes include a miscellany of other provisions, not ordinarily thought of as true "state of the art" provisions, which accomplish the same objective: allowing manufacturers and sellers to defend a products liability claim on the ground of their practicable inability to adopt a design or warning that would have prevented a harm of the kind suffered by the claimant at the time the product was made and sold. For example, New Jersey has an "unavoidably unsafe" defense to claims of defects in design, and North Carolina has one limited to prescription drugs.[186] At least New Jersey, Mississippi, and North Carolina have provisions protecting defendants from design claims for injuries resulting from "an inherent characteristic of the product which is a generic aspect of the product that cannot be eliminated without substantially compromising the product's usefulness or desirability and which is recognized by" an ordinary person.[187] And some statutes define the basis and scope of products liability in negligence terms, based on such concepts as foreseeability or reasonable expectability,[188] reasonable care, and what a reasonably prudent person knew, should have known, or would have done.[189]

## Foreign Law

The spread of the state-of-the-art defense across America is mirrored by its widespread acceptance in other industrial nations. The European Community's *Directive on Liability for Defective Products*[190] provides

**182.** See Idaho Code § [6–1406] 6–1306(4).

**183.** See Miss. Code Ann. § 11–1–63(f)(ii). This statute defines "feasible design alternative" unhelpfully, in terms of the state-of-the-art issue, as "a design that would have to a reasonable probability prevented the harm without impairing the utility, usefulness, practicality or desirability of the product to users or consumers." Id.

**184.** See Tex. Civ. Prac. & Rem. Code Ann. § 82.005(a)(1).

**185.** Id. at (b)(2).

**186.** See N.J. Stat. Ann. § 2A:58c–3a(3); N.C. Gen. Stat. § 99B–6(d).

**187.** This language is from the Mississippi statute. The New Jersey and North Carolina statutes are similar. See Miss. Code Ann. § 11–1–63(b); N.J. Stat. Ann.: 2A:58c–3a(2); N.C. Gen. Stat. § 99B–6(c).

**188.** See Ind. Code § 34–20–4–1(2).

**189.** See Ind. Code §§ 34–20–2–2 & 34–20–4–1; Miss. Code Ann. §§ 11–1–63(c)(ii) & (f)(i); Wash. Rev. Code Ann. § 7.72.030(1).

**190.** 28 O. J. Eur. Comm. (No. L 210) 29 (85/374/EEC, 25 July 1985). On the Directive, see § 1.4, above.

manufacturers with a state-of-the-art defense, referred to in Europe as the "development risk" defense,[191] applicable to most European nations.[192] Article 7(e) of the *Directive* provides a defense for a manufacturer which proves "that the state of scientific and technical knowledge at the time when he put the product into circulation was not such as to enable the existence of the defect to be discovered. . . . " This provision is spawning a diversity of results, with a Dutch court ruling that the development risk defense protects the sellers of HIV-infected blood;[193] a German court holding that this defense does not apply to manufacturing defects;[194] an English court ruling that the defense does not protect suppliers of infected blood, and that it does apply to manufacturing defects until the risk is actually discovered;[195] the European Court of Justice holding that the defense applies even if knowledge of the defect exists but is "inaccessible," as where it resides only in a remote Manchurian scientific journal;[196] and an Australian court, interpreting a similar provision, ruling that the development risk defense applies where the general risk is known but its discovery in a particular product is impossible to detect.[197]

Japan's products liability law, patterned in many respects after the EC *Directive*, adopts an identical principle in Article 4.[198] Interpreting this provision, the Economic Welfare Council of the Economic Planning Agency of Japan has pronounced "that scientific and technological knowledge must be judged against the highest standards of technology applicable at the time and not against the level applied by a specific manufacturer or the industry."[199]

**191.** Some European commentators distinguish the development risk defense from the state-of-the-art defense. See Taschner, Harmonization of Product Liability Law in the European Community, 34 Tex. Int'l L.J. 21 (1999); G. Howells and S. Wetherill, Consumer Protection § 4.1.3, at 201 (2d ed. 2004, Ashgate). Other commentators appear to equate the two. See Wandt, German Approaches to Products Liability, 34 Tex. Int'l L.J. 71 (1999). See generally Howells and Mildred, Infected Blood: Defect and Discoverability. A First Exposition of the EC Product Liability Directive, 65 Mod. L. Rev. 95, 98 (2002); Stapleton, Bugs in Anglo–American Products Liability, 53 S.C. L. Rev. 1225, 1243–52 (2002); Stapleton, Products Liability in the United Kingdom: The Myths of Reform, 34 Tex. Int'l L.J. 45, 53–61 (1999); C.J. Miller and R. Goldberg, Product Liability ch. 13, at 489–528 (Oxford, 2d ed. 2004); J. Stapleton, Product Liability 236–42 (Butterworths, 1994).

**192.** Of the fifteen EU members in early 2004, only Luxembourg and Finland opted to omit this defense entirely, under Article 15(1)(b). Spain excludes from the defense liability for the sale of defective medicines and food, Germany for pharmaceuticals, and France for products (like blood) derived from the human body.

**193.** Scholten v. The Foundation Sanquin of Blood Supply, Amsterdam, Feb. 3, 1999, NJ 621 (ann. DJV), discussed in Stapleton, Bugs in Anglo–American Products Liability, 53 S.C. L. Rev. 1225, 1252–53 (2002).

**194.** BGHZ 129, 353, discussed in Hodges, The Case of the Exploding Bottle of Water, 18 Prod. Liab. Int'l 73 (1996).

**195.** In re Hepatitis C Litigation (A v. National Blood Authority), 3 All E.R. 289 (Q.B. 2001). See Howells and Mildred, Infected Blood: Defect and Discoverability. A First Exposition of the EC Product Liability Directive, 65 Mod. L. Rev. 95, 98 (2002). See generally Feldman, Blood Justice: Courts, Conflicts, and Compensation in Japan, France, and the United States, 34 Law & Society Rev. 651 (2000).

**196.** European Commission v. United Kingdom, Case C–300/95, 1997 E.C.R. I–2649, [1997] All E.R. 481. See C.J. Miller and R. Goldberg, Product Liability 602–04 (Oxford, 2d ed. 2004).

**197.** Ryan v. Great Lakes Council, 78 F.C.R. 309 (1997), on appeal, Graham Barclay Oysters Pty v. Ryan, 102 F.C.R. 307 (2000) (hepatitis-infected oysters).

**198.** See L. Nottage, Product Safety and Liability Law in Japan 124–31 (2004).

**199.** See Kobayashi and Furuta, Products Liability Act and Transnational Litiga-

## The Products Liability Restatement

As earlier discussed, the "state of the art" term has caused considerable confusion because of the widely varying ways in which it is defined, but the underlying proposition that manufacturers should be held responsible only for what they can foresee and reasonably prevent is increasingly accepted in American law. Acknowledging the definitional problem,[200] the *Restatement (Third) of Torts: Products Liability* avoids it altogether by neither defining nor otherwise using the term. Recognizing that manufacturers should only be held to a standard of responsibility they can reasonably achieve,[201] the *Products Liability Restatement* adopts this concept in the precept of reasonableness, based on principles of negligence,[202] used to define the nature and scope of design and warnings responsibility.[203]

### *Warning of Unknowable Risks*

As examined earlier in this section, the most significant state-of-the-art issue is whether manufacturers should be required to warn of unknowable product risks. The *Products Liability Restatement* plainly rejects any such duty as unreasonable and beyond the proper scope of a manufacturer's duty to warn. Section 2(c) provides that a product "is defective because of inadequate instructions or warnings when the foreseeable risks of harm posed by the product could have been reduced or avoided by the provision of reasonable instructions or warnings [the omission of which] renders the product not reasonably safe." It is perfectly clear from this black letter provision that unknowable risks lie outside the duty to warn because they are not "foreseeable," which it justifies on grounds of fairness and efficiency.[204]

tion in Japan, 34 Tex. Int'l L.J. 93, 99–100 (1999). This was the holding of the Tokyo District Court in the "snapper" case, involving the sale of infected snapper fish. The court ruled that the Article 4 defense did not apply because it required that there was no knowledge of the risk in the world, that the applicable standard was "the world's highest standard obtainable" at the time of sale, and there had been some reports of snapper infection in some waters. See L. Nottage, Product Safety and Liability Law in Japan 126 (2004).

**200.** Products Liability Restatement § 2 cmt. *d*.

**201.** See Products Liability Restatement § 2 cmt. *a*, set forth below.

**202.** "Sections 2(b) and 2(c) rely on a reasonableness test traditionally used in determining whether an actor has been negligent." Products Liability Restatement § 1 cmt. *a*.

**203.** These defects are defined for products generally in Products Liability Restatement §§ 2(b) and 2(c), respectively. Design

and warnings defects for pharmaceutical drugs and medical devices are defined in §§ 6(c) and 6(d), respectively.

**204.** Products Liability Restatement § 2 cmt. *a*:

Most courts agree that, for the liability system to be fair and efficient, the balancing of risks and benefits in judging product design and marketing must be done in light of the knowledge of risks and risk-avoidance techniques reasonably attainable at the time of distribution. To hold a manufacturer liable for a risk that was not foreseeable when the product was marketed might foster increased manufacturer investment in safety. But such investment by definition would be a matter of guesswork. Furthermore, manufacturers may persuasively ask to be judged by a normative behavior standard to which it is reasonably possible for manufacturers to conform. For these reasons, Subsections (b) and (c) speak of products being defective only when risks are reasonably foreseeable.

In addition to limiting warning responsibility to foreseeable risks of harm, the *Restatement* also conditions it on "reasonableness."[205] While the foreseeability limitation alone would appear to resolve the unknowable risk warnings question, requiring a plaintiff to prove that some alternative "reasonable" warning could have prevented the accident underscores the necessity that any required warning be within the capabilities of a prudent manufacturer seeking—within the bounds of practically available scientific knowledge—to make its products safe. Warning of unknowable product hazards is impossible by any definition, and so would never be required by a liability standard based on reasonableness.

Various comments buttress these basic provisions in § 2(c). Noting the complexity of the foreseeability of risk issue in connection with products such as prescription drugs, medical devices, and toxic chemicals, comment *m* states that there is no liability for selling such products if their risks are unforeseeable.[206] Further, in addressing the duty to warn of "adverse allergic or idiosyncratic reactions," comment *k* provides that there is no duty to warn of risks of unforeseeable allergic reactions. In short, by limiting the scope of the duty to warn to risks which are foreseeable, the *Restatement (Third) of Torts: Products Liability* rejects any notion that there might be a duty to warn of unknowable product risks.

### Designing to the State of the Art

The *Products Liability Restatement* applies the same general principles of foreseeability and reasonableness used in the warnings context in defining the scope of a manufacturer's responsibility for dangers in design. Section 2(b) provides that a product "is defective in design when the foreseeable risks of harm posed by the product could have been reduced or avoided by the adoption of a reasonable alternative design [the omission of which] renders the product not reasonably safe." As with warning defects, the *Third Restatement* limits the design obligation to "foreseeable" risks and grounds it on principles of reasonableness. Unforeseeable risks are a rarity in design cases,[207] except for the highly dangerous and unusual uses to which products sometimes are subjected. Foreseeability limits responsibility in this type of situation, in design and warnings cases alike.[208]

See also Products Liability Restatement §§ 6(c) and 6(d), which limit design and warnings responsibility for prescription drugs and medical devices to *foreseeable* risks of harm.

**205.** "Subsection (c) adopts a reasonableness test for judging the adequacy of product instructions and warnings." Products Liability Restatement § 2 cmt. *i*.

**206.** Comment *m* makes clear, however, that a seller bears responsibility for performing proper testing to realize such risks as are reasonably capable of discovery.

**207.** See Products Liability Restatement § 2 cmt. *m*.

**208.** "Subsections (b) and (c) impose liability only when the product is put to uses that it is reasonable to expect a seller or distributor to foresee. Product sellers and distributors are not required to foresee and take precautions against every conceivable mode of use and abuse to which their products might be put." Products Liability Restatement § 2 cmt. *m*. See also cmt. *p*, which notes: "The post-sale conduct of the user may be so unreasonable, unusual, and costly to avoid that a seller has no duty to design or warn against [it]. When a court so concludes, the product is not defective within the meaning of Subsection (b) or (c)."

The *Products Liability Restatement*'s most emphatic adoption of a de facto state-of-the-art limitation on the design obligation is in § 2(b)'s black-letter requirement that plaintiffs establish a "reasonable design alternative."[209] By "reasonable," the *Restatement* means feasible, available, and practical: "To establish a prima facie case of defect, the plaintiff must prove the availability of a technologically feasible and practical alternative design that would have reduced or prevented the plaintiff's harm."[210] In other words, the plaintiff must establish "that a reasonable alternative could have been practically adopted."[211] Thus, by restricting liability for design dangers to foreseeable risks that could have been prevented by a reasonable, feasible, available, and practical modification in design, the *Third Restatement* incorporates state-of-the-art principles into the definition of design defectiveness. In short, the definition of design defectiveness in the *Products Liability Restatement* incorporates the underlying tenet of state of the art—that a manufacturer may be held responsible only for failing to avoid foreseeable dangers that it reasonably could have prevented.[212]

### Burden of proof

The *Products Liability Restatement* did not follow the approach of several state reform statutes which adopted state of the art as an affirmative defense. Instead, as noted earlier, the *Restatement* incorporates state-of-the-art components—foreseeability of risk, and the feasibility, availability, and practicality of an alternative design—in the liability definition, as part of the plaintiff's case in chief. Accordingly, the plaintiff has both the burden of pleading and the burden of proof on state-of-the-art issues under the *Products Liability Restatement*.[213]

## § 10.5   PRENATAL HARM

Chemical compounds in prescription drugs and other hazardous substances may directly harm a fetus or may alter chromosomes in the mother or the fetus in a manner that causes genetic defects that may spread from generation to generation. Remote consequences like these naturally raise difficult questions of responsibility for such harm and, more particularly, whether manufacturers of toxic substances should have a duty to guard against birth defects to a fetus injured *in utero* or in subsequent generations. If the child, grandchild—or great grandchild—of a person exposed to some toxin is born with a short finger as a result, or with a handicap more severe, should the descendant have a products liability claim for the disability against the party that manufactured and sold the product generations earlier? Among the various doctrinal vessels into which this problem may be poured are statutes of

---

**209.** That is, in all but a narrow class of cases, most particularly in those involving manifestly unreasonable designs. See Products Liability Restatement § 2 cmt. *e*.

**210.** Id. cmt. *f*. See also cmt. *d*, which states: "Subsection (b) adopts a reasonableness ('risk-utility balancing') test as the standard for judging the defectiveness of product designs. More specifically, the test is whether a reasonable alternative design would, at reasonable cost, have reduced the

foreseeable risks of harm posed by the product. . . . [T]he plaintiff must prove that such a reasonable alternative was, or reasonably could have been, available at time of sale or distribution."

**211.** Id. cmt. *f*.

**212.** Id. cmt. *f*.

**213.** See Products Liability Restatement § 2 comments *d* and *f* (design defects), and comments *i* and *m* (warnings defects).

limitations and repose,[1] proximate cause (including foreseeability of harm),[2] and duty. It is the latter doctrine, duty, which the courts have found most useful for addressing the complex web of policy and legal issues that arise in attempting to figure out whether manufacturers of hazardous substances should be responsible to successive generations of persons who suffer the consequences of harm first inflicted on (and transmitted by the bodies of) their ancestors. This issue in products liability cases is part of the broader, bedeviling subject of recovery for prenatal injury in the law of torts.[3]

If a pregnant woman comes in contact with a toxic drug or other chemical which directly harms a fetus, the normal principles of recovery for foreseeably inflicted harm apply to products liability as to other types of cases involving prenatal harm.[4] So, if a plaintiff can overcome the sometimes daunting problems of establishing proximate causation,[5] there is no special reason why recovery should not be available against a manufacturer or other seller for harm caused by prenatal exposure to a toxic pesticide,[6] fungicide,[7] drug,[8] or other toxic substance.[9]

More difficult are the preconception cases, where the plaintiff had no contact with the toxic substance to which the plaintiff's mother (or

---

**§ 10.5**

**1.** See § 14.5, below.

**2.** See ch. 12, below.

**3.** See Greenberg, Reconceptualizing Preconception Torts, 64 Tenn. L. Rev. 315, 338–40 (1997); Robertson, Toward Rational Boundaries of Tort Liability for Injury to the Unborn: Prenatal Injuries, Preconception Injuries and Wrongful Life, 1978 Duke L.J. 1401; Notes, 69 Fordham L. Rev. 2555 (2001) (preconception tort law); 18 Cardozo L. Rev. 1217 (1996) (DES third-generation liability); 62 U. Cin. L. Rev. 283 (1993) (noting *Grover*); 27 New Eng. L. Rev. 241 (1992); 17 Am. J.L. & Med. 435 (1991); 24 Creighton L. Rev. 1479 (1991); Prosser and Keeton on Torts § 55, at 369; Dobbs on Torts §§ 288–90, at 781 et seq. (thorough and sensitive treatment of tort law issues); 4 J. Lee and B. Lindahl, Modern Tort Law: Liability and Litigation § 31:2 (2d ed. 2003).

**4.** See generally Prosser and Keeton on Torts § 55.

**5.** See, e.g., Merrell Dow Pharmaceuticals, Inc. v. Havner, 953 S.W.2d 706 (Tex. 1997) (Owen, J.) (causation evidence insufficient to establish that prenatal exposure to Bendectin caused child's birth defects); Wintz v. Northrop Corp., 110 F.3d 508 (7th Cir. 1997) (Ill. law) (insufficient evidence to establish that infant's *in utero* exposure to photographic developing chemical containing bromide caused genetic disorder called Prader–Willi Syndrome); National Bank of Commerce (of El Dorado, Ark.) v. Dow

Chemical Co., 965 F.Supp. 1490, 1492 (E.D. Ark. 1996) (plaintiff failed to prove that *in utero* exposure to Dursban pesticide caused injuries).

**6.** Roberti v. Andy's Termite & Pest Control, Inc., 6 Cal.Rptr.3d 827 (Ct. App. 2003) (plaintiff allegedly suffered autism from application of Dursban during mother's pregnancy).

**7.** See, e.g., Brown v. E.I. duPont de Nemours and Co., 820 A.2d 362 (Del. 2003) (birth defects to children of foreign nationals from mothers' prenatal exposure to fungicide in foreign countries).

**8.** See, e.g., Moll v. Abbott Labs., 506 N.W.2d 816 (Mich. 1993) (*in utero* exposure to DES allegedly caused vaginal abnormalities); Hibbs v. Abbott Labs., 814 P.2d 1186 (Wash. Ct. App. 1991) (same); McMahon v. Eli Lilly & Co., 774 F.2d 830 (7th Cir. 1985) (Ill. law) (same, injuries to daughter and, eventually, to daughter's son).

**9.** See, e.g., In re Dow Corning Corp., 255 B.R. 445 (E.D. Mich. 2000) (mentioning claims of children exposed in utero to silicone gel from breast implants). *But see* Wintz v. Northrop Corp., 110 F.3d 508 (7th Cir. 1997) (Ill. law) (denying claim by infant for *in utero* exposure to photographic developing chemical containing bromide that allegedly caused genetic disorder); Widera v. Ettco Wire & Cable Corp., 611 N.Y.S.2d 569 (App. Div. 1994) (denying claim for infant exposed *in utero* to toxic chemicals on father's work clothes, which were washed by pregnant mother) (2–1 decision).

father) is exposed even before the plaintiff is conceived. Perhaps the first preconception products liability case was *Jorgensen v. Meade Johnson Laboratories, Inc.*,[10] a products liability case against the manufacturer of birth control pills for the Down Syndrome suffered by twin girls born to a woman who took the pills for several months before she became pregnant. Plaintiffs claimed that the pills had altered the chromosomal structure of the mother's body causing severe deformities in the twins. Reversing the district court's dismissal of the action, the federal court of appeals allowed a claim for strict liability in tort, ruling that the fact that the defendant's tortious conduct occurred before conception was no reason to bar a claim for foreseeable harm to plaintiffs born thereafter.[11]

In the few preconception products liability cases to follow *Jorgensen*, courts have been less hospitable to claims by plaintiffs who themselves were not exposed, even *in utero*, to the defendant's product. The next such case was *Catherwood v. American Sterilizer Co.*,[12] in which the plaintiff, exposed to ethylene oxide in the course of her employment, conceived and gave birth to a daughter with chromosomal damage, which she attributed to her previous chemical exposure. Dismissing her complaint against the manufacturer and her employers, the trial court reasoned that there is a "policy need for limitation of liability in exposure and ingestion cases." The Appellate Division affirmed. Concurring, Justice Lawton expressed concern over the overwhelming costs that might result from allowing recovery for genetic abnormalities that "pass from generation to generation."[13] The two dissenting justices argued that the law should allow products liability claims for preconception torts to infants when manufacturers of toxic chemicals fail to warn mothers of the dangers of exposure in the workplace, reasoning that liability would be no greater than from any other type of harm from a defective product that occurred many years after marketing.

The preconception issue most pointedly arose in three cases involving the prescription drug, DES, prescribed to pregnant women to prevent miscarriage during the late 1940s, the 1950s, and 1960s.[14] In each case, the plaintiffs ("DES grandchildren") were grandchildren of women to whom DES was given. The plaintiffs claimed that their mothers' reproductive systems were harmed *in utero* when their grandmothers took the drug, eventually injuring the plaintiffs when their mothers became pregnant and, unable to carry their children to term, delivered them prematurely. The premature births caused the plaintiffs to suffer cerebral palsy and other disabilities. In each case, a split appellate court determined that recovery should be denied for such intergenerational harm.[15]

---

**10.** 483 F.2d 237 (10th Cir. 1973) (Okla. law).

**11.** Otherwise, an infant injured by a defective food product, manufactured before his or her conception, would have no remedy. Id. at 240.

**12.** 498 N.Y.S.2d 703 (Sup. Ct. 1986), aff'd, 511 N.Y.S.2d 805 (App. Div. 1987) (3–2 decision), appeal dismissed, 515 N.E.2d 908 (N.Y. 1987).

**13.** See 511 N.Y.S.2d at 806.

**14.** DES is best known in products liability law for spawning the market share liability theory of recovery for use when the manufacturer of a fungible drug cannot be identified. See § 11.3, below.

**15.** A few other cases involving DES grandchildren fail to examine the preconception duty issue. One early case, McMahon v. Eli Lilly & Co., 774 F.2d 830 (7th

In the first case, *Loerch v. Eli Lilly & Co.*,[16] an evenly-divided Minnesota Supreme Court upheld without opinion the trial court's dismissal of a claim for spastic quadriplegia from cerebral palsy occasioned by the plaintiff's premature birth. The trial judge wrote an opinion in the case, "the most difficult and challenging of any" he had encountered "in either an official or personal capacity."[17] Relying heavily on *Palsgraf v. Long Island R.R. Co.*,[18] he reasoned that the plaintiff's case failed under the reasoning of both Chief Judge Cardozo and Judge Andrews. Under a Cardozo analysis, the drug manufacturer owed no duty to the grandchild, a third-generation plaintiff far removed from the original tortious act who was "simply too remote in time to be justifiably within the zone of danger." The same result would obtain under an Andrews analysis, he reasoned, since, as a matter of public policy and "practical politics" (the chilling effect on medical research and development), "a line has to be drawn cutting off liability."

The next case was *Enright v. Eli Lilly & Co.*,[19] in which the New York Court of Appeals rejected negligence and strict liability in tort claims against the drug manufacturer because the child was never exposed to the drug *in utero*. Concerned about the "rippling effects of DES exposure [that] may extend for generations,"[20] the court, drawing on a tradition of using bright-line rules to avoid the perils of limitless liability in tort law,[21] held that liability in such cases must stop with the second-generation plaintiffs actually exposed to the drug, even if that meant leaving third-generation grandchildren harmed by the drug out in the cold.[22] The court reasoned that responsibility for harm to first-and

Cir. 1985) (Ill. law), involved claims of both a DES daughter and her son who was born prematurely and died. Ruling that the foreseeability of the mother's injuries was for the jury, the court allowed the claims to proceed without addressing the question of whether the manufacturer had a duty to the third-generation grandson. See also Bowe v. Abbott Labs., 608 N.E.2d 223 (Ill. App. Ct. 1992) (allowing grandchild to amend complaint to replace market share with alternative liability). One trial court decision on summary judgement does address the remoteness issue in such cases, allowing a grandchild's negligence claim to proceed, but barring the strict liability claim on remoteness grounds. DeMayo v. Schmitt, 1989 WL 234501 (Pa. Commonw. Ct. 1989). *But see* Wood v. Eli Lilly & Co., 38 F.3d 510 (10th Cir. 1994) (Okla. law) (remoteness of injury to grandchild suggested Oklahoma courts would not allow market share liability). Compare Sparapany v. Rexall Corp., 618 N.E.2d 1098 (Ill. App. Ct. 1993), which denied DES grandchildren claims because they arose from conduct occurring before the Illinois Supreme Court first prospectively allowed preconception torts in Renslow v. Mennonite Hosp., 367 N.E.2d 1250 (Ill. 1977), but which explicitly left open general question of whether drug manufacturers may be subject to liability, for conduct after *Renslow*, (for preconcep-

tion third-generation injuries); Sorrells v. Eli Lilly & Co., 737 F.Supp. 678 (D.D.C. 1990) (Md. law) (Maryland does not recognize duty to grandchild).

**16.** 445 N.W.2d 560 (Minn. 1989) (3–3 decision).

**17.** No. 79–8720, Hennepin Cty. Dist. Ct., Minn., 1988 (Schiefelbein, J.), in W.P. Keeton et al., Products Liability and Safety—Cases and Materials 1003–10 (Foundation Press, 2d ed. 1989).

**18.** 162 N.E. 99 (N.Y. 1928).

**19.** 570 N.E.2d 198 (N.Y. 1991) (5–1 decision).

**20.** Id. at 203.

**21.** For example, New York's long-established rule limiting responsibility for fires to the first building. The rule arose in Ryan v. New York Central R.R. Co., 35 N.Y. 210 (1866), discussed in Prosser and Keeton on Torts § 43, at 282.

**22.** 570 N.E.2d at 203 (The issues in the case raise "vexing questions" with " 'staggering implications,' " and "the cause of action plaintiffs ask us to recognize here could not be confined without the drawing of artificial and arbitrary boundaries.... It is our duty to confine liability within manageable limits.... Limiting liability to second-generation victims should provide manufacturers with an adequate incentive to market safe drugs, the safety of which is also regulated by the Food and Drug Administration, and that the tort system should seek to avoid imposing excessive liability that might stifle the development of important new prescription pharmaceuticals that always carry some risk of harm.[23] The Court of Appeals therefore reaffirmed its ruling in an earlier preconception medical malpractice case[24] that tortious injury to a mother causing injury to a later-conceived child does not support a claim by the child against the original tortfeasor.[25]

In the final case, *Grover v. Eli Lilly & Co.*,[26] the Ohio Supreme Court addressed this same issue on a certified question.[27] The court distinguished several medical malpractice cases which had allowed recovery for preconception torts by pointing to the long period of time, in products cases involving third-generation preconception injuries, between the tortious act and plaintiff's injury. The Ohio court reiterated the *Enright* court's conclusion that the "rippling effects" of allowing such claims required a bright-line rule limiting a manufacturer's responsibility to second-generation plaintiffs actually exposed to the drug.[28] Borrowing from *Enright*'s policy analysis and the *Loerch* court's doctrinal reliance on *Palsgraf*, the Ohio court concluded that even if the drug manufacturers could foresee injuries to the reproductive systems of fetuses of mothers who took DES, this general foreseeability was insufficient to extend responsibility to such women's children born nearly thirty years after the harmful exposure. "Because of the remoteness in time and causation," the court concluded that the grandson had no cause of action.[29]

Determining how far liability properly should extend for prenatal harm caused by prescription drugs and other chemicals is vexing, to say the least. To the extent that such harm is foreseeable, courts are surely right to allow recovery to second-generation victims who themselves are harmed *in utero* by such chemicals. Yet, when the harm is caused to an ultimate victim's parents or grandparents, and its consequences are transmitted genetically or otherwise indirectly to subsequent genera-

those who ingested the drug or were exposed to it *in utero* serves this purpose.")

**23.** Id. at 204 ("we are aware of the dangers of overdeterrence—the possibility that research will be discouraged or beneficial drugs withheld from the market").

**24.** Albala v. New York, 429 N.E.2d 786 (N.Y. 1981) (child has no cause of action for doctor's negligence during abortion performed four years prior to child's conception).

**25.** 570 N.E.2d at 204.

**26.** 591 N.E.2d 696 (Ohio 1992) (4–3 decision).

**27.** The question, certified by a federal court, was, "Does Ohio recognize a cause of action on behalf of a child born prematurely, and with severe birth defects, if it can be established that such injuries were proxi-

mately caused by defects in the child's mother's reproductive system, those defects in turn being proximately caused by the child's grandmother ingesting a defective drug (DES) during her pregnancy with the child's mother?" See id. at 697.

**28.** Id. at 699.

**29.** "A pharmaceutical company's liability for the distribution or manufacture of a defective prescription drug does not extend to persons who were never exposed to the drug, either directly or *in utero*." Id. at 700–01. Characterizing the majority treatment of the legal issues surrounding the "devastating" effects of DES as "superficial," the dissent argued that the resulting harm from DES was readily foreseeable to manufacturers and chastised the majority for accepting the defendants' "age-old" floodgates arguments. Id. at 701.

tions, the remoteness problem sharpens. Whether liability ever should extend to third-generation plaintiffs is difficult to answer in the abstract and generally should be answered in the context of a particular toxic substance marketed in a particular situation. While manufacturers normally should not have a duty to avoid such harm, perhaps liability in negligence might be appropriate if the manufacturer foresaw (or clearly could foresee) both the type of harm and class of persons put to risk. In such limited situations, the law might fairly place responsibility for the costs of harm from toxic substances on the makers of such substances rather than on their helpless victims. Yet, beyond such cases, liability must at some point stop. In these situations, where proof of negligence and foreseeability are dim, bright-line no-duty rules may usefully be employed to define liability boundaries for the remote effects of preconception harm to future generations from toxic substances.

## § 10.6　Deterioration

Nothing stays the same.[1] As with lawyers and judges, even the very best of products age and eventually wear out. The fact that products suffer normal wear and tear, and often grow more dangerous over time, presents the law with a challenging set of problems in how to fairly and efficiently allocate responsibility for the harm which older products are bound to cause. How the law of products liability does and should address the safety implications of products aging, deteriorating, and eventually wearing out, is the subject of this section. The problem of product deterioration raises an enormous web of interrelated issues[2] treated elsewhere, such as foreseeability;[3] defectiveness;[4] changes in the state of the art;[5] cause in fact[6] and proximate causation;[7] various user misconduct defenses, including product misuse;[8] statutes of limitations and repose;[9] and a miscellany of evidentiary problems, from circumstantial evidence of product defect, including the "malfunction doctrine,"[10] to the admissibility of evidence on subsequent remedial measures.[11] This section focuses on duty aspects of the deterioration problem.[12]

---

### § 10.6

**1.** Except, perhaps, for the principle that nothing stays the same. See Balido v. Improved Mach., Inc., 105 Cal.Rptr. 890, 896 (Ct. App. 1972) (noting "the inevitability of change").

**2.** See Balido v. Improved Mach., Inc., 105 Cal.Rptr. 890, 896–97 (Ct. App. 1972), involving an injury due to the failure of a non-moving part in a press about fourteen years old:

The problem arises as a by-product of the inevitability of change, for change brought about by time unravels the connection between prior cause and later effect. Did the product fail because it was badly designed or because it was badly manufactured? Because badly manufactured or because it was badly maintained? Badly maintained or abused in use? Abused in use or because it wore out? Here, we find ourselves deep in the labyrinth of causation,

where passage of time almost inevitably brings its concomitant of multiple cause and multiple effect. In working our way out of this labyrinth legal rules, inferences, presumptions furnish little help, for the basic problem is one of reliability of proof.

**3.** See § 10.4, above, §§ 12.2 and 13.5, below.

**4.** See chapters 5–9, above.

**5.** See § 10.4, above.

**6.** See ch. 11, below.

**7.** See ch. 12, below.

**8.** See § 13.5, below.

**9.** See § 14.5, below.

**10.** See § 7.4, above.

**11.** See § 6.4, above.

**12.** See G. Schwartz, New Products, Old Products, Evolving Law, Retroactive Law,

The simple truth that products necessarily decline with age generates a basic legal principle that is logical and fair: "There is no duty upon a manufacturer to furnish a machine that will not wear out."[13] On this principle, in the absence of satisfactory proof that a product was defective when it was first sold, courts have ruled for manufacturers in cases involving a wooden powerline pole that lasted thirteen years before it collapsed from rot;[14] a brake-locking mechanism on a twenty-year-old crane that failed, causing a load of steel pipe to drop upon the plaintiff;[15] the wearing of the steering mechanism that caused a crash of an eleven-year-old truck, driven 186,000 miles and frequently overloaded in a manner that caused the wear;[16] the corrosion of a suspension arm and resulting crash of a car driven for eleven years and 124,000 miles "in the most corrosive environment in the world";[17] and the amputation of a hand in a plastic injection machine which allegedly malfunctioned 35 years after it was manufactured and first sold.[18] These and other cases adopt the principle that manufacturers generally are not responsible for dangers that naturally arise from the normal wear and tear of products that eventually do wear out.[19]

58 N.Y.U. L. Rev. 796 (1983); Note, Limiting Manufacturers' Liability for Aging Products, 39 Drake L. Rev. 713 (1990).

**13.** Auld v. Sears, Roebuck & Co., 25 N.Y.S.2d 491, 493 (App. Div. 1941), aff'd, 41 N.E.2d 927 (N.Y. 1942).

**14.** Triplett v. American Creosote Works, Inc., 171 So.2d 342 (Miss. 1965) ("it cannot be reasonably contended that a preservative applied to a pole such as [this] would make it indestructible or prolong its life indefinitely.... [T]elephone poles and electric power line poles do rot and decay after long exposure to the elements," and the pole lasting thirteen years was long enough).

**15.** Kuisis v. Baldwin–Lima–Hamilton Corp., 319 A.2d 914, 922 (Pa. 1974) ("Section 402A does not make manufacturers and sellers insurers of their products. They are not liable for defects caused by normal wear-and-tear ... however foreseeable these events may be. Here, the vicissitudes of over twenty years of rugged use of the crane make these possible sources of the alleged defect in the locking device no less likely than an error in manufacture or design.").

**16.** Stuckey v. Young Exploration Co., 586 P.2d 726, 731 (Okla. 1978) ("Nearly all automotive parts subject to friction wear out sometime. The fact a part wears out after 186,000 miles does not evidence that a defect existed when the truck left the manufacturer. Plaintiff submitted no evidence as to how long a suspension system should last with overloading present. A manufacturer does not undertake to provide a product that will never wear out, particularly if used in a continually abnormal manner.").

**17.** Navarro v. Fuji Heavy Indus., Ltd., 925 F.Supp. 1323, 1330 (N.D. Ill. 1996) ("Manufacturers will not be held liable for injuries which occur when a product simply wears out."). The car's suspension arm "simply deteriorated over time," and "Fuji was not required to design and manufacture a car that was wholly immune to corrosion." Although "age and worn condition may not be enough by themselves to negate liability, ... increased longevity must yield a progressively stronger inference that a given product ... was not defective, but failed from extrinsic causes." Id.

**18.** Mayorga v. Reed–Prentice Packaging Mach. Co., 656 N.Y.S.2d 652 (App. Div. 1997).

**19.** Compare Blair v. Martin's, 433 N.Y.S.2d 221, 222 (App. Div. 1980). Plaintiff purchased a pair of plastic boots from the defendant for under $10, wore them for months, had new "lifts" installed by her shoemaker, and wore them for several more months. She fell one day, as she was descending the subway steps, and found that the heel had come off one of the boots. *Held,* judgment for defendant, after jury trial, affirmed: "[W]e believe plaintiffs failed to establish, beyond the barest conclusory allegation, that the accident was caused by a defect present in the boots at the time plaintiff purchased them and not by a defect caused as a result of alteration by her shoemaker (who was unavailable to testify at the trial) or by the boots' simply having worn out."

Accord, that manufacturers generally are not liable for accidents from products that wear out from old age, Walker v. General Elec. Co., 968 F.2d 116 (1st Cir. 1992) (Me. law) (solenoid heating element in toaster

Several corollary principles are appended to the basic tenet that a manufacturer has no duty to make products that will not wear out. The first, which really is just the flip side of the basic tenet, is that, as products age, responsibility for accident prevention shifts incrementally from the manufacturer to the user. For much of a product's life, responsibility for harm may be shared between the manufacturer and the user, but at some point it shifts entirely to the user. As a product ages, the user has responsibility to use and maintain the product properly, to inspect the product for the possibility of wear, and to replace such parts as prudence dictates.

In *Mayorga v. Reed–Prentice Packaging Mach. Co.*,[20] which involved the possible malfunction of a 35-year-old industrial machine, the court concluded that the defendant "did not have a duty to design invincible, fail-safe, and accident-proof products that are incapable of wearing out. The remedy remains in having the machinery inspected periodically so that worn parts may be replaced."[21] In *Foster v. Marshall*,[22] a cotter pin holding together the axle assembly on a trailer wore out over time, which caused the assembly to separate and the trailer to veer into oncoming traffic, colliding with the plaintiff's car. Concluding that the cotter pin's wear did not constitute a product defect, the court remarked that "[a] manufacturer cannot be expected to design products with component parts which will never wear out, regardless of the nature of use or maintenance."[23] Many other courts have similarly ruled for manufacturers of aging products on evidence suggesting that the injury is likely to have occurred from improper maintenance by the user, where deterioration is obvious or would be observed by an inspection, rather than from a defect in the product.[24]

Notwithstanding these general principles protecting manufacturers from liability for product deterioration, several related precepts protect consumers who are injured by defects even in products that are very old. The basic liability principle remains the same in every products liability case, regardless of how many years have passed from the time a product was made and sold: if a plaintiff's injury probably was caused by a product defect that existed at the time of sale, the manufacturer is liable;

---

oven used daily for 6 years); Oquendo v. Teledyne Pines, 602 N.E.2d 56, 57 (Ill. App. Ct. 1992) (plaintiff admitted in deposition that hydraulic fluid hose on 33–year-old pipe bending machine ruptured due to "cuts and the wear and tear of old age").

**20.** 656 N.Y.S.2d 652 (App. Div. 1997).

**21.** Id. at 653.

**22.** 341 So.2d 1354 (La. Ct. App. 1977).

**23.** Id. at 1361. "A manufacturer is entitled to anticipate that a consumer purchasing its product will use reasonable care in maintaining it.... All persons who dealt with this particular wagon testified that they knew that cotter keys will wear out and need to be replaced periodically." Id.

**24.** See, e.g., Mitchell v. Ford Motor Co., 533 F.2d 19 (1st Cir. 1976) (N.H. law)

(brake handle on bed of one-year-old dump truck with 25,000 miles allegedly malfunctioned causing plaintiff's injuries; *held*, manufacturer need not foresee that maintenance of product will be neglected where wear and tear are obvious); Kaczmarek v. Mesta Machine Co., 463 F.2d 675 (3rd Cir. 1972) (Pa. law); Courtois v. General Motors Corp., 182 A.2d 545 (N.J. 1962) (wheel came off five-year-old tractor-trailer truck that had travelled over 500,000 miles; no recovery for breach of implied warranty where parts are subject to stress and friction and are known to require maintenance); Gomez v. E. W. Bliss Co., 211 N.Y.S.2d 246 (Sup. Ct. 1961) (wear around the edges of clutch and latch assembly of nine-year-old punch press; duty of inspection and replacement of worn parts was on user, in this case plaintiff's employer).

but, if the defect probably is attributable to other causes, the manufacturer is not responsible. Thus, a plaintiff injured by an old product may recover against the manufacturer if he or she can establish that the product probably was defective when it left the manufacturer, even if the defect did not materialize for many years.

*Mickle v. Blackmon*,[25] a classic case from South Carolina, best illustrates this principle. In 1962, the plaintiff was riding in the front passenger seat of a 1949 Ford automobile hit by another car. The force of the collision threw her against the gearshift lever mounted on the steering wheel, shattering the protective knob and causing the plaintiff's body to become impaled on the exposed spear-like lever. Ford had known that the plastic material it used for the knob weakened from exposure to ultraviolet rays, but it did not switch to an available alternative material resistant to such rays until 1950. In the plaintiff's suit against Ford for negligent design, the jury returned a verdict for the plaintiff, the trial court granted Ford's motion for judgment notwithstanding the verdict, which the Supreme Court reversed, reinstating the plaintiff's verdict.[26] Noting that the plaintiff in a products liability case must prove that the product was defective at the time of sale,[27] and conceding that a manufacturer does not have a duty to make a product which will not wear out, the court nevertheless recognized that a manufacturer remains responsible for a product's original defects long after the product is sold.[28] Because the evidence revealed that the defendant was negligent in selecting the gearshift knob material, which caused it to deteriorate and collapse, the ordinary rule protecting manufacturers from the perils of inevitable product deterioration simply did not fit the facts of the case. While the intervention of thirteen years between a product's manufac-

**25.** 166 S.E.2d 173 (S.C. 1969).

**26.** The court reasoned:

It is implicit in the verdict that the gearshift lever presented an unreasonable risk of injury if not adequately guarded. At the time of plaintiff's injury the knob on the Hill car continued to serve its functional purpose as a handhold, but it had become useless as a protective guard. It is inferable that the condition of the knob did not arise from ordinary wear and tear, but from an inherent weakness in the material of which Ford was aware when the selection was made. In the light of the insidious effect on this material of exposure to sunlight in the normal use of an automobile, it could reasonably be concluded that Ford should have foreseen that many thousands of the one million vehicles produced by it in 1949 would, in the course of time, be operated millions of miles with gearshift lever balls which, while yet serving adequately as handholds, would furnish no protection to an occupant who might be thrown against the gearshift lever. The jury could reasonably conclude that Ford's conduct, in manufacturing a needed safety device of a material which could not tolerate a fre-

quently encountered aspect of the environment in which it would be employed, exposed many users of its product to unreasonably great risk of harm.

Id. at 188.

**27.** Id. at 189.

**28.** The court adopted the following principles from Dean Prosser's tort law treatise:

If the chattel is in good condition when it is sold, the seller is not responsible when it undergoes subsequent changes, or wears out. The mere lapse of time since the sale by the defendant, during which there has been continued safe use of the product, is always relevant, as indicating that the seller was not responsible for the defect. There have been occasional cases in which, upon the particular facts, it has been held to be conclusive. It is, however, quite certain that neither long continued lapse of time nor changes in ownership will be sufficient in themselves to defeat recovery when there is clear evidence of an original defect in the thing sold.

Id., citing Prosser on Torts 667 (3d ed. 1964).

ture and injury-producing failure presents "a formidable obstacle to fastening liability upon the manufacturer," the court concluded that the facts suggested that the knob's advanced age was "coincidental with its failure rather than the cause of it, and that the knob would have shattered upon a comparable impact had it occurred much earlier in the life of the car." In the court's view, the important question was "not how long the knob lasted, but what caused its failure." The passage of time alone did not shield Ford from responsibility, reasoned the court, if its negligence was what caused the knob to fail.[29] Other courts concur that mere passage of time, even over several decades, will not relieve a manufacturer of responsibility for a defect which was present in a product at the time of sale.[30]

In many cases of older products, the evidence may point in both directions, toward normal wear and tear, lack of maintenance, and possible misuse, on the one hand, but toward the possibility of an original product defect, on the other. In cases such as these, rather than holding as a matter of law that the manufacturer had no duty to prevent the harm, or holding alternatively that the product's age and treatment are irrelevant, courts generally have held that a product's age, maintenance, and treatment are important but not decisive factors on the ultimate issue of defectiveness or negligence to be decided by the trier of fact.[31]

While users of aging products must watch and inspect for indications of wear, sometimes products fail unexpectedly. In such cases, where deterioration is likely to cause a product eventually to fail in a dangerous manner without warning to the user, a manufacturer has a duty to warn of the danger and the product's useful life, in order to allow

---

**29.** Id. at 190 (emphasis added).

**30.** See, e.g., Moran v. Eastern Equip. Sales, Inc., 818 A.2d 848, 852 (Conn. App. Ct. 2003) (jury could find that product was within its safe and useful life when fan blade, located close to fuel filler on ten-year-old wheel loader, struck plaintiff's hand; evidence supported finding that injury was caused by defect in design and that wear and tear played no role); Parsons v. Ford Motor Co., 85 S.W.3d 323, 331 (Tex. App. 2002) (fact that car, which burst into flames, was 8-years-old and had 67,000 miles did not relieve manufacturer of strict liability; age and mileage alone are not dispositive); Dorney Park Coaster Co. v. General Elec. Co., 669 F.Supp. 712 (E.D. Pa. 1987) (Pa. law) (27-year-old deep fryer caught fire and damaged plaintiff's property; mere lapse of time alone is not determinative of defect issue).

**31.** See, e.g., Cornelius v. Bay Motors Inc., 484 P.2d 299 (Or. 1971) (plaintiff was rear-ended by seven-year-old car driven 50,-000 miles; jury could conclude that brake malfunction was result of deterioration);

Hawkeye–Security Ins. Co. v. Kelsey–Hayes Co., 174 N.W.2d 672 (Iowa 1970) (brakes on 21-month-old tractor-trailer truck with 31,-602 miles malfunctioned causing crash; rather than defeating plaintiff's claim, lapse of time between manufacture and injury is a relevant factor for jury to consider in determining defectiveness); Tucker v. Unit Crane & Shovel Corp., 473 P.2d 862 (Or. 1970) (nine-year-old crane collapsed, killing plaintiff's intestate; prolonged safe use and substantial lapse of time between manufacture and collapse alone will not defeat liability where there is evidence that original defect in product caused collapse); International Derrick & Equip. Co. v. Croix, 241 F.2d 216 (5th Cir. 1957) (Tex. law) (7-year-old oil drilling derrick collapsed; lapse of time does not per se relieve the manufacturer of liability, especially in the absence of the failure of moving parts that could wear); Pryor v. Lee C. Moore Corp., 262 F.2d 673 (10th Cir. 1959) (Okla. law) (15-year-old oil drilling derrick collapsed; prolonged safe use is not an absolute bar to recovery but is an important factor in determining causation).

the user to manage the product's decline with reasonable safety.[32] However, no such warning is necessary if the danger is obvious.[33]

Finally, if a plaintiff invokes res ipsa loquitur or the malfunction doctrine in an aging product case, relying upon the nature of a product failure to raise an inference that it was caused by a product defect,[34] the plaintiff bears the burden of negating other possible causes, including the possibility that the product merely wore out.[35]

## § 10.7 DISPOSAL AND SALVAGE

All products eventually wear out,[1] after which they must be dismantled, disposed of, recycled, or destroyed.[2] In the process, long after they have outlived their useful lives, "junked" products continue to pose hazards to the community. The largest safety problems surround the disposal of toxic waste.[3] Outside of tort law, the primary control for

**32.** Strauch v. Gates Rubber Co., 879 F.2d 1282, Prod. Liab. Rep. (CCH) 12230 (5th Cir. 1989) (La. law) (where 5-year-old ammonia hose ruptured injuring plaintiff, manufacturer could be liable for failing to warn that hose had only thirty-month useful life); Miller v. Bock Laundry Mach. Co., 568 S.W.2d 648 (Tex. 1977) (where safety device on washing machine wore out before the machine itself, manufacturer has duty to warn); Indiana Nat'l Bank of Indianapolis v. De Laval Separator Co., 389 F.2d 674 (7th Cir. 1968) (Ind. law) (where defendant knows that machine will wear out in an unsafe manner and user is unable to discover wear, defendant has duty to warn); Rosenbusch v. Ambrosia Milk Corp., 168 N.Y.S. 505 (App. Div. 1917) (where the product (milk) is likely to deteriorate in a manner not appreciated by the purchaser, manufacturers have a duty to warn).

**33.** See, e.g., Fluidmaster, Inc. v. Severinsen, 520 S.E.2d 253 (Ga. Ct. App. 1999) (9-year-old toilet tank overflowed damaging plaintiff's property; that the internal component parts of a toilet will deteriorate over time is obvious, so manufacturer had no duty to warn); Perez v. National Presto Indus., Inc., 431 So.2d 667 (Fla. Dist. Ct. App. 1983).

**34.** See §§ 2.5 (res ipsa) and 7.4 (malfunction doctrine), above.

**35.** See, e.g., Crawford v. Sears Roebuck & Co., 295 F.3d 884, 886 (8th Cir. 2002) (Ark. law) (20–year-old ladder collapsed; plaintiff's case failed because he failed to introduce evidence eliminating causes for the failure other than design defect, including ordinary wear and tear or previous misuse); Bourgeois v. Garrard Chevrolet, Inc., 811 So.2d 962 (La. Ct. App. 2002) ("There was no showing that the wear and tear on the brake system was not normal but was caused by a defective design of the brake system."); Hamilton v. Emerson Elec. Co., 133 F.Supp.2d 360, 376–78 (M.D. Pa. 2001) (defective blade brake on miter saw that was one or two years old and had made 1 to 3 thousand cuts; plaintiff produced no evidence of saw's normal life span); Schlier v. Milwaukee Elec. Tool Corp., 835 F.Supp. 839 (E.D. Pa. 1993) (Pa. law) (5- or 6-month-old power saw); Harrison v. Bill Cairns Pontiac of Marlow Heights, Inc., 549 A.2d 385 (Md. Ct. Spec. App. 1988) (5-year-old car driven over 58,000 miles caught fire); Mullen v. General Motors Corp., 336 N.E.2d 338 (Ill. App. Ct. 1975) (tire blowout after 23,600 miles); Quirk v. Ross, 476 P.2d 559 (Or. 1970) (brakes on automobile failed suddenly after 39,500 miles of use); Jakubowski v. Minnesota Mining & Mfg., 199 A.2d 826 (N.J. 1964) (industrial sanding disc broke after extended use).

### § 10.7

**1.** See § 10.6, above.

**2.** "If every product has a finite useful life and eventually reaches a point when it should no longer be used, then at the end of that period of time the commodity must necessarily be recycled, dismantled, or demolished." Cantu, The Recycling, Dismantling, and Destruction of Goods as a Foreseeable Use Under Section 402A of the Restatement (Second) of Torts, 46 Ala. L. Rev. 81, 100 (1994).

**3.** See generally G. Nothstein, Toxic Torts: Litigation of Hazardous Substance Cases (1984); Cantu, The Recycling, Dismantling, and Destruction of Goods as a Foreseeable Use Under Section 402A of the Restatement (Second) of Torts, 46 Ala. L. Rev. 81 (1994) (excellent analysis); DiBenedetto, Generator Liability Under the Common Law and Federal and State Statutes, 39 Bus. Law. 611 (1984); Hall, The Problem of Unending Liability for Hazardous Waste Management, 38 Bus. Law. 593, 606 (1983); Johnson, Hazardous Waste Disposal: Is There Still a Role for Common Law?, 18 Tulsa L.J. 448 (1983); Seltzer, Personal In-

improper disposal of hazardous waste is the Comprehensive Environmental Response, Compensation, and Liability Act (CERCLA),[4] a regulatory statute enacted by Congress in 1980 to clean up the legacy of decades of haphazard hazardous waste disposal and to provide funds to pay for the clean-up costs. CERCLA permits suits for "necessary costs of response" incurred by a private party against a class of persons that CERCLA deems responsible for cleaning up a waste site,[5] but it does not provide recovery for personal injuries from the disposal of toxic substances.[6]

In recent years, courts and commentators have begun to consider whether manufacturers of toxic chemicals, and manufacturers of products that contain toxic chemicals, should be subject to liability under products liability principles. The issue, for example, is whether manufacturers of the acid used in automotive batteries and the polychlorinated biphenyls (PCBs) used in electrical transformers, and manufacturers of the batteries and transformers themselves, should be liable for injuries from the chemicals when such products are disposed of by their users. Thus, several cases have examined the liability issues arising out of injuries to salvage workers and other damage from the release of PCBs from electrical transformers sold as junk.[7] The transformers variously contained copper coils immersed in PCBs or mineral oil containing PCBs, and salvage workers became exposed to the PCBs by transporting the transformers,[8] dismantling them to recover valuable components,[9] or burning the fluid during the winter for warmth or cooking.[10] Each of the courts refused to apply strict liability in tort to the transformer manufacturer,[11] reasoning that the dismantling of a disposed product was not an intended product use, or not a foreseeable use; that the injuries resulted not from the original product but from a substantial alteration in the

jury Hazardous Waste Litigation: A Proposal for Tort Reform, 10 B.C. Envtl. Aff. L. Rev. 797 (1983); Developments in the Law–Toxic Waste Litigation, 99 Harv. L. Rev. 1458, 1462 (1986); Note, The Inapplicability of Traditional Tort Analysis to Environmental Risks: The Example of Toxic Waste Pollution Victim Compensation, 35 Stan. L. Rev. 575 (1983); Kravit, A Duty to Warn Against Improper and Unsafe Disposal: Filling in Where RCRA and CERCLA Leave Off, 18 Prod. Saf. & Liab. Rep. 106 (BNA) (1990); G. Boston and M. Madden, The Law of Environmental and Toxic Torts: Cases, Materials and Problems (2000).

**4.** 42 U.S.C.A. §§ 9601–75.

**5.** 42 U.S.C.A. § 9607(a)(4)(B).

**6.** A few courts have suggested that medical monitoring costs for those exposed to hazardous waste are available under CERCLA. Compare Lykins v. Westinghouse Elec. Corp., Civ. A. No. 85–508, 1988 WL 114522 (E.D. Ky. 1988) (medical testing expenses recoverable when incurred in conjunction with a hazardous waste site clean-up), with Prisco v. New York, 902 F.Supp. 400 (S.D.N.Y. 1995) (damages not allowed

for medical expenses incurred in treatment of personal injuries). See also U.S. v. Union Corp., 277 F.Supp.2d 478, 493 (E.D. Pa. 2003) (CERCLA clean-up action based in part on strict products liability in tort).

**7.** See, e.g., U.S. v. Union Corp., 277 F.Supp.2d 478, 493 (E.D. Pa. 2003) (clean-up action under CERCLA, based in part on strict products liability in tort); Monsanto Co. v. Reed, 950 S.W.2d 811 (Ky. 1997); High v. Westinghouse Elec. Corp., 610 So.2d 1259 (Fla. 1992). See also Kalik v. Allis–Chalmers, 658 F.Supp. 631 (W.D. Pa. 1987) (property damage and clean-up costs).

**8.** See, e.g., High v. Westinghouse Elec. Corp., 610 So.2d 1259 (Fla. 1992).

**9.** See, e.g., U.S. v. Union Corp., 277 F.Supp.2d 478, 493 (E.D. Pa. 2003) (CERCLA clean-up action) (iron casings and copper cores); Monsanto Co. v. Reed, 950 S.W.2d 811, 814 (Ky. 1997) (copper coils).

**10.** Id.

**11.** Note, however, High v. Westinghouse Elec. Corp., 610 So.2d 1259 (Fla. 1992), rev'g 559 So.2d 227 (Fla. Dist. Ct. App. 1990) (both courts rendered split decisions).

product as it had been sold by the defendant; and that such an alteration amounted to an independent intervening cause.[12]

In other contexts, courts are in agreement that the rules of strict products liability generally do not support claims against manufacturers for injuries arising out of dangers created by the dismantling and disposal of their products at the end of the products' useful lives. Courts thus have held that the dismantling and destruction of ductwork is not a reasonably foreseeable product "use";[13] that lead-smelting workers who inhaled harmful fumes from lead used in the smelting process, where the lead had previously been retrieved from automotive batteries, were not "users" of the automotive batteries;[14] and that attempting to discharge a broken fire extinguisher with pliers, in an effort to make it safe for disposal, is not an intended use of such a product.[15] One rather muddled early case,[16] however, did find a strict products liability complaint sufficient in a case involving injuries to a child from the explosion of a can of drain cleaner to which the child added water.

While the early dismantling cases rejected strict products liability largely on the ground that disposal and destruction was unforeseeable to the manufacturer,[17] more recent decisions, sometimes recognizing that manufacturers can indeed foresee the eventual destruction of their products,[18] have generally cast the issue more in terms of duty.[19] In

**12.** The court in Monsanto Co. v. Reed, 950 S.W.2d 811, 815 (Ky. 1997), used all of these arguments to dispose of negligence and other products liability claims against both the manufacturer of the transformer, Westinghouse, and the chemical manufacturer, Monsanto, that supplied the PCBs to Westinghouse.

**13.** See Wingett v. Teledyne Indus., Inc., 479 N.E.2d 51 (Ind. 1985) (summary judgment for manufacturer proper on claim by worker, injured when a portion of the ductwork fell to the floor when he cut the support hangers, that the ductwork had been improperly constructed).

**14.** Johnson v. Murph Metals, Inc., 562 F.Supp. 246, 249 (N.D. Tex. 1983).

**15.** See Boscarino v. Convenience Marine Prods., Inc., 817 F.Supp. 116 (S.D. Fla. 1993).

**16.** In Tucci v. Bossert, 385 N.Y.S.2d 328 (App. Div. 1976) (the purchasers of a can of Drano drain cleaner disposed of it, with some of the contents remaining in the can, in a trash bag placed outside their house. Two children came along, removed the can from the bag, and poured water into the can. The can exploded and injured one of the children. Plaintiffs sued the manufacturer for selling a defectively packaged product with inadequate warnings. The trial court dismissed the complaint. On appeal, *held,* complaint reinstated. See also Hall v. E.I. Du Pont De Nemours & Co., Inc., 345 F.Supp. 353 (E.D.N.Y. 1972) (children injured by lost or abandoned blasting caps; defendants' motion to dismiss denied).

Contrast Venezia v. Miller Brewing Co., 626 F.2d 188, 192 (1st Cir. 1980) (Mass. law), where a child threw a discarded beer bottle against a telephone pole and suffered injury to his eye. *Held,* dismissal of complaint affirmed: "[T]he impact of endorsing a contrary conclusion would be overwhelming, with every discarded glass object holding the potential for generating a future lawsuit."

**17.** See, e.g., Wingett v. Teledyne Indus., Inc., 479 N.E.2d 51 (Ind. 1985); Kalik v. Allis–Chalmers Corp., 658 F.Supp. 631 (W.D. Pa. 1987).

**18.** "While these chemicals were sealed inside transformers, surely Westinghouse cannot now contend that it was 'unforeseeable' these transformers would some day be breached and would release their PCBs. It is obvious and foreseeable that whatever is sealed inside a container some day is likely to be released again." High v. Westinghouse Elec. Corp., 610 So.2d 1259, 1264 (Fla. 1992) (Kogan, J., concurring in part, dissenting in part). See also id. at 1263 (Barkett, J., concurring) (foreseeability jury issue). See generally Cantu, The Recycling, Dismantling, and Destruction of Goods as a Foreseeable Use Under Section 402A of the Restatement (Second) of Torts, 46 Ala. L. Rev. 81, 100 (1994) (arguing that product recycling, dismantling, and demolishing are indeed foreseeable).

**19.** See High v. Westinghouse Elec. Corp., 610 So.2d 1259 (Fla. 1992). The court in Monsanto Co. v. Reed, 950 S.W.2d

addition to the very difficult duty issues, plaintiffs in most such cases also must overcome powerful arguments of superseding causation.[20] For all of these reasons, recent courts have shown no interest whatsoever in holding manufacturers of junked products strictly liable for injuries resulting from disposal or dismantling.

But plaintiffs in such cases may have other avenues of redress. First, at least a couple of decisions (one reversed) have allowed negligence claims to proceed against manufacturers whose products presented unreasonable risks to persons foreseeably endangered by their disposal or destruction.[21] In *High v. Westinghouse Electric Corporation*,[22] the Florida Supreme Court ruled that the manufacturer of electrical transformers, once it discovered the hazard, had a duty of reasonable care to warn its purchasers (the electric companies) of the dangers of PCBs.[23] Moreover, at least a couple of courts have held direct suppliers of dangerous junked products subject to negligence liability, including a manufacturer which itself distributed the potentially dangerous materials to the user.[24]

But the broader issue remains: if manufacturers and other suppliers are not required to take reasonable steps to make products safe for their eventual disposal, the world will become an ever more dangerous place in which to live. Long ago Congress recognized the need to bar the sale of refrigerators equipped with latch doors which, once abandoned, could not be opened by a child who climbed inside to hide.[25] It may well be, as

811 (Ky. 1997), addressed the liability issue principally in terms of duty but slipped up once by asserting that the dismantled transformers were "not being used in a manner intended nor foreseeable." 950 S.W.2d at 813. *But see*, Boscarino v. Convenience Marine Prods., Inc., 817 F.Supp. 116 (S.D. Fla. 1993).

**20.** See, e.g., Monsanto Co. v. Reed, 950 S.W.2d 811, 815 (Ky. 1997) (noting that the alteration, destruction, or mutilation of a product "would be an independent intervening cause of the injury").

**21.** See, e.g., High v. Westinghouse Elec. Corp., 610 So.2d 1259 (Fla. 1992); Boscarino v. Convenience Marine Prods., Inc. 817 F.Supp. 116 (S.D. Fla. 1993) (striking strict liability claims but leaving negligence count). See also Reed v. Westinghouse Elec. Corp., 1995 WL 96819 (Ky. Ct. App. 1995) (allowing negligence claims by 37 salvage workers to go to jury), rev'd, Monsanto Co. v. Reed, 950 S.W.2d 811 (Ky. 1997).

**22.** 610 So.2d 1259 (Fla. 1992).

**23.** "We find that a manufacturer has a duty to warn of dangerous contents in its product which could damage or injure even when the product is not used for its intended purpose. This issue . . . is whether Westinghouse was negligent in [failing to provide a timely warning to Florida Power and Light] of the possible danger of PCB contamination." Id. at 1262–63.

**24.** See, e.g., Jones v. United Metal Recyclers, 825 F.Supp. 1288 (W.D. Mich. 1993) (jury could determine if manufacturer/seller was negligent in selling scrap aluminum without drying it or warning that it might explode if placed in furnace in wet condition).

See also Treadwell Ford, Inc. v. Campbell, 485 So.2d 312 (Ala. 1986) (seller of car, previously junked and later reconditioned by third party, subject to liability for negligent inspection); Ashland Oil, Inc. v. Miller Oil Purchasing Co., 678 F.2d 1293 (5th Cir. 1982) (La. & Miss. law), holding that a waste disposal contractor was not subject to liability under § 402A, for its disposal of a highly dangerous chemical waste product, because it was not in the business of selling such waste. The contractor tried to incinerate the waste, but it turned into hydrochloric acid which damaged the incinerator. In an attempt to disguise and dispose of the waste, the contractor mixed it with crude oil and had it trucked away. This mixture was eventually sold through wholesale and retail vendors of petroleum products as good crude oil to the plaintiff, whose refinery was damaged when the mixture caught fire and exploded. The two vendors of "crude oil" were both held liable under § 402A.

**25.** Household Refrigerator Safety Act, 15 U.S.C.A. §§ 1211–14.

one commentator has suggested, that civilization has come to the end of the "disposable society" era and now must responsibly adjust to a new world in which the reclamation and recycling of products is fully and properly addressed.[26] In such a world, it is the role of law to require properly safe disposal, dismantling, demolition, and recycling of every product sold. Whether responsibility for proper disposal should lie with manufacturers or with users, or whether it should be shared by both must eventually be addressed by legislatures around the world. Until legislatures develop mature and comprehensive disposal responsibility schemes, however, the common law must perform its office. Surely the common law in the twenty-first century will prove robust enough to manage these problems with the kind of creative responsibility it has shown in other contexts at other times.

## § 10.8  POST-SALE DUTIES TO WARN, REPAIR, OR RECALL

A manufacturer or other seller's duties to purchasers, users, and others typically attach at the time a product is sold.[1] Such duties normally extend to persons foreseeably endangered by conditions the manufacturer reasonably should know the product possesses at the time of manufacture and sale. Sometimes, however, manufacturers (and sometimes other sellers) discover defects in their products only *after* they have been sold and put to use. After sale, for example, a manufacturer may discover a hazard that had not previously been foreseeable, either because advances in the state of the art permitted discovery of the hazard[2] or a method for eliminating it[3] only after the product had been sold, or because consumers turned out to use the product in an unexpectedly dangerous way.[4] Although the law on a manufacturer's post-sale duties has been evolving for roughly half a century,[5] and while recent years have witnessed some sharpening of the issues, the law in this area

**26.** See Cantu, The Recycling, Dismantling, and Destruction of Goods as a Foreseeable Use Under Section 402A of the Restatement (Second) of Torts, 46 Ala. L. Rev. 81 (1994) (challenging judicial arguments that these processes are not "foreseeable" and that persons injured are not "users" under Restatement (2d) Torts § 402A, Professor Cantu concludes that manufacturers are best situated to select appropriate materials and provide warnings concerning risks associated with terminal stages of product's life).

### § 10.8

**1.** The post-sale duty discussion here principally addresses manufacturers, but such duties may apply to retailers and other product sellers in particular circumstances. See Products Liability Restatement § 10 cmt. *b*. For post-sale responsibilities of successor corporations, see § 15.5, below.

**2.** See, e.g., Koker v. Armstrong Cork, Inc., 804 P.2d 659, 666 (Wash. Ct. App. 1991) (asbestos; duty to warn of risks reasonably discoverable post-sale even if they were unforeseeable at time of sale). See also

Ragin v. Porter Hayden Co., 754 A.2d 503 (Md. Ct. Spec. App. 2000) (same, by implication; post-sale duty of reasonable care to warn plaintiff arises even if defendant no longer makes product and plaintiff no longer is exposed to it).

**3.** See, e.g., Kozlowski v. John E. Smith's Sons Co., 275 N.W.2d 915, 923–24 (Wis. 1979) (new safety bypass valve for sausage stuffing machine; post-sale duty to warn); Patton v. Hutchinson Wil–Rich Mfg. Co., 861 P.2d 1299, 1311 (Kan. 1993) (no such duty).

**4.** See, e.g., Liriano v. Hobart Corp., 700 N.E.2d 303 (N.Y. 1998) (*Liriano II*) (users would remove guards from commercial meat grinders); Patton v. Hutchinson Wil–Rich Mfg. Co., 861 P.2d 1299, 1311 (Kan. 1993) (farmers sometimes removed lock pin while standing under cultivator wing).

**5.** Comstock v. General Motors Corp., 99 N.W.2d 627 (Mich. 1959) (brake failures), is widely regarded as the progenitor of a manufacturer's post-sale duties. Other early cases include Braniff Airways, Inc. v.

remains somewhat of a muddle.[6] Be that as it may, a manufacturer or other seller which fails to take reasonable steps to protect consumers from harm after discovering that its products are defective may subject itself to liability for compensatory damages and, in certain cases, for punitive damages.[7]

Determining what, if any, duties manufacturers should have after they sell products they reasonably believe to be nondefective is particularly problematic because a manufacturer's duties of product safety normally terminate upon transfer of a product's title and possession. A manufacturer's duties plausibly end at this point due to the impracticality and costs of requiring manufacturers to reduce risk further once products leave their plants and are dispersed widely in the market place. Getting information about product dangers into the hands of consumers after marketing is often difficult and expensive,[8] and product recalls to correct a design or manufacturing flaw are typically only partially successful and may cost tens or even hundreds of millions of dollars.[9]

A manufacturer's post-sale discovery that its product, believed to be reasonably safe when first sold, is in fact dangerously defective may give rise to either of two post-sale duties: (1) a duty to warn consumers, so they can avoid the risk; or (2) a duty to repair ("retrofit") or recall the product, to reduce or eliminate the risk. As will be seen, while a good many jurisdictions recognize a post-sale duty to warn in some circumstances, only a small handful of cases have recognized a common-law duty to repair or recall. Although plaintiffs often assert and courts often

Curtiss–Wright Corp., 411 F.2d 451 (2d Cir. 1969) (N.Y. law); Noel v. United Aircraft Corp., 342 F.2d 232 (3d Cir. 1965) (admiralty law); Balido v. Improved Mach., Inc., 105 Cal.Rptr. 890 (Ct. App. 1973).

**6.** See generally Kennedy and Brock, Postsale Duty to Warn, Retrofit, and Recall, 31 WTR Brief 14 (2002); Madden, Modern Post–Sale Warnings and Related Obligations, 27 Wm. Mitchell L. Rev. 33 (2000); Ross, Post–Sale Duty to Warn: A Critical Cause of Action, 27 Wm. Mitchell L. Rev. 339 (2000); Kulbaski, Statutes of Repose and the Post–Sale Duty to Warn: Time for a New Interpretation, 32 Conn. L. Rev. 1027 (2000); Richmond, Expanding Products Liability: Manufacturers' Post–Sale Duties to Warn, Retrofit and Recall, 36 Idaho L. Rev. 7, 49–70 (1999); Matula, Manufacturers' Post–Sale Duties in the 1990s, 32 Tort & Ins. L.J. 87 (1996); V. Schwartz, The Post–Sale Duty to Warn: Two Unfortunate Forks in the Road to a Reasonable Doctrine, 58 N.Y.U. L. Rev. 892 (1983); Allee, Post–Sale Obligations of Product Manufacturers, 12 Fordham Urb. L.J. 625 (1983–84); Note, 33 Stan. L. Rev. 1087 (1981) (duty to warn of subsequent safety improvements); Annot., 47 A.L.R.5th 395 (1997) (manufacturer's post-sale duty to modify, repair, or recall); 2 Frumer and Friedman, Products Liability § 12.8 (post-sale duty to warn) and ch. 57

(recalls); 1 Madden & Owen on Products Liability §§ 11:1 & 11:2; 3 Am. L. Prod. Liab. 3d 32:79 et seq.

**7.** See, e.g, Barnett v. La Societe Anonyme Turbomeca France, 963 S.W.2d 639 (Mo. Ct. App. 1997) ($87.5 million punitive damage award remitted to $26.5 million); Proctor v. Davis, 682 N.E.2d 1203, 1217 (Ill. App. Ct. 1997) ($124.5 million punitive award remitted to $6 million); Letz v. Turbomeca Engine Corp., 975 S.W.2d 155, 177–80 (Mo. Ct. App. 1997) ($67.5 million punitive award reduced to $41 million). See generally § 18.3, below.

**8.** See, e.g., Products Liability Restatement § 10 cmt. a.

**9.** Id. at § 11 cmt. a (characterizing the costs of recall as "incalculable"). For example, Ford Motor Company some time ago estimated that its recall of 8.7 million autos would cost $300 million after taxes, and that normally about 60% of cars recalled are taken in for repair. See Christian and Nomani, Ford Recalls 8.7 Million Cars to Fix Ignitions, Wall St. J., Apr. 26, 1996, at B1. See also Ross, Post–Sale Duty to Warn: A Critical Cause of Action, 27 Wm. Mitchell L. Rev. 339, 358 (2000) (for ordinary consumer products, experts consider a 25% recall response rate to be "excellent").

address both duties in the same case, it is useful to pull them apart for separate examination.

### Post-Sale Duty to Warn

The seminal case on the post-sale duty to warn was *Comstock v. General Motors Corporation*,[10] decided by the Michigan Supreme Court in 1959. The plaintiff, a mechanic at a Buick dealership, was injured when another employee was unable to stop a 1953 Buick Roadmaster with defective power brakes when he drove the car into a service stall in which the plaintiff was working. Shortly after selling the new model car, Buick discovered that the design and manufacture of the power braking system could lead to brake failures. Buick thereupon issued a "silent recall," sending repair kits to all Buick dealers with instructions to repair the brakes on all such Buicks which came in for service of any type. Because not all Roadmasters were affected by the problem, and for fear of damaging its reputation, Buick management decided not to send warnings to the car owners themselves. On these facts, the court held that General Motors had a duty "to take all reasonable means" to warn Buick purchasers promptly of the latent defect in the brakes.[11]

After *Comstock*, scattered decisions in the 1970s and 1980s began to recognize some form of post-sale duty to warn,[12] particularly in cases involving hazardous drugs.[13] By the 1990s, courts[14] and legislatures[15] had begun to impose a post-sale duty to warn with some frequency, often rejecting the "continuing" duty to warn nomenclature of earlier decisions[16] in favor of the more accurate "post-sale" characterization of the duty.[17] The momentum in favor of this duty in the mid–1990s was such

**10.** 99 N.W.2d 627 (Mich. 1959).

**11.** Id. at 634. The court concluded: "If [a] duty to warn of a known danger exists at point of sale, we believe a like duty to give prompt warning exists when a latent defect which makes the product hazardous to life becomes known to the manufacturer shortly after the product has been put on the market."

**12.** See, e.g., Rekab, Inc. v. Frank Hrubetz & Co., 274 A.2d 107, 110 (Md. 1971) (" 'Even if there is no duty to warn at the time of the sale, facts may thereafter come to the attention of the manufacturer which make it imperative that a warning then be given,' " quoting Frumer and Friedman); doCanto v. Ametek, Inc., 328 N.E.2d 873, 878–79 & n.9 (Mass. 1975); Kozlowski v. John E. Smith's Sons Co., 275 N.W.2d 915 (Wis. 1979); Smith v. F.M.C. Corp., 754 F.2d 873, 877 (10th Cir. 1985) (Okla. law); Island Creek Coal Co. v. Lake Shore, Inc., 832 F.2d 274, 280–81 (4th Cir. 1987) (Va. law); Hodder v. Goodyear Tire & Rubber Co., 426 N.W.2d 826 (Minn. 1988).

**13.** See, e.g., Wooderson v. Ortho Pharm. Corp., 681 P.2d 1038, 1057 (Kan. 1984); Barson v. E.R. Squibb & Sons, Inc., 682 P.2d 832, 835–36 (Utah 1984); McKee v. Moore, 648 P.2d 21, 25 (Okla. 1982).

**14.** See, e.g., Owens–Illinois, Inc. v. Zenobia, 601 A.2d 633, 645–47 (Md. 1992); Walton v. Avco Corp., 610 A.2d 454, 459 (Pa. 1992); Patton v. Hutchinson Wil–Rich Mfg. Co., 861 P.2d 1299 (Kan. 1993); Crowston v. Goodyear Tire & Rubber Co., 521 N.W.2d 401, 406–10 (N.D. 1994); McAlpin v. Leeds & Northrup Co., 912 F.Supp. 207 (W.D. Va. 1996); Vassallo v. Baxter Healthcare Corp., 696 N.E.2d 909 (Mass. 1998); Lovick v. Wil–Rich, 588 N.W.2d 688, 692–96 (Iowa 1999).

**15.** See Ga. Code Ann. § 51–1–11(c); Idaho Code § 6–1406(1); Iowa Code Ann. § 668.12(2); La. Rev. Stat. Ann. § 9:2800.57(C); Mich. Comp. Laws Ann. § 600.2948(4); N.C. Gen. Stat. § 99B–5(a)(2); Ohio Rev. Code Ann. § 2307.76(2); Wash. Rev. Code § 7.72.030(1)(c).

**16.** See, e.g., Kozlowski v. John E. Smith's Sons Co., 275 N.W.2d 915, 923 (Wis. 1979); Cover v. Cohen, 461 N.E.2d 864, 871 (N.Y. 1984).

**17.** See Gregory v. Cincinnati Inc., 538 N.W.2d 325, 328 (Mich. 1995) ("Generally, before there can be any continuing duty— whether it be to warn, repair, or recall— there must be a defect or an actionable problem at the point of manufacture.... If there is no [such] problem at this point,

that the *Products Liability Restatement* adopted the duty unequivocally in § 10(a), which provides that a product seller has a post-sale duty to warn when a reasonable seller in the circumstances would so warn.[18]

Yet, while the existence of a post-sale duty to warn now is quite widely recognized, its scope is not "unbounded,"[19] and its contours vary in jurisdictions which have accepted it. The most fundamental limitation on this duty is that it is preliminarily constrained by principles of negligence, not unlike the more general duty to warn.[20] The *Restatement* provides in § 10(b) that a reasonable seller would provide a post-sale warning if: "(1) the seller knows or reasonably should know that the product poses a substantial risk of harm to persons or property; and (2) those to whom a warning might be provided can be identified and can reasonably be assumed to be unaware of the risk of harm; and (3) a warning can be effectively communicated to and acted on by those to whom a warning might be provided; and (4) the risk of harm is sufficiently great to justify the burden of providing a warning."[21] By listing factors pertinent to the determination of reasonableness, the *Restatement* modestly delimits ordinary negligence liability through particularization of the relevant considerations. That said, the only real limitations on the post-sale duty to warn contained in § 10 are those contained within the basic principles of negligence law that it applies to this particular doctrine, notably that the matter is first and foremost a question of duty for the court.

Most courts that have addressed the post-sale duty to warn have tread more cautiously than the *Restatement*, limiting the duty in various ways.[22] For example, some courts explicitly limit the post-sale duty to warn to products which were defective at the time of sale,[23] while other jurisdictions take the position that the duty to warn may arise after sale even if the product was not originally defective.[24] Most courts addressing the issue have emphatically refused to impose a duty on manufacturers

---

then there can be no continuing duty.... "); Patton v. Hutchinson Wil–Rich Mfg. Co., 861 P.2d 1299, 1310 (Kan. 1993) ("we choose the label 'post-sale' rather than 'continuing' ").

**18.** Section 10(a) provides that a product seller is subject to liability for failing to provide a post-sale warning "if a reasonable person in the seller's position would provide such a warning." See id. cmt. *a.*

**19.** See id.

**20.** See § 9.2, above.

**21.** Products Liability Restatement § 13 describes a parallel warning duty of successor corporations who enter into service relationships with purchasers of their predecessors' products. See § 15.5, below.

**22.** Factors specified by various courts as relevant to whether the duty should be imposed in particular circumstances include the nature of the product market, the type and extent of risk, the product's intended life, the number of products sold, the time between sale and injury, and whether the seller maintains a continuing relationship with the buyer and the industry. See, e.g., Patton v. Hutchinson Wil–Rich Mfg. Co., 861 P.2d 1299 (Kan. 1993). See generally Richmond, Expanding Products Liability: Manufacturers' Post–Sale Duties to Warn, Retrofit and Recall, 36 Idaho L. Rev. 7, 42–47 (1999).

**23.** See, e.g., Wilson v. United States Elevator Corp., 972 P.2d 235, 240 (Ariz. Ct. App. 1998); Gregory v. Cincinnati Inc., 538 N.W.2d 325, 328 (Mich. 1995); Bragg v. Hi–Ranger, Inc., 462 S.E.2d 321, 331 (S.C. Ct. App. 1995); Patton v. Hutchinson Wil–Rich Mfg. Co., 861 P.2d 1299, 1313 (Kan. 1993); Owens–Illinois, Inc. v. Zenobia, 601 A.2d 633, 646 (Md. 1992); Romero v. Int'l Harvester Co., 979 F.2d 1444 (10th Cir. 1992) (Colo. law).

**24.** See, e.g., Lewis v. Ariens Co., 751 N.E.2d 862, 866 n.15 (Mass. 2001); Novak v. Navistar Int'l Transp. Corp., 46 F.3d 844 (8th Cir. 1995) (S.D. law); Walton v. Avco Corp., 610 A.2d 454, 459 (Pa. 1992); Cover v. Cohen, 461 N.E.2d 864, 871 (N.Y. 1984); Ohio Rev. Code Ann. § 2307.76(2); N.C.

to inform product owners of newly developed safety devices[25] or state-of-the-art developments in knowledge, whereas other courts hold that the duty may extend to newly developed safety devices,[26] newly acquired knowledge of improper product use,[27] or newly discovered dangers under the evolving state-of-the-art.[28]

Ploddingly and without much fanfare, the post-sale duty of reasonable care to warn is creeping broadly across the land. While a fair number of states still refuse to accept the post-sale duty to warn,[29] a majority of states[30] now agree with at least the general proposition of the *Third Restatement* that manufacturers (and possibly other sellers) have a post-sale duty of reasonable care to provide warnings of newly-discovered, serious hazards to those who can best avoid the danger, assuming there is a practicable and cost-effective means to distribute the information.[31]

Gen. Stat. Ann. § 99B–5(a)(2). See Products Liability Restatement § 10 cmt. *a*: post-sale duty applies "whether or not the product is defective at the time of original sale."

**25.** See, e.g., Williams v. Monarch Mach. Tool Co., 26 F.3d 228, 232 (1st Cir. 1994) (Mass. law); Patton v. Hutchinson Wil–Rich Mfg. Co., 861 P.2d 1299, 1311 (Kan. 1993); Romero v. Int'l Harvester Co., 979 F.2d 1444 (10th Cir. 1992) (Colo. law).

**26.** See, e.g., Lanclos v. Rockwell Int'l Corp., 470 So.2d 924 (La. Ct. App. 1985); Kozlowski v. John E. Smith's Sons Co., 275 N.W.2d 915 (Wis. 1979) (same; limited to industrial machinery).

**27.** See, e.g., Liriano v. Hobart Corp., 700 N.E.2d 303 (N.Y. 1998) (removal of guards from commercial meat grinders; post-sale duty to warn may arise even when substantial modification defense would bar recovery for design defect).

**28.** See, e.g., Koker v. Armstrong Cork, Inc., 804 P.2d 659, 666 (Wash. Ct. App. 1991) (asbestos; duty to warn of risks reasonably discoverable post-sale even if they were unforeseeable at time of sale).

On the scope of the post-sale duty to warn, compare Richmond, Expanding Products Liability: Manufacturers' Post-Sale Duties to Warn, Retrofit and Recall, 36 Idaho L. Rev. 7, 80 (1999) (extending post-sale duty to warn to development of safer products is bad social policy because it discourages safety improvements), with Products Liability Restatement § 10 Reporters' Note on cmt. *a* ("If a newly discovered risk imposes risk of serious harm and safety improvements can be practically implemented, there may in certain instances be a duty to inform the buyer of the availability of such safety improvements.").

**29.** See, e.g., Irion v. Sun Lighting, Inc., 2004 WL 746823, at *17 (Tenn. Ct. App. 2004) (asserting that majority of states

have not adopted the duty); Noah v. General Motors Corp., 882 So.2d 235, 239 (Miss. Ct. App. 2004) (post-sale duty to warn would conflict with state statute); Smith v. DaimlerChrysler Corp., 2002 WL 31814534, at *5 (Del. Super. Ct. 2002); Miller v. Honeywell Int'l, Inc., 2002 WL 31399793 (S.D. Ind. 2002) (no continuing duty to warn under Indiana products liability statute), aff'd, 107 Fed.Appx. 643 (7th Cir. 2004; Modelski v. Navistar Int'l Transp. Corp., 707 N.E.2d 239, 246–47 (Ill. App. Ct. 1999); DeSantis v. Frick Co., 745 A.2d 624, 632 (Pa. Super. Ct. 1999); Anderson v. Nissan Motor Co., 139 F.3d 599, 601–602 (8th Cir. 1998) (Neb. law). See also Product Liability Desk Reference–A Fifty State Compendium (M. Daller ed., 2004) (listing Illinois, Indiana, Missouri, South Carolina, and Texas to the contrary, to which Delaware, Nebraska, Pennsylvania, and Tennessee may be added, for a total of at least 9 states rejecting the doctrine).

**30.** See Product Liability Desk Reference—A Fifty State Compendium (M. Daller ed., 2004) (revealing that 27 states have some law favoring the post-sale duty to warn, at least in some circumstances, to which another should be added, for a total of at least 28 accepting the doctrine).

**31.** See, e.g., Ostendorf v. Clark Equip. Co., 122 S.W.3d 530, 536 (Ky. 2003) (dictum: "Numerous cases impose a duty to warn of later discovered defects."); Hiner v. Deere and Co., 340 F.3d 1190, 1196 (10th Cir. 2003) (Kan. law) ("even when it may be infeasible for a manufacturer to issue post-sale warnings to consumers, there may still be a duty to issue warnings to retailers"); Couch v. Astec Indus., 53 P.3d 398 (N.M. Ct. App. 2002); Densberger v. United Technologies Corp. 297 F.3d 66, 69–71 (2d Cir. 2002) (Conn. law) (Calabresi, J.) (post-sale duty to warn in negligence compatible with Connecticut products liability act);

## Post-Sale Duty to Retrofit or Recall

Apart from post-sale warnings to consumers, a more aggressive (and expensive) way for a manufacturer to remedy dangerous conditions discovered in its products after sale is to physically eliminate or reduce the danger by some form of repair, upgrade, or "retrofit." Because repairing a defective product often can be performed properly only by a manufacturer or dealer, curing a product hazard by "retrofit" often is preceded by a product "recall,"[32] a notification to consumers of a product hazard and a description of procedures for accomplishing its repair.[33]

Congress has empowered several product safety agencies to order recalls,[34] the violation of which may give rise to liability.[35] At common law, however, there is no general duty to recall defective products. A couple of early cases did suggest that manufacturers might have a duty to recall and repair hazardous conditions discovered after sale,[36] and several more recent decisions have suggested that there may be a duty to retrofit a product if it was defective when originally sold,[37] or if the manufacturer has a special continuing relationship with the buyer based

Lewis v. Ariens Co., 751 N.E.2d 862, 867 (Mass. 2001) (adopting § 10; no duty to second-hand purchaser of 16-year old snow blower who was " 'a member of a universe too diffuse and too large for manufacturers or sellers of original equipment to identify' "); Hollingsworth & Vose Co. v. Connor, 764 A.2d 318, 333–34 (Md. Ct. Spec. App. 2000); Lovick v. Wil–Rich, 588 N.W.2d 688, 692–96 (Iowa 1999) (adopting § 10); Liriano v. Hobart Corp., 700 N.E.2d 303 (N.Y. 1998).

**32.** Some courts and commentators distinguish between these terms. See, e.g., 2 Frumer and Friedman, Products Liability § 57.01; Richmond, Expanding Products Liability: Manufacturers' Post-Sale Duties to Warn, Retrofit and Recall, 36 Idaho L. Rev. 7, 49–70 (1999). Others use the term "recall" generically to describe the post-sale duty of manufacturers and other sellers to physically remedy product hazards. See, e.g., Products Liability Restatement § 11. Compare Madden, Modern Post–Sale Warnings and Related Obligations, 27 Wm. Mitchell L. Rev. 33, 57–58 (2000) (using the terms interchangeably).

**33.** "Silent recalls" are somewhat different, but even this peculiar form of secret retrofit by dealers involves a form of recall via dealers. See, e.g., General Motors Corp. v. Johnston 592 So.2d 1054, 1056 (Ala. 1992) (defendant denied making "silent" or "unpublished" recall by informing dealers to make repairs only on consumer complaints).

**34.** Among the agencies Congress has vested with recall power are the Consumer Product Safety Commission, 15 U.S.C. § 2064(a) (consumer products with "substantial product hazards"); the National

Highway Traffic Safety Administration, 49 U.S.C. §§ 30117–21 (automotive products); the Food and Drug Administration, 21 U.S.C. § 360(h) (medical devices); the Coast Guard, 46 U.S.C. § 1464 (recreational boats with safety defects); and Health and Human Services, 21 U.S.C. § 360ll(f) (electronic products emitting unsafe radiation). See, e.g., United States v. General Motors Corp., 565 F.2d 754 (D.C. Cir. 1977).

**35.** See Products Liability Restatement § 11(a)(1) (liability for negligently recalling product after government-ordered recall). See generally Madden, Modern Post–Sale Warnings and Related Obligations, 27 Wm. Mitchell L. Rev. 33, 66 (2000) (federally mandated recalls).

**36.** See Noel v. United Aircraft Corp., 342 F.2d 232 (3d Cir. 1965) (Del. law) (failure to provide safety device to prevent overspeeding propeller; manufacturer with continuous relationship to owner had continuing duty to provide safety device); Braniff Airways, Inc. v. Curtiss–Wright Corp., 411 F.2d 451, 453 (2d Cir. 1969) (N.Y. law) (cylinder failure from overheated aircraft engine; when manufacturer learns of dangerous design defects after product is sold, it "has a duty either to remedy these or, if complete remedy is not feasible, at least to give users adequate warnings and instructions concerning methods for minimizing the danger"). See also Downing v. Overhead Door Corp., 707 P.2d 1027, 1033 (Colo. Ct. App. 1985) (similar dictum).

**37.** See, e.g., Readenour v. Marion Power Shovel, 719 P.2d 1058 (Ariz. 1986), as explained by Wilson v. U.S. Elevator Corp., 972 P.2d 235 (Ariz. Ct. App. 1998).

on the manufacturer's post-sale undertaking to maintain or even recall the product,[38] and in various other situations.[39]

Yet most decisions, reasoning that governmental regulatory agencies are better suited than courts to forge such complex and onerous duties that might discourage manufacturers from developing new safety technologies, emphatically refuse to impose a common-law duty on manufacturers to recall their products or retrofit them with newly developed safety devices, especially if the product was not defective when sold.[40] This is the position of the *Third Restatement*, which states categorically that there is no common-law duty to recall, even if the product was defective from the start.[41] The *Restatement* provides two exceptions to the broad no-duty-to-recall rule: one for sellers who violate recall orders of government agencies,[42] and the other for sellers who are negligent in performing a recall they voluntarily undertake.[43] The first, government-

**38.** See Couch v. Astec Industries, Inc., 53 P.3d 398 (N.M. Ct. App. 2002) (manufacturer undertook to provide continuing service); Hernandez v. Badger Const. Equip. Co., 34 Cal.Rptr.2d 732 (Ct. App. 1994) ("failure to conduct an adequate retrofit campaign may constitute negligence apart from the issue of defective design"); Blossman Gas Co. v. Williams, 375 S.E.2d 117 (Ga. Ct. App. 1988); Bell Helicopter Co. v. Bradshaw, 594 S.W.2d 519, 532 (Tex. App. 1979) ("[o]nce the duty [to recall and repair] was assumed, Bell had an obligation to complete the remedy by using reasonable means available to it"). See generally V. Schwartz, The Post–Sale Duty to Warn: Two Unfortunate Forks in the Road to a Reasonable Doctrine, 58 N.Y.U. L. Rev. 892, 897–901 (1983); Products Liability Restatement § 11(a)(2).

**39.** See, e.g., Downing v. Overhead Door Corp. 707 P.2d 1027, 1033 (Colo. Ct. App. 1985) (dictum: "[a]fter a product involving human safety has been sold and dangerous defects in design have come to the manufacturer's attention, the manufacturer has a duty either to remedy such defects, or, if a complete remedy is not feasible, to give users adequate warnings and instructions concerning methods for minimizing danger," citing *Braniff Airways* and *Noel*). For a collection of cases both ways, see Annot., 47 A.L.R. 5th 395 (1997) (manufacturer's post-sale duty to modify, repair, or recall).

**40.** See, e.g., Ostendorf v. Clark Equip. Co., 122 S.W.3d 530, 537–40 (Ky. 2003); Tabieros v. Clark Equip. Co., 944 P.2d 1279, 1301 (Haw. 1997) (refusing to impose on manufacturer a "continuing duty to retrofit its products, subsequent to their manufacture and sale, with post-manufacture safety devices that were unavailable at the time of manufacture"); Gregory v. Cincinnati Inc., 538 N.W.2d 325 (Mich. 1995); Eschenburg v. Navistar Int'l Transp. Corp., 829 F.Supp. 210, 214–215 (E.D. Mich. 1993)

(no duty to recall product that was defective at time of sale); Romero v. International Harvester Co., 979 F.2d 1444, 1449–50 (10th Cir. 1992) (Colo. law) (no duty to recall and retrofit product that was nondefective at time of manufacture to improve safety with subsequently developed safety device); Wallace v. Dorsey Trailers Southeast, Inc., 849 F.2d 341, 344 (8th Cir. 1988) (Mo. law); Lynch v. McStome & Lincoln Plaza Assocs., 548 A.2d 1276, 1279 (Pa. Super. Ct. 1988); Patton v. Hutchinson Wil–Rich Mfg. Co., 861 P.2d 1299, 1315 (Kan. 1993) (recognizing post-sale duty to warn, but holding that "product recalls are properly the business of administrative agencies as suggested by federal statutes").

**41.** Products Liability Restatement § 11 cmt. *a*:

If every improvement in product safety were to trigger a common-law duty to recall, manufacturers would face incalculable costs every time they sought to make their product lines better and safer. Moreover, even when a product is defective . . . , an involuntary duty to recall should be imposed on the seller only by a governmental directive issued pursuant to statute or regulation. Issues relating to product recalls are best evaluated by governmental agencies capable of gathering adequate data regarding the ramifications of such undertakings.

**42.** Products Liability Restatement § 11(a)(1).

**43.** Products Liability Restatement § 11(a)(2). Note that sending post-sale hazard information and even retrofit kits to dealers may not amount to an undertaking to recall or retrofit. See Ray v. Rheem Textile Systems, Inc., 2002 WL 433157 (Mich. Ct. App. 2002) (manufacturer did not voluntarily assume duty to retrofit by distributing to its dealers and distributors dealer bulletins and retrofit kits).

recall-order exception, is noncontroversial; but the second, negligent undertaking-to-recall exception, has been rejected as unwisely liberalizing the normal duty-to-rescue requirement that a plaintiff establish detrimental reliance on the negligent undertaking or show how it otherwise increased the plaintiff's risk of harm.[44]

The law on post-sale duties has long been in a muddle, but the issues are beginning to narrow. The *Third Restatement*'s endorsement in § 10 of a post-sale duty to take reasonable and practicable steps to warn users of serious hazards makes good sense, assuming that the duty remains limited to newly discovered hazards and does not expand to include a duty to provide information about routine safety enhancements of a product's design. Yet whether the common law should recognize, and how it should define, a post-sale duty to retrofit or recall is much more difficult to determine. The *Restatement*'s absolute denial in § 11 of any such common-law duty, even if the product originally was defective and despite what special circumstances might exist, seems unduly harsh and rigid, while its provision of a duty of due care for voluntary recalls ignores traditional tort law limitations on responsibility for voluntary undertakings. Yet the *Restatement* is not too far off the mark in describing how the law on the post-sale duty to repair or recall now stands, and much may be said for its clarity and simplicity. So, while the fog is lifting on one side of the post-sale-duty pond, it remains swirling on the other.

---

**44.** See Ostendorf v. Clark Equip. Co., 122 S.W.3d 530, 537–40 (Ky. 2003) (rejecting § 11, noting that the plaintiff had failed to cite a single case relying on § 11 to justify imposing liability for a negligent retrofit campaign). On the duty of affirmative action (to rescue), see Restatement (3d) Torts § 43; Restatement (2d) Torts § 324A (relied upon by *Ostendorf*).

# PART III

# CAUSATION

# Chapter 11

# CAUSE IN FACT

*Table of Sections*

## § 11.1 CAUSE IN FACT—GENERALLY

Few problems are more intriguing, and their solutions more illusive, than causation. Perhaps the most fundamental issue in the universe, and in life, is causation—the causes and effects of molecular actions, biologic activity, and human choices to act and refrain from acting in certain ways.[1] In the words of Leon Green, one of the twentieth century's great tort law scholars, "The attraction of causes is as magnetic for people as flames are for insects, and it is frequently as deadly."[2]

While philosophers, theologians, and scientists may delight in theorizing about the nature of causal agents and their consequences, courts and lawyers do not have this luxury of pure cogitation and hypothesizing.[3] Instead, the law properly demands commonsense proof of a true cause and effect relationship in a court of law before it will assign responsibility for a plaintiff's damages to a defendant allegedly responsible for that harm.[4] Each day of every year, numerous food products go bad, numerous workers are injured in machines, numerous people contract cancer, and numerous cars crash. But most sickness is not caused by bad food, most machine injuries are not caused by defective machines, most cancers are not caused by defective chemicals, and most car crashes are not caused by defective automobile parts. Thus, in products liability litigation, a defendant manufacturer of such a product may be held

---

**§ 11.1**

**1.** "The search for causes must have been an incident of the early awakening of primordial man. There is no human who hesitates to identify the cause of any calamity that touches his life. In the highest echelons of social and scientific research, the vain attempts to reduce to control the causes of war, crime, poverty, cancer, and other barriers to man's happy existence continue with unabated zeal." L. Green, Strict Liability Under Sections 402A and

402B: A Decade of Litigation, 54 Tex. L. Rev. 1185, 1208 (1976).

**2.** Id.

**3.** Williams, Afterward—What Has Philosophy to Learn from Tort Law?, in Philosophical Foundations of Tort Law (D. Owen, ed., Oxford, 1995).

**4.** "The courts ... often insist that the causal questions which they have to face must be determined on common-sense principles." H.L.A. Hart and T. Honoré, Causation and the Law 26 (2d ed., Oxford 1985).

responsible for a plaintiff's injuries only if the plaintiff satisfactorily proves that the injuries were caused, at least in part, by the defendant.[5]

Causation, or "proximate causation," is comprised of two distinct issues: (1) cause in fact, and (2) proximate cause.[6] "Cause in fact" (or "factual cause")[7] is the actual connection between a product defect or the defendant's negligence and the plaintiff's harm. Although this physical (or metaphysical) nexus is not controverted in most cases, a plaintiff must always establish this kind of actual link between his or her injury or disease to a defect in a product which the defendant sold, and, in negligence cases, to the defendant's negligence.[8] "Proximate cause" refers to the *closeness* of whatever actual causal connection has been proven to exist. Although these concepts thus are very different—the one requiring proof that a causal connection *exists*, and the other requiring that the nexus be reasonably *close* (not "remote")—courts and commentators often confusingly use the same terms when talking about these two separate issues.

"Causation" is sometimes used generically to describe both issues.[9] Yet, not infrequently, courts also use the phrase "proximate cause" to

---

**5.** On factual causation in products liability law, see, e.g., Conway–Jones, Factual Causation in Toxic–Tort Litigation: A Philosophical View of Proof and Certainty in Uncertain Disciplines, 35 U. Rich. L. Rev. 875 (2002); Henderson and Twerski, Intuition and Technology in Product Design Litigation: An Essay on Proximate Causation, 88 Geo. L.J. 659 (2000); Symposium, Liability Without Cause? Further Ruminations on Cause–In–Fact as Applied to Handgun Liability, 32 Conn. L. Rev. 1379 (2000); Berger, Eliminating General Causation: Notes Towards a New Theory of Justice and Toxic Torts, 97 Colum. L. Rev. 2117 (1997); Firak, The Developing Policy Characteristics of Cause–In–Fact: Alternative Forms of Liability, Epidemiological Proof and Trans–Scientific Issues, 63 Temp. L. Rev. 311 (1990); V. Schwartz & Mahshigian, Failure to Identify the Defendant in Tort Law: Towards a Legislative Solution, 73 Calif. L. Rev. 941 (1985); Frumer and Friedman, Products Liability ch. 3; Madden & Owen on Products Liability ch. 12.

A rich literature has grown up around the general topic of causation. See, e.g., Stapleton, Legal Cause: Cause-in-Fact and the Scope of Liability for Consequences, 54 Vand. L. Rev. 941 (2001); Wright, Once More Into the Bramble Bush: Duty, Causal Contribution, and the Extent of Legal Responsibility, 54 Vand. L. Rev. 1071 (2001); Robertson, The Common Sense of Cause in Fact, 75 Tex. L. Rev. 1765 (1997); Fischer, Causation in Fact in Omission Cases, 1992 Utah L. Rev. 1335 (1992); Wright, Causation in Tort Law, 73 Cal. L. Rev. 1735 (1985); King, Causation, Valuation, and Chance in Personal Injury Torts Involving Preexisting Conditions and Future Conse-

quences, 90 Yale L.J. 1353 (1981); Calabresi, Concerning Cause and the Law of Torts: An Essay for Harry Kalven, Jr., 43 U. Chi. L. Rev. 69 (1975); Prosser and Keeton on Torts § 41; Dobbs, Law of Torts ch. 9; A. Becht and F. Miller, The Test of Factual Causation in Negligence and Strict Liability Cases (1961); H.L.A. Hart and T. Honoré, Causation and the Law 26 (2d ed., Oxford 1985); J. Mackie, The Cement of the Universe: A Study of Causation (L. Jonathan Cohen ed., 1974).

**6.** See, e.g., Sikora v. AFD Indus., 319 F.Supp.2d 872, 876 (N.D. Ill. 2004) (proximate cause "contains two distinct requirements: cause-in-fact and legal cause"); Citizens Ins. Co. of Am. v. Sears Roebuck and Co., 203 F.Supp.2d 837, 850 (W.D. Mich. 2002) ("Proving cause actually requires proof of two separate elements: (1) cause in fact, and (2) legal cause, also known as proximate cause.").

**7.** "Factual cause" is the term employed by the Restatement (Third) of Torts: Liability for Physical Harm § 26.

**8.** Because a product's defectiveness is an element of almost every negligence claim in products liability litigation, § 2.2, above, proof of causation in a negligence case requires proof that (1) the product was defective, (2) the defendant was negligent in allowing it to be defective, and (3) the defendant's negligence caused the plaintiff's harm.

**9.** See, e.g., Banks v. Eaton Corp., 2002 WL 31951240, at *2 (Mich. Ct. App. 2002) ("causation requires both cause in fact and proximate cause").

refer in umbrella fashion to cause in fact and proximate causation together,[10] and sometimes also when referring to cause in fact alone,[11] since it is part of the umbrella. To complicate matters further, the *Restatement (Second) of Torts* uses the term "legal causation" to embrace both issues,[12] such that this term is sometimes used to refer to factual causation[13] but more commonly to mean proximate cause.[14] The *Third Restatement* helpfully divides these issues clearly in two, calling the one "factual causation"[15] and the other "scope of liability" (proximate cause).[16] Because of the varying terminology applied to these two issues, often in the same jurisdiction and sometimes in the same judicial opinion, a lawyer reading cases involving either of these issues—"factual cause" or "proximate cause"—must read each decision cautiously to ascertain which issue the court truly has addressed. Relying on causation terminology, in other words, is risky business.

In every products liability case, the plaintiff must establish the central element of factual causation—that the plaintiff's harm resulted, at least in part, from some defect in a product that the defendant manufactured or sold.[17] In negligence, the plaintiff's causal proof must further show that the harm resulted from some negligent act or omission by the defendant in making or selling the product in a defective condition.[18] To satisfy the burden of proof on factual causation,[19] a plaintiff must introduce evidence that establishes, more likely than not, that the

**10.**  See, e.g., Sikora v. AFD Indus., 319 F.Supp.2d 872, 876 (N.D. Ill. 2004) (proximate cause "contains two distinct requirements: cause-in-fact and legal cause").

**11.**  See, e.g., 438 Main Street v. Easy Heat, Inc., ___ P.3d ___, 2004 WL 1879598, at *18 (Utah 2004); Tuttle v. Lorillard Tobacco Co., 377 F.3d 917, 924 (8th Cir. 2004) (Minn. law) (proximate cause requires proof that "user would have acted differently had the manufacturers provided adequate warnings").

**12.**  See Restatement (2d) Torts § 431. See, e.g., First Premier Bank v. Kolcraft Enters., 686 N.W.2d 430, 454 (S.D. 2004) ("Proximate or legal cause is a cause that produces a result in a natural and probable sequence and without which the result would not have occurred.").

**13.**  See, e.g., Whiteley v. Philip Morris Inc., 11 Cal.Rptr.3d 807, 858 (Ct. App. 2004) ("A tort is a legal cause of injury only when it is a substantial factor in producing the injury.").

**14.**  See, e.g., Moroney v. General Motors Corp., 850 A.2d 629, 634–35 (Pa. Super. Ct. 2004); Johnson v. Bryco Arms, 304 F.Supp.2d 383, 395 (E.D.N.Y. 2004) (equating proximate and legal cause); Sikora v. AFD Industries, 319 F.Supp.2d 872, 876 (N.D. Ill. 2004) ("Under Illinois law ['proximate cause"] contains two distinct requirements: cause-in-fact and legal cause.").

**15.**  See Restatement (3d) Torts: Liability for Physical Harm ch. 5 and § 26.

**16.**  See id. ch. 6

**17.**  See, e.g., DaimlerChrysler Corp. v. Hillhouse, 2004 WL 1195687, at *2 (Tex. App. 2004) ("Causation is an essential element of a cause of action for products liability."); Vodanovich v. A.P. Green Indus., 869 So.2d 930, 932 (La. Ct. App. 2004) ("A plaintiff seeking to recover under either negligence or strict liability theories must prove that the negligent act or defect complained of was a cause-in-fact of the injury."); Soldo v. Sandoz Pharm. Corp., 244 F.Supp.2d 434, 524 (W.D. Pa. 2003) ("Proof of causation is a necessary element in a products liability action. Absent a causal relationship between the defendant's product and the plaintiff's injury the defendant cannot be held liable on a theory of negligence, strict product liability, or misrepresentation.").

**18.**  See § 2.2, above.

**19.**  See Conway–Jones, Factual Causation in Toxic–Tort Litigation: A Philosophical View of Proof and Certainty in Uncertain Disciplines, 35 U. Rich. L. Rev. 875, 938 (2002) ("In virtually every case, plaintiffs carry the burden of proof on the factual causation element.").

defendant's negligence, or a defective condition in the defendant's product, was a cause of the plaintiff's harm.[20]

This chapter first considers the tests of factual causation, notably the "but-for" and "substantial-factor" tests. Certain recurring issues of proof of causation are also reviewed, including the sufficiency of circumstantial evidence to connect a defendant to an accident product and to connect the accident to a *defect* in that product.[21] Special tests and issues applicable to toxic substance litigation are also examined here. Next discussed are the special issues raised when a plaintiff's proofs point to two or more defendants who possibly caused the harm, including the theory of market share liability.[22] The chapter concludes with a look at some of the special issues of factual causation raised in warnings cases.[23]

## § 11.2  TESTS AND PROOF OF CAUSATION

In order to establish causation, a plaintiff normally must prove two things: (1) that the defendant is the source of the challenged product—that is, that the product most likely was manufactured or sold by the defendant, not by someone else; and (2) that some defective condition in the product (or the defendant's negligence) most likely caused the harm. A plaintiff's causation evidence on the latter point must satisfy the but-for or substantial-factor test for factual causation.

### Defendant Identification

The first step in establishing causation is to show that the challenged product was manufactured or sold by the defendant. Usually, establishing the identity of the manufacturer of a toaster, a punch press, an SUV, or a butane lighter is a simple task, and the issue is not controverted. Yet, after a serious accident, sometimes butane lighters and other products disappear,[1] and memories fade. Many kinds of products—like cleaning solvents, dish towels, and industrial chemicals—may come from sources not remembered or quite unknown.[2] And so the plaintiff's causal responsibility duty is to connect the defendant to the product that caused the plaintiff's harm by establishing that the subject product was manufactured or sold by the defendant.[3]

If the product is destroyed in the accident, lost, or otherwise disappears, a plaintiff may have difficulty in tracing its manufacture (or retail sale) to the defendant. In *Moore v. Mississippi Valley Gas Co.*,[4] for example, the plaintiff was one year old when she was scalded by hot water in a bath tub. Two years later, the heater was discarded. Four years after that, the plaintiff's mother sued the manufacturer of the brand of hot water heater she believed was in her apartment complex at

---

**20.** See, e.g., Richardson v. General Motors Corp., 223 F.Supp.2d 753, 755–56 (M.D.N.C. 2002).

    **21.** See § 11.2, below.

    **22.** See § 11.3, below.

    **23.** See § 11.4, below.

**§ 11.2**

**1.** See, e.g., Flock v. Scripto–Tokai Corp., 319 F.3d 231 (5th Cir. 2003) (Tex.

law) (utility lighter melted in fire that it might have started).

    **2.** For special defendant identification approaches in toxic substance cases, see this section and § 11.3, below.

    **3.** On product identification, see Annot., 51 A.L.R.3d 1344 (1973).

    **4.** 863 So.2d 43 (Miss. 2003).

the time, although the landlord at the time of suit had no record identifying the manufacturer of the heater. In these circumstances, the court upheld summary judgment for the defendant manufacturer. Similarly, in *Brown v. Stone Mfg. Co.*,[5] a child was injured when her nightgown caught fire, but its remnants were discarded at the hospital. The child and her mother remembered that it was pink, but neither could remember the name of the manufacturer. The mother had purchased the nightgown from a store that carried several similar brands. The child thought that a nightgown manufactured by the defendant, which her mother purchased at the same store one year after the accident, was "sort of like" the accident gown, but she thought that it had a different color design on the front. The washing instructions remembered by the mother differed somewhat from those on the defendant's subsequently purchased gown. On these facts, because a jury would be required to resort to guesswork, speculation, and surmise to identify the manufacturer, the court granted the defendant's summary judgment motion. *Moore* and *Brown* illustrate the important point that, if a plaintiff cannot prove that the accident product was most likely produced or sold by the defendant, a jury will not be permitted to speculate on this crucial issue of identification, and the plaintiff's case usually will fail.[6]

Even if the product is lost, however, a plaintiff may be able to establish the product's identity by circumstantial evidence, provided that such evidence establishes "that it is reasonably probable, not merely possible or evenly balanced, that the defendant was the source of the offending product."[7] One especially probative method of identification is proof that the product bears the defendant's name, as by a label or decal of some sort.[8] The memory of the plaintiff or the purchaser of the product's name may sometimes suffice, although such testimony must establish the manufacturer's identity by a preponderance of evidence.[9]

**5.** 660 F.Supp. 454, 458 (S.D. Miss. 1986).

**6.** See, e.g., Clift v. Vose Hardware, Inc., 848 A.2d 1130 (R.I. 2004) (conclusory assertions in summary-judgment affidavit that bungee cord that blinded person was sold by one defendant and manufactured by another defendant were insufficient to connect defendants to the offending bungee cord; affidavit failed to set forth specific facts establishing that defendants actually manufactured and sold the cord that caused the injury.); Hughes v. Smith–Midland Corp., 82 Fed. Appx. 698 (D.C. Cir. 2003) (insufficient proof that defendants designed, manufactured, or supplied concrete barrier or lift from which it fell on plaintiff).

**7.** Healey v. Firestone Tire & Rubber Co., 663 N.E.2d 901, 903 (N.Y. 1996). In *Healey*, the plaintiff's employer failed to keep the truck tire rims, identified by plaintiff's expert as the likely cause of plaintiff's injury, even after a court order requiring they be preserved and an understanding with the employer's insurer that they would

be preserved. *Held*, summary judgment for Firestone affirmed; plaintiff was unable to satisfy the reasonable probability requirement because the product was missing, even though plaintiff's expert had previously narrowed the possible offending tire rims to those made by Firestone.

**8.** See, e.g., Kim v. Ingersoll Rand Co., 921 F.2d 197 (8th Cir. 1990) (Minn. law) (logo on air hammer); Helm v. Pepsi–Cola Bottling Co., 723 S.W.2d 465 (Mo. Ct. App. 1986) (plaintiff's wife and lawyer both read "Mead Corporation" on bottom of defective carton subsequently lost by another lawyer); Smith v. Ariens Co., 377 N.E.2d 954 (Mass. 1978) ("Ariens" decal affixed to defective snowmobile).

**9.** See, e.g., Drayton v. Jiffee Chem. Corp., 395 F.Supp. 1081 (N.D. Ohio 1975), modified and aff'd, 591 F.2d 352 (6th Cir. 1978) (although circumstantial evidence tended to identify drain cleaner as "Mister Plumber," landlady firmly remembered buying "liquid-plumr" manufactured by defendant; *held*, defendant liable).

Another method of identification is testimony by the retailer that it had purchased the product sold to the consumer from a particular supplier.[10] Where there is no direct identifying information, other evidence may point toward the defendant, such as the product's color,[11] composition, or method of construction (like a garment's stitching) that is unique to the defendant.[12]

### Tests of Cause in Fact

Once the defendant's identity is established, connecting a plaintiff's injury to a product defect involves the same kind of causal inquiries involved in other tort law contexts. In ordinary products liability litigation, as in tort law generally,[13] the standard method for establishing factual causation is the "but-for" test. By this test, a manufacturer or other defendant may be found causally responsible for a plaintiff's harm if it would not have occurred but for a defect in the product or the defendant's tortious conduct. Thus, a product defect may be a cause in fact of the plaintiff's injury if the defect was a *sine qua non* of the injury, a necessary antecedent without which the injury would not have occurred.

The but-for issue arises quite clearly in some cases. In *Stewart v. Von Solbrig Hosp., Inc.*,[14] a stainless steel surgical pin made by the defendants was implanted in the plaintiff's broken leg to help align and stabilize the bone, and the leg was put in a cast. When the fracture did not heal in the cast, the plaintiff's doctor removed it but instructed the plaintiff not to walk on the leg. Plaintiff disobeyed, and the pin broke, causing various complications. Plaintiff presented evidence that the pin had inclusions and scratches which reduced its strength by a factor of one third. Yet plaintiff presented no evidence that this defective condition in the pin caused it to break. The defendant's evidence showed that even if the pin had contained no defects, it was not strong enough to support the plaintiff's weight so that it would have broken anyway when he walked, contrary to his doctor's orders, after the cast was removed. Affirming judgments for the defendants, the court ruled that the cause of the pin's break was misuse, not any defect in the pin.

A large majority of courts apply these same but-for principles to exclude claims for injuries which the plaintiff does not establish were a but-for result of a product defect. So, if a driver crashes into a traffic warning sign whose flashing arrow was not working, injuring the plaintiff, recovery is barred if the driver would not have seen a flashing arrow

---

**10.** See, e.g., Daniels v. GNB, Inc., 629 So.2d 595 (Miss. 1993) (batteries always bought from same supplier); Amin v. Knape & Vogt Co., 500 N.E.2d 454 (Ill. App. Ct. 1986) (shelf clips sold to college); Payton v. Abbott Labs., 780 F.2d 147 (1st Cir.1985) (Mass. law) (pharmacist purchased generic drug from supplier who generally purchased that type of drug from defendant).

**11.** See, e.g., Thrasher v. B B Chem. Co., 2 F.3d 995 (10th Cir. 1993) (Okla. law) (barrels of paint stripper); English v. Cren-

shaw Supply Co., 387 S.E.2d 628 (Ga. Ct. App. 1989) (brackets painted red).

**12.** Cf. C.K.S., Inc. v. Helen Borgenicht Sportswear, Inc., 268 N.Y.S.2d 409 (App. Div. 1966) (appearance and composition of blouse).

**13.** See Prosser and Keeton on Torts § 41; Dobbs, Law of Torts §§ 168 and 169; Restatement (3d) Torts: Liability for Physical Harm § 26.

**14.** 321 N.E.2d 428, 432 (Ill. App. Ct. 1974).

because he was asleep.[15] Similarly, if a doctor fails to read a drug manufacturer's warnings about the side-effects of a prescription drug,[16] or a parent fails to heed warnings and instructions in a minivan to seat young children in the rear because they could be killed by the front seat airbag,[17] then it is likely that a better warning would have made no difference, and the plaintiff's case must fail.

Another test for factual causation is the "substantial-factor" test, which the *Second Restatement* employed in an unfortunate attempt to fashion a single test to resolve all factual causation problems. Section 431(a) of the *Second Restatement* defines cause in fact in terms of whether the defendant's negligent conduct "is a substantial factor in bringing about the harm." Observing that this test subsumes the but-for test, the comments to this section note that the substantial-factor test requires a plaintiff to establish, not only that the defendant's tortious conduct was a necessary antecedent of his or her harm, but also that the conduct had a substantial effect in bringing about that harm.[18] The *Second Restatement*'s efforts to include both notions in a single test proved quite unsuccessful, and most courts have pulled the two parts of the causal inquiry in two, using the but-for test for ordinary cases and reserving the substantial-factor test for multiple cause situations in which some question exists as to the materiality of the plaintiff's contribution to the harm. In these latter situations, usually toxic substance cases, the substantial-factor test appears to work quite well.[19] Some courts do use the substantial-factor test as one, or the only, factual causation test in tort and products liability cases.[20] But most courts

**15.** See Lear Siegler, Inc. v. Perez, 819 S.W.2d 470 (Tex. 1991).

**16.** Motus v. Pfizer, Inc., 358 F.3d 659 (9th Cir. 2004) (Cal. law) (no warning that antidepressant posed risk of suicide).

**17.** DaimlerChrysler Corp. v. Hillhouse, ___ S.W.3d ___, 2004 WL 1195687 (Tex. App. 2004). See also Chapman ex rel. Estate of Chapman v. Bernard's Inc., 167 F.Supp.2d 406, 412 (D. Mass 2001) (more warnings not to sit too close to steering wheel probably would have made no difference, since plaintiff ignored the one).

**18.** See Restatement (2d) Torts § 431(a) and cmts. *a* and *b*. California courts acknowledge that the substantial-factor test includes the but-for test, and that it merely adds a substantiality requirement of lesser moment. See, e.g., Rutherford v. Owens–Illinois, Inc., 941 P.2d 1203, 1214 (Cal. 1997) ("Undue emphasis should not be placed on the term 'substantial.'"); Lineaweaver v. Plant Insulation Co., 37 Cal. Rptr.2d 902, 905–06 (Ct. App. 1995) ("the word 'substantial' should not be weighted too heavily"). See also Vodanovich v. A.P. Green Indus., Inc., 869 So.2d 930, 933 (La. Ct. App. 2004).

**19.** See, e.g., Torrejon v. Mobil Oil Co., 876 So.2d 877, 894 (La. Ct. App. 2004) ("in a products liability case, the substantial-

factor test applies to determine whether exposure to a particular asbestos-containing product was a cause in fact of a plaintiff's asbestos-related disease"); Gutteridge v. A.P. Green Servs., Inc., 804 A.2d 643 (Pa. Super. Ct. 2002) (asbestos); Bockrath v. Aldrich Chem. Co., 980 P.2d 398 (Cal. 1999) (substantial-factor test permitted worker to maintain products liability complaint against 55 manufacturers of chemicals that allegedly caused his cancer). See generally § 11.3.

Note, however, that the substantial-factor test is fairly subject to the criticism that it is merely an intuitive device rather than a logical causal test. See Robertson, The Common Sense of Cause in Fact, 75 Tex. L. Rev. 1765, 1780 (1998); Dobbs, Law of Torts 416–17.

**20.** See, e.g., Donald v. Shinn Fu Co. of Am., 2002 WL 32068351, at *7 (E.D.N.Y. 2002) (jack collapse) ("the 'substantial-factor' test assumes that more than one action can cause an accident"); Stevens v. Keller Ladders, 1 Fed.Appx. 452, 460 (6th Cir. 2001) (Ky. law) (ladder collapse) ("Under Kentucky law, the plaintiff in a products liability action has the burden of establishing causation under the substantial-factor test."); General Motors Corp. v. Harper, 61 S.W.3d 118, 130–31 (Tex. App. 2001) (seat-

properly reserve the substantial-factor test for the multiple cause situation and apply the but-for test as the principal, usually the exclusive, test for factual causation in ordinary products liability contexts involving single, durable products. The *Third Restatement* takes this approach, providing a general definition of factual causation in but-for terms[21] and providing a separate standard for multiple causation cases.[22]

It is axiomatic that a plaintiff must establish that a product defect or the defendant's negligent conduct was *a* cause of the plaintiff's harm, not that it was *the* cause of the harm.[23] Every harmful effect has an infinite number of causes,[24] and some number of those causes often are significant. Principles of concurring, multiple causation help plaintiffs establish causation in such cases.[25]

### Proving Causation—In General

A recurring factual causation issue in the reported products liability decisions concerns the sufficiency of a plaintiff's proof connecting his or her damages to some defect in the defendant's product. The classic illustration is *Price v. Ashby's, Inc.*,[26] in which the plaintiff's Star–Chief Pontiac sedan inexplicably ran off the road. Before the accident, the plaintiff noticed that the right front end of the car would settle to within three or four inches above the road after he turned the engine off. Plaintiff took the car back to Ashby's, where he had purchased it, to have the sagging problem diagnosed and repaired, but Ashby's could not

belt design); Rutherford v. Owens–Illinois, Inc., 941 P.2d 1203, 1214 (Cal. 1997) (asbestos, but rule stated generally: "In the context of products liability actions, the plaintiff must prove that the defective products supplied by the defendant were a substantial-factor in bringing about his or her injury.")

**21.** See Restatement (3d) Torts: Liability for Physical Harm § 26 ("Conduct is a factual cause of harm when the harm would not have occurred absent the conduct."). Note that the Products Liability Restatement, in § 15, merely provides that "[w]hether a product defect caused harm to persons or property is determined by the prevailing rules and principles governing causation in tort." Its two illustrations speak in substantial factor terms but rely, to a large extent, on but-for reasoning.

**22.** See id. § 27 ("multiple sufficient causal sets": an actor's tortious conduct is the cause of harm even if there was another but-for cause of the harm).

**23.** See Restatement (3d) Torts: Liability for Physical Harm § 27; id. § 26 cmt. *c*. ("An actor's tortious conduct need only be a factual cause of the other's harm."). See also Reporters' Note to § 26 cmt. *c* ("That a party's tortious conduct need only be a cause of the plaintiff's harm and not the sole cause is well recognized and accepted in every jurisdiction."); Restatement (Second) of Torts § 430 cmt. d. ("It is not

necessary that [the defendant's tortious conduct] be *the* case, using the word 'the' as meaning the sole and even the predominant cause. The wrongful conduct of a number of third persons may also be a cause of the harm ... concurrently with the actor.").

Thus, Reaux v. Deep S. Equip. Co., 840 So.2d 20 (La. Ct. App. 2003), appears wrongly decided. That was an action against the lessor of a lift truck that did not have a backup alarm, and the plaintiff's foot was squashed when the truck backed up. The trial court granted summary judgment to the defendant, and the appellate court affirmed, reasoning that the rental of the truck without a backup alarm was not a cause in fact of the plaintiff's injury. The court would have been correct in this conclusion if it reasoned that there was too much construction noise for a backup alarm to be heard; but it did not. And it might plausibly have ruled that the truck's failure to have an alarm was not a proximate cause of the accident, because of the employer's blatant violation of the OSHA regulation; but it did not.

**24.** See Restatement (3d) Torts: Liability for Physical Harm § 26 cmt. *c* ("there will always be multiple (some say, infinite) factual causes of a harm").

**25.** See id. § 27.

**26.** 354 P.2d 1064 (Utah 1960).

discover the problem. After the accident, the plaintiff discovered a hole in a line connected to the airlift mechanism that appeared to explain the sagging problem, which established the negligence of General Motors in assembling the car and Ashby's negligence in failing properly to repair it. But the plaintiff introduced no proof connecting this defect (or, hence, either defendant's negligence) to the car's failure to stay on the road as it was negotiating a turn. Without proof of this connection, the plaintiff failed to establish that the accident probably was caused by the defect (and the defendants' negligence) rather than driver error.[27] The court upheld dismissal of the plaintiff's case. Plaintiffs frequently lose products liability cases because they provide insufficient proof, by experts or otherwise, establishing that a defect in the defendant's product caused their harm.[28]

Yet, causation need not be proved with certainty, and a plaintiff may establish causation by circumstantial evidence that demonstrates that a defect in the defendant's product most likely caused the harm. The fire cases illustrate this point.[29] Fires may be started by defective products, but they may be started by cigarettes and other things as well. Conflicting experts often provide conflicting hypotheses about a fire's origin from burn patterns and other circumstantial evidence, and the trier of fact will have to weigh the conflicting inferences to determine whether the plaintiff's evidence on balance traces the fire to a defect in the defendant's product.

*Henderson v. Sunbeam Corporation*[30] was an action against the seller and manufacturer of an electric blanket that allegedly caused a fire damaging the plaintiff's property. The plaintiff's fire-origin expert traced the fire to an electrical source on or near the plaintiff's bed, and

**27.** "With two or more possible causes such as an inattentive driver and a mechanical defect that would have made it harder to turn; proof that it may have been either is not proof that it was in fact either. No evidence indicated that either cause was the more probable." Id. at 1065.

**28.** See, e.g., 438 Main Street v. Easy Heat, Inc., ___ P.3d ___, 2004 WL 1879598 (Utah 2004) (insufficient evidence that deicing cable caused fire); Vanover v. Altec Indus., 82 Fed.Appx. 8 (10th Cir. 2003) (Okla. law) (insufficient evidence that defect in aerial lift caused worker's electrocution); Webster v. Pacesetter, Inc., 259 F.Supp.2d 27 (D.D.C. 2003) (insufficient evidence that any defect in pacemaker caused injury to plaintiff's heart); In re Bridgestone/Firestone, Inc., 2003 WL 430491 (S.D. Ind. 2003) (Cal. law) (insufficient evidence that any defect in tires caused traffic accident); Soldo v. Sandoz Pharm. Corp., 244 F.Supp.2d 434 (W.D. Pa. 2003) (insufficient evidence that defendant's drug for control of postpartum lactation caused plaintiff's stroke); Citizens Ins. Co. of Am. v. Sears Roebuck and Co., 203 F.Supp.2d 837 (W.D. Mich. 2002) (insufficient evidence that fire was caused by faulty burner on barbeque gas grill); Ogletree v. Navistar Intern.

Transp. Corp., 535 S.E.2d 545 (Ga. Ct. App. 2000) (insufficient evidence that failure to install back-up alarm on truck that backed over plaintiff caused the injury); Calhoun v. Honda Motor Co., 738 F.2d 126 (6th Cir. 1984) (Ky. law) (insufficient evidence that motorcycle collision with rear of tractor trailer truck was caused by a design defect in the cycle's brakes).

**29.** See, e.g., Speller v. Sears, Roebuck & Co., 790 N.E.2d 252 (N.Y. 2003) (sufficient evidence that defective refrigerator caused fire that killed consumer); Flock v. Scripto–Tokai Corp., 319 F.3d 231, 236–38 (5th Cir. 2003) (Tex. law) (sufficient evidence that allegedly defective Aim 'n Flame utility lighter caused fire); Henderson v. Sunbeam Corp., 46 F.3d 1151 (10th Cir. 1995) (Okla. law) (sufficient evidence that defective electric blanket caused fire). *But see* 438 Main Street v. Easy Heat, Inc., ___ P.3d ___ 2004 WL 1879598 (Utah 2004) (insufficient evidence that deicing cable caused fire); Citizens Ins. Co. of Am. v. Sears Roebuck and Co., 203 F.Supp.2d 837 (W.D. Mich. 2002) (insufficient evidence that fire was caused by faulty burner on barbeque gas grill).

**30.** 1995 WL 39022, 46 F.3d 1151 (table) (10th Cir. 1995) (Okla. law).

concluded that a defect in the electric blanket's control unit caused the fire. The plaintiff's other expert, a specialist in electrical device malfunctions, attributed the fire to a broken connection in the blanket's heating element, igniting the mantle's fabric when it arced, but he could not identify precisely which connection in the mantle's wiring grid had failed. The defendants' experts blamed the fire on the motor in the bed's vibrator, but the motor could run for only fifteen minutes on its timer whereas the fire was first observed nearly three hours after the plaintiff left her house the morning of the fire, a delay the defendants' experts could not explain. The jury rendered a verdict for the plaintiff, the trial court denied the defendants' post-trial motions, and the appellate court affirmed, ruling that the plaintiff had presented sufficient causation evidence, even though the plaintiff's experts had differing theories of the fire's origins.[31] The plaintiff's failure to pinpoint precisely which part had failed was not a problem because the blanket had been destroyed in the fire, permitting the plaintiff to rely on circumstantial evidence indicating that a product defect of some type probably caused the fire.[32] Particularly in cases where an accident may be attributable to a product malfunction, a plaintiff may sometimes prove both cause and defect by circumstantial evidence.[33]

No question is more fundamental than the sufficiency of the evidence on any issue, but this procedural issue plays an especially prominent role in dividing good products liability cases from bad ones when the issue is cause in fact. *Price* well illustrates how a plaintiff must provide a sufficient amount of credible evidence connecting a product defect or the supplier's negligence to the plaintiff's harm to allow a trier of fact reasonably to conclude that the defect or negligence probably caused the harm. Without such evidence, if a jury would be left to speculation and conjecture on what caused a plaintiff's harm, the claim will fail. Yet, as shown by *Henderson*, determinations of factual causation are especially fact intensive, so that the introduction of any credible proof linking the plaintiff's harm to the defendant's negligence or defective product, even by circumstantial evidence, makes cause in fact an issue for the jury.[34]

---

**31.** "A jury question is created, not negated, by disagreement among experts, . . . and the fact that plaintiff's own experts disagreed did not alter the jury's authority to resolve the issue consistently with Dr. Croenwett's view . . . ." Id. at *2.

**32.** "Where, as here, an allegedly defective product has largely destroyed itself, making direct evidence of the precise operative defect unavailable, the plaintiff may prove her case with circumstantial evidence, typically including expert testimony, even though she 'is unable to point an accusing finger at a particular defective component.'" Id. at *2.

**33.** On proof of defect in malfunction cases, see § 7.4, above.

**34.** See, e.g., Speller v. Sears, Roebuck & Co., 790 N.E.2d 252 (N.Y. 2003) (sufficient evidence that defective refrigerator caused fire that killed consumer); Henderson v. Sunbeam Corp., 46 F.3d 1151 (table) (10th Cir. 1995) (Okla. law) (sufficient evidence that defective electric blanket caused fire). See generally First Premier Bank v. Kolcraft Enters., 686 N.W.2d 430, 454 (S.D. 2004) ("Causation is almost always a fact question, except when there are

## Proving Causation—Toxic Substance Litigation

### *In General*

Toxic substance cases typically present a number of serious causation problems,[35] and the substantial-factor test previously mentioned helps plaintiffs in only limited ways. Tracing harmful consequences to asbestos fibers, drugs, and other kinds of chemicals presents perplexing causation problems both in science and the law. Science itself often does not fully understand the biological mechanisms involved in disease causation, rendering it difficult for the law to be confident of evidence that a plaintiff's cancer or other disease was caused by the plaintiff's exposure to a particular product rather than something else. While the but-for test remains at the center of the causal inquiry, courts in toxic substance cases necessarily draw from scientific notions of causation to help make a legal determination of causation. Yet causation is established very differently in science than in law, which often causes a clash between these disciplines when toxic substance causation issues arise in products liability cases. Because the causal issues in such litigation are so arcane, expert testimony is almost always necessary and sits at the center of most disputes.[36] The topic of causation in toxic substance litigation runs wide and deep,[37] and the discussion here just highlights certain causal tests and issues that recur in products liability litigation of this type.

A toxic substance case typically arises when a person is diagnosed with some illness or injury, such as cancer, that his or her doctor may (or may not) believe was caused by some toxic substance, such as asbestos,

no differences of opinion on the interpretation of the facts.'').

**35.** "Causation issues represent a major impediment to the successful resolution of claims based on injuries from hazardous substances." Brennan, Causal Chains and Statistical Links: The Role of Scientific Uncertainty in Hazardous–Substance Litigation, 73 Cornell L. Rev. 469 (1988).

**36.** See § 6.3, above.

**37.** See, e.g., Golanski, General Causation at a Crossroads in Toxic Tort Cases, 108 Penn St. L. Rev. 479 (2003); Pierce and Sexton, Toxicogenomics: Toward the Future of Toxic Tort Causation, 5 N.C. J. L. & Tech. 33 (2003); Conway–Jones, Factual Causation in Toxic Tort Litigation: A Philosophical View of Proof and Certainty in Uncertain Disciplines, 35 U. Rich. L. Rev. 875 (2002); McGarity, Proposal for Linking Culpability and Causation to Ensure Corporate Accountability for Toxic Risks, 26 Wm. & Mary Envtl. L. & Pol'y Rev. 1 (2001); Geistfeld, Scientific Uncertainty and Causation Tort Law, 54 Vand. L. Rev. 1011 (2001); Klein, A Model for Enhanced Risk Recovery in Tort, 56 Wash. & Lee L. Rev. 1173 (1999); Fischer, Successive Causes and the Enigma of Duplicated Harm, 66 Tenn. L. Rev. 1127 (1999); Parascandola, What is Wrong with The Possibility of Causation?, 39 Jurimetrics J. 29 (1998); Bernstein, Formed by Thalidomide: Mass Torts as a

False Cure for Toxic Exposure, 97 Colum. L. Rev. 2153 (1997); Wagner, Choosing Ignorance in the Manufacture of Toxic Products, 82 Cornell L. Rev. 773 (1997); Berger, Eliminating General Causation: Notes Toward a New Theory of Justice and Toxic Torts, 97 Colum. L. Rev. 2117 (1997); Feldman, Science and Uncertainty in Mass Exposure Litigation, 74 Tex. L. Rev. 1 (1995); Sanders, From Science to Evidence: The Testimony on Causation in the Bendectin Cases, 46 Stan. L. Rev. 1 (1993); M. Green, Expert Witnesses and Sufficiency of Evidence in Toxic Substances Litigation: The Legacy of Agent Orange and Bendectin Litigation, 86 Nw. L. Rev. 643 (1992); Brennan, Causal Chains and Statistical Links: The Role of Scientific Uncertainty in Hazardous–Substance Litigation, 73 Cornell L. Rev. 469 (1988); Farber, Toxic Causation, 71 Minn. L. Rev. 1219, 1251–1259 (1987); Frumer and Friedman, Products Liability §§ 3.02[5] ("medical causation") and 3.04[2] (asbestos cases); D. Faigman, D. Kaye, M. Saks, and J. Sanders, Science in the Law—Standards, Statistics and Research Issues (2002); Federal Judicial Center, Reference Manual on Scientific Evidence (2d ed. 2000). For a light but helpful overview, see J. Eggen, Toxic Torts in a Nutshell (2d ed. 2000). For a thorough, scholarly review of many aspects of this problem, see the Restatement (Third) of Torts: Liability for Physical Harm § 28(a) cmt. *c*, and the Reporters' Notes thereto.

silicone gel in a breast implant, a cell phone, or some drug or other chemical. The doctor may suspect that a particular agent caused the illness, yet most physicians are trained principally to diagnose and treat a disease, not to determine its etiology. For a products liability claim to lie, a person suffering from an illness that may have been caused by a toxic substance will have to assemble proof that the substance probably caused the harm. Such proof, for a number of reasons, may be difficult to obtain. Much mystery still surrounds the causes of many illnesses, and much remains unknown about whether (and, if so, how) most substances are hazardous to humans. This problem is exacerbated in many toxic substance cases in which the period between exposure and the onset of symptoms of an illness (the latency period) often is many years, sometimes decades.[38] Thus, proving that any particular toxic agent caused a particular person's injury or illness can be a daunting task.

### General and Specific Causation

Proof of causation in toxic substance cases always involves, at least implicitly, two separate forms of causal proof: (1) general causation, and (2) specific causation.[39] To establish "general causation," a plaintiff must establish that the suspect agent is capable of causing the particular injury or illness suffered by the plaintiff. For example, a plaintiff who seeks to prove that a cell phone caused his brain cancer, that asbestos caused his lung disease, that a silicone-gel breast implant caused her systemic disorders, or that a drug she took during pregnancy caused birth defects in her child, first must establish that the suspect agent in fact is capable of causing the particular type of injury the plaintiff suffers. General causation is sometimes so well established, or its markers so self-evident,[40] that little or no proof of general causation is necessary.[41] Ordinarily, however a plaintiff must affirmatively establish general causation, as by controlled human studies, epidemiological studies of population groups, animal experiments, laboratory studies of the chemistry of an agent and disease, or some combination of these forms of evidence.

General causation is most commonly proved with epidemiological studies of human population groups exposed to the suspect agent.[42]

---

**38.** For example, reproductive anomalies associated with DES are not evident until the victim, exposed to the drug in utero, reaches puberty. See § 11.3, below. The latency period of mesothelioma, a lethal cancer caused by the inhalation of asbestos dust, can reach forty years. See, e.g., Hamilton v. Asbestos Corp., 998 P.2d 403, 405–08 (Cal. 2000) (noting 30–40 year latency period for mesolthelioma).

**39.** This distinction is widely employed. See, e.g., In re Rezulin Products, 331 F.Supp.2d 196, 202 (S.D.N.Y., 2004) ("As in any tort action, plaintiffs are required to establish general and specific causation, viz., that Rezulin was capable of causing, and in fact caused, the injuries they allege."); In re Meridia Prod. Liab. Litig., 328 F.Supp.2d 791, at *798 (N.D. Ohio 2004) ("In toxic tort cases, the causation inquiry is two-pronged. First, a plaintiff must show that the substance to which she was exposed *can cause* the type of injury alleged.

Next, a plaintiff must show that in her case, exposure to the substance *actually caused* the alleged injury.").

**40.** Such as DES. See Farber, Toxic Causation, 71 Minn. L. Rev. 1219, 1251–52 (1987); Abraham and Merrill, Scientific Uncertainty in the Courts, Issues Sci. & Tech., Winter 1986, at 93, 101.

**41.** The causal connections between asbestos and asbestosis and mesothelioma are so strong that courts have long held they are established as a matter of law. See, e.g., Bertrand v. Johns–Manville Sales Corp., 529 F.Supp. 539, 544 (D. Minn. 1982); Flatt v. Johns–Manville Sales Corp., 488 F.Supp. 836, 841 (E.D. Tex. 1980); Karjala v. Johns–Manville Prod. Corp., 523 F.2d 155, 160 (8th Cir. 1975) (Minn. law).

**42.** Controlled human studies may be the most effective way of determining whether a substance can harm human be-

Epidemiological studies yield calculations of the "relative risk" of acquiring a disease from exposure to an agent contrasted to the background risk of contracting the illness or injury from other factors. A relative risk of 1.0 means that the risk of contracting the illness is not increased at all by exposure to the agent; a relative risk greater than 1.0 means that exposure to the agent increases the likelihood of contracting the illness; and a relative risk of 2.0 means that exposure to the agent doubles a person's risk of contracting the disease.[43] With some substances, like Bendectin[44] and silicone-gel breast implants,[45] for which numerous epidemiological studies have revealed no reliable evidence of a causal relationship between exposure and suspected birth defects and systemic disorders, respectively, the insistence by many courts of convincing epidemiologic evidence of causation for a plaintiff to proceed bars recovery. For other types of products, reliable epidemiologic studies may be unavailable, particularly at the beginning of a product's life cycle,[46] and other types of causation evidence often are appropriate.[47]

ings, but such studies are expensive and sometimes are unethical. See McGarity, Proposal for Linking Culpability and Causation to Ensure Corporate Accountability for Toxic Risks, 26 Wm. & Mary Envtl. L. & Pol'y Rev. 1, 14–15 (2001).

**43.** See, e.g., Note, 56 Vand. L. Rev. 1227, 1234–35 (2003).

**44.** See, e.g., Brock v. Merrell Dow Pharms., Inc., 874 F.2d 307, 313 (5th Cir. 1989) (Tex. law) (lack of strong epidemiological proof was fatal to plaintiff's claim that Bendectin caused the plaintiff's birth defects; while convincing epidemiologic proof not required in every toxic substance case, it may be crucial when animal studies, of questionable applicability to humans, are the only other form of proof). See generally J. Sanders, Bendectin on Trial: A Study of Mass Tort Litigation 89 (1998) ("the substantial weight of the scientific evidence fails to support the conclusion that Bendectin causes birth defects"); Boston, A Mass–Exposure Model of Toxic Causation: The Content of Scientific Proof and the Regulatory Experience, 18 Colum. J. Envtl. L. 181 (1993); M. Green, The Road Less Well Traveled (And Seen): Contemporary Lawmaking in Products Liability, 49 DePaul L. Rev. 377 (1999).

**45.** See, e.g., Meister v. Med. Eng'g Corp., 267 F.3d 1123 (D.C. Cir. 2001) (overwhelming epidemiological evidence has established lack of causal connection between silicone breast implants and type of injury plaintiff suffered). See generally Walker and Monahan, Scientific Authority: The Breast Implant Litigation and Beyond, 86 Va. L. Rev. 801 (2000) (examining causation study by National Science Panel).

**46.** See, e.g., Turner v. Iowa Fire Equip. Co., 229 F.3d 1202, 1209 (8th Cir.2000) (Okla. law) ("The first several victims of a new toxic tort should not be barred from

having their day in court simply because the medical literature, which will eventually show the connection between the victims' condition and the toxic substance, has not yet been completed.").

**47.** A "quite substantial body of case law and commentary rejects an epidemiologic threshold for sufficient proof of general causation." Restatement (3d) Torts: Liability for Physical Harm § 28, Reporters' Note to cmt. c (citing cases). See, e.g., Rider v. Sandoz Pharm. Corp., 295 F.3d 1194, 1198 (11th Cir. 2002) ("It is well-settled that while epidemiological studies may be powerful evidence of causation, the lack thereof is not fatal to a plaintiff's case."); Hollander v. Sandoz Pharms. Corp., 289 F.3d 1193, 1211–12 (10th Cir. 2002) (plaintiffs need not always use epidemiological studies to establish general causation); Jennings v. Baxter Healthcare Corp., 14 P.3d 596 (Or. 2001); Kuhn v. Sandoz Pharms. Corp., 14 P.3d 1170, 1184–85 (Kan. 2000) (general causation proof not required where there had been no mass exposure and, hence, no body of epidemiologic evidence).

Commentators are unfriendly to epidemiologic thresholds for causation. See, e.g., Mc Garity, Proposal for Linking Culpability and Causation to Ensure Corporate Accountability for Toxic Risks, 26 Wm. & Mary Envtl. L. & Pol'y Rev. 1 (2001); Geistfeld, Scientific Uncertainty and Causation in Tort Law, 54 Vand. L. Rev. 1011 (2001); Faigman et al., How Good Is Good Enough?: Expert Evidence Under Daubert *and* Kumho, 50 Case W. Res. L. Rev. 645, 663 (2000); Finley, Guarding the Gate to the Courthouse: How Trial Judges Are Using Their Evidentiary Screening Role to Remake Tort Causation Rules, 49 DePaul L. Rev. 335, 339 (1999); Berger, Eliminating General Causation: Notes Towards a

"Specific causation" exists when a plaintiff's exposure to a substance caused his or her particular illness. Establishing specific causation first requires proof of exposure to the defendant's product—normally not a problem in drug litigation, but often a problem in cases where the suspect agent is asbestos or some chemical. Particularly in asbestos litigation, a plaintiff may have worked for many years around asbestos products produced by many manufacturers. In such cases, proving whether any particular manufacturer's asbestos products caused the plaintiff's asbestos disease is difficult if not impossible. To address this problem, the court in *Lohrmann v. Pittsburgh Corning Corp.*[48] crafted a variant of the substantial-factor test[49]—now known as the "frequency, regularity, and proximity test"—for this particular type of litigation. Now widely applied in asbestos litigation,[50] this test allows a causal conclusion—linking a particular asbestos product and the plaintiff's asbestos disease—if the plaintiff produces "evidence of exposure to a specific product on a regular basis over some extended period of time in proximity to where the plaintiff actually worked."[51]

Because the etiology of many diseases is uncertain, courts often turn to epidemiologic evidence to help determine specific as well as general causation. Thus, as proof of specific causation, many courts allow group studies which show at least a doubling in the incidence of a disease in exposed populations (a relative risk of 2.0 or greater); other courts *require* such proof of doubling as a threshold for establishing specific causation; and many recognize the prominence of a two-fold increase, in suggesting that the agent was more likely than not a cause of the plaintiff's injuries, without raising it to threshold status.[52]

Other, more particularized forms of proof are often useful in establishing specific causation.[53] One well-established, if somewhat controversial, scientific method for proving (or helping prove) specific causation is commonly referred to as "differential diagnosis."[54] By this approach, a

New Theory of Justice and Toxic Torts, 97 Colum. L. Rev. 2117 (1997); Wagner, Choosing Ignorance in the Manufacture of Toxic Products, 82 Cornell L. Rev. 773 (1997); Feldman, Science and Uncertainty in Mass Exposure Litigation, 74 Tex. L. Rev. 1, 45 (1995); M. Green, Expert Witnesses and Sufficiency of Evidence in Toxic Substances Litigation: The Legacy of Agent Orange and Bendectin Litigation, 86 Nw. U. L. Rev. 643 (1992). See generally Restatement (3d) Torts: Liability for Physical Harm § 28 cmt. *c.*

**48.** 782 F.2d 1156, 1162–1163 (4th Cir. 1986) (Md. law).

**49.** See, e.g., Hoerner v. ANCO Insulations, Inc., 812 So.2d 45 (La. Ct. App. 2002).

**50.** See, e.g., Chavers v. General Motors Corp., 79 S.W.3d 361, 367 (Ark. 2002) (adopting this "approach to the causation analysis that has been adopted by a majority of courts in dealing with asbestos cases"); Sholtis v. American Cyanamid Co., 568 A.2d 1196, 1207 (N.J. Super. App. Div. 1989) (adopting the "frequency, regularity

and proximity" test as "a fair balance between the needs of plaintiffs (recognizing the difficulty of proving contact) and defendants (protecting against liability predicated on guesswork)").

**51.** *Lohrman*, 782 F.2d 1156, at 1162–63.

**52.** See Restatement (3d) Torts: Liability for Physical Harm § 28, Reporters' Note to cmt. *c.* (collecting cases). See generally Carruth and Goldstein, Relative Risk Greater than Two in Proof of Causation in Toxic Tort Litigation, 41 Jurimetrics J. 195 (2001).

**53.** See, e.g., Alder v. Bayer Corp., AGFA Div., 61 P.3d 1068 (Utah 2002).

**54.** Properly, the term "differential diagnosis" refers to a method for ascertaining the plaintiff's illness, whereas "differential etiology" describes the process for determining the cause of that disease. See, e.g., Note, 56 Vand. L. Rev. 1227, 1228 n.5 (2003), citing Faigman et al., Modern Scientific Evidence: The Law and Science of Ex-

physician attempts to determine the cause of a malady by considering the range of its plausible causes, and ruling them out, one by one, until just one remains.[55] Assuming that a physician applies this technique properly,[56] it can be a particularly useful tool to prove a specific causal link between a defendant's toxic substance and the plaintiff's disease or injury.[57]

## § 11.3  MULTIPLE DEFENDANTS

Most causation problems involving multiple products liability defendants concern toxic substances, and general methods for establishing causation in that type of litigation were just examined.[1] Yet problems arising out of a multiplicity of possible or actual causal agencies extend beyond toxic substance litigation, so that multiple defendant causation issues are of general application. This section first explores the general principles of concurrent causation that apply to multiple defendant situations and then examines "market share liability" and other theories of collective responsibility designed to mitigate a plaintiff's causal difficulties in certain types of cases involving multiple defendants.

### Concurrent Causation

A manufacturer or other seller may be responsible, at least in part, for causing a plaintiff's injuries no matter how many other causes may also combine to cause the harm. If a product defect (or the defendant's negligence) played a material role in causing the plaintiff's injuries, then the defect or conduct was a cause of the harm. This is the principal of

---

pert Testimony § 20–1.1 (2d ed. 2002). Yet the former term is widely used by courts to mean the ruling-out process used to track causation.

**55.** "Differential diagnosis, or differential etiology, is a standard scientific technique of identifying the cause of a medical problem by eliminating the likely causes until the most probable one is isolated." Schafersman v. Agland Coop, 631 N.W.2d 862, 871 (Neb. 2001). See generally Imwinkelried, The Admissibility and Legal Sufficiency of Testimony About Differential Diagnosis (Etiology): Of Under–And Over–Estimations, 56 Baylor L. Rev. 391 (2004); Sanders and Machal–Fulks, The Admissibility of Differential Diagnosis Testimony to Prove Causation in Toxic Tort Cases: The Interplay of Adjective and Substantive Law, 64 L. & Contemp. Probs. 107 (2001); Latimer, A Good Bedside Manner Wouldn't Be Enough, Either: Differential Diagnosis Under *Daubert*, 1 Expert Evid. Rep. 33 (BNA Aug. 1, 2001).

**56.** See, e.g., Glastetter v. Novartis Pharm. Corp., 252 F.3d 986 (8th Cir. 2001) (although differential diagnosis is presumptively admissible, experts lacked basis for "ruling in" Parlodel, drug for suppressing postpartum lactation, as cause of stroke);

Alexander v. Smith & Nephew, 98 F.Supp.2d 1310 (N.D. Okla. 2000) (expert's failure to explain why he eliminated other possible causes rendered methodology unreliable).

**57.** See, e.g., Mattis v. Carlon Elec. Prods., 295 F.3d 856 (8th Cir. 2002) (differential diagnosis admissible to prove causal link between polyvinyl chloride (PVC) cement and the plaintiff's airways dysfunction syndrome); Westberry v. Gislaved Gummi AB, 178 F.3d 257 (4th Cir. 1999) (treating physician's differential diagnosis admissible to prove link between talcum powder used as lubricant in rubber gaskets and plaintiff's sinus infection). In some situations, an expert's failure to apply this diagnostic approach undercuts the validity of his or her conclusions. See, e.g., Turner v. Iowa Fire Equip. Co., 229 F.3d 1202 (8th Cir. 2000) (Okla. law) (expert made no attempt to exclude possible causes of respiratory problems, allegedly caused by accidental discharge of substance from fire suppression equipment, until only one remained).

### § 11.3

**1.** See § 11.2, above.

concurrent causation as well known to tort law generally[2] as it is to the law of products liability.[3] The substantial-factor test was devised to address just this type of multiple defendant situation,[4] as discussed above. So, if a defendant's asbestos,[5] chemical,[6] or tobacco[7] product plays a substantial role in causing a plaintiff's disease, the defendant may be held to have caused that disease, at least in part, even if it was also caused by the asbestos, chemical, or tobacco products of other manufacturers.[8]

It is often difficult to determine which portions of a plaintiff's injuries are attributable to each of two or more responsible parties. If the trier of fact, on some reasonable basis, is able to determine which aspects of the plaintiff's loss are attributable to which defendant, then damages ordinarily must be apportioned on that basis.[9] But where no fair and practicable method for apportioning the loss is available, then, at common law, each defendant whose breach of duty was a substantial factor in producing the damage is held jointly and severally responsible for the total loss.[10]

---

**2.** See Restatement (3d) Torts: Liability for Physical Harm § 27.

**3.** See, e.g., Commonwealth v. United States Mineral Prods. Co., 809 A.2d 1000, 1012 (Pa. Commw. Ct. 2002) ("[a] defendant is not relieved from liability because another concurring cause is also responsible for producing injury"). See generally Restatement (3d) Torts: Products Liability § 3 cmt. *d* (a "defect need not be the only cause of the incident; if the plaintiff can prove that the most likely explanation of the harm involves the causal contribution of a product defect, the fact that there may be other concurrent causes of the harm does not preclude liability").

**4.** "When multiple causes of injury are present, defendant's conduct is a cause in fact of plaintiff's harm if it is substantial factor generating plaintiff's harm." Vodanovich v. A.P. Green Indus., 869 So.2d 930, 932 (La. Ct. App. 2004). See also Commonwealth v. United States Mineral Prods. Co., 809 A.2d 1000, 1012 (Pa. Commw. Ct. 2002) ("[w]here a jury could reasonably believe that a defendant's actions were a substantial factor in bringing about the harm, the fact that there is a concurring cause does not relieve the defendant of liability"). See § 11.2, above.

**5.** See, e.g., Torrejon v. Mobil Oil Co., 876 So.2d 877, 894 (La. Ct. App. 2004) ("in a products liability case, the substantial-factor test applies to determine whether exposure to a particular asbestos-containing product was a cause in fact of a plaintiff's asbestos-related disease"); Rutherford v. Owens–Illinois, Inc., 941 P.2d 1203 (Cal. 1997); Hao v. Owens–Illinois, Inc., 738 P.2d 416 (Haw. 1987) (asbestos manufacturer responsible for its share of plaintiff's lung

damage even though damage was partially caused by smoking).

**6.** See, e.g., Bockrath v. Aldrich Chem. Co., 980 P.2d 398 (Cal. 1999) (substantial-factor test permitted worker to maintain products liability complaint against 55 manufacturers of chemicals that allegedly caused his cancer).

**7.** See, e.g., Burton v. R.J. Reynolds Tobacco Co., 208 F.Supp.2d 1187, 1213 (D. Kan. 2002) (although plaintiff smoked both Camels and Lucky Strikes, he could prevail against the manufacturer of Lucky Strikes by proving that smoking them was a substantial factor in bringing about his disease).

**8.** Note, however, that the substantial-factor test may not be used to undermine comparative fault, which makes a defendant liable even for very small proportions of a plaintiff's injuries. See, e.g., Burton v. R.J. Reynolds Tobacco Co., 208 F.Supp.2d 1187, 1213 (D. Kan. 2002) (substantial-factor test should not be interpreted to undermine principle of comparative fault). Consequently, an attempt to quantify the "size" of the substantial factor in a jury instruction may be reversible error. See Jeter v. Owens–Corning Fiberglas Corp., 716 A.2d 633 (Pa. Super. Ct. 1997) ("considerable" and "significantly large" improperly described required connection). See generally Prosser and Keeton on Torts § 41, at 267 ("The 'substantial factor' formulation is one concerning legal significance rather than factual quantum.").

**9.** Dobbs, Law of Torts § 174, at 422; Restatement (2d) of Torts § 433A(1)(a) and cmt. *b*.

**10.** See, e.g., Smith v. J.C. Penney Co., 525 P.2d 1299 (Or. 1974) (plaintiff suffered

In *Buehler v. Whalen*,[11] for example, the plaintiffs were injured in a fire which erupted when their car was hit by another vehicle driven by Whalen. They sued Whalen for negligent driving and the manufacturer of the car in which they were riding, Ford Motor Company, for designing an uncrashworthy automobile. The other driver argued that all damages should be apportioned to Ford, since the plaintiffs' only injuries were burns caused by the uncrashworthy design of the car's fuel system. Upholding joint and several liability against the other driver as well as Ford, the Illinois Supreme Court reasoned that the other driver's negligent driving caused the collision, which precipitated the fire. Because the injuries were indivisible, the "concurrent" tortfeasors were both jointly and severally responsible for the entire harm.[12]

In recent years, the doctrine of joint and several liability has been widely altered in many jurisdictions (and abolished altogether in a few states) due to the rise of comparative fault and apportionment, together with tort reform. While the general approach of the reform statutes is to apportion damages to a defendant proportionate to its fault or responsibility in causing the plaintiff's harm, variations between the statutes are significant, and there no longer is a majority rule in this area of the law.[13] Accordingly, a lawyer is referred on these issues, first, to the statutory and other law of his or her particular jurisdiction and, second, to specialized texts and the *Apportionment Restatement*.

A special difficulty exists if a plaintiff can trace his or her injuries to a single product manufactured by A, B, or C but is unable to identify which culprit manufactured the offending product. Under conventional principles, since the plaintiff has the burden of proof on causation, the plaintiff's case in this type of situation will fail.[14]

## Multiple Defendants—Theories of Collective Liability

Ordinarily, the law properly requires that a plaintiff identify the manufacturer of the specific product that caused his or her harm, the fundamental causal identification requirement examined earlier.[15] Plaintiffs injured by toxic substances confront a variety of causation problems, some of which were examined above.[16] Sometimes, however, plaintiffs can reliably trace their injuries to a specific drug, chemical, or asbestos product. Yet, if the substance has left no identifying traces, it may be impossible for the plaintiff to identify its manufacturer. When such a

---

severe burns from her excessively flammable imitation fur coat which caught fire when service station operator negligently sprayed gasoline on floor heater). See Dobbs, Law of Torts § 174, at 423; Restatement (2d) Torts § 433B(3).

**11.** 374 N.E.2d 460 (Ill. 1977).

**12.** "We have here a classic case of concurrent tortfeasors whose separate acts combine to produce a single individual injury. Under these circumstances there is no apportionment." Id. at 465. The issue of damages apportionment in indivisible-injury crashworthiness cases is examined in § 17.4, below.

**13.** The Restatement (3d) Torts: Apportionment of Liability (2000), identified at least five variations on the use of joint and several liability. See id. Topic 2, Liability of Multiple Tortfeasors for Indivisible Harm, Introductory note at 98–99 (providing five separate "tracks").

**14.** Garcia v. Joseph Vince Co., 148 Cal. Rptr. 843, 846–47 (Ct. App. 1978) ("Hamlet II"), discussed below in connection with alternative liability. The defendant identification problem is discussed in § 11.2, above.

**15.** See § 11.2, above.

**16.** See id.

product is undoubtedly defective—like asbestos products sold without warnings of their serious health hazards, defective generic drugs like DES, or blood products infected with the AIDS virus—plaintiffs and courts alike have sought to find an equitable way to shift the resulting losses to some or all members of the industry which profited from the sale of the defective products, while still requiring the plaintiff to prove some causal link between the defendants and the harm. The most prominent theory of this type is "market share liability," but plaintiffs have also turned to other collective liability theories, including "alternative liability," "enterprise liability" (sometimes called "industry-wide liability"), "concert of action," and "civil conspiracy."[17] None of these theories has proved particularly helpful in most situations, but a lawyer needs to be aware of their possible existence as well as their benefits and limitations.

### *Market Share Liability*

In *Sindell v. Abbott Laboratories*,[18] the California Supreme Court gave judicial birth to market share liability in 1980. *Sindell* involved class actions by various women for injuries they suffered from taking a synthetic form of the hormone estrogen, diethylstilbesterol, called DES. Manufacturers first marketed DES in the early 1940s as a form of hormone replacement for menopause and for the treatment of senile and gonorrheal vaginitis. During the late 1940s, doctors began to prescribe DES to help prevent miscarriages, and eventually the drug was manufactured generically and sold for this purpose by some 300 pharmaceutical companies.[19] In 1971, the FDA banned the drug when researchers discovered that it could cause a form of vaginal cancer (adenocarcinoma), and precancerous growths in the vagina and cervix (adenosis), in daughters of women who took it during pregnancy.[20] Although DES pills came in all different shapes and colors, each pill was chemically identical, and

---

**17.** See, e.g., Lytton, Tort Claims Against Gun Manufacturers for Crime–Related Injuries: Defining a Suitable Role for the Tort System in Regulating the Firearms Industry, 65 Mo. L. Rev. 1 (2000); Vandall, O.K. Corral II: Policy Issues in Municipal Suits against Gun Manufacturers, 44 Vill. L. Rev. 547 (1999); Leach, Civil Conspiracy: What's The Use?, 54 U. Miami L. Rev. 1 (1999); Giliberti, Emerging Trends for Products Liability: Market Share Liability: Its History and Future, 15 Touro L. Rev. 719 (1999); Klein, Beyond DES: Rejecting The Application of Market Share Liability in Blood Products Litigation, 68 Tul. L. Rev. 883 (1994); K. Owen and Hartline, Industry–Wide Liability: Protecting Plaintiffs And Defendants, 44 Baylor L. Rev. 45 (1992); V. Schwartz & Mahshigian, Failure to Identify the Defendant in Tort Law: Towards a Legislative Solution, 73 Calif. L. Rev. 941 (1985); Fischer, Products Liability—An Analysis of Market Share Liability, 34 Vand. L. Rev. 1623 (1981); Comment, 2000 Wis. L. Rev. 1073 (2000) (lead paint); Notes, 32 Hofstra L. Rev. 1039 (2004) (lead paint), 103 W. Va. L. Rev. 81 (2000) (hand-

guns, noting *Hamilton*), 67 U. Cin. L. Rev. 1331 (1999) (DES, noting *Sutowski*), 37 B.C. L. Rev. 155 (1995) (lead paint), 94 Harv. L. Rev. 668 (1981) (DES, noting *Sindell*); Annot., 63 A.L.R.5th 195 (1998) (concert of activity, alternate liability, market share liability, and enterprise liability); Bernstein, *Hymowitz v. Eli Lilly and Co.*: Markets of Mothers, Torts Stories 151 (R. Rabin & S. Sugarman, eds., 2003); 1 Frumer and Friedman, Products Liability § 3.06.

**18.**   607 P.2d 924 (Cal. 1980).

**19.**   *Sindell* put the total number of manufacturers at about 200, id. at 931, but subsequent opinions state the higher figure. See, e.g., In re DES Litigation, 7 F.3d 20, 21 (2d Cir. 1993) (N.Y. law).

**20.**   Subsequent cases were brought by DES sons. See, e.g., Doe v. Eli Lilly & Co., Prod. Safety & Liab. Rep. (BNA) 604–05 (D.D.C. 1985) (verdict for plaintiff). And DES grandchildren. See, e.g., Grover v. Eli Lilly, 591 N.E.2d 696 (Ohio 1992) (no cause of action). The inter-generational duty issue is examined in § 10.5, above.

pharmacists typically filled prescriptions from whatever stock they had on hand. Thus, most women taking the pills had no idea who manufactured them, and by the time their daughters realized they had been injured by the drug (the reproductive tract injuries did not manifest themselves until puberty), it often was impossible to identify the manufacturer. Unable to identify the manufacturer of the DES taken by her mother, the named plaintiff in *Sindell* sought recovery against ten major manufacturers of the drug (five of whom were on the appeal). Because of her failure to identify the particular manufacturer that made the precise drug ingested by her mother, the trial court dismissed the action.

Adopting a theory of "market share liability,"[21] the California Supreme Court reversed. Because DES manufacturers chose to sell a drug generically that could cause harm long after its sale, allowing them to cover their tracks with the winds of time, the court reasoned that they should be responsible for the share of total harm for which they were statistically responsible.[22] Expanding upon its earlier decision in *Summers v. Tice*,[23] the celebrated quail hunter case in which a pellet from one shotgun of two negligent hunters injured the plaintiff's eye, the *Sindell* court reasoned that the burden of proof on causation could be fairly shifted to the defendants, provided that the plaintiff joined the manufacturers of a "substantial share" of the DES her mother may have taken.[24] Unless a manufacturer could prove that it did not manufacture the drug taken by the plaintiff's mother,[25] each would be severally liable[26] for the share of the plaintiff's injuries represented by the share of the DES market it supplied.[27]

It is difficult to quarrel with the fairness and logic of market share liability: if manufacturers benefit from selling a generic product with

**21.** The court borrowed the market share idea from Comment, DES and a Proposed Theory of Enterprise Liability, 46 Fordham L. Rev. 963 (1978).

**22.** "In our contemporary complex industrialized society, advances in science and technology create fungible goods which may harm consumers and which cannot be traced to any specific producer. The response of the courts can be either to adhere rigidly to prior doctrine, denying recovery to those injured by such products, or to fashion remedies to meet these changing needs." 607 P.2d at 936.

**23.** 199 P.2d 1 (Cal. 1948).

**24.** "If plaintiff joins in the action the manufacturers of a substantial share of the DES which her mother might have taken, the injustice of shifting the burden of proof to defendants to demonstrate that they could not have made the substance which injured plaintiff is significantly diminished." *Sindell*, 607 P.2d at 937. The plaintiff's briefs asserted that six or seven companies had manufactured about 90% of all DES, which, if true, would leave only a 10% chance "that the offending producer would escape liability." Id. at 937. The student

Comment from which the court borrowed the market share idea suggested that the plaintiff should join 75% to 80% of the manufacturers, see 46 Fordham L. Rev. at 995–96, but the court rejected these percentages as too high. See 607 P.2d at 937.

**25.** For example, by proof that its pills all were round and yellow, when the mother testified that all her pills were triangular and white.

**26.** In Brown v. Superior Court, 751 P.2d 470 (Cal. 1988), the court clarified *Sindell* on this point, specifying that a manufacturers' liability under the market share theory is several only, thus limiting a particular manufacturer's liability in any case to the proportion of the plaintiff's damages that corresponds to its percentage share of the pertinent market.

**27.** The court reasoned that it was "reasonable in the present context to measure the likelihood that any of the defendants supplied the product which allegedly injured plaintiff by the percentage which the DES sold by each of them for the purpose of preventing miscarriage bears to the entire production of the drug sold by all for that purpose." Id. at 937.

unduly harmful consequences they know cannot be traced to them, they may be fairly held responsible for the share of harm properly assigned to each. For this reason, variations of market share liability, sometimes under other names, were adopted by the high courts of several states, notably Washington,[28] Wisconsin,[29] Michigan,[30] New York,[31] Florida,[32] and Hawaii,[33] together with a handful of lower state and federal courts.[34] Each of these decisions altered the operational specifics of *Sindell* somewhat, and each except Hawaii applied the doctrine to DES.

But the market share liability theory confronted two enormous hurdles, one practical the other doctrinal. The practical objection, noted but belittled by the *Sindell* court,[35] is the enormous difficulty in ascertaining reasonably accurate market shares for individual manufacturers. Regardless of how one resolves the significant issue of whether to designate the "market" as the plaintiff's pharmacy (or pharmacies), neighborhood, town, city, county, state, nation, or the entire world, other difficulties in locating particularized distribution records from the various manufacturers and retail pharmacies decades after sale may be colossal, to say the least.[36] The doctrinal or policy objection to market share liability is that it simply does too much violence to the fundamental tort law element of factual causation—in particular, to the fundamental requirement that a plaintiff identify the specific product, manufactured by the specific defendant before the court, that probably caused the injuries for which recovery is sought.[37]

**28.** Martin v. Abbott Labs., 689 P.2d 368 (Wash. 1984) ("market share alternate liability").

**29.** Collins v. Eli Lilly Co., 342 N.W.2d 37 (Wis. 1984) ("risk contribution theory").

**30.** Abel v. Eli Lilly & Co., 343 N.W.2d 164 (Mich. 1984) ("alternative liability").

**31.** Hymowitz v. Eli Lilly & Co., 539 N.E.2d 1069 (N.Y. 1989).

**32.** Conley v. Boyle Drug Co., 570 So.2d 275 (Fla. 1990) (for negligence claims).

**33.** Smith v. Cutter Biological, Inc., 823 P.2d 717 (Haw. 1991) (for blood cases).

**34.** See Jackson v. Glidden Co., 647 N.E.2d 879, 883–84 (Ohio Ct. App. 1995) (lead paint); McCormack v. Abbott Labs., 617 F.Supp. 1521 (D. Mass. 1985) (DES); McElhaney v. Eli Lilly & Co., 564 F.Supp. 265 (D.S.D. 1983) (same).

**35.** The court observed that it was "not unmindful of the practical problems involved in defining the market and determining market share," noting that the "[d]efendants assert that there are no figures available to determine market share, that DES was provided for a number of uses other than to prevent miscarriage and it would be difficult to ascertain what proportion of the drug was used as a miscarriage preventative, and that the establishment of a time frame and area for market share would pose problems." 607 P.2d at 938 and n. 29.

**36.** See Fischer, Products Liability—An Analysis of Market Share Liability, 34 Vand. L. Rev. 1623 (1981).

**37.** See § 11.2, above. The Ohio Supreme Court's statement of this objection is typical: "The plaintiff must establish a causal connection between the defendant's actions and the plaintiff's injuries, which necessitates identification of the particular tortfeasor.... Under the market-share theory, the plaintiff is discharged from proving this important causal link. The defendant actually responsible for the plaintiff's injuries may not be before the court. Such a result collides with traditional tort notions of liability by virtue of responsibility, and imposes a judicially created form of industry-wide insurance upon those manufacturers subject to market-share liability. In the end, [this forces manufacturers to pay for injuries their product may not have caused, which is not the law of Ohio where 'manufacturers are not insurers of their products']." Sutowski v. Eli Lilly & Co., 696 N.E.2d 187, 190 (Ohio 1998). In Ferris v. Gatke Corp., 132 Cal.Rptr.2d 819, 828 (Ct. App. 2003), rejecting market share liability in an asbestos case, the court observed: "From *Sindell* onward courts confronting this unique group liability issue have underlined repeatedly the extraordinary departure from conventional tort law doctrine, with its Aristotelian conception of causation, such notions represent....

Largely because of these two obstacles, market share liability has been rejected by a large majority of courts.[38] A small number of decisions from market share states have allowed such claims outside of DES litigation,[39] but most courts have rejected efforts to extend it beyond DES to such contexts as lead paint,[40] asbestos,[41] breast implants,[42] guns,[43] blood,[44] tire rims,[45] and a miscellany of other types of products.[46]

### *Other Theories of Collective Liability*

In addition to market share liability, courts have fashioned a number of other theories of collective liability in an attempt to provide compensation to plaintiffs unable to identify the manufacturers of the specific products that caused their injuries, sometimes (as in the asbestos context) to fix responsibility on members of an industry who still are

[C]ourts should employ such group liability concepts with great caution and only after being satisfied that the circumstances invoked in support of their application are truly compelling."

**38.** See, e.g., Sutowski v. Eli Lilly & Co., 696 N.E.2d 187 (Ohio 1998); Smith v. Eli Lilly & Co., 560 N.E.2d 324 (Ill. 1990); Shackil v. Lederle Lab., 561 A.2d 511 (N.J. 1989) (DPT vaccines for children); Mulcahy v. Eli Lilly & Co., 386 N.W.2d 67 (Iowa 1986) (en banc); Zafft v. Eli Lilly & Co., 676 S.W.2d 241 (Mo. 1984) (en banc). See also Payton v. Abbott Labs., 437 N.E.2d 171 (Mass. 1982).

**39.** See, e.g., In re Methyl Tertiary Butyl Ether ("MTBE") Prod. Liab. Litig., 175 F.Supp.2d 593 (S.D.N.Y. 2001) (MTBE, a toxic additive to gasoline that contaminates groundwater); Jackson v. Glidden Co., 647 N.E.2d 879 (Ohio Ct. App. 1995) (lead paint); Richie v. Bridgestone/Firestone, Inc., 22 Cal.App.4th 335 (Ct. App. 1994) (asbestos in brake products); Ray v. Cutter Labs., 754 F.Supp. 193 (M.D. Fla. 1991) (blood products); Morris v. Parke, Davis & Co., 667 F.Supp. 1332 (C.D. Cal. 1987) (DPT vaccine).

**40.** The landmark case was Santiago v. Sherwin Williams Co., 3 F.3d 546 (1st Cir. 1993) (Mass. law). See also Lewis v. Lead Indus. Ass'n, 793 N.E.2d 869 (Ill. App. Ct. 2003); Brenner v. American Cyanamid Co., 699 N.Y.S.2d 848 (App. Div. 1999); Skipworth by Williams v. Lead Indus. Ass'n, 690 A.2d 169 (Pa. 1997); Jefferson v. Lead Indus. Ass'n, 106 F.3d 1245 (5th Cir. 1997) (La. law); City of Philadelphia v. Lead Indus. Ass'n, Inc., 994 F.2d 112 (3d Cir. 1993) (Pa. law). Compare Setliff v. E.I. Du Pont Nemours & Co., 38 Cal.Rptr.2d 763 (Ct. App. 1995) (paint, solvents, strippers, and glue products).

**41.** See, e.g., Ferris v. Gatke Corp., 132 Cal.Rptr.2d 819, 826 n.3 (Ct. App. 2003) (noting the "phalanx of judicial decisions from across the nation, overwhelmingly declining to apply a *Summers/Sindell*-based

burden-shifting instruction to asbestos-related personal injury tort litigation"); Black v. Abex Corp., 603 N.W.2d 182 (N.D. 1999); University Sys. of New Hampshire v. United States Gypsum Co., 756 F.Supp. 640 (D.N.H. 1991); Leng v. Celotex Corp., 554 N.E.2d 468, 470–71 (Ill. 1990); Gaulding v. Celotex Corp., 772 S.W.2d 66, 70–71 (Tex. 1989); Goldman v. Johns–Manville Sales Corp., 514 N.E.2d 691 (Ohio 1987); Case v. Fibreboard Corp., 743 P.2d 1062 (Okla. 1987); Celotex Corp. v. Copeland, 471 So.2d 533, 537–39 (Fla. 1985). See also Rutherford v. Owens–Illinois, Inc., 941 P.2d 1203 (Cal. 1997).

**42.** See, e.g., In re Dow Corning Corp., 250 B.R. 298, 363 (Bankr. E.D. Mich. 2000) ("no court has permitted a breast implant plaintiff to utilize the market-share theory to prove her claim"); In re New York State Silicone Breast Implant Litig., 631 N.Y.S.2d 491 (Super. Ct. 1995), aff'd, 650 N.Y.S.2d 558 (App. Div. 1996); Lee v. Baxter Health Care Corp., 898 F.2d 146 (4th Cir. 1990) (Md. law).

**43.** See, e.g., District of Columbia v. Beretta U.S.A. Corp., 2002 WL 31811717 (D.C. Super. 2002), rev'd in part on other grounds, 847 A.2d 1127 (D.C. 2004); Hamilton v. Beretta U.S.A. Corp., 750 N.E.2d 1055 (N.Y. 2001).

**44.** See, e.g., Spencer v. Baxter Int'l, Inc., 163 F.Supp.2d 74 (D. Mass. 2001).

**45.** See, e.g., Tirey v. Firestone Tire & Rubber Co., 513 N.E.2d 825 (Ohio Com. Pl. 1986); Cummins v. Firestone Tire & Rubber Co., 495 A.2d 963 (Pa. Super. Ct. 1985).

**46.** See, e.g., Bly v. Tri–Continental Indus., 663 A.2d 1232, 1244 (D.C. 1995) (benzene); York v. Lunkes, 545 N.E.2d 478 (Ill. App. Ct. 1989) (car battery that exploded); Kinnett v. Mass Gas & Elec. Supply Co., 716 F.Supp. 695 (D.N.H. 1989) (Me. law) (heat tape that allegedly caused fire); Bixler v. Avondale Mills, 405 N.W.2d 428 (Minn. Ct. App. 1987) (cotton flannelette).

solvent. Different courts refer to similar theories by different names, and the elements of each theory vary from jurisdiction to jurisdiction, but the contours of the theories are usually roughly similar.

**Alternative liability.** *Sindell* is an outgrowth of the theory that has become known as alternative liability, illustrated by *Summers v. Tice*,[47] which shifts the burden of proof on causation to two or more defendants when their tortious but independent actions cause harm to the plaintiff who cannot establish which particular defendant caused the harm. The *Restatement (Second) of Torts* adopts this principle: "Where the conduct of two or more actors is tortious, and it is proved that harm has been caused to the plaintiff by only one of them, but there is uncertainty as to which one has caused it, the burden is upon each such actor to prove that he has not caused the harm."[48] The *Third Restatement* similarly shifts the burden of proof to the defendants in this type of situation.[49]

A very few courts have applied some form of alternative liability to certain multiple-defendant products liability situations.[50] But the alternative liability theory presumes that there are only two or a small number of defendants who are all before the court,[51] and that the defendants are likely to know who among them caused the harm,[52] both of which conditions reduce the unfairness of shifting to the defendants the burden of establishing causation.[53] Because these conditions normally

**47.** 199 P.2d 1 (Cal. 1948).

**48.** Restatement (2d) Torts § 433(B)(3). Illustration 9, following cmt. *h*, presents the *Summers* quail hunting facts.

**49.** See Restatement (3d) Torts: Liability for Physical Harm § 28(b): "When the plaintiff sues all of two or more defendants whose tortious conduct exposed the plaintiff to a risk of harm and proves that the tortious conduct of one or more defendants caused the plaintiff's harm but cannot reasonably prove which of the defendants caused the harm, the burden of proof, including both production and persuasion, on factual causation is shifted to the defendants."

**50.** See, e.g., Abel v. Eli Lilly & Co., 343 N.W.2d 164 (Mich. 1984) (DES). See also Jackson v. Glidden Co., 647 N.E.2d 879, 883 (Ohio Ct. App. 1995); Poole v. Alpha Therapeutic Corp., 696 F.Supp. 351, 352 (N.D. Ill. 1988) (blood products).

**51.** Even if there are only two defendants, both of their products must have been defective, or the doctrine does not apply. In Garcia v. Joseph Vince Co., 148 Cal.Rptr. 843, 846–47 (Ct. App. 1978) ("Hamlet II"), a college student's eye was injured during a fencing match when his opponent's saber penetrated his mask because its tip was thin and sharp instead of round. The saber was thereafter placed back in the team bag with all the other sabers and was not produced at trial because it had either been lost or "mixed up

with the others in the shuffle." The coach had purchased the sabers from two manufacturers. Since there was no evidence pointing to either manufacturer in particular, plaintiff sued both under the alternative liability theory of *Summers v. Tice*. The plaintiff was nonsuited, and the judgements in favor of both defendants were affirmed. Because the evidence was evenly divided, the jury could only speculate as to which manufacturer had produced the offending saber, and *Summers v. Tice* did not apply to shift the burden of proof because only one of the defendants had acted tortiously toward the plaintiff.

**52.** Such that shifting the burden of proof onto the defendants collectively might "smoke out" the guilty party.

**53.** See, e.g., Snider v. Bob Thibodeau Ford, Inc., 202 N.W.2d 727 (Mich. Ct. App. 1972), where plaintiff was injured when the brakes on his delivery truck failed. Since plaintiff was unable to prove whether the defect had been caused by the manufacturer or the dealer, the trial court dismissed his action against the manufacturer. *Held*, reversed: "True, the burden of proving which of two possible wrongdoers is responsible is generally assigned to the plaintiff. The courts have, however, shown a willingness to consider special circumstances when allocating the burden of proof. This accords with the general view that the placing of that burden is 'merely a question of policy

are not present in litigation on DES and many other products, the
alternative liability theory was rejected by the California Supreme Court
in *Sindell*,[54] as it has been rejected by many other courts in many
contexts in products liability litigation.[55]

**Enterprise liability.** "Enterprise liability," also referred to as
"industry-wide liability," was the first collective theory of liability devised for products liability litigation, initially proposed by Judge Jack B.
Weinstein in *Hall v. E.I. Du Pont De Nemours & Co.*[56] in 1972. *Hall* and
another case involved the liability of the blasting cap industry arising
out of injuries to eighteen children across the nation who could not
identify the manufacturers of the blasting caps that injured them because the caps blew themselves to smithereens in each such incident.
The defendants in *Hall* were the six blasting cap manufacturers (the
entire American industry) and their trade association. Each manufacturer had acted independently, but each adhered to industry-wide safety
standards, and they all delegated to their trade association certain safety
responsibilities, including labeling standards and investigation. Liability
was premised on the defendants' failure to place warnings on individual
caps and to design the caps to make them more difficult for children to
detonate. On motions to dismiss, Judge Weinstein ruled that each
member of the industry could be held jointly liable only if the plaintiffs
established that the defendants (1) were all aware of the risks, and (2)
jointly controlled those risks. Recognizing that enterprise liability could
not fairly be applied to industries that are large and decentralized, Judge
Weinstein limited its application to small industries of five to ten
producers.[57] The enterprise liability theory has not caught on, and other
courts (including the California court in *Sindell*)[58] have uniformly refused to apply this not illogical but clearly radical departure from the
basic causal requirement of product identification.[59]

and fairness' based on experience in the
different situations." In this case, "because
of the technical problems involved in a
brake system, the superior knowledge and
expertise of a manufacturer like Ford, and
the close relationship between the manufacturer and retailer Thibodeau, we conclude
that the burden of negating individual responsibility for the brake failure should be
placed on the defendants." Id. at 732–33.

**54.** See Sindell v. Abbott Labs., 607
P.2d 924, 931 (Cal. 1980).

**55.** See, e.g., Doe v. Baxter Healthcare
Corp., 380 F.3d 399 (8th Cir. 2004) (Iowa
law) (blood products); Doe v. Baxter Healthcare Corp., 178 F.Supp.2d 1003, 1014 (S.D.
Iowa 2001), aff'd, 380 F.3d 399 (8th Cir.
2004) (same); Spencer v. Baxter Int'l, Inc.,
163 F.Supp.2d 74, 79 (D. Mass. 2001)
(same); Burns v. Haines Equip., 726
N.Y.S.2d 516, 519–20 (App. Div. 2001)
(loading machine); Rutherford v. Owens–
Illinois, Inc., 941 P.2d 1203, 1220–21 (Cal.
1997) (asbestos); Setliff v. E.I. Du Pont de
Nemours & Co., 38 Cal.Rptr.2d 763, 767
(Ct. App. 1995) (chemicals, solvents, glues,
strippers, and paints); City of Philadelphia

v. Lead Indus. Ass'n, 994 F.2d 112, 127–28
(3d Cir. 1993) (Pa. law) (lead paint pig-
ments); Gaulding v. Celotex Corp., 772
S.W.2d 66, 69 (Tex. 1989) (asbestos); Hy-
mowitz v. Eli Lilly & Co., 539 N.E.2d 1069,
1074 (N.Y. 1989) (DES); Senn v. Merrell–
Dow Pharm., Inc., 751 P.2d 215 (Or. 1988)
(DPT); Bixler v. Avondale Mills, 405
N.W.2d 428, 430–32 (Minn. Ct. App. 1987)
(flannelette in nightshirt); Mulcahy v. Eli
Lilly & Co., 386 N.W.2d 67 (Iowa 1986)
(DES).

**56.** 345 F.Supp. 353 (E.D.N.Y. 1972).

**57.** Id. at 378.

**58.** Sindell v. Abbott Labs., 607 P.2d
924, 935 (Cal. 1980).

**59.** See, e.g., Lewis v. Lead Indus. Ass'n,
793 N.E.2d 869, 874–75 (Ill. App. Ct. 2003)
(lead paint); In re Methyl Tertiary Butyl
Ether ("MTBE") Prods. Liab. Litig., 175
F.Supp.2d 593, 622 (S.D.N.Y. 2001) (gasoline additive that polluted ground water)
("To invoke the theory of enterprise liability, plaintiffs must allege that (1) the injury-
causing product was manufactured by one

**Concert of action.** The "concert of action" theory of liability results in collective liability when, under a common plan or scheme, a party assists, participates with, or actively encourages one or more wrongdoers who tortiously harm the plaintiff.[60] The classic concert of action cases involved drag races, where one car hit the plaintiff and the driver of the other car was also held liable for tortiously helping create the risk that harmed the plaintiff.[61] Thus, concert of action turns on an actor's participation in and furtherance of group activity that the actor knows to be tortious toward the plaintiff, a kind of "aiding and abetting" of unlawful conduct by a wrongdoer who actively causes the plaintiff's harm.[62] The *Second Restatement* expresses the concert of action principle in § 876, a section on which courts and commentators frequently rely.[63]

A couple of courts, on summary judgment motions in cases where plaintiffs were unable to identify the makers of their drugs, have allowed concert of action claims, holding that "conscious parallelism" by the manufacturers to suppress warnings of side effects,[64] or to promote the sale without warnings of a drug they knew to be ineffective and danger-

---

of a small number of defendants in an industry; (2) the defendants had joint knowledge of the risks inherent in the product and possessed a joint capacity to reduce those risks; and (3) each of them failed to take steps to reduce the risk but, rather, delegated this responsibility to a trade association."); Doe v. Cutter Biological, Div. of Miles, Inc., 852 F.Supp. 909, 918 (D. Idaho 1994) (blood products); City of Philadelphia v. Lead Indus. Ass'n, 994 F.2d 112 (3d Cir. 1993) (Pa. law) (lead paint pigments); Lee v. Baxter Healthcare Corp., 721 F.Supp. 89, 94 (D. Md. 1989) (breast implants); Case v. Fibreboard Corp., 743 P.2d 1062 (Okla. 1987) (asbestos); Martin v. Abbott Labs., 689 P.2d 368, 380 (Wash. 1984) (DES); Collins v. Eli Lilly Co., 342 N.W.2d 37, 47 (Wis. 1984) (DES); Ryan v. Eli Lilly & Co., 514 F.Supp. 1004, 1017 (D.S.C. 1981) (S.C. and N.C. law) (DES) (observing that the "expansive notion of vicarious liability represented by the enterprise concept which would render every manufacturer an insurer not only of the safety of its own products, but of all generically similar products made by others is repugnant to the most basic tenets of tort law").

**60.** "The concerted action theory of liability rests upon the principle that 'those who, in pursuance of a common plan or design to commit a tortious act, actively take part in it, or further it by cooperation or request, or who lend aid or encouragement to the wrongdoer, or ratify and adopt his acts done for their benefit, are equally liable with him. Express agreement is not necessary, and all that is required is that there be a tacit understanding.' W. Prosser, Handbook of the Law of Torts, § 46 at 292 (4th ed. 1970)." Collins v. Eli Lilly Co., 342 N.W.2d 37, 46 (Wis. 1984) (rejecting concert of action theory of liability in DES case).

**61.** See, e.g., Chavers v. Gatke Corp., 132 Cal.Rptr.2d 198, 205 (Ct. App. 2003) (citing drag racing cases); Bierczynski v. Rogers, 239 A.2d 218 (Del. 1968); Ogle v. Avina, 146 N.W.2d 422 (Wis. 1966).

**62.** See, e.g., Shackil v. Lederle Labs., 561 A.2d 511, 515 (N.J. 1989), citing Ryan v. Eli Lilly & Co., 514 F.Supp. 1004, 1015 (D.S.C. 1981). Concert of action thus should be contrasted to alternative liability which presupposes the independence of the actors.

**63.** In the Restatement (2d) Torts chapter on "Contributing Tortfeasors," the general principle of joint and several liability for jointly tortious conduct is expressed in § 875: "Each of two or more persons whose tortious conduct is a legal cause of a single and indivisible harm to the injured party is subject to liability to the injured party for the entire harm." Section § 876, "Persons Acting in Concert," presents the strongest case for joint liability: "For harm resulting to a third person from the tortious conduct of another, one is subject to liability if he

"(a) does a tortious act in concert with the other or pursuant to a common design with him, or

"(b) knows that the other's conduct constitutes a breach of duty and gives substantial assistance or encouragement to the other so to conduct himself, or

"(c) gives substantial assistance to the other in accomplishing a tortious result and his own conduct, separately considered, constitutes a breach of duty to the third person."

**64.** See Dawson v. Bristol Labs., 658 F.Supp. 1036 (W.D. Ky. 1987) (tetracyclines administered to infants eventually stained their primary teeth).

ous,[65] might render them subject to liability to plaintiffs injured by the drugs. And the court in at least one cigarette case allowed the plaintiff to proceed on such a claim.[66] But the great majority of decisions hold to the contrary,[67] agreeing with the *Sindell* court's conclusion that applying the concert of action theory to industry-wide sharing of information and techniques in most situations stretches this joint-liability theory beyond its proper scope "and would render virtually any manufacturer liable for the defective products of an entire industry, even if it could be demonstrated that the product which caused the injury was not made by the defendant."[68]

**Civil conspiracy.** A "civil conspiracy" is a combination of two or more persons for the purpose of accomplishing by concerted action an unlawful purpose or a lawful purpose by unlawful means.[69] A civil conspiracy is not a tort in and of itself, and a plaintiff alleging civil conspiracy must plead and prove an underlying tort (often fraud) or other unlawful act on which the conspiracy claim may rest.[70] Like concert of action, to which it is closely related,[71] a civil conspiracy finding provides a basis for extending liability beyond an active tortfeasor to others who worked together to effectuate the unlawful result,[72] rendering each member of the conspiracy jointly liable for all consequences ensuing from the wrong.[73] Moreover, a civil conspiracy claim may avoid preemption in tobacco litigation.[74]

**65.** See Abel v. Eli Lilly & Co., 343 N.W.2d 164 (Mich. 1984) (DES).

**66.** See Sackman v. Liggett Group, Inc., 965 F.Supp. 391, 396 (E.D.N.Y. 1997) (defendant conspired to repress health risks).

**67.** See, e.g., Chavers v. Gatke Corp., 132 Cal.Rptr.2d 198, 205 (Ct. App. 2003) (asbestos brake products); Brenner v. American Cyanamid Co., 732 N.Y.S.2d 799, 801 (App. Div. 2001) (lead pigment); Christian v. Minnesota Mining & Mfg. Co., 126 F.Supp.2d 951 (D. Md. 2001) (breast implants); Anderson v. Fortune Brands, Inc., 723 N.Y.S.2d 304, 306 (Sup. Ct. 2000) (tobacco); Jodway v. Kennametal, Inc., 525 N.W.2d 883, 890–91 (Mich. Ct. App. 1994) (cobalt dust); Rastelli v. Goodyear Tire & Rub. Co., 591 N.E.2d 222, 225 (N.Y. 1992) (multipiece rim); Smith v. Cutter Biological, Inc., 823 P.2d 717, 726 (Haw. 1991) (blood products); Hymowitz v. Eli Lilly & Co., 539 N.E.2d 1069, 1074–75 (N.Y. 1989) (DES) (without an express or tacit agreement, substantial parallel conduct in developing and marketing product does not suffice); Shackil v. Lederle Labs., 561 A.2d 511, 515–16 (N.J. 1989) (DPT vaccine); Sheffield v. Eli Lilly & Co., 192 Cal.Rptr. 870, 887–88 (Ct. App. 1983) (Salk polio vaccine); Collins v. Eli Lilly Co., 342 N.W.2d 37, 46 (Wis. 1984) (DES).

**68.** *Sindell,* 607 P.2d at 933 (Cal. 1980).

**69.** See, e.g., Lewis v. Lead Indus. Ass'n, 793 N.E.2d 869, 878 (Ill. Ct. App. 2003); Wright v. Brooke Group Ltd., 652 N.W.2d 159, 172–74 (Iowa 2002); Adcock v. Brakegate, Ltd., 645 N.E.2d 888, 894 (Ill. 1994).

**70.** See, e.g., Tuttle v. Lorillard Tobacco Co., 377 F.3d 917, 926 (8th Cir. 2004) (Minn. law) (because fraud claim insufficient for want of proof of reliance, "the civil conspiracy claim, which depends on a viable underlying tort, must fail as well"); Wright v. Brooke Group Ltd., 652 N.W.2d 159, 172 (Iowa 2002); Brown v. Philip Morris Inc., 228 F.Supp.2d 506, 517 (D.N.J. 2002) ("[c]ivil conspiracy is not an independent cause of action, and conspiracy liability depends on the presence of an underlying finding of tort liability").

**71.** Courts often look to § 876 of the Second Restatement as the basis for civil conspiracy claims. See, e.g., Wright v. Brooke Group Ltd., 652 N.W.2d 159, 172–74 (Iowa 2002).

**72.** See, e.g., Wright v. Brooke Group Ltd., 652 N.W.2d 159, 172 (Iowa 2002) ("conspiracy is merely an avenue for imposing vicarious liability on a party for the wrongful conduct or another with whom the party has acted in concert"); Sackman v. Liggett Group, Inc., 965 F. Supp. 391, 394–95 (E.D.N.Y. 1997) ("A claim for civil conspiracy 'is merely the string whereby the plaintiff seeks to tie together those who, acting in concert, may be held responsible in damages for an overt act or acts.'").

**73.** See, e.g., Chavers v. Gatke Corp., 132 Cal.Rptr.2d 198, 201 (Ct. App. 2003) ("It is the essence of common law conspiracy doctrine that the coconspirators are liable in the same way and to the same extent as the principal who actually commits the harmful or outlawed act.").

**74.** See, e.g., Waterhouse v. R.J. Reynolds Tobacco Co., 270 F.Supp.2d 678, 665–

While a defendant's *participation* in an unlawful conspiracy must be intentional,[75] while the underlying wrong *may* be intentional (such as fraud),[76] and while several jurisdictions *require* that the underlying tort or other wrong be intentional,[77] the better view is that the underlying wrong may simply be the sale of a product known to be defective, a tortious act (or breach of warranty) that may be negligent or strict.[78] Although civil conspiracy claims occasionally survive motions to dismiss and for summary judgment,[79] such claims routinely are found wanting in products liability litigation.[80]

A final note is necessary on a company's participation in a trade association.[81] Such participation alone does not subject the member to conspiracy liability for damages from defective products made and sold by other members of the association. First, civil conspiracy requires a showing that the defendant's *purpose* of participating in a group activity was to do something unlawful, whereas the educational, developmental, promotional, and lobbying activities in which trade associations normally engage can hardly be characterized as violative of law. Second, participation in such activities may be constitutionally protected under the

---

866 (D. Md. 2003) (conspiracy to commit fraudulent misrepresentation); Johnson v. Brown & Williamson Tobacco Corp., 122 F.Supp.2d 194 (D. Mass. 2000) (same); Greene v. Brown & Williamson Tobacco Corp., 72 F.Supp.2d 882, 889–90 (W.D. Tenn. 1999).

**75.** "There is no such thing as accidental, inadvertent or negligent participation in a conspiracy." Adcock v. Brakegate, Ltd., 645 N.E.2d 888, 894 (Ill. 1995).

**76.** See, e.g., Waterhouse v. R.J. Reynolds Tobacco Co., 270 F.Supp.2d 678, 685–686 (D. Md. 2003) (fraudulent misrepresentation); Johnson v. Brown & Williamson Tobacco Corp., 122 F.Supp.2d 194 (D. Mass. 2000) (same).

**77.** See, e.g., Flanders v. Garlock, Inc., 2003 WL 22697241, at *3 (S.D. Ga. 2003) (civil conspiracy claim in Georgia must be based on "underlying intentional tortious conduct"); Altman v. Fortune Brands, Inc., 701 N.Y.S.2d 615 (App. Div. 2000); Sonnenreich v. Philip Morris Inc., 929 F.Supp. 416, 419 (S.D. Fla. 1996). These decisions sometimes point to the apparent illogic of conspiring to do a negligent act. While facially appealing, this argument ignores the fact that a defendant may unlawfully conspire to market a product it knows to be defective although that knowledge is unnecessary to the underlying tort of negligence or strict products liability in tort, both of which are surely unlawful acts for purposes of conspiracy. See Wright v. Brooke Group Ltd., 652 N.W.2d 159, 172–73 (Iowa 2002).

**78.** See, e.g., Wright v. Brooke Group Ltd., 652 N.W.2d 159, 172–73 (Iowa 2002); In re Methyl Butyl Ether Prods. Liab. Litig., 175 F.Supp.2d 593, 633–34 (S.D.N.Y. 2001) (Cal., Fla., Ill., and N.Y. law); Adcock v. Brakegate, Ltd., 645 N.E.2d 888, 894–95 (Ill. 1995).

**79.** See, e.g., Lewis v. Lead Ind. Ass'n, Inc., 793 N.E.2d 869 (Ill. App. Ct. 2003) (reinstating civil conspiracy claim; lead paint); Hearn v. R.J. Reynolds Tobacco Co., 279 F.Supp.2d 1096, 1117 (D. Ariz. 2003) (tobacco; denying motion to dismiss); Waterhouse v. R.J. Reynolds Tobacco Co., 270 F.Supp.2d 678, 685–686 (D. Md. 2003) (same).

**80.** See, e.g., Doe v. Baxter Healthcare Corp., 380 F.3d 399 (8th Cir. 2004) (Iowa law) (blood products); Tuttle v. Lorillard Tobacco Co., 377 F.3d 917, 926 (8th Cir. 2004) (Minn. law) (smokeless tobacco); Chavers v. Gatke Corp., 132 Cal.Rptr.2d 198, 201–03 (Ct. App. 2003) (asbestos products); Viguers v. Philip Morris USA, Inc., 837 A.2d 534 (Pa. Sup. Ct. 2003) (tobacco); Brown v. Philip Morris Inc., 228 F.Supp.2d 506 (D.N.J. 2002) (same); Estate of White ex rel. White v. R.J. Reynolds Tobacco Co., 109 F.Supp.2d 424 (D. Md. 2000) (same; no basis for fraudulent concealment claim on which conspiracy claim rested); McClure v. Owens Corning Fiberglas Corp., 720 N.E.2d 242 (Ill. 1999) (asbestos); In re Orthopedic Bone Screw Prods. Liab. Litig., 193 F.3d 781 (3d Cir. 1999) (Pa. law) (bone screws).

**81.** On the liability of trade associations and the First Amendment, see § 15.7, below.

First Amendment, particularly if they involve lobbying for governmental standards.[82] But the First Amendment is not a teflon defense in every case of civil conspiracy, for it provides no protection to manufacturers to conspire to violate the law.[83]

## § 11.4   WARNING CASES—SPECIAL CAUSATION ISSUES

### The Causal Requirement in Warning Cases

As with other types of products liability claims, factual causation is a necessary element of a warning defect claim.[1] No matter how dangerous a defective warning may make a product, the plaintiff must prove that the absence of that safety information caused the plaintiff's injury. In warning cases, like most others, the plaintiff ordinarily must prove causation by the but-for test—that the accident probably would not have occurred but for the absence of adequate warnings, that it probably would have been averted had adequate warnings been provided. If the provision of an adequate warning would have made no difference, if the plaintiff probably would have been injured anyway, then a warning claim will fail on causation grounds.

Sometimes the causal connection between a warning or instruction defect and the plaintiff's harm is clear. If given proper information about serious hazards under their control, people naturally seek to avoid those dangers. It thus is likely that the user of a propane heater, if warned that it might cause asphyxiation if used inside a tent, would use some other means to warm the tent;[2] that a user of a telescope, if instructed

---

**82.** See, e.g., Chavers v. Gatke Corp., 132 Cal.Rptr.2d 198, 206–07 (Ct. App. 2003) (requiring asbestos manufacturer to stand trial for civil conspiracy or concert of action claims without proof of unlawful intent might chill defendant's first amendment freedom of association to contribute to, attend the meetings of, and otherwise associate with trade groups engaging in public advocacy and debate); Hamilton v. Accutek, 935 F.Supp. 1307, 1321 (E.D.N.Y. 1996) (core principle of *Noerr-Pennington* doctrine is that lobbying before federal or state authorities cannot alone support liability); In re Asbestos Sch. Litig., 46 F.3d 1284, 1294 (3d Cir. 1994) (Pa. law) (civil conspiracy and concert of action claims infringed First Amendment freedoms to participate in trade group which engaged in public advocacy by chilling exercise of freedom of association and debate).

**83.** See, e.g., Lewis v. Lead Ind. Ass'n, Inc., 793 N.E.2d 869 (Ill. App. Ct. 2003) (lead paint; reinstating plaintiffs' civil conspiracy claim against defendants); Rogers v. R.J. Reynolds Tobacco Co., 761 S.W.2d 788 (Tex. App. 1988).

### § 11.4

**1.** See, e.g., In re Norplant Contraceptive Prod. Liab. Litig., 215 F. Supp. 2d 795, 830 (E.D. Tex. 2002) ("Causation is a fundamental element of Plaintiffs' failure to

warn claims, as well as any other tort claim."); Estate of White ex rel. White v. R.J. Reynolds Tobacco Co. 109 F.Supp.2d 424, 435 (D. Md. 2000) ("An essential element of plaintiffs' failure-to-warn claims is causation–plaintiffs must show that if an adequate warning had been given (prior to June 1969), Mr. White would have heeded it, and his injury (diagnosed in 1995) would have been avoided.... The evidence shows precisely what Mr. White would have done had he been warned that smoking was dangerous prior to June 1969 [the inception of federally-mandated warnings]: he would have kept on smoking."); Coffman v. Keene Corp., 628 A.2d 710, 716 (N.J. 1993) ("When the alleged defect is the failure to provide warnings, a plaintiff is required to prove that the absence of a warning was a proximate cause of his harm."); Bloxom v. Bloxom, 512 So.2d 839, 850 (La. 1987) ("An essential element of the plaintiff's cause of action for failure to adequately warn of a product's danger is that there be some reasonable connection between the omission of the manufacturer and the damage which the plaintiff has suffered.").

**2.** See Benjamin v. Wal–Mart Stores, Inc., 61 P.3d 257 (Or. 2002).

on how properly to install a sun filter, would install it with utmost care;[3] and that the user of a spermicide contraceptive, if warned that it might cause birth defects if conception did occur, would use a different form of contraceptive.[4] In none of these instances is it certain that proper warnings and instructions would have averted harm, but in all of them it is quite probable, which satisfies the but-for test.

Sometimes causation is plainly absent from a warnings claim. Not infrequently, even the most complete information on product hazards and how to avoid them would not alter a user's actions or avert an accident. Many cases where no causal link exists involve claims that a manufacturer should have warned about a risk of which the plaintiff already was aware. If a user already knows about a hidden danger, warning the user further will almost certainly do no good, for such a user is unlikely to change his or her behavior from receiving information he or she already possesses.[5] A manufacturer still has a *duty* to warn of a material hidden risk of which a particular user happens to be aware,[6] but the absence of causation will undermine a warnings claim by such a user. Thus, a worker who already knows the danger of unjamming a machine without cutting off its power, cannot prove that affixing that same warning to the machine would have caused him to turn it off;[7] nor can a mother, who puts her young child in the front seat despite warnings to seat young children in the rear because the front seat airbag could kill them, show that further warnings of that very risk would have caused her to place her child in the back.[8]

Causation is also clearly missing in other contexts. A driver of a car with a high center of gravity, even if warned that it might roll over if the steering wheel were sharply turned, will probably instinctively turn the wheel sharply to avoid a high-speed collision with a concrete rail, despite the driver's awareness of the risk of rolling over.[9] It is similarly likely that a user of ski bindings, even if warned that they might not release in

---

**3.** See Midgley v. S.S. Kresge Co., 127 Cal.Rptr. 217 (Ct. App. 1976).

**4.** See Wells v. Ortho Pharm. Corp., 788 F.2d 741 (11th Cir. 1986) (Ga law).

**5.** Consider Vallillo v. Muskin Corp., 514 A.2d 528, 530 (N.J. Super. Ct. 1986) ("if the user of a product knows at the moment of use the very danger of which the warning would have apprised him, but chooses to disregard that conscious knowledge, then the presence or absence of the warning is irrelevant," yet if "the danger had been even momentarily forgotten by the user and there is some reasonable possibility that the warning would have triggered his recollection of the danger and thus changed his conduct, then the absence of a warning is a proper ingredient in a proximate cause analysis").

**6.** Because duty arises categorically, it applies to all consumers. See Restatement (3d) Torts: Liability for Physical Harm §§ 6 and 7.

**7.** See Clark v. LR Sys., 219 F.Supp.2d 323 (E.D.N.Y. 2002); Zimmermann v. Bak-

er–Perkins, Inc., 707 F.Supp. 778, 781 (E.D. Pa. 1989).

**8.** DaimlerChrysler Corp. v. Hillhouse, ___ S.W.3d ___, 2004 WL 1195687 (Tex. App. 2004). See also Chapman ex rel. Estate of Chapman v. Bernard's Inc., 167 F.Supp.2d 406, 412 (D. Mass. 2001) (more warnings not to sit too close to steering wheel probably would have made no difference, since plaintiff ignored the one).

**9.** See Greiner v. Volkswagenwerk Ak., 429 F.Supp. 495 (E.D. Pa. 1977) ("It is simply not within the bounds of human reason to suppose that, had there been a warning, Nickel would have recalled it, considered it and then intentionally crashed head-on into a concrete rail."). See also Roy v. Volkswagenwerk Ak., 600 F.Supp. 653 (C.D. Cal. 1985) (VW van rolled over when driver swerved to avoid hitting dog); Conti v. Ford Motor Co., 743 F.2d 195, 196 (3d Cir. 1984) (Pa. law) (driver knew not to start car in gear, without depressing clutch, while his wife was entering the car). Compare Staymates v. ITT Holub Indus., 527

every situation, might use them anyway, and break a leg;[10] that a driver who falls asleep at the wheel, even if warned by a flashing arrow on a malfunctioning traffic sign to go one way, might crash into the sign;[11] and that a doctor who fails to read a drug manufacturer's warnings about the side-effects of an antidepressant, even if told that it posed a risk of suicide, might still prescribe it.[12] Occasionally, the plaintiff,[13] or the plaintiff's doctor,[14] will simply admit that knowing the information that an adequate warning would have provided would not have altered his or her behavior. Sometimes it thus is very clear that warning information would have made no difference.[15] In each such case, the plaintiff has failed to prove but-for causation—that adequate warnings or instructions probably would have averted the harm. Put conversely, the absence of adequate safety information in each such case probably did not cause the plaintiff's harm. Without causation, a warnings claim will fail.

### Special Causal Problems in Warnings Claims

Warning cases present certain *special* causation problems.[16] Unlike the causal examples just provided, where causation appears quite clearly present or quite clearly absent, the causal connection between a warning defect and the plaintiff's injury is usually quite uncertain. This differs from manufacturing and design defect claims, where the factual causation issue typically is clear. The reason for this difference, which explains why figuring causation in warnings cases usually is problematic, lies in the wide gulf between Newtonian physics and Freudian psychology. In

A.2d 140 (Pa. Super. Ct. 1987) (warning could not have prevented "instinctive, knee-jerk reaction").

**10.** See Salk v. Alpine Ski Shop, Inc., 342 A.2d 622, 626 (R.I. 1975) ("[P]laintiff did not allege that had he been warned of the inevitable dangers of skiing, he would not have skied; nor did he allege that he would have purchased other bindings and that other bindings would have prevented his injury. Quite to the contrary, . . . plaintiff has continued to ski.").

**11.** See Lear Siegler, Inc. v. Perez, 819 S.W.2d 470 (Tex. 1991).

**12.** See Motus v. Pfizer, Inc., 358 F.3d 659 (9th Cir. 2004) (Cal. law).

**13.** See, e.g., Neilson v. The Corp. of The Presiding Bishop, 69 P.3d 875 (Wash. Ct. App. 2003) (plaintiff admitted that he still would have tried double somersault on trampoline even if he had read an adequate warning about its dangers).

**14.** See, e.g., Miller v. Pfizer, Inc., 196 F.Supp.2d 1095, 1127–28 (D. Kan. 2002) (doctor testified that different warning would not have affected patient's treatment), aff'd, 356 F.3d 1326 (10th Cir. 2004); Guzman v. Synthes, 20 S.W.3d 717, 718 (Tex. App. 1999) (same).

**15.** See, e.g., Jones v. Hittle Service, Inc., 549 P.2d 1383 (Kan. 1976), where

plaintiffs' decedents were killed in an explosion of gas sold by the defendants. Plaintiffs contended that the defendants had been negligent in adding only one pound of odorant to 10,000 gallons of gas, rather than the nine pounds claimed to be necessary to make the gas reasonably safe. The gas, however, had seeped through the soil prior to passing into the basement where it exploded, and much of the odorizing agent had been leached out as a result. Plaintiffs' expert admitted that even at the nine pound level there would not have been enough odor left in the gas after it had passed through the soil to have been smelled by the victims. *Held*, the inadequate odorization was not a cause of the explosion.

**16.** See, e.g., Geistfeld, Inadequate Product Warnings and Causation, 30 U. Mich. J. L. Reform 309 (1997); Fischer, Causation in Fact in Product Liability Failure to Warn Cases, 17 J. Prod. & Toxics Liab. 271 (1995); Latin, "Good" Warnings, Bad Products, and Cognitive Limitations, 41 UCLA L. Rev. 1193, 1286 n.413 (1994); Henderson and Twerski, Doctrinal Collapse in Products Liability: The Empty Shell of Failure to Warn, 65 N.Y.U. L. Rev. 265 (1990).

Newtonian physics, the principles of cause and effect often are clear. These are the principles used to prove causation in design and manufacturing defect cases. In most such cases, the defect itself often contains a plain causal linkage to the plaintiff's injury: if a machine is defectively designed because its pinch points are unguarded, then guarding the pinch points will probably keep out human limbs; if a tire is defectively designed or manufactured, causing its tread to fly off at highway speeds, then the tread probably will stay affixed to the tire carcass, avoiding an accident, if the design and manufacturing processes both are proper. Experts may dispute whether a machine is defective without a guard, and whether a tread separation was due to a defect or poor maintenance, but once a design or manufacturing defect is established, its causal connection to the plaintiff's injury usually is plain. Causation, in such cases, is proven (and controverted) by hard science.

Causation in a warnings case is an entirely different kettle of fish. Proving that an adequate warning would have prevented the plaintiff's harm depends on the vagaries of human psychology, requiring speculation on whether the user would have read and followed the warning had it in fact been provided.[17] While proving causation in design and manufacturing cases similarly rests on a but-for hypothetical (whether elimination of the defect would have prevented the plaintiff's harm), the warnings hypothetical turns on human responses to information, not hard science. It is one thing to hypothesize that a guard of a certain configuration would have prevented a hand from entering a machine; it is quite another to posit that a teenager, who ignores extensive warnings and instructions on how to use a trampoline, will heed additional, more specific warnings of the dangers;[18] that an adult, warned that a baby left unstrapped in a high chair might get strangled in attempting to slide out, would always remember to strap the child in;[19] or that a mother, warned of a T-shirt's flammability, would keep it from her child.[20]

The point is not that adequate warnings in such cases would have made no difference, only that determining whether they would have averted harm rests on an uncomfortably slender reed. The most typical

**17.** The court well described the causal conundrum in warnings claims in General Motors Corp. v. Saenz, 873 S.W.2d 353, 357 (Tex. 1993) (emphasis omitted): "Proving causation in a failure-to-warn case has peculiar difficulties. Proof that a collision between two cars would not have happened had defendant swerved or braked or driven within the speed limit is mostly a matter of physics. Proof that an accident would not have occurred if defendant had provided adequate warnings concerning the use of a product is more psychology and does not admit of the same degree of certainty. A plaintiff must show that adequate warnings would have made a difference in the outcome, that is, that they would have been followed. In the best case a plaintiff can offer evidence of his habitual, careful adherence to all warnings and instructions. In many cases, however, plaintiff's evidence may be little more than the self-serving assertion that whatever his usual practice may have been, in the circumstances critical to his claim for damages he would have been mindful of an adequate warning had it been given. In the worst case, where the user of the product is deceased, proof of what the decedent would or would not have done may be virtually impossible."

**18.** See Anderson v. Weslo, Inc., 906 P.2d 336, 341 (Wash. Ct. App. 1995) ("because Anderson was aware of the risks of injury, yet paid so little attention to the warnings that were given, it is unlikely that he would have changed his behavior in response to even more detailed warnings").

**19.** See McConnell v. Cosco, Inc., 238 F.Supp.2d 970 (S.D. Ohio 2003).

**20.** Shouey ex rel. Litz v. Duck Head Apparel Co., 49 F.Supp.2d 413 (M.D. Pa. 1999).

form of evidence used to prove causation in a warnings case is the user's own testimony that he or she would have read and heeded an adequate warning or instruction if one had been provided. This forces the user in such cases into an awkward position of having to provide self-serving testimony on a hypothetical situation that requires the user to swear, as convincingly as possible, that a good warning or instruction would have caused him to change his behavior in some manner that would have averted injury. For the legal system to require plaintiffs to provide such highly speculative, self-serving testimony provides the most shallow basis for a finding of causation.

### The "Heeding Presumption"

Beginning in the early 1970s, courts began adopting a "heeding presumption" to help plaintiffs surmount the inherent difficulties, just described, in proving causation in warnings cases.[21] This is a presumption that a plaintiff would have read and heeded adequate warnings and instructions, had they been provided.[22] A heeding presumption relieves a plaintiff of the awkwardness of having to testify affirmatively on this issue, and it provides a basis for a finding of causation where the plaintiff is killed in the accident or otherwise dies before he or she is able to provide testimony in the case.[23] The presumption is rebuttable, so that a defendant may establish that a plaintiff most likely would not have read or heeded an adequate warning in the particular circumstances of the case. For example, a manufacturer may rebut the presumption by showing that "the user was blind, illiterate, intoxicated, . . . irresponsible or lax in judgment"[24] or for some other reason[25] probably would have ignored the warning.[26] Courts in almost half the states have now adopted

---

**21.** See Technical Chem. Co. v. Jacobs, 480 S.W.2d 602, 606 (Tex. 1972) (dictum).

**22.** See, e.g., Daniel, Guide to Defeating the Heeding Presumption in Failure-to-Warn Cases, 70 Def. Couns. J. 250 (2003); Henke, The Heeding Presumption in Failure to Warn Cases: Opening Pandora's Box?, 30 Seton Hall L. Rev. 174 (1999); Geistfeld, Inadequate Product Warnings and Causation, 30 U. Mich. J. L. Reform 309 (1997); Note, The Heeding Presumption and its Application: Distinguishing No Warning from Inadequate Warning, 37 Loy. L.A. L. Rev. 461 (2003); Annot., 38 A.L.R.5th 683 (heeding presumption).

**23.** See id. See, e.g., Tuttle v. Lorillard Tobacco Co., 377 F.3d 917, 925 (8th Cir. 2004) (Minn. law) (baseball player died of oral cancer; recognizing that "application of the heeding presumption would be particularly beneficial in this case, where Tuttle died before testifying under oath that he would have read and heeded warnings had they been provided by the smokeless tobacco manufacturers," but ruling that presumption did not apply).

**24.** Id. But see Sharpe v. Bestop, Inc., 730 A.2d 285, 285–87 (N.J. 1999) (holding that "only evidence of a habit related to the

specific situation of a seat-belt warning, not a character trait, may be offered to rebut the heeding presumption" and "hesitat[ing] to endorse [the Texas court's formulations of] rebuttal evidence that focuses on the product user as one who may be 'illiterate, . . . irresponsible or lax in judgment,' " noting that the latter two descriptions are character traits that may be inadmissible).

**25.** Often, that the plaintiff admits that he or she did not read the label, instruction booklet, or other source of safety information. See, e.g., Mohney v. U.S. Hockey, Inc., 300 F.Supp.2d 556, 578 (N.D. Ohio 2004); Scordill v. Louisville Ladder Group, LLC, 2003 WL 22427981, at *8 (E.D. La. 2003) ("even if the instructions and warnings had been adequate, the accident would have still occurred because Scordill, not having read them, would have proceeded to use the ladder in the same manner in which he did"); Hiner v. Bridgestone/Firestone, Inc., 978 P.2d 505, 509 (Wash. 1999).

**26.** See, e.g., Golonka v. General Motors Corp., 65 P.3d 956, 972 (Ariz. Ct. App. 2003) (decedent never heeded owner's manual warning to set parking break, turn off ignition, and remove key).

the heeding presumption, at least in some types of cases,[27] to help a plaintiff prove causation with warnings claims.[28]

Apart from resolving the causal proof dilemma faced by plaintiffs, for which they have no blame, and avoiding the need for speculative self-serving testimony,[29] two basic rationales have been offered for the heeding presumption, one doctrinal and the other policy. The doctrinal argument draws from a sentence in comment *j* to § 402A of the *Restatement (Second) of Torts* which provides that "[w]here warning is given, the seller may reasonably assume that it will be read and heeded." Because this provision has been viewed as creating a presumption protecting manufacturers when they *do* provide adequate warnings and instructions,[30] many courts have reasoned that this same provision must operate reciprocally as well, by protecting plaintiffs when a manufacturer *fails* to provide a warning and the shoe is on the other foot.[31] The policy argument is that the duty to warn is designed to give an incentive to manufacturers to provide safety information to users and consumers, and manufacturers should not be allowed a large loophole in this vital safety obligation arising out of the causal proof conundrum which victims of product accidents cannot avoid.[32]

While these two arguments have some appeal, they suffer from certain weaknesses. The comment *j* argument, that the heeding presumption is merely a trade-off for the reciprocal presumption afforded manufacturers, is undermined by the fact that the "presumption" comment *j* affords to manufacturers is only a straw horse. Although it is widely read more broadly, comment *j* in fact pertains only to the narrow

---

**27.** Some jurisdictions allow the presumption in cases where the defendant did not warn at all, but not in situations where a substantively inadequate warning was provided. See, e.g., DaimlerChrysler Corp. v. Hillhouse, 2004 WL 1195687 (Tex. App. 2004); Note, The Heeding Presumption and its Application: Distinguishing No Warning from Inadequate Warning, 37 Loy. L.A. L. Rev. 461 (2003).

**28.** See, e.g., Golonka v. General Motors Corp., 65 P.3d 956, 965–72 (Ariz. Ct. App. 2003) (thorough discussion); Needham v. Coordinated Apparel Group, Inc., 811 A.2d 124, 129 (Vt. 2002); Crowston v. Goodyear Tire & Rubber Co., 521 N.W.2d 401, 410 (N.D. 1994); Tune v. Synergy Gas Corp., 883 S.W.2d 10, 14 (Mo. 1994); Coffman v. Keene Corp., 628 A.2d 710–20 (N.J. 1993); Eagle–Picher Indus. v. Balbos, 604 A.2d 445, 468–69 (Md. 1992); Wooderson v. Ortho Pharmaceutical Corp., 681 P.2d 1038, 1057 (Kan. 1984); Seley v. G.D. Searle & Co., 423 N.E.2d 831, 838 (1981); Nissen Trampoline Co. v. Terre Haute First Nat'l Bank, 332 N.E.2d 820, 826 (Ind. Ct. App. 1975), rev'd on other grounds, 358 N.E.2d 974 (Ind. 1976). *But see* Viguers v. Philip Morris USA, Inc., 837 A.2d 534 (Pa. Super. Ct. 2003) (reasons for allowing presumption in asbestos cases do not apply to tobacco cases).

**29.** See, e.g., Coffman v. Keene Corp., 628 A.2d 710, 720 (N.J. 1993) ("The heeding presumption accords with the manufacturer's basic duty to warn; it fairly reduces the victim's burden of proof; and it minimizes the likelihood that determinations of causation will be based on unreliable evidence."); Reyes v. Wyeth Labs., 498 F.2d 1264, 1281 (5th Cir. 1974) (Tex. law) (heeding presumption is beneficial because it avoids plaintiff's testimony that is so self-serving as to be useless).

**30.** See § 6.2, above.

**31.** See, e.g., Technical Chem. Co. v. Jacobs, 480 S.W.2d 602, 606 (Tex. 1972) ("Such a presumption works in favor of the manufacturer when an adequate warning is present. Where there is no warning, as in this case, however, the presumption that the user would have read an adequate warning works in favor of the plaintiff user. In other words, the presumption is that Jacobs would have read an adequate warning.").

**32.** See, e.g., Geistfeld, Inadequate Product Warnings and Causation, 30 U. Mich. J.L. Reform 309 (1997); Latin, "Good" Warnings, Bad Products, and Cognitive Limitations, 41 UCLA L. Rev. 1193 (1994).

category of unavoidably dangerous products such as alcohol, drugs, and cigarettes whose inherently hazardous nature makes warnings the only way to improve their safety.[33] With such products, since there is no way to design the dangers out of the product, providing a warning is all a manufacturer or other seller can do to reduce the risk of harm—after which, a seller has nothing else to do except to "assume [read: "hope"] that [its warning] will be read and heeded." This statement in comment *j* thus means simply that a manufacturer of an inherently hazardous product, one that is "unavoidably unsafe," avoids liability for harm by manufacturing the product properly and providing adequate warnings of its inherent dangers. Thus, the "assumption" of comment *j* does not refer to a legal presumption, nor does comment *j* address normal types of products, but only those that are unavoidably unsafe.[34]

The other problem with the heeding presumption is that it is not logical: in fact, people usually do not read and heed warnings and instructions, no matter how good they may be.[35] As mentioned earlier,[36] studies suggest that warnings alter behavior very little, since few people read or heed them.[37] More recent and sophisticated behavioral studies confirm the hypothesis that consumers process information irrationally.[38]

Finally, the argument that consumers have a fundamental "right" to safety information, so they may decide how to use their products safely and choose to avoid certain dangerous products altogether, certainly is correct.[39] But nothing in the right to adequate safety information confers on users and consumers the right to recover damages from a manufacturer it did not cause. Not only would such a result clash with fundamental fairness and corrective justice, but it has no parallel in design and manufacturing defect cases where plaintiffs have no right to recover damages for harm that manufacturers did not cause. In the end, causation is too important an element to be tossed to the wind without

---

**33.** The meaning of comment *j* is explored in § 6.2, above, and inherently hazardous products are examined in § 10.3, above.

**34.** See Owen, The Puzzle of Comment *j*, 55 Hastings L.J. 1377 (2004).

**35.** See Coffman v. Keene Corp., 628 A.2d 710, 718 (N.J. 1993) ("Although empirical evidence may not demonstrate the soundness of a heeding presumption, an examination of the strong and consistent public policies that have shaped our laws governing strict products liability demonstrates the justification for such a presumption.").

**36.** See § 9.3, above.

**37.** See, e.g., Goldhaber and deTurk, Effects of Consumers' Familiarity With a Product on Attention To and Compliance With Warnings, 11 J. Prod. Liab. 29 (1988); Dorris and Purswell, Warnings and Human

Behavior: Implications for the Design of Product Warnings, 1 J. Prod. Liab. 254 (1977).

**38.** See, e.g., Symposium: Rational Actors or Rational Fools? The Implications of Psychology for Products Liability, 6 Roger Williams U. L. Rev. 1 (2000); Hanson and Kysar, Taking Behavioralism Seriously: The Problem of Market Manipulation, 74 N.Y.U. L. Rev. 630, 724 (1999); Hanson and Kysar, Taking Behavioralism Seriously: Some Evidence of Market Manipulation, 112 Harv. L. Rev. 1420, 1425 (1999); Henderson and Twerski, Doctrinal Collapse in Products Liability: The Empty Shell of Failure to Warn, 65 N.Y.U. L. Rev. 265, 307 (1992). See generally Sunstein, The Laws of Fear, 115 Harv. L. Rev. 1119, 1123 (2002) (reviewing P. Slovic, The Perception of Risk) ("ordinary people often deal poorly with the topic of risk").

**39.** See § 9.1, above.

compelling reasons, for it is the crucible for deciding whether claims of wrongdoing and bad products are real or fancied.[40]

**40.**  See Henderson and Twerski, Doctrinal Collapse in Products Liability: The Empty Shell of Failure to Warn, 65 N.Y.U. L. Rev. 265, 303–08 and 325 (1992) ("a presumption makes no good sense on the merits").

# Chapter 12

# PROXIMATE CAUSE

*Table of Sections*

---

## § 12.1  PROXIMATE CAUSE—GENERALLY

Proximate cause, although linked to factual causation, is a separate element unto itself.[1] The issue that is usually called "proximate cause" is very different from the issue of factual causation. Presupposing some factual connection between a defendant's breach of duty and the plaintiff's injury, proximate cause addresses instead the question of whether in fairness, policy, and practicality the defendant ought to be held legally accountable for the plaintiff's harm which in some manner is "remote" from the defendant's breach.[2] Proximate cause might thus be defined, if somewhat tautologically, as a reasonably close connection between the plaintiff's injury and a defendant's wrong, a connection that is not "remote." More broadly, proximate cause is a doctrine that serves to limit a tortfeasor's responsibility to the consequences of risks viewed fairly as arising from the wrong.[3] Because "[i]t is always to be determined on the facts of each case upon mixed considerations of logic, common sense, justice, policy and precedent,"[4] proximate cause is an "elusive butterfly"[5] that e'er evades a net of rules.[6]

### § 12.1

**1.** "To prevail in a negligence action, the plaintiff must bear the burden of showing that the defendant's negligent conduct was not only a cause in fact of the plaintiff's harm, but also a proximate or legal cause." Dobbs, Law of Torts § 180, at 443. See § 11.1, above.

**2.** See Prosser and Keeton on Torts § 42, at 264 (noting that proximate cause limits legal responsibility to "causes which are so closely connected with the result and of such significance" as to justify liability: "Some boundary must be set to liability for the consequences of any act, upon the basis of some social idea of justice or policy.").

**3.** See Kelley, Restating Duty, Breach, and Proximate Cause In Negligence Law:

Descriptive Theory and The Rule Of Law, 54 Vand. L. Rev. 1039 (2001); Stapleton, Legal Cause: Cause–In–Fact and the Scope of Liability for Consequences, 54 Vand. L. Rev. 941 (2001); Matsuda, On Causation, 100 Colum. L. Rev. 2195 (2000); L. Green, The Causal Relation Issue In Negligence Law, 60 Mich. L. Rev. 543 (1962); James and Perry, Legal Cause, 60 Yale L. Rev. 763 (1951); Pound, Causation, 67 Yale L. Rev. 1 (1957); J. Page, Proximate Cause (2003).

**4.** 1 Street, Foundations of Legal Liability 110 (1906).

**5.** Accordini v. Security Cen., Inc., 320 S.E.2d 713, 714 (S.Ct. App. 1984) (Sanders, C.J.).

**6.** "Proximate cause cannot be reduced to absolute rules." Prosser and Keeton on Torts 279.

Quite like duty, proximate cause provides a broad cauldron into which many factual and legal issues are thrown and mixed together. Yet, while traditionally referred to as "legal cause" (in an effort to distinguish it from factual cause), proximate cause is an issue of "fact" for resolution by a jury.[7]

Proximate cause goes by a variety of names. Some courts still use the "legal cause" term just mentioned, left over from the *Second Restatement*'s use of that umbrella term to describe both factual and "legal" causation in combination, as discussed below.[8] As for umbrella terms, it must be remembered that the term "proximate cause" itself is commonly used to describe both causal issues, factual and proximate alike.[9] This means, of course, that a lawyer reading judicial decisions discussing "proximate cause" needs to be on guard for the possibility that the court is actually addressing the issue of cause in *fact*, not proximate cause at all.[10] And the *Restatement (Third) of Torts*, in an effort to reduce confusion, replaces "proximate cause" with "scope of liability."[11]

By whatever name, proximate cause is an elemental requirement of every products liability claim.[12] In applying proximate cause "principles," such as they may be, products liability law draws from the law of negligence. In the early days of modern products liability law, in an effort to distinguish the then new doctrine of strict products liability in tort from negligence, some courts and commentators sought to eliminate the proximate cause limitations of negligence law (principally, the limita-

---

**7.** See Dobbs, Law of Torts § 182.

**8.** See § 12.2, below.

**9.** See, e.g., First Premier Bank v. Kolcraft Enters., Inc., 686 N.W.2d 430, 454 (S.D. 2004) ("Proximate or legal cause is a cause that produces a result in a natural and probable sequence and without which the result would not have occurred."); Bray v. Marathon Corp., 588 S.E.2d 93, 95 (S.C. 2003) ("Proximate cause requires proof of both causation in fact and legal cause, which is proved by establishing foreseeability."); Meneely v. S.R. Smith, Inc., 5 P.3d 49, 58 (Wash. 2000) (proximate cause has "two distinct elements: cause in fact and legal cause"); see also § 11.1, above.

**10.** See, e.g., Wilkinson v. Duff, 575 S.E.2d 335 (W. Va. 2002); Hanford v. Taco Bell Corp., 2002 WL 570918, at *2 (Wash. Ct. App. 2002) (" 'If an event would have occurred regardless of a defendant's conduct, that conduct is not the proximate cause of the plaintiff's injury.' ").

**11.** See Restatement (3d) Torts: Liability for Physical Harm ch. 6, "Scope of Liability (Proximate Cause)," and § 29 cmt. *b*.

**12.** See, e.g., Cupp, Proximate Cause, The Proposed Basic Principles Restatement, and Products Liability, 53 S.C. L. Rev., 1085 (2002); M. Green, The Unanticipated Ripples of Comparative Negligence: Superseding Cause in Products Liability and Beyond, 53 S.C. L. Rev. 1103 (2002); Henderson and Twerski, Intuition and Technology In Product Design Litigation: An Essay On Proximate Causation, 88 Geo. L.J. 659 (2000); Haley, Paradigms of Proximate Cause, 36 Tort & Ins. L. J. 147 (2000); Zablostky, Eliminating Proximate Cause As An Element of the Prima Facie Case for Strict Products Liability, 45 Cath. U. L. Rev. 31 (1995); Fischer, Products Liability—Proximate Cause, Intervening Cause, and Duty, 52 Mo. L. Rev. 547 (1987); Gillam, Torts—Proximate Cause in Strict–Liability Cases, 50 N.C. L. Rev. 714 (1972); Note, Funds v. Big Tobacco and the Proximate–Cause Issue: A Framework For Derivative Injuries, 80 Tex. L. Rev. 393 (2001); Note, Up In Smoke: How the Proximate Cause Battle Extinguished the Tobacco War, 76 Notre Dame L. Rev. 257 (2000); 1 Frumer and Friedman, Products Liability § 3.03; 1 Madden & Owen on Products Liability ch. 13.

tion of responsibility to foreseeable risks) from the strict tort doctrine.[13] In time, however, this effort proved futile,[14] and proximate cause (with its limiting principle of foreseeable risk) is alive and well today as an element of claims for breach of warranty,[15] strict products liability in tort,[16] and even fraud.[17]

While proximate cause is dealt with here as a separate doctrine, it should be noted that the issue permeates not only duty concepts but indeed *most* of the crucial elements of a products liability case. In a typical products liability action, the ultimate issue is whether, or the degree to which, some "defective" condition of the product, the plaintiff himself, or some third party "caused" the injury. Thus, one court was not far off the mark in noting that whether it labeled the plaintiff's unreasonable encounter with a known danger contributory negligence or assumption of risk was of little consequence because "[t]he controlling factor is causation."[18] Thought of in this broader sense, this issue pervades every products liability action, since each such case is comprised of many issues bound together by proximate causation twine.[19]

**13.** See, e.g., Eshbach v. W. T. Grant's & Co., 481 F.2d 940, (3d Cir. 1973) ("Negligence is of course, tested in terms of foreseeability. The focus of § 402A, however, is not directed to the foreseeability of a given injury, but to whether 'the product is, at the time it leaves the seller's hands, in a condition not contemplated by the ultimate consumer, which will be unreasonably dangerous to him' "). See also Voss v. Black & Decker Mfg. Co., 450 N.E.2d 204, 209 (N.Y. 1983) ("Proximate cause in a products liability case serves a somewhat different role than in a case sounding in negligence because that cause of action seeks to impute liability to the manufacturer not on the basis of his negligence but because the product is not reasonably safe as it was designed."). For a more recent attempt, see Zablostky, Eliminating Proximate Cause As An Element of the Prima Facie Case for Strict Products Liability, 45 Cath. U. L. Rev. 31 (1995).

**14.** See § 10.4, above.

**15.** See, e.g., Accordini v. Security Cen., Inc., 320 S.E.2d 713, 714 (S.C. Ct. App. 1984) (applying principles of proximate cause and foreseeable risk to claims of breach of express and implied warranty, and negligence).

**16.** See, e.g., Fralish v. A.O. Smith Corp., ___ A.2d ___, ___, 2004 WL 1587559, at *6 (Pa. Super. Ct. 2004) ("[i]f the product is defective absent such warnings, and the defect is a proximate cause of the plaintiff's injury, the seller is strictly liable without proof of negligence"); Graham v. American Cyanamid Co., 350 F.3d 496, 513 (6th Cir. 2003) ("To establish strict liability under Ohio law, plaintiffs must produce ex-

pert testimony that the defect at issue 'proximately caused the[ir] claimed injuries.' "); Marzullo v. Crosman Corp., 289 F.Supp.2d 1337, 1347 (M.D. Fla. 2003) (for strict liability in tort under § 402A, "a plaintiff must prove a *defective and unreasonably dangerous condition* of a product was the proximate cause of injury").

**17.** While proximate cause often lies buried in claims for fraud or deceit, it sometimes sits front and center. See, e.g., Goldstein v. Phillip Morris, Inc., 854 A.2d 585, 590–91 (Pa. Super. Ct. 2004) ("To recover on a claim of fraud, the plaintiff must prove [that] the resulting injury was proximately caused by the reliance."); Graham v. American Cyanamid Co., 350 F.3d 496, 507 (6th Cir. 2003) (Ohio law) ("plaintiffs bear the burden of establishing that American Cyanamid's alleged misrepresentation ... proximately caused their injuries," citing Restatement (Second) of Torts § 557A cmt. *a*, which notes that ordinary rules of legal cause govern fraudulent misrepresentation cases involving physical harm).

**18.** See Palmer v. Ford Motor Co., 498 F.2d 952, 953 (10th Cir. 1974) (Kan. law).

**19.** Leon Green may have said it best: "The issues of a 402A action lie as close together as the fingers of one hand, and one issue cannot be considered without holding the other issues in conscious suspense; for all the issues are essential to liability, and each has a part to play in the functioning of all the others. Causal connection runs as a thread through the seller's duty, the violation of its duty, and the use made of the product in its consumption that results in the consumer's injury."L. Green, Strict Liability Under Sections 402A and 402B: A

## § 12.2   FORESEEABILITY AND OTHER "TESTS"

### "Tests" of Proximate Cause

Because proximate cause is little more than a swirling maelstrom of policy, practicality, and case-specific fairness considerations—rather than a meaningful set of rules or even principles—it would seem incapable of being subjected to rational "testing." Yet, lawyers, courts, and juries need some guidance in unraveling the mysteries of this perplexing doctrine, which has led courts and commentators on an eternal search for a proper "test" for deciding whether a plaintiff's injury in any particular case was the proximate result of the defendant's wrong. While various other tests have been tried out over the years, the concept of "foreseeability," in one formulation or another, is the predominant notion informing proximate cause.[1]

### Foreseeability as the Dominant Test

The central notion of proximate cause, often loosely referred to as its "test," is that the responsibility of an actor for the consequences of wrongful action is limited by principles of reasonable "foreseeability." As some courts aptly put it, foreseeability is the "touchstone"[2] or "cornerstone"[3] of proximate cause. This outer boundary of tortious responsibility assures that actors are not held liable for consequences that fall outside the scope of their wrongdoing, beyond their moral accountability.[4] By this perspective, responsibility for consequences should be based on the quality of an actor's choices, decisions whose moral fiber is gauged by the variety of consequences the actor did or should have contemplated as possibilities at the time the choice was made. If some other, "unforeseeable," consequence eventuates from an action, the fact that it lay outside the bundle of consequences the actor reasonably could have contemplated means that it probably did not inform the actor's deliberations and choice. There thus is no moral connection between a person's actions and the unforeseeable consequences of those actions. This suggests that, in evaluating the moral quality of a choice, only the foreseeable consequences of the actor's choices may properly be considered.[5] This is a moral justification for bounding the law of torts by the foreseeable scope of risk.[6]

Decade of Litigation, 54 Tex. L. Rev. 1185, 1208 (1976).

**§ 12.2**

**1.** See Restatement (3d) Torts: Liability for Physical Harm § 29 cmt. *j* (noting that the foreseeable risk approach is the "predominant standard employed to limit liability," that, "[c]urrently, virtually all jurisdictions" employ it "for some range of proximate-cause issues," and asserting that "[t]he risk standard is the best of the available alternatives for providing a standard for limiting liability for tortious conduct that causes harm").

**2.** See, e.g., Walcott v. Total Petroleum, Inc., 964 P.2d 609, 611 (Colo. Ct. App. 1998) ("foreseeability is the touchstone of proximate cause"); Koester v. Carolina Rental Center, Inc., 443 S.E.2d 392, 394 (S.C. 1994).

**3.** See Dillard v. Pittway Corp., 719 So.2d 188, 192 (Ala. 1998).

**4.** See, e.g., Prosser and Keeton on Torts § 43, at 281 ("In so far as the defendant is held liable for consequences which do not lie within the [foreseeable] risk which the defendant [originally] created, a strict liability without fault is superimposed upon the liability that is logically to be attributed to the negligence itself.").

**5.** If a choice is reasonable in view of its foreseeable consequences, an unforeseeable harm that results is a "background" risk of life that victims fairly should protect against and bear. See Owen, Philosophical Foundations of Fault in Tort Law, in Philo-

For these reasons, as in other tort law contexts, the safety obligations of manufacturers and other sellers are limited by principles of reasonable foreseeability. More specifically, in making design and warnings choices, a manufacturer must contemplate and fairly evaluate all risks to all persons that are reasonably foreseeable. The range of risks and persons to be foreseen include how a product may be used, how it may be misused, and the ways in which these risks may endanger users and other persons. Just as foreseeability is an important limiting notion on the duty of a product manufacturer, it is the principal "test" of proximate cause, as mentioned earlier. The "foreseeability" of a product's risks—the "scope" of the product's foreseeable risks—is thus the formal standard for deciding whether responsibility for a defendant's breach of duty should extend to the plaintiff's harm. Put otherwise, the central question of proximate cause in a products liability case is whether the risks which caused the plaintiff's harm were among the foreseeable risks which made the defendant negligent or its product defective.

## Other Tests

### Direct Consequences; Natural and Probable Consequences

As prominent and well-entrenched as foreseeability may be as the standard for determining proximate cause in products liability law, the other tests for proximate cause that long have challenged foreseeability in the law of negligence compete as well in the products liability arena. So, courts still sometimes use the "direct consequences" test of *Polemis* fame,[7] by which proximate cause is defined as a cause which, in natural and continuous sequence, unbroken by any efficient, intervening cause, produces the plaintiff's harm.[8] A variation on this formulation is the "natural and probable consequences" test, also occasionally referred to in products liability decisions.[9] Yet, in the first *Wagon Mound* opinion,[10] *Polemis* was rejected for failing to employ foreseeability as the basic standard, and foreseeability is often woven in, one way or another, when

---

sophical Foundations of Tort Law 201, 226–27 (D. Owen ed., Oxford 1994). See also Owen, The Moral Foundations of Products Liability Law: Toward First Principles, 68 Notre Dame L. Rev. 427, 484 (1993) (utility, freedom, and equality all argue for limiting responsibility to foreseeable risks).

**6.** See Restatement (3d) Torts: Liability for Physical Harm § 29 cmt. *k* (noting that a "risk standard" (meaning a foreseeable risk approach) appeals "to the intuition that it is fair for an actor's liability to be limited to those risks that constituted the basis for the wrongful conduct"). See also id. cmt. *j*.

**7.** In re Polemis, 3 K.B. 560 (1921).

**8.** See, e.g., Stahlecker v. Ford Motor Co., 667 N.W.2d 244, 253 (Neb. 2003); Pickett v. RTS Helicopter, 128 F.3d 925, 929 (5th Cir. 1997) (La. law).

**9.** See, e.g., First Premier Bank v. Kolcraft Enters., Inc., 686 N.W.2d 430, 442 (S.D. 2004) ("Proximate or legal cause is a cause that produces a result in a natural and probable sequence and without which the result would not have occurred."); Stahlecker v. Ford Motor Co., 667 N.W.2d 244, 253–54 (Neb. 2003) (whether injury was "a natural and probable result of the negligence" is another way of stating the "natural and probable sequence" formulation).

**10.** Overseas Tankship (U.K.) Ltd. v. Morts Dock & Eng'g Co., [1961] A.C. 388 (Privy Council) ("Wagon Mound I").

courts dredge up the "natural and probable" standard for proximate cause decisionmaking.[11]

### The Second Restatement

The *Restatement (Second) of Torts* did not really define proximate cause, referring to it obliquely as a set of rules "relieving the actor from liability because of the manner in which his negligence has resulted in the harm."[12] Among these "rules," the *Second Restatement* included a variety of limiting principles, some of which are defined in terms of foreseeability.[13] The *Second Restatement*'s confusing umbrella definition of "legal cause," which defines factual causation in "substantial factor" terms, misled some number of courts to believe that the concept of proximate cause, viewed narrowly, should be conceived of through a substantial-factor lens. This misinterpretation of the *Second Restatement* has contributed to the confusion surrounding the meaning of and relationship between factual causation and proximate cause, and it still infects some products liability decisions.[14]

### The Third Restatement

Drawing from a wealth of judicial and academic support, and rejecting the "proximate cause" phraseology as too confusing,[15] the *Third Restatement* adopts a "scope of risk" or "harm-within-the-risk" test for proximate causation.[16] The doctrine is generally defined in § 29, entitled "Limitations on Liability for Tortious Conduct," which provides: "An actor is not liable for harm different from the harms whose risks made the actor's conduct tortious."[17] Yet such a "risk" test is really little more, as the Reporters acknowledge,[18] than foreseeability in disguise. Yet the Reporters quite plausibly assert that the "scope of risk" formulation more clearly than "foreseeability" reveals that liability is fairly bounded by the risks that made the actor negligent. This argument would be quite compelling if the *Restatement*'s standard were enhanced by adding its single most important defining characteristic: foreseeability. As so enhanced, the "scope of foreseeable risk" formulation well describes the essential concept, nebulous though it may be, of proximate causation.

---

**11.** City of Gary ex rel. King v. Smith & Wesson Corp., 801 N.E.2d 1222, 1244 (Ind. 2003) ("liability may not be imposed on an original negligent actor who sets into motion a chain of events if the ultimate injury was not reasonably foreseeable as the natural and probable consequence of the act or omission"); Koester v. Carolina Rental Ctr., Inc., 443 S.E.2d 392, 394 (S.C. 1994) ("Foreseeability is determined by looking to the natural and probable consequences of the act complained of.").

**12.** Restatement (2d) Torts § 431(b).

**13.** See id. § 435, "Foreseeability of Harm or Manner of Its Occurrence."

**14.** See, e.g., Barry v. Quality Steel Prods., Inc., 820 A.2d 258, 264 (Conn. 2003) (" '[T]he test of proximate cause is whether the defendant's conduct is a substantial fac-

tor in bringing about the plaintiff's injuries.' "); Gonzalez v. Delta Int'l Mach. Corp., 763 N.Y.S.2d 844 (N.Y. App. Div. 2003); Foister v. Purdue Pharm., L.P., 295 F.Supp.2d 693 (E.D. Ky. 2003). See also § 11.1, above.

**15.** See Restatement (3d) Torts: Liability for Physical Harm § 29 cmt. *b*, and the informative Reporters' Note thereto.

**16.** The references here are to the Restatement (Third) of Torts: Liability for Physical Harm. The Products Liability Restatement § 15 takes no position on issues of causation, stating that the causation rules of tort law generally apply as well to products liability.

**17.** Restatement (3d) Torts: Liability for Physical Harm § 29.

**18.** See Restatement (3d) Torts: Liability for Physical Harm § 29 cmt. *k*.

The *Third Restatement* "scope of risk" test comes closest to the mark, and is helpful in many ways, but simple "foreseeability" for many years has been crowding out other competing "tests" for proximate cause, most of which have a quaint appearance of times gone by. None of the traditional "tests" is especially objectionable, except that none provides much guidance to courts or juries attempting to apply whatever principles proximate cause may possess to resolve real-world disputes. No doubt courts for many years will continue to parrot these alternative verbalisms in the jurisdictions where they reside, for they have deep roots in the common law and are doing little in the way of affirmative harm. And foreseeability itself may be faulted for providing little guidance to adjudicators attempting to decide whether a manufacturer or other seller should bear responsibility for some harmful consequence of a defective product that somehow looks remote.[19] Yet, as earlier discussed, at least foreseeability is rooted in fundamental notions of responsibility that, at some basic level, may help decide whether a manufacturer or other seller fairly may be held responsible for a plaintiff's loss.

## Foreseeability and Bizarre Consequences

Perhaps the most intuitively appealing type of case for applying some proximate cause limitation on the harmful consequences of a tortious action is where the consequences appear totally bizarre, even in retrospect,[20] "too cockeyed and far-fetched."[21] If the plaintiff is injured by slipping on the vomit of a friend who was nauseated by the defendant's smelly plate of shrimp, the consequences may simply seem too far outside the foreseeable risks of serving foul food to hold the restaurateur responsible for the plaintiff's injury.[22] And other products liability claims have been rejected on the ground that the consequences are too bizarre.[23]

But courts allow juries to decide the proximate cause issue in some quite extraordinary situations. In one case, for example, the plaintiff was driving at 45–50 mph when he hit a horse that suddenly appeared in front of his car. The horse was thrown into the air and onto the roof, collapsing the roof rail (called the "header") on the passenger side of the car, which instantly killed the plaintiff's wife. Rejecting the defendant's argument that the accident was "freak and bizarre," the court upheld a

---

**19.** How foreseeability may be faulted as a "test" for limiting a manufacturer's responsibility is more deeply probed in the context of misuse. See § 13.5, below.

**20.** See Restatement (2d) Torts § 435 (2) ("where after the event and looking back from the harm" to the tortious conduct they appear "highly extraordinary"). See also id. at § 442(b).

**21.** See Prosser, Palsgraf Revisited, 52 Mich. L. Rev. 1, 19 (1953).

**22.** See Crankshaw v. Piedmont Driving Club, 156 S.E.2d 208 (Ga. Ct. App. 1967).

**23.** In Sidwell v. William Prym, Inc., 730 P.2d 996, 999, 1003 (Idaho 1986), the plaintiff was wearing a dress while her

mother placed a hem in it with brittle, hardened-steel dressmaker pins manufactured by the defendant. Plaintiff bumped a coffee table with her knee, driving a pin into her knee bone where it broke into three pieces. *Held,* no duty to warn of a danger that could not be foreseen. "[T]he manufacturer is asked to anticipate, not only that pins will pierce, but they will be driven into the body with such force as to strike a bone and shatter." The event was "a freak accident that probably could not be duplicated under any condition." One judge dissented: "The 'freak accident' argument might prove not in the least persuasive to a jury."

verdict for the plaintiff.[24] Another case involved a boating accident which began when an outboard motor stalled due to a defective fuel system. While the husband attempted to restart the engine, the anchor line became entangled in the propeller and, as he tried to cut the line, the husband was pulled into the water. While his wife tried to rescue him, an onrush of water washed her inside the boat and below deck. The boat capsized, and the wife, trapped beneath, drowned. Despite this incredible set of freak occurrences, the court ruled that foreseeability was properly for the jury.[25] And courts in other cases quite unusual allow juries to find a product defect and the plaintiff's injuries proximately connected.[26]

### Foreseeability as a Veil

An uncomfortable aspect of foreseeability, even when helpfully modified as *reasonable* foreseeability, is that it, like other "tests" for proximate cause, provides so little guidance that a court or jury can hide behind it all sorts of biases and ideologies that have no proper place in such decisions. Foreseeability, that is, and proximate cause more generally, both serve too often as a veil that shields from view the motivating reasons for allowing or, more typically, disallowing recovery in products liability as other tort law cases. In *Winnet v. Winnet*,[27] for example, a four-year-old child was injured when she placed her hand on a moving conveyor belt on a forage wagon being operated on her grandfather's farm. She settled a suit against her grandfather and pursued a strict tort action against the manufacturer of the forage wagon, alleging that it was defectively designed because it did not have rear-view mirrors or a guard to prevent persons from coming in contact with the conveyor belt. Stating that foreseeability is "that which it is *objectively reasonable* to expect, not merely what might conceivably occur," the Illinois Supreme Court upheld a dismissal of the complaint, ruling that it could not "fairly be said that a manufacturer should reasonably foresee that a four-year-old child will be permitted to approach an operating farm forage wagon or that the child will be permitted to place her fingers in or on the holes in its moving screen." In *Richelman v. Kewanee Machinery & Conveyor Co.*,[28] however, a majority of the Illinois Court of Appeals seemed almost oblivious to the holding in *Winnett*, in ruling that a jury could find in favor of a three-year-old child whose foot was injured when he wandered away from the house and came in contact with a grain auger on his grandfather's farm.[29] Reading between the lines, these inconsistent cases appear to reveal much more about the judges' respective beliefs concerning the balance between parental (and grandparental) responsibility, on

**24.** See Green v. Denney, 742 P.2d 639 (Or. Ct. App. 1987).

**25.** See Greenfield v. Suzuki Motor Co., 776 F.Supp. 698 (E.D.N.Y. 1991).

**26.** See, e.g., Yun v. Ford Motor Co., 669 A.2d 1378 (N.J. 1996), where the plaintiff was killed while trying to cross a rain-slicked highway at night, twice, in violation of state law, to retrieve a bald tire and parts of a broken tire assembly that had fallen off the back of his van because of a defect in the spare tire assembly on the back of the vehicle. Over a vigorous dissent, the majority ruled that a jury could find that this was foreseeable.

**27.** 310 N.E.2d 1 (Ill. 1974).

**28.** 375 N.E.2d 885 (Ill. App. Ct. 1978).

**29.** The dissent in *Richelman* observed: "The only question can be whether this particular plaintiff's injury was reasonably foreseeable. The *Winnett* case held that it was not and we should follow it." Id. at 890.

the one side, and the idea that large manufacturing enterprises may be capable of spreading the costs of accidents, on the other, than about the notion of foreseeability limitations on responsibility for harm.

Often noted (and usually decried) by scholars,[30] the malleability and opaqueness of foreseeability as the "test" for proximate cause has significant implications for lawyers litigating products liability as other tort law cases. Foreseeability becomes a vessel into which a lawyer—in arguing either to a jury or the judge—can pour any number of equitable considerations which are present in the case but which really have no doctrinal home. In this respect, the doctrine of proximate cause, defined in terms of foreseeable risk, can be an especially powerful arrow in a lawyer's quiver of legal tools.

## Foreseeability of Product Use

An important limitation on the scope of a manufacturer's responsibility for product accidents lies in the foreseeability of a product's *use*.[31] While liability is no longer limited to product uses which a manufacturer *intends*, a manufacturer still may be held accountable only for those uses of its products which it reasonably can *foresee*.[32] So, a manufacturer is not liable when a defective elevator stalls six feet short of the floor and a passenger is injured in trying to jump out;[33] a spare tire strap is used to attach curtain rods to the roof of a car;[34] a fertilizer is employed by a terrorist to make a bomb used to try to blow up the World Trade Center;[35] an intoxicated person falls asleep or passes out in a stopped, running vehicle and presses his foot on the accelerator, causing the exhaust system to overheat and ignite;[36] a person attempts to commit

---

**30.** Passwaters v. General Motors Corp., 454 F.2d 1270, 1276 n.5 (8th Cir. 1972) (Iowa law), was an early case extending a manufacturer's liability to include foreseeable risks to foreseeable bystanders: "The difficulty is that 'foreseeability' is a hazardous term to define in the abstract and, like so many other doctrines, must turn on the judgmental process." The court noted the following observations of a leading tort law scholar and legal realist:

> It all depends upon what factors in the evidence a court is willing to isolate and emphasize for the purpose of making this decision, which process in turn depends pretty much on what outcome the court wishes to achieve or thinks to be politic. This factor in the judgment process, in turn, is not usually a matter of conscious choice but may be a function of the judge's accumulated experience in and observations of the world he lives in. Gregory, Proximate Cause in Negligence–A Retreat from "Rationalization," 6 U. Chi. L. Rev. 36, 50 (1938).

The court further observed: "Generally, whether a duty exists is a question of law,

yet when a difficult determination depends on policy values underlying the 'common affairs of life,' it is generally thought that the jury is the best d[i]viner of such values."

**31.** Parks v. AlliedSignal Inc., 113 F.3d 1327, 1333 (3rd Cir. 1997) (Pa. law) ("In strict products liability, the focus is on whether the product was sold in an unreasonably dangerous condition for reasonably foreseeable uses.").

**32.** See the discussion of misuse, in § 13.5, below.

**33.** See Egan v. A. J. Constr. Corp., 724 N.E.2d 366 (N.Y. 1999).

**34.** See Van de Valde v. Volvo of Am. Corp., 744 P.2d 930, 933 (N.M. 1987).

**35.** See Port Authority of New York and New Jersey v. Arcadian Corp., 189 F.3d 305, 318 (3d Cir. 1999) (N.J. law) (plaintiff's allegations regarding past fertilizer explosions, "as a matter of law, simply do not permit a finding of objective foreseeability" so that the product was not defective as designed; "conceivability is not the equivalent of foreseeability").

**36.** See Griffith v. Chrysler Corp., 2003 WL 21500037 (Ohio Ct. App. 2003).

suicide by closing herself in a car trunk without an inside release latch, changes her mind, and is trapped inside for nine days thereafter;[37] a doctor transplants synthetic fibers, normally used for wigs and hair-pieces, into a patient's scalp as a treatment for baldness, causing irritation and infection;[38] a grocery shopper, who trips, hopes that a shopping cart does not scoot away when he grabs for it to save himself from falling;[39] the owner of a riding lawn mower attaches a wooden "dog box" to the mower and places a two-year-old child in the box who falls out and is run over by the mower;[40] a teenage boy hangs himself with a rope on a swing set as a joke to impress the girls;[41] a boy, riding a canister vacuum cleaner like a toy car, is injured when his penis slips through an opening into the cleaner's fan;[42] children play with a gas can without a child-proof top;[43] or a youth tilts or rocks a soft-drink vending machine, to dispense a can without payment, causing the machine to fall upon and kill him.[44] While the product uses in these cases all were deemed unforeseeable, courts in many other cases, involving other kinds of uses beyond the normally expectable, have ruled quite the other way.[45] Because of the inherent elasticity of "foreseeability," no prudent lawyer would attempt to predict how a jury might rule on the foreseeability of any particular product use that seems unusual.[46]

### Conventional Foreseeability Categories

Foreseeability is the controlling issue around which various categories of proximate cause cases cluster. Three categories of foreseeability are conventionally compared: the foreseeability of (1) the extent of harm, (2) the manner of its occurrence, and (3) the type of risk or harm. These three categories may be seen to reside, if roughly, in *Restatement (Second) of Torts* § 435, entitled "Foreseeability of Harm or Manner of Its Occurrence," which provides:

> (1) If the actor's conduct is a substantial factor in bringing about harm to another, the fact that the actor neither foresaw

**37.** See Daniell v. Ford Motor Co., 581 F.Supp. 728 (D.N.M. 1984).

**38.** See Berg v. Underwood's Hair Adaption Process, Inc., 751 F.2d 136, 137 (2d Cir. 1984) (N.Y. law).

**39.** See Smith v. Technibilt, Inc., 791 S.W.2d 247 (Tex. App. 1990).

**40.** See Erkson v. Sears, Roebuck & Co., 841 S.W.2d 207 (Mo. Ct. App. 1992).

**41.** See Smith v. Holmes, 606 N.E.2d 627 (Ill. App. Ct. 1992).

**42.** Larue v. National Union Elec. Corp., 571 F.2d 51 (1st Cir. 1978) (Me. law) (unforeseeable as a matter of law).

**43.** See Simpson v. Standard Container Co., 527 A.2d 1337 (Md. Ct. Spec. App. 1987) (label on can warned against storing in living area). *Contra* Keller v. Welles Dept. Store of Racine, 276 N.W.2d 319, 324 (Wis. Ct. App. 1979) (foreseeable that "incurably curious" children might taste gasoline stored in a can on the floor, or, while playing "mow the lawn" or "gas station," might pour gasoline from the can).

**44.** See Oden v. Pepsi Cola Bottling Co., 621 So.2d 953 (Ala. 1993). *Contra* Morgan v. Cavalier Acquisition Corp., 432 S.E.2d 915 (N.C. Ct. App. 1993) (jury could properly find foreseeable); Ridenour v. Bat 'Em Out, 707 A.2d 1093 (N.J. Super. Ct. App. Div. 1998) (change machine: foreseeable).

**45.** The "misuse" decisions, finding uses to be foreseeable as well as unforeseeable, are collected at § 13.5, below.

**46.** See id.

nor should have foreseen the extent of the harm or the manner in which it occurred does not prevent him from being liable.

(2) The actor's conduct may be held not to be a legal cause of harm to another where after the event and looking back from the harm to the actor's negligent conduct, it appears to the court highly extraordinary that it should have brought about the harm.

Conventional doctrine provides that a manufacturer or other tort defendant remains subject to liability even if it cannot foresee the *extent* or *manner* of harm, but that the defendant is shielded from responsibility if it cannot foresee the *type* of risk that harms the plaintiff.[47]

### Extent of Harm

Myrtle Poplar pricked her finger on the jagged point of a silvery metal star adorning a cosmetic gift box she had received for Christmas. An infection developed, and the finger had to be amputated. The manufacturer argued that it should not be held to anticipate "so extraordinary and unpredictable a result" as an amputation "from the otherwise trivial puncturing of her skin." The court disagreed: "[I]f the plaintiff's injury is traceable to the defendant's negligence without intervention of any other independent, legally operative event—the injured person is entitled to recover for the harm actually suffered even though the precise nature and extent of those injuries, as they finally developed, were more severe than could ordinarily have been foreseen." A defendant is responsible, continued the court, "for all the harm and suffering which his negligent act brought on even though the plaintiff's injuries were aggravated by his own predisposition or weakness or by the intervening mistake or negligence of a physician who treated the original injury."[48]

### Manner of Harm

It generally is agreed that the precise *manner* in which the harm occurs need not be foreseeable. So, a meat packing company that negligently applied a rubber band to bind a shank of lamb was liable even if it could not foresee that a butcher would be hit in the eye when the band flew off as he grasped the lamb to pull it forward along a conveyor rail.[49] And the seller of an improperly designed rotary power lawn mower was liable even if it could not foresee that the mower would eject a stick at high velocity through the open window of a passing police car 26 feet away, into the eye of the officer within.[50]

**47.** See Dobbs, Law of Torts §§ 187–89.

**48.** See Poplar v. Bourjois, 80 N.E.2d 334, 336–37 (N.Y. 1948) (dictum).

**49.** See Katz v. Swift & Co., 276 F.2d 905, 906 (2d Cir. 1960) (N.Y. law) ("It was, of course, not necessary that defendant should have been able to anticipate the particular chain of events that would result in injury in order to be held liable. It was sufficient that it was foreseeable that injury might result if the rubber bands were improperly attached . . . . ").

**50.** See Swearngin v. Sears Roebuck & Co., 376 F.2d 637, 642 (10th Cir. 1967) (Kan. law). See also Stazenski v. Tennant Co., 617 So.2d 344 (Fla. Dist. Ct. App. 1993) (not necessary for plaintiff to prove that manufacturer of industrial sweeper with unnecessarily sharp edges could foresee that worker on another machine would fall off that machine and cut the nerves and tendons in his wrist, only that it was foreseeable that a person might come into con-

### Type of Harm (or Risk of Harm)

**In general.** In contrast to the manner and extent of harm, the foreseeability vel non of the *type* of harm suffered by the plaintiff—or, more properly, the type of *risk* that caused the harm—figures prominently in proximate cause determinations. Indeed, the type-of-harm phraseology is merely the conventional formulation of the harm-within-the-risk idea of the *Third Restatement*, discussed above, which is basically just another window on the scope-of-foreseeable-risk idea that more fully describes the operative principle of proximate causation.

**Emotional distress.** Cases involving claims for emotional distress, while sometimes resolved on duty grounds,[51] frequently are based on whether a manufacturer of a particular type of product should be expected to foresee that some consumers will become distressed, and perhaps even suffer illness as a result, if its products are defective. Thus, a manufacturer might not fairly be required to expect that a person would become so frightened as to have a heart attack from seeing rusty brown water caused by a defect in the manufacturer's water softener.[52] But it might be fair to require a manufacturer to expect that a person would become distressed if, while drinking from a bottle of Coke, he suddenly found himself sucking on a rat;[53] or, at least in the eyes of one court, that a housewife would become hysterical, and ultimately suffer traumatic neurosis, from witnessing her washing machine vibrating violently, like a "robot gone crazy."[54]

**Suicide and Murder.** Cases involving the foreseeability that a product might be used to commit suicide or murder usually involve principles of superseding causation, which itself is grounded in foreseeability,[55] as well as the simpler concept of the foreseeability of the risk of harm. On one of these two grounds, or on some other,[56] most courts deny recovery against manufacturers for product-related suicides and murders.[57]

tact with and be injured by the exposed sharp edges).

**51.** See § 5.3, above (liability for emotional distress under § 402A).

**52.** See Caputzal v. Lindsay Co., 222 A.2d 513 (N.J. 1966) (plaintiff's emotional hypersensitivity was idiosyncratic and hence unforeseeable). Nor that a plaintiff, with a history of heart problems and in poor shape, will suffer a fatal heart attack while engaging in sexual intercourse with his wife after taking the defendant's drug, Viagra. See Brumley v. Pfizer, Inc., 149 F.Supp.2d 305 (S.D. Tex. 2001) (Viagra had merely furnished the condition for the heart attack, not caused it, since it merely did its job).

**53.** See Way v. Tampa Coca Cola Bottling Co., 260 So.2d 288 (Fla. Dist. Ct. App. 1972). Other emotional distress food and drink cases are noted in § 7.5, above.

**54.** See Barnette v. Dickens, 135 S.E.2d 109 (Va. 1964).

**55.** See § 12.3, below.

**56.** See, e.g., Miller v. Pfizer Inc. (Roerig Div.), 196 F.Supp.2d 1095 (D. Kan. 2002) (no cause in fact, because psychiatrist was already aware of suicide risk and would have prescribed anti-depressant medication, Zoloft, even with additional warnings), aff'd, 356 F.3d 1326 (10th Cir. 2004); Martin v. Hacker, 628 N.E.2d 1308 (N.Y. 1993) (warning of risk of suicide provided by manufacturer in drug warnings was adequate as a matter of law).

**57.** See, e.g., Kleen v. Homak Mfg. Co., 749 N.E.2d 26 (Ill. App. Ct. 2001) (unforeseeable to manufacturer of allegedly defective lock on gun case that plaintiff's adult son would break into case with a screwdriver, remove the gun stored inside, and use the gun to kill himself); Watters v. TSR, Inc. 904 F.2d 378 (6th Cir. 1990) (Ky. law) (unforeseeable that Dungeons & Dragons game would cause boy to commit suicide); Moss by Moss v. Meyer, 454 N.E.2d 48 (Ill. Ct. App. 1983) (unforeseeable that child would attempt suicide by swallowing pre-

### Type of Plaintiff

One should recall the lesson of Chief Judge Cardozo's opinion for the majority in the *Palsgraf* case,[58] that the scope of an actor's responsibility extends only to foreseeable plaintiffs, and not to those injured by a product who lie outside the orbit of foreseeable risk. Occasionally a court will rule that a particular type of user is unforeseeable as a matter of law. So, a 14-year-old operator of a meat-grinding machine may be unforeseeable when labor laws prohibit operation by anyone under the age of 16.[59]

One class of plaintiffs encountering special difficulty with proximate cause are hospitals, insurance companies, other institutions, and even nations that have sued cigarette companies for the recovery of health care expenses resulting from the cigarette industry's fraudulent marketing of cigarettes over many years. Often reasoning from a Supreme Court securities law decision,[60] all cigarette health-care expense reimbursement claims have been dismissed,[61] as have many claims by cities against the gun industry for the costs of crime caused by the defendants'

scription capsules delivered by pharmacist to front doorstep of home); Saxton v. McDonnell Douglas Aircraft Co., 428 F.Supp. 1047 (C.D. Cal. 1977) (unforeseeable that mother of passenger killed in plane crash would commit suicide from stress of son's death and subsequent products liability trial).

See also James v. Meow Media, Inc., 300 F.3d 683, 693 (6th Cir. 2002) (Ky. law) (unforeseeable that video game would cause student to shoot other students in school lobby: "it is simply too far a leap from shooting characters on a video screen (an activity undertaken by millions) to shooting people in a classroom (an activity undertaken by a handful, at most) for Carneal's actions to have been reasonably foreseeable to the manufacturers of the media that Carneal played and viewed"); Sanders v. Acclaim Entm't, Inc., 188 F.Supp.2d 1264 (D. Colo. 2002) (unforeseeable that two students would shoot and kill teacher in shooting spree).

*But see* Hooks SuperX, Inc. v. McLaughlin 642 N.E.2d 514 (Ind. 1994) (in action against pharmacist for refilling prescription for dangerous and addictive drug at rate faster than prescribed, whether customer's suicide attempt constituted unforeseeable intervening cause was a jury question).

**58.** See Palsgraf v. Long Island R.R. Co., 162 N.E. 99 (N.Y. 1928).

**59.** See Darsan v. Globe Slicing Mach. Co., 606 N.Y.S.2d 317 (App. Div.1994).

**60.** See Holmes v. Securities Investor Protection Corp., 503 U.S. 258 (1992) (RICO case in which plaintiff's expenses, incurred to reimburse investors who suf-

fered losses due to defendant's fraudulent activity, were "too remote").

**61.** See, e.g., Regence Blueshield v. Philip Morris Inc., 5 Fed.Appx. 651, 653 (9th Cir. 2001) (Wash. law) ("Their claimed damages were not proximately caused by the Tobacco Firms' unlawful conduct, but were instead derivative of the personal injuries of smokers afflicted by tobacco-related illnesses."); United Food and Commercial Workers Unions v. Philip Morris, Inc., 223 F.3d 1271 (11th Cir. 2000) (Ala. law); Laborers Local 17 Health & Benefit Fund v. Philip Morris, Inc., 191 F.3d 229, 236 (2d Cir. 1999) (N.Y. law) ("where a plaintiff complains of injuries that are wholly derivative of harm to a third party, plaintiff's injuries are generally deemed indirect and as a consequence too remote, as a matter of law, to support recovery," citing Holmes v. Sec. Investor Prot. Corp., 503 U.S. 258, 268–69 (1992)); In re Tobacco/Governmental Health Care Costs Litig., 83 F.Supp.2d 125, 130 (D.D.C. 1999) ("[t]he tortured path that one must follow from the tobacco companies' alleged wrongdoing to the [plaintiff's] increased expenditures demonstrates that the [plaintiff's] claims are precisely the type of indirect claims that the proximate cause requirement is intended to weed out," citing Steamfitters Local Union No. 420 Welfare Fund v. Philip Morris, Inc., 171 F.3d 912, 930 (3d Cir. 1999) (Pa. law), aff'd, Service Employees Int'l Union Health and Welfare Fund v. Philip Morris Inc., 249 F.3d 1068 (D.C. Cir. 2001) (claims by Guatemala, Nicaragua, and Ukraine were essentially derivative, too remote, damages were not proximate, and defendants lacked standing).

"negligent marketing,"[62] on grounds (among others) that such "derivative" claims for economic losses suffered by third parties are simply too "remote."[63]

But most courts are quite lenient in finding most types of plaintiffs foreseeable in most situations. Where a paraplegic, with no heat sensitivity in his feet, drove a motor home (with hand controls he had installed) for six hours while his bare feet rested on the steel floorboard that reached 175° Fahrenheit, the court ruled that the plaintiff was a foreseeable consumer;[64] and, a minor biker, who avoided large slots in a drainage grate on a pedestrian-biker pathway by riding into the street, where he was struck by a car, was a foreseeable plaintiff as well.[65] Rescuers, it will be recalled,[66] are considered foreseeable plaintiffs when they provide aid to others, "if only it be not wanton,"[67] when they are themselves injured in the process.[68]

## § 12.3  INTERVENING AND SUPERSEDING CAUSES

### General Principals

The connection between a defendant's breach of duty and the plaintiff's harm may appear tenuous or "remote" because of the intervention of some person or force other than the plaintiff or defendant. Some third party may use the product abusively, or may ignore its warnings or instructions, in a manner that might give rise to a contributory or comparative negligence, assumption of risk, or misuse defense had the conduct been that of the plaintiff. Such conduct by third parties,[1] that combines somehow with a product defect (or its consequences) in a manner that harms the plaintiff, raises a question of how such conduct should affect the manufacturer's or other seller's responsibility for the harm, if at all. The doctrinal question in such cases is whether the third

---

**62.** See, e.g., Camden Cty. Bd. of Chosen Freeholders v. Beretta U.S.A. Corp., 123 F.Supp.2d 245, 257 (D.N.J. 2000) ("in general, 'a plaintiff who complained of harm flowing merely from the misfortunes visited upon a third person by the defendant's acts [is] generally said to stand at too remote a distance to recover' "), aff'd, 273 F.3d 536 (3d Cir. 2001). *But see* James v. Arms Tech., Inc., 820 A.2d 27 (N.J. Super. Ct. App. Div. 2003) (allowing negligence, public nuisance, and punitive damages claims); City of Chicago v. Beretta U.S.A. Corp., 337 Ill.App.3d 1 (App. Ct. 2002) (allowing public nuisance claim); Cincinnati v. Beretta U.S.A. Corp., 768 N.E.2d 1136 (Ohio 2002).

**63.** These issues are touched on in § 10.3, above.

**64.** Goree v. Winnebago Indus., 958 F.2d 1537 (11th Cir. 1992) (Ala. law).

**65.** See Moffat v. U.S. Foundry & Mfg. Corp., 551 So.2d 592 (Fla. Dist. Ct. App. 1989).

**66.** See § 5.3, above.

**67.** See Wagner v. Int'l Ry., 133 N.E. 437, 437–38 (N.Y. 1921).

**68.** See McCoy v. American Suzuki Motor Corp., 961 P.2d 952 (Wash. 1998) (motorist, struck by hit-and-run driver during attempt to aid passengers in overturned vehicle, could proceed with design defect action against manufacturer of overturned vehicle even though plaintiff was injured two hours after accident which prompted his rescue and after police had arrived); Dillard v. Pittway Corp., 719 So.2d 188 (Ala. 1998) (rescuers, injured or killed in a boarding house fire, foreseeable to manufacturer of smoke detectors); Mack v. Ford Motor Co., 669 N.E.2d 608 (Ill. Ct. App. 1996).

**§ 12.3**

**1.** Most courts properly limit the application of principles of intervening and superseding causes to third parties, and do not apply them to plaintiffs, for whom the standard misconduct defenses, including (in unusual cases) the doctrine of "sole proximate cause," should suffice. See ch. 13, below.

party's conduct, intervening upon a set of risks created by the defendant's sale of a defective product, distances the seller from the plaintiff's harm so much that the product defect and the seller's conduct become legally "remote" and, hence, no longer a "proximate" cause of the plaintiff's harm. Stated another way, the issue in products liability cases of this type is whether the third party's conduct is so significant in comparison to the product defect as to trivialize the role of the defect in causing the plaintiff's harm, so that the manufacturer or other seller fairly should be relieved of all responsibility.[2]

The first question in such cases is whether some third party's conduct, which came into existence after the defendant's sale of a defective product, combined in some manner with the product's defective condition so as to cause the plaintiff's injury. If so, the third party's actions are viewed as an "intervening" force or cause.[3] So characterizing the third party's conduct means little more than that it was a "concurring cause," together with the product defect, which normally makes the third party concurrently liable with the seller for the plaintiff's injury.[4] While, traditionally, concurrent tortfeasors were jointly and severally liable for the plaintiff's harm, they now in most jurisdictions may be responsible only for some equitable portion of the plaintiff's damages under principles of comparative fault and apportionment. Even in such apportionment regimes, however, each concurrent tortfeasor is responsible for at least some portion of the plaintiff's damages. Thus, a third party whose conduct joins with a product defect to cause the plaintiff's injuries is subject to liability to the plaintiff anyway, under joint and several liability or comparative fault principles of apportionment, which makes the "intervening cause" classification superfluous unless something else is added to the mix.

That something else is whether the intervening party's conduct is so significant that it "breaks the chain" of proximate causation, insulating the seller from *all* responsibility for the plaintiff's harm. When an intervening cause has such significance that a product seller's responsibility is severed altogether, the intervening cause is denominated "superseding." The *Second Restatement* provides: "A superseding cause is an act of a third person or other force which by its intervention prevents the actor from being liable for harm to another which his antecedent negligence is a substantial factor in bringing about."[5] An intervening cause, which arises after a defendant's tortious conduct and is sufficient in itself to cause the plaintiff's injury, may become a superseding cause if

---

**2.** See, e.g., Gash, The Intersection of Proximate Cause and Terrorism: A Contextual Analysis of the (Proposed) Restatement Third of Torts' Approach to Intervening and Superseding Causes, 91 Ky. L.J. 523 (2003); M. Green, The Unanticipated Ripples of Comparative Negligence: Superseding Cause in Products Liability and Beyond, 53 S.C. L. Rev. 1103 (2002); Note, Dumb As A Matter of Law: The "Superseding Cause" Modification of Comparative Negligence, 79 Tex. L. Rev. 493 (2000); Note, Why Superseding Cause Analysis Should Be Abandoned, 72 Tex. L. Rev. 161 (1993); Note, 59

Temp. L. Rev. 239(1986) (failure to warn as a superseding cause); 1 Frumer and Friedman, Products Liability § 3.05; 1 Madden & Owen on Products Liability, § 13:3.

**3.** "An intervening force is one which actively operates in producing harm to another after the actor's negligent act or omission has been committed." Restatement (2d) Torts § 441(1).

**4.** On concurrent causation, see § 11.3, above.

**5.** Restatement (2d) Torts § 440.

it is an independent force that operates upon, but is not triggered by nor flows from, the defendant's wrongdoing.[6] It is important to note that these common statements characterizing superseding cause merely state the legal consequence of classifying an intervening cause as "superseding." What they do not do is provide a test for determining whether an intervening cause or force should be so classified. In other words, the "superseding cause" term is just a label, not a recipe.

For a recipe, almost every case turns principally or exclusively to a single test—foreseeability. While many courts and commentators elaborate upon foreseeability, explaining how it operates in varying contexts, the underlying analysis remains essentially the same. And, as with proximate cause more generally, commentators continue to object to the vagueness prison from which foreseeability cannot escape, often arguing that courts should use a richer, scope of (foreseeable) risk approach to superseding cause determinations. But this is what courts in fact do, if often they do not say so, and there is less debate about the appropriateness of foreseeability as the test for superseding cause as there is about proximate cause more generally. The courts, at least, seem perfectly content with using foreseeability as the polar star for determining whether a third party's misconduct should sever the responsibility of a manufacturer or other seller of a defective product.[7] "For an intervening force to be a superseding cause that relieves an actor from liability, the intervening cause must be a cause that could not have been reasonably foreseen or anticipated."[8] And the converse is also true: "A third party's acts of negligence do not break the causal chain if the acts are foreseeable."[9]

Some courts enrich the foreseeability inquiry by considering several helpful considerations that the *Second Restatement* suggests may be relevant to this inquiry[10]—(1) whether the intervention brought about a harm different in kind from that risked by the defendant's tortious behavior; (2) whether the operation or consequences of the intervention appear, *after* the event, "extraordinary"; (3) whether the intervention operated "independently" or was a "normal result" of the actor's negligence; and (4) whether the intervening cause was a human wrongdoer and, if so, the degree of that wrongdoing.[11] All of the foregoing

---

**6.** See, e.g., Ontario Sewing Mach. Co. v. Smith, 572 S.E.2d 533, 536 (Ga. 2002); Gaines–Tabb v. ICI Explosives, USA, Inc., 160 F.3d 613, 621 (10th Cir. 1998) (Okla. law); Stephenson by Coley v. S.C. Johnson & Son, Inc., 638 N.Y.S.2d 889, 892 (Sup. Ct. 1996).

**7.** See, e.g., Gaines–Tabb v. ICI Explosives, USA, Inc., 160 F.3d 613, 621 (10th Cir. 1998) (Okla. law).

**8.** Small v. Pioneer Mach., Inc., 494 S.E.2d 835, 844 (S.C. Ct. App. 1997). See also Adams v. Lift–A–Loft Corp., 1999 WL 33105610, at *1 (S.D. Ohio 1999) ("only an intervening act that was unforeseeable was sufficient to break the chain of causation").

**9.** Id. See also Mack v. Ford Motor Co., 669 N.E.2d 608, 613 (Ill. App. Ct. 1996) ("A

foreseeable intervening force does not break the chain of legal causation.").

**10.** See, e.g., Gaines–Tabb v. ICI Explosives, USA, Inc., 160 F.3d 613, 620–21 (10th Cir. 1998) (Okla. law).

**11.** Restatement (2d) Torts § 442, "Considerations Important in Determining Whether an Intervening Force is a Superseding Cause," provides:

The following considerations are of importance in determining whether an intervening force is a superseding cause of harm to another:

(a) The fact that its intervention brings about harm different in kind from that which would otherwise have resulted from the actor's negligence;

principles, it should be noted, although originating in the law of negligence, apply equally to claims in strict products liability.[12] Like most other aspects of proximate cause, whether the defendant should reasonably have foreseen an intervening cause normally is a subject of varying inferences which presents a question for the jury.[13]

### Types of Third Parties

#### Parents

Many, perhaps most, products liability cases in which young children are injured involve inadequate supervision on the part of a parent or other person having custody of the child at the time of the accident. This was true in the two farm accident cases involving young children, *Winnett* and *Richelman*, examined in the previous section.[14] Modern courts are reluctant to hold that a parent's negligent supervision can supersede the responsibility of a manufacturer of a defective product.[15] Yet, in a sense, this is what the court implicitly did in *Winnett,* and what the dissent argued should have been done in *Richelman*. Nevertheless, at least with respect to products intended for use in the home, most courts consider parental neglect—and the resulting wandering and mischief of curious youngsters—part of the "foreseeable environment of use" of such products.[16] While negligent supervision may be viewed as passive misconduct,[17] courts are also loathe to attach a superseding label to a parent's affirmative misbehavior, such as falling asleep at the wheel of a

(b) the fact that its operation or the consequences thereof appear after the event to be extraordinary rather than normal in view of the circumstances existing at the time of its operation;

(c) the fact that the intervening force is operating independently of any situation created by the actor's negligence, or, on the other hand, is or is not a normal result of such a situation;

(d) the fact that the operation of the intervening force is due to a third person's act or to his failure to act;

(e) the fact that the intervening force is due to an act of a third person which is wrongful toward the other and as such subjects the third person to liability to him;

(f) the degree of culpability of a wrongful act of a third person which sets the intervening force in motion.

**12.** See, e.g., Anderson v. Dreis & Krump Mfg. Corp., 739 P.2d 1177, 1185 (Wash. Ct. App. 1987).

**13.** See, e.g., Ontario Sewing Mach. Co., Ltd. v. Smith, 572 S.E.2d 533 (Ga. 2002); Mack v. Ford Motor Co., 669 N.E.2d 608, 613 (Ill. App. Ct. 1996) ("where varying inferences are possible, foreseeability is a question for the jury"); Stephenson by Coley v. S.C. Johnson & Son, Inc., 638 N.Y.S.2d 889, 894 (Sup. Ct. 1996). Compare

McCoy v. American Suzuki Motor Corp., 961 P.2d 952, 957 (Wash. 1998) ("Whether an independent cause is reasonably foreseeable is generally a question of fact for the jury. However, the court will at times take this question from the jury ... if there is no question that the intervening cause was 'totally unforeseeable, in a causal sense, to the original condition attributable to the defendant's conduct.' ").

**14.** See § 12.2, above.

**15.** See, e.g., Talkington v. Atria Reclamelucifers Fabrieken BV, 152 F.3d 254 (4th Cir. 1998) (S.C. law) (plaintiffs died in a house fire that might have been started by infant child with cigarette lighter).

**16.** See, e.g., Spruill v. Boyle–Midway, Inc., 308 F.2d 79 (4th Cir. 1962) (Va. law) (unattended infant drank furniture polish that mother left on bureau beside crib); Eshbach v. W.T. Grant's & Co., 481 F.2d 940 (3d Cir. 1973) (Pa. law) (unbeknownst to father, 9–year-old son drove riding mower with sister riding on back). *But see* Wenzell v. MTD Prods., Inc., 336 N.E.2d 125, 134 (Ill. App. Ct. 1975) (unforeseeable that riding mower would be used by group of young children "virtually as a toy").

**17.** See also McConnell v. Cosco, Inc., 238 F.Supp.2d 970 (S.D. Ohio 2003) (foreseeable that babysitter might neglect baby left unstrapped in high chair).

car in which the child is riding,[18] or knocking over a bottle of liquid drain cleaner onto the child.[19]

### Doctors

A common failing of doctors that quite often leads to serious harm is the failure to provide a patient with drug warnings and instructions provided by the manufacturer to the doctor. *Kirk v. Michael Reese Hosp. & Medical Center*[20] was such a case, where a passenger was injured when the driver of a car lost control of the vehicle and crashed into a tree. Earlier in the day, when the driver was discharged from a psychiatric hospital, his doctors prescribed two drugs, Thorazine and Prolixin, but failed to warn him of the dangers of mixing alcohol with the drugs. After leaving the hospital, he consumed an alcoholic drink which may have interacted with the drugs to cause the loss of control later in the day. On these facts, the court held that the drug manufacturers could not reasonably have foreseen that the drugs would be dispensed without the warnings the companies had furnished to physicians. Nor must a manufacturer foresee that a doctor will use a drug contrary to its express warnings,[21] nor must a manufacturer warn doctors of the risks of prescribing a drug for a non-indicated use.[22]

Yet, if the defect in a medical product is a physical one, courts are more willing to hold manufacturers responsible for the consequences, even if the doctor's intervening conduct substantially aggravates the patient's situation. In *Pharmaseal Labs., Inc. v. Goffe*,[23] a doctor inserted an intestinal tube weighted with a small balloon of mercury through the plaintiff's nostril, down through his stomach, and into his intestines, in order to treat an internal obstruction. As the doctor began to remove the tube, it stuck, leading the doctor to tug at it forcefully several times to pull it out. In the process, the balloon was broken, and it was discovered that the plaintiff had inhaled the mercury into his lungs. The doctor had the plaintiff placed head-down on a tilt table, and the hospital employees pounded on his back for several hours in an attempt to remove the mercury, causing his head constantly to hit the foot of the bed, leading to a heart attack soon thereafter. Reversing a summary judgment for the manufacturer, the court refused to find that the actions of the doctor and hospital employees shielded the manufacturer from liability as a matter of law for selling a balloon of inadequate strength.

### Employers

As examined earlier,[24] a manufacturer of an industrial product sometimes has a duty to communicate warnings and instructions directly to the buyer's employees. If the manufacturer has such a duty, and if the manufacturer provides a warning only to the employer (as by a safety

**18.** See Rossell v. Volkswagen of America, 709 P.2d 517 (Ariz. 1985).

**19.** See Drayton v. Jiffee Chem. Corp., 395 F.Supp. 1081 (N.D. Ohio 1975), aff'd, 591 F.2d 352 (6th Cir. 1978).

**20.** 513 N.E.2d 387, 394 (Ill. 1987).

**21.** See, e.g., Dyer v. Best Pharmacal, 577 P.2d 1084 (Ariz. Ct. App. 1978).

**22.** See Robak v. Abbott Labs., 797 F.Supp. 475 (D. Md. 1992) (renal failure from antibiotic Omniflox prescribed for sinusitis, although drug not indicated for upper respiratory tract conditions).

**23.** 568 P.2d 589 (N.M. 1977).

**24.** See §§ 9.4 and 9.5, above.

information sheet or a technical data manual) and not to the employees (as by a label on the product's container or a warning plate on a machine), the employer's failure to pass along the warning to its employees will not generally supersede the manufacturer's duty to warn them directly.[25] Yet, courts quite generally refuse to hold a manufacturer liable for machinery malfunctions occasioned by an employer's improper maintenance.[26]

**Failing to add guards.** Before the 1970s, the custom was for employers, rather than manufacturers, to install appropriate guards on industrial machinery. Starting with *Bexiga v. Havir Mfg. Corp.*,[27] courts began to hold that manufacturers had a nondelegable duty to equip their machinery with sufficient safety devices. What this means in terms of superseding cause is that, if a manufacturer fails to provide adequate guards, the employer's failure to remedy the danger will not generally shield the manufacturer. This may be true even if the employer blithely ignores warning letters from the manufacturer urging the employer to cure the defect, explaining how to do so, and offering to provide the employer with the necessary devices for a fee.[28]

**Removing or altering guards.** A recurring problem for manufacturers attempting to comply with the *Bexiga* nondelegable duty doctrine occurs when an employer removes or alters a guard provided by the manufacturer.[29] Guards are modified or removed for a variety of reasons: because they malfunction; to facilitate cleaning or maintenance of the machinery; to enhance the usefulness of the machine, as by permitting stock of a particular size or shape to enter the machine; or to speed up production. Most courts hold the manufacturer accountable for injuries attributable to "foreseeable" modifications, provided that a feasible remedy—such as an electrical interlock—was reasonably available to the manufacturer at the time it designed and sold the machine.[30] But if the employer's modification is unforeseeable, the modification is considered

---

**25.** See, e.g., Gordon v. Niagara Mach. & Tool Works, 574 F.2d 1182 (5th Cir. 1978) (Miss. law).

**26.** "The manufacturer is not liable for lack of normal maintenance." Rogers v. Unimac Co., 565 P.2d 181, 184 (Ariz. 1977) (failure to replace worn and cracked parts in automatic car wash mechanism). See also La Plante v. American Honda Motor Co., 27 F.3d 731 (1st Cir. 1994) (R.I. law) (poor maintenance of ATV could constitute statutory defense of alteration). *But cf.* Johnson v. Salem Corp., 477 A.2d 1246, 1255 (N.J. 1984) (where machine defective for not having a guard, employer's negligent maintenance—creating a risk of injury that would have been prevented by guard—does not shield manufacturer from liability).

**27.** 290 A.2d 281 (N.J. 1972). See § 8.9, above.

**28.** See Balido v. Improved Mach., Inc., 105 Cal.Rptr. 890 (Ct. App. 1972). See also Montgomery Elevator Co. v. McCullough, 676 S.W.2d 776 (Ky. 1984). *But see* Hinojo v. New Jersey Mfg. Ins. Co., 802 A.2d 551 (N.J. Super. Ct. App. Div. 2002) (employer's

ignoring of several letters from manufacturer urging employer to replace safety guards on presses entitled employer to instruction on superseding cause). Compare Ontario Sewing Mach. Co., Ltd. v. Smith, 572 S.E.2d 533 (Ga. 2002) (unforeseeable failure to comply with recall would be sole proximate cause, but foreseeability for jury).

**29.** Compare Davis v. Berwind Corp., 690 A.2d 186 (Pa. 1997) (purchaser's removal of safety devices was superseding cause of employee's injury), with Anderson v. Dreis & Krump Mfg. Corp., 739 P.2d 1177, 1185 (Wash. Ct. App. 1987) (purchaser's removal of safety devices was not a superseding cause).

**30.** See, e.g., Cepeda v. Cumberland Eng'g Co., 386 A.2d 816 (N.J. 1978), rev'g 351 A.2d 22 (N.J. 1976) (guard attached to machine with four bolts was not reattached to machine after cleaning; since interlock installation would have cost $25–30, and frequent cleaning was necessary, *held,* foreseeability of removal a jury question). Accord Marois v. Paper Converting Mach. Co., 539 A.2d 621 (Me. 1988); Brown v. United

a superseding cause that shields the manufacturer from liability.[31] In a small number of jurisdictions, even foreseeable alterations may bar recovery.[32]

**"Substantial change."** Courts often examine alteration questions in terms of whether the product was "substantially changed" after it left the manufacturer. This derives from *Restatement (Second) of Torts* § 402A(b) which provides for liability only if the product "is expected to and does reach the user or consumer without substantial change in the condition in which it is sold."[33] While some courts shield manufacturers from injuries from an employer's alteration of safety devices on "substantial change" grounds,[34] other courts refuse to relieve the manufacturer from liability unless the change is deemed "unforeseeable."[35] In addition, courts sometimes bar recovery in alteration cases on grounds of unforeseeable misuse.[36] Courts disagree on whether there should be a duty to warn about foreseeable risks of removing safety devices, some courts refusing to require such a warning,[37] others holding that it makes good sense.[38]

States Stove Co., 484 A.2d 1234, 1240 (N.J. 1984) ("a design defect inherent in a safety feature of a product that foreseeably leads to a substantial alteration and an increased risk of danger can be a basis for strict products liability").

**31.** See, e.g., Fisher v. Walsh Parts & Serv. Co., 296 F.Supp.2d 551 (E.D. Pa. 2003) (unforeseeable modifications by purchaser becomes superseding cause breaking chain of causation).

**32.** See Hines v. Joy Mfg. Co., 850 F.2d 1146, 1151 (6th Cir. 1988) (interpreting Kentucky products liability statute barring recovery for injuries caused by product modifications: "we are not inclined to read the common law concept of foreseeability" into the act). Compare Robinson v. Reed–Prentice Div. of Package Mach. Co., 403 N.E.2d 440, 444 (N.Y. 1980), in which an employee was injured when he stuck his hand through a hole in the safety guard cut by his employer. *Held*: judgment for plaintiff reversed. "The manufacturer's duty . . . does not extend to designing a product that is impossible to abuse or one whose safety features may not be circumvented. . . . Material alterations at the hands of a third party which work a substantial change in the condition in which the product was sold by destroying the functional utility of a key safety feature, however foreseeable that modification may have been, are not within the ambit of a manufacturer's responsibility." *But see* Lopez v. Precision Papers, Inc., 484 N.Y.S.2d 585 (App. Div. 1985), aff'd, 492 N.E.2d 1214 (N.Y. 1986) (allowing recovery for injuries preventable by interlock on forklift guard that could have prevented lift from rising above operator's head.).

**33.** See also caveat (2) and comments *p* and *q*. See, e.g., Davis v. Berwind Corp., 690

A.2d 186, 190 (Pa. 1997) (in disregard of warnings in owner's manual and affixed to machine, plaintiff's employer removed safety devices which "clearly constitutes a substantial change" in the product, thereby relieving manufacturer of liability); Glassey v. Continental Ins. Co., 500 N.W.2d 295 (Wis. 1993) (employer put non-standard replacement cap on pressurized tank).

**34.** See, e.g, Robinson v. Reed–Prentice Div. of Package Mach. Co., 403 N.E.2d 440, 444 (N.Y. 1980) (employee stuck hand through hole in safety guard cut by his employer: "Material alterations at the hands of a third party which work a substantial change in the condition in which the product was sold by destroying the functional utility of a key safety feature, however foreseeable that modification may have been, are not within the ambit of a manufacturer's responsibility.").

**35.** See, e.g., Brown v. United States Stove Co., 484 A.2d 1234, 1240 (N.J. 1984) ("a design defect inherent in a safety feature of a product that foreseeably leads to a substantial alteration and an increased risk of danger can be a basis for strict products liability").

**36.** See, e.g., Westchem Agric. Chem., Inc. v. Ford Motor Co., 990 F.2d 426 (8th Cir. 1993) (N.D. law) (aftermarket electrical equipment, bypassing safety device, spliced into electrical system).

**37.** See, e.g., Huber v. Niagara Mach. & Tool Works, 430 N.W.2d 465 (Minn. 1988) (no duty to warn of danger in removing safety devices).

**38.** See, e.g., Liriano v. Hobart Corp., 700 N.E.2d 303, 307–08 (N.Y. 1998) (*Liriano II*) ("Unlike design decisions that in-

### Other Employees

Employees injure one another with industrial machinery in a variety of ways. A fellow employee's misconduct may or may not supersede the manufacturer's design errors depending on the "foreseeability" of the misconduct and the availability to the manufacturer of a feasible means to prevent it. In *Wieder v. Towmotor Corp.*,[39] for example, a worker left a forklift on an incline and forgot to set the hand brake. The plaintiff was injured when the forklift rolled down the incline and struck him. His theory of liability was that the forklift should have had a passive, "back-up" brake system. The jury rendered a verdict for the plaintiff, which the trial court sustained.

### Other Parties

Although intervening misconduct in products liability cases usually involves parents, doctors, employers, and sometimes fellow workers, other parties are sometimes involved. In *Dugan v. Sears, Roebuck & Co.*,[40] a 5–year-old boy was sitting on the steps to his neighbor's front porch watching her mow the lawn. When the neighbor was about 10 feet from the plaintiff, the lawn mower picked up and ejected at high velocity a small piece of plastic which hit the plaintiff in the eye and blinded him. The neighbor had read the mower manual which warned users in no uncertain terms not to operate the mower if children were in the vicinity and to stop the engine if anyone came near. The plaintiff sued Sears, alleging that it should have sold a mower with a safer alternative design. Upholding a verdict for Sears, the appellate court reasoned that the jury reasonably could have concluded that the neighbor's conduct was unforeseeable and so could be a superseding cause of the plaintiff's injuries. While acknowledging that manufacturers should foresee that people occasionally will disregard their warnings, the court concluded that a reasonable jury still might conclude that the neighbor's conduct in this case was not so "probable, natural, and foreseeable" that the defendant should be held strictly liable.

While the *Dugan* court's holding might be viewed as quite conservative, other courts in superseding cause cases stretch the flexible concept of foreseeable risk the other way. In *Bigbee v. Pacific Tel. & Tel. Co.*,[41] the plaintiff was standing in a telephone booth 15 feet from the street when it was struck by a drunken driver. Plaintiff saw the car coming but could not flee because the door of the telephone booth jammed shut. The plaintiff sued various defendants in connection with the design, location, installation, and maintenance of the booth, and the defendants moved to dismiss, arguing that the drunk driver's conduct was a superseding cause. The trial judge dismissed the complaint, but the appellate court reversed and remanded, concluding that "the risk that a car might hit

volve the consideration of many interdependent factors, the inquiry in a duty to warn case is much more limited, focusing principally on the foreseeability of the risk and the adequacy and effectiveness of any warning.... Thus, although it is virtually impossible to design a product to forestall all future risk-enhancing modifications that could occur after the sale, it is neither infeasible nor onerous, in some cases, to warn of the dangers of foreseeable modifications that pose the risk of injury.").

**39.**   568 F.Supp. 1058 (E.D. Pa. 1983).

**40.**   454 N.E.2d 64 (Ill. App. Ct. 1983).

**41.**   665 P.2d 947 (Cal. 1983).

the telephone booth could be found to constitute one of the hazards to which plaintiff was exposed.''[42]

### Shifting Responsibility

Particularly in the industrial setting, a proximate cause sub-doctrine relied upon occasionally, expressed in § 452 of the *Second Restatement*,[43] is the notion that full responsibility for product safety may sometimes be shifted from the manufacturer to an employer after the passage of many years and the integration of the product into the employer's operations. In *Meuller v. Jeffrey Mfg. Co.*,[44] the plaintiff fell through a three foot square hole in a concrete floor of his employer's foundry building. The opening was part of a sand handling system consisting of a collection of conveyors, elevators, and other equipment. Plaintiff's employer had purchased the sand handling equipment and installation design plans (which prescribed the location of the hole) fifteen years earlier from the defendant, but had done the installation itself, including the construction of the slab floor and the hole. The plaintiff claimed that the system was defectively designed and that the defendant should have warned of the risk. Relying on § 452, the court granted summary judgment for the defendant: the time interval between sale and injury, the obvious nature of the danger, the ability of the employer to remedy the danger without the manufacturer, and the "indisputable duty of the employer to keep the workplace safe and the employer's sole possession and control of the equipment" shifted the duty from the manufacturer to the employer as a matter of law.

### Statutory Reform

Product alteration is one of the key products liability reform issues. Several state reform acts have provisions making product alteration a defense to products liability suits. Kentucky's statute,[45] for example, provides: "In any product liability action, a manufacturer shall be liable only for the personal injury, death or property damage that would have occurred if the product had been used in its original, unaltered and unmodified condition. For the purpose of this section, product alteration or modification shall include failure to observe routine care and maintenance, but shall not include ordinary wear and tear. This section shall

**42.** Id. at 952.

**43.** See Restatement (2d) Torts § 452, "Third Person's Failure to Prevent Harm," which provides that "(1) Except as stated in Subsection (2), the failure of a third person to act to prevent harm to another threatened by the actor's negligent conduct is not a superseding cause of such harm. (2) Where, because of lapse of time or otherwise, the duty to prevent harm to another threatened by the actor's negligent conduct is found to have shifted from the actor to a third person, the failure of the third person to prevent such harm is a superseding cause." Comment *f* provides that a court may "find that all duty and responsibility for the prevention of the harm has passed to the third person. It is apparently impossible to state any comprehensive rule as to when such a decision will be made." Relevant factors include "the degree of danger and the magnitude of the risk of harm, the character and position of the third person who is to take the responsibility, his knowledge of the danger and the likelihood that he will or will not exercise proper care, his relation to the plaintiff or to the defendant, the lapse of time, and perhaps other considerations."

**44.** 494 F.Supp. 275, 278–79 (E.D. Pa. 1980).

**45.** See Ky. Rev. Stat. § 411.320(1).

apply to alterations or modifications made by any person or entity, except those made in accordance with specifications or instructions furnished by the manufacturer." As noted earlier, a federal court of appeals ruled that the protections of this statute are not limited to unforeseeable alterations.[46] Other reform statutes expressly limit the defense of alteration to those that are unforeseeable.[47]

### Intentional and Criminal Misconduct

When the intervening party uses a defective product intentionally to harm the plaintiff, or takes advantage of an opportunity to harm a person because a defective product fails to protect that person in the way he or she had a right to expect, an important issue is whether the doctrine of superseding causation prevents the injured plaintiff from recovering against the manufacturer or seller of the defective product. A number of cases have addressed this issue, most of which have ruled that the intentionally harmful, criminal misconduct of an intervening party was unforeseeable, and that it was accordingly a superseding cause that severed the chain of proximate causation. But courts in several cases have ruled the other way, allowing such cases to proceed if the risk of harm was deemed foreseeable. Foreseeability, or whether the intervening conduct fell within the foreseeable risk that rendered the product defective, is the purported "test" of superseding cause in cases of this type. But the decisions are exceedingly difficult to reconcile, and the best that can be done here is to give some examples and highlight some competing arguments.[48]

If a defect in a product designed for the particular purpose of self-protection, like a burglar alarm or mace,[49] causes the product to malfunction, allowing a criminal to steal from or assault the plaintiff, then the resulting criminal act would appear to fall quite clearly within the foreseeable risk of a product malfunction. But when this envelope is stretched a bit, the foreseeable risk approach begins to waffle. Thus, a locksmith was held not liable for the rape of a woman in an apartment building supposedly protected by the lock.[50] In another case, *Williams v.*

**46.**  See Hines v. Joy Mfg. Co., 850 F.2d 1146, 1151 (6th Cir. 1988) (Ky. law) ("we are not inclined to read the common law concept of foreseeability" into the act).

**47.**  See, e.g., Tenn. Code Ann. § 29–28–108; Or. Rev. Stat. § 30–915.

**48.**  See generally Gash, The Intersection of Proximate Cause and Terrorism: A Contextual Analysis of the (Proposed) Restatement Third of Torts' Approach to Intervening and Superseding Causes, 91 Ky. L.J. 523 (2003); M. Green, The Unanticipated Ripples of Comparative Negligence: Superseding Cause in Products Liability and Beyond, 53 S.C. L. Rev. 1103 (2002).

**49.**  See Klages v. General Ordnance Equip. Corp. 367 A.2d 304 (Pa. Super. Ct. 1976), where plaintiff suffered severe gun-

shot wounds when a mace weapon manufactured by defendant failed to function during a confrontation between the plaintiff and an armed robber. *Held*, because the mace was an instrument of crime prevention, the manufacturer should have foreseen the specific risk that a user would be assaulted if the product failed to function, such that the intervening criminal act was not a superseding cause that would shield the manufacturer from liability.

**50.**  Einhorn v. Seeley, 525 N.Y.S.2d 212, 215 (Ct. App. 1988) (locksmith not liable for failing to properly install door lock: "[T]he act complained of by plaintiff was perpetrated by an intervening person. There will ordinarily be no duty thrust on a defendant to prevent a third party from causing harm to another.").

*RCA Corp.*,[51] a security service guard was injured during a robbery attempt at a restaurant he was guarding. He used his two-way portable receiver manufactured by the defendant to call other security patrols in the area for backup assistance, but the receiver malfunctioned, and he was shot by the robber while trying to make an arrest himself. Because the receiver was designed for communication, not the prevention of criminal attack, the court ruled that the criminal intervening cause was unforeseeable as a matter of law.[52]

In *Stahlecker v. Ford Motor Corp.*,[53] a young woman was driving her Ford Explorer in a remote area of Nebraska when its Firestone Wilderness AT radial tires separated due to a defective condition which subsequently led to a nationwide recall of those tires. Uninjured in the accident, but stranded, she was found alone by an assailant who assaulted and murdered her. Her parents sued Ford and Firestone, alleging that they had long known of the tires' propensity to unexpectedly blow out "causing wide-ranging results that included stranding and rollovers." The Stahlecker's alleged that while Amy's particular assault and murder may not have been foreseeable, "the potential for similar dangerous situations arising as a result of a breakdown of a Ford Explorer and/or its tires resulting in danger to its consumers and users from criminal activity, adverse weather conditions, inability to communicate with others or any combination thereof, were known and/or should have been known to Defendants Ford and Firestone." Relying on *Williams*, the court affirmed summary judgment for the defendants. Yet, it might be argued that an apartment lock, a security officer's phone, and a young woman's car, are similar to burglar alarms and mace in that a purpose of all five types of products is to help the user avoid dangerous situations.

If a product's design is defective because it fails to protect users against a particular type of accidental or natural danger, a court may find that a third party's deliberate misconduct that exposes the plaintiff to that same danger falls within the scope of foreseeable risk. One such case is *Price v. Blaine Kern Artista, Inc.*,[54] where an entertainer at Harrah's Club in Reno who was wearing a large caricature mask of the first President George Bush ("41") was injured when a patron pushed him from behind, causing the weight of the caricature mask to strain and injure his neck as he fell to the ground. He sued the manufacturer of the mask, alleging that it was defectively designed due to the absence of a safety harness to support his head and neck under the heavy weight. The trial court ruled that the patron's push that precipitated the plaintiff's fall constituted an unforeseeable superseding cause, insulating the mask's supplier from liability, but the Supreme Court of Nevada reversed. The court acknowledged that the patron's conduct would be considered a superseding cause of the plaintiff's injuries had it been unforeseeable, yet it reasoned that a trier of fact might find such a push

---

**51.** 376 N.E.2d 37 (Ill. Ct. App. 1978).

**52.** On almost identical facts, but on a misrepresentation claim under § 402B of the Second Restatement, a subsequent court ruled that the seller of a pager marketed to police departments could reasonably foresee such a consequence if a defect in a pager caused it to malfunction. See Hollenbeck v. Selectone Corp., 476 N.E.2d 746 (Ill. App. Ct. 1985).

**53.** 667 N.W.2d 244 (Neb. 2003).

**54.** 893 P.2d 367 (Nev. 1995).

foreseeable if a patron were intoxicated or "politically volatile" and became "ignited by the sight of an oversized caricature of a prominent political figure" with whose abortion rights he might disagree.[55]

In another case, decided on principles similar to *Price*, the plaintiff's decedent and 27 others perished in a hotel fire set by an arsonist. The court refused to shield from liability the manufacturer of excessively flammable acrylic fiber used in the carpeting because it could foresee the dangers if the carpet caught fire.[56] Yet, in *Bellotte v. Zayre Corp.*,[57] a five-year-old plaintiff suffered burns when his pajamas caught fire from a match. Believing that his twelve-year-old brother had deliberately tossed the match on him, the jury returned a verdict for the defendant seller, which the appellate court affirmed. Although many clothing flammability accidents are caused by children playing with matches, "[t]he deliberate setting afire of a child's pajamas by another would not appear to fall within those acts that ought to be anticipated by a clothing supplier." The court approved the trial court's instruction that such a deliberate act constituted an "absolute defense." And many other decisions similarly hold deliberate assaults to be unforeseeable.[58]

A case arising out of the September 11, 2001 terrorist attacks on the World Trade center places more weight on foreseeability than it fairly should be asked to carry. *In re September 11 Litigation*[59] involved a motion to dismiss the claims of about seventy plaintiffs for injuries and deaths for Boeing's failure to design the cockpit doors of two aircraft— American Flight 77 which crashed into the Pentagon and United Flight 93 which crashed in rural Pennsylvania—strongly enough to prevent entry by the terrorist hijackers. Boeing argued that, even if the cockpit doors could be found to have been defectively designed, the acts of the terrorists constituted a superseding cause which defeated proximate cause as a matter of law. In particular, Boeing argued that "the criminal

---

**55.** The court also attempted, heroically but unsuccessfully, to distinguish the effect of superseding cause when applied to claims for strict products liability.

**56.** d'Hedouville v. Pioneer Hotel Co., 552 F.2d 886 (9th Cir. 1977) (Ariz. law) (the defendant manufacturer "was aware of the danger of fire, knew fires are often the result of arson, and knew that in all likelihood its carpeting would be installed in buildings without sprinkler systems, smoke sensors, or fire alarms, and in multi-story homes lacking the safety features the Pioneer Hotel also lacked").

**57.** 531 F.2d 1100 (1st Cir. 1976) (Ariz. law).

**58.** See, e.g., Sanders v. Acclaim Entm't, Inc., 188 F.Supp.2d 1264 (D. Colo. 2002) (unforeseeable that video game would cause shooting incident at Columbine; superseding causes relieve defendants of liability when "the harm is intentionally caused by a third person and is not within the scope of the risk created by the actor's conduct"); James v. Meow Media, Inc., 90 F.Supp.2d 798, 807–08 (W.D. Ky. 2000) (unforeseeable that assailant who watched violent video games would shoot girls as a result), aff'd, 300 F.3d 683 (6th Cir. 2002); Briscoe v. Amazing Prods., Inc., 23 S.W.3d 228 (Ky. Ct. App. 2000) (unforeseeable that man would throw defendant's drain cleaning product at plaintiff during altercation); Horstman v. Farris, 725 N.E.2d 698, 703 (Ohio Ct. App. 1999) (unforeseeable that 16–year–old who inhaled airbrush propellant would deliberately ram plaintiff's car; conduct broke chain of causation between plaintiffs' injuries and any warning defect of the propellant); Walcott v. Total Petroleum Inc., 964 P.2d 609, 612 (Colo. Ct. App. 1998) (unforeseeable that man purchasing cup of gasoline would throw it on plaintiff and set her on fire; "whether analyzed under the rubric of duty or proximate cause, the risk that a purchaser would intentionally throw gasoline on a victim and set the victim on fire was not reasonably foreseeable"); Chapman v. Oshman's Sporting Goods, Inc., 792 S.W.2d 785 (Tex. App. 1990) (murder with handgun sold by defendant retailer). See also the cases on murder in § 12.2, above.

**59.** 280 F.Supp.2d 279 (S.D.N.Y. 2003) (Va. and Pa. law).

acts of the terrorists in hijacking the airplanes and using the airplanes as weapons of mass destruction constituted an 'efficient intervening cause' which broke the 'natural and continuous sequence' of events flowing from Boeing's allegedly inadequate design." The plaintiffs argued that terrorist acts, "including hijackings of airplanes, were reasonably foreseeable," "that the lives of passengers, crew and ground victims would be imminently in danger from such hijackings," and that, "[g]iven the critical nature of the cockpit area, and the inherent danger of crash when a plane is in flight," a jury might find that Boeing should reasonably have foreseen "the risk flowing from an inadequately constructed cockpit door." Agreeing with the plaintiffs, the court denied the motion to dismiss.

The court attempted to distinguish three other cases, *Port Authority of N.Y. and N.J. v. Arcadian Corp.*,[60] *Gaines-Tabb v. ICI Explosives USA, Inc.*,[61] and *Korean Air Lines Disaster of September 1, 1983*,[62] each of which held that an unprovoked terrorist or military attack was an unforeseeable superseding cause as a matter of law. The first two cases involved claims of warning defects against the manufacturers of explosive grade fertilizer used to make the bombs employed in the terrorist attack against the World Trade Center, in 1993, and in the Oklahoma City bombing, in 1995. The third case was brought against Boeing on behalf of passengers killed in Korean Airlines flight 007 which, due to an alleged defect in the plane's navigation systems, flew off course over a sensitive Russian military zone and was shot down by Russian fighter planes. The *September 11* court valiantly attempted to distinguish each case on foreseeability grounds, concluding (with little reasoning) that, unlike the September 11 attacks, the fertilizer manufacturers and aircraft manufacturer could not foresee such unprovoked attacks.

It is difficult not to notice how little decisional power foreseeability has in these superseding cause cases, even when the standard is expanded to the scope of the foreseeable risk. Any of these cases might be decided either way, and courts and lawyers in cases of this type are left with no alternative but to spin foreseeability arguments that shift, and turn, and jump about like the elusive butterfly that is proximate cause.

### Superseding Cause in a Comparative Fault World

Some commentators argue that superseding cause is outmoded in a comparative fault world.[63] Because the doctrine is so blunt, in allowing manufacturers and other sellers to escape liability altogether even if a

---

**60.** 189 F.3d 305 (3d Cir. 1999) (N.J. law).

**61.** 160 F.3d 613 (10th Cir. 1998) (Okla. law).

**62.** 1985 WL 9447 (D.D.C. 1985).

**63.** See generally M. Green, The Unanticipated Ripples of Comparative Negligence: Superseding Cause in Products Liability and Beyond, 53 S.C. L. Rev. 1103 (2002); Cupp, Proximate Cause, the Pro-

posed Basic Principles Restatement and Products Liability, 53 S.C. L. Rev. 1085 (2002); Note, Dumb As A Matter of Law: The "Superseding Cause" Modification of Comparative Negligence, 79 Tex. L. Rev. 493 (2000); Note, Why Superseding Cause Analysis Should Be Abandoned, 72 Tex. L. Rev. 161 (1993). Accord Restatement (3d) Torts: Liability for Physical Harm § 34, and comments thereto.

product defect bears some responsibility for a plaintiff's injuries, the doctrine is seen to conflict with the basic principles of equitable damages apportionment that control comparative fault. Moreover, the basic proximate cause principle of limiting responsibility to the scope of risks that may foreseeably be expected to arise from a tortious act, risks that make the act tortious, sufficiently embrace the ideas of superseding cause without complicating the doctrine. These arguments have some power, and they have been accepted by some courts.[64] In *Barry v. Quality Steel Prods., Inc.*,[65] the jury was instructed that the negligence of the plaintiff, his employer, and his co-workers in connection with certain defective roof brackets could act as a superseding cause of his injury. Rejecting the doctrine of superseding cause, the court stated that "the doctrine of superseding cause no longer serves a useful purpose in our negligence jurisprudence" because its functions are performed by the general principles of proximate cause. "[I]t is inconsistent," reasoned the court, "to conclude simultaneously that all negligent parties should pay in proportion to their fault, but that one negligent party does not have to pay its share because its negligence was somehow 'superseded' by a subsequent negligent act." Nor did the court believe that it should continue "to utilize doctrines that aid fact finders in making policy decisions regarding how to assign liability among various defendants and the plaintiff because those decisions already are inherent in our modern scheme of comparative negligence and apportionment." Thus, under the court's approach, "the question to be answered by the fact finder is whether the various actors' allegedly negligent conduct was a cause in fact and a proximate cause of the plaintiff's injury in light of all the relevant circumstances. If found to be both, each actor will be liable for his or her proportionate share of the plaintiff's damages."

That these few rumblings of discontent with the "doctrine" of superseding cause are well founded is reflected by the inconsistency and lack of meaningful reasoning in the cases discussed above. Over time, other courts may also begin to rethink the role of superseding cause in a comparative fault world, which may be beneficial. It is quite unlikely, however, that courts will soon stampede to abolish the intriguing subdoctrine of superseding cause in the law of proximate cause.

---

**64.** See, e.g., Control Techniques, Inc., v. Johnson, 762 N.E.2d 104 (Ind. 2002); Torres v. El Paso Elec. Co., 987 P.2d 386 (N.M. 1999).

**65.** 820 A.2d 258 (Conn. 2003).

# PART IV

## DEFENSES

# Chapter 13

# USER MISCONDUCT DEFENSES

*Table of Sections*

---

## § 13.1   USER MISCONDUCT DEFENSES—GENERALLY

Product accidents may result more often from consumer misconduct than from a product defect. In the estimation of a former chairman of the Consumer Product Safety Commission, "over 2/3 of all injuries related to consumer products have nothing to do with the design or the performance of the product. They relate to the misuse or abuse of the product."[1] If a product accident is caused in whole or in part by a user's behavior that was by some measure improper, or that was informed and voluntary, the manufacturer or other seller of a defective (or misrepresented) product may avoid responsibility for some or all of the resulting damages. Product sellers are responsible for injuries proximately caused by dangerously defective conditions in their products, not for injuries caused by a user's improper or deliberately-risky use of the product. It would be unfair to the shareholders of a manufacturer, and to other more careful consumers forced to pay higher prices for the product, to require them to subsidize a product user who chose to use a product in a dangerous manner or for an improper purpose and was injured as a consequence.[2] In such cases, the law provides manufacturers and other sellers with at least limited protection through the traditional misconduct defenses, the subject of this chapter. A user's conduct that results in injury to a third party may give rise to an issue of superseding causation, a topic previously addressed.[3]

---

**§ 13.1**

**1.** Fisk, An Interview with John Byington, Trial Magazine 25 (Feb. 1978).

**2.** See, e.g., Owen, The Moral Foundations of Products Liability Law: Toward First Principles, 68 Notre Dame L. Rev. 427, 476 (1993); Holford, The Limits of Strict Liability for Product Design and Manufacture, 52 Tex. L. Rev. 81, 89 (1973).

**3.** See § 12.3, above.

The classic misconduct defenses to products liability negligence claims are contributory negligence[4] and assumption of risk.[5] With the advent of the modern doctrine of strict products liability in tort during the 1960s and 1970s,[6] most jurisdictions added the new defense[7] of product "misuse."[8] While contributory negligence has remained the basic defense to products liability claims grounded in negligence, most jurisdictions in the latter part of the twentieth century renamed the doctrine "comparative negligence," or "comparative fault," and changed its effect from barring a plaintiff's claim altogether to reducing the plaintiff's damages proportionate to his or her fault. The doctrine of comparative fault, an approach to plaintiff misconduct which cuts a broad swathe across the law of torts and products liability, is examined fully in a separate section.[9]

Comparative fault principles to a large extent now define the role of contributory negligence in most jurisdictions, assumption of risk in many jurisdictions, and product misuse in a few jurisdictions, as discussed below. Nevertheless, the traditional user misconduct defenses still apply to products liability claims in the handful of states that continue to reject the doctrine of comparative fault.[10] Moreover, even though the traditional defenses now often operate to reduce a plaintiff's damages, rather than barring them altogether, much of the traditional doctrine surrounding contributory negligence, assumption of risk, and product misuse has survived the conversion to comparative fault.[11]

Although courts in comparative fault jurisdictions generally apply damages-apportioning principles to a plaintiff's contributory negligence, both contributory negligence and assumption of risk remain as *total* bars to recovery in most jurisdictions if the plaintiff's fault equals or, in some states, exceeds the fault of the defendant.[12] In addition, while some

---

**4.** See § 13.2, below.

**5.** See § 13.4, below.

**6.** See § 5.2, above.

**7.** In many jurisdictions, product misuse is technically not a "defense" in the sense of an affirmative defense, but its absence is instead considered part of a plaintiff's prima facie case. In such jurisdictions, the role of misuse in products liability law may be viewed more in the nature of a limitation on defectiveness than a true defense. From whatever perspective, when a user "misuses" a defective product, his or her misconduct may operate as a bar to liability similar to the operation of the traditional defenses of contributory negligence and assumption of risk. For that reason, together with the fact that a number of state reform acts treat product misuse as an affirmative defense, the doctrine of misuse is covered with other misconduct "defenses" in this chapter.

**8.** See § 13.5, below.

**9.** See § 13.3, below.

**10.** As of 2005, the comparative fault doctrine is still rejected in Alabama, Maryland, North Carolina, Virginia, and the District of Columbia.

**11.** For example, the contributory negligence doctrine applicable to strict liability cases that a plaintiff's mere failure to discover a defect or guard against the possibility of its existence does not bar recovery. See, e.g., Jett v. Ford Motor Co., 84 P.3d 219 (Or. Ct. App. 2004) (negligent failure to discover or guard against existence of defect no defense, even under comparative fault); § 13.2, below. Moreover, some courts hold that a plaintiff's fault may sometimes be the sole proximate cause of his or her injury, notwithstanding the doctrine of comparative fault. See §§ 13.2 and 13.3, below.

**12.** See, e.g., King v. Kayak Mfg. Corp., 387 S.E.2d 511 (W. Va. 1989) (assumption of risk remains total bar if plaintiff's fault equals or exceeds fault of other parties). See generally § 13.4, below.

courts, after the adoption of comparative fault, abolished assumption of risk as a separate doctrine, or merged it into the comparative fault scheme, other courts refuse to apply comparative fault principles to assumption of risk or do so only to a limited extent.[13] Finally, in the many jurisdictions that consider the absence of misuse to be an element of the prima facie case of strict liability in tort, a finding of misuse should be entirely unaffected by the doctrine of comparative fault. Similarly, with claims for breach of warranty[14] and misrepresentation,[15] the respective issues of justifiable reliance, proximate cause, and scope of warranty implicated by a user's conduct are part of a plaintiff's case in chief which, if not established, will destroy such claims before they ever arise. In short, most jurisdictions hold that the traditional plaintiff misconduct defenses often still operate in their conventional form as a total bar to liability.

When a plaintiff acts carelessly or adventurously in a manner that causes or contributes to a product accident, the conduct may give rise to two or all three traditional misconduct defenses.[16] So, if a plaintiff proceeds to ignite a pilot light, knowing of a leaking gas valve;[17] attempts to mount a tire, expressly contrary to a warning, on a wheel rim of a different size;[18] falls as a stunt 323 feet onto a cushion rated for 200 feet;[19] or locks herself into a car's trunk, which has no internal release device, in an attempt to commit suicide,[20] a defendant may assert and sometimes successfully defend the case on the basis of some combination of contributory (or comparative) negligence, assumption of risk, and product misuse. Thus, subject to applicable principles of comparative fault, a practitioner representing a defendant seller in a case involving plaintiff misconduct should almost always consider the possible availability of two or all three traditional misconduct defenses. This assumes that the complaint includes claims in both negligence and strict liability, because misuse normally is a strict liability defense,[21] whereas "simple" contributory negligence is not a defense at all to claims for strict liability in tort.[22]

---

**13.** Ohio, for example, merged assumption of risk into comparative fault for negligence claims but left it as a total bar in strict liability in tort. See, e.g., Onderko v. Richmond Mfg. Co., 511 N.E.2d 388 (Ohio 1987); Bowling v. Heil Co., 511 N.E.2d 373 (Ohio 1987).

**14.** See § 13.6, below.

**15.** See § 13.7, below.

**16.** See, e.g., Jett v. Ford Motor Co., 84 P.3d 219, 222 (Or. Ct. App. 2004) (unreasonable use, misuse, and assumption of risk); Ellsworth v. Sherne Lingerie, Inc., 495 A.2d 348, 357 (Md. 1985) ("a defendant may be entitled to instructions on contributory negligence, assumption of risk, and misuse").

**17.** Freislinger v. Emro Propane Co., 99 F.3d 1412 (7th Cir. 1996) (Ill. law) (contributory/comparative negligence and assumption of risk).

**18.** Uniroyal Goodrich Tire Co. v. Hall, 681 So.2d 126 (Ala. 1996) (contributory negligence, assumption of risk, and misuse).

**19.** Bakunas v. Life Pack, Inc., 531 F.Supp. 89 (E.D. La. 1982), aff'd, 701 F.2d 946 (5th Cir. 1983) (assumption of risk and misuse).

**20.** Daniell v. Ford Motor Co., 581 F.Supp. 728 (D.N.M. 1984) (misuse, and possibly assumption of risk and comparative fault).

**21.** See § 13.5, below.

**22.** See, e.g., Cummings v. General Motors Corp., 365 F.3d 944, 952 (10th Cir. 2004) (Okla. law) (contributory negligence not a defense to strict liability in tort). *But see* Mohr v. St. Paul Fire & Marine Ins. Co., 674 N.W.2d 576, 591 (Wis. Ct. App. 2003) (contributory negligence may be defense to a strict product liability claim). See §§ 13.2 and 13.3, below.

The three plaintiff misconduct defenses are fundamental mechanisms by which the law defines the boundaries of liability by allowing manufacturers to avoid responsibility for certain types of product accidents. Accordingly, trial courts have an important obligation to admit appropriate evidence, permit appropriate argument, and submit appropriate instructions to the jury on any misconduct defenses that fairly may be raised in a particular case.[23]

### Reform Legislation

Many states have enacted products liability "reform, or comparative fault," statutes that specifically address the definition, scope, and effect of various defenses based on a plaintiff's conduct. Such statutes variously reduce damages or bar recovery if a product accident is caused by a plaintiff's unreasonable behavior or contributory fault, assumption of risk, misuse of the product, or sometimes specifically designated types of plaintiff misbehavior.[24] Moreover, comparative fault statutes in many states address plaintiff misconduct in general terms, and some such statutes include provisions on the role of a plaintiff's conduct in products liability claims, particularly when the misconduct involves product misuse.[25]

For example, one statutory provision in Connecticut specifies that contributory negligence shall merely diminish damages rather than bar liability,[26] and another specifies that neither contributory nor comparative negligence shall bar liability in strict products liability in tort claims but recognizes the separate defenses of "misuse of the product" and "knowingly using the product in a defective condition."[27] Statutes in both Arizona[28] and North Carolina[29] provide a defense for the use of products contrary to their "express and adequate instructions or warnings . . . if the user knew or with the exercise of reasonable and diligent

**23.** See, e.g., Freislinger v. Emro Propane Co., 99 F.3d 1412 (7th Cir. 1996) (Ill. law), in which the trial court failed to allow the jury to consider certain allegations of contributory negligence asserted by defendants: "In spite of the fact that district courts have substantial discretion in determining whether the evidence at trial warrants submitting theories to the jury, we are disturbed by the court's placing such tight shackles on the jury's ability to consider specific allegations of contributory negligence." Id. at 1418. *Held*, reversed for a new trial "because of the court's decision to exclude certain theories of contributory negligence that were supported by the evidence." Id.

**24.** See, e.g., Wash. Rev. Code § 5.40.060 (plaintiff's drug or alcohol intoxication is complete defense in some cases).

**25.** See, e.g., Wyo. Stat. Ann. § 1–1–109(a)(iv) (" 'Fault' includes acts or omissions, determined to be a proximate cause of death or injury to person or property,

that are in any measure negligent, or that subject an actor to strict tort or strict products liability, and includes breach of warranty, assumption of risk and misuse or alteration of a product.").

**26.** Conn. Gen. Stat. § 52–572h(b).

**27.** Conn. Gen. Stat. § 52–572l.

**28.** Ariz. Rev. Stat. § 12–683(3), which provides that a products liability defendant shall not be liable if the defendant proves that the proximate cause of the incident was "a use or consumption of the product which was for a purpose, in a manner or in an activity other than that which was reasonably foreseeable or was contrary to any express and adequate instructions or warnings appearing on or attached to the product or on its original container or wrapping, if the injured person knew or with the exercise of reasonable and diligent care should have known of such instructions or warnings."

**29.** N.C. Gen. Stat. § 99B–4(1).

care should have known of such instructions, or warnings."[30] Kentucky enacted a contributory negligence defense to products liability actions in 1978[31] but superseded it with a comparative fault act in 1988.[32] A number of products liability reform statutes provide that a plaintiff's damages shall be reduced,[33] or that recovery shall be barred altogether,[34] if a plaintiff voluntarily—sometimes voluntarily and unreasonably[35]— encounters a known (or obvious)[36] product danger. Products liability statutes in several states reduce damages[37] or bar liability[38] when a

**30.** Id.

**31.** Ky. Rev. Stat. Ann. § 411.320. See Reda Pump Co. v. Finck, 713 S.W.2d 818 (Ky. 1986) (holding statute constitutional).

**32.** Ky. Rev. Stat. Ann. § 411.182. See Caterpillar, Inc. v. Brock, 915 S.W.2d 751, 753 (Ky. 1996).

**33.** One source lists Alaska, Arizona, Arkansas, Colorado, Idaho, Iowa, Kansas, Minnesota, Missouri, Montana, New York, North Dakota, Utah, and Washington as strict liability states which provide by statute that assumption of risk merely reduces a plaintiff's recovery rather than serving as a total bar. H. Woods and B. Deere, Comparative Fault § 6:11, at 146–47 (3d ed. 1996). See, e.g., Idaho Code § 6–1305(2)(a) ("When the product seller proves, by a preponderance of the evidence, that the claimant knew about the product's defective condition, and voluntarily used the product or voluntarily assumed the risk of harm from the product, the claimant's damages shall be subject to reduction to the extent that the claimant did not act as an ordinary reasonably prudent person under the circumstances."); Mo. Ann. Stat. § 537.765(3)(3) (damages subject to reduction according to pure comparative fault if plaintiff used product "with knowledge of a danger involved in such use with reasonable appreciation of the consequences and the voluntary and unreasonable exposure to said danger"); Mont. Code Ann. § 27–1–719(5)(a) & (6) (comparative fault applies if "[t]he user or consumer of the product discovered the defect or the defect was open and obvious and the user or consumer unreasonably made use of the product and was injured by it").

**34.** Such legislation includes Conn. Gen. Stat. § 52–572l (assumption of risk and misuse defenses retained for products liability claims based on strict liability in tort); Ind. Code § 34–20–6–3 (defense available if user or consumer "(1) knew of the defect; (2) was aware of the danger in the product; and (3) nevertheless proceeded to make use of the product and was injured"); Mich. Comp. Laws Ann. § 600.2947(3) (defendants not liable if purchaser or user aware that use of product created unreasonable risk of injury and voluntarily exposed himself or herself to that risk); Miss. Code Ann.

§ 11–1–63(d) (defendant not liable if claimant (i) had knowledge of product condition inconsistent with safety; (ii) appreciated the danger in the condition; and (iii) deliberately and voluntarily chose to expose himself to danger in such a manner to register assent on the continuance of the dangerous condition); N.C. Gen. Stat. § 99B–4(2) (no liability if "user knew of or discovered a defect or dangerous condition of the product that was inconsistent with the safe use of the product, and then unreasonably and voluntarily exposed himself or herself to the danger, and was injured by or caused injury with that product"); S.C. Code Ann. § 15–73–20 ("If the user or consumer discovers the defect and is aware of the danger, and nevertheless proceeds unreasonably to make use of the product and is injured by it, he is barred from recovery.").

**35.** Statutes in at least three states define the assumption of risk defense in terms of encounters with dangers which are known, or voluntary, and *unreasonable*. See Mo. Ann. Stat. § 537.765(3)(3); N.C. Gen. Stat. § 99B–4(2); S.C. Code Ann. § 15–73–20.

**36.** Mississippi and Montana both allow a defense in cases of encounters with obvious, as well as known, risks. Compare Miss. Code Ann. § 11–1–63(d) (assumed risks) with (e) (danger is "known or is open and obvious"); Mont. Code Ann. § 27–1–719(5)(a) (allowing defense if "[t]he user or consumer discovered the defect or the defect was open and obvious and the user or consumer unreasonably made use of the product and was injured by it").

**37.** At least Idaho and Missouri have enacted such legislation. See Idaho Code § 6–1405(3) (misuse reduces claimant's damages according to comparative responsibility; "misuse" defined as "when the product user does not act in a manner that would be expected of an ordinary reasonably prudent person who is likely to use the product in the same or similar circumstances"); Mo. Ann. Stat. § 537.765(3) (for purposes of apportionment, plaintiff's "fault" includes product use that is (1) not reasonably anticipated or (2) not intended by the manufacturer).

**38.** At least four states have such provisions. See Ariz. Rev. Stat. § 12–683(3) (un-

plaintiff's use of a product is abnormal or unforeseeable, generally referred to in the statutes as product "misuse."[39]

Finally, most of the reform legislation mentioned above specifically addresses products liability litigation. In all cases, the statutes should be checked carefully for legislative provisions that generally abolish the defense of assumption of risk;[40] that broadly apply comparative fault principles to the doctrines of contributory negligence, assumption of risk, and often product misuse;[41] or that in any other manner affect the definition or role of the traditional plaintiff misconduct defenses of contributory negligence, assumption of risk, and product misuse.

## § 13.2   CONTRIBUTORY NEGLIGENCE

Contributory negligence is the conventional common-law defense[1] to products liability negligence claims.[2] Although most courts considerably restrict the availability of this defense in strict liability in tort claims, as discussed below, they widely apply ordinary contributory negligence principles to products liability claims brought in negligence.[3] In the

---

foreseeable purpose, manner or activity, or contrary to express and adequate instructions or warnings, if injured person knew or with reasonable care should have known of such instructions or warnings); Ind. Code § 34–20–6–4 (misuse is a defense if not reasonably expected by seller at time of sale); Mich. Comp. Laws Ann. § 600. 2947(2) (no liability for harm caused by misuse unless "reasonably foreseeable," which is a legal issue for court); Tenn. Code Ann. § 29–28–108 (no liability for dangers resulting from "unforeseeable alteration, change, improper maintenance or abnormal use").

**39.** The Montana statute defines the conduct in terms of *unreasonable* misuse. See Mont. Code Ann. § 27–1–719(5)(b).

**40.** At least Connecticut, Massachusetts, and Oregon have abolished the defense of assumption of risk legislatively. See Conn. Gen. Stat. § 52–572h (abolished in negligence actions only; retained in strict products liability in tort actions: § 52–572l); Mass. Gen. Laws Ann ch. 231 § 85 ("The defense of assumption of risk is hereby abolished in all actions hereunder."); Or. Rev. Stat. § 18.475(2) ("The doctrine of implied assumption of risk is abolished.").

**41.** The statutory provisions vary widely. See, e.g., Alaska Stat. § 09.17.900 ("fault" defined to include "misuse of a product for which the defendant otherwise would be liable"); Ark. Code Ann. § 16–64–122(c) (" 'fault' as used in this section includes any act, omission, conduct, risk assumed, breach of warranty, or breach of any legal duty which is a proximate cause of any damages sustained by any party"); Iowa Code Ann. § 668.1 (" 'fault' means one or more acts or omissions that are in any measure negligent or reckless toward

the person or property of the actor or others, or that subject a person to strict tort liability" and "also includes breach of warranty, unreasonable assumption of risk not constituting an enforceable express consent, misuse of a product for which the defendant otherwise would be liable, and unreasonable failure to avoid an injury or to mitigate damages"); Wyo. Stat. Ann. § 1–1–109(a)(iv) (" '[f]ault' includes acts or omissions, determined to be a proximate cause of death or injury to person or property, that are in any measure negligent, or that subject an actor to strict tort or strict products liability, and includes breach of warranty, assumption of risk and misuse or alteration of a product").

### § 13.2

**1.** While contributory negligence is a common law doctrine, comparative fault legislation and products liability reform legislation in many states govern the effect of various forms of user misconduct. See § 13.1, above, and § 13.3, below.

**2.** See Noel, Defective Products: Abnormal Use, Contributory Negligence, and Assumption of Risk, 25 Vand. L. Rev. 93 (1972); Epstein, Products Liability: Defenses Based on Plaintiff's Conduct, 1968 Utah L. Rev. 267.

**3.** See, e.g., Hannah v. Gregg, Bland & Berry, Inc., 840 So.2d 839 (Ala. 2002) (in wrongful death action against manufacturer of machine that crushed worker, jury could find worker responsible for his own demise for failing to insert safety pin in machine); Jones v. Ford Motor Co., 559 S.E.2d 592, 605 (Va. 2002); Gillespie v. American Motors Corp., 317 S.E.2d 32 (N.C. Ct. App. 1984) (continuing to drive car for three

products liability context as in others, contributory negligence is defined as conduct of a plaintiff which falls below the standard of reasonable behavior required for a person's own protection which proximately contributes, together with a defendant's negligence or other breach of duty, to cause the person harm.[4]

Contributory negligence operates in much the same manner in products liability cases as in other types of negligence cases. So, unless comparative fault principles dictate to the contrary, a finding that a plaintiff was contributorily negligent will bar the plaintiff altogether from recovering damages from a negligent defendant.[5] Thus, a plaintiff found to have been contributorily negligent in an encounter with a dangerously defective product may not recover from the manufacturer or other seller for negligently making or supplying the product in such a condition.[6] However, if the defendant's misconduct is not merely negligent but rises to the level of reckless, willful, or wanton misbehavior, a plaintiff's recovery will not be barred by contributory negligence, although it will be barred by contributory recklessness.[7]

Contributory negligence operates as a total bar to liability not only in those few jurisdictions that have not adopted comparative fault,[8] but also in certain cases in most other jurisdictions as well. Except for jurisdictions that presently have a system of *pure* comparative fault,[9] most states apply the principles of comparative fault only when a plaintiff's fault was less than (or equal to) the fault of the defendant or defendants. In jurisdictions following such a modified ("50%") approach to comparative negligence, if a plaintiff's fault was greater than (or equal to) that of the defendant(s), the contributory negligence doctrine applies in its conventional form by barring recovery altogether.[10] Thus, the doctrine of contributory negligence remains an important doctrine in modern products liability litigation.

The complex interrelationships between the human brain, the human body, and the myriad different products encountered daily at home

years while knowing of noxious fumes in passenger area: contributorily negligent); Reed v. Carlyle & Martin, Inc., 202 S.E.2d 874 (Va. 1974). See also Duke v. American Olean Tile Co., 400 N.W.2d 677 (Mich. Ct. App. 1986) (in slip-and-fall action against manufacturer of quarry tile used for flooring in fast food restaurant, jury could find that plaintiff was walking unreasonably fast).

**4.** See Prosser and Keeton on Torts § 65, at 451.

**5.** "[I]n the absence of modifying legislation or judicial action, contributory negligence of the plaintiff is a complete bar to his action for any common law negligence of the defendant." Id. at 461. See also W. Prosser, Handbook of The Law of Torts § 102, at 670 (4th ed. 1971) ("There is no doubt that where the plaintiff's action is founded on negligence, his contributory negligence will bar his recovery to the same extent as in any other negligence case.").

**6.** See, e.g., Nicholson v. American Safety Util. Corp., 488 S.E.2d 240, 244 (N.C. 1997) ("contributory negligence in the context of a products liability action operates as a bar to recovery in the same manner as in an ordinary negligence action").

**7.** See, e.g., Koske v. Townsend Eng'g Co., 526 N.E.2d 985 (Ind. Ct. App. 1988), adopted in part and vacated in part on other grounds, 551 N.E.2d 437 (Ind. 1990). See generally Restatement (2d) Torts § 482; Owen, The Highly Blameworthy Manufacturer: Implications on Rules of Liability and Defense in Products Liability Actions, 10 Ind. L. Rev. 769, 787–88 (1977).

**8.** Alabama, Maryland, North Carolina, Virginia, and the District of Columbia.

**9.** See § 13.3, below.

**10.** Id.

and at work result in a vast universe of ways in which user carelessness may result in injury. Consumers may be contributorily negligent for using products in an unreasonably dangerous manner or by using them for an unreasonably dangerous purpose, as by driving an automobile at excessive speed[11] or in an intoxicated condition;[12] reaching into a trash compactor knowing that its door cables are broken;[13] failing to release one's hold of a piece of meat when pushing it into the revolving blade of a meat slicing machine;[14] standing on a slippery substance dangerously close to the exposed moving parts of a machine;[15] operating a spray-painting machine without using an available mask;[16] failing to wear rubber gloves, contrary to label instructions, and splattering a caustic substance on one's hand;[17] failing properly to engage a car's transmission in the "park" position;[18] improperly using a condom;[19] walking too fast on a slippery floor;[20] or carelessly lighting a cigarette with a disposable lighter near one's "big hair" bouffant hairdo held in place with excessive hair spray, the fumes of which ignite.[21]

As is true with negligence claims in general, the issues of contributory negligence are peculiarly grounded in community norms of properly safe behavior in particular circumstances, so that the issue of whether a plaintiff's behavior should be classified as unreasonable is inherently a question of fact especially suited to resolution by a jury.[22] Yet, if a plaintiff's behavior is so evidently reasonable or unreasonable that no rational jury could find to the contrary, a court may rule on contributory negligence as a matter of law.[23]

**11.** See, e.g., Hoelter v. Mohawk Serv., Inc., 365 A.2d 1064 (Conn. 1976).

**12.** See, e.g., Hill v. General Motors Corp., 168 F.3d 482 (4th Cir. 1998) (N.C. law).

**13.** Sears v. Waste Processing Equip., Inc., 695 So.2d 51 (Ala. Civ. App. 1997).

**14.** Koske v. Townsend Eng'g Co., 526 N.E.2d 985 (Ind. Ct. App. 1988), adopted in part and vacated in part on other grounds, 551 N.E.2d 437 (Ind. 1990).

**15.** See, e.g., Reed v. Carlyle & Martin, Inc., 202 S.E.2d 874 (Va. 1974).

**16.** See, e.g., Parris v. M.A. Bruder & Sons, Inc., 261 F.Supp. 406 (E.D. Pa. 1966).

**17.** See Lee v. Crest Chem. Co., 583 F.Supp. 131 (M.D.N.C. 1984) (defendant's motion for summary judgment granted, pursuant to statutory provision barring recovery for use of product contrary to instructions).

**18.** General Motors Corp. v. Sanchez, 997 S.W.2d 584, 594 (Tex. 1999) ("Regardless of any danger of a mis-shift, a driver has a duty to take reasonable precautions to secure his vehicle before getting out of it."); Ray v. Ford Motor Co., 514 S.E.2d 227 (Ga. Ct. App. 1999). Cf. Ford Motor Co. v. Bartholomew, 297 S.E.2d 675 (Va. 1982) (gear shift lever, not fully engaged in park,

slipped into reverse with motor running; jury's finding of no contributory negligence upheld).

**19.** See J.P.M. v. Schmid Lab., Inc., 428 A.2d 515 (N.J. Super. Ct. App. Div. 1981).

**20.** See Duke v. American Olean Tile Co., 400 N.W.2d 677 (Mich. Ct. App. 1986) (in slip-and-fall action against manufacturer of quarry tile used for flooring in fast-food restaurant).

**21.** See McClure v. Wilkinson Sword Consumer Prod., Inc., Prod. Safety & Liab. Rep. (BNA) 394 (Apr. 14, 1995) (Cook Cty. Cir. Ct., Ill.).

**22.** See, e.g., Nicholson v. American Safety Util. Corp., 488 S.E.2d 240, 244 (N.C. 1997) ("Issues of contributory negligence, like those of ordinary negligence are ordinarily questions for the jury and are rarely appropriate for summary judgment.").

**23.** "Only where the evidence establishes the plaintiff's own negligence so clearly that no other reasonable conclusion may be reached is summary judgment to be granted." Id. See, e.g., Hill v. General Motors Corp., 168 F.3d 482 (4th Cir. 1998) (N.C. law) (unpublished opinion); Sears v. Waste Processing Equip., Inc., 695 So.2d 51 (Ala. Civ. App. 1997).

Whereas negligence is defined as the failure to exercise due care toward others, contributory negligence is the failure to exercise due care toward oneself. In most respects, however, contributory negligence is the mirror image of negligence. While theorists may debate whether people properly may be said to have a "duty" to act with reasonable care to protect themselves,[24] the courts are in quite general agreement that the classic elements of negligence[25]—duty,[26] breach,[27] cause in fact,[28] proximate cause,[29] and damage[30]—comprise the defense of contributory negligence as well.

A plaintiff will be contributorily negligent if he or she "fails to exercise such care as an ordinarily prudent person would exercise under the circumstances in order to avoid injury"[31] or simply "fails to use reasonable care with regard to [a] product."[32] Contributory negligence in

**24.** Dean Prosser and other scholars have questioned whether the doctrine of contributory negligence fairly may be said to embrace the notion of a duty. See, e.g., Prosser and Keeton on Torts § 65, at 453 ("Negligence requires a duty, an obligation of conduct to another person. Contributory negligence involves no duty, unless we are to be so ingenious as to say that the plaintiff is under an obligation to protect the defendant against liability for the consequences of the plaintiff's own negligence."). Immanuel Kant believed that the supreme principle of morality (the categorical imperative) included a respect for oneself: "Act so that you treat humanity, whether in your own person or in that of another, always as an end and never as a means only." Immanuel Kant, Foundations of the Metaphysics of Morals (1785) (L. Beck trans., 1959), at 429. However, Kant believed that one's duty to oneself transcended law: "My duty toward myself cannot be treated juridically; the law touches only our relations with other men; I have no legal obligations towards myself. . . . " Immanuel Kant, Duties to Oneself, in Lectures on Ethics 117 (L. Infield trans. 1978 [1930]), quoted in J. M. Finnis, Legal Enforcement of "Duties to Oneself": Kant v. Neo–Kantians, 87 Colum. L. Rev. 433 (1987). See generally Simons, The Puzzling Doctrine of Contributory Negligence, 16 Cardozo L. Rev. 1693, 1728–33 (1995); Simons, Contributory Negligence: Conceptual and Normative Issues, in Philosophical Foundations of Tort Law 461 (D. Owen ed., Oxford 1995) (under current legal doctrine, "the formal criteria defining plaintiff's negligence and defendant's negligence are essentially the same"). Id. at 469.

**25.** See § 2.1, above.

**26.** See, e.g., Jenkins v. Whittaker Corp., 785 F.2d 720, 728–29 (9th Cir. 1986) (Haw. law).

**27.** Prosser and Keeton on Torts § 65, at 453–54:

The plaintiff is required to conform to the same objective standard of conduct, that of the reasonable person of ordinary prudence under like circumstances. The unreasonableness of the risks which he incurs is judged by the same process of weighing the importance of the interest he is seeking to advance, and the burden of taking precautions, against the probability and probable gravity of the anticipated harm to himself.

**28.** "The ordinary negligence principles of cause in fact apply with equal force to contributory negligence." Id. at 456. See also Restatement (2d) Torts § 465(2).

**29.** See, e.g., Jenkins v. Whittaker Corp., 785 F.2d 720, 729 (9th Cir. 1986) (Haw. law) ("Proximate cause is lacking because the alleged [contributory] negligence . . . has no connection with the actual injury. The acts asserted, however much they may have increased the risk of injury [from another source], had absolutely no relation to the risk that actually matured. . . . The duty breached by the alleged [contributory] negligence did not encompass the hazard that actually came about, and any such negligence is therefore irrelevant to the issue of proximate cause."). See also Restatement (2d) Torts § 468.

**30.** On actual damages, see 2 Frumer and Friedman, Products Liability ch. 13; 2 Madden & Owen on Products Liability ch. 17; 4A Am. Law. Prod. Liab. ch. 60.

**31.** Nicholson v. American Safety Util. Corp., 488 S.E.2d 240, 244 (N.C. 1997), quoting Newton v. New Hanover Bd. of Educ., 467 S.E.2d 58, 65 (N.C. 1996). See also Egelhoff v. Holt, 875 S.W.2d 543, 547–48 (Mo. 1994) (en banc) (comparative fault statute, Mo. Ann. Stat. 537.765(3)(5): "failure to undertake the precautions a reasonably careful user of the product would take").

**32.** Uniroyal Goodrich Tire Co. v. Hall, 681 So.2d 126, 129 (Ala. 1996). See also

the products liability setting has been particularized to include the use of a product contrary to adequate warnings and instructions, the unreasonable use of a product known to be defective, or the use of a product in an unreasonable manner.[33] In short, persons have a duty to exercise reasonable care in using products to avoid injuries to themselves.

Although courts rarely examine the notion of contributory negligence explicitly in terms of the Hand formula, by which $B < P \times L$ implies an actor's negligence, this classic "calculus of risk" approach to ascertaining negligence applies as well to contributory negligence as it does to ordinary negligence.[34] Thus, the reasonableness of a plaintiff's exposure of himself to a product hazard is to be ascertained by weighing the burden of avoiding the dangerous conduct, on the one hand, against the likelihood and severity of a foreseeably harmful result, on the other. If the burden of avoiding a risk is large, as in shutting down a machine that takes hours to restart,[35] or very great, such as the possible loss of employment if a worker refuses to engage in a dangerous task as directed by a superior, then an exposure to the risk for such reasons is more likely to be reasonable under the circumstances.[36]

On the other hand, a user's act is more likely to be contributorily negligent if a significant risk may be avoided by a relatively small degree of effort or attention. Contributory negligence may be found, for example, if a substantial risk of harm may be avoided by simply putting on gloves[37] or a face mask,[38] to avoid burns or lung damage; by driving at an appropriate speed for the condition of a tire, to avoid a high speed

Williams v. Delta Int'l Mach. Corp., 619 So.2d 1330, 1332 (Ala. 1993) (failure to exercise reasonable care in using product).

**33.** A North Carolina statute, N.C. Gen. Stat. § 99B–4, describes the form of conduct that may establish contributory negligence in the products liability context:

No manufacturer or seller shall be held liable in any product liability action if:

(1) the use of the product giving rise to the product liability action was contrary to any express and adequate instructions or warnings delivered with, appearing on, or attached to the product or on its original container or wrapping, if the user knew or with the exercise of reasonable and diligent care should have known of such instructions or warnings; provided, that in the case of prescription drugs or devices adequacy of the warning by the manufacturer shall be determined by the prescribing information made available to the health care practitioner; or

(2) the user discovered a defect or unreasonably dangerous condition of the product and was aware of the danger, and nevertheless proceeded unreasonably to make use of the product and was injured by or caused injury with that product; or

(3) the claimant failed to exercise reasonable care under the circumstances in his use of the product, and such failure was a proximate cause of the occurrence that caused injury or damage to the claimant.

See Lienhart v. Dryvit Sys., Inc., 255 F.3d 138, 148 (4th Cir. 2001) (N.C. law) (subsection (1) codifies doctrine of contributory negligence in products liability cases); Nicholson v. American Safety Util. Corp., 488 S.E.2d 240, 243 (N.C. 1997).

**34.** For an explanation of the basic Hand formula, see § 2.2, above.

**35.** As, for example, the printing press in Micallef v. Miehle Co., 348 N.E.2d 571 (N.Y. 1976), which took three hours to restart after shutting it down, superseded by statute on other grounds, see Dewey v. R.J. Reynolds Tobacco Co., 577 A.2d 1239 (N.J. 1990).

**36.** See Suter v. San Angelo Foundry & Mach. Co., 406 A.2d 140, 148 (N.J. 1979), superseded by statute on other grounds, see Dewey v. R.J. Reynolds Tobacco Co., 577 A.2d 1239 (N.J. 1990).

**37.** See Lee v. Crest Chem. Co., 583 F.Supp. 131 (M.D.N.C. 1984).

**38.** See Parris v. M.A. Bruder & Sons, Inc., 261 F.Supp. 406 (E.D. Pa. 1966).

crash;[39] by securely shifting the transmission into the "park" position before getting out of a car parked on an incline, to avoid being squashed by the car;[40] by using a condom in an appropriate manner, to avoid pregnancy and the birth of twins;[41] or by moving cautiously over a slippery floor, to avoid injury from a fall.[42] In sum, the same cost-benefit principles of balance that define negligence define contributory negligence as well.

Other principles governing the negligence standard of care also apply to determinations of contributory negligence. One such principle is the doctrine of negligence per se for violation of a statute.[43] So, an intoxicated driver may be barred from maintaining a negligence claim against an automotive manufacturer if the intoxication violated a DUI statute and contributed to the injury.[44] Another principle is the rescue doctrine,[45] relieving a rescuer of the normal responsibilities of acting according to a standard of reasonable prudence.[46] Additional negligence principles applicable to contributory negligence include the sudden emergency doctrine,[47] and the objective nature of,[48] and role of customary behavior in relation to,[49] the standard of responsibility.

*Reed v. Carlyle & Martin, Inc.*[50] involved negligence claims by a farm hand against the manufacturer, dealer, and repairer of a piece of farm equipment, an ensilage wagon. At the time of the accident, the plaintiff was standing upon and removing a five foot deep load of ensilage from the wagon. A pair of revolving beaters, comprised of metal rods with

**39.** See Noel, Defective Products: Abnormal Use, Contributory Negligence, and Assumption of Risk, 25 Vand. L. Rev. 93, 111 (1972) (mentioning high-speed driving on tire not known to be defective as example of conduct which should bar recovery).

**40.** See, e.g., General Motors Corp. v. Sanchez, 997 S.W.2d 584, 594 (Tex. 1999) ("Regardless of any danger of a mis-shift, a driver has a duty to take reasonable precautions to secure his vehicle before getting out of it."); Ray v. Ford Motor Co., 514 S.E.2d 227 (Ga. Ct. App. 1999). See also Jett v. Ford Motor Co., 84 P.3d 219, 222 (Or. Ct. App. 2004).

**41.** See J.P.M. v. Schmid Lab., Inc., 428 A.2d 515 (N.J. Super. Ct. App. Div. 1981).

**42.** See, e.g., Duke v. American Olean Tile Co., 400 N.W.2d 677 (Mich. Ct. App. 1986); Reed v. Carlyle & Martin, Inc., 202 S.E.2d 874 (Va. 1974).

**43.** See Klinke v. Mitsubishi Motors Corp., 581 N.W.2d 272, 276 (Mich. 1998) (dictum); Zalut v. Andersen & Assocs., Inc., 463 N.W.2d 236 (Mich. Ct. App. 1990) (violation of state OSHA safety regulation is evidence of comparative negligence). See generally Prosser and Keeton on Torts § 36.

**44.** See Hill v. General Motors Corp., 168 F.3d 482 (4th Cir. 1998) (N.C. law) (unpublished opinion) (by implication). See also Smith v. State of N.Y., 742 N.Y.S.2d 792, 798 (Ct. Cl. 2002) (driver's vehicle hit allegedly defective guide rail; because driver's blood alcohol level of .14% violated DWI statute, amounting to negligence per se, court ruled driver 80% at fault).

**45.** See Prosser and Keeton on Torts § 44, at 307–09.

**46.** See, e.g., Dillard v. Pittway Corp., 719 So.2d 188, 193 (Ala. 1998) (person injured in fire while trying to rescue boarder in burning house, even if contributorily negligent, could maintain negligence claim against manufacturer and seller of smoke detector "unless the rescuer's own conduct in attempting the rescue is wanton").

**47.** See, e.g., Jones v. Ford Motor Co., 559 S.E.2d 592, 605 (Va. 2002) ("if the sudden emergency doctrine is to apply, the conditions confronting the operator must be an unexpected happening, an unforeseen occurrence or condition").

**48.** See, e.g., Reed v. Carlyle & Martin, Inc., 202 S.E.2d 874 (Va. 1974).

**49.** Compare Nicholson v. American Safety Util. Corp., 488 S.E.2d 240, 245 (N.C. 1997) (customary behavior is evidence of due care) and Uniroyal Goodrich Tire Co. v. Martinez, 977 S.W.2d 328 (Tex. 1998) (same), with Reed v. Carlyle & Martin, Inc., 202 S.E.2d 874 (Va. 1974) (customary behavior is not conclusive on due care).

**50.** Reed v. Carlyle & Martin, Inc., 202 S.E.2d 874 (Va. 1974).

spikes, located at the front of the wagon deposited the ensilage onto a conveyor belt which then discharged the substance. A co-worker was throwing the ensilage with a pitchfork from the rear of the wagon, but the plaintiff, standing on top of the load, decided that the quickest and easiest way to get the ensilage out of the wagon was to throw it with his pitchfork into the beaters at the front of the wagon. After unloading the ensilage in this manner for some time, the plaintiff found himself standing on a bank of ensilage, which contained "a good bit of sap" and was "right slippery," sloping downward toward the beaters. The bank collapsed, and the plaintiff slid into the beaters.

The trial court granted the defendants' motions for summary judgment on the basis of the plaintiff's contributory negligence, and the Supreme Court of Virginia affirmed. The court applied to the contributory negligence context two of the classic principles of negligence doctrine: the objective nature of the negligence standard of care,[51] and the effect of proof of compliance with customary behavior in ascertaining the standard and its breach.[52] In reply to the plaintiff's argument that he "didn't feel any danger" from working so close to the beaters, the court observed that "the test is not whether the plaintiff *actually* knew of the danger confronting him, but whether, in the exercise of reasonable care, he *should* have known he was in a situation of peril."[53] To the plaintiff's argument that he created a jury issue by showing that farm laborers customarily used a similar technique in unloading ensilage wagons, the court noted the longstanding negligence law principle that "the existence of a custom or usage cannot excuse conduct which is otherwise negligent."[54]

### Warning Cases

Contributory negligence doctrine operates under a special limitation in cases involving products with inadequate warnings of hidden dangers or instructions on safe use. If a warning or instruction is substantively inadequate in failing to inform users of the nature or seriousness of a hidden danger or reason for a particular instructed method of use, then a user who has not otherwise discovered the risk ordinarily will not be contributorily negligent for using the product in disregard of the danger.[55] However, to be contributorily negligent for exposing oneself to a

---

**51.** See § 2.2, above.

**52.** See § 2.4, above.

**53.** Reed v. Carlyle & Martin, Inc., 202 S.E.2d 874, 876 (Va. 1974) (emphasis added). The court ruled that all reasonable persons would conclude that the plaintiff in this case should have known of his peril: "The plaintiff, an experienced farmer, admitted that he was familiar with the operation of the type ensilage wagon in which he was working. Moreover, the revolving beaters were exposed to his plain view. The danger posed by the turning, spike-like mechanism was, therefore, open and obvious to the plaintiff. In exposing himself to this obvious danger, he failed to exercise

reasonable care for his own safety." Id. at 876–77.

**54.** Id. at 877.

**55.** This important point was made by Dillard and Hart in an important, early article:

Though these time-honored defenses [contributory negligence and assumption of risk] are frequently invoked to defeat recovery, they are theoretically inapplicable when the defendant's breach of duty is based on a failure to warn. To allow these defenses is to indulge in circular reasoning, since usually the plaintiff cannot be said to have assumed a risk of which he was ignorant or to have contrib-

hazard, a user generally needs only to be aware of the *general* nature and magnitude of a risk, not the particular chemical or physical attributes of the product and how they specifically may affect the user's various organs. This was the holding in *Parris v. M.A. Bruder & Sons, Inc.*,[56] where a spray painter of more than twenty years claimed that the manufacturer of an epoxy product had failed to warn him that inhaling the epoxy fumes could cause asthma. Because the plaintiff knew generally of the substantial danger of inhaling paint fumes, even if he was not aware of the specific risk of contracting asthma, the court held that the jury properly could find that he was contributorily negligent for failing to wear a mask furnished by his employer.[57]

### Children

Prior to the development of comparative fault, when contributory negligence operated as a complete bar, courts frequently adapted the contributory negligence doctrine in a protective manner for especially vulnerable plaintiffs. Courts and commentators have been particularly solicitous of young children who fail to appreciate product hazards.[58] So, when a five–year–old plaintiff fell and was injured when she attempted to climb into a grocery shopping cart manufactured by the defendant, the court held that she was too young to be contributorily negligent, and that her parents' negligence in failing to instruct or supervise their child should not be imputed to her.[59] As children grow older, however, the child standard of care adjusts according to the child's age, intelligence, and experience.[60] So, one court upheld a jury finding of contributory negligence in the case of a 13–year–old child who, while mowing her parents' lawn with a rotary power lawn mower, hit a pipe imbedded in the ground that protruded 1¾ inches above ground level.[61] The mower

uted to his own injury when he had no way of reasonably ascertaining that the danger of injury existed. On the other hand, if the plaintiff knew of the danger from an independent source, the manufacturer's failure to warn would not be the proximate cause of the injury. Nevertheless, many courts hold that the issue of contributory negligence is involved, and is a question for the jury."

Dillard and Hart, Product Liability: Directions for Use and the Duty To Warn, 41 Va. L. Rev. 145, 163 (1955). See, e.g., Rhodes v. Interstate Battery Sys. of Am., Inc., 722 F.2d 1517, 1519 (11th Cir. 1984) (Ga. law) ("Failure to read a warning does not bar recovery when the plaintiff is challenging the adequacy of the [warning].").

**56.** Parris v. M.A. Bruder & Sons, Inc., 261 F.Supp. 406 (E.D. Pa. 1966).

**57.** Id. at 409.

**58.** See Phillips, Products Liability for Personal Injury to Minors, 56 Va. L. Rev. 1223, 1225 (1970): "The assumption that children will expose themselves to danger in ways that a reasonable adult would not precludes the manufacturer's reliance on

the obviousness of the product's danger to the child plaintiff." Professor Phillips concludes that "even the best of educational efforts cannot be expected to change the essential nature of children, and, unless we are prepared to ignore this fact, in many instances better product design presents the only realistic means available for protecting children against injuries." Id. at 1240–41. See generally Madden, Products Liability, Products for Use by Adults, and Injured Children: Back to the Future, 61 Tenn. L. Rev. 1205, 1207 (1994) ("Lamentably, ... consideration of a child's inherent limitations in judgment and cognition is too often merely an afterthought."); Field, The Young Consumer: A Paradigm Analysis of the Roles of Public and Private Law in Preventing and Redressing Injuries, 29 Mercer L. Rev. 523 (1978).

**59.** Porter v. United Steel & Wire Co., 436 F.Supp. 1376 (N.D. Iowa 1977).

**60.** See Prosser and Keeton on Torts § 32, at 179, and § 65, at 454.

**61.** Siemer v. Midwest Mower Corp., 286 F.2d 381 (8th Cir. 1961) (N.Y. law).

bounced back and over her foot which was injured by the revolving blade. The court held that the jury properly found that the plaintiff either negligently failed to observe the pipe, or that she saw it and negligently failed to avoid it.[62]

Even when older children act very carelessly, courts are not likely to grant summary judgment to product suppliers but instead may be expected to allow juries to decide whether such behavior properly amounts to contributory negligence.[63] But once a child's actions are determined to amount to contributory negligence, the child's contributory negligence may be imputed to the child's parent making a claim for wrongful death, loss of services, or similar injuries.[64]

### Employees

As mentioned earlier, employees are sometimes effectively forced to work with dangerous machines, on dangerous tasks, or in some dangerous manner under an implicit threat of punishment or discharge for refusing to do so. In such situations, if the employee does not have a practical means to avoid the danger without simply refusing to perform the task, his or her exposure to the risk may not be unreasonable under the circumstances. As a means of protecting a worker's rights in this context, some courts "lessen the amount of caution required of him by law in the exercise of ordinary care."[65] And if an employer discovers but fails to inform its employees of a product danger, the employer's knowledge of the danger will not be imputed to its workers for purposes of contributory negligence.[66] But workers do not have a license to act carelessly, and the conduct of a person injured on the job is properly subject to the normal standard of a reasonably prudent employee in the same or similar circumstances.[67]

### As a Defense to Strict Liability in Tort

While contributory negligence is the classic defense to products liability claims brought in negligence, a plaintiff's ordinary contributory

---

**62.** Id. at 384.

**63.** See Morgan v. Cavalier Acquisition Corp., 432 S.E.2d 915 (N.C. Ct. App. 1993) (factual dispute existed on contributory negligence of seventeen-year-old student crushed to death when he tilted soda machine to get soft drink; summary judgment for machine manufacturer and owner reversed).

**64.** And a parent's (or guardian's) own negligence (or assumption of risk) will bar the parent's claim for injuries or the death of the child. See, e.g., Moss v. Crosman Corp., 136 F.3d 1169, (7th Cir. 1998) (Ind. law) (dictum; seven-year-old boy killed by cousin while playing with BB gun manufactured and sold by defendants; wrongful death claim of parents, one of whom bought gun for son, barred). See generally Restatement (3d) Torts: Apportionment of Liability § 6(a) (2000).

**65.** Young v. Aro Corp., 111 Cal.Rptr. 535, 537 (Ct. App. 1973) (worker knowingly operating grinding wheel at excessive speed killed when wheel exploded), quoting the trial court's jury instructions.

**66.** See Jackson v. Coast Paint & Lacquer Co., 499 F.2d 809 (9th Cir. 1974) (Mont. law).

**67.** See, e.g., Sears v. Waste Processing Equip., Inc., 695 So.2d 51 (Ala. Civ. App. 1997) (summary judgment for defendant affirmed where manager reached into trash compactor knowing that door cables were broken); Reed v. Carlyle & Martin, Inc., 202 S.E.2d 874 (Va. 1974) (summary judgment for manufacturer and seller of farm equipment upheld on ground of farmhand's contributory negligence as matter of law for carelessly falling into revolving parts of equipment). See also Hannah v. Gregg, Bland & Berry, Inc. 840 So.2d 839, 860–62 (Ala. 2002) (claims by workers like other plaintiffs, whether for negligence or state's version of strict liability in tort, are barred by contributory negligence).

negligence is not a defense to a claim for strict liability in tort.[68] In cases in which the plaintiff makes claims in both negligence and strict liability in tort, therefore, contributory (or comparative) negligence typically will be an available defense to the negligence claim but not to the strict tort claim.[69] Because of the possibility of confusion by the jury, a court should clearly instruct the jury as to this difference in the applicability of the contributory negligence defense to different types of claims.[70]

Comment *n* to *Restatement (Second) of Torts* § 402A provides that "simple"[71] or "ordinary"[72] contributory negligence—that is, conduct which is merely careless and which does not also amount to a voluntary assumption of risk—does not serve as a bar to liability under § 402A for harm caused by a defective product. Comment *n* provides in full as follows:

> *n. Contributory negligence.* Since the liability with which this Section deals is not based upon negligence of the seller, but is strict liability, the rule applied to strict liability cases (see § 524) applies. Contributory negligence of the plaintiff is not a defense when such negligence consists merely in a failure to discover the defect in the product, or to guard against the possibility of its existence. On the other hand the form of contributory negligence which consists in voluntarily and unreasonably proceeding to encounter a known danger, and commonly passes under the name of assumption of risk, is a defense

**68.** See, e.g., Cummings v. General Motors Corp., 365 F.3d 944, 952 (10th Cir. 2004) (Okla. law) (contributory negligence not a defense to strict liability in tort); Gramex Corp. v. Green Supply, Inc., 89 S.W.3d 432, 439 (Mo. 2002) (en banc) ("Contributory negligence is not a defense to strict liability."); Jay v. Moog Auto., 652 N.W.2d 872 (Neb. 2002) (contributory negligence is not a defense in strict liability, but misuse or assumption of risk could apply where plaintiff used compressor contrary to written instructions); Boerner v. Brown & Williamson Tobacco Corp., 260 F.3d 837 (8th Cir. 2001) (Ark. law) (smoker's claim against tobacco company); Jimenez v. Sears, Roebuck & Co., 904 P.2d 861 (Ariz. 1995) (rejecting contributory negligence in light of comparative fault scheme). *But see* Mohr v. St. Paul Fire & Marine Ins. Co., 674 N.W.2d 576, 591 (Wis. Ct. App. 2003) (contributory negligence may be defense to a strict product liability claim); Hannah v. Gregg, Bland & Berry, Inc. 840 So.2d 839, 860–62 (Ala. 2002) (AEMLD claims, state's version of strict liability in tort, are barred by contributory negligence). *See generally* McNichols, The Relevance of the Plaintiff's Misconduct in Strict Tort Products Liability, the Advent of Comparative Responsibility, and the Proposed Restatement (Third) of Torts, 47 Okla. L. Rev. 201 (1994); Vargo, The Defenses to Strict Liability in Tort: A New Vocabulary with an Old Meaning, 29 Mercer L. Rev. 447 (1978); Noel, Defective Products: Abnormal Use, Contributory Negligence, and Assumption of Risk, 25 Vand. L. Rev. 93 (1972); Epstein, Products Liability: Defenses Based on Plaintiff's Conduct, 1968 Utah L. Rev. 267; Annot., 46 A.L.R.3d 240 (1972) (contributory negligence and assumption of risk as defenses to claim for strict products liability in tort).

**69.** See, e.g., Ray v. Ford Motor Co., 514 S.E.2d 227 (Ga. Ct. App. 1999).

**70.** See, e.g., Ellsworth v. Sherne Lingerie, Inc., 495 A.2d 348, 357 (Md. 1985) ("When theories of negligence and strict liability in tort are being presented to a jury, and the defense of contributory negligence is properly before the jury, a trial judge may well find it helpful to specifically instruct the jury that contributory negligence is not a defense to the strict liability action.").

**71.** See Williams v. Brown Mfg. Co., 261 N.E.2d 305, 309 (Ill. 1970) (characterizing "lack of due care for one's own safety as measured by the objective reasonable-man standard" as "simple contributory negligence").

**72.** See id. at 310. See also Cepeda v. Cumberland Eng'g Co., 386 A.2d 816, 832 (N.J. 1978) (following *Williams* in rejecting "ordinary" contributory negligence as defense to claims for strict products liability in tort).

under this Section as in other cases of strict liability. If the user or consumer discovers the defect and is aware of the danger, and nevertheless proceeds unreasonably to make use of the product and is injured by it, he is barred from recovery.

A couple of early decisions rejected the comment *n* approach and held that contributory negligence in any form would bar liability under strict liability in tort,[73] and at least one prominent early commentator was uncertain of the soundness of abandoning conventional contributory negligence as a defense in strict liability defective product cases.[74] Such courts and commentators reasoned that strict products liability in tort is based in part upon the likelihood that product defects are attributable to a seller's negligence, which, although it usually exists, is often difficult for a plaintiff to prove; that the doctrine functions as a kind of res ipsa loquitur or negligence per se; and that the doctrine rests upon a presumption that injured plaintiffs are incapable of protecting themselves—each of which are rationales consistent with the contributory negligence defense.[75]

Despite comment *n*'s thin reasoning for abandoning the conventional tort law defense of contributory negligence on the ground that this defense has been rejected as a defense to strict liability in tort for harm caused by ultrahazardous activities,[76] courts widely adopted comment *n*'s

---

**73.** See Atkins v. American Motors Corp., 335 So.2d 134, 143 (Ala. 1976); Stephan v. Sears, Roebuck & Co., 266 A.2d 855 (N.H. 1970). See also Codling v. Paglia, 298 N.E.2d 622 (N.Y. 1973) (strict products liability in warranty); Dippel v. Sciano, 155 N.W.2d 55 (Wis. 1967) (comparative fault). Alabama still purports to retain a "contributory negligence" defense to claims for strict products liability in tort, Campbell v. Cutler Hammer, Inc., 646 So.2d 573 (Ala. 1994) (three judges dissenting and one concurring), but its case law is confusing and most of the recent decisions define contributory negligence in assumption of risk terms. This was also true in New Jersey, which had abolished the defense of assumption of risk in Meistrich v. Casino Arena Attractions, Inc., 155 A.2d 90 (N.J. 1959), and McGrath v. American Cyanamid Co., 196 A.2d 238 (N.J. 1963), and so found a need to leave "contributory negligence" available as a strict products liability in tort defense to address cases involving voluntary and unreasonable encounters of product dangers; but it, too, defined the requisite type of contributory negligence in terms of assumption of risk. See generally Cepeda v. Cumberland Eng'g Co., 386 A.2d 816, 831 (N.J. 1978). In addition, New Jersey made an exception for plaintiffs negligently encountering a known danger where the product is defective precisely because of its failure to prevent such negligent encounters. See Bexiga v. Havir Mfg. Co., 290 A.2d 281 (N.J. 1972) (plaintiff's hand crushed in punch press), where the court concluded

that "the interests of justice dictate that contributory negligence be unavailable as a defense to either the negligence or strict liability claims," reasoning as follows:

> The asserted negligence of plaintiff—placing his hand under the ram while at the same time depressing the foot pedal—was the very eventuality the safety devices were designed to guard against. It would be anomalous to hold that defendant has a duty to install safety devices but a breach of that duty results in no liability for the very injury the duty was meant to protect against.

Id. at 286. See also Suter v. San Angelo Foundry & Mach. Co., 406 A.2d 140 (N.J. 1979). Cf. Rivera v. Westinghouse Elevator Co., 526 A.2d 705 (N.J. 1987). *Bexiga* is noted at 86 Harv. L. Rev. 923 (1973).

**74.** See Noel, Defective Products: Abnormal Use, Contributory Negligence, and Assumption of Risk, 25 Vand. L. Rev. 93, 105–19, 128–30 (1972). "If the plaintiff could have discovered the defect in a dangerous product with little effort, it may be that his failure to inspect should be a defense in this new and expanding area of liability." Id. at 117.

**75.** See id. at 105–19.

**76.** See, e.g., McCown v. International Harvester Co., 342 A.2d 381, 382 n.5 (Pa. 1975) (Pomeroy, J., concurring). See generally Noel, Defective Products: Abnormal Use, Contributory Negligence, and Assump-

abandonment of simple contributory negligence as a bar to strict products liability in tort.[77] The courts reasoned that the doctrine of strict liability in tort discarded the concept of fault, that strict liability was premised on requiring suppliers of defective products to internalize the costs of product accidents as a means of risk administration, and that such liability was based on the buyer's reliance upon an implicit representation that the product was safe.[78] The doctrine of comparative fault would seem to complicate the issue, by raising anew the question of whether plaintiffs should still be specially protected from the consequences of their "simple" or "ordinary" contributory negligence, but courts in comparative fault regimes have declined to reduce damages on account of the plaintiff's careless failure to discover a product defect.[79] The *Products Liability Restatement* rejects the idea of exempting from damages apportionment the plaintiff's negligence in failing to discover or guard against the possibility of a defect, but, sympathetic to this type of plaintiff misbehavior, indicates that a plaintiff's simple contributory negligence of this sort rarely will breach the standard of reasonable behavior.[80]

Comment *n*, as mentioned, divides a user's negligent misconduct into two categories: failing to discover or guard against the possibility of a defect, on the one hand, and conduct which amounts to assumption of risk—voluntarily and unreasonably encountering a known and appreciated danger—on the other. Yet, rather than fully occupying the total set

tion of Risk, 25 Vand. L. Rev. 93, 115–17 (1972). It should be noted, however, that comment *n* does faithfully adapt the principles of Restatement of Torts § 524 to the defective product context.

**77.** The leading early case on point was Williams v. Brown Mfg. Co., 261 N.E.2d 305 (Ill. 1970). Other early decisions to this effect included Bachner v. Pearson, 479 P.2d 319 (Alaska 1970); Estabrook v. J.C. Penney Co., 464 P.2d 325 (Ariz. 1970); Perfection Paint & Color Co. v. Konduris, 258 N.E.2d 681, 689 (Ind. 1970); Magnuson v. Rupp Mfg., Inc., 171 N.W.2d 201, 211 (Minn. 1969); Keener v. Dayton Elec. Mfg. Co., 445 S.W.2d 362 (Mo. 1969); Ettin v. Ava Truck Leasing, Inc., 251 A.2d 278 (N.J. 1969); Brown v. Quick Mix Co., 454 P.2d 205, 208 (Wash. 1969); DeFelice v. Ford Motor Co., 255 A.2d 636 (Conn. Super. Ct. 1969); Richard v. H.P. Hood & Sons, 243 A.2d 910 (R.I. 1968); Shamrock Fuel & Oil Sales Co. v. Tunks, 416 S.W.2d 779 (Tex. 1967); Ferraro v. Ford Motor Co., 223 A.2d 746 (Pa. 1966); Martinez v. Nichols Conveyor & Eng'g Co., 52 Cal.Rptr. 842 (Ct. App. 1966); Baker v. Rosemurgy, 144 N.W.2d 660 (Mich. Ct. App. 1966).

**78.** See, e.g., McCown v. International Harvester Co., 342 A.2d 381, 382 (Pa. 1975) (allowing contributory negligence defense "would contradict this normal expectation of product safety"). See generally Noel, Defective Products: Abnormal Use, Contribu-

tory Negligence, and Assumption of Risk, 25 Vand. L. Rev. 93, 105–19, 128–30 (1972). Following Williams v. Brown Mfg. Co., 261 N.E.2d 305 (Ill. 1970), the court in Cepeda v. Cumberland Eng'g Co., 386 A.2d 816, 832 (N.J. 1978), observed that the "acceptance of 'ordinary' contributory negligence as a defense in actions for strict liability in tort would be incompatible with the policy considerations which led to the adoption of strict tort liability in the first instance. The manufacturer's duty is imposed precisely to avert foreseeable inadvertent injury to a user of a product." See also General Motors Corp. v. Sanchez, 997 S.W.2d 584, 594 (Tex. 1999) ("a duty to discover defects, and to take precautions in constant anticipation that a product might have a defect, would defeat the purposes of strict liability"). See generally McNichols, The Relevance of the Plaintiff's Misconduct in Strict Tort Products Liability, the Advent of Comparative Responsibility, and the Proposed Restatement (Third) of Torts, 47 Okla. L. Rev. 201, 260 (1994).

**79.** See, e.g., Jett v. Ford Motor Co., 84 P.3d 219 (Or. Ct. App. 2004); Curtis v. Hoosier Racing Tire Corp., 299 F.Supp.2d 777, 784 (N.D. Ohio 2004); Jay v. Moog Auto., Inc., 652 N.W.2d 872, 882 (Neb. 2002). See § 13.3, below.

**80.** See Products Liability Restatement § 17, Reporters' Note to cmt. *d*, at 259, set forth in § 13.3, below.

of consumer misconduct, these two forms of negligent behavior might instead be seen to occupy only the two extreme ends of the spectrum of consumer mistakes: the first, a type of minimally careless conduct involving a consumer's excessive trust during initial encounters with an unfamiliar product, and the second, a type of deliberately careless decision to encounter known and appreciated hazards of a familiar product. Arguably, neither of these categories adequately describes a consumer's ordinary careless *use* of a defective product, such as operating the product in a careless manner.[81] But comment *n* is not a statute,[82] and its provision excluding contributory negligence for failing to discover or guard against the existence of a defect may be reasonably expanded to include the idea of using a product without due care that it may be defective.[83] In this manner, comment *n*'s two categories of user misconduct may plausibly be viewed as embracing all forms of contributory negligence by product users. Under comparative fault, however, there may be good reason to exclude from damages apportionment a plaintiff's negligence in failing to discover a product's defects, narrowly defined, but to reduce a plaintiff's damages for negligently using the product in a dangerous manner.[84]

### As the Sole Proximate Cause of an Accident

With the loss of the contributory negligence defense in strict liability claims, counsel for defendants lost the most cherished arrow in their quiver. In a case involving appreciable plaintiff misconduct, a plaintiff's lawyer now may style the claim as one of strict liability in tort in order to avoid argument (and possibly evidence) on the plaintiff's negligent misbehavior. But, by rejecting a plaintiff's contributory negligence as a general defense to claims for strict products liability in tort, the law did not abolish the plaintiff's obligation to establish that a defect is a *proximate cause* of the harm.

From an early date, commentators observed that a plaintiff's contributory negligence sometimes is so significant a factor in producing an injury that it may amount to the *sole* proximate cause of the harm.[85] In an appropriate case, therefore, a defendant may properly offer evidence and argument that the plaintiff's behavior—rather than any defect in

---

**81.** See, e.g., McCown v. International Harvester Co., 342 A.2d 381, 383 (Pa. 1975) (Pomeroy, J., concurring).

**82.** Except in South Carolina, which codified the negligent assumption of risk defense embraced in the last sentence of comment *n*. S.C. Code Ann. § 15–73–20.

**83.** See Noel, Defective Products: Abnormal Use, Contributory Negligence, and Assumption of Risk, 25 Vand. L. Rev. 93, 111 (1972) (high-speed driving on tire not known to be defective as example of failing to guard against the possibility of defect). Compare W. Prosser, Handbook of the Law of Torts § 102, at 670–71 (4th ed. 1971), describing the negligent driving on a tire known to be unsafe as the kind of assumption of risk conduct to be distinguished from the simple negligence in failing to discover or guard against the risk that a product might be defective.

**84.** See General Motors Corp. v. Sanchez, 997 S.W.2d 584 (Tex. 1999) (interpreting cmt. *n* of Second Restatement narrowly, and quoting Third Restatement § 17, cmt. *d*: plaintiff's negligence in failing to discover defect should not reduce plaintiff's damages under comparative fault, but negligence in dangerously *using* product should result in such reduction).

**85.** See, e.g., Noel, Defective Products: Abnormal Use, Contributory Negligence, and Assumption of Risk, 25 Vand. L. Rev. 93, 105 (1972).

the product—was the "sole proximate cause" of the harm.[86] Thus, in cases where substantial consumer misconduct was overwhelmingly the predominant force in causing an accident, and where the role of any product defect was manifestly trivial by comparison, evidence and argument that the plaintiff's conduct was the sole proximate cause of the harm is entirely proper and will support a judgment for the defendant in a proper case.[87]

But the sole proximate cause doctrine can be used improperly to drag ordinary contributory negligence back into products liability cases, to operate as a total bar, in situations where a plaintiff's misconduct should reduce damages, not bar recovery altogether.[88] Whether conduct be called "contributory negligence" or something else, it can fairly be described as the *sole* proximate cause of an accident only if it overwhelmed any causal contribution by a product defect which, by comparison, was simply trivial. Without close supervision by the trial court, evidence and argument on the plaintiff's conduct as the sole proximate cause of an accident may slip easily and impermissibly into a thinly veiled revival of the contributory negligence defense.

**86.** On rare occasions, courts speak loosely of a plaintiff's substantial misconduct as amounting to a "superseding" cause of an accident. See, e.g., Sabbatino v. Rosin & Sons Hardware & Paint, Inc., 676 N.Y.S.2d 633, 635 (App. Div. 1998); Madonna v. Harley Davidson, Inc., 708 A.2d 507, 509 (Pa. Super. Ct. 1998); Wagner v. Clark Equip. Co., 700 A.2d 38, 48 (Conn. 1997); Little v. Liquid Air Corp., 37 F.3d 1069, 1079 n.26 (5th Cir. 1994) (Miss. law). However, the concept of superseding causation traditionally refers only to unforeseeable intervening acts of God and behavior by third parties. See generally Restatement (2d) Torts § 440; Prosser and Keeton on Torts § 44, at 312. Accordingly, while a plaintiff's extraordinary behavior may amount to the "sole proximate cause" of a particular accident, it appears preferable not to refer to such behavior as a "superseding" cause of the harm.

**87.** See, e.g., McCarty v. F.C. Kingston Co., 522 P.2d 778 (Ariz. Ct. App. 1974). See also Griffith v. Chrysler Corp., 2003 WL 21500037 (Ohio Ct. App. 2003) (intoxicated person fell asleep or passed out in stopped, running vehicle and pressed foot on accelerator, causing exhaust system to overheat and ignite; proper to instruct jury that vehicle occupant's conduct could be "superseding intervening cause").

Compare Goulah v. Ford Motor Co., 118 F.3d 1478, 1485 (11th Cir. 1997) (Fla. law). In this design defect case involving the rollover of a Bronco II when the trailer it was towing swung around, the manufacturer argued that the "sole legal cause" of the accident was the improper use of the trailer rather than any defect in the vehicle:

Evidence on the issues of the trailer and driving directly refutes Plaintiffs' contention that Ford's negligence caused this accident. Ford was not limited to saying, "we didn't cause this." Ford had every right to tell the jury who or what it believed made this accident happen.

Id. at 1486. *But see* Yun v. Ford Motor Co., 669 A.2d 1378 (N.J. 1996) (plaintiff struck by another vehicle while crossing highway to retrieve spare tire that fell off van; proximate cause for jury), reversing 647 A.2d 841 (N.J. Super. Ct. App. Div. 1994), which had affirmed summary judgement for manufacturer.

**88.** Possibly inappropriate uses of the sole proximate cause doctrine are Wilson v. Vermont Castings, Inc., 170 F.3d 391, 396 (3d Cir. 1999) (Pa. law) (plaintiff's dress caught fire on woodburning stove allegedly defective because of need to leave door open to keep fire going; upholding jury finding that plaintiff's conduct was sole cause of accident); Sabbatino v. Rosin & Sons Hardware & Paint, Inc., 676 N.Y.S.2d 633, 635 (App. Div. 1998) (affirming summary judgment for defendants, where plaintiff failed to heed instructions on drain cleaner to cover opening after pouring cleaner into drain); Wagner v. Clark Equip. Co., 700 A.2d 38, 48 (Conn. 1997) (jury should have been instructed that it could find that plaintiff's failure to pay attention to surroundings, together with forklift operator's failure to look over shoulder as he backed up and employer's failure to maintain safe workplace, all "combined so as to entirely supersede the lack of additional safety devices on the forklift as the proximate cause of the accident").

For example, in *Sheehan v. Anthony Pools*,[89] the plaintiff was injured during a party at his new swimming pool when he fell off the side of the diving board onto the concrete coping at the edge of the pool. In his strict tort action against the pool company, the plaintiff claimed that the non-skid material on the board should have extended to and over the edges of the board and that the design of the pool's diving board-coping area was unsafe. Without using the terms "careless" or "contributory negligence," defense counsel argued essentially that the injury was caused not by any problem with the design of the board or the pool, but by the manner in which the plaintiff used the board.[90] The trial judge denied the defendant's request to instruct the jury that contributory negligence *was* a defense and also denied the plaintiff's request for a charge that the plaintiff's inadvertence in using the board was *not* a defense, and the jury returned a verdict for the defendant. Reversing and remanding, the appellate court held that the trial court should have granted the plaintiff's requested instruction.[91] Arguments by a skillful defense attorney about a plaintiff's contributions to an accident can quite easily mislead a jury as to the proper role of a plaintiff's conduct in establishing liability and damages in a products liability case.[92] This suggests that courts, in addition to closely monitoring such arguments to avoid their abuse, should instruct juries carefully on the effect of consumer carelessness and on the proper, limited role of the doctrine of sole proximate cause in modern products liability litigation.

## § 13.3   COMPARATIVE FAULT

From the late 1960s through the early 1990s, the doctrine of comparative fault swept across America.[1] Its rapid and widespread adoption sprang from the evident unfairness of the all-or-nothing rule of contributory negligence that barred a plaintiff from all recovery against a tortfeasor if the plaintiff was at fault in any way in connection with the accident.[2] The law on comparative fault (otherwise known as "comparative negligence," "comparative responsibility," or "apportionment"),[3]

---

**89.** 440 A.2d 1085, 1090–92 (Md. Ct. Spec. App. 1982).

**90.** In closing argument, defense counsel argued, over objection, as follows:

You must find that this defect proximately caused the accident. The clear testimony here from Mr. Weiner and using your common sense is that if someone steps on the board with about an inch of their foot on it, they will fall off the side. That was the proximate cause, the way the board was used, not the design of the board. I am not willing to concede for a moment that there is anything defective about the board when you use the standards which are customary in the industry and any governmental regulations. Even if you feel there was, I ask you to find that the proximate cause was the way Mr. Sheehan used it, not the way it was designed.

Id. at 1090 (court's emphasis omitted).

**91.** Id. at 1092.

**92.** See the several questionable cases cited in note 88, above.

### § 13.3

**1.** Comparative fault is applied today in every jurisdiction except Maryland, the District of Columbia, Virginia, North Carolina, and Alabama.

**2.** "The hardship of the doctrine of contributory negligence upon the plaintiff is readily apparent. It places upon one party the entire burden of a loss for which two are, by hypothesis, responsible." Prosser and Keeton on Torts § 67, at 468–69.

**3.** See, e.g., Duncan v. Cessna Aircraft Co., 665 S.W.2d 414, 427 (Tex. 1984) ("We choose comparative *causation* instead because it is conceptually accurate in cases based on strict liability and breach of warranty theories in which the defendant's 'fault,' in the traditional sense of culpability, is not at issue."); Daly v. General Mo-

which reduces an accident victim's damages proportionate to his or her fault rather than barring recovery altogether, is now so extensive that it has its own *Restatement (Third) of Torts: Apportionment*[4] and a new uniform law on this topic.[5]

Comparative fault, examined elsewhere in much greater depth,[6] significantly affects modern products liability litigation[7] where it now provides a giant umbrella over the traditional misconduct defenses of contributory negligence,[8] in almost every state; assumption of risk,[9] in many states; and product misuse,[10] in some states. While comparative fault most typically affects claims for negligence and strict liability in tort, its principles of apportionment may also affect claims for breach of warranty[11] and tortious misrepresentation.[12] How the spreading tentacles of comparative fault affect negligence claims was touched on above and how this doctrine affects warranty and misrepresentation claims is considered in sections on these topics, below.

Prior to addressing the specifics of comparative fault, it would be well to note that its widespread adoption still leaves some room for the traditional all-or-nothing misconduct defenses to operate. As mentioned earlier, traditional misconduct defenses continue to govern products actions in the few states that still reject the doctrine of comparative fault.[13] In addition, some secondary misconduct defense doctrine—such as the irrelevance of a plaintiff's contributory negligence in failing to

---

tors Corp., 575 P.2d 1162, 1172 (Cal. 1978) (suggesting "equitable apportionment of loss").

**4.** See Restatement (3d) Torts: Apportionment (2000).

**5.** See Uniform Apportionment of Tort Responsibility Act (2002, revised 2003). See comment to § 3 (2004 electronic pocket part update), discussing history of comparative fault and uniform acts thereon.

**6.** See, e.g., Bublick, Comparative Fault to the Limits, 56 Vand. L. Rev. 977 (2003); Robertson, Love and Fury: Recent Radical Revisions to the Law of Comparative Fault, 59 La. L. Rev. 175, 198–99 (1998); Dobbs, Accountability and Comparative Fault, 47 La. L. Rev. 939 (1987); Cooter & Ulen, An Economic Case for Comparative Negligence, 61 N.Y.U. L. Rev. 1067, 1081–82 (1986); G. Schwartz, Contributory and Comparative Negligence: A Reappraisal, 87 Yale L.J. 697, 721–23 (1978); Prosser, Comparative Negligence, 51 Mich. L. Rev. 465 (1953); Prosser and Keeton on Torts § 67; Dobbs, Law of Torts § 201; V. Schwartz, Comparative Negligence (with E. Rowe, 4th ed. 2002); H. Woods and B. Deere, Comparative Fault (3d ed. 1996); A. Best, Comparative Negligence (1998).

**7.** See, e.g., Henke, Comparative Fault in Products Liability: Comparing California and New Jersey, 19 T.M. Cooley L. Rev. 301 (2002); M. Davis, Individual and Institutional Responsibility: A Vision for Comparative Fault in Products Liability, 39 Vill. L. Rev. 281 (1994); McNichols, The Relevance

of the Plaintiff's Misconduct in Strict Tort Products Liability, the Advent of Comparative Responsibility, and the Proposed Restatement (Third) of Torts, 47 Okla. L. Rev. 201 (1994) (reviewing early draft of Products Liability Restatement); Roszkowski and Prentice, Reconciling Comparative Negligence and Strict Liability: A Public Policy Analysis, 33 St. Louis U. L.J. 19 (1988); Westerbeke & Meltzer, Comparative Fault and Strict Products Liability in Kansas: Reflections on the Distinction Between Initial Liability and Ultimate Loss Allocation, 28 U. Kan. L. Rev. 25 (1979); Twerski, The Use and Abuse of Comparative Negligence in Products Liability, 10 Ind. L. Rev. 797 (1977); Levine, Strict Products Liability and Comparative Negligence: The Collision of Fault and No-Fault, 14 San Diego L. Rev. 337 (1977). See generally 1 and 2 Frumer and Friedman, Products Liability § 8.04[5] (as a defense to strict liability in tort) and § 10.02[3] (as a defense to negligence); 2 Madden & Owen on Products Liability ch. 15; Am. Law Prod. Liab. 3d ch. 40; Dobbs, Law of Torts § 369.

**8.** See § 13.2, above.

**9.** See § 13.4, below.

**10.** See § 13.5, below.

**11.** See § 13.6, below.

**12.** See § 13.7, below.

**13.** Maryland, the District of Columbia, Virginia, North Carolina, and Alabama.

discover a defect, and the role of sole proximate cause—remains largely unaffected by comparative fault. Moreover, in most states, a plaintiff's misconduct remains a *total* bar to recovery if the plaintiff's fault equals (or, in some states, exceeds) that of the defendant.[14] In addition, some courts refuse to apply comparative fault principles to assumption of risk, or do so only to a limited extent,[15] and many still consider the plaintiff's unforeseeable misuse to be a total defense.[16] Finally, in claims for breach of warranty[17] and misrepresentation,[18] a buyer's or user's misconduct often goes to issues—such as scope of warranty, justifiable reliance, and proximate cause—that are part of the plaintiff's case in chief, making the absence of such misconduct essential to the plaintiff's underlying claim. What all this means, of course, is that comparative fault has not beaten the traditional misconduct defenses completely into the ground, that defendants can sometimes still put the traditional all-or-nothing misconduct defenses effectively to use as gladiators against misbehaving plaintiffs, despite the modern urge to shake clear judgments of right or wrong from legal outcomes by fixing responsibility, like Solomon, by division.

Yet, while comparative fault still has competition, let no one doubt its power. This section examines how comparative fault operates in products liability litigation in general and, more particularly, how it affects claims based on strict liability in tort. The specific effects of comparative fault on other doctrines is addressed in later sections.

### Types and Examples of Comparative Fault

#### *"Pure" and "Modified"*

Comparative fault systems applicable to products liability cases come in two basic forms, "pure" and "modified."[19] A comparative fault system is "pure" if the plaintiff may recover damages from a tortfeasor, reduced proportionately by those attributable to the plaintiff's fault, regardless of how great the plaintiff's proportion of the total fault may be. For example, if the plaintiff's fault is 90% and the defendant's fault is only 10%, the plaintiff in a pure comparative fault jurisdiction may still recover the 10% of damages attributable to the defendant.[20] Most states

**14.** See, e.g., King v. Kayak Mfg. Corp., 387 S.E.2d 511 (W. Va. 1989) (assumption of risk). See § 13.4, below.

**15.** Ohio, for example, merged assumption of risk into comparative fault for negligence claims but left it as a total bar to claims for strict liability in tort. See, e.g., Onderko v. Richmond Mfg. Co., 511 N.E.2d 388 (Ohio 1987); Bowling v. Heil Co., 511 N.E.2d 373 (Ohio 1987). See § 13.4, below.

**16.** See § 13.5, below.

**17.** See § 13.6, below.

**18.** See § 13.7, below.

**19.** One state, South Dakota, still has the "slight-gross" system, under which a plaintiff may recover (diminished) damages against a defendant if the plaintiff's contributory negligence is slight, and the defendant's is gross. See S.D. Codified Laws § 20–9–2. Nebraska formerly had this system but switched to a modified system in 1992.

**20.** See, e.g., Thornton v. Gray Auto. Parts Co., 62 S.W.3d 575 (Mo. Ct. App. 2001) (mechanic, 95% at fault for improperly using jack that slipped out from beneath vehicle, could recover against manufacturer of jack who was 5% at fault for not equipping jack with safety feature); Uniroyal Tire Co. v. Trujillo, 711 So.2d 606 (Fla. Dist. Ct. App. 1998) (driver, 99% at fault for speeding, having tire improperly repaired, and failing to wear seatbelt, could recover against tire manufacturer who was 1% responsible), vacated, 757 So.2d 547 (Fla. App. 2000); Winston v. International Harvester Corp., 791 F.2d 430 (5th Cir. 1986) (La. law) (tractor operator 97% negligent

which adopted comparative fault by judicial decision, together with several that adopted it legislatively, adopted the doctrine in this pure form,[21] an approach endorsed by the American Law Institute in 2000,[22] and by the National Conference of Commissioners on Uniform State Laws in 1977[23]—a decision which NCCUSL then reversed in 2002.[24]

A large majority of states, including most which adopted the doctrine legislatively, use some "modified" version of comparative fault. Modified comparative fault systems reduce recoverable damages proportionate to a plaintiff's fault, just as under the pure approach, but such systems continue to bar recovery completely (as under traditional contributory negligence) if the plaintiff's fault *exceeds* the defendant's fault, known as the "New Hampshire system,"[25] or, under the "Georgia system,"[26] if the plaintiff's fault *equals* or exceeds the defendant's fault. So, under either type of modified system, a plaintiff 30% at fault may recover the 70% of damages apportioned to the defendant, but a plaintiff 60% at fault is entitled to no recovery.[27] A plaintiff who is 50% at fault may recover half of his or her damages under the New Hampshire system but nothing whatsoever under the Georgia system. To leave plaintiffs with some recovery in the occasional cases where fault is apportioned 50–50 between plaintiffs and defendants,[28] a number of states have switched to the New Hampshire system, as have two states (Illinois and Iowa) which had been pure. Only eleven states still remain in the Georgia camp,[29] whereas more than twenty states now follow the

could recover 3% of damages against tractor manufacturer).

**21.** The list of "pure" jurisdictions currently includes Alaska, Arizona, California, Florida, Hawaii (applicable to claims for strict liability in tort and warranty, but not negligence), Kentucky, Louisiana, Michigan, Mississippi, Missouri, New Mexico, New York, Rhode Island, Washington, and Puerto Rico. See H. Woods and B. Deere, Comparative Fault § 1.11 (3d ed. 1996, and 2003 Supp.); V. Schwartz, Comparative Negligence § 2.01[a] (4th ed. 2002); Product Liability Desk Reference—A Fifty State Compendium (M. Daller, ed. 2004).

**22.** See Restatement (3d): Apportionment § 7 (2000) which provides that a plaintiff's negligence that is a legal cause of plaintiff's injury "reduces the plaintiff's responsibility in proportion to the share of responsibility the factfinder assigns to the plaintiff."

**23.** See Uniform Comparative Fault Act § 1. Iowa and Washington were the only states to enact the act in any form, and their versions differed from the uniform act materially.

**24.** See Uniform Apportionment of Tort Responsibility Act § 3(b) (2002), and the excellent comment to § 3 (2004 electronic pocket part update).

**25.** Or, in some jurisdictions, compared to the fault of *all* defendants.

**26.** Also known as the (original) "Wisconsin system," but Wisconsin abandoned

this approach for the New Hampshire system in 1971.

**27.** See, e.g., Hernandez v. American Appliance Mfg. Corp., 827 S.W.2d 383 (Tex. App. 1992) (plaintiff, 90% at fault for using adhesive with highly flammable fumes near gas water heater with pilot light, could take nothing against 10% at-fault heater manufacturer). See also Taylor v. Square D Co., 2003 WL 23093835 (Tenn. Ct. App. 2003) (fault of electrician, electrocuted while working on partially energized circuit contrary to supervisor's direct orders, was clearly greater than any negligence of manufacturer); Horton v. American Tobacco Co., 667 So.2d 1289 (Miss. 1995) (jury found tobacco company liable for smoker's death from lung cancer, but awarded damages of $0, presumably because it found the smoker 100% at fault); Gratzle v. Sears, Roebuck & Co., 613 N.E.2d 802 (Ill. App. Ct. 1993) (60% apportionment of causation to plaintiff reversed; jury should have been instructed on effect of finding that plaintiff's conduct accounted for 50% or more of causation).

**28.** Such 50–50 findings are not rare, but, strangely, they are quite uncommon. See, e.g., Kava v. American Honda Motor Co., 48 P.3d 1170 (Alaska 2002); General Motors Corp. v. Sanchez, 997 S.W.2d 584, 592–95 (Tex. 1999).

**29.** Arkansas, Colorado, Georgia, Idaho, Kansas, Maine, Nebraska, North Dakota, Tennessee, Utah, and West Virginia. See H.

increasingly popular New Hampshire approach which allows a 50% at-fault plaintiff to recover.[30]

### Examples of Comparative Fault

Product accidents occur in myriad ways, resulting in myriad divisions of fault between manufacturers and product users. For example, when a defect in a car's steering column caused the steering to lock, after which the plaintiff neglected to apply the brakes, responsibility for the resulting crash was divided 85% to the manufacturer and 15% to the driver;[31] a manufacturer of an aluminum ladder sold without warning of the risk from hitting power lines was 2% responsible for a painter's electrocution, the company that rented the ladder to the painting crew was 3% responsible, and the painter himself, who failed to have the power lines de-energized before painting in their vicinity and failed to use a wooden or fiberglass ladder, was 95% responsible;[32] the manufacturer of a car with a defective door latch, which allowed the door to open when it collided with another car, was 75% responsible, and the plaintiff's responsibility for speeding was 25%;[33] the manufacturer of a potato chip cooker kettle was 52% responsible for a kettle shaft that popped out of place, and the injured Frito Lay employee who attempted to repair the shaft was 48% at fault for conducting the repairs while standing on a board across a kettle of hot oil, and for slipping in;[34] a pharmacy was 51% responsible for failing properly to warn a customer that an anti-depression drug could cause permanent impotency, whereas the customer was 49% at fault for failing for 30 hours to seek medical attention for an erection;[35] and the divisions of responsibility for product accidents go on and on.[36]

Woods and B. Deere, Comparative Fault § 1.11 (3d ed. 1996, and 2003 Supp.); V. Schwartz, Comparative Negligence § 2.01[b] (4th ed. 2002); Product Liability Desk Reference—A Fifty State Compendium (M. Daller, ed. 2004).

**30.** Connecticut, Delaware, Hawaii (negligence claims only), Illinois, Indiana, Iowa, Massachusetts, Minnesota, Montana, Nevada, New Hampshire, New Jersey, Ohio, Oklahoma, Oregon, Pennsylvania, South Carolina, Texas, Vermont, Wisconsin, and Wyoming. See H. Woods and B. Deere, Comparative Fault § 1.11 (3d ed. 1996, and 2003 Supp.); V. Schwartz, Comparative Negligence § 2.01[b] (4th ed. 2002); Product Liability Desk Reference—A Fifty State Compendium (M. Daller, ed. 2004).

**31.** Busch v. Busch Const., Inc., 262 N.W.2d 377 (Minn. 1977).

**32.** Hoeft v. Louisville Ladder Co., 904 S.W.2d 298 (Mo. Ct. App. 1995).

**33.** General Motors Corp. v. Castaneda, 980 S.W.2d 777 (Tex. App. 1998).

**34.** Blaw–Knox Food & Chemical Equip. Corp. v. Holmes, 348 So.2d 604 (Fla. Dist. Ct. App. 1977).

**35.** Cottam v. CVS Pharmacy, 764 N.E.2d 814 (Mass. 2002).

**36.** See, e.g., Jett v. Ford Motor Co., 72 P.3d 71 (Or. 2003) (delivery truck transmission that could slip from park to reverse, 85%; plaintiff's failure to wait for alternative truck and disregard of safety protocols, including walking behind truck with engine running, 15%); Blue v. Environmental Eng'g, Inc., 803 N.E.2d 187 (Ill. App. Ct. 2003) (failing to equip trash compactor with available safety features, 33%; worker's pushing boxes into compactor by foot, 32%; employer's allowing unsafe use of compactor, 35%); Lavergne v. America's Pizza Co., 838 So.2d 845 (La. Ct. App. 2003) (restaurant's negligence in serving hot pizza sauce, 70%; parent-plaintiffs' improper supervision of child burned by sauce, 30%); Lakin v. Senco Prods., Inc., 987 P.2d 463 (Or. 1999) (defective pneumatic air gun that could discharge multiple nails at once, 95%; use of gun while standing on makeshift sawhorse platform, 5%); Delisa v. Stewart Agency, Inc., 515 So.2d 426 (Fla. Dist. Ct. App. 1987) (defective seatbelts, 40%; riding with intoxicated driver, knowing seatbelts did not work, 60%); Miller v. Yazoo Mfg. Co., 26 F.3d 81 (8th Cir. 1994) (Mo. law)

## Strict Liability in Tort

### *Applicability of Comparative Fault*

As one state after another adopted comparative fault in the latter decades of the twentieth century, courts had to decide whether to apply this new form of damages apportionment to claims based on strict liability in tort.[37] The Uniform Comparative Fault Act of 1977 resolved this issue by including "strict tort liability" in its definition of the "fault" to be divided,[38] but only two states adopted versions of this uniform act.[39] In most states, courts have had to interpret statutes which require them to compare the parties' "negligence" or "fault" but fail explicitly to define those terms. And the courts have split on whether such statutory language covers claims for strict products liability in tort. At least Louisiana adopted a functional approach, applying comparative fault when it encourages product users to be more careful, but not when manufacturers need encouragement to make their products safer.[40]

Courts with leeway to decide whether or not to apportion damages in strict liability actions have weighed a number of considerations. Arguments against applying comparative negligence doctrine to strict liability in tort claims have included the "apples-and-oranges" argument, which pointed to the illogic of attempting to compare a plaintiff's fault with a product defect based on no-fault liability, and the "product-safety" or deterrence argument, which rested on strict liability's goal of maximizing product safety by forcing manufacturers to shoulder the costs of accidents caused by product defects. But most courts have set aside such arguments, opting for the apparent justice of making each party to an accident bear responsibility for the losses attributable to that party's breach of good behavior. To the apples and oranges argument, courts replied that factfinders really have no trouble apportioning responsibility between negligent plaintiffs and manufacturers subject to strict liability. To the deterrence argument, courts reasoned that manufacturers still remain responsible for all damages attributable to defects in their products and are shielded only from the portion of losses attributable to a plaintiff's breach of proper behavior for which the plaintiff alone should be responsible. In short, while some courts dis-

---

(designing riding mower with blades that stopped 4.2 seconds after clutch released, 0%; riding so close to top edge of ravine that mower tilted and fell in, 100%); T.H.S. Northstar Assoc. v. W.R. Grace & Co., 860 F.Supp. 640 (D. Minn. 1994) (manufacturing asbestos products, 60%; buying building constructed of such products, 40%); Dafler v. Raymark Indus., Inc., 611 A.2d 136 (N.J. Super. Ct. App. Div. 1992) (manufacturing asbestos products, which caused asbestosis and lung cancer, 30%; smoking, 70%); Delisa v. Stewart Agency, Inc., 515 So.2d 426 (Fla. Dist. Ct. App. 1987); West v. Caterpillar Tractor Co., 336 So.2d 80 (Fla. 1976) (road construction grading machine with poor rear visibility, no rear view mirrors, and no audible warning system for operat-

ing in reverse, 65%; failure to maintain proper lookout around such a machine, 35%).

**37.** See V. Schwartz, above, at ch. 11; Woods and Deere, above, at § 14:42 et seq.

**38.** Uniform Comparative Fault Act § 1(b) (1977). In 2002, the National Conference of Commissioners on Uniform State Laws approved a Uniform Apportionment of Tort Responsibility Act which, in § 3(a), as amended in 2003, dodges this issue entirely. See the excellent comment to § 3 (2004 electronic pocket part update).

**39.** Iowa and Washington.

**40.** See Bell v. Jet Wheel Blast, 462 So.2d 166, 171–72 (La. 1985).

agree,[41] the great majority of courts apply comparative fault to products liability claims based on strict liability in tort.[42]

### Negligent Failure to Discover a Product Defect

As examined earlier, comment *n* to *Restatement (Second) of Torts* § 402A takes the position that a plaintiff's "simple" or "ordinary" contributory negligence in failing to discover a defect, or in failing to guard against the possibility of its existence, should not shield a manufacturer from responsibility for its harmful consequences.[43] But this special category of plaintiff protection arose in the 1960s before the advent of comparative fault when the effect of the misconduct defenses was to bar a plaintiff's claim completely. Once most courts and legislatures abandoned the all-or-nothing effect of contributory negligence in the 1970s and 1980s, one might think they would have reconsidered the role of such simple contributory negligence in products liability actions and thrown it back into the well for consideration with all other types of fault.[44] A number of states avoid the issue by simply stating that all fault must be compared.[45] Yet, almost every court that has considered the matter has chosen to shield consumers from all responsibility for their failure to watch for product defects, by holding that a plaintiff's careless failure to discover that a product is defective lies outside the realm of damages apportionment.[46]

**41.** Refusing to apply comparative fault to strict tort actions, see, e.g., Lutz v. National Crane Corp., 884 P.2d 455 (Mont. 1994); Kimco Dev. Corp. v. Michael D's Carpet Outlets, 637 A.2d 603 (Pa. 1993); Phillips v. Duro–Last Roofing, Inc., 806 P.2d 834 (Wyo. 1991); Bowling v. Heil Co., 511 N.E.2d 373 (Ohio 1987). A very few still bar recovery altogether, even in strict liability, if the plaintiff was contributorily negligent. See, e.g., Campbell v. Cutler Hammer, Inc., 646 So.2d 573 (Ala. 1994) (3 justices dissenting and 1 concurring).

**42.** Applying comparative fault to strict tort actions, see, e.g., Webb v. Navistar Int'l Corp., 692 A.2d 343 (Vt. 1997) ("The overwhelming majority of states have rejected the 'all or nothing' rule ... and have applied principles of comparative liability in strict products liability actions."); Whitehead v. Toyota Motor Corp., 897 S.W.2d 684, 691 (Tenn. 1995) (same, citing cases from Conn., Fla., Haw., Idaho, Ill., Kan., La., Me., Mich., Minn., N.H., N.M., N.D., Or., R.I., Tex., Utah, Wash., W. Va., Wis.; and citing as contra cases from S.D., Colo., Ohio, Okla., and Wyo.). Accord Smith v. Ingersoll–Rand Co., 14 P.3d 990 (Alaska 2000); Elliot v. Sears Roebuck & Co., 642 A.2d 709 (Conn. 1994); Kaneko v. Hilo Coast Processing, 654 P.2d 343 (Haw. 1982); Suter v. San Angelo Foundry & Mach. Co., 406 A.2d 140 (N.J. 1979); Daly v. General Motors Corp., 575 P.2d 1162 (Cal. 1978) (noting that more than 30 states at that time had extended comparative negligence principles to strict products liabili-

ty); Butaud v. Suburban Marine & Sporting Goods, Inc., 555 P.2d 42 (Alaska 1976). See generally Annot., 9 A.L.R.4th 633 (1988) (applicability of comparative fault to strict products liability in tort).

**43.** See § 13.2, above.

**44.** See, e.g., Gillum v. L & J Enterprises, 29 P.3d 266, 270 (Alaska 2001) (negligence claim against warehouse operator for injuries from defective loading dock door; "Failure to discover a hazard can constitute comparative negligence."). See also Minn. Stat. Ann. § 604.01.1a. ("fault" to be apportioned includes "unreasonable failure to avoid an injury").

**45.** See, e.g., Smith v. Toyota Motor Corp., 105 Fed.Appx. 47 (6th Cir. 2004); Byrne v. SCM Corp., 538 N.E.2d 796 (Ill. Ct. App. 1989); Kaneko v. Hilo Coast Processing, 654 P.2d 343 (Haw. 1982); Sandford v. Chevrolet Div. of Gen. Motors, 642 P.2d 624 (Or. 1982); Star Furniture Co. v. Pulaski Furniture Co., 297 S.E.2d 854 (W. Va. 1982); Mulherin v. Ingersoll–Rand Co., 628 P.2d 1301 (Utah 1981); Daly v. General Motors Corp., 575 P.2d 1162 (Cal. 1978); Butaud v. Suburban Marine & Sporting Goods, 555 P.2d 42 (Alaska 1976) (codified in Alaska Stat. §§ 09.17.080, 09.17.900).

**46.** See, e.g., Jett v. Ford Motor Co., 84 P.3d 219 (Or. Ct. App. 2004); Curtis v. Hoosier Racing Tire Corp., 299 F.Supp.2d 777, 784 (N.D. Ohio 2004); Jay v. Moog Automotive, Inc., 652 N.W.2d 872, 882 (Neb. 2002); General Motors Corp. v. San-

The *Third Restatement of Torts* appears to take the opposite view, that courts should not set up special categories of protected plaintiff fault exempt from damages apportionment.[47] Its position appears to be that justice is best served if all types and degrees of plaintiff and defendant fault are thrown into one giant, fault-division cauldron. The *Products Liability Restatement* states in black letter that a plaintiff's damages may be reduced on account of the plaintiff's fault,[48] noting in commentary that "[t]he majority position is that all forms of plaintiff's failure to conform to applicable standards of care are to be considered" on apportionment.[49] While somewhat true, this assertion is misleading with respect to the role of a plaintiff's negligent failure to discover a defect or guard against its existence because, as stated earlier, most courts addressing this particular issue have continued to exempt this form of plaintiff misconduct from apportionment. The *Apportionment Restatement* endorses a general throw-it-all-in-the-cauldron approach, explicitly repudiating "[s]pecial ameliorative doctrines for defining plaintiff's negligence" in § 3's black letter, but nowhere mentioning the ameliorative doctrine concerning a plaintiff's negligent failure to watch for product defects.[50]

The reluctance of both *Restatements* to address this particular issue may possibly reflect the Reporters' sympathy for shielding plaintiffs from their negligence in failing to discover product defects, together with an unwillingness to explicitly "restate" the law on this point contrary to

---

chez, 997 S.W.2d 584, 592–95 (Tex. 1999) (narrowly interpreting cmt. *n* of Second Restatement, and quoting Third Restatement § 17, cmt. *d*); Hernandez v. Barbo Mach. Co., 957 P.2d 147 (Or. 1998); Simpson v. General Motors Corp., 483 N.E.2d 1 (Ill. 1985) (with strong dissent against creating separate categories of plaintiff conduct exempt from comparative fault); Coney v. J.L.G. Indus., Inc., 454 N.E.2d 197, 204 (Ill. 1983) ("a consumer's unobservant, inattentive, ignorant, or awkward failure to discover or guard against a defect should not be compared as a damage-reducing factor"); Sandford v. Chevrolet Div. of Gen. Motors, 642 P.2d 624 (Or. 1982); Star Furniture Co. v. Pulaski Furniture Co., 297 S.E.2d 854, 863 (W. Va. 1982) ("comparative negligence is available as an affirmative defense in a cause of action founded on strict liability so long as the complained of conduct is not a failure to discover a defect or to guard against it"); Busch v. Busch Const., Inc., 262 N.W.2d 377, 394 (Minn. 1977) ("a consumer's negligent failure to inspect a product or to guard against defects is not a defense and thus may not be compared with a distributor's strict liability"); West v. Caterpillar Tractor Co., 336 So.2d 80, 92 (Fla. 1976) ("comparative negligence is a defense in a strict liability action if based upon grounds other than the failure of the user to discover the defect … [or] to guard

against the possibility of its existence"); Idaho Code § 6–1305(1)(a). See also Smith v. Ingersoll–Rand Co., 14 P.3d 990, 993 (Alaska 2000) ("[C]omparative negligence in strict liability is limited to product misuse and unreasonable assumption of risk. Ordinary negligence is generally not sufficient to establish comparative negligence on the part of a products liability plaintiff.").

**47.** See also V. Schwartz, Comparative Negligence § 11.07 (4th ed. 2002) (criticizing this special category of protected misbehavior).

**48.** See Products Liability Restatement § 17(a).

**49.** Id. cmt. *d*, at 259, and Reporters' Note thereto, at 262. See also id. at cmt. *a*, at 256–57, which misleadingly suggests that modern courts have abandoned comment *n*.

**50.** The comments to § 3, and Reporters' Notes thereto, discuss various other ameliorative doctrines but fail to discuss this doctrine. The Reporters specifically mention this doctrine in their notes to § 1 cmt. *b*, at 11, where they assert that, "Most states at least hold that a plaintiff's negligence that constitutes more than a mere failure to discover or guard against the possibility of a product defect supports the factfinder's assigning a percentage of responsibility to the plaintiff."

how courts actually (and not unreasonably) were deciding cases; or it may reflect their reluctance to deviate from a simple, consistent approach to apportionment in which all types of fault are thrown into the mix. Be that as it may, the *Products Liability Restatement* does end up offering a partial back-door escape to plaintiffs in this situation, observing that a plaintiff's simple contributory negligence of this sort rarely will breach the standard of reasonable behavior.[51]

### Sole Proximate Cause

The doctrine of "sole proximate cause"[52] is normally used to deny recovery to a plaintiff injured in an accident caused principally by his or her own misconduct. The problem with the sole proximate cause doctrine in states where contributory negligence is not a defense to strict liability in tort claims, previously discussed, is the risk that defense counsel will use it as an improper back-door means to sneak contributory negligence into the case.[53] In comparative fault jurisdictions, where proof and argument about a plaintiff's fault are entirely fair game, this problem would seem to vanish. If the system is a modified one, a plaintiff even 51% at fault may not recover anyway, so that there would seem to be no need for a doctrine that means, essentially, that the plaintiff should be held 100% responsible for causing injury to himself. If the comparative fault system is pure, the sole proximate cause doctrine might be viewed as infringing the fundamental premise that plaintiffs mostly responsible for accidents in which they are injured are nevertheless entitled to recover whatever small percentage of their damages may be placed upon a defendant's doorstep.[54] In such a case, where a highly reckless plaintiff seeks to recover a tiny portion of his or her damages from a slightly negligent defendant, it might be simpler to sidestep such a nebulous doctrine as sole proximate cause and simply let comparative responsibility do its work. But, just as there is no real harm in the comment *n* doctrine, discussed above, fully protecting plaintiffs from their minor fault, there likewise is no harm in a doctrine that shields defendants from their remote responsibility for injuries that reckless plaintiffs largely bring upon themselves.[55] Indeed, protecting defendants in such situations with the sole proximate cause doctrine injects a refreshing moral clarity to legal problem-solving, pushing aside the moral relativism of comparative fault and permitting a declaration that a plaintiff who recklessly hurts himself is properly accountable for "the

---

**51.** See Products Liability Restatement § 17, cmt. *d*, at 259:

[W]hen the defendant claims that the plaintiff failed to discover a defect, there must be evidence that the plaintiff's conduct in failing to discover a defect did, in fact, fail to meet a standard of reasonable care. In general, a plaintiff has no reason to expect that a new product contains a defect and would have little reason to be on guard to discover it.... In the absence of such evidence courts refuse to submit the plaintiff's conduct to the trier of fact for apportionment based on the principles of comparative responsibility.

**52.** It may give too much credit to the notion of sole proximate cause to call it a

doctrine. See Restatement (3d) Torts: Liability for Physical Harm § 34 cmt. *f.*

**53.** See § 13.2, above.

**54.** See Baker v. City of Ottumwa, Iowa, 560 N.W.2d 578 (Iowa 1997) (modified; sole proximate cause defense is incompatible with doctrine of comparative fault because defense effectively insulates defendant from liability).

**55.** Such as when the doctrine protects the manufacturer of a boat when a drunken boater, who drowns when thrown out of his boat while driving it wildly in a flooded river without a life preserver, claims that the boat's seat is defective. See Norman v. Fisher Marine, Inc., 672 S.W.2d 414 (Tenn. Ct. App. 1984) (Miss. law).

whole damn thing." For reasons such as these, courts in some comparative fault jurisdictions allow proof and argument in appropriate cases that a plaintiff's substantial fault was the sole proximate cause of a product accident.[56]

## § 13.4 ASSUMPTION OF RISK

Originating as a defense to negligence claims about two centuries ago,[1] assumption of risk is a classic defense to products liability claims.[2] As a common law and statutory[3] defense in many jurisdictions, even to claims for strict products liability in tort, assumption of risk remains a total bar to liability in a good number of states, thus significantly distinguishing it from contributory negligence which now serves merely to reduce damages in most cases.[4] Because the situations which give rise to the assumption of risk defense are often quite normal and foreseeable, the assumption of risk defense is not restricted, like the defense of product "misuse,"[5] to product use situations so unusual as to be characterized as unforeseeable. For these reasons, assumption of risk may well

**56.** See, e.g., Labzda v. Purdue Pharma, L.P., 292 F.Supp.2d 1346, 1356 (S.D. Fla. 2003) (Florida courts consistently allow "the doctrine of sole proximate cause, rather than comparative negligence, for the intentional misuse of a product, in spite of warnings of the danger"); Kroon v. Beech Aircraft Corp., 628 F.2d 891 (5th Cir. 1980) (Fla. law) (2–1 decision) (plaintiff's misconduct may serve as sole proximate cause even in comparative fault regime; pilot attempted to take off without removing gust lock pin from steering control column). See generally Hayden, Butterfield Rides Again: Plaintiff's Negligence as Superseding or Sole Proximate Cause in Systems of Pure Comparative Responsibility, 33 Loy. L.A. L. Rev. 887, 901–07 (2000); Note, 79 Tex. L. Rev. 493, 495 (2000) ("The courts use proximate cause to declare the plaintiff 'dumb as a matter of law': so foolish that his actions are legally unforeseeable.").

### § 13.4

**1.** In Cruden v. Fentham, 2 Esp. 685, 170 Eng. Rep. 496 (1799). See Prosser and Keeton on Torts § 68, at 480.

**2.** See Duvall, Plaintiffs' Fault in Products Liability Cases: Why Are They Getting Away with It in Maryland?, 30 U. Balt. L. Rev. 255 (2001); Lukes, The Defense of Assumption of Risk under Montana's Product Liability Law, 58 Mont. L. Rev. 249 (1997); Davis, Individual and Institutional Responsibility: A Vision for Comparative Fault in Products Liability, 39 Vill. L. Rev. 281 (1994); McNichols, The Relevance of the Plaintiff's Misconduct in Strict Tort Products Liability, the Advent of Comparative Responsibility, and the Proposed Restatement (Third) of Torts, 47 Okla. L. Rev. 201 (1994); Vargo, The Defenses to Strict Liability in Tort: A New Vocabulary with

an Old Meaning, 29 Mercer L. Rev. 447 (1978); Twerski, Old Wine in a New Flask– Restructuring Assumption of Risk in the Products Liability Era, 60 Iowa L. Rev. 1 (1974); Noel, Defective Products: Abnormal Use, Contributory Negligence, and Assumption of Risk, 25 Vand. L. Rev. 93 (1972); Epstein, Products Liability: Defenses Based on Plaintiff's Conduct, 1968 Utah L. Rev. 267; W.P. Keeton, Assumption of Products Risks, 19 Sw. L.J. 61 (1965); Keeton, Assumption of Risk in Products Liability Cases, 22 La. L. Rev. 122 (1961); Note, 95 Harv. L. Rev. 872 (1982)(assumption of risk as defense to strict products liability); Annot., 46 A.L.R.3d 240 (1972) (contributory negligence and assumption of risk as defenses to claim for strict products liability in tort). For more general theoretical explorations of the doctrine, see Simons, Reflections on Assumption of Risk, 50 UCLA L. Rev. 481 (2002); Sugarman, Assumption of Risk, 31 Val. U. L. Rev. 833 (1997); Simons, Assumption of Risk and Consent in the Law of Torts: A Theory of Full Preference, 67 B.U. L. Rev. 213 (1987).

**3.** While assumption of risk is a common law doctrine, tort and products liability legislative reform provisions in many states govern the effect of various forms of user misconduct including assumption of risk. For a discussion of such statutes, see § 13.1, above.

**4.** See § 13.2, above. Under the comparative fault reforms of the great majority of states, a plaintiff's contributory negligence, at least if less than the defendant's negligence, serves only to diminish a plaintiff's damages, not to bar the claim altogether. See § 13.3, above.

**5.** See § 13.5, below.

be the most potent of all the plaintiff misconduct defenses of modern products liability law.

Assumption of risk may be distinguished from the other "misconduct" defenses in a more fundamental way. Conduct which gives rise to an assumption of risk *may* be unreasonable; if so, it overlaps the defense of contributory (or comparative) negligence which separately may operate to bar liability (or to reduce the plaintiff's damages). But conventional assumption of risk doctrine does not *require* that a plaintiff's decision to incur a risk be unreasonable; as discussed below, a plaintiff will be barred from maintaining a negligence claim if he or she assumes a risk for reasons and in a manner reasonable in all respects.[6] Nor, as just mentioned, does the assumption of risk defense require that the plaintiff have used a product outside the boundaries of its intended and foreseeable limits of fair use, as required by the misuse defense. Thus, unlike the defenses of contributory negligence and product misuse, which arise from user conduct that may be conceived as "improper"[7]—and so fairly classified as "*mis*conduct"—conduct giving rise to the conventional assumption of risk defense does not always so comfortably fit the "misconduct" mold.

The underlying idea of the assumption of risk defense is that a user has fully consented to incur a risk which he or she fully comprehends.[8] By the act of incurring the risk, the user thus implicitly agrees to take responsibility for any harmful consequences that may result from the encounter and so relieves the person who created the risk from responsibility. In other words, *volenti non fit injuria*.[9]

Thus, a person may assume the risk of injury if he uses his hand instead of a metal stomper to push meat into a grinder;[10] reaches from outside a forklift between horizontal cross bars to engage the throttle and so lowers a bar upon his arm;[11] slips from the top of a tanker truck covered with oil that he knows is "real slick";[12] is run over while jump-starting a tractor that he knows may lurch forward when it starts;[13] slips and is cut by a power mower blade left spinning while he moves an obstacle in the mower's path;[14] inflates a truck tire on a multi-piece rim that he fears may be improperly assembled and could explosively fly

**6.** See, e.g., Rahmig v. Mosley Mach. Co., 412 N.W.2d 56, 74 (Neb. 1987). See generally Prosser and Keeton on Torts § 68, at 481 and 485.

**7.** As arising from conduct which is either unreasonable (contributory negligence) or unforeseeable (misuse). See §§ 13.2, above, and 13.5, below, respectively.

**8.** "[A]ssumption of risk is a user's willingness or consent to use a product which the user actually knows is defective and appreciates the danger resulting from such defect." Rahmig v. Mosley Mach. Co., 412 N.W.2d 56, 74 (Neb. 1987).

**9.** "[A] person is not wronged by that to which he or she consents." Black's Law Dictionary 1605 (8th ed. 2004). See Prosser and Keeton on Torts § 68, at 480.

**10.** Green v. Sanitary Scale Co., 431 F.2d 371 (3d Cir. 1970) (Pa. law).

**11.** See Moran v. Raymond Corp., 484 F.2d 1008 (7th Cir. 1973) (Ill. law).

**12.** Hedgepeth v. Fruehauf Corp., 634 F.Supp. 93, 96 (S.D. Miss. 1986) (oil tanker truck driver, who slipped while walking on rounded top of tanker, testified that he knew top was "real slick and real cruddy").

**13.** See Novak v. Navistar Int'l Transp. Corp., 46 F.3d 844 (8th Cir. 1995) (S.D. law).

**14.** See Denton v. Bachtold Bros., Inc., 291 N.E.2d 229 (Ill. App. Ct. 1972).

apart;[15] or entangles his pants in a moving part of a machine that he knows could injure him if he gets too close.[16]

For a product user[17] to assume responsibility for a risk to the exclusion of the defendant, his or her decision must be based upon an understanding of the nature of the risk, and it must be a choice that is freely made—a person cannot "consent" to what he does not know nor to what is forced upon him. For this reason, assumption of risk arises only when a user's encounter with a risk is both "informed" and "voluntary." These two basic requirements are reflected in the definition, or statement of elements, of the assumption of risk doctrine: first, the plaintiff must know and understand the risk; and, second, the plaintiff's choice to encounter it must be free and voluntary.[18]

Because each aspect of assumption of risk involves an inquiry into a particular person's state of mind—the person's knowledge of risk, appreciation of it, and the extent to which the person's choice to encounter it was free and voluntary—the assumption of risk determination is peculiarly one of fact for a jury to resolve.[19]

The ideas of knowledge and appreciation go together like a horse and carriage: in order to truly "know" something, a person must understand or appreciate it; and knowledge is a *sine qua non* of appreciation, for one cannot "appreciate" what one does not know. Because knowledge and appreciation of a risk are intertwined in this manner, the defense is sometimes defined in terms of two elements: (1) knowledge and understanding, and (2) voluntariness.[20] Yet many courts and commentators subdivide the first element into its two components, and so divide the defense into three separate elements: (1) knowledge, (2) appreciation, and (3) voluntariness.[21] Some courts define this defense in

---

**15.** See Bishop v. Firestone Tire & Rubber Co., 814 F.2d 437, 446 (7th Cir. 1987) (Ind. law) (plaintiff stated, prior to explosion of tire mounted on multi-piece rim, that he "hoped the tire would not explode").

**16.** See Johnson v. Mid–South Distrib., Inc., Prod. Liab. Rep. (CCH) ¶ 7984 (Tenn. Ct. App. 1977).

**17.** While most products liability cases involve product users, the assumption of risk defense may also apply to claims by injured bystanders. See, e.g., Brown v. Link Belt Corp., 565 F.2d 1107 (9th Cir. 1977) (Or. law) (worker run over by crane when worker wandered into area he knew was in crane operator's blind spot); Baker v. Chrysler Corp., 127 Cal.Rptr. 745 (Ct. App. 1976) (pedestrian, hit by allegedly uncrashworthy car with protruding metal headlight protector, ran across street trying to beat oncoming car). *But see* Barr v. Rivinius, Inc., 373 N.E.2d 1063, 1068 (Ill. App. Ct. 1978) (2–1 decision) (worker hit by road-grader/shoulder-spreader machine could not assume risk because he was not user).

**18.** See Prosser and Keeton on Torts § 68, at 486.

**19.** See, e.g., Vaughn v. Daniels Co., 777 N.E.2d 1110, 1131–32 (Ind. Ct. App. 2002); Raimbeault v. Takeuchi Mfg., Ltd., 772 A.2d 1056, 1064 (R.I. 2001) ("Whether a risk of harm has been assumed by plaintiff is a question for a trier of fact."); Rahmig v. Mosley Mach. Co., 412 N.W.2d 56, 74 (Neb. 1987) (ordinarily for jury); Heil Co. v. Grant, 534 S.W.2d 916, 921 (Tex. App. 1976) ("Whether an injured person actually knew of the danger is peculiarly within the province of the jury."). *But see* Frey v. Harley Davidson Motor Co., 734 A.2d 1, 9 (Pa. Super. Ct. 1999) ("assumption of the risk, particularly in product liability cases, is a question of law to be determined by the court").

**20.** See Prosser and Keeton on Torts § 68, at 487 ("first, the plaintiff must know that the risk is present, and he must further understand its nature; and second, his choice to incur it must be free and voluntary").

**21.** See, e.g., Johnson v. Mid–South Distrib., Inc., Prod. Liab. Rep. (CCH) ¶ 7984 (Tenn. Ct. App. 1977) ("assumption of the risk acts in bar of recovery when the proof

slightly varying ways,[22] sometimes without specifically enumerating the elements but usually emphasizing the basic nature of the plaintiff's conduct as reflecting a free and voluntary encounter with a known and appreciated risk.[23]

## Knowledge and Appreciation

"Knowledge," it is said, "is the watchword of assumption of risk."[24] A plaintiff's vague and general understanding that a product may be dangerous if not carefully used is neither "knowledge" nor "appreciation" of a particular risk of harm. If the plaintiff does not know just *how* a product may be hazardous, then the plaintiff cannot assume the risk that he may be injured by that hazard.[25] Particularly in jurisdictions

shows that the plaintiff has (1) knowledge of the danger, (2) an appreciation of that danger, and (3) voluntarily exposed himself to that danger").

**22.** See, e.g., Reimer v. City of Crookston, 326 F.3d 957 (8th Cir. 2003) (Minn. law) ("The elements of primary assumption of risk are: (1) the plaintiff had knowledge of the risk, (2) the plaintiff appreciated the risk, and (3) the plaintiff had a choice to avoid the risk but voluntarily chose to accept the risk."); Gann v. International Harvester Co., 712 S.W.2d 100, 105 (Tenn. 1986) ("it must be shown that the plaintiff, (1) discovered the defect, (2) fully understood the danger it presented, and (3) disregarded this known danger and voluntarily exposed himself or herself to it"); Forrest City Mach. Works, Inc. v. Aderhold, 616 S.W.2d 720, 724 (Ark. 1981) ("assumption of risk bars recovery where (1) a dangerous condition exists which is inconsistent with the injured party's safety, (2) the injured person is actually aware of the condition and appreciates the danger, and (3) the injured person voluntarily exposes himself to the danger which produces the injury").

**23.** See, e.g., Johnson v. Mid–South Distrib., Inc., Prod. Liab. Rep. (CCH) ¶ 7984 (Tenn. Ct. App. 1977). See also Heil Co v. Grant, 534 S.W.2d 916, 920 (Tex. App. 1976) (analyzing facts separately in terms of knowledge, appreciation, and voluntariness, but stating nature of theory in blended fashion: "The theory of the assumption of risk defense is that a person may not recover for an injury received when he voluntarily exposes himself to a known and appreciated danger.").

**24.** Prosser and Keeton on Torts § 68, at 487, citing Cincinnati, New Orleans & Tex. Pac. Ry. Co. v. Thompson, 236 F. 1, 9 (6th Cir. 1916). See also Jara v. Rexworks Inc., 718 A.2d 788, 795 (Pa. Super. 1998) ("Nearly all cases in this area focus on the element of the defense encompassing knowledge of the risk."); Johnson v. Mid–South Distrib., Inc., Prod. Liab. Rep. (CCH) ¶ 7984 (Tenn. Ct. App. 1977) ("Knowledge

on the part of the plaintiff is the keystone of the doctrine.").

**25.** "Knowledge of the general hazard involved in operating a punch-press machine will not support the assumption of risk defense." Rhoads v. Service Mach. Co., 329 F.Supp. 367 (E.D. Ark. 1971). See, e.g., Hopper v. Carey, 716 N.E.2d 566, 575 (Ind. Ct. App. 1999) ("General knowledge of the possibility of an [auto] accident does not constitute knowledge of a specific risk."); Heil Co. v. Grant, 534 S.W.2d 916, 921 (Tex. App. 1976).

See also Burch v. Sears, Roebuck & Co., 467 A.2d 615, 620 (Pa. Super. Ct. 1983). In *Burch*, the plaintiff's electric mower shut off twice and would not restart until he pushed the reset button. The third time the motor shut off, plaintiff leaned the mower on its side, without disturbing the reset button, and reached into the blade area to remove the accumulated clumps of grass. The motor unexpectedly restarted and severely injured plaintiff's hand. Plaintiff's suit was based upon the mower's failure to have a deadman's device that would have stopped the blade automatically once the user stopped pushing the mower. *Held,* the jury could reasonably find that the plaintiff had not assumed the risk because he believed that the motor blade was stopped and could be restarted only if the reset button were depressed.

*Contrast* Denton v. Bachtold Bros., Inc., 291 N.E.2d 229 (Ill. App. Ct. 1972), where the plaintiff understood that the blade of the mower remained spinning. As plaintiff was mowing his grass up an incline with a rotary lawn mower manufactured by defendant, he approached a barrel in his path. He disengaged the driving clutch and stopped pushing the mower, but did not release the clutch controlling the blades. As he worked to move the barrel, his feet slipped on the newly mown grass and into the machine. Plaintiff sued, claiming that the mower was defective because it was not

which do not separately require that the risk be "appreciated," courts sometimes require that the plaintiff know of the *specific* risk.[26] This means the plaintiff must know more than that the product encountered may be dangerous.[27] The plaintiff must further understand with some particularity how the product may cause an injury, so that he or she is able to evaluate the likelihood and seriousness of potential injury and thereby make an informed decision on whether or not to engage the risk.

If one were to apply the appreciation-of-specific-risk requirement quite literally, this aspect of the doctrine would swallow the rule and prevent it from ever being applied. In the first article devoted to assumption of risk in the products liability context,[28] Robert Keeton pointed out the apparent "enigma," or self-contradiction, inherent in the "full appreciation of risk" requirement. " 'Risk' implies a degree of want of appreciation of the forces that are at work in a given factual setting, since if one knew and understood all these forces he would know that injury was certain to occur or that it was certain not to occur."[29] Rejecting the defense, one court made a similar point in a case brought by a wireman who was severely shocked when he began to clean electrical equipment that was not de-energized, due to a defect in the way the equipment was configured.[30] "To conclude that [plaintiff] was aware of the specific defect in this configuration would be tantamount to believing that he intended to commit suicide."[31] But most courts have interpreted the appreciation requirement more loosely, ruling that this element does not require that a plaintiff understand the precise nature and operation of the mechanical, chemical, or biological mechanisms that may result in harm[32] nor the precise manner in which a product may be

equipped with a "deadman's throttle." *Held,* plaintiff had assumed the risk; directed verdict for defendant affirmed.

**26.** See, e.g., Vaughn v. Daniels Co., 777 N.E.2d 1110, 1131 (Ind. Ct. App. 2002) ("The injured party must have been more than merely aware of the potential for mishap and must have had actual knowledge of the specific risk."); Warner Fruehauf Trailer Co. v. Boston, 654 A.2d 1272, 1275 (D.C. 1995) ("in order to establish an assumption of risk defense in a strict liability action, the defendant must show that the plaintiff knew of the specific defect in the product and was aware of the danger arising from it"); Austin v. Lincoln Equip. Assoc., 888 F.2d 934, 937 (1st Cir. 1989) (R.I. law); Jackson v. Harsco Corp., 673 P.2d 363, 366 (Colo. 1983) (en banc) ("The defendant must demonstrate that the plaintiff had actual knowledge of the specific danger posed by the defect in design, and not just general knowledge that the product could be dangerous.").

**27.** See, e.g., Rahmig v. Mosley Mach. Co., 412 N.W.2d 56, 74 (Neb. 1987) ("[a] user's knowledge about the general danger or hazard in using a product will not support the defense"); Heil Co. v. Grant, 534

S.W.2d 916, 921 (Tex. App. 1976); Rhoads v. Service Mach. Co., 329 F.Supp. 367 (E.D. Ark. 1971).

**28.** R. Keeton, Assumption of Risk in Products Liability Cases, 22 La. L. Rev. 122 (1961).

**29.** Id. at 124.

**30.** Campbell v. ITE Imperial Corp., 733 P.2d 969 (Wash. 1987).

**31.** Id. at 976.

**32.** See, e.g., Ensor v. Hodgeson, 615 S.W.2d 519, 525 (Mo. Ct. App. 1981) ("[K]nowledge of the precise engineering explanation of the defect is not necessary. It is sufficient that the user realizes that there is a problem with the product that renders it dangerous to use."); Heil Co. v. Grant, 534 S.W.2d 916, 922 (Tex. App. 1976) ("The assumption of risk defense is based upon the injured person's awareness of the danger of injury rather than an awareness of the producing causes of the injury."). See also Bowen v. Cochran, 556 S.E.2d 530, 532 (Ga. Ct. App. 2001) (plaintiff knew that gas grill might explode if he failed to vent it sufficiently and failed to light it properly, even if he did not understand exactly where and how the unlighted gas might pool).

legally "defective."[33]

For example, in *Heil Co. v. Grant*,[34] the plaintiff's decedent was crushed to death while he and his brother were performing repair work under a dump truck. The raised bed suddenly descended when one of the men accidentally bumped the "pullout cable" attached to the hydraulic valve that controlled the raising and lowering of the bed. Just before the accident, the decedent's brother had warned him that the bed would crash down if he hit the cable. The plaintiff sued the manufacturer, claiming that the hoist mechanism was defectively designed, and the defendant asserted assumption of risk. The trial court excluded certain testimony going to assumption of risk, and the jury found for the plaintiff. On appeal, the court reversed the judgment. To the plaintiff's argument that the decedent had general knowledge that working beneath the dump truck could be dangerous, but had no knowledge of the specific defect involved, the appeals court noted that the specific danger was that hitting the cable would cause the bed to descend, which the decedent knew.[35] To the plaintiff's contention that the requisite knowledge must pertain to a "defect," rather than a danger, the court noted that "the assumption of risk defense is premised upon knowledge of the dangerous condition of a product rather than recognition of its defectiveness."[36]

**33.** See, e.g., Heil Co. v. Grant, 534 S.W.2d 916, 921 (Tex. App. 1976) ("the assumption of risk defense is premised upon knowledge of the dangerous condition of a product rather than recognition of its defectiveness"). *But see* Warner Fruehauf Trailer Co. v. Boston, 654 A.2d 1272, 1275 (D.C. 1995) (evidence failed to show that plaintiff "had actual knowledge of the liftgate's alleged design defect—the lack of a back-up system (e.g., a second cylinder or other safety device) to prevent the heavy liftgate from free-falling in the event of a mechanical failure").

Although the courts in Pennsylvania have purported to require the defendant to prove that the plaintiff knew of the specific "defect" which caused his injury, they appear not really to have meant it. See Mackowick v. Westinghouse Elec. Corp., 541 A.2d 749, 753 (Pa. Super. Ct. 1988) (dissenting opinion):

[U]se of the term "defect," with its mechanical and technological connotations, has caused much confusion among members of the bench and bar. Some have argued that a plaintiff is aware of a specific defect only if he understands the mechanical process which causes the item to be dangerous. This interpretation is an overly technical misstatement of the law. For assumption of the risk to apply, a plaintiff needn't understand the mechanical process, but must be subjectively aware of the nature, character, and extent of the danger posed *by the specific attribute* which is allegedly defective; this requires more than a general awareness by the plaintiff that the product is somehow dangerous.

See also Lonon v. Pep Boys, Manny, Moe & Jack, 538 A.2d 22 (Pa. Super. Ct. 1988), where plaintiff was injured while attaching jumper cables to his battery, which exploded, splashing sulfuric acid into his eyes. His expert theorized that the explosion was caused by a defective weld in the battery; the defendant's expert opined that the explosion was due to the plaintiff's failure to use the spark-free jump-starting procedures specified in the instructions referred to by a warning on the battery. The plaintiff had worked at a service station, knew that batteries contain acid, had jump-started cars fifty times or more, had witnessed sparks created during jump starts, and had heard of batteries exploding. *Held,* he could *not* have assumed the risk of the defect in the battery because he did not know about it. However, he *may* have assumed the more general risk that the battery might explode if he did not use the jumper cables properly.

**34.** 534 S.W.2d 916 (Tex. App. 1976).

**35.** Id. at 922.

**36.** Id. at 921.

In another case, *Haugen v. Minnesota Mining & Mfg. Co.*,[37] the plaintiff was injured when the grinding wheel he was working on exploded into three pieces, one of which hit him in the eye. The plaintiff was not wearing safety goggles at the time of the accident, although two pairs were available in the shop, and he knew of their importance from his prior safety training. The trial court instructed the jury: "It is not enough to bar recovery by the plaintiff on the defense of assumption of risk that the plaintiff knew that there was a general danger connected with the use of the product, but rather it must be shown that the plaintiff actually knew, appreciated, and voluntarily and unreasonably exposed himself to the specific defect and danger which caused his injuries."[38] On appeal, affirming a judgment for the plaintiff, the court held the instruction to be proper because the plaintiff, while knowing that small wood particles might be thrown in the direction of his face, believed that his glasses would provide sufficient protection to his eyes.[39]

Whether, and the extent to which, a plaintiff in fact was aware of a particular risk involves a *subjective* inquiry into the plaintiff's state of mind.[40] Stated otherwise, the knowledge question in such cases concerns the peculiarly factual issue of what the plaintiff himself knew and understood, *not* what a reasonable or normal person would or should have known and understood in similar circumstances. Sometimes courts speak loosely and misstate the principle,[41] but it is plainly wrong for a lawyer to argue, or for a court to instruct a jury, that assumption of risk involves a question of whether the plaintiff "*should* have known" of the risk; the only proper question is what the plaintiff did in fact know.[42] Nor does the plaintiff's age, intelligence, experience, information, or judgment directly help establish, as it does in setting a child's standard of care for negligence and contributory negligence, a standard of proper behavior.[43] The assumption of risk question is properly framed as wheth-

---

**37.** Haugen v. Minnesota Mining & Mfg. Co., 550 P.2d 71 (Wash. Ct. App. 1976), superseded by statute, see Van Hout v. Celotex Corp., 853 P.2d 908 (Wash. 1993).

**38.** Id. at 74.

**39.** The court explained: "If plaintiff assumed any risk at all, it was the risk of having dust or small particles of wood or metal lodged in his eye during the grinding process. He was obviously not aware of the latent defect in the structural integrity of the disc itself and the danger posed by that defect. This latent defect was not and probably could not have been known by the plaintiff. Plaintiff, therefore, could not have assumed the risk engendered by the defect." Id. at 75.

**40.** See, e.g., Jay v. Moog Auto., 652 N.W.2d 872, 882 (Neb. 2002) (finding assumption of risk requires application of subjective standard, even where plaintiff mechanic used compressor contrary to written instructions); Vaughn v. Daniels Co., 777 N.E.2d 1110, 1131 (Ind. Ct. App. 2002) ("Incurred risk involves a mental state of venturousness on the part of the actor and demands a subjective analysis into the actor's actual knowledge and voluntary acceptance of the risk."); Labrie v. Pace Member-

ship Warehouse, Inc., 678 A.2d 867, 872 (R.I. 1996) ("The standard is a subjective one requiring us to review the evidence to determine what this particular plaintiff actually saw, knew, understood, and appreciated at the time of his injury."); Warner Fruehauf Trailer Co. v. Boston, 654 A.2d 1272, 1275 (D.C. 1995); Jackson v. Harsco Corp., 673 P.2d 363, 366 (Colo. 1983) (en banc). See Prosser and Keeton on Torts § 68, at 487.

**41.** See, e.g., Patterson v. Central Mills, Inc., 64 Fed.Appx. 457 (6th Cir. 2003) (Ohio law) (stating that assumption of risk standard asks whether child of similar age, education, and experience would or should have been aware of risks); Bereman v. Burdolski, 460 P.2d 567, 569 (Kan. 1969) (approving instruction that plaintiff was barred if he continued to use vehicle once he was aware of defect in brakes or "should have been aware of it").

**42.** See, e.g., Heil Co. v. Grant, 534 S.W.2d 916, 921 (Tex. App. 1976) ("The fact that the injured person *should have known* of the danger will not support the assumption of risk defense.") (emphasis by court).

**43.** In some cases, a young person may fully understand and voluntarily encounter

er this particular plaintiff *in fact* was subjectively aware of and appreciated this particular risk. That said, a jury is not required to believe the plaintiff's testimony as to his or her state of mind, and the jury may test the plaintiff's avowals of what he or she understood against what the jury believes people with similar personal characteristics—such as "age, or lack of information, experience, intelligence, or judgment"[44]—ordinarily understand when confronting a similar product hazard.[45] This distinction is a fine one, and it is easy for a lawyer or court to confuse the subjective standard that properly is at issue with the kind of objective framework that may help a jury resolve the subjective issue of the plaintiff's state of mind. While such confusion is understandable, it may quite easily upset the outcome of a case and so should be scrupulously avoided.[46]

a product hazard. See, e.g., Garner v. Rite Aid Of Ga., Inc., 595 S.E.2d 582, 587 (Ga. Ct. App. 2004) (teenagers "deliberately chose a perilous course of conduct, appreciated the danger, i.e., had actual and subjective knowledge of the risk, and voluntarily exposed himself or herself to the danger" of inhaling or "huffing" butane). Nevertheless, factors such as the age, intelligence, experience and judgment do provide circumstantial evidence of what the plaintiff may in fact have known and understood. An intelligent adult familiar with the product is more likely to be found to have assumed a risk than is an inexperienced or dim-witted adult, or a child. Compare Walk v. Starkey Mach., Inc., 180 F.3d 937 (8th Cir. 1999) (Minn. law) (experienced worker, nicked by machine previously, assumed risk of hand entanglement by cleaning machine while it was operating); Mackowick v. Westinghouse Elec. Corp., 541 A.2d 749 (Pa. Super. Ct. 1988) (experienced electrician stuck screwdriver into energized capacitor-box–assumption of risk); Barnes v. Harley–Davidson Motor Co., 357 S.E.2d 127 (Ga. Ct. App. 1987) (motorcyclist of nearly 20 years, who collided with stalled car at night, claimed that motorcycle should have been equipped with crash bars as standard equipment, and that head-lamp provided too little light at high-speed—assumption of risk); and Bakunas v. Life Pack, Inc., 531 F.Supp. 89 (E.D. La. 1982) (movie stuntman performed free fall from 323 feet into air-inflated cushion rated only to 200 feet—assumption of risk), with Nettles v. Electrolux Motor AB, 784 F.2d 1574 (11th Cir. 1986) (experienced but dim-witted woodcutter, who was injured when chain saw kicked back, and had been injured by kickbacks before, knew that saws were available which were less likely to cause injury from kickbacks—no assumption of risk); and Forrest City Mach. Works, Inc. v. Aderhold, 616 S.W.2d 720 (Ark. 1981) (climbing off grain cart, eight-year-old caught pants in rotating power take-off shaft attached to tractor—no assumption of risk).

**44.** Restatement (2d) Torts § 496D, cmt. *c*. See also id. §§ 496A cmt. *d* and 496C cmt. *e*.

**45.** The Texas court explains this well:

An injured person's knowledge of a dangerous condition or defect is measured subjectively; i.e., by that person's actual, conscious knowledge. The fact that the injured person *should have known* of the danger will not support the assumption of risk defense. Sometimes, however, that person may know such facts as to be charged with knowledge of the danger. This standard would be applied when it was difficult or impossible to determine the state of the injured person's mind; as it was in the instant case of a fatal injury.

Heil Co. v. Grant, 534 S.W.2d 916, 920–21 (Tex. App. 1976). The Texas court sensitively tested the decedent's probable knowledge against a standard based upon his own level of age, intelligence, experience, and other factors. Id. at 922.

**46.** See, e.g., Prosser and Keeton on Torts § 68, at 76 (Supp. 1988):

[To] state the doctrine in terms of what the plaintiff "knew or should have known" about the danger . . . is calculated at best to confuse the jury, and it is usually seriously misleading, since the apparent question put by such a standard is whether the plaintiff ought to have perceived the danger—by some external, objective standard of proper behavior—rather than the subjective question of whether the plaintiff himself actually knew the risk was present. But this is plainly wrong, and the use of "should have known" language in such instructions to the jury should therefore be prohibited. What the courts have here been searching for is some way to let the jurors know that they do not have to take the plaintiff at his word, but that they may instead test his protestations of ignorance of the risk by some external standard

If a plaintiff does not know of or understand a risk, it is axiomatic that the assumption of risk defense will not bar his damages resulting from that risk, as discussed above. Accordingly, if a product is defective because the manufacturer has not warned of a hidden risk, then a plaintiff unaware of that risk cannot be barred by the doctrine of assumption of risk.[47] If a defendant denies the existence of the risk[48] or conceals it from consumers,[49] as did the manufacturers of cigarettes for several decades, the assumption of risk defense may be disallowed.[50] But a plaintiff's knowledge may come from any source, and assumption of risk may be one reason[51] to bar a claim that a manufacturer failed to provide an adequate warning of a risk which the plaintiff already knows and understands.[52]

## Voluntary Encounter

The second important limitation on the assumption of risk defense is that a plaintiff's decision to encounter a risk must be "free and voluntary."[53] The notions of appreciation and voluntariness to some extent overlap, in that the notion of consent supporting assumption of risk suggests that the plaintiff makes a true and meaningful *choice* to engage a particular risk, presumably to advance an interest (even mere convenience) that the plaintiff considers more valuable than avoidance of the risk. "Choice" in this context means, first, that the plaintiff understands the nature of the risk encountered; second, that the plaintiff has available one or more alternative courses of action by which he or she may reasonably avoid the risk; and third, that the plaintiff then decides that his or her interests will best be served by encountering the danger.

If a plaintiff's only, or best, "choice" is to encounter a known risk, then the encounter is not "voluntary." As just discussed, the voluntary

---

based on ordinary principles of credibility and common sense. It would be much better if the courts would simply say so.

**47.** For the classic statements of this principle, see McClanahan v. California–Spray Chem. Corp., 75 S.E.2d 712, 725 (Va. 1953); Wright v. Carter Prods., Inc., 244 F.2d 53, 60 (2d Cir. 1957) (Mass. law); R. Keeton, Assumption of Risk in Products Liability Cases, 22 La. L. Rev. 122, 145 (1961). A more recent application is Warner Fruehauf Trailer Co. v. Boston, 654 A.2d 1272, 1275 (D.C. 1995).

**48.** See Wilks v. American Tobacco Co., 680 So.2d 839 (Miss. 1996).

**49.** See, e.g., Spain v. Brown & Williamson Tobacco Corp., 872 So.2d 101 (Ala. 2003) (leaving open possibility of question of fact as to whether general warnings are adequate to establish plaintiff's assumption of risk due to tobacco additives); Barnes v. American Tobacco Co., 161 F.3d 127, 146–49 (3d Cir. 1998) (Pa. law) (affirming decertification of Pennsylvania class action).

**50.** *But see* Gilboy v. American Tobacco Co., 582 So.2d 1263, 1265 (La. 1991) (recognizing this defense but denying defendant's

motion for summary judgment on this issue).

**51.** The absence of cause in fact may be another reason. See, e.g., Raimbeault v. Takeuchi Mfg., Ltd., 772 A.2d 1056, 1064 (R.I. 2001) (plaintiff who had used and demonstrated excavator equipment for five years assumed risk and would not have been aided by warning); Haesche v. Kissner, 640 A.2d 89 (Conn. 1994). See also Plummer v. Lederle Labs., 819 F.2d 349, 359 (2d Cir. 1987) (Cal. law) (" 'no harm could have been caused by failure to warn of a risk already known,' " quoting Rosburg v. Minnesota Mining & Mfg. Co., 226 Cal. Rptr. 299, 305 (App. Ct. 1986)). See generally ch. 11, above.

**52.** As in Heil Co. v. Grant, 534 S.W.2d 916, 922–23 (Tex. App. 1976), where the plaintiff alleged that the dump truck was defective because the manufacturer had failed to provide a warning of the pullout cable hazard, but where the decedent's brother had warned him of just that risk.

**53.** Prosser and Keeton on Torts § 68, at 490.

requirement in assumption of risk essentially means that the plaintiff has a true choice, that he or she has *reasonable* options available to avoid the risk. While defining the consensual notions of voluntariness and choice in reasonableness terms may appear to be mixing apples and oranges, it probably is the best way to give content to this requirement. There is something wrong, indeed illogical and perverse, with a doctrine based on a plaintiff's *consent* that permits a defendant to avoid responsibility for causing harm by forcing a danger upon the plaintiff, "forcing" because the plaintiff has no reasonable means to avoid it. "Where the defendant puts him to a choice of evils, there is a species of duress, which destroys the idea of freedom of election.... By placing him in the dilemma, the defendant has deprived him of his freedom of choice, and so cannot be heard to say that he has voluntarily assumed the risk."[54] On the other hand, if a plaintiff has a perfectly reasonable way to avoid a danger created by the defendant, yet knowingly chooses to encounter it, then he cannot complain that he was compelled to take this path, for such a choice is free and voluntary.[55]

The voluntariness aspect of assumption of risk is a chimerical concept, for it is difficult to imagine why a person who truly understands a substantial risk of harm would not avoid it if there were a reasonable way to do so. No doubt there are occasional cases where a plaintiff acts with complete abandon of dangers that he or she full well knows to lie within a product—as when a person sticks his hand into a meat grinder because it is "more convenient" than using the metal stomper that is provided;[56] continues to ride at high speed a motorcycle with a wobbly front end on a pleasure trip without "the slightest compulsion of business or otherwise";[57] or sticks his arm through the cross bars of a fork lift to activate the control lever to lower the bars, rather than going inside the vehicle to do so, because he is "in a hurry and [decides to take] a calculated risk that he could get his hand out of the way before the forks hit him."[58] In "calculated risk" cases such as these, assuming

---

**54.** Id. at 490–91. See, e.g., Vaughn v. Daniels Co., 777 N.E.2d 1110, 1131–32 (Ind. Ct. App. 2002) (employee did not have time to reattach safety belt because of urgent need of coworkers for help); Wallace v. Owens–Illinois, Inc., 389 S.E.2d 155 (S.C. Ct. App. 1989) (Bell, J.) (plaintiff injured while cleaning up effects of soft drink bottle explosion):

The plaintiff's acceptance of a risk is not voluntary if the defendant's wrongful conduct leaves him no reasonable alternative course of conduct in order to avert harm to himself or another.... [T]he explosion of the defective bottle left him with no reasonable alternative. He had a choice between two evils: he could leave the spill on the floor with the risk that he or others might be injured by its presence or he could undertake to remove the spill with the risk that he or another would be injured in the process of cleaning up. In other words, either choice entailed risk.

In these circumstances, his choice to remove the hazard was not a voluntary assumption of risk. The Defendants had created a condition of peril which involved a risk of harm no matter which choice Wallace made. Risk was unavoidable in the circumstances.

Id. at 158–59.

**55.** Prosser and Keeton on Torts § 68, at 491 ("where there is a reasonably safe alternative open, the plaintiff's choice of the dangerous way is a free one, and may amount to assumption of risk, negligence or both").

**56.** See Green v. Sanitary Scale Co., 431 F.2d 371 (3d Cir. 1970) (Pa. law).

**57.** Saeter v. Harley–Davidson Motor Co., 8 Cal.Rptr. 747, 753 (Ct. App. 1960).

**58.** Moran v. Raymond Corp., 484 F.2d 1008, 1016 (7th Cir. 1973) (Ill. law).

that the plaintiff truly appreciates the specific risk, the plaintiff's risk encounter is clearly advertent and so in that sense voluntary.[59]

More typical, however, are cases where the plaintiff may fully understand a specific risk but momentarily forgets about it, or becomes distracted, and then encounters it inadvertently. For example, a plaintiff might appreciate with specificity that if one's foot slips under a power mower with the blade revolving it is likely to be cut,[60] that getting clothing caught in a rotating part of machinery may well cause a limb to become entangled in the machine,[61] or that hitting the pullout cable beneath a dump truck is likely to cause the bed to come crashing down.[62] When such a plaintiff thereafter accidentally engages such a risk, which though earlier appreciated was not in the plaintiff's mind at the time of the accidental encounter, courts often apply the assumption of risk defense on a finding that the encounter was "voluntary."[63]

While it is true that such plaintiffs have the last and sometimes best chance to prevent such injuries,[64] since risk control at the time of the risk encounter lies exclusively with them, inadvertent encounters with the product itself may more appropriately be viewed as careless mistakes than as consensual ("voluntary") decisions to incur particular risks of harm. Plaintiffs in such situations may choose to work around a risk which they understand may cause them harm if they were accidentally to engage certain parts of the machine, and so in this manner they may be said to voluntarily encounter such risks of harm. But the "encounter" of relevance in such cases might more properly be viewed as the *specific* encounter with the unreasonably dangerous aspect of a machine at the time of the accident, rather than the encounter of a *general* risk that such a specific encounter might sometime occur.[65] If an accident results from the plaintiff's inadvertent causative behavior, as from slipping into or otherwise accidentally contacting the dangerous parts of a machine, the plaintiff's operative behavior is purely inadvertent; being inadvertent, it is by definition "involuntary."

The appeal of the assumption of risk doctrine lies in grounding responsibility for accidents in a person's choices concerning risk control. And there are at least two perspectives that help illuminate the signifi-

---

**59.** In workplace settings, such "advertent" encounters may not be truly voluntary if they are compelled in some manner by the employment situation, as discussed below.

**60.** See Denton v. Bachtold Bros., Inc., 291 N.E.2d 229 (Ill. App. Ct. 1972).

**61.** See Johnson v. Mid–South Distrib., Inc., Prod. Liab. Rep. (CCH) ¶ 7984 (Tenn. Ct. App. 1977).

**62.** See Heil Co. v. Grant, 534 S.W.2d 916 (Tex. App. 1976).

**63.** See, e.g., Johnson v. Mid–South Distrib., Inc., Prod. Liab. Rep. (CCH) ¶ 7984 (Tenn. Ct. App. 1977) (pants leg caught in rotating machinery shaft); Heil Co. v. Grant, 534 S.W.2d 916 (Tex. App. 1976) (hitting dump truck pullout cable); Denton

v. Bachtold Bros., Inc., 291 N.E.2d 229 (Ill. App. Ct. 1972) (slip under lawn mower). *But see* Johnson v. Clark Equip. Co., 547 P.2d 132 (Or. 1976) (inadvertently activating control on forklift).

**64.** See Nelson v. Brunswick Corp., 503 F.2d 376, 383 (9th Cir. 1974) (Wash. law) ("the rationale is essentially that when the plaintiff knows and appreciates the danger, he is in a position as good as the defendant's to avoid his injury").

**65.** See, e.g., Jackson v. Harsco Corp., 673 P.2d 363, 367 (Colo. 1983) (en banc) ("There was ... no evidence that plaintiff had actual knowledge of the specific dangers arising out of the precise defect asserted, or that he voluntarily and unreasonably proceeded to encounter those dangers despite his awareness of the defect.").

cance of risk control choices. The first perspective concerns the *reasonableness* of a plaintiff's choice to encounter a risk, which is injected into the concept of voluntariness by defining it in terms of the availability of reasonable alternatives for avoiding the risk, as discussed above. If circumstances force a plaintiff to encounter a product defect, then the plaintiff's encounter is not voluntary because of the absence of choice, as discussed above. And because of the absence of choice resulting from the plaintiff being forced into the encounter, the plaintiff's will is removed from a causative analysis of the accident, leaving the manufacturer's sale of a defective product as the last and sole proximate cause of the accident.

The second perspective on a person's risk control choices concerns the *time* when a person decides to encounter a risk. A product user may understand and voluntarily accept a general risk of harm at the time of employment or when a particular project with a product first begins. Yet, at the precise moment a potential accident victim interacts with a product in a manner that erupts into accidental injury, the victim is rarely deliberating upon the nature and degree of risk in, and the desirability of, the specific interaction. Instead, as mentioned earlier, the actual, physical interactions—the "specific" risk encounters—in most situations are inadvertent mistakes, not deliberative choices. To put the matter slightly differently, while persons often voluntarily decide to encounter future risks in a general way, they rarely encounter particular risks voluntarily at the moment of an accident.

It is only when a person's risk encounter is "voluntary" from both the reasonableness and temporal perspectives that the person fairly may be deemed to have assumed the risk. Thus, accidents caused by a plaintiff's *unreasonable* decision to take a truly calculated risk—one that consciously involves the specific physical interaction with the product that results in injury—may be the only type of case in which the assumption of risk defense provides a proper basis for barring recovery. In such situations, where a prudent person would not knowingly and voluntarily act in such a dangerous manner for such a trivial benefit, the doctrine of sole proximate cause could quite easily be substituted for assumption of risk as a mechanism for placing full responsibility upon the plaintiff.[66]

There are at least two contexts in which courts have been especially open to challenges to the voluntariness of risk encounters: rescues and workplace accidents. In the rescue situation, as with the contributory negligence defense,[67] a number of courts have held that a rescuer of a person endangered by a defective product may not be barred by the defense of assumption of risk.[68]

**66.** The sole proximate cause doctrine, applicable to both contributory and comparative negligence, is discussed in §§ 13.2 and 13.3, above.

**67.** See § 13.2, above.

**68.** See, e.g., Dillard v. Pittway Corp., 719 So.2d 188, 193–94 (Ala. 1998) (collecting the cases) (neither contributory negligence nor assumption of risk available as defense unless rescuer's conduct was "manifestly rash and reckless"). Compare Vaughn v. Daniels Co., 777 N.E.2d 1110, 1131–32 (Ind. Ct. App. 2002) (employee's assumption of risk may not have been voluntary because he did not have time to reattach safety belt before assisting coworkers who were in urgent need of help).

The second context in which courts are more skeptical of the voluntariness of a plaintiff's risk encounter is the employment setting where a worker is injured by a dangerous industrial machine or other workplace product. For example, in *Rhoads v. Service Mach. Co.*,[69] the operator's arm and hand slipped into a large punch press when she lost her balance while activating the press. Upholding the jury's rejection of the assumption of risk defense, despite the plaintiff's knowledge of the unguarded nature of the machine, the court incisively remarked: "The 'voluntariness' with which a worker assigned to a dangerous machine in a factory 'assumes the risk of injury' from the machine is illusory."[70] Other courts[71] and commentators[72] have agreed that such workplace encounters often are not "voluntary." The Supreme Court of Ohio has abolished the assumption of risk defense in the workplace setting on the ground that workers often are effectively trapped into performing dangerous activities, a situation which destroys any voluntariness in many such job-related risk encounters.[73]

However, some courts continue to treat the voluntariness of encounters in the workplace like any other encounter, sometimes without giving adequate consideration to the propriety of its application in this context,[74] and so apply the assumption of risk defense if deemed warranted

**69.** Rhoads v. Serv. Mach. Co., 329 F.Supp. 367 (E.D. Ark. 1971).

**70.** Id. at 381.

**71.** See, e.g., Vaughn v. Daniels Co., 777 N.E.2d 1110, 1131 (Ind. Ct. App. 2002) ("We have recognized that the responsibilities and influences arising from involvement in the workplace can be determinative as to the voluntariness of an employee's actions."); McCalla v. Harnischfeger Corp., 521 A.2d 851, 856 (N.J. Super. Ct. App. Div. 1987) ("an employee engaged in his assigned task . . . has no meaningful choice") (citations and internal quotations omitted). Other courts have found the assumption of risk defense improper in the workplace setting on the ground that such encounters are not unreasonable. See, e.g., Jara v. Rexworks Inc., 718 A.2d 788 (Pa. Super. 1998) (holding, 2–1, that trial court erred in instructing on assumption of risk):

> To suggest that Mr. Jara was required to choose between performing his duties or use the defective product would permit [defendant], by its own wrong, to deny Mr. Jara the right and privilege of his employment. Therefore, he could not voluntarily assume the risk as [defendant] suggests. Where an employee, in doing a job, is required to use equipment as furnished by the employer, this defense is unavailable. An employee who is required to use certain equipment in the course of his employment and who uses that equipment as directed by the employer has no choice in encountering a risk inherent in that equipment.

Id. at 795; Johnson v. Clark Equip. Co., 547 P.2d 132 (Or. 1976).

**72.** See Noel, Defective Products: Abnormal Use, Contributory Negligence, and Assumption of Risk, 25 Vand. L. Rev. 93, 127 (1972):

> When an employee consents to work under dangerous conditions, this consent ordinarily is not regarded as effective in a suit against the employer because of the economic pressure involved. It would seem that when a manufacturer supplies a dangerous machine for use by employees, the workman injured because of the unsafe design is subject to comparable economic pressure and that his consent to use the dangerous machine, perhaps in order to retain his job, is likewise not free and voluntary.

See also Note, 95 Harv. L. Rev. 872, 889–90 n.68 (1982): "It is illogical to prevent the employer from raising the defense of assumption of risk on the ground that the employee lacks freedom of choice, . . . while simultaneously allowing the manufacturer of the product used in the workplace to escape liability on the ground that the employee voluntarily assumed that same risk."

**73.** See Cremeans v. Willmar Henderson Mfg. Co., 566 N.E.2d 1203 (Ohio 1991).

**74.** For example, in Hedgepeth v. Fruehauf Corp., 634 F.Supp. 93 (S.D. Miss. 1986), the driver, whose job required walking on the rounded top of tanker truck to open hatches, complained that the truck's top was "real slick and real cruddy" with

on the facts.[75] These courts sometimes reason that any compulsion comes not from the defendant manufacturer but from a third party, the employer,[76] and that even in this setting workers not infrequently make entirely deliberate (and sometimes entirely foolish) decisions exposing themselves to risks that they fully understand to be unreasonable.[77]

## As a Defense to Strict Liability in Tort

While assumption of risk as classically defined is a standard defense to products liability claims brought in negligence, many jurisdictions alter its definition, and a couple alter its availability[78] and effect,[79] in claims for strict liability in tort.[80] *Restatement (Second) of Torts* § 402A comment *n*, examined above in connection with the contributory negligence defense,[81] provides in part:

> [T]he form of contributory negligence which consists in voluntarily and unreasonably proceeding to encounter a known danger, and commonly passes under the name of assumption of risk, is a defense under this Section as in other cases of strict liability. If the user or consumer discovers the defect and is aware of the danger, and nevertheless proceeds unreasonably to make use of the product and is injured by it, he is barred from recovery.[82]

oil residue and needed to be cleaned. The supervisor ordered him to use the truck anyway, or just to leave. After a delivery, while walking on the top to close a hatch that had been left open, he slipped and fell. Although the driver in this case surely knew of the specific risk, the absence of reasonable alternatives–the compulsion to use the product in its hazardous condition in order to work at all–would seem to render his decision to work completely devoid of choice and hence "*in*voluntary." Yet the court disagreed and held the driver's actions to be "voluntary."

**75.** See, e.g., Hedgepeth v. Fruehauf Corp., 634 F.Supp. 93 (S.D. Miss. 1986); Vargus v. Pittman Mfg. Co., 510 F.Supp. 116 (E.D. Pa. 1981), aff'd, 673 F.2d 1301 (3d Cir. 1981); Campbell v. Nordco Prods., 629 F.2d 1258 (7th Cir. 1980) (Ill. law); Carroll v. Getty Oil Co., 498 F.Supp. 409 (D. Del. 1980), impliedly overruled on other grounds, Figgs v. Bellevue Holding Co., 652 A.2d 1084 (Del. Super. Ct. 1994); Alley v. Praschak Mach. Co., 366 So.2d 661 (Miss. 1979).

**76.** See, e.g., Hedgepeth v. Fruehauf Corp., 634 F.Supp. 93, 99 n.3 (S.D. Miss. 1986) (relying on Restatement (2d) Torts § 496E (cmt. *b*)).

**77.** See, e.g., Karim v. Tanabe Mach., Ltd., 322 F.Supp.2d 578 (E.D. Pa. 2004) (machine operator grabbed control box near moving chain and sprocket, which caught his hand); Walk v. Starkey Mach., Inc., 180 F.3d 937 (8th Cir. 1999) (Minn. law) (experienced worker, who had been nicked previously by machine, assumed risk of hand

entanglement by cleaning machine while it was operating); Moran v. Raymond Corp., 484 F.2d 1008, 1016 (7th Cir. 1973) (Ill. law) (worker stuck his arm through and activated moving cross bars on fork lift: "[w]orkmen often take risks which they should not take").

**78.** Assumption of risk may be abolished as a defense to tort claims generally but be retained to operate as a bar to claims for strict products liability in tort. See, e.g., Rutter v. Northeastern Beaver Cty. Sch. Dist., 437 A.2d 1198, 1209 (Pa. 1981).

**79.** Assumption of risk may operate only to reduce damages on a comparative fault basis, except in strict products liability in tort where it may serve as a total bar. See, e.g., Bowling v. Heil Co., 511 N.E.2d 373 (Ohio 1987); Onderko v. Richmond Mfg. Co., 511 N.E.2d 388 (Ohio 1987).

**80.** See Vargo, The Defenses to Strict Liability in Tort: A New Vocabulary with an Old Meaning, 29 Mercer L. Rev. 447 (1978); Twerski, Old Wine in a New Flask–Restructuring Assumption of Risk in the Products Liability Era, 60 Iowa L. Rev. 1 (1974); Noel, Defective Products: Abnormal Use, Contributory Negligence, and Assumption of Risk, 25 Vand. L. Rev. 93 (1972); Epstein, Products Liability: Defenses Based on Plaintiff's Conduct, 1968 Utah L. Rev. 267; Annot., 46 A.L.R.3d 240 (1972) (contributory negligence and assumption of risk as defenses to claim for strict products liability in tort).

**81.** Comment *n* is set forth in full in § 13.2, above, at text following note 71.

**82.** Restatement (2d) Torts § 402A cmt. *n*.

As discussed above,[83] a few states ignored comment *n* and continued applying the traditional elements of assumption of risk even for claims brought in strict products liability in tort.[84] However, especially before the widespread adoption of comparative fault,[85] many jurisdictions adopted comment *n*'s approach of restricting the availability of the assumption of risk defense in strict products liability in tort to cases of *unreasonable* ("negligent"[86]) assumptions of risk.[87] In effect, such jurisdictions engraft an additional element—unreasonableness—onto the traditional formulation of elements for assumption of risk as applied to claims of negligence. So altered, the assumption of risk defense to claims for strict products liability in tort appears to narrow substantially, requiring that a plaintiff know and appreciate the risk, voluntarily encounter it, and, further, that the plaintiff's decision to encounter it is unreasonable.[88]

---

**83.** See § 13.2, above.

**84.** See, e.g., Jay v. Moog Auto., Inc., 652 N.W.2d 872, 882–84 (Neb. 2002); Vaughn v. Daniels Co. (W. Va.), Inc., 777 N.E.2d 1110 (Ind. Ct. App. 2002). See also Conn. Gen. Stat. § 52–572l ("Nothing in this section shall be construed as barring ... the defense of knowingly using the product in a defective condition in an action based on strict tort liability.").

**85.** After the adoption of comparative fault, many (but not all) jurisdictions saw no need to distinguish between forms of plaintiff fault and so included *all* forms of plaintiff misconduct in the comparative calculus. See V. Schwartz, Comparative Negligence ch. 11 (3d ed. 1994); § 13.3, above.

**86.** See, e.g., Egelhoff v. Holt, 875 S.W.2d 543, 548–49 (Mo. 1994) (en banc) (using "negligent assumption of risk" expression, but applying it to wrong statutory provision).

**87.** Some of the earlier cases adopting this approach include Ferraro v. Ford Motor Co., 223 A.2d 746 (Pa. 1966); Johnson v. Clark Equip. Co., 547 P.2d 132 (Or. 1976); Haugen v. Minnesota Mining & Mfg. Co., 550 P.2d 71 (Wash. Ct. App. 1976). South Carolina did so by adopting a key sentence of comment *n* statutorily. S.C. Code § 15–73–20. Other adoptions, applications, and statements of this principle include Warner Fruehauf Trailer Co. v. Boston, 654 A.2d 1272, 1275 (D.C. 1995); Jimenez v. Sears, Roebuck & Co., 904 P.2d 861, 864 (Ariz. 1995); Berg v. Sukup Mfg. Co., 355 N.W.2d 833, 835 (S.D. 1984); Jackson v. Harsco Corp., 673 P.2d 363, 366 (Colo. 1983) (en banc); Deere & Co. v. Brooks, 299 S.E.2d 704 (Ga. 1983). In Johnson v. Clark Equip. Co., 547 P.2d 132, 138 (Or. 1976), the court explained:

The concept of assumption of risk in a products liability case differs somewhat from the traditional tort doctrine of assumption of risk.... In contrast to the more traditional defense which includes only two elements—subjective knowledge and voluntary encounter—Comment *n* sets forth three elements which must be shown before the plaintiff can be barred from recovery. The defendant must show, first, that the plaintiff *himself* actually knew and appreciated the particular risk or danger created by the defect; second, that plaintiff voluntarily encountered the risk while realizing the danger; and, third, that plaintiff's decision to voluntarily encounter the known risk was unreasonable.

See also Jett v. Ford Motor Co., 84 P.3d 219, 222 (Or. Ct. App. 2004) ("'[u]nreasonable use despite knowledge of the dangerous defect in the product and awareness of the risk posed by that defect" is accurate way to describe assumption of risk defense in products liability action). Compare Milwaukee Elec. Tool Corp. v. San Diego Cty. Super. Ct., 6 Cal.Rptr.2d 423 (Ct. App. 1992) (breach of warranty barred if jury finds that plaintiff used product after discovering defect and that a reasonable person would not have used product knowing of its condition); Allen v. Chance Mfg. Co., Inc., 494 N.E.2d 1324 (Mass. 1986) (implied warranty).

**88.** See, e.g., Berg v. Sukup Mfg. Co., 355 N.W.2d 833, 835 (S.D. 1984), where the court observed that the assumption of risk defense under comment *n* to § 402A requires a manufacturer to establish "(1) That the plaintiff knew and appreciated the risk or danger created by the defect, (2) that the plaintiff voluntarily encountered the risk while realizing the danger, and (3) that the plaintiff's decision to vol-

As with the issue of voluntariness discussed above, some courts have stressed that workplace decisions to encounter risk may be found not to be "unreasonable" if the practical demands of the job sabotage an opportunity for truly consensual decision-making about such encounters.[89] Although there is little recent law on point, it would seem quite clear that, even in the workplace context, a person may unreasonably (and voluntarily) choose to engage a known and appreciated risk.[90]

The reasonableness issue in strict liability in tort cases concerns the plaintiff's *decision* to encounter a particular risk, or to encounter it in a particular way, not the reasonableness of the physical execution of that decision.[91] Unlike the other elements of assumption of risk, the unreasonableness element adds an *objective* determination of whether a prudent person would have decided to encounter the particular risk based on all the surrounding circumstances.[92]

While adding an "unreasonableness" requirement to the definition of assumption of risk for strict liability in tort claims formally narrows and restricts the availability of the defense, and while it may provide a plaintiff's lawyer with a convenient peg on which to hang an argument, the effect of this element may be more apparent than real. No doubt it is true that the orthodox definition of assumption of risk does not require that a plaintiff's choice to incur a known risk be unreasonable, so that the defense may theoretically arise even if an encounter was reasonable in all respects.[93] However, if the "voluntary" element of assumption of risk is defined as the availability of reasonable alternatives, as discussed above, the set of reasonable assumptions of risk essentially disappears.

Assume, for example, that a pregnant woman living deep in the country goes into labor, and her doctor counsels her by telephone that complications in her pregnancy threaten her life if she does not immedi-

---

untarily encounter the risk was unreasonable."

**89.** See, e.g., Brown v. Quick Mix Co., 454 P.2d 205, 208 (Wash. 1969) ("It could never be said as a matter of law that a workman whose job requires him to expose himself to a danger, voluntarily and unreasonably encounters the same."); Johnson v. Clark Equip. Co., 547 P.2d 132, 140–41 (Or. 1976):

> [W]orking conditions and related circumstances are a particularly relevant consideration in an inquiry into the reasonableness of a decision to encounter a job-related danger. Such factors often will have a strong influence on that decision, and, in some cases, they may represent the most important motivational factors. For example, a worker might fear that a slowdown in his individual production would slow down the entire production team and thereby draw the attention of his boss. If he has a history of such slowdowns, or of causing excessive spoilage or ruining machine parts, he may have good cause to fear dismissal. The job market could be tight, and he may have

little hope of being able to find a new job. Moreover, the situation may demand an immediate, hurried decision. It is certainly possible that, under such circumstances, a reasonable jury could find that his decision to encounter a known risk was not unreasonable.

See also Berg v. Sukup Mfg. Co., 355 N.W.2d 833, 835–36 (S.D. 1984).

**90.** See, e.g., Karim v. Tanabe Mach., Ltd., 322 F.Supp.2d 578 (E.D. Pa. 2004) (machine operator grabbed control box near moving chain and sprocket, which caught his hand).

**91.** "We are not concerned with the apparent reasonableness or unreasonableness of the physical conduct through which plaintiff encountered the danger, but rather the reasonableness of his decision to do so." Johnson v. Clark Equip. Co., 547 P.2d 132, 140 (Or. 1976).

**92.** See id. at 138 n.5.

**93.** See, e.g., Rahmig v. Mosley Mach. Co., 412 N.W.2d 56, 74 (Neb. 1987). See generally Prosser and Keeton on Torts § 68, at 481.

ately begin to drive to the distant hospital. When her husband helps her into their only car, he discovers a large bubble defect on the sidewall of a newly purchased front tire on the car. Being a tire salesman, he knows that the bubble may cause the tire to fail at any time. However, because there are no neighbors, nor time to call an ambulance, the husband proceeds to drive slowly and carefully to the hospital. But the tire bursts en route, causing the car to career into a ditch, injuring the husband. No doubt a jury would find that the husband's decision to incur the risk of driving on the defective tire was reasonable, and quite probably that it was informed. But the decision to incur this risk was not voluntary; it was reasonable for the very same reason that it was involuntary—the husband had no choice, no reasonable alternative to attempting the journey (cautiously) on a tire he knew to be dangerously defective.

Thus, if voluntariness rests on the presence of choice, and if choice implies the availability of reasonable alternatives, voluntariness and reasonableness may be seen to collapse into one another, rendering the notion of a reasonable assumption of risk a contradiction in terms and a virtually empty set.[94] In the problem above, the husband would be protected from an assumption of risk defense because his choice to incur the risk was reasonable, but he would avoid it as well because the decision was involuntary. These results would be reversed if the husband had no good reason to drive on the defective tire, that is, if a reasonable alternative *were* available. So, if the husband chose to drive to a baseball game on a tire he knew to be dangerously defective, failing to take the time to change it with an available spare in order to arrive earlier and get a better parking space, then his choice to incur the risk would be voluntary, his decision would also be unreasonable (unless it were a Yankees—Red Sox game), and his assumption of risk would bar recovery. Either way, because reasonableness is bound inextricably to the notion of voluntariness, adding the unreasonableness of a decision to encounter a risk as a formal element to assumption of risk may not materially alter the scope of the defense.[95]

### Reform

Assumption of risk is on the run. The doctrine is plainly problematic: it may unfairly place responsibility for injuries upon a victim whose only fault lay in making a choice, perhaps correctly, that was forced improperly upon him by a tortfeasor. To the extent that a plaintiff truly was at fault in encountering a risk, the doctrines of (no) duty,[96] contribu-

---

**94.** Virtually empty, rather than completely so, because the risks and other costs of an alternative course of action may be equal to, rather than less than, those of the course of action encountered. In such a case, either decision would be reasonable.

**95.** See, e.g., Berg v. Sukup Mfg. Co., 355 N.W.2d 833 (S.D. 1984), where the court, in applying the unreasonableness element of Restatement (2d) Torts § 402A cmt. *n*, defined it in terms of the presence of a reasonable alternative, a standard more typically used to define voluntariness, as

discussed above. The court remarked: "Reasonableness refers to whether the plaintiff had a reasonable opportunity to elect whether or not to subject himself to the danger," id. at 835, and further stated the issue in terms of "[w]hether or not [plaintiff] had a reasonable opportunity to avoid the risk." Id. at 836.

**96.** See, e.g., Bartkewich v. Billinger, 247 A.2d 603 (Pa. 1968) (manufacturer of glass breaking machine had no duty to design machine to prevent operators from

tory (and comparative) negligence,[97] and (sole) proximate causation[98] would appear to cover virtually every case where assumption of risk properly bars recovery. For these reasons, the assumption of risk defense has long been roundly criticized,[99] and it is being abolished, partially[100] or completely,[101] by an increasing number of courts and legislatures. And, with the widespread adoption of comparative fault beginning in the late 1960s, other courts and legislatures have done what amounts to the same thing by "merging" assumption of risk into a broad doctrine of comparative fault.[102] In many of the remaining states which continue to

reaching their hands in machine in an attempt to release a jam).

**97.** See §§ 13.2 and 13.3, above.

**98.** See Horton v. American Tobacco Co., 667 So.2d 1289, 1307 (Miss. 1995) (Lee, P.J., concurring and dissenting in part) ("Under assumption of the risk theory, if a plaintiff is found to have assumed the risk of his own injury, he is, in fact, the sole proximate cause of his injury and thus, no liability lies on the defendant.").

**99.** The critical scholarly literature includes Bohlen, Voluntary Assumption of Risk, 20 Harv. L. Rev. 14 (1906); Wade, The Place of Assumption of Risk in the Law of Negligence, 22 La. L. Rev. 5 (1961); James, Assumption of Risk: Unhappy Reincarnation, 78 Yale L.J. 185 (1968). Simons, Assumption of Risk and Consent in the Law of Torts: A Theory of Full Preference, 67 B.U. L. Rev. 213 (1987) (excellent theoretical inquiry). See generally Prosser and Keeton on Torts at 493–95; 4 Harper, James, and Gray, Law of Torts § 21.8, at 259. For an interesting debate among the tort law scholars of an earlier generation, see "The Battle of the Wilderness," Restatement (2d) Torts § 893, at 70 (Tent. Draft No. 9, 1963).

**100.** For example, a few jurisdictions have abolished the implied assumption of risk defense in all cases except those involving claims of strict products liability in tort. See, e.g., Central Tel. Co. v. Fixtures Mfg. Corp., 738 P.2d 510, 512 (Nev. 1987) (assumption of risk absorbed into comparative fault act except in strict liability cases); Bowling v. Heil Co., 511 N.E.2d 373 (Ohio 1987) (same); Onderko v. Richmond Mfg. Co., 511 N.E.2d 388 (Ohio 1987) (same); Rutter v. Northeastern Beaver Cty. Sch. Dist., 437 A.2d 1198, 1209 (Pa. 1981) (noting 19 other jurisdictions that have abolished or "seriously modified" the defense, and concluding that "the difficulties of using the term 'assumption of risk' outweigh the benefits").

At least Connecticut accomplishes the same result statutorily. Compare Conn. Gen. Stat. § 52–572h(*l* ) (abolishing the doctrine of assumption of risk in negligence actions) with Conn. Gen. Stat. § 52–572l ("Nothing in this section shall be construed

as barring … the defense of knowingly using the product in a defective condition in an action based on strict tort liability.").

**101.** New Jersey was the first such state to do so. See Meistrich v. Casino Arena Attractions Inc., 155 A.2d 90 (N.J. 1959), and McGrath v. American Cyanamid Co., 196 A.2d 238 (N.J. 1963). See also Hornbeck v. Western States Fire Apparatus, Inc., 572 P.2d 620 (Or. 1977) (statute); Bolduc v. Crain, 181 A.2d 641 (N.H. 1962).

The Ohio court abolished the defense for risks encountered by workers in the normal performance of their job-related duties. See Cremeans v. Willmar Henderson Mfg. Co., 566 N.E.2d 1203 (Ohio 1991).

New Jersey, which had abolished the doctrine, had an interesting struggle dealing with aggravated user misconduct in products liability cases without this defense. Its solution was to recognize "a defense of contributory negligence to strict liability in tort based upon a voluntary and unreasonable encountering by the plaintiff of a known safety hazard of a machine where proximately contributive to the accident." Cepeda v. Cumberland Eng'g Co., Inc., 386 A.2d 816, 833 (N.J. 1978). Under New Jersey's system of comparative fault, this is now the only type of plaintiff misconduct that may be used to reduce damages. See, e.g., Lewis v. American Cyanamid Co., 715 A.2d 967, 974–76 (N.J. 1998).

**102.** See, e.g., Blankenship v. CRT Tree, 2002 WL 31195215, at *7 (Ohio Ct. App. 2002) (noting the merger); Smock Materials v. Kerr, 719 N.E.2d 396, 402 (Ind. Ct. App. 1999) (merging assumption of risk into comparative fault for negligence actions, but maintaining it for strict liability actions); Perez v. McConkey, 872 S.W.2d 897 (Tenn. 1994) (implied assumption of risk abolished; fault aspects included in comparative fault); Calderon v. Echo, Inc., 614 N.E.2d 140 (Ill. App. Ct. 1993) (landscaper failed to wear safety goggles while operating trimmer-brush-cutter contrary to instructions, 90% at fault); Larsen v. Pacesetter Sys., Inc., 837 P.2d 1273 (Haw. 1992) (assumption of risk bar, "absurd" in products liability setting, merged into comparative

apply the assumption of risk defense, courts not infrequently recognize its harshness[103] and, refusing to apply it except where clearly mandated by facts and precedent, proclaim that it will not be extended.[104]

The principal *theoretical* benefit of the assumption of risk doctrine is that it grounds the law on choice and so ties legal responsibility at least in part to this important value. But a manufacturer's choices usually are relevant to product accidents as well, and a manufacturer should not necessarily escape all responsibility for accidents when it designs and sells a product that may force consumers to confront difficult choices subjecting themselves to risk. If a product defect leaves a user with no choice of an effective way to avoid a risk of harm, then the manufacturer fairly should shoulder the entire loss. But if a plaintiff knowingly, affirmatively, and voluntarily exercises substantial control over a product hazard, and simply opts to take a calculated and unreasonable risk, then the plaintiff's decision and action—whether viewed as choice, fault, or as both—should usually be considered the sole proximate cause of any resulting harm. Finally, if moral responsibility for a product accident is divided between the choices and conduct of both parties, then comparative fault provides a sound system for dividing damages. Basing responsibility on choice is a two-way street, and it would seem that a system of comparative responsibility generally offers a better method for doing justice when a product user assumes a risk of injury.

Probably the most important *practical* benefit of the assumption of risk doctrine is to provide a basis for summary judgment when a plaintiff is shown to have knowingly engaged an unreasonable risk and so should bear full responsibility for his or her injuries. Although courts are understandably shy to apply comparative fault principles to grant summary judgment against faulty plaintiffs, it would seem that courts might appropriately provide a small window for granting defendants summary judgment when a plaintiff's fault can fairly be characterized as the sole proximate cause of an accident.[105] This will often be the case when the

fault); Austin v. Raybestos–Manhattan, Inc., 471 A.2d 280 (Me. 1984); Zahrte v. Sturm, Ruger & Co., 661 P.2d 17 (Mont. 1983); South v. A.B. Chance Co., 635 P.2d 728 (Wash. 1981) (7–2 decision); Blackburn v. Dorta, 348 So.2d 287, 292–93 (Fla. 1977):

We find no discernible basis analytically or historically to maintain a distinction between the affirmative defense of contributory negligence and assumption of risk.... [Would the fault principles of tort law and comparative negligence be advanced by] a doctrine which would totally bar recovery by one who voluntarily, but reasonably, assumes a known risk while one whose conduct is unreasonable but denominated "contributory negligence" is permitted to recover a proportionate amount of his damages for injury? Certainly not. Therefore, we hold that the affirmative defense of implied assumption of risk is merged into the defense of contributory negligence and the principles of

comparative negligence ... shall apply....

**103.** See, e.g., Forrest City Mach. Works, Inc. v. Aderhold, 616 S.W.2d 720, 724 (Ark. 1981).

**104.** See, e.g., Heil Co. v. Grant, 534 S.W.2d 916, 920 (Tex. App. 1976) (applying it to facts, but stating, "The doctrine of assumed risk is harsh and will not be extended.").

**105.** While courts in pure comparative fault jurisdictions might reasonably be more cautious in so ruling, courts in modified (50%) comparative fault jurisdictions should more often confront situations appropriate for granting summary judgment motions on assumption of risk in favor of defendants. Even in pure comparative fault states, however, a plaintiff's extraordinary misconduct may sometimes authorize summary judgment for the defendant. See § 13.3, above.

facts are clear that the plaintiff knowingly and unreasonably took a calculated risk that resulted in accidental harm.

In conclusion, while the assumption of risk doctrine's grounding in choice theory renders it alluring at some levels, a complete choice theory requires consideration not only of a plaintiff's choices, but of a manufacturer's choices, too. Viewed from a welfare or economic perspective, the doctrine's mischief quite clearly outweighs its benefits.[106] And, viewed on its own terms, courts and legislatures increasingly appreciate the shortcomings of the assumption of risk defense and recognize the availability of reasonable alternative doctrines that well fill the void. Now that the new *Restatement of Apportionment* has taken the position that assumption of risk as a separate doctrine should be abolished,[107] the trend toward abolishing the doctrine and merging it into comparative fault appears inexorable. No doubt assumption of risk will linger on in some jurisdictions for some time, yet it clearly is a doctrine that is doomed.

### Express Assumption of Risk

The discussion above pertains to *implied* assumption of risk, in which context a plaintiff's conduct suggests or implies consent to incur a risk.[108] The issues are quite different when a defendant claims that a product user *expressly* agreed to accept full responsibility for the possibility that the use of a product would result in an injury—usually by means of a written waiver or disclaimer signed by the plaintiff. The principles of express assumption of risk depend upon the theory of recovery: negligence, strict products liability in tort, or warranty.

In negligence, the products liability cases parallel the general tort law principles: a disclaimer is effective only if it clearly and unequivocally relieves the defendant of responsibility for harm caused by the defendant's negligence. To most courts this has meant that the word "negligence" or "fault" (rather than more general words such as "liability") must appear in the disclaimer provision in a manner that makes it entirely clear that the shift of responsibility between the parties includes a shift of liability for harm caused by the defendant's negligence.[109] The negligence disclaimer cases have usually involved commercial parties suffering commercial losses, but the few that have involved garden-variety consumer claims against manufacturers for personal injuries caused by defective products follow similar principles of limitation, as explained below.

**106.** See, e.g., Rutter v. Northeastern Beaver Cty. Sch. Dist., 437 A.2d 1198, 1209 (Pa. 1981) (abolishing implied assumption of risk defense, except for strict tort products liability, on grounds that "the difficulties of using the term 'assumption of risk' outweigh the benefits").

**107.** See Restatement (3d) Torts: Apportionment of Liability §§ 2 cmt. *i*, 3 cmt. *c*.

**108.** See Prosser and Keeton on Torts § 68.

**109.** See, e.g., Johnson v. Zimmer, Inc., 2004 WL 742038 (D. Minn. 2004); Roane v. Greenwich Swim Comm., 330 F.Supp.2d 306 (S.D.N.Y. 2004); Willard Van Dyke Prods., Inc. v. Eastman Kodak Co., 189 N.E.2d 693 (N.Y. 1963), and a case against the same defendant on nearly identical facts, where the disclaimer redrafted in an attempt to comply with *Willard Van Dyke's* requirements was found still inadequate, Posttape Assoc. v. Eastman Kodak Co., 387 F.Supp. 184 (E.D. Pa. 1974), rev'd on other grounds, 537 F.2d 751 (3d Cir. 1976).

Several courts have held that a disclaimer is void if the defendant's negligence resulted in a violation of a duty imposed by statute for the benefit of the public.[110] In addition, as under the principles of warranty law,[111] the plaintiff must be made aware of any disclaimer of negligence responsibility at the time of sale, and such a provision will be ineffective if it is buried in fine print in an owner's manual not given to the plaintiff until after sale.[112] Even if a products liability defendant effectively avoids negligence responsibility toward the user who signed the contractual disclaimer, such a provision will not bar a negligence action brought by an injured third party against the manufacturer or other seller.[113]

As for strict products liability in tort, the law is clear: a seller's attempt to disclaim responsibility to consumers for injuries from new products is against public policy, void, and of no effect.[114] Indeed, the untoward use of disclaimers by sellers of dangerously defective consumer goods, allowable under warranty law, was a principal reason for the development of the doctrine of strict products liability in tort in the 1960s.[115] Both the *Second*[116] and *Third Restatements of Torts*[117] agree that such disclaimers of responsibility for injuries caused by product defects violate the law and are thus invalid.[118] Most of the difficult problems with disclaimers in strict tort involve their effectiveness in commercial contexts involving economic losses, a topic treated elsewhere.[119]

A typical case illustrating the prevailing tort law principles is *Diedrich v. Wright*,[120] in which the plaintiff was severely injured when her parachute failed to open fully because its lines were crossed. In her suit against the parachute center for supplying her with an unsafe parachute, the defendant asserted that she had waived her rights by signing a release form that generally exculpated the defendant from liability for injuries from parachuting. The court held that the release could not bar a strict liability action, and that it did not bar the

---

**110.** See, e.g., Dessert Seed Co. v. Drew Farmers Supply, Inc., 454 S.W.2d 307, 311 (Ark. 1970).

**111.** See §§ 4.7–4.9, above.

**112.** See Omni Flying Club, Inc. v. Cessna Aircraft Co., 315 N.E.2d 885 (Mass. 1974).

**113.** See Blanchard v. Monical Mach. Co., 269 N.W.2d 564 (Mich. Ct. App. 1978) ("as is" sale of used machine from defendant to plaintiff's employer).

**114.** See, e.g., Curtis v. Hoosier Racing Tire Corp., 299 F.Supp.2d 777 (N.D. Ohio 2004).

**115.** See §§ 5.2 and 5.3, above.

**116.** "The consumer's cause of action does not depend upon the validity of his contract with the person from whom he acquires the product, and it is not affected by any disclaimer or other agreement. . . . " Restatement (2d) Torts § 402A cmt. *m.*

**117.** The Products Liability Restatement § 18 provides:

Disclaimers and limitations of remedies by product sellers or other distributors, waivers by product purchasers, and other similar contractual exculpations, oral or written, do not bar or reduce otherwise valid products liability claims against sellers or other distributors of new products for harm to persons.

**118.** See, e.g., Ruzzo v. LaRose Enter., 748 A.2d 261, 268–69 (R.I. 2000) (chattel lessee); McGraw–Edison Co. v. Northeastern Rural Membership Corp., 647 N.E.2d 355 (Ind. Ct. App. 1995) (statute patterned substantially after § 402A); Wheelock v. Sport Kites, Inc., 839 F.Supp. 730 (D. Haw. 1993).

**119.** See 2 Madden & Owen on Products Liability § 17:13. See generally McNichols, Who Says that Strict Tort Disclaimers Can Never Be Effective? The Courts Cannot Agree, 28 Okla. L. Rev. 494 (1975); Note, 10 Tulsa L.J. 612 (1975).

**120.** 550 F.Supp. 805 (N.D. Ill. 1982).

negligence action because it failed clearly to state that the plaintiff was relieving the defendant of liability for *negligence*.[121]

In warranty law, disclaimers are addressed by § 2–316 of the Uniform Commercial Code which is treated in depth in an earlier chapter; basically, disclaimers are allowed under state law, provided they are clearly made pursuant to the requirements of the Code, but their use is substantially restricted by federal law in most significant consumer goods transactions.[122]

### Fireman's Rule

One special, narrow doctrine that concerns assumption of risk in its "primary" or no-duty sense[123] is the "fireman's rule," now sometimes called the "firefighters' rule," which applies to firefighters, police officers, and other professionals trained to rescue and preserve persons and property in emergency situations.[124] Most states still hold that emergency professionals, such as a firefighter injured in fighting a fire, may not recover against a party who tortiously caused the fire or other exigency because the firefighter is deemed to have assumed the normal risks incident to the job.[125] But, the fireman's rule generally will not apply, and so will not bar recovery, if the product's defective condition does not cause the fire or other emergency situation which provided the need for the plaintiff's professional skills.[126]

**121.**　Compare Westlye v. Look Sports, Inc., 22 Cal.Rptr.2d 781 (Ct. App. 1993) (ski equipment rental disclaimer against public policy); Ghionis v. Deer Valley Resort Co., 839 F.Supp. 789 (D. Utah 1993) (notwithstanding release, skier not aware that her rented bindings would fail to release because they were incompatible with her boots); Moore v. Sitzmark Corp., 555 N.E.2d 1305 (Ind. Ct. App. 1990) (skier's signature on release simply acknowledged laws of physics and did not show she knew of defect in bindings). *But see* Johnson v. Paraplane Corp., 460 S.E.2d 398 (S.C. Ct. App. 1995) (release and video fully explained nature and assumption of risks of flying ultralight aircraft).

**122.**　See ch. 4, above.

**123.**　See Prosser and Keeton on Torts § 68, at 481.

**124.**　See Prosser and Keeton on Torts § 61, at 429.

**125.**　See, e.g., Brown v. General Elec. Corp., 648 F.Supp. 470 (M.D. Ga. 1986) (while fighting fire caused by defective coffee pot, fireman injured from jumping off roof of burning building that exploded). Note, however, that courts continue to abol-

ish this doctrine. See, e.g., Roma v. United States, 344 F.3d 352 (N.J. Ct. App. 2003).

**126.**　See, e.g., Holloway v. Midland Risk Ins. Co., 832 So.2d 1004 (La. Ct. App. 2002) (firefighter injured when rescue equipment malfunctioned; doctrine not applied since injury from defective equipment not reasonably within line of duty); McKernan v. General Motor Corp., 3 P.3d 1261 (Kan. 2000) (injured while fighting car fire by explosion of gas filled strut that supported hood, firefighter could maintain products liability action against automaker; firefighter rule did not bar suit); Labrie v. Pace Membership Warehouse, Inc., 678 A.2d 867, 868 (R.I. 1996) (thorough review of rule; fire department employee injured by waterline valve during routine inspection of merchant's sprinkler system: "we conclude that the Superior Court responded to a false alarm when it used the firefighter's rule to torch plaintiff's complaint"); Hauboldt v. Union Carbide Corp., 467 N.W.2d 508 (Wis. 1991) (defective acetylene tank exploded, directly injuring firefighter; doctrine did not apply). *But see* White v. Edmond, 971 F.2d 681 (11th Cir. 1992) (Ga. law) (firefighter injured when car's shock absorbers exploded in fire; doctrine barred recovery).

## § 13.5   MISUSE

A user's "misuse" of a product, putting it to a clearly improper use, generally bars recovery in a products liability action.[1] Thus, like assumption of risk, product misuse is a powerful common law "misconduct defense" in products liability litigation.[2] Although a few jurisdictions have merged misuse into their comparative fault systems,[3] so that some or all forms of product misuse serve only to reduce a plaintiff's damages rather than to bar recovery altogether, a user's[4] *unforeseeable* misuse is widely considered to be an absolute bar to recovery.[5] While product misuse is a common law doctrine,[6] products liability reform statutes in several states reduce damages[7] or bar liability[8] in cases of a plaintiff's product misuse.[9]

The basic idea of the misuse doctrine is that products are necessarily designed to do certain limited tasks, within certain limited environments of use, and that no product can be made safe for every purpose, manner, or extent of use. Considerations of cost and practicality limit every

### § 13.5

**1.** See Calnan, A Consumer–Use Approach to Products Liability, 33 U. Mem. L. Rev. 755 (2003); King, Outlaws and Outlier Doctrines: The Serious Misconduct Bar in Tort Law, 43 Wm. & Mary L. Rev. 1001 (2002); Dell'Osso, Avoiding the 'Misuse' Defense in Products Cases, 38 Trial 68 (Feb. 2002); McNichols, The Relevance of the Plaintiff's Misconduct in Strict Tort Products Liability, the Advent of Comparative Responsibility, and the Proposed Restatement (Third) of Torts, 47 Okla. L. Rev. 201 (1994) (comprehensive review and consideration of early draft of Third Restatement); Fischer, Products Liability—Applicability of Comparative Negligence to Misuse and Assumption of the Risk, 43 Mo. L. Rev. 643 (1978); Twerski, The Many Faces of Misuse: An Inquiry Into the Emerging Doctrine of Comparative Causation, 29 Mercer L.Rev. 403 (1978); Vargo, The Defenses to Strict Liability in Tort: A New Vocabulary with an Old Meaning, 29 Mercer L. Rev. 447 (1978); Noel, Defective Products: Abnormal Use, Contributory Negligence, and Assumption of Risk, 25 Vand. L. Rev. 93 (1972); Dale & Hilton, Use of the Product–When is it Abnormal?, 4 Willamette L. Rev. 350 (1967); Note, 57 Neb. L. Rev. 817 (1978); 42 N.Y.U. L. Rev. 381 (1967); Annot., 65 A.L.R.4th 263 (1988) (comprehensive treatment of misuse "defense" in products liability). On related regulatory issues, see Adler, Redesigning People versus Redesigning Products: The Consumer Product Safety Commission Addresses Product Misuse, 11 J. L. & Pol. 79 (1995).

**2.** While product misuse is a common law doctrine, statutory reform provisions in many states govern the effect of various forms of user misconduct including misuse. For a discussion of such statutes, see § 13.1, above.

**3.** See, e.g., Tober v. Graco Children's Prods., Inc., 2004 WL 1987239 (S.D. Ind.

2004); Jimenez v. Sears, Roebuck & Co., 904 P.2d 861 (Ariz. 1995); Mauch v. Manufacturers Sales & Serv., Inc., 345 N.W.2d 338, 348 (N.D. 1984); General Motors v. Hopkins, 548 S.W.2d 344 (Tex. 1977), overruled on other grounds by Turner v. General Motors Corp., 584 S.W.2d 844 (Tex. 1979), and by Duncan v. Cessna Aircraft Co., 665 S.W.2d 414 (Tex. 1984).

**4.** This chapter addresses the role of product misuse as a *user* misconduct "defense." Misuse by a third party (including product alteration and modification) raises issues of intervening (and possibly superseding) causation and so is examined in the chapter on proximate cause. See § 12.3, above. See generally Annot., 41 A.L.R.3d 1251 (1972).

**5.** See Products Liability Restatement § 2, Reporters' Note to cmt. *p*. While the Uniform Comparative Fault Act includes *foreseeable* misuse as a form of "fault" subject to comparison, this means that *un*foreseeable misuse remains outside of the comparative system as a total bar to liability.

**6.** See Products Liability Restatement § 2, Reporters' Note to cmt. *p*.

**7.** At least Idaho and Missouri have enacted such legislation, and this is the approach of the Uniform Comparative Fault Act which reduces a plaintiff's damages, however, only on account of *foreseeable* product misuse.

**8.** At least Arizona, Indiana, Michigan, Montana, and Tennessee have such statutes. The statutes are set forth in § 13.1, above. The Montana Supreme Court has interpreted that state's ambiguous statute to mean that unforeseeable misuse bars liability. See Hart–Albin Co. v. McLees Inc., 870 P.2d 51, 53–54 (Mont. 1994).

**9.** The statutes use various labels to describe this form of plaintiff misconduct. See,

product's range of effective and safe use, which is a fundamental fact of life that consumers readily understand. Consumers know that products may be used safely only for certain limited purposes; that they should be used properly and within the manufacturer's warnings and instructions; and that using products beyond their capabilities may cause them to break, overheat, or otherwise fail in a possibly dangerous way. If a user chooses to put a product to a type or manner of use that the product cannot fairly be expected to withstand, and the user is injured as a result,[10] he or she cannot reasonably demand that the manufacturer (and, indirectly, other consumers) shoulder the economic consequences of the loss.[11] "We cannot charge the manufacturer of a knife when it is used as a toothpick and the user complains because the sharp edge cuts."[12]

The misuse doctrine is difficult to apply in a principled manner, as discussed below, but the general doctrine is quite easy to state: manufacturers and other sellers are subject to responsibility for harm from product uses which are reasonably foreseeable but not for harm from unforeseeable product use.[13]

e.g., Mont. Code Ann. § 27–1–719(5)(b) (unreasonable misuse).

**10.** See, e.g., Cavanagh v. F.W. Woolworth Co., 32 N.E.2d 256 (Mass. 1941), where the decision suggests that the plaintiff was demanding more from a rubber bottle stopper than he could fairly expect.

**11.** See, e.g., Venezia v. Miller Brewing Co., 626 F.2d 188, 190–91 (1st Cir. 1980) (Mass. law). See generally Findlay v. Copeland Lumber Co., 509 P.2d 28, 31 (Or. 1973) ("Misuse, to bar recovery, must be a use or handling so unusual that the average consumer could not reasonably expect the product to be designed and manufactured to withstand it—a use which the seller, therefore, need not anticipate and provide for."); Holford, The Limits of Strict Liability for Product Design and Manufacture, 52 Tex. L. Rev. 81, 89 (1973):

> If a consumer employs a product in some extraordinary manner, and encounters a known danger in the course of his conduct, the doctrine of product misuse will bar recovery from the manufacturer. The adventurous consumer has voluntarily placed himself in a category distinct from the normal consumer who forgoes the pleasure and convenience of using products in novel but dangerous ways. The rationale of loss distribution does not reach his case because it is unfair to force consumers who forgo these additional benefits to subsidize those individuals who voluntarily take the additional risks. [The misuse defense] fall[s] into the general category of assumption of risk.

See generally Owen, The Moral Foundations of Products Liability Law: Toward First Principles, 68 Notre Dame L. Rev. 427, 476 (1993) (consumer who puts product to "uniquely adventuresome use that he should know may exceed the product's capabilities . . . has no fair claim to compensation from the maker, diminishing the autonomy of the maker's owners and other consumers, because the accident was caused by the victim's greed in demanding greater usefulness from the product than other consumers sought and greater usefulness than was reflected in the price he paid").

**12.** General Motors Corp. v. Hopkins, 548 S.W.2d 344, 349 (Tex. 1977), overruled on other grounds by Turner v. General Motors Corp., 584 S.W.2d 844 (Tex. 1979), and by Duncan v. Cessna Aircraft Co., 665 S.W.2d 414 (Tex. 1984).

**13.** See, e.g., Ricci v. AB Volvo, 106 Fed. Appx. 573 (9th Cir. 2004) (Nev. law); Jameson v. Liquid Controls Corp., 618 N.W.2d 637, 646 (Neb. 2000) ("In the law of products liability, misuse is the use of a product in a way not reasonably foreseeable by the supplier or manufacturer."); Jurado v. Western Gear Works, 619 A.2d 1312, 1318 (N.J. 1993) ("a manufacturer is not under a duty to protect against unforeseeable misuses" yet "has a duty to prevent an injury caused by the foreseeable misuse of its product"). Compare Products Liability Restatement § 2, Reporters' Note to cmt. *p* ("When a product is put to an unforeseeable use and the plaintiff claims that the product should have been designed to avoid injury when put to such a use, the courts agree that liability will not attach."); Armentrout v. FMC Corp., 842 P.2d 175, 188 (Colo. 1992) (en banc) ("regardless of the defective condition of a product, misuse by an injured party which cannot be reasonably anticipated by the manufacturer is a

### Development of the Doctrine

The misuse doctrine runs long and deep through products liability law, having shielded manufacturers from liability for at least a century.[14] For most of the twentieth century, the role of a user's misuse of a product in a personal injury action against the supplier was unclear. Many early courts simply treated product misuse as an issue going to proximate cause.[15] Other courts viewed misuse as limiting the seller's liability to the product's "intended" uses.[16] For example, users in early cases were barred from recovery on claims that cleaning fluid was intended to be applied to inanimate objects, not splashed in the eye;[17] that the entire edge of a grinding wheel was intended to be applied against the object being ground, not just the edge of the edge;[18] and that allegedly uncrashworthy automobiles were intended to be driven on the highway, not for crashing into trees.[19] In the 1950s and 1960s, courts and commentators increasingly framed the issue as whether the user had put the product to an "abnormal" use,[20] although the "intended" use formulation of the misuse principle continued to linger on in some jurisdictions.[21] Through much of the 1960s, 1970s, and even into the 1980s, as the role of product misuse evolved and began to come into focus, all three terms and concepts—intended use, abnormal use, and misuse—shared an uncomfortable coexistence.[22] By the 1980s and 1990s, however, the courts and commentators had worked out a generally accepted definition of the "misuse" doctrine: liability is restricted to the consequences of reasonably "foreseeable" use—a formulation that widely prevails in products liability litigation today.

defense where that conduct actually caused the injury").

**14.** "It seems quite clearly established where the purchaser, actually knowing the defective nature of the article, puts it to a use for which it is unfit and unsafe, any injury received therefrom is due to his misuse and not to the act of him who created the defect." Bohlen, The Basis of Affirmative Obligations in the Law of Tort (pt. 3), 53 U. Pa. L. Rev. 337, 343 (1905).

**15.** See, e.g., Waterman v. Liederman, 60 P.2d 881 (Cal. App. 1936) (wild driving on tire). See generally Prosser, The Fall of the Citadel (Strict Liability to the Consumer), 50 Minn. L. Rev. 791, 824 (1966).

**16.** At least one modern court has clung to this quaint limitation on claims based on strict liability in tort. See Phillips v. Cricket Lighters, 841 A.2d 1000 (Pa. 2003). On foreseeability and "intended use," see also §§ 12.2, above, and 17.3, below.

**17.** Sawyer v. Pine Oil Sales Co., 155 F.2d 855 (5th Cir. 1946) (La. law). Accord Restatement (2d) Torts § 395 cmt. *j. Contra* Haberly v. Reardon Co., 319 S.W.2d 859 (Mo. 1958) (paint).

**18.** Zesch v. Abrasive Co., 193 S.W.2d 581 (Mo. 1946).

**19.** See, e.g., Evans v. General Motors Corp., 359 F.2d 822 (7th Cir. 1966) (Ind.

law), overruled by Huff v. White Motor Corp., 565 F.2d 104, 109 (7th Cir. 1977); General Motors Corp. v. Muncy, 367 F.2d 493 (5th Cir. 1966) (Tex. law). *Contra* Larsen v. General Motors Corp., 391 F.2d 495 (8th Cir. 1968) (Mich. law). The crashworthiness doctrine is addressed in § 17.3, below.

**20.** See W. Prosser, The Law of Torts § 102 (4th ed. 1971); Noel, Defective Products: Abnormal Use, Contributory Negligence, and Assumption of Risk, 25 Vand. L. Rev. 93 (1972).

**21.** See, e.g., Bazerman v. Gardall Safe Corp., 609 N.Y.S.2d 610 (App. Div. 1994); Myers v. American Seating Co., 637 So.2d 771 (La. Ct. App. 1994); Allen v. Chance Mfg. Co., 494 N.E.2d 1324 (Mass. 1986); Codling v. Paglia, 298 N.E.2d 622 (N.Y. 1973); Greenman v. Yuba Power Prods., Inc., 377 P.2d 897, 901 (Cal. 1963).

**22.** See, e.g., Dosier v. Wilcox & Crittendon Co., 119 Cal.Rptr. 135 (Ct. App. 1975) (appearing to equate "intended" and "foreseeable"). See generally, Noel, Defective Products: Abnormal Use, Contributory Negligence, and Assumption of Risk, 25 Vand. L. Rev. 93 (1972). Misuse concepts and nomenclature continue to remain confused in many jurisdictions. See, e.g., Hart–Albin Co. v. McLees Inc., 870 P.2d 51, 53–54 (Mont. 1994) (interpreting statutory "unreasonable misuse" phrase in terms of

## Theory of Liability

Although the precise formulation of the product misuse doctrine was still in ferment in many jurisdictions late into the twentieth century, the correlative ideas of restricting a seller's responsibility to normal or expectable product uses, on the one hand, and making users responsible for their injuries caused by particularly unusual product uses, on the other hand, have been central pillars of products liability law for many years. The *Restatement (Second) of Torts* has long provided that a manufacturer is subject to liability, in negligent manufacturing cases, for harm caused by a chattel's "lawful use in a manner and for a purpose for which it is supplied";[23] in negligent warnings cases, for harm from "use of the chattel in the manner for which ... it is supplied";[24] and in negligent design cases, for harm from "probable use."[25] In warranty law, as examined below,[26] the Uniform Commercial Code built the misuse doctrine into the concept of a product's "merchantability," defined most broadly in terms of a product's being fit for its "ordinary" purposes.[27]

In strict liability in tort, an original premise of manufacturer liability was that the injury arose out of the *proper* use of the product. As Judge Traynor observed, in *Greenman v. Yuba Power Prods., Inc.*[28]:

> Implicit in the machine's presence on the market ... was a representation that it would safely do *the jobs for which it was built.* ... To establish the manufacturer's liability it was sufficient that plaintiff proved that he was injured while using the Shopsmith *in a way it was intended to be used* as a result of a defect in design and manufacture of which plaintiff was not aware that made the Shopsmith *unsafe for its intended use.*[29]

In § 402A of the *Restatement (Second) of Torts*, the scope of strict products liability in tort is limited to injuries from proper product uses: products safe for "normal handling" are not defective, and product sellers are shielded from strict liability for injuries resulting from "mishandling," "over-consumption," "excessive use," and a failure to read and heed an adequate warning.[30] The *Third Restatement* succinctly limits responsibility in black-letter definitions of both design and warnings

intended use, abnormal use, and unforeseeable use).

**23.** See Restatement (2d) Torts § 395.

**24.** See Restatement (2d) Torts § 388.

**25.** Restatement (2d) Torts § 398, special application of § 395.

**26.** See § 13.6, below.

**27.** See UCC § 2–314(2)(c). See generally § 4.3, above.

**28.** Greenman v. Yuba Power Prods., Inc., 377 P.2d 897 (Cal. 1963).

**29.** Id. at 901 (emphasis added). The California court later altered this formulation of the scope of liability to include uses that are reasonably foreseeable as well as intended. See Cronin v. J.B.E. Olson Corp., 501 P.2d 1153, 1157 (Cal. 1972).

**30.** See Restatement (2d) Torts § 402A cmt. *g* (defectiveness not established by harm from "mishandling"); cmt. *h* (product not defective when safe for "normal handling"; no liability for injuries from "abnormal handling" or "abnormal consumption"); cmt. *i* (unreasonable danger not established by harm from "over-consumption"); and cmt. *j* (no duty to warn of generally known risks of excessive use; seller may assume warnings will be read and heeded, and product with adequate warning is neither defective nor unreasonably dangerous).

defects to "the foreseeable risks of harm posed by the product,"[31] and the Reporters make it clear that courts bar recovery in design litigation for injuries that occur "[w]hen a product is put to an unforeseeable use."[32]

## Whether Misuse Is a "Defense"; Burden of Pleading and Proof

One reason the doctrine of misuse is difficult to apply is that there is no agreement on just what kind of legal doctrine it really is. While many lawyers speak loosely of a product misuse "defense," the common law principle of product misuse is more accurately viewed as a liability-limiting principle concerning the scope of a defendant's duty that involves the issues of negligence, product defect, scope of warranty, and proximate causation.[33] As part of the plaintiff's prima facie products liability case in most states,[34] the plaintiff must at least theoretically plead and prove that the accident arose out of a reasonably foreseeable product use[35] which suggests that the plaintiff's unforeseeable misuse cannot be an affirmative defense. Yet, all but one of the several states

---

**31.** Products Liability Restatement §§ 2(b) and (c), respectively. Quite obviously, for a risk to be foreseeable, it must ordinarily result from a foreseeable product use. See id. at cmt. *m*:

> *m. Reasonably foreseeable uses and risks in design and warning claims.* Subsections (b) and (c) impose liability only when the product is put to uses that it is reasonable to expect a seller or distributor to foresee. Product sellers and distributors are not required to foresee and take precautions against every conceivable mode of use and abuse to which their products might be put.

See also id. at cmt. *p.*

**32.** Products Liability Restatement § 2, Reporters' Note to cmt. *p.*

**33.** See, e.g., Jeld–Wen, Inc. v. Gamble, 501 S.E.2d 393 (Va. 1998) (duty); Marshall v. Clark Equip. Co., 680 N.E.2d 1102, 1108 (Ind. Ct. App. 1997) (proximate and intervening causation, involving "foreseeability of an intervening misuse"); Jurado v. Western Gear Works, 619 A.2d 1312, 1319 (N.J. 1993) (duty, product defect, and proximate cause). See generally Wade, On the Nature of Strict Tort Liability for Products, 44 Miss. L.J. 825, 846 (1973) (product defect, proximate cause, and scope of risk); Prosser, The Fall of the Citadel (Strict Liability to the Consumer), 50 Minn. L. Rev. 791, 824 (1966) (product defect and proximate cause); Dobbs, Law of Torts § 370, at 1076; Products Liability Restatement § 2 cmts. *m* and *p,* and Reporters' Note to cmt. *p* (duty):

> When a product is put to an unforeseeable use and the plaintiff claims that the product should have been designed to

avoid injury when put to such a use, the courts agree that liability will not attach. There is widespread understanding that misuse in this context goes to the basic duty issue.

Courts and commentators have had real difficulty in ascertaining and explaining how different forms of misuse figure into the rubrics of duty, defectiveness, proximate cause, and affirmative defenses. The complexity of the issues, particularly in the context of comparative fault, is evident by the confusion in many of the decisions. See, e.g., Jimenez v. Sears, Roebuck & Co., 904 P.2d 861 (Ariz. 1995) (separate opinions by three justices); Jurado v. Western Gear Works, 619 A.2d 1312 (N.J. 1993).

**34.** See, e.g., Ellsworth v. Sherne Lingerie, Inc., 495 A.2d 348 (Md. 1985). See generally Noel, Defective Products: Abnormal Use, Contributory Negligence, and Assumption of Risk, 25 Vand. L. Rev. 93 (1972). Cf. Products Liability Restatement § 2 cmt. *m. But cf.* id. cmt. *p.*

**35.** See, e.g., Newman v. Utility Trailer and Equip. Co., 564 P.2d 674, 676–77 (Or. 1977) (en banc):

> Before a manufacturer or other seller is strictly liable for injury inflicted by a product, the product must have been put to a foreseeable use. As an example: if a shovel is used to prop open a heavy door, but, because of the way the shovel was designed, it is inadequate to the task and the door swings shut and crushes the user's hand, no responsibility for the injury results by reason of the shovel's not being designed to prop open doors since it was not reasonably foreseeable by the

that have enacted statutory reform provisions on misuse define it as an affirmative defense.[36]

Courts and commentators have striven sedulously to work out a clear and sound doctrine of misuse, often without success. The struggle with the meaning of the doctrine is illustrated in many judicial opinions. For example, the Colorado Supreme Court concluded that "the defense of misuse . . . is a particularized defense requiring that the plaintiff's use of the product be unforeseeable and unintended as well as the cause of the injuries"[37] and further observed that "[m]isuse . . . is a question of causation. Regardless of the defective condition, if any, of a manufacturer's product, a manufacturer will not be liable if an unforeseeable misuse of the product caused the injuries."[38] The dissent characterized misuse as an "affirmative defense."[39] By contrast, in another case, the New Jersey Supreme Court concluded that "[t]he absence of misuse is part of the plaintiff's case," that "[m]isuse is not an affirmative defense," and that "the plaintiff has the burden of showing that there was no misuse or that the misuse was objectively foreseeable."[40] Other courts have similarly disagreed as to the true role of plaintiff misuse in products liability litigation, and the perplexities are magnified in jurisdictions that attempt to blend misuse into a system of comparative fault.[41]

When all is said and done, there probably is no logical way to avoid treating the absence of misuse as bearing on the scope of the defendant's responsibility and, hence, as part of the plaintiff's case.[42] Nor does there seem to be any sound reason for a court to try to work around the logic in order to convert the doctrine into an affirmative defense. While one might think at first that plaintiffs would be advantaged if misuse were treated as an affirmative defense (giving the defendant the burden of pleading and proof) rather than as part of the plaintiff's case, the issue ordinarily is of little or no practical consequence in products liability litigation. Defendants typically treat product misuse like any other misconduct defense, offering evidence and argument upon the issue whether or not the plaintiff has pleaded the absence of misuse in the complaint. In a jurisdiction that requires a plaintiff to plead the absence of misuse, it is difficult to imagine a court refusing to allow a plaintiff to amend the complaint to include this aspect of the claim. More importantly, because plaintiffs rarely fail to plead proximate causation—that the defendant's negligence, breach of warranty, or a product defect proximately caused the plaintiff's harm—virtually every complaint includes at least an implicit allegation of the absence of misuse. This is because the

manufacturer or seller that it would be so used.

**36.** See § 13.1, above. Compare Zablotsky, The Appropriate Role of Plaintiff Misuse in Products Liability Causes of Action, 10 Touro L. Rev. 183 (1993) (collecting cases, and stating that most courts properly hold misuse to be an affirmative defense).

**37.** Uptain v. Huntington Lab, Inc., 723 P.2d 1322, 1325 (Colo. 1986).

**38.** Id.

**39.** Id. at 1332.

**40.** Jurado v. Western Gear Works, 619 A.2d 1312, 1317 (N.J. 1993).

**41.** For one court's valiant efforts to unravel the mysteries of how the doctrine of product misuse fits into the comparative fault system, compare the different judges' opinions in Jimenez v. Sears, Roebuck & Co., 904 P.2d 861 (Ariz. 1995).

**42.** See, e.g., Hughes v. Magic Chef, Inc., 288 N.W.2d 542, 546 (Iowa 1980) (abandoning view that misuse is affirmative defense for view that it is part of plaintiff's burden to prove product defect and causa-

absence of misuse is built into the concepts of negligence, breach of warranty, product defectiveness, and, especially, proximate causation. Finally, the burden of proof only infrequently provides a significant tactical advantage, and it would seem that defendants typically would prefer to have a clear-cut misuse "defense," especially one created by the legislature, to argue to the court or jury.

## The Foreseeability Limitation

"The ways in which a product might be misused are, like the stars, an endless number."[43] In order to protect product sellers from liability for accidents caused by adventurous product uses, courts in recent years have almost universally limited responsibility to "foreseeable" product uses.[44] Yet, defining a principle that supposedly is one of limitation in such an amorphous manner creates enormous problems of application, which is a major reason why the misuse defense is so much easier to state than to apply. Indeed, the innate vagueness of "foreseeability" as the one definitional standard for the doctrine—its only limiting basis— renders the definition of misuse virtually meaningless as a device for determining the scope of liability in actual cases. That is, since the doctrine of product misuse is defined in terms of foreseeability, which is an illusory and confusing notion,[45] the doctrine effectively has no real definition. At the end of the day, however, as in "defining" proximate causation in terms of foreseeable risk,[46] there is at least a little comfort in the flexibility provided to the factfinder by framing the scope of responsibility for product use in terms of foreseeability.[47]

The best that the courts have been able to do, in placing at least the appearance of some halter on the foreseeability concept, is to modify it with the word "reasonable," limiting a manufacturer's responsibility to

tion). See also Henkel v. R and S Bottling Co., 323 N.W.2d 185 (Iowa 1982).

**43.** Goodman v. Stalfort, Inc., 411 F.Supp. 889, 894–95 (D.N.J. 1976) (Biunno, J.) (plaintiff burned by flashback when he poured charcoal fluid on grill after enlarging can's opening with tine of garden tool to increase its flow).

**44.** The foreseeability limitation has long been recognized. See James, Products Liability (pt. 1), 34 Tex. L. Rev. 44, 54 (1955) (citing cases from 1852). Recent statements and applications of the principle include Prince v. B.F. Asher Co., 90 P.3d 1020 (Okla. Civ. App. Div. 2004); Romito v. Red Plastic Co., 44 Cal.Rptr.2d 834 (Ct. App. 1995); Slone v. General Motors Corp., 457 S.E.2d 51 (Va. 1995); Lutz v. National Crane Corp., 884 P.2d 455 (Mont. 1994); Hicks v. Commercial Union Ins. Co., 652 So.2d 211 (Ala. 1994); Jurado v. Western Gear Works, 619 A.2d 1312 (N.J. 1993).

**45.** See, e.g., Venezia v. Miller Brewing Co., 626 F.2d 188, 191 (1st Cir. 1980) (Mass. law); Moran v. Faberge, Inc., 332

A.2d 11, 26 (Md. 1975) (O'Donnell, J., dissenting):

> It seems to me that the majority has fallen into the pitfall, recognized by Professor Prosser, who, in undertaking to analyze the treatment by the various courts of the illusory concept of "foreseeability" and noting the confusion resulting therefrom, states:
>
> > "Some 'margin of leeway' has to be left for the unusual and the unexpected. But this has opened a very wide door; and the courts have taken so much advantage of the leeway that it can scarcely be doubted that a great deal of what the ordinary man would regard as freakish, bizarre, and unpredictable has crept within the bounds of liability by the simple device of permitting the jury to foresee at least its very broad, and vague, general outlines." W. Prosser, Torts, § 43, at 269 (4th ed. 1971).

**46.** See § 12.2, above.

**47.** See Twerski, The Many Faces of Misuse: An Inquiry Into the Emerging Doc-

accidents resulting from uses that are "reasonably foreseeable."[48] Surely such a definition of the standard may be faulted for providing no further touchstone for deciding cases, but a reasonableness modification of foreseeability is plainly better than leaving it stark naked. So modifying foreseeability usefully reminds courts and juries that there are indeed reasonable limits to the kinds of uses a manufacturer fairly must consider when making design and warnings decisions.

The intrinsic vagueness of the foreseeability concept in the misuse context, which diminishes its usefulness for either ascribing or predicting liability, has been lamented by the courts.[49] While some uses, especially common ones,[50] are clearly foreseeable, and others, particularly those that are especially bizarre, are clearly unforeseeable, the great majority of uses fall in the "vast middle ground of product uses about which reasonable minds could disagree as to whether they are or should be foreseeable to the manufacturer."[51] The decisions go all over the map on the foreseeability of misuse issue, and the best that can be said is that a prudent judge will almost always recognize product misuse as a question of fact for a jury to decide.[52]

Accordingly, whether advising a seller trying to comply with the law at the time of designing and marketing its products, or a plaintiff

---

trine of Comparative Causation, 29 Mercer L. Rev. 403, 426 (1978).

**48.** See, e.g., Johnson v. Zimmer, Inc., 2004 WL 742038, at *7 (D. Minn. 2004); Brazier v. Hasbro, Inc., 2004 WL 515536, at *5 (S.D.N.Y. 2004) (liability extends to "unintended but reasonably foreseeable use"); Vaughn v. Daniels Co., 777 N.E.2d 1110, 1127 (Ind. Ct. App. 2002) ("reasonably expected uses"); Butz v. Lynch, 762 So.2d 1214 (La. Ct. App. 2000) ("reasonably anticipated use"); Leaf v. Goodyear Tire & Rubber Co., 590 N.W.2d 525 (Iowa 1999) (misuse was "reasonably foreseeable" to manufacturer); Jeld–Wen, Inc. v. Gamble, 501 S.E.2d 393, 397 (Va. 1998) (use not "*reasonably* foreseeable" as a matter of law; emphasis by court); Ellsworth v. Sherne Lingerie, Inc., 495 A.2d 348, 354 (Md. 1985); Henkel v. R and S Bottling Co., 323 N.W.2d 185, 191–92 (Iowa 1982); Newman v. Utility Trailer and Equip. Co., 564 P.2d 674, 676–77 (Or. 1977) (en banc). Compare Jurado v. Western Gear Works, 619 A.2d 1312, 1319 (N.J. 1993) ("objectively" foreseeable).

**49.** See, e.g., Venezia v. Miller Brewing Co., 626 F.2d 188, 191 (1st Cir. 1980) (Mass. law) (" 'In a sense, in retrospect almost nothing is unforeseeable.' ... One with the time and imagination and aided by hindsight no doubt can conjure up all sorts of arguably 'foreseeable' misuses of a variety of otherwise reasonable safe products."). See also Moran v. Faberge, Inc., 332 A.2d 11, 26 (Md. 1975) (O'Donnell, J., dissenting).

**50.** If people regularly use a product in a dangerous, unintended manner, the use likely is foreseeable. See, e.g., Tanner v. Shoupe, 596 N.W.2d 805 (Wis. Ct. App. 1999) (jury might find pounding on battery caps to be foreseeable); Lamer v. McKee Indus., Inc., 721 P.2d 611, 615 (Alaska 1986) ("a manufacturer should not be relieved of responsibility simply because it closes its eyes to the way its products are actually used by consumers"); Gootee v. Colt Indus., Inc., 712 F.2d 1057, 1065 (6th Cir. 1983) (use of revolver half-cock as safety is virtually universal practice).

**51.** Moran v. Faberge, Inc., 332 A.2d 11, 16 (Md. 1975).

**52.** See, e.g., id.; Tunnell v. Ford Motor Corp., 330 F.Supp.2d 748 (W.D. Va. 2004) ("The jury needs to consider all the facts relevant to how the collision happened to resolve the question of fact regarding the misuse defense."); Morgen v. Ford Motor Co., 797 N.E.2d 1146, 1149 (Ind. 2003); In re Sept. 11 Litig., 280 F.Supp.2d 279 (S.D.N.Y. 2003) (Va. law) (declining to grant summary judgment to aircraft manufacturer); Vaughn v. Daniels Co., 777 N.E.2d 1110 (Ind. Ct. App. 2002); Smith v. Bryco Arms, 131 N.M. 87 (N.M. Ct. App. 2001) (although shooting by "friend" is misuse of firearm, foreseeability is for jury); Basford v. Gray Mfg. Co., 11 P.3d 1281 (Okla. Civ. App. 2000) (reversing summary judgment); Haag v. Bongers, 589 N.W.2d 318, 329 (Neb. 1999); Price v. BIC Corp., 702 A.2d 330 (N.H. 1997); Allen v. Minnstar, Inc., 97 F.3d 1365, 1368–69 (10th Cir. 1996) (Utah law); Materials Transp. Co. v.

contemplating a lawsuit, a lawyer can only guess how the foreseeability issue will be resolved at trial. A prudent lawyer would hesitate to predict whether a judge or jury would find that a manufacturer reasonably should foresee that a young boy will hurl a beer bottle against a telephone pole;[53] a teenage girl will scent a candle by pouring cologne upon it below the flame;[54] a woman wearing a cotton flannelette nightgown inside out, with its pockets protruding, will lean over the burner of a stove, causing a pocket to come in contact with a flame;[55] a person will insist on buying shoes that are too small for her feet,[56] on buying automobile tires too large for his rims,[57] on sitting in a chair[58] or an exercise bicycle[59] too frail for one's weight (300 and 500 pounds, respectively), or on standing on an ordinary chair;[60] a car will be driven at 115 m.p.h., go out of control, and injure a third party;[61] a tire, designed for speeds to 85 m.p.h., equipped on a car designed for speeds over 100 m.p.h., will blow out at 100 m.p.h.;[62] a car's emergency brake will be left on undetected at highway speeds long enough to vaporize the hydraulic brake fluid, causing the brakes to fail;[63] the foot of an intoxicated person, who falls asleep or passes out while listening to music in his car with the engine running, will press the accelerator and cause the exhaust system to overheat and ignite;[64] a person will attempt suicide by closing herself in a car trunk without an inside release latch, change her mind, and be trapped inside for nine days thereafter;[65] an empty Clorox container will be used to store gasoline, will tip over, and the gasoline will be ignited by a spark from the motor of an electric appliance in another room;[66] a patient will walk, against doctor's orders, on his broken leg held together with a defective surgical pin designed only to stabilize the fracture, not to support the weight of a man;[67] a machine will not be properly maintained;[68] a person will pour hot Wesson Oil from the skillet back

Newman, 656 So.2d 1199, 1202 (Miss. 1995).

**53.** See Venezia v. Miller Brewing Co., 626 F.2d 188 (1st Cir. 1980) (*unforeseeable* as matter of law).

**54.** See Moran v. Faberge, Inc., 332 A.2d 11 (Md. 1975) (*foreseeable*—jury could properly so find).

**55.** See Ellsworth v. Sherne Lingerie, Inc., 495 A.2d 348 (Md. 1985) (*foreseeable* as matter of law).

**56.** See Restatement (2d) Torts § 395 cmt. *j* (*unforeseeable*). See Dubbs v. Zak Bros. Co., 175 N.E. 626 (Ohio Ct. App. 1931) (same).

**57.** See McDevitt v. Standard Oil Co. of Tex., 391 F.2d 364 (5th Cir. 1968) (Tex. law) (*unforeseeable*—by implication).

**58.** See Horne v. Liberty Furniture Co., 452 So.2d 204 (La. Ct. App. 1984) (*foreseeable*—by implication).

**59.** See Dunne v. Wal–Mart Stores, Inc., 679 So.2d 1034 (La. Ct. App. 1996) (*foreseeable*).

**60.** See Restatement (2d) Torts § 395, cmt. *k* (*foreseeable*).

**61.** See Schemel v. General Motors Corp., 384 F.2d 802 (7th Cir. 1967) (Ind. law) (no duty to foresee such grossly careless misuse), overruled on other grounds by Huff v. White Motor Corp., 565 F.2d 104, 106 n.1, 109–110 (7th Cir. 1977) (Ind. law).

**62.** See LeBouef v. Goodyear Tire & Rubber Co., 451 F.Supp. 253 (W.D. La. 1978) (*foreseeable*).

**63.** Knapp v. Hertz Corp., 375 N.E.2d 1349 (Ill. App. Ct. 1978) (*foreseeable*).

**64.** Griffith v. Chrysler Corp., 2003 WL 21500037 (Ohio Ct. App. 2003) (*unforeseeable*).

**65.** Daniell v. Ford Motor Co., 581 F.Supp. 728 (D.N.M. 1984) (*unforeseeable* as matter of law).

**66.** See Taylor v. General Elec. Co., 505 A.2d 190 (N.J. Super. Ct. App. Div. 1986) (*foreseeable* as matter of law).

**67.** See Stewart v. Von Solbrig Hosp., Inc., 321 N.E.2d 428 (Ill. App. Ct. 1974) (misuse as matter of law).

**68.** See Wilson v. Crouse–Hinds Co., 556 F.2d 870 (8th Cir. 1977) (Iowa law) (*foreseeable*—jury could so find).

into the bottle, and then recap the bottle, causing it to explode;[69] "burning alcohol," sold only for professional dental use, will be drunk by penal farm inmate dental assistants who then go blind;[70] a screen on a second story window will not withstand the pressure of a baby boy waving good-bye to his mother;[71] a doctor will transplant synthetic fibers, normally used for wigs and hairpieces, into a patient's scalp as a treatment for baldness, causing irritation and infection;[72] a grocery shopper who trips will hope that a shopping cart does not scoot away when he grabs for it to save himself from falling;[73] the owner of a riding lawn mower will attach a wooden "dog box" to the mower and place a two-year-old child in the box who will fall out and be run over by the mower;[74] a youth will tilt or rock a soft-drink vending machine, to dispense a can without payment, causing the machine to fall upon and kill him;[75] a teenage boy will hang himself with a rope on a swing set as a joke to impress the girls;[76] a youth, thinking the safety is on, will point a BB gun at his friend's head and pull the trigger;[77] a small child will eat a "spit devil" firework wrapped in plain red paper that looks like candy;[78] a baby will drink bright red furniture polish that looks like a soft drink;[79] an adult will stand on a closet shelf;[80] a child will open and stand on an oven door to see what is cooking on the stove, causing the stove and a pot of boiling water to topple over;[81] a boy, while riding a canister vacuum cleaner like a toy car will be injured when his penis slips through an opening into the cleaner's fan;[82] children will play with a gas can without a child-proof top;[83] or that terrorists will use fertilizer[84] or an airplane[85] to blow up the World Trade Center.

---

**69.** See Chandler v. Hunt Food & Indus., Inc., Prod.Liab.Rep. (CCH) ¶ 5969 (Tenn. 1968) (*unforeseeable*—by implication).

**70.** See Barnes v. Litton Indus. Prod., Inc., 555 F.2d 1184 (4th Cir. 1977) (Va. law) (*foreseeable*—jury could properly so find).

**71.** See Jeld–Wen, Inc. v. Gamble, 501 S.E.2d 393 (Va. 1998) (*unforeseeable* as matter of law).

**72.** See Berg v. Underwood's Hair Adaption Process, Inc., 751 F.2d 136, 137 (2d Cir. 1984) (N.Y. law) (*unforeseeable*—no duty as matter of law).

**73.** See Smith v. Technibilt, Inc., 791 S.W.2d 247 (Tex. App. 1990) (*unforeseeable* as matter of law).

**74.** Erkson v. Sears, Roebuck & Co., 841 S.W.2d 207 (Mo. Ct. App. 1992) (*unforeseeable* as matter of law).

**75.** Compare Oden v. Pepsi Cola Bottling Co., 621 So.2d 953 (Ala. 1993) (*unforeseeable*—one may not impose liability on another for consequences of one's own act of moral turpitude), with Morgan v. Cavalier Acquisition Corp., 432 S.E.2d 915 (N.C. Ct. App. 1993) (*foreseeable*—jury could so find); Ridenour v. Bat 'Em Out, 707 A.2d 1093 (N.J. Super. Ct. App. Div. 1998) (change machine: *foreseeable*).

**76.** See Smith v. Holmes, 606 N.E.2d 627 (Ill. App. Ct. 1992) (*unforeseeable* as matter of law).

**77.** Sherk v. Daisy–Heddon, 450 A.2d 615 (Pa. 1982) (*foreseeable*, but danger was obvious and warned against).

**78.** Victory Sparkler & Specialty Co. v. Latimer, 53 F.2d 3 (8th Cir. 1931) (Mo. law) (*foreseeable*—jury could properly so find).

**79.** Spruill v. Boyle–Midway, Inc., 308 F.2d 79, 83–84 (4th Cir. 1962) (Va. law) (*foreseeable*—jury could properly so find).

**80.** Michael v. G & M Home Builders, Inc., 2003 WL 21634428 (Mich. Ct. App. 2003).

**81.** Ritter v. Narragansett Elec. Co., 283 A.2d 255 (R.I. 1971) (*foreseeable*—jury could properly so find).

**82.** Larue v. National Union Elec. Corp., 571 F.2d 51 (1st Cir. 1978) (Me. law) (*unforeseeable*—as matter of law).

**83.** Compare Simpson v. Standard Container Co., 527 A.2d 1337 (Md. Ct. Spec. App. 1987) (*unforeseeable* as matter of law, where label on can warned against storing in living area), with Keller v. Welles Dept. Store of Racine, 276 N.W.2d 319, 324 (Wis. Ct. App. 1979) (foreseeable that "incurably curious" children might taste gasoline stored in a can on the floor, or, while playing "mow the lawn" or "gas station," might pour gasoline from the can).

---

**84–85.** See notes 84 & 85 on page 852.

If there is a common thread in the decisions on the meaning of the "foreseeability" limitation to product uses, it is one of limiting a seller's responsibility to uses that are *fair*. While the *fairness* of a product's use provides little more direct guidance than the notion of foreseeability, it at least provides a depth and richness for embracing all the equities of a particular case—quite similar to the *reasonableness* of foreseeability of use. An important aspect in evaluating the fairness or foreseeability of particular uses is whether a reasonable consumer might fairly *expect* the product to be able to withstand that use.[86] As one court explained, misuse may be viewed as a "use or handling so unusual that the average consumer could not reasonably expect the product to be designed and manufactured to withstand it—a use which the seller, therefore, need not anticipate and provide for."[87] Applying this principle to deny recovery to a boy whose eye was injured when he threw a discarded beer bottle against a telephone pole shattering the glass bottle, another court concluded that a reasonable consumer could expect nothing else.[88]

While the consumer expectations test has withered considerably as a principal test of product defectiveness,[89] a consumer expectations standard in some cases provides a sound foundation for defining the limits of use for which a manufacturer fairly may be held accountable. Yet the usefulness of a consumer expectation standard in the misuse context, as when ascertaining a product's defectiveness, depends upon the type of product and risk at issue. Consumers have quite well-defined and reasonable expectations about the performance limits of some products, especially more simple ones, but they often have no idea of the limitations of complex products operating in complex environments, such as the extent to which an automobile is or should be able to withstand a particular type of crash.[90] Thus, in a case where the hazards from a particular type of misuse are clear, a court might fairly conclude that the use was not reasonably foreseeable if it was one that a reasonable consumer would not expect the product safely to withstand.

Whether one views the misuse issue in terms of the foreseeability of the plaintiff's use, the presence or absence of a defect, or the presence or absence of proximate cause, the result in each case depends ultimately upon the reasonable foreseeability, or fairness, of the plaintiff's particular use. If the manufacturer or other product seller reasonably should have contemplated and guarded against the risk, the defendant is subject

---

**84.** Port Auth. of N.Y. and N.J. v. Arcadian Corp., 189 F.3d 305 (3d Cir. 1999) (N.J. law) (manufacturers of fertilizer products could not reasonably foresee that their products would be used in 1993 World Trade Center terrorist attack).

**85.** In re Sept. 11 Litig., 280 F.Supp.2d 279, 307 (S.D.N.Y. 2003) (Va. law) (plane manufacturer of airliner might reasonably foresee that failure to design secure cockpit could facilitate hijacking that would substantially increase risk to people and buildings on ground).

**86.** See note 11, above.

**87.** Findlay v. Copeland Lumber Co., 509 P.2d 28, 31 (Or. 1973).

**88.** "No reasonable consumer would expect anything but that a glass beer bottle . . . would fail to safely withstand the type of purposeful abuse involved here." Venezia v. Miller Brewing Co., 626 F.2d 188, 191 (1st Cir. 1980) (Mass. law).

**89.** See § 5.6, above.

**90.** See, e.g., Soule v. General Motors Corp., 882 P.2d 298 (Cal. 1994). See generally § 8.6, above.

to liability for the harm; if the plaintiff put the product to an unforeseeable, unfair use, the defendant simply is not liable.

### Failure to Follow Warnings and Instructions

A user's failure to follow a manufacturer's warnings of danger or instructions on safe use provides a special form of misuse which ordinarily should bar recovery whenever the danger from noncompliance is evident, the noncompliance is a substantial cause of the plaintiff's harm, and there is no simple way or apparent reason for the manufacturer to design the danger out of the product. Despite common knowledge (and hence foreseeability) that users often ignore warnings and instructions, many courts, and a few legislatures,[91] have long had little sympathy with plaintiffs who are injured because they ignore warnings and instructions.[92] Comment *j* to the *Restatement (Second) of Torts* § 402A states the rule quite clearly: "Where warning is given, the seller may reasonably assume that it will be read and heeded; and a product bearing such a warning, which is safe for use if it is followed, is not in a defective condition, nor is it unreasonably dangerous." Accordingly, if there was no practical way or reason for the manufacturer to design the danger away, courts have widely ruled that a user's failure to read or heed adequate instructions for safe use, sometimes characterized as "misuse," bars recovery.[93] It generally is both logical and fair to preclude recovery

**91.** Statutes in at least Arizona, New Jersey, and North Carolina provide blanket protection to a defendant for injuries resulting from the plaintiff's violation of a warning or instruction. See Ariz. Rev. Stat. § 12–683; N.J. Stat. Ann. § 2A:58c–4; N.C. Gen. Stat. 99B–4(1). New Jersey's provision limits this defense to cases involving "adequate" warnings and instructions; Arizona's and North Carolina's do not, although North Carolina's is limited to warnings and instructions of which the user reasonably should have been aware. A Michigan statute's definition of misuse includes uses contrary to warnings and instructions, Mich. Comp. Laws Ann. § 600.2945(e), but it provides an immunity only for unforeseeable misuse. Id. at § 600.2947(2).

**92.** An early example is Fredendall v. Abraham & Straus, Inc., 18 N.E.2d 11 (N.Y. 1938).

**93.** "The seller is entitled to have his warnings and instructions followed; and when they are disregarded, and injury results, he is not liable." W. Prosser, The Law of Torts § 102, at 669 (4th ed. 1971). See, e.g., Barnard v. Saturn Corp., 790 N.E.2d 1023 (Ind. Ct. App. 2003) (motorist jacked up car on incline and crawled underneath in manner expressly warned against on jack, in manual, and on spare tire cover); Jay v. Moog Auto., 652 N.W.2d 872, 881–82 (Neb. 2002) (mechanic's eye injured when he failed to use retaining pin while operating compressor; disregarding warnings and

instructions might be misuse); Halliday v. Sturm, Ruger & Co., 770 A.2d 1072 (Md. 2001) (parent failed to properly store handgun pursuant to warnings provided–unforeseeable misuse); Hood v. Ryobi Amer. Corp., 181 F.3d 608 (4th Cir. 1999) (Md. law) (user ignored seven clear warnings against removing saw blade guards); Kampen v. American Isuzu Motors, Inc., 157 F.3d 306, 309 (5th Cir. 1998) (en banc) (La. law) (plaintiff crushed when jack supporting car collapsed; failed to read instructions in manual and spare tire compartment not to "get beneath the car"); Hughes v. Massey–Ferguson, Inc., 490 N.W.2d 75 (Iowa Ct. App. 1992) (farmer walked on 3" rim over auger without first shutting off corn head as warnings instructed); Bell v. Montgomery Ward, 792 F.Supp. 500 (W.D. La. 1992) (person mowing lawn, who lost two toes in mower when he slipped on wet grass, ignored warnings to keep guards in place and feet away from blade, and not to wear tennis shoes or to mow on wet grass or on slopes steeper than 15 degrees); Uptain v. Huntington Lab, Inc., 723 P.2d 1322, 1326 (Colo. 1986) (housekeeper used bare hands to wring out mop used to apply bathroom cleaning solution containing 23% hydrochloric acid; label warned against skin contact to avoid chemical burns and to wash skin area well if contact occurred); Peterson v. Parke Davis & Co., 705 P.2d 1001 (Colo. Ct. App. 1985) (doctor failed to read or heed warnings and instructions in package insert, leaving patient on toxic

to a user who knowingly ignores the admonitions of a manufacturer's full and fair warnings and instructions, for the user by so doing knowingly pushes the product unfairly beyond its stated safety capabilities. But if the disregarded warning or instruction is itself inadequate, so that the user is not fairly informed about the danger, then the failure to follow warnings or instructions is foreseeable and, generally, excusable as well. In such a case, "if the injury resulting from foreseeable misuse of a product is one which an adequate warning concerning the use of the product would likely prevent, such misuse is no defense."[94] Moreover, because of the foreseeability that warnings may be disregarded, modern courts widely hold that manufacturers have an independent duty to design away dangers if there is a reasonable way to do so.[95]

## Comparative Fault

Whether, and to what extent, "product misuse" should be merged into a jurisdiction's system of comparative fault, and so treated as a damage-reducing factor rather than as a total bar, is a vexing problem which has yet to be carefully addressed by most courts and legislatures. Viewing misuse merely as another plaintiff misconduct "defense," some courts and legislatures have simply merged it into their comparative fault schemes.[96] In those states, misuse will reduce but not bar a plaintiff's recovery, unless, in modified comparative fault states, the plaintiff's fault is found to exceed that of the defendant.[97] Such a merger

drug despite contra-indications); Watson v. Uniden Corp. of Am., 775 F.2d 1514 (11th Cir. 1985) (Ga. law) (failure to follow instructions is not use in "normal" manner for purposes of implied warranty claim but jury issue on negligence and strict liability warnings adequacy claims); Sturm, Ruger & Co. v. Bloyd, 586 S.W.2d 19 (Ky. 1979) (owner of six-shooter revolver left hammer resting on firing pin in line with loaded cartridge, contrary to explicit instructions and warnings; gun discharged when dropped on floor).

**94.** Bristol–Myers Co. v. Gonzales, 548 S.W.2d 416, 422–23 (Tex. App. 1976), rev'd on other grounds 561 S.W.2d 801 (Tex. 1978). See also Lia v. Domaine Mumm, Inc., 2003 WL 21260710 (Cal. Ct. App. 2003) (admonition not to corkscrew champagne bottle did not warn of danger from prying cork fragments with knife); Harless v. Boyle–Midway Div., Am. Home Prod., 594 F.2d 1051, 1055 (5th Cir. 1979) (Fla. law) ("It seems both confusing and internally inconsistent to ask a jury who has previously concluded that the label was *inadequate* to consider the defense of failure to read an *adequate* label."); Johnson v. Johnson Chem. Co., 588 N.Y.S.2d 607 (App. Div. 1992) (failure to read roach bomb instruction to extinguish pilot lights or open flames); Huynh v. Ingersoll–Rand, 20 Cal. Rptr.2d 296 (Ct. App. 1993).

**95.** See, e.g., Lewis v. American Cyanamid Co., 682 A.2d 724, 732 (N.J. Super. Ct. App. Div. 1996):

If there is an objectively foreseeable likelihood that a product will be subject to misuse and that that misuse will endanger users despite appropriate warnings, then warnings alone will not satisfy the manufacturer's duty. In addition to providing warnings, the manufacturer must also take all other feasible measures required by a risk-utility analysis to make even anticipated misusers of the product reasonably safe.

Accord, Products Liability Restatement § 2 cmt. *l*. See § 6.2, above.

**96.** See, e.g., Tungate v. Bridgestone Corp., 2004 WL 771191, *7 (S.D. Ind. 2004); Jett v. Ford Motor Co., 84 P.3d 219, 221 (Or. Ct. App. 2004); Morgen v. Ford Motor Co., 797 N.E.2d 1146, 1148 (Ind. 2003) ("the defense of misuse is not a complete defense, but instead is an element of comparative fault"); Veliz v. Rental Serv. Corp. USA, Inc., 313 F.Supp.2d 1317, 1328 (M.D. Fla. 2003) ("product misuse reduces a plaintiff's recovery in proportion to his or her own comparative fault").

**97.** See, e.g., Barnard v. Saturn Corp., 790 N.E.2d 1023 (Ind. Ct. App. 2003) (motorist jacked up car on incline and crawled underneath in manner expressly warned against on jack, in manual, and on spare tire cover; no reasonable trier of fact could have found that plaintiff was less than 50% at fault); Standard Havens Prod., Inc. v.

requires confronting the issue of what types of misuse will be treated on a comparative fault basis, and whether unforeseeable misuse will still serve as a total bar. At least a couple of courts have ruled mysteriously that a plaintiff's unforeseeable misuse is somehow subject to comparison with the defendant's conduct or a product defect, "that where an unreasonably dangerous defect of a product and the plaintiff's assumption of risk or *unforeseeable misuse* of the product are concurring proximate causes of the injury suffered, the trier of fact must compare those concurring causes to determine the respective percentages" for the apportionment of damages.[98]

However, it seems more logical to view *unforeseeable* misuse as lying entirely outside the scope of responsibility of manufacturers and other sellers and, hence, outside the ambit of comparative fault. Because a seller has no duty to guard against unforeseeable product risks, there ordinarily is no seller fault or product defect in such cases to compare.[99]

To achieve a fair and sensible result in most cases, and to avoid an utterly confusing mixture of doctrines, the best approach (if not prohibited by statute) is to consider a user's *foreseeable* misuse as any other kind of comparative fault for allocation to the plaintiff. On the other hand, if a substantial cause of the plaintiff's injury was his or her *unforeseeable* misuse of a product, then the plaintiff's conduct generally should be considered the sole proximate cause of the harm and so bar any recovery whatsoever.[100] Such a bright-line rule for unforeseeable misuse in comparative fault jurisdictions might seem crude, and juries allowed to allocate responsibility between a product defect and a plaintiff's unforeseeable misuse might conceivably be able to do better justice in some small set of cases. But the number of cases in which the plaintiff's injury is substantially traceable to both a product defect and the plaintiff's unforeseeable misuse (which is not the sole proximate cause of an accident) is surely very small. Like counting angels on a pinhead, the very concept of such combined causation is difficult to grasp and even

Benitez, 648 So.2d 1192 (Fla. 1994) (negligence, following similar holding on strict liability); Elliot v. Sears, Roebuck & Co., 642 A.2d 709 (Conn. 1994) (strict liability).

At least a couple of states have enacted legislation accomplishing this result See Idaho Code § 6–1405(3) (misuse reduces claimant's damages according to comparative responsibility; "misuse" defined as "when the product user does not act in a manner that would be expected of an ordinary reasonably prudent person who is likely to use the product in the same or similar circumstances"); Mo. Ann. Stat. § 537.765(3) (for comparative fault apportionment, plaintiff's "fault" includes product uses (1) not reasonably anticipated by the manufacturer, and (2) for purposes not intended by the manufacturer).

**98.** Mauch v. Manufacturers Sales & Serv., Inc., 345 N.W.2d 338, 348 (N.D. 1984) (emphasis added), citing General Mo-

tors v. Hopkins, 548 S.W.2d 344 (Tex. 1977) (heroic attempt to explicate and justify this nonsense), overruled on other grounds by Turner v. General Motors Corp., 584 S.W.2d 844 (Tex. 1979), and by Duncan v. Cessna Aircraft Co., 665 S.W.2d 414 (Tex. 1984).

**99.** See, e.g., Cigna v. Oy Saunatec Ltd., 241 F.3d 1 (1st Cir. 2001) (Mass. law) (unforeseeable misuse totally bars recovery, whereas foreseeable misuse factors into fault and damages allocation); States v. R.D. Werner Co., 799 P.2d 427 (Colo. Ct. App. 1990) (unlike comparative negligence, which diminishes recovery, unforeseeable misuse of ladder from which plaintiff fell goes to causation and completely bars recovery, regardless of defective condition).

**100.** This is the approach taken by most courts, and it is adopted by the Uniform Comparative Fault Act.

more difficult to put to use.[101] In a real world where the law can only hope to do substantial justice most of the time, rather than perfect justice all of the time, a simple rule that bars liability altogether if a plaintiff's unforeseeable product misuse was a substantial cause of the harm appears to be the fairest way, both within and outside of comparative fault, to resolve most cases in a commonsense and practical way.[102]

## § 13.6  DEFENSES TO WARRANTY CLAIMS

How a plaintiff's misconduct affects liability in warranty is one of the most confused issues in all of products liability law.[1] To a large extent, the confusion springs from the long, uneasy relationship between warranty law and tort. The law of warranty, one must not forget, is "a freak hybrid born of the illicit intercourse of tort and contract."[2] But that origin lies in the distant past, and most courts now view warranty law as a part of the law of contracts.[3] In the contractual warranty context, where breach of warranty is predicated upon the falsity of a seller's representation or the failure of its goods to meet a commercial norm, rather than upon the seller's fault, a defense based upon a user's contributory negligence or dangerously venturous misbehavior seems oddly out of place. Yet, particularly in cases involving personal injuries resulting from a user's unforeseeably hazardous or knowingly dangerous and unreasonable product use, the courts have shown a manifest reluctance to accept the proposition that such misconduct is out of bounds simply because a warranty claim sounds in contract.

A variety of conflicting overlaps in legal categories add to the confusion. While the doctrine of strict products liability in tort (which itself developed from warranty law)[4] is largely a creature of the common law, the law of warranty is now principally enshrined, via Article 2 of the Uniform Commercial Code, in statute.[5] In addition, there are conflicts between differing definitions of the tort-based misconduct defenses of the common law, on the one hand, and the misconduct defenses enacted

**101.** The confusion from combining doctrines (comparative fault and misuse) and sources of law (courts and legislatures) is illustrated by Jimenez v. Sears, Roebuck & Co., 904 P.2d 861 (Ariz. 1995), although Martone, J.'s concurring opinion makes good sense: "[T]rue misuse (unforeseeable, sole cause) continues to be an all or nothing defense. . . . Foreseeable misuse (concurring cause) is really contributory negligence, and is now a comparative defense to a products case." Id. at 873.

**102.** When a product is defective and the user puts it to an unforeseeable use, "then the accident was not proximately caused by the product defect." Prosser and Keeton on Torts § 102, at 711.

### § 13.6

**1.** See B. Clark & C. Smith, The Law of Product Warranties § 12:10, at 12–27 (2d ed. 2002); R. Nordstrom, Law of Sales §§ 81–84 (1970); White and Summers, UCC § 11.8; Levine, Buyer's Conduct as Affecting the Extent of Manufacturer's Liability in Warranty, 52 Minn. L. Rev. 627 (1968); Annot., 4 A.L.R.3d 501 (1965) (warranty misconduct defenses in general); Annot., 75 A.L.R.4th 538 (1989) (§§ 16–20) (warranty misconduct defenses to claims of failure to provide safety devices).

**2.** Prosser, The Assault Upon the Citadel (Strict Liability to the Consumer), 69 Yale L.J. 1099, 1126 (1960). See also Note, 42 Harv. L. Rev. 411, 414–15 (1929). See generally §§ 1.2, 4.3, and 5.2, above.

**3.** See, e.g., Pritchard v. Liggett & Myers Tobacco Co., 350 F.2d 479 (3d Cir. 1965) (Pa. law); Jarnot v. Ford Motor Co., 156 A.2d 568 (Pa. Super. Ct. 1959).

**4.** This development occurred in America during the 1950s and early 1960s. See §§ 5.2 and 5.3, above.

**5.** See ch. 4, above.

in recent products liability reform statutes, on the other. Further, user misconduct is handled in a variety of ways under various systems of comparative fault, most created by legislation but some by common law. In the warranty setting, many courts compound the confusion by altering traditional tort law definitions and effects of various forms of plaintiff misbehavior.[6] In an attempt to avoid this quagmire, some courts have simply abandoned all use of the traditional tort law terms used to describe plaintiff misconduct.[7]

The issue examined here is what the effect should be on a claim for breach of express or implied warranty against a product seller if a plaintiff carelessly uses a product, ignores warnings and instructions, deliberately and unreasonably engages a product danger, or puts a product to an unforeseeably dangerous use. Stated otherwise, do the tort law misconduct defenses of contributory negligence, assumption of risk, and product misuse apply to warranty claims; are there any misconduct defenses unique to warranty claims; and what is the effect of comparative fault doctrine on warranty misconduct defenses? While the developing warranty law on these questions in some states roughly parallels the law applied in strict products liability in tort,[8] and while eventual convergence is not unfathomable,[9] the law on warranty misconduct defenses is teetering at the edge of chaos. The best that can be done here is to describe the principal approaches the courts have taken and to indicate which appear most logical and fair.

### Contributory Negligence; Assumption of Risk

In 1966, Dean Prosser wrote that "[s]uperficially the warranty cases ... are in a state of complete contradiction and confusion as to the defense of contributory negligence."[10] Some early cases held that contributory negligence should simply bar recovery in warranty, reasoning, for example, that "[w]arranty is not insurance, and there is nothing in this contract to indicate that either party supposed the defendant was to

**6.** "Some courts maintain that contributory negligence is no defense but hold that the defendant may parade the same misconduct of the plaintiff before the jury to show a lack of proximate cause." White & Summers § 11–8, at 408, citing Ford Motor Co. v. Lee, 224 S.E.2d 168, 170 (Ga. App. 1976) ("In an action predicated on a breach of warranty, there is no defense per se of contributory negligence, but such defense presents a jury question as to whether the injuries resulted from the breach."), aff'd in part, rev'd in part, 229 S.E.2d 379 (Ga. 1976). See also Imperial Die Casting Co. v. Covil Insulation Co., 216 S.E.2d 532, 534 (S.C. 1975).

**7.** See Huebert v. Federal Pac. Elec. Co., 494 P.2d 1210, 1216 (Kan. 1972) (noting that several courts have abandoned use of "contributory negligence" and "assumption of risk" terms to avoid semantic problems in implied warranty cases, and holding that such concepts "in their normal meaning are

not defenses" to actions for breach of express warranty).

**8.** See, e.g., Duff v. Bonner Bldg. Supply, Inc., 666 P.2d 650 (Idaho 1983) (assumption of risk and misuse are defenses to breach of warranty actions, but contributory negligence is not); Gregory v. White Truck & Equip. Co., 323 N.E.2d 280 (Ind. Ct. App. 1975) (same).

**9.** See H. Woods and B. Deere, Comparative Fault § 14:17, at 339 (3d ed. 1996).

**10.** Prosser, The Fall of the Citadel (Strict Liability to the Consumer), 50 Minn. L. Rev. 791, 838 (1966). On whether contributory negligence is a defense to an implied warranty action, "the authorities are hopelessly divided." Gardner v. Coca Cola Bottling Co., 127 N.W.2d 557, 562 (Minn. 1964). See also Levine, Buyer's Conduct as Affecting the Extent of Manufacturer's Liability in Warranty, 52 Minn. L. Rev. 627 (1968).

answer for the plaintiff's carelessness."[11] Occasional decisions still hold that a plaintiff's contributory negligence should bar recovery.[12] But many courts long have held to the contrary—that a consumer's contributory negligence should be irrelevant to warranty claims, which lie in contract or assumpsit,[13] particularly in cases involving defective food.[14] Many of the more recent cases take the same approach, holding that simple contributory negligence[15] has no effect on a plaintiff's claim for breach of warranty.[16]

Prosser's study of the cases revealed that courts would not bar recovery on grounds of contributory negligence if a plaintiff's only fault lay in failing to inspect or discover a danger in a product, but "if he discovers the defect, or knows the danger arising from it, and proceeds

---

**11.** Razey v. J.B. Colt Co., 94 N.Y.S. 59, 61 (App. Div. 1905) (plaintiff used gas generator in room with lighted gas jet). See also Eisenbach v. Gimbel Bros., Inc., 24 N.E.2d 131 (N.Y. 1939); Finks v. Viking Refrigerators, Inc., 147 S.W.2d 124 (Mo. App. 1940); Walker v. Hickory Packing Co., 16 S.E.2d 668 (N.C. 1941); Natale v. Pepsi–Cola Co., 182 N.Y.S.2d 404 (App. Div. 1959); Posey v. Pensacola Tractor & Equip. Co., 138 So.2d 777 (Fla. Dist. Ct. App. 1962); Dallison v. Sears, Roebuck & Co., 313 F.2d 343 (10th Cir. 1962) (Colo. law) (sole proximate cause of harm to plaintiff, burned when match ignited her nightgown, was her contributory negligence in smoking and using matches in bed while in semiconscious state induced by potent sleeping pill).

**12.** See, e.g., Nicholson v. American Safety Util. Corp., 488 S.E.2d 240, 244 (N.C. 1997) (products liability statute); Cline v. Sawyer, 600 P.2d 725 (Wyo. 1979).

**13.** See, e.g., Pritchard v. Liggett & Myers Tobacco Co., 350 F.2d 479 (3d Cir. 1965) (Pa. law); Jarnot v. Ford Motor Co., 156 A.2d 568 (Pa. Super. Ct. 1959).

**14.** "Contributory negligence, in general, is a defense only to actions grounded on negligence." Kassouf v. Lee Bros., Inc., 26 Cal.Rptr. 276, 278 (Ct. App. 1962) (citing 2 Harper, James, and Gray, Law of Torts § 22.4, at 1210). In Kassouf, after purchasing groceries including a Hershey "Mr. Goodbar" at defendant's food store, plaintiff sat down in a chair to read the newspaper beside a table on which she placed the candy bar. "While reading, she reached with one hand and took the candy bar from the table. Without looking, and with one hand, she opened one end of the wrapper and slid the bar partially out from it. Using this one-handed method, she broke off pieces, one after another, and put them into her mouth. From the outset she noticed that the bar 'didn't taste just right,' but she assumed this was because she hadn't eaten all day. She had consumed about one-third of the candy bar by the time she bit into a mushy worm. When she looked at the bar,

she saw that it was covered with worms and webbing; worms were crawling out of the chocolate and the webbing had little eggs 'hanging onto it.'" Id. at 277. Sickened from ingesting the contaminated candy, plaintiff sued the grocery store for breach of warranty of merchantability, and the jury found for plaintiff. Defendant appealed the trial court's refusal to instruct the jury that plaintiff had a duty "to take reasonable precautions for her own safety in the handling, inspection, and consumption" of the candy bar. Id. *Held,* affirmed. There is no duty to look at and feel a candy bar prior to biting into it.

Compare Coulter v. American Bakeries Co., 530 So.2d 1009 (Fla. Dist. Ct. App. 1988) (metal wire in doughnut—comparative fault generally applicable to implied warranty claims, but sucking on doughnut while sipping milk, rather than chewing the doughnut properly, was not faulty conduct that could reduce recovery).

**15.** On the contributory negligence defense to products liability claims in tort, see § 13.2, above. "Simple" or "ordinary" contributory negligence—negligently failing to discover or guard against the possibility of a defect—is to be distinguished from a plaintiff's assumption of risk in voluntarily, and perhaps unreasonably, encountering a known and appreciated danger. On the assumption of risk defense to products liability claims in tort, see § 13.4, above.

**16.** See, e.g., Jones v. Ford Motor Co., 559 S.E.2d 592, 605 (Va. 2002); Keaton v. A.B.C. Drug Co., 467 S.E.2d 558 (Ga. 1996); Goulet v. Whitin Mach. Works, Inc., 568 N.E.2d 1158 (Mass. App. Ct. 1991); Wallace v. Owens–Illinois, Inc., 389 S.E.2d 155 (S.C. Ct. App. 1989) (illuminating analysis by Bell, J.); Colter v. Barber–Greene Co., 525 N.E.2d 1305 (Mass. 1988); Correia v. Firestone Tire & Rubber Co., 446 N.E.2d 1033 (Mass. 1983) (comparative fault); Williams v. Brown Mfg. Co., 261 N.E.2d 305 (Ill. 1970).

nevertheless deliberately to encounter it by making use of the product, his conduct is the kind of contributory negligence which overlaps assumption of risk; and on either theory his recovery is barred."[17] This is precisely the position taken in *Restatement (Second) of Torts* § 402A comment *n* for strict liability in tort.[18] While there is some thin authority to the contrary,[19] the courts quite widely agree that a plaintiff's negligent assumption of risk—his or her unreasonable decision to encounter a known and appreciated product danger—properly bars recovery in warranty as well.[20]

## Misuse

Many courts have applied a misuse defense to warranty claims quite similarly to how it is applied to products liability claims based in tort.[21] Thus, early warranty cases denied recovery if the injury arose out of a product use not *intended* by the manufacturer.[22] More recently, courts have limited the implied warranty of merchantability, which requires that products be "fit" for their "ordinary purposes,"[23] to uses that are reasonably *foreseeable*.[24] In other words, a seller's implied warranties do

**17.** Prosser, The Fall of the Citadel (Strict Liability to the Consumer), 50 Minn. L. Rev. 791, 838–40 (1966).

**18.** See §§ 13.2 and 13.4, above.

**19.** See, e.g., Wood v. Bass Pro Shops, Inc., 462 S.E.2d 101, 103 (Va. 1995), noting that implied warranty actions are *ex contractu*, and holding that "the tort or *ex delicto* defense of assumption of the risk is not applicable in an action for breach of an implied warranty." Yet, true to principles of warranty, the court held that liability is barred if a defect is "known, visible or obvious" to plaintiff. See §§ 4.3 and 4.7, above.

**20.** Massachusetts has the most extensive jurisprudence on this point. See, e.g., Velleca v. Uniroyal Tire Co., 630 N.E.2d 297 (Mass. App. Ct. 1994); Barry v. Stop & Shop Cos., 507 N.E.2d 1062 (Mass. App. Ct. 1987) (plaintiff's hand cut by rotating blade of lawn mower when she attempted to push misplaced baffle back into place); Allen v. Chance Mfg. Co., 494 N.E.2d 1324 (Mass. 1986); Correia v. Firestone Tire & Rubber Co., 446 N.E.2d 1033 (Mass. 1983). See also Epstein v. Eastman Kodak Co., 638 N.Y.S.2d 490 (App. Div. 1996); Gillespie v. American Motors Corp., 317 S.E.2d 32 (N.C. App. 1984) (where buyers of vehicle complained of noxious fumes in passenger compartment immediately upon purchase, their contributory negligence in driving vehicle for three years thereafter, despite their doctor's advice not to ride therein, barred recovery in warranty for resulting injuries); Hiigel v. General Motors Corp., 525 P.2d 1198 (Colo. App. Ct. 1974), rev'd on other grounds, 544 P.2d 983 (Colo. 1975) (as modified, Feb. 9, 1976); Murphy v. Eaton, Yale & Towne, Inc., 444 F.2d 317 (6th

Cir. 1971) (Mich. law); Williams v. Brown Mfg. Co., 261 N.E.2d 305 (Ill. 1970); Brackett v. Johnson, 273 A.2d 499 (Conn. Super. Ct. 1970) (plaintiff placed hand in chute of snowblower he knew to be defective). Compare Freeman v. Case Corp., 118 F.3d 1011 (4th Cir. 1997) (Va. law) (noting that liability barred if defect was "known, visible or obvious" to plaintiff, but ruling that obviousness was jury issue). See generally Clark and Smith, Product Warranties 2d § 12.10, at 12–28 ("the warranty cases generally parallel the § 402A cases"); White and Summers, UCC § 11.8, at 408–09 ("courts agree that the more specific form of contributory misconduct called 'assumption of the risk' bars a plaintiff's recovery in either strict tort or warranty," consistent with § 402A cmt. *n*).

**21.** On the misuse defense to products liability claims in tort, see § 13.5, above.

**22.** See, e.g., Cheli v. Cudahy Bros. Co., 255 N.W. 414 (Mich. 1934), overruled on other grounds, Hill v. Husky Briquetting, Inc., 223 N.W.2d 290 (Mich. 1974); Ross v. Diamond Match Co., 102 A.2d 858 (Me. 1953); Silverman v. Swift & Co., 107 A.2d 277 (Conn. 1954); Preston v. Up–Right, Inc., 52 Cal.Rptr. 679 (Ct. App. 1966). See generally Levine, Buyer's Conduct as Affecting the Extent of Manufacturer's Liability in Warranty, 52 Minn. L. Rev. 627 (1968).

**23.** In UCC § 2–314(2)(c), discussed below.

**24.** See, e.g., Shuras v. Integrated Project Servs., Inc., 190 F.Supp.2d 194, 199 (D. Mass. 2002) ("The touchstone of a negligent design or warranty analysis is foresee-

not extend to abnormal use, or unforeseeable misuse, whether by the user or another.[25]

For example, in *Venezia v. Miller Brewing Company*,[26] a young boy's eye was injured when he threw a discarded Miller Beer bottle against a telephone pole, shattering the bottle. In his warranty claim against Miller and the bottle manufacturers for failing to make their bottles strong enough to withstand this type of use, the federal appeals court noted that the Massachusetts high court had previously found no breach of warranty of merchantability where a plaintiff was injured by breaking glass while trying to pry the cover off a glass baby food jar with a beer can type of opener.[27] While noting that "[t]he linchpin of the warranty claim ... is thus the proper scope of the term ordinary purpose," and that "at first blush it might appear beyond dispute that throwing a glass container into a telephone pole is by no means an 'ordinary' use of that product,"[28] the court observed that the Massachusetts high court had already rejected the "ordinary use" standard as being devoid of content for deciding misuse cases.[29] Instead, the "manufacturer's warranty of product fitness for ordinary use includes a guarantee that such product will withstand, in a reasonably safe manner, *foreseeable* 'misuse' incident to or arising out of the product's intended use."[30] Applying this standard, the court concluded that "it would be stretching too far to believe that the Massachusetts courts are presently prepared to expand their definition of 'ordinary purposes' to include the deliberate misuse of an otherwise reasonably safe container in a manner totally unrelated to any

ability."); Venezia v. Miller Brewing Co., 626 F.2d 188 (1st Cir. 1980) (Mass. law).

**25.** See, e.g., Patterson v. Central Mills, Inc., 64 Fed.Appx. 457 (6th Cir. 2003) (Ohio law) (jury properly could find that child wearing adult T-shirt unforeseeably misused shirt by climbing onto kitchen counter and reaching for ketchup in cupboard over lit burner on stove); Cigna v. Oy Saunatec Ltd., 241 F.3d 1, 16 (1st Cir. 2001) (Mass. law) (unreasonable use of product is defense to implied warranty of merchantability claim); Carbone v. Alagna, 658 N.Y.S.2d 48 (App. Div. 1997) (boy struck by projectile fired from friend's slingshot could not maintain implied warranty action against suppliers of slingshot); Fournier Furniture, Inc. v. Waltz–Holst Blow Pipe Co., 980 F.Supp. 187, 190 (W.D. Va. 1997) (misuse of product, defined as using it in manner which seller could not reasonably have foreseen, bars breach of warranty claims if misuse is sole proximate cause of harm); Wheeler v. Sunbelt Tool Co., 537 N.E.2d 1332, 1342 (Ill. App. Ct. 1989) (citing UCC § 2–715, and observing that "[m]isuse arises as an issue which may defeat the action in whole or in part by contesting proximate cause"); Global Truck & Equip. Co. v. Palmer Mach. Works, Inc., 628 F.Supp. 641, 650–51 (N.D. Miss. 1986) (improper use negates both implied warranties of merchantability and fitness); Watson v. Uniden Corp. of Am., 775 F.2d 1514 (11th Cir. 1985) (Ga. law) (hearing loss from loud ring of cordless phone when user forgot to switch from standby to talk, as manual instructed, before placing on ear; use of product contrary to instructions is not use of product in normal manner); Daniell v. Ford Motor Co., 581 F.Supp. 728, 731–32 (D.N.M. 1984) (after locking herself in trunk in attempt to commit suicide, buyer could not get out for nine days because of absence of internal release mechanism; use was highly extraordinary rather than "ordinary," and buyer did not think about, much less rely upon, seller's skill or judgment to select automobile suitable for her "unfortunate" purpose); Featherall v. Firestone Tire and Rubber Co., 252 S.E.2d 358, 367 (Va. 1979) (no recovery for breach of implied warranty if use was unforeseeable).

**26.** 626 F.2d 188 (1st Cir. 1980) (Mass. law).

**27.** Id. at 190, citing Vincent v. Nicholas E. Tsiknas Co., 151 N.E.2d 263 (Mass. 1958).

**28.** Id. at 189.

**29.** In Back v. Wickes Corp., 378 N.E.2d 964 (Mass. 1978).

**30.** Venezia v. Miller Brewing Co., 626 F.2d 188, 190 (1st Cir. 1980) (Mass. law) (emphasis added).

normal or intended use of that item.... *A fortiori,* we can see no possible implied fitness warranty that an empty glass bottle discarded by unknown persons would ... safely withstand being intentionally smashed against a solid stationary object."[31]

## UCC Article 2

Since warranty law is now governed in every state by Article 2 of the Uniform Commercial Code,[32] a search for the proper role of user misconduct in warranty law should begin there. But the Code's black-letter ("Official Text") references to consumer misconduct are at best oblique—the scope of warranty liability is defined by whether a product is fit for "normal" use,[33] by whether the buyer is probably aware of the product's dangerous condition,[34] and by whether a breach of warranty "proximately" results in the plaintiff's injuries.[35]

The warranty most frequently litigated in products liability cases, the implied warranty of merchantability, is principally defined in § 2–314(2)(c)'s provision that a merchantable product is "fit for the ordinary purposes for which such goods are used."[36] This provision quite obviously suggests that an implied warranty of merchantability will *not* arise under this subsection[37] if a product's performance capabilities are exceeded by a use which is not "ordinary," however that word may be interpreted. Under § 2–316(3)(b), no warranties arise with respect to defects a buyer does or should discover during a pre-sale examination of a product.[38] Finally, the remedies provision of Article 2 includes, in defining the "consequential damages" available for breach of warranty in § 2–715(2)(b), "injury to person or property proximately resulting from any breach of warranty." While each of these provisions in Article 2 may be interpreted to implicate the role of a buyer's misconduct in warranty litigation, none of them does so in a manner that is clear and to the point.[39]

In contrast to the obscure manner in which buyer misconduct is treated in the UCC's Official Text, the Official Comments specifically address the effect of both a buyer's carelessness and behavior which implies risk acceptance, framing the issue in terms of whether a buyer's

**31.** Id. The court concluded that "the impact of endorsing a contrary conclusion would be overwhelming, with every discarded glass object holding the potential for generating a future lawsuit." Id. at 192.

**32.** On warranty claims in products liability litigation, see ch. 4, above.

**33.** See UCC § 2–314(2)(c).

**34.** See UCC § 2–316(3)(b).

**35.** See UCC § 2–715(2)(b).

**36.** See § 4.3, above.

**37.** Note that UCC § 2–314(2) contains a total of six subsections, so that even if a product is merchantable under one or more subsections it may be found unmerchantable under one or more of the other provisions. So, if opening a Pepsi bottle on a metal fence causing it to explode is not an

"ordinary purpose" under subsection (2), the bottle might still be unmerchantable for not being "adequately contained" under subsection (5). For such facts, see Natale v. Pepsi Cola Co., 182 N.Y.S.2d 404 (App. Div. 1959).

**38.** See, e.g., Light v. Weldarc Co., 569 So.2d 1302 (Fla. Dist. Ct. App. 1990) (no implied warranty that safety glasses would not slip down user's nose, and so fail to protect eye from metal sliver thrown from punch press, when user inspected glasses, knew their propensity to slip, and made "conscious decision" to buy them). See § 4.7, above.

**39.** See Clark and Smith, Product Warranties 2d § 12.10.

loss is "proximately caused" by a product defect or, alternatively, by the buyer's choice or conduct. Comment 13 to § 2–314 provides in part:

> In an action based on breach of warranty, it is of course necessary to show not only the existence of the warranty but the fact that the warranty was broken and that the breach of the warranty was the proximate cause of the loss sustained. In such an action an affirmative showing by the seller that the loss resulted from some action or event following his own delivery of the goods can operate as a defense.... Action by the buyer following an examination of the goods which ought to have indicated the defect complained of can be shown as matter bearing on whether the breach itself was the cause of the injury.

Comment 8 to § 2–316 provides that "if the buyer discovers the defect and uses the goods anyway, or if he unreasonably fails to examine the goods before he uses them, resulting injuries may be found to result from his own action rather than proximately from a breach of warranty." Comment 5 to § 2–715 provides more fully:

> Subsection (2)(b) states the usual rule as to breach of warranty, allowing recovery for injuries "proximately" resulting from the breach. Where the injury involved follows the use of goods without discovery of the defect causing the damage, the question of "proximate" cause turns on whether it was reasonable for the buyer to use the goods without such inspection as would have revealed the defects. If it was not reasonable for him to do so, or if he did in fact discover the defect prior to his use, the injury would not proximately result from the breach of warranty.

This last comment imposes the greatest burden on buyers, for it states that there is no proximate cause, and hence no damages for breach of warranty, if a buyer either (1) unreasonably fails to inspect a product for defects, or (2) uses a product after discovery of a defect, whether such use was unreasonable or not.

*Erdman v. Johnson Bros. Radio & Television Co.*[40] illustrates one court's attempt to harmonize the awkward fit between a plaintiff's contributory negligence and the law of warranty. From the start, the plaintiffs' television-radio-stereo console purchased from the defendant emitted crackling sounds, often accompanied by a tear in the picture, and it sometimes emitted "sparks and heavy smoke shooting out of the back of the set and the smell of burning rubber, wire, or some other substance."[41] The defendants purported to repair the problem, but sparks and smoke still emanated from the rear of the television. After one of these recurring episodes, the plaintiffs turned off (but did not unplug) the television, went to bed, and were later awakened by a fire from the set that destroyed their house. In plaintiffs' warranty and negligence action against the dealers, the trial court ruled for the defendants, finding that the plaintiffs had been contributorily negligent in continuing to use a television that was arcing, smoking, and emitting

---

**40.** 271 A.2d 744 (Md. 1970). **41.** Id. at 745.

sparks and a burning odor for two hours on the night of the fire. The court concluded that the implied warranty of merchantability did not cover the continued use of a television under these conditions since such was not a "normal" use.[42]

On appeal, the Maryland high court affirmed. Pondering whether contributory negligence is a bar to an implied warranty claim under the Uniform Commercial Code, on the one hand, or falls outside the scope of the seller's implied warranty, on the other, the *Erdman* court observed that "[t]he important factor under either theory or an amalgam of them is that, although there may have been a breach of the warranty, that the breach is no longer considered 'the proximate cause of the loss.' "[43] Thus, "the defect in the set, of which the plaintiffs had knowledge, could no longer be relied upon by them as a basis for an action of breach of warranty."[44] The court concluded that "the breach of warranty, if any there was, was not the proximate cause of the fire because of the appellants' continued use of the set after the discovery of the obvious defects," remarking "that such a holding is consistent with the trial judge's characterization of the plaintiffs' conduct as contributory negligence and with the UCC's Official Comment 13 to § 2–314, and Comment 5 to § 2–715."[45]

Despite the specificity of the UCC's Official Comments on how buyer misconduct affects a warranty claim, *Erdman* is one of the few decisions that analyzes these useful comments together with the vague blackletter provisions to resolve the user misconduct issue in a warranty case. Why most courts have failed to use Article 2's misconduct comments in a similarly forthright manner might be because the courts have sensed the rough manner in which the contract law scholars who drafted Article 2 incorporated the tort law concepts of contributory negligence, assumption of risk, misuse, and proximate cause into the warranty law context. Or perhaps the courts, feeling bound only by the UCC's Official Text, have largely ignored the comments to provide more flexibility in their effort to standardize the misconduct defenses applicable to all products liability claims, in tort and warranty alike. Finally, beginning in the late 1960s, courts increasingly may have perceived that the all-or-nothing approach to buyer misconduct exhibited by the comments is inconsistent with the modern comparative fault approach to damages apportionment that swept the nation in the late twentieth century.[46]

The infrequency with which the courts have used the UCC's blackletter provisions to decide consumer misconduct cases is more problematic. Certainly the paucity of this type of analysis is partially explained

---

**42.** The trial court remarked in part:

You have a man of high intelligence, who purchased this television set, who continued to use it, even though he knew and had complained that it was arcing, smoking, with actual sparks and a burning odor. Now using a set which is in that condition is certainly not, in my opinion, a use in a normal manner.... I so hold that, even assuming the fire came about as a result of a defect in the set, that the warranty did not extend to the point,

under the circumstances of this case, of covering the Plaintiff's damages resulting from the fire.

Id. at 747.

**43.** Id. at 749, citing UCC § 2–314, cmt. 13.

**44.** Id.

**45.** Id. at 750–51.

**46.** See § 13.3, above.

by the vague and indirect manner in which these provisions refer to buyer misconduct in terms of ordinary use, discovery of defects, and proximate causation. Moreover, because this Official Text did not explicitly address the subject of buyer misconduct, the enactment of the UCC did not displace prior law. Nor did it interfere with the ongoing development of supplementary law, on how a buyer's misconduct should affect a warranty claim.[47] Thus, courts may have felt authorized by the UCC itself to substitute developing principles of consumer misconduct from the tort law context for the rough, vague, and increasingly anachronistic provisions of Article 2.

Since warranty law claims in most products liability actions are secondary to overlapping claims of strict liability in tort and negligence, many courts and lawyers may simply view these liability claims collectively as lying essentially in tort and so may view the defenses from the same perspective. While the temptation to view tort and warranty claims as falling under a single "products liability action" umbrella for purposes of evaluating available defenses is understandable, it improperly denigrates the legislative prerogative. Until the legislatures themselves choose to unify tort and warranty claims in products liability litigation, as a couple now have done,[48] the courts should clarify how differing forms of consumer misconduct affect claims and damages for breach of warranty under Article 2 of the Uniform Commercial Code.

### Express Warranty

Much of the analysis above applies to express as well as implied warranty claims. But express warranties arise from *explicit* contractual representations, and so the issue of whether a representation was part of the basis of the particular bargain (or whether a plaintiff justifiably relied thereon) is an issue that cannot be ignored.[49]

One special doctrine that has developed in some of the express warranty cases is that contributory negligence is irrelevant if the plaintiff's "misconduct" consists merely in relying on the truthfulness of the defendant's representation. *Hensley v. Sherman Car Wash Equip. Co.*[50] was an action by a car wash employee against the manufacturer of the automobile conveyor unit. On the day of the accident, the pivoting safety hood which ordinarily covered the open pit at the end of the conveyor was not operating, and the plaintiff stepped into the pit. The plaintiff's express warranty claim was based on the assertion in the defendant's information sheet that "[c]ar wash personnel are assured safe working conditions on all areas of the vehicle by the pivoted safety hood [which] eliminates all possibility of persons stepping into an open pit."[51] Holding that the plaintiff's contributory negligence was not a bar to her express warranty claim, the court reasoned that the plaintiff's faulty behavior in

**47.** See UCC § 1–103.

**48.** Connecticut is one example. See Conn. Gen. Stat. § 52–572n(a). See also Mich. Stat. Ann. § 600.2945. Note, however, that some states treat express warranty claims as generating special responsibilities and so exclude them from the general defi-

nition of a "product liability action." See, e.g., N.J. Rev. Stat. § 2A:58c–1(b)(3).

**49.** See § 4.2, above.

**50.** 520 P.2d 146 (Colo. Ct. App. 1974).

**51.** Id. at 147.

failing to observe where she was going was "within the scope of the risk warranted against by defendant," since the stated "purpose of the safety hood was to prevent a person from stepping into the opening at the end of the conveyor unit."[52] Accordingly, "[t]he very risk which defendant warranted not to exist was encountered by plaintiff, and her negligence or lack of due care is irrelevant."[53] Indeed, a person's "fault" in believing a manufacturer's express promise should only rarely be allowed to undercut the manufacturer's fundamental obligation to speak the truth.[54] Other courts have agreed with *Hensley* that a plaintiff's contributory negligence will not bar a breach of express warranty claim if the misconduct merely "puts the warranty to the test."[55]

### Comparative Fault

Only in recent decades have courts and legislatures realized that a plaintiff's misconduct and damages need not be treated in an all-or-nothing manner.[56] Today, whether consumer misconduct should be considered a matter of comparative fault for damages apportionment on a warranty claim depends upon the scope of each particular jurisdiction's comparative fault system.[57] While the development of the comparative fault doctrine is generally beneficial, it has magnified the profound confusion that already existed in fashioning a proper role for user misconduct in warranty litigation.

In states which have enacted "comparative *negligence*" legislation, courts have been properly hesitant to compare a user's misconduct with a defendant's breach of warranty.[58] But in states with legislation which has defined the apportionment system more broadly in terms of compar-

---

**52.** Id. at 148.

**53.** Id.

**54.** See Owen, The Moral Foundations of Products Liability Law: Toward First Principles, 68 Notre Dame L. Rev. 427, 463–65 (1993).

**55.** Hensley v. Sherman Car Wash Equip. Co., 520 P.2d 146, 148 (Colo. App. 1974). See, e.g., Imperial Die Casting Co. v. Covil Insulation Co., 216 S.E.2d 532, 534 (S.C. 1975); Brown v. Chapman, 304 F.2d 149 (9th Cir. 1962) (Haw. law); Hansen v. Firestone Tire & Rubber Co., 276 F.2d 254, 258 (6th Cir. 1960) (Mich. law) ("If the manufacturer chooses to extend the scope of his liability by certifying certain qualities as existent, the negligent acts of the buyer, bringing about the revelation that the qualities do not exist, would not defeat recovery.").

**56.** Perhaps the earliest products liability case in which the court allowed the jury to reduce the plaintiff's recovery for breach of implied warranty on account of contributory negligence, rather than to bar recovery altogether, was Chapman v. Brown, 198 F.Supp. 78 (D. Haw. 1961), aff'd, 304 F.2d 149 (9th Cir. 1962). A helpful, early discus-

sion favoring comparative fault apportionment in warranty cases is Levine, Buyer's Conduct as Affecting the Extent of Manufacturer's Liability in Warranty, 52 Minn. L. Rev. 627 (1968).

**57.** See H. Woods and B. Deere, Comparative Fault §§ 14:16, 14:17 (3d ed. 1996).

**58.** See, e.g., Phillips v. Duro–Last Roofing, 806 P.2d 834, 837 (Wyo. 1991) ("the statute applies only to causes of action arising out of appellee's negligence"). *But see* Larsen v. Pacesetter Sys., Inc., 837 P.2d 1273, 1289 (Haw. 1992) ("merging" breach of implied warranty into pure apportionment products liability scheme). In some jurisdictions, warranty claims may plausibly be included under the "comparative *negligence*" umbrella. "It can be argued that most comparative negligence statutes by using only the term 'negligence' intend to exclude warranty actions. This argument is very tenuous in a jurisdiction recognizing contributory negligence as a defense. It may have some force in a state which has never recognized contributory negligence as a defense to warranty.... " H. Woods and B. Deere, Comparative Fault §§ 14:16, at 336 (3d ed. 1996).

ative "fault"[59] or "culpability,"[60] especially if "fault" is defined to include breach of warranty[61] or something similar,[62] or when the statute provides for apportionment in all cases involving personal injury, death, or damage to property,[63] then courts may or must include breach of warranty as an item to be apportioned.[64] In the two states that have adopted the Uniform Comparative Fault Act,[65] breach of warranty is explicitly included as a type of "fault" to be apportioned.[66] Some state legislatures have enacted special products liability reform statutes that explicitly provide for the comparative fault apportionment of damages in products liability actions generally, regardless of the basis of the claim.[67] Finally, in a number of the ten or so jurisdictions where comparative fault apportionment is a creature of the common law, the courts have generally chosen to include breach of warranty in the apportionment system.[68]

A variety of secondary comparative fault issues arise in connection with warranty claims involving user misconduct. In the majority of comparative fault states that have adopted a "modified" rather than "pure" system of comparative fault, a plaintiff's contributory fault continues to bar recovery altogether, in warranty as in tort, when the plaintiff's fault exceeds the defendant's fault.[69] When comparative fault statutes specify apportionment for claims of personal injury and property damage, such statutes may not be applied to breach of warranty actions seeking recovery of purely economic loss.[70]

**59.** As in Colorado. See Montag v. Honda Motor Co., 75 F.3d 1414, 1419 (10th Cir. 1996) (interpreting products liability apportionment statute, Colo. Rev. Stat. § 13–21–406, to permit comparison of driver's fault with automotive manufacturer's fault in designing defective seatbelt).

**60.** As in New York. See N.Y. Civ. Prac. Law art. 14–A § 1411.

**61.** As in Arkansas. See Ark. Code Ann. § 16–64–122.

**62.** As in Maine, where "fault" includes a "breach of statutory duty." See Me. Rev. Stat. tit. 14, § 156.

**63.** As in Mississippi and Rhode Island. See Miss. Code Ann. § 11–7–15; R.I. Gen. Laws § 9–20–4; Fiske v. MacGregor, Div'n of Brunswick, 464 A.2d 719 (R.I. 1983) (thorough analysis of case law).

**64.** See H. Woods and B. Deere, Comparative Fault §§ 14:16 (3d ed. 1996).

**65.** Uniform Comparative Fault Act (1977). Only Iowa and Washington adopted the Act, and both made changes to the "uniform" provisions. The Uniform Apportionment of Tort Responsibility Act replaced the Uniform Comparative Fault Act in 2002, as amended, 2003. See § 13.3, above.

**66.** Under § 1(b) of the Uniform Comparative Fault Act, "fault" is defined to include "breach of warranty." See id. at 127.

**67.** As in Michigan and Texas. See Karl v. Bryant Air Conditioning Co., 705 F.2d 164 (6th Cir. 1983) (Mich. law); Tex. Civ. Prac. & Rem. Code § 82.001.

**68.** See, e.g., Owens v. Truckstops of Am., 915 S.W.2d 420, 434 (Tenn. 1996); Wheeler v. Sunbelt Tool Co., 537 N.E.2d 1332 (Ill. App. Ct. 1989); Coulter v. American Bakeries Co., 530 So.2d 1009 (Fla. Dist. Ct. App. 1988); Sebring v. Colver, 649 P.2d 932, 935 (Alaska 1982); In re Certified Questions from the United States Court of Appeals for Sixth Circuit, 331 N.W.2d 456 (Mich. 1982).

**69.** See, e.g., Interwest Constr. v. Palmer, 886 P.2d 92 (Utah Ct. App. 1994).

**70.** See, e.g., Ethyl Corp. v. BP Performance Polymers, Inc., 33 F.3d 23 (8th Cir. 1994) (Iowa law); Little Rock Elec. Contractors, Inc. v. Okonite Co., 744 S.W.2d 381, 382 (Ark. 1988) (no apportionment where statute applied to "actions for damages for personal injuries or wrongful death or injury to property in which recovery is predicated upon fault," not because implied warranty was not a form of "fault," but because of type of loss sustained). See also Eastern Mountain Platform Tennis, Inc. v. Sherwin–Williams Co., 40 F.3d 492 (1st Cir. 1994) (N.H. law) (comparative fault not applicable as defense to warranty liability "except in personal injury cases based on dual theories of strict liability in tort and breach

For the many reasons why damages apportionment principles are widely applied to products liability claims in tort,[71] a division of damages based on responsibility in warranty is also sound in principle. Because treating plaintiff misconduct as a basis for apportioning damages was largely nonexistent when the Uniform Commercial Code was drafted in the 1950s, Article 2 fails to address the topic. But Article 2's formulation of buyer misconduct issues in proximate causation terms is compatible with the concept of damages apportionment which assigns responsibility for damages to each party in proportion to the extent to which the party's breach of duty proximately caused the harm.[72]

The widening application of comparative fault principles to warranty actions has occurred mostly in the context of *implied* warranty claims, and there has been a greater reluctance to apply damages apportionment principals to claims for *express* warranty.[73] But the several comparative fault statutes that apply to injury claims generally, together with the products liability statutes that apply comparative fault provisions to all products liability claims, would seem quite clearly to embrace express warranty claims within the ambit of comparative responsibility. However, jurisdictions without these statutes generally should not reduce a plaintiff's damages on account of simple contributory fault, for such behavior usually consists in merely putting the warranty to the test. More egregious misconduct, however, particularly if it involves plaintiff conduct which is knowingly dangerous and unreasonable, or puts a product to an unforeseeable use, unfairly tests the product outside the warranty and so should continue to bar express warranty recovery altogether.

While damages apportionment for consumer misconduct in implied warranty cases is sound as a principle of general application, it needs exceptions. No doubt some forms of consumer misconduct, such as knowingly dangerous and unreasonable behavior and putting products to unforeseeably dangerous use, should be left entirely outside the area of damages apportionment for all warranty claims. Regardless of how user misconduct is characterized, the issue of damages apportionment needs to be addressed only if the product use was within the scope of warranty. And for most products liability claims involving user misconduct, in warranty no less than tort, courts should leave room for a robust doctrine of "sole proximate cause"[74]—often better treated as an issue of

---

of the implied warranty of merchantability").

**71.** See § 13.3, above.

**72.** See, e.g., Frazer v. A.F. Munsterman, Inc., 527 N.E.2d 1248 (Ill. 1988). See generally Levine, Buyer's Conduct as Affecting the Extent of Manufacturer's Liability in Warranty, 52 Minn. L. Rev. 627, 662–63 (1968) (arguing that comparative fault approach "while not a panacea, can serve to substantially ameliorate the harshness of the contributory negligence doctrine while balancing the manufacturer's responsibility to society with the buyer's action in contributing to his injury").

**73.** See, e.g., Coca–Cola Bottling Co. of Cape Cod v. Weston & Sampson Eng'rs, Inc., 695 N.E.2d 688, 695 (Mass. App. Ct. 1998) (comparative negligence statute does not apply to express warranty claims); Ferdig v. Melitta, Inc., 320 N.W.2d 369, 374 (Mich. Ct. App. 1982) ("Contributory negligence has never been an available defense in cases involving express warranties.").

**74.** See, e.g., Fournier Furniture, Inc. v. Waltz–Holst Blow Pipe Co., 980 F.Supp. 187, 190 (W.D. Va. 1997) (misuse of product, defined as using it in manner which seller could not reasonably have foreseen,

"scope of warranty."[75] Both doctrines embrace the same notion that there must be a fair limit to a seller's responsibility, such that both express and implied promises are reasonably construed to exclude responsibility for injuries resulting from the use of a product outside the scope of a warranty.

As an example, assume that a new sport utility vehicle has a high center of gravity, a narrow track width, and a large bubble visible on the sidewall of one tire, and further assume that the buyer is aware of these obvious characteristics of the vehicle. If the buyer chooses to turn the steering wheel sharply at high speed in an effort to spin the vehicle sideways like a movie stuntman, the tire might blow out and the vehicle might roll over, injuring the driver. In such a case, although the tire is clearly defective, and while the safety of the vehicle's stability may fairly be subject to inquiry, the sole proximate cause of the driver's injuries should probably be viewed as the driver's harsh driving rather than any lack of merchantability in the tire or the vehicle. Stated otherwise, the scope of the implied warranty of quality in such a case does not include safe performance when the product is put to such abusive use. The issue of comparative fault should never be reached at all in such a case, because there was no proximate connection between breach of warranty and the plaintiff's harm.

## § 13.7  DEFENSES TO MISREPRESENTATION CLAIMS

The basic misconduct "defense" asserted in tortious misrepresentation actions is that the plaintiff's reliance, if any, was not "justifiable."[1] Indeed, the justifiability of reliance, sometimes referred to as "reasonable reliance" or the "right to rely,"[2] has long been a central element of

---

bars breach of warranty claims if misuse is sole proximate cause of harm).

**75.** See, e.g., Erdman v. Johnson Bros. Radio & Television Co., 271 A.2d 744 (Md. 1971). Professor Nordstrom viewed the user misconduct issue as a question of the nature of the agreement between the parties, addressed in Article 2 in terms of whether the goods "conformed" to the warranty. See UCC § 2–106(2). In view of his focus on the intent of the parties and the nature of their agreement, he preferred among tort law terms the concept of assumption of risk to the vaguer concept of proximate cause. See R. J. Nordstrom, Law of Sales § 84 (1970).

### § 13.7

**1.** See generally 2 Harper, James, and Gray, Law of Torts §§ 7.7 and 7.8; Prosser and Keeton on Torts §§ 108 and 109; Sales, The Innocent Misrepresentation Doctrine: Strict Tort Liability Under Section 402B, 16 Hous. L. Rev. 239 (1979); Comment, 28 Cumb. L. Rev. 177 (1997–98).

**2.** The dominant term is "justifiable." See, e.g., Restatement (2d) Torts §§ 402B, 537(b), 538(1), & 552. The Products Liability Restatement does not really address the issue. Compare id. § 9 cmt. *b* (adopting the principles of Restatement (2d) Torts § 402B), cmt. *c* (referring only to the issue of "contributory fault"), and id. Reporters' Notes 1 and 2 (referring to § 402B's requirement of "justifiable reliance"). But other terms—particularly "reasonable"—are used as well, sometimes interchangeably. See, e.g., Whiteley v. Philip Morris Inc., 11 Cal.Rptr.3d 807, 843 (Ct. App. 2004) (reasonable); Hearn v. R.J. Reynolds Tobacco Co., 279 F.Supp.2d 1096, 1112 (D. Ariz. 2003) (reasonable); IFD Constr. Corp. v. Corddry Carpenter Dietz & Zack, 685 N.Y.S.2d 670, 673 (App. Div. 1999) (reliance was "neither reasonable nor justified"); G & M Farms v. Funk Irrigation Co., 808 P.2d 851, 855 (Idaho 1991) (stating eighth element of fraud claim as plaintiff's "right to rely thereon"); Rowan Cty. Bd. of Educ. v. U.S. Gypsum Co., 407 S.E.2d 860 (N.C. App. 1991) ("justifiable reliance" and "reasonable reliance"); Restatement (2d) Torts § 310 comment *b* (relying on an opinion may make the person's reliance "less reasonable, and so less justified."); Fraud & Deceit, 37 Am. Jur. 2d § 236 et seq. (1968) (classifying issue as plaintiff's "right to rely" and, in § 236, examining basis for

all three forms of tortious misrepresentation: fraud,[3] negligent misrepresentation,[4] and strict products liability in tort for misrepresentation under the *Restatement (Second) of Torts*[5] and the *Restatement (Third) of Torts: Products Liability*.[6]

Probably because the justifiability of a plaintiff's reliance overlaps several other elements of fraud (fact, materiality, plaintiff's ignorance of falsity, and reliance), as discussed below, it is sometimes omitted in recitations of the elements of fraudulent[7] and negligent misrepresentation.[8] This omission might be viewed as suggesting that there exists some uncertainty as to whether the justifiability of a plaintiff's reliance is truly an element of a tortious misrepresentation claim or whether instead a plaintiff's unjustified reliance should be considered an affirmative defense. But the omission is to be explained by its embedded nature in the other elements, and there is essentially no debate that the justifiability of a plaintiff's reliance is an essential component of a common-law[9] claim for tortious misrepresentation.[10]

As an essential element of all three causes of action for tortious misrepresentation, the non-justifiability of the plaintiff's reliance cannot be characterized as an affirmative defense because the plaintiff in all such cases has the burden, as with each element of such claims, to plead and prove the justifiability of his or her reliance upon the defendant's misrepresentation.[11] If a plaintiff is unable to prove that his or her

ascertaining whether reliance is "justifiable or excusable"). Except perhaps on the issue of whether a victim's conduct should be measured objectively or subjectively, discussed below, it matters little which term a court selects to characterize the form of misconduct which will defeat a claim for tortious misrepresentation.

**3.** See Restatement (2d) Torts § 537(b). Although § 537 by its terms applies only to recovery for pecuniary loss, § 557A applies the principles of liability in deceit for pecuniary loss to cases in which the deceit causes physical harm. Restatement (2d) Torts § 557A and cmt. *a.*

**4.** See Restatement (2d) Torts § 552(1).

**5.** Section 402B. See id. cmt. *j.*

**6.** Section 9 of the Products Liability Restatement incorporates the doctrine of § 402B of the Second Restatement. See § 9 cmt. *b.*

**7.** See, e.g., Small v. Lorillard Tobacco Co., 698 N.Y.S.2d 615, 621 (Ct. App. 1999) ("[t]o make out a prima facie case of fraud, the complaint must contain allegations of a representation of material fact, falsity, scienter, reliance and injury"); Sturgeon v. Retherford Publ'ns, Inc., 987 P.2d 1218 (Okla. Civ. App.); Bank of Montreal v. Signet Bank, 193 F.3d 818 (4th Cir. 1999) (Va. law). See also 1 Frumer and Friedman, Products Liability § 2.05 [2], at 2–57 (characterizing element merely as "reliance upon the truth of the representation").

**8.** See, e.g., Restatement (2d) Torts § 310.

**9.** Justifiable reliance is not a required element of certain statutory claims for deceptive business practices and consumer fraud. See, e.g., Small v. Lorillard Tobacco Co., 679 N.Y.S.2d 593, 599 (App. Div. 1998), aff'd, 698 N.Y.S.2d 615 (1999); Gennari v. Weichert Co. Realtors, 691 A.2d 350 (N.J. 1997).

**10.** See, e.g., Gawloski v. Miller Brewing Co., 644 N.E.2d 731 (Ohio Ct. App. 1994); Boyd v. A. O. Smith Harvestore Prods., Inc., 776 P.2d 1125, 1129 (Colo. Ct. App. 1989) ("An essential element of both fraud and negligent misrepresentation is justifiable reliance."); American Safety Equip. Corp. v. Winkler, 640 P.2d 216, 223 (Colo. 1982). *But see* Phinney v. Perlmutter, 564 N.W.2d 532, 546–48 (Mich. App. 1997), narrowly reasoned and not a products liability case, rejected by Novak v. Nationwide Mut. Ins. Co., 599 N.W.2d 546, 554 (Mich. 1999) ("a person who unreasonably relies on false statements should not be entitled to damages for misrepresentation").

**11.** See, e.g., American Safety Equip. Corp. v. Winkler, 640 P.2d 216, 223 (Colo. 1982) (by implication). Compare Kruse v. Bank of Am., 248 Cal.Rptr. 217 (App. Ct. 1988) (fraud pleading insufficient without allegations of justifiable reliance). See generally 37 Am. Jur. 2d Fraud & Deceit § 435 (1968) (plaintiff generally has duty to plead right to rely).

reliance was justifiable, the tortious misrepresentation claim will fail.[12] Similar to the other misconduct defenses examined in this chapter, the justifiability of a plaintiff's reliance is normally a question of fact for the jury to resolve.[13]

## When is Reliance Justifiable?

Whether a plaintiff's reliance is justifiable depends upon the nature of the representation and all of the circumstances of the particular transaction. These include the materiality of the representation;[14] the extent to which it was precise and factual, on the one hand, or vague and subjectively a matter of opinion, on the other;[15] its form and the context in which it was made, as in television advertising, face-to-face negotiations, or in the owner's manual;[16] its apparent plausibility, or its suspiciousness suggesting that the plaintiff should "smell a rat";[17] the availability of other sources of information revealing the falsity of the representation;[18] and any other matter bearing on whether in the cir-

**12.** See, e.g., Baker v. Danek Med., 35 F.Supp.2d 875 (N.D. Fla. 1998) (negligent and strict liability for misrepresentation); Gawloski v. Miller Brewing Co., 644 N.E.2d 731 (Ohio Ct. App. 1994) (fraudulent misrepresentation: no justifiable reliance as a matter of law); Gunsalus v. Celotex Corp., 674 F.Supp. 1149, 1160 (E.D. Pa. 1987) (dismissing claims against tobacco companies for fraud, negligence, and strict liability for misrepresentation on ground that advertisements at issue "are not the kind of representations upon which reasonable people would rely"); American Safety Equip. Corp. v. Winkler, 640 P.2d 216, 223 (Colo. 1982) (4–3 decision) (strict liability).

**13.** See, e.g., Rowan Cty. Bd. of Educ. v. U.S. Gypsum Co., 407 S.E.2d 860 (N.C. App. 1991).

**14.** Section 538 of the Restatement (2d) Torts provides that "[r]eliance upon a fraudulent misrepresentation is not justifiable unless the matter misrepresented is material," and it defines a matter as "material" if:

(a) a reasonable man would attach importance to its existence or nonexistence in determining his choice of action in the transaction in question; or

(b) the maker of the representation knows or has reason to know that its recipient regards or is likely to regard the matter as important in determining his choice of action, although a reasonable man would not so regard it.

**15.** See Prosser and Keeton on Torts § 109, at 755.

**16.** Cf. Restatement (2d) Torts, § 538A, cmt. *c.*

**17.** Thanks to Judge Posner for this colorful phrase. See AMPAT/Midwest, Inc. v. Illinois Tool Works Inc., 896 F.2d 1035, 1041 (7th Cir. 1990) (Ill. law).

**18.** See, e.g., Gawloski v. Miller Brewing Co., 644 N.E.2d 731 (Ohio Ct. App. 1994) (even if Miller beer commercials had represented that prolonged and excessive beer drinking was safe, no justifiable reliance as a matter of law because of common awareness for centuries of risks of alcoholism from prolonged and excessive consumption of alcohol):

Our nation continues to inform its citizens of those dangers, supporting the community's common knowledge with well-documented and highly publicized scientific and statistical information that repeatedly warns of the detrimental physical, psychological, and emotional effects caused by prolonged and excessive alcohol use. Even though we acknowledge that beer advertising is pervasive in our society, we hold that, as a matter of law, a beer manufacturer's commercial images, although enticing, are not enough to neutralize or nullify the immense body of knowledge a reasonable consumer possesses about the dangers of alcohol. Therefore, a reasonable consumer could not, as a matter of law, ignore basic common knowledge about the dangers of alcohol and justifiably rely upon beer advertisements and their idyllic images to conclude that the prolonged and excessive use of alcohol is safe and acceptable.

Id. at 736. Compare Small v. Lorillard Tobacco Co., 679 N.Y.S.2d 593 (App. Div. 1998), aff'd, 698 N.Y.S.2d 615 (1999), where the court decertified a class action against the tobacco industry for fraudulently concealing the addictive nature of cigarette smoking, questioning the plausibility of plaintiff's claim of reliance because of the hundreds of articles published in New York

cumstances the plaintiff, or a reasonable person,[19] could properly believe and base a decision upon the representation.[20] So, a court or jury may conclude that a person can reasonably believe explicit assurances that a golfing practice device is "completely safe" and that the "ball will not hit player,"[21] or that a mace weapon sold for self defense "disables as effectively as a gun" and will "subdue" an attacker "instantly."[22] However, a person, ignoring widespread publicity about the evils of drinking and smoking, may *not* justifiably base personal beer or cigarette consumption decisions upon commercials that glorify drinking or smoking and that somehow convey the idea that the prolonged and excessive consumption of such products is not harmful or addictive.[23]

Reliance itself, apart from its justifiability, involves the entirely factual subjective question of whether the representee personally believed the representation and took action, at least in part, upon it.[24] In contrast, the *justifiability* of that reliance requires an evaluation of the basis for reliance to determine if it was sound or had at least some sensible explanation. Because it gauges the wisdom of a plaintiff's decision to rely upon a particular representation, the justifiability of

---

newspapers during the 1980s and 1990s about nicotine addiction.

**19.** As discussed below, the standard for establishing justifiability of reliance for fraud is tailored to the knowledge and characteristics of the specific plaintiff, in contrast to the objective reasonable person standard for negligent and innocent misrepresentation.

**20.** Representative factors to be considered in evaluating the justifiability of a plaintiff's reliance upon a defendant's fraudulent representations are set forth in Sippy v. Cristich, 609 P.2d 204 (Kan. Ct. App. 1980), an action brought by home purchasers alleging the seller's concealment of a defective roof. There the Kansas Appellate Court stated:

> Many factors must be considered in determining whether a statement is a matter of fact or a matter of opinion and whether or not plaintiff has a right to rely on the statement. Among the facts the court will take into consideration are the intelligence, education, business experience and relative situation of the parties; the general information and experience of the persons involved as to the nature and use of the property; the habits and methods of those in the industry or profession involved; the opportunity for both parties to make an independent investigation as well as the nature, extent, and result of any investigation so made; and any contract the parties knowingly and understandingly entered into.... "A recipient of a fraudulent misrepresentation is justified in relying upon its truth without investigation, unless he knows or has reason to know of facts which make

his reliance unreasonable." ... [T]he test is whether the recipient has "information which would serve as a danger signal and a red light to any normal person of his intelligence and experience."

Id. at 208 (quoting from, inter alia, Restatement (2d) Torts § 540 and comments thereto).

**21.** Hauter v. Zogarts, 534 P.2d 377, 379 (Cal. 1975).

**22.** Klages v. General Ordnance Equip. Corp., 367 A.2d 304, 306 (Pa. Super. Ct. 1976).

**23.** See, e.g., Small v. Lorillard Tobacco Co., 679 N.Y.S.2d 593 (App. Div. 1998), aff'd, 698 N.Y.S.2d 615 (1999); Gawloski v. Miller Brewing Co., 644 N.E.2d 731 (Ohio Ct. App. 1994); Smith v. Anheuser–Busch, Inc., 599 A.2d 320 (R.I. 1991). Compare Hill v. R.J. Reynolds Tobacco Co., 44 F.Supp.2d 837, 845–46 (W.D. Ky. 1999), where the defendant moved to dismiss the fraud claim on grounds that the dangers of smoking were common knowledge. *Held*, motion denied. Common knowledge is no defense to fraud, and it applies thereto, "if at all, by undermining proof of justified reliance upon misinformation" which the fact-finder should compare to the "convincingness" of the misrepresentation. While common knowledge does not "automatically negate the justifiability of reliance," it "introduces a powerful argument against reasonableness" which is more appropriately considered on a motion for summary judgment than on a motion to dismiss. Id. at 846.

**24.** See § 3.2, above.

reliance is often said to be based upon an "objective" determination.[25] In cases involving the intentional tort of fraud, however, the standard differs from the normal objective standard of a reasonable prudent person, since the gullibility or other fault of a person in believing such a misrepresentation cannot in fairness bar a claim against an intentional deceiver who deliberately and shamelessly exploits a person's trust.[26] In such cases, "[j]ustification is a matter of the qualities and characteristics of the particular plaintiff, and the circumstances of the particular case, rather than of the application of a community standard of conduct to all cases."[27] Normally, a person *may* justifiably rely upon a fraudulent misstatement unless the falsity of the representation is so clearly based on the known or obvious facts as to place in doubt his or her own truthfulness, or possibly even sanity, in claiming to have relied upon it.[28] In reality, tailoring the justifiability criteria to the plaintiff's specific characteristics makes the standard look suspiciously subjective,[29] such that it might be best if the courts in fraud cases would abandon pounding and twisting the justifiability standard into an "objective" hole in which it does not fit.

The justifiability requirement is not designed to provide a shield behind which wicked fraudfeasors may hide in order to exploit the

**25.** See, e.g., Rose v. Ford, 2003 WL 21495081, at *3 (Cal. Ct. App. 2003) (unpublished/noncitable) ("whether a reasonable consumer would likely rely"); Gawloski v. Miller Brewing Co., 644 N.E.2d 731, 736 (Ohio Ct. App. 1994). See generally Prosser and Keeton on Torts § 108, at 750 (purpose of justifiable reliance requirement is for "providing some objective corroborations to plaintiff's claim that he did rely").

**26.** "One who justifiably relies upon a fraudulent misrepresentation is not barred from recovery by his contributory negligence in doing so." Restatement (2d) Torts § 545A. "Although the plaintiff's reliance on the misrepresentation must be justifiable . . . , this does not mean that his conduct must conform to the standard of the reasonable man." Id. cmt. *b*. This is the prevailing rule, but there is authority to the contrary. See 37 Am. Jur. 2d, Fraud & Deceit § 249 (1968).

**27.** Restatement (2d) Torts § 545A cmt. *b*. Not unlike the child standard of care in the law of negligence, the standard of justifiability for fraud is often said to conform to the particular attributes of the plaintiff, including his or her age, intelligence, experience, and mental and physical condition. See, e.g., Cheney Bros., Inc. v. Batesville Casket Co., 47 F.3d 111, 115 (4th Cir. 1995) (S.C. law).

**28.** See Prosser and Keeton on Torts § 108:

Rather than contributory negligence, the matter seems to turn upon an individual standard of the plaintiff's own capacity and the knowledge which he has, or which may fairly be charged against him from the facts within his observation in the light of his individual case, and so comes closer to the rules which are associated with assumption of risk. "More succinctly stated, the rule is that one cannot be heard to say he relied upon a statement so patently ridiculous as to be unbelievable on its face, unless he happens to be that special object of the affections of a court of Equity, an idiot."

Id. at 751 (citing Obiter Dicta, 25 Ford. L. Rev. 395, 397 (1956)). Compare AMPAT/Midwest, Inc. v. Illinois Tool Works Inc., 896 F.2d 1035, 1041–42 (7th Cir. 1990) (Ill. law) (Posner, J.):

We think it comes down to this: while the victim of an ordinary accident is required to use the ordinary care of an average person [to avoid being contributorily negligent,] the victim of a deliberate fraud is barred only if he has notice of the fraud, and so he need only avoid deliberate or reckless risk-taking.

Thus, a fraud victim "cannot close his eyes to a known risk," for that would be to "ignore a manifest danger," which would be reckless. Id. at 1042.

**29.** So, justifiability might be said to lie closer to assumption of risk than it does to contributory negligence. See AMPAT/Midwest, Inc. v. Illinois Tool Works Inc., 896 F.2d 1035, 1042 (7th Cir. 1990) (Ill. law) (Posner, J.) ("It differs by only a shade, if that, from . . . assumption of risk that defeats liability under the first aspect of the duty of reasonable reliance as we conceive it."); Prosser and Keeton on Torts § 108.

gullibility of trusting victims, for the law seeks the opposite result.[30] Instead, justifiability overlaps and serves as a useful check on other components of a fraud claim: whether the representation was factual, or merely opinion; whether it was material, or actually quite trivial; whether the plaintiff was ignorant of the falsity of the representation, or truly knew (or at least suspected) that it might be false; and, ultimately, whether the plaintiff in fact relied upon the representation in making a decision to buy or use the product.[31] Even in fraud cases, therefore, the justifiability requirement serves this important validation function of helping weed out claims where the plaintiff unfairly seeks to hold the defendant liable for harm caused principally by the plaintiff's bad judgement rather than any false statement the defendant may have made.[32]

In claims for merely negligent misrepresentation, the standard of conduct for the plaintiff reverts to the normal objective standard of reasonable behavior for a person exercising due regard for his or her own welfare.[33] As for strict liability claims for misrepresentation, the case law is very sparse, but most courts would probably agree that the justifiability of a plaintiff's reliance upon a manufacturer's innocent misrepresentation "involves an objective standard" based upon whether a "reasonable consumer" could rely on the particular representations in dispute.[34]

---

**30.** See Prosser and Keeton on Torts § 108, at 751 (citations omitted):

"The design of the law is to protect the weak and credulous from the wiles and stratagems of the artful and cunning, as well as those whose vigilance and security enable them to protect themselves," and "no rogue should enjoy his ill-gotten plunder for the simple reason that his victim is by chance a fool."

**31.** See, e.g., AMPAT/Midwest, Inc. v. Illinois Tool Works Inc., 896 F.2d 1035, 1042 (7th Cir. 1990) (Ill. law) (Posner, J.) ("The requirement of justifiable reliance backstops the jury's determination of actual reliance."). Compare Miller v. Pfizer Inc., 196 F.Supp.2d 1095 (D. Kan. 2002) (finding plaintiffs failed to raise genuine issue of fact as to reliance upon subtle and subliminal marketing influences, unknown to even prescribing physician himself), aff'd, 356 F.3d 1326 (10th Cir. 2004). Justifiable reliance is conventionally used as an umbrella concept that includes the elements of materiality and fact. See Restatement (2d) Torts § 538 cmt. b; Prosser and Keeton on Torts §§ 108 and 109. See generally Dobbs, Law of Torts § 474, at 1360–61.

**32.** See § 3.2, above.

**33.** See, e.g., Mainline Tractor & Equip. Co. v. Nutrite Corp., 937 F.Supp. 1095, 1105 (D. Vt. 1996) (justifiability of reliance based on objective standard). See generally Restatement (2d) Torts § 552A, stating that "[t]he recipient of a negligent misrepresentation is barred from recovery for pecuniary loss suffered in reliance upon it if he is negligent in so relying," but noting that comparative fault may be applicable to claims involving physical harm. Id. cmt. b.

**34.** Gawloski v. Miller Brewing Co., 644 N.E.2d 731, 736 (Ohio Ct. App. 1994) (prison inmates sued Miller for causing their alcoholism that led to lives of crime, on ground that commercials misrepresented Miller beer as "an enhancer of the quality of life"; held, any reliance not justifiable as matter of law). See also American Safety Equip. Corp. v. Winkler, 640 P.2d 216, 223 (Colo. 1982) (4–3 decision) ("Justifiable reliance contemplates the reasonable exercise of knowledge and intelligence in assessing the represented facts. Unsupportable subjective reliance is inadequate.").

Comment j to Restatement (2d) Torts § 402B (on justifiable reliance) provides scant assistance in discerning the standard for assessing justifiability in the strict liability context. However, comment g suggests an objective standard: "[T]he fact represented must be a material one, of importance to the normal purchaser, by which the ultimate buyer may justifiably be expected to be influenced in buying the chattel."

### Contributory and Comparative Negligence; Assumption of Risk; Misuse

If a plaintiff is justified in relying upon a tortious misrepresentation, there may well be no room for the conventional misconduct defenses to operate. To put the matter another way, the defenses of contributory negligence, assumption of risk, and misuse all logically appear to be absorbed into the requirement that a plaintiff establish the justifiability of his or her reliance upon the defendant's representation.

An example may help to illustrate this point. Assume that a plaintiff purchases a "Golfing Gizmo," a golfers' training device consisting of two metal pegs, two cords (one cotton and one elastic), and a golf ball attached to the cotton cord.[35] The purpose of the device, described by the manufacturer as "completely safe–ball will not hit player," is to return the ball to the golfer, via the elastic cord, after it is hit. If the player sets up the Gizmo device ten feet in front of a brick wall and squarely hits the ball against the wall, the ball might well bounce back and hit the golfer in the head. Using the Gizmo in such an obviously dangerous manner is clearly unreasonable, hence contributorily negligent, and the golfer would appear quite plainly to have assumed the risk. Similarly, if the golfer were to strike the ball with a sledge hammer rather than a golf club, shattering the ball which injured his eye, or if the golfer were injured in a fall when the cord broke as he used it to climb a tree, such unforeseeable misuse should bar recovery. But in each of these situations, the golfer's injuries could not conceivably be said to result from a justifiable reliance on the manufacturer's safety representation.[36] In short, the justifiable reliance element of tortious misrepresentation claims appears to embrace and so supplant the traditional forms of user misconduct defenses.

Over centuries of fraud cases, the courts developed a substantial body of doctrine concerning the misconduct of the representee, largely in cases involving pecuniary loss and mostly involving the effect of a plaintiff's contributory negligence. Although many decisions have required plaintiffs engaged in business transactions to maintain a reasonable vigilance for their own protection, even from fraudulent misrepresentation,[37] the cases widely hold that "contributory negligence" as such is no defense to fraud.[38] The rule is said to be different for claims of

---

**35.** This was the product in fact involved in Hauter v. Zogarts, 534 P.2d 377 (Cal. 1975), an early, prominent case decided under § 402B of the Second Torts Restatement.

**36.** See Sales, The Innocent Misrepresentation Doctrine: Strict Tort Liability Under Section 402B, 16 Hous. L. Rev. 239, 271 (1979). It would also appear to fail on falsity, in that a fair interpretation of the safety representation includes an implicit limitation that the Gizmos be used in a manner that is not patently dangerous.

**37.** See, e.g., Cheney Bros., Inc. v. Batesville Casket Co., 47 F.3d 111, 115 (4th Cir. 1995) (S.C. law) (noting the established

" 'duty on the part of the representee to use some measure of protection and precaution to safeguard his interest,' " quoting Thomas v. American Workmen, 14 S.E.2d 886, 887–88 (S.C. 1941)).

**38.** "That a more cautious buyer might not have relied, might have smelled a rat, does not defeat liability. There is no defense of contributory negligence to an intentional tort, including fraud." AMPAT/Midwest, Inc. v. Illinois Tool Works Inc., 896 F.2d 1035, 1041 (7th Cir. 1990) (Ill. law) (Posner, J.). See generally 37 Am. Jur. 2d, Fraud & Deceit § 247, at 329 (1968) (noting the conflicting policies of suppressing fraud, on the one hand, while not encouraging the ne-

negligent misrepresentation, where contributory negligence is conventionally said to bar the claim.[39] Yet, here as well, these cases have mostly involved business transactions involving pecuniary loss,[40] and there is little case law on whether the contributory negligence defense is applicable to products liability misrepresentation cases involving physical harm.

For claims of strict products liability for misrepresentation, as set forth in § 402B of the *Second Restatement* and § 9 of the *Third Restatement*, the effect of a plaintiff's contributory negligence is unclear. Comment *j* to § 402B, which explicitly addresses justifiable reliance, provides scant assistance in discerning the meaning of justifiability in the strict liability context; it merely mentions that justifiability is a requirement and references the *Second Restatement* sections on justifiable reliance for fraud, "so far as they are pertinent," including the provision that contributory negligence does not bar liability.[41] There is little value in such dated, offhand treatment of important doctrine, and the *Third Restatement* addresses the issue even less.[42] While some isolated case law involving strict liability claims suggests that contributory negligence should not serve as a defense, the authority is old and not entirely on point.[43] Thus, whether a plaintiff's contributory negligence should play some role in strict products liability claims for tortious misrepresentation, or whether contributory negligence is exclusively absorbed into the issue of the justifiability of the plaintiff's reliance, remains a problem to be solved. Surely the most appropriate resolution of this issue, as discussed above, is to view contributory negligence, in all forms of tortious misrepresentation cases, as merged entirely into the justifiability of reliance.

But contributory negligence has been resurrected in recent years in the guise of comparative fault, and so some courts may feel obligated to consider whether and, if so, how the comparative fault doctrine may affect claims for tortious misrepresentation. This issue has received little consideration from either courts or commentators.[44] In cases involving

---

glect of one's own interests, on the other, and observing that the law has opted to protect not only the vigilant but also the gullible "against the machinations of the designedly wicked"); Restatement (2d) Torts § 545A. Although § 545A by its terms applies to recovery for pecuniary loss, it is incorporated by reference into the Restatement's fraud section governing liability for physical harm. See Restatement (2d) Torts § 557A cmt. *a*.

**39.** See Restatement (2d) Torts § 552A.

**40.** See Restatement (2d) Torts § 552A. The principal Restatement section on negligent misrepresentation involving risk of physical harm, § 311, addresses the plaintiff misconduct issue only in terms of the reasonableness of the plaintiff's reliance. See Restatement (2d) Torts § 311 cmt. *c*.

**41.** Restatement (2d) Torts § 545A.

**42.** In short, because of the brevity of explicit discussion of justifiability in either

§ 402B of the Second Restatement or § 9 of the Third Restatement, neither Restatement provides a basis for determining whether, in addition to the justifiable reliance element, the doctrine of strict products liability in tort for misrepresentation may be barred, or damages reduced, on the ground of a plaintiff's contributory negligence.

**43.** See Prosser and Keeton on Torts § 108, n.10 at 750–51.

**44.** The commentary includes a couple of suggestions that comparative fault principles might be applied to negligent misrepresentation claims. See, e.g., Dobbs, Law of Torts 1359–60; Restatement (2d) Torts § 552A cmt. *b. Contra* Comment, 28 Cumb. L. Rev. 177 (1997–98). But such observations probably spring from a desire to reduce the harshness of contributory negligence serving as a total bar, rather than to provide misrepresenters a second bite at the misconduct apple.

intentional misrepresentation, the comparative fault doctrine is widely viewed to be inapplicable[45] for the same reasons of fairness and policy that properly preclude the use of contributory negligence as a bar to fraud recovery discussed above. In negligent misrepresentation cases involving pecuniary loss outside the realm of products liability, the few cases are split, but the better view appears to be that comparative fault should not apply here either.[46] No case has been found applying comparative fault to cases involving strict products liability for misrepresentation under § 402B of the *Second Restatement* or its *Third Restatement* counterpart. Surely comparative fault is inappropriate for strict liability claims where the very idea of a buyer's negligence in relying justifiably upon a manufacturer's product safety representations is a concept that is difficult to grasp.

Because a plaintiff must prove the justifiability of his or her reliance for any tortious misrepresentation claim, the traditional products liability misconduct defenses are simply out of place. Of the few decisions that have addressed this issue, the better reasoned ones have exhibited little tolerance for attempts by defense lawyers to get two bites at the misconduct apple by arguing, first, that the plaintiff's reliance upon the representation was unjustified, and, second, that, even if the reliance in fact was justified, the plaintiff was negligent, assumed the risk, or misused the product.[47] These decisions persuasively conclude that the justifiability (or reasonableness) of a plaintiff's reliance encompasses all forms of plaintiff misconduct addressed by the traditional misconduct defenses.[48] If a statute does not compel a contrary result,[49] little would be lost, except confusion, if the courts would clearly rule that none of the traditional misconduct defenses apply to common law tortious misrepresentation claims in products liability litigation.

---

**45.** "It is probably safe to say that comparative negligence will not apply in deceit cases except in the 'comparative fault' jurisdictions of Arkansas, Maine, and New York." H. Woods and B. Deere, Comparative Fault § 14:51, at 396 (3d ed. 1996). See generally Annot., 18 A.L.R.5th 525 (1995) (applicability of comparative negligence to intentional tort actions).

**46.** See, e.g., Condor Enters., Inc., v. Boise Cascade Corp., 856 P.2d 713 (Wash. App. 1993); Estate of Braswell v. People's Credit Union, 602 A.2d 510 (R.I. 1992); Greycas, Inc. v. Proud, 826 F.2d 1560 (7th Cir. 1987) (Ill. law). See generally Annot., 22 A.L.R. 5th 464 (1995) (applicability of comparative negligence to negligent misrepresentation actions).

**47.** See, e.g., Klages v. General Ordnance Equip. Corp., 367 A.2d 304, 313 (Pa. Super. Ct. 1976) ("the lower court fully charged the jury regarding justifiable reliance, and that instruction encompassed appellant's claim of assumption of the risk"); Schwabe v. Porter, 501 N.W.2d 470 (Wis. Ct. App. 1993) (comparative fault).

**48.** Not all courts or commentators entirely agree. See Daye v. General Motors Corp., 720 So.2d 654 (La. 1998) (sole cause of accident was driver's negligent driving, not defendant's advertising); Nugent v. Utica Cutlery Co., 636 S.W.2d 805, 809–10 (Tex. App. 1982) (misuse defense allowed in defense of § 402B claim). See generally Sales, The Innocent Misrepresentation Doctrine: Strict Tort Liability Under Section 402B, 16 Hous. L. Rev. 239, 269–77 (1979) (acknowledging that the justifiability of reliance requirement fully embraces the assumption of risk defense, but arguing that misuse and comparative fault should be allowed as independent defenses); Comment, 28 Cumb. L. Rev. 177, 190 (1997–98) (assumption of risk and contributory and comparative negligence should not be defenses, but misuse should).

**49.** At least Connecticut has a products liability statute (1) providing that misrepresentation is a products liability claim, and (2) specifying misconduct defenses that apply generally to such claims. Conn. Gen. Stat. §§ 52–572l, m(b), & o.

# Chapter 14

---

# SPECIAL DEFENSES

*Table of Sections*

---

## § 14.1  SPECIAL DEFENSES—GENERALLY

Products liability defenses may be broadly classified into three categories: (1) user-misconduct defenses; (2) no-duty defenses; and (3) other, "special," defenses. The first category of defenses, based on a product user's misconduct—contributory negligence, comparative fault, assumption of risk, product misuse, and unreasonable reliance on a misrepresentation—were addressed in the previous chapter.[1] Those are the most pervasive forms of defense, potentially applicable in nearly every type of products liability case.

The second category of "defense," the no-duty type, gives rise to defensive arguments that a manufacturer may assert but may not be affirmative defenses that a defendant must plead and on which it has the burden of proof. In most states, product misuse falls into the no-duty classification; however, it is treated in the misconduct "defense" chapter because it so centrally concerns consumer misconduct.[2] Another prominent no-duty defensive issue is the state of the art "defense."[3] Like product misuse, most courts consider the state of the art issue to be part of the plaintiff's prima facie case. Thus, a plaintiff ordinarily must prove that, under the prevailing state of the art at the time a product was made and sold, the manufacturer should have reasonably known of the risk and how feasibly to avoid it. Products liability reform statutes in a number of states create true affirmative defenses for product misuse and state of the art, as previously discussed, but the common law of most states views these "defenses" as limitations on the scope of a manufacturer's duty, the breach of which a plaintiff must plead and prove. Issues

§ 14.1

1. See ch. 13, above.

2. See § 13.5, above.

3. See § 10.4, above.

such as product misuse, state of the art, and other no-duty rules (such as the obvious danger rule[4] and the bulk supplier and sophisticated user doctrines[5]) are normally viewed by defendants as "defenses" that may cut off liability as readily[6] as proof of a plaintiff's assumption of risk.[7]

The third category of defenses is a catch-all classification, holding all remaining defenses. Some of these are scattered throughout the book in other chapters, such as the "seat-belt defense," examined in the chapter on automotive products liability litigation;[8] and the "sealed-container defense," treated in the chapter on retailers.[9] The present chapter examines the most important remaining "special" defenses: (1) the contract specifications defense;[10] (2) the government contractor defense;[11] (3) compliance with government standards;[12] (4) federal preemption;[13] and (5) statutes of limitations and repose.[14] Except for the regulatory compliance defense, the other special defenses are affirmative defenses, such that a products liability claim ordinarily will be dismissed entirely if a defendant establishes the applicability of such a defense to the case.

## § 14.2 COMPLIANCE WITH CONTRACT SPECIFICATIONS; GOVERNMENT CONTRACTORS

A manufacturer's responsibility for design defects has always firmly rested on the fact that the manufacturer *created* the bad design, even if only by including a defectively designed component into the larger product over which it had overall design responsibility.[1] Hence, the manufacturer of a *non*defective component that an assembling manufacturer buys and combines with other components in a dangerously defective manner is not subject to liability for resulting injuries unless the component manufacturer helped the assembler design the larger, defective product. A manufacturer's responsibility for injuries caused by defects in its product's design thus rests comfortably on the manufacturer's control over design decisions, and hence, design choices that are somehow flawed. Our sensibilities normally would be jarred if the law were to hold a manufacturer liable for harm for which it was in no fair way responsible.

Two important products liability defenses are based on the idea that the manufacturer, relying entirely on the purchaser's own design specifications, did not participate in decisions resulting in a design defect—a general one, based on a manufacturer's manufacture of a product according to a buyer's precise, contractual terms, and a specific one, where the

**4.** See § 10.2, above.

**5.** See § 9.5, above.

**6.** Or more so, in view of the spreading tentacles of comparative fault which may serve merely to reduce a plaintiff's damages rather than to relieve the defendant of responsibility for the harm. See § 13.3, above.

**7.** See § 13.4, above.

**8.** See § 17.5, below.

**9.** See § 15.2, below.

**10.** See § 14.2, below.

**11.** See id.

**12.** See § 14.3, below.

**13.** See § 14.4, below.

**14.** See § 14.5, below.

**§ 14.2**

**1.** See § 8.1, above.

buyer is the government. The question raised in both situations is whether it is appropriate to hold a manufacturer responsible, if it merely fabricates a product to design specifications supplied by the purchaser, for injuries that result if the design proves defective? For example, General Motors may contract with a punch press manufacturer to construct a press for making hub caps, according to precise design specifications that GM provides to the press manufacturer. If the specifications for the press do not call for guards and a GM worker is injured as a result, should the press manufacturer be subject to liability to the worker for making and selling a defectively designed machine? Or, suppose that Wal–Mart designs a toaster with a dangerously defective heating element, and contracts out production of the toaster to an appliance manufacturer. Should the toaster manufacturer be liable for the harm that results from a fire caused by the toaster when it overheats due to a design defect? Finally, consider the situation of an automotive manufacturer that contracts with the United States Army to produce a number of Jeeps according to a design provided or approved by a federal procurement official. If a roll bar designed according to the contract specifications gives way in a roll-over accident, injuring the driver, should the driver be permitted to maintain a design defect claim against the manufacturer?

Normally manufacturers are responsible for the harmful consequences of design defects in the products that they make and sell.[2] But, as mentioned above, that is because the manufacturer's own engineers ordinarily formulate the designs used to make those products. Where a manufacturer simply follows the design requirements specified by a purchaser, the design and manufacturing functions of product manufacture are separated. When a manufacturer's role is reduced to merely "fabricating" the product, the fairness and logic of holding the manufacturer liable for a dangerous design are called into question. This section surveys the two principal defenses that have developed to address the liability issues that arise in this situation: (1) the contract specifications defense, and (2) the government contractor defense.

### The Contract Specifications Defense

The contract specifications defense shields a manufacturer from liability for injuries caused by a design defect in products it manufactures in accordance with plans and specifications supplied by the purchaser, unless the design is obviously defective.[3] From an early New York case,[4] the contract specifications "defense" evolved as a rule of nonliability for negligence when an independent contractor simply follows its employer's directions on how a product should be built, when the contractor has no reason to know that the directions are unsafe.[5] This widely accepted principle[6] is described in the *Restatement (Second)*

---

**2.** See ch. 8, above.

**3.** See Comments, 33 San Diego L. Rev. 385 (1996); 9 J. Corp. L. 113 (1983).

**4.** Ryan v. Feeney & Sheehan Bldg. Co., 145 N.E. 321 (N.Y. 1924).

**5.** See, e.g., Dorse v. Armstrong World Indus., Inc., 513 So.2d 1265 (Fla. 1987); Bynum v. FMC Corp., 770 F.2d 556 (5th Cir. 1985) (Miss. law).

**6.** Although the principle is widely accepted, not every jurisdiction recognizes it.

*of Torts*, which provides that an independent contractor "is not required to sit in judgment on the plans and specifications or the materials provided by his employer" and is not liable for their insufficiency unless the design or materials specified "is so obviously bad that a competent contractor would realize that there was a grave chance that his product would be dangerously unsafe."[7]

The contract specifications defense rests on the fact that a contractor usually is not negligent in following design specifications provided by a purchaser ("employer") pursuant to the contract.[8] Accordingly, the courts have split over whether the defense should also apply to products liability claims based on strict liability, reasoning that implied warranty claims are based on a product's failure to be in a merchantable condition, not on the seller's fault,[9] and that the defense is inconsistent with the doctrine and policies of strict liability in tort.[10] A growing majority of courts have disagreed, however, holding that even in strict liability, a manufacturer who merely fabricates a product according to the purchaser's design is not responsible, in the absence of an obvious defect, if the design proves bad.[11] "To hold [a contractor] liable for defective design

See, e.g., Collins v. Newman Mach. Co., 380 S.E.2d 314 (Ga. Ct. App. 1989).

**7.** See Restatement (2d) Torts § 404 comment *a*.

**8.** See, e.g., Hunt v. Blasius, 384 N.E.2d 368 (Ill. 1978).

**9.** See Maldonado v. Creative Woodworking Concepts, Inc., 796 N.E.2d 662 (Ill. App. Ct. 2003) (contract specification defense does not apply to breach of warranty claim which is concerned with product's merchantability, not defendant's conduct). *Contra* Sunbeam Constr. Co. v. Fisci, 82 Cal.Rptr. 446 (Ct. App. 1969).

**10.** See, e.g., Hendricks v. Comerio Ercole, 763 F.Supp. 505 (D. Kan. 1991); Dorse v. Armstrong World Indus., Inc., 513 So.2d 1265 (Fla. 1987); Nobriga v. Raybestos–Manhattan, Inc., 683 P.2d 389 (Haw. 1984); McLaughlin v. Sikorsky Aircraft, 195 Cal. Rptr. 764 (Ct. App. 1983); Michalko v. Cook Color & Chem. Corp., 451 A.2d 179 (N.J. 1982); Pust v. Union Supply Co., 561 P.2d 355, 361 (Colo. Ct. App. 1977), aff'd, 583 P.2d 276 (Colo. 1978); Roy v. Star Chopper Co., 442 F.Supp. 1010, 1021–22 (D.R.I. 1977); Challoner v. Day & Zimmermann, Inc., 512 F.2d 77, 83 (5th Cir. 1975) (Tex. law), vacated on other grounds, 423 U.S. 3 (1975) ("a strict liability case, unlike a negligence case, does not require that the defendant's act or omission be the cause of the defect. It is only necessary that the product be defective when it leaves the defendant's control"); Wirth v. Clark Equip. Co., 457 F.2d 1262, 1267 (9th Cir. 1972) (Or. law).

**11.** See, e.g., Spangler v. Kranco, Inc., 481 F.2d 373, 375 n.2 (4th Cir. 1973) (Va. law); Garrison v. Rohm & Haas Co., 492 F.2d 346, 351 (6th Cir. 1974) (Ky. law); Hunt v. Blasius, 384 N.E.2d 368, 371 (Ill. 1978); Moon v. Winger Boss Co., 287 N.W.2d 430, 434 (Neb. 1980) ("a manufacturer is not liable for injuries to a user of a product which it has manufactured in accordance with plans and specifications of one other than the manufacturer, except when the plans are so obviously, patently, or glaringly dangerous that a manufacturer exercising ordinary care under the circumstances then existing would not follow them"); Orion Ins. Co. v. United Tech. Corp., 502 F.Supp. 173, 176–78 (E.D. Pa. 1980); Weggen v. Elwell–Parker Elec. Co., 510 F.Supp. 252, 254 (S.D. Iowa 1981); Housand v. Bra–Con Indus., 751 F.Supp. 541 (D. Md. 1990); Szatkowski v. Turner & Harrison, Inc., 584 N.Y.S.2d 170, 171 (App. Div. 1992) ("a contractor is not responsible for injuries resulting from a defective plan or design if it diligently complies with the specifications furnished to it by the owner"); Bloemer v. Art Welding Co., 884 S.W.2d 55, 56 (Mo. Ct. App. 1994) ("a contractor's compliance with its customer's plans and specifications is, with limited exceptions not applicable to this case, a complete defense to strict liability and negligence claims based on defective design"); Lorenzen v. Bi–State Ford, No. L–93–337, 1994 WL 411511 (Ohio Ct. App. 1994); Austin v. Clark Equip. Co., 48 F.3d 833, 837 (4th Cir. 1995) (Va. law); Duncan v. CRS Sirrine Eng'r., Inc., 524 S.E.2d 115 (S.C. Ct. App. 1999).

would amount to holding a non-designer liable for design defect. Logic forbids any such result."[12]

In recent years, the notion of "strict" products liability in tort has withered substantially as courts and commentators have increasingly recognized the close nexus between negligence and strict liability in cases involving defects in design.[13] As the strict liability straw man continues to unravel, courts which in the past declined to allow the contract specifications defense in actions denominated as "strict" liability should now be more open to recognizing the appropriateness of this defense under modern products liability theory.[14] In short, the soundness of applying the contract specifications defense to design defect claims does not depend on the underlying theory of liability.

Some products liability reform statutes, directly or indirectly, address the effect of compliance with contract specifications. Thus, at least one state statute effectively adopts a contract specifications defense by shielding altogether defendants who manufacture products according to the design specifications of others;[15] a couple of statutes classify such manufacturers as "sellers" and so relieve them from strict products liability entirely[16] or contingently if the designing manufacturer is insolvent or not subject to suit;[17] and a couple of others give a manufacturer a right of indemnity against a seller (such as a large retail chain, like Sears or Wal–Mart) which provides plans and specifications that give rise to a products liability claim.[18]

### The Government Contractor Defense

The government contractor defense is a special doctrine that applies only to manufacturers who contract with the government to build a product according to specifications provided or approved by the government.[19] While some form of government contractor defense has existed for several decades,[20] it gained prominence in the 1980s, particularly

---

**12.** Garrison v. Rohm & Haas Co., 492 F.2d 346, 351 (6th Cir. 1974) (Ky. law).

**13.** See §§ 5.7–5.9, 8.7, and 8.8, above.

**14.** See Comment, 33 San Diego L. Rev. 385 (1996).

**15.** See Wash. Rev. Code § 7.72.010(2) (such a party not a "manufacturer" for purposes of design defect liability). *But cf.* Neher v. II Morrow Inc., 145 F.3d 1339 (9th Cir. 1998).

**16.** See Ga. Code Ann. § 51–1–11.1.

**17.** See N.J. Stat. Ann. §§ 2A:58C–8 and 2A:58C–9(b).

**18.** See Ariz. Rev. Stat. § 12–684(C); Idaho Code § 6–1307(3).

**19.** See Beh, The Government Contractor Defense: When Do Governmental Interests Justify Excusing a Manufacturer's Liability for Defective Products?, 28 Seton Hall L. Rev. 430 (1997); Slawotsky, The Expansion of the Government Contractor Defense, 31 Tort & Ins. L.J. 929 (1996); Davis, The Supreme Court and Our Culture of

Irresponsibility, 31 Wake Forest L. Rev. 1075, 1091–1116 (1996); Cass and Gillette, The Government Contractor Defense: Contractual Allocation of Public Risk, 77 Va. L. Rev. 257 (1991); M. Green and Matasar, The Supreme Court and the Products Liability Crisis: Lessons from *Boyle*'s Government Contractor Defense, 63 S. Cal. L. Rev. 637 (1990); Notes, 33 Pub. Cont. L.J. 649 (Spring 2004), 40 Wm. and Mary L. Rev. 687 (1999); Annot., 53 A.L.R.5th 535 (1997); Note, 70 Tex. L. Rev. 1261 (1992) (applying *Boyle* to vaccine manufacturers). For extensive treatments of this defense, see 4 Frumer and Friedman, Products Liability ch. 31; 3 Am. Law Prod. Liab. 3d ch. 45.

**20.** See, e.g., Sanner v. Ford Motor Co., 381 A.2d 805, 806 (N.J. Super. Ct. App. Div. 1977) (passenger injured in army jeep accident could not maintain suit against jeep manufacturer for failing to equip vehicle with seatbelts and a roll bar "since defendant had no discretion with respect to the installation of seatbelts and since it strictly

after the Supreme Court decided *Boyle v. United Technologies Corp.*[21] in 1988.[22] Having redefined the nature and scope of the defense and clarified its elements, *Boyle* is now the starting point for determining how a products liability claim is affected if the product was fabricated according to specifications provided or approved by a federal (although possibly a state or local) governmental agency.

### The Boyle Case

In *Boyle v. United Technologies Corp.*,[23] the copilot of a Marine Corps helicopter was killed during a training exercise when his helicopter crashed in the ocean. Boyle survived the impact of the crash, but, as the helicopter sank in the water, he was unable to escape and drowned. Boyle's representatives sued the helicopter's manufacturer, the Sikorsky Division of United Technologies, claiming that the escape hatch was defectively designed because (1) it opened out rather than in, which precluded opening the hatch in a submerged craft because of water pressure, and (2) the positioning of various instruments blocked access to the escape hatch handle.[24] Plaintiff won at trial, but the Fourth Circuit Court of Appeals reversed on the basis of that court's version of the "military contractor defense,"[25] and the Supreme Court granted certiorari.[26] The issue before the Court was whether and "when a contractor providing military equipment to the Federal Government can be held liable under state tort law for injury caused by a design defect."[27] As a matter of federal common law, a bare majority of the Court approved a government contractor defense.[28]

Writing for the majority, Justice Scalia reasoned that allowing state products liability claims against military contractors who fabricate products according to designs approved by federal officials would frustrate the purposes of the discretionary function exception to governmental liability in the Federal Tort Claims Act.[29] Because military design specifications involve a host of choices including the "tradeoff between greater safety and greater combat effectiveness,"[30] they involve discretionary decisions with which tort suits against contractors would interfere. If products liability claims challenging such choices were allowed, government contractors would raise their prices to offset this risk of liability,

---

adhered to the plans and specifications owned and provided by the Government").

**21.** 487 U.S. 500 (1988).

**22.** The history of the defense is briefly sketched in 4 Frumer and Friedman, Products Liability § 31.01 (1999).

**23.** 487 U.S. 500 (1988).

**24.** Id. at 502–03.

**25.** Boyle v. United Tech. Corp., 792 F.2d 413 (4th Cir. 1986). The Fourth Circuit had adopted this defense in another case, Tozer v. LTV Corp., 792 F.2d 403 (4th Cir. 1986), that it decided on the same day as *Boyle*.

**26.** 479 U.S. 1029 (1986).

**27.** 487 U.S. at 502.

**28.** Because it was unclear whether the Fourth Circuit had decided whether a jury reasonably could have found each of the elements of the defense as formulated by the Supreme Court, the Court remanded for clarification. See 487 U.S. at 514.

**29.** Although Congress in 28 U.S.C. § 1346(b) waived the sovereign immunity of the United States for negligent or wrongful conduct of federal employees, 28 U.S.C. § 2680(a) retains sovereign immunity for "[a]ny claim ... based upon the exercise or performance or the failure to exercise or perform a discretionary function or duty on the part of a federal agency or an employee of the Government, whether or not the discretion involved be abused."

**30.** 487 U.S. at 511.

passing on the financial burden to the United States.[31] "It makes little sense," reasoned Justice Scalia, "to insulate the Government against financial liability for the judgment that a particular feature of military equipment is necessary when the Government produces the equipment itself, but not when it contracts for the production."[32] Thus, when these federal interests conflict with state products liability law that would allow a design defect claim against a military contractor, the state law must give way.[33]

To protect these federal interests, *Boyle* adopted a three-part test shielding military contractors from design defect liability under state products liability law—when "(1) the United States approved reasonably precise specifications, (2) the equipment conformed to those specifications, and (3) the supplier warned the United States about the dangers in the use of the equipment that were known to the supplier but not to the United States."[34]

### Boyle in the Courts

"Stripped of its essentials," in the words of one court, "the government contractor defense arises when the defendant can prove that 'the government made me do it.' "[35] This may be a fair summary of *Boyle*'s underlying concept, but its interpretation has raised a number of thorny issues. For example, while it is clear that *Boyle*'s first element, the "approval" prong, does not require that the government completely design a product by itself,[36] the Court did not specify the requisite type or extent of government involvement in "approving" a product's design. Thus, it was early held that the defense does not apply if the government merely "rubber stamps" the contractor's design.[37] Yet the government need not participate at all in the actual development of a product's design, so long as it genuinely evaluates the content of the contractor's ultimate design decisions.[38] And even if the government is significantly involved in and approves a product's design as a whole, *Boyle* requires proof that a government officer considered the particular design feature that caused the injury giving rise to the products liability claim.[39]

---

**31.** Id. at 511–12.

**32.** Id. at 512.

**33.** Id.

**34.** Id.

**35.** Gray v. Lockheed Aeronautical Sys. Co., 125 F.3d 1371, 1377 (11th Cir. 1997), vacated by 524 U.S. 924 (1998).

**36.** "The design ultimately selected may well reflect a significant policy judgment by Government officials whether or not the contractor rather than those officials developed the design. In addition, it does not seem to us sound policy to penalize, and thus deter, active contractor participation in the design process.... " 487 U.S. at 513.

**37.** See, e.g., Trevino v. General Dynamics Corp., 865 F.2d 1474 (5th Cir. 1989) (although Navy ultimately "approved" contractor's design of diving hangar, Navy set only general performance standards and

left contractor with complete design discretion). "A rubber stamp is not a discretionary function; therefore, a rubber stamp is not 'approval' under *Boyle*." Id. at 1480. Accord, Johnson v. Grumman Corp., 806 F.Supp. 212 (W.D. Wis. 1992).

**38.** See Haltiwanger v. Unisys Corp., 949 F.Supp. 898 (D.D.C. 1996).

**39.** Miller v. Honeywell Int'l, Inc., 2002 WL 31399125 (S.D. Ind. 2002) (surveying case law on government's role in "approving" design), aff'd, 107 Fed.Appx. 643 (7th Cir. 2004); Jordan v. Ensign–Bickford Co., 20 S.W.3d 847 (Tex. App. 2000) (reversing summary judgment where manufacturer of stun gun grenades for FBI failed to show that FBI provided or approved reasonably precise specifications for grenade's design or warning labels); Boyle v. United States Tech. Corp., 487 U.S. 500, 512 (1988). See, e.g., Shurr v. A.R. Siegler, Inc., 70

*Boyle* raises a host of other issues.[40] For example, the courts are split on whether the government contractor defense applies only to manufacturers of military equipment (military contractors): some hold that the defense is so limited[41] while others hold that *Boyle*'s reasoning protects manufacturers of any type of government equipment (government contractors).[42] As for the types of defects covered by the government contractor defense, *Boyle* by its terms protects a contractor only for *design* defect claims. While the second prong of the *Boyle* test strongly suggests that manufacturing defects lie outside the government contractor defense,[43] leaving manufacturers liable for such defects,[44] some courts take the position that the defense may cover manufacturing defects in certain situations.[45] Warning claims, however, are an entirely different kettle of fish. Assuming that the defendant is able to establish each of the three prongs of the *Boyle* test with respect to the warnings claim, most courts hold that the government contractor defense applies to (and protects the contractor from) such claims, particularly if the federal contract includes warnings requirements that significantly conflict with state products liability law.[46] As for causes of action, the government

F.Supp.2d 900, 912 (E.D. Wis. 1999) (defendant "faces a high evidentiary burden: it must establish that the government approved each specific design feature in question in an exercise of discretion balancing technical, military, social, and safety considerations"); Snell v. Bell Helicopter Textron, 107 F.3d 744 (9th Cir. 1997); Lewis v. Babcock Indus., 985 F.2d 83 (2d Cir. 1993) (reordering product with knowledge of defect constitutes approval).

**40.** See Annot., 53 A.L.R.5th 535 (1997).

**41.** See, e.g., In re Hawaii Fed. Asbestos Cases, 960 F.2d 806, 812 (9th Cir. 1992) (asbestos insulation used in Navy ships not "manufactured with the special needs of the military in mind"); Nielsen v. George Diamond Vogel Paint Co., 892 F.2d 1450 (9th Cir. 1990) (civilian government employee injured by paint manufactured to specifications of Army Corps of Engineers).

**42.** See, e.g., Silverstein v. Northrop Grumman Corp., 842 A.2d 881 (N.J. Super. Ct. App. Div. 2004) (manufacturer of postal vehicle); Wisner v. Unisys Corp., 917 F.Supp. 1501, 1509 (D. Kan. 1996) (Postal Service designed letter sorter that caused repetitive stress injuries); Haltiwanger v. Unisys Corp., 949 F.Supp. 898 (D.D.C. 1996) (same); Carley v. Wheeled Coach, 991 F.2d 1117 (3d Cir. 1993) (defense applicable to manufacturer of ambulance, allegedly with an excessively high center of gravity, manufactured to General Services Administration specifications). In Hercules v. United States, 516 U.S. 417 (1996), the Supreme Court characterized the *Boyle* defense as the "government contractor defense" which "shields contractors from tort liability for products manufactured for the Government in accordance with Government specifica-

tions, if the contractor warned the United States about any hazards known to the contractor but not to the Government." Id. at 422.

**43.** See, e.g., Feldman v. Kohler Co., 918 S.W.2d 615 (Tex. App. 1996); Sundstrom v. McDonnell Douglas Corp., 816 F.Supp. 587 (N.D. Cal. 1993); Mitchell v. Lone Star Ammunition, Inc., 913 F.2d 242 (5th Cir. 1990).

**44.** See, e.g., Snell v. Bell Helicopter Textron, Inc., 107 F.3d 744, 749 (9th Cir. 1997).

**45.** See, e.g., Roll v. Tracor, Inc., 102 F.Supp.2d 1200 (D. Nev. 2000) (recognizing that *Boyle* may apply to manufacturing defect claims but holding that manufacturer of flare failed to establish that government approved reasonably specific manufacturing specifications and that mishap could have been caused by aberrational defect that does not implicate federal interests); Snell v. Bell Helicopter Textron, 107 F.3d 744 (9th Cir. 1997); Bailey v. McDonnell Douglas Corp., 989 F.2d 794 (5th Cir. 1993); Bentzlin v. Hughes Aircraft Co., 833 F.Supp. 1486 (C.D. Cal. 1993) (when government involves itself in manufacturing process of sophisticated military weaponry such as Maverick missile, manufacturer of such equipment may be immunized from manufacturing defect claims).

**46.** See, e.g., In re "Agent Orange" Prods. Liab. Litig., 304 F.Supp.2d 404 (E.D.N.Y. 2004); Kerstetter v. Pacific Scientific Co., 210 F.3d 431 (5th Cir. 2000); Perez v. Lockheed Corp., 81 F.3d 570 (5th Cir. 1996); Tate v. Boeing Helicopters, 55 F.3d 1150 (6th Cir. 1995), on remand, 921

contractor defense logically should apply to negligence, breach of warranty, and strict liability in tort claims alike.[47]

While the *Boyle* government contractor defense is a federal common law rule applicable only to manufacturers supplying equipment to federal agencies, it applies to products liability claims tried in state as well as federal courts.[48] Whether contractors who manufacture and sell products to state and local governments should receive similar protection from both design and warnings defect claims is an entirely separate question that the individual states must answer as a matter of their local products liability law. Most state courts thus are free, as a matter of state common law, to refuse to apply a *Boyle*-type government contractor defense to state and local government contractors.[49] Several states,

F.Supp. 1562 (W.D. Ky. 1996) (defense established where government and contractor had dialogue about warnings and government's approval of operator's manual was more than a rubber stamp); In re Aircraft Crash Litig., 752 F.Supp. 1326 (S.D. Ohio 1990), aff'd, Darling v. Boeing Co., 935 F.2d 269 (6th Cir. 1991) (table) (Air Force required hundreds of changes to aircraft manual prior to approval); Miller v. United Tech. Corp., 660 A.2d 810 (Conn. 1995). Compare Miller v. Diamond Shamrock Co., 275 F.3d 414 (5th Cir. 2001) (*Boyle* only requires manufacturers of Agent Orange to warn government about dangers it actually knew and not should have known); Morgan v. Brush Wellman, Inc., 165 F. Supp. 2d 704 (E.D. Tenn. 2001) (defense to warning claim established where supplier of beryllium oxide to nuclear armament facility showed that government was more aware of the dangers of beryllium than the suppliers); Butler v. Ingalls Shipbuilding, Inc., 89 F.3d 582 (9th Cir. 1996) (defense applicable to warnings claims only if there is conflict between federal contract requirements and state law warnings requirements). See generally Densberger v. United Techs. Corp., 297 F.3d 66 (2d Cir. 2002) (questioning whether *Boyle* applied to claim that manufacturer negligently failed to adequately warn Army, and not end users, of dangers that helicopter could become uncontrollable).

**47.** See, e.g., Feldman v. Kohler Co., 918 S.W.2d 615 (Tex. App. 1996) (warranty); Bailey v. McDonnell Douglas Corp., 989 F.2d 794 (5th Cir. 1993) (warranty); Kern v. Roemer Mach. & Welding Co., 820 F.Supp. 719 (S.D.N.Y. 1992), aff'd without opinion, 996 F.2d 302 (2d Cir. 1993) (summary judgment for defendant on all three claims); In re Aircraft Crash Litig., 752 F.Supp. 1326 (S.D. Ohio 1990), aff'd, Darling v. Boeing Co., 935 F.2d 269 (6th Cir. 1991) (table) (negligent testing).

The result may be different under state law versions of the government contractor

defense. See, e.g., Graham v. Concord Constr., Inc., 999 P.2d 1264, 1266 (Wash. 2000) (contractor immunized from liability only if not negligent).

**48.** See, e.g., Silverstein v. Northrop Grumman Corp., 842 A.2d 881 (N.J. Super. Ct. App. Div. 2004); Graham v. Concord Constr., Inc., 999 P.2d 1264 (Wash. 2000); Feldman v. Kohler Co., 918 S.W.2d 615 (Tex. App. 1996) (thorough review of doctrine); Miller v. United Tech. Corp., 660 A.2d 810 (Conn. 1995); Anzalone v. Westech Gear Corp., 661 A.2d 796 (N.J. 1995). While applicable in state courts, *Boyle* appears to allow defendants sued in state courts to remove the case to federal court whether or not federal claims are alleged or if there is diversity of citizenship. See, e.g., Madden v. Able Supply Co., 205 F.Supp.2d 695 (S.D. Tex. 2002) (clothing the manufacturer of turbine generator on Navy vessel with "federal officer" status under federal officer removal statute); Miller v. Diamond Shamrock Co., 275 F.3d 414 (5th Cir. 2001) (clothing an Agent Orange manufacturer protected by *Boyle* with the status of a "federal officer" entitled to remove cases to federal court under 28 U.S.C. § 1442(a)(1)).

**49.** See, e.g., Conner v. Quality Coach, Inc., 750 A.2d 823 (Pa. 2000) (rejecting defense). "[T]here are a range of other considerations that would compete with protection of the government's economic interests, not the least of which is that the insulation of the Commonwealth from indirect costs on grounds of public interest has the perverse effect of permitting a government officer to minimize as a consideration in procurement decisions (at least as a matter of financial concern) external societal costs, particularly in terms of potential diminishment to public safety." Id. at 834. See also Nickolson v. Alabama Trailer Co., Inc., 791 So.2d 926 (Ala. 2000) (reversing summary judgment where plaintiff produced expert testimony that state's design of trailer for its power com-

however, have enacted products liability reform statutes that protect government contractors who comply with mandatory government contract specifications.[50]

## § 14.3   COMPLIANCE WITH STATUTES AND REGULATIONS

### The Dual Regulation Problem

Manufacturers of many types of products are subject to two (or even three) different forms of safety regulation—by federal (and possibly state) administrative agencies, *ex ante*, and by the judicial products liability system, *ex post*. For example, manufacturers of cars and airplanes first must meet the often detailed design safety standards of the National Highway Traffic Safety Administration or the Federal Aviation Administration only to be second-guessed by juries passing on the very same issues, years later, when a person injured in a crash complains in court. Producers of other products, such as industrial materials, have to endure a third layer of regulation, first having to conform to safety standards of the federal agency, like the Occupational Safety and Health Administration, then to the standards of each state's industrial safety department, and finally to a state's judicial standards of "defectiveness" if the product causes harm and ends up as the subject of a products liability case in court. Thus, manufacturers understandably question the logic and fairness of having to conform to safety regulations imposed by the government's executive-administrative branch before marketing a product only to have the government's judicial branch declare the conforming product illegal thereafter.

The idea of a government standards (or "regulatory compliance") defense,[1] that would shield a manufacturer from liability in a products liability action if the product complied with relevant regulations of a safety agency, is a "close cousin" of the federal preemption defense.[2] However, the two defenses are fundamentally distinct. The government standards defense concerns the standard by which a state's substantive products liability law determines whether a product is deemed defective.

---

pany was so obviously dangerous that no competent manufacturer would follow specifications).

**50.** See Ind. Code § 34–20–5–1(2) (rebuttable presumption of nonliability); Kan. Stat. Ann. § 60–3304(c) (absolute defense); Wash. Rev. Code § 7.72.050(2) (same); Mich. Comp. Laws Ann. § 600.2946(4) (rebuttable presumption).

#### § 14.3

**1.** See Rabin, Reassessing Regulatory Compliance, 88 Geo. L. J. 2049 (2000); M. Green and Schultz, Tort Law Deference to FDA Regulation of Medical Devices, 88 Geo. L. J. 2119 (2000); Noah, Rewarding Regulatory Compliance: The Pursuit of Symmetry in Products Liability, 88 Geo. L.J. 2147 (2000); T. Schwartz, Regulatory Standards and Products Liability: Striking the Right Balance Between the Two, 30 U. Mich. J.L. Reform 431 (1997); Ausness, The Case for a

"Strong" Regulatory Compliance Defense, 55 Md. L. Rev. 1210 (1996); D'Angelo, Effect Of Compliance With Applicable Governmental Product Safety Regulations On a Determination Of Product Defect, 36 S. Tex. L. Rev. 453 (1995); T. Schwartz, The Role of Federal Safety Regulations in Products Liability Actions, 41 Vand. L. Rev. 1121 (1988); Note, 26 Harv. J. on Legis. 175 (1989); Products Liability Restatement § 4(b); Frumer and Friedman, Products Liability § 18.05; 2 Madden & Owen on Products Liability § 16:3.

**2.** See Rabin, Reassessing Regulatory Compliance, 88 Geo. L.J. 2049, 2053 (2000); Products Liability Restatement § 4(b) cmt. *e*. A closer cousin is the negligence doctrine governing the effect of compliance with a safety statute or regulation. See § 2.4, above. A more distant cousin is the government contractor defense. See § 14.2, above. On federal preemption, see § 14.4, below.

When a manufacturer in a products liability case asserts that it complied with certain government standards of product safety, the regulatory compliance issue is whether the court should borrow the safety standards of the regulatory agency (or statute) as the formal test of product defectiveness. By contrast, the federal preemption defense concerns the constitutional issue, under the Supremacy Clause, of when federal law (normally safety regulations of federal agencies) overrides state products liability law (normally the standards set by courts in defectiveness adjudications) with which it may conflict.[3] While the two defenses share in common the issue of whether statutory and regulatory safety standards should bar products liability actions, the government standards defense is a state-law defense recognized narrowly in only a small minority of jurisdictions, whereas the federal preemption defense is a federal-law defense that binds all courts when Congress so intends.

A government standards defense, that would bar a products liability action if the accident product complied with all relevant governmental safety standards at the time it was sold, has a superficial appearance of fair play and common sense. However, arguments favoring the defense are more than offset by a large number of problems: statutes (and sometimes regulations) tend to be abstract, vague, limited in scope, and incapable of adequately addressing the myriad factual situations that may arise in individual cases; conversely, regulations may be so narrow and specific that they fail to capture related activities at the margins of the regulation, leaving large categories of similar activities unregulated; statutes and regulations are both difficult to amend to reflect changes over time, and those dealing with science and technology quickly become obsolete; both are often shaped more by lobbyists for the regulated parties than by detached and objective decision makers neutrally balancing all affected interests in pursuit of optimal safety; and, unlike the inherent flexibility of the common law, the rigidity of regulatory safety standards tends to stifle creativity and innovation.[4] For these and other reasons, the courts have never seen fit to create a common-law regulatory compliance defense. As discussed below, however, courts in rare instances do recognize a kind of government standards defense, and several states have legislated various narrow forms of the defense as a part of tort reform.

### Judicial Rejection of Government Standards Defense

The issue of whether there should be a government standards defense is not unique to products liability law. For many years, many types of actors, in many types of situations where conduct is subjected to governmental regulation *ex ante*, have sought to assert a government standards defense to liability in tort *ex post*. Courts[5] and commentators[6]

---

**3.** On federal preemption, see § 14.4, below.

**4.** "Common law tort courts have long provided a safer haven from the corruption that can accompany the making of statutes and regulations; among institutional actors, judges are relatively likely to treat injured persons fairly." Bernstein, Products Liability in the United States Supreme Court: A Venture in Memory of Gary Schwartz, 53 S.C. L. Rev. 1193, 1219 (2002). See T. Schwartz, The Role of Federal Safety Regulations in Products Liability Actions, 41 Vand. L. Rev. 1121 (1988).

**5.** See, e.g., Grand Trunk Ry. Co. v. Ives, 144 U.S. 408, 419–27 (1892). "Courts

---

**6.** See note 6 on page 888.

long ago rejected the idea that an actor whose conduct comports with a safety standard required by statute or administrative regulation is automatically protected from tort liability for harm resulting from that conduct. Courts on infrequent occasions do make an exception to the general rule in limited situations where a defendant conformed its behavior precisely as directed by an especially well-considered government standard.[7] But it is fundamental law that governmental safety standards adopt only a minimum safety floor below which an actor may face criminal sanctions but above which due care may require the actor to be more cautious.[8]

Following these fundamental tort law principles, virtually all courts reject the general idea of a regulatory compliance defense to products liability actions, whether based on negligence, warranty, or strict liability in tort.[9] Compliance with a relevant governmental safety standard is some evidence of a manufacturer's non-negligence and a product's non-defectiveness, but it is not conclusive on those issues.[10] Compliance evidence is not unimportant,[11] but in a products liability case it serves

have generally not looked with favor upon the use of statutory compliance as a defense to tort liability." Ramirez v. Plough, Inc., 863 P.2d 167, 173 (Cal. 1993).

**6.** See, e.g., Morris, The Role of Criminal Statutes in Negligence Actions, 49 Colum. L. Rev. 21, 42 (1949).

**7.** See Prosser and Keeton on Torts § 36, at 233.

**8.** "Such a standard is no more than a minimum, and it does not necessarily preclude a finding that the actor was negligent in failing to take additional precautions." Id. See Restatement (2d) Torts § 288C: "Compliance with a legislative enactment or an administrative regulation does not prevent a finding of negligence where a reasonable man would take additional precautions."

**9.** See, e.g., Red Hill Hosiery Mill, Inc., v. MagneTek, Inc., 582 S.E.2d 632 (N.C. Ct. App. 2003) (compliance not determinative of defectiveness; implied warranty); Abadie v. Metropolitan Life Ins. Co., 784 So.2d 46 (La. Ct. App. 2001) (jury charge that "[c]ompliance with government standards is but one element or item of proof of whether of not the product is defective" accurately stated the law); Doyle v. Volkswagenwerk AK., 481 S.E.2d 518 (Ga. 1997) (all three liability theories); Wagner v. Clark Equip. Co., 700 A.2d 38, 48–51 (Conn. 1997) (negligence and strict liability in tort); Ake v. General Motors Corp., 942 F.Supp. 869, 873–74 (W.D.N.Y. 1996) (same).

The only apparent exception to this universal rule is where a plaintiff brings a design defect claim based solely on the consumer expectation test and the manufacturer has complied with governmentally mandated warnings. A few courts have held that

compliance with the government's warning standards precludes a design defect claim based solely on consumer expectations because it would be "anomalous" for a consumer to expect a product to perform more safely than its government-mandated warnings indicate. This narrow exception was first employed in cases alleging toxic shock syndrome from tampons but has now been applied to other products. See e.g., Eriksen v. Mobay Corp., 41 P.3d 488 (Wash. Ct. App. 2002); Murphy ex rel. Murphy v. Playtex Family Prods. Corp., 176 F.Supp.2d 473 (D. Md. 2001), aff'd on point, 69 Fed.Appx. 140 (4th Cir. 2003); Haddix v. Playtex Family Prods. Corp., 138 F.3d 681 (7th Cir. 1998) (Ill. law); Papike v. Tambrands Inc., 107 F.3d 737 (9th Cir. 1997) (Cal. law).

**10.** Nor is compliance conclusive on liability for punitive damages where the manufacturer knows that the standard is insufficient. See, e.g., Clark v. Chrysler Corp., 310 F.3d 461 (6th Cir. 2002) (Ky. law) (compliance with door latch safety standard did not preclude punitive damages award where manufacturer knew that standard did not test design defect proven at trial); Nissan Motor Co., Ltd. v. Armstrong, 32 S.W.3d 701 (Tex. App. 2000) ("no safety defect" finding by NHTSA did not preclude punitive damages award where manufacturer failed to advise NHTSA of defect), rev'd on other grounds, 145 S.W.3d 131 (Tex. 2004); Dorsey v. Honda Motor Co., 655 F.2d 650, 656–57 (5th Cir. 1981) (Fla. law); Gryc v. Dayton–Hudson Corp., 297 N.W.2d 727, 733–35 (Minn. 1980). See generally § 18.6, below.

**11.** See, e.g., Gable v. Gates Mills, 784 N.E.2d 739 (Ohio Ct. App. 2003) (compliance with statutory regulation is relevant

only as "a piece of the evidentiary puzzle" rather than as "an impenetrable shield from liability."[12] This has been the rule since the early days of modern products liability law,[13] and, except for some relatively minor legislative retrenchments in several states, discussed below, the rule is as firmly entrenched today as ever.[14] The *Restatement* provides quite simply that "a product's compliance with an applicable product safety statute or administrative regulation is properly considered in determining whether the product is defective with respect to the risks sought to be reduced by the statute or regulation, but such compliance does not preclude as a matter of law a finding of product defect."[15]

An occasional court asserts that regulatory compliance carries more weight than mere evidence of due care and a product's nondefectiveness—that compliance with government safety standards provides "strong evidence" of the manufacturer's nonliability.[16] And sometimes courts note that "where no special circumstances require extra caution, a court may find that conformity to the statutory standard amounts to due care as a matter of law."[17] While this is true, it is also tautological to say that a defendant who complies with a statutory standard is not liable for acting more safely than required by the statute if there was no

and probative of what a reasonable consumer would expect when evaluating purchase but does not immunize manufacturer from liability); Wagner v. Clark Equip. Co., 700 A.2d 38, 51 (Conn. 1997) ("compliance with a federal regulation may carry more weight with a jury than compliance with an industrial standard, because federal regulation has the imprimatur of the federal government").

**12.** Doyle v. Volkswagenwerk AK., 481 S.E.2d 518, 521 (Ga. 1997).

**13.** Early cases include Sherman v. M. Lowenstein & Sons, Inc., 282 N.Y.S.2d 142 (App. Div. 1967) (Flammable Fabrics Act, flammability standard); LaGorga v. Kroger Co., 275 F.Supp. 373 (W.D. Pa. 1967), aff'd, 407 F.2d 671 (3d Cir. 1969) (same); Berkebile v. Brantley Helicopter Corp., 281 A.2d 707 (Pa. Super. Ct. 1971) (FAA, airworthiness standard); Jonescue v. Jewel Home Shopping Service, 306 N.E.2d 312 (Ill. App. Ct. 1973) (Federal Hazardous Substance Labeling Act, determination of whether substance is harmful or toxic); Stevens v. Park, Davis & Co., 507 P.2d 653 (Cal. 1973) (FDA, drug labeling); Raymond v. Riegel Textile Corp., 484 F.2d 1025 (1st Cir. 1973) (Flammable Fabrics Act, flammability standards); Hill v. Husky Briquetting, Inc., 220 N.W.2d 137 (Mich. Ct. App. 1974) (warnings on bags of charcoal for home use prescribed by state statute), aff'd, 223 N.W.2d 290 (Mich. 1974); Wilson v. Piper Aircraft Corp., 577 P.2d 1322 (Or. 1978) (FAA, approval of general model design and airworthiness).

**14.** More recent cases include Red Hill Hosiery Mill, Inc., v. Magnatek, Inc., 582 S.E.2d 632 (N.C. Ct. App. 2003) (implied

warranty); Abadie v. Metropolitan Life Ins. Co., 784 So.2d 46, 81–82 (La. Ct. App. 2001) (negligence; jury charge that "[c]ompliance with government standards is but one element or item of proof of whether or not the product is defective" was correct); Edwards v. Basel Pharms., 933 P.2d 298 (Okla. 1997) (strict liability in tort; FDA direct-to-consumer warning requirements of risk of heart attack from nicotine patches); Doyle v. Volkswagenwerk AK., 481 S.E.2d 518 (Ga. 1997) (NHTSA Standard 208 on passive restraints); Wagner v. Roche Labs., 671 N.E.2d 252 (Ohio 1996) (FDA approval of package insert); Brooks v. Beech Aircraft Corp., 902 P.2d 54, 63 (N.M. 1995) (no FAA requirement of shoulder harnesses in general aviation aircraft like Musketeer when it was designed); Washington State Physicians Ins. Exch. & Assoc. v. Fisons Corp., 858 P.2d 1054, 1069 (Wash. 1993) (FDA labeling and warning regulations); United Blood Services v. Quintana, 827 P.2d 509, 520 (Colo. 1992) (AIDS; standards for processing blood).

**15.** Products Liability Restatement § 4(b). See cmt. *a*, noting that this principle concerns design and warnings defects, but not manufacturing defects.

**16.** See, e.g., Sims v. Washex Mach. Corp., 932 S.W.2d 559, 565 (Tex. App. 1995) ("Compliance with government regulations is strong evidence, although not conclusive, that a machine was not defectively designed.").

**17.** Beatty v. Trailmaster Prods., Inc., 625 A.2d 1005, 1014 (Md. 1993). See also Jones v. Hittle Serv., Inc., 549 P.2d 1383, 1390 (Kan. 1976).

reason to act more safely—which circles back to basing liability on the defendant's lack of negligence, not on the defendant's compliance with the statutory standard.[18]

Denying manufacturers a full-fledged regulatory compliance defense may appear to be unfair because it forces them to meet the safety standards of both governmental regulators and the courts, but this dual approach to product safety oversight generally makes good sense. Most product safety statutes, and most product safety regulations promulgated thereunder, are designed to prohibit (and criminalize) only the clearest and most egregious hazards. In addition to the problems with a regulatory compliance defense noted earlier, the limited budgets and other resources of safety agencies generally preclude them from being effective arbiters of optimal, rather than minimal, safety. Consequently, the law allocates responsibility for product safety, first, to manufacturers, to make their products reasonably safe and so conforming to the safety obligations of both the regulators and the courts; second, to governmental regulators, to set minimum safety standards for products whose special dangers require regulatory intervention; and, finally, to the courts, to test a manufacturer's safety decisions, in case of product accident, against the common-law safety standards based on balance, reason, and fairness.[19] Admittedly, this multi-layered allocation of safety responsibility is somewhat complicated, and burdensome on manufacturers, but it normally works quite well to minimize government intrusion into product design and labeling decisions while protecting the basic safety rights of product consumers.[20]

Litigation involving industrial machinery raises an interesting question of the admissibility of evidence that a manufacturer's industrial product complied with safety regulations of the Occupational Safety and Health Administration (OSHA), the federal agency which regulates the safety of products in the workplace.[21] Manufacturers normally are eager to introduce such evidence, not only to show that their products met these safety standards, and so are at least arguably nondefective, but also to help focus the jury's attention, first, on the employer's role in causing (or at least in not preventing) the injury, perhaps by failing to equip a machine with a safety device, and, second, on the possibility that the employee may have received workers' compensation. Manufacturers generally are barred from introducing evidence or argument directly on these issues,[22] and using evidence of compliance with OSHA standards

---

**18.** See Restatement (2d) Torts § 288C cmt. *a.* Thus, in *Beatty,* the court, applying the statutory standard as a matter of law, ruled for the defendant because the plaintiff had failed to prove that the product, "either for negligence or strict liability purposes, was foreseeably unsafe, defective, or unreasonably dangerous." 625 A.2d at 1014.

**19.** See Owen, The Moral Foundations of Products Liability Law: Toward First Principles, 68 Notre Dame L. Rev. 427 (1993).

**20.** "It has long been the concern of this state to protect the health and safety of its

citizens. . . . It is the widely held view that the FDA sets minimum standards for drug manufacturers as to design and warnings. We conclude that compliance with these minimum standards does not necessarily complete the manufacturer's duty." Edwards v. Basel Pharms., 933 P.2d 298, 302 (Okla. 1997).

**21.** See the Occupational Safety and Health Act of 1970, 29 U.S.C. § 651 et seq.

**22.** Workers' compensation statutes bar employees from suing their own employers in tort for workplace injuries, of course, in exchange for guaranteed compensation un-

may permit a manufacturer's counsel to get the jury thinking about these other factors related to the larger responsibility and compensation issues present in such cases. For these same reasons, plaintiffs' counsel seek to exclude evidence on an industrial machine's compliance with OSHA standards, in order to keep attention focused on the manufacturer's responsibility for the injury.

But cases involving compliance with OSHA regulations are different from other types of regulatory compliance cases because OSHA standards on design and warnings requirements of industrial machinery impose requirements for *employers*, not manufacturers.[23] Nevertheless, such standards do set safety minimums for industrial products, which would seem to have some relevance to the issue of product defectiveness in products liability litigation. Because such regulations do have at least some minimal relevance to product defectiveness, with respect to a manufacturer's risk-benefit analysis[24] and possibly to a user's safety expectations,[25] many courts allow evidence of a product's compliance with relevant OSHA standards in a products liability action against the manufacturer.[26] Because of the limited relevance and probable prejudice of such evidence, other courts hold that OSHA safety standards are generally inadmissible in products liability litigation.[27]

### Special Situations Where Compliance with Safety Standards May Be Conclusive

In certain limited situations, federal and state regulators study and regulate the safety of particular aspects of particular products especially closely. In such situations, if an agency has reasonably settled on a specific safety standard that appears optimal at the time, then much may be said for foreclosing products liability actions that demand more safety of manufacturers than the agency determined was appropriate. The CPSC, for example, after conducting a major study of the problem of

der such insurance systems. See Weiler, Workers' Compensation and Product Liability: The Interaction of a Tort and a Non–Tort Regime, 50 Ohio St. L.J. 825 (1989); § 15.6, below.

**23.** See, e.g., Hughes v. Lumbermens Mut. Cas. Co., 2 S.W.3d 218 (Tenn. Ct. App. 1999); Minichello v. U.S. Indus., Inc., 756 F.2d 26, 29 (6th Cir. 1985).

**24.** See Doyle v. Volkswagenwerk AK., 481 S.E.2d 518, 521 (Ga. 1997); Knitz v. Minster Mach. Co., 1987 WL 6486, at *31–33 (Ohio Ct. App. 1987).

**25.** See Wagner v. Clark Equip. Co., 700 A.2d 38, 50 (Conn. 1997).

**26.** See, e.g., Couch v. Astec Indus., Inc., 53 P.3d 398 (N.M. Ct. App. 2002) (failure to comply with OSHA regulations relevant to prove that manufacturer was negligent); Wagner v. Clark Equip. Co., 700 A.2d 38, 48–51 (Conn. 1997); Sims v. Washex Mach. Corp., 932 S.W.2d 559 (Tex. App. 1995); Vaughn v. Cannon USA, Inc., Prod. Liab. Rep. (CCH) ¶ 12,578 (W.D. Mich. 1990); Saphore v. Clark Equip. Co., Prod. Liab. Rep.

(CCH) ¶ 12,574 (Pa. Super. Ct. 1989); Knitz v. Minster Mach. Co., 1987 WL 6486, at *27–33 (Ohio Ct. App. 1987) (evidence of OSHA standards and those of Ohio's Industrial Commission, while not conclusive of liability, are relevant and admissible to prove feasibility of design, availability of alternative safeguards, and other factors relevant to a risk-benefit determination of defectiveness); Gideon v. Johns–Manville Sales Corp., 761 F.2d 1129, 1144 (5th Cir. 1985); Deyoe v. Clark Equip. Co., 655 P.2d 1333, 1337 (Ariz. Ct. App. 1982).

**27.** See, e.g., Hughes v. Lumbermens Mut. Cas. Co., 2 S.W.3d 218 (Tenn. Ct. App. 1999). See generally 3 Frumer and Friedman, Products Liability § 18.05[3] (citing cases both ways); R. Hogan and R. Moran, Occupational Safety and Health Act, ch. 12, The Use of OSHA in Private Litigation (Matthew Bender); Siris, OSHA Compliance: Can it be Used to Show that a Product is Safe?, 4 Prod. Liab. L.J. 156 (1993).

injuries to operators of power mowers, adopted a regulation requiring that manufacturers design their mowers so that the blades will stop rotating within three seconds of the time an operator releases the control handle.[28] Apart from the possibility of federal preemption,[29] and assuming that technology has not advanced sufficiently to resolve the problem in a clearly better way, a court might reasonably decide not to permit an operator, injured when his foot slips beneath the mower, to attempt to prove that the mower's design was defective because the blade did not stop within *two* seconds after the handle was released.

A rare situation where a court chose to adopt a regulatory standard as a matter of law is *Ramirez v. Plough, Inc.*[30] In this case, a four-month-old child contracted Reye's Syndrome after his Spanish-speaking mother gave him some St. Joseph's Aspirin for Children to relieve his symptoms of a cold. The aspirin's label warned of the risk only in English, not in Spanish. Although the FDA specifically permitted English-only labeling, the plaintiff claimed that the failure to warn in Spanish was inadequate. After considering the web of rules on foreign-language labeling requirements in various other contexts adopted by the California legislature; the FDA's quite specific rules governing foreign-language labeling that permitted, but did not require, such labeling; and the multiplicity of health, social, cost, and practicability factors, the court concluded that foreign-language labeling requirements were better determined by legislatures and regulatory agencies than by the courts. For this reason, the court chose to adopt the legislative/regulatory rule permitting English-only warnings as the safety standard that properly should be applied in the case.[31]

The Food and Drug Administration closely reviews applications submitted by pharmaceutical manufacturers for new prescription drugs. Scrupulously evaluating the clinical data provided by the manufacturer, the agency balances the safety and efficacy of each proposed new drug and evaluates the adequacy of proposed warnings and usage information to be provided to doctors who will prescribe the drug. If the FDA fully and fairly evaluates all of this information, and approves for sale the drug and warnings, then it would seem to make little sense to let a jury reevaluate the same information and find the drug or warnings "defective."[32] On this basis, at least two states have immunized manufacturers of prescription drugs from strict liability,[33] and another has ruled that a

---

**28.** Details of the study and regulation are examined in Southland Mower Co. v. Consumer Prod. Safety Comm'n, 619 F.2d 499 (5th Cir. 1980), which upheld the CPSC's three-second blade-stop criterion.

**29.** See § 14.4, below.

**30.** 863 P.2d 167 (Cal. 1993). *Ramirez* is also examined in § 9.3, above.

**31.** Noting that the FDA stresses the importance of "uniformity of presentation and clarity of message," the court concluded: "To preserve that uniformity and clarity, to avoid adverse impacts upon the warning requirements mandated by the

federal regulatory scheme, and in deference to the superior technical and procedural lawmaking resources of legislative and administrative bodies, we adopt the legislative/regulatory standard of care that mandates nonprescription drug package warnings in English only." Id. at 177.

**32.** See Noah, Rewarding Regulatory Compliance: The Pursuit of Symmetry in Products Liability, 88 Geo. L.J. 2147 (2000).

**33.** See Brown v. Superior Court, 751 P.2d 470 (Cal. 1988); Grundberg v. Upjohn Co., 813 P.2d 89 (Utah 1991). See § 8.10, above.

manufacturer's compliance with FDA regulations for warnings in direct-to-consumer advertising of pharmaceuticals gives rise to a rebuttable presumption that the warnings satisfy the duty to warn.[34] When a plaintiff is harmed by an aspect of a product that met an applicable safety standard which the FDA or other regulatory agency scrupulously investigated and approved, and the perfect agency model fits the situation quite closely, then a court may properly conclude that the product's compliance with the governmentally approved safety standard conclusively establishes that the challenged aspect of the product was not defective.[35] Such cases, however, will be unusual.

The model of a perfect FDA—fully informed of a drug's foreseeable hazards before the drug is marketed, kept fully informed thereafter of adverse drug-reactions, fully funded by Congress, and with no political pressure to expedite the approval of new drugs—does not closely fit the real world.[36] For this reason, courts should almost always base defectiveness determinations on broader considerations than a manufacturer's compliance with an administrative agency's product safety regulation—even if the safety standard applies directly to the product feature of which the plaintiff complains, and even if the agency's procedures normally are rigorous and precise—because of the probability of imper-

---

**34.** See Perez v. Wyeth Labs., Inc., 734 A.2d 1245, 1259 (N.J. 1999). "For all practical purposes, absent deliberate concealment or nondisclosure of after-acquired knowledge of harmful effects, compliance with FDA standards should be virtually dispositive of such claims. By definition, the advertising will have been 'fairly balanced.'" Id.

**35.** See, e.g., Dentson v. Eddins & Lee Bus Sales, Inc., 491 So.2d 942, 944 (Ala. 1986) ("in this context, involving school transportation, an area traditionally reserved for the legislature, we find that the legislature's pronouncement is conclusive: a school bus in Alabama may not be found defective ... because it is not equipped with passenger seat belts"). The *Restatement* provides:

Occasionally, after reviewing relevant circumstances, a court may properly conclude that a particular product safety standard set by statute or regulation adequately serves the objectives of tort law and therefore that the product that complies with the standard is not defective as a matter of law. Such a conclusion may be appropriate when the safety statute or regulation was promulgated recently, thus supplying currency to the standard therein established; when the specific standard addresses the very issue of product design or warning presented in the case before the court; and when the court is confident that the deliberative process by which the safety standard was established was full, fair, and thorough and reflected substantial expertise.

Products Liability Restatement § 4 cmt. *e.*

**36.** See Rabin, Keynote Paper: Reassessing Regulatory Compliance, 88 Geo. L.J. 2049 (2000); T. Schwartz, The Role of Federal Safety Regulations in Products Liability Actions, 41 Vand. L. Rev. 1121 (1988).

An example is Tobin v. Astra Pharm. Prods., Inc., 993 F.2d 528, 538 (6th Cir. 1993) (Ky. law), where plaintiff "presented an articulable basis for disregarding the FDA's finding that ritodrine was effective ... : the individual studies relied on by the FDA were insufficient to support a finding of efficacy as found by the FDA Advisory Committee, and the pooled data requested by the Advisory Committee was statistically invalid." Although its safety decisions may be better than those of other agencies, the FDA is not immune to criticism. See, e.g., Pollack, Drug to Treat Bowel Illness is Approved by the FDA, N.Y. Times, July 25, 2002, at A12 (quoting Dr. Sidney Wolfe, Director of the Public Citizen Health Research Group, who characterized the FDA's approval as "a very bad decision" because of its marginal effectiveness, the fact that it appears to increase the risk of ovarian cysts, and the availability of over-the-counter medicines to treat the condition). Despite its real-world shortcomings, the FDA's safety standards are probably closer to optimal than any other agency. See, e.g., Schultz, Tort Law Deference to FDA Regulation of Medical Devices, 88 Geo. L.J. 2119 (2000).

fections in the safety standard or the agency's procedures in any particular case. Thus, courts and juries should give only such weight to a product's compliance with a governmental safety standard as is warranted by the particular circumstances of each case.[37]

## State Reform Legislation

About a dozen states have enacted products liability reform statutes concerning the effect of a manufacturer's compliance with a governmental safety standard. Commonly, the statutes create a rebuttable[38] presumption that a product was not defective—or not defective and that the manufacturer or seller was not negligent—if the product complied with applicable state or federal safety statutes or agency regulations. For example, Michigan's statute provides that "there is a rebuttable presumption that the manufacturer or seller is not liable if ... the aspect of the product that allegedly caused the harm was in compliance with standards relevant to the event causing the death or injury set forth in a federal or state statute or ... regulations.... "[39] Taking a slightly different approach, the Kansas statute provides that, if a product conforms to a governmental safety standard, the plaintiff must prove "that a reasonably prudent product seller could and would have taken additional precautions."[40] Three statutes restate the common law rule on compliance, stating merely that a manufacturer's compliance with government standards may be considered by the trier of fact.[41] Several statutes are directed at drugs that comport with FDA standards, one raising a rebuttable presumption that complying warnings are adequate,[42] another giving manufacturers of complying drugs complete immunity,[43] and several barring punitive damages for drugs marketed with

---

**37.**  See Rabin, 88 Geo. L.J. 2049 (2000).

**38.**  Since the plaintiff has the burden of proof on negligence and product defect anyway, it is difficult to understand what if any additional proof a plaintiff must offer to rebut such a presumption. In Duffee v. Murray Ohio Mfg. Co., 879 F.Supp. 1078 (D. Kan. 1995), the court suggested that a plaintiff's rebuttal could consist of proof that (1) the regulatory standards were outdated, or (2) that a reasonable manufacturer would know of dangers in the product's use not contemplated by the standard. Alternatively, it would seem that rebuttal evidence could lie in the plaintiff's proofs on negligence or defectiveness in the prima facie case. Expert testimony is not necessarily required to rebut such a presumption. See, e.g., Cansler v. Mills, 765 N.E.2d 698, 706–07 (Ind. Ct. App. 2002) (airbag that met Standard 208 failed to inflate in crash; circumstantial evidence of defectiveness sufficient to overcome presumption).

A Tennessee Court has held that compliance with OSHA regulations does not create a rebuttable presumption of nondefectiveness under that state's statute because the regulations apply to employers, not manufacturers. See Hughes v. Lumbermens

Mut. Cas. Co., 2 S.W.3d 218 (Tenn. Ct. App. 1999).

**39.**  Mich. Comp. L. § 600.2946(4). See also Colo. Rev. Stat. § 13–21–403(1)(b); Ind. Code § 34–20–5–1(2); N.D. Cent. Code § 28–01.3–09; Tenn. Code Ann. § 29–28–104; Utah Code Ann. § 78–15–6(3). For an example of decisions applying these presumptions, see Ehlis v. Shire Richwood, Inc., 233 F.Supp.2d 1189 (D.N.D. 2002) (evidence that prescription drug Adderall was used for "off-label" illnesses overcame statutory presumption of no defect from compliance with FDA standards), aff'd on other grounds, 376 F.3d 1013 (8th Cir. 2004); Rogers v. Cosco, Inc., 737 N.E.2d 1158 (Ind. Ct. App. 2000) (plaintiff overcame statutory presumption of no defect from compliance with government standard for child booster seats).

**40.**  Kan. Stat. Ann. § 60–3304(a).

**41.**  Ark. Code Ann. § 16–116–105(a); Ohio Rev. Code Ann. § 2307.75(B)(4); Wash. Rev. Code § 7.72.050(1).

**42.**  N.J. Stat. Ann. § 2A:58C–4.

**43.**  Mich. Comp. L. § 600.2946(5). This statutory immunity has survived constitu-

FDA approval.[44]

## § 14.4  FEDERAL PREEMPTION

### Nature of Federal Preemption

No issue in modern products liability law is more important, or more inscrutable, than the doctrine of federal preemption. The doctrine is important because the defense of federal preemption in recent years has grown from little more than a blip on the radar screen to one of the most powerful defenses in all of products liability law. The doctrine is inscrutable because it is a formless and elusive creature, based on ephemeral notions of federalism and the oft-obscure intent of Congress, that vacillates according to shifting political sentiments of the courts—views on federal versus states rights, on Congress versus the courts, and on regulatory versus products liability law.[1] Despite the best efforts of courts and commentators to bring order to the chaos,[2] the law on federal preemption has obstinately refused to set anchor in enduring principles.

tional attack. See Taylor v. Smithkline Beecham Corp., 658 N.W.2d 127 (Mich. 2003); Garcia v. Wyeth–Ayerst Labs., 265 F.Supp.2d 825 (E.D. Mich. 2003).

**44.** Ariz. Rev. State § 12–701; N.J. Stat. Ann. § 2A:58C–5(c); Ohio Rev. Stat. Ann. § 2307.80(C); Or. Rev. Stat. § 30.927, Utah Code Ann. § 78–18–2. The statutes provide that protection from punitive damages is lost if the manufacturer knowingly withholds or misrepresents pertinent information.

### § 14.4

**1.** See, e.g., Nelson, Preemption, 86 Va. L. Rev. 225, 229 (2000) (noting that "the politics of preemption are complicated"); Smith and Grage, Federal Preemption of State Products Liability Actions, 27 Wm. Mitchell L. Rev. 391 (2000) (predicting that "the preemption defense is almost certain to remain highly politicized"). On preemption generally, see 1 L. Tribe, American Constitutional Law § 6–28 et seq. (3d ed. 2000); J. Nowak and R. Rotunda, Constitutional Law § 9.1 et seq. (6th ed. 2000); Spence and Murray, The Law, Economics, and Politics of Federal Preemption Jurisprudence: A Quantitative Analysis, 87 Cal. L. Rev. 1125, 1129 (1999) ("For most judges, whether liberal or conservative, these cases pit one dimension of their ideology, their principles of federalism, against another, their policy preferences or attitudes toward the particular local regulation at issue.").

**2.** See, e.g., Davis, On Preemption, Congressional Intent, and Conflict of Laws, 66 U. Pitt. L. Rev. ___ (2004); Ausness, Preemption of State Tort Law by Federal Safe-

ty Statutes: Supreme Court Preemption Jurisprudence Since *Cipollone*, 92 Ky. L.J. 913, 968 (2004); Owen, Federal Preemption of Products Liability Claims, 55 S.C. L. Rev. 411 (2003); Raeker–Jordan, A Study in Judical Sleight of Hand: Did Geier v. American Honda Motor Co. Eradicate the Presumption Against Preemption, 17 BYU J. Pub. Pol'y 1 (2002); Davis, Unmasking the Presumption in Favor of Preemption, 53 S.C. L. Rev. 967 (2002); Scordato, Federal Preemption of State Tort Claims, 35 U.C. Davis L. Rev. 1 (2001); Madden, Federal Preemption of Inconsistent State Safety Obligations, 21 Pace L. Rev. 103 (2000); Nelson, Preemption, 86 Va. L. Rev. 225 (2000); Dinh, Reassessing the Law of Preemption, 88 Geo. L.J. 2085 (2000) [hereinafter Dinh]; Rabin, Reassessing Regulatory Compliance, 88 Geo. L.J. 2049 (2000); Smith and Grage, Federal Preemption of State Products Liability Actions, 27 Wm. Mitchell L. Rev. 391 (2000); Raeker–Jordan, The Pre–Emption Presumption That Never Was: Pre–Emption Doctrine Swallows the Rule, 40 Ariz. L. Rev. 1379, 1418 (1998); Leflar and Adler, The Preemption Pentad: Federal Preemption of Products Liability Claims After Medtronic, 64 Tenn. L . Rev. 691 (1997); Grey, Make Congress Speak Clearly: Federal Preemption of State Tort Remedies, 77 B.U. L. Rev. 559 (1997); Noah, Reconceptualizing Federal Preemption of Tort Claims As the Government Standards Defense, 37 Wm. & Mary L. Rev. 903 (1996); Ausness, Federal Preemption of State Products Liability Doctrines, 44 S.C. L. Rev. 187 (1993). See generally 4 Frumer and Friedman, Products Liability ch. 24; 2 Madden & Owen on Products Liability ch. 28; 4A Am. Law Prod. Liab. ch. 64; Prod. Liab. Rep. (CCH) ¶ 2810.

Instead, it continues to wallow in a state of utter chaos—"ad hoc, unprincipled . . . , seemingly bereft of any consistent doctrinal basis,"[3] "a muddle,"[4] "inexplicable,"[5] "confusing and chaotic,"[6] "terrible,"[7] "indeterminate,"[8] and "in a state of disarray"[9]—quite simply, in a "mess."[10]

Federal preemption is an affirmative defense, subject to waiver, on which the defendant has the burden of proof.[11] The federal preemption defense arises, and a products liability claim is foreclosed, when the claim somehow conflicts with a federal product safety statute or regulation specifying design, marketing, or manufacturing standards. When enacting product safety legislation, Congress normally vests regulatory authority over the matter in a federal administrative agency, often specifying, in a preemption clause, that state law may not interfere with safety standards or "requirements" in the statute itself or, more typically, as promulgated by the federal agency. Whether or not Congress in any particular statute expressly prohibits the states from interfering with implementation of the legislation, any state law that *in fact* interferes with the operation of a federal statute or regulation thereunder contravenes the Supremacy Clause of the United States Constitution. This clause provides that federal law "shall be the supreme law of the Land; and the Judges in every State shall be bound thereby, any Thing in the Constitution or Laws of any State to the Contrary notwithstanding."[12]

State statutes and administrative regulations are of course governed by the Supremacy Clause, but so too are products liability actions which can interfere, if less directly, with the administration of a federal safety statute. "[R]egulation can be as effectively exerted through an award of damages as through some form of preventive relief. The obligation to pay compensation can be, indeed is designed to be, a potent method of governing conduct and controlling policy."[13] Thus, a products liability claim is preempted if it is prohibited by or conflicts in some way with a

---

**3.** Note, 75 Colum. L. Rev. 623, 624 (1975).

**4.** Nelson, Preemption, 86 Va. L. Rev. 225, 232 (2000).

**5.** Smith and Grage, Federal Preemption of State Products Liability Actions, 27 Wm. Mitchell L. Rev. 391, 415 (2000).

**6.** Id. at 392.

**7.** Ausness, Preemption of State Tort Law by Federal Safety Statutes: Supreme Court Preemption Jurisprudence Since *Cipollone*, 92 Ky. L.J. 913, 968 (2004).

**8.** Dinh, above note 2, at 2085.

**9.** Scordato, Federal Preemption of State Tort Claims, 35 U.C. Davis L. Rev. 1, 7 (2001). See Raeker–Jordan, A Study in Judicial Sleight of Hand: Did Geier v. American Honda Motor Co. Eradicate the Presumption Against Preemption, 17 BYU J. Pub. L. 1, 33 (2002) (the doctrine is "still in disarray").

**10.** Dinh, above note 2, at 2085.

**11.** See, e.g., Colon v. BIC USA, Inc., 136 F.Supp.2d 196, 199–200 (S.D.N.Y.

2000) (but a statement in the answer that the product met government standards may suffice); Hawkins v. Leslie's Pool Mart, Inc., 184 F.3d 244, 256 (3d Cir. 1999) (affirmative defense on which defendant has burden of proof); Williams v. Ashland Eng'g Co., 45 F.3d 588, 592 n.7 (1st Cir. 1995). See also Milanese v. Rust–Oleum Corp., 244 F.3d 104 (2d Cir. 2001). Hence, a defendant who fails to assert preemption in a timely manner may waive the defense. See, e.g., Violette v. Smith & Nephew Dyonics, Inc., 62 F.3d 8, 10–12 (1st Cir. 1995) (although pleaded in answer, defendant did not raise defense substantively until after adverse verdict); Gonzales v. Surgidev, 899 P.2d 576, 581–83 (N.M. 1995) (waived if not raised before end of trial). *But see* Kennan v. Dow Chem. Co., 717 F.Supp. 799 (M.D. Fla. 1989) (not affirmative defense subject to waiver).

**12.** U.S. Const. art. IV, cl. 2.

**13.** San Diego Bldg. Trades Council v. Garmon, 359 U.S. 236, 247 (1959).

federal statute or regulation.[14] In determining whether a products liability claim conflicts with federal law, courts must interpret the statute to ascertain its aims. " 'The purpose of Congress is the ultimate touchstone' in every preemption case."[15] Put otherwise, statutory construction is the cornerstone of preemption analysis.[16]

In general, federal courts are more willing than state courts to find preemption. State courts normally are more focused on protecting the right to compensation of their citizens harmed by the unlawful behavior of others (a right often protected by state constitutions), whereas federal courts of limited jurisdiction generally are more concerned about the doctrine of federal supremacy.[17]

### Types of Preemption

Federal preemption of state law may be "express" or "implied." That is, preemption "is compelled whether Congress's command is explicitly stated in the statute's language or implicitly contained in its structure and purpose."[18] Express preemption may helpfully be viewed as *textual*, in contrast to implied preemption which may be thought of as *contextual*. What this means is that express preemption is discernable from the explicit language of a federal statute, whereas implied preemption must be deduced from the broader purposes of a statute—whether or not it contains an express preemption clause.[19]

**Express preemption.** Congress by statute may *expressly* preempt state law with a preemption clause that explicitly states the statute's preemptive scope—the extent to which it precludes state law.[20] In legislation regulating product safety, enacted mostly in the late 1960s, Congress was less concerned with common-law damage claims in products liability cases than with the possibility that state statutes or administrative regulations might somehow undermine the federal legislation.[21] Accordingly, as discussed below, preemption clauses in federal statutes typically provide that the states may not adopt conflicting "requirements" or "standards." Phrasing of this sort has raised the question of whether the words "requirements" and "standards" mean only legislative and regulatory requirements and standards, or whether Congress

**14.** Federal administrative agencies may be authorized to preempt state law by regulation. Hillsborough Cty., Fla. v. Automated Medical Labs. Inc., 471 U.S. 707, 713 (1985) ("state laws can be pre-empted by federal regulations as well as by federal statutes"). See also Medtronic, Inc. v. Lohr, 518 U.S. 470, 503, 505 (1996) (Breyer, J., concurring).

**15.** Gade v. National Solid Wastes Mgt. Ass'n, 505 U.S. 88, 96 (1992) (quoting Allis–Chalmers Corp. v. Lueck, 471 U.S. 202, 208 (1985)).

**16.** See 1 L. Tribe, American Constitutional Law § 6–28, at 1176–79 (3d ed. 2000); J. Nowak and R. Rotunda, Constitutional Law § 9.1, at 348 (6th ed. 2000).

**17.** See Smith and Grage, Federal Preemption of State Products Liability Actions, 27 Wm. Mitchell L. Rev. 391, 412 (2000).

**18.** Jones v. Rath Packing Co., 430 U.S. 519, 525 (1977). See also Medtronic, Inc. v. Lohr, 518 U.S. 470, 486 (Stevens, J.).

**19.** See Madden, Federal Preemption of Inconsistent State Safety Obligations, 21 Pace L. Rev. 103, 106 (2000).

**20.** State law is expressly preempted "[w]hen Congress has considered the issue of preemption and has included in the enacted legislation a provision explicitly addressing that issue, and when that provision provides a 'reliable indicium of congressional intent with respect to state authority[.]' " Cipollone v. Liggett Group, Inc., 505 U.S. 504, 517 (1992).

**21.** See, e.g., Leflar and Adler, The Preemption Pentad: Federal Preemption of Products Liability Claims After *Medtronic*, 64 Tenn. L. Rev. 691, 746–48 (1997).

intended these terms more broadly to include judicial rulings on common-law damages claims. As mentioned earlier, the Supreme Court has ruled definitively that these phrases in preemption clauses can indeed preclude products liability judgments, as well as more obvious and direct kinds of state action, through legislation and administrative regulation. Accordingly, to the extent that allowing a products liability claim would establish a form of common-law safety standard different from that imposed by federal law, an express preemption clause may preclude the claim.

Two types of clauses are particularly relevant in determining whether a statute expressly preempts a state law products liability claim: (1) preemption clauses, and (2) savings clauses. A "preemption clause" describes the extent to which a statute precludes the application of state law, and a "savings clause" provides that compliance with a statute does not exempt a person from liability under common law. These two provisions thus generally point in opposite directions: preemption clauses tend to deny, and savings clauses tend to allow, state law products liability claims. Normally, therefore, the express preemption issue should be clearer if a federal safety statute has only a preemption clause,[22] or only a savings clause.[23] Preemption determinations are complicated in statutes that contain *neither* type of clause, and thus are silent on the matter,[24] and in statutes that contain *both* types of clause,[25] and so appear internally conflicted.

**Implied preemption.** Even if a federal statute is silent with respect to the preemption issue, a products liability claim may be foreclosed by the doctrine of *implied* preemption. There are two forms of implied preemption, "implied *field* preemption" and "implied *conflict* preemption." Implied *field* preemption arises (a) when federal regulation of a field is so complete and "so pervasive as to make reasonable the inference that Congress left no room for the States to supplement it,"[26] or (b) when Congress legislates in a field in which "the federal interest is so dominant that the federal system [must] be assumed to preclude the enforcement of state laws on the same subject."[27] Implied *conflict* preemption may arise in one of two ways: (a) where federal and state provisions directly conflict, so that it is impossible for a person to comply with both requirements,[28] or (b) when the state law "stands as an obstacle to the accomplishment and execution of the full purposes and objectives of Congress."[29] Thus, even if a federal product safety statute

---

**22.** Such as the Federal Insecticide, Fungicide and Rodenticide Act (FIFRA), discussed below.

**23.** Such as the Occupational Safety and Health Act. As discussed below, however, a federal agency (as OSHA) may, by regulation, preempt state law with respect to particular matters.

**24.** Such as the Food, Drug and Cosmetic Act, discussed below. Like OSHA, however, the FDA expressly preempts state law on certain issues.

**25.** Such as the National Traffic and Motor Vehicle Safety Act, discussed below.

**26.** Rice v. Santa Fe Elevator Corp., 331 U.S. 218, 230 (1947).

**27.** Id.

**28.** See Weinberg, The Federal–State Conflict of Laws: "Actual" Conflicts, 70 Tex. L. Rev. 1743, 1751 (1992).

**29.** Hines v. Davidowitz, 312 U.S. 52, 67 (1941). See also Perez v. Campbell, 402 U.S. 637, 649 (1971). This last form of conflict preemption is often aptly termed "obstacle" or "frustration-of-purpose" preemption. In addition to the conventional divisions, implied preemption also may result from fed-

does not contain a clause expressly preempting damages claims under state law, the statute still may impliedly preempt such claims.[30]

### The Presumption Against Preemption

Principles of federalism command congressional respect for the sovereignty of the states,[31] including their authority to render damages judgments in products liability and other litigation. In the words of the Supreme Court, "because the States are independent sovereigns in our federal system, we have long presumed that Congress does not cavalierly pre-empt state-law causes of action."[32] From this premise, the Court has relied upon an "assumption that the historic police powers of the States were not to be superseded by a Federal Act unless that was the clear and manifest purpose of Congress."[33] At bottom, this "presumption against preemption" rests on the precept that the Constitution constrains the federal government, the powers of which are limited and specifically enumerated, from trampling on the reserved powers of the states.[34] In the first two products liability preemption cases, the Court interpreted the federal product safety statutes against this backdrop assumption that disfavored preemption.[35]

Recently, however, the Court has moved away from the presumption against preemption, noting its inapplicability when the matter regulated implicates federal interests[36] at least as much as matters traditionally addressed by state law. As the Supreme Court has strayed from its former regard for the presumption against preemption, commentators have increasingly questioned the meaning, strength, and legitimacy of any such presumption.[37] It is true, of course, that Congress should be guided by principles of federalism in enacting legislation on health and safety, subjects that traditionally have resided largely under state control. However, if Congress has authority under the Commerce Clause to enact particular legislation regulating health and safety, then the Su-

eral common law and from the "dormant" commerce clause. See Dinh, above note 2, at 2109 et seq.

**30.** See, e.g., Buckman Co. v. Plaintiffs' Legal Comm., 531 U.S. 341, 352 (2001); Geier v. American Honda Motor Co., 529 U.S. 861, 869 (2000).

**31.** See Dinh, above note 2, at 2085–86.

**32.** Medtronic, Inc. v. Lohr, 518 U.S. 470, 485 (1996) (Stevens, J.).

**33.** Rice v. Santa Fe Elevator Corp., 331 U.S. 218, 230 (1947). See 1 L. Tribe, Constitutional Law § 6–28, at 1175 (3d ed. 1999).

**34.** See Gade v. National Solid Wastes Mgt. Ass'n, 505 U.S. 88, 109, 111 (1992), a workplace safety standards case in which state standards were challenged as preempted under OSHA. Justice Kennedy concurred only in the result because he believed the plurality's broad resort to implied preemption principles contradicted "two basic principles of our pre-emption jurisprudence. First, we begin with the assumption that the historic police powers of the States [are] not to be superseded ...

unless that was the clear and manifest purpose of Congress. Second, the purpose of Congress is the ultimate touchstone in all pre-emption cases."

**35.** See Medtronic, Inc. v. Lohr, 518 U.S. 470, 485 (1996); Cipollone v. Liggett Group, Inc., 505 U.S. 504, 516 (1992). See generally Dinh, above note 2, at 2085–86.

**36.** Such as regulating fraud on a federal agency, see *Buckman*, below, or boat safety, traditionally the domain of the Coast Guard. See *Sprietsma*, below.

**37.** See, e.g., Raeker–Jordan, A Study in Judicial Sleight of Hand: Did Geier v. American Honda Motor Co. Eradicate the Presumption Against Preemption, 17 BYU J. Pub. L. 1 (2002); Davis, Unmasking the Presumption in Favor of Preemption, 53 S.C. L. Rev. 967 (2002); Scordato, Federal Preemption of State Tort Claims, 35 U.C. Davis L. Rev. 1, 29–32 (2001); Dinh, above note 2; Raeker–Jordan, The Pre–Emption Presumption That Never Was: Pre–Emption Doctrine Swallows the Rule, 40 Ariz. L. Rev. 1379, 1418 (1998).

premacy Clause might seem to certify, automatically, the legitimacy of this federal incursion into a domain normally controlled by the states. If this view is correct, then the responsibility of courts is merely to interpret such a statute, untrammeled by any presumption for or against preemption, to determine whether, and the extent to which, Congress intended to restrict common-law claims.[38] Rather than being an independent principle of federalism, therefore, the doctrine of federal preemption might more accurately be viewed as a doctrine governing ·the interpretation of legislation which itself should be animated and bounded by principles of federalism lying within the Commerce Clause.[39] Put another way, principles of federalism may help determine whether a federal statute is proper under the Commerce Clause, but, once a statute is found proper under the Commerce Clause, the statute properly occupies whatever space might otherwise have been occupied by state law and so is not further subject to challenge on federalism grounds. That said, however, where exactly principles of federalism may lie within the Constitution may be less important than the fact that such principles do oblige the Congress, when considering legislation on matters of health and safety, to respect the traditional sovereignty of the states. So, if federal legislation on product safety does not clearly state whether products liability claims under state law are prohibited or permitted, and if such claims do not truly conflict with federal regulation, it seems likely that Congress intended to leave unmolested the traditional state control over matters in this realm.[40] Whether or not a "presumption against preemption" is the best way to articulate this kind of backdrop deference that Congress should exhibit when it enters a field traditionally ruled by the states, the presumption idea does capture important structural truths about the republic that reside somewhere in the Constitution.

### Development of Preemption Doctrine—Federal Safety Legislation for Particular Products

Rooted in statutory construction, the federal preemption defense rests upon a determination that Congress in a particular statute intended to preclude particular products liability claims. The preemption issue thus is both statute-specific and claim-specific, meaning that the resolution of this issue is governed in any given case by an interpretation of the relevant provisions of the particular federal statute in relation to the particular claims involved.[41] While preemption analysis in every case will therefore turn on the meaning and purposes of a specific statute—as revealed by its express provisions, its structure, and its legislative history[42]—the basic issue in every case remains the same: whether

**38.** Cf. 1 L. Tribe, American Constitutional Law §§ 6–28, at 1177 (3d ed. 2000) ("Perhaps, the most important point to remember is that preemption analysis is, or at least should be, a matter of precise statutory construction rather than an exercise in free-form judicial policymaking."). *But see* id. at 1195 n.74.

**39.** See Dinh, above note 2.

**40.** See, e.g., Raeker–Jordan, The Pre-Emption Presumption That Never Was:

Pre–Emption Doctrine Swallows the Rule, 40 Ariz. L. Rev. 1379, 1468–69 (1998).

**41.** See, e.g., Dinh, above note 2, at 2085; Scordato, Federal Preemption of State Tort Claims, 35 U.C. Davis L. Rev. 1, 31 (2001).

**42.** See, e.g., Gade v. National Solid Wastes Mgt. Ass'n, 505 U.S. 88, 98 (1992)

Congress intended, expressly or implicitly, to prohibit products liability claims of the type asserted by the plaintiff. Because preemption doctrine has thus evolved on a statute-specific basis,[43] the preemption defense in products liability litigation is helpfully informed by an examination of the doctrine's development over time as the courts have investigated the preemptive effect of particular federal statutes regulating the safety of particular types of products.

### Pesticides and Insecticides—Pre-Cipollone

Prior to the Supreme Court's initial foray into the application of preemption doctrine to products liability law in 1992,[44] federal preemption rarely figured seriously in this type of litigation. Indeed, prior to this time, the Supreme Court had decided only a handful of preemption cases involving common-law damage claims of any type.[45] During the 1980s, as manufacturers scrambled for ways to avoid the rigors of products liability judgments, they increasingly asserted the preemption defense.[46] In part because of the Supreme Court's skeptical attitude at the time toward the preemption of state tort-law claims,[47] assertions of the preemption defense during most of this decade generally fell on deaf judicial ears.[48]

The first reported decision concerning the preemptive effect of the Federal Insecticide, Fungicide and Rodenticide Act (FIFRA), was *Ferebee v. Chevron Chemical Co.*,[49] a prominent decision by the Court of Appeals for the District of Columbia that involved a products liability claim against the distributor of a herbicide, Paraquat, on behalf of an agricultural worker who allegedly died from breathing and contacting the herbicide.[50] In FIFRA, Congress established a comprehensive scheme for registering and labeling herbicides and other toxic products, adminis-

---

(the "ultimate task in any pre-emption case is to determine whether state regulation is consistent with the structure and purpose of the statute as a whole"); Medtronic, Inc. v. Lohr, 518 U.S. 470, 486 (courts must look to structure and purpose of statute as whole "as revealed not only in the text, but through the reviewing court's reasoned understanding of the way in which Congress intended the statute and its surrounding regulatory scheme to affect business, consumers, and the law") (Stevens, J.); Wisconsin Public Intervener v. Mortier, 501 U.S. 597, 617 (1991) (Scalia, J., concurring). See generally Ausness, Federal Preemption of State Products Liability Doctrines, 44 S.C. L. Rev. 187, 240–52 (1993) (model for interpreting federal regulations by evaluating text, history, and legislative policy).

**43.** See, e.g., Dinh, above note 2, at 2085.

**44.** The first products liability preemption case was Cipollone v. Liggett Group, Inc., 505 U.S. 504 (1992), discussed below.

**45.** Davis, Unmasking the Presumption in Favor of Preemption, 53 S.C. L. Rev. 969 n.9 (2002); Scordato, Federal Preemption of

State Tort Claims, 35 U.C. Davis L. Rev. 1 (2001).

**46.** Davis, 53 S.C. L. Rev. at 998.

**47.** Notably in Silkwood v. Kerr–McGee Corp., 464 U.S. 238 (1984) (plutonium-contamination claim by worker at nuclear power plant not preempted by Atomic Energy Act). *Silkwood* is examined in Davis, 53 S.C. L. Rev. at 990–94.

**48.** "[D]efendants had rarely been successful in arguing that the existence of a federal statutory standard totally preempted the plaintiff's state law based allegations of defectiveness or negligence." Davis, 53 S.C. L. Rev. at 998. See Ausness, Federal Preemption of State Products Liability Doctrines, 44 S.C. L. Rev. 187 (1993).

**49.** 736 F.2d 1529 (D.C. Cir. 1984), cert. denied, 469 U.S. 1062 (1984).

**50.** See Watnick, Federal Preemption of Tort Claims Under FIFRA: The Erosion of a Defense, 36 U. Mich. J.L. Reform 419 (2003); Madden, Federal Preemption of Inconsistent State Safety Obligations, 21 Pace L. Rev. 103, 120–28 (2000).

tered by the EPA.[51] Under the Act, a manufacturer must submit proposed labels to the EPA to assure that they are "adequate to protect health and the environment" and "likely to be read and understood."[52] FIFRA expressly prohibits the states from imposing any "requirements for labeling or packaging in addition to or different from those required" under the Act's provisions. In *Ferebee*, the plaintiff claimed that the label warnings on Paraquat were inadequate and caused the decedent's death, and the jury agreed. Rejecting the defendant's federal preemption arguments, the Court of Appeals concluded that the Act did not expressly preclude state common-law actions, nor did implied field or conflict preemption apply. Although a damages award for inadequate warnings might impose a dual obligation on the defendant, the court concluded that the defendant could comply with both federal and state law by using the EPA-approved warning labels while paying damages for insufficient warnings as required by the state products liability judgment.[53]

Despite a growing minority of cases ruling against plaintiffs on the preemption issue,[54] most courts through the 1980s and early 1990s followed the *Ferebee* approach in holding that neither FIFRA[55] nor other federal safety statutes[56] preempted products liability claims. However, once the Supreme Court in 1992 energized the federal preemption defense in products liability litigation, the lower courts began to rethink the role of preemption under federal statutes such as FIFRA. In recent years, the FIFRA decisions have turned sharply in the other direction. In cases where a manufacturer has complied with an EPA-required warning under FIFRA, courts are now nearly unanimous[57] in holding that the Act

---

**51.** See 7 U.S.C. § 136–136y.

**52.** See id. at §§ 136(q)(1)(F), 136a(d); and id. at 136(q)(1)(E).

**53.** Ferebee, 736 F.2d at 1540.

**54.** See, e.g., Papas v. Upjohn Co., 926 F.2d 1019 (11th Cir. 1991) (impliedly preempted), vacated, 505 U.S. 1215 (1992), on remand, 985 F.2d 516 (11th Cir. 1993) (expressly preempted); Taylor v. General Motors Corp., 875 F.2d 816 (11th Cir. 1989) (no-airbag claim); Fitzgerald v. Mallinckrodt, Inc., 681 F.Supp. 404 (E.D. Mich. 1987) (FIFRA).

**55.** See, e.g., Montana Pole & Treating Plant v. I.F. Laucks & Co., 775 F.Supp. 1339 (D. Mont. 1991); Riden v. ICI Am., Inc., 763 F.Supp. 1500 (W.D. Mo. 1991); Evenson v. Osmose Wood Preserving, Inc., 760 F.Supp. 1345 (S.D. Ind. 1990); Cox v. Velsicol Chem. Corp., 704 F.Supp. 85 (E.D. Pa. 1989); Roberts v. Dow Chem. Co., 702 F.Supp. 195 (N.D. Ill. 1988).

**56.** See, e.g., Abbot v. American Cyanamid Co., 844 F.2d 1108 (4th Cir. 1988) (neurological injuries from inoculation of DTP vaccine manufactured by defendant; *held*, no express preemption by Public Health Service Act or Federal Food, Drug, and Cosmetic Act, nor any implied preemption because common-law vaccine claims do

not frustrate federal statutory goals); MacDonald v. Ortho Pharm. Corp., 475 N.E.2d 65 (Mass. 1985) (compliance with FDA labeling requirements on birth control pills–no preemption).

**57.** One important case to the contrary, holding that FIFRA does not preempt warnings claims, is Sleath v. West Mont Home Health Services, 16 P.3d 1042 (Mont. 2000). In *Sleath*, the Court relied heavily on an amicus curiae brief that the EPA filed in Etcheverry v. Tri–Ag Serv., Inc., 993 P.2d 366 (Cal. 2000) (also holding that FIFRA does not preempt warnings claims). In that brief, the EPA took the position that FIFRA does not preempt any state law theories of liability, including failure to warn claims that implicate pesticide labels. The Montana Supreme Court granted deference to the EPA's view because it is the agency responsible for administering FIFRA. Other courts have declined to grant the EPA deference, holding that the plain terms of 7 U.S.C. § 136v(b) expressly preempt state law claims based on the failure to warn. See, e.g., Eyl v. Ciba–Geigy Corp., 650 N.W.2d 744 (Neb. 2002); Netland v. Hess & Clark, Inc., 284 F.3d 895 (8th Cir. 2002); Etcheverry v. Tri–Ag Serv., Inc., 993 P.2d 366 (Cal. 2000).

preempts at least tort-law[58] warnings claims, the most common type of FIFRA claim.[59] However, the courts are generally in accord that FIFRA neither expressly nor impliedly preempts claims that pertain to matters not regulated by the EPA, such as claims that truly are not based on labeling but on the defectiveness of a pesticide's design, packaging, or manufacture.[60] Yet, the courts will not be fooled by artful pleading efforts to disguise warnings claims under cover of assertions of negligent testing, defective manufacture, defective design, or other claims that indirectly challenge EPA-approved labeling information, and all such claims will be preempted.[61]

**58.** Most courts also bar warranty and tortious misrepresentation claims if based on an EPA-required warning. See, e.g., Williams v. Dow Chemical Co., 255 F.Supp.2d 219 (S.D.N.Y. 2003); Akee v. Dow Chem. Co., 272 F.Supp.2d 1112 (D. Haw. 2003); Andrus v. Agrevo USA Co., 178 F.3d 395 (5th Cir. 1999); National Bank of Commerce v. Dow Chem. Co., 165 F.3d 602 (8th Cir. 1999); Grenier v. Vermont Log Bldgs., Inc., 96 F.3d 559, 563 (1st Cir. 1996); Papas v. Upjohn Co., 985 F.2d 516, 520 (11th Cir. 1993). *Contra*, Arnold v. Dow Chem. Co., 110 Cal.Rptr.2d 722, 731–32 (Ct. App. 2001) (citing cases holding that implied warranty claims are not preempted); Goeb v. Tharaldson, 615 N.W.2d 800 (Minn. 2000) (FIFRA does not preempt negligent misrepresentation or negligent testing claims).

Courts addressing claims based on off-label statements generally hold that such claims are not preempted if the statement differs from the label, but that such claims are preempted if the statements merely reiterate language on the label. See, e.g., Anderson v. Dow Agrosciences, 262 F.Supp.2d 1280 (W.D. Okla. 2003); Diehl v. Polo Coop. Ass'n, 766 N.E.2d 317 (Ill. App. Ct. 2002) (FIFRA does not preempt claims based on off-label recommendations that differ from label); Dillon v. Zeneca Corp., 42 P.3d 598 (Ariz. Ct. App. 2002) (FIFRA preempts claims based on off-label statements that merely reiterate language on label); Sun Valley Packing v. Consep, Inc., 114 Cal.Rptr.2d 237 (Ct. App. 2001) (FIFRA does not preempt implied warranty of fitness for particular purpose claim based on off-label statements about matters outside scope of required label).

**59.** See, e.g., Anderson v. Dow Agrosciences, 262 F.Supp.2d 1280 (W.D. Okla. 2003); Eyl v. Ciba–Geigy Corp., 650 N.W.2d 744 (Neb. 2002) (citing cases); Lowe's Home Ctrs., Inc. v. Olin Corp., 313 F.3d 1307 (11th Cir. 2002); Netland v. Hess & Clark, Inc., 284 F.3d 895 (8th Cir. 2002); Arnold v. Dow Chem. Co., 110 Cal.Rptr.2d 722 (Ct. App. 2001); Etcheverry v. Tri-Ag Serv., Inc., 993 P.2d 366 (Cal. 2000) (citing cases); Hawkins v. Leslie's Pool Mart, Inc., 184

F.3d 244, 251 (3d Cir. 1999); National Bank of Commerce v. Dow Chem. Co., 165 F.3d 602 (8th Cir. 1999); Lewis v. American Cyanamid Co., 715 A.2d 967, 973 (N.J. 1998); Kuiper v. American Cyanamid Co., 131 F.3d 656, 662 (7th Cir. 1997); Greiner v. Vermont Log Bldgs., Inc., 96 F.3d 559, 563–64 (1st Cir. 1996). *But see* Dow Chem. Co. v. Ebling ex rel. Ebling, 753 N.E.2d 633 (Ind. 2001) (FIFRA does not preempt claim that pest control applicator negligently failed to convey to pesticide's ultimate user information found on required label).

**60.** See, e.g., Southern States Coop. Inc., v. I.S.P. Co., Inc., 198 F.Supp.2d 807 (N.D. W.Va. 2002) (FIFRA does not preempt claim that horse feed was adulterated with rat poison); Arnold v. Dow Chem. Co., 110 Cal.Rptr.2d 722 (Ct. App. 2001) (true design claims not preempted; full discussion), noted, 31 Sw. U. L. Rev. 441 (2002); Jeffers v. Wal–Mart Stores, Inc., 171 F.Supp.2d 617 (S.D. W.Va. 2001) (design defect claims not preempted); National Bank of Commerce v. Dow Chem. Co., 165 F.3d 602, 609 (8th Cir. 1999) ("defectively manufactured or designed products properly labeled under FIFRA may still be subject to state regulation, in the form of common-law or other claims"); Hawkins v. Leslie's Pool Mart, Inc., 184 F.3d 244 (3d Cir. 1999) (gaseous fumes from chlorinator tablets used in pools; packaging claims not preempted); Ackerman v. American Cyanamid Co., 586 N.W.2d 208, 215 (Iowa 1998).

Courts disagree on whether FIFRA preempts claims based on a product's *efficacy*—whether a herbicide harms rather than helps a crop—that are outside the realm the EPA chooses to regulate. Compare American Cyanamid Co. v. Geye, 79 S.W.3d 21 (Tex. 2002) (no preemption), with Etcheverry v. Tri-Ag Serv., Inc., 93 Cal.Rptr.2d 36 (2000) (preemption).

**61.** See, e.g., Dow Agrosciences L.L.C. v. Bates, 332 F.3d 323, 332 (5th Cir. 2003) (FIFRA preempts breach of express warranty claim and warnings claims "disguised" as defective design and negligent testing claims); Akee v. Dow Chem. Co., 272

### Cigarettes—Cipollone

In *Cipollone v. Liggett Group, Inc.*,[62] the Supreme Court in 1992 for the first time applied federal preemption doctrine to a products liability case.[63] *Cipollone* was an action against three cigarette manufacturers on behalf of Rose Cipollone who died of lung cancer after smoking the defendants' cigarettes from 1942 to 1984. The products liability claims included design defectiveness; failure to provide adequate warnings; negligent research, testing, and marketing; breach of express warranties in advertising; fraudulent misrepresentation of the hazards of smoking; and conspiracy to defraud by depriving the public of medical and scientific information on smoking.[64]

At issue in *Cipollone* was the preemptive effect of two cigarette labeling statutes. The preemption clause in the 1965 Cigarette Labeling and Advertising Act (the "1965 Act") provided, "No statement relating to smoking and health" other than that required by the Act, "shall be required" on cigarette packages or in advertising.[65] In 1969, Congress amended the 1965 Act in the Public Health Cigarette Smoking Act of 1969 (the "1969 Act") to make the labeling requirements more stringent, to ban electronic cigarette advertising, and to modify the preemption provision to read:

> No requirement or prohibition based on smoking and health shall be imposed under State law with respect to the advertising or promotion of any cigarettes the packages of which are labeled in conformity with the provisions of this chapter.[66]

Prior to *Cipollone*, the Supreme Court justices, and hence the lower courts, were badly split on the role of both express and implied preemption in barring common-law claims.[67] Even in cigarette warnings cases, most pre-*Cipollone* decisions had rejected *express* preemption claims in favor of *implied* preemption.[68] Turning that approach on its head, *Cipollone* ruled that, where Congress speaks expressly to the preemption issue, a largely textual express preemption analysis—not implied preemption—should control.[69]

F.Supp.2d 1112 (D. Haw. 2003) (FIFRA preempts any claims that challenge adequacy of pesticide product's labels, directly or indirectly); Netland v. Hess & Clark, Inc., 284 F.3d 895 (8th Cir. 2002) (FIFRA preempted manufacturing defect and design defect claims that were factually premised on inadequate labeling); Traube v. Freund, 775 N.E.2d 212 (Ill. App. Ct. 2002) (FIFRA preempts nuisance and ultra-hazardous activity claims based on allegedly deficient label); Eriksen v. Mobay Corp., 41 P.3d 488 (Wash. Ct. App. 2002) (consumer expectations design defect claim was effectively a warnings claim); Johnson v. Monsanto Chem. Co., 129 F.Supp.2d 189, 195 (N.D.N.Y. 2001) ("Claims of misdesign or mismanufacture which the Court regards as thinly veiled labeling or failure to warn claims will not stand.").

**62.**   505 U.S. 504 (1992).

**63.**   See Galligan, Products Liability—Cigarettes and Cipollone: What's Left? What's Gone?, 53 La. L. Rev. 713 (1993); Note, 80 Va. L. Rev. 979 (1994).

**64.**   505 U.S. at 508–10.

**65.**   15 U.S.C. § 5.

**66.**   15 U.S.C. § 5(b). See 505 U.S. at 514–15.

**67.**   See Davis, Unmasking the Presumption in Favor of Preemption, 53 S.C. L. Rev. 967 (2002).

**68.**   Cipollone, 505 U.S. at 508 n.2.

**69.**   "When congress has considered the issue of pre-emption and has included in the enacted legislation a prevision explicitly addressing that issue, and when that provision provides a 'reliable indicium of congressional intent with respect to state authority, there is no need to infer con-

The Court held that the narrower 1965 Act did not preempt state-law damages actions, but that the broader 1969 Act—which barred not simply "statement[s]" but rather "requirement[s] or prohibition[s] imposed under State law"—barred at least some products liability claims because it imposed stiffer requirements on cigarette manufacturers in exchange for explicit limitations on the right to sue.[70] Reasoning that a products liability claim should be considered a "requirement" or "prohibition" under the Act,[71] and that the plaintiff's inadequate warnings claim effectively asserted that the manufacturers' "post-1969 advertising or promotions should have included additional, or more clearly stated, warnings," the Court concluded that the 1969 Act preempted the plaintiff's warnings claim.[72] However, that Act did *not* preempt claims for *fraud*, or *conspiracy to defraud*—which were not "predicated upon a duty based on smoking and health, but rather on a more general obligation—the duty not to deceive,"[73] nor those based upon *express warranty*, because "the 'requirement[s]' imposed by an express warranty claim are not 'imposed under state law,' but rather imposed by the warrantor."[74] Concurring and dissenting, Justices Blackmun, Kennedy, and Souter reasoned that the 1969 Act did not speak clearly enough to deny the petitioner's common-law claims,[75] while Justices Scalia and Thomas asserted that the 1965 Act preempted the warnings claims and the 1969 Act barred them all.[76] Although the justices thus were widely split, *Cipollone* appears to put to rest most preemption issues in most cigarette litigation.

### Motor Vehicles— Myrick and Geier

**Anti-lock braking systems in trucks.** After *Cipollone*, the next Supreme Court case to address preemption in the products liability context was *Freightliner Corp. v. Myrick*[77] which concerned the preemptive effect of the National Traffic and Motor Vehicle Safety Act of 1966[78] and safety standards issued by its corresponding regulatory agency, the National Highway Traffic Safety Agency (NHTSA). Congress enacted the Safety Act to regulate the safety of motor vehicles in an effort to reduce the toll of injuries and deaths from traffic accidents.[79] The Safety Act's preemption clause prohibits the states from maintaining "motor vehicle

gressional intent to pre-empt state laws from the substantive provisions' of the legislation." Id. at 517 (citations omitted).

**70.**  505 U.S. at 520.

**71.**  In rejecting petitioner's argument that the 1969 Act's preemption provision did not reach common-law actions, the Court observed that "the phrase '[n]o requirement or prohibition' sweeps broadly and suggests no distinction between positive enactments and common law." Id. at 521.

**72.**  This is the conventional interpretation of *Cipollone*. See, e.g., Waterhouse v. R.J. Reynolds Tobacco Co., 270 F.Supp.2d 678 (D. Md. 2003) ("failure-to-warn allegations are quintessentially claims preempted by the Labeling Act"). *But see* M. Green, Cipollone Revisited: A Not So Little Secret About the Scope of Cigarette Preemption, 82 Iowa L. Rev. 1257 (1997) (arguing that "claims asserting inadequate warnings on cigarette packages are not preempted" under *Cipollone*).

**73.**  505 U.S. at 528–29.

**74.**  Nor does the Act preempt claims "that rely solely on respondents' testing or research practices or other actions unrelated to advertising or promotion." Id. at 524–25.

**75.**  Id. at 531–44.

**76.**  Id. at 544–56.

**77.**  514 U.S. 280 (1995).

**78.**  15 U.S.C. § 1381 et seq., now recodified at 49 U.S.C. § 30101 et seq. (1994).

**79.**  Id.

safety standards" that are not identical to any federal standards "in effect."[80] The Act also contains a savings clause, which provides: "Compliance with any Federal motor vehicle safety standard issued under this subchapter does not exempt any person from any liability under common law."[81]

In 1970, NHTSA's predecessor agency issued Standard 121, which imposed certain stopping distances for trucks that could be achieved only if trucks were equipped with anti-lock braking systems (ABS). Various truck manufacturers challenged Standard 121, and the Ninth Circuit suspended it pending further study. *Myrick* involved design defect claims by plaintiffs who attributed their injuries to the absence of ABS in eighteen-wheel trucks. Notwithstanding the fact that Standard 121 had been previously suspended, the district court ruled that the plaintiffs' design defect claims were preempted by federal Standard 121 and the Safety Act. The Eleventh Circuit reversed, holding that the plaintiffs' claims were not expressly preempted, nor were they impliedly preempted because of "*Cipollone*'s clear instruction that when there is an express preemption provision we should not consider implied pre-emption."[82]

The Supreme Court affirmed.[83] Speaking for a unanimous court, Justice Thomas reasoned that express preemption could not apply because no federal safety standard was "in effect" as required by the Safety Act's preemption clause. Nor were plaintiffs' design defect claims impliedly preempted because there was no conflict with the Act. Thus, because there was no federal standard with which the plaintiffs' products liability claims could conflict, *Myrick* may be viewed as a "false preemption" case. *Myrick*'s importance lies not in its holding but in its dictum which resurrects and applies the doctrine of *implied* preemption to federal statutes containing express preemption clauses. Rejecting the court of appeals' interpretation of *Cipollone* "that implied pre-emption cannot exist when Congress has chosen to include an express pre-emption clause in a statute,"[84] the Court inscrutably observed: "At best, *Cipollone* supports an inference that an express pre-emption clause forecloses implied pre-emption; it does not establish a rule."[85]

**Airbags.** Five years after *Myrick*, the Supreme Court tackled the preemption issue in another motor vehicle safety case, *Geier v. American Honda Motor Company*,[86] which involved the preemptive effect of certain NHTSA regulations on the use of airbags in passenger cars.[87] *Geier*

---

**80.** Id. at § 1392(d), recodified at 49 U.S.C. § 30103(b)(1).

**81.** Id. at § 1397(k).

**82.** Myrick v. Freuhauf Corp., 13 F.3d 1516, 1522 (11th Cir. 1994).

**83.** Freightliner Corp. v. Myrick, 514 U.S. 280 (1995).

**84.** Id. at 287.

**85.** Id. at 289.

**86.** 529 U.S. 861 (2000).

**87.** See Bough and Johnson, Crossing the Center Line: Preemption in Automobile Product Liability Cases, 57 J. Mo. B. 30 (Jan.–Feb. 2001); Raeker–Jordan, The Pre-Emption Presumption That Never Was: Pre-Emption Doctrine Swallows the Rule, 40 Ariz. L. Rev. 1379, 1445–68 (1998); Lichtenstein and Ferrera, Airbag Products Liability Litigation: State Common Law Tort Claims Are Not Automatically Preempted by Federal Legislation, 45 Clev. St. L. Rev. 1 (1997); Nader and Page, Automobile–Design Liability and Compliance with Federal Standards, 64 Geo. Wash. L. Rev. 415 (1996); Notes, 30 Ind. L. Rev. 827 (1997), 75 Wash. U. L.Q. 1677 (1997).

revealed the latent strength and resilience of the *implied* preemption doctrine that *Myrick* had suggested.

*Geier* involved the preemptive effect of Federal Motor Vehicle Safety Standard 208 (entitled "Occupant Crash Protection"), a NHTSA regulation pertaining to airbags and other passive restraints.[88] From its initial formulation in 1967, when it required only lap belts, Standard 208 has evolved in fits and starts.[89] Beginning in 1975, Standard 208 began to offer manufacturers an evolving menu of passive restraint options, including airbags or various combinations of passive restraints, shoulder harnesses, lapbelts, and warning systems. It was not until 1997 that NHTSA finally mandated dual front-seat airbags in all (1998 model) passenger cars.[90] Beginning in the late 1980s, an increasing number of automotive products liability claims were based on the failure of manufacturers to equip their cars with airbags during this transitional period, before NHTSA required such devices in all cars. The courts were divided on the preemption issue, many state courts ruling that such airbag claims were not preempted[91] while all the federal circuit courts ruling that such claims were.[92]

The plaintiffs in *Geier* claimed that the driver's injuries were aggravated by a design defect in their 1987 Honda Accord because it was not equipped with a driver's-side airbag. Honda argued that such an airbag claim was preempted by Standard 208 which, during the transitional period, permitted manufacturers to choose between seatbelts and airbags. The district court granted summary judgment for Honda, ruling that the plaintiffs' no-airbag claims were *expressly* preempted, and the court of appeals affirmed on the basis that such claims were *impliedly* preempted because they conflicted with the objectives of federal Standard 208.[93]

The Supreme Court affirmed, agreeing with the court of appeals that "no-airbag" claims are impliedly preempted because they conflict with FMVSS 208.[94] The Court again was badly split, and Justice Breyer spoke for the five-judge majority which reasoned from "three subsidiary questions:"

> First, does the Act's express pre-emption provision pre-empt this lawsuit? [No.] Second, do ordinary [implied] pre-emption principles nonetheless apply? [Yes.] Third, does this lawsuit

**88.**　49 C.F.R. § 571.208.

**89.**　"Passive restraint regulation (Standard 208) has advanced over the years along a protracted, winding, sometimes perilous course." Public Citizen v. Steed, 851 F.2d 444, 445 (D.C. Cir. 1988). Its history is chronicled in Hernandez–Gomez v. Leonardo, 884 P.2d 183 (Ariz. 1994), and Motor Vehicle Mfrs. Ass'n v. State Farm Mut. Auto. Ins. Co., 463 U.S. 29, 34–38 (1983).

**90.**　Actually, those manufactured on or after September 1, 1997. 49 CFR § 571.208.S4.1.5.3.

**91.**　See, e.g., Drattel v. Toyota Corp., 699 N.E.2d 376 (N.Y. 1998); Minton v. Honda of Am. Mfg., Inc., 684 N.E.2d 648 (Ohio 1997); Munroe v. Galati, 938 P.2d 1114 (Ariz. 1997); Wilson v. Pleasant, 660 N.E.2d 327 (Ind. 1996); Tebbetts v. Ford Motor Co., 665 A.2d 345 (N.H. 1995).

**92.**　See, e.g., Harris v. Ford Motor Co., 110 F.3d 1410 (9th Cir. 1997) (express preemption); Montag v. Honda Motor Co., 75 F.3d 1414 (10th Cir. 1996) (implied preemption); Pokorny v. Ford Motor Co., 902 F.2d 1116 (3d Cir. 1990) (same); Taylor v. General Motors Corp., 875 F.2d 816 (11th Cir. 1989) (same); Wood v. General Motors Corp., 865 F.2d 395 (1st Cir. 1988) (same).

**93.**　166 F.3d 1236 (D.D.C. 1999).

**94.**　529 U.S. at 866.

actually conflict with FMVSS 208, hence with the Act itself? [Yes.][95]

The Safety Act did not expressly preempt products liability claims, the Court reasoned, because the savings clause suggests that Congress believed that there were common-law claims that needed to be saved. For this reason, the Court narrowly construed the phrase "safety standard" in the express preemption clause to exclude common-law claims.[96] But the savings clause does not reach further, thought the majority, to foreclose the operation of *implied* preemption where common-law claims actually conflict with a statute or regulation.[97] Because the plaintiffs alleged that the car was defectively designed because the manufacturer *failed* to equip it with an airbag, while the Safety Act *permitted* manufacturers at the time to choose between airbags and alternative passive restraints, the no-airbag claims actually conflicted with the federal standard and so were impliedly preempted.[98]

### Food, Drugs, Cosmetics, and Medical Devices—Medtronic and Buckman

**Food, drugs, and cosmetics.** The federal Food and Drug Administration (FDA) regulates the preparation and labeling of food,[99] drugs, and cosmetics under the Food, Drug and Cosmetic Act (FDCA).[100] Because the FDCA does not contain a preemption clause relevant to drugs, the statute itself does not expressly preempt defective warning and other products liability claims against pharmaceutical manufacturers.[101] Nor,

---

**95.** Id. at 867.

**96.** Id. at 867–68.

**97.** Id. at 869. Applying *Geier*, courts have since focused on whether the claimed defect actually conflicts with a relevant FMVSS. See, e.g., Ysbrand v. Daimler Chrysler Corp., 81 P.3d 618 (Okla. 2003) (finding no conflict with FMVSS 208 and no preemption of claim that airbag that was installed was defectively designed); Volkswagen of Am., Inc. v. Gentry, 564 S.E.2d 733 (Ga. Ct. App. 2002) (finding no conflict with FMVSS 208 and no preemption of claim that seatbelt system was defectively designed by the improper placement and angle of the shoulder strap and placement of the knee bolster); Mejia v. White GMC Trucks, Inc., 784 N.E.2d 345 (Ill. App. Ct. 2002) (finding actual conflict with relevant standard and preemption of design defect claim based on design of doors and door handles of garbage truck); Stewart v. General Motors Corp., 222 F.Supp.2d 845 (W.D. Ky. 2002) (finding actual conflict with FMVSS 208 and preemption of claim that airbag warning should have included language beyond that required by FMVSS 208), aff'd on other grounds, 102 Fed.Appx. 961 (6th Cir. 2004); Great Dane Trailers, Inc. v. Estate of Wells, 52 S.W.3d 737 (Tex. 2001) (finding no conflict with FMVSS 108 and no preemption of claim that tractor-trailer was defectively designed for failing

to have lighting in addition to lighting required by FMVSS 108).

**98.** Id. at 874. "Because the rule of law for which petitioners contend would have stood 'as an obstacle to the accomplishment and execution of' the important means-related federal objectives that we have just discussed, it is pre-empted." Id. at 881. A number of courts have applied *Geier* to likewise hold that claims based on the failure to equip a car with lapbelts or passenger side airbags are preempted under FMVSS 208. See, e.g., Griffith v. General Motors Corp., 303 F.3d 1276 (11th Cir. 2002) (lapbelt); Nelson v. Ford Motor Co., 761 N.E.2d 1099 (Ohio Ct. App. 2001) (passenger-side airbag).

**99.** In Jones v. Rath Packing Co., 430 U.S. 519 (1977), the Supreme Court held that the Fair Packaging and Labeling Act and its regulations impliedly preempt inconsistent state food labeling regulations. See also Boulahanis v. Prevo's Family Market, Inc., 583 N.W.2d 509 (Mich. Ct. App. 1998) (claim for illness from E. coli bacteria preempted by Federal Meat Inspection Act).

**100.** 21 U.S.C. § 301 et seq.

**101.** "The portion of the FDCA that is applicable to drugs does not contain a preemption provision." Eve v. Sandoz Pharm. Corp., 2002 WL 181972, at *2 (S.D. Ind. 2002); Bell v. Lollar, 791 N.E.2d 849 (Ind.

in general, have courts found that the FDCA *impliedly* preempts products liability claims against manufacturers of prescription drugs.[102] However, the statute delegates authority to the FDA to preempt state law,[103] and the agency by regulation has expressly preempted state law by mandating certain warnings for over-the-counter drugs,[104] but generally not for prescription drugs.[105] Because preemption may so emanate from the edict of a mere administrative agency, a court will not find that an FDA regulation preempts state law unless the regulation clearly says so.[106] Courts traditionally have taken the view, as until recently the FDA did itself,[107] that FDA drug labeling regulations generally impose only minimum standards—these regulatory provisions provide merely a safety floor—and that state tort law beneficially supplements federal regulatory efforts to promote drug safety.[108] More recently, however, the FDA has

Ct. App. 2003) (ditto; failure to warn of risk of mixing acetaminophen and alcohol). On the preemption defense in claims against drug manufacturers, see 2 Madden & Owen on Products Liability § 28:6; Frost, 54 Food & Drug L.J. 367 (1999); Geiger and Rosen, Rationalizing Product Liability for Prescription Drugs: Implied Preemption, Federal Common Law, and Other Paths to Uniform Pharmaceutical Safety Standards, 45 DePaul L. Rev. 395 (1996).

**102.** See, e.g., Bell v. Lollar, 791 N.E.2d 849 (Ind. Ct. App. 2003) (acetaminophen, risk of mixing with alcohol); Ohler v. Purdue Pharma, L.P., 2002 WL 88945 (E.D. La. 2002) (OxyContin); Caraker v. Sandoz Pharm. Corp., 172 F.Supp.2d 1018 (S.D. Ill. 2001) (Parlodel); Abbot v. American Cyanamid Co., 844 F.2d 1108 (4th Cir. 1988) (DTP vaccine); MacDonald v. Ortho Pharm. Corp., 475 N.E.2d 65 (Mass. 1985) (birth control pills).

**103.** See Hillsborough Cty., Fla. v. Automated Med. Labs., Inc., 471 U.S. 707, 713, 721 (1985). Since the FDA is authorized to preempt state law, its failure explicitly to do so "should be taken as a strong sign that the state action does not threaten national policy and is not *impliedly* preempted." 1 L. Tribe, American Constitutional Law §§ 6–32, at 1213 n.1 (3d ed. 2000). See *Hillsborough*, 471 U.S. at 721.

**104.** See, e.g., Kanter v. Warner-Lambert Co., 122 Cal.Rptr.2d 72 (Ct. App. 2002) (inadequate warnings claim with respect to head lice treatment); Green v. BDI Pharm., 803 So.2d 68 (La. Ct. App. 2001) (failure to warn of addictive nature of Ephedrine in "Mini Thins"). See also Ohler v. Purdue Pharma, L.P., 2002 WL 88945, at *12–13 (E.D. La. 2002), quoting 63 Fed. Reg. 66383–84 (concerning direct-to-patient warnings).

**105.** See Ohler v. Purdue Pharma, L.P., 2002 WL 88945, at *12 (E.D. La. 2002).

**106.** See id. at *13 n.34.

**107.** See id. (warnings on prescription pain medication, OxyContin); Caraker v. Sandoz Pharm. Corp., 172 F.Supp.2d 1018, 1036 (S.D. Ill. 2001) (quoting FDA's recognition of tort litigation's value and desire not to impede it).

**108.** See, e.g., Eve v. Sandoz Pharm. Corp., 2002 WL 181972, at *5 (S.D. Ind. 2002); Caraker v. Sandoz Pharm. Corp., 172 F.Supp.2d 1018, 1033 (S.D. Ill. 2001) ("Because there is no evidence that either Congress or the FDA intended on scrap[p]ing state products liability claims based on a failure to warn . . . , it is reasonable to find that the FDA has imposed a minimum—as opposed to conclusive—standard of safety."); Motus v. Pfizer, Inc., 127 F.Supp.2d 1085 (C.D. Cal. 2000) (Zoloft; court observed that manufacturer was unable to cite a single decision holding that FDA prescription drug requirements preempted state law claims), aff'd on other grounds, 358 F.3d 659 (9th Cir. 2004); Merrell Dow Pharm., Inc. v. Oxendine, 649 A.2d 825, 828 (D.C. 1994) (Bendectin).

One aberrant trial court decision concluded that FDA labeling requirements for the drug Adderall preempted a failure to warn claim, reasoning that the FDA prohibited the manufacturer from changing the FDA-approved warning without prior FDA approval, except in limited circumstances for a limited period of time. See Ehlis v. Shire Richwood, Inc., 233 F.Supp.2d 1189 (D.N.D. 2002), aff'd on other grounds, 367 F.3d 1013 (8th Cir. 2004). The court did not address the relevant regulations which indicate that manufacturers may strengthen their drug warnings without prior FDA approval, that the FDA encourages manufacturers to take such initiatives on their own, and that a former FDA Commissioner memorialized the FDA's view at the time that manufacturers may be under a state law duty to do so. See Caraker v. Sandoz Pharm. Corp., 172 F.Supp.2d 1018 (S.D. Ill. 2001) (extensive discussion of FDA's views

reversed its view on the desirability of products liability litigation which it now views as frustrating, rather than beneficially complementing, the agency's goal of promoting the public health.[109] Reasoning that even a federal agency has the right to change its mind, and that an agency's present views on preemption are entitled to respect, a couple of recent decisions have held that FDA approval of a manufacturer's design, manufacturing processes, and labeling in fact preempt products liability claims.[110]

**Medical devices.** Prior to the mid–1970s, the FDA had limited regulatory power over manufacturers of medical devices.[111] In response to a number of safety problems with various medical devices during the early 1970s—including an IUD called the Dalkon Shield, catheters, artificial heart valves, defibrillators, and pacemakers—Congress enacted the Medical Device Amendments of 1976 (the MDA) to the FDCA, directing the FDA to classify and regulate the safety and effectiveness of medical devices.[112] The FDA divides medical devices among three categories, depending on the potential health and safety implications of the device: Class I devices, such as tongue depressors and stethoscopes, contain minimal risk and are subject to minimal regulation; Class II devices, such as hearing aids and tampons, are potentially more harmful and so are subject to "special controls;" Class III devices, such as

on preemption and history of 1965 amendment to FDA regulations that allows supplemental warnings without prior FDA approval).

**109.** See Pear, In a Shift, Bush Moves to Block Medical Suits, www.nytimes.com (July 25, 2004) (quoting former Director of Bush administration's Domestic Policy Council as saying that the new FDA litigation strategy is "good health policy and good tort reform"); Amicus Brief for FDA in Motus v. Pfizer, Inc., 358 F.3d 659 (9th Cir. 2004), brief at 2002 WL 32303084; Miller, "Failure to Warn"—Blocking Bad Claims, Nat'l L.J. 31 (Nov. 10, 2003) (describing FDA filings of amicus briefs in some cases arguing that FDA approval of labeling for prescription drugs preempts failure-to-warn claims against manufacturers); O'Reilly, A State of Extinction: Does Food and Drug Administration Approval of a Prescription Drug Label Extinguish State Claims for Inadequate Warning?, 58 Food & Drug. L.J. 287 (2003). See also Opinion, Blocking Medical Product Suits, nytimes.com (Aug. 1, 2004) ("It seems poor policy to assume that once the agency has judged a product safe enough to use, the manufacturer should be insulated forever from lawsuits that could force improvements.").

**110.** See, e.g., Horn v. Thoratec Corp., 376 F.3d 163, 173 (3rd Cir. 2004) (2–1 decision) (quoting the FDA's Amicus Curiae Letter Brief in the case, which argued that the plaintiff's claims of defects in the de-

sign, manufacture, and labeling of the heart pump which met FDA requirements suggest that products liability law may require that the device be designed, manufactured, and marketed differently from the way approved by FDA). According to the FDA, products liability actions "threaten the statutory framework" for regulating medical devices, particularly the agency's review and approval of a product's labeling. Rather than being based on "centralized expert evaluation of device regulatory issues," products liability actions require "lay judges and juries to second-guess the balancing of benefits and risks of a specific device to their intended patient population–the central role of FDA." The threat of large damage awards "creates pressure on manufacturers to add warnings that FDA has neither approved, nor found to be scientifically required, or withdrawal of FDA-approved products from the market in conflict with the agency's expert determination that such products are safe and effective. This situation can harm the public health by retarding research and development and by encouraging 'defensive labeling' by manufacturers to avoid state liability, resulting in scientifically unsubstantiated warnings and underutilization of beneficial treatments."

**111.** See Medtronic, Inc. v. Lohr, 518 U.S. 470, 475–80 (1996) (history of medical device regulation, and FDA safety controls under MDA).

**112.** See 21 U.S.C. § 360.

pacemakers and artificial hearts, pose considerable potential risk and thus are subject to substantial regulatory control.[113]

Prior to marketing a new Class III device, the manufacturer must submit the device to a rigorous, time-consuming, and expensive "premarket approval" (PMA) process in order to assure the FDA that the device is safe and effective and, so, proper for sale. Congress provided two exemptions to the premarket approval process: (1) a "grandfathering" exemption for devices marketed prior to the 1976 enactment of the MDA, until such time as the FDA initiates and completes the requisite PMA; and (2) an exemption for post–1976 devices that are "substantially equivalent" to pre–1976 devices, in order to prevent manufacturers of the grandfathered devices from obtaining an unfair competitive advantage over manufacturers of new devices, and to facilitate improvements to the designs of existing devices. Prior to marketing an exempted device under this second exemption, a manufacturer must submit a premarket notification to the FDA[114] to permit the agency to determine the new device's "substantial equivalence" to an existing device. Quite simple and inexpensive, the "premarket notification" (or "§ 510(k)") process usually results in prompt FDA approval of the new device.

Unlike the FDCA's non-preemptive approach to regulating prescription drugs, the MDA expressly preempts inconsistent state law, providing that the states may not enforce any requirement for a medical device which is "different from or in addition to" any federal requirement "applicable ... to the device."[115] The FDA has interpreted this provision to mean that state requirements are preempted only if the agency has a "specific" counterpart regulation or requirement, thereby rendering any divergent state requirements "different from or in addition to" the specific FDA requirements[116] although, more recently, the agency appears to have changed its position on this point.[117]

In *Medtronic, Inc. v. Lohr*,[118] the plaintiffs alleged that the defendant's pacemaker, which the FDA had approved under the substantial-equivalence § 510(k) process, failed due to a defectively designed and manufactured wire lead,[119] and that the manufacturer failed to warn of this risk despite knowing of earlier failures. The district court dismissed the action, concluding that the MDA preempted all of the plaintiffs' claims, and the court of appeals reversed in part, ruling that the design defect claims were preempted, but that the manufacturing and warning defect claims were not.

The Supreme Court reversed in part, concluding that the MDA did not preempt *any* of the plaintiffs' products liability claims. Applying an express preemption analysis, the *Medtronic* Court reasoned that, for a state safety requirement to be "different from or in addition to" a

---

**113.** See Fowler v. Smith & Nephew Richards, Inc., 1999 WL 1132967 (M.D. Fla. 1999).

**114.** See 21 U.S.C. § 360(k).

**115.** Id.

**116.** 21 C.F.R. § 801.1(d).

**117.** See Plaintiff, Device Maker Differ on Significance of Government's New Stand on Preemption, 32 Prod. Saf. & Liab. Rep. (BNA) (June 21, 2004).

**118.** 518 U.S. 470 (1996).

**119.** The lead carries the current into the heart muscle. See Martin v. Medtronic, Inc., 254 F.3d 573 (5th Cir. 2001).

corresponding FDA regulation, the federal regulation would have to be "specific" to the device, not a regulation of general applicability. With respect to the plaintiffs' design defect claims, the Court ruled that the FDA did not impose any specific design safety "requirements" by its cursory § 510(k) determination that the defendant's product was a "substantially equivalent" device.[120] As for the defective manufacturing and warnings claims, the Court reasoned that both the FDA's general "Good Manufacturing Practices" regulations, as well as its general labeling regulations that required manufacturers of almost every device to provide warnings appropriate to the device, were simply too general to be either "applicable ... to the device," as required in the preemption clause, or "specific" to a "particular device," as required by the FDA's interpretation of that clause.[121]

Consistent with *Medtronic*'s holding that generalized FDA safety regulations are not preemptive, courts have ruled that state law products liability claims are indeed preempted where the FDA's regulations are exacting or specific to a particular product.[122] For example, in a case involving a pacemaker that was an investigational device,[123] a context where the FDA imposes quite exacting standards,[124] the Sixth Circuit Court of Appeals held that the FDA's specific approval of the product's design was preemptive because a state-law design-defect claim "would thwart [the federal] goals of safety and innovation."[125] So, too, because the FDA labeling requirement for tampons (Class II devices) are specific to tampons, the Ninth Circuit has ruled that this "device-and-disease-specific" requirement accordingly preempts a products liability claim.[126]

*Medtronic* does not directly address the preemption issue with respect to medical devices approved under the rigorous PMA process. A number of lower courts have found products liability claims concerning such devices to be preempted,[127] while other courts have not.[128]

*Split*

---

**120.** 518 U.S. at 492–94.

**121.** Id. at 497–502. Nor were the plaintiffs' claims based on violation of FDA regulations preempted because the preemption clause precluded safety requirements that are "different from," not identical to, the federal standards. Id. at 494–97.

**122.** "Most courts of appeal have interpreted *Lohr* to mean that the MDA preempts common-law claims to the extent that they interfere or conflict with specific federal requirements." Brooks v. Howmedica, Inc., 273 F.3d 785, 795 (8th Cir. 2001) (en banc).

**123.** The MDA exempts investigational devices from the PMA process "to encourage, and to the extent consistent with the protection of public health and safety and with ethical standards, the discovery and development of useful devices intended for human use." 21 U.S.C. § 360j(g).

**124.** See, e.g., 21 C.F.R. §§ 812.20, 812.25.

**125.** Martin v. Telectronics Pacing Sys., Inc., 105 F.3d 1090, 1099 (6th Cir. 1997). See also Chambers v. Osteonics Corp., 109 F.3d 1243 (7th Cir. 1997). *But see* Baird v. American Medical Optics, 713 A.2d 1019 (N.J. 1998)

**126.** Papike v. Tambrands, Inc., 107 F.3d 737, 740 (9th Cir. 1997) (tampon caused toxic shock syndrome; failure to warn and design defect claim based on consumer expectations preempted by labeling requirements). Accord, Murphy v. Playtex Family Prods. Corp., 69 Fed.Appx. 140 (4th Cir. 2003) (Md. law) ("federal regulators considered exactly the risk that [plaintiff] was exposed to and determined how best to warn consumers of this risk through product labeling").

**127.** *Preempted*: see, e.g., Horn v. Thoratec Corp., 376 F.3d 163 (3d Cir. 2004); Brooks v. Howmedica, Inc., 273 F.3d 785 (8th Cir. 2001) (en banc, 7–2 decision); Kemp v. Medtronic, Inc., 231 F.3d 216, 226 (6th Cir. 2000); Mitchell v. Collagen Corp., 126 F.3d 902 (7th Cir. 1997); Fry v. Allergan Med. Optics, 695 A.2d 511, 517 (R.I. 1997); Green v. Dolsky, 685 A.2d 110 (Pa. 1996).

---

**128.** See note 128 on page 913.

In 2001, the Supreme Court decided a quite different medical device preemption case, *Buckman Co. v. Plaintiffs' Legal Committee.*[129] In the mid–1980s, the FDA rejected a § 510(k) substantial equivalency application by the Acromed Corporation for a variable screw spinal plate fixation system for use in spinal surgery, determining that the device was a Class III device that was not substantially equivalent to any other device. Acromed hired a regulatory consultant, the Buckman Company, to refile the application which the FDA again rejected. Acromed and Buckman then split the device in two and filed two new § 510(k) applications, one for the bone plates and one for the bone screws, and changed the intended use from the spine to the long bones of the arms and legs. Finding that the devices, when applied to these uses met the test of substantial equivalence, the FDA approved the bone-plate and bone-screw devices for these purposes.

Once Acromed marketed the bone-plate and bone-screw devices, surgeons widely began to use the devices for spinal surgery; thousands of persons eventually were injured from the implantation of orthopedic bone screws into the pedicles of their spines. During the 1990s, thousands of suits were filed, and over 2,000 actions were consolidated for pre-trial proceedings in the District Court for the Eastern District of Pennsylvania.[130] Many of the claims against Acromed and Buckman, styled "fraud on the FDA," alleged that the defendants fraudulently misrepresented the product's intended use to the FDA by seeking agency " 'approval of its VSP plates and screws for use in long bones simply as a pretext in order to market the device for its true intended use in the spine.' "[131] The district court dismissed the fraud-on-the-FDA claims as preempted by the MDA, but the court of appeals reversed, ruling in a split decision that the claims were not preempted.[132]

Reversing, the Supreme Court held that the plaintiffs' fraud-on-the-FDA claims were *impliedly* preempted because they conflicted with federal law.[133] There was no "presumption against the preemption" of state law claims, reasoned the Court, because "[p]olicing fraud against federal agencies is hardly 'a field which the States have traditionally occupied.' "[134] The state law claims conflicted with federal law since "the federal statutory scheme amply empowers the FDA to punish and deter fraud against the Administration, and that this authority is used by the Administration to achieve a somewhat delicate balance of statutory objectives."[135] Because the FDCA expressly approves "off-label" use of medical devices by medical practitioners, "the FDA is charged with the

**128.** *Not preempted*: see, e.g., Woods v. Gliatech, Inc., 218 F.Supp.2d 802 (W.D. Va. 2002) (citing split of authority); Weiland v. Teletronics Pacing Sys., Inc., 721 N.E.2d 1149 (Ill. 1999); Goodlin v. Medtronic, Inc., 167 F.3d 1367, 1375 (11th Cir. 1999); Haidak v. Collagen Corp., 67 F.Supp.2d 21 (D. Mass. 1999).

**129.** 531 U.S. 341 (2001).

**130.** See In re Orthopedic Bone Screw Liab. Litig., 159 F.3d 817 (3d Cir. 1998).

**131.** Id. at 820.

**132.** Id. at 829.

**133.** The Court in *Buckman* reiterated the point it made in Geier v. American Honda Motor Co., 529 U.S. 861 (2000), that the presence in a federal statute of an express preemption clause in no way precludes the operation of implied ("ordinary") preemption principles. *Buckman*, 531 U.S. at 352.

**134.** Id. at 347.

**135.** Id. at 348.

difficult task of regulating the [safety] of medical devices without intruding upon decisions statutorily committed to the discretion of health care professionals."[136] The Court reasoned that fraud-on-the-FDA claims would interfere with the FDA's judgment on how best to achieve a sensitive balance between policing fraud without discouraging § 510(k) applications for "devices with potentially beneficial off-label uses for fear that such use might expose the manufacturer or its associates [such as Buckman] to unpredictable civil liability."[137]

*Buckman* left unresolved the question whether the MDA impliedly preempts normal products liability claims, those grounded solely on state tort or warranty law rather than on a violation of federal law. Although the Court in its earlier *Medtronic* decision had only ruled on express preemption, the Court in *Buckman* distinguished *Medtronic* on the ground that "the *Medtronic* claims arose from the manufacturer's alleged failure to use reasonable care in the production of the product, not solely from the violation of FDCA requirements."[138] The Court thus observed that *Medtronic* might be read to shelter from implied-preemption attack state-law claims that parallel federal safety regulations.[139] So reasoning, several courts have held that *Buckman* should be read to allow traditional products liability claims,[140] even fraud claims that are based on a manufacturer's misrepresentations to the plaintiff rather than to the FDA.[141]

### Recreational Boats—Sprietsma

In an effort to stem an increasing number of boat-related injuries and fatalities, Congress enacted the Federal Boat Safety Act of 1971 (FBSA)[142] to establish "a coordinated national boating safety program." The FBSA gives the Coast Guard authority to promulgate safety standards for boating equipment and recreational boats, thereby creating a uniform safety regulatory scheme to guide manufacturers in designing such equipment.[143] Before issuing a boat-safety regulation, the Coast Guard is required to consult with the National Boating Safety Advisory Council (Advisory Council) to help determine whether the regulation is appropriate.[144] A recurring safety problem in recreational boating is the risk, to swimmers and persons falling from boats, of being struck by the rapidly moving propeller blades on boat motors. Addressing this risk, the Coast Guard in 1988 decided to investigate the possibility of requiring manufacturers to install propeller guards to minimize the propeller

---

**136.** Id. at 350.

**137.** Id.

**138.** Id. at 352.

**139.** Id. at 353.

**140.** See, e.g., Bryant v. Hoffman–La Roche, Inc., 585 S.E.2d 723 (Ga. Ct. App. 2003) (allowing design and warnings claims against drug manufacturer which argued that such claims were effectively fraud-on-FDA claims and hence preempted).

**141.** See, e.g., Eve v. Sandoz Pharm. Corp., 2002 WL 181972 (S.D. Ind. 2002) (citing other cases). See also Dawson v. Ciba–Geigy Corp., 145 F.Supp.2d 565, 572–

73 (D.N.J. 2001); Caraker v. Sandoz Pharm. Corp., 172 F.Supp.2d 1018 (S.D. Ill. 2001) (holding that *Buckman* did not alter wealth of authority holding that FDA regulations do not impliedly preempt state law claims).

**142.** 46 U.S.C. § 4301 et seq.

**143.** S. Rep. No. 92–248 (1971), in 1971 U.S.C.C.A.N. 1331, 1333–35. Regulatory authority was delegated by the Secretary of Transportation to the Coast Guard. 49 C.F.R. § 1.46(n)(1).

**144.** 46 U.S.C. § 4302(c).

danger to persons in the water.[145] The Coast Guard directed the Advisory Council to study the data, feasibility, advantages, and disadvantages of minimizing propeller-strike injuries with propeller guards. After studying the issue and holding public hearings, the Propeller Guard Subcommittee unanimously determined that the Coast Guard should *not* require propeller guards for reasons of safety,[146] economics, and feasibility.[147] The Advisory Committee adopted the Subcommittee report and recommended to the Coast Guard that manufacturers not be required to install propeller guards, and the Coast Guard adopted the Advisory Committee recommendation in 1990.[148]

The FBSA contains both a preemption clause and a savings clause. The preemption clause prohibits state laws and regulations that are not identical to federal regulations promulgated under the Act.[149] The savings clause provides that "[c]ompliance with this chapter or standards, regulations, or orders prescribed under this chapter does not relieve a person from liability at common law or under State law."[150]

During the 1990s and early 2000s, a number of "no-propeller-guard" claims were asserted against manufacturers of boats and motors for failing to equip boat motors with propeller guards. A large majority of courts, but not all,[151] held that the FBSA preempted such claims—most on the basis of express preemption,[152] but several, influenced by the savings clause, on implied conflict preemption grounds.[153] On both bases, many courts concluded that the Coast Guard's deliberative decision *not* to require propeller guards was preemptive of no-propeller-guard claims, which effectively would require manufacturers to install such guards—a state "requirement" not "identical" to the federal requirement,[154] indeed, "in direct contravention to the Coast Guard's policy against

---

**145.** See Note, 68 Fordham L. Rev. 487 (1999) (preemption of propeller strike injuries).

**146.** The Subcommittee found that propeller guards tend to hinder steering, increase the risk of blunt contact with persons in the water, and create a risk that a person's arm or leg could be caught between the guard and propeller blades. See, e.g., Sprietsma v. Mercury Marine, 757 N.E.2d 75, 78–79 (Ill. 2001), rev'd, 537 U.S. 51 (2002).

**147.** See Sprietsma v. Mercury Marine, 537 U.S. 51, 61 (2002).

**148.** See, e.g., Sprietsma v. Mercury Marine, 757 N.E.2d 75, 78–79 (Ill. 2001), rev'd, 537 U.S. 51 (2002).

**149.** "Unless permitted by the Secretary . . . , a State . . . may not establish, continue in effect, or enforce a law or regulation establishing a recreational vessel . . . safety standard . . . that is not identical to a regulation prescribed under section 4302 of this title." 46 U.S.C. § 4306.

**150.** Id. at § 4311(g).

**151.** See, e.g., Ard v. Jensen, 996 S.W.2d 594 (Mo. Ct. App. 1999) (waterskier); Moore v. Brunswick Bowling & Billiards Corp., 889 S.W.2d 246 (Tex. 1994) (swimmer).

**152.** See, e.g., Ryan v. Brunswick Corp., 557 N.W.2d 541 (Mich. 1997) (swimmer struck by propeller); Moss v. Outboard Marine Corp., 915 F.Supp. 183, 187 (E.D. Cal. 1996) (passenger fell from boat and struck by propeller; emotional distress claim by other passenger); Carstensen v. Brunswick Corp., 49 F.3d 430 (8th Cir. 1995) (same); Shield v. Bayliner Marine Corp., 822 F.Supp. 81 (D. Conn. 1993) (same).

**153.** See, e.g., Sprietsma v. Mercury Marine, 757 N.E.2d 75, 78–79 (Ill. 2001), rev'd, 537 U.S. 51 (2002) (fall from boat); Lady v. Neal Glaser Marine, Inc., 228 F.3d 598 (5th Cir. 2000) (jet skier collided with boat); Lewis v. Brunswick Corp., 107 F.3d 1494 (11th Cir. 1997) (plaintiff thrown from boat).

**154.** See, e.g., Carstensen, 49 F.3d at 432 (express preemption).

mandating such a device in favor of affording manufacturers flexibility in the matter."[155]

In *Sprietsma v. Mercury Marine*,[156] the plaintiff's wife fell from a boat and was killed when struck by the motor's propeller blades. The plaintiff sued the manufacturer of the motor, claiming that it was unreasonably dangerous for not being equipped with a propeller guard. The trial court held that the claims were impliedly preempted by the FBSA; the appellate court affirmed on the basis of express preemption; and the Illinois Supreme Court affirmed, ruling that the plaintiff's claims conflicted with the Coast Guard's no-propeller-guard decision and so were barred on implied preemption grounds.[157] Reversing, the Supreme Court unanimously held that the Boat Safety Act neither expressly nor implicitly preempted the plaintiff's common-law products liability claims. The Court reasoned that, first, the Act's *express* preemption clause, which referred to "a" state "law or regulation," appeared to preempt only a state's positive regulatory law, not common-law compensation claims, particularly in view of the savings clause provision that compliance with the Act "does not relieve a person from liability at common law or under State law." Nor was the plaintiff's claim *impliedly* preempted by *conflict* or *field* preemption principles. The plaintiff's products liability claim did not conflict with the Coast Guard's decision not to require propeller guards, consistent with its policy of leaving state law regulations in place until the Coast Guard adopted a conflicting regulation under the Act—which it had not done. Finally, Congress's effort to promote uniformity in boat safety regulation had to yield to the Act's primary goal of boat safety, a goal served by both the Coast Guard's policy of allowing broad state regulation of boat safety and by products liability claims like those in this case.

### Other Types of Products

The preemption issue has arisen in the lower courts in connection with a large number of other federal statutes that regulate the safety of many different types of products, and the diversity of approaches in the decisions reflects the failure of Congress to speak clearly to this issue together with the confused evolution of preemption in the Supreme Court.[158] The two most important categories of products subject to safety

---

**155.** See, e.g., Lady v. Neal Glaser Marine, Inc., 228 F.3d 598, 611 (5th Cir. 2000) (implied preemption).

Courts have found not preempted (and hence allowed) other types of claims against boat manufacturers based on unsafe features that the Coast Guard has not addressed. See, e.g., LaPlante v. Wellcraft Marine Corp., 114 Cal.Rptr.2d 196 (Ct. App. 2001) (child thrown from boat; failure to equip boat with handrails).

**156.** 537 U.S. 51 (2002).

**157.** 757 N.E.2d 75, 82–88 (Ill. 2001), rev'd, 537 U.S. 51 (2002).

**158.** See, e.g., Darby v. A–Best Prod. Co., 811 N.E.2d 1117 (Ohio 2004) (5–2 decision) (Federal Locomotive Boiler Inspection Act (BIA) preempts tort law claims against manufacturers of locomotives for injuries from asbestos contained in locomotives); Adkins v. Illinois Cent. R.R. Co., 326 F.3d 828 (7th Cir. 2003) (BIA can give rise to conflict preemption but not field preemption); General Motors v. Kilgore, 853 So.2d 171 (Ala. 2002) (Locomotive Inspection Act preempts claim based on asbestos exposure from locomotive components because Act occupies entire field of locomotive equipment and safety); Scheiding v. General Motors Corp., 993 P.2d 996 (Cal. 2000) (same); In re Wireless Tel. Radio Frequency Emissions Prods. Liab. Litig., 248 F.Supp.2d 452 (D. Md. 2003) (*cellular phones*: claim that phones emitted unsafe levels of radiation impliedly preempted because suit would necessarily require judge and jury to usurp the regulatory functions that Congress en-

regulation by federal agencies are consumer products and workplace products.

**Consumer products.** Consumer products are regulated by the Consumer Product Safety Commission (CPSC) under the Consumer Product Safety Act (CPSA),[159] the Federal Hazardous Substances Act,[160] and two other statutes.[161] The CPSA contains both a preemption clause[162] and a savings clause.[163] The preemption defense has arisen only infrequently in consumer products liability litigation. A couple of decisions involving warnings and design defect claims against power mower manufacturers have held that the plaintiffs' warnings claims were preempted, because the CPSC had promulgated a specific regulation governing such warnings, but that the design claims were not,[164] and one court has ruled that the CPSA preempts all such claims.[165] In several cases involving injuries from fires caused by children playing with lighters, some courts have found no preemption,[166] while one court has ruled that the CPSA

trusted to FCC under Telecommunications Act); King v. Aventis Pasteur, Inc., 210 F.Supp.2d 1201 (D. Or. 2002) (*vaccines*: National Childhood Vaccine Injury Compensation Act, autism—no preemption); Lucia v. Teledyne Cont'l Motors, 173 F.Supp.2d 1253 (S.D. Ala. 2001) (*general aviation aircraft*: FAA, defective crankshafts—no preemption; distinguishing "complete preemption" doctrine, for assessing federal removal jurisdiction, from "ordinary preemption," which precludes state-law claims); Seaman v. A.P. Green Indus., 707 N.Y.S.2d 299 (Sup. Ct. 2000) (*locomotives*: Boiler Inspection Act, asbestos—preemption); Choate v. Champion Home Builders Co., 222 F.3d 788 (10th Cir. 2000) (*mobile homes*: National Manufactured Housing Construction and Safety Standards Act does not preempt design defect and warnings claims based on lack of battery-powered backup in smoke detectors); Schiffner v. Motorola, Inc., 697 N.E.2d 868 (Ill. App. Ct. 1998) (*cellular phones*: Electronic Product Radiation Control Act, diminished value from defects—no preemption); Symens v. SmithKline Beecham Corp., 152 F.3d 1050 (8th Cir. 1998) (*animal vaccines*: USDA, cattle infections—preemption); Hall v. Fairmont Homes, Inc., 664 N.E.2d 546 (Ohio Ct. App. 1995) (*mobile homes*: NMHCSSA, level of formaldehyde emissions violated HUD regulations—no preemption); Olson v. Prosoco, Inc., 522 N.W.2d 284 (Iowa 1994) (*mortar cleaner* containing hydrochloric acid: Hazardous Materials Transportation Act—no preemption); Cleveland v. Piper Aircraft Corp., 985 F.2d 1438 (10th Cir. 1993) (*general aviation aircraft*: FAA, crash—no preemption). See generally Comment, 28 Transp. L.J. 107 (2000) (FAA, air crash litigation).

**159.** 15 U.S.C. § 2051 et seq.

**160.** Id. § 1261 et. seq.

**161.** The Federal Flammable Fabrics Act (FFA), id. § 1191 et seq., and the Poi-

son Prevention Packaging Act (PPPA), id. § 1471 et seq. Despite a preemption clause, the courts have ruled that the FFA does not preempt products liability claims for flammable clothing. See, e.g., O'Donnell v. Big Yank, Inc., 696 A.2d 846, 853 (Pa. Super. Ct. 1997); Wilson v. Bradlees of New England, Inc., 96 F.3d 552, 553 (1st Cir. 1996); Raymond v. Riegel Textile Corp., 484 F.2d 1025, 1028 (1st Cir. 1973).

**162.** The preemption clause provides that, if the CPSC has established federal safety standards for a product, the states may not adopt a safety standard or regulation "which prescribes any requirements as to the performance, composition, design, finish, construction, packaging, or labeling of such product which are designed to deal with the same risk of injury associated with such consumer product, unless such requirements are identical to the requirements of the Federal standard." 15 U.S.C. § 2075(a).

**163.** The savings clause provides: "Compliance with consumer product safety rules or other rules or orders under this Act shall not relieve any person from liability at common law or under State statutory law to any other person." 15 U.S.C. § 2074.

**164.** See Cortez v. MTD Prod., Inc., 927 F.Supp. 386 (N.D. Cal. 1996); Moe v. MTD Prod., Inc., 73 F.3d 179 (8th Cir. 1995).

**165.** Frazier v. Heckingers, 96 F.Supp.2d 486 (E.D. Pa. 2000).

**166.** See, e.g., Frith v. BIC Corp., 852 So.2d 592 (Miss. Ct. App. 2002); Phillips v. Cricket Lighters, 773 A.2d 802 (Pa. Super. Ct. 2001), appeal granted, 790 A.2d 1018 (Pa. 2001) (table); Hittle v. Scripto–Tokai Corp., 166 F.Supp.2d 142 (M.D. Pa. 2001); Colon v. BIC USA, Inc., 136 F.Supp.2d 196 (S.D.N.Y. 2000).

preempted the design defect claim but not the warnings claim.[167] And in a case involving injuries from the shattering of a glass shower door, the Ninth Circuit ruled that the CPSA did not preempt either the design or warnings claims.[168]

Pursuant to the Federal Hazardous Substances Act (FHSA), the CPSC establishes mandatory labeling requirements for certain hazardous substances intended for household use.[169] Because the structure and purpose of the FHSA are similar to the CPSA, the CPSC applies a single preemption regulation to both acts, interpreting the preemption of state "requirements" to mean statutory and regulatory requirements, not common-law holdings by the courts.[170] Although early decisions found no preemption,[171] courts in recent years have quite uniformly found that the FHSA preempts warnings claims when the manufacturer's warning complies with federal requirements,[172] but that the Act does not preempt design (or manufacturing defect) claims[173] or "misbranding" claims based on violation of FHSA regulations.[174]

**Workplace products.** The safety of workplace products is regulated by the Occupational Safety and Health Administration (OSHA) under the Occupational Safety and Health Act (OSHA).[175] OSHA does not contain an express preemption clause,[176] but it does contain a savings clause that seems to make clear that it does not displace state tort-law

**167.** See Ball v. BIC Corp., 2000 WL 33312192 (E.D. Mo. 2000).

**168.** Leipart v. Guardian Indus., 234 F.3d 1063 (9th Cir. 2000).

**169.** 15 U.S.C. § 1261.

**170.** See Leflar and Adler, The Preemption Pentad: Federal Preemption of Products Liability Claims After *Medtronic*, 64 Tenn. L. Rev. 691, 745 (1997), citing 56 Fed. Reg. 3414, 3415 (1991) (preamble to 16 C.F.R. § 1061).

**171.** See, e.g., Burch v. Amsterdam Corp., 366 A.2d 1079, 1084–86 (D.C. 1976) (explosive floor tile adhesive); Jonescue v. Jewel Home Shopping Serv., 306 N.E.2d 312, 316 (Ill. App. Ct. 1973) (toxic cleaning agent).

**172.** See, e.g., West v. Mattel, Inc., 246 F.Supp.2d 640 (S.D. Tex. 2003) (child's toy; Child Safety Protection Act amendment to FHSA preempts claim for inadequate warning of choking hazard, but not design defect claims); Schrader v. Sunnyside Corp., 747 N.Y.S.2d 26 (App. Div. 2002) (warning on can of denatured alcohol); Milanese v. Rust–Oleum Corp., 244 F.3d 104, 109 (2d Cir. 2001); Pennsylvania Gen. Ins. Co. v. Landis, 96 F.Supp.2d 408, 414–15 (D.N.J. 2000), aff'd, 248 F.3d 1131 (3d Cir. 2000) (table); Kirstein v. W.M. Barr & Co., 983 F.Supp. 753, 761 (N.D. Ill. 1997), aff'd, 159 F.3d 1065 (7th Cir. 1998); Comeaux v. National Tea Co., 81 F.3d 42 (5th Cir. 1996); Busch v. Graphic Color Corp., 662 N.E.2d 397, 408–09 (Ill. 1996); Jenkins v. James B. Day & Co., 634 N.E.2d 998, 1004 (Ohio

1994); Moss v. Parks Corp., 985 F.2d 736, 740 (4th Cir. 1993).

**173.** See Smith and Grage, Federal Preemption of State Products Liability Actions, 27 Wm. Mitchell L. Rev. 391, 408–09 (2000). The Act probably does not preempt design and manufacturing defect claims that are bona fide, that is, claims that are not merely warnings claims dressed in sheep's clothing in an attempt to circumvent the Act's preemption of warnings claims. See generally Beadling v. William Bowman Assocs., 809 A.2d 188 (N.J. Ct. App. 2002) (FHSA did not preempt design defect claim alleging that government-mandated warning for methanol should have been placed on side of drum rather than top); Arnold v. Dow Chem. Co., 110 Cal. Rptr.2d 722 (Ct. App. 2001) (full resolution of issue in FIFRA context), noted, 31 Sw. U. L. Rev. 441 (2002), and discussion of issue in FIFRA context, above.

**174.** See, e.g., Milanese v. Rust–Oleum Corp., 244 F.3d 104, 109 (2d Cir. 2001) ("a state cause of action alleging non-compliance with the FHSA would not be preempted by the Act"); Kirstein v. W.M. Barr & Co., 983 F.Supp. 753, 761 (N.D. Ill. 1997), aff'd, 159 F.3d 1065 (7th Cir. 1998); Canty v. Ever–Lasting Supply Co., 685 A.2d 1365, 1374 (N.J. Super. Ct. Law Div. 1996).

**175.** 29 U.S.C. § 651(b).

**176.** But the Occupational Safety and Health Administration has adopted certain preemption regulations. See 29 C.F.R. § 1910.1200(a), (f)(1).

claims for injuries.[177] When the savings clause is considered together with the fact that OSHA applies only to employers, not manufacturers, it is difficult to escape the conclusion that OSHA does not preempt injury claims against manufacturers of products in the workplace.[178] Were it not for one dubious case suggesting a contrary result,[179] it would be clear that OSHA has no preemptive effect on third-party products liability claims by injured workers against manufacturers of industrial products.

### Concluding Thoughts on Federal Preemption

The ever-shifting law of federal preemption is rife with perplexities. In attempting to unravel these perplexities, the first thing a judge or lawyer should do in any particular case is to determine if the Supreme Court has spoken definitively on the issue. If the Supreme Court has not done so, one must try to discern whether the particular products liability claims involved would contravene either an express preemption clause or the purposes of the particular act of Congress. Because regulatory objectives (and the phrasing of preemption and savings clauses) differ among the various federal product safety statutes, preemption issues normally are resolved by the growing jurisprudence specific to the particular statute relevant to the plaintiff's particular products liability claims.

Because product safety is federally regulated to quite a large extent, widening the reach of the preemption doctrine erases more and more areas of products liability law. Such a shift toward safety regulation in substitution for compensating injuries caused by defective products, similar to the current European approach,[180] may make some sense in terms of broad-scale social engineering. But efforts to protect the common good through federal regulation of product safety must not trample the state-law compensatory rights of persons injured by defective products to judicial remedies,[181] remedies protected by both federal and state constitutions. In enacting most of the product safety statutes during the consumer protection period of the late 1960s and early 1970s, Congress probably intended only to preempt state regulatory law, not broadly to immunize manufacturers from their duties to consumers under state products liability law.[182] And there is in fact no reason, as a general matter, why product safety regulation and products liability litigation cannot comfortably co-exist.

**177.** 29 U.S.C. § 653(b)(4). "There is a solid consensus that section 4(b)(4) operates to save state tort rules from preemption." Pedraza v. Shell Oil Co., 942 F.2d 48, 53 (1st Cir. 1991), quoting Notes, 88 Colum. L. Rev. 630, 641 (1988), and 101 Harv. L. Rev. 535, 543 (1987) (extent of OSHA preemption).

**178.** See, e.g., Cotto v. Estado Libre Asociado De Puerto Rico, 2002 WL 1009685, at *12 (P.R. 2002); Pedraza, 942 F.2d at 54 n.6; Wickham v. American Tokyo Kasei, Inc., 927 F.Supp. 293 (N.D. Ill. 1996); York v. Union Carbide Corp., 586 N.E.2d 861, 866 (Ind. Ct. App. 1992). See

also Jones v. Cincinnati, Inc., 589 N.E.2d 335, 340 (Mass. App. Ct. 1992).

**179.** Torres–Rios v. LPS Labs., Inc., 152 F.3d 11 (1st Cir. 1998). See also Smith and Grage, Federal Preemption of State Products Liability Actions, 27 Wm. Mitchell L. Rev. 391, 408–09 (2000).

**180.** See § 1.4, above.

**181.** See Rabin, Reassessing Regulatory Compliance, 88 Geo. L.J. 2049 (2000).

**182.** See Leflar and Adler, The Preemption Pentad: Federal Preemption of Products Liability Claims After *Medtronic*, 64 Tenn. L. Rev. 691, 746–48 (1997).

Congress, if it wanted to do so, could largely clean up the current "preemption mess." That is, if Congress truly desired to leave damages actions intact for persons injured by product hazards subject to federal regulation, it could explicitly limit the preemptive reach of its product safety statutes to legislative and regulatory activity while simultaneously providing, in a savings clause, that damages actions do not conflict with (indeed, may be complementary to) congressional purpose. While Congress fairly may be urged to speak clearly on whether federal legislation is intended to preempt common-law claims,[183] it seems quite unrealistic to expect Congress now to amend the product safety statutes of the 1960s and 1970s to cure the problem. As a practical matter, there is just no simple route out of the preemption thicket in which we now are largely lost. In any single case, courts and lawyers must simply do their best to ascertain whether the language of particular federal legislation or regulations bearing on a particular product safety issue in fact appear to bar particular products liability claims, and, if not, whether such claims do or do not reasonably appear to interfere substantially with the particular statute's goals. In this, it is worth remembering that the key to federal preemption begins and ends with statutory interpretation— with figuring congressional intent.

## § 14.5 STATUTES OF LIMITATIONS AND REPOSE

### Nature of Time–Limitation Statutes

Statutes of limitations and statutes of repose impose maximum time limits on products liability claims. Both forms of time-limitation statute cut off a plaintiff's rights after a particular period of time, although the period within which a plaintiff must file a claim may be extended in certain, limited circumstances. If the plaintiff files a products liability claim after the statutory period has run, the time-limitation statute simply bars the claim. A statute of *limitations* is an affirmative defense, and the defendant must raise it in a timely manner, which ordinarily means that it must be pled in the answer.[1] By contrast, because a statute of *repose* cuts off the plaintiff's rights at the expiration of the time period, rather than just the remedy, the defendant does not waive the running of a statute of repose by failing to raise it in a timely manner.[2] Statutes of limitations and repose provide a potent defense to products

---

**183.** See, e.g., Davis, 53 S.C. L. Rev. at 72; Raeker–Jordan, The Pre-Emption Presumption That Never Was: Pre-Emption Doctrine Swallows the Rule, 40 Ariz. L. Rev. 1379, 1381 (1998); Grey, Make Congress Speak Clearly: Federal Preemption of State Tort Remedies, 77 B.U. L. Rev. 559, 615–18 (1997).

**§ 14.5**

**1.** See Fed. R. Civ. P. 8(c); 2 C. Corman, Limitations of Actions § 15.2.1, at 349 (1991) (noting "the uniform requirement that when the statute of limitations is used as a defense it must be set forth affirma-tively in a party's responsive pleading"). But a court in its discretion may allow the defendant to amend its answer to include the defense if doing so is not unfair or prejudicial to the plaintiff. See id. § 15.3, at 355–58. If the running of the statute is apparent on the face of the complaint, the defendant may raise the defense by a motion to dismiss. See, e.g., Albrecht v. General Motors Corp., 648 N.W.2d 87, 89 (Iowa 2002). See generally Corman, above, § 15.1.3, at 345.

**2.** Id. § 15.2.3, at 355.

liability actions that a plaintiff's lawyer must seek to avoid and a defendant's lawyer must be sure not to overlook.[3]

As creatures of state legislation (with one exception),[4] time-limitation statutes vary widely in their provisions—the time periods, what starts the clock running, what stops it running, what types of claims they affect, and many others. Moreover, courts vary over time in how they interpret and apply similar provisions of similar statutes. Accordingly, each state has developed its own complex set of rules, both statutory and judicial, detailing the time periods within which various types of products liability claims must be filed to escape the time limitation defenses. More so than with many other issues in products liability litigation, therefore, the law on time-limitation issues in products liability cases tends to be unusually twisted and particularly localized. Thus, outcomes in particular cases involving time-limitation statutes are controlled by the language of particular statutes as interpreted by courts of varying persuasions in particular jurisdictions, according to particular common-law rules, and applied in varying fashions to the facts of particular cases. Because so many cases have been decided so many different ways on limitations issues in every jurisdiction,[5] little can be said about statutes of limitations and repose for which there is not contrary authority. For this reason, a lawyer must study the local statutory and case law especially closely in an attempt to fathom how a court might rule on a limitations issue in any particular case. Nevertheless, a general description of some of the recurring issues in this area of the law may be useful to a lawyer getting started on a limitations problem.

### Reasons for Time Limitations

It may seem unjust for a legislature to terminate the legal responsibility of a party who has wrongfully caused harm to another person, no

---

**3.** On statutes of limitations and repose in products liability litigation, see M. Green, The Paradox of Statutes of Limitations in Toxic Substances Litigation, 76 Cal. L. Rev. 965, 976–78 (1988) (limitation statutes should be abolished in toxic substance cases to promote more accurate fact finding, efficiency, and fairness); Epstein, The Temporal Dimension in Tort Law, 53 U. Chi. L. Rev. 1175 (1986); G. Schwartz, New Products, Old Products, Evolving Law, Retroactive Law, 59 N.Y.U. L. Rev. 796 (1983); Phillips, An Analysis of Proposed Reform of Products Liability Statutes of Limitations, 56 N.C. L. Rev. 643 (1978); 4 Frumer and Friedman, Products Liability ch. 26; 2 Madden & Owen on Products Liability § 16:1 and ch. 31; Am. Law Prod. Liab. 3d ch. 47. See generally Prosser and Keeton on Torts § 30; C. Corman, Limitations of Actions (1991) (2 vols.); 2 Prod. Liab. Rep. (CCH) ¶¶ 3100 and 3200; Annot., 4 A.L.R.3d 821, § 4 (1965) (products liability statutes of limitations); Annot., 30 A.L.R.5th 1 (1995) (products liability statutes of repose); Annot., 30 A.L.R.5th 1 (1995) (latent industrial diseases).

**4.** The General Aviation Revitalization Act (GARA), 49 U.S.C. § 40101, Note, examined below, is the one federal time-limitation statute applicable to products liability litigation. Congress has enacted a discovery rule for personal injury and property damages actions brought under the Comprehensive Environmental Response, Compensation, and Liability Act. 42 U.S.C. § 9658. For a variety of reasons, the courts have held that this statute does not apply in product liability actions. See, e.g., Rivas v. Safety–Kleen Corp., 119 Cal.Rptr.2d 503 (Ct. App. 2002) (CERCLA federal discovery rule does not preempt state time limits in toxic tort claims asserted against third party manufacturers because Congress did not have such actions in mind when drafting the relevant CERCLA provisions). The discovery rule is discussed in more detail below.

**5.** "It would be a laborious and unprofitable task to examine all the cases which have been decided on the statute of limitations." Fries v. Boisselete, 9 Serg. & Rawle 128, 130 (Pa. 1822).

matter how much time has passed since the harmful event occurred. Yet the law has recognized across the ages—from early Hebrew law,[6] to late Roman law,[7] thence into early German law,[8] early English law,[9] and in the early law of this nation[10]—that there is good reason to call a halt to legal responsibility for most wrongs after some period of time. In the products liability context, a major reason for eventually calling an end to litigation about old products is the simple fact that the available proofs— of the manufacturer's alleged wrongdoing, the product's alleged defectiveness, the plaintiff's alleged harms, and the alleged causal connection between them all—diminish over time. The legal system thus operates less accurately and hence less fairly in attempting to ascertain responsibility for harm as the years roll by after damaging events:[11] witnesses (and the parties and their agents) forget important facts, move, grow old, and eventually die; defendant manufacturers change their personnel, merge, and otherwise become transformed in myriad ways; and physical objects pertinent to a particular case—the product, its environment of use and failure, and documentary evidence of its creation, the accident, and the plaintiff's injuries—deteriorate, are discarded, or otherwise disappear. In addition to these practical reasons of diminishing proof for time-limitation statutes, they are substantively supported by the fact that the needs served by the justice system—deterrence, retributive justice, and even compensation—tend to lessen over time. Similarly, the economic logic of loss-shifting to manufacturers and their insurers diminishes with time, not only with respect to the goal of efficiently deterring wrongdoing but also because manufacturers and their insurers

**6.** See Deuteronomy 15:1 (7 years— money debts should be cancelled).

**7.** See R. Sohm, The Institutes—A Textbook of the History and System of Roman Private Law § 54. at 282–85 (J. Ledlie trans., 3d ed. 1970) (temporal limitations on civil actions were "quite exceptional" prior to 424 A.D., but from that date forward most claims were barred after 30 years, some after 40 years, and some after shorter periods). See also L. Wenger, Institutes of the Roman Law of Civil Procedure § 16(7), at 170, and § 29(V), at 302–03 (O. Fisk trans, 1940).

**8.** R. Sohn, above, at 284.

**9.** See T. Plucknett, A Concise History of the Common Law 719 (5th ed. 1956) (after 1540, "no seisin could found a claim in a writ of right unless it was within sixty years of the date of the writ").

**10.** See United States v. Kubrick, 444 U.S. 111, 117 (1979) (White, J.) (citing Bell v. Morrison, 26 U.S. (1 Pet.) 351, 360 (1828) and other cases):

Statutes of limitations, which "are found and approved in all systems of enlightened jurisprudence," Wood v. Carpenter, 101 U.S. 135, 139 (1879), represent a pervasive legislative judgment that it is unjust to fail to put the adversary on

notice to defend within a specified period of time and that "the right to be free of stale claims in time comes to prevail over the right to prosecute them." Railroad Telegraphers v. Railway Express Agency, 321 U.S. 342, 349 (1944). These enactments are statutes of repose; and although affording plaintiffs what the legislature deems a reasonable time to present their claims, they protect defendants and the courts from having to deal with cases in which the search for truth may be seriously impaired by the loss of evidence, whether by death or disappearance of witnesses, fading memories, disappearance of documents, or otherwise.

See generally Corman, Limitations of Actions § 1.1 (1991).

**11.** "The process of discovery and trial which result in the finding of ultimate facts for or against the plaintiff by the judge or jury is obviously more reliable if the witness or testimony in question is relatively fresh. Thus in the judgment of most legislatures and courts, there comes a point at which the delay of a plaintiff in asserting a claim is sufficiently likely either to impair the accuracy of the fact-finding process or to upset settled expectations that a substantive claim will be barred without respect to whether it is meritorious." Board of Regents v. Tomanio, 446 U.S. 478, 487 (1980).

can organize their resources more efficiently if they have some reasonable basis for estimating their exposure to liability for past occurrences. Finally, the equities of providing judicial remedies to persons who have long neglected to use them—who have "sat upon their rights"—weaken as the years progress. In short, after *some* period of time, in fairness to potential defendants and recognition of the limits of the courts, victims of wrongdoing who have long ignored their rights can fairly be required to accept their bygone losses as their own.[12]

### Types of Time–Limitation Statutes

As further explained below, time-limitation statutes come in a variety of forms. The two basic types of time-limitation statutes are statutes of *limitations* and statutes of *repose*. While both forms of statute cut off a defendant's products liability exposure after a period of time, they operate quite differently. The time periods of statutes of limitations are shorter—from as short as 1 year to as long as 6 years, depending on the jurisdiction—than those of statutes of repose, which run from 5 or 6 years, in a few jurisdictions, to as long as 18 or 20 years, in others. But there are a number of other important differences between these two types of time-limitation statutes. For example, statutes of limitations begin to run at the time an injury occurs or is discovered (actually or constructively), whereas statutes of repose generally begin to run when a product is sold; statutes of limitations normally may be delayed or "tolled" by certain equitable circumstances, such as a plaintiff's infancy or failure to discover an injury, whereas statutes of repose ordinarily may not; a number of other important differences distinguish the two basic forms of time-limitation statutes.[13]

Statutes of *limitations* come in various forms. All states have statutes of limitations applicable to personal injury torts, and separate statutes of limitations for wrongful death. In the absence of a more specific statute, such as a products liability statute of limitations,[14] these general statutes of limitations govern products liability claims for both negligence and strict liability in tort. In addition, most states have statutes of limitations in their commercial codes applicable to warranty claims. An increasing number of states, now a slight majority, have special statutes of limitations applicable specifically to products liability claims.

**12.** See, e.g., Albrecht v. General Motors Corp., 648 N.W.2d 87, 91 (Iowa 2002). See generally Note, Developments in the Law—Statutes of Limitations, 63 Harv. L. Rev. 1177, 1185 (1950), citing Order of R.R. Telegraphers v. Railway Express Agency, Inc., 321 U.S. 342, 349 (1944):

The primary consideration underlying such legislation is undoubtedly one of fairness to the defendant. There comes a time when he ought to be secure in his reasonable expectation that the slate has been wiped clean of ancient obligations, and he ought not to be called on to resist a claim when "evidence has been lost, memories have faded, and witnesses have disappeared."

**13.** For example, as stated earlier, a statutes of limitations defense, being remedial, may be waived if not raised in a timely manner; but a statute of repose defense, based on the termination of a plaintiff's rights, may not.

**14.** Specific statutes of limitations, such as those governing products liability actions, normally take precedence over general statutes of limitations for personal injuries or wrongful death. See, e.g., Kambury v. Daimler Chrysler Corp., 50 P.3d 1163, 1166 (Or. 2002); Harper v. Holiday Inns, Inc., 498 F.Supp. 910 (D. Tenn. 1978), aff'd, 633 F.2d 215 (6th Cir. 1980).

Statutes of *repose* also come in a number of forms. The most basic form of repose statute pertains to products liability claims generally, but some such statutes make exceptions for particular types of products, such as asbestos. A quite different form of repose statute, called a "useful-life" statute, bars a plaintiff's claim at the expiration of the product's useful-life rather than after a set period of time. In addition, some states apply repose statutes governing improvements to realty to cases involving products attached to land, such as large grain silos or overhead cranes. Finally, a federal statute of repose places outer time limits on products liability claims against manufacturers of small planes.

## Statutes of Limitations

### In General

**Tort law statutes.** Every jurisdiction has a statute of limitations governing claims for personal injuries or tortiously caused harm, with time periods ranging from 1 year (in California, Kentucky, Louisiana, and Tennessee) to 6 years (in Maine and North Dakota). The most common periods are 2 and 3 years.[15] Separate statutes of limitations governing wrongful death and survival claims normally are of the same duration as the injury statutes, but they are sometimes shorter[16] and occasionally longer.[17] Although a state may have a special statute of limitations for fraud or tortious misrepresentation, the statute of limitations governing personal injuries, wrongful death, or tortious misconduct may apply when the misconduct results in personal injury or death, because the defendant's misrepresentation "wrongfully" or "tortiously" produces the result.[18] And if the gist or gravamen of a products liability claim is really negligence or strict liability in tort for selling a defective product, a court may not allow a plaintiff to circumvent a shorter personal injury statute by alleging fraud.[19]

Traditionally, tort law claims begin to run when the claim "accrues," which is when the tort is complete because all of its elements have occurred. The last element in a tort is the plaintiff's damage—harm that is proximately caused by the defendant's breach of duty. For this reason, the traditional rule was that a tort-law statute of limitations begins to run at the time the plaintiff is injured.[20] A number of limita-

---

**15.** Time periods for and citations to each jurisdiction's statute of limitations for personal injuries are collected in Prod. Liab. Rep. (CCH) ¶ 3210. For limitations applicable to strict products liability in tort, see Annot., 91 A.L.R.3d 455 (1979).

**16.** See D.C. (injuries—3 years, death—1 year); Fla. (injuries—4 years, death—2 years); Maine (injuries—6 years, death—2 years); Mo. (injuries—5 years, death—3 years); Nebraska (injuries—4 years, death—2 years); N.C. (injuries—3 years, death—2 years); Utah (injuries—4 years, death—2 years); Wyo. (same). Time periods for and citations to each jurisdiction's statute of limitations for wrongful death are collected in Prod. Liab. Rep. (CCH) ¶ 3240.

**17.** See Minn. (injuries—2 years, death—3 years); N.H. (injuries—3 years, death—6 years); Or. (injuries—2 years, death—3 years).

**18.** See, e.g., Clark v. Baxter Healthcare Corp., 100 Cal.Rptr.2d 223, 226 n.2 (Ct. App. 2000) (allergic reaction to latex gloves; applying 1–year personal injury statute rather than 3–year fraud statute).

**19.** See, e.g., Larkins v. Glaxo Wellcome, Inc., 1999 WL 360204, at *9 (E.D.N.Y. 1999) (side effects from drug; fraud claim incidental to negligence and strict liability claims).

**20.** See Prosser and Keeton on Torts § 30; Annot., 4 A.L.R.3d 821, § 4 (1965).

tions statutes, even special products liability statutes, still are phrased in terms of when the tort or products liability cause of action arises or accrues,[21] and some actually specify that the statutory period begins when the damage occurs.[22] However, a majority of states now have jettisoned the traditional accrual rule based on the time of injury, in favor of the discovery rule discussed below.

**Warranty law statutes.** State commercial law statutes contain statutes of limitations for warranty claims, based on Uniform Commercial Code § 2–725(1), Statute of Limitations in Contracts for Sale.[23] In the absence of other agreement, this section specifies a 4–year limitation period[24] for Article 2 breach of warranty claims.[25] This provision is quite specific, and it would seem that courts would be bound to apply this statutory period—which often is longer than the jurisdiction's limitation period for torts—to products liability claims brought in warranty. Duly considering themselves so bound, many courts apply the Article 2 limitations provision to products liability claims brought in warranty.[26] But a number of courts, sometimes drawing on the warranty-law derivations of the doctrine of strict products liability in tort, reason that modern products liability actions for personal injuries (and death) sound more properly in tort than in warranty.[27] So flouting the legislature's prerogative to define warranty statutes of limitations however it may choose,[28] these courts thus have held that the *tort* law statutes of limitations apply to *warranty* as well as tort claims in ordinary products liability actions.[29]

---

**21.** See, e.g., Colo. Rev. Stat. § 13–80–107 (products liability claims, except in warranty, 2 years after claim arises); Idaho Code § 6–1403 (products liability claims, 2 years after claim accrues); Ind. Code § 33–1–1.5–5 (products liability claims, 2 years after claim accrues); Mich. Comp. Laws 1979 § 600.5805 (products liability claims, 3 years after claim accrues).

**22.** See, e.g., Ala. Code § 6–5–502 (all products liability actions must be brought within 1 year of time of injury, death, or property damage); Ark. Rev. Stat. § 16–116–104 (same—3 years); Neb. Rev. Stat. 25–224 (products liability claims—4 years after death, injury or other damage); Ore. Rev. Stat. § 30.905 (products liability claims—2 years after injury, death, or property damage); Tenn. Code Ann. § 29–28–103 (products liability claims—6 years after injury, death, or property damage).

**23.** See Clark and Smith, Product Warranties ch. 11; White and Summers, UCC § 11.9; Annot., 49 A.L.R.5th 1 (1997).

**24.** Except in Oklahoma (5 years), Mississippi (6 years), South Carolina (6 years), Wisconsin (6 years), and Rhode Island (10 years).

**25.** UCC § 2–725(1) provides: "An action for breach of any contract for sale must be commenced within four years after the cause of action has accrued. By the original agreement the parties may reduce the peri-

od of limitation to not less than one year but may not extend it."

**26.** See, e.g., Hughes v. Allegiance Healthcare Corp., 152 F.Supp.2d 667, 675 (E.D. Pa. 2001); Strange v. Keiper Recaro Seating, Inc., 117 F.Supp.2d 408, 410 (D. Del. 2000). See generally Frumer and Friedman, Products Liability § 26.03[4][a][iv] (noting that a majority of courts apply § 2–725 to all breach of warranty actions).

**27.** Courts that ignore the legislature in this respect struggle to find a convincing rationale for this imperious behavior, often attempting to justify their decisions by drawing upon such dubious factors as the nature of the injury (if the injuries are tort-like, then the tort-law statute is supposedly appropriate) and whether the parties are in privity of contract (if not, then the tort-law statute may be applied). Neither of these rationales is sound. See Clark and Smith, Product Warranties § 11.05.

**28.** See id. § 11.05[3] (characterizing a court's ignoring of UCC § 2–725 as "legislative destruction"). "In all cases the court should invoke the statute of limitations applicable to the cause of action." Id.

**29.** See, e.g., Fritchie v. Alumax, Inc., 931 F.Supp. 662 (D. Neb. 1996); Taylor v. Ford Motor Co., 408 S.E.2d 270 (W. Va. 1991) (state's 2–year tort law statute barred

Section 2–725(2) of the Code provides that the statute of limitations on breach of warranty claims under Article 2 "accrues" when the *breach* occurs, which generally is when the product is "tendered for delivery" unless the seller has explicitly extended the warranty to future performance:

> A cause of action accrues when the breach occurs, regardless of the aggrieved party's lack of knowledge of the breach. A breach of warranty occurs when tender of delivery is made, except that where a warranty explicitly extends to future performance of the goods and discovery of the breach must await the time of such performance the cause of action accrues when the breach is or should have been discovered.[30]

This means that the 4–year statute of limitations on warranty claims normally begins to run when the seller tenders delivery to a buyer— which usually is when the buyer first takes delivery of a product— whether or not the buyer or other plaintiff has reason to know at that time that the product is unmerchantable or an express warranty is false. In other words, the Code explicitly rejects the discovery rule. However, as with the 4–year time period in § 2–725(1), courts applying § 2–725(2) to personal injury cases sometimes ignore its explicit language and apply the discovery rule to warranty actions involving personal injuries.[31]

Section 2–725(2) contains some ambiguous wrinkles. First is the issue concerning a product's "shelf-life," a problem which results when a manufacturer tenders delivery of a product to a retailer who places it on a shelf for three years before selling it and tendering delivery to a buyer. If the product malfunctions and injures the buyer two years thereafter (5 years after the manufacturer tendered delivery to the retailer, but only 2 years after the retailer tendered delivery to the injured purchaser) and if the injured buyer thereupon sues the manufacturer for breach of warranty, a court will have to determine which tender of delivery started the 4–year time limitations clock ticking under § 2–725(2). On this point the courts disagree, some ruling that the period begins to run on the manufacturer's tender of delivery[32] in order to promote commercial certainty, others holding that the period begins only when delivery by somebody is tendered to the buyer[33] in order to spread the risk of loss and allow an injured plaintiff at least some chance to bring an action for breach of warranty.[34]

---

plaintiff's breach of warranty claim for personal injuries brought within 4 years of product's delivery). See generally Clark and Smith, Product Warranties § 11.05[1], at S11–39 (1998 Supp.) ("Unfortunately, some courts are willing to ignore the plain language of Section 2–725 when personal injury is sought under a warranty banner, thus fuzzing the line between tort and warranty.").

**30.** UCC § 2–725(2). See the nonuniform variations in Alabama and Maine, where claims for personal injury accrue when the injury occurs; in South Carolina, which substitutes the discovery rule.

**31.** See discussion of discovery rule, below.

**32.** See, e.g., Heller v. U.S. Suzuki Motor Corp., 477 N.E.2d 434 (N.Y. 1985) (4–2 decision).

**33.** See, e.g., Patterson v. Her Majesty Indus., 450 F.Supp. 425 (E.D. Pa. 1978), discussed in Case Comment, 17 Am. Bus. L.J. 221 (1979).

**34.** This latter approach "appears correct." Clark and Smith, Product Warranties § 11.01[2][d], at 11–20. See Heller v. U.S. Suzuki Motor Corp., 465 N.Y.S.2d 822 (Sup. Ct. 1983) (endorsing this approach) rev'd,

A second interpretative wrinkle in § 2–725(2) concerns the question of when a seller's warranty "extends to future performance," in which event the 4–year time period does not begin to run until the plaintiff does or should discover the breach of warranty, (normally the time of injury). Because the discovery-rule exception applies only to warranties that "explicitly" extend to future performance, the courts are quite clear in holding that this exception cannot logically apply to *implied* warranties.[35] And while *express* warranties would in a sense seem *always* to extend to a product's future performance, most courts have been reluctant to rule that normal express warranties "explicitly" so extend.[36] Consequently, unless an express warranty (as distinguished from a remedy, such as repair or replacement)[37] provides that it will last for a specified period of time,[38] most courts hold that such a warranty does *not* extend to future performance, which means that the 4–year limitations period begins to run when delivery is tendered rather than when plaintiff discovers the harm.[39]

**Products liability statutes.** An increasing majority of states have enacted special statutes of limitations, usually as part of a larger products liability reform act, that specifically govern products liability claims.[40] Because they apply specially to products liability claims, such provisions take precedence over more general statutes of limitations covering torts, personal injuries, and wrongful death.[41] Products liability

475 N.Y.S.2d 146 (App. Div. 1985), aff'd, 477 N.E.2d 434 (N.Y. 1985).

**35.** See Clark and Smith, above, § 11.01[2][b][ii], at 11–16 ("The courts have consistently ruled that implied warranties of merchantability and fitness do not explicitly extend to future performance."). See, e.g., Selzer v. Brunsell Bros., Ltd., 652 N.W.2d 806 (Wis. Ct. App. 2002) (implied warranties cannot extend to future performance); Marvin Lumber and Cedar Co. v. PPG Indus., Inc., 223 F.3d 873 (8th Cir. 2000) (Minn. law) (same).

**36.** See id. § 11.01[2][b][i], at 11–7 et seq. (noting that the great bulk of cases refuse to find that warranties extend to future performance).

**37.** See, e.g., Tittle v. Steel City Oldsmobile GMC Truck, Inc., 544 So.2d 883 (Ala. 1989) ("repair-or-replacement" warranty for 36,000 miles or 36 months addresses remedy, not warranty, and so does not explicitly extend to future performance). *But see* Mississippi Chem. Corp. v. Dresser–Rand Co., 287 F.3d 359 (5th Cir. 2002) (Miss. law) (limitations period based on "repair or replace" provision did not begin to run until the promise to repair or replace failed of its essential purpose); Krieger v. Nick Alexander Imports, Inc., 285 Cal.Rptr. 717 (Ct. App. 1991) (promise to repair defects that occur within 36,000 miles or 36 months explicitly extends to future performance; discovery rule applied).

**38.** Such as a two-year limited express warranty, or a limited automotive warranty for the lesser of 3 years or 36,000 miles.

**39.** See, e.g., Sherman v. Sea Ray Boats, Inc., 649 N.W.2d 783 (Mich. Ct. App. 2002) (reference in boat manual to "years of trouble free boating" and "family fun for many years to come" did not create a warranty of future performance); Selzer v. Brunsell Bros., Ltd., 652 N.W.2d 806 (Wis. Ct. App. 2002) (statement that "all exterior wood is deep-treated to permanently protect against rot and decay" did not create warranty of future performance); Snyder v. Boston Whaler, Inc., 892 F.Supp. 955 (W.D. Mich. 1994) (boat warranted to be "unsinkable"). *But see* Marvin Lumber and Cedar Co. v. PPG Indus., Inc., 223 F.3d 873 (8th Cir. 2000) (Minn. law) (warranty may extend to future performance even if length of coverage is imprecise; warranty that product would last as long as other manufacturers' products and longer than similar product that plaintiff already owned created jury issue on whether warranty of future performance was created).

**40.** The statutes are listed and described at Prod. Liab. Rep. (CCH) ¶ 3210.

**41.** See, e.g., Kambury v. Daimler Chrysler Corp., 50 P.3d 1163 (Or. 2002) (applying ordinary canon of statutory construction, *held*, 2–year products liability statute of limitations, being more specific, trumps 3–year wrongful death statute). *But see* Alder v. Bayer Corp., AGFA Div., 61

statutes of limitations typically apply to all "products liability claims," including claims for breach of warranty and wrongful death.[42] Yet, because of Article 2's special statute of limitations for warranty claims in UCC § 2–725, it is unclear whether a legislature's enactment of a statute of limitations for "products liability claims" captures warranty claims under that umbrella. Many products liability statutes cure this ambiguity by specifying the types of claims included, as by expressly including or excluding breach of warranty and possibly other types of claims, such as those for wrongful death. Colorado's products liability statute, for example, specifies that all products liability actions for personal injury or death, other than in warranty, must be brought within two years after a claim for relief arises.[43] Some special products liability statutes combine statutes of limitations with statutes of repose.[44]

### Stopping the Clock

Certain conduct by a defendant, or a plaintiff's status or reasonable ignorance of an injury or a products liability claim, may "toll"—stop the running of—the statute of limitations clock. Some statutes explicitly so provide, and courts sometimes apply the doctrine of equitable tolling to achieve the same result.[45] Moreover, a statute of limitations clock may be delayed until the plaintiff's final exposure to a toxic substance; and long after the plaintiff first suffers an initial injury from such a substance, the limitations clock may begin to run anew if the plaintiff subsequently suffers another separate type of harm.

**Tolling.** The running of a statutory limitations period may be delayed on account of certain wrongful conduct by a defendant. If a defendant fraudulently prevents a plaintiff from learning that he or she has a products liability claim against the defendant, a court may apply the equitable doctrine of tolling to delay a statute of limitations from running until the plaintiff does, or should, discover the existence of the claim.[46] For a defendant's fraudulent concealment to be sufficient to toll a limitations statute, the defendant must act affirmatively to hide facts necessary to the plaintiff's claim and thereby prevent the plaintiff from discovering its existence.[47] Silence alone, including a failure to warn of a

---

P.3d 1068 (Utah 2002) (4–year statute of limitations for negligence actions, and not 2–year statute of limitations for products liability actions, governed claim that manufacturer negligently installed and serviced its machine).

**42.** See, e.g., Ark. Rev. Stat. § 16–116–104 (3 years—all products liability actions or injury, death, or damage); Neb. Rev. Stat. 25–224 (4 years—all products liability actions for injury, death, or damage).

**43.** See, e.g., Colo. Rev. Stat. § 13–80–106.

**44.** See, e.g., Conn. Gen. Stat. Ann. § 52–577a(a).

**45.** See Corman, above, at chs. 8–10; 4 Frumer and Friedman, Products Liability § 26.07.

**46.** See Corman, above, § 9.7.2, at 67: "Fraudulent concealment involves the use of artifice to prevent inquiry or investigation and to mislead or hinder the acquisition of information that would disclose a right of action. Postponing the accrual of the cause of action is based on the concealing party's wrongdoing and the plaintiff's blameless ignorance of the cause of action." See generally Marcus, Fraudulent Concealment in Federal Court: Toward a More Disparate Standard?, 71 Geo. L.J. 829 (1983).

**47.** See, e.g., Hatfield v. Dyncorp., Inc., 187 F.3d 647 (9th Cir. 1999) (Ariz. law) (limitations statute not tolled where no allegation of positive act by defendant); Curlee v. Mock Enter., Inc., 327 S.E.2d 736 (Ga. Ct. App. 1985); Curry v. A. H. Robins Co., 775 F.2d 212 (7th Cir. 1985) (Ill. law). See also State Farm Mut. Auto. Ins. Co. v. Ford Motor Co., 572 N.W.2d 321 (Minn. Ct. App.

known defect, is insufficient.[48] As a predicate for tolling on the basis of fraudulent concealment, most jurisdictions require that the plaintiff prove the defendant's intent to deceive the plaintiff.[49] Even in the absence of an intent to deceive, however, a defendant whose misrepresentation is relied upon by a plaintiff may be equitably estopped from relying on a statute of limitations.[50]

By statute and case law, most states toll statutes of limitations for claims by plaintiffs whose disabilities interfere with a fair opportunity to pursue a legal claim. Most states, but not all, also toll statutes of limitations for a minor's claims until he or she reaches the age of majority.[51] In addition, at least when the defendant's product causes a person to become mentally incompetent, a plaintiff's incompetency may toll the statute of limitations.[52] Further, federal law provides for the tolling of claims by persons on active duty in the armed services.[53]

Various jurisdictions toll statutes of limitations in a miscellany of other situations. Statutes in some states protect retailers and other nonmanufacturing defendants from strict liability unless, among other things, the manufacturer is (or is likely to become) insolvent.[54] In a state with such a statute, if a plaintiff after diligent investigation chooses not to join a nonmanufacturing defendant because the manufacturer (or its successor) reasonably appears likely to remain solvent, a court may toll the statute of limitations against the nonmanufacturing seller until the plaintiff should discover the manufacturer's insolvency.[55] And, while a class action is pending certification, most courts toll the statute of limitations provisionally, in case the petition fails, for the individual claims of persons who would have been class members had the class action been approved.[56]

1997) (no tolling where claim of fraudulent concealment was mere conjecture). See generally Corman, above, at § 9.7.

**48.** See, e.g., Martin v. Arthur, 3 S.W.3d 684, 690 (Ark. 1999); Curlee v. Mock Enter., Inc., 327 S.E.2d 736, 741 (Ga. Ct. App. 1985); Cazalas v. Johns–Manville Sales Corp., 435 So.2d 55, 58 (Ala. 1983).

**49.** See, e.g., Curry v. A.H. Robins Co., 775 F.2d 212 (7th Cir. 1985) (Ill. law). See generally Corman, above, § 9.7.1, at 61.

**50.** See, e.g., Northwestern Pub. Serv. v. Union Carbide Corp., 115 F.Supp.2d 1164, 1171 (D.S.D. 2000); Anane v. Pettibone Corp., 560 N.E.2d 1088 (Ill. App. Ct. 1990).

**51.** See, e.g., Mueller v. Parke Davis, 599 A.2d 950, 955 (N.J. App. Div. 1991) (applying N.J. or Va. law, both of which tolled statute for plaintiff's infancy, rather than that of Conn., which did not); Macku v. Drackett Prods. Co., 343 N.W.2d 58 (Neb. 1984); Smith v. Sturm, Ruger and Co., 643 P.2d 576 (Mont. 1982).

In contrast to a statute of limitations, a plaintiff's minority will *not* toll a statute of repose. See, e.g., Albrecht v. General Motors Corp., 648 N.W.2d 87 (Iowa 2002).

**52.** See, e.g., Pardy v. United States, 548 F.Supp. 682 (S.D. Ill. 1982) (reviewing the law nationally). *But see* Penley v. Honda Motor Co., 31 S.W.3d 181 (Tenn. 2000) (statute not tolled for plaintiff who was on nearly constant pain medication in hospital after accident and often did not know where she was).

**53.** See the Soldiers' and Sailors' Civil Relief Act of 1940, 50 U.S.C. App. § 501 et seq.

**54.** See § 15.2, below.

**55.** See, e.g., Braswell v. AC and S, Inc., 105 S.W.3d 587 (Tenn. Ct. App. 2002) (statute which precluded strict liability in tort claim against seller unless manufacturer is insolvent tolled statute of limitations until manufacturer filed for bankruptcy); Crego v. Baldwin–Lima–Hamilton Corp., 1998 WL 80240 (Ohio Ct. App. 1998), and 1999 WL 1043887 (Ohio Ct. App. 1999). See generally Frumer and Friedman, Products Liability § 26.07[5].

**56.** See, e.g., Vaccariello v. Smith & Nephew Richards, Inc., 763 N.E.2d 160 (Ohio 2002) (filing of class action in Ohio or federal court system tolls statute of limita-

**The discovery rule.** In products liability actions involving toxic substances (such as asbestos, dangerous drugs, or other toxic chemicals) and medical devices implanted in the human body, a plaintiff may have no way to know that he or she has suffered injury until long after it first occurs. For example, the incubation period for mesothelioma, a form of lung cancer resulting from inhaling asbestos dust, may be as long as 40 years.[57] If a statute of limitations begins to run on a plaintiff's claim for harm from a toxic substance at the time the plaintiff first suffers harm, the conventional accrual point for tort-law claims as discussed above, then the limitations statute would bar the legal rights of many persons injured by toxic substances before they even knew that they were injured. Applying the traditional accrual rule to cases of this type, as courts used to do, snuffed out the products liability rights of many consumers and workers to recover for grievous injuries caused by the most insidious kinds of defective products.[58]

Beginning in the 1960s and 1970s,[59] several courts began to remedy this problem by extending the "discovery rule" from medical malpractice litigation, where it had been incubating,[60] to products liability litigation.[61] Under the discovery rule, a cause of action accrues not when the plaintiff is injured but when the plaintiff *discovers*, or in the exercise of reasonable diligence should discover, pertinent facts about the injury. Today, courts in the vast majority of jurisdictions apply the discovery rule to products liability cases,[62] and some states have codified the rule, either

tions as to all asserted members of class who would have been parties had suit been permitted to continue as class action; discussing cases on cross-jurisdictional tolling based on class action filings); In re Norplant Contraceptive Prods. Liab. Litig., 961 F.Supp. 163, 166–67 (E.D. Tex. 1997); Burton v. American Home Prods. Corp., 173 F.R.D. 185 (E.D. Tex. 1997) (refusing to vacate order in preceding Norplant case); American Pipe & Const. Co. v. Utah, 414 U.S. 538, 551 (1974). *But see* Maestas v. Sofamor Danek Group, Inc., 1999 WL 74212, at *4 (Tenn. Ct. App. 1999) (in bone screw litigation, statute not tolled for subsequent state claims filed after federal class certification denied; state does not recognize "cross-jursidictional tolling"), aff'd, 33 S.W.3d 805 (Tenn. 2000); Jolly v. Eli Lilly & Co., 751 P.2d 923 (Cal. 1988) (refusing to toll statute during DES putative class action, where variance among individual claims made class certification very unlikely). But a suspension of the statute of limitations in such litigation does not revive claims on which the statute already has run. See Michals v. Baxter Healthcare Corp., 289 F.3d 402 (6th Cir. 2002) (Ky. law) (6–month suspension of statutes of limitations and repose designated in opt-out form accompanying settlement notifications in silicone breast implant class action). See generally Frumer and Friedman, Products Liability § 26.07[6].

**57.** See Hamilton v. Asbestos Corp., 998 P.2d 403, 405–08 (Cal. 2000) (noting 30–40 year latency period for mesolthelioma).

**58.** See, e.g., Locke v. Johns–Manville Corp., 275 S.E.2d 900, 905–06 (Va. 1981).

**59.** A progenator case was Urie v. Thompson, 337 U.S. 163 (1949) (FELA compensation claim for silicosis).

**60.** See Prosser and Keeton on Torts § 30.

**61.** Early cases include R.J. Reynolds Tobacco Co. v. Hudson, 314 F.2d 776 (5th Cir. 1963) (La. law); Breaux v. Aetna Cas. & Sur. Co., 272 F.Supp. 668 (E.D. La. 1967); Gilbert v. Jones, 523 S.W.2d 211 (Tenn. Ct. App. 1974); Raymond v. Eli Lilly & Co., 371 A.2d 170, 174 (N.H. 1977) (Kenison, C.J.) ("we do not think the drug company can reasonably expect to be immune to suit before its customer has a fair opportunity to discover the company's tortious conduct"); Louisville Trust Co. v. Johns–Manville Prod. Corp., 580 S.W.2d 497 (Ky. 1979). See generally Annot., 4 A.L.R.3d 821 (1965).

**62.** See, e.g., Zamboni v. Aladan Corp., 304 F.Supp.2d 218 (D. Mass 2004); In re Bridgestone/Firestone, Inc., 200 F.Supp.2d 983 (S.D. Ind. 2002) (Cal. and Ariz. law) (finding for plaintiffs); Russo v. Cabot Corp., 2002 WL 1833348 (E.D. Pa. 2002) (finding for defendants), overruled on other grounds, Debiec v. Cabot Corp., 352 F.3d

for tort actions generally[63] or for products liability actions in particular.[64] Some courts and statutes specify that the discovery rule, or some particular version of it, applies to cases involving injuries or illnesses from toxic substances, cases where the rule is needed most.[65]

Courts and legislatures are widely split on precisely what type of facts a plaintiff must discover to trigger a limitations statute and start the clock ticking. Some jurisdictions start the clock when the plaintiff learns or should be aware that he or she is ill or injured,[66] while others hold that the clock does not begin to run until the plaintiff discovers both the injury and its cause.[67] Even these latter courts cannot agree on

117 (3d Cir.2003); Degussa Corp. v. Mullens, 744 N.E.2d 407 (Ind. 2001). See generally Frumer and Friedman, Products Liability § 26.04[2][a] ("It has become the near unanimous rule."). Some courts apply the discovery rule in product liability actions on a case-by-case basis while others hold that their states' various statutes of limitation do not allow a discovery rule. See Hoffman v. Orthopedic Sys., Inc., 765 N.E.2d 116 (Ill. App. Ct. 2002) (case-by-case basis); Griffith v. Blatt, 51 P.3d 1256 (Or. 2002) (discovery rule does not apply to 2–year products liability statute of limitations); Colormatch Exteriors, Inc. v. Hickey, 569 S.E.2d 495 (Ga. 2002) (discovery rule does not apply to 4–year statute for damage to realty).

**63.** See, e.g., S.C. Code Ann. § 15–3–535, applied to toxic substance products liability case in Grillo v. Speedrite Prod., Inc., 532 S.E.2d 1 (S.C. Ct. App. 2000); Colo. Rev. Stat. § 13–80–108(I), similarly applied in Salazar v. American Sterilizer Co., 5 P.3d 357 (Colo. Ct. App. 2000).

**64.** See, e.g., Conn. Gen. Stat. Ann. § 52–577a(a); Fla. Stat. Ann. § 95.031(2); Utah Code Ann. § 78–15–3; Wash. Rev. Code § 7.72.060.

**65.** See, e.g., Carter v. Brown & Williamson Tobacco Corp., 778 So.2d 932 (Fla. 2000) (discovery rule applies to "creeping diseases" such as lung cancer); Barnes v. A.H. Robins Co., 476 N.E.2d 84 (Ind. 1985) (discovery rule adopted for use in limited context of claims of injuries from "protracted exposure to a foreign substance"—Dalkon Shield IUD); N.Y. C.P.L.R. 214–c(2) (discovery rule applies to harm "caused by the latent effects of exposure to any substance or combination of substances, in any form, upon or within the body or upon or within property").

Statutes: See, e.g., Or. Rev. Stat. § 30.907 (claims for asbestos injuries to be brought within 2 years of when injuries were or should have been discovered, in contrast to 2 years from date of injury for normal products liability claims, id. § 30.905); N.Y. C.P.L.R. 214–c[2] (claims for injuries to body or property from latent effects of exposure to substance must be brought within 3 years of when injury was

or should have been discovered through exercise of reasonable diligence).

**66.** See, e.g., Wiggins v. Boston Scientific Corp., 1999 WL 94615 (E.D. Pa. 1999) (broken guide wire in heart; statute began to run when plaintiff learned or reasonably should have learned of objective and ascertainable injury); Wetherill v. Eli Lilly & Co., 678 N.E.2d 474 (N.Y. 1997) (DES; discovery of primary condition); Adams v. Armstrong World Indus., 847 F.2d 589 (9th Cir. 1988) (Idaho law) (asbestos; when asbestosis or other injury was "objectively ascertainable"); Cavanaugh v. Abbott Labs., 496 A.2d 154 (Vt. 1985) (DES; when vaginal cancer was discovered); Bendix Corp. v. Stagg, 486 A.2d 1150 (Del. 1984) (asbestosis; when harmful effect was manifested, physically ascertainable); Condon v. A.H. Robins Co., 349 N.W.2d 622 (Neb. 1984) (Dalkon Shield).

Statutes to this effect include Conn. Gen. Stat. § 52–577a(a); Mo. Ann. Stat. § 516.100; S.D. Codified Laws Ann. § 15–2–12.2; Vt. Stat. Ann. tit. 12, § 512(4).

**67.** See, e.g., Brown v. E.I. duPont de Nemours and Co., Inc., 820 A.2d 362 (Del. 2003) (fungicide; plaintiff knew or should have known both of the injury and that injury may have been caused by the defendant's tortious conduct); Baldwin v. Badger Mining Corp., 663 N.W.2d 382 (Wis. Ct. App. 2003) (allegedly defective respirator masks; plaintiff must know or should have known both of his injury and that injury probably was caused by defendant's product or conduct); Dorman v. Osmose, Inc., 782 N.E.2d 463 (Ind. Ct. App. 2003) (chromated copper arsenate used in treating wood; plaintiff must know or should have known both of his injury and that it was caused by product or acts of another); Johnson v. Sandoz Pharm. Corp., 24 Fed.Appx. 533 (6th Cir. 2001) (Ky. law) (prescription drug Parlodel; statute not triggered until plaintiff has reasonable opportunity to discover causal relationship between drug and stroke); Carter v. Brown & Williamson Tobacco Corp., 778 So.2d 932 (Fla. 2000) (statute does not begin to run on latent injury

how specific the plaintiff's discovery of "cause" must be. Some courts start the clock only when the plaintiff discovers a causal connection between the injury and a particular product;[68] others start the clock only when the plaintiff discovers the identity of the party responsible for causing the injury (the defendant);[69] and some require that the plaintiff must discover the defendant's wrongdoing—that he or she has a cause of action, or at least be put on notice of that reasonable possibility.[70] One reasonable way to formulate a discovery rule, capturing the essence of what many courts have ruled, is to hold a statute triggered when an injured person acquires facts reasonably suggesting that a likely cause of the injury was a particular product that plausibly may have been defective.[71] Knowledge of this type should put most people on notice that they should see a lawyer to determine if they have a legal remedy.[72]

As seen above, the Uniform Commercial Code is perfectly clear in stating that claims for breach of warranty under the Code accrue on breach, defined as when tender of delivery occurs, "regardless of the aggrieved party's lack of knowledge of the breach."[73] It is hard to imagine how the Code's drafters could have been any more explicit in rejecting the discovery rule. Yet, for whatever reason,[74] some courts have

---

for "creeping disease," like lung cancer from smoking, until plaintiff is on notice of causal connection between exposure to product and an injury). See generally Frumer and Friedman, Products Liability §§ 26.04[4][b] and 26.04[4][f] (listing, as following this rule, Arkansas, California, Connecticut, Georgia, Illinois, Kentucky, Louisiana, Massachusetts, Michigan, Minnesota, Missouri, New Hampshire, Ohio, Oklahoma, Pennsylvania, Tennessee, and Utah).

**68.** See, e.g., Stewart v. Philip Morris, Inc., 205 F.3d 1054 (8th Cir. 2000) (Ark. law) (connection between cigarette smoking and breathing and coughing problems); Bowen v. Eli Lilly & Co., 557 N.E.2d 739 (Mass. 1990) (connection between DES and cancer.

**69.** See, e.g., Michals v. Baxter Healthcare Corp., 289 F.3d 402 (6th Cir. 2002) (Ky. law) (breast implants; plaintiff must know or should have known that she has been wronged and by whom wrong has been committed). See generally Frumer and Friedman, Products Liability §§ 26.04[4][b] and 26.04[4][f] (listing, as following this rule, Arizona, New Hampshire, Oregon, Puerto Rico, Washington, and West Virginia).

**70.** See, e.g., Collin v. Securi Int'l, 322 F.Supp.2d 170 (D. Conn. 2004); Clark v. Baxter Healthcare Corp., 100 Cal.Rptr.2d 223, 227 (Ct. App. 2000) (" 'Under the discovery rule, the statute of limitations begins to run when the plaintiff suspects or should suspect that her injury was caused by wrongdoing, that someone has done something wrong to her.' "); Welch v. Celo-

tex Corp. 951 F.2d 1235 (11th Cir. 1992) (Ga. law) (plaintiff must discover both injury and its causal connection to wrongful conduct). See generally Frumer and Friedman, Products Liability § 26.04[4][f] (listing, as following this rule, Alaska, Florida, Hawaii, Iowa, Michigan, Montana, New Jersey, North Dakota, and South Carolina). At least South Carolina's rule is by statute. See S.C. Code Ann. § 15–3–535, applied in Grillo v. Speedrite Prod., Inc., 532 S.E.2d 1, 3–6 (S.C. Ct. App. 2000) (factual question whether circumstances would have put plaintiff on notice that some claim against another party might exist).

**71.** See, e.g., Dennis v. ICL, Inc., 957 F.Supp. 376 (D. Conn. 1997) (focus is on plaintiff's knowledge of facts, not discovery of applicable legal theories); Jolly v. Eli Lilly & Co., 751 P.2d 923, 927–28 (Cal. 1988) (DES; "[o]nce the plaintiff has a suspicion of wrongdoing, and therefore an incentive to sue, she must decide whether to file suit or sit on her rights"). For a case purporting to reject "inquiry notice" as the trigger for the discovery rule, see Salazar v. American Sterilizer Co., 5 P.3d 357, 363 (Colo. Ct. App. 2000).

**72.** Demanding any greater confidence in the existence of a products liability claim might require the plaintiff to have the expertise of a reader of this book, a result which would be monstrously unfair to normal plaintiffs.

**73.** UCC § 2–725(2).

**74.** For example, some courts read § 2–725(2) as applying only to buyers rather than third parties. See, e.g., Salvador v.

ignored the clear language and applied the discovery rule to products liability claims for breach of warranty involving personal injury or death.[75]

**Splitting claims—The "single-action" vs. "separate-injury" rules.** A special statute of limitations issue arises when a single defective condition in a product harms a person in two or more separate ways at different times. A problematic question in such cases is when the statute of limitations should begin to run on the *second* injury—at the time the plaintiff discovered the first injury, or at the time he or she discovers the second. Normally, because each breach of duty by a defendant is thought to generate a single, indivisible cause of action, a plaintiff is required to seek all damages caused thereby at the time the complaint is filed; thereafter, the plaintiff is precluded from suing the defendant again for damages arising from the same transaction.[76] So, if the operator of a defective punch press recovers damages for resulting injuries to his hand and arm in an action against the manufacturer, he cannot later maintain a second action against the manufacturer for injuries from the same accident that he subsequently discovers in his back. Underlying res judicata, this principle of claim preclusion is sometimes called the single-action rule, or the rule against claim-splitting.[77]

Although the claim-splitting issue can arise in traumatic injury cases, such as the punch press situation just discussed, it most frequently and acutely arises in cases involving injuries and illnesses from toxic substances like asbestos. Two decades after exposure,[78] an asbestos worker may suffer asbestosis (or pleural thickening) for which damages may be available against the asbestos supplier, perhaps for failing to warn of the risk. Another one or two decades later,[79] long after the initial asbestosis claim is resolved, the very same worker may contract a deadly form of lung cancer, mesothelioma. In this context, some courts have applied the single-action rule to bar the second claim, holding that the

Atlantic Steel Boiler Co., 389 A.2d 1148 (Pa. Super. Ct. 1978) (2–year tort statute, not UCC § 2–725, applicable to all third party personal injury actions, tort and warranty, because "[i]t takes a very strained reading of Section 2–725 to conclude that it was ever meant to apply to persons other than the contracting parties"). This approach itself seems rather strained. However, in a state with a special statute of limitations for products liability claims, a court might reasonably conclude that a products liability statute of limitations trumps the Article 2 statute of limitations because the former is more specific than the latter.

**75.** See Clark and Smith, Product Warranties § 11.05, at S11–38–39 (1998 Supp.).

**76.** See Henderson and Twerski, Asbestos Litigation Gone Mad: Exposure–Based Recovery for Increased Risk, Mental Distress, and Medical Monitoring, 53 S.C. L. Rev. 815, 819–20 (2002):

In most tort cases, the law provides a plaintiff one indivisible cause of action for all damages arising from a defendant's breach of duty. This hoary rule against splitting a cause of action is designed to prevent vexatious and repetitive litigation of a single underlying claim when plaintiff's injuries eventually result in damages that are more serious than originally contemplated. [Despite the real problem of proof and risks of undercompensation facing injured plaintiffs,] the specter of repetitive litigation and the lack of finality to litigation present unacceptable costs to the legal system. Thus, the single-action rule is deeply embedded in the jurisprudence of this country.

**77.** See F. James, G. Hazard, and J. Leubsdorf, Civil Procedure § 11.8 et seq. (5th ed. 2001).

**78.** See, e.g., Hamilton v. Asbestos Corp., 998 P.2d 403, 405–08 (Cal. 2000) (noting the 20–year average latency period of asbestosis).

**79.** See id. (noting the 30– to 40–year average latency period of mesothelioma).

statute of limitations on *all* claims runs from the first injury or its discovery.[80] However, "[g]iven the harshness of the single-action rule, ... the overwhelming majority of courts abandoned the single-action rule and now allow separate causes of action later, when a plaintiff actually develops asbestosis, lung cancer, or mesothelioma."[81] Thus, in place of the old single-action rule, courts in latent or "creeping" disease cases are rapidly switching over to a converse doctrine—the separate-injury or two-disease rule—which starts the limitations clock ticking on separate and distinct diseases at the time of their discovery.[82]

## Statutes of Repose

### *Origin*

The discovery rule, which courts and legislatures widely adopted in products liability litigation in the 1970s and 1980s, protects injury victims from losing their claims before they know that they have been harmed or that they may have a means of legal redress. But by delaying the running of statutes of limitations, sometimes for many years past the time of injury (and long after the product was manufactured), the discovery rule undermines the central purpose of limitations statutes. It will be recalled that limitations statutes are designed to provide a point

---

**80.** See, e.g., Gideon v. Johns–Manville Sales Corp., 761 F.2d 1129, 1136 (5th Cir. 1985) ("a plaintiff may not split this cause of action by seeking damages for some of his injuries in one suit and for later developing injuries in another"). Compare Kemp v. G.D. Searle & Co., 103 F.3d 405 (5th Cir. 1997) (Miss. law) (IUD caused pelvic inflammatory disease that eventually led to infertility; *held*, statute ran from discovery of PID 8 years prior to diagnosis of scarred fallopian tubes that caused plaintiff's infertility).

In smoking cases, courts have likewise applied the "first injury" rule, holding that the alleged addiction to cigarettes is the injury which triggers the statute of limitations on the subsequently developed illnesses. See Spain v. Brown & Williamson Tobacco Corp., 872 So.2d 101 (Ala. 2003) ("Artful pleading such as presented here, where Spain disavows seeking recovery for all pre-cancer injuries, should not defeat the operation of the first injury rule."); Soliman v. Philip Morris Inc., 311 F.3d 966 (9th Cir. 2002) (Cal. law) (smoker's claims accrued when he knew or should have known that smoking is addictive; "the injury he should have known about first is the one that starts the statute of limitations").

**81.** Henderson and Twerski, Asbestos Litigation Gone Mad: Exposure–Based Recovery for Increased Risk, Mental Distress, and Medical Monitoring, 53 S.C. L. Rev. 815, 821 (2002) (citing cases).

**82.** The fountainhead case was Wilson v. Johns–Manville Sales Corp., 684 F.2d 111, 120–21 (D.C. 1982) (diagnosis of asbestosis did not trigger limitations statute for other injuries from same exposure to asbestos). See also Potts v. Celotex Corp., 796 S.W.2d 678, 685 (Tenn. 1990) (same; good summary of rationales). For examples of recent cases, see, e.g., Parks v. A.P. Green Indus., 754 N.E.2d 1052, 1058 (Ind. Ct. App. 2001) (asbestos claim did not trigger statute of limitations for cancer claim since they are separate diseases); Hamilton v. Asbestos Corp., 998 P.2d 403, 405–08 (Cal. 2000) (use of single-action rule in asbestos cases precluded by state statute); Pustejovsky v. Rapid–Am. Corp., 35 S.W.3d 643, 648 (Tex. 2000) ("[T]he single action rule is a catch 22 for victims of multiple latent diseases [because] '[a] plaintiff who sues for asbestosis is precluded from any recovery for a later-developing lethal mesothelioma. But the discovery rule would preclude a plaintiff with asbestosis from waiting to see if an asbestosis-related cancer later develops.... '"); Carroll v. Owens–Corning Fiberglas Corp., 37 S.W.3d 699, 703 (Ky. 2000) (although Kentucky has never been a "two disease" state, a cancer claim accrues on date of its diagnosis, not date of asbestosis diagnosis, since the diseases are separate and distinct); Sopha v. Owens–Corning Fiberglas Corp., 601 N.W.2d 627, 642 (Wis. 1999) ("The diagnosis of a malignant asbestos-related condition creates a new cause of action and the statute of limitations governing the malignant asbestos-related condition begins when the claimant discovers, or with reasonable diligence should discover, the malignant asbestos-related condition.").

in time after which both actors and courts can avoid having to address claims for injuries allegedly caused by actors and suffered by victims many years in the past. So, while promoting fairness for injured plaintiffs, the discovery rule promotes unfairness for manufacturers and inconvenience for the courts.

In an attempt to reinstate some portion of the defendant-fairness objectives of limitations statutes in a world committed to the plaintiff-fairness objectives of the discovery rule, many state legislatures from the 1960s through the early 1980s enacted statutes of "repose."[83] A major pillar of the tort "reform" movement, these special limitations statutes addressed problems with long-delayed claims by three particular groups disadvantaged by the discovery rule: doctors, who wanted an eventual end to the threat of malpractice suits for medical accidents; architects, engineers, and contractors, who wanted an end to potential liability for injuries from buildings and other structures that might last for centuries;[84] and manufacturers of products, who may have to answer products liability claims for products manufactured many decades in the past.[85]

### Distinguished from Statutes of Limitations

Like statutes of limitations, products liability and other statutes of repose terminate a plaintiff's right to bring a claim after a period of time;[86] but statutes of repose are different in two principal respects. First, statutes of repose *begin to run* at a *time certain*: products liability statutes of this type typically run from the time the manufacturer first sells the product, and realty improvement statutes normally run from when the structure is completed. This aspect of repose statutes gives manufacturers much more confidence that their potential liability eventually will stop some number of years after a product has been manufactured and sold. Second, statutes of repose have a much greater *duration* than statutes of limitations, varying in length from state to state, from 5 or 6 years to as long as 10, or 12, or even 20 years. The much longer periods within which a claim may be filed under statutes of repose

**83.** See, e.g., Note, 1989 Duke L.J. 1689, 1697–1702.

**84.** "The pyramids of Egypt, the Colosseum in Rome, the Parthenon in Greece are only now, at the end of the twentieth century, starting to succumb to the ravages of time. Consequently, it would be easy to imagine ten-, twenty-, fifty- or even one-hundred-year-old buildings and other structures as potential liability problems. So too are the products that are an integral part of them, such as elevators, furnaces, heavy machinery and the like." 4 Frumer and Friedman, Products Liability § 26.05[5][a], at 26–138.

**85.** On statutes of repose in general, see, e.g., Note, 38 Vand. L. Rev. 627 (1985). On products liability statutes of repose, see McGovern, The Variety, Policy and Constitutionality of Product Liability Statutes of Repose, 30 Am. U. L. Rev. 579 (1981); Martin, A Statute of Repose for Product Liability Claims, 50 Fordham L. Rev. 745 (1982); Frumer and Friedman, Products Liability

§ 26.05; 4 Am. Law Prod. Liab. § 47:38— § 47:50; Prod. Liab. Rep. (CCH) ¶ 3100; Annot., 30 A.L.R.5th 1 (1995) (products liability statutes of repose).

**86.** Statutes of limitations and repose often are contrasted on the ground that a limitations statute merely limits a plaintiff's right to seek a remedy for a defendant's breach of duty, whereas a repose statute limits the duty itself. That is, the former merely limits the time for bringing a claim after it has accrued, whereas the latter extinguishes the claim after a fixed period of time. See, e.g., Albrecht v. General Motors Corp., 648 N.W.2d 87, 91 (Iowa 2002) ("a statute of limitations affects only the remedy, not the right, whereas a statute of repose affects the right itself, extinguishing existing rights or preventing rights from arising"); Martin, A Statute of Repose for Product Liability Claims, 50 Fordham L. Rev. 745, 749 (1982).

reflects a deference to the discovery rule's objective of providing most persons injured by most products with an opportunity to assert their claims once they discover their injuries. While repose statutes bar some claims, sometimes even before they are discovered or otherwise accrue,[87] such claims normally are infrequent and generally quite old. Moreover, as time marches on after particular products are made and sold, one must weigh the decreasing hardships of barring plaintiffs from making legitimate, but aging, claims against the increasing burdens on manufacturers and courts in responding to such claims long after the fact—a balance that at some point tips in favor of terminating claims after a reasonable, but arbitrary period of time.[88] For this reason, repose statutes do not normally allow for the kind of equitable tolling applied to statutes of limitations.[89]

### Choice of Law

Differences between statutes of limitations and repose may affect the choice of law.[90] Limitations and repose statutes often are contrasted on the ground that statutes of limitations are "procedural," because they merely limit a plaintiff's right to seek a remedy for a defendant's breach of duty, whereas statutes of repose are "substantive," because they limit the duty itself. Stated otherwise, this traditional view characterizes statutes of limitation as procedural because they merely limit the time for bringing claims after they have accrued, whereas statutes of repose are characterized as substantive because, after a fixed period of time, they extinguish claims altogether.[91] This procedural/substantive distinction is important in states that adhere to traditional conflict of laws principles and that lack an applicable borrowing statute. Traditionally, a forum state applied its own "procedural" statute of limitation even if another state's law governed the parties' substantive rights.[92] Over time, many state legislatures altered this traditional rule by enacting "borrowing statutes" which typically provide that the forum state's court will borrow the statute of limitations of another state where the cause of action arose or accrued, or where the defendant resided or was domiciled.[93] Courts adhering to the traditional procedural/substantive distinc-

---

**87.** See, e.g., Albrecht v. General Motors Corp., 648 N.W.2d 87, 91 (Iowa 2002) (15-year statute of repose barred claim before car accident involving minor plaintiff).

**88.** See G. Schwartz, New Products, Old Products, Evolving Law, Retroactive Law, 58 N.Y.U. L. Rev. 796, 842–51 (1983).

**89.** See, e.g., Albrecht v. General Motors Corp., 648 N.W.2d 87 (Iowa 2002) (no tolling for infancy). Cf. Lantzy v. Centex Homes, 73 P.3d 517, 522 (Cal. 2003) (builder statute of repose not subject to judicial doctrine of equitable tolling).

**90.** See, e.g., 4 Frumer and Friedman, Products Liability ch. 25; 2 Madden & Owen on Products Liability Law ch. 30; 4 Am. Law Prod. Liab. 3d ch. 46; L. McDougal, III, R. Felix, and R. Whitten, American Conflicts Law §§ 116–18 (5th ed. 2001).

**91.** See, e.g., Albrecht v. General Motors Corp., 648 N.W.2d 87, 91 (Iowa 2002) ("a

statute of limitations affects only the remedy, not the right, whereas a statute of repose affects the right itself, extinguishing existing rights or preventing rights from arising"); Martin, A Statute of Repose for Product Liability Claims, 50 Fordham L. Rev. 745, 749 (1982).

**92.** See, e.g., Sun Oil Co. v. Wortman, 486 U.S. 717 (1988) (because statutes of limitation are traditionally characterized as procedural, a state may apply its own statute of limitation to a claim governed by another state's law without violating due process or the full faith and credit clause).

**93.** See Giest v. Sequoia Ventures, Inc., 99 Cal.Rptr.2d 476 (Ct. App. 2000) (applying California borrowing statute to hold that California lawsuit was barred by Montana's realty statute of repose); Annot., 41 A.L.R.4th 1025 (1985) (borrowing statutes).

tion which lack an applicable borrowing statute are divided on several points: whether a statute of repose is procedural or substantive;[94] whether the traditional conflict of laws rule applies to its or another state's statutes of repose;[95] and whether the forum state is bound by the other state's characterization of its statute of repose.[96]

Characterizing statutes of repose as procedural or substantive is less important for choice of law purposes in jurisdictions that have adopted some form of the modern "most significant relationship" or "governmental interests" tests. Under this approach, courts generally apply the statute of limitations or repose of the state where the injury occurred unless the place of the injury is insignificant or another state has a greater interest in applying its time bars.[97] For breach of warranty

**94.** Compare Walls v. General Motors, Inc., 906 F.2d 143 (5th Cir. 1990) (Or. law) (repose statute is substantive), with Baxter v. Sturm, Ruger & Co., 32 F.3d 48 (2d Cir. 1994) (Conn. law) (repose statute is procedural).

**95.** See, e.g., Thornton v. Cessna Aircraft Co., 886 F.2d 85 (4th Cir. 1989) (S.C. law) (under lex loci delicti rule of forum state, substantive law of place where accident occurred applied, including its statute of repose which barred tort claim; but warranty claim could proceed according to forum state law under UCC § 1–105 "appropriate relation" test).

**96.** See e.g., Etheredge v. Genie Indus., Inc., 632 So.2d 1324 (Ala. 1994) (North Carolina products liability statute of repose is procedural and thus inapplicable in Alabama lawsuit governed by North Carolina substantive law even though North Carolina characterizes its statute of repose as substantive); Baxter v. Strum, Ruger & Co., Inc., 32 F.3d 48 (2d Cir. 1994) (Conn. law) (Oregon products liability statute of repose is procedural and thus inapplicable in Connecticut lawsuit governed by Oregon's substantive law); Walls v. General Motors, Inc., 906 F.2d 143 (5th Cir. 1990) (Miss. law) (Oregon products liability statute of repose is substantive, and thus applicable in Mississippi lawsuit governed by Oregon substantive law, because Mississippi is bound to apply Oregon's view that its statute of repose is substantive); Terry v. Pullman Trailmobile, a Division of Pullman, Inc., 376 S.E.2d 47 (N.C. Ct. App. 1989) (North Carolina's 6–year products liability statute of repose did not apply to tort claims brought in a North Carolina lawsuit governed by New York's substantive law); Boudreau v. Baughman, 368 S.E.2d 849 (N.C. 1988) (Florida's 12–year products liability statute of repose, and not North Carolina's 6–year product liability statute of repose, applied because both statutes are substantive and the North Carolina lawsuit was governed by Florida's substantive law).

**97.** See, e.g., Martin v. Goodyear Tire & Rubber Co., 61 P.3d 1196 (Wash. Ct. App. 2003) (Washington's 12–year useful life statute of repose, and not Oregon's 8–year products liability statute of repose, applied where injury occurred in Washington and Oregon did not have a more significant relationship); Nelson v. Sandoz Pharm. Corp., 288 F.3d 954 (7th Cir. 2002) (N.J. law) (Indiana law on the discovery rule applied and not New Jersey law on the discovery rule where the injury occurred in Indiana and New Jersey did not have a more significant relationship); Land v. Yamaha Motor Corp., 272 F.3d 514 (7th Cir. 2001) (Ind. law) (Indiana's 10–year products liability statute of repose applied where injury occurred in Indiana and the place of the injury was not insignificant); Tune v. Philip Morris Inc., 766 So.2d 350 (Fla. Ct. App. 2000) (Florida's 4–year statute of limitations, and not New Jersey's 2–year statute of limitations, applied where injury occurred in Florida and New Jersey did not have more significant relationship); Tanges v. Heidelberg N. Am., Inc., 710 N.E.2d 250 (N.Y. 1999) (applying Connecticut statute of repose to bar claim); Hall v. General Motors Corp., 582 N.W.2d 866 (Mich. Ct. App. 1998) (North Carolina's 6–year products liability statute of repose applied where injury occurred in North Carolina and Michigan's only connection to lawsuit was that plaintiff moved there after injury); Gantes v. Kason Corp., 679 A.2d 106 (N.J. 1996) (Georgia's 10–year products liability statute of repose did not apply even though injury occurred in Georgia because New Jersey's interest in deterring tortious conduct by New Jersey manufacturers outweighed Georgia's interest in enforcing its statute of repose); Jaurequi v. John Deere Co., 986 F.2d 170 (7th Cir. 1993) (Tex. law) (Indiana's 10–year products liability statute of repose did not apply where injury occurred outside Indiana and Indiana did not have more significant relationship). *Gantes* is examined in E. Scoles, P. Hay, P. Borchers, and S. Symeonides, Conflict of Laws § 17.70 (3d ed. 2000).

claims, the *Uniform Commercial Code* contains a choice of law provision providing that the law of the forum "applies to transactions bearing an appropriate relation to this State."[98] This provision is generally construed as employing a standard similar to the "most significant relationship" test described above with one significant difference: the focus is on the place of contracting or manufacture rather than the place of the injury.[99]

### *Products Liability Statutes of Repose*

There are two basic types of products liability statutes of repose, depending on how the statute defines the period of time before repose. The most common type of statute, "time-certain" statutes, define the time period with certainty as a particular number of years after the sale or purchase of the product. Another form of statute, called a "useful-life" statute, measures the time period variously, according to whatever a court or jury determines the particular product's useful, safe life to be. Presently, about a dozen states[100] have time-certain products liability statutes of repose in effect, and six states[101] have some form of useful-life statute of repose.[102] The most fundamental issue regarding statutes of repose concerns their constitutionality, discussed below.

**Time-certain statutes.** The limitations periods of most products liability statutes of repose are absolute, and a plaintiff's rights to sue are terminated after a set period of time, ranging from 6 to 15 years, but most typically 10 years after the manufacturer first sold the product.[103] For example, Indiana's statute provides that "a product liability action must be commenced: ... within ten (10) years after the delivery of the product to the initial user or consumer." This 10–year repose provision does not apply to asbestos claims, and it may be extended up to 2 years for claims accruing after 8 years.[104] Indiana's statute is atypical of the

---

**98.** UCC § 1–105. See, e.g., Thornton v. Cessna Aircraft Co., 886 F.2d 85 (4th Cir. 1989).

**99.** See Terry v. Pullman Trailmobile, a Division of Pullman, Inc., 376 S.E.2d 47 (N.C. App. 1989) (North Carolina's 6–year product liability statute of repose did not apply to tort claims brought in a North Carolina lawsuit governed by New York's substantive law but did apply to the breach of warranty claims because the sale and distribution of the product occurred in North Carolina).

For more thorough discussions of choice of law in product liability cases, including statutes of limitation and repose, see R. Felix and the great conflicts masters, above.

**100.** Arizona, Colorado, Connecticut, Georgia, Indiana, Iowa, Kentucky, Nebraska, North Carolina, Oregon, Tennessee, and Texas. The statutes in Connecticut and Tennessee have some combination of time-certain and useful-life statutes of repose.

**101.** Connecticut, Idaho, Kansas, Minnesota, Tennessee, and Washington.

**102.** One might question the characterization of useful-life statutes as statutes of repose, but that is what they are. See Frumer and Friedman, Products Liability § 26.05[3][a] (distinguishing time-certain statutes, which it calls "true" statutes of repose, from useful-life statutes). While the limitation period of useful-life statutes is uncertain, these statutes do indeed put an end to (and hence place in "repose") products liability claims at some point. The useful life of a flashlight battery, for example, might be 3 to 5 years. If acid from a flashlight battery leaks and causes injury after 20 years, a useful-life statute surely would preclude a claim for such an injury.

**103.** See McGovern, The Variety, Policy and Constitutionality of Product Liability Statutes of Repose, 30 Am. U. L. Rev. 579 (1981); Frumer and Friedman, Products Liability § 26.05; Annot., 30 A.L.R.5th 1 (1995).

**104.** See Ind. Code § 34–20–3–1(b)(2). The Indiana Supreme Court has held that its repose statute's exception for certain asbestos claims is constitutional. See Allied-

repose statutes, most of which are qualified in a number of respects. For instance, Arizona's 12–year statute does not apply to negligence or express warranty actions;[105] Colorado's 10–year statute establishes a rebuttable presumption that an older product was not defective;[106] Georgia's 10–year statute does not bar negligence claims resulting in "disease or birth defect, or arising out of conduct which manifests a willful, reckless, or wanton disregard for life or property," nor does it bar actions for breach of the post-sale duty to warn;[107] Iowa's 15–year statute does not apply to asbestos, tobacco, and other types of products;[108] Nebraska's 10–year statute does not apply to warranty actions subject to UCC § 2–725 nor does it apply to asbestos claims;[109] Oregon's 8–year statute does not apply to claims arising out of asbestos or silicone breast implants; Tennessee's 10–year statute applies if it is shorter than that state's useful-life statute and does not apply to minors, nor does it apply to claims from asbestos or silicone gel breast implants which have a 25–year period;[110] and Texas's 15–year statute applies only to the sale of manufacturing equipment that has not been warranted to last longer.[111] In addition, several statutes have exceptions for the defendant's fraudulent conduct;[112] and other statutes specify applicable causes of action, defendants, and other circumstances to which they do or do not apply.[113] One noteworthy exception to repose statutes allowed by a few courts has been for a manufacturer's breach of its post-sale duty to warn.[114] The post-sale duty to warn exception rests on the reasonable hypothesis that the purpose of repose legislation is to provide a manufacturer with eventual relief from liability for any errors it may have made at the time it designed, made, and sold its products—not for the negligent failure to observe its safety obligations that arise thereafter.

Products liability statutes of repose are drafted quite differently from state to state, and the courts have passed on a large variety of interpretative issues. For example, courts have ruled that while the

Signal, Inc. v. Ott, 785 N.E.2d 1068 (Ind. 2003).

**105.** See Ariz. Rev. Stat. § 12–551.

**106.** See Colo. Rev. Stat. § 13–21–403(3).

**107.** See Ga. St. § 51–1–11(c).

**108.** See Iowa Code Ann. § 614.2A.

**109.** See Neb. Rev. St. § 25–224.

**110.** See Tenn. Code Ann. § 29–28–103.

**111.** See Tex. Civ. Prac. & Rem. § 16.012.

**112.** See, e.g., Colo. Rev. Stat. § 13–80–107(1)(c); Conn. Gen. Stat. § 52–577a(5)(d); Idaho Code § 6–1303(2)(b)(2); Iowa Code § 614.1(a); Kans. Stat. Ann. § 60–3303(b)(2)(B).

**113.** See Frumer and Friedman, Products Liability § 26.05[3][b]. See, e.g., Masters v. Hesston Corp., 291 F.3d 985 (7th Cir. 2002) (Ill. law) (construing repose exception for products modified after they were originally made and sold and holding

that hay baler was not modified within meaning of exception); Vickery v. Waste Mgmt. of Ga. Inc., 549 S.E.2d 482 (Ga. Ct. App. 2001) (plaintiff failed to prove that defendant fell within repose exception for willful, reckless, or wanton conduct).

**114.** See Sharp v. Case Corp., 595 N.E.2d 380, 385 (Wis. 1999); Hodder v. Goodyear Tire & Rubber Co., 426 N.W.2d 826 (Minn. 1988); Erickson Air–Crane v. United Tech. Corp., 735 P.2d 614, 618 (Or. 1987). See also Parks v. Hyundai Motor Am., Inc., 575 S.E.2d 673 (Ga. Ct. App. 2002) (applying failure to warn exception to state's 10–year products liability statute of repose); Sherwood v. Danbury Hosp., 746 A.2d 730, 737–38 (Conn. 2000) (continuing duty to warn; plaintiff not warned that blood she received in transfusion had not been tested for HIV). See generally Kulbaski, Statutes of Repose and the Post–Sale Duty to Warn: Time for a New Interpretation, 32 Conn. L. Rev. 1027 (2000) (advocating that repose statutes be construed as containing exception for post-sale duty to warn).

discovery rule does not normally apply to statutes of repose,[115] it may apply in cases involving latent diseases such as asbestos;[116] that a repose statute is not tolled for mental incompetency[117] or infancy;[118] that it may be tolled by a continuing breach of duty to warn;[119] that it may bar a claim by a governmental plaintiff notwithstanding a contrary rule for statutes of limitations;[120] and that it does or does not apply in a host of other situations.[121]

**Useful-life statutes.** Following an approach recommended in the late 1970s by the Commerce Department's Interagency Task Force on Products Liability,[122] several states adopted some form of "useful-life" statute,[123] which is a weak form of statute of repose. Standing between rigid statutes of repose (that conclusively terminate liability after a set number of years from a product's sale) and open-ended statutes of limitations (that keep a manufacturer's responsibility open indefinitely), "useful-life" statutes cut off a manufacturer's liability conclusively after a period of time, but only after a product's "useful safe life" has expired. For this reason, useful-life statutes are viewed as something of a compromise,[124] but a compromise filled with interpretative land mines and subject to criticism for being ambiguous.[125]

**115.** See, e.g., Albrecht v. General Motors Corp., 648 N.W.2d 87, 91 (Iowa 2002).

**116.** See Wilder v. Amatex Corp., 336 S.E.2d 66 (N.C. 1985). Some statutes specifically address the problem of latent disease. See, e.g., Tex. Civ. Prac. & Rem. § 16.012 (d)(3) (excepting claims for disease manifested after 15–year period expires).

**117.** See Penley v. Honda Motor Co., 31 S.W.3d 181 (Tenn. 2000) (plaintiff, who was on constant pain medication in hospital after accident often did not know where she was).

**118.** See Albrecht v. General Motors Corp., 648 N.W.2d 87, 91 (Iowa 2002).

**119.** See Sherwood v. Danbury Hosp., 746 A.2d 730, 737–38 (Conn. 2000) (plaintiff not warned that blood she received in transfusion had not been tested for HIV).

**120.** See Shasta View Irrigation Dist. v. Amoco Chem. Corp., 986 P.2d 536 (Or. 1999). *But see* People v. Asbestospray Corp., 616 N.E.2d 652 (Ill. App. Ct. 1993) (holding that nullum tempus doctrine immunizes the State from both statutes of limitation and repose).

**121.** See, e.g., Henderson v. Park Homes Inc., 555 S.E.2d 926 (N.C. Ct. App. 2001) (defective synthetic stucco covered by products liability statute of repose, not real property improvement statute of repose; products liability statute of repose not equitably tolled by class action filing); Jones v. Methodist Healthcare, 83 S.W.3d 739 (Tenn. Ct. App. 2001) (human blood is "product" within meaning of products liability statute of repose even though blood otherwise exempted from strict liability claims); Richardson v. Gallo Equip. Co., 990

F.2d 330 (7th Cir. 1993) (Ind. law) (Posner, J.) (statute of repose clock begins again once product is reconstructed—after backup alarm added to forklift).

**122.** See Model Uniform Product Liability Act § 110(A) (1979), 44 Fed. Reg. 62, 417 (1979). The Model Act provided that a seller would not be subject to products liability if it proved that the harm occurred "after the product's useful safe life had expired," unless it had "expressly warranted the product for a longer period." The term " 'useful safe life' begins at the time of delivery of the product and extends for the time during which the product would normally be likely to perform or stored in a safe manner." Evidence on any particular product's "useful safe life" may include: (a) the amount of its wear and tear; (b) its deterioration; (c) the types and frequency of its use, repair, renewal, and replacement; (d) any representations, warnings, or instructions about its maintenance, storage, use, or expected life; and (e) whether it was modified or altered.

**123.** See Cantu, The Useful Life Defense: Embracing the Idea that All Products Grow Old and Die, 80 Neb. L. Rev. 1 (2001); Note, The Evolution of Useful Life Statutes in the Products Liability Reform Effort, 1989 Duke L.J. 1689; Frumer and Friedman, Products Liability § 26. 05[4].

**124.** See Frumer and Friedman, Products Liability § 26.05[4][a].

**125.** See Hodder v. Goodyear Tire & Rubber Co., 426 N.W.2d 826, 830 (Minn. 1988) ("ambiguous"; although jury found that useful life of corroded 26–year-old multi-piece rim for truck tire had expired, court held that statute placed no limits on

First enacted in Minnesota,[126] useful-life statutes have also been adopted in a handful of other states.[127] Most of the statutes provide that, at the end of its period of safe life, a product is presumed nondefective. A typical useful-life statute is Washington's, which provides: "If the harm was caused more than twelve years after the time of delivery, a presumption arises that the harm was caused after the useful safe life had expired. This presumption may only be rebutted by a preponderance of the evidence."[128] Among the various differences between the statutes, Connecticut's normal 10–year period is extended to 60 years for asbestos claims;[129] and the presumption of nondefectiveness does not arise at all if workers' compensation benefits are unavailable, provided that the injury occurs during the product's useful safe life.[130]

Tennessee, which has a one-year statute of limitations,[131] blends a useful-life statute with a statute of repose, terminating liability at the lesser of ten years or one year after the end of a product's anticipated life.[132] The statutes in two other states, Kentucky and Colorado, while not using the "useful-life" concept, borrow the approach of creating a presumption of nondefectiveness but apply the presumption after a set period of time.[133]

### Realty Improvement Statutes

Many states have another entirely different form of statute of repose that may bar products liability claims with respect to a narrow category of old products—those attached to realty. During the 1950s and early 1960s, most state legislatures enacted real property improvement statutes of repose in an effort to stem the tide of rising liability claims confronting architects, engineers, and contractors who designed and built buildings and other structures that could last for decades if not centuries.[134] Like time-certain products liability statutes of repose, realty improvement statutes of repose begin to run, not on the accrual of a plaintiff's cause of action, but upon the occurrence of a designated event—usually the substantial completion of the improvement—without regard to when the injury occurs or is discovered. The length of time before repose varies in these statutes from as short as 5 years in

duty to warn); G. Schwartz, New Products, Old Products, Evolving Law, Retroactive Law, 58 N.Y.U. L. Rev. 796, 848 (1983) (expressing some sympathy for concept, but criticizing such statutes as drafted for being "incoherent both theoretically and operationally").

**126.** Minn. Stat. Ann. § 6.04.03.

**127.** See Conn. Gen. Stat. § 52–577a (default rule for a time-certain statute of repose); Idaho Code § [6–1403] 6–1303; Kan. Stat. Ann. § 60–3303 (rebuttably presuming that a product has exceeded its useful life 10 years after delivery); Tenn. Code Ann. § 28–3–104; Wash. Rev. Code. Ann. § 7.72.060(1)-(2), applied in Pardo v. Olson & Sons, Inc., 40 F.3d 1063 (9th Cir. 1994) (Wash. law) (summary judgment for manufacturer of 21–year-old dump truck reversed and remanded where plaintiff's expert's af-

fidavit asserted useful safe life was 30 years, putting matter in contention).

**128.** Wash. Rev. Code. Ann. § 7.72.060(2).

**129.** Conn. Gen. Stat. § 52–577a(e).

**130.** Conn. Gen. Stat. § 52–577a(c).

**131.** Tenn. Code Ann. § 28–3–104.

**132.** Tenn. Code Ann. § 28–3–103.

**133.** Ky. Rev. Stat. Ann. § 411.310(1); Colo. Rev. Stat. § 13–21–403(3).

**134.** See, e.g., McGovern, The Variety, Policy and Constitutionality of Product Liability Statutes of Repose, 30 Am. U. L. Rev. 579 (1981); Frumer and Friedman, Products Liability § 26.05[5]; Note, 57 N.D. L. Rev. 43 (1981); Comment, 18 Cath. U. L. Rev. 361 (1969); Annot., 93 A.L.R.3d 1242 (1979).

Virginia, to as long as 20 years in Maryland, with a number of statutes at 6 years and the great majority at 10 years before the repose begins.[135]

Although some of the realty improvement repose statutes expressly provide that they are applicable only to the building professions, and not to products,[136] most of the statutes do not provide explicitly one way or the other, leaving their application to products liability defendants to the courts. On this issue the courts have split, some construing their statutes as *not* applying to products liability defendants,[137] others holding that their statutes *do* apply to manufacturers of products that are part of improvements to land.[138] Several courts apply a more contextual approach, applying this type of statute of repose to manufacturers who also participate in some manner in installing or otherwise constructing a real estate improvement.[139]

Perhaps the central issue litigated concerning realty improvement statutes of repose is whether a particular product qualifies as an "improvement" to real property, often generally defined as a permanent addition to realty that enhances its value.[140] Courts have applied these statutes and barred liability after the expiration of the period of repose in cases involving such products as precast concrete used in the structural framework of a garage;[141] an outdoor incline conveyor;[142] a glass vestibule attached to an airport terminal building;[143] a mounting plate

**135.** The statutes are summarized, and annotated, at Prod. Liab. Rep. (CCH) ¶ 3100.

**136.** See, e.g., D.C. Code § 12–310(3); Mo. Rev. Stat. § 516.097; Wash. Rev. Code § 4.16.300. Compare Va. Code § 8:01–250 (repose statute does not apply to manufacturers or suppliers of machinery or equipment installed in real property structures). *But see* Cape Henry Towers, Inc. v. National Gypsum Co., 331 S.E.2d 476, 479–80 (Va. 1985) (statute excluded only equipment and machinery, not ordinary building materials such as building's exterior panels).

**137.** Such statutes do *not* apply to products liability defendants: Arkansas, Montana, Nevada, New Jersey, New Mexico, and North Dakota. See Frumer and Friedman, Products Liability § 26.05[5][a].

**138.** Such statutes *do* apply to products liability defendants: Florida, Iowa, Louisiana, Maryland, Massachusetts, Minnesota, and Utah. See id.

**139.** Such statutes *may* apply to products liability actions if defendant participates in design or construction of improvement: Colorado, Illinois, Michigan, Mississippi, Missouri, Oklahoma, Pennsylvania, and Texas. Id. See, e.g., Meiser v. Otis Elevator Co., CCH Prod. Liab. Rep. ¶ 16,786 (N.D. Tex. 2003).

See, e.g., J.M. Foster, Inc. v. Spriggs, 789 N.E.2d 526 (Ind. Ct. App. 2003) (statute protects manufacturer that installed asbestos products in foundry); Biniek v. Exxon Mobil Corp., 818 A.2d 330 (N.J. Super. Ct.

Law Div. 2002) (statute does not protect manufacturer of mass produced underground storage tanks); Lay v. P & G Health Care, Inc., 37 S.W.3d 310 (Mo. Ct. App. 2000) (statute does not protect elevator company that assembled, sold, and installed prefabricated dumbwaiter); Two Denver Highlands LLLP v. Stanley Structures, Inc., 12 P.3d 819, 822 (Colo. Ct. App. 2000) (statute protects manufacturer that is substantially involved in construction); Adcock v. Montgomery Elevator Co., 654 N.E.2d 631 (Ill. App. Ct. 1995) (statute may protect elevator manufacturer that engaged in substantial installation work at site). See also Noll v. Harrisburg Area YMCA, 643 A.2d 81, 86–87 (Pa. 1994) (statute protects manufacturer that provides "individual expertise" on appropriateness of product for incorporation into property improvement). Cf. Meneely v. S.R. Smith, Inc., 5 P.3d 49 (Wash. Ct. App. 2000) (statute does not protect trade association that promulgated safety standards for swimming pool).

**140.** As in Michigan and Pennsylvania. See, e.g., Dominguez v. Lanham Mach. Co., 122 F.Supp.2d 852 (W.D. Mich. 2000) (oven was "improvement").

**141.** See Two Denver Highlands LLLP v. Stanley Structures, Inc., 12 P.3d 819, 822 (Colo. Ct. App. 2000).

**142.** See Anderson v. M.W. Kellogg Co., 766 P.2d 637 (Colo. 1988).

**143.** See Enright v. City of Colorado Springs, 716 P.2d 148 (Colo. Ct. App. 1985).

for an overhead garage door in a warehouse;[144] a larry car for shuttling coal at a coke processing plant;[145] a custom crane;[146] a manufactured home;[147] an ordinary house;[148] a home furnace;[149] an automatic garage door opener;[150] an in-ground swimming pool;[151] an above-ground swimming pool surrounded by an elaborate 3–tier deck;[152] asbestos products;[153] a concrete block curing machine;[154] a 27–foot grain bin structure;[155] gas transmission lines;[156] a sorting conveyor at a farm;[157] a glass door installed in a school;[158] and a "Spin Around" playground amusement ride anchored to the ground.[159]

Among the many types of products held *not* to be protected under various realty improvement statutes of repose are asbestos insulation[160] and asbestos fireproofing[161] sold as standard, not custom, products; fiberglass insulation;[162] a standardized (rather than custom) switch installed in an electrical supply system;[163] a steel tube mill;[164] a rubber calender machine;[165] a grass-seed mixer;[166] a machine for removing doors from coke-ovens at a coke steel plant;[167] formaldehyde-generating ply-

**144.** Garner v. Kinnear Mfg. Co., 37 F.3d 263 (7th Cir. 1994) (Ill. law).

**145.** See Herriott v. Allied Signal, Inc., 998 F.2d 487 (7th Cir. 1993) (Ill. law).

**146.** See, e.g., Bilbow v. Kochs Crane, Inc., Prod. Liab. Rep. (CCH) ¶ 13,958 (E.D. Pa. 1994) (several hundred tons, several stories high, at marine terminal); Ball v. Harnischfeger Corp., 877 P.2d 45 (Okla. 1994) (customized overhead crane); Witham v. Whiting Corp., 975 F.2d 1342 (7th Cir. 1992) (40–ton crane at steel plant).

**147.** See Frankenmuth Mut. Ins. Co. v. Marlette Homes, Inc., 573 N.W.2d 611 (Mich. 1998).

**148.** See Jaworsky v. Frolich, 850 P.2d 1052 (Okla. 1992).

**149.** See Dedmon v. Stewart–Warner Corp., 950 F.2d 244 (5th Cir. 1992) (Tex. law).

**150.** See Ablin v. Morton Southwest Co., 802 S.W.2d 788 (Tex. App. 1990).

**151.** See, e.g., Jackson v. Coldspring Terrace Prop. Owners Ass'n, 939 S.W.2d 762 (Tex. App. 1997); Rose v. Fox Pool Corp., 643 A.2d 906 (Md. 1994).

**152.** See Fleck v. KDI Sylvan Pools, Inc., 981 F.2d 107 (3d Cir. 1992) (Pa. law).

**153.** See, e.g., Tallman v. W.R. Grace & Co., 558 N.W.2d 208 (Iowa 1997); Pendzsu v. Beazer East, Inc., 557 N.W.2d 127 (Mich. Ct. App. 1997); Trust Co. Bank v. U.S. Gypsum Co., 950 F.2d 1144 (5th Cir. 1992) (Miss. law).

**154.** See Freeman v. Paco Corp., Prod. Liab. Rep. (CCH) ¶ 15, 822 (E.D. Pa. 2000).

**155.** See Theunissen v. GSI Group, 109 F.Supp.2d 505 (N.D. Miss. 2000).

**156.** See S.C. Pipeline Corp. v. Lone Star Steel Co., 546 S.E.2d 654 (S.C. 2001) (13–year statute; natural gas pipeline lay peacefully before exploding 38 years after installation); MBA Enterprises, Inc. v. Northern Ill. Gas Co., 717 N.E.2d 849 (Ill. 1999) (10–year statute; explosion 33 years after installation).

**157.** See Cross v. Ainsworth Seed Co., 557 N.E.2d 906 (Ill. App. Ct. 1990); Uricam Corp. v. W.R. Grace & Co., 739 F.Supp. 1493 (W.D. Okla. 1990).

**158.** See Mahathy v. George L. Ingram & Assoc., 584 S.W.2d 521 (Tex. App. 1979).

**159.** See Schmoyer v. Mexico Forge, Inc., 621 A.2d 692 (Pa. Super. Ct. 1993).

**160.** See Krueger v. A.P. Green Refractories Co., 669 N.E.2d 947 (Ill. App. Ct. 1996).

**161.** See State Farm Mut. Auto. Ins. Co. v. W.R. Grace & Co., 24 F.3d 955 (7th Cir. 1994) (Ill. law).

**162.** See Petro Stopping Ctrs., Inc. v. Owens–Corning Fiberglas Corp., 906 S.W.2d 618 (Tex. App. 1995).

**163.** See Garrison v. Gould, Inc., 36 F.3d 588 (7th Cir. 1994) (Ill. law).

**164.** See Ritter v. Abbey–Etna Mach. Co., 483 N.W.2d 91 (Minn. Ct. App. 1992).

**165.** See McIntyre v. Farrel Corp., 97 F.3d 779 (5th Cir. 1996) (Miss. law).

**166.** See Christ v. Prater Indus., Inc., 67 F.Supp.2d 491 (E.D. Pa. 1999).

**167.** See Vargo v. Koppers Co., 715 A.2d 423 (Pa. 1998).

wood used as a component in a home;[168] an escalator;[169] and a diving platform.[170]

### Federal Repose Statute for Private Airplanes—"GARA"

More than manufacturers of most other types of products, manufacturers of general aviation aircraft were especially hard hit by the rapid expansion of products liability law during the 1980s, a time when the industry was facing a number of other serious problems. Within about fifteen years, from the late 1970s to the early 1990s, the general aviation industry was "decimated."[171] Whereas some twenty-nine manufacturers of general aviation aircraft (led by Piper, Cessna, and Beech) had manufactured more than 14,000 light piston airplanes per year in the late 1970s, by 1993, the remaining nine manufacturers produced only about 500 small planes.[172] Congress finally responded, amending the Federal Aviation Act with the General Aviation Revitalization Act of 1994 (GARA).[173] GARA provides an 18–year statute of repose, from the date of first delivery,[174] for manufacturers of "general aviation aircraft and the components, systems, subassemblies, and other parts of such aircraft."[175] This federal statute[176] makes exception for (and hence does not bar) claims for fraud,[177] breach of express warranty, and those brought by passengers being transported for medical emergencies or by persons injured or killed on the ground.[178]

For each new component added to an existing aircraft, GARA's 18–year repose period starts anew, a provision aptly referred to as the statute's "rolling" feature.[179] The clock thus starts ticking again for

**168.** See Ferricks v. Ryan Homes, Inc., 578 A.2d 441 (Pa. Super. 1990).

**169.** See Homrighausen v. Westinghouse Elec. Corp., 832 F.Supp. 903 (E.D. Pa. 1993).

**170.** See Noll Harrisburg Area YMCA, 643 A.2d 81 (Pa. 1994).

**171.** See V. Schwartz and Lorber, The General Aviation Revitalization Act: How Rational Civil Justice Reform Revitalized an Industry, 67 J. Air L. & Com. 1269 (2002); McAllister, A "Tail" of Liability Reform: General Aviation Revitalization Act of 1994 & The General Aviation Industry in the United States, 23 Transp. L.J. 301, 304–07 (1995); Casenotes, 68 J. Air L. & Com. 631 (2003) (noting case allowing immediate appeal of trial court's refusal to allow GARA defense).

**172.** See id. at 306.

**173.** 49 U.S.C. § 40101, Note. "Congress decided that the economic health of the general aviation aircraft manufacturing industry depended on lifting the requirement that manufacturers abide the possibility of litigation for the indefinite future when they sell an airplane." Lyon v. Agusta S.P.A., 252 F.3d 1078, 1089 (9th Cir. 2001).

**174.** Id. § 2(a). See Estate of Kennedy v. Bell Helicopter Textron, Inc., 283 F.3d 1107 (9th Cir. 2002) (GARA clock begins to run on date of first delivery of helicopter to Navy, not when helicopter later sold as military surplus and resold as general aviation aircraft).

**175.** See id. § 3(3). A "general aviation aircraft" is defined as a plane having less than 20 passenger seats and not engaged in scheduled passenger-carrying operations at the time of the accident. Id. at § 2(c).

**176.** By simply placing a federal repose on certain old products liability claims, GARA neither raises a substantial federal issue, establishes a federal cause of action, nor otherwise "arises under" federal law for purposes of federal question jurisdiction. See Wright v. Bond–Air, Ltd., 930 F.Supp. 300 (E.D. Mich. 1996).

**177.** See, e.g., Butler v. Bell Helicopter Textron, Inc., 135 Cal.Rptr.2d 762 (Ct. App. 2003) (manufacturer's failure to report tail rotor yoke failure in violation of FAA's reporting requirement triggered fraud exception to GARA); Rickert v. Mitsubishi Heavy Indus., Ltd. 929 F.Supp. 380 (D. Wyo. 1996) (knowing misrepresentations exception to GARA requires plaintiff to offer evidence on knowledge, misrepresentation, concealment or withholding required information to or from FAA, materiality, relevance, and causation). Compare Campbell v. Parker–Hannifin Corp., 82 Cal.Rptr.2d 202, 210 (Ct. App. 1999) (insufficient evidence of fraudulent representations to FAA).

**178.** See id. § 2(b).

**179.** See Legis. hist., 1994 U.S. Code Cong. & Admin. News, at 1647; H.R. No. 103–525(II), 103d Cong., 2d sess. (1994), at

manufacturers of replacement parts,[180] including a successor of a predecessor company that actually made the part,[181] at the time the part is installed in an existing plane.[182] In an important decision, the Ninth Circuit Court of Appeals ruled that each aircraft's *flight manual* is a "part" of an aircraft falling within GARA's rolling provisions.[183] Accordingly, the limitations clock for each *revision* of a flight manual, if causally responsible for an accident, starts ticking on the date of the revision.[184] But a manufacturer's revision of a manual on one point will not stop the clock ticking on other inadequacies in the original manual, whether misrepresentations or the absence of adequate warnings or instructions.[185] Thus, a manufacturer's post-sale or continuing failure to warn does not begin the clock anew, because such an interpretation of GARA could keep the limitations clock forever ticking and so undermine the basic objective of the statute.[186]

### *Constitutionality of Repose Statutes*

By imposing an absolute cut-off to products liability claims after a set period of time, time-certain statutes of repose sometimes extinguish

1647. GARA extends the limitation period "with respect to any new component, system, subassembly, or other part which replaced another component, system, subassembly, or other part originally in, or which was added to, the aircraft, and which is alleged to have caused such death, injury, or damage." GARA § 2(a)(2). See generally Caldwell v. Enstrom Helicopter Corp., 230 F.3d 1155, 1156 (9th Cir. 2000).

**180.** But the clock starts anew only for the manufacturer of the defective component, not for the manufacturer of the aircraft into which it is installed, even if the latter's name is stamped on the replacement parts together with that of the actual manufacturer of the parts. See Campbell v. Parker–Hannifin Corp., 82 Cal.Rptr.2d 202, 209 (Ct. App. 1999) (twin 1975 Cessna 310R crashed due to failure of both engine-driven vacuum pumps, causing loss of supply to air-driven gyroscopic flight instruments which thereupon provided erroneous altitude and directional data; although Cessna did not manufacture replacement parts, "Cessna" name stamped on vacuum pumps, replaced in 1984, and gyroscopic artificial horizon, replaced in 1994).

**181.** See Burroughs v. Precision Airmotive Corp., 93 Cal.Rptr.2d 124, 132–34 (Ct. App. 2000). "The central objective of GARA would be materially undermined if its protection did not apply to a successor to the manufacturer who, as part of its ongoing business, acquired a product line long after the particular product had been discontinued and years after the statute of repose had run as to the original manufacturer." Id. at 132.

**182.** See GARA § 2(a)(2). But the clock is reset only for the replaced part, not for

other parts of the particular system. See Hiser v. Bell Helicopter Textron Inc., 4 Cal.Rptr.3d 249 (Ct. App. 2003).

**183.** See Caldwell v. Enstrom Helicopter Corp., 230 F.3d 1155, 1156–58 (9th Cir. 2000). *Contra*, Alter v. Bell Helicopter Textron, Inc., 944 F.Supp. 531 (S.D. Tex. 1996).

**184.** See id.

**185.** See, e.g., Carolina Indus. Prods., Inc. v. Learjet, Inc., 189 F. Supp. 2d 1147 (D. Kan. 2001) (manufacturer's issuance of new maintenance manual sections did not restart repose period on owner's claims of failing to warn owners of a defect in landing gear, and of failing to instruct on proper repair, since owner failed to allege that landing accident was proximately caused by any information in manual); Caldwell v. Enstrom Helicopter Corp., 230 F.3d 1155 (9th Cir. 2000).

**186.** See Lyon v. Agusta S.P.A., 252 F.3d 1078, 1088 (9th Cir. 2001), where the court rejected plaintiffs' argument "that a failure to warn about a newly perceived problem also amounts to something like replacement of a component part because it breaches an alleged continuing duty to upgrade and update [which would gut GARA] because the plaintiff could always argue that an 18–year period commenced if the manufacturer did nothing at all, while simultaneously arguing that if the manufacturer did do something that, too, would start a new 18–year period running.... [A] failure to warn is decidedly not the same as replacing a component part with a new one." See also Burroughs v. Precision Airmotive Corp., 93 Cal.Rptr.2d 124 (Ct. App. 2000) (limitations clock is not tolled by post-sale or continuing duty to warn).

claims before they can be discovered, and sometimes even before injuries occur and claims exist at all. For this reason, some courts[187] and commentators have denounced statutes of repose as fundamentally illogical and unfair, often invoking Judge Jerome Frank's celebrated critique of statutes of limitations for generating such an "Alice in Wonderland" effect:[188]

> Except in topsy-turvy land, you can't die before you are conceived, or be divorced before you marry, or harvest a crop never planted, or burn down a house never built, or miss a train running on a non-existent railroad. For substantially similar reasons, it has always heretofore been accepted, as a sort of legal "axiom," that a statute of limitations does not begin to run against a cause of action before that cause of action exists, *i.e.*, before a judicial remedy is available to the plaintiff.

So reasoning, several courts have struck down products liability statutes of repose for being unconstitutional,[189] sometimes as applied to particular types of products liability claims.[190] The typical constitutional objection is that repose statutes violate the due process or equal protection clauses of the federal or a state constitution, or that they abrogate the open courts provision of a state constitution.[191] Nevertheless, most courts have upheld products liability statutes of repose against a variety of these and other constitutional challenges.[192] Similarly, while some realty improve-

**187.** See, e.g., Heath v. Sears, Roebuck & Co., 464 A.2d 288, 295–96 (N.H. 1983) (Douglas, J.).

**188.** See Dincher v. Marlin Firearms Co., 198 F.2d 821, 823 (2d Cir. 1952) (Conn. law) (Frank, J., dissenting).

**189.** In addition to the *Heath* case in New Hampshire, see Hazine v. Montgomery Elev. Co., 861 P.2d 625 (Ariz. 1993); Hanson v. Williams Cty., 389 N.W.2d 319 (N.D. 1986); Berry v. Beech Aircraft Corp., 717 P.2d 670 (Utah 1985); Kennedy v. Cumberland Eng'g Co., 471 A.2d 195 (R.I. 1984); Lankford v. Sullivan, Long & Hagerty, 416 So.2d 996 (Ala. 1982); Battilla v. Allis Chalmers Mfg. Co., 392 So.2d 874 (Fla. 1980). See also Dickie v. Farmers Union Oil Co., 611 N.W.2d 168 (N.D. 2000) (holding unconstitutional statute of repose reenacted in 1995 after *Hanson*); Wells v. Thomson Newspaper Holdings, Inc., 183 F.R.D. 225, 227–30 (S.D. Ohio 1998).

Products liability statutes of repose have been repealed in at least two states, Florida and South Dakota.

See McGovern, The Variety, Policy and Constitutionality of Product Liability Statutes of Repose, 30 Am. U. L. Rev. 579 (1981); Frumer and Friedman, Products Liability § 26.05[2][a] (products liability statutes of repose) and § 26.05[5][d] (realty improvement statutes of repose); Annot., 30 A.L.R.5th 1 (1995); Note, The Constitutionality of Statutes of Repose: Federalism Reigns, 38 Vand. L. Rev. 627 (1985).

**190.** See, e.g., Jurich v. Garlock, Inc., 759 N.E.2d 1066, 1077 (Ind. Ct. App. 2001) (unconstitutional as applied to asbestos claim), adopted in part, vacated in part, 785 N.E.2d 1093 (Ind. 2003). But other courts have held that a repose statute's exception for certain asbestos claims is constitutional. See, e.g., AlliedSignal, Inc. v. Ott, 785 N.E.2d 1068 (Ind. 2003).

**191.** See, e.g., Estate of Branson v. O.F. Mossberg & Sons, Inc., 221 F.3d 1064, 1065 (8th Cir. 2000) (Iowa law) (rejecting challenges on all three grounds); Olsen v. J.A. Freeman Co., 791 P.2d 1285 (Idaho 1990) (same).

**192.** See, e.g., Land v. Yamaha Motor Corp., 272 F.3d 514 (7th Cir. 2001) (Ind. law) (Indiana's product liability statute of repose does not violate state's equal protection or due process provisions); Branson v. O.F. Mossberg & Sons, Inc., 221 F.3d 1064 (8th Cir. 2000) (federal and Iowa law) (Iowa's 15–year repose statute for products liability actions does not violate equal protection, due process, or state's open courts provision); McIntosh v. Melroe Co., 729 N.E.2d 972 (Ind. 2000) (10–year repose statute violates neither open courts provision nor privileges and immunities provision of state constitution); Sealey v. Hicks, 788 P.2d 435 (Or. 1990) (repose statute does not violate minor's right to jury trial under state constitution, among other constitutional challenges); Tetterton v. Long

ment statutes of repose have been held unconstitutional,[193] most have withstood constitutional scrutiny.[194] To date, GARA has proved immune to constitutional attack.[195]

Mfg. Co., 332 S.E.2d 67 (N.C. 1985) (repose statute does not violate "exclusive or separate emoluments or privileges" clause of state constitution); Mathis v. Eli Lilly & Co., 719 F.2d 134 (6th Cir. 1983) (federal and Tenn. law) (repose statute does not violate constitutional prohibition against impairing contractual obligations).

**193.** See, e.g., Brennaman v. R.M.I. Co., 639 N.E.2d 425 (Ohio 1994) (violates open courts provision of state constitution); Perkins v. Northeastern Log Homes, 808 S.W.2d 809 (Ky. 1991) (statute arbitrary, and violates open courts and limits on legislative power provisions).

**194.** See, e.g., Baugher v. Beaver Corp., 791 So.2d 932 (Ala. 2000); 1519–1525 Lakeview Blvd. Condo. Ass'n v. Apartment Sales Corp., 6 P.3d 74 (Wash. Ct. App. 2000); Craftsman Builder's Supply, Inc. v. Butler Mfg. Co., 974 P.2d 1194 (Utah 1999); Blaske v. Smith & Entzeroth, Inc., 821 S.W.2d 822 (Mo. 1991); Patton v. Yarrington, 472 N.W.2d 157 (Minn. Ct. App. 1991); Wise v. Bechtel Corp., 766 P.2d 1317 (Nev. 1988).

**195.** See Lyon v. Agusta S.P.A., 252 F.3d 1078, 1085–88 (9th Cir. 2001) (although GARA was not passed until after accident, it violated neither due process nor equal protection).

\*

# PART V

---

# SPECIAL ISSUES

# Chapter 15

## SPECIAL TYPES OF DEFENDANTS

*Table of Sections*

## § 15.1   SPECIAL TYPES OF DEFENDANTS—GENERALLY

In most products liability cases, the principal defendant is the manufacturer that designed, manufactured, and marketed the product which injured the plaintiff. For this reason, most cases, and most discussion in this book, concern the responsibility of such manufacturing enterprises. Yet parties in the product distribution chain other than ordinary manufacturers, notably retail sellers, play significant roles in moving potentially dangerous products from factories to consumers and so may bear some responsibility when product hazards cause injuries to consumers. While a defendant's role in the chain of distribution often has no bearing on what liability theories may be available to users and consumers injured by defective products, a number of variations in policy and doctrine do arise in products liability litigation when the defendant is not the primary manufacturer.

The types of defendants considered in this chapter display a diversity of interests, concentrations of economic power, and methods of doing business. Retailers, for example, vary in size from small, corner stores to major and even multi-national enterprises like Wal–Mart and Sears; in function from serving primarily as conduits for products made by others to imposing on manufacturers their own design specifications and quality control programs; and in range of services from sale alone to sale plus substantial services.[1] Wholesalers and distributors exhibit corresponding diversities.[2] Other defendants examined in this chapter include suppliers of raw materials and component parts, enterprises which ordinarily have

### § 15.1

**1.** See § 15.2, below.

**2.** See Id.

no control over how their products will be put to use;[3] parent and apparent manufacturers, who may benefit from products sold by a subsidiary corporation or trademark licensee;[4] successor corporations, who benefit from the durable assets and goodwill of predecessor enterprises which may have manufactured and sold defective products;[5] employers, who specially design and manufacture products for their own internal use, such as solvents, tools, and machinery which may injure their employees if dangerously defective;[6] and a miscellany of other types of non-manufacturing defendants.[7]

Sometimes the special roles of defendants such as these call for liability principles that differ from those applied to principal manufacturers, but often the rules remain the same. Surely the most enduring issue in the cases involving such special defendants is the applicability of the doctrine of strict liability in tort. But negligence, breach of warranty, tortious misrepresentation, and other theories of liability[8] can also be important claims in cases brought against the special types of defendants examined in this chapter.

A product's normal chain of distribution begins with suppliers of raw materials, moves to manufacturers of component parts, then to the principal manufacturer, a wholesaler or other distributor, the retailer, and finally to the consuming purchaser. Apart from principal manufacturers, retailers are typically the most significant defendants in products liability actions, and so their liability (together with that of wholesalers and other distributors) is examined first.

## § 15.2   RETAILERS AND OTHER NON-MANUFACTURING SELLERS

Retail dealers and other non-manufacturing sellers of ordinary types of products are subject to liability for negligence,[1] tortious misrepresentation,[2] breach of warranty,[3] and, in most states, for strict liability in tort.[4] In general, the elements of these basic products liability causes of action are the same whether the defendant is a manufacturer, a retailer, a wholesale distributor, or some other party in the chain of distribution. Thus, the first step in understanding the legal responsibility of a retailer, wholesaler, or other distributor of an ordinary product[5] is to examine the underlying liability principles applicable to the particular type of claim.

### Retailers—Negligence in General

Like other product suppliers, retail sellers have a duty to exercise reasonable care, in supplying products, not to injure their customers or

---

**3.** See § 15.3, below.

**4.** See § 15.4, below.

**5.** See § 15.5, below.

**6.** See § 15.6, below.

**7.** See § 15.7, below.

**8.** Such as negligent entrustment, in the case of retail dealers. See § 15.2, below.

**§ 15.2**

**1.** See ch. 2, above.

**2.** See ch. 3, above.

**3.** See ch. 4, above.

**4.** See ch. 5, above.

**5.** The liability of a pharmacist for dispensing prescription drugs is addressed in the warnings context, in § 9.6, above.

others.[6] Unlike manufacturers, however, who typically design, manufacturer, package, and affirmatively market their products, most retailers ordinarily have little or no knowledge of, or control over, whether the products they sell may be dangerously defective. Also unlike manufacturers, retailers usually have no practical way to test products to discover hidden dangers; as a result, they ordinarily have no reason to know about latent dangers and, hence, no reason to warn consumers about them. In short, a "seller who reasonably believes that the chattel he is selling is safe for use is not, in selling and delivering the chattel, doing anything which is foreseeably likely to cause harm."[7] Thus, most jurisdictions hold as a general rule that a retailer who has no reason to know that a product may be dangerous has no duty to test or inspect it before sale.[8] Many of the cases, particularly the older ones, express this rule in terms of the absence of a duty on the retail dealer to test or inspect its products for latent defects.[9] Nor, of course, does the retailer have a duty to warn consumers of hidden dangers of which it has no reason to know,[10] nor dangers that are as obvious to the consumer as to the retailer.[11] Put simply, in the absence of some reason to believe that a product may be defective, a retailer is not negligent in merely passing it along to the consumer.[12]

Courts long have held that this general no-duty rule is particularly applicable when the retail seller serves merely as a conduit of a product

---

**6.** See Annot., 6 A.L.R.3d 12 (1966).

**7.** Restatement (2d) Torts § 402 cmt. *d.*

**8.** See, e.g., Jackson v. Sears Authorized Retail Dealer Store, 821 So.2d 590, 593 (La. Ct. App. 2002) (retailer has no duty to inspect for defects); Krumpek v. Millfeld Trading Co., 709 N.Y.S.2d 265, 267 (App. Div. 2000) (vendor who purchases products from reputable source has reasonable grounds to believe products to be free from defects); Baird v. Mervyn's, Inc., 2000 WL 295616 (N.D. Tex. 2000) (hypodermic needle in pocket of blue jeans bought at defendant department store); Ream Tool Co. v. Newton Freeborn Tool Co., 433 S.E.2d 67 (Ga. Ct. App. 1993) (no duty to test when nothing calls attention to danger; seller may assume manufacturer made and sold product in safe condition); Curry v. Sile Distribs., 727 F.Supp. 1052 (N.D. Miss 1990) (no duty to inspect).

Restatement (Second) of Torts § 402, entitled "Absence of Duty to Inspect Chattel," provides that a nonmanufacturing seller "who neither knows nor has reason to know that it is, or is likely to be, dangerous, is not liable in an action for negligence for harm caused by the dangerous character or condition of the chattel because of his failure to discover the danger by an inspection or test of the chattel before selling it."

**9.** See, e.g., Levis v. Zapolitz, 178 A.2d 44 (N.J. Super. Ct. App. Div. 1962) (weak arm of plastic slingshot that broke); Washburn Storage Co. v. General Motors Corp., 83 S.E.2d 26 (Ga. 1954) (pitted groove on

truck axle). See generally Annot., 6 A.L.R.3d 12 (1966).

**10.** See, e.g., Sanns v. Butterfield Ford, 94 P.3d 301 (Utah Ct. App. 2004) (automobile dealership, as a passive retailer, had no duty in negligence law to warn customers of a manufacturing defect of which it was unaware); Bren–Tex Tractor Co. v. Massey Ferguson, Inc., 97 S.W.3d 155 (Tex. App. 2002) (tractor without ROPS rolled over; no duty to warn if retailer unaware of defect or danger); Federal Ins. Co. v. Farmer's Supply Store, 555 S.E.2d 238 (Ga. Ct. App. 2001) (vibration in generator caused unexpected movement closer to house resulting in fire); Baird v. Mervyn's, Inc., 2000 WL 295616 (N.D. Tex. 2000) (hypodermic needle in pocket of blue jeans bought at defendant department store); Malone v. Schapun, Inc., 965 S.W.2d 177, 185–86 (Mo. Ct. App. 1997).

**11.** See, e.g., Bren–Tex Tractor Co. v. Massey–Ferguson, Inc., 97 S.W.3d 155 (Tex. App. 2002) (no duty to warn customer of risk of tractor without a rollover protection system); Zamora v. Mobil Corp., 704 P.2d 584 (Wash. 1985) (distributor). See generally § 10.2, above.

**12.** See, e.g., Hester v. Human, 439 S.E.2d 50, 53 (Ga. Ct. App. 1993) (retailer not liable under negligence theory since it "was entitled to assume that the manufacturer has done its duty in properly constructing the equipment and in not placing on the market a defective machine").

that arrives at the retailer in a pre-packaged condition, like a can of peas, a toaster in a sealed box, a bottle of Coke,[13] a honeybun sold in a sealed cellophane package,[14] a bottle of face cream,[15] or some other product in a sealed container.[16] In such cases, the consumer understands that the retailer has no way to inspect or test the product so that the only party who may be relied upon for the quality of the goods is the manufacturer.[17] Some states have a doctrine that shields retail sellers and other distributors from liability for negligence when selling goods in their original, sealed containers or packages, variously known as the "sealed-container" or "original-package" doctrine or defense.[18]

But the general no-duty to inspect, test, or warn rule has exceptions in situations where the retail seller knows,[19] or has reason to know,[20] of the danger, in which case the seller has a duty of reasonable care to test, inspect, or warn. For example, if a retailer knows or should know that a space heater can dangerously overheat if it is used in a poorly insulated house trailer, the retailer has a duty to give warning of this fact if it learns that the purchaser intends to use it for this purpose.[21] Moreover, if the retail seller acts affirmatively to prepare, install, repair, test, or inspect a product, it no longer acts merely as a conduit, and it will have a duty to exercise reasonable care in its actions.[22] Thus, a retail tractor seller is liable in negligence for injuries caused by its failure to tighten the grab handle it loosens prior to touching up the paint job on the tractor and by its failure to inspect the job after the painting is complete.[23] So, too, some courts find an exception to the no-duty rule for retail sellers of *used* goods, especially automobiles, holding that such

**13.** See, e.g., Coca–Cola Bottling Co. v. Swilling, 57 S.W.2d 1029 (Ark. 1933) (bottle contained partially-decomposed centipede).

**14.** See Sirmons v. Derst Baking Co., 470 S.E.2d 515 (Ga. Ct. App. 1996) (plaintiff bit into honeybun containing dime; since store owner held not liable, no discussion of whether plaintiff's damage recovery would have been reduced by the 10¢ she received in bun).

**15.** See Bel v. Adler, 11 S.E.2d 495 (Ga. Ct. App. 1940).

**16.** See, e.g., Federal Ins. Co. v. Farmer's Supply Store, 555 S.E.2d 238, 240 (Ga. Ct. App. 2001); Jones v. GMRI, Inc., 551 S.E.2d 867 (N.C. Ct. App. 2001) (plaintiff broke tooth when she bit into meatball at restaurant; restaurant protected by sealed-container statute); Annot., 6 A.L.R.3d 12, § 4, at 25 (1966).

**17.** See, e.g., Jones v. GMRI, Inc., 551 S.E.2d 867 (N.C. Ct. App. 2001); Holman Motor Co. v. Evans, 314 S.E.2d 453 (Ga. Ct. App. 1984); Davis v. Siloo, Inc., 267 S.E.2d 354 (N.C. Ct. App. 1980); Pierce v. Liberty Furniture Co., 233 S.E.2d 33 (Ga. Ct. App. 1977); Ross v. Spiegel, Inc., 373 N.E.2d 1288 (Ohio Ct. App. 1977).

**18.** See, e.g., Jones v. GMRI, Inc., 551 S.E.2d 867 (N.C. Ct. App. 2001) (meatballs purchased by restaurant in package); Annot., 6 A.L.R.3d 12, § 4, at 25 (1966).

**19.** See, e.g., Edwards v. Hop Sin Inc., 140 S.W.3d 13 (Ky. Ct. App. 2003) (restaurant owner could be liable for failing to pass along manufacturer's warning of risk of eating raw oysters). See Restatement (2d) Torts § 399. See also Restatement (2d) Torts §§ 388–90 and § 401.

**20.** See Restatement (2d) Torts § 401 (liability of seller who knows chattel is or is likely to be dangerous). See, e.g., Arslanian v. Volkswagen of Am., Inc., 493 N.Y.S.2d 588 (App. Div. 1985) (brake system with defect that could be visually detected).

**21.** See Frey v. Montgomery Ward & Co., 258 N.W.2d 782 (Minn. 1977).

**22.** See, e.g., Coulon v. Wal–Mart Stores, Inc., 734 So.2d 916 (La. Ct. App. 1999) (Wal–Mart considered manufacturer under Louisiana Products Liability Act because its employees or its independent contractor assembled bicycle); Nicholson v. American Safety Util. Corp., 476 S.E.2d 672, 676 (N.C. Ct. App. 1996). See generally Annot., 6 A.L.R.3d 12, § 8, at 36 (1966).

**23.** See Schweich v. Ziegler, Inc., 463 N.W.2d 722 (Minn. 1990).

sellers have a duty of reasonable care to test or inspect,[24] while other courts apply the normal retailer negligence rules to dealers in used products.[25]

### Retailers—Negligent Entrustment

Retailers may be liable for negligently entrusting dangerous products to children or other persons likely to use them in an unsafe manner under the theory of negligent entrustment.[26] The doctrine of negligent entrustment is expressed in § 390 of the *Restatement (Second) of Torts*, which is entitled "Chattel for Use by Person Known to be Incompetent":

> One who supplies directly or through a third person a chattel for the use of another whom the supplier knows or has reason to know to be likely because of his youth, inexperience, or otherwise, to use it in a manner involving unreasonable risk of physical harm to himself and others whom the supplier should expect to share in or be endangered by its use, is subject to liability for physical harm resulting to them.

So, if a retail dealer sells a gun,[27] fireworks,[28] or a jet ski to an intoxicated person, a young child, or a mental incompetent; an automobile to a person known to be an unlicensed driver[29] or perhaps to an habitual drunkard; or gasoline to a very young child[30] or a clearly intoxicated driver,[31] the seller may be subject to liability for negligently supplying a chattel to a person who is likely to use it in an unreasonably

---

**24.** See, e.g., Realmuto v. Straub Motors, Inc., 322 A.2d 440 (N.J. 1974); Thrash v. U–Drive–It Co., 110 N.E.2d 419 (Ohio 1953). See generally Annot., 6 A.L.R.3d 12, § 4, at 25 (1966).

**25.** See, e.g., Crothers v. Cohen, 384 N.W.2d 562 (Minn. Ct. App. 1986) (duty to discover latent defects only).

**26.** See Woods, Negligent Entrustment: Evaluation of a Frequently Overlooked Source of Additional Liability, 20 Ark. L. Rev. 101 (1966); Note, The Negligent Commercial Transaction Tort: Imposing Common Law Liability on Merchants for Sales and Leases to "Defective" Customers, 1988 Duke L.J. 755; Comment, 46 U. Cin. L. Rev. 1047 (1977) (noting *Moning v. Alfono*, below).

**27.** See Salvi v. Montgomery Ward & Co., 489 N.E.2d 394 (Ill. App. Ct. 1986) (despite prominent warning that air gun should not be used by children under 16 without adult supervision, retailer sold one to 14–year-old boy who accidentally shot younger brother in eye while cleaning gun).

But a retail seller ordinarily is not liable for the criminal use of a gun or ammunition. See, e.g., Buczkowski v. McKay, 490 N.W.2d 330 (Mich. 1992) (plaintiff injured when intoxicated man, who bought ammunition from defendant retailer, tried to shoot out back window of plaintiff's parked truck, and shot ricocheted and hit plaintiff). *But see* Ireland v. Jefferson Cty. Sheriff's

Dep't, 193 F.Supp.2d 1201, 1229 (D. Col. 2002) (plaintiff injured in shooting spree at Columbine High School sued retailers who sold shotgun to minors through "straw man purchase"; intervening criminal acts of minors does not absolve defendant if third-party's conduct is reasonably foreseeable).

**28.** See, e.g., Schmidt v. Capital Candy Co., 166 N.W. 502, 503 (Minn. 1918) (dictum). Compare Collins v. Arkansas Cement Co., 453 F.2d 512 (8th Cir. 1972) (Ark. law) (six-year-old girl injured while playing with cherry bomb that exploded; listing and applying elements to negligent entrustment claim, court allowed action against company which used cherry bombs in its business).

**29.** See, e.g., Dillon v. Suburban Motors, Inc., 212 Cal.Rptr. 360 (Ct. App. 1985), dismissed as moot, 705 P.2d 1260 (Cal. 1985); Roland v. Golden Bay Chevrolet, 207 Cal.Rptr. 413 (Ct. App. 1984), dismissed as moot, 704 P.2d 175 (Cal. 1985).

**30.** Jones v. Robbins, 289 So.2d 104 (La. 1974) (service station subject to liability to young child burned when she threw match into gasoline sold by defendant to another six-year-old child). The result will be different if the child is older. See Daniels v. Dauphine, 557 So.2d 1062 (La. Ct. App. 1990) (not negligent to sell gasoline to 12-year-old boy to use to destroy ant hill, causing injury to younger child).

**31.** O'Toole v. Carlsbad Shell Serv. Station, 247 Cal.Rptr. 663 (Ct. App. 1988) (af-

dangerous manner. In *Moning v. Alfono*,[32] for example, a retail merchant sold a slingshot to an 11-year-old boy who shot a pellet which ricocheted off a tree into his friend's eye. In a negligent entrustment action against the retailer, wholesaler, and manufacturer of the slingshot for marketing the slingshot directly to children, the Michigan Supreme Court held that a jury could find that such a sale created an unreasonable risk of harm to the injured boy.[33]

But neither *Moning*, decided in 1977 by a split court, nor the more general doctrine of negligent entrustment has been widely applied by the courts to hold retailers liable for harm caused by a " 'defective' customer,"[34] and at least some commentators are wary of extending the negligent entrustment doctrine into the realm of product sales.[35] While courts in California[36] and a few other jurisdictions[37] have applied the negligent entrustment doctrine to retailers in certain limited situations, most courts have refused to apply, much less expand, the principle of *Moning*. While the basic idea of allowing a cause of action against retailers for negligent entrustment makes good sense, most courts, troubled by the implications of broadly allowing such claims, have held that it is not negligent simply to sell to children bows and arrows,[38] $CO_2$ cartridges,[39] ordinary darts,[40] lawn darts,[41] and even slingshots.[42] While the sale of a

ter buying gas from defendant gas station, inebriated driver struck motorcycle, killing driver and passenger).

**32.** 254 N.W.2d 759 (Mich. 1977).

**33.** "Entrusting potentially dangerous articles to a child may pose an unreasonable risk of harm not only because the child may not appreciate the risk or may not have the skill to use the article safely but even if he does appreciate the risk and does have the requisite skill because he may recklessly ignore the risk and use the article frivolously due to immaturity of judgment, exuberance of spirit, or sheer bravado." Id. at 769. The court allowed the negligent entrustment claim against each member of the marketing chain, including the retailer, wholesaler, and manufacturer.

**34.** Vic Potamkin Chevrolet, Inc. v. Horne, 505 So.2d 560, (Fla. Dist. Ct. App. 1987) (en banc), aff'd, 533 So.2d 261 (Fla. 1988). See Note, 1988 Duke L.J. 755, 776–79 (discussing case).

**35.** See, e.g., Note, The Negligent Commercial Transaction Tort: Imposing Common Law Liability on Merchants for Sales and Leases to "Defective" Customers, 1988 Duke L.J. 755 (arguing against applying negligent entrustment doctrine to commercial transactions); Comment, 46 U. Cin. L. Rev. 1047, 1054 (1977) (criticizing *Moning*, arguing that the case would "have a devastating effect on the merchandisers of inexpensive toys and games. In effect, the court has banned the marketing of any such products that have even a slight propensity to cause physical injury.").

**36.** See, e.g., O'Toole v. Carlsbad Shell Service Station, 247 Cal.Rptr. 663 (Ct. App. 1988) (sale of gasoline to clearly inebriated driver); Dillon v. Suburban Motors, Inc., 212 Cal.Rptr. 360 (Ct. App. 1985) (same), dismissed as moot, 705 P.2d 1260 (Cal. 1985); Roland v. Golden Bay Chevrolet, 207 Cal.Rptr. 413 (Ct. App. 1984) (unlicensed driver), dismissed as moot, 704 P.2d 175 (Cal. 1985).

**37.** See, e.g., Barsness v. General Diesel & Equip. Co., 383 N.W.2d 840, 845–46 (N.D. 1986) (construction company hired inexperienced supervisor to oversee crane operations at construction site); Tosh v. Scott, 472 N.E.2d 591 (Ill. Ct. App. 1984) (suit against father for selling car to son); Fowler v. Park Corp. 673 S.W.2d 749, 753–54 (Mo. 1984) (en banc) (railroad company allowed untrained and incompetent employees to operate switching engine in railyard); Flieger v. Barcia, 674 P.2d 299, 301 (Alaska 1983) (private sale of automobile to used car dealer who sold car to driver without requiring proper documentation); Killeen v. Harmon Grain Products, Inc., 413 N.E.2d 767 (Mass. App. Ct. 1980) (jury might find retailer negligent for selling cinnamon flavored toothpicks to 10-year-old girl who fell, face down, while sucking on one while playing).

**38.** Morris v. Toy Box, 22 Cal.Rptr. 572 (Ct. App. 1962) (dismissing failure to warn complaint against retailer).

**39–42.** See notes 39–42 on page 956.

potentially dangerous implement such as a slingshot to a child who is very young,[43] or a shotgun to a child under suspicious circumstances,[44] might fairly give rise to a negligent entrustment claim, both courts[45] and commentators[46] have emphasized that such a claim will not lie unless the seller has reason to believe that the particular purchaser is likely to dangerously misuse the product.

Today, many courts might be inclined to follow *Vic Potamkin Chevrolet, Inc. v. Horne*,[47] which refused to apply the negligent entrustment doctrine to a claim arising out of a dealer's sale of a car to a clearly incompetent driver for fear of creating a slippery slope of commercial uncertainty over the extent to which retailers might have to investigate the fitness of their buyers.[48] However, while the slippery slope problem is very real, it is likely that most courts will appropriately leave their doors slightly ajar for negligent entrustment claims against retailers of particularly dangerous products for use in cases where the incompetence or irresponsibility of the purchaser is clear and the unreasonable danger is accordingly apparent.[49]

**39.** Warren ex rel. Brassell v. K–Mart Corp., 765 So.2d 235 (Fla. Dist. Ct. App. 2000) (used in pellet gun).

**40.** See Stanford v. Wal–Mart Stores, Inc., 600 So.2d 234 (Ala. 1992) (store sold dart game to nine-year-old child). See also Pitts v. Basile, 219 N.E.2d 472 (Ill. 1966) (action against wholesaler).

**41.** See Atkins v. Arlans Dep't Store Inc., 522 P.2d 1020 (Okla. 1974).

**42.** See, e.g., Carbone v. Alagna, 658 N.Y.S.2d 48 (App. Div. 1997); Bojorquez v. House of Toys, Inc., 133 Cal.Rptr. 483 (Ct. App. 1976).

**43.** For example, to a four-year-old child.

**44.** See, e.g., Ireland v. Jefferson Cty. Sheriff's Dep't, 193 F.Supp.2d 1201, 1229–30 (D. Col. 2002) (plaintiff injured in shooting spree at Columbine High School; gun retailer had reason to know shotgun was to be used by minors accompanying 18-year-old supposed purchaser, and retailer advised minors on how to saw off gun's barrel).

**45.** See, e.g., Troncoso v. Home Depot, U.S.A., Inc., 685 N.Y.S.2d 797, 798 (App. Div. 1999) (store not negligent in entrusting saw blade to experienced power tool user who attached blade to power grinder in dangerous manner as instructed by defendant's employee); Horstman v. Farris, 725 N.E.2d 698 (Ohio Ct. App. 1999) (plaintiff injured in collision with minors high from "huffing" airbrush propellant; retailer had no reason to believe boys would use airbrush propellant to get high); Carbone v. Alagna, 658 N.Y.S.2d 48, 50 (App. Div. 1997) ("While the misuse of a slingshot certainly carries with it grave potential dangers, the weight of authority supports a finding that slingshots constitute toys used

by adolescents. Therefore, the entrustment of a slingshot to an adolescent is not actionable absent further evidence of the unsuitability of the user and the seller's knowledge thereof."). See also Hilberg v. F.W. Woolworth Co., 761 P.2d 236 (Colo. Ct. App. 1988) (not negligent entrustment to sell .22 rifle to father even though retailer knew father intended to give gun to his 14-year-old son for Christmas, absent reason to believe father or son would act improperly).

**46.** "It is essential to an entrustment case that the claiming party establish that the entrustor knew or should have known of the entrustee's condition or propensities." Woods, Negligent Entrustment: Evaluation of a Frequently Overlooked Source of Additional Liability, 20 Ark. L. Rev. 101, 106–07 (1966).

**47.** 505 So.2d 560, (Fla. Dist. Ct. App. 1987) (en banc), aff'd, 533 So.2d 261 (Fla. 1988) (examined approvingly in Note, 1988 Duke L.J. 755, 776–79).

**48.** Compare Messer Griesheim Ind., Inc. v. Cryotech of Kingsport, Inc., 45 S.W.3d 588 (Tenn. Ct. App. 2001) (defendant financial lessor not liable for negligent entrustment; "negligent entrustment should not be used as a shortcut to establish the duty and breach elements of a negligence action in every instance where the defendant, by loaning funds, enables another to obtain the instrument of a tort"); Leslie v. United States, 986 F.Supp. 900 (D.N.J. 1997) (retailer not liable for negligently selling Black Talon hollow-point bullets, used by robber to shoot postal customers, two days after manufacturer's press release that it was withdrawing bullets from general public marketing).

**49.** *But cf.* 1 Frumer and Friedman, Products Liability § 6.02[4], at 6–38 ("It is extremely difficult for a plaintiff to succeed

### Retailers—Tortious Misrepresentation

A retail dealer is subject to liability for tortious misrepresentation, including fraud, negligence, and strict liability in tort for misrepresentation. Thus, the tortious misrepresentation liability principles examined previously[50] apply as readily to retailers as they do to manufacturers.

### Retailers—Warranty

Retailers, of course, are as liable as manufacturers or any other seller for breach of warranty under the Uniform Commercial Code, a topic addressed in detail earlier.[51] Consequently, retailers are subject to liability for breach of express warranty,[52] the implied warranty of merchantability,[53] and the implied warranty of fitness for particular purpose[54]—subject to the normal limitations based on disclaimers,[55] privity,[56] notice,[57] and limitations on remedies,[58] all as previously addressed.

Although a retail seller is subject to liability for breaching its own express warranties, it normally bears no responsibility for the failure of a *manufacturer*'s express warranties. This ordinarily makes sense since retailers normally have no control over the content of such warranties, and buyers normally have no reason to expect that a retail dealer is personally responsible if the manufacturer's warranty proves false. But there are a couple of exceptions to a retailer's ordinary immunity from the failure of a manufacturer's express warranty. One rather large exception is for a manufacturer's express warranties made on the container or label of a product. Uniform Commercial Code § 2–314(2)(f) provides that such warranties must be true in order for a product to be merchantable.[59] Stated otherwise, if representations on a product's con-

---

in such a lawsuit, however, because most courts have exonerated retailers by determining that a duty does not exist.").

**50.** See ch. 3, above.

**51.** See ch. 4, above.

**52.** Under UCC § 2–313. See, e.g., Jones v. Kellner, 451 N.E.2d 548 (Ohio Ct. App. 1982) (used car sold as "mechanically A–1"). See generally § 4.2, above.

**53.** Under UCC § 2–314. See, e.g., Hollister v. Dayton Hudson Corp., 201 F.3d 731 (6th Cir. 2000) (Mich. law) (plaintiff's shirt caught fire; failure to warn claim allowed); Patterson v. Central Mills, Inc., 112 F.Supp.2d 681 (N.D. Ohio 2000) (child's T-shirt caught fire; design and warnings defect claims allowed); Maybank v. S.S. Kresge Co., 266 S.E.2d 409 (N.C. Ct. App. 1980), modified on other grounds and aff'd, 273 S.E.2d 681 (N.C. 1981) (sealed flashcube, in package of flashcubes plaintiff bought at K–Mart); Pierce v. Liberty Furniture Co., 233 S.E.2d 33 (Ga. Ct. App. 1977) (defective porch swing collapsed; retailer liable although swing kit purchased in sealed container from reputable manufacturer and re-

sold to plaintiff in original package). See generally § 4.3, above.

**54.** Under UCC § 2–315. See, e.g., Klein v. Sears Roebuck & Co., 773 F.2d 1421 (4th Cir. 1985) (Md. law) (riding mower tipped over on hilly property inspected by retail dealer who assured buyers that mower was appropriate for property); Barb v. Wallace, 412 A.2d 1314 (Md. Ct. Spec. App. 1980) (sale of used engine for use in go-cart). See generally § 4.4, above.

In the consumer goods products liability context, claims for breach of the implied warranty of fitness for a particular purpose arise in the retail context more than any other.

**55.** Under UCC § 2–316. See §§ 4.7 and 4.8, above.

**56.** Under UCC § 2–318. See § 4.5, above.

**57.** Under UCC § 2–607(3). See § 4.6, above.

**58.** Under UCC § 2–719. See § 4.8, above.

**59.** "Goods to be merchantable must be at least such as . . . (f) conform to the promises or affirmations of fact made on

tainer or label are false, the product is unmerchantable, and a seller is subject to liability for breach of the implied warranty of merchantability under UCC § 2–314 for selling such a mislabeled product.[60] A retail dealer will also be subject to liability for selling a product accompanied by a manufacturer's express warranty which indicates that both the manufacturer and the retail dealer are making and are responsible for the express warranties, in which case the retailer may be treated as a co-warrantor together with the manufacturer.[61]

An alternative method for holding a retailer responsible for a manufacturer's express warranty is to establish that the retailer "adopted" the manufacturer's warranty.[62] It is reasonable, of course, to hold a retailer liable for the failure of an express warranty of another that the retailer has undertaken to support. But "adoption" logically requires that the retailer affirmatively communicate to the purchaser the idea that the retailer stands behind the manufacturer's warranty,[63] for otherwise the purchaser has no fair claim to hold the retailer to a warranty it did not make.[64] Thus, the mere resale of a product carrying a manufacturer's express warranty does not alone constitute adoption, even if the retailer explains its terms to the buyer.[65] Nor does making repairs on behalf of the manufacturer pursuant to the terms of the latter's warranty amount to an adoption.[66] Some courts have expanded the adoption notion further than it logically should extend,[67] and such stretching misconceives the nature of the buyer's separate relationships with the manufacturer and the retail dealer and does violence to fundamental principles of warranty and agency law.[68]

### Retailers—Strict Liability in Tort

The most significant issue in modern products liability litigation is whether retailers are subject to strict liability in tort for the sale of

the container or label if any." UCC § 2–314(2)(f).

**60.** While a comment to § 2–314 suggests that this particular provision is intended to protect dealers against the risk of receiving mislabeled articles from manufacturers, see UCC § 2–314 Official Comment 10, on its face it appears as well to protect consumers against the risk of purchasing mislabeled products from retailers. So interpreted, this section to some extent serves "to overturn the 'adoption' of warranty rule which sometimes has shielded the retailer." See W. Hawkland, A Transactional Guide to the U.C.C. 69–70 (1964).

**61.** See B. Clark and C. Smith, The Law of Product Warranties § 4.05[3], at 4–46 (1984).

**62.** See, e.g., Scovil v. Chilcoat, 424 P.2d 87 (Okla. 1967) (new VW engine).

**63.** See, e.g., Hillcrest Country Club v. N.D. Judds Co., 461 N.W.2d 55 (Neb. 1990) (distributor contracted with buyer that product would meet manufacturer's warranty).

**64.** Recall, however, that a seller may nevertheless be liable for a manufacturer's express warranties on the container or label under UCC § 2–314(2)(f), as discussed above.

**65.** See, e.g., Import Motors, Inc. v. Matthews, 557 S.W.2d 807 (Tex. App. 1977). This is especially true if the retail seller effectively disclaims all warranties. See, e.g., Frank Griffin Volkswagen, Inc. v. Smith, 610 So.2d 597 (Fla. Dist. Ct. App. 1992) (thorough discussion of adoption cases). Compare Thorpe v. Hammons Sheet Metal Co., 991 S.W.2d 157 (Mo. Ct. App. 1999) (no adoption of distributor's warranty).

**66.** See, e.g., Carbo Indus. Inc. v. Becker Chevrolet Inc., 491 N.Y.S.2d 786 (App. Div. 1985).

**67.** See, e.g., Riley v. Ken Wilson Ford, Inc., 426 S.E.2d 717 (N.C. Ct. App. 1993) (by telling buyers about manufacturer's 12–month/12,000 mile warranty, dealer adopted warranty).

**68.** See B. Clark and C. Smith, The Law of Product Warranties § 4.05 (1984).

defective products.[69] In 1964, a year after the California Supreme Court decided *Greenman v. Yuba Power Products, Inc.* and only a few weeks before the American Law Institute approved § 402A of the *Restatement (Second) of Torts*, the California court rendered its landmark decision in *Vandermark v. Ford Motor Co.*[70] In *Vandermark*, the plaintiff was injured when the brakes failed on his new car causing it to crash into a pole. In actions against the retail dealer and manufacturer of the automobile, the court ruled that the retail dealer was strictly liable in tort for injuries caused by a defect in the car.[71] Writing for the court, Justice Roger Traynor reasoned that retailers are just as much engaged in the business of distributing goods to the public as manufacturers. As "an integral part of the overall producing and marketing enterprise," and as sometimes the only member of that enterprise available to injured consumers, retailers properly should "bear the cost of injuries resulting from defective products." Because retailers sometimes can and do pressure manufacturers to ensure product safety, "the retailer's strict liability thus serves as an added incentive to safety." In sum, imposing strict liability on both retailers and manufacturers "affords maximum protection to the injured plaintiff and works no injustice to the defendants, for they can adjust the costs of such protection between them in the course of their continuing business relationship."[72]

*Vandermark's* application of the doctrine of strict products liability in tort to retailers was validated by the American Law Institute in a comment to § 402A of the *Restatement (Second) of Torts* which specifically provides that retail dealers are covered by the strict liability doctrine.[73] Thereafter, with little dissent,[74] the courts quite quickly applied the strict tort doctrine to retailers and other non-manufacturing distributors of defective products,[75] which many courts still do.[76] Al-

---

**69.** See Cavico, The Strict Tort Liability of Retailers, Wholesalers, and Distributors of Defective Products, 12 Nova L. Rev. 213 (1987).

**70.** 391 P.2d 168, 171–72 (Cal. 1964).

**71.** Id. at 172.

**72.** Id. at 171–72. See also Godoy v. Abamaster of Miami, Inc., 754 N.Y.S.2d 301, 307 (App. Div. 2003) (imposing strict liability on retailers and distributors enhances product safety; distributors and importers, closest to the manufacturer, are in the best position to advance this goal).

**73.** "The rule stated in this Section applies to any person engaged in the business of selling products for use or consumption. It therefore applies to any manufacturer of such a product, to any wholesale or retail dealer or distributor, and to the operator of a restaurant." Restatement (2d) Torts § 402A cmt. f.

**74.** For an example of the sprinkling of dissent, see Bailey v. Montgomery Ward & Co., 431 P.2d 108, 114 (Ariz. Ct. App. 1967) (Molloy, J., dissenting): "As to the non-negligent distributor, wholesaler, and retailer, the new doctrine is heavy-handed to

point of injustice.... The new philosophy of liability without fault will mean the difference between survival and extinction to many a small businessman." Id. at 117–18.

In Sam Shainberg Co. of Jackson v. Barlow, 258 So.2d 242 (Miss. 1972), the Mississippi court applied the original package doctrine and so refused to hold the retail dealer or wholesaler strictly liable in tort. *Shainberg*, criticized in 1 Frumer and Friedman, Products Liability § 6.04[2], at 6–47, appears to have been rejected in a subsequent decision. See Coca Cola Bottling Co. v. Reeves, 486 So.2d 374, 379 (Miss. 1986).

**75.** See, e.g., Webb v. Zern, 220 A.2d 853, 854 (Pa. 1966); McKisson v. Sales Affiliates, Inc., 416 S.W.2d 787, 796 (Tex. 1967); Dippel v. Sciano, 155 N.W.2d 55, 61–63 (Wis. 1967); Bailey v. Montgomery Ward & Co., 431 P.2d 108, 111 (Ariz. Ct. App. 1967); Dunham v. Vaughan & Bushnell Mfg. Co., 247 N.E.2d 401, 403–04 (Ill. 1969); Keener v. Dayton Elec. Mfg. Co., 445 S.W.2d 362, 365 (Mo. 1969); Cottom v. McGuire Funeral Serv., Inc., 262 A.2d 807, 809 (D.C. 1970); Moss v. Plyco, 522 P.2d 622, 626–27 (Okla. 1974); Seattle First Nat'l Bank v. Volks-

---

**76.** See note 76 on page 960.

though the *Restatement (Third) of Torts: Products Liability* speaks approvingly of the statutory reform discussed below, it reaffirms the *Second Restatement*'s unqualified rule of strict tort liability for retailers and other non-manufacturing sellers in the chain of distribution.[77]

In recent years, however, at least an occasional court has begun to refuse to apply strict liability principles to retailers for defects they neither caused nor could have known about.[78] In addition, legislative tort reformers have increasingly questioned the fairness of holding retailers strictly liable for design and other defects over which they have no control, such as an uncrashworthy automobile sold to a consumer by a retail dealer. The result has been the enactment of statutory provisions in many states that serve to shield retail dealers and other non-manufacturing distributors from some or all forms of strict products liability;[79] furthermore, in at least a couple instances statutory provisions exempt non-manufacturers unconditionally from strict products liability in tort.[80] A number of the statutes follow the approach of the Model Uniform Product Liability Act,[81] to a greater or lesser extent, by relieving non-manufacturing product sellers[82] of strict products liability (except for express warranty), unless the manufacturer (1) is not subject to the jurisdiction of the court,[83] or (2) is, or is likely to become, insolvent.[84] The

wagen of Am., Inc., 525 P.2d 286, 289 (Wash. Ct. App. 1974), aff'd, 542 P.2d 774 (Wash. 1975); Berkebile v. Brantly Helicopter Co., 337 A.2d 893, 898 n.3 (Pa. 1975); Mead v. Warner Pruyn Div. Finch Pruyn Sales, Inc., 394 N.Y.S.2d 483 (App. Div. 1977).

**76.** See, e.g., Donald v. Shinn Fu Co. of America, 2002 WL 32068351, at *15 (E.D.N.Y. 2002) (retailer of goods over which it has no control as to hidden or latent defects is subject to strict products liability simply for selling such goods); Clay v. Brown & Williamson Tobacco Corp., 77 F.Supp.2d 1220 (M.D. Ala. 1999); Marcon v. Kmart Corp., 573 N.W.2d 728 (Minn. Ct. App. 1998) (retailer subject to strict liability in tort for manufacturer's failure to warn); Adkins v. K–Mart Corp., 511 S.E.2d 840, 846 (W. Va. 1998) (circumstantial evidence of defect in gas grill that exploded; retailer subject to strict liability in tort for defective design or manufacture); Dunn v. Kanawha Cty. Bd. of Educ., 459 S.E.2d 151 (W. Va. 1995).

**77.** See Products Liability Restatement § 1 cmt. *e*:

The rule stated in this Section provides that all commercial sellers and distributors of products, including nonmanufacturing sellers and distributors such as wholesalers and retailers, are subject to liability for selling products that are defective. Liability attaches even when such nonmanufacturing sellers or distributors do not themselves render the products defective and regardless of whether they are in a position to prevent defects from occurring.

**78.** See, e.g., Baird v. Mervyn's, Inc., 2000 WL 295616 (N.D. Tex. 2000) (hypodermic needle in pocket of blue jeans bought at defendant department store). To recover under strict liability in tort (as well as negligence) for failure to warn, a plaintiff must establish "that the defendant knew or should have known that the jeans were defective so as to render them unreasonably dangerous at the time they were sold." Id. at *2.

**79.** Sachs, Product Liability Reform and Seller Liability: A Proposal for Change, 55 Baylor L. Rev. 1031 (2003).

**80.** See Ga. Code Ann. § 51–1–11.1; Neb. Rev. Stat. § 25–21,181.

**81.** See Model Uniform Product Liability Act § 105, reprinted in vol. 3 of Madden & Owen on Products Liability. On such statutes, see generally 1 Frumer and Friedman, Products Liability § 6.01[2][c], at 6–10; Culhane, Real and Imagined Effects of Statutes Restricting the Liability of Non-manufacturing Sellers of Defective Products, 95 Dick. L. Rev. 287 (1991).

**82.** See, e.g., Kennedy v. Guess, Inc., 806 N.E.2d 776 (Ind. 2004) (question of fact whether defendant was a "principal distributor" under statute).

**83.** See, e.g., Williams v. REP Corp. 302 F.3d 660 (7th Cir. 2002) (Ind. law); Malone v. Schapun, Inc., 965 S.W.2d 177, 185–86 (Mo. Ct. App. 1997) (retailer could not get dismissal under "innocent seller statute" where plaintiff had earlier settled with manufacturer and distributor who were

**84.** See note 84 on page 961.

statutes vary in their formulations,[85] and the particular provisions of an applicable statute should be examined carefully in every case.[86] Several states have enacted sealed container defenses, usually with an exception for the manufacturer's insolvency and sometimes for breach of warranty, which serve as a practical matter to shield retailers and other non-manufacturing sellers from the rigors of strict liability in tort,[87] and a miscellany of other state statutes may affect a retailer's liability.[88]

thereafter voluntarily dismissed, after which court no longer had jurisdiction over them).

**84.** See, e.g., Marcon v. K–Mart Corp., 573 N.W.2d 728 (Minn. Ct. App. 1998) (retailer, although found 0% at fault (vs. manufacturer's 100% fault), was liable for all damages assigned to bankrupt manufacturer). See also Hawks v. EPI Prods. USA, Inc., 923 P.2d 988 (Idaho 1996) (retailer protected from direct liability but responsible for bankrupt manufacturer's share of damages).

**85.** See, e.g., Ga. Code Ann. § 51–1–11.1 (non-manufacturer seller is not liable as manufacturer in action based on strict liability in tort); 735 Ill. Comp. Stat. § 5/2–621 (non-manufacturer seller released from suit upon identification of manufacturer unless recovery from manufacturer not possible); Ind. Code Ann. § 34–6–2–77 (seller who knows of defect, provides product specifications, alters product, or owns or is owned by manufacturer is liable as manufacturer); Iowa Code Ann. § 613.18 (non-manufacturer seller not liable as manufacturer in action based on strict liability in tort); Kan. Stat. Ann. § 60–3306 (seller not liable for harm caused by product unless seller breaches duty proximately causing injuries, including breach of express or implied warranties); Minn. Stat. Ann. § 544.41 (non-manufacturer seller released from strict liability in tort suit upon identifying manufacturer unless manufacturer insolvent or not subject to process or if seller knew of defect or exercised control over manufacturing process); Mo. Ann. Stat. § 537.762 (non-manufacturer seller dismissed if manufacturer properly before court in same action); Neb. Rev. Stat. § 25–21,181 (non-manufacturer seller liable only for negligence or breach of warranty unless manufacturer is insolvent, not subject to process, or owns or is owned by seller, or if seller exercises control over manufacturing process, alters product, markets product under its own label or trade name, or fails to timely identify manufacturer); S.D. Codified Laws § 20–9–9 (non-manufacturer seller not liable for latent defects unless it

knew or should have known of defect); Wash. Rev. Code § 7.72.040 (non-manufacturer seller liable only for negligence or breach of warranty unless seller owns or is owned by manufacturer, provides specs for product, markets product under seller's trade or brand name, or if manufacturer insolvent).

**86.** For examples of these types of statutes, see, e.g., Colo. Rev. Stat. § 13–21–402; Del. Code Ann. tit. 18 § 7001; Ind. Code § 6–1407; 735 Ill. Comp. Stat. Ann. 5/2–621(a)-(c); Ind. § 33–1–1.5–3(d); Iowa Code § 613.18; Kan. Stat. Ann. § 60–3306; Ky. Rev. Stat. Ann. § 411.340; Md. Code Ann., Cts. & Jud. Proc. § 5–311; Minn. Stat. Ann. § 544.41; Mo. Rev. Stat. § 537.762; N.D. Cent. Code § 28–01.1–06.1; N.J. Stat. Ann. § 2A: 58C–9; Ohio Rev. Code Ann. 2307.78; Tenn. Code Ann. § 29–28–106; Wash. Rev. Code Ann. § 7.72.040. The statutes are collected in vol. 3 of Madden & Owen on Products Liability.

**87.** See, e.g., Del. Code Ann. tit. 18 § 7001; Idaho Code § 6–1307; Ky. Rev. Stat. Ann. § 411.340; Md. Code Ann. Cts. & Jud. Proc. § 5–405; and Tenn. Code Ann. § 29–28–106. North Carolina does not recognize the doctrine of strict products liability in tort, but it does have a sealed container statutory defense. See N.C. Gen. Stat. § 99B–2(a).

**88.** For example, a number of states have statutes requiring manufacturers to indemnify retailers for the amount of judgment and attorneys fees unless the retailer provided defective specifications for the product. See, e.g., Ariz. Rev. Stat. § 12–684; Cal. Civ. Code § 1792; Idaho Code § 6–1307; Miss. Code Ann. § 11–1–63; N.J. Stat. Ann. § 2A:58C–9; N.D. Cent. Code § 28–01.3–05; Tex. Civ. Prac. & Rem. Code Ann. § 82.002.

Three states have statutes holding motor vehicle manufacturers liable for products liability damages incurred by dealers. See Del. Code Ann. tit. 6 § 4905; Idaho Code § 49–1622; Me. Rev. Stat. Ann. tit. 10 § 1175.

## Wholesalers and Other Distributors

The principles examined above applicable to retail dealers generally apply to wholesalers and other non-manufacturing distributors as well.[89] Thus, subject to the same limitations protecting retailers,[90] many states hold that wholesalers and other distributors ordinarily are subject to liability for negligence,[91] warranty,[92] and strict liability in tort.[93] Some states, however, offer non-manufacturing distributors common-law protection from strict liability in tort (and, implicitly, from negligence) if they act as mere conduits of goods that they have no reason to believe may be defective.[94] Moreover, the reform statutes discussed above that conditionally protect retailers also apply to wholesalers and other non-manufacturing distributors.[95]

**89.** See Cavico, The Strict Tort Liability of Retailers, Wholesalers, and Distributors of Defective Products, 12 Nova L. Rev. 213 (1987).

**90.** See, e.g., Farmer v. Brannan Auto Parts, Inc., 498 S.E.2d 583 (Ga. Ct. App. 1998) (distributor not liable for negligent failure to warn if not aware of danger); Thomasson v. Rich Prods. Corp., 502 S.E.2d 289 (Ga. Ct. App. 1998) (no liability, under sealed container doctrine, for injuries from staple baked by third-party baker into bagel); Vanderlune v. 4B Elevator Components Unlimited, 148 F.3d 943, 947 (8th Cir. 1998) (Iowa law) (no negligence duty to inspect for latent defects unless reason to suspect existence of dangerous defect); Townsend v. General Motors Corp., 642 So.2d 411, 424–25 (Ala. 1994) (no liability of mere "middleman" distributor who is unaware of defect and who has no better opportunity to inspect product than consumer); Curry v. Sile Distribs., 727 F.Supp. 1052 (N.D. Miss. 1990) (no negligence duty to inspect for latent defects unless reason to suspect existence of dangerous defect); Zamora v. Mobil Corp., 704 P.2d 584 (Wash. 1985) (distributor which purchased propane gas from reputable supplier had no duty to test or inspect gas to determine if it was odorized, nor did it have duty to warn retailer of obvious risk if gas were in fact not odorized).

**91.** See, e.g., Kennedy v. Guess, Inc., 806 N.E.2d 776 (Ind. 2004) (umbrella distributor); Mills v. Allegiance Healthcare Corp., 178 F.Supp.2d 1 (D. Mass. 2001); Bishop v. Farhat, 489 S.E.2d 323 (Ga. Ct. App. 1997) (distributor of gloves could be liable for failing to warn if it reasonably should have known of latex allergies); Beam v. Omark Indus., Inc., 237 S.E.2d 607 (Ga. Ct. App. 1977) (wholesaler removed product from container and failed to pass along warnings and instructions).

**92.** See, e.g., Mills v. Allegiance Healthcare Corp., 178 F.Supp.2d 1 (D. Mass. 2001) (distributor of latex gloves could be liable for breach of implied warranty for failing to warn of latex allergies); Peris v. Western Reg'l Off–Track Betting Corp., 680 N.Y.S.2d 346 (App. Div. 1998); Fleming Farms v. Dixie Ag Supply, Inc., 631 So.2d 922 (Ala. 1994); Jones v. Cranman's Sporting Goods, 237 S.E.2d 402 (Ga. Ct. App. 1977) (distributor subject to express and implied warranties for "fully guaranteed" rifle that exploded).

**93.** See, e.g., Kennedy v. Guess, Inc., 806 N.E.2d 776 (Ind. 2004); Levey v. Yamaha Motor Corp., 825 A.2d 554 (N.J. Super. Ct. App. Div. 2003) (distributor of jet boat failed adequately to warn of risks); Fronckowiak v. King–Kong Mfg. Co., 735 N.Y.S.2d 294 (App. Div. 2001) (bicycle); Giuffrida v. Panasonic Indus. Co., 607 N.Y.S.2d 72 (App. Div. 1994) ("[d]istributors of defective products, as well as retailers and manufacturers, are subject to potential strict products liability"); Lawrence v. Brandell Prod., Inc., 619 So.2d 427 (Fla. Dist. Ct. App. 1993) (even though defective golf club warm-up weight was shipped directly from manufacturer to retailer); Promaulayko v. Johns Manville Sales Corp., 562 A.2d 202, 205 (N.J. 1989); Zamora v. Mobil Corp., 704 P.2d 584 (Wash. 1985); Smith v. Fiat–Roosevelt Motors, Inc., 556 F.2d 728 (5th Cir. 1977) (Fla. law) (uncrashworthy car). See also Bittler v. White & Co., 560 N.E.2d 979 (Ill. App. Ct. 1990) (manufacturer's sales rep).

**94.** See, e.g., Townsend v. General Motors Corp., 642 So.2d 411 (Ala. 1994); Wolfgram v. Neveln, 502 N.W.2d 617 (Wis. Ct. App. 1993) (motorcycle's distributor not liable for design defects).

**95.** For the statutes, see vol. 3 of Madden & Owen on Products Liability.

## § 15.3   RAW MATERIAL AND COMPONENT PART SUPPLIERS

In contrast to retailers who sit at the bottom of the chain of product distribution, suppliers of raw materials and component parts stand at the top. But similar to retailers, these suppliers generally have little control over the safety of the final product which incorporates the raw materials and component parts because the design, assembly, and packaging of the finished product is usually in the exclusive hands of the manufacturer-assembler. An automobile manufacturer, for example, which obtains sheet metal, plastic, screws, glass, carpeting, tires, batteries, and radios from a wide diversity of suppliers of raw materials and component parts, makes most of the design decisions and conducts most of the production and marketing operations that bear on the safety of the finished car. While cases against suppliers of raw materials and component parts are much less common than against manufacturer-assemblers of finished products, and while the rules applicable to component suppliers are in a state of some confusion, the law in this area has begun to settle in a logical fashion.[1]

### Theories of Liability

Since suppliers of raw materials and component parts are always remote from the ultimate consumer, the privity of contract requirement of negligence as well as warranty law precluded claims against such defendants well into the twentieth century. But with the crumbling of the privity bar in negligence law in the early to mid-1900s,[2] courts began to allow negligence claims against suppliers of dangerously defective component parts that caused consumer harm.[3] Although privity of con-

---

**§ 15.3**

1. See, e.g., Fischer, Product Liability: A Commentary on the Liability of Suppliers of Component Parts and Raw Materials, 53 S.C. L. Rev. 1137 (2002); Parshall, For Want of a Nail: Component Supplier Products Liability, 30–SPG Brief 48 (2001); Madden, Component Parts and Raw Materials Sellers: From the Titanic to the New Restatement, 26 N. Ky. L. Rev. 535 (1999); Madden, Liability of Suppliers of Natural Raw Materials and the Restatement (Third) of Torts: Products Liability—A First Step Toward Sound Public Policy, 30 U. Mich. J.L. Reform 281, 308 (1997) (asserting that Products Liability Restatement should have excluded bulk sellers of naturally occurring raw materials from design and warning duties "absent a showing of defect in the product itself that poses an unreasonable risk of personal physical injury"); Mansfield, Reflections on Current Limits on Component and Raw Material Supplier Liability and the Proposed Third Restatement, 84 Ky. L.J. 221 (1995–96); Hager, Don't Say I Didn't Warn You (Even Though I Didn't): Why the Pro-Defendant Consensus on Warning Law Is Wrong, 61 Tenn. L. Rev. 1125 (1994); Liebman, Strict Tort Liability

for Unfinished Products, 19 Am. Bus. L.J. 407 (1982) (no reason to bar § 402A actions when product is unfinished or is to be incorporated into larger product); Kennelly, Trial of a General Aviation Aircraft Case Against Manufacturer, Component-Part Maker, and Overhaul Company—Defective 5¢ Screws Result in $660,000 Aggregate Awards for Two Deaths, 15 Tr. Law. Guide 281 (1971); Comment, Apportionment Between Partmakers and Assemblers in Strict Liability, 49 U. Chi. L. Rev. 544, 547 (1982) (apportionment of liability should rest on cheapest cost avoider); Casenote, 31 Creighton L. Rev. 617 (1998) (liability of manufacturers of raw materials and component parts, focusing on TMJ implant litigation); Annot, 39 A.L.R.4th 6 (1985) (duty of component part supplier to warn of danger).

2. See § 1.2, above.

3. See, e.g., Smith v. Peerless Glass Co., 181 N.E. 576 (N.Y. 1932); Spencer v. Madsen, 142 F.2d 820 (10th Cir. 1944) (Kan. law); Carson v. Weston Hotel Corp., 97 N.E.2d 620 (Ill. App. Ct. 1951); Maryland ex rel Woodzell v. Garzell Plastics Indus., Inc., 152 F.Supp. 483 (D. Mich. 1957) (Md. law);

tract in many jurisdictions still remains an important requirement of warranty law, vertical privity is no longer an absolute requirement to warranty claims in every state, as discussed above.[4] Accordingly, courts have occasionally begun to allow warranty claims against component part suppliers.[5] The principal liability question in the 1960s and 1970s, however, was whether the doctrine of strict products liability in tort should be allowed against manufacturers of raw materials and component parts. While a prominent early decision held that strict products liability claims against component part manufacturers were inappropriate,[6] at least when the manufacturer of the final product was available to answer to the victims of a product accident, courts in recent decades have found no difficulty in finding the doctrine of strict products liability in tort applicable in appropriate cases to suppliers of raw materials[7] and component parts.[8] Several state products liability reform statutes provide

Edison v. Lewis Mfg. Co., 336 P.2d 286 (Cal. Ct. App. 1959). More recently, see, e.g., Thorndike v. DaimlerChrysler Corp., 2003 WL 21212591 (D. Me. 2003) (defective bolt used to secure spare tire to van floor); Torres v. Mactac Trading Corp., 1995 WL 21612 (N.D. Ill. 1995).

**4.** See § 4.5, above.

**5.** See, e.g., Thorndike v. DaimlerChrysler Corp., 2003 WL 21212591 (D. Me. 2003) (defective bolt used to secure spare tire to van floor); Shaw v. General Motors Corp., 727 P.2d 387 (Colo. Ct. App. 1986); Favors v. Firestone Tire & Rubber Co., 309 So.2d 69 (Fla. Dist. Ct. App. 1975); Clark v. Bendix Corp., 345 N.Y.S.2d 662 (App. Div. 1973). But the normal defenses apply to component part makers, and the finished product manufacturer's disclaimer may protect unnamed suppliers of component parts. See Moore v. Coachmen Indus., Inc., 499 S.E.2d 772, 778–80 (N.C. Ct. App. 1998).

**6.** See Goldberg v. Kollsman Instrument Corp., 191 N.E.2d 81 (N.Y. 1963) (defective altimeter caused crash of plane). See generally Hunt, A Reporter at Large: The Case of Flight 320, The New Yorker (Apr. 30, 1960, at 119) (fascinating account of *Goldberg* crash and subsequent investigation into its cause). Although *Goldberg* played a role in the development of strict products liability in tort, see § 5.2, above, it characterized the claim in warranty terms. It did lay the basis, however, for the debate that followed over whether the new doctrine of strict liability in tort should be extended to manufacturers of component parts.

**7.** See, e.g., Arena v. Owens–Corning Fiberglas Corp., 74 Cal.Rptr.2d 580 (Ct. App. 1998) (supplier of raw asbestos subject to liability for design defect); Hammond v. North Am. Asbestos Corp., 454 N.E.2d 210 (Ill. 1983) (strict liability in tort for sale of raw asbestos fiber, which defendant mined, milled, and packaged, without adequate warnings); Suchomajcz v. Hummel Chemi-

cal Co., 524 F.2d 19, 25–27 (3d Cir. 1975) (Pa. law) (chemical supplier subject to liability for selling its products to manufacturer-assembler knowing that its chemicals would be used to manufacture and sell firecracker assembly kits prohibited by law). But these cases are unusual, and most courts hold that suppliers ordinarily are *not* subject to strict products liability for providing raw materials for use by another manufacturer as an ingredient in a finished product. See, e.g., Haase v. Badger Mining Corp., 669 N.W.2d 737 (Wis. Ct. App. 2003), aff'd on other grounds, 682 N.W.2d 389 (Wis. 2004) (supplier of silica sand not subject to strict liability); Walker v. Stauffer Chem. Corp., 96 Cal.Rptr. 803 (Ct. App. 1971) (supplier of sulfuric acid, used as ingredient in drain cleaner which exploded, not subject to strict liability).

**8.** See, e.g., Thorndike v. DaimlerChrysler Corp., 2003 WL 21212591 (D. Me. 2003) (defective bolt used to secure spare tire to van floor); Jimenez v. Superior Ct., 58 P.3d 450, 454 (Cal. 2002) (windows for mass-produced homes); Buonanno v. Colmar Belting Co., 733 A.2d 712 (R.I. 1999); House v. Armour of Am., 886 P.2d 542 (Utah Ct. App. 1994), aff'd, 929 P.2d 340 (Utah 1996); Depre v. Power Climber, 635 N.E.2d 542 (Ill. Ct. App. 1994); Butchkosky v. Enstrom Helicopter Corp., 855 F.Supp. 1251 (S.D. Fla. 1993), aff'd without opinion, 66 F.3d 341 (11th Cir. 1995); Gifaldi v. Jefferson Chem. Co., 1992 WL 76980 (W.D.N.Y. 1992); Neofes v. Robertshaw Controls Co., 409 F.Supp. 1376 (S.D. Ind. 1976); Leahy v. Mid–West Conveyor Co., 507 N.Y.S.2d 514 (App. Div. 1986); Michalko v. Cooke Color & Chem. Corp., 451 A.2d 179 (N.J. 1982); Mott v. Callahan AMS Mach. Co., 416 A.2d 57 (N.J. Super. Ct. 1980); Union Supply Co. v. Pust, 583 P.2d 276, 281–83 (Colo. 1978) (en banc); City of Franklin v. Badger Ford Truck Sales, Inc., 207 N.W.2d 866 (Wis. 1973); Burbage v. Boiler Eng'g & Supply

for the liability of manufacturers of component parts.[9] A narrow, federal statute protects suppliers of biomaterials used by medical device manufacturers in medical implants from liability for harm caused by the implants.[10]

## Liability Principles

The fulcrum on which the liability issue usually rests is whether the dangerously defective condition resides in the component itself, in which case the component supplier generally is liable for resulting harm, or whether the defect arises from the manner in which the manufacturer-assembler of the final product combines the component into the integrated product, in which case the component supplier usually is *not* responsible for resulting harm.[11] It is clear that suppliers of component parts (including raw materials) are subject to liability for harm proximately caused by defects in the components at the time they are sold, notwithstanding the fact that the defective components are integrated into final products that ultimately cause the harm.[12] If a wheel or tire manufacturer supplies a defective wheel or tire to the assembler of a vehicle, and the defect causes the vehicle to crash, then the supplier of the defective wheel[13] or tire[14] is properly liable (in addition to the manufacturer-assembler of the entire vehicle) for the harmful consequences of the crash. Component suppliers thus are subject to liability for manufacturing defects[15] and for defects in design[16] proximately caused[17] by supplying the component.

---

Co., 249 A.2d 563 (Pa. 1969); Barth v. B.F. Goodrich Tire Co., 71 Cal.Rptr. 306 (Ct. App. 1968); Suvada v. White Motor Co., 210 N.E.2d 182 (Ill. 1965), overruled on other grounds, Dixon v. Chicago & N.W. Transp. Co., 601 N.E.2d 704 (Ill. 1992).

**9.** Arizona accomplishes this result by including component parts in the definition of "product." See Ariz. Rev. Stat. § 12–681(2). Other states include manufacturers of component parts in the definition of a "manufacturer." See, e.g., Ark. Code Ann. § 16–116–102(1); Colo. Rev. Stat. Ann. § 13–21–401(1); Idaho Code § [6–1402] 6–1302(2); Kan. Stat. Ann. § 60–3302(b).

**10.** This is the Biomaterials Access Assurance Act of 1998, 21 U.S.C.A. § 1601 et seq. The Act is included in vol. 3 of Madden & Owen on Products Liability.

**11.** See, e.g., White v. ABCO Eng'g Corp., 221 F.3d 293 (2d Cir. 2000) (N.J. law) (question turns on whether component part itself was defective).

**12.** The logic of this point has been evident from the inception of modern products liability law. See Restatement (2d) Torts § 402A cmt. *q* ("where there is no change in the component part itself, but it is merely incorporated into something larger, the strict liability will be found to carry through to the ultimate user or consumer").

**13.** See, e.g., City of Franklin v. Badger Ford Truck Sales, Inc., 207 N.W.2d 866 (Wis. 1973).

**14.** See, e.g., Harbor City Disc. Auto Ctr., Inc. v. Firestone Tire & Rubber Co., 157 Cal.Rptr. 438 (Ct. App. 1979).

**15.** See, e.g., Thorndike v. Daimler-Chrysler Corp., 2003 WL 21212591 (D. Me. 2003) (defectively manufactured bolt used to secure spare tire to van floor); Jimenez v. Superior Court, 58 P.3d 450 (Cal. 2002) (defective windows in manufactured home); Sipes v. General Motors Corp., 946 S.W.2d 143, 159–60 (Tex. App. 1997) (automotive airbag component); Jones v. Aero–Chem Corp., 680 F.Supp. 338 (D. Mont. 1987) (tear gas canister valve); Kaneko v. Hilo Coast Processing, 654 P.2d 343 (Haw. 1982) (service platform); Bradford v. Bendix–Westinghouse Auto. Air Brake Co., 517 P.2d 406 (Colo. Ct. App. 1973) (truck brake pedal assembly); Burbage v. Boiler Eng'g & Supply Co., 249 A.2d 563 (Pa. 1969) (defective replacement valve in boiler); Suvada v. White Motor Co., 210 N.E.2d 182 (Ill. 1965) (truck brake), overruled on other grounds, Dixon v. Chicago & N.W. Transp. Co., 601 N.E.2d 704, 711 (Ill.1992).

**16.** See, e.g., White v. ABCO Eng'g Corp., 221 F.3d 293 (2d Cir. 2000) (N.J. law) (unguarded line conveyor of recycling machine may not have been defective);

---

**17.** See note 17 on page 966.

Courts quite frequently assert that manufacturers of component parts have no duty to warn of possible dangers from integrating the part into another product unless the component supplier is involved in the design of the integrated product.[18] But such assertions overstate the principle, for suppliers of raw materials and component parts surely are subject to liability for failing to adequately warn or instruct in certain situations.[19] If a component contains an inherent hidden danger of which the manufacturer-assembler of the finished product is likely to be unaware, then the component supplier quite clearly has a duty to provide a warning of the danger.[20] But if the danger is unforeseeable;[21] or if it is obvious, commonly known,[22] or otherwise likely to be known by

Dougherty v. Edward J. Meloney, Inc., 661 A.2d 375 (Pa. Super. Ct. 1995) (shut-off valve used in boilers); Parkins v. Van Doren Sales, Inc., 724 P.2d 389, 392 (Wash. Ct. App. 1986) (conveyor components defectively designed because they always presented risk to users); Gryc v. Dayton–Hudson Corp., 297 N.W.2d 727 (Minn. 1980) (flammable cotton flannelette fabric made into children's nightgowns); d'Hedouville v. Pioneer Hotel Co., 552 F.2d 886 (9th Cir. 1977) (Ariz. law) (flammable acrylic fiber made into carpeting).

**17.** So, the doctrine of proximate cause barred liability in a products liability action against the manufacturers of otherwise safe fertilizer products used by terrorists to construct the explosive device used to bomb the World Trade Ctr. Port Auth. of N.Y. & N.J. v. Arcadian Corp., 189 F.3d 305, 317–19 (3d Cir. 1999) (N.Y. and N.J. law). See also Davis v. Berwind Corp., 640 A.2d 1289, 1299–1300 (Pa. Super. Ct. 1994) (removal of safety interlock from component product was unforeseeable); Temple v. Wean United, Inc., 364 N.E.2d 267, 271 (Ohio 1977) (employer's dangerous installation and use of component was "sole responsible cause" of accident).

**18.** See, e.g., Artiglio v. General Elec. Co., 71 Cal.Rptr.2d 817 (Ct. App. 1998) (supplier of silicone used in breast implants had no duty to warn breast implant recipients of risks); Schaffer v. A.O. Smith Harvestore Prods., Inc., 74 F.3d 722, 729 (6th Cir. 1996) (Ohio law) ("a manufacturer of a non-defective component part has no duty to warn about dangers that may result when the part is integrated into another product or system, where the component manufacturer was not involved in the design or assembly of the integrated product of system."); In re Silicone Gel Breast Implants Prods. Liab. Litig., 887 F.Supp. 1463 (N.D. Ala. 1995) (manufacturer of polyurethane foam used in breast implants had no duty to warn recipients of potential hazards).

**19.** See, e.g., J. Meade Williamson and F.D.I.B., Inc. v. Piper Aircraft Corp., 968 F.2d 380 (3d Cir. 1992) (Pa. law) (manufac-

turer of standby vacuum pump for aircraft engine had duty to provide warnings to manufacturer of aircraft about dangers of design and instructions on safe method for attaching pump to engine); Fleck v. KDI Sylvan Pools, Inc., 981 F.2d 107, 118 (3d Cir. 1992) (Pa. law) (replacement pool-liner supplier had duty to provide diving warnings and depth markers—warning obligation was more logically affixed to supplier of pool liner than to manufacturer of finished pool); Gryc v. Dayton–Hudson Corp., 297 N.W.2d 727 (Minn. 1980) (flammable cotton flannelette fabric made into children's nightgowns that parents could flame-retard at home); Hill v. Wilmington Chem. Corp., 156 N.W.2d 898, 902 (Minn. 1968).

Probably most courts hold that the duty to warn is limited to the manufacturer-assembler and does not include providing warnings directly to end users of the final, integrated product. See, e.g., Smith v. Walter C. Best, Inc., 927 F.2d 736 (3d Cir. 1990) (Ohio law); Goodbar v. Whitehead Bros., 591 F.Supp. 552 (W.D. Va. 1984); Jones v. Hittle Serv., Inc., 549 P.2d 1383 (Kan. 1976).

**20.** See, e.g., Hammond v. North Am. Asbestos Corp., 454 N.E.2d 210 (Ill. 1983) (strict liability in tort for sale of raw asbestos fiber, which defendant mined, milled, and packaged, without adequate warnings). See generally Products Liability Restatement § 5 cmt. b. But see id. cmt. c (raw material supplier has no duty to warn).

**21.** Zaza v. Marquess & Nell, Inc., 675 A.2d 620 (N.J. 1996) (no strict liability for failure to warn where risk was unforeseeable); Schaffer v. A.O. Smith Harvestore Prods., Inc., 74 F.3d 722, 731 (6th Cir. 1996) (Ohio law) (no duty to warn of unforeseeable risk).

**22.** See, e.g., Wood v. Phillips Petroleum Co., 119 S.W.3d 870 (Tex. App. 2003) (dangers of benzene commonly known in petrochemical industry); Gray v. Badger Mining Corp., 664 N.W.2d 881, 884 (Minn. Ct. App. 2003) (supplier of silica sand had no duty to warn; "it was common knowledge in the

the manufacturer-assembler of the final product;[23] or if the large variety of possible uses of a generic component product make it impractical to warn of a large and amorphous bundle of speculative risks,[24] then the component supplier has no reason or obligation to provide a warning. When a supplier of raw materials or other component parts supplier does have a duty to warn of hidden dangers, most cases hold that the duty is fulfilled by providing the information to the manufacturer-assembler, so that the component supplier ordinarily has no duty to warn the end user[25]—at least if the component part supplier does not participate in designing the integrated product. In unusual cases, however, a court may find a duty to warn the consumer when a component supplier has strong reason to expect that the only practical way to assure the effectiveness of a warning is to provide it directly to the ultimate user.[26]

foundry industry that silica dust could pose a health risk"), rev'd, 676 N.W.2d 268 (Minn. 2004); Fluidmaster, Inc. v. Severinsen, 520 S.E.2d 253 (Ga. Ct. App. 1999) (obvious that seal on toilet-tank's flush valve could deteriorate over time).

**23.** See, e.g., Artiglio v. General Elec. Co., 71 Cal.Rptr.2d 817 (Ct. App. 1998) (supplier of silicone used in breast implants had no duty to warn recipients of risk; implant manufacturers were sophisticated buyers); Zaza v. Marquess & Nell, Inc., 675 A.2d 620, 633 (N.J. 1996) (manufacturer of component part, not dangerous in itself, has no duty to warn employee of immediate purchaser of component which itself is aware of need to attach safety devices). See generally § 9.4, above.

**24.** See, e.g., Pomplun v. Rockwell Int'l Corp., 552 N.W.2d 632 (Wis. Ct. App. 1996) (manufacturer of foot switch did not know how manufacturer of press might integrate switch into overall design of press).

**25.** See, e.g., Wood v. Phillips Petroleum Co., 119 S.W.3d 871 (Tex. App. 2003) (manufacturers of benzene did not have duty to warn decedent of dangers of exposure because decedent's employer knew of such dangers); Gray v. Badger Mining Corp., 664 N.W.2d 881, 886 (Minn. Ct. App. 2003) ("a bulk supplier of silica sand to a sophisticated purchaser has no duty to warn the user of the dangers of exposure to silica dust"), rev'd, 676 N.W.2d 268 (Minn. 2004); Artiglio v. General Elec. Co., 71 Cal.Rptr.2d 817 (Ct. App. 1998) (supplier of silicone to manufacturer of defective breast implant did not have duty to warn patient-victims of dangers of using silicon in medical applications); In re TMJ Implants Prods. Liab. Litig., 872 F.Supp. 1019 (D. Minn. 1995) (summary judgment in multidistrict case granted in favor of manufacturer of Teflon, a product with numerous industrial uses that was utilized by a surgical-implant manufacturer as a component in jaw implants; *held*, raw-material supplier or component-part manufacturer has no duty to

warn consumers directly of defects in the integrated products, purportedly the rule in all jurisdictions); Smith v. Walter C. Best, Inc., 927 F.2d 736 (3d Cir. 1990) (Ohio law); Lee v. Electric Motor Div., 215 Cal.Rptr. 195 (Ct. App. 1985); Goodbar v. Whitehead Bros., 591 F.Supp. 552 (W.D. Va. 1984); Jones v. Hittle Serv., Inc., 549 P.2d 1383 (Kan. 1976).

**26.** See, e.g., White v. ABCO Eng'g Corp., 221 F.3d 293 (2d Cir. 2000) (N.J. law) (summary judgment for component-part supplier reversed; defendant may have had a duty to warn foreseeable users of product hazard); Beauchamp v. Russell, 547 F.Supp. 1191 (N.D. Ga. 1982) (manufacturer of air valve component used in pneumatically-run palletizer had duty to provide warnings and instructions to users concerning the release of compressed air, particularly when suppliers of other valves did so): "The responsibility for information collection and dissemination should rest on the party who has the greatest access to the information and who can make it available at the lowest cost. Where a component part is incorporated into another product, without material change, the manufacturer of the part is in the best position to bear this responsibility." Id at 1197; Gryc v. Dayton–Hudson Corp., 297 N.W.2d 727 (Minn. 1980) (manufacturer of cotton flannelette sold for use in making young girls' nightgowns had duty to warn consumers directly, as on hang-tags provided to clothing manufacturers, of the flammability risk and methods of reducing it); Suchomajcz v. Hummel Chem. Co., 524 F.2d 19, 25–27 (3d Cir. 1975) (Pa. law) (chemical supplier subject to liability for selling its products to manufacturer-assembler knowing that its chemicals would be used to manufacture and sell firecracker assembly kits prohibited by law). See also Restatement (2d) Torts § 388 cmt. *n*.

It has been suggested that the duty to warn end users may be more appropriate

If a component material or product is not itself dangerously defective, but becomes so only because of the manner in which a manufacturer-assembler incorporates it into a finished product, then the component supplier generally is not liable for harm caused by the defect in the integrated product.[27] In *Temple v. Wean United, Inc.*,[28] for example, the manufacturer of a dual-button operating control panel, Square D, sold a control panel to the plaintiff's employer who proceeded to install it on a power press incorrectly, with the control buttons facing upwards. The installation of the control panel in this position created an unreasonable risk that stock could fall upon and accidentally activate the buttons, which subsequently occurred. Holding Square D free of responsibility for the accident, the court observed that "the obligation that generates the duty to warn does not extend to the speculative anticipation of how manufactured components, not in and of themselves dangerous or defective, can become potentially dangerous dependent upon the nature of their integration into a unit designed and assembled by another. Because of limited contact with [the employer], there is no indication that Square D could have known that its components were to be fashioned or fabricated into the power press in the particular manner that they were."[29] Courts widely agree that suppliers of nondefective components have no duty to police the manner in which their components are integrated into finished products and, accordingly, have held that such suppliers are not liable for dangers that manufacturer-assemblers introduce into finished products containing the components,[30] unless the

with respect to component materials that are inherently dangerous, or because the component is "toxic or otherwise dangerous for normal handling." Mansfield, Reflections on Current Limits on Component and Raw Material Supplier Liability and the Proposed Third Restatement, 84 Ky. L.J. 221, 229–230 (1995–96). See, e.g., Hunnings v. Texaco, Inc., 29 F.3d 1480 (11th Cir. 1994) (Fla. law) (manufacturers and suppliers of "inherently dangerous" mineral spirits sold in bulk, which they knew retailers were routinely repackaging and selling in milk containers without adequate warnings, were subject to negligence liability). But such vague, outdated characterizations are unhelpful in determining when the duty to warn should extend to end users, and the more relevant questions would seem to be the degree of risk to end users, the likelihood that the intermediate manufacturer will not provide the warnings, the feasibility for the component supplier to provide warnings directly to end users, and the component supplier's knowledge of each of these facts. See generally Restatement (2d) Torts § 388 cmt. *n*.

**27.** See, e.g., Thorndike v. Daimler-Chrysler Corp., 2003 WL 21212591, at *5 (D. Me. 2003) (defective bolt used to secure spare tire to van floor: "Because component parts manufacturers are neither designers nor manufacturers of the finished, composite product, they are to be held liable for defects in the composite product only if their component part was itself defective."); Hothan v. Herman Miller, Inc., 742 N.Y.S.2d 104 (App. Div. 2002) (manufacturer of nondefective work surface, which did not install it, not liable); Cipollone v. Yale Indus. Prods., Inc., 202 F.3d 376, 379 (1st Cir. 2000) (Mass. law) ("When a component of an integrated product is not itself defective, the maker of the component is not liable for injury that results from a defect in the integrated product.").

**28.** 364 N.E.2d 267 (Ohio 1977).

**29.** Id. at 272.

**30.** See, e.g., Hothan v. Herman Miller, Inc., 742 N.Y.S.2d 104 (App. Div. 2002) (manufacturer of nondefective work surface not liable); Jacobs v. E.I. Du Pont De Nemours & Co., 67 F.3d 1219, 1241 (6th Cir. 1995) (Ohio law) (manufacturer of Teflon, integrated by medical device manufacturer into jaw implant prosthesis which disintegrated from foreign-body reaction to commercial-grade plastic being implanted in human jaws, not subject to liability for harmful results); Apperson v. E.I. Du Pont De Nemours & Co., 41 F.3d 1103 (7th Cir. 1994) (Ill. law) (same); Crossfield v. Quality Control Equip. Co., 1 F.3d 701, 704 (8th Cir. 1993) (Mo. law) (supplier of chain for chitterlings cleaning machine not liable for failing to provide warning decal or interlock

component supplier participates in the design of the finished product.[31]

The pivotal issue in most of the cases is whether the supplier of the component product or the manufacturer of the finished product was substantially responsible for creating the unreasonable risk of harm that injured the plaintiff. The *Restatement (Second) of Torts* and many of the cases[32] address this issue in terms of whether the dangerous defect was

guard to cover chain that ripped off worker's fingers):

> To impose responsibility on the supplier of the chain in the context of the larger defectively designed machine system would simply extend liability too far. This would mean that suppliers would be required to hire machine design experts to scrutinize machine systems that the supplier had no role in developing. Suppliers would be forced to provide modifications and attach warnings on machines which they never designed nor manufactured. Mere suppliers cannot be expected to guarantee the safety of other manufacturers' machinery.

Lee v. Butcher Boy, 215 Cal.Rptr. 195, 199 (Ct. App. 1985) (motor manufacturer, which played no role in design of meat grinder into which motor was integrated, not liable for plaintiff's injuries when hand caught and injured in machine—component part manufacturers who play no role in designing finished products who supply non-defective component parts not liable for the defective design of finished product); Shawver v. Roberts Corp., 280 N.W.2d 226 (Wis. 1979) (manufacturer of conveyor not liable for injury caused by conveyor's integration with electrical control system). See also Zaza v. Marquess & Nell, Inc., 675 A.2d 620, 629 (N.J. 1996) (fabricator of sheetmetal tank for complex machine not liable for failing to supply safety devices which specifications showed would be provided by owner) (most courts hold that "a manufacturer of a component part, which is not dangerous until it is integrated by the owner into a larger system, cannot be held strictly liable to an injured employee for the failure of the owner and/or assembler to install safety devices, so long as the specifications provided are not so obviously dangerous that it would be unreasonable to follow them"):

> Holding defendant liable would impose upon a component part fabricator . . . the duty to investigate whether the use of its non-defective product would be made dangerous by the integration of that product into the complex system designed and installed by experts. Component fabricators would become insurers for the mistakes and failures of the owners and installers to follow their own plans. Defendant would have to retain an expert to determine whether each and every inte-

grated manufacturing system that incorporates one of its sheet metal products is reasonably safe for its intended use.

Id. at 634; Childress v. Gresen Mfg. Co., 888 F.2d 45, 49 (6th Cir. 1989) (Mich. law) (manufacturer of hydraulic valve not liable for its use in log-splitting machine) (noting the "marked difference between knowing the identity of the equipment into which a component part will be integrated and anticipating any hazardous operation by that equipment that might be facilitated by the addition of the component part. Indeed, extending the duty to make a product safe to the manufacturer of a non-defective component part would be tantamount to charging a component part manufacturer with knowledge that is superior to that of the completed product manufacturer").

**31.** See, e.g., Springmeyer v. Ford Motor Co., 71 Cal.Rptr.2d 190, 194–97 (Ct. App. 1998) (supplier of defective fan blade used on engines in Ford trucks liable for resulting injuries because it helped Ford in design and testing of blade); Pasquale v. Speed Prods. Eng'g, 654 N.E.2d 1365 (Ill. 1995) (supplier of can for bellhousing used in race car engine may have participated in design of can with bellhousing manufacturer).

**32.** See, e.g., Haase v. Badger Mining Corp., 669 N.W.2d 737 (Wis. Ct. App. 2003), aff'd on other grounds, 682 N.W.2d 389 (Wis. 2004); Artiglio v. General Elec. Co., 71 Cal.Rptr.2d 817 (Ct. App. 1998) (supplier of silicone used in breast implants had no duty to warn); Davis v. Pak–Mor Mfg. Co., 672 N.E.2d 771 (Ill. App. Ct. 1996); Depre v. Power Climber, Inc., 635 N.E.2d 542 (Ill. App. Ct. 1994); Davis v. Berwind Corp., 640 A.2d 1289, 1299–1300 (Pa. Super. Ct. 1994); Shawver v. Roberts Corp., 280 N.W.2d 226, 232–33 (Wis. 1979); Union Supply Co. v. Pust, 583 P.2d 276, 281–83 (Colo. 1978) (en banc); Burbage v. Boiler Eng'g & Supply Co., 249 A.2d 563 (Pa. 1969); Suvada v. White Motor Co., 210 N.E.2d 182 (Ill. 1965).

Some courts shield the component supplier from liability in such cases only if the change or alteration is unforeseeable. See, e.g., Davis v. Pak–Mor Mfg. Co., 672 N.E.2d 771 (Ill. App. Ct. 1996); Gabler v. Robbins & Myers, Inc., 895 S.W.2d 79 (Mo. Ct. App. 1995) (because substantial alterations to hoist when integrated into dumbwaiter

in the component at the time it left the component supplier's control, or whether the danger was introduced into the product through "further processing or other substantial change" by the manufacturer-assembler of the finished product.[33] Indeed, § 402A declares that a seller is subject to strict products liability in tort only if the product "is expected to and does reach the user or consumer without substantial change in the condition in which it is sold."[34] The *Restatement (Third) of Torts: Products Liability* focuses more precisely on the circumstances that may give rise to liability for suppliers of component parts. Section 5 provides that a component part supplier is subject to liability caused by a product into which the component is integrated only if (1) the component itself is defective, or (2) the seller "substantially participates" in a dangerously defective integration of the component into the design of the finished product.[35]

---

were foreseeable and did not substantially change the operation of the hoist, hoist supplier was subject to liability). But if the change in the component is extensive (even if it is foreseeable), the component supplier may be protected from liability by the doctrine of proximate cause. See, e.g., Woods v. Graham Eng'g Corp., 539 N.E.2d 316, 319–20 (Ill. App. Ct. 1989).

**33.** See Restatement (2d) Torts § 402A cmt. *p*, entitled "Further processing or substantial change," which provides in part:

It seems reasonably clear that the mere fact that the product is to undergo processing, or other substantial change, will not in all cases relieve the seller of liability under the rule stated in this Section. If, for example, raw coffee beans are sold to a buyer who roasts and packs them for sale to the ultimate consumer, it cannot be supposed that the seller will be relieved of all liability when the raw beans are contaminated with arsenic, or some other poison.... On the other hand, the manufacturer of pig iron, which is capable of a wide variety of uses, is not so likely to be held to strict liability when it turns out to be unsuitable for the child's tricycle into which it is finally made by a remote buyer. The question is essentially one of whether the responsibility for discovery and prevention of the dangerous defect is shifted to the intermediate party who is to make the changes. No doubt there will be some situations, and some defects, as to which the responsibility will be shifted, and others in which it will not.

Comment *q*, entitled "Component parts," provides in part that a question which arises in such cases is "whether the responsibility is not shifted to the assembler. It is no doubt to be expected that where there is no change in the component part itself, but it is merely incorporated into something larger, the strict liability will be found to

carry through to the ultimate user or consumer."

Compare, with comment *p*'s pig iron tricycle example, States Steamship Co. v. Stone Manganese Marine, Ltd., 371 F.Supp. 500 (D.N.J. 1973). This was a suit brought by a shipowner against the manufacturer of alloy ingots which were cast into propellers and installed on plaintiff's ships by a third party shipyard. The alloy was inadequate for the job, and several of the propeller blades fractured causing various damage. Defendant argued that casting the ingots into propellers was a "substantial change" in their condition, precluding liability under § 402A. The court thought this "too simplistic a reading of Section 402A(1)(b)," pointing out that at issue were "the qualities of the alloy, regardless of its shape." Id. at 505

**34.** Restatement (2d) Torts § 402A (1)(b).

**35.** Products Liability Restatement § 5, entitled "Liability of Commercial Seller or Distributor of Product Components for Harm Caused by Products Into Which Components Are Integrated" provides in full:

One engaged in the business of selling or otherwise distributing product components who sells or distributes a component is subject to liability for harm to persons or property caused by a product into which the component is integrated if:

(a) the component is defective in itself, as defined in this Chapter, and the defect causes the harm; or

(b)(1) the seller or distributor of the component substantially participates in the integration of the component into the design of the product; and

(2) the integration of the component causes the product to be defective, as defined in this Chapter; and

(3) the defect in the product causes the harm.

Because § 5 clearly and faithfully distills much of the rather confused prior case law, the courts have begun to rely upon this section of the *Products Liability Restatement* as an authoritative statement of applicable principles of law.[36] For example, in *Buonanno v. Colmar Belting Co.*,[37] a worker's arm was caught and injured in the unguarded nip point of a conveyor belt system at the point where the belt moved over the stationary "wing pulley." In a negligence and strict products liability in tort action against both the manufacturer of the wing pulley and the supplier of the various component parts of the conveyor system, principally for failing to shield the conveyor system's nip point, a majority of the court upheld summary judgment for the wing pulley manufacturer, ruling that the wing pulley component was not "defective in itself," under § 5(a):

> [T]he nip point is created only when the belt meets the wing pulley after the entire conveyor belt system is assembled. There was no evidence presented to suggest that a single, isolated wing pulley presents a danger. Therefore, the wing pulley is not defective "in itself" or "at the time of sale or distribution," but only creates the potential for injury when integrated into the conveyor-belt system.[38]

As for § 5(b), the court ruled that there was some evidence that the distributor of the various component parts had substantially participated in the conveyor system design but no evidence that the wing pulley manufacturer had participated at all in the design of the integrated system. Hence, the court reversed the summary judgment for the distributor of the conveyor system's various component parts, remanding for a trial on the issue of whether it had substantially participated in the conveyor system's design.[39]

The *Buonanno* decision was split, however, on two issues, illustrating the difficulty of many of the cases dealing with the liability of component part manufacturers. Two of the justices thought that, in the case against the wing pulley manufacturer, the plaintiff had presented sufficient evidence that the pulley could have been designed in a safer manner that would have reduced the risk of harm, rendering the pulley defectively designed "in itself" under § 5(a).[40] And, while four of the justices thought that the wing pulley manufacturer "had no duty to warn against any injuries caused by the final integrated product since it had no involvement with the design of the entire system,"[41] one justice asserted that there was sufficient evidence to find the pulley defective in itself under § 5(a) because of the absence of a "warning on the pulley itself that would alert users to the nip-point danger."[42]

---

**36.** See, e.g., Bostrom Seating, Inc. v. Crane Carrier Co., 140 S.W.3d 681 (Tex. 2004); Gray v. Badger Mining Corp., 676 N.W.2d 268 (Minn. 2004); Jimenez v. Superior Court, 58 P.3d 450 (Cal. 2002); Scheman–Gonzalez v. Saber Mfg. Co., 816 So.2d 1133 (Fla. Dist. Ct. App. 2002); Davis v. Komatsu Am. Indus. Corp., 42 S.W.3d 34 (Tenn. 2001); Buonanno v. Colmar Belting Co., Inc., 733 A.2d 712 (R.I. 1999).

**37.** 733 A.2d 712 (R.I. 1999).

**38.** Id. at 717.

**39.** See id. at 719–20.

**40.** See id. at 717–18.

**41.** Id. at 714.

**42.** Id. at 721.

Indeed, § 5 is not entirely clear with respect to the most difficult issue in many component part cases—the component supplier's duty to warn the manufacturer-assembler and, possibly, even ultimate users. Section 5(a) provides that a component supplier is liable for providing a component that is defective in itself, and a product may be defective under *Products Liability Restatement* § 2(c) if the supplier fails to provide adequate warnings or instructions, a point made clear in § 5 comment *b*. But comment *b* also asserts that "when a sophisticated buyer integrates a component into another product, the component seller owes no duty to warn either the immediate buyer or ultimate consumers of dangers arising because the component is unsuited for the special purpose to which the buyer puts it," even if the component supplier is aware of "the component purchaser's lack of expertise and ignorance of the risks of integrating the component into the purchaser's product."[43]

While much of the case law supports the view that component part makers have no duty to warn beyond the manufacturer-assembler,[44] reason suggests that, for warnings to be effective, they sometimes will have to be transmitted through, over, or around the manufacturer-assembler directly to end users.[45] Comment *b* to § 5 does acknowledge that such cases may be covered by the doctrine of negligent entrustment, which is ordinarily a better vehicle for addressing this small subset of cases concerning component supplier liability. But courts may wish to define a general duty for suppliers of raw materials and component parts to warn of dangers they know are likely to injure consumers from the manner in which manufacturer-assemblers integrate the components into finished products.[46] However the law chooses to protect consumers in cases of this type, surely component suppliers will not be immunized from liability for failing to provide effective warnings of serious product hazards by permitting them to hide behind the coattails of finished product manufacturers in every case.[47]

---

**43.** Products Liability Restatement § 5 cmt. *b*.

**44.** Particularly the spate of cases shielding Du Pont from responsibility for the massive injuries resulting from the inappropriate use of Du Pont's Teflon, by a small medical device company that promptly went bankrupt, in jaw implants for treating TMJ syndrome. See, e.g., In re TMJ Implants Prod. Liab. Litig., 872 F.Supp. 1019 (D. Minn. 1995), aff'd 97 F.3d 1050 (8th Cir. 1996) (summary judgment in multidistrict case granted in favor of Du Pont; *held*, raw-material supplier or component-part manufacturer has no duty to warn consumers directly of defects in the integrated products, purportedly the rule in all jurisdictions); Hoyt v. Vitek, Inc., 894 P.2d 1225 (Or. Ct. App. 1995); Apperson v. E.I. Du Pont De Nemours & Co., 41 F.3d 1103 (7th Cir. 1994) (Ill. law); Klem v. E.I. Du Pont De Nemours Co., 19 F.3d 997 (5th Cir. 1994) (La. law); Bond v. E.I. Du Pont De Nemours & Co., 868 P.2d 1114 (Colo. Ct. App. 1994); Longo v. E.I. Du Pont De Nem-

ours & Co., 632 So.2d 1193 (La. Ct. App. 1993). See also In re Silicone Gel Breast Implants Prods. Liab. Litig., 887 F.Supp. 1463 (N.D. Ala. 1995).

**45.** See, e.g., Beauchamp v. Russell, 547 F.Supp. 1191, 1197 (N.D. Ga. 1982); Gryc v. Dayton–Hudson Corp., 297 N.W.2d 727 (Minn. 1980); Suchomajcz v. Hummel Chem. Co., 524 F.2d 19, 25–27 (3d Cir. 1975) (Pa. law). See Restatement (2d) Torts § 388 cmt. *n*.

**46.** See, e.g., Hunnings v. Texaco, Inc., 29 F.3d 1480 (11th Cir. 1994) (Fla. law) (manufacturers and suppliers of mineral spirits sold in bulk, which they knew retailers were routinely repackaging and selling in milk containers without adequate warnings, were subject to negligence liability).

**47.** "[M]anufacturers do not enjoy blanket protection from liability simply because others in the chain of distribution may repackage or reformulate the product before it reaches the ultimate consumer." Id. at 1485.

In summary, a supplier of raw materials or component parts normally has no duty to warn end users of risks arising out of the incorporation of the component into a larger, finished product. But on rare occasions, when a component supplier knows that a manufacturer-assembler has used or intends to use its components in a way that is likely to be unreasonably dangerous to consumers,[48] the component supplier should not be shielded by a blanket no-duty rule but should be required to take reasonable steps to protect consumers from an unreasonable risk of harm. Often these steps may involve no more than effectively notifying the manufacturer-assembler of the safety problem, how to remedy it, and the manufacturer-assembler's obligation to do so. If the danger is great enough, however, and if the component supplier knows that the manufacturer-assembler is unlikely to address the danger effectively, then logic suggests that the component supplier should have a duty to monitor the situation and, if the problem is not resolved, to take whatever steps may reasonably be required of a component supplier in the circumstances to protect consumers from unreasonable risks of harm arising from the component's use in the finished product.[49]

## § 15.4  PARENT AND APPARENT MANUFACTURERS; FRANCHISERS

Sometimes a plaintiff injured in a product accident seeks recovery beyond the manufacturer from some other, perhaps more solvent, defendant who profitably exploited another company's manufacture and sale of the accident product. Parent corporations of manufacturing subsidiaries are one such possible defendant, as are trademark-holders who license their mark to other companies who make and sell a product. Parent corporations and trademark-holders reap the commercial benefits of products designed, manufactured, and/or marketed substantially or wholly by their subsidiaries or trademark licensees. The latter, as product manufacturers, are of course subject to the normal rules of products liability law, but sometimes subsidiaries are thinly capitalized, and trademark licensees and franchisees typically are small enterprises in comparison to their licensors or franchisers. This section briefly examines when a parent corporation, trademark-holder, or franchiser which profits from the manufacture and sale of products by a related company is insulated from liability, and when such a nonmanufacturing but related enterprise may be subject to liability for product-caused harm.

### Parent Corporations—Alter Ego Liability

Ordinarily, of course, fundamental principles of corporate law shield shareholders from the debts and other liabilities of the corporation.

---

**48.** Perhaps by prior lawsuits concerning the same danger in which they both were defendants. See, e.g., Speer v. Wheelabrator Corp., 826 F.Supp. 1264, 1272–73 (D. Kan. 1993).

**49.** Sometimes reasonable care will require providing warnings directly to end users; other times it may require terminating sales to the offending manufacturer-assembler of the finished product; and on rare occasions it may require informing safety agencies or law enforcement authorities. See, e.g., Hunnings v. Texaco, Inc., 29 F.3d 1480 (11th Cir. 1994) (Fla. law); Suchomajcz v. Hummel Chem. Co., 524 F.2d 19 (3d Cir. 1975) (Pa. law).

Indeed, shareholder immunity from the enterprise's liabilities is an essential pillar of the corporate form of organization,[1] and courts are exceedingly reluctant to allow inroads into this basic tenet of corporate limited liability.[2] Thus, when a parent corporation owns much, or all, of the stock of a financially unstable subsidiary corporation, the separate identities of the two corporations normally precludes creditors of the subsidiary from obtaining relief from the parent corporation.

As strong as the limited shareholder liability principle may be, a court may nevertheless allow the "corporate veil" to be "pierced" in certain limited situations.[3] Among the various theories for holding a parent corporation responsible for the defective products of its manufacturing subsidiary,[4] the principal derivative basis is "alter ego" liability, a theory grounded in the idea that the parent so dominates the subsidiary that they are essentially a single economic entity.[5] "[W]hen a corporation is so controlled as to be the alter ego or mere instrumentality of its stockholder, the corporate form may be disregarded in the interests of justice."[6] This "disregarding" of the corporate form, allowing a subsidiary corporation's creditor to reach the parent corporation, is often called "piercing the corporate veil."[7]

For the plaintiff to prevail on an "alter ego" claim, many jurisdictions require that the plaintiff show *both* that (1) the parent and subsidiary acted as a single economic entity, and (2) some injustice,

---

**§ 15.4**

**1.** "Limited liability is a distinguishing feature of corporate law—perhaps *the* distinguishing feature." F. Easterbrook and D. Fischel, The Economic Structure of Corporate Law 40 (1991). See generally 1 W. Fletcher, Fletcher Cyclopedia Corporations § 41.35 (Perm. ed.) (1999); 1 J. Cox and T. Hazen, Corporations § 7.07 at 271 (2d ed., 2003) ("limited shareholder liability is not simply a principle of corporate law, but a cornerstone of capitalism"); H. Henn and J. Alexander, Law of Corporations and other Business Enterprises § 202, 547 (3d ed. 1983) ("limited liability of shareholders is probably the most significant attribute of the modern corporation").

**2.** "Limited liability," according to Justice Douglas, "is the rule not the exception; and on that assumption large undertakings are rested, vast enterprises are launched, and huge sums of capital attracted." Anderson v. Abbott, 321 U.S. 349, 362 (1944).

**3.** See F. Gevurtz, Corporation Law § 1.5 (2000); F. Easterbrook and D. Fischel, The Economic Structure of Corporate Law 54 et seq. (1991); P. Blumberg, The Law of Corporate Groups—Substantive Law ch. 13 (1987); R. Clark, Corporate Law § 2.4, at 71 n.1 (1986) (collecting articles); Hansmann and Kraakman, Toward Unlimited Shareholder Liability for Corporate Torts, 100 Yale L.J. 1879 (1991); Thompson, Piercing the Corporate Veil: An Empirical Study, 76 Cornell L. Rev. 1036, 1058 (1991) (courts pierce veil about thirty percent of time in tort cases); Notes, 1996 U. Ill. L. Rev. 1059 (veil piercing); 29 Rutgers L.J. 121 (1997) (breast implant victims' efforts to reach Dow Chemical); Annot., 7 A.L.R.3d 1343 (1966) (liability of corporation for torts of subsidiary).

**4.** For examples of both derivative and direct theories of recovery, see, e.g., Dow Chem. Co. v. Mahlum, 970 P.2d 98, 106 (Nev. 1998) (reversing findings on (1) fraudulent concealment of dangers in silicone breast implants, (2) concert of action, and (3) aiding and abetting, but allowing claim on negligent undertaking); Fletcher v. Atex, Inc., 68 F.3d 1451 (2d Cir. 1995) (Del. law) (affirming summary judgment for defendant on each of four theories of liability: (1) alter ego, (2) agency and apparent agency, (3) apparent manufacturer, and (4) concerted tortious action). See also In re Silicone Gel Breast Implants Products Liab. Litig., 887 F.Supp. 1447 (N.D. Ala. 1995) (allowing alter ego and negligent undertaking claims against Bristol–Meyers Squibb).

**5.** See, e.g., Fletcher v. Atex, Inc., 68 F.3d 1451, 1456 (2d Cir. 1995) (Del. law).

**6.** In re Silicone Gel Breast Implants Prods. Liab. Litig., 887 F.Supp. 1447, 1452 (N.D. Ala. 1995).

**7.** See, e.g., Patin v. Thoroughbred Power Boats Inc., 294 F.3d 640, 647–49 (5th Cir. 2002) (Fla. law).

unfairness, or improper conduct by the defendant.[8] Whether a parent and subsidiary acted as a single economic entity depends upon a variety of factors, including: whether they had common directors and officers; whether the subsidiary was adequately capitalized for its undertaking; whether it was solvent at the relevant time; whether it paid dividends, kept corporate records, and observed other corporate formalities; whether its officers and directors operated according to regular corporate form; whether the parent siphoned off the subsidiary's funds; and whether, more generally, the subsidiary corporation served merely as "a facade for the dominant shareholder."[9]

The opinions of Chief Judge Pointer in *In re Silicone Gel Breast Implants Products Liability Litigation*[10] illustrate the "substantial domination" rule in action. Arising out of injuries resulting from the surgical implantation of silicone gel breast implants in many thousands of women over many years,[11] *In re Breast Implants* was a consolidated multi-district action in federal court in which thousands of plaintiffs sought recovery from the implant manufacturers and related companies for systemic autoimmune system diseases caused by silicone leaking from the implants into the body. The principal implant supplier, Dow Corning, was jointly owned by Dow Chemical Company and Corning Incorporated, and another implant supplier, Medical Engineering Corporation (MEC), was solely owned by Bristol–Meyers Squibb Company. Because neither Dow Corning nor MEC had sufficient assets to meet the massive

---

**8.**  Fletcher v. Atex, Inc., 68 F.3d 1451, 1456 (2d Cir. 1995) (Del. law). "[F]raud or wrongdoing is not necessary under an alter ego theory, but the plaintiff must demonstrate an overall element of injustice or unfairness." Id. at 1458. "It is well settled that a parent corporation, even one that owns all the stock of a subsidiary corporation is not subject to liability for the acts of its subsidiary unless the parent so controls the operation of the subsidiary as to make it a mere adjunct, instrumentality, or alter ego of the parent corporation. However, the mere domination or control of a corporation by its stockholder cannot be enough to allow a piercing of the corporate veil; rather, there must be the added elements of misuse and harm or loss resulting from the misuse." In re Birmingham Asbestos Litig., 619 So.2d 1360, 1362 (Ala. 1993) (citations omitted). See, e.g., Patin v. Thoroughbred Power Boats Inc., 294 F.3d 640, 647 (5th Cir. 2002) (Fla. law) ("a plaintiff must prove both: (1) that the corporation is a 'mere instrumentality' or alter ego of the defendant; and (2) that the defendant engaged in 'improper conduct' in the formation or use of the corporation"); Binder v. Bristo–Squibb, Co., 184 F.Supp.2d 762, 772 (N.D. Ill. 2001) (Del. law) (alter-ego relationship may exist if parent exercises complete domination and control over subsidiary, or if it fails to pay attention to corporate formalities and engages in "fraud or something like it"). See generally F. Ge-

vurtz, Corporation Law § 1.5, at 76 (2000) (discussing second, "fraud, wrong or injustice," prong).

**9.**  See, e.g., McConkey v. McGhan Med. Corp., 144 F.Supp.2d 958, 962–63 (E.D. Tenn. 2000) (listing eleven relevant factors); Fletcher v. Atex, Inc., 68 F.3d 1451, 1458 (2d Cir. 1995) (Del. law); In re Silicone Gel Breast Implants Prods. Liab. Litig., 887 F.Supp. 1447, 1452 (N.D. Ala. 1995) (listing eleven substantial-domination factors). See generally F. Gevurtz, Corporation Law § 1.5 (2000) (discussing the requirements).

See also In re Birmingham Asbestos Litig., 619 So.2d 1360 (Ala. 1993) (no liability for subsidiary's actions unless parent exerts so much control over subsidiary's operations as to render parent its alter ego).

**10.**  837 F.Supp. 1128 (N.D. Ala. 1993); 887 F.Supp. 1447 (N.D. Ala. 1995).

**11.**  See Hellwege, Plaintiffs Score Victories in Breast Implant Cases, 35 Trial 16 (March 1999); Notes, Breast Implants as Beauty Ritual: Woman's Sceptre and Prison, 9 Yale J.L. & Feminism 157 (1997); 'Milking the Dow': Compensating the Victims of Silicone Gel Breast Implants at the Expense of the Parent Corporation, 29 Rutgers L.J. 121 (1997) (examining breast implant victims' efforts to reach Dow Chemical); Silicone, Science and Settlements: Breast Implants and a Search for Truth, 63 Def. Couns. J. 491 (1996).

damages claims of thousands of plaintiffs,[12] relief was also sought from the implant suppliers' much larger parent corporations.

Judge Pointer's treatment of the two parent-subsidiary sets in these cases is instructive in understanding when a court may allow a plaintiff to reach a parent corporation in products liability litigation. First dismissing the derivative, alter-ego claims against both parent corporations of Dow Corning,[13] Judge Pointer later allowed such a claim against MEC's parent, Bristol–Meyers Squibb,[14] and also allowed the plaintiffs to maintain direct liability claims against Dow Chemical based on that parent corporation's own alleged misconduct in researching silicone toxicity.[15]

In the litigation involving Dow Corning, owned jointly by Dow Chemical and Corning, Judge Pointer found that the parent corporations did not dominate the control of their subsidiary. "Dow Corning," wrote Judge Pointer, "has observed all corporate formalities, including but not limited to, maintaining its own books, filing its own tax returns; hiring its own auditor; employing its own officers, management, and workers; owning and operating its own plants in seven states and nine countries; holding its own stockholders' and directors' meetings; and, in recent years, paying regular dividends."[16] Such facts, in Judge Pointer's view, "clearly demonstrate a separate corporate existence for Dow Corning, recognized and respected by it and its parent corporations."[17] Accordingly, Dow Chemical and Corning were not derivatively liable for the actions of their subsidiary.[18]

In the litigation involving MEC, owned entirely by Bristol–Meyers Squibb, the facts concerning the relationship between parent and subsidiary were quite different. Applying the substantial-domination factors listed above,[19] the evidence revealed that "two of MEC's three directors were Bristol directors; MEC was part of Bristol's Health Care group and used Bristol's legal, auditing, and communications departments; MEC and Bristol filed consolidated federal tax returns and Bristol prepared consolidated financial reports; Bristol operated as MEC's finance company . . . ; Bristol effectively used MEC's resources as its own by obtaining interest on MEC's money and requiring MEC to make requests for capital appropriations to obtain its own funds; some members of MEC's board were not aware that MEC has a board of directors, let alone that they were members; and the senior Bristol member of MEC's board could not be out-voted by the other two directors."[20] In short, a jury

---

**12.** Dow Corning petitioned for bankruptcy protection on May 15, 1995. See, e.g., Dow Chem. Co. v. Mahlum, 970 P.2d 98, 106 (Nev. 1998).

**13.** In re Silicone Gel Breast Implants Prods. Liab. Litig., 837 F.Supp. 1128 (N.D. Ala. 1993).

**14.** In re Silicone Gel Breast Implants Prods. Liab. Litig., 887 F.Supp. 1447 (N.D. Ala. 1995).

**15.** Id. at 1455.

**16.** In re Silicone Gel Breast Implants Prods. Liab. Litig., 837 F.Supp. 1128, 1133 (N.D. Ala. 1993).

**17.** Id. at 1134.

**18.** Id. at 1138.

**19.** The court applied many of a list of eleven separate factors relevant to the substantial domination issue. 887 F.Supp. at 1452.

**20.** Id. at 1452–53.

"could—and, under the laws of many states probably should—find that MEC was but the alter ego of Bristol."[21]

While it is difficult for a plaintiff injured by a subsidiary's product to prevail against the parent corporation on the alter-ego theory of liability,[22] other theories of liability may be available. In the breast implant litigation in particular, both Judge Pointer[23] and the Nevada Supreme Court[24] allowed claims against Dow Chemical on a negligent performance of an undertaking theory, under *Restatement (Second) of Torts § 324A*, based on Dow Corning's reliance for many years on Dow Chemical's negligent toxicity testing of Dow Corning's silicones.[25] "[A] cause of action under § 324A does not involve an assertion of derivative liability but one of direct liability, since it is based on the actions of the defendant itself."[26] So, while the alter-ego theory may be the traditional derivative liability route for reaching the parent of an underfunded manufacturing subsidiary, a parent's active participation in the subsidiary's affairs can make it vulnerable on some other, direct theory of liability.[27]

### Apparent Manufacturers

The "apparent manufacturer" theory imposes liability on a manufacturer or seller if it holds itself out to the public as the manufacturer of a product. For a statement of this theory, most courts turn to *Restatement (Second) of Torts § 400*: "One who puts out as his own product a chattel manufactured by another is subject to the same liability as though he were its manufacturer."[28] This doctrine would apply, for example, to the sale by Sears of a power drill manufactured by Black and Decker, but sold by Sears under its "Kenmore" brand name. If the drill were defective and injured a user, the user could hold Sears liable as if it were Black and Decker. So, if Black and Decker were subject to either negligence or strict liability, Sears, derivatively, would be liable as well.[29] While some courts have held parent and other up-stream defendants

---

**21.**  Id. at 1452.

**22.**  Nelson v. International Paint Co., 734 F.2d 1084 (5th Cir. 1984) (Tex. law) (ruling no alter ego).

**23.**  In re Silicone Gel Breast Implants Prods. Liab. Litig., 887 F.Supp. 1455 (N.D. Ala. 1995).

**24.**  Dow Chem. Co. v. Mahlum, 970 P.2d 98 (Nev. 1998).

**25.**  On the negligent undertaking theory, plaintiffs alleged that Dow Chemical was negligent in marketing silicone-gel implants without having conducted reasonable tests and research on the toxicity, biological activity, and safety of silicones to determine their safety for use in breast implants. 887 F.Supp. at 1460.

**26.**  Id.

**27.**  Other claims in In re Silicone Gel Prods. Liab. Litig., 887 F.Supp. 1455 (N.D.

Ala. 1995), which Judge Pointer did not then address, included "strict liability, corporate conspiracy, concert of action, aiding and abetting, fraud, and fraudulent concealment." Id. at 1462.

**28.**  Restatement (2d) Torts § 400.

**29.**  The actor puts out a chattel as his own product in two types of cases. The first is where the actor appears to be the manufacturer of the chattel. The second is where the chattel appears to have been made particularly for the actor. In the first type of case the actor frequently causes the chattel to be used in reliance upon his care in making it; in the second, he frequently causes the chattel to be used in reliance upon a belief that he has required it to be made properly for him and that the actor's reputation is an assurance to the user of the quality of the product.

Restatement (2d) Torts § 400 cmt. *d*.

liable on this basis, most of the cases involve retailers or other distributors holding themselves out as the product's manufacturer.[30]

An underlying rationale for the apparent manufacturer doctrine is that a retail seller or other defendant cannot avoid responsibility as a manufacturer if it represents itself to be the product's manufacturer, or sponsor, in order to induce consumers to buy the product. Being a species of estoppel, liability resting on a defendant's "holding out" itself as a product's manufacturer[31] is based upon the idea that a "vendor who, through its labeling or advertising of a product, caused the public to believe that it was the manufacturer and to buy the product in reliance on the vendor's reputation and care in making it, was held to have assumed the obligations of a manufacturer and to be estopped to deny its identity as the manufacturer."[32]

Courts have allowed recovery on the basis of a defendant's holding itself out as the manufacturer, or sponsor, of a product in a variety of cases. Courts allow recovery where a manufacturer places the retailer's label in garments sold by the retailer;[33] where a seller places its private label on a product without disclosing the actual manufacturer;[34] where a retailer holds out a defective attic stairway to the public as its own by listing the product in its catalogue, and providing its own name and model number on the product instruction sheet;[35] where a retailer places an assembled product on a sales rack without giving any notice that another entity assembled the product;[36] and in other similar situations.[37]

When the apparent manufacturer doctrine was first set forth in § 400 of the *Restatement of Torts* in 1934, it expressed a bold new way to hold sellers strictly liable in tort for production errors made by manufac-

---

**30.** See Hebel v. Sherman Equip., 442 N.E.2d 199, 201 (Ill. 1982).

**31.** " 'Holding out' cases usually involve either (a) a defendant's labeling or affixing to the product its own name, trade name, or trademark; or (b) advertising identifying the defendant as the maker of the product." Id. at 202.

**32.** Id. at 201. See also id. at 201–02 ("where a defendant puts out a product as its own, the purchaser has no means of ascertaining the identity of the true manufacturer, and it is thus fair to impose liability on the party whose actions effectively conceal the true manufacturer's identity").

**33.** Morgan v. Sears, Roebuck & Co., 693 F.Supp. 1154 (N.D. Ga. 1988), superseded by 700 F.Supp. 1574 (N.D. Ga. 1988).

**34.** See, e.g., Kennedy v. Guess, Inc., 765 N.E.2d 213, 222 (Ind. Ct. App. 2002) (defendant subject to liability for placing logo on defective umbrella manufactured by another company: "Where one labels a product as a 'designer label' product and places it into the stream of commerce, the consumer is induced to believe that the product he receives is of a superior quality."); Yoder v. Honeywell, Inc., 104 F.3d 1215 (10th Cir. 1997) (Colo. law).

**35.** Landry v. State Farm Fire & Cas. Co., 504 So.2d 171 (La. Ct. App. 1987).

**36.** Long v. United States Brass Corp., 333 F.Supp.2d 999 (D. Colo. 2004) (pipe manufactured by third party was sold together with bolts stamped with defendant's logo); Lou ex rel. Chen v. Otis Elevator Co., 2004 WL 504697 (Mass. Super. 2004) (defendant granted another company right to use its name on escalator); Coulon v. Wal–Mart Stores, Inc., 734 So.2d 916 (La. Ct. App. 1999).

**37.** See, e.g., Andujar v. Sears, Roebuck & Co., 597 N.Y.S.2d 78 (App. Div. 1993) (retailer of table saw that held itself out as manufacturer owed duty to customers to test saw for design defects); Warzynski v. Empire Comfort Sys., Inc., 401 S.E.2d 801 (N.C. Ct. App. 1991) (advertisements referred only to distributor, warranty bore only distributor's name, and product packaging did not name manufacturer). *But see* CSX Transp. v. Matweld, Inc., 828 So.2d 910 (Ala. 2002) (Fla. law) (although defendant's label affixed to product, apparent-manufacturer statute was inapplicable because defendant did not assemble product but merely sold it in same condition it received it from manufacturer).

turers who were often hard to identify and who were still immunized even from negligence liability in many jurisdictions by privity of contract. But with the fall of the privity defense, with the spread of effective discovery techniques for uncovering both the identity and production methods of manufacturers, and, most importantly, with the adoption of a general doctrine of strict products liability in tort in the 1960s and 1970s, § 400 and the apparent manufacturer doctrine has now become quaintly obsolete.[38] Although the principle has some lingering, secondary value as a component issue in the trademark-licensor and franchiser doctrines discussed below, the apparent manufacturer doctrine has little remaining independent value as a theory of liability. Thus, there seems little reason for a court to adopt the rule if it has not already done so.[39] Perhaps because a majority of jurisdictions are said to follow the rule,[40] but acknowledging that the rule has "little practical significance,"[41] the American Law Institute curiously readopted this harmless but now essentially hollow doctrine one more time in the *Third Restatement*.[42] And while the apparent manufacturer doctrine may find sporadic service from time to time in peculiar contexts, one may confidently predict that it will not appear in the *Fourth Restatement*.

### Trademark Licensors; Franchisers

Cases involving trademarks and franchises are a species of apparent manufacturer cases—the consumer is led to believe by the mark or name that the trademark holder or franchiser is responsible for the quality of the product. Owners of trademarks and trade names license their marks, names, and processes in order to induce consumers to buy or use a product based on the reputation for product quality possessed by the holder of the mark or name. Consumer reliance on the owner's reputation rests on an assumption, based on an implicit representation of the owner (often a franchiser), that the owner has contributed in substantial measure to the quality of the product sold by the licensee or franchisee. If a person is injured by a product manufactured by one company, but bearing the name or logo of another, a question that arises is whether the trademark owner is subject to the responsibility of the manufacturer despite the fact that the product was manufactured by someone else. The central issue in this type of case is whether the trademark owner or franchiser should be permitted to commercially exploit the value of its reputation without a corresponding responsibility—whether such a party should be accountable for defects in products sold under its name or mark. If the licensor exercised substantial control over the production, marketing, or distribution of a product, the licensor is subject to liability

**38.** See Hebel v. Sherman Equip., 442 N.E.2d 199, 202 (Ill. 1982) (the purpose of the doctrine was to provide a remedy against the retailer, who now is subject to strict liability in tort: "The function of the apparent-manufacturer doctrine has, as it were, been absorbed by the theory of sellers' strict liability in tort for injuries caused by unreasonably unsafe products.").

**39.** See, e.g., Seasword v. Hilti, Inc., 537 N.W.2d 221 (Mich. 1995) (no reason to adopt apparent manufacturer doctrine since jurisdiction holds nonmanufacturing sellers strictly liable anyway).

**40.** Products Liability Restatement § 14 Reporters' Note.

**41.** Products Liability Restatement § 14 cmt. *b.*

**42.** Products Liability Restatement § 14.

for injuries caused by a defect in the product distributed by a licensee.[43] The case for the franchiser's liability is enhanced, of course, if it designed the product itself.[44]

The liability principles applicable to trademark licenses are illustrated in an early case, *Kosters v. Seven–Up Co.*,[45] where the plaintiff was blinded in one eye when a bottle of 7–Up slipped out of a defectively designed carton supplied to the franchisee bottling company by a third party. Seven–Up's liability as a franchiser, the court declared, depended upon a variety of factors: "(1) the risk created by approving for distribution an unsafe product likely to cause injury, (2) the franchisor's ability and opportunity to eliminate the unsafe character of the product and prevent the loss, (3) the consumer's lack of knowledge of danger, and (4) the consumer's reliance on the trade name which gives the intended impression that the franchisor is responsible and stands behind the product."[46] In sum, the court concluded that "[l]iability is based on the franchisor's control and the public's assumption, induced by the franchisor's conduct, that it does in fact control and vouch for the product."[47] Based on these principles, and because the Seven–Up Company had contractually retained control over the design of the cartons, the court held that it was subject to strict liability (in implied warranty) for the carton's design.

The courts widely agree that trademark owners and franchisers that substantially control product safety may be subject to liability for injuries from defective products made and sold by their licensees.[48] The

**43.**   See authorities cited below.

**44.**   See, e.g., Cook v. Branick Mfg., Inc., 736 F.2d 1442 (11th Cir. 1984) (Ala. law).

**45.**   595 F.2d 347 (6th Cir. 1979) (Mich. law).

**46.**   Id. at 353.

**47.**   Id. See also Miller v. McDonald's Corp., 945 P.2d 1107 (Or. Ct. App. 1997) (franchiser could be liable under right to control test for injury from heart-shaped sapphire stone found in Big Mac).

**48.**   See, e.g., Bridgestone/Firestone North America Tire, L.L.C. v. A.P.S. Rent–A–Car & Leasing, Inc., 88 P.3d 572 (Ariz. Ct. App. 2004); Miller v. McDonald's Corp., 945 P.2d 1107 (Or. Ct. App. 1997) (franchiser could be liable under right-to-control test for injury from heart-shaped sapphire stone found in Big Mac); Harrison v. ITT Corp., 603 N.Y.S.2d 826 (App. Div. 1993) (licensor's ability to control quality sufficient); Torres v. Goodyear Tire & Rubber Co., 786 P.2d 939 (Ariz. 1990) (Goodyear subject to strict liability in tort for defects in tires of its subsidiary, Goodyear Great Britain); Cook v. Branick Mfg., Inc., 736 F.2d 1442 (11th Cir. 1984) (Ala. law) (franchiser designed product); Harris v. Aluminum Co. of Am., 550 F.Supp. 1024 (W.D. Va. 1982) (Coke bottle's cap flew off into plaintiff's eye; implied warranty); Connelly v. Uniroyal, Inc., 389 N.E.2d 155, 164 (Ill.

1979) ("A licensor is an integral part of the marketing enterprise, and its participation in the profits reaped by placing a defective product in the stream of commerce presents the same public policy reasons for the applicability of strict liability which supported the imposition of such liability on wholesalers, retailers and lessors."); Kosters v. Seven–Up Co., 595 F.2d 347, 353 (6th Cir. 1979) (Mich. law) (Seven–Up subject to implied warranty liability for defective carton design: "[l]iability is based on the franchiser's control and the public's assumption, induced by the franchiser's conduct, that it does in fact control and vouch for the product"); Carter v. Joseph Bancroft & Sons Co., 360 F.Supp. 1103 (E.D. Pa. 1973) (defendant owners of BAN–LON trademark used on fabrics, garments and articles, made per specifications and quality standards trademark owners prescribed and controlled, liable as manufacturer for flammability of dress that ignited during dinner party); Kasel v. Remington Arms Co., 101 Cal.Rptr. 314, 325 (Ct. App. 1972) (plaintiff, injured when his shotgun exploded, sued Remington because shotgun shells bore Remington trademark; although shells in fact were made by Mexican company, Remington held liable because of its overwhelming control of design and manufacture of the shells). See generally Products

reverse is true, of course, if the trademark owner or franchise licensor does not substantially control a product's safety. While some courts disagree,[49] a trade name franchiser or trademark licensor is not responsible for a product defect merely because the product carries the defendant's name or logo; liability does not attach, in other words, from simply selling a name or mark to a licensee who places it on an unsafe product.[50] This is simply the flip side of the liability coin that bears substantial-control-over-product-safety on its obverse side.

At least one court, *Kennedy v. Guess, Inc.*,[51] has taken an interesting, comparative responsibility approach to the liability of the owners of trademarks and trade names. In *Kennedy*, the plaintiff was injured by a defective umbrella, that bore a "Guess" logo, given to his wife as a gift by a retailer when she purchased a Guess watch. The plaintiff sued Guess for his injuries. Guess defended on the ground that the umbrella had been manufactured by a Hong Kong company, and that Guess had merely sold the use of its logo to a licensee. Unwilling to allow trademark owners and licensors to escape responsibility by avoiding participation in product safety decisions, the court rejected the traditional rule that shields such parties from liability. Instead, the court adopted a principle of comparative responsibility in which a trademark licensor's damages reflect the degree it participated in the product's design, advertising, manufacturing, and distribution.[52] This comparative ap-

---

Liability Restatement § 14 cmt. *d*; 1 Frumer and Friedman, Products Liability § 5.14.

**49.**  See, e.g., Kasel v. Remington Arms Co., 101 Cal.Rptr. 314 (1972) (Remington liable for explosion of shotgun shells, bearing Remington trademark, manufactured by Mexican company), noting that "California has utilized the enterprise-stream of commerce liability concept in the strict liability field without regard for the individual defendant's control over the cause of defect in the product, although such control, if it exists, would remain a significant factor." Id. at 323–24. "[A]s long as the franchisor or trademark licensor can be said to be a link in the marketing enterprise which placed a defective product within the stream of commerce, there is no reason in logic for refusing to apply strict liability in tort to such an entity." Id. at 323.

**50.**  See, e.g., Harrison v. B.F. Goodrich Co., 881 So.2d 288, 292 (Miss. Ct. App. 2004) ("there is no liability for an allegedly defective product on the part of a trademark licensor who was not involved in the design, manufacture, or sale of the product"); Patterson v. Central Mills, Inc., 112 F.Supp.2d 681, 692 (N.D. Ohio 2000) ("Numerous courts have held that a trademark licensor—who does nothing more than permit the use its trademark—is not liable in tort for potential defects in the final product."); Firestone Steel Prod. Co. v. Barajas, 927 S.W.2d 608, 614 (Tex. 1996) (noting that "[a] mere licensor is not subject to strict products liability" and that "[m]ost

jurisdictions require more than the mere act of licensing a design to impose strict products liability," requiring further proof that the licensor also engaged in "some purposeful activity with respect to the design"); Yoder v. Honeywell, Inc., 900 F.Supp. 240 (D. Colo. 1995) (without reliance by plaintiff, trademark on back of keyboard not enough to hold trademark owner liable for wrist injuries); Kealoha v. E.I. Du Pont De Nemours & Co., 82 F.3d 894 (9th Cir. 1995) (Haw. law) (defective TMJ proplast implants carried defendant's "Teflon" trademark); Porter v. LSB Indus., Inc., 600 N.Y.S.2d 867 (App. Div. 1993); Burket v. Petrol Plus of Naugatuck, Inc., 579 A.2d 26, 30–35 (Conn. 1990) (GM was merely trademark licensor and did not exert enough control for liability); Tyler v. Pepsico, Inc., 400 S.E.2d 673 (Ga. Ct. App. 1990). See Products Liability Restatement § 14 cmt. *d*; 1 Frumer and Friedman, Products Liability § 5.14.

**51.**  806 N.E.2d 776 (Ind. 2004).

**52.**  See id. at 786 (The "law should treat trademark licensors as having responsibility for defective products ... , but only so much of the liability for those defects as their relative role in the larger scheme of design, advertising, manufacturing, and distribution warrants. Consumers rightly expect that products bearing logos like 'Guess' have been subject to some oversight by those who put their name on the product, but those same consumers can well

proach to a duty issue is quite creative: it might encourage licensors to play at least a minor role in reviewing the safety of products they want the public to believe are connected with them in some respect, and, if not, it will extract from licensors a kind of safety penalty for misleading the public into thinking it knew something about products in which it pretended to have some role.

## § 15.5 SUCCESSOR CORPORATIONS

When a manufacturer goes out of business, it is obligated under the dissolution statutes of most states to make provisions for its existing creditors, including products liability judgement creditors, prior to distributing its remaining assets to its shareholders.[1] Once a corporation is properly dissolved, however, its shareholders are generally immune from responsibility for the firm's liabilities, and there usually is no remaining entity subject to responsibility for injuries caused by defective products the corporation may have made and sold.[2] Yet, sometimes a part or all of a dissolving company is sold to another, successor enterprise that puts some portions of the predecessor's productive assets—its equipment, capital, labor force, marketing apparatus, and goodwill—to some continued use. Indeed, sometimes the successor corporation will use the predecessor's productive assets to continue making and selling the same products to the same customers. When a predecessor company[3] is acquired by another firm, it typically will dissolve at, or immediately after, the transfer of stock or assets to the successor firm.[4] After such a corporate transfer of ownership, if a person is injured by a product made and sold by the predecessor before the transfer, the only viable enterprise from whom the victim may seek recovery is the successor corporation.[5] Whether and when a successor corporation may be liable for its

imagine that in modern commerce the products they buy may have actually been manufactured by someone else.").

### § 15.5

**1.** See, e.g., 16A W. Fletcher, Fletcher Cyclopedia of the Law of Private Corporations § 8129 (perm. ed., rev. vol. 2003) (hereinafter Fletcher, Corporations).

**2.** "Tort claimants who, as a result of defective products sold by a predecessor corporation, seek recovery only after transfer of assets to a successor corporation often face difficulty [in collecting on their claims which] typically accrue after the predecessor corporation has lawfully distributed to its shareholders the proceeds from the transfer of assets and has ceased to exist. Under these circumstances, tort claimants who were not existing creditors at the time of the transfer of assets ordinarily have no recourse against the predecessor's shareholders." Products Liability Restatement § 12 cmt. *a.*

**3.** Usually, both the buying and selling companies are corporations, but they need not be, and the principles of liability

discussed in this section generally should apply without regard to the form of the successor's or predecessor's business organization. See, e.g., Tift v. Forage King Indus., Inc., 322 N.W.2d 14 (Wis. 1982). *But see* Lundell v. Sidney Mach. Tool Co., 236 Cal.Rptr. 70 (Ct. App. 1987) (sole proprietorship purchaser not liable as successor because it was unable to assume predecessor's risk-spreading role). See generally 15 Fletcher, Corporations §§ 7122, at 227, and 7123.10, at 264–65 (1999 rev. ed.); Annot., 32 A.L.R.4th 196 (1984).

**4.** "Almost all of the reported decisions applying the bases of successor liability stated in this Section involve predecessors that transfer all of their assets to successors and then dissolve or otherwise cease operations. Indeed, the predecessor's termination is the circumstance that, as a practical matter, most often gives rise to the need for a post-transfer tort plaintiff to look to the successor for recovery." Products Liability Restatement § 12 cmt. *h.*

**5.** See Products Liability Restatement § 12 cmt. *a.*

predecessor's defective products, the topic of this section, has generated a spate of litigation[6] and commentary.[7]

## General Rule of Nonliability with Specific Exceptions

Under general corporate law principles, when one company acquires the assets of another, the successor entity is generally not responsible for the obligations of the predecessor.[8] This rule of successor corporation nonliability applies generally to the predecessor's debts and other liabilities, including products liability claims and judgments from defective products made and sold by the predecessor before the transfer.[9] "A corporate successor is not a seller and bears no blame in bringing the product and the user together. It seems patently unfair to require such a

**6.** Among the many judicial decisions thoroughly examining this issue are Ammend v. BioPort, Inc., 322 F.Supp.2d 848 (W.D. Mich. 2004) (successor's predecessor was state of Michigan); Paradise Corp. v. Amerihost Dev., Inc., 848 So.2d 177 (Miss. 2003); Meadows v. Amsted Indus., Inc., 760 N.Y.S.2d 604 (App. Div. 2003); Kradel v. Fox River Tractor Co., 308 F.3d 328 (3d Cir. 2002) (Pa. law); Fisher v. Allis–Chalmers Corp. Prod. Liab. Trust, 116 Cal. Rptr.2d 310 (Ct. App. 2002); Arevalo v. Saginaw Mach. Sys., Inc., 782 A.2d 931, 937 (N.J. 2001); Lockheed Martin Corp. v. Gordon, 16 S.W.3d 127 (Tex. App. 2000) (Del. law); Savage Arms, Inc. v. Western Auto Supply Co., 18 P.3d 49 (Alaska 2000); Guerrero v. Allison Engine Co., 725 N.E.2d 479 (Ind. Ct. App. 2000); Foster v. Cone–Blanchard Mach. Co., 597 N.W.2d 506 (Mich. 1999); Fish v. Amsted Indus., Inc., 376 N.W.2d 820 (Wis. 1985) (4 opinions thoroughly examining the pros and cons of expanding successor liability); Ramirez v. Amsted Indus., Inc., 431 A.2d 811 (N.J. 1981); Leannais v. Cincinnati, Inc., 565 F.2d 437 (7th Cir. 1977) (Wis. law); Ray v. Alad Corp., 560 P.2d 3 (Cal. 1977); Turner v. Bituminous Cas. Co., 244 N.W.2d 873 (Mich. 1976).

**7.** See, e.g., Reilly, Making Sense of Successor Liability, 31 Hofstra L. Rev. 745 (2003); Epstein, Imperfect Liability Regimes: Individual and Corporate Issues, 53 S.C. L. Rev. 1153 (2002); Cupp, Redesigning Successor Liability, 1999 U. Ill. L. Rev. 845; Slawotsky, The Impropriety of Levying Punitive Damages on Innocent Successor Corporations, 38 Duq. L. Rev. 49 (1999); Blumberg, The Continuity of the Enterprise Doctrine: Corporate Successorship in United States Law, 10 Fla. J. Int'l L. 365 (1996); M. Green, Successors and CERCLA: The Imperfect Analogy to Products Liability and an Alternative Proposal, 87 Nw. U. L. Rev. 897, 909 (1993); Rogala, Nontraditional Successor Product Liability: Should Society Be Forced to Pay the Cost?, 68 U. Det. Mercy L. Rev. 37 (1990) (economic

analysis); Cantu and Goldberg, Products Liability: An Argument for Product Line Liability in Texas, 19 St. Mary's L.J. 621 (1988); M. Green, Successor Liability: The Superiority of Statutory Reform to Protect Products Liability Claimants, 72 Cornell L. Rev. 17 (1986); Roe, Mergers, Acquisitions, and Tort: A Comment on the Problem of Successor Corporation Liability, 70 Va. L. Rev. 1559 (1984); Yamin, The Achilles Heel of the Takeover: Nature and Scope of Successor Corporations Product Liability in Asset Acquisitions, 7 Harv. J.L. & Pub. Pol'y 185 (1984); Phillips, Product Line Continuity and Successor Corporation Liability, 58 N.Y.U. L. Rev. 906 (1983); Phillips, Products Liability of Successor Corporations: A Corporate and Commercial Law Perspective, 11 Hofstra L. Rev. 249 (1982); Comments, 30 Wake Forest L. Rev. 889 (1995); 71 Marq. L. Rev. 815 (1982); Notes, 87 Colum. L. Rev. 1048 (1987); 21 Ohio N.U. L. Rev. 297 (1994); Annot., 66 A.L.R.3d 824 (1975).

See generally 15 Fletcher, Corporations §§ 7122 and 7123; P. Blumberg, The Law of Corporate Tort, Contract, and Other Common Law Problems in Substantive Law of Parent and Subsidiary Corporations ch. 13 (1987); 1 Frumer and Friedman, Products Liability § 7.1 et seq.; 1 Am. Law Prod. Liab. 3d § 7.1 et seq. The whole topic of successor corporation liability in the products liability context is exceptionally well examined in the comments and Reporters' Notes to Products Liability Restatement §§ 12 and 13. Note, however, that its conclusions differ materially from the more recent study by Professor Cupp, noted above, the results of which are discussed below.

**8.** "The general rule, which is well settled, is that where one company sells or otherwise transfers all its assets to another company, the latter is not liable for the debts and liabilities of the transferor." 15 Fletcher, Corporations § 7122, at 218.

**9.** See id. § 7123.10, at 264–65.

party to bear the cost of unassumed and uncontemplated products liability claims primarily because it is still in business and is perceived as a 'deep pocket.' "[10] In such cases, injury victims and other late-discovered creditors of a predecessor enterprise are sometimes prejudiced by the protective mantle thrown over successor corporations, but this result is seen as not unfair and a reasonable cost for the offsetting benefits to the economic system believed to flow from a rule providing successor enterprises security from unexpected debts following a good-faith acquisition of the assets of another enterprise.[11]

Notwithstanding the general rule of nonliability, the courts have recognized that a successor fairly should be responsible for the liabilities of a predecessor if the successor *consents* to undertake the predecessor's liabilities, if the successor and predecessor are essentially *the same entity*, or if a transfer is *fraudulently designed* to avoid liability.[12] Thus, where one company sells its assets to another, the purchaser is not liable for the seller's products liability obligations unless: (1) the purchaser expressly or impliedly assumes such liability;[13] (2) the transaction amounts to a consolidation or merger of the two companies;[14] (3) the purchaser is a mere continuation of the seller;[15] or (4) the transaction is a fraudulent

---

**10.** Nissen Corp. v. Miller, 594 A.2d 564, 569 (Md. 1991).

**11.** See Products Liability Restatement § 12 cmts. *a* and *b*.

**12.** See 15 Fletcher, Corporations § 7122; Products Liability Restatement § 12.

**13.** See, e.g., Ammend v. BioPort, Inc., 322 F.Supp.2d 848 (W.D. Mich. 2004); Fisher v. Allis–Chalmers Corp. Prod. Liab. Trust, 116 Cal.Rptr.2d 310 (Ct. App. 2002); Lockheed Martin Corp. v. Gordon, 16 S.W.3d 127 (Tex. App. 2000) (Del. law); T.H.S. Northstar Assocs. v. W.R. Grace & Co., 840 F.Supp. 676 (D. Minn. 1998); Dobbelaere v. Cosco, Inc., 697 N.E.2d 1016 (Ohio Ct. App. 1997).

**14.** See, e.g., Gamradt v. Federal Labs., Inc., 380 F.3d 416 (8th Cir. 2004) (Minn. law); T.H.S. Northstar Assocs. v. W.R. Grace & Co., 840 F.Supp. 676 (D. Minn. 1998) (transfer held to be merger rather than mere asset purchase based on merger agreement; continuity of management, personnel, assets, and operations; and purchaser's provision of stock for assets, such that shareholders of acquired company became shareholders of successor). "The key factor in distinguishing between a merger and an asset purchase is the ... continuity of shareholders resulting from an exchange of stock, rather than cash, for assets." Id. at 678.

Indeed, some courts hold that "when a corporation acquires or merges with a company manufacturing a product that is known to create serious health hazards, and the successor corporation continues to produce the same product in the same manner,

it may be found liable for punitive damages for liabilities incurred by the predecessor company in its manufacture of such product." Davis v. Celotex Corp., 420 S.E.2d 557, 564 (W. Va. 1992). "[I]t is the acquisition or merger of a company, along with the express assumption of liability, that makes a successor corporation liable for punitive damages." Id. at 563.

[C]orporations are in a very real sense, "molders of their own destinies" in acquisition transactions, with the full panoply of corporate transformations at their disposal. When a corporation ... voluntarily chooses a formal merger, it will take the "bad will" along with the "good will." ... We will not allow such an acquiring corporation to "jettison inchoate liabilities into a never-never land of transcorporate limbo."

Celotex Corp. v. Pickett, 490 So.2d 35, 38 (Fla. 1986).

**15.** See, e.g., Arevalo v. Saginaw Mach. Sys., Inc., 782 A.2d 931, 937 (N.J. 2001) (corporation merely reorganized); Roll v. Tracor, Inc., 140 F.Supp.2d 1073 (D. Nev. 2001) (same officers and directors served both corporate entities); Savage Arms, Inc. v. Western Auto Supply Co., 18 P.3d 49 (Alaska 2000) (recovery under mere continuation exception available to distributor in indemnity claim against successor); Farmex Inc. v. Wainwright, 501 S.E.2d 802 (Ga. 1998); Pancratz v. Monsato Co., 547 N.W.2d 198 (Iowa 1996) (absence of key element of continuation, identity of management and shareholders, precluded successor liability).

effort to avoid such liability.[16] While the question of whether successor liability should be limited to the four traditional exceptions is not without continuing controversy,[17] all products liability decisions accept the general rule of nonliability and most still subject it to the conventional four exceptions.[18] Proclaiming that these principles of successor corporation liability are "supported by fairness and efficiency considerations,"[19] the *Restatement (Third) of Torts: Products Liability* adopts the traditional rule of nonliability with the standard four exceptions.[20]

### Product Line and Continuity of Enterprise Exceptions

Due to the general rule of nonliability and narrowness of the standard four exceptions, a number of courts have applied one or both of

---

**16.** See, e.g., Nichols v. Roper–Whitney Co., 843 F.Supp. 799 (D.N.H. 1994). A finding of fraud or other bad faith in these cases is highly unusual. See, e.g., Reina v. Ginerale Corp., 472 So.2d 530 (Fla. Dist. Ct. App. 1985) (fraud alleged but not proved). See generally Reilly, Making Sense of Successor Liability, 31 Hofstra L. Rev. 745 (2003); Annot., 66 A.L.R.3d 824 § 4(d) (1975).

On the four exceptions, see generally 15 Fletcher, §§ 7122, 7123; Annot., 66 A.L.R.3d 824 (1975).

**17.** See, e.g., Cupp, Redesigning Successor Liability, 1999 U. Ill. L. Rev. 845.

**18.** See, e.g., Winsor v. Glasswerks PHX, L.L.C., 63 P.3d 1040, 1048 (Ariz. Ct. App. 2003); Meadows v. Amsted Ind., Inc., 760 N.Y.S.2d 604 (App. Div. 2003); Lockheed Martin Corp. v. Gordon, 16 S.W.3d 127, 134–35 (Tex. App. 2000) (Del. law); Pancratz v. Monsanto Co., 547 N.W.2d 198 (Iowa 1996); Costello v. Unipress Corp., 1996 WL 106215 (Minn. Ct. App. 1996); Bozell v. H & R 1871, Inc., 916 F.Supp. 951 (E.D. Mo. 1996); Cooper v. Lakewood Eng'g & Mfg. Co., 45 F.3d 243 (8th Cir. 1995) (Minn. law); Jordan v. Ravenswood Aluminum Corp., 455 S.E.2d 561 (W. Va. 1995); Welco Indus., Inc. v. Applied Co., 617 N.E.2d 1129 (Ohio 1993); Harris v. T.I., Inc., 413 S.E.2d 605 (Va. 1992); LeSane v. Hillenbrand Indus., 791 F.Supp. 871, 873–74 (D.D.C. 1992); Johnston v. Amsted Indus., Inc., 830 P.2d 1141 (Colo. Ct. App. 1992); Nissen Corp. v. Miller, 594 A.2d 564 (Md. 1991); Guzman v. MRM/Elgin, 567 N.E.2d 929 (Mass. 1991); Florom v. Elliott Mfg., 867 F.2d 570 (10th Cir. 1989) (Colo. law); Budd Tire Corp. v. Pierce Tire Co., 370 S.E.2d 267 (N.C. Ct. App. 1988); Swayze v. A.O. Smith Corp., 694 F.Supp. 619, 623 (E.D. Ark. 1988); Conn v. Fales Div. of Mathewson Corp., 835 F.2d 145 (6th Cir. 1987) (Ky. law); Hamaker v. Kenwel–Jackson Mach., Inc., 387 N.W.2d 515 (S.D. 1986); Polius v. Clark Equip. Co., 802 F.2d 75 (3d Cir. 1986) (V.I. law); Mudgett v. Paxson Mach. Co., 709 S.W.2d 755 (Tex.

App. 1986); Fish v. Amsted Indus., Inc., 376 N.W.2d 820 (Wis. 1985); Bullington v. Union Tool Corp., 328 S.E.2d 726 (Ga. 1985); Griggs v. Capitol Mach. Works, Inc., 690 S.W.2d 287 (Tex. App. 1985); Downtowner Inc. v. Acrometal Prods., Inc., 347 N.W.2d 118 (N.D. 1984); Goucher v. Parmac, Inc., 694 P.2d 953 (Okla. Ct. App. 1984); Ostrowski v. Hydra–Tool Corp., 479 A.2d 126 (Vt. 1984); Gonzalez v. Rock Wool Eng'g & Equip. Co., 453 N.E.2d 792 (Ill. App. Ct. 1983); Bernard v. Kee Mfg. Co., 409 So.2d 1047 (Fla. 1982); Jones v. Johnson Mach. & Press Co., 320 N.W.2d 481 (Neb. 1982).

From the fourth, fraud exception, a small number of courts have spun out a fifth exception for transactions made in bad faith or with inadequate consideration. See, e.g., Man v. Raymark Indus., 728 F.Supp. 1461 (D. Haw. 1989); Everest v. American Transp. Corp., 685 F.Supp. 203 (D. Minn. 1988); Ostrowski v. Hydra–Tool Corp., 479 A.2d 126 (Vt. 1984).

**19.** Products Liability Restatement § 12 cmt. *b*.

**20.** Section 12 of the Products Liability Restatement, entitled "Liability of Successor for Harm Caused by Defective Products Sold by Predecessor," provides:

A successor corporation or other business entity that acquires assets of a predecessor corporation or other business entity is subject to liability for harm to persons or property caused by a defective product sold or otherwise distributed commercially by the predecessor if the acquisition:

(a) is accompanied by an agreement for the successor to assume such liability; or

(b) results from a fraudulent conveyance to escape liability for the debts or liabilities of the predecessor; or

(c) constitutes a consolidation or merger with the predecessor; or

(d) results in the successor becoming a continuation of the predecessor.

two new exceptions to the general rule of nonliability to provide broader opportunities for redress to persons injured by defective products manufactured by defunct corporations. Building upon the fairness and logic of allowing liability when the successor and predecessor are essentially the same entity (the idea behind the standard merger and mere-continuation exceptions), the new nonstandard exceptions extend a successor's liability well beyond the traditional four exceptions.

In 1976, the Michigan Supreme Court, in *Turner v. Bituminous Casualty Company*,[21] adopted the first new exception of this type, called the "continuity of enterprise" exception.[22] Explaining its rationale for expanding beyond the traditional four exceptions, the majority remarked:

> [I]t seems both unfair and unbelievable that a corporate combination or acquisition decision would be principally or exclusively made on the basis of cutting off the contingent right to sue of a products liability victim. . . . First, it would seem illogical that a merger or de facto merger be encumbered by liability for a products liability suit while a cash acquisition of corporate assets is free from such liability. [Second], if there are no real business reasons for choosing a cash acquisition of corporate assets and the only real reason is to avoid products liability suits, then it would seem that the machinery of corporate law is unreasonably geared up to accomplish a purpose not really intended for it or in the public interest.

An increasing number of other courts have adopted the continuity of enterprise exception,[23] but most courts still reject it for unfairly holding one entity liable for the acts of another contrary to the traditional set of principles applied to the liability of successor corporations.[24]

The year after *Turner* was decided, in *Ray v. Alad Corp.*,[25] the Supreme Court of California promulgated the "product line" exception

---

**21.** 244 N.W.2d 873 (Mich. 1976) (3–2 decision).

**22.** For an earlier case along similar lines, see Cyr v. B. Offen & Co., 501 F.2d 1145 (1st Cir. 1974) (N.H. law).

**23.** See, e.g., Paradise Corp. v. Amerihost Dev., Inc., 848 So.2d 177 (Miss. 2003); Savage Arms, Inc. v. Western Auto Supply Co., 18 P.3d 49 (Alaska 2000); Asher v. KCS Int'l, 659 So.2d 598 (Ala. 1995); McCaffrey v. Weaver Jack Corp., 1992 WL 266923, at 2* (E.D.N.Y. 1992); Flaugher v. Cone Automatic Mach. Co., 507 N.E.2d 331, 334 (Ohio 1987); Mozingo v. Correct Mfg. Corp., 752 F.2d 168, 174–76 (5th Cir. 1985) (Miss. law); Salvati v. Blaw–Know Food & Chem. Equip., Inc., 497 N.Y.S.2d 242, 247 (Sup. Ct. 1985); Holloway v. John E. Smith's Sons Co., 432 F.Supp. 454, 455 (D. S.C. 1977); Cyr v. B. Offen & Co., 501 F.2d 1145, 1152–54 (1st Cir. 1974) (N.H. law). See also Foster v. Cone–Blanchard Mach. Co., 597 N.W.2d 506 (Mich. 1999) (over three dissenting justices, majority found continuity of enterprise theory inapplicable when

plaintiff able to recover from purchaser); MacCleery v. T.S.S. Retail Corp., 882 F.Supp. 13 (D.N.H. 1994) (listing eight factors relevant to liability under this doctrine).

**24.** See, e.g., Winsor v. Glasswerks PHX, L.L.C., 63 P.3d 1040, 1048 (Ariz. Ct. App. 2003) ("the issue is one of policy for the legislature"); Pancratz v. Monsanto Co., 547 N.W.2d 198, 201 (Iowa 1996) ("Such a radical departure from traditional corporate principles . . . should be left to the legislature."); Johnston v. Amsted Indus., Inc., 830 P.2d 1141 (Colo. Ct. App. 1992); Nissen Corp. v. Miller, 594 A.2d 564 (Md. 1991) (5– 2 decision); Niccum v. Hydra Tool Corp., 438 N.W.2d 96 (Minn. 1989). ("Like the majority of our sister states, we adhere to the general rule of nonliability of successor corporations, with its four traditional exceptions, in products liability cases."). Id. at 573 (citing cases from Colo., Ky., Mo., Ark., Fla., Ill., Iowa, Minn., Neb., N.D., Okla., S.D., Vt., and Wis.).

**25.** 560 P.2d 3 (Cal. 1977).

to the general rule of a successor's nonliability for defective products produced by a predecessor company: "a party which acquires a manufacturing business and continues the output of its line of products ... assumes strict tort liability for defects in units of the same product line previously manufactured and distributed by the entity from which the business was acquired."[26] The California court provided three rationales for its new product line exception:

> (1) the virtual destruction of the plaintiff's remedies against the original manufacturer caused by the successor's acquisition of the business, (2) the successor's ability to assume the original manufacturer's risk-spreading role, and (3) the fairness of requiring the successor to assume a responsibility for [its predecessor's] defective products that was a burden necessarily attached to the original manufacturer's good will being enjoyed by the successor in the continued operation of the business.[27]

An increasing number of courts have followed *Ray* in adopting a product line exception,[28] but most courts that have addressed the issue have rejected this new exception, too.[29] For example, in *Guzman v. MRM/Elgin*,[30] the Massachusetts Supreme Judicial Court systematically rejected each of *Ray*'s three reasons for adopting a product line exception. It criticized *Ray*'s first rationale on the ground that "the plaintiff's lack of a remedy against the original manufacturers is not a justification for imposing liability on another absent fault and causation."[31] *Guzman* criticized Ray's second, "risk-spreading" rationale as being contrary to modern products liability theory[32] which is based instead on the notion of deterrence or risk control effected by placing liability on the party

---

**26.** Id. at 11.

**27.** Id. at 9.

**28.** See, e.g., Ramirez v. Amsted Indus., Inc., 431 A.2d 811 (N.J. 1981); Dawejko v. Jorgensen Steel Co., 434 A.2d 106 (Pa. Super. Ct. 1981); Martin v. Abbott Lab., Inc., 689 P.2d 368 (Wash. 1984). See also Fox v. Sunmaster Prods., Inc., 821 P.2d 502 (Wash. Ct. App. 1991) (product that harms plaintiff must come from continued product line); Sullivan v. A.W. Flint Co., 1996 WL 469716, at *7–*8 (Conn. Super. Ct. 1996); Garcia v. Coe Mfg. Co., 933 P.2d 243 (N.M. 1997); Rothstein v. Tennessee Gas Pipeline Co., 664 N.Y.S.2d 213, 220–21 (Sup. Ct. 1997), rev'd in part by 696 N.Y.S.2d 528 (App. Div. 1999); Rosales v. Thermex–Thermatron, Inc., 78 Cal.Rptr.2d 861 (Ct. App. 1998); Mettinger v. Globe Slicing Mach. Co., 709 A.2d 779 (N.J. 1998) (retailers and distributors may use product line exception to seek indemnification from successor corporations); Guerrero v. Allison Engine Co., 725 N.E.2d 479, 487 (Ind. Ct. App. 2000) (product line exception may be an appropriate rule, but successor liability inappropriate where predecessor continues to exist); Huff v. Shopsmith, 786 So.2d 383 (Miss. 2001) (listing elements necessary for product line exception); Kradel v. Fox River

Tractor Co., 308 F.3d 328 (3d Cir. 2002) (Pa. law); Mitchell v. Powermatic Corp., 2004 WL 292479 (E.D. Pa. 2004). Cf. Farmex Inc. v. Wainwright, 501 S.E.2d 802 (Ga. 1998) (approving underlying concept in dictum).

**29.** See, e.g., Winsor v. Glasswerks PHX, L.L.C., 63 P.3d 1040, 1049 (Ariz. Ct. App. 2003); Pearson v. National Feeding Sys., Inc., 90 S.W.3d 46 (Ky. 2002); Savage Arms, Inc. v. Western Auto Supply Co., 18 P.3d 49 (Alaska 2001); Johnston v. Amsted Indus., Inc., 830 P.2d 1141 (Colo. Ct. App. 1992); Simoneau v. South Bend Lathe, Inc., 543 A.2d 407 (N.H. 1988); Flaugher v. Cone Automatic Mach. Co., 507 N.E.2d 331 (Ohio 1987); Polius v. Clark Equip. Co., 802 F.2d 75 (3d Cir. 1986) (V.I. law). See generally 1 Am. Law of Prod. Liab. 3d § 7:27, at 44–45 n.95 (1999) (citing cases rejecting the doctrine from Ala., Ark., Fla., Ill., Iowa, Ky., La., Md., Mich., Minn., Mo., Neb., N.H., N.D., Ohio, Or., S.D., Tex., Vt., and Wis.).

**30.** 567 N.E.2d 929 (Mass. 1991).

**31.** Id. at 931.

**32.** The rise and decline of the risk-spreading (insurance) rationale for strict products liability is traced in § 5.4, above.

responsible for making and selling the product.[33] The Massachusetts court criticized *Ray*'s third rationale for failing to recognize that a purchaser pays fair value for the seller's good will.[34] Finally, *Guzman* explained that the product line exception ignored the financial burden it forced on successors, who often would be unable to insure effectively against the risk, noting that "the threat of potential liability would inhibit the free alienability of corporate assets, forcing some small businesses to liquidate rather than transferring their assets, to the detriment of the economy in general."[35]

Conventional wisdom,[36] and the position taken by the *Products Liability Restatement*,[37] holds that the traditional four exceptions are deeply entrenched in American products liability jurisprudence and that the two upstart exceptions, the "continuity of enterprise" and "product line" exceptions, were only temporary aberrations in what is otherwise an unwavering set of exceptions to the general nonliability rule for successor corporations. At least until quite recently, it appears quite true that most courts have rejected one or both of the two new liability-expanding approaches and adhered to the traditional four exceptions.[38] More recently, however, one scholar has discovered that "the evolution toward loosening restrictions has fitfully continued,"[39] and believes that "[t]he less restrictive approaches now operate in almost as many jurisdictions, and probably in more actual lawsuits, as does the traditional approach,"[40] a development he applauds.[41] It is difficult to discern whether this creeping expansion in exceptions is continuing apace,[42] or whether instead it has been largely halted by the *Restatement*'s unequivocal adherence to the conventional list of four exceptions.[43] Be that as it may,

---

**33.** 567 N.E.2d at 932.

**34.** Id. *Ray*'s third rationale, that a successor ought to bear the burdens along with the benefits of the predecessor's good will is characterized as "specious" in M. Green, Successor Liability: The Superiority of Statutory Reform to Protect Products Liability Claimants, 72 Cornell L. Rev. 17, 29–30 (1986).

**35.** 567 N.E.2d at 933.

**36.** See, e.g., M. Green, Successors and CERCLA: The Imperfect Analogy to Products Liability and an Alternative Proposal, 87 Nw. U. L. Rev. 897, 909 (1993) (stating that the expansion of corporate successor liability "fizzled in the 1980s and 1990s"); Henderson and Eisenberg, The Quiet Revolution in Products Liability: An Empirical Study of Legal Change, 37 UCLA L. Rev. 479, 492 and n.64 (1990) (citing six state supreme court cases decided in the mid-to-late 1980s rejecting product line exception).

**37.** See Products Liability Restatement § 12 cmt. *b*.

**38.** See, e.g., Johnston v. Amsted Indus., Inc., 830 P.2d 1141 (Colo. Ct. App. 1992) (rejecting both product line and continuity of enterprise exceptions to traditional rule of nonliability of successor corporations). See generally Products Liability Re-

statement § 12 cmt. *b*, citing M. Green, Successors and CERCLA: The Imperfect Analogy to Products Liability and an Alternative Proposal, 87 Nw. U. L. Rev. 897, 909–10 (1993); Henderson and Eisenberg, The Quiet Revolution in Products Liability: An Empirical Study of Legal Change, 37 UCLA L. Rev. 479, 492 and n.64 (1990).

**39.** See Cupp, Redesigning Successor Liability, 1999 U. Ill. L. Rev. 845, 894.

**40.** Id.

**41.** Professor Cupp concludes: "Courts should not rest from their fitful redesigning of successor liability until they settle on the less restrictive approaches that both protect tortiously injured consumers, and at the same time allow innocent successors to channel responsibility back to the original manufacturers." Id. at 896.

**42.** See, e.g, Paradise Corp. v. Amerihost Dev., Inc., 848 So.2d 177 (Miss. 2003) (adopting continuity of enterprise exception); Huff v. Shopsmith, Inc., 786 So.2d 383, 386–88 (Miss. 2001) (adopting product line exception, but ruling that it did not apply to facts).

**43.** See, e.g., Winsor v. Glasswerks PHX, L.L.C., 63 P.3d 1040, 1049 (Ariz. Ct. App. 2003) (declining to adopt either new

it at least is clear that "much evolution remains ahead."[44]

### Successor Corporation's Duty to Warn

The issue just examined concerns the liability of a successor firm for harm caused by defective goods produced by a predecessor, solely because the successor acquired the predecessor's assets. An entirely different issue is whether a successor corporation should have an independent duty, when it discovers that a predecessor's products are dangerously defective, to *warn* the predecessor's consumers of the danger.[45] "[B]y virtue of succeeding to the predecessor's interests, the successor is often in a good position to learn of problems arising from use of the predecessor's product and to prevent harm to persons or property. When the relationship between the successor and pre-transfer purchasers of the predecessor's products gives rise to actual or potential economic benefit to the successor, it is both fair and efficient to require the successor to act reasonably to prevent such harm."[46] For these reasons, many courts have concluded that a successor does have an independent duty to warn such parties, dependent upon various factors, even if none of the four traditional exceptions apply.[47]

Adopting basically a negligence standard, the *Products Liability Restatement* provides that a successor corporation is subject to liability for failure to warn of risks in products sold by its predecessor if (1) the successor enters into a maintenance, repair, or similar product service

exception; "a fundamental tenet of our products liability law is that compensation for injury is tied to those who have a causal connection to placing the product into the stream of commerce [but the] product line and continuity of enterprise exceptions at issue overlook or minimize this causal link"); Pearson ex rel. Trent v. Nat'l Feeding Sys., Inc., 90 S.W.3d 46, 52 (Ky. 2002) (declining to adopt product-line exception; "whether or not strict liability in tort policy should be substantially altered by also changing established principles of corporate succession transactions involves broad public policy issues which are more appropriately left to legislative determination").

**44.** See Cupp, Redesigning Successor Liability, 1999 U. Ill. L. Rev. 845, 894.

**45.** See Kommer, The Successor Corporation's Continuing Duty to Warn, 23 Prod. Safety & Liab. Rep. (BNA) No. 36, p. 990 et seq. (Sept. 15, 1995).

**46.** Products Liability Restatement § 13 cmt. *a.*

**47.** Cases holding that successor corporations have a duty to warn if they maintain a substantial continuing relationship with their predecessor's customers include Huff v. Shopsmith, 786 So.2d 383 (Miss. 2001); Foster v. Cone–Blanchard Mach. Co., 597 N.W.2d 506 (Mich. 1999); Sherlock v. Quality Control Equip. Co., 79 F.3d 731

(8th Cir. 1996) (Mo. law); Patton v. TIC United Corp., 77 F.3d 1235 (10th Cir. 1996) (Kan. law); Kaleta v. Whittaker Corp., 583 N.E.2d 567 (Ill. App. Ct. 1991); Tracey v. Winchester Repeating Arms Co., 745 F.Supp. 1099 (E.D. Pa. 1990); Florom v. Elliott Mfg., 867 F.2d 570, 577 (10th Cir. 1989) (Colo. law); Flaugher v. Cone Automatic Mach. Co., 507 N.E.2d 331, 337–38 (Ohio 1987); Polius v. Clark Equip. Co., 802 F.2d 75, 84 (3d Cir. 1986) (V.I. law); Mozingo v. Correct Mfg. Corp., 752 F.2d 168, 177 (5th Cir. 1985) (Miss. law); Downtowner, Inc. v. Acrometal Prods. Inc., 347 N.W.2d 118, 125 (N.D. 1984); Ostrowski v. Hydra–Tool Corp., 479 A.2d 126, 127–28 (Vt. 1984); Stratton v. Garvey Int'l, Inc., 676 P.2d 1290 (Kan. Ct. App. 1984); Gonzalez v. Rock Wool Eng'g & Equip., 453 N.E.2d 792 (Ill. App. Ct. 1983); Schumacher v. Richards Shear Co., 451 N.E.2d 195 (N.Y. 1983); Pelc v. Bendix Mach. Tool Corp., 314 N.W.2d 614, 621 (Mich. Ct. App. 1981); Tucker v. Paxson Mach. Co., 645 F.2d 620 (8th Cir. 1981) (Mo. law); Gee v. Tenneco, Inc., 615 F.2d 857, 866 (9th Cir. 1980) (Cal. law); Travis v. Harris Corp., 565 F.2d 443, 449 (7th Cir. 1977) (Ind. law); Leannais v. Cincinnati, Inc., 565 F.2d 437, 441–42 (7th Cir. 1977) (Wis. law); Wilson v. Fare Well Corp., 356 A.2d 458 (N.J. Super. Ct. Law Div. 1976); Shane v. Hobam, Inc., 332 F.Supp. 526 (E.D. Pa. 1971). See Annot. 92 A.L.R.5th 227 (2001).

relationship with its predecessor's customers,[48] and (2) "a reasonable person in the position of the successor would provide a warning."[49] Whether a reasonable person in such a position would provide a warning depends upon a variety of factors, distilled from the cases, which the *Restatement* describes as whether (1) the successor reasonably should know that the product is dangerous; (2) the persons to whom a warning might be provided can be identified and are likely to be unaware of the risk; (3) there is an effective way to convey a warning, and the recipients can practically act upon it; and (4) the risk is great enough to justify the burden of providing a warning.[50] Because the *Restatement*'s formulation of these commonsense principles of responsibility developed by the courts seems reasonable and fair, other courts may be expected to impose a similar duty to warn on successor corporations, unless requiring such a warning would be unreasonable.[51]

## § 15.6 EMPLOYERS AS MANUFACTURERS

In bringing products and workers together, employers stand at the "nip point" of product safety in the industrial setting.[1] Employers have virtually exclusive control over many product safety matters, such as selecting industrial machinery and specifying guards for that machinery; allocating particular employees to operate particular machines; training workers to use dangerous chemicals and machinery; designing the production process, including the speed of the assembly line; and supervising all of these production activities. With such extensive control over product safety in the workplace, employers bear principal responsibility for many injuries to workers from industrial tools, chemicals, and machines. For this reason, Congress in 1970 enacted legislation imposing

---

**48.** "For example, a successor may sell or offer to sell spare parts to the predecessor's customers for machinery sold by the predecessor when the successor knows or should know the machinery is defective." Products Liability Restatement § 13 cmt. *b*. See, e.g., Sherlock v. Quality Control Equip. Co., 79 F.3d 731 (8th Cir. 1996) (Mo. law) (upholding verdict for plaintiff against successor corporation, that sold replacement parts for machine sold by predecessor, for failing to warn of dangers successor learned about after asset transfer).

"The critical element required for the imposition of the duty is a continuing relationship between the successor and the predecessor's customers for the benefit of the successor." 15 Fletcher, Corporations § 7123.40, at 290. In determining whether there is a sufficient continuing relationship between the successor and the predecessor's customers, many of the cases consider the existence of an ongoing service contract to be critical. See, e.g., Florom v. Elliott Mfg. Co., 867 F.2d 570 (10th Cir. 1989) (Colo. law); Polius v. Clark Equip. Co., 802 F.2d 75 (3d Cir. 1986) (V.I. law); Mozingo v. Correct Mfg. Corp., 752 F.2d 168 (5th Cir. 1985) (Miss. law); Stratton v. Garvey Int'l, Inc., 676 P.2d 1290 (Kan. Ct. App. 1984);

Tucker v. Paxson Mach. Co., 645 F.2d 620 (8th Cir. 1981) (Mo. law). *But see* Schumacher v. Richards Shear Co., 451 N.E.2d 195 (N.Y. 1983). Yet, while the existence of such a service contract is one important basis for imposing a duty to warn upon a successor corporation, it should not be a sine qua non for the creation of such a duty. See Products Liability Restatement § 13 cmt. *b*.

**49.** See Products Liability Restatement § 13(a)(2).

**50.** See Products Liability Restatement § 13(b).

**51.** See, e.g., Huff v. Shopsmith, Inc., 786 So.2d 383, 389 (Miss. 2001) ("In the present case, contacting the Huffs would have been a virtual impossibility.").

### § 15.6

**1.** See Weiler, Workers' Compensation and Product Liability: The Interaction of a Tort and a Non-Tort Regime, 50 Ohio St. L.J. 825 (1989); Weisgall, Product Liability in the Workplace: The Effect of Workers' Compensation on the Rights and Liabilities of Third Parties, 1977 Wis. L. Rev. 1035; Annot., 9 A.L.R.4th 873 (1981).

major safety responsibilities upon employers under the regulatory supervision of the Occupational Safety and Health Administration.[2]

### Employers as Suppliers of Dangerous Equipment; Workers' Compensation Acts

Because of their commercial exploitation of workers, together with
their tenacious hold on industrial safety, employers are properly held
responsible for on-the-job injuries to workers from dangerous products
supplied by the employer.[3] It was for just this reason that state legislatures enacted "workmen's compensation" acts in the early 1900s.[4] Prior
to such legislation, a worker injured on the job could sue his or her
employer for negligence, but the difficulties of proving an employer's
fault, together with the rigorous defenses of contributory negligence,
assumption of risk, and the fellow servant rule, prevented recovery in
"by far the greater proportion" of cases.[5] In place of protracted common
law actions which had little chance of success, the workers' compensation statutes substituted speedy and assured no-fault compensation from
employers[6] for workplace accidents.[7] The legislative trade-offs for providing workers with these benefits was to restrict the amounts of compensation paid and to abolish negligence and other common-law claims against
employers for workplace accidents.[8] Thus, a central feature of all workers' compensation statutes is that the benefits legislatively prescribed
are the worker's "exclusive remedy" against the employer for injuries on
the job.[9] Over time, the level of worker compensation benefits have failed
to keep pace with even the basic needs of injured workers, while the size

**2.** See the Occupational Safety and Health Act of 1970, 29 U.S.C. § 651 et seq.

**3.** "The theory underlying the workers' compensation acts never has been stated better than in the old campaign slogan, 'the cost of the product should bear the blood of the workman.'" Prosser and Keeton on Torts § 80, at 573, quoting Bohlen, A Problem in the Drafting of Workmen's Compensation Acts, 25 Harv. L. Rev. 328 (1911).

**4.** See Prosser and Keeton on Torts § 80; Beauchamp v. Dow Chem. Co., 398 N.W.2d 882, 884–85 (Mich. 1986) (tracing the background of Michigan's workers' compensation act enacted in 1912).

**5.** Prosser and Keeton on Torts § 80, at 572 (citing various estimates of uncompensated industrial accident injuries from seventy to ninety-four percent). See also Comment, Bell v. Industrial Vangas: The Employer-Manufacturer and the Dilemma of Dual Capacity, 34 Hastings L.J. 461, 463–70 (1982).

**6.** And, as a practical matter, from their workers' compensation insurance carriers.

**7.** See Dobbs, Law of Torts §§ 392–96.

**8.** "The chief benefit of the workers' compensation system for the injured employee is that it provides a much speedier and more certain recovery than a suit at

law. By abolishing the requirement of proving negligence on the part of the employer, workers' compensation also makes some recovery available for injured workers in a large number of cases where employer fault would be difficult to establish. In contrast, the benefits of the system for industrial employers lie in the protection from excessive liability in tort for employee injuries. In a more general sense, workers' compensation also benefits society by providing incentives for employers to run safe operations." Comment, Bell v. Industrial Vangas: The Employer–Manufacturer and the Dilemma of Dual Capacity, 34 Hastings L.J. 461, 467–68 (1982).

**9.** Mississippi's provision is typical: "The liability of an employer to pay compensation shall be exclusive and in place of all other liability of such employer to the employee." Miss. Code Ann. § 71–3–9 (1972). See Rader v. United States Rubber Reclaiming Co., 617 F.Supp. 1045 (S.D. Miss. 1985) (quoting this provision and asserting that "workers' compensation is an employee's exclusive remedy for work-related injuries"). See generally Prosser and Keeton on Torts § 80, at 574; 6 A. Larson and A. Larson, Larson's Workers' Compensation Law § 100.01 et seq. (2000) [hereinafter Larson's Workers' Compensation Law].

of tort recoveries for accidents outside the workplace have mushroomed. For these reasons, workers have once again looked to the common law for help in obtaining greater compensation for workplace injuries.

Since industrial and other workplace accidents usually involve some kind of hazardous product (some kind of material,[10] tool,[11] machine,[12] vehicle,[13] process,[14] or chemical[15]), and since many workplace product hazards (as many consumer product hazards) are excessive and unnecessary, workers not infrequently seek compensation from the manufacturers of those products to supplement workers' compensation benefits which usually are quite inadequate. Employers most often are not directly involved in such products liability claims by workers against manufacturers of workplace products, so that such third-party actions lie largely outside the workers' compensation system. An employer,[16] however, ordinarily may recoup its workers' compensation payments and obligations from any recovery the worker might obtain from such a products liability lawsuit.[17]

### Employers as Manufacturers; the "Dual Capacity" Doctrine

Not infrequently, industrial employers design and manufacture products for their own use. Often these are specialty tools used only in the employer's own business and not manufactured and sold widely to the public. Yet, some manufacturers make products not only for their own use but also for sale to the general public: a press manufacturer may use its own presses on its own assembly line to make parts for presses sold to others, and a tire manufacturer may equip the trucks it uses around its factories with tires from its normal production inventory.[18] Because such an enterprise in a real sense wears two hats, it may be said to act in a "dual capacity"—both as a manufacturer and employer. Normally, as discussed above, if an employee is injured on the job by an

---

**10.** See, e.g., Estate of Blakely v. Asbestos Corp., 766 F.Supp. 721 (E.D. Ark. 1991) (asbestos); Franco v. United Wholesale Lumber Co., 196 Cal.Rptr. 430 (Ct. App. 1983) (wood board kicked back while being cut).

**11.** See, e.g., Caraccioli v. KFC Mfg. Corp., 761 F.Supp. 119 (M.D. Fla. 1991) (automatic cooker); Toth v. Westinghouse Elevator Co., 449 N.E.2d 1005 (Ill. App. Ct. 1983) (elevator); Windham v. Blount Int'l, Ltd., 423 So.2d 194 (Ala. 1982) (safety belt).

**12.** See, e.g., Duffy v. Liberty Mach. Co., 562 N.Y.S.2d 769 (App. Div. 1990) (tile planisher machine); Hyman v. Sipi Metals Corp., 509 N.E.2d 516 (Ill. App. Ct. 1987) (smelter exploded); Horne v. General Elec. Co., 716 F.2d 253 (4th Cir. 1982) (N.C. law) (hydraulic press).

**13.** See, e.g., Coello v. Tug Mfg. Corp., 756 F.Supp. 1258 (W.D. Mo. 1991) (industrial tow tractor); Gurry v. Cumberland Farms, Inc., 550 N.E.2d 127 (Mass. 1990) (sand buggy used in farming business); Christman v. Allison Gas Turbine, 702 F.Supp. 369 (D. Mass. 1989) (helicopter).

**14.** See, e.g., Estate of Coates v. Pacific Eng'g, 791 P.2d 1257 (Haw. 1990) (diver employed by engineering firm that designed powerful water sucking process for elaborate "water features" at hotel swimming pool).

**15.** See, e.g., Ervin v. Great Dane Trailers, Inc., 393 S.E.2d 467 (Ga. Ct. App. 1990) (workers alleged that their cancers resulted from workplace exposure to hazardous chemicals); White v. E.I. Du Pont De Nemours & Co., 523 F.Supp. 302 (W.D. Va. 1981) (employee in Orlon-making plant alleged that his liver damage was caused by chemical made by defendant employer).

**16.** Or, typically, the employer's workers' compensation insurance carrier.

**17.** See 6 Larson's Workers' Compensation Law § 117.01 et seq.

**18.** Compare Mercer v. Uniroyal, Inc., 361 N.E.2d 492 (Ohio Ct. App. 1977) (dual capacity recovery allowed), with Schump v. Firestone Tire & Rubber Co., 541 N.E.2d 1040 (Ohio 1989) (dual capacity doctrine disapproved and recovery not allowed).

unguarded punch press or a defective tire blowout, the employee may recover workers' compensation benefits from the employer and damages in a products liability action from the manufacturer. But what if the product manufacturer is also the employee's employer? May the injured employee maintain an ordinary products liability action against the company in its capacity as manufacturer? Or is the employee precluded from maintaining such a suit against the company because of its capacity as his or her employer? This situation raises what is called the "dual capacity" (or "dual persona")[19] issue.

The dual capacity doctrine had an interesting, but quite short and narrow, life in products liability law. A California appellate court first recognized the doctrine in *Duprey v. Shane*,[20] a 1952 case in which the defendant chiropractor treated his nurse for an injury. The treatment aggravated the injury, and the nurse sued for malpractice. Notwithstanding the exclusive remedy rule of the workers' compensation statute, the court permitted the action because the defendant had removed the mantle of employer, and assumed the obligations of a chiropractor, when he undertook to treat his employee as a patient. A quarter of a century later, in *Mercer v. Uniroyal, Inc.*,[21] an Ohio appellate court first applied the dual capacity doctrine to a products liability case. In *Mercer*, while driving a company truck equipped with Uniroyal tires, a Uniroyal employee was injured when a tire blew out. Relying on *Duprey v. Shane*[22] and other cases outside the products liability context, and reasoning that "[i]t was only a matter of circumstance that the tire on the truck in which the plaintiff was riding was a Uniroyal tire rather than a Sears, Goodyear or Goodrich,"[23] the Ohio court allowed the Uniroyal employee to maintain a products liability action against his employer.[24]

Twelve days after the Ohio court rendered *Mercer*, a California appellate court similarly extended the dual capacity doctrine to the products liability context. In *Douglas v. E. & J. Gallo Winery*,[25] the plaintiffs were injured by the collapse of scaffolding on which they were working, scaffolding that their employer also manufactured and sold to the general public. Allowing the workers to maintain a products liability suit against their own employer, the court held that the dual capacity doctrine permitted the claim in this context, despite the exclusive remedy doctrine which normally precludes tort claims by workers against their employers. Noting that "[t]here is nothing ghostly or fictional about two capacities,"[26] the court explained that "[a]n employer *qua* employer enjoys the cloak of immunity waived by the Workers' Compensation Law. But when an employer engages in the dual capacity

---

**19.** While most courts refer to the doctrine as the "dual capacity" doctrine, at least in the products liability context, the principal workers' compensation treatise argues cogently that "dual persona" is the better name for the narrower, proper conception of the doctrine, a position which has had its effect on the courts. See 6 Larson's Workers' Compensation Law §§ 113.01[2] and 113.03.

**20.** 249 P.2d 8 (Cal. 1952).

**21.** 361 N.E.2d 492 (Ohio Ct. App. 1976).

**22.** 249 P.2d 8 (Cal. 1952).

**23.** 361 N.E.2d at 496.

**24.** See also Guy v. Arthur H. Thomas Co., 378 N.E.2d 488, 490–92 (Ohio 1978).

**25.** 137 Cal.Rptr. 797, 802–03 (Ct. App. 1977).

**26.** Id. at 801.

of manufacturer of a product for sale to the public, the employer assumes all of the duties and liabilities of such manufacturer."[27] While an employee may surrender his or her rights to sue the employer for workplace hazards as part of the workers' compensation tradeoff, the court reasoned that the employment relationship does not require that a worker also surrender his or her rights as a product consumer.[28] Four years later, in *Bell v. Industrial Vangas, Inc.*,[29] the California Supreme Court reaffirmed the use of the dual capacity doctrine in products liability cases asserting that "there is naught to commend a rule of the law which would encourage manufacturers to do less in the area of product safety if by chance the product is to be used by their own employees."[30]

Outside of California and Ohio, the dual capacity doctrine experienced a much cooler reception. Troubled by the doctrine's obvious conflict with the exclusive remedy rule, and fearful that it would undermine the long-established balance the legislatures had struck in the workers' compensation legislation,[31] courts in other states widely rejected the doctrine. In 1980, for example, characterizing the dual capacity doctrine as "fundamentally unsound," the New York Court of Appeals explained that "[w]e would be seriously undermining the salutary social purposes underlying the existing workers' compensation scheme if we

---

**27.** Id.

**28.** "When an employee is hired, he assumes all of the hazards and risks of employment which naturally flow from that employment. He does not as employee give up his rights as a user against a manufacturer." Id. The court concluded:

> Limitations on the remedy of an injured employee should not be extended beyond the purposes of the Workers' Compensation Law. Failure to apply the dual capacity doctrine to the manufacturer who sells to the public would unduly restrict the injured person's remedy. There is no reason to relieve a manufacturer who sells to the public of liability *as a manufacturer* by the chance circumstance that the defendant manufacturer also happens to be an employer of the injured person. The deterrent value of a manufacturer's liability to promote the manufacture of safe products is effectively reduced if recovery is limited to Workers' Compensation.

Id. at 803.

The *Douglas* court limited application of the doctrine "to a defendant who engaged in manufacturing for sale to the general public." Other courts agreed that the dual capacity doctrine only applied to products also made available to the general public. See, e.g., Bibby v. Central Indus. Eng'g Co., 200 Cal.Rptr. 412 (Ct. App. 1984); Simpkins v. Delco, 444 N.E.2d 1064 (Ohio Ct. App. 1981).

**29.** 637 P.2d 266 (Cal. 1981).

**30.** Id. at 273.

**31.** See, e.g., Vineyard v. Southwest Eng'g & Contracting Co., 570 P.2d 823, 824 (Ariz. Ct. App. 1977) ("in view of the exclusivity provisions of the [workers' compensation] Statute which are 'part of the *quid pro quo* in which the sacrifices and gains of employees and employers are to some extent put in balance,' absent an express agreement, the workmen's compensation laws should offer the exclusive remedy"). One commentator at the time argued that the courts were more solicitous of the workers compensation system than was warranted:

> [M]ost courts have yielded to a perception that any breach in the exclusive remedy rule would betray the bargain implicit in the enactment of the original workers' compensation laws and thereby impair, if not destroy, the compensation system itself. In view of the outdated terms of the bargain and the inconsistency of these terms with major goals of compensation law, courts should not feel compelled to apply the exclusive remedy rule rigidly in the borderline cases not squarely within the scope of the bargain. Judicial recognition of reasonable exceptions to the rule would itself contribute to the achievement of safety, compensation, and equity goals while encouraging legislatures to undertake necessary reform of the workers' compensation system.

Note, 96 Harv. L. Rev. 1641, 1661 (1983).

were to permit common law recovery outside of that scheme on the basis of such illusory distinctions."[32] Following "[t]he vast majority of courts [that] have rejected the dual capacity doctrine and have held that an employer who designs, manufactures or distributes a product used by its employees cannot be held liable to an injured employee on the theory of products liability,"[33] a Mississippi federal district court in 1985 observed: " 'Imagine how much would remain of employer immunity if it were forfeited every time an employer adjusted or tinkered with a machine.' "[34]

Even in California and Ohio, the states that spawned the dual capacity doctrine in products liability cases, the doctrine quickly ran out of steam. In 1982, the year after the California Supreme Court approved the doctrine in *Bell*, the California legislature effectively abolished it,[35] and the Ohio Supreme Court restricted the doctrine substantially in the following year.[36] Thus, "[t]he dual capacity doctrine, in spite of widespread and varied attempts to invoke it as a way to defeat exclusiveness, flourished in only two states, Ohio and California, and even there for only a few years, from 1977 to 1983."[37] Recent courts have continued to reject the rule,[38] and it seems safe to proclaim that the dual capacity

---

**32.** Billy v. Consolidated Mach. Tool Corp., 412 N.E.2d 934, 939 (N.Y. 1980). The court further remarked:

The Workers' Compensation Law was designed to spread the risk of industrial accidents through [insurance] coverage and, more specifically, to [provide a swift and sure source of benefits to injured employees] without regard to fault in most instances. In exchange for the security of knowing that fixed benefits will be paid without the need to resort to expensive and sometimes risky litigation, however, the employee has been asked to pay a price [by surrendering] his common-law right to sue his employer in tort and perhaps to enjoy a more substantial recovery through a jury award. The legislative implementation of this "trade-off" is embodied in section 11 of the Workers' Compensation Law, which precludes suits against the employer and limits [an employee] to the recompense afforded under the statute when he is injured in the course of his employment.

We cannot sanction the circumvention of this clear legislative plan by approving a theory which would permit the employer to be sued in his capacity as property owner or manufacturer of equipment used on the job site. As we have previously observed, "an employer remains an employer in his relations with his employees as to all matters arising from and connected with their employment. He may not be treated as a dual legal personality, 'a sort of Dr. Jekyl and Mr. Hyde.' " Employers are expected to provide their employees with a safe workplace that is reasonably free of hazards. This obli-

gation to provide a safe workplace simply cannot be separated in a logical and orderly fashion from the duties owed by the employer to his employees by reason of his ownership of the premises or his manufacture of the equipment with which the employees must work. Indeed, these duties are merely subcategories within the complex of obligations that arise in connection with the employment relation.

Id.

**33.** Rader v. United States Rubber Reclaiming Co., 617 F.Supp. 1045, 1046 (S.D. Miss. 1985) (citing 2A Larson, Workmens' Compensation Law, § 72.81, and noting that "[t]he Mississippi Supreme Court has consistently rejected attempts to circumvent the exclusive remedy of workers' compensation").

**34.** Id.

**35.** See Cal. Lab. Code § 3602.

**36.** See Freese v. Consolidated Rail Corp., 445 N.E.2d 1110 (Ohio 1983). See also Bakonyi v. Ralston Purina Co., 478 N.E.2d 241 (Ohio 1985). Compare Estep v. Rieter Auto. N. Am., 774 N.E.2d 323 (Ohio Ct. App. 2002) (refusing to apply dual capacity rule because defective product not for sale to general public but only for use by employees).

**37.** 6 Larson's Workers' Compensation Law § 113.01[4], at 113–16.

**38.** See, e.g., Minton v. Ralston Purina Co., 47 P.3d 556 (Wash. 2002); Suburban Hosp. v. Kirson, 763 A.2d 185 (Md. Ct. App. 2000) (nurse unable to assert dual capacity claim against employer-hospital for aggra-

doctrine essentially is dead.[39]

## Post-Merger Accidents

Although the dual capacity doctrine appears now to have been put to rest, the "dual persona" doctrine, applicable to a small set of products liability cases, has properly remained alive. A manufacturer may be considered a third person for purposes of the workers' compensation statutes if it possessed "a second persona completely independent from and unrelated to its status as employer"[40] at the time an accident product was manufactured. In the merger context, a number of decisions have held that the dual persona doctrine allows a worker to maintain a products liability claim against his or her employer if the worker is injured by a defective product manufactured by a firm acquired by the employer.[41] In such cases, the courts have reasoned that the exclusive remedy rule of the workers' compensation statutes is not subverted by holding the successor corporation[42] responsible for the liability it assumed as a result of the merger.[43] Indeed, a successor company which expressly undertakes to assume a predecessor's liabilities cannot in fairness or equity be allowed to use the merger as tool for depriving its own employees of the very liabilities it expressly agreed to assume in the merger agreement.

## Intentional Employer Misconduct

One possible escape from the exclusive remedy rule, applicable to a narrow class of cases in which an employee is injured by a dangerously defective product supplied by his or her employer, is to prove that the employer *intended* to harm the employee. If an employer intentionally harms a worker, the worker in most states may maintain a tort action against the employer.[44] The workers' compensation statutes in some

vation of injuries); Hedglin v. Stahl Specialty Co., 903 S.W.2d 922 (Mo. Ct. App. 1995); Ritchie v. Bridgestone/Firestone, Inc., 621 So.2d 288 (Ala. 1993).

**39.** "It is now held with virtual unanimity that an employer, who is also the manufacturer . . . of a product used in the work, cannot be held liable in damages to his own employee on a theory of products liability." 6 Larson's Workers' Compensation Law § 113.03, at 113–14.

**40.** See 6 Larson's Workers' Compensation Law § 113.01[1].

**41.** The seminal case for this proposition is Billy v. Consolidated Mach. Tool Corp., 412 N.E.2d 934 (N.Y. 1980). See also Milford v. Commercial Carriers, Inc., 210 F.Supp.2d 987 (N.D. Ill. 2002) (dual persona exception applied where employer was successor to company that designed defective product); Oliver v. N.L. Indus., Inc., 566 N.Y.S.2d 128 (App. Div. 1991); Gurry v. Cumberland Farms, Inc., 550 N.E.2d 127 (Mass. 1990). Compare Percy v. Falcon Fabricators, Inc., 584 So.2d 17, 18 (Fla. Dist. Ct. App. 1991) (adopting "dual persona"

doctrine for successor corporations: "an injured employee may sue her employer in tort when that employer is the corporate successor of the manufacturer of the defective product that caused the injury, and the product was manufactured before the corporate merger"); Duffy v. Liberty Mach. Co., 562 N.Y.S.2d 769 (App. Div. 1990) (exclusive remedy rule barred employee's claim against employer for injuries from product manufactured by firm that sold product line to employer). *But see* Bland v. IMCO Recycling, Inc., 67 S.W.3d 673 (Mo. Ct. App. 2002) (no liability because parent company, as surviving corporation following merger, was actual employer of worker).

**42.** On the liability of successor corporations generally, see § 15.5, above.

**43.** See, e.g., Billy v. Consolidated Mach. Tool Corp., 412 N.E.2d 934 (N.Y. 1980). See also Gurry v. Cumberland Farms, Inc., 550 N.E.2d 127 (Mass. 1990).

**44.** See, e.g., Caldwell v. Petersburg Stone Co., 2003 WL 21443746 (Ohio Ct. App. 2003) (discussing elements of inten-

states expressly exclude intentional tort actions (or "wilful misconduct") from the exclusive remedy bar.[45] In states with statutes that do not expressly exclude such misconduct from coverage, courts generally hold that the statutes do not cover an employer's intentional misconduct.[46] Typically, such courts reason persuasively that the workers' compensation laws are intended to cover only "accidental" injuries to employees in the workplace, not to shield an employer from civil litigation for injuries it intentionally inflicts on its employees.[47]

For example, *Handley v. Unarco Industries, Inc.*[48] was an action by workers and the representatives of deceased workers at an asbestos company against their employer, alleging claims of intentional murder, fraud, and battery: the murder claim alleged that the defendant "intended to kill plaintiff and his coworkers in that it knew that exposing plaintiffs and his coworkers to huge amounts of asbestos caused a strong probability of death;" the fraud claim asserted that the defendant "fraudulently concealed the dangers of working with asbestos" from the plaintiffs and that the defendant fraudulently represented to the plaintiffs that asbestos was not harmful; and the battery claim charged that the defendant, "intend[ing] bodily harm to the plaintiffs," had a "conscious purpose . . . that asbestos would become trapped in the lungs and bodies of the workers."[49] Allowing the workers claims, the court reasoned that no matter how clearly the state's workers' compensation act stated that compensation under the act was the exclusive remedy against an employer, "the legislature could not be presumed to have intended to permit an intentional tortfeasor to shift his liability to a fund paid for with premiums collected from innocent employers."[50] Similarly, in a carefully reasoned opinion,[51] the Michigan Supreme Court allowed a Dow

---

tional employer tort in Ohio); Laidlow v. Hariton Mach. Co., 790 A.2d 884 (N.J. 2002) (exception would apply if plaintiff could prove that employer desired or knew with substantial certainty that tying up of safety guard would injure an employee); Beauchamp v. Dow Chem. Co., 398 N.W.2d 882 (Mich. 1986). See generally 6 Larson's Workers' Compensation Law § 103.01 et seq.

**45.** See, e.g., N.J. Stat. Ann. § 34:15–8; Ky. Rev. Stat. Ann. ¶ 342.610; Or. Rev. Stat. § 656.156; Wash. Rev. Code § 51.24.020; La. Rev. Stat. Ann. § 23:1032; W. Va. Code § 23–4–2; S.D. Codified Laws Ann. § 62–3–2. *But see* 6 Larson's Workers' Compensation Law § 103.05[5], at 103–35 (warning that "equating wilful and wanton negligence with intent to injure" is "dipping [one's] toe into . . . treacherous waters").

At least Ohio's statute provides that a deliberate removal of safety guards or misrepresentation of hazardous substances is evidence of an "act committed with the intent to injure another." See Ohio Rev. Code Ann. § 4121.80, as amended. See generally 6 Larson's Workers' Compensation Law § 103.05[3].

**46.** See, e.g., Birklid v. Boeing Co., 904 P.2d 278 (Wash. 1995) (toxic chemicals; intentional infliction of emotional distress falls outside of exclusive remedy bar as exempt "deliberate intent to injure"); Potter v. Firestone Tire & Rubber Co., 863 P.2d 795 (Cal. 1993) (recovery allowable for cancerphobia); Beauchamp v. Dow Chem. Co., 398 N.W.2d 882 (Mich. 1986); Pleasant v. Johnson, 325 S.E.2d 244 (N.C. 1985); Mingachos v. CBS, Inc., 491 A.2d 368 (Conn. 1985); Blankenship v. Cincinnati Milacron Chem., 433 N.E.2d 572 (Ohio 1982), rev'd on other grounds, 433 N.E.2d 572 (Ohio 1982) (knowingly exposing employees to noxious chemicals); In re Johns–Manville Asbestosis Cases, 511 F.Supp. 1229 (N.D. Ill. 1981).

**47.** See 6 Larson's Workers' Compensation Law § 103.01.

**48.** 463 N.E.2d 1011 (Ill. App. Ct. 1984).

**49.** Id. at 1020.

**50.** Id. at 1022. See generally 6 Larson's Workers' Compensation Law § 103.05[6].

**51.** For a thorough analysis and critique of *Beauchamp*, cited note 52, below, see 6 Larson's Workers' Compensation Law

Chemical Company research scientist and his wife to maintain various intentional tort claims—for intentional misrepresentation, fraudulent concealment, assault, and intentional infliction of emotional distress—against Dow for injuries from the researcher's on-the-job exposure to Agent Orange.[52]

However, fearful that a flexible intentional harm exception might cause a precipitous erosion of the exclusive remedy principle, most courts interpret this exception narrowly as allowing common law claims only if the plaintiff is able to prove that the employer truly intended to harm the employee, at least in the sense of knowing to a substantial certainty that the employee would be injured.[53] Thus, most courts scrupulously refuse to allow the intentional injury exception to be "stretched to include accidental injuries caused by the gross, wanton, wilful, deliberate, intentional, reckless, culpable, or malicious negligence, breach of statute, or other misconduct of the employer short of a conscious and deliberate intent directed to the purpose of inflicting an injury."[54]

## Scope of Exclusive Remedy Rule

The exclusive remedy rule has various inherent limitations, such as barring a worker's tort recovery against an employer if the worker is a "statutory employee,"[55] but not if he or she is not.[56] Also, the rule may not bar a spouse's claim for loss of consortium.[57] And while the rule will bar a claim against the manufacturer, it may not always bar a claim against a supervisor who directly caused the harm, depending on the particular circumstances and the particular statutory provision.[58] Here, as elsewhere, claims against an employer involve the interpretation of the applicable workers' compensation statute against the backdrop of a

§ 103.05[5] (carefully examining the workers' compensation issues, but recklessly characterizing a hypothetical in Prosser and Keeton on Torts as "silly" while amusingly displaying an utter lack of understanding of basic tort law principles).

**52.** Beauchamp v. Dow Chem. Co., 398 N.W.2d 882 (Mich. 1986). See also Golec v. Dries & Krump Mfg. Co., 551 N.W.2d 132 (Mich. 1996) (allowing action for injuries from explosion of aerosol can, even on tightened statutory standard requiring employer's knowledge that injury was certain—as opposed to substantially certain—to occur).

**53.** See, e.g., Morocco v. Rex Lumber Co., 805 A.2d 168, 173 (Conn. App. Ct. 2002) (employee failed to show that employer knew with substantial certainty that employee would be hurt); Estep v. Rieter Auto. N. Am., 774 N.E.2d 323 (Ohio Ct. App. 2002) (employee failed to prove employer's intent where employer failed to install additional safety guards). See generally Prosser and Keeton on Torts § 80, at 576 ("The vast majority of courts have held that conduct that falls short of an intent to injure will not permit an employee to overcome the exclusivity provision."); 6 Larson's Workers Compensation Law § 103.03.

**54.** Larson's Workers' Compensation Law §§ 103–6 to –7. See, e.g., Sarocco v. General Elec. Co., 879 F.Supp. 156 (D. Mass. 1995) (statute barred claims for all personal injuries, even if arising from fraudulent concealment); Poyser v. Newman & Co., 522 A.2d 548 (Pa. 1987) (statute barred claim for deliberately failing to guard saw blades).

**55.** See, e.g., DuBose v. Flightsafety Int'l, Inc., 824 S.W.2d 486 (Mo. Ct. App. 1992).

**56.** See, e.g., Willison v. Texaco Ref. & Mktg., Inc., 848 P.2d 1062 (Nev. 1993) (defendant might not have had requisite control over employee of wholly-owned subsidiary); Duvon v. Rockwell Int'l, 807 P.2d 876 (Wash. 1991) (former employee).

**57.** See, e.g., Lynn v. Haybuster Mfg., Inc., 627 A.2d 1288 (Conn. 1993).

**58.** See, e.g., Hedglin v. Stahl Specialty Co., 903 S.W.2d 922 (Mo. Ct. App. 1995) (supervisor's actions in dangling plaintiff's decedent by chain over vat of scalding water to retrieve object that had fallen in were outside scope of employment; supervisor might be personally liable). See generally 6

broad scheme of workers compensation law principles, so that a lawyer with such a case should consult authorities on that topic.[59]

## § 15.7  MISCELLANEOUS MARKETING PARTICIPANTS

This chapter so far has examined the major types of nonmanufacturing product suppliers who often play an important role in the chain of distribution. In addition to such key parties, there are a number of other types of marketing participants who sometimes contribute in a secondary way to the sale and distribution of products in society. This section examines the responsibility of some of these secondary parties, including certifiers and endorsers, safety inspectors, trade associations, and various other incidental marketing participants.

### Product Certifiers and Endorsers

Some enterprises, notably Underwriters Laboratories, stimulate the demand for particular products by certifying or endorsing the safety or general quality of products that pass their inspection process. Certain tools, and other products (such as stepladders) are marketed with a "UL" seal of approval. Although Underwriters Laboratories is nominally a nonprofit testing organization, financial support for this large enterprise comes from manufacturers whose product marketing is materially enhanced by a UL certification. Because endorsements by Underwriters Laboratories and other certifiers of product quality may figure prominently in a consumer's purchasing decisions, and because such certifications sometimes may mislead consumers as to a particular product's safety, courts from time to time have addressed the nature and scope of a product certifier's responsibility for injuries from products it has endorsed.[1]

The most cited products liability case concerning a product endorser's liability is *Hanberry v. Hearst Corp.*[2] The plaintiff purchased a pair of shoes that were defective in manufacture and design in that they had a low co-efficient of friction on vinyl surfaces making them slippery and unsafe, which caused her to slip and fall injuring herself on her kitchen floor. The shoes had been advertised in the defendant Hearst Corporation's magazine, Good Housekeeping, as meeting the "Good Housekeeping's Consumers' Guaranty Seal" which the magazine claimed was its "Consumers' Guaranty." The magazine further represented that "[w]e satisfy ourselves that products advertised in Good Housekeeping are good ones and that the advertising claims made for them in our magazine are truthful." The seal itself represented that "[i]f the product or

Larson's Workers Compensation Law § 103.06.

**59.** Larson's Workers Compensation Law, despite its failure to accord proper obeisance to the preeminent field of tort law, see note 51, above, is of course the classic work.

**§ 15.7**

**1.** See Baby, Liability of a Product Endorser as Certifier: A Tort Whose Time Has Come and Gone, 20 Trial 38 (April 1984); Comments, Tort Liability for Nonlibellous Negligent Statements: First Amendment Considerations, 93 Yale L.J. 744 (1984); Note, Publisher Liability for Material that Invites Reliance, 66 Tex. L. Rev. 1155 (1988); Annot., 1 A.L.R.5th 431 (1992) (products liability of endorsers, trade associations, certifiers, and similar parties).

**2.** 81 Cal.Rptr. 519 (Ct. App. 1969).

performance is defective, Good Housekeeping guarantees replacement or refund to consumer."[3]

The plaintiff sued the Hearst Corporation for negligent misrepresentation, breach of warranty, and strict liability in tort. She alleged that she bought the shoes on the strength of the advertisement in the magazine; that the Good Housekeeping seal was affixed to the shoes and the box in which they came; that Hearst either failed to test, investigate, or even examine the type of shoes she bought or, that if it did, it did so negligently; and that "Hearst's issuance of its seal and certification as to the shoes was not warranted by the information it possessed."[4] The trial court dismissed the plaintiff's complaint on demurrer.

On appeal, the *Hanberry* court allowed the negligent misrepresentation claim but denied the claims for breach of warranty and strict liability in tort. On the negligent misrepresentation claim, the court observed that the Good Housekeeping seal enhances the value of its advertisements "because its seal and certification tend to induce and encourage consumers to purchase products advertised in the magazine and which bear that seal and certification," which was their very purpose. "Implicit in the seal and certification is the representation respondent has taken reasonable steps to make an independent examination of the product endorsed, with some degree of expertise, and found it satisfactory."[5] In this situation, the court concluded that a negligent misrepresentation claim was proper: "Having voluntarily involved itself into the marketing process, having in effect loaned its reputation to promote and induce the sale of a given product, ... we think respondent Hearst has placed itself in the position where public policy imposes upon it the duty to use ordinary care in the issuance of its seal and certification of quality so that members of the consuming public who rely on its endorsement are not unreasonably exposed to the risk of harm."[6] But the claims for breach of warranty and strict liability in tort were inappropriate, in the court's view, because the seal implied merely that the defendant had approved the general type of product (presumably its design and possibly its warnings and instructions), not the particular pair of shoes purchased by the plaintiff. If the plaintiff's shoes had a manufacturing defect, the defendant's endorsement could not fairly be interpreted to cover such a defect.[7]

**3.** Id. at 521.

**4.** Id.

**5.** Id. at 522.

**6.** Id.

**7.** The representation associated with the defendant's seal of approval, the court observed, does not suggest that the defendant had tested or examined the particular pair of shoes purchased by the plaintiff.

The most that can be implied from respondent's representation is that it has examined or tested samples of the product and found the general design and materials used to be satisfactory. Applica-tion of either warranty or strict liability in tort would subject respondent to liability even if the general design and material used in making this brand of shoe were good, but the particular pair became defective through some mishap in the manufacturing process. We believe this kind of liability for individually defective items should be limited to those directly involved in the manufacturing and supplying process, and should not be extended through warranty or strict liability to a general endorser who makes no representation it has examined or tested each item marketed.

Id. at 524.

Although the cases are quite sparse,[8] other courts have agreed that certifiers and endorsers are subject to liability for negligent misrepresentation, but that such defendants ordinarily are not subject to liability for breach of warranty or strict liability in tort.[9] This appears to be the correct approach: a certifier should not be permitted to escape responsibility for negligent misrepresentation, and especially not for fraud, for falsely representing the safety of a product. Yet certifiers do not "sell" products nor otherwise directly participate in product sales transactions, nor can they effectively improve product safety or properly spread the cost of injuries from defective products.[10] Accordingly, product certifiers generally should not be held accountable for manufacturing defects or other product dangers that lie outside the scope of a fair interpretation of their endorsements.[11] Nor, of course, are publishers liable merely for advertising products that turn out to be defective.[12]

### Safety Inspectors

Insurance companies and gas utilities having the duty to inspect products for safety, such as industrial machinery, furnaces, or service lines, may be liable for negligent inspection.[13] The courts are split on this issue, however, and many courts hold that such inspectors have no duty or liability to third parties, with whom they are not in privity of contract, for injuries arising out of negligent inspections.[14] The extent of

**8.** See generally Annot., 1 A.L.R.5th 431 (1992).

**9.** See, e.g., U.S. Lighting Serv., Inc. v. Llerrad Corp., 800 F.Supp. 1513 (N.D. Ohio 1992), vacated by 807 F.Supp. 439 (N.D. Ohio 1992) (defective lighting equipment approved by Underwriters Laboratories, a nonprofit testing organization, which was negligent in applying its own internal testing procedures):

> The raison d'etre of the UL mark is to show that a product has met safety standards. By offering its mark to manufacturers, UL has placed itself into the stream of commerce.... The UL seal does not guarantee that a manufacturer has acted with ordinary care but sound public policy requires that UL act with ordinary care in the conduct of its own business—the certification process.

Id. at 1517. The court emphasized, however, that liability against a product endorsement service is limited to negligence, and that it should not extend to strict liability. Id.

See also Hempstead v. General Fire Extinguisher Corp., 269 F.Supp. 109 (D. Del. 1967), where UL allowed the use of its inspection and testing label on a manufacturer's fire extinguishers. *Held,* UL could be held liable, for injuries from the explosion of an extinguisher carrying its label, for negligent approval of its design.

**10.** See, e.g., Bay Summit Cmty. Ass'n. v. Shell Oil Co., 59 Cal.Rptr.2d 322 (Ct. App. 1996).

**11.** See Kurtz and Ohanian, Recent Trends in the Law of Endorsement Advertising: Infomercials, Celebrity Endorsers, and Nontraditional Defendants in Deceptive Advertising Cases, 19 Hofstra L. Rev. 603 (1991); Baby, Liability of a Product Endorser as Certified: A Tort Whose Time Has Come and Gone, 20 Trial 38 (April 1984).

**12.** See, e.g., Walters v. Seventeen Magazine, 241 Cal.Rptr. 101 (Ct. App. 1987) (no liability for advertising tampons that caused toxic shock syndrome); Yuhas v. Mudge, 322 A.2d 824 (N.J. Super. Ct. App. Div. 1974) (no liability for advertising fireworks in Popular Mechanics magazine). See generally § 16.8, below.

**13.** See, e.g., Huggins v. Aetna Cas. & Sur. Co., 264 S.E.2d 191 (Ga. 1980) (providing there is reliance; adopting Restatement (2d) Torts § 324A); Jackson v. New Jersey Mfg. Ins. Co., 400 A.2d 81 (N.J. Super. Ct. App. Div. 1979) (insurer liable to third persons only if it has undertaken to make safety inspections upon which insured has relied); O'Laughlin v. Minnesota Natural Gas Co., 253 N.W.2d 826 (Minn. 1977) (gas furnace). See generally Weinberger, Inspection Companies as Defendants, 130 Products Liability Advisory 8 (Dec. 1999).

**14.** See, e.g., Mueller v. Daum & Dewey, Inc., 636 F.Supp. 192 (E.D.N.C. 1986); Scott v. City of Detroit, 318 N.W.2d 32 (Mich. Ct. App. 1982); Matthews v. Liberty Mut. Ins. Co., 238 N.E.2d 348 (Mass. 1968); De Jesus v. Liberty Mut. Ins. Co., 223 A.2d 849 (Pa. 1966).

a safety inspector's duty to third parties is dependent on the extent to which a jurisdiction has expanded the tort law duties of persons contracting to perform services for others to include the prevention of risk of harm to third parties foreseeably placed at risk by the negligent performance of an inspection undertaking.[15]

Various federal agencies have testing and inspection responsibilities, but the discretionary function exception to liability in the Federal Tort Claims Act often,[16] but not always,[17] will defeat recovery against the government.[18]

### Trade Associations

Trade associations are nonprofit organizations variously composed of manufacturers, retailers, and other product suppliers (often competitors) who share a mutual interest in gathering information about, and promoting, the products that they make or sell.[19] Manufacturers and retailers often form industry-wide trade associations to perform a variety of functions, from serving merely as an information clearing house to performing a wide-ranging assortment of services, such as conducting and sponsoring product testing, research studies, workshops, and technical symposia; developing and recommending design specifications, construction techniques, and packaging and handling procedures; promoting plant safety; collecting, analyzing, and furnishing various safety and other information; and lobbying governmental entities for beneficial legislation.[20] Trade associations are sometimes defendants in products liability litigation.[21]

Compare Lacy v. State Accident Ins. Fund, Inc., 832 P.2d 1268 (Or. Ct. App. 1992) (after accident, workers' compensation insurer does not have duty to inform injured employee that he might have products liability claim against manufacturer of product involved).

**15.** As such, this topic is basically a question of general tort law, to which the reader is referred. See, e.g., Comment, 66 Ky. L.J. 910 (1977–78) (insurers); Annots., 93 A.L.R.2d 598 (1964) (workmen's compensation insurance carriers); 26 A.L.R.2d 136 (1952) (gas companies). See generally Boynton and Evans, What Price Liability for Insurance Carriers Who Undertake Voluntary Safety Inspections, 43 Notre Dame L. Rev. 193 (1967); Prosser and Keeton on Torts § 56, at 381; Restatement (2d) Torts § 324A.

**16.** See, e.g., Irving v. United States, 162 F.3d 154 (1st Cir. 1998) (discretionary function exception barred claim against United States by injured factory worker for negligent OSHA inspection, given broad discretion of OSHA compliance officers in conducting inspections); Cassens v. St. Louis River Cruise Lines, Inc., 44 F.3d 508 (7th Cir. 1995) (Coast Guard's failure to notice absence of handrail on river excursion cruise boat fell within discretionary function exception); United States v. S.A. Empresa de Viacao Aerea Rio Grandense (Varig Airlines), 467 U.S. 797 (1984) (FAA's negligence in certifying aircraft fell within discretionary function).

**17.** See, e.g., In re Sabin Oral Polio Vaccine Prods. Liab. Litig., 984 F.2d 124 (4th Cir. 1993) (FDA failed to follow its own inspection procedures on lot of polio vaccine); Berkovitz v. United States, 486 U.S. 531 (1988) (same). See also Myers v. United States, 17 F.3d 890 (6th Cir. 1994) (discretionary function exception did not bar claim of negligent inspection by Mine Safety and Health Administration, but government not liable for mine owners' safety violations).

**18.** See 1 Am. Law Prod. Liab. 3d § 5:49 et seq.

**19.** See Annot., 1 A.L.R. 5th 431 (1992); 1 Frumer and Friedman, Products Liability § 5.15.

**20.** The trade association defendants in Arnstein v. Manufacturing Chemists Ass'n, 414 F.Supp. 12 (E.D. Pa. 1976) (trade association for chemical suppliers), and Meneely v. S.R. Smith, Inc., 5 P.3d 49 (Wash. Ct. App. 2000) (trade association for swimming pool companies), each performed many of these functions, and each was held subject to negligence liability.

**21.** See Feldmeier, The Risk of Negligence Liability for Trade Associations Engaged in Standards Setting or Product Cer-

Because trade associations do not make or sell products, they are not subject to strict liability in tort[22] or for breach of warranty[23] for defective products sold by members of such associations.[24] Whether trade associations owe a duty of care to customers of their members, subjecting them to claims of negligence for harm to such third parties, is a more difficult question. Many of the negligence duty cases involve an interpretation of the negligent undertaking provision in the *Restatement (Second) of Torts*, § 324A, which concerns negligence that foreseeably endangers third parties. Section 324A provides that one who undertakes to render a service to another, which the actor should recognize as necessary for the protection of a third person, is subject to liability for physical harm to the third person resulting from the failure to exercise reasonable care if: (a) the negligence increases the risk of harm; (b) the actor has undertaken to perform a duty owed by the other to the third person; or (c) the third person relies on the actor's undertaking.[25]

All courts agree that a trade association which neither designs, tests, conducts safety research on, sets standards for, manufactures, nor sells its members' products does not owe an affirmative duty of care to protect the customers of its member companies from defects in the products that the companies make and sell.[26] Indeed, while some courts

---

tification, 34 Tort & Ins. L.J. 785 (1999); Schotland and Rhyne, Products Liability Implications of Trade Association Activities, 7 J. Prod. Liab. 215 (1984); Comment, Trade Association and Product Liability, 16 Cap. U. L. Rev. 581 (1988); 5 Frumer and Friedman, Products Liability § 5.15; 1 Am. Law Prods. Liab. 3d § 5:37.

**22.** See, e.g., Swartzbauer v. Lead Indus. Ass'n, 794 F.Supp. 142 (E.D. Pa. 1992); Evenson v. Osmose Wood Preserving, Inc., 760 F.Supp. 1345 (S.D. Ind. 1990); Harmon v. National Auto. Parts Ass'n, 720 F.Supp. 79 (N.D. Miss. 1989); Howard v. Poseidon Pools, Inc., 506 N.Y.S.2d 523 (Sup. Ct. 1986).

**23.** See, e.g., Hughes v. Tobacco Institute, Inc., 278 F.3d 417, 424 (5th Cir. 2001) (Tex. law) (only sellers, not trade associations, could be liable for breach of express warranty); Evenson v. Osmose Wood Preserving, Inc., 760 F.Supp. 1345 (S.D. Ind. 1990); Harmon v. National Auto. Parts Ass'n, 720 F.Supp. 79 (N.D. Miss. 1989) (trade association not a "seller" under UCC § 2–103(1)(d)); Howard v. Poseidon Pools, Inc., 506 N.Y.S.2d 523 (Sup. Ct. 1986) (trade association did not place product in stream of commerce); Klein v. Council of Chem. Ass'n, 587 F.Supp. 213 (E.D. Pa. 1984) (neither trade association nor industry research institute placed any chemical product into stream of commerce); Albin v. Illinois Crop Improvement Ass'n, 174 N.E.2d 697 (Ill. App. Ct. 1961), disapproved on other grounds by Rozny v. Marnul, 250 N.E.2d 656 (Ill. 1969) (no privity of contract).

**24.** A trade association normally cannot be considered a "seller" under a state products liability statute. See, e.g., Jefferson v. Lead Indus. Ass'n, 930 F.Supp. 241, 247–48 (E.D. La. 1996), aff'd per curiam, 106 F.3d 1245 (5th Cir. 1997) (trade association not subject to suit under Louisiana Products Liability Act).

**25.** Compare, for example, FNS Mortgage Serv. Corp. v. Pacific Gen. Group, Inc., 29 Cal.Rptr.2d 916 (Ct. App. 1994) (finding undertaking under § 324A), King v. National Spa & Pool Inst., Inc., 570 So.2d 612 (Ala. 1990) (same), and Arnstein v. Manufacturing Chemists Ass'n, 414 F.Supp. 12 (E.D. Pa. 1976) (same), with Bailey v. Edward Hines Lumber Co., 719 N.E.2d 178 (Ill. App. Ct. 1999) (no undertaking under § 324A; thorough review of cases and policy issues); Meyers v. Donnatacci, 531 A.2d 398 (N.J. Super. Ct. Law Div. 1987) (no undertaking under § 324A), Klein v. Council of Chem. Assn's., 587 F.Supp. 213 (E.D. Pa. 1984) (same).

In Meneely v. S.R. Smith, Inc., 5 P.3d 49 (Wash. Ct. App. 2000), the trial court found a duty in both § 324A and the duty to rescue, but the intermediate appellate court rested its decision solely on the duty to rescue since the state supreme court had not yet adopted § 324A. See id. at 58 n.4.

**26.** See, e.g., Bailey v. Edward Hines Lumber Co., 719 N.E.2d 178 (Ill. App. Ct. 1999) (2–1 decision); Evenson v. Osmose Wood Preserving, Inc., 760 F.Supp. 1345 (S.D. Ind. 1990). Even King v. National Spa & Pool Inst., Inc., 570 So.2d 612, 614 (Ala.

have found industry trade associations to have a duty of care to ultimate customers when they promulgate standards for use by association members,[27] most courts, reluctant to force such useful organizations to don the burdensome mantle of rule-making organizations,[28] have refused to find a duty even when the trade association plays some role in the development and promulgation of safety standards.[29]

But the greater a trade association's participation in the development and promulgation of safety standards, the more likely it is that the individual members of the association will come to rely upon and defer to the standards of the association. In such cases, a trade association may effectively undertake design and warnings responsibilities for an entire industry, a circumstance that may make it reasonable to hold the association responsible for negligently failing to perform its responsibilities in a manner protective of the safety of consumers of products manufactured to association specifications by members of the trade association. Thus, in *Meneely v. S.R. Smith, Inc.*,[30] the court upheld a judgment against the trade association for swimming pool suppliers for negligently failing to revise its industry-wide safety standard, which permitted the use of a particular type of diving board in a particular type of pool, when its own testing revealed that certain divers risked serious injury from this particular combination and further knew that pool and board manufacturers relied upon the trade association standard. Similar-

1990), agreed with this basic tort law principle: "There is no duty imposed by judicial decision on trade associations to promulgate industry standards." Yet *King* turned on an alternative principle captured in Justice Cardozo's precept that "one who assumes to act, even though gratuitously, may thereby become subject to the duty of acting carefully." Glanzer v. Shepard, 135 N.E. 275, 276 (N.Y. 1922). Hence, once a trade association undertakes to formulate a standard, it is obligated to exercise reasonable care in doing so. *Held*, swimming pool trade association was subject to negligence liability for the construction and installation standards that it promulgated that were relied upon by manufacturer or installer of pool. 570 So.2d at 614–16.

**27.**   Meneely v. S.R. Smith, Inc., 5 P.3d 49 (Wash. Ct. App. 2000); Weigand v. University Hosp. of N.Y. Univ. Med. Ctr., 659 N.Y.S.2d 395 (Sup. Ct. 1997); Snyder v. American Ass'n of Blood Banks, 676 A.2d 1036 (N.J. 1996); Prudential Prop. & Cas. Ins. Co. v. American Plywood Ass'n, 1994 WL 463527 (S.D. Fla. 1994) (construction standards proved far too lax by Hurricane Andrew); King v. National Spa & Pool Inst., Inc., 570 So.2d 612 (Ala. 1990); Arnstein v. Manufacturing Chemists Ass'n, Inc., 414 F.Supp. 12 (E.D. Pa. 1976).

**28.**   See, e.g., Meyers v. Donnatacci, 531 A.2d 398, 405 (N.J. Super. Ct. Law Div. 1987).

**29.**   See, e.g., Tuttle v. Lorillard Tobacco Co., 2003 WL 1571584 (D. Minn. 2003) (ab-

sent proof Smokeless Tobacco Council manufactured, sold, or designed cigarettes, or set standards, no duty), aff'd, 377 F.3d 917 (8th Cir. 2004); Bailey v. Edward Hines Lumber Co., 719 N.E.2d 178 (Ill. App. Ct. 1999) (2–1 decision) (truss plate manufacturing industry trade association provided recommendations on truss installation); Friedman v. F.E. Myers Co., 706 F.Supp. 376 (E.D. Pa. 1989) (no duty even if trade association disseminated misleading information to members about dangers of PCBs); Meyers v. Donnatacci, 531 A.2d 398 (N.J. Super. Ct. Law Div. 1987) (swimming pool trade association promulgated suggested minimum standards); Howard v. Poseidon Pools, Inc., 506 N.Y.S.2d 523 (Sup. Ct. 1986) (no duty even if trade association made design change recommendations); Beasock v. Dioguardi Enter., Inc., 494 N.Y.S.2d 974 (Sup. Ct. 1985) (no duty to warn of danger of mismatching tire on wrong size rim, despite trade association's role in promoting and maintaining dimensional standards for tires and rims among its members); Klein v. Council of Chem. Ass'n, 587 F.Supp. 213 (E.D. Pa. 1984) (four trade associations and research institute; no duty). Compare Harmon v. National Auto. Parts Ass'n, 720 F.Supp. 79 (N.D. Miss. 1989) (no duty although association permitted members to fund national advertising under its name).

**30.**   5 P.3d 49 (Wash. Ct. App. 2000).

ly, in view of the heavy reliance placed by blood banks, hospitals, and patients on the American Association of Blood Bank's recommended procedures for assuring the quality of blood, at least a couple of courts have held this organization subject to liability for negligence in its recommended procedures.[31]

Sometimes plaintiffs claim that trade associations are basically a front for civil conspiracies to obstruct legislation and litigation and, more generally, to frustrate the principles of products liability and safety.[32] Normally courts reject such claims, on both substantive[33] and First Amendment grounds,[34] but the litigation against the tobacco industry more plausibly supports such claims.[35]

### Other Marketing Participants

A large miscellany of other types of defendants are sometimes involved in products liability litigation.[36] Certain important products liability defendants—automotive manufacturers, and manufacturers of prescription drugs, blood and biological products, and of medical devices, instruments, and equipment—are treated later in sections of their own.[37] The following chapter covers many different types of transactions and products, such as product leases, bailments, and the sale of used products—supplied to consumers by lessors, bailors, and used product sellers—and the responsibilities of those special types of defendants are treated there.[38] The remaining part of the present section summarizes principles applicable to certain miscellaneous defendants whose liability is not addressed elsewhere in this work.

Most participants in product marketing, particularly product suppliers who directly place a product in the marketing chain, are subject to

**31.** See, e.g., Jappell v. American Ass'n of Blood Banks, 162 F.Supp.2d 476 (E.D. Va. 2001); Weigand v. University Hosp. of N.Y. Univ. Med. Ctr., 659 N.Y.S.2d 395 (Sup. Ct. 1997); Snyder v. American Ass'n of Blood Banks, 676 A.2d 1036 (N.J. 1996) (negligence in failing to recommend surrogate testing for AIDS virus). But cf. N.N.V. v. American Ass'n of Blood Banks, 89 Cal. Rptr.2d 885 (Ct. App. 1999) (but blood bank only liable for negligence, and not liable if it could not reasonably have known of danger); In re Factor VIII or IX Concentrate Blood Prods. Litig., 25 F.Supp.2d 837 (N.D. Ill. 1998) (nonprofit organization which provided information to hemophiliacs about blood products entitled to First Amendment free press protections).

**32.** Civil conspiracy claims are examined in § 11.3, above.

**33.** See, e.g., James v. National Shooting Sports Found., Inc., 2003 WL 1843975 (N.J. Super. App. Div. 2003) (no proof that handgun manufacturer trade associations engaged in activities amounting to public nuisance).

**34.** See, e.g., Chavers v. Gatke Corp., 132 Cal.Rptr.2d 198 (Ct. App. 2003) (requiring asbestos manufacturer to stand trial for civil conspiracy or concert of action claims without proof of unlawful intent might chill defendant's first amendment freedom of association to contribute to, attend the meetings of, and otherwise associate with trade groups engaging in public advocacy and debate; In re Asbestos Sch. Litig. (Pfizer Inc. v. Giles), 46 F.3d 1284 (3d Cir. 1994) (2–1 decision) (membership in trade association does not support civil conspiracy and concert of action claims and is protected by first amendment).

**35.** See, e.g., Rogers v. R.J. Reynolds Tobacco Co., 761 S.W.2d 788 (Tex. App. 1988). See also Lewis v. Lead Ind. Ass'n, Inc., 793 N.E.2d 869 (Ill. App. Ct. 2003) (reinstating plaintiffs' civil conspiracy claim against defendants associated with lead paint).

**36.** For discussions of such miscellaneous defendants, see generally 1 Frumer and Friedman, Products Liability §§ 5.06–.17; 1 Am. Law Prods. Liab. §§ 5:22–52.

**37.** See §§ 8.10 and 9.6 (Prescription Drugs and Medical Devices), above, and ch. 17 (Automotive Litigation), below.

**38.** See ch. 16, below.

liability in negligence for failing to exercise reasonable care to avoid conduct that foreseeably endangers product users.[39] However, as a party's connection with the chain of product distribution (and hence with the ultimate consumer or user) grows more remote, the likelihood that the party will owe a duty of care to product users attenuates and eventually disappears. Thus, secondary participants in the chain of product distribution may or may not have a duty of care to product users, depending on the nature and degree of their control over the safety and marketing of particular injury-producing products.[40]

Many of the cases involving miscellaneous defendants involve the issue of whether the particular type of defendant is subject to strict products liability in tort or liability for breach of warranty. Because most secondary participants in product marketing do not design, manufacture, market, or sell products to consumers, they generally are not subject to strict liability either in tort or for breach of the implied warranty of merchantability. Such defendants ordinarily are not "engaged in the business of selling" or "otherwise distributing" such products, as required by both *Restatement (Second) of Torts* § 402A[41] and *Restatement (Third) of Torts: Products Liability* § 1.[42] Section 402A clearly does not apply to isolated product sales by ordinary individuals,[43] such as an individual's one-time sale of a used car,[44] nor does it apply to "sales of the stock of merchants out of the usual course of business, such as execution sales, bankruptcy sales, bulk sales, and the like."[45] Nor does the Uniform Commercial Code usually apply to such secondary products liability defendants who ordinarily do not qualify as "merchant" sellers for purposes of the implied warranty of merchantability.[46] In short, the principles of strict products liability normally apply only to commercial sellers, and even then only to their regular,[47] rather than occasional,[48] products sales.

**39.** Negligence liability is examined generally in ch. 2, above.

**40.** Compare Wissel v. Ohio High Sch. Athletic Ass'n, 605 N.E.2d 458 (Ohio Ct. App. 1992) (nonprofit safety-standards organization was subject to liability in negligence under Restatement (2d) Torts § 324A), with Meyers v. Donnatacci, 531 A.2d 398 (N.J. Super. Ct. Law Div. 1987) (trade association not subject to liability under § 324A).

**41.** See Restatement (2d) Torts § 402A(1)(a) and cmt. *f.*

**42.** See also Products Liability Restatement § 20.

**43.** Section 402A does not apply to "the ordinary individual who makes the isolated sale, and he is not liable to a third person, or even to his buyer, in the absence of his negligence." Restatement (2d) Torts § 402A cmt. *f.*

**44.** See, e.g., Griffin Indus., Inc. v. Jones, 975 S.W.2d 100 (Ky. 1998).

**45.** Restatement (2d) Torts § 402A cmt. *f.*

**46.** Under UCC § 2–314(1)(a), the implied warranty of merchantability applies to goods only "if the seller is a merchant with respect to goods of that kind." UCC §§ 2–313 (express warranties) and 2–315 (implied warranties of fitness for particular purpose) apply to "sellers" generally. Section 2–103(1)(d) defines "seller" as "a person who sells or contracts to sell goods." See generally ch. 4, above.

**47.** For example, in Nutting v. Ford Motor Co., 584 N.Y.S.2d 653 (App. Div. 1992), Hewlett Packard regularly resold its fleet of more than 3,000 cars:

[O]ne who regularly purchases a substantial quantity of new cars for use by its employees and regularly disposes of those vehicles by auction sales to used car dealers for resale to the public after the vehicles have been used for approximately one year is in the regular business of a used car dealer for the purposes of imposing strict products liability.

Id. at 656.

**48.** If the seller does not regularly deal in used good sales, but only does so infre-

For these reasons, strict liability in tort does not apply to nonprofit standards-setting organizations which merely establish safety standards for products but which neither manufacture nor sell such products.[49] Such entities may be subject to liability in negligence, however, under *Restatement (Second) of Torts* § 324A.[50]

Auctioneers are not strictly liable in tort for the products that they auction,[51] but they may be subject to liability for fraudulent misrepresentation[52] or for breach of implied warranty of merchantability if they regularly auction merchandise of a particular type and hold themselves out as being experts in the field,[53] particularly if they fail to reveal the identity of their principal.[54]

The liability of sales representatives and agents, and brokers, is less clear, although normally they are not subject to strict products liability.[55] But sales representatives and agents, particularly if they serve in an exclusive capacity, may be subject to strict liability for harm from defective products if they participate directly in and profit from a sales transaction, thereby becoming an important link in the product's distri-

---

quently, it will not be considered a "seller" of the used goods. See, e.g., Stiles v. Batavia Atomic Horseshoes, Inc., 613 N.E.2d 572 (N.Y. 1993); Sukljian v. Charles Ross & Son Co., 503 N.E.2d 1358, 1361 (N.Y. 1986) (G.E. each year sold at auction two or three used machines of a particular type that it had purchased new and used for many years: "strict liability was inapposite because [G.E. had not] *regularly* engaged in the business of selling the equipment in issue"). But compare Sprung v. MTR Ravensburg Inc., 788 N.E.2d 620, 623 (N.Y. 2003) ("'casual' or 'occasional' sales are not subject to claims of strict liability"; but custom fabricator of retractable floor sold in ordinary course of business subject to strict liability).

**49.** See, e.g., Wissel v. Ohio High Sch. Athletic Ass'n, 605 N.E.2d 458 (Ohio Ct. App. 1992) (nonprofit organization engaged in setting safety standards for athletic equipment, including setting minimum impact requirements for football helmets, was not a "seller" for purposes of strict liability in tort but was subject to liability in negligence under Restatement (2d) Torts § 324A).

**50.** Id.

**51.** See, e.g., Pelnar v. Rosen Sys., Inc., 964 F.Supp. 1277 (E.D. Wis. 1997) (machinery auctioneer); Musser v. Vilsmeier Auction Co., 562 A.2d 279 (Pa. 1989); Tauber–Arons Auctioneers Co. v. Superior Ct., 161 Cal.Rptr. 789 (Ct. App. 1980). See generally Annot., 83 A.L.R.4th 1188 (1991) (liability of auctioneers for strict products liability).

**52.** See Werremeyer v. K.C. Auto Salvage Co., Inc., 2003 WL 21487311 (Mo. Ct. App. 2003), rev'd in part on other grounds, 134 S.W.3d 633 (Mo. 2004) (en banc) (car auctioneer subject to liability for fraudulent misrepresentation for car that contained stolen chassis of one car and stolen body of another).

**53.** See, e.g., Bradford v. Northwest Ala. Livestock Ass'n, 379 So.2d 609 (Ala. Civ. App. 1980).

**54.** See Powers v. Coffeyville Livestock Sales Co., 665 F.2d 311 (10th Cir. 1981) (Kan. law).

**55.** See, e.g., Memphis Bank & Trust Co. v. Water Serv., Inc., 758 S.W.2d 525 (Tenn. 1988) (sales representative); Alvarez v. Koby Mach. Co., 516 N.E.2d 930 (Ill. App. Ct. 1987) (sales facilitator); Lyons v. Premo Pharm. Labs, Inc., 406 A.2d 185 (N.J. Super. Ct. App. Div. 1979) (passive role of broker, who never had control over product, prevents him from being strictly liable). See also Dillard Dep't Stores, Inc. v. Associated Merch. Corp., 782 P.2d 1187 (Ariz. Ct. App. 1989) (non-profit merchandising organization).

The relationship of auctioneers to products is similar to that of sales personnel; thus auctioneers also are not held strictly liable. See, e.g., Musser v. Vilsmeier Auction Co., 562 A.2d 279, 283 (Pa. 1989) ("[An] auctioneer is . . . an ad hoc salesman of the goods of another. . . . He bears no relationship to the manufacturer or the goods, beyond their immediate sale."); Tauber–Arons Auctioneers Co., v. Superior Ct., 161 Cal.Rptr. 789 (Ct. App. 1980) (treating auctioneer as dealer in used machinery).

bution.[56] For example, in *Brumbaugh v. CEJJ, Inc.*,[57] the plaintiff brought a strict liability action against the exclusive marketing agent of a trash compactor to recover for fatal injuries of a worker when a dumpster swung loose from the trash compactor. A New York appeals court permitted the action explaining that imposing liability against such defendants "would provide injured consumers with a greater opportunity to commence an action against the party responsible, fix liability on one who is in a position to exert pressure on the manufacturer to improve the safety of the product, [and] ensure that the burden of accidental injuries ... be treated as a cost of production by placing liability upon those who market them."[58] Even if the agent never takes possession of the product, controls it, or takes title to it, the agent still may be strictly liable.[59]

While the broker involved in the sale of an airplane was held to be a product supplier in one case,[60] brokers generally are viewed as mere go-betweens whose only duty is to effect a sales agreement between the parties.[61] Often they do not take physical control over the products that they broker and usually do not otherwise qualify as the type of "sellers" to which strict liability appropriately attaches.[62] In a case concerning a spice broker who arranged sales of recleaned and treated peppercorns between an importer and a seller, the court found that a plaintiff could not bring a strict liability claim against a broker unless he had such control over the transaction that he could control or eliminate the risk, or pressure the parties responsible for the defect to improve the safety of the product.[63]

---

**56.** See, e.g., Bittler v. White & Co., 560 N.E.2d 979 (Ill. App. Ct. 1990) (exclusive sales rep of truck-mounted vacuum loader could be strictly liable in tort because agent had sufficient "participatory connection" with the marketing of the product); Brumbaugh v. CEJJ, Inc., 547 N.Y.S.2d 699, 701 (App. Div. 1989) (exclusive marketing agent); Weber v. Johns–Manville Corp., 630 F.Supp. 285 (D.N.J. 1986); Hoffman v. Loos & Dilworth, Inc., 452 A.2d 1349 (Pa. Super. Ct. 1982).

**57.** 547 N.Y.S.2d 699 (Sup. Ct. 1989).

**58.** Id. at 701.

**59.** See, e.g., Brumbaugh v. CEJJ, Inc., 547 N.Y.S.2d 699 (Sup. Ct. 1989).

**60.** See Alaskan Oil, Inc. v. Central Flying Serv., Inc., 975 F.2d 553 (8th Cir. 1992) (Ark. law).

**61.** See Straley v. United States, 887 F.Supp. 728 (D.N.J. 1995) (but broker may be subject to liability for taking title to product in its own name, even briefly).

**62.** See, e.g., Geboy v. TRL Inc., 159 F.3d 993 (7th Cir. 1998) (Wis. law); Ankum v. White Consol. Indus., 1992 WL 314904 (E.D. La. 1992); Oscar Mayer Corp. v. Mincing Trading Corp., 744 F.Supp. 79 (D.N.J. 1990) (N.J. and N.Y. law); Lyons v. Premo Pharm. Labs, Inc., 406 A.2d 185 (N.J. Super. Ct. App. Div. 1979).

**63.** Oscar Mayer Corp. v. Mincing Trading Corp., 744 F.Supp. 79 (D.N.J. 1990) (N.J. and N.Y. law).

# Chapter 16

<hr>

# SPECIAL TYPES OF TRANSACTIONS
# AND PRODUCTS

*Table of Sections*

<hr>

## § 16.1  Special Types of Transactions and Products— Generally

Some products liability litigation involves transactions other than the typical sale of a new chattel, the paradigm around which most products liability law is centered. The principal issue involved in many of the cases examined in this chapter is whether the usual principles of products liability law, particularly the doctrine of strict products liability, should be extended from the new chattel sale situation to another context in which other policies and principles may predominate. In some of these situations, the differing objectives and doctrinal borderlines of products liability, premises liability, professional malpractice, environmental protection, free speech, public health, and other areas of the law are brought into sharp relief.

This chapter thus considers a number of special types of transactions and products that differ from the paradigm. Section 16.2 examines the major types of non-sale transactions—those involving leases, bailments, and licenses—that may implicate products liability principles. Section 16.3 addresses the extent to which traditional products liability rules may apply to transactions in which a supplier provides services together with a product. Sections 16.4 and 16.5 consider how legal principles may change if the product sold is not new—if it has been repaired, rebuilt, reconditioned, or is simply used. And the remaining sections examine the legal principles surrounding the provision of a variety of particular products and transactions that sometimes prove harmful, including the supply of electricity,[1] hazardous buildings,[2] dangerous types of publications (including certain computer games),[3] infected blood,[4] and dangerous animals.[5] Disposal and salvage transactions were examined previously as limitations on defectiveness.[6]

## § 16.2   LEASE, BAILMENT, AND LICENSE TRANSACTIONS

### Leases

Lease transactions[1] are an increasingly common method by which consumers take possession of the products they put to daily use, such as cars, trucks, cranes and other chattels that are likely to be dangerous if defective.[2] Indeed, consumers and businesses to a large extent are shifting away from purchasing many types of products, notably automobiles, and are obtaining them instead by means of short-term and long-term leases.[3] In general, the products liability principles that presently control a supplier's *sale* of a product apply with equal force to those applicable to product *leases*. But the law has taken some time to evolve to this point, and some jurisdictions have yet to complete the process of breaking down the barriers separating the law governing product sales and leases.

### *Theory of Liability*

**Negligence.** Ordinary negligence principles govern the liability of lessors of defective products that injure lessees and other people. *Restatement (Second) of Torts* § 408 provides that a lessor is subject to liability to lessees and others foreseeably endangered by the lessor's failure to exercise due care to make the leased product safe for its probable uses and for failing to warn of any hidden dangers the product may possess.[4]

### § 16.1

1. See § 16.6, below.
2. See § 16.7, below.
3. See § 16.8, below.
4. See § 16.9, below.
5. See § 16.10, below.
6. See § 10.6, above.

### § 16.2

**1.** " 'Lease' means the transfer of the right to possession and use of goods for a term in return for consideration. . . . " UCC § 2A–103(j).

**2.** See, e.g., Samuel Friedland Family Enters. v. Amoroso, 630 So.2d 1067, 1070 (Fla. 1994) (court was "[m]indful of the recent growth of the commercial leasing business in recent years"); Martin v. Ryder Truck Rental, Inc., 353 A.2d 581, 587 (Del. 1976) (noting the "present day magnitude of the motor vehicle rental business"); Price v. Shell Oil Co., 466 P.2d 722, 726 (Cal. 1970) (noting "the widespread use of the lease of personalty in today's business world"); Cintrone v. Hertz Truck Leasing & Rental Serv., 212 A.2d 769, 776 (N.J. 1965)

(Francis, J.) (taking judicial notice of growth in vehicular rental business). See generally Ausness, Strict Liability for Chattel Leasing, 48 U. Pitt. L. Rev. 273 (1987); Henszey, Application of Strict Liability to the Leasing Industry, 33 Bus. Law. 631 (1978); Annot., 52 A.L.R.3d 121 (1974) (applicability of strict liability in tort to chattel lessors); 1 Frumer and Friedman, Products Liability § 5.07.

**3.** See Ausness, above note 2, at 274–76 (detailing boom in both short-term and long-term leasing in America); 3 Anderson, Uniform Commercial Code § 2–314:64, at 276.

**4.** Restatement (2d) Torts § 408 provides in full:

One who leases a chattel as safe for immediate use is subject to liability to those whom he should expect to use the chattel, or to be endangered by its probable use, for physical harm caused by its use in a manner for which, and by a person for whose use, it is leased, if the lessor fails to exercise reasonable care to make it safe for such use or to disclose its actual

The lessor's duty of care includes subjecting its products to appropriate inspections, from initial purchase throughout the product's periodic use.[5] Indeed, a commercial lessor's duty of care is said to include, in the absence of an agreement to the contrary, an implied promise "that the article is leased as fit for immediate use."[6] In addition to other claims, plaintiffs commonly include allegations of negligence in products liability actions against lessors of dangerously defective products.[7]

**Warranty—Article 2.** By its terms, "Article 2—Sales" of the Uniform Commercial Code applies only to true sales transactions,[8] which suggests that it was not intended to apply to lease transactions in which the lessor retains title to the goods. In *Leake v. Meredith*,[9] for example, the plaintiff was injured by the collapse of an aluminum extension ladder he had rented from the defendant. In his suit against the lessor, the plaintiff alleged negligence and breach of an implied warranty of fitness. The trial court ruled for the defendant on the negligence claim but submitted the implied warranty claim to the jury which found for the plaintiff. On appeal, the court reversed the judgment, ruling that a literal reading of the relevant sections of the Code "indicates that the implied warranty of fitness for a particular purpose . . . applies to sales only, and not to bailments or chattel lease transactions."[10] Other courts have similarly construed Article 2 strictly as not applying to lease transactions.[11]

By one means or another, however, most courts have extended the principles of Article 2 to lease transactions.[12] Some courts[13] have relied upon a comment to UCC § 2–313 which disclaims any effort to displace developing case law on this issue;[14] some courts have applied Article 2 to

condition to those who may be expected to use it.

But to be liable for negligently failing to warn, a lessor must be shown to have had reason to know of the defect. See, e.g., Evans v. Byers Enter., Inc., 2000 WL 522469 (Ohio Ct. App. 2000) (no proof that lessor knew or had reason to know that trunk could unexpectedly fall and injure user).

**5.** See Restatement (2d) Torts § 408 cmt. *a*.

**6.** Id. cmt. *b*.

**7.** See, e.g., Evans v. Byers Enter., Inc., 2000 WL 522469 (Ohio Ct. App. 2000) (not liable); Kemp v. Miller, 453 N.W.2d 872 (Wis. 1990); Bachner v. Pearson, 479 P.2d 319 (Alaska 1970).

**8.** UCC § 2–106(1) provides that "[a] 'sale' consists in the passing of title from the seller to the buyer," and § 2–103(1)(d) provides that " 'Seller' means a person who sells or contracts to sell goods."

**9.** 267 S.E.2d 93 (Va. 1980).

**10.** Id. at 95.

**11.** See, e.g., Bechtel v. Paul Clark, Inc., 412 N.E.2d 143 (Mass. App. Ct. 1980) (injuries from defective brakes on rental car not recoverable in claim for breach of warranty under UCC § 2–314). Although the state legislature had subsequently amended Article 2 to include lessors within its scope, the court refused to apply it retroactively to cover the plaintiff's transaction. Id. at 149–50. Cf. Dicintio v. DaimlerChrysler Corp., 97 N.Y.2d 463 (2002) (holding that Magnuson Moss Act, enacted against backdrop of UCC Article 2, does not apply to lease transactions). See generally 3 Anderson, Uniform Commercial Code § 2–314:62, at 274.

**12.** See, e.g., Cucchi v. Rollins Protective Servs. Co., 574 A.2d 565, 571 (Pa. 1990) (alarm system: "lessees rely upon implied and express representations of lessors as to the quality, merchantability, and fitness of goods to the same extent and in the same manner as buyers rely upon similar representations by sellers").

**13.** See, e.g., Cintrone v. Hertz Truck Leasing & Rental Serv., 212 A.2d 769, 775–76 (N.J. 1965).

**14.** See UCC § 2–313 cmt. 2:

[T]he warranty sections of this Article are not designed in any way to disturb those lines of case law growth which have recognized that warranties need not be

leases when a transaction is in the nature of a disguised sale;[15] while other courts have applied Article 2 by analogy, reasoning that such transactions are closely similar to sales,[16] an approach criticized by commentators for being at once too narrow and too vague.[17] Some courts, applying a policy-oriented approach, extend Article 2's warranty protections to lessees when such an approach is consistent with underlying policies of the law. For example, the Washington Supreme Court used this approach in extending Article 2's warranty provisions to a plaintiff's claim for injuries resulting when defective brakes on his rental golf cart caused the cart to overturn,[18] as did the Florida Supreme Court in an action against the lessor of a defective forklift hoist which malfunctioned while lifting a wheelchair passenger from an airplane.[19] Many other courts have similarly applied a policy-based perspective,[20] an approach applauded by the commentators.[21]

**Warranty—Article 2A.** The problem of whether Article 2 should be applied to lease transactions was resolved in 1987, when a new "Article 2A—Leases" was promulgated and promptly enacted into law in a number of jurisdictions. The article was amended in a number of respects in 1990,[22] and almost all states enacted this new article of the Uniform Commercial Code which explicitly applies to personal property "lease" transactions.[23] In 2002–03, Article 2A was revised again, and most states eventually should adopt this version.[24] Article 2A's key

confined ... to sales contracts.... They may arise in other appropriate circumstances such as in the case of bailments for hire, whether such bailment is itself the main contract or is merely a supplying of containers under a contract for the sale of their contents. [T]he matter is left to the case law with the intention that the policies of this Act may offer useful guidance in dealing with further cases as they arise.

**15.** See 3 Anderson, Uniform Commercial Code § 2–314:63, at 275.

**16.** See 3 Anderson, Uniform Commercial Code § 2–314:64, at 276.

**17.** See, e.g., Murray, Under the Spreading Analogy of Article 2 of the Uniform Commercial Code, 39 Fordham L. Rev. 447, 451 (1971); Ausness, Strict Liability for Chattel Leasing, 48 U. Pitt. L. Rev. 273, 293 (1987).

**18.** Baker v. City of Seattle, 484 P.2d 405 (Wash. 1971).

**19.** See W.E. Johnson Equip. Co. v. United Airlines, Inc., 238 So.2d 98, 100 (Fla. 1970) ("The reasons for imposing the warranty of fitness in sales cases are often present in lease transactions. Public policy demands that is this day of expanding rental and leasing enterprises the consumer who leases be given protection equivalent to the consumer who purchases. Although a sale transfers ownership and a lease or bailment merely transfers possession and anticipates future return of the chattel to the owner, there may be as much or more reli-

ance on the competence or expertise of the lessor than on the competence of the seller.").

**20.** See, e.g., Owens v. Patent Scaffolding Co.—Div. of Harsco, 354 N.Y.S.2d 778, 784 (Sup. Ct. 1974), rev'd on other grounds, 376 N.Y.S.2d 948 (App. Div. 1975) (Article 2 warranty provisions applied to lease transactions since "there is no real commercial or economic difference to a contractor-user of scaffolding equipment between buying equipment and leasing it for use on a job").

**21.** See, e.g., Ausness, above note 2, at 295 (this approach "correctly focuses on the policies that underlie warranty protection instead of applying a mechanical test"); Krasnow, The Extension of Warranty Protection to Lease Transactions, 10 B.C. Ind. & Com. L. Rev. 127, 138 (1968).

**22.** See UCC § 2A–101 Official Comment (History).

**23.** UCC § 2A–103(j) provides: " 'Lease' means a transfer of the right to possession and use of goods for a term in return for consideration.... " See cmt. to id. ("a lease is created when the lessee agrees to furnish consideration for the right to the possession and use of goods over a specified period of time," citing Mooney, Personal Property Leasing: A Challenge, 36 Bus. Law. 1605, 1607 (1981)).

**24.** In 2002, the National Conference of Commissioners on Uniform State Laws (NCCUSL) approved the revision of Article

provisions closely mimic Article 2's provisions governing the law of sales, including similar provisions on express and implied warranties, damages, and the various bases for contractual limitations.[25] While it is still too early to know how courts will apply Article 2A to products liability actions involving personal injuries, its widespread enactment has undoubtedly relieved the courts of having to decide whether, how, and to what extent they should apply Article 2 to lease transactions.

**Strict Liability in Tort.** The landmark case extending strict liability in tort to lessors of motor vehicles was *Cintrone v. Hertz Truck Leasing & Rental Serv.*,[26] in which a passenger in a rental truck was injured when the brakes failed. The plaintiff sued the rental company, Hertz, for breach of implied warranty and negligence in failing properly to maintain the brakes. The trial court dismissed the warranty claim, and the jury found for Hertz on the negligence claim. On appeal, the New Jersey Supreme Court reversed the dismissal of the warranty claim, holding that the commercial rental of a truck included an implied warranty that the truck was fit and would remain so throughout the rental period. Writing for the majority, Judge Francis, who had authored *Henningsen v. Bloomfield Motors, Inc.*[27] five years earlier, reasoned that the policies underlying implied warranties in sales transactions applied with equal or greater force to commercial rentals of motor vehicles: rental vehicles are subjected to harder use than new vehicles offered for sale, and commercial lessors have a greater opportunity to inspect the vehicles for defects than the consuming public who necessarily rely upon the expertise of the lessor to discover and correct any defects prior to leasing such vehicles to the public; advertising and the nature of short-term lease transactions include a lessor's implied representation that its vehicles are fit for use and will remain so throughout the rental period; and, because defective vehicles present widespread and substantial risks to persons on the highways, the law should place maximum incentives on renters of cars and trucks to assure that they will be put in a safe condition before their release to the public. For all these reasons, Judge Francis concluded that commercial lessors should be subject to strict liability in tort just like sellers of new products.[28]

Although a few early decisions were reluctant to apply strict liability in tort to lease transactions,[29] courts widely followed *Cintrone*'s application of strict liability in tort to short-term[30] commercial leases of defec-

2A, as did the American Law Institute (ALI) in 2003. See 25 ALI Reporter 1 (Summer 2003). Article 2A should soon be introduced as legislation in the various states.

**25.** For example, see § 2A–210 (express warranties), § 2A–212 (implied warranty of merchantability), § 2A–213 (implied warranty of fitness for particular purpose), § 2A–214 (exclusion or modification of warranties), § 2A–216 (third party beneficiaries, including alternatives A, B, and C), § 2A–503 (modification or impairment of rights and remedies, including prima facie unconscionability for injury to the person in the case of consumer goods), § 2A–520 (les-

see's incidental and consequential damages, including injury to person or property proximately resulting from breach).

**26.** 212 A.2d 769 (N.J. 1965).

**27.** 161 A.2d 69 (N.J. 1960). For a discussion of *Henningsen*, see § 5.2, above.

**28.** Id. at 775–81.

**29.** See, e.g., Bona v. Graefe, 285 A.2d 607 (Md. 1972); Speyer, Inc. v. Humble Oil & Ref. Co., 403 F.2d 766 (3d Cir. 1968) (Pa. law). See generally Ausness, above note 2, at 300–02.

**30.** Although most of the cases involve short-term leases, and the Restatement limits its provision in this regard, see Products

tive products, frequently relying on the same policy rationales.[31] A noteworthy example is *Price v. Shell Oil Co.*,[32] in which a mechanic was injured when a ladder on a rental truck gave way. Relying heavily on *Cintrone*'s reasoning, supplemented by its own risk-spreading rationale,[33] the California Supreme Court extended strict products liability in tort to commercial lessors because it could discern "no substantial difference between *sellers* of personal property and *non-sellers*, such as bailors and lessors."[34] In both cases, the product supplier places a product on the market knowing that it will not be inspected for defects. In view of "the market realities and the widespread use of the lease of personalty in today's business world," the court concluded that it made good sense to impose responsibility for physical harm on lessors as well as sellers of defective products.[35] On similar reasoning, many other courts have followed suit, and commercial lessors[36] of new and like-new[37] products

Liability Restatement § 20 cmt. *c*, several cases do extend strict liability to the long-term lease situation. See, e.g., Berman v. Watergate W., Inc., 391 A.2d 1351 (D.C. 1978); Coleman v. Hertz Corp., 534 P.2d 940 (Okla. 1975); Price v. Shell Oil Co., 85 Cal.Rptr. 178 (Ct. App. 1970); Cintrone v. Hertz Truck Leasing & Rental Serv., 212 A.2d 769, 784 (N.J. 1965) (dissent troubled by lease's long-term nature). See also Bainter v. Lamoine LP Gas Co., 321 N.E.2d 744 (Ill. App. Ct. 1974) (propane gas tank provided to customer). The problem with long-term leases is that maintenance responsibilities, and to this extent risk control, may lie principally with the lessee who thus may be the better party to bear responsibility for at least certain types of defects which arise during the period of the lease. See P. Sherman, Products Liability § 8.06, at 241 (1981). "However, a distinction based solely on whether a lease is 'long-term' or 'short-term' is likely to be arbitrary and unrelated to the policies that underlie strict liability." Ausness, above note 2, at 323.

**31.** Other early decisions include Bachner v. Pearson, 479 P.2d 319 (Alaska 1970) (Piper Comanche aircraft); Stewart v. Budget Rent–A–Car Corp., 470 P.2d 240 (Haw. 1970); Galluccio v. Hertz Corp., 274 N.E.2d 178 (Ill. App. Ct. 1971); Stang v. Hertz Corp., 497 P.2d 732 (N.M. 1972); Hawkins Const. Co. v. Matthews Co., 209 N.W.2d 643 (Neb. 1973); Rourke v. Garza, 530 S.W.2d 794 (Tex. 1975); Martin v. Ryder Truck Rental, Inc., 353 A.2d 581 (Del. 1976) (nicely summarizing policy rationales for extending strict products liability in tort to commercial lease transactions); Francioni v. Gibsonia Truck Corp., 372 A.2d 736 (Pa. 1977) (reviewing early cases).

In *Martin*, the Delaware Supreme Court observed that, because rentals were non-sale transactions not addressed by Article 2 of the Uniform Commercial Code, the Code could not have preempted the field in the

product lease context. 353 A.2d at 583–84. Subsequently, however, this court refused to apply the doctrine of strict liability in tort to sales transactions reasoning that, by enacting Uniform Commercial Code Article 2, the legislature had preempted the field of products liability arising out of sales transactions. See Cline v. Prowler Indus. of Md., Inc., 418 A.2d 968 (Del. 1980). See § 5.3, above.

**32.** 466 P.2d 722 (Cal. 1970).

**33.** Id. at 725–26 ("the paramount policy to be promoted by the rule is the protection of otherwise defenseless victims of manufacturing defects and the spreading throughout society of the cost of compensating them").

**34.** Id. at 726.

**35.** Id.

**36.** Most courts have limited the extension of strict products liability to commercial lessors, such that strict liability has been held not to apply to "private" lease transactions. See, e.g., Burns v. Haines Equip., Inc., 726 N.Y.S.2d 516 (App. Div. 2001) (as casual lessor, crane owner who leased crane to plaintiff's employer could not be strictly liable in tort); Brescia v. Great Rd. Realty Trust, 373 A.2d 1310, 1312 (N.H. 1977) (lease of defective crane between two companies closely held by same person; "defendant does not deal in cranes, and its role as lessor was due solely to [lessee's] shortage of funds").

**37.** The Restatement limits the applicability of strict liability to products rented in a new or like-new condition, reasoning that the rental of older, clearly used property, like the sale of such property, displaces many of the rationales for imposing strict liability on the supplier. See Products Liability Restatement § 8 cmt. *j* ("when the rental units are in obviously used condition, and rented under circumstances in which a

today are routinely held subject to strict liability in tort[38] to the same extent as manufacturers and other sellers, an approach that is certified by the *Products Liability Restatement*.[39]

### *Financial Lease Transactions*

Strict liability principles do not apply to financial lease transactions except in the unusual case where the financial lessor actively participates in marketing the product.[40] In a financial lease transaction, a financial institution takes title to a chattel and leases it to the user, as an alternative to simply loaning funds to the purchaser and taking a security interest in the chattel. While financial lessors thus do "lease" chattels, their role is to provide financial services to their "lessees," not to assure the safety of the products. Despite some protestations to the contrary,[41] courts have widely refused to hold financial lessors liable for injuries caused by defects in the products they finance, reasoning that such financial institutions rarely participate directly in the chain of product distribution and have little control over product safety.[42]

reasonable person would not expect the risk of defect to be substantially the same as if the rental units were new, liability of the lessor will depend upon a showing of fault"). See also id. at § 20 cmt. *c*.

**38.** See, e.g., Ruzzo v. LaRose Enters., 748 A.2d 261 (R.I. 2000) ("the policy considerations that impel imposition of strict liability upon manufacturers and sellers of dangerously defective goods apply with equal or greater force to lessors of potentially dangerous products or instrumentalities."); Junge v. Smyrna Rental & Repair, Inc., 1998 WL 960716 (Del. Super. Ct. 1998); Tabieros v. Clark Equip. Co., 944 P.2d 1279 (Haw. 1997) (straddle carrier); Black v. Gorman–Rupp, 655 So.2d 717 (La. Ct. App. 1995) (water pump); Samuel Friedland Family Enter. v. Amoroso, 630 So.2d 1067 (Fla. 1994) (sailboat); Ghionis v. Deer Valley Resort Co., 839 F.Supp. 789 (D. Utah 1993) (ski equipment); Westlye v. Look Sports, Inc., 22 Cal.Rptr.2d 781 (Ct. App. 1993) (same); Kemp v. Miller, 453 N.W.2d 872 (Wis. 1990) (commercial lessor strictly liable for design and manufacturing defects and for defects arising after product leaves manufacturer—1984 Ford Tempo). See generally Ausness, above note 2; Henszey, Application of Strict Liability to the Leasing Industry, 33 Bus. Law. 631 (1978); Annot., 52 A.L.R.3d 121 (1974) (applicability of strict liability in tort to chattel lessors).

**39.** See Products Liability Restatement § 20 cmt. *c*, declaring that "[a] commercial lessor of new and like-new products is generally subject to the rules governing new product sellers." The Restatement explicitly includes "lessors, bailors, and those who provide products to others as a means of promoting either the use of or consumption of such products or some other commercial

activity" as parties subject to the basic liability principles of §§ 1 and 2. Products Liability Restatement § 20(b).

**40.** See Products Liability Restatement § 20 cmt. *e* and Reporters' Note to cmt. *c*. See generally Ausness, above note 2, at 347 (1987); Annot., 28 A.L.R.4th 326 (1984).

**41.** See, e.g., Nath v. National Equip. Leasing Corp., 439 A.2d 633, 636 (Pa. 1981) (Larsen, J., dissenting, joined by Flaherty and Kauffman, JJ.); Ausness, above note 2, at 349–50; Annot., 28 A.L.R.4th 326 (1984).

**42.** See, e.g., Potts v. UAP–GA AG Chem, Inc. 567 S.E.2d 316 (Ga. Ct. App. 2002); Messer Giesheim Indus., Inc. v. Cryotech of Kingsport, Inc., 45 S.W.3d 588 (Tenn. Ct. App. 2001); Dominguez Mojica v. Citibank, N.A., 830 F.Supp. 668 (D.P.R. 1993); Starobin v. Niagara Mach. & Tool Works Corp., 577 N.Y.S.2d 327 (App. Div. 1991) (Owen, J.); Agristor Leasing v. Meuli, 634 F.Supp. 1208, 1216 (D. Kan. 1986) (lease-purchase of grain storage system; noting distinction between " 'commercial' lessors and 'finance' lessors, with strict liability being imposed on the former but not the latter"); Rivera v. Mahogany Corp., 494 N.E.2d 660 (Ill. App. Ct. 1986) (lease-purchase of plastic molding machine); Wright v. Newman, 735 F.2d 1073 (8th Cir. 1984) (Mo. law); Abco Metals Corp. v. Equico Lessors, Inc., 721 F.2d 583 (7th Cir. 1983) (Ill. law); Nath v. National Equip. Leasing Corp., 439 A.2d 633, 636 (Pa. 1981) (4–3 decision) ("[A] finance lessor is not in the business of selling or marketing merchandise. A finance lessor is in the business of circulating funds. Such an activity cannot possibly produce reasonable reliance upon the safety of the merchandise."); Cole v. Elliott Equip. Co., 653 F.2d 1031 (5th Cir.

## Bailments

### *In General*

Traditionally, product leases were regarded as "bailments for hire."[43] In modern practice, lease transactions often are set forth in formalized contracts, whereas product bailment transactions normally are much more casual.[44] Typical product bailment transactions involve a hotel providing chairs in its rented rooms,[45] a bowling alley that provides balls for its customers to use,[46] a skating center that rents roller skates to the skaters,[47] a restaurant that provides wine glasses and other implements for its patrons' use,[48] a supplier of propane gas that supplies its customers with tanks to hold the gas,[49] and a sports complex that rents go-carts to its patrons.[50] Not only do such transactions in many ways resemble short-term leases, but they generally overlap the category of product license transactions, considered next.

Because some courts have extended the doctrine of strict liability in tort to bailments as well as to lease transactions,[51] a plaintiff injured while using a product that he did not buy or lease generally will seek to establish that he was a bailee.[52] For example, in *Golt v. Sports Complex, Inc.*,[53] the renter of a go-cart at a sports complex was injured when rammed from behind by another cart. Claiming that the cart's design was uncrashworthy, the plaintiff sued the complex for negligence and strict liability in tort. The court defined a bailment as the transfer of possession, but not title, of a chattel from the bailor to the bailee to use

---

1981) (Tex. law); Brescia v. Great Rd. Realty Trust, 373 A.2d 1310 (N.H. 1977).

**43.** "At common law a lease of personal property is a bailment for hire." UCC 2A–103(j) cmt. *j*. See, e.g., Cintrone v. Hertz Truck Leasing & Rental Serv., 212 A.2d 769 (N.J. 1965).

**44.** On product bailment transactions, see, e.g., Ausness, above note 2, at 313–17 and 335–39; Products Liability Restatement § 20 cmt. *f* and Reporters' Note thereto; Annot., 48 A.L.R.3d 668 (1973).

**45.** See, e.g., Jones v. Keetch, 200 N.W.2d 227 (Mich. 1972) (motel subject to common-law implied warranty of fitness, as to the nondefectiveness and suitability of goods for their intended use, for injuries to guest from chair that collapsed), citing Schnitzer v. Nixon, 439 F.2d 940 (4th Cir. 1971) (Va. law), and 8 Am. Jur. 2d Bailments § 144 [now 8A Am. Jur. 2d Bailments § 101] (implied warranty of fitness). *But see* Ferrucci v. Atlantic City Showboat, Inc., 51 F.Supp.2d 129 (D. Conn. 1999) (no bailment of hotel bed over which plaintiff tripped because hotel never surrendered exclusive possession and control, precluding plaintiff's recovery under Connecticut's products liability statute).

**46.** See, e.g., Dixon v. Four Seasons Bowling Alley, Inc., 424 A.2d 428 (N.J. Super. Ct. App. Div. 1980).

**47.** See Wilson v. Dover Skating Ctr., Ltd., 566 A.2d 1020 (Del. Super. Ct. 1989).

**48.** See, e.g., Shaffer v. Victoria Station, Inc., 588 P.2d 233 (Wash. 1978) (restaurant liable in both warranty and strict tort for injuries to patron from wine glass shattering in his hand).

**49.** See, e.g., Bainter v. Lamoine LP Gas Co., 321 N.E.2d 744 (Ill. App. Ct. 1974). See also Fulbright v. Klamath Gas Co., 533 P.2d 316 (Or. 1975).

**50.** Golt v. Sports Complex, Inc., 644 A.2d 989, 992–93 (Del. Super. Ct. 1994).

**51.** See, e.g., Martin v. Ryder Truck Rental, Inc., 353 A.2d 581, 586–87 (Del. 1976); Thomas v. St. Joseph Hosp., 618 S.W.2d 791, 796–98 (Tex. App. 1981) (hospital provided flammable gown to patient).

**52.** See, e.g., Ferrucci v. Atlantic City Showboat, Inc., 51 F.Supp.2d 129 (D. Conn. 1999) (no bailment of hotel bed over which plaintiff tripped because hotel never surrendered exclusive possession and control; thus, products liability statute did not apply); Kalumetals, Inc. v. Hitachi Magnetics Corp., 21 F.Supp.2d 510 (W.D. Pa. 1998) (supplier of grinding swarf with retort tube that exploded was bailor and hence subject to strict liability).

**53.** 644 A.2d 989 (Del. Super. Ct. 1994).

for some purpose during which the bailee's possession is exclusive.[54] Applying these principles to the rental of the go-cart, the court concluded that the go-cart drivers had full control and possession of the go-carts during each lap around the track, subject only to certain normal restrictions. Accordingly, and consistent with the underlying policies of risk distribution and deterrence,[55] the court ruled that the defendant was subject to strict liability in tort as a bailor of the go-cart.[56]

Because a bailment is not a sale, however, the warranties provided by Article 2 of the Uniform Commercial Code have been held not to apply to such a transaction. In *Garfield v. Furniture Fair–Hanover*,[57] for example, a woman was injured when a bed collapsed that had been loaned to her and her husband by the defendant furniture store pending the delivery of a new bed they had purchased. The court held that since the plaintiffs had never taken title to the loaned bed, and since they were bound to return it upon delivery of the purchased bed, the transaction was a bailment rather than a sale under UCC § 2–106(1).[58]

### Demonstrators, Loaners, and Giveaways

If a seller provides a user with a demonstrator,[59] a loaner,[60] or even a product giveaway[61] as part of its marketing scheme, then the transaction probably should be viewed as having entered the stream of commerce,

**54.** Id. at 992.

**55.** See id. at 994:

The cost of supplying a defective go-cart should be imposed on the party profiting from the public's use of the go-cart. The owner of the go-cart can best spread the risk of injury through the prices of tickets. From the very nature of the go-cart transaction, the owner implies a representation that the go-cart is fit to travel around the track and adequately absorb the energy created from a collision of two go-carts. Placing liability on the owner will also ensure the go-cart owner will take care in selecting responsible manufacturers who design and construct safe go-carts, resulting in general risk-reduction.

**56.** "Buying an amusement ticket and using the ticket to gain control and possession of a go-cart creates a bailment.... Since strict liability applies to bailments, ... strict liability applies to this transaction." Id.

**57.** 274 A.2d 325 (N.J. Super. Ct. Law Div. 1971).

**58.** Nor did the court think that the bailment had become integrated into the sale of the new bed so as to extend the warranties attaching to the sale to the bailment as well. See id. at 326.

**59.** See, e.g., Beattie v. Beattie, 786 A.2d 549, 551 (Del. Super. Ct. 2001) (dealership subject to strict liability for "demonstrator vehicle" which salesperson furnished to customer for test drive); Robert F.

Bullock, Inc. v. Thorpe, 353 S.E.2d 340 (Ga. 1987), aff'g 348 S.E.2d 55 (Ga. Ct. App. 1986) (supplier placed deep-fat fryer in restaurant kitchen on trial basis); First Nat'l Bank v. Cessna Aircraft Co., 365 So.2d 966, 967 (Ala. 1978) (strict tort doctrine applies to the crash of a demonstrator airplane: "having placed the product on the market, if the manufacturer still retains some measure of control, he should be liable under the doctrine"); Delaney v. Towmotor Corp., 339 F.2d 4 (2d Cir. 1964) (N.Y. law) (forklift truck). *But see* Mason v. General Motors Corp., 490 N.E.2d 437 (Mass. 1986) (dealer which allowed customer to test drive automobile not subject to warranty of merchantability).

**60.** See, e.g., Johnson v. Stanley–Bostitch, Inc., 2000 WL 709480 (E.D. Pa. 2000) (pneumatic nail gun loaner provided by manufacturer as business incentive to customers who purchased large quantities of nails and fasteners).

**61.** "[A] commercial entity is subject to strict liability for products it distributes free of charge, since title has passed to the consumer." Products Liability Restatement § 20 Reporters' Note to cmt. *b*. See, e.g., Levondosky v. Marina Assocs., 731 F.Supp. 1210 (D.N.J. 1990) (casino served free drink in defective glass); Perfection Paint & Color Co. v. Konduris, 258 N.E.2d 681 (Ind. Ct. App. 1970) (free lacquer thinner supplied following sale of lacquer that failed to bond); McKisson v. Sales Affiliates, Inc., 416 S.W.2d 787 (Tex. 1967) (free sample of permanent hair solution).

rendering the supplier strictly liable in tort. However, if a supplier provides a product for use exclusively in a commercial context, a court may find that it never enters the stream of commerce so that strict liability should not apply. In *Armstrong Rubber Co. v. Urquidez*,[62] for example, the court held that strict liability in tort did not apply to an action brought for the death of a test driver caused by the blowout of an allegedly defective tire manufactured by the defendant, Armstrong. The defendant had supplied the tire in question to the plaintiff's employer, a tire-testing facility, as a "non-interest spare" to be used on test vehicles along with whatever tires were actually being tested at the time. Ruling that the tire had never entered the stream of commerce, the court held that strict liability in tort did not apply.[63]

### License Transactions

#### *In General*

Two separate types of license situations arise in products liability litigation: (1) trademark or trade name licenses, by which the owner of a valuable mark or name, such as 7–Up, Goodyear, or McDonald's, sells the rights to use its mark or name to a manufacturer or other supplier further down the chain of product distribution; and (2) product-use licenses, by which the owner of a product, such as a laundromat with washing machines and driers, or an amusement park with rides, charges customers to use its products. The present discussion addresses the topic of licenses for product use. Trademarks and trade-name licenses have been previously addressed.[64]

Product-use licenses and commercial bailments frequently overlap and are often indistinguishable. Transactions include a laundromat providing washing machines,[65] a hotel providing chairs[66] and bath mats,[67] a bowling alley providing balls,[68] a skating center renting roller skates,[69] a restaurant providing wine glasses and other eating implements,[70] a supplier of propane gas supplying tanks to hold the gas,[71] and an amusement park providing rides.[72] These transactions in many respects

---

**62.** 570 S.W.2d 374 (Tex. 1978).

**63.** Id. at 377 ("Armstrong never released the non-interest spare to an ordinary user or consumer within the meaning of the Restatement. The defective tire, although not itself the subject of the test, always remained within the industrial, testing process.").

**64.** See Madison v. American Home Prods. Corp., 595 S.E.2d 493 (S.C. 2004); § 15.4, above.

**65.** See, e.g., Garcia v. Halsett, 82 Cal. Rptr. 420 (Ct. App. 1970).

**66.** See, e.g., Jones v. Keetch, 200 N.W.2d 227 (Mich. 1972) (motel subject to common-law implied warranty of fitness, as to the nondefectiveness and suitability of goods for their intended use, for injuries to guest from chair that collapsed), citing Schnitzer v. Nixon, 439 F.2d 940 (4th Cir. 1971) (Va. law), and 8 Am. Jur. 2d Bail-

ments § 144 [now 8A Am. Jur. 2d Bailments § 101] (implied warranty of fitness).

**67.** See Wagner v. Coronet Hotel, 458 P.2d 390 (Ariz. Ct. App. 1969) (strict liability in tort does not apply).

**68.** See, e.g., Dixon v. Four Seasons Bowling Alley, Inc., 424 A.2d 428 (N.J. Super. Ct. App. Div. 1980).

**69.** See Wilson v. Dover Skating Ctr., Ltd., 566 A.2d 1020 (Del. Super. Ct. 1989).

**70.** See, e.g., Shaffer v. Victoria Station, Inc., 588 P.2d 233 (Wash. 1978) (restaurant liable in both warranty and strict tort for injuries to patron from wine glass shattering in his hand).

**71.** See, e.g., Bainter v. Lamoine LP Gas Co., 321 N.E.2d 744 (Ill. App. Ct. 1974). See also Fulbright v. Klamath Gas Co., 533 P.2d 316 (Or. 1975) (vine burner).

**72.** See, e.g., Greenwood v. Busch Entm't Corp., 101 F.Supp.2d 292 (E.D. Pa.

resemble short-term product leases,[73] but true license transactions have a number of distinguishing characteristics: (1) they generally are less formal than true chattel lease transactions; (2) the user often does not pay a specific fee for the product's use; (3) and the product's use is often restricted to the supplier's premises. But, most of these situations are more properly classified as license transactions, or possibly as bailments.[74]

When a defect in such a product injures the user, courts sometimes attempt to determine whether the transaction should be classified as a bailment or a license, on the belief that the classification may have some bearing on whether the doctrine of strict liability in tort properly applies to the transaction. This was in fact the situation in *Golt v. Sports Complex, Inc.*,[75] the go-cart case examined previously, in which the court declared that classifying the go-cart rental as a bailment (or "lease-bailment") was crucial to its application of strict liability in tort. Other courts, however, proceed in products liability cases to examine such non-sale transactions without ever attempting to classify the precise type of property transaction involved.[76] While most of these transactions fairly may be characterized as bailments,[77] they often are better classified as license transactions because such transactions do not involve a transfer of "legal" possession to the user who typically has a limited right of possession, to use the product in restricted ways on the premises of the licensor.[78] While the distinction may possibly be relevant to whether Article 2A of the Uniform Commercial Code applies to a transaction,[79] courts would be better advised to avoid becoming ensnared in fine

---

2000); Bobryk v. Lincoln Amusements, Inc., 1996 WL 24566 (Conn. Super. Ct. 1996). See also Siciliano v. Capitol City Shows, Inc., 475 A.2d 19 (N.H. 1984); cf. Allen v. Nicole, Inc., 412 A.2d 824, 826 (N.J. Super. Ct. Law Div. 1980).

Other examples of licenses might include a woodworking shop that charges a fee for users to use its table saws and a batting practice operation that for a fee allows batters to use its pitching machines.

**73.** See above.

**74.** On product license and bailment transactions, see, e.g., Ausness, Strict Liability for Chattel Leasing, 48 U. Pitt. L. Rev. 273, 313–17 and 335–39 (1987); Products Liability Restatement § 20 cmt. *f* and Reporters' Note thereto; Annot., 48 A.L.R.3d 668 (1973). Bailments are separately examined above.

**75.** 644 A.2d 989, 992–93 (Del. Super. Ct. 1994).

**76.** See, e.g., Safeway Stores, Inc. v. Nest–Kart, 579 P.2d 441 (Cal. 1978) (grocery shopping cart); Keen v. Dominick's Finer Foods, Inc., 364 N.E.2d 502 (Ill. App. Ct. 1977) (same).

**77.** See, e.g., Golt v. Sports Complex, Inc., 644 A.2d 989, 992–93 (Del. Super. Ct.

1994) (go-cart rented to plaintiff constituted bailment).

**78.** See, e.g., Reeder v. Bally's Total Fitness Corp., 963 F.Supp. 530 (E.D. Va. 1997) (health club patron injured on stomach curl machine was merely a business invitee on defendant's premises; no bailment or lease of the machine): "[W]hat plaintiff purchased with the membership agreement was a right to use the Club and its exercise equipment during business hours, provided the equipment was not being used by any other members of the Club. Plaintiff did not purchase the right to possess and use specific equipment for a specific period of time to the exclusion of all others." Id. at 533. Garcia v. Halsett, 82 Cal. Rptr. 420, 422 (Ct. App. 1970). See also Wagner v. Coronet Hotel, 458 P.2d 390, 395 (Ariz. Ct. App. 1969). ("a license differs from a chattel lease in that legal possession of the product is transferred to the lessee in a lease relationship, but remains with the licensor in a license arrangement"). See generally Ausness, above note 2, at 335, citing Comment, 28 Sw. L.J. 575, 597 (1974).

**79.** See, e.g., Rotshteyn v. Klos Const., Inc., 2004 WL 1576637 (E.D. Pa. 2004); Reeder v. Bally's Total Fitness Corp., 963

distinctions of property law in tort-law cases involving personal injuries.[80]

### Theory of Liability

**Negligence.** Licensors of course are subject to negligence liability for failing to submit their products to such inspections as are reasonable under the circumstances, for failing to exercise care to repair or replace products that become damaged or worn, and for failing to exercise reasonable care to warn users of dangers in the products that they license.[81]

**Warranty.** Neither Article 2 nor Article 2A of the Uniform Commercial Code expressly applies to product license transactions: "Article 2—Sales" by its terms applies only to "sales" transactions,[82] and "Article 2A—Leases" by its terms is limited to product "lease" transactions.[83] Because both sales and leases ("bailments for hire")[84] involve the transfer of rights to the exclusive use and possession of a product, and because such "legal" possession by hypothesis is *not* transferred to a licensee, as mentioned earlier, a license cannot logically be considered within the scope of either a sale or lease transaction. In short, a literal construction of the terms of Articles 2 and 2A excludes license transactions from coverage.[85] Nevertheless, a court might extend Article 2, or apply it by analogy, to license transactions similar to how many courts have approached lease transactions under Article 2.[86] In addition, a court might find that a product license contains a common-law implied warranty of quality,[87] similar to the rulings of a few courts in bailment cases, as discussed above.

**Strict liability in tort.** The distinctions between leases, bailments,[88] and licenses are often blurred in products liability cases, as

---

F.Supp. 530 (E.D. Va. 1997) (Article 2A did not apply because health club did not bail its equipment to patrons).

**80.** Because of the overlap and imprecision among classifications, this admonition applies to bailment and license transactions alike.

**81.** See Restatement (2d) Torts §§ 388–93 and 405–06.

**82.** UCC § 2–106(1) provides that "[a] 'sale' consists in the passing of title from the seller to the buyer," and § 2–103(d) provides that " 'Seller' means a person who sells or contracts to sell goods."

**83.** UCC § 2A–103(j) provides that " 'Lease' means a transfer of the right to possession and use of goods for a term in return for consideration. . . . "

**84.** See UCC § 2A–103 cmt. *j.* "[A] lease is created when the lessee agrees to furnish consideration for the right to the possession and use of goods over a specified period of time." Id., citing Mooney, Personal Property Leasing: A Challenge, 36 Bus. Law. 1605, 1607 (1981). See also note 43, above.

**85.** See 3 Anderson, Uniform Commercial Code § 2–314:62, at 274.

**86.** Note that UCC § 2–313 cmt. 2 appears to authorize courts to extend the warranty principles of Article 2 beyond sales transactions, as discussed in the lease context above.

**87.** See, e.g., Hurley v. Larry's Water Ski Sch., 762 F.2d 925 (11th Cir. 1985) (Fla. law) (tow rope and handle attached to defendant ski school's boat), citing Washwell, Inc. v. Morejon, 294 So.2d 30, 32–33 (Fla. Dist. Ct. App. 1974) (patron injured while using washing machine in laundromat).

**88.** The court in Bobryk v. Lincoln Amusements, Inc., 1996 WL 24566 (Conn. Super. Ct. 1996), attempted to distinguish these different forms of transaction:

A lease is a contract under which the lessor, for a fee or other valuable consideration, transfers an interest or estate in real or personal property to the lessee for a stated period of time, with a reversion in the owner after the expiration of the lease. A lease is distinguishable from a license. While the former confers a right,

noted earlier,[89] but courts sometimes do decide to allow or deny a strict liability in tort, warranty, or other claim on the basis of its characterization of the particular transaction.[90] Most courts, however, in deciding whether strict products liability in tort applies to a non-sale transaction, ignore the niceties of property-law classification distinctions. Instead, courts generally base their decisions of whether to apply strict liability in tort to such transactions on basic tort-law considerations: whether the product supplier is in the business of supplying such products, whether it has placed its products into the "stream of commerce," and sometimes on the policy goals supporting strict products liability.[91] Property law technicalities, in other words, are usually subordinated in such cases to the principles and goals of higher law, the law of torts.

Yet the fact that courts in products liability cases do not dwell on the fine points of the law of chattel transactions does not mean that the doctrine of strict liability in tort is applied in every product license case. In fact, courts sometimes refuse to apply strict liability principles, and the cases are difficult to distinguish or to classify. Because product licenses generally are limited to the premises of the licensor, and because they often are provided as a service to customers, the license cases are often complicated by overlapping principles governing the liability of landowners or providers of services. In both of the latter contexts, as examined later,[92] courts have generally applied traditional negligence principles rather than the doctrine of strict liability in tort.

One of the first modern cases to examine a product license transaction was *Garcia v. Halsett*.[93] The eleven-year-old plaintiff injured his arm while trying to remove clothes from a washing machine belonging to the

during the term of the lease, to exercise exclusive possession of an control over the property in question, assertable even against the lessor, the latter extends but a [privilege of possession].
Id. at *4 (citations omitted). Further, the court defined a bailment in terms of the owner's surrender of property to another for some particular purpose for some period of time during which the bailor retains the right of control. Id. at *5. See generally Ausness, Strict Liability for Chattel Leasing, 48 U. Pitt. L. Rev. 273 (1987).

**89.** See, e.g., Jones v. Keetch, 200 N.W.2d 227, 228 (Mich. 1972) (noting that "it matters not that the chattel comes to the possession of the plaintiff either as lessee or bailee" and citing sources as to liability of bailors and lessors). See generally Ausness, above note 14, at 335–39.

**90.** For example, in Hurley v. Larry's Water Ski Sch., 762 F.2d 925 (11th Cir. 1985) (Fla. law), plaintiff was injured while taking water skiing lessons from the defendant when the wooden tow handle he was holding broke. In plaintiff's action against the ski school, the court held that since the tow rope and handle were at all times attached to the boat, he never had complete possession and control over them and so

never had a bailment. Although plaintiff's strict liability in tort claim thus would not lie, his breach of warranty claim could. Implicit in the defendant's agreement to provide ski lessons to the plaintiff was "an implied warranty that the equipment supplied by Larry's was fit for the purpose of teaching an individual to ski." Id. at 929.

Compare Ferrucci v. Atlantic City Showboat, Inc., 51 F.Supp.2d 129 (D. Conn. 1999) (no bailment of hotel bed over which plaintiff tripped because hotel never surrendered exclusive possession and control; consequently, products liability statute did not apply); Kalumetals, Inc. v. Hitachi Magnetics Corp., 21 F.Supp.2d 510 (W.D. Pa. 1998) (supplier of grinding swarf with retort tube that exploded was a bailor and hence subject to strict liability); Golt v. Sports Complex, Inc., 644 A.2d 989, 992–93 (Del. Super. Ct. 1994) (finding that go-cart rented to plaintiff was a bailment, thereby allowing claim for strict liability in tort).

**91.** See Ausness, above note 2, at 335–39.

**92.** See § 16.3 (service transactions), and § 16.7 (real estate), below.

**93.** 82 Cal.Rptr. 420 (Ct. App. 1970).

defendant laundromat when a defect in the machine caused it unexpectedly to start up, entangling the boy's arm in the clothing. The trial court refused to instruct the jury on strict liability in tort, but the appellate court reversed, ruling that strict liability in tort properly applied to a license transaction of this type. Reasoning that a licensee of a product may be in a worse position than a buyer, because the licensee has less opportunity or motivation to inspect the product for defects, the court concluded that such suppliers "play more than a random and accidental role in the overall marketing enterprise of the product in question."[94] Like manufacturers and lessors, thought the court, licensors " 'are an integral part of the overall . . . marketing enterprise that should bear the cost of injuries resulting from defective products.' "[95] Courts in other cases in which a fee was charged for the use of a defective product have also applied strict liability in tort, including cases involving the use of defective roller skates at a skating center[96] and the use of a defective go-cart at an amusement park.[97] But other courts have refused to apply strict liability in tort to defective amusement rides, finding that they principally involve a service.[98]

When a licensor (or bailor) provides a product as a service to its customers without charging a separate fee for the use of the product, whether strict liability in tort should apply is more difficult to determine. If the use of the licensed (or bailed) product is necessary or "integral" to the sale of some other product, then courts generally have considered the provision of the tie-in product subject to strict liability in tort. So, a defective propane gas container provided by the gas company,[99] a wine glass provided by a restaurant,[100] or a ladder provided by a pick-it-yourself orchard[101] all must be provided if the defendants expect to sell their primary products. In each such case, the courts have reasoned that the providers of such tie-in products are appropriately subject to strict products liability for defects in those products.[102]

However, when a product seller allows its customers to use an ancillary product without charge and merely as a convenience, courts have been more reluctant to impose strict liability in tort. For example,

**94.** Id. at 423.

**95.** Id., citing Vandermark v. Ford Motor Co., 391 P.2d 168 (Cal. 1964).

**96.** See Wilson v. Dover Skating Ctr., Ltd., 566 A.2d 1020, 1024 (Del. Super. Ct. 1989).

**97.** See Golt v. Sports Complex, Inc., 644 A.2d 989, 992–93 (Del. Super. Ct. 1994) (transaction classified as bailment).

**98.** See, e.g., Greenwood v. Busch Entm't Corp., 101 F.Supp.2d 292 (E.D. Pa. 2000) (by providing plaintiff license to use its water slides, defendant provided service, not product); Siciliano v. Capitol City Shows, Inc., 475 A.2d 19 (N.H. 1984) (arm of octopus ride broke off while in operation); cf. Allen v. Nicole, Inc., 412 A.2d 824, 826 (N.J. Super. Ct. Law Div. 1980) (occa-

sional sale of amusement ride to another amusement ride operator; "it is not the sale but the use of the equipment which constitutes his business").

**99.** See, e.g., Bainter v. Lamoine LP Gas Co., 321 N.E.2d 744 (Ill. App. Ct. 1974). See also Fulbright v. Klamath Gas Co., 533 P.2d 316 (Or. 1975) (vine burner).

**100.** See, e.g., Shaffer v. Victoria Station, Inc., 588 P.2d 233 (Wash. 1978) (restaurant liable in both warranty and strict tort for injuries to patron from wine glass shattering in his hand).

**101.** See, e.g., Gabbard v. Stephenson's Orchard, Inc., 565 S.W.2d 753 (Mo. Ct. App. 1978).

**102.** See Products Liability Restatement § 20 cmt. f Reporters' Note.

in *Keen v. Dominick's Finer Foods, Inc.*,[103] the plaintiff was injured while using a grocery cart in the defendant's grocery store when she grabbed the cart in an attempt to prevent it from overturning. Plaintiff sued the grocery store for strict liability in tort and other claims, alleging that the cart was dangerously defective, and the store defended on the ground that it could not be held strictly liable since it had not placed the cart into the stream of commerce. Agreeing with the defendant, the trial court dismissed the claim for strict liability in tort. On appeal, a divided court affirmed dismissal of the plaintiff's strict liability in tort claim, reasoning that the doctrine of strict liability in tort does not require an actual sales transaction but does require that the supplier be in the chain of distribution.[104] Although the dissent argued that the store was the final link in the chain of distribution,[105] the majority concluded that the store, like the injured customer, was merely a user of the cart. Distinguishing *Bainter v. Lamoine LP Gas Co.*,[106] in which strict liability in tort had been applied to the supplier of propane gas in a defective tank, the majority reasoned that in the *Bainter* case "the fluidity of the product compelled supplying the tank as a necessary concomitant of the sale of gas," whereas a shopping cart "can be classified only as a convenient receptacle which the customer may temporarily utilize to move groceries to the checkout" or to a car.[107] "Public policy considerations," concluded the court, "do not demand that the duty of a storekeeper to keep its premises in a safe condition be elevated beyond the traditional standard of reasonable care."[108] Most courts have agreed that, by allowing customers to use an ancillary product as a convenience, a defendant generally does not place the product into the chain of distribution sufficient to support a strict liability in tort claim, especially if the product must remain on the defendant's premises.[109]

---

**103.** 364 N.E.2d 502 (Ill. App. Ct. 1977).

**104.** "One of the underlying reasons for imposing strict liability is to ensure that losses are borne by those who have created the risk and subsequently reaped the profit of marketing the allegedly defective product. Liability will not be imposed upon a defendant who is not a part of the original producing and marketing chain." Id. at 504.

**105.** See id. at 505:

Dominick's was part of the stream of commerce flowing from the cart's manufacturer to the plaintiff. The cart was intended for use by customers of grocery supermarkets. It reached the plaintiff through Dominick's. Therefore, the stream of commerce did not stop, as the majority views it, with the parties who distributed the cart to Dominick's, but continued until the cart reached the customers who were intended to use it and for whose use Dominick's supplied it. . . . I regard Dominick's as the supplier of the carts to its customers and, therefore, as a conduit in the marketing chain which brought the carts to their ultimate users, Dominick's customers.

**106.** 321 N.E.2d 744 (Ill. 1974).

**107.** 364 N.E.2d at 504.

**108.** The court noted that its ruling did not deny plaintiff her claim for negligence against the grocery store nor her claim for strict liability in tort against the manufacturer of the cart. Id. at 505.

**109.** See, e.g., Ranalli v. Edro Motel Corp., 690 A.2d 137, 140 (N.J. Super. Ct. App. Div. 1997) (frying pan in motel room kitchenette: "to apply the broad brush of strict liability to motel owners would impose an unusual and unjust burden"); Dixon v. Four Seasons Bowling Alley, Inc., 424 A.2d 428 (N.J. Super. Ct. App. Div. 1980) (bowling alley not subject to strict liability for defective bowling ball); Gilliland v. Rothermel, 403 N.E.2d 759, 761 (Ill. App. Ct. 1980) (tire gauge loaned to customer "was neither a necessary incident of the products which the defendant offered for sale nor an integral part of defendant's marketing operation"). Compare Ferrucci v. Atlantic City Showboat, Inc., 51 F.Supp.2d 129 (D. Conn. 1999) (no bailment of hotel bed over which plaintiff tripped because hotel never surrendered exclusive possession and control; consequently, products liability statute did not apply); Reeder v. Bal-

## Statutory Reform

Products liability reform statutes often cover lease, bailment, and license transactions either directly or indirectly. A popular products liability reform measure, previously examined,[110] exempts nonmanufacturing product suppliers from strict liability if the manufacturer is solvent and subject to the jurisdiction of the court. Such statutes have obvious applicability to product lessors who rarely manufacture the products they sell. For example, in *Saieva v. Budget Rent–A–Car of Rockford,*[111] which involved a leased van with defective brakes, the court granted summary judgment for the lessor on the plaintiff's negligence claim for lack of proof that the lessor reasonably should have discovered the safety defect, and also held the lessor exempt from strict liability under the Illinois statute conditionally protecting nonmanufacturing sellers from such liability. *Saieva* is a good example of the impact statutes of this type can have in shielding lessors from liability for defects in the products that they lease.[112]

These nonmanufacturing supplier shield statutes also apply to product bailment and license transactions. As with commercial lessors, to the extent that such statutes apply to bailors and licensors, such nonmanufacturing defendants should be conditionally protected from the rigors of strict liability in tort. Accordingly, while courts which have reasoned that the policies of strict liability in tort apply alike to sellers, bailors, and licensors may be correct, reform statutes which relieve nonmanufacturing defendants of strict liability convert the liability issue from a question of policy to one of statutory interpretation.

Non-sales transactions may affect recovery under other types of products liability statutes that apply only to qualifying sellers or suppliers. For example, *Bobryk v. Lincoln Amusements, Inc.*[113] was a claim against a carnival ride provider for injuries to a child who rode the defendant's "Flying Chairs." Seeking recovery under Connecticut's products liability act as well as negligence, the plaintiff was required to prove that the defendant was a "product seller" as defined in the act.[114] While holding that the statutory term included lessors and bailors of products

---

ly's Total Fitness Corp., 963 F.Supp. 530 (E.D. Va. 1997) (health club patron injured on stomach curl machine was merely business invitee on defendant's premises; no bailment or lease of machine); Wagner v. Coronet Hotel, 458 P.2d 390, 395 (Ariz. Ct. App. 1969) (plaintiff slipped on allegedly defective rubber shower mat provided by defendant hotel: "Of all the various policy views expressed for the theory of strict liability, none are applicable to the Coronet Hotel.").

*But see* Safeway Stores, Inc. v. Nest-Kart, 579 P.2d 441 (Cal. 1978), where a supermarket shopping cart broke and fell on plaintiff's foot. The jury found the supermarket liable, in negligence and strict liability in tort, and the cart manufacturer strictly liable, apportioning 80% to the su-

permarket and 20% to the manufacturer. Without discussing the propriety of the strict liability claim against the supermarket, the Supreme Court approved the verdict.

**110.** See § 15.2, above.

**111.** 591 N.E.2d 507 (Ill. App. Ct. 1992).

**112.** Note that Illinois' products liability statute of repose specifically provides that a product's initial lease triggers the running of the statute. See Garza v. Navistar Int'l Transp. Corp., 666 N.E.2d 1198, 1200 (Ill. 1996).

**113.** 1996 WL 24566 (Conn. Super. Ct. 1996).

**114.** See Conn. Gen. Stat. § 52–572m(a).

engaged in the business of leasing or bailing goods,[115] the court ruled that the selling of rides did not amount to a bailment of the Flying Chairs because the defendant never relinquished control.[116] Thus, because the plaintiff acquired no more than a license to use a Flying Chair, the products liability statute did not apply and plaintiff was left to the negligence claims.[117]

## § 16.3   SERVICE TRANSACTIONS

### In General

The law of "*products* liability" concerns the responsibility of manufacturing, retail, and other enterprises for harm caused by products they supply to others who put the products to use.[1] As examined earlier, modern products liability law is constituted by the confluence of warranty and tort law principles governing accountability for selling harmful chattels.[2] If an actor harms a person in a manner other than by supplying a dangerous chattel, more general principles of tort and contract law—not the law of products liability—define the nature and extent to which the actor may be liable for the harm. In short, supplying harmful chattels is what defines products liability as a discrete area of the law.[3]

General principles of tort law, principally negligence, define the responsibilities of people for harmful interactions with other people while *using* products. If a driver runs over a pedestrian with a car, this incident implicates the law of negligence, not the law of products liability. If, instead, a person buys and is injured by a dangerously designed car, these events implicate the law of products liability. But the modern world increasingly requires specialists to help select, adapt, and install the products that consumers need and want. Architects, engineers, and building contractors create structures to house people and business firms; doctors and other health professionals select drugs, use hypodermic needles, and implant medical devices and prostheses for health care; and plumbers and electricians select and install home heaters for warmth. When such specialists make mistakes, or when they use or install defective products, negligence law (including professional malpractice) establishes their basic responsibilities for resulting harm.[4]

---

**115.** 1996 WL 24566, at *2.

**116.** Id. at *5.

**117.** Id. Compare Ferrucci v. Atlantic City Showboat, Inc., 51 F.Supp.2d 129 (D. Conn. 1999) (no bailment of hotel bed over which plaintiff tripped because hotel never surrendered exclusive possession and control; consequently, Connecticut's products liability statute did not apply).

### § 16.3

**1.** See § 1.1, above.

**2.** See § 5.2, above.

**3.** "A premise of strict products liability is that product injuries constitute a discrete, integral problem that merits special

treatment. Otherwise, it would be inappropriate to distinguish product injuries from other personal injuries, liability for which is governed by negligence." Powers, Distinguishing Between Products and Services in Strict Liability, 62 N.C. L. Rev. 415, 418 (1984). Compare Stapleton, Bugs in Anglo–American Products Liability Law, 53 S.C. L. Rev. 1225, 1255 (2002) ("there does not seem to be any particular moral, economic, or social reason why the victims of [product] injuries should have been accorded any more special treatment than the victims of [other types of] disasters").

**4.** See Prosser and Keeton on Torts ch. 5.

The special question addressed in this section is whether and when architects, doctors, plumbers, and other service providers should also be subject to strict products liability.[5]

As a starting point, it is axiomatic that products liability principles apply to the commercial distribution of new chattels. At the other end of the spectrum, strict liability doctrine does *not* apply to the provision of pure services. In between, of course, lie a large number of sales-service hybrid transactions; in between resides the devil.[6]

### The Classic Cases

Two sets of cases, all classics in this field, illuminate how courts address the basic liability issues involving service providers. The first two cases were both decided in 1954, one in California and the other in New York. *Gagne v. Bertran*[7] was an action against a test hole driller for providing incorrect information as to the depth of fill on lots purchased by the plaintiffs in reliance on his report. Writing for the majority, Judge Traynor ruled that negligence, not strict liability, was the proper basis of liability for a specialist of this type. Strict liability was inappropriate, reasoned Judge Traynor, because the defendant had in no way assumed responsibility to guarantee that the information he provided was correct.[8] The size of the defendant's fee, together with the fact that he charged by the hour, suggested that he was selling and the buyer was buying "service and not insurance."[9] For these reasons, the court applied the general rule that providers of services are not subject to strict liability for providing defective services but are only required to meet the standard of reasonable care, according to ordinary levels of skill and care of members of their profession.[10]

---

**5.** Normally, a plaintiff is interested in being able to recover under a rule of strict liability rather than negligence and is thus indifferent to whether strict liability is available in warranty or tort. While distinctions in secondary doctrine (such as applicable statutes of limitations, other defenses, and the availability of punitive damages) sometimes are important, decisions examining the sales-service issue typically do not dwell upon differences between these separate theories of strict products liability.

**6.** See Lannetti, Toward a Revised Definition of "Product" under the Restatement (Third) of Torts: Products Liability, 55 Bus. Law. 799 (2000), reprinted in, 35 Tort & Ins. L.J. 845 (2000); Taylor, Applicability of Strict Liability Warranty Theories to Service Transactions, 47 S.C. L. Rev. 231 (1996); Cantu, A New Look at an Old Conundrum: The Determinative Test for the Hybrid Sales/Service Transaction under Section 402A of the Restatement (Second) of Torts, 45 Ark. L. Rev. 913 (1993); Cantu, The Illusive Meaning of the Term "Product" Under Section 402A of the Restatement (Second) of Torts, 44 Okla. L. Rev. 635 (1991); Vandall, Applying Strict Liability to Pharmacists, 18 U. Tol. L. Rev. 1

(1986); Powers, Distinguishing Between Products and Services in Strict Liability, 62 N.C. L. Rev. 415 (1984); Crump and Maxwell, Should Health Service Providers be Strictly Liable for Product Related Injuries? A Legal and Economic Analysis, 36 Sw. L. J. 831 (1982); Reynolds, Strict Liability for Commercial Service—Will Another Citadel Crumble?, 30 Okla. L. Rev. 298 (1977); 1 Frumer and Friedman, Products Liability §§ 5.10–.13; 3 Anderson, UCC § 2–314:35 et seq.

**7.** 275 P.2d 15 (Cal. 1954).

**8.** "The evidence in the present case does not justify the imposition of the strict liability of a warranty. There was no express warranty agreement, and there is nothing in the evidence to indicate that defendant assumed responsibility for the accuracy of his statements.... The amount of his fee and the fact that he was paid by the hour also indicate that he was selling service and not insurance." Id. at 20.

**9.** Id.

**10.** Id. at 20–21.

Two months later, across the continent, the New York Court of Appeals decided another service-provider case, *Perlmutter v. Beth David Hospital*,[11] this one involving the provision of a defective product. The plaintiff was a patient who sued the hospital for breach of warranty under the Sales Act for injuries resulting from "the transfusing of 'bad' blood, supplied by the hospital for a price as part of the customary services rendered by the hospital to its patients."[12] Holding that the hospital's provision of blood to the patient was a service rather than a sale, a majority of the New York Court of Appeals reasoned that the hospital's principal role was to promote the healing of its patients, not to sell them medicines, drugs, or blood. That title to such items may be transferred "from the hospital to the patient during the course of medical treatment does not serve to make each such transaction a sale,"[13] explained Judge Fuld, and "[i]t has long been recognized that, when service predominates, and transfer of personal property is but an incidental feature of the transaction, the transaction is not deemed a sale within the Sales Act."[14] Applying that standard to the facts before the court, Judge Fuld concluded that "the main object sought to be accomplished in this case was the care and treatment of the patient," such that the hospital's supply of blood was "entirely subordinate to its paramount function of furnishing trained personnel and specialized facilities in an endeavor to restore plaintiff's health."[15] Nor should the transaction be split in two, dividing the doctor's provision of services from the hospital's sale of blood, since what mattered was the essence of the transaction as a whole.[16] The food warranty cases were not analogous at all because people enter restaurants to buy food in contrast to patients who enter hospitals "to obtain a course of treatment in the hope of being cured."[17] Because sales law warranties did not apply to the hospital's provision of the contaminated blood, the plaintiff was left to his remedies under the law of negligence.[18]

The second important set of sales-service cases were decided by the New Jersey courts in the late 1960s. In *Magrine v. Krasnica*,[19] while a dentist was injecting an anesthetic into a patient's gum, the needle broke from the syringe leaving the entire $1\frac{5}{8}$ inch needle in the plaintiff's jaw. The needle was defective, and surgery was required to remove it. The dentist could not determine from whom he had purchased the needle, and the plaintiff sued him for strict liability, breach of warranty, and breach of contract. Inspired by *Cintrone*, the New Jersey Supreme Court's earlier decision extending the doctrine of strict liability in

**11.**   123 N.E.2d 792 (N.Y. 1954).

**12.**   Id. at 793. See § 16.9 (blood), below.

**13.**   Id. at 794.

**14.**   Id. at 794.

**15.**   "It was not for blood—or iodine or bandages—for which plaintiff bargained, but the wherewithal of the hospital staff and the availability of hospital facilities to provide whatever medical treatment was considered advisable. The conclusion is evident that the furnishing of blood was only an incidental and very secondary adjunct to the services performed by the hospital and,

therefore, was not within the provisions of the Sales Act." Id. at 795.

**16.**   Id.

**17.**   Id. at 795.

**18.**   Id.

**19.**   227 A.2d 539 (Hudson Cty. Ct. 1967), aff'd (implicitly on the basis of Judge Lynch's opinion) sub nom. Magrine v. Spector, 241 A.2d 637 (N.J. Super. Ct. App. Div. 1968) (2–1 decision), aff'd (largely on same basis), 250 A.2d 129 (N.J. 1969) (Francis, J.) (7–0 decision).

warranty and tort beyond sales transactions to commercial lessors,[20] and apparently thinking that "the gates are wide open," the plaintiff argued that the doctrine should be extended to service contracts involving the use of defective products.[21]

The plaintiff was wrong. Unlike cases against manufacturers, retailers, lessors, and other commercial distributors of products, the court thought that the dentist was in no better position than the plaintiff to discover or control the risk.[22] Further, traditional products liability defendants are all in the business of supplying chattels to consumers whereas the essence of the defendant dentist's business was providing professional services.[23] Moreover, to the extent that risk spreading might be considered a legitimate goal of strict products liability, it is premised on the assumption that defendants are large-scale enterprises engaged in wide-spread product distribution as distinguished from the one-on-one nature of a dentist-patient relationship. Nor would shifting the risk of loss to a dentist or doctor's insurers be appropriate in view of the rapidly increasing costs of medical insurance and care.[24] And it would not be fair to allow the plaintiff to use the dentist as a mere conduit to reach the manufacturer of the defective needle when the plaintiff, through discovery, had a means to identify the manufacturer, if identification were possible at all. Finally, the court reasoned that because the law of professional malpractice limits a health care provider's liability to negligence, it would be illogical to expand responsibility to strict liability for merely *using* (not selling) an instrument that happens to be defective.

Shortly after *Magrine*, the New Jersey courts were asked to decide whether a "beauty parlor" should be subject to strict liability for applying a defective permanent wave solution to a patron's hair and scalp, causing contact dermatitis to her scalp and causing her hair to fall out. In *Newmark v. Gimbel's, Inc.*,[25] nearly a decade after penning his landmark decision in *Henningsen v. Bloomfield Motors, Inc.*,[26] Justice Francis had an opportunity to explore how far the principles of strict products liability law should extend. Holding that Gimbel's was a retailer subject to strict liability in both warranty and tort, and that Mrs. Newmark was a consumer of a defective product entitled to protection, Justice Francis addressed the defendants' argument that *Magrine* afforded them protection against strict liability because the same principles applied to all service providers, whether dentists, doctors, or dispensers of beauty. The court saw vast differences between the "commercial enterprise" of a beauty parlor and the "profession" of a dentist or a doctor. While the former caters to "convenience or luxury," the latter,

---

**20.** See Cintrone v. Hertz Truck Leasing & Rental Serv., 212 A.2d 769 (N.J. 1965); § 16.2, above.

**21.** 227 A.2d at 541.

**22.** Id. at 542–43.

**23.** "[T]he *essence* of the transaction between the retail seller and the consumer relates to the *article sold*. The seller is *in the business* of supplying the product to the consumer. It is that, and that alone, for which he is paid. A dentist or a physician

offers, and is paid for, his professional services and skill. That is the essence of the relationship between him and his patient." Id. at 543.

**24.** Id. at 545–46.

**25.** 258 A.2d 697 (N.J. 1969) (Francis, J.), aff'g 246 A.2d 11 (N.J. Super. Ct. App. Div. 1968).

**26.** 161 A.2d 69 (N.J. 1960). See § 5.2, above.

who cannot advertise for patients, addresses the "felt necessity" of the patient. Unlike the "mechanical and routine" nature of a beautician's services, highly trained and skilled medical care professionals must apply individualized study and judgment to the particular medical condition of each patient.[27] A doctor or dentist neither guarantees results nor sells a product in any reasonable sense of that word. Instead, the "paramount function" of such professionals, licensed after many years of study to fulfill their "special and essential role" of diagnosing and relieving ailments, must be viewed as "the furnishing of opinions and services."[28] Thus, the court concluded that negligence is the only appropriate standard of liability for doctors and dentists, professionals whose services are fundamentally distinguishable from beauty parlors.[29] The latter type of commercial enterprise, as a retailer of consumer products, is subject to strict liability, both in warranty and tort, for supplying defective products that harm their customers.[30]

### General Principles

The preceding cases illustrate most of the important principles about service transactions in products liability law. The first principle, illustrated by *Gagne*, is that pure service transactions merely involve a service provider's *conduct* and so must be judged according to the law of negligence. While a small handful of courts have found common-law implied warranties in the provision of pure services,[31] and while a number of early commentators argued for the expansion of strict liability to service transactions,[32] the vast majority of courts have rejected out of hand any thought of applying strict liability to such transactions.[33]

The second point, illustrated by *Perlmutter*, *Magrine*, and *Newmark*, is the way in which the courts often rely upon a blend of doctrine and policy analysis in deciding whether to apply strict liability to mixed sales-service transactions. In sales-service hybrid cases, most courts search for the "essence" of the transaction to ascertain whether the sale or service aspect predominates.[34] If the transaction predominantly involves a prod-

**27.** 258 A.2d at 702–03.

**28.** Id. at 703 (citing Gagne v. Bertran, 275 P.2d 15 (Cal. 1954)).

**29.** The "unique status" of health care professionals, and "the utility of and the need for them, involving as they do, the health and even survival of many people, are so important to the general welfare as to outweigh in the policy scale any need for the imposition on dentists and doctors of the rules of strict liability in tort." Id.

**30.** Id. at 705.

**31.** See, e.g., Broyles v. Brown Eng'g Co., 151 So.2d 767 (Ala. 1963) (as to routine engineering survey of subdivision drainage requirements); Bloomsburg Mills, Inc. v. Sordoni Constr. Co., 164 A.2d 201 (Pa. 1960); Hill v. Polar Pantries, 64 S.E.2d 885 (S.C. 1951).

**32.** See, e.g., Schmidt, Ince, and Richbourg, Piercing the Aluminum Overcast: A

Case for Strict Liability for Commercial Air Carriers, 9 Lincoln L. Rev. 37 (1974); Comment, 22 UCLA. L. Rev. 401, 450 (1974) ("The extension of enterprise liability to all services would have a sound basis in economic and justice considerations.").

**33.** For example, doctors uniformly have been held not subject to strict liability for medical accidents arising purely from their treatment. Barton v. Owen, 139 Cal. Rptr. 494 (Ct. App. 1977); Hoven v. Kelble, 256 N.W.2d 379 (Wis. 1977).

**34.** For more recent examples, see, e.g., Brandt v. Sarah Lincoln Health Ctr., 792 N.E.2d 296 (Ill. 2003) (where hospital surgically implanted in plaintiff pubovaginal sling, "thrust" of transaction was provision of service, not sale of good); Wallace v. Gerard Med., Inc., 2003 WL 1995910 (Conn. Super. Ct. 2003); ACMAT Corp. v. Jansen & Rogan Constr. Eng'rs, 1999 WL 701814

uct sale, then strict liability principles are appropriate; if service aspects dominate the transaction, then negligence alone should be applied. The essence-of-the-transaction or predominant-factor "test,"[35] together with the very distinction between products and services on which the test is based, have both been criticized by the commentators who call for courts to abandon mechanical distinctions in favor of a policy analysis that looks to whether the principles of strict products liability are appropriate in any given case.[36] But in this respect, many courts were ahead of the commentators: in *Perlmutter v. Beth David Hospital*, Judge Fuld recognized that determining "whether the essence of a particular contract is for the rendition of services or for the sale of property, may at times be troublesome and vexatious,"[37] and a large number of decisions (including *Perlmutter* and the other early decisions considered above) have applied policy analysis (often blending it with the "essence" test) to help determine whether a case should be located in the "sale" or "service" category.[38] Indeed, one must be cautious of reposing too much confidence in "policy analysis" as a panacea; what with the numerous and diverse policies said to support modern products liability law (many of which are hotly controverted),[39] a lawyer or court may reach virtually any result desired by manipulating the panoply of theories that lie behind the righteous veil of "policy analysis."[40] In the final analysis, courts often appropriately return to boundary definitions that distinguish products liability from other types of cases—whether the defendant was instru-

---

(Conn. Super. Ct. 1999); ACandS, Inc. v. Abate, 710 A.2d 944, 999 (Md. 1998); Ayyash v. Henry Ford Health Sys., 533 N.W.2d 353 (Mich. Ct. App. 1996); Parker v. St. Vincent Hosp., 919 P.2d 1104 (N.M. Ct. App. 1996); Porter v. Rosenberg, 650 So.2d 79 (Fla. Dist. Ct. App. 1995); Sapp v. Morton Bldgs., Inc., 973 F.2d 539, 541 (7th Cir. 1992) (Ind. law) (Indiana Product Liability Act does not apply to "a transaction that, by its nature, involves wholly or predominantly the sale of a service rather than a product"; *held*, providing customized stable was a "service"); Podrat v. Codman–Shurtleff, Inc., 558 A.2d 895, 895–98 (Pa. Super. Ct. 1989).

**35.** This approach is also referred to as the gravamen-of-the-action test. See Taylor, Applicability of Strict Liability Warranty Theories to Service Transactions, 47 S.C. L. Rev. 231, 253 (1996).

**36.** See, e.g., Stapleton, Bugs in Anglo–American Products Liability Law, 53 S.C. L. Rev. 1225, 1253 (2002) (noting "the artificiality of any product/service distinction in our law of obligations and the incoherence of the idea that products liability can sensibly look at the product and not the human behaviour surrounding its production and handling"); Lannetti, Toward a Revised Definition of "Product" under the Restatement (Third) of Torts: Products Liability, 55 Bus. Law. 799 (2000), reprinted in, 35 Tort & Ins. L.J. 845 (2000); Taylor, Applicability of Strict Liability Warranty Theories

to Service Transactions, 47 S.C. L. Rev. 231 (1996); Powers, Distinguishing Between Products and Services in Strict Liability, 62 N.C. L. Rev. 415 (1984).

**37.** 123 N.E.2d 792, 794 (N.Y. 1954).

**38.** The older classics include Gagne v. Bertran, 275 P.2d 15 (Cal. 1954); Perlmutter v. Beth David Hosp., 123 N.E.2d 792 (N.Y. 1954); Magrine v. Krasnica, 227 A.2d 539 (Hudson Cty. Ct. 1967); Newmark v. Gimbel's, Inc., 258 A.2d 697 (N.J. 1969) (Francis, J.), aff'g 246 A.2d 11 (N.J. Super. Ct. App. Div. 1968). Modern examples abound. See, e.g., Wallace v. Gerard Med., Inc., 2003 WL 1995910 (Conn. Super. Ct. 2003); Condos v. Musculoskeletal Transplant Found., 208 F.Supp.2d 1226 (D. Utah 2002); Cafazzo v. Central Med. Health Servs., Inc., 668 A.2d 521 (Pa. 1995) (Montemuro, J.), and id. at 527 (Cappy, J., dissenting); Porter v. Rosenberg, 650 So.2d 79 (Fla. Dist. Ct. App. 1995); Hector v. Cedars–Sinai Med. Ctr., 225 Cal.Rptr. 595, 597–601 (Ct. App. 1986).

**39.** See § 5.4, above.

**40.** See, e.g., Cafazzo v. Central Med. Health Servs., Inc., 668 A.2d 521, 527 (Pa. 1995) (Cappy, J., dissenting) (criticizing the majority's "distorted" and "muddled" application of the jurisdiction's multiple-policy test to improperly protect the defendant hospital and doctor from liability for selling and implanting a defective TMJ prosthesis).

mental in moving a harm-producing "product" through the stream of commerce[41] and whether the chain of distribution ended effectively with a defendant who was more of a product user than supplier.[42]

This last issue, whether a defendant is fairly to be regarded as more of a product *user* than supplier, is another especially important perspective highlighted by the court in *Magrine*. Refusing to apply strict liability to the dentist for using a defective hypodermic needle, the court explained that a contrary holding would require it to apply strict liability "to any user of a tool, other equipment or any article which, through no fault of the user, breaks due to a latent defect and injures another. It would apply to any physician, artisan or mechanic and to any user of a defective article—even to a driver of a defective automobile." The court was aware of no rationale for intruding so deeply into the domain of negligence law.[43] This slippery-slope problem is very real, and no American court has held a driver subject to strict liability in tort merely for driving a defective car.[44] Such a holding would turn accident law entirely on its head, converting the basic liability principle from negligence to strict liability. In the field of products liability, the product "use" vs. "supply" distinction is perhaps the most fundamental divide between negligence and strict liability—since using a product implicates a person's conduct, which the law of torts judges only according to the law of negligence,[45] whereas selling or otherwise supplying a product is what provides the very foundation for strict products liability.[46]

All four of the decisions discussed above, from *Gagne* through *Newmark*, resolutely refuse to impose a strict liability standard on doctors in particular, and professionals more generally. As discussed below, subsequent decisions have adhered closely to these principles, exempting doctors and other professionals from the rigors of strict products liability. Yet *Newmark*, the final case examined above, reveals a couple of related loopholes that may be available in a sales-service case to help a plaintiff injured by a specialist's use of a defective product avoid the general rule that service providers are not subject to strict liability. First, a plaintiff may be permitted to apply the principles of strict products liability to a sales-service hybrid transaction if the defendant specialist is classified as a *non*-professional, like the beautician in

---

**41.** See, e.g., Cafazzo v. Central Med. Health Servs., Inc., 668 A.2d 521 (Pa. 1995) (TMJ implant); Hector v. Cedars–Sinai Med. Ctr., 225 Cal.Rptr. 595, 597–601 (Ct. App. 1986) (pacemaker); Silverhart v. Mount Zion Hosp., 98 Cal.Rptr. 187 (Ct. App. 1971) (defective surgical needle).

**42.** See, e.g., Bhardwaj v. 24 Hour Fitness, Inc., 2002 WL 373563 (Cal. Ct. App. 2002) (exercise equipment; chain of distribution ended not with plaintiff, but with health club, as there was no evidence that health club played role in manufacture, design, or marketing of product); Podrat v. Codman–Shurtleff, Inc., 558 A.2d 895 (Pa. Super. Ct. 1989) (pituitary forceps that broke); Silverhart v. Mount Zion Hosp., 98

Cal.Rptr. 187 (Ct. App. 1971) (defective surgical needle).

**43.** 227 A.2d at 547.

**44.** Compare Hammontree v. Jenner, 97 Cal.Rptr. 739 (Ct. App. 1971) (driver not strictly liable for driving accidents); Maloney v. Rath, 445 P.2d 513 (Cal. 1968) (Traynor, C.J.) (driver not strictly liable for bad brakes but has nondelegable duty rendering owner vicariously liable for mechanic's negligence).

**45.** See Prosser and Keeton on Torts ch. 5.

**46.** See ch. 5, above. See also Products Liability Restatement § 20.

*Newmark*, or a plumber or electrician. This distinction has been criticized as "elitist,"[47] as it may well be, but it serves an important function that is well described in the cases discussed above.

*Newmark* suggests a second and related loophole for plaintiffs seeking to impose strict liability on service providers—the distinction between simple, routine, mechanical tasks, for which strict liability might arguably be appropriate, and discretionary judgments that involve complex and multi-faceted decisions, for which only negligence responsibility is proper. There is an analogy here to the protected realm of policy decisionmaking lying at the core of governmental[48] and family[49] management decisions which traditionally have been held off-limits to judicial oversight. But behind the governmental and parental exemptions for core decisions lies a basic rule of negligence for the misconduct of such special parties, not a rule of strict liability. And while a very occasional decision has allowed strict liability recovery for service providers,[50] most courts properly refuse to apply strict liability to providers of pure services for making even "simple" mistakes, reasoning that the normal principles of professional negligence adequately protect persons harmed by errors of this type.[51]

### Professional Services

For the many reasons developed in the early decisions discussed above, and those examined below, courts have broadly refused to apply strict liability rules to doctors, dentists, hospitals, and other health care providers,[52] or to architects, engineers, and other design professionals,[53]

---

**47.** See Murphy v. E.R. Squibb & Sons, Inc., 710 P.2d 247, 258 (Cal. 1985) (Bird, J., dissenting) (protecting pharmacists as "professionals" creates "elitist distinctions").

**48.** Policy decisions are protected in this context by the "discretionary function" exception to governmental liability. See Prosser and Keeton on Torts § 131.

**49.** See id. at § 122.

**50.** See, e.g., Broyles v. Brown Eng'g Co., 151 So.2d 767 (Ala. 1963) (implied warranty of fitness for intended use as to routine engineering survey of subdivision drainage requirements). See also Bloomsburg Mills, Inc. v. Sordoni Constr. Co., 164 A.2d 201 (Pa. 1960); Hill v. Polar Pantries, 64 S.E.2d 885 (S.C. 1951).

**51.** See, e.g., City of Mounds View v. Walijarvi, 263 N.W.2d 420, 424–25 (Minn. 1978), which reexamined the majority rule holding professionals only to a negligence standard:

The city suggests that many of the design-related tasks performed by modern architects are routine and carry no risk of error if they are performed with professional due care. It is argued that with respect to such tasks, the premise on which the traditional rule rests is inoperative, making the adoption of the implied warranty theory fully proper. [But]

architectural errors in relatively simple matters are quite easily handled under the existing cause of action for professional negligence.

Moreover, if implied warranties are held to accompany only uncomplicated architectural endeavors, the finder of fact will be forced in every case to determine, as a preliminary matter, whether the alleged architectural error was made in the performance of a sufficiently simplistic task. [T]he net effect would be the interjection of substantive ambiguity into the law of professional malpractice without a favorable trade-off in procedural expedience.

**52.** See discussion below.

**53.** See, e.g., G.J. Palmer v. Espey Huston & Assocs., 84 S.W.3d 345 (Tex. App. 2002) (engineering firms that designed artificial harbor not liable for strict products liability or breach of implied warranty); Milford v. Commercial Carriers, Inc., 210 F.Supp.2d 987 (N.D. Ill. 2002) (designer of auto trailer, who had no role in manufacture, was not subject to strict products liability); Bruzga v. PMR Architects, P.C., 693 A.2d 401, 404–06 (N.H. 1997) (architects who designed facility not strictly liable for suicide in psychiatric cell because they pro-

for damages from providing professional services. *Audlane Lumber & Builders Supply, Inc. v. D.E. Britt Associates, Inc.*[54] involved the question of whether an engineering firm which prepared design specifications for a chattel could be liable for breach of implied warranty for damages to a third party for defects in the specifications. The court saw no room for implied warranty principles in cases involving professional responsibility. Engineers and other professionals normally do not "warrant" the quality of their work as sellers warrant the quality of their goods. "Rather, in the preparation of design and specifications as the basis of construction, the engineer or architect 'warrants' that he will or has exercised his skill according to a certain standard of care, that he acted reasonably and without neglect." But this is nothing more than saying that a professional who is negligent breaches his or her warranty of quality, which conflates the separate concepts of negligence and warranty and sows confusion in "an area of law where confusion abounds."[55]

A later decision, *City of Mounds View v. Walijarvi*,[56] which involved a claim for defects in a building against the firm of architects and engineers responsible for its design, explained that all professionals—including architects, doctors, engineers, and lawyers—are immune from strict liability largely because they deal in "inexact sciences" involving "random factors which are incapable of precise measurement" which require the exercise of skilled judgment by the professional.[57] The indeterminate nature of professional decisions precludes accuracy in every case,[58] such that "doctors cannot promise that every operation will be successful; a lawyer can never be certain that a contract he drafts is without latent ambiguity; and an architect cannot be certain that a structural design will interact with natural forces as anticipated."[59] Clients are adequately protected against simple, routine architectural errors by the law of negligence,[60] and the principles of modern products liability cannot be borrowed because the contexts are so different. Unlike mass producers of defective products, architects work one-on-one with their clients; and, because architects ordinarily build only a single "product," they do not have a manufacturer's opportunity for testing prototypes to discover latent defects.[61] For these reasons, the court concluded that the standard negligence malpractice action was sufficient protection against architectural errors in design and rejected an implied

vided professional service); Hunt v. ESI Eng'g, Inc., 808 P.2d 1137, 1139–40 (Utah Ct. App. 1991); Industrial Risk Insurers v. Creole Prod. Servs., Inc., 746 F.2d 526, 527 (9th Cir. 1984) (Alaska law) (pumping station engineering services for pumping station on Trans–Alaska Pipeline); Chubb Group of Ins. Cos. v. C.F. Murphy & Assocs., Inc., 656 S.W.2d 766, 780 (Mo. Ct. App. 1983) (products liability claims unavailable against consulting structural engineers for roof collapse of arena); Del Mar Beach Club Owners Ass'n v. Imperial Contracting Co., 176 Cal.Rptr. 886, 894 (Ct. App. 1981).

**54.**  168 So.2d 333 (Fla. Dist. Ct. App. 1964).

**55.**  Id. at 335.

**56.**  263 N.W.2d 420 (Minn. 1978).

**57.**  Id. at 424.

**58.**  Id.

**59.**  Id. "If every facet of structural design consisted of little more than the mechanical application of immutable physical principles, we could accept the rule of strict liability which the city proposes." Id.

**60.**  Id.

**61.**  Id.

warranty rule of strict liability that would guarantee the client good results.[62]

In a number of cases, patients have tried to hold doctors and hospitals liable for "selling" defective medical products for which the patients must pay, either directly or indirectly. In almost every case,[63] the courts have rejected strict products liability claims (in both tort and warranty) against doctors, hospitals, and other healthcare providers for providing defective pharmaceutical drugs,[64] pacemakers,[65] silicone breast implants,[66] jaw implants,[67] joint prostheses,[68] and other products surgically implanted, prescribed, used, or provided by health-care professionals.[69]

**62.** Id. at 425.

**63.** A scattered miscellany of cases are to the contrary. See, e.g., Garcia v. Edgewater Hosp., 613 N.E.2d 1243 (Ill. App. Ct. 1993) (hospital charged patient for defective heart valve engaged in sale subject to implied warranty liability); Malawy v. Richards Mfg. Co., 501 N.E.2d 376 (Ill. App. Ct. 1986) (hospital—implied warranty for defective bone plate). Several lower court decisions in Missouri formerly allowed strict products liability claims against health care providers, but the Supreme Court has put a halt to that. See Budding v. SSM Healthcare Sys., 19 S.W.3d 678 (Mo. 2000) (en banc), overruling Mulligan v. Truman Med. Ctr., 950 S.W.2d 576 (Mo. Ct. App. 1997), Bell v. Poplar Bluff Physicians Group, Inc., 879 S.W.3d 618, 619 (Mo. Ct. App. 1994), and other cases.

**64.** See, e.g., Kohl v. American Home Prods. Corp., 78 F.Supp.2d 885 (W.D. Ark. 1999) ("fen-phen" diet drug—pharmacist); Coyle v. Richardon–Merrell, Inc., 584 A.2d 1383 (Pa. 1991) (Bendectin—pharmacist); Murphy v. E.R. Squibb & Sons, Inc., 710 P.2d 247 (Cal. 1985) (Mosk, J.) (DES—pharmacist); Batiste v. American Home Prods. Corp., 231 S.E.2d 269, 272–73 (N.C. Ct. App. 1977) (contraceptives—doctor). On pharmacist liability in negligence for incorrectly filling drug prescriptions, see Annot., 3 A.L.R.4th 270 (1981). For a pharmacist's liability for harm from properly filling a prescription, see Annot., 44 A.L.R.5th 393 (1996). For pharmacist liability for failure to warn, see § 9.6, above.

**65.** See, e.g., St. Mary Med. Ctr., Inc. v. Casko, 639 N.E.2d 312 (Ind. Ct. App. 1994); Hector v. Cedars–Sinai Med. Ctr., 225 Cal. Rptr. 595, 597–601 (Ct. App. 1986).

**66.** See, e.g., In re Breast Implant Prod. Liab. Litig., 503 S.E.2d 445 (S.C. 1998) (Toal, J.), noted, 50 S.C. L. Rev. 463, 465 (1999); Porter v. Rosenberg, 650 So.2d 79 (Fla. Dist. Ct. App. 1995). For an illuminating explanation of why certain medical professionals might properly be held subject to strict products liability for the serious com-plications from breast implants, see Cupp, Sharing Accountability for Breast Implants: Strict Products Liability and Medical Professionals Engaged in Hybrid Sales/Service Cosmetic Products Transactions, 21 Fla. St. U. L. Rev. 873 (1994). See also Spanbauer, Breast Implants as Beauty Ritual: Woman's Sceptre and Prison, 9 Yale J.L. & Feminism 157 (1997); Note, 50 S.C. L. Rev. 463 (1999).

**67.** See, e.g., Budding v. SSM Healthcare Sys., 19 S.W.3d 678 (Mo. 2000) (en banc) (overruling earlier cases); Ayyash v. Henry Ford Health Sys., 533 N.W.2d 353 (Mich. Ct. App. 1996); Parker v. St. Vincent Hosp., 919 P.2d 1104 (N.M. Ct. App. 1996); Cafazzo v. Central Med. Health Servs., Inc., 668 A.2d 521 (Pa. 1995).

**68.** See, e.g., Royer v. Catholic Med. Ctr., 741 A.2d 74 (N.H. 1999) (knee); Hoff v. Zimmer, Inc., 746 F.Supp. 872 (W.D. Wis. 1990) (hip).

**69.** See, e.g., Brandt v. Sarah Lincoln Health Ctr., 792 N.E.2d 296 (Ill. 2003) (surgically implanted pubovaginal sling); Wallace v. Gerard Med., Inc., 2003 WL 1995910 (Conn. Super. Ct. 2003) (porta catheter); Condos v. Musculoskeletal Transplant Found., 208 F.Supp.2d 1226 (D. Utah 2002) (bone tissue); Cobb v. Dallas Fort Worth Med. Ctr.—Grand Prairie, 48 S.W.3d 820 (Tex. App. 2001) (implantation of pedicular hardware in plaintiff's back); Betro v. GAC Int'l, Inc., 551 N.Y.S.2d 72 (App. Div. 1990) (orthodontic night brace); North Miami Gen. Hosp., Inc. v. Goldberg, 520 So.2d 650, 652 (Fla. Dist. Ct. App. 1988) (electro-surgical grounding pad supplied by hospital—burns); Probst v. Albert Einstein Med. Ctr., 440 N.Y.S.2d 2 (App. Div. 1981) (defective metal rod inserted in spinal column for scoliosis); Carmichael v. Reitz, 95 Cal.Rptr. 381 (Ct. App. 1971) (oral contraceptive); Silverhart v. Mount Zion Hosp., 98 Cal. Rptr. 187 (Ct. App. 1971) (surgical needle that broke and became imbedded in plaintiff's lower pelvic area during vaginal hysterectomy); Barbee v. Rogers, 425 S.W.2d

In such cases, drawing on the principles developed above, courts reason that strict products liability is inappropriate because the defendants are predominantly providing medical services, not selling products, and because they are themselves merely product users, not suppliers.[70]

The rule against holding healthcare providers strictly liable for injuries to patients logically is limited, however, to injuries directly related to medical treatment of the plaintiff. Thus, a Texas court held a hospital subject to strict liability for providing a patient with a flammable gown.[71] A California court, however, properly concluded that it would stretch strict products liability too far to extend it to a patient's wife who made a products liability claim against the hospital for injuries from tripping on defective carpeting in her husband's hospital room.[72]

### Non-Professionals—Product Installers

Like professionals, non-professionals are also subject to the normal rules of negligence.[73] Perhaps the two largest classes of non-professionals who routinely deal with products are those who install products and those who repair them, two different forms of service often performed by the same tradesperson. So, a plumber, electrician, or contractor may either install or repair a water heater that blows up. Product installation is treated here, and product repair is addressed below.[74]

To a considerable extent, the product installation cases mirror the service and sale-service hybrid cases discussed above. Thus, most courts appear to search for the essence or predominant purpose of the transaction in an effort to determine whether it was more in the nature of a service transaction, involving at most an incidental sale of a defective product, or primarily a sales transaction in which the installer was in the chain of product distribution.[75] If a homeowner buys a new hot water heater from a plumbing contractor who installs it, the transaction probably will include significant aspects of both sales and service. If the water heater explodes because of a manufacturing defect, the homeowner may seek to recover from the plumber for "selling" a defective

342 (Tex. 1968) (contact lens prescribed and fitted by optometrist); W.P. Keeton, Torts, 23 Sw. L.J. 1, 6–9 (1969) (discussing *Barbee*).

**70.** See Annot., 65 A.L.R.5th 357 (1999) (strict liability in tort or warranty of doctor or hospital for harm to patients from products used in treatment).

**71.** See, e.g., Thomas v. St. Joseph Hosp., 618 S.W.2d 791, 796–97 (Tex. App. 1981) (smoking in bed, plaintiff died from burns when his gown caught fire).

**72.** Pierson v. Sharp Mem'l Hosp., Inc., 264 Cal.Rptr. 673 (Ct. App. 1989).

**73.** See, e.g., Couch v. Astec Indus., Inc., 71 F.Supp.2d 1145 (D.N.M. 1999).

**74.** See § 16.4, below.

**75.** See, e.g., Maack v. Resource Design & Constr., Inc., 875 P.2d 570, 581 (Utah Ct. App. 1994) (stucco installer not in business of selling stucco, although it included costs thereof in its bill, but merely used it in its work). See also Hidalgo v. Fagen, Inc., 206 F.3d 1013 (10th Cir. 2000) (Colo. law) (construction of plant's conveyor system was not sale of product but, rather, sale of contractor's services). Compare ACandS, Inc. v. Abate, 710 A.2d 944, 999 (Md. 1998) (jury could find that predominant purpose of contract was sale of asbestos fireproofing spray where defendant's employees delivered spray to job sites, defendant included cost of spray in each job bid, and defendant was a major applicator (installer) of the spray; but court erred in not instructing jury that contractor was not subject to strict liability in tort if its predominant purpose was provision of service rather than a sale), with Scordino v. Hopeman Bros., 662 So.2d 640, 645 (Miss. 1995) (because subcontractor who installed asbestos paneling in ships was not a "seller" of such materials, but "merely supplied the materials to complete the service for which it was hired," it was not subject to strict liability in tort). See generally 1 Frumer and Friedman, Products Liability § 5.13[2].

product. Especially if the plumber separated the heater price from the plumbing services in billing for the project,[76] the transaction to a large extent will have involved the supply of a defective product, and the plumber will have played a significant role in the chain of distribution. In such a case, the plumber could not in any way be viewed merely as a user, but should instead be considered the necessary final link in the chain of distribution to the ultimate consumer. Just as a tire dealer that sells and installs a defective tire is subject to the strict liability of a retailer,[77] so too is a plumber, electrician, contractor, or other tradesperson properly subject to strict products liability for selling a defective product that it installs.[78] But if a product installer supplies a defective product only incidentally to his or her provision of services, and so cannot fairly be classified as a member of the chain of distribution, then most courts decline to apply either warranty or strict liability in tort.[79]

Many of the cases involving product installers concern the applicability of implied warranty and strict liability in tort theories to the defective installation of a *non*defective product. *State Stove Manufacturing Company v. Hodges*[80] was an early case of this type, in which a plumber and the contractors that hired him were both held strictly liable in tort for the destruction of a home from an explosion of the water heater due to its defective installation.[81] Several other courts have similarly allowed implied warranty or strict liability in tort claims against suppliers of nondefective products who install them in a dangerously defective manner.[82] In most instances, however, courts properly refuse to apply strict products liability to claims of improper installation of a nondefective product, concluding that the service component of the

---

**76.** See Parker v. St. Vincent Hosp., 919 P.2d 1104 (N.M. Ct. App. 1996); Products Liability Restatement § 20 cmt. *d*.

**77.** See, e.g., Barth v. B. F. Goodrich Tire Co., 71 Cal.Rptr. 306 (Ct. App. 1968).

**78.** See, e.g., ACandS, Inc. v. Abate, 710 A.2d 944, 999 (Md. 1998) (supplier-applier of asbestos fireproofing spray); Hinojasa v. Automatic Elevator Co., 416 N.E.2d 45 (Ill. 1980) (defective elevator); Court v. Grzelinski, 379 N.E.2d 281 (Ill. 1978) (defendant sold used car with defective fuel tank it had installed). See also Prompt Air, Inc. v. Firewall Forward, Inc., 707 N.E.2d 235 (Ill. App. Ct. 1999) (aircraft engine overhauler subject to strict tort liability for forced landing caused by reconditioned turbocharger procured, paid for, and installed by, defendant). See generally Products Liability Restatement § 20(a) and (c).

**79.** See, e.g., Scordino v. Hopeman Bros., 662 So.2d 640, 645 (Miss. 1995) (because subcontractor who installed asbestos paneling in ships was not "seller" of such materials, but "merely supplied the materials to complete the service for which it was hired," it was not subject to strict liability in tort; "a contractor/subcontractor is not a seller [for § 402A] and is therefore not lia-

ble for any component parts it may supply in compliance with the performance of a job or service"); Maack v. Resource Design & Constr., Inc., 875 P.2d 570, 581 (Utah Ct. App. 1994) (stucco installer); Monte Vista Dev. Corp. v. Superior Ct., 277 Cal.Rptr. 608 (Ct. App. 1991) (subcontractor who installed defective soap dish in house not strictly liable because not in business of selling soap dishes); Chenango Ind. Dev. Agency v. Lockwood Greene Eng'rs, Inc., 494 N.Y.S.2d 832, 834 (App. Div. 1985), appeal dismissed, 490 N.E.2d 1233 (N.Y. 1986); Delta Ref. Co. v. Procon, Inc., 552 S.W.2d 387 (Tenn. Ct. App. 1976) (contractor installed defective pump at oil refinery). See also Hunt v. Guarantee Elec. Co. of St. Louis, 667 S.W.2d 9, 11–12 (Mo. Ct. App. 1984) (electrical contractors who installed nondefective timer in electrical system that may have been defectively designed not subject to strict liability in tort).

**80.** 189 So.2d 113 (Miss. 1966).

**81.** Id. at 123–24.

**82.** See, e.g., O'Laughlin v. Minnesota Natural Gas Co., 253 N.W.2d 826 (Minn. 1977) (defective installation of furnace by plumbing and heating contractor); Worrell v. Barnes, 484 P.2d 573 (Nev. 1971).

transaction must be judged according to traditional principles of the law of negligence.[83]

## Other Services

In other contexts, courts have refused to extend the principles of strict products liability to a large miscellany of service providers who in some respect provide "products" to their patrons. For example, courts have refused to apply strict liability to health clubs, for providing patrons with defective exercise equipment;[84] amusement ride operators, for providing defective rides;[85] ski facilities, for providing defective equipment for transporting skiers up the mountain;[86] travel agents, for providing defective trips fraught with unexpected dangers;[87] baseball stadiums, for providing spectators with defective protection from foul balls;[88] and school districts, for providing defective lunches to students.[89] Such providers are liable, of course, for negligence.[90] But, because they are not commercial suppliers of products in the chain of distribution, they appropriately are immune from strict products liability.

**83.** This principle is axiomatic. See, e.g., Conger v. Tel Tech, Inc., 798 P.2d 279 (Utah Ct. App. 1990). See also Ramos v. Silent Hoist & Crane Co., 607 A.2d 667 (N.J. Super. Ct. App. Div. 1992) (Dreier, J.A.D.), an action against an electrician for improperly installing an electrical system, which included conduit, switches, winches, a motor, starter, and stop-start station. Based on the fundamental "proposition that negligence in installing a particular piece of equipment has a different basis of liability than strict liability for the sale of the equipment itself," and reasoning that the defendant's "design of the electrical system and its professional choice of where to place the controls" principally involved the installation of another's product, the court concluded that negligence rather than strict liability in tort was the proper standard. Id. at 670–71. However, the court then determined that the design responsibilities in negligence and strict liability in tort, both based on reasonableness, are essentially the same. See generally Calloway v. City of Reno, 993 P.2d 1259 (Nev. 2000), overruling Worrell v. Barnes, 484 P.2d 573 (1971); Hoover v. Montgomery Ward & Co., 528 P.2d 76 (Or. 1974).

**84.** See, e.g., Bhardwaj v. 24 Hour Fitness, Inc., 2002 WL 373563 (Cal. Ct. App. 2002) ("Hack Squat" machine); Reeder v. Bally's Total Fitness Corp., 963 F.Supp. 530 (E.D. Va. 1997) (stomach curl machine); Watford v. Jack LaLanne Long Island, Inc., 542 N.Y.S.2d 765, 767 (App. Div. 1989) (rowing machine).

**85.** See, e.g., Greenwood v. Busch Entm't Corp., 101 F.Supp.2d 292 (E.D. Pa. 2000) (water slide—service); Rossetti v. Busch Entm't Corp., 87 F.Supp.2d 415

(E.D. Pa. 2000) (same); Marsh v. Dixon, 707 N.E.2d 998, 1001–02 (Ind. Ct. App. 1999) (ride not "product" under products liability act); Bobryk v. Lincoln Amusements, Inc., 1996 WL 24566 (Conn. Super. Ct. 1996); Siciliano v. Capitol City Shows, Inc., 475 A.2d 19, 24–25 (N.H. 1984).

**86.** See, e.g., Bolduc v. Hebert Schneider Corp., 374 A.2d 1187, 1189–90 (N.H. 1977) (child fell from tramway); Lewis v. Big Powderhorn Mountain Ski Corp., 245 N.W.2d 81 (Mich. Ct. App. 1976) (2–1 decision) (Burns, J.) (tow rope).

**87.** See, e.g., Pena v. Sita World Travel, Inc., 152 Cal.Rptr. 17, 18 (Ct. App. 1978). See also Birmingham v. Fodor's Travel Publ'ns, Inc., 833 P.2d 70 (Haw. 1992) (travel guide not "product" subjecting publisher to strict liability for failing to warn body-surfing tourist of ocean surf conditions at beach).

**88.** See Romeo v. Pittsburgh Assocs., 787 A.2d 1027 (Pa. Super. Ct. 2001) (sale of ticket to baseball game is sale of service, not product, precluding strict products liability).

**89.** See Almquist v. The Finley Sch. Dist., 57 P.3d 1191 (Wash. Ct. App. 2002) (school lunch is "product" under Washington products liability statute, not service).

**90.** For example, operators of ski resorts and similar facilities are subject to liability in negligence, apart from statutes that commonly place the inherent risks of skiing on skiers. See, e.g., Morgan v. State, 618 N.Y.S.2d 967 (Ct. Cl. 1994) (design of bobsled run); Clover v. Snowbird Ski Resort, 808 P.2d 1037 (Utah 1991) (negligent design of ski trails).

### Statutory Reform

Products liability reform statutes are playing an increasingly significant role in cases involving providers of product services. The scope of many products liability statutes is limited to product "sellers," a category from which pure service transactions, together with some sales-service hybrid transactions, generally are excluded.[91] Some statutes more specifically exclude claims arising out of transactions that predominantly involve product services.[92] Moreover, in cases involving healthcare providers, medical malpractice reform statutes must be considered as well, and a number of cases have ruled that the statutory malpractice negligence standard, rather than that of strict products liability, governs mixed sales-services cases involving such providers.[93]

## § 16.4  REPAIRED, REBUILT, AND RECONDITIONED PRODUCTS

### Repaired Products

Those who repair products are subject to liability for their negligence that causes injury.[1] A number of early cases held that the rendition of personal services included a common-law implied warranty that the services would be provided in a workmanlike manner,[2] defined simply as a duty of due care.[3] But pure repair transactions cannot give rise to implied warranties under the Uniform Commercial Code because they involve pure services and do not involve the sale of goods.[4] Similarly, because the repair process is merely a service transaction not involv-

---

**91.** See, e.g., ACMAT Corp. v. Jansen & Rogan Constr. Eng'rs, 1999 WL 701814; In re Breast Implant Prod. Liab. Litig., 503 S.E.2d 445 (S.C. 1998) (Toal, J.) (healthcare providers not "sellers" for purposes of state's products liability act), noted, 50 S.C. L. Rev. 463, 465 (1999); Zbras v. St. Vincent's Med. Ctr., 1998 WL 144996, at *1 (Conn. Super. Ct. 1998) (orthopedic surgeon not "seller" of hardware he ordered and used in surgery); Paul v. McPhee Elec. Contractors, 698 A.2d 354, 357 (Conn. App. Ct. 1997) (installer); Ramos v. Silent Hoist & Crane Co., 607 A.2d 667, 671–72 (N.J. Super. Ct. App. Div. 1992) (electrician not seller or manufacturer).

**92.** See, e.g., Whitaker v. T.J. Snow Co. 151 F.3d 661 (7th Cir. 1998) (Ind. law) (applying Ind. Code § 33–1–1.5–2(6)).

**93.** See, e.g., Budding v. SSM Healthcare Sys., 19 S.W.3d 678 (Mo. 2000) (en banc) (overruling earlier cases); Huffaker v. ABC Ins. Co., 659 So.2d 544 (La. Ct. App. 1995); Porter v. Rosenberg, 650 So.2d 79 (Fla. Dist. Ct. App. 1995); St. Mary Med. Ctr., Inc. v. Casko, 639 N.E.2d 312 (Ind. Ct. App. 1994); Rogers v. Synthes, Ltd., 626 So.2d 775 (La. Ct. App. 1993).

**§ 16.4**

**1.** See, e.g., Holt v. Deere Co., 24 F.3d 1289 (10th Cir. 1994) (Okla. law); Swenson Trucking & Excavating, Inc. v. Truckweld Equip. Co., 604 P.2d 1113, 1117–18 (Alaska 1980) (repair of dump truck; defective ram assembly); Hunt v. Ford Motor Co., 341 So.2d 614, 619–20 (La. Ct. App. 1977) (repair of car; defective steering). See generally 1 Frumer and Friedman, Products Liability § 5.13; Restatement (2d) Torts § 404.

**2.** "In circumstances involving the rendition of personal services the duty upon the actor is to perform the services in a workmanlike manner." Hoffman v. Simplot Aviation, Inc., 539 P.2d 584, 590 (Idaho 1975), noted, 42 J. Air L. & Com. 919 (1976). Accord, Pepsi Cola Bottling Co. v. Superior Burner Serv., Co., 427 P.2d 833 (Alaska 1967).

**3.** See, e.g., Hoffman v. Simplot Aviation, Inc., 539 P.2d 584 (Idaho 1975); Pepsi Cola Bottling Co. v. Superior Burner Serv., 427 P.2d 833, 840–41 (Alaska 1967) (for both negligence law and the implied warranty of workmanlike performance, standard of care for provider of personal services is identical).

**4.** See, e.g., Stafford v. International Harvester Co., 668 F.2d 142, 146–47 (2d Cir. 1981) (N.Y. law) (predominantly service contract for repairing truck, not sale of goods); Lemley v. J & B Tire Co., 426 F.Supp. 1378 (W.D. Pa. 1977) (defective brakes). See § 16.3, above.

ing a product sale, strict liability in tort does not apply to faulty product repairs which are governed by negligence alone.[5] Some courts have pointed to *Restatement (Second) of Torts* § 404's use of negligence as the standard of liability for repairers,[6] distinct from § 402A's "special rule applicable to sellers of products,"[7] as further support for the proposition that strict liability in tort does not apply to product repairers.[8]

### Refurbished, Reconditioned, Rebuilt, and Remanufactured Products

While all products eventually wear out, sometimes in a dangerous manner,[9] some products can be reconditioned to substantially increase their useful lives.[10] Such processes range from simple "refurbishing" and "reconditioning" to "rebuilding" and "remanufacturing" the product altogether.[11] These descriptions are terms of art that carry special meaning: each level implies greater work by the renovator and generates a heightened expectation of reliability and safety by purchasers of such goods. The type and extent of product improvement thus moves along a sliding scale, from a basic clean-up and minor fix-up, at the refurbishing end, to a major remake, often accompanied by a product sale and warranty, at the remanufacturing end.[12]

**5.** See, e.g., Carlson v. Trailer Equip. and Supply, Inc., 600 N.W.2d 54 (Wis. Ct. App. 1999) (defective handle on semi-tractor cab repaired by defendant); Micciche v. Eastern Elevator Co., 645 A.2d 278, 280 (Pa. Super. Ct. 1994) (elevator system repairer not "seller"); Martinez v. Gouverneur Gardens Hous. Corp., 585 N.Y.S.2d 23 (App. Div. 1992) (warnings accompanying retrofit kit for commercial washing machine); Lemley v. J & B Tire Co., 426 F.Supp. 1378 (W.D. Pa. 1977) (defective brakes). See generally Note, 8 Pac. L.J. 865 (1977).

If a repairer was also the original retail *seller*, however, it may be subject to strict products liability. See Winters v. Sears, Roebuck & Co., 554 S.W.2d 565, 572 (Mo. Ct. App. 1977) ("Upon completion of servicing the product, whether it is done on the seller's premises or on the premises of the purchaser, the effect is a re-delivery of the product with the same assurances and with the same obligations as the original sale."). A repairer who was also the original *manufacturer* may also be subject to strict products liability. See, e.g., Young v. Aro Corp., 111 Cal.Rptr. 535, 538 (Ct. App. 1973) ("Whatever may be the strict liability exposure of a repairer who also happens to be a manufacturer in general, this particular case appears to be well within the justification for manufacturers' strict liability"). *But see* Winans v. Rockwell Int'l Corp., 705 F.2d 1449, 1452 (5th Cir. 1983) (La. law) (because original manufacturer which overhauled jet engine "acted not as a manufacturer but as a repairer of the engines," it was not subject to strict liability).

**6.** Restatement (2d) Torts § 404, "Negligence in Making, Rebuilding, or Repairing Chattel," provides: "One who as an independent contractor negligently makes, rebuilds, or repairs a chattel for another is subject to the same liability as that imposed upon negligent manufacturers of chattels."

**7.** Restatement (2d) Torts § 402A cmt. *a.* Section 402A is entitled "Special Liability of Seller of Product for Physical Harm to User or Consumer."

**8.** See, e.g., Nickel v. Hyster Co., 412 N.Y.S.2d 273, 274–76 (Sup. Ct. 1978); Lemley v. J & B Tire Co., 426 F.Supp. 1378 (W.D. Pa. 1977).

**9.** See § 10.6, above.

**10.** See, e.g., Whitaker v. T.J. Snow Co., 953 F.Supp. 1034, 1038 (N.D. Ind. 1997) ("Part of the purpose of refurbishing a machine is to increase its useful life.").

**11.** "Refurbishing entails work which is less extensive than reconditioning, which in turn, entails work which is less extensive than remanufacturing. Normally, a refurbishing is 'just an upgrade' of a product, a very minimal amount of work is performed on equipment that is refurbished. In contrast, when a machine is remanufactured, its frame is completely torn down and all of the component parts are removed and inspected individually during reassembly." Id. at 1037.

**12.** See Hogan and Colonna, Products Liability Implications of Reprocessing and Reuse of Single–Use Medical Devices, 53 Food Drug Cosm. L.J. 385 (1998).

If a product is simply refurbished, few if any major parts are likely to be replaced or substantially altered, and the addition of any new or rebuilt parts will likely be incidental to a transaction that both parties understand to be essentially a product improvement service transaction. For this reason, simple reconditioning or refurbishing generally will give rise to negligence liability alone, and strict products liability generally will not be available with respect to products furnished with only such basic upgrades.[13]

At the other end of the spectrum lie rebuilt and remanufactured products, which frequently are sold or otherwise placed in the stream of commerce by their restorers to compete with new products. Purchasers fairly expect such products to have nearly the reliability and overall quality of new goods,[14] and rebuilders and remanufacturers have the opportunity and obligation to rebuild or remanufacture their products to demanding standards, subjecting them to whatever testing and quality control is reasonably called for in the circumstances. Buyers of rebuilt and remanufactured products thus are entitled to the same legal protection from harm from manufacturing defects as buyers of new products.[15]

In between simple refurbishing and complete remanufacturing lie a broad range of product upgrade services, sometimes called reconditioning, overhauling, or something else. Because of the wide scope of possible services, including a lesser or greater repair or replacement of worn parts, the cases are very fact-specific, making it difficult to generalize how the law does or should treat such transactions. It may be said, however, that courts generally use some rough form of the essence-of-the-transaction or predominant-factor test examined earlier.[16] Thus, if a particular renovation called for mostly skill and effort inputs from the product renovator, so that it is predominantly a service transaction, then such a renovation (by whatever name) should be treated as a service transaction for which negligence, not strict products liability, will apply.[17] If, on the other hand, a product renovator substantially transforms

---

**13.** See, e.g., Whitaker v. T.J. Snow Co., 953 F.Supp. 1034, 1038 (N.D. Ind. 1997); Rolph v. EBI Cos., 464 N.W.2d 667, 671 (Wis. 1991) (Busch "simply 'reconditioned'" the machine, a process the record shows is nothing more than a very thorough cleaning and repair job that includes taking a machine apart, replacing worn parts, and reassembling the machine. Any profit Busch reaped was from reconditioning the machine, not from placing it in the stream of commerce."). See also Strasser v. Transtech Mobile Fleet Serv., Inc., 613 N.W.2d 142 (Wis. 2000) (crane reconditioner subject to negligence liability for lack of safety treads on new ladder it fabricated and installed on crane).

**14.** See, e.g., Stillie v. AM Int'l, Inc., 850 F.Supp. 960, 962 (D. Kan. 1994) (a "purchaser of a 'like new' rebuilt machine is more justified in expecting performance and safety commensurate with that of a new

machine than is a purchaser of an 'as is' used machine").

**15.** See id.

**16.** See § 16.3, above.

**17.** See, e.g., Levine v. Sears Roebuck & Co., Inc., 200 F.Supp.2d 180 (E.D.N.Y. 2002) (repair of dishwasher door); Turbines, Inc. v. Dardis, 1 S.W.3d 726 (Tex. App. 1999) (rebuilt aircraft engine; evidence suggested pilot error); Micciche v. Eastern Elevator Co., 645 A.2d 278 (Pa. 1994) (elevator repaired and modernized by defendant misaligned with floor landing); Watts v. Rubber Tree, Inc., 848 P.2d 1210 (Or. Ct. App. 1993) (recapped tire); Swenson Trucking & Excavating, Inc. v. Truckweld Equip. Co., 604 P.2d 1113, 1117–18 (Alaska 1980) (faulty weld in dump truck ram assembly). See also Heart of Tex. Dodge v. Star Coach, LLC, 567 S.E.2d 61 (Ga. Ct. App. 2002) (predominant purpose of contract was modification, not sale of goods, so Article 2 of UCC did not create implied warranty).

a product from a used one into basically a new one—as by reconfiguring and/or replacing many important parts, rewiring, and otherwise reconstructing important aspects of the product—then the transaction will be one of rebuilding or remanufacturing that should ordinarily subject the supplier to the normal rules of strict products liability for manufacturing defects in such products.[18] The cases do not always divide nicely along these lines, but this classification is consistent with broader liability principles that subject manufacturers, but not service providers, to a rule of strict products liability for defective manufacture.

Most of the cases and the discussion to this point have concerned manufacturing defects; design and warnings defects raise questions of a different kind. Buyers understand that rebuilders and remanufacturers have no magic wand to eliminate most inherent product dangers. Consequently, some courts understandably have shielded product reconditioners from any obligation, even in negligence, to correct or warn of design defects lurking in the machines they recondition.[19] Yet, by undertaking to rebuild or remanufacture products and to re-introduce them into the stream of commerce, such suppliers in a sense step into the shoes of the original manufacturer, and rebuilders and occasionally even refurbishers sometimes undertake to assure that their reconditioned products are properly guarded and otherwise meet appropriate safety requirements.[20] Nevertheless, negligence, rather than any form of strict products liability, appears to be the preferable standard of liability in such cases.

**18.** See, e.g., Bell v. Precision Airmotive Corp., 42 P.3d 1071 (Ala. 2002) (overhauler of engine held subject to strict products liability for selling and installing, during course of overhaul, used and defective component part that overhauler had subjected to extensive inspection, repair, and testing); R.R. Donnelley & Sons Co. v. North Tex. Steel Co., 752 N.E.2d 112 (Ind. Ct. App. 2001) (defendant created "new product," and did not merely provide service, when it transformed raw material into components that differed substantially from original raw material); Stillie v. AM Int'l, Inc., 850 F.Supp. 960, 962 (D. Kan. 1994) (a "purchaser of a 'like new' rebuilt machine is more justified in expecting performance and safety commensurate with that of a new machine than is a purchaser of an 'as is' used machine"); Anderson v. Olmsted Util. Equip., Inc., 573 N.E.2d 626, 629 (Ohio 1991) (reconditioner remanufactured cherry picker per contract requiring "100% tear down, inspection and rebuild"; "When a product is totally remanufactured or rebuilt, it becomes, for all intent[s] and purposes, a new product."); Gentile v. MacGregor Mfg. Co., 493 A.2d 647 (N.J. Super. Ct. Law Div. 1985) (reconditioner of defective football helmet); Michalko v. Cooke Color & Chem. Corp., 451 A.2d 179 (N.J. 1982) (rebuilt molding machine).

The Illinois courts have an unusually strong tradition of holding providers of sales-service hybrid transactions subject to strict products liability, see § 16.3, above, and the overhaul situation is no different. See Prompt Air, Inc. v. Firewall Forward, Inc., 707 N.E.2d 235 (Ill. App. Ct. 1999) (aircraft engine overhauler which procured, paid for, and installed reconditioned turbocharger that was defective and caused forced landing was subject to strict tort liability for resulting damage).

**19.** See, e.g., Rodriguez v. Riddell Sports, Inc., 242 F.3d 567 (5th Cir. 2001) (Tex. law) (reconditioner of football helmet had no obligation to upgrade helmet to safer alternative, even if it knew that helmet was unsafe at time); Rolph v. EBI Cos., 464 N.W.2d 667, 673 (Wis. 1991): ("Imposing liability on Busch for failing to correct a design defect simply because it reconditioned the machine would make all repairers who disassemble a product in order to repair it insurers against design defects created by manufacturers."). Accord, Barry v. Stevens Equip. Co., 335 S.E.2d 129 (Ga. Ct. App. 1985); Johnson v. William C. Ellis & Sons Iron Works, 604 F.2d 950 (5th Cir. 1979) (Miss. law).

**20.** See, e.g., Whitaker v. T.J. Snow Co., 953 F.Supp. 1034 (N.D. Ind. 1997) (per agreement with regular buyer, refurbisher was to determine if guarding was needed and either bring welding machine into compliance with OSHA regulations or inform buyer).

Whether suppliers of rebuilt or remanufactured products should be liable for failing to supply warnings of inherent dangers is a difficult question. Because of the fact-specific nature of product overhauling and rebuilding,[21] courts should be prepared in particular cases to rule that in certain contexts a supplier has no duty to design away a particular danger, such as an obvious inherent danger, nor any duty to warn of risks of which the reconditioner did not know or that were clearly evident to intended purchasers.[22] In cases when a reconditioner fairly should be obligated to provide a warning,[23] the duty should be limited to one of reasonable care.

Not distinguishing between different type of defects, the *Products Liability Restatement* in no uncertain terms provides that remanufactured products are subject to the normal rules of products liability applicable to sellers of new products.[24]

Statutes of limitations and repose are treated elsewhere,[25] but it may be noted here that a substantially rebuilt or remanufactured product may be treated as a "new" product that will start a statute of limitations or repose running anew from the date the product is sold in its refurbished condition.[26] Yet, such a statute will not begin to run again, of course, if the defect lay in the product's original manufacture and if the rebuilder did not have some responsibility to find or cure it.[27]

### Reform Statutes

If a state products liability act limits coverage to product "sellers," a defendant who merely repairs or otherwise reconditions a product owned by another is not subject to the act's provisions.[28] However, if a statute

---

**21.** See Gentile v. MacGregor Mfg. Co., 493 A.2d 647, 652 (N.J. Super. Ct. Law Div. 1985) (service transactions not subject to strict liability "because of the individuality of the service rendered").

**22.** See, e.g., Strasser v. Transtech Mobile Fleet Serv., Inc., 613 N.W.2d 142 (Wis. 2000) (no duty to warn of absence of safety treads on ladder of reconditioned crane).

**23.** See, e.g., Slaid v. Evergreen Indem., Ltd., 745 So.2d 793, 798 (La. Ct. App. 1999) (bank that sold mobile home to purchaser had duty to warn of defective window after inspection).

**24.** Products Liability Restatement § 8, covering the liability of suppliers of defective used products, provides that such suppliers are subject to liability for resulting harm "if the defect: . . . (c) is a defect under § 2 or § 3 in a used product remanufactured by the seller. . . . " Comment *i* to § 8 explains:

> When one undertakes to remanufacture a used product and bring it to market as a product that meets current design and production standards, it is fair to subject the seller of the remanufactured product to liability for harm caused by §§ 2 and 3 defects existing at the time

of sale of the remanufactured used product. The fact that the remanufactured product is sold at a discount compared to a new product does not relieve the seller of responsibility for such defects. In part the imposition of liability for §§ 2 and 3 defects arises because of heightened consumer expectations. . . .

**25.** See § 14.5, above.

**26.** See, e.g., Richardson v. Gallo Equip. Co., 990 F.2d 330 (7th Cir. 1993) (Ind. law); Fugate v. AAA Mach. & Equip. Co. 593 F.Supp. 392 (E.D. Tenn. 1984). See also Rollins v. Cherokee Warehouses, Inc., 635 F.Supp. 136 (E.D. Tenn. 1986).

**27.** See, e.g., Divis v. Clarklift of Neb., Inc., 590 N.W.2d 696 (Neb. 1999).

**28.** See, e.g., Watts v. Rubber Tree, Inc., 848 P.2d 1210, 1213 (Or. Ct. App. 1993) (tire recapper only affixed new tread on client's casing; strict liability statute inapplicable to service providers). See also Rollins v. Cherokee Warehouses, Inc., 635 F.Supp. 136, 138 (E.D. Tenn. 1986) ("in order for a rebuilder or reconditioner of products to be held liable as a seller under the Act, it must be 'engaged in the business' of selling such products").

does not expressly limit its scope to new products, a court may interpret the statute as including the sale of products that have been rebuilt or remanufactured.[29] Moreover, statutes in at least four states include "remanufacturer" or "rebuilder" in the definition of "manufacturer," subjecting such parties to the principal provisions of such statutes.[30]

## § 16.5  USED PRODUCTS

Sellers of used products are subject to liability in negligence.[1] While early courts held that the sale of a used product did not carry an implied warranty,[2] the situation is different today. Both express warranties[3] and implied warranties[4] may arise in appropriate cases[5] under Article 2 of the Uniform Commercial Code.

The big question in modern products liability litigation is whether the seller of a used product is subject to strict liability in tort.[6] On this

**29.** See, e.g., Rollins v. Cherokee Warehouses, Inc., 635 F.Supp. 136, 138 (E.D. Tenn. 1986).

**30.** See, e.g., Idaho Code § 6–1402(2); Kan. Stat. Ann. § 60–3302(b); Tex. Civ. Prac. & Rem. Code Ann. § 82.001(4); Wash. Rev. Code § 7.72.010(2). See Stillie v. AM Int'l, Inc., 850 F.Supp. 960, 962 (D. Kan. 1994) ("remanufacturers and sellers in the chain of distribution after remanufacture are subject to strict liability").

### § 16.5

**1.** See, e.g., Meyering v. General Motors Corp., 275 Cal.Rptr. 346 (Dist. Ct. 1990); Treadwell Ford, Inc. v. Campbell, 485 So.2d 312 (Ala. 1986) (negligent inspection); Wilkinson v. Hicks, 179 Cal.Rptr. 5, 8 (Ct. App. 1981). *But see* Zavala–Pizano v. Industrial Handling Equip. Co., 847 F.Supp. 621, 623 (C.D. Ill. 1994) ("policy and cost/benefit considerations should preclude any duty on dealers of used equipment" because "the sale of used products does not generate the kind of expectations of safety associated with new products and the imposition of a duty on the sellers of used products would sacrifice the used products market in order to gain marginal gains in safety," unless used product seller assumed more aggressive role by warranting, inspecting, reconditioning, or rebuilding product).

**2.** See, e.g., Bayer v. Winton Motor Car Co., 160 N.W. 642 (Mich. 1916).

**3.** See, e.g., Limited Flying Club, Inc. v. Wood, 632 F.2d 51, 55–57 (8th Cir. 1980) (Iowa law) (repair and inspection history stated in log book of used airplane); Barb v. Wallace, 412 A.2d 1314, 1316–18 (Md. Ct. Spec. App. 1980) (statement that used engine sold for go-cart ran "real good"; engine promptly exploded).

**4.** See, e.g., Gaston v. Bobby Johnson Equip. Co., 771 So.2d 848 (La. Ct. App. 2000) ("Although this warranty does not

apply as extensively as with new products, it requires that even used equipment operate reasonably well for a reasonable period of time."); Fernandes v. Union Bookbinding Co., 507 N.E.2d 728 (Mass. 1987) (implied warranty of merchantability); Hoort v. Oklahoma Truck Parts, Inc., 650 P.2d 71 (Okla. Ct. App. 1981) (implied warranty of merchantability "reasonably appropriate to the particular goods sold"); Barb v. Wallace, 412 A.2d 1314 (Md. Ct. Spec. App. 1980) (implied warranty of fitness for particular purpose accompanied sale of used engine for use in go-cart); Roupp v. Acor, 384 A.2d 968 (Pa. Super. Ct. 1978) (both implied warranties accompanied sale of used truck); Rose v. Epley Motor Sales, 215 S.E.2d 573 (N.C. 1975) (implied warranty of merchantability).

*But see* Fuquay v. Revels Motors, Inc., 389 So.2d 1238 (Fla. Dist. Ct. App. 1980) (implied warranty not applicable if seller did not know, have reason to know, nor have superior knowledge of latent defect); Valley Datsun v. Martinez, 578 S.W.2d 485 (Tex. App. 1979) (no implied warranty of merchantability where purchaser knows goods are used).

**5.** See UCC § 2–314, Official Comment 3: "A contract for the sale of second-hand goods, however, involves only such obligation as is appropriate to such goods.... "

**6.** On the applicability of strict liability in tort to sellers of used products, see Notes, 16 Okla. City U. L. Rev. 373 (1991) (strict liability should be available on case-by-case basis, although rebuttable presumption of such liability should normally arise); 33 Stan. L. Rev. 535 (1981) (strict liability should not apply to sellers of unmodified used products); Annot., 9 A.L.R. 5th 1 (1993); 1 Frumer and Friedman, Products Liability § 5.06; Products Liability Restatement § 8 Reporters' Note to cmt. *b* (thorough summary and analysis of cases).

issue, the decisions are sharply split. Following the position taken in an early Illinois case,[7] a majority of courts have held that strict liability in tort ordinarily does *not* apply[8] to the sale of used products.[9] Courts following this majority approach often rely upon an influential early case, *Tillman v. Vance Equipment Company*,[10] which held that a dealer who sold a used crane "as is," without making any inspection or repairs, was not strictly liable for design and warnings defects that had originated with the manufacturer.[11] Of the three principal policies the court thought were served by strict liability—risk spreading, protecting a user's expectations, and risk reduction—the court concluded that only risk spreading would be served by holding used product sellers strictly liable. Buyers do not expect new-product quality from used products, and buyers can bargain for safety assurances if they so desire. Imposing strict products liability on sellers of used products would raise the price of such products and otherwise disrupt markets in those goods. Nor can a seller of used products, being entirely outside the chain of new product distribution, pressure manufacturers to improve product safety.[12] Probably reflecting these rationales, at least a couple of products liability

**7.** Peterson v. Lou Bachrodt Chevrolet Co., 329 N.E.2d 785 (Ill. 1975) (used car dealer not subject to strict liability in tort for defects arising after car's original manufacture because such a rule would make dealer insurer for defects arising while car is under control of others). See also Court v. Grzelinski, 379 N.E.2d 281 (Ill. 1978); Bruce v. Martin–Marietta Corp., 544 F.2d 442 (10th Cir. 1976) (Okla. law).

**8.** "Strict liability does not apply unless the seller repaired or modified the product, caused the defect, or made some representation about the product's quality." These are the normal provisos to the general rule of no strict liability. See Annot., 9 A.L.R.5th 1, 24 (1993).

**9.** See, e.g., Kotz v. Hawaii Elec. Light Co., 83 P.3d 743 (Haw. 2004); Harber v. Altec Indus., Inc., 812 F.Supp. 954 (W.D. Mo. 1993) (excellent review; declining to impose strict liability in tort on seller of used product); Peterson v. Idaho First Nat'l Bank, 791 P.2d 1303, 1306 (Idaho 1990) (no strict liability for sellers of used products); Gorath v. Rockwell Int'l, Inc., 441 N.W.2d 128, 131–32 (Minn. Ct. App. 1989) (no strict liability on used product seller unless it exercised control over design, manufacture, or warnings, had actual knowledge of defect, or created defect); Harrison v. Bill Cairns Pontiac, Inc., 549 A.2d 385, 392 (Md. Ct. Spec. App. 1988) (used product dealer who did not create defect not strictly liable); Grimes v. Axtell Ford Lincoln–Mercury, 403 N.W.2d 781, 785 (Iowa 1987) (where defect not caused by dealer, nor discoverable by reasonable inspection, strict liability does not apply); Keith v. Russell T. Bundy & Assocs., Inc., 495 So.2d 1223, 1227 (Fla. Dist. Ct. App. 1986) ("Strict liability does

not apply to a dealer in used equipment."); Kodiak Elec. Assoc., Inc. v. DeLaval Turbine, Inc., 694 P.2d 150, 154 n.6 (Alaska 1984) (used product seller not strictly liable unless seller has subjected product to extensive repair, inspection, and testing); Sell v. Bertsch & Co., 577 F.Supp. 1393, 1399 (D. Kan. 1984) (seller of defective used product who has not repaired or remanufactured product not strictly liable); Crandell v. Larkin & Jones Appliance Co., 334 N.W.2d 31, 34 (S.D. 1983) (used product sellers not strictly liable unless they rebuilt or reconditioned product); Wilkinson v. Hicks, 179 Cal.Rptr. 5, 8 (Ct. App. 1981) (strict liability does not apply to dealer of used goods); Tillman v. Vance Equip. Co., 596 P.2d 1299, 1304 (Or. 1979) (used equipment dealer not strictly liable for defective used equipment sold "as is"); Brigham v. Hudson Motors, Inc., 392 A.2d 130, 135 (N.H. 1978) (used car dealers not subject to strict liability); Peterson v. Lou Bachrodt Chevrolet Co., 329 N.E.2d 785, 787 (Ill. 1975) (no strict liability for used car seller who did not create defects). See also King v. Damiron Corp., 113 F.3d 93 (7th Cir. 1997) (Conn. law) (examining cases both ways, and holding that Connecticut would follow majority approach), rejected in Stanton v. Carlson Sales, Inc., 728 A.2d 534 (Conn. Super. Ct. 1998).

**10.** 596 P.2d 1299 (Or. 1979).

**11.** *Tillman* is examined in Owen, Rethinking the Policies of Strict Products Liability, 33 Vand. L. Rev. 681, 696–99 (1980) (applauding high quality of court's policy analysis, but lamenting court's choice of policy objectives).

**12.** 596 P.2d at 1203.

reform statutes explicitly exclude sellers of used products from coverage.[13]

Following an early New Jersey case,[14] a fairly large minority of courts have held that strict liability in tort *does* apply to used product sales.[15] *Jordan v. Sunnyslope Appliance Propane & Plumbing Supplies Company*,[16] which involved an explosion of a used propane storage tank with a defective shut-off valve, outlined the rationales for applying strict liability in tort to used product sales. Pointing out that *Restatement (Second) of Torts* § 402A by its terms applies to the sale of "any" product, not merely to any *new* product, the court addressed the *Tillman* court's arguments for rejecting strict liability in tort for used product sales. The *Jordan* court first challenged the view that buyers of used products have lower safety expectations, arguing that such buyers do not expect unreasonably dangerous defects in used products that they buy. And as for risk reduction, the *Jordan* court reasoned that strict liability in tort should encourage sellers of used products to increase their maintenance and inspections of such products before offering them for sale. Sellers of used goods are very much in the chain of distribution, thought the court, because they offer their goods for sale and profit therefrom. Finally, the *Jordan* court reasoned that "[t]here is no justification for finding that used good dealers as a class cannot shift losses, distribute costs, or insure against losses."[17]

Some courts limit strict liability in the used product situation to cases where a seller reconditions or rebuilds the product prior to sale;[18]

---

**13.** See, e.g., Idaho Code § 6–1302(1)(b) (used product seller not included in definition of "product seller"); Wash. Rev. Code § 7.72.010(1)(b) (same).

**14.** Turner v. International Harvester Co., 336 A.2d 62, 69 (N.J. Super. Ct. Law Div. 1975) (observing that "realistic expectations of quality and durability will be lower for used goods, commensurate with their age, appearance and price. However, safety of the general public demands that when a used motor vehicle, for example, is sold for use *as a serviceable motor vehicle* (and not as junk parts), absent special circumstances, the seller will be responsible for safety defects whether known or unknown at time of sale, present while the machine was under his control."). Although *Turner* is the principal early case adopting this position, it was preceded by Realmuto v. Straub Motors, Inc., 322 A.2d 440 (N.J. 1974). See also Hovenden v. Tenbush, 529 S.W.2d 302 (Tex. App. 1975).

**15.** In addition to *Turner*, see also Frey v. Harley Davidson Motor Co., 734 A.2d 1, 9 (Pa. Super. Ct. 1999) (new-used dealer which cut jumper wire subject to strict liability in tort); Stanton v. Carlson Sales, Inc., 728 A.2d 534 (Conn. Super. Ct. 1998) (used product sellers strictly liable); Stiles v. Batavia Atomic Horseshoes, Inc., 579 N.Y.S.2d 790, 792 (App. Div. 1992) (same); Nelson v. Nelson Hardware, Inc., 467

N.W.2d 518, 524 (Wis. 1991) (used product sellers strictly liable "even though completely innocent or completely uninvolved in creating the defect"); Thompson v. Rockford Mach. Tool Co., 744 P.2d 357, 361 (Wash. Ct. App. 1987) (same); Jordan v. Sunnyslope Appliance Propane & Plumbing Supplies, Co., 660 P.2d 1236, 1241 (Ariz. Ct. App. 1983) (used product seller subject to strict liability in tort); Hovenden v. Tenbush, 529 S.W.2d 302, 310 (Tex. App. 1975) (same); Mixter v. Mack Trucks, Inc., 308 A.2d 139, 142 (Pa. Super. Ct. 1973) (used truck seller strictly liable for defective tire rim).

**16.** 660 P.2d 1236 (Ariz. Ct. App. 1983).

**17.** Id. at 1242.

**18.** See, e.g., Bell v. Precision Airmotive Corp., 42 P.3d 1071 (Ala. 2002) (seller of used component part strictly liable because of his extensive repair of part); Harber v. Altec Indus., Inc., 812 F.Supp. 954, 961 (W.D. Mo. 1993) (excellent review) (declining to impose strict liability in tort on seller of used product) ("Once a dealer in used goods takes substantial steps to change the nature of the good sold, the justifications for imposing enhanced liability change markedly."); Crandell v. Larkin & Jones Appliance Co., 334 N.W.2d 31 (S.D. 1983) (dealer, who reconditioned and guaranteed

other courts limit strict liability to defects of which the seller is aware;[19] and some courts condition strict liability on *both* the seller's reconditioning of the product together with the opportunity to discover the defect prior to the product's sale.[20] Finally, even in states that hold sellers of used products subject to strict liability, such liability requires that the seller regularly deal in used good sales.[21] So, if the dealer sells such goods infrequently, it will not be considered a "seller" of the used goods.[22]

The *Products Liability Restatement* basically adopts the majority approach.[23] Section 8 provides that sellers of defective used products are subject generally to liability for negligence;[24] for manufacturing defects and product malfunctions in cases where the seller's marketing causes buyers to expect the safety of a new product;[25] for any type of defect in a remanufactured product;[26] and for noncompliance with an applicable safety statute or regulation.[27]

## § 16.6   ELECTRICITY

Invisible and elusive, electricity is hard to comprehend. Its mysterious character puts in question whether electricity should be considered a "product" at all, subject to the principles of products liability law.[1]

used clothes dryer which caught fire, liable in strict tort, express warranty, and implied warranty of merchantability). Compare Allenberg v. Bentley Hedges Travel Servs., Inc., 22 P.3d 223 (Okla. 2001) (strict liability does not apply to commercial sellers of used products if alleged defect was not created by seller and product was sold in essentially same condition in which seller acquired it).

**19.** See, e.g., Stump v. Indiana Equip. Co., 601 N.E.2d 398 (Ind. Ct. App. 1992) (former owner had hot-wired starter on grader that cut off operator's legs; duty of due care to inspect and warn not breached since defect was latent); Grimes v. Axtell Ford Lincoln–Mercury, 403 N.W.2d 781 (Iowa 1987) (no strict liability for latent defects).

**20.** See, e.g., Wynia v. Richard–Ewing Equip. Co., 17 F.3d 1084 (8th Cir. 1993) (S.D. law).

**21.** See, e.g., Nutting v. Ford Motor Co., 584 N.Y.S.2d 653, 656 (App. Div. 1992), where Hewlett Packard regularly resold its fleet of more than 3,000 cars: "[O]ne who regularly purchases a substantial quantity of new cars for use by its employees and who regularly disposes of those vehicles by auction sales to used car dealers for resale to the public after the vehicles have been used for approximately one year is in the regular business of a used car dealer for the purposes of imposing strict products liability."

**22.** See, e.g., McCabe v. Allied Prods. Corp., 2000 WL 1805687 (D. Me. 2000) (defendant who had sold only two brake presses in two years not "engaged in the busi-

ness of selling" such products); Stiles v. Batavia Atomic Horseshoes, Inc., 613 N.E.2d 572 (N.Y. 1993); Sukljian v. Charles Ross & Son Co., 503 N.E.2d 1358, 1361 (N.Y. 1986) (G.E. each year sold at auction two or three used machines of particular type that it had purchased new and used for many years: "strict liability was inapposite because [G.E. had not] *regularly* engaged in the business of selling the equipment in issue").

**23.** The Reporters' Note to cmt. *b* contains a particularly thorough and useful summary and analysis of the used product cases.

**24.** Products Liability Restatement § 8(a).

**25.** Id. § 8(b). Comment *h* explains that such reasonable expectations may be influenced by a large variety of factors, such as the product's age and condition; price; representations that the product has been rebuilt, reconditioned, or repaired; any guarantees, warranties, and disclaimers and limitations thereof; and any information provided on the product's condition or prior use.

**26.** See id. § 8(c). See § 16.4, above.

**27.** Id. § 8(d).

### § 16.6

**1.** See Ferry, Defining Power: Electrons and the Law, 32 Envtl. L. Rep. 10038 (2002); Myers, The Sale of Electricity in a Deregulated Industry: Should Article 2 of the Uniform Commercial Code Govern?, 54 SMU L. Rev. 1051 (2001); Cantu, Twenty-

"What is electricity? Simply stated, it is a force, like the wind.... "[2] Electricity is "a form of energy that can be made or produced by men, confined, controlled, transmitted and distributed to be used as an energy source for heat, power and light and is distributed in the stream of commerce."[3] On this reasoning, a majority of courts hold that electricity is a "product" that may subject its suppliers, electrical utility companies, to strict liability in tort[4] for selling it in a defective condition.[5] These courts, sometimes calling on policy rationales,[6] reason that once electricity passes through a customer's meter, it is a product that has been sold into the stream of commerce and so is subject to strict liability.[7] Such cases typically involve power surges, causing personal injury or property loss by the excessive flow of electricity into a building.[8] Yet a quite substantial minority of courts refuse to apply strict liability to electrical injuries, reasoning that the provision of electricity is a service rather than the sale of a product, whether the harm is caused before or after the current passes through a consumer's meter.[9]

Five Years of Strict Product Liability Law: The Transformation and Present Meaning of Section 402A, 25 St. Mary's L.J. 327 (1993); Cantu, The Illusive Meaning of the Term "Product" Under Section 402A of the Restatement (Second) of Torts, 44 Okla. L. Rev. 635 (1991); Annot., Products Liability: Electricity, 60 A.L.R.4th 732 (1988); Note, 29 Suffolk U. L. Rev. 161 (1995); Comment, 26 Cap. U. L. Rev. 421 (1997); 10 Am. Law Prod. Liab. 3d ch. 117 (electricity and electrical equipment); Restatement of Products Liability § 19 and cmt. d.

**2.** Pierce v. Pacific Gas & Elec. Co., 212 Cal.Rptr. 283, 288 n.3 (Ct. App. 1985) (holding that electricity is a product under § 402A).

**3.** Ransome v. Wisconsin Elec. Power Co., 275 N.W.2d 641, 643 (Wis. 1979).

**4.** Compare Myers, The Sale of Electricity in a Deregulated Industry: Should Article 2 of the Uniform Commercial Code Govern?, 54 SMU L. Rev. 1051 (2001) (arguing that electricity should be treated as a "good" for Article 2 purposes).

**5.** See, e.g., Hanus v. Texas Utils. Co., 71 S.W.3d 874 (Tex. App. 2002); Bryant v. Tri–County Elec. Membership Corp., 844 F.Supp. 347 (W.D. Ky. 1994); Pierce v. Pacific Gas & Elec. Co., 212 Cal.Rptr. 283 (Ct. App. 1985) (electricity's intrinsic nature does not disqualify it as product); Carbone v. Connecticut Light & Power Co., 482 A.2d 722 (Conn. Super. Ct. 1984); Aversa v. Public Serv. Elec. & Gas Co., 451 A.2d 976 (N.J. Super. Ct. Law Div. 1982); Elgin Airport Inn, Inc., v. Commonwealth Edison Co., 410 N.E.2d 620 (Ill. App. Ct. 1980); Ransome v. Wisconsin Elec. Power Co., 275 N.W.2d 641 (Wis. 1979); Williams v. Detroit Edison Co., 234 N.W.2d 702 (Mich. Ct. App. 1975).

**6.** The rationales are summarized in 10 Am. Law Prod. Liab. 3d § 117:4.

**7.** See Annot., Products Liability: Electricity, 60 A.L.R.4th 732 (1988); Note, 29 Suffolk U. L. Rev. 161 (1995). This position is endorsed by the Products Liability Restatement § 19(a) cmt. d ("the distinction drawn between pre- and post-delivery is reasonable"); 10 Am. Law Prod. Liab. 3d § 117:2.

**8.** See, e.g., Pierce v. Pacific Gas & Elec. Co., 212 Cal.Rptr. 283 (Ct. App. 1985) (plaintiff injured by surge of 7,000 volts of electricity into her home, traced to defective component in utility's system); Carbone v. Connecticut Light & Power Co., 482 A.2d 722 (Conn. Super. Ct. 1984) (high-voltage surge of electric current overwhelmed electrical service panel, causing arc and fire which damaged plaintiff's home). See also Bryant v. Tri–County Elec. Membership Corp., 844 F.Supp. 347 (W.D. Ky. 1994) (series of voltage spikes destroyed electrical transformer switch over time, causing it to explode, setting saw mill on fire; claims for warranty and strict liability in tort, in addition to negligence, allowed).

If the surge is caused by lightening, however, it is not marketed or placed in the stream of commerce by any act of the utility. See Mancuso v. Southern Cal. Edison Co., 283 Cal.Rptr. 300, 308 (Ct. App. 1991).

**9.** See, e.g., Universal Underwriters Ins. Group v. Public Serv. Elec. & Gas Co., 103 F.Supp.2d 744 (D.N.J. 2000) (defendant not subject to strict liability for failure to shut off electricity in response to emergency); Balke v. Central Mo. Elec. Coop., 966 S.W.2d 15 (Mo. Ct. App. 1997); Wyrulec Co. v. Schutt, 866 P.2d 756 (Wyo. 1993) (electricity is service, not product); Bowen v. Niagara Mohawk Power Corp., 590 N.Y.S.2d 628 (App. Div. 1992); Otte v. Dayton Power & Light Co., 523 N.E.2d 835

As for electrical injuries from high-voltage transmission lines, typically incurred when the plaintiff hits a power line with some tall object,[10] the courts are in general agreement that negligence alone is the proper basis of liability[11] and that neither strict liability for an abnormal activity,[12] nor strict products liability,[13] is an appropriate basis for recovery. The courts reason that electricity in high-voltage lines is still under the ownership and control of the supplier, and that neither the high-power line nor the electricity in it have been prepared or made available for consumption or sale.[14] Thus, courts consider electricity in this form not yet to be a "product" in the "stream of commerce"[15] or reason simply that it is not "sold" until it passes through the meter of a customer.[16]

The courts are split, however, on the liability of a electrical utility for damage to dairy herds from naturally occurring stray voltage from

(Ohio 1988); Rodgers v. Chimney Rock Pub. Power Dist., 345 N.W.2d 12 (Neb. 1984); Wood v. Public Serv. Co., 317 A.2d 576 (N.H. 1974). The *Otte* court explained its position:

> A "product" is anything made by human industry or art. Electricity appears to fall outside this definition. This is so because electricity is the flow of electrically charged particles along a conductor. [A utility] does not manufacture electrically charged particles, but rather, sets in motion the necessary elements that allow the flow of electricity. What we have here is a purported defect in the distribution system. Such a system is, in our view, a service.

523 N.E.2d at 838.

**10.** See, e.g., Hayes v. Entergy Corp., 850 So.2d 916 (La. Ct. App. 2003) (logging shear); Smith v. Florida Power & Light Co., 857 So.2d 224 (Fla. Dist. Ct. App. 2003) (boom of crane); Monroe v. Savannah Elec. & Power Co., 471 S.E.2d 854 (Ga. 1996) (towed boat); Martinez v. Grant Cty. Pub. Util. Dist. No. 2, 851 P.2d 1248 (Wash. Ct. App. 1993) (farmhand touched 7,620 volt wire located 27½ feet off ground with 32 foot irrigation pipe); Fuller v. Central Me. Power Co., 598 A.2d 457 (Me. 1991) (ladder); Priest v. Brown, 396 S.E.2d 638 (S.C. Ct. App. 1990) (deceased tried to move downed power line); Smith v. Home Light & Power Co., 734 P.2d 1051, 1055 (Colo. 1987) (portable grain auger); Hedges v. Public Serv. Co., 396 N.E.2d 933 (Ind. Ct. App. 1979) (ladder); Petroski v. Northern Ind. Pub. Serv. Co., 354 N.E.2d 736 (Ind. Ct. App. 1976) (child grabbed power line in tree).

**11.** See, e.g., Martinez v. Grant Cty. Pub. Util. Dist. No. 2, 851 P.2d 1248, 1250 (Wash. Ct. App. 1993) ("Washington recognizes the societal necessity of transmitting lethal amounts of electricity through uninsulated overhead power lines through rural areas; it does not impose strict liability on electrical power companies for injuries arising out of contact with those power lines." *Held*, jury finding of no negligence affirmed.)

Although some courts have held that electric companies are under a duty to exercise the highest degree of care to prevent injury, see, e.g., Cerretti v. Flint Hills Rural Elec. Coop. Ass'n, 837 P.2d 330 (Kan. 1992), the better view is that the standard of care is reasonable care under all the circumstances. See, e.g., Wyrulec Co. v. Schutt, 866 P.2d 756, 762 (Wyo. 1993). See generally Prosser and Keeton on Torts § 34.

**12.** See, e.g., Wyrulec Co. v. Schutt, 866 P.2d 756, 761 (Wyo. 1993); Wirth v. Mayrath Indus., Inc., 278 N.W.2d 789 (N.D. 1979); Wertz v. Holy Cross Elec. Ass'n, 512 P.2d 286 (Colo. Ct. App. 1973).

**13.** See cases in note 9, above.

**14.** See 10 Am. Law Prod. Liab. 3d § 117:3.

**15.** See, e.g., Fuller v. Central Me. Power Co., 598 A.2d 457 (Me. 1991) (electricity in high-voltage transmission line hit by plaintiff's ladder was not "product" for purposes of state's products liability statute); Smith v. Home Light and Power Co., 734 P.2d 1051, 1055 (Colo. 1987). Compare Butler v. City of Peru, 714 N.E.2d 264 (Ind. Ct. App. 1999) (electricity can be "product," but school maintenance worker electrocuted while meddling with high voltage facility not "user" or "consumer" for purposes of state's products liability act).

**16.** See, e.g., Darling v. Central Vt. Pub. Serv. Corp., 762 A.2d 826 (Vt. 2000) (no strict liability because electricity escaping from storm-damaged power lines was never "sold" to plaintiffs); Monroe v. Savannah Elec. & Power Co., 471 S.E.2d 854 (Ga. 1996) (no strict liability for death resulting when towed boat hit high power line).

transmission lines or other sources,[17] some courts allowing strict liability and other claims for such losses,[18] other courts ruling that strict liability in tort or warranty is not appropriate.[19]

Finally, courts have held that the use of x-rays[20] and other forms of radiation therapy[21] for medical treatment is the provision of a service, not the sale of a product that will support a claim for strict products liability.

## § 16.7  REAL ESTATE

### In General

Products liability law conventionally is defined as the liability of suppliers for defects in their chattels. Chattels, of course, are personal property, as classically distinguished from real property. Thus real estate, including any fixtures attached to it,[1] would not appear to be a proper subject of "products" liability law. Accordingly, many courts refuse to apply the doctrine of strict products liability in tort to claims involving defects in land, houses, and other structures attached to the land.[2] Similarly, because Article 2 of the Uniform Commercial Code

**17.** See Annot., 60 A.L.R.4th 732, § 18 at 765 (1988); Products Liability Restatement § 19 Reporters' Note to cmt. *d.*

**18.** See, e.g., ZumBerge v. Northern States Power Co., 481 N.W.2d 103 (Minn. Ct. App. 1992) (verdict upheld on claims of negligence, breach of warranty, and strict liability); Public Serv. Ind., Inc. v. Nichols, 494 N.E.2d 349, 355 (Ind. Ct. App. 1986); Schriner v. Pennsylvania Power & Light Co., 501 A.2d 1128 (Pa. Super. Ct. 1985). See also James v. Beauregard Elec. Coop., Inc., 736 So.2d 353 (La. Ct. App. 1999).

**19.** See, e.g., Hoffman v. Wisconsin Elec. Power Co., 671 N.W.2d 853 (Wis. 2003) (applying negligence principles to determine liability for injuries to dairy herd caused by stray voltage); Pillow v. Entergy Corp., 828 So.2d 83 (La. Ct. App. 2002); G & K Dairy v. Princeton Elec. Plant Bd., 781 F.Supp. 485 (W.D. Ky. 1991) (allowing claim for negligence but denying claims for breach of warranty and strict liability in tort because stray voltage not "good" or "product" which defendant sold to plaintiff); Kolpin v. Pioneer Power & Light Co., 453 N.W.2d 214 (Wis. Ct. App. 1990) (stray voltage, a natural byproduct of electric power transmission, is not a product nor is it sold or even used by consumers); Otte v. Dayton Power & Light Co., 523 N.E.2d 835 (Ohio 1988).

**20.** See, e.g., Dubin v. Michael Reese Hosp. & Med. Ctr., 415 N.E.2d 350, 352 (Ill. 1980) ("the true object of [the complaint] is the alleged error in professional judgment and not . . . the nature of X-radiation itself"). See also Greenberg v. Michael Reese Hosp., 415 N.E.2d 390 (Ill. 1980); Pitler v.

Michael Reese Hosp., 415 N.E.2d 1255 (Ill. App. Ct. 1980).

**21.** See, e.g., Nevauex v. Park Place Hosp., Inc., 656 S.W.2d 923 (Tex. App. 1983) (radiation burns from cobalt therapy).

### § 16.7

**1.** For an article to be a fixture, as opposed to a product, it must be actually annexed to the realty or something appurtenant thereto; it must have been appropriated to the use or purpose of the part of the realty to which it is connected; and the party making the annexation must intend to make the article a permanent accession to the freehold. Wireman v. Keneco Distrib., Inc., 661 N.E.2d 744, 747 (Ohio 1996) (defectively designed vapor recovery system attached to above-ground gasoline storage tank, causing explosion that killed worker, was "product" for purposes of products liability statute, not fixture, because oil company did not intend to make system a permanent addition to plant and had previously sold it along with tanks by bill of sale: "when property is sold by bill of sale, the property is presumed to be personalty"). See also Pamperin v. Interlake Cos., 634 So.2d 1137 (Fla. Dist. Ct. App. 1994) (if improvement to real property is not permanent, and can be disassembled and removed with ease, it is not fixture and may be considered "product" for purposes of strict liability).

**2.** See, e.g., Martens v. MCL Constr. Corp., 807 N.E.2d 480, 493 (Ill. App. Ct. 2004) ("buildings and indivisible component parts of the building structure itself,

applies only to "goods," it does not apply to real estate transactions.[3] Also, a number of products liability reform statutes explicitly provide that real estate is not a covered "product,"[4] and other statutes use other means to exclude real estate and fixtures from coverage.[5]

Notwithstanding the general rule excluding real property from the strict liability principles applied to defective chattels, *Schipper v. Levitt & Sons, Inc.*[6] began a judicial drift toward applying products liability doctrine to various real estate transactions. Accordingly, the mere fact that a defective article is connected in some way with real estate does not in every jurisdiction preclude the application of certain products liability principles.[7]

such as bricks, supporting beams and railings, are not deemed products for the purpose of strict liability in tort."); Keck v. Dryvit Sys., Inc., 830 So.2d 1 (Ala. 2002) (items "part of the structural integrity of the house or building" are not products for purposes of strict liability); Calloway v. City of Reno, 993 P.2d 1259 (Nev. 2000) (townhouses are not "products" for purposes of strict products liability); Kennedy v. Vacation Internationale Ltd., 841 F.Supp. 986 (D. Haw. 1994) (buildings and fixtures contained in them not "products" for strict liability); Moore v. Jesco, Inc., 531 So.2d 815 (Miss. 1988) (component parts of steel chicken houses constituted improvements to real property and thus were not products for purposes of strict liability); Edward M. Chadbourne, Inc. v. Vaughn, 491 So.2d 551 (Fla. 1986) (paving materials not product).

**3.** See UCC § 2–105(1) (defining goods as movable things).

**4.** Statutes in New Jersey and Washington explicitly exclude real estate from the definition of "product," and statutes in Georgia and Indiana define "product" in terms of "personal property" and "personalty," respectively. See Ga. Code Ann. § 51–1–11(b)(1) ("personal property"); Ind. Code § 34–6–2–114(a) ("personalty"); N.J. Stat. Ann. § 2A:58C–8(1); Wash. Rev. Code § 7.72.010(1)(a). See, e.g., Seely v. Loyd H. Johnson Constr. Co., 470 S.E.2d 283, 288 (Ga. Ct. App. 1996) (plaintiff slipped in puddle of water from home's plumbing; strict liability claim dismissed because case did not involve "the manufacture of defective personal property").

**5.** Statutes in Arkansas and Tennessee define "product" as "any tangible object or goods produced." See Tenn. Rev. Code § 29–28–102(5); Ark. Code § 16–116–102 (2). See, e.g., McMichael v. United States, 856 F.2d 1026 (8th Cir. 1988) (Ark. law) (building without lightening protection was not "product" for purposes of Arkansas statute). Compare Blagg v. Fred Hunt Co., 612 S.W.2d 321, 324 (Ark. 1981) ("in construing the Arkansas strict liability statute,

we hold that the word 'product' is as applicable to a house as to an automobile").

**6.** 207 A.2d 314 (N.J. 1965) (infant severely scalded by excessively hot water from faucet in bathroom sink due to failure of developer to add inexpensive mixing valve to reduce temperature of water drawn from boiler; strict liability applied).

**7.** See Lannetti, Toward a Revised Definition of "Product" Under the Restatement (Third) of Torts: Products Liability, 55 Bus. Law. 799 (2000); Morgan, When the Walls Come Tumbling Down—Theories of Recovery for Defective Housing, 56 St. John's L. Rev. 670 (1982) (arguing for strict liability for defects in houses); Love, Landlord's Liability for Defective Premises: Caveat Lessee, Negligence, or Strict Liability?, 1975 Wis. L. Rev. 19 (excellent overview); Ursin, Strict Liability for Defective Business Premises—One Step Beyond Rowland and Greenman, 22 UCLA L. Rev. 820 (1975); Moscovitz, Implied Warranty of Habitability: A New Doctrine Raising New Issues, 62 Cal. L. Rev. 1444 (1974); Roberts, The Case of the Unwary Home Buyer: The Housing Merchant Did It, 52 Cornell L.Q. 835 (1967); Haskell, The Case for an Implied Warranty of Quality in Sales of Real Property, 53 Geo. L.J. 633 (1965); Notes, 99 Harv. L. Rev. 1861 (1986) (real estate broker liable for defective housing); 17 Land & Water L. Rev. 467 (1982) (unsafe homesites); 32 Stan. L. Rev. 607 (1980) (used homes); 25 S.D. L. Rev. 333 (1980) (new and used housing); Comments, 33 Land & Water L. Rev. 329 (1998) (implied warranty of habitability); 33 Emory L.J. 175 (1985) (strict liability and the building industry); Annot., 25 A.L.R.4th 351 (1983) (strict liability for defects in buildings and land); Annot., 75 A.L.R.5th 413 (2000) (tort liability of building contractors). The whole matter is examined comprehensively in J. Page, The Law of Premises Liability (2d ed. 1988); 3 Am. Law Prod. Liab. 3d ch. 38; Restatement of Products Liability § 19 cmt. e; 1 Frumer and Friedman, Products Liability § 5.08. See also Nolan and Ursin, Un-

## Homes and Related Structures—Strict Liability in Tort

In the landmark case of *Schipper v. Levitt & Sons, Inc.*,[8] an infant was severely scalded by excessively hot water from a faucet in the bathroom sink because the developer had failed to install an inexpensive mixing valve to reduce the temperature of water drawn from the boiler. The court held the developer strictly liable for the injuries, reasoning that mass-builders can better bear the risk of construction defects than consumers, that "there are no meaningful distinctions between Levitt's mass production and sale of homes and the mass production and sale of automobiles, and that pertinent overriding policy considerations are the same."[9] Following *Schipper*, a handful of courts have applied strict liability in tort to builder-vendors of residential homes[10] and to manufacturers of prefabricated homes and structures.[11] A lower New Jersey court extended the *Schipper* principle to a small developer of custom homes,[12] but the New Jersey legislature subsequently excluded real estate from coverage in its products liability act.[13] Even with respect to mass-produced tract homes, some courts have rejected *Schipper*, reasoning that developers and building contractors generally are not as financially capable as manufacturers of mass-produced chattels to absorb and spread the costs of accidents.[14]

A few courts have extended strict liability to defects in less standardized structures. For example, the doctrine has been applied to a defective sewage system,[15] a single family home,[16] condominiums,[17] and a

derstanding Enterprise Liability (1995) (proposing rule of strict business premises liability).

**8.** 207 A.2d 314 (N.J. 1965).

**9.** Id. at 325.

**10.** See, e.g., Bednarski v. Hideout Homes & Realty, Inc., 711 F.Supp. 823, 225–26 (M.D. Pa. 1989) (plaintiff's son killed and home destroyed in fire originating in electrical outlet); Bastian v. Wausau Homes, Inc., 620 F.Supp. 947, 950 (N.D. Ill. 1985); Vincent v. Jim Walter Homes, Inc., Prod. Liab. Rep. (CCH) ¶ 8278 (Tenn. Ct. App. 1978); Kriegler v. Eichler Homes, Inc., 74 Cal.Rptr. 749 (Ct. App. 1969) (strict liability applied to builder of mass-produced tract homes for replacement costs of heating system made of steel tubing which corroded). See also Oliver v. Superior Court, 259 Cal.Rptr. 160, 161–62 (Ct. App. 1989) ("the doctrine of strict liability has been applied to defendants who were characterized as mass-producers . . . not to occasional or isolated construction"); La Jolla Vill. Homeowners' Ass'n v. Superior Court, 261 Cal.Rptr. 146 (Ct. App. 1989).

**11.** See, e.g., Bastian v. Wausau Homes, Inc., 620 F.Supp. 947 (N.D. Ill. 1985) (Ill. law) (defective baseboard heater); Kaneko v. Hilo Coast Processing, 654 P.2d 343 (Haw. 1982) (temporary weld in prefabricated building failed, and iron worker injured in collapse). See generally Model Uni-

form Product Liability Act § 102(A)(1), 44 Fed. Reg. 62,714, 62,717–19 (1979) (builder-vendor strictly liable only if mass producer and seller of standardized dwellings, including modular homes); Annot., 4 A.L.R.5th 667 (1993) (products liability and prefab buildings).

**12.** See Patitucci v. Drelich, 379 A.2d 297, 298 (N.J. Super. Ct. Law Div. 1977) (defective sewage disposal system in twelve homes).

**13.** See N.J. Stat. Ann. § 2A:58C–8(1).

**14.** See, e.g., Chapman v. Lily Cache Builders, Inc., 362 N.E.2d 811 (Ill. App. Ct. 1977).

**15.** See Patitucci v. Drelich, 379 A.2d 297, 298 (N.J. Super. Ct. Law Div. 1977) (strict liability extends to professional builder-vendor because "[t]he buyer of a home from a builder vendor can no more dig up the ground to inspect the sewage system than the buyer of an automobile can cause the car to be disassembled and tested").

**16.** See Salka v. Dean Homes of Beverly Hills, Inc., 864 P.2d 1037 (Cal. 1993); Blagg v. Fred Hunt Co., 612 S.W.2d 321, 324 (Ark. 1981).

**17.** See Towers Tenant Ass'n. v. Towers Ltd. P'ship, 563 F.Supp. 566 (D.D.C. 1983) (converted condominiums; strict liability in tort).

residential building.[18] California courts have applied strict liability in tort to "defective" residential lots which subsided from inadequate compaction of the fill or erosion,[19] and to the defective "design" of a house by locating the hot water heater in the garage.[20]

Many courts apply strict products liability to defective products that are incorporated as fixtures in homes or other structures on real property. Strict liability thus applies to defects in a storage rack system,[21] an air-conditioning system,[22] a gas floor furnace,[23] a heat exchanger,[24] an entire heating and air conditioning system,[25] a hot water heater,[26] concrete panels,[27] a window,[28] a roof covering system,[29] and driveway paint.[30] Some courts arrive at their decisions on a simple "product" vs. "real estate" division, while others reason by policy analysis as to whether the goals of strict products liability are served by extending strict liability to the particular situation.[31]

### Homes—Implied Warranty

While most courts have been reluctant to extend strict liability in tort to defective homes and fixtures, and while the Uniform Commercial Code warranties do not apply to real estate transactions, as mentioned earlier, most states have now replaced the traditional rule of *caveat emptor* in the sale of new homes with a common-law implied warranty of reasonable quality—often referred to as a warranty of "habitability."[32]

**18.** See Hyman v. Gordon, 111 Cal.Rptr. 262 (Ct. App. 1973).

**19.** See Avner v. Longridge Estates, 77 Cal.Rptr. 633 (Ct. App. 1969). See also Stearman v. Centex Homes, 92 Cal.Rptr.2d 761 (Ct. App. 2000) (shifting land under house foundation deformed slab and caused extensive cracks); GEM Developers v. Hallcraft Homes of San Diego, Inc., 261 Cal. Rptr. 626, 633 (Ct. App. 1989) (soil subsidence; "a developer who mass grades land into finished lots for sale to the public for residential housing has produced a product and is strictly liable to the consumer for any defects in the design or manufacture of the lots"); Del Mar Beach Club Owners Ass'n v. Imperial Contracting Co., 176 Cal. Rptr. 886 (Ct. App. 1981) (erosion of bluff on which apartment complex was situated).

**20.** See Hyman v. Gordon, 111 Cal.Rptr. 262 (Ct. App. 1973).

**21.** See Pamperin v. Interlake Cos., 634 So.2d 1137 (Fla. Dist. Ct. App. 1994) (storage rack system that can be disassembled and resold is thus product rather than permanent fixture).

**22.** See Berman v. Watergate W., Inc., 391 A.2d 1351 (D.C. 1978).

**23.** See O'Laughlin v. Minnesota Natural Gas Co., 253 N.W.2d 826 (Minn. 1977).

**24.** See Smith v. Fluor Corp., 514 So.2d 1227 (Miss. 1987).

**25.** See Trent v. Brasch Mfg. Co., 477 N.E.2d 1312 (Ill. App. Ct. 1985) (whether

HVAC system is a product is based on policy analysis, not whether article is "attached" to real estate). See also Loughridge v. Goodyear Tire & Rubber Co., 207 F.Supp.2d 1187 (D. Colo. 2002) (heating system constitutes "product" under Colorado products liability law).

**26.** See, e.g., Nichols v. Agway, Inc., 720 N.Y.S.2d 691 (App. Div. 2001); State Stove Mfg. Co. v. Hodges, 189 So.2d 113 (Miss. 1966).

**27.** See Trustees of Columbia Univ. v. Exposaic Indus., Inc., 505 N.Y.S.2d 882 (App. Div. 1986).

**28.** See, e.g., Jimenez v. Superior Court, 58 P.3d 450 (Cal. 2002); Soproni v. Polygon Apartment Parts., 971 P.2d 500 (Wash. 1999).

**29.** See Federal Ins. Co. v. HPG Int'l, Inc., 758 N.E.2d 261 (Ohio Ct. App. 2001).

**30.** See Halpryn v. Highland Ins. Co., 426 So.2d 1050 (Fla. Dist. Ct. App. 1983).

**31.** For an excellent discussion of these two approaches, together with the court's own policy analysis, see Menendez v. Paddock Pool Constr. Co., 836 P.2d 968 (Ariz. Ct. App. 1991) (inapplicability of policies precluded application of strict liability to installer of custom swimming pool).

**32.** Compare Centex Homes v. Buecher, 95 S.W.3d 266 (Tex. 2002) (recognizing both warranty of good workmanship and

Reasoning that new home sale transactions involve primarily the sale of a house rather than the conveyance of land, courts have justified this warranty on the basis of "the disparity of bargaining positions between the seller and purchaser, reliance by the purchaser on the skill of the builder, and the inability of the purchaser to inspect the house for latent defects."[33] Such a warranty has been applied to leaky pipes, and smelly floors and toilets;[34] water with a high iron content that stained fixtures "chocolaty brown," had an offensive odor, fizzled like Alka–Seltzer, and emitted methane gas;[35] a smelly carpet;[36] a flooded basement;[37] leaky and overflowing septic tanks;[38] a fire from a defective fireplace;[39] cracking walls;[40] and numerous other defective conditions.[41] A few courts have disagreed, fearing to venture into uncharted seas.[42] Warranty and other products liability principles have also been held applicable to cooperative apartments,[43] condominiums,[44] and mobile homes.[45]

warranty of habitability); Council of Unit Owners of Breakwater House Condo. v. Simpler, 603 A.2d 792 (Del. 1992) (warranty of good quality and workmanship, distinguishing warranty of habitability).

**33.** Lane v. Trenholm Bldg. Co., 229 S.E.2d 728, 729 (S.C. 1976).

**34.** See, e.g., Hoke v. Beck, 587 N.E.2d 4 (Ill. App. Ct. 1992) (and a dozen other problems).

**35.** McDonald v. Mianecki, 386 A.2d 1325 (N.J. Super. Ct. App. Div. 1978), aff'd, 398 A.2d 1283 (N.J. 1979).

**36.** See Blagg v. Fred Hunt Co., 612 S.W.2d 321 (Ark. 1981).

**37.** See, e.g., Hartley v. Ballou, 209 S.E.2d 776 (N.C. 1974) (implied warranty of freedom from major, latent structural defects).

**38.** See, e.g., Trien v. Croasdale Constr. Co., 874 S.W.2d 478 (Mo. Ct. App. 1994) (leaky and dusty house); Rutledge v. Dodenhoff, 175 S.E.2d 792 (S.C. 1970) (overflowing).

**39.** See Humber v. Morton, 426 S.W.2d 554 (Tex. 1968).

**40.** See Carpenter v. Donohoe, 388 P.2d 399 (Colo. 1964).

**41.** See, e.g., Berish v. Bornstein, 770 N.E.2d 961 (Mass. 2002) (condominium complex contained defective sliding doors, chimneys, decks, and roofs); Council of Unit Owners of Breakwater House Condo. v. Simpler, 603 A.2d 792 (Del. 1992); Vincent v. Jim Walter Homes, Inc., Prod. Liab. Rep. (CCH) ¶ 8278 (Tenn. Ct. App. 1978).

**42.** See, e.g., Snow Flower Homeowners Ass'n v. Snow Flower, Ltd., 31 P.3d 576 (Utah Ct. App. 2001); Maack v. Resource Design & Constr., Inc., 875 P.2d 570 (Utah Ct. App. 1994); Bruce Farms, Inc. v. Coupe,

247 S.E.2d 400, 403–404 (Va. 1978) (cracking bricks). In *Bruce Farms*, the court reasoned that the "modern rule" would open too many questions: "Should it apply only when the seller is the builder? Should it be confined to the sale of houses under construction or those newly constructed or extended to the sale of renovated homes? Should it be limited to single-family detached dwellings or should it also reach owner-occupied condominium units or duplex houses? Should the warranty cover materials, fixtures, and other physical appurtenances?" The court also saw troubles in determining the duration of such warranties and damages for their breach. "[T]he decision ... is one properly within the province of the General Assembly. The issue involves a multitude of competing economic, cultural, and societal values which courts are ill-equipped to balance, a fact best illustrated by the disparate conclusions reached by the several courts which have tinkered with the common law rule." Id. at 404.

**43.** See, e.g., Berman v. Watergate W., Inc., 391 A.2d 1351 (D.C. 1978) (implied warranty).

**44.** See, e.g., Council of Unit Owners of Breakwater House Condo. v. Simpler, 603 A.2d 792 (Del. 1992) (conversion from apartments; negligence and warranty). *Contra* Association of Unit Owners of Bridgeview Condos. v. Dunning, 69 P.3d 788 (Or. Ct. App. 2003) (refusing to extend definition of "product" to include 18–unit condominiums); Messier v. Association of Apartment Owners, 735 P.2d 939 (Haw. Ct. App. 1987).

**45.** See, e.g., Gautheir v. Mayo, 258 N.W.2d 748 (Mich. Ct. App. 1977) (implied warranty).

## Other Structures

Courts generally have refused to apply strict liability in tort to non-dwelling structures on real property. For example, an Illinois court refused to apply strict liability principles to the design of a parking garage.[46] The plaintiff's decedent was killed when he fell from an upper level of an open-air parking garage that allegedly had insufficient walking space around the vehicles and no railings to prevent such falls.[47] Similarly, a Pennsylvania court ruled that strict liability in tort is applicable only to defective components of a building, not the entire building.[48] And an Arizona court refused to apply strict liability principles to the installation of a custom swimming pool in the common area of a subdivision, persuasively reasoning that the policies of strict products liability did not apply to the custom construction on real estate of a single structure of this type.[49] On this basis, the Arizona court distinguished an Iowa decision that had applied strict liability in tort to the design, manufacture, and sale of a prefabricated fiberglass pool.[50] Other courts have refused to apply strict liability in tort to a crude oil refinery,[51] a jail,[52] an enclosed public arena,[53] a petroleum separator facility,[54] and many other kinds of structures on real property.[55]

## Landlords

### *Negligence*

For centuries, the rule of caveat emptor, or more precisely "caveat lessee," dominated the law of real estate leases as it did the law of real estate sales. Because of the dominant position of the landowner in medieval society, landlords were cloaked at an early date with a mantle of immunity from liability for injuries caused by defective conditions in premises that were leased. As time progressed, however, various exceptions grew up around the general rule of nonliability, so that landlords became subject to liability in negligence for: (1) hidden dangers known to the lessor but not to the lessee, (2) injuries to persons off the premises,

---

**46.** See Lowrie v. City of Evanston, 365 N.E.2d 923 (Ill. App. Ct. 1977).

**47.** The court distinguished *Schipper* and *Kriegler* on the ground that they "do not deal with a defect in the home *per se* but with a defect with some product installed therein. Thus, it appears to us that these builder-vendor cases apply strict liability to a contractor who sells a defective product along with the home, as distinguished from holding that a home is itself a product." Id. at 928.

**48.** See Cox v. Shaffer, 302 A.2d 456 (Pa. Super. Ct. 1973) (plaintiff asphyxiated in silo from lack of ventilation).

**49.** See Menendez v. Paddock Pool Constr. Co., 836 P.2d 968 (Ariz. Ct. App. 1991) (excellent analysis; collecting cases). See also Jackson v. City of Franklin, 554 N.E.2d 932 (Ohio Ct. App. 1988) (strict liability in tort inapplicable to custom-designed public swimming pool).

**50.** See Duggan v. Hallmark Pool Mfg. Co., 398 N.W.2d 175 (Iowa 1986).

**51.** See McClanahan v. American Gilsonite Co., 494 F.Supp. 1334 (D. Colo. 1980).

**52.** See Easterday v. Masiello, 518 So.2d 260 (Fla. 1988) (jail).

**53.** See Chubb Group of Ins. Cos. v. C.F. Murphy & Assocs., Inc., 656 S.W.2d 766 (Mo. Ct. App. 1983).

**54.** See Papp v. Rocky Mountain Oil & Minerals, Inc., 769 P.2d 1249 (Mont. 1989).

**55.** See, e.g., Brooks v. Eugene Burger Mgmt. Corp., 264 Cal.Rptr. 756 (Ct. App. 1989) (young child who wandered off unfenced grounds of apartment complex struck by car; entire complex could not be defective product). See generally Annot., 25 A.L.R.4th 351 (1983).

(3) defects in premises leased for admission of the public, (4) defects in "common areas" retained under the landlord's control, (5) failure to keep the premises in good repair when the landlord had covenanted so to do, (6) negligence in making repairs, and (7) defects constituting violations of building or housing code provisions.[56] Then, in a spectacular decision in 1973, the New Hampshire Supreme Court turned the general rule of nonliability on its head in *Sargent v. Ross*[57] by holding a landlord subject to the general principles of negligence liability. A number of other courts have followed this eminently sound approach.[58]

### Warranty

On the warranty side of the matter, while a warranty of habitability had been implied into short-term leases of furnished dwellings by a few courts for some time, courts began to find a general implied warranty of habitability in leases of residential premises in the 1960s and early 1970s.[59] While most of the cases have involved essentially contractual disputes surrounding the nonpayment of rent and other economic complaints,[60] occasional cases concern more typical products liability claims involving personal injuries.[61] Quite recently, a Maryland decision held that a landlord was subject to liability for breach of warranty under that state's consumer protection act for injuries to a child who ingested lead-

**56.** See Prosser and Keeton on Torts § 63.

**57.** 308 A.2d 528 (N.H. 1973) (Kenison, C.J.).

**58.** See, e.g., Tenney v. Atlantic Assocs., 594 N.W.2d 11 (Iowa 1999) (plaintiff raped by stranger in her own apartment; landlord negligent in not securing spare apartment keys in office). Other cases following *Sargent* include Newton v. Magill, 872 P.2d 1213 (Alaska 1994); Favreau v. Miller, 591 A.2d 68 (Vt. 1991); Chi Turpel v. Sayles, 692 P.2d 1290 (Nev. 1985); Stephens v. Stearns, 678 P.2d 41 (Idaho 1984); Young v. Garwacki, 402 N.E.2d 1045 (Mass. 1980); Curry v. New York City Hous. Auth., 430 N.Y.S.2d 305 (App. Div. 1980); Pagelsdorf v. Safeco Ins. Co. of Am., 284 N.W.2d 55 (Wis. 1979); Stephenson v. Warner, 581 P.2d 567 (Utah 1978); Brennan v. Cockrell Invs., Inc., 111 Cal.Rptr. 122 (Ct. App. 1973). See also Mansur v. Eubanks, 401 So.2d 1328 (Fla. 1981) (holding residential landlord has duty to reasonably inspect and repair in order to deliver a reasonably safe dwelling to tenant); Shroades v. Rental Homes, Inc., 427 N.E.2d 774 (Ohio 1981) ("abrogation of this [landlord] immunity has been advocated by legal commentators, and the overwhelming majority of states have abolished, either in whole or in part, the traditional immunity."). *But see* Thomas v. Stewart, 60 S.W.3d 415, 420 (Ark. 2001) (noting that *Sargent* was rejected in the past, but suggesting that it might be followed in the future); Propst v. McNeill, 932 S.W.2d 766 (Ark. 1996) (plaintiff's aircraft damaged in

leased hangar during windstorm; although a majority of states have done so, abandoning doctrine of caveat lessee is for legislature); Ortega v. Flaim, 902 P.2d 199 (Wyo. 1995).

**59.** See, e.g., Pines v. Perssion, 111 N.W.2d 409 (Wis. 1961); Lemle v. Breeden, 462 P.2d 470 (Haw. 1969); Javins v. First Nat'l Realty Corp., 428 F.2d 1071 (D.C. Cir. 1970). See generally Comment, 33 Land & Water L. Rev. 329 (1998).

**60.** See, e.g., Wade v. Jobe, 818 P.2d 1006 (Utah 1991).

**61.** See, e.g., Joyner v. Durant, 716 N.Y.S.2d 221 (App. Div. 2000) (plaintiff's daughter contracted lead poisoning); Richardson v. Simone, 712 N.Y.S.2d 672 (App. Div. 2000) (plaintiff injured while standing on staircase that separated from building and fell to ground); Old Town Dev. Co. v. Langford, 349 N.E.2d 744 (Ind. Ct. App. 1976), set aside without opinion, 369 N.E.2d 404 (Ind. 1977) (explosion of defective furnace in apartment building). See also Richwind Joint Venture 4 v. Brunson, 645 A.2d 1147 (Md. 1994) (plaintiff's infant contracted lead poisoning from ingesting paint chips that fell from ceiling; notice to landlord of lead-based paint chips necessary to both warranty and negligence claims); Alharb v. Sayegh, 604 N.Y.S.2d 243 (App. Div. 1993) (same; lack of notice of dangerous condition may be defense: by implication); Rivera v. Selfon Home Repairs and Improvements Co., 439 A.2d 739 (Pa. Super. Ct. 1982).

based paint chips existing in the dwelling at the inception of the lease in violation of a local housing code.[62]

### *Strict Liability in Tort*

At the height (and close to the end) of the tort expansionary era in the mid–1980s, the California Supreme Court in *Becker v. IRM Corporation*[63] adopted a rule of landlord strict tort liability for injuries from defects in leased dwellings, reasoning that an apartment itself may be considered a "product" placed in the stream of commerce by the landlord.[64] Louisiana, by statute, was the only other state to have such a rule.[65] No court followed *Becker*, and courts and commentators widely rejected it as an excessive extension of the principles of products liability law.[66] Hawaii, for example, which has a strong tradition of protecting plaintiffs' rights, would have nothing to do with the *Becker* approach.[67] Shortly after *Becker* was decided, the composition of the California Supreme Court changed substantially, and the newly constituted court eventually found an opportunity to revisit *Becker* when asked to extend its strict liability rule to hoteliers. In *Peterson v. Superior Court*,[68] the court declared that landlords have no duty "to insure the safety of their tenants in situations in which injury is caused by a defect of which the landlord neither knew nor should have known."[69] Admitting that it had erred in *Becker*, the court ruled that strict liability in tort does *not* apply to either landlords or hoteliers for injuries to tenants or guests caused by defects in the premises.[70]

### Statutes of Repose

Many states have special statutes of repose for improvements to real property.[71] These statutes, some of which are quite short,[72] protect

---

**62.** Benik v. Hatcher, 750 A.2d 10, 26 (Md. 2000) (4–3 decision) ("the landlord who leases premises for human habitation is presumed to have knowledge of any defective condition that a reasonable inspection would have disclosed").

**63.** 698 P.2d 116 (Cal. 1985).

**64.** Earlier, the California court had held that a landlord negligence disclaimer violated public policy. See Henrioulle v. Marin Ventures, Inc., 573 P.2d 465 (Cal. 1978).

**65.** See Marcantel v. Karam, 601 So.2d 1 (La. Ct. App. 1992).

**66.** See, e.g., Leong v. Sears Roebuck & Co., 970 P.2d 972 (Haw. 1998); Ortega v. Flaim, 902 P.2d 199 (Wyo. 1995); Armstrong v. Cione, 738 P.2d 79 (Haw. 1987) (shower door made of ordinary glass); Duncavage v. Allen, 497 N.E.2d 433 (Ill. App. Ct. 1986) (broken lock on window permitted murderer to enter); Young v. Morrisey, 329 S.E.2d 426 (S.C. 1985) (electrical system); Livingston v. Begay, 652 P.2d 734 (N.M. 1982) (gas heater in hotel room emitted carbon monoxide); Dwyer v. Skyline Apartments, Inc., 301 A.2d 463 (N.J. Super. Ct. App. Div. 1973), aff'd, 311 A.2d 1 (N.J. 1973) (hot water faucet in bathtub).

**67.** See Armstrong v. Cione, 738 P.2d 79 (Haw. 1987).

**68.** 899 P.2d 905 (Cal. 1995).

**69.** Id. at 912 (noting that "every other jurisdiction that has considered this issue expressly has rejected the approach followed by *Becker*").

**70.** The court noted that it had "erred in *Becker* in applying the doctrine of strict products liability to a residential landlord that is not a part of the manufacturing or marketing enterprise of the allegedly defective product that caused the injury in question," and that for similar reasons strict products liability should not apply to hoteliers for defects in the premises that the hotelier did not create or market. Id. at 906. Compare Serna v. New York State Urban Dev. Corp., 586 N.Y.S.2d 413 (App. Div. 1992) (plaintiff tripped when exiting elevator that stopped below floor level; strict products liability principles inapplicable to commercial lessor of building).

**71.** See § 14.5, above.

**72.** See, e.g., Trust Co. Bank v. U.S. Gypsum Co., 950 F.2d 1144 (5th Cir. 1992) (Miss. law) (6–year statute barred claim for

building contractors from suits long after a structure has been completed, but manufacturers of component products used in the structure may not be protected under the more narrowly drawn statutes.[73] Yet some of the statutes are drawn more broadly, thus protecting component manufacturers. In *Krull v. Thermogas Company*,[74] a gas control valve in the furnace of the plaintiffs' home malfunctioned, causing an explosion and fire that destroyed their home. The furnace had been purchased in 1969 and the explosion occurred in 1990. Iowa's repose statute provided that "an action arising out of the unsafe or defective condition of an improvement to real property based on tort and implied warranty ... shall not be brought more than fifteen years after" the act complained of.[75] Since "[t]he furnace—including its component valve—was an integral part of the house," it was an "improvement" to realty, such that its manufacturer was shielded by the repose statute which barred all such claims after 1984, 15 years after the purchase of the furnace.[76] As in most states, the Iowa court in *Krull* held its statute constitutional.[77]

## § 16.8  PUBLICATIONS

Harmful publications have always been subject to the law of defamation[1] as well as to the law of tortious misrepresentation[2] and breach of express warranty.[3] In recent years, however, publishers have been subjected to an additional type of claim, one based on products liability. A number of claims have been brought against publishers for injuries attributable to information or thoughts communicated in books, magazine articles, films, records, computer games, websites, and aeronautical charts. Plaintiffs in these cases have alleged that the publishers, producers, and distributors of the materials breached a duty to persons put at risk by the information or ideas communicated in these various forms and that the law of products liability, or the broader law of torts, provides a basis for recovery.[4]

Except for cases involving defective navigational charts and publications providing contract killer information, these actions have all been barred. In some cases, courts have ruled that books cannot be classified

asbestos abatement costs against manufacturer of materials).

**73.** See, e.g., Dziewiecki v. Bakula, 824 A.2d 241 (N.J. Super. Ct. App. Div. 2003) (New Jersey's statute of repose was intended "to protect those who contribute to the design, planning, supervision or construction of a structural improvement to real estate," not manufacturers and sellers of products used in or incorporated into improvement); Noll v. Harrisburg Area YMCA, 643 A.2d 81 (Pa. 1994).

**74.** 522 N.W.2d 607 (Iowa 1994).

**75.** Iowa Code § 614.1(11).

**76.** 522 N.W.2d at 611.

**77.** Accord, Coleman v. United Eng'rs & Constructors, Inc., 878 P.2d 996 (N.M.

1994). *Contra*, Brennaman v. R.M.I. Co., 639 N.E.2d 425 (Ohio 1994) (holding Ohio's similar statute unconstitutional).

### § 16.8

**1.** See Prosser and Keeton on Torts ch. 19.

**2.** See ch. 3, above.

**3.** See § 4.2, above.

**4.** "Plaintiffs allege that the information delivered was false and misleading, causing harm when actors relied on it. They seek to recover against publishers in strict liability in tort based on product defect, rather than on negligence or some form of misrepresentation." Products Liability Restatement § 19 cmt. *d.*

as "products," but many of the decisions are troubled at a deeper level with the First Amendment implications of such potential liability.[5]

### Books, Magazines, and Print Media

In products liability actions against publishers of books and other printed media, the fault is generally claimed to lie with the intangible information contained in the publication, not the physical book itself.[6] For example, in *Winter v. G.P. Putnam's Sons*,[7] the plaintiff mushroom hunters suffered liver damage from eating mushrooms they thought were safe to eat based on mushroom descriptions in "The Encyclopedia of Mushrooms." The mushroom eaters sued the publisher, alleging products liability, breach of warranty, negligence, negligent misrepresentation, and false representations. The trial court granted the publisher's summary judgment motion, and the Ninth Circuit affirmed, reasoning that the materials that physically comprise the book may be a product, but the ideas expressed inside are not.[8] The court ruled that principles of products liability law, especially strict liability, may not be applied to the written word.[9] "We place a high priority on the unfettered exchange of ideas. We accept the risk that words and ideas have wings we cannot clip and which carry them we know not where. The threat of liability without fault . . . could seriously inhibit those who wish to share thoughts and theories."[10]

Other courts have similarly refused to apply products liability principles, particularly a rule of strict liability, to the publication of dangerously false information. The decisions typically conclude that the message, as distinct from the packaging of the message, is not a "product" within the meaning of *Restatement (Second) of Torts* § 402A.[11] On this basis,

---

**5.** See, e.g., Sanders v. Acclaim Entm't, Inc., 188 F.Supp.2d 1264 (D. Colo. 2002). See generally Gilles, "Poisonous" Publications and Other False Speech Physical Harm Cases, 37 Wake Forest L. Rev. 1073 (2002); Ausness, The Application of Product Liability Principles to Publishers of Violent or Sexually Explicit Material, 52 Fla. L. Rev. 603 (2000); Noah, Authors, Publishers, and Products Liability: Remedies for Defective Information in Books, 77 Or. L. Rev. 1195 (1998); Mince, Strict Liability for Commercial Intellect, 41 Cath. U. L. Rev. 617 (1992); Powell, Products Liability and the First Amendment: The Liability of Publishers for Failure to Warn, 9 J. Prod. Liab. 159 (1986); Notes, "Exceedingly Vexed and Difficult": Games and the First Amendment, 112 Yale L.J. 361 (2002); The Persistence of Caveat Emptor: Publisher Immunity from Inaccurate Factual Information, 53 U. Pitt. L. Rev. 777 (1992); Comments, Tort Liability for Nonlibellous Negligent Statements: First Amendment Considerations, 93 Yale L.J. 744 (1984); Tort Liability of the Media for Audience Acts of Violence: A Constitutional Analysis, 52 S. Cal. L. Rev. 529 (1979); Note, Publisher Liability for Material that Invites Reliance, 66 Tex. L. Rev. 1155 (1988); 10 Am. Law Prod. Liab. 3d ch. 119.

**6.** "Although a tangible medium such as a book, itself clearly a product, delivers the information, the plaintiff's grievance in such cases is with the information, not with the tangible medium." Products Liability Restatement § 19 cmt. *d*.

**7.** 938 F.2d 1033 (9th Cir. 1991) (Cal. law), noted, 105 Harv. L. Rev. 255, 261 (1992).

**8.** "A book containing Shakespeare's sonnets consists of two parts, the material and print therein, and the ideas and expression thereof. The first may be a product, but the second is not. . . . Products liability law is geared to the tangible world." Id. at 1034.

**9.** "Strict liability principles even when applied to products are not without their costs. Innovation may be inhibited. We tolerate these losses. They are much less disturbing than the prospect that we might be deprived of the latest ideas and theories." Id. at 1035.

**10.** Id.

**11.** See, e.g., James v. Meow Media, Inc., 300 F.3d 683 (6th Cir. 2002) (Ky. law); Sanders v. Acclaim Entm't, Inc., 188 F.Supp.2d 1264 (D. Colo. 2002); Wilson v.

courts have rejected strict liability claims against publishers of a liquid diet book, for the death of a woman from complications associated with the diet;[12] a medical textbook, for injuries to a nursing student from following a constipation remedy described in the textbook;[13] a travel guide, for injuries to a swimmer injured in hazardous beach conditions not mentioned in the guide;[14] a metalsmithing book, for injuries from the explosion of a caustic substance mixed according to the book's instructions;[15] and other publishers, for harmful results spurred by the written word.[16] Reasoning that book merchants should not be required to evaluate the thought processes of every author of the thousands of books they sell, a court disallowed an implied warranty action against the retail seller of a cookbook which failed to warn that an ingredient was poisonous if not cooked.[17]

The one very limited situation in which courts have allowed tort claims against publishers of books and magazines is for the promotion of contract killing. Several courts have allowed claims against *Soldier of Fortune Magazine* for publishing advertisements of contract killers.[18] In one,[19] a husband hired the person who placed such an ad in the magazine to kill his wife, and the job was done. In view of the nature of the magazine, and the fact that other ads explicitly offered criminal services, the district court allowed a negligence action for failure to investigate, reasoning that the First Amendment was not a bar because this form of commercial speech was not as stringently protected as core speech.[20] Without addressing the First Amendment issue, the court of appeals reversed, ruling that the advertisement was sufficiently ambiguous not

Midway Games, Inc., 198 F.Supp.2d 167 (D. Conn. 2002). Compare Kercsmar v. Pen Argyl Area Sch. Dist., 1 Pa. D. & C. 3d 1 (1976) (action for injuries to secondary school student while conducting chemistry experiment described in textbook; *held*, textbook was "good" under UCC § 2–105); Roccaforte v. Nintendo of Am., Inc., 802 So.2d 764, 766 (La. Ct. App. 2001) (by implication).

**12.** See Smith v. Linn, 563 A.2d 123, 126 (Pa. Super. Ct. 1989), aff'd, 587 A.2d 309 (Pa. 1991).

**13.** See Jones v. J.B. Lippincott Co., 694 F.Supp. 1216 (D. Md. 1988).

**14.** See Birmingham v. Fodor's Travel Publ'ns, Inc., 833 P.2d 70 (Haw. 1992).

**15.** See Lewin v. McCreight, 655 F.Supp. 282 (E.D. Mich. 1987).

**16.** See, e.g., Way v. Boy Scouts of Am., 856 S.W.2d 230 (Tex. App. 1993) (content of *Boys Life* magazine, and advertising supplement for shooting sports, held not "products"); Appleby v. Miller, 554 N.E.2d 773 (Ill. App. Ct. 1990) (strict liability in tort did not apply to defective standardized medical history intake forms, on which doctor relied in making diagnosis, allegedly resulting in improper treatment; forms were

service, not product); Herceg v. Hustler Magazine, Inc., 565 F.Supp. 802, 803–04 (S.D. Tex. 1983) (boy died from trying "autoerotic asphyxiation" described in magazine article); Walter v. Bauer, 439 N.Y.S.2d 821, 822–23 (Sup. Ct. 1981) (student injured doing science project described in textbook), rev'd in part on other grounds, 451 N.Y.S.2d 533 (App. Div. 1982); Walters v. Seventeen Magazine, 241 Cal.Rptr. 101 (Ct. App. 1987) (publishers not liable for plaintiff's toxic shock syndrome caused by Playtex tampons advertised in Seventeen Magazine).

**17.** See Cardozo v. True, 342 So.2d 1053 (Fla. Dist. Ct. App. 1977) (the Dasheen plant, commonly known as "elephant's ears").

**18.** See Braun v. Soldier of Fortune Magazine, Inc., 968 F.2d 1110 (11th Cir. 1992) (Ga. law); Eimann v. Soldier of Fortune Magazine, Inc., 680 F.Supp. 863 (S.D. Tex. 1988), rev'd, 880 F.2d 830 (5th Cir. 1989) (2–1 decision); Norwood v. Soldier of Fortune Magazine, Inc., 651 F.Supp. 1397 (W.D. Ark. 1987).

**19.** Eimann v. Soldier of Fortune Magazine, Inc., 680 F.Supp. 863 (S.D. Tex. 1988).

**20.** Id. at 865–66.

to give rise to a duty by the defendant to refrain from publishing it.[21]

More recently, in *Rice v. Paladin Enterprises*,[22] the Fourth Circuit allowed a tort-law aiding-and-abetting claim against the publisher of a "how-to" book for contract killers, including precise instructions on every gruesome detail of such projects. "[R]eadied by these instructions and steeled by these seductive adjurations from *Hit Man: A Technical Manual for Independent Contractors*, a copy of which was subsequently found in his apartment, James Perry brutally murdered Mildred Horn, her eight-year-old quadriplegic son Trevor, and Trevor's nurse."[23] Mildred Horn's ex-husband had hired Perry, the contract killer, so he could receive his son's $2 million settlement for injuries that had left him paralyzed. In conducting the murders, Perry meticulously followed numerous details from the *Hit Man* manual. Since the defendant publisher stipulated that it targeted the book to murderers and would-be murderers and that it knew and intended that the manual would be used for contract murders, the court found no difficulty in ruling that a jury could find that *Hit Man* had "little, if any, purpose beyond the unlawful one of facilitating murder," and so was unprotected by the First Amendment.[24] After the court allowed the action to proceed, the publisher settled the case for millions of dollars.[25]

### Games, Music, Video Games, and Websites

First Amendment protection for published materials has extended to distributors of games, recordings, movies, video games, and Internet websites.[26] In an action against the publisher and manufacturer of the game "Dungeons and Dragons" for the suicide death of an adherent thereto, the court upheld the defendants' First Amendment defense and further ruled that the defendant-publishers had no duty to warn mentally fragile persons of the possibly dangerous consequences of playing the game.[27] Likewise, in an action against musician Ozzy Osbourne, his composer, and CBS Records for damages arising from the suicide of a listener, the court held that music is also entitled to First Amendment protection, that the song did not fall within the incitement exception, and that the listener's suicide was unforeseeable.[28] For similar reasons, the trial court granted summary judgment to Tupac Shakur, a rap

**21.** Eimann v. Soldier of Fortune Magazine, Inc., 880 F.2d 830, 838 (5th Cir. 1989) (Tex. Law) ("we decline to impose on publishers the obligation to reject all ambiguous advertisements for products or services that might pose a threat of harm").

**22.** 128 F.3d 233 (4th Cir. 1997) (Md. law).

**23.** Id. at 239.

**24.** Id. at 266. See also Wilson v. Paladin Enters., 186 F.Supp.2d 1140, 1144 (D. Or. 2001) (similar case against publisher of *Hit Man*).

**25.** Liability Week 6 (May 24, 1999).

**26.** See Swartz and Swartz, Holding the Electronic Game Industry Accountable for the Deleterious Effects Violent Video Games Can Have on Our Children, 147 Products Advisory 1 (West, May 2001); Interactive Digital Software Ass'n v. St. Louis Cty., Mo., 329 F.3d 954 (8th Cir. 2003) (video games protected under First Amendment), reversing 200 F.Supp.2d 1126 (E.D. Mo. 2002).

**27.** See Watters v. TSR, Inc., 715 F.Supp. 819 (W.D. Kan. 1989), aff'd, 904 F.2d 378, 380 (6th Cir. 1990) (Kan. law) ("the doctrine of strict liability has never been extended to words or pictures [and] other courts have looked in vain for decisions so expanding the scope of the strict liability doctrine").

**28.** See Jack McCollum v. CBS, Inc., 249 Cal.Rptr. 187 (Ct. App. 1988).

"artist," and the record companies that produced and distributed his recording, "2Pacalypse Now," for the murder of a police officer in a manner suggested by the recording.[29]

Courts have rejected a number of claims against manufacturers of video games and other visual entertainment products, often concluding that products liability principles do not apply to them because they simply are not "products."[30] *James v. Meow Media, Inc.*[31] was a case arising out of the massacre of Kentucky high school students by a fellow student who took six guns to school and shot other students after their prayer session. In a products liability suit against makers and distributors of violent video games, a violent movie, and obscene Internet websites of which the assailant was an avid consumer, the parents of the murdered students claimed that the defendants made and distributed these materials in a defective and unreasonably dangerous condition giving rise to strict liability in tort under *Restatement (Second) of Torts* § 402A.[32] Not claiming that the tangible materials themselves were defective, the parents' claim instead was that intangible and subliminal thoughts, ideas, and messages contained within the products presented a danger of which the defendants had a duty to warn. Finding that the few analogous cases and the *Products Liability Restatement* unanimously opposed extending products liability law to such a situation, the court ruled that "intangible thoughts, ideas, and messages contained within games, movies, and website materials are not products for purposes of strict products liability."[33]

### Computer Software

Whether manufacturers of computer software should be subject to products liability for personal injuries caused by defective software is an intriguing question. While commentators widely favor the application of products liability theories in such situations,[34] the case law is as yet

**29.** See Davidson v. Time Warner, Inc., 1997 WL 405907, at *15–*22 (S.D. Tex. 1997) (finding all case law against a products liability claim, together with constitutional problems).

**30.** See, e.g., James v. Meow Media, Inc., 300 F.3d 683 (6th Cir. 2002) (Ky. law); Sanders v. Acclaim Entm't, Inc., F.Supp.2d 1264 (D. Colo. 2002); Wilson v. Midway Games, Inc., 198 F.Supp.2d 167 (D. Conn. 2002). Compare Kercsmar v. Pen Argyl Area Sch. Dist., 1 Pa. D. & C. 3d 1 (1976) (action for injuries to secondary school student while conducting chemistry experiment described in textbook; *held*, textbook was "good" under UCC § 2–105); Roccaforte v. Nintendo of Am., Inc., 802 So.2d 764, 766 (La. Ct. App. 2001) (by implication).

**31.** 90 F.Supp.2d 798 (W.D. Ky. 2000), aff'd, 300 F.3d 683, 700 (6th Cir. 2002) (noting that plaintiffs' products liability theory was "deeply flawed").

**32.** 90 F.Supp.2d at 809.

**33.** 90 F.Supp.2d at 810.

**34.** See Kathrein, Class Actions in Year 2000 Defective Software and Hardware Litigation, 18 Rev. Litig. 487, 513–17 (1999); Wolpert, Products Liability and Software Implicated in Personal Injury, 60 Def. Couns. J. 519 (1993); Gemignani, Product Liability and Software, 8 Rutgers Computer & Tech. L.J. 173, 196–99 (1981); Note, Bad Bytes: The Application of Strict Products Liability to Computer Software, 66 St. John's L. Rev. 469 (1992); Note, Strict Products Liability and Computer Software: Caveat Vendor, 4 Computer/L.J. 373 (1983); Note, Negligence: Liability for Defective Software, 33 Okla. L. Rev. 848, 855 (1980) ("when software is distributed to the public through mass merchandising, strict liability in tort should be an available theory for a consumer who is injured because of a defect in the software"); Note, Computer Software and Strict Products Liability, 20 San Diego L. Rev. 439 (1983); Note, Easing Plaintiffs' Burden of Proving Negligence for Computer Malfunction, 69 Iowa L. Rev. 241 (1983).

nonexistent.[35] One commentator,[36] however, has noted four scenarios implicating products liability claims arising hypothetically from actual cases in which the computer programming issues were not developed by the parties or the courts: a program for an energy management system that failed to activate a chemistry lab fan, causing a teacher to inhale chlorine gas;[37] a defective computer-generated warning label for a prescription drug;[38] a system that failed to inform an arraignment judge of an arrestee's prior violent crimes, leading to a victim's injuries after the arrestee's release;[39] and a software program's erroneous calculation of the proper doses of radiation for radioactive seeds implanted in a prostate cancer patient.[40] Because these cases conceptually appear to fall somewhere between mushroom cookbooks and navigational charts, it is difficult to know how they should be classified. At least when the defect lies solely in the software program design, rather than the substantive information fed into the program, a defective software program might seem to lie closer to a defective navigational chart for which a producer should be subject to strict responsibility for resulting harm.

## Navigational Charts

One type of case in which the courts have allowed claims against a publisher involves the publication of aeronautical charts containing false information, causing a pilot, for example, to fly into a mountain not shown on the chart.[41] "[A]lthough a sheet of paper might not be dangerous, per se, it would be difficult indeed to conceive of a salable commodity with more inherent lethal potential than an aid to aircraft

**35.** In the commercial law context, there is case law holding mass-marketed software to be a "good" under the Uniform Commercial Code. See, e.g., Advent Sys. Ltd. v. Unisys Corp., 925 F.2d 670 (3d Cir. 1991) (Pa. law); Systems Design & Mgmt. Info., Inc. v. Kansas City Post Office Employee Credit Union, 788 P.2d 878 (Kan. Ct. App. 1990); RRX Indus., Inc. v. Lab–Con, Inc., 772 F.2d 543 (9th Cir. 1985) (Cal. law). Software developed specifically for a customer, however, has been found to be a "service." See, e.g., Micro–Managers, Inc. v. Gregory, 434 N.W.2d 97 (Wis. Ct. App. 1988); Data Processing Servs., Inc. v. L.H. Smith Oil Corp., 492 N.E.2d 314 (Ind. Ct. App. 1986). But see Analysts Int'l Corp. v. Recycled Paper Prods., Inc., 1987 WL 12917, at *3 (N.D. Ill. 1987) (custom software was a "good"). See generally Note, Computer Software as a Good Under the Uniform Commercial Code: Taking a Byte Out of the Intangibility Myth, 65 B.U. L. Rev. 129 (1985); Comment, The Warranty of Merchantability and Computer Software Contracts: A Square Peg Won't Fit in a Round Hole, 59 Wash. L. Rev. 511 (1984); Products Liability Restatement § 19 Reporters' Note to cmt. d.

**36.** Wolpert, Product Liability and Software Implicated in Personal Injury, 60 Def. Couns. J. 519 (1993).

**37.** This scenario is based on Sparacino v. Andover Controls Corp., 592 N.E.2d 431 (Ill. App. Ct. 1992).

**38.** This scenario is based on Frye v. Medicare–Glaser Corp., 579 N.E.2d 1255 (Ill. App. Ct. 1991).

**39.** This scenario is based on Akins v. District of Columbia, 526 A.2d 933 (D.C. 1987).

**40.** This scenario is based on Jones v. Minnesota Mining & Mfg. Co., 669 P.2d 744 (N.M. Ct. App. 1983).

**41.** See, e.g., Fluor Corp. v. Jeppesen & Co., 216 Cal.Rptr. 68, 71–72 (Ct. App. 1985) (jet pilot crashed into mountain not depicted on approach chart, although lower mountain was). See also Times Mirror Co. v. Sisk, 593 P.2d 924 (Ariz. Ct. App. 1978). In Saloomey v. Jeppesen & Co., 707 F.2d 671 (2d Cir. 1983) (Colo. law), the chart showed the Martinsburg, W. Va., airport as having a full ILS instrument approach, including a glideslope (providing pilots with vertical descent information), rather than only a localizer (providing pilots only with horizontal guidance information). While attempting an approach, an off-duty commercial pilot flew his personal Beechcraft Sierra into a 1,600–foot ridge. Martinsburg airport (MRB) now has a full ILS.

navigation that, contrary to its own design standards, fails to list the highest land mass immediately surrounding a landing site."[42] Noting that the total reliance pilots necessarily place on the accuracy of navigational charts can directly cause a fatal crash if the information proves false,[43] courts have distinguished navigational charts from other types of publications because the very purpose of such charts is to portray physical phenomena rather than ideas.[44] While such cases may fit more comfortably in the law of misrepresentation and express warranty,[45] there seems little harm in allowing these meritorious claims under the conventional product defect umbrella.

## Products Liability and Freedom of Expression

Whether and to what extent the law of products liability should provide recovery for persons injured by the improper transmission of information and ideas involves a host of intriguing questions, including the propriety of extending legal principles designed to provide a remedy for injuries caused by defective chattels to injuries resulting from the dissemination of thought. Once private law begins to press upon the freedom of expression, First Amendment rights are implicated.

While the menace of products liability claims to free expression is real, the threat to First Amendment interests may be overdrawn. If the challenged information is false or incites violence, then it may well fall outside the protected sphere of freedom of expression.[46] In any event, plaintiffs in such cases face a major hurdle in showing how the provision of such information might have been a proximate cause of violently inflicted harm.[47] The courts appear to have drawn a sound distinction between the expression of thoughts and ideas, which needs constitutional protection, and the communication of factual information (the accura-

**42.** 216 Cal.Rptr. at 71–72.

**43.** "In those cases, the charts were physically used in the operation of the aircraft at the time of the accident. The inaccurate data directly caused or was alleged to have caused the accidents in question in the same manner in which a broken compass or an inaccurate altimeter would have caused a plane to crash." Way v. Boy Scouts of Am., 856 S.W.2d 230, 238–39 (Tex. App. 1993) (distinguishing charts from magazines).

**44.** See Brocklesby v. United States, 767 F.2d 1288, 1298 (9th Cir. 1985) (Cal. law) ("Jeppesen converts a government procedure from text into graphic form and represents that the chart contains all necessary information."); Aetna Cas. & Sur. Co. v. Jeppesen & Co., 642 F.2d 339, 341 (9th Cir. 1981) (Nev. law) (approach chart defective because, contrary to custom, it changed the scale on plan and profile views; "The [landing] specifications prescribed are set forth by the FAA in tabular form. Jeppesen acquires this FAA form and portrays the information therein on a graphic approach chart. This is Jeppesen's 'product.' ").

**45.** See Products Liability Restatement § 19 Reporters' Note to cmt. *d.* See Phillips, Information Liability: The Possible Chilling Effect of Tort Claims Against Producers of Geographic Information Systems Data, 26 Fla. St. U. L. Rev. 743 (1999).

**46.** *But see* Davidson v. Time Warner, Inc., 1997 WL 405907, at *15–*22 (S.D. Tex. 1997) (thorough discussion, rejecting claim that cop-killing rap song was unprotected expression).

**47.** Even if the provision of information or entertainment in some way stimulates a violent act, the violence itself nearly always supersedes any responsibility of the publisher. See, e.g., James v. Meow Media, Inc., 300 F.3d 683, 699 (6th Cir. 2002) (Ky. law) (recovery against makers and distributors of video games, violent movie, and obscene Internet websites for student murders at Kentucky school precluded by superseding cause; discussing other cases); Sanders v. Acclaim Entm't, Inc., 188 F.Supp.2d 1264 (D. Colo. 2002) (criminal acts of killers were superseding cause).

cy of which is capable of objective determination), which needs no breathing space. While line drawing of this type may invite error and abuse,[48] it may be necessary to accommodate the competing goals of tort law and freedom of expression.

Of the various types of injury claims arising out of publications for which plaintiffs have sought recovery under products liability law, only two are clearly deserving of protection. Claims for publishing inaccurate aeronautical charts and manuals for contract murder both deserve a private remedy, and neither form of conduct needs constitutional protection. Closely analogous claims, such as publishing false information about poisonous mushrooms and advertisements for contract killers, also may be proper for tort law treatment, but evaluating such claims requires considerable caution.[49] The proper basis for false safety information claims appears to lie in the law of tortious misrepresentation and breach of express warranty; and the contract killer cases fit most comfortably within tort law rules on aiding and abetting,[50] which is the essence of those claims. Thus, while the "strict" liability rules of products liability law may offer a tempting haven to plaintiffs in either type of case, other bases of recovery may be preferable to conventional theories of products liability.

## § 16.9  BLOOD

No "product" could be further distanced from a typical, commercially manufactured product than human blood. Yet blood is "sold" for use by thousands of patients each year, often for purposes of transfusion, by hospitals, blood banks, and manufacturers of blood products.[1] Less commonly, other forms of human tissue—such as bones, tendons, and

---

**48.** In Winter v. G.P. Putnam's Sons, 938 F.2d 1033, 1035 (9th Cir. 1991) (Cal. law), the court rejected such a distinction:

> Plaintiffs suggest, however, that our fears would be groundless were strict liability rules applied only to books that give instruction on how to accomplish a physical activity and that are intended to be used as part of an activity that is inherently dangerous. We find such a limitation illusory. Ideas are often intimately linked with proposed action, and it would be difficult to draw such a bright line. While "How To" books are a special genre, we decline to attempt to draw a line that puts "How To Live A Good Life" books beyond the reach of strict liability while leaving "How To Exercise Properly" books within its reach.

**49.** The court in Winter v. G.P. Putnam's Sons, 938 F.2d 1033, 1036 (9th Cir. 1991) (Cal. law), rejected the plaintiff's argument that the Encyclopedia of Mushrooms was analogous to an aeronautical chart because the purpose of both was to describe natural features to promote safety:

> Aeronautical charts are highly technical tools. They are graphic depictions of technical, mechanical data. The best anal-

ogy to an aeronautical chart is a compass. Both may be used to guide an individual who is engaged in an activity requiring certain knowledge of natural features. Computer software that fails to yield the result for which it was designed may be another. In contrast, The Encyclopedia of Mushrooms is like a book on how to use a compass or an aeronautical chart. The chart itself is like a physical "product" while the "How to Use" book is pure thought and expression.

Compare Schultz, Application of Strict Products Liability to Aeronautical Chart Publishers, 64 Air L. & Com. 431 (1999) (criticizing *Winter* court's analogy of chart to compass).

**50.** See Restatement (2d) Torts § 876.

### § 16.9

**1.** Blood products include "whole blood and its component parts, such as red blood cells, platelets, and plasma, and coagulation products derived from blood plasma, such as factor concentrates." Comment, 3 J. Pharm. & L. 129 n.5 (1994).

organs—are sold to and inserted into human beings.[2] Despite the difficulty of trying to fit such human components into normal products liability doctrinal pigeon-holes, courts and legislatures have been forced to address the question of legal responsibility for infected blood or tissue that is transfused or otherwise implanted in a patient.[3]

While the first reported transfusion of human blood was in 1795, the use of blood transfusions in surgery did not become common and reliable until the middle of the twentieth century.[4] The widespread medical use of blood transfusions created a market which impelled the rise of blood banks—firms that collect, store, and distribute blood products—a development considered one of the great advances in the history of medicine. If supplies of whole blood were not readily available at hospitals across the land, many important medical procedures which now are common would be impossible.[5] But with this boon came the dreadful risk that blood gathered from other persons may be infected with some serious, possibly deadly, disease. Especially since the early to mid–1980s, the transfusion risk of greatest concern has been the risk of HIV and AIDS. Prior thereto, the most troubling risk in transfused blood was serum hepatitis.

**2.** In the few cases involving claims of infected human tissue other than blood, courts have applied similar rules to those applied in cases involving blood, notably, holding that the supply of human tissue is not a service and that human tissue is not a "product" for purposes of products liability law. See, e.g., Cryolife, Inc. v. Superior Court, 2 Cal.Rptr.3d 396 (Ct. App. 2003) (infected cadaver tendon used in knee surgery; supply of human tissue under tissue shield statute is a service, and statute immunizes suppliers from strict liability); Condos v. Musculoskeletal Transplant Foundation, 208 F.Supp.2d 1226 (D. Utah 2002) (dismissing claims against supplier and processor of bone tissue, infected with hepatitis C virus, implanted in plaintiff; bone tissue not a "product," and defendants not negligent). Some "blood shield" statutes are written broadly to include other human tissue and organs. See, e.g., Pa. Stat. Ann. § 8333; Mont. Code Ann. § 50–33–102. See also Products Liability Restatement § 19 (c) ("Human blood and human tissue, even when provided commercially, are not subject to the rules of this Restatement."). Because of the similarity of treatment, and for simplicity, the discussion in this section is limited to blood.

**3.** Earlier literature on blood transfusion liability focused on serum hepatitis. See, e.g., Kessel, Transfused Blood, Serum Hepatitis, and the Coase Theorem, 17 J.L. & Econ. 265 (1974); Franklin, Tort Liability for Hepatitis: An Analysis and a Proposal, 24 Stan. L. Rev. 439 (1972); Franklin, Hepatitis, Blood Transfusions, and Public Action, 21 Cath. U. L. Rev. 683 (1972); Most of the more recent literature on liability for selling infected blood has concerned the risk of contracting AIDS from receiving the blood products of others. See, e.g., Eckert, The AIDS Blood–Transfusion Cases: A Legal and Economic Analysis of Liability, 29 San Diego L. Rev. 203 (1992); Note, 36 Ariz. L. Rev. 473 (1994) (liability for transfusion-transmitted disease). See also Reser and Radnofsky, New Wave of Tainted Blood Litigation: Hepatitis C Liability Issues, 67 Def. Coun. J. 306 (2000). Cases are collected in Annots., 24 A.L.R. 4th 136 (1983) (liability of hospitals and doctors for harm from blood transfusions); 24 A.L.R. 4th 508 (1983) (liability of blood suppliers for harm from blood transfusions). See generally Feldman, Blood Justice: Courts, Conflict, and Compensation in Japan, France, and the United States, 34 L. & Soc'y Rev. 651 (2000); Trebilcock, House, and Daniels, Do Institutions Matter? A Comparative Pathology of the HIV–Infected Blood Tragedy, 82 Va. L. Rev. 1407 (1996), critiqued, Glied, Markets Matter: U.S. Responses to the HIV–Infected Blood Tragedy, 82 Va. L. Rev. 1493 (1996); Salbu, AIDS and the Blood Supply: An Analysis of Law, Regulation, and Public Policy, 74 Wash. U.L.Q 913 (1996); Klein, A Legislative Alternative to "No Cause" Liability in Blood Products Litigation, 12 Yale J. on Reg. 107 (1995).

**4.** See Banks, Legal and Ethical Safeguards: Protection of Society's Most Vulnerable Participants in A Commercialized Organ Transplantation System, 21 Am. J.L. & Med. 45, 48 n.20 (1995).

**5.** See Annot., 24 A.L.R. 4th 508, at § 2 (1983).

In the 1960s, one-third of blood transfusion recipients contracted hepatitis.[6] By 1970, it was estimated that 1.25 million patients received transfusions of 5 million units of blood each year in the United States, about 80% of which was then supplied by volunteer donors.[7] Studies showed that the 20% of blood collected from paid donors in large cities was 10–15 times more likely to be infected with hepatitis than that collected from volunteers.[8] It was estimated that some 30,000 serious, overt hepatitis cases resulted from transfusions in the U.S. each year (some 5–10% of which were fatal) together with 150,000 additional subclinical cases.[9] Nearly 25% of persons over 40 who contract the illness die.[10] To make matters worse, there was then no reliable test to determine whether blood was infected with hepatitis.

The growth of widespread blood transfusions and blood banks in the middle of the twentieth century was coincident with the rise of modern products liability law with its strict liability doctrines for the sale of defective products.[11] In an early case, *Perlmutter v. Beth David Hospital*,[12] the plaintiff was a patient who sued the hospital for breach of implied warranty for injuries resulting from "the transfusing of 'bad' blood, supplied by the hospital for a price as part of the customary services rendered by the hospital to its patients."[13] Holding that the hospital's provision of blood to the patient was a service rather than a sale, a majority of the New York Court of Appeals reasoned in 1954 that the hospital's principal role was to promote the healing of its patients, not to sell them medicines, drugs, or blood.[14] A similar claim arose in Florida, in *Community Blood Bank v. Russell*,[15] where the Florida Supreme Court in 1967 remanded for a determination of whether it was possible for the defendant blood bank to have detected hepatitis in the blood it sold. While the court explicitly took no position on whether the detectability of hepatitis in the blood would affect the outcome, Justice Roberts strongly argued in a concurring opinion that the sale of blood by a blood bank was every bit as much of a "sale" for purposes of strict warranty liability as the sale of any other product, and that neither the fact that hepatitis might not be discoverable before the sale nor any other policy should prevent blood suppliers from being strictly liable for harm from defects in the blood they sold.[16] Relying heavily on *Russell*, and persuaded that hepatitis-infected blood was undeniably "defective," the Illinois Supreme Court in *Cunningham v. MacNeal Memorial Hospi-*

---

**6.** See Note, Strict Liability, Negligence and the Standard of Care for Transfusion-Transmitted Disease, 36 Ariz. L. Rev. 473, 513 (1996), citing Langdale, Infectious Complications of Blood Transfusions, 6 Infectious Disease Clinics of North America 731, 732 (1992).

**7.** See Franklin, Tort Liability for Hepatitis: An Analysis and a Proposal, 24 Stan. L. Rev. 439 (1972).

**8.** Id.

**9.** Id.

**10.** Id.

**11.** See § 5.3, above.

**12.** 123 N.E.2d 792 (N.Y. 1954).

**13.** Id. at 793.

**14.** *Perlmutter* is further examined in the sales-service context, at § 16.3, below.

**15.** 196 So.2d 115 (Fla. 1967).

**16.** See id. at 118, 121 (Roberts, J. specially concurring) ("it is more consonant with right and justice to require the Blood Bank to be held absolutely and strictly answerable to the consumers of its product for defects therein, so that the burden of the losses resulting therefrom may be spread among all who benefit from the operation of the blood bank, rather than to require such losses to be borne by the innocent victims alone").

*tal* ruled in 1970 that the supplying hospital was strictly liable in tort regardless of the defendant's inability to detect or prevent the virus.[17]

These developments, and particularly *Cunningham*, were widely criticized on the policy ground that imposing strict liability on blood suppliers who had no way to detect the hepatitis virus would deter the collection and sale of blood and undermine the market in this uniquely valuable commodity that had become so necessary to public health.[18] Not only did other state courts refuse to apply strict liability in tort or warranty to the sale of blood,[19] but the Illinois legislature promptly overruled *Cunningham* by statute.[20] Other state legislatures around the nation, if they had not already done so,[21] enacted similar statutes restricting the responsibility of blood suppliers to negligence. Today, every state exempts blood suppliers from strict liability, in warranty or tort, for supplying infected blood. Almost all states accomplish this exemption from strict products liability through "blood shield statutes," legislation which prohibits strict liability actions by providing that the supply of blood is a service (rather than a sale), or more directly, by stating that the supply of blood does not give rise to liability unless the supplier was at fault.[22] Blood shield statutes may apply broadly to all

**17.** 266 N.E.2d 897 (Ill. 1970). "To allow a defense to strict liability on the ground that there is no way, either practical or theoretical, for a defendant to ascertain the existence of impurities in his product would be to emasculate the doctrine and in a very real sense would signal a return to a negligence theory." Id. at 902. *Cunningham* is examined elsewhere in the context of state of the art. See § 10.4, above.

**18.** See, e.g., Notes, 69 Mich. L. Rev. 1172 (1971); 66 Nw. U.L. Rev. 80 (1971); 24 Vand. L. Rev. 645 (1971).

**19.** See, e.g., McMichael v. American Red Cross, 532 S.W.2d 7 (Ky. 1975); Brody v. Overlook Hosp., 317 A.2d 392 (N.J. Super. Ct. App. Div. 1974), aff'd, 332 A.2d 596 (N.J. 1975). The trial court in *Brody*, reversed on appeal, examined the policy issues and allowed a claim for strict liability in tort. See 296 A.2d 668 (N.J. Super. Law Div. 1972).

**20.** See 745 Ill. Comp. Stat. Ann. 40/2, enacted in 1971, discussed in Glass v. Ingalls Mem. Hosp., 336 N.E.2d 495 (Ill. App. Ct. 1975).

**21.** By the time *Cunningham* was decided in 1970, half the states had already enacted blood shield statutes. See *Cunningham*, 266 N.E.2d at 902.

**22.** See, e.g., Cal. Health & Safety Code § 1606 (procuring and distributing blood is a service); Colo. Rev. Stat. § 13–22–104 (liability without fault inapplicable to blood transactions); Fla. Stat. Ann. § 672.316(5) (procuring, processing, or distributing blood is service); Haw. Rev. Stat. Ann. § 325–91 (no implied warranty that blood is pure in absence of scientific technology to detect possible impurities); Idaho Code § 39–3702 (service, unless provider operates blood bank for profit); 745 Ill. Comp. Stat. Ann. 40/2 (service, not sale, and no warranties or strict liability in tort apply); Ind. Code Ann. § 16–41–12–11 (service); Kan. Stat. Ann. § 65–3701 (no liability without negligence); La. Civ. Code Ann. art. 2322.1 (strict liability inapplicable to nonprofit blood banks); Md. Code Ann., Cts. & Jud. Proc. § 5–630 (no strict liability); Mass. Gen. Laws Ann. ch. 106, § 2–316(5) (service); Mich. Comp. Laws Ann. § 333.9121(2) (service, whether remuneration paid or not); Minn. Stat. Ann. § 525.9221 (service); Nev. Rev. Stat. Ann. 460.010 (no liability without negligence or willful misconduct); N.H. Rev. Stat. Ann. § 507:8–b (no strict liability); N.Y. Pub. Health Law § 580(4) (public health service); Ohio Rev. Code Ann. § 2108.11 (service); 42 Pa. Cons. Stat. Ann. § 8333(a) (no liability without negligence); S.C. Code Ann. § 44–43–10 (implied warranties of merchantability and fitness do not apply); Tex. Civ. Prac. & Rem. Code. Ann. § 77.003 (no liability except for negligence, gross negligence, or intentional tort); Vt. Stat. Ann. 9A § 2–108 (service); Va. Code Ann. § 32.1–297 (no implied warranty actions); Wash. Rev. Code Ann. § 70.54.120 (only negligent or willful conduct); Wis. Stat. Ann. § 146.31 (service, not sale). The statutes are collected in Cantu, A Continuing Whimsical Search for the True Meaning of "Product" in Products Liability Litigation, 35 St. Mary's L. Rev. 331, 345 n.7 (2004). See also Roberts v. Suburban Hosp. Ass'n, Inc., 532 A.2d 1081, 1086 n.3 (Md. Ct. Spec. App. 1987) (AIDS) (listing blood shield law citations for all jurisdictions except N.J.,

kinds of blood and human tissue products, including those manufactured by commercial enterprises.[23]

More recently, litigation has mostly involved AIDS transmitted by transfused blood and blood products. Since the outset of the AIDS epidemic in the late 1970s and early 1980s, about 10,000 people in the United States have contracted HIV/AIDS by blood transfusion, blood components, or tissue.[24] Not until 1984 did the medical community learn that AIDS was transmitted by blood, and a reliable test for the presence of the virus in blood first became available in 1985.[25] The various collection, testing, and heat-treating procedures devised during the mid–1980s now permit virtually 100% assurance of avoiding, killing, or detecting the virus if due care is exercised. Hence, most such cases today are decided on the basis of negligence, and, because of the blood shield statutes, strict liability in tort or warranty generally is not involved at all.[26] Yet, because of the difficulties of proof of negligence, such claims generally fail.[27]

Vt., & D.C.); Annot., 75 A.L.R.5th (2000) (validity and construction of blood shield statutes).

New Jersey and the District of Columbia appear to be the only jurisdictions without blood shield statutes, and their case law accomplishes the same result. See Fisher v. Sibley Mem'l Hosp., 403 A.2d 1130, 1134 (D.C. App. 1979) ("characterizing blood plasma as a product governed by strict tort liability is as unnatural as forcing a blood transfusion into the commercial sales mode"); Brody v. Overlook Hosp., 317 A.2d 392 (N.J. Super. App. Div. 1974), aff'd, 332, 596 (N.J. 1975) (no liability under strict liability in tort for undiscoverable defect). Some courts have held that strict liability is applicable in certain situations. See, e.g., JKB v. Armour Pharm. Co., 660 N.E.2d 602, 605 (Ind. Ct. App. 1996) (statute does not protect pharmaceutical company when production is for commercial use); Rogers v. Miles Lab., Inc., 802 P.2d 1346, 1349 (Wash. 1991) (statute does not protect paid donors).

**23.** See, e.g., Scher v. Bayer Corp., 258 F.Supp.2d 190 (E.D.N.Y. 2003) (strict liability in tort and warranty claims dismissed against commercial supplier of allegedly defective blood derivative product, Hyp–Rho(D), used to prevent hemolytic disease in newborn children of Rh–Negative mothers and Rh–Positive fathers; case allowed to proceed on negligence claims). See Products Liability Restatement § 19(c) ("Human blood and human tissue, even when provided commercially, are not subject to the rules of this Restatement.").

**24.** See United States HIV & AIDS Statistics, by Exposure Category, www.avert. org, (statistics through Dec. 2002).

**25.** For public health responses to AIDS, see Trebilcock, House, and Daniels, Do Institutions Matter? A Comparative Pathology of the HIV–Infected Blood Tragedy, 82 Va. L. Rev. 1407 (1996), critiqued, Glied, Markets Matter: U.S. Responses to the HIV–Infected Blood Tragedy, 82 Va. L. Rev. 1493 (1996); Eckert, The AIDS Blood–Transfusion Cases: A Legal and Economic Analysis of Liability, 29 San Diego L. Rev. 203, 295–98 (1992) (chronology); Kozup v. Georgetown Univ., 663 F.Supp. 1048 (D.D.C.1987), rev'd on other grounds, 851 F.2d 437 (D.C. Cir. 1988) (chronicling developments in AIDS research).

**26.** See, e.g., Christiana v. Southern Baptist Hosp., 867 So.2d 809 (La. App. 2004) (blood shield law in effect at time of transfusion protected hospital that supplied blood from patient's strict liability claim); Spann v. Irwin Mem. Blood Centers, 40 Cal.Rptr.2d 360 (Ct. App. 1995); Brown v. United Blood Services, 858 P.2d 391 (Nev. 1993).

**27.** See, e.g., Johnson v. American Nat'l Red Cross, 578 S.E.2d 106 (Ga. 2003) (negligence claims against blood bank for HIV and fear of HIV failed); Advincula v. United Blood Services, 678 N.E.2d 1009 (Ill. 1996) (blood bank's conduct should have been measured against professional standard of care according to state of the art at time of injury). *But see* Snyder v. American Ass'n of Blood Banks, 676 A.2d 1036 (N.J. 1996) (allowing claim against association of blood banks for negligently setting standards for prevention of AIDS).

## § 16.10  MISCELLANEOUS TRANSACTIONS AND PRODUCTS

Because of the attraction of not having to prove negligence in strict products liability cases, plaintiffs often attempt to stretch the strict liability doctrine well beyond the paradigm case of a commercial sale of a new chattel.[1] Most recurring types of miscellaneous transactions and products have been treated in this and the previous chapter. Already examined, for example, is the applicability of strict products liability to franchise transactions,[2] auction sales,[3] financial lease arrangements, electricity, real estate, publications, blood, and various other non-sale transactions.[4] Two special, recurring situations remain to be considered here: casual sales and animals.

### Casual Sales

It is fundamental that strict liability in tort[5] is applicable only to harm from products that have been commercially distributed. The *Restatement (Second) of Torts* § 402A applies only if "the seller is engaged in the business of selling such a product,"[6] and the *Products Liability Restatement*, which applies only to commercial transactions in the normal course of business, explicitly excludes "casual sales."[7] Accordingly, as discussed above,[8] courts have refused to apply strict products liability to occasional commercial sales of a used tractor,[9] an airplane,[10] or machinery of various types.[11] There is even less reason, of course, to

### § 16.10

**1.** See generally Cantu, A Continuing Whimsical Search for the True Meaning of the Term "Product" in Products Liability Litigation, 35 St. Mary's L.J. 341 (2004); Lannetti, Toward a Revised Definition of "Product" under the Restatement (Third) of Torts: Products Liability, 55 Bus. Law. 799 (2000); Cantu, Twenty–Five Years of Strict Product Liability Law: The Transformation and Present Meaning of Section 402A, 25 St. Mary's L.J. 327 (1993); Cantu, The Illusive Meaning of the Term "Product" Under Section 402A of the Restatement (Second) of Torts, 44 Okla. L. Rev. 635 (1991).

**2.** See § 15.4, above.

**3.** See § 15.7, above.

**4.** See §§ 16.2–16.9, above.

**5.** The same principle applies to claims for breach of the implied warranty of merchantability, under Article 2 of the Uniform Commercial Code, which applies to sales of goods only "if the seller is a merchant with respect to goods of that kind." UCC § 2–314(1).

**6.** Restatement (2d) Torts § 402A(1)(a).

**7.** See Products Liability Restatement § 1 cmt. *c* (stating that defect rule "applies only to manufacturers and other commercial sellers and distributors who are engaged in the business of selling or otherwise distributing the type of product that harmed the plaintiff"):

It is not necessary that a commercial seller or distributor be engaged exclusively or even primarily in selling or otherwise distributing the type of product that injured the plaintiff, so long as the sale of the product is other than occasional or casual. Thus, the rule applies to a motion picture theater's routine sales of popcorn or ice cream, either for consumption on the premises or in packages to be taken home. Similarly, a service station that does mechanical repair work on cars may also sell tires and automobile equipment as part of its regular business. Such sales are subject to the rule in this Section. However, the rule does not cover occasional sales (frequently referred to as "casual sales") outside the regular course of the seller's business. Thus, an occasional sale of surplus equipment by a business does not fall within the ambit of this rule. Whether a defendant is a commercial seller or distributor within the meaning of this Section is usually a question of law to be determined by the court.

**8.** See §§ 5.3 and 15.7, above.

**9.** See, e.g., Clute v. Paquin, 631 N.Y.S.2d 463 (App. Div. 1995).

**10.** See, e.g., Nastasi v. Hochman, 396 N.Y.S.2d 216 (App. Div. 1977) (isolated lease of plane with defective strobe light system by lingerie manufacturer which owned plane).

**11.** See, e.g., McGraw v. Furon Co., 812 So.2d 273 (Ala. 2001) (occasional sellers are not "manufacturers" under Alabama

apply strict products liability against a private party who, on one occasion, sells his neighbor a pound of sugar or his car.[12]

## Animals

The cases are split on whether strict liability in tort applies to animals.[13] Most courts have held that "living things do not constitute 'products' within the scope of the strict tort liability doctrine which requires that a product's nature be fixed when it leaves the manufacturer's or seller's control."[14] Thus, courts have been particularly reluctant to hold defendants subject to liability for the natural proclivities in animals, such as the tendency of a "fractious" horse to expand its chest while being saddled[15] or a dog to bite.[16] But negligence remains a viable claim in the case of a fractious horse,[17] and most courts have allowed recovery on some basis for the sale of animals infected with diseases that are transmitted to the owner, sometimes on the theory that the animal is a defective product[18] and sometimes on simple negligence principles

products liability statute); Gebo v. Black Clawson Co., 703 N.E.2d 1234 (N.Y. 1998) (embossing machine; casual seller's only obligation is to warn of hidden defects known to seller); Griffin Indus., Inc. v. Jones, 975 S.W.2d 100, 103 (Ky. 1998) (screw conveyor system; no strict liability when product sold only on occasion or incident to seller's business); Geboy v. TRL Inc., 159 F.3d 993, 997 (7th Cir. 1998) (Wis. law) (vertical boring mill; "a seller who does not place or maintain a product in the stream of commerce and who has neither created nor assumed the risk of harm for a defective product is not strictly liable"). See also Sprung v. MTR Ravensburg Inc., 788 N.E.2d 620, 623 (N.Y. 2003) (" 'casual' or 'occasional' sales are not subject to claims of strict liability"; but custom fabricator of retractable floor sold in ordinary course of business subject to strict liability); Burns v. Haines Equip., Inc., 726 N.Y.S.2d 516 (App. Div. 2001) (casual lessor not strictly liable for injury caused by product).

**12.** See Restatement (2d) Torts § 402A cmt. *f.*

**13.** See Annot., 63 A.L.R.4th 127 (1988) (live animal as "product" for products liability).

**14.** Kaplan v. C Lazy U Ranch, 615 F.Supp. 234 (D. Colo. 1985) (horse not "product"). See also Malicki v. Koci, 700 N.E.2d 913, 915 (Ohio Ct. App. 1997) (parakeet not product; sellers should not be held "as absolute insurers of the health of a living organism whose health can be affected by many factors totally outside the defendant's control"); Latham v. Wal–Mart Stores, Inc., 818 S.W.2d 673, 676 (Mo. Ct. App. 1991) (parrot not product; "due to their mutability and their tendency to be affected by the purchaser, animals should

not be products under § 402A as a matter of law"); Anderson v. Farmers Hybrid Cos., 408 N.E.2d 1194 (Ill. App. Ct. 1980) (unbred female pigs not products); Whitmer v. Schneble, 331 N.E.2d 115 (Ill. App. Ct. 1975) (dog not product).

**15.** See Kaplan v. C Lazy U Ranch, 615 F.Supp. 234 (D. Colo. 1985).

**16.** See, e.g., Blaha v. Stuard, 640 N.W.2d 85, 89 (S.D. 2002) (yellow Labrador retriever: "living creatures have no fixed nature and cannot be products as a matter of law"); Whitmer v. Schneble, 331 N.E.2d 115 (Ill. App. Ct. 1975) (after giving birth, Doberman bit child).

**17.** See Kaplan v. C Lazy U Ranch, 615 F.Supp. 234 (D. Colo. 1985).

**18.** See, e.g., Johnson v. William Benedict, Inc., 1993 WL 408058 (Conn. Super. Ct. 1993) (ducklings infected with salmonella bacteria passed disease to plaintiff's child; "products" under state products liability statute); Worrell v. Sachs, 563 A.2d 1387 (Conn. Super. Ct. 1989) (child suffered eye damage from diseased, parasite-carrying puppy purchased from defendant's pet shop; puppy was "product" under products liability statute); Sease v. Taylor's Pets, Inc., 700 P.2d 1054 (Or. Ct. App. 1985) (pet shop skunk was "product"); Beyer v. Aquarium Supply Co., 404 N.Y.S.2d 778, 779 (Sup. Ct. 1977) ("[t]he risk presented to human well being by a diseased animal is as great and probably greater than that created by a defectively manufactured product").

Animals may be considered "goods" under the Uniform Commercial Code. See, e.g., Blaha v. Stuard, 640 N.W.2d 85 (S.D. 2002) (dog); Flanagan v. Consolidated Nutrition, L.C., 627 N.W.2d 573 (Iowa Ct. App. 2001) (pigs); Trad Inds., Ltd. v. Brogan, 805

such as the failure to warn.[19] The *Products Liability Restatement* takes the position that "when a living animal is sold commercially in a diseased condition and causes harm to other property or to persons, the animal constitutes a product for purposes of this Restatement."[20]

P.2d 54 (Mont. 1991) (elk); Claxton v. Boothe, 790 P.2d 1201 (Or. Ct. App. 1990) (horse); Vince v. Broome, 443 So.2d 23 (Miss. 1983) (cattle).

**19.**  See, e.g., Malicki v. Koci, 700 N.E.2d 913 (Ohio Ct. App. 1997) (plaintiffs caught parrot fever from parakeet bought from pet store).

**20.**  Products Liability Restatement § 19 cmt. *b*.

# Chapter 17

---

# AUTOMOTIVE LITIGATION

*Table of Sections*

---

## § 17.1  AUTOMOTIVE LITIGATION—GENERALLY

Many cases involve claims against manufacturers of cars, sport utility vehicles, vans, trucks, motorcycles, and other vehicles alleging that defective conditions in such products caused injuries to the plaintiffs.[1] The usual victims in such accidents are drivers and passengers in the defective vehicles, but sometimes an accident vehicle (or some portion thereof) injures someone in another vehicle[2] or who is merely standing nearby.[3] Automotive products liability cases may be divided into two major categories: (1) accidents caused by automotive defects,[4] and

---

### § 17.1

**1.** On automotive products liability generally, see Nader and Page, Automobile–Design Liability and Compliance with Federal Standards, 64 Geo. Wash. L. Rev. 415 (1996); Sugarman, Nader's Failures?, 80 Cal. L. Rev. 289 (1992) (reviewing J. Marshaw and D. Harfst, The Struggle for Auto Safety (1990)); DeDominicis, No Duty at Any Speed?: Determining the Responsibility of the Automobile Manufacturer in Speed–Related Accidents, 14 Hofstra L. Rev. 403 (1986); Symposium, Products Liability Law and Motor Vehicle Design, 14 U. of Tol. L. Rev. 301 (1983); Nader and Page, Automobile Design and the Judicial Process, 55 Cal. L. Rev. 645 (1967); Katz, Liability of Automobile Manufacturers for Unsafe Design of Passenger Cars, 69 Harv. L. Rev. 863 (1956); 7 Am. Law Prod. Liab. 3d. ch. 95 Automobiles.

**2.** See Great Dane Trailers, Inc. v. Estate of Wells, 52 S.W.3d 737 (Tex. 2001) (products liability and negligence action by

estate of motorist killed in collision with tractor-trailer that was allegedly defective because it was not equipped with "conspicuity" devices); Duren v. Paccar, Inc., 549 S.E.2d 755 (Ga. Ct. App. 2001)(products liability claim for motorist killed in collision with jack-knifed tractor-trailer that was allegedly defective because it was not equipped with anti-lock brakes).

**3.** See e.g., Bourgeois v. Garrard Chevrolet, Inc., 811 So.2d 962 (La. Ct. App. 2002) (products liability claim by police officer injured by police vehicle with allegedly defective brakes); Ogletree v. Navistar Int'l Transp. Corp., 535 S.E.2d 545 (Ga. Ct. App. 2000) (negligence action for pedestrian killed when backed over by fertilizer spreader that was allegedly defective because it was not equipped with back-up alarm); Haumersen v. Ford Motor Co., 257 N.W.2d 7 (Iowa 1977) (strict liability claim for child in school yard struck by defective car).

**4.** See § 17.2, below.

(2) aggravated injuries caused by a vehicle's failure to be sufficiently "crashworthy" to protect its occupants in an accident.[5]

In many respects, automotive products liability cases are no different from any other type of products liability case: a plaintiff normally must prove that some manufacturing, design, or warning defect, or some false assertion by the manufacturer, caused the plaintiff's harm. An automotive manufacturer typically defends cases of this type in conventional fashion, by claiming that the accident was attributable to something other than a product defect, such as the driver's careless use. But the issues that often control the outcome of automotive products liability litigation—automotive crashworthiness, apportionment of damages, and the role of plaintiff fault—frequently involve certain special applications of, and limitations on, the general rules of products liability law. Thus, while much of the applicable doctrine in products liability cases involving automobiles is identical to that applied in other types of products liability cases, enough special issues occur in the automotive context to warrant their separate examination.

This chapter explores the most important, recurring issues in automotive products liability law.[6] By causing crashes, defects in tires and other automotive components may become integral to automotive products liability litigation, as illustrated by the rash of accidents involving Ford Explorers and other vehicles equipped with defective Firestone tires some time ago.[7] Since liability issues for manufacturers of tires and other automotive components are generally the same as in cases involving components of other types of products,[8] the discussion here does not address the liability of manufacturers of such components. This chapter instead is limited to an examination of the principal recurring theories of liability and of defense based on driver fault in accident litigation against manufacturers of automotive vehicles.[9] A number of more general issues examined in other chapters, such as product recalls,[10] federal preemption,[11] and punitive damages,[12] often play a major role in automotive products liability litigation, and the treatment of those issues in other chapters should be referred to as appropriate.

Section 17.2 examines the kinds of automotive defects, such as defects in a vehicle's steering, brakes, acceleration system, transmission, and other design features that can cause automotive accidents. Section 17.3 considers the nature and historical development of the doctrine of

---

**5.** See § 17.3, below.

**6.** Crashworthiness and other liability principles and defenses ordinarily apply to a manufacturer's responsibility for accidents involving other types of vehicles, such as airplanes, tractors, and boats. See, e.g., Deere & Co. v. Grose, 586 So.2d 196 (Ala. 1991) (tractor should have been equipped with ROPS); Rose v. Mercury Marine, 483 So.2d 1351 (Miss. 1986) (swimmer injured by propeller of boat allowed to assert claim against manufacturer of boat's engine); Bruce v. Martin–Marietta Corp., 544 F.2d 442 (10th Cir. 1976) (Md. law) (airplane); 3 Frumer and Friedman, Products Liability § 21.02 (collecting cases regarding various

products and crashworthiness claims). The liability principles applied in these cases are generally identical or analogous to those applied in cases involving automotive vehicles.

**7.** See Yates, Tire Hysteria Veers Out of Control, Wall St. J., Aug. 15, 2000, at A18.

**8.** See § 15.3, above.

**9.** Liability issues involving used car dealers are examined in § 16.5, above.

**10.** See § 10.8, above.

**11.** See § 14.4, above.

**12.** See ch. 18, below.

automotive crashworthiness. Section 17.4 explores apportionment issues that arise when responsibility for an accident is shared by an automotive manufacturer and another party. Finally, § 17.5 examines the role of plaintiff fault in automotive products liability litigation, including the effect of a driver's intoxication and the consequence of a plaintiff's failure to use a seatbelt or other safety device.

## § 17.2  DEFECTS WHICH CAUSE ACCIDENTS

Many automotive products liability cases involve accidents that allegedly result from some defect in the vehicle. As discussed below, many of these cases allege that the accident was caused by a manufacturing defect, some allege that the vehicle was defectively designed, and others allege that the manufacturer failed to provide adequate warnings or instructions. Although a vehicle's general design features may lead to accidents in certain situations, as by generating a propensity to roll over, most of the cases considered in this section involve claims of defects in one of a vehicle's essential control mechanisms or components, such as its steering, brakes, accelerator, transmission, engine, suspension system, and wheels or tires.

### Manufacturing Defect Claims

Two of the most renowned products liability cases of all time, *MacPherson v. Buick Motor Co.*[1] and *Henningsen v. Bloomfield Motors, Inc.*,[2] arose out of manufacturing defects in automobiles which caused the cars to crash. *MacPherson* involved a twenty-two horsepower Buick runabout equipped with wooden wheels, one of which was made of brittle, coarse-grained hickory, which caused the wheel to break and the car to crash.[3] The plaintiff claimed that Buick Motor Company had been negligent in failing to test or inspect the wheel sufficiently for defects, and Buick contended that its limited testing and inspection process was sufficient because of the reputation of its supplier, a wheel manufacturer, for making high quality wheels.[4] A modern analogue is Ford Motor Company's plight from having equipped its Explorer SUVs with Firestone tires with treads that had a tendency to peel off at highway speeds.[5] The other classic products liability case, *Henningsen*, involved a mechanical defect in the steering mechanism of a Plymouth Plaza 6 Club Sedan which caused the car to veer off the highway and hit a brick wall, injuring Mrs. Henningsen and destroying the car.[6]

**§ 17.2**

**1.** 111 N.E. 1050 (N.Y. 1916). Affirming judgment on a verdict for the plaintiff, Judge Cardozo concluded:

> We think the defendant was not absolved from a duty of inspection because it bought the wheels from a reputable manufacturer.... It was a manufacturer of automobiles. It was responsible for the finished product. It was not at liberty to put the finished product on the market without subjecting the component parts to ordinary and simple tests.

Id. at 1055. *MacPherson* is discussed in § 1.3, above.

**2.** 161 A.2d 69 (N.J. 1960) (Francis, J.). *Henningsen* is discussed in § 5.2, above.

**3.** See D. Peck, Decision at Law 40–64 (1961). For other discussions of this case, see § 1.3 note 72, above.

**4.** See id.; MacPherson v. Buick Motor Co., 111 N.E. 1050 (N.Y. 1916).

**5.** States Launch Investigation of Tire Recall, Wall St. J., Sept. 26, 2000, at A3.

**6.** 161 A.2d at 75.

When the sudden malfunction of a new vehicle leads to a crash, as in both *MacPherson* and *Henningsen*, the cause of the accident is usually some type of manufacturing defect, although it may be some defect in design. Especially if the vehicle is badly damaged, it may be difficult (if not impossible) to discover precisely what went wrong. In such cases, a plaintiff may be assisted by res ipsa loquitur[7] or the malfunction doctrine,[8] previously discussed. Although accident reconstructionists frequently disagree, such experts are usually able to ascertain the precise manufacturing or design defect that caused a crash. Cases involving claims that manufacturing defects caused an accident include claims of defects in a vehicle's steering,[9] brakes,[10] accelerator,[11] transmission,[12] engine,[13] suspension system,[14] and wheels or tires.[15]

**7.** See § 2.5, above.

**8.** See § 7.4, above.

**9.** See, e.g., Smith v. Ford Motor Co., 215 F.3d 713 (7th Cir. 2000) (Ind. law) (driver lost control of Ford Econoline 150 van; design and manufacturing defects in steering gearbox); Morehead v. Ford Motor Co., 694 So.2d 650 (La. Ct. App. 1997) (1997 Ford F–150 pickup rolled over when driver lost control due to steering malfunction allegedly caused by defect of intermediate steering shaft comprised of two tubes that pulled apart at joint between them); Roman v. General Motors Corp., 727 F.Supp. 1153 (N.D. Ill. 1989) (driver lost control of 1987 Chevy Spectrum); Landahl v. Chrysler Corp., 534 N.Y.S.2d 245 (App. Div. 1988); Hill v. International Harvester Co., 798 F.2d 256 (7th Cir. 1986) (Ill. law) (driver of truck lost control when he heard snap from right front of truck; front tires splayed when truck came to rest); Stackiewicz v. Nissan Motor Corp., 686 P.2d 925 (Nev. 1984) (plaintiff heard clicking noise in steering column of Datsun B210 and steering locked); Annot., 3 A.L.R.3d 158 (1980) (defects in steering systems); 7 Am. Law Prod. Liab. 3d §§ 95.137–95.163 (defects grouped by elements of steering system).

**10.** See, e.g., Bombard v. General Motors Corp., 238 F.Supp.2d 464 (N.D.N.Y. 2002) (claim that anti-lock braking switch was negligently designed and manufactured); Aldridge v. King's Colonial Ford, Inc., 550 S.E.2d 439 (Ga. Ct. App. 2001) (claim that brakes were defective because brake pedal had improper resistance and would touch floor); MacDonald v. General Motors Corp., 784 F.Supp. 486 (M.D. Tenn. 1992) (claim that brakes of van defective in that axle seal allowed fluid to enter brake system); Kirchoff v. International Harvester Co., 526 N.Y.S.2d 238 (App. Div. 1988) (claim that truck brake failure was caused by hole in brake line); Arslanian v. Volkswagen of Am., Inc., 493 N.Y.S.2d 588 (App. Div. 1985) (claim that master cylinder union in brake system improperly assembled); Bohannon v. Chrysler Motors Corp., 366

F.Supp. 802 (S.D. Miss. 1973) (defective brake drum out of round from manufacture); Annot., 99 A.L.R.3d 179 (1980) (brake system defects); 7 Am. Law Prod. Liab. 3d, §§ 95.55–95.73 (defects grouped by elements of braking system).

**11.** See, e.g., Ferro v. Volkswagen of Am., Inc., 588 A.2d 1047 (R.I. 1991) (claim of manufacturing defect in accelerator pedal in 1978 Audi 5000S); Foster v. Craig Equip. Co., 550 So.2d 818 (La. Ct. App. 1989) (misaligned accelerator pedal on school bus could slide past stop and cause throttle to remain in open position); Treadwell Ford, Inc. v. Campbell, 485 So.2d 312 (Ala. 1986) (defective accelerator linkage caused truck to surge forward); Wright v. General Motors Corp., 717 S.W.2d 153 (Tex. App. 1986) (rubber flap cut off accelerator pedal which allowed pedal to stick under floor covering); Annot., 60 A.L.R.4th 20 (1988) (sudden or unexpected acceleration of motor vehicle); 7 Am. Law Prod. Liab. 3d § 95.106 (acceleration problems).

**12.** See, e.g., Davis v. Ford Motor Co., 128 F.3d 631 (8th Cir. 1997) (Ark. law) (parking gear released in defective Ford transmission); Ford Motor Co. v. Burdeshaw, 661 So.2d 236 (Ala. 1995) (claim of defective manufacture of transmission in 1978 Ford pick up); Hall v. Chrysler Corp., 526 F.2d 350 (5th Cir. 1976) (La. law) (misrouted transmission cable on truck); Ault v. International Harvester Co., 528 P.2d 1148 (Cal. 1974) (failure in gear box of Scout); Annot., 100 A.L.R.3d 471 (1980) (transmission defects); 7 Am. Law Prod. Liab. 3d § 95.170 (self-shifting transmissions).

**13.** See, e.g., Delvecchio v. General Motors Corp., 625 N.E.2d 1022 (Ill. App. Ct. 1993) (engine stall caused by malfunction in engine throttle system); Nutting v. Ford Motor Co., 584 N.Y.S.2d 653 (App. Div. 1992) (claim that manufacturing defect caused engine to stall).

**14.** See, e.g., Norton v. Ford Motor Co., 470 F.2d 992 (5th Cir. 1972) (Tex. law)

**15.** See note 15 on page 1076.

### Design Defect Claims

Design defects are the other principal cause of automotive accidents claimed in products liability litigation. Since design defects by their nature infect the entire product line, threatening the safety of thousands of persons, some have become quite notorious. Control problems in the Corvair, publicized by Ralph Nader in the 1960s in *Unsafe at Any Speed*, is one example.[16] Accelerator sticking problems in certain Audis led to claims in the 1970s,[17] as did the roll-over tendencies of certain Jeeps[18] in the 1970s and 1980s; the Suzuki Samurai,[19] the Ford Bronco II,[20] and other SUVs[21] in the 1980s and 1990s;[22] and the Ford Explorer in the late 1990s and early 2000s.[23] This latter form of litigation resulted from the relatively high center of gravity in many SUVs, combined with their narrow track width and sometimes light weight, which made some models quite unstable and apt to roll over in sharp steering maneuvers at highway speeds.[24]

Ford Motor Company[25] encountered a rash of litigation during the 1970s and 1980s from the tendency of some of its transmissions to slip

(spindle nut on right front wheel defectively manufactured); Annot., 100 A.L.R.3d 912 (1980) (collecting cases); Jenkins v. General Motors Corp., 446 F.2d 377 (5th Cir. 1971) (Ga. law) (improperly tightened nut in suspension system); Ford Motor Co. v. Conrardy, 488 P.2d 219 (Colo. Ct. App. 1971) (corroded control arm); 7 American Law of Products Liability 3d §§ 95.137–95.163 (collecting cases).

**15.** See, e.g., Cooper Tire and Rubber Co. v. Tuckier, 826 So.2d 679 (Miss. 2002) (tire); MacPherson v. Buick Motor Co., 111 N.E. 1050 (N.Y. 1916) (wheel); Annot., 81 A.L.R.3d 318 (1977) (collecting cases).

**16.** See e.g., Faust v. General Motors Corp., 377 A.2d 885 (N.H. 1977); Chart v. General Motors Corp., 258 N.W.2d 680 (Wis. 1977); Cardulo v. General Motors Corp., 378 F.Supp. 890 (E.D. Pa. 1974); Jenkins v. General Motors Corp., 446 F.2d 377 (5th Cir. 1971) (Ga. law); Selmo v. Baratono, 184 N.W.2d 367 (Mich. Ct. App. 1970).

**17.** See, e.g., Ferro v. Volkswagen of Am., Inc., 588 A.2d 1047 (R.I. 1991); Bradofsky v. Volkswagen of Am., Inc., 17 Prod. Liab. Advisory 5 (N.D. Ohio 1988); Rose v. Volkswagen of Am., Inc., 17 Prod. Liab. Advisory 5 (La. Super. Ct. 1988); Gibbs v. Volkswagen, 13 Prod. Liab. Advisory 5 (N.J. Super. St. 1988).

**18.** See, e.g., 7A Am. Law Prod. Liab. 3d § 97.29 (Jeep roll-over accidents).

**19.** See, e.g., Rodriguez v. Suzuki Motor Co., 936 S.W.2d 104 (Mo. 1996) ($50 million punitive damages verdict for passenger injured in rollover of Suzuki Samurai); 7A Am. Law Prod. Liab. 3d § 97.30 (Suzuki Samurai).

**20.** See, e.g., Clay v. Ford Motor Co., 215 F.3d 663, 671 (6th Cir. 2000) (Ohio law); Ford Motor Co. v. Ammerman, 705 N.E.2d 539 (Ind. Ct. App. 1999); 7A Am. Law Prod. Liab. 3d § 95.27 (Ford Bronco II's).

**21.** See, e.g., Jonas v. Isuzu Motors Ltd., 210 F.Supp.2d 1373, 1381 (M.D. Ga. 2002) (1993 Isuzu Rodeo); McCathern v. Toyota Motor Corp., 23 P.3d 320, 333 (Or. 2001) (1994 Toyota 4Runner); Dorsett v. American Isuzu Motors, Inc., 805 F.Supp. 1212 (E.D. Pa. 1992) (Isuzu Trooper II); 7A Am. Law Prod. Liab. 3d § 95.28 (Isuzu Trooper IIs).

**22.** See Bradsher, Auto Industry Lessens its Resistance to Rollover Ratings, N.Y. Times, Sept. 19, 2000 (rollovers kill 9,500 of 42,000 Americans who die each year).

**23.** Most of these resulted from blowouts of allegedly defective Firestone tires. See, e.g., In re Bridgestone/Firestone, Inc., Tires Prods. Liab. Litig., 287 F.Supp.2d 943, 943 (S.D. Ind. 2003); McDonald, Don't Tread on Me: Faster Than a Tire Blowout, Congress Passes Wide-Sweeping Legislation That Treads on the Thirty-Five Year Old Motor Vehicle Safety Act, 49 Buff. L. Rev. 1163 (2001); Bradsher, Ford Begins a Recall of 13 Million Tires, N.Y. Times, May 23, 2001, at C1; White et al., Ford Intends to Replace Millions of Tires, Wall. St. J., May 23, 2001, at A3.

**24.** See, e.g., McCathern v. Toyota Motor Corp., 23 P.3d 320, 333 (Or. 2001); Clay v. Ford Motor Co., 215 F.3d 663, 671 (6th Cir. 2000) (Ohio law).

**25.** Ford transmissions may have had the biggest problem along these lines, but transmissions in other vehicles sometimes

from Park to Reverse. Accidents could occur when the driver tried to place the gear shift lever in Park but mispositioned it on the gatepost between Park and Reverse. If the driver then left the car with the engine running, the vibration from the engine or the door slamming could cause the transmission to slip into Reverse. In particular, plaintiffs' experts testified that the shape and height of the gatepost and the design of the springs involved made it much more likely that the Ford FMX transmission would accidentally slip into Reverse as compared to transmissions in other cars. For example, in *Ford Motor Co. v. Nowak*,[26] the plaintiff's decedent drove into her driveway, stopped the car, attempted to shift the car into Park, stepped out of the car, and went behind it to close the driveway gate. The transmission slipped from Park to Reverse, and the car ran over the decedent. Many other cases were based on similar claims.[27]

Other cases in which a design defect allegedly caused an accident include claims of defects in a vehicle's steering,[28] brakes,[29] accelerator,[30] transmission,[31] engine (stalls),[32] suspension system,[33] and wheels or tires.[34]

---

experience similar problems. See, e.g., General Motors Corp. v. Sanchez, 997 S.W.2d 584 (Tex. 1999) (1990 Chevy pickup); Klein v. BMW of North Am., Inc., 705 So.2d 1200 (La. Ct. App. 1997); Hunter v. Benson Chevrolet Co., 572 So.2d 672 (La. Ct. App. 1990) (1983 Chevrolet Citation); 7 Am. Law Prod. Liab. 3d. § 95.170 (self-shifting transmissions).

**26.** 638 S.W.2d 582 (Tex. App. 1982) (5–1 decision) (affirming $400,000 pecuniary damages and $4,000,000 punitive damages awards). The gatepost is diagramed in id. at 586–87.

**27.** See, e.g., Sand Hill Energy, Inc. v. Ford Motor Co., 83 S.W.3d 483, 494 (Ky. 2002) (transmission slipped from park to reverse, crushing to death employee who was unloading bags from bed of F–250 pickup truck), vacated and remanded, Sand Hill Energy, Inc. v. Smith, 142 S.W.3d 153 (Ky. 2004); Pappas v. Ford Motor Co., 7 F.Supp.2d 22 (D.D.C. 1998) (transmission slipped into reverse, crushing plaintiff attempting to help jump-start another car); Davis v. Ford Motor Co., 128 F.3d 631 (8th Cir. 1997) (Ark. law) (plaintiff injured when Ford Explorer parked on 3.5% grade rolled backward and crushed her leg); Ford Motor Co. v. Burdeshaw, 661 So.2d 236 (Ala. 1995) (garbage truck shifted from neutral to reverse, shot backward, and crushed employee); Kallio v. Ford Motor Co., 407 N.W.2d 92 (Minn. 1987) (plaintiff crushed while stopped in middle of road when pickup shifted to reverse); Ford Motor Co. v. Bartholomew, 297 S.E.2d 675 (Va. 1982) (affirming but remitting damages of person slightly injured when she fell while chasing car that slipped into reverse); Ford Motor Co. v. Nowak, 638 S.W.2d 582 (Tex. App.

1982) (woman crushed when car rolled over her while attempting to open garage door). See generally Branton, From "Park" to "Reverse"—The Costly Slip, Trial 42 (Nov. 1978).

**28.** See, e.g., Halvorsen v. Ford Motor Co., 522 N.Y.S.2d 272 (App. Div. 1987).

**29.** See, e.g., Bourgeois v. Garrard Chevrolet, Inc., 811 So.2d 962, 963 (La. Ct. App. 2002) (worn tire and low air pressure, combined with sticking caliper, allegedly caused ABS brakes to function improperly); Duren v. Paccar, Inc., 549 S.E.2d 755 (Ga. Ct. App. 2001) (tractor-trailer allegedly defective because it was not equipped with anti-lock brakes); Brooks v. Chrysler Corp., 786 F.2d 1191 (D.C. Cir. 1986) (lip-in dust boot permitted junk to enter caliper bore).

**30.** See, e.g., Jarvis v. Ford Motor Co., 283 F.3d 33 (2d Cir. 2002) (N.Y. law) (design defect in cruise control allegedly caused sudden acceleration in six-day-old minivan); Nissan Motor Co., Ltd. v. Armstrong, 32 S.W.3d 701 (Tex. App. 2000) (design defect allegedly caused unintended acceleration), rev'd, 145 S.W.3d 131 (Tex. 2004); Smith v. Ford Motor Co., 215 F.3d 713 (7th Cir. 2000) (Ind. law) (design defect in steering gearbox); Roman v. General Motors Corp., 727 F.Supp. 1153 (N.D. Ill. 1989) (loss of steering in toll booth); Annot., 100 A.L.R.3d 158 (1980) (collecting cases).

**31.** See, e.g., General Motors Corp. v. Sanchez, 997 S.W.2d 584 (Tex. 1999) (defective design allowed transmission to slip into "hydraulic neutral"); Pappas v. Ford Motor Co., 7 F.Supp.2d 22 (D.D.C. 1998) (design defect in gearbox caused shift from park to reverse); Kallio v. Ford Motor Co., 407 N.W.2d 92 (Minn. 1987) (improper design of

**32–34.** See notes 32–34 on page 1078.

## Warning and Instruction Defect Claims

Warning and instruction defect claims are less common than manufacturing and design defect claims in this context. Indeed, in automotive as well as other types of products liability litigation,[35] defective warning claims normally piggy-back on underlying claims of some deficiency in a vehicle's design. For example, although the Park–Reverse litigation against Ford mentioned earlier involved an allegedly defective design of the transmission's gatepost and springs, the danger would have been reduced had drivers known that their transmissions could slip out of gear if they did not take particular caution to assure that their shift levers were carefully secured in Park before leaving their vehicles. Accordingly, in addition to allegations of design defectiveness, the transmission-slip cases typically included claims that Ford failed to provide adequate warnings and instructions to operators of the vehicles.[36]

Similarly, roll-over cases properly involve warning and instruction defect claims in addition to allegations of a vehicle's design deficiency. For example, the manufacturer's failure to warn of the risk was a central claim in *Greiner v. Volkswagenwerk Aktiengesellschaft*,[37] which involved the propensity of old-model Volkswagen beetles to roll over on sharp steering maneuvers. The failure to warn of this propensity was also a principal claim in the roll-over litigation involving the Bronco II,[38] discussed above, especially before prominent warnings were required by the National Highway Traffic Safety Administration.[39] Other claims of an automotive manufacturer's failure to adequately warn or instruct

automatic transmission shifting mechanism); Ford Motor Co. v. Bartholomew, 297 S.E.2d 675 (Va. 1982) (defective design allowed transmission to slip into "hydraulic neutral"); Ford Motor Co. v. Nowak, 638 S.W.2d 582 (Tex. App. 1982) (defective design of transmission control system); Harrell Motors, Inc. v. Flanery, 612 S.W.2d 727 (Ark. 1981) (Chrysler van with self-shifting design problem); Annot., 100 A.L.R.3d 471 (1980) (collecting cases).

**32.** See, e.g., Delvecchio v. General Motors Corp., 625 N.E.2d 1022 (Ill. App. Ct. 1993) (design flaw caused engine stall); Nutting v. Ford Motor Co., 584 N.Y.S.2d 653 (App. Div. 1992) (same).

**33.** See, e.g., Thomasson v. A.K. Durnin Chrysler–Plymouth, Inc., 399 So.2d 1205 (La. Ct. App. 1981) (short length of longitudinal member beam did not provide optimal strength in 1983 Nissan Pulsar); Chart v. General Motors Corp., 258 N.W.2d 680 (Wis. 1977) (evidence of differently designed suspension in 1964 Corvair was evidence of defective design in 1962 Corvair); Julander v. Ford Motor Co., 488 F.2d 839 (10th Cir. 1973) (Utah law) (solid front axle instead of independent front suspension caused oversteer in Ford Bronco); Annot., 100 A.L.R.3d 912 (1980) (suspension cases).

**34.** See, e.g., Connelly v. General Motors Corp., 540 N.E.2d 370 (Ill. App. Ct. 1989); Jolley v. General Motors Corp., 285 S.E.2d 301 (N.C. Ct. App. 1982).

**35.** See § 9.1, above.

**36.** See, e.g., Kallio v. Ford Motor Co., 407 N.W.2d 92, 93–94 (Minn. 1987) (failure to provide adequate warnings); Ford Motor Co. v. Nowak, 638 S.W.2d 582, 585 (Tex. App. 1982) ("Ford failed to adequately warn its consumers about this problem."); Ford Motor Co. v. Bartholomew, 297 S.E.2d 675, 680 (Va. 1982) (Ford officials were aware by interoffice memoranda).

**37.** 540 F.2d 85 (3rd Cir. 1976) (Pa. law) (passenger's failure to warn claim warranted submission to jury).

**38.** See, e.g., Ford Motor Co. v. Ammerman, 705 N.E.2d 539, 563 (Ind. Ct. App. 1999) (upholding punitive damages judgment of $13.8 million, remitted by trial judge from verdict of $58 million); Watkins v. Ford Motor Co., 190 F.3d 1213, 1217 (11th Cir. 1999) (Ga. law); Greco v. Ford Motor Co., 937 F.Supp. 810, 816 (S.D. Ind. 1996) (denying Ford's motion for summary judgment).

**39.** See Fisher v. Ford Motor Co., 224 F.3d 570 (6th Cir. 2000) (Ohio law).

involve dangers in a vehicle's steering,[40] brakes,[41] accelerator,[42] transmission,[43] suspension system,[44] and wheels or tires.[45]

## § 17.3 CRASHWORTHINESS

The previous section examined the ways in which automotive defects may result in vehicular accidents. Yet automotive accidents have many causes, including driver error,[1] collisions caused by other drivers, and dangerous highway conditions. An issue that cuts across nearly every automotive accident, regardless of its cause, is the extent to which the design of the vehicle protected the safety or aggravated the injuries of the occupants during a vehicular accident. This is the issue of automotive crashworthiness, one of the most important aspects of design defectiveness in modern American products liability law.[2]

**40.** See, e.g., Superior Indus. Int'l v. Faulk, 695 So.2d 376 (Fla. Dist. Ct. App. 1997) (failure to warn driver that defective lift block might compromise steering); Fordham v. Garrett–Scharwtz Motor Co., 173 S.E.2d 450 (Ga. Ct. App. 1970) (failure to warn that steering was defective); Annot., 100 A.L.R. 3d 158 (1980) (steering defects); 7 Am. Law Prod. Liab. 3d §§ 95.137–95.163 (steering cases grouped by specific elements).

**41.** See, e.g., Rougeau v. Hyundai Motor Am., 805 So.2d 147 (La. 2002) (failure to warn of defective braking system); Jenkins v. General Motors Corp., 524 S.E.2d 324 (Ga. Ct. App. 1999); Moran v. Volkswagen of Am., Inc., 519 So.2d 871 (La. Ct. App. 1988); Hasson v. Ford Motor Co., 564 P.2d 857 (Cal. 1977); Thornton v. Toyota Motor Sales, Inc., 397 F.Supp. 476 (N.D. Ga. 1975); Annot., 99 A.L.R.3d 179 (1980); 7 Am. Law Prod. Liab. 3d. §§ 95.55–95.73.

**42.** See, e.g., Babb v. Ford Motor Co., 535 N.E.2d 676 (Ohio Ct. App. 1987); 66 A.L.R.4th 20 (1988); 7 Am. Law Prod. Liab. 3d § 95.106.

**43.** See, e.g., Klein v. BMW of North Am., Inc., 705 So.2d 1200 (La. Ct. App. 1997); Davis v. Ford Motor Co., 128 F.3d 631 (8th Cir. 1997) (Ark. law); Kallio v. Ford Motor Co., 407 N.W.2d 92 (Minn. 1987); Ford Motor Co. v. Bartholomew, 297 S.E.2d 675 (Va. 1982); Ford Motor Co. v. Nowak, 638 S.W.2d 582 (Tex. App. 1982); Annot., 100 A.L.R. 3d 471 (1980); 7 Am. Law Prod. Liab. 3d Ch. 95.170.

**44.** See, e.g., Haberkorn v. Chrysler Corp., 533 N.W.2d 373 (Mich. Ct. App. 1995); Bond v. Fruehauf Corp., Prod. Liab. Rep. (CCH) 8830 (Tenn. App. 1978); Farner v. Paccar, Inc., 562 F.2d 518 (8th Cir. 1977) (S.D. law); Annot., 100 A.L.R.3d 912 (1980); 7 Am. Law Prod. Liab. 3d §§ 95:137–95:163.

**45.** See, e.g., Rougeau v. Hyundai Motor Am., 805 So.2d 147 (La. 2002); Gray v. Cannon, 807 So.2d 924, 929 (La. Ct. App. 2002); Connelly v. General Motors Corp., 540 N.E.2d 370 (Ill. App. Ct. 1989); Jolley v. General Motors Corp., 285 S.E.2d 301 (N.C. Ct. App. 1982)

### § 17.3

**1.** See § 17.5, below.

**2.** See, e.g., Latin and Kasolas, Bad Designs, Lethal Profits: The Duty to Protect Other Motorists Against SUV Collision Risks, 82 B. U. L. Rev. 1161 (2002); Mudgett, Exploding Liability: Creating a Cause of Action for Defectively Designed Airbags Under the Restatement (Third) of Torts, 78 Or. L. Rev. 827, 833 (1999); Norton, What Happens When Airbags Kill: Automobile Manufacturers' Liability for Injuries Caused by Airbags, 48 Case W. Res. L. Rev. 659 (1998); Langdon, Recognizing Enhanced Injury Cases, 55 J. Mo. B. 149 (1999); Nader and Page, Automobile–Design Liability and Compliance with Federal Standards, 64 Geo. Wash. L. Rev. 415 (1996); Hogan, The Crashworthiness Doctrine, 18 Am. J. Trial Advoc. 37 (1994); Sugarman, Nader's Failures?, 80 Cal. L. Rev. 289 (1992) (reviewing J. Mashaw and D. Harfst, The Struggle for Auto Safety (1990)); DeDominicis, No Duty at Any Speed? Determining the Responsibility of the Automobile Manufacturer in Speed–Related Accidents, 14 Hofstra L. Rev. 403 (1986); Harris, Enhanced Injury Theory: An Analytic Framework, 62 N.C. L. Rev. 643 (1984); Symposium, Products Liability Law and Motor Vehicle Design, 14 U. of Tol. L. Rev. 301 (1983); Hoenig, Resolution of "Crashworthiness" Design Claims, 55 St. John's L. Rev. 633 (1981); Hoenig and Goetz, A Rational Approach to "Crashworthy" Automobiles: The Need for Judicial Responsibility, 6 Sw. U. L. Rev. 1 (1974); Nader and Page, Automobile Design and the Judicial Process, 55 Cal. L. Rev. 645 (1967); Katz, Liability of Automobile Manufacturers for Unsafe Design of Passenger Cars, 69 Harv. L. Rev. 863 (1956); 3 Frumer and Friedman, Products Liability ch. 21.

## Crashworthiness in General

Automotive "crashworthiness" is aptly defined by Congress as "the protection a passenger motor vehicle gives its passengers against personal injury or death from a motor vehicle accident."[3] A vehicle's capacity to offer such protection is a function of its ability to withstand and absorb the physical stresses of a collision combined with its ability to prevent additional ("enhanced" or "aggravated") injuries the occupants may sustain in a "second collision" with the vehicle's interior.[4] Thus, a vehicle's crashworthiness is improved or diminished by the extent that its structure can absorb the forces of a crash without collapsing into the passenger compartment against the occupants; that its dashboard and head restraints are appropriately padded, rather than being made of solid steel; that the glass in its windows crumbles harmlessly, rather than fracturing into lethal slivers; that the steering wheel telescopes to absorb the force of a collision with the driver's chest, rather than remaining rigid as a wall; that the edges and ends of knobs, levers, and other protrusions are rounded and covered by protective material, rather than being left as sharp, pointed steel; that the fuel tank is located in a safe position and securely protected against the varying insults it may encounter in different types of collisions; that the doors and windows have sufficient latches to hold them closed in accident situations, to keep the occupants contained, rather than popping open and allowing the occupants to be flung outside; that airbags protect the occupants from injury, rather than activating spontaneously or with explosive force; and that safety belts, harnesses, and head rests effectively restrain and protect the occupants rather than serving as instruments of death.

## The Crashworthiness Duty

Whether manufacturers have a duty to design crashworthy vehicles was a major issue of products liability law in the late 1960s and early 1970s. The controversy originated with the 1966 decision in *Evans v. General Motors Corporation*,[5] where the driver of a 1961 Chevrolet station wagon manufactured by the defendant was killed when the side of his car collapsed on him when it was struck by another vehicle. The plaintiff alleged that the car's frame was defective because it was designed in the shape of an "X" without the kind of steel perimeter railing used in other cars. But the court disagreed. While it might be desirable for manufacturers to construct automobiles to be safe in collisions, the court viewed the imposition of such a requirement to be a

**3.** 49 U.S.C.A. § 32301(1) (the Motor Vehicle Information and Cost Savings Act). While this definition is limited to passenger vehicles, common-law crashworthiness principals apply more broadly to other types of vehicles. See, e.g., Colville v. Crown Equipment Corp. 809 A.2d 916 (Pa. Super. 2002) (forklift); Duren v. Paccar, Inc., 549 S.E.2d 755 (Ga. Ct. App. 2001) (tractor-trailer); Black v. M & W Gear Co. 269 F.3d 1220 (10th Cir. 2001) (Okla. law) (riding tractor lawnmower); Schroeder v. Com., Dept. of Transp., 710 A.2d 23 (Pa. 1998) (truck); Kupetz v. Deere & Co., 644 A.2d 1213 (Pa. Super. 1994) (bulldozer). See also Miller v. Todd, 551 N.E.2d 1139, 1141 n.1 (Ind.

1990) (noting that crashworthiness doctrine has been applied to motorcycles, airplanes, snowmobiles, pleasure boats, and tractors).

**4.** The crashworthiness concept might be viewed as broader than "second-collision" liability, in that the latter term suggests interior collision injuries to the exclusion of injuries from ejection, see, e.g., Lee v. Volkswagen of Am., Inc., 688 P.2d 1283 (Okla. 1984) (ejected occupant "collided" with street), and from burns caused by defective fuel systems, as discussed below. See Mazda Motor Corp. v. Lindahl, 706 A.2d 526, 530 n.12 (Del. 1998).

**5.** 359 F.2d 822 (7th Cir. 1966) (Ind. law).

legislative function,[6] and "[a] manufacturer is not under a duty to make his automobile accident-proof or fool-proof."[7] Reasoning that the "intended purpose" of automobiles does not include their participation in collisions,[8] a split panel[9] of the Seventh Circuit Court of Appeals ruled that General Motors did not have a duty to equip its cars with side frames to protect the occupants from foreseeable collisions.

Two years later, after critical reviews of *Evans* in the law journals,[10] the Eighth Circuit joined issue in *Larsen v. General Motors Corporation.*[11] The plaintiff was injured in a head-on collision, the force of which propelled the steering mechanism, the front shaft of which protruded 2.7 inches in front of the forward tires, back into his head. Citing *Evans,* General Motors argued once again that its design obligation was limited to making cars safe for their intended use of driving on the highways and did not extend to designing them for safety in head-on collisions. But the argument was wearing thin, and the Eighth Circuit was markedly unimpressed:

> We think the "intended use" construction urged by General Motors is much too narrow and unrealistic. Where the manufacturer's negligence in design causes an unreasonable risk to be imposed upon the user of its products, the manufacturer should be liable for the injury caused by its failure to exercise reasonable care in the design. These injuries are readily foreseeable as an incident to the normal and expected use of an automobile.... The sole function of an automobile is not just to provide a means of transportation, it is to provide a means of safe transportation or as safe as is reasonably possible under the present state of the art.[12]

**6.** Id. at 824.

**7.** Id.

**8.** "The intended purpose of an automobile does not include its participation in collisions with other objects, despite the manufacturer's ability to foresee the possibility that such collisions may occur. As defendant argues, the defendant also knows that its automobiles may be driven into bodies of water, but it is not suggested that defendant has a duty to equip them with pontoons." Id. at 825. On the rise and fall of the intended use doctrine, see § 13.5, above.

**9.** Judge Kiley's persuasive dissenting opinion, 359 F.2d at 825, foreshadowed (and was relied upon by) Larsen v. General Motors Corp., 391 F.2d 495, 499 (8th Cir. 1968) (Mich. law).

**10.** See, e.g., Nader and Page, Automobile Design and the Judicial Process, 55 Cal. L. Rev. 645, 655 (1967); Notes, 80 Harv. L. Rev. 688 (1967); 32 Iowa L. Rev. 953 (1967), all cited at 391 F.2d at 505 n.9.

**11.** 391 F.2d 495 (8th Cir. 1968) (Mich. law).

**12.** Id. at 502. The court also remarked:

> While automobiles are not made for the purpose of colliding with each other, a frequent and inevitable contingency of normal automobile use will result in collisions and injury-producing impacts. No rational basis exists for limiting recovery to situations where the defect in design or manufacture was the causative factor of the accident, as the accident and the resulting injury, usually caused by the 'second collision' of the passenger with the interior part of the automobile, are all foreseeable. Where the injuries or enhanced injuries are due to the manufacturer's failure to use reasonable care to avoid subjecting the user of its products to an unreasonable risk of injury, general negligence principles should be applicable.

Id.

Citing data on the high rate of serious injuries and deaths from automotive accidents,[13] including the fact that many or most cars eventually are involved in at least one accident causing injury or death,[14] the *Larsen* court concluded that car manufacturers have a duty of due care, as an extension of their general duty to make their products reasonably safe for normal use,[15] including reasonable safety for the crash environment.[16]

While a small handful of cases followed the *Evans* no-duty approach for a brief period,[17] an increasingly large majority adopted *Larsen's* view that automotive manufacturers have a duty of reasonable care to design crashworthy vehicles. If there ever was any doubt as to the final outcome of the controversy, it was put to rest in 1977 when the Seventh Circuit swung over, repudiating its own decision in *Evans*[18] and adopting *Larsen's* reasoning and result.[19] While the Supreme Court of Virginia purported to reject the crashworthiness doctrine in a 1995 decision involving the rollover of a truck,[20] it proceeded to apply the doctrine's principles by allowing the plaintiff's claim that the truck's cab, crushed in the rollover, was inadequately braced and padded to protect its occupants against such a risk.[21] Thus, it seems safe to say that the crashworthiness doctrine is now the law in every American jurisdiction.[22]

### Ascertaining Crashworthiness

Establishing that manufacturers have a duty to design their cars to be crashworthy does not of course resolve the far more complex problem of deciding what the limits of that design obligation should be. All courts start with the premise that manufacturers are not expected to make

**13.** Including National Safety Council motor vehicle accident data revealing 49,000 deaths and 1.8 million disabling injuries in 1965, rising to 52,500 deaths and 1.9 million disabling injuries in 1966. 391 F.2d at 502 n.4. The court also noted: "In automobile accidents since the advent of the horseless carriage up to the end of 1965, 1.5 million people have been killed in the United States." Id.

**14.** Id. (citing O'Connell, Taming the Automobile, 58 Nw. U. L. Rev. 299, 348 (1963), for proposition that "between one-fourth to two-thirds of all automobiles during their use at some time are involved in an accident producing injury or death").

**15.** Id. at 504. See also Mazda Motor Corp. v. Lindahl, 706 A.2d 526, 531 (Del. 1998).

**16.** "We perceive of no sound reason, either in logic or experience, nor any command in precedent, why the manufacturer should not be held to a reasonable duty of care in the design of its vehicle consonant with the state of the art to minimize the effect of accidents." 391 F.2d at 503.

**17.** See, e.g., Shumard v. General Motors Corp., 270 F.Supp. 311 (S.D. Ohio 1967); Willis v. Chrysler Corp., 264 F.Supp. 1010 (S.D. Tex. 1967); Walton v. Chrysler Corp., 229 So.2d 568 (Miss. 1969).

**18.** "In light of an expanding extension of protection for consumers in products liability cases, the 'intended purpose' rationale in Evans as to motor vehicles is unrealistically narrow. [M]anufacturers must anticipate and take precautions against reasonably foreseeable risks in the use of their products." Huff v. White Motor Co., 565 F.2d 104, 108 (7th Cir. 1977) (Ind. law) (death by fire from rupture of fuel tank).

**19.** "There is no rational basis for limiting the manufacturer's liability to those instances where a structural defect has caused the collision and a resulting injury.... Since collisions [from] whatever cause are foreseeable events, the scope of liability should be commensurate with the scope of foreseeable risks." Id. at 109. Indiana finally adopted the crashworthiness doctrine in Miller v. Todd, 551 N.E.2d 1139 (Ind. 1990).

**20.** Slone v. General Motors Corp., 457 S.E.2d 51 (Va. 1995).

**21.** Id. at 52.

**22.** The crashworthiness duty "controversy" is now settled. Although accidents are not intended uses of products, they are generally foreseeable. A manufacturer has a duty to design and manufacture its product so as reasonably to reduce the foreseeable harm that may occur in an accident brought about by causes other than a product defect. Products Liability Restatement § 16 cmt. *a*.

their vehicles crash-proof and able to protect occupants in accidents of every type, such as when a small car crashes head-on into an 18–wheeler truck at highway speeds.[23] Even *Larsen* recognized that "manufacturers are not insurers,"[24] that "all risks cannot be eliminated nor can a crash-proof vehicle be designed,"[25] and that the crashworthiness duty extends only to eliminating *unreasonable* risks and requires only "*reasonable* steps in design . . . to minimize the injury-producing effect of impacts."[26] All courts now agree that a manufacturer's obligation to produce a "crashworthy" vehicle is bounded by a reasonable balance of the costs and benefits of reducing various risks of injury.[27] In short, automotive crashworthiness is not an absolute concept but a matter of degree. This point might best be understood if courts and commentators discarded the notion that vehicles must be designed in a "crashworthy" manner and rephrased the manufacturer's duty in terms of an obligation to design vehicles that are "*sufficiently* crashworthy" in view of the balance of costs and benefits involved in removing (or reducing) the hazard that caused (or aggravated) a particular injury. While the term "crashworthy" remains unmodified in explicit legal discourse, the concept is understood to include this silent modifier. Thus, courts and lawyers understand that a vehicle's "crashworthiness" is a function of the costs and benefits (and, to a lesser extent, of consumer expectations) of various safety features, some included and others left out. In short, "crashworthy" means *optimal*—not perfect—automotive safety.[28]

Determining what types and severity of accidents any particular vehicle reasonably should be expected to withstand is sometimes quite easy. For example, if a low-speed collision causes a steering wheel hub cover to pop off, exposing sharp prongs that injure a passenger's face, no such car could be found reasonably safe for the crash environment.[29] As the initial impact increases in severity, however, the crashworthiness issue becomes increasingly more difficult. In cases involving collisions at higher speeds, it generally is not self-evident whether the vehicle should

**23.** For this basic proposition, see, e.g., Dreisonstok v. Volkswagenwerk AG, 489 F.2d 1066, 1073 (4th Cir. 1974) (Va. law); Dyson v. General Motors Corp., 298 F.Supp. 1064, 1073 (E.D. Pa. 1969).

**24.** 391 F.2d at 503.

**25.** Id.

**26.** Id. (Emphasis added.)

**27.** See, e.g., Carillo v. Ford Motor Co., 759 N.E.2d 99, 107 (Ill. App. Ct. 2001) (seat design); Nissan Motor Co. v. Nave, 740 A.2d 102 (Md. Ct. Spec. App. 1999) (design of steering column); Soule v. General Motors Corp., 882 P.2d 298 (Cal. 1994) (design of floorboard and wheel assembly). Compare Alabama's standard jury instruction for crashworthiness cases, which requires a plaintiff to prove that:

[t]he utility of the alternative design outweighed the utility of the design actually used. In deciding [this issue], factors which may be considered would include the intended use of the vehicle, its styling, cost, desirability, safety aspects, the foreseeability of the particular accident, the likelihood of injury, the probable seriousness of the injury if that accident occurred, the obviousness or not of the defect, and the manufacturer's ability to eliminate the defect.

Flemister v. General Motors Corp., 723 So.2d 25, 27 (Ala. 1998). Consumer expectations may also play a role in determining the scope of automotive crashworthiness. Cf. Bruce v. Martin–Marietta Corp., 544 F.2d 442, 447 (10th Cir. 1976) (Okla. law) (aircraft crashworthiness: "A consumer would not expect a Model T to have the safety features which are incorporated in automobiles made today.").

**28.** This specific proposition rests on more general notions of the nature of a manufacturer's duty of (reasonably) safe design. See chs. 2, 5, and 8, above.

**29.** See Horn v. General Motors Corp., 551 P.2d 398, 402 (Cal. 1976) (plaintiff, while attempting to avoid collision at speed of 25–mph, brushed hand over horncap, dislodging it and exposing prongs); Ellithorpe v. Ford Motor Co., 503 S.W.2d 516 (Tenn. 1973) (prong designed in emblem).

have been reasonably designed to protect its occupants against various injuries, and the fact finder in each such instance will have to carefully evaluate the various safety-utility-cost tradeoffs to determine if the plaintiff has fairly made a case that the particular design feature of the vehicle was uncrashworthy.[30] Cases involving moderate to severe crashes and injuries almost always require the plaintiff to show by expert engineering testimony how the injuries were caused, how particular design enhancements would have prevented such injuries, and the costs and feasibility of such preventive measures.[31]

*Dreisonstok v. Volkswagenwerk AG,*[32] an early influential case, helped to set the limits of the crashworthiness doctrine and to illustrate the necessary tradeoffs between safety, cost, and function inherent in all aspects of a vehicle's design. The plaintiff was injured while riding as a passenger in the front seat of a Volkswagen microbus when the vehicle collided with a telephone pole head-on at 40 mph. The plaintiff sued the manufacturer for defective design, based on the relative weakness of the vehicle's passenger compartment in front-end collisions compared to the greater ability of standard American passenger cars to withstand such collisions. The district court found for the plaintiff, concluding that the vehicle's design was defective for failure to have "sufficient energy-absorbing materials or devices or 'crush space' ... so that at 40 miles an

---

**30.** For example, a jury question on crashworthiness was held to have been properly presented in Clark v. Chrysler Corp., 310 F.3d 461, 478 (6th Cir. 2002)(Ky. law) (allegedly-defective door latch on Dodge Ram truck caused death of driver in low speed accident), Poliseno v. General Motors Corp., 744 A.2d 679, 683 (N.J. Super. Ct. App. Div. 2000) (tree protruded 20 inches through door in collision at delta-V speed between 10–23 mph), and Seattle–First Nat'l Bank v. Volkswagen of Am., Inc., 525 P.2d 286 (Wash. Ct. App. 1974), aff'd, 542 P.2d 774 (Wash. 1975) (VW microbus struck rear end of flatbed truck at relative speed of 20 mph).

**31.** See, e.g., Gray v. General Motors Corp., 312 F.3d 240, 242 (6th Cir. 2002) (Ky. law) ("despite his voluminous testimony before the district court, the plaintiff's expert was unable to identify any 'probable' defect in the seatbelt mechanism that caused the injury, as is required by Kentucky products liability law"); Walters ex rel. Walters v. General Motors Corp., 209 F.Supp.2d 481, 490 (W.D. Pa. 2002) (court granted defendants' summary judgment motion because plaintiff failed to provide expert testimony and instead opted to proceed solely on a malfunction theory; "[p]laintiffs have had more than sufficient time to procure the use of an accident reconstruction expert, an airbag design expert or a biomechanical injury expert"); Batiste v. General Motors Corp., 802 So.2d 686, 690 (La. Ct. App. 2001) (court granted defendant summary judgment because plaintiff failed to present expert testimony on tech-

nical matters related to claim that airbag failed to inflate properly); Hayles v. General Motors Corp., 82 F.Supp.2d 650, 658–59 (S.D. Tex. 1999) (court granted defendant's motion for summary judgment on plaintiff's claim, unsubstantiated by expert testimony, that airbag should have deployed); Mazda Motor Corp. v. Lindahl, 706 A.2d 526, 533 (Del. 1998) (defendant contested survivability of crash if yielding seat had not permitted decedent to be partially ejected; accident forces on decedent and corresponding injuries not evident, so jurors needed expert testimony "in order to reach a reasoned conclusion on ... proximate cause"); Whitted v. General Motors Corp., 58 F.3d 1200, 1206 (7th Cir. 1995) (Ind. law) ("to allow a plaintiff to establish the existence of a design defect by his mere assertion is ludicrous"); Soule v. General Motors Corp., 882 P.2d 298 (Cal. 1994) (adequacy vel non of design of floorboard and wheel assembly testified to by numerous experts). On expert testimony generally, see § 6.3, above.

*But see* Silvestri v. General Motors Corp., 210 F.3d 240 (4th Cir. 2000) (N.Y. law) (airbag, said in owner's manual to deploy in 9–14 mph collisions, failed to deploy in 24 mph collision; under malfunction doctrine applied by New York courts, a plaintiff need only prove "that the product did not perform as intended and must exclude all causes of his enhanced injuries not attributable to the defendant").

**32.** 489 F.2d 1066 (4th Cir. 1974) (Va. law).

hour the integrity of the passenger compartment would not be violated.''[33] Rejecting the plaintiff's comparison as invalid, the Court of Appeals reversed, reasoning that this multipurpose van was designed to provide users with maximum space for cargo or passengers, while keeping its dimensions as small as possible for easy maneuverability and its cost as low as possible. To achieve these goals, the manufacturer brought the front seat as far forward as possible to leave as much space for cargo or passengers in the rear. While this design reduced the space between the front of the vehicle and the driver's compartment, this aspect of the design was not only evident but was the very design feature that made the vehicle unique. The court noted that the usefulness of the VW microbus design was vouchsafed by its popularity; indeed, after the accident, the driver's father purchased another VW microbus to replace the one destroyed in the collision with the pole. Finally, the court observed that the plaintiff had offered no evidence of any practical way to improve the safety of the microbus for front-end collisions without interfering with its many uses for carrying light cargo, serving as a family camper, and as a conveyor of more passengers than could be carried by a normal car.[34]

As *Dreisonstok* illustrates, there can be no single standard for automotive crashworthiness; instead, crashworthiness determinations necessarily involve evaluations of the varying trade-offs between safety and utility inherent in the design of each particular type of vehicle.[35] So, consumers may not fairly expect a convertible to be as safe in a rollover situation as a "standard four-door sedan with center posts and full-door frames."[36] And the necessary tradeoffs are not restricted to safety and utility, but extend as well to cost or price—like most goods, safety has a cost.[37] "Price is, also, a factor to be considered, for, if a change in design would appreciably add to cost, add little to safety, and take an article out of the price range of the market to which it was intended to appeal, it may be 'unreasonable' as well as 'impractical' for the Courts to require the manufacturer to adopt such change."[38] The public, thought the court, surely expects less crashworthiness in an economy car than in a Cadillac.[39] For these reasons, the court properly concluded that the plaintiff

**33.** Id. at 1068–69.

**34.** Id. at 1074.

**35.** The court noted that Congress, in the National Traffic and Motor Vehicle Safety Act of 1966, pronounced that specific automotive safety regulations must take into account what is "reasonable, practicable and appropriate for the particular type of motor vehicle." Id. at 1072, quoting 15 U.S.C. 1392(f)(3), now recodified at 49 U.S.C.A. § 30111.

**36.** Dyson v. General Motors Corp., 298 F.Supp. 1064, 1073 (E.D. Pa. 1969).

**37.** See, e.g., Whitted v. General Motors Corp., 58 F.3d 1200, 1205 (7th Cir. 1995) (Ind. law):

[C]ar makers have a duty within economic reason to ensure that their vehicles will protect occupants against injury following

the initial collision. Given the reality that safety technology is expensive, the operative consideration in defining a crashworthiness defect is the balance between reasonable safety and economics.... [T]he law does not require manufacturers to follow ... economically suffocating measures.

**38.** *Dreisonstok*, 489 F.2d at 1072–73.

**39.** Id. at 1073. Compare Products Liability Restatement § 2 cmt. *f*, Illus. 9: "Given that the risk and benefits associated with relative automobile size are generally known, decisions regarding which sizes to purchase and use should be left to purchasers and users in the market."

had failed to show that the manufacturer of the VW microbus had been negligent in its design.[40]

Because of the different ways in which accidents can occur, automotive engineers are forced to balance a vehicle's safety in one type of crash against its safety in other types of crashes; making it safer for one type of accident may make it more dangerous for another type of accident. It is thus axiomatic that a design which allows or enhances one type of hazard in order to prevent another, greater hazard is not defective. This widely accepted principle of design defectiveness[41] receives unequivocal expression in the *Products Liability Restatement*: "When evaluating the reasonableness of a design alternative, the overall safety of the product must be considered. It is not sufficient that the alternative design would have reduced or prevented the harm suffered by the plaintiff if it would also have introduced into the product other dangers of equal or greater magnitude."[42]

---

**40.** Id. at 1073–76. Compare Seattle–First Nat'l Bank v. Volkswagen of Am., Inc., 525 P.2d 286 (Wash. Ct. App. 1974), aff'd, 542 P.2d 774 (Wash. 1975), where the court held that a jury should be permitted to pass on the crashworthiness of the front end of a VW microbus which struck the rear end of a flatbed truck at a relative speed of 20 mph. *Dreisonstok* was distinguished on the basis of the difference in speed at the time of the collisions.

**41.** For a short while, Dawson v. Chrysler Corp., 630 F.2d 950 (3d Cir. 1980) (N.J. law), put the principle somewhat in doubt. In *Dawson*, plaintiff lost control of his 1974 Dodge Monaco, which "slid off the highway, over a curb, through a small sign, and into an unyielding steel pole that was fifteen inches in diameter. The car struck the pole in a backwards direction at a forty-five degree angle on the left side of the vehicle; the point of impact was the left rear wheel well. As a result of the force of the collision, the vehicle literally wrapped itself around the pole. The pole ripped through the body of the car and crushed Dawson between the seat and the 'header' area of the roof, located just above the windshield." Id. at 954. Dawson's collision with the interior of the car ruptured his fifth and sixth cervical vertebrae, rendering him a quadriplegic.

The plaintiffs alleged that the car was defectively designed "because it did not have a full, continuous steel frame extending through the door panels, and a cross-member running through the floor board between the posts located between the front and rear doors of the vehicle. Had the vehicle been so designed, the Dawsons alleged, it would have 'bounced' off the pole following relatively slight penetration by the pole into the passenger space." Id. Chrysler's experts testified that the vehicle's propensity to deform was in fact a safety feature in most crashes because deformation "absorbs the impact of the crash and decreases the rate of deceleration on the occupants of the vehicle." Id. For this reason, Chrysler's experts claimed that the plaintiff's alternative design was actually *more* dangerous than the existing design for most types of automobile accidents. Nevertheless, the jury returned a verdict for the plaintiffs, a result which the Court of Appeals found unfair and inefficient: "[W]hile the jury found Chrysler liable for not producing a rigid enough vehicular frame, a factfinder in another case might well hold the manufacturer liable for producing a frame that is too rigid. . . . In effect, this permits individual juries applying varying laws in different jurisdictions to set nationwide automobile safety standards and to impose on automobile manufacturers conflicting requirements." Id. at 962. Against its better instincts, however, the Court of Appeals felt compelled to affirm, ruling that the jury could find the car "not reasonably fit, suitable and safe" under then-prevailing New Jersey law. Id. at 959–60.

**42.** Products Liability Restatement § 2 cmt. *f*. See also id. § 16 cmt. *b*, repeating this principle in the context of a defendant's liability for enhanced injury. The Reporters' Note to § 2 cmt. *f* observes:

> The proposition that, in order to determine that a design is not reasonably safe, the alternative must contribute to greater overall safety needs no citation; it is axiomatic. If the alternative design proffered by the plaintiff does not make the product safer, let alone if it makes it more dangerous, such an alternative is not reasonable. In such a case the fact that the alternative design would have avoided injury in a specific case is of no moment.

The Third Restatement explicitly rejects *Dawson* in § 16 cmt. *b*, Illus. 5.

Proof that a vehicle is uncrashworthy is not in itself, however, sufficient to make out a crashworthiness case. As in all products liability cases,[43] the plaintiff must connect his or her allegation of product defect with the injury claimed. Thus, an essential element in every crashworthiness case is that the uncrashworthy aspect of the vehicle proximately caused the plaintiff's harm.[44] What this means, at a minimum, is that the plaintiff must prove that the uncrashworthy design was a substantial factor in enhancing the plaintiff's injuries.[45]

### Theories of Liability and Defect Tests

Although *Larsen* was based on negligence, crashworthiness principles apply more broadly, and courts have applied the doctrine without hesitation to claims based on breach of implied warranty[46] and on strict

**43.** See chs. 11 and 12, above.

**44.** See, e.g., Harris v. General Motors Corp., 34 Fed. Appx. 487, 490 (7th Cir. 2002) (Ill. law) (while affirming summary judgment for defendant, court observed that plaintiff "has not provided concrete evidence that the airbag system in her particular vehicle was defective, nor, even if we assumed that all late deployments are defective, has she shown that the late deployment caused her injuries"); Bombard v. General Motors Corp., 238 F.Supp.2d 464, 468 (N.D.N.Y. 2002) (summary judgment for defendant; "[m]erely establishing a defect as a possible cause of an accident is not adequate to prove liability"); Stewart v. General Motors Corp., 222 F.Supp.2d 845, 848–49 (W.D. Ky. 2002) (holding that plaintiff failed to prove that tethered airbag would have prevented or minimized her injuries or how her injuries were enhanced by untethered nature of her airbag), aff'd, 102 Fed.Appx. 961 (6th Cir. 2004); General Motors Corp. v. Iracheta, 90 S.W.3d 725 (Tex. App. 2002) (holding that evidence was both factually and legally sufficient to support jury's finding that defect in vehicle was producing cause of injury); Jensen v. American Suzuki Motor Corp., 35 P.3d 776, 779 (Idaho 2001) ("If the record does not establish facts that demonstrate the plaintiffs' injuries were enhanced or intensified by the alleged defect or if the allegations are merely conclusory, a claim under this theory cannot prevail."); Morton Int'l v. Gillespie, 39 S.W.3d 651, 656 (Tex. App. 2001) (affirming judgment for plaintiff, court held that evidence was legally and factually sufficient to support findings that airbag malfunctioned and that delay in airbag's deployment was a producing cause of motorist's injuries); Yard v. DaimlerChrysler Corp., 44 S.W.3d 238, 243 (Tex. App. 2001) (court, affirming summary judgment for defendant, observed that "evidence that the airbag failed is not evidence that this failure caused Bradley's injuries and

death"); Norwest Bank N.M., N.A. v. Chrysler Corp., 981 P.2d 1215, 1219 (N.M. Ct. App. 1999) (affirming defense verdict in defective tailgate latch case, where defendant's evidence showed that "the force of the minivan striking the guardrail was so great that no latch could have withstood such an impact, no matter how safe the design, and thus, this particular latch, no matter how defective, did not cause Plaintiff's injuries"); Nissan Motor Co. Ltd. v. Nave, 740 A.2d 102 (Md. Ct. Spec. App. 1999) (insufficient proof that safer design would have made accident survivable); Mazda Motor Corp. v. Lindahl, 706 A.2d 526, 533 (Del. 1998) (plaintiff "introduced no evidence linking the design defect to the specific causes of death identified on the death certificate"); Burgos v. Lutz, 512 N.Y.S.2d 424 (App. Div. 1987).

**45.** See, e.g., Carrasquilla v. Mazda Motor Corp., 197 F.Supp.2d 169, 180 (M.D. Pa. 2002) (court adopted burden of proof in crashworthiness cases requiring "plaintiff to prove only that a defect was a substantial factor in producing damages over and above those which were probably caused as a result of the original impact or collision"); Poliseno v. General Motors Corp., 744 A.2d 679, 683 (N.J. Super. Ct. App. Div. 2000); Lally v. Volkswagen AG, 698 N.E.2d 28 (Mass. App. Ct. 1998). This is the apportionment issue developed in § 17.4, below.

**46.** See, e.g., Harris v. General Motors Corp., 34 Fed. Appx. 487, 490 (7th Cir. 2002) (Ill. law) (res ipsa loquitur doctrine, strict liability, negligence, and breach of warranty); Stewart v. General Motors Corp., 222 F.Supp.2d 845, 848–49 (W.D. Ky. 2002) (strict products liability, negligence and breach of warranty), aff'd, 102 Fed. Appx. 961 (6th Cir. 2004); Silvestri v. General Motors Corp., 210 F.3d 240 (4th Cir. 2000) (N.Y. law) (implied warranty, express warranty, strict liability in tort, negligence,

liability in tort.[47] This follows logically from the proposition that "strict" liability is in effect a lesser included offense of negligence liability, in that negligence in design usually means the negligent sale of a defectively designed product.[48]

More difficult is the question of the appropriate theory of defectiveness for crashworthiness cases. The basic contest here, as elsewhere, is between the consumer expectations and risk-utility tests.[49] From the start, courts experienced difficulty in attempting to apply the consumer expectations test to questions of automotive design safety that by nature involve the kinds of trade-offs between safety, usefulness, and cost discussed above. In a very early case, *Heaton v. Ford Motor Co.*,[50] a 5–6 inch rock struck a wheel on the plaintiff's 4–wheel-drive pickup truck that was traveling at normal highway speed. Half an hour later, the wheel came apart, causing the truck to leave the highway and tip over, injuring the plaintiff. Although the court used the case to adopt § 402A of the *Second Restatement*, together with the consumer expectations test for product defectiveness, it affirmed the trial court's refusal to submit the case to the jury, reasoning that a jury could only speculate, in the absence of "data concerning the cost or feasibility of designing and building" a stronger wheel, on what consumers in fact would expect under circumstances such as these.[51]

*Heaton* illustrates the courts' recognition, which has strengthened over time, that an intelligent evaluation of the appropriateness of the complex safety-usefulness-cost tradeoffs involved in design engineering generally requires use of the kind of cost-benefit analysis embraced by the risk-utility test.[52] While a number of courts have attempted to apply

and res ipsa loquitur); Lally v. Volkswagen AG, 698 N.E.2d 28 (Mass. App. Ct. 1998) (no breach of implied warranty of merchantability on facts); Elsasser v. American Motors Corp., 265 N.W.2d 339 (Mich. Ct. App. 1978) (common-law implied warranty).

**47.** See, e.g., Lattrell v. Chrysler Corp., 79 S.W.3d 141 (Tex. App. 2002) (strict liability); Harris v. General Motors Corp., 34 Fed.Appx. 487 (7th Cir. 2002) (Ill. law) (res ipsa loquitur, strict liability, negligence, and breach of warranty); Green v. General Motors Corp., 709 A.2d 205, 209 (N.J. Super. Ct., App. Div. 1998) (Dreier, P.J.A.D.) (New Jersey's products liability act consolidates claims for negligence, strict liability, and implied warranty into single products liability claim "the essence of which is strict liability"); Bass v. General Motors Corp., 150 F.3d 842 (8th Cir. 1998) (Mo. law); Miller v. Todd, 551 N.E.2d 1139 (Ind. 1990); Turcotte v. Ford Motor Co., 494 F.2d 173, 181 (1st Cir. 1974) (R.I. law). See also Hyundai Motor Co. v. Rodriguez, 995 S.W.2d 661, 665 (Tex. 1999) (failure to instruct on "defect" under implied warranty in addition to strict liability in tort was proper):

> [I]n a crashworthiness case . . . , strict-liability's and breach-of-warranty's concepts of "defect" are functionally identical. The claim in a crashworthiness case

is that a defect in the vehicle caused an occupant to sustain injuries in an accident that he or she would not otherwise have suffered. A defect in a vehicle that makes it uncrashworthy and thus causes occupants to be exposed to an unreasonable risk of harm in the event of an accident is both "unfit for the ordinary purposes for which [it is] used because of a lack of something necessary for adequacy" and unreasonably dangerous. An uncrashworthy vehicle cannot be unfit for ordinary use but not unreasonably dangerous, nor can it be unreasonably dangerous but fit for ordinary use; it must be both or neither.

**48.** See, e.g., Hayles v. General Motors Corp., 82 F.Supp.2d 650, 658–59 (S.D. Tex. 1999); Oanes v. Westgo, Inc., 476 N.W.2d 248, 253 (N.D. 1991). See generally § 5.9, above.

**49.** See chs. 5 and 8, above.

**50.** 435 P.2d 806 (Or. 1967).

**51.** Id. at 809.

**52.** See, e.g., Bowman v. General Motors Corp., 427 F.Supp. 234, 242 (E.D. Pa. 1977) (adopting "a risk-utility balancing test pursuant to which the jury makes a judgment as to the social acceptability of

the consumer expectations test in crashworthiness cases,[53] courts increasingly have turned to cost-benefit analysis to test the reasonableness of a vehicle's design for particular types of accident environments.[54]

Perhaps the case example of the risk-utility test's supremacy in crashworthiness cases is *Soule v. General Motors Corp.*,[55] decided by the California Supreme Court in 1994.[56] The plaintiff's ankles were fractured when the Chevrolet Camaro she was driving collided with another vehicle at a closing speed of 50–60 miles per hour. She sued the manufacturer, asserting that the design of her automobile was defective in allowing the left front wheel to break free, collapse rearward, and smash the toe pan and floorboard into her feet. In particular, she claimed that the configuration of the car's frame, and the bracket attaching the wheel assembly to it, were defectively designed because they did not limit the wheel's rearward travel in the event the bracket should fail. At trial, the parties disagreed on the angle and force of the impact and the extent to which the toe pan had actually deformed. To testify on design defectiveness and causation, both parties employed numerous experts on biomechanics, metallurgy, orthopedics, design engineering, crash-test simulation, and other matters. The plaintiff's experts testified, on the basis of crash tests, metallurgical analysis, and other bases, as to how the damage to her car would have been minimized had it been alternatively designed. The defendant's experts attempted to refute these claims and explained how the plaintiff's ankle injuries were caused by the force of the collision and her failure to wear a seatbelt rather than any defect in the car. The jury rendered a verdict for the plaintiff, the intermediate appellate court affirmed, and the defendant appealed.

The question before the California Supreme Court was whether an "ordinary consumer expectations" instruction may be used in a case where the question of how safely the product should have performed cannot be answered by the common experience of its users. In a prior

---

the conscious design choice trade-off"). See § 8.4, above.

**53.** See, e.g., Force v. Ford Motor Co., 879 So.2d 103 (Fla. Dist. Ct. App. 2004); Jackson v. General Motors Corp., 60 S.W.3d 800 (Tenn. 2001) (court held that consumer expectations test might be used to determine if restraint system was unreasonably dangerous); Higgs v. General Motors Corp., 655 F.Supp. 22 (E.D. Tenn. 1985), aff'd, 815 F.2d 80 (6th Cir. 1987); Leichtamer v. American Motors Corp., 424 N.E.2d 568, 576–77 (Ohio 1981) (Jeep roll bar collapsed); Hancock v. Paccar, Inc., 283 N.W.2d 25 (Neb. 1979). Compare Bresnahan v. Chrysler Corp., 38 Cal.Rptr.2d 446 (Ct. App. 1995), on subsequent appeal, 76 Cal.Rptr.2d 804 (Ct. App. 1998) (deployment of airbag in low-impact collision, breaking driver's elbow; ordinary consumer could form expectation of how airbag would perform in such situations, which authorized consumer expectations test), with

Pruitt v. General Motors Corp., 86 Cal. Rptr.2d 4 (Ct. App. 1999) (deployment of airbag in low-impact collision, breaking driver's weak jaw, was *not* part of everyday experience of consuming public, so trial court correctly refused to give consumer expectations instruction).

**54.** See, e.g., Nissan Motor Co. Ltd. v. Nave, 740 A.2d 102 (Md. Ct. Spec. App. 1999); Green v. General Motors Corp., 709 A.2d 205 (N.J. Super. Ct. App. Div. 1998) (Dreier, P.J.A.D.). See also Flemister v. General Motors Corp., 723 So.2d 25, 28 (Ala. 1998) (Alabama's mixed consumer-expectations-risk-utility standard jury instruction "ultimately requires, in resolving the issue of an alleged design defect, a balancing of the risk of harm to the consumer against the utility of the product's design").

**55.** 882 P.2d 298 (Cal. 1994).

**56.** *Soule* is examined in detail in § 8.6, above.

case, *Barker v. Lull Engineering Co.,*[57] the court had pronounced its celebrated two-pronged defect test which provided for a finding of design defectiveness if either the product's design failed to meet consumer expectations or if its risks outweighed its benefits.[58] While *Barker* was widely interpreted as holding that a plaintiff could recover on either prong,[59] the *Soule* court pointed to *Barker*'s admonition that "when the ultimate issue of design defect calls for a careful assessment of feasibility, practicality, risk, and benefit, the case should not be resolved simply on the basis of ordinary consumer expectations" but should turn instead upon "the balancing or weighing of competing considerations" provided in the risk-utility test.[60] On the facts of *Soule*, therefore, because consumers normally have no meaningful expectations about how the complex mechanisms of physics and mechanics may combine in violent automotive crashes,[61] the court concluded that the risk-utility test was the only appropriate standard for use in a crashworthiness case of this type.[62]

### Contexts

Courts have applied the crashworthiness doctrine in a large variety of contexts. Probably the most recurring type of case, including most of those discussed above, involve the structural integrity of a vehicle: *Evans* and *Dawson* involved the resistance of vehicles to impacts from the side, *Dreisonstok* and *Soule* involved the vehicles' resistance to head-on collisions, and *Heaton* concerned an impact to a wheel. Other cases have similarly involved the integrity of a vehicle's exterior in impact situations,[63] while many others have involved the ability of a vehicle's roof,[64]

---

**57.** 573 P.2d 443 (Cal. 1978).

**58.** Id. at 457–58.

**59.** See § 8.6, above.

**60.** 882 P.2d at 305.

**61.** "[A] complex product, even when it is being used as intended, may often cause injury in a way that does not engage its ordinary consumers' reasonable minimum assumptions about safe performance. For example, the ordinary consumer of an automobile simply has 'no idea' how [safely] it should perform in [various] situations." Id. at 308.

**62.** Consequently, on the facts before it, the court concluded that the jury should not have been instructed on the consumer expectations test:

An ordinary consumer of automobiles cannot reasonably expect that a car's frame, suspension, or interior will be designed to remain intact in any and all accidents. Nor would ordinary experience and understanding inform such a consumer how safely an automobile's design should perform under the esoteric circumstances of the collision at issue here. Indeed, both parties assumed that quite complicated design considerations were at issue, and that expert testimony was necessary to illuminate these matters. There-

fore, injection of ordinary consumer expectations into the design defect equation was improper.

Id. at 310. Nevertheless, because of the "voluminous evidence on the risks and benefits of the Camaro's design," the court saw no reason to believe that the jury ignored such evidence and instead relied upon the consumer expectations test. Id. at 311. Accordingly, the court held that the trial court's error in instructing the jury on the consumer expectations prong was harmless. Id.

**63.** See, e.g., General Motors Corp. v. McGee, 837 So.2d 1010, 1017 (Fla. Dist. Ct. App. 2002) (fuel tank exploded in low impact collision with trailer that had broken free of pickup truck); Poliseno v. General Motors Corp., 744 A.2d 679 (N.J. Super. Ct. App. Div. 2000) (tree penetrated 20 inches through driver's door in low-medium impact collision).

**64.** See, e.g., Romo v. Ford Motor Co., 122 Cal.Rptr.2d 139 (Ct. App. 2002) (fiberglass roof of sport utility vehicle was negligently designed; manufacturer's safety engineers had previously concluded that unreinforced fiberglass should never be used for part of vehicle intended to en-

liftgate latch,[65] or some other component,[66] to withstand the forces of a rollover.

Some of the most notorious crashworthiness cases have involved the ability of a vehicle's fuel system to withstand certain types of collisions. It was the vulnerability of the Ford Pinto's fuel system that formed the basis for a California jury's assessment of $125 million in punitive damages against Ford in *Grimshaw v. Ford Motor Co.*,[67] a 1979 verdict that was eclipsed two decades later by another California jury's levy of a $4.8 *billion* punitive damages assessment against General Motors for locating the 1979 Chevrolet Malibu gas tank behind the rear axle close to the rear bumper, causing the car to burst into flames when hit at high speed from the rear.[68] Both punitive damages verdicts were substantially reduced by the trial courts, but both were partially allowed to stand.[69] Other crashworthiness cases have also involved the integrity of a vehicle's fuel system.[70]

Some crashworthiness cases have involved dangerous design aspects of a vehicle's *interior*, such as a seat latch unable to withstand the forces of a collision,[71] or the presence of sharp or hard objects inside a vehicle

close passenger compartment), vacated by Ford Motor Co. v. Romo, 538 U.S. 1028 (2003), on remand, 6 Cal.Rptr.3d 793 (2003); Hyundai Motor Co. v. Rodriguez, 995 S.W.2d 661 (Tex. 1999) (car roof collapse not caused by design defect); Slone v. General Motors Corp., 457 S.E.2d 51 (Va. 1995) (truck cab roof). See also Green v. General Motors Corp., 709 A.2d 205, 209 (N.J. Super. Ct. App. Div. 1998) (Dreier, P.J.A.D.) (collapse of car roof in non-rollover crash).

**65.** See, e.g., Clark v. Chrysler Corp., 310 F.3d 461 (6th Cir. 2002) (Ky. law), vacated by Chrysler Corp. v. Clark, 540 U.S. 801, on remand Clark v. Chrysler, 80 Fed. Appx. 453 (6th Cir. 2003); Jimenez v. DaimlerChrysler Corp., 269 F.3d 439, 458 (4th Cir. 2001) (S.C. law); Norwest Bank N.M., N.A. v. Chrysler Corp., 981 P.2d 1215 (N.M. Ct. App. 1999).

**66.** See, e.g., Alami v. Volkswagen of Am., Inc., 766 N.E.2d 574 (N.Y. 2002) (defectively designed sub-frame reinforcement); Rossell v. Volkswagen of Am., 709 P.2d 517 (Ariz. 1985) (battery located inside passenger compartment of VW beetle where it could drip acid on occupants if vehicle rolled on back).

**67.** 174 Cal.Rptr. 348 (Ct. App. 1981).

**68.** Anderson v. General Motors Corp., 1999 WL 1466627 (L.A. Cty. Super. Ct. 1999). See White, Jury Orders GM to Pay $4.9 Billion (AP), The State, Columbia, S.C., at A1 (July 10, 1999).

**69.** The trial court in *Grimshaw* reduced the punitive award to $3.5 million, which the appellate court affirmed. Grim-

shaw v. Ford Motor Co., 174 Cal.Rptr. 348 (Ct. App. 1981). *Anderson* was not reviewed by an appellate court, but the trial court remitted the punitive verdict to $1.09 billion. See Germain, Judge Cuts Billions from GM Fine (AP), The State, Columbia, S.C., at A9 (Aug. 27, 1999). *Anderson* and *Grimshaw* are considered in the chapter on punitive damages in ch. 18, below.

**70.** See, e.g., General Motors Corp. v. Iracheta, 90 S.W.3d 725 (Tex. App. 2002) (lack of proper fuel shut-off valve or other anti-siphoning device allowed gasoline to siphon, causing fatal fire); General Motors Corp. v. McGee, 837 So.2d 1010, 1017 (Fla. Dist. Ct. App. 2002) (placement of fuel tank between rear axle and bumper made tank vulnerable to breach and puncture); Gerow v. Mitch Crawford Holiday Motors, 987 S.W.2d 359 (Mo. Ct. App. 1999) ("underslung" fuel tank positioned one-quarter inch above floor pan in front of rear bumper, rendering tank vulnerable to puncture in accidents); In re General Motors Corp. Pick-Up Fuel Tank Prods. Liab. Litig., 55 F.3d 768 (3d Cir. 1995) (rejecting coupon settlement between GM and owners of pickups equipped with dangerous side-saddle fuel tanks); General Motors Corp. v. Edwards, 482 So.2d 1176 (Ala. 1985); Ford Motor Co. v. Stubblefield, 319 S.E.2d 470 (Ga. Ct. App. 1984) (Ford Pinto-type fuel tank used in Mustang II); Huff v. White Motor Corp., 565 F.2d 104 (7th Cir. 1977) (Ind. law) (truck tractor fuel tank).

**71.** See, e.g., Sumnicht v. Toyota Motor Sales, 360 N.W.2d 2 (Wis. 1984). See also Sasser v. Ford Motor Co. (Ga. Super. Ct. 2004), in Ford to Appeal $48 Million Jury Award in Suit Over Faulty Lincoln LS Seat

which can aggravate injuries to occupants in a collision.[72] Other cases have involved claims challenging the safety of a vehicle's *exterior* design for presenting untoward risks to innocent bystanders who may come in contact with sharp or unyielding parts of an automotive vehicle.[73]

Safety devices in vehicles, such as head restraints, lap and shoulder belts, and airbags are all designed to protect occupants in the event of collisions—in short, to make a vehicle more crashworthy. Normally such devices do indeed improve occupant safety, but sometimes they fail or otherwise expose an occupant to an unexpected and unreasonable risk of harm. Thus, a vehicle is uncrashworthy if its roll bar collapses;[74] its headrest contains a sharp metal edge that strikes the driver's skull and kills him when the vehicle is rear-ended;[75] its lap or shoulder belts cause severe abdominal injuries, paralysis, brain damage, or death;[76] or its airbag activates unnecessarily, with excessive force, fails to deploy, or deploys too late, injuring or killing an unsuspecting occupant.[77]

Latch, 32 Prod. Saf. & Liab. Rep. (BNA) (March 29, 2004).

**72.** See, e.g., Carillo v. Ford Motor Co., 759 N.E.2d 99, 107 (Ill. App. Ct. 2001) (driver suffered serious back injury when her seat collapsed during rear-end collision); Ellithorpe v. Ford Motor Co., 503 S.W.2d 516 (Tenn. 1973) (wheel hub popped off exposing sharp prongs that injured driver's face); Mickle v. Blackmon, 166 S.E.2d 173 (S.C. 1969) (passenger impaled on gear shift lever mounted on steering column when plastic knob cover shattered in side-impact collision). See also Lally v. Volkswagen AG, 698 N.E.2d 28 (Mass. App. Ct. 1998) (evidence did not support claims that driver's head hit unpadded pillar between front windshield and side window, and that baby's head hit glove box door that opened in collision); Ford Motor Co. v. Zahn, 265 F.2d 729 (8th Cir. 1959) (Minn. law) (passenger's eye struck sharp edge or jagged burr on corner of ash tray when driver jammed on brakes to avoid collision).

**73.** See, e.g., Threats v. General Motors Corp., 890 S.W.2d 327 (Mo. Ct. App. 1994) (rigid side-view mirror unreasonably dangerous to pedestrians); Knippen v. Ford Motor Co., 546 F.2d 993 (D.C. Cir. 1976); Green v. Volkswagen of Am., Inc., 485 F.2d 430 (6th Cir. 1973) (Mich. law) (finger of young girl, walking by parked van, severed by sharp side vent); Passwaters v. General Motors Corp., 454 F.2d 1270 (8th Cir. 1972) (Iowa law) (motorcycle passenger's leg injured by Ben–Hur-type wheel cover of passing motorist). Compare Kahn v. Chrysler Corp., 221 F.Supp. 677 (S.D. Tex. 1963) (Chrysler had no duty to protect child riding bike from injury from protruding fins of 1957 Dodge); Hatch v. Ford Motor Co., 329 P.2d 605 (Cal. Ct. App. 1958) (boy walked into hood ornament which pierced eye).

Not to be forgotten in this context is Guido Calabresi's classic discussion of a car designed without a spongy bumper. G. Calabresi, The Costs of Accidents 133–40 (1970).

See also Latin and Kasolas, Bad Designs, Lethal Profits: The Duty to Protect Other Motorists Against SUV Collission Risks, 82 B. U. L. Rev. 1161 (2002).

**74.** Leichtamer v. American Motors Corp., 424 N.E.2d 568 (Ohio 1981) (Jeep).

**75.** See, e.g., Huddell v. Levin, 537 F.2d 726 (3d Cir. 1976) (N.J. law).

**76.** See, e.g., Babcock v. General Motors Corp., 299 F.3d 60 (1st Cir. 2002) (N.H. law) (seatbelt failed to latch properly); Nelson v. Ford Motor Co., 761 N.E.2d 1099 (Ohio Ct. App. 2001) (seatbelt designed with comfort feature that allowed for slack in shoulder-belt portion of three-point system; passenger suffered severe and permanent spinal cord injury); Tracy v. Cottrell, 524 S.E.2d 879 (W. Va. 1999) (lap and shoulder belts); Bass v. General Motors Corp., 150 F.3d 842 (8th Cir. 1998) (Mo. law) ("window shade comfort feature," eliminating constant tension, allowed excessive slack to develop in driver's shoulder strap; driver suffered brain damage when his head hit windshield); Johnson v. General Motors Corp., 438 S.E.2d 28 (W. Va. 1993) (rear-seat lap belt); Garrett v. Ford Motor Co., 684 F.Supp. 407 (D. Md. 1987) (same). Hundreds of cases have been brought on whether the standard rear-seat lap belt used on older cars, as opposed to the three point shoulder belt used in the front, renders a vehicle uncrashworthy. See generally Sakayan, Holtz, and Kelley, More Than a Case About a Car—An Analysis of Garrett v. Ford Motor Company, Trial 34 (Feb. 1989); Swartz, Swartz, and Cantor, Seat–Belt Injury Litigation, Trial 47 (Nov. 1988).

**77.** See, e.g., Cansler v. Mills, 765 N.E.2d 698 (Ind. Ct. App. 2002) (airbag did not deploy in injurious accident at 45–50 mph); Harris v. General Motors Corp., 34 Fed. Appx. 487 (7th Cir. 2002) (Ill. law) (airbag failed to deploy after minor collision); Walters ex rel. Walters v. General

Automotive airbags present a special problem.[78] "Airbag technology has been available to automobile manufacturers for over 30 years. There is now general agreement on the proposition 'that, to be safe, a car must have an airbag.' Indeed, current federal law imposes that requirement on all automobile manufacturers."[79] In 1976, a National Highway Traffic Safety Administration regulation, FMVSS 208, provided manufacturers with the option of installing (1) lap and shoulder belts (with a belt warning system), (2) airbags, or (3) both.[80] Amending Standard 208 in 1984, NHTSA conditionally mandated a gradual phase-in of passive restraints, including airbags, in passenger automobiles. The deadline, originally set at 1989, was subsequently extended.[81] By 1989, only a few manufacturers[82] had begun to equip some of their models with airbags as standard equipment, but most manufacturers began to equip their automobiles with airbags over the next several years. By the mid–1990s Volvo, Ford, and several other manufacturers had begun to develop airbags for side impacts, and airbag technology and the extent of airbag protection has continued to improve in the twenty-first century.

During the phase-in period, particularly during the 1990s, many persons injured in cars not equipped with airbags brought "no-airbag" claims against manufacturers alleging that the absence of airbags in their cars unreasonably aggravated their injuries in accidents, thereby rendering the vehicles defective in design. Many state courts allowed such claims,[83] but most federal courts denied the no-airbag claims on grounds of federal preemption.[84] The Supreme Court finally took up the

---

Motors Corp., 209 F.Supp.2d 481, 489 (W.D. Pa. 2002) (manufacturing defect in airbag safety restraint system caused airbags to fail to deploy); Silvestri v. General Motors Corp., 210 F.3d 240 (4th Cir. 2000) (N.Y. law) (airbag, said in owner's manual to deploy in 9–14 mph collisions, failed to deploy in 24 mph collision, causing disfigurement); Pruitt v. General Motors Corp., 86 Cal.Rptr.2d 4 (Ct. App. 1999) (deployment of airbag in low-impact collision broke driver's weak jaw); Cruze v. Ford Motor Co., 1999 WL 1206798 (Tenn. Ct. App. 1999) (late deployment of airbag broke plaintiff's neck); Bresnahan v. Chrysler Corp., 38 Cal. Rptr.2d 446 (Ct. App. 1995) (deployment of airbag in low-impact collision broke driver's elbow).

**78.** On airbag litigation, see Raeker–Jordan, The Pre–Emption Presumption That Never Was: Pre–Emption Doctrine Swallows the Rule, 40 Ariz. L. Rev. 1379 (1998); Chadwell, Automobile Passive Restraint Claims Post–Cipollone: An End to the Federal Preemption Defense, 46 Baylor L. Rev. 141 (1994); § 14.4, above.

**79.** Geier v. American Honda Motor Co., 529 U.S. 861, 886 (2000) (Stevens, J., dissenting) (citing 49 U.S.C. § 30127; 49 C.F.R. § 571.208, S4.1.5.3 (1998)).

**80.** 49 C.F.R. § 571.208, S4.2.2 (1998).

**81.** "Passive restraint regulation (Standard 208) has advanced over the years along a protracted, winding, sometimes perilous course." Public Citizen v. Steed, 851 F.2d 444, 445 (D.C. Cir. 1988). The history of FMVSS 208 is chronicled in Hernandez–Gomez v. Leonardo, 884 P.2d 183 (Ariz. 1994), and Motor Vehicle Mfr. Ass'n v. State Farm Mut. Auto. Ins. Co., 463 U.S. 29, 34–38 (1983).

**82.** Notably Mercedes Benz, Honda (Acura), and BMW.

**83.** See, e.g., Tebbetts v. Ford Motor Co., 665 A.2d 345 (N.H. 1995); Heiple v. C.R. Motors, Inc., 666 A.2d 1066 (Pa. Super. Ct. 1995) (no-airbag claim not expressly nor impliedly preempted, reaffirming Gingold v. Audi–NSU–Auto Union AG, 567 A.2d 312 (Pa. Super. Ct. 1989)); Loulos v. Dick Smith Ford., Inc., 882 S.W.2d 149 (Mo. Ct. App. 1994) (no-airbag claim not expressly nor impliedly preempted); Hernandez–Gomez v. Leonardo, 884 P.2d 183 (Ariz. 1994) (no express preemption based on Standard 208; saving clause "explicitly shelters common law claims"; implied preemption not available). But see Cooper v. General Motors Corp., 702 So.2d 428 (Miss. 1997) (6–3 decision).

**84.** See, e.g., Harris v. Ford Motor Co., 110 F.3d 1410, 1413–15 (9th Cir. 1997) (express preemption).

issue and, in *Geier v. American Honda Motor Company*,[85] it ruled that the National Traffic and Motor Vehicle Safety Act of 1966, and FMVSS 208 promulgated thereunder, impliedly preempted state common-law no-airbag actions. As a result, no-airbag claims are now prohibited under the federal preemption doctrine.[86]

## § 17.4 INDIVISIBLE HARM AND DAMAGES APPORTIONMENT

Damages apportionment broadly concerns how damages should be divided between the plaintiff, defendant, and any third parties. General principles of damages apportionment applicable to products liability litigation are examined elsewhere in treatments of the extent to which a plaintiff's fault or other form of misconduct may bar or reduce the plaintiff's damages[1] and the extent to which defendants may share responsibility for damages with other defendants.[2] In many respects, the normal damages apportionment principles applicable to products liability cases apply as well to automotive products cases. Yet, a number of special apportionment issues have arisen in the automotive product context that require separate examination. This section considers the question of who has the burden of proving apportionment in crashworthiness cases, the plaintiff or the defendant.[3] The next section considers the role of plaintiff fault in automotive products liability cases.

As examined in the preceding section, the crashworthiness doctrine maintains that vehicular manufacturers have a duty to afford as much protection as reasonably possible against the risks of "second collisions" between a vehicle's occupants and its interior.[4] More generally, the duty is one of affording reasonable protection to occupants against defects in design[5] that may enhance or aggravate injuries in a collision or other

---

**85.** 529 U.S. 861 (2000).

**86.** *Geier* and federal preemption are examined in depth in § 14.4, above.

### § 17.4

**1.** See ch. 13, above.

**2.** See 2 Madden & Owen on Products Liability ch. 25 (multiple defendants—contribution and indemnity).

**3.** See Chadwick, "Causing" Enhanced Injuries in Crashworthiness Cases, 48 Syracuse L. Rev. 1223 (1998); Vickles and Oldham, Enhanced Injury Should Not Equal Enhanced Liability, 36 S. Tex. L. Rev. 417 (1995); O'Donnell, Public Policy and the Burden of Proof in Enhanced Injury Litigation: A Case Study in the Dangers of Trends and Easy Assumptions, 17 W. St. U. L. Rev. 325 (1990); Tietz, Bushman, and Podraza, Crashworthiness and *Erie*: Determining State Law Regarding the Burden of Proving and Apportioning Damages, 62 Temple L.Q. 587 (1989); Levanstam and Lapp, Plaintiff's Burden of Proving Enhanced Injury in Crashworthiness Cases: A Clash Worthy of Analysis, 38 Depaul L. Rev. 55 (1988); Clark, Second Collision Liability: A Critique of Two Approaches to

Plaintiff's Burden of Proof, 68 Iowa L. Rev. 811 (1983); Foland, Enhanced Injury: Problems of Proof in "Second Collision" and "Crashworthy" Cases, 16 Washburn L. J. 600 (1977); Note, Apportionment of Damages in the "Second Collision" Case, 63 Va. L. Rev. 475 (1977) (excellent analysis); Annot., 9 A.L.R. 4th 494 (1981) (sufficiency of proof of injuries in second collision cases). 3 Frumer and Friedman, Products Liability § 21.04. The Products Liability Restatement § 16, including its comments and Reporters' Notes, contains one of the best treatments of this entire issue.

**4.** See § 17.3, above.

**5.** Although the vast majority of crashworthiness cases involve defects in design, they may be based on other types of defect or on a manufacturer's false representations. See, e.g., Gable v. Gates Mills, 784 N.E.2d 739, 741 (Ohio Ct. App. 2003) (failure to provide adequate warnings of "lethal potential" of airbags); Chandler v. Gene Messer Ford, Inc., 81 S.W.3d 493, 503–04 (Tex. App. 2002) (failure to warn of possible risks from airbag deployment to child riding in front passenger seat); Carlson v. Hyundai Motor Co., 164 F.3d 1160 (8th Cir.

accident situation. If a manufacturer breaches this duty, it is axiomatic that the manufacturer will be responsible for any resulting harm—that is, any harm proximately resulting from the uncrashworthy design of the vehicle.[6] But liability for such additional ("enhanced" or "aggravated") injuries does not render the manufacturer responsible for other injuries that the occupant would have suffered anyway from the first collision. Thus, assuming that the first collision was caused by something other than an automotive defect, such as driver error or dangerous highway conditions, the manufacturer of an uncrashworthy vehicle is *not* responsible for the injuries caused in the initial accident but *is* responsible for any *additional* injuries attributable to the uncrashworthy feature of the vehicle.

This fundamental rule of causal responsibility was first enunciated in *Larsen v. General Motors Corporation*,[7] the case which first imposed the crashworthiness duty on manufacturers of automotive vehicles.[8] "Any design defect not causing the accident would not subject the manufacturer to liability for the entire damage, but the manufacturer should be liable for that portion of the damage or injury caused by the defective design *over and above* the damage or injury that probably would have occurred as a result of the impact or collision absent the defective design."[9] This basic apportionment principle is simple, logical, and fair: a manufacturer should pay for the damage caused by defects in its vehicles, but not for damages caused by something else. When this kind of division of injuries between the first and second collisions is feasible, it clearly must be done, and the manufacturer's responsibility will be limited to those damages resulting from the uncrashworthy aspect of the vehicle. For example, if a truck is driven through a red light and smashes into the passenger door of a car entering the intersection, the force of the first collision may break the arm of a passenger in the car and may also cause the car to roll over, injuring the passenger's head when the roof collapses. Assuming that a properly designed roof structure would not have collapsed, the passenger, in a crashworthiness action against the manufacturer of the car, may recover for his head injuries caused by the uncrashworthy roof but not for his broken arm caused by the first collision. Probably all courts would agree with this commonsense result, which is also embraced by the *Products Liability Restatement*.[10]

---

1999) (bad door welds); Jimenez v. Chrysler Corp., 74 F.Supp.2d 548 (D.S.C. 1999), rev'd, Jimenez v. DaimlerChrysler Corp., 269 F.3d 439 (4th Cir. 2001) (manufacturer negligently misrepresented that minivans equipped with flimsy liftgate latch were safe); Crispin v. Volkswagenwerk AG, 591 A.2d 966, 976–98 (N.J. Super. Ct. App. Div. 1991) (failure to warn that occupants should wear seatbelts to reduce risk of injury in collisions); Lahocki v. Contee Sand & Gravel Co., 398 A.2d 490 (Md. Ct. Spec. App. 1979) (bad roof welds).

**6.** Products Liability Restatement § 16, "Increased Harm Due to Product Defect," provides in part: "(a) When a product is

defective at the time of commercial sale or other distribution and the defect is a substantial factor in increasing the plaintiff's harm beyond that which would have resulted from other causes, the product seller is subject to liability for the increased harm."

**7.** 391 F.2d 495 (8th Cir. 1968) (Minn. law).

**8.** See § 17.3, above.

**9.** *Larsen*, 391 F.2d at 503 (emphasis added).

**10.** Products Liability Restatement § 16(b) provides: "If proof supports a determination of the harm that would have resulted from other causes in the absence of

In violent collision situations involving severe injuries, however, determining which injuries were caused by the first collision and which are attributable only to the second collision is often difficult or impossible.[11] Thus, whether the injured plaintiff or the defendant manufacturer has the burden of proof on damages apportionment—on proving which damages were caused by the vehicle's uncrashworthy feature—may effectively determine whether recovery is allowable in serious injury cases in which the vehicle's crashworthiness is challenged.

The first case to expressly address the apportionment burden-of-proof problem in crashworthiness cases was *Huddell v. Levin*,[12] decided in 1976 by the Third Circuit Court of Appeals. Plaintiff Huddell was killed when his Chevrolet Nova, which had run out of gas, was hit from behind at 50–60 miles per hour by another car. The plaintiff died from brain injuries caused by the impact of his head against the head restraint which contained "a relatively sharp, unyielding metal edge, covered by two inches of soft, foam-like material."[13] In an action against General Motors, the manufacturer of the Nova, the plaintiff contended that the head restraint was defective " 'because its relatively sharp edge of unyielding metal allowed for excessive concentration of forces against the rear of the skull,' " and that it " 'was designed much like an airplane wing, with the front "ax-like" portion aimed directly at the rear of the head.' "[14] The jury decided in favor of the plaintiff. In General Motors' appeal, the Third Circuit reversed, ruling that plaintiffs in design defect crashworthiness cases must prove three things: (1) the existence of a feasible, alternative, safer design; (2) the injuries that would have resulted from such an alternative design; and (3) "the extent of enhanced injuries attributable to the defective design."[15] Because the plaintiff's expert had only testified that a properly designed head restraint would have been "survivable," and because the plaintiff offered no proof of the probable extent of injury had such a restraint been used,[16] a majority of the court[17] ruled that the plaintiff had failed to carry his burden of proof showing the extent to which the design defect had caused his damages.[18]

the product defect, the product seller's liability is limited to the increased harm attributable solely to the product defect."

**11.** See Note, Apportionment of Damages in the "Second Collision" Case, 63 Va. L. Rev. 475, 476 (1977) ("Courts will hold the manufacturer liable for the plaintiff's loss in the second collision only if defective design of the automobile caused or exacerbated the plaintiff's injury. Yet, if a court finds that defective automobile design did cause some injury, determining where one defendant's liability ends and another's begins may be virtually impossible. Both those injuries for which the manufacturer should be liable and those attributable to other causes, such as another driver's negligence, occurred during the very brief time span of the second collision.").

**12.** 537 F.2d 726 (3rd Cir. 1976) (N.J. law).

**13.** Huddell v. Levin, 395 F.Supp. 64, 68 (D.N.J. 1975).

**14.** 537 F.2d at 735.

**15.** Id. at 738.

**16.** "It was not established whether the hypothetical victim of the survivable crash would have sustained no injuries, temporary injuries, permanent but insignificant injuries, extensive and permanent injuries, or, possibly, paraplegia or quadriplegia." Id.

**17.** Over Judge Rosenn's persuasive concurring opinion arguing that the burden of proof should have been shifted to the defendant. See id. at 744.

**18.** "Without proof to establish what injuries would have resulted from a non-defective head restraint, the plaintiff could not and did not establish what injuries resulted from the alleged defect in the head restraint." Id. at 738.

One year after *Huddell*, in 1977, the federal circuits began to split. In *Smith v. Fiat–Roosevelt Motors, Inc.*,[19] the plaintiff was injured when the Fiat he was driving was rear-ended causing his seat to collapse. In a crashworthiness action against the supplier of a car, the district court granted the defendant's summary judgment motion because the plaintiff's doctor admitted his inability to apportion the injuries between those caused by the initial rear-ending and those caused by the collapse of the plaintiff's seat. Reversing, the Fifth Circuit ruled that the plaintiff's inability to apportion the damages was not fatal to his crashworthiness case, since "[i]n Florida, where an injury is indivisible and apportionment is impossible, plaintiff may recover his entire damages from either tortfeasor."[20]

During the next year, 1978, the split among the circuits widened. *Fox v. Ford Motor Company*[21] involved the deaths of two rear-seat passengers who were killed in a 1970 Ford Thunderbird when they were thrown forward in a head-on collision. Both plaintiffs suffered fractured spines and fatal abdominal injuries caused by the seatbelts they were wearing.[22] Their case alleged that Ford had designed the car in an uncrashworthy condition by failing to install shoulder harnesses in the rear passenger compartment, setting the seatbelts at the wrong angle, and failing to provide adequate padding on the backs of the front seats.[23] The trial court refused Ford's requested jury instruction that it was liable only for that portion of the damage caused by the defective design over and above the injury attributable to the initial impact. Rejecting the defendant's argument from *Huddell* that the plaintiffs should have been required to prove with specificity the injuries caused by the alleged design defects, and reasoning that the "duty to prove so-called enhanced damages is simply a part of the plaintiff's responsibility to prove proximate cause,"[24] a split panel of the Tenth Circuit ruled that the trial court had sufficiently instructed the jury that the plaintiffs were required to establish the alleged defects proximately caused the deaths.[25]

Over the next few years, the split among the circuits deepened further. In 1981, a divided panel of the Second Circuit followed *Huddell* in a thinly reasoned decision, *Caiazzo v. Volkswagenwerk AG*.[26] The

---

**19.**  556 F.2d 728 (5th Cir. 1977) (Fla. law).

**20.**  Id. at 729. The year before, the Fifth Circuit had ruled ambiguously on the apportionment issue in Higginbotham v. Ford Motor Co., 540 F.2d 762, 772–74 (5th Cir. 1976) (Ga. law).

**21.**  575 F.2d 774 (10th Cir. 1978) (Wyo. law) (Doyle, J.).

**22.**  Id. at 778. The head of one plaintiff hit an unpadded portion of the front seat which broke her neck.

**23.**  Id. at 783.

**24.**  Id. at 787.

**25.**  See id. at 788.

**26.**  647 F.2d 241 (2d Cir. 1981) (N.Y. law). The court summarized its rationale:

We realize that a plaintiff's burden of offering evidence of what injuries would have resulted absent the alleged defect will be heavy in some instances and perhaps impossible in others. Where it is impossible, however, the plaintiff has merely failed to establish his prima facie case, i.e., that it is more probable than not that the alleged defect aggravated or enhanced the injuries resulting from the initial collision. Moreover, in those instances in which the plaintiff cannot offer any evidence as to what would have occurred but for the alleged defect, the plaintiff has not established the fact of enhancement at all.

Id. at 251.

following year, in *Mitchell v. Volkswagenwerk, AG,*[27] the Eighth Circuit followed the *Fox* approach, lucidly explaining how automotive manufacturers and other defendants are jointly and severally liable for indivisible injuries (such as paraplegia and death) where there is no reasonable basis for determining causation between them.[28] Thereafter, the number of jurisdictions following the *Huddell* approach of burdening plaintiffs with apportionment has been diminishing[29] and a growing majority of courts—including an intermediate appellate court in New Jersey, the state whose law was predicted in *Huddell*—now follow the *Fox-Mitchell* approach of holding manufacturers of uncrashworthy vehicles responsible for indivisible injuries.[30]

Proponents of the *Fox-Mitchell* method of shifting the burden of apportionment to defendant manufacturers often point to the established common-law principle that two or more tortfeasors whose actions combine to cause a single injury are jointly and severally liable for the

---

**27.** 669 F.2d 1199 (8th Cir. 1982) (Minn. law).

**28.** See id. at 1206:

[T]he plaintiffs' burden of proof should be deemed satisfied against the manufacturer if it is shown that the design defect was a substantial factor in producing damages over and above those which were probably caused as a result of the original impact or collision. [T]he extent of the manufacturer's liability depends upon whether or not the injuries involved are divisible such that the injuries can be clearly separated and attributed either to the manufacturer or the original tortfeasor. If the manufacturer's negligence is found to be a substantial factor in causing an indivisible injury such as paraplegia, death, etc., then absent a reasonable basis to determine which wrongdoer actually caused the harm, the defendants should be treated as joint and several tortfeasors.

**29.** See, e.g., Sumner v. General Motors Corp., 538 N.W.2d 112 (Mich. Ct. App. 1995); Brooks v. Beech Aircraft Corp., 902 P.2d 54 (N.M. 1995); Kupetz v. Deere & Co., 644 A.2d 1213 (Pa. Super. Ct. 1994); Chretien v. General Motors Corp., 959 F.2d 231 (4th Cir. 1992) (Va. law); Garcia v. Rivera, 553 N.Y.S.2d 378 (App. Div. 1990); Duran v. General Motors Corp., 688 P.2d 779 (N.M. Ct. App. 1983), overruled on other grounds; Caiazzo v. Volkswagenwerk AG, 647 F.2d 241 (2d Cir. 1981) (N.Y. law); Wernimont v. International Harvester Corp., 309 N.W.2d 137 (Iowa Ct. App. 1981); Stonehocker v. General Motors Corp., 587 F.2d 151 (4th Cir. 1978) (S.C. law); Huddell v. Levin, 537 F.2d 726 (3rd Cir. 1976) (N.J. law).

**30.** See, e.g., Carrasquilla v. Mazda Motor Corp., 197 F.Supp.2d 169, 180 (M.D. Pa. 2002); Stecher v. Ford Motor Co., 779 A.2d 491, 497 (Pa. Super. Ct. 2001) (dicta); Trull v. Volkswagen of Am., Inc., 761 A.2d 477 (N.H. 2000); Poliseno v. General Motors Corp., 744 A.2d 679 (N.J. Super. Ct. App. Div. 2000); Tracy v. Cottrell, 524 S.E.2d 879 (W. Va. 1999); General Motors Corp. v. Farnsworth, 965 P.2d 1209 (Alaska 1998); Kudlacek v. Fiat S.P.A., 509 N.W.2d 603 (Neb. 1994); DePaepe v. General Motors Corp., 33 F.3d 737 (7th Cir. 1994) (Ill. law); Oakes v. General Motors Corp., 628 N.E.2d 341 (Ill. App. Ct. 1993); Polston v. Boomershine Pontiac–GMC Truck, 423 S.E.2d 659 (Ga. 1992); Blankenship v. General Motors Corp., 406 S.E.2d 781 (W. Va. 1991); Czarnecki v. Volkswagen of Am., 837 P.2d 1143 (Ariz. Ct. App. 1991); Doupnik v. General Motors Corp., 275 Cal.Rptr. 715 (Ct. App. 1990); McDowell v. Kawasaki Motors Corp. USA, 799 S.W.2d 854 (Mo. Ct. App. 1990); Jackson v. Warrum, 535 N.E.2d 1207, 1220 (Ind. Ct. App. 1989); General Motors Corp. v. Edwards, 482 So.2d 1176, 1189 (Ala. 1985), overruled on other grounds, Schwartz v. Volvo North Am. Corp., 554 So.2d 927 (Ala. 1989); Shipp v. General Motors Corp., 750 F.2d 418 (5th Cir. 1985) (Tex. law); Sumnicht v. Toyota Motor Sales U.S.A., Inc., 360 N.W.2d 2 (Wis. 1984); Lee v. Volkswagen of Am., Inc., 688 P.2d 1283 (Okla. 1984); Fouche v. Chrysler Motors Corp., 692 P.2d 345 (Idaho 1984); McLeod v. American Motors Corp., 723 F.2d 830 (11th Cir. 1984) (Fla. law); Mitchell v. Volkswagenwerk AG, 669 F.2d 1199 (8th Cir. 1982) (Minn. law); Buehler v. Whalen, 374 N.E.2d 460 (Ill. 1978); Chrysler Corp. v. Todorovich, 580 P.2d 1123 (Wyo. 1978); Fox v. Ford Motor Co., 575 F.2d 774 (10th Cir. 1978) (Wyo. law). See also May v. Portland Jeep, Inc., 509 P.2d 24 (Or. 1973).

harm unless they can prove a basis for apportionment.[31] Indeed, the *Restatement (Second) of Torts* provides for a general shift in the burden of proof to defendants in such cases,[32] and the *Third Restatement* adopts essentially the same approach.[33] Following the reasoning of the *Second Restatement*,[34] the *Third Restatement* explains that "[t]he defendant, a wrongdoer who in fact has caused harm to the plaintiff, should not escape liability because the nature of the harm makes such a determination impossible."[35] Following *Fox-Mitchell* and most other courts,[36] the *Third Restatement* provides that if the plaintiff establishes that an uncrashworthy feature of a vehicle was a substantial factor in aggravating his or her injuries, the defendant bears responsibility for all such injuries which are incapable of apportionment.[37]

In short, a large and growing majority of courts, most objective scholars,[38] and the *Second* and *Third Restatements of Torts*, all maintain that the *Huddell* approach provides an unfair escape for wrongdoing manufacturers when the extent of harm they have caused to innocent plaintiffs[39] is by nature impossible to ascertain.[40] Thus, subject to a

---

**31.** "[W]here wrongdoers each play a substantial role in creating an indivisible harm, they are treated as joint and several tortfeasors." Mitchell v. Volkswagenwerk AG, 669 F.2d 1199, 1207 (8th Cir. 1982) (Minn. law). See Products Liability Restatement § 16, Reporters' Note to cmt. *d*; Prosser and Keeton on Torts § 52; Dobbs, Law of Torts § 174.

**32.** Restatement (2d) Torts § 433B(2) provides: "Where the tortious conduct of two or more actors has combined to bring about harm to the plaintiff, and one or more of the actors seeks to limit his liability on the ground that the harm is capable of apportionment among them, the burden of proof as to the apportionment is upon each such actor."

**33.** The Products Liability Restatement § 16(c) provides: "If proof does not support a determination under Subsection (b) of the harm that would have resulted in the absence of the product defect, the product seller is liable for all of the plaintiff's harm attributable to the defect and other causes." The Reporters avowal that subsection (c) does not formally shift the burden of proof to the defendant is unpersuasive. See Reporters' Note to cmt. *d*.

**34.** See Restatement (2d) Torts § 433B cmt. *d*, justifying "the exceptional rule placing the burden of proof as to apportionment upon the defendant or defendants," rather than upon the innocent plaintiff, by pointing to "the injustice of allowing a proved wrongdoer who has in fact caused harm to the plaintiff to escape liability merely because the harm which he has inflicted has combined with similar harm inflicted by other wrongdoers," rendering causal attribution impossible. See also Products Liability Restatement § 16 Reporters' Note to cmt. *d*.

**35.** Products Liability Restatement § 16 cmt. *d*.

**36.** *But see* Chadwick, "Causing" Enhanced Injuries in Crashworthiness Cases, 48 Syracuse L. Rev. 1223, 1258–61 (1998) (criticizing the *Third Restatement* for adopting a confusing position lying somewhere between *Huddell* and *Fox-Mitchell*).

**37.** In addition to proving defect, "[t]he plaintiff must also establish that the defect was a substantial factor in increasing the plaintiff's harm beyond the harm that would have occurred from other causes," and "when proof does not support a determination of increased harm, the product seller is liable for all harm suffered by the victim." Products Liability Restatement § 16 cmt. *b*.

Cases involving multiple defendants are governed by the applicable apportionment rules of joint and several liability. See Products Liability Restatement § 16(d) ("A seller of a defective product ... is jointly and severally liable or severally liable with other parties who bear legal responsibility for causing the harm, determined by applicable rules of joint and several liability.").

**38.** Much of the writing on this topic, some of it cogently argued, was authored by defense counsel.

**39.** If the plaintiff affirmatively causes an accident by his or her own fault, as by driving recklessly while intoxicated, it seems less unfair to require him or her to apportion damages. But a plaintiff's merely passive failure to wear a seatbelt does not in any respect diminish his or her fairness claim to have the defendant apportion damages. For a contrary view, see Caiazzo v. Volkswagenwerk AG, 647 F.2d 241, 253 (2d Cir. 1981) (N.Y. law) (Mansfield, J., concurring).

**40.** See, e.g., Stecher v. Ford Motor Co., 779 A.2d 491, 497 (Pa. Super. Ct. 2001)

weakening minority to the contrary, the courts now widely hold that automotive manufacturers are responsible for both the divisible and indivisible harm caused by uncrashworthy features of their vehicles. The plaintiff must establish that the feature was a substantial factor in aggravating his or her injuries, after which the manufacturer is liable for all such injuries that it is unable to prove were not caused by the vehicle's uncrashworthy design.

## § 17.5   Plaintiff Fault

### Plaintiff Fault—In General

For various reasons, defendant manufacturers often seek to introduce evidence of the plaintiff's fault in automotive products liability litigation.[1] Whether the evidence concerns the driver's intoxication, speeding, erratic driving, failing to wear an available seatbelt, falling asleep, overloading the vehicle, failing to keep the tires inflated or otherwise to maintain the vehicle, or any other form of misbehavior, the manufacturer of the vehicle will often seek to strengthen its own case, and weaken the plaintiff's, with evidence that the plaintiff used the vehicle improperly. Such evidence may undercut the plaintiff's prima facie case on cause in fact and proximate causation, establish affirmative defenses, and diminish the plaintiff's damages. Moreover, evidence of the plaintiff's misbehavior may intangibly tarnish his or her standing in the eyes of the jury and so tip the balance of the scales of justice in favor of the manufacturer.

The general role of plaintiff fault in products liability litigation, including the defenses of contributory negligence, assumption of risk, product misuse, and comparative fault, is considered elsewhere.[2] But courts and legislatures have confronted a number of special issues involving the fault of drivers and other plaintiffs in automotive products liability cases. General aspects of plaintiff fault in automotive products liability litigation are examined first, followed by a consideration of the role of a driver's intoxication and the effect of a plaintiff's failure to wear a seatbelt or other safety devices.

### *Accident Causation*

Evidence of a driver's misconduct is relevant in a products liability action only if it contributed in some way to cause the accident. Assume, for example, that a drunken driver is injured while driving at excessive

---

(dicta); Williams v. Ford Motor Co., 1986 WL 110681, at *2 (W.D. Tenn. 1986); Lee v. Volkswagen of Am., Inc., 688 P.2d 1283, 1288 (Okla. 1984); Tietz, Bushman, and Podraza, Crashworthiness and *Erie*: Determining State Law Regarding the Burden of Proving and Apportioning Damages, 62 Temple L.Q. 587, 620 (1989). See generally Products Liability Restatement § 16 Reporters' Note to cmt. *d* (collecting authorities).

**§ 17.5**

**1.** See DeDominicis, No Duty at Any Speed?: Determining the Responsibility of the Automobile Manufacturer in Speed–Related Accidents, 14 Hofstra L. Rev. 403 (1986); Davis, Individual and Institutional Responsibility: A Vision for Comparative Fault in Products Liability, 39 Vill. L. Rev. 281 (1994).

**2.** See ch. 13, above.

speed when one of his tires blows out. If the plaintiff can establish that the tire failed solely because it was manufactured in a defective condition, and that neither the speed nor erratic driving caused by his intoxication contributed in any way to the tire's failure, then the driver's misconduct simply has no bearing on any issue in the case. Surely it has no relevance to the defectiveness of the tire, nor to the manufacturer's negligence in making and selling it in such a condition. Nor, assuming that the defect was latent, does it have any relevance to assumption of risk (which requires that a plaintiff appreciate the specific risk), to contributory or comparative negligence, or to product misuse, all of which require that the misconduct was a contributing cause of the plaintiff's harm. In a case like this, a court should exclude all such evidence of the driver's misconduct simply because it has no bearing on accident causation. Stated otherwise, evidence of a plaintiff's bad behavior must be excluded if it was not a cause in fact of the accident or resulting injuries.

To help avoid the defense of contributory negligence, a negligent driver typically will base a products liability claim on strict liability in tort. As previously discussed, courts widely hold that a plaintiff's simple contributory negligence is not a bar to a claim for strict products liability in tort.[3] Thus, if a drunken driver, injured when his fast and erratic driving causes his sport utility vehicle to roll over, asserts that the SUV was too susceptible to rolling over, he normally should limit his claim to strict liability in tort and ask the court to exclude evidence of his intoxication, speed, and erratic driving. However, a court may refuse to keep out some or all of this misconduct evidence for at least three reasons. First, in replacing the absolute bar of contributory negligence with the damages-reducing feature of comparative fault,[4] most states now have eliminated the principal reason for ousting a plaintiff's contributory fault from consideration in strict products liability in tort.[5] A second, related reason for admitting such misconduct evidence in the SUV hypothetical is that, unlike the defective tire situation, such evidence might possibly be relevant to the defenses of misuse and assumption of risk defense. The third reason this kind of evidence may properly be admissible is that the SUV in the previous example may have rolled over because the forces placed on it were too great for any SUV, not because of any defect in its design. While the mere fact of the driver's intoxication may have no direct bearing on the vehicle's roll-over propensities, certainly both the driver's speed and erratic maneuvering are highly relevant to how and why the accident occurred and, so, to proximate causation, and possibly to the defectiveness of its design. Thus, the SUV driver's misconduct may not bar liability on grounds of contributory negligence, but it may be relevant to comparative fault, misuse, assumption of risk, proximate causation, and product defectiveness.

A driver's misconduct implicates two principal causation issues—cause in fact and proximate cause. Sometimes the actual cause of an

---

**3.** See § 13.2, above.

**4.** See § 13.3, above.

**5.** See Annot., 9 A.L.R.4th 633 (1981) (applicability of comparative fault to strict liability in tort).

accident is hotly in dispute, with the plaintiff typically claiming that the accident was caused by some defect in the vehicle and the manufacturer asserting that the failed component in the vehicle was caused by the violence of the accident which itself was caused by the driver's misbehavior. In *Hardy v. General Motors Corporation*,[6] for example, the driver of a Corvette was injured when he lost control of his car and struck a tree while attempting to negotiate a curve at between 104 and 111 miles per hour. The plaintiff's expert testified that the loss of control resulted when a tie rod broke due to a fatigue fracture, while the defendant's engineers testified that the tie rod broke when the vehicle hit the tree. Affirming a directed verdict for the defendant, the court determined that the evidence clearly established that the loss of control was caused by the driver's dangerous driving, not by any defect in the car. Other courts similarly have allowed evidence of the driver's speeding and erratic driving,[7] or recklessly jamming on the brakes in a high-speed turn,[8] to support the defendant's theory of accident causation, but not to prove the plaintiff's contributory fault.

The other principal causation issue to which driver fault is relevant is *proximate* causation, as distinguished from factual causation. If a driver's misconduct is clearly the dominant cause of the injuries, and any uncrashworthy aspect of the vehicle is trivial by comparison, the driver's claim may be barred on grounds that his misconduct was the sole proximate cause of the accident.[9] Often characterized merely as a "sole cause" or "proximate cause" issue, courts sometimes admit evidence of a driver's grossly careless driving to bar the claim on some such basis. On this ground, for example, courts have allowed evidence of a driver's speeding while intoxicated,[10] or speeding at 110–20 miles per hour on underinflated tires.[11]

### Relevance in Crashworthiness Cases

Most of the cases involving the role of a driver's fault discussed above involve manufacturing defects alleged to have caused the initial accident. A difficult issue that has sharply split the courts[12] is whether the fault of the driver or other occupant in causing an accident may be considered, as a matter of proximate cause or comparative fault, in apportioning damages for enhanced injuries in crashworthiness cases.[13]

---

**6.** 710 N.E.2d 764 (Ohio Ct. App. 1998).

**7.** See, e.g., Reidelberger v. Highland Body Shop, Inc., 416 N.E.2d 268 (Ill. 1981).

**8.** See Daye v. General Motors Corp., 720 So.2d 654, 660 (La. 1998) ("In reality, plaintiff's vigorous application of the brakes while driving through a blind curve on a substandard two-lane country road at a breakneck speed—and not his reliance on the promotional information—was the cause of the accident.").

**9.** See ch. 13, above.

**10.** See, e.g., Mazda Motor Corp. v. Lindahl, 706 A.2d 526 (Del. 1998) (driver killed when car failed to negotiate curve and plunged down embankment, tumbling end over end through air, and striking ground several times before it came to rest; claim for defective design of seats denied).

**11.** Hegwood v. General Motors Corp., 286 N.W.2d 29 (Iowa 1979) (tire blowout; jury properly could find that no failure of manufacturer was proximate cause of accident).

**12.** See Products Liability Restatement § 16 Reporters' Note to cmt. *f* (characterizing driver fault as "more difficult" and noting that courts are "sharply split").

**13.** See Annot., 69 A.L.R.5th 625 (1999) (collecting cases on driver's comparative fault as defense to second collision claims). More generally, most courts now reduce a plaintiff's damages on account of his or her comparative fault. See ch. 13, above.

Some courts take the position that evidence of the plaintiff's fault in causing the first collision is simply irrelevant to the issue of a manufacturer's duty to protect occupants against statistically inevitable second collisions.[14] Other courts disagree, reasoning that the role of plaintiff fault in crashworthiness cases logically is no different than in other contexts.[15]

A closely divided decision, *Reed v. Chrysler Corporation*,[16] illustrates the two perspectives. The plaintiff, riding as a passenger, injured his arm in the rollover of a Jeep CJ–7. The plaintiff's claim against Jeep's manufacturer was that the vehicle was uncrashworthy because its top was made of brittle fiberglass rather than the much stronger steel used by other manufacturers. Both the driver and plaintiff were intoxicated at the time of the collision, evidence which Chrysler introduced. Ruling that the intoxication evidence should have been excluded, a five judge majority of the court, overruling an earlier decision to the contrary, reasoned that a driver's misconduct in causing an accident is "beside the point" because the role of the crashworthiness duty is to reduce damages in "accidents precipitated for myriad reasons."[17] The four judges in dissent thought that the majority entirely missed the point: "Because under settled principles of proximate cause a claimant's fault that produces an injury-producing occurrence will also be a proximate cause of the enhanced injuries sustained, the usual rules for fault comparison should apply to the enhanced injury portion of the claim."[18]

This issue is a close and difficult one, as illustrated not only by the sharp division of the court in *Reed*, but by the nearly equal division of the decisions which continue to go both ways. It is sometimes said that a majority of courts allow evidence of a driver's comparative fault to be considered in crashworthiness enhanced injury cases.[19] In truth, however, the decisions are quite evenly divided.[20] Many of the cases, particularly the older ones, fail to focus on the precise issue,[21] and many of the

---

**14.** For cases prior to 1995, see, e.g., Volkswagen of Am., Inc. v. Marinelli, 628 So.2d 378, 385 (Ala. 1993); Pree v. Brunswick Corp., 983 F.2d 863, 866 n.3 (8th Cir. 1993) (Mo. law) ("evidence of intoxication is irrelevant in a strict tort liability action for enhancement of injury"); Reed v. Chrysler Corp., 494 N.W.2d 224 (Iowa 1992); Andrews v. Harley Davidson, Inc., 796 P.2d 1092, 1095 (Nev. 1990); Cota v. Harley Davidson, 684 P.2d 888 (Ariz. Ct. App. 1984); Ford Motor Co. v. Hill, 404 So.2d 1049 (Fla. 1981). Cases from 1995 are listed at note 22 below.

**15.** For cases prior to 1995, see, e.g., Harvey v. General Motors Corp., 873 F.2d 1343 (10th Cir. 1989) (Wyo. law) (drinking and reckless driving); Dahl v. Bayerische Motoren Werke, 748 P.2d 77 (Or. 1987); Day v. General Motors Corp., 345 N.W.2d 349 (N.D. 1984); Keltner v. Ford Motor Co., 748 F.2d 1265 (8th Cir. 1984) (Ark. law) (intoxication); Hinkamp v. American Motors Corp., 735 F.Supp. 176 (E.D.N.C.

1989), aff'd, 900 F.2d 252 (4th Cir. 1990); Daly v. General Motors Corp., 575 P.2d 1162, 1174 (Cal. 1978) (intoxication). Cases from 1995 are listed at note 22 below.

**16.** 494 N.W.2d 224 (Iowa 1992).

**17.** Id. at 230.

**18.** Id. at 231.

**19.** See, e.g., Whitehead v. Toyota Motor Corp., 897 S.W.2d 684, 693 (Tenn. 1995); Kidron, Inc. v. Carmona, 665 So.2d 289 (Fla. Dist. Ct. App. 1995); Products Liability Restatement § 16 Reporters' Note to cmt. *f*; 2 Prod. Liab. Rep. (CCH) ¶ 3030, at 6903 (1997).

**20.** See Annot., 69 A.L.R.5th 625 (1999) (collecting cases on driver's comparative fault as defense to second collision claims).

**21.** See Meekins v. Ford Motor Co., 699 A.2d 339, 343 (Del. Super. Ct. 1997) ("[m]any of the decisions on both sides of the issue reach a conclusion but fail to analyze the issue in depth").

more recent ones exclude evidence of driver fault in cases of this type.[22] At present, therefore, a simple head count of decisions is a hollow exercise that diverts attention from the difficult issues of fairness and policy that need attention.

The commentators are also hopelessly divided, some viewing driver fault as irrelevant to claims for enhanced injuries,[23] others viewing such conduct as no different from other types of plaintiff (or third party) fault.[24] The *Third Restatement* addresses this issue ambiguously. The Reporters favored a rule excluding evidence of driver fault in crashwor-

**22.** Since 1995, the cases have continued to split, but most of the very recent cases explicitly examining this issue have ruled that driver negligence should not be considered on a manufacturer's liability for enhanced injuries in a crashworthiness case.

*Allowing* evidence of driver fault in crashworthiness cases, see General Motors Corp. v. Farnsworth, 965 P.2d 1209 (Alaska 1998); Meekins v. Ford Motor Co., 699 A.2d 339 (Del. Super. Ct. 1997) (balanced presentation of both positions); Montag v. Honda Motor Co., 75 F.3d 1414 (10th Cir. 1996) (Colo. law) (driving car equipped with defective seatbelt into path of train); Whitehead v. Toyota Motor Corp., 897 S.W.2d 684 (Tenn. 1995); Kidron, Inc. v. Carmona, 665 So.2d 289 (Fla. Dist. Ct. App. 1995); Boutte v. Nissan Motor Corp., 663 So.2d 154, 161 (La. Ct. App. 1995) (falling asleep; but defendant's "fault should have been assessed in relation to the injury sustained by [plaintiff] rather than the cause of the accident"). See also Estate of Hunter v. General Motors Corp., 729 So.2d 1264 (Miss. 1999) (dictum); Bravo v. Ford Motor Co. 2001 WL 477275, at *6 (Conn. Super. Ct. 2001); .

*Disallowing* evidence of driver fault, see Gable v. Gates Mills, 784 N.E.2d 739, 741 (Ohio Ct. App. 2003); Alami v. Volkswagen of Am., Inc., 766 N.E.2d 574, 577 (N.Y. 2002); D'Amario v. Ford Motor Co., 806 So.2d 424, 426 (Fla. 2001); Jimenez v. DaimlerChrysler Corp., 269 F.3d 439, 452–54 (4th Cir. 2001) (S.C. law) (child passenger injured when mother ran red light); Mercurio v. Nissan Motor Corp., 81 F.Supp.2d 859 (N.D. Ohio 2000); Gerow v. Mitch Crawford Holiday Motors, 987 S.W.2d 359 (Mo. Ct. App. 1999) (falling asleep); Norwest Bank N.M., N.A. v. Chrysler Corp., 981 P.2d 1215 (N.M. Ct. App. 1999); Binakonsky v. Ford Motor Co., 133 F.3d 281 (4th Cir. 1998) (Md. law) (driver's intoxication irrelevant to whether allegedly defective fuel tank enhanced his injuries when vehicle crashed); Green v. General Motors Corp., 709 A.2d 205, 216 (N.J. Super. Ct. App. Div. 1998); Kritzberg v. Chrysler Corp., No. 1:97 CV 03579, Tr. at 17 (N.D. Ill. May 15, 1997) (Posner, J.). On *D'Amario*, compare Roth, 78 Fla. B.J. 20

(Apr. 2004) (critical), with Ricci, Leopold, and Salzillo, id. at 14 (June 2004) (favorable).

**23.** See, e.g., DiPaola and Ricci, Evolution of the Automobile Crashworthiness Doctrine in Florida, 69 Fla. Bar J. 40, 44 (Oct. 1995) (emphasis added) ("Logically, where a plaintiff proceeds solely on a crashworthiness claim, the defendant should not have a defense based on the cause of the *accident* because the plaintiff is not making a claim that the *accident* was caused by the defendant. Instead, pure crashworthiness cases should focus on the cause of the enhancement of the plaintiff's *injuries* and eliminate operator error or third party negligence as a defense."); Hogan, The Crashworthiness Doctrine, 18 Am. J. Trial Advoc. 37, 52–53 (1994) ("The crashworthiness doctrine, by taking driver actions out of the case, can also restrict available defenses. The logic seems unassailable that where the plaintiff makes no claim that the accident was caused by the defendant, the defendant should not have a defense based on the cause of the accident."); Harris, Enhanced Injury Theory: An Analytic Framework, 62 N.C. L. Rev. 643, 673–74 (1984) ("[i]n enhanced injury cases, unlike ordinary products liability cases, a claimant's fault in causing the accident is not a basis for reducing his recovery [because] a manufacturer's duty is that of minimizing the injurious effects of contact however caused [and a] negligent operator is entitled to the same protection against unnecessary injury as the careful user"); Reichert, Limitations on Manufacturer Liability in Second Collision Actions, 43 Mont. L. Rev. 109 (1982).

**24.** See, e.g., Vickles and Oldham, Enhanced Injury Should Not Equal Enhanced Liability, 36 S. Tex. L. Rev. 417 (1995) (plaintiff's conduct affecting severity of accident affects severity of injuries and thus constitutes proximate cause of enhanced injuries which should be considered in damages apportionment); Thomas, Comparative Fault in Crashworthiness or "Second Collision" Cases, 22 Prod. Safety & Liab. Rep. (BNA) No. 20, 520 (April 29, 1994) (plaintiff's fault should be considered in enhanced injury cases); Bowbeer and Borkon, Recent Developments in Crashworthiness Litigation, 450 Prac. Law Inst.—Litigation 9, 37 (1992); V. Schwartz, Comparative Negligence § 12.5, at 204–05 (5th ed. 1986).

thiness cases, cogently explained in an early draft comment[25] which the American Law Institute Council tentatively approved and presented to the general membership for consideration in 1994.[26] But the automotive defense bar had been forewarned, and a polished brief was presented to the membership advocating the other way.[27] Despite an impassioned explanation by the Reporters of the logic of their view,[28] a slight majority of the membership voted to deny the Reporters' exemption of driver fault from apportionment of enhanced injuries in crashworthiness cases.[29] Dutifully deleting this enhanced injury exception from the comments to the apportionment rule,[30] together with the relevant portion of their persuasive Reporters' Note,[31] the Reporters artfully redrafted the

---

**25.** Their discussion remains the most considered analysis of this issue. After explaining that the black letter general rule "provides that all forms of plaintiff fault are to be considered by the trier of fact for the purposes of apportioning liability between the plaintiff and the product seller" without exempting, for example, a plaintiff's failure to discover a product defect, they summarized the case for excepting driver fault from apportionment in enhanced injury cases:

> Cases of increased harm require a different rule. The requirement that an automobile be reasonably crashworthy, for example, aims to protect the plaintiff from increased harm arising from harm-causing uses of the product that defendant should have foreseen and protected against. An automobile, not otherwise defective, does not become defective because it fails to protect a plaintiff against harm-causing conduct where the risks exceed those that defendant could reasonably have protected against. However, if the risks created by plaintiff's conduct are within the range that justifies crashworthiness protection, plaintiff's conduct creates the very situation in which the plaintiff has a legitimate right to expect the automobile to provide reasonable protection. This is so regardless of the nature of the plaintiff's conduct. Accordingly, plaintiff's fault should not be taken into account in determining the defendant's liability for the defect-caused increase in harm.

> Ignoring the role of plaintiff's fault in connection with increased harm in cases where the proof supports causal apportionment has troubled many courts who find it objectionable that drunken drivers or drug abusers be allowed full recovery for increased harm when the initial accident was brought about by such egregious conduct. The issue is admittedly a difficult one. On balance, however, the theoretical justification for requiring a defendant to provide reasonable protection against increased harm when a plaintiff is fully dependent on the product

to mitigate harm makes it difficult to distinguish between the forms of conduct that brought the plaintiff to the state of dependency.

Products Liability Restatement § 6 cmt. *f, Plaintiff's fault in cases of increased harm* (Tent. Draft No. 1, 1994). See also the Reporters' Note to comment *f*, note 4, below, which further explicated their position. The Reporters might have continued: We would not say that a drunken college student who stumbles and hits his head is entitled to any less protection from the rules of damages for medical malpractice than an elderly person who stumbles and hits his head.

**26.** See Products Liability Restatement § 6 cmt. *f* (Tent. Draft No. 1, 1994).

**27.** By a memorandum and oral presentation, both exceptionally well crafted, presented to the ALI membership by a defense attorney member of the Institute. See 71 ALI Proc. 207–08 (1994).

**28.** See id. at 208–214.

**29.** See id. at 214.

**30.** See Products Liability Restatement § 11 cmt. *f* (Tent. Draft No. 2, 1995).

**31.** Products Liability Restatement § 6 Reporters' Note to cmt. *f* (Tent. Draft No. 1, 1994):

> Although we recognize that the arguments supporting taking into consideration a plaintiff's fault in bringing about the accident have validity, we believe that strong policy considerations support the position taken in Comment *f*. Consider, for example, a plaintiff who was injured when either a seatbelt or an air bag failed because it was either defectively manufactured or defectively designed. Should negligent conduct, on the part of the plaintiff in causing the first collision be taken into account to reduce the plaintiff's recovery? We suggest that to do so would make little sense. The purpose of the seatbelt or air bag is to function when the plaintiff is involved in an accident

pertinent comment to leave wiggle room for courts to apportion enhanced injuries *in toto* to manufacturers of uncrashworthy vehicles.[32]

The *Restatement* Reporters are not the only conservative scholars who believe that driver fault should be immune from enhanced injury apportionment in crashworthiness cases. No less an authority than Chief Judge (and professor) Richard Posner, not generally viewed as a mindless protecter of plaintiff interests, ruled that evidence of driver fault should be excluded in a crashworthiness case because a contrary conclusion "wouldn't make any sense."[33] Indeed, if one accepts the proposition that many, perhaps most, automotive accidents giving rise to crashworthiness claims are caused entirely by driver fault, allowing a driver's

and to offer protection when the plaintiff can no longer do anything in self protection. The seatbelt or air bag is designed to protect the plaintiff in a crash situation. How the plaintiff got into the situation is of little relevance. No manufacturer would say that its seatbelts or air bags are there only for the protection of the non-negligent. A crashworthiness claim is very much like a defective seatbelt or defective air bag claim. It demands of the manufacturer that it provide a reasonable design to protect a plaintiff when an auto has been involved in a collision. If plaintiff's conduct has been such that the auto need not protect against it, then the auto is simply not defective. No auto manufacturer has to design a car to protect a plaintiff who drives a car going over a cliff. However, once an auto has been found to be defectively designed and hence not crashworthy, it should not lie in the mouth of the auto manufacturer to claim that the plaintiff put itself in the position that it had to make use of the very aspect of the product that made it non-crashworthy. This is reminiscent of the common law doctrine that contributory fault should not be taken into account when the plaintiff made use of a product and tested the express warranty of the defendant-manufacturer. The plaintiff here has, so to speak, put the product to its reasonableness test. When it fails, the plaintiff's conduct should not be considered in apportioning fault.

An argument can be made that it behooves us to seek to deter plaintiffs from acting negligently even though the product provides them with inadequate crashworthiness protection. There are several reasons why the deterrent value of comparative fault is of lesser importance in this class of cases. First, before plaintiffs encounter enhanced injuries, they first encounter accident injuries. These injuries will be borne in whole or part by a negligent plaintiff. Second, where other defendant tortfeasors are involved in an

accident, the plaintiff's conduct will operate to reduce recovery against those tortfeasors. Plaintiffs cannot, in advance, plan on the absence of first collision injuries or on the likelihood that other tortfeasors may be present on the scene. In short, significant deterrence incentives already exist to encourage safe conduct on the part of plaintiffs.

**32.** In their redraft of comment *f*, the Reporters excluded an explicit exemption of driver fault from apportionment of enhanced injuries and stated that "the nature of the product defect [is] relevant in allocating the appropriate percentages between the plaintiff and the product seller, but should not serve automatically to absolve the plaintiff from fault." The comment further provided that "the contributory fault of the plaintiff in causing the accident that resulted in defect-related increased harm is relevant in apportioning damages between or among the parties, according to applicable apportionment law. In apportioning damages in these cases, it may be important that requiring a product to be designed reasonably to prevent increased harm aims to protect the plaintiff from harm when the plaintiff is in a position where self-protection is no longer possible." Products Liability Restatement § 11 cmt. *f* (Tent. Draft No. 2, 1995). The final version, approved by the ALI in 1997 and published in 1998, is nearly identical. See Products Liability Restatement § 16 cmt. *f*.

**33.** Kritzberg v. Chrysler Corp., No. 97 C 3579, Tr. at 17 (N.D. Ill. Dec. 1, 1999, Hr'g). Temporally assigned (by himself) as a district judge, Judge Posner reasoned: "[I]f you have an accident, no matter how much it's your fault, [the manufacturer's duty to build a crashworthy vehicle is] going to minimize the consequence of it. So I can't see as a matter of basic tort theory how the [plaintiff's] negligence in falling asleep [while driving] has anything to do with the case." Id. at 15. See also Haugh v. Jones & Laughlin Steel Corp., 949 F.2d 914, 920–21 (7th Cir. 1991) (Ind. law) (discuss-

fault to reduce his or her damages appears to go a long way to "emasculate second collision liability."[34] But the siren call of comparative fault, which has beguiled many a busy court into surrendering to juries responsibility for resolving difficult issues of responsibility, continues its seductive draw of tort law issues into the clutches of its greedy grasp.[35] Advocates on both sides of the driver-fault crashworthiness debate assert that logic supports only their position, but doctrinal logic does not lead ineluctably to an evident, true conclusion, such that courts and commentators have much work remaining to reach a reasoned resolution of this perplexing problem.

## Plaintiff's Intoxication

### In General

In products liability claims against the manufacturer or other seller of an automotive vehicle, evidence that the plaintiff driver[36] was intoxicated is often relevant and admissible.[37] Because intoxication obviously reduces the skill and judgment a driver needs to operate a vehicle safely, and because driving under the influence of intoxicants is widely criminalized for just this reason,[38] intoxication evidence logically bears on the driver's failure to exercise reasonable care for his or her own safety. Thus, a driver's intoxication (but not necessarily the mere fact that he had been drinking)[39] generally is proof of a driver's contributory negligence[40] that may bar recovery, or comparative fault that may reduce the

ing policy reasons for not requiring plaintiffs to anticipate negligence of others).

**34.** Comment, 43 Mont. L. Rev. 109 (1982).

**35.** See Prosser & Keeton on Torts § 67, at 479 (observing that "[c]ourts need to be cautious not to become caught up by the sheer momentum of the [comparative fault] movement, and with the facile simplicity of the doctrine, but instead should apply deliberate thought to each new call for its further extension").

**36.** While normally it is the driver's intoxication that may be relevant in a products liability action against the manufacturer or other seller of a vehicle, a passenger's intoxication sometimes may also be relevant to the passenger's claim against the manufacturer. See, e.g., Truchan v. Nissan Motor Corp., 720 A.2d 981 (N.J. Super. Ct. App. Div. 1998) (rear-seat passenger allegedly lay down in seatbelt and was too drunk to heed warnings about seatbelt system); Rodriguez v. Suzuki Motor Corp., 936 S.W.2d 104, 109 (Mo. 1996) (passenger's alcohol consumption relevant to her comparative fault in deciding to enter and remain in vehicle operated by intoxicated driver); Harvey v. General Motors Corp., 873 F.2d 1343 (10th Cir. 1989) (Wyo. law) (passenger's drinking relevant to lack of care for his own safety and to whether he had negligently encouraged driver's misconduct).

**37.** See 3 Am. Law Prod. Liab. 3d § 40.19.

**38.** Hence, operating an automotive vehicle in violation of a state's prohibitions against driving under the influence may be considered (contributory) negligence per se. See, e.g., Salinas v. General Motors Corp., 857 S.W.2d 944 (Tex. App. 1993).

**39.** The fact of ultimate relevance in civil litigation ordinarily is intoxication, not any particular level of blood alcohol. See, e.g., Miles v. General Motors Corp., 262 F.3d 720, 723 (8th Cir. 2001) (Ark. law) ("Given the circumstances surrounding the accident, the jury was entitled to consider whether Miles's alcohol consumption contributed to the accident."); Hunter v. General Motors Corp., 729 So.2d 1264 (Miss. 1999) (proper to admit evidence of driver's intoxication even if below statutory level of legal intoxication); Surowiec v. General Motors Corp., 672 A.2d 333, 336 (Pa. Super. Ct. 1996) ("where recklessness or carelessness is at issue, proof of intoxication is relevant, but the mere fact of consuming alcohol is inadmissible as unfairly prejudicial unless it reasonably establishes intoxication").

**40.** See, e.g., Hinkamp v. American Motors Corp., 735 F.Supp. 176 (E.D.N.C. 1989), aff'd, 900 F.2d 252 (4th Cir. 1990); Jarrell v. Ford Motor Co., 327 F.2d 233 (4th Cir. 1964) (W. Va. law). On contributory negligence generally, see § 13.2, above.

driver's damages proportionate to his or her fault.[41] Indeed, in the majority of jurisdictions that have adopted modified (as opposed to "pure") comparative fault, a driver's intoxication will bar recovery altogether if it exceeds the fault of the manufacturer.[42] Moreover, under any form of comparative fault, a driver's intoxication will operate as a total bar to recovery if it is determined to have been the sole cause of an accident.[43]

A driver's intoxication also may establish the defense of assumption of risk.[44] If an intoxicated driver is aware of and understands the risks of a particular defect in a vehicle, his or her decision to operate the vehicle, or to use it in a particular manner, may bar (or reduce)[45] recovery because of the driver's voluntary decision to encounter the risk.[46] But if the driver does not know of and voluntarily encounters a particular defect, the assumption of risk defense will fail.[47]

Evidence of a driver's intoxication has also been held admissible for the purpose of establishing a driver's misuse of an automotive vehicle.[48] Yet driving under the influence is such a common problem that it must be viewed as a foreseeable risk against which a manufacturer is duty-bound to guard.[49] Put otherwise, a driver's intoxication cannot *ipso facto* bar a products liability action under the common-law misuse doctrine. Yet, in states that have merged the misuse defense into their general systems of comparative fault,[50] evidence of driving while intoxicated may serve to reduce a driver's damages or possibly to bar the claim entirely.[51]

**41.** See, e.g., Rodriguez v. Suzuki Motor Corp., 936 S.W.2d 104, 107 (Mo. 1996) (since apportionment of fault and damages is factual by nature, jury should be as fully informed as possible to determine relative fault of parties, and comparative fault system better accommodates alcohol evidence than contributory negligence system); Ake v. General Motors Corp., 942 F.Supp. 869, 875 (W.D.N.Y. 1996) (driving while intoxicated could be considered "culpable conduct" under comparative fault statute). See also Daly v. General Motors Corp., 575 P.2d 1162, 1173–74 (Cal. 1978) (by implication). On comparative fault generally, see § 13.3, above.

**42.** See id.

**43.** See, e.g., Wallace v. Ford Motor Co., 723 A.2d 1226 (N.J. Super. Ct. App. Div. 1999).

**44.** On assumption of risk generally, see § 13.4, above.

**45.** The plaintiff's recovery will be reduced rather than barred, at least if the plaintiff's fault is less than the manufacturer's, in jurisdictions which have merged assumption of risk into their general systems of comparative fault. See id.

**46.** See, e.g., Davis v. Brooks Transp. Co., 186 F.Supp. 366, 371 (D. Del. 1960).

**47.** See, e.g., Mercurio v. Nissan Motor Corp., 81 F.Supp.2d 859, 861–62 (N.D. Ohio

2000) (no evidence that intoxicated driver knew that vehicle's subfloor posed unreasonable risk of buckling, nor that he voluntarily exposed himself to vehicle's uncrashworthy condition); LeBouef v. Goodyear Tire & Rubber Co., 623 F.2d 985 (5th Cir. 1980) (La. law) (insufficient evidence that intoxicated driver killed in accident caused by tread separation knew that tire could not be used safely at speeds in excess of 100 mph); DeFelice v. Ford Motor Co., 255 A.2d 636 (Conn. Super. Ct. 1969).

**48.** See, e.g., Tunnell v. Ford Motor Co., 330 F.Supp.2d 748 (W.D. Va. 2004); Kirkland v. General Motors Corp., 521 P.2d 1353, 1367 (Okla. 1974) (driving under intoxication is "an abnormal use or misuse of the product and is a complete defense to strict liability theory"); General Motors Corp. v. Walden, 406 F.2d 606 (10th Cir. 1969) (Ariz. law). On misuse generally, see § 13.5, above.

**49.** See, e.g., Mercurio v. Nissan Motor Corp., 81 F.Supp.2d 859 (N.D. Ohio 2000); Reed v. Chrysler Corp., 494 N.W.2d 224, 230 (Iowa 1992), quoted below.

**50.** See § 13.5, above.

**51.** In modified comparative fault jurisdictions, a plaintiff's recovery may be barred entirely, rather than reduced, if the plaintiff's fault is found to have exceeded that of the manufacturer. See § 13.1, above.

Apart from the misconduct defenses, evidence of a driver's intoxication may be admissible on proximate causation, including both cause in fact and proximate or legal cause. With respect to cause in fact, intoxication may bear on whether the driver's improper driving technique (brought about by the intoxication), rather than some problem in the vehicle, such as a defective axle, caused the accident.[52] Such evidence is especially relevant if the plaintiff proceeds under the "malfunction theory" of liability,[53] since that theory requires a plaintiff to negate reasonable secondary causes of the accident.[54] In addition, if a driver's severe intoxication results in a violent collision, the drunk driving, rather than some defect in the vehicle, may be found to be the sole proximate cause of the resulting injuries.[55]

Finally, it is important to remember that some courts hold that evidence of a driver's intoxication is irrelevant to an enhanced injury claim based on some uncrashworthy aspect of an automotive vehicle. Although many courts disagree,[56] as previously discussed,[57] some courts view the manufacturer's duty broadly to require that vehicles be designed and manufactured in a manner that reasonably protects all its occupants from second collision injuries regardless of the cause of the initial accident, whether from the driver's intoxication or something else.[58]

**52.** See, e.g., Wallace v. Ford Motor Co., 723 A.2d 1226 (N.J. Super. Ct. App. Div. 1999) (intoxication evidence admissible, relevant to "proximate cause" or comparative fault, to establish that cause of vehicle's rollover was bad driving rather than defect in axle); Hansen v. General Motors Corp., 915 F.Supp. 118 (E.D. Mo. 1996); Swajian v. General Motors Corp., 916 F.2d 31, 34 (1st Cir. 1990) (R.I. law) (evidence of intoxication admissible to show causation):

> Armed with this evidence, the jury could have concluded that driver error contributed significantly to, if not caused, decedent's accident. As it was, the jury was presented with the following factual scenario: the two month old vehicle was travelling down a straight, flat road in good weather when it swayed and went out of control for no apparent reason. The only explanation proffered was that there was a defect in one of the axles. Without the evidence of intoxication the jury was left with no reason for the loss of control other than [plaintiff's] allegations.

See also Truchan v. Nissan Motor Corp., 720 A.2d 981, 989 (N.J. Super. Ct. App. Div. 1998) (rear-seat passenger claimed to be sitting upright when injured by seatbelt in collision: "evidence of plaintiff's intoxication may be admitted both to prove that she was in a 'slumped' position at the time of impact and to show that she would not have heeded warnings pertaining to the dangers posed by the seatbelt system had they been given").

**53.** See § 7.4, above. See also § 2.5 (res ipsa loquitur), above.

**54.** See, e.g., Surowiec v. General Motors Corp., 672 A.2d 333, 336–37 (Pa. Super. Ct. 1996).

**55.** See, e.g., Timmons v. Ford Motor Co., 982 F.Supp. 1475, 1479 (S.D. Ga. 1997) ("when the circumstances of the crash itself rise to such an extreme level of violence that manufacturers cannot reasonably and cost-effectively protect consumers," the consequences of such high-speed collision are unforeseeable and driver's drunk driving is sole proximate cause of deaths in collision); Goodman v. General Motors Corp., 652 N.Y.S.2d 626 (App. Div. 1997) (sole proximate causes of accident were driver's intoxication, together with plaintiff's standing in dark roadway, not design of plaintiff's delivery van whose rear lights were blocked by open doors of van).

**56.** Some courts allow intoxication evidence in crashworthiness cases without appearing to recognize the issue. See, e.g., Ake v. General Motors Corp., 942 F.Supp. 869 (W.D.N.Y. 1996) (intoxication evidence admitted, without discussion of appropriateness in this context, in claim of uncrashworthy fuel system design).

**57.** See this section, above.

**58.** See, e.g., Reed v. Chrysler Corp., 494 N.W.2d 224, 230 (Iowa 1992) ("The theory, which presupposes the occurrence of accidents precipitated for myriad reasons, focuses alone on the enhancement of

### Statutes

Many states in recent decades have enacted driving-under-the-influence statutes that specifically address the role of a driver's intoxication in civil litigation. Several statutes provide broadly that the results of breath tests are admissible evidence in any civil action,[59] and others provide more specifically that such evidence is admissible in civil (or criminal) actions arising out of driving under the influence.[60] An Alaska statute provides that a driver's *refusal* to submit to the prescribed DUI chemical test is admissible evidence in an action arising out of an accident allegedly resulting from his or her driving while intoxicated.[61] Ohio has a statute providing that proof of a plaintiff's violation of its DUI statute, coupled with proof that the plaintiff at the time in fact was under the influence, creates a rebuttable presumption that "the alcohol or drug abuse was the proximate cause of the harm for which the plaintiff seeks to recover damages."[62] Statutes in at least Michigan and Washington provide an absolute defense to claims for injury or death in accidents in which the plaintiff's intoxication was at least,[63] or more than,[64] 50% responsible for the accident.

## Failure to Use Seatbelts and Other Safety Devices

One of the easiest and most effective ways to increase one's life expectancy, and to improve the general level of automotive safety,[65] is to

resulting injuries [so that] any participation by the plaintiff in bringing the accident about is quite beside the point."); Andrews v. Harley Davidson, Inc., 796 P.2d 1092, 1095 (Nev. 1990) ("[a] major policy reason behind holding manufacturers strictly liable for failing to produce crashworthy vehicles is to encourage them to do all they reasonably can do to design a vehicle which will protect a driver in an accident," and manufacturers can foresee that intoxicated drivers will drive negligently and cause accidents); Mercurio v. Nissan Motor Corp., 81 F.Supp.2d 859, 861 (N.D. Ohio 2000):

> The fact that a collision may have been caused by the driver's intoxication, as opposed to another form of negligence, does not reduce the manufacturer's duty to provide a reasonably safe vehicle. The Court is reminded of the old adage that "[a] drunken man is as much entitled to a safe street as a sober one, and much more in need of it." Robinson v. Pioche, Bayerque & Co., 5 Cal. 460, 461 (1855).

See also Smothers v. General Motors Corp., 40 Cal.Rptr.2d 618 (Ct. App. 1995) (in crashworthiness case in which plaintiff did not dispute that accident was caused by his intoxication, trial judge could exclude intoxication evidence because such evidence is relevant to cause of accident rather than cause of plaintiff's injuries).

**59.** See, e.g., Ariz. Rev. Stat. Ann. § 28–1323; Okla. Stat. Ann. tit. 47 § 752(J); Or. Rev. Stat. § 813.320.

**60.** New Mexico's statute is typical:

The results of a test performed pursuant to the Implied Consent Act [66–8–105 to 66–8–112 NMSA 1978] may be introduced into evidence in any civil action or criminal action arising out of the acts alleged to have been committed by the person tested for driving a motor vehicle while under the influence of intoxicating liquor or drugs.

N.M. Stat. Ann. § 66–8–110A. Similar statutes include: Fla. Stat. Ann. § 316.1934(2); Ga. Code Ann. § 40–6–392(a); 625 Ill. Comp. Stat. Ann. 5/11–501.1(c); Minn. Stat. Ann. § 169.121 subd. 6(b).

**61.** Alaska Stat. § 28.35.032(e).

**62.** Ohio Rev. Code Ann. § 2353.59.

**63.** Mich. Comp. Laws. Ann. § 600. 2955a.

**64.** Wash. Rev. Code Ann. § 5.40.060.

**65.** Using automotive seatbelts is one of the most effective ways to improve one's life expectancy. For passengers over 4 years old on American highways, seatbelts saved over 11,000 lives in 1998 alone, and over 110,000 lives from 1975 through 1998. See NCSA Fact Sheet: Traffic Safety Facts 1998–Occupant Protection, National Highway Traffic Vehicle Administration, DOT HS 808 954, at 2 <http://www.nhtsa.dot.gov/people/ncsa/pdf/OccPrt98.pdf> (hereinafter Traffic Safety Facts). When they are used,

buckle up one's seatbelt.[66] Put another way, occupants of automotive vehicles who fail to use their seatbelts significantly increase the risk of being seriously injured or killed in accident situations.[67] For these reasons, automobile manufacturers began equipping some vehicles with seatbelts in the 1950s,[68] states legislatures began requiring manufacturers to install seatbelts in automobiles in the early 1960s,[69] and, by 1966, the automotive industry began equipping the entire fleet of automobiles with seatbelts.[70]

But equipping cars with seatbelts did not mean that people would use them. As late as the mid–1980s, a pathetically low 13% of Americans voluntarily wore their seatbelts.[71] To hasten seatbelt usage, NHTSA in 1984 issued a rule requiring that all new cars be equipped with automatic seatbelts or airbags by 1990, unless by 1989 states comprising two-thirds of the nation's population enacted qualifying mandatory seatbelt use laws.[72] One qualifying criterion was the jurisdiction's adoption of the seat-belt defense, reducing damages in civil actions for seatbelt nonuse.[73] From 1984 through 1987, thirty-one states enacted mandatory seatbelt use laws, and seatbelt usage correspondingly increased from 14% to 42%.[74] By 1998, seatbelt usage had increased to 62% in states with secondary enforcement laws and 79% in states with primary enforcement laws.[75] By 2003, all states except New Hampshire[76] had adopted mandatory seatbelt use statutes applicable to adults[77] and the national seat-belt usage rate had risen to nearly 80%.[78]

lap/shoulder safety belts reduce the risk of death to front-seat car occupants by 45%, their risk of moderate to critical injury by 50%, the risk of death to light truck occupants by 60%, and their risk of moderate to critical injury by 65%. Id. at 1.

**66.** See, e.g., Waterson v. General Motors Corp., 544 A.2d 357, 373 (N.J. 1988) ("the effectiveness of seatbelts in reducing death and injury from automobile accidents cannot reasonably be disputed at this point [and] this Court is willing to take judicial notice of the efficacy of seatbelts [as o]ther courts have done"); Dunn v. Durso, 530 A.2d 387, 393 n. 8 (N.J. Super Ct. Law Div. 1986) ("[p]roperly worn, seatbelts may be the most significant source of automobile crash protection for automobile occupants"); Spier v. Barker, 323 N.E.2d 164, 168 (N.Y. 1974) (emphasis omitted) ("[t]he seatbelt, properly installed and properly worn, still offers the single best protection available to the automotive occupant exposed to an impact").

**67.** In 1998, nearly 10,000 people killed in automotive accidents in America could have survived by wearing seatbelts. Traffic Safety Facts, above, at 1.

**68.** The first seatbelt was installed in an automobile in 1955. 3 Frumer and Friedman, Products Liability § 21.06, at 21–111.

**69.** New York was the first state to require seatbelts in 1962. See Comment, 36 Hous. L. Rev. 1371, 1378 n.33 (1999).

**70.** See id. at 1378.

**71.** See Note, 64 N.C. L. Rev. 1127, 1131 (1986).

**72.** See Federal Motor Vehicle Safety Standard; Occupant Crash Protection, 49 Fed. Reg. 28,962–63 (1984), codified at 49 C.F.R. § 571.208.

**73.** Id. at S4.1.5.1(c)(2).

**74.** Comment, 36 Hous. L. Rev. 1371, 1378 n.43 (1999).

**75.** See Traffic Safety Facts, above, at 1.

**76.** New Hampshire's motto is "Live Free or Die." See Wooley v. Maynard, 430 U.S. 705 (1977).

**77.** All fifty states, including New Hampshire, have mandatory child restraint use laws. New Hampshire reports a seatbelt use rate of 56%. See Traffic Safety Facts, above, at 1.

**78.** Seat–Belt Use Rises to 79% Across U.S., Topping Expectations, Wall St. J., Aug. 26, 2003, at D4.

### Seatbelt Defense; Common–Law Development

From the time seatbelts first began to be widely available in 1960s, defendants in car accident litigation have sought to introduce evidence that the plaintiff failed to use an available seatbelt.[79] In defending a vehicular accident case, the "seat-belt defense" is used to try to establish that the plaintiff, rather than the defendant, is responsible for those injuries which a seatbelt would have prevented.[80] Depending on the underlying claim and the nature of the particular collision and injuries,[81] a defendant may seek to introduce evidence of seatbelt nonuse on any number of legal issues, including the plaintiff's comparative fault,[82] assumption of risk,[83] or failure to mitigate damages;[84] the proximate cause of the accident[85] or the injuries;[86] or, in a products liability case,

---

**79.** The first use of the seat-belt defense may have been in Stockinger v. Dunisch, No. 981 (Wis. Cir. Ct. 1964), in which the jury reduced the plaintiff's damages by 10% for failing to use an available seatbelt. See Westenberg, Buckle Up or Pay: The Emerging Safety Belt Defense, 20 Suffolk U. L. Rev. 867, 869 n.4 (1986).

**80.** On the seatbelt defense generally, see, e.g., Mobley, Revisiting Alabama's Seatbelt Defense: Is the Failure to Buckle Up a Defense in AEMLD Claims?, 53 Ala. L. Rev. 963 (2002); Bomer, The Seatbelt Defense: A Doctrine Based in Common Sense, 38 Tulsa L. Rev. 405 (2002); Nielsen, Tort Litigation—The New Case For the "Seat Belt Defense"—Norwest Bank, N.A. v. Chrysler Corporation, 30 N.M. L. Rev. 403 (2000); Scaff, The Final Piece of the Seat Belt Evidence Puzzle, 36 Hous. L. Rev. 1371 (1999); LeBel, Reducing the Recovery of Avoidable "Seat–Belt Damages": A Cure for the Defects of Waterson v. General Motors Corporation, 22 Seton Hall L. Rev. 1 (1991); L. Schwartz, The Seat–Belt Defense and Seatbelt Mandatory Usage: Law, Ethics, and Economics, 24 Idaho L. Rev. 275 (1988); Westenberg, Buckle Up or Pay: The Emerging Safety Belt Defense, 20 Suffolk U. L. Rev. 867 (1986); Ackerman, The Seat–Belt Defense Reconsidered: A Return to Accountability in Tort Law?, 16 N.M. L. Rev. 221 (1986); Benguerel, Mandatory Seat Belt Legislation: Panacea for Highway Traffic Fatalities?, 36 Syracuse L. Rev. 1341 (1986); Werber, A Multi–Disciplinary Approach to Seat Belt Issues, 29 Clev. St. L. Rev. 217 (1980); Hoglund and Parsons, Caveat Viator: The Duty to Wear Seat Belts Under Comparative Negligence Law, 50 Wash. L. Rev. 1 (1974); Kircher, The Seat–Belt Defense—State of the Law, 53 Marq. L. Rev. 172 (1970); Comment, 36 Hous. L. Rev. 1371 (1999); Annot., Nonuse of Seatbelt as Reducing Amount of Damages Recoverable, 62 A.L.R.5th 537 (1998).

For an excellent overview of the role of seatbelts in automotive products liability litigation, see 3 Frumer and Friedman, Products Liability § 21.06.

**81.** And depending, of course, on the jurisdiction, since many jurisdictions preclude use of the defense entirely or for certain purposes. See Annot., 62 A.L.R.5th 537 (1998); Comment, 36 Hous. L. Rev. 1371, 1380 (1990).

**82.** See, e.g., Gable v. Gates Mills, 784 N.E.2d 739 (Ohio Ct. App. 2003); Waterson v. General Motors Corp., 544 A.2d 357 (N.J. 1988), noted, 102 Harv. L. Rev. 925 (1989); Dahl v. Bayerische Motoren Werke (BMW), 748 P.2d 77 (Or. 1987); Bentzler v. Braun, 149 N.W.2d 626 (Wis. 1967).

**83.** See, e.g., Walsh v. Emergency One, 1992 WL 180134 (N.D. Ill. 1992), aff'd, 26 F.3d 1417 (7th Cir. 1994). See also Mac-Donald v. General Motors Corp., 784 F.Supp. 486 (M.D. Tenn. 1992). See generally Ackerman, The Seat–Belt Defense Reconsidered: A Return to Accountability in Tort Law?, 16 N.M. L. Rev. 221, 227 (1986) (calling "quite plausible" application of assumption of risk defense to seatbelt nonuse "in light of the well-known dangers of the highway").

Yet, to establish assumption of risk, many courts require a defendant to establish that the plaintiff was aware of the particular risk that caused injury which renders it difficult to apply this defense to the seatbelt nonuse situation. "It is the opinion of this court that the failure to buckle up does not constitute a self-willed and knowing exposure to the specific risk of sustaining enhanced injuries originally set in motion by another person's negligence or undetectable product defect." Swajian v. General Motors Corp., 559 A.2d 1041, 1046–47 (R.I. 1989).

**84.** See, e.g., Hutchins v. Schwartz, 724 P.2d 1194 (Alaska 1986); Spier v. Barker, 323 N.E.2d 164 (N.Y. 1974).

**85.** See, e.g., Jimenez v. DaimlerChrysler Corp., 269 F.3d 439, 458 (4th Cir. 2001) (S.C. law); Floyd v. General Motors Corp., 960 P.2d 763 (Kan. Ct. App. 1998) (plaintiff claimed that broken steering mechanism caused accident, but defendant contended that mechanism was broken in driver-

**86.** See note 86 on page 1113.

the crashworthy nature[87] or the plaintiff's misuse[88] of the vehicle. The law concerning the seatbelt defense is fragmented and ever-shifting,[89] and the best that can be done here is to highlight some of its central features.

In early attempts to invoke the seatbelt defense, most courts were hostile to the concept in any form. In rejecting the defense, courts reasoned that tort law does not impose a pre-accident duty on plaintiffs to take protective measures to minimize damages to themselves that might result if other people are negligent; that a plaintiff's failure to wear a seatbelt does not meet the requirements of any of the traditional tort law defenses or other tort law doctrine; that, at the time, most people did not in fact use seatbelts, so that the failure to do so did not deviate from the norm of a person of ordinary prudence; that the efficacy of seatbelts was questionable; that allowing the defense would raise substantial administrative problems, including the difficulty of connecting seatbelt nonuse with actual damages; and that the matter was better left for legislative determination.[90]

Notwithstanding these arguments, a small number of courts did adopt some version of the seatbelt defense during the 1960s and the early 1970s.[91] In the products liability context, an important decision was

caused accident by force of unbelted driver thrown against steering wheel; nonuse evidence not allowable to show comparative fault or mitigation of damages, but could be used to help establish causation).

**86.** See, e.g., General Motors Corp. v. Wolhar, 686 A.2d 170 (Del. 1996).

**87.** See, e.g., Daly v. General Motors Corp., 575 P.2d 1162, 1174–75 (Cal. 1978).

**88.** See, e.g., Morgen v. Ford Motor Co. 762 N.E.2d 137, 142 (Ind. Ct. App. 2002); Melia v. Ford Motor Co., 534 F.2d 795, 797 (8th Cir. 1976) (Neb. law); General Motors Corp. v. Walden, 406 F.2d 606, 608–09 (10th Cir. 1969) (Ariz. law). *But see* MacCuish v. Volkswagenwerk AG, 494 N.E.2d 390, 395 (Mass. App. Ct. 1986); Daly v. General Motors Corp., 575 P.2d 1162, 1174 (Cal. 1978).

**89.** See, e.g., LaHue v. General Motors Corp., 716 F.Supp. 407, 410 (W.D. Mo. 1989):

Enough has been written about the "seatbelt defense" to show the body of law related to it is split, fragmented and changing. It varies in time, place, rationale, effect and implementation. No doubt the law varies so much because the theory does not fit neatly into traditional tort doctrines of negligence (including duty, breach of duty and causation), strict liability, contributory negligence, mitigation of damages, avoidance of consequences, and comparative fault.

**90.** See generally Swajian v. General Motors Corp., 559 A.2d 1041 (R.I. 1989)

(refusing to allow the defense); Waterson v. General Motors Corp., 544 A.2d 357, 367–68 (N.J. 1988) (allowing the defense); Cochran, New Seat Belt Defense Issues: The Impact of Air Bags and Mandatory Seat Belt Use Statutes on the Seat Belt Defense, and the Basis of Damage Reduction under the Seat Belt Defense, 73 Minn. L. Rev. 1369, 1381–1408 (1989) (carefully examining arguments in light of modern developments).

**91.** See, e.g., Sams v. Sams, 148 S.E.2d 154 (S.C. 1966); Kavanagh v. Butorac, 221 N.E.2d 824 (Ind. Ct. App. 1966); Bentzler v. Braun, 149 N.W.2d 626 (Wis. 1967); Mount v. McClellan, 234 N.E.2d 329 (Ill. App. Ct. 1968); Truman v. Vargas, 80 Cal.Rptr. 373 (Ct. App. 1969); Glover v. Daniels, 310 F.Supp. 750 (N.D. Miss. 1970); Tiemeyer v. McIntosh, 176 N.W.2d 819 (Iowa 1970); Spier v. Barker, 323 N.E.2d 164 (N.Y. 1974); Pritts v. Walter Lowery Trucking Co., 400 F.Supp. 867 (W.D. Pa. 1975); Horn v. General Motors Corp., 551 P.2d 398 (Cal. 1976). A federal court in New York applied *Spier v. Barker* to reduce the plaintiffs' damages for nonuse of their seatbelts in Caiazzo v. Volkswagenwerk AG, 468 F.Supp. 593 (E.D.N.Y. 1979), aff'd on point and rev'd on other grounds, 647 F.2d 241 (2d Cir. 1981). See also Wilson v. Volkswagen of Am., Inc., 445 F.Supp. 1368 (E.D. Va. 1978) (seatbelt nonuse admissible for mitigation of damages in crashworthiness case).

The spread of the seatbelt defense ground to a halt in the mid–1970s, and no new

*Daly v. General Motors Corporation*,[92] decided by the California Supreme Court in 1978. In *Daly*, an attorney was driving his Opel on a Los Angeles freeway in the early hours of the morning when his car struck a metal divider fence, causing the latch button on the exterior door handle of the driver's door to depress. The collision with the fence spun the car out of control, throwing the driver's door open and hurling him from the car, resulting in fatal injuries to his head. In a products liability action brought by his representative against the manufacturer of the vehicle,[93] the defendant introduced evidence that the plaintiff was intoxicated, that he had failed to lock the door or use his seatbelt-shoulder harness, and that use of the seatbelt-shoulder harness would have saved his life.[94] Appealing a judgment on a verdict for General Motors, the plaintiff challenged the admissibility of the seatbelt nonuse evidence. Extending the comparative fault doctrine to claims based on strict liability in tort, the court reversed, ruling that the jury may have believed that the plaintiff's failure to use his seatbelt constituted contributory negligence that barred recovery altogether.[95]

Another issue in *Daly* was the propriety of the trial court's instruction that "[i]n determining whether or not the vehicle was defective you should consider all of the equipment on the vehicle including any features intended for the safety of the driver."[96] The plaintiff challenged this instruction, arguing that the jury could only consider the defectiveness of the challenged design feature that allegedly had malfunctioned, the latch on the driver's door.[97] Concluding that the defectiveness of a vehicle's design "is to be determined with respect to the product as a whole,"[98] the *Daly* court reasoned that a "jury could properly determine whether the Opel's overall design, including safety features provided in the vehicle, made it 'crashworthy,' thus rendering the vehicle nondefective. . . . [A] product's components are not developed in isolation, but as part of an integrated and interrelated whole."[99]

While plaintiffs in defective design cases ordinarily must assert some deficiency in a particular feature of a product's design,[100] manufacturers logically should be permitted to defend the safety of their products viewed as a whole; it is difficult to deny that "safety belts are an essential part of the total safety package provided by the manufacturer."[101] Thus, the availability of seatbelts of a particular design is surely relevant to the overall crashworthiness of a particular vehicle, as other courts have held.[102] Yet the appropriateness of evidence of seatbelt

---

appellate court decisions adopted the defense from 1975 until 1984. See Westenberg, Buckle Up or Pay: The Emerging Seat–Belt Defense, 20 Suffolk U. L. Rev. 867, 875 (1986).

**92.** 575 P.2d 1162 (Cal. 1978).

**93.** The plaintiff claimed that the vehicle's door latch was defectively designed. Id. at 1164.

**94.** Id. at 1164–65.

**95.** Id. at 1174.

**96.** Id.

**97.** See id.

**98.** Id.

**99.** Id. at 1175.

**100.** See Owen, Toward a Proper Test for Design Defectiveness: "Micro–Balancing" Costs and Benefits, 75 Tex. L. Rev. 1661 (1997).

**101.** Westenberg, Buckle Up or Pay: The Emerging Seat–Belt Defense, 20 Suffolk L. Rev. 867, 878 (1986).

**102.** See, e.g., Lowe v. Estate Motors Ltd., 410 N.W.2d 706, 707 (Mich. 1987);

*nonuse* (as opposed to availability) raises difficult issues apart from the defectiveness *vel non* of a vehicle's design, and the propriety of such evidence is not so clear.

During the 1980s, two important developments served to reinvigorate the seatbelt defense and propel it forward in the courts.[103] The first development was the increasingly rapid spread of the doctrine of comparative fault.[104] One of the biggest conceptual hurdles to the adoption of a seatbelt defense had been tort law's all-or-nothing approach to liability and damages, resulting in the courts' reluctance to shift the entire loss from a negligent tortfeasor to an innocent plaintiff who had merely failed before an accident to reduce potential damages to himself. Because the emerging comparative fault doctrine rested upon the pillar of damages apportionment, it much more easily accommodated the damages reduction aspect of the seatbelt defense.

The second development affecting the adoption of the seatbelt defense was NHTSA's prodding of the states to enact mandatory seatbelt use laws. By the late 1980s, most states had enacted mandatory seatbelt use laws, some containing a seatbelt nonuse defense providing for the reduction of damages in civil actions. As discussed below, however, many of the statutes explicitly prohibited use of seatbelt nonuse evidence in civil actions, and several limited the amount of damages reduction to five percent. Nevertheless, in states where legislation did not prohibit evidence of seatbelt nonuse, the seatbelt laws facilitated the adoption of the seatbelt defense by undercutting some of the traditional arguments against adopting it: mandatory use laws imposed a duty on occupants of self protection before an accident and converted seatbelt use into the practice of a reasonable person.

Thus spurred by the spread of comparative fault and the adoption of mandatory seatbelt legislation around the nation, a number of courts in the late 1980s and 1990s adopted some form of seatbelt defense,[105] some in products liability cases against vehicle manufacturers.[106] Today, much of the litigation on seatbelt nonuse has shifted to questions of statutory interpretation, and so the statutes need to be examined.

General Motors Corp. v. Wolhar, 686 A.2d 170 (Del. 1996).

**103.** See Westenberg, Buckle Up or Pay: The Emerging Seatbelt defense, 20 Suffolk U. L. Rev. 867, 875–85 (1986).

**104.** See § 13.3, above.

**105.** See, e.g., Insurance Co. of N. Am. v. Pasakarnis, 451 So.2d 447 (Fla. 1984); Smith v. Goodyear Tire & Rubber Co., 600 F.Supp. 1561 (D. Vt. 1985); Hutchins v. Schwartz, 724 P.2d 1194 (Alaska 1986); Law v. Superior Court, 755 P.2d 1135 (Ariz. Ct. App. 1988); Wemyss v. Coleman, 729 S.W.2d 174 (Ky. 1987).

**106.** See, e.g., Jordan v. General Motors Corp., 624 F.Supp. 72 (E.D. La. 1985); Maskrey v. Volkswagenwerk AG, 370 N.W.2d 815 (Wis. Ct. App. 1985); Dahl v. Bayerische Motoren Werke (BMW), 748 P.2d 77 (Or. 1987); Waterson v. General Motors Corp., 544 A.2d 357 (N.J. 1988); LaHue v. General Motors Corp., 716 F.Supp. 407 (W.D. Mo. 1989); Charles v. Bill Watson Hyundai Inc., 559 So.2d 872 (La. Ct. App. 1990); McElyea v. Navistar Int'l Transp. Corp., 788 F.Supp. 1366 (E.D. Pa. 1991); Barron v. Ford Motor Co. of Canada, Ltd., 965 F.2d 195 (7th Cir. 1992) (N.C. law); Tiner v. General Motors Corp., 909 F.Supp. 112 (N.D.N.Y. 1995); Gardner v. Chrysler Corp., 89 F.3d 729 (10th Cir. 1996) (Kan. law); General Motors Corp. v. Wolhar, 686 A.2d 170 (Del. 1996); Rodriguez v. Hyundai Motor Co., 944 S.W.2d 757, 773 n.17 (Tex. App. 1997), rev'd on other grounds, Hyundai Motor Co. v. Rodriguz, 995 S.W.2d 661 (Tex. 1999).

### Seatbelt Use Statutes

As mentioned earlier, all states except New Hampshire eventually enacted some form of legislation requiring the use of seatbelts.[107] The statutes may usefully be classified into four categories: those that prohibit the use of seatbelt nonuse evidence in civil litigation to reduce ("mitigate") a plaintiff's damages; those that permit such evidence to reduce a plaintiff's damages; those that permit such evidence to reduce a plaintiff's damages, but cap the reduction; and those that leave the matter to the courts.[108]

Seatbelt use statutes in most states provide that the "[f]ailure to wear a seat safety belt shall not be considered as contributory negligence nor shall such failure be admissible evidence in any civil action"[109] or words to similar effect.[110] But the statutes vary in certain significant respects, and it is difficult to generalize on whether or how such statutes may be specifically applicable to automotive products liability litigation.[111]

A smaller group of states have statutes allowing evidence of a person's failure to wear a seatbelt in mitigation of damages in any civil action,[112] and a few states limit the admissibility of such evidence to products liability actions.[113] Several states allow the reduction of a plaintiff's damages, but cap the reduction at a generally nominal percentage of the plaintiff's total damages.[114] Statutes in at least a couple of states appear to leave the matter to the courts.[115]

---

**107.** See notes 76 and 77, above.

**108.** This is the classification used in Products Liability Restatement § 16 Reporters' Note to cmt. *f.* The Products Liability Restatement does not take a position on the seatbelt defense issue, but notes that the Restatement (Third) of Torts: Apportionment, in § 3 (illus. 3) approves of the defense as part of its broad approach to apportionment in general.

**109.** Conn. Gen. Stat. Ann. § 14–100a(c)(4).

**110.** Statutes of this type include Ala. Code § 32–5B–7; Conn. Gen. Stat. Ann. § 14–100a(c)(4); Del. Code Ann. tit. 21 § 4802(i); D.C. Code Ann. § 41–1607; Ga. Code Ann. § 40–8–76.1(d); Idaho Code § 49–673(6); 625 Ill. Comp. Stat. 5/12–603.1(c); Kan. Stat. Ann. § 8–2504(c); Ky. Rev. Stat. Ann. § 189.125(5); La. Rev. Stat. Ann. § 32:295.1(E); Me. Rev. Stat. Ann. tit. 29–A § 2081(5); Md. Code Ann. [Transportation] § 22–412.3(h); Mass. Gen. Laws Ann. ch. 90 § 7AA; Minn. Stat. Ann. § 169.685(4)(a); Miss. Code Ann. § 63–2–3; Mont. Code Ann. § 61–13–106; Nev. Rev. stat. § 484.474(4); N.M. Stat. Ann. § 66–7–373(A); N.C. Gen. Stat. § 20–135.2A(d); Okla. Stat. tit. 47 § 11–1112(E); 75 Pa. Cons. Stat. Ann. § 4581(e); R.I. Gen. Laws § 31–22–22(b)(ii); S.C. Code Ann. § 56–5–6540(C); Tex. [Transportation] Code Ann. § 545.413(g);Vt. Stat. Ann. tit. 23, § 1259(d)(e); Va. Code Ann. § 46.2–1092; Wash. Rev. Code Ann § 46.61.688(6); W. Va. Code § 17C–15–49(d); Wyo. Stat. Ann. § 31–5–1402(f).

**111.** Contrast with Connecticut's quite terse provision the one in Georgia: "The failure of an occupant of a motor vehicle to wear a seat safety belt in any seat of a motor vehicle which has a seat safety belt or belts shall not be considered by the finder of fact on any question of negligence or causation, shall not be otherwise considered by the finder of fact on any question of liability of any person, corporation, or insurer, shall not be any basis for cancellation of coverage or increase in insurance rates, and shall not be evidence used to diminish any recovery for damages arising out of the ownership, maintenance, occupancy, or operation of a motor vehicle." Ga. Code Ann. § 40–8–76.1(d).

**112.** Statutes of this type include Cal. [Veh.] Code § 27315(j); Colo. Rev. Stat. § 42–4–237(b)(7); Fla. Stat. Ann. § 316.614(9); N.Y.[Veh. & Traf.] Law 1229–§c(8); and Ohio Rev. Code Ann. § 4513.263(F).

**113.** Statutes of this type include Ark. Code Ann. § 27–37–703; Ind. Code § 9–19–10–7(c); and Tenn. Code Ann. § 55–9–604.

**114.** Statutes of this type include Iowa Code Ann. § 321.445(4) (5%); Mich. Comp. Laws Ann. § 257.710e(h)(6) (5%) (*but see Klinke*, discussed below); Mo. Rev. Stat. § 307.178(3)(2) (1%); Neb. Rev. Stat. § 60–6,273 (5%), and Wis. Stat. Ann. § 347.48(2m)(g) (15%).

**115.** Statutes of this type include N.J. Stat. Ann. § 39:3–76.2(h) and Haw. Rev. Stat. Ann. § 291–11.6(5)(d).

One recurring issue of statutory interpretation is whether statutes that prohibit evidence of seatbelt nonuse (or that cap the reduction of damages) apply to crashworthiness claims against automotive manufacturers.[116] For example, the Michigan Supreme Court has ruled that that state's capping of mitigated damages does not apply to products liability claims because the statute by its terms applies only to cases "arising out of the ownership, maintenance, or operation of a motor vehicle."[117] Similarly, some courts have ruled that their statutes which do not allow evidence of seatbelt nonuse to show contributory negligence or "as evidence in a trial of any civil action,"[118] or which prohibit the use of such evidence as proof of negligence or "in mitigation of damages of whatever nature,"[119] do not bar the use of seatbelt nonuse evidence on causation and other matters. But other courts disagree, holding that the plain meaning of similar statutes requires their application to products liability actions like any other action[120] and to issues of proximate cause as well as comparative fault.[121] One court taking this approach reasoned that carving out a crashworthiness exception to the seatbelt nonuse law would frustrate the statutory policy of encouraging manufacturers "to design cars in a crashworthy manner in spite of the fact that drivers and passengers often fail to wear their seatbelts."[122]

Another interpretation issue on which the courts have split is whether a statutory prohibition of seatbelt use evidence applies against a plaintiff in an action against the manufacturer of an allegedly defective seatbelt that malfunctioned. At least a couple of cases have ruled that Minnesota's seatbelt "gag rule" prohibited plaintiffs from making crashworthiness claims based on defective seatbelts because the plaintiff's seatbelt use was necessary to the claim.[123] But the Minnesota seatbelt law has now been amended to allow such claims,[124] and other courts have

**116.** At least Oregon's statute explicitly excludes products liability cases from operation of its 5% reduction provision. See Or. Rev. Stat. § 18.590 (5%).

**117.** See Klinke v. Mitsubishi Motors Corp., 581 N.W.2d 272 (Mich. 1998) (jury found that decedent was 90% at fault for wearing her lap belt but not her shoulder harness; *held*, damages reduced by 90%). Accord, LaHue v. General Motors Corp., 716 F.Supp. 407, 412 (W.D. Mo. 1989) (legislature's reference to "any action to recover damages arising out of the ownership, common maintenance or operation of a motor vehicle" in statute "was not intended to prevent evidence of failure to use seatbelts in a product liability case").

**118.** MacDonald v. General Motors Corp., 784 F.Supp. 486 (M.D. Tenn. 1992).

**119.** Brown v. Ford Motor Co., 67 F.Supp.2d 581 (E.D. Va. 1999) (construing state statute as procedural and nonbinding to extent that it limited admissibility of nonuse evidence for matters other than (contributory) negligence or damages mitigation, court allowed such evidence on issues of defendant's negligence, vehicle's defectiveness, and on product misuse).

**120.** See, e.g., Milbrand v. Daimler-Chrysler Corp., 105 F.Supp.2d 601, 608 (E.D. Tex. 2000); Newman v. Ford Motor Co., 975 S.W.2d 147 (Mo. 1998).

**121.** See, e.g., Ulm v. Ford Motor Co., 750 A.2d 981 (Vt. 2000).

**122.** Estate of Hunter v. General Motors Corp., 729 So.2d 1264, 1270 (Miss. 1999).

**123.** See, e.g., Carlson v. Hyundai Motor Co., 164 F.3d 1160 (8th Cir. 1999); Olson v. Ford Motor Co., 558 N.W.2d 491, 494 (Minn. 1997).

**124.** See Minn. Stat. Ann. § 169. 685(4)(b).

interpreted their statutes more sensibly to allow this type of action.[125] Other seatbelt statutory interpretation issues abound,[126] providing grist galore for future litigation.

### Other Safety Devices

While the discussion to this point has concerned an occupant's failure to wear a seatbelt, a person's failure to use other kinds of safety devices may raise similar issues in products liability litigation. Thus, a parent's failure to buckle up a child in a child-restraint seat logically may bar or reduce the parent's claim for medical expenses and other derivative damages arising out of injury to the child to the same extent as if the parent had failed to use his or her own seatbelt. Yet, the child's own claim for injuries should not of course be affected by the parent's failure to perform his or her parental duties.[127] But many of the state seatbelt use laws that prohibit the use of seatbelt nonuse evidence are broad enough to include a parent's failure to use child restraints,[128] and many others specifically provide that evidence of the nonuse of child restraints is not admissible in civil actions.[129]

Motorcycle helmets are another safety device mandated in many but not all jurisdictions,[130] and the failure of a motorcycle rider to wear a helmet logically raises issues similar to those applicable to the seatbelt nonuse situation.[131]

**125.** See, e.g., Milbrand v. Daimler-Chrysler Corp., 105 F.Supp.2d 601, 608 (E.D. Tex. 2000) (allegation that seatbelt is defective creates only exception to statutory prohibition on seatbelt evidence); Chapman v. Mazda Motor of Am., Inc., 7 F.Supp.2d 1123 (D. Mont. 1998) (plaintiff may not use seatbelt usage to prove the absence of contributory fault, but may use such evidence to prove the defectiveness of the seatbelt); Bridgestone/Firestone, Inc. v. Glyn–Jones, 878 S.W.2d 132 (Tex. 1994).

**126.** For simply one example, see Hopper v. Carey, 716 N.E.2d 566 (Ind. Ct. App. 1999) (fire truck was not "passenger motor vehicle" for purposes of mandatory seatbelt statute).

**127.** A contrary result would indirectly resurrect the long-discredited and "hideous" doctrine of imputed contributory negligence from a parent to the child. See Prosser & Keeton on Torts § 74, at 531–32.

**128.** See, e.g., Ky. Rev. Stat. Ann. § 189.125(5); Me. Rev. Stat. Ann. tit. 29A § 2081(5); N.M. Stat. Ann. § 66–7–373(a); 75 Pa. Cons. Stat. Ann. § 4581(e); R.I. Gen. Laws § 31–22–22(b)(ii).

**129.** See, e.g., Ky. Rev. Stat. Ann. § 189.125(5); Me. Rev. Stat. Ann. tit. 29–A § 2081(5); N.J. Stat. Ann. § 39:3–76.2a; N.M. Stat. Ann. § 66–7–373(A); R.I. Gen. Laws § 31–22–22(b)(ii).

**130.** See, e.g., N.J. Stat. Ann. § 39:3–76.7. See also N.J. Stat. Ann. § 39:3–76.8–39:3–76.9 (riders of motorcycles without wind screens required to wear goggles or face shields).

**131.** Compare Rogers v. Frush, 262 A.2d 549 (Md. 1970) (rejecting motorcycle helmet defense on analogy to seatbelt defense), with Halvorson v. Voeller, 336 N.W.2d 118, 121 (N.D. 1983) (allowing mitigation of motorcyclist's damages based on helmet nonuse). Cf. Thurel v. Varghese, 621 N.Y.S.2d 633 (App. Div. 1995). See Annot., 40 A.L.R.3d 856 (1971) (failure of motorcyclist to wear helmet as contributory negligence, assumption of risk, or failure to avoid consequences of accident). See, e.g., N.J. Stat. Ann. § 39:3–76.7. See also N.J. Stat. Ann. § 39: 3–76.8, .9 (riders of motorcycles without wind screens required to wear goggles or face shields).

# Chapter 18

## PUNITIVE DAMAGES

*Table of Sections*

---

### § 18.1  PUNITIVE DAMAGES—GENERALLY

Manufacturers have a powerful hold on product safety. Through product design, testing, inspection, and collection of field performance data, manufacturers have virtually exclusive access to much of the information necessary for effective control of product hazards. Indeed, the doctrine of strict products liability in tort evolved in part to motivate manufacturers to use this information to help combat the massive problem of product accidents.[1]

Most manufacturers, from a desire to avoid liability and loss of reputation, act prudently to prevent defective products from reaching or remaining on the market. Occasionally, however, manufacturers abuse their control over product safety and market defective products in flagrant disregard of public safety. One manufacturer of color televisions, for example, knowingly included in each set a high voltage transformer that was prone to catch fire and, when informed that its sets were causing frequent fires, refused to spend the one dollar per unit it knew would eliminate the hazard.[2] In another case, a major drug company submitted fabricated test data to the Food and Drug Administration to obtain approval for the sale of a dangerous new drug. Approval was granted, and hundreds of persons developed cataracts as a result.[3]

---

**§ 18.1**

**1.** See §§ 5.2 and 5.4, above. The number of product accidents in America each year is conservatively estimated to be 50 million, at an annual cost to the nation of $100 billion. See D. Owen, J. Montgomery, and M. Davis, Products Liability & Safety 2 (4th ed. 2004).

**2.** See Gillham v. Admiral Corp., 523 F.2d 102 (6th Cir. 1975) (Ohio law).

**3.** See Toole v. Richardson–Merrell, Inc., 60 Cal.Rptr. 398 (Ct. App. 1967). Cf. Roginsky v. Richardson–Merrell, Inc., 378 F.2d 832 (2d Cir. 1967) (N.Y. law).

The liability rules of products liability law address the question of when a manufacturer or other supplier should bear responsibility for actual damages suffered by the victim of a product accident. Much of modern products liability law is based at least nominally on no-fault principles,[4] and the normal liability rules do not address problems at the other end of the culpability scale when harm results from a manufacturer's sale of a defective product in conscious or reckless disregard of consumer safety. Nor has the criminal law filled this void.[5] Punitive damages help to expose this form of gross misconduct, to punish manufacturers guilty of such flagrant misbehavior, and to deter all manufacturers from acting with similar disregard for public safety.

## Nature of Punitive Damages

"Punitive" or "exemplary" damages[6] are money damages awarded to a plaintiff in a private civil action, in addition to and apart from compensatory damages, assessed against a defendant guilty of flagrantly violating the plaintiff's rights.[7] The principal purposes of such damages are usually said to be (1) to punish a defendant for outrageous conduct, and (2) to deter the defendant and others from similarly misbehaving in the future.[8] The law and commentary on punitive damages is vast, rich, and expanding exponentially.[9]

**4.** See ch. 5, above.

**5.** See National Commission on Product Safety, Final Report 95 (1970).

**6.** The terms "punitive" and "exemplary" damages today generally are used interchangeably. Black's Law Dictionary 396 (7th ed. 1999). Such damages have also been referred to as "punitory," "penal," "additional," "aggravated," "plenary," "imaginary," and "smart money." See Freifield, The Rationale of Punitive Damages, 1 Ohio St. L.J. 5, 5 (1935). In civil law nations, "extra" damages serving similar functions are referred to as "moral" damages, "satisfaction," or "private fines." See Stoll, Penal Purposes in the Law of Tort, 18 Am. J. Comp. L. 3, 13–19 (1970).

**7.** The basic principles are set forth in Restatement (2d) Torts § 908.

**8.** "Punitive damages are damages, other than compensatory or nominal damages, awarded against a person to punish him for his outrageous conduct." Restatement (2d) Torts § 908(1). "The purposes of awarding punitive damages ... are to punish the person doing the wrongful act and to discourage him and others from similar conduct in the future." Id. cmt. *a.* See, e.g., Ford Motor Co. v. Ammerman, 705 N.E.2d 539, 563 (Ind. Ct. App. 1999); BMW of N. Am., Inc. v. Gore, 517 U.S. 559, 593 (1996). The functions of punitive damages are explored in greater depth in § 18.2, below.

**9.** Three helpful treatises are J. Kircher and C. Wiseman, Punitive Damages: Law and Practice (2000) (hereinafter Kircher

and Wiseman, Punitive Damages); L. Schlueter and K. Redden, Punitive Damages (4th ed. 2000); and Gerald W. Boston, Punitive Damages in Tort Law (1993). See also D. Dobbs, Law of Remedies § 3.11 (2d ed. 1993); Dobbs, Law of Torts § 381 et seq. For a state-by-state survey, see Richard L. Blatt et al., Punitive Damages: A State-By-State Guide to Law and Practice (2003).

The law review literature continues to grow apace. See, e.g., Gash, Solving the Multiple Punishment Problem: A Call for a National Punitive Damages Registry, 99 Nw. U.L. Rev. ___ (2005); Gash, Punitive Damages, Other Acts Evidence, and the Constitution, 2004 Utah L. Rev. ___ (2004); Sharkey, Punitive Damages as Societal Damages, 113 Yale L.J. 347 (2003); Madden, Renegade Conduct and Punitive Damages in Tort, 53 S.C. L. Rev. 1175 (2002); Colby, Beyond the Multiple Punishment Problem: Punitive Damages As Punishment for Individual, Private Wrongs, 87 Minn. L. Rev. 583 (2003); Eisenberg, LaFountain, Ostrom, Rottman, and Wells, Juries, Judges, and Punitive Damages: An Empirical Study, 87 Cornell L. Rev. 743 (2002); Schkade, Erratic by Design: A Task Analysis of Punitive Damages Assessment, 39 Harv. J. on Legis. 121 (2002); Sunstein, Kahneman, Schkade, and Ritov, Predictably Incoherent Judgements, 54 Stan. L. Rev. 1153 (2002); Eisenberg, Rachlinski, and Wells, Reconciling Experimental Incoherence with Real-World Coherence in Punitive Damages, 54 Stan. L. Rev. 1239 (2002); Kelman, Problematic Perhaps, But

A jury (or judge, in the absence of a jury) may, in its discretion, render such an award in cases in which the defendant is found to have injured the plaintiff maliciously, intentionally, or with a "conscious," "reckless," "willful," "wanton," or "oppressive" disregard of the plaintiff's rights. Punitive damages may be assessed against an employer vicariously for the misconduct of its employees, although some states restrict such awards to instances where a managing officer of the enterprise ordered, participated in, or consented to the misconduct.[10] The damage to the plaintiff may involve physical, emotional, property, or financial harm.[11] The amount of the award is determined by the jury[12] upon consideration of the seriousness of the wrong, the seriousness of

Not Irrational, 54 Stan. L. Rev. 1273 (2002); Robbennolt, Determining Punitive Damages: Empirical Insights and Implications for Reform, 50 Buff. L. Rev. 103 (2002); Eisenberg, Damage Awards in Perspective: Behind the Headline—Grabbing Awards in *Exxon Valdez* and *Engle*, 36 Wake Forest L. Rev. 1129 (2001); Sunstein, Schkade & Kahneman, Do People Want Optimal Deterrence?, 29 J. Legal Stud. 237 (2000); Eisenberg and Wells, The Predictability of Punitive Damages Awards in Published Opinions, the Impact of *BMW v. Gore* on Punitive Damages Awards, and Forecasting Which Punitive Awards Will Be Reduced, 7 Sup. Ct. Econ. Rev. 59 (1999); Polinsky and Shavell, Punitive Damages: An Economic Analysis, 111 Harv. L. Rev. 869 (1998); Sunstein et al., Assessing Punitive Damages (with Notes on Cognition and Valuation in Law), 107 Yale L.J. 2071 (1998); Owen, A Punitive Damages Overview: Functions, Problems and Reform, 39 Vill. L. Rev. 363 (1994); Galanter and Luban, Poetic Justice: Punitive Damages and Legal Pluralism, 42 Am. U. L. Rev. 1393, 1418 (1993); Rustad and Koenig, The Historical Continuity of Punitive Damages Awards: Reforming the Tort Reformers, 42 Am. U. L. Rev. 1269 (1993) (hereinafter Historical Continuity); Christie, Current Trends in the American Law of Punitive Damages, 20 Anglo–Am. L. Rev. 349 (1991); Daniels and Martin, Myth and Reality in Punitive Damages, 75 Minn. L. Rev. 1 (1990) (hereinafter Myth and Reality); Galligan, Jr., Augmented Awards: The Efficient Evolution of Punitive Damages, 51 La. L. Rev. 3, 34 (1990); Kuklin, Punishment: The Civil Perspective of Punitive Damages, 37 Clev. St. L. Rev. 1 (1989); Owen, The Moral Foundations of Punitive Damages, 40 Ala. L. Rev. 705 (1989) (hereinafter Moral Foundations); Ellis, Jr., Fairness and Efficiency in the Law of Punitive Damages, 56 S. Cal. L. Rev. 1 (1982); Owen, Civil Punishment and the Public Good, 56 S. Cal. L. Rev. 103 (1982) (hereinafter Civil Punishment). See generally Symposia: Engle v. R.J. Reynolds Tobacco Co.:

Lessons in State Class Actions, Punitive Damages, and Jury Decision-Making, 36 Wake Forest L. Rev. 871 (2001); Punitive Damages, 87 Geo. L.J. 285 (1998); The Future of Punitive Damages, 1998 Wis. L. Rev. 1; Punitive Damages Awards in Product Liability Litigation: Strong Medicine or Poison Pill?, 39 Vill. L. Rev. 353 (1994); Civil Justice Reform, 42 Am. U. L. Rev. 1245 (1993); Punitive Damages, 40 Ala. L. Rev. 687 (1989); Punitive Damages, 56 S. Cal. L. Rev. 1 (1982); Viscusi, Jurors, Judges, and the Mistreatment of Risk by the Courts, 30 J. Legal Stud. 107 (2001). For articles pertaining specifically to products liability, see note 60, below.

**10.** The Restatements (Second) of Torts and Agency both take the narrower approach, permitting assessments of punitive damages against employers only in cases where the employer authorized or ratified the act, was reckless in employing or retaining the agent, or the agent was in a managerial capacity and acting in the scope of employment. Restatement (2d) Torts § 909; Restatement (Second) of Agency § 217C. This issue is examined in greater detail in § 18.4, below.

**11.** All general assertions about punitive damages have exceptions in some states. In Minnesota, for example, such damages are not available for property damage alone, at least not in products liability cases. See Independent Sch. Dist. No. 622 v. Keene Corp., 511 N.W.2d 728 (Minn. 1994). As another example, Kansas, as many states, prohibits such awards in wrongful death (but not survival) actions. Smith v. Printup, 866 P.2d 985, 998–99 (Kan. 1993) (reviewing national status of rule).

**12.** Courts quite frequently order the remittitur of punitive damage verdicts deemed excessive, but the additur of such awards may improperly invade the province of the jury. See, e.g., Bozeman v. Busby, 639 So.2d 501 (Ala. 1994). See generally Annot., 12 A.L.R.5th 195 (1993) (excessiveness or inadequacy of punitive damages for personal injury or death).

the plaintiff's injury, and the extent of the defendant's wealth.[13]

Straddling the civil and the criminal law, punitive damages are a form of "quasi-criminal"[14] penalty: they are "awarded" as "damages" to a plaintiff against a defendant in a private lawsuit; yet their purpose in most jurisdictions is explicitly held to be noncompensatory and in the nature of a penal fine. Because the gravamen of such damages is considered civil, the procedural safeguards of the criminal law (such as the beyond-a-reasonable-doubt burden of proof and prohibitions against double jeopardy, excessive fines, and compulsory self-incrimination) have generally been held not to apply.[15] This strange mixture of criminal and civil law objectives and effects—creating a form of penal remedy inhabiting (some would say "invading") the civil-law domain—is perhaps the principal source of the widespread controversy that has always surrounded the allowance of punitive damages awards.

The punitive damages doctrine is partly judicial and partly legislative. While the doctrine is fundamentally a creature of the common law, both its historical roots and many current sources are found in statutory, and even constitutional,[16] provisions.[17] Many western states,[18] whose legal systems are codified to a large extent, have express legislative provisions which generally authorize punitive damages in appropriate cases involving aggravated misconduct.[19] In addition, a large miscellany of statutes, both federal and state, expressly provide for punitive or multiple damages in a great variety of particular situations,[20] including products

---

**13.** "In assessing punitive damages, the trier of fact can properly consider the character of the defendant's act, the nature and extent of the harm to the plaintiff that the defendant caused or intended to cause and the wealth of the defendant." Restatement (2d) Torts § 908(2). Compare the Supreme Court's list of three excessiveness "guideposts" in *Gore* which tracks the first two common-law measurement factors but which substitutes, in the third, other types of available penalties for the defendant's wealth. See § 18.7, below.

**14.** This apt characterization of punitive damages is quite common. See, e.g., Cooper Indus., Inc. v. Leatherman Tool Group, Inc., 532 U.S. 424, 432 (2001) ("[Punitive damages], which have been described as 'quasi-criminal,' operate as 'private fines' intended to punish the defendant and to deter future wrongdoing."); Pacific Mut. Life Ins. Co. v. Haslip, 499 U.S. 1, 19 (1991).

**15.** However, the excessive fines clause may possibly apply to claims in jurisdictions where the state shares with the private plaintiff in such an award. See § 18.7, below.

**16.** See, e.g., Tex. Const. art. 16, § 26 ("homicide through wilful act, or omission, or gross neglect").

**17.** See Owen, Punitive Damages in Products Liability Litigation, 74 Mich. L.

Rev. 1257, 1262–64 (1976) (hereinafter Punitive Damages).

**18.** States with legislation expressly authorizing punitive damages in cases involving aggravated misconduct include California, Nevada, Montana, Oklahoma, North Dakota, and South Dakota.

**19.** See, e.g., Cal. Civ. Code § 3294 (allowing punitive damages in non-contract claims for sake of example and to punish defendant guilty of oppression, fraud, or malice); Mont. Code Ann. § 27–1–221 (where defendant guilty of actual fraud or actual malice); Nev. Rev. Stat. Ann. § 42.005 (listing situations where punitive damages proper); Okla. Stat. Ann. tit. 23, § 9 (where no direct evidence of fraud, malice, or gross negligence but where malice may be inferred from defendant's wanton disregard of rights); S.D. Codified Laws § 21–3–2 (where defendant guilty of oppression, fraud, or malice).

**20.** See, e.g., 15 U.S.C. § 15a (treble damages for antitrust violations); id. § 1681n (actual and punitive damages available for willful violations of consumer credit reporting law); Cal. Civ. Code § 3340 (punitive damages available for willful or grossly negligent wrongful injury to animal); S.C. Code Ann. § 39–5–140 (treble damages available for knowing practice of unfair or deceptive trade practices). In addition to such express statutory provisions, courts have inferred punitive damages into a number of federal statutes. See, e.g., 42

liability cases.[21] By contrast, many states, either statutorily or constitutionally, prohibit punitive damages in a vast array of contexts, including commercial transactions under the Uniform Commercial Code.[22] More broadly, five states prohibit all awards of punitive damages unless specifically authorized by statute.[23] Since the 1980s, punitive damages have been a favorite target of tort reformers, so that most states now have some form of tort reform legislation limiting punitive damages in a variety of ways.[24] And, beginning largely with the Supreme Court's 1991 decision in *Pacific Mutual Life Insurance Co. v. Haslip*,[25] punitive damages awards have been increasingly subjected to federal constitutional review and control.[26]

### History

Punitive damages have a deep history in the law.[27] Their early ancestor was the doctrine of multiple damages, a form of punitive damages measured according to a predetermined scale. Babylonian law provided for such damages nearly 4000 years ago in the Code of Hammurabi, the earliest known legal code.[28] Such damages were also recognized in the Hittite Laws of about 1400 B.C.,[29] the Hebrew Covenant Code of Mosaic law dating back to about 1200 B.C.,[30] and the Hindu Code of Manu of about 200 B.C.[31] The very basis of early Roman civil law, beginning with the Twelve Tables of 450 B.C., was punitive in nature, and several provisions of Roman law prescribed double, treble, and quadruple damages.[32]

U.S.C. § 1983 (1988) (punitive damages available for deprivations of civil rights under color of state law).

**21.** Connecticut, for example, provides for punitive damages in appropriate products liability cases. Conn. Gen. Stat. § 52–240b.

**22.** "[P]enal damages may [not] be had except as specifically provided in this Act or by other rule of law." UCC § 1–106(1). See § 18.4, below.

**23.** Louisiana, Massachusetts, Nebraska, New Hampshire, and Washington.

**24.** See § 18.6, below.

**25.** 499 U.S. 1 (1991).

**26.** See § 18.7, below.

**27.** This historical sketch is drawn from Owen, Punitive Damages, 74 Mich. L. Rev. 1277 (1976). See also DeMendoza v. Huffman, 51 P.3d 1232, 1239–42 (Or. 2002) (extensive historical review); Rustad and Koenig, Historical Continuity, 42 Am. U. L. Rev. at 1284–97; Rustad and Koenig, Taming the Tort Monster: The American Civil Justice System as a Battleground for Social Theory, 68 Brook. L. Rev. 1 (2002); Ellis, Jr., Fairness and Efficiency in the Law of Punitive Damages, 56 S. Cal. L. Rev. 1, 12–20 (1982); Daniels and Martin, Myth and Reality, 76 Minn. L. Rev. 1, 6–7 (1990).

**28.** 1 G. Driver and J. Miles, The Babylonian Laws 500–01 (1952). See also R. Ver-Steeg, Early Mesopotamian Law 39, 112–13, 126–28 (2000) (multiple damages commonly assessed for theft during Ur III period, about 2100 B.C., and suggesting possibility of such assessments even earlier under Sumerian law, citing H. Saggs, The Greatness That Was Babylon 200 (1962)).

**29.** M. Belli, Modern Damages 75 (1959).

**30.** See Exodus 22.1 (thief who slaughters or sells ox or sheep shall restore five oxen or four sheep for each one stolen; if animal is found alive in thief's possession, he shall restore two animals for each one stolen).

**31.** Belli, above, at 84; see also Owen, Punitive Damages, 74 Mich. L. Rev. at 1262 n.17.

**32.** See, e.g., D. Pugsley, The Roman Law of Property and Obligations 111–12 (1972); W. W. Buckland, A Text–Book of Roman Law 581–84 (3d rev. Stein ed. 1966); W. W. Buckland and A. McNair, Roman Law and Common Law 344–45 (2d rev. Lawson ed. 1965).

Perhaps the first English provision for multiple damages was enacted by Parliament in 1275. "Trespassers against religious persons shall yield double damages."[33] Including this first statute, Parliament enacted at least sixty-five separate provisions for double, treble, and quadruple damages between 1275 and 1753.[34]

"Exemplary" damages were first explicitly authorized in England in *Huckle v. Money*,[35] decided in 1763. The doctrine was promptly transported to America, where the South Carolina Supreme Court allowed such an award twenty-one years later in *Genay v. Norris*,[36] a case involving a plaintiff who became ill after drinking a glass of wine that the defendant as a practical joke had laced with Spanish Fly. By the mid-nineteenth century, punitive damages had become an established fixture in American law. In *Day v. Woodworth*,[37] the Supreme Court asserted, without citation (and with some exaggeration), that the doctrine was supported by "repeated judicial decisions for more than a century."[38] By the early part of the twentieth century, all but five states provided generally for such awards upon appropriate proof.[39] Yet, even in these few renegade states (with the possible exception of Nebraska),[40] punitive damages have been legislatively authorized in a variety of specific situations.[41]

### Controversial Nature of Punitive Damages

Controversy has followed punitive damages throughout their history in this nation. "Punitive damages like class actions have been highly praised and roundly denounced depending on who is paying the piper."[42] Two leading treatise writers in nineteenth century America, Sedgwick and Greenleaf, engaged in a long-standing scholarly debate over whether

**33.** Synopsis of Statute of Westminster I, 3 Edw., ch. 1. (Eng.), in 24 Great Britain Statutes at Large 138 (Pickering Index 1761).

**34.** See id. at 138–41. See generally 2 F. Pollock and F. Maitland, The History of the English Law 522 (2d ed. 1899) (referring to these multiple damage provisions as "penal and exemplary damages").

**35.** 95 Eng. Rep. 768, 769 (K.B. 1763) (false imprisonment and trespass action by journeyman printer against agents of the King). Accord, Wilkes v. Wood, 98 Eng. Rep. 489 (C.P. 1763) (allowing such damages in similar case).

**36.** 1 S.C.L. 6, 1 Bay 6 (1784) (awarding "vindictive damages" to plaintiff despite defense of drunken frolic).

**37.** 54 U.S. 363 (1851).

**38.** Id. at 371. This would indicate the existence of punitive damages awards twelve years prior to *Huckle*, which appears erroneous.

**39.** See C. McCormick, Law of Damages 278–79 (1935) (listing Louisiana, Massachusetts, Nebraska, and Washington as the only states without such general doctrine).

New Hampshire also generally prohibits such awards. N.H. Rev. Stat. Ann. § 507.16 ("No punitive damages shall be awarded in any action, unless otherwise provided by statute.").

**40.** See Distinctive Printing & Packaging Co. v. Cox, 443 N.W.2d 566, 574 (Neb. 1989) (noting that punitive damages prohibited by state constitution).

**41.** See, e.g., La. Civ. Code Ann. art. 2315.4 (punitive damages authorized for wanton or reckless drunk driving), id. at § 2800.63 and 2800.76 (reckless disregard for safety by distributors of illicit drugs); Mass. Gen. Laws Ann. ch. 93, § 63 (failure to comply with consumer reporting agency statute); id. at ch. 111, § 199 (failure to correct dangerous lead levels upon premises); N.H. St. Ann. § 359–B:16 and D:11 (violating consumer credit reporting act); id. at § 570–A:11 (unauthorized wiretapping); Wash. Rev. Code Ann. § 9A.36.083 (malicious harassment due to race, gender, etc.).

**42.** In re Paris Air Crash, 427 F.Supp. 701, 705 (C.D. Cal. 1977) (California ban on punitive damages in wrongful death actions unconstitutional), rev'd, 622 F.2d 1315 (9th Cir. 1980).

such damages should be allowed at all.[43] The depth of the early philosophical disagreement is colorfully portrayed by characterizations offered by different state supreme court justices. In a nineteenth century New Hampshire case, the court remarked: "The idea is wrong. It is a monstrous heresy. It is an unsightly and unhealthy excrescence, deforming the symmetry of the body of law."[44] In contrast, the Wisconsin Supreme Court shortly after the turn of the century characterized the law of punitive damages as "an outgrowth of the English love of liberty regulated by law. It tends to elevate the jury as a responsible instrument of government, discourages private reprisals, restrains the strong, influential, and unscrupulous, vindicates the right of the weak, and encourages recourse to, and confidence in, the courts of law by those wronged or oppressed by acts or practices not cognizable in, or not sufficiently punished, by the criminal law."[45] Courts critical of this form of damages often recite that punitive damages are "not favored in the law."[46]

Once the number and size of punitive damage verdicts and judgments began to increase in the 1970s, particularly in products liability litigation, such awards became a central, highly politicized part of the broader "tort reform" movement.[47] This movement arose out of supposed "crises" in the areas of medical malpractice and products liability—particularly in the availability and affordability of liability insurance—first in the mid-1970s and again in the mid-1980s. As has been true with tort reform in general, the debate on punitive damages has also been highly charged.[48] Claiming that "runaway" punitive damage awards have become routine, especially in products liability cases, businesses and insurance companies carried their message to the legislatures and the courts.[49] Many courts, together with about thirty state legislatures, responded by adopting a variety of laws "reforming" punitive

---

**43.** Compare 1 Theodore Sedgwick, A Treatise on the Measures of Damages § 355 (9th ed. 1912) with 2 Simon Greenleaf, A Treatise on the Law of Evidence § 253 (16th ed. 1899). Greenleaf adamantly opposed punitive damages, believing that they were not part of the American tradition and had no doctrinal basis. Sedgwick, on the other hand, was a staunch proponent of exemplary damages and believed they were an effective way of setting an example for the community. See Rustad and Koenig, Historical Continuity, 42 Am. U. L. Rev. at 1298–1302 (summarizing the Greenleaf–Sedgwick debate).

**44.** Fay v. Parker, 53 N.H. 342, 382 (1872) (criticizing and setting aside jury's punitive damages award in assault and battery action).

**45.** Luther v. Shaw, 147 N.W. 18, 20 (Wis. 1914) (allowing punitive damages in action for breach of promise to marry).

**46.** See, e.g., Bachman v. General Motors Corp., 776 N.E.2d 262, 301 (Ill. App. Ct. 2002) ("Because of their penal nature, punitive damages are not favored in the law."); Stevens v. Owens–Corning Fiberglas

Corp., 57 Cal.Rptr.2d 525, 533 (Ct. App. 1996); Kansas City v. Keene Corp., 855 S.W.2d 360, 378 (Mo. 1993) (affirming j.n.o.v. for defendant on punitive damages award) (Holstein, J., concurring); Ross v. Black & Decker, Inc., 977 F.2d 1178, 1190 (7th Cir. 1992) (Ill. law) (reducing a $10 million punitive award to $5 million in products liability case); Lyons v. Jordan, 524 A.2d 1199, 1204 (D.C. 1987) (punitive damages are disfavored, but allowable on facts).

**47.** See Rustad, In Defense of Punitive Damages in Products Liability: Testing Tort Anecdotes with Empirical Data, 78 Iowa L. Rev. 1, 24 (1992) (hereinafter In Defense of Punitive Damages); Daniels and Martin, Myth and Reality, 75 Minn. L. Rev. at 10–14.

**48.** See, e.g., Galanter, Shadow Play: The Fabled Menace of Punitive Damages, 1998 Wis. L. Rev. 1, 14 ("punitive damages has become an issue like gun control or abortion, generating heated rhetoric and an unwillingness to undertake sustained and dispassionate analysis").

**49.** See Rustad, In Defense of Punitive Damages, at 2.

damages in various respects,[50] and a restrictive Model State Punitive Damages Act was formulated along these lines.[51]

There is no doubt that the number of large, sometimes very large, punitive damage verdicts in products liability cases has increased substantially in recent decades.[52] Yet, such jury awards are still uncommon and, even when awarded, they frequently are reduced or eliminated altogether by the trial or appellate court. This is especially true with the largest of the awards, as discussed below. One of the first important empirical studies of punitive damages in products liability cases was conducted by Professors Michael Rustad and Thomas Koenig.[53] Their study showed "that punitive damages are generally working appropriately,"[54] and they concluded that "[p]unitive damages are rarely awarded and even more rarely collected" and that "[w]hen they are awarded, they are generally richly deserved" because the defendants knew about, yet chose not to cure, a dangerous product defect.[55] One of their "most striking finding[s]" was that they could only locate a total of 355 punitive damage verdicts in the many thousands of products liability actions over the quarter century of their survey.[56] Their study confirmed the small number of such awards reported by other empirical investigators,[57] and it concluded that punitive damages are assessed in a very small percentage of the cases.[58] Other evaluators of large numbers of

**50.** See Galligan, Jr., Augmented Awards: The Efficient Evolution of Punitive Damages, 51 La. L. Rev. 3, 34–35 (1990); Rustad, In Defense of Punitive Damages, at 6 n.22. Legislative reform is discussed at § 18.6, below.

**51.** See Rustad and Koenig, Historical Continuity, 42 Am. U. L. Rev. at 1278–81 (setting forth Model Act).

**52.** See Daniels and Martin, Myth and Reality, at 28–62; Owen, Problems in Assessing Punitive Damages Against Manufacturers of Defective Products, 49 U. Chi. L. Rev. 1, 1–6 (1982).

**53.** See Thomas Koenig and Michael Rustad, The Quiet Revolution Revisited: An Empirical Study of the Impact of State Tort Reform of Punitive Damages in Products Liability, 16 Just. Sys. J. 21 (1993); Rustad, In Defense of Punitive Damages, at 24; Rustad and Koenig, Historical Continuity, at 1308 (examining empirical data).

**54.** Michael Rustad and Thomas Koenig, Punitive Damages in Products Liability: An Empirical Study of the Last Quarter Century of Verdicts 14 (Nov. 14, 1991) ("An Empirical Study").

**55.** Id. at 14–15.

**56.** Id. at 16.

**57.** "Landes and Posner found two percent of the products cases resulting in punitive damages, while the Rand study found only 1/10th of one percent in Cook County and even less in San Francisco." Id. at 7–8. See, e.g., Vidmar and Rose, Punitive Damages by Juries in Florida: In Terrorem and

in Reality, 38 Harv. J. on Legis 469, 472 (2001) (noting empirical studies that demonstrate "strikingly low" frequency of punitive damages in products liability cases); Rustad, Unraveling Punitive Damages: Current Data and Further Inquiry, 1998 Wis. L. Rev. 15 (examining empirical studies); Eisenberg, Goerdt, Ostrom, Rottman and Wells, The Predictability of Punitive Damages, 26 J. Legal Stud. 623, 633–41 (1997) (empirical study revealing infrequency of punitive damages in products liability litigation).

**58.** During the quarter century covered by the survey, the CCH Products Liability Reporter reported roughly 10,000 products liability judicial decisions, and many such decisions go unreported. Thus, assuming conservatively that the total number of products liability verdicts over the period was twice the number reported in CCH, the 355 punitive damage verdicts represent roughly only 2% of the total. However, it is important to note that the frequency and judicial approval of such awards increased rather substantially over this protracted period, particularly in the 1970s and early 1980s. See Owen, Problems in Assessing Punitive Damages Against Manufacturers of Defective Products, 49 U. Chi. L. Rev. 1 (1982). But the trend of punitive damage awards in non-asbestos products liability cases may have turned downward. Koenig and Rustad, The Quiet Revolution Revisited: An Empirical Study of the Impact of State Tort Reform of Punitive Damages in Products Liability, 16 Just. Sys. J. 21 (1993).

punitive damages cases agree that decisions to award punitive damages almost always appear sound, that most awards are moderate, and that unreasonably large awards are likely to be overturned.[59] In short, punitive damages play a prominent but relatively minor role in products liability cases as in other types of litigation.

### Use in Products Liability Cases

Despite their infrequency, punitive damages have clamorously invaded the field of products liability. Indeed, there is probably no other aspect of modern products liability doctrine provoking as much spirited controversy as large awards of punitive damages.[60] Quite probably the most notorious verdict of this type in recent years was the $2.7 million in punitive damages awarded to a woman scalded when she spilled a cup of McDonald's hot coffee in her lap.[61] The claim was based on McDonald's

**59.** See Eisenberg, Damage Awards in Perspective: Behind the Headline—Grabbing Awards in *Exxon Valdez* and *Engle*, 36 Wake Forest L. Rev. 1129, 1131 (2001).

**60.** See, e.g., Sunstein, Hastie, Payne, Schkade, and Viscuci, Punitive Damages: How Juries Decide (U. Chi. Press 2002); Colby, Beyond the Multiple Punishment Problem: Punitive Damages As Punishment for Individual, Private Wrongs, 87 Minn. L. Rev. 583 (2003); Eisenberg, LaFountain, Ostrom, Rottman, and Wells, Juries, Judges, and Punitive Damages: An Empirical Study, 87 Cornell L. Rev. 743 (2002); Schkade, Erratic by Design: A Task Analysis of Punitive Damages Assessment, 39 Harv. J. on Legis. 121 (2002); Robbennolt, Determining Punitive Damages: Empirical Insights and Implications for Reform, 50 Buff. L. Rev. 103 (2002); Sunstein, Kahneman, Schkade, and Ritov, Predictably Incoherent Judgements, 54 Stan. L. Rev. 1153 (2002); Eisenberg, Rachlinski, and Wells, Reconciling Experimental Incoherence with Real-World Coherence in Punitive Damages, 54 Stan. L. Rev. 1239 (2002); Kelman, Problematic Perhaps, But Not Irrational, 54 Stan. L. Rev. 1273 (2002); Viscusi, Jurors, Judges, and the Mistreatment of Risk by the Courts, 30 J. Legal Stud. 107 (2001); Sunstein, Schkade, and Kahneman, Do People Want Optimal Deterrence?, 29 J. Legal Stud. 237 (2000); Viscusi, Corporate Risk Analysis: A Reckless Act?, 52 Stan. L. Rev. 547 (2000); Garber, Product Liability, Punitive Damages, Business Decisions and Economic Outcomes, 1998 Wis. L. Rev. 237; Viscusi, The Social Costs of Punitive Damages Against Corporations in Environmental and Safety Torts, 87 Geo. L.J. 285 (1998); Daughety and Reinganum, Everybody Out of the Pool: Products Liability, Punitive Damages, and Competition, 13 J.L. Econ. & Org. 410 (1997); Boston, Punitive Damages in Products Liability Cases: Facts and Inferences, Prod. Liab. Advisory 12 (June 1995) (reviewing 7 empirical studies); Symposium, Punitive Damages Awards in Product Liability Litigation: Strong Medicine or Poison Pill?, 39 Vill. L. Rev. 353 (1994) (essays by Twerski, Owen, G. Schwartz, Phillips, and Widiss); Koenig and Rustad, The Quiet Revolution Revisited: An Empirical Study of the Impact of State Tort Reform of Punitive Damages in Products Liability, 16 Just. Sys. J. 21 (1993); T. Schwartz, Punitive Damages and Regulated Products, 42 Am. U. L. Rev. 1335 (1993); Rustad, In Defense of Punitive Damages in Products Liability: Testing Tort Anecdotes with Empirical Data, 78 Iowa L. Rev. 1 (1992); Bernstein, Punitive Damages in Mass Products Liability, 1 Prod. Liab. L.J. 327 (1990); Ausness, Retribution and Deterrence: The Role of Punitive Damages in Products Liability Litigation, 74 Ky. L.J. 1 (1986); Seltzer, Punitive Damages in Mass Tort Litigation: Addressing the Problems of Fairness, Efficiency and Control, 52 Fordham L. Rev. 37 (1983); Owen, Problems in Assessing Punitive Damages Against Manufacturers of Defective Products, 49 U. Chi. L. Rev. 1 (1982) (hereinafter Problems); Owen, Punitive Damages in Products Liability Litigation, 74 Mich. L. Rev. 1257 (1976); Annot., 13 A.L.R.4th 52 (1982) (punitive damages in products liability cases). Much of chapter 18 draws from the my prior writings on this topic cited here.

**61.** Liebeck v. McDonald's Rests., P.T.S., Inc., No. CV–93–02419, 1995 WL 360309 (D. N.M. 1994). Mrs. Liebeck, a passenger in her grandson's car, spilled her coffee when she placed it between her legs and tried to remove the plastic lid. See Mead, Punitive Damages and the Spill Felt Round the World: A U.S. Perspective, 17 Loy. L.A. Int'l & Comp. L. Rev. 829 (1995); Gerlin, A Matter of Degree: How a Jury Decided that a Coffee Spill Is Worth $2.9 Million, Wall Street Journal A1 (Sept. 1,

failure to warn customers that it served its coffee exceedingly hot, at 180–90 degrees, and the evidence revealed that the company kept it far hotter than coffee sold by most of its competitors despite receipt of more than 700 complaints of burns, sometimes in the third degree. While upholding the jury's finding that punitive damages were warranted on these facts, the trial court remitted the award to $480,000, three times the amount of the compensatory award.[62]

Punitive damages have been awarded in a wide range of products liability cases. For example, juries have rendered such assessments for the manufacture and sale of an interuterine device especially prone to cause septic abortions and even death;[63] a tire knowingly made from bad stock rubber that could cause the tread to separate;[64] an asthma medication, Theo–Dur, that caused brain damage when taken with certain antibiotics;[65] a water heater susceptible to improper installation causing death from carbon monoxide poisoning;[66] a power miter box saw without a guard sufficient to prevent the amputation of a user's hand;[67] an automatic nail gun that activated too easily;[68] a disposable butane cigarette lighter which a child could use to start a fire;[69] an unstable three-wheel all-terrain vehicle that could too easily tip over;[70] a surgical anesthesia ventilator whose hoses could easily be attached to the wrong air port;[71] an overly-absorbent tampon that caused toxic shock syndrome;[72] a helicopter that was prone to engine failure;[73] cotton flannelette fabric for a child's nightgown that was not treated with flame

1994); Morgan, McDonald's Burned Itself, Legal Times, Sept. 19, 1994, at 26; Two Hot Verdicts Were Distorted by Critics, 20 ATLA Advocate 3 (Oct. 1994). *Liebeck* is examined further in § 18.3, below. See also Greene v. Boddie–Noell Enters., Inc., 966 F.Supp. 416, 418 n.1 (W.D. Va. 1997) (discussing *Liebeck*). Compare Immormino v. J & M Powers, Inc., 698 N.E.2d 516 (Ohio Ct. Common Pleas 1998), a hot tea spill case, where the court granted the defendant's motion for summary judgment, ruling that consumers are commonly aware of the dangers of hot liquid spills.

**62.** The plaintiff, 79 years old at the time of the accident, suffered third degree burns over six percent of her body on her inner thighs, buttocks, genital, and groin area, requiring skin grafts and debridement over seven or eight days in the hospital. The jury's punitive verdict represented two days of McDonald's national coffee sales. The jury calculated the plaintiff's compensatory damages at $200,000, but found her 20% at fault, reducing her compensatory award to $160,000. See articles cited in note 61, above.

**63.** E.g., Palmer v. A.H. Robins Co., 684 P.2d 187 (Colo. 1984) ($6.2 million); Tetuan v. A.H. Robins Co., 738 P.2d 1210 (Kan. 1987) ($7.5 million).

**64.** Cooper Tire and Rubber Co. v. Tuckier, 826 So.2d 679 (Miss. 2002) ($3 million).

**65.** Bocci v. Key Pharm., Inc., 35 P.3d 1106 (Or. Ct. App. 2001) ($35 million to one plaintiff, $22 million to other plaintiff).

**66.** Sears, Roebuck & Co. v. Harris, 630 So.2d 1018 (Ala. 1993) ($2.5 million).

**67.** Ross v. Black & Decker, Inc., 977 F.2d 1178 (7th Cir. 1992) (Ill. law) ($10 million remitted on appeal to $5 million).

**68.** E.g., Lakin v. Senco Products, 925 P.2d 107 (Or. Ct. App. 1996) ($4 million).

**69.** American Nat'l Bank & Trust Co. v. BIC Corp., 880 P.2d 420 (Okla. Civ. App. 1994) (more than $3.6 million for each of three children remitted by appellate court to $1 million each).

**70.** Oberg v. Honda Motor Co., 851 P.2d 1084 (Or. 1993) ($5 million), rev'd, 512 U.S. 415 (1994), reaffirmed on remand, 888 P.2d 8 (Or. 1995).

**71.** Airco, Inc. v. Simmons First Nat'l Bank, 638 S.W.2d 660, 662–63 (Ark. 1982) ($3 million).

**72.** West v. Johnson & Johnson Prods., Inc., 220 Cal.Rptr. 437 (Ct. App. 1985) (affirming trial court's remittitur of $10 million to $1 million).

**73.** Barnett v. La Societe Anonyme Turbomeca France, 963 S.W.2d 639 (Mo. Ct. App. 1997) ($175 million, remitted by trial judge to $87.5 million, further remitted by appellate court to $26.5 million).

retardant chemicals;[74] a multi-piece truck tire rim which could easily be misassembled and explosively fly apart;[75] a football helmet that failed to protect a high school football player against brain damage;[76] a forklift with an operator cabin designed without doors;[77] a television transformer that tended to catch fire;[78] and a large number of pharmaceutical drug cases in which manufacturers marketed dangerous pharmaceutical drugs or medical devices without warning about their hazards and sometimes with outright fraudulent representations to the medical profession, the public, and the FDA.[79] Such decisions represent only a sampling of the several hundred cases in which juries have awarded punitive damages in products liability litigation.[80]

Not only are punitive damages awarded in a wide variety of situations, but sometimes the awards are very large. Juries have returned a number of enormous punitive damages awards in automotive crashworthiness cases, beginning in 1978 with an award of $125 million, in *Grimshaw v. Ford Motor Company*, reduced by the trial court to $3.5 million.[81] The young plaintiff in *Grimshaw* was severely burned when the Ford Pinto in which he was riding burst into flames when its gas tank ruptured upon being struck from the rear by another vehicle.[82] The verdict was based on jury findings that Ford knew of dangers in the fuel system before the car was placed on the market and, although the company also knew that it could remedy the problem through inexpensive design changes, chose instead to sell the car in its dangerous condition to save on costs.[83] Since *Grimshaw*,[84] juries have awarded

---

**74.** Gryc v. Dayton–Hudson Corp., 297 N.W.2d 727 (Minn. 1980) ($1 million).

**75.** Hodder v. Goodyear Tire & Rubber Co., 426 N.W.2d 826 (Minn. 1988) ($12.5 million remitted on appeal to $4 million).

**76.** Rawlings Sporting Goods Co. v. Daniels, 619 S.W.2d 435 (Tex. App. 1981) ($750,000).

**77.** McEuin v. Crown Equip. Corp., 328 F.3d 1028, 1032 (9th Cir. 2003) (Or. law) ($1.25 million).

**78.** Gillham v. Admiral Corp., 523 F.2d 102 (6th Cir. 1975) (Ohio law) ($100,000).

**79.** Arrow Intern., Inc. v. Sparks, 98 S.W.3d 48 (Ark. Ct. App. 2003) (medical device: $4 million); Axen v. American Home Prod. Corp., 974 P.2d 224 (Or. Ct. App. 1999) (drug: $20 million). For a critical discussion and listing of punitive damages awards in pharmaceutical cases, see Viscusi, Corporate Risk Analysis: A Reckless Act?, 52 Stan. L. Rev. 547, 579–86 (2000) (listing the cases at 596–97, Table 5).

**80.** See Annot., 13 A.L.R.4th 52 (1982) (punitive damages in products liability cases).

**81.** No. 19–77–61 (Super. Ct., Orange Cty., Cal., Feb. 7, 1978), aff'd as amended, 174 Cal.Rptr. 348 (Ct. App. 1981). On *Grimshaw* and the Pinto fuel system design problem, see G. Schwartz, The Myth of the Ford Pinto Case, 43 Rutgers L. Rev. 1013

(1991); Owen, Problems in Assessing Punitive Damages Against Manufacturers of Defective Products, 49 U. Chi. L. Rev. 1, 47 (1982); Bruck, How Ford Stalled the Pinto Litigation, The American Lawyer 23 (June 1979); James S. Kunen, Reckless Disregard 249 et seq. (1994); Schmitt and May, Beyond Products Liability: The Legal, Social, and Ethical Problems Facing the Automobile Industry in Producing Safe Products, 56 U. Det. J. Urb. L. 1021 (1979); and the Pulitzer Prize-winning article by Dowie, Pinto Madness, Mother Jones 18 (Sept./Oct. 1977). On the criminal prosecution of Ford for its manufacture and sale of the Pinto, see L. Stobel, Reckless Homicide? (1980); Epstein, Is Pinto a Criminal? Regulation 15 (Mar./ Apr. 1980); Tybor, How Ford Won Pinto Trial, Nat'l L.J. 1 (Mar. 24, 1980); and a series of five articles by Wheeler, beginning with In Pinto's Wake, Criminal Trials Loom for More Manufacturers, Nat'l L.J. 27 (Oct. 6, 1980).

**82.** 174 Cal.Rptr. 348, 359.

**83.** See id. at 359–62. The danger alleged in the fuel system's design was its particular vulnerability to rupture when hit from the rear at relatively low speeds, with the resulting risk of fire if escaping fuel ignited. Specific claims of design inadequacy that allegedly aggravated the situation included the location of the fuel tank within

---

**84.** See note 84 on page 1130.

punitive damages in a substantial number of crashworthiness cases,[85] including verdicts against Ford for $58 million,[86] $150 million,[87] $246 million,[88] and $290 million;[89] Suzuki for $60 million;[90] General Motors for $101 million;[91] and Chrysler for $250 million.[92] But the largest award by far against an automotive manufacturer was the $4.8 *billion* punitive damages verdict levied against General Motors in 1999, remitted by the trial court to $1.09 billion, for locating the gas tank of a 1979 Chevrolet

---

only nine or ten inches (of "crush space") from the rear bumper, the flimsiness of the bumper itself, the absence of reinforcing members in the rear frame, and the positioning of the fuel tank just behind the differential housing with sharp protrusions pointing directly at the unshielded tank. Id. at 360. In addition, there was evidence of a variety of corrective design changes (safety "fixes") found to be feasible and economical. See id. at 361.

**84.** For a consideration of the cases before *Grimshaw*, see Owen, Crashworthiness Litigation and Punitive Damages, 4 J. Prod. Liab. 221 (1981). For a helpful policy analysis, see Schmitt and May, Beyond Products Liability: The Legal, Social, and Ethical Problems Facing the Automobile Industry in Producing Safe Products, 56 U. Det. J. Urb. L. 1021 (1979).

**85.** For other fuel tank cases, see, e.g., Ford Motor Co. v. Durrill, 714 S.W.2d 329 (Tex. App. 1986), vacated on motion of parties, 754 S.W.2d 646 (Tex. 1988) ($100 million punitive damages verdict, remitted by trial court to $20 million, further remitted on appeal to $10 million, and then settled, for design of Ford Mustang II fuel system); Ford Motor Co. v. Stubblefield, 319 S.E.2d 470 (Ga. Ct. App. 1984) ($8 million: Mustang II); Toyota Motor Co., Ltd. v. Moll, 438 So.2d 192 (Fla. Dist. Ct. App. 1983) ($3 million punitive damages award upheld); American Motors Corp. v. Ellis, 403 So.2d 459 (Fla. Dist. Ct. App. 1981) (punitive damages claim for jury).

Non-fuel tank cases include Clark v. Chrysler Corp., 310 F.3d 461 (6th Cir. 2002) (Ky. law) ($3 million: insufficient pillar in Dodge Ram pickup); Hasson v. Ford Motor Co., 650 P.2d 1171, 1180 (Cal. 1982) ($4 million: brake system); Ford Motor Co. v. Nowak, 638 S.W.2d 582 (Tex. App. 1982) ($4 million: park-reverse transmission slip); General Motors Corp. v. Johnston, 592 So.2d 1054 (Ala. 1992) ($15 million, reduced to $7.5 million: stalling problem for which GM issued only "silent" or "unpublished" recall); Dorsey v. Honda Motor Co., 655 F.2d 650 (5th Cir. 1981) (Fla. law) ($5 million: frontal design of small Honda).

**86.** Remitted by the trial court to $13.8 million, and upheld on appeal. Ford Motor Co. v. Ammerman, 705 N.E.2d 539 (Ind. Ct. App. 1999). In *Ammerman*, which involved the rollover of a Bronco II sport utility

vehicle (SUV), the jury found that Ford knew when it designed the vehicle in the early 1980s that it was unstable, but that the company "decided against spending extra money to widen the vehicle and lower its center of gravity in order to meet a production schedule" and thereafter sought to cover up the danger. Prod. Liab. Advisory 3 (Nov. 1995). The punitive damages verdict was divided equally between the driver and passenger who were both severely injured. Id. In another Bronco II rollover case, a Texas jury assessed Ford $22.5 million, reduced by the trial judge in that case to the statutory maximum of $4 million, four times the compensatory award. Cammack v. Ford Motor Co., Tex. Dist. Ct., 61st Dist. Harris Cty. (Aug. 25, 1995). Prod. Saf. & Liab. Rep. 958 (Sept. 8, 1995).

**87.** White v. Ford Motor Co., 312 F.3d 998 (9th Cir. 2002) (Nev. law) ($150 million punitive damages verdict ($\frac{1}{2}$ of 1% of Ford's net worth of $30 billion), remitted by district court to $69 million, reversed), amended, 335 F.3d 833 (9th Cir. 2003).

**88.** Wilson v. Ford Motor Co., 2004 WL 1574107 (Cal. Super. Ct. 2004) in 32 Prod. Saf. & Liab. Rep. (BNA) 535 (June 14, 2004) (Explorer rollover suit).

**89.** Romo v. Ford Motor Co., 122 Cal. Rptr.2d 139 (Ct. App. 2002) (affirming verdict), vacated and remanded, 538 U.S. 1028 (2003), remitted to $27 million on remand, 6 Cal.Rptr.3d 793 (Ct. App. 2003).

**90.** Rodriguez v. American Suzuki Motor Co., 936 S.W.2d 104 (Mo. 1996) (verdict July 7, 1995) (passenger injured in rollover of Suzuki Samurai).

**91.** General Motors Corp. v. Moseley, 447 S.E.2d 302 (Ga. Ct. App. 1994) ($101 million punitive verdict, for death of youth in fiery crash of GM side-saddle pickup truck, vacated and remanded for new trial for improper argument by plaintiff's counsel). Cf. In re: General Motors Corporation Pick-Up Fuel Tank Prod. Liab. Litig., 55 F.3d 768 (3d Cir. 1995) (Pa. law) (rejecting coupon settlement with owners of pickups equipped with dangerous side-saddle fuel tanks).

**92.** Jimenez v. Chrysler Corp., 74 F.Supp.2d 548 (D.S.C. 1999), rev'd, Jimenez v. DaimlerChrysler Corp., 269 F.3d 439 (4th Cir. 2001).

Malibu behind the rear axle close to the rear bumper, causing the car to burst into flames when it was hit at high speed from behind.[93]

While the absolute size of individual punitive damages verdicts in the automotive cases until recently dwarfed such assessments against manufacturers of other types of products, the exaction and threat of repeated punitive assessments across the nation have made the largest impact in the toxic substance mass litigation setting. Beginning in the 1980s, large and recurring punitive damages awards began to play a significant role in the eventual bankruptcy of the asbestos industry.[94] In the tobacco litigation, the specter of massive punitive damages awards played a major role in forcing an industry not known for its tractability to settle the numerous cases brought against it by all 50 states to recover for their health care costs. In 1997 and 1998, the industry settled the cases for $246 billion, most to be paid over twenty-five years.[95] Large punitive damages awards are assessed from time to time in individual tobacco cases,[96] all of which are dwarfed by the $145 billion verdict

**93.** Anderson v. General Motors Corp., No. BC116926, 1999 WL 1466627 (L.A. Cty. Super. Ct. 1999). See White, Jury Orders GM to Pay $4.9 Billion (AP), The State (Columbia, S.C.) July 10, 1999, at A1; Germain, Judge Cuts Billions from GM Fine (AP), The State (Columbia, S.C.) Aug. 27, 1999, at A9.

**94.** As of the early 2000s, some 60 asbestos manufacturers have filed bankruptcy. See § 10.3, above. For a small sampling of the many cases, see, e.g., Hoskins v. Business Men's Assurance, 116 S.W.3d 557 (Mo. Ct. App. 2003) (affirming $7 million punitive damages award); Owens–Corning Fiberglas Corp. v. Malone, 972 S.W.2d 35 (Tex. 1998) (affirming $3.7 million punitive award); Stevens v. Owens–Corning Fiberglas Corp., 57 Cal.Rptr.2d 525 (Ct. App. 1996) (affirming $2 million punitive award); Dunn v. HOVIC, 1 F.3d 1371 (3d Cir. 1993) (2–1 decision) (V.I. law) (district court reduced $25 million punitive to $2 million, and court of appeals reduced it to $1 million), modified, 13 F.3d 58 (3d Cir. 1993); Spaur v. Owens–Corning Fiberglas Corp., 510 N.W.2d 854 (Iowa 1994) (affirming $1.5 million punitive award).

Although punitive damages are more common in asbestos cases than any other context, they are not allowed in every asbestos case. See, e.g., Kasun v. Owens–Illinois, Inc., 635 N.W.2d 26 (Wis. Ct. App. 2001) (affirming verdicts for asbestos manufacturers); In re Asbestos Litigation, 986 F.Supp. 761 (S.D.N.Y. 1997) (upholding jury's refusal to assess punitive damages in multidistrict litigation); ACandS, Inc. v. Godwin, 667 A.2d 116 (Md. 1995) (reversing punitive damages for insufficient proof of defendants' malice). See also In re Asbestos Products Liability Litigation, 170 F.Supp.2d

1348 (Jud. Pan. Mult. Lit. 2001) (noting Court of Appeals' approval of multidistrict panel's withholding of punitive damages claims on remand, effectively barring them).

**95.** See § 10.3, above. Van Voris, A Carton of New Tobacco Trials, Nat'l L.J., Apr. 24, 2000, at A1; R.J. Reynolds Slowly Checks Decline in Cigarette Sales, Wall St. J., Apr. 17, 2000, at B4; Brickman, Want to Be a Billionaire? Sue a Tobacco Company, Wall St. J., Dec. 30, 1998, at A11. See generally Viscusi, A Postmortem on the Cigarette Settlement, 29 Cumb. L. Rev. 523 (1999); LeBel and Ausness, Toward Justice in Tobacco Policymaking: A Critique of Hanson and Logue and an Alternative Approach to the Cost of Cigarettes, 33 Ga. L. Rev. 693 (1999); Jacobson and Warner, Litigation and Public Health Policy Making: The Case of Tobacco Control, 24 J. Health Pol. Pol'y & L. 769 (1999) (suggesting litigation take back seat to regulation in controlling tobacco); Symposia: Torts and Tobacco, 33 Ga. L. Rev. 693 (1999) (articles by LeBel and Ausness, Rachlinski, Rendleman, Wagner, and Weber); Tobacco Regulation: The Convergence of Law, Medicine & Public Health, 25 Wm. Mitchell L. Rev. 373 (1999) (twelve articles); LeBel, Introduction, Florida Tobacco Litigation Symposium–Putting the 1997 Settlement into Context, 25 Fla. St. U. L. Rev. 731 (1998); Tobacco: The Growing Controversy, 24 N. Ky. L. Rev. 397 (1997) (articles by Wertheimer, Ausness, LeBel, Eases, O'Reilly, Jevicky, Redish, and Valauri); Note, 49 S.C. L. Rev. 311 (1998).

**96.** See, e.g., Henley v. Philip Morris Inc., 5 Cal.Rptr.3d 42 (Ct. App. 2003), review granted and cause transferred, 81 P.3d 223 (Cal. 2003) ($50 million award to

returned by a Florida jury, subsequently reversed, in that state's class action litigation against the tobacco industry.[97]

Though sometimes awarded in large amounts, punitive damages verdicts of any size are rendered in only a tiny fraction of products liability litigation, as previously discussed. Moreover, the largest punitive damages awards typically are remitted substantially by trial or appellate courts, or both,[98] particularly now that the Supreme Court has declared that excessive punitive damages awards may violate due process of law.[99] For example, in a case against the manufacturer of a helicopter that crashed due to a defect that the manufacturer knew about but concealed, the jury assessed punitive damages of $175 million, which the trial court remitted to $87.5 million and which the appellate court remitted further to $26.5 million.[100] Even twice reduced, however, $26.5 million remains a very large award. Thus, the threat of massive punitive damage awards truly is the "big stick" of modern products liability litigation.

## § 18.2  FUNCTIONS OF PUNITIVE DAMAGES

In order to determine whether punitive damages are appropriate in particular cases, it is necessary to understand the objectives of such damages that may justify their award.[1] Although courts typically refer only to "punishment" and "deterrence" as the purposes of such damages,[2] this commonly stated duality of goals masks the nuanced variety

smoker, remitted by trial judge to $25 million, further remitted by appellate court to $9 million); Burton v. R.J. Reynolds Tobacco Co., 205 F.Supp.2d 1253, 1264 (D. Kan. 2002) (upholding $15 million award to smoker); Williams v. Philip Morris Inc., 48 P.3d 824 (Or. Ct. App. 2002) ($79.2 million verdict for smoker, reduced by trial judge to $32.8 million, reinstated on appeal), vacated and remanded for reconsideration, Philip Morris USA, Inc. v. Williams, 540 U.S. 801 (2003), reconsidered and reinstated, 92 P.3d 126 (Or. Ct. App. 2004) (concluding that $79.5 million punitive award was reasonable, proportionate to the wrong to the plaintiff and the public in the state, and hence comported with Supreme Court due process guidelines); Annot., Liability of Cigarette Manufacturers for Punitive Damages, 108 A.L.R.5th 343 (2003) (summarizing cases in which courts have determined cigarette manufacturer liability for punitive damages).

**97.** See Liggett Group Inc. v. Engle, 853 So.2d 434 (Fla. Dist. Ct. App. 2003). See, e.g., Bragg, Jurors in Florida Give Record Award in Tobacco Case—A $144.8 Billion Verdict, N.Y. Times, July 15, 2000, at A1 (New England ed.); Geyelin and Fairclough, Taking a Hit—Yes, $145 Billion Deals Tobacco a Huge Blow, But Not a Killing One, Wall St. J., July 17, 2000, at A1. See also Bragg and Kershaw, Juror Says a 'Sense of Mission' Led to Huge Tobacco Damages—Panel Saw Industry as Dishonest and Arro-

gant, N.Y. Times, July 16, 2000, at A1 (New England ed.).

**98.** Remittitur is examined in § 18.6, below.

**99.** See § 18.7, below. Excessiveness in general is examined in § 18.5, below.

**100.** Barnett v. La Societe Anonyme Turbomeca France, 963 S.W.2d 639 (Mo. Ct. App. 1997).

### § 18.2

**1.** Indeed, the Supreme Court now ties the constitutionality of punitive damages to their being assessed according to their functions. See Pacific Mut. Life Ins. Co. v. Haslip, 499 U.S. 1, 19 (1991).

**2.** See, e.g., Cooper Indus., Inc. v. Leatherman Tool Group, Inc., 532 U.S. 424, 432 (2001) (punitive damages "operate as 'private fines' intended to punish the defendant and to deter future wrongdoing"); Owens–Corning Fiberglas Corp. v. Malone, 972 S.W.2d 35, 40 (Tex. 1998) ("the purpose of punitive damages is to punish a party"); BMW of N. Am., Inc. v. Gore, 517 U.S. 559, 611 (1996); Pacific Mut. Life Ins. Co. v. Haslip, 499 U.S. 1 (1991); Ford Motor Co. v. Ammerman, 705 N.E.2d 539, 563 (Ind. Ct. App. 1999), Miss. Code Ann. § 11–1–65(f)(i) (purpose is "to punish what occurred giving rise to the award and to deter its repetition by the defendant and others"); Restatement (2d) Torts § 908(1). See also Ga. Code Ann. § 51–12–5.1(a).

of specific functions served by punitive damages.[3] While the various overlapping functions may be formulated and subdivided in any number of ways, it may be helpful to identify five separate objectives: (1) retribution, (2) education, (3) deterrence, (4) compensation, and (5) law enforcement.[4]

## Retribution

When courts refer to the "punishment" function of punitive damages, they generally mean retribution, perhaps the most fundamental basis for punishment in any form.[5] Some commentators are troubled by the idea that modern law might be based in part on a kind of private revenge,[6] but logic and fundamental fairness suggest that it is entirely appropriate to allow a person injured by the wanton misconduct of another to vent his or her outrage by extracting from the wrongdoer a judicial fine.[7] This form of judicial retribution is appropriate because it protects and promotes two fundamental values that support the law: freedom and equality.[8]

Punitive damages are designed to punish conduct that is quasi-criminal,[9] and an understanding of their basis in retributive justice is facilitated by examining the doctrine in terms of a metaphor based on theft.[10] The wrongdoer (the "thief") deserves to be punished because he or she has "stolen" things of value, from both the individual and society, that need to be returned in order to prevent the unjust impoverishment

---

**3.** On the functions of punitive damages, see, e.g., Madden, Renegade Conduct and Punitive Damages in Tort, 53 S.C. L. Rev. 1175 (2002); Owen, A Punitive Damages Overview: Functions, Problems and Reform, 39 Vill. L. Rev. 363 (1994) (hereinafter Punitive Damages Overview); Kuklin, Punishment: The Civil Perspective of Punitive Damages, 37 Clev. St. L. Rev. 1 (1989); Ausness, Retribution and Deterrence: The Role of Punitive Damages in Products Liability Litigation, 74 Ky. L.J. 1 (1986); Seltzer, Punitive Damages in Mass Tort Litigation: Addressing the Problems of Fairness, Efficiency and Control, 52 Fordham L. Rev. 37 (1983); Ellis, Fairness and Efficiency in the Law of Punitive Damages, 56 S. Cal. L. Rev. 1 (1982); Owen, Punitive Damages, 74 Mich. L. Rev. at 1257. See also Gash, Solving the Multiple Punishment Problem: A Call for a National Punitive Damages Registry, 99 Nw. U. L. Rev. ___ (2005) (using the five functions discussed in this section to analyze appropriateness of proposed solution to multiple punishment problem).

**4.** Much of the discussion here is adapted from Owen, Punitive Damages Overview; Owen, The Moral Foundations of Punitive Damages, 40 Ala. L. Rev. 705 (1989) (hereinafter Moral Foundations); and Owen, Punitive Damages.

**5.** Punishment itself is merely a means to a variety of ends, such as retribution and deterrence.

**6.** Some commentators view retribution and revenge as inappropriate in modern legal systems. See, e.g., Rubin, Punitive Damages: Reconceptualizing the Runcible Remedies of Common Law, 1998 Wis. L. Rev. 131, 138–41 (questioning appropriateness of retribution in modern law); Viscusi, Why There is No Defense of Punitive Damages, 87 Geo. L.J. 381, 395 (1998) ("vengeance . . . is not a constructive function for our legal system").

**7.** See, e.g., Galanter and Luban, Poetic Justice: Punitive Damages and Legal Pluralism, 42 Am. U. L. Rev. 1393 (1993); Hampton, Correcting Harm versus Righting Wrongs—The Goal of Retribution, 39 UCLA L. Rev. 1659 (1992); Owen, Punitive Damages, at 1279.

**8.** The retributive rationale for punitive damages is explored in Owen, Moral Foundations, at 708–13. See H.L.A. Hart, Punishment and Responsibility 235–37 (1982); Kuklin, Punishment: The Civil Perspective of Punitive Damages, 37 Clev. St. L. Rev. 1 (1989); Owen, Punitive Damages, at 1279–82.

**9.** See § 18.1, above.

**10.** This metaphor is developed in Owen, Moral Foundations, at 708–13.

of the victim and society as well as the unjust enrichment of the thief. The scales of justice, thrown out of balance by the offense, can only be restored by corresponding punishment. In this respect, the offender's punishment serves as a form of "restitution" for the theft.[11]

When an actor intentionally violates the rights of another person, the actor "steals" the victim's autonomy and thus asserts that the thief is more worthy than the victim. If such autonomy thefts were not subjected to penalties in addition to requiring that the thief restore the stolen goods (compensatory damages), the rectification of the transaction would be incomplete. This is because such theft transactions contain two distinct components: (1) the transfer of goods from the victim to the thief, and (2) the deliberately wrongful nature of the transfer in violation of the plaintiff's vested rights—the illicit transfer of freedom from the victim to the thief. Punishment, through punitive damages, serves to restore the equality of the victim in relation to the thief by diminishing the extra worth and freedom held illicitly by the thief that was stolen from the victim.[12] By vindicating the plaintiff's right to remain free from flagrantly inflicted harm,[13] the law in this manner reaffirms the equal worth of all and the duty of each person to respect the equal rights and worth of others.

Punitive damages also serve an important retributive, restitutionary function for society as a whole. The theft of goods and freedom diminishes the worth of all law-abiding members of society in relation to the thief. When persons in the community agree to rules establishing the boundaries of their legal rights, they each surrender their freedom to violate other persons' boundaries in pursuit of their own personal objectives. This is, of course, a reciprocal sacrifice which contemplates that all citizens share equally in this restriction upon their individual freedoms. When a thief intentionally intrudes into another person's zone of rights, he assigns to himself more than the equal share of freedom the community assigned by law to him. In comparison to the thief, law-abiding members of society are impoverished by the gain appropriated by the law-breaker. In this respect, the thief has stolen value from society by breaking the reciprocal security pact based on equal rights. By punishing intentional law-breakers, society restores all its members to a position of equal worth, and reinforces the confidence of law-abiders in the basic fairness of the legal system and in the utility of their personal decisions to obey the law.[14] Punitive damages thus have an important

---

**11.** "A person who is unjustly enriched at the expense of another is liable in restitution to the other." Restatement (3d) of Restitution and Unjust Enrichment § 1 (Discussion Draft, March 31, 2000).

**12.** "A person who interferes with the legally protected rights of another, acting without justification and in conscious disregard of the other's rights, is liable to the other for any profit realized by such interference." Restatement (3d) Restitution and

Unjust Enrichment § 3 (Discussion Draft, March 31, 2000).

**13.** See, e.g., Clark v. Cantrell, 529 S.E.2d 528, 533 (S.C. 2000) ("punitive damages [provide] vindication ... and compensate or satisfy for the willfulness with which the private right was invaded").

**14.** See C. Fried, An Anatomy of Values 121–26 (1970); L. Fuller, Anatomy of the Law 29 (1968); H.L.A. Hart, The Concept of Law 193 (1961); 10 Halsbury, The Laws of England 306 (1909).

restitutionary role in forcing flagrant offenders to repay their "debts" to, and restore the equality of, both their victims and society.

These general retributive objectives of punitive damages apply to cases of flagrant misbehavior by manufacturers. The retributive needs of victims and society may be substantial when manufacturers sell defective products in flagrant disregard of serious risks of injuries to consumers. Awards of punitive damages in such cases help assuage a victim's feelings of helplessness and frustration over the apparent futility of holding an anonymous corporation accountable for its damaging misdeeds.[15] Further, such awards express the public's condemnation of the misconduct[16] and remind manufacturers of their responsibility for consumer safety.[17] Finally, punishing manufacturers guilty of intentional or reckless breaches of their safety obligations should tend to diminish whatever unfair competitive advantages such companies otherwise might obtain.[18]

### Education

Punitive damages serve to educate individual offenders and society in general in two significant respects. First, punitive damages certify the existence of a particular legally protected right or interest belonging to the plaintiff, on the one hand, and a correlative legal duty on the part of the defendant to respect that interest, on the other. Second, punitive damages proclaim the special importance the law attaches to the plaintiff's particular invaded right, and the corresponding condemnation that society attaches to its flagrant invasion by the kind of conduct engaged in by the defendant.[19]

Much more so than with assessments of responsibility for actual damages, punitive damages assessments sensationalize the consequences of improper behavior in a manner that informs and reminds defendants and society at large that a particular right–duty legal value not only exists, but that it is given staunch protection by the law. Society's most important rules governing how people are to live together, and the boundaries of their respective spheres of freedom to pursue their person-

---

**15.** See R. Heilbroner, Controlling the Corporation, In the Name of Profit 191, 200 (R. Heilbroner ed., 1973) (A "feeling of individual impotence in the face of massive organizations" is in part "[w]hat fuels the public protest against corporate misbehavior. . . . It is an aspect of a widely shared frustration with respect to all bastions of power that are immense, anonymous and impregnable, and yet inextricably bound up with the industrial society that few of us wish to abandon."); A. Linden, Canadian Negligence Law 487 (1972).

**16.** See Fischer v. Johns–Manville Corp., 512 A.2d 466, 472 (N.J. 1986) (the punitive damages doctrine "continues to serve the useful purposes of expressing society's disapproval of intolerable conduct and deterring such conduct where no other remedy would suffice").

**17.** Punishment serves "the symbolic function of reinforcing the public sense that there are certain acts that are fundamentally wrong, that must not be done." L. Fuller, Anatomy of the Law 28 (1968).

**18.** By forcing flagrant law violators to disgorge their illicit profits, as discussed below.

**19.** For this reason, the retributive function may aptly be referred to as "condemnation." See, e.g., Haralson v. Fisher Surveying, Inc., 31 P.3d 114, 116 (Ariz. 2001) (recognizing that societal condemnation is a valid ground for assessing punitive damages); The Law Commission (Great Britain), Aggravated, Exemplary and Restitutionary Damages—A Consultation Paper 114, 123 (Consultation Paper No. 132, 1993) (condemnation is legitimate function of punitive damages).

al interests that sometimes conflict, are publicly declared and certified as fundamental by punitive damage awards. This form of judicial punishment serves to publicize the community's condemnation of flagrant breaches of the rules of proper behavior which reaffirms society's commitment to its moral and legal standards.

The education objective appears particularly relevant to the products liability context. Many manufacturers fail to understand the basic rules of product safety. Because the principal liability rules are normally based on a balancing of incommensurable values,[20] product "defectiveness" can often look quite different from separate points of view.[21] Due to the elusive nature of design defectiveness,[22] it is often difficult for a design engineer or manager to know just how much safety the law requires. In such an environment, where the line of lawful conduct is obscured by mist, there must be great temptation for manufacturers driven by the profit motive to push ever closer toward the amorphous line that separates lawful from unlawful conduct, to push toward greater profits at the expense of safety. Yet, while such behavior may be understandable, manufacturers should not be permitted blithely to close their eyes to the safety consequences of their design and warnings decisions which they know may unreasonably endanger many persons. Accordingly, occasional judicial declarations that certain types of product safety decisions are not only improper but intolerable provide useful information; the publicity afforded large assessments of punitive damages serves to remind the manufacturer, the industry, other victims of the same misconduct, and society generally that the push for profit must always leave fair room for safety.[23]

**Deterrence**

In their retributive role, punitive damages serve to rectify some of the negative effects of a wrongdoer's prior misconduct. In many ways, retributive justice is the most important goal of punitive damages. Yet, many courts and commentators believe that the predominant purpose of punishment in general, and punitive damages in particular, is deterrence—the prevention of similar misconduct in the future.[24] While the practical effectiveness of punishment in deterring misbehavior remains a source of study and debate,[25] few would disagree with the premises of

**20.** See ch. 5, above.

**21.** "A rose is often not a rose in such an environment, and what looks like acceptable if not praiseworthy conduct to one person may look flagrantly improper to another: one person's sound engineering is another person's trading lives for profits." Owen, Problems in Assessing Punitive Damages Against Manufacturers of Defective Products, 49 U. Chi. L. Rev. 1, 47 (1982).

**22.** See ch. 8, above.

**23.** Among those who may be informed are engineering faculty at universities, who educate future engineers, and governmental regulators of product safety. On the effect

of publicity on the latter, and on other victims of the same misconduct, see generally Garber, Product Liability, Punitive Damages, Business Decisions and Economic Outcomes, 1998 Wis. L. Rev. 237; Bailis and MacCoun, Estimating Liability Risks with the Media as Your Guide, 80 Judicature 64 (Sept./Oct. 1996).

**24.** See Restatement (2d) Torts § 908(1); H.L.A. Hart, Punishment and Responsibility 128–29 (1982); Owen, Punitive Damages, above, at 1283.

**25.** See, e.g., Garber, Product Liability, Punitive Damages, Business Decisions and Economic Outcomes, 1998 Wis. L. Rev. 237; Viscusi, The Social Costs of Punitive Dam-

both the law of torts and crimes that liability and punishment do achieve some measure of deterrence in many cases.[26]

The effectiveness of punitive damages in deterring gross misconduct depends significantly upon two related factors: (1) the regularity with which the law catches and punishes persons who flagrantly violate the rights of other persons, and (2) the extent to which potential offenders understand that the law proscribes, and that enforcers are likely to punish, their contemplated misbehavior.[27] Because potential offenders well know that misconduct often goes undetected and unpunished, punitive damages deter misconduct by serving to sensationalize, and hence to publicize, the apprehension and punishment of offenders found guilty of egregious misconduct.[28] Potential offenders are thereby informed of several important things: (1) the kinds of rights the law recognizes and protects, and the kinds of conduct that will violate those rights; (2) that rights violations which are intentional or otherwise flagrant may be punished in amounts exceeding the return of the stolen goods; and (3) that, although punishment may be uncertain, it is likely enough (because of the monetary incentive for victims to prosecute such offenses) and may be large enough to take the apparent profitability out of contemplated thefts. In sum, the deterrence message directed at would-be thieves is that the price of getting caught, discounted by the risk thereof, exceeds the value of the booty.

This deterrence rationale is especially applicable to repetitive profit-seeking behavior when its wrongfulness is not readily apparent. The manufacture and sale of thousands of consumer products across the nation involves the potential for this type of hidden misbehavior. If a manufacturer makes and sells a product it knows to have a deficient design or warning, many persons may be injured without their realizing that the vague and otherwise arcane rules of products liability law were violated at all, much less that they were violated in a flagrant manner.[29] When such a manufacturer is caught and punished with a punitive damage assessment, such damages serve in part as a kind of surrogate "filler" for the compensatory damages of those other victims of the same misconduct who do not successfully pursue claims against the manufac-

---

ages Against Corporations in Environmental and Safety Torts, 87 Geo. L.J. 285, 336 (1998) ("[p]unitive damages generate no statistically significant deterrent effects"); Elliott, Why Punitive Damages Don't Deter Corporate Misconduct Effectively, 40 Ala. L. Rev. 1053, 1072 (1989) ("punitive damages probably have very little effect on corporate behavior").

**26.** See G. Schwartz, Reality in the Economic Analysis of Tort Law: Does Tort Law Really Deter?, 42 UCLA L. Rev. 377 (1994). See also Wells, Comments on Why Punitive Damages Don't Deter Corporate Misconduct Effectively, 40 Ala. L. Rev. 1073, 1076 (1989) ("Economic analysis suggests that punitive damages do influence decision making. Rational actors attempt to minimize their costs, and hence will avoid con-

duct that generates punitive damages. Punitive damages may deter too much, rather than too little.").

**27.** See Owen, Punitive Damages, 74 Mich. L. Rev. at 1283.

**28.** See Garber, Product Liability, Punitive Damages, Business Decisions and Economic Outcomes, 1998 Wis. L. Rev. 237, 279 ("an award of roughly $2 million that includes a punitive component is as likely to receive newspaper coverage as a $25 million award that is entirely compensatory").

**29.** Moreover, as discussed below, injury victims often do not seek legal redress and may be unsuccessful when they do. See Polinsky and Shavell, Punitive Damages: An Economic Analysis, 111 Harv. L. Rev. 869, 888–89 (1998).

turer.[30] In this way, manufacturers are informed that they may ultimately be forced to pay in full, albeit very roughly, the price of all the harm resulting from their sale of products known to be defective, and maybe more. The two-part message provided by punitive damages awards is (1) that the law will not tolerate a manufacturer's acquisition of illicit profits from exploiting the vagueness and resulting under-enforcement of the liability rules; and (2) that the law instead will force an enterprise which has marketed a product in flagrant disregard of consumer safety to disgorge all ill-gotten gains, and possibly much more.

One final matter should be mentioned that probably diminishes the deterrent effect of punitive damages assessments: the impossibility of predicting the *amount* of a manufacturer's aggregate punitive damages liability. For a variety of reasons, there is no way for a manufacturer to know in advance the magnitude of total punitive damages liability for marketing a particular dangerously defective product. Predicting the aggregate amount of punitive damages is virtually impossible, first, because of the difficulty of predicting the number or extent of injuries likely to result from any kind of product defect. Second, while an informed lawyer might hazard a prediction of the likelihood that a jury might return a punitive damages verdict in a particular case, only a daring lawyer would be willing to predict the size of such an award.[31] The method the law prescribes for determining amounts of punitive damages[32] introduces such perplexing imponderables that it is truly impossible for a manufacturer to forecast the amounts of such awards in any meaningful way. Depending on how a jury evaluates the gravity of a manufacturer's wrongdoing, the number and severity of the resulting injuries, and how a jury measures a manufacturer's wealth, a punitive damages verdict in a particular case could range from nothing at all to hundreds of millions, or even billions, of dollars. In short, even with detailed information on the nature and flagrancy of the marketing misconduct, no sober lawyer would be willing to estimate the total amount of punitive damages liability that a manufacturer would likely incur from selling a particular dangerously defective product across the nation.

Thus, predicting punitive damages liability is futile, which quite probably undercuts the deterrent effect of such awards. In most cases, however, a manufacturer well advised by counsel and acting rationally should be influenced to some extent by the possibility of the largely open-ended liability of punitive damages verdicts for flagrantly disregarding consumer safety in its design and marketing decisions.[33]

**30.** See id.

**31.** Empirical research suggests that it may be far easier to predict whether punitive damages may be assessed in a particular situation than to predict their amount. See Sunstein, Kahneman, and Schkade, Assessing Punitive Damages (with Notes on Cognition and Valuation in Law), 107 Yale L.J. 2071 (1998).

**32.** See § 18.5, below.

**33.** Of course, one might question the hypothesis that all activity within the enterprise is rationally directed toward profit maximization. See, e.g., J. Galbraith, The New Industrial State (1967); C. Stone, Where the Law Ends: The Social Control of Corporate Behavior (1975).

**Compensation**

Although it is frequently asserted that punitive damages are not designed to compensate the plaintiff,[34] such damages do indeed serve a variety of important compensatory roles.[35] As seen above, such awards serve the restitutionary purpose that underlies the retributive function,[36] and their provision of "extra" money is what fuels the private prosecutor engine of the law-enforcement function, as discussed below. More directly, such awards also serve to reimburse the plaintiff for losses not ordinarily recoverable as compensatory damages—actual losses the plaintiff is unable to prove or for which the rules of damages do not provide relief including, most importantly, attorneys' fees and other costs of bringing suit.

Many of a plaintiff's actual losses, particularly those involving intangible harm, are not compensable under the ordinary rules of compensatory damage liability. For example, a severely injured person who is rendered immobile for many months may lose a number of important interpersonal relationships and will probably suffer a large variety of missed (and often unknown) opportunities. There is no practical way for the law to measure such speculative or at least non-quantifiable losses, as real as they may be. Ordinarily, therefore, in fairness to the injurer, such losses are excluded from the accident compensation system and left to remain instead upon the plaintiff as a risk of life. Yet, when the defendant inflicts injury intentionally or pursues his or her private interests in a manner that he knows will expose the plaintiff to substantial undue risk, the equities of the situation change considerably, and responsibility for ordinarily nonrecoverable emotional and other intangible losses properly may be placed upon the guilty party.

While the payment of attorneys' fees and other costs of litigation ordinarily is not articulated as an explicit purpose for punitive damages, it sometimes is,[37] and requiring a plaintiff to incur these substantial costs in order to rectify an aggravated wrong appears fundamentally unfair. Because at least one-third of a plaintiff's recovery ordinarily is expended on legal fees, a verdict that does not include a sum for these expenses almost always leaves the plaintiff substantially worse off financially than he or she was before the injury. And whether or not requiring

**34.** See, e.g., Oros v. Hull & Assocs., 302 F.Supp.2d 839 (N.D. Ohio 2004); Bachman v. General Motors Corp., 776 N.E.2d 262, 301 (Ill. App. Ct. 2002) ("purpose of punitive damages is not compensation"); Ga. Code Ann. § 51–12–5.1(c) ("Punitive damages shall be awarded not as compensation to a plaintiff but solely to punish, penalize, or deter a defendant.").

**35.** See, e.g., In re Simon II Litig., 211 F.R.D. 86, 159 (E.D.N.Y. 2002) (cigarette class action litigation; punitive damages "compensate for social damages not likely to be fully reflected in compensatory damages to individuals"); Clark v. Cantrell, 529

S.E.2d 528, 533 (S.C. 2000) ("there is a compensatory aspect to punitive damages").

**36.** See, e.g., Clark v. Cantrell, 529 S.E.2d 528, 533 (S.C. 2000) ("such damages in a measure compensate or satisfy for the willfulness with which the private right was invaded").

**37.** See, e.g., St. Luke Evangelical Lutheran Church, Inc. v. Smith, 568 A.2d 35 (Md. 1990); Triangle Sheet Metal Works, Inc. v. Silver, 222 A.2d 220, 225 (Conn. 1966). See also Cox v. Stolworthy, 496 P.2d 682 (Idaho 1972), overruled in part by Cheney v. Palos Verdes Inv. Corp., 665 P.2d 661 (Idaho 1983).

the injured plaintiff to suffer this significant detriment makes sense in an ordinary case, it is plainly illogical and unjust in a situation where punitive damages are proper. Surely it is the thief in such cases—not the victim—who should pay the costs of activating and driving the legal system to restore the stolen goods to their rightful owner. It seems self-evident that a defendant who has intentionally or wantonly injured another should fairly be required, as much as a money judgment is capable of doing, to make the plaintiff truly whole again.[38]

All of these compensatory purposes of punitive damages awards are applicable in the products liability context. Plaintiffs injured by product defects are as deserving of full compensation for their losses as any other class of plaintiffs. It is true that persons injured by defective products do not usually suffer the personal humiliation and embarrassment caused by the dignitary torts that sparked the punitive damages remedy in the eighteenth and nineteenth centuries.[39] While product accident victims may not need the same form of legal "satisfaction" traditionally afforded by the law for maliciously inflicted personal insults, such persons are no less deserving of satisfaction for the flagrant manner in which their personal injuries were inflicted. And many seriously injured persons are quite likely to suffer more tangible, economic losses that the tort law litigation system often undercompensates.[40] Further, accident victims often suffer damage to their emotional well-being, family harmony, and employment security that is particularly difficult to prove and generally not compensable. Moreover, the large reduction in an award for attorneys' fees may be especially burdensome to an injured person who may need most of the verdict to pay for medical, rehabilitation, and special living expenses.[41] Punitive damages thus play a valuable compensatory role in products liability cases as in other tort law contexts.

### Law Enforcement

Punitive damages are frequently criticized for providing "windfalls" to plaintiffs in addition to compensating them for losses they actually sustained.[42] In a sense this characterization is accurate, but in another sense it is not. The windfall objection to punitive damages ignores the crucial restitutionary and compensatory effects of such awards and overlooks the important fact that the very purpose of prospective windfalls is to help motivate reluctant victims (and their lawyers) to press their claims and so enforce the rules of law. In so energizing the law through increased enforcement, punitive damage

---

**38.** See Owen, Punitive Damages, at 1297–98.

**39.** See, e.g., Stoll, Penal Purposes in the Law of Torts, 18 Am. J. Comp. L. 3, 15–16 (1970).

**40.** See Franklin, Replacing the Negligence Lottery: Compensation and Selective Reimbursement, 53 Va. L. Rev. 774, 780 (1967) ("in big damage cases very few victims get as much as twenty-five percent of their real economic loss").

**41.** Damages for pain and suffering and other intangible losses often indirectly serve

to fund attorneys' fees and other litigation expenses, but such damages sometimes are insufficient to cover all costs of litigation.

**42.** See, e.g., Roginsky v. Richardson–Merrell, Inc., 378 F.2d 832, 841 (2d Cir. 1967) (N.Y. law); Mogin, Why Judges, Not Juries, Should Set Punitive Damages, 65 U. Chi. L. Rev. 179, 222 (1998); Comment, Taking the Punitive Damages Windfall Away from the Plaintiffs: An Analysis, 86 Nw. U. L. Rev. 1130 (1992); Prosser and Keeton on Torts § 2, at 13.

assessments serve instrumentally, through retribution, education, deterrence, and compensation, to maximize compliance with the obligations imposed on manufacturers by the substantive law of products liability. Thus, punitive damages have a vital procedural function, "law enforcement," which provides a mechanism for increasing compliance with the underlying rules of products liability law.[43]

While the law enforcement goal is closely intertwined with each of the other functions of punitive damages, it is most closely connected to deterrence. In a sense, law enforcement is the opposite side of the deterrence coin. Deterrence may be viewed as operating *ex ante*, in discouraging prospective wrongdoers from violating the rules, whereas law enforcement may be seen as operating *ex post*, in catching and punishing wrongdoers who are not deterred. Yet, it is the enforcement of the law that provides deterrence, so that law enforcement may itself be viewed as operating *ex ante*, in providing a warning to persons contemplating wrongdoing of the consequences of such misconduct. If law enforcement proves successful in this respect, then prospective wrongdoing will have been deterred, *ex post*. And so the deterrence-law enforcement coin forever turns.

As is true with the deterrence function, law enforcement serves to increase compliance with the rules of law.[44] No doubt few, if any, legal rules are perfectly obeyed or enforced.[45] Violations are apt to be especially prevalent when the unlawful activity is profitable for the violator, when violations are difficult to detect or to prove, when violations appear morally neutral, when the rules are vague, when enforcement of the rules is infrequent, and when punishment is light.[46] By helping to finance the detection, proof, and punishment of flagrant violations of the rules, punitive damages increase the likelihood that wrongdoers will be identified in the first instance and adequately punished in the second. To the extent that potential wrongdoers who are acting rationally perceive this increase in the probability and size of penalties and the commensurate reduction in the profitability of their contemplated misconduct, violations of the substantive rules of law should be deterred and, hence, compliance with the law should be improved.

More particularly, the law enforcement function of punitive damages operates as follows. After an injury occurs, if the victim (or the victim's attorney) suspects or discovers that the injurer flagrantly disregarded the victim's rights, the prospect of a punitive damage recovery serves as a compensatory incentive for the victim (and attorney) to pursue the matter against the flagrant offender. Since punitive damages are not recoverable on their own, but are dependent upon the flagrant violation

---

**43.** See Rustad and Koenig, The Historical Continuity of Punitive Damages Awards: Reforming the Tort Reformers, 42 Am. U. L. Rev. 1269, 1322–26 (1993) (private attorney general function); Chapman and Trebilcock, Punitive Damages: Deterrence in Search of a Rationale, 40 Ala. L. Rev. 741, 779–81 (1989) (private enforcement of law); Owen, Punitive Damages, at 1287.

**44.** By discouraging rule violations, punitive damages accordingly enhance compliance with law and promote the public good. Owen, Moral Foundations, at 715.

**45.** See, e.g., Becker and Stigler, Law Enforcement, Malfeasance, and Compensation of Enforcers, 3 J. Legal Studies 1, 2 (1974).

**46.** See Owen, Punitive Damages, at 1289–90.

of some underlying substantive right and duty,[47] the recovery of such damages requires that the victim prove and enforce the substantive rules of liability which otherwise might go unprosecuted. Thus, punitive damage awards serve as a kind of bounty, inducing injured victims to serve as "private attorneys general," increasing the number of wrong-doers who are pursued, prosecuted, and eventually "brought to justice."[48] This assistance is important because many serious misdeeds deserving punishment are beyond the reach of the criminal law and the public prosecutor. Thus, a limitation of the realm of criminal justice[49] is partially remedied, and the "private prosecutor" is rewarded with a "private fine" for his "public service in bringing the wrongdoer to account."[50]

Perhaps the most fundamental principle of products liability law is that a product containing a danger that may reasonably be eliminated is "defective," and that the manufacturer of such a product should pay for any harm occasioned by the defect.[51] Since this is a rule of tort rather than criminal law, it is cast in terms of post-accident loss distribution rather than as an absolute prohibition. This does not mean, however, that a manufacturer should be permitted to abuse the rule flagrantly and with impunity by treating the payment of accident costs merely as a " 'license fee for the conduct of an illegitimate business.' "[52] Experience has shown that manufacturers are sometimes tempted to maximize profits by marketing products known to be defective and to absorb resulting injury claims as a cost of doing business.[53] To the extent that manufacturers act as rational economic entities, they understand that sacrificing safety to limit costs is often profitable substantially beyond the point where a product becomes legally "defective" and the manufac-turer becomes obligated to pay compensatory damages to persons injured by the defect. Yet flagrantly improper marketing misconduct violates the basic rules of products liability law as well as fundamental principles of fairness and morality.[54] This nation has criminalized many forms of

---

**47.** See, e.g., Berczyk v. Emerson Tool Co., 291 F.Supp.2d 1004, 1016 (D. Minn. 2003); Oliver v. Raymark Indus., Inc., 799 F.2d 95 (3d Cir. 1986) (N.J. law); Lindquist v. Ayerst Labs., Inc., 607 P.2d 1339 (Kan. 1980). See generally Note, 63 Notre Dame L. Rev. 63 (1988) (noting *Oliver*).

**48.** See, e.g., Jackson v. Johns–Manville Sales Corp., 781 F.2d 394, 403 (5th Cir. 1986) (Miss. law) (punitive damages serve to motivate private attorneys general to bring suit); Fay v. Parker, 53 N.H. 342, 347 (1872) (punitive damages encourage prosecution of lawsuits). See generally Owen, Punitive Damages, at 1287–88.

**49.** This limitation on the role of criminal law is often proper because of strong reasons for preferring the civil to the criminal justice systems in marginal areas. See § 18.5, below.

**50.** Neal v. Newburger Co., 123 So. 861, 863 (Miss. 1929).

**51.** See ch. 5, above.

**52.** See United States v. Dotterweich, 320 U.S. 277, 282–83 (1943), quoted in United States v. Park, 421 U.S. 658, 669 (1975).

**53.** This tendency by some manufactur-ers led the National Commission on Prod-uct Safety to propose that consumers in-jured by "knowing or willful" violations of safety standards be awarded treble damages and attorneys' fees. See Proposed Consum-er Product Safety Act § 30, National Com-mission on Product Safety, Final Report, App. at 29. "Such statutory redress will add powerful private support to public safety programs." Id. at 118. Congress omitted this particular proposal from the Consumer Product Safety Act as it was enacted in 1972. See 15 U.S.C. §§ 2051–2081.

**54.** See Owen, The Moral Foundations of Products Liability Law: Toward First Principles, 68 Notre Dame L. Rev. 427 (1993); Owen, The Moral Foundations of Punitive Damages, 40 Ala. L. Rev. 705 (1989).

conduct that pose particular dangers to the public safety,[55] and the magnitude of accident costs attributable to defective products suggests a need for mechanisms such as punitive damages to improve compliance with the substantive rules of product safety.

It may be profitable for a manufacturer knowingly to market a defective product for at least two reasons. First, manufacturers generally are not called upon to pay for all of the injuries caused by their products, as mentioned earlier. This is because a product's "defectiveness" often is invisible to the injured consumer, particularly if the injury is attributable to some inadequacy in a warning or the product's design. In such cases, because the accident victim frequently is unaware that the injury resulted from a violation of law by the manufacturer, he or she often may never discover the existence of, much less assert, a compensation claim.[56] Even if an injury victim is aware of his or her legal rights, the assertion of those rights is expensive, not only because of the complex nature of such litigation (often requiring expert technical assistance),[57] but also because of costly attorneys' fees.[58] Even in cases in which liability is fairly clear, the vagaries of the litigation process insure that some valid claims will go completely or partially unpaid. For these and other reasons, manufacturers avoid paying for a large proportion of the accident costs which the rules of liability presume that they will shoulder.[59]

Second, manufacturers may choose to market products known to be defective because safety measures often cause a decrease in profit margins and sales. Adding a safety device to a product typically increases its cost and possibly its price[60] and so may cause a decline in sales. Sales

---

**55.** See, e.g., Federal Insecticide, Fungicide, and Rodenticide Act, 7 U.S.C. § 136l (criminalizing various acts and omissions, including misbranding registered pesticides); Flammable Fabrics Act, 15 U.S.C. § 1192 (prohibiting manufacture or sale of fabrics failing to meet certain safety standards); Federal Hazardous Substances Act, 15 U.S.C. § 1263 (prohibiting sale of misbranded or banned hazardous substances); Consumer Product Safety Act, 15 U.S.C. § 2068 (proscribing manufacture or sale of products violating certain safety standards); Federal Food, Drug and Cosmetic Act, 21 U.S.C. § 331 (prohibiting sale of adulterated or misbranded foods, drugs, devices, and cosmetics). In addition to federal statutes, there are an "infinite variety" of state statutes criminally proscribing various forms of hazardous conduct, such as selling impure food, selling firearms to minors, and failing to guard elevators, machinery, and other dangerous devices. See Prosser and Keeton on Torts § 36, at 225.

**56.** Whitford, Products Liability, in National Commission on Product Safety, 3 Supplemental Studies—Product Safety Law & Administration: Federal, State, Local and Common Law 221, 223 (1970). See also Final Report, National Commission on

Product Safety, at 74 ("Small wonder that some manufacturers do not even respond to letters claiming compensation for injuries: they know that more than two-thirds will never pursue the claim"); Rheingold, The MER/29 Story—An Instance of Successful Mass Disaster Litigation, 56 Cal. L. Rev. 116, 141 (1968). A RAND study revealed that very few injury victims hire lawyers. See D. Hensler et al., Compensation for Accidental Injuries in the United States 127 (RAND 1991) (only 9% of workers injured on the job by products, and 3% of seriously injured persons in other product accidents, hire lawyers). See generally Polinsky and Shavell, Punitive Damages: An Economic Analysis, 111 Harv. L. Rev. 869, 888–89 (1998).

**57.** See § 6.3, above.

**58.** See Black, The Mobilization of Law, 2 J. Legal Studies 125, 139 (1973).

**59.** Accident cost internalization by manufacturers was a principal rationale for the development of strict products liability in tort. See § 5.4, above.

**60.** See Morris, Enterprise Liability and the Actuarial Process—The Insignificance of Foresight, 70 Yale L.J. 554, 585 (1961).

may also decline because safety measures often reduce a product's usefulness or psychological appeal. While the dollar cost of affixing adequate warnings to a product is usually minimal, an effective warning may frighten away potential consumers.[61] For reasons such as these, a manufacturer may rationally choose to bolster sales by marketing a product in a defective condition and simply absorb ensuing injury claims.

Regardless of what actually motivates manufacturers to market products known to be defective, such conduct amounts to a conscious flouting of the law. If public confidence in the legal system is to be maintained, flagrant breaches of the rules of behavior need to be punished and deterred. Law enforcement and the various other punitive damages functions combine to present a compelling case for allowing such awards in situations where the profit motive has blinded a manufacturer to its product safety obligations. By undercutting a manufacturer's ability to accumulate illicit profits, punitive damages are a powerful instrument in enforcing compliance with the basic safety principles of products liability law.

## § 18.3   Forms of Manufacturer Misconduct

The previous section explored the variety of useful purposes served by punitive damages in general and in products liability cases in particular. This section examines the different ways manufacturers have marketed dangerous products that juries and courts have found flagrantly improper and, hence, deserving of punitive damages.[1] A study of the cases reveals six types of manufacturer misconduct that recur with some frequency: (1) fraud; (2) knowingly violating safety standards; (3) failing to conduct adequate tests to uncover dangerous defects; (4) failing to design away known dangers; (5) failing to warn of known dangers; and (6) failing, post-sale, to warn or recall.[2] Most cases in which punitive damages are assessed involve some combination of these different forms of marketing misbehavior.

### Fraud

Many products liability cases in which punitive damages have been assessed against manufacturers involve the concealment of known de-

---

**61.** See Spruill v. Boyle–Midway, Inc., 308 F.2d 79, 87 (4th Cir. 1962) (Va. law) ("had the warning been in a form calculated ... to convey a conception of the true nature of the danger, this mother ... might not have purchased the product at all").

**§ 18.3**

**1.** This section examines the type of behavior that may properly support a punitive damages claim in a products liability case. For discussions of when such claims may be inappropriate, see, e.g., Montgomery and Nahrstadt, How to Defend Punitive Damages Claims Effectively—And Maybe Successfully, 66 Def. Couns. J. 347 (1999); Owen, Problems in Assessing Punitive Damages Against Manufacturers of Defective Products, 49 U. Chi. L. Rev. 1 (1982).

**2.** Except for the addition of one new category, (4), this is essentially the list set forth in Owen, Punitive Damages in Products Liability Litigation, 74 Mich. L. Rev. 1257 (1976). Other commentators have used similar classifications. See, e.g., Rustad, Unraveling Punitive Damages: Current Data and Further Inquiry, 1998 Wis. L. Rev. 15, 49; Rustad, In Defense of Punitive Damages in Products Liability: Testing Tort Anecdotes with Empirical Data, 78 Iowa L. Rev. 1, 66 (1992). For a broader classification, and descriptions of a number of cases, see Rustad, How the Common Good is Served by the Remedy of Punitive Damages, 64 Tenn. L. Rev. 793 (1997).

fects from consumers. While in some circumstances the mere failure to warn of a known danger has been labeled "fraudulent concealment,"[3] the cases considered here involve affirmative communications by a manufacturer designed to mislead the public.

An appropriate starting point is an examination of a trio of early cases, *Toole v. Richardson–Merrell Inc.*,[4] *Roginsky v. Richardson–Merrell, Inc.*,[5] and *Ostopowitz v. William S. Merrell Co.*[6] These were among the more than 1500 actions brought against Richardson–Merrell for the manufacture and sale of the drug triparanol, marketed under the trade name MER/29, between April 1960 and April 1962.[7] MER/29 was purported to reduce the level of blood cholesterol to aid in the treatment of arteriosclerosis and thus reduce the incidence of heart attacks and strokes. Regardless of whether the drug actually worked,[8] it did in fact seriously injure thousands of persons.[9] The most serious of the drug's side effects was its propensity to cause cataracts, and by 1967 some 490 reported cases of this condition had been attributed to the use of MER/29.[10]

The juries awarded punitive damages in these three cases because they found that Richardson–Merrell had acted in a manner calculated to deceive the Food and Drug Administration (FDA), the medical profession, and consumers concerning the safety of MER/29. In order to obtain FDA approval for the drug and improve its marketability, the director of the defendant's Biological Science Division ordered the falsification of data in a test conducted on monkeys, including the fabrication of data for a nonexistent monkey. In its 1959 new drug application to the FDA, Richardson–Merrell incorporated the falsified monkey data and other significant misrepresentations, including a claim that only four of eight

**3.** Particularly in the asbestos cases. See, e.g., Rowan Cty. Bd. of Educ. v. U.S. Gypsum Co., 418 S.E.2d 648, 661 (N.C. 1992); Nicolet, Inc. v. Nutt, 525 A.2d 146, 149 (Del. 1987). For non-asbestos cases, see Burton v. R.J. Reynolds Tobacco Co., 205 F. Supp.2d 1253, 1260 (D. Kan. 2002) (fraudulent concealment of tobacco's addictive capacity). See generally § 3.2, above.

**4.** 251 Cal.App.2d 689, 60 Cal.Rptr. 398 (1967).

**5.** 378 F.2d 832 (2d Cir. 1967), rev'g in part 254 F.Supp. 430 (S.D.N.Y. 1966).

**6.** N.Y.L.J., Jan. 11, 1967, at 21, col. 3 (Sup. Ct. Westchester County, N.Y.).

**7.** See Rheingold, The MER/29 Story– An Instance of Successful Mass Disaster Litigation, 56 Cal. L. Rev. 116, 121 (1968) (hereinafter The MER/29 Story). Only eleven of the 1500 MER/29 claims resulted in jury verdicts, and seven of the verdicts were rendered in favor of the plaintiffs in amounts ranging from $20,000 to $1.2 million. Id. at 133. The three cases of these eleven in which the published decisions discussed the punitive damages awards were *Toole, Roginsky* and *Ostopowitz*. The *Toole* jury awarded the plaintiff $175,000 general

damages and $500,000 punitive damages. The trial judge remitted the punitive damages verdict to $250,000, and the appellate court affirmed. *Toole*, 60 Cal.Rptr. at 418. The jury in *Roginsky* rendered a compensatory damages verdict of $17,500 and punitive damages of $100,000. *Roginsky*, 254 F.Supp. at 430. Judge Friendly, writing for the majority in a 2–1 decision of the Second Circuit, affirmed the compensatory damages award but reversed the award of punitive damages. 378 F.2d at 851. The *Ostopowitz* jury awarded $350,000 in compensatory damages and $850,000 in punitive damages to the injured party and $5000 to her husband for loss of services. On a motion to set aside the verdict, the trial judge approved the compensatory damages verdict and ordered a reduction in the punitive damages award to $100,000. *Ostopowitz*, N.Y.L.J., Jan. 11, 1967, at 21, cols. 3–4.

**8.** There was some doubt that it did. See *Toole*, 60 Cal.Rptr. at 403.

**9.** The trustee of the MER/29 litigation group, Paul D. Rheingold, estimated that the drug caused a minimum of 5000 injuries. Rheingold, note 7, above at 121.

**10.** *Toole*, 60 Cal.Rptr. at 408.

rats had died in one study when in fact all eight had died. Even so, the FDA still concluded that the drug appeared to be excessively hazardous and insisted that the manufacturer run additional tests, to which the defendant responded with further falsifications of test data. In three additional animal tests on rats and dogs, nine of ten rats in one test developed eye opacities, as did twenty-five of thirty-six in another, and one of the dogs went blind. The defendant deleted all of this information from subsequent reports submitted to the FDA. On the basis of the false and misleading information provided to it by the defendant, the safety agency approved the drug for marketing in April 1960.[11]

From initial marketing until sales were terminated in 1962, evidence mounted rapidly that MER/29 could cause eye damage and other harm to both test animals and humans. Despite its knowledge of the increasing evidence of the drug's dangerous side effects, Richardson–Merrell continued to advertise the product as "a proven drug, remarkably free from side effects, virtually non-toxic . . . and completely safe"[12] and assured its salesman that "[t]here is no longer any valid question as to its safety or lack of significant side effects."[13] Moreover, in response to inquiries from doctors concerned that MER/29 might be responsible for the hair loss or eye problems of their patients, the company falsely claimed to be unaware of such side effects or similar complaints.[14] When urged in late 1961 by both the FDA and the British government to remove the drug from the market, the defendant stubbornly refused. Only after the FDA seized all of the company's animal experiment records in an unannounced raid on Richardson–Merrell laboratories in April 1962, did the company finally suspend sales of the drug. The FDA withdrew its approval of the unsafe drug the following month.[15]

During the two years it was on the market, MER/29 was administered to approximately 400,000 persons, several thousand of whom suffered eye injuries, hair loss, and skin disorders, even though most of them had been taking the drug for less than three months. Most of the 400,000 users probably would have developed cataracts had they continued taking it.[16]

If Richardson–Merrell had been truthful with the FDA from the start, it is likely that MER/29 would never have been marketed. However, this dangerously defective drug reached the market and stayed there long enough to injure many persons because its manufacturer actively deceived the public. Undoubtedly Richardson–Merrell acted so irresponsibly because the drug promised to be especially profitable.[17] The juries in *Toole*, *Roginsky*, and *Ostopowitz* determined that this fraudulent-type behavior needed to be punished and discouraged and so awarded substantial punitive damages,[18] thus initiating the era of such awards in modern products liability litigation.[19]

**11.** See id. at 404–05.

**12.** Id. at 416.

**13.** Id. at 406.

**14.** See Rheingold, above, at 119.

**15.** See *Toole*, 60 Cal.Rptr. at 408.

**16.** See id.

**17.** MER/29 was " 'the biggest and most important drug in Merrell history. . . . ' " Id. at 407.

**18.** See Rheingold, above, at 132–34 n.46.

Since the MER/29 litigation in the late 1960s, many other punitive damages assessments in products liability cases have been based on fraudulent misrepresentations by manufacturers. The facts in *Axen v. American Home Products Corp.*,[20] decided in 1999, were in some respects similar to those involved in the sale of MER/29. In *Axen*, a pharmaceutical company sold a drug called amiodarone, marketed under the tradename Cordarone, used for heart conditions. Like MER/29, a side-effect of Cordarone was damage to the eyes. Although Cordarone's manufacturer knew for years that the drug could permanently injure people's eyes, and despite repeated letters from the FDA threatening criminal prosecution unless the company stopped promoting Cordarone, "an extraordinarily hazardous drug, in a manner we consider clearly misrepresentative of its known hazards,"[21] the company continued to market the drug as carrying merely a possibility of eye nerve inflammation. The plaintiff took the drug for three months and went blind.[22] Concluding that the jury could find that the defendant "deliberately placed misleading information on its packaging in order to preserve sales,"[23] the court upheld a punitive damages verdict of $20 million.

Punitive damages have been assessed in many other products liability cases at least in part because the manufacturers were shown to have deliberately and affirmatively deceived consumers by concealing serious product hazards in order to profit from sales to consumers who believed the products to be safer than the manufacturers knew to be true. For example, punitive damages verdicts have been levied against manufacturers of such products as a minivan advertised as safe despite the manufacturer's knowledge that many persons were being killed in accidents when thrown through the rear opening when the liftgate popped open due to a defective latch;[24] asbestos products promoted as "non-irritating and non-toxic" after the manufacturer's discovery of the lethal effects of inhaling asbestos dust;[25] silicone gel breast implants marketed for years as safe when tests and experience suggested they could cause irreversible autoimmune disease;[26] and an intrauterine device, the Dalkon Shield, marketed as safe and highly effective while the manufacturer knew for a decade that it was neither and could cause pelvic inflammato-

**19.** The only previously reported products liability personal injury case in which a court upheld a punitive damages award was Fleet v. Hollenkemp, 52 Ky. 219, 13 B. Mon. 219 (1852), which involved the sale of an adulterated drug.

**20.** 974 P.2d 224 (Or. Ct. App. 1999).

**21.** Id. at 230.

**22.** See id. at 228.

**23.** See id. at 242.

**24.** See Jimenez v. Chrysler Corp., 74 F.Supp.2d 548, 563 (D.S.C. 1999) ($250 million punitive damages awarded in part on underlying claim of negligent misrepresentation), rev'd, 269 F.3d 439 (4th Cir. 2001). Evidence showed "that Chrysler consciously placed a defective product containing a known defect in the stream of commerce, misrepresented that product as safe, and concealed for years its knowledge of the defect." Id. at 563.

**25.** See, e.g., Owens–Corning Fiberglas Corp. v. Golightly, 976 S.W.2d 409 (Ky. 1998).

**26.** See Hopkins v. Dow Corning Corp., 33 F.3d 1116 (9th Cir. 1994) (Cal. law) ($6.5 million punitive damages). Evidence showed that "Dow was aware of possible defects in its implants, that Dow knew long-term studies were needed, that Dow concealed this information as well as the negative results of the few short-term laboratory tests performed, and that Dow continued for several years to market its implants as safe despite this knowledge." Id. at 1127.

ry disease (PID) that sometimes required a total hysterectomy.[27] In addition, the tobacco industry's fraudulent concealment of the carcinogenic and addictive qualities of cigarettes over many years has been a principal basis for the punitive damages awards assessed against that industry, including the $145 billion verdict in the Florida smoker class action (subsequently reversed),[28] in various litigations around the nation.[29]

### Knowingly Violating Safety Standards

Thousands of standards prescribing minimally acceptable safety characteristics for many types of products have been issued by various legislatures, regulatory agencies, and private organizations.[30] Sometimes a plaintiff can prove that a product marketed in violation of such a standard injured him or her and that the injury probably would have been averted had the manufacturer followed the standard.[31] Further evidence that the manufacturer knew its product violated a safety standard, yet marketed it anyway, is proof that the manufacturer acted in conscious disregard that the product might be dangerously defective. In this way a manufacturer's knowing violation of a safety standard has figured prominently in several cases in which juries have assessed punitive damages verdicts.

An early case involving the breach of a federal safety regulation is *Rosendin v. Avco Lycoming Division*,[32] a consolidated action for the deaths of four persons and injuries to a fifth caused by the crash of an executive jet due to engine failure in 1967. The airplane's engine was first manufactured by the defendant in 1957 and then remanufactured and resold by the defendant in 1960 and again in 1963. On each occasion that the remanufactured engine was resold it was ostensibly "zero timed"; the new owner was given a new warranty and a certificate

**27.** See, e.g., Tetuan v. A.H. Robins Co., 738 P.2d 1210 (Kan. 1987) ($7.5 million punitive damages). Evidence showed that "Robins knew of a high rate of PID and septic abortion associated with the Dalkon Shield; that Robins misled doctors through claims of safety and efficacy while it knew there was no basis for a claim of safety. . . . " Id. at 1240.

**28.** Liggett Group Inc. v. Engle, 853 So.2d 434 (Fla. Dist. Ct. App. 2003). See Bragg and Kershaw, Juror Says a 'Sense of Mission' Led to Huge Tobacco Damages—Panel Saw Industry as Dishonest and Arrogant, N.Y. Times, July 16, 2000, at A1 (New England ed.) (foreman reported that jury thought verdict "would put the companies on notice—not just the tobacco companies, all companies—concerning fraud or misrepresentation of the American public"). Id.

**29.** See, e.g., Henley v. Philip Morris Inc., 5 Cal.Rptr.3d 42 (Ct. App. 2003) ($50 million to smoker, remitted by trial judge to $25 million, further remitted by appellate court to $9 million), review granted and

cause transferred, 831 P.3d 223 (Cal. 2003); Williams v. Philip Morris Inc., 48 P.3d 824 (Or. Ct. App. 2002) ($79.2 million verdict for smoker, reduced by trial judge to $32.8 million, reinstated on appeal), vacated and remanded for reconsideration, Philip Morris USA, Inc. v. Williams, 540 U.S. 801 (2003), reconsidered and reinstated, 92 P.3d 126 (Or. Ct. App. 2004) (concluding that $79.5 million punitive award was reasonable, proportionate to the wrong to the plaintiff and the public in the state, and hence comported with Supreme Court due process guidelines). See § 18.1, above.

**30.** See §§ 2.3 and 6.4, above.

**31.** See, e.g., Axen v. American Home Products Corp., 974 P.2d 224, 234–36 (Or. Ct. App. 1999).

**32.** No. 202,715 (Super. Ct. Santa Clara County, Cal., March 8, 1972), noted in 15 A.T.L.A.N.L. 103 (1972), and 16 Jury Verdicts Weekly 49 (Feb. 18, 1972), aff'd, Civil No. 32,999, Cal. Ct. App., 1st App. Dist., June 23, 1976.

stating that the engine complied with "all Federal Aviation Administration [FAA] regulations concerning zero timing engines."[33] Strict federal regulations governed the tolerances of parts in zero-timed engines represented to be "rebuilt," and the defendant's service manager conceded that the 1963 resale violated FAA regulations because the company had "remanufactured" its engines with secondhand parts that met only the lower tolerances permitted by the FAA for "overhauled" engines rather than the safer tolerances required for genuinely "rebuilt" zero-timed engines. The testimony also indicated that the defendant had ignored the regulations governing "rebuilt" engines because it considered them too stringent and too expensive, and further suggested that the manufacturer possibly used the term "remanufactured" to deceive purchasers into thinking that their engines had in fact been "rebuilt" while avoiding the more expensive reconditioning required by the FAA for engines so represented.[34] Upon this evidence of an intentional breach of a governmental regulatory safety standard, together with some evidence of a fraudulent-type effort to mislead consumers, the jury awarded substantial compensatory damages to each plaintiff and $10.5 million in punitive damages to the sole survivor.[35]

While some safety standards are quite formally developed by professional industrial organizations, other standards evolve informally over time by industry custom. In *Miller v. Solaglas California, Inc.*,[36] the plaintiff-driver suffered paralysis when the windshield of his GMC truck popped out during a collision causing the plaintiff to be ejected through the opening. When the defendant, a manufacturer and installer of replacement windshield systems, had replaced the truck's cracked windshield three months before the accident, it secured the windshield with silicone, pursuant to its policy, rather than with urethane glue, as required by industry standards. The jury returned a punitive damages verdict on evidence that the defendant knew that the GMC manual required the use of urethane but deliberately installed the windshield without it, despite a "parts list and price guide indicating that urethane could be required in windshield installation, despite industry publications and conventions discussing the use of urethane, and despite indus-

---

**33.** Brief for Plaintiffs at 11–13, Rosendin v. Avco Lycoming Div., cited above. "In effect, the certificate said that the engine had been remanufactured or rebuilt, that it could be treated as a zero-timed engine and could have a new record without previous operating history as provided in the [FAA] regulations." Id. at 13. "[O]wners and mechanics rely on these log book entries when an engine is rebuilt ... and it is important whether an engine is zero-timed or whether it has a previous history." Id. at 14–15.

**34.** See id. at 10–12. "Lycoming adopted a semantics scheme to avoid compliance in a manner which constituted a fraud on the public." Id. at 5.

**35.** The jury awarded approximately $2.8 million compensatory damages to the representatives of the pilot and three passengers killed in the crash and approximately $1.1 million compensatory damages in addition to the punitive damages to the permanently disabled survivor. In an unpublished opinion dated June 7, 1972, the trial court denied the defendant's motions for j.n.o.v. and for a new trial on compensatory damages but granted its motion for a new trial on punitive damages, ruling that the verdict was excessive and that the plaintiffs had failed to establish their reliance upon the defendant's fraudulent conduct. The decisions were affirmed on appeal. Rosendin v. Avco Lycoming Div., cited above.

**36.** 870 P.2d 559 (Colo. Ct. App. 1993).

try safety standards requiring the use of urethane.''[37] Not only did the defendant fail to use the proper sealant, but it charged customers as if it had, billing 2.8 hours of labor for installing a windshield which took only 30 minutes without the use of urethane.[38] Proof of a manufacturer's failure to adopt private industry safety standards has supported punitive awards in other cases, too.[39]

Evidence demonstrating that a manufacturer knowingly marketed a product in violation of an industrial safety standard is certainly pertinent to whether the factfinder should award punitive damages, but it should never be determinative.[40] Manufacturers should be entitled to challenge the appropriateness of safety standards promulgated by private organizations. Because formal industry standards are entitled to less deference than standards promulgated by safety agencies, and customary standards even less so, a manufacturer's reasons for disagreement with an industry standard should be examined closely. For example, in a case involving an automobile that crashed when a defective tire blew out,[41] General Motors representatives testified that the company had intentionally disregarded the maximum carrying capacity standards of the Tire and Rim Association because the company considered the standards too stringent.[42] While industry safety organizations may occasionally promulgate standards that are indeed more stringent than demanded for public safety, and while GM in this case may have been correct, common sense suggests that courts and juries generally should examine such protestations skeptically.

Proof of an intentional breach of a safety standard often is compelling evidence that a manufacturer marketed a product in flagrant disregard of the rights or interests of consumers. But the weight of such evidence depends on the circumstances, and a number of factors influence the weight that should be given to such evidence in particular cases: the authoritativeness and expertise of the body promulgating the standard; the clarity of the standard; the clarity of the violation of the standard; the nature of the danger the standard seeks to prevent; the degree of increased danger resulting from its violation; the standard's apparent effectiveness in averting the danger; the economic and practical feasibility of complying with the standard; any benefits that may have accrued to consumers from its violation; the extent of the manufactur-

---

**37.** Id. at 569.

**38.** See id.

**39.** See, e.g., Clark v. Chrysler Corp., 310 F.3d 461, 482 (6th Cir. 2002) (Ky. law) ($3 million punitive damages award against automobile manufacturer because door latches failed to meet industry standards), vacated by Chrysler Corp. v. Clark, 540 U.S. 801 (2003); Sears, Roebuck and Co. v. Kunze, 996 S.W.2d 416, 428 (Tex. App. 1999) ($2 million punitive damages award appropriate for failing to equip radial arm saw with lower blade guard as standard feature, as did rest of industry; amputation of four fingers); Wussow v. Commercial Mechanisms, Inc., 293 N.W.2d 897, 906 (Wis. 1980) (approving punitive damages

verdict awarded to fourteen-year-old plaintiff struck in head by arm of automatic baseball pitching machine not equipped with safety guards its manufacturer knew were on its competitors' machines).

**40.** A rule of punitive damages liability as a matter of law in such cases would conflict with the fundamental principle that punitive damages are awarded only in a jury's discretion and never as a matter of right. See 1 Kircher and Wiseman, Punitive Damages § 5.23.

**41.** See Barth v. B.F. Goodrich Tire Co., 71 Cal.Rptr. 306 (Ct. App. 1968).

**42.** Id. at 311.

er's awareness that it was violating the standard; and, finally, the manufacturer's reasons for violating the standard.[43]

Proof that a manufacturer marketed a product it knew violated a product safety standard is always relevant to whether the manufacturer acted in flagrant disregard of consumer safety because the standard puts the manufacturer on notice that its product falls below an established safety norm and thus may be excessively hazardous. If a defendant chooses to ignore this notice, the burden of explanation fairly shifts to it to explain its reasons for violating the standard. The absence of a good explanation for the violation suggests a conscious disregard of public safety that may render punitive damages appropriate.

### Failing to Conduct Adequate Tests to Uncover Dangerous Defects

When negligence was the predominant theory of liability for defective products, injured plaintiffs frequently claimed that the manufacturer failed to conduct adequate tests or inspections.[44] *MacPherson v. Buick Motor Co.*[45] firmly established a manufacturer's duty of ordinary care to consumers to search for and remedy whatever unreasonable dangers might be hidden in its products. Ordinary care requires that the diligence of the search reflect the product's potential for harm.[46] The rationale behind such searches, of course, is that manufacturers will remedy defects uncovered by tests and inspections before marketing their products so that consumers will not be used as unsuspecting subjects for marketplace safety test programs.[47]

The formulation of strict products liability principles for compensatory damages, however, shifted the crucial determination from whether a manufacturer had diligently searched for hidden defects to whether the product was sold in a defective condition.[48] The analysis of punitive damages claims requires that attention be shifted back once again to the manufacturer's diligence in searching for defects in its products. The inquiry here is whether the manufacturer's research, testing, and quality control procedures were so inadequate as to manifest a flagrant indifference to the possibility that the product might expose consumers to unreasonable risks of harm.

Certain types of products are especially hazardous, such as devices placed in sensitive locations in the human body (such as IUDs, tampons, penile implants, and pacemakers), automobiles driven at high speeds, and flammable clothing worn by young children. A manufacturer of products like these will be keenly aware of the substantial risks to life and limb if such products are defective, and so will be duty bound to take

---

**43.** See Owen, Punitive Damages in Products Liability Litigation, 74 Mich. L. Rev. 1257, 1339 (1976).

**44.** See § 2.6, above.

**45.** 111 N.E. 1050 (N.Y. 1916).

**46.** See id. at 1055; § 2.2, above.

**47.** See Dalehite v. United States, 346 U.S. 15, 52 (1953) (Jackson, J., dissenting);

Morris, Negligence in Tort Law—With Emphasis on Automobile Accidents and Unsound Products, 53 Va. L. Rev. 899, 909 (1967) ("Pernicious products should be scrapped in the factory rather than dodged in the home.").

**48.** See ch. 5, above.

special care to assure that they are marketed in a safe condition.[49] Consequently, due care requires manufacturers of such inherently dangerous products to institutionalize procedures for discovering, minimizing, and correcting hazards in their products prior to sale,[50] and a palpable inadequacy of testing or research would indicate a plain indifference to consumer safety.[51] Punitive damages have been upheld in at least one case in which the manufacturer failed to have in place a "formal safety review committee" that probably would have detected and eliminated the hazard,[52] and other courts have concluded that companies which ignore the safety concerns and recommendations of such committees and the company's own engineers and scientists may be found to exhibit a conscious indifference to consumer safety.[53]

In *Deemer v. A.H. Robins Co.*,[54] for example, the jury awarded $10,000 in compensatory damages and $75,000 in punitive damages to a woman injured when the defendant's intrauterine contraceptive device (IUD), the Dalkon Shield, had to be surgically removed after perforating her uterine wall. Among other things, the complaint alleged inadequate

**49.** This special duty of care derives from the basic calculus of risk principle of cost-benefit analysis. See §§ 2.2 , 5.7, and 8.4, above.

**50.** Reasonable attention to safety normally includes, at a minimum, conducting premarketing engineering studies and prototype testing, instituting assembly line quality controls, warning and instructing as appropriate, and monitoring a product's performance in the field.

**51.** See, e.g., Romo v. Ford Motor Co., 122 Cal.Rptr.2d 139 (Ct. App. 2002) (defendant decided to forgo normal testing to rush product to market, evidencing indifference to consumer safety), vacated and remanded, Ford Motor Co. v. Romo, 538 U.S. 1028 (2003), on remand, 6 Cal.Rptr.3d 793 (Ct. App. 2003) (remitting punitive damages award to $23,723,287); North Am. Refractory Co. v. Easter, 988 S.W.2d 904, 919 (Tex. App. 1999) (manufacturer's failure to test its asbestos-containing products for many years after becoming aware of asbestos dangers warranted large punitive damages award); Hopkins v. Dow Corning Corp., 33 F.3d 1116, 1119 (9th Cir. 1994) (Cal. law) (failure to research long-term safety of silicone gel breast implants; longest study, which revealed adverse effects, lasted only 80 days). See also Gonzales v. Surgidev Corp., 899 P.2d 576, 589 (N.M. 1995) (manufacturer of intraocular lens implants seeking premarket approval "failed to keep adequately informed of the data that would have indicated potential problems").

**52.** Wussow v. Commercial Mechanisms, Inc., 293 N.W.2d 897, 906 (Wis. 1980).

**53.** See, e.g., Sand Hill Energy, Inc. v. Ford Motor Co., 83 S.W.3d 483, 493 (Ky. 2002) (manufacturer ignored its engineers who forcefully informed company that transmission in its automobiles was dangerous), vacated and remanded, Ford Motor Co. v. Smith 538 U.S. 1028 (2003); Ford Motor Co. v. Ammerman, 705 N.E.2d 539, 547 (Ind. Ct. App. 1999): "After the advent of production Ford engineers continued to raise questions concerning Bronco II's stability.... Another Ford engineer recommended consideration of more permanent methods of improving the Bronco's stability, including lowering the vehicle's center of gravity, adding more weight, and widening the track width. The engineers were essentially ignored. By placing the Bronco II on the market, Ford failed to meet its own design criteria." See also Jimenez v. Chrysler Corp., 74 F.Supp.2d 548, 558–61 (D.S.C. 1999) (management ignored repeated pleas by engineers, including "liftgate latch work team," to strengthen latch to reduce risk that it would pop open in accidents), rev'd, 269 F.3d 439 (4th Cir. 2001); Hopkins v. Dow Corning Corp., 33 F.3d 1116, 1119 (9th Cir. 1994) (Cal. law) (manufacturer ignored internal proposals to strengthen silicone breast implant envelopes to reduce risk of rupture and leakage); Mack Trucks, Inc. v. Conkle, 436 S.E.2d 635, 640 (Ga. 1993) (marketing division repeatedly vetoed proposals by engineering division to reinforce truck frames).

**54.** No. C–26420 (Dist. Ct. Sedgwick Cty., Kan., filed Oct. 1972, verdict, March 1, 1975). *Deemer* was the first action against A.H. Robins for the marketing of the Dalkon Shield to go to judgment. See Tetuan v. A.H. Robins Co., 738 P.2d 1210, 1246 (Kan. 1987) (upholding $7.5 million punitive damages award). See also Palmer v. A.H. Robins Co., 684 P.2d 187 (Colo. 1984) (upholding $6.2 million punitive damages award).

testing. Testimony before a congressional committee investigating the cause of the many injuries and deaths from IUDs revealed that A.H. Robins had marketed the Dalkon Shield after clinically testing the product for a "pathetic" average insertion time of only 5.5 months.[55] Considering the delicacy and importance of the human organ into which the device was to be inserted for extended periods, and the risks involved if the device proved dangerously defective, proof that pre-marketing clinical testing had been seriously inadequate strongly suggests the manufacturer's flagrant disregard of consumer safety.

In another case, *Gryc v. Dayton–Hudson Corp.*,[56] a young girl was severely burned when her cotton flannelette nightgown caught fire. Upholding a $1 million punitive damages award against the fabric manufacturer for failing to flame retard its product,[57] the court pointed to the defendant's "minimal" efforts in its "surveillance of developments in the flame-retardant field," noted that the defendant kept no records of its research and development on flammability prevention and critically observed that from 1967 to 1969 the company had spent but $140,000 on this type of research out of its total research and development budget of $1.8 million.[58]

In cases involving the design safety of automobiles and other types of high-speed vehicles, courts sometimes cite insufficient crash-testing of prototypes in support of a punitive award.[59] Thus, in *Sabich v. Outboard Marine Corp.*,[60] a passenger on a "trackster" snow vehicle manufactured by the defendant was seriously injured when the vehicle traversed a rock and rolled over while descending a slope varying in grade from twenty-four to thirty-eight degrees. Despite promotional representations that the vehicle could be operated on slopes of up to forty-five degrees and that it would run smoothly over rocks and stones, the manufacturer admitted that it had never tested the trackster on inclines to determine the point at which the vehicle would overturn.[61] Accordingly, the jury awarded substantial compensatory damages and more than $1 million in punitive damages.[62]

---

**55.** Hearings on Regulation of Medical Devices (Intrauterine Contraceptive Devices) Before the Subcomm. of the House Comm. on Governmental Operations 93d Cong. 61 (1973) (testimony of Russell J. Thomsen, M.D.). In addition to its inadequate tests, the company engaged in a grossly misleading promotional campaign based on the results of the deficient tests. "[T]he Dalkon Shield and its promotion provide the classic example of the misuse of statistics to market an item." Id. See Note, The Intrauterine Device: A Criticism of Governmental Compliance and an Analysis of Manufacturer and Physician Liability, 24 Clev. St. L. Rev. 247, 287–90 (1975).

**56.** 297 N.W.2d 727 (Minn. 1980).

**57.** At the time, this was the largest punitive damages award in a products liability case to have been upheld by a state high court.

**58.** See *Gryc*, 297 N.W.2d at 740.

**59.** See, e.g., Ford Motor Co. v. Ammerman, 705 N.E.2d 539, 547 (Ind. Ct. App. 1999) (noting that one type of stability test on the Bronco II "was halted because it was too dangerous for the engineers and test drivers"); Jimenez v. Chrysler Corp., 74 F. Supp.2d 548, 558 (D.S.C. 1999) (jury could properly find that defendant's failure to test flimsy latch design of rear liftgate was "reckless and provided sufficient support for a finding of punitive damages"), rev'd, 269 F.3d 439 (4th Cir. 2001); Leichtamer v. American Motors Corp., 424 N.E.2d 568, 580 (Ohio 1981) (pitch-over of Jeep CJ–7).

**60.** 131 Cal.Rptr. 703 (Ct. App. 1976).

**61.** Owen, Punitive Damages in Products Liability Litigation, 74 Mich. L. Rev. 1257, 1342 (1976).

**62.** See *Sabich*, 131 Cal.Rptr. at 705. On appeal, the court emphasized that the defendant had knowingly designed the vehicle

In *Sabich*, a punitive damages award may have been appropriate in view of the manufacturer's failure to subject its potentially lethal yet relatively inexpensive product to simple crash-testing, coupled with its misrepresentations of the vehicle's performance capabilities—representations calculated to deceive consumers who would naturally assume that the manufacturer had a reasonable basis to support its performance assertions. If a particular type of foreseeable risk is substantial, as the risk that dozens of young children and other people may die when ejected through a minivan's rear liftgate that pops open in accidents due to a particularly flimsy latch,[63] basic respect for human safety requires that the manufacturer crash test the vehicle to discover the true nature and extent of the risk. But crash tests are expensive, and a manufacturer cannot be expected to conduct such experiments to test the durability of its vehicles in all the myriad contexts in which crashes can occur.[64]

In addition to testing prototypes for design defects, a manufacturer may uncover physical flaws in individual products at various points in the manufacturing process. The effectiveness of a manufacturer's quality control procedures will determine both the type and percentage of flaws discovered and permitted to remain in a product line. A manufacturer may make an erroneous risk-benefit judgment by devoting too few resources to quality control in view of the injuries likely to result. In such a case, the manufacturer would be liable in negligence for any actual injuries to consumers resulting from its erroneous decision.[65] On occasion, a manufacturer's failure to establish adequate quality control procedures may be in flagrant disregard of the possibility that consumers may be injured as a result. A manufacturer's failure to make inexpensive quality control improvements upon learning that existing procedures are failing to detect defects causing consumers substantial harm is compelling evidence of the manufacturer's conscious indifference to consumer safety. Punitive damages thus may be appropriate when a manufacturer's testing or quality control procedures are so grossly inadequate in view of the known risks as to constitute a reckless indifference to public safety.[66]

### Failing to Design Away Known Dangers

A number of punitive damages assessments have been based largely upon a manufacturer's failure to adopt a simple design solution to a

---

to climb slopes steeper than those it could descend, as well as having failed to warn consumers adequately of this hazard. Id. at 707–09. The court nevertheless reversed the punitive damages award because of the trial court's erroneous instruction on the burden of proof required to sustain the underlying fraud cause of action. Id. at 709–11.

**63.** See Jimenez v. Chrysler Corp., 74 F.Supp.2d 548, 558 (D.S.C. 1999), rev'd, 269 F.3d 439 (4th Cir. 2001).

**64.** See, e.g., Faniola v. Mazda Motor Corp., 2004 WL 1354469, at *5–*7 (D.N.M. 2004) (risk of injuries from auto fires from auto collisions not great enough to characterize defendant's failure to conduct further

tests as reckless); Owen, Problems In Assessing Punitive Damages Against Manufacturers of Defective Products, 49 U. Chi. L. Rev. 1, 35 n.163 (1982).

**65.** See § 2.2, above.

**66.** See, e.g., Sufix, U.S.A., Inc. v. Cook, 128 S.W.3d 838 (Ky. Ct. App. 2004) ($3 million punitive damages award upheld for grossly deficient testing of defective weed trimmer); Shurr v. A.R. Siegler, Inc., 70 F.Supp.2d 900, 940 (E.D. Wis. 1999) ("defective testing alone can justify punitive damages"); International Armament Corp. v. King, 674 S.W.2d 413, 417 (Tex. App. 1984).

substantial safety problem plainly demanded by the simplicity and economy of the easy "fix."[67] Thus, a manufacturer of silicone gel breast implants which knows they are prone to leak and break may be subject to punitive damages if it refuses to "dip" the envelope more than once (which would reduce the risk of rupture) and retains the "single dip method" of manufacture because it was "easier" and "cheaper."[68] Punitive damages may be assessed against a radial saw manufacturer which knows that a lower blade guard is necessary to prevent amputations, if it refuses to follow the rest of the industry in installing the guard as standard equipment rather than selling it merely as an optional accessory "because of the nominal additional cost."[69] And punitive damages have been assessed in other cases on similar evidence that the manufacturer failed to adopt simple and inexpensive design improvements that it knew were necessary to eliminate a serious danger.[70]

While a manufacturer's conscious refusal to adopt simple and inexpensive design improvements is often strong evidence of indifference to public safety, the simplicity and expense of such improvements must be examined carefully. Thus, in *Grimshaw v. Ford Motor Co.*,[71] the famous Ford Pinto case involving fuel tanks which could explosively ignite in relatively low-speed rear-end collisions, the jury and the court were both impressed that the company refused to adopt a variety of "inexpensive fixes," each costing only several dollars, which supposedly could have solved the Pinto's gas tank problem.[72] On this evidence, the jury awarded $125 million in punitive damages.[73] Although Ford's design decisionmaking was roundly condemned at the time,[74] commentators have questioned

---

**67.** See, e.g., Gillham v. Admiral Corp., 523 F.2d 102, 107 n.3 (6th Cir. 1975) (Ohio law) (change in high voltage transformer materials at cost of $0.60–1.20 per color television unit).

**68.** Hopkins v. Dow Corning Corp., 33 F.3d 1116, 1119 (9th Cir. 1994) (Cal. law) (affirming $6.5 million punitive award).

**69.** Sears, Roebuck and Co. v. Kunze, 996 S.W.2d 416, 429 (Tex. App. 1999) (affirming $2 million punitive award to man who lost four fingers while using defendant's power saw).

**70.** See, e.g., Airco, Inc. v. Simmons First Nat'l Bank, 638 S.W.2d 660, 661 (Ark. 1982) (failure to remove dangerous selector valve from anesthesia ventilator, or to eliminate the dangerous connecting port); Mack Trucks, Inc. v. Conkle, 436 S.E.2d 635, 640 (Ga. 1993) (marketing division repeatedly vetoed proposals by engineering division to reinforce unsafe truck frames that would cost about $100 per truck).

**71.** 174 Cal.Rptr. 348 (Ct. App. 1981).

**72.** Design changes that would have enhanced the integrity of the fuel tank system at relatively little cost per car included "[l]ongitudinal side members and cross members at $2.40 and $1.80, respectively; a single shock absorbent 'flak suit' to protect

the tank at $4; a tank within a tank and placement of the tank over the axle at $5.08 to $5.79; a nylon bladder within the tank at $5.25 to $8; placement of the tank over the axle surrounded with a protective barrier at a cost of $9.95 per car; substitution of a rear axle with a smooth differential housing at a cost of $2.10; imposition of a protective shield between the differential housing and the tank at $2.35; improvement and reinforcement of the bumper at $2.60; addition of eight inches of crush space [at] a cost of $6.40," changes that would have made the fuel tank safe in collisions up to 50 miles per hour. 174 Cal.Rptr. at 361.

**73.** Remitted by the trial court to $3.5 million, and affirmed on appeal. See *Grimshaw*, 174 Cal.Rptr. 348 (Ct. App. 1981).

**74.** See, e.g., L. Stobel, Reckless Homicide? (1980); J. Kunen, Reckless Disregard: Corporate Greed, Government Indifference, and the Kentucky School Bus Crash 249 (1994); Bruck, How Ford Stalled the Pinto Litigation, in The American Lawyer 23 (June 1979); Schmitt and May, Beyond Products Liability: The Legal, Social, and Ethical Problems Facing the Automobile Industry in Producing Safe Products, 56 U. Det. J. Urb. L. 1021 (1979); Dowie, Pinto Madness, Mother Jones 18 (Sept./Oct. 1977).

the logic and fairness of the punitive damages award.[75] The problem in cases like *Grimshaw* lies in the readiness of juries and courts to accept a plaintiff's claim that a proposed design solution was indeed simple and inexpensive, without considering real-world costs and practicalities. For example, the *Grimshaw* court appeared to accept the plaintiff's argument that Ford should have added a rubber or nylon bladder to the inside of the gas tank.[76] Yet, such bladders were simply not used in commercially produced cars (with the temporary exception of one sports car during the late 1970s), partially due to servicing and durability problems, which raises questions of whether this particular fix was feasible from a practical point of view.[77]

In addition to the practicability problems with a proposed remedial design, the monetary cost of such alternatives must also be examined carefully. In a complex product such as a car, there are always hundreds of design changes that can be made to enhance the safety of the vehicle in a particular type of crash situation, ranging in cost per unit from pennies to hundreds of dollars. Although the cost of any one change may be small in isolation, each separate design choice is of course only a small sub-decision in the overall safety-cost-utility mix that must be tailored to the special needs and limitations of each particular type of product.[78] For example, a proper examination of Ford's decision in the early 1980s not to widen the track width of its Bronco II SUV by two to four inches, in order to improve its stability,[79] must include a consideration not only of the monetary cost of altering the size of the frame but also of the other costs of such a change—any sacrifices in performance, safety in other situations, and practicality. Dollar cost alone, in other words, is usually only a small part of the much larger picture of a manufacturer's reasons for failing to improve the design safety of a product in any particular way.[80]

A manufacturer's failure to design away an evident danger in a product sometimes is a result of rushing the product to the market in an effort to meet a deadline scheduled by upper management for competitive purposes early in the product's developmental process, or perhaps to fit with a scheduled model turnover. As such deadlines approach, management is likely to be more and more resistant to suggestions by its engineers that the product's design be altered to make it safer. While such real-world considerations are understandable, such pressures need to give way to safety if a particular hazard is found to substantially endanger public safety. In a number of cases, courts and juries have

---

**75.** See G. Schwartz, The Myth of the Ford Pinto Case, 43 Rutgers L. Rev. 1013 (1991); Owen, Problems in Assessing Punitive Damages Against Manufacturers of Defective Products, 49 U. Chi. L. Rev. 1 (1982); Epstein, Is Pinto a Criminal? Regulation 15 (Mar./Apr. 1980); Wheeler, beginning with In Pinto's Wake, Criminal Trials Loom for More Manufacturers, Nat'l L.J. 27 (Oct. 6, 1980) (first of five articles in series).

**76.** See *Grimshaw*, 174 Cal.Rptr. at 360–61.

**77.** See Owen, Problems in Assessing Punitive Damages Against Manufacturers of Defective Products, 49 U. Chi. L. Rev. at 33–34.

**78.** See id. at 24–25.

**79.** See, e.g., Ford Motor Co. v. Ammerman, 705 N.E.2d 539, 546–47 (Ind. Ct. App. 1999).

**80.** See Owen, Problems in Assessing Punitive Damages Against Manufacturers of Defective Products, 49 U. Chi. L. Rev. 1 (1982).

found such "rush to market" explanations for design defects indicative of a greater concern for profit than for safety, thus warranting punitive damages if a consumer is seriously injured or killed as a result.[81]

### Failing to Warn of Known Dangers

It is axiomatic that a manufacturer owes a duty to consumers to warn them adequately of hidden dangers in its products and to instruct them on methods of safe use.[82] If a manufacturer knows its products contain a hidden danger which may be communicated to consumers effectively and at reasonable expense, the failure to do so may evidence a flagrant indifference to public safety which may warrant punitive damages. If a manufacturer is further shown to have consciously withheld from consumers information about a serious product hazard in order to protect the marketing and profitability of its products, a punitive damages assessment would appear not only appropriate but necessary, both to punish the defendant and to make it clear that such behavior will be neither tolerated by society nor profitable for the manufacturer. A large proportion of punitive damages verdicts awarded in products liability cases have been based at least in part on the manufacturer's failure to warn consumers of a serious product hazard of which it was aware.

A particularly notorious punitive damages verdict illustrates this type of case. In *Liebeck v. McDonald's Restaurants, P.T.S., Inc.*,[83] the jury awarded $2.7 million to a woman scalded when she spilled a cup of McDonald's hot coffee on her lap. The 81-year-old plaintiff, who spilled the coffee while attempting to remove the lid, suffered third-degree burns over six percent of her body on her inner thighs, buttocks, and genital and groin areas, requiring skin grafts and debridement during a week of hospitalization. The plaintiff's claim was based on McDonald's failure to warn its customers that the company served its coffee exceedingly hot, at 180–90°. At 190°, coffee causes third-degree burns to human skin in less than three seconds. The evidence revealed that McDonald's knew that its coffee was so hot that it was not "fit for consumption" when served, some 20–40° hotter than coffee sold by most other restaurants. The plaintiff also proved that the company continued its policy of keeping the coffee temperature so hot despite receipt of some 700 complaints of burns, some in the third degree. And yet, until after the verdict in this case, the company chose not to warn its customers of the danger. A McDonald's executive testified at trial that the company "had decided not to warn customers about the possibility of severe burns, even though most people wouldn't think it possible," and that the company

---

**81.** "The continued push to production of this product after all of the internal protestation to the contrary, is the crassest form of corporate indifference to the safety of the ultimate user or consumer and constitutes gross negligence." Ford Motor Co. v. Ammerman, 705 N.E.2d 539, 557 (Ind. Ct. App. 1999), quoting the trial court and concluding that Ford's conduct "[a]t the very least ... showed an utter indifference for the rights of consumers." Ford's efforts to rush the Pinto to market was also a factor in Grimshaw v. Ford Motor Co., 174

Cal.Rptr. 348 (Ct. App. 1981). See also Hopkins v. Dow Corning Corp., 33 F.3d 1116, 1119 (9th Cir. 1994) (Cal. law) ("Dow rushed development of the silicone gel implants," charging its Mammary Task Force to get the product to market in under five months).

**82.** See Products Liability Restatement § 2(b); ch. 9, above.

**83.** No. CV–93–02419, 1995 WL 360309, at *1 (D.N.M. 1994).

had no intention to change any of its policies.[84] On post-trial motions, the trial court upheld the jury's finding that punitive damages were warranted on the facts but remitted the jury's punitive damages award, which represented two days of McDonald's national coffee sales, to $480,000—three times the amount of the plaintiff's final compensatory award.[85]

Punitive damage awards in other cases have also been based at least in part upon a manufacturer's failure to provide consumers with adequate information about a serious and hidden product hazard. Such cases include, for example, a heart medication manufacturer's "deliberate choice not to warn that its product might cause vision loss because it feared that such a warning would affect its profits";[86] a silicone breast implant manufacturer's failure to warn of the suspected defectiveness of its implants and the adverse results of its laboratory tests;[87] an intraocular lens implant manufacturer's failure to warn of the higher risks it knew existed from implanting its lens using a particular medical procedure;[88] a chemical preservative manufacturer's warning merely of irritation, burns, and allergic reaction, and its failure to warn that inhalation could be deadly, after discovering nine other incidents of death or injury;[89] a fish bowl manufacturer's failure to warn of the danger of shattering;[90] and the asbestos product manufacturers' failure to warn of the extreme hazards of inhaling asbestos dust for years after they learned of the often fatal risk.[91]

Warnings may be inadequate not only in substance, but also in the manner in which they are communicated. Even the best of warnings will be worthless unless the warning is likely to reach the consumer or

---

**84.** See Gerlin, A Matter of Degree: How a Jury Decided That One Coffee Spill Is Worth $2.9 Million, Wall St. J., Sept. 1, 1994, at A1.

**85.** The jury awarded the plaintiff $200,000, reduced by 20% to $160,000 on account of the plaintiff's fault. See Mead, Punitive Damages and the Spill Felt Round the World: A U.S. Perspective, 17 Loy. L.A. Int'l & Comp. L. Rev. 829, 847 (1995); Gerlin, A Matter of Degree: How a Jury Decided That One Coffee Spill Is Worth $2.9 Million, Wall St. J., Sept. 1, 1994, at A1; Morgan, McDonald's Burned Itself, Legal Times, Sept. 19, 1994, at 26; Two Hot Verdicts Were Distorted by Critics, 20 ATLA Advocate 3 (Oct. 1994).

For a similar case, see, e.g., Greene v. Boddie–Noell Enters., Inc., 966 F.Supp. 416, 418 n.1 (W.D. Va. 1997) (discussing Liebeck). Compare Immormino v. J & M Powers, Inc., 698 N.E.2d 516 (Ohio Ct. C.P. 1998), a hot tea spill case, where the court granted the defendant's motion for summary judgment, ruling that consumers are commonly aware of the dangers of hot liquid spills.

**86.** Axen v. American Home Prods. Corp., 974 P.2d 224, 242 (Or. Ct. App. 1999) (affirming $20 million punitive award).

**87.** See Hopkins v. Dow Corning Corp., 33 F.3d 1116, 1127 (9th Cir. 1994) (Cal. law).

**88.** See Gonzales v. Surgidev Corp., 899 P.2d 576, 589 (N.M. 1995) (affirming two $350,000 punitive damages awards).

**89.** See General Chemical Corp. v. De La Lastra, 852 S.W.2d 916, 921–22 (Tex. 1993) (affirming two punitive damages awards to estates of deceased shrimpers, but reducing both awards from $15 million to $4 million in compliance with the statutory maximum of four times the compensatory awards).

**90.** See Waddill v. Anchor Hocking, Inc., 78 P.3d 570 (Or. Ct. App. 2003) ($403,416).

**91.** See, e.g., North Am. Refractory Co. v. Easter, 988 S.W.2d 904, 919 (Tex. App. 1999) (affirming $1.5 million punitive award); Owens–Corning Fiberglas Corp. v. Golightly, 976 S.W.2d 409 (Ky. 1998) (affirming $435,000 punitive damages award). *But see*, e.g., holding that manufacturers were insufficiently aware of risk for punitive damages, ACandS, Inc. v. Asner, 686 A.2d 250 (Md. 1996); ACandS, Inc. v. Godwin, 667 A.2d 116 (Md. 1995).

someone who will act on his or her behalf unless it is transmitted in a way likely to attract that person's attention and is communicated in a form that he or she is likely to understand.[92] In *Hoffman v. Sterling Drug, Inc.*,[93] an action was brought against a drug manufacturer for eye injuries attributable to the use of chloroquine phosphate, a prescription drug marketed under the trade name "Aralen." The plaintiff's claim for punitive damages was based on allegations that the manufacturer had inadequately warned the FDA and the medical profession that the drug could cause retinal damage. Sterling Drug showed in defense that, once it learned of the danger, its salespersons warned physicians by mailing or personally delivering product cards and promotional brochures containing the necessary warning. Nevertheless, the Third Circuit Court of Appeals overruled the district court's refusal to submit the punitive damages claim to the jury and remanded on that issue, holding that the manufacturer's duty was to warn of the danger "in a manner which could be expected to alert the medical profession." Pointing to evidence that many physicians pay little attention to comments of drug company salespersons or to promotional literature received in the mail, the court stated that a drug manufacturer "must be charged with knowledge of the workings of the distribution system" it selects to convey its warnings to the medical community.[94] The court concluded that on these facts a jury could properly find that Sterling's "failure to take action reasonably calculated to warn physicians of a risk of great magnitude was in reckless disregard of the public's health" and that a jury thus would have grounds for a punitive damages award.[95]

### Failing to Warn or Recall Post-Sale

Only reluctantly, and in carefully measured respects, has the law in recent years subjected a manufacturer to liability even for compensatory damages for failing to correct dangerous conditions first discovered (and only discoverable) after a product had been placed on the market. Consequently, the post-sale failure-to-remedy cases in which the possibility of punitive damages are raised generally involve an important preliminary issue of whether a manufacturer is under any duty at all to remedy defects in its products already sold and in use, a topic examined earlier.[96] Here, the issue is the manufacturer's exposure to punitive damages for flagrantly failing to perform its post-sale safety obligations.

When a dangerous defect is discovered after initial marketing, the defect is of course much easier to remedy in products as yet unsold, especially in those still to be produced, than in products already in the field. But manufacturers confront a variety of disincentives to making safety changes even in their unsold products. Production can be stopped to make a safety alteration in the current production line, but the cost of

---

**92.** See ch. 9, above.

**93.** 485 F.2d 132 (3d Cir. 1973) (Pa. law).

**94.** Id. at 146.

**95.** *Hoffman*, 485 F.2d at 147. After five weeks of retrial the case was settled for $600,000 (see 18 A.T.L.A.N.L. 120 (1975)),

$163,000 in excess of the original verdict for compensatory damages. See *Hoffman*, 485 F.2d at 135. Several pretrial matters on the remand of the case are reported in 374 F.Supp. 850 (M.D. Pa. 1974).

**96.** See § 10.8, above.

retooling and otherwise altering the assembly line may be substantial, and production schedules may be substantially upset. Moreover, once a product has gone to market, the horse is out of the barn, so to speak, and those responsible for permitting its escape in a defective condition are likely to be reluctant to admit that the release was a mistake. Apart from the natural embarrassment in admitting that a product already sold in fact is dangerously defective, the responsible employees might face sanctions by their employer for causing it extra trouble and expense. Not only will the enterprise be required to confront retooling and other direct costs of eliminating the defective condition, but also, by so doing, the manufacturer will be perceived as implicitly admitting that there was something wrong with all the products sold before the change.

Once the public discovers that a manufacturer has improved the safety of a product line, the manufacturer may encounter all kinds of problems: existing litigation may be rendered more difficult to defend; new litigation may be stimulated; competitors may be advantaged; product demand may fall; and a regulatory safety agency may be prompted to investigate the problem and ultimately order a recall.[97] In short, once a product has been sold, efforts to remedy a discovered defect usually are at least inconvenient, generally expensive, and otherwise very damaging to both the manufacturing enterprise and its responsible employees. For these reasons, managers of manufacturing enterprises are quite likely first to ignore and later to deny developing safety problems well past the point at which ordinary prudence, good morals, and common sense dictate that post-sale steps be taken to protect consumer safety.[98]

The failure of a manufacturer to remedy a known defect in an already marketed product has given rise to punitive damages in a good many products liability cases.[99] Punitive damages are sometimes based on a manufacturer's failure to issue a post-sale warning about a product defect,[100] and such awards are occasionally based at least in part on the

---

**97.** This was essentially the scenario of the litigation surrounding the Chrysler minivan, sold from 1984 with an especially flimsy liftgate latch which the company partially improved as a "running change" in 1988. See Jimenez v. Chrysler Corp., 74 F.Supp.2d 548, 558–59 (D.S.C. 1999), rev'd, 269 F.3d 439 (4th Cir. 2001).

**98.** See, e.g., Eichenwald, Guidant Admits That It Hid Problems of Artery Tool, nytimes.com (June 13, 2003) (medical device manufacturer pleaded guilty to 10 felonies, admitting it lied to FDA, concealing thousands of adverse reports including 12 deaths).

**99.** See, e.g., Sharp ex rel. Gordon v. Case Corp., 595 N.W.2d 380, 390 (Wis. 1999) (punitive damages require a showing of reckless disregard for the rights of others and "a manufacturer may be found to have acted in reckless disregard if, after having gained specific knowledge of a product's defect and its potential harm, the manufac-

turer fails to take some action that the defect demands, such as ... post-sale warnings."); Lovick v. Wil–Rich, 588 N.W.2d 688 (Iowa 1999) (punitive damages warranted in action against manufacturer of cultivator, where manufacturer failed to institute post-sale warning campaign, despite its knowledge of numerous similar accidents involving its cultivators); Patton v. TIC United Corp., 859 F.Supp. 509, 512 (D. Kan. 1994) (noting a "trend [to] recognize a post-sale duty to warn, the 'egregious' breach of which might result in a punitive damages award").

**100.** See, e.g., Patton v. TIC United Corp., 859 F.Supp. 509 (D. Kan. 1994) (failure to provide post-sale warnings of danger in agricultural machine after learning of a number of serious accidents); Tetuan v. A.H. Robins Co., 738 P.2d 1210 (Kan. 1987) (failure to warn or recall defective IUD); Wooderson v. Ortho Pharm. Corp., 681 P.2d 1038 (Kan. 1984) (prescription drug).

manufacturer's refusal to repair a defectively designed product. Thus, punitive damages have been assessed for a manufacturer's failure to warn consumers of, and repair, a defect that was causing a product to fail dangerously in normal use;[101] to accept its engineering staff's recommendations on how to simply and inexpensively remedy a dangerous defect;[102] to study how to eliminate a recurring design problem that the manufacturer knew to be injuring its customers;[103] or simply to stop selling a product that the company knew to be seriously injuring users.[104]

An early example of a post-sale misconduct case, *Gillham v. Admiral Corp.*,[105] illustrates the kind of circumstances that fairly may raise a punitive damages claim. In *Gillham*, an action against a television manufacturer by a seventy-five-year-old woman burned when her television caught fire, the Sixth Circuit approved a verdict for punitive damages (and attorneys' fees) assessed against the manufacturer.[106] The evidence indicated that the fire had been caused by a defectively designed high voltage transformer; that the defendant had known of at least 91 similar fires, some of which had likewise burned homes and caused personal injuries, over the four-year period preceding the fire in the plaintiff's set; that two years before the plaintiff's injury all 16 transformers tested by one of the defendant's own engineers had caught fire;[107] and that the manufacturer not only failed to recall the sets or even to warn consumers of the hazard, but also systematically attempted through its complaint manager and even counsel[108] to conceal the defect from consumers and to frustrate inquiries about the danger. When a manufacturer refuses to take any steps whatsoever to remedy a hazard

---

**101.** See, e.g., Barnett v. La Societe Anonyme Turbomeca France, 963 S.W.2d 639 (Mo. Ct. App. 1997) (helicopter pilot killed when helicopter engine failed in flight due to defect; aware that defect was causing in-flight engine failures, manufacturer failed to warn owners, notify FAA, or recall, in order to delay replacements of defective parts until owners could be charged for them during normally scheduled overhauls); Hodder v. Goodyear Tire & Rubber Co., 426 N.W.2d 826, 835–37 (Minn. 1988)(tire changer injured by exploding multi-piece wheel rim; aware of its explosive tendencies manufacturer failed to issue adequate post-sale warnings).

**102.** See, e.g., Jimenez v. Chrysler Corp., 74 F.Supp.2d 548 (D.S.C. 1999) (manufacturer of minivan, knowing of dangerous design defect, for years ignored pleas by engineers to strengthen flimsy liftgate latch, destroyed videotapes of crash tests, obstructed NHTSA investigation, and, when finally forced to issue post-sale warning, misled consumers about the danger), rev'd, 269 F.3d 439 (4th Cir. 2001); Mack Trucks, Inc. v. Conkle, 436 S.E.2d 635, 640 (Ga. 1993) (for years, marketing division vetoed engineering division's proposal to reinforce inadequate frame rail).

**103.** See, e.g., Sears, Roebuck & Co. v. Kunze, 996 S.W.2d 416, 428–29 (Tex. App. 1999) (for many years, manufacturer failed to equip radial saw with lower blade guard to prevent amputations it knew its customers were experiencing).

**104.** See, e.g., Tetuan v. A.H. Robins Co., 738 P.2d 1210 (Kan. 1987) (dangerously defective IUD); O'Gilvie v. International Playtex, Inc., 609 F.Supp. 817 (D. Kan. 1985) (dangerously defective tampon), rev'd, 821 F.2d 1438 (10th Cir. 1987) (reinstating $10 million punitive damages award).

**105.** 523 F.2d 102 (6th Cir. 1975) (Ohio law).

**106.** See id. at 109.

**107.** See id. at 105–06.

**108.** See id. at 106–07. One of Admiral's in-house legal counsel sent a memorandum to the company's official in charge of "product safety" asking whether Admiral "could keep claimants under better 'control' " by informing them "that the matter has been referred to [the company's] insurance company who will contact them shortly. Alternatively, [the company] could inform them that a representative of National Service will make contact.... [S]o informed, claimant would be less inclined to get a lawyer involved." Brief for Plaintiff at 34.

as serious as that in *Gillham*, even though it clearly knows of both the specific defect and the seriousness of the risk to consumers, a punitive damages assessment appears particularly appropriate.[109]

The determinative factors in awarding punitive damages for post-marketing misconduct of manufacturers are largely the same as those in the other categories of marketing misconduct previously examined. The distinguishing feature of the post-marketing cases is that the ultimate test of a product's safety—its performance during use by consumers—is ascertainable to help determine whether the product in fact is excessively dangerous. If its products are failing in a manner likely to produce or in fact producing severe injuries, particularly if the producer is aware of both the product's defectiveness and a reasonable remedy, as in *Gillham*, the failure of the manufacturer to act promptly and decisively to reduce the danger is strong evidence that the manufacturer has little concern for consumer safety. But sending warning letters and recalling products are expensive procedures. Accordingly, punitive damages are appropriate in post-marketing cases only when the probable reduction in the risk of harm from such remedial measures clearly outweighs the manufacturer's costs.

## § 18.4   BASIS OF LIABILITY

For manufacturers and other product suppliers to know what type of conduct is subject to civil punishment, and for courts and juries to be able to assess such punishment in a fair and logical manner, the law must state in a general way what is necessary and sufficient for a punitive damages determination; the law, that is, must specify the basis of liability for punitive damages. This requires, first, a determination of which underlying theories of liability may support a punitive award in addition to an award for compensatory damages. Second, the nature of the conduct that properly gives rise to liability for punitive damages must be described. These are the two topics treated here. A related issue, which concerns the standard of measurement for determining the proper *amount* of punitive damages, is considered later.[1]

### Basis of Underlying Claim

Punitive damages are awarded to remedy a conscious, reckless, or willful and wanton violation of a person's rights.[2] Accordingly, punitive damages are not recoverable on their own, but rest instead upon the flagrant violation of some underlying substantive right and duty.[3] There

---

**109.** Plaintiff's counsel argued on appeal: "The only inferable motive for Admiral's conduct is that Admiral consciously decided to perpetuate the hazard, because to eliminate it might have been costly, and to warn its customers might have adversely affected sales. Thus, solely for financial gain, Admiral deliberately exposed Mrs. Gillham to the fire hazard which [foreseeably] caused a fire, burned her severely, and permanently ruined her life." Brief for Plaintiff at 45; Id.

**§ 18.4**

**1.** See § 18.5, below.

**2.** See § 18.1, above.

**3.** See, e.g., Graham v. American Cyanamid Co., 2000 WL 1911431 (S.D. Ohio 2000), aff'd, 350 F.3d 496 (6th Cir. 2003); Oliver v. Raymark Indus., Inc., 799 F.2d 95 (3d Cir. 1986) (N.J. law); Lindquist v. Ayerst Labs., Inc., 607 P.2d 1339 (Kan. 1980). See generally Note, 63 Notre Dame L. Rev. 63 (1988) (noting *Oliver*).

is, in other words, no independent cause of action for punitive damages; such damages must piggy-back instead upon one of the traditional products liability claims for compensatory damages.[4] Thus, the plaintiff's entitlement to compensatory damages is widely held to be a prerequisite to recovery on a punitive damages claim.[5]

A question then arises as to whether a punitive damages claim may attach to *any* underlying products liability cause of action, assuming there is sufficient extra proof to support a punitive claim, or whether there are some underlying causes of action to which punitive damages must, or cannot, attach. One problematic cause of action is for the death of a person killed in a product accident or who otherwise dies before bringing a products liability action. Wrongful death and survival statutes vary in their particular provisions,[6] and some such statutes provide expressly or by interpretation that punitive damages may or may not be recoverable after the plaintiff has died. In a slight majority of jurisdictions, the wrongful death act is held to exclude recovery of punitive damages.[7] However, survival statutes offset this obstacle in most states by authorizing a decedent's personal representative or estate to bring most or all claims for tortiously caused harm, including claims for punitive damages, that the decedent could have maintained had he or she remained alive.[8]

---

**4.** This is well explained by Professors Kircher and Wiseman:

> Initially, a "cause of action" must be defined.... Generally, a cause of action includes facts showing the plaintiff's right, the defendant's corresponding duty, and the defendant's breach of that duty. A punitive damage claim, standing alone, does not contain a statement of the facts necessary to establish the defendant's breach of duty owed to the plaintiff.

1 Kircher and Wiseman, Punitive Damages § 6.16, at 71.

**5.** See, e.g., Messer v. Amway Corp., 106 Fed.Appx. 678 (10th Cir. 2004) (Kan. law); Liggett Group Inc. v. Engle, 853 So.2d 434, 451 (Fla. Dist. Ct. App. 2003); Robinson v. Audi NSU Auto Union Ak., 739 F.2d 1481 (10th Cir. 1984) (Okla. law) (in strict products liability action, proof of actual damages prerequisite to punitive damages). See generally 1 Kircher and Wiseman, Punitive Damages §§ 5.37 and 6.16.

**6.** See Prosser and Keeton on Torts ch. 23; Dobbs, Law of Torts ch. 19.

**7.** See, e.g., Forte v. Connerwood Healthcare, Inc., 745 N.E.2d 796 (Ind. 2001); Simeone v. Charron, 762 A.2d 442 (R.I. 2000); Figgie Int'l, Inc., Snorkel–Economy Div. v. Tognocchi, 624 A.2d 1285 (Md. Ct. App. 1993); Fellows v. Superior Prods. Co., 506 N.W.2d 534 (Mich. Ct. App. 1993); General Chem. Corp. v. De La Lastra, 852 S.W.2d 916, 922 (Tex. 1993) ("At common law, a cause of action for personal injuries and the right to exemplary damages for the willful or wanton conduct of the tortfeasor terminated with the deceased."); Smith v. Printup, 866 P.2d 985, 998–99 (Kan. 1993). See generally Gerald W. Boston, Punitive Damages in Tort Law § 5.11 et seq. (1993); 1 Kircher and Wiseman, Punitive Damages § 5.19.

**8.** See, e.g., Thomas v. Thomas, 254 B.R. 879 (D.S.C. 1999); General Chem. Corp. v. De La Lastra, 852 S.W.2d 916, 922–24 (Tex. 1993). See generally Gerald W. Boston, Punitive Damages in Tort Law §§ 5.15–5.17 (1993); 1 Kircher and Wiseman, Punitive Damages § 9.08.

While the issue usually does not arise in products liability litigation, there is a split of authority as to whether punitive damages should be recoverable against the estate of a deceased tortfeasor. See, e.g., Estate of Farrell v. Gordon, 770 A.2d 517, 521 (Del. 2001) (Delaware Survival Act allows plaintiffs to assert claim for punitive damages against deceased defendant's estate); Haralson v. Fisher Surveying, Inc., 31 P.3d 114, 117 (Ariz. 2001) ("While a punitive award cannot punish a deceased wrongdoer for his or her reprehensible conduct, it may deter its future occurrence by others."); Doe v. Colligan, 753 P.2d 144, 145 (Alaska 1988) ("Death of the tortfeasor renders meaningless the punitive aspect of damages."); Restatement (2d) Torts § 908 cmt. *a. Contra*, Hofer v. Lavender, 679 S.W.2d 470, 474 (Tex. 1984) (punitive damages also serve as an example and to compensate for

Whether or not the plaintiff makes a claim for punitive damages, products liability complaints usually contain a variety of substantive causes of action, including negligence, violation of statute, misrepresentation, breach of warranty, and strict liability in tort.[9] Except for claims of breach of warranty and strict liability in tort, as discussed below, courts usually do not focus on the appropriateness of attaching punitive damages to individual theories of recovery. When courts do address the separate underlying liability claims, the inquiry usually is whether the evidence was sufficient to establish the particular causes of action, and whether the defendant's conduct was sufficiently egregious to support a punitive damages verdict, rather than whether punitive damages properly attach to a particular products liability cause of action.

It is quite clear that any tort law products liability cause of action can support a punitive damages claim. Such damages are thus recoverable, based on proof of the requisite misconduct as discussed below, in actions brought for negligence;[10] negligence per se;[11] fraud and deceit;[12] negligent misrepresentation;[13] and, in all but one jurisdiction,[14] strict liability in tort.[15] No punitive damages cases have been located in which the underlying theory of recovery was strict liability in tort for misrepresentation, under § 402B of the *Restatement (Second) of Torts*, but there is no logical reason why a punitive damages claim should not be held to attach to this particular cause of action.[16] The one common products liability claim that quite clearly will *not* independently support a puni-

---

inconvenience and attorney's fees, so that they are recoverable from the estate of a deceased tortfeasor under the Texas Survival Statute; thorough review).

**9.** See, e.g., Ford Motor Co. v. Ammerman, 705 N.E.2d 539, 549 (Ind. Ct. App. 1999) (negligence, breach of warranty, and strict liability in tort); Palmer v. A.H. Robins Co., 684 P.2d 187 (Colo. 1984) (negligence, negligence per se, strict liability in tort, breach of express warranty, implied warranty of merchantability, and implied warranty of fitness for a particular purpose); Toole v. Richardson–Merrell, Inc., 60 Cal.Rptr. 398 (Ct. App. 1967) (fraud and deceit, breach of express and implied warranties, negligence, negligence per se, and strict liability in tort).

**10.** See, e.g., Jimenez v. Chrysler Corp., 74 F.Supp.2d 548 (D.S.C. 1999), rev'd, 269 F.3d 439 (4th Cir. 2001); North Am. Refractory Co. v. Easter, 988 S.W.2d 904 (Tex. App. 1999) (negligent failure to test or to warn); Mack Trucks, Inc. v. Conkle, 436 S.E.2d 635 (Ga. 1993) (negligent failure to warn or recall).

**11.** See, e.g., Werremeyer v. K.C. Auto Salvage Co., 134 S.W.3d 633 (Mo. 2004); Axen v. American Home Prod. Corp., 974 P.2d 224, 234–36 (Or. Ct. App. 1999); Palmer v. A.H. Robins Co., 684 P.2d 187, 210–13 (Colo. 1984).

**12.** See, e.g., Smith v. Morris, Manning & Martin, LLP, 589 S.E.2d 840 (Ga. Ct. App. 2003); Tetuan v. A.H. Robins Co., 738 P.2d 1210 (Kan. 1987); Toole v. Richardson–Merrell, Inc., 60 Cal.Rptr. 398 (Ct. App. 1967).

**13.** Jimenez v. Chrysler Corp., 74 F.Supp.2d 548, 563 (D.S.C. 1999) ($250 million punitive damages awarded in part on underlying claim of negligent misrepresentation), rev'd, 269 F.3d 439 (4th Cir. 2001).

**14.** South Carolina, as discussed below.

**15.** See, e.g., Ford Motor Co. v. Miles, 141 S.W.3d 309 (Tex. App. 2004); Hoskins v. Business Men's Assurance, 116 S.W.3d 557 (Mo. Ct. App. 2003); Ford Motor Co. v. Ammerman, 705 N.E.2d 539 (Ind. Ct. App. 1999); Owens–Corning Fiberglas Corp. v. Golightly, 976 S.W.2d 409 (Ky. 1998); Hopkins v. Dow Corning Corp., 33 F.3d 1116 (9th Cir. 1994) (Cal. law) (strict liability in tort for defects in design, warning, and manufacture).

**16.** That fraud would also typically be an appropriate cause of action in such a case does not render the strict liability claim for misrepresentation inappropriate, for in either case the plaintiff, in order to make out a punitive damages claim, will have to prove that the defendant flagrantly disregarded the plaintiff's rights to safety.

tive damages award is a breach of warranty claim under the Uniform Commercial Code, as discussed below.

### Strict Liability in Tort

Early in the development of products liability law, a number of commentators argued that punitive damages claims are logically inconsistent with claims for strict products liability in tort.[17] "Strict liability and punitive damages," it was asserted, "will not mix. In strict liability the character of the defendant's act is of no consequence; in the punitive damages claim the character of the act is paramount."[18] The argument put forth, still sometimes made today, is that a punitive damages claim based upon allegations of aggravated fault is conceptually incompatible with a strict products liability action where the manufacturer's care, or absence thereof, is irrelevant to a determination of liability for compensatory damages. The crux of this argument is that strict liability focuses exclusively upon the product's condition, as defective or nondefective, to the exclusion of the manufacturer's fault or conduct.[19]

While the incompatibility argument contains some superficial appeal, it fails for several reasons. First, its primary contention that liability in strict tort precludes consideration of a defendant manufacturer's fault is misguided. Rather than dispensing with the notion of fault from products liability law, strict tort theory may be viewed as *expanding* the concept of fault to include the "innocent" manufacture of defective products,[20] in a manner analogous to negligence per se.[21] Indeed, modern products liability law is increasingly perceived as resting largely on fault.[22] Yet even acknowledging that the doctrine of strict products liability in tort formally eliminates the requirement of proving a manufacturer's fault, this is so only with respect to establishing liability for compensatory damages. As a liability doctrine designed to compensate product accident victims for their actual losses, strict tort theory does not address (and certainly does not limit) the remedies that may be appropriate if a plaintiff's injuries are attributable to some aggravated fault of the manufacturer.[23]

---

**17.** See, e.g., Tozer, Punitive Damages and Products Liability, 39 Ins. Couns. J. 300 (1972); Haskell, The Aircraft Manufacturer's Liability for Design and Punitive Damages—The Insurance Policy and the Public Policy, 40 J. Air L. & Com. 595, 618–20 (1974); Ghiardi and Koehn, Punitive Damages in Strict Liability Cases, 61 Marq. L. Rev. 245, 247 (1977); Fulton, Punitive Damages in Product Liability Cases, 15 Forum 117, 128–32 (1979).

**18.** Tozer, Punitive Damages and Products Liability, 39 Ins. Couns. J. 300, 301 (1972).

**19.** Strict liability is conventionally distinguished from negligence on the ground that the former type of claim is based on the condition of the product rather than on the seller's fault. See § 5.3, above.

**20.** Cf. R. Keeton, Conditional Fault in the Law of Torts, 72 Harv. L. Rev. 401 (1959).

**21.** See, e.g., Wade, On the Nature of Strict Tort Liability for Products, 44 Miss. L.J. 825, 835, 850 (1973) ("The time will probably come when courts are ready to declare that one who supplies a product which is unduly unsafe is negligent per se. Selling a product which is not duly safe is negligence within itself, and no more needs to be proved. Whether this is called negligence or strict liability is not really significant.") Id. at 850.

**22.** See §§ 2.6, 5.9, and 6.5, above.

**23.** "Strict liability was intended to compensate victims, not to limit their remedies." Gerald W. Boston, Punitive Damages in Tort Law § 19:10, at 24 (1993).

Second, the incompatibility argument rests upon the invalid assumption that punitive damages claims must be established by facts identical to those supporting the underlying claim for compensatory damages. Punitive damages claims have long been deemed compatible with the negligence cause of action despite the fact that considerably more, and sometimes different, proof is required to establish that a defendant's conduct was "willful and wanton" or "malicious" rather than merely negligent.[24] And punitive damages awards have been held appropriate in a number of cases involving various other causes of action based on strict principles of liability: nuisance,[25] liability for ultra-hazardous activities,[26] negligence per se,[27] defamation,[28] and implied warranty in the sale of drugs.[29]

The incompatibility argument was repudiated a century and a half ago in *Fleet v. Hollenkemp*,[30] the earliest reported products liability case involving punitive damages. Addressing the question of whether punitive damages could be awarded in an action brought in case as well as one brought in trespass, the court responded that "whether exemplary damages should or should not be given does not depend upon the form of action so much as upon the extent and nature of the injury done and the manner in which it was inflicted, whether by negligence, wantoness [sic], or with or without malice."[31] In an even earlier punitive damages case in which the defendant raised the trespass-case distinction, the court remarked that "[s]uch [a] distinction would be as arbitrary and unjust, as it is technical."[32]

The first modern products liability case to address the strict products liability in tort incompatibility argument, *Drake v. Wham–O Manufacturing Co.*,[33] reasoned similarly to the court in *Fleet*: "Where the principal claim is based on strict liability in tort and there is an additional claim of wanton disregard of the plaintiff's rights, it is a simple matter to allow the plaintiff to make a supplementary showing of

---

**24.** In two of the very few cases to accept the incompatibility argument, the courts expressly stated that such damages were still recoverable on a negligence claim. See Scott v. Fruehauf Corp., 396 S.E.2d 354, 357 (S.C. 1990); Doe v. Miles Labs., Inc., 675 F.Supp. 1466, 1482 n.8 (D. Md. 1987), aff'd, 927 F.2d 187 (4th Cir. 1991).

**25.** See, e.g., Seale v. Pearson, 736 So.2d 1108 (Ala. Civ. App. 1999) (low overflights over plaintiff's house); Lovejoy Specialty Hospital, Inc. v. Advocates for Life, Inc., 855 P.2d 159 (Or. Ct. App. 1993) (action by abortion clinic against protesters).

**26.** See, e.g., Fallowfield Dev. Corp. v. Strunk, 1991 WL 280264 (E.D.Pa. 1991); SKF Farms v. Superior Court, 200 Cal.Rptr. 497 (Ct. App. 1984) (aerial cropdusting damaged adjoining lettuce growers); McGregor v. Barton Sand & Gravel, Inc., 660 P.2d 175 (Or. Ct. App. 1983).

**27.** See, e.g., Austin v. Specialty Transp. Servs. Inc., 594 S.E.2d 867 (S.C. Ct. App.

2004); McCain v. Beverly Health and Rehabilitation Servs. 2002 WL 1565526 (E.D. Pa. 2002); Axen v. American Home Prod. Corp., 974 P.2d 224, 234–36 (Or. Ct. App. 1999); Palmer v. A.H. Robins Co., 684 P.2d 187, 210–13 (Colo. 1984).

**28.** See, e.g., Central Bering Sea Fishermen's Assoc. v. Anderson, 54 P.3d 271 (Ala. 2002); Aken v. Plains Elec. Generation & Transmission Coop., Inc., 49 P.3d 662 (N.M. 2002); Rogers v. Florence Printing Co., 106 S.E.2d 258 (S.C. 1958); Reynolds v. Pegler, 123 F.Supp. 36 (S.D.N.Y. 1954), aff'd, 223 F.2d 429 (2d Cir. 1955). Cf. Dun & Bradstreet v. Greenmoss Builders, Inc., 472 U.S. 749 (1985).

**29.** See Fleet v. Hollenkemp, 52 Ky. 219 (1852).

**30.** 52 Ky. 219 (1852).

**31.** Id. at 225–26.

**32.** Merrills v. Tariff Mfg. Co., 10 Conn. 384, 388 (1835).

**33.** 373 F.Supp. 608 (E.D. Wis. 1974).

aggravating conduct for the purpose of proving entitlement to punitive damages."[34] The *Drake* court reasoned that this was an appropriate approach since "a claim for punitive damages is considered a prayer for a specific type of relief in Wisconsin, not a part of the claim itself.... "[35]

Notwithstanding the paucity of logical support for the proposition that punitive damages should not be allowable in strict liability actions, defense lawyers,[36] and even one otherwise intelligent products liability scholar,[37] vigorously continued to advance the incompatibility argument into the 1980s and even the 1990s, perhaps bedazzling but certainly misguiding a small number of federal district courts.[38] But the holdings in those district courts have now been repudiated,[39] and all of the state and federal appellate courts to examine the issue have rejected the incompatibility argument.[40] The only appellate court to prohibit punitive damages in strict products liability in tort claims based its ruling on a narrow interpretation of that state's products liability statute.[41] Thus, the incompatibility argument may now be viewed as a quaint historical relic with no logical or legal force leaving punitive damages recoverable today, in almost all jurisdictions,[42] in products liability actions brought in strict liability in tort.

**34.**   Id. at 611.

**35.**   Id.

**36.**   See, e.g., Sales, The Emergence of Punitive Damages in Product Liability Actions: A Further Assault on the Citadel, 14 St. Mary's L.J. 351 (1983).

**37.**   See Wertheimer, Punitive Damages and Strict Products Liability: An Essay in Oxymoron, 39 Vill. L. Rev. 505 (1994).

**38.**   Rejecting punitive damages in strict liability, see Butcher v. Robertshaw Controls Co., 550 F.Supp. 692 (D. Md. 1981); Doe v. Miles Labs., Inc., 675 F.Supp. 1466 (D. Md. 1987), aff'd on other grounds, 927 F.2d 187 (4th Cir. 1991); Gold v. Johns–Manville Sales Corp., 553 F.Supp. 482 (D. N.J. 1982); Sanford v. Celotex Corp., 598 F.Supp. 529 (M.D. Tenn. 1984).

**39.**   By Owens–Illinois, Inc. v. Zenobia, 601 A.2d 633, 654–55 (Md. 1992); Fischer v. Johns–Manville Corp., 512 A.2d 466, 475 (N.J. 1986); and Cathey v. Johns–Manville Sales Corp., 776 F.2d 1565 (6th Cir. 1985) (Tenn. law).

**40.**   See, e.g., Owens–Illinois, Inc. v. Zenobia, 601 A.2d 633, 654–55 (Md. 1992) (collecting the cases); Lockley v. Deere & Co., 933 F.2d 1378 (8th Cir. 1991) (Ark. law); Home Ins. Co. v. American Home Prods., 550 N.E.2d 930, 935 (N.Y. 1990); Masaki v. General Motors Corp., 780 P.2d 566 (Haw. 1989); Racich v. Celotex Corp., 887 F.2d 393, 397 (2d Cir. 1989) (N.Y. law); Fischer v. Johns–Manville Corp., 512 A.2d 466, 475 (N.J. 1986) (collecting cases), aff'g 472 A.2d 577 (N.J. Super. Ct. App. Div. 1984) (Pressler, J.); Cathey v. Johns–Manville Sales Corp., 776 F.2d 1565 (6th Cir. 1985) (Tenn. law); Hansen v. Johns–Manville Prods. Corp., 734 F.2d 1036 (5th Cir. 1984) (Tex. law); Palmer v. A.H. Robins Co., 684 P.2d 187 (Colo. 1984); Johns–Manville Sales Corp. v. Janssens, 463 So.2d 242 (Fla. Dist. Ct. App. 1984); Thiry v. Armstrong World Indus., 661 P.2d 515 (Okla. 1983); Neal v. Carey Canadian Mines, Ltd., 548 F.Supp. 357 (E.D. Pa. 1982), aff'd, 760 F.2d 481 (3d Cir. 1985); Acosta v. Honda Motor Co., 717 F.2d 828 (3d Cir. 1983) (V.I. law) (Becker, J.); Leichtamer v. American Motors Corp., 424 N.E.2d 568 (Ohio 1981); Wangen v. Ford Motor Co., 294 N.W.2d 437 (Wis. 1980); Gryc v. Dayton–Hudson Corp., 297 N.W.2d 727, 732 (Minn. 1980); Sturm, Ruger & Co. v. Day, 594 P.2d 38, 46–47 (Alaska 1979).

**41.**   South Carolina does not permit punitive damages in claims brought under its strict products liability statute for reasons of statutory construction, not incompatibility. See Barnwell v. Barber–Colman Co., 393 S.E.2d 162, 164 n.4 (S.C. 1989) (such damages not recoverable because statute codifying § 402A, providing for strict liability "for physical harm caused to the ultimate user or consumer, or to his property," did not provide for punitive damages).

**42.**   Except in South Carolina and the handful of states that prohibit such damages altogether.

### Warranty

Sometimes a plaintiff injured by a defective product is able to bring an action only in warranty because other claims are blocked by a shorter tort statute of limitation or for some other reason. Such a plaintiff faces a substantial doctrinal barrier to the recovery of punitive damages no matter how serious the manufacturer's misconduct and despite the likelihood that punitive damages would be appropriate were the action framed and recoverable in negligence or strict liability in tort. The obstacle is the long-established rule that punitive damages may not be awarded in contract actions,[43] a rule which reflects the importance of maintaining certainty and predictability in commercial transactions.[44] Since warranty actions today are widely viewed as sounding principally in contract rather than in tort,[45] punitive damages claims are presumptively inappropriate in products liability actions brought for breach of warranty.[46]

In most states today, warranty claims in products liability cases are cognizable under the Uniform Commercial Code, which provides for warranties of quality in §§ 2–313, 2–314, and 2–315.[47] The recoverability of punitive damages in claims brought under the Code is specifically addressed in § 1–106(1), which provides:

> The remedies provided by this Act shall be liberally administered to the end that the aggrieved party may be put in as good a position as if the other party had fully performed but neither consequential or special nor penal damages may be had except as specifically provided in this Act or by other rule of law.

Official Comment 1 to UCC § 1–106(1) states that this section seeks "to make it clear that compensatory damages are limited to compensation. They do not include consequential or special damages, or penal damages. . . . "[48]

Because Article 2's remedial provisions[49] for breach of warranty do not "specifically provide" for punitive ("penal") damages, the availabili-

---

**43.** See Restatement of Contracts § 342 (1932). See generally 11 A. Corbin, Corbin on Contracts § 1077 (2003); 10 Halsbury, The Laws of England, Damages § 566, at 207 (1909); Simpson, Punitive Damages for Breach of Contract, 20 Ohio St. L.J. 284 (1959); Notes, 8 Ind. L. Rev. 668 (1975); 7 Willamette L. Rev. 137 (1971). The rule was so clearly established and incontrovertible by 1930 that it was not discussed at all when presented to the American Law Institute for inclusion in the Restatement of Contracts. See 8 ALI Proceedings 340 (1929–1930).

**44.** See 5 A. Corbin, Contracts § 1077, at 440 (1964); Simpson, Punitive Damages for Breach of Contract, 20 Ohio St. L.J. 284 (1959). By limiting a promisor's liability for breach to the promisee's foreseeable loss, the law permits the promisor to predict its liability with some certainty and to weigh this cost against the benefits of employing its resources elsewhere.

**45.** See § 4.1, above.

**46.** See, e.g., Robinson Helicopter Co., Inc. v. Dana Corp., 129 Cal.Rptr.2d 682, 700 (Ct. App. 2003) ("This rule is based in part upon the important policy concern of providing predictability in commercial transactions and respecting the freedom of contract by restricting a contracting party to its contractual remedies for breach."), review granted and opinion superseded, 68 P.3d 344 (Cal. 2003); Cancun Adventure Tours, Inc. v. Underwater Designer Co., 862 F.2d 1044 (4th Cir. 1988) (Va. law) (noting strong presumption against punitive damages in contract cases, and holding punitive damages available in warranty action only if awardable under a tort or other cause of action; breach of warranty could not be converted into tort action for fraud).

**47.** See ch. 4, above.

**48.** UCC § 1–106(1).

**49.** See UCC §§ 2–714 and 2–715.

ty of punitive damages for breach of warranty under the Code thus depends upon whether such damages are "specifically provided ... by other rule of law."[50] No products liability cases have been found ruling whether UCC § 1–106(1) prohibits or allows a punitive damages claim when the only underlying cause of action is for breach of warranty. One early commentator suggested that § 1–106's "other rule of law" exception permits courts to continue awarding punitive damages in cases in which "the failure to perform a promise (such as a warranty of quality) is combined with tortious conduct (such as wanton failure to determine whether the goods measured up to their warranted quality)."[51] Other early commentators suggested that the courts "will have to find or make up the 'other rule of law,' by extrapolation from the fraud cases."[52]

Outside of the products liability area, most courts in Uniform Commercial Code actions, as in common law contract actions,[53] prohibit punitive damages unless the plaintiff also establishes the defendant's liability for an independent tort (the "other rule of law" under the Code), such as fraud, that separately supports the punitive damages claim.[54] A small number of non-products liability warranty cases have allowed punitive damages on this basis.[55] Yet the reason for this exception to the general rule is unclear; if an independent tort-law cause of action supports a punitive damages claim, there ordinarily would appear to be no need for punitive damages to attach to the warranty claim as well.

Warranty's tort-law background and its special role in the development of modern products liability law[56] might argue for a liberal extrapolation from the common law in personal injury cases brought under the Code despite the admonition that "the other rule of law" must "specifically" provide for punitive damages. The marketing of a defective product in willful and wanton disregard of consumer safety might then be broadly classified as "tortious conduct"—sufficiently tortious, at least, to serve as the "other rule of law"—and thus provide a basis for allowing punitive damages awards in products liability actions brought solely for breach of warranty under the Code. This kind of broad interpretation of § 1–106 may possibly make sense in states such as Delaware and Virginia which chose to broaden the principles of liability for breach of the implied warranty of merchantability under the Uniform Commercial Code rather than adopting an independent theory of strict products liability in tort.[57]

---

**50.** UCC § 1–106(1).

**51.** R. Nordstrom, Handbook of the Law of Sales 475–76 (1970).

**52.** J. White & R. Summers, Handbook of the Law Under the Uniform Commercial Code 133 (1972).

**53.** See Simpson, Punitive Damages for Breach of Contract, 20 Ohio St. L.J. 284 (1959).

**54.** See, e.g., Dominion Bank of Richmond, N.A. v. Star Five P'ship, 1991 WL 835184, at *1 (Va. Cir. Ct. 1991) (negotiable instrument transaction).

**55.** See, e.g., Vintage Enter., Inc. v. Jaye, 547 So.2d 1169 (Ala. 1989); Fousel v. Ted Walker Mobile Homes, Inc., 602 P.2d 507 (Ariz. Ct. App. 1979) (relying partially on UCC § 2–721's fraud remedy provision). See also Halprin v. Ford Motor Co., 420 S.E.2d 686 (N.C. Ct. App. 1992).

**56.** See §§ 4.1 and 5.2, above.

**57.** See § 5.3, above.

However, while such a creative expansion of the independent tort requirement might make sense in the context of a common law warranty claim, it most probably would stretch § 1–106(1) further than its drafters intended it to go. Moreover, now that tort law in most jurisdictions has quite properly won its protracted battle with contract law for control of personal injury products liability cases,[58] much may be said for leaving creative flexibility to tort law while retaining the more rigid warranty law principles pure and uncontaminated by the law of torts. That is, because tort law generally provides all appropriate protection to physically injured persons, it may be best to leave warranty law to the resolution of commercial transactions and those personal injury cases in which the plaintiff is willing to accept the generally more restrictive principles of the law of contract. On this view, UCC § 1–106 reasonably may be interpreted as barring punitive damages in products liability claims brought solely for breach of warranty under the Uniform Commercial Code.

### Basis of Punitive Damages Claim

Section 18.3 explored a number of recurring products liability situations in which punitive damages have been found appropriate. Remaining to be examined is the formal punitive damages liability standard that should be used in products liability cases. In states where general punitive damages statutes specify the standard of liability for punitive damages claims,[59] the courts must of course apply the statutory standard to a products liability case as any other. Statutes in a couple of states specifically address the availability of punitive damages in products liability cases, and such a statute may tailor the general punitive damages liability standards to this particular type of litigation.[60]

In the many states in which the standard of liability for punitive damages remains a matter of common law, courts are free to craft the standard to fit the special circumstances of products liability cases.[61]

---

**58.** See §§ 4.3, 5.2, and 5.9, above. Except in states that still use warranty law as the basis for modern "strict" products liability law—Delaware, Massachusetts, Michigan, North Carolina, and Virginia (see § 5.3, above), and perhaps in New York, which cannot quite seem to make up its mind. See Denny v. Ford Motor Co., 662 N.E.2d 730 (N.Y. 1995).

**59.** Such as "that the defendant maliciously intended to cause the injury or consciously and flagrantly disregarded the rights or interests of others in causing the injury." Uniform Law Commissioners' Model Punitive Damages Act § 5(a)(2), 14 U.L.A. 121 (cum. ann. pocket part 2004).

**60.** See, e.g., Conn. Gen. Stat. § 52–240b: "Punitive damages may be awarded if the claimant proves that the harm suffered was the result of the product seller's reckless disregard for the safety of product users, consumers or others who were injured by the product."

**61.** See, e.g., Kansas City v. Keene Corp., 855 S.W.2d 360, 374 (Mo. 1993) ("Punitive damages may be awarded only where the defendant knew of the defect and danger of the product and, by selling the product, showed complete indifference to or conscious disregard for the safety of others."); Leichtamer v. American Motors Corp., 424 N.E.2d 568, 580 (Ohio 1981) (punitive damages appropriate where quality control is "so inadequate as to manifest a flagrant indifference to the possibility that the product might expose consumers to unreasonable risks of harm"). In Missouri, punitive damages may be awarded in negligence "if the defendant showed complete indifference to or a conscious disregard for the safety of others," which the plaintiff must also establish in strict liability together with proof that "the defendant introduced the offending product into commerce with actual knowledge of the product's defects." Barnett v. La Societe Anonyme Tur-

Such a standard must be based upon the state's general punitive damages jurisprudence, but it may incorporate features specially applicable to the products liability setting to render it especially useful in this particular context; it should be broad enough to permit flexibility in its application, yet sufficiently specific to provide manufacturers with at least some basic notion of the type of conduct subject to quasi-criminal punishment.[62] Indeed, adequate notice is essential if punitive damages awards are to be effective in deterring the proscribed misconduct,[63] and fair notice is now a constitutional imperative.[64]

In order for punitive damages to be properly assessed, a manufacturer must be proven to have grossly abused the power flowing from its position of control over product safety in one of three ways: (1) by failing to acquire sufficient product safety information about a substantial product danger that a product is quite likely to possess, through tests, inspections, or post-marketing safety monitoring; (2) by failing to warn about or design away a product hazard it knows to be excessive and reasonably avoidable; or (3) by knowingly misleading the public concerning the product's safety.[65]

Since the third form of misconduct is characterized by an intent to deceive and thus is akin to fraud, it almost always will justify punitive damages liability. However, the first two forms of misconduct described above overlap and easily slide into mere negligence and thus are not always appropriate for punitive damages liability. Indeed, misbehavior akin to negligence and misbehavior deserving of punitive damages are similar in products liability cases in that both are based on selling defective products that present unreasonable risks of harm. Two additional elements are necessary, however, before a manufacturer may appropriately be punished with a punitive assessment. First, the manufacturer must be either aware of, or culpably indifferent to, a significant possibility that its products pose a substantial and unnecessary risk of injury because of their defectiveness. Second, knowing that its products are or may well be defective, the manufacturer must brazenly refuse to

---

bomeca France, 963 S.W.2d 639, 659 (Mo. Ct. App. 1997).

See also Owens–Illinois, Inc. v. Zenobia, 601 A.2d 633 (Md. 1992). In nonintentional tort cases, Maryland requires proof of the defendant's "actual malice" for the recovery of punitive damages. Adapting this standard to products liability cases, the Maryland court held that "actual malice" in this context requires a plaintiff to prove "(1) actual knowledge of the defect on the part of the defendant, and (2) the defendant's conscious or deliberate disregard of the foreseeable harm resulting from the defect." Id. at 653. For the first element, "[t]he plaintiff must show that the defendant actually knew of the defect and of the danger of the product at the time the product left the defendant's possession or control." Id. at 653–54. A defendant will be deemed to have knowledge if it deliberately shuts its eyes to avoid discovering a danger-

ous defect. Id. at 654 n.23. The second element "requires a bad faith decision by the defendant to market a product, knowing of the defect and danger, in conscious or deliberate disregard of the threat to the safety of the consumer." Id. at 654. In ACandS, Inc. v. Godwin, 667 A.2d 116 (Md. 1995), a consolidation of actions brought by injured workers against asbestos suppliers, the court applied the *Zenobia* standard to strike down the punitive damages awards.

**62.** See § 18.7, below.

**63.** See § 18.2, above.

**64.** See BMW of N. Am., Inc. v. Gore, 517 U.S. 559, 574 (1996). See also § 18.7, below.

**65.** The recurring forms of misconduct that have generated punitive damages awards in the products liability context are examined in § 18.3, above.

ascertain the danger or to adopt appropriate measures to reduce a known danger to an acceptable level.[66] Punitive damages are appropriate in such cases if a manufacturer is proven to have known that the product was exposing customers to an unnecessarily high risk of serious harm and, further, that the risk could be substantially reduced at relatively small cost. In short, a manufacturer which fails to test for, warn about, or design away a danger may properly be subject to punitive damages if the manufacturer not only knew that its product was inflicting or likely to inflict substantial injury, but also was then aware of a means to reduce the risk which was simple, inexpensive, and readily available at the time.[67]

A liability standard for punitive damages in products liability cases should be broad enough to cover the variety of ways in which a manufacturer may deliberately or recklessly disregard consumer safety. Most of the products liability decisions addressing punitive damages have applied the traditional common law and statutory general standards for punitive damages liability, such as "willful and wanton;"[68] "malice, oppression, or gross negligence;"[69] or "ill will, . . . actual malice, or . . . under circumstances amounting to fraud or oppression."[70] But

**66.** See, e.g., Gonzales v. Surgidev Corp., 899 P.2d 576, 590 (N.M. 1995), citing Baker v. Firestone Tire & Rubber Co., 793 F.2d 1196, 1200 (11th Cir. 1986) (Fla. law); Leichtamer v. American Motors Corp., 424 N.E.2d 568, 580 (Ohio 1981). See also Boehm v. Fox, 473 F.2d 445, 447 (10th Cir. 1973) (Kan. law) ("Wantonness is characterized by a realization of the imminence of damage to others and a restraint from doing what is necessary to prevent the damage because of indifference to whether it occurs.").

**67.** See, e.g., General Motors Corp. v. Sanchez, 997 S.W.2d 584 (Tex. 1999). The textual assertion, which refers to the ordinary case, should not be taken to suggest that the plaintiff must always prove the defendant's actual knowledge of either the product's harmfulness or the feasibility of reducing the harm, since a manufacturer completely indifferent to consumer safety may well have no idea of the extent of a product's dangers or how to eliminate them. See, e.g., Barnett v. La Societe Anonyme Turbomeca France, 963 S.W.2d 639, 665 (Mo. Ct. App. 1997) (defendant, aware of helicopter engine failure problem for several years, failed to investigate extent of problem until after plaintiffs' fatal accident). Moreover, in most cases an established manufacturer may fairly be presumed to have expert knowledge in its particular field and thus to be aware of the feasibility of reducing a particular danger, especially when the feasibility is clear.

**68.** See, e.g., Moore v. Jewel Tea Co., 253 N.E.2d 636, 648 (Ill. App. Ct. 1969), aff'd, 263 N.E.2d 103 (Ill. 1970). "The question of willful and wanton conduct is essen-

tially whether the failure to exercise care is so gross that it shows a lack of regard for the safety of others." 253 N.E.2d at 649. See also Axen v. American Home Prods. Corp., 974 P.2d 224, 238 (Or. Ct. App. 1999) ("constitute 'wanton disregard' for the safety of others"); Patton v. TIC United Corp., 859 F.Supp. 509, 513 n.4 (D. Kan. 1994) ("'wantonness' . . . means . . . that the defendant realized the imminence of danger and showed complete indifference or reckless disregard for it"). The standard in some states is willful or wanton. See, e.g., Bocci v. Key Pharm., Inc., 76 P.3d 669, 674 (Or. Ct. App. 2003) ("wanton disregard"); Ford v. GACS, Inc. 265 F.3d 670, 678 (8th Cir. 2001) (Mo. law) (wantonness required to justify punitive damages); Hundley v. Rite Aid, 529 S.E.2d 45, 60 (S.C. Ct. App. 2000) ("willful, wanton, or reckless conduct"); Iowa Code § 668A.1 ("willful or *wanton* disregard for the rights or safety of another").

**69.** See, e.g., Ford Motor Co. v. Miles, 141 S.W.3d 309 (Tex. App. 2004); Vollert v. Summa Corp., 389 F.Supp. 1348, 1352 n.13 (D. Haw. 1975).

**70.** See, e.g., Isabel v. Velsicol Chemical Co., 327 F.Supp.2d 915 (W.D. Tenn. 2004) ("a court may award punitive damages if the plaintiff proves by clear and convincing evidence that the defendant acted either intentionally, fraudulently, maliciously, or recklessly"); Dewick v. Maytag Corp., 296 F.Supp.2d 905, 905 (N.D. Ill. 2003) ("fraud, actual malice, deliberate violence or oppression, or when the defendant acts willfully, or with such gross negligence as to indicate a wanton disregard of the rights of oth-

these traditional liability standards were originally formulated to cover interpersonal intentional torts or oppressive misconduct by government officials exhibiting personal hostility or a callous abuse of power.[71] In cases where a manufacturer's marketing misconduct is sufficiently culpable to deserve the sanction of punitive damages, the particular misconduct may fairly be characterized as "wanton" or "oppressive."[72] Such phrases, however, are at best vague and imprecise, and they do little to help a manufacturer conform to the law or to help a court or jury apply the standard to concrete cases.

Courts in products liability cases sometimes define the proscribed marketing behavior as conduct that is in "conscious" or "reckless" disregard of consumer safety or product danger or defect.[73] The formula-

ers"); Toole v. Richardson–Merrell, Inc., 60 Cal.Rptr. 398, 414 (Ct. App. 1967). See also Palmer v. A.H. Robins Co., 684 P.2d 187, 219 (Colo. 1984) (" 'attended by circumstances of fraud' and/or constituted a 'wanton and reckless disregard of the injured party's rights and feelings' "); Gillham v. Admiral Corp., 523 F.2d 102 (6th Cir. 1975) (Ohio law) ("so intentional, reckless, wanton, willful, or gross that an inference of malice could be drawn," id. at 109; "reckless indifference to the safety of others," id. at 109 n.4); G.D. Searle & Co. v. Superior Ct., 122 Cal.Rptr. 218, 225 (Ct. App. 1975) ("conscious disregard of the safety of others"); Pease v. Beech Aircraft Corp., 113 Cal.Rptr. 416, 426 (Ct. App. 1974) ("willful and wanton indifference to the safety of persons who might use the [product]"); Hoffman v. Sterling Drug, Inc., 485 F.2d 132 (3d Cir. 1973) (Pa. law) ("reckless indifference to the public's safety," id. at 146; "reckless disregard of the public's health," id. at 147); Kritser v. Beech Aircraft Corp., 479 F.2d 1089, 1097 (5th Cir. 1973) (Tex. law) ("conscious indifference toward the public which generally typifies gross negligence"); Boehm v. Fox, 473 F.2d 445, 447 (10th Cir. 1973) (Kan. law) ("malice, fraud, or a willful and wanton disregard of the rights of others"); Fleet v. Hollenkemp, 52 Ky. 219, 226 (1852) (exemplary damages should depend on the "nature and extent of the injury done and the manner in which it was inflicted, whether by negligence, wantonness, or with or without malice").

In Ford Motor Co. v. Ammerman, 705 N.E.2d 539, 557 (Ind. Ct. App. 1999), the trial court defined some of the basic punitive damages terms:

Willful and wanton misconduct: A course of action which shows an actual or deliberate intention to cause injury or which, under existing conditions, shows either an utter indifference or conscious disregard for the rights of others. Gross negligence: The intentional failure to perform a manifest duty in reckless disregard of the consequences as affecting the life or

property of another, such a gross want of care and regard for the rights of others as to justify [a finding of] willfulness and wantonness. Recklessness is characterized ... by highly unreasonable conduct or a gross departure from ordinary care, in a situation where a high degree of danger is apparent. A person acts recklessly when one disregards a substantial risk of danger, that either is known or would be apparent to a reasonable person in the same position.

**71.** See 1 T. Sedgwick, A Treatise on the Measure of Damages § 350, at 689–92 (9th ed. 1912).

**72.** "Oppression" ensues from an abuse of power over the welfare of others, which accurately describes the misconduct in the first case in Anglo–American law expressly allowing punitive damages, Huckle v. Money, 2 Wils. 205 (K.B. 1763). Oppression also fairly characterizes flagrant marketing misconduct in products liability cases. In this context, a manufacturer's power derives from its virtually monopolistic control over the means for gathering and applying crucial information necessary for consumer safety.

**73.** See, e.g., Sufix, U.S.A., Inc. v. Cook, 128 S.W.3d 838, 841 (Ky. Ct. App. 2004) ("a manufacturer's failure to test for defects that pose a risk of serious injury and that are susceptible to adequate pre-release testing can amount to a conscious or reckless disregard for the rights and safety of others and thus can justify an award of punitive damages"); Shurr v. A.R. Siegler, Inc., 70 F.Supp.2d 900, 937 (E.D. Wis. 1999) ("To be awarded punitive damages, a plaintiff must establish 'malice, vindictiveness, ill-will, or wanton, willful or reckless disregard of plaintiff's rights.' ") (quoting Wangen v. Ford Motor Co., 294 N.W.2d 437 (Wis. 1980)); Owens–Illinois, Inc. v. Zenobia, 601 A.2d 633, 654 (Md. 1992) ("conscious or deliberate disregard of the threat to the safety of the consumer"); Barnett v. La

tion of a liability standard in forms like these lies close to the mark, but the precise wording is important to avoid ambiguity. Phrasing the standard in terms of disregarding a product "defect" is specific and correct, since the wrongfulness of the conduct lies in the manufacturer's conscious or reckless sale of a product in violation of the law—a product, in other words, that is "defective." But if the test is formulated more loosely in terms of disregarding a product's "danger," or, far broader still, in terms of "consciously disregarding" the consequences of one's actions,[74] the liability standard becomes so broad and ambiguous that its integrity is subverted. The ambiguity springs from the fact that a design engineer properly should eliminate only those dangers that may be avoided feasibly and cost effectively and should leave all other dangers in the product. Thus, the design process necessarily involves considering ("regarding") all significant dangers, and a judge or jury after the fact may all too easily view the manufacturer's failure to cure a particular, known danger as "consciously disregarding" it.[75]

One way to tailor general punitive damages standards to products liability cases is to define the standard of liability in terms of marketing a product in flagrant disregard of the rights of consumers.[76] Adding "flagrancy" to a punitive damages standard in any type of case helpfully emphasizes that the defendant's conduct ordinarily must be proven to have deviated substantially from acceptable behavior before it fairly may be punished.[77] By emphasizing to judges and juries that punitive damages are available only for extreme departures from the norm, a flagrant disregard test provides fair breathing space[78] for manufacturers to make

Societe Anonyme Turbomeca France, 963 S.W.2d 639, 659 (Mo. Ct. App. 1997) ("conscious disregard for the safety of others" based upon "actual knowledge of the product's defects"); Acosta v. Honda Motor Co., 717 F.2d 828, 841 (3d Cir. 1982) (V.I. law) ("reckless disregard for the safety of users"); Grimshaw v. Ford Motor Co., 174 Cal.Rptr. 348, 387 (Ct. App. 1981) ("conscious and callous disregard of a substantial likelihood of injury to others").

**74.** See, e.g., Mack Trucks, Inc. v. Conkle, 436 S.E.2d 635, 640 (Ga. 1993) ("conscious indifference to consequences"). This was also the standard applied by the trial court in the famous Ford Pinto case, Grimshaw v. Ford Motor Co., 174 Cal.Rptr. 348, 385 (Ct. App. 1981) (jury instructions that punitive damages appropriate if conduct was "wilful, intentional, and done in conscious disregard of its possible results").

**75.** See Owen, Problems In Assessing Punitive Damages Against Manufacturers of Defective Products, 49 U. Chi. L. Rev. 1, 20–28 (1982).

**76.** Or, since consumers have a right not to have their safety threatened by defective products, the standard may be phrased in terms of selling a product in flagrant disregard of consumer safety. See Owen, Punitive Damages in Products Liability Litigation, 74 Mich. L. Rev. 1257,

1367 (1976) (proposing "flagrant indifference" standard). Cf. Ford Motor Co. v. Ammerman, 705 N.E.2d 539, 557 (Ind. Ct. App. 1999) ("utter indifference for the rights of consumers").

**77.** Serving to limit the standard's scope, the word "flagrant" connotes misconduct significantly more serious than inadvertent negligence and thus assures that only the most egregious misbehavior is punished. Yet it does not call for proof of a subjective awareness of wrongdoing that the word "conscious" implicitly requires. Instead, the word imputes such awareness to the manufacturer when its conduct is obviously and seriously wrong; it suggests that punitive damages are appropriate only in cases of extreme departure from accepted safety norms, that is, only if a product was very defective, and plainly so, at the time it was sold. Owen, Problems in Assessing Punitive Damages Against Manufacturers of Defective Products, 49 U. Chi. L. Rev. 1, 27, 38 (1982). "A plaintiff usually should be entitled to a directed verdict on defectiveness, or close thereto, before the punitive damages issue is properly before the jury at all." Id. at 38.

**78.** From quasi-criminal punishment, not against responsibility for compensatory damages. See Owen, Civil Punishment and

good faith mistakes.[79] Recognizing the advantages of this conception, a number of courts have adopted some form of flagrant disregard formulation.[80] Yet there is nothing magical in the word "flagrant," and a court may achieve the same beneficial results by enhancing the more conventional liability formulations to stress that a manufacturer's conduct should be found to have extended far outside the bounds of normal and proper conduct in order to be branded quasi-criminal.[81] For example, such a standard might frame the prohibited misconduct as the conscious or reckless disregard of consumer safety which constituted an extreme departure from proper conduct,[82] or something similar.[83]

As frequently is true whenever a complex matter is reduced to a simple test, any standard may be better administered if its elements are isolated. The following factors[84] may properly be considered to help determine whether a manufacturer's marketing misconduct flagrantly disregarded consumer rights to reasonable safety:[85]

the Public Good, 56 S. Cal. L. Rev. 103, 115–16 (1982).

**79.** See Owen, Problems In Assessing Punitive Damages Against Manufacturers of Defective Products, 49 U. Chi. L. Rev. 1, 27–28 (1982).

**80.** See, e.g., Owens–Corning Fiberglas Corp. v. Golightly, 976 S.W.2d 409, 412 (Ky. 1998) ("flagrant indifference to the rights of the Plaintiff"); Loitz v. Remington Arms Co., 563 N.E.2d 397, 407 (Ill. 1990) (recognizing both " 'flagrant indifference' to public safety" standard used in products liability cases and "the more traditional phrasing of willful and wanton misconduct"); Palmer v. A.H. Robins Co., 684 P.2d 187, 218 (Colo. 1984) (referring to "marketing of a product in flagrant disregard of consumer safety," but applying statutory standard of conduct that was " 'attended by circumstances of fraud' or a 'wanton and reckless disregard of the injured party's rights and feelings' "); Moore v. Remington Arms Co., 427 N.E.2d 608, 617 (Ill. App. Ct. 1981) (adopting standard of " 'conduct that reflects a flagrant indifference to the public safety' " for products liability cases); Leichtamer v. American Motors Corp., 424 N.E.2d 568, 580 (Ohio 1981) (quality control "so inadequate as to manifest a flagrant indifference to the possibility that the product might expose consumers to unreasonable risks of harm").

**81.** See, e.g., Owens–Illinois, Inc. v. Zenobia, 601 A.2d 633, 654 (Md. 1992), where the court recognized yet curiously rejected the inspired flagrant indifference standard because, "[w]e prefer the characterization 'conscious or deliberate disregard,' and emphatically state that negligence alone, no matter how gross, wanton, or outrageous, will not satisfy this standard. Instead the test requires a bad faith decision by the

defendant to market a product, knowing of the defect and danger, in conscious or deliberate disregard of the threat to the safety of the consumer."

**82.** For discussions of the extreme departure notion, see Owen, A Punitive Damages Overview: Functions, Problems and Reform, 39 Vill. L. Rev. 363, 407 (1994); Owen, The Moral Foundations of Punitive Damages, 40 Ala. L. Rev. 705, 730 (1989); Owen, Problems In Assessing Punitive Damages Against Manufacturers of Defective Products, 49 U. Chi. L. Rev. 1, 27–28 (1982); Owen, Civil Punishment and the Public Good, 56 S. Cal. L. Rev. 103, 115–16 (1982).

**83.** See, e.g., Bachman v. General Motors Corp., 776 N.E.2d 262, 301 (Ill. App. Ct. 2002) (punitive damages permitted when "the defendant acts willfully, or with such gross negligence as to indicate a wanton disregard of the rights of others"); Ford Motor Co. v. Ammerman, 705 N.E.2d 539, 557 (Ind. Ct. App. 1999) ("[r]ecklessness is characterized by . . . a gross departure from ordinary care, in a situation where a high degree of danger is apparent").

**84.** This is a slightly reformulated list of factors proposed in Owen, Punitive Damages in Products Liability Litigation, 74 Mich. L. Rev. 1257, 1369–70 (1976).

**85.** The factors relevant to the basic determination of whether punitive damages should be assessed at all in products liability cases reflect many of the considerations pertinent to the measurement of such awards. See § 18.5, below. The flagrancy of the manufacturer's misconduct is the key to both. See BMW of N. Am., Inc. v. Gore, 517 U.S. 559, 575 (1996) ("degree of reprehensibility").

(1) the magnitude of the product danger;

(2) the practical and economic feasibility of reducing the danger to an acceptable level;

(3) the manufacturer's awareness of the danger, its magnitude, and how it feasibly could be reduced;

(4) the nature, reasons for, and duration of the manufacturer's failure to act appropriately to discover or reduce the danger; and

(5) the extent to which the manufacturer purposefully created the danger.

An examination of these factors often should help determine in particular cases whether a manufacturer's misconduct was so egregious as to make it fairly subject to punitive damages liability.[86] First, a manufacturer's fault in failing to minimize a product hazard increases with the likelihood and magnitude of the potential harm to consumers.[87] Second, the easier and cheaper it is to reduce a hazard to an acceptable level, the greater will be a manufacturer's fault for failing to do so.[88] Third, as a manufacturer's awareness of the existence, magnitude, and means to reduce a product hazard increases, so too does its duty to address the problem in a responsible way, and its culpability for failing to do so.[89] Fourth, the nature and duration of a manufacturer's failure to respond appropriately to a product hazard, its reasons for not responding more appropriately, and the nature of any measures actually taken, all shed light on the extent to which the enterprise values profits over safety,[90] and, accordingly, on its culpability.[91] Finally, if the manufacturer created a product danger deliberately, as by knowingly deceiving the public about the product's safety, it usually will be especially blameworthy and deserving of punishment.[92]

**86.** See, e.g., Mead, Punitive Damages and the Spill Felt Round the World: A U.S. Perspective, 17 Loy. L.A. Int'l & Comp. L. Rev. 829, 847 (1995).

**87.** See, e.g., Gonzales v. Surgidev Corp., 899 P.2d 576, 590 (N.M. 1995).

**88.** See, e.g., Grimshaw v. Ford Motor Co., 174 Cal.Rptr. 348, 361 (Ct. App. 1981).

**89.** See, e.g., Axen v. American Home Prod. Corp., 974 P.2d 224 (Or. Ct. App. 1999). An enterprise will be put on notice of a product danger upon receipt of a complaint of injury or near-injury from a single consumer. The more complaints received by the manufacturer concerning a specific danger, the greater will be its awareness of the existence, magnitude, and possible excessiveness of the hazard. Failing to have an organized method for collecting, analyzing, and responsibly addressing complaints of serious product hazards would itself suggest a manufacturer's indifference to public safety. See, e.g., Gillham v. Admiral Corp., 523 F.2d 102 (6th Cir. 1975) (Ohio law).

**90.** See, e.g., North Am. Refractory Co. v. Easter, 988 S.W.2d 904, 921 (Tex. App. 1999) (jury could properly find that defendant was "more concerned with maintaining profits than the health and safety of individuals").

**91.** Tetuan v. A.H. Robins Co., 738 P.2d 1210 (Kan. 1987).

**92.** See, e.g., Williams v. Philip Morris Inc., 48 P.3d 824 (Or. Ct. App. 2002) (evidence showed that defendant publicly asserted that health issue was unresolved while knowing that smoking indeed caused lung cancer and other health hazards; $79.2 million verdict for smoker, reduced by trial judge to $32.8 million, reinstated on appeal), vacated and remanded for reconsideration, Philip Morris USA, Inc. v. Williams, 540 U.S. 801 (2003), reconsidered and reinstated, 92 P.3d 126 (Or. Ct. App. 2004) (concluding that $79.5 million punitive award was reasonable, proportionate to the wrong to the plaintiff and the public in the state, and hence comported with Supreme Court due process guidelines); Burton v. R.J. Reynolds Tobacco Co., 205 F. Supp. 2d 1253 (D. Kan. 2002); Toole v. Richardson–Merrell, Inc., 60 Cal.Rptr. 398 (Ct. App. 1967) (fraud). Cases of true fraud are rare in products liability litigation, and flagrant

## § 18.5   PROBLEMS AND RECURRING CRITICISMS

Punitive damages suffer from a variety of problems, and such awards are subject to a number of criticisms, some with merit and some without. The criticisms are raised in one form or another, time and time again, and the punitive damages doctrine cannot be fully understood without considering each of the major criticisms to which it is exposed.[1] While certain objections are examined further in a later section in connection with reform proposals,[2] the inquiry here explores some of the basic problems and recurring criticisms of punitive damages applicable to products liability litigation: that punitive damages result in a confusion of tort and criminal law; that manufacturers and innocent shareholders are unfairly subjected to vicarious liability for punitive damages; that insurance against punitive damages destroys their punitive effect; that the legal standards for determining punitive damages liability are hopelessly vague; and that the methods for determining and controlling the amounts of punitive damages awards are unfair.

### Confusion of Tort and Criminal Law

Because punitive damages are designed to punish a defendant and deter gross misbehavior rather than to provide a plaintiff with compensation, one of the oldest criticisms of such assessments is that they intrude into the realm of criminal law and thus may be seen as deforming the symmetry of the law.[3] This objection, which developed in the nineteenth century, is based on a pure and abstract model of the law in which the law of torts and the law of crimes are defined in perfect exclusion of one another. The idea here is that each legal domain should be entirely unique unto itself, such that there can be no valid overlap of functions between different categories of law. With the advent of legal realism in the early twentieth century, this kind of focus on architectural purity and symmetry in the design of a society's legal structure resoundingly collapsed in American legal thought; and thus, formalist arguments of this type carry little persuasive force today.[4] Moreover, this type of

misconduct sufficient for punitive damages ordinarily may be established in the absence of deliberate deception. See § 18.3, above.

### § 18.5

**1.** See, e.g., Gash, Solving the Multiple Punishment Problem: A Call for a National Punitive Damages Registry, 99 Nw. U.L. Rev. ___ (2005); Colby, Beyond the Multiple Punishment Problem: Punitive Damages As Punishment for Individual, Private Wrongs, 87 Minn. L. Rev. 583 (2003); Schkade, Erratic by Design: A Task Analysis of Punitive Damages Assessment, 39 Harv. J. on Legis. 121 (2002); Eisenberg and Wells, The Predictability of Punitive Damages Awards in Published Opinions, the Impact of *BMW v. Gore* on Punitive Damages Awards, and Forecasting Which Punitive Awards Will Be Reduced, 7 Sup. Ct. Econ. Rev. 59 (1999); Polinsky & Shavell, Punitive Damages: An Economic Analysis, 111 Harv. L. Rev. 869 (1998); Sunstein et al., Assessing Punitive Damages (with Notes on Cognition and Valuation in Law), 107 Yale L.J. 2071 (1998). Critiquing the critiques, see, e.g., Owen, A Punitive Damages Overview: Functions, Problems and Reform, 39 Vill. L. Rev. 363, 407 (1994); Daniels and Martin, Myth and Reality in Punitive Damages, 75 Minn. L. Rev. 1 (1990); Comment, 86 Nw. U. L. Rev. 1130, 1130–34 (1992) (listing criticisms).

**2.** For a discussion of reform proposals, see § 18.6, below.

**3.** Fay v. Parker, 53 N.H. 342, 382 (1872). See also Fluke Corp. v. Hartford Accident & Indem. Co., 34 P.3d 809, 814 (Wash. 2001) (noting that punitive damages "encroach upon criminal sanctions").

**4.** "[M]ore is at stake in legal theory than elegance and symmetry." Fletcher, Corrective Justice for Moderns, 106 Harv. L. Rev. 1658, 1678 (1993).

structural critique fails to recognize the deep historical and functional nexus between the law of torts and the law of crimes,[5] and it ignores in particular the traditional and central role of admonition in the law of torts.[6]

A related, substantive argument against punitive damages is that criminal law is designed to punish and deter, whereas the principal purpose of tort law is to compensate injured persons for wrongfully inflicted harm, so that the purposes of punitive damages are already and better accomplished by and within criminal law. This criticism rests uncomfortably upon the disturbing premise that the criminal law is superior to the civil law when the functions of the two areas of law overlap, and that the domain of criminal law should be expanded to be the exclusive mechanism for remedying all forms of serious misbehavior. In any nation devoted to the promotion of personal freedom, this premise should be rejected as a pernicious heresy. The criminal law is far more intrusive to personal liberty than is the civil law, and criminal sanctions should be reserved for only the most extreme forms of misbehavior that most clearly harm the public good. Where the private law can as cheaply and successfully accomplish the same objectives, and where public condemnation in the extreme by a criminal conviction (and possibly imprisonment) is not required, the civil law should be allowed to perform its offices. Not only is the punitive damages doctrine likely to perform the retributive, deterrent, and law-enforcement functions more cheaply than the criminal law, because of its partial funding by the wrongdoer, but it is also apt to perform them better because of the personal and monetary incentives that punitive damages provide to victim-enforcers and their lawyers.[7]

But there is a final aspect to the overlap between tort and criminal law inherent in punitive damages that is quite troubling. While punitive damages are in the nature of criminal fines, defendants generally are denied the procedural safeguards of the criminal law, such as the benefit of a higher burden of proof.[8] For this reason, many courts and legislatures have been adopting a "mid-level" burden of proof, such as "clear and convincing evidence," as necessary to protect the interests of the "accused."[9] But the law has been less successful in finding a solution to the fairness problem of allowing a defendant to be punished too severely in a single adjudication, or over and over again by different private

---

**5.** See Prosser and Keeton on Torts § 2.

**6.** For one early article emphasizing the important role of punishment in tort law, see, Morris, Rough Justice and Some Utopian Ideas, 24 Ill. L. Rev. 730 (1930).

**7.** See § 18.2, above.

**8.** The burden of proof in the civil system is "preponderance of the evidence," which is less than the "beyond a reasonable doubt" standard required by the criminal system. Other criminal safeguards which are unavailable in the civil law include the right to counsel, the role and size of the jury, and the prohibitions against self-incrimination, cruel and unusual punishment,

double jeopardy, and excessive fines. See Colby, Beyond the Multiple Punishment Problem: Punitive Damages As Punishment for Individual, Private Wrongs, 87 Minn. L. Rev. 583 (2003); Daniels and Martin, Myth and Reality in Punitive Damages, 75 Minn. L. Rev. 1 (1990); Ellis, Jr., Punitive Damages, Due Process, and the Jury, 40 Ala. L. Rev. 975 (1988); Peters, Punitive Damages in Oregon, 18 Willamette L. Rev. 369, 406–25 (1982); Comment, Criminal Safeguards and the Punitive Damages Defendant, 34 U. Chi. L. Rev. 408 (1967).

**9.** See § 18.6, below.

attorneys general prosecuting separately what was arguably a single act, such as the design and sale of a particular type of product. The criminal law generally addresses these problems through prohibitions against excessive fines and double jeopardy, but punitive damages law has been less successful in protecting defendants against these problems. As addressed below in the discussion of mass disaster cases, this very serious problem of repetitive punitive damage awards remains without a satisfactory judicial or legislative resolution.[10]

### Vicarious Liability and the Innocent Shareholder

The logic and fairness of assessing punitive damages against a corporation for the misconduct of its employees has long been questioned by both courts and commentators.[11] In the final analysis it is the shareholders who feel the brunt of a punitive verdict against the corporation,[12] yet they are almost invariably innocent of personal wrongdoing and incapable of exerting any effective control over the manufacturing enterprise.[13] Why innocent shareholders should be made to suffer for the misconduct of employees of the enterprise is perhaps the most serious conceptual problem concerning the use of punitive damages in products liability litigation.

As a general proposition, the law should avoid inflicting improper punishment upon innocent shareholders of manufacturing enterprises. Ordinarily, however, imposing punitive damages upon manufacturers, and indirectly upon their shareholders, for the flagrantly improper safety decisions made by corporate employees in the scope of their employment does not result in improper shareholder punishment. The corporation's vicarious liability for punitive damages generally is proper in such cases because the misconduct ordinarily is approved by management of the enterprise, even if only tacitly. If a manufacturer's senior engineers and management team rush a product to the market without sufficient testing, or if, in an effort to cut costs or maintain a market, they decide not to eliminate a hazard they know is causing serious injury and could be remedied simply and inexpensively, their employer reaps the benefits of such flagrantly improper decisions by its employees. Obtaining profits in this manner may be likened to a theft of consumer safety, and an enterprise should not be permitted to retain the benefits of such thefts. Manufacturing enterprises may act, of course, only through their employees, and management may encourage employees to pursue the firm's

---

**10.** See id.

**11.** See, e.g., Roginsky v. Richardson–Merrell, Inc., 378 F.2d 832 (2d Cir. 1967) (N.Y. law); Lake Shore & M.S. Ry. v. Prentice, 147 U.S. 101 (1893); C. McCormick, Law of Damages § 80 (1935); 1 T. Sedgwick, Measure of Damages 738–43 (9th ed. 1912); Collier, Exemplary Damages in Actions Against Corporations, 55 Cent. L.J. 105 (1902); Morris, Punitive Damages in Personal Injury Cases, 21 Ohio St. L.J. 216 (1960); Morris, Punitive Damages in Tort Cases, 44 Harv. L. Rev. 1173, 1199–205 (1931); Notes, 70 Yale L.J. 1296 (1961); Notes, 30 Geo. L.J. 294 (1942). Cf. Edgerton, Corporate Criminal Responsibility, 36 Yale L.J. 827, 836–40 (1927). More recently, see generally 1 Kircher and Wiseman, Punitive Damages § 6.10; Richard L. Blatt et al., Punitive Damages: A State-by-State Guide to Law and Practice ch. 5 (2003).

**12.** See, e.g., Roginsky v. Richardson–Merrell, Inc., 378 F.2d 832, 841 (2d Cir. 1967) (N.Y. law). See generally Model Penal Code § 2.07(1)(c), comment at 335 (1985).

**13.** See Model Penal Code § 2.07(1)(c), comment at 335 (1985).

business with excessive zeal, in conscious violation of consumer safety, if it knows that the company is shielded from accountability for the harmful consequences of such illicit decisions.[14]

Principles of restitution argue for a firm's vicarious responsibility for punitive assessments. To the extent that an employee's misconduct in pursuit of corporate profit flagrantly violates consumer rights, profits "earned" by such activities may be viewed as tainted and hence as not properly belonging to the enterprise. "Innocent" shareholders[15] thus have no fair claim to such "illicit profits" which may be seen as a form of unjust enrichment not belonging to them at all.[16] Although precise measurement of such profits will no doubt be highly problematic, punitive damages in such cases serve roughly to recoup from a manufacturer's coffers the unjust rewards of its employee's misdeeds and to return some of the stolen booty to a victim, one of its rightful owners. Nor will the market ordinarily allow the company to slough off such resulting "losses" upon its innocent customers, because the pricing policies of the company's law-abiding competitors will remain unaffected. Finally, the punishment of some innocent shareholders may be a price that has to be paid in order to deter the conscious and reckless endangerment of the public safety. Because shareholders feel the brunt of a punitive damages award, they have an incentive to encourage management to avoid flagrant misconduct of the type that may lead to punitive damages against the corporate enterprise. For these reasons, a number of early, well-reasoned cases rejected the argument that punitive damages awards against manufacturers of defective products are unfair to innocent shareholders.[17]

Between the shareholders and a wrongdoing employee lies the enterprise itself. Courts divide into two conflicting camps on how to determine when an employee's seriously wrongful acts appropriately may be imputed to the enterprise.[18] Some courts, following the 1893 Supreme Court decision in *Lake Shore & Michigan Southern Railway Co. v. Prentice*,[19] have adopted a narrow rule of enterprise liability for punitive damages arising out of malicious acts of corporate employees.[20] This doctrine, which Professor Clarence Morris dubbed the "complicity rule,"[21] imposes liability for punitive damages upon a corporation only

---

**14.** See Comment, 28 Hastings L.J. 431, 466 (1976).

**15.** See Robinson and Kane, Punitive Damages in Product Liability Cases, 6 Pepp. L. Rev. 139, 143 (1979) ("[I]t is precisely on behalf of their 'innocent' shareholders that corporate manufacturers seek to maximize profits at the expense of public safety, and it is the shareholders who ultimately enjoy the rewards of such conduct. Shareholders of errant corporations are thus hardly more 'innocent' than the absentee shareholder who hires an overseer to drive his slaves and to forward resulting profits, but who claims 'innocence' because he has not himself wielded the whip.").

**16.** Cf. Uniform Law Commissioners' Model Punitive Damages Act § 6(c), 14 U.L.A. 126, 127 (cum. ann. pocket pt. 2003) (limiting vicarious liability for punitive

damages to profit or gain in excess of amounts necessary to pay compensatory damages or restitution).

**17.** See, e.g., Wangen v. Ford Motor Co., 294 N.W.2d 437, 453–54 (Wis. 1980); Martin v. Johns–Manville Corp., 469 A.2d 655, 666–67 (Pa. Super. Ct. 1983), vacated on other grounds, 494 A.2d 1088 (Pa. 1985); Fischer v. Johns–Manville Corp., 512 A.2d 466, 476 (N.J. 1986).

**18.** See 2 Kircher and Wiseman, Punitive Damages ch. 24.

**19.** 147 U.S. 101 (1893).

**20.** See Prosser and Keeton on Torts ch. 12.

**21.** Morris, Punitive Damages in Personal Injury Cases, 21 Ohio St. L.J. 216, 221 (1960).

when a superior officer ordered, participated in, or ratified the miscon-duct.[22] This rule imposes liability on an enterprise in the event of such direct involvement by a superior officer because "the imposition of punitive damages serves as a deterrent to the employment of unfit persons in important positions."[23] But this narrow rule of corporate responsibility protects a firm from punitive damages liability arising out of the actions of lower-level employees because of the supposed inequity of punishing a blameless corporation and its shareholders for malicious acts of such employees when the corporation's interests are in fact often undermined by the misconduct.[24] The complicity rule was adopted by the *Second Restatement*[25] and by the Model Punitive Damages Act.[26]

Other courts have adopted the so-called "vicarious liability rule"[27] which holds a corporation liable for punitive damages for the wanton misconduct of *all* employees acting within the general scope of their employment.[28] This approach, "broadly accepted because of its liberal allowance of damages to injured persons,"[29] postulates that strict enter-prise liability for wanton misbehavior of low-level employees will encour-age care in the selection and supervision of such personnel.[30] The debate between supporters of the complicity and vicarious liability rules of

**22.** Id. See, e.g., Roginsky v. Richard-son–Merrell, Inc., 378 F.2d 832, 842 (2d Cir. 1967) (N.Y. law). Some courts have permit-ted ratification to be established by a show-ing that the corporation retained the em-ployee after discovery of his misdeed. See Morris, Punitive Damages in Tort Cases, 44 Harv. L. Rev. 1173, 1203–04 (1931). But this may no longer be accepted practice. See Restatement (Second) of Agency § 217C, cmt. *b* (1958).

**23.** Restatement (2d) Torts § 909, cmt. *a* at 86 (Tent. Draft No. 19, 1973). Discour-aging the employment of unfit persons is also a principal rationale of the broader vicarious liability rule.

**24.** See, e.g., Notes, 41 N.Y.U. L. Rev. 1158, 1166–67 (1966); 70 Yale L.J. 1296, 1306–07 (1961).

**25.** Restatement (2d) Torts § 909, "Pu-nitive Damages Against a Principal," pro-vides that punitive damages may be as-sessed against a principal for an act by an agent if (a) the doing and manner of the agent's act was authorized by the principal (or managerial agent); (b) the principal was reckless in employing an unfit agent; (c) the agent held a managerial position and acted in the scope of employment; or (d) the prin-cipal ratified or approved the act. Restate-ment (Second) of Agency § 217C (1958) (contains an identical section). Yet the drafters of these sections in both Restate-ments were unenthusiastic about the rule. Compare "Note to Institute," following Re-statement (2d) Torts § 909 (Tent. Draft No. 19, 1973), with Restatement (Second) of Agency § 217C, cmt. *a*.

**26.** See Uniform Law Commissioners' Model Punitive Damages Act, 14 U.L.A. 118 (cum. ann. pocket pt. 2003).

**27.** See Morris, Punitive Damages in Personal Injury Cases, 21 Ohio St. L.J. 216, 220 (1960) (asserting it to be the majority rule).

**28.** See Prosser and Keeton on Torts ch. 13.

**29.** See 10 W. Fletcher, Fletcher Cy-clopedia of the Law of Private Corporations § 4906.30, at 547 (2003 cum. supp.), so characterizing it.

**30.** See, e.g., Prosser and Keeton on Torts 13; C. McCormick, Handbook on the Law of Damages 284–85 (1935). The classic expression of this reasoning was set forth in Goddard v. Grand Trunk Ry. of Canada, 57 Me. 202, 224 (1869) ("There is but one vulnerable point about ... corporations; and that is, the pocket of the monied power that is concealed behind them; and if that is reached they will wince. When it is thor-oughly understood that it is not profitable to employ careless and indifferent agents, or reckless and insolent servants, better men will take their places, and not be-fore."). Two other considerations support the broad rule. First, "the practical difficul-ty of proving employer authorization neces-sitates a presumption conclusive of such conduct." Note, 70 Yale L.J. 1296, 1301 (1961). See McCormick, above, at 285. Sec-ond, "the rule of unrestricted corporate lia-bility has the great merit of workable sim-plicity." Id.

punitive damages, and concern for the innocent shareholder, entered products liability litigation when courts first began to consider whether to allow punitive damages in this context.[31] But as punitive damages in products liability cases became increasingly well established in the 1980s, discussion of whether the complicity or vicarious liability rule for punitive damages should be applied in products liability cases disappeared from judicial decisions.

Why debate on the two versions of the rule died is somewhat of a mystery. Perhaps the persuasive power of an early article,[32] which argued for the vicarious liability rule in products liability cases, simply devastated the forces that favored the complicity rule. Or the evaporation of debate may suggest that the vicarious liability issue had little relevance to normal products liability litigation. The kind of case presumed in the debate involved corporate responsibility for punitive damages to a person injured by a razor blade maliciously inserted by a soap factory assembly line worker into a bar of soap. But this scenario is entirely removed from the kinds of situations in which punitive damages have been awarded in products liability cases.[33] In the case of a low-level employee secreting a razor blade in a bar of soap, arguments for shielding the manufacturer from liability are much stronger than in the typical kind of punitive damages case in which various employees conjoin to maximize profits at the expense of consumer safety.[34]

In almost every products liability case in which punitive damages are awarded, the evidence gives rise to reasonable inferences that management at some level[35] consciously decided to cut safety corners in order to increase income for the manufacturer. Even if upper management is not actually shown to have been involved in making the operative decisions, the evidence in products liability cases in which punitive damages are assessed typically suggests that middle management knows what upper management expects when safety and profitability conflict, as they often do. As far as modern products liability law has progressed, and as noble as most employees of manufacturers may be, the corporate profit ethic has if anything intensified over time. In the competitive global economy, when push comes to shove over whether limited corporate dollars should be directed into product safety or toward the bottom

**31.** Compare Roginsky v. Richardson–Merrell, Inc., 378 F.2d 832, 841 (2d Cir. 1967) (N.Y. law) ("a sufficiently egregious error as to one product can end the business life of a concern that has wrought much good in the past and might otherwise have continued to do so in the future, with many innocent stockholders suffering extinction of their investments for a single management sin"), with Pease v. Beech Aircraft Corp., 113 Cal.Rptr. 416, 427 (Ct. App. 1974) ("No sufficient reason appears why shareholders should be seen as captive innocent hostages to the inhuman management of a corporate juggernaut.").

**32.** See Owen, Punitive Damages in Products Liability Litigation, 74 Mich. L. Rev. 1257, 1299–308 (1976).

**33.** See § 18.3, above.

**34.** See Note, 70 Yale L.J. 1296 (1961).

**35.** "Whether an employee acts in a 'managerial capacity' does not necessarily depend on his 'level' in the corporate hierarchy." Grimshaw v. Ford Motor Co., 174 Cal.Rptr. 348, 385 (Ct. App. 1981) (although Ford claimed that its Assistant Chief Engineer of Research and Chief Chassis Engineer did not occupy managerial positions, both of whom said they were powerless to change the Pinto's rear-end design, court found that both possessed discretion to make policy decisions and so exercised managerial authority sufficient to find corporate malice under complicity rule).

line, middle managers have generally come to understand that upper management has no objection to safety so long as it is largely costless, but that safety must be pushed decisively to the rear once it begins to intrude on profitability in any measurable degree.[36] In an environment such as this, the very foundations of the complicity rule[37] crumble in products liability cases, and nothing remains to debate.

### Punitive Damages Insurance as Against Public Policy

To the extent that liability for a punitive damages award is insured, the impact of such an award is transferred to the insurer and thereby avoided by the wrongdoer, which undercuts the supposed punitive and deterrent effects of such awards.[38] However, premium rates of many institutional insurers are based at least partially on the particular insured's loss experience, which makes such insurers pay in the long-run for at least some of such "insured" losses.[39] In addition, at least some insurers, who formerly insured against such losses under the general liability provisions of insurance contracts, now avoid the risk altogether by explicitly excluding coverage for punitive damages liability. Thus, the insurance market (large segments of which suffered enormous losses from punitive damages assessed in thousands of asbestos cases) has itself addressed the punitive damages insurance problem to some extent.

The law could make the matter simple, however, by prohibiting the insurance of such damages on grounds of public policy. The law certainly would not tolerate or enforce insurance policies against the risk of a jail sentence or a criminal fine, at least not where the crime involved moral turpitude. The cases[40] are almost evenly split on the insurability of punitive damages,[41] but it would appear that the better-reasoned deci-

---

**36.** See § 18.3, above.

**37.** Such as assumptions that only low-level employees typically are involved in flagrant misconduct that violates the rights of others; that such misconduct is usually outside the scope of employment; that gross misconduct is usually driven by personal ill-will and, hence, is inherently contrary to the best interests of the employer and the shareholders; and that, accordingly, punishment of the enterprise is illogical and unfair.

**38.** See Widiss, Liability Insurance Coverage for Punitive Damages? Discerning Answers to the Conundrum Created by Disputes Involving Conflicting Public Policies, Pragmatic Considerations and Political Actions, 39 Vill. L. Rev. 455 (1994) (comprehensive review); Giesel, The Knowledge of Insurers and the Posture of the Parties in the Determination of the Insurability of Punitive Damages, 39 U. Kan. L. Rev. 355, 383–84 (1991); Priest, Insurability and Punitive Damages, 40 Ala. L. Rev. 1009 (1989); Owen, Punitive Damages in Products Liability Litigation, 74 Mich. L. Rev. 1257, 1308 (1976); Comment, 28 Hastings L.J. 431, 459 (1976).

**39.** See Owen, Punitive Damages in Products Liability Litigation, 74 Mich. L. Rev. 1257, 1309 (1976).

**40.** Some states have statutes on point. In at least two states, statutes provide that insurance contracts are to be construed as *not* covering punitive damages (as in policy clauses, for example, that provide insurance for "all sums which the Insured shall become legally obligated to pay as damages") unless such contracts expressly so provide. See, e.g., Haw. Rev. Stat. § 431:10–240; Mont. Code Ann. § 33–15–317.

**41.** See R. Blatt et al., Punitive Damages: A State-by-State Guide to Law and Practice ch. 5 (2003); Giesel, The Knowledge of Insurers and the Posture of the Parties in the Determination of the Insurability of Punitive Damages, 39 U. Kan. L. Rev. 355, 383–84 nn.136–43 (1991) (compiling cases on insurability of punitive damages). The majority approach—33 states and 2 territories—allows directly and vicariously assessed punitive damages to be insurable. Blatt et al., at 186. However, some 20 states follow the minority approach, under which punitive damages are not insurable if assessed directly against the wrong-

sions favor outlawing insurance contracts for punitive damages liability,[42] at least in the case of flagrantly improper behavior by corporations and malicious misconduct by individuals.[43]

One important caveat undercuts the desirability of a general rule prohibiting insurance against punitive damages liability. Although the Supreme Court has recently helped alleviate the problem,[44] some courts in the last couple of decades appeared to liberalize the availability of punitive damages, awarding them on vague standards without meaningful judicial oversight. When the law is poorly defined and poorly administered in these respects, the risk of undeserved punitive damage awards is substantial, making insurance contracts for such events more reasonable. While insurance against properly defined and administered punitive damages awards should quite clearly be forbidden, fairness requires the allowance of insurance against punitive awards that are randomly assessed or based on conduct that is not truly reprehensible.[45] Yet, it is doubtful that a court would admit that its own punitive damages standards are so vague, and its oversight over punitive damages verdicts so wanting, that it should allow insurance against punitive damages to cure the unfairness caused by its poorly crafted rules of law and deficient administration of justice under those rules. Accordingly, it would seem best for courts simply to formulate and administer fair and effective punitive damages rules and then to prohibit punitive damages insurance agreements.

doer. Id. One treatise states that the trend, at present, appears to be in favor of allowing insurance of punitive damages. 2 L. Schlueter and K. Redden, Punitive Damages 231 (4th ed. 2000). This conclusion appears questionable, and there would appear to be no ascertainable "trend" at this time, either way. The jurisdictions remain strongly split, and the nature of the issue has been changing recently in ways that undermine any intelligible reference to the notion of a trend. For a general examination of the insurability of punitive damages, see 1 Kircher and Wiseman, Punitive Damages ch. 7. See also id. at § 6:11 (insurability in products liability context).

**42.** See, e.g., Bohrer v. Church Mut. Ins. Co., 12 P.3d 854, 856 (Colo. Ct. App. 2000) ("Because punitive damages are intended to punish the defendant for wrongful acts and to deter similar conduct in the future, public policy prohibits an insurance carrier from providing insurance coverage for punitive damages."); United States Fire Ins. Co. v. Goodyear Tire & Rubber Co., 920 F.2d 487, 490 (8th Cir. 1990) (insurance coverage for punitive damages is void as against Minnesota public policy); Home Ins. Co. v. American Home Prods. Corp., 902 F.2d 1111, 1113 (2d Cir. 1990) (New York public

policy does not allow punitive damage insurance).

Recognizing that principals usually are not personally at fault in most instances of vicarious liability, some states which generally prohibit punitive damages insurance allow it in cases of true vicarious liability. See generally Giesel, The Knowledge of Insurers and the Posture of the Parties in the Determination of the Insurability of Punitive Damages, 39 U. Kan. L. Rev. 355, 357 n.11 (1991) (noting that eight jurisdictions allow insurance of vicariously imposed punitive damages).

**43.** A court might reasonably decide that public policy does not prohibit insurance coverage of punitive damages for automobile accidents in the absence of truly reprehensible behavior by the driver.

**44.** See § 18.7, below.

**45.** In recognition of this problem, a number of states which generally prohibit punitive damages insurance allow it in the absence of truly reprehensible behavior. See Widiss, Liability Insurance Coverage for Punitive Damages? Discerning Answers to the Conundrum Created by Disputes Involving Conflicting Public Policies, Pragmatic Considerations and Political Actions, 39 Vill. L. Rev. 455 (1994).

**Vagueness in Liability Standards for Punitive Damages**

The typical liability standards for punitive damages—such as "malicious," "oppressive" or "outrageous" behavior, or a "conscious," "willful," "wanton," or "reckless" disregard of safety—were examined in the previous section.[46] Unfortunately, such broadly pejorative characterizations of misbehavior contain little descriptive power for ascertaining whether punitive damages are appropriate in particular cases. It frequently is argued that liability standards so vaguely drawn fail to provide a legitimate basis for punitive damages assessments, a condition which invites juries to award such damages on the basis of passion, bias, and prejudice rather than on the law.[47] The problem in a nutshell is that vagueness in the prevailing legal standards for punitive damages recovery deprives not only juries but also judges of any meaningful "tests" to determine when punitive damages are proper.[48]

This criticism is to a large extent well founded, and it requires serious attention by the courts and perhaps the legislatures. An important first step in addressing the vagueness problem is to reduce the ambiguity in the prevailing verbal standards by sharpening their specificity, as discussed above.[49] However, the nature of flagrant misconduct, like ordinary misconduct (negligence), is that it is unsusceptible to precise and particularized definition. Consequently, although the formulation of definitional standards for punitive damages generally may be improved, vagueness is an inherent aspect of punitive damages liability standards, as is true with many general definitions in the law.[50]

The vagueness in such standards as "reckless" and "willful or wanton" is both good and bad. The advantage to such vague standards lies in the discretion it provides to the trier of fact to apply the punitive damages doctrine flexibly to achieve justice on individualized facts. The problem, of course, is that this same flexibility can just as easily be used by a biased jury to subvert justice in any particular case. But vagueness and jury discretion can be directed and controlled by a variety of

---

**46.** See § 18.4, above.

**47.** See, e.g., BMW of N. Am., Inc. v. Gore, 517 U.S. 559, 586, 588–89 (1996) (Breyer, J., concurring); Pacific Mut. Life Ins. Co. v. Haslip, 499 U.S. 1, 42 (1991) (O'Connor, J., dissenting); Ellis, Fairness and Efficiency in the Law of Punitive Damages, 56 S. Cal. L. Rev. 1, 34–39 (1982); Owen, The Moral Foundations of Punitive Damages, 40 Ala. L. Rev. 705, 727–30 (1989); Owen, Problems in Assessing Punitive Damages Against Manufacturers of Defective Products, 49 U. Chi. L. Rev. 1, 18–20 (1982). See generally Owen, A Punitive Damages Overview: Functions, Problems and Reform, 39 Vill. L. Rev. 363, 384 (1994).

**48.** See § 18.4, above. The due process implications of the vagueness problem are examined in § 18.7, below.

**49.** See § 18.4, above. See also § 18.6, below.

**50.** See Romo v. Ford Motor Co., 122 Cal.Rptr.2d 139 (Ct. App. 2002) ("It is empirically impossible, of course, to know exactly the level of punitive damages that would have a sufficient punitive and deterrent effect without unduly stifling innovation and competition in the marketplace."), vacated and remanded, Ford Motor Co. v. Romo, 538 U.S. 1028 (2003), on remand, 6 Cal.Rptr.3d 793 (Ct. App. 2003) (remitting punitive damages award to $23,723,287); Pacific Mut. Life Ins. Co. v. Haslip, 499 U.S. 1, 20 (1991) ("The discretion allowed under Alabama law in determining punitive damages is no greater than that pursued in many familiar areas of the law as, for example, deciding 'the best interests of the child,' or 'reasonable care,' or 'due diligence,' or appropriate compensation for pain and suffering or mental anguish. As long as the discretion is exercised within reasonable constraints, due process is satisfied.").

measures to help assure that the general standards, which by their nature must remain quite vague, are applied in a manner that is as fair and accurate as possible. This requires, first, that trial judges instruct juries precisely and completely on the nature of punitive damages, the standards for their availability, and the conditions under which such damages may or may not be applicable to the facts of the particular case.[51] In addition, juries will have a much sounder basis for rendering principled decisions if judges instruct them on the types of factors generally relevant to culpability.[52] An important way that both trial and appellate courts can manage the vagueness problem is to scrutinize the sufficiency of the evidence for the award, from motions for summary judgment and directed verdict through post-trial motions and appeal.[53] Finally, both trial and appellate courts should explicitly particularize why the award was or was not deserved in light of the legal standards, the doctrine's goals, and the facts of the particular case.[54]

### Amount of Punitive Damages Awards

One of the most perplexing problems for courts and juries has been how to determine an appropriate *amount* for a punitive damages award. Measuring and controlling punitive damages award amounts is difficult in all tort cases, but products liability litigation adds a particularly high risk that excessive verdicts will be levied against defendant manufacturers. For example, a California jury in 1999 levied a punitive damages assessment of $4.8 billion against General Motors for locating the gas tank of a 1979 Chevrolet Malibu behind the rear axle close to the rear bumper, which caused the car to burst into flames when hit at high speed from the rear.[55] Although the trial court remitted the award by a factor of almost five, to $1.09 billion,[56] even the remitted assessment is an enormous civil fine on any scale. Multiple lawsuits compound the

---

**51.** See §§ 18.6 and 18.7, below.

**52.** In her dissent in Pacific Mut. Life Ins. Co. v. Haslip, 499 U.S. 1, 42, 52 (1991), Justice O'Connor referred to the list of culpability factors (the so-called *Green Oil* factors) which Alabama appellate courts use for reviewing punitive awards: "By giving these factors to juries, the State would be providing them with some specific standards to guide their discretion. This would substantially enhance the fairness and rationality of the State's punitive damages system." Id. at 57. *But cf.* BMW of N. Am., Inc. v. Gore, 517 U.S. 559, 586, 589–97 (1996) (Breyer, J., concurring). A list of culpability factors in products liability cases is provided in § 18.4, above.

**53.** See, e.g., Sturm, Ruger & Co. v. Day, 594 P.2d 38, 48 (Alaska 1979) ("[J]udicial scrutiny over the awards provides a partial justification for allowing such awards in the first place. The spectre of bankruptcy and excessive punishment can be in part dispelled to the extent that trial and appellate courts exercise their powers of review."). See also American Laundry Mach. Indus. v. Horan, 412 A.2d 407, 417–

19 (Md. Ct. Spec. App. 1980); Wangen v. Ford Motor Co., 294 N.W.2d 437, 461 (Wis. 1980); Rinker v. Ford Motor Co., 567 S.W.2d 655, 668–69 (Mo. Ct. App. 1978). See generally Mallor & Roberts, Punitive Damages: Toward a Principled Approach, 31 Hastings L.J. 639, 670 (1980) ("the very power of the remedy demands that judges exercise close control over the imposition and assessment of punitive damages"); Owen, Problems in Assessing Punitive Damages Against Manufacturers of Defective Products, 49 U. Chi. L. Rev. 1, 50–59 (1982).

**54.** The provision of written reasons for judicial action on punitive damages awards is an especially important reform development, discussed in § 18.6, below.

**55.** Anderson v. General Motors Corp., No. BC116926, 1999 WL 1466627 (L.A. Cty. Super. Ct. 1999). See White, Jury Orders GM to Pay $4.9 Billion (AP), The State (Columbia, S.C.), July 10, 1999, at A1.

**56.** See Biddle, G.M. Verdict Cut $3.9 Billion in Suit Over Explosion, Wall St. J., Aug. 27, 1999, at B5.

problem of measuring and controlling amounts of punitive damages assessments, as illustrated by the asbestos litigation in recent decades (which probably helped to bankrupt that industry),[57] and by the cigarette litigation which most spectacularly included a $145 billion verdict against tobacco manufacturers in a Florida cigarette smoker class action that eventually was reversed.[58]

Various measurement problems concerning the calculation of proper amounts of punitive damages awards are examined below, including standards of measurement; the admissibility of post-marketing, post-accident, and other types of evidence; and the risk of overpunishment in mass-disaster litigation. Additionally, certain judicial control techniques for dealing with these problems are briefly discussed.

### Standards of Measurement

Under the *Restatement (Second) of Torts*, followed in most jurisdictions,[59] the trier of fact determines the amount of a punitive damages award based upon a consideration of "the character of the defendant's act, the nature and extent of the harm to the plaintiff which the defendant caused or intended to cause, and the wealth of the defendant."[60] As with the standards of *liability* for punitive damages just discussed, courts and commentators long have criticized the vague standards governing the *amount* of such awards.[61] As with the liability standards defining when punitive damages are appropriate, there really is no entirely satisfactory answer to the vagueness problem in determining the amount of such damages.

The flagrancy of the misconduct (reprehensibility) is thought to be the primary consideration in determining the amount of a punitive damages award,[62] but putting the reprehensibility notion to principled use in ascertaining proper amounts of such damages is probably even more difficult than in rendering the underlying liability determination.

**57.** See § 10.3, above.

**58.** Liggett Group Inc. v. Engle, 853 So.2d 434 (Fla. Dist. Ct. App. 2003). The jury in Engle v. R.J. Reynolds Tobacco Co. rendered a punitive damages award against five cigarette manufacturers, the Council for Tobacco Research, and the Tobacco Institute, the latter two of which "had provided false data that refuted medical research of the dangers of smoking." Bragg, Jurors in Florida Give Record Award in Tobacco Case—A $144.8 Billion Verdict, N.Y. Times, July 15, 2000, at A1 (New England ed.).

**59.** See, e.g., Owens–Corning Fiberglas Corp. v. Malone, 972 S.W.2d 35, 41–42 (Tex. 1998); Spaur v. Owen–Corning Fiberglas Corp., 510 N.W.2d 854, 867–68 (Iowa 1994); Herman v. Sunshine Chem. Specialties, Inc., 627 A.2d 1081, 1086 (N.J. 1993); Ross v. Black & Decker, Inc., 977 F.2d 1178, 1189 (7th Cir. 1992) (Ill. law). See generally Pace, Recalibrating the Scales of Justice Through National Punitive Damage Reform, 46 Am. U. L. Rev. 1573, 1583 (1997)

("The many factors that legislators and judges have created can be reduced to three basic considerations: (1) the character of the defendant's act; (2) the nature and extent of the plaintiff's injuries; and (3) the defendant's wealth.").

**60.** Restatement (2d) Torts § 908(2).

**61.** See, e.g., C. McCormick, Law of Damages 296 (1935); Morris, Punitive Damages in Tort Cases, 44 Harv. L. Rev. 1173, 1189 (1931). See also Browning–Ferris Industries of Vt. v. Kelco Disposal, Inc., 492 U.S. 257, 281 (1989) (Brennan, J., concurring) ("Guidance like this is scarcely better than no guidance at all."); Owen, The Moral Foundations of Punitive Damages, 40 Ala. L. Rev. 705, 731 (1989) ("a more vague basis for measurement could hardly be devised").

**62.** See, e.g., BMW of N. Am., Inc. v. Gore, 517 U.S. 559, 574 (1996). See also Barnett v. La Societe Anonyme Turbomeca France, 963 S.W.2d 639, 662 (Mo. Ct. App. 1997).

Yet, similar problems of indeterminacy surround the basis of liability for other forms of damages in private law, such as pain and suffering, mental anguish, and loss of reputation. Moreover, the criminal law has always had to deal with the problem of determining proper levels of punishment for serious misconduct based upon a host of intangible considerations, including the heinousness of the crime. If juries, trial judges, and appellate courts earnestly seek to apply the standards of measurement (such as they may be) to the factual circumstances of each case, with the purpose of achieving the goals of punitive damages, the determination of the amount of such awards should have at least a basic grounding in principle.

In fixing the size of a punitive damages award, the trier of fact is principally guided by the functions of punitive damages, often summarized as punishment and deterrence[63] but including compensation and the other specific purposes discussed above.[64] Thus, the three conventional standards for ascertaining an appropriate award—reprehensibility, actual and potential harm, and the defendant's wealth—together embrace the central objectives of punitive damages awards. Because each of the separate punitive damages functions—retribution, education, deterrence, compensation, and law enforcement—requires an assessment of a different amount, selecting a particular amount for any punitive damages award requires finding a balance of how the various objectives in the aggregate may most effectively and fairly be achieved on the facts of a particular case. While measuring punitive damages assessments according to the combined objectives of such awards may be exceedingly complex, it is only fair and logical[65] and now is almost certainly a constitutional requirement.[66]

As discussed above,[67] one might well view restitution as the first important function of punitive damages, a goal which requires that the plaintiff ends up with his or her entire compensatory award after payments of attorneys fees and litigation expenses.[68] In cases where the defendant is found to have flagrantly, perhaps intentionally, invaded the plaintiff's rights, it is only fair that the defendant be required to pay all costs incurred by the plaintiff in rectifying the harmful consequences of the defendant's gross misdeed.[69] Accordingly, once it is established that a defendant's misconduct warrants punitive damages liability, a punitive damages award at a minimum should include an amount that covers attorney's fees and litigation costs. In many cases involving serious injury, a punitive damages award equal to the plaintiff's compensatory damages would roughly cover the depletion of the plaintiff's judgment

---

**63.** See, e.g., Ross v. Black & Decker, Inc., 977 F.2d 1178, 1189 (7th Cir. 1992) (Ill. law).

**64.** See § 18.2, above.

**65.** See Owen, The Moral Foundations of Punitive Damages, 40 Ala. L. Rev. 705, 731–38 (1989); Owen, Punitive Damages in Products Liability Litigation, 74 Mich. L. Rev. 1257, 1314–19 (1976).

**66.** This theoretically perfect basis for determining punitive damages amounts

may logically give way to more practical, second-best measurement approaches, such as using a multiple of the plaintiff's compensatory award. See Owen, The Moral Foundations of Punitive Damages, 40 Ala. L. Rev. 705, 735–38 (1989).

**67.** See § 18.2, above.

**68.** This point is well explained in Bowden v. Caldor, Inc., 710 A.2d 267, 282–83 (Md. 1998).

**69.** See id.; § 18.2, above.

from litigation expenses and other noncompensable losses. In short, without regard to the other functions, the starting point for determining a proper amount for a punitive damages award should be to make the plaintiff truly whole.

The accurate measurement of punitive damages is also promoted by examining the effects of awards of particular amounts on the related goals of deterrence and law enforcement.[70] Thus, if a plaintiff's injuries are relatively mild, the punitive award should be sufficient, together with a recompense of litigation expenses, to encourage the plaintiff to bring a lawsuit.[71] Secondly, as the magnitude of a product hazard increases, so too does the need to deter such behavior and therefore the need to increase the penalty. In addition, and especially important in most products liability cases, punitive damages should be used to attack directly the excessive profit incentive that generated the marketing misconduct. Punitive damages assessments (in the aggregate) should extract the profit realized from all sales of the product in its dangerous condition.[72] Further, the probability at the time of sale that the manufacturer would avoid liability altogether should be factored in as well, so that the profits from the misconduct ordinarily need to be multiplied several times to optimize the deterrent effect.[73]

Any evidence bearing on the likelihood that the particular defendant or other manufacturers might repeat the misbehavior should also be carefully considered. For example, if a defendant proves that it has stopped making an offending product altogether, or that it has otherwise voluntarily cured the defect[74] (especially if the termination occurred prior to the litigation),[75] the need for specific deterrence is correspondingly diminished.[76] Corrective measures taken in good faith, such as overhauling relevant operating procedures and disciplining or discharging em-

---

**70.** See § 18.2, above.

**71.** See, e.g., Fischer v. Johns–Manville Corp., 512 A.2d 466, 482 (N.J. 1986).

**72.** The extent to which a punitive damages award in a particular case should include recovery for the risks and harms to other persons is a particularly difficult problem. See, e.g., Owen, Punitive Damages in Products Liability Litigation, 74 Mich. L. Rev. 1257, 1316 n.286 (1976). It may not be farfetched to conclude that the Supreme Court eventually might rule that due process limits plaintiffs to the recovery of profits (or some multiple thereof) from the defendant's sale of similar products into the jurisdiction. See § 18.7, below.

**73.** See § 18.2, above.

**74.** Or has stopped making misleading representations, in fraudulent misrepresentation cases.

**75.** In one case, the trial court conditioned remittitur of a $10 million punitive damages verdict against the manufacturer of over-absorbent tampons that caused toxic shock syndrome (TSS) on the defendant's removal of the product from the market. The defendant agreed, and the court remitted the verdict to $1.35 million, but the court of appeals reversed on the ground that the trial judge did not have authority to remit on that basis. See O'Gilvie v. International Playtex, Inc., 609 F.Supp. 817 (D. Kan. 1985), rev'd (2–1 decision), 821 F.2d 1438 (10th Cir. 1987).

**76.** This is particularly true if the voluntary termination was accomplished by new management immediately after discovery of the misconduct. See, e.g., Drayton v. Jiffee Chem. Corp., 395 F.Supp. 1081, 1098 (N.D. Ohio 1975). The same principles apply to general deterrence where the entire industry has stopped making or selling products in a defective condition. The asbestos industry in fact is a case in point, but the defendants' efforts in the Florida smoker class action case to convince the jury that the industry had reformed itself fell on twelve deaf ears. See, e.g., Fairclough and Geyelin, Tobacco Companies Rail Against Verdict, Plan to Appeal $144.87 Billion Award, Wall St. J., July 17, 2000, at A3, A6.

ployees responsible for the misconduct,[77] ordinarily should also demonstrate a reformed attitude that reduces the need for specific deterrence. Recalcitrance and cover-up by the manufacturer, on the other hand, either prior to or during the litigation, would indicate an excessive concern with profits and reputation at the expense of the public safety. In such a case, the deterrent and law enforcement functions of punitive damages require that a punitive damages assessment be expanded to teach the lesson soundly that knowingly or recklessly marketing defective products will not pay.

A manufacturer's punishment should correspond to its degree of awareness of both the presence of an excessive risk in its product and the seriousness of the risk of injury presented. Thus, the greater the manufacturer's awareness that its product is excessively hazardous, and the more dangerous that particular hazard is,[78] the more serious its misconduct in marketing the product and the more severe its punishment should be. Also bearing on the seriousness of the offense, and hence on the amount of punishment needed, are the number and level of employees whose actions or conscious inactions contributed to the marketing misconduct or its cover-up. Furthermore, since the number of consumers potentially harmed by a defect increases as more and more products are sold, a manufacturer's culpability and the need for greater punishment commensurately increase as the company fails to remedy the problem over time.[79]

The penalty should not only be proportional to the nature and extent of the misconduct and harm (that is, to reprehensibility together with the actual and potential harm),[80] but it also should be tailored to the wealth of the particular defendant to optimize punishment and deterrence. "The theory is that a penalty which would be sufficient to reform a poor man is likely to make little impression on a rich one; and therefore the richer the defendant is the larger the punitive damages

**77.** If such action is taken in good faith, it should go a long way to refute a claim that the manufacturer had ratified the misconduct and so should undercut a claim of enterprise responsibility for the discharged employees' misconduct in states following the vicarious liability complicity rule.

**78.** The amount of harm actually caused the plaintiff as a result of the defendant's misconduct has some minor relevance to the determination of the amount of punitive damages properly to be assessed in a given case "by analogy to the doctrine of the criminal law by which the seriousness of a crime may depend upon the harm done.... " Restatement (2d) Torts § 908, cmt. *e*. However, more relevant are the magnitude of the aggregate risk of harm to the public created by the misbehavior and the extent of the defendant's awareness that its marketing behavior would generate a major risk to public safety. See Owen, Punitive Damages in Products Liability Litigation, 74 Mich. L. Rev. 1257, 1317 n.291

(1976); Morris, Punitive Damages in Tort Cases, 44 Harv. L. Rev. 1173, 1181 (1931).

**79.** See, e.g., Tetuan v. A.H. Robins Co., 738 P.2d 1210 (Kan. 1987).

**80.** It is fundamental in punishment theory, in punitive damages measurement as much as in sentencing in criminal law, that the punishment should match the "crime." See, e.g., Sand Hill Energy, Inc. v. Ford Motor Co., 83 S.W.3d 483, 493 (Ky. 2002) (emphasizing especially culpable conduct of defendant in reinstating $15 million award of punitive damages), vacated by Ford Motor Co. v. Smith, 538 U.S. 1028 (2003), vacated and remanded, Sand Hill Energy, Inc. v. Smith, 142 S.W.3d 153 (Ky. 2004); Bowden v. Caldor, Inc., 710 A.2d 267, 278 (Md. 1998) ("The most important legal rule in this area, applicable to every punitive damages award, is that the amount of punitive damages 'must not be disproportionate to the gravity of the defendant's

award should be.''[81] The financial condition of a manufacturer thus should be ascertained together with the probable impact thereon of a proposed punitive damages assessment.[82]

Finally, the punitive damages assessment should reflect other "punishment" already or likely to be imposed upon the manufacturer as a result of its marketing misconduct. This other punishment might possibly be viewed as including compensatory damages awards to the plaintiff

wrong.' ''); BMW of N. Am., Inc. v. Gore, 517 U.S. 559, 575 (1996).

**81.** Morris, Punitive Damages in Tort Cases, 44 Harv. L. Rev. 1173, 1191 (1931). " 'Based upon the theory that it will take a greater penalty to dissuade the rich than the poor from oppressive conduct, the wealth of the defendant may be shown so that the jury will assess damages which will punish it.' '' Ford Motor Co. v. Ammerman, 705 N.E.2d 539, 561 (Ind. Ct. App. 1999). See also Henley v. Philip Morris Inc., 5 Cal.Rptr.3d 42, 86 (Ct. App. 2003) ("The wealthier the wrongdoer, the larger the punitive damages must be."), review granted and cause transferred, 81 P.3d 223 (Cal. 2003).

**82.** This principle is rooted in logic and justice and is accepted by most courts today. See, e.g., Liggett Group Inc. v. Engle, 853 So.2d 434, at 458 (Fla. Dist. Ct. App. 2003) ("A defendant's financial capacity is a crucial factor in determining the appropriateness of a punitive damages award."); Williams v. Philip Morris Inc., 48 P.3d 824, 841 (Or. Ct. App. 2002) ("the defendant's wealth is an important consideration; an award that might be serious punishment for one defendant could be only a minor inconvenience for another"), vacated and remanded for reconsideration on other grounds, Philip Morris USA, Inc. v. Williams, 540 U.S. 801 (2003), punitive award reconsidered and reinstated, 92 P.3d 126 (Or. Ct. App. 2004) (concluding, again based in part on defendant's wealth, including net worth of $17 billion and annual profits of $1.6 billion, that $79.5 million punitive award was reasonable, proportionate to the wrong to the plaintiff and the public in the state, and hence comported with Supreme Court due process guidelines); In re New Orleans Train Car Leakage Fire Litig., 795 So.2d 364, 388 (La. Ct. App. 2001) ("The importance of the defendant's financial situation to the goals of punishment and deterrence is obvious: What may be awesome punishment for an impecunious individual defendant [may be] wholly insufficient to influence the behavior of a prosperous corporation."); Bryant v. Waste Mgmt., Inc., 536 S.E.2d 380, 386 (S.C. Ct. App. 2000) ("Although a defendant's net worth has been the standard to prove a corporation's ability to pay punitive damages, net worth is merely one indicia of a corporation's financial condition."); Bow-

den v. Caldor, Inc., 710 A.2d 267, 278 (Md. 1998) (a "very important principle, long recognized under Maryland law, is that the amount of punitive damages 'should not be disproportionate to . . . the defendant's ability to pay.' ''); Robertson Oil Co. v. Phillips Petroleum Co., 14 F.3d 373, 380–81 (8th Cir. 1993) (Ark. law) (use of such evidence not unconstitutional). See generally Restatement (2d) Torts § 908(2) and cmt. e. Compare the civil penalties provision of the National Traffic and Motor Vehicle Safety Act of 1966: "In determining the amount of a civil penalty or compromise, the appropriateness of the penalty or compromise to the size of the business of the person charged and the gravity of the violation shall be considered." 49 U.S.C.A. § 30165(c).

In the case of corporate enterprises, wealth generally has been considered provable by a showing of the institution's net worth. See, e.g., Dewick v. Maytag Corp., 324 F.Supp.2d 889 (N.D. Ill. 2004); Liggett Group Inc. v. Engle, 853 So.2d 434 (Fla. Dist. Ct. App. 2003); Nevada Cement Co. v. Lemler, 514 P.2d 1180, 1183 (Nev. 1973); Richards Co. v. Harrison, 262 So.2d 258, 264 (Fla. Dist. Ct. App. 1972). Other financial data have also been accepted as relevant to the determination of wealth. See, e.g., Herman v. Sunshine Chem. Specialties, Inc., 627 A.2d 1081 (N.J. 1993) (gross sales as well as net worth are sufficient evidence for establishing a corporation's ability to pay punitive damages); Dunn v. HOVIC, 1 F.3d 1371 (3d Cir. 1993) (V.I. law) (annual average after-tax earnings used to determine ability to pay); Barnett v. La Societe Anonyme Turbomeca France, 963 S.W.2d 639, 654–55 (Mo. Ct. App. 1997) (gross sales, as well as net worth, legitimate evidence of manufacturer's "financial status"); Vollert v. Summa Corp., 389 F.Supp. 1348, 1352 (D. Haw. 1975) (authorized or stated capital; net worth; gross income; and net income); Herman v. Hess Oil V.I. Corp., 379 F.Supp. 1268, 1277 (D. V.I. 1974), aff'd, 524 F.2d 767 (3d Cir. 1975) (net worth and net income; balance sheet and income statement both admitted into evidence). The logical and constitutional appropriateness of considering manufacturer wealth evidence in setting punitive damages awards is explored in § 18.7, below.

and to other injured consumers,[83] but it most certainly includes punitive damages awarded to other plaintiffs and any criminal penalties.[84]

In summary, proper measurement of a punitive damages award in a products liability case is advanced by a careful consideration of factors such as the following:

(1)  the amount of the plaintiff's litigation expenses;

(2)  the seriousness of the hazard to the public;

(3)  the profitability of the marketing misconduct (increased by an appropriate multiple);

(4)  the attitude and conduct of the enterprise upon discovery of the misconduct;

(5)  the degree of the manufacturer's awareness of the hazard and of its excessiveness;

(6)  the number and level of employees involved in causing or covering up the marketing misconduct;

(7)  the duration of both the improper marketing behavior and its cover-up;

(8)  the financial condition of the enterprise and the probable effect thereon of a particular judgment; and

(9)  the total punishment the enterprise probably will receive from other sources.

Precise measurement of a punitive damages award simply is not possible because of the indeterminate nature of the disparate goals it serves. Yet a number of courts,[85] legislatures,[86] commentators,[87] the Commerce Department's Model Uniform Products Liability Act,[88] and the Model Punitive Damages Act[89] all agree that the careful use of

**83.** See Morris, Punitive Damages in Tort Cases, 44 Harv. L. Rev. 1173, 1188 (1931). However, one might well think that such compensatory damages payments should be viewed as restitution rather than as punishment. Compare Fischer v. Johns–Manville Corp., 512 A.2d 466, 477 (N.J. 1986).

**84.** See Bowden v. Caldor, Inc., 710 A.2d 267, 281–82 (Md. 1998); Dunn v. HOVIC, 1 F.3d 1371, 1385–91 (3d Cir. 1993) (V.I. law); Owen, Punitive Damages in Products Liability Litigation, 74 Mich. L. Rev. 1257, 1319 (1976); Morris, Punitive Damages in Tort Cases, 44 Harv. L. Rev. 1173, 1187–88, 1195–98 (1931); Restatement (2d) Torts § 908 cmt. *e.*

**85.** See, e.g., Coffey v. Fayette Tubular Prods., 929 S.W.2d 326 (Tenn. 1996); Jonathan Woodner Co. v. Breeden, 665 A.2d 929, 941 n.19 (D.C. 1995). Early products liability cases taking this approach were Sturm, Ruger & Co. v. Day, 594 P.2d 38, 48 n.17 (Alaska 1979), on rehearing, 615 P.2d 621 (Alaska 1980); Wangen v. Ford Motor Co., 294 N.W.2d 437, 460 (Wis. 1980). See also

BMW of N. Am., Inc. v. Gore, 517 U.S. 559, 586 (1996) (Breyer, J., concurring) (noting that use of specific measurement factors reduces risk of arbitrary awards).

**86.** See, e.g., Minn. Stat. § 549.20(3); Or. Rev. Stat. § 30.925; Kan. Stat. Ann. § 60–3701(b), § 60–3702(b); Miss. Code Ann. § 11–1–65(e); Or. Rev. Stat. § 30.925; Mont. Code Ann § 27–1–221(2).

**87.** See, e.g., Pace, Recalibrating the Scales of Justice Through National Punitive Damage Reform, 46 Am. U. L. Rev. 1573, 1581–85, 1632–64 (1997). See id. at 1638 ("Most importantly, federal reform should articulate a uniform set of factors for mandatory consideration in calculating punitive damage awards.").

**88.** See Model Uniform Product Liability Act § 120(B) (U.S. Dep't of Commerce 1979), reprinted in 44 Fed. Reg. at 62,714, 62,748 (1979).

**89.** Uniform Law Commissioners' Model Punitive Damages Act § 7, 14 U.L.A. 128, 129 (cum. ann. pocket pt. 2003).

factors such as those above[90] should help considerably to reduce the risk of capriciously determined awards and to assure that punitive damages awards assessed in products liability cases are more consistent with their underlying objectives.

### Post-Event and Other Types of Evidence

As previously discussed, one of the most important aspects of punitive damages is retributive justice, an objective which looks backward in an effort to punish a defendant according to its just deserts. To fulfill this function, a punitive damages award should assure that the defendant is required to fully compensate the plaintiff for any loss, that the defendant is deprived of any profit from the misconduct, and that the defendant's suffering is proportionate to the grievousness of the act, all as discussed above.[91] Evidence pertinent to each of these sub-goals of punitive damages is relevant and ordinarily should be admissible. While evidence of the plaintiff's losses and the defendant's profits often will be concrete, evidence supporting the other aspects of the retributive justice function ordinarily must rest circumstantially upon the particulars of the defendant's conduct and attitude toward the relevant safety issues at the time it made and sold the product.

Deterrence is widely viewed as another central purpose of punitive damages, and such awards should be large enough to discourage both the defendant and potential offenders from similarly misbehaving in the future, as previously discussed.[92] As with the retributive justice function, deterrence requires, for a start, that the defendant be made to disgorge its entire profit from the particular act of misconduct. But optimal deterrence requires further that the amount of actual profit be multiplied, sometimes many-fold, to serve as a "filler" for similarly harmful acts of misconduct that were not caught and punished and thus to reflect the probability that the defendant would escape punishment for its flagrant misbehavior. Determining what multiplier will fulfill this role in particular cases is exceedingly difficult, and the endeavor is filled with quagmires. In every case, the multiplier should reflect the particular defendant's specific-deterrence needs as well as the amount of punishment necessary to discourage other potential offenders (general deterrence) and to achieve the other goals of punitive damages.[93]

The principal deterrence focus, in fairness to defendants, ordinarily should be on the specific-deterrence issue of how much punishment is necessary to discourage the defendant from repeating the misconduct for which it is being held responsible. For example, a defendant may have voluntarily terminated the misbehavior, as by warning of the danger, curing an unsafe design or misrepresentation, or recalling the product. If a manufacturer proves that it promptly took such remedial action upon discovery of a serious product hazard, especially if it did so before or

**90.** These factors were originally proposed in Owen, Punitive Damages in Products Liability Litigation, 74 Mich. L. Rev. 1257, 1319 (1976). See also Owen, Problems in Assessing Punitive Damages Against Manufacturers of Defective Products, 49 U. Chi. L. Rev. 1, 50–52 (1982).

**91.** In addition, awards should be large enough to catch the attention of potential offenders in order to achieve the educational function of punitive damages.

**92.** See § 18.2, above.

**93.** See id.

early in any litigation, then the need for specific deterrence is eliminated or at least diminished.[94] Similarly, if a manufacturer shows that it voluntarily undertook other corrective measures—as by disciplining or discharging employees responsible for the misconduct, or instituting new safety procedures or improving old ones—such evidence normally will demonstrate a reformed attitude that diminishes the need for specific deterrence. On the other hand, a manufacturer which recalcitrantly denies the existence of a serious safety hazard, especially if the enterprise affirmatively tries to conceal the hazard, shows an unrepentant corporate heart. Sometimes such evidence is very strong, as when a manufacturer denies the existence of, hides, or even destroys[95] important documentary evidence revealing the defendant's knowledge of a serious safety hazard (and possibly a cheap and simple way to fix it), or when it improperly obstructs the efforts of a governmental regulatory safety agency investigating a product hazard.[96]

Because evidence of an enterprise's continued marketing misbehavior, as well as evidence of a cover-up of earlier misbehavior, concerns conduct that occurs *after* a defendant's initial marketing decision, and sometimes even after the plaintiff's accident, courts must determine the relevance of such post-marketing and post-accident evidence. Such post-event misconduct evidence normally is irrelevant to the underlying claim for *compensatory* damages, since that claim must be established by evidence that culminates in the defendant's legally wrongful act or omission and the plaintiff's harm. Similarly, the question of a defendant's liability for *punitive* damages—based on its conscious or reckless violation of the plaintiff's rights—logically must be based upon how and why the defendant acted in a way that resulted in the plaintiff's harm.[97] Yet, post-sale conduct may be relevant to the punitive damages liability issue if the defendant could and should have warned the plaintiff or recalled the product after sale, and wrongfully failed to do so.[98] Indeed, flagrant post-marketing indifference to consumer safety has been a dominant ground for punitive damages against manufacturers of defective products from the inception of such awards in products liability cases in the 1960s.[99] Moreover, evidence of post-sale and even post-accident misconduct toward other plaintiffs may be relevant circumstan-

**94.** This is particularly true if the voluntary termination was accomplished by new management immediately after discovery of the misconduct. See, e.g., Drayton v. Jiffee Chem. Corp., 395 F.Supp. 1081, 1098 (N.D. Ohio 1975).

**95.** See, e.g., Jimenez v. Chrysler Corp., 74 F.Supp.2d 548 (D.S.C. 1999) (defendant destroyed videotapes of crash tests), rev'd, 269 F.3d 439 (4th Cir. 2001); Tetuan v. A.H. Robins Co., 738 P.2d 1210, 1240 (Kan. 1987) (defendant "consigned hundreds of documents to the furnace").

**96.** See, e.g., Jimenez v. Chrysler Corp., 74 F.Supp.2d 548 (D. S.C. 1999) (defendant obstructed NHTSA investigation into liftgate latch defect), rev'd, 269 F.3d 439 (4th Cir. 2001).

**97.** See, e.g., Barnett v. La Societe Anonyme Turbomeca France, 963 S.W.2d 639, 651 (Mo. Ct. App. 1997) (punitive damages liability requires "a showing that the defendant had actual knowledge of the defect and danger at the time the product was sold").

**98.** See, e.g., Gonzales v. Surgidev Corp., 899 P.2d 594, 598 (N.M. 1995) (post-sale evidence relevant to defendant's mental state in continuing to market its product despite mounting evidence of safety problems).

**99.** See Rustad, Unraveling Punitive Damages: Current Data and Further Inquiry, 1998 Wis. L. Rev. 15, 49–50; Owen, Punitive Damages in Products Liability Litigation, 74 Mich. L. Rev. 1257, 1352–61 (1976); § 18.3, above.

tially to show a course of conduct that is probative of the defendant's pre-event state of mind. On whatever ground, however, post-event misconduct evidence must be tied in some fair way to the defendant's violation of the plaintiff's rights to be admissible on the issue of a manufacturer's *liability* for punitive damages.

But once a plaintiff introduces sufficient evidence of a manufacturer's conscious or reckless indifference to the plaintiff's rights to allow a jury to assess a punitive award, evidence of *post*-event misconduct is logically relevant and admissible on the issue of the *amount* of punishment that may be appropriate. Unlike retribution, the deterrence goal of punitive damages is *forward*-looking, which fairly opens up a much broader realm of inquiry into a variety of factors—the defendant's attitude toward a product hazard and its consequences; the defendant's financial condition; and other matters from the moment the product is first placed on the market, through the defendant's first receipt of information concerning product safety failures, to the very date of trial. Indeed, from a deterrence perspective, the most relevant type of evidence may well be the defendant's state of mind (and financial status) proved to exist at the time of trial. While some courts have disagreed,[100] a manufacturer's obstruction of litigation,[101] or unrepentant testimony by its top executives,[102] would appear to show a present unwillingness to accept responsibility that requires a higher punitive award to achieve the retributive and deterrent goals of punitive damages. Similar to the breadth of coverage in pre-sentencing reports on actors convicted of crimes,[103] any evidence relevant to how much punishment may be neces-

**100.** Litigation misdeeds "are not proper grist for an award of punitive damages. Punitive damages must derive from the wrongful conduct giving rise to a cause of action. Such damages are not to be awarded as a sanction for a party's misconduct during litigation. Rather, the remedy for such wrongdoing may be found in the trial court's contempt power and rules of court...." Kopczick v. Hobart Corp., 721 N.E.2d 769, 779 (Ill. App. Ct. 1999). See also Gonzales v. Surgidev Corp., 899 P.2d 594, 598 (N.M. 1995).

**101.** See, e.g., Hundley v. Rite Aid of S.C., Inc., 529 S.E.2d 45, 55 (S.C. Ct. App. 2000) (defendant's conduct throughout discovery and litigation revealed a "clear pattern of abusive and obstructionist behavior"); Cloroben Chem. Corp. v. Comegys, 464 A.2d 887, 889–92 (Del. 1983).

**102.** Conversely, if responsible executives prove to be truly repentant of prior marketing misbehavior, particularly if the misconduct was engaged in by employees who have since left the company, there ordinarily is much less need for specific deterrence. In the Florida class action litigation against the tobacco industry, the chief executive officers of the tobacco companies took the stand in an effort to convince the jury that they were repentant, listing the ways in which their companies had changed, how they had begun to try to stop youth smoking, and how they had (finally) become forthright about the dangers of smoking. See Kaufman (Wash. Post), Jury Orders Tobacco Firms to Pay $145B—Florida Verdict Is Record Penalty, Boston Globe, July 15, 2000, A1 at A10. The $145 billion punitive damages verdict suggests the jury was not convinced.

**103.** See, e.g., United States v. Lee, 540 F.2d 1205 (4th Cir. 1976) (for sentencing, federal court may conduct a broad, largely unlimited inquiry). See generally 21A Am. Jur. 2d Criminal Law § 808, at 73–74 (1998) (there is no limitation on information about the background, character, or conduct of a convict that a federal court may consider for sentencing; "any circumstance that aids the sentencing court in deriving a more complete and true picture regarding the convicted person's background, history, or behavior is properly considered"). In BMW of N. Am., Inc. v. Gore, 517 U.S. 559, 573 n.19 (1996), the Supreme Court compared the kinds of evidence proper in determining an amount of punitive damages to the broad kinds of evidence habitual offender statutes allow for sentencing criminals, including prior convictions, convictions in other jurisdictions, and past criminal behavior that did not result in a

sary for retribution or deterrence-without any artificial temporal limitation-is logically admissible for determining the amount of a punitive damages assessment.[104]

### *Risk of Over–Punishment in Mass–Disaster Litigation*

One of the most troublesome aspects of punitive damages awards in products liability litigation is their potential not only to punish an offending enterprise but also to impair its finances severely or even to bankrupt it.[105] If a product is dangerously defective because of inadequate warnings or design, or because of a recurring flaw in manufacture, hundreds or thousands of similar injuries may result from a single defect in the product line. Such a result can be a "mass disaster" for both the consuming public and the manufacturer. In such situations, as presently in the asbestos industry, the manufacturer may be overwhelmed by the resulting liability for compensatory damages alone; massive additional awards of punitive damages to each plaintiff may virtually ensure the manufacturer's bankruptcy, destroying the enterprise and depriving plaintiffs of corporate funds to cover even their actual damages.[106] Since the purpose of punitive damages is to punish a defendant, not to bankrupt it,[107] and since the law's first objective should be to compensate victims for their losses before punishing the offending enterprise, fashioning a proper role for punitive damages in mass-disaster litigation is a profoundly complex problem that scholars have studied and debated at length.[108]

The best example of the kinds of problems punitive damages can raise in mass-disaster products liability cases is the asbestos litigation arising out of the sale by suppliers of a useful but insidiously dangerous product over many decades without warning of its dangers. Tens of thousands of persons have died of asbestos diseases already, and many thousands more will die from mesothelioma or become disabled from

---

conviction, and even lawful behavior relevant to the defendant's prospects for rehabilitation.

**104.** See, e.g., Bowden v. Caldor, Inc., 710 A.2d 267, 279 (Md. 1998) ("repeated or frequent misconduct of the same nature, misconduct of long duration, attempts to conceal or cover-up the misconduct, failure to take corrective action, and similar circumstances, support the deterrence value of a significant award"). See also Mattison v. Dallas Carrier Corp., 947 F.2d 95, 109–110 (4th Cir. 1991) (S.C. law).

**105.** See Roginsky v. Richardson–Merrell, Inc., 378 F.2d 832, 839–41 (2d Cir. 1967) (N.Y. law). See generally Carroll, Hensler, Abrahamse, Gross, White, Ashwood, and Sloss, Asbestos Litigation Costs and Compensation, RAND (2002).

**106.** See, e.g., Fischer v. Johns–Manville Corp., 512 A.2d 466, 478 (N.J. 1986); Roginsky v. Richardson–Merrell, Inc., 378 F.2d 832, 839–40 (2d Cir. 1967) (N.Y. law). See generally Carroll, Hensler, Abrahamse, Gross, White, Ashwood, and Sloss, Asbestos

Litigation Costs and Compensation, RAND (2002).

**107.** See, e.g., Bowden v. Caldor, Inc., 710 A.2d 267, 278 (Md. 1998); In re Northern Dist. of Cal. "Dalkon Shield" IUD Prods. Liab. Litig., 526 F.Supp. 887, 899 (N.D. Cal. 1981).

**108.** See Gash, Solving the Multiple Punishment Problem: A Call for a National Punitive Damages Registry, 99 Nw. U.L. Rev. ___ (2005); Phillips, Multiple Punitive Damages Awards, 39 Vill. L. Rev. 433 (1994); G. Schwartz, Mass Torts and Punitive Damages: A Comment, 39 Vill. L. Rev. 415 (1994); Bernstein, Punitive Damages in Mass Products Liability, 1 Prod. Liab. L.J. 327 (1990); Saks and Blanck, Justice Improved: The Unrecognized Benefits of Aggregation and Sampling in the Trial of Mass Torts, 44 Stan. L. Rev. 815 (1992); Seltzer, Punitive Damages in Mass Tort Litigation: Addressing the Problems of Fairness, Efficiency and Control, 52 Fordham L. Rev. 37 (1983); Owen, Punitive Damages in Products Liability Litigation, 74 Mich. L. Rev. 1257, 1322–25 (1976).

asbestosis (a serious lung disorder) for decades to come. Compensatory damages alone will amount to many billions of dollars, and courts have assessed hundreds of millions of dollars in punitive damages against many asbestos companies for failing to warn of a danger they knew existed. More than a dozen manufacturers (most notably Johns–Manville, or Manville) have gone into bankruptcy, in part because of liability for punitive damages on top of a crushing liability for the actual losses of so many plaintiffs.[109] More recently, the tobacco industry has increasingly felt the bite of large punitive damages on account of its fraudulent concealment for decades of the addictive nature and health risks of smoking cigarettes.[110] In the Florida smokers class action litigation, the jury assessed the industry $145 billion in punitive damages (subsequently reversed),[111] far more than the combined assets of the entire industry.[112]

A host of problems with punitive damages arise in the mass-disaster context, which have been examined at length by commentators[113] and the courts,[114] and only a couple aspects of the problems can be touched on here. A recurring proposal for resolving such problems is the so-called "one-bite," "single-shot," or "first-comer" approach to punitive damages by which a defendant would be subjected to only one punitive damages assessment for a single marketing decision and would be shielded thereafter from any further liability for punitive damages.[115] This approach,

**109.** On the asbestos litigation, see, e.g., Cimino v. Raymark Indus., Inc., 751 F.Supp. 649 (E.D. Tex. 1990), aff'd in part, vacated in part, 151 F.3d 297 (5th Cir. 1998); Dunn v. HOVIC, 1 F.3d 1371 (3d Cir. 1993) (V.I. law); Jackson v. Johns–Manville Sales Corp., 781 F.2d 394 (5th Cir. 1986) (Miss. law) ("Jackson III," terminating lengthy litigation); Fischer v. Johns–Manville Corp., 512 A.2d 466 (N.J. 1986); and other cases collected in § 18.1, note 88, above. See generally Edley & Weiler, Asbestos: A Multi-Billion Dollar Crisis, 30 Harv. J. on Legis. 383 (1993); Page, Asbestos and the Dalkon Shield: Corporate America on Trial, 85 Mich. L. Rev. 1324 (1987) (hereinafter, Asbestos and the Dalkon Shield); Saks & Blanck, Justice Improved: The Unrecognized Benefits of Aggregation and Sampling in the Trial of Mass Torts, 44 Stan. L. Rev. 815, 816 (1992).

Another mass-disaster products liability litigation involving punitive damages concerned the Dalkon Shield, an intrauterine device that injured thousands of women, bankrupting its manufacturer, the A.H. Robins Company. See, e.g., In re A.H. Robins Co. v. Mabey, 880 F.2d 769, 776 (4th Cir. 1989) (Va. law) (discussing personal injury trust fund created to process claims of parties injured by bankrupt debtor's Dalkon Shields); In re N. Dist. of Cal. "Dalkon Shield" IUD Prods. Liab. Litig., 526 F.Supp. 887, 899 (N.D. Cal. 1981). See generally Page, Asbestos and the Dalkon Shield, above; Seltzer, Punitive Damages in

Mass Tort Litigation: Addressing the Problems of Fairness, Efficiency and Control, 52 Fordham L. Rev. 37, 72 (1983) (discussing Dalkon Shield class actions).

**110.** See §§ 18.1 and 18.3, above.

**111.** Liggett Group Inc. v. Engle, 853 So.2d 434 (Fla. Dist. Ct. App. 2003).

**112.** See Bragg, Jurors in Florida Give Record Award in Tobacco Case—A $144.8 Billion Verdict, N.Y. Times, July 15, 2000, at A1 (New England ed.); Kaufman (Wash. Post), Jury Orders Tobacco Firms to Pay $145B—Florida Verdict Is Record Penalty, Boston Globe, July 15, 2000, at A1.

**113.** See articles collected above.

**114.** See, e.g., Dunn v. HOVIC, 1 F.3d 1371, 1385–86 (3d Cir. 1993) (V.I. law), modified in part, 13 F.3d 58 (3d Cir. 1993) (asbestos; collecting cases); Jackson v. Johns–Manville Sales Corp. ("Jackson III"), 781 F.2d 394, 396 (5th Cir. 1986) (Miss. law) (asbestos); Fischer v. Johns–Manville Corp., 512 A.2d 466, 481 (N.J. 1986) (same); Roginsky v. Richardson–Merrell, Inc., 378 F.2d 832, 838 (2d Cir. 1967) (N.Y. law) (Friendly, J.) (MER/29, cholesterol-lowering drug litigation). See generally Annot., 11 A.L.R.4th 1261 (1993) (collecting cases on propriety of multiple assessments of punitive damages from common occurrence).

**115.** See Annot., 11 A.L.R.4th 1261, 1262 (1993) (noting the bankruptcy concern, but concluding that bankruptcy nor-

appealing to tort reformers, has been legislatively adopted in at least a couple of states,[116] but it is far too arbitrary and easy to manipulate by defendants to be a sound solution to the mass-disaster problem. Accordingly, the one-bite approach to punitive damages claims in mass disaster litigation has virtually no support in the courts.[117]

A variation on the one-bite approach is to limit punitive damages to a single, aggregate punitive award for division among the entire class of victims.[118] While it may well be that this approach might make sense in a well-administered national class action,[119] any type of aggregative approach to punitive damages is fraught with difficulties of fairness and administration, even in the context of a comprehensive class action. One of the biggest problems with an aggregative approach is the all-or-nothing gamble for both the plaintiffs and defendants. Proof of a flagrantly improper marketing scheme often takes years or even decades

mally is unlikely because of judicial controls).

**116.** Such legislation has been enacted at least in Florida and Georgia. See § 18.6, below.

**117.** See, e.g., Owens–Corning Fiberglas Corp. v. Malone, 972 S.W.2d 35, 49 (Tex. 1998) (stating that rule may "allow only those plaintiffs who win the 'race to the courthouse' to recover punitive damages."); Owens–Corning Fiberglas Corp. v. Golightly, 976 S.W.2d 409 (Ky. 1998); Spaur v. Owens–Corning Fiberglas Corp., 510 N.W.2d 854, 865 (Iowa 1994) ("The vast majority of state and federal courts 'that have addressed the issue have declined to strike punitive damages awards merely because they constituted repetitive punishment for the same conduct.' "); W.R. Grace & Co.—Conn. v. Waters, 638 So.2d 502 (Fla. 1994); Dunn v. HOVIC, 1 F.3d 1371 (3d Cir. 1993), modified in part, 13 F.3d 58 (3d Cir. 1993) (V.I. law); Davis v. Celotex Corp., 420 S.E.2d 557, 565 (W. Va. 1992) ("it seems highly illogical and unfair for courts to determine at what point punitive damage awards should cease"); Juzwin v. Amtorg Trading Corp., 718 F.Supp. 1233 (D.N.J. 1989). See generally, Annot. 11 A.L.R.4th 1261 (1982) (examining one-bite doctrine); Glasscock v. Armstrong Cork Co., 946 F.2d 1085 (5th Cir. 1991) (Tex. law); State ex rel. Young v. Crookham, 618 P.2d 1268, 1272 (Or. 1980) (refusing to "endorse a system of awarding punitive damages which threatens to reduce civil justice to a race to the courthouse steps").

A number of courts have pointed to the irony of a rule that would allow a manufacturer to escape punitive damages liability because its misconduct was so great that it managed to maim and kill enormous quantities of people. See, e.g., Froud v. Celotex Corp., 437 N.E.2d 910, 913 (Ill. App. Ct. 1982), rev'd on other grounds, 456 N.E.2d 131 (Ill. 1983); Fischer v. Johns–Manville

Corp., 512 A.2d 466, 478 (N.J. 1986); Owens–Corning Fiberglas Corp. v. Golightly, 976 S.W.2d 409, 413 (Ky. 1998).

Although the nature of the underlying policy discussion has remained essentially unchanged over the years, the framework of the debate has shifted in recent years from the common law to the Constitution. See, e.g., Owens–Corning Fiberglas Corp. v. Wasiak, 972 S.W.2d 35 (Tex. 1998) (thorough analysis, concluding that punitive damages award in case did not violate due process when considered in aggregate with prior awards). As discussed below, the Supreme Court has ruled that repetitive punitive damage assessments for a single course of behavior are not generally proscribed by the prohibitions against double jeopardy or excessive fines, at least if none of the "penal fine" goes to the state. Although the Court has indicated that the due process clause places some constraints on such awards, it has to date avoided ruling on whether due process in some manner restrains repetitive assessments of this type. For the Supreme Court's recent punitive damages jurisprudence, see § 18.7, below.

**118.** Cf. Ga. Code Ann. § 51–12–5.1 (e)(1) (only one punitive damages award may be recovered from defendant in products liability action, regardless of number of suits brought). Compare McBride v. General Motors Corp., 737 F.Supp. 1563, 1580 (M.D. Ga. 1990) (holding § 51–12–5.1(e)(1) unconstitutional), with Mack Trucks, Inc. v. Conkle, 436 S.E.2d 635 (Ga. 1993) (contra). See also Cabrasser, Unfinished Business: Reaching the Due Process Limits of Punitive Damages in Tobacco Litigation through Unitary Classwide Adjudication, 36 Wake Forest L. Rev. 979 (2001).

**119.** See, e.g., Fischer v. Johns–Manville Corp., 512 A.2d 466, 478–80 (N.J. 1986) (suggesting class actions as best solution).

of litigation before the full story of the defendant's misconduct comes to light, so that plaintiffs' counsel in a single lawsuit early in the litigation usually would be unable to assemble more than a small fraction of the evidence of misconduct that in fact exists. Moreover, most corporate enterprises prefer to divide and conquer, taking their cases one at a time rather than risking total defeat with a catastrophic judgment in a single lawsuit. Accordingly, while plaintiffs' class counsel ordinarily would be delighted to handle a mass-disaster case on a one-shot basis for a potentially enormous fee, and while many courts as a matter of administrative convenience might also be happy to have the punitive damages issue dispensed with in a single shot, virtually no one else would benefit from such an approach. Accordingly, the one-bite aggregate approach has been rejected by almost every court that has considered it.[120]

An interesting approach applied in at least a couple of aggregated asbestos cases has been to have the jury assign a multiplier (perhaps no higher than three) to the compensatory awards assessed against each defendant liable for punitive damages.[121] This type of mass multiplier approach has the very decided advantage of being administratively convenient, and hence efficient, as well as assuring the equal treatment of each of the aggregated plaintiffs in regard to one another and in regard to each defendant. By its very nature, however, it exposes future plaintiffs to a particular risk of being unable to recover even their actual damages if the corporate tills run dry. Thus, courts must be cautious in assigning or allowing multipliers when the aggregate payouts might bankrupt the defendants. By standardizing amounts of punitive damages awards proportionate to each plaintiff's actual damages, the multiplier approach deprives the parties of fully individualized punitive damages computations, a result which has caused at least one state's high court to reject this method as inconsistent with its common law.[122]

Regardless of whether courts adopt a multiplier approach, or simply administer punitive damages claims independently of one another in separate cases over time, they should maintain especially close supervision of punitive damages assessments over the progression of mass-disaster products liability litigation. To protect defendants against the risk of bankruptcy, for the benefit of later plaintiffs as well as the defendants, the courts should be prepared to reduce punitive damages assessments—and ultimately to eliminate them altogether—if and when

---

**120.** See Annot., 11 A.L.R.4th 1261, 1262 (1993).

**121.** See, e.g., Cimino v. Raymark Indus., Inc., 751 F.Supp. 649, 657–58 (E.D. Tex. 1990) (jury assessed punitive damages multipliers ranging from 1.5 to 3.0 depending on defendant), aff'd on point but vacated in part on other grounds, 151 F.3d 297 (5th Cir. 1998). See also ACandS, Inc. v. Godwin, 667 A.2d 116 (Md. 1995) (reversing punitive damages multiplier assessments against two asbestos defendants, one in amount of 1.5 and the other in amount of .35 times compensatory damages, for insuf-

ficient evidence of malice). Note, however, that the Maryland courts have since rejected the use of punitive damages multipliers. See Philip Morris Inc. v. Angeletti, 752 A.2d 200, 249 (Md. 2000). See generally Robinson & Abraham, Collective Justice in Tort Law, 78 Va. L. Rev. 1481, 1490–96 (1992) (discussing the *Cimino* approach); Saks and Blanck, Justice Improved: The Unrecognized Benefits of Aggregation and Sampling in the Trial of Mass Torts, 44 Stan. L. Rev. 815, 816, 821 (1992) (same).

**122.** Philip Morris Inc. v. Angeletti, 752 A.2d 200, 249 (Md. 2000).

a mass-disaster defendant's financial viability becomes truly threatened by the litigation and the payouts.[123]

The risk that defendants may be excessively punished is very real. But so too is the need for the punitive damages remedy in products liability cases involving the marketing of dangerously defective products in flagrant disregard of consumer safety. The risk of excessive punishment, similar to the other punitive damages problems examined in this section, generally can be reduced to an acceptable level through responsible judicial control, as discussed below.[124] On occasion, punitive damages awards will over-punish a manufacturer or otherwise be imposed unfairly. But the benefits to the public from the general use of such awards in products liability cases, even in the mass-disaster context, outweigh the risk of occasional unfair treatment of defendants guilty of flagrant misbehavior.[125]

## § 18.6 JUDICIAL AND LEGISLATIVE REFORM

The various problems with punitive damages explored in the previous section, some only imagined but others very real, suggest a rather compelling need to reform the law of punitive damages in a variety of ways. A number of "reform" proposals are indeed afoot, all supposed to improve the logic and fairness of punitive damages law. It is important to note at the outset, however, that the various reforms are designed to adjust various aspects of how the law of punitive damages is administered, not to eliminate it as a remedy available in appropriate cases. With few exceptions,[1] neither the courts nor the community of scholars has urged that the institution of punitive damages be abolished. In this nation,[2] punitive damages are still considered an important remedy that checks, rectifies, and helps prevent extreme misconduct. In recent decades, however, both courts and legislatures have initiated a series of reforms in an effort to reduce as much as possible the most serious problems with the law and administration of punitive damages.

This section outlines the major types of punitive damages reforms and controls that courts and legislatures have adopted in recent years. The presentation here is intended merely as a survey, and one must turn to the reform literature for comprehensive discussions of particular reforms.[3] The focus here is on common law and statutory reform;

**123.** Thus, multipliers should perhaps be subject to opening for reconsideration on a change in circumstances—such as a substantial and unanticipated increase in claims threatening the defendant's financial viability.

**124.** See § 18.6, below.

**125.** See Owen, Punitive Damages, 74 Mich. L. Rev. 1257, 1325 (1976).

### § 18.6

**1.** For the exceptions, see Kircher and Wiseman, Punitive Damages § 21.18.

**2.** Although most other nations do not have a general doctrine of punitive damages, the British Law Commission has recommended widening their use in Great Britain. See The Law Commission, Aggravated, Exemplary and Restitutionary Damages—A Consultation Paper 114, 173–78 (Consultation Paper No. 132, 1993) (detailing recommendations for expanding use of punitive damages).

**3.** See Kircher and Wiseman, Punitive Damages ch. 21; Rustad and Koenig, The Historical Continuity of Punitive Damages Awards: Reforming the Tort Reformers, 42 Am. U. L. Rev. 1269 (1993) (arguing that punitive damages reform is unnecessary); V. Schwartz and Behrens, Punitive Damages Reform—State Legislatures Can and

constitutional reform of punitive damages, under the due process clause in particular, is examined later.[4]

### Refining the Standards of Liability and Measurement

One of the first and most important reforms that some courts and legislatures have taken is to narrow and refine the standard of liability for punitive damages, sometimes specifying the types of flagrant marketing misbehavior deserving punishment and the culpability factors that a trier of fact might consider in a products liability case, as discussed above.[5] In similar fashion, to assist triers of fact in assessing particular amounts of punitive damages, a number of jurisdictions have specified the factors relevant to the proper measurement of such awards.[6] Both the definitions of the proscribed misconduct and the standards for determining amounts for such awards may be improved by expressly tying them to the goals of punitive damages applicable to the products liability context.[7]

### Prima Facie Case and Other Pretrial Showings; Evidentiary Rulings

Although all courts do not have the power to do so without legislative authorization,[8] California and several other states have legislation[9] requiring a plaintiff to make a prima facie showing of the defendant's liability for punitive damages before punitive damages may be pleaded,[10] discovery of wealth may proceed, evidence of wealth may be admitted, a provisional cap on the amount of a punitive damages award may be removed, or the amount of punitive damages may be argued to the jury.[11] Because considerable financial data on publicly-held corporations is available to plaintiffs' counsel in annual reports and 10-K reports filed with the SEC, protecting a manufacturer's wealth from pretrial discovery probably accomplishes very little in most cases. However, the other reforms beneficially force a court to examine the pleadings and evidence to assure that the plaintiff has a fair case of punitive damages before the jury is exposed to prejudicial and otherwise improper evidence and argument on a defendant's wealth. The prima facie proof requirement also usefully prevents the practice of some plaintiffs' lawyers of routinely asking for punitive damages in every case.[12]

Should Meet the Challenge Issued by the Supreme Court of the United States in Haslip, 42 Am. U. L. Rev. 1365 (1993).

**4.** See § 18.7, below.

**5.** See § 18.5, above.

**6.** See id.

**7.** See §§ 18.2, above, and 18.7, below.

**8.** See, e.g., Nichols v. Hocke, 297 N.W.2d 205 (Iowa 1980).

**9.** See, e.g., Cal. Civ. Code § 3295; Fla. Stat. § 768.72; Minn. Stat. § 549.191.

**10.** See, e.g., Minn. Stat. § 549.191; Fla. Stat. § 768.72. See generally Olson v. Snap Prods., Inc., 29 F.Supp.2d 1027 (D. Minn.

1998) (thorough analysis of Minnesota's requirement).

**11.** See, e.g., Sides v. John Cordes, Inc., 981 P.2d 301, 306 (Okla. 1999) (showing of misconduct necessary for removing cap on punitive damages); Olson v. Snap Prods., Inc., 29 F.Supp.2d 1027 (D. Minn. 1998); Leidholt v. District Court, 619 P.2d 768, 771 (Colo. 1980). See generally Note, Pretrial Discovery of Net Worth in Punitive Damages Cases, 54 S. Cal. L. Rev. 1141, 1148–49 (1981).

**12.** See Rosener v. Sears, Roebuck & Co., 168 Cal.Rptr. 237, 250 (Ct. App. 1980) (Elkington, J., concurring) (noting the "present-day practice of seeking punitive

## Judgments on the Merits

Trial courts generally are reluctant to exercise their powers to grant summary judgment, directed verdicts, judgments notwithstanding verdicts, and new trials; such powers, being in derogation of the judgment of the jury, are properly exercised only with studied care.[13] Yet to avoid the special risks of erroneous jury awards of punitive damages in products liability cases, trial courts should give especially careful consideration to motions of this type. Courts should make every effort to cut through the morass of proof, the semantics of the rules of liability, and the rhetoric of counsel to pass judgment at the earliest reasonable time on whether a fair case really has been made that the manufacturer's conduct was flagrant. If such a fair case has not been made—if, for example, a manufacturer's design choice should instead be placed in the large, gray realm of "close calls" short of moral reprehensibility (as usually will be the case)—the court should relieve the jury of the temptation to base its decision on passion and prejudice, or it should correct the error if the jury in its verdict succumbed to such emotions. In recent decades, trial courts in products liability cases increasingly have ruled for manufacturers on punitive damages claims, on motions for summary judgement,[14] directed verdict,[15] and judgment notwithstanding the verdict.[16]

damages in substantially *all* damage actions"). A former president of the Association of Trial Lawyers of America concurs: "We almost always include a count for punitive damages." Cartwright, Products Liability: Trial Strategy and Tactics, Trial, July 1980, at 38, 39. See also Levit, Punitive Damages: Yesterday, Today and Tomorrow, 1980 Ins. L.J. 257, 259 (1980) ("whereas 25 years ago, the punitive damages case was a rarity, today it is an anomaly when one sees a complaint which does *not* seek punitive damages"). Some plaintiffs' lawyers, however, urge restraint. See, e.g., Igoe, Punitive Damages in Products Liability Cases Should be Allowed, 22 Trial Law. Guide 24, 29 (1978); Kreindler, Punitive Damages in Aviation Litigation—An Essay, 8 Cumb. L. Rev. 607, 617 (1978).

**13.** See C. Wright, Law of Federal Courts § 95 at 640, § 99 at 666 (4th ed. 1983).

**14.** See, e.g., Estep v. Rieter Auto. N. Am., Inc., 774 N.E.2d 323, 329 (Ohio Ct. App. 2002) ("Nothing in the record indicates that any of the parties demonstrated either ill will or a conscious disregard for the safety of others, which would entitle appellant to an award of punitive damages."); Robles v. Shoreside Petroleum, Inc., 29 P.3d 838 (Alaska 2001); Lashlee v. White Consol. Indus., Inc., 548 S.E.2d 821 (N.C. Ct. App. 2001). See also Wagner v. International Harvester Co., 611 F.2d 224, 233 (8th Cir. 1979) (Minn. law) (district court's denial of plaintiff's motion to amend

complaint to include punitive damages issue was proper, and appeal of issue was deemed "to border on the frivolous").

**15.** See, e.g., Mack Trucks, Inc. v. Tackett, 841 So.2d 1107 (Miss. 2003) (affirming trial court's refusal to submit punitive damages claim to jury); Couch v. Astec Indus., Inc., 53 P.3d 398, 411 (N.M. Ct. App. 2002) (evidence that defendant failed to follow formal, written product safety program was insufficient to sustain plaintiff's punitive damages claim); Eiland v. Westinghouse Elec. Corp., 58 F.3d 176, 178 (5th Cir. 1995) (Miss. law) (affirming directed verdict for manufacturer on punitive damages); Turney v. Ford Motor Co., 418 N.E.2d 1079, 1085 (Ill. App. Ct. 1981) (affirming trial court's decision to strike punitive damages count at end of plaintiff's case); Knippen v. Ford Motor Co., 546 F.2d 993, 1003 (D.C. Cir. 1976) (same). See also Wangen v. Ford Motor Co., 294 N.W.2d 437, 457 (Wis. 1980) ("Unless there is evidence from which a jury could find that the wrongdoer's conduct was 'outrageous,' the trial court should not submit the issue of punitive damages to the jury.").

**16.** See, e.g., Ford v. GACS, Inc. 265 F.3d 670, 678 (8th Cir. 2001) (Mo. law) (defendant entitled to j.n.o.v. because evidence did not show that defendant acted with the requisite wantonness); HillRichs v. Avco Corp., 514 N.W.2d 94, 100 (Iowa 1994) (affirming trial court's order granting manufacturer's motion for j.n.o.v. on $1 million punitive damages award).

Particularly since the Supreme Court began its examination of punitive damages awards on due process grounds during the 1990s,[17] but also earlier,[18] appellate courts have shown an increased sense of obligation to subject punitive damage awards to close scrutiny and to reverse them when unwarranted on the record.[19] Scrupulous appellate review is especially important because it is a defendant's final protection against the infliction of punishment that may be very large and unfairly imposed. On the appeal of such awards, the trial record should be scrutinized with special care for the propriety of the evidence, jury argument, jury instructions, and for the sufficiency of the evidence as a whole.[20]

## Standard of Proof

"Because punitive damages are extraordinary and harsh,"[21] many courts[22] and legislatures[23] in recent years have raised the standard of proof from "preponderance of the evidence," the ordinary standard used in civil law litigation, to a "clear and convincing"[24] standard of

**17.** See § 18.7, below.

**18.** See, e.g., Forrest City Mach. Works, Inc. v. Aderhold, 616 S.W.2d 720 (Ark. 1981); Ellis v. Golconda Corp., 352 So.2d 1221 (Fla. Dist. Ct. App. 1977); Moore v. Remington Arms Co., 427 N.E.2d 608 (Ill. App. Ct. 1981); Harley–Davidson Motor Co. v. Wisniewski, 437 A.2d 700, 704–05 (Md. Ct. Spec. App. 1981); American Laundry Mach. Indus. v. Horan, 412 A.2d 407 (Md. Ct. Spec. App. 1980); Johnson v. Husky Indus., Inc., 536 F.2d 645 (6th Cir. 1976) (Tenn. law).

**19.** See, e.g., Quigley Co., Inc. v. Calderon, 2003 WL 77256 (Tex. App. 2003) (reversing $750,000 award, remitted from $15 million, for insufficient evidence of "conscious indifference malice"); Jimenez v. DaimlerChrysler Corp., 269 F.3d 439 (4th Cir. 2001) (S.C. law) (reversing $250 million punitive award; insufficient proof of conduct that was reckless, willful, or wanton); General Motors Corp. v. Sanchez, 997 S.W.2d 584 (Tex. 1999) (reversing $8.5 million punitive award; insufficient evidence of gross negligence); General Motors Corp. v. Moseley, 447 S.E.2d 302 (Ga. Ct. App. 1994) (reversing $101 million punitive award for death of youth in fiery crash of GM pickup truck for improper argument by plaintiff's counsel).

**20.** See Owen, Problems in Assessing Punitive Damages Against Manufacturers of Defective Products, 49 U. Chi. L. Rev. 1, 57–58 (1982). The Supreme Court is finding more and more appellate obligations on the review of punitive awards. See § 18.7, below.

**21.** Rodriguez v. Suzuki Motor Corp., 936 S.W.2d 104, 111 (Mo. 1996) (en banc).

**22.** See, e.g., Wal–Mart, Inc. v. Stewart, 990 P.2d 626 (Alaska 1999); Chicago Hardware & Fixture Co. v. Letterman, 510

S.E.2d 875 (Ga. Ct. App. 1999); General Motors Corp. v. Bell, 714 So.2d 268 (Ala. 1996); Rodriguez v. Suzuki Motor Corp., 936 S.W.2d 104, 109–11 (Mo. 1996) (overruling earlier case; thorough discussion); Jonathan Woodner Co. v. Breeden, 665 A.2d 929,, 932 (D.C. 1995); Kleinschmidt v. Morrow, 642 A.2d 161 (Me. 1994); Hodges v. S.C. Toof & Co., 833 S.W.2d 896 (Tenn. 1992); Lawyers Title Ins. Corp. v. Pokraka, 595 N.E.2d 244 (Ind. 1992); Owens–Illinois, Inc. v. Zenobia, 601 A.2d 633 (Md. 1992); Masaki v. General Motors Corp., 780 P.2d 566, 575 (Haw. 1989); Linthicum v. Nationwide Life Ins. Co., 723 P.2d 675, 681 (Ariz. 1986); Wangen v. Ford Motor Co., 294 N.W.2d 437 (Wis. 1980). See also Roginsky v. Richardson–Merrell, Inc., 378 F.2d 832 (2d Cir. 1967) (N.Y. law) (Friendly, J.).

**23.** See, e.g., Ala. Code § 6–11–20(a); Alaska Stat. § 09.17.020(b); Cal. Civ. Code § 3294(a); Fla. St. Ann. § 768.725; Ga. Code Ann. § 51–12–5.1(b); Ind. Code Ann. § 34–51–3–2; Iowa Code Ann. § 668A.1.1a; Kan. Stat. Ann. § 60–3701(c); Ky. Rev. Stat. Ann. § 411.184(2); Minn. Stat. Ann. § 549.20.1(a); Miss. Code Ann. § 11–1–65(1)(a); Mont. Code Ann. § 27–1–221(5); Nev. Rev. Stat. § 42.005(1); N.J. Stat. Ann. § 2A:15–5.12(a); N.C. Gen. Stat. § 1D–15(b); N.D. Cent. Code § 32–03.2–11(1); Ohio Rev. Code Ann. § 2315.21(D)(3)(b)(i); Okla. Stat. Ann. tit. 23, § 9.1(C) & (D); Or. Rev. Stat. § 18.537(1); Or. Rev. Stat. § 30.925; S.C. Code Ann. § 15–33–135; S.D. Codified Laws § 21–1–4.1; Tex. Civ. Prac. & Rem. Code Ann. § 41.003(a); Utah Code Ann. § 78–18–1(a). Colorado raises the standard of proof for punitive damages to "beyond a reasonable doubt." Colo. Rev. Stat. Ann. § 13–25–127(2).

**24.** Isabel v. Velsicol Chem. Co., 327 F.Supp.2d 915 (W.D. Tenn 2004); "Clear-

proof.[25] This is an important reform that reflects the intermediate position of punitive damages, a "quasi-criminal" remedy,[26] between the civil and criminal law. This salutary adjustment of the standard of proof should serve to focus the decision-maker on the importance of careful deliberation on the merits of the case, and it appears to provide courts with both the authority and obligation to review carefully the sufficiency of the evidence for such awards.

## Compliance with Government Standards

Some states have enacted legislation providing an absolute defense for manufacturers of pharmaceutical drugs to punitive damages for selling drugs that comply with applicable regulations of the Food and Drug Administration.[27] Some states have broader statutes that shield manufacturers of all types of products; but these statutes merely raise a rebuttable presumption that a manufacturer complying with an applicable governmental safety standard is not negligent, or that a product meeting such standards is not defective.[28] Assuming that such a presumption is applicable to the manufacturer,[29] and that it is not rebutted, such a statute should serve to bar punitive as well as compensatory damages.[30]

The basic concept of the compliance-with-law punitive damages defense appears logical and fair, for ordinarily a manufacturer or other

and-convincing evidence is that measure or degree of proof which will produce in the mind of the trier of fact a firm belief or conviction as to the truth of the allegation sought to be established." Sides v. John Cordes, Inc., 981 P.2d 301, 306 n.15 (Okla. 1999). See also Mont. Code Ann. § 27–1–221(b)(5) ("Clear and convincing evidence means evidence in which there is no serious or substantial doubt about the correctness of the conclusions drawn from the evidence."); Ala. Code § 6–11–20(b)(4), defining "clear and convincing evidence" as "[e]vidence that, when weighed against evidence in opposition, will produce in the mind of the trier of fact a firm conviction as to each essential element of the claim and a high probability as to the correctness of the conclusion. Proof by clear and convincing evidence requires a level of proof greater than a preponderance of the evidence or the substantial weight of the evidence, but less than beyond a reasonable doubt."

**25.** See Kircher and Wiseman, Punitive Damages § 21.14; Development in the Law-The Civil Jury, 110 Harv. L. Rev. 1408, 1531 (1997); Annot., 58 A.L.R.4th 878 (1987).

**26.** See § 18.1, above.

**27.** See, e.g., Ariz. Rev. Stat. Ann. § 12–701 (compliance with FDA regulations; proviso where manufacturer knowingly withheld or misrepresented information required by agency); N.J. Stat. Ann. § 2A:58C–5(c) (same); Or. Rev. Stat.

§ 30.927 (same); Utah Code Ann. § 78–18–2 (same).

See generally T. Schwartz, Punitive Damages and Regulated Products, 42 Am. U. L. Rev. 1335 (1993); V. Schwartz and Behrens, Punitive Damages Reform—State Legislatures Can and Should Meet the Challenge Issued by the Supreme Court of the United States in Haslip, 42 Am. U. L. Rev. 1365, 1383–84 (1993); Owen, Problems in Assessing Punitive Damages Against Manufacturers of Defective Products, 49 U. Chi. L. Rev. 1, 41–42 (1982).

**28.** See, e.g., Colo. Rev. Stat. § 13–21–403; Kan. Stat. Ann. § 60–3304(a); Tenn. Code Ann. § 29–28–104; Utah Code Ann. § 78–15–6. The prevailing common-law rule is that compliance with governmental safety provisions is merely some evidence of due care and nondefectiveness. See §§ 2.3 and 6.4, above.

**29.** See Tuggle v. Raymond Corp., 868 S.W.2d 621 (Tenn. Ct. App. 1992) (OSHA safety regulations apply to employers, not manufacturers).

**30.** This conclusion is not only logical, in that it cannot be quasi-criminal (in the absence of fraud or selling to known incompetents) to sell a nondefective product, but it is also supported by the rule prevailing in almost every state that punitive damages are not recoverable in the absence of a compensatory award. See § 18.1, above.

product supplier is far from quasi-criminal in doing what the government explicitly permitted or required it to do. However, sometimes a government agency, such as the FDA, regulates according to information fraudulently supplied to or concealed from it by a manufacturer,[31] which is why the statutory FDA regulation compliance statutes have a proviso for this situation. Frequently, perhaps typically, legislatures and administrative agencies regulate safety at a floor that is so low that it prohibits only a small, select class of only some of the very most dangerously defective products of a certain type.[32] In such cases, a manufacturer may know that its products, while meeting the letter of the governmental safety standard, still are dangerously defective.[33] In such cases, notwithstanding its compliance with a governmental safety regulation, the manufacturer still should be subject to punitive damages upon a proper showing that it marketed its products in flagrant disregard of consumer safety. Because legislatures and regulatory agencies often have much less information than manufacturers on specific safety problems, and because such public institutions move much more slowly and with far less flexibility than private manufacturers, the presumptive approach is generally preferable to an absolute defense for complying with government safety regulations.[34]

### Remittitur

Another common mechanism of judicial control, which courts have exercised from the very inception of punitive damages in products liability litigation, is the remittitur of excessive awards—by granting a defendant's request for a new trial (or by reversing and remanding for a new trial, in the case of an appellate court) unless the plaintiff accepts a reduction in the punitive damages award to some specified amount.[35] The experience of the California courts with the remittitur of excessive punitive damages awards in products liability cases illustrates this method of judicial control over the entire span of time in which punitive damages have been awarded in products liability cases. In the first decision by an appellate court to uphold a punitive damages verdict in modern products liability litigation, *Toole v. Richardson–Merrell, Inc.*,[36] decided in 1967, the Court of Appeals affirmed the trial court's order remitting a punitive damages jury award from $500,000 to $250,000.[37] In

**31.** See § 18.3, above.

**32.** See Prosser and Keeton on Torts § 36, at 233.

**33.** See, e.g., Gryc v. Dayton–Hudson Corp., 297 N.W.2d 727 (Minn. 1980) (compliance with Flammable Fabrics Act no defense to punitive damages).

**34.** At least outside of the special FDA situation.

**35.** See, e.g., Bocci v. Key Pharms. Inc., 76 P.3d 669 (Or. Ct. App. 2003) (denying defendant's motion for new trial conditioned on plaintiff's failure to accept remittitur of punitive damages verdict of $57 million to $3.5 million); Hobart Corp. v. Scoggins, 776 So.2d 56 (Ala. 2000) (denying

defendant's motion for new trial conditioned on plaintiff's failure to accept remittitur of punitive damages verdict of $10 million to $7.5 million); Romo v. Ford Motor Co., 6 Cal.Rptr.3d 793 (Ct. App. 2003) (reversing $290 million punitive award unless plaintiff accepts reduction to $23,723,287); Mack Trucks, Inc. v. Witherspoon, 867 So.2d 307 (Ala. 2003) (reversing $7.5 million punitive award unless plaintiff accepts reduction to $6 million).

**36.** 60 Cal.Rptr. 398 (Ct. App. 1967).

**37.** The manufacturer marketed a drug as "safe" that it knew might cause cataracts in people's eyes. This litigation, surrounding a drug called MER/29, is discussed in § 18.3, above.

1981, in *Grimshaw v. Ford Motor Co.*,[38] the renowned case involving the fiery eruption of a Ford Pinto fuel tank,[39] the Court of Appeals affirmed the trial court's order remitting a $125 million punitive damages award to $3.5 million.[40] In 1999, in *Anderson v. General Motors Corp.*,[41] the trial court remitted a $4.8 *billion* punitive damages verdict against General Motors to $1.09 billion.[42] Finally, after the trial court reduced a punitive damages verdict awarded to a smoker against a tobacco company from $50 million to $25 million, the Court of Appeals in 2003 remitted it further to $9 million.[43] Many other trial and appellate courts have ordered or approved the remittitur of excessive punitive damages awards in products liability litigation.[44]

Perhaps the most imaginative remittitur order was entered by the trial court in *O'Gilvie v. International Playtex, Inc.*[45] in which the jury returned a $10 million punitive damages verdict against the defendant for selling a high-absorbency tampon that could cause toxic shock syndrome. The court offered to reduce or eliminate the punitive verdict if the defendant would remove the product from the market, which

---

**38.** 174 Cal.Rptr. 348 (Ct. App. 1981).

**39.** See G. Schwartz, The Myth of the Ford Pinto Case, 43 Rutgers L. Rev. 1013 (1990–91); Owen, Problems in Assessing Punitive Damages Against Manufacturers of Defective Products, 49 U. Chi. L. Rev. 1 (1982).

**40.** The *Grimshaw* case is discussed in § 18.3, above. See also Ford Motor Co. v. Durrill, 714 S.W.2d 329 (Tex. App. 1986), vacated and remanded on settlement of parties, 754 S.W.2d 646 (Tex. 1988) (fuel system of Mustang II, a close cousin of the Pinto) ($100 million punitive damages verdict, remitted by trial court to $20 million, further remitted on appeal to $10 million).

**41.** No. BC116926, 1999 WL 1466627 (L.A. Cty. Super. Ct. 1999).

**42.** See Biddle, G.M. Verdict Cut $3.9 Billion in Suit Over Explosion, Wall St. J., Aug. 27, 1999 at B5. Similar to *Grimshaw*, the claim in *Anderson* was based upon the manufacturer's placement of the gas tank in a 1979 Chevrolet Malibu behind the rear axle in close proximity to the rear bumper, which caused the car to burst into flames when hit at high speed from the rear. See generally, White, Jury Orders GM to Pay $4.9 Billion (AP), The State (Columbia, S.C.) Aug. 27, 1999, at A9.

**43.** Henley v. Philip Morris Inc., 5 Cal. Rptr.3d 42 (Ct. App. 2003) ($50 million to smoker, remitted by trial judge to $25 million, further remitted by appellate court to $9 million), review granted and cause transferred, 81 P.3d 223 (Cal. 2003).

**44.** Other remittitur examples include Boeken v. Philip Morris, Inc., 19 Cal. Rptr.3d 101 (Ct. App. 2004); White v. Ford Motor Co., 312 F.3d 998 (9th Cir. 2002)

(Nev. law) ($150 million punitive damages verdict (½ of 1% of Ford's net worth of $30 billion plus $1 for each defective truck recalled), remitted by district court to $69 million; reversed); Horton Homes, Inc. v. Brooks, 832 So.2d 44 (Ala. 2001) (remitting $600,000 award to $150,000); Boeken v. Philip Morris, Inc., 2001 WL 1894403 (Cal. Super. Ct. 2001) ($3 billion award remitted to $100 million), aff'd as modified, 19 Cal. Rptr.3d 101 (Ct. App. 2004); Ford Motor Co. v. Ammerman, 705 N.E.2d 539 (Ind. Ct. App. 1999) ($58 million remitted by superior court to $13.8 million); Barnett v. La Societe Anonyme Turbomeca France, 963 S.W.2d 639 (Mo. Ct. App. 1997) ($175 million punitive damages verdict, remitted by trial court to $87.5 million, further remitted by appellate court to $26.5 million), noted, 64 Mo. L. Rev. 205 (1999); American Nat'l Bank & Trust Co. v. BIC Corp., 880 P.2d 420 (Okla. Ct. App. 1994) (more than $3.6 million for each of three children remitted by appellate court to $1 million each); Ross v. Black & Decker, Inc., 977 F.2d 1178 (7th Cir. 1992) (Ill. law) ($10 million remitted by appellate court to $5 million); Hodder v. Goodyear Tire & Rubber Co., 426 N.W.2d 826, 837 (Minn. 1988) (multi-piece tire rim exploded) ($12.5 million punitive damages verdict reduced to $4 million) ("it is because of the unique, public aspect of punitive damages that the court exercises a much closer supervision over these awards than is the case with compensatory awards"); West v. Johnson & Johnson Prods., Inc., 220 Cal.Rptr. 437 (Ct. App. 1985) (affirming trial court's remittitur of $10 million to $1 million).

**45.** 609 F.Supp. 817 (D. Kan. 1985) (Kelly, J.), rev'd, 821 F.2d 1438 (10th Cir. 1987).

Playtex agreed to do, whereupon the trial judge remitted the verdict to $1.35 million. Reversing and reinstating the full $10 million award, a split Court of Appeals held that the defendant's post-trial conduct was irrelevant to the amount of the award[46] and that the trial court had no authority to remit on that basis.

Although punitive damages verdicts should be closely scrutinized for excessiveness, and should be remitted (or reversed) when awards truly are excessive, courts should disturb punitive damages awards only on clear evidence that the damages verdicts are excessive as a whole. Special caution is required because juries not infrequently include some or all of the plaintiff's general compensatory damages in the punitive damages award.[47] Thus, remitting an apparently excessive punitive award may improperly reduce the composite award intended by the jury as much to compensate the plaintiff fully as to punish the defendant.

## Multipliers and Other Caps

In an effort to bridle jury discretion[48] so as to prevent runaway punitive damages awards, some jurisdictions[49] have adopted various arbitrary types of measurement approaches that reduce or remove discretion from the trier of fact.[50] The most common form of limitation is to cap punitive damages at some multiple of the plaintiff's compensatory award, at one,[51] two,[52] three,[53] four,[54] or five[55] times compensatory damages. Some jurisdictions use other measures to cap punitive awards, such

---

**46.** This basis for the holding appears to be incorrect. See § 18.5, above.

**47.** For example, in Gillham v. Admiral Corp., 523 F.2d 102 (6th Cir. 1975) (Ohio law), the trial court rendered a j.n.o.v. setting aside verdicts against the manufacturer of $100,000 in punitive damages and $50,000 in attorneys' fees, but left intact a compensatory damages verdict of $125,000. Plaintiff had incurred out-of-pocket medical expenses to the date of trial amounting to $128,000 and would require medical expenses including full-time nursing care for the remainder of her life, costing $13,624 annually. Since there was no real issue on liability in the case, at least not for compensatory damages, it appears quite likely that the jury arrived at a total amount intended to compensate the plaintiff for her actual damages, past and future, and then divided this amount between the compensatory and punitive damages awards and perhaps the attorneys' fees award as well.

**48.** See Wackenhut Applied Tech. Ctr., Inc. v. Sygnetron Prot. Sys., Inc., 979 F.2d 980, 985 (4th Cir. 1992) (Virginia's statutory cap constitutional).

**49.** See, e.g., Ala. Code § 6–11–21 ($250,000 unless misconduct was "highly aggravated"), held unconstitutional, Hartsfield v. Alabama Power Co., 627 So.2d 878 (Ala. 1993); Colo. Rev. Stat. § 13–21–102(1)(a) (punitive damages may not exceed compensatory damages); Ford Motor Co. v. Cammack, 999 S.W.2d 1 (Tex. App. 1998) ($22.5 million award reduced to $4 million, pursuant to statutory cap of 4 times actual damages). See generally BMW of N. Am., Inc. v. Gore, 517 U.S. 559, 615 (1996) (describing punitive damages cap statutes in Colorado, Connecticut, Florida, Georgia, Kansas, Nevada, North Dakota, and Virginia, and bills (some enacted) in Delaware, Illinois, Indiana, Maryland, Minnesota, New Jersey, and Texas).

**50.** See Sunstein, Kahneman, and Schkade, Assessing Punitive Damages (with Notes on Cognition and Valuation in Law), 107 Yale L.J. 2071, 2126–27 (1998); Note, 49 S.C. L. Rev. 293 (1998); Development in the Law—The Civil Jury, 110 Harv. L. Rev. 1408, 1533 (1997).

**51.** As in Colorado. See BMW of N. Am., Inc. v. Gore, 517 U.S. 559, 615 (1996).

**52.** As in Connecticut, North Dakota, Oklahoma (in certain instances), and Texas. See id.

**53.** As in Florida and Nevada, and in bills in Delaware, Illinois, and Indiana (enacted). See id.

**54.** As in a Maryland bill. See id.

**55.** As in New Jersey. See N.J. Stat. Ann. § 2A:15–5.14(b) (greater of 5 times compensatory damages or $350,000).

as absolute dollar amounts,[56] the defendant's gross income,[57] a percentage of the defendant's net worth,[58] or the amount (or some multiple thereof) by which the defendant profited from the misconduct.[59] Most statutes include more than one limitation. While the most common form of combined-cap provision limits such damages to the greater of some dollar amount, such as $250,000,[60] or to some multiple of the compensatory damages, such as three times that award, the statutes vary considerably in their complexity and ingenuity in combining various caps for different situations. At least a couple of the caps build in an exception for especially egregious or profit-motivated behavior, but even these provisions fail to fully implement deterrence theory by failing to multiply the defendant's expected profit by the defendant's expected probability of getting caught and punished for the wrongful behavior.[61] Most of the caps apply generally to punitive damages awarded in any type of case, but some apply specifically to products liability litigation,[62] and a couple *exclude* products liability cases from the general caps.[63]

In all but three or four states, punitive damages are awarded solely within the discretion of the factfinder, such that there is no right or entitlement to punitive damages, as previously discussed.[64] For this reason, legislative caps on the amounts of punitive damages would seem to be constitutional in most jurisdictions.[65] Indeed, caps quite clearly reduce the due process threat of unbridled jury discretion.[66] By their nature, however, caps do deprive juries of authority to fix an amount of

**56.** Such as $350,000, in Virginia, see Va. Code Ann. § 8.01–38.1; or $5 million, in certain cases, in Kansas. See Kan. Stat. Ann. § 60–3702(e)(2).

**57.** See Kan. Stat. Ann. § 60–3701(e) and (f) (lesser of defendant's annual gross income, or $5 million, subject to profitability of defendant's misconduct).

**58.** See Miss. Code Ann. § 11–1–65 (providing distinct caps on punitive damages for various brackets of net worth); Kan. Stat. Ann. § 60–3702(e) (lesser of 50% of defendant's net worth, if necessary to penalize defendant, otherwise highest annual gross income over five years preceding punishable act, or $5 million).

**59.** See Okla. Stat. Ann. tit. 23, § 9.1(C); Kan. Stat. Ann. § 60–3702(f) (1½ times amount of profit defendant gained or is expected to gain). For a considered proposal to tailor punitive damages assessments to the profitability of the misconduct, see Dobbs, Ending Punishment in "Punitive" Damages: Deterrence-Measured Remedies, 40 Ala. L. Rev. 831 (1989).

**60.** The dollar amounts range from $50,000 in Indiana to $7 million in Alaska. Compare Ind. Code § 34–51–3–5(2) with Alaska Stat. § 09.17.020(g)(3).

**61.** See § 18.2, above. However, punitive damages assessments in individual products liability cases ordinarily should not seek to punish a manufacturer for its entire course of misconduct over time and

across the nation. Apart from constitutional extraterritoriality problems, see § 18.7, below, manufacturers guilty of truly reprehensible marketing behavior generally will be assessed punitive damages in multiple cases. See § 18.5, above.

**62.** See Conn. Gen. Stat. § 52–240b.

**63.** See Ga. Code Ann. § 51–12–5.1(e)(1); Nev. Rev. Stat. § 42.005(2)(a).

**64.** See § 18.1, above.

**65.** "Because a plaintiff does not have a right to punitive damages, the legislature could, without infringing upon a plaintiff's basic constitutional rights, abolish punitive damages. If the legislature may abolish punitive damages, then it also may, without impinging upon the right to trial by jury, accomplish anything short of that, such as requiring the court to determine the amount of punitive damages or capping the amount of the punitive damages." Smith v. Printup, 866 P.2d 985, 994 (Kan. 1993). See also Rhyne v. K–Mart Corp., 562 S.E.2d 82, 88 (N.C. Ct. App. 2002) (because "the legislature has the power to create, modify, or eliminate other common law remedies," it "necessarily has the power to limit punitive damages."), aff'd on point, 594 S.E.2d 1 (N.C. 2004).

**66.** See Wackenhut Applied Tech. Ctr., Inc. v. Sygnetron Prot. Sys., Inc., 979 F.2d 980, 985 (4th Cir. 1992) (Va. law).

punitive damages they deem appropriate in particular cases, so that there may be a question of whether this form of legislative control may abridge a state's constitutional right to jury trial.[67] However, it seems more logical to conclude that a legislature generally should have the power to limit or even eliminate an extra-compensatory remedy to which plaintiffs have no entitlement, as previously discussed. Thus, except in the very few states in which plaintiffs have a right or entitlement to punitive damages, such as Alabama,[68] caps on punitive damages awards should not be constitutionally objectionable.

Some combination of arbitrary limitations on punitive damages awards are a partial solution to the risk of over-punishment, if an imperfect one. As in a number of state statutes, exceptions to caps might provide for particularly reprehensible misconduct, and for cases in which the defendant has continued the misconduct after getting caught and appears likely to continue it in the future. Yet there is virtue as well as vice in the vagueness of the standards for determining the size of punitive damage assessments; the very vagueness that permits their abuse permits as well their enlightened use to achieve individualized justice tailored to the parties and the circumstances of the case. Legislatures thus should be cautious in adopting arbitrary measurement-control rules to avoid over-mechanizing the administration of justice in cases involving flagrant misconduct.[69]

### Single Award

A recurring problem with punitive damages awards in products liability litigation is that a defendant may be subject to punishment over and over again for a single design or warning defect.[70] While punitive damages awards in some amount are justifiable in every case of flagrant misconduct on retribution and restitution grounds,[71] very large, repetitive awards are more difficult to justify. Accordingly, a small number of states (at least Georgia and Florida) have enacted "one-bite" reform legislation that limits punitive damages to one punishment for a single act or course of conduct.[72] Georgia's statute limits punitive damages awards in products liability litigation to one award without exception,[73] whereas Florida's statute allows subsequent awards "if the court deter-

---

**67.** See State ex rel. Ohio Acad. of Trial Lawyers v. Sheward, 715 N.E.2d 1062, 1091 (Ohio 1999) (holding punitive damages caps unconstitutional). See also Henderson v. Alabama Power Co., 627 So.2d 878 (Ala. 1993) ($150,000 cap on punitive damage awards imposed an unconstitutional, arbitrary limit on jury awards).

**68.** See Henderson v. Alabama Power Co., 627 So.2d 878 (Ala. 1993).

**69.** "Overall, statutory caps provide a certain and administratively easy solution to the perceived problem of excess in punitive damages awards, but they may prove to be too crude a reform measure, sacrificing flexibility and precision in the imposition of punishment and deterrence for the sake of greater control over the size of awards."

Development in the Law—The Civil Jury, 110 Harv. L. Rev. 1408, 1534 (1997).

**70.** See § 18.5, above.

**71.** See § 18.2, above.

**72.** See Annot., 11 A.L.R.4th 1261 (1993).

**73.** See Ga. Code § 51–12–5.1(e)(1). This provision was held unconstitutional in McBride v. General Motors Corp., 737 F.Supp. 1563, 1576–80 (M.D. Ga. 1990), the court reasoned that limiting punitive damages to one award is both arbitrary and unreasonable. This provision was subsequently upheld, however, by the Georgia Supreme Court in Mack Trucks, Inc. v. Conkle, 436 S.E.2d 635 (Ga. 1993).

mines by clear and convincing evidence that the amount of prior punitive damages awarded was insufficient to punish that defendant's behavior.''[74] In such a case, the court must reduce the amount of any such subsequent award by the amount of any earlier awards, so that the defendant is still ultimately liable only for a single, ultimate punishment for the same act or course of conduct.[75]

Although limiting punitive damages to a single assessment may superficially appear logical and fair, this approach may too easily be manipulated by defendants and otherwise is likely to work poorly in mass products liability litigations in which claims mount over time, as discussed above.[76] Even assuming the feasibility of establishing a proper aggregate amount for a single punitive damages award, a quite unlikely possibility, the "one-bite" or "single-shot" approach denies the importance of the functions of compensation and restitutionary retribution to plaintiffs not included in the single punitive damages recovery. For this and other reasons, courts have uniformly refused to adopt a common law one-bite approach to punitive damages awards, as previously discussed.[77] In the absence of legislative mandate, therefore, courts should reject the single-shot approach in mass products liability ongoing-claim situations, on grounds of both principle and practicality.[78] Yet, the one-bite approach appears desirable in single-event disasters, such as airplane or train crashes and hotel fires, where a defendant's aggregate liability is reasonably determinable within a finite period of time, especially if it is determinable in a single proceeding. In such a context, the adjudication of a single judgment for punitive damages would seem feasible and efficient, and the court could assure that each victim received a fair share of the aggregate award.

### Splitting Awards With the State

A reform adopted in some states, designed to capture the supposed "windfall" aspect of punitive damages awards from plaintiffs[79] and in recognition of the public policy purposes of punitive damages,[80] is to provide that some portion of punitive damages assessments go to the state.[81] The statutes, variously called "split-recovery" or "state-extrac-

---

**74.** See Fla. Stat. ch. § 768.73(2)(b).

**75.** Id. See also Gash, Solving the Multiple Punishment Problem: A Call for a National Punitive Damages Registry, 99 Nw. U.L. Rev. ___ (2005) (proposing federal legislation that would allow defendants to register punitive damages awards and settlement and thereby receive a credit against future punitive damages awards the defendants prove involved the same act or course of conduct).

**76.** See § 18.5, above.

**77.** See id.

**78.** A multiplier approach, perhaps determined once and for all in an aggregate claims proceeding, appears to be a preferable approach in such ongoing mass tort situations. See § 18.5, above.

**79.** See Ford v. Uniroyal Goodrich Tire Co., 476 S.E.2d 565, 570 (Ga. 1996). For an examination of the ways in which punitive damages are *not* a windfall, see § 18.2, above.

**80.** See § 18.1, above.

**81.** See V. Schwartz, Behrens, and Silverman, I'll Take That: Legal and Public Policy Problems Raised by Statutes that Require Punitive Damages Awards to be Shared with the State, 68 Mo. L. Rev. 525 (2003); Development in the Law–The Civil Jury, 110 Harv. L. Rev. 1408, 1534 (1997); Stevens, Split–Recovery: A Constitutional Answer to the Punitive Damages Dilemma, 21 Pepp. L. Rev. 857 (1994); Toy, Statutory Punitive Damages Caps and the Profit Motive: An Economic Perspective, 40 Emory L.J. 303 (1991); Notes, 80 Cornell L. Rev.

tion" statutes, have varied in the amount of the award provided to the state: 35 percent of a punitive damages award goes to the state in Florida;[82] 50 percent in Alaska, Kansas, Missouri, and Utah;[83] 60 percent in Oregon;[84] 75 percent in Georgia and Iowa,[85] and a percentage within the court's discretion in Illinois.[86] Some of the statutes deduct attorneys' fees and other litigation costs prior to calculating the amount to go to the state,[87] and the statutes vary on whether particular state agencies are designated as the recipients of such recoveries[88] or whether the state's share simply goes into its general treasury.[89] This kind of statutory division of punitive damages awards has been successfully attacked on state constitutional grounds in one state,[90] but split-recovery punitive damages statutes have been upheld against a variety of state and federal constitutional attacks in a number of other states.[91] Because this reform provides that the state shares in the punitive damages award, very large awards may violate the excessive fines clause of the eighth amendment, an issue left open by the Supreme Court.[92]

Whether this reform is desirable depends to a large extent on the absolute size of particular compensatory and punitive awards. While requiring that such awards be split between the plaintiff and the state may reduce somewhat a plaintiff's incentive to pursue such claims, this reform otherwise appears sensible in cases involving very large punitive assessments.[93] Awards of punitive damages, being "quasi-criminal," are

104 (1994); 50 Wash. & Lee L. Rev. 843 (1993); Recent Case, 106 Harv. L. Rev. 1691 (1993); Annot., 16 A.L.R.5th 129 (1994); Developments in Missouri Law 1997–1998, 63 Mo. L. Rev. 511 (1998); Kircher and Wiseman, Punitive Damages § 21.17.

**82.** See Fla. Stat. ch. 768.73(2)(a) (repealed 1997).

**83.** See Alaska Stat. § 09.17.020(j); Kan. Stat. Ann. § 60–3402(e) (expired 1989); Mo. Rev. Stat. § 537.675(2); Utah Code Ann. § 78–18–1(3).

**84.** See Or. Rev. Stat. § 18.540(1)(b).

**85.** See Ga. Code Ann. § 51–12–5.1(e)(2); Iowa Code § 668A.1(2)(b).

**86.** See Ill. Comp. Stat. Ann. ch. 735, § 5/2–1207.

**87.** See, e.g., Iowa Code § 668A.1(2)(b); Mo. Rev. Stat. § 537.675.

**88.** See, e.g., Iowa Code § 668A.1(2)(b) (to civil reparations trust fund); Mo. Rev. Stat. § 537.675 (Tort Victims' Compensation Fund).

**89.** See, e.g., Alaska Stat. § 09.17.020(j) (to general fund); Ga. Code § 51–12–5.1(e)(2) (to state treasury).

**90.** See Colo. Rev. Stat. § 13–21–102(4) (one-third to state), declared unconstitutional and subsequently repealed. See Kirk v. Denver Publ'n. Co., 818 P.2d 262 (Colo. 1991).

**91.** See Fust v. Attorney General of Mo. 947 S.W.2d 424 (Mo. 1997); State v. Moseley, 436 S.E.2d 632 (Ga. 1993); Gordon v.

State, 608 So.2d 800 (Fla. 1992) (but statute providing 60 percent to state subsequently repealed); Shepherd Components, Inc. v. Brice Petrides–Donohue & Assoc., Inc., 473 N.W.2d 612 (Iowa 1991). See generally Developments in Missouri Law 1996–1997, 63 Mo. L. Rev. 511 (1998).

**92.** See Browning–Ferris Indus., Inc. v. Kelco Disposal, Inc., 492 U.S. 257, 276 n.21 (1989). Although the matter was left undecided, Justice O'Connor expressed little doubt that the Excessive Fines Clause would indeed apply to punitive damages assessments paid to the government. See id. at 298–99 (O'Connor, J., concurring in part and dissenting in part). See generally McAllister, A Pragmatic Approach to the Eighth Amendment and Punitive Damages, 43 U. Kan. L. Rev. 761 (1995); Massey, The Excessive Fines Clause and Punitive Damages: Some Lessons from History, 40 Vand. L. Rev. 1233 (1987).

One commentator has argued that state extraction statutes as drawn generally violate the takings clause of the fifth and fourteenth amendments. Burrows, Apportioning a Piece of a Punitive Damage Award to the State: Can State Extraction Statutes Be Reconciled With Punitive Damages Goals and the Takings Clause, 47 U. Miami L. Rev. 437 (1992).

**93.** See State v. Moseley, 436 S.E.2d 632 (Ga. 1993) (holding Georgia statute, which apportions 75% of punitive damages awards

by their nature "quasi-public"; therefore, the public logically should share in very large awards. But split-recover statutes do suffer from a number of theoretical and practical problems,[94] including the infection of the jury's deliberations with extraneous information if it is improperly informed that the public will share in the award.[95] The first and foremost office of punitive damages should be to achieve justice between the parties in the "private" lawsuit, such that the victim ought to be truly fully compensated—both in terms of actual losses and retribution—before the public should have a claim at all. Thus, in cases where the amount of such damages is relatively modest, a plaintiff fairly should have a prior, exclusive claim to the total award.

## Bifurcation

Some courts[96] and legislatures[97] require or permit, upon the defendant's (or any party's) motion, that the punitive damages issue be bifurcated at trial, so that the jury's decision on liability and compensatory damages will not be contaminated by the plaintiff's evidence of the defendant's wealth, and possibly by other punitive damages evidence and argument.[98] Some jurisdictions bifurcate all punitive damages issues from the basic liability and compensatory damages issues; others segregate only the determination of the *amount* of punitive damages, leaving the issue of liability therefor to be decided in the preliminary proceeding along with liability for (and the amount of) compensatory damages. The Federal Rules of Civil Procedure accommodate bifurcation of punitive damages in its rule permitting federal courts to order separate trials of

to state, is constitutional); Mack Trucks, Inc. v. Conkle, 436 S.E.2d 635 (Ga. 1993) (same). *Contra*, Kirk v. Denver Publ'n Co., 818 P.2d 262 (Colo. 1991) (holding such a statute unconstitutional).

**94.** See Development in the Law—The Civil Jury, 110 Harv. L. Rev. 1408, 1535–36 (1997).

**95.** See Ford v. Uniroyal Goodrich Tire Co., 476 S.E.2d 565, 570 (Ga. 1996) (such an instruction was reversible error); Burke v. Deere & Co., 6 F.3d 497, 513 (8th Cir. 1993) (Iowa law); Honeywell v. Sterling Furniture Co., 797 P.2d 1019, 1021–23 (Or. 1990).

**96.** See, e.g., W.R. Grace & Co. v. Waters, 638 So.2d 502 (Fla. 1994) (bifurcation on motion by party); Transportation Ins. Co. v. Moriel, 879 S.W.2d 10 (Tex. 1994) (noting that at least thirteen states then provided for bifurcation); Hodges v. S.C. Toof & Co., 833 S.W.2d 896, 901–02 (Tenn. 1992) (establishing rules for bifurcation of punitive damages amounts). Compare Uniroyal Goodrich Tire Co. v. Martinez, 977 S.W.2d 328, 342–43 (Tex. 1998) (failure to bifurcate was harmless error where plaintiff did not introduce evidence of defendant's wealth).

**97.** See, e.g., Cal. Civ. Code Ann. § 3295(d); Mo. Ann. Stat. § 510.263 (bifurcation required; net worth evidence admissible only in punitive damages portion of trial). See generally BMW of N. Am., Inc. v. Gore, 517 U.S. 559, 618 (1996) (describing bifurcation statutes in California, Georgia, Kansas, Missouri, Montana, Nevada, New Jersey, North Dakota, and Oklahoma, and bills in Delaware, Illinois, and Virginia).

**98.** See, e.g., W.R. Grace & Co. v. Waters, 638 So.2d 502, 506 (Fla. 1994) (holding that trial court, on motion, should bifurcate punitive damages from remaining issues). See generally Kircher and Wiseman, Punitive Damages § 12.01 (noting danger that evidence regarding defendant's reckless or malicious conduct and financial status may prejudice the jury's determination of liability for compensatory damages); Seltzer, Punitive Damages in Mass Tort Litigation: Addressing the Problems of Fairness, Efficiency and Control, 52 Fordham L. Rev. 37, 90 (1983) (maintaining that bifurcated trial would allow jury to receive all relevant evidence regarding amount of punitive damages without prejudicing defendant on other disputed issues); Development in the Law—The Civil Jury, 110 Harv. L. Rev. 1408, 1530 (1997).

claims and issues in the interests of convenience, expedition, economy, or to avoid prejudice.[99]

For many years, conventional wisdom held that bifurcation, by fractionizing the issues in the case, benefits defendants.[100] Consequently, during the late twentieth century, permitting or requiring bifurcation of some or all aspects of punitive damages from liability for compensatory damages was a central feature of both state and federal products liability legislative reform initiatives.[101] But experience and recent studies suggest that the blessings of bifurcation may be mixed. The bifurcated Florida smokers class action trial against the tobacco industry, which ended in a punitive damages verdict of $145 billion, although subsequently reversed, is the most dramatic illustration of the risks to defendants of bifurcating punitive damages liability.[102] Surely the conduct of the tobacco companies during the last half of the twentieth century was unacceptable, and the result of the Florida case may have been substantially the same even if all issues had been litigated in a single proceeding. But the case does demonstrate the risks that a separate punitive damages trial creates, especially where the only remaining issue is the selection of a proper amount of money damages to punish a defendant already found flagrantly at fault for subjecting consumers to a lethal hazard for many decades.[103]

In any products liability litigation, restricting the issues at a second, independent trial to liability for and the amount of a punitive damages award (or, what may be even more difficult for defendants, solely to how large a punitive damages award should be) may provide a jury solely concerned with a manufacturer's culpability with an inquisitorial frame of mind. Moreover, in a second, punitive damages phase of a protracted trial, the jury will be asked to examine an artificially narrow slice of the manufacturer's marketing decisions which are drained of the broad real-world range of considerations contextually at play in institutional deci-

---

**99.** See Fed. R. Civ. P. 42(b).

**100.** See, e.g., 2 Harper and James, Jr., The Law of Torts 894 (1956) (" '[a]ny procedural device which effectively keeps the jury within their theoretical sphere tends to restrict liability' "), quoted in Weinstein, Routine Bifurcation of Jury Negligence Trials: An Example of the Questionable Use of Rule Making Power, 14 Vand. L. Rev. 831, 834 n.10 (1961); Mallor & Roberts, Punitive Damages: Toward a Principled Approach, 31 Hastings L.J. 639, 663–66 (1980); Owen, Problems in Assessing Punitive Damages Against Manufacturers of Defective Products, 49 U. Chi. L. Rev. 1, 52–53 (1982); Wheeler, The Constitutional Case for Reforming Punitive Damages Procedures, 69 Va. L. Rev. 269, 272 (1983). See generally Landsman, Diamond, Dimitropoulos, and Saks, Be Careful What You Wish For: The Paradoxical Effects of Bifurcating Claims for Punitive Damages, 1998 Wis. L. Rev. 297, 300–03.

**101.** See, e.g., Pace, Recalibrating the Scales of Justice Through National Punitive Damage Reform, 46 Am. U. L. Rev. 1573, 1620 (1997).

**102.** See, Liggett Group Inc. v. Engle, 853 So. 2d 434 (Fla. Dist. Ct. App. 2003).

**103.** For examples of other cases in which bifurcation appeared to be disastrous for the defendant, see, e.g., Barnett v. La Societe Anonyme Turbomeca France, 963 S.W.2d 639, 653–54 (Mo. Ct. App. 1997), cert. denied, 525 U.S. 827 (1998) ($175 million punitive damages verdict in second phase of trial, remitted by trial court to $87.5 million, further remitted by appellate court to $26.5 million), noted, 64 Mo. L. Rev. 205 (1999); General Motors Corp. v. Moseley, 447 S.E.2d 302 (Ga. Ct. App. 1994) ($101 million punitive damages verdict in phase 2). See also Gensler, Bifurcation Unbound, 75 Wash. L. Rev. 705 (2000) (review of bifurcation studies demonstrates that bifurcation is not necessarily advantageous to defendants).

sionmaking over time.[104] While the courts may no longer question whether bifurcation unconstitutionally deprives a non-consenting party of the right to jury trial,[105] this procedure does substantially restrict the freedom of the parties in deciding how to present their claims and defenses.

Empirical studies suggest that bifurcating compensatory and punitive damages liability is likely to produce two important effects in jury trials: (1) the defendant is indeed more likely to prevail in the preliminary, compensatory damages stage of the litigation; but (2) in the second phase, a punitive damages award is both more likely to be rendered and to be considerably higher than in a unitary trial.[106] In short, "if the defendant has lost at the stage of compensatory liability, the chance becomes very great that the defendant will lose at the punitive liability stage."[107] Thus, not only is the bifurcation device procedurally awkward, but also it presents defendants with a significant strategic dilemma of whether to gamble with a higher chance of success in the compensatory damages phase in exchange for a higher risk of disaster in the punitive damages phase. The data suggest that a defendant should opt to bifurcate only if its case on compensatory damages is strong, especially if the case against it on punitive damages is quite weak. Either way, bifurcating the punitive damages issue in major products liability litigation may be likened to playing with fire in the vicinity of kerosene.

### Judicial Determination of Amount of Punitive Damages Awards

At least three states, Connecticut,[108] Kansas,[109] and Ohio,[110] have enacted legislation allowing juries to determine whether a defendant should be liable for punitive damages but transferring to the court responsibility for determining the *amount* of such awards.[111] This shift of responsibility is designed to prevent the perceived risk of biased juries

---

**104.** These considerations may help explain the defendant's decision not to move to bifurcate in Owens–Corning Fiberglas Corp. v. Rivera, 683 So.2d 154 (Fla. Dist. Ct. App. 1996), and it may also help explain the large verdict in Moseley v. General Motors, which involved the explosion risk from side-mounted gas tanks on certain G.M. pickup trucks. See General Motors Corp. v. Moseley, 447 S.E.2d 302 (Ga. Ct. App. 1994). In Phase I of the *Moseley* trial, hearing evidence on liability for compensatory damages and also on the propriety of a punitive damages award, the jury found the truck design defective and that punitive damages were warranted. Id. at 305. In Phase II, the jury assessed General Motors $101 million in punitive damages. The Georgia Court of Appeals found this bifurcated proceeding to have improperly influenced the jury. Id. However, because the case was remanded on other grounds, this opinion is merely dicta. See id. at 306.

**105.** See 9 Charles Alan Wright and Arthur R. Miller, Federal Practice and Procedure § 2391, at 512–15 (2d ed. 1985); Landsman, Diamond, Dimitropoulos, and Saks, Be Careful What You Wish For: The Paradoxical Effects of Bifurcating Claims for Punitive Damages, 1998 Wis. L. Rev. 297, 299.

**106.** Empirical findings indicated that while "bifurcation may offer defendants significant protection from prejudice arising out of the misuse of information relevant only to the punitive damages decisions," "not only does the incidence of punitive liability increase, but the size of the punitive award grows substantially if the case is bifurcated." Landsman, Diamond, Dimitropoulos, and Saks, Be Careful What You Wish For: The Paradoxical Effects of Bifurcating Claims for Punitive Damages, 1998 Wis. L. Rev. 297, 335.

**107.** Id. at 330.

**108.** See Conn. Gen. Stat. Ann. § 52–240b.

**109.** See Kan. Stat. Ann. § 60–3701(a).

**110.** Ohio Rev. Code Ann. § 2307.80(B).

**111.** See Development in the Law—The Civil Jury, 110 Harv. L. Rev. 1408, 1527 (1997).

rendering run-away punitive damage awards. Challenges to these statutes in two of the three states on grounds that they violated the state constitutional right to a jury trial met with mixed results: the Ohio Supreme Court struck down its statute,[112] while the Kansas Supreme Court upheld the constitutionality of its statute, reasoning that punitive damages were merely a discretionary remedy of the common law not subject to the right to jury trial.[113]

In some ways it makes good sense to shift decisions on the amounts of punitive damages to the courts, for such determinations are in the nature of quasi-criminal sentencing, and judges are generally more qualified than jurors—in training, temperament, and experience—to fix the amounts of punitive sanctions.[114] This reform, which has been advocated for many years,[115] offers several advantages over the traditional method of allowing the jury to determine the amounts of such awards. First, it reduces the probability that punitive damages awards are unduly influenced by emotion, since most judges are more detached in their deliberations and therefore more likely to render objective damages assessments. Additionally, evidence of the defendant's wealth that could prejudice the jury on the issue of liability could then be excluded from jury consideration without bifurcating the jury trial. Further, judges would be able to call upon their experience in criminal sentencing, unavailable to jurors, in evaluating the need for particular levels of punishment and deterrence in particular cases.[116] Finally, trial judges usually have a more sophisticated appreciation than jurors of the often far-reaching effects that punitive damages awards may have on the operations of particular corporate defendants. On the other hand, even judges may be biased and ideologically committed, one way or the other, and the institution of the jury at least requires a compromise among extremes. Instead of relieving the jury of its historic task of determining the amount of punitive damage awards, the most practical, second-best solution to the measurement problem may lie in formulating a combination of procedural and arbitrary measurement devices of the sort considered above.

### Written Explanations

Many punitive damages problems may be minimized if courts are required to provide explicit justifications—in the record or by opinion—for allowing, upsetting, or remitting punitive damage assessments. Such justifications, tying the evidence to the facts and the principles of punitive damages, should assure that the courts work through the smoke of rhetoric and emotion at the trial to determine if such damages truly

---

**112.** See Zoppo v. Homestead Ins. Co., 644 N.E.2d 397, 401 (Ohio 1994).

**113.** See Smith v. Printup, 866 P.2d 985, 997–98 (Kan. 1993). See note 65, above.

**114.** See Owen, Punitive Damages in Products Liability Litigation, 74 Mich. L. Rev. 1257, 1320–22 (1976) (advocating shifting measurement function from jury to judge).

**115.** See DuBois, Punitive Damages in Personal Injury, Products Liability and Professional Malpractice Cases: Bonanza or Disaster, 43 Ins. Counsel J. 344, 352–53 (1974); See also Morris, Punitive Damages in Tort Cases, 44 Harv. L. Rev. 1173, 1179–80 (1931).

**116.** See Note, 41 N.Y.U. L. Rev. 1158, 1171 (1966); Note, 70 Harv. L. Rev. 517, 530 (1957).

are deserved on the evidence, and, if they are, whether the amounts of such awards are truly warranted. In response to the Supreme Court's insistence that punitive damages be based on fair procedures,[117] a number of jurisdictions now require judicial explanations of punitive damages rulings, some requiring appellate courts[118] and others requiring trial courts[119] to explain their rulings. The importance of this reform should not be underestimated, and it would seem to be a necessary procedural bedrock for substantive fairness in the administration of the law of punitive damages.

## § 18.7  CONSTITUTIONAL LIMITATIONS

Courts and commentators long have questioned the fairness of assessing civil penalties for conduct described so vaguely as "malicious," "reckless," or "willful and wanton," with no real ceiling on the size of the assessments, and without the procedural safeguards used in criminal cases to assure the propriety of punishment.[1] Yet, until quite recently, due process and other constitutional challenges to punitive damages fared poorly in the courts.[2] Toward the end of the twentieth century, in a string of cases which constitutionalized the law of punitive damages, the United States Supreme Court began to examine these issues in some detail.[3] In a series of decisions, the Supreme Court addressed concerns

**117.** See Pacific Mut. Life Ins. Co. v. Haslip, 499 U.S. 1 (1991). See generally § 18.7, below.

**118.** See, e.g., Transportation Ins. Co. v. Moriel, 879 S.W.2d 10 (Tex. 1994). In order for an appellate court to provide the type of post-trial scrutiny of punitive damages awards required by *Haslip*, a fair reading of that case might well lead to the conclusion that appellate courts must provide written explanations for upholding punitive damages awards in every case.

**119.** See, e.g., Gamble v. Stevenson, 406 S.E.2d 350 (S.C. 1991). Although in *Moriel*, 879 S.W.2d at 32–33, the Texas court concluded that it could not require its already overburdened and understaffed trial courts to provide a written explanation on punitive damages rulings in every case, that court did urge its trial courts to do so to the extent feasible, indicating that "at least eight jurisdictions now expressly require the trial court to articulate its reasons for refusing to disturb a punitive damage award," citing cases from Alabama, Idaho, Maryland, Minnesota, South Carolina, Tennessee, Utah, and West Virginia.

### § 18.7

**1.** See Wheeler, The Constitutional Case for Reforming Punitive Damages Procedures, 69 Va. L. Rev. 269 (1983); Comment, Criminal Safeguards and the Punitive Damages Defendant, 34 U. Chi. L. Rev. 408 (1967).

**2.** See Comment, 34 U. Chi. L. Rev. at 464–65. The Supreme Court refused due

process challenges to punitive damage awards as early as 1889. See Minneapolis & St. Louis Ry. Co. v. Beckwith, 129 U.S. 26, 36 (1889) ("The imposition of punitive or exemplary damages in such cases cannot be opposed as in conflict with the prohibition against the deprivation of property without due process of law.... [I]ts propriety and legality have been recognized ... by repeated judicial decisions for more than a century."). Early rejections of due process challenges in products liability cases include Grimshaw v. Ford Motor Co., 174 Cal.Rptr. 348, 383–84 (Ct. App. 1981); Sturm, Ruger & Co. v. Day, 594 P.2d 38, 46 (Alaska 1979), overruled by, 703 P.2d 396 (1985); Toole v. Richardson–Merrell, Inc., 60 Cal.Rptr. 398, 417–18 (Ct. App. 1967).

**3.** The Supreme Court's venture into the punitive damages arena has generated a spate of commentary in the law reviews. See, e.g., Weddle, A Practitioner's Guide to Litigating Punitive Damages After BMW of North America, Inc. v. Gore, 47 Drake L. Rev. 661 (1999); Olson, Boutrous, and Perry, Constitutional Challenges to Punitive Damages After BMW v. Gore, 2 Briefly ... Perspectives on Legislation, Regulation and Litigation 1 (No. 5, May 1998); Robinson and Abraham, Collective Justice in Tort Law, 78 Va. L. Rev. 1481, 1507 (1992) (substantive due process aspects of aggregating mass tort claims); Volz and Fayz, Punitive Damages and the Due Process Clause: The Search for Constitutional Standards, 69 U. Det. Mercy L. Rev. 459 (1992); Riggs, Con-

over the increase in multi-million dollar awards of punitive damages and the widespread perception that such damages are too often assessed arbitrarily and unfairly.[4]

In the first decision, *Browning–Ferris Industries of Vermont v. Kelco Disposal, Inc.*,[5] an unfair business practices case, the Court rejected an excessive fines clause challenge to a $6 million punitive damages award, holding that the Eighth Amendment does not apply to punitive damages assessments in civil cases where the state does not share in the recovery.[6] Yet the decision leaves open the possibility that large punitive damages awards might be challenged on an excessive fines basis in states that do take part of a plaintiff's punitive award.[7]

### *Pacific Mutual Life Insurance Co. v. Haslip*

The next decision was an insurance fraud case, *Pacific Mutual Life Insurance Co. v. Haslip*,[8] in which the jury had returned a compensatory damages verdict of $200,000 and a punitive damages verdict of $840,000. Ruling on the applicability of the Fourteenth Amendment's due process clause to punitive damages assessments, a five justice majority concluded that (1) the imposition of punitive damages on a vicarious liability basis is not fundamentally unfair,[9] (2) the common law method for determining punitive damages is not per se unconstitutional,[10] and (3) the punitive damages award in the case, about four times larger than the compensatory damages verdict, was "close to the [constitutional] line"[11] but not so disproportionately large as to violate due process.[12] While observing that "unlimited jury discretion ... in the fixing of punitive damages may invite extreme results that jar one's constitutional sensibilities,"[13] the Court refused to "draw a mathematical bright line between the constitutionally acceptable and the constitutionally unacceptable that would fit every case."[14] Nevertheless, the Court did observe that

stitutionalizing Punitive Damages: The Limits of Due Process, 52 Ohio St. L.J. 859 (1991) (punitive damages should not be regulated by due process); Zwier, Due Process and Punitive Damages, 1991 Utah L. Rev. 407 (due process analysis unnecessary); Note, The Shadow of BMW of North America, Inc. v. Gore, 1998 Wis. L. Rev. 427. See generally G. Boston, Punitive Damages in Tort Law ch. 4 (1993).

**4.** See Browning–Ferris Indus. of Vt., Inc. v. Kelco Disposal, Inc., 492 U.S. 257 (1989); Pacific Mut. Life Ins. Co. v. Haslip, 499 U.S. 1 (1991); TXO Prod. Corp. v. Alliance Resources Corp., 509 U.S. 443 (1993); Honda Motor Co. v. Oberg, 512 U.S. 415 (1994); BMW of N. Am., Inc. v. Gore, 517 U.S. 559 (1996); Cooper Indus. Inc. v. Leatherman Tool Group, Inc., 532 U.S. 424 (2001); State Farm Mut. Auto. Ins. Co. v. Campbell, 538 U.S. 408 (2003).

**5.** 492 U.S. 257 (1989).

**6.** See id. at 260.

**7.** See Appendix II to Justice Ginsburg's dissenting opinion in BMW of N. Am., Inc. v. Gore, 517 U.S. 559, 616 (1996), listing

thirteen state statutes to this effect. These statutes are discussed in § 18.6, above.

**8.** 499 U.S. 1 (1991).

**9.** See id. at 14–15 (upholding Alabama common law doctrine of respondeat superior as rationally advancing state goal of minimizing fraud by imposing incentives for principals to oversee actions of their agents).

**10.** See id. at 17 (noting that this method was in use before Fourteenth Amendment was enacted and that courts have consistently upheld it against constitutional attack).

**11.** Id. at 23.

**12.** See id. at 23–24 (justifying disparity between this punitive damages award and fines imposed for insurance fraud because state insurance fraud statute permits imprisonment to supplement any monetary fine).

**13.** Id. at 18.

**14.** Id.

"general concerns of reasonableness and adequate guidance from the court when the case is tried to a jury properly enter into the constitutional calculus."[15]

The *Haslip* majority concluded that Alabama's process for assessing punitive damages met the due process requirement that punitive damages decisionmaking be rational and constrained.[16] The tripartite process that passed constitutional muster in *Haslip* included, first, jury instructions on the punitive damages purposes of retribution and deterrence; second, post-verdict review by the trial court to determine that a punitive award was in fact based upon the law's objectives; and, third, appellate review of such awards to check the jury's or trial court's discretion, including a comparative analysis of the verdict and a consideration of a list of factors bearing on the appropriateness of the particular punitive assessment in light of the law's objectives.[17] The majority concluded that, in combination, these three components of the Alabama system for assessing punitive damages, particularly the procedures for trial and appellate court review,[18] reasonably assured that punitive damages would be "reasonable in their amount and rational in light of their purpose to punish [and] deter"[19] so that such awards "are not grossly out of proportion to the severity of the offense" and to the compensatory damages.[20] In this manner, *Haslip* established a due process structure for punitive damages determinations.[21]

### *TXO Production Corp. v. Alliance Resources Corp.*

The Supreme Court's next case was *TXO Production Corp. v. Alliance Resources Corp.*,[22] another unfair business practices case.[23] On evidence that the defendant had tried to cheat the plaintiff out of millions of dollars in a business transaction, the Court in *TXO* upheld, against a charge of constitutional excessiveness, a $10 million punitive damage verdict—some 526 times greater than the compensatory award of $19,000.[24] Following so closely on the heels of *Haslip*, the Court's

**15.** Id.

**16.** See id. at 20.

**17.** The punitive damages factors reviewed on appeal, listed in Green Oil Co. v. Hornsby, 539 So.2d 218, 223–24 (Ala. 1989), include the relationship between the punitive award and the actual and likely harm from the defendant's misconduct; the reprehensibility of the defendant's conduct, its duration, any concealment, and the frequency of any similar past conduct; the profitability of the misconduct and desirability of removing the profit and causing the defendant to suffer a loss; the defendant's financial position; the costs of litigation; any criminal sanctions suffered by the defendant for the misconduct; and other civil awards against the defendant for the same misconduct. See *Haslip*, 499 U.S. at 21.

**18.** It has been held that the vagueness in traditional review standards that condition reversal of a punitive damages awards

on a "shock the conscience of the court" standard, or on a determination that the jury was motivated by "passion or prejudice," does not affront due process if the reviewing court makes particularized *Haslip*-type findings in addition to applying the traditional standards of review. See Robertson Oil Co. v. Phillips Petroleum Co., 14 F.3d 373 (8th Cir. 1993) (en banc).

**19.** *Haslip*, 499 U.S. at 21.

**20.** Id. at 22.

**21.** See id. at 18–22.

**22.** 509 U.S. 443 (1993).

**23.** Nominally a slander of title case because defendant obtained and filed a worthless quitclaim deed to property owned by the plaintiff solely to deceive and obtain an unfair advantage in negotiations over the purchase of the plaintiff's valuable oil and gas rights. See id. at 448–49.

**24.** See id. at 460–65.

upholding of such a large award was somewhat unexpected because of Haslip's emphasis on guarding against assessments of punitive damages that appear unfairly large.

In the evolving Supreme Court jurisprudence on punitive damages and the due process clause, *TXO* clarified a couple of important points. First, reaffirming its inability to " 'draw a mathematical bright line' " for evaluating the propriety of large punitive awards,[25] the Court refused to adopt formal standards for testing the constitutionality of the size of such awards, whether in the form of a comparative approach based on prior awards[26] or a particular ratio of punitive to compensatory damages.[27] Second, in comparing the size of the punitive award to harm, the Court widened the relevant harm beyond the plaintiff's actual damages alone, as measured by compensatory damages, to "the magnitude of the *potential harm* that the defendant's conduct" could have made upon the intended victim "as well as the possible harm to other victims that might have resulted if similar future behavior were not deterred."[28] More fundamentally, *TXO* also helped to clarify the Court's alignment on the role of due process in punitive damages cases. All nine justices were now on record as holding that punitive damages assessments are constrained by certain *procedural* due process requirements of appropriate jury instructions and meaningful judicial review. The case further established that seven justices (those other than Scalia and Thomas, JJ.)[29] believed there to be certain *substantive* due process limits to the *size* of such awards, based on principles of "reasonableness" and/or the underlying goals of punitive damages law—punishment, deterrence, and (in a few states) compensation.[30]

Unfortunately, *TXO* further establishes that due process does *not* require trial courts to explain their decisions on post-trial motions to uphold punitive damage assessments, even $10 million ones.[31] But without such an explicit application of the law to the evidence by the judge who presided at the trial, it is unclear how the Supreme Court expects

---

**25.** Id. at 458, quoting *Haslip*, 499 U.S. at 18.

**26.** The court was unwilling to test the constitutionality of a particular award by comparing it to prior punitive assessments because punitive awards "are the product of numerous, and sometimes intangible, factors; a jury imposing a punitive damages award must make a qualitative assessment based on a host of facts and circumstances unique to the particular case before it." Id. at 457.

**27.** See id. at 460 (noting that it had "eschewed an approach that concentrates entirely on the relationship between actual and punitive damages").

**28.** Id. (emphasis by the Court).

**29.** See id. at 471 (contending that procedural due process requires judicial review of punitive damages for reasonableness, but that there is no constitutional right to a substantively correct reasonableness determination).

**30.** Presumably, the "punishment" goal includes the goals of retribution, restitution, and education; the "deterrence" goal includes the goal of law enforcement; and the "compensation" goal includes compensation for both actual (but otherwise noncompensable) damages and attorneys' fees (and other litigation expenses).

**31.** See id. at 464–65. After *Haslip*, courts in at least eight states, and several federal courts of appeal, adopted a requirement that trial courts explain their refusal to disturb jury awards of punitive damages. See, e.g., Transportation Ins. Co. v. Moriel, 879 S.W.2d 10 (Tex. 1994) (refusing to impose this requirement on already over-burdened Texas trial courts, but imposing it on state's intermediate appellate courts). See also Morgan v. Woessner, 997 F.2d 1244 (9th Cir. 1993) (remanding punitive damage award for district court to analyze its ruling in light of appellate court's opinion and to provide reasons for its ultimate conclusion).

appellate courts, as required under *Haslip*, to determine if a particular defendant subjected to a large punitive damages assessment was in fact highly culpable and hence deserving of such a penalty. Without written decisions from the trial bench, appellate courts are forced to decide such cases solely from the trial transcript and appellate argument without the benefit of the trial court's reflective insights, as the Supreme Court was forced to do in *TXO*.[32] The risk is that appellate courts remote from trial courtrooms will be reluctant to second guess the decisions of juries (and silent trial courts) in such cases, leading them to accord a de facto presumptive validity to such awards. Before *Haslip*, there was little true judicial review of punitive damage awards in most jurisdictions, which appeared to be a major part of the problem that the *Haslip* majority sought to remedy. In removing this important explanatory arrow from *Haslip*'s due process quiver, *TXO* may have the unfortunate effect of systemically weakening *Haslip*'s procedural due process structure that was designed to help assure that punitive damage judgments are based on proper considerations.

### Honda Motor Co. v. Oberg

In the fourth case, *Honda Motor Co. v. Oberg*,[33] the Court ruled that procedural due process requires that judicial review be available for defendants to challenge punitive damage awards on grounds of excessiveness. *Oberg* was a products liability design defect case, involving a three-wheel all-terrain vehicle that overturned and injured the plaintiff. The jury awarded the plaintiff $5 million in punitive damages in addition to about $900,000 in compensatory damages, the latter reduced by 20% on account of the plaintiff's contributory negligence. A unique state constitutional provision in Oregon effectively precluded judicial review of the amount of punitive damage assessments. On this authority, and notwithstanding *Haslip*'s emphasis on the importance of judicial review, the Oregon appellate courts in *Oberg* upheld the award without reviewing the defendant's claim that it was excessive. The United States Supreme Court reversed, holding that punitive damages awards cannot constitutionally be committed to the unreviewable discretion of a jury.[34]

On its face, *Oberg* is a trivial case. It is difficult to understand why the Supreme Court rendered a decision on such a clear and narrow punitive damages judicial review issue—one that was plainly and strongly implicit in *Haslip* and applicable only to a single state. The importance of *Oberg* may lie in its tone. In justifying the reversal of the award, Justice Stevens for the majority underscored once again the potential dangers of unchecked punitive damages verdicts and the availability of the due process clause to remedy arbitrary awards. "Punitive damages pose an acute danger of arbitrary deprivation of property, since jury

**32.** Except, of course, in those jurisdictions otherwise requiring trial courts to specify reasons for their rulings on punitive assessments. See § 18.6, above.

**33.** 512 U.S. 415 (1994).

**34.** "The common-law practice, the procedures applied by every other State, the strong presumption favoring judicial review that we have applied in other areas of the law, and elementary considerations of justice all support the conclusion that such a decision should not be committed to the unreviewable discretion of a jury." Id. at 435.

instructions typically leave the jury with wide discretion in choosing amounts and since evidence of a defendant's net worth creates the potential that juries will use their verdicts to express biases against big businesses."[35] *Oberg* further pronounced in no uncertain terms that "the Constitution imposes a substantive limit on the size of punitive damages awards"[36] which the courts have a constitutional duty to review.[37] In sum, *Oberg* realigned the Court's focus back to the two principal *Haslip* themes: (1) that punitive damages may be assessed against defendants for the wrong reasons and otherwise unfairly, and (2) that the due process clause requires courts to remedy such arbitrary and improper awards. The effect of the Court's resuscitation of *Haslip* in this manner may be to color *TXO*, sandwiched in between, as an aberration in the developing Supreme Court jurisprudence on the constitutional limits of punitive damages law.

### BMW of North America, Inc. v. Gore

Until 1996, the Supreme Court had been vague about how a court might apply due process to strike down a large punitive damages assessment. But in *BMW of North America, Inc. v. Gore*,[38] the Court specifically addressed how courts should determine whether an award of punitive damages is constitutionally excessive. An Alabama dentist recovered $4,000 in compensatory damages against BMW for selling him a car as "new" without disclosing that it had been repaired and partially repainted after being damaged in transit by acid rain. Following the suggestion of plaintiff's counsel, the jury calculated punitive damages by multiplying the compensatory damages times 1000, the approximate number of cars BMW had refinished and sold as new across America, for a total punitive award of $4 million.[39] The Alabama Supreme Court, concluding that the jury could not properly have based its award on the defendant's conduct outside the state, reduced the punitive damages award to a "constitutionally reasonable" amount of $2 million.[40] The United States Supreme Court acknowledged that a state may use punitive damages assessments to punish and deter misconduct, asserting that "[o]nly when an award can fairly be categorized as 'grossly excessive' in relation to these interests does it enter the zone of arbitrariness that violates the Due Process Clause of the Fourteenth Amendment."[41] Nevertheless, a 5–4 majority of the Court reversed, finding the $2 million punitive award to be grossly excessive.[42]

The Supreme Court agreed with the Alabama high court that a jury could not properly impose extraterritorial punishment on the defendant in such a case, and it was troubled by the fact that legislation in about half the states does not require disclosure (and so implicitly authorizes nondisclosure) of minor repairs of new cars. This led the Court to

**35.** Id. at 416.

**36.** Id. at 420.

**37.** This holding is grounded in history. "Judicial review of the size of punitive damages awards has been a safeguard against excessive verdicts for as long as punitive damages have been awarded." Id. at 421.

**38.** 517 U.S. 559 (1996).

**39.** See BMW of N. Am., Inc. v. Gore, 646 So.2d 619 (Ala. 1994).

**40.** Id. at 629.

**41.** *Gore*, 517 U.S. at 568.

**42.** See id. at 585.

conclude that the jury's punitive damages verdict, based in part upon conduct in states where the conduct was legal, violated principles of state sovereignty and comity.[43] While Alabama may require whatever disclosure it deems appropriate within its borders, its effort to change (deter) BMW's policies that were lawful in other states "would be infringing on the policy choices of other States."[44] Ruling that one state may not impose extra-territorial punishment on a defendant for conduct that is lawful in other states, the *Gore* majority viewed the $2 million penalty as grossly excessive when Alabama's state interests alone were considered.[45]

Actors must be provided with fair notice, the Court reasoned, not only of the type of conduct that is punishable "but also of the severity of the penalty that a State may impose."[46] For this purpose, the *Gore* Court identified three "guideposts" or "indicia" of adequate notice in an effort to help indicate whether a particular punitive award is "grossly excessive" and, hence, violative of due process: (1) the degree of reprehensibility of the defendant's conduct, the most important guidepost;[47] (2) the reasonableness of the relationship (the "ratio") of the punitive to the compensatory award; and (3) a comparison of the punitive award with other civil and criminal penalties authorized in such cases. Although the Court reiterated that it was "not prepared to draw a bright line marking the limits of a constitutionally acceptable punitive damages award,"[48] it concluded that the $2 million punitive award in *Gore* was out of all proportion to the goals of punitive damages under each of the three indicia.[49]

### Cooper Industries, Inc. v. Leatherman Tool Group, Inc.

The next punitive damages case the Supreme Court decided was *Cooper Industries, Inc. v. Leatherman Tool Group, Inc.*,[50] which changed the standard of federal appellate review of the constitutionality of punitive damages awards from abuse of discretion to *de novo* review. The plaintiff, Leatherman, sued Cooper Industries for trademark infringement, false advertising, and unfair competition for copying its Pocket Survival Tool and its advertising thereof. The jury found for the plaintiff, awarding compensatory damages of $50,000 and punitive damages of $4.5 million. Employing the normal abuse of discretion standard for reviewing the district court's due process analysis of the punitive award, the circuit court affirmed. Reversing, the Supreme Court concluded that a court of appeals must apply *de novo* review to a district court's determination of the constitutionality of a punitive damages award.[51] The eight-judge majority[52] reasoned that, because a punitive damages award operates as a quasi-criminal private fine designed to punish a defendant, rather than to assess actual damage suffered by a plaintiff,

---

**43.** See id. at 568–74.

**44.** Id. at 572.

**45.** See id. at 572–74.

**46.** Id. at 574.

**47.** "The most important indicium of the reasonableness of a punitive damages award is the degree of reprehensibility of the defendant's conduct." Id. at 575.

**48.** Id. at 585.

**49.** See id. at 574–85.

**50.** 532 U.S. 424 (2001).

**51.** Id. at 436.

**52.** Justice Stevens wrote for an 8-judge majority. Thomas and Scalia, JJ., concurred, and Ginsburg, J., dissented.

the standard of appellate review of district court due process determinations of punitive damages awards is not constrained by the Seventh Amendment right to jury trial.[53]

While *Cooper Industries* has been decried as effecting a radical shift of control over punitive damages decisionmaking from juries to courts,[54] it probably should be read narrowly to merely address the appropriate standard of federal appellate court review of district court determinations on the constitutionality of punitive damages awards. The dissenting[55] and even majority[56] opinions suggested that the change in the standard of review would likely have little practical impact, and neither state[57] nor federal[58] courts have accorded it much significance.

### State Farm Mutual Automobile Insurance Co. v. Campbell

The Court's most recent treatment of the constitutional aspects of punitive damages law is *State Farm Mutual Automobile Insurance Co. v. Campbell*.[59] This was a bad faith failure-to-settle case in which the plaintiff's insurance company, State Farm, failed to settle within the policy limits tort claims against the plaintiff for causing a serious car accident. Although there was no doubt of the plaintiff's negligence in causing the accident in which one driver died and another was disabled, State Farm told him that he did not need independent representation, assured him that his personal assets were safe, and refused to settle the case for the policy limits of $50,000. The jury returned a verdict for more than $185,000, leaving the plaintiff with excess liability of more than $135,000.

Initially, State Farm refused to cover the plaintiff's excess liability or even to post bond to permit the plaintiff to appeal. Thereafter, plaintiff and his wife sued the company for bad faith failure to settle, fraud, and intentional infliction of emotional distress. At the trial of these claims, plaintiff introduced evidence that State Farm's denial of the plaintiff's claim was part of the company's nation-wide scheme over 20 years to limit claim payouts improperly in order to improve profitabil-

---

**53.** 532 U.S. at 432–40.

**54.** See, e.g., Litwiller, Has the Supreme Court Sounded the Death Knell for Jury Assessed Punitive Damages? A Critical Reexamination of the American Jury, 36 U.S.F. L. Rev. 411 (2002); Dosaneo, Reexamining the Right to Trial by Jury, 54 SMU L. Rev. 1695, 1733 (2001).

**55.** See 532 U.S. at 450 (stating suspicion that *de novo* review standard "will yield different outcomes in few cases").

**56.** See 532 U.S. at 441 (acknowledging possibility of same).

**57.** See, e.g., Time Warner Entm't Co. v. Six Flags Over Ga., 563 S.E.2d 178 (Ga. Ct. App. 2002) (abuse of discretion proper standard of review where defendant did not challenge constitutionality of punitive award); Williams v. Philip Morris, 48 P.3d 824, 837 (Or. Ct. App. 2002) (Or. Ct. App.

2002) (*Cooper Industries* does not alter criteria by which trial court reviews punitive award), vacated and remanded for reconsideration on other grounds, Philip Morris USA, Inc. v. Williams, 501 U.S. 801 (2003), award reconsidered and reinstated, 92 P.3d 126 (Or. Ct. App. 2004); Seitzinger v. Trans–Lux Corp., 2001 WL 1748893, at *11 (N.M. Ct. App. 2002) ("We do not interpret *Cooper Industries, Inc.* to impose de novo review as a matter of constitutional imperative. Rather, it appears to be an appellate procedural option for the federal courts. We are thus free to apply our own standard as a matter of constitutional law.").

**58.** See, e.g., Todd v. Roadway Express, Inc., 178 F.Supp.2d 1244 (M.D. Ala. 2001) (*Cooper Industries* has no bearing on how punitive damages are awarded, only on how a jury's award is reviewed).

**59.** 538 U.S. 408 (2003).

ity. On this evidence, the jury returned verdicts of $2.6 million in compensatory damages and $145 million in punitive damages which the trial judge remitted, respectively, to $1 million and $25 million. Reinstating the full $145 million punitive damages verdict, the Utah Supreme Court concluded that it was warranted under the three *Gore* measurement guideposts because the defendant's nation-wide scheme to cheat its policyholders was reprehensible, coupled with the company's "massive wealth" and the improbability of its being caught and punished due to the clandestine nature of its activities.[60]

State Farm appealed the case to the Supreme Court, arguing that the $145 million punitive damages assessment was excessive and violative of due process because the Utah courts had improperly considered conduct outside the state and had otherwise violated the due process principles set forth in *Gore*.[61] Agreeing, the Supreme Court reversed and remanded, stating that the case was "neither close nor difficult" under Gore's guideposts for avoiding constitutionally excessive punitive damages awards.[62] As for reprehensibility, the first and most important guidepost, the court acknowledged the impropriety of the defendant's scheme but explained that due process precluded courts from basing punitive awards on misconduct, especially conduct outside the state, unrelated to the plaintiff's harm.[63] So long as a defendant's misconduct to other persons is similar to the conduct that harmed the plaintiff, courts and juries may properly consider it as showing that the defendant is a repeat offender and hence deserving of greater punishment, but the majority concluded that the record in this case revealed scant evidence of repeated misconduct of the kind that injured the plaintiff—the denial of third-party liability claims. Noting that a much lower award would have adequately protected Utah's interest in punishing and deterring State Farm's relevant misconduct that occurred in Utah, the Court observed that the case was improperly "used as a platform to expose, and punish, the perceived deficiencies of State Farm's operations throughout the country."[64] Unfortunately, the majority ignored considerable reprehensi-

---

**60.** See Campbell v. State Farm Mut. Auto. Ins. Co., 65 P.3d 1134 (Utah 2001), reversed and remanded, 538 U.S. 508 (2003).

**61.** 538 U.S. 408 (2003).

**62.** Id. at 417. The majority decision was authored by Kennedy, J. Justices Scalia, Thomas, and Ginsburg reasoned in separate dissents that the Supreme Court should not review state court punitive damages judgments.

**63.** "Lawful out-of-state conduct may be probative when it demonstrates the deliberateness and culpability of the defendant's action in the State where it is tortious, but that conduct must have a nexus to the specific harm suffered by the plaintiff." Id. at 418. Nor did the Court think that a punitive damages award could be supported by substantially dissimilar conduct by the defendant that harmed persons other than the plaintiffs:

A defendant should be punished for the conduct that harmed the plaintiff, not for being an unsavory individual or business. Due process does not permit courts, in the calculation of punitive damages, to adjudicate the merits of other parties' hypothetical claims against a defendant under the guise of the reprehensibility analysis.... Punishment on these bases creates the possibility of multiple punitive damages awards for the same conduct....

Id. at 423.

**64.** Id. at 420. "The reprehensibility guidepost does not permit courts to expand the scope of the case so that a defendant may be punished for any malfeasance, which in this case extended for a 20-year period. In this case, because the Campbell's have shown no conduct by State Farm similar to that which harmed them, the conduct that harmed them is the only conduct rele-

bility evidence of serious State Farm misconduct, much of which was directly relevant to the company's abusive practices in this case.[65]

As for the second guidepost, the ratio between punitive and compensatory damages, the Court "decline[d] again to impose a bright-line ratio which a punitive damages award cannot exceed."[66] While signaling that "few awards exceeding a single-digit ratio ... will satisfy due process,"[67] the Court observed that due process may permit greater ratios in certain circumstances—for particularly egregious misconduct resulting in small economic damages,[68] where the injury is hard to detect, or where the misconduct causes physical injuries. In all cases, however, "courts must ensure that the measure of punishment is both reasonable and proportionate to the amount of harm to the plaintiff and to the general damages recovered."[69] Because State Farm eventually paid the plaintiffs' excess liability, their losses were mostly emotional, leading the Court to determine that the generous $1 million compensatory damages award contained a substantial punitive component such that a large punitive award would be constitutionally inappropriate.[70] Finally, the Court explained that the very large punitive damages award was unjustified by the third and final *Gore* guidepost which compares the punitive award to other civil and criminal penalties that may also apply to the defendant's misconduct which, in Utah, was a mere $10,000 fine for fraud. For these reasons, the Court concluded that the $145 million punitive damages assessment in this case was "neither reasonable nor proportionate to the wrong committed, and it was an irrational and arbitrary deprivation of the property of the defendant."[71]

---

vant to the reprehensibility analysis." Id. at 424. As pointed out in Justice Ginsburg's dissent, discussed in the following footnote, the majority's last assertion is simply wrong.

**65.** In dissent, Justice Ginsburg summarized evidence, conveniently ignored by the majority, of the defendant's truly intolerable business practices, some of which the company employed in this case, that were in fact highly relevant to an assessment of the defendant's reprehensibility. See id. at 431–37. "[O]n the key criterion 'reprehensibility,' there is a good deal more to the story than the Court's abbreviated account tells." Id. at 431. The evidence revealed an ongoing, company-wide scheme to falsify records and use trickery and other dishonest techniques—such as unjustly attacking a claimant's character, reputation, and credibility by making false and prejudicial notations in the file—to pay less both first-party and third-party claims at less than fair value. Two of the defendant's Utah employees testified to "intolerable" and "recurrent" pressure to reduce payouts below fair value, id. at 432, and the local manager ordered the adjuster for the Campbell case to falsify company records by inventing a story that the driver who died in the accident was speeding to see a pregnant

girlfriend who did not exist. Several former State Farm employees testified "that they were trained to target 'the weakest of the herd'—'the elderly, the poor, and other consumers who are least knowledgeable about their rights and thus most vulnerable to trickery or deceit, or who have little money and hence have no real alternative but to accept an inadequate offer to settle a claim at much less than fair value.' " The plaintiffs fell into this vulnerable claimant category—economically, emotionally, and physically, Mr. Campbell (since deceased) having suffered from a stroke and Parkinson's disease. Id. at 433.

**66.** Id. at 425.

**67.** Id. at 426.

**68.** Conversely, "[w]hen compensatory damages are substantial, then a lesser ratio, perhaps only equal to compensatory damages, can reach the outermost limit of the due process guarantee." Id. at 425.

**69.** Id. at 426.

**70.** "When compensatory damages are substantial, then a lesser ratio, perhaps only equal to compensatory damages, can reach the outermost limit of the due process guarantee." Id. at 425.

**71.** Id. at 429.

## Applying Constitutional Doctrine to the Products Liability Context

One must question how meaningfully the due process excessiveness principles of *Gore* and its progeny may be applied to products liability cases involving personal injury or death. In *Gore*, the Supreme Court noted that the reprehensibility of misconduct is affected by certain "aggravating factors," including whether the conduct threatened merely economic interests or health and safety,[72] and whether the defendant acted with "trickery and deceit"—with "deliberate false statements, acts of affirmative misconduct, or concealment of evidence of improper motive."[73] In *TXO*, trickery was the only aggravating factor, and the Court there upheld a $10 million punitive award that was ten times the amount of potential harm and 527 times the actual harm. Products liability cases ordinarily involve a significant threat to human safety,[74] and trickery and concealment frequently pervade those products liability cases in which punitive damages are fairly imposed.[75] Another of Gore's aggravating factors is whether the defendant had engaged in repetitive misbehavior, whether it was a repeat offender.[76] Products liability cases in which the manufacturer continues to market a product despite increasing proof that it is dangerously defective, particularly if it also continues to tout the product's safety,[77] involve precisely this form of aggravated misbehavior.[78]

The fact that each of Gore's aggravating factors commonly exists in products liability cases involving large punitive damages awards—cases in which multi-million dollar punitive damages awards are assessed against multi-billion dollar, multi-national manufacturers of defective products—frustrates their usefulness in this context. Stated otherwise, Gore's excessiveness guideposts provide manufacturers and the courts with little useful guidance as to how due process may limit punitive damage awards in products liability cases.[79] The only really helpful lesson from *Gore* is its central theme, underscored by the Court's shift to a standard of *de novo* review in *Cooper Industries*, that reviewing courts must closely examine the culpability and other punitive damages evidence in relation to the rules and goals of punitive damages law—

**72.** See id. at 575–76. "The harm BMW inflicted on Dr. Gore was purely economic in nature.... BMW's conduct evinced no indifference to or reckless disregard for the health and safety of others." Id. at 576. See also *State Farm*, 538 U.S. at 410 (discussing *Gore*'s second guidepost).

**73.** Id. at 579.

**74.** Even if only property damage in fact results.

**75.** See § 18.3, above.

**76.** "Certainly, evidence that a defendant has repeatedly engaged in prohibited conduct while knowing or suspecting that it was unlawful would provide relevant support for an argument that strong medicine is required to cure the defendant's disrespect for the law.... Our holdings that a

recidivist may be punished more severely than a first offender recognize that repeated misconduct is more reprehensible than an individual instance of malfeasance." *Gore*, 517 U.S. at 576–77.

**77.** See, e.g., Jimenez v. Chrysler Corp., 74 F.Supp.2d 548, 579–80 (D.S.C. 1999) (although defendant was "fully cognizant of the grave risk and fact of serious injuries and deaths," it "continued to sell the 'safety' of its minivans, reaping billions of dollars in profits along the way"), rev'd, 269 F.3d 439 (4th Cir. 2001).

**78.** See § 18.3, above.

**79.** See Justice Scalia's observation that "the 'guideposts' mark a road to nowhere; they provide no real guidance at all." *Gore*, 517 U.S. at 605 (Scalia, J., dissenting).

particularly if the size of a particular award raises "a suspicious judicial eyebrow,"[80] which may indeed be all that due process truly should require.[81] Yet one should not minimize the importance of this due process requirement, commenced in *Haslip*[82] and continued in *Gore, Cooper Industries*, and *State Farm*, that courts scrutinize the evidence closely to assure that the procedures by which punitive damages are assessed are fair to the defendant.

Conspicuously absent from the Court's listing of due process excessiveness guideposts in *Gore* and its progeny is the matter of the defendant's financial condition or "wealth." While defendants and economic theorists vigorously challenge the relevance of such evidence to punitive damages determinations,[83] common law courts long have considered it to be an important guidepost for establishing the proper size of punitive damages assessments,[84] a customary approach to measurement acknowledged by the Court.[85] The point quite simply is that a $1 million punitive damages award that may be trivial for General Motors may bankrupt a small automotive parts company.[86] For this reason, some courts actually *require* proof of a defendant's wealth before a punitive damages award properly may be assessed.[87] In its latest pronouncement, the majority in *State Farm* seems to shift from recognizing the states' conventional and legitimate use of wealth, for helping ascertain an appropriate amount of a punitive damages assessment, to viewing evidence of the defendant's wealth almost as perverse.

If a guidepost list for determining the excessiveness of punitive damages awards is to be limited to three indicia, as it most assuredly need not,[88] it would be much improved if the Court were to substitute

---

**80.** Id. at 583.

**81.** See id. at 598 (Scalia, J., dissenting).

**82.** See *Haslip*, 499 U.S. at 9–10.

**83.** See, e.g., Polinsky and Shavell, Punitive Damages: An Economic Analysis, 111 Harv. L. Rev. 869, 910 (1998) (irrelevant to deterrence in case of economic harms); Abraham and Jeffries, Punitive Damages and the Rule of Law: The Role of Defendant's Wealth, 18 J. Legal Stud. 415 (1989).

**84.** See § 18.4, above.

**85.** See, e.g., TXO Prod. Corp. v. Alliance Res. Corp., 509 U.S. 443, 462 and n. 28 (1993), specifying the "petitioner's wealth" as one basis for upholding large punitive damages award, and recognizing that reliance on evidence of a defendant's wealth is "typically considered" and allowable under "well-settled law." See also id. at 464; Pacific Mut. Life Ins. Co. v. Haslip, 499 U.S. 1, 21–22 (1991) (finding defendant's "financial position" a legitimate factor). *But see* Honda Motor Co. v. Oberg, 512 U.S. 415, 432 (1994) ("evidence of a defendant's net worth creates the potential that juries will use their verdicts to express biases against big businesses").

**86.** See, e.g., BMW of N. Am., Inc. v. Gore, 517 U.S. 559, 586, 591 (1996) (Breyer, J., concurring) ("Since a fixed dollar award will punish a poor person more than a wealthy one, one can understand the relevance of this factor to the state's interest in retribution.") (citations omitted).

**87.** See, e.g., Adams v. Murakami, 813 P.2d 1348, 1351 (Cal. 1991) (information on defendant's wealth is necessary for appellate review of alleged excessiveness of punitive award; trial court should instruct jury to consider defendant's financial condition); Herman v. Sunshine Chem. Specialties, Inc., 627 A.2d 1081, 1087 (N.J. 1993) (holding in a non-products liability case that "a jury must consider evidence of a defendant's financial condition in determining the amount of punitive damages" and noting state statute mandating such evidence in products liability actions).

**88.** Although Justice Stevens' majority opinion in *Gore* does not address this point directly, Justice Scalia observes that "the Court nowhere says that these three 'guideposts' are the only guideposts; indeed, it makes very clear that they are not...."

the defendant's *wealth* for a comparison of the punitive award with other sanctions.[89] Just as due process fairly requires that punitive damages awards be tied to the overall objectives of such assessments, the ultimate due process fairness question pertaining to the size of an award is the overall *appropriateness* of any given award on all the facts of the particular case. Unlike the concept of "excessiveness," which seems more narrowly to focus on the size of an award in numerical terms, the concept of appropriateness more embracingly includes all aspects of a defendant's and plaintiff's situations relevant to the amount of punishment proper in any given case. Particularly in the products liability context, there may be as many as *nine* separate considerations ("guideposts") that properly bear on the measurement issue.[90] Confining the measurement criteria to only three of the many relevant factors forces the underlying fairness inquiry awkwardly into an incomplete and rigid mold. If substantive due process is to be revivified, as now it surely has, it should not be used to make the states recraft their law according to a structure that is flawed. At least in products liability cases, the marked deficiencies in Gore's guidepost list robs it of usefulness and validity for testing the fairness of a punitive damages award of a given size.

The extra-territoriality aspect of *Gore*,[91] underscored in *State Farm*,[92] is important in products liability litigation where a manufacturer's sale of thousands or even millions of similarly defective products across the nation (or throughout the world) is often argued by plaintiff's counsel as aggravating the misconduct and as so providing in the aggregate a proper foundation for calculating an appropriate punitive assessment proportionate to the wrong. But the *Gore* majority's analysis of the extra-territorial punishment issue translates poorly into products liability cases where the sale of a seriously defective product is patently unlawful and contrary to the public policy of every state in the nation. While the purpose of a punitive damages award in an individual case

*Gore*, 517 U.S. at 606. See, e.g., Barnett v. La Societe Anonyme Turbomeca France, 963 S.W.2d 639, 666 (Mo. Ct. App. 1997); Patton v. TIC United Corp., 859 F.Supp. 509 (D. Kan. 1994).

**89.** See, e.g., Note, The Shadow of BMW of North America, Inc. v. Gore, 1998 Wis. L. Rev. 427, 460 ("While a comparison to legislative sanctions may be quite objective, and thus desirable from a defendant's point of view, a small legislative sanction often warrants a higher punitive award when the conduct is fairly egregious. Thus, the defendant's wealth would have provided a better guidepost than legislative sanctions for excessiveness review."). Justice Breyer's attempt in *Gore* to explain why wealth is not included on the excessiveness constraint list, 517 U.S. at 591, fails to recognize that the concept of excessiveness is but a part of the broader concept of appropriateness: if for some reason (the defendant's wealth or other factual indicium omitted from Gore's short list) a "large" punitive award is warranted, it can hardly be "excessive."

**90.** See § 18.4, above. In *Gore*, Justice Breyer criticized Alabama's "*Green Oil*" list of seven such factors (summarized in note 17, above) on the ground that the Alabama courts in practice had not used the factors to restrain excessive punitive awards. See *Gore*, 517 U.S. at 586 and 592 (Breyer, J., concurring) ("the state courts neither referred to, nor made any effort to find, nor enunciated any other standard that either directly, or indirectly as background, might have supplied the constraining legal force that the [seven factors] lack"). While the Alabama courts may well not have applied their seven factors with sufficient vigor, drastically cutting the list to the bone, and including in it the most arbitrary factors (guideposts 2 and 3), would seem to exacerbate the problem rather than to help resolve it.

**91.** See *Gore*, 517 U.S. at 568–74.

**92.** 538 U.S. at 420–25.

should not be to provide an optimal punitive assessment for a manufacturer's entire marketing misconduct across the entire nation, rarely can a manufacturer's marketing behavior be evaluated intelligently solely from a narrow state-oriented perspective. Many products (especially automobiles) first sold into one state are later transported into others, and major manufacturers make engineering, safety, marketing, and profitability decisions on a national (or international) basis. At the time of making decisions of this type that may improperly expose consumers across the nation (or globe) to an excessive risk of harm, a manufacturer has no idea which consumers in which states its products will likely injure. Accordingly, in judging the flagrancy of a defendant's misconduct that eventually injures a particular plaintiff in a particular state, and in ascertaining the proper level of retribution and deterrence for that misconduct, it would seem that punitive damages factfinders would necessarily have to consider the manufacturer's entire misconduct and decisionmaking as it extended nation-wide.[93]

From *Haslip* to *Gore* and *State Farm*, the Supreme Court has continued to emphasize the due process problems in punitive damage assessments many times the size of the compensatory awards. Lower courts seem to be getting the message, reflected in their lowering high-multiple punitive awards, in an attempt to comport with due process ratio principles, to much lower "reasonable" multiples of compensatory damages.[94]

**93.** Ruling on the admission of similar incidents evidence from other states against the backdrop of BMW of N. Am., Inc. v. Gore, 517 U.S. 559 (1996), the court in Smith v. Ingersoll–Rand Co., 214 F.3d 1235, 1253 (10th Cir. 2000) (N.M. law) had "no trouble concluding the district court did not exceed New Mexico's legitimate interest in punishing and deterring the production of defective products by permitting the jury to consider incidents occurring outside the state. Not only were the out-of-state incidents offered to illustrate the reprehensibility of Ingersoll–Rand's conduct, but the manufacture of defective products is not a lawful activity in any of the jurisdictions where the other incidents occurred." In State Farm, while the majority claimed to recognize the relevance of a defendant's extra-state conduct for some purposes, the narrowness of the evidence it considered relevant to reprehensibility on the facts of that case, as explained in Justice Ginsburg's dissent, casts serious doubt on the genuineness of the majority's claim.

**94.** Shortly after the Supreme Court handed down its decision in State Farm, the Court vacated and remanded for reconsideration four products liability decisions for reconsideration in light of that case: Romo v. Ford Motor Co., 122 Cal.Rptr.2d 139 (Ct. App. 2002), which approved a $290 million punitive damages award, on a compensatory award of $5 million, in a Ford Bronco roll-over case; Bocci v. Key Pharm., Inc., 35

P.3d 1106 (Or. Ct. App. 2001), which approved two punitive damages awards including one for $22.5 million, in a drug fraud case, on a compensatory award of $500,000; Williams v. Philip Morris Inc., 48 P.3d 824 (Or. Ct. App. 2002), which remitted a $79.5 million punitive award to $32.8 million, on a compensatory award of slightly over $800,000, in a smoker cancer death case; Sand Hill Energy, Inc. v. Ford Motor Co., 83 S.W.3d 483 (Ky. 2002), which approved a $15 million punitive damages award, on a compensatory award of $3 million, in a Park-to-Reverse transmission slip case.

On remand in *Romo*, the California Court of Appeals remitted the punitive award to $23.7 million, Romo v. Ford Motor Co., 6 Cal.Rptr.3d 793 (Ct. App. 2003); on remand in *Bocci*, the Oregon Court of Appeals reduced the punitive award to $3.5 million, Bocci v. Key Pharm. Inc., 79 P.3d 908 (Or. Ct. App. 2003) (cutting treating physician's $22.5 million punitive damages award, on compensatory damages of $500,000, to $3.5 million—thereby reducing ratio from 45:1 to 7:1); on remand in *Williams*, the Oregon Court of Appeals reinstated the full $79.5 million punitive award, concluding that it in fact was reasonable, proportionate to the wrong to the plaintiff and to the public in the state, and hence comported with Supreme Court due process guidelines, Williams v. Philip Morris Inc., 92 P.3d 126

Additional due process (and other constitutional) questions remain unresolved that the Supreme Court may one day choose to answer. Probably the most significant unresolved issue is whether the Constitution imposes any restraints on the repetitive imposition of punitive damages in mass disaster cases, such as the litigation that has confronted the asbestos industry for many years.[95] Indeed, it is difficult to understand why the Court has failed to review this most important matter when presented with what appeared to be the perfect opportunity.[96] Many other fairness questions about punitive damages may (or may not) have due process implications, such as whether the burden of proof for punitive damages may properly be set at only a preponderance of the evidence,[97] the propriety of basing punitive assessments upon the defendant's wealth,[98] and many others.

However one views the claim that punitive damages awards have "run wild,"[99] one may question whether the United States Supreme Court ever should have begun to constitutionalize state tort law in this area.[100] But *Haslip* decidedly crossed that Rubicon in 1991, since which time the Court has continued its march toward Rome. It is difficult to predict how far the Supreme Court ultimately may extend its foray of substantive due process into the punitive damages lair, and one must hope that the Court will be cautious in attempting to reform this unruly beast.[101] While recent years have witnessed occasional punitive damages

(Or. Ct. App. 2004); on remand in *Sand Hill*, the Kentucky Supreme Court vacated the award and remanded for a new trial on punitive damages which would have to exclude extraterritorial punishment, Sand Hill Energy, Inc. v. Smith, 142 S.W.3d 153 (Ky. 2004).

**95.** For a further discussion of these issues, see § 18.5, above.

**96.** In Dunn v. HOVIC, 1 F.3d 1371 (3d Cir. 1993) (en banc), modified in part, 13 F.3d 58 (3d Cir.). Collecting the state and federal cases to that date, the court in *Dunn* observed that virtually every court to address the issue has "declined to strike punitive damages awards merely because they constituted repetitive punishment for the same conduct," noting that "[i]n concluding that multiple punitive damage awards are not inconsistent with the due process clause or substantive tort law principles, both state and federal courts have recognized that no single court can fashion an effective response to the national problem flowing from mass exposure to asbestos products." 1 F.3d at 1386. Accord, Spaur v. Owens–Corning Fiberglas Corp., 510 N.W.2d 854 (Iowa 1994); W.R. Grace & Co.—Conn. v. Waters, 638 So.2d 502 (Fla. 1994) (noting the problems of successive awards in mass tort litigation, but refusing to limit their imposition). Although the opportunity for consideration of the multiplicity of awards issue was less appropriate in *Gore* than in *Dunn*, the issue was presented

to and sidestepped by the Court in *Gore*. See BMW of N. Am., Inc. v. Gore, 517 U.S. 559, 607, 612 n.4 (1996) (Ginsburg, J., dissenting).

**97.** *Haslip* suggests that such a higher standard of proof may not be constitutionally required. Pacific Mut. Life Ins. Co. v. Haslip, 449 U.S. 1, 23 n.11 (1991).

**98.** The Supreme Court to date has tolerated evidence and argument on the defendant's wealth, see note 64, above, but the defense bar continues to argue its unconstitutionality and, in *State Farm*, the Court noted that a defendant's wealth "cannot justify an otherwise unconstitutional punitive damages award." 538 U.S. at 427. The allowance of such evidence was challenged as a denial of due process in the defendant's petition for certiorari in Ford Motor Co. v. Ammerman, 705 N.E.2d 539, 563 (Ind. Ct. App. 1999), where the jury rendered a $58 million punitive assessment, reduced by the trial court to $13.8 million, which was upheld on appeal.

**99.** See *Haslip*, 499 U.S. 1, 18 (1991).

**100.** See Riggs, Constitutionalizing Punitive Damages: The Limits of Due Process, 52 Ohio St. L.J. 859 (1991); Zwier, Due Process and Punitive Damages, 1991 Utah L. Rev. 407.

**101.** Surely an unruly beast, see § 18.5, above, but not without redeeming value. See § 18.2, above.

awards that by any standards are extremely large,[102] the accelerated growth and consolidation of corporate institutions is making more and more multi-national enterprises wealthier and more powerful than many nations on the planet.[103] In this rapidly changing world, substantive due process should not require that people be deprived of what may be their most effective protection against the abuses of megalithic enterprises which may trample, sometimes flagrantly and always in the pursuit of profit, the safety and other interests of private individuals. The Constitution ought not be read to prohibit states from using all available resources, including the possibility of large assessments of punitive damages, to teach such enterprises that profitability at some point must give way to public safety and to provide an effective level of retribution and deterrence for flagrantly improper conduct that harms the citizens of this nation.

Justice Scalia has charged that the Supreme Court's punitive damages jurisprudence is "insusceptible of principled application,"[104] a view that contains some truth and is shared by some tort law scholars.[105] In time, perhaps, the Court may recognize the perils of treading too deeply into this particular quagmire of state tort law, as it eventually saw the error of excessive constitutional zeal in reforming the law of defamation.[106] If so, the Court may then begin at least a partial retreat from its current path of substantively second-guessing the size of punitive damages awards that survive Haslip's proper procedural due process net.[107] Yet *State Farm* suggests the opposite, that the Court has decided to continue the enterprise begun in *Gore* of evaluating the constitutional propriety of "large" punitive awards in particular cases. This should come as no surprise, what with the staggering size of some awards and the inability of courts and legislatures to impose coherent limits. Logic suggests that punitive damage awards at some point become *too* large, and the Supreme Court has felt impelled to wield the powerful due process sword in an effort to lop off the most extreme excesses that have cried out for real reform.

Whatever path it ultimately may follow, it is clear for now that the Supreme Court takes seriously the idea that the due process clause

---

**102.** Justice O'Connor's observation in 1989 that such awards were "skyrocketing" was not inapt. See Browning–Ferris Indus. v. Kelco Disposal, Inc., 492 U.S. 257, 282 (O'Connor, J., concurring in part and dissenting in part).

**103.** Pursuant to Congressional authorization, a court subjected Iran to $300 million in punitive damages for wantonly abusing the human rights of a hostage, Terry Anderson. New York Times, Mar. 25, 2000, at A28.

**104.** State Farm Mut. Auto. Ins. Co. v. Campbell, 538 U.S. 408, 429 (Scalia, J., dissenting).

**105.** See, e.g., Gash, Punitive Damages, Other Acts Evidence, and the Constitution, 2004 Utah L. Rev. ___ (2004).

**106.** Realizing that it had gone too far in Rosenbloom v. Metromedia, Inc., 403 U.S. 29 (1971), in extending the free speech and press principles of New York Times Co. v. Sullivan, 376 U.S. 254 (1964), the Supreme Court began to accord greater respect to countervailing state tort law interests in Gertz v. Robert Welch, Inc., 418 U.S. 323 (1974), and Dunn & Bradstreet, Inc. v. Greenmoss Builders, Inc., 472 U.S. 749 (1985).

**107.** See, e.g., BMW of N. Am. v. Gore: A Misplaced Guide for Punitive Damage Awards, 18 N. Ill. U. L. Rev. 219 (1997); BMW v. Gore: Why the States (Not the U.S. Supreme Court) Should Review Substantive Due Process Challenges to Large Punitive Damage Awards, 46 U. Kan. L. Rev. 395 (1998).

limits the size of punitive awards, a development that is beginning to ripple through punitive damages awards in products liability cases.[108] As a consequence, courts and lawyers will have to continue to make what sense they can of the growing constitutional jurisprudence on the law of punitive damages. State and lower federal courts now must focus closely on the various constitutional dimensions of punitive damages, from the fairness of the procedures by which such assessments are made and reviewed, pursuant to *Haslip*,[109] to the various standards for testing their excessiveness developed in and applied by *Gore* and *State Farm*.[110]

**108.** See footnote 57, above.

**109.** Pursuant to *Haslip*, many courts have imposed a variety of procedural requirements on awards of punitive damages in an effort to tighten up the standards by which they are assessed and reviewed, such as requiring judges to provide written (or recorded) justification of such awards in ruling on post-trial motions. See, e.g., Gamble v. Stevenson, 406 S.E.2d 350 (S.C. 1991) (trial judges); Transportation Ins. Co. v. Moriel, 879 S.W.2d 10 (Tex. 1994) (appellate judges, but not trial judges; trials to be bifurcated).

**110.** Following *Gore*, courts have diligently applied that decision's three excessiveness guideposts to claims of excessiveness. See, e.g., Ford Motor Co. v. Ammerman, 705 N.E.2d 539, 563 (Ind. Ct. App. 1999) (holding that jury's $58 million punitive assessment violated due process but upholding trial court's remitted award in amount of $13.8 million). Following *State Farm*, in examining the excessiveness of a punitive award under the due process clause, courts have more closely focused on the ratio of punitive damages to compensatory damages, par-

ticularly after the Supreme Court vacated and remanded high ratio punitive awards. See, e.g., Frankson v. Brown & Williamson Tobacco Corp., 781 N.Y.S. 2d 427 (Sup. Ct. 2004); Suffix, U.S.A., Inc. v. Cook, 128 S.W.3d 838 (Ky. Ct. App. 2004); Werremeyer v. K.C. Auto Salvage Co., 134 S.W.3d 633 (Mo. 2004); Romo v. Ford Motor Co., 6 Cal.Rptr.3d 793 (Ct. App. 2003) (punitive damages totaling $290 million, on compensatory damages of somewhat under $5 million, reduced to $23.7 million, a ratio of about 5:1); Henley v. Philip Morris Inc., 5 Cal. Rptr.3d 42 (Ct. App. 2003) ($50 million punitive damages verdict, remitted by trial court to $25 million, reduced on appeal to $9 million, lowering ratio from 17:1 to 6:1), review granted and cause transferred, 81 P.3d 223 (Cal. 2003); Waddill v. Anchor Hocking, Inc., 78 P.3d 570 (Or. Ct. App. 2003) (reducing $1 million punitive damages award to $400,000, lowering ratio from 10:1 to 4:1). See also Bocci v. Key Pharm., Inc., 76 P.3d 669 (Or. Ct. App. 2003) (punitive damages reduced to $3.5 million, lowering ratio from 45:1 to 7:1).

# Westlaw Appendix

# Researching Products Liability Law

---

## Section 1. Introduction

*Products Liability Law* provides a strong base for analyzing even the most complex problem involving issues related to products liability law. Whether your research requires examination of case law, statutes, administrative decisions, expert commentary, or other materials, West books and Westlaw are excellent sources of information.

To keep you informed of current developments, Westlaw provides frequently updated databases. With Westlaw, you have unparalleled legal research resources at your fingertips.

## Additional Resources

If you have not previously used Westlaw or if you have questions not covered in this appendix, call the West Reference Attorneys at 1–800–REF–ATTY (1–800–733–2889). The West Reference Attorneys are trained, licensed attorneys, available 24 hours a day to assist you with your Westlaw search questions. To subscribe to Westlaw, call 1–800–344–5008 or visit westlaw.com at **www.westlaw.com**.

## Section 2. Westlaw Databases

Each database on Westlaw is assigned an abbreviation called an *identifier*, which you can use to access the database. You can find identifiers for Westlaw databases in the online Westlaw Directory and in the printed *Westlaw Database Directory*. When you need to know more detailed information about a database, use Scope. Scope contains coverage information, lists of related databases, and valuable search tips.

The following chart lists selected Westlaw databases that contain information pertaining to products liability law. For a complete list of products liability law databases, see the online Westlaw Directory or the printed *Westlaw Database Directory*. Because new information is continually being added to Westlaw, you should also check the tabbed Westlaw page and the online Westlaw Directory for new database information.

### Selected Products Liability Law Databases on Westlaw

| Database | Identifier | Coverage |
| --- | --- | --- |
| **Case Law** | | |
| Federal Products Liability—Cases | FPL–CS | Begins with 1789 |
| Federal Products Liability—Supreme Court Cases | FPL–SCT | Begins with 1790 |
| Federal Products Liability—Courts of Appeals Cases | FPL–CTA | Begins with 1891 |
| Federal Products Liability—District Courts Cases | FPL–DCT | Begins with 1789 |
| Products Liability Cases | PL–CS | Begins with 1945 |
| Multistate Products Liability Cases | MPL–CS | Varies by state |
| Individual State Products Liability Cases | XXPL–CS (where XX is a state's two-letter postal abbreviation) | Varies by state |

| Database | Identifier | Coverage |
|---|---|---|
| Multistate Tort Law Cases | MTRT–CS | Varies by state |
| Individual State Tort Law Cases | XXTRT–CS (where XX is a state's two-letter postal abbreviation) | Varies by state |
| Daubert Citator | DAUBERT | July 1993–December 2000 |

## Briefs, Pleadings, and Other Court Documents

| | | |
|---|---|---|
| Andrews Asbestos Litigation Reporter Court Documents | ANASBLR–DOC | Begins with 2000 |
| Andrews Automotive Litigation Reporter Court Documents | ANAUTOLR–DOC | Begins with 2000 |
| Andrews Class Action Litigation Reporter Court Documents | ANCALR–DOC | Begins with 2000 |
| Andrews Drug Recall Litigation Reporter Court Documents | ANDRLR–DOC | Begins with 2000 |
| Andrews Food Health and Safety Litigation Reporter Court Documents | ANFOODLR–DOC | Begins with 2004 |
| Andrews Gun Industry Litigation Reporter Court Documents | ANGUNLTGR–DOC | Begins with 2000 |
| Andrews Medical Devices Litigation Reporter Court Documents | ANMDLR–DOC | Begins with 2000 |
| Andrews Pharmaceutical Litigation Reporter Court Documents | ANPHARLR–DOC | Begins with 2000 |
| Andrews Product Liability Litigation Reporter Court Documents | ANPRODLLR–DOC | Begins with 2000 |

| Database | Identifier | Coverage |
|---|---|---|
| Andrews Tire Defect Litigation Reporter Court Documents | ANTDLR–DOC | Begins with 2000 |
| Andrews Tobacco Industry Litigation Reporter Court Documents | ANTILR–DOC | Begins with 2000 |
| Minnesota Tobacco Case Transcripts | MNTOBAC–TRANS | Begins with January 1998 |
| Products Liability Briefs | PL–BRIEF | Begins with 1963 |
| Products Liability Trial Motions | PL–MOTIONS | Begins with 1997 |
| Products Liability Trial Pleadings | PL–PLEADINGS | Begins with 1997 |

## Statutes, Legislative History, and Rules

| | | |
|---|---|---|
| Products Liability Statutes | PL–ST | Varies by jurisdiction |
| United States Code Annotated® | USCA | Current data |
| Legislative History— U.S. Code, 1948 to Present | LH | Begins with 1948 |
| State Statutes—Annotated | ST–ANN–ALL | Current data |
| Individual State Statutes—Annotated | XX–ST–ANN (where XX is a state's two-letter postal abbreviation) | Current data |
| Federal Rules | US–RULES | Current data |
| Federal Orders | US–ORDERS | Current data |
| State Court Rules | RULES–ALL | Current data |
| Individual State Court Rules | XX–RULES (where XX is a state's two-letter postal abbreviation) | Current data |
| State Court Orders | ORDERS–ALL | Current data |

| Database | Identifier | Coverage |
|---|---|---|
| Individual State Court Orders | XX–ORDERS (where XX is a state's two-letter postal abbreviation) | Current data |

## Administrative Materials

| | | |
|---|---|---|
| Code of Federal Regulations | CFR | Current data |
| Federal Register | FR | Begins with July 1980 |
| Federal Antitrust and Trade Regulation—Consumer Product Safety Commission Materials | FATR–CPSC | Begins with 1981 |
| Federal Products Liability—Products Liability Regulations | FPL–CFR | Current data |

## Legal Texts, Periodicals, and Practice Materials

| | | |
|---|---|---|
| Products Liability—Law Reviews, Texts, and Bar Journals | PL–TP | Varies by publication |
| Products Liability Texts and Periodicals | PL–TEXTS | Varies by publication |
| Tort Law—Law Reviews, Texts, and Bar Journals | TRT–TP | Varies by publication |
| ALR®—Products Liability | PL–ALR | Current data |
| Am Jur® Pleading and Practice Forms—Products Liability | PL–PP | Current data |
| Am Jur Proof of Facts—Products Liability | PL–POF | Current data |
| Am Jur Trials—Products Liability | PL–TRIALS | Current data |
| American Law of Products Liability 3d | ALPL | Current data |
| ATLA's Litigating Tort Cases | ATLA–TORT | Current data |

| Database | Identifier | Coverage |
|---|---|---|
| Automobile Design Liability 3d | AUTODLIAB | Current data |
| Aviation Tort and Regulatory Law | AVIATION | Second edition |
| Causes of Action—Products Liability | PL–COA | Current data |
| Corporate Compliance Series: Product Liability | CORPC–PL | Current data |
| Crashworthiness Litigation | CRASH | Current data |
| Evidence in Negligence Cases | PLIREF–NEGEVD | 10th edition |
| Georgia Products Liability Law | GAPRODLIAB | Third edition |
| Kentucky Products Liability Law | KYPRODL | Current data |
| Law of Product Warranties | PRODWARR | Current data |
| Madden and Owen on Products Liability | MOPL | Current data |
| Modern Tort Law: Liability and Litigation 2d | MTLLL | Current data |
| New York Products Liability 2d | NYPRODL | Current data |
| Pattern Discovery: Products Liability 3d | PDPRODL | Current data |
| National Evaluator Multibase | NATEVAL–ALL | Varies by source |
| Product Liability: Winning Strategies and Techniques | PRODLIAB | Current data |
| Products Liability: Design and Manufacturing Defects | PL–DESIGN | Second edition |
| Products Liability Restatements | PL–REST | Current data |

| Database | Identifier | Coverage |
|---|---|---|
| Punitive Damages: A State-by-State Guide to Law and Practice | PUNITIVE | Current data |
| Restatement of the Law—Torts | REST–TORT | Current data |

## News and Information

| Database | Identifier | Coverage |
|---|---|---|
| Andrews Asbestos Litigation Reporter | ANASBLR | Begins with November 1996 |
| Andrews Automotive Litigation Reporter | ANAUTOLR | Begins with November 1996 |
| Andrews Class Action Litigation Reporter | ANCALR | Begins with November 1996 |
| Andrews Drug Recall Litigation Reporter | ANDRLR | Begins with October 1996 |
| Andrews Food Health and Safety Litigation Reporter | ANFOODLR | Begins with September 2004 |
| Andrews Gun Industry Litigation Reporter | ANGUNLTGR | Begins with September 1999 |
| Andrews Medical Devices Litigation Reporter | ANMDLR | Begins with November 1996 |
| Andrews Pharmaceutical Litigation Reporter | ANPHARLR | Begins with November 1996 |
| Andrews Product Liability Litigation Reporter | ANPRODLLR | Begins with November 1996 |
| Andrews Tire Defect Litigation Reporter | ANTDLR | Begins with January 2001 |
| Andrews Tire Defect Report | ANTDR | Begins with September 2000 |
| Andrews Tobacco Industry Litigation Reporter | ANTILR | Begins with November 1996 |
| California Tort Reporter | CATRTR | Begins with January 2000 |
| Consumer Product Safety Information | CPSCPRESS | Current data |

| Database | Identifier | Coverage |
|----------|-----------|----------|
| LJN's Product Liability Law and Strategy | LJNPLLST | Begins with March 1995 |
| Medical/Legal Aspects of Breast Implants | MLABI | Begins with July 1995 |
| Products Liability Advisory | PLADVISORY | Begins with January 1994 |
| Westlaw Topical Highlights—Products Liability | WTH–PL | Current data |

**Directories**

| | | |
|----------|-----------|----------|
| Expert Witness Résumés | EXPTRESUME | Current data |
| ExpertNet | EXPNET | Current data |
| Forensic Services Directory | FSD | Current data |
| National Expert Transcript Service | NETS | Begins with April 1993 |
| West Legal Directory®—Products Liability | WLD–PL | Current data |

## Section 3. Retrieving a Document with a Citation: Find and Hypertext Links

### 3.1 Find

Find is a Westlaw service that allows you to retrieve a document by entering its citation. Find allows you to retrieve documents from any page in westlaw.com without accessing or changing databases. Find is available for many documents, including case law (state and federal), the *United States Code Annotated®* (USCA®), state statutes, administrative materials, and texts and periodicals.

To use Find, simply type the citation in the *Find this document by citation* text box at the tabbed Westlaw page and click **GO**. The following list provides some examples:

| **To find this document:** | **Access Find and type:** |
|----------------------------|---------------------------|
| *Buckman Co. v. Plaintiff's Legal Committee* 121 S. Ct. 1012 (2001) | **121 sct 1012** |
| *Romo v. Ford Motor Co.* 6 Cal. Rptr. 3d 793 (Cal. Ct. App. 2003) | **6 calrptr3d 793** |

| To find this document: | Access Find and type: |
|---|---|
| 15 U.S.C.A. § 2301 | **15 usca 2301** |
| 26 C.F.R. § 1.172–13 | **26 cfr 1.172–13** |
| Cal. Civ. Code § 1714.45 | **cal civ s 1714.45** |

For a complete list of publications that can be retrieved with Find and their abbreviations, click **Find** on the toolbar and then click **Publications List**.

### 3.2   Hypertext Links

Use hypertext links to move from one location to another on Westlaw. For example, use hypertext links to go directly from the statute, case, or law review article you are viewing to a cited statute, case, or article; from a headnote to the corresponding text in the opinion; or from an entry in a statutes index database to the full text of the statute.

### Section 4. Searching with Natural Language

**Overview:** With Natural Language, you can retrieve documents by simply describing your issue in plain English. If you are a relatively new Westlaw user, Natural Language searching can make it easier for you to retrieve cases that are on point. If you are an experienced Westlaw user, Natural Language gives you a valuable alternative search method to the Terms and Connectors search method described in Section 5.

When you enter a Natural Language description, Westlaw automatically identifies legal phrases, removes common words, and generates variations of terms in your description. Westlaw then searches for the concepts in your description. Concepts may include significant terms, phrases, legal citations, or topic and key numbers. Westlaw retrieves the documents that most closely match the concepts in your description, beginning with the document most likely to match.

### 4.1   Natural Language Search

Access a database, such as the Federal Products Liability–Cases database (FPL–CS). Click **Natural Language** and type the following description in the text box:

**risk benefit design analysis**

### 4.2   Browsing Search Results

**Best Mode:** To display the best portion (the portion that most closely matches your description) of each document in a Natural Language search result, click the **Best** arrows at the bottom of the right frame.

**Term Mode:** Click the **Term** arrows at the bottom of the right frame to display portions of the document that contain your search terms.

**Previous/Next Document:** Click the left or right **Doc** arrow at the bottom of the right frame to view the previous or the next document in the search result.

## Section 5. Searching with Terms and Connectors

**Overview:** With Terms and Connectors searching, you enter a query consisting of key terms from your issue and connectors specifying the relationship between these terms.

Terms and Connectors searching is useful when you want to retrieve a document for which you know specific details, such as the title or the fact situation. Terms and Connectors searching is also useful when you want to retrieve all documents containing specific terms.

### 5.1   Terms

**Plurals and Possessives:** Plurals are automatically retrieved when you enter the singular form of a term. This is true for both regular and irregular plurals (e.g., **child** retrieves *children*). If you enter the plural form of a term, you will not retrieve the singular form.

If you enter the nonpossessive form of a term, Westlaw automatically retrieves the possessive form as well. However, if you enter the possessive form, only the possessive form is retrieved.

**Compound Words and Abbreviations:** When a compound word is one of your search terms, use a hyphen to retrieve all forms of the word. For example, the term **along-side** retrieves *along-side, alongside,* and *along side.*

When using an abbreviation as a search term, place a period after each of the letters to retrieve any of its forms. For example, the term **f.d.a.** retrieves *FDA, F.D.A., F D A,* and *F. D. A.* Note: The abbreviation does not retrieve the phrase *Food and Drug Administration,* so remember to add additional alternative terms such as **"food and drug administration"** to your query.

**The Root Expander and the Universal Character:** When you use the Terms and Connectors search method, placing the root expander (!) at the end of a root term generates all other terms with that root. For example, adding the ! to the root *manufactur* in the query

**manufactur! /s defect**

instructs Westlaw to retrieve such terms as *manufacture, manufactured, manufacturer,* and *manufacturing.*

The universal character (*) stands for one character and can be inserted in the middle or at the end of a term. For example, the term

**withdr*w**

will retrieve *withdraw* and *withdrew.* Adding three asterisks to the root *elect*

**elect* * ***

instructs Westlaw to retrieve all forms of the root with up to three additional characters. Terms such as *elected* or *election* are retrieved by this query. However, terms with more than three letters following the root, such as *electronic,* are not retrieved. Plurals are always retrieved, even if the plural form of the term has more than three letters following the root.

**Phrase Searching:** To search for an exact phrase, place it within quotation marks. For example, to search for references to *res ipsa loquitur*, type **"res ipsa loquitur"**. When you are using the Terms and Connectors search method, you should use phrase searching only if you are certain that the terms in the phrase will not appear in any other order.

### 5.2　Alternative Terms

After selecting the terms for your query, consider which alternative terms are necessary. For example, if you are searching for the term *admissible*, you might also want to search for the term *inadmissible*. You should consider both synonyms and antonyms as alternative terms. You can also use the Westlaw thesaurus to add alternative terms to your query.

### 5.3　Connectors

After selecting terms and alternative terms for your query, use connectors to specify the relationship that must exist between search terms in your retrieved documents. The connectors are described below:

| Type: | To retrieve documents with: | Example: |
|---|---|---|
| **&**　(and) | both terms | **duty & warn!** |
| a space (or) | either term or both terms | **implied express** |
| /p | search terms in the same paragraph | **defense /p misrepresent!** |
| /s | search terms in the same sentence | **design /s specification** |
| +s | the first search term preceding the second within the same sentence | **burden +s prov! proof** |
| /n | search terms within *n* terms of each other (where *n* is a number from 1 to 255) | **standard /3 care** |
| +n | the first search term preceding the second by *n* terms (where *n* is a number from 1 to 255) | **proximate +3 cause"** |
| " " | search terms appearing in the same order as in the quotation marks | **"class action"** |

| Type: | To exclude documents with: | Example: |
|---|---|---|
| % (but not) | search terms following the % symbol | **fraud % "statute of frauds"** |

### 5.4　Field Restrictions

**Overview:** Documents in each Westlaw database consist of several segments, or *fields*. One field may contain the citation, another the title, another the synopsis, and so forth. Not all databases contain the same fields. Also depending on the database, fields with the same name may contain different types of information.

To view a list of fields and their contents for a specific database, see Scope for that database. Note that in some databases not every field is available for every document.

To retrieve only those documents containing your search terms in a specific field, restrict your search to that field. To restrict your search to a specific field, type the field name or abbreviation followed by your search terms enclosed in parentheses. For example, to retrieve a U.S. Supreme Court case titled *Medtronic, Inc. v. Lohr*, access the Federal Products Liability–Supreme Court Cases database (FPL–SCT) and search for your terms in the title field (ti):

**ti(medtronic & lohr)**

The fields discussed below are available in Westlaw case law databases you might use for researching issues related to products liability law.

**Digest and Synopsis Fields:** The digest (di) and synopsis (sy) fields summarize the main points of a case. The synopsis field contains a brief description of a case. The digest field contains the topic and headnote fields and includes the complete hierarchy of concepts used by West's editors to classify the headnotes to specific West digest topic and key numbers. Restricting your search to the synopsis and digest fields limits your result to cases in which your terms are related to a major issue in the case.

Consider restricting your search to one or both of these fields if

● you are searching for common terms or terms with more than one meaning, and you need to narrow your search; or

● you cannot narrow your search by using a smaller database.

For example, to retrieve state products liability cases that discuss defective tire design, access the Multistate Products Liability Cases database (MPL–CS) and type the following query:

**sy,di(defect! /p design! /p tire)**

**Headnote Field:** The headnote field (he) is part of the digest field but does not contain the topic names or numbers, hierarchical classification information, or key numbers. The headnote field contains a one-sentence summary for each point of law in a case and any supporting citations given by the author of the opinion. A headnote field restriction is useful when you are searching for specific statutory sections or rule numbers. For example, to retrieve headnotes from federal district court cases that cite 15 U.S.C.A. § 2301, access the Federal Products Liability–District Courts Cases database (FPL–DCT) and type the following query:

**he(15 +s 2301)**

**Topic Field:** The topic field (to) is also part of the digest field. It contains the hierarchical classification information, including the West digest topic names and numbers and the key numbers. You should restrict search terms to the topic field in a case law database if

- a digest field search retrieves too many documents; or
- you want to retrieve cases with digest paragraphs classified under more than one topic.

For example, the topic Products Liability has the topic number 313A. To retrieve U.S. Supreme Court cases that discuss preemption of state law claims by the Medical Device Amendments (MDA), access the FPL–SCT database and type a query like the following:

**to(313a) /p pre-empt! /p "medical device amendment" m.d.a.**

To retrieve cases classified under more than one topic and key number, search for your terms in the topic field. For example, to retrieve recent federal cases discussing strict liability, which may be classified to such topics as Evidence (157), Negligence (272), and Products Liability (313A), access the FPL–CS database and type a query like the following:

**to(strict! /3 liab!) & da(aft 2002)**

For a complete list of West digest topics and their corresponding topic numbers, access the Custom Digest by choosing **Key Numbers and Digest** from the *More* drop-down list on the toolbar.

---

*Note*: Slip opinions and cases from topical services do not contain the West digest, headnote, and topic fields.

---

**Prelim and Caption Fields:** When searching in a database containing statutes, rules, or regulations, restrict your search to the prelim (pr) and caption (ca) fields to retrieve documents in which your terms are important enough to appear in a section name or heading. For example, to retrieve federal statutes regarding penalties for violating consumer product safety laws, access the United States Code Annotated database (USCA) and type the following query:

**pr,ca("product safety" & penalty)**

### 5.5  Date Restrictions

You can use Westlaw to retrieve documents *decided* or *issued* before, after, or on a specified date, as well as within a range of dates. The following sample queries contain date restrictions:

**da(2003) & duty /5 warn**

**da(aft 1998) & duty /5 warn**

**da(11/5/1990) & duty /5 warn**

You can also search for documents *added to a database* on or after a specified date, as well as within a range of dates, which is useful for updating your research. The following sample queries contain added-date restrictions:

**ad(aft 2002) & duty /5 warn**

**ad(aft 11/9/2001 & bef 6/23/2002) & duty /5 warn**

### Section 6. Searching with Topic and Key Numbers

To retrieve cases that address a specific point of law, use topic and key numbers as your search terms. If you have an on-point case, run a search using the topic and key number from the relevant headnote in an appropriate database to find other cases containing headnotes classified to that topic and key number. For example, to search for federal cases containing headnotes classified under topic 313A (Products Liability) and key number 46.4 (Vaccines and Immunization), access the FPL–CS database and type the following query:

**313ak46.4**

For a complete list of West digest topics and their corresponding topic numbers, access the Custom Digest by choosing **Key Numbers and Digest** from the *More* drop-down list on the toolbar.

---

*note*: slip opinions and cases from topical services do not contain West topic and key numbers.

---

### 6.1 Custom Digest

The Custom Digest contains the complete topic and key number outline used by West attorney-editors to classify headnotes. You can use the Custom Digest to obtain a single document containing all case law headnotes from a specific jurisdiction that are classified under a particular topic and key number.

Access the Custom Digest by choosing **Key Numbers and Digest** from the *More* drop-down list on the toolbar. Select up to 10 topics and key numbers from the easy-to-browse outline and click **Search selected**. Then follow the displayed instructions.

For example, to research issues involving products liability, scroll down the Custom Digest page until topic *313A Products Liability* is displayed. Click the plus symbols ( + ) to display key number information. Select the check box next to each key number you want to include in your search, then click **Search selected**. Select the jurisdiction from which you want to retrieve headnotes and, if desired, type additional search terms and select a date restriction. Click **Search**.

### 6.2 KeySearch

KeySearch is a research tool that helps you find cases and secondary sources in a specific area of the law. KeySearch guides you through the selection of terms from a classification system based on the West Key Number System® and then uses the key numbers and their underlying concepts to provide a query for you.

To access KeySearch, click **KeySearch** on the toolbar. Then browse the list of topics and subtopics and select a topic or subtopic to search by clicking the hypertext links. For example, to search for cases that discuss assumption of risk, click **Products Liability** at the first KeySearch page. Then click **Assumption of Risk** at the next page. Select the source from which you want to retrieve documents and, if desired, type additional search terms. Click **Search**.

## Section 7. Verifying Your Research with Citation Research Services

**Overview:** A citation research service, such as KeyCite, is a tool that helps you ensure that your cases, statutes, regulations, and administrative decisions are good law; retrieve cases, legislation, articles, or other documents that cite them; and verify the spelling and format of your citations.

### 7.1  KeyCite for Cases

**KeyCite for cases** covers case law on Westlaw, including unpublished opinions. KeyCite for cases provides the following:

- direct appellate history of a case, including related references, which are opinions involving the same parties and facts but resolving different issues
- negative indirect history of a case, which consists of cases outside the direct appellate line that may have a negative impact on its precedential value
- the title, parallel citations, court of decision, docket number, and filing date of a case
- citations to cases, administrative decisions, secondary sources, and briefs and other court documents on Westlaw that have cited a case
- complete integration with the West Key Number System so you can track legal issues discussed in a case

### 7.2  KeyCite for Statutes and Regulations

**KeyCite for statutes and regulations** covers the USCA, the *Code of Federal Regulations* (CFR), statutes from all 50 states, and regulations from selected states. KeyCite for statutes and regulations provides

- links to session laws or rules amending or repealing a statute or regulation
- statutory credits and historical notes
- citations to pending legislation affecting a statute
- citations to cases, administrative decisions, secondary sources, and briefs and other court documents that have cited a statute or regulation

### 7.3  KeyCite for Administrative Materials

**KeyCite for administrative materials** includes the following:

- National Labor Relations Board decisions beginning with 1935
- Board of Contract Appeals decisions (varies by agency)
- Board of Immigration Appeals decisions beginning with 1940
- Comptroller General decisions beginning with 1921
- Environmental Protection Agency decisions beginning with 1974
- Federal Communications Commission decisions beginning with 1960

- Federal Energy Regulatory Commission (Federal Power Commission) decisions beginning with 1931
- Internal Revenue Service revenue rulings beginning with 1954
- Internal Revenue Service revenue procedures beginning with 1954
- Internal Revenue Service private letter rulings beginning with 1954
- Internal Revenue Service technical advice memoranda beginning with 1954
- *Public Utilities Reports* beginning with 1974
- U.S. Merit Systems Protection Board decisions beginning with 1979
- U.S. Patent and Trademark Office decisions beginning with 1984
- U.S. Tax Court (Board of Tax Appeals) decisions beginning with 1924
- U.S. patents beginning with 1976

### 7.4  KeyCite Alert

**KeyCite Alert** monitors the status of your cases, statutes, regulations, and administrative decisions and automatically sends you updates at the frequency you specify when their KeyCite information changes.

### Section 8. Researching with Westlaw: Examples

### 8.1  Retrieving Law Review Articles

Recent law review articles are often a good place to begin researching a legal issue because law review articles serve as an excellent introduction to a new topic or review for an old one, providing terminology to help you formulate a query; as a finding tool for pertinent primary authority, such as cases, statutes, and rules; and in some instances, as persuasive secondary authority.

Suppose you need to gain background information on the defense of assumption of the risk in a product liability claim.

*Solution*

- To retrieve law review articles relevant to your issue, access the Products Liability–Law Reviews, Texts, and Bar Journals database (PL–TP). Using the Natural Language search method, type a description like the following:

**assumption of risk as a defense**

- If you have a citation to an article in a specific publication, use Find to retrieve it. (For more information on Find, see Section 3.1 of this appendix.) For example, to retrieve the article found at 58 Mont. L. Rev. 249, access Find and type

**58 mont l rev 249**

- If you know the title of an article but not the journal in which it was published, access the PL–TP database and search for key terms in the title field. For example, to retrieve the article "The Defense of Assumption of Risk Under Montana's Product Liability Law," type the following Terms and Connectors query:

**ti(assumption & risk & montana)**

## 8.2 Retrieving Case Law

Suppose you need to retrieve federal district court cases discussing the consumer expectations test.

*Solution*

- Access the FPL–DCT database. Type a Terms and Connectors query such as the following:

**consumer /5 expectation /5 test**

- When you know the citation for a specific case, use Find to retrieve it. For example, to retrieve *Conley v. R.J. Reynolds Tobacco Co.,* 286 F. Supp. 2d 1097 (N.D. Cal. 2002), access Find and type

**286 fsupp2d 1097**

- If you find a topic and key number that is on point, run a search using that topic and key number to retrieve additional cases discussing that point of law. For example, to retrieve federal district court cases containing headnotes classified under topic 313A (Products Liability) and key number 8 (Nature of Product and Existence of Defect or Danger), access the FPL–DCT database and type the following query:

**313ak8**

- To retrieve opinions written by a particular judge, add a judge field (ju) restriction to your query. For example, to retrieve federal district court opinions written by Judge Gwin that contain headnotes classified under topic 313A (Products Liability), access the FPL–DCT database and type the following query:

**ju(gwin) & to(313a)**

- You can also use KeySearch and the Custom Digest to retrieve cases and headnotes that discuss the issue you are researching.

## 8.3 Retrieving Statutes and Regulations

Suppose you need to retrieve federal statutes dealing with the National Vaccine Injury Compensation Program.

*Solution*

- Access the USCA database. Search for your terms in the prelim and caption fields using the Terms and Connectors search method:

**pr,ca(national & vaccine & compensation)**

- When you know the citation for a specific statute or regulation, use Find to retrieve it. For example, to retrieve 42 U.S.C.A. § 300aa–13, access Find and type

**42 usca 300aa–13**

- To look at surrounding sections, use the Table of Contents service. Click **Table of Contents** on the Links tab in the left frame. To display a section listed in the Table of Contents, click its hypertext link. You can also use Documents in Sequence to retrieve the sections following 42 U.S.C.A. § 300aa–13 even if the subsequent sections were not retrieved with your search or Find request. Choose **Documents in Sequence** from the Tools menu at the bottom of the right frame.

## 8.4 Using KeyCite

Suppose one of the cases you retrieve in your case law research is *Phillips v. Kimwood Mach. Co.*, 525 P.2d 1033 (Or. 1974). You want to make sure it is good law and retrieve a list of citing references.

*Solution*

- Use KeyCite to retrieve direct and negative indirect history for *Phillips*. Access KeyCite and type **525 p2d 1033**.

- Use KeyCite to display citing references for *Phillips*. Click **Citing References** on the Links tab in the left frame.

## 8.5 Following Recent Developments

If you are researching issues related to products liability law, it is important to keep up with recent developments. How can you do this efficiently?

*Solution*

One of the easiest ways to follow recent developments in products liability law is to access the Westlaw Topical Highlights–Products Liability database (WTH–PL). The WTH–PL database contains summaries of recent legal developments, including court decisions, legislation, and materials released by administrative agencies. When you access the WTH–PL database, you automatically retrieve a list of documents added to the database in the last two weeks.

You can also use the WestClip® clipping service to stay informed of recent developments of interest to you. WestClip will run your Terms and Connectors queries on a regular basis and deliver the results to you automatically. You can run WestClip queries in legal and news and information databases.

# Table of Statutes and Rules

## UNITED STATES CODE ANNOTATED
### 21 U.S.C.A.—Food and Drugs

|  | This Work | |
|---|---|---|
| Sec. | Sec. | Note |
| 301—392 | 9.6 | 22 |
| 301 et seq. | 1.1 | 6 |
| 301 et seq. | 14.4 | 100 |
| 321(g)(1)(C) | 9.6 | 21 |
| 331 | 18.2 | 55 |
| 331(a) | 9.6 | 23 |
| 352 | 9.6 | 25 |
| 352(e) | 9.6 | 26 |
| 352(f) | 9.6 | 27 |
| 352(n) | 9.6 | 28 |
| 353 | 9.6 | 25 |
| 353(b)(1)(B) | 9.6 | 29 |
| 353(b)(4) | 9.6 | 29 |
| 355 | 9.6 | 24 |
| 360 | 14.4 | 112 |
| 360(h) | 10.8 | 34 |
| 360(k) | 14.4 | 114 |
| 360j(g) | 14.4 | 123 |
| 360ll(f) | 10.8 | 34 |
| 1601 et seq. | 15.3 | 10 |

### 27 U.S.C.A.—Intoxicating Liquors

|  | This Work | |
|---|---|---|
| Sec. | Sec. | Note |
| 213—219 | 10.3 | 195 |
| 215 | 10.2 | 88 |
| 215 | 10.3 | 196 |

### 28 U.S.C.A.—Judiciary and Judicial Procedure

|  | This Work | |
|---|---|---|
| Sec. | Sec. | Note |
| 1346(b) | 14.2 | 29 |
| 1442(a)(1) | 14.2 | 48 |
| 2680(a) | 14.2 | 29 |

### 29 U.S.C.A.—Labor

|  | This Work | |
|---|---|---|
| Sec. | Sec. | Note |
| 651 et seq. | 1.1 | 7 |
| 651 et seq. | 14.3 | 21 |
| 651 et seq. | 15.6 | 2 |
| 651(b) | 14.4 | 175 |
| 653(b)(4) | 6.4 | 75 |
| 653(b)(4) | 14.4 | 177 |

### 42 U.S.C.A.—The Public Health and Welfare

|  | This Work | |
|---|---|---|
| Sec. | Sec. | Note |
| 300aa–1 et seq. | 8.10 | 18 |
| 300aa–2 | 8.10 | 18 |
| 1983 | 18.1 | 20 |
| 7412 | 1.1 | 9 |
| 9267 | 10.3 | 185 |
| 9601—9675 | 10.7 | 4 |
| 9607(a)(4)(B) | 10.7 | 5 |
| 9658 | 14.5 | 4 |

## UNITED STATES CODE ANNOTATED
### 46 U.S.C.A.—Shipping

|  | This Work | |
|---|---|---|
| Sec. | Sec. | Note |
| 1464 | 10.8 | 34 |
| 4301 et seq. | 14.4 | 142 |
| 4302(c) | 14.4 | 144 |
| 4306 | 14.4 | 149 |

### 49 U.S.C.A.—Transportation

|  | This Work | |
|---|---|---|
| Sec. | Sec. | Note |
| 1301 et seq. | 1.1 | 8 |
| 30101 et seq. | 14.4 | 78 |
| 30103(b)(1) | 14.4 | 80 |
| 30111 | 17.3 | 35 |
| 30117—30121 | 10.8 | 34 |
| 30127 | 17.3 | 79 |
| 30165(c) | 18.5 | 82 |
| 32301(1) | 17.3 | 3 |
| 32710 | 3.2 | 76 |
| 32710 | 3.3 | 35 |
| 40101 | 14.5 | 4 |
| 40101 | 14.5 | 173 |

### 50 U.S.C.A.App.—War and National Defense

|  | This Work | |
|---|---|---|
| Sec. | Sec. | Note |
| 501 et seq. | 14.5 | 53 |

## POPULAR NAME ACTS

————

### MAGNUSON–MOSS WARRANTY ACT

|  | This Work | |
|---|---|---|
| Sec. | Sec. | Note |
| 104(a)(3) | 4.9 | 59 |
| 108 | 4.9 | |
| 108 | 4.9 | 44 |
| 108 | 4.9 | 59 |
| 111(b) | 4.9 | 59 |

### MODEL STATE PUNITIVE DAMAGES ACT

|  | This Work | |
|---|---|---|
| Sec. | Sec. | Note |
| 5(a)(2) | 18.4 | 59 |
| 6(c) | 18.5 | 16 |
| 7 | 18.5 | 89 |

### MODEL UNIFORM PRODUCT LIABILITY ACT

|  | This Work | |
|---|---|---|
| Sec. | Sec. | Note |
| 110(A) | 14.5 | 122 |
| 120(B) | 18.5 | 88 |

## WEST'S ANNOTATED CALIFORNIA VEHICLE CODE

| Sec. | This Work Sec. | Note |
|------|------|------|
| 27315(j) | 17.5 | 112 |

## WEST'S COLORADO REVISED STATUTES ANNOTATED

| Sec. | This Work Sec. | Note |
|------|------|------|
| 13–21–102(1)(a) | 18.6 | 49 |
| 13–21–102(4) | 18.6 | 90 |
| 13–21–401 et seq. | 1.3 | 6 |
| 13–21–401(1) | 15.3 | 9 |
| 13–21–402 | 15.2 | 86 |
| 13–21–403 | 18.6 | 28 |
| 13–21–403(1) | 2.4 | 66 |
| 13–21–403(1) | 6.4 | 101 |
| 13–21–403(1) | 10.4 | 175 |
| 13–21–403(1)(a) | 10.4 | 57 |
| 13–21–403(1)(b) | 14.3 | 39 |
| 13–21–403(2) | 2.4 | 49 |
| 13–21–403(2) | 6.4 | 68 |
| 13–21–403(2) | 6.4 | 91 |
| 13–21–403(3) | 14.5 | 106 |
| 13–21–403(3) | 14.5 | 133 |
| 13–21–404 | 10.4 | 176 |
| 13–21–406 | 13.6 | 59 |
| 13–21–1101 | 10.3 | 203 |
| 13–22–104 | 16.9 | 22 |
| 13–25–127(2) | 18.6 | 23 |
| 13–80–106 | 14.5 | 43 |
| 13–80–107 | 14.5 | 21 |
| 13–80–107(1)(c) | 14.5 | 112 |
| 13–80–108(I) | 14.5 | 63 |
| 42–4–237(b)(7) | 17.5 | 112 |

## CONNECTICUT GENERAL STATUTES ANNOTATED

| Sec. | This Work Sec. | Note |
|------|------|------|
| 14–100a(c)(4) | 17.5 | 109 |
| 14–100a(c)(4) | 17.5 | 110 |
| 19–425 (repealed) | 1.1 | 1 |
| 42a–2–316(5) | 4.9 | 15 |
| 52–240b | 18.1 | 21 |
| 52–240b | 18.4 | 60 |
| 52–240b | 18.6 | 62 |
| 52–240b | 18.6 | 108 |
| 52–572h | 13.1 | 40 |
| 52–572h et seq. | 5.3 | 132 |
| 52–572h(b) | 13.1 | 26 |
| 52–572h(l) | 13.4 | 100 |
| 52–572l | 13.1 | 27 |
| 52–572l | 13.1 | 34 |
| 52–572l | 13.1 | 40 |
| 52–572l | 13.4 | 84 |
| 52–572l | 13.4 | 100 |
| 52–572l | 13.7 | 49 |
| 52–572l et seq. | 1.3 | 6 |
| 52–572m | 7.2 | 6 |
| 52–572m et seq. | 1.3 | 6 |
| 52–572m(a) | 16.2 | 114 |
| 52–572m(b) | 13.7 | 49 |
| 52–572n | 7.2 | 6 |

## CONNECTICUT GENERAL STATUTES ANNOTATED

| Sec. | This Work Sec. | Note |
|------|------|------|
| 52–572n(a) | 13.6 | 48 |
| 52–572o | 13.7 | 49 |
| 52–572q(d) | 9.5 | 20 |
| 52–577a | 14.5 | 127 |
| 52–577a(5)(d) | 14.5 | 112 |
| 52–577a(a) | 14.5 | 44 |
| 52–577a(a) | 14.5 | 64 |
| 52–577a(a) | 14.5 | 66 |
| 52–577a(c) | 14.5 | 130 |
| 52–577a(e) | 14.5 | 129 |

## DELAWARE CODE

| Tit. | This Work Sec. | Note |
|------|------|------|
| 6, § 4905 | 15.2 | 88 |
| 18, § 7001 | 15.2 | 86 |
| 18, § 7001 | 15.2 | 87 |
| 21, § 4802(i) | 17.5 | 110 |

## DISTRICT OF COLUMBIA CODE

| Sec. | This Work Sec. | Note |
|------|------|------|
| 2–316 | 4.9 | 17 |
| 2–316.1 | 4.9 | 17 |
| 6–2381 et seq. | 1.3 | 6 |
| 6–2391 et seq. | 1.3 | 6 |
| 6–2392 (former) | 10.3 | 201 |
| 7–2551.02 | 10.3 | 201 |
| 12–310(3) | 14.5 | 136 |
| 28.2–316.1 | 4.9 | 17 |
| 41–1607 | 17.5 | 110 |

## WEST'S FLORIDA STATUTES ANNOTATED

| Sec. | This Work Sec. | Note |
|------|------|------|
| 90.407 | 6.4 | 166 |
| 95.031(2) | 14.5 | 64 |
| 316.614(9) | 17.5 | 112 |
| 316.1934(2) | 17.5 | 60 |
| 672.316(5) | 16.9 | 22 |
| 768.37 | 10.3 | 203 |
| 768.72 | 18.6 | 9 |
| 768.72 | 18.6 | 10 |
| 768.73(2)(a) (repealed) | 18.6 | 82 |
| 768.73(2)(b) | 18.6 | 74 |
| 768.725 | 18.6 | 23 |
| 768.1257 | 10.4 | 59 |
| 768.1257 | 10.4 | 172 |
| 768.1257 | 10.4 | 176 |

## OFFICIAL CODE OF GEORGIA ANNOTATED

| Sec. | This Work Sec. | Note |
|------|------|------|
| 26–2–430 | 10.3 | 203 |
| 40–6–392(a) | 17.5 | 60 |
| 40–8–76.1(d) | 17.5 | 110 |

## IOWA CODE ANNOTATED

| Sec. | This Work Sec. | Note |
|---|---|---|
| 5.407 | 6.4 | 168 |
| 321.445(4) | 17.5 | 114 |
| 613.18 | 1.3 | 6 |
| 613.18 | 15.2 | 85 |
| 613.18 | 15.2 | 86 |
| 614.1(11) | 16.7 | 75 |
| 614.1(a) | 14.5 | 112 |
| 614.2A | 14.5 | 108 |
| 668.1 | 13.1 | 41 |
| 668.12 | 1.3 | 6 |
| 668.12 | 10.4 | 174 |
| 668.12(2) | 10.8 | 15 |
| 668A.1 | 18.4 | 68 |
| 668A.1(2)(b) | 18.6 | 85 |
| 668A.1(2)(b) | 18.6 | 87 |
| 668A.1(2)(b) | 18.6 | 88 |
| 668A.1.1a | 18.6 | 23 |

## KANSAS STATUTES ANNOTATED

| Sec. | This Work Sec. | Note |
|---|---|---|
| 8–2504(c) | 17.5 | 110 |
| 50–623 et seq. | 4.8 | 21 |
| 50–623 et seq. | 4.9 | 26 |
| 50–639 | 4.9 | 26 |
| 60–3301 et seq. | 1.3 | 6 |
| 60–3302(b) | 15.3 | 9 |
| 60–3302(b) | 16.4 | 30 |
| 60–3303 | 14.5 | 127 |
| 60–3303(b)(2)(B) | 14.5 | 112 |
| 60–3304(a) | 6.4 | 101 |
| 60–3304(a) | 14.3 | 40 |
| 60–3304(a) | 18.6 | 28 |
| 60–3304(b) | 2.4 | 49 |
| 60–3304(b) | 6.4 | 68 |
| 60–3304(b) | 6.4 | 91 |
| 60–3304(c) | 14.2 | 50 |
| 60–3305 | 9.5 | 22 |
| 60–3305(c) | 10.2 | 48 |
| 60–3306 | 15.2 | 85 |
| 60–3306 | 15.2 | 86 |
| 60–3307 | 10.4 | 176 |
| 60–3307 | 10.4 | 177 |
| 60–3307(a)(1) | 6.4 | 176 |
| 60–3307(a)(1) | 10.4 | 62 |
| 60–3402(e) | 18.6 | 83 |
| 60–3701(a) | 18.6 | 109 |
| 60–3701(b) | 18.5 | 86 |
| 60–3701(c) | 18.6 | 23 |
| 60–3701(e) | 18.6 | 57 |
| 60–3701(f) | 18.6 | 57 |
| 60–3702(e) | 18.6 | 58 |
| 60–3702(e)(2) | 18.6 | 56 |
| 60–3702(f) | 18.6 | 59 |
| 65–3701 | 16.9 | 22 |

## KENTUCKY REVISED STATUTES

| Sec. | This Work Sec. | Note |
|---|---|---|
| 189.125(5) | 17.5 | 110 |
| 189.125(5) | 17.5 | 128 |
| 189.125(5) | 17.5 | 129 |

## KENTUCKY REVISED STATUTES

| Sec. | This Work Sec. | Note |
|---|---|---|
| 342.610 | 15.6 | 45 |
| 411.182 | 13.1 | 32 |
| 411.184(2) | 18.6 | 23 |
| 411.300 et seq. | 1.3 | 6 |
| 411.310(1) | 14.5 | 133 |
| 411.310(2) | 2.3 | 53 |
| 411.310(2) | 6.4 | 48 |
| 411.310(2) | 10.4 | 57 |
| 411.310(2) | 10.4 | 175 |
| 411.320 | 13.1 | 31 |
| 411.320(1) | 12.3 | 45 |
| 411.340 | 15.2 | 86 |
| 411.340 | 15.2 | 87 |

## KENTUCKY RULES OF EVIDENCE

| Rule | This Work Sec. | Note |
|---|---|---|
| 407 | 6.4 | 168 |

## LOUISIANA STATUTES ANNOTATED— REVISED STATUTES

| Sec. | This Work Sec. | Note |
|---|---|---|
| 9:2799.6 | 10.3 | 203 |
| 9:2800.51 et seq. | 1.3 | 6 |
| 9:2800.51 et seq. | 5.3 | 134 |
| 9:2800.52 | 7.2 | 6 |
| 9:2800.54 | 5.3 | 22 |
| 9:2800.54 | 5.3 | 27 |
| 9:2800.55 | 7.3 | 12 |
| 9:2800.56 | 5.3 | 122 |
| 9:2800.56 | 8.5 | 25 |
| 9:2800.56 | 10.4 | 179 |
| 9:2800.56(2) | 2.6 | 25 |
| 9:2800.57 | 9.2 | 34 |
| 9:2800.57 | 9.5 | 21 |
| 9:2800.57(B) | 10.2 | 48 |
| 9:2800.57(C) | 10.8 | 15 |
| 9:2800.57A | 2.6 | 28 |
| 9:2800.59 | 10.4 | 174 |
| 9:2800.60 | 10.3 | 199 |
| 23:1032 | 15.6 | 45 |
| 32:295.1(E) | 17.5 | 110 |

## LOUISIANA STATUTES ANNOTATED— CIVIL CODE

| Art. | This Work Sec. | Note |
|---|---|---|
| 2315.4 | 18.1 | 41 |
| 2322.1 | 16.9 | 22 |

## MAINE REVISED STATUTES ANNOTATED

| Tit. | This Work Sec. | Note |
|---|---|---|
| 10, § 1175 | 15.2 | 88 |
| 11, § 2–316 | 4.9 | 19 |
| 11, § 2–316(2) | 4.9 | 18 |
| 11, § 2–316(3) | 4.9 | 18 |
| 11, § 2–316(4) | 4.9 | 18 |

## NEW JERSEY STATUTES ANNOTATED

## NEW JERSEY REVISED STATUTES

## NEW MEXICO STATUTES ANNOTATED

## NEW YORK, MCKINNEY'S CIVIL PRACTICE LAW

## NEW YORK, MCKINNEY'S CIVIL PRACTICE LAW AND RULES

## NEW YORK, MCKINNEY'S GENERAL BUSINESS LAW

## NEW YORK, MCKINNEY'S PUBLIC HEALTH LAW

## NEW YORK, MCKINNEY'S VEHICLE AND TRAFFIC LAW

## NORTH CAROLINA GENERAL STATUTES

## NORTH DAKOTA CENTURY CODE

## NORTH DAKOTA RULES OF EVIDENCE

| Rule | This Work Sec. | Note |
|------|------|------|
| 407 | 6.4 | 166 |

## OHIO REVISED CODE

| Sec. | This Work Sec. | Note |
|------|------|------|
| 2108.11 | 16.9 | 22 |
| 2305.10 et seq. | 5.3 | 137 |
| 2307.71 et seq. | 1.3 | 6 |
| 2307.71 et seq. | 5.3 | 137 |
| 2307.71(M) | 5.3 | 82 |
| 2307.73(A) | 5.3 | 27 |
| 2307.73(A)(1) | 5.3 | 22 |
| 2307.73(A)(1) | 6.2 | 7 |
| 2307.74 | 7.3 | 12 |
| 2307.75(A) | 8.3 | 12 |
| 2307.75(A) | 8.3 | 32 |
| 2307.75(A) | 8.6 | 45 |
| 2307.75(B)(4) | 14.3 | 41 |
| 2307.75(F) | 8.5 | 25 |
| 2307.75(F) | 10.4 | 179 |
| 2307.76 | 2.6 | 32 |
| 2307.76 | 9.2 | 34 |
| 2307.76 | 9.2 | 35 |
| 2307.76(2) | 10.8 | 15 |
| 2307.76(2) | 10.8 | 24 |
| 2307.76(A)(1) | 2.6 | 22 |
| 2307.76(B) | 10.2 | 48 |
| 2307.77 | 6.2 | 7 |
| 2307.78 | 15.2 | 86 |
| 2307.80(B) | 18.6 | 110 |
| 2307.80(C) | 14.3 | 44 |
| 2315.21(D)(3)(b)(i) | 18.6 | 23 |
| 2353.59 | 17.5 | 62 |
| 4121.80 | 15.6 | 45 |
| 4513.263(F) | 17.5 | 112 |

## OKLAHOMA STATUTES ANNOTATED

| Tit. | This Work Sec. | Note |
|------|------|------|
| 23, § 9 | 18.1 | 19 |
| 23, § 9.1(C) | 18.6 | 23 |
| 23, § 9.1(C) | 18.6 | 59 |
| 23, § 9.1(D) | 18.6 | 23 |
| 47, § 11–1112(E) | 17.5 | 110 |
| 47, § 752(J) | 17.5 | 59 |

## OREGON REVISED STATUTES

| Sec. | This Work Sec. | Note |
|------|------|------|
| 18.475(2) | 13.1 | 40 |
| 18.537(1) | 18.6 | 23 |
| 18.540(1)(b) | 18.6 | 84 |
| 18.590 | 17.5 | 116 |
| 30.900 | 6.2 | 8 |
| 30.900 et seq. | 1.3 | 6 |
| 30.905 | 14.5 | 22 |
| 30.905 | 14.5 | 65 |
| 30.907 | 14.5 | 65 |
| 30–915 | 12.3 | 47 |
| 30.920 | 5.3 | 28 |

## OREGON REVISED STATUTES

| Sec. | This Work Sec. | Note |
|------|------|------|
| 30.920 | 5.3 | 130 |
| 30.920 | 8.3 | 12 |
| 30.920 | 8.7 | 41 |
| 30.920(3) | 8.6 | 56 |
| 30.925 | 18.5 | 86 |
| 30.925 | 18.6 | 23 |
| 30.927 | 14.3 | 44 |
| 30.927 | 18.6 | 27 |
| 72.8010 et seq. | 4.9 | 26 |
| 72.8050 | 4.9 | 26 |
| 656.156 | 15.6 | 45 |
| 813.320 | 17.5 | 59 |

## PENNSYLVANIA STATUTES

| Tit. | This Work Sec. | Note |
|------|------|------|
| 8333 | 16.9 | 2 |

## PENNSYLVANIA CONSOLIDATED STATUTES ANNOTATED

| Sec. | This Work Sec. | Note |
|------|------|------|
| 42, § 8333(a) | 16.9 | 22 |
| 75, § 4581(e) | 17.5 | 110 |
| 75, § 4581(e) | 17.5 | 128 |

## PENNSYLVANIA RULES OF EVIDENCE

| Rule | This Work Sec. | Note |
|------|------|------|
| 407 | 6.4 | 167 |

## RHODE ISLAND GENERAL LAWS

| Sec. | This Work Sec. | Note |
|------|------|------|
| 6A–2–329(2) | 4.9 | 23 |
| 6A–2–329(2)—(3)(a) | 4.9 | 23 |
| 9–1–13 | 1.3 | 6 |
| 9–1–32 | 1.3 | 6 |
| 9–20–4 | 13.6 | 63 |
| 31–22–22(b)(ii) | 17.5 | 110 |
| 31–22–22(b)(ii) | 17.5 | 128 |
| 31–22–22(b)(ii) | 17.5 | 129 |
| 62–2–329 | 4.9 | 26 |

## RHODE ISLAND RULES OF EVIDENCE

| Rule | This Work Sec. | Note |
|------|------|------|
| 407 | 6.4 | 155 |

## SOUTH CAROLINA CODE

| Sec. | This Work Sec. | Note |
|------|------|------|
| 15–3–535 | 14.5 | 63 |
| 15–3–535 | 14.5 | 70 |
| 15–33–135 | 18.6 | 23 |
| 15–73–10 | 5.3 | 28 |

## VERMONT STATUTES ANNOTATED

|  |  | This Work |
|---|---|---|
| Tit. | Sec. | Note |
| 9A, § 2–108 | 16.9 | 22 |
| 9A, § 2–316(2) | 4.9 | 24 |
| 9A, § 2–316(3) | 4.9 | 24 |
| 9A, § 2–316(4) | 4.9 | 24 |
| 9A, § 2–316(5) | 4.9 | 24 |
| 12, § 512(4) | 14.5 | 66 |
| 23, § 1259(d)(e) | 17.5 | 110 |

## VIRGINIA CODE

|  |  | This Work |
|---|---|---|
| Sec. | Sec. | Note |
| 8.01–38.1 | 18.6 | 56 |
| 8.01–250 | 14.5 | 136 |
| 8.2–318 | 4.5 | 33 |
| 15.2–915.1 | 10.3 | 135 |
| 15.2–915.1 | 10.3 | 200 |
| 32.1–297 | 16.9 | 22 |
| 46.2–1092 | 17.5 | 110 |

## WEST'S REVISED CODE OF WASHINGTON ANNOTATED

|  |  | This Work |
|---|---|---|
| Sec. | Sec. | Note |
| 4.16.300 | 14.5 | 136 |
| 5.40.060 | 13.1 | 24 |
| 5.40.060 | 17.5 | 64 |
| 7.72.010 | 7.2 | 6 |
| 7.72.010 et seq. | 1.3 | 6 |
| 7.72.010 et seq. | 5.3 | 139 |
| 7.72.010(1)(a) | 16.7 | 4 |
| 7.72.010(1)(b) | 16.5 | 13 |
| 7.72.010(2) | 14.2 | 15 |
| 7.72.010(2) | 16.4 | 30 |
| 7.72.010(6) | 5.3 | 82 |
| 7.72.030 | 10.3 | 199 |
| 7.72.030 | 10.4 | 43 |
| 7.72.030 | 10.4 | 179 |
| 7.72.030(1) | 2.6 | 24 |
| 7.72.030(1) | 10.4 | 189 |
| 7.72.030(1)(a) | 8.3 | 32 |
| 7.72.030(1)(a) | 8.5 | 25 |
| 7.72.030(1)(a) | 8.6 | 19 |
| 7.72.030(1)(a) | 8.6 | 41 |
| 7.72.030(1)(c) | 10.8 | 15 |
| 7.72.030(2) | 5.3 | 22 |
| 7.72.030(2) | 5.3 | 27 |
| 7.72.030(2)(a) | 7.3 | 11 |
| 7.72.030(3) | 8.3 | 32 |
| 7.72.030(3) | 8.5 | 25 |
| 7.72.030(3) | 8.6 | 19 |
| 7.72.030(3) | 8.6 | 41 |
| 7.72.040 | 15.2 | 85 |
| 7.72.040 | 15.2 | 86 |
| 7.72.050 | 2.3 | 51 |
| 7.72.050 | 6.4 | 44 |
| 7.72.050 | 10.4 | 43 |
| 7.72.050 | 10.4 | 176 |
| 7.72.050(1) | 6.4 | 47 |
| 7.72.050(1) | 6.4 | 90 |
| 7.72.050(1) | 6.4 | 99 |

## WEST'S REVISED CODE OF WASHINGTON ANNOTATED

|  |  | This Work |
|---|---|---|
| Sec. | Sec. | Note |
| 7.72.050(1) | 14.3 | 41 |
| 7.72.050(2) | 14.2 | 50 |
| 7.72.060 | 14.5 | 64 |
| 7.72.060(1)—(2) | 14.5 | 127 |
| 7.72.060(2) | 14.5 | 128 |
| 7.72.070 | 10.3 | 203 |
| 9A.36.083 | 18.1 | 41 |
| 46.61.688(6) | 17.5 | 110 |
| 51.24.020 | 15.6 | 45 |
| 62A.2–316(4) | 4.9 | 25 |
| 70.54.120 | 16.9 | 22 |

## WEST VIRGINIA CODE

|  |  | This Work |
|---|---|---|
| Sec. | Sec. | Note |
| 17C–15–49(d) | 17.5 | 110 |
| 23–4–2 | 15.6 | 45 |
| 46A–6–107 | 4.9 | 26 |

## WISCONSIN STATUTES ANNOTATED

|  |  | This Work |
|---|---|---|
| Sec. | Sec. | Note |
| 146.31 | 16.9 | 22 |
| 347.48(2m)(g) | 17.5 | 114 |

## WYOMING STATUTES ANNOTATED

|  |  | This Work |
|---|---|---|
| Sec. | Sec. | Note |
| 1–1–109(a)(iv) | 13.1 | 25 |
| 1–1–109(a)(iv) | 13.1 | 41 |
| 31–5–1402(f) | 17.5 | 110 |

---

## FEDERAL RULES OF CIVIL PROCEDURE

|  |  | This Work |
|---|---|---|
| Rule | Sec. | Note |
| 8(c) | 14.5 | 1 |
| 9(b) | 3.2 | 14 |
| 11 | 7.3 | 25 |
| 26(a)(2) | 6.3 | 9 |
| 42(b) | 18.6 | 99 |

## FEDERAL RULES OF EVIDENCE

|  |  | This Work |
|---|---|---|
| Rule | Sec. | Note |
| 104(a) | 6.3 | 119 |
| 402 | 6.4 | 149 |
| 403 | 2.3 | 17 |
| 403 | 6.4 | 131 |
| 403 | 6.4 | 164 |
| 407 | 6.4 |  |
| 407 | 6.4 | 156 |
| 407 | 6.4 | 158 |
| 407 | 6.4 | 164 |
| 407 | 6.4 | 165 |
| 407 | 6.4 | 167 |
| 407 | 6.4 | 169 |
| 407 | 6.4 | 175 |

## FEDERAL RULES OF EVIDENCE

| Rule | This Work Sec. | Note |
|------|------|------|
| 407 | 6.4 | 189 |
| 407 | 10.4 | |
| 701 | 6.3 | |
| 701 | 6.3 | 6 |
| 702 | 6.3 | |
| 702 | 6.3 | 42 |
| 702 | 6.3 | 60 |
| 702 | 6.3 | 63 |
| 702 | 6.3 | 90 |
| 702 | 6.3 | 129 |
| 703 | 6.3 | |
| 703 | 6.3 | 64 |
| 803(18) | 2.3 | 17 |

## UNIFORM APPORTIONMENT OF TORT RESPONSIBILITY ACT

| Sec. | This Work Sec. | Note |
|------|------|------|
| 3(a) | 13.3 | 38 |
| 3(b) | 13.3 | 24 |

## UNIFORM COMPARATIVE FAULT ACT

| Sec. | This Work Sec. | Note |
|------|------|------|
| 1 | 13.3 | 23 |
| 1(b) | 13.3 | 38 |
| 1(b) | 13.6 | 66 |

## UNIFORM SALES ACT

| Sec. | This Work Sec. | Note |
|------|------|------|
| 12 | 4.2 | |
| 15(2) | 1.2 | 52 |
| 15(2) | 4.3 | |
| 15(3) | 4.4 | |
| 49 | 4.6 | 1 |
| 69(3) | 4.6 | 1 |

## UNIFORM COMMERCIAL CODE

| Sec. | This Work Sec. | Note |
|------|------|------|
| 1–102(2)(b)(3) | 4.8 | 9 |
| 1–103 | 13.6 | 47 |
| 1–105 | 14.5 | 95 |
| 1–105 | 14.5 | 98 |
| 1–106 | 18.4 | |
| 1–106(1) | 18.1 | 22 |
| 1–106(1) | 18.4 | |
| 1–106(1) | 18.4 | 48 |
| 1–106(1) | 18.4 | 50 |
| 1–201(10) | 4.7 | |
| 1–205(1) | 4.7 | 95 |
| 1–205(2) | 4.7 | 96 |
| Art. 2 | 1.3 | |
| Art. 2 | 4.1 | |
| Art. 2 | 4.1 | 14 |
| Art. 2 | 4.2 | |
| Art. 2 | 4.2 | 78 |
| Art. 2 | 4.2 | 94 |
| Art. 2 | 4.2 | 99 |

## UNIFORM COMMERCIAL CODE

| Sec. | This Work Sec. | Note |
|------|------|------|
| Art. 2 | 4.3 | |
| Art. 2 | 4.3 | 27 |
| Art. 2 | 4.5 | 40 |
| Art. 2 | 4.7 | |
| Art. 2 | 4.8 | |
| Art. 2 | 4.8 | 8 |
| Art. 2 | 4.8 | 33 |
| Art. 2 | 4.9 | |
| Art. 2 | 5.3 | |
| Art. 2 | 5.9 | |
| Art. 2 | 13.6 | |
| Art. 2 | 13.6 | 75 |
| Art. 2 | 14.5 | |
| Art. 2 | 16.2 | |
| Art. 2 | 16.2 | 11 |
| Art. 2 | 16.2 | 17 |
| Art. 2 | 16.2 | 20 |
| Art. 2 | 16.2 | 31 |
| Art. 2 | 16.2 | 86 |
| Art. 2 | 16.4 | 17 |
| Art. 2 | 16.5 | |
| Art. 2 | 16.7 | |
| Art. 2 | 16.10 | 5 |
| Art. 2 | 18.4 | |
| 2–103(1) | 4.2 | 100 |
| 2–103(1)(d) | 15.7 | 23 |
| 2–103(1)(d) | 15.7 | 46 |
| 2–103(1)(d) | 16.2 | 8 |
| 2–103(3) | 4.8 | 33 |
| 2–104 | 4.3 | 12 |
| 2–104 | 4.3 | 17 |
| 2–105 | 16.8 | 11 |
| 2–105 | 16.8 | 30 |
| 2–105(1) | 16.7 | 3 |
| 2–106(1) | 4.3 | 33 |
| 2–106(1) | 16.2 | |
| 2–106(1) | 16.2 | 8 |
| 2–106(1) | 16.2 | 82 |
| 2–106(2) | 13.6 | 75 |
| 2–209 | 4.7 | |
| 2–209 | 4.7 | 64 |
| 2–301 | 4.8 | 3 |
| 2–302 | 4.7 | |
| 2–302 | 4.7 | 113 |
| 2–302 | 4.8 | 23 |
| 2–302(1) | 4.7 | 112 |
| 2–302, Com. 1 | 4.7 | |
| 2–302, Com. 1 | 4.7 | 103 |
| 2–313 | 1.3 | |
| 2–313 | 3.1 | 1 |
| 2–313 | 4.1 | |
| 2–313 | 4.1 | 3 |
| 2–313 | 4.1 | 12 |
| 2–313 | 4.1 | 15 |
| 2–313 | 4.2 | |
| 2–313 | 4.2 | 67 |
| 2–313 | 4.2 | 69 |
| 2–313 | 4.2 | 101 |
| 2–313 | 4.3 | |
| 2–313 | 4.5 | 40 |
| 2–313 | 4.5 | 46 |
| 2–313 | 6.5 | |
| 2–313 | 7.2 | 20 |
| 2–313 | 15.2 | 52 |

# Table of Cases

Dunne v. Wal–Mart Stores, Inc., 679 So.2d 1034 (La.App. 1 Cir.1996)—§ **13.5, n. 59.**

Duprey v. Shane, 39 Cal.2d 781, 249 P.2d 8 (Cal.1952)—§ **15.6;** § **15.6, n. 20, 22.**

Dura Corp. v. Harned, 703 P.2d 396 (Alaska 1985)—§ **2.4, n. 37.**

Duran v. General Motors Corp., 101 N.M. 742, 688 P.2d 779 (N.M.App.1983)— § **17.4, n. 29.**

Duren v. Paccar, Inc., 249 Ga.App. 758, 549 S.E.2d 755 (Ga.App.2001)—§ **17.1, n. 2;** § **17.2, n. 29;** § **17.3, n. 3.**

Dutsch v. Sea Ray Boats, Inc., 845 P.2d 187 (Okla.1992)—§ **5.3, n. 12.**

Duvall v. Bristol–Myers–Squibb Co., 103 F.3d 324 (4th Cir.1996)—§ **4.2, n. 21.**

Duvon v. Rockwell Intern., 116 Wash.2d 749, 807 P.2d 876 (Wash.1991)—§ **15.6, n. 56.**

Dwyer v. Skyline Apartments, Inc., 123 N.J.Super. 48, 301 A.2d 463 (N.J.Super.A.D.1973)—§ **16.7, n. 66.**

Dyer v. Best Pharmacal, 118 Ariz. 465, 577 P.2d 1084 (Ariz.App. Div. 1 1978)— § **12.3, n. 21.**

Dyson v. General Motors Corp., 298 F.Supp. 1064 (E.D.Pa.1969)—§ **17.3, n. 23, 36.**

Dziewiecki v. Bakula, 361 N.J.Super. 90, 824 A.2d 241 (N.J.Super.A.D.2003)— § **16.7, n. 73.**

# E

Eagle–Picher Industries, Inc. v. Balbos, 326 Md. 179, 604 A.2d 445 (Md.1992)— § **11.4, n. 28.**

Eagle–Picher Industries, Inc. v. Balbos, 84 Md.App. 10, 578 A.2d 228 (Md.App. 1990)—§ **5.9, n. 34.**

Early–Gary, Inc. v. Walters, 294 So.2d 181 (Miss.1974)—§ **5.6, n. 3;** § **5.8, n. 16.**

Easterday v. Masiello, 518 So.2d 260 (Fla. 1988)—§ **16.7, n. 52.**

Eastern Mountain Platform Tennis, Inc. v. Sherwin–Williams Co., Inc., 40 F.3d 492 (1st Cir.1994)—§ **13.6, n. 70.**

Easton v. Chevron Industries, Inc., 602 So.2d 1032 (La.App. 4 Cir.1992)—§ **9.3, n. 40.**

East River S.S. Corp. v. Transamerica Delaval, Inc., 476 U.S. 858, 106 S.Ct. 2295, 90 L.Ed.2d 865 (1986)—§ **5.3, n. 81.**

Eaton Corp. v. Wright, 281 Md. 80, 375 A.2d 1122 (Md.1977)—§ **7.4, n. 34.**

Ebenhoech v. Koppers Industries, Inc., 239 F.Supp.2d 455 (D.N.J.2002)—§ **7.1, n. 33.**

Edison v. Lewis Mfg. Co., 168 Cal.App.2d 429, 336 P.2d 286 (Cal.App. 2 Dist. 1959)—§ **15.3, n. 3.**

Edward M. Chadbourne, Inc. v. Vaughn, 491 So.2d 551 (Fla.1986)—§ **16.7, n. 2.**

Edwards v. Basel Pharmaceuticals, 933 P.2d 298 (Okla.1997)—§ **14.3, n. 14, 20.**

Edwards v. California Chemical Co., 245 So.2d 259 (Fla.App. 4 Dist.1971)—§ **9.3, n. 15.**

Edwards v. Hop Sin, Inc., 140 S.W.3d 13 (Ky.App.2003)—§ **9.4, n. 21;** § **15.2, n. 19.**

Edwards v. Safety–Kleen Corp., 61 F.Supp.2d 1354 (S.D.Fla.1999)—§ **6.3, n. 109.**

Efron v. Embassy Suites (Puerto Rico), Inc., 223 F.3d 12 (1st Cir.2000)—§ **3.2, n. 82.**

Egan v. A.J. Const. Corp., 702 N.Y.S.2d 574, 724 N.E.2d 366 (N.Y.1999)—§ **12.2, n. 33.**

Egelhoff v. Holt, 875 S.W.2d 543 (Mo. 1994)—§ **13.2, n. 31;** § **13.4, n. 86.**

Ehlis v. Shire Richwood, Inc., 367 F.3d 1013 (8th Cir.2004)—§ **9.6, n. 38.**

Ehlis v. Shire Richwood, Inc., 233 F.Supp.2d 1189 (D.N.D.2002)—§ **5.9, n. 6;** § **14.3, n. 39;** § **14.4, n. 108.**

80 South Eighth Street Ltd. Partnership v. Carey–Canada, Inc., 486 N.W.2d 393 (Minn.1992)—§ **5.3, n. 83.**

Eiland v. Westinghouse Elec. Corp., 58 F.3d 176 (5th Cir.1995)—§ **18.6, n. 15.**

Eimann v. Soldier of Fortune Magazine, Inc., 880 F.2d 830 (5th Cir.1989)— § **16.8, n. 21.**

Eimann v. Soldier of Fortune Magazine, Inc., 680 F.Supp. 863 (S.D.Tex.1988)— § **16.8, n. 18, 19.**

Einhorn v. Seeley, 136 A.D.2d 122, 525 N.Y.S.2d 212 (N.Y.A.D. 1 Dept.1988)— § **12.3, n. 50.**

Eisenbach v. Gimbel Bros., 281 N.Y. 474, 24 N.E.2d 131 (N.Y.1939)—§ **13.6, n. 11.**

Eisenbeiss v. Payne, 42 Ariz. 262, 25 P.2d 162 (Ariz.1933)—§ **2.5, n. 3;** § **7.5, n. 17, 43.**

Elgin Airport Inn, Inc. v. Commonwealth Edison Co., 88 Ill.App.3d 477, 43 Ill.Dec. 620, 410 N.E.2d 620 (Ill.App. 2 Dist. 1980)—§ **16.6, n. 5.**

Ellington v. Coca Cola Bottling Co. of Tulsa, Inc., 717 P.2d 109 (Okla.1986)— § **7.5, n. 162.**

Elliot v. Sears, Roebuck and Co., 229 Conn. 500, 642 A.2d 709 (Conn.1994)—§ **13.3, n. 42;** § **13.5, n. 97.**

Elliott v. Brunswick Corp., 903 F.2d 1505 (11th Cir.1990)—§ **10.2, n. 97.**

Elliott v. City of New York, 724 N.Y.S.2d 397, 747 N.E.2d 760 (N.Y.2001)—§ **2.4, n. 35, 50, 52.**

Elliott v. Kraft Foods North America, Inc., 118 S.W.3d 50 (Tex.App.-Hous. (14 Dist.) 2003)—§ **7.5, n. 61.**

Elliott v. Lachance, 109 N.H. 481, 256 A.2d 153 (N.H.1969)—§ **7.4, n. 62.**

Ellis v. C.R. Bard, Inc., 311 F.3d 1272 (11th Cir.2002)—§ **9.6, n. 45.**

Ellis v. Golconda Corp., 352 So.2d 1221 (Fla.App. 1 Dist.1977)—§ **18.6, n. 18.**

Ellis v. K–Lan Co., Inc., 695 F.2d 157 (5th Cir.1983)—§ **6.4, n. 85, 90.**

# F

# G

Kirchoff v. International Harvester Co., 138 A.D.2d 820, 526 N.Y.S.2d 238 (N.Y.A.D. 3 Dept.1988)—§ **17.2, n. 10.**

Kircos v. Holiday Food Center, Inc., 191 Mich.App. 82, 477 N.W.2d 130 (Mich. App.1991)—§ **10.4, n. 6.**

Kirk v. Denver Pub. Co., 818 P.2d 262 (Colo.1991)—§ **18.6, n. 90, 93.**

Kirk v. Michael Reese Hosp. and Medical Center, 117 Ill.2d 507, 111 Ill.Dec. 944, 513 N.E.2d 387 (Ill.1987)—§ **5.3, n. 53; § 9.4, n. 12; § 12.3; § 12.3, n. 20.**

Kirkland v. General Motors Corp., 521 P.2d 1353 (Okla.1974)—§ **5.3; § 5.3, n. 117; § 17.5, n. 48.**

Kirsch v. Picker Intern., Inc., 753 F.2d 670 (8th Cir.1985)—§ **9.6, n. 46.**

Kirstein v. W.M. Barr & Co., Inc., 983 F.Supp. 753 (N.D.Ill.1997)—§ **14.4, n. 172, 174.**

Kisor v. Johns–Manville Corp., 783 F.2d 1337 (9th Cir.1986)—§ **10.4, n. 42.**

Klages v. General Ordnance Equipment Corp., 240 Pa.Super. 356, 367 A.2d 304 (Pa.Super.1976)—§ **3.4, n. 11; § 12.3, n. 49; § 13.7, n. 22, 47.**

Klanseck v. Anderson Sales & Service, Inc., 426 Mich. 78, 393 N.W.2d 356 (Mich. 1986)—§ **2.4, n. 49.**

Kleen v. Homak Mfg. Co., Inc., 321 Ill. App.3d 639, 255 Ill.Dec. 246, 749 N.E.2d 26 (Ill.App. 1 Dist.2001)—§ **12.2, n. 57.**

Klein v. BMW of North America, Inc., 705 So.2d 1200 (La.App. 5 Cir.1997)—§ **17.2, n. 25, 43.**

Klein v. Council of Chemical Associations, 587 F.Supp. 213 (E.D.Pa.1984)—§ **15.7, n. 23, 25, 29.**

Klein v. Sears Roebuck and Co., 773 F.2d 1421 (4th Cir.1985)—§ **4.4; § 4.4, n. 5, 8; § 5.3, n. 76; § 15.2, n. 54.**

Kleinschmidt v. Morrow, 642 A.2d 161 (Me. 1994)—§ **18.6, n. 22.**

Klem v. E.I. DuPont De Nemours & Co., 19 F.3d 997 (5th Cir.1994)—§ **15.3, n. 44.**

Klen v. Asahi Pool, Inc., 268 Ill.App.3d 1031, 205 Ill.Dec. 753, 643 N.E.2d 1360 (Ill.App. 1 Dist.1994)—§ **10.2, n. 116.**

Klinke v. Mitsubishi Motors Corp., 458 Mich. 582, 581 N.W.2d 272 (Mich. 1998)—§ **13.2, n. 43; § 17.5, n. 117.**

Klinke v. Mitsubishi Motors Corp., 219 Mich.App. 500, 556 N.W.2d 528 (Mich. App.1996)—§ **2.2, n. 34; § 7.1, n. 39; § 7.2, n. 11.**

Klootwyk v. DaimlerChrysler Corp., 2003 WL 21038417 (N.D.Ill.2003)—§ **5.3, n. 18.**

Klug v. Keller Industries, Inc., 328 N.W.2d 847 (S.D.1982)—§ **6.4, n. 169.**

Knab v. Alden's Irving Park, Inc., 49 Ill. App.2d 371, 199 N.E.2d 815 (Ill.App. 1 Dist.1964)—§ **4.4, n. 37.**

Knapp v. Hertz Corp., 59 Ill.App.3d 241, 17 Ill.Dec. 65, 375 N.E.2d 1349 (Ill.App. 1 Dist.1978)—§ **13.5, n. 63.**

Kneibel v. RRM Enterprises, 506 N.W.2d 664 (Minn.App.1993)—§ **7.5, n. 98.**

Knight v. Just Born, Inc., 2000 WL 924624 (D.Or.2000)—§ **2.5, n. 22, 38, 66, 74; § 5.3, n. 76; § 7.5, n. 55, 67, 75, 152, 163.**

Knipp v. Weinbaum, 351 So.2d 1081 (Fla. App. 3 Dist.1977)—§ **4.7, n. 73.**

Knippen v. Ford Motor Co., 546 F.2d 993, 178 U.S.App.D.C. 227 (D.C.Cir.1976)— § **17.3, n. 73; § 18.6, n. 15.**

Knitz v. Minster Mach. Co., 69 Ohio St.2d 460, 432 N.E.2d 814 (Ohio 1982)—§ **5.8, n. 31; § 8.6, n. 40.**

Knitz v. Minster Machine Co., Prod. Liab. Rep. (CCH) ¶ 6486 (Ohio App. 6 Dist. 1987)—§ **8.1, n. 11; § 14.3, n. 24, 26.**

Knox v. Delta Intern. Machinery Corp., 554 So.2d 6 (Fla.App. 3 Dist.1989)—§ **10.2, n. 107.**

Kociemba v. G.D. Searle & Co., 707 F.Supp. 1517 (D.Minn.1989)—§ **7.1, n. 35.**

Kodiak Elec. Ass'n, Inc. v. DeLaval Turbine, Inc., 694 P.2d 150 (Alaska 1984)— § **16.5, n. 9.**

Koellmer v. Chrysler Motors Corp., 6 Conn. Cir.Ct. 478, 276 A.2d 807 (Conn.Cir.A.D. 1970)—§ **4.7; § 4.7, n. 47.**

Koepke v. Crosman Arms Co., 65 Ohio App.3d 1, 582 N.E.2d 1000 (Ohio App. 1 Dist.1989)—§ **10.2, n. 64.**

Koester v. Carolina Rental Center, Inc., 313 S.C. 490, 443 S.E.2d 392 (S.C.1994)— § **12.2, n. 2, 11.**

Kohl v. American Home Products Corp., 78 F.Supp.2d 885 (W.D.Ark.1999)—§ **16.3, n. 64.**

Kohler v. Ford Motor Co., 187 Neb. 428, 191 N.W.2d 601 (Neb.1971)—§ **5.3, n. 96.**

Koker v. Armstrong Cork, Inc., 60 Wash. App. 466, 804 P.2d 659 (Wash.App. Div. 1 1991)—§ **10.8, n. 2, 28.**

Kolpin v. Pioneer Power & Light Co., Inc., 154 Wis.2d 487, 453 N.W.2d 214 (Wis. App.1990)—§ **16.6, n. 19.**

Kopczick v. Hobart Corp., 308 Ill.App.3d 967, 242 Ill.Dec. 490, 721 N.E.2d 769 (Ill.App. 3 Dist.1999)—§ **6.4, n. 116; § 18.5, n. 100.**

Koperwas v. Publix Supermarkets, Inc., 534 So.2d 872 (Fla.App. 3 Dist.1988)—§ **7.5, n. 8, 138.**

Korean Air Lines Disaster of Sept. 1, 1983, In re, 1985 WL 9447 (D.D.C.1985)— § **12.3; § 12.3, n. 62.**

Koske v. Townsend Engineering Co., 526 N.E.2d 985 (Ind.App. 2 Dist.1988)— § **13.2, n. 7, 14.**

Koster v. Scotch Associates, 273 N.J.Super. 102, 640 A.2d 1225 (N.J.Super.L.1993)— § **7.5, n. 46.**

Kosters v. Seven–Up Co., 595 F.2d 347 (6th Cir.1979)—§ **15.4; § 15.4, n. 45, 48.**

Kotz v. Hawaii Elec. Light Co., Inc., 83 P.3d 743 (Hawai'i 2004)—§ **16.5, n. 9.**

Kozlowski v. John E. Smith's Sons Co., 87 Wis.2d 882, 275 N.W.2d 915 (Wis. 1979)—§ **10.8, n. 3, 12, 16, 26.**

# L

# M

## N

# O

# U

# V

# Index

References are to page numbers

**1369**

†

0–314–21175–6